A
PORTUGUESE-ENGLISH
DICTIONARY

A
Portuguese-English
Dictionary

REVISED

James L. Taylor

WITH CORRECTIONS AND ADDITIONS
BY THE AUTHOR
AND PRISCILLA CLARK MARTIN

STANFORD UNIVERSITY PRESS
STANFORD, CALIFORNIA
1970

First published 1958. Second printing,
with corrections and additions by the author, 1963.
Third printing, with further corrections
and additions by the author and
Priscilla Clark Martin, 1970.

Stanford University Press
Stanford, California
© 1958 by the Board of Trustees of the
Leland Stanford Junior University
Printed in the United States of America
ISBN 0–8047–0480–5

CONTENTS

ACKNOWLEDGMENTS

Whatever merit this dictionary may have is due in large measure to the help so freely given by many kind persons, among them Dr. Oscar Bandeira, Dr. and Mrs. Roberto Barthel-Rosa, Jorge V. Bérard, Mrs. Carmen Chang, Dr. Reinaldo A. Forster, Charles A. Gauld, Dr. Jorge da Costa Lino, A. C. Mosser, Dr. J. O. Nascimento, Dr. Heraldo P. de Oliveira, Dr. Sansão Campos Pereira, Dr. and Mrs. João Baptista Pinheiro, Miss Hedy Schroder, Mrs. Gwendolyn Taylor, my daughter Sally Taylor, Érico Veríssimo, and Dr. M. A. Zeitlin.

In addition to these, I am especially indebted to Armando S. Pires for his editing of countless pages of the draft copy and for much of the proofreading; to Mrs. Leontina Figner and Dr. Maurício Wellisch for much close collaboration during the early stages; to Dr. George Sprague Myers, of Stanford University, for his help with the entries on fishes; to Dr. Robert F. Murphy, of the University of California, for his review of Indian tribal names; to Dr. James S. Holton, of Sacramento State College, for his authorship of the Appendix on verbs and for his review of the section on pronunciation; to the editorial staff of Stanford University Press for their expert guidance; to Nancy Morgan and Ruth Randle, who did much of the typing, and especially to Corrine Mason, who did most of it.

And finally, my deepest gratitude to Dr. Ronald Hilton, Director of the Institute of Hispanic American and Luso-Brazilian Studies at Stanford University, for his years of active help and stimulating interest in the work, and to Agnes, to whom this book is affectionately dedicated, for her cheerful renunciation of wifely claim to thousands of hours of my leisure time while the work was in progress.

JAMES L. TAYLOR

INTRODUCTION

The need for a good Portuguese-English dictionary has long been felt, and it is the aim of this work to satisfy that need. Although several English-Portuguese dictionaries are available— notably two excellent ones published in Brazil since 1950[1]—the same cannot be said of Portuguese-English works. In fact, with the lone exception of the now quite old Michaelis (published in 1887) no comprehensive Portuguese-English dictionary has heretofore appeared.

This lacuna having now been filled, it is the compiler's ardent hope that this volume will facilitate the use and enjoyment of the Portuguese language to an ever greater number of English-speaking persons. It will be useful also to Brazilians and Portuguese in writing and speaking English.

In the preparation of this dictionary a number of points had to be decided upon at the outset. The first, of course, was the nature and scope of the work contemplated. In this respect my aim has been to provide an everyday working tool for as large a number of persons as possible, ranging from beginning students of the language to teachers of Portuguese; from travelers, translators, exporters and importers, to technicians, engineers, scientists, professional people, government officials and diplomats—anyone, in fact, who for any reason may wish to "look up" a word in Portuguese.

Among other things, this utilitarian aim has meant providing for most of the entry words not alone their closest equivalents in English but one or more synonyms as well, with further clarification in many cases by examples of usage. In cases where equivalents do not exist in English, definitions have been supplied, sometimes by lifting them verbatim from the Merriam-Webster[2] and the *Glossary of Brazilian-Amazonian Terms*.[3] See, for example, *aval* and *mata-feijão*.

Large numbers of technical words in the arts and sciences have been included, and many colloquialisms, idioms, slang words, and expressions are given along with their counterparts in English. Further, in keeping with the richness of the Brazilian fauna and flora, the vernacular names of many plants and animals are supplied, accompanied not alone by their common names or descriptions in English but by their Latin scientific names as well, which in practically every case were checked against the latest authorities and brought up to date where necessary. In the case of plants, the spelling of the common names in English is that adopted and recommended by the American Joint Committee on Horticultural Nomenclature; thus, jackinthepulpit instead of jack-in-the-pulpit; dutchmanspipe instead of dutchman's-pipe.

It should be pointed out in this connection that Brazilian common names for plants and animals are exceedingly varied, and just as any one species may be known by different names in various parts of the country, each of these in turn may refer to more than one species. It is certain, therefore, that many of the common names appearing in the vocabulary are applicable to one or more species in addition to those listed.

An example, and not an unusual one, of the multiplicity of vernacular names is the equivalents for skunk, taken from three Brazilian sources. In addition to *cangambá*, which is perhaps the term most widely used, the following nineteen synonyms or variants are offered, of which no fewer than twelve (those in italics) appear in the official orthographic vocabulary: iritacaca, *iritataca, jaguané, jaguaré*, jaguarecaca, jaguarecagua, *jaguaritaca, jaratataca, jaraticaca, jaritacaca, jaritataca*, jeraticaca, jeritacaca, jeritataca, *maritacaca, maritafede*, maritataca, *tacaca* and *zorrilho*.

This profusion of variants is not limited to names of plants and animals but exists in relation to many other words. The word *alvanel*, for instance, meaning stonemason or bricklayer, has eight variants; the verb *relampaguear* (to flash like lightning) has six variants. Though many variants have been included in the vocabulary, with cross-reference to the main word, it was obviously impossible to include them all, and in fact no attempt was made to do so.

Another basic matter which had to be decided upon at the beginning of the work was the approximate number of words to be listed. The largest Portuguese dictionary in existence[4] is a work of five volumes with 171,046 main entries. At the other end we have the word count sponsored in the early 1940's by the Committee on Modern Languages of the American Council of Education, and, as far as I know, the only word count ever made of Portuguese. The *Graded*

---

[1] Leonel Vallandro and Lino Vallandro, *Dicionário Inglês-Português*. Pôrto Alegre: Editôra Globo, 1954. 1135 pp.

J. L. Campos Júnior, *Dicionário Inglês-Português*. São Paulo: Edições LEP Ltda, 1951. 1100 pp.

[2] *Webster's New International Dictionary of the English Language*. Springfield, Mass.: G. & C. Merriam Company, Publishers, 1943. 2d ed., 3210 pp.

[3] *Glossary of Brazilian-Amazonian Terms*, compiled by the Research Division of the Coordinator of Inter-American Affairs, Washington, 1943. 22 pp.

[4] Laudelino Freire and J. L. de Campos, *Grande e Novíssimo Dicionário da Língua Portuguêsa*. Rio de Janeiro: A Noite, S.A., Editôra, 1943. 5 vols., 5283 pp.

Word Book[5] published as the result of this count supplies a list of only 9,345 words having a range and frequency of five or more. Somewhere between these two extremes—9,345 and 171,046—lay the optimum number for my purpose, and I arbitrarily set 60,000 as the ideal number, or about one-third of the main entries in the large

dictionary cited above. This number of 60,000, incidentally, is about one-half the number of words listed in the official *Pequeno Vocabulário da Língua Portuguêsa* published in 1943 by the Brazilian Academy of Letters.

In this dictionary the 9,345 words listed in the *Graded Word Book* are of course included, as they were certain to be in any case, even without the word count. The remaining fifty thousand had to be selected subjectively, but not altogether without some aid from informants.

[5] Charles B. Brown, Wesley M. Carr, and Milton L. Shane, *A Graded Word Book of Brazilian Portuguese*. New York: F. S. Crofts & Co., 1945. 252 pp.

ORTHOGRAPHY

The simplified and, for all practical purposes, unified systems of orthography now prevailing in Brazil and Portugal are the happy result of a series of agreements and disagreements extending as far back as 1915.

In 1940 the Lisbon Academy of Sciences published its official and definitive simplified vocabulary, and by agreement and official government endorsement, this was used by the Brazilian Academy of Letters as the basis for the compilation of its own vocabulary published in 1943.

Although the differences between the two vocabularies were minor, an attempt was made in 1945 by a dissident group in Brazil to force a closer approximation to the Portuguese model, particularly in the matter of accentuation, and an arbitrary decree by the then dictator government of Brazil was in fact handed down to this effect. This decree, however, met with strong popular resistance and was never ratified by the Brazilian Congress, though it was not until 1956 that the Congress got around to declaring it of no effect. Thus, the official Brazilian orthography is and has been since 1943 the one issued on August 12 of that year by the Brazilian Academy of Letters, and is the one followed in this work. As previously stated, however, the differences between the orthographies of the two countries are minor.

From the standpoint of simplification, the principal gains achieved by the reformed spelling are: elimination of most silent letters, and of most double letters except *rr* and *ss;* the dropping of *k*, *w*, and *y*, and almost entirely of *h*; the replacement of *ph* by *f*, and a wider use of accent marks.

Because of these and other changes, persons not entirely familiar with the new system may sometimes have difficulty in finding in this dictionary words appearing in the older literature. In such cases, the following table will afford clues to possible respellings under which the search may be continued.

Examples of

Instead of:	Try:	Old or Variant Spelling	New or Variant Spelling
b	v	basculhar	vasculhar
bb	b	abbade	abade
c	omitting	tecto	teto
ca	qua	catorze	quatorze

Examples of

Instead of:	Try:	Old or Variant Spelling	New or Variant Spelling
cc	c	occulto	oculto
cç	ç	funcção	função
ch	x or qu	chicara; chimica	xícara; química
dd	d	addenda	adenda
e	i	enebriar	inebriar
ff	f	difficil	dificil
g	j	geito	jeito
gg	g	aggravo	agravo
gn	n	signal	sinal
gy	gi	gyneceu	gineceu
gymn	gin	gymnasio	ginásio
gyp	gi	Egypto	Egito
h	omitting	inhabil	inábil
hym	hi	hymno	hino
j	g	jirafa	girafa
k	qu or c	kilo; kaolin	quilo; caulim
ll	l	fallar	falar
mm	m	gramma	grama
mn	n	amnistia	anistia
mpc	nc	assumpcionista	assuncionista
mph	nf	triumpho	triunfo
mpt	nt	prompto	pronto
nn	n	anno	ano
oi	ou	oiro	ouro
ou	oi	cousa	coisa
ph	f	phosphoro	fósforo
pt	t	baptismo	batismo
quo	co	quota	cota
s	c or z	setim; resingar	cetim; rezingar
sc	c	sciencia	ciência
sch	esqu	schema	esquema
ss	ç	assucar	açúcar
th	t	cathedral	catedral
tt	t	matto	mato
v	b	assovio	assobio
w	u	sandwich	sanduíche
x	ch or s	ximarrão; mixto	chimarrão; misto
y	i	tympano	tímpano
z	s	Brazil	Brasil

ACCENTUATION

1. If a word bears an acute accent (which indicates open vowel quality), or a circumflex accent (which indicates close vowel quality), stress the syllable so marked: *até, açúcar, ambíguo, francês, âmbar.*

2. If a word bears a tilde (which indicates nasal vowel quality) stress the syllable so marked, unless the word bears also an acute or circumflex accent: *irmã, manhã, capitão,* but *acórdão, bênção.*

Exceptions to (1) and (2): derivatives in *-mente*, or words having a suffix beginning with *z*, are stressed on the next-to-last syllable, regardless of the accent mark which then is retained merely to indicate vowel quality. (In such cases, the grave accent is used in place of the acute.) Examples: terrìvel*mente* [ter*rível*], cômodo*mente* [*cômodo*], chã*mente* [*chão*], opùsculo*zinho* [*opúsculo*], dendê*zeiro* [den*dê*], irmã*zinha* [*irmã*].

3. If there is no written accent:

a) Stress the next-to-last syllable of words ending in *a(s), e(s), o(s), am, em,* or *ens.* Note that the final groups *ua, uo, ia,* and *io* will ordinarily be stressed on the *i* or *u,* forming two syllables (unless, of course, the word bears a written accent on another syllable, as in *ambíguo* above). Examples: *casa(s), antes, aprende, comem, cansados, imagens, partia, continua, doentio.*

b) Stress the last syllable of all other words: fa*zer,* ca*ir,* si*ri,* ta*tu,* a*qui,* pa*pel,* ja*mais,* i*guais.*

c) Stressed last syllables ending in open *a, e, o,* bear the acute accent (ca*já,* jaca*ré,* go*gó*), and those ending in close *e* or *o* bear the circumflex (sa*ruê,* a*vô*). But stressed last syllables ending in *i* or *u* do not take an accent mark: si*ri,* tu*pi,* ta*tu,* ja*cu.* [Many persons find it strange no longer to write si*ri,* tu*pí,* ta*tú,* ja*cú.*]

4. Note that the grave accent (`) indicates open-vowel quality but not stress. In addition to its use on derivatives (as shown above) it is used also to indicate contractions of the preposition *a* with the article *a* or with demonstrative adjectives or pronouns: *à* [*a+a,* to the], *àqueles* [*a+aquêles,* to those], *àqueloutras* [*a+aqueloutras,* to those other ones].

5. The dieresis (¨) does not indicate stress but the fact that unstressed *u* is to be pronounced in the combinations *qüe, qüi, güe* and *güi.* When stressed and pronounced in these combinations, *u* bears the acute accent: ar*güi,* averi*güe,* etc.

SYLLABIFICATION

The rules governing the division of words are few and simple:

1. An initial consonant group is not divided but begins the first syllable: *mne-mô-ni-ca, pneu-má-ti-co.* [Note: such initial consonants are not silent, as in English, but are pronounced.]

2. A medial consonant not followed by a vowel remains with the preceding syllable: *ab-di-car, nup-ci-al, des-li-gar.*

3. The digraphs *ch, lh,* and *nh* are never divided: bi*chi-nho,* fi*-lhi-nho,* nhe*-nhe-nhém.*

4. An occlusive or stopped consonant (*p, b, t, d,* hard *c* and *g*) plus a liquid consonant (*l* or *r*) remain together unless the first consonant belongs to the prefix: a-*blu*-ção, a-*bra*-sar, but sub-*lin*-gual.

5. The letters *s* and *x* remain with the prefix when followed by a consonant: *bis*-ne-to, *ex*-tra-ir; but when followed by a vowel they become the first letter of the second syllable: bi-sa-vô, e-xér-ci-to.

6. All double letters are divided: pror-ro-gar, as-sen-tir.

7. Vowels in hiatus, whether different or alike, are divided: fri-ís-si-mo, du-e-lo.

8. Diphthongs, and the combinations *qu* and *gu,* always remain together: a-ni-ma*is,* e-*qui*-va-ler, am-bí-*guo.*

PRONUNCIATION

THE ALPHABET

Letters	Names* in Portuguese	IPA Symbols†
A	á	[ɑ], [a], [ɐ̃]
B	bê	[b]
C	cê	[k], [s]
D	dê	[d]
E	é	[ɛ], [e], [ɛ̃], [i], [I]
F	efe	[f]
G	gê	[g], [ʒ]
H	agá	silent
I	i	[i], [I], [j]
J	jota	[ʒ]
L	ele	[l]
M	eme	[m]
N	ene	[n]
O	ó	[ɔ], [o], [õ], [u]
P	pê	[p]
Q	quê	[k]
R	erre	[r], [rr]
S	esse	[s], [z], [ʃ], [ʒ]
T	tê	[t]
U	u	[u], [ũ], [w]
V	vê	[v]
X	xis	[s], [z], [ʃ], [ks]
Z	zê	[z], [ʃ], [ʒ]

* The names are all masculine.

† In phonetic transcription the tilde [~] indicates nasalization only, whereas in written words it indicates both stress and nasalization. Stress in phonetic transcription is indicated by the mark (´) in *front* of the stressed syllable.

Although there is no standard Portuguese, the language of cultured persons in Rio de Janeiro and Coimbra or Lisbon is frequently regarded as such, and since this dictionary relates mainly to Brazilian Portuguese, so will this brief exposition relate mainly to the language of the *carioca.*

The tables are intended merely to provide a key to the symbols of the International Phonetic Association (IPA) which will be used in transcribing the examples given in the ensuing paragraphs.

VOWELS

IPA Symbols	Examples in Portuguese	Approximate Equivalents in English and Other Languages
[ɑ]	cal, falso, aula, auto	father; Fr. pas; Sp. cal
[a]	mala, lá, dar, casa	aunt (intermediate between ant and ahnt); Fr. mal, gare; Sp. pato
[ɐ̃]	lã, ama, plano, banha	lung, with g silent
[ɛ]	pé, mel, chefe, leva	pear; Fr. père; It. era
[e]	sêda, mêdo, parede	Sp. mes; Fr. thé; It. sera; Scottish way
[ẽ]	sem, bem, lenha	Roughly, aing with g silent
[i]	ida, cidade, depois	pique; Fr. and Sp. si
[I]	sim, embora, enfim	Roughly, eeng with g silent
[ɔ]	norte, farol, gosto	north; Fr. nord; Sp. norte
[o]	tôda, gôsto, fôro	toad; Fr. tôt; Sp. noche
[õ]	bom, vontade	Fr. bon
[u]	tudo, vulto, nulo	to; Fr. tout; Sp. tubo
[ũ]	uma	Rhymes with oom-ah

CONSONANTS

p, b, t, d, m, n, l, f, and *v* have their common English values. (See, however, remarks in paragraphs headed *M, N,* and *L* concerning special functions of these letters.)

IPA Symbols	Examples in Portuguese	Approximate Equivalents in English and Other Languages
[g]	ga*g*o, la*g*o	ga*g*
[ʒ]	*g*íria, *j*ejum, des*d*e	vi*si*on; Fr. *g*entil, dé*j*à
[r]	ca*r*o, pê*r*a	Sp. & It. ca*r*o; Scottish ve*r*y
[rr]	ca*rr*o, *r*oda	Sp. trilled *r* (ca*rr*o), or Fr. velar *r* (ca*rr*eau)
[s]	so*ss*êgo, *c*iência	*c*ease
[w]	g*u*arda, mág*o*a	*w*alk; Fr. o*u*i, d*o*it
[j]	sér*i*o, rád*i*o	*y*ou; Fr. *y*eux, v*i*ens; Ger. *J*ahr
[z]	ca*s*a, *z*agueiro	*z*ig*z*ag; Fr. ro*s*e, *z*èle
[ʃ]	*ch*u*ch*u, nó*s*, lu*z*	*sh*ush; Fr. *ch*ez; It. pe*sc*e
[ʎ]	fi*lh*o, toa*lh*a	fi*li*al; It. e*gl*i
[ɲ]	ni*nh*o, ti*nh*a	o*ni*on; Fr. oi*gn*on; Sp. ni*ñ*o; It. o*gn*i

THE VOWELS

A

In Brazil, *a* has three possible values: [ɑ], [a], and [ẽ] (In Portugal, there is a fourth value [ɐ] discussed later.)

The first value is like *a* in arm, and occurs when followed in the same syllable (which is not very often) by *u* or *l*: *aumento* [ɑu'mẽ.tu], *balde* ['bɑl.di].

The second value [a] is the most troublesome for English-speaking persons, especially Americans, mainly because they do not recognize the difference between it and [ɑ], which indeed it closely resembles, and also because [a] is less used in English than any other *a*.

This [a] is never as in *a*rm, *a*le, c*a*re, or *a*dd, but is intermediate between *a*rm and *a*dd, and is often so pronounced in America in *au*nt, *a*sk, gr*a*ss, d*a*nce, st*a*ff, p*a*th, etc., in northern England in b*a*ck, p*a*n; French p*a*tte, m*a*l, g*a*re; Spanish g*a*to, p*a*to.

[a] occurs in both stressed and unstressed syllables. When unstressed its quality approximates that of *a* in sof*a* or ide*a*. In narrow phonetic transcription its IPA symbol would be [ə], but here we are using the same symbol [a] for both stressed and unstressed [a]: *barata* [ba'ra.ta], *saltar* [sɑl'tar], *sapataria* [sa.pa.ta'ri.a].

The third value—nasal *a*—is not easy to acquire nor can it be described on paper. It is somewhat like French *un* [œ̃e], but not like *enfant* [ã] nor *vin* [ɛ̃], neither of which sounds occurs in Brazil. Nor is it simply [a] nasalized, but a close variety of *a* [ɐ] heard in Portugal in such words as c*a*da, *a*tacar, p*a*ra, but not in Brazil except when nasalized; hence the symbol [ẽ]: *lã* [lẽ], *ano* ['ẽ.nu], *mama* ['mẽ.ma].

E

Stressed *e* has three values: [ɛ] open, [e] close, and [ẽ] nasal.

Open *e* [ɛ] is somewhat like *e* in pear, but it is better compared with French p*è*re, Italian *e*ra. Many words having [ɛ] are marked with the acute accent (é), but many are not so marked and must be learned one by one. Examples: *pé* [pɛ], *sede* ['sɛ.di] (cf. *sêde* below), *papel* [pa'pɛl].

Close *e* [e] approximates the *e* sound in Scottish day, French parl*er*. When marked with the circumflex accent (ê), it is always close, as well as in other cases not so

marked and which must be learned individually. Examples: *mês* [meʃ], *mesa* ['me.za], *sêde* ['se.di] (cf. *sede* above).

(For remarks concerning certain regular shifts in the quality of *e* in verb conjugations, see the section on verbs in the Appendix.)

When [e] is followed by *m, n,* or *nh*, it is nasalized and becomes [ẽ]. Its correct sound cannot be described but roughly may be compared to uttering *eng* without the *g*. It does not resemble any of the French nasals. Examples: *tempo* ['tẽ.pu], *mente* ['mẽ.ti], *venho* ['vẽ.ɲu].

In the prefixes *em-* and *en-*, when unstressed and followed by a consonant, [ẽ] generally but not always becomes [ĩ]: *embora* [ĩ'bɔ.ra], *encanto* [ĩ.'kẽ.tu].

Unstressed *e* generally becomes unstressed [i], as *y* in lady: *vale* ['va.li]. It should be pointed out in this connection that many Brazilians, notably the Paulistas, resist this change of unstressed [e] to [i].

I

This letter is never pronounced as *i* in ice, but if stressed resembles the *i* in pique, and if unstressed, it is like *y* in ready. A better illustration is French, Spanish, and Italian *si*. In the following examples [i] is used in both stressed and unstressed syllables: *livro* ['li.vru], *juruti* [ʒu.ru'ti], *fitar* [fi'tar], *médico* ['mɛ.di.ku].

Nasal *i* [ĩ] is formed when [i] precedes *m, n,* or *nh*, and is pronounced as stressed oral *i* but through the nose, somewhat as in *sing* with *g* silent: *fim* [fĩ], *intriga* [ĩ'tri.ga], *vinho* ['vĩ.ɲu].

O

Stressed *o* has three values: [ɔ] open, [o] close, and [õ] close and nasalized.

Open *o* [ɔ] is never pronounced as in old, dog, or anatomy, but approximately as in north, orb, hot. Italian poca cosa is a better example, and so is French nord and Spanish norte. When *o* bears the acute (ó) or grave (ò) accent it is always open: *cobra* ['kɔ.bra], *código* ['kɔ.di.gu], *sòmente* [sɔ'mẽ.ti].

Close *o* [o] approaches English note, Scottish coat, French tôt, Italian dove. It is always close when it bears the circumflex accent and often when it does not: *côrte* ['kor.ti], *valioso* [va.li'o.zu].

Tonic *o* in many words changes from [o] in the masculine to [ɔ] in the feminine (if there is one), and in both plurals. The most common and unexceptional examples of this are the adjectives ending in *-oso* (see table, p. xiii).

[For remarks concerning regular shifts in the quality of *o* in verb conjugations, see the section on verbs in the Appendix.]

Pretonic [o] followed by a vowel with which it does not form a diphthong, posttonic [o], and unstressed final [o], generally change to [u]: *doente* [du'ẽ.ti], *pérola* ['pɛ.ru.la], *eterno* [e'tɛr.nu]—but, as in other instances, many Brazilians outside of Rio de Janeiro resist this change. The Carioca says ['por.tu] but the Paulista sticks to ['por.to].

Posttonic [o] followed by a vowel changes to [w]: *páscoa* ['paʃ.kwa], but careful speakers often interpose a hiatus: ['paʃ.ku.a]. In this connection, see remarks under "Deceptive Diphthongs."

Nasal *o*: when unstressed [o] is followed by *m, n,* or *nh*, in the same word, it becomes nasalized, roughly as in French bon, which, however, is [bɔ̃], whereas Portuguese *bom* is [bõ]. Examples: *conde* ['kõ.di], *nome* ['nõ.mi], *medonho* [me'dõ.ɲu].

Many Brazilians, however, do not nasalize pretonic [o] or any other vowel in an open syllable followed by *m* or *n*+vowel: *tomate* [tõ'ma.ti] or [to'ma.ti], *nacional* [na.si.õ'nal] or [na.si.o'nal].

	Masc. sing.	Masc. plural	Fem. sing.	Fem. plural
valioso	[va.li'ɔ.zu]	[va.li'ɔ.zuʃ]	[va.li'ɔ.za]	[va.li'ɔ.zaʃ]

Some other everyday words in which this shift occurs:

corpo	['kor.pu]	['kɔr.puʃ]		
esforço	[iʃ'for.su]	[iʃ'fɔr.suʃ]		
fogo	['fo.gu]	['fɔ.guʃ]		
grosso	['gro.su]	['grɔ.suʃ]	['grɔ.sa]	['grɔ.saʃ]
jôgo	['ʒo.gu]	['ʒɔ.guʃ]		
morto	['mor.tu]	['mɔr.tuʃ]	['mɔr.ta]	['mɔr.taʃ]
ôlho	['o.ʎu]	['ɔ.ʎuʃ]		
osso	['o.su]	['ɔ.suʃ]		
ôvo	['o.vu]	['ɔ.vuʃ]		
povo	['po.vu]	['pɔ.vuʃ]		
torto	['tor.tu]	['tɔr.tuʃ]	['tɔr.ta]	['tɔr.taʃ]

U

U has two values: oral [u] and nasal [ũ].

Oral [u], both stressed and unstressed, is usually like *ou* in French *tout*, never like *u* in *cube*, *urn*, or *up*: *cura* ['ku.ra], *puxar* [pu'ʃar]. Sometimes, and optionally, when followed by a vowel, [u] becomes [w]: *mútua* ['mu.twa] or ['mu.tu.a].

U is silent in the combinations *gue*, *gui*, *que*, and *qui*, but must be pronounced when it bears a dieresis: *guerra* ['ge.rra], *quilo* ['ki.lu], but *eloqüente* [e.lo'kwẽ.ti].

Stressed *u* becomes [ũ] when followed by *m*, *n*, or *nh*: *cumba* ['kũ.ba], *dunga* ['dũ.ga], *punho* ['pũ.ɲu].

Unstressed *u* in an open vowel followed by *m* or *n* may be nasalized or not: *túmor* [tũ'mor] or [tu'mor].

THE DIPHTHONGS

Oral diphthongs

In Portuguese there are eleven strong or falling diphthongs, consisting of any one of the vowels plus a weaker *i* or *u*, which in phonetic transcription will be marked thus: ĭ, ŭ. They are:

ai [aɪ̆]—rhymes with pie: *pai* [paɪ̆]
éi [ɛɪ̆]—open *e*: *papéis* [pa'pɛɪ̆ʃ]
ei [eɪ̆]—rhymes with day: *lei* [leɪ̆]
ói [ɔɪ̆]—open *e*: *dodói* [do.dɔɪ̆]
oi [oɪ̆]—close *o*, rhymes with *bo-ee*, not boy: *boi* [boɪ̆]
ui [uɪ̆]—rhymes with *oo-ee*, without hiatus: *fui* [fuɪ̆]

Note: when any of the foregoing diphthongs is followed by a vowel, there is interposed a slight [j]-glide; that is, the sound of *y* as in *yet* is formed by the speech organs in "gliding" from the diphthong to the vowel: *saia* ['saɪ̆.ja], *feio* ['feɪ̆.ju].

au [aŭ]—formerly written *ao*—rhymes with cow: *mau* [maŭ]

Note: not all combinations of *a+u* are diphthongs—see remarks under "Deceptive Diphthongs."

éu [ɛŭ]—open *e*—rhymes more or less with *eh-oo*, without hiatus: *chapéu* [ʃa'pɛŭ]
eu [eŭ]—close *e*—does not rhyme with few but with Spanish *feudo*: *comeu* [kõ'meŭ]
ou [oŭ]—rhymes with owe, but many speakers rhyme it with the close *o* [o]: *louco* ['loŭ.ku] or ['lo.ku]
iu [iŭ]—rhymes, very roughly, with *ee-oo*, without hiatus: *subiu* [su'biŭ]

Nasal diphthongs

Though few in number, the nasal diphthongs constitute the most difficult hurdle in pronunciation for English-

speaking persons. They bear little resemblance to the sounds of any other common language and cannot be adequately described on paper.

ão [ẽŭ]—roughly like *oun* in ounce, nasalized, leaving the *n* unarticulated. It occurs in a great many words: *são*, *não*, *sabichão*, etc. [When used as an augmentative, as in this last word, it changes to *-ona* in the feminine form: *sabichona*.]
am [ẽŭ]—this is the unstressed form of *ão*, and occurs only when final in such words as *falam*, *tocam*, etc. [The *m* is silent.]
ãe [ẽɪ̆]—suggestive of *uh-eeng*, with g silent and no hiatus: *mãe* [mẽɪ̆], *cães* [kẽɪ̆ʃ].
em [ẽɪ̆]—roughly, rhymes with *ay-ing* (without hiatus and with g silent). Occurs only when final in such words as *bem*, *também*, *viagem*, etc. The plural form is *-ens*.
õe [õɪ̆]—roughly like *oh-eeng*, without hiatus and with g silent: *põe* [põɪ̆], *lições* [li'sõɪ̆ʃ].

Semi-diphthongs

At the end of many words there occur certain two-vowel combinations, of which the first vowel is the weaker, which are sometimes referred to as semi- or rising diphthongs.

Although these endings may correctly be uttered as diphthongs, it is considered more elegant to make a hiatus. As a matter of fact, words like *gloria*, *mágoa*, *régua*, etc. are classed as three-syllable words and are accented as such. The following are examples of the ten recognized semi-diphthongs:

ea, as in *áurea* ['au.rja] or ['au.ri.a]
eo, as in *níveo* ['ni.vju] or ['ni.vi.u]
ia, as in *Itália* [i'ta.lja] or [i'ta.li.a]
ie, as in *espécie* [iʃ'pɛ.sji] or [iʃ'pɛ.si.i]
io, as in *canário* [kẽ'na.rju] or [kẽ'na.ri.u] or [kẽ'na.ri.o]
oa, as in *páscoa* ['paʃ.kwa] or ['paʃ.ku.a] or ['pas.co.a]
ua, as in *régua* ['rrɛ.gwa] or ['rrɛ.gu.a]
ue, as in *tênue* ['tẽ.nwi] or ['te.nu.i]
ui, as in *sangüíneo* [sẽ'gwi.nju] or [sẽ.gu'i.ni.u] or [sẽ.gu'i.nju]
uo, as in *fátuo* ['fa.twu] or ['fa.tu.u] or ['fa.tu.o]

Deceptive diphthongs

These are not diphthongs at all but have only the appearance of being so; at best they might be called equal-stress diphthongs. They occur in many Portuguese words, and careful speakers pronounce them with a distinct hiatus. When one of the vowels bears an accent mark, as many of them do, a hiatus is always called for: *aéreo* [a'ɛ.rju], *saúde* [sa'u.di]. More often, however, no accent mark is provided, as in the following examples, all of which require hiatus:

ae—*baeta* [ba′e.ta]
ao—*aorta* [a′ɔr.ta]
au—*paul* [pa′ul] [but *Paulo* is [′paŭ.lu]
ea—*ideal* [i.di′al]
ean—*meandro* [me′ẽ.dru]
ee—*reeleger* [rre.e.le.′ʒer]
eo—*teologia* [te.o.lo′ʒi.a]
ia—*periferia* [pe.ri.fe′ri.a]
ian—*persiana* [per.si′ẽ.na]
ie—*piedade* [pi.e′da.di]
ien—*odiento* [o.di′ẽ.tu]
io—*doentio* [du.ẽ′ti.u]
iu—*miudezas* [mi.u′de.zaʃ]
oa—*lagoa* [la′go.a]
oan—*coando* [ko′ẽ.du]
oe—*joelho* [ʒu′e.ʎu]
oen—*doente* [du′ẽ.ti]
oo—*coordenar* [ko.ɔr.de′nar]
ua—*falua* [fa′lu.a]
uan—*aguando* [a.gu′ẽ.du]
uo—*averiguo* [a.ve.ri′gu.o]
uim—*ruim* [rru′ĩ]

THE CONSONANTS

B

IPA symbol [b], as in English *bub*, not as in Spanish *saber* [sa′ßer].

C

Always hard [k] before, *a*, *o*, *u*, or another consonant, except when marked with a cedilla (ç). It is uttered as in English, but is more staccato.

Before *e* and *i*, and when marked with a cedilla (ç), it is soft, as in *cease*. IPA symbol [s].

Whenever the [k] sound occurs before *e* or *i*, it is written *qu*. See comments under letter Q.

Before a, o, u, or consonant

hard	soft
caco [′ka.ku]	*caça* [′ka.sa]
côco [′ko.ku]	*coço* [′kɔ.su]
cutucar [ku.tu′kar]	*açúcar* [a′su.kar]
crítica [′kri.ti.ca]	

Before e and i: soft

cêrca [′ser.ka]
ciência [si′ẽ.sja]
criancice [kr.ẽ′si.si]

When *c* occurs before *h*, it is a digraph and is pronounced as *sh* in shush, shoe, shave—IPA symbol [ʃ]. It is never pronounced as [k] in chemistry, but before 1931 it did have that value in such words as *chimica*, *machina*, *character*, modernly spelled *química*, *máquina*, *caráter*.

In a few words of optional spelling (*seção* or *secção*, *aspeto* or *aspecto*) both the *cç* (ks) and the *ct* (kt) must be pronounced if so written. The general practice in Brazil is to omit the *c*.

D

IPA symbol [d]. With slight differences, the pronunciation is the same as in English. Speakers of Spanish should avoid rendering *d* fricative between vowels: *cidade* is [si′da.di] not [si′ða.ðe] as in Spanish *cada* [′ka.ða].

F

As in English *fife*—IPA [f].

G

Before *a*, *o*, *u*, or any consonant—hard as in *gag*. IPA [g]: *gago* [′ga.gu], *glosa* [′glɔ.za].

Before *e* or *i*, the sound of *g* is like *s* in *vision*. IPA [ʒ]: *gelo* [′ʒe.lu]

When followed by *a* or *o*, *gu* is pronounced [gw], but as [g] when followed by *e* or *i*: *água* [′a.gwa], *guerra* [′ge.rra].

When the *u* of *gu* bears a dieresis (gü), as it does in a few instances, a hiatus is required before the next vowel: *sangüento* [sẽ.gu′en.tu].

H

The letter *h* is nearly always initial and, except in the digraphs *ch*, *lh*, and *nh*, has no phonetic value. It was retained in the official system of simplified spelling purely for etymological and traditional, not to say sentimental, reasons. It goes against the grain to write *Baía* instead of *Bahia*.

J

Always as *s* in vision [ʒ] or like French *j*, but never as *j* in *judge*; nor is it pronounced as in Spanish [IPA x]. Examples: *já* [ʒa], *jeito* [ʒeĭ.tu], *junta* [′ʒũ.ta].

K

This letter is not a part of the Portuguese alphabet, but is retained in international symbols (kg, kl, km, kw, etc.) and in proper names: Kubitschek.

L

As in English, there is a "clear" *l* and a "dark" *l*, but there is not enough distinction between them to justify making it here; hence, in all examples only the IPA symbol [l] will be used.

lh is a digraph used in many Portuguese words. It is something like English *li* in *filial*, but exactly like *gl* in Italian *egli*, and Castillian Spanish *ll* in *allá*. IPA symbol [ʎ]: *filho* [′fi.ʎu], *toalha* [to′a.ʎa], *fôlha* [′fo.ʎa].

M

In addition to its normal value [m] as in English, *m* has a nasalizing function but is not itself pronounced; that is, when final, or medial before a consonant, the preceding vowel is nasalized but the *m* nearly or totally disappears: *tocam* [′tɔ.kẽŭ], *bom* [bõ], *amplo* [′ẽ.plu].

N

When followed by a vowel, *n* is [n] as in English, but when followed by a consonant it is silent, merely serving to nasalize the preceding vowel: *nada* [′na.da], *tanto* [′tẽ.tu], *findo* [′fĩ.du].

nh is a digraph—IPA [ɲ]—and corresponds roughly to *ni* in *onion*, but is the same as French *gn* (oignon), Italian *gn* (ogni), and Spanish *ñ* (niño). It always nasalizes the preceding vowel: *vinho* [′vĩ.ɲu], *tinha* [′tĩ.ɲa].

P

P is the same as in English—[p].

Q

As in English, *q* occurs only in combination with *u* (qu) and when followed by *a* or *o* is pronounced *kwa* [kwa] or *kwo* [kwo]: *quatro* [′kwa.tru], *quanto* [′kwẽ.tu].

When followed by *e* or *i*, the pronunciation of *qu* is [k], except when the *u* bears a dieresis (qü), which makes it [kw] also: *queda* ['ke.da], *quindim* [kɪ'dɪ], *freqüente* [fre'kwɛ̃.ti], *tranqüilo* [trẽ'kwi.lu].

R

Single intervocalic *r* [r] is not pronounced at all as in English *rear, roar, rat*, etc., but as in Scottish *very*, Spanish *pero*, Italian *vero: caro* ['ka.ru].

Double *r* [rr], or initial *r*, on the other hand, is strongly trilled as in Spanish *carro*, but more often as Parisian uvular *r* in *carreau*. In fact, it often sounds like a strongly aspirated *h* as in hate, or as German *ch* in Bach: *porre* ['pɔ.rri].

Single *r* is pronounced in the same strong manner when initial, or after *l* or *n: rua* ['rru.wa], *chalrar* [ʃal'rrar] *honra* ['õ.rra].

Final *r* is generally weak and tends to drop off entirely. It should, however, be pronounced with a single flip of the tongue.

S

This letter has four values: two unvoiced, *s* [s] as in *sin*, and *sh* [ʃ] as in *shoe*, and two voiced: *z* [z] as in *zero*, and *s* as in *vision* [ʒ]. Double *s*, and *sc* followed by *e* or *i*, are always [s].

1. *s* is generally [s]:
   a) when initial: *safado* [sa'fa.du];
   b) after consonants: *falso* ['fɑl.su]; but in the prefix *trans-* it is [z] when followed by a vowel: *trânsito* ['trẽ.zi.tu];
   c) when final and followed by a word beginning with *s: os sêlos* [us'se.luʃ].
2. *s* is generally [ʃ]:
   a) before *p, k, t* and *f: esposo* [iʃ'po.zu];
   b) when followed immediately by a word beginning with any of these letters: *os pelegos* [uʃ.pe'le.guʃ];
   c) when final before a period or other pause in a sentence.
3. *s* is generally [z]:
   a) when intervocalic: *ca.sa* ['ka.za];
   b) when final if followed immediately by another word beginning with a vowel or with *z: belos olhos* [be.lu'zɔ.ʎuʃ], *os zorros* [uz'zo.rruʃ].
4. *s* is generally [ʒ]:

a) before *b, g, d, v, l, r, m, n: desmentir* [diʒ.mɪ'tir];
b) when final if followed immediately by a word beginning with any of these letters: *Minas Gerais* ['mɪ.naʒ.ʒe'raiʃ].
Most Brazilians outside of Rio de Janeiro resist these [ʃ] and [ʒ] varieties of *s* sounds, and retain [s] and [z] in all cases.

T

The same as in English—symbol [t].

V

The same as in English *vivid*—symbol [v].

W and Y

These letters are not part of the Portuguese alphabet, but are retained for internationally recognized symbols and for proper names: Werneck, Yolanda, etc.

X

This letter is officially stated to have five different values, but there are no set rules by which they can be learned.

The most common value of *x* is *sh* [ʃ]. It occurs both initially and medially in a great many words: *xarope* [ʃa'rɔ.pi], *xilindró* [ʃi.lĩ'drɔ], *xixixi* [ʃi.ʃi'ʃi], *deixa* ['dei.ʃa], *desenxabido* [diz.ẽ.ʃa'bi.du].

The second value of *x* is *ks* [ks] and it occurs usually within and at the end of words: *sexual* [sek.su'al], *taxi* ['tak.si].

A third value is [z] in the prefix *ex-* followed by a vowel: *exemplo* [e'zẽ.plu].

Fourth is the sound of double *s* as in *hiss*, occurring in such words as *aproximar, auxiliar, máxime, proximidade, sintaxe*, etc.

Fifth is simple [s]: *pretexto* [pre'tes.tu], *sexto* ['ses.tu].

Z

Z is pronounced as in English [z]. If a Brazilian palatalizes final *s* he will also palatalize final *z*.

CONTINENTAL VS.
BRAZILIAN PORTUGUESE

The differences between the pronunciation of Portuguese on opposite sides of the ocean occur chiefly in the vowels, and are due in part to the existence of two vowel sounds unknown in Brazil.

1. The first of these is [ɐ]. It is a relaxed close *a* which has been described as resembling the vowel sound of *bird* of South England. In Portugal it occurs generally where in Brazil it is [a], but when nasalized [ẽ] it is the same in both countries:

	Portugal	Brazil
atacar	[ɐ.tɐ'kar]	[a.ta'kar]
palavra	[pɐ'la.vrɐ]	[pa'la.vra]
dançar	[dẽ'sar]	[dẽ'sar]

2. The second vowel sound not used in Brazil is [ə]. This approximates French mute *e*, and corresponds generally to Brazilian pretonic [e]:

	Portugal	Brazil
levar	[lə'var]	[le'var]
beber	[bə'ber]	[be'ber]

3. In Portugal, however, pretonic *e* is frequently dropped altogether in words such as *querer* and *menino*,

which are pronounced as if written *qu'rer* and *m'nino*.
4. In Portugal, but not in Brazil, unstressed final *e* and *o* are usually dropped, and such words as *noute, gente, cidade, levo, fixo, peixe, leite* are pronounced as if written *nout', gent', cidad', lev', fix', peix', and leit'.*
5. Pretonic *e* and *o* are kept open in many cases where in Brazil they are close:

	Portugal	Brazil
espetáculo	[iʃ.pɛ'ta.ku.lu]	[iʃ.pe'ta.ku.lu]
mezinha	[mɛ'zɪ.ɲɐ]	[me'zɪ.ɲa]
freguês	[frɛ'geʃ]	[fre'geʃ]
corar	[kɔ'rar]	[ko'rar]

6. In Portugal, but not in Brazil, a distinction is made both in writing and in pronunciation between the verbal ending *–amos* of the present and preterite tenses:

	Portugal	Brazil
Present Ind.	*falamos* [fɐ'lẽ.muʃ]	*falamos* [fa'lẽ.muʃ]
Preterite	*falámos* [fɐ'la.muʃ]	*falamos* [fa'lẽ.muʃ]

7. *e* and *o* preceding *m, n*, and *nh* followed by a vowel are not nasalized and therefore remain open, whereas in Brazil just the opposite occurs:

	Portugal	Brazil
fome	['fɔ.m]	['fõ.mi]
comodo	['kɔ.mu.du]	['kõ.mu.du]
(written)	*cômodo*	*cômodo*
genio	['ʒɛ.nju]	['ʒẽ.nju]
(written)	*gênio*	*gênio*

8. *a* preceding *m*, *n*, and *nh* followed by a vowel is not nasalized but remains close, whereas in Brazil it is both close and nasalized:

	Portugal	Brazil
banho	['bɐ.ɲu]	['bẽ.ɲu]
lama	['lɐ.mɐ]	['lẽ.ma]
cama	['kɐ.mɐ]	['kẽ.ma]

9. Final *s* and *z* are noticeably more strongly palatalized than Brazilian [ʃ] and [ʒ], which in most of Brazil are not palatalized at all.

10. Many words of optional spelling with the diphthongs *ou* or *oi*, such as *couro, coiro, ouro, oiro, louro, loiro,* are differently preferred in the two countries. Of the examples given, the words with *ou* are preferred in Brazil and the ones with *oi* in Portugal. On the other hand, the reverse is true in many other cases, such as *doudo* and *cousa*, which in Brazil are generally *doido* and *coisa*. The point is that when *ou* is preferred in one country, *oi* is preferred in the other, and vice-versa.

EXPLANATORY NOTES

1. Parts-of-speech labels, accompanied in many cases by subject and usage labels, are supplied in parentheses for all entry words:

    situar (*v.t.*)
    sucinato (*m., Chem.*)
    lero-lero (*m., slang*)

2. Although subject labels are not used when the limitation is obvious, they may on the other hand include more than one subject:

    hilo (*m., Bot., Anat., Zool.*)

3. Irregular plural endings are shown in brackets immediately after the entry word:

    papel [–péis] (*m.*)

4. A number referring to the model conjugations in the Appendix is supplied for each irregular verb:

    fazer [47] (*v.t.*)
    ir [53] (*v.i.*)
    pôr [63] (*v.t.*)
    ser [76] (*v.i.*)

5. Irregular forms of the more common verbs are listed as separate entries, with cross reference to the infinitive and to the verb model in the Appendix:

    fomos, form of SER [76] and of IR [53]

6. A clue to correct pronunciation, especially of the tonic vowel, is supplied in brackets for words concerning which there may be doubt. [The indication is by means of ordinary letters and accent marks, as if the word were so written, and not by phonetic symbols.]

    letra [ê] (*f.*)
    pegada [gá] (*f.*)

7. The pronunciation of the letter *x* is shown in brackets when it is *ks:*

    ataxia [ks] (*f.*)

8. Vowels in hiatus are shown in brackets:

    baiano –**na** [a–i] (*adj.; m.,f.*)
    bainha [a–í] (*f.*)
    saudade [a–u] (*f.*)

9. Alphabetically-close variants or synonyms are entered on the same line, either in full or (to save space) in abbreviated form:

    cominativo –**va**, **cominatório** –**ria** (*adj.*)
    literataço, –**teiro,** –**telho,** –**tiço,** –**tiqueiro** (*m.*)

10. In a few instances, where there is a difference of but one letter between two alphabetically-close words of identical meaning and validity, the variant letter is written between brackets:

    descarril[h]ar

11. Variants which are not close alphabetically are entered separately and cross-referenced:

    sector (*m.*) = SETOR
    setor (*m., Mil., Geom., Astron.*) sector. Var. SECTOR

12. When two or more words are entered on the same line all forms to the left of a part-of-speech label are grammatically the same:

    helícidas, helicídeos (*m.pl.*)
    abalroação, –**ada,** –**adela** (*f.*), –**amento** (*m.*)

13. When words entered on the same line are not of equal validity, the more usual or preferred one is entered first even though alphabetically it is second:

    alojamento (*m.*), **alojação** (*f.*)

14. Words of the same spelling are combined in a single entry, regardless of variation in part of speech, subject, usage, meaning or etymology:

    gôta (*f.*) drop; tear; dewdrop; (*colloq.*) epilepsy; (*Med.*) gout; (*Arch.*) gutta.

15. Adverbs formed by the simple addition of –**mente** to feminine adjectives are not listed except in a few instances where it seemed desirable to include them; e.g., **absoluta-mente.**

16. The feminine form of adjectives is shown if it is different from the masculine form, which is always placed first:

    gordo –**da**
    vão, vã

17. The feminine form is shown of many nouns which ordinarily are thought of as masculine only, and as in the case of adjectives, the masculine form is placed first:

    deputado –**da**
    doutor –**tora**

18. When the masculine and feminine forms of nouns and adjectives are well-established, or when there is a wide difference in their spelling, they are entered separately:

    meu (*adj.; poss. pron. masc.*)
    minha, fem. of MEU.
    ator (*m.*)
    atriz (*f.*)
    juiz [u–i] (*m.*)
    juíza (*f.*)

19. Most compound words in Portuguese, whether hyphenated or not, begin with a noun, and in this dictionary will be found in one article grouped alphabetically under the noun. See, for instance, the groupings under **bôca, cipó, pau, pé.** Such compound words are themselves nouns and have all the same gender as the noun.

Compound words in which the first element is not a noun are all hyphenated and, unlike compound nouns, will vary from one another both in gender and part of speech. They have therefore been entered separately in regular alphabetical order. See, for instance, the entries immediately following **bem.**

As regards hyphenation, the general rule is that hyphens are to be used when not to do so would create a doubt or convey a wrong meaning, but authors and reference books are anything but consistent on this point.

20. Proper names and nouns are included in alphabetical order. In Portuguese orthography, proper names are always capitalized but their derivatives are not:

    Itália, italiano −na
    Brasil, brasileiro −ra
    América, americano −na

21. All cities, states, regions, rivers, etc., whose names appear in the vocabulary or in the definitions, are situated in Brazil, unless indicated or obviously otherwise.

22. Abbreviations are included in the vocabulary in regular alphabetical order.

23. Synonyms in Portuguese are supplied in brackets, in many cases, either at the end of or within the body of an article. In the latter case, the synonym applies only to that portion of the article lying within semicolons:

    açotéia (*f.*) roof terrace [= SOTÉIA].
    abatis [−tises] (*m., Fort.*) abatis; stew made of chicken necks, wings, feet and giblets [= CABIDELA]; felling of trees [= DERRUBADA].

24. Locutions, idioms, and examples of usage, are listed within articles in alphabetical order. See **dar,** for example.

WORKS OF REFERENCE

My indebtedness for help received extends in large measure also to the authors and publishers of the following works:

AGARD, Frederick B., LOBO, Hélio, and WILLIS, Raymond S. Jr., *Brazilian Portuguese from Thought to Word.* Princeton: Princeton University Press, 1944. 277 pp.

AMARAL, Afrânio do, *Nomes Vulgares de Ofídios do Brazil.* Boletim do Museu Nacional do Rio de Janeiro, Vol. II, 1926.

BANDEIRA, Oscar, *Dificuldades e Idiotismos da Língua Inglêsa.* Rio de Janeiro: Of. Graf. Fábrica de Bonsucesso, 1947. 414 pp.

BARNHART, Clarence L., Editor, *The American College Dictionary.* New York: Random House, 1947. 1432 pp.

BENNETT, H., Editor, *Concise Chemical and Technical Dictionary.* Brooklyn: Chemical Publishing Company, Inc., 1947. 1055 pp.

BREDER, Charles M., Jr., *Field Book of Marine Fishes of the Atlantic Coast.* New York: G. P. Putnam's Sons, 1929. 332 pp.

BOURLIÈRE, François, *Mammals of the World.* New York: Alfred A. Knopf, Inc., 1955. 223 pp.

BROWN, Charles B., CARR, Wesley M., and SHANE, Milton L., *A Graded Book of Brazilian Portuguese.* New York: F. S. Crofts & Co., 1945. 252 pp.

BROWN, Charles B. and SHANE, Milton L., *Brazilian Portuguese Idiom List.* Nashville: The Vanderbilt University Press, 1951. 118 pp.

CASCUDO, Luis da Câmara, *Dicionário do Folclore Brasileiro.* Rio de Janeiro: Ministério da Educação e Cultura, Instituto Nacional do Livro, 1954. 660 pp.

COUTO DE MAGALHÃES, Agenor, *Monographia Brazileira de Peixes Fluviaes.* São Paulo: Graphicars, 1931. 260 pp.

———— *Ensaio sobre a Fauna Brasileira.* São Paulo: Secretaria da Agricultura, Indústria e Comércio do Estado de São Paulo, Diretoria de Publicidade Agrícola, 1939. 336 pp.

CRUZ, Pe. Antônio da, C. M., *Regimes de Substantivos e Adjetivos.* Petrópolis: Editôra Vozes Ltda., 1941. 307 pp.

CRUZ LIMA, Eládio da, *Mammals of Amazonia* (Translation by Agnes Chagas). Rio de Janeiro: Livraria Agir Editôra, 1945. 274 pp. XLII plates.

D'ALBUQUERQUE, A. Tenório, *O Nosso Vocabulário.* Rio de Janeiro: Editôra Getulio Costa, 1945. 283 pp.

DESCOURTILZ, Dr. J. T., *Ornitologia Brasileira ou História Natural das Aves do Brazil* (Translated by Eurico Santos). Rio de Janeiro: Kosmos Editôra, 1944. 228 pp.

DITMARS, Raymond L., *Snakes of the World.* New York: The Macmillan Co., 1931. 207 pp.

EMRICH, Karl, *Os Nomes Populares das Plantas do Rio Grande do Sul.* Pôrto Alegre: Edição da Livraria do Globo, 1935. 76 pp.

FARQUHAR, Donald, MACMILLAN, Helen, and SIEGEL, Bernard, Compilers, *Glossary of Brazilian-Amazonian Terms,* compiled from the Strategic Index of the Americas. Washington: Office of the Coordinator of Inter American Affairs, Research Division, 1943. 22 pp.

FARQUHAR, Donald, and SIEGEL, Bernard J., Compilers, *A Glossary of Useful Amazonian Flora,* based on material deposited in the files of the Strategic Index of the Americas. Washington: Office of the Coordinator of Inter-American Affairs, Research Division, 1944. 117 pp.

FERNANDES, Francisco, *Dicionário de Verbos e Regimes.* Pôrto Alegre: Livraria do Globo, 1944. 623 pp.

———— *Dicionário de Sinônimos e Antônimos da Língua Portuguêsa.* Pôrto Alegre: Livraria do Globo, 1946. 919 pp.

FERREIRA, Pe. Júlio Albino, *Dicionário Português-Inglês.* Pôrto: Domingos Barreira, Editor, 1943. 745 pp.

HELLMAYR, Charles E., and CONOVER, Boardman, *Catalogue of Birds of the Americas.* Chicago: Field Museum of Natural History, 11 vols.

FREIRE, Laudelino, and CAMPOS, J. L. de, *Grande e Novíssimo Dicionário da Língua Portuguêsa.* Rio de Janeiro: A Noite, S.A., Editôra, 1943. 5 vols., 5283 pp.

FÜRSTENAU, Eugênio E., *Dicionário Técnico Brasileiro da Língua Portuguêsa.* Rio de Janeiro: Gertum Carneiro, Editôra, 1949. 474 pp.

GÓIS, Carlos, *Dicionário de Galicismos.* Rio de Janeiro: Edição do Autor, 1940. 3d ed., 196 pp.

GUENTHER, Konrad, *A Naturalist in Brazil* (Translated by Bernard Miall). Boston: Houghton Mifflin Company, 1931. 400 pp.

HILLS, E. C., FORD, J. D. M., and COUTINHO, J. de S., *Portuguese Grammar,* revised by L. G. Moffatt. Boston: D. C. Heath and Company, 1944. 352 pp.

IHERING, Rodolpho von, *Dicionário dos Animais do Brasil.* São Paulo: Secretaria da Agricultura, Indústria e Comércio do Estado de São Paulo, Diretoria de Publicidade Agrícola, 1940. 898 pp.

JORDAN, David Starr, *Fishes.* New York: D. Appleton and Company, 1925. 773 pp.

KELSEY, Harlan P., and DAYTON, William A., Editors, *Standardized Plant Names.* Harrisburg: J. Horace McFarland Company, 1942. 2d ed., 675 pp.

LIMA, Hildebrando de, BARROSO, Gustavo, and others, *Pequeno Dicionário Brasileiro da Língua Portuguêsa.* Rio de Janeiro: Editôra Civilização S/A, 1951. 9th ed., 1310 pp.

MAGALHÃES, Alvaro, *Enciclopédia do Curso Secundário.* Pôrto Alegre: Livraria do Globo, 1941. 732 pp.

———— *Dicionário Enciclopédico Brasileiro.* Pôrto Alegre: Livraria do Globo, 1943. 1557 pp.

MELLO-LEITÃO, Candido de, *Glossário Biológico.* São Paulo: Companhia Editôra Nacional, 1946. 646 pp.

―――― *Zoo-Geografia do Brasil.* São Paulo: Companhia Editôra Nacional, 1937. 416 pp.

MESQUITA DE CARVALHO, J., *Dicionário Prático da Língua Nacional.* Pôrto Alegre: Livraria do Globo, 1945. 1109 pp.

MITCHELL, Margaret H., *Observations on Birds of Southeastern Brazil.* Toronto: University of Toronto Press, 1957. 258 pp.

MOTA, Otoniel, *Lições de Português.* São Paulo: Companhia Editôra Nacional, 1941. 359 pp.

NASCENTES, Antenor, *A Gíria Brasileira.* Rio de Janeiro: Livraria Acadêmica, 1953. 181 pp.

―――― *O Idioma Nacional.* Rio de Janeiro: Companhia Editôra Nacional, 1941. 312 pp.

PENNA, Meira, *Dicionário Brasileiro de Plantas Medicinais.* Rio de Janeiro: Livraria Kosmos Editôra, 1946. 3d ed., 409 pp.

PEREIRA, Huascar, *Dicionário das Plantas Úteis do Estado de S. Paulo.* São Paulo: Typographia Brasil de Rothschild & Co., 1929. 779 pp.

PEREIRA, Eduardo Carlos, *Gramática Expositiva, Curso Superior.* São Paulo: Companhia Editôra Nacional, 1941. 419 pp.

PEREIRA, Manuel da Cunha, and others, *Vocabulário Ortográfico Brasileiro da Língua Portuguêsa.* Rio de Janeiro: S.A. O Livro Vermelho dos Telefones, Editôra, 1954. 2d ed., 447 pp.

PINTO, Pedro A., *Brasileirismos e Supostos Brasileirismos.* Rio de Janeiro: Tip. S. Benedito, 1931. 139 pp.

―――― *Têrmos de Economia.* Rio de Janeiro: Editôra Científica, 1947. 141 pp.

POPE, Clifford H., *The Reptile World.* New York: Alfred A. Knopf, Inc., 1955. 325 pp.

ROCHA, Pe. Edgard de Aquino, S.D.B., *Manual de Economia Política.* São Paulo: Companhia Editôra Nacional, 1955. 13th ed., 221 pp.

ROGERS, Julia Ellen, *The Shell Book.* Boston: Charles T. Bradford Co., 1951. 503 pp.

ROSSI, P. Carlo, S.J., Ph.D., *Portuguese, The Language of Brazil.* New York: Henry Holt and Company, 1945. 379 pp.

SÁ PEREIRA, Maria de Lourdes, *Brazilian Portuguese Grammar,* with Phonetic Introduction and Transcription by Robert A. Hall, Jr. Boston: D. C. Heath and Company, 1948. 403 pp.

SANTOS, Eurico, *Anfíbios e Répteis do Brasil.* Rio de Janeiro: F. Briguiet & Cia., Editôres, 1942. 279 pp.

―――― *Da Ema ao Beija-flor.* Rio de Janeiro: F. Briguiet & Cia., Editôres, 1952. 335 pp.

―――― *Entre o Gambá e o Macaco.* Rio de Janeiro: F. Briguiet & Cia., Editôres, 1945. 298 pp.

―――― *Nossos Peixes Marinhos.* Rio de Janeiro: F. Briguiet & Cia., Editôres, 1952. 265 pp.

―――― *Os Moluscos.* Rio de Janeiro: F. Briguiet & Cia., Editôres, 1955. 136 pp.

―――― *Pássaros do Brasil.* Rio de Janeiro: F. Briguiet & Cia., Editôres, 1940. 301 pp.

―――― *Peixes da Água Doce.* Rio de Janeiro: F. Briguiet & Cia., Editôres, 1954. 270 pp.

SEGUIER, Jayme de, *Diccionário Prático Illustrado.* Pôrto: Lello & Irmão, 1944. 1820 pp.

SENNA, Nelson Coelho de, *A Influência do Indio na Linguagem Brasileira,* C.N.P.I., Separata da Publicação No. 101, 1947. 34 pp.

SOUZA, Bernardino José de, *Dicionário da Terra e da Gente do Brasil.* São Paulo: Companhia Editôra Nacional, 1939. 433 pp.

SOUZA LIMA, Mario Pereira de, *Gramática Portuguêsa.* Rio de Janeiro: Livraria José Olympio, Editôra, 1945. 413 pp.

STAVROU, Christopher, *Brazilian-Portuguese Pronunciation.* Philadelphia: David McKay Company, 1947. 152 pp.

STEWARD, Julian H., Editor, *The Handbook of South American Indians.* Washington: Bureau of American Ethnology Bulletin 143, Vols. 1 & 3, 1948.

VALLANDRO, Leonel, and VALLANDRO, Lino, *Dicionário Inglês-Português.* Pôrto Alegre: Editôra Globo, 1954. 1135 pp.

VIOTTI, Manuel, *Dicionário da Gíria Brasileira.* São Paulo: Editôra Universitária, Ltda., 1945. 372 pp.

WEBSTER's *New International Dictionary,* 2d ed. Springfield, Mass.: G. & C. Merriam Company, 1943. 3210 pp.

WILLIAMS, Edwin B., *An Introductory Portuguese Grammar.* New York: F. S. Crofts & Co., 1942. 168 pp.

―――― *First Brazilian Grammar.* New York: F. S. Crofts & Co., 1944. 194 pp.

WRIGHT, Albert Hazen, and WRIGHT, Anna Ellen, *Handbook of Frogs and Toads.* Ithaca: Comstock Publishing Co., 1949. 640 pp.

ABBREVIATIONS

abbrev.	abbreviation	aug.	augmentative
absol.	absolute	Autom.	Automobile
adj.	adjective	Avn.	Aviation
adv.	adverb	Bact(eriol).	Bacteriology
Aeron.	Aeronautics	Bibliog.	Bibliography
Af., Afr.	Africa, African	Biochem.	Biochemistry
Agr(ic).	Agriculture	Biog.	Biography
Alg.	Algebra	Biogeog.	Biogeography
Am(er).	American	Biol.	Biology
Amaz.	Amazon(ian), Amazonas	Bot.	Botany
Anat.	Anatomy	Br.	British
ant.	antonym	Braz.	Brazil(ian)
Anthrop(ol).	Anthropology	Brit.	Britain, British
Anthropom.	Anthropometry	c.a.	called also
App.	Appendix	Calif.	California(n)
Arch.	Architecture	Can.	Canada, Canadian
Archaeol.	Archaeology	Carp.	Carpentry
Arg.	Argentina	Cartog.	Cartography
Arith.	Arithmetic	Cath.	Catholic
art.	article	cf.	compare
Astrol.	Astrology	Ch.	Church
Astron.	Astronomy	Chem.	Chemistry, Chemical

Civ. Eng.	Civil Engineering	Immunol.	Immunology
colloq.	colloquial(ly), -ism	imper.	imperative
Com.	Commerce; commercial	imperf.	imperfect (tense)
comp.	comparative	impers.	impersonal
cond.	conditional	in.	inch(es)
conj.	conjunction; conjugation	Ind.	Indian
Const.	Construction	indef.	indefinite
contr.	contraction	indic.	indicative
corrup.	corruption	inf(in).	infinitive
Craniol.	Craniology	inter.	interrogation
Craniom.	Craniometry	interj.	interjection
Cryst.	Crystallography	intrans.	intransitive
def.	definite; definition	irreg.	irregular
dem.	demonstrative	Jap.	Japan(ese)
Dent.	Dentistry	Join.	Joinery
deriv.	derivative	kg.	kilogram(s)
derog.	derogatory	km.	kilometer(s)
dial.	dialect(ical)	L., Lat.	Latin
Dict.	Dictionary	lb.	pound(s)
dim.	diminutive	ling.	linguistic(s)
dir.	direct	lit.	literally
E.	East, Eastern, English	Lithog.	Lithography
East.	Eastern	Locom.	Locomotive
Eccl.	Ecclesiastical	Log.	Logic
Econ.	Economics	m.	masculine noun
Educ.	Educational	Mach.	Machinery
e.g.	for example	Man.	Manège
Elec.	Electricity, electric(al)	Mar.	Marine, Maritime
Embryol.	Embryology	masc.	masculine
Eng.	England, English	Math.	Mathematics
Engin.	Engineering	Mech.	Mechanics
Entom.	Entomology	Med.	Medicine
erron.	erroneous	Metal.	Metallurgy
esp.	especially	Metaph.	Metaphysics
etc.	et cetera	Meteor(ol).	Meteorology
Ethnog.	Ethnography	Mex.	Mexico, Mexican
Ethnol.	Ethnology	m., f.	masculine and feminine noun
Etym(ol).	Etymology	Mfg.	Manufacturing
exclam.	exclamation	mfr.	manufacture(r)
ext.	extension	M.G.	Minas Gerais
f.	feminine noun	mi.	mile(s)
F., Fr.	French	Micros.	Microscopy
fem.	feminine	Mil(it).	Military
fig.	figurative(ly)	Min.	Mineral(ogy)
Fin.	Finance	m.pl.	masculine noun plural
Fort.	Fortification	Mt. Gr.	Mato Grosso
f.pl.	feminine noun plural	Mus.	Music
fr.	from	Myth.	Mythology
ft.	foot, feet	N.	North; New
fut.	future	n.	noun
g.	gram(s)	Nat. Hist.	Natural History
gal.	gallon(s)	Naut.	Nautical
GBAT	Glossary of Brazilian-Amazonian Terms	Nav.	Navy, Naval
Geod.	Geodesy	Navig.	Navigation
Geog.	Geography	N.E.	Northeast(ern)
Geol.	Geology	neg.	negative
Geom.	Geometry	Neol.	Neologism
Ger.	German(y)	No., no.	North(ern); number
Govt.	Government	Numis.	Numismatics
Gr.	Greek	N.W.	Northwest(ern)
Gt. Br.	Great Britain	obj.	object; objective
GUAF	Glossary of Useful Amazonian Flora	obs.	obsolete
Gun.	Gunnery	Oceanog.	Oceanography
Hist.	History, historical	Ophth.	Ophthalmology
Homeop.	Homeopathy	Opt.	Optics
Horol.	Horology	Optom.	Optometry
Hort.	Horticulture	ord.	ordinary
h.p.	horsepower	Ord.	Ordnance
Hunt.	Hunting	Orthog.	Orthography
Hydr(aul).	Hydraulics	O.W.	Old World
Hydrog.	Hydrography	p.	participle; page
Hydros.	Hydrostatics	P.	Portuguese
i.e.	that is	Paleobot.	Paleobotany

Paleog.	Paleography	S.	South(ern); Santo; São
Paleontol.	Paleontology	s.	substantive
Par.	Paraná	S.A.	South America
part.	participle	S.C.	Santa Catarina
Path.	Pathology	Sci.	Science
perf.	perfect.	Sculp.	Sculpture
Pern.	Pernambuco	S.E.	Southeast(ern)
pers.	person(al)	Seismol.	Seismology
pert.	pertaining	S.I.A., SIA	Strategic Index of the Americas
Petrog.	Petrography	sing.	singular
Petrol.	Petroleum Industry	sl.	slang
Pg.	Portuguese	So.	South(ern)
Pharm.	Pharmacopoeia, Pharmacy, Pharmaceutics	Sociol.	Sociology
Philol.	Philology	sp.	species (singular)
Philos.	Philosophy	S.P.	São Paulo
Phonet.	Phonetics	Span.	Spanish
Phot(og).	Photography	specif.	specifically
Photoeng.	Photoengraving	spp.	species (plural)
Photom.	Photometry	sq.	square
Phys.	Physics	St.	Saint
Phys. Chem.	Physical Chemistry	Stat.	Statistics
Phys. Geog.	Physical Geography	subj.	subjunctive
Physiog.	Physiography	suff.	suffix
Physiol.	Physiology	superl.	superlative
Phytogeog.	Phytogeography	Surg.	Surgery
pl.	plural(s)	Surv.	Surveying
plup.	pluperfect	S.W.	Southwest(ern)
Pol. Econ.	Political Economy	syn.	synonym
Pol. Sci.	Political Science	Tech.	Technical; Technology
Port.	Portugal, Portuguese	Teleg.	Telegraphy
poss.	possessive	Teleph.	Telephony
p.p.	participle past	Theol.	Theology
p. pr.	participle present	Therap.	Therapeutics
pred.	predicate	Thermodyn.	Thermodynamics
pref.	prefix	Topog.	Topography
prep.	preposition	Trig.	Trigonometry
pres.	present	Typog.	Typography
pret.	preterit	TV	Television
prin.	principal(ly)	U.S., U.S.A.	United States of America
Print.	Printing	v.	verb
pron.	pronoun	var.	variant(s)
Pros.	Prosody	Veter.	Veterinary Science
Prot.	Protestant	v.i.	verb intransitive
Psychol.	Psychology	vocab.	vocabulary
Psychopathol.	Psychopathology	v.r.	verb reflexive
q.v.	which see	vs.	versus
Rad.	Radio	v.t.	verb transitive
R.C.Ch.	Roman Catholic Church	W.	West(ern)
ref.	referring (to); reference	Web.	Webster's New International Dictionary, 2nd. Ed.
refl(ex).	reflexive		
R.G.S.	Rio Grande do Sul	West.	Western
rel. pron.	relative pronoun	Zool.	Zoology
Rhet.	Rhetoric	&	and
R.J.	Rio de Janeiro	&c	et cetera
R.R.	Railroad(ing)	+	plus; and; combined with
		=	the same as; equals

A
PORTUGUESE-ENGLISH
DICTIONARY

A PORTUGUESE-ENGLISH DICTIONARY

A

A, a, the first and most-often used letter of the Portuguese alphabet. [It occurs in most of the words.]
A= AMPÈRE INTERNACIONAL (international ampere).
A.= AUTOR (author).
a= ARE (a land measure).
a.= ARRÔBA (a dry measure).
(a)= ASSINADO (signed).
a (*art. fem.*) the; (*dir. obj. pron.*) her; (*dem. pron.*) she; the one (**que**, who).
a (*prep.*) to, at, on, by, for, from, with, etc. Used also in forming many adverbial and prepositional phrases:— **bem de,** for the good of.—**bem dizer,** in truth, strictly speaking.—**braços com,** struggling with (a problem, a difficulty).—**cabo,** finally; to conclusion.—**cada instante,** or—**cada momento,** every minute; all the time.—**cada passo,** at every step.—**cântaros,** (to rain) in buckets; (to rain) cats and dogs.—**caráter,** characteristically, typically; also, as befits the occasion (referring to mode of dress, etc.).—**cargo de,** under the charge (responsibility) of.—**cavaleiro de,** overlooking (from a high point).—**cavalo,** on horseback.—**cem léguas de,** fig., a million miles from.—**céu aberto,** under open skies. [**Mineração a céu aberto,** open-pit mining.]—**chamado,** by invitation.—**chumbo,** [receive, attack, kill] with bullets.—**coberto,** safely under cover; [to draw] against credit balance.—**coberto de,** safe from; free of.—**conselho de,** on the advice of.—**contar de,** beginning with (date); counting from (date or time).—**contento** (or **contamento**), to (one's) heart's content.—**contra-gôsto,** unwillingly; against the grain.—**contrapêlo,** the wrong way, against the grain, against the fur.—**corta-mato,** by a short-cut.—**crédito,** on credit.—**custo,** with difficulty. —**dedo,** with the finger; in detail; painstakingly.— **dentadas,** with bites; with (one's) teeth.—**dente,** by force.—**descoberto,** in view; without funds. [**Sacar a descoberto,** to overdraw one's account.]—**despeito de,** despite, in spite of.—**Deus e à aventura,** aimlessly, haphazardly, at random; for cash; for payment on delivery.—**dois dedos de,** two steps from.— **dois de fundo,** in double file.—**dois passos de,** two steps from.—**duas amarras,** doubly protected.—**duas vozes,** (*Music*) in two (singing) parts. [**As Invenções a duas vozes, de Bach,** Bach's Two-part Inventions.]—**duras penas,** painfully.—**escâncaras,** wide-open.—**êsmo,** haphazardly, adrift, aimlessly, at random; right and left. —**esta(s) hora(s),** at this time; by this time. [**Amanhã a estas horas estarei longe,** Tomorrow by this time I'll be far away.]—**estibordo,** to starboard.—**exemplo de,** following the example of.—**expensas de,** at the expense of.—**extremos,** to extremes.—**facadas,** with knife-stabbings.—**ferro frio,** [to kill] with cold steel.—**fim de,** in order that.—**fio,** uninterruptedly. [**Dias a fio,** days on end, day after day.]—**fartar,** to (one's) fill; to satiety.— **favor,** favorably.—**favor da maré,** with the help of the tide.—**favor de,** in favor of.—**ferro e fogo** (or **a fogo e ferro**), killing and burning; violently.—**fogo lento,** on a slow fire (i.e., slowly, little by little).—**fôlhas tantas,** at a given moment; lit., on such and such a page.—**fórceps,** with difficulty; lit., with forceps.—**frio,** coldly; (in surgery) without anesthesia.—**fundo,** deeply, profoundly; thoroughly; to the bottom.—**galope,** at a gallop.— **garnel,** see A GRANEL.—**gôsto,** as one wishes. [**Esteja a gôsto,** Make yourself at home.]—**grado de,** at the pleasure of.—**granel,** in bulk.—**horas mortas,** or—**horas velhas da noite,** late at night.—**horas tantas,** after a while; presently; unexpectedly.—**intervalos,** from time to time; at intervals.—**jusante,** downstream.—**la bruta,** roughly.—**lanços,** from time to time.—**leite de pato,** "for free" (gratis).—**lufadas,** in spurts.—**machado,** with ax-blows (violently).—**mais,** to excess; left over, surplus, too many. [**Tem um lugar a mais,** There's one seat too many.]—**mais e melhor,** to perfection. [**take, judge, think, consider, etc.**] wrongly.—**manadas,** in handfuls; in droves.—**mancheias,** see A MÃOS CHEIAS.— **mandado de,** on order of.—**mando de,** under orders of. —**mãos cheias,** by the handful.—**mãos largas,** generously, open-handedly.—**mãos lavadas,** with clean hands. —**mãos plenas,** in handfuls.—**mãos rasgadas** (or **rotas**), openhandedly, generously.—**marcha forçada,** by forced marches.—**marche-marche,** [marching] quickly.—**martelo,** with hammer-blows.—**más horas,** late at night.— **mau grado,** in spite of.—**meia luz,** in a half light.— **meia rédea,** with reins held fairly loosely; prudently.— **meia vêrga,** at half-mast. Cf. A MEIO PAU.—**meia voz,** in a low voice.—**meio caminho,** midway.—**meio pano,** with lowered sails; at half-mast.—**meio pau,** at half-mast.—**menos que,** or **a não ser que,** unless.—**mil e mil,** by the thousands.—**miúde** (or **miúdo**) frequently; often. —**mole e mole,** softly, gradually.—**montante,** upstream. —**montante de,** above.—**montão** (or **aos montões**), in heaps.—**muito custo,** with much difficulty; at great cost.—**muque,** by main force.—**murros,** by blows.—**não ser** (**serem**), except (for). [**Vieram todos a não ser(em) o(s) convidado(s) de honra,** Everyone came except the guest(s) of honor.]—**não ser que,** unless.—**ôlho,** visibly, clearly.—**ôlho armado,** with the aided eye.—**ôlho nu,** with the naked eye.—**olhos vistos,** manifestly, clearly.— **palmos,** [to know something] minutely (as the palm of one's hand).—**panos largos,** under full sail.—**pão e água,** on bread and water.—**pão e laranja,** in reduced circumstances.—**par de,** beside; in comparison with; in addition to.—**par e passo,** pari passu.—**par e passo com,** step by step with.—**partir de,** dating from; starting with.— **passo,** slowly.—**passo de anjo,** nodding while walking.— **passo de gigante,** with giant strides.—**passo e passo,** slowly, step by step.—**passo igual,** keeping pace, simultaneously.—**passo medido,** with cautious step; with measured step.—**passos agigantados,** with rapid strides. —**passos contados,** with measured step.—**passos descansados** (or **lentos**), with slow steps.—**passos largos,** with rapid strides.—**pàzadas,** with spade-blows; in spadefuls.—**pé,** on foot.—**pé enxuto,** with dry feet.— **pé firme,** steadfastly.—**pedaços,** piecemeal.—**peito,** seriously, to heart; resolutely, decisively.—**peito descoberto,** with bared breast.—**perna sôlta,** freely.—**pêso de ouro,** very expensively.—**pino,** straight up.—**pique,** to the bottom (of the ocean); in danger; straight up.— **pique de,** on the verge of.—**poder de,** by dint of.— **ponto de,** almost, at the point of; on the verge of.— **poucos passos,** at a short distance; shortly.—**prestações,** in instalment payments.—**pretêxto de,** under pretext of. —**princípio,** at first.—**propósito,** by the way.—**propósito de,** apropos of.—**prumo,** straight up; perpendicularly. —**pulso,** with fist-blows.—**quatro,** in or by fours.—**quatro mãos,** four-handed (piano playing).—**queima-roupa,** point-blank (gunshot) fig., a sudden and pointed statement or question.—**rabo-de-andorinha,** dovetailed.— **reboque,** in tow; trailing behind.—**respeito de,** with re-

spect to.—**risco aberto**, with open danger.—**rôdo**, copiously.—**rôgo**, by request (de, of).—**saber**, to wit.—**salvo**, out of danger.—**salvo de**, free of (danger); shielded from.—**sangue frio**, coolly; coldbloodedly.—**são e salvo**, safe and sound.—**seguir**, to follow; following.—**sério**, seriously; to heart.—**sete chaves**, [locked] tight.—**sete pés**, hurriedly.—**sete sêlos**, sealed tight.—**seu tempo**, in (one's) own time; in due time.—**só(s)**, alone.—**sôcos**, with fist-blows.—**sôldo**, for hire.—**sono sôlto**, [to sleep] soundly.—**tal ponto que**, to such a point that; to the extent that.—**tempo**, timely, on time.—**tempo de**, in time to or for.—**têrmo**, [goods bought or sold] for future delivery.—**tiracolo**, slung over the shoulder and across the chest (as a rifle sling).—**título de**, under pretext of; by way of.—**tôda a brida**, at full tilt.—**tôda a pressa**, with all haste; hotfoot.—**tôda prova**, proof against anything.—**tôda tira**, by every means.—**tôda hora** (or **tôdas as horas**), all the time.—**todo custo** (or **todo transe**), at all costs.—**todo o galope**, at full gallop.—**todo instante** (or **todo tempo**) at every minute.—**todo o pano**, at all costs.—**todo passo**, at every step.—**todo o pulso**, with all strength.—**todo risco**, at all risks.—**todo o tempo**, at every minute.—**todo transe** (or **todo custo**), at all costs.—**todo vapor**, full speed ahead.—**toque de caixa**, on the instant, immediately.—**torto e a direito**, rightly or wrongly; by hook or by crook; as best you can.—**trancos e barrancos**, tumbling and bumping; with difficulty.—**três de fundo**, in triple file.—**trôco de**, in exchange for.—**trôco de que?** What on earth for?—**trote**, trotting.—**trote largo**, at a fast trot.—**trouxe-mouxe**, haphazardly.—**um de fundo**, in single file.—**um tempo**, at one (or the same) time.—**uma voz**, in one voice.—**vapor**, with steam; by steamer.—**venda**, for sale.—**ver navios**, [left] empty-handed; [left] in the lurch.

à (*contraction of prep.* **a**+*article* **a**) to the, at the, on the, etc. Used also in forming numerous adverbial and prepositional phrases. Cf. AO.—**alta noite**, late at night.—**altura de**, with capacity for, capable of; up to (a standard of excellence); up to the height or level of; at a given latitude or longitude.—**americana**, in the American manner.—**antiga**, in the olden manner.—**aposta**, on a bet; purposely.—**aventura**, aimlessly.—**baila**, [to call, to come] up for discussion.—**baioneta**, with bayonets.—**bala**, [to kill, to receive] with bullets.—**bandoleira**, [to wear, carry] over the shoulder (as a bandoleer).—**beira de**, at the edge of; alongside of.—**beira-mar**, along the seashore or sea coast.—**beira-rio**, along the river bank; at river's edge.—**bessa**, in great abundance.—**boa(s) hora(s)**, in good time; at a proper time.—**boa voz**, in a loud voice.—**bolina**, [to sail] close to the wind; obliquely.—**boquinha da noite**, at twilight.—**borda de**, on the edge of.—**brasileira**, in the Brazilian manner.—**bruta**, savagely; roughly; by force; abundantly.—**burguêsa**, in a bourgeois manner.—**busca de**, in search of.—**cabeça**, on (top of) the head.—**cabeceira**, at the bedside (**de**, of).—**caça de**, in search of.—**canhota**, lefthandedly.—**carga**, [to attack] in a charge.—**carga cerrada**, [to fire] in a volley.—**carreira**, hurriedly; [also **às carreiras**].—**cata de**, in search of.—**cautela**, cautiously.—**cena** on stage.—**chave**, [to fasten, bolt] with a key.—**cinta**, [hanging] from the belt (knife, gun, etc.).—**conclusão**, to conclusion.—**concorrência**, [to put] in competition; [to offer] to highest bidder.—**condição**, conditionally.—**conta**, on account.—**conta de**, to the account of; under the care of.—**corda**, at the will of.—**cunha**, chock full, chockablock.—**custa de**, by dint of; at the expense of.—**custa dos outros**, at others' expense.—**derradeira**, or **derradeiro**, at the end.—**descoberta**, on the lookout; in the open.—**desfilada**, headlong, pell-mell.—**desforra**, in revenge.—**destra** (or **destro**), to the right.—**determinação de**, under the orders of.—**diferença de**, contrary to.—**direita**, to the right.—**direita e**—**esquerda**, right and left.—**discrição de**, at the discretion of.—**disparada**, headlong, pell-mell; hotfoot.—**disposição**, available; at one's disposition.—**disposição de**, at the disposal of.—**distância**, at a distance, (**de**, from); afar.—**divina**, divinely.—**escôlha**, with free choice.—**escôlha do freguês**, at customers' choice.—**escoteira**, lightly equipped (as a scout).—**escovinha**, like a brush (referring to a "crew" haircut).—**escuta**, alertly, attentively.—**espanhola**, in the Spanish manner.—**evidência**, patently.—**exceção de**, with the exception of.—**expiração de**, at the expiration of.—**extremidade**, to (an) extreme.—**espera**, awaiting.—**espera de**, waiting for.—**espora**, in a spurt.—**espreita**,

on the lookout.—**esquerda**, on the left.—**face de**, in view of; in the face of.—**face da igreja**, or **do altar**, at the foot of the altar.—**fala**, within hailing distance.—(**or na**) **falta de**, for want of.—**falta do homem**, for want of the right man.—**farta**, abundantly; to satiety.—**fé de**, for the honor of.—**fé de quem sou**, on my word of honor.—**feição de**, in the image of; iike; in the fashion of.—**fina fôrça**, by main force.—**flor de**, on the surface of (water, ground).—**fôrça**, by force.—**fôrça aberta**, by naked force.—**fôrça de**, by force of.—**fôrça de vela**, under full sail.—**fôrro**, intimately.—**francêsa**, in the French manner. [**sair à francêsa**, to take French leave.]—**frente (de)**, at the front (of).—**fresca**, lightly dressed.—**garra**, adrift.—**grande**, grandly, ostentatiously; abundantly; a great deal.—**hora**, at the moment; punctually; [to pay] by the hour.—**imitação de**, like; after.—**laia de**, like; of the same ilk.—**larga**, freely, generously.—**letra**, literally.—**lufa-lufa**, hurriedly.—**luz de**, by the light of (a lamp, candle, etc.); in the light (knowledge) of.—**maneira de**, in the manner of.—**mão**, by hand; at hand, within reach.—**mão armada**, by force of arms.—**mão direita (esquerda)**, on the right (left) hand.—**mão larga**, liberally.—**máquina**, by machine. [**feito à** (or **a**) **máquina**, machine-made.]—**maravilha**, marvelously.—**margem**, to one side (abandoned).—**margem de**, at the side of, near to.—**marinheira**, or—**maruja**, in sailor fashion.—**medida**, to the full.—**medida de**, according to.—**medida que**, as, while.—**melhor parte**, to the better side.—**mercê de**, at the mercy of.—**mesa**, at table.—**míngua**, in destitution.—**míngua de**, without, wanting, lacking.—**mira**, with eyes open.—(or **na**) **moda**, modishly; in keeping with fashion.—**moda de**, in the mode of, after.—**moderna**, in the modern manner.—**mostra de**, face to face with.—**nascença**, at birth.—**noitinha**, at nightfall.—**orla de**, at the edge of.—**ourela de**, on the edge of.—**paisana**, in plain (civilian) clothes.—**parte**, separately; secretly; aside from; for one's part.—**pluralidade**, by plurality.—**porfia**, with rivalry; unceasingly.—**presença de**, to the presence of.—**primeira enxadada**, at the first blow.—**primeira vista**, at first sight.—**proporção de**, in proportion with.—**proporção que**, as, when or while; at the same rate as.—**prova de**, proof, impervious to.—**prova de água**, waterproof.—**prova de bomba**, bomb-proof.—**prova de fogo**, fireproof.—**pura fôrça**, by main force.—**queima roupa**, or—**queima bucha**, point-blank.—**razão de**, in virtue of; by reason of; at the rate of; at the price of.—**rédea larga**, or **rédea sôlta**, at full tilt.—**revelia (de)**, (*Law*) in default (of); also, unbeknownst to; without the knowledge or approval of.—**risca**, to the letter.—**saciedade**, to satiety.—**semelhança de**, similar to, like.—**simples vista**, in plain sight; intuitively.—**soalheira de**, at the threshold of.—**socapa**, furtively; softly.—**sôfrega**, greedily.—**solapa**, secretly.—**sombra**, in the shade; (*colloq.*) in jail.—**sombra de**, in the shadow of; beneath; under the protection of.—**superfície**, on the surface.—**surda**, or—**surdina**, quietly, softly.—**tarde**, in the afternoon.—**testa (de)**, at the front or head (of).—**toa**, in tow; adrift; aimlessly; without reason; at random.—**-toa**, (*adj.*) worthless.—**tona (de)**, on the surface of.—**traição**, treacherously.—**tripa fôrra**, [to eat] hugely.—**última**, to the extreme.—**última extremidade**, to the last extremity.—**última hora**, at the last minute.—**uma**, as one, all together.—**valentona**, ruffianly.—**vela**, under sail; in shirttails.—**vela sôlta**, under full sail.—(or **a**) **venda**, for sale.—**ventura**, haphazardly.—**vista**, in sight; [pay, payment] at sight; [cash] on delivery.—(or **em**) **vista de**, in view of.—**vista desarmada**, with the naked eye.—(or **em**) **vista disto**, therefore, in view of this; in that case; if that's so.—**viva fôrça**, by main force.—**volta**, on returning.—(or **por**) **volta de**, about (referring esp. to the hour).

AA. = AUTORES (authors).

Aarão (*m.*) Aaron.

aba (*f.*) rim, brim; skirt; tab; overhang.—**do chapéu**, hat brim.—**da sela**, flap of a saddle.

ababangaí (*m*) India trumpetflower (*Oroxylum indicum*).

ababelado -da (*adj.*) Babelic.

ababone (*f.*) the tallowwood (*Ximenia americana*).

abaçaí (*m.*) Indian evil spirit.

abaçanado -da (*adj.*) dusky, swarthy.

abacataia (*f.*) = ARACANGUIRA (threadfish).

abacate (*m.*) avocado, alligator pear.

abacateiro (*m.*) avocado tree (*Persea americana*).

abacatuaia (*f.*) moonfish (*Argyreiosus vomer* or *Vomer* *setapinnis*), c.a. PEIXE-CAVALO, PEIXE-GALO, ALFAQUIM, ABACATUIA.

abacaxi [í] (*m.*) pineapple; (*sl.*) dud, lemon; tiresome thing; difficult, delicate situation.

abacelar (*v.t.*, *Hort.*) to heel in cuttings.

abacharelar-se (*v.r.*) = BACHARELAR-SE.

abacial (*adj.*) abbatial.

ábaco (*m.*) abacus.

abáculo (*m.*) abaculus; tessera.

abada (*f.*) apronful; eaves of a roof.

abadavina (*f.*) = PINTASSILGO-VERDE.

abade (*m.*) abbot; fig., fat man.

abadejo (*m.*) a codfish (*Gadus pollackius*), c.a. ABADIVA, BADEJO; the yellow meal worm (*Tenebrio molitor*), c.a. VACA-LOURA.

abadêssa (*f.*) abbess.

abadia (*f.*) abbey.

abafadiço –ça (*adj.*) sultry, close.

abafado –da (*adj.*) stuffy, stifling; hidden; repressed, subdued; distressed, upset; annoyed; very busy.

abafador –dora (*adj.*) stifling; (*m.*) muffler (of sound); damper (of stove or piano); mute (of a musical instrument); teapot cozy; hoodwinker.

abafar (*v.t.*) to smother, stifle; to choke, strangle; to deaden (sound); to repress, subdue; to restrain; to swathe, wrap up; (*colloq.*) to swipe (steal); (*colloq.*) to make good, be a winner, shine in one's job.—**a banca**, to break the bank.—**o fogo**, to smother the fire.—**a voz**, to muffle the voice.—**uma revolta**, to quell a rebellion. —**um escândalo**, to hush up a scandal.

abafo (*m.*) sultriness; muffler; affectionate holding, hugging or sheltering (as of a child).

abagum (*m.*) a hornbill (*Buceros*).

abaí (*m.*) the wintersweet (*Chimonanthus praecox*).

abaianado –da [a-i] (*adj.*) having the habits, manners, etc., of the people of Bahia.

abainhar [a-i] (*v.t.*) to hem (a garment).

abaionetar (*v.t.*) to bayonet.

abairrar (*v.t.*) to divide (a town) into districts; to classify (voters, etc.) by districts.

abaixador –dora (*adj.*) lowering, reducing, depressing; (*m.*) depressor (muscle).

abaixa-língua (*m.*) tongue depressor.

abaixamento (*m.*) lowering; lessening; falling; reduction (of prices); submission; humiliation; degradation.—**da madre**, (*Med.*) prolapse of the uterus.—**da temperatura**, drop in temperature.—**da trajetória**, the vertical distance, at any point, between the sight line and the trajectory of a bullet.—**do solo**, a cave-in or other lowering of the ground level.—**do som**, lowering of a sound.

abaixar (*v.t.*) to lower; to let (bring, take, pull) down; to drop; to diminish, reduce; to humiliate; to degrade; (*v.i.*) to sink, settle; (*v.r.*) to stoop, bend down.—**a cabeça**, to bow the head; to duck.—**a crista** (**proa**, **topête**), to lower one's flag; draw in one's horns; eat crow.—**(alguma coisa) à terra**, to lower (something) to the ground.—**a vista sôbre**, to look down on (at).—**a voz**, to lower the voice.—**os olhos**, to drop the eyes.— **-se a**, to condescend to.—**se adiante de (alguém)**, to grovel before (someone).

abaixo (*adv.*) beneath, under, underneath; down, downward; (*prep.*)—**de**, under, below; (*interj.*) Down with (him, it, etc.)!—**e acima**, up and down. **deitar**, **por**—, to raze. **mais**—, lower down. **vir**—, to come (fall) down.

abaixo-assinado (*m.*) signed petition, round robin; the undersigned (person).

'**abajur** (*m.*) lampshade. [Fr. *abat-jour*.]

abalada (*f.*) hasty flight.

abaladiço –ça (*adj.*) unstable, easily upset.

abalado –da (*adj.*) loose, unsteady, insecure; shaken, moved, disturbed; weakened; upset; threatened with danger. **alma**—, shaken soul. **dente**—, loose tooth. **nervos**—**s**, upset nerves. **reputação**—, tottering reputation. **saúde**—, enfeebled health.

abalador –dora (*adj.*) shaking, rocking; moving.

abalaiado –da (*adj.*) basket-like.

abalamento (*m.*) a shaking or rocking; agitation; hurried flight.

abalançar (*v.t.*) to weigh (goods); to balance (accounts); to swing, rock; (*v.i.*) to swing, sway. —**a**, to actuate, impel.—**contra**, to go against, attack.—**se a**, to dare (venture) to.

abalar (*v.t.*) to rock, jolt, stagger, shake (loose, down); to upset; to move, affect (emotionally); to weaken; (*v.i.*) to rush off; (*v.r.*) to become unsteady. **não se**—,

to sit tight.

abalaustrado –da [a-u] (*adj.*) provided with balusters.

abalável (*adj.*) "that can be shaken, etc. See the verb ABALAR.

abalizado –da (*adj.*) competent, capable, noted, distinguished.

abalizador (*m.*) surveyor; measuring rod.

abalizar (*v.t.*) to demarcate, measure, stake out (land); to mark with buoys; to define, delimit; (*v.r.*) to distinguish oneself.

abalo (*m.*) jolt, shock; commotion; upset.—**sísmico**, earthquake.

abalonado –da (*adj.*) balloon-like; puffed out.

abaloar (*v.t.*) to balloon, inflate; to puff up or out.

abalroação, **–ada**, **–adela** (*f.*), **–amento** (*m.*) crash, collision (esp. of ships).

abalroador –dora (*adj.*) colliding; (*m.*) ship which caused collision.

abalroar (*v.t.*) to grapple; to crash; (*v.i.*) to crash into, collide with, bump against.

abanação, **–adela**, **–adura** (*f.*), **–amento** (*m.*) act of fanning or winnowing; a shaking.

abanador –dora (*m.,f.*) fanner; winnower; (*m.*) fan.

abana-moscas (*m.*) a fly whisk.

abananado –da (*adj.*) banana-like; simple, stupid.

abanar (*v.t.*) to fan; to agitate; to wag.—**(com) a cabeça**, to shake the head.

abancar (*v.t.*) to seat on a bench; (*v.i.*) to sit on a bench or at table; (*v.r.*) to sit down.

abandalhar (*v.t.*) to disgrace (-se, oneself).

abandar (*v.t.*) to provide with bands or stripes; to set aside, allot, apportion; to band together; (*v.r.*) to unite with a band or party; to flock together.

abandear (*v.*) = BANDEAR.

abandeirar (*v.*) = EMBANDEIRAR.

abandidar-se (*v.r.*) to turn bandit.

abandoar-se (*v.r.*) to band together.

abandonado –da (*adj.*) abandoned; left behind; forsaken.

abandonamento (*m.*) = ABANDONO.

abandonar (*v.t.*) to abandon, forsake; to relinquish; (*v.r.*) to give oneself over (to excesses).—**o campo**, to quit the field.

abandono (*m.*) abandonment; relinquishment.—**da herança**, relinquishment of an inheritance.—**de causa**, (*Law*) discontinuance.—**de emprêgo**, throwing up of one's job.—**de menores**, child abandonment.—**de pôsto**, (*Mil.*) abandonment of post or duty.—**do lar conjugal**, (*Law*) desertion of one spouse by the other.

abaneiro (*m.*) a clusia (*C. fluminensis*) which yields a medicinal resin, c.a. ABANO, MANGUE-BRAVO, MANGA-DA-PRAIA.

abanicar (*v.t.*) to fan (-se, oneself).

abanico (*m.*) a small fan; (*pl.*) fine words, gallantries.

abano (*m.*) a fan. [*GBAT*: "A type of fan without a handle, woven of TUCUMÃ fibers and used to fan fires, etc.; a gum-bearing tree (*Clusia fluminensis*)."]

abaporu [ú] (*m.*) Indian cannibal.

abará (*m.*) a dish of beans mixed with pepper and DENDÊ-palm oil.

abaraíba (*f.*) = AROEIRA.

abaratar (*v.*) = BARATEAR.

abarbado –da (*adj.*) very busy; swamped with work; struggling; in a tight spot.—**com a morte**, at the point of death.

abarbar (*v.t.*) to face, oppose; to put up against; to go (come) up to or abreast of; to overload with work.

abarbarado –da (*adj.*) barbarous, brutish.

abarbarizar (*v.*) = BARBARIZAR.

abarcador –dora (*adj.*) encompassing; monopolistic; (*m.,f.*) monopolist.

abarcamento (*m.*) encompassment; monopoly.

abarcar (*v.t.*) to embrace, encompass, encircle; to take on many duties; to monopolize.—**a lua com uma joeira**, to try to hide plain facts; lit., to hide the moon with a sieve. —**o mundo com as pernas**, to attempt everything at once.

abaré (*m.*) Indian name for a Christian missionary. Var. AVARÉ.

abaritonado –da (*adj.*) baritone-like.

abarracado –da (*adj.*) tentlike; hutlike; lodged in tents, huts, or sheds; of a space, divided up into stalls.

abarracamento (*m.*) group of tents, huts, sheds, or stalls temporary military quarters or camp.

abarracar (*v.t.*) to provide with, or lodge in, tents.

abarrancar (*v.t.*) to block (roads, ideas); to overturn, ditch (train, automobile).

abarreirado –da (*adj.*) fortified or surrounded by barriers and trenches.

abarreirar (*v.t.*) to erect barriers; to bar passage; to fortify, defend.

abarrotado –da (*adj.*) crammed, filled full; stuffed with food.

abarrotamento (*m.*) act of cramming, filling, stuffing.

abarrotar (*v.t.*) to cram, fill full.

abarticulaçao (*f.*, *Anat.*) articulation, especially diarthrosis.

abasia (*f.*, *Med.*) abasia.

abastado –da (*adj.*) well-to-do; well-supplied.

abastamento (*m.*) supplying, provisioning; ample supply. [More usual: ABASTECIMENTO.]

abastança (*f.*) abundance, wealth; (*pl.*) riches, goods; large promises.

abastar (*v.t.*) to supply, provision. Cf. ABASTECER.

abastardado –da (*adj.*) debased, degraded, corrupt.

abastardar (*v.t.*) to debase, degrade.

abastecedor –dora (*adj.*) supplying; (*m.*,*f.*) supplier.

abastecer (*v.t.*) to supply, provision; to lay in (stores).

abastecido –da (*adj.*) full, well-supplied.

abastecimento (*m.*) supply; act of supplying or provisioning.—de água, water supply.

abastoso –sa (*adj.*) plentiful, abundant.

abatedor –dora (*adj.*) abating, lowering, depressing; (*m.*,*f.*) abater; reducer.—de gado, butcher.

abatedouro (*m.*) = MATADOURO.

abater (*v.t.*) to lower, let down; to floor, knock down; to fell (trees); to raze; to slaughter (cattle); to humble, crush; to browbeat; to enfeeble; (*v.i.*) to drop, fall; (*v.r.*) to sag; to despond.—a bandeira, to strike the flag. —as armas, to lay down arms.—de (or em), to rebate, discount, take off.—os fumos, to come down a peg.—-se a, to prostrate onself before (another).

abati [í] (*m.*) Indian word for corn.

abatiapé (*m.*) wild rice.

abatido –da (*adj.*) prostrate; downcast, downhearted; crestfallen, dejected, depressed; blue; enfeebled; of cattle, slaughtered.

abatimento (*m.*) abatement; depression; dejection; despondency, the blues; weakness, debility; felling (of trees); slaughter (of cattle); razing (of buildings); discount, rebate.

abatinar-se (*v.r.*) to put on a cassock.

abatis [-tises] (*m.*, *Fort.*) abatis; stew made of chicken necks, wings, feet and giblets [= CABIDELA]; felling of trees [= DERRUBADA].

abatocar (*v.t.*) to insert a bung in (a cask, etc.).

abatumado –da (*adj.*) in low spirits; of bread, sad soggy.

abatumar (*v.*) = ABETUMAR.

abaúbo (*m.*) tattler (a bird), c.a. ABONAXI.

abaulado –da [a-u] (*adj.*) convex, cambered.

abaulamento [a-u] (*m.*) convexity; camber(ing).

abaular [a-u, 10] (*v.t.*) to camber, bend or curve upward in the middle (as a roadway). [The word derives from BAÚ, an old-fashioned round-topped trunk.]

abaúna (*m.*,*f.*) pure-blooded Indian. Var. ABARUNA.

abaunilhado –da (*adj.*) having the scent of vanilla.

abaxial [ks] (*adj.*) abaxial.

abdicação (*f.*) abdication.

abdicador –catriz (*adj.*) abdicating, renouncing; (*m.*,*f.*) abdicator, abdicant.

abdicar (*v.t.*) to abdicate; to renounce, forgo.—à pátria, to exile oneself.

abdicativo –va (*adj.*) abdicative.

abdicatriz, fem. of ABDICADOR.

abdicável (*adj.*) abdicable.

abdome, **abdômen** (*m.*) abdomen.

abdominal (*adj.*) abdominal. tifo—, typhoid fever.

abdominoscopia (*f.*, *Med.*) abdominoscopy.

abdômino-torácico –ca (*adj.*, *Anat.*) abdomino-thoracic.

abdômino-uterotomia (*f.*, *Surg.*) abdomino-uterotomy, Caesarian section.

abdominoso –sa (*adj.*) abdominous, big-bellied.

abdução (*f.*, *Physiol.*, *Logic*) abduction.

abducente (*adj.*) abducent.

abdutor –tora (*adj.*, *Physiol.*, *Anat.*) abducting; (*m.*, *Anat.*) abductor nerve or muscle.

abduzir (*v.t.*, *Physiol.*) to abduct.

abeatado –da (*adj.*) sanctimonious.

abeberar (*v.t.*) to water (cattle); to soak; (*v.r.*) to immerse oneself (in work, study)

abecar (*v.t.*) to buttonhole, seize by the lapels.

a-bê-cê (*m.*) the ABC's.

abecedar (*v.t.*) to alphabetize.

abecedário –ria (*adj.*) abecedarian; alphabetically arranged; rudimentary; (*m.*) the ABC's, alphabet; primer, first speller; alphabetical index; rudiments of anything. —manual, manual alphabet (of deaf-mutes).—telegráfico, Morse alphabet; (*f.*) a spot-flower (*Spilanthes acmella*), c.a. ABEADÁRIA, ACMELA, AGRIÃO-DO-PARÁ, AGRIÃO-DO-BRASIL, ERVA-DAS-CRIANÇAS, JAMBU, MASTRUÇO; the century plant (*Agave americana*), c.a. ALOÉS-DOS-CEM-ANOS, BABOSA-BRAVA, PITA, PITEIRA.

abegão (*m.*) farm hand; farm overseer; drone [= ABELHÃO, ZANGÃO.]

abegoa (*f.*) farm hand's, or overseer's, wife.

abegoaria (*f.*) stable, barn; farm animals and equipment.

abeirante (*adj.*) bordering on.

abeirar (*v.t.*) to approach, come near to; to bring near to; (*v.i.*,*v.r.*) to draw near or nearer.

abelha (*f.*) any bee.—-amarela, or —-italiana, the yellow Italian honeybee.—-caga-fogo (—-de-fogo), a stingless bee (*Melipona tataira*), c.a TATAIRA. —-comum (—-doméstica, —-do-reino), the common honeybee (*Apis mellifera*, syn. *mellifica*). —-da-terra, any burrowing bee.—-de-cachorro, a small stingless bee (*Melipona ruficus*), c.a. ARAPUÁ, IRAPUÁ; also either *M. argentata* or *M. fulviventris*.—-de-cupim, any bee which nests in termitaries; c.a. BÔCA-DE-BARRO.—-de-mel, honeybee. —-do-chão = MULATINHA.—-do-pau, any of numerous bees that nest in tree hollows.—-flor, a butterfly orchid (*Orchis papillionacea*), c.a. ABELINHA, ABELHEIRA, ERVA-ABELHA.—-limão = IRAXIM.—-macho, drone, c.a. ZANGÃO.—-mestra, queen bee.—-mirim (—-mosquito), the tiny black-and-yellow stingless bee (*Melipona minima*), c.a. JATÍ, JATAÍ-MOSQUITO, JATAÍ-PRETA.—-mulata, a stingless bee (*Melipona quadripunctata*), c.a. GUIRUÇU, PAPA-TERRA.—s sociais, social bees.—s solitárias, solitary bees.

abelhal (*m.*) beehive.

abelhão (*m.*) drone; bumblebee.

abelhar-se (*v.r.*) to be busy as a bee.

abelharuco (*m.*) bee eater (a bird).

abelheira (*f.*) bee nest (as in a tree); beehive; an orchid [= ABELHA-FLOR].

abelheiro (*m.*) beehive; bee nest; beekeeper; the European bee eater (*Merops apiaster*), c.a. ABELHARUCO, ABELHUCO, MELHARUCO.

abelhinha (*f.*) = ABELHA-FLOR.

abelhudar (*v.t.*) to pry into (another's affairs).

abelhudice (*f.*) intrusiveness, nosiness.

abelhudo –da (*adj.*) prying, nosey, meddlesome.

abélia (*f.*, *Bot.*) abelia.

abeliana (*f.*, *Bot.*) common balm (*Melissa*).

abelícea (*f.*) bastard sandalwood (*Zelkova abelicea*).

abelmosco (*m.*) muskmallow (*Hibiscus abelmoschus*), c.a. AMBARINA, AMBRETA; common okra (*Hibiscus esculentus*), c.a. QUIABO.

abeloura (*f.*) common foxglove (*Digitalis purpurea*), c.a. DEDALEIRA, DIGITAL, ERVA-DEDAL. Var. ABELOIRA.

abemolado –da (*adj.*, *Mus.*) flat; of voice, dulcet.

abemolar (*v.t.*, *Mus.*) to lower a pitch; to render (the voice) dulcet.

abençoadeiro –ra (*m.*) shaman; (*f.*) witch.

abençoado –da (*adj.*) blessed; blest.

abençoador –dora (*adj.*) blessing; (*m.*,*f.*) one who blesses.

abençoamento (*m.*) act of blessing; a blessing.

abençoante (*adj.*) blessing.

abençoar (*v.t.*) to bless; to bestow good upon.

abendiçoar (*v.t.*) to bless.

aberdim (*m.*) Aberdeen Angus (beef cattle).

aberem (*m.*) a cornmeal- or rice-cake, wrapped in banana leaf. Var: ABARÉM.

aberração (*f.*) aberrance; aberrancy; aberration (all senses).—biológica, (*Biol.*) mutation.—cromática, (*Opt.*) chromatic aberration.—de esfericidade, (*Opt.*) spherical aberration.—da natureza, a freak of nature.

aberrante (*adj.*) aberrant.

aberrar (*v.i.*) to deviate, stray (from normal).

aberto –ta (*adj.*; *irreg. p.p.* of ABRIR) open; clear; overt; manifest; frank, honest; (*f.*) an opening, open space; gap; clearing (as in a forest); fig., way out of a difficulty.—de água, leak (in a ship).—de tempo, a clearing of the weather. em—, open; unsettled.

abertamente (*adv.*) openly; aboveboard.

abertura (*f.*) opening; aperture; gap; hole, orifice; inauguration; sincerity.—**de falência**, declaration of bankruptcy.—**de concorrência**, opening of bids.—**de crédito**, opening of credit.—**de testamento**, opening of a will.—**de uma ópera**, (*Mus.*) overture.—**do pulso**, spraining of the wrist.

abesourar (*v.t.*) to annoy with humming or buzzing, or by dinning or insistent repetition.

abespinhado –**da** (*adj.*) waspish; touchy.

abespinhar-se (*v.r.*) to become irritated; to bristle.

abestalhado –**da** (*adj.*) dull, stupid.

abestruz (*f.,m*) = AVESTRUZ.

abetarda (*f.*) the great bustard (*Otis tarda*), c.a. ABETARDA-BARBUDA (or -GRANDE), BATARDA, BATARDÃO, BETARDA, PERU-SELVAGEM.—-**anã**, the little bustard (*Otis tetrax*), c.a. ABETARDA-PEQUENA, ABETARDINHA.

abeto [ê] (*m.*) any fir (*Abies*).

abetouro (*m.*) a bittern (*Botaurus stellaris*); the tree heath (*Erica arborea*).

abetumado –**da** (*adj.*) smeared, coated (as with tar); gloomy, in the dumps; soggy [bread].

abexim (*adj.*) = ABISSÍNIO.

ABI = ASSOCIAÇÃO BRASILEIRA DE IMPRENSA (Brazilian Press Association).

abibe (*m.*) a lapwing (*Vanellus vanellus*), c.a. ABITONINHA, VENTOINHA.

abibura (*f.*) a poisonous mushroom (*Agaricus pisonianus*).

abicar (*v.t.*) to touch land, moor, cast anchor.

abichito (*m., Min.*) clinoclasite [= AFANESITO].

abieiro (*m., Bot.*) the abiu (*Pouteria caimito*), c.a. CAIMITEIRO.

abietato (*m., Chem.*) abietate.

abietena (*f., Chem.*) abietene.

abietico –**ca** (*adj., Chem.*) abietic.

abietina (*f.*) rosin, colophony.

abietíneo –**nea** (*adj.*) abietineous; (*f.pl.*) the *Abietineae* (pines, spruces, hemlocks, firs).

ábiga (*f., Bot.*) a bugle (*Ajuga iva*); a germander (*Teucrium chamaepites*).

abiogênese, –genesia, –genia (*f., Biol.*) abiogenesis.

abiogenésico –**ca** (*adj.*) abiogenetic.

abiogenista (*m.,f., Biol.*) abiogenist.

abiologia (*f.*) abiology.

abiose (*f.*) abiosis.

abiótico –**ca** (*adj.*) abiotic.

abiotrofia (*f., Med.*) abiotrophy.

abirritação (*f., Med.*) abirritation.

abirritante (*adj.*) abirritant.

abirritar (*v.t., Med.*) to abirritate.

abiscoitado –**da** (*adj.*) obtained by stealth, etc.;—see the verb ABISCOITAR.

abiscoitar (*v.t.*) to get, gain, win (somewhat luckily or by stealth); to swipe. Var. ABISCOUTAR.

abismado –**da** (*adj.*) engulfed; astounded; thunder-struck; bewildered; lost, ruined.—**em cismos**, buried in thought.

abismal (*adj.*) abysmal.

abismar (*v.t.*) to amaze, astound; to bewilder; (*v.r.*) to become engrossed, absorbed (in).

abismo (*m.*) abysm, abyss, chasm; limbo, bottomless pit; the deep, the depths; profound riddle. **à beira do**—, on the brink of ruin.

abissal (*adj.*) abyssal.

abissínio –**nia** (*adj.; m.,f.*) Abyssinian [= ABEXIM].

abisso (*m.*) abyss.

abitas (*f.pl., Naut.*) bitts.

abitolar (*v.t.*) to measure with a gauge.

abitoninha (*f.*) = ABIBE.

abiu (*m.*) fruit of the ABIEIRO.

abiurana (*f.*) any of several trees of genus *Lucuma*.

abjeção (*f.*) abjection, meanness, degradation.

abjeto –**ta** (*adj.*) abject, base, vile, despicable.

abjudicar (*v.t.*) to abjudge (take away by judicial decision).

abjugar (*v.t.*) to unyoke.

abjuração (*f.*) abjuration, forswearing.

abjurar (*v.t.*) to abjure, renounce; to retract, recant; to reject; (*v.i.*) to apostatize, backslide.

ablabe (*m.*) = LABE-LABE.

ablação (*f., Surg., Geol.*) ablation; (*Gram.*) aphaeresis.

ablactar (*v.*) = DESMAMAR.

ablativo –**va** (*adj.; m.*) ablative.—**s de viagem**, last-minute preparations for a journey.

ablegar [ab-le] (*v.t.*) to deport; to send (a cardinal) as a pontifical delegate.

ablepsia (*f., Med.*) ablepsia.

ablução (*f.*) act of washing; (*Eccl.*) ablution.

abluir [72] (*v.t.*), to wash, cleanse; to restore (ancient manuscripts) by cleaning.

abnegação (*f.*) abnegation, self-denial.

abnegado –**da** (*adj.*) altruistic, unselfish; (*m.,f.*) one who denies self, who sacrifices for others.

abnegar (*v.t.*) to abnegate, renounce; to give up; (*v.r.*) to deny (sacrifice) oneself.

abóboda (*f.*) dome, cupola; arch; canopy; vault; camber, convexity.—**abatida** (—**de volta**,—**de sarapanel**,—**elíptica**,—**de asa-de-cesto**), a three-centered or basket-handle arch.—**celeste**, the vault of heaven.—**chata**, flat (French, Dutch) arch.—**cilíndrica** (—**de berço**,—**de volta-de-berço**,—**de um só centro**,—**de canudo**,—**de tubo**,—**de tumba**,—**mestra**) barrel vault.—**craniana**, upper part of the skull.—**de ângulo**, cylindrical intersecting or cross vault.—**de aresta**, groined vault.—**de barrete-de-clérigo**, cloister or coved vault.—**ogival** (—**gótica**,—**à moderna**), ogee arch.—**palatina**, roof of the mouth (palate).

abobadado –**da** (*adj.*) arched, vaulted; domelike.

abobado –**da** (*adj.*) idiotic, stupid, "dumb".

abobar-se (*v.r.*) to play stupid.

abóbora (*f.*) pumpkin, squash, gourd; (*colloq.*) a "weak sister."—-**cabaça** (—-**de-romeiro**), a bottle or calabash gourd (*Lagenaria*).—-**cheirosa** (—**almiscar**,—**catinga**,—**melão**), the cushaw or winter crook-neck squash (*Cucurbita moschata*).—-**chila**, Malabar gourd (*Cucurbita ficifolia*).—-**d'água**, summer squash.—-**do-campo**, the cranberry gourd (*Abobra tenuifolia*).—-**do-mato**, a tropical herbaceous vine (*Melothria fluminensis*), c.a. ABOBREIRA-DO-MATO, CEREJA-DE-PURGA, GUARDIÃO, MELÃO-DE-MORCEGO, TAIUIÁ-MIÚDO.—-**menina** (—-**gigante**,—-**grande**), winter squash (*Cucurbita maxima*).—-**moganga** (—-**carneira**,—**de-porco**,—**moranga**,—**porqueira**) common pumpkin (*Cucurbita pepo*).—-**ovos** (—-**pêra**), the yellow-flower gourd (*Cucurbita ovifera*), c.a. CABACINHA-RISCADA.—-**serpente**, the edible snake-gourd (*Tricosanthes anguina*). Var. ABOBRA.

aboboreira (*f.*) pumpkin (gourd), squash) vine.

abobrinha, aboborinha (*f.*) summer squash.

abocamento (*m.*) inosculation; anastomosis.

abocanhar (*v.t.*) to seize with the jaws; to tear (slash) with the teeth; to devour, wolf; to seize possession of; to defame, malign.—**um bom emprêgo**, to grab off a good job.

abocar (*v.t.*) to seize with the mouth; to arrive at the mouth of (a river); to point (a gun); (*Physiol.*) to inosculate, anastomose.

aboiado (*m.*) = ABOIO.

abolar (*v.i.*) to sing out while herding cattle.

aboio (*m.*) cowboy's calls or shouts while herding cattle; sometimes, a chant.

aboiz [aboízes] (*f.*) snare, noose; trap.

abolachar (*v.t.*) to make flat like a biscuit.

abolar (*v.t.*) to render like a cake [BÔLO], or like a ball [BOLA].

aboletar (*v.t.*) to billet, quarter.—**-se em**, to lodge oneself in.

abolição (*f.*) abolition; abolishment.—**da sensibilidade**, (*Med.*) anesthesia.—**do movimento**, (*Med.*) paralysis.

abolicionismo (*m.*) abolitionism.

abolicionista (*adj.; m.,f.*) abolitionist.

abolido –**da** (*adj.*) abolished; annulled.

abolim (*m.*) a leatherleaf (*Chamaedaphne*, syn. *Cassandra*) whose flowers are used for garlands.

abolinar (*v.i.*) to sail close-hauled.

abolir [25] (*v.t.*) to abolish; to abrogate, repeal.

abolorecer (*v.i.*) to become moldy.

abolorecido –**da** (*adj.*) mildewed, moldy.

abomaso (*m., Zool.*) abomasum.

abombachado –**da** (*adj.*) like BOMBACHAS.

abombado –**da** (*adj.*) jaded, fagged, worn out (referring esp. to horses).

abombador (*m.*) one who jades a horse.

abombamento (*m.*) exhaustion.

abombar (*v.i.,v.r.*) to become jaded.

abominação (*f.*) abomination; outrage.

abominado –**da** (*adj.*) abominated, hated.

abominador –**dora** (*m.,f.*) abominator.

abominar (*v.t.*) to abominate, abhor, execrate; (*v.r.*) to hate oneself.

abominável (*adj.*) abominable, hateful, odious.

abominoso –**sa** (*adj.*) abominable, detestable.

abonação (*f.*) warranty, surety; security; assurance.

abonado –da (*adj.*) reputable, creditable; in good standing; bona fide.

abonador –dora (*adj.*) guaranteeing, confirming, approving; (*m.,f.*) guarantor, surety, bondsman.

abonamento (*m.*) = ABONAÇÃO.

abonançar (*v.t.*) to quiet, lull, tranquilize; (*v.i.,v.r.*) to grow calm, quiet, tranquil.

abonar (*v.t.*) to guarantee, warrant; to vouch for; to go bail for; to endorse, sanction; to justify; to sell on credit; (*colloq.*) to advance money to; in this sense = ADIANTAR.

abonatório –ria (*adj.*) that warrants or vouches for (something or someone).

abonável (*adj.*) warrantable.

abonaxi [í] (*m.*) = ABAÚBO.

abono (*m.*) warranty; an advance or allowance of money; bonus, payment; praise; (*Mil.*) commutation of quarters; (*pl.*) playing chips [= FICHAS].—**de Natal,** Christmas bonus.—**familiar,** in Brazil, a system of extra compensation for heads of families, paid for by joint contributions of employers and all employees; family allowance.

aboquejar (*v.*) = ABOCANHAR.

aborbulhar (*v.i.*) to bubble, foam.

aborcar (*v.*) = EMBORCAR.

abordagem, abordada (*f.*) act of attacking, etc. See the verb ABORDAR.

abordar (*v.t.*) [from BORDO, board] to attack and board ship; to make land or a landing; [from BORDA, border] to approach the edge (of a lake, river, etc.); [from Fr. *aborder*] to accost or address another; to tackle, come to grips with (a problem, subject, etc.).

abordoar (*v.t.*) to strike with a heavy cane; (*v.r.*) to rest on a cane; to stand on (reasons, principles).

aborígine (*adj.*) aboriginal; (*m.,f.pl.*) aborigines.

aborrecer (*v.t.*) to bore, annoy; to abhor, loathe; (*v.r.*) to become bored, annoyed (**com,** with, at). **Aborreço os ignorantes,** I detest stupid people. **Não se aborreça,** Don't (you) worry.

aborrecido –da (*adj.*) irksome, boresome, wearisome, tiresome, tedious; pesky; bored, fed up; dejected, gloomy; worried; peeved, cross.—**da vida,** bored with life, sick of living. **andar,** or **estar,—,** to be blue, in the dumps; also, to be preoccupied; to be sore at (someone).

aborrecimento (*m.*) annoyance, nuisance; irritation; unpleasantness; boredom, tedium; worry, anxiety, concern; aversion, disgust; serious setback or very bad news.

aborrir (*v.*) = ABORRECER.

abortado –da (*adj.*) aborted; frustrated, thwarted.

abortamento (*m.*) abortion, miscarriage.

abortar (*v.i.*) to abort, miscarry; to fail; (*v.t.*) to cause to fail.

aborticídio (*m.*) aborticide, feticide.

abortífero –ra (*adj.*) abortifacient.

abortivo –va (*adj.*) abortive; (*m.*) abortifacient.

abôrto (*m.*) abortion; (*colloq.*) a botch.—**da natureza,** freak of nature.

abostelar (*v.i.*) to become pustulous.

abotoação (*f.*) budding, sprouting, burgeoning.

abotoadeira (*f.*) buttonhook; buttonhole; woman who makes or sews on buttons, or who makes buttonholes.

abotoado –da (*adj.*) buttoned up; bud-covered; of eyes, bugging; (*m.*) a giant fresh-water catfish (*Doras granulosus*).

abotoador (*m.*) buttonhook [= ABOTOADEIRA].

abotoadura (*f.*) a set of buttons; (*pl.*) cuff buttons.

abotoar (*v.t.*) to button (up); to buckle (on); (*v.i.*) to bud, burgeon.—**se com alguém,** to buttonhole someone, take him by the lapels.

abra (*f.*) cove, bay.

Abraão (*m.*) Abraham.

abracadabra (*f.*) abracadabra.

abraçadeira (*f.*) bracket, brace, clip, clasp; tie-back for drapes and curtains; (*pl.*) parentheses.

abraçar (*v.t.*) to embrace, clasp, hug; to enfold, encompass (**em,** in); to adopt, accept, espouse.—**se a,** to cling to.—**se com alguém,** to embrace another.—**uma carreira,** to adopt a career.—**uma opinião,** to embrace an opinion.

abraço (*m.*) embrace, hug.—**de tamanduá,** a treacherous show of friendship.

abrandamento (*m.*) act of softening; mitigation; quieting.

abrandar (*v.t.*) to soften; to assuage, moderate; to allay; to mitigate, appease; to mollify, placate; to quell; (*v.i.*) to tone down, quiet down, cool down; to grow gentle; to become tranquil; (*v.r.*) to relent.—**a dor,** to

ease the pain. **O tempo abrandou depois da chuva,** The weather cooled off after the rain.

abrandecer (*v.*) = ABRANDAR, EMBRANDECER.

abranger (*v.t.*) to encircle, enfold, embrace; to embody; to comprehend, enclose, include; to take in (the whole of); to reach, extend to. **Isto não abrange todos,** This does not apply to everyone.

abrânquio –quia (*adj., Zool.*) abranchial, abranchiate, without gills; (*m.pl.*) the *Abranchiata.*

abrasado –da (*adj.*) glowing, flaming; ruddy.

abrasador –dora (*adj.*) inflammatory; combustible; devouring, consuming. **calor—,** burning heat. **sol—,** blazing sun.

abrasamento (*m.*) burning; ardor.

abrasante (*adj.*) = ABRASADOR.

abrasão (*f.*) abrasion; erosion; (*Dent., Med.*) abrasion.

abrasar (*v.t.*) to burn (up), consume (with fire); to cremate; to heat; to inflame, excite; (*v.i.*) to blaze, flame, glow; (*v.r.*) to get on fire (fig.).

abrasileirado –da (*adj.*) Brazilian-like; Brazilianized.

abrasileirar (*v.t.*) to Brazilianize; (*v.r.*) to turn Brazilian; to acquire Brazilian traits, manners, etc.

abrasivo –va (*adj.; m.*) abrasive.

abrastol (*m., Chem., Pharm.*) abrastol [= ASSAPROL].

abraxas [ks] (*m.pl.*) abraxas stones.

Abr. = ABRIL (April).

abre-cartas (*m.*) letter opener; paper knife.

abre-ilhós (*m.*) eyelet punch.

abrejar (*v.t.*) to flood, make into a swamp; (*v.i.*) to enter a swamp.

abre-latas (*m.*) can opener.

abrenunciar (*v.t.*) to reject, renounce; to repel.

abreu (*m.*) a stingless bee (*Melipona angustata*); also = MOÇA-BRANCA.

abreviação (*f.*) act of abbreviating, shortening, abridging. Cf. ABREVIATURA.

abreviadamente (*adv.*) briefly.

abreviado –da (*adj.*) abbreviated; brief.

abreviador –dora (*adj.*) abbreviating; (*m.,f.*) one who abbreviates; (*m., R.C.Ch.*) abbreviator.

abreviar (*v.t.*) to abbreviate, shorten, curtail; to abridge, epitomize, condense; to hasten, expedite.

abreviatura (*f.*) abbreviation. Cf. ABREVIAÇÃO.

abricó (*m.*) the fruit of the ABRICOTEIRO, or mammee apple, c.a. ABRICOTE, ABRICÓ-DO-PARÁ, ABRICÓ-DE-SÃO DOMINGOS, ABRICÓ-SELVAGEM. [Though sometimes called tropical apricot, it is not related to the true apricot, which in Port. is DAMASCO.]—**amarelo** = ABRICOTEIRO-DO-MATO.—**das-antilhas,** a lucuma (*L. pauciflora*), c.a. ABRICOTEIRO.—**de-macaco,** the Guiana cannonball tree (*Couroupita guianensis*), c.a. CASTANHA-DE-MACACO.—**-do-pará** = ABRICOTEIRO.

abricoque (*m.*) = ALBRICOQUE, ALBRICOQUEIRO.

abricote (*m.*) = ABRICÓ.

abricoteiro [cô] (*m.*) the mamey or mammee apple (*Mammea americana*), c.a. ABRICÓ-DAS-ANTILHAS, ABRICÓ-DO-PARÁ.—**do-mato,** the elengi bulletwood (*Mimusops elengi*), c.a. ABRICÓ-AMARELO, ABRICOTEIRO-DO-BRASIL.

abrideira (*f.*) aperitif.

abridor –dora (*adj.*) opening; of liquor, serving as an appetizer; (*m.*) opener; burin (engraver's tool).—**de garrafas,** bottle opener.

abrigado –da (*adj.*) sheltered; protected; warmly clothed; (*m.,f.*) inmate; (*f.*) shelter, refuge; cove.

abrigador –dora (*adj.*) sheltering; protecting; (*m.,f.*) one who protects, defends, gives shelter to.

abrigadouro (*m.*) = ABRIGADA.

abrigar (*v.t.*) to shelter, shield (**sob,** under); to lodge, harbor (**em,** in); to protect, defend; to safeguard; (*v.r.*) to take shelter, seek refuge.

abrigo (*m.*) shelter, cover; refuge, asylum; harbor, haven. —**à prova de bombas,** bomb-proof shelter.—**anti-aéreo,** air-raid shelter.—**de barcos,** covered shed for boats.—**de trincheira,** dugout.—**individual,** foxhole. **ao—,** protected, sheltered. **barraca de—,** pup tent. **sem—,** shelterless.

Abril (*m.*) April; (fig.) springtime; youth. **primeiro de—,** April Fool's Day.

abrilhantado –da (*adj.*) polished, bright, shining.

abrilhantamento (*m.*) polishing, shining, brightening, beautifying.

abrilhantar (*v.t.*) to brighten; to illumine; to add to the brilliance of (an occasion, a gathering, as by one's presence).

abrimento (*m.*) act of opening. [=ABERTURA]

abrir [26] (*v.t.*) to open (up); to unclose; to uncork; to unseal; to unfold; to break (lay, stretch, dig, tear) open; to unfasten, untie; to loose(n); to clear (the way); to free from obstacles; to open wide; to reveal, disclose; to begin, enter upon, initiate; to split, cleave; to bore, pierce; to engrave, carve, chisel; to unroll; to spread out; to roll out (dough); (*v.i.*, *v.r.*) to open; to come asunder; to begin, start; to disclose.—**a bôca**, to open the mouth; to speak, break the silence; to yawn; to grumble; to scold; to weep.—**a bôlsa a (alguém)**, to open one's pocketbook to (another).—**a cabeça de (alguém)**, to crack (another's) head.—**a campanha**, to begin military operations.—**a estrada**, to clear the way.—**água**, to spring a leak.—**alas**, to open up a lane (through a crowd).—**a marcha**, to lead the way.—**a porta**, to open the door, fig., to ease the way.—**as asas**, to spread the wings (fly).—**as mãos**, to be freehanded; to accept a bribe.—**as velas**, to spread sail.—**brecha**, to breach.—**caminho**, to make way, clear the way.—**campo a**, to give an opportunity to, permit.—**cancha**, to open up the way.—**conta**, to open an account; to start a new account (in the ledger).—**crédito**, to give credit.—**de par em par**, to open wide (doors, windows).—**falência**, to take (declare) bankruptcy.—**fileiras**, (*Mil.*) to open ranks.—**gestões**, to open negotiations.—**mão de**, to forego, let go, desist.—**o apetite**, to whet the appetite.—**o bico**, to speak up, speak out.—**o chambre**, to run away. —**o coração**, to open one's heart to; welcome; to confide in (another).—**o espírito a (alguém)**, to enlighten (another's) understanding.—**o fôgo**, to open fire; to assail.—**o jôgo**, to open the pot (in poker).—**o ôlho**, to keep one's eyes peeled.—**o pulso**, to sprain the wrist. —**os braços**, to welcome with open arms.—**os olhos a (alguém)**, to open (another's) eyes, undeceive, disillusion (him).—**os ouvidos**, to give ear, listen.—**para fora**, to open out on, as a window opens out on the garden.—**passagem**, to force a passage.—**praça**, to make way; to make a place.—**-se**, to open (by itself); to leave, take off.—**-se com (alguém)**, to unbosom oneself to (another). —**-se para o estrangeiro**, to go abroad.—**vaga**, to create a vacancy (as by resignation of one's job).—**via**, to clear the way. **não—o bico**, not to let out a peep. **num e fechar de olhos**, in the twinkling of an eye.

ab-rogação (*f.*) abrogation, repeal.

ab-rogar (*v.t.*) to abrogate, rescind, repeal, void.

ab-rogatório -ria, -tivo -va (*adj.*) abrogative.

abrolhado -da (*adj.*) prickly, thorny.

abrolhal (*m.*) thistle-covered ground.

abrolhar (*v.i.*) to sprout, bud. burgeon.

abrôlho (*m.*) the star thistle (*Centaurea calcitrapa*), c.a. CALCITRAPA, CARDO-ESTRELADO; the puncturevine (*Tribulus terrestris*), c.a. TRÍBULO; (*pl.*, *Mil.*) caltrops; (*Naut.*) underwater rocks; fig., difficulties.

abrolhoso -sa (*adj.*) prickly; full of difficulties.

abronemose (*f.*, *Veter.*) habronemiasis.

abrônia (*f.*) pink sandverbena (*Abronia umbellata*).

abronzeado -da (*adj.*) bronzed, tanned.

abroquelar (*v.t.*) to shield; to protect, defend (-se, oneself).

abrótea (*f.*) the squirrel ling (*Phycis chuss*) and other fishes of this genus, c.a. ABROTE, BROTA, BRÓTOLA, BACALHAU-DO-BRASIL; (*Bot.*) asphodel [= ASFODELO].

abrótono-fêmea (*m.*) cypress lavender cotton (*Santolina chamaecyparissus*).

abrótono-macho (*m.*) old-man wormwood (*Artemisia abrotanum*), c.a. AURÔNIA, ERVA-LOMBRIQUEIRA, ALFA-CINHA-DO-RIO.

abrumado -da (*adj.*) foggy, misty; gloomy.

abrumar (*v.t.*) to envelop as with fog; to darken.

abrunhal (*m.*) a growth of blackthorns.

abrunheiro-bravo (*m.*) the sloe or blackthorn (*Prunus spinosa*), c.a. AMEIXA-BRAVA, ACÁCIA-DOS-ALEMÃES.

abrunheiro-manso (*m.*) garden plum (*Prunus domestica*).

abrunho (*m.*) sloe (fruit of ABRUNHEIRO-BRAVO).

abrupto -ta [ab-rup] (*adj.*) abrupt, steep; sudden, unexpected; precipitate; brusk, blunt.

abrutalhado -da (*adj.*) brutish, coarse.

abrutalhar (*v.t.*) to brutalize; (*v.r.*) to become brutish.

abrutecer (*v.*) = EMBRUTECER, ABRUTALHAR.

absceder (*v.i.*) to become abscessed.

abscesso (*m.*) abscess.

abscissão (*f.*) abscission.

abscissa (*f.*, *Geom.*) abscissa.

absconder (*v.*) = ESCONDER.

absconsa (*f.*, *R.C.Ch.*) absconce.

absenteísmo (*m.*) abstention from voting.

absenteísta (*m.*, *f.*) habitual nonvoter.

ábside (*f.*, *Arch.*) apse; (*Astron.*) apsis.

absintina (*f.*, *Chem.*) absinthin.

absintismo (*m.*, *Med.*) absinthism.

absinto (*m.*) absinthe; common wormwood (*Artemisia absinthium*), c.a. LOSNA, LOSNA-MAIOR, ACINTRO.—**-marítimo**, the maritime wormwood (*A. maritima*).—**-menor**, Roman wormwood (*A. pontica*).

absolto -ta, irreg. p.p. of ABSOLVER.

absolutamente (*adv.*) absolutely; absolutely not.

absolutismo (*m.*) absolutism; despotism.

absolutista (*adj.*; *m.*,*f.*) absolutist.

absoluto -ta (*adj.*) absolute. **Em—!** Absolutely not!

absolver (*v.t.*) to absolve, acquit (**de**, of); to exonerate, excuse, forgive.

absolvição (*f.*), **absolvimento** (*m.*) absolution, acquittal, remission.

absorção (*f.*) absorption; assimilation; engrossment.

absorciômetro (*m.*, *Physics.*) absorptiometer.

absortivo -va (*adj.*) absorptive.

absorto -ta (*adj.*) absorbed; intent; spell-bound; (*m.pl.*) ecstasies.

absorvedor -dora (*adj.*) = ABSORVENTE.

absorvedouro (*m.*) gulf, abyss, whirlpool. Var. ABSORVE-DOIRO.

absorvência (*f.*) absorbency.

absorvente (*adj.*, *m.*) absorbent; absorbing, engrossing.

absorver (*v.t.*) to absorb; to imbibe; to assimilate; to consume; to engulf; to engross, occupy.

abstemia (*f.*) abstemiousness.

abstêmio -mia (*adj.*) abstemious; (*m.*,*f.*) teetotaler.

abstenção (*f.*) abstention, abstinence.

abster-se [78] (*v.r.*) to abstain, refrain (**de**, from); to forbear, desist; to deny oneself.

abstergente (*adj.*; *m.*) abstergent, detergent.

absterger (*v.t.*) to absterge, clean; to purge.

abstersão (*f.*) abstersion, cleansing, purging.

abstinência (*f.*) abstinence; self-denial.

abstinente (*adj.*) abstinent, abstemious; continent; temperate.

abstração (*f.*) abstraction, separation; preoccupation.

abstraído -da (*adj.*) absent-minded; aloof.

abstrair [75] (*v.t.*) to abstract, dissociate; to separate, isolate, detach.—**-se em pensamentos**, to lose oneself in thought.

abstrato -ta (*adj.*) abstract; (*m.*) an abstraction; the abstract. [An abstract is EXTRATO.]

abstruso -sa (*adj.*) abstruse.

absurdez, **-deza**, **-didade** (*f.*) = ABSURDO.

absurdo -da (*adj.*) absurd, ludicrous, preposterous; (*m.*) an absurdity.

abugalhar (*v.t.*) to bug (the eyes).

abuirana (*f.*) "A tree producing gutta percha (*Palaquim gutta*); called SACHACAIMITO in Peru and COQUIMO-COLORADO in Bolivia." [*GBAT*]

abulia (*f.*, *Med.*) abulia.

abúlico -ca (*adj.*) abulic; irresolute.

abumom (*m.*, *Bot.*) a crinum (*C. africanum*).

abuna (*m.*) Tupian name for Jesuit missionaries in early Brazil.

abundância (*f.*) abundance; affluence. **côrno de—**, horn of plenty.

abundante (*adj.*) abundant; rich.

abundar (*v.i.*) to abound (**em**, in, with); to super-abound.

aburria (*f.*) the black-wattled guan (*Aburria aburi*).

abusado -da (*adj.*) impertinent, presumptuous; credulous, superstitious; of a word, poorly employed.

abusador -dora (*adj.*) abusing; (*m.*,*f.*) abuser.

abusão (*f.*) abuse; gross error; fallacy; catachresis.

abusar (*v.t.*) to abuse; to misuse; to maltreat, harm, injure; to deceive; to impose on; to ravish, rape.—**com (alguém)**, to provoke, stir up trouble with (another). —**da paciência de (alguém)**, to try (another's) patience. —**de**, to make ill use of; to take improper advantage of; to outrage.

abusivo -va (*adj.*) abusive (of power, etc.).

abuso (*m.*) abuse, misuse; lie; error, fallacy; importunity, annoyance; outrage, insult; rape.—**de autoridade (poder)**, abuse of authority (power).—**de confiança**, breach of trust; betrayal of confidence.

abutilão (*m.*, *Bot.*) kinds of abutilon, esp. the Brazilian (*A. megapotamicum*) and the redvein (*A. striatum*).

abutinha (*f.*) = CIPÓ-DE-COBRA.

abutre (*m.*) vulture (fig. & lit.).—**-do-egito**, the Egyptian vulture (*Neophron percnopterus*).—**-do-mundo-novo**, the condor (*Vultur gryphys*).—**-negro**, turkey buzzard [= URUBU].

abutua (*f.*) woody tropical vines of moonseed family. specif.: *Abutua rufescens*, which yields the white pareira brava, c.a. ENREDIÇA-AMARGA, PARREIRA-BRAVA, BEJUCO-AMARGO; and *Abutua selloana*, c.a. BAGA-DE-CABOCLO, BUTUA, UVA-SÊCA, UVA-DE-GENTIO.—**-de-batata** = BA-TATA-BRAVA.—**-do-amazonas**, a snailseed (*Cocculus amazonum*).—**-do-rio**, a moonseed vine (*Cissampelos fluminensis*), c.a. PARREIRA-BRAVA-DO-RIO.—**-grande** (—**-preta**,—**-legítima**,—**-da-terra**), a pareiraroot (*Chondodendron platyphyllum*), c.a. BAGA-DA-PRAIA, BATATA-BRAVA, BUTUA, JABOTICABA-DE-CIPÓ, ORELHA-DE-ONÇA, UVA-DO-MATO.—**-miúda**, a snailseed (*Cocculus filipendula*) which yields an edible fruit but whose bitter root is poisonous though used in medicine; also = CIPÓ-DE-COBRA. Var. BUTUA.

abuzinado –**da** (*adj.*) flaring (as the mouth of a trumpet); bell-bottom [trousers].

abuzinar (*v.t.*) to make a din; to honk an automobile horn. Cf. BUZINAR.

A.C. = ANTES DE CRISTO (B.C., Before Christ); also = ANO CORRENTE (current year).

A/C = AO(S) CUIDADO(S) DE, (in care of).

aca (*m.*) stink; (*Bot.*) a lucuma (*L. torta*).

aça (*adj.*) albinic; (*m.,f.*) albino. Cf. SARARÁ.

acabaçado –**da** (*adj.*) gourdlike.

acabadiço –**ça** (*adj.*) tending to end quickly; of short duration; weakly, sickly, broken.

acabado –**da** (*adj.*) complete(d), finished; done; spent; worn-out; exhausted; aged; (*m.*) final touch.

acabador –**dora** (*adj.*) finishing; (*m.,f.*) finisher.

acabadote (*adj.*) of persons, about done for.

acabamento (*m.*) finish(ing); polish(ing); final touch.

acabar (*v.t.*) to end, conclude, terminate, finish; to bring to an end, close, wind up; to put an end to; to kill, destroy; to consume, use up, exhaust; to put finishing touches on, polish, perfect; (*v.i.,v.r.*) to come to an end; to die.—**com**, to end or put an end to.—**de** + an infinitive = to have just + a past participle; *e.g.*, **Êle acaba de matar um homem**, He has just killed a man.—**em**, to end up in; *e.g.*, **Isto acaba em briga**, This will end up in a fight.—**mal**, to end up badly; come to no good; come to grief.—**por**, to end up by (doing something). **Acabe com isso!** Stop that! I have done with it! **Acabo de vê-lo**, I have just seen him. **Acabou-se**, It is all over, finished; that's all, there is no more. **Acabou por comprá-lo**, He finally bought it. **Não há bem que sempre dure, nem mal que nunca se acabe**, It's a long lane that has no turning. **para—com isso (com o assunto)**, to end it (the matter) once for all. **que não acaba mais**, endless.

acabável (*adj.*) finishable, endable, terminable.

acabelar (*v.i.,v.r.*) to grow hair.

acaboclado –**da** (*adj.*) rural, rustic; having the ways, looks, etc. of a CABOCLO.

acaboclar-se (*v.r.*) to become like a CABOCLO (rustic).

acabramar (*v.t.*) to curb (a bull, etc.) by connecting a horn and a front foot with a short rope.

acabrunhado –**da** (*adj.*) crushed, bowed down; grief-stricken; dejected; humbled.

acabrunhador –**dora** (*adj.*) crushing, overwhelming; afflictive; humbling.

acabrunhar (*v.t.*) to afflict; to distress; to crush, humble; to harass; (*v.r.*) to despond.

acaçá (*m.*) an Afro-Brazilian dish popular in Bahia, consisting of a sort of rice and cornmeal cake wrapped in banana leaf; when dissolved in water with sugar it serves as a cooling drink, said to be beneficial to nursing mothers.

acaçalar (*v.t.*) to sharpen (swords, wits).

acacalote (*m.*) = ACALOTE.

acaçapado –**da** (*adj.*) hunched down (as in an easy chair); crouching; squat, dumpy, thickset, low.

acaçapar (*v.t.*) to make low, squat; to crush, flatten; to hide; (*v.r.*) to crouch, squat; to become crushed; to hide.

acacetina (*f.*, *Chem.*) acacetin.

acachaçado –**da** (*adj.*) smelling of CACHAÇA (rum).

acachaçar (*v.t.*) to serve (food) with CACHAÇA; to make

(another) drunk on CACHAÇA; (*v.r.*) to get drunk on CACHAÇA.

acachapado –**da** (*adj.*) = ACAÇAPADO.

acachapar (*v.*) = ACAÇAPAR.

acachar (*v.*) = ACAÇAPAR, ESCONDER.

acachoeirado –**da** (*adj.*) of a river, having falls and rapids.

acachoeirar-se (*v.r.*) of a river, to run to falls and rapids.

acácia (*f.*, *Bot.*) acacia.—**-arábica** (—**-verdadeira**), the babul acacia (*A. arabica*).—**-asiática**, the molucca albizzia (*A. moluccana*).—**-bastarda** (—**-falsa**,—**-pára-sol**), the black locust (*Robinia pseudoacacia*).—**-de-flores-vermelhas**, a rattlebox (*Daubentonia punicea*).—**-do-japão**, pagoda tree (*Sophora japonica*).—**-do-méxico**, an apes-earring (*Pithecellobium albicans*).—**-dos-alemães**, the sloe or blackthorn (*Prunus spinosa*), c.a. ABRUN-HEIRO.—**-meleira** = ESPINHEIRO-DA-VIRGÍNIA (honey locust).—**-mimosa**, pearl acacia (*A. podalyriaefolia*).—**-negra**, the black green-wattle acacia (*A. decurrens mollis*).—**-unha-de-gato**, catclaw acacia (*A. greggi*).

acaciano –**na** (*adj.*) trite, hackneyed, "corny".

acacifar (*v.t.*) to put (something) in a CACIFO (strongbox, drawer, box).

acacina (*f.*) acacin, gum arabic.

acácio (*m.*) a person given to trite utterances.

açacu [ú] (*m.*) sandbox tree (*Hura crepitans*) which has a poisonous sap and yields possumwood.

açacurana (*f.*) a coralbean (*Erythrina glauca*).

açacuzeiro (*m.*) = AÇACU.

acadeirar-se (*v.r.*) to take a chair.

academia (*f.*) academy; scientific, literary or artistic body; college of higher learning.

acadêmia (*f.*) plaster model; academic figure.

academicismo (*m.*) academicism.

acadêmico –**ca** (*adj.*) academic; (*m.,f.*) member of an academy; college student.

academismo (*m.*) academism.

acadimar-se (*v.r.*) to take a liking to.

acadiro (*m.*) the palmyra palm (*Borassus flabellifer*).

acafajestado –**da** (*adj.*) low-down, coarse, vulgar.

acafajestar-se (*v.r.*) to become degraded.

açafata (*f.*) lady-in-waiting.

açafate (*m.*) small open basket.—**-de-ouro**, (*Bot.*) the goldentuft alyssum (*A. saxatile*).—**-de-prata**, the sweet alyssum (*Lobularia maritima*), c.a. ALICE, ESCUDINHA.

acafelar (*v.t.*) to parget; to bolt (a door); to cover up, feign, dissemble.

açaflor (*m.*) = AÇAFROEIRA.

açafrão (*m.*) the color saffron; (*Bot.*) the saffron crocus (plant or flower).—**-agreste** (—**-bravo**) = AÇAFROL.—**-bastardo** (—**-espúrio**), false saffron (*Carthamus tinctorius*), c.a. AÇAFROA.—**-da-índia** (—**-da-terra**), common turmeric (*Curcuma longa*), c.a. AÇAFROEIRA(-DA-ÍNDIA), BATATINHA-AMARELA, GENGIBRE-DOURADA, MANGARA-TAIA.—**-da-primavera**, common crocus (*C. vernus*), c.a. AÇAFROL-DA-PRIMAVERA.—**-do-campo** (—**-do-mato**), a plant of the figwort family (*Escobedia scabrifolia*) from whose roots a saffron dye is extracted.—**-do-outono** (—**-palhinha**) a crocus (*C. autumnalis*), c.a. AÇAFROL-DO-OUTONO, AÇAFROL-PALHINHA.

açafroa (*f.*) = AÇAFRÃO-BASTARDO, CARRAPÊTA.

açafroado –**da** (*adj.*) deep orange-colored; curried [food].

açafroal (*m.*) place growing crocuses.

açafroar (*v.t.*) to color or flavor with saffron; (*v.r.*) to turn pale (as with hate).

açafroeira (*f.*) crocus plant.—**-da-índia** = AÇAFRÃO-DA-ÍNDIA.—**-da-terra** (—**-do-brasil**,—**-indígena**) a night jasmine (*Nyctanthes arbor-tristis*), c.a. ÁRVORE-TRISTE, SONÂMBULA, URUCU.—**-de-pernambuco**, a Brazilian plant (*Melasthanus tinctorius*) whose white flowers yield a saffron-like condiment.

açafroína (*f.*, *Chem.*) crocin.

açafrol (*m.*, *Bot.*) a crocus (*C. clusisi*), c.a. AÇAFRÃO-BRAVO, AÇAFRÃO-AGRESTE, PÉ-DE-BURRO.—**-da-primavera** = AÇAFRÃO-DA-PRIMAVERA.—**-do-outono** = AÇAFRÃO-DO-OUTONO.

acagüete (*m.*) = ALCAGÜETE.

açaí (*m.*) the fruit of the AÇAÍZEIRO, or the tree itself; a cooling drink made from the fruit.

acaiá-açu [ú] (*m.*) = CAJÁ-MANGA.

acaiaca (*m.*, *Bot.*) a Braz. cedrela (*C. brasiliensis*).

açaimar (*v.t.*) to muzzle. Var. AÇAMAR.

açaimo (*m.*) muzzle. Var. AÇAMO.

acaina (*f.*) = AQUÊNIO.

acaipirado -da (*adj.*) like a CAIPIRA (rustic); countrified; timid.

acaipirar-se (*v.r.*) to become like a CAIPIRA (rustic).

açairana [a-i] (*f.*) a shadowpalm (*Geonoma camana*).

acairelar (*v.t.*) to edge with braid.

acaiura [a-i] (*f.*) an astrocaryum palm (*A. aculeatum*).

açaizeiro (*m.*) the assai euterpe palm (*Euterpe oleracea*), c.a. AÇAÍ, JUÇARA.

acajá (*m.*), –jaíba, –jàzeira (*f.*) = CAJÀZEIRA.

acaju [ú] (*m.*) a mahogany-like wood; an old name for the fruit of the CAJU (cashew); (*Bot.*) American muskwood (*Guarea trichilioides*); also = CEDRO-CHEIROSO. **cabelo côr de—**, Titian hair.

acajueiro (*m.*) = CAJUEIRO.

acalantar (*v.*) = acalentar

acalcanhado -da (*adj.*) run-down at the heels (shoes); well-trod (path).

acalcanhar (*v.t.*) to crush with the heel; to tread on (lit. & fig.); (*v.i.*) to walk on one's heels; to run down or over at the heels.

acalentador -dora (*adj.*) lulling.

acalentar (*v.t.*) to hushaby, lull to sleep; to cuddle.

acalento (*m.*) a rocking or lulling to sleep. **cantiga de—**, lullaby.

acalicino -na (*adj.*, *Bot.*) acalycine.

acaliculado -da (*adj.*, *Bot.*) acalyculate.

acálifa (*f.*) the copperleaf (*Acalypha*).

acalmação (*f.*) act of calming, quieting.

acalmado -da (*adj.*) calm(ed), quiet(ed), still(ed).

acalmar (*v.t.*) to calm, tranquilize; to lull, soothe; to still; to allay; (*v.r.*) to grow calm; to quiet down; to subside. Cf. ABONANÇAR.

acalmia (*f.*) lull, respite.

acalorado -da (*adj.*) heated; excited, inflamed.

acalorar (*v.t.*) to warm, heat (up); (*v.r.*) to become heated (as a discussion).

acalote (*m.*) the wood ibis (*Mycteria*), c.a. ACACALOTE, CORVO-AQUÁTICO, MARTINETE-PESCADOR.

acamado -da (*adj.*) sick abed; lying stretched out; (*Geol.*) stratified.

acamar (*v.t.*) to put (someone) to bed; to lay (something) flat or low; to arrange in layers or in windrows; to seat or set (a machine, etc.) on a solid base or bed (as of concrete); (*v.i.*) to fall sick abed; (*v.r.*) to lie down.

açamar (*v.*) = AÇAIMAR.

acamaradar-se (*v.r.*) to become friendly.**—se com**, to associate with (another) as a pal.

açambarcador -dora (*adj.*) monopolizing; (*m.,f.*) monopolizer; profiteer.

açambarcamento (*m.*) act of monopolizing.

açambarcar (*v.t.*) to monopolize; to corner (goods).

açamo (*m.*) = AÇAIMO.

acampamento (*m.*) encampment; camp, bivouac.

acampar (*v.t.*) to camp, encamp, pitch camp.

acampsia (*f.*, *Med.*) acampsia.

acamurçado -da (*adj.*) like chamois.

acamutanga (*f.*) = AJURÚ-ETÊ.

acanã (*f.*) = ACAUÃ.

açanã (*f.*) kinds of waterfowl.

acanáceo -cea (*adj.*, *Bot.*) acanaceous, prickly.

acanalado -da (*adj.*) grooved, fluted.

acanaladura (*f.*) grooves, fluting.

acanalar (*v.t.*) to groove, provide with fluting.

acanalhado -da (*adj.*) coarse, vulgar; ridiculed, insulted.

acanalhador -dora (*adj.*) degrading; (*m.,f.*) one who degrades, coarsens, cheapens (something).

acanalhamento (*m.*) debasement, degradation.

acanalhar (*v.t.*) to debase, degrade (-se, oneself); (*colloq.*) to ridicule, make fun of.

acanati [í] (*m.*) = MÃE-DE-PORCO (a bird).

acanaveado -da (*adj.*) thin, broken, sickly, done in.

acanavear (*v.t.*) to make sick, weak, thin.

acandes (*m.*, *Zool.*) a remora (*Echeneis remora*).

acangatara (*m.*) Indian headdress [= CANITAR.]

acanguçu [çú] (*m.*) a jaguar (*Felis onca*), c.a. CANGUÇU, ONÇA-PINTADA.

acanhado -da (*adj.*) timid, bashful; diffident, restrained; narrow-minded; tight, narrow [space].

acanhamento (*m.*) timidity, shyness; abashment; restraint; diffidence.

acanhar (*v.t.*) to stunt, dwarf; to restrain, restrict; to belittle; to abash; to make ashamed; (*v.r.*) to become bashful, shy, fearful.

acanjarana (*f.*) a kind of jaguar.

acanoado -da (*adj.*) of boards, curled, warped lengthwise.

acantáceo -cea (*adj.*, *Bot.*) acanthaceous; (*f.pl.*) the Acanthaceae.

acantia (*f.*, *Zool.*) the genus Cimex (bedbugs).

acântico -ca (*adj.*) prickly.

acântidas, acântides (*m.pl.*) the Cimicidae (bedbugs and their relatives).

acântino -na (*adj.*, *Bot.*) acanthine, prickly; (*f.*, *Zool.*) acanthin.

acantita (*f.*, *Min.*) acanthite.

acanto (*m.*, *Arch.*) acanthus foliage; (*Bot.*) the genus Acanthus.**—bastardo**, the Scotch cottonthistle (*Onopordum acanthium*).**—bravo** (**—espinhoso,—selvagem**) spiny acanthus (*A. spinosus*).**—mole**, soft acanthus (*A. mollis*), c.a. ERVA-GIGANTE.

acantoado -da (*adj.*) hidden away (as in a corner).

acantoar (*v.t.*) to put in a corner (lit. & fig.); to set aside, separate, isolate; (*v.r.*) to withdraw, isolate oneself.

acantocarpo -pa (*adj.*, *Bot.*) acanthocarpous.

acantocéfalo -la (*adj.*) acanthocephalous; (*m.pl.*) the Acanthocephala (intestinal worms).

acântofe, acântofis (*m.*) the death adder (*Acanthophis antarticum*).

acantolimo (*m.*) the prickly thrift (*Acantholimon*).

acantoma (*f.*, *Med.*) acanthoma.

acantonamento (*m.*, *Mil.*) cantonment, billet.

acantonar (*v.t.*) to billet, quarter (troops).

acantopana (*m.*, *Bot.*) the castor aralia (*Acanthopanax ricinifolium*).

acantopterígios (*m.pl.*) the Acanthopterygii (teleost fishes).

acantose (*f.*, *Med.*) acanthosis.

acanturo (*m.*) surgeonfish (*Acanthurus*).

acanudado -da (*adj.*) tubelike.

ação (*f.*) action, activity, act, deed, feat; battle, engagement; encounter; acting, enacting; share of stock; plot (of a story or play); lawsuit, court action.**—à ordem**, a stock certificate endorsed in blank.**—ao portador**, unregistered stock certificate (payable to bearer).**—de graças**, act of thanksgiving.**—entre amigos**, pool, raffle [= RIFA].**—judicial**, lawsuit.**—liberada**, fully paid-for share of stock.**—nominativa**, registered stock certificate.**—preferencial** (**—de prioridade**), preferred share of stock.**—química**, chemical action.**—reflexa**, reflex action.**—sumária**, (*Law*) summary proceeding or procedure. **intentar, or promover, uma—**, to bring suit. **morto em—** killed in action. **pôr em—**, to put in motion, set going. **raio de—**, range of action. **uma boa—**, a good deed.

acapachar (*v.t.*) to humble, make a CAPACHO (door-mat) of; (*v.r.*) to humble oneself.

acapalti (*m.*) the bigleaf sumpweed (*Iva frutescens*).

acapelar (*v.t.*) to raise whitecaps (referring to the wind); to overwhelm with waves; (*v.r.*) to become covered with whitecaps.

acapitã (*f.*) the yellow-billed cardinal (*Paroaria capitata*).

acapnia (*f.*, *Med.*) acapnia.

acapora (*f.*) marrow, pith; (*Bot.*) elder tree (*Sambucus*); [= SABUGUEIRO.]

acapu [ú] (*m.*) the cabbage angelintree (*Andira inermis* syn. *Vouacapoua americana*) which yields a teak-like, dark chocolate-brown wood, much used for construction work, esp. flooring; prized also for its insect and fire-resisting qualities.

acará (*m.*) a cake of cooked beans fired in DENDÊ-palm oil [= ACARAJÉ]; an egret [= GARÇA-GRANDE]; any of numerous small fresh-water cichlids, esp. of the genus Cichlasoma.**—aia** = VERMELHO (red snapper).**—bandeira**, the scalare (*Pterophyllum scalare*) popular in home aquariums.**—cascudo**, the chanchito (*Cichlasoma facetus*).**—moçó** = CANGULO (triggerfish).

acarajé (*m.*) = ACARÁ.

acaranguejado -da (*adj.*) crab-like.

acarapicu [ú] (*m.*) = CARAPICU.

acarapitanga (*f.*) = VERMELHO (a fish).

acarar (*v.*) = ENCARAR.

acaratinga (*m.*) = GARÇA-GRANDE.

acardia (*f.*, *Med.*) acardia.

acardumar-se (*v.r.*) to shoal; to throng.

acareação (*f.*) confrontation.

acarear (*v.t.*) to bring face to face; to confront (witnesses); to cajole.**—com**, to collate with.

acaríase (*f.*) acariasis, infestation with mites.

acariciador -dora (*adj.*) caressing; flattering; (*m.,f.*) one who caresses or flatters.

acariciamento (*m.*) caressing, etc. See the verb ACARICIAR.

acariciar (*v.t.*) to caress, fondle, cuddle, pet; to cherish; to cajole, flatter; to comfort, console; to touch or stroke lightly (as a pet).—**esperanças**, to cherish hopes.

acariçoba (*f.*, *Bot.*) a pennywort (*Hydrocotyle umbellata*), c.a. ERVA-DO-CAPITÃO.

acaridar-se (*v.r.*) to have charity, compassion, pity (de, for).

acarídeos (*m.pl.*, *Zool.*) the Acarina (mites, ticks).

acarima (*f.*, *Zool.*) the silky tamarin (*Leontocebus rosalia*), c.a. MACACO-LEÃO, MARIQUINA.

acarinhar (*v.t.*) to caress; to cherish; to fondle, pet.

acarino (*m.*) any acarid (mite, tick, etc.).

ácaro (*m.*) acarus, mite, tick.—**da sarna**, itch mite (*Sarcoptes*).—**terrestre**, red mite, chigger (*Trombidium*).

acarofobia (*f.*, *Med.*) morbid dread of the itch.

acaróide (*adj.*, *Zool.*) acaroid. **resina**—, acaroid gum or resin.

acarpelado (*f.*, *Bot.*) acarpelous.

acárpico –ca, **acarpo** –pa (*adj.*, *Bot.*) acarpous.

acarraçar-se (*v.r.*) to stick (a, to) like a CARRAÇA (tick); to importune.

acarrar (*v.i.*,*v.r.*) of cattle, to rest in the shade; of persons, to be still; to sleep (while sick, tired or drunk).

acarretado –da (*adj.*) carted; carried; occasioned.

acarretador –dora (*adj.*) carting; carrying; giving rise to (something); (*m.*) porter.

acarretamento (*m.*), **acarretadura** (*f.*) act of carting, etc.; See the verb ACARRETAR.

acarretar (*v.t.*) to cart; to carry; bear; to bring about, give rise to.—**conseqüências**, to entail consequences.—**lágrimas**, to bring tears.—**razões**, to bring up reasons.

acasalamento (*m.*) act of pairing or mating.

acasalar (*v.t.*) to mate (animals); to match.

acaso (*m.*) casualty, chance; unforeseen event, contingency; stroke of luck (good or bad); fate, hazard; (*adv.*) perchance, perhaps. **ao**—, at random, aimlessly, haphazardly.—**feliz**, lucky break; fluke. **por**—, by chance.

acasquilhar-se (*v.r.*) to spruce up.

acastanhar (*v.t.*) to make (the hair) chestnut-brown.

acastelado –da (*adj.*) castellated, castle-like.

acastelar (*v.t.*) to build or fortify, as a castle.—**-se**, fig., to protect oneself. Cf. ENCASTELAR-SE.

acastelhanado –da (*adj.*) Castilian-like.

acatá (*m.*) plantain banana (*Musa paradisiaca*).

acatado –da (*adj.*) respected, esteemed.

acatador –dora (*adj.*) respectful, regardful.

acatafasia (*f.*) syntactical aphasia.

acataia (*f.*) a medicinal knotweed (*Polygonum antihemmorhoidale*), c.a. CATAIA, ERVA-DO-BICHO, PIMENTA-D'ÁGUA, PERSICÁRIA-MORDAZ; also = CAPITIÇOVA.

acataléctico –ca (*adj.*, *Pros.*) actalectic.

acatalepsia (*f.*, *Med.*) acatalepsia.

acataléptico –ca (*adj.*; *m.*,*f.*) acataleptic.

acatamatesia (*f.*, *Med.*) acatamathesia.

acatamento (*m.*) respect; deference; veneration.

acatápose (*f.*, *Med.*) dysphagia.

acatar (*v.t.*) to respect, esteem, honor, revere; to heed (reason, advice, etc.); to observe (a rule).—**a autoridade**, to respect authority.—**a lei**, to obey the law.

acatarrado –da (*adj.*) affected by catarrh.

acatarroar-se (*v.r.*) to become catarrhed.

acatarsia (*f.*, *Med.*) acatharsia.

acatassolado –da (*adj.*) watered [silk]; kaleidoscopic.

acatassolar (*v.t.*) to water (silk); to fleck with light; to switch, change (color, ideas) rapidly.

acatastasia (*f.*, *Med.*) acatastasia.

acatável (*adj.*) worthy of respect, deserving of regard.

acatechili (*m.*) a finch (*Fringilla mexicana*).

acatingado –da (*adj.*) having a strong smell (as of a goat, or as of certain plants).

acatitar-se (*v.r.*) = AJANOTAR-SE.

acatólico –ca (*adj.*; *m.*,*f.*) non-Catholic (person).

acauã (*m.* or *f.*) the snake-eating laughing hawk (*Herpetotheres c. cachinnans*), c.a. MACAUÃ, MACAGUÁ, MACAÁ, ACANÃ.

acaudalado –da (*adj.*) of rivers, heavy-flowing; of persons, moneyed.

acaudilhar (*v.t.*) to lead, rule, as a CAUDILHO (military leader or chieftain); (*v.r.*) to place oneself under the leadership of a CAUDILHO.

acaule, acaulescente (*adj.*, *Bot.*) acaulescent.

acautelado –da (*adj.*) cautious, wary.

acautelador –dora (*adj.*) cautioning, warning; (*m.*,*f.*) one who warns or cautions.

acautelamento (*m.*) act of warning, forewarning; cautioning.

acautelar (*v.r.*) to caution, warn, forewarn; (*v.t.*) to be wary.—**-se contra**, to safeguard oneself against.—**os interesses da companhia**, to watch out for the company's interests. **Acautele-se!** Watch out!

acavalado –da (*adj.*) astride of; atop of; sitting on top; big (as a horse).

acavalar (*v.t.*) of horses, to serve (cover) mares; to pile (things) up.

acavaleirado –da (*adj.*) astraddle; piled up.

acavaleirar (*v.t.*) to place (a house, etc.) in a commanding position, high up; to pile (things) up.

ACB = AUTOMÓVEL CLUBE DO BRASIL (Brazilian Automobile Club).

acc-, for words formerly spelled with double-c look under ac-.

acebolado –da (*adj.*) like an onion; onion-flavored.

acedência (*f.*) acquiescence.

acedente (*adj.*) acquiescent.

aceder (*v.i.*) to accede, acquiesce; to yield assent to; to become added by way of accession.

acedia (*f.*) sloth; spiritual torpor or apathy. Var. ACÍDIA.

acediamina (*f.*, *Chem.*) acediamine, acetamidine.

acefálico –ca, **acéfalo** –la (*adj.*) acephalous, headless; idiotic.

acefalociste (*m.*, *Med.*, *Zool.*) acephalocyst.—**ramoso**, hydatiform mole.

aceiração (*f.*) clearing away of woods and undergrowth, as for a firebreak or fence line; act of watching, looking on, observing with curiosity.

aceirar (*v.t.*) to acierate, convert into steel; to remove woods and undergrowth, as for a wagon road, fence line or firebreak; to spy, watch, look on, observe with curiosity; to pack figs, raisins, etc. in frails; to engage (someone) for work.

aceiro –ra (*adj.*) of metal, steely; (*m.*) steel bar; firebreak; [*GBAT*: "A wide band of ground between the boundaries of the cacao plantation to facilitate the tasks of overseeing and defending the trees against incursions of animal pests."]; (*pl.*) compass needles.

aceitabilidade (*f.*) acceptability.

aceitação (*f.*) acceptance; approval. **ter**—**na sociedade**, to be accepted socially. **ter boa**—, to meet with approval; find a ready market; be in demand.

aceitador –dora (*adj.*) accepting; *m.*,*f.*) acceptor.

aceitamento (*m.*) = ACEITAÇÃO.

aceitante (*m.*,*f.*) drawee (of a bill of exchange); acceptor; one who accepts (by endorsement) a draft or bill of exchange; (*adj.*) accepting.

aceitar [24] (*v.t.*) to accept; to take (what is offered); to admit, assent to, agree to; to acquiesce in; to accommodate oneself to; to receive, welcome; to accept (a bill of exchange) by endorsement.—**de bom grado**, to accept with pleasure; to welcome.—**por honra da firma**, to agree to something but only because "noblesse oblige". —**um desafio**, to accept a challenge. **Aceita um charuto?** Will you have a cigar?

aceitável (*adj.*) acceptable; admissible.

aceite (*m.*) acceptance (by endorsement) of a draft or bill of exchange.—**em branco**, endorsement in blank; (*adj.*) a popular form of ACEITO.

aceito –ta (*adj.*; *irreg. p.p.* of ACEITAR) accepted. **O livro foi bem**—, The book was well received. **A letra foi**—, The draft was accepted.

aceleração (*f.*) acceleration; haste, speed.—**da gravidade**, (*Physics*) acceleration of gravity.—**da lua**, acceleration of the moon.—**da maré**, priming of the tide.—**do pulso**, (*Med.*) tachycardia.—**das planetas**, acceleration of the planets.—**negativa**, deceleration. **em plena**—, at full speed, at full throttle.

acelerado –da (*adj.*) hasty, quick, rapid, speedy; **em**—, quickened. **passo**—, (*Mil.*) quick step.

acelerador –atriz (*adj.*) accelerating; (*m.*,*f.*) one who, or that which, accelerates; (*m.*, *Chem.*, *Photog.*, *Autom.*) accelerator.

aceleramento (*m.*) = ACELERAÇÃO.

acelerando (*adj.*, *adv.*, *Music*) accelerando.

acelerar (*v.t.*) to accelerate, hasten, speed up; to urge forward; (*v.i.*) to increase in speed.—**o passo**, to quicken one's step.

aceleratório –ria (*adj.*) accelerative.

aceleratriz (*adj.*) fem. of ACELERADOR; (*f.*) accelerative force.

acelerógrafo (*m.*, *Mil.*, *Seismol.*) accelerograph.

acelerômetro (*m.*) accelerometer.

acelga (*f.*) beet, chard.—**-brava**, leaf beet (*Beta cicla*); sea-lavender (*Limonium*), c.a. LIMÔNIO.—**-vermelha**, common beet (*Beta vulgaris*).

acenafteno (*m.*, *Chem.*) acenaphthene.

acenaftileno (*m.*, *Chem.*) acenaphthylene.

acenar (*v.i.*) to beckon; to signal, invite.—**a**, to hold out (hope promise, etc.) to.—**com a cabeça**, to nod (to or toward).—**com a mão**, to signal or beckon with the hand.—**para**, to wave to.—**um taxi**, to hail a cab.

acendalha (*f.*) kindling.

acendedor –**dora** (*adj.*) lighting; igniting; inflaming; (*m.*,*f.*) lighter (person or thing); inciter; inflamer.

acender [24] (*v.t.*) to ignite, kindle, set fire to; to light; to arouse, excite, inflame. [Do not confuse with ASCENDER]. (*v.r.*) to catch (on) fire; to light up; to become incensed.—**um cigarro**, to light a cigarette.—**um fósforo**, to strike a match.—**uma vela a Deus e outra ao diabo**, to double-deal, be two-faced. **Acenda a luz**, Turn on the light.

acendido –**da** (*adj.; reg. p.p.* of ACENDER) lit, ignited, inflamed, glowing. Cf. ACESO.

acendrado –**da** (*adj.*) refined, pure.—**patriotismo**, high patriotism.

acendramento (*m.*) act of cleansing, scouring, purifying, refining.

acendrar (*v.t.*) to scour (with ashes); to scrub; to refine, cleanse, purify.

aceno (*m.*) nod, beckon, wave of the hand, signal with the eyes; a gesture of calling or invitation.

acento (*m.*) accent; accent mark; stress (on a syllable); intonation, modulation (of the voice);—**ortográfico**, grammatical or graphic accent.—**tônico**, phonetic accent.—**prosódico**, prosodic or orthoepic accent.

acentor (*m.*) the genus which includes the hedge sparrow or hedge accentor (*Prunella modularis*).

acentorídeos (*m.pl.*) the Prunellidae (hedge sparrows).

acêntrico –**ca** (*adj.*) excentric.

acentuação (*f.*) accentuation; emphasis, stress.

acentuadamente (*adv.*) emphatically.

acentuado –**da** (*adj.*) accented; stressed; emphatic.

acentuar (*v.t.*) to accentuate, accent; to stress, emphasize, underscore; to enunciate clearly; (*v.r.*) to become accentuated.

acentuável (*adj.*) that can be or should be accentuated or accented.

acepção (*f.*) acceptation (of the sense or meaning of a word or expression); preference. **na plena—da palavra**, in the fullest sense of the word.

acepilhado –**da** (*adj.*) smoothed or dressed with a CEPILHO (plane); polished, finished, perfected.

acepilhador –**dora** (*adj.*) smoothing, dressing; polishing; (*m.*,*f.*) one who, or that which, smoothes, dresses, polishes.

acepilhadura (*f.*) act of planing, smoothing, dressing; wood shavings.

acepilhar (*v.t.*) to smoothe or dress with a CEPILHO (plane); to polish, finish, perfect.

acepipe (*m.*) delicacy, tidbit, dainty; appetizing dish.

acepipeiro –**ra** (*adj.*) fond of tidbits and tasty dishes.

acéquia (*f.*) irrigation ditch or canal.

ácer (*m.*) the genus Acer (maples and box elders).

aceração (*f.*) acieration; steeling; cementation.

aceráceo –**cea** (*adj.*) aceraceous; (*f.*) a maple or box elder; (*f.pl.*) the Aceraceae (maple family).

acerado –**da** (*adj.*) steel; steely; steel-faced.

acerador –**dora** (*adj.*) steelworking; (*m.*) steelworker.

aceragem (*f.*), **aceramento** (*m.*) = ACERAÇÃO.

acerar (*v.t.*) to acierate, convert (iron) into steel; to temper; to toughen; to whet.

aceraria (*f.*) steel mill; cutlery factory.

aceratose, **aceratia** (*f.*, *Med.*) aceratosis.

acerbamente (*adv.*) bitterly, harshly.

acerbidade (*f.*) acerbity.

acerbo –**ba** (*adj.*) bitter; sour; severe, harsh, cruel.

acêrca (*adv.*) near.—**de**, (*prep.*) about, relating to, with respect to, concerning.

acercamento (*m.*) act of nearing or surrounding.

acercar (*v.t.*) to surround; (*v.r.*) to draw near (**de**, **a**, to); to approach; to surround oneself with.

acerdésio (*m.*) = MANGANITA.

acerdol (*m.*, *Pharm.*) acerdol, calcium permanganate.

acerejado –**da** (*adj.*) cherrylike; ripe; oven-brown.

acerejar (*v.t.*) to give a cherry color to; to redden; to polish like a cherry; to brown (in the oven); (*v.i.*,*v.r.*) to turn red.

ácero –**ra** (*adj.*, *Zool.*) acerous.

aceroso –**sa** (*adj.*, *Bot.*) acerose, needle-shaped.

acérrimo –**ma** (*absol. superl.* of ACRE) most bitter, most sour; most acrid.

acertado –**da** (*adj.*) judicious, wise, sensible; having (using, showing) good judgment; right; accurate, correct; well-advised.

acertador –**dora** (*adj.*) adjusting, fitting, righting; (*m.*,*f.*) adjuster, fitter; horse trainer.

acertamento (*m.*) act of hitting the mark, etc. See the verb ACERTAR.

acertar (*v.t.*) to find, hit upon (the right answer, the right way); to hit the mark, the nail on the head; to fit, adjust, make right.—**na loteria**, to pick a prize-winning number in the lottery.—**no alvo**, to hit the bull's-eye.—**o passo**, to get in step.—**o relógio**, to set one's watch. **Acertou!** You're right! You guessed it! **Não acertei com a porta no escuro**, I couldn't find the door in the dark. **Não acertei com o endereço**, I couldn't find the right address. **Quantas palavras você acertou?** How many words did you get right?

acêrto (*m.*) discernment, discretion; rightness; commonsense; skill; a hit (on the target).

acervar (*v.t.*) to heap up.

acervo (*m.*) heap, pile; clutter; property; heritage, inheritance, patrimony. **um—de asneiras**, a lot of nonsense.—**de bens**, or **da herança**, the estate of a decedent.

acérvulo (*m.*) little heap. (pl., *Anat.*, *Med.*) acervulus cerebri, brain sand.

acescência (*f.*) acescence; (*Med.*) stomach acidity.

acescente (*adj.*) acescent.

aceso –**sa** [ê] (*adj.; irreg. p.p.* of ACENDER) lit, lit up; burning; inflamed, excited; flaming, blazing. Cf. ACENDIDO.

acessão (*f.*) accession.

acessibilidade (*f.*) accessibility.

acessional (*adj.*) accessional, additional.

acessível (*adj.*) accessible; approachable; affable.

acesso (*m.*) access, entrance; approach; attack, fit, seizure; outburst; promotion.—**de cólera (fúria, raiva)**, fit of anger, outburst of fury.—**de tosse**, a fit of coughing. **de fácil—**, of easy access. **vias de—a (uma ponte)**, approaches to (a bridge).

acessório –**ria** (*adj.*) accessory; added, additional, extra; (*m.*) accessory, fitting, attachment, spare part; appurtenance.

acetabulado –**da** (*adj.*) cup-shaped.

acetabulária (*f.*, *Bot.*) Acetabularia (green algae).

acetabulífero –**ra** (*adj.*, *Zool.*) acetabuliferous; (*m.pl.*) the Dibranchia (squids, octopuses).

acetabuliforme (*adj.*) acetabuliform, cup-shaped.

acetábulo (*m.*) acetabulum (all senses).

acetabuloso –**sa** (*adj.*) = ACETABULIFORME.

acetacetato (*m.*, *Chem.*) acetoacetate.

acetacético –**ca** (*adj.*) = ACETILACÉTICO.

acetamida (*f.*, *Chem.*) acetamide.

acetamidina (*f.*, *Chem.*) acetamidine.

acetamido (*m.*) = ACETAMIDA.

acetanilida (*f.*), –**do** (*m.*, *Chem.*) acetanilide.

acetar (*v.*) = ACETIFICAR.

acetato (*m.*, *Chem.*) acetate.

aceteno (*m.*) = ETANA.

acético –**ca** (*adj.*) acetic.

acetificação (*f.*) acetification.

acetificar (*v.t.*) to acetify.

acetil-, a combining form of acetyl-.

acetila (*f.*) = ACETILO.

acetilacetona (*f.*, *Chem.*) acetylacetone.

acetilamina (*f.*, *Chem.*) acetylamine.

acetilbenzina (*f.*) = ACETOFENONA.

acetilbenzóico –**ca** (*adj.*) acetylbenzoic.

acetilcarbinol (*m.*, *Chem.*) acetyl carbinol, acetol, methyl ketol.

acetilênico –**ca** (*adj.*) actylenic.

acetileno (*m.*, *Chem.*) acetylene.

acetilógeno (*m.*) acetylene producer.

acetílico –**ca** (*adj.*) = ACÉTICO.

acetilo (*m.*, *Chem.*) = acetyl.

acetilogênio (*m.*) acetylene burner.

acetilsalicílico –ca (*adj.*) acetylsalicylic.
acetimetria (*f.*) acetometry.
acetímetro (*m.*) acetometer.
acetina (*f.*, *Chem.*) acetin.
acetinado –da (*adj.*) satiny; satin-finished.
acetinar (*v.t.*) to make smooth as satin.
acetoacetato (*m.*, *Chem.*) acetoacetate.
acetoacético –ca (*adj.*, *Chem.*) acetoacetic.
acetofenona (*f.*, *Chem.*) acetophenone, phenyl methyl ketone; hypnone.
acetol (*m.*, *Chem.*) acetol.
acetolar (*v.t.*) to acidulate.
acetometria (*f.*) = ACETIMETRIA.
acetômetro (*m.*) = ACETÍMETRO.
acetona (*f.*, *Chem.*) acetone.
acetonaftona (*f.*, *Chem.*) acetonaphthone.
acetonemia (*f.*, *Med.*) acetonemia.
acetônico –ca (*adj.*) acetonic.
acetonilacetona (*f.*, *Chem.*) acetonylacetone.
acetonúria, acetonuria (*f.*, *Med.*) acetonuria.
acetopirina (*f.*, *Chem.*) acetopyrin.
acetoso –sa (*adj.*) sour, vinegary; (*f.*, *Bot.*) garden sorrel (*Rumex acetosa*).
acetoxima [ks] (*f.*, *Chem.*) acetoxime.
acetúrico –ca (*adj.*) aceturic.
acevadar (*v.t.*) to feed CEVADA (barley corn) to animals.
acha (*f.*) a piece of firewood.—**de armas**, poleax.
achacadiço –ça (*adj.*) sickly, given to aches and pains, complaining.
achacar (*v.t.*) to blame, censure; to find fault with; to accuse; to pretend to, lay claim to; to fall sick; (*slang*) to hold up (rob); to panhandle.
achacoso –sa (*adj.*) valetudinarian.
achada (*f.*) a find or act of finding; a plateau.
achadão (*m.*, *colloq.*) an excellent find.
achadiço –ça (*adj.*; *m.*) (something) easy to find.
achado –da (*adj.*) found; discovered; verified; (*m.*) a find; (*colloq.*) bargain; windfall, godsend.—**de vento**, something found whose owner is not known to the finder. **não se dar por**—, to pretend not to understand.
achador –dora (*adj.*) finding, discovering; (*m.,f.*) finder, discoverer.
achadouro (*m.*) place where something is or was found. Var. ACHADOIRO.
achafurdado –da (*adj.*) filthy, dirty as a pig.
achamalotado –da (*adj.*) like camlet.
achamalotar (*v.t.*) to give a smooth, silken, camlet-like surface to.
achamboado –da (*adj.*) coarse, rough; crude.
achamboar (*v.t.*) to bungle, botch; (*v.i.,v.r.*) to grow coarse, vulgar.
achamento (*m.*) a finding or discovery
achanado –da (*adj.*) smooth, level (as the ground); razed; won over; made easy to deal with.
achanar (*v.t.*) to make smooth and level (as the ground); to clear the way; to render tractable; to placate.
achaparrado –da (*adj.*) chunky, thickset, dumpy; stunted.
achaparrar (*v.t.*) to make short or thickset—(from CHAPARRO, dwarf oak); (*v.i.*) to become so.
achaque (*m.*) chronic ailment, esp. of old age; fig., besetting sin. **cheio de**—**s**, full of aches and pains.
achaqueira (*f.*, *colloq.*) form of ACHAQUE.
achaquento –ta (*adj.*) chronically ailing.
achaquilho (*m.*) minor ailment; flaw.
achar (*v.t.*) to find (by chance or by searching); to encounter, meet with; to discover; to hit upon; to deem (que, that); to feel (que, that); (*v.r.*) to be; to feel or believe oneself to be; to find oneself (em, in; com, with). —**bom**, to consider desirable, deem good.—**direito**, to deem (it) right.—**graça em**, to find (it) amusing.—**o fio da meada**, to find a clue.—**para si**, to judge for oneself.— **por acaso**, to hit upon, come across by chance.—**que dizer**, to have something to say (in criticism of).—**que não**, to think not.—**que sim**, to think so.—**se em jôgo**, to be at stake.—**ruim**, to be displeased. **Acha-se aqui**, Here it is. **Acho graça nisso**, I think that's funny. **Não acho grande coisa**, I don't think much of it.
acharoar (*v.t.*) to paint with CHARÃO (lacquer).
achatadela (*f.*, *colloq.*) a flattening out or down; a flooring (in an argument).
achatadura (*f.*), **achatamento** (*m.*) act of flattening.
achatar (*v.t.*) to flatten, squash; (*colloq.*) to squelch.
achavascado –da (*adj.*) coarse, rough, crude.
achavascar (*v.t.*) to bungle; to disfigure; to coarsen;

(*v.r.*) to become coarse, rough-mannered.
achega (*f.*) an advance of money; subsidy, subvention; grant; help; small extra profit or income; supplementary material.
achegado –da (*adj.*) close; kin.
achegar [17a] (*v.t.*) to bring (draw) near or together;—**-se** (a, para, de) to approach, get closer to.—**-se a uma pessoa influente**, to get close to an influential person. **Achegue-se a mim**, Come close(r) to me.
achego [ê] (*m.*) = ACHEGA.
achicanar (*v.*) = CHICANAR.
achicar (*v.t.*) to bail out (a boat); to swab.
achinado –da (*adj.*) Chinese-like
achincalhação (*f.*) act of scoffing or ridiculing.
achincalhador –dora (*adj.*) ridiculing; (*m.,f.*) one who ridicules.
achincalhamento (*m.*) = ACHINCALHAÇÃO.
achincalhar (*v.t.*) to scoff at, mock, ridicule.
achincalhe (*m.*) = ACHINCALHAÇÃO.
achinesado –da (*adj.*) Chinese-like
achinesar (*v.t.*) to make Chinese-like (as the eyes).
achiota (*f.*) fruit of the ACHIOTE, from whose pulp a yellowish-red dyestuff is extracted.
achiote (*m.*) the anatto tree (*Bixa orellana*).
achite (*m.*) catigua bitterwood (*Trichilia catigua*).
achoar (*v.t.*) to tread on, step on.
achocalhado –da (*adj.*) provided with a cowbell.
achocolatado –da (*adj.*) chocolate-like.
achouriçado –da (*adj.*) resembling CHOURIÇO (smoked sausage). Var. ACHOIRIÇADO.
achumbar (*v.t.*) to render leaden; (*v.r.*) of the atmosphere, to grow heavy.
aciacatura (*f.*, *Mus.*) acciaccatura.
aciano (*m.*, *Bot.*) the mountain bluet (*Centaurea montana*), c.a. CIANO, ESCOVINHA.
acianoblepsia (*f.*, *Med.*) acyanopsia.
acibara (*f.*) = AGAVE.
acicatar (*v.t.*) to spur; to prod; to incite; to "needle".
acicate (*m.*) spur, goad; fig., incentive.
acíclico –ca (*adj.*) acyclic; (*Chem.*) aliphatic.
acícula (*f.*) acicula; (*Zool.*) aciculum.
aciculado –da (*adj.*) aciculate.
acicular (*adj.*) acicular.
acidação (*f.*) acidification.
acidade (*f.*) acidity.
acidado –da (*adj.*) acid.
acidalbumina (*f.*, *Biochem.*) acid albumine, albuminate.
acidar (*v.t.*) to acidify.
acidável (*adj.*) acidifiable.
acidemia (*f.*, *Med.*) acidemia.
acidência (*f.*) accidency, fortuitousness.
acidentação (*f.*) unevenness (of topography).
acidentado –da (*adj.*) of ground surface, rugged, rough, bumpy, broken; of a trip, eventful, adventuresome. **carro**—, a car involved in an accident. **uma vida**—, a checkered career, an adventurous life; (*m.,f.*) victim of an accident.
acidental (*adj.*) accidental; fortuitous.
acidentalidade (*f.*) accidentality.
acidentalismo (*m.*, *Med.*) accidentalism.
acidentalista (*adj.*, *m.,f.*) accidentalist.
acidentar (*v.t.*) to make (topography) accidented, irregular (as by an earthquake); to provide (as a painting) with sharp contrasts; to make a sudden change (as in plans); to injure accidentally.
acidentável (*adj.*) liable to accident.
acidente (*m.*) accident, disaster, mishap, casualty; mischance; (*Phys. Geog.*) accident, irregularity; (*Gram.*) accident; (*Med.*) unfavorable or unexpected symptom; (*colloq.*) epileptic fit; stroke; faint.—**artificial**, man-made changes in the earth's surface.—**de tiro**, shooting accident.—**de trabalho**, industrial accident.—**natural**, natural changes in the earth's surface.—**primário**, (*Med.*) initial symptom.—**sérico**, (*Med.*) serum sickness.— **terapêutico**, therapeutic accident.—**terminal**, (*Med.*) terminal accident.—**vacinal**, (*Med.*) vaccinal accident. **por**—, by accident.
acidez [ê] (*f.*) acidity, acidness; sourness, tartness.—**de estômago**, stomach acidity, heartburn.
acídia (*f.*) = ACEDIA.
acídico –ca (*adj.*, *Petrog.*) acid, persilicic.
acidífero –ra (*adj.*) acidiferous.
acidificação (*f.*) acidification.
acidificante (*adj.*) acidifying; (*m.*) acidifier.

acidificar (*v.t.*) to acidify.
acidimetria (*f.*, *Chem.*) acidimetry.
acidímetro (*m.*, *Chem.*) acidimeter.
ácido –**da** (*adj.*; *m.*) acid.—**acético**, acetic acid.—**acrílico**, acrylic acid.—**adípico**, adipic acid; fatty acid.—**arsênico**, arsenic acid.—**arsenioso**, arsenious acid.—**benzóico**, benzoic acid.—**bórico**, boric acid.—**butírico**, butyric acid.—**carbólico**, carbolic acid.—**carbônico**, carbonic acid.—**ciânico**, cyanic acid.—**cianídrico**, hydrocyanic acid.—**cítrico**, citric acid.—**clorídrico**, hydrochloric acid.—**cresílico**, cresylic acid.—**crômico**, chromic acid.—**esteárico**, stearic acid.—**fixo**, fixed acid.—**fluorídrico**, hydrogen fluoride.—**fórmico**, formic acid.—**fosfórico**, phosphoric acid.—**graxo**, fatty acid.—**lático**, lactic acid.—**maléico**, maleic acid.—**muriático**, muriatic acid.—**nítrico**, nitric acid.—**oléico**, oleic acid.—**oxálico**, oxalic acid.—**péctico**, pectic acid.—**perclórico**, perchloric acid.—**pícrico**, picric acid.—**prússico**, prussic acid.—**salicílico**, salicylic acid.—**selenídrico**, hydrogen selenide.—**silícico**, silicic acid.—**sulfídrico**, hydrogen sulphide.—**sulfônico**, sulphonic acid.—**sulfúrico**, sulphuric acid, oil of vitriol.—**tânico**, tannin.—**tartárico**, tartaric acid.—**úrico**, uric acid.
acidófilo –**la** (*adj.*, *Biol.*) acidophilic.
acidose (*f.*, *Med.*) acidosis.
acidósico –**ca** (*adj.*) acidotic.
acidosteófito (*m.*) acidosteophyte.
acidulação (*f.*) acidulation.
acidulado –**da** (*adj.*) acidulous.
acidular (*v.t.*) to acidulate.
acídulo –**la** (*adj.*) acidulous.
aciesia (*f.*, *Med.*) acyesis.
aciforme (*adj.*) shaped like a needle.
aciganado –**da** (*adj.*) gypsy-like.
acima (*adv.*) above, overhead, aloft; of a higher rank or order; on high; (*prep.*) —**de**, on top of; atop of; above, higher than, more than, superior to, beyond. **abaixo e**—, up and down; (*interj.*) Upward! **Acima, corações, acima!** Lift up your hearts!
acinacifólio –**lia** (*adj.*, *Bot.*) acinacifolius.
acinaciforme (*adj.*, *Bot.*) acinaciform.
acinário –**ria** (*adj.*, *Bot.*) acinarious; (*f.*) a sea grape; gulfweed.
acinesia (*f.*, *Med.*) akinesia.
acinético –**ca** (*adj.*) akinesic.
acineto (*m.*) a genus (*Acineta*) of epiphytic orchids.
aciniforme (*adj.*) aciniform.
ácino (*m.*, *Bot.*, *Anat.*) acinus.
acinoso –**sa** (*adj.*) acinose, acinous.
acinte (*adv.*) purposely, deliberately, intentionally, with premeditation; spitefully; (*m.*) premeditated act, esp. a malevolent one; a spiteful taunt.
acintoso –**sa** (*adj.*) spiteful, malevolent; of a remark, pointed; nasty; deliberately malicious.
acinzar (*v.*) & derivs. = ACINZENTAR & derivs.
acinzentado –**da** (*adj.*) ashen, grayish.
acinzentar (*v.t.*) to make ash-colored; (*v.r.*) to turn ashen.
acionabilidade (*f.*) liability to court action.
acionado –**da** (*adj.*) charged to appear in court; of a speech, accompanied by suitable gestures; (*m.pl.*) speaker's gestures.
acionador –**dora** (*adj.*) moving, actuating; suing; incorporating; (*m.,f.*) mover; driver; suer; incorporator.
acionamento (*m.*) action; (*Mach.*) drive.
acionar (*v.t.*) to actuate, set in motion; (*Mach.*) to drive; (*Law*) to sue; to form a stock company; (*v.i.*) to gesticulate.—**um adversário**, to sue a rival.—**uma máquina**, to drive a machine.
acionável (*adj.*, *Law*) liable to court action.
acionista (*m.,f.*) shareholder, stockholder.
acipênser (*m.*) the sturgeon (*Acipenser*).
acipitrídeos (*m.pl.*, *Zool.*) the Falconidae.
acirrado –**da** (*adj.*) exasperated, irritated, annoyed; obstinate, contumacious.
acirramento (*m.*) incitement, irritation, provocation, exasperation.—**de ódios**, stirring up of hatreds.
acirrante (*adj.*) exasperating, provoking; stimulating (to the appetite); (*m.*) an apéritif.
acirrar (*v.t.*) to incite, provoke, stir up; to irritate; to exasperate, infuriate, annoy; to embitter; to stimulate; (*v.r.*) to become exasperated, annoyed, infuriated.
acisa (*f.*) excise tax.
acistia (*f.*, *Med.*) acystia.
aclamação (*f.*) acclamation.

aclamar (*v.t.*) to acclaim, applaud; to shout welcome to; to hail; to proclaim (ruler); to declare; to elect by acclamation; to cheer for.
aclaração (*f.*) elucidation.
aclarador –**dora** (*adj.*) elucidative; (*m.,f.*) elucidator.
aclaragem (*f.*) clarification (of wine).
aclaramento (*m.*) = ACLARAÇÃO.
aclarar (*v.t.*) to light up, illuminate; to make clear, elucidate, clarify, explain; (*v.r.*) to become clear.
aclasto –**ta** (*adj.*, *Optics.*) aclastic.
aclerizar-se (*v.r.*) to become a priest or like one.
aclidiano –**na** (*adj.*, *Anat.*) acleidian.
aclimação (*f.*) acclimation.
aclimado –**da** (*adj.*) acclimated.
aclimamento (*m.*) acclimatement, acclimation.
aclimar, aclimatar, aclimatizar (*v.t.*) to acclimate; acclimatize; to habituate; (*v.r.*) to accustom oneself (**a**, to); to become acclimated.
aclínico –**ca** (*adj.*, *Physics.*) aclinic.
aclise (*f.*) vanilla leaf (*Achlys*).
aclivado –**da** (*adj.*) acclinate.
aclive (*adj.*) acclivous, sloping upward; (*m.*) acclivity, upward slope; hillside.
aclividade (*f.*) acclivity.
aclivoso –**sa** (*adj.*) acclivous, acclivitous.
acloroblepsia (*f.*, *Psychol.*) achloropsia.
aclorofiláceo –**cea** (*adj.*, *Bot.*) achlorophyllous.
acme (*f.*) acme.
acméia (*f.*) a genus of limpets (*Acmaea*).
acmela (*f.*) = AGRIÃO-DO-PARÁ.
acmena (*f.*) lillipilli tree (*Acmena*).
acmita (*f.*, *Min.*) acmite.
acne (*f.*, *Med.*) acne.—**mentagra**, sycosis.—**caparrosa** (—**eritematosa**,—**rosácea**) acne rosacea.—**sebácea concreta**, acneiform epithelioma.—**sifilítica**, a pustulous syphiloderm.—**vulgar**, common acne [= ESPINHAS].
acnemia (*f.*, *Med.*) acnemia.
acnisto (*m.*) wild tobacco (*Acnistus*).
aço (*m.*) steel; an albino [= AÇA]; (*colloq.*) booze [= CACHAÇA].—**ácido**, acid steel.—**austenítico**, austenitic steel.—**autotemperante**, self-hardening steel.—**Bessemer**, Bessemer steel.—**de cadinho**, crucible steel.—**ao carbono**, carbon steel.—**de cementação**, casehardening steel.—**ao cromo**, chrome steel.—**elétrico**, electric steel.—**de ferramentas**, tool steel.—**fundido**, cast steel.—**hipereutectóide**, hyper-eutectoid steel.—**inoxidável**, stainless steel.—**ao manganês**, manganese steel.—**de molas**, spring steel.—**ao molibdênio**, molybdenum steel.—**ao níquel**, nickel steel.—**padrão**, standard steel.—**rápido**, high-speed steel.—**ao silício**, silicon steel.
acobardado –**da** (*adj.*) cowardly; fearful; timid. Var. ACOVARDADO.
acobardamento (*m.*) cowardice, pusillanimity. Var. ACOVARDAMENTO.
acobardar (*v.t.*) to cow, intimidate, frighten; to unnerve; to daunt, discourage; (*v.r.*) to lose courage; become cowardly. Var. ACOVARDAR.
acobertado –**da** (*adj.*) covered; protected; hidden.
acobertar (*v.t.*) to cover; to protect; to disguise, conceal; to dress.
acobilhar (*v.*) = ACOVILHAR.
acobrear (*v.t.*) to render coppery.
açoca (*f.*, *Bot.*) common saraca (*S. indica*).
acocar (*v.t.*) to pet; = ACOCORAR.
acochar (*v.t.*) to lay, squeeze and twist together (strands of a rope or cable); to place or pack (objects) tightly together; to compress, press upon, squeeze in (as the belly with a belt); to twist; (*v.r.*) to tighten one's belt; to crouch.
acocorado –**da** (*adj.*) squatting; crouching.
acocorar (*v.t.*, *v.r.*) to squat (down), crouch.
açodado –**da** (*adj.*) precipitate.
açodamento (*m.*) precipitation, rush.
açodar (*v.t.*) to urge on, drive on; (*v.r.*) to hasten.
açofeifa (*f.*) jujube (the fruit), c.a. JUJUBA.—-**maior**, the common jujube or Chinese date tree (*Zizyphus jujuba*), c.a. ANÁFEGA, JUJUBEIRA.
açofeifeira (*f.*) jujube tree, c.a. JUJUBEIRA.
acognosia (*f.*) materia medica.
acografia (*f.*) acology.
acogulado –**da** (*adj.*) heaped up (as grain in a measure).
acogular (*v.t.*) to heap up (as grain in a measure), fill to overflowing.
açoiaba (*f.*) Brazilian Indian feather mantle.

acoimador –dora (*adj.*) fining; punishing; (*m.,f.*) one who fines or punishes.
acoimamento (*m.*) act of fining; amount of damages payable; punishment.
acoimar (*v.t.*) to fine, esp. for property damage; to punish; to accuse, criticize, condemn; (*v.i.*) to take revenge for injury.
acoína (*f., Pharm.*) acoin(e).
acoirelar (*v.t.*) to divide (land) into COIRELAS (narrow strips for planting).
açoita-cavalos (*m.*) the common whiptree (*Luhea divaricata*), c.a. IVANTIJI. Var. AÇOUTA-CAVALOS.
açoitador –dora (*adj.*) whipping, etc. See the verb AÇOITAR; (*m.,f.*) whipper, etc.; See the verb. Var. AÇOUTADOR.
acoitar (*v.t.*) to harbor, shelter, give asylum to; (*v.r.*) to seek shelter. Var. ACOUTAR.
açoitar (*v.t.*) to whip, lash, thrash, flog, scourge. Var. AÇOUTAR.
açoite (*m.*) whip, lash; whipping, lashing; a smack on a child's bottom. Var. AÇOUTE.
açoiteira (*f.*) short whip; whip lash. Var. AÇOUTEIRA.
acolá (*adv.*) there, over there, way over there.
acolchetar (*v.t.*) to fasten with a COLCHETE (hook-and-eye or other clasp); to provide (a dress) with the same.
acolchoadeira (*f.*) quilter.
acolchoadinho (*m.*) a light quilted coverlet, as for a baby.
acolchoado –da (*adj.*) quilted; (*m.*) any quilted bedcover.
acolchoador –deira (*adj.*) quilting; (*m.,f.*) quilter.
acolchoar (*v.t.*) to fill, pad, or line, as a quilt; to stitch or sew, as quilts.
acolhedor –dora (*adj.*) cordial, heartwarming. um sorriso—, inviting smile. (*m.,f.*) one who greets or welcomes.
acolher (*v.t.*) to receive, accept, take in; to welcome; to greet; to shelter, protect, harbor; (*v.r.*) to take shelter.
acolherar (*v.t.*) to harness together; (*v.r.*) to tie oneself to another.
acolhido –da (*adj.*) given asylum; sheltered; welcomed; (*f.*) = ACOLHIMENTO.
acolhimento (*m.*) reception; welcome; shelter, asylum, ter bom—, to be well-received.
acolia (*f., Med.*) acholia.
acolitar (*v.t.*) to assist (a priest) as an acolyte; (*v.i.*) to serve as an acolyte.
acolitato (*m.*) acolythate.
acólito (*m.*) acolyte; attendant; altar-boy; assistant; henchman.
acologia (*f.*) acology.
acolúria, acoluria (*f., Med.*) acholuria.
acolúrico –ca (*adj.*) acholuric.
acomadrar-se (*v.r.*) of a woman, to become a COMADRE to another; by ext., to become her close friend.
acometedor –dora (*adj.*) attacking, assailing, aggressive; (*m.,f.*) assailant, aggressor; entrepreneur.
acometer (*v.t.,v.i.*) to attack, assail, assault; (*v.t.*) to provoke a fight; to undertake (something).
acometida (*f.*), acometimento (*m.*) unexpected attack; aggression; onslaught; onset (of a disease); risky undertaking or commitment.
acomia (*f.*) acomia, baldness.
acômico –ca (*adj.*) acomous, bald.
acomodação (*f.*) accommodation; adaptation; adjustment; comfortable lodging; (*Physiol.*) accommodation of the eye.
acomodadiço –ça (*adj.*) accommodative.
acomodado –da (*adj.*) suitable, fit; adapted.
acomodamento (*m.*) comprise; reconciliation; accommodation.
acomodar (*v.t.*) to accommodate; to make comfortable; to suit, fit, adapt; to harmonize, adjust, settle; to lodge; (*v.r.*) to lodge oneself; to retire to one's quarters; to adapt oneself; to withdraw from a lawsuit.
acomodatício –cia (*adj.*) accommodating.
acomodatismo (*m.*) willingness to adjust to any situation; want of positive opinions or attitudes; indifference.
acomodável (*adj.*) accommodable.
acompadrado –da (*adj.*) on intimate terms (with); (*m.*) intimate friendship, close association.
acompadrar (*v.t.*) to make a COMPADRE or close friend of; —se com, to become very close to.
acompanhadeira (*f.*) woman companion; accompanist.
acompanhador –dora (*adj.*) accompanying; (*m.,f.*) companion; escort, (*Music*) accompanist.
acompanhamento (*m.*) retinue, escort, entourage;

(*Music*) accompaniment.
acompanhante (*m.,f.*) escort; (*adj.*) escorting.
acompanhar (*v.t.*) to accompany (all senses); to escort; to keep up with.—ao piano, to accompany at the piano. —de perto, to follow closely.
acompridar (*v.t.*) to stretch, make longer; (*v.r.*) to stretch out.
aconchavar (*v.*) = CONCHAVAR.
aconchear (*v.t.*) to cup (the hands).
aconchegar [17a] (*v.t.*) to bring close together; to ensconce; (*v.r.*) to huddle together; to snuggle, cuddle up.
aconchego [ê] (*m.*) comfort; convenience; shelter.
acôncias (*f.pl.*) Acontias (a genus of limbless lizards).
acondicionação (*f.*) = ACONDICIONAMENTO.
acondicionado –da (*adj.*) packed; packaged, wrapped; arranged; preserved.
acondicionador –dora (*adj.*) packaging; wrapping; packing; (*m.,f.*) packer.
acondicionamento (*m.*) —de mercadorias, packing of goods (for shipment).
acondicionar (*v.t.*) to package; to pack (goods) for shipment; to protect from spoilage. Cf. CONDICIONAR.
acôndilo –la (*adj., Anat.*) acondylous, jointless.
acondimentar (*v.*) = CONDIMENTAR.
acondroplasia (*f., Med.*) achondroplasia.
acônico –ca (*adj., Chem.*) aconic.
aconina (*f., Chem.*) aconine.
aconítico –ca (*adj., Chem.*) aconitic.
aconitina (*f., Chem.*) aconitin(e).
acônito (*m., Bot.*) aconite monkshood (*Aconitum napellus*).
aconselhadeira, fem. of ACONSELHADOR.
aconselhado –da (*adj.*) prudent, heedful. mal—, ill-advised.
aconselhador –deira (*adj.*) counseling; (*m.,f.*) counselor.
aconselhar (*v.t.*) to counsel, advise; to admonish; (*v.r.*) to seek counsel; to take counsel.
aconselhável (*adj.*) advisable; expedient. não—, inadvisable, not wise.
aconsoantar (*v.t.*) to render (verses) consonous or symphonious.
acontecer (*v.i.*) to happen, chance, occur; to befall, betide; to come about, come to pass; to turn out, eventuate. Aconteça o que—, Come what may. acontece que, it (so) happens that. Aconteceu eu estar ali, I chanced to be there. conforme aconteceu ao pai dêle, as happened to his father. como geralmente acontece, as generally happens; as is usually the case. Êle diz que faz e acontece, He talks big. Que lhe aconteceu? What happened to him? [But for What became of him? one would say Que fim levou êle?]
acontecido –da (*adj.*) that occurred; (*m.*) something that happened, an occurrence, an incident.
acontecimento (*m.*) a happening; event.
aconurese (*f., Med.*) aconuresis.
acópico –ca (*adj., Med.*) acopic.
acoplador (*m., Elec.*) coupler.—variável, vario-coupler.
acoplamento (*m., Elec.*) coupling.—capacitativo, capacitive coupling.—direto, direct coupling.—indutivo, inductive coupling.
acoplar (*v.t.*) to couple (circuits and wires).
ácopo –pa (*adj.*) acopic, relieving weariness; (*m., Med.*) a restorative or anodyne to relieve fatigue.
açor [açôres] (*m.*) goshawk, falcon (*Accipiter*).
açorar (*v.t.*) to arouse passion in.
acorçoar (*v.*) = ACOROÇOAR.
acorcovar (*v.*) = CORCOVAR.
açorda (*f.*) panada (bread boiled and flavored); fig., a milquetoast, milksop.
acordado –da (*adj.*) awake, wide-awake; fig., attentive, watchful; recollected; harmonious, in tune; in accord.
acordamento (*m.*) an awakening or rousing.
acordante (*adj.*) harmonious.
acôrdão [-ãos] (*m., Law*) collective judgment or sentence (of a court of appeals).
acordar (*v.t.,v.i.*) to awake(n), wake (up), rouse; (*v.t.*) to arouse, excite, stir up, call forth; (*v.i.*) to accord with, agree with; (*v.r.*) to remember; to agree.
acorde (*adj.*) harmonious, concordant; (*Music*) in tune; (*m., Music*) chord.
acordeão (*m.*) accordion [= SANFONA, HARMÔNICA; in So. Braz. = GAITA (DE FOLES)].
acordeonista (*m.,f.*) accordionist.
acôrdo (*m.*) accord, agreement, covenant, treaty; har-

mony, unison; good sense.—**comercial**, commercial treaty.—**de credores**, creditors' composition.—**financeiro**, financial treaty.—**trabalhista**, labor agreement. **chegar a (entrar em, vir a)**—, to come to terms; to reach an agreement. **De**— !Agreed! **de**—**com**, according to; in agreement with. **de comum**—, by common consent; with one accord; **pôr de**—, to reconcile.
acordoar (v.) = ENCORDOAR.
Açôres (m.pl.) the Azores.
acoria (f., Med.) acoria, insatiable hunger.
açoriano –na (adj.; m.,f.) Azorian.
acornado –da (adj.) horn-shaped.
ácoro (M., Bot.) a sweetflag (Acorus calamus), c.a. CÁLAMO-AROMÁTICO.—-**bastardo** (—-falso), the yellow-flag iris (iris pseudacorus), c.a. LIRIO-AMARELO-DOS-CHARCOS.—-**gramíneo**, Japanese sweetflag (Acorus aramineus).
Acoroá (m.,f.) = ACROÁ.
acoroçoado –da (adj.) heartened, encouraged, hopeful. Var. ACORÇOADO.
acoroçoador –dora (adj.) heartening, encouraging; (m.,f.) one who or that which heartens, encourages, animates, inspires. Var. ACORÇOADOR.
acoroçoar (v.t.) to encourage, inspire. Var. ACORÇOAR.
acorrentado –da (adj.) in chains; enslaved.
acorrentamento (m.) enchaining.
acorrentar (v.t.) to chain, enchain; to enslave.
acorrer (v.i.) to gather, come together; to run (go) to the aid of (someone) or to the scene of (an accident or the like); to take refuge.
acorrilhar (v.t.) to place in, or drive into, a corner.
acortinar (v.t.) to curtain.
acoruchar (v.t.) to peak (as a roof).
acosmismo (m.) acosmism.
acossador –dora (adj.) harassing; (m.,f.) one who harasses, harries, persecutes, hunts down.
acossar (v.t.) to chase, hunt; to pursue, hound, harry, harass; to goad, badger; to beset. **acossado pela necessidade, pela fome**, harassed by want, by hunger.
acostar (v.i.) to come alongside (a, of); to run aground; (v.t.) to place next to; to attach to; (v.r.) to lean back (on, against, upon).
acostumado –da (adj.) accustomed; customary.
acostumar (v.t.) to accustom, habituate (a, to);—**-se a**, to get used to.—**mal**, to spoil, pamper.
açotéia (f.) roof terrace [= SOTÉIA].
acotiar (v.t.) to frequent; to do (something) daily.
acotiledone (f., Bot.) acotyledon.
acotoar (v.t.) to cover with lint or dust.
acotonar-se (v.r.) to become fuzzy (as a peach).
acotovelado –da (adj.) elbowed; elbow-shaped.
acotovelador –dora (adj.) elbowing; jogging, nudging; (m.,f.) elbower.
acotoveladura (f.) nudge or jog with the elbow.
acotovelamento (m.) a nudging with the elbow.
acotovelar (v.t.) to nudge, poke, jog (with the elbow); (v.r.) to elbow (jostle) one another.
açougada (f.) loud shouts and curses.
açougue (m.) meat market, butcher shop; slaughter house.—-**de-Vênus**, brothel.
açougueiro (m.) butcher; (colloq.) clumsy surgeon.
açoutar (v.) = AÇOITAR.
açoute (m.) = AÇOITE.
acovardar (v.) = ACOBARDAR.
acovilhar (v.t.) to shelter, as in a den.
Acrá (m.,f.) = ACROÁ.
acracia (f.) acracy, anarchy; acratia, impotence; acrasia, intemperance.
acrânio –nia (adj.) acranial.
acraniota (adj.) acraniate.
acrasia (f., Med.) acrasia.
acraturese (f., Med.) acraturesis.
acre (adj.) acrid, biting, bitter; acrimonious, severe, harsh; (m.) a measure of land.
acreano –na (adj.; m.,f.) (person) of the territory of Acre, in Brazil.
acreditado –da (adj.) believed, credited; worthy of confidence; accredited; recognized by a foreign power (as an ambassador).
acreditar (v.t.) to believe; to accredit, provide with credentials; to place to the credit of; (v.i.) to believe.—**em**, to trust, believe in, put faith in. **ao que se acredita**, according to general belief. **Dito, ninguem acredita!** You wouldn't believe it if I told you! **Não acredito nisso,** I

don't believe it.
acreditável (adj.) believable, credible.
acre-doce (adj.) = AGRIDOCE.
acrescência (f.) enlargement; accretion.
acrescentador –dora (adj.) enlarging; (m.,f.) one who, or that which, enlarges or betters.
acrescentamento (m.) enlargement, increase, addition [= ACRÉSCIMO]; (pl.) betterments; improvements.
acrescentar (v.t.) to enlarge.—**a**, to add to.
acrescentável (adj.) susceptible of increase.
acrescente (adj., Bot.) accrescent.
acrescento (m.) something added.
acrescer (v.t.) to increase, enlarge, add to; (v.i.) to increase, be added. **acresce que**, furthermore, furthermore.
acrescido –da (adj.) added to, increased; (m.) increase; annex; (pl.) additions, accretions.
acrescimento (m.) additament, growth, increase.
acréscimo (m.) increase, addition.
acriançado –da (adj.) like a child; childish.
acridez [ê], **acridão** (f.) acridity; acrimony.
acrídia (f.) grasshopper, locust.
acridiano –na (adj.) acridian.
acrídidas (m.,pl.) the Acrididae (locusts, grasshoppers).
acridina (f., Chem.) acridin(e).
acridínico –ca (adj.) acridinic, acridic.
acrídio –dia (adj.; m.) acridian.
acridófago –ga (adj.) acridophagous; (m.,f.) locust-eater.
acridona (f., Chem.) acridone.
acrilato (m., Chem.) acrylate.
acrílico –ca (adj.) acrylic.
acrimônia (f.) acrimony, harshness.
acrimonioso –sa (adj.) acrimonious.
acrisia, acrise (f., Med.) acrisia.
acrisolado –da (adj.) purified, refined.
acrisolador –dora (adj.) purifying, refining; (m.,f.) refiner, purifier.
acrisolar (v.t.) to refine, purify; to cleanse.
acríssimo –ma (absol. superl. of ACRE) most sour; most acrid.
acrítico –ca (adj., Med.) acritical.
acro –cra (adj.) brittle, fragile; also = ACRE.
Acroá (m.,f.) an Indian of the Acroá, of the Central Ge family, who were settled on the Corrente River in the State of Goiás; (adj.) pert. to or designating the Acroá. Vars. ACOROÁ, ACRÁ
acroácito (m.) achroacyte, lymphocyte.
acroama (m.) acroama.
acroamático –ca (adj.) acroamatic, oral; esoteric, abstruse, profound.
acroartite (f., Med.) acroarthritis.
acroasfixia [ks] (f., Med.) acroasphyxia.
acrobacia (f.) acrobatics.—**aérea**, stunt flying.
acrobata, acróbata (m.,f.) acrobat, clown, tightrope walker.—**contorcionista**, contortionist.—**equilibrista**, juggler.—**voador**, or **volante**, flying acrobat, aerialist.
acrobático –ca (adj.) acrobatic.
acrobatismo (m.) acrobatism, acrobatics.
acrobistite (f., Med.) acrobystitis.
acroblasta (m., Zool.) acroblast.
acrobrioso –sa (adj., Bot.) acrobryous.
acrocárpeas (f.pl., Bot.) the Acrocarpi (mosses).
acrocárpico –ca (adj.) acrocarpous.
acrocefalia (f., Craniol.) acrocephaly.
acrocefálico –ca (adj.) acrocephalic.
acrocéfalo –la (adj.) acrocephalous; (m.,f.) acrocephalic person.
acróceros (m., pl.) a genus (Acrocera) of two-winged flies.
acrocianose (f., Med.) acrocyanosis.
acrocômia (f., Bot.) a genus (Acrocomia) of palms.
acroconídea (f., Bot.) acroconidium.
acrocoracóide (adj., Zool.) acrocoracoid.
acrocórdone (m., Med.) achrocordon.
acrodáctila (f., Zool.) acrodactylum.
acrodermatite (f., Med.) acrodermatitis.
acrodinia (f., Med.) acrodynia.
acrodonte (adj., m., Zool.) acrodont.
acrodrômico –ca (adj., Bot.) acrodrome.
acroesclerodermia (f.) = ACROSCLERODERMIA.
acroesfácelo (m.) = ACROSFÁCELO.
acrofobia (f., Med.) acrophobia.
acrofonia (f.) acrophony.
acrogamia (f., Bot.) acrogamy.
acrogâmico –ca (adj.) acrogamous.
acrogênias (f.,pl.) the Acrogynae (leafy liver-worts).

acrógeno -na (*adj.*, *Bot.*) acrogenic, acrogenous.
acrografia (*f.*) acrography.
acroíta (*f.*, *Min.*) achroite.
acroleína (*f.*, *Chem.*) acrolein.
acrolítico -ca (*adj.*) acrolithic.
acrólito (*m.*) acrolith.
acrologia (*f.*) acrology.
acroma (*f.*, *Med.*) achroma.
acromacia (*f.*, *Micros.*) achromasia.
acromácito (*m.*, *Anat.*) achromacyte [= ACROMATÓCITO].
acromania (*f.*) incurable insanity.
acrómano -na (*m.*,*f.*) incurably insane person.
acromasia (*f.*) = ACROMACIA.
acromastite (*f.*, *Med.*) achromastitis.
acromatia (*f.*) = ACROMASIA.
acromaticidade (*f.*) achromaticity.
acromático -ca (*adj.*) achromatic.
acromatina (*f.*, *Biol.*) achromatin.
acromatismo (*m.*) achromatism.
acromatização (*f.*) achromatization.
acromatizar (*v.t.*) to achromatize, deprive of color.
acromatócito (*m.*, *Anat.*) achromacyte [= ACROMÁCITO].
acromatólise (*f.*, *Med.*) achromatolysis.
acromatope (*m.*) achromatope.
acromatopsia (*f.*, *Med.*) acromatopsia.
acromatose, -tosia (*f.*, *Med.*) achromatosis.
acromaturia (*f.*, *Med.*) achromaturia.
acromegalia (*f.*, *Med.*) acromegaly.
acromegálico -ca (*adj.*) acromegalic.
acromegalismo (*m.*) = ACROMEGALIA.
acromelalgia (*f.*, *Med.*) acromelalgia.
acromia (*f.*, *Med.*) achroma, achromia.
acromial (*adj.*) acromial.
acromico -ca (*adj.*) achromic; acromial.
acromicria (*f.*, *Med.*) acromicria.
acrômio (*m.*, *Anat.*) acromion.
acrômio-clavicular (*adj.*) acromioclavicular.
acrômio-coracoídeo -dea (*adj.*) acromiocoracoid.
acrômio-torácico -ca (*adj.*) acromiothoracic.
acrômio-umeral (*adj.*) acromiohumeral.
acromo -ma (*adj.*) achromic, colorless.
acromodermia (*f.*, *Med.*) leucoderma.
acromonogramático -ca (*adj.*, *Pros.*) acromonogrammatic.
acromotriquia (*f.*) achromotrichia.
acronarcótico -ca (*adj.*; *m.*) acronarcotic.
acroneurose (*f.*, *Med.*) acroneurosis.
acrônico -ca (*adj.*, *Astron.*) acronical.
acronicto -ta (*adj.*, *Astron.*) acronyctous, acronical.
acroparalisia (*f.*, *Med.*) acroparalysis.
acroparestesia (*f.*, *Med.*) acroparesthesia.
acropatia (*f.*, *Med.*) acropathy.
acropatologia (*f.*, *Med.*) acropathology.
acropetal (*adj.*, *Bot.*) acropetal.
acropódio (*m.*) acropodium (pedestal).
acrópole (*f.*) acropolis.
acróporo (*m.*, *Zool.*) a genus (*Acropora*) of madrepores.
acropostite (*f.*) = ACROBISTITE.
acrorrágio (*m.*, *Zool.*) acrorhagus.
acrosclerodermia (*f.*, *Med.*) acroscleroderma.
acroscópico - ca (*adj.*, *Bot.*) acroscopic.
acrose (*f.*, *Chem.*) acrose.
acrosfácelo (*m.*, *Med.*) acrosphacelus.
acrosômio (*m.*, *Zool.*) acrosome.
acrospira (*f.*, *Bot.*) acrospire.
acrospório, acrósporo (*m.*, *Bot.*) acrospore.
acrossarco (*m.*, *Bot.*) acrosarcum.
acrossomo (*m.*, *Zool.*) acrosome.
acróstico -ca (*adj.*; *m.*) acrostic.
acrotarso (*m.*, *Zool.*) acrotarsium, instep.
acroteléutico (*m.*, *Eccl.*) acroteleutic.
acrotério (*m.*, *Arch.*) acroterium.
acrótico -ca (*adj.*, *Med.*) acrotic.
acrotismo (*m.*, *Med.*) acrotism.
acrótomo -ma (*adj.*, *Min.*) acrotomous.
acrotreta (*m.*, *Paleontol.*) Acrotreta (shells).
act-, words not listed may be found under at-.
acteáceas (*f.pl.*) the Acteaceae (baneberries).
acteão (*m.*, *Zool.*) a genus (*Actaeon*) of gastropods.
actéia (*f.*) baneberry (*Actaea*), c.a. ÉBULO, ERVA-DE-SÃO-CRISTÓVÃO.
actinéia, actinela (*f.*) the genus *Actinea*, syn. *Actinella*, of the thistle family.
actinênquimia (*f.*, *Bot.*) actinenchyma.
actínia (*f.*) actinia, sea anemone.

actinianos, actiniários (*m.pl.*) the Actiniaria (sea anemones).
actínico -ca (*adj.*) actinic.
actinídea (*f.*) a genus (*Actinidia*) comprising the silver vine (*A. polygama*).
actinífero -fera (*adj.*) actiniferous.
actiniforme (*adj.*) actiniform.
actinimorfo -fa (*adj.*) = ACTINOMORFO.
actínio (*m.*, *Chem.*) actinium.
actinismo (*m.*) actinism.
actinoblasto (*m.*, *Zool.*) scleroblast.
actinocárpico (*f.*, *Bot.*) actinocarp.
actinocarpo -pa (*adj.*) actinocarpous.
actinodermatite, actinodermite (*f.*, *Med.*) actinodermatitis.
actino-elétrico -ca (*adj.*, *Physics*) actinoelectric.
actinofore (*m.*, *Physics*) actinophore.
actinofônico -ca (*adj.*) actinophonic.
actinogonídeo -dea (*adj.*, *Zool.*) actinogonidiate.
actinógrafo (*m.*) actinograph.
actinóide (*adj.*) actinoid, raylike.
actinolítico -ca (*adj.*) actinolitic.
actinólito (*m.*, *Min.*) actinolite [= ACTINOTO].
actinometria (*f.*) actinometry.
actinométrico -ca (*adj.*) actinometric.
actinômetro (*m.*) actinometer.
actinomicete (*m.*, *Bot.*) actinomycete.
actinomicose (*f.*, *Veter.*, *Med.*) actinomycosis.
actinomicósico -ca (*adj.*) actinomycotic.
actinomorfo -fa, actinomórfico -ca (*adj.*) actinomorphic, actinomorphous, radiosymmetrical.
actinonêmo (*m.*, *Bot.*) a form genus (*Actinonema*) of imperfect fungi.
actinoneurite (*f.*, *Med.*) actinoneuritis.
actinoquímica (*f.*) actinochemistry.
actinosférico (*m.*, *Zool.*) a genus (*Actinosphaerium*) of large fresh-water protozoans.
actinoterapia (*f.*, *Med.*) actinotherapy.
actinoto (*m.*, *Min.*) actinolite [= ACTINÓLITO].
actinotríquio (*m.*, *Zool.*) actinotrichium.
actinozoários (*m.pl.*) the Anthozoa (corals, sea anemones, etc.).
actínula (*f.*, *Zool.*) actinula.
actite (*f.*) the spotted sandpiper (*Actitis macularia*).
açu [ú] (*adj.*) a Tupian word meaning large [= GUAÇU]— used alone or in combination.
acuação (*f.*) act of cornering, bringing to bay.
acuado -da (*adj.*) brought to bay; trapped, cornered; of an animal, sitting on its haunches; balky.
acuador -dora (*adj.*) of horses, balky.
acuamento (*m.*) = ACUAÇÃO.
acuar (*v.i.*) of an animal, to crouch or sit on its hindquarters; to balk; to hesitate, draw back, back up; (*v.t.*) to drive into a corner, bring to bay.
açúcar (*m.*) sugar; by ext., sweetness, sweet words.—areado, finely powdered sugar.—branco, or refinado, white, refined sugar.—bruto, raw sugar.—cande, rock candy—confeiteiro, confectioner's sugar.—cristal, or cristalizado, crystallized sugar.—de beterraba, beet sugar.—de cana, cane sugar.—de leite, lactose.—de pedra, rock candy.—de-saturno, salt of Saturn, sugar of lead, hydrated lead acetate.—de uvas, grape sugar, glucose, dextrose.—em pó, powdered sugar.—invertido, invert sugar.—mascavado, or mascavo, raw sugar; brown sugar.—mascavinho, light brown sugar. Pão de—, Sugar Loaf (the famous granite monolith at the entrance to the harbor of Rio de Janeiro). plantação de—, sugar plantation. refinaria de—, sugar refinery. usina de—, sugar mill.
açucarado -da (*adj.*) sugared, sweetened. palavras—s, honeyed words, sweet talk.
açucarador -dora (*adj.*) sweetening; (*m.*,*f.*) sweetener.
açucarar (*v.t.*) to sugar; to sweeten.
açucareiro -ra (*adj.*) sugar-yielding; sugar-making; (*m.*) sugar bowl; sugar dealer or refiner.
açucena (*f.*) madonna lily (*Lilium candidum*); Easter lily (*L. longiflorum*), c.a. COPO-DE-LEITE, LÍRIO-BRANCO, PALMA-DE-SÃO-JOSÉ; the tall amaryllis (*A. procera*), c.a. FLOR-DA-IMPERATRIZ; fig., candlestick socket; chastity, purity.—da-água, the carib crinum (*Crinum erubescens*).—do-jardim, the Barbados lily (*Amaryllis vittata*), c.a. LÍRIO-BRANCO.—do-mato, Panama posqueria (*P. latifolia*), c.a. FLOR-DE-MICO, ARAÇÁ-DA-PRAIA, BACUPARI-DE-CAPOEIRA, MARIA-PEIDORREIRA, PAPA-TERRA, POSO-QUERI, PURUÍ.—do-campo, parrot amaryllis (*A. psit-*

tacina).—-**encarnada,** belladonna amaryllis (*A. belladonna*), c.a. BELADONA-DOS-ITALIANOS, CEBOLA-CECÉM. —-**formosa,** Aztec lily (*Amaryllis formosissima*).

acuchí (*m., Zool.*) acouchy, a small species of agouti (*Myoprocta acouchy*).

acuchilar (*v.*) = ACUTILAR.

acucular (*v.*) = ACOGULAR.

açudada (*f.*) water held back by a dam; swamp drainage ditch.

açudagem (*f.*), **açudamento** (*m.*) act of damming (up).

açudar (*v.t.*) to dam (up) a stream.

açude (*m.*) dam; weir.

acudir [22] (*v.t.*) to aid, assist, help, succor; to take measures; to reply quickly, retort; (*v.i.*) to come (go, run) to the aid or rescue of; to come running (as to the scene of an accident); to have recourse to.—**à mente,** to come to mind. **Acode!** Help! **Deus me acuda!** God help me! **Isso não acode à cabeça de ninguém,** No one (with any sense) would ever think of such a thing.

acué (*m.,f.*) an Indian of the Akwĕ, the western branch of the Central Ge, comprising the Xacriabá, Xerente and Xavante of the State of Goiás; (*adj.*) pert. to or designating the Acué.

acuiari [rí] (*m.*) acuyari wood, a fragrant S.A. wood obtained from *Bursera altissima*.

acuidade [u-i] (*f.*) acuity, acuteness.

acuiuru [ui-u] (*f.*) an Astrocaryum palm (*A. aculeatum*).

açulado –**da** (*adj.*) instigated, incited, provoked; egged on; of dogs, sicked on.

açulador –**dora** (*adj.*) instigating, inciting; irritating; (*m.,f.*) instigator.

açulamento (*m.*) instigation (to quarrel); incitement (esp. of dogs).

açular (*v.t.*) to instigate, incite (**contra,** against); to egg on; to sick on (dogs).

aculeado –**da** (*adj.*) aculeate; (*m.pl., Zool.*) the Aculeata (bees, wasps, ants).

aculear (*v.t.*) to provide with a sharp point.

aculeiforme (*adj.*) aculeiform.

acúleo (*m.*) sharp point, prickle; (*Bot., Zool.*) aculeus.

aculturação (*f., Anthropol.*) acculturation.

acumã (*m.*) the field syagrus palm (*Syagrus campestris*), c.a., COCO-DA-SERRA, COQUEIRO-DO-CAMPO, COQUEIRO-DE-VASSOURA, COQUEIRINHO-DO-CAMPO.—**rasteiro** is *Syagrus petraea*, c.a. GUIRIRI, INDAIÁ-RASTEIRO, INDAIÁ-DO-CAMPO.

acumatanga (*f.*) = AJURUETÉ.

acume, acúmen (*m.*) acumen.

acumetria (*f.*) = ACUOMETRIA.

acúmetro (*m.*) = ACUÔMETRO.

acuminação (*f.*) acumination.

acuminado –**da** (*adj.*) acuminate, pointed.

acuminar (*v.t.*) to acuminate; (*v.r.*) to end in a sharp point.

acuminoso –**sa** (*adj.*) acuminate.

acumpliciar (*v.t.*) to make an accomplice of; (*v.r.*) to become an accomplice.

acumulação (*f.*) accumulation, pile, heap; accrual; accretion; cumulus cloud formation.

acumulado –**da** (*adj.*) accumulated; heaped (up).

acumulador –**dora** (*adj.*) accumulating; collecting; (*m.*) accumulator; collector.—**de vapor,** steam accumulator. —**elétrico,** electric battery.—**hidráulico,** hydraulic accumulator.

acumular (*v.t.*) to accumulate, amass; to pile up; to store up.—**de,** to heap with.—**sôbre,** to pile on. (*v.r.*) to accumulate; of interest, to accrue.

acumulativo –**va** (*adj.*) accumulative.

acumulável (*adj.*) accumulative.

acúmulo (*m.*) = ACUMULAÇÃO.

acunã (*f.*) an *Orbignya* palm whose small hard fruit are used as beads; c.a. VINTE-PÉS.

acunhar (*v.t.*) to wedge tight; to shape like a wedge; to split with a wedge; to jam full.

acunheado –**da** (*adj.*) wedge-shaped.

acunhear (*v.t.*) to shape like a wedge.

acuofonia (*f., Med.*) acouphonia.

acuometria (*f., Psychophysics*) acoumetry. Var. ACUMETRIA.

acuômetro (*m.*) acoumeter. Var. ACÚMETRO.

acupremir (*v.t.*) to acupress.

acupressão, acupressura (*f., Surg.*) acupressure.

acurado –**da** (*adj.*) done or made with great care—said esp. of plans, studies, reports, etc.; painstaking. [The

cognate, accurate, is translated EXATO, PRECISO].

acurana, acuraua (*f.*), **acurau** (*m.*) = BACURAU.

acurar (*v.t.*) to treat with care; to perfect (as style).

acuré (*f.*) a species of S.A. tapir (*Tapirus roulini* or *T. pinchaque*), c.a. ANTA-XURÉ.

acuri [í] (*m.*) = CUTIA.

acurralar (*v.*) & derivs. = ENCURRALAR & derivs.

acuravado –**da** (*adj.*) curved; sagging; bowed down.

acurvamento (*m.*) a curving; a bowing down.

acurvar (*v.t.*) to bow; to subdue; (*v.r.*) to stoop, bend; to yield.

acurvilhar (*v.i.*) to stumble—said of horses.

acusação (*f.*) accusation; reproach; charge, indictment; arraignment.—**de si mesmo,** self-blame.

acusado –**da** (*adj.*) accused, charged; arraigned; (*m.,f.*) accused person; defendant. **feições bem**—**s,** pronounced (facial) features. **sotaque**—, strong (foreign) accent.

acusador –**dora** (*adj.*) accusing; (*m.,f.*) accuser; informer. —**particular,** private prosecutor.—**público,** public prosecutor.

acusante (*m.,f.*) accuser; (*adj.*) accusing.

acusar (*v.t.*) to accuse (**de,** of); to charge (**de,** with); to blame; to indict, incriminate; to show, betray, reveal; to number.—-**se de,** to confess oneself guilty of, or in the wrong about, (something).—**o recebimento de uma carta,** to acknowledge receipt of a letter. **acusando cinco mil,** numbering (to the number of) 5,000. **As receitas acusam um aumento de dez por cento,** The income shows an increase of ten per cent.

acusativo –**da** (*adj.*) accusatory; (*m., Gram.*) accusative case.

acusatório –**ria** (*adj.*) accusatory.

acusável (*adj.*) accusable, blamable.

acústico –**ca** (*adj.*) acoustic; (*f.*) acoustics.

acutangulado –**da** (*adj.*) acute-angled.

acutenáculo (*m., Surg.*) needle holder.

acuti [í] (*f.*) = CUTIA.

acutifoliado –**da** (*adj., Bot.*) acutifoliate.

acutiguepo (*m., Bot.*) an exotic thalia (*T. geniculata*).

acutiladiço –**ça** (*adj.*) slashing, cutting; susceptible of slashing or of being slashed.

acutilado –**da** (*adj.*) slashed, cut, gashed.

acutilador –**dora** (*adj.*) slashing; (*m.*) swordsman; bully, slasher.

acutilamento (*m.*) slash, slit; slashing, gashing.

acutilar (*v.t.*) to slash, gash, hack, chop (as with a sword or large knife); of tigers, etc., to slash, tear, with the fangs; to cut ornamental slits in a garment; (*v.r.*) to slash one another.

acutilobado –**da** (*adj., Bot.*) acutilobate.

acutinodoso –**sa** (*adj., Bot.*) acutonodose.

acutipuru [rú] (*m.*) a palm squirrel (*Sciurus aestuans*).

acutiranha (*f.*) an agouti's tooth used by Brazilian Indians as a lancet.

acutíssimo –**ma** (*absol. superl. of* AGUDO) most sharp; most acute.

acutorsão (*f., Surg.*) acutorsion.

ada (*f., Bot.*) an orchid (*Ada sp.*).

adactilia (*f.*) adactylia.

adáctilo –**la** (*adj., Zool.*) adactylous.

adaga (*f.*) dagger.

adagada (*f.*) a stab with a dagger.

adagial (*adj.*) adagial, proverbial.

adagiar (*v.i.*) to quote adages and proverbs.

adágio (*m.*) adage; (*Music*) adagio.

Adalberto (*m.*) Adalbert.

adali [í] (*m., Bot.*) a sp. of lippia (*L. nodiflora*).

adamado –**da** (*adj.*) ladylike; womanish, effeminate; **um vinho**—, a sweet, smooth wine.

adamantino –**na** (*adj.*) adamantine.

adamantinoma (*f., Med.*) adamantinoma.

adamantoblasto (*m., Anat.*) adamantoblast.

adamar-se (*v.r.*) to become effeminate.

adamascado –**da** (*adj.*) of fabric or color, damask; of taste, like a damson plum.

adamascar (*v.t.*) to damask.

adamasquinado –**da** (*adj.*) damascened.

adamelito (*m., Petrog.*) adamellite.

adâmico –**ca** (*adj.*) Adamic.

adamina (*f., Min.*) adamite.

adansônia (*f., Bot.*) baobab (*Adansonia digitata*).

Adão (*m.*) Adam; [*not cap.*] Adam's apple.

adaptabilidade (*f.*) adaptability; versatility.

adaptação (*f.*) adaptation.

adaptado –da (*adj.*) adapted; adjusted.
adaptador –dora (*adj.*) adapting; (*m.,f.*) adapter.
adaptar (*v.t.*) to adapt; suit (**a**, to); to fit; to match; to adjust (**-se**, oneself).
adaptivo –va (*adj.*) adaptive.
adaptável (*adj.*) adaptable; versatile; accommodative.
adarga (*f.*) ancient leather shield.
adargar (*v.t.*) to shield, shelter; (*v.r.*) to protect oneself.
adarve (*m.*) battlement.
adastra (*f.*) triblet, mandrel.
adátoda (*f.*) Brazil bower plant (*Adhatoda cydoniaefolia*).
add-, see under **ad-**.
adeant-, see under **adiant-**.
adéfago –ga (*adj., Med., Zool.*) adephagous; (*m.pl.*) the Adephaga (predacious beetles).
adega (*f.*) cellar; wine cellar. Cf. BODEGA.
adegar (*v.t.*) to put or keep in the cellar; to visit the wine cellar too often.
adeira (*f., Bot.*) edible canna (*C. edulis*).
adejar (*v.i.*) to flutter, flicker, flap.—(por) sôbre, to hover over.
adejo [ê] (*m.*) flying, fluttering, hovering (of birds and butterflies).
Adelaide (*f.*) Adelaide.
adeleiro (*m.*) second-hand dealer.
adelfa (*f.*) = ESPIRRADEIRA.
adelfogamia (*f., Zool.*) adelphogamy.
adelgaçado –da (*adj.*) thin, slender, slim; sharp.
adelgaçar (*v.t.*) to make thin or slender; to scatter (clouds, darkness); to sharpen (voice, wits); (*v.r.*) to grow thin; to grow less.
adélia (*f., Bot.*) the genus Adelia (spurge family).
adelita (*f., Min.*) adelite.
adelo (*m.*) = ADELEIRO.
adelócero –ra (*adj., Zool.*) adelocerous.
adelomorfo –fa (*adj., Biol.*) adelomorphic, -phous.
adelope (*m.*) a genus (*Adelops*) of blind cave beetles.
ademais (*adv.*) besides, furthermore.
ademanes (*m.pl.*) gestures, flourishes, mannerisms, affectations.
ademão (*m.*) a helping hand, a house-raising or other "bee".
adenalgia (*f., Med.*) adenalgia.
adenantero (*m.*) a beadtree (*Adenanthera*).
adenastenia (*f., Med.*) adenasthenia.
adenda (*f.*) addendum, supplement.
adendo (*m.*) addendum.
adenectomia (*f., Surg.*) adenectomy.
adenectopia (*f., Med.*) adenectopy.
adenenfraxia [ks] (*f., Med.*) adenemphraxis.
adenia (*f., Med.*) adenia.
adenina (*f., Biochem.*) adenine.
adenite (*f., Med.*) adenitis.
adenocarcinoma, adenocancro (*m., Med.*) adenocarcinoma.
adenocarpo (*m., Bot.*) the faltpods (*Adenocarpus*).
adenocaule (*m., Bot.*) the genus Adenocaulon.
adenocondroma (*m., Med.*) adenochondroma.
adenodiástase (*f., Med.*) adenodiastasis.
adenofaríngeo –gea (*adj., Med.*) adenopharyngeal.
adenofaringite (*f., Med.*) adenopharyngitis.
adenofibroma (*f., Med.*) adenofibroma.
adenofilo –la (*adj., Bot.*) adenophyllous.
adenofima (*f., Med.*) adenophyma.
adenoflegmão (*m., Med.*) adenophlegmon.
adenóforo –ra (*adj.*) adenophorous; (*f., Bot.*) the ladybells (*Adenophora*).
adenoftalmia (*f., Med.*) adenophthalmia.
adenóide (*adj.*) adenoid(al).
adenoidectomia (*f., Surg.*) adenoidectomy.
adenoidismo [ò-i] (*m., Med.*) adenoidism.
adenoidite [ò-i] (*f., Med.*) inflammation of the adenoids.
adenolipomatose (*f., Med.*) adenolipomatosis.
adenologadite (*f., Med.*) adenologaditis.
adenologia (*f.*) adenology.
adenoma (*m., Med.*) adenoma.
adenomalacia (*f., Med.*) adenomalacia.
adenomeníngeo –gea (*adj., Med.*) adenomeningeal.
adenomioma (*m., Med.*) adenomyoma.
adenomixoma [ks] (*m., Med.*) adenomyxoma.
adenomorfo –fa (*adj.*) adeniform, like a gland.
adenopatia (*f., Med.*) adenopathy.
adenosclerose (*f., Med.*) adenosclerosis.
adenoso –sa (*adj.*) adenose.

adenossarcoma (*m., Med.*) adenosarcoma.
adenostêmone (*adj., Bot.*) adenostemonous.
adenotomia (*f., Med.*) adenotomy.
adensado –da (*adj.*) dense; compacted.
adensador –dora (*adj.*) densifying, condensing; (*m.,f.*) condensor; (*m.*) a rammer or "stomper" for concrete.
adensamento (*m.*) densification, condensing, thickening; slumping (of concrete).
adensar (*v.t.*) to densify; to ram or "stomp" (concrete); (*v.i.*) of concrete, to slump or settle; (*v.r.*) to become dense.
adentar (*v.t.*) to provide with teeth (as a saw or gear); (*v.i.*) to teethe.
adentrar (*v.t.*) to push in, cause to enter; (*v.i.*) to enter; (*v.r.*) to enter in, penetrate.
adentro (*adv.*) indoors; inside (**de**, of). **pela porta—**, in through the door. Cf. DENTRO.
adepto (*m.*) follower, adherent, admirer; henchman.
adequado –da (*adj.*) fit, suitable, appropriate (**a**, to).
adequar [27] (*v.t.*) to suit, fit, render appropriate (**a**, to).
aderecar (*v.t.*) to adorn, to prepare; to address; (*v.r.*) to deck oneself out.
adereço (*m.*) ornament, adornment; address; (*pl.*) regalia, trappings; household goods; theatrical props.
aderência (*f.*) adhesion; adherence. Cf. ADESÃO.
aderente (*adj.; m.,f.*) adherent.
adergar (*v.*) = ADREGAR.
aderir [22a] (*v.i.*) to join (with); to adhere (to); to stick, cling (to), to be attached (to); to subscribe (to), agree (with).—**a um partido**, to join a party.—**a uma teoria**, to subscribe to a theory.
adermia (*f., Med.*) adermia.
adernado –da (*adj.*) of ships, careened, heeled over; sunk (low in spirits); low, small.
adernamento (*m.*) careening, heeling over, listing.
adernar (*v.i., Naut.*) to heel (over), careen, list.
aderno (*m.*) a startree (*Astronium spectabilis*).—prêto (—verdadeiro), is *Astronium concinnum*, c.a. ADERNE, GONÇALO-ALVES, GUARABU-PRÊTO.
adesão (*f.*) adherence, attachment; concurrence, assent, adhesion. Cf. ADERÊNCIA.
adesividade (*f.*) adherency, steady attachment (to other persons, ideas, principles, etc.).
adesivo –va (*adj.*) adhesive; **sêlo—**, gummed stamp; (*m.*) adhesive plaster.
adeso –sa (*adj.*) adherent.
adestrado –da (*adj.*) trained; dexterous.
adestrador –dora (*adj.*) training; (*m.,f.*) trainer (esp. of horses).
adestramento (*m.*) training; drilling; dexterity.
adestrar (*v.t.*) to train, drill, coach; to break in (horses),
adestro –tra (*adj.*) spare, in reserve;—said esp. of horses.
adeus [-es] (*m.*) a farewell; (*exclam.*) Goodby! Farewell! Adieu!—**de mão fechada**, a threatening or insulting farewell gesture with the closed fist.—**eterno**, eternal farewell.—**minhas encomendas!** It's all gone! All over! That's the end of it!
adeuzinho! Ta-ta! See you soon!
adiabático –ca (*adj.*) adiabatic; (*f., Thermodyn.*) adiabatic process.
adiabilidade (*f.*) possibility of postponement.
adiadococinesia (*f., Med.*) adiadochokinesis.
adiáfono –na (*adj.*) adiaphanous, not transparent.
adiaforese (*f., Med.*) adiaphoretic.
adiáforo –ra (*adj.*) adiaphorous.
adiamantado –da (*adj.*) diamond-like.
adiamantar (*v.t.*) to make (something) brilliant; to adorn with diamonds.
adiamantino –na (*adj.*) adamantine.
adiamento (*m.*) adjournment; postponement.
adiantáceo –cea (*adj.*) like maidenhair fern.
adiantadamente (*adv.*) ahead of time; beforehand; in advance.
adiantado –da (*adj.*) advanced, ahead; forward, presumptuous, brazen; of time, early; of timepiece, fast. —**na idade**, advanced in years.—**nos estudos**, ahead in one's studies. **chegar—**, to arrive ahead of time. **grau, or estagio,—**, advanced stage. **estar—**, to be (well) ahead. **o—da hora**, the lateness of the hour. **pagamento—**, payment in advance; (*m.*) provincial governor.
adiantamento (*m.*) advancement; progress; advance payment.
adiantar (*v.t.*) to advance, push forward; to set ahead;

to improve; to further, promote; to pay in advance; to state beforehand; (*v.r.*) to advance, go forward, get ahead; to come forward; to be forward, presumptuous; of a timepiece, to gain time, run fast.—**uma idéia,** to advance (offer, put forth) an idea. **A viagem não adiantou,** The effort (attempt) accomplished nothing. **Adianta-se que,** it is revealed (said, disclosed) that. **Êle pode falar que não adianta (nada),** He can talk all he wants, it won't do any good. **Isso não adianta nada,** That doesn't help at all. **Não adianta insistir,** It's no use insisting. **Não se adiante muito,** Don't get too far ahead. **O trabalho está se adiantando,** The work is getting on. **Que é que adianta?** What's the use?

adiante (*adv.*) ahead, in advance, in front, forward; later on; farther on; (*exclam.*) Forward! **levar**—, to carry on, carry forward. **mais**—, further on, farther ahead. **pelo tempo**—, in time to come; in the days ahead. **pouco**—, a little farther (on).

adianto (*m.*) maidenhair ferns (*Adiantum*).

adiar (*v.t.*) to adjourn; to postpone; to defer, put off.

adiatermancia (*f., Physics*) adiathermancy.

adiatermia (*f.*) adiathermancy.

adiatérmico —**ca** (*adj., Physics*) athermanous.

adiatésico —**ca** (*adj., Med.*) adiathetic.

adiável (*adj.*) postponable.

adição (*f.*) addition; adding, joining; increase; bill (in a restaurant). [In the latter sense, a gallicism.]

adicidade (*f., Chem.*) adicity, valence.

adicionação (*f.*) addition; additament.

adicionado —**da** (*adj.*) added, increased; sick or injured [horse].

adicionador —**dora** (*adj.*) adding, increasing.

adicional (*adj.*) additional; (*m.*) something added.

adicionamento (*m.*) addition; additament.

adicionar (*v.t.*) to add, join (a, to); to increase in number; to augment; (*v.r.*) of a horse, to get hurt.

adicionável (*adj.*) addible.

adicto —**ta** (*adj.*) addicted (to), devoted (to); adjunct, auxiliary.

adido —**da** (*adj.*) adjoined, attached; (*m.*) assistant (in civil service); attaché.—**comercial (militar, naval),** commercial (military, naval) attaché.

adietar (*v.t.*) to put on a diet; (*v.r.*) to go on a diet.

adimplir (*v.t., Law*) to carry out a court order.

adina (*f.*) the heartleaf adina (*Adina cordifolia*).

adinamia (*f., Med.*) adynamia.

adinâmico —**ca, adínamo** —**ma** (*adj.*) adynamic.

adinole (*f., Petrog.*) adinole.

adioés (*m.pl.*) one of the seven tribes composing Guaycuruan linguistic family of S.A. Indians.

adipato (*m., Chem.*) adipate.

ádipe (*f.* or *m.*) **ádipo** (*m.*) animal fat.

adípico —**ca** (*adj., Chem.*) adipic.

adipínico —**ca** (*adj., Chem.*) adipinic, adipic.

adipocele (*f.*) adipocele.

adipocera (*f.*) adipocere.

adipofibroma (*m., Med.*) adipofibroma, lipofibroma.

adipogênico —**ca** (*adj.*) adipogenic.

adipólise (*f.*) adipolysis.

adipoma (*m., Med.*) adipoma, lipoma.

adipopexia [ks] [*f., Med.*] adipopexia.

adipose (*f., Med.*) adiposis.

adiposidade (*f., Med.*) adiposity.—**dolorosa,** Dercum's disease.

adiposo —**sa** (*adj.*) adipose, fatty. **panículo**—, fatty layer. **tecido**—, fatty tissue.

adiposuria (*f., Med.*) adiposuria.

adipsia (*f., Med.*) adipsia.

adir [46] (*v.t.*) to add to; to adjoin.

aditamento (*m.*) additament; addendum; supplement.

aditar (*v.t.*) to add to; to attach to.

aditivo —**va** (*adj.; m.*) additive.

adito —**ta** (*adj.*) attached to; (*m.*) = ADIDO.

adivinha (*f.*) fortune-teller; riddle, enigma.

adivinhação (*f.*) fortune-telling, soothsaying, divination; riddle, conundrum, puzzle; guesswork.

adivinhadeira (*f.*) fortune-teller.

adivinhador —**dora** (*adj.*) divinatory; (*m.*) soothsayer, diviner; (*f.*) divineress.

adivinhar (*v.t.*) to guess; to decipher; to divine.

adivinhável (*adj.*) divinable; that can be guessed.

adivinho (*m.*) fortune-teller, soothsayer.

adjacência (*f.*) adjacency; nearness, proximity; (*pl.*) environs.

adjacente (*adj.*) adjacent, adjoining, neighboring.

adjeção (*f.*) adjection; addition.

adjetivação (*f.*) use of adjectives, esp. to excess.

adjetivado —**da** (*adj.*) adjectived.

adjetival (*adj.*) adjectival.

adjetivamento (*m.*) = ADJETIVAÇÃO.

adjetivar (*v.t.*) to adjective; to dress up (speech, style) with adjectives.

adjetivo —**va** (*adj.; m.*) adjective.

adjeto —**ta** (*adj.*) added. **pacto**—, supplemental agreement.

adjudicação (*f.*) adjudication; award.

adjudicador —**dora** (*m.,f.*) adjudicator.

adjudicar (*v.t.*) to adjudicate; to decide (settle) by law; to judge, adjudge; to award to.

adjudicativo —**va,** —**tório** —**ria** (*adj.*) adjudicative.

adjunto —**ta** (*adj.*) adjunct, conjoined, annexed, adjoined; (*m.*) assistant, associate; assistant teacher; (*Gram.*) adjunct; (*colloq.*) a house-raising or other "bee".

adjuração (*f.*) adjuration.

adjurador —**dora** (*adj.*) adjuring; (*m.,f.*) adjurer.

adjurar (*v.t.*) to adjure.

adjutor —**tora** (*m.,f.*) one who helps.

adjutorar (*v.t.*) to give help to.

adjutório (*m.*) help, aid; a helping hand; enema.

adjuvante (*adj.*) helping; (*m.,f.*) assistant; something that assists; (*m., Pharm., Med.*) adjuvant.

adligar-se [ad-li] (*v.r.*) of a plant, to attach itself to another.

adlúmia (*f.*), **adlúmio** (*m.*) the mountain fringe or climbing fumitory (*Adlumia fungosa*).

adlumidina [ad-lu] (*f., Chem.*) adlumidin(e).

adlumina [ad-lu] (*f., Chem.*) adlumin(e).

administração (*f.*) administration, management; administration building; executive department.

administradeira (*f.*) administratress.

administrador —**dora** (*adj.*) administering, managing; (*m.*) manager, director; superintendent; steward; overseer of an estate; administrator.—**de bens,** property manager.

administrante (*adj.*) administrant.

administrar (*v.t.*) to administer; to administrate, direct, manage, conduct, rule, govern.—**a,** to dispense to.—**justiça,** to administer justice.

administrativo —**va** (*adj.*) administrative.

admirabilidade (*f.*) admirability, admirableness.

admiração (*f.*) admiration; wonder, astonishment, amazement, surprise. **cheio de**—**por,** filled with wonder at. **ponto de**—, exclamation point[!].

admirado —**da** (*adj.*) surprised, amazed; admired.

admirador —**dora** (*adj.*) admiring; (*m.,f.*) admirer.

admirar (*v.t.*) to admire; to praise; to wonder (marvel) at; (*v.r.*) to be astonished (**de,** at). **admira-me que,** it surprises me that. **admiro-me que,** I am surprised that. **não admira que,** it is not surprising that.

admirável (*adj.*) admirable; wonderful; beautiful.

admissão (*f.*) admission; admittance; intake; pre-college year; college-entrance exam; (*Mach.*) inlet.

admissibilidade (*f.*) admissibility.

admissível (*adj.*) admissible, allowable; bearable, tolerable; not unlikely, not impossible.

admitância (*f., Elec.*) admittance.

admitido —**da** (*adj.*) admitted; accepted.

admitir (*v.t.*) to admit, concede, grant, acknowledge; to let in, take in; to permit (allow, admit) of.

admoestação (*f.*) admonition, admonishment.

admoestador —**dora** (*adj.*) admonishing; (*m.,f.*) admonisher.

admoestar (*v.t.*) to admonish; to rebuke (lightly); to advise, caution, warn.

admoestativo —**va, admoestatório** —**ria** (*adj.*) admonitive, admonitorial.

admoestável (*adj.*) susceptible of, or deserving of, admonishment.

admonição (*f.*) admonition.

admonitivo —**va** (*adj.*) admonitory.

admonitor (*m.*) admonitor, admonitioner.

admonitório —**ria** (*adj.*) admonitory; (*m.*) admonition.

adm.ᵒʳ = ADMIRADOR (admirer)—used as a complimentary close in letters.

adnascente (*adj.*) growing on something else.

adnato —**ta** (*adj., Bot., Zool.*) adnate, grown or growing together.

adnerval (*adj., Physiol.*) adnerval.

adnexo —**xa** [ks] (*adj., Bot.*) adnexed.

adnumerar (*v.t.*) to number; to enumerate.
adôbe, adôbo (*m.*) adobe (brick).
adoçado –da (*adj.*) sweetened; softened.
adoçamento (*m.*) sweetening; mitigation; (*Arch.*) fascia; (*Engin.*) fairing.—**de tintas**, toning down of colors.
adoçante (*adj.*) sweetening; (*m.*) soothing syrup.
adoção (*f.*) adoption; acceptance, avowal. [The verb is ADOTAR, not ADOÇAR.]
adoçar (*v.t.*) to sweeten; to mitigate, lessen, soothe, soften; to moderate; to temper.
adocicado –da (*adj.*) sweetish.
adocicar (*v.t.*) to sweeten slightly.
adoecer (*v.i.*) to sicken; (*v.t.*) to make sick.
adoentado –da (*adj.*) somewhat sick, indisposed.
adoentar (*v.t.*) to make ill.
adoidado –da (*adj.*) senseless, crack-brained; touched (in the head). Var. ADOUDADO.
adoidar (*v.t.*) to make crazy or crazy-like; (*v.i.,v.r.*) to go crazy. Var. ADOUDAR.
adolescência (*f.*) adolescence; youth.
adolescente (*adj.; m.,f.*) adolescent.
adolescer (*v.i.*) to adolesce.
Adolfo (*m.*) Adolph; Adolphus.
adomingado –da (*adj.*) dressed up in one's best.
adomingar-se (*v.r.*) to dress up (as for Sunday).
adonairar (*v.t.*) to embellish, lend gracefulness to.
adonde, often wrongly used in place of AONDE or ONDE.
adônico –ca (*adj.*) Adonic.
adonidina (*f., Pharm.*) adonidin.
adonina (*f., Chem.*) adonin.
adônio –nia (*adj.*) = ADÔNICO.
adônis (*m., Bot.*) the spring adonis (*A. vernalis*), c.a. ADÔNIS-VERNAL, ADÔNIS-DA-ITÁLIA.
adonisar (*v.t.*) to adonize, beautify, dandify; (*v.r.*) to deck oneself out.
adonita (*f.*) adonital (*m., Chem.*) adonitol.
adoperar (*v.t.*) to employ, make use of.
adoração (*f.*) adoration, worship.—**da Cruz**, adoration of the Cross.—**do Santíssimo Sacramento**, adoration of the Blessed Sacrament.
adorado –da (*adj.*) adored; loved.
adorador –dora (*adj.*) adoring; (*m.,f.*) adorer; worshipper.
adorar (*v.t.*) to adore; to love; to worship; to venerate.
adoratório (*m.*) a place of adoration.
adorável (*adj.*) adorable.
adoreto (*m.*) a genus (*Adoretus*) of beetles.
adormecente (*adj.*) soporific.
adormecer (*v.i.*) to fall asleep; (*v.t.*) to put (lull) to sleep; to still.
adormecido –da (*adj.*) dormant; sleeping.
adormecimento (*m.*) dormancy; lethargy.
adormentado –da (*adj.*) sleeping; quiet; insensible.
adormentador –dora (*adj.*) soporiferous.
adormentar (*v.t.*) to lull to sleep; to render insensible; (*v.i.*) to sleep.
adornado –da (*adj.*) embellished; ornate.
adornador –dora (*adj.*) adorning; (*m.,f.*) adorner.
adornamento (*m.*) adornment; adorning.
adornar (*v.t.*) to adorn, bedeck, trim, embellish (**com, de,** **with**).
adôrno (*m.*) ornament, adornment.
adotante (*adj.*) adopting; (*m.,f.*) adopter.
adotar (*v.t.*) to adopt, appropriate; to approve, accept. avow; to take (a child) as one's own.
adotável (*adj.*) adoptable.
adotivo –va (*adj.*) adoptive. **filho—**, adopted son (or child).
adoudado –da (*adj.*) = ADOIDADO.
adoxa [ks] (*f.*) muskroot (*Adoxa moschatellina*), c.a. ERVA-ALMISCARADA.
adquirente (*adj.*) acquiring; (*m.,f.*) acquirer.
adquirição (*f.*) = AQUISIÇÃO.
adquirido –da (*adj.*) acquired.
adquiridor –dora (*adj.*) acquiring; (*m.,f.*) acquirer.
adquirir (*v.t.*) to acquire, gain, obtain; to achieve, attain; to purchase.
adquirível (*adj.*) acquirable.
adquisição (*f.*) = AQUISIÇÃO.
adraganta (*f.*), **–to** (*m.*) tragacanth gum.
adragantina (*f., Chem.*) tragacanthin, bassorin.
adrede (*adv.*) purposely, intentionally, designedly.—**preparado**, of scheme, trap, plot, intentionally set up (prepared) in advance.
adregar (*v.i.*) to happen by chance; (*v.r.*) to come upon.

Var. ADERGAR.
ad-renal (*adj.; f., Anat.*) adrenal.
adrenalina (*f., Pharm., Biochem.*) adrenaline.
ad-retal (*adj., Anat., Zool.*) adrectal.
Adriana (*f.*) Adrienne.
adriático –ca (*adj.*) Adriatic.
adriça (*f.*) halyard.
adriçar (*v.t.*) to haul up or in; to trim ship.
adro (*m.*) church plaza.
ad-rogar (*v.t., Rom. Law*) to arrogate.
ad-rostal (*adj., Zool.*) adrostral.
adscrever (*v.t.*) to add to in writing.
adscrição (*f.*) something added in writing; transcription, inscription.
adscrito –ta (*adj.*) added in writing; (*m.,f.*) an adscript serf.
adsorção (*f., Physical Chem.*) adsorption.
adsorvente (*adj.; m.,f.*) adsorbent.
adstringência (*f.*) astringency.
adstringente (*f.*) astringent; clinging.
adstringir (*v.t.*) to astringe, constrict, compress, squeeze.
adstrito –ta (*adj.; irreg. p.p. of* ADSTRINGIR) tied (to); connected (with), in liaison (with).
aduana (*f.*) customhouse. [More usual: ALFÂNDEGA].
aduanar (*v.t.*) to clear through the customhouse.
aduaneiro –ra (*adj.*) customhouse. **direitos—s**, customs duties. **união—**, tariff union; (*m.,f.*) customhouse employee.
aduar (*v.t.*) to divide irrigation waters.
adubação, –bagem (*f.*) fertilizing (of land); spicing, seasoning (of food).—**sideral**, green manuring.
adubar (*v.t.*) to fertilize, manure (the land); to season, spice (food).
adubo (*m.*) fertilizer, manure.—**químico**, or **mineral**, chemical fertilizer.—**orgânico**, organic fertilizer.—**s prêtos**, the general term for spices such as cinnamon, peppers and cloves.—**verde**, green manure, cover crop.
adução (*f.*) adduction, bringing forward. [Verb ADUZIR]. **canal de—de águas**, water canal.
aducente (*adj.*) adducent.
aduchar (*v.t.*) to coil a rope or cable.
aduchas (*f.pl.*) coils of rope or cable.
aduela (*f.*) barrel stave; (*Arch.*) arch brick or stone, voussoir, springer. **ter uma—de menos**, to have a screw loose (in the head).
adufa (*f.*) window shutter; flood gate; sluice gate; stone wheel for pressing olives.
adufar (*v.t.*) to provide with shutters.
adulação (*f.*) adulation; toadyism; blarney, applesauce.
adulador –dora (*adj.*) flattering; (*m.,f.*) adulator.
adulão –lona (*adj.*) flattering; (*m.,f.*) servile flatterer; sycophant; toady.
adular (*v.t.*) to flatter, cajole, blandish; to fawn upon, curry favor with.
adularescência (*f.*) adularescence.
adulária (*f., Min.*) adularia, moonstone.
adulatório –ria (*adj.*) adulatory.
adulçorar (*v.*) = DULCIFICAR.
adulona, fem. of ADULÃO.
aduloso –sa (*adj.*) flattering; (*m.,f.*) adulator.
adúltera (*f.*) adulteress.
adulteração (*f.*) adulteration.—**de gêneros**, adulteration of foodstuffs.
adulterado –da (*adj.*) adulterated; spurious.
adulterador –dora (*m.,f.*) adulterator.
adulterar (*v.t.*) to adulterate, debase; (*v.i.*) to commit adultery.
adulterino –na (*adj.*) adulterine; spurious; illegal. **filho—**, illegitimate child.
adultério (*m.*) adultery.
adulterioso –sa (*adj.*) adulterous.
adúltero –ra (*adj.*) adulterous; illicit; spurious; (*m.*) adulterer; (*f.*) adulteress.
adulteroso –sa (*adj.*) adulterous.
adulto –ta (*adj.; m.,f.*) adult.
adumbração (*f.*) adumbration; faint sketch; vague portrayal; illusion.
adumbrar (*v.t.*) to adumbrate; to shade; to sketch.
adunar (*v.t.*) to make as one, unite, bring together; (*v.r.*) to come together (as one).
aduncidade (*f.*) aduncity, hookedness.
adunco –ca (*adj.*) aduncous, curved inward; hooked. **nariz—**, hooknose.
adurir (*v.t.*) to cauterize.

adustão (f.) act of burning or parching, or state of being burned or parched.

adustez (f.) excessive heat.

adusto -ta (adj.) burnt or scorched; fiery; sunburnt; tanned.

adutor -tora (adj.) adductor; adducing; conveying; (m., Anat., Zool.) adductor (muscle); (f.) water main, pipe line, aqueduct.

aduzir [36] (v.t.) to adduce, bring forward, cite, allege; to carry forward, convey (as water in an aqueduct); (Physiol.) to adduct.

ádvena (m.,f.) foreigner, stranger, newcomer.

adventício -cia (adj.) adventitious; adventive; accidental, casual; supervenient; foreign; (Anat.) of or relating to an adventitia. **raiz**—, adventitious root; (m.,f.) foreigner, stranger; upstart.

adventismo (m.) Adventism.

adventista (adj.; m.,f.) Adventist.

advento (m.) advent, coming, arrival; (Eccl.) advent.

adverbial (adj.) adverbial.

adverbializar (v.t.) to adverbialize.

adverbialmente (adv.) adverbially.

adverbiar (v.t.) to adverbialize, give the force or form of an adverb to.

advérbio (m.) adverb.

adversante (adj.) adverse.

adversão (f.) word of warning or advice; opposition; contrariety; adverseness.

adversar (v.t.) to oppose.

adversário -ria (adj.) adverse, opposed, antagonistic; (m.,f.) adversary, opponent; (m.pl.) adversaria (miscellaneous collection of notes, remarks, commentaries, etc.).

adversativo -va (adj.) adversative; (f.) an adversative word or proposition.

adversidade (f.) adversity, hardship, misfortune, calamity; bad luck; mishap.

adversifólio -lia (adj., Bot.) adversifoliate.

adverso -sa (adj.) adverse, contrary; antagonistic; unlucky; (m.,f.) adversary.

advertência (f.) advertence; admonition; warning; reproach; instruction, advice.

advertido -da (adj.) admonished; heedful.

advertimento (m.) admonishment.

advertir [21A] (v.t.) to admonish; to warn; to remind; to explain; to give heed to.—**de** (sôbre, a respeito de), to warn of (about). (v.i.) to advert; to take heed or notice; to realize.

advindo -da (adj.) supervened.

advir [82] (v.i.) to supervene; to befall, happen, occur, take place, come to pass.—**de**, to result from. **donde advem que**, or **advem dai que**, whence, wherefore; in consequence of that (fact).

advocacia (f.) advocacy (legal profession); act of advocating.

advocatório -ria (adj.) advocatory.

advocatura (f.) advocacy.

advogado (m.) lawyer, attorney(-at-law), counsel, counsellor; advocate, defender, patron.—**da acusação**, attorney for plaintiff or prosecution.—**da defesa**, attorney for defendant or defense.—**do diabo**, Devil's advocate. —**oficioso**, or **ex-ofício**, a lawyer appointed by the court in behalf of a defendant.—**provisionado**, a licensed attorney though not a law graduate. **Ordem dos Advogados**, Bar Association. **ser—de causa própria**, to act as one's own lawyer; to plead one's own cause.

advogar (v.i.) to practice law; (v.t.) to advocate, support; to defend in court.

aegirina (f., Min.) aegirite.

aeração, aeragem (f.) aeration. **poço de**—, air-shaft.

aeremia (f.) the bends, caisson disease.

aerênquima (f., Bot.) aerenchyma.

aerenterectasia (f., Med.) aerenterectasia.

aéreo -rea (adj.) aerial; ethereal. **acrobacia**—, stunt flying. **ataque**—, air raid. **carta**—, airmail letter. **correio**—, airmail.

aeretmia (f., Med.) emphysema.

aéride, aérida (f.) a genus (Aerides) of epiphytic orchids.

aérido -da (adj.) epiphytic.

aerífero -ra (adj.) conveying air.

aerificação (f.) aerification.

aerificar (v.t.) to aerify.

aeriforme (adj.) aeriform, gaseous.

aeróbio -bia (adj.) aerobic; (m.) aerobe.

aerobioscópio (m., Med.) aerobioscope.

aerobiose (f., Biol.) aerobiosis.

aerociste (m., Bot.) aerocyst (of algae).

aerodermectasia (f., Med.) aerodermectasia, interstitial emphysema.

aerodinâmico -ca (adj.) aerodynamic; streamlined. **plano**—, airfoil; (f.) aerodynamics.

aeródromo (m.) airdrome; flying field.—**base**, air base. —**de combate**, combat air field.—**de recurso**, emergency air field.—**de trabalho**, major air base.—**militar**, military air base.—**particular**, private flying field.—**público**, public flying field.

aeroduto (m.) air duct.

aerofagia (f.) aerophagy.

aerofíceas (f.pl., Bot.) lichens.

aerófito -ta (adj., Bot.) epiphytic; (m.) epiphyte.

aerofobia (f.) aerophobia.

aerófilo -la (adj.) airminded, fond of flying.

aerofólio (m.) airfoil.

aerofone, aerofono (m.) aerophone.

aeróforo (m.) miner's aerophore.

aerofotografia (f.) aerophotography.

aerofotogrametria (f.) aerophotogrammetry.

aerófugo -fa (adj.) airtight.

aerogênese (f.) aerogenesis.

aerogênico -ca (adj.) aerogenic.

aerografia (f.) aerography.

aeroidro -dra (adj., Min.) aerohydrous.

aeroidroterapia [o-i] (f., Med.) aerohydrotherapy.

aerólito (m.) aerolite; meteorite. [Often incorrectly pronounced AEROLITO.]

aerologia (f.) aerology.

aerológico -ca (adj.) aerologic(al).

aerólogo (m.) aerologist.

aeromancia (f.) aeromancy.

aeromecância (f.) aeromechanics.

aerometria (f.) aerometry.

aerométrico -ca (adj.) aerometric.

aerômetro (m.) aerometer.

aeromoça (f.) air stewardess.

aeromoço (m.) air steward.

aeromodelo (m.) model airplane.

aeromotor (m.) aeromotor.

aeron. = AERONÁUTICA (Aeronautics).

aeronauta (m.,f.) aeronaut.

aeronáutico -ca (adj.) aeronautic(al); (f.) aeronautics.

aeronave (f.) airship, aircraft.

aeronavegação (f.) aerial navigation.

aeroplanar (v.i.) to travel by plane.

aeroplania (f.) airplaning, flying.

aeroplano (m.) airplane.

aeroporto (m.) airport.—**aduaneiro**, airport of entry from foreign countries.

aeroposta (f.) pneumatic mail carrier; airmail.

aeropostal (adj.) airmail.

aeroscepse (f., Zool.) aeroscepsis.

aeroscopia (f.) aeroscopy.

aeroscópico -ca (adj.) aeroscopic.

aeroscópio (m.) aeroscope.

aerosfera (f.) aerosphere, atmosphere.

aeróstata (m.,f.) aeronaut.

aerostático -ca (adj.) aerostatic(al); (f.) aerostatics.

aeróstato (m.) aerostat, airship, balloon.—**cativo**, captive balloon.—**dirigível**, dirigible airship.—**livre**, free balloon.—**papagaio**, kite balloon.—**pilôto**, pilot balloon.

aerotaxia [ks] (f.) aerotaxis.

aerotécnico -ca (adj.) aerotechnical; (f.) technic of aeronautics.

aeroterapêutica (f.) aerotherapeutics.

aeroterapia (f.) aerotherapy.

aerotropismo (m., Plant Physiol.) aerotropism.

aerovia (f.) air lane.

aetita (f., Min.) eaglestone, c.a. PEDRA-DE-ÁGUIA.

afã (m.) ado, bustle; diligence, assiduousness; toil; craving; zeal; anxiety, concern, care; fatigue.

afabilidade (f.) affability.

afabilíssimo -ma (absol. superl. of AFÁVEL) most affable.

afacia (f.) = AFAQUIA.

afadigado -da (adj.) fatigued, tired.

afadigador -dora (adj.) fatiguing, tiring.

afadigar (v.t.) to fatigue; to importune; (v.r.) to tire; to drudge.

afadigoso -sa (adj.) fatiguing.

afagador -dora (adj.) caressing, fondling; (m.,f.) caresser.

afagante (*adj.*) cherishing, caressing.
afagar (*v.t.*) to caress, fondle, pet, cuddle; to coax; to cherish; to nourish; to smoothe (down).—**com os olhos**, to caress with the eyes.
afagia (*f., Med.*) aphagia.
afago (*m.*) caress; expression of affection; blandishment.—**da fortuna**, Fortune's smile.
afaimado –**da** (*adj.*) famished, starving.
afaimar (*v.t.*) to starve.
afalar (*v.t.*) to shout at animals.
afalcaçar (*v.t.*) to whip or wrap (the end of a rope).
afamado –**da** (*adj.*) famed.
afamar (*v.t.*) to make famous or renowned; (*v.r.*) to become famous.
afamilhar-se (*v.r.*) to acquire a large family.
afanado –**da** (*adj.*) toilsome, laborious; anxious; eager; financially embarrassed.
afanar-se (*v.r.*) to toil, grub, struggle.
afanésio (*m., Min.*) aphanesite, clinoclasite.
afanítico –**ca** (*adj.*) aphanitic.
afanita (*f., Petrog.*) aphanite.
afano (*m.*) = AFÃ.
afanoso –**sa** (*adj.*) anxious, solicitous; toilsome, grueling.
afaquia (*f., Med.*) aphakia.
afasia (*f., Med.*) aphasia.—**motora**, motor, or Broca's, aphasia; aphemia.—**ótica**, or **sensorial**, auditory, or sensory, aphasia.
afásico –**ca** (*adj.*) aphasic.
afasta! (*interj.*) Out of the way! Stand back!
afastado –**da** (*adj.*) distant, remote, far-away; far-removed; away from; outlying; long ago; sequestered; separated, parted. **manter-se**—, to stand aloof. **parentes** —**s**, distant relations.
afastador –**dora** (*adj.*) pushing aside, removing, routing, averting, dispelling; (*m.,f.*) one who or that which pushes aside, etc. See the verb AFASTAR.
afastamento (*m.*) separation, dissociation; departure; withdrawal; distance from; estrangement; removal.— **das rodas**, wheel base.—**efetivo**, (*Aeron.*) effective pitch; —**típico**, or—**quadrático médio**, (*Stat.*) standard deviation [= DESVIO PADRÃO.]
afastar (*v.t.*) to push away (aside, back); to remove; to separate; to disaffect; to parry, ward off; to avert; to rout, dispel; (*v.i.*) to deviate; (*v.r.*) to move (go) away; to swerve; to step back (away, aside); to keep away; to withdraw, retire.—**-se do assunto**, to stray from the subject, digress.—**-se do** (**seu**) **dever**, to swerve from (one's) duty.—**a multidão**, to push back the crowd.— **suspeitas**, to dispel suspicion. **Afasta!** Get back! Stand aside!
afatiar (*v.t.*) to cut slices.
afável (*adj.*) affable, courteous (**para com**, toward); urbane; **de natureza**—, kindly, gentle.
afazendado –**da** (*adj.*) rich; owning FAZENDAS.
afazendar-se (*v.r.*) to get rich.
afazer [47] (*v.t.*) to habituate; (*v.r.*) to accustom oneself, get used to.—**-se aos costumes do país**, to adapt, adjust, oneself to the ways of the country.
afazeres (*m.pl.*) chores, tasks.—**caseiros**, or **domésticos**, household duties.
afeado –**da** (*adj.*) disfigured, somewhat ugly.
afeador –**dora** (*adj.*) uglifying; (*m.,f.*) uglifier.
afear (*v.t.*) to uglify, disfigure; deface, deform; (*v.r.*) to become ugly or disfigured.
afecção, **afeção** (*f.*) affection (disease).
afect-, see under **afet-**.
afegane (*adj.; m.,f.*) Afghan.
Afeganistão (*m.*) Afghanistan.
afeiar, wrong spelling of AFEAR.
afeição (*f.*) affection, love, fondness, liking. **com**—, dearly. **provas de**—, tokens of affection. **tomar-se de**—**por**, to take a liking to.
afeiçoado –**da** (*adj.*) fond of, addicted to, devoted to; appropriate; properly fashioned; well made; (*m.,f.*) close friend.
afeiçoar [from FEIÇÃO, form, and AFEIÇÃO, affection] (*v.t.*) to form, fashion, shape, mold; to adapt, adjust to.—**-se** (**a, de, por**) to develop a liking for, become attached to, addicted to.
afeito –**ta** (*adj.; irreg. p.p. of* AFAZER) accustomed (**a**, to); inured (**a**, to).—**aos maus tratos**, used to ill-treatment. —**ao trabalho**, used to hard work.
afélio (*m., Astron.*) aphelion.
afeliotropismo (*m., Plant Physiol.*) apheliotropism.
afemia (*f., Med.*) aphemia, motor aphasia.

afeminar (*v.*) = EFEMINAR.
aferente (*adj., Physiol.*) afferent.
aférese (*f., Gram.*) apheresis.
aferético –**ca** (*adj.*) apheretic.
aferição (*f.*) checking, comparing, esp. weights and measures.
aferidor (*m.*) checker, inspector (of weights and measures); a gauge.
aferimento (*m.*) = AFERIÇÃO.
aferir [21a] (*v.t.*) to compare with a standard (as of weights and measures); to check; to collate (with); to gauge. Cf. CONFERIR.
aferrado –**da** (*adj.*) fixed, fastened (as with iron); persistent; obstinate, dogged, stubborn.
aferrar (*v.t.*) to anchor; to harpoon; to fasten, secure;—**-se a**, to clutch, grab hold of, hang on to; to cling to; to persist in (obstinately).
aferrenhar (*v.t.*) to make hard as iron; (*v.r.*) to become obdurate.
aferretoar (*v.t.*) to jab or prod with a goad; to spur, stimulate; to slur, disparage.
afêrro (*m.*) obstinacy; strong attachment.
aferroar (*v.t.*) to prick, sting; to stimulate.
aferrolhar (*v.t.*) to bolt, lock.
aferventar (*v.t.*) to boil, parboil; to excite.
afervoar (*v.t.*) to arouse fervor in; to excite; to boil.
afestoar, **afestonar** (*v.t.*) to festoon.
afetação (*f.*) affectation, affectedness; pretension, airs; affected manner.
afetado –**da** (*adj.*) affected, unnatural; prissy; finical; namby-pamby; pretentious; stilted; touched, moved; infected (with), diseased.
afetante (*adj.*) given to false show.
afetar [24] (*v.t.*) to affect, pretend, feign, put on; to impress, touch, move; to concern, interest.
afetivo –**va** (*adj.*) affective, emotional; affectionate.
afeto –**ta** (*adj.*) affectionate, friendly.—**a**, under the care or charge of; submitted to (for action, for decision); (*m.*) affection, fondness, liking.
afetuoso –**sa** (*adj.*) affectionate, fond, tender, loving.
aff-, see under **af-**.
afiação (*f.*) **afiamento** (*m.*) sharpening.
afiado –**da** (*adj.*) sharp, sharpened.
afiador (*m.*) sharpener, grinder.—**de navalhas**, razor strop.
afiançado –**da** (*adj.*) bonded, under bond, vouched for; (*m.,f.*) person under bond, or one vouched for by another.
afiançador –**dora** (*adj.*) guaranteeing, vouching for; (*m.,f.*) person who vouches for another.
afiançar (*v.t.*) to guarantee, vouch for, answer for; to assure.—**a**, to declare to, vow to, warrant.
afiançável (*adj.*) bailable, bondable.
afiar (*v.t.*) to sharpen, grind; to make keen; to strop (a razor).
aficionado –**da** (*adj.*) very fond of (sports, etc.); (*m.,f.*) a sports enthusiast, fight fan, etc.; ardent follower (as of a hobby).
afidalgar (*v.t.*) to raise to the rank of nobility; to enoble; (*v.r.*) to put on airs of nobility.
afidífago –**ga** (*adj.*) aphidivorous.
afídios (*m.pl., Zool.*) the Aphididae (aphids).
afiguração (*f.*) imagination; conjecture.
afigurar (*v.t.*) to represent, delineate, draw a figure of; to form an image of; (*v.r.*) to seem, appear. **afigura-se-me que**, it seems to me that. **afigurou-se-nos que**, it appeared to us that.
afilado –**da** (*adj.*) slender; tapering.
afilanta (*f.*) a liliaceous plant, *Aphyllanthes monspeliensis*.
afilantropia (*f.*) aphilanthropy.
afilantropo [trô] (*m.*) misanthrope.
afilar (*v.t.*) to check weights and measures [= AFERIR]; to sharpen, make keen [= AFIAR]; to make thin, tapering, slender; to sick on (dogs) [= AÇULAR].
afilhada (*f.*) goddaughter; protegée.
afilhadismo (*m.*) nepotism.
afilhado (*m.*) godson; protegé.
afilhar (*v.i.*) to sprout.
afiliação (*f.*) affiliation.
afiliar (*v.t.*) to affiliate.
afilo –**la** (*adj., Bot.*) aphyllous, leafless.
afim (*adj.*) having affinity with or resemblance to.—**de**, related to, allied to. [Do not confuse with A FIM DE, in order to.]; (*m.,f.*) a relation by marriage.

afinação (*f.*) refining, refinement; purification; tuning (of a musical instrument); accurate pitch; harmonious accordance; concert of parts; final touch.

afinado -da (*adj.*) refined; tuned.

afinador -dora (*adj.*) refining; tuning; (*m.,f.*) tuner (of pianos, etc.); refiner; checker, gauger.

afinal (*adv.*) after all, finally, at last [= POR FIM, ENFIM, FINALMENTE].—**de contas**, taking all in all. **até que**—, at last.

afinar (*v.t.*) to tune (piano, etc.); to pitch (the voice); to sharpen; to refine; to polish; to purify, refine (metals); to harmonize.

afincar (*v.t.*) to stick in (as a pin), plunge in (as a dagger), drive in (as a stake);—more usual: FINCAR; (*v.r.*) to persevere, persist doggedly.

afinco (*m.*) perseverance, steadfastness, "stick-to-itiveness." **trabalhar com**—, to work perseveringly. **fazer (alguma coisa) com**—, to work at (something) earnestly.

afinidade (*f.*) affinity; relationship by marriage; **irmão por**—, half-brother.

afírico -ca (*adj., Petrog.*) aphyric.

afirmação (*f.*) affirmation, assertion.

afirmador -dora (*adj.*) affirming, confirming; (*m.,f.*) affirmer.

afirmar (*v.t.*) to affirm, declare, assert; to uphold. (*v.r.*) to make certain of; to gaze at. **afirma-se que**, it is said that.

afirmativo -va (*adj.*) affirmative, declaratory; (*f.*) affirmation, declaration, assertion, statement; affirmative. **ser pela**—, to be for the affirmative. **responder pela**—, to answer in the affirmative.

afirmável (*adj.*) affirmable.

afistulado -da (*adj.*) fistulous.

afivelar (*v.t.*) to buckle (on).

afixar [ks] (*v.t.*) to affix, fasten; to post (bills, notices). **É proibido—cartazes**, Post no bills.

afixo [ks] (*m.*) affix (prefix or suffix).

afiar (*v.t.*) to breathe on or blow on; to inspire; (*v.i.*) to breathe hard, pant; to flutter.

aflato (*m.*) afflatus; afflation.

aflautado -da (*adj.*) flutelike.

aflautar (*v.t.*) to make (the voice) flutelike.

afleimar-se (*v.r.*) to become upset, irritated, annoyed.

afleumar-se (*v.r.*) to become phlegmatic.

aflição (*f.*) afflication, woe, tribulation; hardship; sorrow, distress; irritation.

afligido -da (*adj.*) afflicted, tormented.

afligidor -dora (*adj.*) afflicting; (*m.,f.*) afflicter.

afligimento (*m.*) = AFLIÇÃO.

afligir (*v.t.*) to afflict, grieve, distress; to try, torment; to scourge; to badger, plague, worry, trouble; (*v.r.*) to grieve; to fret.—**se com**, to be saddened by; to be worried by. **Não o aflija**, Don't be too hard on him. **Não se aflija**, Don't worry (yourself).

aflitivo -va (*adj.*) afflictive, distressing; heart-rending, grievous; harrowing; nerve-racking.

aflito -ta (*adj.*) afflicted; distressed; worried, anxious.

aflogístico -ca (*adj.*) aphlogistic, flameless.

afloração (*f.*) **afloramento** (*m.*) outcropping (of minerals); levelling (of surfaces); (*Geol.*) basset.

aflorar (*v.i.*) to outcrop, appear on the surface; (*v.t.*) to make level (flush) with.

afluência (*f.*) affluence, abundance; rushing stream. **um dia de**—, a day of large crowds. **uma grande—de pessoas**, a large throng of people.

afluente (*adj.*) affluent, abundant, plenteous; (*m.*) tributary stream.

afluir [72] (*v.i.*) to flow, run, stream (**a**, to; **de**, from); to flock together.

afluxo [ks] (*m.*) afflux, flowing.

af.° = AFETUOSO (affectionate)—used ín closing a letter.

afobação (*f.*) hurry, flurry, scurry; fluster; hustle and bustle.

afobado -da (*adj.*) flustered; hurried; "hot and bothered."

afobamento (*m.*) = AFOBAÇÃO.

afobar (*v.t.*) to annoy, upset; (*v.r.*) to become flustered, upset, bothered. **Não se afobe!** Relax¹ Take it easy! Keep your shirt on!

afocinhar (*v.t.*) to muzzle; to root with the nose (as a pig); (*v.i.*) to fall on one's nose; to nose down.

afódio (*m.*) dung beetle (*Aphodius*).

afofado -da (*adj.*) fluffy.

afofar (*v.t.*) to fluff, make fluffy.

afogadilho (*m.*) haste, hurry, impetuosity. **de**—, precipitately, hastily, slap-bang, slapdash. **obra feita de**—, a rush job.

afogado -da (*adj.*) drowned; sunk; muffled; overwhelmed; (*m.,f.*) drowned person.

afogador -dora (*adj.*) drowning; suffocating; (*m.*) choker (necklace); (*Autom.*) choke.

afogamento (*m.*) drowning; suffocating; choking.

afogar (*v.t.*) to drown; to suffocate, asphyxiate; to extinguish; to stifle; to choke.—**se em pouca água**, to be upset by trifles; to raise a tempest in a teacup.

afôgo (*m.*) suffocation; oppression; hurry.

afogueado -da (*adj.*) flame-colored; fiery, burning, aglow. **com o rosto**—, with cheeks aglow.

afoguear (*v.t.*) to set ablaze; (*v.r.*) to blush, redden.

afoitar (*v.t.*) to encourage, embolden; (*v.r.*) to dare to. Var. AFOUTAR.

afoiteza (*f.*) boldness, courage, valor. Var. AFOUTEZA.

afoito -ta (*adj.*) bold, daring; fearless, dauntless; (*m.*) daredevil. Var. AFOUTO.

afolhamento (*m.*) crop rotation.

afolhar (*v.t.*) to divide (land) into fields for rotation of crops; (*v.i.*) to put forth leaves.

afonia (*f., Med.*) aphonia.

áfono -na, afônico -ca, afono -na (*adj.*) aphonic, voiceless.

Afonso (*m.*) Alfonso; Alphonso; Alonzo.

afora (*prep.*) except, excepting, excluding, but, save, leaving out, with the exception of.—**um, todos os outros ganharam**, All but one won. (*adv.*) outside. **pela vida**—, throughout life. **por este mundo**—, throughout the world. **rua**—, out into the street. Cf. FORA.

aforação (*f.*) **aforamento** (*m.*) long-term lease of real property. Cf. FÔRO, FOREIRO.

aforar (*v.t.*) to rent, lease.

aforçurar (*v.*) = APRESSURAR.

aforismo (*m.*) aphorism.

aforístico -ca (*adj.*) aphoristic.

aformosear (*v.t.*) to embellish, beautify, adorn, decorate; (*v.r.*) to grow beautiful; to embellish oneself; to preen.

aforquilhado -da (*adj.*) forked; branched.

aforrado -da (*adj.*) of slaves, free. Cf. FÔRRO, ALFORRIADO.

aforrar (*v.t.*) to provide (as, a garment) with a lining; to free (slaves).

afortalezar (*v.t.*) to fortify.

afortunado -da (*adj.*) lucky, blessed, fortunate; thriving, prosperous.

afortunar (*v.t.*) to make fortunate, happy; (*v.r.*) to become so.

afótico -ca (*adj.*) aphotic, lightless.

afoutar (*v.*) & derivs. = AFOITAR & derivs.

afracar (*v.t.,v.i.*) to weaken.

afrancesado -da (*adj.*) Frenchified.

afrancesar (*v.t.*) to Frenchify.

afrasia (*f., Med.*) aphrasia, dumbness.

afreguesado -da (*adj.*) well-frequented (by customers).

afreguesar (*v.t.*) to make a client or customer of; to fill (a place) with customers; to obtain customers; (*v.r.*) to become a customer

afrescar (*v.*) = REFRESCAR.

afretador (*m., Maritime Law*) the one to whom a ship (or a part of one) is leased by charter party.

afretar (*v.t.*) to charter a ship.

áfrica (*f.*) exploit, feat, stunt; (*cap.*) Africa.

africânder (*adj.*; *m.,f.*) Afrikander.

africanismo (*m.*) word of African origin.

africano -na (*adj.*; *m.,f.*) African; (*m.*) a small live-bearing tropical fish (*Epiplatys chaperi*), seen in home aquaria; (*f.pl.*) large gold earrings, such as worn by Moorish women.

afrita (*f., Min.*) aphrite.

afrizita (*f., Min.*) aphrizite.

afrodisia (*f.*) aphrodisia.

afrodisíaco -ca (*adj.*; *m.*) aphrodisiac.

afroixar (*v.*) & derivs. = AFROUXAR & derivs.

afronesia, afronia (*f., Psychiatry*) aphronia.

afronta (*f.*) affront, insult; outrage; indignity; slight; assault. **reparar uma**—, to make amends for an affront.

afrontação (*f.*) affronting.

afrontado -da (*adj.*) affronted; short of breath ; of horses, winded.

afrontador -dora (*adj.*) affronting; (*m.,f.*) affronter.

afrontamento (*m.*) affronting.

afrontar (*v.t.*) to affront, insult; to strike, attack; to face, front, oppose; to defy (death, danger, trouble, etc.); to tire; fatigue; to meet (face to face) with; to engage with; to measure up to.

afrontoso -sa (*adj.*) affrontive, outrageous, offensive; abusive.

afrossiderita (*f.*, *Min.*) aphrosiderite.

afrouxado -da (*adj.*) slack, loose. Var. AFROIXADO.

afrouxamento (*m.*) loosening, slackening. Var. AFROIXA-MENTO.

afrouxar (*v.t.*) to loosen, unfasten (rope, fetter, belt, etc.); to slacken (speed); (*v.i.*) to become loose or looser; to slow down; to sag; (*v.r.*) to become loose or slack; to give way.—o garrão,—os quartos, (*slang*) to give up, poop out. Var. AFROIXAR.

afrouxelado -da (*adj.*) down-covered. Var. AFROIXELADO.

afrutar (*v.i.*) to bear fruit.

aftas (*f.pl.*, *Med.*, *Veter.*) aphthae.

aftongia (*f.*, *Med.*) aphthongia.

aftoso -sa (*adj.*) aphthous. **febre**—, aphthous fever, hoof-and-mouth disease.

afugentar (*v.t.*) to put to flight; to chase, drive away (**de**, from); to dispel.—môscas, to shoo flies.—um mau pensamento, to banish an evil thought.

afumaçado -da (*adj.*) smoky, smoke-filled.

afumado -da (*adj.*) full of smoke.

afumar (*v.t.*) to fill with smoke; (*v.i.*) to smoke.

afumegar (*v.*) = FUMEGAR.

afundado -da (*adj.*) sunk.

afundamento (*m.*) act of sinking.

afundar (*v.t.*) to sink, send to the bottom; to submerge; to sink (a well, post, etc.); to make deep or deeper. (*v.r.*) to sink, founder; to be swallowed up (as in darkness).

afunilado -da (*adj.*) funnel-shaped.

afunilar (*v.t.*) to shape like a funnel; to splay.

afuroar (*v.t.*) to ferret, search out; (*v.i.*) to nose about.

afusado -da (*adj.*) tapered; spindle-shaped.

afusão (*f.*, *Med.*) affusion.

afusar (*v.t.*) to taper; to sharpen at one end; to pique (curiosity, interest, etc.).

afuzilar (*v.*) = FUZILAR.

afzélia (*f.*, *Bot.*) African afzelia (*A. africana*).

agacés (*m.pl.*) the southern division of a Guaycuruan or Payaguan tribe formerly dwelling along the Paraguay River.

ag. = AGÔSTO (August).

agachada (*f.*) dodge, side spring, spurt forward; (*Zool.*) a snipe [= NARCEJA].

agachadeira (*f.*) a snipe (*Capella p. paraguaiae*), c.a. NARCEJA; the ruddy turnstone (*Arenaria interpres morinella*); Azara's collared plover (*Charadrinus collaris*), c.a. MAÇARICO-DE-COLEIRA.

agachar-se (*v.r.*) to crouch, squat, stoop low; to cringe, cower. Cf. ACAÇAPAR-SE.

agadanhar (*v.t.*) to seize (as with the claws); (*colloq.*) to grab (steal).

agaí (*m.*, *Bot.*) a thevetia (*T. ahovai*).

agaiatar-se (*v.r.*) to become urchinlike.

agalactia (*f.*, *Med.*, *Veter.*) agalactia.

agaláctico -ca (*adj.*) agalactic.

agalacto -ta (*adj.*) agalactous.

agalanar (*v.*) = ENGALANAR.

agalancéia (*f.*) the dog rose (*Rosa canina*).

agalaxia [ks] (*f.*) = AGALACTIA.

agalegado -da (*adj.*) like the Gallicians; (*colloq.*) a disparaging term meaning coarse, rude, brutish, stupid.

agalena (*f.*) a grass spider (*Agalena*).

agalita (*f.*, *Min.*) agalite.

agalmotolita (*f.*, *Min.*) agalmotolite, figure stone, pagodite.

agaloar (*v.t.*) to adorn or trim with galloons, gold braid, insignia of rank, etc.

agaloche (*m.*) agalloch or aloeswood. Cf. ALOÉS.

agamá (*m.*) the starred lizard (*Agama stellio*).

agami [í] (*f.*) = JACAMIM.

agâmico -ca (*adj.*, *Biol.*) agamic, asexual, parthenogenic; (*Bot.*) cryptogamic.

ágamo -ma (*adj.*, *Bot.*) agamous, cryptogamous.

agamogênese (*f.*, *Biol.*) agamogenesis.

agamonte (*f.*, *Zool.*) agamont, schizont.

agapanto (*m.*, *Bot.*) any agapanthus, esp. *A. africanus*.

ágape, ágapa (*m.* or *f.*) primitive love-feast; modern-day political banquet or business luncheon.

Agar (*f.*) Hagar.

ágar-ágar (*m.*) agar-agar.

agaricáceo -cea (*adj.*) agaricaceous; (*f.*, *Bot.*) an agaric.

agarícico -ca (*adj.*, *Chem.*) agaric, agaricic, agaricinic. **ácido**—, agaric acid.

agaricina (*f.*, *Pharm.*) agaricin.

agárico (*m.*) a genus (*Agaricus*) of gill fungi, comprising the edible meadow mushroom (*A. campestris*) which is known in Brazil by its common French name *champignon*.—branco, a shelf fungus (*Polyporus officinalis*).

agarístidas (*f.pl.*) the Agaristidae (diurnal moths).

ágaro (*m.*, *Bot.*) the sea colander (*Agarum turneri*).

agarotado -da (*adj.*) roguish, mischievous.

agarração (*f.*) act of seizing, grabbing, clutching.

agarradiço -ca (*adj.*) clinging; importunate.

agarradinho -nha (*adj.*) of persons, esp. children and sweethearts, displaying strong attachment to one another, as by hugging, holding hands, etc.; clinging, inseparable.

agarrado -da (*adj.*) caught, held fast; clinging; of friends, inseparable; tight, close-fisted.—com o chão, of plants, close to (hugging) the ground.

agarrador -dora (*adj.*) seizing, clutching; (*m.*) one who, or that which, grabs, holds, clutches, etc.; (*Zool.*) a suckfish (remora). c.a. PIRAQUIBA, PEIXE-PIOLHO, PIOLHO-DE-TURBARÃO, RÊMORA, IPIRUQUIBA, UPERUQUIBA.

agarramento (*m.*) seizure; strong attachment between persons, esp. sweethearts.

agarrar (*v.t.*) to seize, grab, clutch; to catch hold (of); to lay (grab, take) hold of.—com, to grasp with.—por, to catch by.—-se (com), to cling, hold fast (to).—-se a, to seize (fasten) upon; to grasp, cling to.—-se às abas de, to hang on to the coattails of.—-se com o chão, to hug the ground. "Devemos agarrar-nos uns aos outros ou seremos agarrados um de cada vez"; "We must hang together or surely we shall hang separately."

agarrochar (*v.t.*) to goad; to incite.

agasalhado -da (*adj.*) protected, sheltered.

agasalhador -dora (*adj.*) sheltering, welcoming; (*m.,f.*) one who takes in, welcomes, shelters another.

agasalhar (*v.t.*) to shelter; to receive, welcome, take in (with kindness or affection); to nourish; to wrap up, muffle up, swathe.—-se bem, to wrap (oneself) up warmly.—-se com, to lodge with, take shelter with.

agasalho (*m.*) shelter(ing); lodgement; welcome; a wrap (as a shawl).—de pele, fur wrap.

agasflide (*m.*) giant fennel (*Ferula brevifolia*), c.a. CANA-FRECHA.

agastadiço -ça (*adj.*) peevish, cranky, irritable, cantankerous.

agastado -da (*adj.*) upset; irate; irked.

agastamento (*m.*) tiff, quarrel.

agastar (*v.t.*) to irritate, nettle, chafe; to spite; (*v.r.*) to become upset.—-se com, to get peeved with.

agástrico -ca (*adj.*, *Zool.*) agastric.

agastronervia (*f.*, *Med.*) agastroneuria.

ágata (*f.*, *Min.*) agate; [*cap.*] Agatha.

agatanhar (*v.t.*,*v.i.*) to claw, scratch (as a cat).

agateado -da (*adj.*) of eyes, like a cat's; bluish.

agáteo -tea (*adj.*) agate; agaty.

agati [í] (*f.*, *Bot.*) the agati sesbania (*S. grandiflora*).

agatífero -ra (*adj.*) agatiferous.

agatinhar (*v.i.*) to crawl (as a kitten); (*v.r.*) to climb (as a cat.)

agatino -na (*adj.*) agatine; (*f.*, *Pharm.*) agathin.

agatis [í] (*m.*, *Bot.*) the genus (*Agathis*) of dammar pines.

agatismo (*m.*, *Metaph.*) agathism.

agatóide (*adj.*) agatelike.

agatologia (*f.*, *Ethics*) agathology.

agauchado -da [a-u] (*adj.*) GAÚCHO-like.

agauchar-se [a-u] (*v.r.*) to become like a GAÚCHO.

agave (*f.*) the century plant (*Agave americana*), c.a. PITA, PITEIRA, ABECEDÁRIA, ALOÉS-DOS-CEM-ANOS, BABOSA-BRAVA.

agavelar (*v.*) = ENGAVELAR.

agência (*f.*) agency; agentry; branch office; agent's pay.—de câmbio, money exchanger's office.—de empregos, employment agency.—de navios, steamship agency.—de publicidade, advertising agency.—noticiosa, news agency. Vive de sua—, he makes his living at odd jobs.

agenciador (*m.*) -deira (*f.*,) canvasser; salesman; agent.

agenciar (*v.t.*) to solicit, seek, endeavor to obtain; to canvass; to tout for; to be an agent for.

agenda (*f.*) agenda; memorandum book.

agente (*m.*, *f.*) agent—all senses; (*adj.*) acting.

agérato (*m.*, *Bot.*) the Mexican ageratum (*A. houston-*

ianum) and others of this genus; the sweet yarrow (*Achillea ageratum*), c.a. ERVA-DE-SÃO-JOÃO, MACELA-DE-SÃO-JOÃO, MACELA-FRANCESA.

agermanar (*v.t.*) to couple, link, connect (one thing with another).

agérrimo –**ma** (*absol. superl. of* AGRE *and of* AGRO) most sour; most acid.

ageusia, ageustia (*f., Med.*) ageusia.

agg-, see under **ag-.**

agigantado –**da** (*adj.*) gigantic, huge.

agigantar (*v.t.*) to greatly enlarge something; (*v.r.*) to loom.

ágil [**ágeis**] (*adj.*) agile, lively, nimble, lithe; clever.

agilidade (*f.*) agility; alertness; sprightliness.

agílimo –**ma, agilíssimo** –**ma,** absol. superls. of ÁGIL.

agilitar (*v.t.*) to make agile (as by exercise); (*Milit.*) to exercise troops.

aginário –**ria** (*adj., Bot.*) agynary.

ágio (*m.*) agio; broker's fee; premium or discount on foreign exchange; money-changing; usury.

agiota (*m.,f.*) speculator; moneylender; pawnbroker; usurer; sharper.

agiotagem (*f.*) agiotage; speculation on the market; sharp dealing; usury.

agiotar (*v.t.*) to engage in sharp dealings; to speculate.

agiotista (*m.,f.*) speculator.

agir (*v.i.*) to act, do, perform; to behave, proceed.—**bem** (**mal**), to do right (wrong); to behave well (badly).—**em prejuizo de,** to discriminate against.—**sem discernimento,** to act without understanding. **Está na hora de—,** It is time for action. **fazer—,** to set (something) going.

agitação (*f.*) agitation, shaking; disturbance; fluster; turmoil; boisterousness; excitement, emotion, perturbation, jitters; trouble.

agitadiço –**ça** (*adj.*) excitable.

agitado –**da** (*adj.*) agitated; restless; hectic; jittery, upset; of sleep, uneasy; of sea, rough; deranged, insane.

agitador –**dora** (*m.,f.*) agitator (person or implement); trouble-maker; (*Mach.*) shaker.

agitamento (*m.*) = AGITAÇÃO.

agitante (*adj.*) agitating.

agitar (*v.t.*) to agitate, shake; to jar; to wave; to wag; to brandish; to sway; to excite, rouse, stir up; to bring up for discussion; to debate; to exercise (make anxious); to disturb; (*v.r.*) to stir, move (about), flit (about); to mill around; to busy oneself; to bestir oneself. **Agite antes de usar,** Shake well before using.

agitato (*adj., Music*) agitato.

agitável (*adj.*) shakeable; susceptible of agitation.

áglifo –**fa** (*adj., Zool.*) aglyphous; (*m.*) one of the Aglypha.

aglobulia (*f., Med.*) aligocythenia.

aglomeração (*f.*) agglomeration, conglomeration.

aglomerado –**da** (*adj.*) agglomerate, gathered together; (*m.*) aggregate (of crushed rock, gravel, cement, etc.); (*Geol.*) agglomerate; coal briquette; (*f., Geol.*) agglomerate rocks.

aglomerador –**dora** (*adj.*) agglomerating; (*m.,f.*) agglomerator.

aglomerante (*adj.*) agglomerative.

aglomerar (*v.t.*) to agglomerate, mass (together); to lump together; (*v.r.*) to heap up, pile up, pile together, crowd together.

aglomerativo –**va** (*adj.*) agglomerative.

aglossia (*f., Med.*) aglossia.

aglosso –**sa** (*adj., Zool.*) aglossate; (*m.*) one of the Aglossa.

aglutição (*f., Med.*) aglutition.

aglutinabilidade (*f.*) aglutinability.

aglutinação (*f.*) agglutination.—**por grupo,** (*Immunol.*) group or cross agglutination [= COAGLUTINAÇÃO].

aglutinado –**da** (*adj.*) agglutinate.

aglutinador (*m.*) agglutinant.

aglutinamento (*m.*) = AGLUTINAÇÃO.

aglutinante (*adj.; m.*) agglutinant.

aglutinar (*v.t.*) to agglutinate, bind together, cause to stick (as with glue); (*v.r.*) to cling.

aglutinativo –**va** (*adj.*) agglutinate, adhesive.

aglutinável (*adj.*) agglutinable.

aglutinina (*f., Immunol.*) agglutinin.

aglutinogênico –**ca** (*adj., Immunol.*) agglutinogenic.

aglutinogênio (*m., Immunol.*) agglutinogen.

aglutinóide (*f., Immunol.*) agglutinoid.

aglutinômetro (*m., Immunol.*) agglutinoscope.

agmatina (*f., Biochem.*) agmatine.

agmatologia (*f., Surg.*) agmatology.

agmíneo –**nea, agminado** –**da** (*adj.*) agminate, grouped together.

agnação (*f.*) agnation, kinship.

agnado –**da** (*adj.*) agnate, akin; (*m.,f.*) agnate.

ágnato –**ta** (*adj.*) agnathous; (*m., Zool.*) one of the Agnatha.

agnocasto (*m.*) the lilac chastetree (*Vitex agnuscastus*), c.a. ÁRVORE-DA-CASTIDADE, PIMENTEIRO-SILVESTRE.

agnoiologia (*f., Metaph.*) agnoiology.

agnominação (*f., Rhet.*) agnomination, paronomasia.

agnosia (*f., Psychopathol.*) agnosia.

agnosticismo (*m.*) agnosticism.

agnosticista (*m.,f.*) agnostic.

agnóstico –**ca** (*adj.; m.,f.*) agnostic.

agnotozóico –**ca** (*adj., Geol.*) agnotozoic, Algonkian.

agoirar (*v.*) & derivs. = AGOURAR & derivs.

agoirentar (*v.*) & derivs. = AGOURENTAR & derivs.

agomã (*m.*) evil spirit in primitive Braz. folklore.

agomar (*v.i.*) to bud, sprout.

agomia (*f.*), **agomil** (*m.*) = GOMIL.

agonfíase, –**fose** (*f., Med.*) agomphiasis.

agongorado –**da** (*adj.*) of literary style, gongoristic.

agonia (*f.*) agony, distress, severe pain; death pangs; anguish; torment. **na—,** moribund.

agoniada (*f.*) = ARAPUÉ.

agoniadina (*f., Chem.*) agoniadin, plumieride.

agoniado –**da** (*adj.*) agonied; disturbed; upset.

agoniador –**dora** (*adj.*) agonizing.

agoniar (*v.t.*) to agonize, distress, torture; to afflict, grieve; to annoy, harry; (*v.r.*) to be upset.

agônico –**ca** (*adj.*) agonic.

agonis (*m.*) peppermint tree (*Agonis flexuosa*).

agonístico –**ca** (*adj.*) agonistic, combative; (*f.*) agonistics.

agonizado –**da** (*adj.*) agonized, suffering.

agonizante (*adj., m.,f.*) dying, moribund (person).

agonizar (*v.i.*) to agonize; to be at the point of death, on one's death bed; to be decadent, in decline; (*v.t.*) to agonize, torment, torture, rack.

ágono –**na** (*adj.*) agonic.

agonóstoma (*m.*) a genus (*Agonostomus*) of tropical freshwater mullets.

agora (*adv.*) now, at this time, at this moment, at present; after this, things being so; (*conj.*) but; (*interj.*) now! —**agora,** right now.—**é que eu quero ver!** Now we'll see!—, **isso é que não!** Yes, but not that!—**mesmo,** right now; just now.—**não,** not now; no longer.—**ou nunca,** now or never.—**que,** now that. **ainda—,** just now. **até—,** until now, hitherto. **de—em diante,** from now on. **E—?** And now what? **já—,** now. **por—,** for now, for the present, for the time being. **Que há—?** What's the matter now?

ágora (*f.*) agora, place of assembly; market place (in ancient Greece).

agorafobia (*f.*) agoraphobia.

agorentar (*v.t.*) to cut short.

agorinha (*adv.*) just now, a minute ago.

agostar (*v.i.,v.r.*) to wilt.

agostinho –**nha** (*adj.; m.*) Augustinian; (*f.pl.*) Augustinian nuns; (*m.*) [*cap*]. Augustin(e).

agôsto (*m.*) the month of August. Cf. AUGUSTO.

agoural (*adj.*) augural, ominous. Var. AGOIRAL.

agourar (*v.t.,v.i.*) to augur, portend, forebode; to predict, foretell. Var. AGOIRAR.

agoureiro –**ra, agourento** –**ta** (*adj.*) premonitory, portentous, ominous, foreboding; superstitious; (*m.,f.*) augur, soothsayer, diviner (esp. of evil). Var. AGOIREIRO.

agourentar (*v.t.*) to forebode evil. Var. AGOIRENTAR.

agouro (*m.*) augury, omen, sign, portent. **de mau—,** ominous (of evil). **mau—,** ill omen. Var. AGORRO.

agraciação (*f.*) an honoring; decoration.

agraciado –**da** (*adj.; m.,f.*) (person) honored with a decoration; (person) absolved, pardoned.

agraciar (*v.t.*) to grace, dignify, honor; to pardon, absolve. —**com,** to honor or decorate (as with a medal).

agradabilíssimo –**ma** (*absol. superl. of* AGRADÁVEL) most agreeable.

agradado –**da** (*adj.*) pleased, gratified; pleasantly greeted or received.

agradar (*v.t.*) to gratify, please; to delight; to give pleasure to.—**-se de,** to be pleased with; to like; to take a liking or fancy to. **Isso não me agrada,** I don't like it; it doesn't please me.

agradável (*adj.*) agreeable, pleasing, pleasant. **pouco—,**

unpleasant. **notícia**—, welcome news. **uma noite**—, a pleasant evening.
agradecer (v.t.) to thank (**por**, for); to return thanks (**a**, to); to express thanks (**por**, for).
agradecido –**da** (adj.) grateful, thankful. **mal**—, ungrateful.
agradecimento (m.) thanks, expression of gratitude; thankfulness.
agrado (m.) liking; delight; pleasure; charm; amiability, courtesy; (pl., Bot.) a fuchsia (F. integrifolia), c.a. BRINCOS-DE-PRINCESA.
agrafo (m.) surgical clip.
agramatismo (m.) agrammatism, syntactical aphasia.
agranulocitose (f., Med.) agranulocytosis.
agrar (v.t.) to level land for planting.
agrário –**ria** (adj.) agrarian.
agrarismo (m.) agrarianism.
agraudar (a-u] (v.i.) to grow big.
agravação (f.) aggravation; grievance.
agravado –**da** (adj.) of condition, aggravated; aggrieved; (m.,f.) one who has a grievance.
agravador –**dora** (adj.) aggravating; (m.,f.) aggravator.
agravamento (m.) aggravation.
agravante (adj.) aggravating; (f.) aggravating circumstance; (m.) one who or that which aggravates; (Law) appellant.
agravar (v.t.) to aggrieve; to aggravate; to heighten (the evil of); to make worse; to oppress, overburden; to provoke; to offend; to irritate; (Law) to appeal to a higher court; (v.r.) to grow worse.—**se de**, to be offended by or with.
agravista (m., Law) judge of an appellate court.
agravo (m.) wrong; offense; grievance; gravamen; appeal to a higher court.
agravoso –**sa** (adj.) grievous, oppressive.
agre (adj.) acrid; sour [= ACRE, AGRO].
agredido –**da** (adj.) attacked, assailed; offended; (m.,f.) victim of aggression.
agredir [21b] (v.t.) to attack, assail, assault; to commit aggression against; to affront, offend. [The noun is AGRESSÃO.]
agregação (f.) aggregation.
agregado –**da** (adj.) aggregate; adjunct; (m.) tenant farmer; share cropper; ranch hand; (Geol.) aggregate rock. (pl., Zool.) the Aggregata (genus of protozoans).
agregar (v.t.) to aggregate, bring together; to add, annex. —**se a**, to join (a party, etc.).
agregativo –**va** (adj.) aggregative, collective.
agremente (adv.) bitterly, harshly.
agremiação (f.) guild, association, society, body; act of assembling or gathering (of people).
agremiado –**da** (adj.) belonging (as a member) to an association; (m.,f.) member.
agremiar (v.t.) to assemble, bring (persons) together, as members of an association; (v.r.) to form a guild.
agressão (f.) aggression, offense, injury.
agressina (f., Immunol.) aggressin.
agressividade (f.) aggressiveness.
agressivo –**va** (adj.) aggressive, offensive. [The verb is AGREDIR.]
agressor –**sora** (m.,f.) aggressor, attacker.
agreste (adj.) agrestic; rustic, rural; countrified; agrestal, wild. **flores**—**s**, wild flowers. (m.) rustic; (Biogeog.) a zone of bare rocky soil in N.E. Brazil; (Bot.) = CAPIM-SAPÉ (a grass).
agrestia, agrestidade (f.) rusticity; boorishness.
agrião (m.) watercress (Rorippa nasturtium-aquaticum); (Veter.) capped hock.—**bravo** (—**falso**) a bittercress (Cardamine amara); a spotflower (Spilanthes uliginosa). —**da-terra** (—**dos-jardins**), a wintercress (Barbarea praecox).—**dos-prados**, the cuckoo bittercress or lady's-smock (Cardamine pratensis).—**do-brasil** (—**do-pará**), a spotflower (Spilanthes acmella), c.a. ABECEDÁRIA, ACMELA, BOTÃO-DE-OURO, MASTRUÇO, JAMBU-AÇU, JAMBU-RANA.—**do-méxico** = CAPUCHINHA-GRANDE.—**do-pântano**, bog marshcress (Rorippa palustris).
agrícola (adj.) agricultural; (m.,f.) agriculturist.
agricolita (f., Min.) agricolite.
agricultado –**da** (adj.) cultivated, tilled.
agricultar (v.t.) to till the soil; (v.i.) to farm.
agricultável (adj.) tillable.
agricultor –**tora** (adj.) farming; (m.,f.) farmer.
agricultura (f.) agriculture, farming.
agricultural (adj.) agricultural.

agridoce [AGRE+DOCE] (adj.) bitter-sweet.
agridoçura (f.) bittersweetness.
agrilhoar (v.t.) to fetter, shackle, hamper; to enslave.
agrimensão (f.) = AGRIMENSURA.
agrimensar (v.t.) to survey (land).
agrimensor (m.) land surveyor.
agrimensura (f.) land surveying.
agrimônia (f.) acrimony; (Bot.) common agrimony.
agrinaldar (v.) = ENGRINALDAR.
agripalma (f., Bot.) common motherwort (Leonurus cardiaca), c.a. CARDÍACA, CAUDA-DE-LEÃO, CORDÃO-DE-FRADE.
agripnia (f., Med.) agrypnia, insomnia.
agrisalhado –**da** (adj.) white-haired.
agríssimo –**ma** (absol. superl. of AGRE and AGRO) most sour; most acrid, bitter; most rough.
agro –**ra** (adj.) acrid, sour, bitter; rough, uneven; (m.) field; tilled ground; bitter taste, sourness.
agrodoce (adj.) = AGRIDOCE.
agrogeologia (f.) agricultural geology.
agrologia (f.) agrology.
agromiza (f.) a genus (Agromyza) of minute 2-winged flies.
agronomia (f.) agronomy.
agronômico –**ca** (adj.) agronomic.
agrônomo (m.) agronomist. **engenheiro**—, (in Brazil) a graduate in agronomics.
agropecuária (f.) farming and cattle-raising.
agropiro (m.) wheatgrass (Agropyron).
agror (m.) bitterness, sourness.
agroste, agróstide (f.) bent grass (Agrostis).
agrostema (f.) corncockle (Agrostemma).
agrostiografia (f., Bot.) agrostography.
agrostiógrafo (m.) agrostographer.
agrostiologia (f., Bot.) agrostology.
agrotídeos (m.pl.) a genus of noctuid moths (Agrotis) whose larvae are cutworms.
agrumar-se (v.r.) to clot.
agrumelar (v.t.,v.r.) to clot.
agrupação (f.), **agrupamento** (m.) grouping.
agrupar (v.t.) to group; to bunch; to cluster; (v.r.) to gather together, form a group.
agrura (f.) hardship; sorrows; roughness.
ag.ᵗᵒ = agôsto (August).
água (f.) water; body of water; any aqueous liquid (as tears, saliva, sweat, urine, etc.); sap; fruit juice; one side or slope of a roof; limpidity of diamonds; (slang) drunken spree.—**abaixo**, downstream.—**acima**, or **arriba**, upstream; against the current.—**benta**, holy water.—**-brava**, or—**-de-goma**, manioc-root juice, used as a condiment.—**-bruta**, or—**-de-briga**, (slang) "fire water" (rum).—**choca**, bad-smelling stagnant water.—**clorada**, chlorinated water.—**corrente**, running water.—**crua**, or **dura**, hard water.—**da bica**, tap water.—**-da-guerra**, (Med.) Dakin's solution.—**de barrela**, (slang) flop, failure.—**-de-cheiro**, (colloq.) perfume.—**-de-colônia**, eau de Cologne.—**de sabão**, soapsuds.—**doce**, fresh water. —**dormente**, still water.—**dos diamantes**, limpidity of diamonds.—**e sal**, a strict diet.—**fervente**, boiling water. —**flórida**, a perfumed toilet water.—**forte**, aqua fortis, nitric acid; an etching.—**-fortista** = AQUA-FORTISTA.—**-fria-na-fervura**, (colloq.) a wet-blanket, a kill-joy. —**furtada**, garret, attic.—**gasosa**, soda water; sparkling water.—**mãe**, mother liquor.—**marinha**, aquamarine. —**mel**, hydromel, mead.—**mole em pedra dura, tanto dá** (or **bate**) **até que fura**, Constant dripping bores the stone.—**morna**, mild-mannered person; a "milque-toast"; a shiftless fellow; (pl.) palliatives, half-measures. —**oxigenada**, peroxide, hydrogen dioxide.—**parada**, still water.—**parada cria bicho**, Idleness breeds mischief. —**potável**, drinking water.—**-que-gato** (or **-passarinho**) **-não-bebe**, (colloq.) liquor, booze.—**redonda**, lake, lagoon.—**régia**, aqua regia.—**salobra**, brackish water. —**-só** = NARCEJÃO (a snipe).—**suja**, (colloq.) squabble; quarrel; free-for-all; a bawling out.—**vem**—**vai**, Easy come, easy go.—**viva**, a large jelly fish; (pl.) spring tide.—**s caldas**, hot springs.—**s-de-setembro**, (colloq.) booze, liquor.—**s-emendadas**, confluence of two streams. —**s-férreas**, chalybeate mineral springs.—**s-mestras**, a trapezoid roof slope, as of a mansard roof.—**s-mortas**, neap tide.—**s paradas são as mais fundas**, Still waters run deep.—**s passadas não movem moinho**, It's water under the bridge, let bygones be bygones.—**s-puladeiras**, river rapids.—**s termais**, thermal waters, hot springs.

—s turvas, troubled waters. à flor da—, between wind and water (just on the surface of the water). a pão e—, on bread and water; on short rations; on a strict diet. abrir (or fazer)—, to spring a leak. afogar-se em pouca— (or num copo d'água), to be upset by trifles, to cause a tempest in a teacup. aquentar—para o mate dos outros, to do another's work for him. beber—de chocalho, to rattle (talk too much). beber—nas orelhas dos outros, to tittle-tattle. dar—pela barba de alguém, to cause serious trouble to someone. dar em—de barrela, (slang) to flop, fail. estação de—s, watering place, resort. como peixe dentro d'—, like a pig in clover. fazer vir—à bôca, to make one's mouth water. Gato escaldado tem medo de—fria, A scalded cat dreads cold water. ir nas—s de alguém, to follow in another's footsteps. ir para as—s, to visit a spa. ir(-se) por—abaixo, to come to naught, fail. lançar (or jogar)—no mar, to carry coals to New-castle. lançar (or deitar, or jogar)—na fervura, to pour oil on troubled waters. levar—no bico, (colloq.) to have a preconceived notion, a fixed idea. navegar entre duas—s, to keep to the middle of the road. pescar em—s turvas, to fish in troubled waters. poeta d'—doce, a poetaster. tirar—da pedra, to get blood from a turnip. transporte por—, water transportation.

aguaçal (m.) swamp, marsh; puddles of rainwater; flow of water.

aguaceiro (m.) sudden shower; squall, downpour, cloud-burst.

aguacento -ta (adj.) watery; marshy.

aguaçu [cú] (m.) = GUAÇU (a palm).

aguada (f.) water supply (for ships); watering place.

aguadeiro (m.), -ra (f.) water carrier; water seller.

aguadilha (f.) serous fluid.

aguado -da (adj.) watered; watery, diluted; of pleasure, spoiled; of horses, foundered.

aguador (m.) watering can; sprinkler.

aguagem (f.) watering (of milk, wine, etc.); bore, race (powerful current, heavy sea).

aguaí (m.) a starapple (Chrysophyllum).

aguamento (m.) watering; (Veter.) founder, laminitis.

águano (m.) a giant Amazonian tree (Swietenia macro-phylla) whose wood is known in the trade as Honduras mahogany.

aguapé (f.) weak wine; (m.) any of various waterlilies (Nymphaea) which form huge floating masses in the lakes and rivers of northern Brazil; c.a. GÓLFÃO, GIGÓIA. —-da-meia-noite, the Rudge waterlily (Nymphaea rudgeana), c.a. APÉ.—-do-amazonas, the Amazon water-lily (N. amazonum).—-do-grande, the dotleaf waterlily (N. ampla).

aguapeaçoca (f.) = JAÇANÃ.

aguapèzal (m.) large area of water covered with floating masses of waterlilies.

aguar [8] (v.t.) to water, wet; to irrigate (plants); to dilute (wine, milk, etc.); to dampen (another's pleasure); to tone down (colors); (v.i., Veter.) to founder; (v.r.) to water at the mouth.

aguará (m., Zool.) an agouara (Canis jubatus); also, the scarlet ibis (Guara rubra).

aguarapondá (f., Bot.) a false valerian (Stachytarpheta dichotoma).

aguaraquiá (m., Bot.) black nightshade (Solanum nigrum), c.a. ERVA-MOURA.

aguaraquinha (f.) a heliotrope used medicinally (H. elon-gatum).

aguaraxaim [a-i] (m.) a kind of wild dog (Canis brasilien-sis), c.a. GUARAXAIM. Cf. AGUARÁ.

aguardado -da (adj.) awaited, expected; guarded; re-spected; tolerated.

aguardar (v.t.) to await, wait for; to expect, look for; to respect (laws); to watch over; to stand (tolerate); (v.i.) to wait.

aguardentaria (f.) warehouse or distillery of AGUARDENTE.

aguardente [ÁGUA+ARDENTE, firewater] (f.) an inferior brandy; sugar cane rum; loosely, any distilled alcoholic drink [= CACHAÇA, PINGA].

aguardenteiro (m.) maker of, or dealer in, AGUARDENTE; habitual drinker.

aguarela (f.) aquarelle; water color (paint or picture).

aguarelar (v.i.) to paint in water colors.

aguarelista (m.,f.) aquarellist; water-colorist.

aguarentar (v.t.) to shorten or trim all around (as the bottom of a skirt); to cut short (lit. & fig.).

aguarrás (f.) oil of turpentine.

aguateiro (m.) = AGUADEIRO.

aguaxima (f.) = GUAXUMA.

aguazil (m.) formerly, a high ranking officer of justice in Spain; now, a warrant officer, constable, bailiff. Var. ALGUAZIL.

aguçado -da (adj.) sharp, keen-edged.

aguçador -dora (adj.) sharpening; (m.,f.) sharpener.

aguçadura (f.) aguçamento (m.) act of sharpening.

aguçar (v.t.) to sharpen, make keen; to make pointed; to make eager, excite, stimulate.—a língua, to sharpen the tongue.—a vista, to keep a sharp lookout; to keep one's eyes peeled.—os dentes, to get ready to eat heartily. (v.r.) to become sharp or pointed.

agudez[a] [ê] (f.) sharpness, keenness; acuity; a quip; wit; acuteness; shrewdness; severity.—de espirito, acumen, perspicacity.

agudo -da (adj.) sharp, keen; pointed; astute; discerning; acute, penetrating; witty; alert, quick; high-pitched, shrill. acento—, acute accent. ângulo—, acute angle; (m., Music) a sharp.

Águeda (f.) Agatha.

agüeiro (m.) road ditch; roof gutter.

agüentador -dora (adj.) supporting, bearing, enduring, withstanding; (m.,f.) one who sustains, etc.;—see the verb AGÜENTAR.

agüentar (v.t.) to sustain, undergo, bear, support; to stand, endure; to put up with; to withstand; (v.i.) to stand firm; to hold out, last, endure.—firme, to face the music; to stand up and "take it".—o repuxo, or o tirão, (colloq.) to stand the racket; to stand the gaff; to bear the brunt.—o tempo, to withstand adversity.

aguerrear (v.) = AGUERRIR.

aguerrido -da (adj.) bellicose, warlike; accustomed to war; embattled; courageous.

aguerrilhar (v.t.) to make guerrillas of (persons).

aguerrir [46] (v.t.) to inure (to war, hardships, etc.); (v.r.) to become inured (to war, etc.).

águia (f.) eagle; the standard of the ancient Romans; a U. S. gold coin (eagle, $10.00); (Astron.) Aquila; (Zool.) a drumfish or croaker (Sciaena aquila); (m.) sharper, crook.—-chilena, a buzzard eagle (Buteo fuscescens). —-pescadora, the osprey or fish hawk (Pandion haliaetus carolinensis), c.a. GAVIÃO-PESCADOR, GAVIÃO-PAPA-PEIXE.

aguião (m.) rascal, crook.

aguieta [ê] (f.) eaglet.

águila (f., Bot.) the agalloch eaglewood (Aquilaria agallocha).

aguilhada (f.) ox goad.

aguilhão (m.) sting; prick; spike; goad; stimulus; the poisonous sting of a bee, wasp, etc.—da carne, or dos sentidos, carnal temptation, carnal desires.—da miséria, the goad of poverty. aguilhões acesos, burning desires. aguilhões da morte, mortal dangers. aguilhões de ferro, pointed iron spikes (as along the top of a wall or fence).

aguilhoada (f.) sting(ing), prick(ing), prod(ding).

aguilhoar (v.t.) to goad, poke, jab, prod; to incite, spur (on).

agulha (f.) needle (of any kind); pointer; spire; obelisk; needlework; common name for rutile found in diamond beds, c.a. FERRAGEM and FUNDINHO; railroad switch point; an eel; any needlefish or swordfish; withers; chuck of beef; firing pin (of a gun).—branca (—crioula,— -preta), a halfbeak (Hemiramphus sp.).—de cerzir, darning needle.—de coser, sewing needle.—de crochê, crocheting needle.—de enfardar, packing needle. —de máquina, sewing-machine needle.—de marear, mariner's compass.—de mato, (Bot.) pigeonwings (Clitoria linearis).—de meia, knitting needle.—-de-pastor (—-de-raposa), (Bot.) the Venuscomb shepherds-needle (Scandix pecten-veneris), c.a. ERVA-AGULHEIRA. —-de-pastor-moscada, (Bot.) the musk heronbill (Ero-dium moschatum), c.a. AGULHEIRA-MOSCADA, BICO-DE-CEGONHA-MOSCADA.—de sutura, suturing needle.—do mar=CACHIMBO (pipefish).—em palheiro, needle in a haystack.—ferrugenta, a meddler.—magnética, mag-netic needle. trabalho(s) de—, needlework.

agulhada (f.) needle prick.

agulhão (m.) swordfish (Xiphius gladius), c.a. AGULHA. —-atum, the saury (Scombresox saurus), c.a. TIRAVIRA. —-bandeira (—-de-vela), a sailfish (Istiophorus nigri-cans or I. volador), c.a. BICUDO, FRAGATA, GUEBUÇU, MACAÍRA, PEIXE-LEQUE, PEIXE-VELA.—-branco (—-comum), a garfish (Belone trachurs).—-lambaio, a large gar or needlefish (Tylosurus raphidoma).—-trom-

beta, a flutemouth fish (*Fistularia*), c.a. TROMBETA, PETIMBUABA, PETUMBO.

agulhar (*v.t.*) to prick; to prod; to sting.

agulheado –da (*adj.*) needle-shaped.

agulheira (*f.*) fishing line and hook.—**-menor,** (*Bot.*) a shepherds-needle (*Scandix australis*).—**-moscada,** the musk heronbill (*Erodium moschatum*), c.a. AGULHA-DE-PASTOR-MOSCADA, BICO-DE-GROU, BICO-DE-CEGONHA-MOSCADA, ERVA-ALMISCAREIRA.

agulheiro (*m.*) pin cushion; railroad switchman; any of various spouts, holes or openings in walls, buildings, ships' hulls, etc., as for drainage or for letting in light and air.

agulhêta (*f.*) aglet, metal tag at the end of a lace; bobbin needle; tape needle; spray or jet nozzle (as on a garden or fire hose); aiguillete (ornamental tag on military or naval uniforms); (*m.*) fire hoseman.

aguti [í] (*m.*) = CUTIA.

agutiguepe (*f.*) = ARARUTA.

agutipuru [rú] (*m.*) = ACUTIPURU.

ah! Ah! Aha!

ahn! Hum! Ahem!

ai-ai! Oh! Alas! Ouch! **ai-ai!** Oh, oh! Oh my! Ai dêles! Woe to them! **Ai gente!** Well, of all things! Well, I'll be!

aí (*adv.*) there (near you); in that place; thereupon;—**por,** about. **por—,** around there, out there, over there, yonder, thereabout, here and there.—**menino!** Attaboy! **Espera—!** Wait there! also: Just you wait and see! (*m., Zool.*) the S.A. 3-toed sloth (*Bradypus tridactylus*) better known as PREGUIÇA. [The 3-toed sloth (*Bradypus torquatus*), with a sort of mane, is AÍ-IGAPÓ or AÍ-PIXUNA; the unau or 2-toed sloth (*Choloepus hoffmanni*) is AÍ-MIRIM or PREGUIÇA-PEQUENA.]

aia (*f.*) nursemaid; governess; companion; chambermaid.

aiaçá, aiacá (*f.*) any of various small fresh-water turtles of genus Podocnemis, esp. *P. sextuberculata*.

aiaia (*f.*) toy; child's dress.

aiapaina (*f., Bot.*) a sp. of eupatorium (*E. ayapana*) believed by Braz. Indians to yield an antidote for snake poison.

aiar (*v.i.*) to moan, groan.

aiereba (*f.*) a sting ray (*Dasyastis orbicularis*).

aifano (*m.*) a rufflepalm (*Aiphanes*).

ai-jesus (*m.*) darling, idol, pet; (*exclam.*) Heavens! (in pain) Oh my God!

ailanto (*m., Bot.*) tree-of-heaven ailanthus (*A. altissima*).

aileron (*m.*) aileron (of an airplane.).

aimoré (*m.,f.*) an Indian of the Aimore, called also BOTOCUDO, a few thousands of whom still wander in the forest parts of Brazil. Vars. AIMBIRÉ and AIMBORÉ; also, a prehensile-tailed monkey of Amazonia (*Lagothrix sp.*); (*adj.*) pert. to or designating either.

ainda (*adv.*) still, (as) yet, (up) till now, to this time; besides, further, in addition; also, moreover; even, but also; again.—**agora,** just now, just a moment ago.—**assim,** even so; just the same, nevertheless.—**bem que,** fortunately, luckily; it's a good thing that; it's just as well that.—**em (por) cima,** on top of all that; to boot; in addition; into the bargain; over and above.—**mais que,** all the more; still more; especially that.—**mal,** worse yet. —**não,** not yet.—**há pouco,** not so long ago.—**pior,** yet worse.—**quando,** even when; even though; although, while still.—**quando fosse (verdade),** even though it were (true).—**quando o quisesse,** even if he wanted to (he couldn't).—**que,** even though; although; though; even if.—**que fosse,** even if it were so.—**uma vez,** once more; once again; one more time. **mais—,** still further; moreover; even more. **melhor—,** better still, better yet, even better. **pior—,** worse still, worse yet, even worse.

aio (*m.*) private tutor, teacher; chamberlain.

aió (*m.*) fiber hunting bag.

aipé (*m.*) = IPÊ-DA-FÔLHA-MIÚDA.

aipim (*m., Bot.*) the aipi cassava (*Manihot aipi*), c.a. MACAXEIRA, MANDIOCA-DOCE. Cf. MANDIOCA.

aipo (*m.*) celery (*Apium*).—**do banhado,** yelloweye-grass (*Xyris*).

aiquinito (*m., Min.*) aikinite.

aira (*f.*) hairgrass (*Aira*).

airado –da (*adj.*) airy, aerial; light-headed, rattle-brained; deranged; suffering from a cold. **rapariga da vida—,** strumpet.

airela (*f.*) myrtle whortleberry (*Vaccinium myrtillus*).

airi (*f.*), **airiri** (*m.*) an astrocaryum palm (*A. airy*) from which is obtained a useful fiber and edible fruit; c.a.

BREJAÚBA, BREJAÚVA, COQUEIRO-AIRI, COQUEIRO-IRI.

airiticum (*m.*) cord for weaving hammocks, made from the fiber of the AIRI palm.

airo (*m., Zool.*) an auk or murre (*Uria a. aalge*).

airoso –sa (*adj.*) graceful, elegant, comely; jaunty; refined, courteous; decorous.

aíte (*f.*) Indian paint.

aiuara-aiuara [ai-u] (*f.*) = MÃE-D'ÁGUA (a river siren).

aiveca (*f.*) moldboard of a plow.

aizoáceas (*f.pl.*) the carpetweeds (Aizoaceae).

aj., aj.te = AJUDANTE (assistant).

ajaezar (*v.t.*) to harness; to adorn. **ajaezada de joias,** bejewelled.

ajaja (*f., Zool.*) the roseate spoonbill (*Ajaia ajaia*), c.a. COLHEREIRO.

ajanotado –da (*adj.*) dandyish, foppish.

ajanotar-se (*v.r.*) to become foppish, dandified.

ajantarado –da (*adj.*) dinner-like.

ajardinado –da (*adj.*) landscaped.

ajardinamento (*m.*) landscape gardening.

ajardinar (*v.t.*) to landscape; to make into a garden.

ajaré (*m.*) a plant of *Tephrosia*, c.a. TIMBÓ-CAÁ.

ajax [ks] (*m.*) the zebra swallowtail or Ajax butterfly.

ajeitação (*f.*) act of adjusting, arranging, adapting, fitting.

ajeitado –da (*adj.*) adjusted, arranged, fixed.

ajeitamento (*m.*) act or result of adjusting or suiting (something) to a given end or purpose.

ajeitar (*v.t.*) to adjust, arrange; to fit, adapt, suit; to make ready.—**a,** or **com,** to make conformable to or with; to arrange with or for.

ajeurarana (*f., Bot.*) a hirtella (*H. ciliata*).

ajoelhação (*f.*) act of kneeling.

ajoelhado –da (*adj.*) kneeling.

ajoelhar-se (*v.r.*) to kneel.

ajoujar (*v.t.*) to leash.

ajoujo (*m.*) leash; team (of animals); yoke (of oxen).

ajuda (*f.*) aid, assistance, help; succor; (*m.*) helper.—**ao estrangeiro,** foreign aid.—**de custo,** expense allowance.—**externa,** foreign aid. **prestar—,** to lend aid.

ajudador –deira (*adj.*) helping; (*m.,f.*) helper.

ajudante (*m.,f.*) aider, helper, assistant; (*Milit.*) adjutant.—**de campo,** or **de ordens,** aide-de-camp.—**de missa,** acolyte.—**-general,** adjutant general.

ajudar (*v.t.*) to aid, assist, help (**a,** to; **com,** with); to befriend.—**a bem morrer,** to give spiritual comfort to a dying person.—**à missa,** to assist at mass.—**-se de pés e mãos,** to leave no stone unturned; to make every effort to help oneself. **A língua não lhe ajuda o pensamento,** His mind works faster than his tonge. **Ajuda-te, que Deus te ajudará,** Heaven helps those who help themselves. **Deus ajuda a quem cedo madruga,** Early to bed and early to rise make a man healthy, happy and wise. **Todo empurrão ajuda,** Every little bit helps. **Você é quem deve ajudá-lo,** It is up to you to help him.

ajuga (*m., Bot.*) carpet bugle (*Ajuga reptans*), c.a. ERVA-DE-SÃO-LOURENÇO.

ajuizado –da [u-i] (*adj.*) judicious; sober; sensible; reasonable.

ajuizar [u-i] (*v.t.*) to judge; to form an opinion about; to bring (someone) to his senses; (*Law*) to take (a matter) to court.

ajuntamento (*m.*) assembling; collection; assemblage, meeting, congregation, gathering.

ajuntar (*v.t.*) to join, unite; to amass; to gather, collect, assemble; to add, annex, attach; to augment; to gather (heap, pile) up; to lay up (by), hoard; (*v.r.*) to come together.—**dinheiro,** to hoard money.—**o dia com a noite,** to work day and night.—**os pés,** to turn up one's toes (die).

ajuramentar (*v.t.*) to put under oath; to swear in (witnesses); to swear to; (*v.r.*) to take an oath.

ajuri [í] (*m.*) a corn-shucking, house-raising, or other "bee" [=MUXIRÃO].

ajuru [rú] (*m.*) any of various trees and shrubs of *Hirtella* and *Licania*, some of which yield tan bark and valuable timber; any of various Brazilian parrots, esp. *Amazona aestiva* which has red upper-wing coverts.—**-açu,** the largest Brazilian parrot (*Amazona farinosa*), c.a. MOLEIRO.—**-catinga,** a small parrot (*Ara modesta*), c.a. ARARINHA, MACAVANA.—**-curau** (—**-curuca**), a parrot (*Amazona amazona*), c.a. CURICA, ENCONTROS-VERDES, PAPAGAIO-DOS-MANGUES.—**-etê,** a parrot (*Amazona dufresnii*), c.a. ACAMUTANGA, ACUMATANGA, CAMATANGA

JAUÁ, PAPAGAIO-GREGO, PAPAGAIO-VERDADEIRO.—-**juba-canga,** a parrot (*Conurus auricapillus*).

ajurujuba (*f.*) = GUARUBA (a paroquet).

ajurujurá, ajurujurau, ajurujuru, ajurupura (*m.*) kinds of parrots.

ajustado -da (*adj.*) adjusted; adapted; fitted; harmonized; agreed upon; (*m.*) agreement.

ajustador (*m.*) fitter, mechanic.

ajustagem (*f.*) adjustment or fitting (of parts).

ajustamento (*m.*) adjustment; agreement; settlement (of accounts); reconciliation.

ajustar (*v.t.*) to adjust, conform, adapt; to suit (one thing to another); to accommodate; to arrange, settle; to prearrange; to agree upon; to fix or regulate (as a watch); to tune up (a motor).—**com,** to make conformable with. —**contas,** to settle accounts (lit. & fig.).—**-se a,** to accommodate oneself to. **Eu tenho contas a—contigo,** I have a bone to pick with you.

ajustável (*adj.*) adjustable.

ajuste (*m.*) adjustment, accommodation, settlement, agreement; compromise; in criminal law, a conspiracy to commit a crime, fraud or other wrongful act.—**comercial,** commercial agreement.—**de contas,** settlement of accounts; fig., settlement of a dispute (by fighting).

ajutório (*m.*) help, aid, assistance; a house-raising or other "bee".

AL = ALAGOAS (State of).

Al. = ALAMÊDA (street name).

ala (*f.*) aisle; file or row; wing (of a building); (*Mil.*) wing, flank; (*Soccer*) wing. [But wing of a bird is ASA.]

alabama (*m.*) drummer (traveling salesman); a showy but inferior diamond; a tout or runner for a hotel.

alabandina (*f.*) almandine (a violet variety of the ruby spinel), c.a. RUBI-NEGRO.

alabandita (*f., Min.*) alabandite.

alabar-se (*v.r.*) to boast.

alabarda (*f.*) halberd; poleax.

alabardeiro (*m.*) halberdier; a coarse shoe.

alabastrino -na (*adj.*) alabastrine.

alabastro (*m.*) alabaster.

alacaiado -da (*adj.*) like a lackey.

alacaiar (*v.t.*) to serve (others) as a lackey.

alacrau (*m.*) = LACRAU.

álacre (*adj.*) cheerful, eager; sprightly; blithe.

alacreatina (*f., Chem.*) alacreatin(e).

alacreatinina (*f., Chem.*) alacreatinin(e).

alacridade (*f.*) alacrity, cheerfulness, liveliness, good spirits; sprightliness; mirth.

aladeirado -da (*adj.; m.*) steep (road or street).

alado -da (*adj.*) winged.

aladroar (*v.t.*) to cheat, esp. on weights and measures.

alagação (*f.*) flooding; overflowing (of a river).

alagadeiro (*m.*) flooded or marshy land.

alagadiço -ça (*adj.*) swampy, low, wet, marshy.

alagado -da (*adj.*) flooded, marshy; waterlogged; (*m.*) swamp, marsh.

alagamar (*m.*) cove, inlet.

alagamento (*m.*) flooding; flooded paddy field.

alagar (*v.t.*) to flood, deluge; to overflow; to overwhelm.

alagite (*f., Min.*) allagite.

alagoa (*f.*) = LAGOA.

alagoado -da (*adj.*) like a lake.

alagoano -na (*adj.*) of or pert. to the State of Alagoas, ·Brazil; (*m.,f.*) a native of the same.

alagoar (*v.t.*) to flood or fill with water; (*v.r.*) to become flooded.

alagoso -sa (*adj.*) laky, flooded.

alalia (*f., Med.*) alalia, motor aphasia.

alálito (*m., Min.*) alalite.

alamal (*m.*) a row or growth of poplars.

alamanda (*f., Bot.*) the common allamanda (*A. cathartica*).

alamar [-es] (*m.*) frog (ornamental braid loop).

alambari [í] (*m.*) lambari.

alambazar-se (*v.r.*) to be gluttonous.

alambicado -da (*adj.*) prim, prissy, finical. **estilo—,** over-refined, affected, pretentious style (of speech or writing).

alambicar (*v.t.*) to distill; (*v.r.*) to put on frills.

alambique (*m.*) alembic, still, retort.

alambiqueiro (*m.*) distiller.

alambor [ô] (*m.*) footing (spreading or enlargement) of a foundation wall.

alambrar (*v.t.*) to wire-fence (an area of land).

alambre (*m.*) = ÂMBAR, ARAME.

alamêda (*f.*) a tree-lined street; a row of trees, esp. poplars.

alamiré (*m.*) = LAMIRÉ.

álamo (*m.*) white poplar (*Populus alba*), c.a. CHOUPO-BRANCO, FAIA-BRANCA.—**-prêto** (—**-negro**), black poplar (*P. nigra*), c.a. CHOUPO-PRÊTO, CHOUPO-NEGRO.

alancear (*v.t.*) to pierce with a lance.

alangião (*m.*) the planeleaf alangium (*A. platanifolium*) and others of this genus.

alanguidar-se (*v.r.*) = LANGUESCER-SE.

alanhar (*v.t.*) to slash (open), rip (open) as with a knife; to gut (fish); to inflict a deep hurt. Cf. LANHAR.

alanina (*f., Chem.*) alanine.

alanita (*f., Min.*) allanite.

alantíase (*f.*) allantiasis, sausage poisoning, botulism.

alântico -ca (*adj., Chem.*) alantic.

alantina (*f., Chem.*) alantin, inulin.

alantóico -ca (*adj.*) allantoic.

alantóide (*m.*), **-tóidea** (*f., Anat.*) allantosis.

alantoidiano -na (*adj.*) allantoid.

alantoína (*f., Biochem.*) allantoin.

alantol [-tóis] (*m., Chem.*) alantol.

alantolactona (*f., Chem.*) alantolactone.

alantólico -ca (*adj.*) allantolic, alanic.

alantotóxico [ks] (*m., Biochem.*) botulismus toxin.

alantoxânico -ca [ks] (*adj.*) **ácido—,** allantoxanic acid, oxonic acid.

alantúrico -ca (*adj., Chem.*) allanturic.

alanzoar (*v.i.*) to blather, talk at random.

alão [-ãos, -ães, ões] (*m.*) mastiii; [*cap.*] Alan, Allan, Allen.

alapado -da (*adj.*) hidden behind or beneath something; hidden in a cave or den; crouching.

alapar (*v.t.*) to hide (something) as in a den; (*v.r.*) to hide behind or under (something).

alapardar-se (*v.r.*) to hide; to cover.

alar (*v.t.*) to hoist, raise, lift, haul up; to pull, tug, haul on (at); (*v.r.*) to lift (raise) oneself up. [The etymology is the same as of English haul.]—**à lupa,** to pull (up) by snubbing the rope.—**de leva arriba,** to pull (up) by walking away with one end of the rope.—**de mão em mão,** to pull (up) hand over hand. (*v.t.*) [from ALA, wing] to give wings to (imagination, etc.); (*v.r.*) to grow wings; to fly, wing, soar; (*adj.*) alar, wing-shaped.

alaranjado -da (*adj.*) orange-colored, orange-shaped, orange-tasting.

alarar (*v.t.*) to place (as wood) on the LAR (hearth).

alardar (*v.*) = ALARDEAR, LARDEAR.

alarde (*m.*) boasting, blustering, brag; vainglory; splurge. **fazer—de,** to boast of (about); to flaunt. Var. ALARDO.

alardear (*v.t.*) to flaunt, boast, show off.—**-se de,** to boast of, brag about.

alargadeiras (*f.pl.*) shoe stretchers.

alargador -dora (*adj.*) enlarging, dilating, etc. See the verb ALARGAR. (*m., Mach.*) reamer.—**cônico,** tapered reamer.—**de expansão,** expanding reamer.

alargamento (*m.*) enlargement; widening, broadening; expansion.

alargar (*v.t.*) to enlarge, extend, widen, broaden; to stretch; to dilate; to expand; to prolong; to slacken, relax; (*v.r.*) to stretch, widen, broaden; to spread, scatter; to put to sea.—**a bôlsa,** to stretch the purse.—**a língua,** to loosen the tongue.—**as gâmbias,** to take to one's heels in a hurry.—**as rédeas,** to slacken the reins (used fig.). —**o coração,** to lift up one's heart, take on new courage. —**o passo,** to quicken one's step.—**os cordões à bôlsa,** to loosen the pursestrings.—**os olhos,** to stretch the eyesight, look afar.

alária (*f.*) bladderlocks wingkelp (*Alaria esculenta*).

alarido (*m.*), **alarida** (*f.*) clamor, hue and cry; adb, hubbub; tumult; din, hullabaloo.

alarma (*m.*) alarm, alarum; alert.—**aéreo,** air alarm. **dar—,** to raise the alarm. **sinal de—,** alarm signal; burglar alarm; fire alarm.

alarmado -da (*adj.*) alarmed, frightened.

alarmante (*adj.*) alarming; startling.

alarmar (*v.t.*) to alarm; (*v.r.*) to become alarmed.

alarmista (*adj.; m.,f.*) alarmist.

alarpar-se (*v.r.*) = ALAPADAR-SE.

alarve (*adj.*) boorish; loutish; savage; gluttonous; (*m.,f.*) such a person; (*m.*) formerly, a Bedouin.

alascaíte (*f., Min.*) alaskaite, galenobismutite.

alassotônico -ca (*adj., Plant Physiol.*) allassotonic.

alastrado -da (*adj.*) ballasted; littered; strewn (**de,** with).

alastramento (*m.*) ballasting; spreading.

alastrante (*adj.*) spreading.
alastrar (*v.t.*) to ballast; to litter, strew, scatter; to spread abroad; (*v.r.*) of rumor or epidemic, to spread. **A epidemia alastrou-se pela cidade,** the epidemic spread throughout the city.
alastrim (*m., Med.*) alastrim, mild form of smallpox.
alaterno (*m.*) Italian buckthorn (*Rhamnus alaternus*).
alatinado –**da** (*adj.*) Latinized [= LATINIZADO].
alatinar (*v.t.*) to Latinize.
alatoar (*v.t.*) to trim with brass.
alauate [a-u] (*m.*) alouatte, the howling monkey.
alaúde (*m.*) lute.
alaudídeos (*m.pl.*) the true larks (*Alaudidae*).
alavanca (*f.*) lever; crowbar; street-car trolley pole.—**de alimentação,** feed lever.—**de comando,** control stick (of an airplane).—**de cotovêlo,** bell crank.—**de mudanças,** gearshift lever (of an automobile).—**de unha,** pinch bar.—**interfixa,** or—**do primeiro gênero,** lever of the first kind.—**interresistente,** or—**do segundo gênero,** lever of the second kind.—**interpotente,** or—**do terceiro gênero,** lever of the third kind.—**manual,** hand crank.
alavercar (*v.t.*) to humiliate, humble; (*v.i.,v.r.*) to humble oneself, bow down.
alazão [-zães, -zões] –**zã** [-zãs] (*adj.; m.,f.*) sorrel (horse). Var. LAZÃO.
alba (*f.*) daybreak.
albacora (*f.*) the long-finned albacore (*Germo alalunga*), c.a. ALBACORA-BRANCA, ALVACORA, ATUM-BRANCO, BANDOLIM, CAROROCOATÁ.
albanês –**nesa** (*adj.; m.,f.*) Albanian.
albará, albará (*m., Bot.*) Indian shot (*Canna flaccida*), c.a. COQUILHO, BANANEIRINHA-DA-ÍNDIA.
albarda (*f.*) a crude sort of straw-filled pack-saddle; an ill-fitting coat; (*colloq.*) annoyance.
albardar (*v.t.*) to packsaddle (animals); to fry (bread) in egg batter; to bungle, botch.
albarelo (*m.*) albarello (a majolica jar).
albarrã (*f., Bot.*) the sea onion (*Urginea maritima*); (*f.*) donjon, keep. Var. ALVARRÃ.
albatroz (*m.*) the wandering albatross (*Diomedea exulans*), c.a. CARNEIRO-DO-CABO, ALCATRAZ, NAVIO-DE-GUERRA.
alberca (*f.*) a hollow place containing water; water hole; water pocket.
albergado –**da** (*adj.*) lodged; sheltered; (*m.,f.*) inmate of a charitable institution.
albergar (*v.t.*) to lodge, harbor, quarter; to shelter; to provide lodging for; to give asylum to; (*v.i.*) to lodge; (*v.r.*) to lodge; to take lodging (**em, in**); to take or seek shelter or asylum (**em, in**).
albergue (*m.*) auberge, inn, hostel(ry); lodging place; shelter.—**noturno,** a flophouse.
albergueiro (*m.*) innkeeper.
Alberta (*f.*) Alberta.
Albertina (*f.*) Alberta, Albertina; Albertine.
albertita (*f., Min.*) albertite.
Alberto (*m.*) Albert.
albescente (*adj.*) albescent.
albibarbo –**ba** (*adj.*) white-bearded.
albicaude (*adj.*) white-tailed.
albiduria (*f., Med.*) albinuria, chyluria.
albificar (*v.t.*) to whiten.
albina (*f., Bot.*) the yellow alder or sweet turnera (*T. ulmifolia*), c.a. CHANANA.
albinismo (*m.*) albinism.
albino –**na** (*adj.; m.,f.*) albino.
albinuria (*f.*) = ALBIDURIA.
albita (*f., Min.*) albite.
albitófiro (*m., Petrog.*) albitophyre.
albízia (*f.*) the silktree (*Albizzia julibrissin*).
albo (*m.*) a salmon (*Salmo albula*).
albor [ô] (*m.*) = ALVOR.
alboranita (*f., Petrog.*) alboranite.
alborcar (*v.t.*) to swap.
albornoz (*m.*) burnoose.
alborque (*m.*) trade, swap.
albuca (*m.*) a genus (*Albuca*) of liliaceous plants, closely related to the star-of-Bethlehem.
albugem (*f., Med.*) albugo, leucoma, c.a. BELIDA; (*Bot.*) the white rusts (*Albugo, syn. Cystopus*).
albugínea (*f.*) albugineous tissue.
albugíneo –**nea, albuginado** –**da, albuginoso** –**sa** (*adj.*) albugineous.
albugo (*m.*) = ALBUGEM.
álbum [-uns] (*m.*) album.—**de recortes,** scrap-book.
albume, albúmen (*m.*) albumen.

albumina (*f.*) albumin.
albuminato (*m.*) albuminate.
albuminífero –**ra** (*adj.*) albuminiferous.
albuminiforme (*adj.*) albuminiform.
albuminimetria (*f., Biochem.*) albuminimetry.
albuminímetro (*m., Biochem.*) albuminimeter.
albuminocolia (*f., Med.*) albuminocholia.
albuminôide (*adj., Biochem.*) albuminoid.
albuminose (*f., Med.*) albuminosis.
albuminoso –**sa** (*adj.*) albuminous.
albuminúria, –nuria (*f., Med.*) albuminuria.
albuminúrico –**ca** (*adj.*) albuminuric.
albumóide (*adj.; m.*) albuminoid.
albumose (*f., Biochem.*) albumose.
albumosúria, –suria (*f., Med.*) albumosuria.
alburnete (*m., Zool.*) the bleak or blay (*Alburnus lucidus*).
alburno (*m., Bot.*) alburnum, sapwood.
alca (*f., Zool.*) a penguin, c.a. COTETO, SOTILICÁRIO.
alça (*f.*) a ring or handle for pulling or lifting; lug; tab, tag; shoulder strap; bootstrap; (*Firearms*) sight; range; (*Law*) appeal.—**de lança-bombas,** bombsight.—**de mira,** rear (gun) sight.—**de platina,** (*Bacteriol.*) platinum loop.—**sigmóide,** (*Anat.*) sigmoid flexure.—**telescópica,** telescopic gun sight.
alcácer, alcáçar (*m.*) alcazar, Moorish castle, palace or fortress.
alcachinar-se (*v.r.*) to bow.
alcachôfra (*f.*) artichoke (*Cynara scolymus*), c.a.—-COMUM,—-DE-COMER,—-HORTENSE.—-**brava** = CARDO.—-**dos-telhados,** hen-and-chickens, roof houseleek (*Sempervivum tectorum*).
alcaçuz (*m., Bot.*) common licorice (*Glycyrrhiza glabra*); (*Pharm.*) licorice root, c.a. REGOLIZ.—-**da-américa** (—-**indiano,**—-**silvestre**) Indian licorice, better known as JEQUIRITI.—-**da-terra** (—-**do-brasil**) a plant of the pea family (*Periandra dulcis*), c.a. CIPÓ-EM-PAU-DOCE, RAIZ-DOCE.—-**bravo** = BOI-GORDO.
alçado –**da** (*adj.*) of cattle, stray, runaway, wild; (*m.*) vertical projection (drawing); (*f.*) jurisdiction; in olden days, a circuit court; precinct; compe'ncy. **Isso não é da minha—,** That is beyond my control, outside of my jurisdiction.
alçadura (*f.*) act of lifting or hoisting.
alçagem (*f.*) act of drawing printed sheets from the press.
alcagüete (*m.*) procurer.—**da polícia,** stoolpigeon.
alcaidaria (*f.*) position of an ALCAIDE (person).
alcaide (*adj.*) of horses, poor; of persons, homely; (*m.*) any old, useless article; a sleeper (article of unsalable merchandise on the shelves); a drug on the market; a nag; a bird, better known as TIETÊ or GATURAMO-SERRADOR; an ancient (very old person); in former times, commander of a castle or governor of a province; warden or keeper of a jail; bailiff; nowadays, mayor of a Spanish town. **ter pai—,** to have a rich father, or to have the backing of a powerful person.
alcaidia (*f.*) = ALCAIDARIA.
alcaidessa, –dina (*f.*) wife of the ALCAIDE.
alcaiota (*f.*) procuress.
alcaiote (*m.*) procurer; pimp; a go-between (in shady transactions).
alcaixa (*f., Shipbuilding*) strake.
alcalamida (*f., Chem.*) alkalamide.
alcalescência (*f.*) alkalescence.
alcalescente (*adj.*) alkalescent.
álcali (*m., Chem.*) alkali.—**terroso,** alkaline earth.—**vegetal,** vegetable alkali.—**volátil,** volatile alkali, ammonia. (*Bot.*) the saltwort (*Salsola kali*).
alcalicidade (*f.*) alkalinity.
alcálico –**ca** (*adj.*) = ALCALINO.
alcalificar (*v.t.*) to alkalify.
alcalígeno –**na** (*adj.*) alkaligenous.
alcalimetria (*f.*) alkalimetry.
alcalímetro (*m.*) alkalimeter.
alcalinar (*v.t.*) to alkalize.
alcalinicidade (*f.*) alkalinity.
alcalinizar (*v.t.*) to alkalinize, alkalize.
alcalino –**na** (*adj.*) alkaline.
alcalinúria (*f., Med.*) alkalinuria.
alcalização (*f.*) alkalization.
alcalizar (*v.t.*) to alkalize.
alcalóide (*m.*) alkaloid.
alcaloidometria (*f., Pharm.*) alkalometry.
alcalose (*f.*) alkalosis.
alçamento (*m.*) act of raising, lifting, hoisting.

alcamonia (f.) a sweet confection made of manioc meal and molasses. Var. ALCOMONIA.

alcana (f., Bot.) alkanet (Alkanna tinctoria).

alcançadiço -ça (adj.) easily reached, obtained, attained, etc. See the verb ALCANÇAR.

alcançado -da (adj.) obtained, attained; in debt; in arrears.—em meios, formerly rich, now poor.

alcançadura (f., Veter.) attaint; overreach.

alcançamento (m.) attainment.

alcançar (v.t.) to reach, arrive at, come to, get to; to get, obtain, attain to; to overtake, catch up with, come up with; (Naut.) to overhaul.—o trem, to catch the train. até onde a vista alcança, as far as eye can see. Quem corre cansa, quem anda alcança, Make haste slowly. Quem espera sempre alcança, Everything comes to him who waits.

alcançável (adj.) attainable; obtainable; reachable.

alcance (m.) reach; extent; capacity, grasp; embezzlement. ao—da mão, within reach. ao—de, within reach of. ao—da vista, within eyeshot. ao—da voz, within hearing, within earshot. de curto—, short-range. de grande—, long-range. medidas de grande—, far-reaching measures.

alcândor (m.) summit; peak.

alcândora (f.) perch (for falcons or parrots).

alcandorado -da (adj.) high-flown; perched high.

alcandorar-se (v.r.) to rise or perch on high; to soar; fig., to exalt oneself.

alcanfor [ô] (m.), alcânfora (f.) = CÂNFORA.

alcanforar (v.) = CANFORAR.

alcanforeira (f.) camphor tree (Cinnamomum camphora), c.a. CANFOREIRA.

alcanina (f., Chem.) alkannin, orcanet.

alcantil (m.) crag; cliff, bluff, precipice. Cf. CANTIL.

alcantilado -da (adj.) steep, bluff, precipitous, abrupt; slanting, sloping (steeply); of roofs, high-pitched.

alcantilar (v.t.) to cant steeply; (v.r.) to rise steeply.

alcantiloso -sa (adj.) = ALCANTILADO.

alçapão (m.) trap door; a figure-four trap, esp. for birds. ninho—, trap-nest.

alcaparra (f.) common caper (Capparis spinosa)—plant, bud or berry.

alçaprema (f.) crowbar; dentist's forceps.

alçapremar (v.t.) to lift with a crowbar.

alcaptona (f., Biochem.) alkapton.

alcaptonúria, -nuria (f., Med.) alkaptonuria.

alcaptonúrico -ca (adj.) alkaptonuric.

alçar (v.t.) to lift (up), raise (up), elevate; to hoist, heave; (v.i.) of cattle, to stray and grow wild; (v.r.) to rebel, rise up.—vôo, of an airplane, to take off; of a bird, to take flight.

alcaravão (m.) a tiger heron (Trigrosoma brasiliense) c.a. MARIA-MOLE, SOCÔZINHO.

alcaravia (f., Bot.) caraway (Carum carvi).

alcaraviz (f.) tuyère (of a blast furnace;) blow pipe (of a forge).

alcatear-se (v.r.) to band together.

alcatéia (f.) pack (of wolves); gang (of evil-doers) de—, on the lookout; lurking.

alcatifa (f.) large carpet; carpet-like covering.

alcatifado -da (adj.) carpeted.

alcatifar (v.t.) to carpet.

alcatira (f.) tragacanth gum; (Bot.) the tragacanth milk-vetch (Astragalus gummifer).

alcatrão (m.) tar.—mineral, or—de hulha, coal tar.—vegetal, wood tar.

alcatraz (m.) frigate bird, man-of-war bird (Fregata magnificens or F. aquila), c.a. GRAPIRÁ, JOÃO-GRANDE, FRAGATA, TESOURA; formerly, a pelican or albatross; (colloq.) a bonesetter, c.a. ALGEBRISTA.

alcatre (m.) loin end, rump (of beef); a piece of the round (of beef) for roasting.

alcatroado -da (adj.) tarred.

alcatroamento (m.) act of tarring.

alcatroar (v.t.) to tar.

alcatroeiro (m.) maker of, or dealer in, tar.

alcatruz (m.) bucket.

alcatruzar (v.t.) to crook, bend (over); (v.i.) to bend over (with age).

alce (m.) European moose or elk; halt, rest; truce.

alcedídeos (m.pl.) = ALCEDONÍDEOS.

alcedo [ê] (m.) the small, brightly colored European king-fisher (Alcedo) and other birds of this genus.

alcédone (f.) = ALCIÃO.

alcedonídeos (m.pl.) the kingfishers (Alcedinidae).

alcião (m.) = ALCÍONE.

alcicórnio (m.) staghorn fern (Platycerium, syn. Alcicornium).

alcídeos (m.pl.) the Alcidae (auks, puffins, etc.).

alcíone, alcíona (f.) halcyon (fabled bird); modernly, the kingfisher, called MARTIM-PESCADOR or PICA-PEIXE; an alcyonarian coral; (Astron.) Alcyone (the brightest star in the Pleiades). Vars. ALCÍON, ALCIÃO.

alcionário (m., Zool.) any alcyonarian.

alcíoneo -nea, alciônico -ca (adj.) halcyon, calm, peaceful.

alco (m.) a small, long-haired, domesticated dog, with pendulous ears, of tropical America.

alcobaça (f.) large, red, cotton handkerchief, used principally by persons taking snuff.

alcôfa (f.) creel or other small basket; (m.) procurer; (f.) procuress.

alcofar (v.) = ALCOVITAR.

alcoice (m.) bawdyhouse. Var. ALCOUCE.

alcofla (f.), alcoflio (m., Chem.) alkyl .

alcoilizar [o-i] (v.t., Chem.) to alkylate.

alcomonia (f.) = ALCAMONIA.

álcool [álcoois (òis)] (m.) alcohol; liquor.—absoluto, absolute alcohol.—alflico, allyl alcohol.—amílico, amyl alcohol [= AMILÁLCOOL].—anidro, anhydrous or absolute alcohol.—benzílico, benzyl alcohol.—butílico, butyl alcohol.—butílico normal, normal butyl alcohol, 1-butanol.—butílico secundário, secondary butyl alcohol, 2-butanol.—canfólico, borneol, bornyl alcohol, camphol.—cerílico, ceryl alcohol.—cetílico, cetyl alcohol, ethal.—cinâmico, cinnamic alcohol.—colestérico, (Biochem.) cholesterol.—comum, common alcohol, spirit of wine, ethyl alcohol.—de indústria, industrial alcohol.—de queimar, denatured alcohol.—desnaturado, denatured alcohol.—de vinho, spirit of wine, common alcohol.—etálico, cetyl alcohol, ethal.—etílico, ethyl or common alcohol.—fênico, phenol, phenyl alcohol, carbolic acid, hydroxy-benzene [= FENOL].—isobutílico, isobutyl alcohol, 2-methyl-1-propanol, isopropyl carbinol.—melícico or mirícico, myricyl or melissal alcohol.—mentólico, menthol, 3-p-menthanol, peppermint camphor [= MENTOL].—metílico, methyl alcohol, methanol, wood alcohol [= METANOL].—ordinário, common alcohol, spirit of wine, ethyl alcohol [= ÁLCOOL COMUM].—poliatômico, polyalcohol, polyhydric alcohol.—primário, primary alcohol.—propargílico, propargyl alcohol, 2-propyn-1-ol.—propílico, propyl alcohol.—propílico primário, normal propyl alcohol, 1-propanol.—propílico secundário, isopropyl alcohol, 2-propanol.—secundário, secondary alcohol.—terciário, tertiary alcohol.—tricloro-isopropílico, tricholoro isopropyl alcohol, isopral.—vanílico, vanillic alcohol, vanillyl alcohol.—vínico, spirit of wine, common alcohol.

alcoolato (m., Chem., Pharm.) alcoholate.

alcoólatra (m.,f.) an alcoholic.

alcoolatura (f.) alcoholature.

alcooleiro (m.) alcohol manufacturer.

alcoólico -ca (adj.; m.,f.) alcoholic.

alcoolismo (m.) alcoholism.

alcoolista (m.,f.) alcoholist, alcoholic.

alcoolizado -da (adj.) treated with, or saturated with, alcohol; drunk.

alcoolizar (v.t.) to alcoholize; to inebriate.

alcoolizável (adj.) alcoholizable.

alcoolomania (f.) dipsomania.

alcoolometria (f.) alcoholometry.

alcoolométrico -ca (adj.) alcoholometric(al).

alcoolômetro, alcoolometro (m.) alcoholometer.

alcorânico -ca (adj.) Alcoranic, Koranic.

alcoranista (m.,f.) Alcoranist.

Alcorão [-rões, -rães] (m.) Alcoran, Koran.

alcorça [ô] (f.), alcorce [ô] (m.) icing (for cakes).

alcorcovar (v.) = CORCOVAR.

alcorque (m.) cork-soled shoes.

alcouce (m.) = ALCOICE.

alcouceiro (m.) whoremonger; pimp. Var. ALCOICEIRO.

alcova [ô] (f.) alcove; small (windowless) bedroom.

alcovista (m.) whoremonger; woman chaser.

alcovista (m.) whoremonger; woman chaser.

alcovitar (v.t.) to procure (women); (v.i.) to intrigue.

alcoviteirice, alcovitice (f.) pandering, procuring, pimping; intrigue.

alcoviteiro -ra (adj.) pandering; intriguing; (m.) pander, bawd, pimp, procurer [= ALCAIOTE and ALCAGÜETE];

small kerosene lamp; a parakeet, c.a. MEXERIQUEIRO; (*f.*) bawd, procuress.
alcunha (*f.*) nickname, epithet (esp. a contemptuous or derogatory one).
alcunhar (*v.t.*) to nickname, dub.
aldeamento (*m.*) village, rural settlement; Indian settlement.
aldeão [-deãos, -deões, -deães] **-deã** (*m.,f.*) villager; peasant. (*adj.*) village; rustic.
aldear (*v.t.*) to settle in villages.
aldeia (*f.*) village, hamlet, settlement.
aldeidase [e-i] (*f., Biochem.*) aldehydase.
aldeídico -ca (*adj.*) aldehydic.
aldeidina [e-i] (*m., Chem.*) aldehydine.
aldeído (*m., Chem.*) aldehyde.—**acético,** acetaldehyde, ethanal.—**acíclico,** acyclic or aliphatic aldehyde.—**aromático,** aromatic aldehyde.—**benzílico,** or **benzóico,** benzaldehyde, benzene carbonal, artificial essential oil of almond.—**butírico,** butyraldehyde, butanal, butyric aldehyde.—**cinâmico,** cinnamaldehyde, 3-phenyl propenal, cinnamic aldehyde, cinnamol, cinnamyl aldehyde.—**crotônico,** croton(ic) aldehyde, 2-butenal, propylene aldehyde.—**cumínico,** cumaldehyde, cuminal.—**etílico,** ethyl aldehyde, acetaldehyde [= ALDEÍDO ACÉTICO].—**fórmico,** formaldehyde, methanal, oxomethane, oxymethylene, formic aldehyde, methylene oxide, formalith [= FORMOL].—**glicério,** glyceraldehyde.—**glicólico,** glycoaldehyde, glycolic aldehyde, hydroxy ethanal.—**metílico** = —FÓRMICO.—**ordinário** = —ACÉTICO.—**oxálico,** glyoxal, ethanedial, oxaldehyde, biformyl.—**piromúcico,** pyromucic aldehyde, furfural, furfuraldehyde (= FURFUROL).—**silicílico,** salicyl(ic) aldehyde.—**valérico,** valeraldehyde, pentanal, valeral.—**vínico** = — ACÉTICO.
aldeola (*f.*) tiny village, hamlet.
aldimina (*f., Chem.*) aldimin(e), aldime.
aldino -na (*adj., Bibliog.*) Aldine.
aldo (*m.*) an Aldine book or edition.
aldol (*m., Chem.*) aldol.
aldolização (*f., Chem.*) aldolization.
aldolizar (*v.t., Chem.*) to aldolize.
aldose (*f., Chem.*) aldose.
aldoxímio [ks] (*m., Chem.*) aldoxime.
aldraba (*f.*) = ALDRAVA; (*pl.*) leather leggings.
aldrabar (*v.*) & derivs. = ALDRAVAR & derivs.
aldrava (*f.*) latch; door bolt; door knocker.
aldravado -da (*adj.*) of doors and windows, bolted, latched; of work, bungled, botched; (*f.*) a knock with the door knocker.
aldravão (*m.*) large door bolt; blusterer; bungler.
aldravar (*v.t.*) to provide (a door) with a bolt or knocker; to bolt (a door); to bungle, botch; to knock (on a door); (*v.i.*) to lie; to ramble.
aldrovanda (*f., Bot.*) the waterbug trap (*Aldrovanda vesciculosa*).
alé (*m.*) a shrike or butcherbird.
álea (*f.*) = ALÉIA.
alealdar (*v.*) = LEALDAR.
aleatório -ria (*adj.*) aleatory, uncertain, conditional; fortuitous, accidental. **contrato—,** aleatory contract.
alécito -ta (*adj.*) alecithal, without yolk.
alecrim (*m.*) rosemary (*Rosmarinus officinalis*).—**bravo,** a St. John's-wort (*Hypericum*).—**da-praia,** a sedge (*Bulbostylis capillaris*).—**de-são-josé,** jump-up-and-kiss-me, the shaggy portulaca (*P. pilosa*) c.a. AMOR-CRESCIDO, BELDROEGA, CAAPONGA.—**do-campo,** a lantana (*L. microphylla*).—**do-mato,** a baccharis thistle (*B. silvestris*).—**do-norte,** the sweet gale (*Myrica gale*).
alecrinzeiro (*m.*) rosemary shrub.
alectória (*f.*) a genus (*Alectoria*) of lichens.
alectorólofo (*m., Bot.*) a rattlepot (*Alectorolophus*); the cockscomb rattleweed (*Phinanthus crista-galli*).
alectoromancia (*f.*) alectryomancy.
alegação (*f.*) allegation.
alegado -da (*adj.*) alleged; cited; (*m.*) allegation.
alegar (*v.t.*) to allege, affirm; to plead, offer in excuse; to cite, quote.
alegoria (*f.*) allegory.
alegórico -ca (*adj.*) allegoric.
alegorizar (*v.t.*) to allegorize.
alegrado -da (*adj.*) glad, joyful, happy, gay.
alegrador -dora (*adj.*) gladdening, cheering.
alegrar (*v.t.*) to gladden, make glad; to rejoice, delight; to cheer; to make tipsy; (*Masonry*) to point.—**-se com,** to be gladdened by.—**-se em,** to be glad to; to rejoice in.

Isso me alegra, I am glad of that. **muito me alegra saber que,** I am very glad to know that.
alegre (*adj.*) glad, happy; cheerful, joyous, blithe, merry; cheery, gladdening; jovial, jolly; showy, bright; racy, piquant; tipsy; gay (wanton).
alegrete [grê] (*adj.*) tipsy; (*m.*) flower box; flower pot; (*colloq.*) tipsiness.
alegria (*f.*) joy, gladness; happiness; elation; cheerfulness; merriment, festivity; mirth.—**indizível,** unspeakable joy. **nos páramos,** or **no auge, da—,** in the seventh heaven. **não se conter de—,** to be beside oneself with joy. **pular de—,** to jump for joy. **transbordar de—,** to be overjoyed.
alegrinho (*m.*) the white-crested flycatcher (*Serpophaga subscristata*).
alegro (*m., Music*) allegro.
aleguá, guá, guá! Rah! rah! rah!
aléia (*f.*) narrow passage; garden path, lane, walk; a bordered way; alley. Var. ALEA.
aleijado -da (*adj.*) lame, crippled; (*m.,f.*) cripple.
aleijamento (*m.*) crippling; deformity.
aleijão (*m.*) deformity (of body or character); a blunder.
aleijar (*v.t.*) to maim, cripple.
aieiloar (*v.t.*) to sell at auction; to auction off (something).
aleirar (*v.*) = LEIRAR.
aleitação (*f.*), **aleitamento** (*m.*) lactation.—**materno,** breastfeeding.
aleitado -da (*adj.*) milk-fed; milky.
aleitar (*v.t.*) to milk-feed; to suckle; to make white as milk.
aleive (*m.*) calumny, slander, defamation.
aleivosia (*f.*) treachery, perfidy; duplicity, double-dealing.
aleivoso -sa (*adj.*) caluminous, slanderous; treacherous, false.
Aleixo (*m.*) Alexis.
alelomorfismo (*m., Bot.*) allelomorphism.
aleluia (*m.*) halieluia; a certain small white butterfly; a swarm of flying ants; (*Bot.*) a senna (*Cassia bacillaris*); the wood sorrel (*Oxalis acetosella*).
além (*adv.*) beyond, yonder, at a distance, over there.—**muito—,** far beyond.—**de,** (*prep.*) beyond, on the other side of, past; above, superior to; besides, except, save, over and above, in addition to. **para—de,** beyond.—**de que,**—**disso,**—**disto,** (*conj.*) moreover, besides, furthermore, over and above that.—**de tudo,** above all.—**do que,** besides. (*m.*) the beyond.
alemã, fem. of ALEMÃO.
Alemanha (*f.*) Germany.
alemânico -ca (*adj.; m.*) Germanic.
alemanismo (*m.*) Germanism.
alemanizar-se (*v.r.*) to Germanize.
alemão [-mães] **-mã** [mãs] (*adj.; m.,f.*) German (person); (*m.*) a sea catfish.
além-mar (*adv.*) overseas; (*m.*) lands overseas.
além-mundo (*m.*) the next world, the hereafter.
alemoado -da (*adj.*) German-like; (*f.*) a bunch of Germans. [*Derogatory*].
alemoar-se (*v.*) = ALEMANIZAR-SE.
alemontite (*f., Min.*) allemontite.
além-túmulo (*m.*) life beyond the grave.
alênio (*m., Chem.*) allene.
alentado -da (*adj.*) brave, courageous, valiant; bold, daring; stout; vigorous.
alentar (*v.t.*) to animate, encourage; to quicken; to invigorate; to stimulate, enliven, arouse; to nourish (hopes, etc.); (*v.i.*) to breath, pant; (*v.r.*) to take on new life, courage.
alentecer (*v.i.*) to slow down (up).
alentilhado -da (*adj.*) lenticular.
alento (*m.*) respiration, breath; breeze, gust; boldness, daring, courage. **lutar até o último—,** to fight to one's dying breath.
aleócar (*f.*) a genus (*Aleochara*) of rove beetles.
aleonado -da (*adj.*) lion-like; tawny.
alepídoto (*adj.; m.*) alepidote, (fish) without scales.
alequeado -da (*adj.*) fan-shaped.
alerce (*m., Bot.*) the Patagonian fitzroya (*F. cupressoides*).
alérgeno (*m., Immunol.*) allergen.
alergia (*f., Immunol.*) allergy.
alérgico -ca (*adj.*) allergic.
alergina (*f.*) = ALÉRGENO.
alerta (*adv.*) on the alert; on guard; (*m.*) alarm; alert, watchword; alertness; (*exclam.*) Watch out! Look out!

alertar (*v.t.*) to alert; (*v.i.*) to be alert.
alestar (*v.t.*) to lighten (a ship); to make nimble, quick, agile; (*v.r.*) to become so.
alestesia (*f.*, *Med.*) allochiria.
aleta [ê] (*f.*) little wing; (*Anat.*) ala, wing of the nose. (*Arch.*) alette.
aleto [ê] (*m.*) = ARACANGUIRA.
aletologia (*f.*) alethiology.
aletoscópio (*m.*) alethoscope.
aletradar-se (*v.r.*) to become lettered.
aletrado –da (*adj.*) lettered, literate.
aletria (*f.*) vermicelli; (*Zool.*) silversides, sand smelt (*Menidia brasiliensis*), c.a. MANJUBA, PITITINGA.
aletriaria (*f.*) vermicelli factory.
alétride (*f.*), **alétris** (*m.*) the colicroot or whitetube stargrass (*Aletris farinosa*).
aleucemia (*f.*, *Med.*) leucopenia.
aleucêmico –ca (*adj.*, *Med.*) aleukemic; leucopenic.
aleurite (*f.*) the candlenut tree (*Aleurites moluccana*); the tungoil tree (*A. fordi*), and others of this genus.
aleurode (*m.*) a genus (*Aleyrodes*) of white flies.
aleuródida (*f.*, *Zool.*) any aleyrodid.
aleurômetro (*m.*) aleurometer.
aleurona (*f.*, *Bot.*, *Biochem.*) aleurone grains.
aleuroscópio (*m.*) aleuroscope.
alevantar (*v.*) & derivs. = LEVANTAR & derivs.
alevante (*m.*) horse mint (*Mentha longifolia*).
alevedar (*v.*) = LEVEDAR.
alevim (*m.*) alevin (newly-hatched fish, esp. salmon).
Alexandre (*m.*) Alexander.
alexandrino –na (*adj.*; *m.*,*f.*) Alexandrine (verse, person).
alexandrita (*f.*, *Min.*) alexandrite.
alexia [ks] (*f.*, *Psycopathol.*) alexia, word blindness.
alexifármaco –ca [ks] (*adj.*) antidotal; (*m.*) antidote, counterpoison.
alexina [ks] (*f.*, *Immunol.*). alexin.
alexipirético –ca [ks] (*adj.*, *Med.*) alexipyretic, febrifuge.
alfa (*m.*) alpha (all the usual senses); **alfa e ômega**, alpha and omega, the beginning and ending; the chief; the whole; (*Bot.*) alfa grass or esparto needlegrass (*Stipa tenacissima*) of Spain and North Africa.
alfabetação (*f.*), **alfabetamento** (*m.*) alphabetizing.
alfabetado –da (*adj.*) alphabetized.
alfabetar (*v.t.*) to alphabetize.
alfabetário –ria (*adj.*) alphabetic.
alfabético –ca (*adj.*) alphabetic.
alfabetismo (*m.*) alphabetism; early stage of learning.
alfabetista (*m.*,*f.*) alphabetist.
alfabetização (*f.*) the teaching of reading.
alfabetizado –da (*adj.*) able to read, literate; (*m.*,*f.*) one who can read.
alfabetizar (*v.t.*) to teach to read.
alfabeto (*m.*) alphabet; the abc's of anything.—**manual**, sign language.
alface (*f.*) garden lettuce (*Lactuca sativa*).—**d'água**, water lettuce (*Pistia stratiotes*) c.a.—**d'AGUA.**—**de-cordeiro**, African valerian (*Fedia cornucopiae*).—**de-cordeiro**, European cornsalad (*Valerianella olitoria*).
alfacinha (*f.*) young lettuce plant; (*m.*) nickname for natives of Lisbon.—**do-rio** = ABRÓTANO-MACHO.
alfafa (*f.*) alfalfa.—**arbórea**, Australian saltbush (*Atriplex semibaccata*).—**da-suécia**, sickle alfalfa (*Medicago sativa falcata*), c.a. CASSOA, LUZERNA-DE-SEQUEIRO.—**-de-flor-amarela**,—**lupulina**, black medic (*Medicago lupulina*), c.a. LUZERNA-AMARELA, LUZERNA-LUPULINA.—**-de-fôlhas-manchadas**, the spotted medic (*Medicago arabica*).—**espinhosa**, the calvary medic (*Medicago echinus*).—**-gigante** or—**sempre-verde**, the tree medic (*Medicago arborea*).—**verdadeira**,—**-de-flor-roxa**,—**-de-provença**, lucerne or common alfalfa (*Medicago sativa*), c.a. LUZERNA, MELGA-DOS-PRADOS.
alfafal (*m.*) alfalfa field.
alfaia (*f.*) furniture, furnishings; ornament; household utensils; tableware; jewelry.
alfaiar (*v.t.*) to decorate, adorn, ornament, embellish.
alfaiata (*f.*) woman tailor; dressmaker; tailor's wife.
alfaiatar (*v.t.*,*v.i.*) to tailor.
alfaiataria (*f.*) tailoring shop, the tailor's.
alfaiate (*m.*) tailor; a small bird (better known as SERRA-SERRA); a water spider, c.a. CABRA; (*Zool.*) the European avocet (*Recurvirostra avosetta*) c.a. FRADE, SOVELA.
alfândega (*f.*) customhouse. **despachante de**—, customhouse agent or broker. **direitos de**—, customs duties. **tarifa**, or **pauta**, **de**—, customs tariff.

alfandegar (*v.t.*) to store in or clear through customs.
alfandegário –ria (*adj.*; *m.*,*f.*) customhouse (employee).
alfaneque (*m.*) the kestrel (*Falco t. tinnunculus*).
alfanje (*m.*) scimitar; cutlass Cf. CIMITARRA.
alfaque (*m.*) deep place near the shore; mud bank.
alfaquim (*m.*) a moonfish [= ABACATUAIA].
alfarrábio (*m.*) old book.
alfarrabista (*m.*,*f.*) collector of, or dealer in, old books. **casa de**—, second-hand bookstore. Cf. SEBO.
alfarrôba (*f.*) pod of the ALFARROBEIRA.
alfarrobeira (*f.*, *Bot.*) the carob, or St.-John's-bread, or locust (*Ceratonia siliqua*), c.a. FAVA-RICA, ALGAROBA.
alfarva (*f.*, *Bot.*) fenugreek (*Trigonella foenumgraecum*), c.a. ALFORVA, ALFÔRRA, ERVINHA.
alfavaca (*f.*, *Bot.*) basil (*Ocimum*).—**cheirosa**, sweet basil (*O. basilicum*) c.a. BASÍLICO-GRANDE, MANGERICÃO-DE-MÔLHO, MANGERICÃO-DOS-COZINHEIROS, MANGERICÃO-GRANDE, ERVA-REAL.—**-da-guiné**, fever basil (*O. viride*), c.a. QUIOIÔ.—**-de-cobra**, a rue (*Monnieria trifolia*), c.a. JABORANDI.—**-do-campo**, savory (*Satureia*).
alfazema (*f.*, *Bot.*) true lavender (*Lavandula officinalis*).—**-brava**, a bushmint (*Hyptis racemulosa*).—**-de-caboclo** = SAMBACAETÁ.
alféloa (*f.*) candymaker's plastic mass of sugar; pull candy; taffy.
alfena, **alfeneira** (*f.*) **alfeneiro** (*m.*) European privet (*Ligustrum vulgare*).—**-do-japão**, Japanese privet (*L. japonicum*).
alfenim (*m.*) sugar coating; person of delicate complexion; milksop, mollycoddle; fop, dandy.
alfeninar-se (*v.r.*) to become effeminate or dandified.
alferes (*m.*) former military rank corresponding to second lieutenant or ensign.
alfinetada (*f.*) pin-prick; a "dig".
alfinetar (*v.t.*) to prick with a pin; to satirize; to "needle".
alfinête (*m.*) pin; tie pin; brooch, breast pin; hatpin; a wireworm called BICHA-AMARELA; a pikelike fish called GUARANÁ-PEQUENA. (*pl.*) pin money.—**de ama** (**de dama**, **de gancho**, **de passador**, **de segurança**) safety pin.—**de cabelo**, bodkin.—**de peito**, breast pin; tie pin; —**-do-mato** = CUARI-BRAVO. (*pl.*, *Bot.*) the Jupiter's-beard centranthus (*C. ruber*); the sweet william silene (*S. ameria*).—**s-da-terra**, the French silene (*S. gallica*).—**s-de-dama**, the drooping silene (*S. pendula*).
alfinetear (*v.*) = ALFINETAR.
alfineteira (*f.*) pincushion.
alfobre [ô] (*m.*) hotbed.
alfol (*m.*, *Pharm.*) alphol.
alfombra (*f.*) carpet; lawn, turf, (green)sward.
alfombrado –da (*adj.*) carpeted; (*m.*) a carpeted surface; lawn, turf.
alfonsia (*f.*) = ALFÔRRA.
alforjar (*v.t.*) to put (something) in a saddlebag; to pocket (something).
alforje (*m.*) saddlebag; valise.
alfôrra (*f.*) plant rust; blight, blast.
alforreca (*f.*) jellyfish.[= ÁGUA-VIVA].
alforria (*f.*) freeing of slaves. **carta de**—, a certificate of freedom issued to an ex-slave.
alforriado –da (*adj.*) of slaves, freed.
alforriar (*v.t.*) to free (slaves); (*v.r.*) to free oneself.
alforva [ô] (*f.*) plant rust, blight, blast; (*Bot.*) an euphorbia (*E.seget alis*).
alfôstigo (*m.*, *Bot.*) the common pistache (*P. vera*) c.a. PISTÁCIA.—**da**(**terra** = AMENDOIM (peanut).
alfredo (*m.*) kerosene lamp; (*cap.*).Alfred.
alfurja (*f.*) lair; inner court; open sewer; manure pile.
Álg. = ÁLGEBRA (Algebra).
alga (*f.*, *Bot.*) alga; (*pl.*) algae; seaweeds.—**das-lagoas** = FITA-DO-MAR (eel grass).—**vesiculosa** = BODELHA (rockweed).
algáceo –cea (*adj.*) algal.
algália (*f.*, *Med.*) catheter [= CANDELINHA].
algalia (*f.*) musk; civet cat.
algaliaçao (*f.*, *Med.*) catheterization.
algaliar (*v.t.*, *Med.*) to catheterize.
algar (*m.*) ravine; cave; crater.
algaravia (*f.*) Arabic language; gibberish, rigamarole.
algaraviar (*v.t.*) to jargonize; to jabber.,
algarismo (*m.*) digit.—**s aproximados**, approximate figures.—**s arábicos**, Arabic numerals.—**s romanos**, Roman numerals.—**s significativos**, significant figures.
algaroba (*f.*) = ALFARROBEIRA.
algarobeira (*f.*), **algarobo** (*m.*, *Bot.*) mesquite (*Prosopis*).

algarobilho (*m.*, *Bot.*) a Caesalpinia (*C. brevifolia*) whose pods are used in tanning.

algarroba [ô] (*f.*) = ALFARROBA.

algazarra (*f.*) clamor, hullabaloo, hub-bub, din, uproar, row, racket, roughhouse, shindy.

algazarrar (*v.i.*) to be loud, noisy, obstreperous.

algazarrento –ta, **algazarreiro** –ra (*adj.*) loud, noisy, vociferous, obstreperous.

álgebra (*f.*) algebra; bonesetting.

algébrico –ca (*adj.*) algebraic.

algebrista (*m.,f.*) algebraist; (*colloq.*) bonesetter; = ALCATRAZ and ENDIREITA.

algebrizar (*v.t.*) to algebraize.

algedo [ê], **algédone** (*m.*) algedo (severe pain in the region of the urinary and genital organs).

algema (*f.*) handcuff, manacle, shackle.

algemar (*v.t.*) to manacle, handcuff; to hamper, trammel.

algerianc, incorrect variant of ARGELINO.

algeroz [ó] (*m.*) downspout; gutter.

algesia (*f.*) algesia, sensitiveness to pain.

algesiógeno –na (*adj.*, *Med.*) algogenic, producing pain. Var. ALGOGÊNICO.

algia (*f.*) pain.

algibe (*m.*) cistern.

algibebe (*m.*) cheap tailor; dealer in ready-made clothes.

algibeira (*f.*) pocket. **pergunta de**—, trick question.

algidez [ê] (*f.*) coldness, chilliness.

álgido –da (*adj.*) algid, chilly, cold.

algina (*f.*, *Chem.*) algin(e).

algínico –ca (*adj.*, *Chem.*) alginic.

alginurese (*f.*, *Med.*) alginuresis, painful urination.

algo (*pron.*) something, anything; (*adv.*) somewhat, a little, to some extent.

algodão (*m.*) cotton; cotton wool, cloth, thread or goods. —**beneficiado**, ginned cotton.—**bravo**, a poisonous morning glory (*Ipomoea fistulosa*), c.a. CAMPAINHA-DE-CANUDO, CANUDO, MATA-CABRAS, MATA-PINTO, SALSA-BRANCA; also, an okra-like hibiscus (*H. furcellatus*).—-colódio, gun-cotton.—**cravo** = BUTUÁ-DE-CORVO.—**cru**, raw cotton, unbleached cotton.—**de-vidro**, spun glass. —**do-brejo**, forkleaf hibiscus (*H. bifurcatus*), c.a. ALGODOEIRO-BRAVO, AMANDURANA, MAJORANA, VINA-GREIRA.—-do-mato = BUTUÁ-DE-CORVO.—**doce**, spun sugar.—**em pasta**, cotton batting.—**em rama**, raw cotton. —**enfardado**, baled cotton.—**estampado**, cotton print. —**hidrófilo**, absorbent cotton.—**macaco**, American long-staple cotton (*Gossypium hirsutum religiosum*).—-pólvora, gun-cotton. **fazenda de**—, cotton cloth. **fio de**—, cotton thread, cotton yarn. **tecido de**—, cotton fabric.

algodãorana (*f.*, *Bot.*) a mallow (*Pavonia paniculata*).

algodãozinho (*m.*) calico.—**do-campo** = CAPITÃO-DA-SALA.

algodoal (*m.*) cotton plantation.

algodoar (*v.t.*) to fill, stuff or cover with, or as with, cotton.

algodoaria (*f.*) cotton (goods) mill.

algodoeiro –ra (*adj.*) pert. to cotton; (*m.*) cotton plant. —-americano,—-crioulo,—-da-costa,—-de-guiné,— —-das-barbadas,—-de-pernambuco,—-folha-de-parreira: all names for sea-island cotton (*Gossypium barbadense*). —-da-índia, or —-da-praia, the linden hibiscus (*H. tili-aceus*), c.a. UÁCIMA-DA-PRAIA.—**-da-terra-alta**, upland cotton (*G. hirsutum*) or Levant cotton (*G. herbaceum*).— -do-campo, or—-do-mato = BUTUÁ-DE-CORVO.—**gigante**, Asiatic tree cotton (*G. arboreum*).—**silvestre**, wild cotton.

algodoento –ta (*adj.*) cottony.

algodoim [o-ím] (*m.*) cotton duck.

algodonita (*f.*, *Min.*) algodonite.

algofilia (*f.*, *Psychopathol.*) algophilia, algolagnia.

algófilo –la (*m.,f.*) algophilist.

algofobia (*f.*) algophobia, morbid dread of pain.

algogênico –ca (*adj.*) = ALGESIÓGENO.

algóide (*adj.*) algoid.

algol (*m.*, *Astron.*) algol.

algolagnia (*f.*, *Psychopathol.*) algolagnia.

algolagnista (*m.,f.*, *Psychopathol.*) algolagnist.

algologia (*f.*, *Bot.*) algology, phycology.

algológico —ca (*adj.*) algological.

algologista (*m.,f.*) algologist.

algólogo –ga (*m.,f.*) algologist.

algomania (*f.*) = ALGOFILIA.

algômetro (*m.*, *Psychol.*) algometer.

algonquiano –na (*adj.*; *m.,f.*) Algonquian.

algor [ô] (*m.*) intense cold; (*Med.*) algor, a chill.

algorítmico –ca (*adj.*) algorithmic, arithmetical, algorismic.

algose (*f.*, *Med.*) algosis.

algoso –sa (*adj.*) algous, full of algae or seaweeds.

algoz (*m.*) hangman, executioner; torturer; a cruel, inhuman person.—-das-árvores, (*Bot.*) the American bittersweet (*Celastrus scandens*).

alguém (*pron.*) someone, somebody, anyone, anybody.

alguergar (*v.t.*) to decorate with mosaic work (as the sidewalks in Rio de Janeiro).

alguergue (*m.*) small piece of stone used in mosaic or inlay work; an old game similar to checkers, or the stones with which it is played; the large stone of an olive press.

alguidar (*m.*) shallow earthen pan or bowl.

algum [-guns] —**ma** [-gumas] (*adj.*) a, an, any, one; (*pl.*) some, several, various, diverse; a few. [When placed after a noun in a negative phrase, ALGUM is the equivalent of no, none, not any, not one, as in the examples below.] —**dia**, some day, any day.—**espaço**, a while.—**tanto**, somewhat, a little.—**tempo**, awhile; for a time; for sometime; for awhile.—**coisa**, something, anything.—**hora**, sometime.—**pessoa**, someone, somebody.—**vez**, sometime.—**as vezes**, sometimes, now and then. **coisa**—, nothing. **de modo**—, in no wise; not at all. **de**—**modo**, in some way. **em**—**lugar**, somewhere. **em lugar**—, nowhere. **em tempo**—, at no time; never. **pessoa**—, no one, nobody.

algures (*adv.*) somewhere, in some place. [Frequently confused with ALHURES, elsewhere.]

alhage (*m.*, *Bot.*) the camelthorn (*Alhagi pseudalhagi*) and other plants of this genus.

alhada (*f.*) mess of garlic; dish of garlic; tangled affair.

alhal (*m.*) garlic field.

alheamento (*m.*) estrangement, separation; aloofness.

alhear [13] (*v.t.*) to alienate; to estrange; to separate;—-se de, to turn away from.

alheio –lheia (*adj.*) strange, inappropriate; foreign; deprived; remote; extraneous; of others; (*m.*) that which belongs to another.—**de si**, rapt in thought. **amigo do**—, a thief. **direitos**—s, the rights of others. **falar da vida**—, to talk about others; to gossip. **opiniões**—s, others' opinions.

alheta [ê] (*f. Naut.*) buttocks. **na**—**de**, on the trail of, close behind.

alho (*m.*) garlic; (*Bot.*)—-do-mato, the Trinidad cipura (*C. paludosa*), c.a.—-DA-CAMPINA,—-DO-CAMPO, CEBO-LINHA-DO-CAMPO, COQUEIRINHO, COQUINHO, VARETA. —-grosso-de-espanha, giant garlic (*Allium scorodo-prasum*), c.a.—-ESPANHOL,—-MOURISCO,—-ROCAMBOLE. —-porro, leek (*Allium porrum*).—-sem-mau-cheiro, —-silvestre, false garlic (*Nothoscordum*).

alhures (*adv.*) elsewhere. [Frequently confused with ALGURES, elsewhere.]

ali (*adv.*) there, in that place; over there; yonder.—**acima**, up there, up yonder.—**dentro**, in there.—**em baixo**, down there, down yonder.—**mesmo**, right there. **aqui e**—, here and there. **por**—, that way, in that direction, there somewhere, around there, over there.

aliáceo –cea (*adj.*) alliaceous; (*f.pl.*, *Bot.*) the garlic or onion family (*Alliaceae*).

aliado –da (*adj.*) allied; (*m.,f.*) ally.

aliamba (*f.*) = DIAMBA.

aliança (*f.*) alliance; engagement ring; wedding ring.

aliar (*v.t.,v.r.*) to ally, unite, join (a, com, with).—**metais**, to alloy metals. Cf. LIGAR.

aliária (*f.*, *Bot.*) garlic mustard (*Sisymbrium alliaria*), c.a. ERVA-ALHEIRA.

aliás (*adv.*) besides, moreover, too, also, furthermore; rather (preferably); otherwise, in other respects; incidentally; as a matter of fact. [The term is not used, as in English, to denote an alias (assumed name), which in Port. is OUTRO NOME or NOME SUPOSTO.]

aliável (*adj.*) susceptible of being allied or alloyed.

alibi [á] (*m.*) alibi; (*colloq.*) plausible excuse.

alíbil (*adj.*) nutritive, nourishing.

álica (*f.*) = ESPELTA.

alicantina (*f.*) cheating at gambling; trickery, deceit.

alicantineiro –ra (*m.,f.*) crook, sharper.

alicatão (*m.*) forging tongs.

alicate (*m.*) pliers.—**de unhas**, nail clipper.—**de pontas redondas**, roundnose pliers.—**para tubos**, pipe wrench.

Alice (*f.*) Alice; Alicia.

alicerçado –da (*adj.*) having a foundation; based.

alicerçar (*v.t.*) to lay a foundation; to base (as opinions) on something.
alicerce (*m.*) foundation; basis, base; support.
aliciação (*f.*) = ALICIAMENTO.
aliciador –**dora** (*adj.*) beguiling; attractive; alluring; seductive; bribing; (*m.,f.*) enticer; briber.—**de freguezes**, tout.
aliciamento (*m.*) allurement, enticement, seduction; attractiveness; bribery.
aliciar (*v.t.*) to lure, entice, attract; to seduce; to bribe; to mislead.—**eleitores**, to beguile voters.
aliciante (*adj.*) attractive, alluring; (*m.,f.*) that which attracts; seduction.
alicorne (*m.*) = ANHUMA.
alicuí (*f.*) arikury palm (*Arikuryoba schizophylla*), c.a. ARICUÍ.
alicuri (*m.*) = ARICURI.
alidade (*f.*) alidade (surveying instrument).
alienabilidade (*f.*) alienability.
alienação (*f.*) alienation, transfer, conveyance (of property); estrangement; insanity, derangement.—**mental**, psychosis.
alienado –**da** (*adj.*) alienated; separated; carried away; (*m.,f.*) insane person. **hospício de**—**s**, mental hospital; insane asylum.
alienador –**dora** (*adj.*) alienating; (*m.,f.*) alienator; one who conveys property to another.
alienante (*adj.*) alienating; (*m.,f.*) alienor (transferer of property).
alienar (*v.t.*) to alienate, transfer, convey, make over (to); to estrange; to make unfriendly; to hallucinate; (*v.r.*) to become insane or degraded.
alienatário –**ria** (*m.,f.*) alienee; assignee, consignee, transferee.
alienatório –**ria** (*adj.*) of property, alienable, transferable, conveyable.
alienável (*adj.*) alienable.
alienígena (*adj.; m.,f.*) alien; foreign(er).
alienismo (*m.*) alienism, psychiatry.
alienista (*adj.*) relating to diseases of the mind; (*m.,f.*) alienist, psychiatrist.
alifafe (*m.*, *Veter.*) bog spavin.
alifático –**ca** (*adj.*, *Chem.*) aliphatic.
alífero –**ra** (*adj.*) aliferous, winged.
aliforme (*adj.*) aliform, wing-shaped.
aligátor [-gatores] (*m.*) alligator. Cf. JACARÉ.
aligeirar (*v.t.*) to quicken (steps); to lighten (a burden, a ship); to make light-stepping (as troops and horses, by training); to mitigate (pain, sorrow);—**-se de**, to rid oneself of.
alígero –**ra** (*adj.*) aligerous, winged.
alijamento (*m.*) jettisoning.
alijar (*v.t.*) to jettison, throw overboard; to push out or aside.—**de si**, to rid oneself of.—**-se de**, to be (or get) rid of.
alil (*Chem.*) allyl (combining form). Cf. ALILO.
alilamina (*f.*, *Chem.*) allylamine.
alileno (*m.*, *Chem.*) allylene, propyne, methyl acetylene.
alílico –**ca** (*adj.*) allylic.
alilo (*m.*, *Chem.*) allyl. Cf. ALIL.
alimária (*f.*) dumb animal, brute; by ext., a stupid person.
alimentação (*f.*) alimentation, nourishment, nutrition; food, nutriment; (*Mach.*) feed.—**forçada**, forced feeding. —**materna**, breast feeding.—**por gravidade**, gravity feed.
alimentador –**dora** (*adj.*) feeding; nourishing; (*m.,f.*) feeder.
alimentar (*adj.*) alimentary; (*v.t.*) to nourish, feed; to support, maintain; to encourage, foster, promote.—**esperanças**, to cherish hopes.—**ódio**, to harbor hatred.—**-se de carne**, to live on meat.
alimentício –**cia**, **alimentário** –**ria** (*adj.*) nutritive, nourishing. **produtos alimentícios**, food products.
alimento (*m.*) food, nutriment; (*pl.*) provisions; allowance for support, alimony (but not necessarily related to divorce).—**s de origem animal**, animal food products.
alimentoso –**sa** (*adj.*) alimentative, nutritive.
alimpa, **alimpação** (*f.*) weeding, pruning.
alimpaduras (*f.pl.*) screenings, chaff.
alimpar (*v.*) = LIMPAR.
alindar (*v.t.*) to make (-se, oneself) beautiful.
alínea (*f.*) the first line of a paragraph; each separate item in an article or section of law, usually indicated by a letter, as (a), (b), etc.

alinfia (*f.*, *Med.*) alymphia.
alinhado –**da** (*adj.*) aligned, lined up, in line; (*colloq.*) spruce, well-dressed; well-behaved.
alinhamento (*m.*) alignment. **fora do**—, out of line.
alinhar (*v.t.*) to align; to line up; to form a line; (*v.r.*) to spruce up.
alinhavar (*v.t.*) to baste (sew); to trace, delineate; to make a rough sketch of; to cook up, improvise.
alinhavo (*m.*) act of basting; basting stitches; outline; rough sketch.
alinho (*m.*) alignment; neatness; spruceness.
aliônia (*f.*, *Bot.*) the genus (*Allionia*) of the four-o'clock family.
alípede (*adj.*, *Zool.*) aliped, wingfooted (as the bat).
aliquanta (*adj.*, *Math.*) aliquant.
alíquota [quo = co] (*adj.*, *Math.*) aliquot, factor, submultiple.
alisadeira (*f.*) smoother.
alisado –**da** (*adj.*) smooth; smoothed down; polished; (*m.*) trade wind [= ALISEU].
alisador –**dora** (*adj.*) smoothing; (*m.,f.*) polisher.
alisamento (*m.*) smoothing, polishing.
alisar (*v.t.*) to smooth (down, over, away); to unwrinkle; to polish; to soften.
aliseu, **alísio** (*m.*) trade wind [= ALISADO].
alisma (*f.*) water plantain (*Alisma plantago*).
alismáceas (*f.pl.*) the water plantains (*Alismaceae*).
alismóide (*adj.*) alismoid.
alisonita (*f.*, *Min.*) alisonite.
alisso (*m.*, *Bot.*) any alyssum, esp. goldentuft (*A. saxatile*) called **açafate-de-ouro**.
alistado –**da** (*adj.*) enlisted; (*m.*) enlisted man.
alistamento (*m.*) enlistment, recruiting; enrollment. —**eleitoral**, registration of voters.
alistando (*m.*) one who is eligible for military service.
alistar (*v.t.*) to list; to enlist, enroll; to register; to draft, recruit; (*v.r.*) to enlist.
alita (*f.*) alite (Portland-cement clinker).
aliteração (*f.*) alliteration.
aliterar (*v.t.*) to alliterate.
aliteratar-se (*v.r.*) to make a pretense of literacy.
aliviação (*f.*) alleviation.
aliviador –**dora** (*adj.*) alleviating, mitigating; (*m.,f.*) alleviator.
aliviamento (*m.*) alleviation.
aliviar (*v.t.*) to alleviate, lighten; to allay, assuage; to moderate; to relieve; to ease; (*v.i.*) of pain, to diminish; (*v.r.*) to relieve oneself.
alívio (*m.*) alleviation; relief; easement.
alizarato (*m.*, *Chem.*) alizarate.
alizares (*m.pl.*) doorframe, windowframe; casing; wainscot.
alizari [rí] (*m.*) madder root (for dyeing).
alizarina (*f.*, *Chem.*) alizarin(e).
aljamia (*f.*) vernacular Spanish of Jews and Moors; Spanish written in Hebrew or Arabic characters.
aljava (*f.*) quiver (for arrows) [= CARCÁS, FÁRETRA].
aljofareira (*f.*, *Bot.*) the common gromwell (*Lithospermum officinale*).
aljofrado –**da** (*adj.*) pearly; dewy. Var. ALJOFARADO.
aljofrar (*v.t.*) to decorate with seed pearls; to bedew. Var. ALJOFARAR.
aljôfres (*m.pl.*) seed pearls; (*Poetical*) tears; beads of sweat; dew drops. Var. ALJÔFARES.
aljuba (*f.*) doublet [= GIBÃO].
aljube (*m.*) dungeon, prison; den; cavern.
alm. = ALMIRANTE (admiral).
alma (*f.*) soul, mind, spirit; heart, center, core; essence, meaning; courage, fortitude; a person; web (of a steel beam); bore (of a gun); core (of a cable).—**aflita**, troubled soul.—**danada** (—**-de-cântaro**,—**-de-púcaro**,—**-do-diabo**), an evil, mean, hard-hearted person.—**de-ferro**, an iron-willed person.—**-de-gato** (or **-de-caboclo**) robust heath; also, the large-tailed squirrel cuckoo (*Piaya cayana macroura*), c.a. MARIA-CARAÍBA, RABO-DE-PALHA, RABO-DE-ESCRIVÃO, RABILONGA, MEIA-PATACA, PATO-PATACA, CHINCOÃ, ATINGAÚ, ORACA; also = ANUM-BRANCO.—**-de-mestre**, Wilson's petrel (*Oceanites oceanicus*), c.a. ANDORINHÃO-DAS-TORMENTAS.—**do outro mundo**, a ghost.—**-de-padeiro**, large air hole in a loaf of bread.—**errada**, a lost (wandering) soul.—**grande**, a big-hearted, noble person.—**-mater**, alma mater.—**-negra**, Bulwer's petrel (*Bulweria bulweri*), c.a. ANJINHO. —**nova**, new life, renewed courage.—**parens**, fatherland. —**-penada**, or, **-perdida**, a wandering soul.—**viva**, living

soul, living creature. **boa—**, a good soul (person). **de corpo e—**, with body and soul. **Dia das—s**, All Souls Day. **do fundo da—**, from the bottom of the heart. **pela—que Deus me deu**, upon my soul.

almácego (*m.*) hotbed.

almaço (*adj.*) **papel—**, foolscap paper.

almadraque (*m.*) tick, straw mattress.

almadrava (*f.*) tuna fishing; tuna-fishing grounds; tuna-fishing equipment.

almagre, –gro (*m.*) **–gra** (*f.*) Indian red, purplish-red ocher (clay); fig., plebeian blood.

almajarra (*f.*) = ALMANJARRA.

almalha (*f.*) heifer [= NOVILHA].

almalho (*m.*) yearling, young bull [= NOVILHO].

almanaque (*m.*) almanac.

almandina (*f., Min.*) a deep-red variety of garnet (almandite); also, precious garnet.

almandita (*f., Min.*) almandite.

almanjarra (*f.*) a sweep (long pole) attached to a horse-drawn device for raising water; fig., any ungainly, large, odd thing, person or vehicle. Var. ALMAJARRA.

almécega (*f.*) mastic resin.

almecegueira (*f., Bot.*) any resintree (*Protium*); also the mastic or lentisk pistache (*Pistacia lentiscus*).—**cheirosa,—de-cheiro,—vermelha**, Brazil resintree (*Protium heptaphyllum*), c.a. ALMECEGUEIRA-BRAVO, BREU-BANCO-VERDADEIRO, ICICA-AÇU.—**da-praia** is *Protium brasiliense*.—**de-minas** is *P. warmingianum*.—**mansa** is *P. elegans*, c.a. ALMISCAR, BREU-BRANCO, PAU-DE-BREU.

almeida (*f., Naut.*) counter, overhang (of a vessel's stern).

almeirão (*m.*) common chicory (*Cichorium intybus*), c.a. CHICÓRIA-AMARGA, CHICÓRIA-SELVAGEM.—**da-terra**, a hawkweed (*Hieracium commersonii*).

almeiroa [ô] (*f., Bot.*) a hawksbeard (*Crepis taraxacifolia*).

almejante (*adj.*) craving.

almejar (*v.t.*) to crave, covet; to set one's heart on; (*v.i.*) to be at the point of death.—**a**, to wish well to (someone).—**por**, to long (yearn) for; to hanker (lust) after.

almejável (*adj.*) to be desired, desirable.

almejo [ê] (*m.*) yearning, burning desire.

almilha (*f., Carp.*) tenon.

almiranta (*f.*) flagship.

almirantado –da (*adj.*) under Admiralty orders; (*m.*) Admiralty.

almirante (*m.*) admiral; opium poppy; the common red admiral butterfly (*Vanessa, syn. Parameis, atalanta*).

almirantear (*v.i.*) to serve as an admiral.

almíscar [-es] (*m.*) musk; musklike odor; bad smell; fish smell; (*Bot.*) a resin tree (*Protium*), c.a. ALMECEGUEIRA; a snowbell (*Styrax*).

almiscarado –da (*adj.*) perfumed.

almiscarar (*v.t.*) to perfume (**-se**, oneself) with musk.

almiscareira (*f., Bot.*) the musk heron bill (*Erodium moschatum*).

almiscareiro (*m.*) the musk deer (*Moschus moschiferous*).

almocadém (*m.*) commander; chief.

almocafre (*m.*) miner's pick.

almocântara (*f., Astron.*) almucantar.

almoçar (*v.t.*) to eat (something) for lunch; (*v.i.*) to have lunch.

almôço (*m.*) lunch; (*Port.*) breakfast; (*fig.*) the first event of the day.—**ajantarado**, a late, heavy lunch. **pequeno**, or **primeiro,—**, breakfast.

almocrevar (*v.t.*) to transport on pack animals; (*v.i.*) to work as a muleteer.

almocrevaria (*f.*) occupation of a muleteer; transport by pack animals [= RECOVAGEM].

almocreve (*m.*) mule-driver, muleteer.

almoeda (*f.*) auction, public sale.

almoedar (*v.t.*) to auction off.

almofaça (*f.*) currycomb.

almofaçar (*v.t.*) to currycomb.

almofada (*f.*) cushion, pillow, pad, bolster; (*Arch.*) panel. **—de tinta**, ink pad.—**de ar**, air cushion.

almofadado –da (*adj.*) cushioned; paneled; (*m.*) paneling.

almofadar (*v.t.*) to cushion; to pad; to panel (as a door).

almofadinha (*f.*) small pillow or cushion; pin cushion; sachet; cotton wad; porter's head pad; (*m.*) dude, dandy, fop, effeminate young man.

almofadismo (*m.*) dandyism, dudishness, effeminacy.

almofariz (*m.*) mortar.

almofate (*m.*) shoemaker's punch or awl [= SOVELA].

almofeira (*f.*) a dark liquid which oozes from olives in vats; olive juice.

almofreixe (*m.*) large trunk.

almôndega (*f.*) meatball; croquette.

almorreimas (*f.pl.*) hemorrhoids.

almotaçar (*v.t.*) to tax; to regulate, fix prices.

almotolia (*f.*) oil can.—**de pistola**, oil gun.—**de pressão**, squirt oil can.

almoxarifado (*m.*) storehouse; depot; storekeeper's job or department.

almoxarife (*m.*) storekeeper; stock clerk.

almude (*m.*) a measure of dry or liquid capacity in Portugal, Brazil and certain other countries, varying widely in dimensions.

almuédão, almuadem (*m.*) muezzin.

alno (*m., Bot.*) alder (*Alnus*).

aló (*adv.*) windward.

alô! Hello!

alocásia (*f., Bot.*) a genus (*Alocasia*) of the arum family.

alocinesia (*f., Physiol.*) allokinesis.

alocinético –ca (*adj.*) allokinetic.

aloclasita (*f., Min.*) alloclasite.

aloclorofila (*f., Biochem.*) allochlorophyll.

alocríptico –ca (*adj., Zool.*) allocryptic.

alocróico –ca (*adj., Med.*) allocroic.

alocroíte (*f., Min.*) allochroite.

alocrômico –ca , alocromático –ca (*adj.*) allochromatic.

alóctone (*adj., Geol.*) allochthonous.

alocução (*f.*) allocution, brief address.

alodesmismo (*m., Chem.*) allodesmism.

alodial (*adj., Law*) allodial; of land, clear, unencumbered. **propriedade—**, allodial property.

alodialidade (*f.*) allodiality.

alódio (*m.*) allodium, land which is the absolute property of the owner.

aloendro (*m.*) = ESPIRRADEIRA.

aloerotismo (*m., Psychoanalysis*) alloerotism.

aloés (*m.*) any plant of the genus *Aloe*, esp. *A. succotrina*, c.a. AZEVRE or ERVA-BABOSA; the juice of this plant, used in medicine.—**dos-cem-anos**, the century plant (*Agave americana*), c.a. ABECEDÁRIA or AGAVE.

aloético –ca (*adj., m.,f.*) aloetic (medicine).

aloexilo [ks] (*m.*) agalloch eaglewood (*Aquilaria agallocha*), c.a. CALAMBUCO.

alofana (*f.*) = ALOFÂNIO.

alofanamida (*f., Chem.*) allophanamid(e), biuret.

alofanato (*m., Chem.*) allophanate.

alofânico –ca (*adj., Chem.*) allophanic.

alofânio (*m., Min.*) allophane.

alofilo –la (*adj.; m.,f.*) allophyllian (person); (*m.*) a large genus (*Allophyllus*) of tropical trees.

alogamia (*f., Bot.*) allogamy, cross-fertilization.

alógamo –ma (*adj.*) allogamous.

alógeno –na (*adj.*) allogeneous; (*Geol.*) allogenic; (*Petrog.*) allothogenic.

alogia (*f.*) unreasonableness; (*Med.*) alogia.

alógico –ca (*adj., Logic*) alogical.

alogismo (*m.*) alogism.

aloína (*f., Pharm., Chem.*) aloin.

aloirar (*v.*) = ALOURAR.

aloísia (*f.*) = LÍPIA.

Aloísio (*m.*) Aloysius.

aloisomerismo [o-i] (*m., Chem.*) alloisomerism.

aloja (*f., Bot.*) a mesquite (*Prosopis dulcis*).

alojamento (*m.*) **alojação** (*f.*) lodging, housing; accomodation; quartering, billeting.—**da guarnição**, crew's quarters. **problema do—**, housing problem.

alojar (*v.t.*) to lodge, give lodging to; to harbor; to quarter. to billet; (*v.t., v.i.*) to vomit; (*v.r.*) to lodge.

alôjo (*m.*) vomit; also = ALOJAMENTO.

alombado –da (*adj.*) indolent; convex; broken-backed.

alombar (*v.t.*) to arch, curve, round off (a surface); to provide (a book) with a spine.

alomérico –ca (*adj., Chem., Min.*) allomerous.

alomerismo (*m., Chem., Min.*) allomerism.

alomorfia (*f.*) metamorphosis.

alomórfico –ca (*adj.*) allomorphic.

alomorfismo (*m.*) allomorphism.

alomorfita (*f., Min.*) allomorphite.

alomorfo (*m., Min.*) allomorph.

alongado –da (*adj.*) elongated; far off.

alongador –dora (*adj.*) prolonging; (*m.,f.*) prolonger.

alongamento (*m.*) elongation, prolongation.

alongar (*v.t.*) to lengthen, elongate, stretch out; to put off (away, afar); to prolong; to estrange; (*v.r.*) to withdraw, go away; to remain (stay longer).—**o tiro,** to raise the sights of a gun.

alônimo –**ma** (*adj.*) allonymous; (*m.,f.*) allonym.

alônomo –**ma** (*adj.*) allonomous.

alônsoa (*f.*) any maskflower (*Alonsoa*).

alopata, alópata (*m.,f.*) allopath.

alopatia (*f.*) allopathy.

alopático –**ca** (*adj.*) allopathic.

alopecia (*f.*) alopecia, baldness.

alopecura (*f.*) foxtail grass (*Alopecurus*).

alópias (*m.*) the thresher shark (*Alopias*).

aloplasma (*m., Biol.*) alloplasm.

aloprado –**da** (*adj.*) jittery; nutty, screwball.

alopsíquico –**ca** (*adj., Psychol.*) allopsychic.

aloquezia (*f., Med.*) allochezia.

aloquia (*f., Med.*) alochia.

aloquiria (*f., Med.*) allochiria.

alorcínico –**ca** (*adj. Chem.*) alorcic or alorcinic.

alorritmia (*f., Med.*) allorrhythmia.

alorrítmico –**ca** (*adj.*) allorrhythmic.

alose (*f., Chem.*) allose.

alosna (*f.*) = LOSNA.

alosomo (*m., Biol.*) heterochromosome.

alotador (*m.*) stud horse, stallion [= GARANHÃO].

alótipo (*m., Zool.*) allotype.

alotriodontia (*f., Med.*) allotriodontia.

alotriofagia (*f., Med.*) allotriophagy.

alotrófico –**ca** (*adj., Biochem., Physiol.*) allotrophic.

alotropia (*f., Chem.*) allotropy.

alotrópico –**ca** (*adj.*) allotropic.

alotropismo (*m., Chem.*) allotropy.

aloucado –**da** (*adj.*) crazylike, half-crazy.

aloucar-se (*v.r.*) to go crazy.

alourado –**da** (*adj.*) blondish.

alourar (*v.t.*) to make (the hair) blond; to brown (meat) in the oven. Var. ALOIRAR.

aloxana [ks] (*f., Chem.*) alloxan

aloxanato [ks] (*m., Chem.*) alloxanate.

aloxânico –**ca** [ks] (*adj.*) alloxanic.

aloxantina [ks] (*f., Chem.*) alloxantin.

aloxuremia [ks] (*f.*) alloxuremia.

aloxúrico –**ca** [ks] (*adj., Biochem.*) alloxuric.

alozoóide (*m., Zool.*) allozooid.

alpaca (*f.*) alpaca (animal, wool or cloth); also, a silver-plated nickel alloy used in the manufacture of tableware.

alpão (*m., Bot.*) the alpamroot bragantia (*B. wallichi*), c.a. FRUTA-TRILHA.

alparca (*f.*) a sandal, esp. one with a hemp sole and canvas upper. Var. ALPERCATA.

alpataco (*m., Bot.*) a mesquite (*Prosopis campestris*).

alpechim (*m.*) olive juice; dregs of olive oil.

alpedo [ê] (*adv.*) aimlessly.

alpendrado (*m.*) a large shed or covered porch.

alpendrar (*v.t.*) to cover (as a porch) with a shed.

alpendre (*m.*) shed, lean-to; veranda, porch; canopy.

alpense (*adj.*) Alpine.

alpercata (*f.*) = ALPARCA.

alperceiro-do-japão (*m.*) = CAQUIZEIRO.

alpestre (*adj.*) alpine.

alpígena (*adj., Bot.*) alpigene.

alpínia (*f., Bot.*) galangal (*Alpinia*) esp. *A. galanga* and *A. officinarum*, which yield galingale or chinaroot.

alpinismo (*m.*) mountain climbing.

alpinista (*adj.*) mountain-climbing; (*m.,f.*) alpinist, mountain climber.

alpino –**na** (*adj.*) alpine.

alpista (*f.*), **alpiste** (*m.*) canary grass (*Phalaris canariensis*); also, its seed (alpist) used as birdseed.—**-miúdo,** timothy canary grass (*P. angusta*).

alpisto (*m.*) = APISTO.

alpivre (*m.*) a terrestrial orchid (*Listera speculum*), c.a. ERVA-ABELHA.

alpondras (*f.pl.*) stepping stones.

alporca (*f., Hort.*) layer; (*Med.*) scrofula.

alporcado –**da** (*adj., Hort.*) layered; (*Med.*) scrofulous.

alporcamento (*m., Hort.*) layering.

alporcar (*v.t., Hort.*) to layer.

alporque (*m., Hort.*) layer; layering.

alporquento –**ta** (*adj.*) scrofulous.

alq. = ALQUEIRE (a dry or liquid measure; a land measure).

alquebrado –**da** (*adj.*) decrepit.

alquebrar (*v.t.,v.i.*) to bend, break (as with age or weakness); to break amidships; (*v.r.*) to break down.

alqueire (*m.*) a dry or liquid measure of capacity, of

widely varying dimensions. It is also a measure of area, varying according to the locality.—**do norte,** 272.25 ares.—**mineiro,** 484 ares.—**paulista,** 242 ares, c.a. QUARTEL PAULISTA.

alqueive (*m.*) fallow land; fallow state.

alquemila (*f., Bot.*) ladysmantle (*Alchemilla*).

alquequenje (*m.*) strawberry groundcherry (*Physalis alkekengi*), c.a. ERVA-NOIVA.—**-amarelo,** downy ground-cherry (*P. pubescens*), c.a. CAMAPU, BALÃOZINHO, JOÁ-DE-CAPOTE.

alquifol, –fu (*m.*) alquifou, galena.

alquilação (*f., Chem.*) alkylation.

alquilador (*m.*) one who keeps a livery stable; horse trader.

alquilar (*v.t.*) to rent out (horses); (*Chem.*) to alkylate.

alquilato (*m., Chem.*) alkylate.

alquimão (*m.*) a purple gallinule or sultana bird (*Porphyrio veterum*).

alquime (*m.*) tombac; pinchbeck.

alquimia (*f.*) alchemy.

alquimista (*m.,f.*) alchemist.

alquirívia (*f.*) caraway (*Carum carvi*); = ALCARAVIA.

alquitira (*f.*) = ALCATIRA.

alrute (*m.*) = ABELHEIRO.

alsaciano –**na** (*adj.; m.,f.*) Alsatian.

alseuôsmia (*f., Bot.*) crimsonbead (*Alseuosmia*).

álsina (*f., Bot.*) starwort (*Stellaria*), c.a. ESTELÁRIA, ORELHA-DE-TOUPEIRA.

alsináceas, alsíneas (*f.pl.*) the chickweeds (*Alsinaceae*).

alsófila (*f.*) a genus (*Alsophila*) of tree ferns.

alstônia (*f.*) a genus (*Alstonia*) of trees and shrubs of the dogbane family.

alstonidina (*f., Chem.*) alstonidine.

alstonina (*f., Chem.*) alstonine.

alstroméria (*f.*) a genus (*Alstromeria*) of showy herbs of the amaryllis family.

alta (*f.*) rise (in prices); increase; release or discharge from hospital or military service; halt; (*colloq.*) high society. **receber—,** to be discharged (from hospital, etc.).

alta-fidelidade (*f., Radio*) high fidelity.

alta-freqüência (*f.*) high frequency.

altamente (*adv.*) highly; greatly; loudly.

altamisa (*f., Bot.*) a baccharis (*B. artemisioides*).

altanado –**da** (*adj.*) haughty; uprisen.

altanar-se (*v.r.*) to become arrogant; to rise up (mutiny).

altaneiro –**ra** (*adj.*) lofty, towering; haughty, supercilious, "snooty"; high-flown; high-flying.

altar (*m.*) altar.—**-mor,** high altar.

altaragem (*f., Eccl.*) altarage, altar dues.

altarrão –**rona** (*adj., m.,f.*) very tall (person).

alta-tensão, alta-voltagem (*f., Elec.*) high voltage.

altazimute (*m., Astron.*) altazimuth.

alteamento (*m.*) act of raising; act of increasing the height of (a wall, etc.).

altear (*v.t.*) to raise, lift (up); to enhance, heighten, increase; (*v.i.*) to rise, grow; (*v.r.*) to grow higher; to rise; to elevate oneself.

altéia (*f., Bot.*) marshmallow (*Althaea officinalis*); [*cap.*] Althea.

alteína (*f., Biochem.*) althein.

alterabilidade (*f.*) alterability.

alteração (*f.*) alteration, change, modification; shift; deterioration; altercation, dispute, war of words; run-in; disturbance.

alterado –**da** (*adj.*) altered, changed; angry; upset; in revolt.

alterador –**dora** (*adj.*) altering; alterative; (*m.,f.*) alterer; counterfeiter; disturber.

alterante (*adj.*) alterant; (*Med.*) alterative.

alterar (*v.t.*) to alter, change, vary, modify; to adulterate; to disturb, agitate; to anger, inflame; (*v.r.*) to become upset, excited, disturbed; to lose one's temper; to change.

alterativo –**va** (*adj.*) alterative.

alteratriz, fem. of ALTERADOR.

alterável (*adj.*) alterable, changeable.

altercação (*f.*) altercation, angry dispute; quarrel, wrangle; brawl; squabble.

altercador –**dora** (*adj.*) altercating, altercative; (*m.,f.*) one who altercates.

altercar (*v.i.*) to wrangle, quarrel, bicker; to have words; to have a falling out; to squabble.

alternação (*f.*) alternation.

alternado –**da** (*adj.*) alternate; every other.

alternador –**dora** (*adj.*) alternating; (*m., Elec.*) alternator.

alternância (*f.*) alternance; rotation of crops.

alternante (*adj.*) alternating.
alternantera (*f.*, *Bot.*) a genus (*Alternanthera*) of the amaranth family.
alternar (*v.t.*) to alternate, interchange; to reverse; to reciprocate; to rotate; (*v.i.*) to alternate; (*v.r.*) to occur alternately; to rotate.
alternária (*f.*) a genus (*Alternaria*) of imperfect fungi.
alternariose (*f.*, *Plant Pathol.*) alternariose.
alternativo **-va** (*adj.*) alternative, alternating; (*f.*) alternation; alternative.
alternato (*m.*) alternation; rotation of crops.
alternável (*adj.*) susceptible of alternation.
alternifólio **-lia** (*adj.*, *Bot.*) alternifoliate.
alternipene (*adj.*, *Bot.*) alternipinnate.
alternipétalo **-la** (*adj.*, *Bot.*) alternipetalous.
alterno **-na** (*adj.*) alternate.
alteroso **-sa** (*adj.*) towering, lofty; grand, sublime, stately.
alteza [ê] (*f.*) loftiness; height; elevation; sublimity, grandeur.—**imperial**, Imperial Highness;—**real**, Royal Highness.—**sereníssima**, Most Serene Highness. **Vossa—**, Your Highness.
altibaixos [ALTOS+BAIXOS] (*m.,pl.*) ups and downs; vicissitudes.
altica (*f.*) a genus (*Altica*) of flea beetles.
alticolúnio **-nia** (*adj.*) high-columned.
altígrafo (*m.*) altigraph.
altiloqüência (*f.*) great eloquence [but not altiloquence].
altiloqüente (*adj.*) very eloquent [but not altiloquent].
altiloqüentíssimo **-ma** (*absol. superl. of* ALTILOQÜENTE) most eloquent.
altimetria (*f.*) altimetry.
altimétrico **-ca** (*adj.*) altimetrical.
altímetro (*m.*) altimeter.
altimurado **-da** (*adj.*) high-walled.
altiplano (*m.*) a high plateau.
altíssimo **-ma** (*absol. superl. of* ALTO) very high, most high; (*m.*) the Most High.
altissonante, **altíssono** **-na** (*adj.*) altisonant, high-sounding; lofty or pompous.
altista (*adj.*) bullish; (*m.,f.*) bull (speculator). [A bear is BAIXISTA]; player of an alto (musical instrument).
altitude (*f.*) altitude. **grande** (**pequena**)—, high (low) altitude.—**de vôo**, flight altitude.—**zero**, sea level.
altitudinal (*adj.*) altitudinal.
altivez[a] [ê] (*f.*) hauteur; arrogance; pride.
altivo **-va** (*adj.*) haughty, supercilious, arrogant; contemptuous; proud, lofty.
alto **-ta** (*adj.*) high, lofty, elevated; tall; loud; eminent, prominent, superior; distinguished; noble; dear (high-priced); upper; (*adv.*) aloud, loudly; (*interj.*) Halt!; (*m.*) top, summit, crest; upper part, elevation, height; head, chief; alto (voice or instrument); viola; halt, standstill, stop.—**da serra**, top of the mountain range.—**dia**, broad daylight.—**lá!** Stop! That's enough!—**Amazonas**, the upper Amazon.—**manhã**, late morning.—**noite**, late at night.—**traição**, high treason. **ao—**, on high. **de—a baixo**, from top to bottom; from head to foot. **de—teor**, having a high content (of something); of ore, high-grade. **do—**, from above. **do—de**, from the top of. **em—e bom som**, loudly and clearly (to speak thus). **em—mar**, on the high seas. **falar—**, to speak loudly. **fazer—**, to come to a halt. **Mãos ao—**! Hands up! Stick 'em up! **no—**, aloft. **os —s da casa**, the upper parts of a house (attic, garret). **os—da cidade**, the heights of the town. **passar por—**, to overlook, pass over, skip over. **por—**, superficially, casually.
altocúmulus (*m.*, *Meteor.*) alto-cumulus.
alto-falante (*m.*) loud speaker; megaphone.
alto-forno (*m.*) blast furnace.
alto-relêvo (*m.*,) high relief (sculpture).
altostratus (*m.*, *Meteor.*) altostratus.
altrose (*f.*, *Chem.*) altrose.
altruísmo (*m.*) altruism.
altruísta (*adj.*) altruistic; (*m.,f.*) altruist.
altruístico **-ca** (*adj.*) altruistic.
altura (*f.*) height, elevation; depth; altitude; pitch (of sound); stature; loftiness; eminence; top; superiority, excellence; importance; sky. **à—de**, abreast of; within reach of; at a height of; at a latitude of; on a level with; in keeping with; capable of; up to, equal to; up to expectations. **a certa—**, at a certain distance, at a certain point. **a esta—**, at this point (state of affairs). **Êle é da minha—**, He is as tall as I. **nessa—**, then; at that state

(of the situation). **nesta—**, at this juncture. **pelas—s de 1940**, along about 1940. **salto de—**, high jump (in athletics).
aluado **-da** (*adj.*) lunatic, moonstruck, "loony"; of animals, in heat.
aluamento (*m.*) lunacy; estrus, rut.
aluar-se (*v.r.*) to turn lunatic; of animals, to become in the condition of rut.
aluato (*m.*) the ursine howling monkey of Brazil (*Alouatta ursina*) and others of this genus.
alucinação (*f.*) hallucination.
alucinado **-da** (*adj.*) hallucinated, delirious; (*m.,f.*) lunatic.
alucinador **-dora** (*adj.*) hallucinating.
alucinamento (*m.*) hallucination.
alucinar (*v.t.*) to hallucinate; (*v.r.*) to become hallucinated; to go out of one's head, become temporarily deranged.
alucinose (*f.*, *Psychiatry*) hallucinosis.
alude (*m.*) avalanche.
aludel [-déis] (*m.*, *Chem.*) aludel.
aludir (*v.t.*) to allude (**a**, to), hint (**a**, at), touch (**a**, upon), make allusion to, intimate, imply.
alugado **-da** (*adj.*) rented, leased; hired.
alugamento (*m.*) renting, leasing; hiring.
alugar (*v.t.*) to rent (from or to); to let; to hire. **Aluga-se**, For rent (sign on a building). **Alugam-se quartos**, Rooms to let. **Esta casa está para—**, This house is for rent.
aluguel [-guéis], **aluguer** (*m.*) renting, letting, hiring; rent, rental. **cavalo de—**, a hack (horse let for hire).
aluição [u-i] (*f.*), **aluimento** [u-i] (*m.*) ruin; overthrow; collapse; landslide; demolition; crumbling.
aluir [72] (*v.t.*) to raze, ruin; to overthrow, overturn; to demolish, destroy; (*v.i.*) to collapse; to crumble; to fall; to cave in.
álula (*f.*, *Zool.*) alula, bastard wing.
alum (*m.*, *Bot.*) taro (*Colocasia antiquorum*); (*Chem.*) = ALÚMEN.
alumagem (*f.*) = IGNIÇÃO.
alume, **alúmen** (*m.*) alum[= PEDRA-UME].
alumiação (*f.*) illumination, lighting.
alumiado **-da** (*adj.*) illuminated, light, luminous, bright.
alumiamento (*m.*) illumination; enlightenment.
alumiar (*v.t.*) to illumine, illuminate; to light (up); to enlighten; (*v.i.*) to shine, give light.
alumina (*f.*, *Chem.*) alumina, aluminum oxide.
aluminar (*v.t.*) to aluminate.
aluminato (*m.*, *Chem.*) aluminate.
alumínico **-ca** (*adj.*) aluminic.
aluminídio (*m.*, *Chem.*) aluminide.
aluminífero **-ra** (*adj.*) aluminiferous.
aluminiforme (*adj.*) aluminiform.
alumínio (*m.*, *Chem.*) aluminum, aluminium.
aluminita (*f.*, *Min.*) aluminite.
aluminoférrico **-ca** (*adj.*) aluminoferous.
aluminografia (*f.*) aluminography.
aluminose (*f.*, *Med.*) aluminosis.
aluminoso **-sa** (*adj.*) aluminous.
aluminotermia (*f.*, *Metal.*) aluminothermy.
aluminotérmico **-ca** (*adj.*) aluminothermic.
aluminôxido [ks] (*m.*, *Chem.*) aluminum oxide.
aluna, fem. of ALUNO.
alundo (*m.*) alundum.
alunita (*f.*, *Min.*) alunite.
aluno **-na** (*m.*) pupil, student.—**externo**, day pupil.—**interno**, boarding (resident) student.
alunogênio (*m.*, *Min.*) alunogen, feather alum.
alusão (*f.*) allusion, reference, passing mention; hint.—**maliciosa**, innuendo.
alusivo **-va** (*adj.*) allusive.
aluvial, **aluviano** **-na** (*adj.*) alluvial.
aluvião (*m.*) alluvium; alluvion.
alva (*f.*) dawn, daybreak; white of the eye; alb. **estrêla d'alva**, morning star; (*pl.*) paddles of a water wheel.
alvação **-çã** (*adj.*) white [steer or cow].
alvacento **-ta**, **alvadio** **-dia** (*adj.*) whitish, light-gray.
alvacora (*f.*) = ALBACORA.
alvado (*m.*) eye (of a hammer, axe, etc.); tooth socket; entrance to a beehive.
alvaiade (*m.*) white lead (pigment).—**de zinco**, zinc oxide.
alvanel [-néis] (*m.*) mason, bricklayer.
alvar (*adj.*) stupid; silly, foolish, ingenuous; whitish.
alvará (*m.*) judicial writ or warrant; charter.—**de construção**, building permit.—**de soltura**, court order releasing a prisoner.

alvarado (m.) a razor sedge (Scleria hirtella).
alvarádoa (f.) the Mexican alvaradoa (A. amorphoides) or other plant of this genus.
alvaraz[o] (m.) leucoderma and other white spots on the skin of man or beast.
alvarenga (f.) a lighter, esp. one used for ferrying goods between ship and shore; a steel barge used on the Amazon River for transporting goods.
alvarengueiro (m.) lighterman, bargeman.
alvarilho (m.) tallow wood (Ximenia americana).
alvarinho (m.) English oak (Quercus robur), c.a. CARVALHO-DA-EUROPA.
alvarizado –da (adj.) suffering from leucoderma.
alvaroz [ó] (m.) overalls.
alvarrã (f.) = ALBARRÃ.
alvear (v.) = CAIAR.
alveário (m.) beehive; honeycomb; (Anat.) alveary.
alvedrio [drí] (m.) free will.
alveiro (m.) a white milestone; a baker's apron.
alveitar (m.) a "horse doctor" (practical veterinarian); farrier; quack.
alveitarar (v.i.) to function as an ALVEITAR; (v.t.) to patch up (something).
alveitaria (f.) practical treatment of animals; horseshoeing.
alvejar (v.t.) [from ALVO, target] to aim at, point a gun at; [from ALVO, white] to bleach (as cloth); to purify, whiten (as sugar); (v.i.) to lose color, whiten; to bleach in the sun (as clothes on a line, bones on the desert); to loom white in the distance (as a house on a hill); to gleam white (as snow-covered ground, or a white-covered table); of dawn, to grow light.
alveloz [ó] (m.) a Brazilian plant (Euphorbia heterodoxa or E. insulana) whose caustic milky sap is used in the treatment of skin cancers.
alvenaria (f.) stonemasonry; rough stonework; brickwork, masonry.—de argamassa, masonry laid up with mortar.—ciclópica, cyclopean concrete.—insôssa, dry masonry.—de pedra, or—poliédrica, rubble masonry.—de tijolo, brickwork.
álveo (m.) river bed; pit.
alveolado –da (adj.) pitted; honeycombed.
alveolar (adj.) alveolar.
alveolariforme (adj.) alveoliform.
alvéolo (m.) alveolus; tooth socket; cell of a honeycomb; any small pit or cavity.—s pulmonares, lung cavities, alveoli.
alverca (f.) pool, pond, fishpond; water tank.
alvião (m.) mattock; pickax.
alvinegro –gra (adj.) black-and-white.
alvinitente (adj.) of an immaculate whiteness.
alvirrubro –bra (adj.) white-and-red.
alvissarar (v.t.) to announce (bring news).
alvíssaras (f.pl.) finder's reward; gift for a bearer of good news.
alvissareiro –ra (adj.) bearing glad tidings, announcing good news. notícias—s, happy news, glad tidings; (m.,f.) one who promises, gives or receives a reward (esp. for good news).
alvitrar (v.t.) to suggest, move, propose; to arbitrate.
alvitre (m.) suggestion, reminder; proposal, scheme; expedient; opinion.
alvo –va (adj.) white, snow-white; pure, limpid; (m.) target; aim, end, design, object, goal. atingir o, or dar no, —, to hit the mark (target, bull's-eye). centro (or espêlho) do—, bull's-eye. tiro ao—, target practice.
alvor [ó] (m.) dawn; whiteness, snow-whiteness.
alvorada (f.) dawn, break of day, cockcrowing; fig., blossoming of youth.—do século, dawn of the century. toque de—, reveille (bugle call).
alvorecer (v.i.) to dawn; to appear, begin to appear; of a feeling, idea, etc., to be manifest. ao—, at daybreak. Vars. ALVARAR, ALVOREJAR.
alvoroçado –da, alvorotado –da (adj.) excited, agog, aflutter; aroused, stirred up; riotous; ruffled.
alvoroçar, alvorotar (v.t.) to excite, stir up; to elate, exhilarate; to incite, rouse (to action); (v.r.) to become excited; to riot.
alvorôço, alvorôto (m.) agitation, commotion, tumult, turmoil; disturbance; row; excitement, emotion; fuss, bustle, hurry, flurry; rut, oestrus [= CIO].
alvura (f.) whiteness; purity.
a.m.= ANTES DO MEIO-DIA, (before noon).
A.M.= ave-maria (hail Mary).

AM = Amazonas (State of).
am.ᵃ = AMIGA (friend).
ama (f.) nurse; housekeeper; governess; (Bot.) the lavender ruellia (R. macrantha).—-sêca, nursemaid.—de leite or—de peito, wet nurse. Cf. AMO.
amabile (adj., Music) amabile.
amabilidade (f.) amiability, affability, kindliness; amenity.
amabilíssimo –ma (absol. superl. of AMÁVEL) most amiable, etc. See AMÁVEL.
amacacado –da (adj.) monkeylike; fig., of skimpy proportions.
amachucar (v.t.) to crush.
amaciar (v.t.) to soften; to assuage, soothe.
amacrático –ca (adj.) = AMASTÊNICO.
amacrino –na (adj.; m., Anat.) amacrine.
amadeirado –da (adj.) like wood.
amadeirar (v.t.) to give the appearance of wood to.
amadelfo –fa (adj., Zool.) amadelphous, gregarious.
amado –da (adj.) loved; (m.,f.) beloved, loved one; sweetheart.
amador –dora (adj.) loving; (m.,f.) lover; amateur.
amadorismo (m.) amateurism.
amadornar, amadorrar (v.) = AMODORRAR.
amadrinhado –da (adj.) that herd together;—said esp. of horses.
amadrinhar (v.t.) of a bell horse, to lead a string of pack animals; to yoke, tether, harness (animals) together.
amadurecer, amadurar (v.t.,v.i.) to mature, ripen.
amadurecido –da (adj.) ripe, mature.
âmago (m.) pith; essence, substance, gist; kernel, marrow. o—do problema, the heart of the problem.
amainar (v.i.) to abate, subside, die down, diminish (wind, waves, storm, rain, anger, etc.); (v.t.) to furl (sail).
amaldiçoado –da (adj.) accursed, execrable, hateful.
amaldiçoador –dora (adj.) cursing; (m.,f.) curser.
amaldiçoar (v.t.) to curse, execrate; to damn.
amálgama (m.) amalgam.
amalgamação (f.), amalgamamento (m.) amalgamation; (Ore dressing) almagamation process.
amalgamador (m.) almagamator.
amalgamar (v.t.) to amalgamate, mix, blend; (v.r.) to amalgamate, blend.
amalgamável (adj.) amalgamable.
amalhar (v.t.) to pen animals, esp. sheep; (v.i.,v.r.) to enter the fold.
amálico (adj., Chem.) ácido—, amalic acid.
amaltar (v.t.) to form a gang of evil-doers.
amaltas (m.pl.) golden-shower senna or drumstick tree (Cassia fistula), c.a. CANAFÍSTULA-VERDADEIRA.
amalucado –da (adj.) cracked, crazy, "nuts"; touched (in the head); flighty.
amalucar-se (v.r.) to go crazy.
amamentação (f.) lactation, breast-feeding.
amamentadora (f.) woman who suckles her child.
amamentar (v.t.) to suckle.
amaná (f.) = ARUANÁ.
amanaçaia (f.) = MANDAÇAIA.
amanajé (m.,f.) an Indian of the Amanajé or Manajó, an extinct Tupian tribe which occupied territory in the western part of what is now the State of Maranhão; some were called Ararandeuaras; (adj.) pert. to or designating the Amanaje.
amancebado –da (adj.) cohabiting; (m.,f.) paramour.
amancebamento (m.) concubinage; cohabitation.
amancebar-se [17a] (v.r.) to take a mistress.
amandina (f., Biochem.) amandin.
amandurana (f.) ALGODÃO-DO-BREJO.
amaneirado –da (adj.) affected; prissy, finical.
amaneirar-se (v.r.) to put on airs.
amanhã (adv.) tomorrow; in the future; (m.) tomorrow, the next day; the future.—à noite, tomorrow night.—de manhã, tomorrow morning.—de tarde, tomorrow afternoon.—mesmo, tomorrow for sure. até—, until tomorrow. depois de—, day after tomorrow.
amanhado –da (adj.) prepared; cultivated.
amanhar (v.t.) to till, cultivate; to put in order; to garner.
amanhecente (adj.) about to appear.
amanhecer (v.i.) to dawn; to awake; to start the morning; to begin to appear. ao—, at daybreak.
amanho (m.) preparation; cultivation; (pl.) farming tools.
amaninhar (v.t.) to lay waste.
amanita (f.) any fungus of the genus Amanita.

amanitina (*f.*, *Biochem.*) amanitine, choline.

amaniú (*m.*) sea island cotton (*Gossypium barbadense*), c.a. ALGODÃO-AMERICANO.

amansadela (*f.*) act of taming; a lesson.

amansador (*m.*) tamer. Cf. DOMADOR.

amansar (*v.t.*) to tame, domesticate; to break in (animals); to placate, pacify; (*v.i.*) to grow tame; (*v.r.*) to grow quiet.

amansa-senhor (*m.*) garlic guineahen weed (*Petiveria alliacea*).

amantar (*v.t.*) to cover with, or as with, a blanket.

amante (*adj.*) fond of, addicted to; (*m.,f.*) sweetheart; paramour.

amanteigado –da (*adj.*) like butter.

amanteigar (*v.t.*) to butter; to make like butter.—a opinião publica, to soften up public opinion.

amantelar (*v.t.*) to fortify, wall in.

amantético –ca (*adj.*) amorous.

amantíssimo –ma (*absol. superl. of* AMANTE) most devoted.

amanuense (*m.,f.*) amanuensis, clerk, copyist.

amapá (*m.*) the amapa (*Parahancornia*) a large Amazon tree which yields a chicle-like gum.

amapola [ô] (*f.*) a cactus (*Pereskia sacharosa*).

amar (*v.t.,v.r.*) to love; (*v.t.*) to like very much.

amara (*m.*) a large genus (*Amara*) of beetles.

amarado –da (*adj.*) brimming; out at sea; of hydroplanes, afloat.

amaragem (*f.*) of hydroplanes, act of alighting.

amarantáceo –cea (*adj.*, *Bot.*) amaranthaceous; (*f.pl.*) the amaranth family (Amaranthaceae).

amarantino –na (*adj.*) amaranthine.

amarantita (*f.*, *Min.*) amarantite.

amaranto (*m.*) any plant of the genus Amaranthus.— -branco, the feather cockscomb (*Celosia argentea*), c.a. CELÓSIA-BRANCA, CRISTA-DE-GALO, VELUDO-BRANCO.— -verde = CARURU-VERDE.

amarar (*v.i.*) of a hydroplane, to alight on water; (*v.r.*) to put out to sea; of eyes, to brim with tears.

amarela (*f.*) a gold coin; a large tree (*Terminalia australis*); also, the tart polygala (*P. amara*).

amarelaço –ça (*adj.*) yellowish.

amarelado –da (*adj.*) yellowish; sallow; faded.

amarelão (*m.*) hookworm disease.

amarelar, **amarelecer** (*v.t.*) to make yellow; (*v.i.,v.r.*) to turn yellow.

amarelejar (*v.i.*) to show yellow; to grow yellow (as with age).

amarelento –ta (*adj.*) yellowish.

amarelidão (*m.*), –lidez [ê] (*f.*) yellowness; paleness.

amarelinha (*f.*) hopscotch; the blackeyed clockvine (*Thunbergia alata*), c.a. ERVA-DE-CABRITA, BUNDA-DE-MULATA.

amarelinho (*m.*) a sweetleaf (*Symplocos speciosa*); a Braz. timber tree (*Raputia magnifica*) whose wood, esteemed for boat ribs, tool handles, etc., closely resembles American hickory.—-da-serra = ANGUSTURA.

amarelo –la (*adj.*; *m.*) yellow (color, dye, person).—de cádmio, cadmium yellow, cadmium sulphide.—de cromo, chrome yellow, lead chromate, Paris yellow.—de Nápoles, Naples yellow (a pigment).—de ôvo, egg yolk.

amarfanhar, **amarfalhar** (*v.t.*) to crumple, rumple, wrinkle; to dishevel.

amargado –da (*adj.*) bitter; embittered.

amargar (*v.t.*) to embitter; to rue, regret bitterly; (*v.i.*) to be bitter or disagreeable. de—, terrible, horrible.

amargo –ga (*adj.*) bitter, acrid, sour; severe, harsh; (*m.*) bitter taste; unsweetened mate tea [= CHIMARRÃO]; (*pl.*) bitters.

amargor [ô] (*m.*) bitterness; pain, grief; asperity, acrimony.

amargoseira (*f.*) China tree (*Melia azedarach*).

amargoso –sa (*adj.*) galling, sorrowful.

amarguíssimo –ma (*absol. superl. of* AMARGO) most bitter.

amargura (*f.*) bitterness; sorrow, grief.

amargurar (*v.t.*) to grieve, afflict, hurt, distress; to embitter; (*v.r.*) to suffer anguish.

amaricado –da (*adj.*) effeminate, womanish.

amaricar-se (*v.r.*) to become effeminate.

amarilho (*m.*) a large tropical timber tree (*Terminalia australis* or *T. obovata*).

amarilidáceo –cea (*adj.*, *Bot.*) amaryllidaceous; (*f.pl.*) the amaryllis family (Amaryllidaceae), c.a. AMARILÍDEAS.

amarílide, **amarílis** (*f.*, *Bot.*) any amaryllis.

amarina (*f.*, *Chem.*) amarin(e).

amarinhar (*v.t.*) to equip (a ship) with a crew; to command a ship; (*v.r.*) to sign up as a sailor; to get one's sea legs; to take on a crew.

amaríssimo –ma (*absol. superl. of* AMARGO) most bitter.

amaro –ra (*adj.*) = AMARGO.

amarra (*f.*) cable, line, rope, hawser; fig., support, protection. largar as—s, to cast off.

amarra-pinto (*m.*) = AGARRA-PINTO.

amarração (*f.*) anchorage; mooring; lashing; tangled love affair; (*Masonry*) bond. cabo de—, mooring rope.

amarrado –da (*adj.*) tied, bound; (*colloq.*) married; committed to something; (*m.*) a tied bundle.—ao dever, bound to one's duty. com a cara—, frowning, crosslooking.

amarradouro (*m.*) mooring place. Var. AMARRADOIRO.

amarradura (*f.*) mooring cable.

amarrar (*v.t.*) to tie, bind, fasten (a, to); to lash together, tie together; to furl (sails); to moor, secure; to engage, pledge; of a hunting dog, to point game; (*v.r.*) to become attached (to); to get "tied" (married); to commit oneself (to something).

amarrilho (*m.*) tie, twine, string.

amarroar (*v.t.*) to strike with a sledge hammer; (*v.i.*) to feel beat (done in).

amarrotado –da (*adj.*) crumpled; bruised; beaten (in an argument).

amarrotar (*v.t.*) to wrinkle, crease, crumple; to dishevel. "muss"; to smash (another's argument . . . or nose).

amartelar (*v.t.*) to strike with a hammer.

ama-sêca (*f.*) nursemaid.

amasesia (*f.*, *Med.*) amasesis.

amasia (*f.*) mistress, paramour, ladylove.

amasiar-se (*v.r.*) = AMANCEBAR-SE.

amasio (*m.*) illicit cohabitation [= MANCEBIA].

amásio (*m.*) paramour [= AMANTE].

amasisa (*f.*) a coralbean (*Erythrina*).

amasônia (*f.*) any plant of the genus Amasonia.

amassa-barro (*m.*) the twice-banded oven-bird (*Furnarius f. figulus*); the pale-legged oven-bird (*F. l. leucopus*), c.a. MARIA-DE-BARRO; also = JOÃO-DE-BARRO.

amassadeira (*f.*) kneading machine; crusher.

amassadela (*f.*) act of kneading; act of flattening.

amassador (*m.*) mixer; mixing table; crusher.

amassadouro (*m.*) kneading table or trough; trough; mortar trough. Var. AMASSADOIRO.

amassadura (*f.*) act of kneading; batch of dough; a beating.

amassamento (*m.*) act of smashing, or of crushing.

amassar (*v.t.*) to knead (dough); mix (mortar); to batter; to crush, mash, smash.

amastênico –ca (*adj.*, *Photog.*) amasthenic.

amastia (*f.*, *Med.*) amastia.

amatalotar-se (*v.r.*) to go to sea; to bunk with another seaman or buddy.

amatilhar (*v.t.*) to congregate, group together (persons, esp. evildoers, as in a gang or pack); (*v.r.*) to so congregate.

amatividade (*f.*) amativeness.

amativo –va (*adj.*) amative.

amatório –ria (*adj.*) amatory.

amatular-se (*v.r.*) to join a band of evildoers.

amatutado –da (*adj.*) like a rustic (in manners, speech, etc.).

amatutar-se (*v.r.*) to become like a backwoodsman or rustic, in manners, speech, etc.

amaurose (*f.*, *Med.*) amaurosis.

amaurótico –ca (*adj.*) amaurotic.

amável (*adj.*) amiable, lovable; kind, gracious, friendly pleasant, likeable; engaging, courteous.

amavios (*m.pl.*) love charms.

amavioso –sa (*adj.*) charming, seductive; amorous.

amazelado –da (*adj.*) covered with sores.

amazelar-se (*v.r.*) to break out in sores.

amazia (*f.*) = AMASTIA.

amazona (*f.*) Amazon (female warrior); by ext., a horsewoman; woman's riding habit; parrots of the genus Amazona.

amazonense (*adj.*) Amazon; (*m.,f.*) a person of Amazonas. Var. AMAZONIENSE.

amazônico –ca (*adj.*) of the Amazon River.

amazônio –nia (*adj.*) of the Amazon region.

amazonita (*f.*) amazonite (semi-precious stone), c.a. PEDRA-DAS-AMAZONAS.
ambages (*m.pl.*) quibblings, circumlocutions.
ambagioso –sa (*adj.*) circuitous; circumlocutory.
ambaíba (*f.*) = AMBAÚBA.
ambaló (*m.*) a mombin (*Spondias mangifera*) or its fruit.
ambapaia (*f.*) = MAMOEIRO.
âmbar (*m.*) amber; ambergris. Var. AMBRE.
ambarina (*f.*) = ABELMOSCO.
ambatoarinito (*m., Min.*) ambatoarinite.
ambaúba (*f.*) the shieldleaf pumpwood (*Cecropia peltata*), c.a. UMBAÚBA. Var. AMBAÍBA.
amberboa (*f.*) the spiny amerboa (*A. muricata*) or other plant of this genus.
ambição (*f.*) ambition; zeal, craving, longing.
ambicionar (*v.t.*) to crave, desire, long for, hanker after.
ambicioso –sa (*adj.*) ambitious, strongly desirous of; (*m.,f.*) one who is ambitious, aspiring, covetous.
ambidestro –tra [ê] (*adj.*) ambidextrous.
ambiência (*f.*) environment, milieu.
ambientar (*v.t.*) to adapt (**-se**, oneself) to a new environment.
ambiente (*adj.*) ambient, surrounding, encircling; (*m.*) atmosphere, surroundings, milieu.—**doméstico**, home environment. **ar**—, surrounding atmosphere.
ambiesquerdo –da [êr] (*adj.*) ambisinister, clumsy in the use of both hands.
ambígeno –na (*adj., Bot.*) ambigenous.
ambigüidade (*f.*) ambiguity; ambiguous expression.
ambíguo –gua (*adj.*) ambiguous, equivocal; not plain, not clear.
ambiopia (*f., Med.*) diplopia.
ambíparo –ra (*adj., Bot.*) ambiparous.
ambissêxuo –ua [ks] (*adj.*) ambosexous, hermaphrodite.
âmbito (*m.*) ambit; circuit, compass; extent, scope; field of action; confine, enclosure.
ambívio (*m.*) crossroads [= ENCRUZILHADA].
amblicéfalo (*m.*) a genus (*Amblycephalus*) of blunthead, nonpoisonous snakes.
amblígono –na (*adj.*) obtuse-angled.
ambligonita (*f., Min.*) amblygonite, hebromite.
amblíope, ambliope (*m.,f., Med.*) one having amblyopia.
amblipia (*f., Pathol.*) amblyopia.
ambliopsis (*m.*) blindfish (*Amblyopsis spelaeus*).
amblistegita (*f., Min.*) amblystegite, a variety of hypersthene.
amblótico –ca (*adj.; m., Med.*) amblotic (agent).
amboceptor (*m., Immunol.*) amboceptor.
ambó (*m.*) = CAJÀZEIRA.
ambone (*m., Anat.*) ambon.
amboré (*m.*) a small fresh-water goby.
ambos –bas (*pron.*) both, both of them, the two; (*adj.*) both.—**a dois,—de dois,—dois,—e dois,** all mean the same as AMBOS (both).—**os dois (as duas),** the two of them, both of them.—**nós,** both of us.
ambre (*m.*) = ÂMBAR.
ambrear (*v.t.*) to scent with ambergris; to render amber in color.
ambreta [ê] (*f., Bot.*) the muskmallow (*Hibiscus abelmoschus*), c.a. ABELMOSCO.
ambrite (*f.*) ambrite.
ambrosia (*f.*) ambrosia; hence, any food "fit for the gods", esp. a certain very sweet Brazilian dessert.
ambrósia (*f.*) the wormseed goosefoot (*Chenopodium ambrosioides*), c.a. CHÁ-DO-MÉXICO, ERVA-FORMIGUEIRA.—**americana,** common ragweed (*Ambrosia artemisifolia*).—**das-farmácias,** the Jerusalem oak goosefoot (*Chenopodium botrys*).
ambrosiáceo –cea (*adj., Bot.*) ambrosiaceous; (*f.pl.*) the ragweed family (*Ambrosiaceae*).
ambrosíaco –ca (*adj.*) ambrosial, delicious.
ambrósio (*m.*) ambrose.
ambuí (*m.*) = AMEIXEIRA-DO-BRASIL.
ambuia-embo (*f., Bot.*) a dutchmanspipe (*Aristolochia labiosa*).
âmbula (*f.*) ampulla.
ambulacro (*m., Zool.*) ambulacrum.
ambulância (*f.*) ambulance.
ambulante (*adj.*) roving, wandering, vagabond; vagrant; traveling. **vendedor**—, street peddler.
ambular (*v.i.*) to ambulate.
ambulativo –va (*adj.*) ambulant.
ameaça (*f.*) menace, threat.
ameaçador –dora (*adj.*) threatening, menacing; (*m.,f.*) threatener.
ameaçante (*adj.*) menacing, threatening.
ameaçar (*v.t.,v.i.*) to threaten, menace; (*v.t.*) to portend, presage; to warn; to use threats; (*v.i.*) to impend, be imminent; to lower, look black. **Está ameaçando chuva,** It looks like rain.
ameaço (*m.*) threat; fig., symptom.
amealhar (*v.t.*) to save (money); to parcel out; (*v.i.*) to haggle.
ameba (*f.*) amoeba. Var. AMIBA.
amebiano –na (*adj.*) amoebic.
amebiforme (*adj.*) amoebiform, amoeboid.
amebíase (*f., Med.*) amoebiasis; amoebic dysentery.
amebicida (*m.*) amoebicide.
amébico –ca (*adj.*) amoebic.
amebídeo (*m., Zool.*) amoebid.
amebócito (*m., Zool.*) amoebocyte.
amebóide (*adj.*) amoeboid.
amedrontado –da (*adj.*) frightened, afraid.
amedrontar (*v.t.*) to frighten, scare, terrify; to intimidate; (*v.r.*) to take fright.
ameia (*f.*) battlement; crenel.
ameigador –dora (*adj.*) caressing; (*m.,f.*) caresser.
ameigar (*v.t.*) to fondle, pet; to coax, wheedle, cajole; to soothe; to soften (the voice); (*v.r.*) to become gentle, caressing.
ameigo (*m.*) caress; blandishment.
amêijoa (*f.*) in Portugal, a tellin shell; in Brazil, a lucina (*Phacoides pectinata*), better known as SERNAMBI.
ameijoar (*v.t.*) to drive (cattle) into a pen; (*v.i.,v.r.*) to bed down for the night.
ameiva (*f.*) kinds of small inoffensive lizards of the genus Ameiva, having long, whip-like tails.
ameixa (*f.*) any plum or prune; a spiny shrub (*Ximenia coriacea*) related to the mountain plum.—**amarela,**—**-do-canadá,** the loquat (*Eriobotyra japonica*).—**caranguejeira** = RAINHA-CLÁUDIA.—**-da-bahia,**—**-da-terra,**—**-de-espinho,**—**-do-brasil,**—**-do-pará,** all = AMEIXEIRA-DO-BRASIL.—**-de-madagascar,** ramontchi or governor's plum (*Flacourtia indica*).—**passada,** or **prêta,** dried prune.
ameixal (*m.*) plum orchard.
ameixeira (*f.*) the garden plum (*Prunus domestica*), c.a. AMEIXEIRA-MANSA.—**americana,** hortulan plum (*Prunus hortulana*).—**brava** = ABRUNHEIRO.—**-da-pérsia,** the wild myrobalan plum (*Prunus cerasifera divaricata*).—**-de-pôrto-natal,** the karanda carissa (*C. carandas*).—**-do-brasil,** the mountain plum or tallow wood (*Ximenia americana*), c.a. AMBUÍ, AMEIXA-DA-BAHIA, AMEIXA-DA-TERRA, AMEIXA-DE-ESPINHO, AMEIXA-DO-PARÁ, ESPINHEIRO-DE-AMEIXA.—**-do-japão,** Japanese plum (*Prunus salicina*).
amelaçar (*v.t.*) to sweeten with, or as with, syrup.
amelhorado –da (*adj.*) = MELHORADO.
Amélia (*f.*) Amelia.
ameloado –da (*adj.*) like a melon; "In Pará, a species of cacao tree having 42 round seeds in a large smooth pod, sometimes 18 centimeters long." [GBAT].
amem (*adv.; m.*) amen. **dizer—a tudo,** to agree to everything, say yes to everything.
amência (*f., Med.*) amentia.
amêndoa (*f.*) almond or other similar nut; (*Petrog.*) amygdule; (*pl.*) Easter gifts of coated almonds or other dainties.—**-dos-andes** = CASTANHA-DE-MACACO (a tree).—**s mondadas,** shelled almonds.
amendoadô –da (*adj.*) almond-shaped; (*f.*) an orgeat prepared with an emulsion of almonds; pastry or cake flavored with almonds.
amendoeira (*f.*) almond tree (*Prunus amygdalus*).—**-da-américa** = CASTANHEIRO-DO-PARÁ (Brazil nut).—**-da-índia,** the Malabar almond, or tropical-almond terminalia (*T. catappa*), c.a. CASTANHOLA, CHAPÉU-DE-SOL, GUARDA-SOL.—**-do-japão,** a flowering almond or almond cherry (*Prunus japonica*).
amendoeirana (*f.*) a tick clover (*Desmodium*), c.a. AMÔRES-DO-CAMPO (or -DO-MATO), BICO-DE-CORVO, CARRAPICHO-RASTEIRO, MANDUBIRANA.
amendoim [o-ím] (*m.*) the peanut plant (*Arachis hypogaea*), c.a.—COMUM,—VERDADEIRO, ARÁQUIDA, ALFÓSTIGO-DA-TERRA, MANDUBI, MENDOBI; the peanut pod or seed.—**-de-veado,** a pinnate-leaved climber (*Teramnus uncinatus*), c.a. FAVEIRA, FAVINHA-DE-CAPOEIRA, JEQUIRANA.—**-rasteiro,**—**-do-maranhão,**—**-rajado,**—**-roxo,** a peanut plant (*Arachnis prostrata*).

amendoína (f.) almond lotion.
amenidade (f.) amenity, pleasantness, agreeableness; suavity, affability.
ameninado –da (adj.) childish; weak; tender.
amenista (m.,f.) one who says amen (yes) to everything, who has no opinions of his own.
amenizado –da (adj.) bland, soft, pleasant.
amenizar (v.t.) to render bland, soft, gentle, pleasant; to render less difficult or arduous; (v.r.) to become thus.
ameno –na (adj.) mild, gentle; suave; pleasant.
amenorréia (f., Med.) amenorrhea.
amentáceo –cea (adj., Bot.) amentaceous.
amentar (v.t.) to recollect, remember; to pray for the dead; to make crazy [= DEMENTAR].
amentífero –ra (adj.) amentiferous.
amentiforme (adj., Bot.) amentiform.
amentilho, amento (m., Bot.) ament, catkin.
amerceamento (m.) pity, compassion; pardon; commutation of a sentence.
amercear-se (v.r.) to have mercy, take pity. **Que Deus se amercie de nós!** May God have pity on us!
americanada (f.) bunch of Americans; characteristic American action or idea. [Somewhat derogatory.]
americanismo (m.) Americanism.
americanista (adj.) Americanistic; (m.,f.) Americanist.
americanização (f.) Americanization.
americanizar (v.t.) to Americanize; (v.r.) to become Americanized.
americano –na (adj.; m.,f.) American.
americanomania, americomania (f.) excessive attachment to America or things American.
ameríndio –dia (adj.; m.,f.) Amerind(ian).
amerismo (m., Biol.) amerism.
amerissagem (f.) = AMARAGEM.
amerissar (v.) = amarar.
amerístico –ca (adj., Biol.) ameristic.
amérstia (f., Bot.) the flame amherstia (A. nobilis).
amesito (m., Min.) amesite.
amesquinhado –da (adj.) belittled, disparaged.
amesquinhador –dora (adj.) belittling.
amesquinhamento (m.) belittling, disparagement.
amesquinhar (v.t.) to depreciate, disparage, belittle; (v.r.) to belittle oneself; to show oneself small (stingy).
amestrado –da (adj.) trained, skilled.
amestrador –dora (m.,f.) trainer, teacher.
amestramento (m.) training.
amestrar (v.t.) to train, teach, coach; (v.r.) to become expert, skilled.
ametabólico –ca (adj., Zool.) ametabolic.
ametabolismo (m., Zool.) ametabolism.
ametalar (v.t.) to metalize.
ametista (f.), **ametiste** (m.) amethyst.
ametístea (f.) a plant of the mint family (Amethystia coerulea).
ametístico –ca (adj.) amethystine.
ametria (f., Med.) ametria.
ametrômetro (m., Med.) ametrometer.
ametropia (f., Med.) ametropia.
ametrópico –ca (adj.) ametropic; (m.,f.) ametrope.
amezinhar [ê] (v.t.) to treat with a home remedy.
âmia (f.) the mudfish or bowfin (Amia calva).
amiântia (f.) the fly poison or crow poison (Amianthium muscaetoxicum) and related herbs.
amiantino –na (adj.) amianthine.
amianto (m., Min.) amianthus, fine silky asbestos.
amicíssimo –ma (absol. superl. of AMIGO) most friendly.
amiantóide (adj.) amianthoid(al).
amiba (f.), **amibo** (m.) & derivs. = AMEBA & derivs.
amida (f., Chem.) amide.—**primária,** primary amide.—**secundária,** secondary amide.—**terciária,** tertiary amide.
amídala (f.) & derivs. = AMÍGDALA & derivs.
amidina (f., Chem.) amidin; amidine.
amido, âmido (m.) starch; (Chem.) amidogen.—**solúvel,** soluble starch, amylodestrin.
amidofenol (m., Chem.) amidophenol, aminophenol.
amidogênio (m., Chem.) amidogen.
amieiro (m.) European alder (Alnus glutinosa).—**-negro,** the alder buckthorn (Rhamnus frangula).
amiga (f.) friend; mistress.
amigação (f.) illicit cohabitation.
amigado –da (adj.) in a state of illicit cohabitation.
amigalhaço, –lhão (m.) big (close) friend (generally somewhat derogatory).
amigalhote (m.) fair-weather friend.

amigar (v.t.) to make friendly; (v.r.) to become friendly; to take (or become) a mistress. Cf. AMASIAR-SE.
amigável (adj.) amicable, friendly.
amígdala (f., Anat.) amygdala, tonsil; (Petrog.) amygdule. Var. AMÍDALA.
amigdaláceas (f.pl.) the Amygdalaceae (peach or almond family). Var. AMIDALÁCEAS.
amigdalectomia (f., Surg.) tonsillectomy. Var. AMIDALECTOMIA.
amigdálico –ca (adj., Chem.) amygdalic. Var. AMIDÁLICO.
amigdalato (m., Chem.) amygdalate. Var. AMIDALATO.
amigdalino –na (adj.) amygdaline; (f., Chem.) amygdalin. Var. AMIDALINO.
amigdalite (f., Med.) tonsillitis. Var. AMIDALITE.
amigdalóide (adj.) amygdaloidal; almond-shaped; (m., Petrog.) amygdaloid. Var. AMIDALÓIDE.
amigdalotomia (f., Surg.) amygdalotomy. Var. AMIDALOTOMIA.
amigdofinina (f., Pharm.) amygdophenin. Var. AMIDOFININA.
amigo –ga (adj.) friendly; fond of; (m.) friend; paramour, lover. Cf. AMIGA.—**da onça,** a supposedly good friend who, in a showdown, sides with one's adversary.—**do coração,** or **do peito,** bosom friend.—**particular,** close personal friend.—**urso,** false friend.—**s do alheio,** light-fingered gentry. **Amigos, amigos, negócios à parte,** Business is business; Friendship is one thing, business another. **É na necessidade que se conhece os—s,** A friend in need is a friend indeed. **sem—s,** friendless. **ter cara de poucos amigos,** to have a sinister look.
amiguinho –nha (m.,f.) little friend.—**de folguedos,** playmate.
amila (f., Chem.) amyl.
amiláceo –cea (adj.) amylaceous; starchy.
amilálcool (m., Chem.) amyl alcohol, [= ÁLCOOL AMÍLICO].
amilamina (f., Chem.) amylamine.
amílase (f., Biochem.) amylase.
amilênio, –leno (m., Chem.) amylene.
amilfenol (m., Chem.) amyl phenol.
amíloco –ca (adj., Chem.) amylic.
amilo (m.) = AMIDO.
amilodextrina (f., Chem.) amylodextrin, soluble starch.
amilogênio (m.) amylogen.
amilóide (adj.; m., Chem., Biochem.) amyloid.
amilólise (f., Chem.) amylolysis.
amilolítico –ca (adj., Chem.) amylolytic.
amilômetro (m.) amylometer.
amilopsina (f., Biochem.) amylopsin, panchreatic amylase.
amilose (f., Chem.) amylose.
amilsulfato (m., Chem.) amyl sulfate, pentyl sulfate.
amimalhar (v.t.) to indulge, spoil; to mollycoddle.
amimar (v.t.) to pamper, coddle, pet, spoil; to humor.
amimia (f., Med.) amimia.
amina (f., Chem.) amine.—**primária,** primary amine.—**secundária,** secondary amine.—**terciária,** tertiary amine.
aminguar (v.) = MINGUAR.
amino (m.) = AMINA.
aminoácido, aminácido (m., Chem.) amino acid.
aminobenzeno, –benzol. (m., Chem.) aminobenzene, aniline.
aminofenol (m., Chem.) aminophenol.
aminofórmio (m.) = LEXAMINA.
aminose (f., Pathol.) aminosis.
amiólito (m., Min.) ammiolite.
amiostenia (f., Med.) amyosthenia.
amiotaxia [ks] (f., Med.) amyotaxia.
amiotonia (f., Med.) amyotonia.
amiotrofia (m., Med.) amyotrophy.
amirina (f., Chem.) amyrin.
amírio (m.) the Jamaica rosewood (Amyris balsamifera).
amíris (f.) a genus (Amyris) of tropical American trees and shrubs of the rue family.
amiserar-se (v.r.) to feel miserable; to feel pity.
amistar (v.t.) to bring together as friends; (v.r.) to become friendly with.
amistoso –sa (adj.) friendly, cordial; (m.) friendly soccer game.
amiudado –da [i-u] (adj.) frequent, oft-repeated.
amiudar [i-u] (v.t.) to redouble, repeat with frequency; (v.i.,v.r.) to occur often, become frequent; (v.i.) of cocks, to crow frequently as day breaks.
amiúde (adv.) often, frequently, repeatedly, at short intervals. Var. AMIÚDO.

amixia [ks] (*f.*) amixia.
amizade (*f.*) friendship, fellowship; deep regard.
amnésia, amnesia (*f., Psychiatry*) amnesia.
amnéstico –ca, amnésico –ca (*adj.*) amnestic, amnesic.
âmnico –ca (*adj., Anat.*) amnic, amniac, amniotic.
âmnio (*m., Anat., Zool.*) amnion.
amniótico –ca, amniático –ca (*adj.*) amniotic.
am.º = AMIGO (friend).
amo (*m.*) master, head of household; landlord.
amóbio (*m.*) the wing-everlasting (*Ammobium alatum*) and related herbs.
amocambar (*v.t.*) to hide (cattle) in a MOCAMBO (thickly wooded place); (*v.r.*) to hide oneself in the woods.
amocete [cê] (*m., Zool.*) ammocoetes.
amochar-se (*v.r.*) to hide away, withdraw from contact with others.
amodelar (*v.*) = MODELAR.
amodernar (*v.t.*) to modernize.
amódite, –to (*m., Zool.*) a sand launce (*Ammodytes*).
amodorrar (*v.t.*) to put to sleep; (*v.r.*) to become sleepy, drowsy, lethargic.
amoedar (*v.t.*) to mint (gold, etc.).
amoedável (*adj.*) coinable.
amófila (*f.*) beach grass (*Ammophila*).
amófilos (*m.pl.*) sand wasps of the genus Ammophila (syn. Sphex).
amofinação (*f.*) fretfulness, uneasiness.
amofinado –da (*adj.*) distressed; upset, jittery.
amofinar (*v.t.*) to afflict; to vex; to pester, badger; (*v.r.*) to become upset; to fret, chafe. **Não se amofine**, Relax, take it easy.
amoiriscar (*v.*) & derivs. = AMOURISCAR & derivs.
amoitar-se (*v.r.*) to hide as in a thicket. Var. AMOUTAR-SE.
amojar (*v.t.,v.i.*) to fill with milk or sap.
amolação (*f.*) whetting, sharpening; (*colloq.*) botheration, annoyance. **Que**—! What a nuisance!
amolado –da (*adj.*) keen, sharp; worried; annoyed.
amolador –deira (*adj.*) sharpening; annoying; (*m.*) sharpener, grinder; annoyer, pesterer, plaguer.
amoladura (*f.*) act of sharpening or grinding.
amolar (*v.t.*) to whet, sharpen, grind; to bother, annoy, plague, pester.—**facas**, to sharpen knives. **Não me amole!** Don't bother me! **pedra de**—, grindstone, whetstone. **Vá**—**o boi**, or **vá**—**outro**, (*slang*) Go away, go bother someone else.
amoldar (*v.t.*) to mold, fashion, model; to adapt; (*v.r.*) to conform oneself (**a**, to).
amoldável (*adj.*) conformable, adaptable.
amolecado –da (*adj.*) rascally. **modos**—**s**, coarse manners, low behavior.
amolecar (*v.t.*) to treat like a rascal; (*v.r.*) to turn rascal.
amolecedor –dora (*adj.*) softening; enervating; (*m.*) softener.
amolecer (*v.t.*) to make soft; (*v.i.*) to soften; to relent.
amolecido –da (*adj.*) soft; kind, tender.
amolecimento (*m.*) act of softening.
amolegar (*v.*) = AMOLGAR.
amolentar (*v.t.*) to soften, assuage; to enervate.
amolestar (*v.*) = MOLESTAR.
amolgado –da (*adj.*) smashed, battered; crushed, defeated.
amolgadela, amolgadura (*f.*) crushing defeat; dent, bump, nick, crease.
amolgar (*v.t.*) to flatten; to smash, crush; to bruise, batter; to subdue, master; to force, compel; (*v.i.*) to give up, yield.—**a espada**, to dull or bend one's sword. Var. AMOLEGAR.
amolgável (*adj.*) susceptible of being crushed, etc.—See the verb AMOLGAR.
amomo (*m.*) the cardamon amomum (*A. cardamon*) or other plant of this genus.
amônia (*f., Chem.*) ammonia, volatile alkali.
amoniacado –da (*adj.*) ammoniated.
amoniacal (*adj.*) ammoniacal.
amoníaco –ca (*adj.*) ammoniacal; (*m.*) ammonia (gas); (*f.*) gum ammoniac.—**cáustico**, caustic ammonia.
amonieto, amonito (*m., Chem.*) ammoniate.
amoniemia (*f., Med.*) ammoniemia.
amonificação (*f.*) ammonification.
amonificar (*v.t.*) to ammonify.
amonímetro (*m.*) = AMONÔMETRO.
amônio (*m., Chem.*) ammonium.
amonita (*f.*) ammonite (explosive).

amonite (*m., Paleontol.*) ammonite.
amoniúria, amoniuria [i-u] (*f., Med.*) ammoniuria.
amonjeaba (*f.*) = CAPIM-AMONJEABA.
amonômetro (*m., Chem.*) ammonia meter.
amontanhar (*v.i.*) to form or rise in a hill.
amontar (*v.*) = MONTAR.
amontoa (*f.*) act of hilling, heaping or drawing soil around the base of plants.
amontoação (*f.*) = AMONTOAMENTO.
amontoado (*m.*) heap, pile, mass. **um**—**de asneiras**, a heap of nonsense.
amontoador (*m., Agric. Mach.*) hiller.
amontoamento (*m.*) heap(ing); accumulation.
amontoar (*v.t.*) to heap (pile up; to amass, accumulate; (*v.i.*) to rise in a hill, pile up; to save, accumulate (as money); (*v.r.*) to multiply (increase in number); to pile up.
amonturar (*v.t.*) to gather in a pile (as garbage or manure).
amoque (*m.*) amuck, amok.
amor [*pl.* **amôres**] (*m.*) love; affection, fondness, attachment; tenderness; sweetheart; lover; (*pl.*) love affairs, amours.—**à pátria**, love for one's fatherland.—**à primeira vista**, love at first sight.—**-agarrado**, the mountainrose coralvine (*Antigonon leptopus*) c.a. AMOR-ENTRELAÇADO, AMÔRES-AGARRADINHOS, CORAL, CORÁLIA, ENTRADA-DE-BAILE, GEORGINA, MIMO-DO-CÉU, ROSÁLIA, VIUVINHA.—**com amor se paga**, One good turn deserves another.—**conjugal**, conjugal love.—**-crescido**, the jump-up-and-kiss-me or shaggy portulaca (*P. pilosa*) c.a. ALECRIM-DE-SÃO-JOSÉ; the common portulaca (*P. grandiflora*) c.a. CAVALHEIRO-DAS-ONZE-HORAS.—**-das-onze-horas**, the common Star of Bethlehem (*Ornithogalum umbellatum*).—**de Deus**, love of God.—**-de-hortelão**, the catchweed bedstraw (*Galium aparine*).—**-de-moça**, the yellow cosmos (*C. sulphureus*).—**-de-negro**, the Paraguay star-bur (*Acanthospermum australe*) c.a. CARRAPICHO-RASTEIRO, ESPINHO-DE-AGULHA, ESPINHO-DE-CARNEIRO, FEL-DA-TERRA, MATA-PASTO, PICÃO-DA-PRAIA, POEJO-DA-PRAIA; the spiny cocklebur (*Xanthium spinosum*) c.a. ERVA-DE-CARNEIRO.—**-de-sogra**, (*slang*) pain or tingling caused by a blow on the funny bone.—**-de-um-dia**, the dwarf glorybind (*Convolvulus tricolor*).—**-de-vaqueiro**, a tickclover (*Desmodium*).—**-do-campo**, a tickclover (*Desmodium*) c.a. AMORZINHO-SÊCO, TREVO-DO-CAMPO, CARRAPICHO.—**do próximo**, love of one's neighbor, of one's fellowman.—**-dos-homens**, the cottonrose (*Hibiscus mutabilis*).—**filial**, filial love.—**livre**, free love.—**maternal** or **materno**, maternal love, mother-love.—**paternal** or **paterno**, paternal love.—**-perfeito**, pansy.—**-perfeito-azul**, the altai violet (*Viola altaica*).—**-perfeito-bravo**, wild pansy (*Viola tricolor*).—**-perfeito-da-China**, the blue torenia (*T. fournieri*).—**-perfeito do mato**, any pansy orchid (*Miltonia*).—**-platônico**, platonic love.—**-próprio**, self-respect, self-esteem, pride.—**-sêco**, a tickclover (*Desmodium*); also a Christmasbush (*Alchornea*).—**-es-agarradinhos** = CORAL (coralvine).—**es-do-campo**.—**es-do-mato** = AMENDOEIRANA.—**es-sécos**, the redspot stinglily (*Blumenbachia insignis*). **consumir-se de**—, to be lovesick. **estar a morrer de**—**es por alguém**, to be dying-in-love for someone. **não ter**—**à vida**, to be reckless, heedless of danger. **O**—**é cego**, Love is blind. **por**—**de**, for the sake of, for love of. **perdido de**—, head-over-heels in love; lovesick. **Simpatia é quase**—, To like is almost to love. **ter**—**à pele**, to be careful of one's skin, wary of danger. **viver de**—**e brisas**, to live on bread and cheese and kisses.
amora (*f.*) any of various berries, esp. the mulberry.—**-brava**, a wild blackberry (*Rubus imperialis*).—**-preta**, European blackberry (*Rubus fruticosus*).—**-vermelha**, the roseleaf raspberry (*Rubus rosaefolius*). Cf. AMOREIRA.
amoral (*adj.*) amoral, nonmoral.
amoralidade (*f.*) unmorality.
amoralismo (*m.*) amoralism.
amorangado –da (*adj.*) like a strawberry.
amorável (*adj.*) lovable, loving.
amordaçamento (*m.*) act of muzzling or gagging.
amordaçar (*v.t.*) to gag; to silence; to muzzle.
amoréia (*f.*) = BABOSA (a fish).
amoreira (*f.*) mulberry tree; blackberry vine.—**-branca**, the white mulberry (*Morus alba*).—**-do-brasil**, Brazilian blackberry (*Rubus brasiliensis*), c.a.—**-DA-SILVA** (or -DO-MATO), SARÇA-AMOREIRA, SILVA-BRANCA.—**-negra** (or **-preta**), black mulberry (*Morus nigra*). Cf. AMORA.

amoreiral (*m.*) a growth of mulberry trees or of black-berry vines.

amorenado –**da** (*adj.*) brunet-ish, of dark complexion. Cf. MORENO.

amorenar (*v.t.*) to tan the complexion; (*v.r.*) to get deeply tanned.

amorfa (*f.*) the false indigo or indigobush amorpha (*A. fruticosa*) or other plant of this genus.

amorfia (*f.*) amorphia, amorphism.

amorfismo (*m.*) amorphism.

amorfo –**fa, amórfico** –**ca** (*adj.*) amorphous, shapeless.

amorfófalo (*m., Bot.*) the East Indian giant arum (*Amorphophallus*).

amoricos, amorinhos (*m.pl.*) passing love affairs; casual amours.

amoriscar-se (*v.r.*) to fall in love.

amornado –**da** (*adj.*) warm, tepid.

amornar (*v.t.*) to warm (up).

amorosidade (*f.*) fondness, amorosity, amorousness.

amoroso –**sa** (*adj.*) loving, affectionate, inclined or disposed to love [but not amorous, in the sense of passionate or ardent, which is ARDENTE, APAIXONADO]; (*m.*) the "heavy lover" in a play; (*adv., Music*) amoroso, tenderly.

amorrinhar-se (*v.r.*) of cattle, to become affected with a plague; of persons, to grow weak, infirm.

amorsegar (*v.*) = MORSEGAR.

amortalhado –**da** (*adj.*) shrouded.

amortalhador –**dora** (*adj.*) shrouding; (*m.,f.*) one who dresses a corpse for the grave.

amortalhamento (*m.*) act of shrouding.

amortalhar (*v.t.*) to shroud; to lay out a corpse for burial; (*v.r.*) to put on sackcloth.

amortecedor –**dora** (*adj.*) deadening; shock-absorbing; (*m.*) shock absorber; muffler (of sound).

amortecer (*v.t.*) to deaden; to dull, dampen, muffle, mute; (*v.i.*) to grow dim; to die away.

amortecido –**da** (*adj.*) weak, dim, dull; deadened; muffled.

amortecimento (*m.*) act of deadening, weakening, dimming, muffling.

amortiçar (*v.t.*) to extinguish.

amortização (*f.*) amortization.—**mensal,** a monthly installment payment.

amortizar (*v.t.*) to amortize (a debt); to alienate (property) in mortmain; (*v.r.*) to die down.

amortizável (*adj.*) amortizable.

Amós (*m.*) Amos.

amossar (*v.t.*) to dent, notch, nick.

amostardado –**da** (*adj.*) seasoned with mustard.

amostra (*f.*) sample, specimen, example, instance, model, pattern; (*pl.*) threats.—**do pano,** a sample of one's ability; free sample.

amostrar (*v.*) = MOSTRAR.

amota (*f.*) = MOTA.

amotar (*v.t.*) to hill (plants); to protect (land) with dikes or levees.

amoterapia (*f., Med.*) ammotherapy.

amotinação (*f.*) mutiny, riot, revolt, rebellion.

amotinado –**da** (*adj.*) mutinous, unruly, rebellious, insurgent.

amotinador –**dora** (*m.,f.*) mutineer, rebel, rioter.

amotinar (*v.i.*) to mutiny, revolt.

amoucado –**da** (*adj.*) somewhat deaf.

amoucar-se (*adj.*) to turn deaf.

amouriscado –**da** (*adj.*) Moorish, Moorish-looking. Var. AMOIRISCADO.

amouriscar (*v.t.*) to give a Moorish look to (a house, roof, etc.). Var. AMOIRISCAR.

amoutar-se (*v.r.*) = AMOITAR-SE.

amover (*v.t.*) to dismiss or remove (from office).

amovibilidade (*f.*) removableness; revocableness, revocability.

amovível (*adj.*) removable (as from office); revocable.

amoxamar (*v.t.*) to smoke-dry (fish, meat).

ampangabeíto (*m., Min.*) ampangabeite.

amparado –**da** (*adj.*) sustained, upheld; sheltered, protected; backed.

amparar (*v.t.*) to support, sustain, uphold; to protect, shield; to provide for; to shelter; (*v.r.*) to seek shelter; to protect oneself; to lean on.—**-se na lei,** to stand on, or under the protection of, the law.

amparo (*m.*) support, aid, help, assistance; patronage; sustenance; relief; prop, stay. **buscar—,** to seek refuge,

protection.

ampelidáceas, ampelídeas (*f.pl.*) the Vitaceae (grape or vine family).

ampelito (*m.*) ampelite.

ampelopse (*m.*) a genus (*Ampelopsis*) of the grape family.

ampeloterapia (*f., Med.*) the grape cure.

amperagem (*f., Elec.*) amperage.

ampere (*m., Elec.*) ampere.—**-espira, or—-volta,** ampere turn.—**-hora,** ampere-hour.—**internacional,** international ampere.

amperímetro, amperômetro (*m., Elec.*) ampere-meter, ammeter.—**térmico,** or—**de fio quente,** thermal, or hot-wire, ammeter.

ampletivo –**va, amplexátil** [ks] (*adj., Bot.*) amplectant.

amplexicaude [ks] (*adj., Zool.*) amplexicaudate.

amplexicaule [ks] (*adj., Bot.*) amplexicaul(ine).

amplexifólio –**lia** [ks] (*adj., Bot.*) amplexifoliate.

amplexo [ks] (*m.*) amplexus, embrace [= ABRAÇO].

ampliação (*f.*) amplification, enlargement; exaggeration; (*Photog.*) enlargement.—**dos fatos,** exaggeration of the facts.

ampliado –**da** (*adj.*) amplified; (*Photog.*) enlarged.

ampliador –**dora** (*adj.*) amplifying; (*m.,f.*) amplifier, enlarger.

ampliar (*v.t.*) to amplify, enlarge, extend, augment, magnify; (*v.r.*) to expand, dilate.

ampliativo –**va, -tório** –**ria** (*adj.*) serving to amplify or expand.

ampliável (*adj.*) susceptible of enlargement.

amplidão (*f.*) amplitude, spaciousness; scope, extent; breadth; vastness.

amplificação (*f.*) amplification, dilation, expansion; diffuseness, prolixity.

amplificador –**dora** (*adj.*) amplifying; (*m., Elec.*) amplifier.

amplificar (*v.t.*) to amplify, dilate, expand.

amplificativo –**va** (*adj.*) amplificative, -tory.

amplificável (*adj.*) = AMPLIÁVEL.

amplitude (*f.*) amplitude, extent; fullness.

amplo –**pla** (*adj.*) ample, wide, broad, roomy.

ampola [ô] (*f.*) ampoule; blister; (*Anat., Zool., Bot.*) ampulla.—**retal,** the rectum.

ampula (*f.*) ampulla; cruet; flask.

ampuláceo –**cea** (*adj.*) ampullaceous.

ampular (*adj.*) ampular, ampullary.

ampulária (*f.*) = ARUÁ.

ampulheta (*f.*) hourglass, sandglass.

amputação (*f.*) amputation.

amputado –**da** (*adj.*) amputated, mutilated; (*m.,f.*) an amputee.

amputar (*v.t.*) to amputate, sever, cut off; to mutilate; to lop, curtail.

Amsterdão (*m.*) Amsterdam.

amuado –**da** (*adj.*) moody, sullen, surly, grouchy; of assets, frozen.

amuar (*v.t.*) to vex, annoy; (*v.i.*) to pout, sulk, scowl; (*v.r.*) to become sullen.

amulatado –**da** (*adj.*) mulatto-like. **um branco meio—,** a white man with negroid features.

amuleto (*m.*) amulet, talisman.

amulherado –**da** (*adj.*) effeminate, womanish.

amulherar-se, amulherengar-se (*v.r.*) to become effeminate.

amumiado –**da** (*adj.*) mummy-like.

amunhecar (*v.i.*) of a horse, to develop a weakness in the feet.

amunicionamento (*m.*) = MUNICIONAMENTO.

amunicionar, amuniciar (*v.*) = MUNICIONAR.

amuo (*m.*) peevishness, ill-humor, sullenness; tiff; a pout.

amura (*f. Naut.*) tack.

amurada (*f.*) gunwale, ship's rail; bulwark; wall.

amuralhar, amurar (*v.t.*) to enclose with a wall or fence.

amurchecer (*v.*) = MURCHAR.

amusia (*f.*) amusia, loss of ability to follow music.

Ana (*f.*) Ann, Anne, Anna; Hannah.

aná (*f.*) anna (coin of India); (*Pharm.*) ana.

anã (*f.*) fem. of ANÃO (dwarf).

anabático –**ca** (*adj., Med., Meteor.*) anabatic.

anabatista (*adj.; m.,f.*) Anabaptist.

Anabela (*f.*) Annabel, Annabelle.

anabiose (*f.*) resuscitation.

anablepso (*m.*) any four-eyes (*Anableps*)—a top minnow.

anabólico –**ca** (*adj., Biol.*) anabolic.

anabolismo (*m., Biol.*) anabolism.

anabrose (*f., Med.*) anabrosis.

anabrótico –ca (adj.) anabrotic; (m.) an anabrotic substance.

anacã, anacá (m.) a large Brazilian macaw (Ara severa), c.a. MARCANÃ-GUAÇU; the Braz. hawk-headed parrot (Deroptyus accipitrinus fuscifrons), c.a. PAPAGAIO-DE-COLEIRA (or -DE-COLÊTE).

anacâmpsero (m.) the shy sedum (S. anacampseros).

anacantinos (m.pl.) the Acanthini (codfish, hakes, etc.).

anaçar (v.t.) to stir, beat (eggs, cream, etc.).

anacarado –da (adj.) nacreous.

anacardiáceo –cea (adj., Bot.) anacardiaceous; (f.pl.) the sumac or cashew family (Anacardiaceae), c.a. TEREBINTÁCEAS.

anacárdico –ca (adj.) ácido—, anacardic acid.

anacárdio (m.) the cashew marking-nut tree (Semecarpus anacardium), c.a.—-DO-MALABAR,—-DO-ORIENTE; also its fruit (the cashew or anacardium nut) known as —-DAS-BOTICAS.—-da-américa, the common cashew (Anacardium occidentale), c.a.—-DO-OCIDENTE, but is better known as CAJUEIRO or CAJUZEIRO.

anácaris (m.) the waterweeds (Anachris) of North America, or (Elodea) of South America.

anacatarse (f., Med.) anacatharsis.

anacatártico –ca (adj.; m.,f.) anacathartic.

anacauita [a-u] (f., Bot.) anacahuita (Cordia boissieri).

anacefaleose (f.) recapitulation, summary.

anacinesia (f., Chem.) anakinesis.

anáclase (f.) anaclasis.

anaclástico –ca (adj.) anaclastic; (f., Optics.) anaclastics, dioptrics.

anaclisia (f., Med.) anaclisis, decubitus.

anacoluto (m., Gram.) anacoluthon.

anaconda (f., Zool.) anaconda (Eunectes murinus).

anacoreta [ê] (m.) anchorite, hermit, recluse.

anacrônico –ca (adj.) anachronic, anachronistic.

anacronismo (m.) anachronism.

anacronizar (v.t.) to make an anachronism of.

anacrótico –ca (adj.) anacrotic.

anacrotismo (m., Physiol.) anacrotism.

anacrusa, anacruse (f., Pros.) anacrusis.

anactesia (f., Med.) convalescence.

anacusia (f.) anacusia, absolute deafness.

anadicrotismo (m., Physiol.) anadicrotism.

anadiplose (f., Rhet.) anadiplosis.

anadipsia (f., Med.) anadipsia, excessive thirst.

anádromo –ma (adj., Zool.) anadromous.

anaeróbio –bia (adj.) anaerobic; (m.) anaerobe.

anaerobiose (f.) anaerobiosis.

anafa (f.) yellow sweet clover (Melilotus officinalis), c.a. ANAFA-CHEIROSA, TREVO-CHEIROSO, TREVO-DE CARVALHO, COROA-DO-REI, MELILOTO. Cf. ÂNAFE.

anafado –da (adj.) of cattle, sleek, well-fed.

anáfalo (m.) the pearly everlasting (Anaphalis margaritacea) or other plants of this genus.

anafar (v.t.) to fatten (cattle); to rub with ointment.

anáfase (f., Biol.) anaphase.

ânafe (m.) kinds of sweet clover (Melilotus). Cf. ANAFA.

anáfega (f.) jujube tree (Zizphus jujuba), c.a. AÇOFEIFEIRA, JUJUBA.

anafia (f. Med.) anaphia.

anafilatina (f., Biochem.) anaphylactin.

anafilactogêneo –nea (adj., Biochem.) anaphylactogenic.

anafilaxia [ks] (f., Med., Biol.) anaphylaxis.

anáfora (f., Rhet.) anaphora.

anaforese (f., Chem.) anaphoresis.

anaforia (f., Med.) anaphoria.

anafrodisia (f., Med.) anaphrodisia.

anafrodisíaco –ca (adj.; m.,f., Med.) anaphrodisiac.

anafrodítico –ca (adj., Biol.) anaphroditic.

anagal, anagálide (f., Bot.) pimpernel (Anagalis), c.a. MORRIÃO.

anagênese (f., Physiol.) anagenesis.

anagenético –ca (adj.) anagenetic.

anagirina (f., Chem.) anagyrine.

anágire (f.), anagíris, anágiro (m.) the bean trefoil or Mediterranean stinkbush (Anagyris foetida).

anáglifo (m.) anaglyph.

anaglipto (m.) anaglypton.

anagogia (f.) anagoge.

anagógico –ca (adj.) anagogic.

anagogismo (m.) anagogistics.

anagrama (m.) anagram.

anagramático –ca (adj.) anagrammatic(al).

anagramatismo (m.) anagrammatism.

anagramatizar (v.t.) to anagrammatize.

anágua (f.) petticoat, slip, underskirt.

anais (m.pl.) annals, chronicles.

anajá (m.) either of two palms: Pindarea concinna, c.a. INDAIÁ, INAIÁ, CÔCO-DE-INDAIÁ, and Scheelea amylacea, c.a. CATOLÉ.—-brava, a maximilian palm.—-mirim, a small attalea palm (A. humilis), c.a. CÔCO-CATOLÉ, CÔCO-DE-PINDOBA, PALMEIRA-CATOLÉ, PALMEIRIM, PALMEIRINHA, PINDOBA; [GBAT: "a palm (Maximiliana regia) whose shoots yield a fiber used in the manufacture of mats, baskets, screens, and hats."]

anal (adj.) anal; annual.

analagmático –ca (adj., Math.) anallagmatic.

análcimo (m.) analcita (f., Min.) analcime, analcite.

analectos (m.pl.) analects, collectanea.

analema (m., Geom., Astron.) analemma.

analepsia (f., Med.) convalescence.

analéptico –ca (adj.; m.,f., Med.) analeptic.

analérgico –ca (adj.) anallergic.

analfabetismo (m.) illiteracy.

analfabeto –ta (adj.; m.,f.) illiterate.

analgene (m., Pharm.) analgen.

analgesia (f., Med.) analgesia.

analgésico –ca, –gético –ca (adj.; m.) analgesic.

analisador –dora (adj.) analyzing; (m.,f.) analyzer.

analisar (v.t.) to analyze; to examine, study.

analisável (adj.) susceptible of analysis.

análise (f.) analysis, separation of elements; assay; algebra.—de esforço, stress analysis.—qualitativa, (quantitativa), qualitative, (quantitative), analysis.—química, chemical analysis.—sintática, (Gram.) parsing of a sentence. em última—, in the final analysis.

analista (m.,f.) analyst; algebraist.

analítico –ca (adj.) analytic(al).

analogia (f.) analogy.

analógico –ca (adj.) analogic(al).

analogismo (m.) analogism.

analogista (m.,f.) analogist.

análogo –ga (adj.) analogous, similar, alike; akin.

anambé (m.,f.) an Indian of the Anambé, a little-known Tupian tribe who lived on the left bank of the Tocantins River; (adj.) pert. to or designating this tribe; (m., Zool.) any of numerous chatterers (Cotingidae) such as: the pompadour chatterer (Xipholena punicea); the red chatterer (Phoenicircus carnifex), c.a. PAPA-AÇAÍ, UIRA-TATÁ, SAURÁ.—-açu, the bar-necked grackle (Gymnoderus foetidus), c.a. POMBO-ANAMBÉ, PITIÚ.—-azul, the purple-breasted cotinga (Cotinga cotinga), c.a. CURUÁ, CURURÁ; the Cayenne cotinga (C. cayana).—-branco, the Cayenne tityra (Tityra c. cayana); LaFresnaye's chatterer (Xipholena lamellipennis), c.a. BACACU, PRÊTO.—-grande, the large, high-flying crimson fruit-crow (Haematoderus militaris), c.a. PÁSSARO-SOL.—-prêto, the umbrella-bird (Cephalopterus o. ornatus), c.a. PAVÃO-DO-MATO, TOROPIXI; the purple-throated fruit-crow (Querula purpurata), c.a. ANAMBÉ-UNA.

anambi (m.) the hog-gum or mawna tree (Symphonia globulifera). Var. ANAMI.

anamesito (m., Petrog.) a variety of common basalt.

anamirtina (f., Chem.) anamirtin.

anamirto (m.) the Malay fishberry (Anamirta cocculus) which yields cocculus indicus.

anamnésia, anamnese (f., Med., Eccl.) anamnesis.

anamniano –na (adj., Zool.) anamniotic.

anamniota (adj., Zool.) anaminiote, anamniotic; (m.) anamniote.

anamórfico –ca (adj.) anamorphic; anamorphous.

anamorfoscópio (m., Optics.) anamorphoscope.

anamorfose (f., Biol.) anamorphosis.

ananaí (m.) the Brazilian teal (Nettion brasiliensis), c.a. MARRECA-ANANAÍ.

ananás (m., Bot.) the pineapple (Ananas sativus or A. comosus) better known as ABACAXI; other names for it are:—-de-caraguatá,—-do-mato,—-selvagem, ananaseiro, nanás; also, any of several bromelias.—-de-agulha, a bromelia (B. muricata), c.a. GRAVATÁ-DE-AGULHA.

ananaseiro (m.) pineapple plant.

anandria (f., Med.) anandria.

anândrino –na, anândrio –dria, anandro –dra (adj., Bot.) anandrous, having no stamens.

ananerá (m.) a timber tree (Licania macrophylla).

ananicado –da (adj.) dwarfish; pygmy; fig., mean, sordid. Cf. NANICO.

ananicar (v.t.) to dwarf.

ananico –ca (adj.) = NANICO.
anânico –ca (adj.) dwarfish.
ananismo (m.) nanism, dwarfishness, esp. of plants.
ananto –ta (adj., Bot.) ananthous, flowerless.
anão [anãos, anões] (adj.; m.) dwarf. [fem. anã(s).]
anapirático –ca (adj., Med.) anapeiratic.
anapesto (m., Pros.) anapaest.
ana-pinta (f.) = CAPITÃO-DO-MUNDO.
anaplasia (f., Biol.) anaplasia; (Surg.) anaplasty, plastic surgery [= ANAPLASTIA].
anaplasma (m.) a genus (Anaplasma) of parasitic protozoans which live in the blood of cattle.
anaplasmose (f., Veter.) anaplasmosis, tick fever.
anaplastia (f.) plastic surgery.
anaplástico –ca (adj., Surg.) anaplastic.
anaplerose (f., Med.) anaplerosis.
anaplerótico –ca (adj., Med.) anaplerotic.
anapnóico –ca (adj., Med.) anapnoic.
anapnômetro (m.) anapnometer.
anaptí[c]tico –ca (adj., Phonet.) anaptyctic.
anaptixe [ks] (f., Phonet.) anaptyxis.
anarco, anarca (m.) anarchist.
anarquia (f.) anarchy, disorder, confusion; lawlessness; demoralization.
anárquico –ca (adj.) anarchic; chaotic.
anarquismo (m.) anarchism.
anarquista (adj.) anarchic; (m.,f.) anarchist.
anarquização (f.) act of reducing to anarchy or of inciting to disorder.
anarquizador –dora (adj.) serving to anarchize.
anarquizar (v.t.) to anarchize; to incite to disorder; to throw into confusion; to demoralize.
anárrico (m.) the sea wolf or wolf fish (Anarhicas lupus), c.a. LÔBO-MARINHO, GATO-MARINHO.
anartria (f., Med.) anarthria.
anartro –tra (adj., Zool.) anarthrous.
anasarca (f., Med.) anasarca, dropsy.
anasárcico –ca, anasártico –ca (adj.) anasarcous, dropsical.
anastácio (m., colloq.) dunce.
anastalse (f., Med.) anastalsis.
anastáltico –ca (adj.) anastaltic, styptic.
anástase (f., Med.) anastasis.
anastática (f.) the Jericho resurrection plant (Anastatica hierochuntica) c.a. ROSA-DE-JERICÓ.
anastático –ca (adj., Med.) anastatic.
anastigmático –ca (adj., Optics) anastigmatic.
anástomo (m.) the open-bill storks (genus Anastomus).
anastomosar (v.t.) to anastomose; to inosculate; to interjoin.
anastomose (f., Anat., Biol.) anastomosis; inosculation; (Radio, TV) hook-up.
anastomótico –ca (adj.) anastomotic.
anástrofe (f., Rhet.) anastrophe.
anata (f., Eccl. Law) annates.
anatado –da (adj.) cream-like; cream-colored.
anatar (v.t.) to make like cream; to cover with cream.
anatásio (m., Min.) anatase, octahedrite.
anate (f.) annatto tree (Bixa orellana), c.a. URUCU, URUCUEIRO; the dye annatto.
anateirado –da (adj.) covered with river mud.
anátema (adj.) cursèd; (m.) anathema, curse, malediction; excommunication.
anatemático –ca (adj.) anathematic.
anatematismo (m.) anathematism.
anatematização (f.) anathematization.
anatematizador –dora (adj.) anathematizing; (m.,f.) anathematizer.
anatematizar (v.t.) to anathematize, curse; to condemn, proscribe, ban.
anatídeo –dea (adj., Zool.) anatine.
anátides (f.,pl.) the Anatidae (ducks, geese, swans).
anatifa (f.), anatifo (m.) goose barnacle.
anato (m.) anatto (dye).
anatocismo (m., Law) anatocism.
anatomia (f.) anatomy (the science of); art of dissecting; minute analysis. [Anatomy in the sense of structure of an animal or plant is ESTRUTURA ANATÔMICA].—descritiva, descriptive anatomy.—geral, general anatomy.—patológica, pathological or morbid anatomy.—topográfica, regional or topographical anatomy.
anatômico –ca (adj.) anatomic.
anatomista (m.,f.) anatomist.
anatomização (f.) anatomization.

anatomizar (v.t.) to anatomize.
anatomo-patológico –ca (adj., Med.) anatamopathologic.
anatoxina [ks] (f.) anatoxin, toxoid.
anatripsia (f., Med.) anatripsis.
anátropo –pa (adj., Bot.) anatropous.
anaudia (f.) loss of voice.
anauerá (f.) = ANANERÁ.
anauquá (m.,f.) = NAUGUÁ (an Indian).
anauxita [ks] (f., Min.) anauxite.
anavalhado –da (adj.) slashed with a razor; sharp as a razor.
anavalhar (v.t.) to slash with a razor.
ana-velha (f.) = SOCÔZINHO.
anavinga (f.) a cosmopolitan tropical tree (Casearia ovata).
anazotúria, –turia (f., Med.) anazoturia.
anca (f.) haunch, flank; rump, hindquarters.
ançarinha (f.) the silverweed cinquefoil (Potentilla anserina), c.a. ARGENTINA, POTENTILA.—-branca, lamb's-quarters goosefoot (Chenopodium album).—-vermífuga, the drug wormseed goosefoot (Chenopodium ambrosioides anthelminticum).
ancestral (adj.) ancestral.
ancestre (m.) ancestor.
anchieta [ê] (f.) the mercury anchietea (A. salutaris), whose bark is used in treating erysipelas; c.a. PIRAGUAIA.
anchietina [ê] (f., Pharm.) anchietin(e).
ancho –cha (adj.) broad, wide; large, ample; (colloq.) haughty, vain. todo—, all puffed up.
anchova (f.) = ENCHOVA.
anchura (f.) width.
anciã, fem. of ANCIÃO.
ancião [-ães, -ões, -ãos] anciã (adj.; m.) ancient, venerable (man).
ancila (f.) maidservant.
anciloblefaria (f., Med.) ankyloblepharon.
anciloglossia, –glossa (f., Med.) ankyloglossia.
ancilômelo (m., Surg.) ankylomele, curved probe.
ancilomerismo (m., Med.) ankylomerism.
ancilopodia (f., Med.) ankylopodia.
anciloproctia (f., Med.) ankyloproctia.
anciloquilia (f., Med.) ankylocheilia.
ancilorrinia (f., Med.) ankylorrhinia.
ancilosar (v.t.) to ankylose.
ancilose (f., Med.) ankylosis.
ancilostomíase (f., Med.) ancylostomiasis, hookworm disease, c.a. UNCINARIASE, AMARELÃO, OPILAÇÃO.
ancilóstomo (m.) the typical hookworm (Ancylostoma).
ancilostomose (f.) = ANCILOSTOMÍASE.
ancilótomo (m., Surg.) ankylotome.
ancinhar (v.t.) to rake.
ancinho (m.) rake (garden tool).
ancipitado –da (adj., Bot.) ancipital.
anciróide (adj., Anat.) ankyroid, hook-shaped.
anco (m.) any elbow, angle or bend, esp. in the coastline.
ancólia (f.) = ERVA-POMBINHA.
anconagra (f.) gouty pain in the elbow.
ancôneo –nea (adj.) of or pert. to the elbow; (m., Anat.) anconeus.
anconite (f., Med.) anconitis.
âncora (f.) anchor; security, stay, hold; last resource.—-de misericórdia,—-de-salvação,—-de-salvamento,—-sagrada, sheet anchor (lit. & fig.). lançar (levantar)—, to drop (weigh) anchor.
ancoração (f.) anchoring; anchorage.
ancorado –da (adj.) at anchor, anchored.
ancoradouro (m.) anchorage (place).
ancoragem (f.) dropping of the anchor; anchorage fee.
ancorar (v.t.,v.i.) to anchor.
ancoreta [ê] (f.) a small anchor; a small water keg.
ancorete [rê] (m.) a small anchor, kedge.
ancudo –da (adj.) haunchy, big-hipped.
ancusa (f.) the alkanet or common bugloss (Anchusa officinalis) and other plants of this genus.
ancusina (f., Chem.) alkannin [= ORÇANETINA].
anda! (imperative of ANDAR) Move! Get out of the way! Get a move on! Hurry up!
andá-açu [ú] (f.) the Joannesia princeps, a large and handsome tree of the spurge family, sole species of its genus, prized in Brazil as a shade tree because of its size and many branches. The kernel of its large stone-fruit yields a powerful cathartic, whence its other name CÔCO-DE-PURGA. Still other common names are: ANDÁ-GUAÇU, FRUTA-DE-ARARA, INDÁ-GUAÇU.

andaca (*f.*, *Bot.*) a spiderwort (*Tradescantia diuretica*), c.a. TRAPOERABA, MARIANINHA.
andacaá [a-á] (*m.*) = CAPIM-ANDACAÁ.
andaço (*m.*) contagious disease; epidemic. **um—de resfriados**, a mild epidemic of colds.
andadeiro -ra (*adj.*) of horses, pacing, easy-riding.
andado -da (*adj.*) of distance, walked; of time, gone by; (*f.*) act of walking, esp. a long distance.
andador -dora (*adj.*) fast-walking; of horses, pacing; (*m.,f.*) walker.
andadura (*f.*) gait, pace. **cavalo de boa—**, well-gaited horse.
andá-guaçu [ú] (*m.*) = ANDA-AÇU.
andaiá (*f.*) a palm (*Attalea compta*), c.a. INDAIÁ.
andaime (*m.*) scaffolding.
andaina (*f.*) a suit of clothes; a row or string of objects.
andaluz -luza (*adj.*; *m.,f.*) Andalusian.
andaluzita (*f.,m.*) andalusite (semi-precious stone).
andamento (*m.*) progress, course, movement; performance (of a machine); (*Music*) tempo. **dar—a alguma coisa**, to start a matter on its way (esp. through government channels).
andante (*adj.*) errant, wandering , straying. **cavaleiro—**, knight-errant; (*adj.*; *adv.*; *m.*; *Music*) andante; (*m.,f.*) walker, transient.
andantino (*adj.*; *adv.*; *m.*; *Music*) andantino.
andar (*m.*) walk, manner of walking, pace, step, stride; floor (story of a building). **o—de cima**, the upper floor. **—térreo**, ground floor. **primeiro—**, second floor; (*v.i.*) to walk, step, march, tramp; (of machinery, clock, automobile, etc.) to run; to move; to go; to wander, rove; to proceed, progress, advance, go on, go ahead; of time, to elapse; to act, behave, live (in a given manner). With prep. **a** or **de**, **andar** indicates mode of action, as in:—**a cavalo**, to ride horseback.—**a passo**, of horses, to pace.—**a pé**, to go afoot.—**à roda**, to go around and around.—**ao acaso, a esmo, à toa, ao léu**, to walk aimlessly about.—**ao laré**, to loaf; to be on the ragged edge.—**às turras com alguém**, to be at sword's point with someone.—**de caranguejo**, to walk like a crab (sideways or backwards).—**de esguelha**, to sidle.—**de ronda**, to go the rounds; to prowl. **Andar** is frequently employed instead of **estar** to indicate a successive or continual state of being, as in:—**aborrecido, melancólico, pre-ocupado, triste**, etc., to be blue, in the dumps, worried, etc.—**alegre**, to be happy.—**ao corrente**, to be au courant [= ESTAR AO PAR].—**às voltas com**, to be having trouble with (something or someone). —**atravessado com alguém**, to be at outs with someone. —**com a cara amarrada**, to be cross, grouchy, illtempered.—**emburrado**, to be out of humor, crabby, peevish.—**em dia**, to be up to date (referring to bills, accounts, books). Other examples of **andar:—com a pedra no sapato**, to feel uneasy (about something).—**com a pulga atrás da orelha**, or **no ouvido**, to smell a rat, be suspicious.—**com pés de lã**, to be overly cautious.— **como unha e carne com alguém**, to be hand and glove with someone.—**de azar**, or **com falta de sorte**, or **com caveira de burro**, to be down on one's luck.—**de gatinhas**, [from GATINHO, kitten), to crawl, go on all fours.— (or **ir**) **de mal a pior**, to go from bad to worse.—**de pé coxo**, or **coxinho**, to limp; to hop on one foot.—**depressa**, to hasten, hurry (up).—**descalço**, to go barefoot(ed).— **fazendo alguma coisa**, to be at, or about, or up to something.—(or **fiar**) **fino**, to proceed warily.—**mal de dinheiros**, or **de finanças**, to be hard up for money.—**na bôca do povo**, of an incident, a scandal, etc., to be known and discussed by "everybody".—**na rua**, to be out of a job, down and out.—**na corda bamba**, to be in difficulties; lit., to walk a tight rope.—**na ponta dos pés**, to tiptoe.— **numa azáfama (dobadeira, lufa-lufa, roda-viva)**, to be flustered, flurried, not know whether one is coming or going.—**pelas ruas**, to walk the streets.—**sem dinheiro**, to be broke (practically all of the time).—**sôbre brasas**, to be on pins and needles, greatly worried.—**um pedacinho**, to go for a short walk. **Anda** (the imperative form) can range from a threat to an exhortation, depending on the tone of voice: Move! Move on! Get out! Get out of the way! Get a move on! Hurry! Hurry up! Hurry, please! **Anda depressa**, Hurry up! Get a move on! **Anda devagar!** Go slow! Slow down! **Dize-me com quem andas e dir-te-ei quem és**, Tell me with whom you associate and I will tell you who you are; A man is known by the company he keeps. **fazer alguém—com a cabeça à roda**, to turn a person's head. **Os que se parecem** (or, **que se**

entendem) **andam juntos**, Birds of a feather flock together. **Quem corre cansa, quem anda alcança**, Haste makes waste; Make haste slowly. **saber a quantas anda**, to get one's bearings; to know what one is about. **Por onde é que você tem andado?** Where have you been keeping yourself? **Vamos andando!** Let's get going! Let's get started!
andarengo -ga (*adj.*; *m.,f.*) given to moving about, traveling from place to place.
andarilhar (*v.i.*) to hike; to go here and there.
andarilho (*m.*) walker; tramp, vagrant.
andas (*f.,pl.*) stilts [= PERNAS DE PAU]; litter.
andebol (*m.*) handball.
andejar (*v.i.*) to wander, ramble, roam; to gad about.
andejo -ja [ê] (*adj.*) gadabout, roving, rambling, on the go; (*m.*) walker.
andesita (*f.*, *Min.*) andesine.
andesito (*m.*, *Petrog.*) andesite.
andinista (*m.,f.*) mountain climber.
andino -na (*adj.*) Andean.
andira (*f.*, *Bot.*) any angelin tree (*Andira*) esp. the cabbage tree (*A. inermis*), the Goa andira (*A. araroba*) which yields Goa powder, and the Brazilian angelin tree (*A. vermifuga*).—-**ibá** = ANGELIM-DE-FÔLHA-LARGA.
andirá (*m.*, *Zool.*) a leaf-nosed bat (*Phyllostoma hastatum*), c.a. GUANDIRÁ.
andiroba (*f.*) the Guiana crabwood (*Carapa guianensis*), c.a. ANDIROBEIRA. [*GBAT*: "Brazilian mahogany, providing medium-hard lumber resistant to termites; the seeds contain oil used by the natives for insect bites and lighting purposes, and is employed commercially for the manufacture of soap, stearine, and lubricants."]
ândito (*m.*) passage, corridor, walk; footpath.
andô (*adj.*) of beards, pointed.
andor (ô) (*m.*) a litter with poles, used for conveying images in religious street processions.
andorinha (*f.*) any swallow; moving van; launch; traveling saleswoman (of ladies' wear); (*colloq.*) prostitute; (*f.*) any swallow or martin; any of various swifts, esp. *Chaetura brachyura* (the short-tailed swift) or *Chaetura c. cinereiventris* (the ash-vented swift).—**-do-mato**, a swallow-wing puff-bird (*Chelidoptera t. tenebrósa*) c.a. TATERA, URUBÚZINHO.—-**das-chaminés**, the chimney swallow (*Hirundo rustica*).—-**de-pescoço-vermelho**, the barn swallow (*Hirundo rustica erythrogaster*).—-**de-rabo-branco**, the white-winged swallow (*Iridoprocne albiventer*).—-**do-campo**, the brown-chested martin (*Phaeoprogne t. tapera*) c.a. TAPERA, TAPERÁ, UIRIRI.— **-do-mar**, the long-billed tern (*Phaetusa simplex*) c.a. GAIVINHA, TRINTA-RÉIS.—-**do-ôco-do-pau**, the cinereous warbling finch (*Poospiza cinerea*).—-**fusca-do-mar**, the noddy tern (*Anous s. stolidus*).—-**grande**, or **-da-casa**, Azara's martin (*Progne chalybea domestica*).—-**pequena**, or **-de-bando**, the blue-and-white swallow (*Pygochelidon c. cyanoleuca*). **Uma—não faz verão**, One swallow does not a summer make.
andorinhão (*m.*) any of various swifts, esp. the Cayenne swift (*Panyptila cayanensis*) c.a. UIRIRI; the collared swift (*Streptoprocne z. zonaris*) c.a. TAPERUÇU; the biscutellated swift (*Streptoprocne biscutata*).—-**das-tormentas**, a petrel (*Oceanodroma castro*) c.a. ALMA-DE-MESTRE; a tern called gaivão.
andorita (*f.*, *Min.*) andorite.
andrade (*m.*, *Bot.*) a laurel (*Persea venosa*).
andradita (*f.*, *Min.*) andradite.
andrajo (*m.*) rags, tatters; (*pl.*) ragged clothes.
andrajoso -sa (*adj.*) tattered, ragged; seedy, threadbare, shabby.
andranatomia (*f.*) andranatomy, anthropotomy.
André (*m.*) Andrew.
andréia (*f.*) a genus (*Andreaea*) of Alpine mosses.
andrena (*f.*) a genus (*Andrenas*) of solitary bees.
andrequicé [drè] (*m.*) the clubhead cutgrass (*Leersia hexandra*); = CAMARÉ-DE-CAVALO.
androceu (*m.*) **androcia** (*f.*, *Bot.*) androecium.
androdínamo -ma (*adj.*, *Bot.*) androdynamous.
andrófago -ga (*adj.*) androphagous, man-eating [= ANTROPÓFAGO].
androfobia (*f.*) androphobia.
androfonomania (*f.*, *Med.*) androphonomania.
andróforo (*m.*, *Bot.*) androphore.
androgenesia, -genia (*f.*, *Biol.*) androgenesis.
androginário -ria (*adj.*, *Bot.*) androgynary.
androginia (*f.*) androgyny.

androginismo (*m.*) androgynism, hermaphroditism.
andrógino –na (*adj.*) androgynous.
andróide (*m.*) android.
androlepsia (*f.*, *Law*) androlepsia.
andromania (*f.*, *Med.*) andromania, nymphomania.
andrômeda (*f.*) the moorwart or bog-rosemary andromeda (*A. polifolia*) and other plants of this genus; [*cap.*] (*Astron.*) Andromeda.
andromedotoxina [ks] (*f.*, *Chem.*) andromedotoxin.
andromonóico –ca (*adj.*, *Bot.*) andromonoecious.
andropetalar (*adj.*, *Bot.*) andropetalous.
andropogão (*m.*) the genus (*Andropogon*) of bluestem grasses.
androsemo (*m.*, *Bot.*) the tutsan St. Johnswort (*Hypericum androsaemum*).
androspório (*m.*, *Bot.*) androspore.
andróssaco (*m.*, *Bot.*) rock jasmine (*Androsace*).
andu (*m.*) the pigeon pea (*Cajanus cajan*) or its edible seeds; c.a. ANDUZEIRO, GUANDO, GUANDU, GUANDEIRO.
andurrial (*m.*) unfrequented, solitary place.
anediar (*v.t.*) to stroke the head or hair of.
anedota (*f.*) anecdote; joke.
anedotário (*m.*) a collection of stories.
anedótico –ca (*adj.*) anecdotic.
anedotista (*m.,f.*) anecdotist.
anedotizar (*v.t.*) to relate anecdotes; to give an anecdotic twist or style to a narrative.
anegalhar (*v.t.*) to tie with a piece of string.
anegar (*v.t.*) to submerge, drown.
anegrar (*v.t.*) to blacken.
aneiro –ra (*adj.*) seasonal; uncertain; of trees and plants, bearing every other year.
anejo –ja (*adj.*) one-year-old.
anel [-éis] (*m.*) ring; loop, link; curl, ringlet.—**de casamento**, wedding ring.—**de chuveiro**, or **de formatura**, a graduation ring consisting of brilliants surrounding a stone that identifies the wearer's profession, as: emerald for physicians, ruby for lawyers, sapphire for civil engineers, turquoise for military engineers, topaz for pharmacists, almandite garnet for dental surgeons. For teachers it is a platinum star set in black onyx (symbolizing light in darkness).—**de noivado**, engagement ring.—**de segmento**, piston ring.—**do Pescador**, Pope's ring.—**pastoral**, bishop's ring.
anelacão (*f.*) labored breathing.
anelado –da (*adj.*) ring-like, curled. **cabelos—s**, curly hair; (*m.*) = ANELÍDEO.
anelante (*adj.*) yearning; panting, gasping.
anelão (*m.*) a heavy finger ring, usually of gold, engraved with the wearer's coat of arms or initials, or with a diamond set in it.
anelar [from ANELO, craving] (*v.t.*) to long (**por**, for) to yearn (**por**, for), to pine (**por**, for); to lust after; (*v.i.*) to pant, gasp; to breathe hard; [from ANEL, ring] (*v.t.*) to form into a ring; to curl.
anelástico –ca (*adj.*) unelastic.
anelétrico –ca (*adj.*, *Physics*) anelectric.
aneletrotônico –ca (*adj.*, *Physiol.*) anelectrotonic.
aneletrótono (*m.*, *Physiol.*) anelectrotonus.
anelídeo –dea (*adj.; m.*, *Zool.*) annelid.
aneliforme (*adj.*) ring-shaped.
anelo (*m.*) longing, desire, craving, eagerness to possess.
anemia (*f.*, *Med.*, *Physiol.*) anemia.
anêmico –ca (*adj.*) anemic.
anemizar (*v.t.*) to render anemic.
anemófilo –la (*adj.*, *Bot.*) anemophilous.
anemografia (*f.*) anemography.
anemologia (*f.*) anemology.
anemometria (*f.*) anemometry.
anemômetro (*m.*) anemometer, wind gauge.
anemometrógrafo (*m.*) anemometrograph.
anêmona (*f.*, *Bot.*) any anemone; (*Zool.*) sea anemone, polyp.—**-dos-bosques**, the European wood anemone (*A. nemorosa*), c.a. SÍLVIA.—**-pulsatila**, European pasqueflower.
anemônico –ca (*adj.*, *Chem.*) **ácido—**, anemonic acid.
anemonina (*f.*, *Chem.*) anemonin.
anemoscópio (*m.*) anemoscope.
anemotropismo (*m.*, *Biol.*) anemotropism.
anencefálico –ca (*adj.*, *Zool.*) anencephalic.
anencefalotrofia (*f.*) anencephalotrophia.
anenergia (*f.*, *Med.*) anergy, anergia; = ANERGIA.
anepigráfico –ca (*adj.*) anepigraphic.
anepiplóico –ca (*adj.*, *Anat.*) anepiploic.

anepitimia (*f.*, *Med.*) anepithymia.
anequim (*m.*) the huge man-eater or great white shark (*Cancharodon carcharias*), c.a. CAÇÃO-ANEQUIM [The largest in Brazilian waters, it attains a length of 30 feet.]
aneretisia (*f.*, *Med.*) anerethisia.
anergia (*f.*) = ANENERGIA.
anestesia (*f.*) anesthesia; insensibility.—**raquidiana**, spinal anesthesia.
anestesiante (*adj.*) anesthesiant, anesthetic.
anestisiar (*v.t.*) to anesthetize.
anestesiômetro, anestesímetro (*m.*, *Med.*) anesthesimeter.
anestesista (*m.,f.*) anesthetist.
anestético –ca, **anestésico** –ca (*adj.; m.*) anesthetic.
anete [nê] (*m.*) a shackle or coupling, as for an anchor.
aneto (*m.*, *Bot.*) the dill (*Anethum graveolens*).
anetol (*m.*, *Chem.*) anethole, anise camphor.
aneuria (*f.*) deficiency of nervous energy.
aneurisma (*m.*, *Med.*) aneurysm.
aneurismal (*adj.*, *Med.*) aneurysmal.
aneurismático –ca (*adj.*, *Med.*) aneurysmatic.
anexação [ks] (*f.*) annexation; incorporation (of territory).
anexado –da [ks] (*adj.*) annexed, joined, connected; of territory, incorporated.
anexar [ks] (*v.t.*) to annex, affix, attach; to add (to); to join, unite, connect; to incorporate (territory).
anexim (*m.*) popular saying.
anexite [ks] (*f.*, *Med.*) adnexitis.
anexo –xa [ks] (*adj.*, *irreg. p.p. of* ANEXAR) annexed, attached, joined, connected; (*Bot.*) adnexed; (*m.*) an annex; a sheet or document attached to another; (*pl.*, *Anat.*) adnexa, conjoined parts (as of the uterus).
anfarístero –ra (*adj.*) clumsy in the use of both hands. [Anton. AMBIDEXTRO].
anfiartrose (*f.*, *Anat.*) amphiarthrosis.
anfiaster (*m.*, *Biol.*) amphiaster.
anfibianos (*m.pl.*, *Zool.*) the Amphibia [= BATRÁQUIOS].
anfíbio –bia (*adj.*) amphibious; (*m.,f.*) amphibian.
anfibiologia (*f.*) amphibiology.
anfiblástula (*f.*, *Biol.*) amphiblastula.
anfiblestroidite (*f.*, *Med.*) retinitis.
anfibolia (*f.*, *Logic*) amphibology; (*Med.*) amphibolia.
anfibólico –ca (*adj.*, *Med.*) amphibolic.
anfibólio (*m.*, *Min.*) amphibole.
anfibolito (*m.*, *Min.*) amphibolite.
anfíbolo (*m.*) = ANFIBÓLIO.
anfibologia (*f.*) amphibology.
anfibologismo (*m.*) amphibologism.
anfíbraco (*m.*, *Pros.*) amphibrach.
anficarpo –pa (*adj.*, *Bot.*) amphicarpic.
anficeliano –na (*adj.*, *Zool.*) amphicoelous.
anficêntrico –ca (*adj.*, *Anat.*) amphicentric.
anficítula (*f.*, *Zool.*) amphicytula.
anficreatina (*f.*, *Biochem.*) amphicraetinine.
anfigástrio (*m.*, *Bot.*) amphigastrium.
anfigástrula (*f.*, *Zool.*) amphigastrula.
anfigonia (*f.*) amphigony, sexual propagation.
anfiguri [í] (*m.*) amphigory.
anfimixia [ks] (*f.*, *Biol.*) amphimixis; interbreeding.
anfioxo [ks] (*m.*) the common European lancelet (*Branchiostoma lanceolatum*); also, a Brazilian species (*B. caribaeum*) called MARIA-MOLE.
anfipirenina (*f.*, *Biol.*) amphipyrenin.
anfipneusto –ta (*adj.*, *Zool.*) amphipneustic; (*m.pl.*) the Perennibrachiata.
anfípode (*adj.*, *Zool.*) amphipodal; (*m.*) an amphipod; (*m.pl.*) the Amphipoda.
anfipróstilo –la (*adj.*, *m.*, *Arch.*) amphiprostyle.
anfisarca (*m.*, *Bot.*) amphisarca.
anfisbena (*f.*,) a limbless lizard (*Amphisbaena*) with concealed eyes and ears, whence the common name: COBRA-DE-DUAS-CABEÇAS (two-headed snake).
anfíscio –cia (*m.,f.*) an amphiscian (inhabitant of the tropics).
anfispório (*m.*, *Bot.*) amphispore.
anfístomo (*m.*) an amphistomous trematode worm.
anfiteatral, anfiteátrico –ca (*adj.*) amphitheatric.
anfiteatro (*m.*) amphitheater.
anfitrião (*m.*) host.
anfítrico –ca (*adj.*, *Bacteriol.*) amphitrichous.
anfitrioa (*f.*) hostess.
anfitrites (*m.pl.*) a genus (*Amphitrite*) of tube-inhabiting marine annelid worms.
anfítropo –pa, **anfitrópico** –ca (*adj.*, *Bot.*) amphitropous.

anfiúma (f.) a congo snake or blind eel (*Amphiuma*).
anfodiplopia (f., *Med.*) amphodiplopia.
anfófilo –la (*adj.*, *Biol.*) amphophilic.
anfólito (m., *Chem.*) ampholyte.
ânfora (f.) amphora (ancient Greek vase); a measure of capacity; (*Bot.*) amphora.
anfórico –ca (*adj.*, *Med.*) amphoric. **sôpro**—, amphoric breathing or resonance of the lungs.
anforofonia (f., *Med.*) amphorophony.
anfótero –ra (*adj.*, *Chem.*) amphoteric.
anfracto –ta (*adj.*) anfractuous, winding, sinuous; (*Bot.*) anfractuose; (m.) a circuitous way.
anfractuosidade (f.) anfractuosity; roughness, unevenness, as of the bark of a tree or of a rock wall.
anfractuoso –sa (*adj.*) anfractuous.
anga (f.) evil eye.
angareira (f.) a type of small net adapted for taking mullets.
angariação (f.) act or instance of procuring, securing, canvassing, etc. See the verb ANGARIAR.
angariador –dora (*adj.*) canvassing, soliciting; (m.,f.) canvasser, solicitor, collector.
angariamento (m.) = ANGARIAÇÃO.
angariar (*v.t.*) to procure, get, obtain; to attract, induce; to win, secure; to canvass, solicit; to tout for.—**anúncios**, to solicit advertisements (as for a newspaper).—**donativos** or **esmolas**, to solicit small gifts or alms.
angarilha (f.) a straw cover for bottles.
angaturama (m.) a good spirit (in Tupian mythology).
Ângela (f.) Angela.
angelato (m., *Chem.*) angelate.
angélica (f.) the garden angelica (*A. archangelica*); the tuberose (*Polianthes tuberosa*); (f.) Angelica.—**branca**, the plantainlily (*Hosta plantaginea*).—**de-rama** = CIPÓ-DE-SAPO.—**do-mato**,—**mansa**, a velvetseed (*Guettarda angelica*).—**do-pará**, the Pará angelwood (*Dicorynia paraensis*).
angelícico –ca (*adj.; Chem.*) angelic, angelicic.
angélico –ca (*adj.*) angelical; (*Chem.*) angelic.
angelicó (m., *Bot.*) the Brazil dutchmanspipe (*Aristolochia brasiliensis*), c.a. CAÇAÚ, JARRINHA, MILHOMENS, CAPAHOMEM, PAPO-DE-PERÚ, URUBUCAÁ; also another species (*A. cordigera*), c.a. CIPÓ-DE-CORAÇÃO, GUACO-BRAVO.
angelim (m.) an anjelywood (*Artocarpus hirsutus*); any of several trees of the pea family, esp. of the genus Andira; the seed of some, used in medicine.—**amargoso**, the Brazilian andira (*Andira vermifuga*), c.a. ANGELIM-DO-CAMPO.—**araroba**, the Goa andira (*A. araroba*) from which Goa powder is obtained; c.a. ANGELIM-AMARELO, ANGELIM-AMARGOSO, ARAROBA.—**côco**, is *Andira stipulacea* and is c.a. MAREMA, PAU-PINTADO.—**de-espinho**, the spiny andira (*A. spinulosa*), c.a. MARI, UMARI.—**de-fôlha-larga**, or **-de-fôlha-grande**, probably the same as ANGELIM-AMARGOSO, and c.a. ANGELIM-PRÊTO, ANDIRA-IBÁ, ARACUI, PAU-DE-MORCEGO.—**doce**, is *Andira faxinfolia* and is c.a. ANGELIM-DO-MATO, MATA-BARATAS, PINHÃO-DO-MATO, PAU-DE-MORCEGO.—**pedra**, the cabbage tree or showy andira (*A. spectabilis*).—**rajado**, an apesearring (*Pithecellobium racemosum*).
Angelina (f.) Angelina.
angelologia (f.) angelology.
angico (m., *Bot.*) any of certain S.A. trees of the mimosa family, genus *Piptadenia*, whose hard wood is much used in Brazil for heavy construction, railroad ties, fence posts, etc. It is also exported in trimmed logs of 6–10″ in diameter for use by cabinet makers and turners. The bark of some species is used medicinally and for tanning. The best-known species is *P. rigida* some common names for which are—**amarelo**,—**cedro**,—**de-banhado**,—**demontes**,—**verdadeiro**,—**vermelho**.—**surucucu** = CATANDUBA.
angiectasia (f., *Med.*) angiectasis.
angiectopia (f., *Med.*) angiectopia.
angiefraxia [ks] (f., *Med.*) angiemphraxis.
angiite [i-í] (f., *Med.*) angiitis.
angina (f., *Med.*) angina.—**de garganta**, quinsy.—**de peito**, angina pectoris.—**diftérica**, croup.—**estreptocócica**, septic sore throat.
anginóide (*adj.*, *Med.*) anginoid.
anginoso –sa (*adj.*, *Med.*) anginose, anginous.
angiocardite (f., *Med.*) angiocarditis.
angiocarpo (m., *Bot.*) an angiocarpous plant.
angioceratoma (f., *Med.*) angiokeratoma.

angioclasto (m., *Surg.*) angioclast.
angiocolecistite (f., *Med.*) angiochelecystitis.
angiocolite (f., *Med.*) angiocholitis.
angiodermatite (f., *Med.*) angiodermatitis.
angiofibroma (f., *Med.*) angiofibroma.
angiogênese (f.) angiogenesis.
angiogenia (f.) angiogeny.
angiografia (f., *Anat.*) angiography.
angiohidrotomia (f., *Surg.*) angiohydrotomy.
angioleucita, angiolinfite (f., *Med.*) lymphangitis.
angiolinfoma (f., *Med.*) angiolymphoma.
angiolipoma (f., *Med.*) angiolipoma.
angiólito (m., *Med.*) angiolith.
angiologia (f., *Anat.*) angiology.
angioma (f., *Med.*) angioma.
angiomalacia (f., *Med.*) angiomalacia.
angiomatose (f., *Med.*) angiomatosis.
angiomatoso –sa (*adj.*, *Med.*) angiomatous.
angiomioma (f., *Med.*) angiomyoma.
angiomiosarcoma (f., *Med.*) angiomyosarcoma.
angioneurose (f., *Med.*) angioneurosis.
angioneurótico –ca (*adj.*, *Med.*) angioneurotic.
angiônoma (f., *Med.*) angionoma.
angionose (f.) = ANGIOSE.
angioparalisia (f., *Med.*) angioparalysis.
angioparesia (f., *Med.*) angioparesis.
angiopatia (f., *Med.*) angiopathy.
angioplania (f., *Med.*) angioplany.
angioplerose (f., *Med.*) angioplerosis.
angiopteris (f.) a vessel fern (*Angiopteris*).
angiorrafia (f., *Surg.*) angiorrhaphy.
angiorragia (f., *Med.*) angiorrhagia.
angiorréia (f., *Med.*) angiorrhea.
angiorrexe [ks] (f., *Med.*) angiorrhexis.
angiosclerose (f., *Med.*) angiosclerosis.
angioscópio (m., *Med.*) angioscope.
angiose (f.) angionosis.
angiospermas (m.pl., *Bot.*) the Angiospermae.
angiospérmico –ca, **angiospérmo** –ma (*adj.*, *Bot.*) angiospermic, angiospermous.
angiósporo –ra, **angiosporado** –da (*adj.*, *Bot.*) angiosporous.
angiostenose (f., *Med.*) angiostenosis.
angiostrofia (f., *Med.*) angiostrophy.
angiotomia (f., *Surg.*) angiotomy.
angiotônico –ca (*adj.*, *Med.*) angiotonic.
angiótribo (f., *Surg.*) angiotribe.
angiotripsia (f., *Surg.*) angiotripsy.
angiotrófico –ca (*adj.*, *Med.*) angiotrophic.
anglesita (f.) anglesite, lead sulfate, ore of lead.
anglicanismo (m.) Anglicanism; the Anglican Church.
anglicano –na (*adj.; m.,f.*) Anglican.
anglicismo (m.) Anglicism.
anglicista (m.,f.) Anglicist.
anglicizar, anglizar (*v.t.*) to anglicize.
ânglico –ca (*adj.*) Anglo, English; (m.) Old English.
anglo –gla (*adj.*) Anglo, (m.pl.) the Angles.
anglo-americano –na (*adj.*) Anglo-American.
anglo-brasileiro –ra (*adj.*) Anglo-Brazilian.
anglo-canadense (*adj.*) Anglo-Canadian.
anglo-dinamarquês –quêsa (*adj.*) Anglo-Danish.
anglo-espanhol –la (*adj.*) Anglo-Spanish.
anglofilia (f.) friendship, admiration, etc., for England and things English.
anglófilo –la (*adj.*) Anglophile.
anglofobia (f.) Anglophobia.
anglófobo –ba (*adj.*) Anglophobe.
anglo-francês –cesa [ê] (*adj.*) Anglo-French.
anglo-indiano –na (*adj.*) Anglo-Indian.
anglo-luso –sa (*adj.*) Anglo-Portuguese.
anglomania (f.) Anglomania.
anglomaníaco –ca (*adj.*) Anglomaniacal.
anglômano –na (m.,f.) Anglomane, Anglomaniac.
anglo-normando –da (*adj.*) Anglo-Norman.
anglo-russo –sa (*adj.*) Anglo-Russian.
anglo-saxão –xã, **anglo-saxônio** –nia [ks] (*adj.*) Anglo-Saxon.
angófora (f.) a genus (*Angophora*) of gum myrtles.
angola (m.,f.) a native of Angola; (m.pl.) the Angolese people; (m.) guinea grass, c.a. CAPIM-DE-ANGOLA or CAPIM-GUINÉ; (f.) guinea fowl, c.a. ANGOLINHA.—**açu**, a panicum grass (*P. spectabilis*), c.a. ANGOLÃO, ANGOLAÇU.
angolano –na (*adj.; m.,f.*) a native of Angola.

angolense (*adj.*) Angolese; (*m.,f.*) a native of Angola; (*m.*) Angolese language.

angolinha, angolista (*f.*) = GALINHA-D'ANGOLA.

Angora (*f.*) Angora; Ankara.

angorá (*adj.*) Angora (goats, rabbits, cats, wool, etc.).

angra (*f.*) cove, inlet, small bay.

angu [ú] (*m.*) mush, porridge; (*colloq.*) mess, hodge-podge; also = JAPACANIM (a bird).—**-de caroço**, (*colloq.*) plight, muddle, predicament; melee, shindy, free-for-all.

angüídeos (*m.pl.*) a family (*Anguidae*) of lizards.

angüiforme (*adj.*) snake-shaped.

angüílula (*f.*) the vinegar eel (*Anguillula aceti*).

angüino -na (*adj.*) anguine.

angulado -da (*adj.*) angular.

angular (*adj.*) angular. **pedra—**, cornerstone.

angularidade (*f.*) angularity.

angulífero -ra (*adj.*) anguliferous.

angulinvervado -da (*adj., Bot.*) angulinerved.

ângulo (*m.*) angle; corner.—**agudo**, acute angle.—**crítico**, (*Optics, Aeron.*) critical angle.—**de adiantamento** = ÂNGULO DE AVANÇO.—**de aproximação**, (*Aeron., Mach.*) angle of approach.—**de ascensão**, (*Aeron.*) angle of climb.—**de ataque**, (*Aeron.*) angle of attack.—**de aterragem**, (*Aeron.*) landing angle.—**de atraso**, (*Elec.*) angle of lag, phase angle.—**de atrito**, (*Mach.*) angle of friction.—**de avanço** (*Elec.*) angle of lead or of lag; (*Steam Eng.*) angle of lead, angular advance.—**de contingência**, (*Math.*) angle of contingence or curvature.—**de declinação**, angle of declination.—**de deriva**, (*Aeron.*) angle of crab.—**de descida**, (*Aeron.*) angle of descent.—**de desvio**, (*Physics*) angle of deviation.—**de elevação**, angle of elevation.—**de guinada**, (*Aeron.*) angle of yaw.—**de incidência**, (*Physics*) angle of incidence; (*Aeron.*) angle of attack.—**de inclinação**, angle of dip (of the needle).—**de obliqüidade**, (*Mach.*) angle of obliquity, angle of pressure.—**de planeio**, or **de planeamento**, (*Aeron.*) angle of glide.—**de polarização**, angle of polarization.—**de posição**, (*Astron.*) angle of position.—**de reflexão**, angle of reflection.—**de refração**, angle of refraction.—**de repouso**, (*Civ. Eng.*) angle of repose, angle of rest.—**de retardamento** = —DE ATRASO.—**descendente**, (*Geod.*) angle of depression.—**de subida**, (*Aeron.*) angle of climb.—**de talude**, angle of slope, angle of slide.—**de tiro**, (*Gun.*) angle of elevation.—**de torção**, angle of torsion, angle of twist.—**de tração**, angle of draft.—**do ôlho**, corner of the eye.—**reentrante**, re-entrant angle.—**reto**, right angle.—**s adjacentes**, adjacent angles.—**s alternos**, alternate angles.

angúloa (*f.*) a genus (*Anguloa*) of cradle orchids.

angulômetro (*m.*) angulometer.

anguloso -sa (*adj.*) angulous, angular.

angústia (*f.*) anguish, agony, acute distress, pang, severe pain; distressing narrowness (of space); briefness (of time).

angustiado -da (*adj.*) anguished; anxious.

angustiante (*adj.*) harrowing; distressing; (*m.,f.*) one who causes anguish.

angustiar (*v.t.*) to anguish, afflict, distress, torment; (*v.r.*) to torture oneself.

angustifoliado -da, angustifólio -lia (*adj., Bot.*) angustifoliate, angustifolious, narrow-leaved.

angustioso -sa (*adj.*) anguishing; feeling or causing anguish; grievous, heart-rending.

angustirrostro -tra (*adj., Zool.*) angustirostrate.

angustissepto -ta (*adj., Bot.*) angustiseptal, -tate.

angustura (*f.*) narrow pass; angostura bark; (*Bot.*) any of various trees from which angostura bark is obtained, esp. *Cusparia angostura* and *Galipea cusparia*.

anguzada (*f., colloq.*) a pickle (predicament).

anhangá, anhanga (*m.*) a Tupian Indian word meaning evil spirit or devil—used frequently in compounding words; (*Zool.*) the variegated tinamou (*Crypturellus v. variegatus*).

anhangüera (*adj.*) fearless; (*m.*) an evil spirit.

anhapa (*f.*) = JAPA and INHAPA.

anhima (*f.*) = ANHUMA.

anhinga (*f.*) the American snakebird (*Anhinga anhinga*), c.a. CARARÁ, BIGUÁ-TINGA.

anho (*m.*) lamb. **O—de Deus**, the Lamb of God.

anhuma (*f., Zool.*) the horned screamer (*Anhima cornuta*), c.a. INHUMA, CAMETAÚ, CAMIXI, ALICORNE, ANHIMA.

anhumapoca (*f.*) = TACHÃ.

aniagem (*f.*) burlap, sacking. **saco de—**, gunny sack.

anião (*m.*) = ANIONTE.

aniba (*f., Bot.*) the cotobark (*Aniba sp.*).

anibu [ú] (*m.*) the garlic guineahen weed (*Petiveria alliacea*).

anicavara (*f.*) = TIÉ-TINGA.

anichado -da (*adj.*) in, or hidden away as in, a niche; well-placed in a good job.

anichar (*v.t.*) to place in a niche; to give shelter to.

anidremia (*f., Med.*) anhydremia.

anídrico -ca (*adj.*) anhydrous, waterless.

anidrido, anídrido (*m., Chem.*) anhydride.—**acético**, acetic anhydride.—**benzóico**, benzoic anhydride, benzoyl oxide.—**bórico**, boric a., boron oxide.—**carbônico**, carbonic anhydride, carbon dioxide, carbonic acid gas.—**crômico**, chromic anhydride, chromium trioxide, chromic acid.—**fosfórico**, phosphoric anhydride, phosphorus pentoxide.—**ftálico**, phthalic anhydride, phthalandione.—**iódico**, iodic anhydride, iodine pentoxide.—**nítrico**, nitric anhydride, nitrogen pentoxide.—**nitroso**, nitrous anhydride, nitrogen oxide.—**silícico**, silicic anhydride, silicon dioxide.—**sulfúrico**, sulfuric anhydride, sulfur trioxide.

anidrita (*f., Min.*) anhydrite, anhydrous calcium sulfate.

anidro -dra (*adj.*) anhydrous.

anidromielia (*f., Med.*) anhydromyelia.

anielar (*v.t.*) to inlay or ornament with niello.

anigozanto (*m., Bot.*) kangaroo paw (*Anigozanthos manglesi*).

aniilar [i-i] (*v.*) = ANIQUILAR.

aniju-acanga [j-ú] (*m.*) a Brazilian lizard (*Enyalius catenatus*) of the iguana family.

anil (*adj.*) anile, old-womanish; (*m.*) indigo; laundry bluing.—**-açu**, (*Bot.*) a eupatorium (*E. laeve*).—**-bravo**, the ashen tephrosia (*T. cinerea*).—**-do-mato**, an indigo (*Indigofera microcarpa*).—**-trepador**, the waterwithe treebine (*Cissus sicyoides*), c.a. TINTA-DO-GENTIO.

anilado -da (*adj.*) indigo-blue or bluish.

anilar (*v.t.*) to dye with indigo.

anileira (*f., Bot.*) the anil indigo (*Indigofera suffruticosa*).

anilha (*f.*), **-lho** (*m.*) [dim. of ANEL] any of a number of small metal rings for various purposes.

anilina (*f.*) aniline (dye).

anilismo (*m., Med.*) anilinism.

animação (*f.*) animation, elation, liveliness, "pep".

animado -da (*adj.*) active, sprightly, lively, chipper, jolly; boisterous.

animador -dora (*adj.*) animating, encouraging; (*m.,f.*) one who or that which animates, stimulates or encourages.

animadversão (*f.*) animadversion, criticism, blame, censure.

animal (*adj.*) animal; carnal; (*m.*) animal; beast; horse; fig., a coarse, brutish person; (*exclam.*) Stupid ass! Idiot!—**de carga**, pack animal.—**de corte**, beef cattle.—**de estimação**, a pet animal.—**de tiro**, draft animal.—**irracional**, dumb animal.—**racional**, man. **animais domésticos**, domestic animals, stock (on a farm). **animais daninhos**, vermin.

animalaço, -lão (*m.*) very stupid person.

animalada (*f.*) large herd of animals, esp. horses.

animálculo, animalejo [ê] (*m.*) animalcule.

animalesco -ca [ê] (*adj.*) animal, bestial.

animália (*f.*) dumb animal, brute, beast.

animalidade (*f.*) animality.

animalismo (*m.*) animalism.

animalista (*m.,f.*) painter or sculptor of animals.

animalizar (*v.t.*) to animalize (convert into animal matter by assimilation); to sensualize. [In this sense = BESTIALIZAR.]

anima-membeca (*f.*) a calathea (*C. grandifolia*) of the arrowroot family, c.a. BANANEIRINHA-DO-MATO, BANANEIRINHA-COMUM, CAITÉ-AÇU.

animante (*adj.*) animating, heartening.

animar (*v.t.*) to animate, quicken, give life to; to stimulate, pep up, enliven, activate; to encourage, inspire, hearten; (*v.r.*) to take heart; to buck-up, cheer up, perk up; to be emboldened (a, to).

animável (*adj.*) capable of being animated.

anímico -ca (*adj.*) pertaining to the soul.

animismo (*m.*) animism.

animista (*adj.; m.,f.*) animist.

ânimo (*m.*) life, vitality, animation; soul, spirit; courage, bravery; mind, intention; animus; (*exclam.*) Courage! **desafogado**, carefree spirit. **cobrar—**, to regain one's spirits; to cheer up. **dar—**, to encourage. **perder o—**, to lose heart. **Ela procurou levantar-me o—**, She tried to cheer me up.

animosidade (*f.*) animosity, animus, bitterness, rancor, persistent hostility.

animoso -sa (*adj.*) full of spirit; mettlesome; brave; spunky; cheerful.

aninado -da (*adj.*) snugly wrapped up.

aninar (*v.t.*) to bundle up, wrap up snugly.

aninga (*f.*, *Bot.*) a philodendron (*P. speciosum*) c.a. ANINGAÍBA.—-**da-água**, a caladium (*C. sororium*).—-**de-espinho**,—-**do-pará**, = ANINGAÚBA.—-**perê** = ANINGAÚBA.

aningaçu [ú] (*f.*) a plant of the arum family (*Montrichardia linifera*) c.a. LINGA.

aningafba (*f.*) = ANINGA.

aningal (*m.*) a place abounding in plants of the arum family.

aningapara (*f.*) the variable tuftroot (*Dieffenbachia picta*); the poisonous seguin tuftroot (*D. seguine*) c.a. CANA-DE-IMBÊ, CANA-MARONA.

aningaúba, -gaúva (*f.*) a plant of the arum family (*Montrichardia arborescens*), c.a. ANINGA-DE-ESPINHO, ANINGA-DO-PARÁ, ANINGA-PERÊ, BANANA-DE-MACACO, IMBÊ-DA-PRAIA, IMBERANA.

aninhar (*v.t.*) to put in a nest; to shelter, protect; (*v.r.*) to nestle; to snuggle up (as in a bed or blanket), cuddle up.

aninheiro (*m.*) nest egg.

anionte (*m.*, *Physical Chem.*) anion. Vars. ANIÃO, ANION.

aniquilação (*f.*) annihilation.

aniquilacionismo (*m.*, *Theol.*) annihilationism.

aniquilado -da (*adj.*) annihilated; ruined; defeated, crushed.—**pelo mêdo**, prostrated by fear.

aniquilador -dora (*adj.*) annihilating, destroying (*m.,f.*) annihilator, destroyer.

aniquilamento (*m.*) annihilation, extermination, obliteration.

aniquilar (*v.t.*) to annihilate, destroy, extinguish; to blot out, obliterate.

aniquilável (*adj.*) capable of being annihilated.

aniridia (*f.*) congenital absence or defect of the iris.

anis [í] (*m.*, *Bot.*) anise (*Pimpinella anisum*); aniseed; anise cordial.—-**doce**, common fennel (*Foeniculum vulgare*).—-**estrelado**, the Japanese star anise tree (*Ilicium anisatum*) an evergreen with poisonous fruit, c.a. BADIANA.

anisado -da (*adj.*) anisated.

anisar (*v.t.*) to anisate.

aniseta [ê] (*f.*) anisette (liqueur).

anísico -ca (*adj.*) anisic.

anisidina (*f.*, *Chem.*) anisidin(e).

anisocárpico -ca (*adj.*, *Bot.*) anisocarpic, -pous.

anisocitose (*f.*, *Med.*) anisocytosis.

anisocoria (*f.*, *Med.*) anisocoria.

anisocromático -ca (*adj.*) anisochromatic.

anisocromia (*f.*, *Med.*) anisochromia.

anisodáctilo -la (*adj.*) anisodactylous.

anisófilo -la (*adj.*, *Bot.*) anisophyllous.

anisogamia (*f.*, *Biol.*) anisogamia.

anisógino -na (*adj.*, *Bot.*) anisogynous.

anisoína (*f.*, *Chem.*) anisoin.

anisol (*m.*, *Chem.*) anisol(e).

anisômero -ra (*adj.*, *Bot.*) anisomerous.

anisométrico -ca (*adj.*) anisometric.

anisometropia (*f.*) anisometropia.

anisomiário (*m.*) anisomyarian (a mollusk).

anisopétalo -la (*adj.*, *Bot.*) anisopetalous.

anisospório (*m.*, *Bot.*) anisospore.

anisostêmone (*adj.*, *Bot.*) anisostemonous.

anisotênico -ca (*adj.*) anisothenic.

anisóstico (*m.*) = BIGNÔNIA.

anisotropia (*f.*) anisotropy.

anisotrópico -ca (*adj.*; *Physics*) anisotropic.

anisótropo (*m.*, *Physics*) anisotrope.

anistia (*f.*) amnesty, general pardon.

anistiar (*v.t.*) to grant amnesty to, pardon.

Anita (*f.*) Anita.

aniversàriamente (*adv.*) anniversarily.

aniversariante (*adj.*; *m.,f.*) (one) having a birthday.

aniversariar (*v.i.*) to have a birthday.

aniversário -ria (*adj.*) anniversary; (*m.*) anniversary, birthday.—**de casamento**, wedding anniversary.—**natalício**, birthday.

anixo (*m.*) an S hook.

anjinho (*m.*) cherub; child; child dressed as a little angel

(in a religious procession); a dead baby; a petral, c.a. ALMA-NEGRA.

anjo (*m.*) angel; a cherubic child or adult.—**da guarda**, guardian angel.—**do-mar** or—-**viola**, an angeifish, c.a. CAÇÃO-ANJO. **salto de—**, swan dive.

ankerite (*f.*, *Min.*) ankerite.

ano (*m.*) year; (*pl.*) age; birthday.—**a—**, year by year. —**agrícola**, the farming months of the year; that is, from seed to harvest.—**astronômico**, astronomical year.—**bissexto**, bissextile (leap) year.—**bom**, New Year [= ANO NOVO]; prosperous year; a year of good rainfall in the drouth areas of northern Brazil.—**civil**, calendar year.—**commercial**, twelve months of 30 days each; 360 days.—**comum**, common year; 365 days.—**corrente**, the current year.—**cristão**, Christian year, church year; also, holy year, jubilee year. [In the latter sense = ANO SANTO].—**de graça**, year of grace.—**de jubileu**, jubilee year, holy year [= ANO SANTO].—**eclesiástico**, ecclesiastical year, Christian year.—**econômico**, fiscal year.—**embolísmico**, embolismic year (13 lunar months, or 384 days).—**emergente**, any up-coming twelve-month period.—**escolar**, school year.—**fiscal**, fiscal year.—**intercalar**, bissextile year.—**judicial**, the period of the year when the courts are in session.—**letivo**, school year. —**lunar**, lunar year.—**luz**, light-year.—**Novo**, New Year; New Year's Day.—**que vem**, next year.—**santo**, holy year, jubilee year.—**secular**, the last year of a century.—**sideral**, sidereal year, astral year.—**sim,—não**, every other year.—**solar**, solar year, tropical year. —**trás—**, year after year.—**trópico**, tropical year, solar year.—**vem,—vai**, year after year; year in, year out.—**s atrás**, years ago.—**s da era de** (or **do nascimento de**) **Cristo**, years of the Christian era.—**s maduros**, years of maturity. **antes dum—**, inside of a year. **ao—**, per year. **aos**, or **com, (cinco)—s (de idade)**, when I (you, he, she) was (five). **conta (trinta)—s**, he (she) is (thirty). **daqui a (dois)—s**, (two) years hence. **de—em—**, from year to year. **de (dois) em (dois)—s**, every (two) years. **de (vinte)—s**, (twenty) years old. **dentro de (dez)—s**, within (ten) years. **Dia de—Bom**, New Year's Day. **durante todo o—**, all during the year; the year 'round; all year long. **entra—, sai—**, year in, year out; year after year. **entrado em—s**, getting on in years. **faz um—, a year ago. **fazer—s**, to have a birthday. **Feliz—Novo**, Happy New Year. **há de haver um—**, it must be about a year ago. **há um—**, a year ago. **havia um—**, a year earlier, a year prior. **no—atrasado**, year before last. **no—passado**, last year. **no—próximo** (or—**que vem**), next year; during the coming year. **no—seguinte**, in the following year. **o pêso dos—s**, the burden of the years; old age. **por—**, yearly; per annum. **quadra do—**, season of the year. **Quando você faz—s?** When is your birthday? **Quantos —s você tem?** How old are you? **todo—**, every year. **todo o—**, or **o—todo**, the whole year. **todos os—s**, every year, yearly. **um—antes**, a year before.

anococcígeo -gea (*adj.*) anococcygeal.

anodal (*adj.*, *Elec.*) anodic.

anodinia (*f.*, *Med.*) anodynia.

anódino -na (*adj.*) anodyne; insignificant, unimportant (*m.*) anodyne.

ânodo, anódio (*m.*, *Elec.*) anode.

anodontes (*m.pl.*) a large genus (*Anodanta*) of freshwater mussels.

anodontia (*f.*) anodontia, absence of the teeth.

anófele (*m.*) the genus (*Anopheles*) of malaria-carrying mosquitoes.

anoftalmia (*f.*, *Med.*) anophthalmia.

anoitar (*v.*) = ANOITECER, ENOITAR.

anoitecer, anoutecer (*v.i.*) to grow dark; to come night. **ao—**, at nightfall.

anojado -da (*adj.*) nauseated; disgusted; in mourning.

anojador -dora (*adj.*) nauseating.

anojamento (*m.*) nausea; mourning; grief.

anojar (*v.t.*) to nauseate, disgust; to displease, annoy; (*v.r.*) to become sick of; to go into mourning.

anôjo (*m.*) nausea; disgust; ennui.

anólis (*m.*) a lizard of the genus *Anolis*, popularly called chameleon.

anólito (*m.*) anolyte.

anomalia (*f.*) anomaly, irregularity.—**média**, (*Astron.*) mean anomaly.—**verdadeira**, true anomaly.

anomalípede (*adj.*, *Zool.*) anomaliped, syndactylous.

anomalístico -ca (*adj.*) anomalistic.

anômalo –la (adj.) anomalous, irregular, abnormal, anomalistic.

anomateca (f., Bot.) red false freesia (Lapeirousia cruenta).

anomite (f., Min.) anomite.

anomocarpo –pa (adj., Bot.) anomocarpous.

anona (f.) the sugar apple or sweetsop (Annona squamosa), better known as ATEIRA; also its fruit, better known as ATA, FRUTA-DO-CONDE, PINHA.—-do-chile, the cherimoya (A. cherimola), c.a. QUERIMÓLIA.

anonáceo –cea (adj., Bot.) annonaceous; (f.pl.) the Annonaceae (custard apple family).

anonimato (m.) anonymity.

anonímia (f.) anonymousness.

anônimo –ma (adj.) anonymous, nameless; (m.,f.) one who retains anonymity. sociedade—, a corporation (stock company).

anopia (f., Med.) anopia; defective vision.

anopistógrafo –fa (adj.) anopistographic.

anoplanta (f., Bot.) the genus (Thalesia) which includes the ghost pipe (T. uniflora).

anopluros (m.pl.) the order (Anoplura) which comprises the true lice.

anopsia (f., Med.) anopsia, blindness.

anorco –ca (adj., Med.) anorchus.

anordestar (v.t.) to steer northeast.

anorexia [ks] (f., Med.) anorexia.

anorganologia (f.) abiology.

anormal (adj.) abnormal, anomalous, irregular; mentally defective; (m.,f.) abnormal person.

anormalidade (f.) abnormality.

anorquia (f., Med.) anorchia, anorchism.

anortear (v.t.) to steer north; fig., to guide, govern, direct (the destiny of anything).

anórtico –ca (adj., Min.) anorthic, triclinic.

anortita (f., Min.) anorthite.

anortoclásio (m., Min.) anorthoclase.

anortografia (f., Med.) anorthography, motor agraphia.

anortoscópio (m.) anorthoscope.

anortosito (m., Petrog.) anorthosite.

anoscópio (m., Med.) anoscope.

anosfresia (f., Med.) anosphresia, anosmia.

anosidade (f.) state of old age.

anosmático –ca (adj.) anosmatic.

anosmia (f., Med.) anosmia.

anoso –sa (adj.) getting on in years, old.

anotação (f.) annotation, note, comment.

anotado –da (adj.) annotated; registered.

anotador –dora (adj.) annotating; (m.,f.) annotator.

anotar (v.t.) to annotate, comment on, make notes on; to mark (write) down.

anovear (v.t.) to multiply by nine; to charge an excessively high price for something.

anovelar (v.) = ENOVELAR.

anoxibiose [ks] (f., Physiol.) anoxybiosis, anaerobiosis.

anoxiemia, anoxemia [ks] (f., Med.) anoxemia.

anquilosar (v.) & derivs. = ANCILOSAR & derivs.

anquinhas (f.pl.) pannier (of a skirt).

ansarinha-malhada (f.) = CICUTA-DA-EUROPA.

anseio (m.) longing, craving, yearning; anxiety.

ansélia (f.) a genus (Ansellia) of orchids.

ânser (m.) any goose of the genus Anser.

anseriformes (m.pl.) the Anseriformes (ducks, geese, swans, mergansers and the screamers).

anseríneos (m.pl.) the Anserinae (geese).

anserino –na (adj.) anserine, gooselike. pele—, gooseflesh.

ânsia (f.) anguish, agony, throes; anxiety, uneasiness; burning desire; (pl.) qualms of nausea.

ansiado –da (adj.) yearned for; qualmish.

ansiar [16] (v.t.) to crave; to yearn, long, pine (por, for); to hanker after.

ansiedade (f.) anxiety, worry, apprehension; anguish, longing, craving; eagerness.

ansiforme (adj.) shaped like the handle of a basket or of a jug.

ansioso –sa (adj.) anxious, eager (por, for), desirous (por, of); uneasy.

anspeçada (m.) a military rank corresponding to private first-class.

anta (f.) prehistoric stone monument, dolmen; leather made from tapir hide; (Arch.) anta; (Zool.) the Brazilian tapir (Tapirus terrestris, syn. Americanus).—-xuré, the Andean tapir (T. roulini or T. pinchaque) c.a. ACURÉ.

côr de—, buff color.

antafrodisíaco –ca (adj.) = ANTIAFRODISÍACO.

antagônico –ca (adj.) antagonistic, opposing, adverse, opposite, contrary.

antagonismo (m.) antagonism, opposition, clashing, incompatability.

antagonista (adj.) antagonistic; (m.,f.) antagonist, opponent, adversary, competitor.

antanho (adv.) last year; in days of yore. tempos de—, bygone days; the good old days.

antarquismo (m.) antarchism.

antarquista (adj.) antarchistic; (m.,f.) antarchist.

antártico –ca (adj.) antarctic.

ante (prep.) before, in the presence of; in view of; in the face of; ere.

anteaurora (f.) antedawn.

anteavante (m.) foredeck.

anteboca [ô] (f.) fore part of the mouth.

antebraço (m., Anat.) antebrachium, forearm.

antebraquial (adj.) antebrachial.

antecâmara (f.) antechamber, antecabinet, anteroom, vestibule, waiting room.

antecedência (f.) antecedence, precedence. com—, beforehand, in advance. com duas semanas de—, two weeks ahead of time.

antecedente (adj.) antecedent, preceding; precedent, previous, prior; (m., Gram.) a word, phrase or clause referred to by a pronoun; (Math.) the first term of a ratio; (pl.) antecedents.

anteceder (v.t.) to antecede, precede; to be (go, come) before or in front of; to be earlier than.

antecessor (m.) antecessor, predecessor; (pl.) ancestors [= ANTEPASSADOS].

antecipação (f.) anticipation, expectation; forestalling. com três mezes de—, three months ahead of time.

antecipado –da (adj.) beforehand, in advance.

antecipar (v.t.) to anticipate; to experience beforehand; to do or use in advance; to advance, move up (a date); to pay in advance; to precipitate, accelerate; to expect, foresee; to forestall; (v.i.) to act precipitately; to speak out of turn; (v.r.) to be in advance, ahead of time.—-se a, to go ahead of, precede another; to forestall.

antecoro [cô] (m., Arch.) antechoir.

antedata (f.) antedate.

antedatar (v.t.) to antedate.

antediluviano –na (adj.) antediluvian; very old.

antedito –ta (p.p. of ANTEDIZER) foretold.

antedizer (v.t.) to foretell.

antedorsal (adj.) antedorsal.

antefirma (f.) concluding words of esteem, affection, courtesy, etc., in a letter, just before the signature.

antefixas ks] (f.pl., Arch.) antefix.

anteflexão [ks] (f., Med.) anteflexion.

antéfora (f.) a genus (Antephora) of panicum grasses.

antegozar, –gostar (v.t.) to anticipate the pleasures of; foretaste.

antegôzo, –gôsto (m.) foretaste, anticipation.

anteguarda (f.) = VANGUARDA.

antehipófise (f., Anat.) antehypophysis.

antehistórico –ca (adj.) antehistoric, prehistoric.

anteiro (m.) a dog trained to hunt ANTAS (tapirs).

antela (f., Bot.) panicle, compound raceme.

antelação (f.) preference; priority.

antélice (f., Anat.) antihelix.

antélio (m., Meteorol.) anthelion, antisun.

antelmíntico –ca (adj.; m., Med.) anthelmintic (remedy).

antelo (m., Bot.) anthela, the panicle of certain rushes, esp. of the genus Juncus.

antelóquio (m.) prologue; preface.

antemanhã (adv., f.) pre-dawn.

antemão (adv.) de—, previously, beforehand, in advance.

antemeridiano –na (adj.) antemeridian.

antemina (f., Chem.) anthemene.

ântemis (f., Bot.) camomile (Anthemis).

antemostrar-se (v.r.) to show (self) prematurely.

antemover (v.t.) to move (as a chess piece) too soon.

antemurar (v.t.) to provide with an outer wall; to defend, protect.

antemuro (m.) outside wall; rampart.

antena (f., Zool., Radio) antenna; (Naut.) spar, yard.

antenal (adj.) antennal; (m., Zool.) the wandering albatross (Diomedea exulans).

antenária (f., Bot.) the genus of pussytoes or cat's-foot (Antennaria).

antenário (m.) a frogfish (*Antennarius scaber*) c.a. PEIXE-SAPO, GUAPERVA.

antenífero –ra (*adj., Zool.*) antenniferous.

anteniforme (*adj., Zool.*) antenniform.

antenome (m.) first or given name, as MAURÍCIO; also, a title of rank, nobility, etc., as PRÍNCIPE, DOUTOR, TENENTE, etc.

antênula (f., *Zool.*) antennule.

antenupcial (*adj.*) antenuptial.

anteocupar (v.) = PREOCUPAR.

anteolhos [eó] (*m.pl.*) horse blinders; eyeshade.

anteontem (*adv.*) day before yesterday.

antepagar (v.t.) to pay ahead of time.

antepara (f.) = ANTEPARO.

anteparar (v.t.) to place something in front of, as a shield or protection (**contra**, against); to bring (a horse, train, automobile, etc.) to a sudden stop.

anteparo (m.) anything in the nature of a screen or shield. [This may range from a bulkhead to a fan before a lady's eyes]; (*Mach.*) baffle plate.—**de chicana,** baffle wall (as of a furnace).

anteparto (m.) ante partum.

antepassado –da (*adj.*) foregone, bygone; former, previous; (*m.pl.*) ancestors, forefathers.

antepassar (v.t.) to precede.

antepasto (m.) hors d'oeuvres, relish, appetizer.

antepenúltimo –ma (*adj.*) antepenult.

antepor [63] (v.t.) to place or put before or ahead of; to prefer.

anteporta (f.) outer door; screen.

anteposição (f.) anteposition, a placing before.

anteprojeto (m.) preliminary sketch or plan; draft.

antepróstata (f., *Anat.*) anteprostate.

antera (f., *Bot.*) anther.

anteral (*adj.*) antheral.

antérico (m.) a large genus (*Anthericum*) of plants of the lily family.

anterídio (m., *Bot.*) antheridium.

anterífero –ra (*adj., Bot.*) antheriferous.

anteriforme (*adj., Bot.*) antheriform.

anterior [ô] (*adj.*) anterior, prior, previous; fore, front, in front.

anterioridade (f.) anteriorness.

anteriormente (*adv.*) hitherto, previously.

anterodorsal (*adj., Anat.*) anterodorsal.

ântero-exterior (*adj., Anat.*) anteroexternal.

ântero-inferior (*adj., Anat.*) anteroinferior.

ântero-interior, –**interno** (*adj., Anat.*) anterointerior, anterointernal.

anterolateral (*adj., Anat.*) anterolateral.

anteroposterior (*adj., Anat.*) anteroposterior.

ante-rosto (m.) frontispiece of a book.

ântero-superior (*adj., Anat.*) anterosuperior.

anterozóide (m., *Bot.*) spermatozoid.

antes (*adv.*) before, formerly, previously; aforetime; rather, preferably; (*adj.*) before.—**daquela época,** before that time, before then.—**de,** before, prior to; sooner, rather than. [antes de+an infinitive = before+a present participle, as: **antes de partir,** before leaving].—**de então,** before that time.—**de mais nada,** before anything else; first of all.—**de tempo,** ahead of time.—**de tudo,** first of all; before everything; before all else; above all.—**-de-ontem,** = ANTEONTEM.—**dum ano,** inside of a year, before the year is or was up.—**fôsse,** would that he (she, it) were!—**pelo contrário,** rather the contrary.—(**de) que,** before, ahead of.—**que cases, vê o que fazes,** Look before you leap.—**só do que mal acompanhado,** Better alone than in bad company.—**tarde do que nunca,** Better late than never. **ou—,** or rather. **quanto—,** as soon as possible, right away, at once, immediately. **Quisera—isto do que aquilo,** I would rather this than that.

ante-sala (f.) = ANTECÂMARA.

ante-sazão (*adv.*) out of season, prematurely.

antese (f.) anthesis, full bloom.

ante-sala (f.) anteroom, waiting room.

antestatura (f.) an improvised entrenchment or work of palisades, sacks of earth, etc.

antetempo (*adv.*) ahead of time.

antever [81] (v.t.) to foresee.

anteversão (f., *Med.*) anteversion.

anteverter (v.t.) to precede; to prevent; (*Med.*) to antevert.

antevéspera (f.) the day before the eve; (*pl.*) the period just preceding any event.

antevidência (f.) foresight.

antevidente (*adj.*) foreseeing.

antevieiro –ra (*adj., colloq.*) meddling, nosey.

antevisão (f.) foresight, foreseeing.

antevisto –ta (*adj.*) foreseen.

antevocálico –ca (*adj.; Phonet.*) antevocalic.

antiabrasivo –va (*adj.*) antiabrasion.

antiabrina (f., *Immunol.*) antiabrin.

antiácido –da (*adj.; m., Chem., Med.*) antacid.

antiaéreo –rea (*adj.*) anti-aircraft.

antiafrodisíaco –ca (*adj., m.*) antiaphrodisiac.

antiaglutinante (*adj.*) antiagglutinating.

antiaglutinina (f.) antiagglutinin.

antialcoólico –ca (*adj.*) antialcoholic.

antialcoolismo (m.) antialcoholism.

antialcoolista (*m.,f.*) antialcoholist.

antialexina [ks] (f.) antialexin.

antiamarílico –ca (*adj.*) preventive of yellow fever.

antianafilaxia [ks] (f., *Immunol.*) antianaphylaxis.

antiar (f.) the upas tree (*Antiaris toxicaria*) of the mulberry family, c.a. ÁRVORE-VENENO, ÁRVORE-DA-MORTE, UPAS-ANTIAR; also, a poisonous gum resin and arrow poison prepared from its sap. Cf. UPAS.

antiarina (f., *Chem.*) antiarin.

antiaristocrata (*m.,f.*) antiaristocrat.

antiartrítico –ca (*adj., Med.*) antiarthritic.

antiasmático –ca (*adj., Med.*) antiasthmatic.

antibilioso –sa (*adj., Med.*) antibilious.

antibiose (f., *Biol.*) antibiosis.

antibiótico –ca (*adj.; m., Biol.*) antibiotic.

antiblenorrágico –ca (*adj., Med.*) antiblennorrhagic.

antibotrópico –ca (*adj.*) of an antivenum serum, efficacious against bites of the JARARACA, the fer-de-lance, and other venomous serpents of the Bothrops family. Cf. ANTICROTÁLICO.

antibrasileiro –ra (*adj.*) anti-Brazilian.

antibritânico –ca (*adj.*) anti-British.

antibrômico –ca (*adj.*) antibromic, deodorant.

anticanceroso –sa (*adj.*) anticancer.

anticárdio (m., *Anat.*) anticardium, pit of the stomach.

anticatalisador (m., *Physical Chem.*) anticatalyst.

anticatalítico (m., *Physical Chem.*) anticatalyst.

anticatarral (*adj.; m., Med.*) anticatarrhal.

anticatódio, –**cátodo** (m., *Physical Chem.*) anti-cathode.

anticatólico –ca (*adj.*) anti-Catholic.

anticefalálgico –ca (*adj.*) anticephalalgic.

anticéptico –ca (*adj.*) antiskeptical.

anticiclone (m., *Meteorol.*) anticyclone.

anticientífico –ca (*adj.*) unscientific.

anticitolisina (f., *Biochem.*) anticytolysin.

anticívico –ca (*adj.*) anticivic.

anticivismo (m.) anticivism.

anticlerical (*adj.; m.,f.*) anticlerical (person).

anticlericalismo (m.) anticlericalism.

anticlímax [ks] (m.) anticlimax.

anticlinal (f., *Geol.*) anticline, (*adj.,*) anticlinal.

anticloro (m., *Chem.*) antichlor.

anticoagulante (*adj.; m.*) anticoagulant.

anticoagulina (f., *Biochem.*) anticoagulin.

anticolagogo –ga (*adj.; m., Med.*) antichologogue.

anticoncepcional (*adj.*) contraceptive.

anticongelante (*adj.; m.*) antifreeze (mixture).

anticonstitucional (*adj.*) anticonstitutional.

anticonstitucionalismo (m.) anticonstitutionalism.

anticonstitucionalissimamente (*adv.*) most anticonstitutionally. [Said to be the longest word in the Portuguese language.]

anticontagionista (*m.,f.*) anticontagionist.

anticontagioso –sa (*adj.*) anticontagious.

anticonvulsivo –va (*adj.; m., Med.*) anticonvulsive.

anticorpo (m., *Chem., Immunol.*) antibody, antitoxin.

anticorrosivo –va (*adj.; m.*) anticorrosive (agent).

anticosmético –ca (*adj.*) anticosmetic.

anticosta (f.) an opposite shore.

anticrepúsculo (m.) anticrepuscule.

anticrese (f., *Law*) antichresis.

anticrético –ca (*adj.*) antichretic.

anticristão –tã [-tãos, -tãs] (*adj.; m.,f.*) anti-Christian.

anticristianismo (m.) anti-Christianism.

anticristo (m.) Antichrist.

anticrítica (f.) anticritique.

anticrítico –ca (*adj.*) anticritic.

anticrotálico –ca (adj.) of an antivenum serum, effective against rattlesnake bites. Cf. ANTIBOTRÓPICO.
antictérico –ca (adj.; Med.) anti-icteric.
antidáctilo (m.) antidactyl, anapest.
antideflagrante (adj.) explosion-proof; flame-proof.
antidemocrata (m.,f.) antidemocrat.
antidemocrático –ca (adj.) antidemocratic(al).
antiderrapante (adj.) antiskid.
antidesma (f.) a genus (Antidesma) of China laurels.
antidetonante (adj.) of gasoline, antiknock.
antidiabético –ca (adj.; m., Med.) antidiabetic.
antidiftérico –ca (adj.; m., Med.) antidiphtheric.
antidinástico –ca (adj.) antidynastic.
antidisentérico –ca (adj.; m., Med.) antidysenteric.
antidivino –na (adj.) antidivine.
antidivorcista (adj.) antidivorce; (m.,f.) one who opposes divorce.
antidogmático –ca (adj.) antidogmatic.
antidotal (adj.) antidotal.
antidotar (v.t.) to antidote.
antidotário (m.) a book of antidotes.
antídoto (m.) antidote.
antidrômico –ca (adj.; Physiol.) antidromic.
antídromo (m., Bot.) antidromy.
antiemético –ca (adj.; m., Med.) antiemetic.
antiepiléptico –ca (adj.; m., Med.) antiepileptic.
antiescravista (adj.; m.,f.) (one) opposed to slavery.
antiescriturário –ria (adj.) anti-Scriptural.
antiestafilocócico –ca (adj., Med.) antistaphylococcic.
antiestatismo (m.) antistatism.
antiestético –ca (adj.) antiaesthetic.
antievangélico –ca (adj.) antievangelic(al).
antievolucionista (adj.; m.,f.) antievolutionist.
antifebril (adj., Med.) antifebril.
antifeminismo (m.) antifeminism.
antifeminista (adj.; m.,f.) antifeminist.
antifermentescível (adj.) antifermentative.
antifermento (m.) antiferment.
antiferruginoso –sa (adj.) anti-rust.
antifilosófico –ca (adj.) antiphilosophic(al).
antifísico –ca (adj.) antiphysical.
antiflatulento –ta (adj., Med.) antiflatulent.
antiflogístico –ca (adj.; m., Med.) antiphlogistic.
antífona (f.) antiphon.
antifonal (adj.) antiphonal.
antifonia (f.) antiphony.
antifônico –ca (adj.) antiphonic.
antifônio (m.) ear plug.
antiformoso –sa (adj.) ugly.
antifrancês –cesa [ê] (adj.) anti-French.
antífrase (f., Rhet.) antiphrasis.
antifricção (f.) antifriction metal. metal de—, Babbit metal.
antigalactico –ca (adj.) antigalactic.
antigalha (f.) antique, old thing; curio.
antigamente (adv.) formerly; in former days; in days of old; aforetime.
antigênico –ca (adj., Immunol.) antigenic.
antigênio, antígeno (m., Immunol.) antigen.
antigermânico –ca (adj.) anti-German.
antigo –ga (adj.) ancient, old; antique, antiquated, old-time, old fashioned; former, pre-existing; (m.pl.) the ancients.—Testamento, Old Testament. à antiga, in the olden manner. estilo—, old-fashioned style. História Antiga, Ancient History.
antigorita (f., Min.) antigorite.
antigotoso –sa (adj., Med.) antipodagric.
antigovernamental (adj.) antigovernment.
antigramatical (adj.) antigrammatical.
antiguado –da (adj.) = ANTIQUADO.
antigualha (f.) = ANTIGALHA.
antiguidade, –güidade (f.) antiquity; ancient or remote times, days of yore; ancientness; seniority (in job-rating); (pl.) ancients (people); antiques (relics); antiquities. por ordem de—, in order of seniority.
antiguíssimo –ma (absol. superl. of ANTIGO) most ancient.
antihalo (m., Photog.) antihalation.
anti-helmíntico –ca (adj., Med.) anthelmintic.
anti-hemorrágico –ca (adj., Med.) antihemorrhagic.
anti-hemorroidal (adj., Med.) antihemorrhoidal.
anti-hidrofóbico –ca (adj., Med.) antihydrophobic, antilyssic.
anti-higiênico –ca (adj.) antihygienic; unsanitary.
anti-hipocondríaco –ca (adj.) antihypochondriac.

anti-histérico –ca (adj.) antihysteric.
anti-humano –na (adj.) antihuman [= DESHUMANO].
antiictérico –ca [i-i] (adj., Med.) anti-icteric.
antiimigrantista [i-i] (adj.) anti-immigrationist.
antiinfalibilista [i-i] (m.,f.) anti-infallibilist.
antilatino –na (adj.) anti-Latin.
antilêmico –ca (adj., Med.) antiloimic.
antilepse (f., Med.) antilepsis.
antiléptico –ca (adj.) antileptic.
antiletárgico –ca (adj.) antilethargic.
antilhano –na, –lhense, (adj.; m.,f.) Antillean; West Indian.
Antilhas (f.pl.) Antilles.
antiliberal (adj.) antiliberal.
antilisina (f., Biochem.) antilysin.
antilíssico –ca (adj., Biochem.) antilyssic, preventive of hydrophobia.
antilítico –ca (adj.) antilytic; (Med.) antilithic.
antilogaritmo (m., Math.) antilogarithm.
antilogia (f.) antilogy.
antilógico –ca (adj.) antilogical.
antílogo –ga (adj., Physics) pôlo—. antilogous pole.
antilombrigóide (adj.) anthelmintic, vermifuge.
antílope (m.) antelope.
antiluético –ca (adj., Med.) antiluetic.
antimalárico –ca (adj.) antimalarial.
antimedical (adj.) antimedical.
antimefítico –ca (adj.) antimephitic.
antimelancólico –ca (adj.) antimelancholic.
antimeningocócico –ca (adj., Med.) antimeningococcic.
antímero (m., Zool.) antimere.
antimetábole, antimetalepse (f., Rhet.) antimetabole.
antimetátese (f., Rhet.) antimetathesis.
antimetropia (f.) antimetropy.
antimiasmático –ca (adj.) antimiasmatic.
antimilitar (adj.) antimilitary.
antimilitarismo (m.) antimilitarism.
antimilitarista (adj.) antimilitarist.
antiministerial (adj.) antiministerial.
antimonárquico –ca (adj.) antimonarchic(al).
antimonarquista (adj.; m.,f.) antimonarchist.
antimoniado –da (adj.) antimoniated.
antimonial (adj.; m.) antimonial.
antimoniato (m., Chem.) antimonate.
antimônico –ca (adj.; Chem.) antimonic.
antimonieto (m., Chem.) antimonide.
antimonífero –ra (adj.) antimoniferous.
antimonilo (m., Chem.) antimonyl.
antimônio (m., Chem.) antimony.—diaforético, diaphoretic antimony, potassium antimonate.—tartarizado, tartrated antimony, antimony potassium tartrate, potassium antimonyl tartrate, tartar emetic.
antimonioso –sa (adj.; Chem.) antimonious.
antimonita (f., Chem.) antimonite; (Min.) stibnite.
antimoral (adj.) antimoral.
antimoralismo (m.) antimoralism.
antinacional (adj.) antinational.
antinarcótico –ca (adj.) antinarcotic.
antinatural (adj.) unnatural.
antinefrítico –ca (adj.; Med.) antinephritic.
antineurálgico –ca, antinevrálgico –ca (adj.; Med.) antineuralgic.
antinipônico –ca (adj.) anti-Japanese.
antino –na (adj.) anthine.
antinodo (m., Physics) antinode.
antinódoa (f.) spot remover.
antinomia (f.) antinomy.
antinômico –ca (adj.) antinomic(al).
antinomismo (m.) antinomianism.
antinomista (m.,f.) antinomian.
antinupcial (adj.) opposed to marriage.
antiodontálgico –ca (adj.; m., Med.) antiodontalgic.
antiofídico –ca (adj.) against snake bites.
antíopa (f.) a butterfly of the genus Vanessa.
Antioquia (f.) Antioch.
antioxidante [ks] (adj.) antirust; (m.) rust preventive.
antipalustre (adj.) antimalarial.
antipapa (m.) antipope.
antipapismo (m.) antipapism.
antipapista (m.,f.) antipapist.
antiparelelo –la (adj., Geom.) antiparallel (line).
antiparalítico –ca (adj.) antiparalytic(al).
antiparlamentar (adj.) antiparliament(al), -tary.
antipatários (m.pl., Zool.) the Antipatharia (black corals).

antipatia (*f.*) antipathy, repugnance, aversion; instinctive dislike. [Anton. SIMPATIA].
antipático –ca (*adj.*) antipathetic; obnoxious; uncongenial. [Anton. SIMPÁTICO].
antipatizar (*v.t.*) to feel antipathy for, dislike instinctively.
antipatriótico –ca (*adj.; m.,f.*) unpatriotic (person).
antipatriotismo (*m.*) unpatriotism.
antipelicular (*adj., Med.*) anti-dandruff.
antipepsina (*f., Biochem.*) antipepsin.
antipeptona (*f., Biochem.*) antipeptone.
antiperiódico –ca (*adj.; m., Med.*) (a remedy) effective against intermittent fevers.
antiperistáltico –ca (*adj., Med.*) antiperistaltic.
antipestilencial (*adj.*) antibubonic; antimephitic.
antipestoso –sa (*adj.; m., Med.*) antibubonic (agent).
antipíico –ca [í-i] (*adj., Med.*) antipyic.
antipirético –ca (*adj.; m., Med.*) antipyretic, febrifuge.
antipirina (*f.*) Antipyrine (an analgesic drug).
antipirótico –ca (*adj.*) antipyrotic.
antiplástico –ca (*adj.*) that diminishes plasticity; (*m.*) antiplastic agent.
antipleurítico –ca (*adj., Med.*) antipleuritic.
antipneumocócico –ca (*adj., Med.*) antipneumococcic.
antípoda (*adj.*) antipodal, diametrically opposite; (*m.*) antipode; (*pl.*) persons living on opposite sides of the globe.
antipodal (*adj.*) antipodal.
antipódico –ca (*adj.*) antipodean, antipodal.
antipoético –ca (*adj.*) antipoetic.
antipolítico –ca (*adj.*) antipolitical,
antipopular (*adj.*) antipopular.
antipráctico –ca (*adj.*) impractical.
antiproibicionista [o-i] (*adj.*) antiprohibitionist.
antiproibitivo –va [o-i] (*adj.*) antiprohibition.
antiprotestante (*m.,f.*) anti-Protestant.
antipsórico –ca (*adj., Med.*) antipsoric.
antiptose (*f., Gram.*) antiptosis.
antipuritano –na (*adj.*) antipuritan.
antipútrido –da (*adj.*) antiputrid.
antiquado –da (*adj.*) antiquated, archaic, obsolete; superannuated, out-of-date, old-fashioned.
antiqualha (*f.*) = ANTIGALHA.
antiquar [28] (*v.t.*) to render antique; (*v.r.*) to become antiquated.
antiquário –ria (*adj.*) antiquated; (*m.,f.*) antiquary.
antiqüíssimo –ma (*absol. superl. of* ANTIGO) most ancient.
anti-rábico –ca (*adj.*) antirabies, antihydrophobic.
anti-racional (*adj.*) antirational.
anti-racionalista (*adj.*) antirationalistic.
anti-raquítico –ca (*adj., Med.*) antirachitic, anti-rickets.
anti-real (*adj.*) unreal.
anti-realismo (*m.*) antirealism.
anti-realista (*adj.*) antirealistic.
anti-reformista (*adj.*) antireformist.
anti-religioso –sa (*adj.; m.,f.*) antireligious (person).
anti-republicano –na (*adj.*) antirepublican.
anti-reumático –ca (*adj., Med.*) antirheumatic.
anti-revisionista (*adj.*) antirevisionist.
anti-revolucionário –ria (*adj.*) antirevolutionary.
antirrináceas (*f.pl.*) = ESCROFULARIÁCEAS.
antirrino (*m.*) the genus (*Antirrhinum*) of snapdragons; the common snapdragon (*A. majus*) is called ERVA-BEZERRA, BÔCA-DE-DRAGÃO, BÔCA-DE-LEÃO.
antiscorbútico –ca (*adj., Med.*) antiscorbutic.
antiscrofuloso –sa (*adj., Med.*) antiscrofulous.
anti-semita (*adj.*) anti-Semitic; (*m.,f.*) anti-Semite.
anti-semítico –ca (*adj.*) anti-Semitic.
anti-semitismo (*m.*) anti-Semitism.
anti-sifilítico –ca (*adj., Med.*) antisyphilitic (remedy).
anti-social (*adj.*) antisocial; unsocial.
anti-sociável (*adj.*) unsociable.
anti-sofista (*adj.*) antisophist.
anti-sôro (*m., Immunol.*) antiserum.
antíspase (*f., Med.*) revulsion.
antispasmódico –ca (*adj., Med.*) antispasmodic.
antispástico –ca (*adj., Med.*) antispasmodic.
antispasto (*m., Pros.*) antispast.
antisplenético –ca (*adj., Med.*) antisplenetic.
antissepsia (*f.*) antisepsis.
antisséptico –ca (*adj.; m., Med.*) antiseptic.
antissialgogo –ga (*adj., Med.*) antisialogogue.
antistreptocócico –ca (*adj., Med.*) antistreptococcic.
anti-sudoral (*adj., Med.*) antisudoral.
antitanque (*adj., Milit.*) antitank.

antiteísmo (*m.*) antitheism.
antiteísta (*m.,f.*) antitheist.
antitenar (*adj., Anat.*) antithenar; hypothenar.
antiteológico –ca (*adj.*) antitheological.
antitérmico –ca (*adj., Med.*) antipyretic; (*m., Pharm.*) antithermin.
antítese (*f.*) antithesis, direct opposite.
antitetânico –ca (*adj., Med.*) antitetanic, antitetanus.
antitético –ca (*adj.*) antithetic(al).
antitífico –ca (*adj., Med.*) antityphus.
antitipia (*f.*) antitypy.
antítipo (*m.*) antitype.
antitísico –ca (*adj., Med.*) antituberculosis.
antitóxico –ca [ks] (*adj.*) antitoxic; (*Med.*) antidote.
antitoxina [ks] (*f., Immunol.*) antitoxin.
antitradicional (*adj.*) antitraditional.
antítrago (*m., Anat.*) antitragus.
antitrinitário –ria (*adj.; m.,f.*) anti-Trinitarian.
antituberculoso –sa (*adj.*) antituberculosis.
antivariólico –ca (*adj., Med.*) antivariolous. **certificado de vacina—**. certificate of vaccination against smallpox.
antivenéreo –rea (*adj., Med.*) antivenereal.
antiverminoso –sa (*adj.*) vermifuge.
antivirulento –ta (*adj.*) antivirus.
antivivisecção (*f.*) antivivisection.
antiviviseccionista (*m.,f.*) antivivisectionist.
antizímico –ca (*adj.*) antizymic.
Ant.º = ANTÔNIO (Anthony).
anto (*m., Zool.*) the genus (*Anthus*) of the pipits and the titlark.
antocarpo (*m., Bot.*) anthocarp.
antócera (*f., Bot.*) a genus (*Anthocerus*) of horned liverworts.
antocianina (*f., Biochem.*) anthocyanin, anthocyan.
antócloa (*f., Bot.*) colusa grass (*Anthocloa*).
antódio (*m., Bot.*) anthodium.
antófago –ga (*adj.*) anthophagous.
antofilita (*f., Min.*) anthophyllite.
antófilo –la (*adj., Zool.*) anthophilous; (*pl.*) the Anthophila (bees).
antofobia (*f., Med.*) anthophobia.
antóforo –ra (*adj., Bot.*) anthophorous; (*m.*) anthophore.
antojar, antolhar (*v.t.*) to place before the eyes; to stir the imagination; to covet.
antôjo, [-ôjos] antôlho [-olhos(ólh)] (*m.*) whim, fancy; bizarre craving or appetite exhibited by a pregnant woman.
antólisa (*f.*) the genus (*Antholyza*) of madflowers.
antólise (*f., Bot.*) antholysis.
antologia (*f.*) anthology.
antológico –ca (*adj.*) anthological; (*m., Eastern Church*) anthologion, anthology.
antologista (*m.,f.*) anthologist.
antomania (*f.*) anthomania.
antonímia (*f.*) antonymy.
antônimo –ma (*adj.*) antonimous; (*m.*) antonym.
Antônia (*f.*) Antonia.
Antonieta (*f.*) Antoinette.
Antônio (*m.*) Anthony; Antony; Antonio.
antonomásia (*f., Rhet.*) antonomasia.
antospermo (*m.*) a genus (*Anthospermum*) of rubiaceous herbs and shrubs.
antossiderita (*f., Min.*) anthosiderite.
antoxantina [ks] (*f., Biochem.*) anthoxanthin.
antoxanto [ks] (*m.*) the vernal grass (*Anthoxantum odoratum*), c.a. FLAVA, FENO-DE-CHEIRO.
antozoário (*m., Zool.*) anthozoan.
antracemia (*f., Med.*) anthracemia; (*Veter.*) anthrax.
antracênio, –ceno (*m., Chem.*) anthracene.
antrácia (*f., Med.*) anthracia.
antrácico –ca (*adj.*) anthracic.
antracífero –ra (*adj.*) anthraciferous.
antracito, –te (*m.*) anthracite (coal).
antracitoso –sa (*adj.*) anthracitous.
antracnose (*f., Plant Pathol.*) anthracnose, -nosis, bitter rot, ripe rot; c.a. MOLÉSTIA-NEGRA.
antracóide (*adj.*) coal-colored; (*Med.*) anthracoid.
antracômetro (*m.*) anthracometer.
antraconecrose (*f., Med.*) anthraconecrosis, dry gangrene.
antraconita (*f., Min.*) anthraconite.
antracose (*f., Med.*) anthracosis, miner's phthisis.
antracotério (*m., Paleontol.*) anthracothere.
antracrisona (*f., Chem.*) anthrachrysone.
antragalol (*m., Chem.*) anthragallol.

antramina (*m.*, *Chem.*) anthramine.
antranilato (*m.*, *Chem.*) anthranilate.
antranílico –ca (*adj.*, *Chem.*) anthranilic.
antranol (*m.*, *Chem.*) anthranol.
antraquinona (*f.*, *Chem.*) anthraquinone.
antrarrufina (*f.*, *Chem.*) anthrarufin.
antraz (*m.*, *Med.*, *Veter.*) anthrax.
antreno (*m.*) the genus (*Anthrenus*) which includes the museum pest (*A. varius*) and the carpet beetle or buffalo bug.
antribídeos (*m.pl.*, *Zool.*) a family of snout beetles (*Platystomidae*, *syn. Anthribidae*).
antrisco (*m.*, *Bot.*) the beak chervil (*Anthriscus*).
antro (*m.*) cavern; lair; abyss; den of vice; dive; gambling hell.
antrop. = ANTROPOLOGIA.
antropocêntrico –ca (*adj.*) anthropocentric.
antropocentrismo (*m.*) anthropocentrism.
antropofagia (*f.*) anthropophagy, cannibalism.
antropofágico –ca (*adj.*) anthropophagic.
antropófago –ga (*adj.*) anthropophagous, cannibal, man-eating; (*m.,f.*) cannibal.
antropófilo –la (*m.,f.*) an anthropophilous person.
antropofobia (*f.*) anthropophobia.
antropófobo –ba (*adj.*) misanthropic(al); (*m.,f.*) misanthrope.
antropoforme (*adj.*) = ANTROPOMORFO.
antropogênese (*f.*) anthropogenesis.
antropogeografia (*f.*) anthropogeography.
antropognosia (*f.*) = ANTROPOLOGIA.
antropografia (*f.*) anthropography.
antropóide (*adj.*, *m.*) anthropoid (ape).
antropolatria (*f.*) anthropolatry.
antropólito (*m.*, *Paleontol.*) anthropolith.
antropologia (*f.*) anthropology.
antropológico –ca (*adj.*) anthropological.
antropologista, antropólogo –ga (*m.,f.*) anthropologist.
antropometria (*f.*) anthropometry.
antropométrico –ca (*adj.*) anthropometric(al).
antropômetro (*m.*) anthropometer.
antropomórfico –ca (*adj.*) anthropomorphic(al).
antropomorfismo (*m.*) anthropomorphism.
antropomorfista (*adj.*; *m.,f.*) anthropomorphist.
antropomorfizar (*v.t.,v.r.*) to anthropomorphize.
antropomorfo –fa (*adj.*) anthropomorphous; (*m.,f.*) an anthropoid ape.
antropomorfologia (*f.*) anthropomorphology.
antropopatia (*f.*) anthropopathy.
antropopiteco (*m.*, *Paleontol.*) Anthropopithecus.
antropossociologia (*f.*) anthroposociology.
antropossofia (*f.*) anthroposophy.
antropoteísmo (*m.*) anthropotheism.
antropotomia (*f.*) anthropotomy.
antropotoxina [ks] (*f.*, *Biochem.*) anthropotoxin.
antropozóico –ca (*adj.*, *Geol.*) Anthropozoic.
Antuérpia (*f.*) Antwerp.
antúrio (*m.*, *Bot.*) a genus (*Anthurium*) of the arum family.
anu [ú] (*m.*) = ANUM.—-coroca,—-da-serra,—-galego,—-guaçu = ANUNGUAÇU.
ânua (*f.*) yearly report.
anual (*adj.*) annual, yearly.
anualidade (*f.*) = ANUIDADE.
anuário (*m.*) yearbook; directory.
anuência (*f.*) assent, consent, concurrence, acquiescence.
anuente (*adj.*) assenting, concurring.
anuição [u-i] (*f.*) concurrence, acquiescence.
anuidade [u-i] (*f.*) annuity; membership dues.
anuir [72] (*v.t.*) to assent, consent, agree (a, to); to acquiesce, concur (em, in).
anujá (*m.*) a fresh-water catfish (*Trachycoristes galeatus*), c.a. CUMBACA, CHORÃO, CACHORRO-DE-PADRE, CABEÇA-DE-FERRO, MANDI-CHORÃO.
anulação (*f.*) annulment, cancellation, invalidation; abrogation; (*Law*) defeasance.
anulador –dora (*adj.*) nullifying; (*m.,f.*) annuller, nullifier.
anulamento (*m.*) annulment, abolishment.
anulante (*adj.*) nullifying.
anular (*v.t.*) to annul, cancel, abrogate, repeal, abolish, nullify; to annihilate, reduce to naught; (*Law*) disaffirm; (*adj.*) annular, ring-shaped; (*m.*) the ring finger.
anulatório –ria (*adj.*) annulling, nullifying.
anulável (*adj.*) voidable; (*Law*) defeasible.
ânulo (*m.*, *Arch.*) annulet.

anuloso –sa (*adj.*) annulate, ringed; ring-shaped.
anum (*m.*, *Zool.*) the common ani (*Crotophaga ani*), c.a. ANU, ANUÍ, ANUM-PEQUENO, ANUM-PRETO.—-branco, the guira cuckoo (*Guira guira*), c.a. PILÓ, PELINCHO, QUIRIRU, ANUM-DO-CAMPO, ALMA-DE-GATO, PIRIRIGUÁ, PIRITÁ.—-do-brejo,—-grande,—-peixe, all = ANUNGUAÇU
anunciação (*f.*) announcement; the Annunciation.
anunciada (*f.*) announcement.
anunciador –dora (*adj.*) annunciating; announcing; (*m.,f.*) annunciator.—de rádio, radio announcer.
anunciante (*adj.*) announcing; (*m.,f.*) advertiser; announcer.
anunciar (*v.t.*) to announce; to advertise; to presage, foretell.
anunciativo –va (*adj.*) annunciatory.
anúncio (*m.*) announcement; advertisement; notice; augury.—a neon, neon sign.—luminoso, electric light sign.—s nos jornais, newspaper ads. agência de—s, advertising agency. pequenos—s, classified newspaper ads.
anunguaçu (*m.*, *Zool.*) the greater ani (*Crotophaga major*), c.a. ANU-DE-ENCHENTE, ANU-GALEGO, ANU-COROCA, ANU-DA-SERRA, ANU-GUAICURU, ANUGUAÇU, ANUM-PEIXE, ANUM-DO-BREJO, ANUM-GRANDE, COROIA, GROLÓ.
ânuo –a (*adj.*) annual.
anuro –ra (*adj.*, *Zool.*) anurous, having no tail; (*m.*) one of the Salientia (syn. Anura).
ânus (*m.*, *Anat.*, *Zool.*) anus.
anuviado –da (*adj.*) cloudy, clouded, overcast.
anuviador –dora (*adj.*) clouding; that renders melancholy, gloomy.
anuviar (*v.t.*) to cloud; to blur; to render unhappy or gloomy; (*v.r.*) to grow cloudy; to grow dark.
anvali (*m.*) the emblic leafflower (*Phyllanthus emblica*).
anvaló (*m.*) the fruit emblic or myrobalan.
anverso (*m.*) obverse (head) of a coin.
anzol [-óis] (*m.*) fishhook.—de lontra, (*Bot.*) a climber of the nightshade family (*Strychnos ericetina*) having claw-like tendrils.
anzolado –da (*adj.*) shaped like a fishhook.
ao (*contraction of prep.* a + *article* o) to the, at the, for the, in the, etc. Cf. à.—acaso, casually; at random.—alcance de, within reach of; within the understanding (ability, power, etc.) of.—alto, on high.—anoitecer, at nightfall. —ar livre, in the open, outdoors.—arrepio, against the grain; the wrong way; against the current.—auge, to the highest degree.—avêsso, backwards.—cabo, at the end, at the last.—cabo de, at the end of.—cabo de contas, or de tudo, after all.—cair da noite, at nightfall.—cair da tarde, at sunset.—cantar do galo, at cockcrow (dawn). —capricho de, at the pleasure of.—certo, for certain.— chegar, on arrival; when (I) arrived.—cimo, to the top. —compasso, harmoniously, at the same time.—compasso de, in harmony with.—compasso que, as, while. —comprido, lengthwise; extensively, in full.—comum, habitually.—contrário, on the contrary.—contrário de, contrary to; in contrast to.—correr de, alongside of.— correr da pena, (to write) without pausing to think.— correr do martelo, at auction.—critério de, at the will of. —cúmulo, to the highest.—cúmulo de, to the limit of.— custo, at cost.—de leve, lightly, superficially.—demais, furthermore, moreover.—demais disso, besides that.— desbarato, anyhow; at any price; confusedly.—descuido, carelessly.—desdém, negligently—desespêro, obstinately.—desmazelo, slovenly.—Deus dará, aimlessly adrift.—dispor de, at the disposal of.—encalço de, in pursuit of.—entrar, (sair), on (upon) entering (leaving). —envés, on the contrary.—envés de, instead of.— escurecer, at nightfall.—extremo, to the extreme.— extremo de, to the point of.——faro, in search.—faro de, on the track of.—fazer de, at the will of.—figurado, figuratively.—fim, finally.—fim de, at the end of.—fim de contas, or de tudo, finally, after all.—fresco, in the open, outdoors; in the clear.—fundo (de), at the other end (of), at the rear (of), at the bottom (of).—galante, gallantly.—galope, at a gallop.—gôsto de, according to the taste, liking, or choice of.—infinito, infinitely; to infinity.—inverso, inversely.—inverso de, instead of.— invés (de), instead (of).—jeito de, in the manner of.— jugo de, under the yoke of.—juízo de, in the judgment of.—justo, exactly, precisely.—lado, near, close.—lado de, beside.—largo, afar; out to sea.—largo de, far from. —léu, aimlessly.—léu de, at the whim of.—longe, afar, in the distance.—longo de, alongside of.—lusco-fusco,

or **lusque-fusque**, at twilight.—**mais**, furthermore.—**mandado de**, on orders of.—**mando de**, under the orders of.—**martelo**, at auction.—**máximo**, to the maximum; at most.—**meio**, in the middle.—**menos**, at least.—**passo**, at the same time.—**tempo**, at the same time.—**mínimo**, to the minimum; at least.—**modo de**, in the manner of.—**natural**, au naturel.—**nível**, on a level.—**nível de**, at the level of.—**nuto de**, at the nod (whim, pleasure) of.—**oposto**, contrarily.—**ouvido**, secretly, in whispers.—**paladar de**, to the taste (liking) of.—**par**, at par.—**par de**, along with; aware of.—**parecer**, seemingly.—**passo que**, as, when, while; whereas.—**pé de**, near, nearby, close to; at the foot of; at the edge of.—**pé da letra**, literally; letter for letter; word for word.—**perto**, near.—**pintar**, opportunely, just right.—**ponto de**, to the point of.—**presente**, presently.—**primeiro**, at first.—**primeiro aspeto**, or **primeiro lance**, at first sight or glance.—**primeiro lance de olhos**, or **de vista**, at first glance.—**princípio**, at first.—**que(dizem)**, as (they say).—**redor**, about, around.—**redor de**, around.—**relento**, exposed to the night air; without shelter.—**rés de**, level with.—**revés**, on the contrary; in reverse; against the grain.—**revés de**, contrary to.—**romper da aurora**, or **da madrugada**, at daybreak.—**romper do dia**, at daybreak.—**sabor das ondas**, adrift, rudderless, at the mercy of the waves.—**sabor de**, at the caprice (whim, will, pleasure) of.—**salto**, assaulting.—**saque**, sacking.—**sereno**, in the night air; outdoors.—**serviço de**, at the service of.—**sumo grau**, to the highest degree.—**talante de**, at the will (whim, pleasure) of.—**tempo**, outdoors, in the weather; at the time.—**tempo que**, at the same time that.—**término de**, at the end of.—**têrmo (de)**, at the end (of).—**tiracolo**, (to carry) like a bandoleer, slung over the shoulder.—**todo**, in all, altogether.—**través (de)** = ATRAVÉS (DE).

ão, a shortened form of HÃO, used in forming the fut. ind. of all verbs: DARÃO, VIRÃO, etc.; a masc. suffix forming adjectives and nouns and suggesting origin, nationality and relationship: CIDADÃO, PAGÃO, FOLGAZÃO, CRISTÃO, ALEMÃO, SULTÃO. [The fem. form is -Ã or -ANA (sometimes -OA or -ONA): CRISTÃ, PAGÃ, ALEMÃ, SULTANA, CIDADOA, FOLGAZONA.] The regular plural of -ÃO is -ÃOS: CIDADÃOS, PAGÃOS, CRISTÃOS, but frequently it is -ÃES or -ÕES: ALEMÃES, CAPITÃES, MELÕES.

aolo (*m.*) = PAPAGAIO-CAMPEIRO.
aonde [a+onde] (*adv.*) where; whither; wherever.
aoristo (*m., Gram.*) aorist tense.
aorta (*f., Anat.*) aorta.
aórtico -**ca** (*adj.*) aortic.
aortoclasia, -**clastia** (*f., Med.*) aortoclasia.
aortomalacia (*f., Med.*) aortomalacia.
aortoptosia (*f., Med.*) aortoptosia.
aos (contraction of prep. **a**+article pl. **os**) to the, in the, etc. Cf. **às**.—**(dois) anos de idade**, when he was (two).—**bambaleios**, swaying, weaving.—**bamboleios**, swaggering.—**berros**, screaming, yelling.—**borbotões**, or **cachões**, gushing (out).—**brados**, clamorously; shouting.—**cântaros**, in buckets [rain]. [More commonly, **a cântaros**.]—**cardumes**, in schools [fish].—**centos**, by hundreds.—**cochichos**, whispering.—**empurrões**, stumbling; shoving.—**fins de**, toward the end of. [More commonly, **em fins de**.]—**jatos**, in jets, in streams.—**jorros**, in gushes.—**magotes**, in bands; in heaps.—**milhares**, by the thousand; in thousands.—**montes**, in profusion; in heaps.—**montões**, copiously.—**olhos de**, in the eyes of.—**pares**, in pairs.—**pés de**, at the feet of. [**Não chega aos pés de**, He doesn't even come near to; is much inferior to.]—**poucos**, little by little, gradually.—**princípios**, at first, in the beginning. [More commonly, **a princípios**.]—**quatros ventos**, to the four winds.—**racimos**, in bunches.—**recuos**, backwards [= DE RECUO].—**tombos**, tumbling; clumsily.—**trambolhões**, shoving, pushing; helter-skelter.—**trancos**, in leaps; tumbling.—**trancos e barrancos**, tumbling and bumping; with difficulty; catch as catch can.—**tropelões**, staggering and stumbling; shoving.—**ziguezagues**, in zigzags.
aoto (*m.*) the genus (*Aotus*, syn. *Nyctipithecus*) of night apes.
ap. = APARTAMENTO (apartment); [L.] APUD (according to); APROVADO (approved).
APA = Associação Protetora de Animais (Society for Protection of Animals).
apá (*m.*) a kind of seive; a shovel [= PÁ]; (*colloq.*) the thick part of the leg; (*Bot.*) the soft wallabatree (*Eperua*

falcata), c.a. APÀZEIRO, ESPADEIRA.
apacanim (*m.*) a hawk-eagle (*Spizaëtus ornatus*), c.a. URUTAURANA, GAVIÃO-DE-PENACHO; the tyrant hawk-eagle (*Spizaëtus tyrannus*), c.a. GAVIÃO-PEGA-MACACO; the harpy eagle (*Harpia harpyja*), c.a. HARPIA, GAVIÃO-REAL.
apache (*m.*) Apache Indian; in Paris, a member of a criminal gang.
apachorrar-se (*v.r.*) to become apathetic, sluggish, phlegmatic.
apadrinhado -**da** (*adj.*) sponsored, protected, favored.
apadrinhador -**dora** (*adj.*) sponsoring, protecting, favoring, backing; (*m.*) sponsor, protector, backer.
apadrinhar (*v.t.*) to sponsor; to act as godfather of; to favor, protect; to defend, uphold.—**-se com**, to seek another's favor or protection; to appeal to another's authority.
apadroar (*v.t.*) to patronize; to sponsor.
apagado -**da** (*adj.*) extinguished, quenched, put out; in darkness; dim, dark, unlit; vague, faded, faint. **uma figura**—, an obscure, uncultured person.
apagador -**dora** (*adj.*) extinguishing; (*m.*) one who or that which extinguishes; candle snuffer.—**de quadro negro**, blackboard eraser.
apagamento (*m.*) extinguishment, effacement, erasure.
apaga-pó (*m.*) a light drizzle [= CHUVISCO, XIXIXI].
apagar (*v.t.*) to extinguish, quench, put out (as a light or fire); to destroy, nullify; to efface, obliterate, erase; to expunge, to blot out; to obscure, dim; (*v.r.*) to go out (as a light or fire); to grow weak, dim.
apaí (*m.*) = IRERÊ.
apaiari [rí] (*m.*) a foot-long, vicious cichlid (*Astronotus ocelatus*) sometimes seen in home aquaria; c.a. ACARÁ-AÇU, ACARÁ-GRANDE, CARÁ-GRANDE.
apainelado -**da** (*adj.*) paneled; (*m.*) panel work.
apainelamento (*m.*) paneling.
apainelar (*v.t.*) to panel.
apaisanado -**da** (*adj.*) like a civilian in dress or manners (as opposed to the military).
apaisanar (*v.t.,v.r.*) to dress as a civilian.
apaixonado -**da** (*adj.*) passionate, impassioned; enthusiastic; intense, excited; hectic; fervent, zealous; ardent, very much in love, heels over head in love, desperately in love; stuck on (someone); infatuated; amorous; (*m.*) sweetheart, lover. **Ela está**—**por êle**, She is madly in love with him. **Êle é**—**pela música**, He is crazy about music. **Êle ficou muito**—**com a má notícia que recebeu**, He was deeply affected by the bad news which he received. **Não se pode discutir com êle: é um**—, You can't argue with him, he is too impassioned.
apaixonar (*v.t.*) to fill with passion; to infatuate; to inspire, exalt, fill with enthusiasm; (*v.r.*) to fall (madly) in love (**por**, **de**, with).
apalachina (*f., Bot.*) the yaupon (*Ilex vomitoria*).
apalacianar (*v.t.,v.r.*) to turn into a PALACIANO (courtier).
apaladar (*v.t.*) to render pleasing to the taste.
apalai (*m.,f.*) = APARAI.
apalavrado -**da** (*adj.*) agreed upon orally; pledged by word of mouth; betrothed.
apalavramento (*m.*) oral agreement; pledge.
apalavrar (*v.t.*) to pledge, bind (by word of mouth).—**para casar**, to betroth.
apalear (*v.t.*) to beat with a stick.
apalermado -**da** (*adj.*) fatuous, foolish, stupid.
apalermar-se (*v.r.*) to grow foolish.
apalhaçado -**da** (*adj.*) clownish; zany.
apalpadela, **apalpação** (*f.*) act of touching or feeling. **andar às apalpadelas**, to grope, feel one's way.
apalpadeira (*f.*) a woman employed at a custom-house, etc.; to "frisk" women suspects.
apalpador -**dora** (*adj.*) touching, feeling; (*m., Mach.*) a feeler gauge.
apalpar (*v.t.*) to palpate; to feel of; to grope, feel one's way; to sound, probe; to try, put to the test; (*v.r.*) to feel of oneself.—**as costelas de**, to drub, pommel, wallop (another's) ribs.—**o terreno**, to survey the ground; to feel out the situation.
apalpo (*m.*) = APALPADELA.
apanágio (*m.*) an outstanding personal characteristic or natural attribute; [*Rare*] appanage.
apandilhar-se (*v.r.*) to join in a scheme to swindle.
apanha, **apanhação** (*f.*) (act of) gathering or picking; harvest(ing).

apanhadeira (*f.*) harvest woman; coffee picker; dust pan.
apanhadiço –ça (*adj.*) easily picked, plucked, gathered, etc. See the verb APANHAR.
apanhado –da (*adj.*) picked, gathered, caught, taken; (*m.*) summary, résumé; tuck, pleat, fold; a handful; a grab sample.
apanhador (*m.*) coffee picker; rubber gatherer; dust pan.
apanhamento (*m.*) picking, harvesting; a handful.
apanha-môscas (*m.*, *Bot.*) the Venus flytrap (*Dionaea muscipula*); the catchfly silene (*S. muscipula*).
apanhar (*v.t.*) to gather, pluck, pick (coffee, cotton, fruit, flowers, etc.); to grasp, clasp; to seize, lay hold of, nab, catch; to lift (pick, gather) up; to take, net, entrap, ensnare, bag (game, fish); to catch up with, overtake; to get, gain, win; to catch (punishment, disease); to surprise, catch in the act, take unawares; to catch on, understand, get the idea; to tuck, fold, pleat; (*v.i.*) to take a beating (lose a game); (*v.r.*) to find oneself (in a given situation or place).—**a luva**, to take up the gauntlet (challenge).—**a dente**, to learn something by rote.—**chuva**, to get caught in the rain.—**como o holandês, pagando o mal que não fêz**, to suffer for wrong-doing of which one is innocent.—**em taquigrafia**, to take down in shorthand.—**môscas**, to waste time on trifles.—**num jôgo**, to take a licking in a game.—**no laço**, to ensnare.—**o sentido de**, to catch the meaning of.—**pancada**, to take a beating (blows with a stick).—**que nem boi ladrão**, to take a severe beating.—**uma chuvarada**, to get caught in a shower.—**uma constipação, um resfriado**, to catch a cold.—**uma multa**, to draw a fine. **Êle merece (está precisando)**—, He deserves (needs) to be licked. **Quando o político se apanhou no poder, nunca mais o quis largar**, When the politico found himself in power, he never afterwards wanted to give it up.
apanha-saia (*f.*) = GANHA-SAIA.
apaniguado (*m.*) follower, dependent; creature; protégé; henchman.
apaniguar (*v.t.*) to protect, sponsor.
apapá (*m.*) any of various fresh-water herrings and shad-like fishes of the family Clupeidae found in the Amazon River.
apaparicar (*v.t.*) to pet, caress, give candy to; to flatter.
apapocuva (*m.*,*f.*) An Indian of the modern Guarani or Cainguá who lived originally in the southern tip of Mato Grosso on the Iguatemi River, later spreading in small groups to the adjoining states of São Paulo and Paraná; (*adj.*) pert. to or designating the Apapocuva.
apar (*m.*, *Zool.*) an armadillo (*Dasypus apara*), c.a. TATU-BOLA.
apara (*f.*) shred, scrap, fragment, chip, bit; (*pl.*) shavings, filings, clippings, parings, left-overs.
aparadeira (*f.*) untrained midwife; bed pan.
aparado –da (*adj.*) caught (as a ball); stopped (as a blow); cut, trimmed, clipped, pared; sharpened; planed. **bem**—, well groomed.
aparador [ô] (*m.*) sideboard, buffet.
aparafusar (*v.t.*) to fasten with a screw or screws; also = PARAFUSAR.
aparai (*m.*,*f.*) an Indian of the Aparai, a Cariban tribe dwelling between the Tumucumac Mountains and the north bank of the Amazon; (*adj.*) pert. to or designating this tribe.
apara-lápis (*m.*) pencil sharpener.
aparar (*v.t.*) to catch (as a ball); to parry (a blow); to smooth, plane; to pare; to chip; to trim; to cut, shear, clip; to sharpen (as a pencil); to flatter; to coax; to endure, bear.—(or **cortar**) **o cabelo**, to get a hair-cut.
aparatar (*v.t.*) to adorn, ornament, bedeck; to make pompous, magnificent.
aparato (*m.*) ostentation, pomp, magnificence; swank, show, display, fanfare. [But not apparatus, which is APARELHO].
aparatoso –sa (*adj.*) showy, swanky; ornate.
aparceirar (*v.t.*) to take (someone) as a partner; (*v.r.*) to enter into a partnership.
aparcelar (*v.t.*) to divide into parcels.
aparecer (*v.i.*) to appear, emerge, come into sight; to show up; to arise, occur; (*v.t.*) to make or put in an appearance. **Apareça lá por casa**, Drop around some time. **Este livro acaba de**—, This book has just been published. **Este jornal aparece às quartas-feiras**, This paper comes out on Wednesdays.
aparecido –da (*adj.*) appeared; manifested.
aparecimento (*m.*) appearance.

apareíba (*f.*) the American mangrove (*Rhizophora mangle*), c.a. MANGUE-VERMELHO (-VERDADEIRO,-PRÊTO).
aparelhado –da (*adj.*) ready, prepared, in readiness, fitted, equipped, rigged; (of lumber) finished. **bem**—, well-equipped. **mal**—, ill-equipped.
aparelhador (*m.*) rigger; fixer; construction foreman.
aparelhagem (*f.*) gear, tackle; a set of appliances; finishing (of lumber).
aparelhamento (*m.*) rigging, tackle; act of equipping; equipment.
aparelhar (*v.t.*) to prepare, make ready; to harness; to rig, accoutre; to apparel; to finish (lumber); to cut (stone); (*v.r.*) to get ready.
aparelho [ê] (*m.*) preparation, arrangement; rigging, tackle, gear; harness, trappings; appliance, tool, instrument; device, contrivance, gadget; apparatus, utensils; a set of things used together, as a set of china, a silver teaset, etc.; a telephone instrument; radio receiving set; splint, bandage.—**alimentar**, feed system (of a boiler).—**contra incêndios**, fire-fighting equipment.—**de alarme**, alarm signal,—**de audição**, hearing aid.—**de cinema**, motion picture camera or projector.—**de endireitar os dentes**, metal band for straightening the teeth. —**de ensaio**, testing machine.—**de gesso**, plaster cast (for broken limbs).—**de pilotagem automática**, robot pilot.—**de rádio**, radio set.—**de salvação**, life-saving equipment.—**de segurança**, safety device.—**de televisão**, TV set.—**digestivo**, (*Anat.*) digestive system.—**genital**, (*Anat.*) genital organs.—**lacrimal**, (*Anat.*) lachrymal organs (tear glands and ducts).—**linfático**, (*Anat.*) lymphatic system.—**receptor**, radio receiving set.—**respiratório**, (*Anat.*) respiratory system.—**trans-missor**, radio transmitting set.—**urinário**, (*Anat.*) urinary system.—**visual**, (*Anat.*) sight organs. —**s de casa**, household goods, household equipment.
aparência (*f.*) appearance, aspect; semblance; affectation. **em**—, seemingly, apparently.
aparentado –da (*adj.*) kin, related by blood.
aparentar (*v.t.*) to seem to; to give the appearance of; to pretend to; to affect. **Ela não aparenta sua idade**, She does not look her age.—**riqueza**, to act rich. (*v.t.*) to establish kinship with.—**se com**, to become related to.
aparente (*adj.*) apparent, seeming, specious, not real; visible, perceptible. [But not apparent, in the sense of manifest or clear, which is EVIDENTE.]
apárgia (*f.*, *Bot.*) the hawkbit (*Leontodon*).
aparição (*f.*) appearance; advent; apparition; ghost.
aparo (*m.*) pen point; a paring.
aparrado –da (*adj.*) squat, dumpy.
aparreirar (*v.t.*) to cover with vines.
apart. = APARTAMENTO.
apartação (*f.*) separation; a cutting out (of one or more head of cattle from a herd).
apartado –da (*adj.*) separated, set apart; gone astray; far away, secluded.
apartador –dora (*adj.*) separating; (*m.*,*f.*) separator.
apartamento (*m.*) apartment; separation.
apartar (*v.t.*) to part, divide; to separate; to set apart; to part (combatants); to divorce; to call aside; (*v.r.*) to get away from, move away from, withdraw, part (from another); to straggle.—**se do assunto**, to digress, stray from the subject.—**o grão da palha**, to separate the wheat from the chaff.
aparte (*m.*) an aside; an interrupting remark. **dizer—s**, to make side remarks.
aparteador –dora, aparteante, apartista (*adj.*) interrupting; heckling; (*m.*,*f.*) one who interrupts or heckles (a speaker).
apartear (*v.t.*) to interrupt or heckle (a speaker).
apartidário –ria (*adj.*) non-partisan.
aparvalhado –da (*adj.*) foolish; oafish; puzzled; bewildered.
aparvalhamento (*m.*) bewilderment, puzzlement.
aparvalhar (*v.t.*) to make silly; to bemuddle; to confound, puzzle.
aparvoado –da (*adj.*) idiotic.
apascentador (*m.*) cattle herder, sheep herder.
apascentamento (*m.*) herding; pasturing.
apascentar (*v.t.*) to herd, lead to pasture; to delight, feast (the eye, the ear, the soul); (*v.r.*) to take delight in; to feast on.
apassamanar (*v.t.*) to provide with braids, cords, beads, etc.

apassivar (*v.t.*) to render passive; to change (a verb) to the passive; (*v.r.*) to become passive.

apatacado –da (*adj.*) having plenty of money; lit., having many PATACAS (an old silver coin).

apatetado –da (*adj.*) daft, deranged.

apatetar (*v.t.*) to render daft, crazy; to besot.

apatia (*f.*) apathy.

apático –ca (*adj.*) apathetic; torpid; shiftless; listless.

apatifar (*v.t.*) to turn (someone) into a rascal; (*v.r.*) to become one.

apatita (*f.*, *Min.*) apatite.

apatizar (*v.t.*) to render apathetic; (*v.r.*) to become so.

apátrida (*m.,f.*) foreign refugee, displaced person.

apatriotismo (*m.*) want of patriotism.

apatrulhar (*v.t.*) to patrol; (*v.r.*) to join a patrol.

apaulado –da [a-u] (*adj.*) swampy, marshy, boggy.

apaular [a-u] (*v.t.*) to make into a swamp; (*v.r.*) to turn into one.

apaulistado –da (*adj.*) like a Paulista (native of São Paulo) in manners, habit, speech, etc.

apavesar (*v.*) = EMPAVESAR.

apavonar-se (*v.t.*) to become vain; to strut, show off.

apavorado –da (*adj.*) terror-stricken; appalled; aghast; dismayed.

apavorador –dora, **apavorante** (*adj.*) fearful, appalling, dismaying.

apavorar (*v.t.*) to appall, terrify; (*v.r.*) to become appalled, dismayed.

apàzeiro (*m.*) = APÁ.

apaziguado –da (*adj.*) pacified, appeased.

apaziguador –dora (*adj.*) pacifying, appeasing; disarming; (*m.,f.*) peacemaker.

apaziguamento (*m.*) pacification, appeasement.

apaziguante (*adj.*) pacifying, conciliatory.

apaziguar (*v.t.*) to pacify, conciliate, appease; to disarm, to allay; (*v.r.*) to grow peaceful; to quiet down.

apé (*m.*) the rudge waterlily (*Nymphaea rudgeana*), c.a. AGUAPÉ-DA-MEIA-NOITE; the royal water-platter or giant Amazon waterlily (*Victoria regia*).

apeadeira (*f.*) horseblock (for mounting or dismounting).

apeadeiro (*m.*) railroad flag stop.

apeadouro, **–doiro** (*m.*) = APEADEIRA; APEADEIRO.

apeamento (*m.*) act of dismounting.

apeanhar (*v.t.*) to place on a pedestal.

apear (*v.i.*) to dismount (from a horse); to get off (a train or streetcar); (*v.t.*) to help to dismount; to unhorse; to unhitch; to raze (a wall or building); to dethrone; to oust; (*v.r.*) to get off, dismount, alight (de, from); to stop and rest on a journey.—de, to deprive, divest of (power, position, riches), Eu apeio na próxima estação, I get off at the next station.

apeçonhar (*v.*) & derivs.= EMPEÇONHAR & derivs.

apedantado –da (*adj.*) somewhat pedantic.

apedantar-se (*v.r.*) to play the pedant.

apedeuta, **apedeuto** (*m.*) ignoramus.

apedeutismo (*m.*) ignorance.

apedido (*m.*) a paid notice, statement or letter published in a newspaper "by request" of its author, who assumes full responsibility therefor.

apedrar (*v.t.*) to stone, throw rocks at; (*v.i.*) to turn hard as a rock.—com, to set with precious stones.

apedrajado –da (*adj.*) injured or killed by stoning; insulted, cursed.

apedrejamento (*m.*) stoning.

apedrejar (*v.t.*) to stone; to injure by stoning; to chase with rocks; to rain (things or insults) upon.

apegação (*f.*) attachment.

apegadiço –ça (*adj.*) sticky; said also of persons who become easily or quickly attached to others.

apegado –da (*adj.*) attached; joined; contiguous; having strong attachment (for someone or something).

apegamento (*m.*) attachment.

apegar (*v.t.*) to attach to; to transmit (a disease) to by contagion.—-se a, to adhere (cling, cleave) to; to attach oneself to; to stick close to; to join with; to become attached to, fond of (a person, pet or thing); to adhere to, stick to (as to a principle).

apêgo (*m.*) tenacity; adherence, adhesion, fondness; addiction; plow beam.

apeíba (*f.*) = PAU-DE-JANGADA.

apeiragem (*f.*) gear for yoking oxen; farm equipment.

apeirar (*v.t.*) to yoke, harness (a, to); to equip (as a farm).

apeiro (*m.*) gear, rigging, tackle; farm equipment; harness, trappings; paraphernalia.

apelação (*f.*) appellation, designation; appeal; recourse. Côrte de—, Court of Appeals.

apelado –da (*adj.*) appealed; designating one against whom an appeal is taken; designating the judge to whom an appeal is made; (*m.,f.*) appellee.

apelamento (*m.*) = APELAÇÃO.

apelante (*adj.*) appealing; (*m.,f.*) appellant.

apelar (*v.i.*) to appeal (de, from; **para**, to); to call for assistance.—**de uma sentença**, to appeal from a court decision.—**para os bons sentimentos de alguém**, to appeal to a person's better nature.—**para um tribunal superior**, to appeal to a higher court.

apelativo –va (*adj.*) of nouns, common, as opposed to proper; (*m.*) a common noun.

apelatório –ria (*adj.*) relating to an appellant or an appeal.

apelável (*adj.*) appealable.

apelidação (*f.*) appellation, designation.

apelidar (*v.t.*) to name, call, term; to dub, nickname; to summon; to invoke; (*v.r.*) to be called, dubbed.—-se de, to be known by the name of.

apelido (*m.*) appellation; surname; family name; given name, nickname, pet name; qualifying word or term.

apelidor –dora (*adj.*) naming; calling; (*m.,f.*) namer; caller.

apêlo (*m.*) appeal, plea; call for help.

apenas (*adj.*) barely, hardly, scarcely, only, merely; as soon as.—isto, merely this.

apender (*v.t.*) to append (a, to).

apendicalgia (*f.*, *Med.*) appendicalgia.

apêndice (*m.*) appendix, appendage; addendum; supplement; annex to a building (*Anat.*, *Zool.*) appendix.

apendicectomia (*f.*, *Surg.*) appendectomy.

apendicite (*f.*, *Med.*) appendicitis.—**fulminante**, fulminating appendicitis.—**perfurante**, perforative a.

apendicostomia (*f.*, *Surg.*) appendicostomy.

apendicular (*adj.*) appendicular.

apendículo (*m.*) appendicule.

apendoar (*v.t.*) to deck with pennants; (*v.i.*) to put forth tassels or inflorescences, as corn.

apenhascado –da (*adj.*) craggy.

apensar (*v.t.*) to append, annex.

apenso –sa (*adj.*) appended; (*m.*) thing appended.

apepinar (*v.t.*) to ridicule.

apepsia (*f.*, *Med.*) apepsia, indigestion.

apequenado –da (*adj.*) smallish.

apequenar (*v.t.*) to make smaller; (*v.r.*) to become so.

aperaltar-se (*v.r.*) to play the dandy.

aperalvilhar (*v.t.*) to make a dandy of; (*v.r.*) to become one.

aperana (*f.*, *Bot.*) a floatingheart (*Nymphoides sp.*)

aperceber (*v.t.*) to perceive, note, discern; to make ready, equip, prepare; (*v.r.*) to prepare oneself (**para**, for); to provide oneself (de, with);—-se de, to perceive, note, see. Apercebeu-se do êrro, he saw his mistake. Cf. PERCEBER.

apercebimento (*m.*) perceiving, noting; preparation; equipment; (*pl.*) supplies; munitions.

apercepção (*f.*) apperception, perception.

aperceptível (*adj.*) perceptible.

apereá (*m.*) = PREÁ.

aperema (*m.*) an amphibious turtle (*Geomyda punctilaria*) c.a. CÁGADO-DO-AMAZONAS, JABUTI-APEREMA.

aperfeiçoado –da (*adj.*) perfected, improved.

aperfeiçoador –dora (*adj.*) perfecting, improving; (*m.,f.*) one who or that which improves or perfects.

aperfeiçoamento (*m.*) improvement, perfecting. curso de—, post-graduate course.

aperfeiçoar (*v.t.*) to perfect, bring to perfection; to improve, better; (*v.r.*) to improve oneself.

aperfeiçoável (*adj.*) capable of being improved or perfected.

apergaminhado –da (*adj.*) parchment-like.

aperiente (*adj.*) = APERITIVO.

aperiódico –ca (*adj.*, *Physics: Elec.*) aperiodic; deadbeat.

aperispérmico –ca (*adj.*, *Bot.*) aperispermic, exalbuminous.

aperitivo –va (*adj.*) serving to stimulate the appetite; (*m.*) an apéritif.

aperos [ê] (*m.pl.*) trappings; harness, equipment.

aperrar (*v.t.*) to cock (a firearm).

aperreação (*f.*) harassment; oppression; trouble; financial difficulties.

aperreado –da (*adj.*) treated like a dog; harassed; oppressed; stunted; depressed.

aperreador –**dora** (*adj.*) harassing, tormenting, bullying; (*m.,f.*) person who harasses, torments, ill-treats, picks on, bullies, pesters.
aperreamento (*m.*) = APERREAÇÃO.
aperrear (*v.t.*) to vex, torment, harry; to dominate, bully.
aperreio (*m.*) = APERREAÇÃO.
aperta-chico (*m., colloq.*) fracas, free-for-all.
apertada (*f.*) mountain pass, gap; a "tight squeeze".
apertadela (*f.*) a squeeze, a tightening.
apertado –**da** (*adj.*) tight, close; close fitting; narrow; pressing, rigorous; (*colloq.*) tight, stingy; short of money; pressed for money; (*m.*) narrow gap.
apertador –**dora** (*adj.*) tightening, squeezing; (*m.,f.*) tightener.
apertadouro, –**doiro** (*m.*) band, girth, cinch, girdle, belt, strap, etc., used for tightening.
apertão (*m.*) squeeze, crush; crowd.
apertar (*v.t.*) to squeeze, compress, contract, constrict; to tighten; to clasp, clutch, grip; to narrow; to press; to restrict, cramp.—**a mão a**, to shake hands with.—**ao peito**, to clasp to the bosom, hug.—**com alguém**, to press, urge, harry, someone.—**com perguntas**, to grill.—**o cêrco,** to narrow the circle, tighten the ring, surround, close in on (a wild animal, criminal, etc).—**o coração**, to afflict, grieve, someone.—**o crânio a alguém**, to beat another in an argument; to put him in an awkward position.—**o passo**, to quicken one's step, hurry along.—**-se o peito**, to have a heartache. **É ahí que aperta o sapato**, That's where the shoe pinches.
aperta-ruão (*m.*) a climbing jointed shrub (*Piper aduncum*) of the pepper family.
apêrto (*m.*) pressure, squeeze, crush, stress; throng, crowd; tight spot, plight, predicament; stinginess; urgency; affliction.—**de cabeça**, headache.—**de mãos**, handclasp.—**do cinto**, tightening of the belt. **estar em (grande)**—, to be in a fix, in a tight spot, in a pickle. **sair-se dum**—, to get oneself out of a scrape.
apertura (*f.*) = APÊRTO.
aperuar (*v.*) & derivs. = PERUAR & derivs.
apesar (*adv.*)—**de**, notwithstanding; despite, in spite of. —**de que**, in spite of which.—**de todos os pesares**, or —**dos pesares**, notwithstanding, for all that, even so, in spite of everything.
apesentar-se (*v.r.*) to grow heavy.
apessoado –**da** (*adj.*) **bem**—, well-favored; well-groomed; tall and handsome. **mal**—, ill-favored.
apestar (*v.*) = EMPESTAR.
apétalo –**la** (*adj., Bot.*) apetalous.
apetecedor –**dora** (*adj.*) appetizing, inviting.
apetecer (*v.t.*) to hunger for; to crave, desire, long for; (*v.i.*) to tempt the appetite. **Apetece-me comer agora**, I should like to eat now. **Esta fruta está me apetecendo,** This fruit is tempting me. **Quando bem lhe apetece**, Whenever it pleases him; in his own good time.
apetecível (*adj.*) tempting, alluring, enticing; desirable.
apetência (*f.*) appetence.
apetente (*adj.*) tempting.
apetitar (*v.t.*) to appetize.
apetite (*m.*) appetite, hunger; longing, craving; lust.
apetitível (*adj.*) = APETECÍVEL.
apetitivo –**va** (*adj.*) appetizing.
apetitoso –**sa** (*adj.*) delectable; covetous.
apetrechar (*v.t.*) to equip, furnish, provide, arm, fit out, rig.
apetrecho [ê] (*m.*) equipment, accoutrement, appurtenance; gear, outfit, rigging. *Cf.* **petrechos**.
âpex [ks] (*m.*) = APICE.
apezinhar (*v.*) = ESPEZINHAR.
apiabar (*v.t., slang*) to borrow money in a game.
apiacá (*m.,f.*) an Indian of the Apiacá, a once-numerous but now extinct Tupian people who lived in the region between the junction of the Arinos and Juruema Rivers in Mato Grosso; also, an Indian of a Cariban tribe dwelling near the mouth of the Tocantins River; (*adj.*) pert. to or designating either of these tribes.
apiançado –**da** (*adj., colloq.*) asthmatic.
apiário –**ria** (*adj.*) apian; (*m.*) apiary.
apiastro (*m.*) = ERVA-CIDREIRA.
apicaçar (*v.*) ESPICAÇAR.
apicado –**da**, **apical** (*adj.*) apical.
ápice (*m.*) apex, acme, top; (*pl.*) diaeresis [¨]; = TREMA.
apicoectomia (*f., Dental Surg.*) apicoectomy.
apicu [ú] (*m.*) = APICUM.
apicuí (*m.*) the talpacoti dove (*Columbigallina t. talpacoti*)

c.a. CALDO-DE-FEIJÃO, RÔLA-DE-SANGUE-DE-BOI, RÔLA-ROXA, RÔLA-CABOCLA, ROLINHA, POMBA-RÔLA.
apícula (*f.*) –**lo** (*m.*) apiculus.
apiculado –**da** (*adj., Bot.*) apiculate.
apicultor –**tora** (*m.,f.*) apiarist, beekeeper.
apicultura (*f.*) apiculture, beekeeping.
apicum (*m.*) salt marsh.
apídeos (*m.,pl., Zool.*) the Apidae (social bees).
apiedado –**da** (*adj.*) moved to pity.
apiedador –**dora** (*adj.*) pitying; (*m.,f.*) one who pities.
apiedar-se [29] (*v.r.*) to feel sorry for, pity, take pity on.
apifarado –**da** (*adj.*) resembling a PÍFARO (fife); (*colloq.*) tall and skinny.
apiina [i-í] (*f., Chem.*) apiin.
apiloar (*v.t.*) to pound (grain) with a PILÃO (pestle).
apimentado –**da** (*adj.*) peppery, spicy; malicious.
apimentar (*v.t.*) to spice with pepper; to stimulate, excite.
apimpolhar-se (*v.r.*) to put forth PIMPÔLHOS (shoots).
apinajé (*m.,f.*) an Indian of the Apinayé, a subbranch of the Northwestern Ge between the Araguaia and Tocantins Rivers in the State of Goiás; (*adj.*) pert. to or designating this tribe.
apinar (*v.*) = EMPINAR.
apincelar (*v.t.*) to whitewash.
apinhado –**da** (*adj.*) heaped up, crowded, jammed, chockablock, chock-full [= LOTADO].
apinhar (*v.t.*) to heap up, crowd together; (*v.r.*) to jam together; to cluster.
apinhoar (*v.*) = APINHAR.
apintalhar (*v.t.*) to mark off or stake out (a boundary).
ápio (*m.*) celery (*Apium*); = AIPO.
apióide (*adj., Med.*) apinoid.
apiol (*m., Chem., Pharm.*) apiole.
apiolina (*f., Pharm.*) apiolin.
apionol (*m., Chem.*) apionol.
apipado –**da** (*adj.*) barrel-shaped.
apirético –**da** (*adj., Med.*) apyretic, without fever.
apirene (*adj., Biol.*) apyrene.
apirexia [ks] (*f., Med.*) apyrexia.
ápiro –**ra** (*adj.*) apyrous, incombustible, fire-resistant.
apis (*m.*) a genus (*Apis*) of common honey-bees.
apisoamento (*m.*) fulling (of cloth); tamping (of soil).
apisoar (*v.t.*) to full (cloth); to pound, tamp (soil).
apisto (*m.*) beef juice; pap; comfort.
apitã (*m.*) a turkey buzzard (*Cathartes foetens*).
apitar (*v.t.*) to blow a whistle; (*v.i.*) to whistle. **ficar apitando**, (*colloq.*) to be left whistling (chagrined).
apito (*m.*) whistle (instrument, sound).
apívoro –**ra** (*adj., Zool.*) bee-eating.
aplacação (*f.*) placation, appeasement.
aplacador –**dora** (*adj.*) placating, appeasing; (*m.,f.*) placater, appeaser.
aplacar (*v.t.*) to placate, appease; to calm (down); to lull; to mitigate; (*v.r.*) to relent.
aplacável (*adj.*) placable, appeasable.
aplacentário –**ria** (*adj.*) aplacental; (*m., Zool.*) one of the Aplacentalia.
aplainador –**dora** (*adj.*) smoothing, planing.
aplainamento (*m.*) act of planing, smoothing.
aplainar (*v.t.*) to plane, make smooth; to level, flatten.
aplanação (*f.*) levelling.
aplanado –**da** (*adj.*) plane, level, flat.
aplanador –**dora** (*adj.*) levelling; (*m.,f.*) leveller; grader (ground-leveling machine).
aplanamento (*m.*) = APLANAÇÃO.
aplanar (*v.t.*) to level; to flatten; to smooth the way.
aplanático –**ca** (*adj., Optics*) aplanatic.
aplanatismo (*m.*) aplanatism.
aplasia (*f., Med.*) aplasia.
aplastamento (*m., Aeron.*) belly-landing.
aplastar (*v.t.*) to unfurl (a sail); (*Aeron.*) to make a belly-landing.
aplástico –**ca** (*adj.*) not plastic; (*Biol., Med.*) aplastic.
aplastrar (*v.*) = ABOMBAR.
aplaudente (*adj.*) applauding, approving.
aplaudidor –**dora** (*adj.*) applauding; (*m.,f.*) applauder.
aplaudir (*v.t.*) to applaud, cheer, clap; to acclaim; to laud, praise; (*v.r.*) to pat oneself on the back.
aplausível, aplaudível (*adj.*) worthy of applause, praiseworthy.
aplauso (*m.*) applause; acclamation.
aplicabilidade (*f.*) applicability.
aplicação (*f.*) application (of something); [but not application for something, which is REQUERIMENTO, PEDIDO];

appliance, use; exertion; diligence, intense study; appliqué.

aplicante (*adj.*) applicant, applying (*m.,f.*) applier. [But not an applicant for something, which is PRETENDENTE, CANDIDATO, REQUERENTE, PETICIONÁRIO].

aplicar (*v.t.*) to apply, lay on; to put to use, employ; to bring to bear; to set, employ with attention; to be pertinent to. [But not to apply *for* something, which is REQUERER, SOLICITAR, PEDIR.]—**a,** to put on, apply to, affix to.—**a atenção a,** to devote attention to.—**se a,** to apply oneself to.—**um ensinamento,** to put a lesson into practice.—**uma compressa de água fria na cabeça,** to apply a cold compress to the head.—**uma estampilha,** to affix a tax stamp to.—**uma multa em,** to impose a fine against. **Nem todas as regras se aplicam aos mesmos casos,** The same rules do not apply in every case. **Isto não se aplica a você,** This does not apply to you.

aplicável, aplicativo –va (*adj.*) applicable.

aplito (*m., Petrog.*) aplite.

aplotomia (*f., Surg.*) aplotomy, simple incision.

apnéia (*f., Med.*) apnea.

apneumatose (*f., Med.*) atelectasis.

apoaconitina (*f., Chem.*) apoaconitine.

apoatropina (*f., Chem.*) atropine, atropamine.

apocalipse (*f.*) revelation; (*m.*) [*cap.*] the Apocalypse.

apocalíptico –ca (*adj.*) apocaliptic(al); occult, cryptic.

apocarpo –pa (*adj.; Bot.*) apocarpous; (*m.*) apocarp.

apoceiro (*m.*) a shallow watering basin dug around a tree or shrub.

apocináceas, apocíneas (*f.,pl., Bot.*) the Apocynaceae (dogbane family).

apócino (*m., Bot.*) any dogbane (*Apocynum*).

apocodeína (*f., Chem.*) apocodeine.

apocopar (*v.t., Gram.*) to apocopate.

apócope (*f., Gram., Med.*) apocope.

apocópico –ca (*adj.*) apocopic.

apocrênico –ca (*adj.; Chem.*) apocrenic.

apócrifo –fa (*adj.*) apocryphal.

apocromático –ca (*adj.; Optics*) apochromatic.

apocrústico –ca (*adj.; Med.*) apocrustic.

apodadeira (*f.*) a taunter.

apodador –dora (*adj.*) taunting; (*m.*) taunter.

apodadura (*f.*) taunt, quip.

apodar (*v.t.*) to taunt; to poke fun at; to deride; to call names; to liken to; to make a rough guess.

ápode (*adj., Zool.*) apodal ; (*m.*) an apodal animal.

apodema (*m., Zool.*) apodeme.

apoderar-se (*v.r.*) to seize control of; to take possession of.

apodíctico –ca (*adj.*) incontestable; absolutely certain.

apodixe [ks] (*f.*) apodixis, absolute demonstration.

apôdo (*m.*) biting jest, taunt; nickname, tag.

apódose (*f., Gram.*) apodosis.

apodrecer (*v.i.*) to rot, decay; (*v.t.*) to corrupt; to taint.

apodrecido –da (*adj.*) putrefied; tainted, spoiled.

apodrecimento (*m.*) putrefaction; corruption.

apodrentar (*v.*) = APODRECER.

apodrido –da (*adj.*) = APODRECIDO.

apófase (*f., Rhet.*) apophasis.

apófige (*f., Arch.*) apophyge.

apofilita (*f., Min.*) apophylite.

apofisado –da (*adj.*) having an apophysis.

apofisário (*m.*) apophysary, apophyseal.

apófise (*f., Anat., Bot.*) apophysis.—**basilar,** (*Anat.*) basilar process.—**espinhosa,** (*Anat.*) apophyseal process of the spine.—**mastóide,** (*Anat.*) the mastoid process.—**s pterigoídeas** (*Anat.*) pterygoid processes.

apofisite (*f., Med.*) apophysitis.

apoflegmático –ca (*adj., Med.*) apophlegmatic.

apofonia (*f., Phonet.*) apophony, ablaut.

apogamia (*f., Bot.*) apogamy.

apogeotropismo (*m., Bot.*) negative geotropism.

apogeu [é] (*m.*) apogee, apex, acme, zenith. **no—da glória,** at the peak of glory.

apoginia (*f., Bot.*) apogeny.

apogínico –ca (*adj., Bot.*) apogenous.

apogitaguara (*f.*) a medicinal plant (*Esenbeckia intermedia*) of the family Rutaceae.

apogone (*adj.*) beardless; (*m., Zool.*) a genus (*Apogon, syn. Amia*) of marine fishes consisting of the cardinal fishes.

apogôndias, apogonídeos (*m.pl., Zool.*) the Apogonidae (family of marine fishes).

apógrafo (*m.*) apograph, transcript.

apoiado –da (*adj.*) propped, supported; approved; backed; (*m.*) applause, approval; (*exclam.*) Hear! Hear!

apoiar (*v.t.*) to support, sustain, uphold; to approve, applaud; to patronize, champion, abet; to back up (a person, plan, idea, etc.); to protect, defend; to bolster; to buttress; to second (a motion).—(**-se) em** or **sôbre,** to lean (rest, depend, rely) on.—**se sôbre os cotovêlos,** to lean on one's elbows.—**um candidato,** to back a candidate.

apoio (*m.*) foundation, basis, support; prop, brace, strut, stay; applause, approval, endorsement; patronage; (*Mach.*) bearing.—**financeiro,** financial backing.—**moral,** moral support. **ponto de—,** bearing point.

apoitar (*v.*) = APOUTAR.

apojadura (*f.*) an afflux of milk in the breast.

apojar (*v.t.*) to intumesce (the breasts with milk); of a calf, to suck.

apolar (*adj.*) having no pole.

apolear (*v.t.*) to pillory.

apolegar (*v.t.*) to crumble (as tobacco) with the POLEGAR (thumb) and other fingers.

apólice (*f.*) bond, share (of stock).—**de seguro,** insurance policy.

apolíneo –nea (*adj.*) Apollo-like.

apólise (*f., Eastern Ch.*) apolysis, dismissal.

apologal (*adj.*) apologal.

apologético –ca (*adj.*) panegyric(al), eulogistical [But not apologetic in the ordinary sense, which is ESCUSATÓRIO]; (*f.*) apologetics.

apologia (*f.*) **apologismo** (*m.*) apology (but only in the sense of a formal defense in speech or writing); eulogy, encomium. [Apology in the ordinary sense is DESCULPAS, ESCUSA.]

apologista (*m.,f.*) apologist.

apologizar (*v.t.*) to make a formal defense of, in speech or writing. [To apologize in the ordinary sense is DESCULPAR-SE.]

apólogo (*m.*) apologue, allegory.

apoltronar-se (*v.r.*) to take a POLTRONA (armchair); to become a poltroon.

apolvilhar (*v.*) = POLVILHAR.

apombocado –da (*adj.*) silly, stupid.

apomecômetro (*m.*) apomecometer.

apomixia [ks] (*f., Biol.*) apomixis.

apomorfina (*f., Chem., Pharm.*) apomorphin(e).

aponeurologia, aponevrologia (*f., Anat.*) aponeurology.

aponeurose, aponevrose (*f., Anat.*) aponeurosis.

aponeurosite, aponevrosite (*f., Med.*) aponeurositis.

aponeurótico, aponevrótico –ca (*adj.; Anat.*) aponeurotic.

aponeurótomo, aponevrótomo (*m., Surg.*) aponeurotome.

apontar (*v.t.*) to point at, aim at; to point out, indicate; to mention; to show; to head for; to prompt (actors); to mark, record; to make note of; to place a bet; to sketch out; (*v.i.*) to emerge, peep out; (*v.r.*) to burgeon.—**a,** to aim at, point at, point out.—**para,** to point toward, aim at.

apontoado –da (*adj.*) basted (sewn) together.

apontoar (*v.t.*) to baste (sew); to cite, enumerate.

apopléctico –ca (*adj.*) apoplectic; choleric; (*m.,f.*) one liable to, or having, apoplexy.

apoplexia [x= ss] (*f., Med.*) apoplexy, stroke; (*Plant Pathol.*) apoplexy (of grapevines).

apoquentação (*f.*) worry, vexation, annoyance.

apoquentado –da (*adj.*) troubled, upset; annoyed.

apoquentador –dora (*adj.*) troublesome; (*m.,f.*) one who or that which annoys.

apoquentar (*v.t.*) to worry, plague, annoy, devil; pester, tease, "needle," badger, nag; (*v.r.*) to get worried and upset; to get "hot and bothered".

apor [63] (*v.t.*) to appose; to affix (signature, tax stamp).

aporfiar (*v.*) = PORFIAR.

aporia (*f., Rhet.*) aporia.

aporismar (*v.*) = APOSTEMAR.

aporreado –da (*adj.*) cudgeled; pestered; of a horse, not properly broken.

aporrear (*v.t.*) to cudgel; to pester; to break (a horse) inexpertly; (*v.r.*) of a horse, to become wild or dangerous because of improper handling.

aporretar (*v.t.*) to beat with a PORRETE (cudgel).

aporrinhação (*f.*) **aporrinhamento** (*m.*), pestering, "botheration"; annoyance, disgust.

aporrinhar (*v.t., colloq.*) to bother, pester, annoy.

aportar (*v.t.*) to enter port; (*v.i.*) to arrive in port.

aportuguesado –da (*adj.*) Portuguese-like.

aportuguesar (*v.t.*) to render Portuguese; to assimilate to the Portuguese, esp. in the matter of language.

após (*prep.*) after; behind; (*adv.*) after.
aposentação (*f.*) accommodation; retirement (from employment).
aposentador (*m.*) -dora (*f.*) one who provides lodgings.
aposentadoria (*f.*) retirement; lodgings. **proventos de—,** retirement income, pension.
aposentar (*v.t.*) to retire, pension off; to give lodging to; (*v.r.*) to retire from employment; to take lodgings.
aposento (*m.*) room, bedroom, apartment; dwelling-house.
aposia (*f., Med.*) aposia, adipsia.
aposição (*f.*) apposition.
aposiopese (*f., Rhet.*) aposiopesis.
apositia (*f.*) apositia, aversion to food.
aposítico -ca (*adj., Med.*) apositic.
apósito -ta (*adj.*) apposite.
apossador -dora (*adj.*) possessing; (*m.,f.*) possessor.
apossar-se (*v.r.*) to take possession (of).
aposta (*f.*) wager, bet; amount wagered; challenge; breast of chicken.
apostado -da (*adj.*) decided, resolved; wagered.
apostador -dora (*adj.*) betting; (*m.,f.*) bettor.
apostar (*v.t.*) to wager, bet; to aver, assert; to vie with; to challenge comparison with; (*v.r.*) to bind, pledge, oneself; to get ready.—**corrida,** to challenge to a race.
apóstase (*f., Med.*) apostasis.
apostasia (*f.*) apostasy.
apóstata (*adj.; m.,f.*) apostate; turncoat.
apostatar (*v.i.*) to apostatize.
apostema (*m., Med.*) aposteme, abscess, boil.
apostemar (*v.i.,v.r.*) to fester; to form an abscess.
apostemático -ca (*adj.*) pert. to abscesses.
apostemeira (*f., colloq.*) a crop of boils.
apostemoso -sa (*adj.*) apostematous.
apostia (*f., Med.*) aposthia.
apostil(h)a (*f.*) study outline, class notes; annotation; marginal note; postscript; rider (addition to a document).
apostilar (*v.t.*) to annotate.
apôsto, aposta (*p.p. of* APOR) apposed.
apóstola (*f.*) a woman apostle.
apostolado (*m.*) apostleship.
apostolar (*v.t.*) to evangelize; to preach; (*v.i.*) to serve as an apostle.
apostólico -ca (*adj.*) apostolic.
apostolizar (*v.*) = APOSTOLAR.
apóstolo (*m.*) apostle.
apóstrofe (*f.*) apostrophe (digression from a discourse.)
apóstrofo (*m.*) apostrophe [the mark '].
apostura (*f.*) posture.
apotegma (*m.*) apothegm, terse aphorism.
apotegmático -ca (*adj.*) apothegmatic.
apótema (*m., Math.*) apothem.
apoteosar (*v.t.*) to apotheosize, glorify, exalt.
apoteose (*f.*) apotheosis.
apótese (*f., Surg.*) apothesis, setting of a fractured limb.
apoucado -da (*adj.*) mean, petty; narrow-minded; belittled.
apoucador -dora (*adj.*) belittling; (*m.,f.*) detractor.
apoucamento (*m.*) narrowness, meanness.
apoucar (*v.t.*) to reduce; to belittle, run down; (*v.r.*) to underrate oneself.
apoutar (*v.t.,v.i.*) to anchor. Var. APOITAR; Cf. POITAR.
apôzema (*f., Pharm.*) apozem, a decoction.
aprático -ca (*adj., Med.*) apraxic.
aprauá (*f.*) a bulletwood (*Mimusops brasiliensis*).
àpraxia [ks] (*f., Med.*) apraxia.
aprazador (*m.*) one who sets the time (as for a meeting).
aprazamento (*m.*) designation of time, date or place (as for a meeting).
aprazar (*v.t.*) to fix, determine (the time or day or length of time); to designate, agree on (the place); to adjourn.
aprazer [30] (*v.t.*) to please, give pleasure to; (*v.r.*) to be pleased (**com,** with). **Apraz-me levar ao conhecimento de V. Ex. que,** I am pleased to inform Your Excellency that. . . . **Apraz-me satisfazer ao seu pedido,** I am happy to comply with your request. **Declarou que só faria o que bem lhe aprouvesse,** He said he would do only as he pleased. **Disse-me que eu aprovasse quanto me aprouvesse,** He told me to approve whatever I pleased.
aprazibilidade (*f.*) pleasurable quality.
aprazimento (*m.*) pleasure, enjoyment, delight.
aprazível (*adj.*) delightful, pleasant, pleasurable, agreeable.

apre! (*interj.*) Dammit! Doggonit! The devil!
apreçador -dora (*adj.*) pricing; (*m.,f.*) pricer.
apreçamento (*m.*) pricing.
apreçar (*v.t.*) to price; to appraise.
apreciação (*f.*) appreciation, valuation, appraisal.
apreciador -dora (*adj.*) appreciating, appraising; (*m.,f.*) appraiser.
apreciar (*v.t.*) to appreciate, value, prize; to take delight in, derive pleasure from; to enjoy; to appraise, rate, size up.—**o valor de uma jóia,** to appraise the value of a jewel. —**os fatos,** to evaluate the facts.
apreciativo -va (*adj.*) appreciative.
apreciável (*adj.*) appreciable; worthy of esteem.
aprêço (*m.*) esteem, high regard; opinion. **o assunto em—,** the business in hand; the matter under discussion. **ter muito—a (por),** to hold in high esteem, have high regard for.
apreendedor -dora (*adj.*) = APREENSOR.
apreender [e-e] (*v.t.*) to apprehend, seize, arrest; to grasp mentally; (*Law*) to distrain; (*v.r.*) to be apprehensive.
apreensão (*f.*) apprehension; seizure, arrest; dread, misgiving; (*Law*) distraint; attachment.
apreensível (*adj.*) apprehensible.
apreensivo -va (*adj.*) apprehensive, uneasy, anxious.
apreensor -sora (*m., f.*) apprehender.
apreensório -ria (*adj., Law*) arresting, seizing.
aprefixar [ks] (*v.t.*) to prefix.
apregoado -da (*adj.*) proclaimed.
apregoador -dora (*adj.*) proclaiming; (*m.*) crier; barker.
apregoar (*v.t.*) to announce, publish, proclaim; to cry (wares); (*v.r.*) to boast.
apremar (*v.*) = OPRIMIR.
apremer (*v.*) = PREMER.
aprender (*v.t.*) to learn (**a,** to).
aprendiz (*m*) apprentice, beginner.
aprendizado (*m.*) **aprendizagem** (*f.*) apprenticeship; trade school; the learning process.
apresamento (*m.*) capture, seizure.
apresar (*v.t.*) to seize as prey; to seize (enemy vessel, goods, etc.) as booty.
apresentação (*f.*) presentation, introduction; letter of introduction; bearing, deportment; personal appearance; get up (as of a book). **de boa—,** of good address (appearance). **fazer a—,** to make an introduction (of one person to another).
apresentador -dora (*adj.*) presenting; (*m.,f.*) one who or that which presents.
apresentante (*adj.*) presenting; (*m.,f.*) bearer of a draft, check or note presented for payment.
apresentar (*v.t.*) to present, introduce, make known; to exhibit, offer; to present to view; to submit, refer; to show, reveal; to expound, explain; (*v.r.*) to present oneself; to appear.—**argumentos,** to present arguments, offer reasons.—**credenciais,** to present one's credentials.—**defesa,** to offer a defense (in court).—**desculpas,** to offer apologies.—**os seus respeitos (as suas homenagens),** to pay one's respects.—**provas,** to present evidence, offer proof.—**se bem,** to make a good personal appearance, make a good impression.—**se como voluntário,** to offer oneself as a volunteer.
apresentável (*adj.*) presentable.
apresilhar (*v.t.*) to fasten with a buckle or clasp.
apressado -da (*adj.*) hurried, hasty, quick; pressed for time.
apressador -dora (*adj.*) hastening, hurrying; (*m.,f.*) one who hastens.
apressamento (*m.*) hastening; urgency.
apressar (*v.t.*) to hurry, hasten, expedite, speed, push on; to urge forward; to urge, press; (*v.r.*) to hasten, make haste, hurry (**a, em, por, para,** to).
apressurado -da (*adj.*) hasty; up and stirring; pressed for time.
apressuramento (*m.*) rush, speed, haste.
apressurar (*v.t.*) to hasten, speed, urge; (*v.r.*) to hurry; to get ready in a hurry.
aprestador -dora (*adj.*) preparing, making ready; (*m.,f.*) one who prepares or makes ready promptly.
aprestamento (*m.*) preparation; equipment.
aprestar (*v.t.*) to make ready; to equip; (*v.r.*) to get ready.
apresto (*m.*) equipment; preparation.
aprilino -na (*adj.*) April.
aprimorado -da (*adj.*) exquisite, of rare excellence or refinement; perfect; painstakingly executed.

aprimorador –dora (*adj.*) perfecting; (*m.,f.*) one who perfects or strives to perfect (something).
aprimoramento (*m.*) refinement, betterment.
aprimorar (*v.t.*) to refine, perfect, make excellent; (*v.r.*) to strive for perfection, do one's best.
apriorismo (*m.*) apriorism.
apriorista (*m.,f.*) apriorist.
apriorístico –ca (*adj.*) aprioristic.
aprisco (*m.*) sheepfold, pen, corral.
aprisionador –dora (*adj.*) imprisoning; (*m.,f.*) imprisoner.
aprisionamento (*m.*) imprisonment.
aprisionar (*v.t.*) to imprison.
aproamento (*m.*) act of heading for (land, etc.).
aproar (*v.t.*) to steer for, head for.
aprobativo –va, –tório, –ria (*adj.*) approbative, approving. Var. APROVATIVO.
aproctia (*f., Med.*) aproctia.
aproejar (*v.*) = APROAR.
aprofundamento (*m.*), **aprofundação** (*f.*) getting at the bottom of; making deeper.
aprofundar (*v.t.*) to deepen; to make a deep study of.— –se em, to delve deeply into (a subject).
aprontação (*f.*) act of making ready.
aprontar (*v.t.*) to make ready, put in order; to finish (a job); (*v.r.*) to get ready (**para**, to).
apropinquar [9] (*v.t.*) to carry or advance closer to; to cause to approach; (*v.r.*) to come nearer.
apropositado –da (*adj.*) appropriate, pertinent; suitable, convenient.
apropositar (*v.t.*) to suit, make appropriate; to speak to the point; (*v.r.*) to present itself opportunely.—**os meios aos fins,** to suit the means to the end.
apropriação (*f.*) appropriation, seizure; application (to a particular use).—**indébita,** unlawful seizure.
apropriado –da (*adj.*) appropriate, proper, suitable.
apropriador –dora (*adj.*) appropriating; (*m.,f.*) one who appropriates.
apropriar (*v.t.*) to apportion, allot to; to make suitable.— –se de, to appropriate, take as one's own that which belongs to another.
aprosexia [ks] (*f.*) aprosexia, inability to pay attention.
aprouv+verb endings=forms of APRAZER [30].
aprovação (*f.*) approval, approbation; ratification, endorsement; praise, commendation.—**no exame,** passing in an exam.
aprovado –da (*adj.*) approved, sanctioned; (*exclamation*) Agreed! Done!
aprovador –dora (*adj.*) approving.
aprovar (*v.t.*) to approve, commend; to think well (highly, favorably) of; to sanction, assent to, concur in; to pass (a student, in an exam).
aprovativo –va (*adj.*) = APROBATIVO.
aprovável (*adj.*) approvable.
aproveitadeira, fem. of APROVEITADOR.
aproveitado –da (*adj.*) fully utilized; turned to profit or advantage; thrifty.
aproveitador –deira (*adj.*) that takes full advantage of; (*m.,f.*) one who does so.—**de guerra,** war profiteer.
aproveitamento (*m.*) utilization, turning to account, making good use of, seizing the opportunity; improvement.— **de tempo,** making good use of time.—**nos estudos,** profiting from school work.
aproveitar (*v.t.*) to profit by, benefit by, take advantage of, improve the opportunity, turn to good account; to utilize fully; (*v.i.*) to be of use.—**-se de,** to take advantage of, avail oneself of.—**a maré,** to sail with the tide; strike while the iron is hot; make hay while the sun shines.
aproveitável (*adj.*) utilizable.
aprovisionador –dora (*adj.*) provisioning, supplying; (*m.,f.*) provisioner, supplier.
aprovisionamento (*m.*) provisioning, supply.—**de víveres,** stock of food.
aprovisionar (*v.t.*) to provision, stock, supply. Cf. ABASTECER.
aproximação [x=ss] (*f.*) approximation; close estimate; approach. **ângulo de**—, (*Aeron.*) angle of approach.
aproximadamente [x=ss] (*adv.*) approximately, about.
aproximado –da [x=ss] (*adj.*) close, near.
aproximar [x=ss] (*v.t.*) to approximate; to approach; to carry or advance near to; to bring closer; (*v.r.*) to draw closer (**a, de,** to).—**-se do têrmo,** to draw to a close. Êle aproximou-se de mim, He came up to me.
aproximativo –va [x=ss] (*adj.*) approximate.

aprumação (*f.*) act of setting upright, making plumb.
aprumado –da (*adj.*) plumb, upright, erect. **um homem—,** an upstanding man.
aprumar (*v.t.*) to plumb; to stand (something) straight up; (*v.r.*) to stand (straighten) up.—**uma mesa,** to steady a table (keep it from wobbling).
aprumo (*m.*) upright position; uprightness; haughtiness; aplomb.
apselafesia (*f., Med.*) apselaphesia.
apside (*f., Astron.*) apsis; (*pl.*) apsides.
apsiquia (*f., Med.*) apsychia.
aptar (*v.t.*) to render apt; (*v.r.*) to become apt.
apteira (*f., Bot.*) a sp. of Bauhinia (*B. parviflora*).
aptenoditas (*m.pl.*) the genus (*Aptenodytes*) of king and emperor penguins.
aptéria (*f., Zool.*) apterium.
aptérix [ks] (*f., Zool.*) apteryx.
áptero –ra (*adj., Zool.*) apterous, without wings.
aptialia (*f.*), –**lismo** (*m., Med.*) aptyalia, aptyalism.
aptiano (*m., Geol.*) Aptian.
aptidão, aptitude (*f.*) aptitude, aptness, knack.—**profissional,** professional or vocational ability.
aptificar (*v.*) = APTAR.
apto –ta (*adj.*) apt, able; capable, skillful.
apuar (*v.t.*) to pierce with a sharp point.
apuf (*m.*) = APUÎZEIRO.
apuirana [u-i] (*m.*) a poison nut (*Strychnos rouhamon*).
apuizeiro (*m.*) either of two epiphytic strangler trees: *Ficus fagifolia,* of the mulberry family, or the waxflower, *Clusia insignis.*
apunhalar (*v.t.*) to stab with, or as with, a dagger; to wound the feelings of.
apunhar (*v.t.*) to grasp (a sword) by the hilt.
apupada (*f.*) jeers, boos.
apupar (*v.t.*) to jeer (hoot) at; to boo, hiss.
apupo (*m.*) jeer; shouting, clamor.
.apuração (*f.*) purification; verification; investigation; checking.—**de votos,** counting of votes.
apurado –da (*adj.*) accurate; choice, select, fine, elegant, trim; (*colloq.*) hard up. **um caldo de galinha bem—,** a rich chicken broth; (*f.*) a kind of rich red soil in Brazil.
apurador –dora (*adj.*) purifying; verifying; (*m.,f.*) purifier; checker.
apuramento (*m.*) settlement (of accounts); purification.
apurar (*v.t.*) to purify, cleanse; to choose, pick out; to ascertain by investigation, find out, learn, discover, trace; to confirm, verify; to perfect; to edit, correct; to raise money by selling something; to thicken (as soup) by boiling; to refine (metals); to wash (diamond-bearing gravel); to speed up; (*v.r.*) to become purer; to preen oneself; to get into financial or other difficulties; to become "riled" (**com alguém,** at someone).—**as contas,** to settle accounts.—**a memória,** to search one's memory.—**o ouvido,** to prick up one's ears.—**a situação,** to investigate and determine the situation.—**a vista,** to sharpen one's eyes.—**os fatos,** to determine the facts.—**os votos,** to count (check) the votes. Apurou bom dinheiro na venda do automóvel, He got a good price for his car.
apurativo –va (*adj.*) = DEPURATIVO.
apuro (*m.*) act of counting, checking, verifying; carefulness (in dress, speech, etc.); strait, plight, predicament, state of distress; the sum total. **em—s,** up against it.
aquadrilhar (*v.t.*) to form an armed band; (*v.r.*) to enlist in an armed band.
aquaforte (*f.*) = AGUAFORTE.
aquafortista (*m.,f.*) aquafortist, etcher. Var. ÁGUAFORTISTA.
aquapun[c]tura (*f., Med.*) aquapuncture.
aquarela (*f.*) = AGUARELA.
aquarelista (*m.,f.*) = AGUARELISTA.
aquário (*m.*) aquarium.
aquarterlar (*v.t.*) to quarter, billet, lodge.
aquático –ca (*adj.*) aquatic; (*m.,f.*) a frequenter of spas.
aquátil (*adj.*) = AQUÁTICO.
aquecedor –dora (*adj.*) heating; (*m.*) heater; water heater.—**de ar,** air heater.—**elétrico,** electric heater.— **de gás,** gas heater.—**de óleo,** oil heater.
aquecer (*v.t.*) to get warm or hot; (*v.r.*) to warm oneself.— –se com, to get angry at. Cf. AQUENTAR, ESQUENTAR
aquecimento (*m.*) heating.—**central,** central heating. **superfície de**—, heating surface.
aquecível (*adj.*) capable of being heated.
aqueduto (*m.*) aqueduct.—**subterrâneo,** underground water main.

aquela [é] (*fem.*), **aquêle** (*masc.*) (*adj., pron.*) that, that one, that one yonder, that one over there; the former; (*pl.*) those. **sem mais**—, without further ado.

àquela [é] (*fem.*), **àquele** [êl] (*masc.*) [*contr. of prep.* A +*pron.* AQUELA, AQUÊLE] to her (him); to that; to the former; (*pl.*) to those; to them.

aqueloutra [AQUELA+OUTRA], **aqueloutro** [AQUÊLE+OUTRO] that other one (over there).

àqueloutra [ÀQUELA+OUTRA], **àqueloutro** [ÀQUELE+OUTRO] to that other one (over there).

aquém (*adv.*) on this side.—**de**, (*prep.*) this side of; less than, not up to; short of; below, beneath; inferior to. **muito**—**das minhas esperanças**, far short of my hopes.

aquênio (*m., Bot.*) achene.

aquenódio (*m., Bot.*) achenodium, cremocarp.

aquentar (*v.t.*) to warm, heat; to stimulate, animate; (*v.r.*) to warm oneself. Cf. AQUECER, ESQUENTAR.

aquerenciar-se (*v.r.*) to get used to a place (as a pet gets used to a new home).

aqui (*adv.*) here, herein.—**dentro**, in here.—**e ali**, here and there.—**mesmo**, right here.—**e ali**, just between us.—**por perto**, hereabout. **eis**—, behold; here you have; here (it) is. **para**—, here. **por**—, hereabout. **um**—, **outro acolá**, one here, another there. **Por**—, **faça o favor**, This way, please.

aqüícola (*adj.*) aquicolous.

aqüicultura (*f.*) aquiculture.

aqui-del-rei (*exclam.*) an old form of cry for help;—something like Help! Police! Murder!

aquiscência (*f.*) acquiescence, assent, consent.

aquiescente (*adj.*) acquiescent.

aquiescer (*v.t.*) to acquiesce, assent, consent, agree.—**em**, to abide by.

aquietação (*f.*) quieting; appeasing.

aquietador –**dora** (*adj.*) quieting; (*m.,f.*) one who or that which quiets or appeases.

aquietar (*v.t.*) to quiet (down), tranquilize, calm; to lull; to soothe; to allay; to appease; (*v.i.*) to be still; (*v.r.*) to grow quiet; to subside.

aqüífero –**ra** (*adj.*) aquiferous.

aqüifoliáceo –**cea** (*adj., Bot.*) ilicaceous; (*f.*) a holly.

aqüifólio (*m.*) English holly (*Ilex aquifolium*), better known as AZEVINHO or AZEVIM.

aquilatação (*f.*) act of assaying.

aquilatador –**dora** [ô] (*adj.*) assaying; (*m.,f.*) assayer.

aquilatar (*v.t.*) to appraise, assay, value; to improve, add to the worth of.—**os fatos**, to weigh the facts.

aqüilégia (*f.*) the European columbine (*Aquilegia vulgaris*) c.a. ANCÓLIA, ERVA-POMBINHA.

aquiléia (*f., Bot.*) yarrow (*Achillea millefolium*).

aquileína (*f., Chem.*) achileine.

Aquiles (*m.*) Achilles.

aquilhado –**da** (*adj.*) having a keel.

aquilia (*f., Med.*) achylia.

aquilino –**na** (*adj.*) aquiline.

aquilo (*dem. pron.*) that, those; (*derog.*) that thing (meaning, that person).

àquilo (*contr. of prep.* A+*pron.* AQUILO), to that.

aquilodinia (*f., Med.*) achillodynia.

aquimia (*f., Med.*) achymia.

aquinhoado –**da** (*adj.*) apportioned. **bem**—**pela sorte**, well-favored by fortune. **o mais bem**—, the one who receives the largest share.

aquinhoador –**dora** (*adj.*) sharing, allotting; (*m.,f.*) allotter, sharer.

aquinhoamento (*m.*) allotment.

aquinhoar (*v.t.*) to parcel out, apportion, portion out, mete. Var. QUINHOAR.

aquisição (*f.*) acquisition.

aquisitivo –**va** (*adj.*) acquisitive. [But not in the sense of rapacious, which is RAPACE, but of ability to make acquisitions, as in the term PODER AQUISITIVO, purchasing power.]

aquocapsulite (*f., Med.*) aquocapsulitis.

aquosidade (*f.*) state of being watery.

aquoso –**sa** (*adj.*) aqueous, watery; hydrous.

ar [-es] (*m.*) air, atmosphere; climate; breeze, zephyr, gentle wind; behavior, demeanor, manner; countenance, mein, look, aspect; paralysis, stroke.—**ambiente**, ambient air.—**atmosférico**, the atmosphere.—**atrevido**, bold, brazen, look.—**coado**, a draft of air.—**comprimido**, compressed air.—**condicionado**, conditioned air.—**de bêsta**, or **de bobo**, a feigned look of innocence.—**de riso**, a smiling face.—**do mar**, sea air.—**empestado**, foul, in-

fected air.—**encanado**, a draft (current of air).—**espantado**, an astonished look.—**líquido**, liquid air.—**livre**, the open air.—**trágico**, tragic mien.—**triunfante**, triumphant air. **ao**—**livre**, out-of-doors, in the open. **aos**—**es**, into the air, up into the sky. **apanhar um**—, to catch a cold. **armar castelos no**—, to build air-castles; to day-dream. **atirar (com) tudo pelos**—**es**, to blow up (in a rage). **bôlha de**—, air bubble. **bomba de**—, air pump. **câmara de**—, inner tube. **dar um**—, or **dar**—**es, com**, to favor (resemble) another person. **dar-se**—**es**, to put on airs. **dar-se**—**es de**, to pose as. **dar um**—**de sua graça**, to smile; to show up (on a visit); to put in an appearance. **falar no**—, to talk idly. **fazer as coisas no**—, to do things in a scatterbrained sort of way. **golpe de**—, a draft of air. **impermeável ao**—, airtight. **ir pelos**—**es**, to burst, blow up (into the air). **ir tomar**—, to go for an airing. **mudar de**—**es**, to make a change (of place). **Não deu um**—**de gua graça**, He did not (even) show up. **palavras no**—, empty words.

ara (*f.*) sacrificial altar; (*interj.*) = ORA.

ará (*f.*) the common caladium (*C. bicolor*), c.a. TINHORÃO.

arabaiana (*m.*) an amber fish (*Seriola dumerili*), c.a. ÔLHO-DE-VIDRO, FOGUEIRA; also = ÔLHO-DE-BOI, OLHETE.

árabe (*adj.*) Arabian; (*m.*) Arab; Arabic.

Arabela (*f.*) Arabella; Arabel.

arabêsco (*m.*) arabesque; scrollwork; tracery.

arabi [í] (*m.*) = RABINO.

arábico –**ca**, –**bigo** –**ga** (*dj.*) Arabic, Arabian; (*m.*) Arabic (the language).

arabina (*f., Chem.*) arabic acid.

arabinose (*f., Chem.*) arabinose.

arábio –**bia** (*adj.*) = ARÁBICO.

árabis (*f., Bot.*) rockcress (*Arabis.*)

arabismo (*m.*) Arabicism.

arabista (*m.,f.*) Arabist.

arabite (*f., Chem.*) arabite, arabitol.

arabizar (*v.t.*) to Arabize.

arabóia (*f.*) a rat snake (*Chironius fuscus*), c.a. CANINANA.

arabutã (*m.*) the prickly Brazilwood (*Caesalpinia echinata*); = PAU-BRASIL.

araçá (*f.*) having black markings (referring to a yellow steer); (*m.*) any of numerous tropical American shrubs or small trees, or their fruit, esp. the following:—-**de coroa**,—**da-praia**,—**de-comer**,—**do-campo**,—**do-mato**,—-**pêra**,—**piranga**,—**rosa**,—**vermelho**, all are the Cattley or strawberry guava (*Psidium littorale*).—-**do-campo**,—**pedra**,—**mirim**, are the Brazilian guava (*P. guineense*) c.a. ARAÇAÍ, ARAÇAIBA, ARAÇAEIRO, ARAÇAZEIRO.—-**do-pará**, is the paraguava (*Britoa acida*).

aracaju [ú] (*m.,f.*) one of the Aracaju, a little-known Tupian tribe of the lower Amazon and now extinct; (*adj.*) pert. to or designating this tribe.

araçanga (*f.*) a club used by JANGADEIROS for killing fish brought in on a hook.

aracanga (*f., Zool.*) the red-and-blue macaw (*Ara macao*).

aracanguira (*m.*) the threadfish (*Alectis ciliaris*) c.a. ABACATAIA, ALETO, GALO-FITA, PEIXE-GALO-DO-BRASIL; also = PEIXE-GALO, the look-down (*Selene vomer*).

aração (*f.*) plowing; ravening of food.

araçari [í] (*m., Zool.*) any aracari, esp. the following: the curl crested aracari (*Bauharnaisius bauharnaisius*) and the many-banded aracari (*Pteroglossus pluricinctus*), both of the upper Amazon.—-**banana**, the saffron-colored aracari of southeastern Brazil (*Baillonius bailloni*).—(-**do**)-**minhoca**, the black-necked aracari (*Pteroglossus a. aracari*) c.a. TUCANUÍ.—-**poca**, Gould's toucanet (*Selenidera maculirostris gouldii*), and the spotted-billed toucanet (*Selenidera m. maculirostris*).

araçazeiro (*m.*) the Brazilian guava (*Psidium guineense*). [The common guava, called GOIABEIRA, is *Psidium guajava.*]

arácea (*f.*) any plant of the Araceae (arums).

araciurá [i-ui] (*m.*) = PAPA-AÇAÍ.

aracnídeos (*m.pl.*) the Arachnida (spiders and scorpions).

aracnismo (*m.*) arachnidism or arachism (condition resulting from the poisonous bite of a spider or other arachnid).

aracnóide (*adj.*) arachnid; cobweblike; (*Zool.*) Arachnidian; (*f., Anat.*) the arachnoid membrane; (*m., Zool.*) one of the Arachnida.

aracnoídeo –**dea** (*adj.*) resembling a spider's web; (*Anat.; Bot.*) arachnoid.

aracnoidismo (*m.*) = ARACNISMO.

aracnologia (*f., Zool.*) arachnology.

araçóia (*f.*) Indian belt made of feathers. Var. ARAZÓIA

araçoiaba (*f.*) Indian skirt or apron made of feathers; a group of iron-ore mountains in the State of São Paulo.

aracoram (*m.*) = GALO (moonfish).

araçuaiava (*m.*) = SABIACICA.

aracuã (*f., Zool.*) any of various chachalacas (genus Ortalis, family Cracidae), esp. the white-bellied one (*O. araucuan*) and the Guiana chachalaca (*O. motmot*), the latter c.a. ARACUÃ-DE-CABEÇA-VERMELHA.

aracuão (*m.*) = MÃE-DE-PORCO.

aracuí (*m.*) = ANGELIM-DE-FÔLHA-LARGA.

arada (*f.*) plowing; a plowed field.

arado (*m.*) a plow.—**de discos**, disk plow.

arador (*m.*) plowman.

aradura (*f.*) plowing; plowed land.

aragem (*f.*) breeze, zephyr, gentle wind, breath of air, current of air; aura; favorable time.

aragonita (*f., Min.*) aragonite.

araguaguá (*m.*) the common sawfish (*Pristis pectinatus*), c.a. PEIXE-SERRA, PIRAGUAGUÁ.

araguaí, araguari [í] (*m., Zool.*) a macaw (*Conurus leucophthalmus*).

araguato (*m.*) the ursine howling monkey of northern Brazil (*Alouatta*, syn. *Mycetes, ursina*).

araguirá (*m.*) = TICO-TICO-REI.

arajuba (*m.*) = GUARUBA.

araliáceas (*f., Bot.*) the Araliaceae (ginseng family).

aramã, aramã (*m.*) an angry black bee, having yellow wings and a disagreeable odor (*Melipona heideri*), c.a. BORÁ, BORÁ-BOI, BORÁ-CAVALO, VORÁ.

aramaça, -maçã (*m.*) = LINGUADO (a flounder).

aramado -da (*adj.*) enclosed with a wire fence.

aramador (*m.*) manufacturer of wire and wire netting.

aramagem (*f.*) wire netting.

aramanjaiá (*f.*) a snout beetle (*Rhyncophorus palmarum*).

aramar (*v.t.*) to enclose with wire.

arambóia (*f.*) the bojobi or dog-headed boa of the Amazon (*Xiphosoma caninum*).

arame (*m.*) wire; alloy; (*pl., slang*) dough (money).—**farpado**, barbed wire.—**recouto**, or **recozido**, annealed wire. **andar no—**, to walk a tightrope. **cortina de—**, wire screen. **estai de—**, guy wire. **estar sem—s**, (*slang*) to be strapped, broke. **ir aos—s**, to lose one's temper.

arameiro (*m.*) a wire worker; wire netting.

aramifício (*m.*) wire factory.

aramina (*f.*) the fiber of the cadillo (*Urena lobata*).

aramista (*m.,f.*) tightrope acrobat.

aramudo -da (*adj.; slang*) having much "dough" (money).

arancim (*m.*) = ARIXIM.

arandela (*f.*) bobêche of a candlestick; lampholder; wall light fixture; gaslight jet; guard of a sword hilt.

arandéua (*f., Bot.*) an apesearring (*Pithecellobium cauliflorum*), c.a. INGARANA, INGÀZINHO.

arando (*m.*) the myrtle whortleberry (*Vaccinium myrtillus*), c.a. UVA-DO-MONTE.

araneídeos (*m.,pl.*) the order Araneida (spiders).

araneiforme (*adj.*) araneiform, like a spider.

araneologia (*f.*) = ARACNOLOGIA.

aranha (*f.*) spider; any of various things resembling or suggesting a spider; a spider phaeton (light two-wheeled carriage or trap); a slow-moving person; (*Naut.*) crowfoot; (*Bot.*) an orchid (*Renanthera coccinea*); a glorylily (*Gloriosa simplex*); (*m., slang*) a nitwit, sap.—**do-linho**, black widow spider.—**do-mar**, spider crab. **em palpos de—**, in hot water, in a mess, behind the 8-ball, in a jam, stumped. **prender-se com teias de—**, to be balked by trifles.

aranhagato (*m., Bot.*) the catclaw apesearring (*Pithecellobium unguiscati*).

aranhão (*m.*) a large spider.

aranhar (*v.i.*) to move slowly, like a spider.

aranheiro (*m.*) spider's nest.

aranhento -ta (*adj.*) spidery; full of spiders.

aranhiço (*m.*) a small spider.

aranhol [-óis] (*m.*) a spider's hole; a fine net for trapping birds.

aranhoso -sa (*adj.*) spidery; spider-like.

aranhuço (*m.*) a huge spider.

aranzel [-zéis] (*m.*) long-winded discourse; rigmarole; balderdash; (*colloq.*) brawl.

arão (*m.*) = JARRO (a plant).

arapabaca (*f.*) any herb of genus Spigelia.

arapaçu [ú] (*m.*) any of various birds of the Dendrocolaptidae, esp. the buff-throated wood-hewer (*Xiphorphynchus g. guttatus*); the flat-billed wood-hewer (*Dendro-* *colaptes p. platyrostris*), c.a. ARAPAÇU-GRANDE, SUBIDEIRA, TARASCA; the red-billed sickle-bill (*Campylorhamphus t. trochilirostris*) c.a. ARAPAÇU-DE-BICO-TORTO; Riker's pointed tail (*Berlepschia rikeri*), c.a. ARAPAÇU-DOS-COQUEIROS. The name **arapaçu** applies also to two oven birds: the cinnamon-rumped philydor (*P. pyrrhodes*) and the lower Amazon autumolus (*A. infuscatus paraensis*).

arapaima (*m.*) = PIRARUCU.

arapapá (*m.*) the boat-billed heron (*Cochlearius cochlearius* or *Cancroma cochlearia*), c.a. ARATIAÇU, COLHEREIRO, REI-DOS-QUÁ, SAVACU, TAMATIÁ.—**de-bico-comprido** = SOCOÍ.

arapatão (*m.*) the garden pea (*Pisum sativum*); = ERVILHA.

araponga (*f.*) the naked-throated bell-bird (*Procnias nudicollis*) of southwestern and southern Brazil, c.a. FERREIRO, FERRADOR, GUIRAPONGA, UIRAPONGA.—**da-horta** = ARAPONGUINHA.—**de-asa-preta**, Marcgrave's black-winged bell-bird (*Procnias a. averano*) of northeastern Brazil; fig., a strident-voiced person.

araponguinha (*f.*) either of two birds: the crested sharpbill (*Oxyruncus c. cristatus*), c.a. ARAPONGA-DA-HORTA, CHIBANTE; or the inquisitive tityra (*Tityra inquisitor*).

araponguira (*f.*) a bird—the Brazilian tityra (*T. cayana brasiliensis*), c.a. SANJICA.

arapuá, arapuã (*f.*) disheveled hair; a bee, c.a. TORCECABELO, IRAPUÁ, ABELHA-DE-CACHORRO.

arapuca (*f.*) a figure-four (bird) trap; any trap or pitfall; a tumble-down, ramshackle house; a gambling house; a "gyp joint"; a racket.

arapuçá (*f.*) a fresh-water turtle (*Podocnemis lewyayana*).

arapuê (*m., Bot.*) a frangipani (*Plumeria*), c.a. AGONIADA.

arapuru [rú] (*m.*) any of numerous small, bright-colored songless birds, esp. manakins, common in Brazil, notably in the Amazon region; also = UIRAPURU (a wren).

aráquida (*f., Bot.*) the peanut (*Arachis*); = AMENDOIM.

araquina (*f., Chem.*) arachin.

arar (*v.t.*) to plow; to work the land; (*v.i.*) to be without air; to be ravenously hungry; to be in a fix.

arara (*f.*) any macaw (large, long-tailed parrot); (*colloq.*) a fib or false rumor; (*m.,f.*) a dumbbell (stupid person); (*Bot.*) the Joseph's coat amaranth (*A. tricolor*).—**azul**, or—**preta**, the blue macaw (*Anodorhynchus hyacinthus*), c.a. ARARAÚNA.—**canindé** = CANINDÉ.—**vermelha**, the scarlet macaw (*Ara macao*) or the red-blue-and-green macaw (*Ara chloroptera*), c.a. ARARACANGA, ARARAMACAU, ARARAPIRANGA.

arará (*m.,f.*) an Indian of the Arará, comprising several Cariban tribes, now extinct, who lived on both sides of the lower Xingu River; (*adj.*) pert. to or designating the Arará.

araracanga (*f.*) = ARARA-VERMELHA.

araracangaçu [ú] (*m.*) = CABEÇUDA (a turtle).

ararandeuaras, see AMANAJÉ.

ararajuba (*f.*) = GUARUBA (a paroquet).

araramacau, ararapiranga (*f.*) = ARARA-VERMELHA.

araratucupé, araratucupi [i] (*f.*) a nitta tree (*Parkia oppositifolia*), c.a. VISGUEIRO, the fruits of which are enjoyed by the ARARAS (macaws).

araraúba (*f.*) = ARARIBÁ-ROSA.

araraúva (*f.*) = ARARIBÁ-AMARELO.

araréua (*f.*) = ARARIBA.

arari [í] (*m.*) a macaw (*Ara arauana*), c.a. CANINDÉ; (*Bot.*) the beaked velvetbean (*Stizolobium rostratum*).

arariba (*f.*) any of several S.A. timber trees of genus Sickingia (madder family), with heavy dark-red wood; some yield dyes and medicinal alkaloids.—**vermelha** (*Sickingia rubra*), c.a. QUINA-VERMELHA-DO-BRASIL, ARARIBÁ-ROXO, yields arabine.

araribá (*m.*) any of various porcupine podtrees of the pea family, genus Centrolobium.—**amarelo**, or—**grande**, is Brazilian zebra wood (*C. robustum*), c.a. ARARAÚVA, IRIRIBÁ, PUTUMUJU-AMARELO.—**rosa** is *C. tomentosum* and is c.a. ARARAÚBA, ARARUVA, CARIJÓ, IRIRIBÁ-ROSA, TIPIRI.—**roxo** = ARARIBA-VERMELHA.

araribina (*f.*) aribine, a crystallized alkaloid found in the bark of the Brazilian plant called ARARIBA-VERMELHA (*Sickingia rubra*).

ararinha (*f.*) Cassin's macaw (*Ara' auricollis*), c.a. MARACANÃ.

araroba (*f., Pharm.*) Goa powder; (*Bot.*) the Goa andira (*A. araroba*), c.a. ANGELIM-ARAROBA.

araruna (*f.*) = ARARAÚNA.

araruta (*f.*) arrow-root starch, or the plant (*Maranta arundinacea*) from whose roots it is obtained.
araruva (*f.*) = ARARIBÁ-ROSA.
aratabola (*f.*) = GALHUDO.
arataca (*f.*) a wild-animal trap; (*m.*) a person from north Brazil, c.a. CABEÇA-CHATA.
aratalaçu [ú] (*m.*) = ARAPAPÁ.
aratauá (*m.*) = IRATAUÁ.
araticum (*m.*) any of numerous shrubs and small trees of the genus Annona. (custardapple family); also their fruit.—-**de-cheiro** the bullocksheart custardapple (*Annona reticulata*); also its fruit.—-**do-mangue,** the pond or alligator apple (*A. glabra*); also its fruit.
aratinga (*f.*) any green parrot of genus Conurus; the Brazilian macaw (*Ara severa*).
aratório –**ria** (*adj.*) plowing.
aratu [ú] (*m.*) a small, squarish, marine land crab (*Aratus pisoni*) with short eyestalks and a very wide postabdomen, c.a. MARINHEIRO.
arauá (*m.,f.*) an Indian of an Arawakan tribe of western Brazil, or of any of the group of tribes constituting the Arauan branch of that stock; (*adj.*) Arauan.
arauanã (*m.*) = AMANÁ.
araucária (*f.*) the Brazilian pine or Paraná araucaria (*A. angustifolia*), c.a. PINHO-DO-PARANÁ, PINHEIRO-NACIONAL. [The trees occur in vast forests in southern Brazil and in addition to timber yield large edible seeds (PINHÕES), one of which is found in each scale of the trees' cones. Swine are fattened in ARAUCÁRIA woods.]—-**da-austrália,** the bunyabunya araucaria of Australia (*A. bidwilli*).—-**da-caledônia,** the columnar araucaria (*A. columnaris*).—-**do-chile,** the monkeypuzzle araucaria (*A. araucana*).—-**do-japão** = CEDRO-JAPONÊS.
araúja (*f.*), **araújo** (*m.*) the white bladderflower (*Araujia sericifera*).
araúna (*f.*) = GRAÚNA.
arauto (*m.*) herald; harbinger; crier.
araveça (*f.*) a plow having only one moldboard.
arável (*adj.*) arable.
aravela (*f.*) plow handle.
aravia (*f.*) = ALGARAVIA.
aravine (*m.,f.*) an Indian of the Arawine, a Tupian tribe on the Culuene River, a tributary of the Upper Xingu; (*adj.*) pert. to or designating this tribe.
araxá (*m.*) tableland; (*cap.*) town in Minas Gerais.
arazóia (*f.*) = ARAÇOIA.
arbitração (*f.*) arbitration, arbitrament.
arbitrador –**dora** (*adj.*) arbitrating; (*m.*) arbitrator, arbiter, umpire, referee.
arbitragem (*f.*) arbitration, arbitrament.—**de câmbio,** arbitrage (of foreign exchange).
arbitral (*adj.*) pert. to arbitration.
arbitramento (*m.*) arbitrament.
arbitrar (*v.t.*) to arbitrate, decide, determine; to mediate; to award.—**um jôgo de futebol,** to referee a soccer game.
arbitrariedade (*f.*) arbitrariness, despotism; outrage; capriciousness, wilfulness.
arbitrário –**ria** (*adj.*) arbitrary, peremptory; despotic, overbearing; wanton.
arbítrio (*m.*) will, pleasure, choice.—**livre,** free will. **ao**— **de,** at the mercy (pleasure, will, discretion) of.
árbitro (*m.*) arbiter, arbitrator, umpire, judge, referee; sovereign; criterion.—**de futebol,** referee (umpire) of a soccer game.
arbóreo –**rea** (*adj.*) arboreal.
arborescente (*adj.*) arborescent.
arborescer (*v.i.*) to grow into a tree; to flourish.
arboreto [ê] (*m.*) arboretum.
arborícola (*adj., Zool.*) arboricole; arboreal.
arboricultor –**tora** (*m.,f.*) arboriculturist.
arboricultura (*f.*) arboriculture.
arboriforme (*adj.*) tree-shaped.
arborização (*f.*) tree planting.
arborizar (*v.t.*) to plant with trees.
arbúsculo (*m.*) a dwarf tree or treelike shrub.
arbusto (*m.*) shrub, bush.
arbutina (*f., Chem.*) arbutin.
árbuto (*m., Bot.*) the genus Arbutus (madrone).
arca (*f.*) chest, large box, coffer; treasure; ark; chest, thorax.—**da Aliança,** Ark of the Covenant.—**de Noé,** Noah's Ark. **As**—**s do Tesouro,** or **da Nação,** the Nation's coffers.
arcabouço (*m.*) skeleton, framework. Var. ARCABOIÇO
arcabuz (*m.*) harquebus (ancient musket).

arcada (*f.*) arcade; arch; arched vault.—**zigomática,** (*Anat.*) zygomatic arch. (*pl.*) heavings (of the chest) = ARQUEJOS.
árcade (*adj.; m.,f.*) Arcadian.
arcado –**da** (*adj.*) arched [= ARQUEADO].
arcadura (*f.*) curvature, arching (as of a bow).
arcaico –**ca** (*adj.*) archaic.
arcaísmo (*m.*) archaism (obsolete or old-fashioned idiom or diction).
arcaizar [a-i] (*v.t.*) to use archaisms.
arcal (*m., Bot.*) a rockrose (*Cistus sp.*).
arcanjo (*m.*) archangel.
arcano –**na** (*adj.*) arcane, secret, hidden, mysterious; (*m.*) arcanum, secret, mystery.
arção (*m.*) bow of a saddle.
arcar (*v.t.*) to arch, bend, bow, curve [= ARQUEAR]; (*v.i.*) —**com,** to grapple, struggle, cope with (difficulties, problems, etc.).—**com a responsabilidade,** to shoulder the responsibility.—**com os ônus (dum negócio, duma decisão)** to bear the burden of responsibility (of a business, of making a decision, etc.).
arcebispado (*m.*) archbishopric.
arcebispo (*m.*) archbishop.
arcediago (*m.*) archdeacon.
arcediagado (*m.*) archdeaconry.
arch-, archi-, see also under **arque-, arqui-.**
archa (*f.*) halberd.
archeiro (*m.*) halberdier [but not archer, which is ARQUEIRO].
archotada (*f.*) torch-light parade.
archote (*m.*) torch; flambeau.
arciforme (*adj.*) having the form of an arch; bowed.
arcipreste (*m.*) archpriest.
arc.º = ARCEBISPO (archbishop).
arco (*m.*) arc; arch; bow (for arrows or violin); hoop (of a barrel); goal (in soccer).—**abatido,** a three-center or basket-handle arch.—**afrechado,** inflected or counter-curved arch.—**angular** or **quebrado,** indented arch.— **(a)viajado,** or **rampante,** rampant arch.—**campanulado,** reversed ogee arch.—-**celeste,**—-**de-deus,**—-**da-chuva,** —-**da-velha,**—-**íris,** are all names for the rainbow.—**de centro cheio,** or **de volta redonda,** surmounted arch.—**de pipa,** barrel hoop; also, a cocaine tree (*Erythroxylum pulchrum*).—**de pua,** brace for holding a boring bit.—**de serra,** hacksaw-frame.—**de triunfo,** or **triunfal,** triumphal arch.—**de violino,** violin bow.—**deprimido,** depressed arch.—**diastáltico,** or **reflexo,** (*Physiol.*) reflex arc.— **do pé,** arch of the foot.—**elíptico,** elliptical arch.—**em ferradura,** or **mourisco,** horseshoe arch.—**em forma de lança,** lance-shaped arch.—**ogival,** ogival arch.—**trilobado,** three-lobed arch.—**Tudor,** Tudor or four-center pointed arch.—**voltaico,** voltaic arc. **coisas do arco-da-velha,** incredible adventures. **corda do**—, bow string. **pau-d'arco** = IPÊ (a tree).
arcobotante (*m.*) abutment; flying buttress.
arcocele (*m., Med.*) archocele, rectal hernia.
arcoptoma (*m., Med.*) archoptoma.
arcoptose (*f., Med.*) archoptosis.
arcorragia (*f., Med.*) archorrhagia.
arcorréia (*f., Med.*) archorrhea.
arcostenose (*f., Med.*) archostenosis.
arctação (*f., Med.*) arctation.
arcto (*m., Astron.*) the constellation Ursa Major.
arctocéfalo (*m.*) a fur seal (*Arctocephalus*) of the southern hemisphere, c.f. FOCA.
arctótis (*m.*) the African daisy (*Arctotis stoechadifolia*).
Arcturo (*m., Astron.*) Arcturus.
ardacina (*f.*) ardassine (fine Persian silk fabric).
árdea (*f.*) a genus (*Ardea*) of herons.
árdego –**ga** (*adj.*) ardent, fiery, spirited. **um corcel**—, a fiery steed.
ardeídeos (*m.pl.*) the herons (*Ardeidae*).
ardelião (*m.*) a "buttinsky", intermeddler, pest.
ardência (*f.*) ardency; ardor, fervency.
ardente (*adj.*) ardent, hot, burning, fiery, ablaze, afire; warm, impassioned, eager, intense. **câmara**—, chamber where a body lies in state.
ardenita (*f., Min.*) ardennite.
ardentia (*f.*) glow, gleam; burning heat.
arder (*v.i.*) to burn with a flame; to blaze, flame, glow; to smart; to rage.—**contra alguém,** to rage against another person.—**de vontade de (or de desejo de),** to burn with desire for.—**em cólera,** to boil with rage.—**em febre,** to have a burning fever.—**por,** to desire ardently.

ardidez [ê] (f.) eagerness; dauntlessness.
ardido –da (adj.) burned; brave, bold. **um gôsto**—, a rancid taste. (m.) a small skin infection.
ardil (m.) ruse, stratagem, trick, artifice, wile; trap, snare.
ardileza (f.) trickery, cunning.
ardiloso –sa (adj.) cunning, crafty, guileful, artful; astute, wily, tricky, crooked.
ardimento (m.) ardency, ardor; eagerness.
ardor (m.) ardor, zeal, fierceness, passion, "pep", "snap"; heat, hotness; an itching or burning sensation.
ardoroso –sa (adj.) ardent; strenuous; spunky.
ardósia (f.) slate.
ardoso –sa (adj.) pungent, piquant.
árduo –dua (adj.) arduous, steep; hard, onerous, beset with difficulties; tough.
are (m.) are. [A unit of superficial measure = 100 sq. meters = 119.6 sq. yards = 0.02471 acre.]
área (f.) area; surface; areaway, inner court.—**de baixa pressão,** (Meteor.) low-pressure area.
areação (f.) scouring with sand.
areado –da (adj.) bewildered, dazed, "up in the air"; scoured with sand; sand-covered.
areal (m.) sand dune, desert, beach; sandpit.
areamento (m.) sand blasting.
areão (m.) a large AREAL.
arear (v.t.) to sand blast; to scour with sand; (v.i.) to become bewildered, dazed. **pó** (or **pasta**) **para**—**metais,** metal-polishing powder (or paste).
areca (f.) any Areca palm, esp. the betel nut palm (A. cathecu), c.a. AREQUEIRA; also its fruit.—**-banguá,** the Bungua Areca palm.
arecaína, arecadeína (f., Chem.) arecaidine, arecaine.
areia (f.) sand, grit, fine gravel; (colloq.) foolishness.—**de construção,** building sand.—**de fundição,** foundry sand. —**de metais,** powdered metal.—**engulideira (gulosa, movediça),** quicksand.—**fervente,** very fine, clean sand. —**lavada,** river sand.—**nos rins,** "sand" or "gravel" in the kidneys.—**s amarelas,** or **monazíticas,** monazitic sands or cerium group minerals, which usually contain thorium. —**s brancas,** zirconium group minerals.—**s gordas,** rich sandy loam.—**s pretas,** titanium group minerals (wrongly called monazite). **baixio de**—, sandy shoal. **banco de**—, sandbank. **caixa de**—, sandbox. **jato de**—, sand blast. **jogar**—**nos** (or **aos**) **olhos de alguém,** to throw dust in someone's eyes (deceive him). **semear na**—, to labor in vain. **ter**—, to be crazy, mentally unbalanced.
arejado –da (adj.) aerated, aired, ventilated.
arejador –dora (adj.) aerating, airing; (m.) ventilator pipe.
arejamento (m.) airing, ventilation.
arejar (v.t.) to air, expose to the air, ventilate, aerate; (v.i.) to breathe; of fruit, to wither, dry up; (v.r.) to go for an airing.
arejo [ê] (m.) airing, ventilation, aeration.
arena (f.) arena, circus ring; scene of action; sand.
arenáceo –cea (adj.) arenaceous, sandy.
arenado –da (adj.) sandy, sand-covered.
arenal (m.) = AREAL.
arenária (f., Bot.) a genus (Arenaria) of sandworts.
arenário –ria (adj., Bot.) arenaceous, growing in sandy places.
arendalita (f., Min.) arendalite.
arenga (f.) harangue, tirade; tedious discourse.
arengada (f.) a long harangue.
arengador (m.) long-winded talker; "windbag"; soap-box orator; haranguer.
arengar (v.i.) to harangue; to hold forth; to declaim, spout; to blab.
arenícola (adj., Zool.) arenicolous; (m.) a sandworm.
arenífero –ra (adj.) sand-bearing.
areniforme (adj.) sandlike.
arenito (m.) sandstone.
arenoso –sa (adj.) sandy. **pedra**—, sandstone. **terreno**—, sandy soil.
arenque (m.) herring; anchovy [= MANJUBA].—**-defumado,** or **de fumeiro,** smoked herring.
areocó (m.) = VERMELHO-HENRIQUE.
aréola (f.) areola (all senses).
areolado –da (adj.) = AREOLAR.
areolar (adj.) areolar.
areometria (f.) hydrometry.
areômetro (m., Physics) hydrometer [= HIDRÔMETRO].
areópago (m.) any tribunal or group of persons whose judgments are decisive or authoritative.
areostilo (m., Arch.) areostyle.

arequeira (f.) the betel nut palm (Areca cathecu), c.a. ARECA.
arerê (m.,f.) = IRERÊ.
aresta (f.) corner, angle, edge; slender bristle; shoe tack; glazier's point; crest, peak; (Arch.) arris. **polir as—s,** to smooth the rough edges; to smooth over matters.
aresto (m.) judgment, sentence; legal decision; a case which has been tried.
arestoso –sa (adj.) sharp, prickly, bristly.
aretino –na (adj.) mercenary, venal—said of one who writes for hire; (m.) such a writer.
aréu (adj.) perplexed.
arfada, –dura, –fagem (f.) rolling, pitching (of a ship); heaving, gasping.
arfante (adj.) heaving, gasping, panting; of a ship, rolling, pitching.
arfar (v.i.) to heave; to gasp, pant, labor for breath; to roll and pitch (as a ship).—**de cansaço,** to pant from exhaustion.—**de emoção,** to heave with emotion.
argala (f.) the adjutant bird.
argalf [i] (m., Zool.) the argali (Ovis ammon).
argamassa (f.) mortar, building cement.—**gorda,** mortar having more lime than sand,—**hidráulica,** hydraulic (water-setting) mortar.—**magra,** mortar having more sand than lime.
argamassador (m.) plasterer.
argamassar (v.t.) to plaster; to stir and mix (as mortar).
arganaz (m.) a wood rat; dormouse; (colloq.) a very tall man.
argas (m.) a genus (Argas) of ticks.
argau (m.) a pipette used in sampling wine, etc.
argel [-éis] (adj.) of a horse, having both hind feet white; clumsy; slovenly; (f., cap.) Algiers.
argelino –na (adj.; m.,f.) Algerian.
argemona (f.) the Mexican pricklepoppy (Argemone mexicana), c.a. CARDO-SANTO.
argentado –da (adj.) silvered; silvery.
argentador (m.) silver-plater.
argentão (m.) German silver.
argentar (v.t.) to silver; to silver-plate.
argentaria (f.) table silverware [= PRATARIA].
argentário (m.) a wealthy man.
argênteo –tea (adj.) argentine, silver, silvery.
argentífero –ra (adj.) silver-bearing.
argentina (f.) see ARGENTINO.
argentinar (v.i.) to gleam like silver.
argentino –na (adj.) argentine, silvery; Argentine; (m.,f.) an Argentine or Argentinean; (f.) the silverweed cinquefoil (Potentilla anserina), c.a. ANÇARINHA; [cap.] Argentina.
argentita (f., Min.) argentite.
argentoso –sa (adj.) silvery.
argento-vivo (m.) quicksilver.
argila (f.) argil, clay.—**refratária,** fire clay.
argiláceo –cea (adj., Petrog.) argillaceous.
argileira (f.) clay pit.
argilífero –ra (adj., Petrog.) argilliferous.
argilito (m., Petrog.) argillite.
argiloso –sa (adj.) clayey.
arginina (f., Biochem.) arginin(e).
árgio (m., Chem.) argon. Vars. ÁRGON, ARGÔNIO.
argiréia (f., Bot.) the genus Argyreia (Asia glory).
argiria, argiríase (f., Med.) argyria.
argírico –ca (adj.) argyric, argentic,
argirita (f., Min.) argyrite, argentite.
argiritrósio (m., Min.) argyrythrose, pyrargyrite.
argirodita (f., Min.) argyrodite.
argirol (m., Pharm.) Argyrol.
argironeta (f.) a genus (Argyroneta) of water spiders.
argirósio (m., Min.) argyrose, argyrite, argentite; (Med.) argyria.
argivo –va (adj.; m.,f.) = GREGO.
argo (m.) = ARGÔNIO.
argô (m.) argot.
argol (m., Chem.) crude cream of tartar.
argola (f.) metal ring, hoop; door knocker; dog collar; (pl.) round earrings.
argolar (v.t.) to fasten with rings; to provide with rings.
argolinha (f.) a children's game played with little hoops.
árgon (m.) = ÁRGIO.
argonauta (m.) argonaut; (Zool.) the argonaut or paper nautilus (Argonauta argo).
argônio (m., Chem.) argon; = ÁRGIO.
argos (m.) an Argus-eyed person; an argus pheasant.
argúcia (f.) astuteness, shrewdness; acuteness; smartness; subtlety; jest, witticism.

arguciar (*v.i.*) to argue shrewdly.
argucioso –sa (*adj.*) shrewd, artful, subtle.
argueireiro –ra (*adj.*) hairsplitting, quibbling.
argueiro (*m.*) trifle, drop in the bucket; mote; speck of dust; a straw, a nothing.
argüente (*m.,f.*) arguer; argumentator.
argüição (*f.*) arguing; censure, rebuke, reproof; argument, argumentation.
argüidor –dora (*m.,f.*) arguer; accuser, blamer.
argüir [31] (*v.t.*) to reprehend, condemn; to reveal, disclose; to question; to impugn; to allege; (*v.i.*) to argue, reason, plead; to conclude, infer.—**se de,** to accuse oneself of, blame oneself for.—**de** to accuse of. —**por,** to blame for.
argüitivo –va (*adj.*) demonstrative, conclusive; accusing.
argumentação (*f.*) argumentation; argument, controversy.
argumentador –dora (*adj.*) arguing; (*m.,f.*) argumentator, controversialist; arguer.
argumentante (*adj.*) arguing; (*m.,f.*) arguer; argumentator.
argumentar (*v.i.*) to argue; to dispute, debate; to hold or carry on an argument; to deduce, conclude, infer (**de,** from); (*v.t.*) to argue (a cause); to argue that. —**com alguém,** to dispute with someone.—**contra,** to use arguments against. **argumenta-se que,** it is argued that.
argumentativo –va (*adj.*) argumentative.
argumento (*m.*) argument, reason; dispute; story, plot; subject, topic; summary, outline.—**casuístico (sibilino, bizantino),** clever but false reasoning.—**convincente** (or **definitivo**), sound argument; cogent reason.—**contundente,** an argument accompanied by blows.—**de esmagar** (or **esmagador,** or **de rachar**), a smashing argument.—**de filme,** the plot of a motion picture story. **como—,** as evidence, as an example. **dar volta a um—,** to twist an argument around.
argus (*m.*) a genus (*Argus*) of pheasants.
arguto –ta (*adj.*) quick, bright, astute, ingenious, subtle, acute; shrewd, sharp; shrill; high-toned.
aria (*f.*) = CAUAÇU.
ária (*f.*) aria, song, tune; (*m.pl.*) Aryans.
ariá (*f.*) a plant (*Thalia lutea*) of the arrowroot family.
arianismo (*m.*) Aryanism; Arianism.
arianista (*m.,f.*) Aryanist.
arianizar (*v.t.*) to Aryanize.
ariano –na (*adj.*) Aryan; Arian; (*m.,f.*) a devotee of Aryanism or of Arianism.
aribina (*f.*) aribine, a crystalline alkaloid found in the bark of the Brazilian plant arariba vermelha (*Sickingia rubra*), c.a. ARARIBINA.
aricó (*m.*) = VERMELHO-HENRIQUE.
aricuí (*f.*) = ALICUÍ.
aricuri [curí] (*m.*) the uricury syagrus palm (*Syagrus coronata*), c.a. OURICURI, ARICORI, URICURI, NICURI, COQUEIRO-DO-CAMPO.
aricuriroba (*m.*) the arikury palm (*Arikuryroba schizophylla*), c.a. NICURIOBA, NICURIROBA, URICURIROBA.
aridez [ê] (*f.*) aridity, dryness; barrenness; dulness.
árido –da (*adj.*) arid, dry, parched; barren; dull, pointless.
arieta [ê] (*f.*) arietta (a short aria).
ariete (*m.*) battering ram; hydraulic ram.
arietino –na (*adj.*) shaped like a ram's head.
arila (*f., Chem.*) aryl.
arilado –da (*adj., Bot.*) arillate.
arilo (*m., Bot.*) aril.—**falso,** a false aril.
arilódio (*m., Bot.*) arillode, false aril.
arimaru (ú) (*m.*) a poison nut (*Strychnos cogens*).
arimbá (*m.*) a glazed clay jar.
arimético –ca (*adj.*) = ARITMÉTICO; (*f.*) = ARITMÉTICA.
ariocó (*m.*) = VERMELHO-HENRIQUE.
ariramba (*m.*) any of various kingfishers, esp. those specified under MARTIM-PESCADOR (which see).
ariranha (*f., Zool.*) the giant river otter of Brazil (*Pteroneura brasiliensis*), which attains an overall length of six feet or more; c.a. LONTRA, ONÇA-D'AGUA.
ariri (*m.*) a palm (*Allagoptera campestris*) which yields a useful fiber; c.a. BURI-DO-CAMPO, CÔCO-DE-VASSOURA, COQUEIRO-PIÇANDÓ, EMBURI, GURIRI-DO-CAMPO, PICANDÓ, PICANDÚ.
arisco –ca (*adj.*) sandy; cross, peevish; sulky, wild, rough; stray; skittish; (*m.*) a type of fertile sandy soil. **cavalo—,** a skittish horse. **criança—,** a fretful child.
aristado –da (*adj.; Bot.*) aristate.
aristarco (*m.*) a severe but just censor; a critic.
aristocracia (*f.*) aristocracy, nobility; distinction, superi-

ority.
aristocrata (*adj.*) aristocratic; (*m.,f.*) aristocrat.
aristocrátrico –ca (*adj.*) aristocratic; (*m.,f.*) noble.
aristodemocracia (*f.*) aristodemocracy.
Aristol (*m., Pharm.*) Aristol.
aristolóquia (*f.*) any plant of the genus Aristolochia.—**-vulgar,** the birthwort dutchmanspipe (*Aristolochia clematitis*).
aristoloquiáceo –cea (*adj., Bot.*) aristoloquiaceous; (*f.*) any birthwort.
aristoso –sa (*adj.*) = ARISTADO.
aristélia (*f.*) a genus (*Aristotelia*) of wineberries.
aristotélico –ca (*adj.*) Aristotelian.
aristotelismo (*m.*) Aristotelians, Aristotelianism.
aristótipo (*m., Photog.*) aristotype.
ariteno-epiglótico –ca (*adj., Anat.*) aryteno-epiglottic.
aritenóide (*adj.; f.; Anat.*) arytenoid.
aritenoídeo –dea (*adj., Anat.*) arytenoidal.
aritmético –ca (*adj.*) arithmetic(al); (*m.,f.*) arithmetician; (*f.*) arithmetic. Var. ARIMÉTICO.
aritmografia (*f.*) arithmography.
aritmomania (*f., Med.*) arithmomania.
aritmômetro (*m.*) calculating machine.
arizonita (*f., Min.*) arizonite.
arlequim (*m.*) harlequin.
arlequinada (*f.*) harlequinade.
arma (*f.*) arm, weapon; gun; power, might; branch of military service; resource, expedient; (*pl.*) arms, armed forces; feat of arms; coat of arms.—**branca,** any blade (sword, dagger, etc).—**de arremêsso,** any missile weapon (dart, arrows, etc).—**de caça** hunting weapon.—**de dois gumes,** two-edged sword.—**de fogo,** firearm.—**de longo alcance,** long-range gun.—**de salão,** any small rifle, pistol, etc. for indoor target-shooting.—**de serra,** hardwood timber tree.—**s proibidas,** forbidden arms. **às—s!** to arms! **carreira das—s,** military career or profession. **depor as—s,** to lay down arms. **estar em—s,** to be up in arms. **feito de—s,** military feat, exploit. **homem de—s,** man-at-arms. **mestre de—s,** fencing master. **pegar em —s,** to take up (bear) arms. **por força das—s,** by force of arms. **praça de—s,** military parade ground. **sala de—s,** fencing school or room. **suspensão de—s,** armed truce.
armação (*f.*) arming; gear, rigging, tackle; furniture, appointments; equipment, outfit; armature; structure, frame, framework; showcase; fishing tackle; horns, claws, teeth (of wild animals).—**de aço,** steel frame.—**de armazém,** store fixtures.—**de cama,** bedstead.—**de janela,** window frame.—**de pescaria,** fishing gear.—**dos ossos,** skeleton.
armada (*f.*) armada, fleet, navy.
armadilha (*f.*) trap, snare, pitfall; trick, wile, swindle; booby-trap.
armadilho (*m.*) armadillo—better known as TATU.
armado –da (*adj.*) armed, equipped, outfitted; harnessed; forewarned; **chapéu—,** cocked hat; (*m.*) a fish better known as BACU.
armador (*m.*) one who arms; outfitter, rigger; animal trapper; hammock hook; ship's chandler, supplier or outfitter; undertaker.
armadura (*f.*) armor; suit of armor; shield; casing; armature; framework; animals' horns, teeth, claws.
armamentário (*m.*) armamentarium, paraphernalia (esp. of a surgeon or dentist).
armamento (*m.*) armament; arming; accoutrements; equipment of a ship.
armão (*m.*) futchel (of a wagon); (*Milit.*) limber.
armar (*v.t.*) to arm; to equip with arms; to get or make ready; to outfit, rig (up); to supply with armament; to mount, set (up), fix, fit or arrange something in a particular manner; to cock (a trigger); (*v.r.*) to arm oneself (**de,** with).—**a cauda,** to spread the tail (as a peacock). —**ao afeito,** to do something for effect, play to the gallery.—**a fôrça,** to set a trap.—**baioneta,** to fix bayonets.—**barracas,** to pitch tents.—**castelos no ar,** to build castles in the air.—**pleitos** or **demandas,** to cavil.—**-se com o sinal da cruz,** to protect oneself from temptation. —**-se de paciência,** to fortify oneself with patience.—**um brinquedo,** to assemble a toy.—**uma armadilha,** to set a trap.—**uma ratoeira,** to set a rat trap.—**uma traição,** to hatch a treacherous plot.
armaria (*f.*) armory; coat of arms.
armarinheiro –ra (*m.,f.*) keeper of an ARMARINHO.
armarinho (*m.*) small dry goods or notions store.
armário (*m.*) cupboard, closet, locker, cabinet.—**de louça,**

china closet.—**de remédios**, medicine cabinet.—**de roupa**, clothes closet.

armazém (*m.*) store, shop; storehouse, warehouse; depot; magazine; (*pl.*) department store.—or **trapiche da Alfândega**, customs warehouse.—**de atacado**, wholesale warehouse.—**de retém**, storage warehouse.—**de sêcos e molhados**, grocery store; [=MERCEARIA in Portugal.]—**s gerais**, bonded warehouse.

armazenagem (*f.*) warehousing, storage; storage charges; demurrage charges.

armazenamento (*m.*) warehousing, storing.

armazenar (*v.t.*) to store (in a warehouse); to garner.

armazenário (*m.*) one who warehouses (cotton, sugar, etc.) pending resale.

armazeneiro (*m.*) one who warehouses; owner of a warehouse.

armazenista (*m.*) warehouseman.

armeiro (*m.*) armorer; gunsmith; armory.

armela (*f.*) a metal ring or hoop serving any of several purposes.

armelina (*f.*) ermine (fur).

armelino (*m.*) ermine (the animal) = ARMINHO.

armênio –**nia**, **armênico** –**ca** (*adj.; m.,f.*) Armenian (person or language).

arméria (*f., Bot.*) the genus Armeria (thrift).

armezim (*m.*) a kind of taffeta.

armífero –**ra** (*adj.*) bearing arms or weapons.

armígero (*m.*) formerly, an armor-bearer; now, one who bears arms.

armila (*f.*) bracelet or anklet; (*Arch.*) torus; (*Anat., Bot.*) armilla; (*Astron.*) armil.

armilar (*adj.*) armillary; ringed. **esfera—**, (*Astron.*) armillary sphere.

arminho (*m.*) ermine (the animal or its fur); (*pl.*) titles of nobility, position or rank.

armistício (*m.*) armistice.

armolão (*m., Bot.*) the blite goosefoot (*Chenopodium capitatum*); also, spinach (*Spinacia*).

armorácia (*f.*) horseradish (*Armoracia lapathifolia*), c.a. RÁBANO-BASTARDO, RÁBANO-RÚSTICO, RÁBANO-SILVES-TRE-MAIOR, SARAMAGO-MAIOR.

armorial (*adj.; m.*) armorial.

arnado, –**nedo** [ê], –**neiro** (*m.*) barren sandy soil.

arnela (*f.*) stump (snag) of a tooth.

arnês (*m.*) harness; trappings; armor; by ext., protection.

arnesar (*v.t.*) to equip (a horse) with armor. [To harness a horse is ARREAR]; (*v.r.*) to put on armor.

arni [ní] (*m.*) water buffalo.

arnica (*f., Bot.*) mountain arnica (*A. montana*); also, the tincture of arnica obtained from the rhizome and roots of this plant.

arnote (*m.*) the anatto tree (*Bixa orellana*), c.a. URUCU-ZEIRO.

aro (*m.*) a wood or metal hoop; rim of a wheel; steel tire of a railroad car wheel; door, window or eyeglass frame; (*Bot.*) arum.—**de expansão**, expanding ring.

aroeira (*f.*) the California pepper tree (*Schinus molle*), c.a.—-DE-FÔLHA-DE-SALSO,—-SALSO, PIMENTEIRA-BASTARDA, PIMENTEIRA-DO-PERU.—-branca (—-brava,—-da-capueira), are all *Lithraea molleoides*, c.a. AROEIRINHA, is *Schinus areira*.—-da-praia, the lentisk pistache (*Pistacia lentiscus*), c.a. LENTISCO.—-da-serra is *Schinus glazioviana*.—-de-bugre, (—-do-mato) is a plant of the sumac or cashew family (*Lithraea brasiliensis*), c.a. AROEIRINHA-PRETA, CORAÇÃO-DE--BUGRE, PAU-DE-BUGRE.—-de-fôlha-branca is *Schinus argentifolia*.—-de-goiás (—-do-rio-grande,—-do-campo) are the pinkberry pepper tree (*Schinus lentiscifolia*), c.a. AROEIRINHA.—-do-campo, (—-rasteira) is *Schinus weinmanniaefolia*, c.a. AROEIRINHA-DO-CAMPO.—-do-sertão (—-preta) is a star tree (*Astronium urundeuva*), c.a. URUNDEÚVA.—-mansa (—-vermelha) is the Brazil peppertree (*Schinus terebinthifolia*), c.a. CAMBUI, FRUTO-DE-SABIÁ.—-raiada is *Schinus pohliana*.

aroeirinha (*f.*) any of various peppertrees (*Schinus*) or related plants; c.a. AROEIRA.

aroma (*m.*) aroma; fragrance; perfume; flavor; (*pl., Bot.*) the sweet acacia (*A. farnesiana*), c.a. ESPONJEIRA.

aromar (*v.t.*) to fill with fragrance; (*v.i.*) to exhale it.

aromático –**ca** (*adj.*) aromatic, fragrant, sweet-smelling; (*Chem.*) aromatic. **vinagre—**, aromatic spirits of ammonia.

aromatização (*f.*) aromatization.

aromatizador –**dora**, –**zante** (*adj.*) aromatizing.

aromatizar (*v.t.*) to aromatize.

arpado –**da** (*adj.*) barbed [=FARPADO].

arpão (*m.*) harpoon; gaff, grapnel.

arpar, arpear (*v.*) = ARPOAR.

arpejar (*v.t., Music*) to play (chords, etc.) in arpeggio.

arpejo [ê] (*m., Music*] arpeggio.

arpéu (*m.*) grappling hook; small harpoon; (*pl.*) hands, nails, claws.

arpoação (*f.*) harpooning.

arpoador (*m.*) harpooner.

arpoar (*v.t.*) to harpoon; to gaff; to spear; fig., to seduce.

arqueação (*f.*) arching, bowing, bending; curvature; gauging of the cubic content of a cask, ship, etc.

arqueado –**da** (*adj.*) arched, bowed, curved; of cubic content, gauged.

arqueadura (*f.*), –**amento** (*m.*) curvature; camber; sag.

arquear (*v.t.*) to arch, bend, bow, curve; to gauge the displacement of a ship, the cubic capacity of a barrel, etc.

arquégono (*m., Bot.*) archegonium.

arqueio (*m.*) = ARQUEAÇÃO.

arqueira (*f.*) a woman archer.

arqueiro (*m.*) archer; (*Soccer*) goalkeeper.

arquejante (*adj.*) panting, puffing, gasping; out of breath.

arquejar (*v.i.*) to gasp, pant, puff, blow, labor for breath, wheeze. Cf. ARFAR.

arquejo [ê] (*m.*) shortness of breath; labored breathing, gasp.

arqueologia (*f.*) archeology.

arquentério (*m., Zool.*) archenteron.

arqueogeologia (*f.*) archaeogeology.

arqueografia (*f.*) archaeography.

arqueolítico –**ca** (*adj., Archaeol.*) archaeolithic.

arqueologia (*f.*) archaeology.

arqueológico –**ca** (*adj.*) archaeological.

arqueólogo –**ga** (*m.,f.*) archaeologist.

arqueozóico –**ca** (*adj., Geol.*) Archeozoic.

arqueta [ê] a poor box; a small chest or safe.

arquete [ê] (*m.*) burial urn.

arquétipo –**pa** (*adj.*) archetypical, archetypal; (*m.,f.*) archetype, pattern, model.

arquiapóstata (*m.,f.*) archapostate.

Arquibaldo (*m.*) Archibald.

arquibancada (*f.*) tiers of seats or benches as in a circus or amphitheater; bleachers; grandstand.

arquiblastoma (*f., Med.*) archiblastoma.

arquiblástula (*f., Zool.*) archiblastula.

arquicantor (*m.*) archicantor.

arquidiaconato (*m.*) archidiaconate.

arquidiácono (*m.*) archdeacon [= ARCEDIAGO].

arquidiocese (*f.*) archdiocese.

arquiducado (*m.*) archduchy.

arquiduque (*m.*) archduke.

arquiduquesa [ê] (*f.*) archduchess.

arquiespicopado (*m.*) archiepiscopate; archbishopric.

arquiepiscopal (*adj.*) archiepiscopal.

arquieunuco (*m.*) head eunuch.

arquigástrula (*f., Zool.*) archigastrula.

arquiinimigo [i-i] –**ga** (*m.,f.*) archenemy, archfoe.

arquilha (*f.*) a small chest; coachman's box.

arquilho (*m.*) a wood or metal hoop.

arquiloquiano (*m.*) an Archilochian verse.

arquimagiro (*m.*) chef, head cook.

arquimago (*m.*) head wizard, archmagician.

arquimilionário (*m.*) multimillionaire.

arquipélago (*m.*) archipelago.

arquiplasma (*m., Biol.*) archiplasm, archoplasm.

arqui-rabino (*m.*) chief rabbi.

arqui-sátrapa (*m.*) archsatrap.

arquispermas (*f.pl., Bot.*) the Gymnospermae.

arquite (*f., Med.*) architis, proctitis.

arquitetar (*v.t.*) to plan, project, scheme, plot; to trump up (an excuse); to build; (*v.i.*) to conceive, dream; to work as an architect.

arquiteto (*m.*) architect; dreamer; creator.

arquitetônico –**ca** (*adj.*) architectonic; (*f.*) the science of architecture; (*Philos.*) architectonic.

arquitetura (*f.*) architecture; plan, project.

arquitetural (*adj.*) architectural.

arquitrave (*f.*) architrave.

arquivamento (*m.*) filing, safekeeping (of papers).

arquivar (*v.t.*) to file (away) papers, etc.—**um assunto**, (*colloq.*) to forget a subject (not mention it again).

arquivista (*m.,f.*) file clerk, recorder, registrar, archivist.

arquivo (*m.*) archives, file, record, register.—**de aço**, steel filing cabinet.

arquivolta (*f.*, *Arch.*) archivolt.

arr. = ARRÔBA.

arrabalde (*m.*) suburbs, environs, outskirts, neighborhood, district.

arrabídea (*f.*) the genus Arrabidea (funnelvine).

arrabio (*m.*) = RABIJUNCO.

arracimado –**da** (*adj.*, *Bot.*) racemed.

arracimar-se (*v.r.*, *Bot.*) to bear racemes.

arraçoar (*v.t.*) to ration.

arraia (*f.*) any batoid fish (ray, skate, etc); border frontier; a paper kite.—**elétrica**, the electric ray (*Narcine brasiliensis*), c.a. TREME-TREME.—**borboleta**, butterfly ray (*Pteroplatea micrura*), c.a. BORBOLETA.—**chita** = RAIA-CHITA (a skate).—**manteiga** = RAIA-MANTEIGA (a sting ray).—**miúda**, riff-raff.—**sapo** = RAIA-SAPO (a ray). —**viola** = VIOLA (guitar fish).

arraial (*m.*) camping ground; hamlet; country festivity.

arraiar (*v.*) = RAIAR.

arraigado –**da** (*adj.*) deep-rooted; inveterate; ingrained.

arraigar (*v.t.*) to root; (*v.i.*, *v.r.*) to take root.

arramalhar (*v.i.*) to rustle (as the branches of a tree).

arramar (*v.i.*, *v.r.*) to spread, branch out (as a tree).

arrambóia (*f.*) the green tree boa (*Boa canina*), c.a. COBRA-PAPAGAIO.

arrampadouro (*m.*) sloping ground.

arrancada (*f.*) jerk, yank, sudden pull; quick get-away (referring to automobile, horse, etc.); land from which stumps have been pulled. **de uma só—**, at a stretch; at one sitting. Cf. ARRANCO, ARRANQUE.

arrancadeira (*f.*) machine for digging potatoes, etc.

arrancadela (*f.*) = ARRANCADURA.

arrancador (*m.*) puller, jerker.

arrancadura (*f.*) act of uprooting or pulling out something.

arranca-estrepe (*m.*, *Bot.*) the barbifruit pavonia (*P. spinifex*).

arrancamento (*m.*) = ARRANCADA.

arranca-milho (*m.*) the chopi grackle (*Gnorimopsar c. chopi*), c.a. ARUMARÁ, PÁSSARO-PRÊTO, CHOPIM, VIRA-BOSTA.

arranca-pregos (*m.*) nail puller.

arrancar (*v.t.*) to pull out (up, away, off); to yank; to jerk; to snatch; to wrench; to uproot; to grub (up); to tear up or away; to extract, extort; (*v.i.*) to emit dying gasps; (*v.i.*, *v.r.*) to depart in haste or excitement.—**a espada**, to draw out one's sword quickly.—**à morte**, to snatch from death.—**a verdade**, to drag out the truth (from someone).—**com** or **contra**, to attack.—**lágrimas**, to draw tears.—**o motor**, to start the motor.—**os cabelos**, to pull out hair by the roots.—**pelas raízes**, to pull something up or out by the roots.—**um dente**, to pull a tooth, or to have one pulled.—**um grito**, to let out a cry of pain or rage.—**o vôo**, of an airplane, to take off.

arranca-rabo (*m.*) quarrel, heated discussion; rough-and-rumble fight.

arranca-sonda (*m.*) a device for fishing out lost tools, drill bits, etc., from oil wells, drill holes, mine shafts, etc.

arranca-tocos (*m.*) a stump puller; a bully; (*colloq.*) free-for-all, shindy, melee.

arranco (*m.*) sudden start, jerk, yank; spurt; a clearing in the woods (from which stumps have been pulled); automobile starter; a violent protest or revolt against tyranny, injustice, etc.; (*pl.*) paroxysm, convulsion, gasps. **de—**, with a jerk, violently. Cf. ARRANCADA, ARRANQUE.

arrancorar-se (*v.r.*) to become rancorous.

arranha-céu (*m.*) skyscraper.

arranhadela (*f.*) = ARRANHADURA.

arranhador –**dora** (*adj.*) scratching, scraping; (*m.*, *f.*) scratcher, scraper.

arranhadura (*f.*) **arranhão** (*m.*) a scratch; a light cut or wound.

arranhar (*v.t.*) to scratch (as with nails or claws); to "scrape" (a violin); to "get by" (in a foreign language); (*v.r.*) to suffer a scratch or slight wound. [To scratch oneself is COÇAR-SE.]

arranjadeiro –**ra** (*adj.*) tidy, neat.

arranjado –**da** (*adj.*) arranged, fixed; well-off.

arranjador –**dora** (*adj.*) arranging; (*m.*, *f.*) arranger.

arranjamento (*m.*) arrangement; arranging. Cf. ARRANJO.

arranjar (*v.t.*) to arrange, set in order; to adjust, settle; to mend; to obtain; to contrive; to wangle; to fix

(matters); (*v.r.*) to arrange matters, fix things well for oneself; to fend for oneself; to take care of oneself.—**a vida**, to order one's life; to feather one's nest.—**uma colocação**, to get a job.—**-se bem**, to get out of a tight spot; to get an easy job.—**-se na vida**, to make a (good) living; to order one's private affairs. **Arranje-se!** That's your lookout! **Deixe, que eu arranjo isso,** Leave it to me, I'll fix it (up) for you. **Êle arranjou um bom emprêgo,** He got himself a good job. **Êle que se arranje (como puder),** Let him do the best he can (it's his problem). **Êle sempre se arranja,** He always lands on his feet. **Isso tudo há de se arranjar,** Everything will come out all right (in the end).

arranjista (*m.*) go-getter, hustler; fixer-upper.

arranjo (*m.*) arrangement, disposition; adjustment, settlement; a "deal"; solution; (*colloq.*) kept woman.

arranque (*m.*) automobile self-starter; spurt; sudden start; (*Arch.*) spring of an arch. Cf. ARRANCO.

arraque (*f.*) arrack (a distilled spirit).

arras (*f.pl.*) earnest money; pledge, token; down payment; dowry; handicap (advantage given); occasion, opportunity.—**de casamento**, marriage settlement.

arrás (*m.*) Arras tapestry.

arrasadeira (*f.*) a strickle [= RASOURA].

arrasado –**da** (*adj.*) razed; levelled; overthrown; crushed; ruined; filled to overflowing (as eyes with tears).—**de humilhação**, crushed with humiliation.

arrasador –**dora** (*adj.*) crushing; razing; ruining; (*m.*) plunderer, ravager, destroyer; a strickle. **um argumento—**, a shattering argument.

arrasamento (*m.*) razing, demolition, overthrow; wearing down (of an animal's teeth).

arrasar (*v.t.*) to raze, ruin; to demolish; to level; to overthrow; to fill to overflowing; to drag down; to crush, humble (with words).

arrastadeiro –**ra** (*adj.*) dragging.

arrastadiço –**ça** (*adj.*) easily influenced; lit., easily dragged.

arrastado –**da** (*adj.*) dragged; dragging; laggard; drawling; wretched; **fala—**, a drawl. **sentido—**, forced meaning.

arrastador (*m.*) any rough forest trail, as for traveling between clearings or for dragging out logs.

arrastadura (*f.*), –**tamento** (*m.*) act of dragging.

arrastão (*m.*) tug, wrench, jerk; plant sucker; dragnet, trawl; trawling. **peixe de—**, fish taken in nets (i.e., not hooked).

arrasta-pé (*m.*, *colloq.*) a hop (dance).

arrastar (*v.t.*) to drag, draw, pull, haul, tug; (*v.i.*) to trail, creep; (*v.r.*) to creep, crawl; to trudge, plod along.—**a asa**, (*colloq.*) to woo, pay court to; lit., to drag the wing, as a cock in courtship.—**a voz**, or **as palavras**, to drawl. —**na lama**, or **no lôdo**, or **pela rua da amarguna**, to drag in the mud (someone's name or reputation).—**os pés**, to drag the feet; (*colloq.*) to dance.—**pelo chão**, to drag along the ground; to sweep the ground (as a woman's gown). **O velho está arrastando os pés,** The old man is on his last legs.

arrasto (*m.*) a haul; a hauling or towing; trawl, dragnet; a load of logs skidded out of the woods; transportation (as of ore) by endless bucket-chain; a shallow place where a boat scrapes the bottom. **barco de—**, trawler.

arrastre (*m.*) a revolving cylinder for crushing and screening ore.

arrátel [-teis] (*m.*) an old Portuguese unit of weight, equivalent to about one pound.

arrazoado –**da** (*adj.*) reasonable, sensible; reasoned; justified; (*m.*) plea, defense.

arrazoador –**dora** (*adj.*) reasoning; (*m.*, *f.*) reasoner; pleader (in court).

arrazoamento (*m.*) reasoning, argumentation.

arrazoar (*v.t.*) to reason, argue, to plead a cause; (*v.i.*) to argue, dispute.

arre! (*interj.*) Dammit! Also: Giddap!

arreação (*f.*) gashes made in tapping a rubber tree; also = ARREAMENTO.

arreador (*m.*) harnesser; muleteer.

arreamento (*m.*) act of harnessing; trappings; furniture.

arrear (*v.t.*) to harness; to deck, array (**-se**, oneself); to provide with furniture. [Do not confuse with ARRIAR.]

arreata (*f.*) halter rope; hitching rope.

arreatar (*v.t.*) to bind or tie (as a load on a wagon), by passing a rope over and around it.

arrebanhador –**dora** (*adj.*) herding; (*m.*, *f.*) herder.

arrebanhar (*v.t.*) to herd, gather together.—**votos, elei-tores,** to round up votes, voters.—**restos,** to salvage re-mainders, pick up left-overs.
arrebatado –da (*adj.*) impetuous, precipitate; rash, hasty; hot-headed; rapt, ecstatic, rapturous, "carried away".
arrebatador –dora (*adj.*) ravishing, enchanting; eloqüên-cia—, stirring eloquence. (*m.,f.*) snatcher.
arrebatamento (*m.*) rapture, ecstasy; spell, trance; ravish-ment; rashness; fit of anger.
arrebatar (*v.t.*) to take from, grab, snatch; to drag away, carry off; to ravish; to impel, drive; to entrance; (*v.r.*) to become enraptured; to fly into a rage.
arrebém (*m., Naut.*) a reef point or other short line.
arrebenta-boi, arrebenta-cavalo (*m.*) the longflower shrub harebell (*Isotoma longiflora*), c.a. CEGA-ÔLHO, JASMIN-DA-ITALIA; the soda-apple nightshade (*Solanum aculeatissimum*).
arrebentação (*f.*) bursting; breaking of waves; pounding of surf.
arrebentadela (*f.*) a bursting.
arrebentadiço –ca (*adj.*) easily burst or broken; explosive.
arrebentamento (*m.*) burst, bursting, blast, explosion.
arrebentão (*m.*) offshoot (of a plant).
arrebenta-panela (*f.*) = PIRAMBU.
arrebenta-pedra (*f.*) the flyroost leafflower (*Phyllanthus niruri*), c.a. ERVA-POMBINHA, QUEBRA-PEDRA, SAXÍ-FRAGA.
arrebentar (*v.t.,v.i.*) to burst, break, explode.—**a banca,** to break the bank (at gambling).—**um pneu,** to blow out a tire. Cf. REBENTAR.
arreblcado –da (*adj.*) made-up (face painted), over-dressed, gaudy; tawdry; affected.
arrebicar (*v.t.,v.r.*) to make up (paint) the face; to over-dress; to bedizen; to dandify.
arrebique (*m.*) rouge (for the face); fripperies; garishness; affected style.
arrebitado –da (*adj.*) turned up, cocked up; ill-tempered; bold, cocky. **nariz—,** snub nose.
arrebitar (*v.t.*) to turn up, cock up (as a hat); to clinch (a nail); (*v.r.*) to become stuck up; to become angry.
arrebita-rabo (*m.*) = SABIÁ-DO-CAMPO, JAPACANIM.
arrebito (*m.*) upturn; clinched nail; cockiness.
arrebol [-bóis] (*m.*) redness in the sky at sunrise or sunset; afterglow.
arrebolar (*v.t.*) to make round as a ball; to sharpen on a grindstone; to make red as the sunset.
arre-burrinho (*m.*) see-saw; butt (of jokes).
arrecadas (*f.pl.*) earrings.
arrecadação (*f.*) depository, depot; custody; prison; ex-action, collection (of taxes).—**fiscal,** tax collection.
arrecadado –da (*adj.*) in custody, in safekeeping; thrifty, frugal.
arrecadador –dora (*m.,f.*) collector, tax collector.
arrecadamento (*m.*) collecting; gathering; safe-keeping.
arrecadar (*v.t.*) to take care of; to collect (taxes); to take possession of; to receive for safekeeping; to take into custody.
arrecear (*v.*) = RECEAR.
arrecife (*m.*) = RECIFE.
arredado –da (*adj.*) removed, set aside.
arredamento (*m.*) removal, withdrawal, pushing aside.
arredar (*v.t.*) to draw back, push back, push aside, turn away.—**se de,** to withdraw from; to turn from; to get back.—**pé,** to give ground; to leave, move away. **Arreda!** Get back! Out of the way! **não—pé,** to stand one's ground. **não se—,** to sit tight, stand pat, refuse to budge.
arre-diabo (*m., Bot.*) the drug treadsoftly (*Cnidoscolus urens*), c.a. CANSANÇÃO-DE-LEITE, QUEIMADEIRA, PINHA-QUEIMADEIRA.
arredio –dia (*adj.*) strayed, wandering; apart, retired; aloof, standoffish, unsociable, uncompanionable.
arredondado –da (*adj.*) round, rounded, roundish.
arredondar (*v.t.*) to round (off, out); (*v.r.*) to become round.—**cifras,** to round out figures.
arredor (*adv.*) nigh, about, around.—**de,** (*prep.*) around [= AO REDOR DE].
arredores (*m.pl.*) environs, surroundings, outskirts.
arrefecer (*v.t.,v.i.*) to cool; (*v.r.*) to cool off; to grow luke-warm (indifferent). Cf. ESFRIAR, RESFRIAR.
arrefecido –da (*adj.*) cooled (off); lukewarm.
arrefecimento (*m.*) a cooling (off); refrigeration. **sistema de—,** cooling system.
arregaçada (*f.*) lapful, apronful.

arregaçar (*v.t.*) to roll up (as shirt sleeves), turn up (as trouser legs); to tuck up (as an apron or skirt); to draw back (as the lips).
arregaço (*m.*) state of being rolled up or tucked up (as shirt sleeves); free-for-all, shindy, melee; reproof, reprimand.
arregalar (*v.t.*) to open wide the eyes, stare. **de olhos arregalados,** wide-eyed.
arreganhar (*v.t.*) to grin; to draw back the lips and bare the teeth (as in anger or scorn); (*v.i.*) to split, burst open (as ripe fruit); (*v.r.*) to laugh and joke; to shiver with cold; to sneer.
arreganho (*m.*) grin; intrepidity; threat; sneer.
arregimentar (*v.t.*) to regiment.
arregoar (*v.t.*) to furrow; to plow; (*v.i.*) of fruit, to split.
arreio (*m.*) ornament; (*pl.*) harness, trappings, gear, breeching.
arreitar (*v.t.*) to arouse lust in.
arrejeitar (*v.*) = REJEITAR.
arrelia (*f.*) anger, vexation; bad omen; spree. **Que—! How annoying! What rotten luck!**
arreliação (*f.*) annoyance.
arreliado –da (*adj.*) peeved; (*colloq.*) mischievous.
arreliador –dora (*adj.*) vexatious; (*m.,f.*) teaser.
arreliante (*adj.*) annoying.
arreliar (*v.t.*) to annoy; to tease; to "needle"; (*v.r.*) to get peeved.
arreliento –ta, arrelioso –sa (*adj.*) irritating, annoying.
arrelique (*m.*) summer vetch (*Vicia angustifolia*).
arrelvar (*v.t.*) to cover with sward; (*v.r.*) to become grass-covered.
arremangar (*v.t.*) to roll up the sleeves; to raise the arm in a threatening way.
arrematar (*v.t.*) to put an end to, finish up, wind up; to put a finishing touch on; to buy or sell at auction. Cf. REMATAR.
arremate (*m.*) = REMATE.
arremedador –dora (*adj.*) mimicking; (*m.,f.*) mimic; copy-cat.
arremedar (*v.t.*) to mimic, ape, mock, impersonate.
arremêdo (*m.*) mimicry, take-off; imitation.
arremessador –dora (*adj.*) hurling, etc. See the verb ARREMESSAR; (*m.,f.*) thrower, pitcher, hurler.
arremessão (*m.*) any missile or thrown weapon; act of throwing, hurling, flinging, etc. See the verb ARREMESSAR.
arremessar (*v.t.*) to hurl, fling, throw, cast, pitch, sling, toss; (*v.r.*) to rush, run headlong (**a, em,** to, into; **após, atrás,** after); to hurl oneself (**contra,** against; **sôbre,** upon).
arremêsso (*m.*) act of hurling, etc. See the verb ARREMES-SAR; a throw (as of a ball); a thrust; act of rushing; a threat; boldness, daring; attack; (*pl.*) flights of fancy; appearances.—**de criança,** childish display of bad temper.—**de dardo (disco, pêso),** javelin (disk, weight) throwing.—**de poeta,** poetical flight. **aos, or em, —s, in jerks, by fits and starts; in headlong fashion. arma de—, spear, lance or other missile weapon. fazer—de,** to make a show of (doing something).
arremetedor –dora (*adj.*) aggressive; (*m.,f.*) attacker.
arremetente (*adj.*) assaulting, assailing.
arremeter (*v.t.*) to assail, set upon; to rush violently at; to instigate, incite.—**contra,** to dash against.—**para,** to rush upon, lunge at.
arremetida (*f.*), arremetimento (*m.*) onset, attack, on-slaught, charge, thrust, dash, lunge.
arrenal (*m., Pharm.*) arrhenal.
arrendação (*f.*) = ARRENDAMENTO.
arrendado –da (*adj.*) leased, rented; adorned with lace.
arrendador –dora (*adj.*) renting, leasing; (*m.f.*), renter, leaser, hirer; lessor.
arrendamento (*m.*) renting, lease, rent, hire.—**e empres-timo,** lend-lease. **contrato de—,** a lease contract.
arrendar (*v.t.*) to rent, lease (to or from); to let; to hire; to furnish with lace.
arrendatário –ria (*m.,f.*) lessee, renter, tenant.
arrendável (*adj.*) capable of being leased (to or from).
arrenegação (*f.*) anger, irritation.
arrenegado –da (*adj.; m.,f.*) renegade; apostate.
arrenegador –dora (*m.,f.*) one who renounces or curses.
arrenegar (*v.t.*) to renounce; to execrate; to curse; (*v.r.*) to get mad.
arrenêgo (*m.*) apostasy; renunciation; execration; anger.
arrepanhado –da (*adj.*) wrinkled, creased; close-fisted.

arrepanhar (*v.t.*) to crease, wrinkle; to tuck (up); to pick up; to snatch; to hoard.

arrepelão (*m.*) violent pull or push.

arrepelar (*v.t.*) to pull out hair, feathers, etc.; (*v.r.*) to pull one's hair or beard; to blubber.

arrepender-se (*v.r.*) to repent (of), be sorry (for), regret; to rue; to change one's mind.

arrependido –**da** (*adj.*) repentant, penitent, sorry, regretful, contrite.

arrependimento (*m.*) repentance, penitence, contrition, regret; change of mind.

arrepiado –**da** (*adj.*) hispid, bristly; terrified.

arrepiador –**dora** (*adj.*) frightening; hair-raising.

arrepiadura (*f.*) –**amento** (*m.*) act of ruffling, etc. See the verb ARREPIAR.

arrepiar (*v.t.*) to ruffle, dishevel, muss (hair, feathers, fur); to scare, frighten; to make hair stand on end; to cause gooseflesh; (*v.r.*) to shiver with cold or fear.—**caminho**, to backtrack; to retract.—**carreira**, to abandon one career in order to take up another; to change horses in midstream. **de**—**cabelo**, hair-raising.

arrepio (*m.*) shiver; thrill; (*pl.*) goose pimples, gooseflesh [= GASTURA]. **ao**—, against the grain, the wrong way.

arrestado –**da** (*adj.*) under distraint or embargo; (*m.,f.*) person under a distraint.

arrestante (*m.,f., Law*) distrainer.

arrestar (*v.t., Law*) to seize, appropriate, confiscate; to lay an embargo on; to put under distraint.

arresto (*m.*) seizure, confiscation, embargo; (*Law*) attachment; distraint.

arrevesado –**da** (*adj.*) confused, intricate, enigmatic; tongue-twisting [words]. **estilo**—, a tortuous style. **palavras**—**s**, twisted words.

arrevesar (*v.t.*) to reverse; to turn inside out or upside down; to make intricate; to twist the meaning (of words).

arriar (*v.t.*) to lower (flag, sails); to lay down (arms); to set (a burden) on the ground; (*v.i.*) to let down (in exertion); to give up (effort); (*v.r.*) to sink to the ground, fall of its own weight. [Do not confuse with ARREAR.]

arriaria (*f.*) harness maker's shop or occupation.

arriba (*adv.*) above, up, upward.—**de**, upwards of. **água**—, upstream. **Arriba!** (*interj.*) Up! Onward!.

arribaçã (*f.*) = POMBA-DE-BANDO.

arribação (*f.*) arrival (in port); a putting into port; migration (of birds and animals). **aves de**—, migratory birds; birds of passage. **pomba-de**—, see POMBA-DE-BANDO.

arriba-coelha (*f.*) = RABILA.

arribada (*f.*) arrival (in port); convalescence.

arribadiço –**ça** (*adj.*) of birds, etc., migratory; of persons, alien, foreign, strange.

arribana (*f.*) a thatched hut or shed.

arribar (*v.i.*) to arrive in, or put into, port; to touch land; to arrive at the top (as of a mountain); to depart; to take French leave; to run away; of cattle, to stampede; to be above, exceed; to get well.

arribe (*m.*) arrival; importation.

arriçar (*v.t.*) to reef, lash.

arrida (*f.*) lanyard.

arrieiro (*m.*) driver of pack animals; muleteer [= ARRE-EIRO].

arrimadiço –**ça** (*adj.*) given to leaning on others.

arrimar (*v.t.*) to prop (up); to support; to heap (something) up; (*v.f.*) to lean on or against.—**-se a alguém**, to lean on (depend on) someone.—**dinheiro**, to pile up money.—**os pés à parede**, to stand pat, refuse to budge.

arrimo (*m.*) prop, support.—**de família**, the support (breadwinner) of a family.

arrincoar (*v.t.*) to pen up (animals); (*v.r.*) to hole up.

arrinia (*f., Med.*) arrhinia.

arriosca (*f.*) trap; hoax; game played with pebbles.

arriscado –**da** (*adj.*) risky, dangerous; ticklish; unsafe; bold, daring; venturesome.

arriscar (*v.t.*) to risk, endanger, hazard, jeopardize; (*v.r.*) to expose oneself to danger.—**-se a perder**, to run the risk of losing.—**a sorte**, to try one's luck. **Quem não arrisca, não petisca**, Nothing ventured, nothing gained.

arritmia (*f., Pathol.*) arrhythmia.

arrítmico –**ca** (*adj.*) arrhythmic(al).

arritmo (*m.*) want of rhythm; irregularity.

arrivismo (*m.*) practice of social or financial climbing by unworthy means.

arrivista (*m.*) upstart, parvenu; climber.

arrizar (*v.*) = ARRIÇAR.

arrizo –**za** (*adj.*) rootless; (*Bot.*) arrhizal.

arrizotônico –**ca** (*adj.*) designating words stressed after the root vowel.

arrôba (*f.*) an old Portuguese measure of weight used in Brazil: equivalent nowadays to 15 kilograms.

arrôbe (*m.*) rob (fruit juice syrup).

arrochada (*f.*) cudgel-blow.

arrochar (*v.t.*) to tighten (by lacing, pulling, or twisting with a tourniquet); to be severe and exacting. **um exame arrochado**, a stiff examination.

arrôcho (*m.*) club, cudgel; garrote; piece of stick used to twist a tourniquet; difficulty, hard nut to crack; (*pl.*) turns of a rope; beckets.

arrodelar (*v.t.*) to cover, protect, defend, as with a buckler.

arrogador –**dora** (*adj.*) arrogating; usurping; (*m.,f.*) one who arrogates; usurper.

arrogância (*f.*) arrogance; pride.

arrogante (*adj.*) arrogant; haughty; high and mighty; "snooty", uppish; cocky; overweening, overbearing.

arrogar (*v.t.*) to arrogate, claim, seize, usurp.—**-se o direito de**, to arrogate to oneself the right to.

arroio (*m.*) arroyo, gully; a small stream.

arrojadiço –**ça** (*adj.*) daring, fearless; of weapons, missile.

arrojado –**da** (*adj.*) plucky; undaunted; daring, reckless, fearless; rash, daredevil.

arrojamento (*m.*) act of dragging, etc. See verb ARROJAR.

arrojar (*v.t.*) to drag (along the ground); to throw violently; to repel, reject.—**a**, to throw at, in, on, to.—**contra**, to let fly at.—**de**, to hurl from.—**em**, to throw into.—**para**, to throw to.—**para longe**, to fling away, hurl afar; (*v.r.*) to throw oneself (**a**, at; **para**, on; **contra**, against; **sôbre**, upon).—**-se a fazer alguma coisa**, to dare to do something.

arrôjo (*m.*) daring, boldness; derring-do; assurance; flight (of imagination, etc.); act of hurling; ostentation; (*pl.*) pieces of wreckage thrown up on the beach.

arrolar [from ROL, list] (*v.t.*) to enroll, list, make a list of.—**bens**, to make an inventory of an estate. [from RÔLO, roll] (*v.t.,v.i.*) to roll; [from RÔLA, dove] (*v.t.*) to croon (a child) to sleep; (*v.i.*) to coo.

arrolhador –**dora** (*adj.*) corking; designating a person who is easily silenced; (*m.*) bottle-corker; person who prevents another from speaking out; worker who strips leaves from MATE shrubs.

arrolhamento (*m.*) operation of stripping leaves from MATE shrubs.

arrolhar (*v.t.*) to cork (bottles, etc.); to silence another person.

arrôlo (*m.*) lullaby.

arromba (*f.*) lively guitar tune. **de**—, (*slang*) swell, great, wonderful.

arrombada (*f.*) a breaking in, forced entry.

arrombador –**dora** (*adj.*) forcing, breaking in; (*m.,f.*) one who breaks in or forces (something) open; housebreaker, burglar.—**de cofres**, safe-cracker.

arrombamento (*m.*) forced entry; act of breaking in (into, down).

arrombar (*v.t.*) to break into (as a house); to break down, batter in (as a door); to crack open (as a safe); to crush (another's spirits).

arrostar (*v.t.*) to face, front; to brave, defy.—**com**, to cope with.—**o perigo**, to brave danger.

arrotador (*m.*) belcher; fig., blusterer, boaster.

arrotar (*v.i.*) to belch; to bluster, brag.—**grandeza**, to brag about what one is (has, or has done).

arrotear (*v.t.*) to clear and cultivate land; to bring land under cultivation; to teach rudimentally.

arrotéia (*f.*) newly cleared land.

arrôto (*m.*) belch.

arroubar (*v.*) = ARREBATAR.

arroubo (*m.*) ecstasy, rapture; delirium; flight (of imagination, etc.); trance; ravishment. **um**—**de eloqüência**, a burst of eloquence.

arroxeado –**da** (*adj.*) purplish, violaceous.

arroz [ô] (*m.*) rice.—**-bravo** (or **-da-guiana**, or **-de-caiena**, or **-do-méxico**), the clubhead cutgrass (*Leersia hexandra*), c.a. ANDREQUICÉ, CAPIM-ANDREQUICÉ, SERRA-PERNA; also = MAÇAMBARÁ.—**de-auçá**, a dish consisting of rice, jerked beef and pepper.—**-de-cachorro** (or **-de-cutia**) = CAPIM-BAMBU.—**-de-espinho** (or **-bravo**, or **-do-mato**, or **-silvestre**), a species of rice (*Oryza subulata*).—**de forno**, baked rice.—**-de-função**, a sweet dessert made with rice and cinnamon.—**-de-rato**, (*Bot.*) white stonecrop (*Sedum album*).—**-de-telhado**, (*Bot.*) nodding navelwort (*Umbilicus pendulinus*), c.a. CONCHELO, PINHÕES-DE-RATO.—-**doce** (or **-de-leite**), rice pudding.— -**doce-de-pagode** (or **-de-festa**), an inveterate party-goer or amusement-seeker.

arrozal (*m.*) rice paddy.

arrozeiro –**ra** (*adj.*) rice; fond of rice; (*m.*) rice grower; rice merchant; (*f.*) rice field.

arruã (*adj.*) wild, undomesticated, untamed; skittish.

arruaça (*f.*) street riot, tumult, commotion.

arruação (*f.*) street lay-out. [Verb: ARRUAR not ARRU-AÇAR.]

arruaçar (*v.i.*) to riot in the streets.

arruaceiro (*m.*) street rioter; roughneck, hooligan, hood-lum, rowdy.

arruadeira (*f.*) a gadabout; a street-walker.

arruado –**da** (*adj.*) having streets; (*m.*) a one-street hamlet; on a plantation, a row of workers houses.

arruador (*m.*) street loafer; street rioter; man who lays out streets.

arruamento (*m.*) laying out of streets; alignment of build-ings on a street; a grouping of like businesses on a same street.

arruar (*v.t.*) to divide into streets; to lay out streets; (*v.i.*) to gad about; (*v.r.*) of the people, to come out into the streets; to open one's office or establish one's business in a given street.

arruda (*f.*, *Bot.*) common rue (*Ruta graveolens*).—-**de-campinas**, an indigo (*Indigofera campinaria*).—-**de-fôlhas-miúdas**, fringed rue (*Ruta chalepensis*).—-**de são-paulo** (—-**do-campo**), a St. John's-wort (*Hypericum teretiusculum*).—-**do-mato**, a pilocarpus (*P. officinals*); a prickly ash (*Zanthoxylum peckoltianum*); also, an indigo (*Indigo similruta*).—-**dos-muros**, the wall rue spleen-wort (*Asplenium ruta-muraria*), c.a. PARONÍQUIA.

arruela (*f.*) washer (flat ring of iron, etc.).—-**de apêrto**, or **de fêcho**, or **de pressão**, lock washer.—-**de espaceja-mento**, spacing washer.

arrufadiço –**ça** (*adj.*) touchy, easily ruffled.

arrufar (*v.t.*) to irritate; to ruffle (feathers, water, etc.); (*v.r.*) to become ruffled, irritated.

arrufo (*m.*) peevish mood; pique; tiff; lover's spat.

arrugar (*v.*) = ENRUGAR.

arruinação [u-i] (*f.*) ruination.

arruinado –**da** [u-i] (*adj.*) ruined; delapidated.

arruinador –**dora** [u-i] (*adj.*) ruinous; (*m.*,*f.*) one who or that which ruins.

arruinamento [u-i] (*m.*) = ARRUINAÇÃO.

arruinar [u-i] (*v.t.*) to ruin, destroy, demolish; to beggar, impoverish; (*v.i.*) to fall into ruin; to spoil, decay; (*v.r.*) to ruin oneself; to go broke.

arruivado –**da** (*adj.*) reddish (referring esp. to hair).

arrulhar (*v.i.*) to coo; (*v.t.*) to utter gentle words; to croon to sleep.

arrulho (*m.*) a cooing; lullaby. ɔ—**das pombas**, cooing of doves.

arrumá (*f.*, *Bot.*) an arrowroot (*Maranta arouma*).

arrumação (*f.*) arrangement, placing in proper order; packing (of baggage); stowing, stowage; situation, em-ployment; listing in proper order; logbook entry; position on the map; a jumble; sharp practice.

arrumadeira (*f.*) housemaid; a neat housekeeper.

arrumador (*m.*) houseman.

arrumar (*v.t.*) to arrange, put in proper order; to tidy up (a room); to pack (baggage); to stow (cargo); to place (in a job); to come by, get (something); to steer (a given course); (*v.r.*) to get settled (fixed up, placed in a good job).—**a trouxa (e ir-se embora)**, to pack up one's things (and leave).—**a gravata**, to straighten one's tie.—**as contas, os livros**, to keep accounts, books, in good order. —**emprêgo**, to dig up a job.—**as malas**, to pack one's bags.—**os móveis**, to arrange the furniture.

arrumo (*m.*) = ARRUMAÇÃO.

arrunhar (*v.t.*) to trim around the edge of.

arsamina (*f.*) = ATOXIL.

arsanílico –**ca** (*adj.*, *Chem.*) **ácido**—, arsanilic acid, atoxy-lic acid.

arsenal (*m.*) arsenal.—**de Guerra**, Army Arsenal.—**de Marinha**, Navy Yard.

arsenamina (*f.*, *Chem.*) arsenic hydride, arsine.

arseníaco –**ca** (*adj.*, *Chem.*) arsenic.

arseniado –**da** (*adj.*) = ARSENICADO.

arseníase (*f.*, *Med.*) arseniasis.

arseniato (*m.*, *Chem.*) arsenate.

arsenicado –**da** (*adj.*, *Chem.*) arseniureted.

arsenicalismo (*m.*) = ARSENÍASE.

arsenicíase (*f.*), –**cismo** (*m.*, *Med.*) arsenism, chronic arsenical poisoning.

arsênico –**ca** (*adj.*, *Chem.*) arsenical; (*m.*) arsenic.

arsenicofagia (*f.*) the habit of eating arsenic.

arsenicóxido [ks] (*m.*, *Chem.*) arsenic oxide.

arsenido (*m.*, *Chem.*) arsenide.

arsenieto (*m.*, *Chem.*) arsenide.

arsenífero –**ra** (*adj.*) arseniferous.

arsênio (*m.*, *Chem.*) arsenium, arsenic.

arsenioso –**sa** (*adj.*) arsenious.

arsenito (*m.*, *Chem.*) arsenite.

arseniureto [i-u] (*m.*) = ARSENIETO.

arsenobenzol (*m.*, *Chem.*) arsphenamine, salvarsan, "606".

arsenocrocita (*f.*) = ARSENOSSIDERITA.

arsenolamprita (*f.*, *Chem.*) arsenolamprite, mineral arsenic.

arsenólito (*m.*, *Min.*) arsenolite, arsenic oxide, white arsenic.

arsenopirite (*f.*) = ARSENOSSIDERITA.

arsenossiderita (*f.*, *Min.*) arsenopyrites, mispickel.

arsenoterapia (*f.*, *Med.*) arsenotherapy.

arsina (*f.*, *Chem.*) arsine [= ARSENAMINA].

arsis (*f.*, *Pros.*; *Music*) arsis.

arsônico –**ca** (*adj.*, *Chem.*) arsonic.

arsônio (*m.*, *Chem.*) arsonium.

artabótris, –**bótrio** (*m.*, *Bot.*) the genus Artabotrys (tail-grape).

artanita (*f.*) the European cyclamen (*C. europaeum*), c.a. VIOLETA-DOS-ALPES, PÃO-PORCINO, PÃO-DE-PORCO; a medicinal ointment made from this plant.

arte (*f.*) art; skill; trade, craft; cunning, artfulness, arti-fice; childish mischief.—**cerâmica**, ceramic art.—**culi-nária**, culinary art.—**dramática**, dramatic art.—**mágica**, black magic, necromancy.—**s do Diabo**, the Devil's wiles. —**s liberais**, liberal arts.—**s mecânicas**, handcrafts, handicrafts.—**plásticas**, plastic arts (esp. sculpture). **belas—s**, fine arts. **com**—, artistically. **de tal**—, **dess'arte, dest'arte**, thus , consequently, in such a man-ner. **obra de**—, work of art, masterpiece; a work of masonry or other construction (bridge, culvert, under-pass, etc.) along a highway or railroad. **sem**—, artless.

artefato (*m.*) artifact; (*pl.*) manufactured goods.—**s de couro**, leather goods. Var. ARTEFACTO.

arteirice (*f.*) artifice, subtlety; childish wile, trick.

arteiro –**ra** (*adj.*) artful, cunning, crafty, wily; sly, tricky; mischievous.

artelho [ê] (*m.*) ankle, anklebone [but not toe, as it is sometimes taken to mean].

artêmia (*f.*) a brine shrimp (genus *Artemia*).

artemigem, artemija (*f.*) = ARTEMÍSIA.

artemísia (*f.*) the mugwort wormwood (*Artemisia vul-garis*), c.a. ARTEMÍSIA-VERDADEIRA, ERVA-DE-SÃO-JOÃO; also the oriental wormwood (*A. scoparia*).—-**brava** = CRAVORANA (a ragweed).—-**de-praia**, a ragweed (*Ambrosia humilis*).—-**do-campo**, the sagewort worm-wood (*Artemisia campestris*).

artemisina (*f.*, *Chem.*) artimisin.

artéria (*f.*, *Anat.*) artery; arterial highway.

arterial (*adj.*) arterial.

arterializar (*v.t.*) to arterialize (venous blood).

arteriarctia (*f.*, *Med.*) arteriarctia.

arteriectasia (*f.*, *Med.*) arteriectasia.

arteriectopia (*f.*, *Med.*) arteriectopia.

arterioflebotomia (*f.*, *Med.*) arteriophlebotomy

arteriografia (*f.*, *Med.*) arteriography.

arteríola (*f.*) arteriole.

arteriólito (*m.*, *Med.*) ateriolith.

arteriomalacia (*f.*, *Med.*) arteriomalacia.

arterionecrose (*f.*, *Med.*) arterionecrosis.

arteriopatia (*f.*, *Med.*) arteriopathy.

arterioplania (*f.*, *Med.*) arterioplania.

arteriorrafia (*f.*, *Surg.*) arteriorrhaphy.

arteriorragia (*f.*, *Med.*) ateriorrhagia.

arteriorrexe [ks] (*f.*, *Med.*) arteriorrhexis.

arteriosclerose (*f.*, *Med.*) arteriosclerosis.

arterioscleroso –**sa** (*adj.*, *Med.*) arteriosclerotic.

arterioso –**sa** (*adj.*, *Physiol.*) arterious, arterial.

arterioso-venoso –**sa** (*adj.*, *Anat.*) arteriovenous.

arteriostenose (*f.*, *Med.*) arteriostenosis.

arteriotomia (*f.*, *Surg.*) arteriotomy.

arteriotrepsia (*f.*, *Surg.*) arteriotrepsis.

artesanato (*m.*) artistic technique or skill.

artesão [-sãos] (m.) artisan;=ARTÍFICE.
artesiano –na (adj.) (of wells) artesian.
artético –ca (adj.) = ARTRÍTICO.
ártico –ca (adj.) arctic.
articulação (f.) articulation; enunciation; joint, knuckle; (colloq.) dressing-down, scolding.—condiliana, (Anat.) condylarthrosis.—em sela, or por encaixe recíproco, (Anat.) articulation by reciprocal reception, or saddle-joint, as, e.g., the calcaneocuboid in the foot, or the carpo-metacarpal joint of the thumb.—esférica, ball joint.—imóvel, (Anat.) immovable articulation, synarthrosis.—móvel, (Anat.) movable articulation, diarthrosis.—semimóvel, (Anat.) mixed articulation, amphiarthrosis.—troclear, (Anat.) articulation as of the trochlea with the patella.—trocóide, (Anat.) a trochoid, or pivot-joint, articulation, as, e.g., the radioulnar.
articulado –da (adj.) articulated, jointed; pronounced.
articular (adj.) articular; (v.t.) to articulate; to utter; to enunciate, pronounce; to put (link) together; to set down in articles, clauses or paragraphs.—acusações não comprovadas contra, to forge (hatch, concoct, trump up) false charges against.
articulista (m.,f.) newspaper writer; feature writer.
artículo (m.) joint, knuckle; internode; article (of a contract, treaty, etc.).
artífice (m.) artificer, skilled workman, artisan; craftsman; author, inventor.
artificial (adj.) artificial; far-fetched; fictitious.
artificialidade (f.), artificialismo (m.) artificiality; affectation.
artificiar (v.t.) to employ skill (in the making of something); to plot, scheme, contrive artfully.
artifício (m.) artifice, skill, craft; device, contrivance; makeshift; trickery; ruse; guile.—de cálculo, a mathematical shortcut.—de idéias, cleverness of ideas. fogos de—, fireworks.
artificioso –sa (adj.) ingenious; expert; designing; crafty.
artigo (m.) article, item, commodity, piece of merchandise; clause, paragraph; piece of writing; (Gram.) article. —de fé, article of faith.—definido, (Gram.) definite article.—de fundo, principal editorial or feature article in a newspaper.—estrangeiro, foreign (imported) merchandise.—indefinido, (Gram.) indefinite article.—nacional, domestic goods.—partitivo, (Gram.) partitive article.—s alimentícios, food products.—s de consumo, consumer goods.—s de fantasia, fancy goods.—s de importação, imported goods.—s de luxo, luxury items.—s para escritório, office supplies.—s para viagem, travel goods. em—de morte, at the point of death.
artiguelho [ê] (m.) an insignificant, worthless article; a scurrilous newspaper article.
artilhar (v.t.) to arm with artillery.
artiharia (f.) artillery (guns, men); gunnery.—de campanha, field artillery.—da costa, coast artillery.—de montanha, mountain artillery.—de sítio, siege guns.—ligeira, light artillery.—pesada, heavy artillery. parque de—, artillery park. peça de—, a cannon.
artilheiro (m.) artilleryman, gunner; center forward (soccer player).
artimanha (f.) artifice, ruse, wile; gadget.
artista (adj.) artistic; (m.,f.) artist, actor, actress; artisan, artificer.
artístico –ca (adj.) artistic.
artitude (f., Med.) arctation.
artocarpo (m.) the genus Artocarpus, which includes the breadfruit (A. altilis) called FRUTA-PÃO, and the jakfruit (A. heterophyllus).
artragra (f., Med.) arthragra.
artralgia (f., Med.) arthralgia.
artrectomia·(f., Surg.) arthrectomy.
artrite (f., Med.) arthritis.
artrítico –ca (adj.; m.,f.) arthritic.
artritismo (m., Med.) arthritism.
artrobrânquia (f., Zool.) arthrobranch, -branchia.
artrócace (f., Med.) arthrocace.
artrocele (f., Med.) arthrocele.
artrocondrite (f., Med.) arthrochondritis.
artródese (f., Surg.) arthrodesis.
artrodia (f., Anat.) arthrodia.
artrogastros (m.pl.) the Arthrogastra (scorpions, etc.).
artrografia (f.) arthrography.
artrogripose (f., Med.) arthrogryposis.
artrólito (m., Med.) arthrolith.
artrologia (f.) arthrology.

artromeral, –mérico –ca (adj., Zool.) arthromeric.
artrômero (m., Zool.) arthromere.
artropatia (f., Med.) arthropathy.
artropiose (f., Med.) arthropiosis.
artroplastia (f., Surg.) arthroplasty.
artrópode (m., Bot.) the genus Arthropodium; (Zool.) an arthropod; (pl.) the Arthropoda.
artrose (f., Anat.) arthrosis.
artrossinovite (f., Med.) arthrosynovitis.
artrotifo (m., Med.) arthrotyphoid.
artrozoário (m., Zool.) arthrozoan.
Artur (m.) Arthur.
aruã (m.,f.) an Indian of an extinct Arawakan tribe which at one time occupied a part of the Marajó Island, and of other islands, in the Amazon estuary. [The same name is used to designate an unrelated tribe on the Rio Branco in southwestern Mato Grosso.]; (adj.) pert. to or designating either of these tribes.
aruã (m.) any amphibious flask snail, esp. Pomacea nobilis of Amazonia, or the paper apple snail (P. papyracea), c.a. ARUÁ-DO-BREJO, AMPULÁRIA, CARAMUJO-DO-BANHADO.—do mangue, a neritina (N. virginea).
aruaí (m.) the white-eyed paroquet (Aratinga l. leucophthalmus). Cf. PERIQUITO.
aruanã, aruanã (m.) a large river-fish (Osteoglossum bicirrhosum), c.a. ARAUANÁ, AMANÁ. [It is closely related to the PIRARUCU (Arapaima gigas).]
arubatã (m.) = PAU-BRASIL.
arubé (m.) a condiment made of manioc with salt, pepper, garlic and fish oil.
aruca (f., Bot.) the orangeleaf tabernaemontana (T. citrifolia).
árum (m., Bot.) the genus Arum. Cf. ARÃO and JARRO.
arumã (m., Bot.) a tirite (Ischnosiphon sp.).
arumá (m.,f.) = JARUMÁ (Indian).
arumará (m.) = ARRANCA-MILHO.
arumarana (f., Bot.) a thalia (T. geniculata), c.a. CAETÉ.
arumbeba (f.) the common pricklypear (Opuntia vulgaris) = OPÚNCIA.
arunco (m., Bot.) the sylvan goatsbeard (Aruncus sylvester), c.a. BARBA-DE-CABRA, BARBA-DE-PACA.
arunda (f.) the giant reed (Arundo donax).
arundináceo –cea (adj., Bot.) arundinaceous.
arundinária (f.) a genus (Arundinaria) of large bamboo grasses.
arundíneo –nea (adj.) arundineous, reedy.
aruru [urú] (m.) a resin tree (Protium decandrum), c.a. ÁRVORE-DE-CHIPA.
arúspice (m.) haruspex, soothsayer.
arval (adj.) pert. to the land or fields; rustic.
arvícola (adj.) arvicoline; (m.) a worker on the land; a field mouse.
aviicultor –tora (m.,f.) a grower of field crops.
avicultura (f., Agric.) aviculture.
arvoado –da (adj.) giddy, dazed.
arvoamento (m.) dizziness, giddiness.
arvoar (v.i.) to feel dizzy; (v.t.) to make giddy.
arvoeiro (m.) = JEQUIRITI.
arvorado –da (adj.) tree-planted; lifted, raised (as a flag); promoted to a higher post; (m.) a private acting as corporal.
arvorar (v.t.) to hoist, raise (flag); to lift, set up; to elevate, promote; to arrogate (to oneself); to plant with trees; (v.i.) to run away.—se (em alguma coisa) to lay claim (to being something).—se em (advogado), to pretend to be, set oneself up as (a lawyer).—uma doutrina, to proclaim a doctrine.
árvore (f.) tree; mast; (Mach.) arbor; spindle; axle; shaft.—celeste, the tree-of-heaven ailanthus (A. altissima).—da-borracha, Pará rubbertree (Hevea brasiliensis).—da-cânfora, camphortree (Cinnamomum camphora), c.a. CANFOREIRA.—da-cera, southern waxmyrtle (Myrica cerifera).—da-chuva = BARAÚNA.—da-cera-do-japão, waxtree (Toxicodendron succedaneum).—da-chipa = ARURU.—da ciência do bem e do mal, the Biblical tree of the knowledge of good and evil.—da cruz, the Holy Cross.—da-fortuna, a ginseng (Panax fructicosum).—da-goma-arábica, the gumarabic acacia (A. senegal).—da-goma-elástica, the Indiarubber ficus (F. elastica).—da-independência, a variegated leafcroton (Codiaeum variegatum) having green-and-yellow leaves.—de-judéia, or -de-judas, the Judastree (Cercis siliquastrum).—da-lã, or -de-paina, the floss-silktree (Chorisia speciosa).—da-laca, Japanese lacquertree (Toxicoden-

dron verniciſluum).—**-da-manteiga,** a butter tree (_Pentadesma butyracea_).—**-da-morte** = ÁRVORE-VENENO, ANTIAR.—**-da-preguiça** the shieldleaf pumpwood (_Cecropia peltata_), or the silverleaf pumpwood (_C. palmata_), c.a. UMBAÚBA.—**-da-pureza,** the Spanish dagger or moundlily yucca (_Y. gloriosa_).—**-da-raspa,** a fig (_Ficus asperrima_) whose leaves are used as rasps.—**-da-vaca,** a bulletwood (_Mimusops elata_), c.a. MAÇARANDUBA; the cow breadnut tree (_Brosimum utile_), c.a.BROSIMO. —**-da-vida,** eastern arborvitae (_Thuja occidentalis_); also = CEDRO-DO-BUGAÇO.—**-de-caroço,** any drupaceous tree. —**-de-castidade,** or **-da-pimenta,** the lilac chastetree (_Vitex agnus-castus_), c.a. AGNOCASTO, PIMENTEIRO-SILVESTRE.—**-de-coral,** a coralbean (_Erythrina poianthes_). —**-de-costados** = ÁRVORE GENEALÓGICA. —**-de-cuia** = CUEIRA.—**-de-espinho,** any prickly tree.—**de fruta,** or **-frutífera,** any fruit tree.—**-de-geração** = ÁRVORE GENE-ALÓGICA.—**-de-gralha,** the banyan fig (_Ficus benghalensis_).—**-de-leite,** cowtree (_Tabernaemontana utilis_); cowbreadnut tree (_Brosimum utile_,) c.a. ÁRVORE-DA-VACA. —**-de-lotus,** the European hackberry (_Celtis australis_). —**-de-mosquito** = CARAPANAÚBA. —**-de-neve,** white fringetree (_Chionanthus virginicus_).—**-de-sant'ana,** the palimara alstonia (_A. scholaris_).—**-de-são sebastião,** the milk-bush or malabartree euphorbia (_E. tirucalli_), c.a. COROA-DE-CRISTO.—**-de-são-tomaz,** the mountain ebony or buddhist bauhinia (_B. variegata_).—**de transmissão,** transmission shaft.—**-de-tucano,** a chastetree (_Vitex montevidense_).—**-de-umbrela,** the umbrella magnolia (_M. tripetala_).—**-de-velas,** Panama candletree (_Parmentiera cereifera_).—**-do-brasil,** brazilwood (_Caesalphina brasiliensis_), or the prickly brazilwood (_C. echinata_), c.a. PAU-BRASIL.—**-do-dragão,** the dragon dracaena (_D. draco_), c.a. DRAGO(N)EIRO.—**-do-natal,** Christmas tree; the common chinafir (_Cunninghamia lanceolata_); Japanese cryptomeria (_C. japonica_).—**-do-pão,** the breadfruit tree (_Artocarpus altilis_), c.a. ARTOCAROPO, FRUTA-PÃO, FRUTEIRA-DE-PÃO.—**-do-pão-do-macaco,** the baobab (_Adansonia digitata_).—**-do-papel,** a spiderflower (_Tibouchina papyrifera_), c.a. PAU-PAPEL.—**-do-papel-arroz,** the ricepaper plant (_Tetrapanax papyriferus_).—**-do-rosário** = ÁRVORE-SANTA.—**-do-sabão,** southern soapberry or Chinaberry tree (_Sapindus saponaria_).—**-do-sebo,** Chinese tallowtree (_Sapium sebiferum_).—**-do-viajante,** Madagascar travelerstree (_Ravenala madagascariensis_), c.a. BANANEIRA-DE-LEQUE.—**-dos-feiticeiros,** Guiana zebrawood (_Connarus guianensis_).—**-dos-pagodes,** Japanese pagodatree (_Sophora japonica_).—**-dos-sobreiros** = PALMEIRA-DAS-VASSOURAS. — **genealógica,** family tree; pedigree.—**-mãe** = PORTA-SEMENTES.—**-motora,** drive shaft.—**-santa,** or **-do(s)-rosário(s),** the holy tree, bead tree or China tree (_Melia azederach_), c.a. AZEDERAQUE, CINAMOMO, JASMIM-DE-SOLDADO, LILÁS-DA-ÍNDIA.—**-sêca,** (_Naut._)bare mast.—**-triste,** or **-da-noite,** nightjasmine (_Nyctanthes arbor-tristis_), c.a. AÇAFROEIRA-DO-BRASIL.—**-vaca** = ÁRVORE-DE-LEITE.—**-veneno,** upastree (_Antiaris toxicaria_), c.a. ÁRVORE-DA-MORTE, ANTIAR. **correr em—sêca,** (_Naut._) to scud.
arvoredo [ê] (_m._) a grove of trees; the masts of a ship.
arvorejar-se (_v.r._) to become covered with trees.
arzola (_f._) spiny cocklebur (_Xanthium spinosum_).
as (_fem. def. art. pl._) the; (_pron._) those, them, the ones. [The masc. form is OS.]
ás (_m._) ace (flier, playing card, etc.).
às (_contraction of prep._ a+_fem. article pl._ **as**) to the, at the, etc. Cf. AOS.—**apaldeladas,** gropingly.—**armas!** to arms!—**arrecuas,** backing away.—**avançadas,** little by little.—**ave-marias,** at the hour of the evening Angelus. —**avessas,** backwards, inside out.—**bandeiras despregadas,** [to laugh] without restraint.—**barbas de,** face to face with.—**boas** (com), on good terms (with).—**braçadas,** in armfuls, abundantly.—**bulhas,** in a turmoil. —**cabriolas,** skipping about.—**cabritas,** astride the shoulders of.—**caladas,** secretly, quietly.—**canastradas,** or **canastras,** in basketfuls.—**canchas,** on (one's) back. —**canhas,** lefthandedly.—**carrachas (carrachuchas, carrancholas),** piggyback.—**carreiras,** on the run; hurriedly. —**cavaleiras (cavaletas, cavalinhas, cavalitas),** astride (de, of).—**cegas,** blindly.—**chusmas,** in swarms.— **claras,** openly, clearly.—**costas,** on the back or shoulders (of); piggyback.—**curvetas,** curvetting, jumping.— **cutiladas,** [to slash] with knife or sword.—**declaradas,** publicly.—**de Vila Diogo,** running away.—**dezenas,** in tens, by tens.—**direitas,** right, just, correct.—**dúzias,**

by the dozen; in dozens.—**encobertas,** clandestinely.— **escâncaras,** wide-open (as windows).—**escondidas,** secretly, hiddenly.—**escuras,** in the dark.—**espadeiradas,** with sabre blows—**estopinhas,** excessively.—**expensas de,** at the expense of.—**fornadas,** in batches.— **furtadas,** or **furtadelas,** furtively.—**horas,** at the moment; [pay] by the hour.—**horas de estalar,** at the last minute.—**investidas,** thrusting, by thrusts.—**legiões,** in legions.—**léguas,** far away.—**manadas,** by the handful; in droves.—**mãos ambas,** with both hands.—**mãos cheias** (or **a mancheia**), by the handful, prodigally.—**mãos de,** at the hands of.—**mãos lavadas,** easily; gratis.—**maravilhas,** marvelously.—**margens de,** on the sides or edges of.—**marradas,** bumping, butting.—**marteladas,** with hammer blows.—**más,** on bad terms; by force.—**matinas,** at matins.—**migalhas,** or **migas,** bit by bit.—**mil maravilhas,** marvelously well.—**môscas,** empty of customers; doing nothing.—**noites,** at night.—**nuvens,**[to praise] to the skies.—**ocultas,** secretly.—**ordens,** under orders.— **ordens de,** at the disposal of.—**pencas,** in bunches (as bananas); in heaps.—**perdidas,** losing.—**porções,** in small doses.—**portas da morte,** at death's door.—**pressas,** hurriedly.—**públicas,** publicly.—**rajadas,** in gusts.— **recuadas,** [to move] backwards.—**resmas,** in reams.— **revoadas,** now and then.—**ribeiradas,** [to flow] in streams.—**rimas,** in heaps.—**rinchavelhadas,** with horselaughs.—**sabidas,** publicly.—**sêcas,** drily.—**singelas,** alone.—**sôltas,** freely; without restraint.—**súbitas,** suddenly.—**surdas,** softly, quietly.—**tartufas,** hypocritically.—**temporadas,** from time to time.—**tontas,** dizzily.— **turras,** disputatiously.—**últimas,** to extremes.—**upas,** leaping.—**upas e arrifadas,** with leaps and bounds.— **vésperas de,** on the eve of.—**vezes,** at times, sometimes. —**voltas com,** busy with; involved with; engaged in; up to one's ears in (a problem, etc.).
asa (_f._) wing; lobe, fin; lug, handle; (_colloq._) arm; (_Soccer_) half-back.—**-branca,** the Picazuro pigeon (_Columba p. picazuro_), c.a. POMBA-TROCAZ, JACAÇU.—**da orelha,** (_Anat._) the auricle or pinna.—**de cêsto,** (_Geom._) baskethandle (arch).—**de papagaio,** (_Bot._) a poinsettia = FÔLHA-DE-SANGUE.—**-de-telha,** the bay-winged cowbird (_Molothrus b. badius_).—**negra,** Jonah, jinx, hoodoo.—**s do nariz,** sides of the nostrils. **arrastar a—,** to court, woo, make love to; lit., to drag the wing, as do some male birds when engaged in courtship. **dar—s à imaginação,** to give free rein to fancy. **extremidade da—,** (_Aeron._) wing tip. **voar com as próprias—s,** to go ahead under one's own steam.
asado -da (_adj._) winged; having ears (as a jug).
asafia (_f._) asaphia, indistinct utterance.
asarabácara (_f., Bot._) asarabacca, c.a. ÁSARO.
ásaro (_m., Bot._) European wild ginger (_Asarum europaeum_), c.a. ASARABÁCARA, NARDO-SILVESTRE, ORELHA-HUMANA.
asarona (_f., Chem._) asaron, asarum camphor.
asbestiforme (_adj._) asbestiform.
asbestino -na (_adj._) asbestine.
asbesto (_m., Min._) asbestos. Cf. AMIANTO.
asbolano (_m., Min._) asbolite, c.a. ASBOLITA, COBALTO OXIDADO NEGRO.
asbolina (_f., Pharm._) asbolin.
asca (_f._) aversion; disgust [= ASCO]; bad smell; unpleasant body odor.
ascalônia (_f., Bot._) the shallot (_Allium ascalonicum_).
ascaricida (_adj._) ascaricidal; (_f._) ascaricide.
ascáride, ascárida (_f._) any roundworm of the genus Ascaris, esp. _A. lumbricoides_ which is parasitic in human intestines [= LOMBRIGA].
ascárides, ascaríeos (_m.pl._) a family (_Ascaridae_) of nematode worms.
ascaridíase, ascaridiose (_f., Med._) ascaridiasis, ascariasis.
ascendência (_f._) ascendancy; ancestry, genealogy. **ângulo de—,** (_Aeron._) climbing angle.
ascendente (_adj._) ascendant; ascending, climbing; increasing; (_m.,f._) ancestor, forebear.—**em linha reta,** a direct ancestor.
ascender (_v.i._) to ascend, rise, mount, climb. Do not confuse with ACENDER.]
ascensão (_f._) ascension, ascent, rise, climb; (_Astron._)— **oblíqua,** oblique ascension.—**reta,** right ascension.
ascensional (_adj._) ascensional.
ascensionário -ria (_adj._) ascensive.
ascensionista (_m.,f._) mountain climber; balloonist.
ascensor (_m._) elevator. [British: lift].

ascensorista (*m.,f.*) elevator operator.
asceta (*m.,f.*) ascetic.
ascético –ca (*adj.*) ascetic, self-denying; (*m.,f.*) ascetic.
ascetismo (*m.*) ascetism.
ascídia (*f., Bot.*) ascidium; (*Zool.*) a genus (*Ascidia*) of sea squirts.
ascidiado –da (*adj., Bot.*) ascidiate.
ascidiforme (*adj., Bot.*) ascidiform, pitcher-shaped.
ascígero –ra (*adj., Bot.*) ascigerous.
áscio –cia (*adj.*) without shadow; (*m.pl.*) ascians (inhabitants of the torrid zone.)
ásciro (*m., Bot.*) St. Andrew's-cross (*Ascyrum hypericoides*).
ascite (*f., Med.*) ascites.
ascítico –ca (*adj.*) ascitic(al).
asclépia, asclepíade (*f.*) any milkweed of the genus Asclepias.
asclepiadáceas, –piáceas, –píadas, –piádeas (*f.pl.*) the milkweed family (*Asclepiadaceae*).
asclepiadina (*f., Pharm.*) asclepidin, asclepin extract (from the root of *Asclepias tuberosa*).
asclepiona (*f., Chem.*) asclepion (from the sap of *Asclepias syriaca*).
asco (*m.*) loathing, disgust, repugnance, aversion, revulsion, [= ASCA]; (*Bot.*) ascus.
ascocarpo (*m., Bot.*) ascocarp.
ascóforo (*m., Bot.*) ascophore.
ascoliquene (*m., Bot.*) ascolichen.
ascoma (*m., Bot.*) ascoma.
ascomicete (*m., Bot.*) an ascomycete.
ascoroso –sa, **ascoso** –sa (*adj.*) = ASQUEROSO.
ascospóreo –rea (*adj., Bot.*) ascosporous.
ascósporo (*m., Bot.*) ascospore.
áscua (*f.*) ember.
aselha [ê] (*f.*) a little wing; a loop which forms a catch, as for a button; tab, tag.
aselho (*m.*) = ASELO.
asélidos (*m.pl.*) a family (*Asellidae*) of fresh-water isopod crustaceans.
aselo (*m.*) a genus (*Asellus*) of fresh-water isopod crustaceans.—-de-água-doce, a fresh-water "pill bug" (*Asellus vulgaris*), c.a. BICHO-DE-CONTA-AQUÁTICO; (*pl., Astron.*) the Aselli.
asfaltado –da (*adj.*) covered or paved with asphalt.
asfaltador (*m.*) asphalter.
asfaltagem (*f.*), **asfaltamento** (*m.*) asphalting.
asfaltar (*v.t.*) to cover or pave with asphalt.
asfaltaria (*f.*) asphalt plant.
asfalteno (*m.*) asphaltene.
asfalto (*m.*) asphalt.
asfixia [ks] (*f., Med., Physiol.*) asphyxia.
asfixiante, asfixiador –dora [ks] (*adj.*) asphyxiating, suffocating.
asfixiar [ks] (*v.t.*) to asphyxiate; to choke.
asfíxico –ca, **asfixioso** –sa [ks] = ASFIXIANTE.
asfódelo (*m., Bot.*) asphodel, c.a. ABRÓTEA.
asiano –na (*adj., m.,f.*) Asian.
asiaticismo (*m.*) Asiaticism.
asiático –ca (*adj.*) Asiatic; luxurious, voluptuous; prolix, high-flown; (*m.,f.*) an Asiatic.
asilado –da (*adj.*) that has been given asylum; refugee; (*m.,f.*) inmate of an asylum; refugee.
asilar (*v.t.*) to give asylum to; to shelter; (*v.r.*) to seek asylum; to take refuge.
asilídeos (*m.pl.*) a family (*Asilidae*) of robber flies.
asilo (*m.*) asylum, shelter, retreat, haven, place of refuge, sanctuary; (*Zool.*) a robber fly (*Asillus*).—de alienados, insane asylum.—de órfãos, orphanage.—dos velhos, or —da velhice desamparada, old folks' home.
asimina (*f.*) the common pawpaw (*Asimina triloba*).
asinal (*adj.*) ass-like.
asinino –na, **asinário** –ria (*adj.*) asinine.
asinha (*f.*) winglet.
asma (*f., Med.*) asthma.
asmático –ca (*adj., m.,f.*) asthmatic.
asmento –ta (*adj.*) asthmatic.
asmo –ma (*adj.*) var. of ÁZIMO.
asna (*f.*) a she-donkey; (*Const.*) triangular roof truss; (*Heraldry*) chevron.
asnada (*f.*) a piece of asininity, gross blunder; a drove of donkeys.
asnal (*adj.*) ass-like.
asnamento (*m.*) timbers of a gable roof.
asnaria (*f.*) drove of donkeys; also = ASNAMENTO.

asnático –ca (*adj.*) stupid, asinine.
asnear (*v.i.*) to behave stupidly, play the fool; to flounder.
asneira (*f.*) blunder, piece of stupidity, "howler"; bosh, nonsense; folly.
asneirada (*f.*) a bigger ASNEIRA.
asneirão (*m.*) dolt, a big ass.
asneirento –ta (*adj.*) stupid, blundering; doltish.
asneirista (*adj.*) given to uttering ASNEIRAS.
asneiro –ra (*adj.*) ass-like; mule-like; (*m.*) donkey driver . or tender.
asneirola (*f.*) an obscenity; an equivocal or vulgar statement.
asnice (*f.*) = ASNEIRA.
asnidade (*f.*) asininity.
asnilho (*m.*) a little ass.
asno (*m.*) ass, donkey; dolt, dunce, fool; stupid or ignorant person.—quadrado, utter fool, complete ass.
aspa (*f.*) St. Andrew's cross [X]; (*pl.*) quotation marks; inverted commas; arms of a windmill; horns.
aspaço (*m.*) a horn-thrust.
aspálato (*m., Bot.*) the genus Aspalathus.
aspar (*v.t.*) to set with inverted commas; to crucify; to erase, eliminate.
asparagina (*f., Chem.*) asparagine.
aspárago (*m.*) = ESPARGO.
aspartato (*m., Chem.*) aspartate.
aspártico –ca (*adj., Chem.*) aspartic.
aspásia (*f.*) a genus (*Aspasia*) of orchids.
aspecto (*m.*) aspect, appearance; look, mien; point of view.—de doente, sick-looking. ao primeiro—, at first sight. de bom (mau)—, good- (bad-) looking. sob êste—, from this viewpoint. Var. ASPETO.
aspelina (*f., Bot.*) a groundsel (*Senecio sp.*).
asperamente (*adv.*) unkindly; harshly.
aspereza (*f.*) asperity, roughness, ruggedness, harshness, severity, sharpness, abruptness, bluntness.
asperges (*m., Eccl.*) Asperges (ceremony, anthem); an aspergillum.
aspergiliário –ria, **aspergiliforme** (*adj., Bot.*) aspergilliform.
aspergilo (*m., Bot.*) an aspergilliform organ; any fungus of the genus Aspergillus, esp. *A. fumigatus*; (*Zool.*) a genus (*Brechites, syn. Aspergillum*) of marine bivalve mollusks —the watering-pot shells.
aspergilose (*f.*) aspergillosis.
aspergimento (*m.*) = ASPERSÃO.
aspergir [24, 21-a] (*v.t.*) to sprinkle.
asperidade, asperidão (*f.*) = ASPEREZA.
asperifólio –lia (*adj.*) asperifoliate, rough-leaved.
aspérrimo –ma (*absol. superl. of* ÁSPERO) most rough, etc.;—see the adjective.
aspermatismo (*m., Med.*) aspermatism.
aspermia (*f., Bot.*) condition of being seedless; (*Med.*) aspermatism.
aspermo –ma (*adj.*) seedless.
áspero –ra (*adj.*) rough, uneven, scabrous; tart, sour [wine]; harsh, severe; rude, coarse.
aspérrimo –ma (*absol. superl. of* ÁSPERO), most rough, etc. —see the adjective.
aspersão (*f.*) aspersion, sprinkling. [But not aspersion in the sense of a calumnious remark, which is CALÚNIA.]
asperso –sa, irreg. p.p. of ASPERGIR.
aspersório (*m.*) aspergillum; stoup.
asperugo (*m., Bot.*) German madwort (*Asperugo procumbens*).
aspérula (*f., Bot.*) sweet woodruff (*Asperula odorata*).
aspeto (*m.*) = ASPECTO.
áspide (*f.*) asp, viper.
aspídia (*f.*), –dio (*m.*) a genus (*Dryopteris, syn. Aspidium*) of ferns.
aspidiota (*m.*) a genus (*Aspidiotus*) of armored scale insects.
aspidobrânquios (*m.pl.*) an order (*Aspidobranchia*) of marine snails.
aspidospermo (*m., Bot.*) white quebracho (*Aspidosperma quebracho*), c.a. QUEBRACHO-BRANCO.
aspidospermina (*f., Chem., Pharm.*) aspidospermine.
aspiração (*f.*) breathing, inhaling; aspiration, longing, yearning; (*Gas. Engine*) suction stroke.
aspirado –da (*adj.*) inhaled, sucked in; (*adj.; f., Gram.; Phonet.*) aspirate.
aspirador –dora (*adj.*) aspirating; (*m.*) aspirator.—de pó, vacuum cleaner.
aspirante (*adj.*) that employs suction (as a pump);

(*m.,f.*) candidate, aspirant.—**a oficial,** officer-candidate. —**de escola militar,** cadet.—**de marinha,** naval cadet, midshipman.

aspirar (*v.t.*) to breathe (in), inhale, suck in (air, smoke); to aspirate (sounds).—**a,** to aspire to, be a candidate for; to aim at.

aspirativo –**va** (*adj.*) aspirate.

aspirina (*f., Pharm.*) aspirin.

asplâncnico –**ca** (*adj., Zool.*) asplanchnic.

asplênio (*m.*), **asplênia** (*f.*) a genus (*Asplenium*) of spleenworts.

aspleniôide (*adj., Bot.*) asplenioid.

ásporo –**ra** (*adj., Bot.*) without true spores.

aspredo [ê] (*m.*) a genus (*Aspredo*) of So. American catfishes.

aspudo –**da** (*adj.*) having big horns.

asquerosidade (*f.*) loathesomeness, repulsiveness.

asqueroso –**sa** (*adj.*) nauseous, disgusting, repellent, loathesome, nasty, foul [= ASCOROSO].

assacadilha (*f.*) calumny, slander, defamation.

assacador –**dora** (*adj.*) imputing; (*m.,f.*) imputer.

assacar (*v.t.*) to impute (faults).—**injúrias contra,** to utter slander against.

assadeira (*f.*) roasting pan; baking pan; woman who roasts and peddles chestnuts.

assadeiro (*m.*) roasting pan, baking pan.

assado –**da** (*adj.*) roasted, baked; (*colloq.*) in a fix; (*slang*) burned up, angry; (*m.*) a roast.—**ao (de) sol,** sunburned. —**de carneiro,** roast lamb.—**de terneiro,** roast veal. **assim ou—,** in this way or that. **banana—,** baked banana [but baked potatoes are BATATAS COZIDAS, not ASSADAS.] **peru—,** roast turkey.

assador (*m.*) roaster.

assadura (*f.*) roasting; a piece of meat for roasting; blister. —**das crianças,** infants' chafing.

assa-fétida (*f.*) asafetida giantfennel (*Ferula assafoetida*).

assalariado –**da** (*adj.*) employed for wages; in the pay of; subsidized (in the sense of bribed); (*m.*) henchman, retainer.

assalariador –**dora** (*m.,f.*) employer.

assalariamento (*m.*) employment for wages.

assalariar (*v.t.*) to hire for wages; to bribe; (*v.r.*) to take employment for wages; to accept bribes.

assaltada (*f.*) assault, attack, onset.

assaltador –**dora, assaltante** (*adj.*) assaulting; (*m.*) assailant, aggressor; housebreaker.

assaltar (*v.t.*) to assault, assail, attack, charge, fall upon, storm.

assaltear (*v.*) = ASSALTAR.

assalto (*m.*) assault, attack, onslaught; (*Boxing*) round; (*Milit.*) push, charge, storm.—**à mão armada,** armed assault; holdup.—**à traição,** sneak attack.—**de esgrima,** fencing bout.—**do demônio,** strong temptation. **carro de—,** armored car.

assanhadiço –**ça** (*adj.*) irascible.

assanhado –**da** (*adj.*) raging; excited; in turmoil.

assanhamento (*m.*) anger, rage, fury.

assanhar (*v.t.*) to anger, irritate, stir up, enrage. (*v.r.*) to rage.

assa-peixe (*m.*) a falsenettle (*Boehmeria caudata*); an ironweed (*Vernonia sp.*).

assaprol (*m.*) = ABRASTOL.

assapuva (*f.*) a rosewood (*Dalbergia viciabilis*).

assaque (*m.*) calumnious imputation. [Verb: ASSACAR].

assar (*v.t.*) to roast, bake.—**na grelha,** to broil.—**no forno,** to bake.—**-se ao sol,** to sunburn.

assarapantar (*v.t.*) to frighten; to upset; (*v.r.*) to become upset, confused.

assassinador –**dora** (*adj.; m.,f.*) = ASSASSINO.

assassinar (*v.t.*) to assassinate, murder, kill; (*colloq.*) to "murder" a piece of music; to "butcher" a foreign language.

assassinato (*m.*) a murder.

assassínio (*m.*) murder.

assassino –**na** (*adj.*) murderous; (*m.*) assassin, murderer; (*f.*) murderess.

assaz (*adv.*) enough, sufficiently.

assazmente (*adv.*) sufficiently; more than enough.

assazonar (*v.*) = SAZONAR.

asseado –**da** (*adj.*) neat, clean, cleanly, trim, tidy, spruce. **pouco—,** dirty, untidy.

assear (*v.t.*) to clean up, tidy up; to deck, adorn.

assecla (*m.,f.*) partisan, sectarian.

assecuratório –**ria** (*adj.*) assuring, reassuring.

assedar (*v.t.*) to render smooth as silk; to card, comb (flax).

assedentado –**da** (*adj.*) thirsty.

assediador –**dora, –diante** (*adj.*) besieging; (*m.,f.*) besieger.

assediar (*v.t.*) to besiege; to importune, beset; to obsess; to haunt.

assédio (*m.*) siege, blockade; importunity, insistence; entreaty, pleading, beseeching.

asseguração (*f.*) = SEGURANÇA.

assegurado –**da** (*adj.; m.,f.*) = SEGURADO.

assegurador –**dora** (*adj.*) assuring, reassuring; assurer; insurer.

assegurar (*v.t.*) to asseverate, assert, aver, affirm; to safeguard; to assure, make sure (**de,** of).

asseio (*m.*) cleanliness, neatness; spruceness; perfection.

asselar (*v.*) = SELAR.

asselvajado –**da** (*adj.*) savage, wild, rough.

asselvajar (*v.t.*) to make savage, wild, brutish; (*v.r.*) to become so.

assembléia (*f.*) assembly, meeting, convention, gathering; (*pl., Bot.*) globe candytuft [*Iberis umbellata*].—**constituinte,** constitutional convention.—**de credores,** creditors' meeting.—**geral,** general assembly.—**legislativa,** legislative assembly.

assemelhação (*f.*) assimilation.

assemelhar (*v.t.*) to assimilate, make similar to; to liken to.—**-se a (com, em)** to be like (something or someone); to take after (someone).

assemia (*f., Med.*) asymbolia.

assenhorear-se (*v.r.*) to take possession (**de,** of).

assentado –**da** (*adj.*) seated; based; agreed upon; (*f.*) sitting, session (as of a board of inquiry). **ler (um livro) de uma—,** to read (a book) at one sitting.

assentador (*m.*) recorder; machine fitter; bricklayer; smith's flatter; razor strop.

assentamento (*m.*) a seating, a settling down; a putting in or into place; registry, registration; enrollment.—**de trilhos,** tracklaying.—**de tijolos,** bricklaying.

assentar [24] (*v.t.*) to seat (**em,** on); to lay, place; to base (**em,** on); to jot down, make a note of; to settle upon; to agree to (as the terms of a contract); to decide; to assent to, acquiesce in, concede; to deem, suppose; to fit (as a garment); to strop (a razor); (*v.i.*) to be suited (**a,** to); to be becoming (**a,** to); to look well (**a,** on); to be seated; of liquids, to settle, become clear; to settle down (become sedate); (*v.r.*) to sit down.—**a mão,** to develop skill; to get into one's stride.—**a primeira pedra de um edifício,** to lay a cornerstone.—**as bases de um acôrdo,** to lay the bases for, agree upon the terms of, an agreement.—**as despesas,** to jot down the expenses.—**bem, mal,** to fit well, badly.—**morada,** to settle down.—**no papel,** to enter in the books.—**o visto em (um passaporte, um documento),** to visa (a passport); to O.K. (a document). —**praça,** to enlist (in the army).—**os cabelos,** to smooth down one's hair.—**tijolos,** to lay bricks.—**uma bofetada,** to land a blow.

assente (*irreg. p.p. of* ASSENTAR) seated on; placed upon; agreed, settled; of liquids, settled.

assentimento (*m.*) assent.

assentir [21a] (*v.i.*) to assent (**em,** to); to concur (**a, em, in**).

assento (*m.*) any seat (chair, bench, etc.); place to sit; base (on which something rests); foundation; rump; sedateness; bookkeeping entry; sediment.

assepsia (*f.*) asepsis.

assepsiar (*v.t.*) to asepticize.

asséptico –**ca** (*adj.*) aseptic.

asseptol (*m., Pharm.*) aseptol.

asseptulina (*f., Pharm.*) aseptolin.

asserção (*f.*) assertion.

asserenar (*v.*) = SERENAR.

assertivo –**va** (*adj.*) assertive; (*f.*) assertion.

asserto (*m.*) assertion.

assertório –**ria** (*adj.*) of the nature of an assertion; assertive; (*m.*) sworn statement.

assessor –**sôra** (*m.,f.*) assessor, adviser. [But not a tax assessor which is LANÇADOR DE IMPOSTOS.]—**técnico,** technical adviser.

assessorar (*v.t.*) to assist, advise (with special knowledge)

assessorial, assessório –**ria** (*adj.*) assessorial.

assestar (*v.t.*) to aim, point, train (gun, telescope).

assetear (*v.t.*) to wound or kill with arrows; to shoot arrows at.

asseveração (f.) asseveration.
asseverador –**dora** (adj.) asserting; (m.,f.) asserter.
asseverante (adj.) asseverating.
asseverar (v.t.) to asseverate, assert; to allege.
asseverativo –**va** (adj.) affirmative.
assexuado –**da**, **assexo** –**xa**, **assexual** [ks] (adj.) asexual, sexless.
assexualizar [ks] (v.t.) to unsex.
assialia (f., Med.) assialia, aptyalism.
assibilar (v.t.; Phonet.) to assibilate.
assidente (adj., Med.) assident.
assiduidade [u-i] (f.) assiduity; diligence.
assíduo –**dua** (adj.) assiduous, unremitting, sedulous.
assifôneo (m.) an asiphonate mollusk, as an oyster.
assilabia (f., Psychiatry) asyllabia.
assim (adv.) thus, so, in this manner, like this, like that, this way, that way; also; so very; then, consequently, therefore. **assim, assim**, so, so; fairly well.—**como**, as well as, like, such as, just as.—**como**—, in any case, in that case, be that as it may.—**é que**, so that, consequently.—**mesmo**, just the same, exactly like that; thus, just so, even so; anyway, in any case, notwithstanding.—**na terra como no céu**, on earth as in heaven.—**ou assado**, in this way or that, in one way or another, thus or so.—**pois**, thus.—**que**, as soon as.—**seja!** So be it! Let's hope so! **ainda**—, even so. **bem**—, as well as (same as BEM COMO). **Como**—? How so? How come? **e**—**por diante**, and so on, and so forth. **Ela é bonita mas não é tão bonita**—, She is pretty but not as pretty as all that. **já que (a coisa) é**—, such being the case. **mesmo**—, even so, nevertheless. **Não é**—? Isn't that so? Isn't that the way it is? **para (por)**—**dizer**, so to speak, as it were. **sendo**—, or—**sendo**, that being so, in such case. **tanto**—**que**, so much so that.
assimbolia (f., Med.) assymbolia.
assimetria (f.) asymmetry.—**negativa (positiva)**, (Stat.) negative (positive) skewness.
assimétrico –**ca** (adj.) asymmetric(al); uneven; lopsided.
assimilabilidade (f.) assimilability.
assimilação (f.) assimilation, digestion, absorption, appropriation.
assimilador –**dora** (adj.) assimilating; (m.,f.) assimilator.
assimilar (v.t.) to assimilate, digest; to make similar. Cf. ASSEMELHAR.
assimilativo –**va** (adj.) assimilative.
assimilável (adj.) assimilable.
assimptota (f.) = ASSÍNTOTA.
assinação (f.) assignment; summons; signing; assignation; consignment.
assinado –**da** (adj.) signed; (m.) a signed paper. **abiaxo**—, undersigned. **um abaixo**—, a signed petition, a round robin.
assinalação (f.) signalizing; sign, mark.—**das estradas**, road markers.
assinalado –**da** (adj.) signal, eminent, notable, remarkable; marked, branded. **O inimigo foi**—**a pouca distância**, The enemy was spotted a short distance away.
assinalador –**dora** (adj.) marking; (m.) marker.
assinalamento (m.) signalment; earmark.
assinalar (v.t.) to mark, brand, label, earmark; to characterize, designate; to signalize, make notable; to denote, signify; (v.r.) to distinguish oneself.
assinante (m.,f.) subscriber (to a periodical).
assinar (v.t.) to sign; to fix the time and place; to assign, adduce; to specify, determine, designate; to apportion, allot (a, to); to pledge (a, to); (v.r.) to sign one's name.—**de cruz**, to make one's mark in lieu of a signature; by ext., to approve a thing blindly.—**e beber não se faz sem ver**, Look before you leap.—**em branco**, to sign in blank.—**o gado**, to brand cattle.—**o ponto**, to sign in and out (at a place of employment).—**um jornal, uma revista**, to subscribe to a newspaper, to a magazine.—**vencido**, to sign under protest.
assinatura (f.) signature; subscription. **tomar de**—, to subscribe to (a periodical); to buy a season ticket. **tomar**—**em cima de alguém**, (colloq.) to pick on someone.
assinável (adj.) assignable; signable.
assíncrono –**na** (adj.) asynchronous.
assíndeto [n] (m., Rhet.) asyndeton.
assinergia (f.) asynergia, asynergy.
assíntota (f., Math.) asymptote.
assírio –**ria** (adj.; m.,f.) Assyrian.
assisado –**da** (adj.) = SISUDO.
assistência (f.) attendance, presence (at a gathering);

audience (persons in attendance); first aid, succor, relief; first-aid station. [But assistance in the ordinary sense of help is AUXÍLIO.]—**à infância**, or **aos menores**, child welfare work.—**divina**, divine grace.—**judiciária**, free legal aid.—**pública**, public ambulance and first-aid service.—**social**, social welfare work.
assistente (m.,f.) person present (member of an audience); spectator; looker-on; assistant, helper; (f.) midwife; (adj.) assisting, assistant.—**de professor**, teaching assistant, **médico**—, attending physician.
assistido –**da** (adj.) helped, aided, succored; attended; said of a parturient who is assisted in labor by a midwife.
assistir (v.t.) to attend, be present at; to live in a given place; to assist, aid, help; to minister to, do service; to succor, nurse, comfort.—**a um jogo, a um casamento, a uma festa**, to go to a game, a wedding, a party. **assiste-lhe o direito de**, he has the right to.
assistolia (f., Physiol.) asystole.
assitia (f., Med.) asitia.
assoalhado –**da** (adj.) having a wooden floor; exposed to the sun, sun-dried; divulged, publicized.
assoalhador –**dora** (adj.) newsmongering, tale-bearing; (m.,f.) tale-bearer; (m.) floorlayer.
assoalhadura (f.), –**lhamento** (m.) laying of a floor; revelation, divulging, exposing; exposure to the sun.
assoalhar (v.t.) to lay a wood floor; to expose to the sun to dry; to divulge, make public, spread abroad (maliciously); to "blab": (v.r.) to show off.
assoalho (m.) = SOALHO.
assoante (adj.) assonant; assonanced.
assoar-se (v.r.) to blow one's nose.
assoberbado –**da** (adj.) haughty, lofty; overawed; overloaded with work.—**de pânico**, panic-stricken.—**de serviço**, swamped with work.
assoberbador –**dora** (adj.) overawing; overwhelming.
assoberbamento (m.) overawing; overwhelming.
assoberbante (adj.) overawing; overloading.
assoberbar (v.t.) to treat with hauteur; to overcome, overwhelm; to threaten, intimidate; to dominate, overlook; to overload with work; (v.i.) to act haughtily.
assobiadeira (f.) the yellow-billed teal (Nettion f. flavirostre), c.a. PIADEIRA. Var. ASSOVIADEIRA.
assobiado –**da** (adj.) whistled; booed, jeered at (f.) hissing, booing, whistling. Var. ASSOVIADO.
assobiador –**dora** (adj.) whistling; (m.,f.) whistler; (m.) the tijuca, a large black-and-yellow, cotingine bird (Tijuca atra), c.a. PIADEIRA; also = CHIBANTE. Var. ASSOVIADOR.
assobiante (adj.) whistling. Var. ASSOVIANTE.
assobiar (v.i.) to whistle; to hiss; (v.t.) to jeer at by whistling. [Instead of being a form of approval or applause, as in the U.S.A., whistling and stamping of the feet at a public performance in Brazil and other parts of Latin America is a demonstration of strong displeasure.] Var. ASSOVIAR.
assobio (m.) whistle (the sound, act or instrument); hiss. **refeição de**—, a hurried snack. Var. ASSOVIO.
assobradado –**da** (adj.) of a building, having two or more stories. Cf. SOBRADO.
associação (f.) association; act of associating.—**Cristã de Moços**, Y.M.C.A.—**de assistência**, or **de beneficência**, welfare agency.—**de idéias**, association of ideas.—**de pais e professores**, P.T.A.—**positiva**, (Stat.) positive association.
associado –**da** (adj.) associated; (m.,f.) associate.
assocializar (v.) = SOCIALIZAR.
associar (v.t.) to associate (com, with); to join (a, to); to combine (com, with); to form into a society; to join hands with; to take as partner.—**-se a**, to take part in, join.—**-se com**, to enter into partnership with. **Associo-me à sua dôr**, I share your sorrow.
associativo –**va** (adj.) sociable. **espírito**—, social-mindedness.
assolação (f.) desolation, devastation, ravaging.
assolador –**dora** (adj.) devastating; (m.,f.) desolater.
assolamento (m.) desolation, devastation; laying waste.
assolapar (v.) = SOLAPAR.
assolar (v.t.) to desolate, devastate, lay waste.
assoldadar (v.t.) to hire for wages; (v.r.) to hire (oneself) out for wages.
assomada (f.) appearance (on a high place); summit; angry outburst.—**do seculo**, dawn of the century.
assomadiço –**ça** (adj.) irascible.

assomado –**da** (*adj.*) irascible; skittish; on high, at the top.
assomar (*v.i.*) to appear; to dawn; to emerge; to loom; (*v.t.*) to enrage; (*v.r.*) to become angry: to let oneself be seen in public; to get "lit" (tipsy).—**a**, to appear at (a window, balcony, or other high place); to scale, climb up on (a high place).
assombração (*f.*) blind terror; specter, spook.
assombradiço –**ca** (*adj.*) scary, easily frightened.
assombrado –**da** (*adj.*) somber, shady; dismayed, terrified, amazed; haunted. **casa mal—**, haunted house. **cavalo—**, skittish horse.
assombramento (*m.*) astonishment; consternation; terror; shading, darkening.
assombrar (*v.t.*) to shade, darken; to astonish, amaze; to startle; to frighten, terrify; (*v.r.*) to startle.
assombrear (*v.*) = SOMBREAR.
assombro (*m.*) amazement, astonishment; marvel, wonder; fright, terror; terrible thing.
assombroso –**sa** (*adj.*) amazing; frightful.
assomo (*m.*) beginning, dawn, emergence; irritation, exasperation.—**de cólera**, outburst (fit) of anger, tantrum.
assonância (*f.*) assonance.
assoprador (*m.*) blower, esp. a glass blower.
assoprar (*v.t.*) to blow on; (*v.i.*) to blow. Cf. SOPRAR.
assoreamento (*m.*) a silting up (of a bay or mouth of a river).
assorear (*v.t.,v.i.*) to silt up.
assossegar (*v.*) = SOSSEGAR.
assovelar (*v.t.*) to prick with, or as with, an awl; to "needle" (someone).
assoviar (*v.*) derivs. = ASSOBIAR & derivs.
assovinar-se (*v.r.*) to be sordid, mean, stingy.
assuada (*f.*) mob, gang; riot, uproar, hurly-burly; hoots and jeers. **fazer—**, to kick up a row.
assumir (*v.t.*) to assume, take on; to take over; to take upon oneself; to take charge. [To assume, in the sense of taking for granted, is ADMITIR.]
assunção (*f.*) assumption; elevation to high office.—**de Nossa Senhora**, the Assumption of our Blessed Lady.
assungar (*v.*) = SUNGAR.
assuntar (*v.t.*) to give heed to; to hearken to; (*v.i.*) to listen, observe closely.—**em**, to ponder on, reflect upon.
assunto (*m.*) subject, topic, theme, matter in hand; plot, argument.—**aborrecido**, boresome subject.—**de dinheiro**, a money matter.—**obrigatório** or **obrigado**, a forced or routine topic of conversation. **afastar-se**, or **apartar-se**, **do—**, to stray from the subject, digress. **conhecer o—**, to know one's subject. **dar por concluído o—**, to consider a matter closed. **entender do—**, to know all about a given subject. **instalar-se num**, or **tomar conta dum**,**—**, to dwell at length upon a subject, monopolize the conversation. **Isso não tem nada a ver com o—**, That has nothing to do with the question. **liquidar o—**, to have it out with someone, settle the matter. **matar de vez o—**, to settle a matter once for all. **o—em questão**, **o—em apreço**, **o—de que se trata** (or **do qual se trata**), the business in hand. **resolver um—amigàvelmente**, to settle a matter amicably (in private, out of court.)
assustadiço –**ca** (*adj.*) easily frightened.
assustado –**da** (*adj.*) timid, fearful, afraid, timorous; (*m. colloq.*) impromptu dance.
assustador –**dora** (*adj.*) frightening, alarming startling, terrifying; (*m.,f.*) one who or that which frightens, alarms, etc.
assustar (*v.t.*) to frighten, terrify; to startle; (*v.r.*) to become frightened, get scared. **Não se assuste**, Don't be afraid, don't be alarmed.
ástaco (*m.*) crayfish (*Astacus*).
astasia (*f.*, *Med.*) astasia.
astasia-abasia (*f.*, *Med.*) astasia-abasia.
astático –**ca** (*adj.*) astatic.
asteatose (*f.*, *Med.*) asteatosis.
asteca (*adj.; m.,f.*) Aztec.
asteísmo (*m.*, *Rhet.*) asteism.
astenia (*f.*, *Med.*) asthenia.
astênico –**ca** (*adj.*, *Med.*) asthenic.
astenologia (*f.*, *Med.*) asthenology.
astenopia (*f.*, *Med.*) asthenopia.
astenópico –**ca** (*adj.*, *Med.*) asthenopic.
áster (*m.*, *Eastern Ch.*) asterisk; (*Biol.*) aster rays; (*Bot.*) aster.
astereognosia (*f.*, *Med.*) astereognosis.
astéria (*f.*) starfish; star sapphire; (*Cryst.*) asterism.

asterídeos (*m.pl.*) the Asteriidae (family of starfishes).
asterisco, **asterístico** (*m.*) asterisk [*].
asterismo (*m.*) asterism, constellation.
asternal (*adj.*, *Anat.*) asternal.
asteróide (*m.*) asteroid; (*adj.*) asteroidal.
asteroídeos (*m.pl.*) = ASTERÍDEOS.
astiano –**na** (*adj.*, *Geol.*) Astian.
astigmático –**ca** (*adj.*) astigmatic.
astigmatismo (*m.*, *Optics*, *Med.*) astigmatism.
astigmômetro (*m.*, *Optics*, *Med.*) astigmometer.
astilbe (*m.*, *Bot.*) the genus Astilbe.
astômato –**ta** (*adj.*) astomatous.
ástomo –**ma** (*adj.*) astomous, astomatous.
astracã (*m.*) astrakhan wool; Persian lamb.
astracanito (*m.*, *Min.*) astrakanite.
astragalectomia (*f.*, *Surg.*) astragalectomy.
astragáleo-calcâneo –**nea** (*adj.*, *Anat.*) astragalocalcaneal.
astragáleo-escafóide (*adj.*, *Anat.*) astragaloscaphoid.
astrágalo (*m.*, *Arch.*) astragal; (*Anat.*) astragalus, anklebone, talus; (*Bot.*) loco, milkvetch, poisonvetch (*Astragalus*).
astral (*adj.*) astral, heavenly.
astrância (*f.*) the genus (*Astrantia*) of masterworts.
astrapéia (*f.*, *Bot.*) scarlet dombeya (*D. wallichi*).
astrapofobia (*f.*, *Med.*) astrapophobia.
astréia (*f.*) a genus (*Astraea*) of star corals.
ástreo –**trea** (*adj.*) starry.
astricção (*f.*, *Med.*) astriction.
astro (*m.*) star, heavenly body; famous person, luminary. **—vespertino**, evening star. **o—-rei**, the sun. **um—da tela**, a movie star.
astrocário (*m.*) a genus (*Astrocaryum*) of palms.
astrofísica (*f.*) astrophysics.
astrofobia (*f.*, *Med.*) astrophobia.
astrofotografia (*f.*) astrophotography.
astrografia (*f.*) astrography.
astróide (*adj.*) astroid, star-shaped.
astrol. = ASTROLOGIA.
astrolábio (*m.*) astrolabe.
astrólatra (*m.,f.*) astrolater.
astrologia (*f.*) astrology.
astrológico –**ca** (*adj.*) astrologic(al).
astrólogo –**ga** (*m.,f.*) astrologer.
astromancia (*f.*) astromancy.
astrometria (*f.*) astrometry.
astronauta (*m.,f.*) astronaut.
astronáutica (*f.*) astronautics.
astronomia (*f.*) astronomy.
astronômico –**ca** (*adj.*) astronomic(al).
astrônomo –**ma** (*m.,f.*) astronomer.
astropólio (*m.*, *Bot.*) aster.
astroscopia (*f.*) astroscopy.
astroso –**sa** (*adj.*) ill-starred.
astúcia (*f.*) astuteness, artfulness, subtlety; cunning, guile, craftiness; trick, wile, deceit.
astuciar (*v.i.*) to plan or act shrewdly, astutely.
astucioso –**sa** (*adj.*) astute, shrewd, cunning; artful, crafty, wily, "slick".
asturiano –**na** (*adj.; m.,f.*) Asturian.
astuto –**ta** (*adj.*) astute, cunning; cagey; guileful; designing; artful, wily, tricky, shifty, crafty, sly, shrewd, sharp, foxy. **um ladrão—**, a clever thief.
ata (*f.*) a sugarapple (fruit of the ATEIRA), c.a. FRUTA-DO-CONDE, CONDÊSSA, PINHA; any leaf-cutting ant of the genus Atta, of which *A. cephalotes* (the SAÚVA) is the most widely distributed in Brazil and causes great losses to agriculture; (*pl.*) minutes of a meeting.
atá (*adv.*) **ao—**, aimlessly.
atabacado –**da** (*adj.*) like tobacco in color.
atabafar (*v.t.*) to cover; to suppress; to steal; (*v.i.*) to breathe with difficulty. Cf. ABAFAR.
atabale (*m.*) kettledrum.
atabalhoado –**da** (*adj.*) confused, disorderly, chaotic, helter-skelter.
atabalhoar (*v.i.*) to act or speak in a precipitate, disorganized fashion, without thinking.
atabular (*v.t.*) to quicken one's steps; (*v.i.*) to wrangle; to ramble.
atacadista (*m.,f.*) wholesaler, wholesale merchant.
atacado –**da** (*adj.*) attached; tied, laced (as a corset). **por—**, wholesale.
atacador (*n.*) attacker; ramrod; lace (of a shoe, corset, leather belting, etc.).
atacamita (*f.*, *Min.*) atacamite.

atacante (*adj.*) attacking, aggressive; (*m.,f.*) offensive player.

atacar (*v.t.*) to attack, assail, assault, make aggression on; to tackle, have a go at; to impugn; to corrode; to lace (shoes, etc.); to ram, stuff in; to speed up an airplane motor.

atacável (*adj.*) assailable.

atado –da (*adj.*) tied; timid, restrained; (*m.*) a bundle of clothes, sticks, etc.; (*m.,f.*) a tied bundle.

atador –dora (*m.,f.*) one who ties or laces something.

atadura (*f.*) tie, cord, band, string, etc., used for tying; bandage; swaddling band; link, connection.

atafal (*m.*) crupper (of a saddle).

atafona (*f.*) handmill; water mill; = TAFONA.

atafular-se (*v.r.*) to dress up [= TUFULHAR-SE].

atafulhado –da (*adj.*) replete, crammed; gorged.

atafulhar (*v.t.*) to plug (up); to cram, stuff; (*v.r.*) to gorge oneself.

atagantar (*v.t.*) to lash with a TAGANTE (rawhide whip); to afflict, torment.

atalaia (*f.*) sentinel; watch tower; crow's nest; (*m.*) watchman; lookout point. **estar de**—, to be on the lookout.

atalaiar (*v.i.*) to stand watch; (*v.t.*) to watch, observe, look out over, spy.

atálamo –ma (*adj., Bot.*) athalamous.

atalanta (*f.*) Atalanta butterfly, red admiral.

ataléia (*f.*) a genus (*Attalea*) of palms.

atalhada (*f.*) a firebreak cut through the woods.

atalhador –dora (*m.,f.*) one who impedes.

atalhamento (*m.*) obstruction; moat.

atalhar (*v.t.*) to check, thwart, block; to stop, intercept; to interrupt, cut off; to shorten (distance); to take a short cut; to cut in on another's remarks.

atalho (*m.*) any short cut; by-path, side trail; a cutting short (of time, distance, etc.); hindrance, obstruction.

atamancar (*v.t.*) to botch, bungle; to work unskilfully or clumsily at anything; to tinker.

atanado –da (*adj.*) tanned; (*m.*) tanbark; tanned hide

atanar (*v.t.*) to tan (hides).

atanazer (*v.*) = ATENAZAR.

atangará (*m.*) = TANGARÁ.

atangaratinga (*f.*) a bird—the white-bearded manakin (*Manacus. m. manacus*), c.a. BILREIRA, RENDEIRA.

atapetar (*v.t.*) to carpet.

atapu [ú] (*m.*) any unspecified large triton shell, c.a. BÚZIO, esp. one used as a horn by Indians and fishermen to call customers; a sea diver.

atapulhar (*v.t.*) to stop with a TAPULHO (plug); to cram, stuff (as the stomach).

ataque (*m.*) attack, assault, onslaught; charge, accusation; seizure (of sickness); fit, convulsion.—**aéreo**, air raid.—**cardíaco**, heart attack.—**de apoplexia**, stroke of paralysis.—**de nervos**, nervous attack.—**epiléptico**, epileptic fit.—**falso**, feint, mock attack. **dar**, or **ter, um**—, to suffer an attack (of sickness); to have a fit.

atar (*v.t.*) to tie (up), bind, fasten, knot; to unite, join, link; to hitch; to lace up (as shoes).—**a**, to bind to. —**com**, to link up with.—**de pés e mãos**, to bind hand and foot.—**o fio da conversa**, to take up the thread of conversation; to return to the subject.—**relações com alguém**, to establish relations with someone. **louco (doido, maluco) de**—, raving mad, "fit to be tied". **não— nem desatar**, to waver, shilly-shally.

atarantação (*f.*) fluster, bewilderment.

atarantado –da (*adj.*) stunned, bewildered.

atarantar (*v.t.*) to bewilder, rattle, (*v.r.*) to flounder, become confused.

ataraxia [ks] (*f.*) ataraxia, imperturbability.

atarefado –da (*adj.*) busy, burdened with work.

atarefar (*v.t.*) to burden or overload with work.

atarracado –da (*adj.*) squat, stocky, chunky, dumpy, thickset.

atarracar (*v.t.*) to tie down; to hammer (something) on the anvil.

atarraxar (*v.t.*) to screw or rivet together.

atascadeiro (*m.*) mud flat, mudhole, quagmire.

atascar-se (*v.r.*) to mire, to bog down.

atasqueiro (*m.*) = ATASCADEIRO.

atassalhar (*v.t.*) to rend, lacerate, tear to pieces; to calumniate, defame.

ataúba (*f.*) a muskwood (*Guarea tuberculata*).

ataúde (*m.*) coffin, casket; bier; tomb; tombstone.

atauxiar (*v.t.*) to decorate, as iron, steel, etc., with TAUXIAS (damascene work); = TAUXIAR.

ataviamento (*m.*) = ATAVIO.

ataviar (*v.t.*) to trim, dress, array, deck out, trick out; to embellish; (*v.r.*) to spruce up.

atávico –ca (*adj.*) atavic; atavistic.

atavio (*m.*) array, adornment; ornament; (*pl.*) fripperies; preparations (as for war).

atavismo (*m.*) atavism, throwback.

ataxia [ks] (*f., Med.*) ataxia.—**locomotora**, locomotor ataxia.

atáxico –ca [ks] (*adj.; m.,f., Med.*) ataxic.

ataxito [ks] (*m., Petrog.*) ataxite.

ataxofemia [ks] (*f., Med.*) ataxophemia.

até (*prep.*) to, till, until, as far as, up to, to the point of; (*adv.*) even, likewise, in like manner; not only so, but also.—**a**, to, till, until, as far as.—**à medula dos ossos**, to the marrow of one's bones.—**à ponta**, or **à raiz, dos cabelos**, to the tips, or to the roots, of one's hair.—**à vista**, au revoir.—**à volta**, until your return.—**agora**, hitherto, till now, to (up to, until) this time; thus far.—**altas horas da noite**, far into the night.—**amanhã**, until tomorrow.—**ao infinito**, to the infinite.—**aos alhos**, up to the eyes.—**aqui**, to here, thus far.—**às últimas**, to the very last.—**bem pouco**, until quite recently.—**breve**, see you soon [= ATÉ LOGO].—**então**, till then.—**eu não posso**, Even I can't.—**já**, I'll be right back, see you in a minute. —**logo**, See you soon, goodby.—**mais tarde**, See you later. —**mais ver**, Till I see you again.—**não poder mais**, to the limit of (one's) capacity.—**o fim do ano**, by the end of the year.—**onde?** How far?—**os adversários o admiram**, Even his enemies admire him.—**quando?** How long? Until when?—**que**, till, until, to the time when, to the time that.—**que enfim**, finally, at last. **daqui—lá**, between now and then; between here and there. **Disse— que não iria**, He even said he would not go. **Eu te acompanho—à esquina**, I'll go with you as far as the corner. **Venha—cá**, Come over here.

atear (*v.t.*) to kindle, light, ignite; to inflame, excite, arouse, foment; to provoke, enrage.—**fogo a**, to set fire to.

atecnia (*f.*) lack of technical knowledge.

atécnico –ca (*adj.*) without technical knowledge.

atediar (*v.t.*) to bore [= ENTEDIAR].

atéia fem. of ATEU.

ateimar (*v.*) = TEIMAR.

ateira (*f.*) the sugar apple or sweetsop (*Annona squamosa*) whose fruit is called FRUTA-DO-CONDE, ATA, PINHA, CONDÉSSA.

ateísmo (*m.*) atheism.

ateísta (*m.,f.*) atheist.

ateístico –ca (*adj.*) atheistic.

átele (*m.*) the genus (*Ateles*) of spider monkeys, called MACACOS-ARANHAS.

atelectasia (*f., Med.*) atelectasis.

atelia (*f., Anat.*) athelia.

atemorizador –dora (*adj.*) scary, frightening; (*m.,f.*) one who or that which frightens.

atemorizamento (*m.*) act of frightening; fright.

atemorizar (*v.t.*) to scare, frighten, daunt; (*v.r.*) to become frightened.

atempar (*v.t.*) to postpone, put off.

Atenas (*f.*) Athens.

atenazar (*v.t.*) to torture (as with pincers); to afflict; to importune.

atenção (*f.*) attention, care, heed, regard, notice; courtesy, politeness; respect; kindness; application, study; (*exclam.*) Watch out! Take care! **em**—a, in consideration of; on account of; in view of. **falta de**—, heedlessness. **prestar**, or **dar,**—, to pay attention.

atencioso –sa (*adj.*) attentive; polite, courteous; thoughtful, considerate; deferential; mindful.

atender (*v.t.*) to consider, mind, heed, give (pay) attention to; give heed to, take heed (notice) of, listen to; to be attentive to.—**a**, to take care of.—**a uma pergunta**, to respond to a question.—**à porta**, to answer the door.—**ao telefone**, to answer the telephone.—**às necessidades**, to meet the needs.—**pelo nome de**, to answer to the name of. **atendendo a isto**, owing to this, in view of this. **atendendo a que**, in view of which; by reason of which. **Já lhe dei muitos conselhos mas ela não me atende**, I have given her a lot of good advice but she pays no attention to it. [To attend, in the sense of to accompany or escort is ACOMPANHAR; to watch, have in keeping, is CUIDAR DE; to minister to, is ACUDIR; to frequent, be present at, is ASSISTIR A.]

atendimento (*m.*) attention to.

atendível (*adj.*) worthy of being noticed.
ateneu (*m.*) athenaeum.
ateniense (*adj.; m.,f.*). Athenian.
atenrar (*v.t.*) to make tender.
atentado –da (*adj.*) attentive; (*m.*) criminal assault; outrage.
atentamente (*adv.*) attentively, closely.
atentar (*v.t.*) to attend, notice, perceive, observe; to heed, consider.—a, to be mindful of, give thought to, heed. —**contra**, to attempt (a criminal act) against.—**contra a moral**, to commit a moral outrage.—**contra a vida de alguem**, to make an attempt against someone's life.—**em alguma coisa**, to look into a matter; to direct one's attention to a subject.—**para**, to look at.
atentatório –ria (*adj.*) contrary to law; offensive.—**à moral**, offensive to moral decency.
atentivo –va (*adj.*) attentive.
atento –ta (*adj.*) attentive; alert; studious; mindful; thoughtful; regardful; deferential—**que**, seeing that, since. **de olhos abertos e ouvidos**—s, with eyes and ears open.
atenuação (*f.*) attenuation.
atenuado –da (*adj.*) attenuated, diminished.
atenuador –dora (*adj.*) attenuating.
atenuante (*adj.*) attenuating; (*f., Law*) an attenuating circumstance.
atenuar (*v.t.*) to attenuate, make thin, make slim or slender; to lessen (the gravity or importance of); to reduce, diminish, weaken, water down.
atenuativo –va (*adj.*) serving to attenuate.
atenuável (*adj.*) that may be attenuated.
ateréua (*f., Bot.*) manbarklak (*Eschweilera corrugata*), c.a. ATIRIBA.
aterina (*f.*) any of numerous small fishes of the family Atherinidae (ATERINÍDEOS)—silversides, sand smelts.
atermal, atérmano –na (*adj.*) = ATÉRMICO.
atermar (*v.t.*) to put a term, limit, to.
atermia (*f., Med.*) absence of heat; (*Physics*) adiathermancy.
atérmico –ca (*adj., Physics*) athermanous, adiathermic.
ateroma (*m., Med.*) atheroma.
ateromasia (*m., Med.*) atheromasia.
ateromatoso –sa (*adj., Med.*) atheromatous.
aterrado –da (*adj.*) dirt-filled; level with the ground; (of aircraft) landed; panic stricken; terrified; aghast; (*m.*) a dirt fill; filled-in land; piece of high ground in a marshy region.
aterrador –dora (*adj.*) terrifying, appalling.
aterragem (*f.*) landing (of aircraft); filling with dirt.—**às cegas**, blind landing.—**noturna**, night landing.—**sem motor**, dead-stick landing. **farol de**—, landing light. **trem de**—, landing gear. **velocidade de**—, landing speed.
aterraplenar, aterraplanar (*v.t.*) to level the ground (as with a bulldozer) = TERRAPLENAR.
aterrar (*v.t.*) [from TERRA, dirt, ground] to fill (in) or cover with dirt; to make a dirt fill; to fell; (*v.t.,v.i.*) to land (aircraft); (*v.t.*) [from TERROR, terror] to terrorize, frighten, appal; to dismay.
aterrissagem (*f.*) = ATERRAGEM.
aterrissar (*v.*) = ATERRAR (to land aircraft).
atêrro (*m.*) dirt-fill; filling with earth; earth embankment.
aterrorizador –dora (*adj.*) terrifying.
aterrorizar (*v.t.*) to terrify; to terrorize; to appal.
ater-se [78] (*v.r.*) to lean against (a wall, etc.); to cling to (a habit, an attitude, etc.); to depend (rely) on (the advice of a friend, etc.); to hold to, stick to (a belief, a reason, an idea, etc.); to abide by (a tradition, etc.).
atesar (*v.*) = ENTESAR.
atesia (*f.*) = ATETOSE.
atestação (*f.*) attestation; testimony.
atestado –da (*adj.*) certified; witnessed; filled to the top; (*m.*) certificate; voucher; testimonial; credential.—**de casamento**, marriage certificate.—**de nascimento**, birth certificate.—**de óbito**, death certificate.
atestador –dora (*adj.*) testifying; (*m.,f.*) testifier; certifier.
atestante (*m.,f.*) person who signs a certificate or other written evidence.
atestar (*v.t.*) to attest, witness, certify; to prove, exhibit; to bear witness to; to fill to the top.
atestatório –ria (*adj.*) attesting, certifying.
atetose (*f., Med.*) athetosis.
ateu –téia (*adj.*) atheistic; (*m.,f.*) atheist.
ati [i] (*m.*) the Patagonian brown-headed gull (*Larus ridibundus maculpinnis*).

atiçador –dora (*adj.*) provocative, provoking, inciting; (*m.,f.*) inciter, instigator; (*m.*) fire poker.
atiçamento (*m.*) act of kindling a fire.
atiçar (*v.t.*) to stir up; to poke (the fire); to instigate, incite, arouse.
aticismo (*m.*) simple elegance, incisive intelligence and delicate wit (in the use of language).
ático –ca (*adj.*) Attic; (*m., Anat., Arch.*) attic.
atijolar (*v.t.*) to pave with bricks; to brick up.
atilado –da (*adj.*) intelligent, alert, clever, smart, wise; careful; well-advised.
atilar (*v.t.*) to execute with care; to finish, polish, perfect; to embellish.
atilho (*m.*) anything used for tying, such as a piece of string or a shoe lace.
atímia (*f.*) athymia, despondency, melancholy.
átimo (*m.*) instant; tiny bit. **num**—, in a jiffy.
atinado –da (*adj.*) sharp, shrewd, wise, discreet.
atinar (*v.t.*) to guess (**com, em**, at); to fathom (by conjecture); to hit upon, catch on; to discover, detect.
atincal (*m., Min.*) borax [= TINCAL].
atinente (*adj.*) respecting, pertaining (**a**, to).
atingaú (*f.*) = ALMA-DE-GATO.
atingir (*v.t.*) to touch, reach; to attain; to grasp the meaning of; to affect, concern.—**maioridade**, to come of age.—**o alvo**, to hit the target.—**o cume**, to reach the top. **Êle não atingiu o meu pensamento**, He did not grasp my meaning. **Esta lei não atinge os professores**, This law does not affect teachers. [This verb is often though erroneously employed with preposition A to mean: attain to, come up to, amount to, as in the following examples: **A população do país atinge a 45 milhões de habitantes**, The population of the country amounts to 45 millions. **Ela não atinge à inteligência dêle**, She does not come up to him in intelligence.]
atingível (*adj.*) touchable; attainable.
atípico –ca (*adj.*) atypic(al).
atiradiço –ca (*adj.*) adventurous, daring (esp. in affairs of the heart).
atirado –da (*adj.*) thrown, hurled; (*colloq.*) bold-faced, impudent, audacious.
atirador –dora (*adj.*) shooting; (*m.*) shooter, sharpshooter, rifleman, marksman.—**de tocaia**, sniper.
atirar (*v.t.*) to throw, hurl, cast, fling, pitch (an object)—**a**, at; **em**, in, into; **contra**, on, against; **para**, to; **para cima de**, on top of; **para longe**, away, far away; **sôbre**, on, on top of; to shoot (**em, at**); to fire (**contra**, on); (*v.r.*) to throw oneself; to rush, plunge (**a, para, em**, into).—**a luva**, to fling down the gauntlet, issue a challenge.—**a primeira pedra**, to cast the first stone.—**ao alvo**, to shoot at a target.—**ao mundo**, to cast out, cast away.—**às urtigas**, to cast aside as worthless.—**com a porta**, to slam the door.—**(com) tudo pelos ares**, to blow up (in anger).—**de arco**, to shoot with bow and arrow.—**de pistola**, to shoot with a pistol.—**fora aos quatro ventos**, to throw to the four winds.—**o** (or **com o**) **livro no chão**, to throw the book to the ground.—**para matar**, to shoot to kill.—**para o ar**, to shoot into the air.—**pérolas aos porcos**, to cast pearls before swine. **Quem tem telhado de vidro não atira no do vizinho**, Those who live in glass houses should not throw stones.
atireoidia [o-i] (*f., Med.*) athyreosis.
atiria (*f., Med.*) athyria.
atiriba (*f.*) = ATERÉUA.
atitar (*v.i.*) (of birds) to scold.
atitude (*f.*) attitude, position; disposition, mood; intent, purpose; body posture, pose.
ativa (*f.*) see under ATIVO.
ativação (*f.*) activation.
ativar (*v.t.*) to activate, actuate; (*v.r.*) to become active.
atividade (*f.*) activity. **em**—, in active service.
ativo –va (*adj.*) active, busy, diligent, alert, energetic, agile, spry.—**concorrência**, keen competition. **ter voz**—**num assunto**, to have an active voice in a matter; (*m.*) assets; record (of past performance).—**e passivo**, assets and liabilities.—**s correntes**, current assets.—**mobilizado**, fixed assets; (*f.*) state of being on active military duty. (*Gram.*) active voice. **oficial da**—, officer on active duty.
atlântico –ca (*adj.; m.*) Atlantic (ocean).
atlas [pl. atlas] (*m.*) atlas; [*cap.*] Atlas; (*Anat.*) atlas.
atleta (*m.,f.*) athlete.
atlética (*f.*) athletics.
atleticismo (*m.*) = ATLETISMO.
atlético –ca (*adj.*) athletic.

atletismo (m.) athletics.
atmiatria (f.) treatment of disease by inhalation of vapors or gases.
atmidômetro (m.) atmidometer, atmometer.
atmólise (f.) atmolysis.
atmometria (f.) atmometry.
atmosfera (f.) atmosphere.
atmosférico –ca (adj.) atmospheric.
atmosferologia (f.) atmospherology.
at.º = ATENTO or ATENCIOSO ([your] attentive [servant]— at your service—complimentary close to a letter).
ato (m.) act, action, deed.—contínuo, immediately thereafter; right away.—de contrição, an Act (prayer) of Contrition.—jurídico, legal action; court action.—solene, rite. fazer—de presença, to put in an appearance. no mesmo—, simultaneously.
à-toa (adj.) heedless; worthless, good-for nothing; trifling. Cf. À TOA (adv.)
atoalhado (m.) table cloth; (pl.) table linen.
atoalhar (v.t.) to cover with, or as with, a table cloth.
atoar (v.t.) to tow, take in tow; to balk, refuse to budge. —-se a alguém, to follow another person blindly.
atobá (m.) the white-bellied booby (Sula leucogaster), c.a. MERGULHÃO.
atocaiar (v.t.) to ambush, waylay.
atochado –da (adj.) tight, wedged in; overloaded.
atochador –dora (adj.) tightening, squeezing.
atochar (v.t.) to force in (as a cork); to squeeze in; to wedge in; to crowd in; to pack in.
atôcho (m.) chock, wedge, scotch; importunate insistence.
atocia (f., Med.) atocia.
à-toinha [o-i] (adj.) very easy; (adv.) at every step, all the time.
atol [atóis] (m.) atoll.
atoladiço –ca (adj.) miry.
atolado –da (adj.) stuck in the mud; crazy, foolish.
atolar (v.t.) to mire (em, in); to stick in mire; to get involved in difficulties. (v.r.) to stall, bog down; to sink in the mire (of loose living).
atoleimado –da (adj.) foolish, simple; dazed.
atoleimar (v.t.) to make silly or foolish; to besot. (v.r.) to become thus.
atoleiro (m.) mudhole; quagmire; immorality; predicament, fix, mess. sair da lama e meter-se no—, to jump out of the frying pan into the fire.
atomatado –da (adj.) tomato-like.
atomatar (v.t.) to abash; to squash (as a tomato).
atomicidade (f., Physics, Chem.) atomicity.
atômico –ca (adj.) atomic. bomba—, atomic bomb.
atomismo (m., Philos.) atomism.
atomizar (v.t.) to atomize; to pulverize.
átomo (m.) atom.
atomoelétrico –ca (adj.) atomic-electric. usina—, atomic energy plant.
atomologia (f.) atomology.
atonalidade (f., Music) atonality.
atonia (f., Med.) atony.
atônico –ca (adj., Med., Gram.) atonic.
atônito –ta (adj.) astonished, dumfounded.
átono –na (adj., Med., Gram.) atonic.
atontar (v.) = ENTONTECER.
atopetar (v.t.) to haul to the top (of a mast); to arrive at the top; to cram, fill full (as a store with goods).
atópico –ca (adj., Med.) atopic, displaced.
atopite (f., Min.) atopite.
ator [atôres] (m.) actor, [fem. ATRIZ]; an agent, one who acts for another.
atorar (v.t.) to make TOROS (logs) out of trees; to cut (a log, etc.) in two; (v.i.) to take a short cut; of a stream, to dry up; to leave, go away.
atorás (m.pl.) an Arawakan tribe in the region between northern Amazonas and southern Br. Guiana, recently absorbed by the Wapisianas.
atorçalar (v.t.) to trim with TORÇAL (twisted silk or gold braid).
atordoado –da (adj.) dizzy; stunned, dazed.
atordoador –dora (adj.) stunning.
atordoamento (m.) stunning, loss of consciousness, fainting spell, daze.
atordoar (v.t.) to stun, make senseless, make dizzy; to shock; to dumfound; to daze.
atormentação (f.) tormenting; affliction.
atormentadiço –ça (adj.) easily afflicted; worrisome.
atormentado –da (adj.) tormented; tortured; afflicted, worried.
atormentador –dora (adj.) tormenting, harrowing; (m.,f.) tormenter.
atormentar (v.t.) to torment, torture, afflict; to grieve; to vex, worry; to harass; to tease, badger; to obsess, pester; (v.r.) to fret.—com bagatelas, to nag.
atormentativo –va (adj.) tormenting.
atouco (m.) a hole in a tree.
atoxiar (v.) = ENTOXICAR; ENVENENAR.
atóxico –ca [ks] (adj.] non-poisonous.
atoxil [ks] (m., Chem.) Atoxyl (used in medicine).
atrabiliário –ria, –lioso –sa (adj.) atrabilious, melancholic; splenetic, spiteful; peevish, irritable; disagreeable; hypochondriac; violent.
atracação (f.) mooring, docking (of a ship.)
atracado –da (adj.) moored; overloaded.
atracador –dora (adj.) mooring; (m.) mooring line; (colloq.) tout for a gambling joint.
atração (f.) attraction, affinity; (pl.) amusements.—elétrica, electrical attraction.—magnética, magnetic attraction.—molecular, cohesion or adhesion.—química, chemical affinity.—sintática, (Gram.) attraction.—terrestre, terrestrial gravitation.—universal, gravitation.
atracar (v.t.) to moor, berth, tie up (a ship); (v.i.,v.r.) to come alongside, to make fast.—alguém na rua, to accost someone importunately on the street.—-se com alguém, to bump into someone; to grapple with (come to blows with) someone.
atraente (adj.) attractive, fascinating, captivating; engaging.
atrafegar-se (v.r.) to overburden oneself with work, responsibilities, etc.
atrágena (f., Bot.) the genus Clematis.
atraiçoado –da (adj.) betrayed; treacherous.
atraiçoador –dora (adj.) treacherous, traitorous, treasonable; (m.,f.) traitor, betrayer, deceiver.
atraiçoar (v.t.) to betray; to double-cross; to mislead.
atraidor –dora [a-i] (adj.) = ATRAENTE.
atraimento [a-i] (m.) = ATRAÇÃO.
atrair [75] (v.t.) to attract; to draw, pull (to oneself); to allure, entice, lure.—simpatias, to arouse liking and admiration (not sympathy) for oneself.
atralhoar (v.t.) to yoke (oxen).
atrancar (v.) = TRANCAR.
atrapalhação (f.) confusion, fluster.
atrapalhado –da (adj.) mixed-up, jumbled; fumbling; non-plussed, flustered. com a vida—, beset with personal problems.
atrapalhador –dora (m.,f.) one who causes confusion.
atrapalhar (v.t.) to upset, disconcert, disturb, perturb, embarrass; to cause confusion; (v.r.) to get mixed up, tangled, confused; to flounder.—-se com pouca coisa, to be upset by trifles.—os planos de alguém, to upset another's plans.
atrás (adv.) behind, back, in back (de, of), at the back, in the rear, backward, rearward; aft, astern; ago, in times past, formerly. anos—, years ago. dar para—em, to oppose, set oneself against, object strongly to, obstruct (business matter, plans, agreement, etc.). deixar—, to leave behind. Êle não te fica—, He is in no way your inferior. estar de pé—com alguém, to be on one's guard against someone, be mistrustful of him. ir—de, to go after. Não há nada como um dia—do outro, There is nothing like one day after another (in which to get even). voltar para—, to turn back.
atrasado –da (adj.) behindhand, backward, late, tardy, behind time; overdue, in arrears; antiquated; retarded (in growth); (m.,f.) a retarded child; (m.pl.) overdue payments; ancestors.—nos estudos, no serviço, behind in (his) studies, (his) work. no ano (mês)—, year (month) before last. O seu relógio está—, Your watch is slow. O trem está—, The train is late. número—, back number (of a magazine). um povo—, a backward people.
atrasador –dora (adj.) delaying; (m.,f.) delayer.
atrasar (v.t.) to put (turn, set) back; to delay, retard, impede; (v.i.) (of a timepiece) to run slow; (v.r.) to be slow or tardy.—-se nos estudos, to fall behind in one's studies.—-se nos pagamentos, to get in arrears in payments due.
atraso (m.) delay; tardiness; setback; backwardness; hindrance; (pl.) arrears, overdue payments. chegar com—, to arrive late. em—, late; in arrears.
atrativo –va (adj.) attractive; (m.) attraction, affinity; (pl.) attractions, charms, graces.

atravancado –**da** (*adj.*) jammed, crammed.
atravancador –**dora** (*adj.*) cumbersome (as a piece of heavy furniture).
atravancamento (*m.*) obstruction, obstacle; clog.
atravancar (*v.t.*) to clog, obstruct; to jam (the streets); to clutter up (a room).
atravanco (*m.*) = ATRAVANCAMENTO.
através (*adv.*) through, across, over, athwart, from one side or part of to another; transversely.—**de**, (*prep.*) through, across, from one side, part or end to the other; within, among, in the midst of.—**dos tempos**, over the years.
atravessadiço –**ça** (*adj.*) opposing, thwarting.
atravessado –**da** (*adj.*) unruly; (of animals) crossbred. **estar**—**com alguém**, to be at odds with someone. **ter alguma coisa**—**na garganta**, to have something stuck in the throat.
atravessador (*m.*) profiteer, monopolizer.
atravessar (*v.t.*) to traverse, cross (over), pass over; to pierce, transfix, run through (as with a sword); to bar, hinder, thwart; to lay across; to undergo, go through, pass through (dangers, bad times); (*v.r.*) to get stuck (as a fishbone in the throat).—**a**, to cross, oppose.—**a fronteira**, to cross the frontier.—**alguém com o olhar**, to pierce someone with a look.—**por**, to pierce through. —-**se no caminho de alguém**, to block another's path, interfere in his affairs.—**mercadorias**, to buy up merchandise for purposes of profiteering.
atreguar (*v.i.*,*v.r.*) to cease hostilities, declare a truce.
atreito –**ta** (*adj.*) prone to, disposed to; accustomed to.
atrelar (*v.t.*) to lease, hitch, tie (together); to hitch (a horse to a wagon); to yoke (oxen); to control.—-**se a alguém**, to stick close to someone.
atremar (*v.i.*) to use good judgment.
atrepsia (*f.*, *Med.*) athrepsia.
atresia (*f.*, *Med.*) atresia.
atrever-se (*v.r.*) to dare (**a**, to), venture, risk, make bold (**de**, to).—-**se contra**, to dare to oppose.
atrevidaço –**ça**, **atrevidão** –**dona** (*adj.*) insolent, highly impertinent.
atrevido –**da** (*adj.*) daring, brave, intrepid; familiar, too free, impertinent, impudent, presumptuous, fresh, cheeky, brash, cocky; (*m.,f.*) such a one.
atrevimento (*m.*) insolence, impertinence, effrontery, impudence; daring, boldness.
atribuição [u-i] (*f.*) attribution; prerogative, privilege; rights.
atribuir [72] (*v.t.*) to attribute, assign, ascribe, impute, charge; to grant, confer, bestow; (*v.r.*) to arrogate to oneself.
atribuível (*adj.*) attributable.
atribulação (*f.*) tribulation.
atribulado –**da** (*adj.*) distressed, troubled, afflicted, wretched.
atribulador –**dora** (*adj.*) distressing; (*m.,f.*) one who distresses another.
atribular (*v.t.*) to afflict, grieve, distress, trouble, try, torment; (*v.r.*) to be distressed, troubled, etc.
atributivo –**va** (*adj.*) attributive.
atributo (*m.*) attribute, characteristic, peculiarity; symbol, emblem; (*Gram.*) an attributive adjunct, esp. an adjective.
atrição (*f.*) attrition, friction, abrasion [more usual: ATRITO, FRICÇÃO, ABRASÃO]; (*Theol.*) attrition, contrition.
atril (*m.*) reading desk, lectern.
atrincheirar (*v.*) = ENTRINCHEIRAR.
átrio (*m.*) atrium; courtyard; living-room, vestibule.
atriquia (*f.*, *Med.*) atrichia, baldness.
atristar (*v.*) = ENTRISTECER.
atritar (*v.t.*) to cause attrition.
atrito (*m.*) attrition, friction, abrasion, rubbing; misunderstanding, dissension; (*pl.*) personal clashes.—**de arrastamento**, sliding friction.—**de rolamento**, rolling friction.
atriz (*f.*) actress. [actor is ATOR].
átro –**tra** (*adj.*) atrous, black; dark, dismal, gloomy.
atroado –**da** (*adj.*) of persons, loud and fast-talking; foolish; (*f.*) loud noise; a roar or roaring.
atroador –**dora** (*adj.*) thundering; deafening.
atroamento (*m.*) a thundering; stunning (as by shock or deafening noise); lack of good sense.
atroante (*adj.*) thundering.
atroar (*v.t.*) to cause to shake and tremble (as by thunder); to stun (with noise); to roar, thunder.

atrocidade (*f.*) atrocity, outrage.
atrocíssimo –**ma** (*absol. superl. of* ATROZ) most atrocious.
atrofia (*f.*) atrophy.
atrofiado –**da** (*adj.*) atrophied.
atrofiador –**dora** (*adj.*) atrophying.
atrofiamento (*m.*) wasting away.
atrofiante (*adj.*) atrophying.
atrofiar (*v.t.*) to atrophy; (*v.r.*) to waste away.
atrombetado –**da** (*adj.*) shaped like a trumpet.
atrôo (*m.*) = ATROADA.
átropa (*f.*, *Bot.*) belladonna (*Atropa belladonna*).
atropelacão (*f.*), –**amento**, –**pêlo** (*m.*) act of trampling etc. See the verb ATROPELAR.
atropelante (*adj.*) trampling.
atropelar (*v.t.*) to trample, knock down, run over, trip up, upset; to treat with scorn, set at naught; to crowd (someone) with work; (*v.r.*) to get crushed (in a crowd); of thoughts, to crowd in one after another; to smash against each other (as waves).—**léguas** (**o chão, o caminho**), to "eat up" the miles, "burn up" the road.
atropina (*f.*, *Chem.*, *Pharm.*) atropine.
atropismo (*m.*, *Med.*) atropism.
átropo –**pa** (*adj.*) atropous.
atroz (*adj.*) atrocious; of pain, excruciating.
at.te = ATENCIOSAMENTE (attentively).
atuação (*f.*) actuation, operation; performance.
atual (*adj.*) present, now existing, at this moment, here and now, present-day. [But not actual, in the sense of real or true, which is REAL, VERDADEIRO.]
atualidade (*f.*) the present time; present state of affairs; (*pl.*) news of the moment; current events; (*colloq.*) newsreel. [But not actuality, in the sense of reality, which is REALIDADE.]
atualização (*f.*) modernization; up-to-dating.
atualizar (*v.t.*) to bring up to date; to modernize.
atualmente (*adv.*) nowadays, now, at present. [But not actually, in the senses of really, truly, which is NA VERDADE, NA REALIDADE, REALMENTE.]
atuante (*adj.*) active, acting, in action; (*m.,f.*) one who is being, or is to be, quizzed.
atuar (*v.t.*) to act on or upon; to actuate; to influence, have effect on; to take steps (to do something); to thee-and-thou, address as TU [= French *tutoyer*]; (*v.i.*) of animals, to balk; to act (in a play).
atuarial (*adj.*) actuarial.
atuário –**ria** (*m.,f.*) actuary.
atuável (*adj.*) that can be done; that can be acted upon; easy to handle.
atucanar (*v.t.*) to "needle" (someone).
atufar (*v.t.*) to fill (as sails); to fill full; (*v.r.*) to dive into (water, a crowd, woods, etc.).
atulhamento (*m.*) a heaping up, filling.—**de carros**, traffic jam.
atulhar (*v.t.*) to fill up; to cram, stuff full; to block, choke (a passageway); (*v.r.*) to become crowded (with people, animals).
atulho (*m.*) = ATULHAMENTO.
atum (*m.*) tuna (fish).—-**branco** = ALBACORA.
atumultuar (*v.t.*) to cause a tumult.
atuoso –**sa** (*adj.*) active, busy.
aturá (*m.*) an Indian basket carried on the back and held by a strap across the forehead. [GBAT: "A large cylindrical basket used for transporting Brazil nuts."]
aturado –**da** (*adj.*) persistent, persevering.
aturar (*v.t.*) to endure, brook, tolerate, submit to, put up with, withstand, stomach; to bear (up under); to suffer, undergo; (*v.i.*) to endure.
aturável (*adj.*) bearable, endurable.
aturdido –**da** (*adj.*) amazed, dumfounded.
aturdidor –**dora** (*adj.*) amazing.
aturdimento (*m.*) amazement; fluster; daze.
aturdir [25] (*v.t.*) to confound, muddle, rattle, confuse; to astound; to stun; to daze, dazzle; to deafen; (*v.r.*) to get worked up, excited; to become confused.
aturiá (*f.*) = CIGANA.
aubriécia (*f.*, *Bot.*) the common aubretia.
aucuba (*f.*, *Bot.*) the Japanese aucuba (*A. japonica*) and other species of this genus.
audácia (*f.*) audacity, boldness; effrontery, "brass".
audacioso –**sa** (*adj.*) audacious.
audacíssimo –**ma** (*absol. superl. of* AUDAZ) most audacious.
audaz (*adj.*) audacious, bold.
audibilidade (*f.*) audibility.

audição (f.) audition, hearing; recital.
audiência (f.) audition, audience, hearing, formal interview or reception; court session. [But not audience in the sense of assembly of listeners, which is ASSISTÊNCIA.]—**secreta**, private hearing.
áudio –dia (adj., Radio.) audio. **freqüência de—** or **audiofreqüência**, audio frequency.
audiograma (m., Acoustics.) audiogram.
audiometria (f., Acoustics) audiometry.
audiômetro (m., Acoustics) audiometer.
áudion (m.) audion (radio tube).
auditivo –va (adj.) auditory.
auditor (m.) hearer, listener; magistrate, judge. [But not auditor in the sense of one who audits accounts, which is FISCAL, CONTADOR, VERIFICADOR DE CONTAS.]
auditoria (f.) judgeship; courtroom.
auditório –ria (adj.) auditory; (m.) audience; auditorium.
audível (adj.) audible.
aueté (m.,f.) an Indian of the Auetö, a Tupian tribe on the upper Xingu River in Mato Grosso; (adj.) pert. to or designating this tribe.
auferir [21a] (v.t.) to benefit; to draw, receive (benefits).—**lucros**, to make (obtain) profits.
auge (m.) summit, highest point, acme, pinnacle. **ao**, or **no**,—, to, or in, the highest degree. **o—da alegria**, seventh heaven.
augite (f., Min.) augite.
augitito (m., Petrog.) augitite.
Aug⁰ = AUGUSTO (August—proper name).
augural (adj.) augural.
augurar (v.t.,v.i.) to augur, portend, forebode.
áugure (m.) augurer.
augúrio (m.) augury. **de bom—**, auspicious.
augusto –ta (adj.) august, majestic, venerable; [cap.] (m.) August; (f.) Augusta.
auíba (f., Bot.) a manzanillo (Xylosma).
aula (f.) class; classroom; lecture; recitation. **dar uma—**, to give, or to have, a lesson. **faltar à—**, to be absent from class. **sala de—s**, classroom.
áulico –ca (adj.) court; (m.) courtier.
aulido (m.) howl(ing) of animals.
aulista (m.,f.) pupil, student.
aulo (m.) aulos (Greek wood-wind instrument).
aumentação (f.) = AUMENTO.
aumentador –dora, aumentante (adj.) augmenting; (m.,f.) one who or that which augments.
aumentar (v.t.) to augment, enlarge, increase (em, in), swell, magnify; to better; to raise; (v.i.,v.r.) to increase, grow larger.—**a**, to add to.
aumentativo –va (adj.) augmentative; (m., Gram.) an augmented word; e.g., NARIGÃO = a big NARIZ.
aumentável (adj.) augmentable.
aumento (m.) enlargement, increase, rise; accession; addition to; accretion, increment; expansion, growth; (pl.) good fortune.—**de ordenado**, salary increase. **vidro de—**, magnifying glass.
aunar [a–u] (v.t.) to make as one; (v.r.) to become as one.
aura (f.) zephyr; breath. [But not aura in the sense of emanation or exhalation, which is EFLÚVIO.]—**vital**, breath, breathing.—**popular**, public favor, popularity.
auramina (f., Chem.) auramine.
auranciâceo –cea (adj., Bot.) auranciaceous.
aurato (m., Chem.) aurate.
aurélia (f.) a chrysalis; a genus (Aurelia) of large jellyfishes.
áureo –rea (adj.) aureate, golden.
auréola (f.) aureole, halo, glory.
aureolar, –lizar (v.t.) to glorify; to surround with a halo.
auriazul (adj.) gold-and-blue.
auricalcite (f., Min.) aurichalcite.
auricalco (m.) tombac, Dutch metal.
áurico –ca (adj., Chem.) ácido—, auric acid.
auricolor [lôr] (adj.) golden-colored.
aurícomo –ma (adj.) golden-haired.
aurícula (f., Anat., Zool.) auricle; pinna; (Anat.) atrium; (Bot.) auricle, auricula (primrose); (Zool.) auricula (snail).
auricular (adj.) auricular. **confissão—**, auricular confession. **dedo—**, the little finger (in allusion to the fact that one uses it to allay an itching inside the ear). **testemunha—**, ear witness.
auriculista (m.,f., Med.) ear specialist.
aurículo-occipital, -parietal, -temporal, -ventricular (adj.,

Anat., Craniom.) auriculooccipital, auriculoparietal, auriculotemporal, auriculoventricular.
aurífero –ra (adj.) auriferous, gold-bearing.
aurificar (v.t.) to gold-fill teeth.
aurífice (m.) goldsmith.
aurífico –ca (adj.) aurific.
auriflama (f.) oriflame; banner, flag.
aurifrigiado –da, –giato –ta (adj.) adorned with orphrey.
auriluzir (v.i.) to glitter like gold.
aurino (m., Chem.) aurin, (para)rosolic acid.
aurirrubro –bra (adj.) gold-and-red.
auriscálpio (m.) an earpick.
auriverde [vêr] (adj.) gold-and-green. **o pendão**, or **o pavilhão,—**, the flag of Brazil, poetically so called because of its dominant green and yellow colors.
aurocianeto (m., Chem.) aurocyanide.
aurônia (f.) = ABRÓTANO-MACHO.
auroque (m.) the aurochs (Bison bonasus).
aurora (f.) dawn, daybreak, sunrise; beginning or rise of anything; advent; (Bot.) the cottonrose hibiscus (H. mutabilis), c.a. ROSA-DA-CHINA.—**boreal**, aurora borealis. **ao romper da—**, at break of day.
auroral (adj.) auroral.
aurorescer, aurorejar (v.i.) to dawn.
aurotelurite (f., Min.) aurotellurite, sylvanite.
auscultação (f.) auscultation.—**direta** or **immediata**, (Med.) immediate ausculation.—**instrumental** or **mediata** (Med.) mediate ausculation.
auscultador –dora [ô] (adj.) listening; (m.) listening device; telephone receiver; stethoscope; listener.
auscultar (v.t., Med.) to auscultate; to sound out another's opinion; (colloq.) to get at the bottom of a matter.
ausência (f.) absence; want, lack (de, of); (pl.) remarks (good or bad) about one who is absent.—**sem licença**, absence without leave; class cutting.
ausentar-se (v.r.) to absent oneself, leave, depart. **dar licença para—**, to grant leave of absence.
ausente (adj.) absent, away, gone; (m.,f.) absentee.
áuspice (m.) augurer, soothsayer.
auspiciar (v.t.) to augur.
auspício (m.) auspice, omen. **sob os—s de**, under the auspices of.
auspicioso –sa (adj.) auspicious, favorable.
aúste (m., Naut.) splice.
austeridade (f.) austerity, severity, strictness.
austero –ra [é] (adj.) austere, severe, strict, straitlaced, stern, rigid, harsh, rugged.
austral (adj.) austral, southern.
australasiano –na, –lásio –sia (adj., m.,f.) Australasian.
australeno (m., Chem.) australene, dextropinene.
austrália (f.,Bot.) the blackwood acacia (A. melanoxylon); [cap.] Australia.
australiano –na, –trálio –lia, –tralês –lesa (adj.; m.,f.) Australian.
australite (f., Min.) australite.
austríaco –ca (adj., m.,f.) Austrian.
autacóide (m., Physiol.) autacoid.
autarcia (f.) self-satisfaction; self-sufficiency; frugality.
autarquia (f.) autarchy, autonomy, self-government.
autenticação (f.) authentication.
autenticar (v.t.) to authenticate, verify, attest; to countersign (a document).
autenticidade (f.) authenticity.
autêntico –ca (adj.) authentic, genuine, real.
auto (m.) public ceremony; a document pertaining to a trial or lawsuit; an official report; short for automobile; a kind of short play or drama; (pl.) legal proceedings.—**de investigação**, an investigation or hearing of witnesses preliminary to a formal indictment.—**de praça**, a "for hire" automobile.—**particular**, private automobile.—**jurídico**, legal brief. **não estar pelos—s**, to be in a bad humor; to be "agin" a thing. **os—s de um processo**, the papers in a lawsuit.
autobiografar-se (v.r.) to write one's autobiography.
autobiografia (f.) autobiography.
autobiográfico –ca (adj.) autobiographic(al).
autocaminhão (m.) motor truck.
autocatálise (f., Chem.) self-catlysis.
autocerrador –dora (adj.) self-closing.
autocinesia (f., Physiol.) autokinesis.
autoclave (f.) autoclave; pressure cooker.
autocoesor (m., Radio) autocoherer.
autocolimador (m., Physics) autocollimator.
autoconfiante (adj.) self-confident.

autocontrole (*m.*) automatic control.
autocópia (*f.*) a polygraphic copy.
autocracia (*f.*) autocracy.
autocrata, autócrata (*m.*) autocrat; (*adj.*) autocratic. [fem AUTOCRATRIZ].
autocrático –ca (*adj.*) autocratic.
autocronógrafo (*m.*) automatic chronograph.
autóctone (*adj.*) autochthonous; aboriginal; (*m.*) autochthon.
autoctonia (*f.*) autochthony.
autoctonismo (*m.*) autochthonism.
auto-de-fé (*m.*) public ceremony accompanying the passing of sentence by the Inquisition.
autodidata (*adj.; m.,f.*) self-taught (person).
autodidáxia [ks] autodidática (*f.*) self-instruction.
autodinâmico –ca (*adj.*) autodynamic.
autodino (*m., Radio*) autodyne.
autodomínio (*m.*) self-control, self-possession.
autoenrolador –dora (*adj.*) self-winding.
autoerotismo (*m., Psychoanalysis*) autoerotism.
auto-excitador (*m., Élec.*) self-exciter.
autofagia (*f., Med.*) autophagia.
autófago –ga (*adj.*) autophagous, self-devouring.
autofecundação (*f., Biol.*) self-fertilization.
autofilismo (*m.*) exaggerated self-love.
autofobia (*f., Psychol.*) autophobia.
autofonia (*f., Med.*) autophony.
autogamia (*f., Bot., Zool.*) autogamy, self-fertilization.
autógamo –ma (*adj.*) autogamous.
autógeno –na, autogêneo –nea (*adj.*) autogenous, self-generated.
autogiro (*m.*) autogiro.
autognose, autognosia (*f., Psychopathol.*) autognosis, self-knowledge, self-understanding.
autogoverno [ê] (*m.*) self-government.
autografar (*v.t.*) to autograph.
autográfico –ca (*adj.*) autographic.
autógrafo –fa (*adj.*) autographic; (*m.*) autograph.
autografômetro (*m., Surv.*) autographometer.
auto-idolatria (*f.*) self-idolatry.
auto-ignição (*f.*) self-ignition.
auto-indução (*f., Élec.*) self-induction.
auto-infecção (*f., Med.*) self-infection.
auto-inoculação (*f., Med.*) self-inoculation.
auto-intoxicação [ks] [*f.*) self-intoxication.
auto-lagarta (*m.*) a half-track truck.
autolatria (*f.*) self-worship.
autólise (*f., Biochem.*) autolysis
autolítico –ca (*adj.*) autolytic.
autolotacão (*f.*) a jitney bus.
autolubrificador –dora, –cante (*adj.*) self-lubricating, self-oiling.
automação (*f.*) automation.
automatia (*f.*) automaticity.
automático –ca (*adj.*) automatic.
automatismo (*m.*) automatism.
automatização (*f.*) automation.
automatizar (*v.t.*) to automatize; (*v.r.*) to become an automaton.
autômato –ta (*m.,f.*) automaton.
automatógrafo (*m.*) automatograph.
automobilismo (*m.*) automobile racing.
automobilista (*m.,f.*) automobilist.
automolite (*f., Min.*) automolite, a variety of gahnite.
automotor (*m.*) a self-propelled vehicle or mechanism.
automotriz (*adj.*) self-propelling; (*f., R.R.*) motor coach, c.a. LITORINA.
automóvel (*adj.*) automotive, self-propelling; (*m.*) automobile, motor car.—aerodinâmico, streamlined automobile.—blindado, or couraçado, armored car.
autonomia (*f.*) autonomy.
autonomista (*m.,f.*) autonomist.
autônomo –ma (*adj.*) autonomous.
auto-ônibus (*m.*) omnibus.
auto-oxidação [ks] (*f.*) self-oxidation.
autoplastia (*f., Surg.*) autoplasty.
autopneumático –ca (*adj.*) autopneumatic.
autópsia, autopsia (*f.*) autopsy.
autopsiar (*v.t.*) to conduct an autopsy upon.
autor –tora (*m.,f.*) author(ess), originator, maker, creator, inventor, writer, composer; (*Law*) complainant, plaintiff.
autoral (*adj.*) of authors. direitos autorais, authors' copyright.
auto-regulação (*f.*) self-regulation.

auto-retrato (*m.*) self-portrait.
autoria (*f.*) authorship.
autoridade (*f.*) authority, power, dominion; influence, prestige; person of commanding knowledge; police magistrate; (*pl.*) the authorities.
autoritário –ria (*adj.*) authoritarian, despotic; overbearing.
autoritarismo (*m.*) authoritarianism.
autorização (*f.*) authorization, permission.
autorizado –da (*adj.*) authorized; having authority or permission; worthy of credence.
autorizador –dora (*adj.*) authorizing; (*m.,f.*) one who or that which authorizes.
autorizamento (*m.*) = AUTORIZAÇÃO.
autorizar (*v.t.*) to authorize, sanction, justify, warrant; to empower, permit, allow; to give permission (**a, para, to**); (*v.r.*) to justify oneself.
autorizável (*adj.*) permissible.
autoscopia (*f., Med., Psychol.*) autoscopy.
auto-suficiência (*f.*) self-sufficiency.
auto-sugestão (*f.*) auto-suggestion.
autoterapia (*f.*) self-treatment.
autotipografia (*f.*) autotypography.
autotrófico –ca (*adj., Plant Physiol.*) autotrophic.
autuar (*v.t.*) to reduce to (put in) writing; to draw up a written statement, report, charge, etc.
autunita (*f., Min.*) autunite, lime uranite.
aux. = AUXILIAR (assistant).
auxanômetro [ks] (*m.*) auxanometer.
auxese [ks] (*f., Rhet., Physiol.*) auxesis.
auxiliador –dora, auxiliante [x = ss] helping; (*m.,f.*) helper.
auxiliar [x = ss] (*v.t.*) to help, relieve, succor; to assist, aid (**em**, in); (*adj.*) auxiliary. **linha**—, branch line (of a railroad); (*m.,f.*) assistant.—**de escritório**, office clerk.—**de expedição**, shipping clerk.—**de revisor**, (*Print.*) copyholder.
auxiliário [x = ss] (*m.*) instalment-payments plan. [= CREDIÁRIO and FACILITÁRIO].
auxílio [x = ss] (*m.*) aid, help, assistance.
aux.º = AUXÍLIO (assistance).
auxocardia [ks] (*f., Biol.*) auxocardia.
auxócito [ks] (*m., Biol.*) auxocite.
auxógrafo [ks] (*m., Physics*) auxograph.
auxósporo [ks] (*m., Bot.*) auxospore.
av. = AVENIDA (avenue); AVIADOR (aviator).
avacalhado –da (*adj., colloq.*) demoralized; sloppy; cowardly.
avacalhar (*v.t., colloq.*) to demoralize, to ridicule; (*v.r.*) to turn coward; to cringe.
aval (*m., Law*) aval. [*Webster*: "A written engagement by one not a drawer, acceptor, or indorser of a note or bill of exchange that it will be paid at maturity."] (*fig.*) moral support.
avalancha (*f.*) avalanche.
avaliação (*f.*) appraisal, valuation.
avaliado –da (*adj.*) evaluated, appraised (**em**, at).
avaliador –dora (*adj.*) appraising; (*m.,f.*) appraiser.
avaliamento (*m.*) = AVALIAÇÃO.
avaliar (*v.t.*) to appraise, evaluate, value (**em**, at); to set a value on; to assess (taxes); to value rightly, rate; (*v.r.*) to rate oneself as, deem oneself to be.—**por alto**, to make an offhand appraisal of. **a—pelas inúmeras cartas recebidas**, judging by the many letters received. **Você não avalia!** You can't imagine!
avalista (*m.,f.*) one who gives an AVAL (which see).
avalizar (*v.t.*) to give an AVAL (which see).
avaluar (*v.t., Colloq.*) = AVALIAR.
avançada (*f.*) advance; assault, onset; vanguard, advance guard. **às—s**, little by little, step by step. **de uma—**, all at once, in a rush.
avançado –da (*adj.*) advanced; forward. **companhias—s**, (*Milit.*) front-line companies. **guarda—**, advance guard. **hora—**, late hour.
avançamento (*m.*) advance, act of going forward. [But not advancement, in the sense of promotion, which is PROMOÇÃO.]; overhang of a building.
avançar (*v.t.*) to advance (**contra**, against); to attack; to push (bring, move, send) forward; to progress; (*v.r.*) to push oneself forward.—**o sinal**, to jump the traffic signal.—**uma idéia**, to venture, put forward, an idea. **Êle avançou por cima do outro**, He rushed at the other fellow. **Não avance nas minhas coisas!** Don't you go taking my things!
avanço (*m.*) advance, progress, improvement, enhancement; (*Mach.*) feed.—**automático**, automatic feed.

avantajado -da (*adj.*) superior, better-than-average; (*colloq.*) of big proportions, corpulent. **de tamanho—**, good-sized; on the heavy side.—**no porte**, stout.

avantajar (*v.t.*) to surpass (**em**, in); to have the advantage (**a**, over); to give the advantage (**a**, to); to better, improve; (*v.r.*) to exceed, excel, outdo, outstrip.

avante (*adv.*) forward, onward, ahead; (*interj.*) Forward! Go ahead! **de ora—**, henceforth.

avará (*m.*) the awarra Astrocarium palm.

avarandado -da (*adj.*) having a porch or veranda; (*m.*) veranda [= VARANDA].

avaremotemo (*m., Bot.*) an apes-earring (*Pithecellobium avaremotemo*); also = BORDÃO-DE-VELHO.

avarento -ta (*adj.*) miserly, covetous, avaricious, niggardly, stingy, closefisted; (*m.,f.*) miser, skinflint, tightwad.

avareza [ê] (*f.*) avarice, greed, covetousness; jealousy.—**sórdida**, sordidness.

avaria (*f.*) average (damage to ship or cargo); any damage or spoilage; expense of salvage.—**grossa**, or **comum**, (*Marine Ins.*) general average.—**particular**, (*Marine Ins.*) particular average. **causar—a**, to damage, esp. ship or cargo. **indenizar de (por) uma—**, to make good an average (damage). **pequena—**, (*Marine Ins.*) petty average.

avariado -da (*adj.*) damaged, impaired, spoiled; (*colloq.*) syphilitic.—**do juízo**, demented.

avariador -dora (*adj.*) damaging; (*m.,f.*) damager.

avariar (*v.t.*) to damage, impair, mar; (*v.i.*) to suffer damage; to spoil.

avariose (*f., Med.*) syphilis; pox.

avaro -ra [vá] (*adj.*) avaricious; niggardly, mean; (*m.,f.*) a miser.

avassalador -dora (*adj.*) overpowering, overwhelming; dire.

avassalamento (*m.*) enslavement.

avassalante (*adj.*) enslaving.

avassalar (*v.t.*) to make vassal, enslave, subdue, subjugate; (*v.r.*) to turn vassal; to subject oneself.

avatar (*m.*) avatar.

ave (*f.*) bird; fowl; swindler, sharper; a "queer bird"; (*interj.*) Hail!—**agoureira** (agourenta, de máu agouro), bird of ill omen.—**de alto vôo**, high-flying bird.—**de arribação**, bird of passage.—**aquática**, waterfowl.—**canora**, song bird.—**de rapina**, bird of prey.—**do-paraíso** bird of paradise.—**fênix**, phoenix.—**fragata**, frigate bird.—**palmípede**, web-footed bird.—**passeriforme**, passerine bird.—**rara**, a "rara avis", a rarity.—**s domésticas**, domestic fowl, poultry.

aveia (*f.*) oats; oatmeal; (*Bot.*)—**amarela**, the yellow trisetum (*T. flavescens*).—**comum**, the common oat (*Avena sativa*).—**doida**, wild oat (*Avena fatua*).—**do-rosário**, tall oat grass (*Arrhenatherum elatius*).—**estéril**, animated oat (*Avena sterilis*).—**grande**, an oatgrass (*Arrhenatherum avenaceum*).—**silvestre**, wild oats [but not the kind sown by young men, which are EXTRAVAGÂNCIAS PRÓPRIAS DA MOCIDADE]. **mingau de—**, oatmeal porridge.

avejão (*m.*) evil spirit.

aveicoma (*m.,f.*) any Indian of the Aweikoma-Caingang of Santa Catarina, called also Botocudo; (*adj.*) pert. to or designating these people.

avelã (*f.*) filbert, hazel nut. **cabeça de—**, (*colloq.*) a "nut".

avelar (*v.i.,v.r.*) to become wrinkled (as a prune); to grow old and wrinkled.

aveleira (*f.*) European filbert (*Corylus avellana*).

avelhado -da [ê], **avelhentado** -da (*adj.*) grown old, aged.

avelhentar (*v.t.*) to age, make old; (*v.r.*) to grow old.

avelórios (*m.pl.*) beads; bagatelles.

avelós (*m.*) a Brazilian plant (*Euphorbia heterodoxa*) whose irritant juice is used medicinally.

aveludado -da (*adj.*) velvety.

aveludar (*v.t.*) to make like velvet; (*v.r.*) to become velvety.

ave-maria (*f.*) a prayer (Hail Mary); one of the small beads of a rosary by which Hail Marys are counted; (*pl.*) Angelus bell, nightfall.

avena (*f.*) the genus Avena (oats); (*Poetical*) flute.

avenáceo -cea (*adj.*) avenaceous.

avenaína (*f., Biochem.*) avenin.

avenca (*f., Bot.*) the common name for the maidenhair and other polypodies. Cf. AVENCÃO, FETO.—**branca**, silverfern (*Pityrogramma calomelanos*).—**cabelo-de-**

vênus, southern maidenhair (*Adiantum capillus-veneris*).—**-da-grande**, a maidenhair (*Adiantum subcordatum*), c.a. AVENCÃO.—**-da-serra**, a maidenhair (*Adiantum regulare*).—**-da-terra**, a lipfern (*Chielanthes chlorophylla*).—**-de-espiga**, a pinefern (*Anemia fraxinifolia*).—**-de-fôlha-miúda**, the delta maidenhair (*Adiantum cuneatum*), c.a. AVENCÃO.—**-de-minas** = AVENCA-ESTRELADA.—**-do-rio-grande**, a brake (*Pteris liptophylla*).—**-dourada**, the golden polypody (*Polypodium aurea*).—**-estrelada**, a lipfern (*Cheilanthes radiata*).—**-negra**, a spleenwort (*Asplenium adiantum nigrum*).—**-paulista**, the diamond maidenhair (*Adiantum trapeziforme*), c.a. AVENCÃO.

avença (*f.*) adjustment, settlement; reconciliation; stipend, allowance; excise tax.

avencão (*m.*) any of various ferns, esp. the maidenhair spleenwort (*Asplenium trichomonoides*); a polypody (*Acrostichum aureum*), c.a. FETO-GRANDE, and several maidenhairs specified in the article on AVENCA.

avençar-se (*v.r.*) to adjust, come to agreement.

avenida (*f.*) avenue; wide, tree-lined street; court (a number of small houses grouped around a yard).

avental (*m.*) apron.

aventar (*v.t.*) to winnow; to air, ventilate; to hurl; to venture, suggest, put forth (idea, opinion); to descry; to raise the scent of; (*v.i.*) of a board, to split while being sawed; of a horse, to bloat.

aventura (*f.*) adventure, hazard, risk; exploit, hazardous enterprise; romantic adventure; a "lucky break". **à—**, aimlessly. **ter uma—**, to have a love affair.

aventurado -da (*adj.*) adventurous; fortunate. **bem—**, blessed.

aventurar (*v.t.*) to venture, hazard, risk; to put forth (an opinion); (*v.r.*) to run the risk (**a**, of); to take one's chances; to venture (**a**, to).

aventureiro -ra (*adj.*) adventuresome; rash, reckless; (*m.*) adventurer; (*f.*) adventuress.

aventurina (*f.*) aventurine (glass; mineral).

aventuroso -sa (*adj.*) venturesome; risky. **vida—**, eventful life.

averbamento (*m.*) registration; notation; marginal note.

averbar (*v.t.*) to write or sign in the margin; to state facts in writing; to draw up, register; to initial (papers); to point the finger of scorn at; (*Gram.*) to use as a verb.—**em conta**, to reckon.

avergalhar (*v.t.*) to whip with a pizzle (dried penis of a horse or bull).

avergar (*v.*) = VERGAR.

avergoar (*v.t.*) to raise stripes on the skin with a whip.

avergonhar (*v.*) = ENVERGONHAR.

averiguação (*f.*) inquiry, investigation.

averiguador -dora (*adj.*) investigating; (*m.,f.*) investigator.

averiguar (*v.t.*) to investigate, màke inquiry about; to verify, confirm, attest; to inquire (**de**, about, into).

averiguável (*adj.*) determinable, verifiable.

avermelhado -da (*adj.*) reddish.

avermelhar (*v.t.*) to make red; (*v.r.*) to blush, turn red.

aversão (*f.*) aversion.—**de morte**, intense (deep-seated) hatred.

averter (*v.t.*) to divert (as a stream from its channel, but not to avert, in the ordinary sense of warding off or preventing, which is PREVENIR, EVITAR, OBSTAR, OBVIAR).

avessar (*v.t.*) to do something **às avessas** (wrong or backwards).

avessas (*f.pl.*) contraries, opposites. **às—**, backwards, wrong. **tomar tudo às—**, to misconstrue everything.

avêsso -sa (*adj.*) opposite, converse, contrary; (*m.*) the underside, bottom side, bad side, other side, wrong side, reverse; back, tail. **ao—**, inside out; on the reverse. **o—duma fazenda**, the wrong side of a piece of material (cloth). **não ter—nem direito**, fig., to have no head or tail.

avestruz (*m.,f.*) ostrich; emu; rhea; (*colloq.*) a "queer bird".

avexar (*v.*) = VEXAR.

avezado -da (*adj.*) accustomed to, in the habit of.

avezar (*v.t.*) to accustom to, inure to; (*v.r.*) to become used to.

aviação (*f.*) aviation. **arma da—**, air corps. **campo de—**, airfield, flying field.

aviado -da (*adj.*) hurried, unencumbered; on the way; (*m.*) business agent; a rubber tapper who has others working for him in the same area.

aviador (*m.*) aviator, airman, flyer; shipper and forwarder of merchandise to rubber gatherers in Braz. [*GBAT:* "The name applied to intermediaries who formerly supplied the rubber producer or PATRÃO with the merchandise necessary for the year's operations and received on consignment the rubber collected on the SERINGAL. (The practice has largely died out, and his functions have been taken over by the warehouse itself, to which the term is still often applied)."]

aviadora (*f.*) aviatress, woman flyer.

aviajado –da (*adj.*) rampant [arch].

aviamento (*m.*) shipment, dispatch; forwarding (of merchandise); the wherewithal for carrying out any sort of job (such as tools, accessories, supplies, etc.); (*pl.*) notions (for dressmaking).

avião (*m.*) airplane; any heavier-than-air flying machine. Cf. AEROPLANO—**a hélice**, propeller plane.—**a jato**, jet airplane.—**anfíbio**, amphibian plane.—**correio**, or **-postal**, mail plane.—**de carreira**, airliner.—**de combate**, fighter plane.—**de jato-propulsão**, or **de retropropulsão**, jet plane.—**de observação**, spotter plane.—**de reconhecimento**, scout plane.—**de saúde**, ambulance plane.—**de transporte**, transport plane.—**de turismo**, light plane for private flying.—**-escola**, or—**de treinamento**, trainer plane.—**leve**, light bomber.—**médio**, medium bomber.—**pesado**, heavy bomber.—**-foguete**, rocket plane.—**quadrimotor**, four-motor plane. **porta-aviões**, plane carrier.—**sem cauda**, flying wing.

aviar (*v.t.*) to dispatch, ship, send on its way; to put up (a prescription); to get rid of; to do away with (kill); (*v.i.*) to engage in the supply of goods to rubber tappers; (*v.r.*) to hurry, get a move on.

aviário –ria (*adj.*) avian; (*m.*) aviary, bird house.

aviatório –ria (*adj.*) pert. to aviation.

avicênia (*f.*) a genus (*Avicennia*) of tropical shrubs or trees whose bark is used in tanning.

avícola (*adj.*) avian; (*m.*) = AVICULTOR; (*f.*) = AVICULTORA.

avícula (*f.*) any small bird; the genus (*Avicula*) of pearl oysters.

avicultor (*m.*), **–tora** (*f.*) poultry raiser, bird fancier.

avicultura (*f.*) poultry raising.

avidez [ê] (*f.*) avidity, eagerness; greediness.

ávido –da (*adj.*) avid, eager; greedy.

avifauna (*f., Zool.*) avifauna.

avigorar (*v.t.*) to invigorate, fortify.

aviltação (*f.*) degradation, vileness.

aviltado –da (*adj.*) disgraced, debased.

aviltador –dora (*adj.*) degrading.

aviltamento (*m.*) degradation, ignominy.

aviltante (*adj.*) debasing; degrading; ignominious.

aviltar (*v.t.*) to degrade, debase, disgrace, dishonor; to vilify, smear, sully; (*v.r.*) to degrade (debase, demean) oneself; to cringe; to eat humble pie.

avinagrado –da (*adj.*) sourish; vinegar-like.

avinagrar (*v.t.*) to season with vinegar.

avincar (*v.*) = VINCAR.

avindo –da (*p.pr.* of AVIR) agreed; (*m.,f.*) client.

avindor –dora (*adj.*) mediating; (*m.,f.*) mediator.

avinhado –da (*adj.*) drunk; tipsy; wine-like; (*m.*) a bird c.a. BICUDO, CURIÓ.

avinhar (*v.t.*) to make like wine; to mix with wine; to toast with wine.

avir [82] (*v.t.*) to adjust, reconcile, harmonize.—**se com**, to get along with.

avisadamente (*adv.*) advisedly.

avisado –da (*adj.*) sensible, wise, discreet; warned.

avisador –dora (*adj.*) warning; (*m.,f.*) informer; one who warns or notifies.

avisar (*v.t.*) to warn, inform, notify, let know, advise, acquaint, apprise (**de que**, that); to give warning (**a**, to); (*v.r.*) to be well-advised; to take counsel (**de**, concerning). **—contra**, to warn against.

aviso (*m.*) notice, advice, warning, caution, admonition; an official (government) communication.—**afixado**, placard, poster. **sem prévio—**, without prior notice.

avistar (*v.t.*) to sight, see, perceive in the distance, catch sight of, discern, descry, behold, glimpse.—**-se com**, to have a face-to-face meeting with, to have an interview with.—**ao longe**, to espy in the distance. **Êles avistaram-se mas não se cumprimentaram**, They caught sight of each other but did not speak. **Os chefes avistaram-se ontem para entabolarem negociações**, The leaders came together (in a meeting) yesterday to begin negotiations.

avistável (*adj.*) discernible; visible.

avitaminose (*f.*) vitamin deficiency.

avitualhar (*v.t.*) to provide with victuals.

avivamento (*m.*) revival.

avivar (*v.t.*) to revive, give new life to, wake, rouse; (*v.r.*) to cheer up, regain one's spirits.

aviventar (*v.t.*) to revive, give new life to, reanimate; (*v.r.*) to come to life.

avizinhação (*f.*) approximation, approach.

avizinhar (*v.t., v.r.*) to approach; to come (bring, draw, go) near or nearer (**a**, **de**, **com**, to).

avo [á] (*m.*) an "eenth": a fractional part above one-tenth. **três dezessete avos**, 3/17th.

avô (*m.*) grandfather.—**materno**, **paterno**, maternal paternal, grandfather.—**tôrto**, step grandfather.

avó (*f.*) grandmother; (*m.pl.*) grandparents; forefathers.

avoado –da (*adj.*) giddy, dizzy; giddy-brained; light-headed.

avoante (*f.*) the Paraguayan eared dove (*Zenaidura auriculata chrysauchenia*), known also by many other names, for which see POMBA-DE-BANDO.

avoar (*v.*) = VOAR.

avocação (*f.*) appeal to a higher court. [But not avocation, in the sense of hobby, which is DIVERSÃO, nor vocation, which is OCUPAÇÃO.]

avocar (*v.t.*) to attract (**a**, to); to arrogate (**a si**, to oneself); to take an appeal to a higher court; to evoke.—**a si a culpa de um êrro**, to take upon oneself the blame for a mistake.

avoceta [ê] (*f., Zool.*) an avocet (*Recurvirostra sp.*).

avocétula (*f.*) Swainson's hummingbird (*Avocettula recurvirostris*). Cf. BEIJA-FLOR.

avoejar (*v.*) = VOEJAR.

avoengo –ga (*adj.*) ancestral; (*m.pl.*) ancestors.

avolumar (*v.t.*) to increase the volume of, augment, enlarge, add to; (*v.i.*) to take up much space; (*v.r.*) to become voluminous, grow larger, increase.

avulsão (*f.*) yank, jerk; extraction of a tooth.

avulso –sa (*adj.*) torn asunder, loose; detached, separate(d); odd, sundry; vague; inconsistent; inauthentic. **papéis—s**, sundry papers; (*m.pl.*) odds and ends, sundries.

avultado –da (*adj.*) voluminous, large, bulky. **soma—**, large sum.

avultar (*v.t.*) to cause to stand out; to augment, increase; (*v.i.*) to loom up; to stand out.

avultoso –sa (*adj.*) = AVULTADO.

avuncular (*adj.*) avuncular.

axadrezado –da (*adj.*) checkered.

axadrezar (*v.t.*) to checker.

axe [ks] (*m.*) = EIXO.

axenus [ks] (*m.*) = NIGELA-DOS TRIGOS.

axial (*adj.*) axial.

áxil [ks] (*adj., Bot.*) axile.

axila [ks] (*f., Anat., Zool.*) axilla; armpit; (*Bot.*) axil.

axilante [ks] (*adj., Bot.*) axillant.

axilar [ks] (*adj.*) axillary.

axinite [ks] (*f., Min.*) axinite.

axioma [ks or ss] (*m.*) axiom.

axiomático –ca [ks or ss] (*adj.*) axiomatic.

axiômetro [ks] (*m., Naut.*) telltale.

áxis [ks] (*m., Anat.*) axis; (*Zool.*) an axis deer (*Cervus axis*). [Axis in the ordinary sense is EIXO.]

axodendrito [ks] (*m., Anat.*) axodendrite.

axófito [ks] (*m., Bot.*) axophyte, cormophyte.

axóide, axoídeo –dea [ks] (*adj., Anat.*) axoid.

axolotle (*m., Zool.*) axolotl.

axômetro [ks] (*m.*) = AXIÔMETRO.

axônio [ks] (*m., Anat.*) axon.

axonometria [ks] (*f.*) axonometry.

az [-es] (*m.*) squadron; wing of an army. [Do not confuse with **ás**, ace.]

azado –da (*adj.*) opportune, suitable. **o momento—**, the right moment.

azáfama (*f.*) hurry, flurry, bustle, ado, to-do, fuss.

azafamado –da (*adj.*) busy, bustling.

azafamar (*v.t.*) to hurry, hasten, expedite; (*v.r.*) to hurry up, be in a flurry.

azagaia (*f.*) assagai. [Webster: "A slender hardwood spear tipped with iron, used by tribes in South Africa as a missile for throwing or for stabbing; a kind of light javelin."]

azálea (*f.*) any species of Azalea. [Often wrongly pronounced AZALÉIA.]

azamboar (*v.t.*) to make giddy.

azambuja (*f.*) wild common olive (*Olea europaea oleaster*).
azambujeiro, -bujo (*m.*) a buckthorn (*Rhamnus lycioides*) c.a. ZAMBUJEIRO, ZAMBUJO, OLIVEIRA-BRAVA. Vars. ZAMBUJEIRO, ZAMBUJO.
azar (*m.*) bad luck; jinx; [= CAIPORISMO]; outsider (race horse) (*v.t.*) to cause, give rise to. **estar,** or **andar, de—,** to be down on one's luck. **jogo de—,** game of chance. **Que—**! What rotten luck!
azarado -da (*adj.*) unlucky, luckless; (*m.,f.*) victim of persistent bad luck, steady loser.
azarar (*v.t.*) to cause or bring bad luck to.
azarento -ta (*adj.*) unlucky; hoodoo.
azaroleira (*f.*) the azarole hawthorn (*Crataegus azarolus*) which yields a pleasant fruit.
azebrar (*v.i.*) to become covered with verdigris.
azêbre (*m.*) verdigris; (*Bot.*) = ALOÉS.
azebuado -da (*adj.*) zebu-like [cattle].
azêda (*f.*) woodsorrel oxalis (*Oxalis acetosella*).—**-romana,** French sorrel (*Rumex scutatus*). **sal de—s,** oxalic acid.
azedado -da (*adj.*) sour; acrimonious.
azedador -dora (*adj.*) souring; irritating; (*m.,f.*) one who or that which irritates.
azedamento (*m.*) souring; irritation.
azedar (*v.t.*) to render sour; to cause ill-humor; to embitter; (*v.i.,v.r.*) to turn sour.
azederaco, azederaque (*m., Bot.*) the margosa (*Melia azadirachta*).
azedete [ê] (*adj.*) sourish.
azedinha (*f.*) the creeping oxalis (*O. corniculata*) and other species of this genus; also, the roselle (*Hibiscus sabdariffa*), c.a. CARURU-AZÊDO.—**-do-brejo,** the perpetual begonia (*B. semperflorens*), c.a. CORAÇÃO-DE-ESTUDANTE.
azêdo -da (*adj.*) sour, vinegary, acid, tart; cross, acrimonious, peevish; (*m.*) sourness.
azedume (*m.*) sourness, bitterness; acrimony, peevishness.
azeitão -tona (*adj.*) sleek [cattle]; (*f.*) an olive.
azeitar (*v.t.*) to oil; to season with oil; (*colloq.*) to woo.
azeite (*m.*) olive oil; vegetable or animal oil; (*colloq.*) dalliance, courtship.—**-de-cheiro,** or **-de-dendê,** oil extracted from the fruits of the DENDÊZEIRO [African oil-palm (*Elaeis guineensis*)] extensively used in north Brazilian cookery.—**doce,** olive oil [= ÓLEO DE OLIVA];—**virgem,** virgin olive oil. **estar com os seus—s,** (*colloq.*) to be worried, upset.
azeiteira (*f.*) oil can; oil cruet.
azeiteiro -ra (*adj.*) pert. to oil; (*m.*) oil merchant; oil extractor; (*colloq.*) a ladies' man.
azeitona (*f.*) olive.—**-recheada,** stuffed olive.—**-da-terra,** (*Bot.*) a cuphea (*C. pseudovaccinium*).—**-do-mato,** a raphanea (*R. ferruginosa*), c.a. CAMARÁ.
azeitonado -da (*adj.*) olive-colored.
azeitoneira (*f.*) olive dish.
azemel [-méis] (*m.*) muleteer [= ALMOCREVE and RECOVEIRO].
azêmola (*f.*) pack animal; fig., a moron.
azenha (*f.*) water wheel.
azeotropia (*f., Physical Chem.*) azeotropy.
azerar (*v.*) = ACERAR.
azereiro (*m.*) Port. laurelcherry (*Prunus lusitanica*).
azevém (*m.*) perennial ryegrass (*Lolium perenne*).
azeviche (*m.*) jet, pitch coal. **negro como o—,** pitch black.
azevim, azevinho (*m.*) English holly (*Ilex aquifolium*), c.a. AZEVINHEIRA, AQÜIFÓLIO.
azevrar (*v.*) = AZEBRAR.
azêvre (*m.*) = AZEBRE.
azia (*f.*) heart-burn, sour stomach; belch.
aziago -ga [iá] (*adj.*) ill-omened; ill-fated; unlucky.
aziar (*m.*) barnacles (for pinching a horse's lip to restrain him).
ázigo -ga (*adj.*) azygous. **veia—,** azygous vein.
ázimo -ma (*adj., m.*) unleavened (bread). Var. ASMO.
azimutal (*adj.*) azimuthal.
azimute (*m.*) azimuth.
azinha (*f.*) acorn [= BOLOTA].
azinhaga (*f.*) narrow trail.
azinhal (*m.*) a grove of holm oaks.
azinhavrar (*v.i.*) to become tarnished with verdigris.
azinhavre (*m.*) verdigris.

azinheira (*f.*) the holm or holly oak of southern Europe (*Quercus ilex*).
azinheiral (*m.*) = AZINHAL.
azinheiro (*m.*) = AZINHEIRA.
azinho (*m.*) acorn; holm oak.
azinhoso -sa (*adj.*) abounding in holm oaks.
aziumar [i-u] (*v.*) = AZEDAR.
azo (*m.*) opportunity; fitting occasion; pretext.
azoado -da (*adj.*) bothered; dizzy.
azoar (*v.t.*) to stun; to bother, annoy, pester.
azobenzóico -ca (*adj., Chem.*) azobenzoic.
azobenzol (*m., Chem.*) azobenzene, azobenzol.
azofenol (*m., Chem.*) azophenol.
azóico -ca (*adj., Geol.*) azoic.
azoinar (*v.t.*) to stun, make dizzy.
azolitmina (*f., Chem.*) azolitmin.
azoospermia (*f.*) azoospermia.
azoraque (*m.*) the dwarf glorybind (*Convolvulus tricolor*).
azoratar, azoretar (*v.*) = ENTONTECER.
azorite (*f., Min.*) azorite.
azorragar (*v.t.*) to scourge.
azorrague (*m.*) scourge, whip.
azotar (*v.t.*) to nitrogenate.
azotato (*m.*) = NITRATO.
azote (*m.*) = AZOTO.
azotemia (*f., Med., Veter.*) azotemia.
azótico -ca (*adj.*) = NÍTRICO.
azotito (*m.*) a nitrite.
azôto (*m.*) nitrogen.
azotômetro (*m., Chem.*) nitrometer.
azotorréia (*f., Med.*) azotorrhea.
azotoso -sa (*adj.*) nitrous.
azotúria (*f., Med.*) azoturia.
azougado -da (*adj.*) quick, lively; sly; irritable.
azougar (*v.t.*) to silver (a mirror); to enliven (someone); to disturb (someone); to wilt (plants).
azougue (*n.*) quick-silver, mercury; (*colloq.*) a quick, lively fellow.—**-do-campo,** a red dyewood tree (*Erythroxylum tuberosum*), c.a. GALINHA-CHOCA.
azucrim (*m.*) an imp; a pestiferous person.
azucrinante (*adj.*) annoying, pestiferous.
azucrinar (*v.t.*) to pester, plague, annoy (esp. with tears, as children).
azul (*adj.*) blue, azure; in a daze; tipsy; (*m.*) the color blue.—**acinzentado,** grayish blue.—**-celeste,** (or—**do céu,** or—**-fino,** or—**-pombinho),** sky blue.—**claro,** light blue.—**-cobalto,** cobalt blue, azure blue.—**-da-armênia,** azurite blue (bice).—**-da-prússia,** Prussian blue.—**-de-metileno,** (*Chem.*) methylene blue.—**escuro,** dark blue. —**ferrête,** or **turqui,** navy blue, dark blue.—**-marinho,** ultra-marine, deep blue.—**-pavão,** peacock blue.—**-sêda,** a butterfly (*Morpho anaxibia*), c.a. CORCOVADO;—**-turquesa,** turquoise blue. **com borda—,** blue-bordered, blue edged. **sangue—,** blue blood. **Tudo—**! Everything's rosy!
azulado -da (*adj.*) bluish; hazy.
azulão (*m.*) blue denim; a butterfly (*Morpho laerte*); any of various birds, such as the southern blue grosbeak (*Cyanocompsa cyanea sterea*), c.a. GUARANDI-AZUL, AZULÃO-BICUDO; the Brazilian blue grosbeak (*C. cyanea cyanea*); Rothchild's blue grosbeak (*C. cyanoides rothschildii*).—**-bicudo** (—**-da-serra,**—**-de-cabeça-encarnada**) = SANHAÇO-FRADE (a tanager).—**-boia,** a harmless tree snake (*Leptophis sp.*).
azular (*v.t.*) to make blue; (*v.i.*) to turn blue; to run like a blue streak.
azulejado -da (*adj.*) bluish.
azulejador (*m.*) tile-setter.
azulejar (*v.t.*) to dye blue; to set tiles.
azulejista (*m.*) = AZULEJADOR.
azulejo [ê] (*m.*) an ornamental tile, a Dutch tile.
azulinho (*m.*) the glaucous grosbeak (*Cyanoloxia glaucocaerulea*).
azulino -na (*adj.*) bluish, azurine.
azulóio -loia (*adj.*) violet-blue.
azumbrar (*v.i.*) to become stooped.
azumbre (*m.*) a Spanish liquid measure of between 2 and 3 liters.
azurite (*f.*) azurite (blue copper ore).
azurrar (*v.i.*) to bray [= ZURRAR, ORNEAR].

B

B, the second letter of the Portuguese alphabet; as abbrev. = BÊCO (Alley—name of a street) ; BOM (good).

BA = Bahia (State of).

bá (*f.*) an old nurse (for children); wet nurse.

baba (*f.*) slobber, dribbling saliva.—-**de-boi,** a queen palm (*Arecastrum romanzoffianum*), c.a. COQUINHO, JERIBÁ, JERIBÀZEIRO.—-**de-boi-da-campina,** a waxmallow (*Malvaviscus babata*), c.a. CORAÇÃOZINHO.—-**de-môça,** a delicious and popular Braz. confection made with eggs, sugar and coconut milk.

babá (*m.*) a nightshade (*Solanum agrarium*), c.a. MELAN-CIA-DA-PRAIA, BOMBÃO.

bababi [í] (*m., colloq.*) a beating; melee, free-for-all.

babaça (*m.,f.*) = MABAÇA.

babaçu [ú] (*m.*) either of two large palms (*Orbignya martiana* or *O. oleifera*), native to northeastern Brazil and highly prized for their several products, esp. the oil extracted from the nuts and which is valuable as food, as fuel, as a lubricant and in the manufacture of soap. The hard, ivory-like nuts can be made into buttons, and the husks used as fuel; the leaves furnish a fiber for hat and basket weaving and the flower stalk yields a fermented beverage.

babado -**da** (*adj.*) wet with slobber; drooling; (*colloq.*) head-over-heels in love; (*m.pl.*) ruffles, flounces.

babadouro, babador (*m.*) child's bib.

babão -**ona** (*adj.*) drooling; fond, doting; (*m.*) driveler, idiot.

babaquara (*m.,f.*) simpleton; (*m.*) a rustic.

babar-se (*v.r.*) to slobber, drool; to froth at the mouth. —**por alguém,** to "drool" over someone.

babatar (*v.i.*) to grope.

babau! (*interj.*) Gone!

babeira (*f.*) gorget (of a suit of armor).

babel [-béis] (*f.*) babel, confusion, noise.

babélico -**ca** (*adj.*) babelic, confused, disordered.

babésia (*f.*) = PIROPLASMA.

babiana (*f., Bot.*) baboonroot (*Babiana*).

babirrussa (*f.*) the babirusa (a large hoglike quadruped of the East Indies), c.a. PORCO-VEADO. [The wart hog of Africa, which it somewhat resembles, is called JAVALI-AFRICANO.]

babona, fem. of BABÃO.

baboré (*m.*) a nightshade (*Solanum papillosum*), c.a. BANBORÉ, LARANJINHA-DO-CAMPO.

babosa (*f.*) see BABOSO.

baboseira, babosice (*f.*) drivel, twaddle, nonsense, piffle; slush.

baboso -**sa** (*adj.*) drooling (doting)￼; enamoured, infatuated; slushy; stupid; (*f.*) the mapo (*Bathygobius soporator*), a tropical shore fish, c.a. MARIA-DA-TOCA, PEIXE-FLOR, FLORETE, MUÇURUNGO, AMOREIA, MOREIA; also = ABECEDÁRIA (century plant).

babugem (*f.*) slobber; spume; left-overs (as of food).

babuíno (*m.*) baboon.

babujar (*v.t.*) to wet with slobber; to flatter abjectly; to corrupt, pollute.

babul (*m., Bot.*) the babul acacia (*A. arabica*).

babunha (*f.*) a peachpalm (*Gulielma insignis*).

bacaaí [a-a] (*m.*) = SARACURA.

bacaba (*f.*) any palm of the genus Oenocarpus, esp. *O. distichus* and *O. bacaba,* abundant throughout the Amazon valley. The pulp of their drupaceous fruits is used in making a pleasant drink, and the kernels furnish an olivelike cooking oil.

bacacu [ú] (*m.*) = ANAMBÉ.

bacafuzada (*f.*) hubbub; confusion.

bacairi [ca-irí] (*m.,f.*) an Indian of the Bacairi, a Cariban tribe dwelling on the upper Xingu River in Mato Grosso; (*adj.*) pert. to or designating this tribe.

bacaiúva (*f.*) an acrocomia palm (*A. glaucophilla*).

bacalaureato (*m.*) = BACHARELADO.

bacalhau (*m.*) dried codfish; a rawhide whip used on slaves in early Brazil; (*colloq.*) an emergency tire patch; (*pl.*) old-fashioned collars with very long tips; lace neckerchief; (*Zool.*) a common collective term for codfish. [The true cod (*Gadus*) does not occur in South American waters; the term is applied, however, to a number of unrelated Brazilian fishes, such as MANGAGÁ-LISO.]—-**de-porta-de-venda,** (*colloq.*) an extremely thin

person. [The allusion is to dried salt codfish exposed for sale at the entrance to food stores.]—-**do-brasil** = ABRÓ-TEA.—**frescal,** codfish barreled in brine.

bacalhoada (*f.*) codfish stew.

bacalhoeiro (*m.*) codfish merchant; cod fisherman.

bacamarte (*m.*) blunderbuss; (*colloq.*) a worthless chap.

bacana (*adj., slang*) smart, elegant; first-rate, "tops".

bacanal (*adj., f.*) bacchanal; (*f.pl.*) Bacchanalia.

bacano (*m., slang*) person "loaded" with money.

bacante (*f.*) bacchante; (*fig.*) dissolute woman.

bacântico -**ca** (*adj.*) bacchanalian, bacchic.

bacará (*m.*) baccarat; cut and etched crystal ware.

bacarejo [ê] (*m.*) needlegrass.

bacêlo (*m.*) a cutting from a grapevine (for planting).

bacento -**ta** (*adj.*) dull, dim.

bacharel [-réis] (*m.*) bachelor (graduate of a FACULDADE: a school of law, or other school, at the university level); (*colloq.*) a lawyer.

bacharela (*f.*) a woman bachelor (graduate); (*colloq.*) a pretentious-talking woman.

bacharelado -**da** (*adj.*) designating one on whom the degree of bachelor has been conferred; (*m.*) baccalaureate; college course leading to the degree of bachelor; (*f.*) grandiloquent speech; tedious talk.

bacharelando (*m.*), -**da** (*f.*) senior student.

bacharelar-se (*v.r.*) to bachelorize.—**em ciências e letras,** to receive an academic degree.—**em direito,** to graduate in law.

bacharelato (*m.*) = BACHARELADO.

bacharelice (*f.*) = BACHARELADA.

bacharelismo (*m.*) exaggerated importance attached to academic degrees.

bacia (*f.*) basin; wash-bowl; pelvic cavity; an area enclosed by higher surrounding ground.

baciada (*f.*) a basinful.

baciano -**na** (*adj., Bot.*) baccate, pulpy, berrylike.

bacífero -**ra** (*adj., Bot.*) bacciferous, bearing berries.

baciforme (*adj., Bot.*) bacciform.

bacilar, -**lário** -**ria** (*adj.*) bacillary, rod-shaped.

bacilemia (*f.*) bacillemia.

bacilicida (*adj., Bacteriol.*) bacillicide.

baciliforme (*adj.*) bacilliform, rod-shaped.

bacilíparo -**ra** (*adj.*) bacilliparous.

bacilo (*m.*) bacillus.—**virgula,** The bacterium of Asiatic cholera (*Vitrio comma*).

bacilofobia (*f.*) bacillophobia.

bacilose (*f., Med.*) bacillosis.

baciluria (*f., Med.*) bacilluria.

bacinete [nê] (*m., Anat.*)￼ pelvis of the ureter; (*Armor*) basinet.

bacio (*m.*) chamber pot.

bacívoro -**ra** (*adj.*) baccivorous (eating or subsisting on berries).

baco (*m.*) a trough used for washing damond-bearing sand and gravel; (*m.*) Bacchus.

baço -**ça** (*adj.*) dull, dim, lusterless; pale, wan; (*m., Anat.*) the spleen.

baconiano -**na** (*adj.*) Baconian.

bacopa (*f., Bot.*) a water hyssop (*Bacopa aquatica*).

bacopari-de-capoeira (*m.*) = AÇUCENA-DO-MATO.

bácora, fem. of BÁCORO.

bacorá (*m.*) the So. Amer. coral snake (*Micrurus, syn. Elaps, corallinus*). Cf. BOICORÁ.

bacorejar (*v.t.*) to forebode; to have a presentiment of; to suggest; (*v.i.*) to grunt like a pig.

bacorejo [ê] (*m., colloq.*) a premonition, a "hunch".

bacorinha (*f.*) an old-fashioned high hat; a derby hat; a transient workman's bundle of personal belongings.

bacorinho, bacorim (*m.*) a young pig, suckling pig.

bácoro (*m.*) a suckling pig, young pig.

bactéria (*f.*) bacterium; (*pl.*) bacteria.

bacterial (*adj.*) bacterial.

bactericida (*adj.*) bactericidal.

bacteriemia (*f., Med.*) bacteriemia.

bacterina (*f., Immunol.*) bacterin.

bacteriólise (*f.*) bacteriolysis.

bacteriologia (*f.*) bacteriology.

bacteriológico -**ca** (*adj.*) bacteriological.

bacterilogista (*m.,f.*) bacteriologist.

bacterioscopia (*f.*) bacterioscopy.
bacteriose (*f.*) bacteriosis.
bacterioterapia (*f.*) bacteriotherapy.
bacteriotoxina [ks] (*f.*) bacteriotoxin.
bacteriúria, bacteriuria (*f., Med.*) bacteriuria.
bactris (*m.*) a genus (*Bactris*) of spiny club palms which yield an oil and sometimes edible fruit.
bacu [ú] (*m.*) "an edible fish (*Doras dorsalis*) about a meter in length, caught with a hook, and much advertised in the fish-shops of Belém because of the fine quality of its meat." [*GBAT*]; a variant name is VACU; (*colloq.*) a big-bellied man.
bacubixá (*m.*) = BACUMIXÁ.
bacucu [ucú] (*m.*) a horse mussel (*Modiola brasiliensis*), c.a. SURURU; also, the tulip modiola (*M. tulipa*); (*colloq.*) a name applied to the beach fishermen and other natives around São Francisco in the State of Santa Catarina.
bacuçu [uçú] (*m.*) a type of outrigger canoe (in Bahia).
baculífero –ra (*adj., Bot.*) baculiferous.
baculiforme (*adj.*) baculiform, rod-shaped.
báculo (*m.*) baculus; crozier.
bacumixá (*m.*) a jungleplum (*Sideroxylon vastum*).
bacupari [í] (*m.*) any of various tropical shrubs and trees of the genus Salacia.—-açu, or—-grande, is a gardenia (*G. suavolens*), c.a. JASMIN-DO-MATO, LIMÃO-DO-MATO.—-miúdo is a posoqueria (*P. acutifolia*), c.a. PAU-DE-MACACO, FRUTA-DE-MACACO; also, a rheedia (*R. gardneriana*).
bacurau (*m.*) any goatsucker, whippoorwill or nighthawk, esp. the following: the nacunda nighthawk (*Podager nacunda*), c.a. SEBASTIÃO, ACURANA; the So. Amer. nighthawk (*Chordeiles a. acutipennis*); the sand-colored nighthawk (*Chordeiles r. rupestris*); the semi-collared nighthawk (*Lucoralis semitorquatus*); the banded nighthawk (*Hydropsalis climacocerca*), c.a. ACURAU, ACURANA; the cuiejo or parauque (*Nyctidroma a. albicollis*), c.a. CURIANGO, IBIJAÚ, MEDE-LÉGUAS; the rufous goatsucker (*Antrostomus r. rufus*) c.a. JOÃO-CORTA-PAU; by ext., a nighthawk (person who habitually goes out at night); (*slang* in Rio) a Negro.
bacuri [í] (*m.*) bacury, "A tree (*Platonia insignis*) with fine, grey wood, and fruit resembling an orange, the pulp being used for preserves and the seeds for oil used in the manufacture of soap." [*GBAT*]. c.a. BACURIZEIRO; the fruit of the bacury.
bacuripari [rí-rí] (*m.*) the bakupari rheedia (*R. brasiliensis*) whose edible fruit has a snow-white, slightly acid pulp.
bacurizeiro (*m.*) the bacury Guiana orange (*Platonia insignis*). c.a. BACURI.
bacurubu (*m.*) a large Braz. tree (*Schizolobium parahybum*) of the senna family, c.a. BAQUERUBU, BAQUERUVU, GUAPIRUVU, GUAPURUBU, PAU-VINTÉM.
badalada (*f.*) the sound (clang) of a bell.
badaladal (*m.*) peal, ringing.
badalão (*m.*) senseless gabbler, [Fem. BADALONA].
badalar (*v.t.*) to blab; (*v.t.,v.i.*) to ring, peal, toll.
badaleiro (*m.*), **–ra** (*f.*) blabber.
badalejar (*v.i.*) to ring, peal; to chatter (with cold or fear).
badalim (*m.*) the characteristic smell of unwashed laundry.
badalo (*m.*) clapper (of a bell). **correr o—**, or **dar ao—**, to blab, gabble, jabber.
badalona, fem. of BADALÃO.
badame (*m.*) = BEDAME.
badameco (*m.*) nobody, nonentity, cipher; whippersnapper; presumptuous child.
badana (*f.*) an old ewe; a fold of loose, hanging skin; whale bone; a fool; a sheep skin.
badanal (*m.*) hubbub, racket, hullabaloo.
badejete [jê] (*m.*) a young BADEJO.
badejo [é] (*m.*) any of various groupers and related fishes of family Serranidae.—-branco (—-bicudo,—-saltão.—-sapateiro), the gag (*Mycteroperca microlepis*).—-ferro, the black grouper (*Mycteroperca bonaci*), c.a. BADEJO-PRÊTO, SERIGADO-PRÊTO.—-mira, a small grouper (*Mycteroperca rubra*) which despite the name is never red, c.a. MIRA.—-pintado, the rock hind (*Epinephelus adscenscionis*), c.a. GAROUPA-PINTADA, PEIXE-GATO.—-sabão, the 3-spined soapfish (*Rypticus saponaceous*), c.a. SERIGADO-SABÃO.
badeleíta (*f., Min.*) baddeleyite.
baderna (*f.*) a "bunch of fellows"; a gang; a rowdy escapade; ruckus, row, rumpus, shindy.

badiana (*f.*) the Japanese star anise (*Illicium anisatum*) —an evergreen with poisonous fruit—c.a. ANÍS-ESTRELADO.—-da-china, the Chinese anise (*I. verum*) which yields the carminative fruit, badian.
badulaque (*m.*) a hash of lights and liver; trinket, trifle; cosmetics; a sweet made of coconut and honey.
baeta [a-ê] (*f.*) flannelette, baize; (*m.,f.*) a nickname applied to the inhabitants of Minas Gerais.
baetão [a-ê] (*m.*) thick, fleecy woolen cloth; wool blanket.
baetilha [a-ê] (*f.*) a kind of flannel.
bafafá (*f.*) uproar, ruckus, street fight.
bafagem (*f.*) zephyr, light breeze; a breathing out.
bafejado –da (*adj.*) beloved; favorite.
bafejar (*v.t.*) to warm with the BAFO (breath); to favor, smile upon; to breath into or upon; (*v.i.*) to exhale; to blow gently.
bafejo [ê] (*m.*) gentle breeze; smile of fortune.
bafio (*m.*) mustiness, fustiness.
bafo (*m.*) breath; favor, protection; smile of fortune.
baforada (*f.*) bad breath; puff, cloud (of smoke); whiff; gust, blast; disturbance; blustering. **tirar—s**, to puff (a cigar, etc.).
baforar (*v.i.*) to expel the breath; to puff, blow; to boast, brag.
baforeira (*f.*) wild fig tree; the castor bean.
baga (*f.*) any berry or small, pulpy fruit, such as the grape; a bead of sweat; a castor bean.—-da-praia, the common seagrape (*Coccolobis uvifera*) c.a. ABUTUA-GRANDE.—-de-caboclo = ABUTUA.
bagaçada (*f.*) a pile of crushed sugar-cane husks; a pile of kindling; empty words.
bagaceira (*f.*) a place where sugar-cane husks are dumped; the general atmosphere of a sugar-cane mill; rum; riff-raff; wood pile; a heap of useless things; empty talk; (*slang*) prostitute.
bagaceiro (*m.*) a workman who feeds sugar-cane husks into the furnace or disposes of them elsewhere; the place where he dumps them; a low-down person; cattle which feed on sugar-cane husks.
bagaço (*m.*) bagasse (the refuse matter of crushed sugar cane, grapes, etc.); frolic, romp; a loose woman. **ter dinheiro como—**, (*colloq.*) to be "filthy rich".
bagada (*f.*) large tear drop; beads of sweat.
bagageira (*f.*) a bluish pebble, characteristic of diamond-bearing gravel; (*slang*) a baggage (wench).
bagageiro (*m.*) baggageman; baggage car; the last horse in a race; a person who associates with the lowest class of people.
bagagem (*f.*) baggage, equipment; author's works; low-class persons.
bagana (*f.*) a cigar or cigarette butt.
baganha (*f.*) skin; hull, husk; (*colloq.*) a bargain.
bagata (*f.*) witchcraft; voodooism.
bagatela (*f.*) bagatelle, trifle, bauble. **atiçar**, or **atormentar, com—s**, to nag.
bagauri [í] (*m.*) = BAGUARI.
bagaxa (*f., slang*) prostitute.
bago (*m.*) single grape or grapelike fruit; berry; seed; bird shot; (*slang*) "dough" (money); testicle.
bagre (*m.*) any marine or fresh-water catfish.—-amarelo (—-de-areia), a very common Brazilian sea cat (*Arius spixii*).—-bandeira, either of two gaff-topsail cats (*Bagre marina* or *B. bagre*).—-branco, = BÔCA-LISA.—-cabeçudo and—-de-corso, unspecified cats.—-do-mar, a large sea catfish (*Arius barbus*).
bagual, baguá (*adj.*) skittish; unsociable; (*m.*) a wild young horse.
baguaçu [çú] (*m.*) a palm (*Scheelea lauromulleriana*).
baguari [í] (*m.*) the cocoi heron (*Ardea cocoi*), c.a. BAGAURI, MANGUARI, JOÃO-GRANDE; also = JABURU-MOLEQUE (a stork).
bagueta [ê] (*f., Arch.*) baguette.
bagulho (*m.*) pip (as of a pear or grape).
bagunça (*f.*) bulldozer; (*slang*) confusion, disorder. **Que—!** What a mess!
bagunçada (*f.*) row, disturbance.
bagunceiro –ra (*adj., slang*) rowdy, disorderly.
Bahia (*f.*) Bahia (city and state).
baia (*f.*) stall in a stable.
baía (*f.*) bay; river lake; drainage ditch.
baiacu [ú] (*m.*) any of various fishes.—-arara (—-ara, —-dondon,—-guaiama), the smooth or silvery puffer (*Lagocephalus laevigatus*), c.a. PEIXE-COELHO.—-de-chifre, the cowfish (*Lactophrys tricornis*), c.a. PEIXE-BOI,

PEIXE-VACA, TAOCA.—-de-espinho, a porcupine fish (*Diodon hystrix*); a spiny boxfish (*Chilo spinosus*).—-mirim, West Indian swellfish (*Spheroides testudineus*).—-panela, a globefish (*Spheroides sp.*).—-sem-chifre (—-caixão), common trunkfish (*Lactophrys trigonus*), c.a. COFRE, OSTRACIÃO, TAOCA, VACA-SEM-CHIFRE.

baíagu [ú] (*m.*) = BATUÍRA.

baiana [a-i] (*f.*) see BAIANO.

baianada [a-i] (*f.*) a group of persons from Bahia;—[somewhat pejorative]; a mistake, mistep or fumble in horsemanship, round-up of cattle, etc., according to GAÚCHO standards.

baiano -na (*adj.*) of or pert. to Bahia; (*m.*) a native of Bahia; in Rio, a Negro who is careful of his dress and manner of speech; in Rio Grande do Sul, a foot soldier; a poor horseman; anyone from the north of Brazil; (*f.*) a woman of Bahia; in Rio, a Negro woman street vender of home-made sweets.

baião (*m.*) a "rock-and-roll" type of music and dance.

baié (*m.*) a type of small pig in northern Brazil.

baiense [a-i] (*adj.; m.,f.*) = BAIANO.

baila (*f.*) barrier (as a net or fence); ball, dance; ballet. **vir à—**, to come up for consideration or discussion.

bailadeira (*f.*) a woman dancer.

bailado (*m.*) ballet, stage dance; any ball or dance.

bailador (*m.*) dancer.

bailar (*v.i.*) to dance.

bailarico (*m.*) informal dancing party.

bailarim (*m.*) = BAILARINO.

bailarina (*f.*) ballerina.

bailarino (*m.*) professional dancer; fig., a man who walks with mincing steps.

baile (*m.*) dance, dancing party, ball.—**de fantasia**, fancy dress ball.—**de máscaras**, masked ball.—**público**, public dance hall. **corpo de—**, ballet (the dancers). **dar um— em alguém**, (*slang*) to give someone a drubbing, a bawling out, "the works".

bailéu (*m.*) painter's or bricklayer's scaffold; (*Naut.*) gangway.

bailio (*m.*) bailiff.

bainha [a-í] (*f.*) sheath, scabbard; hem; (*Bot.; Anat.*) sheath.—**da espada**, sword scabbard.—**de costura**, hem (of a garment).—**de laçada**, hemstitch.

bainhar [a-i, 11] (*v.t.*) to hem.

baio -aia (*adj.*) bay, reddish-brown; (*m.*) bay horse.

baioneta [ê] (*f.*) bayonet; (*Bot.*)—-**espanhola**, the datil yucca (*Y. baccata*).—**calada**, fixed bayonet.

baionetada (*f.*) a bayonet thrust or wound.

baionetar (*v.t.*) to bayonet.

bairari [rí] (*m.*) = POMBA-DE-BANDO.

bairrismo (*m.*) parochialism, narrowness (of interests, opinions, etc.); provincialism.

bairrista (*adj.*) provincial, parochial, narrow; (*m.,f.*) a person whose interests, opinions, etc., are narrow and local.

bairro [áí] (*m.*) neighborhood, district, part of town.

bairu [ú] (*m.*) = MUSSURANA.

baita (*adj., colloq.*) whopping, enormous; grown-up.

baitaca (*f.*) any parrot of the genus Pionias.

baitatá (*m.*) = BOITATÁ.

baiúca (*f.*) small tavern; low eating house [= TABERNA].

baiuqueiro -ra [ai-u] (*adj.*) tavern; (*m.,f.*) tavern-keeper; a tavern's steady customer.

baixa (*f.*) see BAIXO.

baixada (*f.*) lowland; flat stretch of land.

baixadão (*m.*) = BAIXÃO.

baixamar (*f.*) tide low point.

baixão (*m.*) bassoon.

baixar (*v.t.*) to lower, drop, let down, bring down, take down; to lessen, reduce, decrease; (*v.i.*) to grow less, subside; to go down, descend; (*v.r.*) to stoop; to lower oneself.—**a cabeça**, to lower the head; fig., to submit, obey.—**à sepultura**, to lower to the grave.—**à terra**, to lower to the ground; also, to the grave.—**a vista, os olhos**, to lower the eyes.—**ao hospital**, to enter the hospital.—**um decreto, uma sentença**, etc., to hand down a decree, a sentence, etc.

baixeira (*f.*) first picking of cotton.

baixeiro (*m.*) saddlecloth.

baixela (*f.*) tableware.—**de prata**, silver tableware, silver service.

baixeza [ê] (*f.*) lowness; meanness, vileness; abjection.

baixinho (*adv.*) softly, quietly; in secret; (*adj.*) not tall, quite low.

baixio (*m.*) shoal.—**de areia**, sandbank.

baixista (*adj.*) bearish (tending to fall in price); (*m.,f.*) bear (speculator).

baixo -xa (*adj.*) low, lower, not high or tall, short; shallow, mean, sordid, base, vile; abject; disreputable; despicable; vulgar, cheap; (*adv.*) low, at low pitch; softly; (*f.*) decrease, reduction, decline, abatement; fall, descent; low ground shallow place; drop in price; (*Meteor.*) a low; [*GBAT*: "A lowering in the level of land water; a shallow region in a sea or river; specifically, a flooded depression in the VÁRZEA."]; (*pl.*) war casualties; (*m.*) bottom, lower part; shoal; bass (voice or musical instrument); pace (of a horse).—**freqüência**, (*Elec.*) low frequency.—**tensão** or **voltagem**, low voltage. **água—**, shallow water. **altos e—s**, ups and downs. **de—**, lower. **de cabeça para—**, upside down. **de cima para—**, from top to bottom. **em—**, below. **em—de**, under, underneath, beneath, below. **lá por—**, down over (around) there. **lá em—**, down there; downstairs. **maré—**, low tide. **os—s de uma casa**, the lower or main floor of a house. **para—**, down(ward), below , to the bottom. **para cima e para—**, up and down. **por—**, under(neath), below. **por—de**, under.

baixo-império (*m.*) the Byzantine Empire.

baixo-latim (*m.*) Low Latin.

baixo-relêvo (*m.*) bas (low) relief.

baixo-ventre (*m.*) the lower belly.

baixote -ota (*adj.*) low, short, not tall, dumpy.

bajacu [ú] (*m.*) the common name for a puffer or globefish [= BAIACU].—-**de-espinho**, a spiny globefish or porcupine fish.

bajoujar (*v.t.*) to pet, fondle, make much of; to flatter.

bajoujice (*f.*) flattery.

bajoujo (*m.*) sycophant, base flatterer; infatuated lover; driveler; simpleton.

bajulação (*f.*) flattery, blarney; obsequiousness, toadyism.

bajulador -dora (*adj.*) flattering; (*m.,f.*) base flatterer, fawner, lickspittle, toady.

bajular (*v.t.*) to flatter in a cringing, fawning manner; to kowtow to.

bajulatório -ria (*adj.*) flattering.

bajulice (*f.*) = BAJULAÇÃO.

bala (*f.*) bullet, shot, ball; bale; 32 reams of paper; piece of hard candy. **a—**, with bullets; by gunfire. **à prova de—**, bulletproof.—**, or fardo, de algodão**, bale of cotton.—**de altéia**, marshmallow candy.—**de estalo**, a cracker bonbon.—**fumígena**, smoke bomb.—**incendiária**, incendiary bullet.—**morta**, spent bullet.—**perdida**, stray bullet.—**traçadora**, tracer bullet. **ferimento de—**, bullet wound.

Balaão [a-ão] (*m.*) Balaam.

balaço (*m.*) shot, gunshot.

balada (*f.*) ballad; ditty.

baladeira (*f.*) slingshot.

balaieiro -ra (*m.,f.*) street vender of farm produce carried in BALAIOS (hampers).

balaio (*m.*) hamper, small basket; a box lunch; a sort of Negro fandango.

balalaica (*f.*) balalaika, Russian guitar.

balança (*f.*) balance, pair of scales; fig., moral or mental equilibrium, equipoise.—**de mola**, spring balance.—**de precisão**, balance of precision.—**de torção**, torsion scale.—**química**, (*Chem.*) analytical balance.—**romana**, steelyard. **fiel da—**, beam or pointer of a scale. **pratos da—**, dishes of a scale. **tara da—**, tare of a scale.

balançar (*v.t.*) to balance; to weigh (mentally), compare; to cast accounts; (*v.i.*) to hesitate, waver; (*v.r.*) to swing, sway, rock back and forth, teeter.

balanceador -dora (*m.,f.*) scale inspector [= BALANCISTA].

balanceamento (*m.*) balancing of accounts, swinging, rocking.

balancear (*v.*) = BALANÇAR.

balanceio (*m.*) balancing; (*Aeron.*) banking.

balanceiro -ra (*m.,f.*) weigher, weight checker; (*m., Mach.*) rockshaft, rocker arm, valve rocker, walking beam [= BALANCIM].

balancete [cê] (*m.*) trial balance, balance sheet.

balancim (*m.*) whiffletree; a swinging gate; (*Mach.*) rockshaft, rocker arm [= BALANCEIRO]; (*pl., Zool.*) halteres, balancers of Diptera.

balancista (*m.,f.*) scale inspector.

balanço (*m.*) oscillation, vibration, swinging; rolling (of a ship); balance sheet; checking of accounts; swing rocker, swing, see-saw. [But not balance in the sense of surplus or remainder, which is RESTO or SALDO.]—de compensação, (*Horol.*) compensation balance.—térmico, heat balance.

balandra (*f.*) a Spanish ocean-going ship of burden with a single mast.

balandrau (*m.*) frock coat; a long, sleeveless garment worn by lay brethren; a large mantle or cloak, esp. such as worn by travelers in the Middle Ages; (*slang*) overcoat; revelry, merrymaking.

balangandã (*m.*) a type of ornamental silver buckle, with amulets and trinkets attached, worn on feast days by the Negro women of Bahia; by ext., any ornamental trinket, bauble or gewgaw; c.a. BARANGANDÃ, BERENGUENDÉM, CAMBIO, PENCA. [Usually used in the plural.]

balanídeos (*m.pl.*) the Balanidae (acorn barnacles).

balanífero –ra (*adj.*) balaniferous, bearing acorns.

balanismo (*m.*) balanism (application of pessaries or suppositories).

balanita (*f.*) balanite (a kind of precious stone not certainly identified); (*Bot.*) a plant of the genus Balanites (family Zygophyllaceae).

balanite (*f.*, *Med.*) balanitis.

bálano (*m.*, *Anat.*) glans; (*Zool.*) an acorn barnacle.

balanoforáceo –cea (*adj.*, *Bot.*) balanophoraceous.

balanóforo –ra (*adj.*) balanophore; (*m.*, *Bot.*) the genus Balanophora.

balanóide (*adj.*) balanoid, acorn-shaped.

balanopostite (*f.*, *Med.*) balanoposthitis.

balano-prepucial (*adj.*, *Anat.*) balanopreputial.

balanorragia (*f.*, *Med.*) balanorrhagia.

balanquinho (*m.*) the slender oat (*Avena barbata*).

balantas (*m.pl.*) the Balante (a Sudanese Negro tribe in French Senegal and Portuguese West Africa).

balante (*adj.*) bleating.

balantídio (*m.*, *Zool.*) a genus (*Balantidium*) of large parasitic ciliate protozoans, one species of which (*B. coli*) infests the intestines of swine and other mammals, and is believed to cause a form of dysentery in man.

balantos (*m.pl.*) = BALANTAS.

balão (*m.*) balloon; globe; hoop skirt; false rumor; charcoal kiln; (*Chem.*) flask.—cativo, captive balloon.—de ensaio, trial balloon; test balloon (in a laboratory).—dirigível, dirigible balloon.—livre, free balloon.—pilôtô, (*Meteor.*) pilot balloon.—sonda (*Meteor.*) sounding balloon.—veneziano, paper lantern. balões de São João, balloons made of colored tissue paper, often several feet high, and released on St. John's eve (June 23rd).

balãozinho [í] (*m.*) a small balloon; (*Bot.*) = ALQUEQUENJE-AMARELO or CHUMBINHO.

balar (*v.i.*) to bleat (as sheep).

balastragem (*f.*) ballasting.

balastrar (*v.t.*) to fill (a railroad bed) with ballast.

balastreira (*f.*) a ballast train.

balastreiro (*m.*) a ballast dump car.

balastro (*m.*) ballast [= LASTRO].

balata (*f.*) the common balata or bully tree (*Manilkara bidentata*) which yields balata gum—an important item of export from the Amazon region.—rosada, an ironwood tree (*Sideroxylon resiniferum*).

balateiro –ra (*m.f.*) gatherer of balata gum.

baláustio (*m.*) any fruit which resembles the pomegranate.

balaustrada [a-u] (*f.*) balustrade, banisters; railing.

balaustrar [a-u] (*v.t.*) to provide with balusters or railing.

balaústre (*m.*) baluster; handrail.

balbuciação (*f.*) stuttering, stammering, lisping; faltering; prattle.

balbuciante (*adj.*) stuttering, stammering; confused.

balbuciar (*v.i.*,*v.t.*) to stammer, stutter, falter, lisp; to babble, prattle.

balbúcie, balbuciência (*f.*) difficulty in speaking, gagging, stammering.

balbucio (*m.*) = BALBUCIAÇÃO.

balbúrdia (*f.*) hubbub, racket, noisy tumult; bedlam; uproar, riot.

balburdiar (*v.t.*) to confuse, confound.

balça (*f.*) thicket; coppice. [Do not confuse with BALSA.]

balcão (*m.*) store counter; window balcony; theater balcony.

balcedo [ê] (*m.*) a ticket; large area of floating vegetation. Var. BALSEDO.

balconista (*m.,f.*) sales clerk.

balda (*f.*) failing, foible; bad habit (of a horse); the suit

---

of cards missing in a player's hand.

baldado –da (*adj.*) vain, useless, ineffectual, unavailing. esforços—s, fruitless efforts.

baldão (*m.*) affront, outrage, reproach; misadventure, ill luck, reverse; fruitless effort, indecorum; large wave, breaker. de—, precipitately.

baldaquino, baldaquim (*m.*) canopy, marquee.

baldaquinado –da (*adj.*) canopied.

baídar (*v.t.*) to frustrate, defeat, thwart, foil; to employ in vain, (*v.r.*) to be useless (in vain); to run out of trumps or other suit.

balde (*m.*) bucket, pail; dam wall; a type of paper kite.

baldeação (*f.*) transshipment.

baldear (*v.t.*) to decant; to bail (water); to transship merchandise; to transfer passengers or baggage; to wet with buckets of water; to throw, hurl (em, in); (*v.r.*) to move oneself (de, from; para, to).

baldio –dia (*adj.*) uncultivated, unused. terreno—, waste land; vacant lot, fallow ground.

baldo –da (*adj.*) unsuccessful; useless; lacking; devoid; short-suited (at cards).

baldoar (*v.t.*) to shout insults at.

baldoso –sa (*adj.*) of horses, vicious.

baldrame (*m.*) foundation, base; floor beam; sill; girder.

baldréu (*m.*) kid leather.

baldroca (*f.*) fraud, trick, cheat.

baldrocar (*v.t.*) to trick, deceive; to cheat at cards.

balduína (*f.*) a (Baldwin) locomotive.

balear (*v.t.*) to shoot (inflict a bullet wound).

baleárico –ca, baleário –ria (*adj.*) balearic.

baleato (*m.*) a baby whale.

baleeiro –ra [e-ei] (*adj.*) pert. to whales, (*m.*) whaler (boat or man); (*f.*) whaleboat.

baleia (*f.*) whale; baleen, whale bone; an obese woman.—azul, the blue whale or rorqual (*Sibbaldus musculus*).—branca, the bowhead or Greenland whale (*Balaena mysticetus*).

baleiro (*m.*) street vender of BALAS (hard candies).

balela (*f.*) false rumor.

balenídeos (*m.pl.*) the Balaenidae (family of right whales).

baleote (*m.*) = BALEATO.

balgado (*m.*) a rorqual or finback (*Balaenoptera rostrata*).

balido (*m.*) bleat(ing) (of lambs); fig., complaints of parishioners against their pastor.

balieira (*f.*) = CATINGA-DE-PRÊTO.

balir [25] (*v.i.*) to bleat.

balista (*f.*) crossbow.

balístico –ca (*adj.*) ballistic; (*f.*) ballistics.

balistita (*f.*) Balistite (a smokeless powder).

baliza (*f.*) landmark, boundary stake, monument; beacon; buoy; levelling rod; range pole; wooden keel.

balizador (*m.*) surveyor, land marker.

balizagem (*f.*) balizamento (*m.*) delimitation, marking (of boundaries). luzes de balizamento, landing lights (at an airport).

balizar (*v.t.*) to delimit (areas); to stake out (boundaries); to determine the greatness of; to distinguish from.

balnear (*adj.*) balneal, bath, bathing. estância—, bathing beach; (*v.i.*) to bathe.

balneário (*m.*) balneary, bathing place. hotel—, a beach hotel, or one at a spa.

balneatório –ria (*adj.*) balneatory.

balneografia (*f.*) balneography.

balneologia (*f.*) balneology.

balneoterapia (*f.*) balneotherapy.

balofo –fa [lô] (*adj.*) fluffy; puffed up, bloated; vain; of deceitful appearance.

balota (*f.*, *Bot.*) the black hoarhound (*Ballota nigra*), c.a. MARROIO-PRÊTO.

balote (*m.*) small ball; bale of cotton; (*Fireworks*) torpedo.

baloiçador –dora (*adj.*) swaying, rocking; (*m.*) a hardtrotting horse; (*f.*) a rocking chair.

baloiçamento (*m.*) act of swinging, rocking.

baloiçar (*v.t.*,*v.i.*) to balance, swing, sway, rock. Var. BALOIÇAR.

baloiço (*m.*) balance, balancing; swaying, rocking; a child's swing. Var. BALOIÇO.

balroar (*v.*) = ABALROAR.

balsa (*f.*) raft, float; river ferry; slabs of salted beef to be dried; wine vat; [*GBAT*:] "(1) a raft made of rubber tied together with wire, used by the rubber gatherers when the rivers are too low for boats and canoes; (2) a raft on which the Indians live; (3) timber used in the construction of small rafts used for navigation on the upper rivers of the Amazon Basin; for several purposes can be used as a cork substitute; is especially good for loud speaker mountings; is also good as an insulator; (the fruit yields a material resembling kapok)."] Cf. BALÇA.

balsamar (*v.t.*) to balsam; to aromatize with balsam.

balsâmico –ca (*adj.*) balsamic(al).

balsamífero –ra (*adj.*) producing balsam.

balsamificar (*v.*) = BALSAMAR.

balsâmina (*f., Bot.*) the garden balsam (*Impatiens balsamina*), c.a. BEIJO-DE-FRADE.—**-de-purga**, the balsam apple (*Momordica balsamina*).—**-longa** = CARAMELO.

balsamináceo –cea, –míneo –nea (*adj., Bot.*) balsaminaceous.

balsamizar (*v.*) = BALSAMAR.

bálsamo (*m.*) balsam; balm; (*Bot.*)—**-de-cheiro**, common heliotrope (*H. arborescens*).—**-de-tolu**, tolubalsam balmtree (*Myroxylon balsamum*).—**-de-jardim**, garden balsam (*Impatiens balsamina*), c.a. BALSÂMINA, BEIJO-DE-FRADE, NÃO-ME TOQUES.—**-do-canadá**, balsam fir (*Abies balsamea*).—**-do-peru**, Peru balsam balmtree (*Myroxylon pereirae*).—**-de-copaíba**, copaiba balsam (a pharmaceutical product).—**-tranqüilo**, a soothing oil for massage.

balsedo [ê] (*m.*) = BALCEDO.

balseiro –ra (*adj.*) woody, wild; (*m.*) river boatman, raftsman; grape pressing vat; (*f.*) = BALSA.

balso (*m.*) hawser, cable.

baluarte (*m.*) fortress, bastion, bulwark, rampart; safeguard, palladium; fig., a safe place.

baluda (*f., colloq.*) a heavy-gauge gun.

bamba (*m.*) braggadocio, blusterer, roisterer; (*slang*) a "shark" (expert, master).

bambá (*m.*) a Negro handclapping and dance; a card game; disorder, commotion; a game played with peach stones.

bambalear (*v.*) & derivs. = BAMBOLEAR & derivs.

bambalhão –lhona (*adj.*) very slack; careless, slouchy, lazy.

bambaquerê (*m.*) shindig; shindy.

bambar (*v.*) = BAMBEAR.

bambaré (*m.*) hubbub, uproar, din, racket; outcry.

bambear (*v.t.*) to slacken, loosen; (*v.i.*) to become loose or slack; to sag.

bambeza [ê] (*f.*) slackness.

bambinar (*v.i.*) to shake, quiver.

bambinela (*f.*) window curtain.

bambo –ba (*adj.*) slack, lax, dilatory, loose, relaxed, floppy, limp, limber; (*m.*) see BAMBA above.

bamboar (*v.*) = BAMBOLEAR.

bambochata (*f.*) spree, revel(ry); folly; orgy; picture of a grotesque scene.

bamboleadura (*f.*), **–leamento** (*m.*) act of swaying, reeling, tottering.

bamboleante (*adj.*) swaying, rocking.

bambolear (*v.i.*) to sway; to waver; to walk with mincing steps; to shake the hips; to swagger.

bamboleio (*m.*) shimmy (of front wheels); BAMBOLEA-MENTO.

bambolim (*m.*) flounce, valance.

bambolina (*f.*) the upper crosspieces of theatrical scenery.

bamboré (*m.*) = BABORÉ.

bambu [ú] (*m.*) bamboo; any species of Bambusa, esp. *B. arundinacea* and *B. vulgaris*.—**-balde** or —**-gigante**, the giant bamboo (*Dendrocalamus giganteus*).—**-cheio-chinês** or —**-maciço** is *Dendrocalamus strictus*, sometimes called the male bamboo.—**-imperial** is the castillo bamboo (*Phyllostachys castilloni*), whose round slender culms are used for furniture, walking sticks, etc.—**-japonês**, the fern asparagus (*Asparagus plumosus*), c.a. BAMBUZINHO.—**-prêto**, black bamboo (*Phyllostachys nigra*).

bambual (*m.*) a growth of bamboos.

bamburral (*m.*) a bamboo thicket; tangled, shrubby growth, esp. along a river bank; land with sparse vegetation; grazing land; a bushmint (*Hyptis umbroza*).

bambúrrio (*m.*) lucky break, piece of luck, fluke.

bamburrista (*m.,f.*) lucky person.

bamburro (*m.*) = BAMBÚRRIO.

bambusa (*f.*) the bamboo genus (*Bambusa*.)

bambuzal (*m.*) = BAMBUAL.

bambuzinho (*m.*) fern asparagus (*A. plumosus*), c.a. BAMBU-JAPONES, CANA-DE-PASSARINHO; also = CAPIM-RABO-DE-RAPÔSA (a grass).

banal (*adj.*) banal, commonplace, trite, "corny".

banalidade (*f.*) banality, triviality.

banalizar (*v.t.*) to render banal.

banana (*f.*) banana; an obscene gesture of contempt made with clenched fist; (*m.*) a wishy-washy person, a milksop.—**-de-macaco** = ANIN-GAÚBA.—**-de-são-tomé**, plantain banana (*Musa paradisiaca*).—**-do-brejo**, the ceriman (*Monstera deliciosa*).—**-mãe**, India banana (*Musa rosacea*), c.a. BANANEIRA-DE-SEMENTES.—**-nanica**, the dwarf (low-growing) Chinese banana (*Musa nana*), c.a. BANANA-CHINESA, BANANEIRA-ANÃ.

bananada (*f.*) a confection made of bananas and sugar.

bananal (*m.*) a banana plantation.

bananeira (*f.*) banana tree.—**-anã**, dwarf (low-growing) Chinese banana, (*Musa nana*), c.a. BANANA-CHINESA, BANANEIRA-CHINESA, BANANEIRA-DE-ITALIANO, BANA-NEIRA-NANICA.—**-brava**, a heliconia (*H. sylvestris*).—**-de-abissínia**, Abyssinian banana (*Musa ensete*).—**-da-rainha**, the queen's bird-of-paradise flower (*Strelitzia reginae*).—**-de-corda**, the abaca banana (*Musa textilis*), c.a. BANANEIRA-DE-FLOR. [It is the source of Manila hemp.]—**-de-jardim**, the Arnold banana (*Musa arnoldiana*).—**-de-leque**, the Madagascar travelerstree (*Ravenala madagascariensis*), c.a. ÁRVORE-DO-VIAJANTE.—**-de-sementes**, India banana (*Musa rosacea*), c.a. BANANA-MÃE.—**-do-mato**, the Carib heliconia (*H. bihai*) c.a. BANANEIRINHA-DO-MATO, BIAÍ, CAETÉ, PACOVA-BRAVA; also, the Brazilian canna (*C. polyclada*), c.a. BANANEIRINHA, CAETÉ-MIRIM; also = COQUILHO.

bananeiral (*m.*) = BANANAL.

bananeirinha (*f.*) the common name for any canna, the leaves of which somewhat resemble those of a small banana tree; a heliconia (*H. angustifolia*); the Brazilian canna (*C. polyclada*), c.a. BANANEIRA-DO-MATO.—**-comum**, a calathea (*C. grandifolia*), c.a. BANANEIRINHA-DO-MATO, ANIMA-MEMBECA, CAETÉ-AÇU.—**-da-índia**, the India canna (*C. indica*), c.a. BANANEIRINHA-DE-FLOR, BANANEIRINHA-DO-MATO, ALBARÁ, CAETÉ-DOS-JARDINS, CANA-DA-ÍNDIA.—**-de-touceira**, an arrowroot (*Maranta prolifera*).—**-do-mato**, the scarlet canna (*C. coccinea*), c.a. CAETÉ-VERMELHO; also = BANANEIRA-DO-MATO, ARUMÁ.

bananeiro (*m.*) banana grower; banana merchant.

bananicultor –tora (*m.,f.*) banana grower.

bananista (*adj.*) banana; (*m.,f.*) banana grower.

bananívoro –ra (*adj.*) banana-eating.

bananose (*f.*) banana flour.

banatito (*m., Petrog.*) banatite.

banazola, bananzola (*m.,f.*) a nobody; a milksop.

banca (*f.*) table; writing desk; examining board; a certain card game; market stall; the bank (at gambling); law office; lawyer's profession.—**de carpinteiro**, carpenter's bench.—**de jornais**, newsstand.—**examinadora**, examining board.—**francesa**, a certain dice game. **abrir—de advogado**, to hang out one's shingle.

bancada (*f.*) long bench; carpenter's bench; row of benches; tier; a congressional bloc.

bancal (*m.*) cloth cover for a bench.

bancalé (*m.*) a screwpine (*Pandanus astrocarpus*).

bancar (*v.t.*) to bank (a gambling game); to pretend, put on, feign.—**o difícil**, to play hard to get.—**o importante, o sabido**, (*slang*) to pretend to be a big shot, a wise guy. **Você está bancando o trouxa**, You are playing the fool, being a sucker.

bancário –ria (*adj.*) bank; banking; (*m.,f.*) bank employee. Cf. BANQUEIRO.

bancarrota (*f.*) bankruptcy, failure.

bancarrotear (*v.i.*) to go bankrupt.

bancarroteiro –ra (*adj.; m.,f.*) bankrupt (person).

banco (*m.*) a commercial bank; bank building: any kind of bench, seat or pew; stool; footstool; work bench; shoal; the outclinic at a hospital; privy.—**agrícola**, farm bank.—**comercial**, commercial bank.—**de areia**, sandbank;—**de carpinteiro**, carpenter's bench.—**de circulação**, bank of issue.—**de depósito**, depository bank.—**de emissão**, bank of issue.—**de ensaio**, or **de prova**, testing bench.—**de gêlo**, ice bank;—**de igreja**, church bench.—**de sangue**, blood bank.—**de três pés**, three-legged stool.—**dos réus**, defendant's bench.—**emissor**, bank of issue—**giratório**, revolving piano stool.—**hipotecário**, land bank.—**industrial**, industrial bank—**por ações**, joint-stock bank.—**prestamista**, personal loan bank. **caderneta de—**, bank book. **nota de—**, bank note.

banda (*f.*) side, flank; rear; officer's belt; stripe; sash (ribbon); strap; broadside; band of people, faction, party.—de música, band of musicians.—militar, military band. à—, (fallen, tilted) to one side; apart, privily. pôr de—, to cast aside. sair de—, to sneak out. Cf. BANDO.

bandada (f.) big flock of birds. Cf. DEBANDADA.

banda-fôrra (m.) son of a white man and negro slave woman.

bandagem (f.) bandage; striping.

bandalheira (f.) low behavior.

bandalho (m.) a no-good fellow; a rag; a tatterdemalion.

bandar (v.t.) to sew on stripes, ribbons, etc.

bandarilha (f.) barbed dart used in bullfighting—Spanish *banderilla*.

bandarra (m.) loafer, idler, sluggard.

bandarrear (v.i.) to loaf.

bandear (v.t.) to band together, unite, gather persons together; to incline to the side; to consider from every angle; (v.r.) to join, unite with (a faction, party, etc.); to band (contra, against).—-se para, to swing over (to the other side).

bandeira (f.) flag, banner, ensign, colors; lampshade, lightshade; transom; flagman; an armed band of adventurers during the XVIIth and XVIIIth centuries in Brazil—called BANDEIRANTES; (colloq.) a house-raising or other "bee".—a meio-pau, or a meia-haste, flag at half mast.—alemã, the tetra ulreyi (*Hemigrammus ulreyi*), a small tropical fish.—desfraldada, unfurled flag.—em funeral, a flag draped with crape.—paulista, the small zebra fish (*Brachydanio rerio*). arriar—, (slang) to quit, give up. arriar a—, to strike the colors. continência à—, salute to the colors. hastear, or içar, a—, to raise the colors. pau (mastro, haste) de—, flagpole. rir a—s despregadas, to laugh uproariously.

bandeirante (m.) member of an armed band of early explorers in Brazil; (f.) a Girl Scout.

bandeirinha (f.) a streamer (little flag); (m., Soccer) linesman.

bandeirista (m.) railroad flagman.

bandeirola (f.) banderole, any small flag, pennant, or streamer; corn tassel.—de sinais, wigwag flag.

bandeja (f.) tray, salver; large winnowing fan.—d'água, lily pad.—de óleo, oil pan.—de tôrre, (Petrol.) bubble tray.

bandido (m.) bandit, outlaw, desperado.

banditismo (m.) banditry.

bando (m.) band, party, faction; bevy; crowd; gang (of loafers or evil-doers); flock; ban, proclamation.—de andorinhas, a cloud of swallows. Cf. BANDA.

bandola (f.) cartridge belt.

bandoleiro -ra (adj.) unstable, erratic, lazy; (m.) highwayman, bandit; liar; (f.) bandoleer, rifle sling. à—, slung over the shoulder and across the chest, as a rifle sling.

bandolim (m.) mandolin; also = ALBACORA (a fish).

bandolinista (m.,f.) mandolin player.

bandulho (m., colloq.) belly [= PANDULHO].

bandurra (f.) bandore (old guitar-like instrument).

bangalô (m.) bungalow.

bangue, bango (m.) hemp (*Cannabis sativa*); = CÂNHAMO.

bangüê (m.) stretcher, litter; sled, skid; handbarrow; sugar-mill furnace and boilers; an old-fashioned sugarmill, esp. one using animal power; a sugar plantation.

banguela (adj.; m.,f.) (person) having one or more front teeth missing, or of defective speech. [The term is derived from the name of a tribe of Portuguese West Africa—the Benguelas—many of whose members were shipped as slaves to Brazil. It was the custom of this tribe to knock out their children's front teeth.]

banguelê (m., colloq.) fracas, melee.

bangüêzeiro, -zista (m.) owner of a BANGÜÊ (sugar mill) in northeastern Brazil.

bangula (f.) fishing boat.

bangulê (m.) an obscene Negro song and dance.

banha (f.) animal fat, esp. lard; hair pomade.—de cheiro, perfumed lard used as a hair dressing.—de porco, lard. criar—, to grow fat, put on weight.

banhadal (m.) a large tract of low, wet land.

banhado -da (adj.) bathed; drenched.—em lágrimas, em sangue, steeped in tears, in blood; (m.) a grassy marsh, esp. one which remains green during the dry season; [GBAT: "a pool covered with vegetation."].

banhar (v.t.) to bathe, give a bath to; to drench; (v.r.) to bathe, take a bath.—se em água de rosas, to be very pleased with oneself.

banheira (f.) bathtub.

banheiro (m.) bathroom; a cattle-dipping trough.

banhista (m.,f.) sea-bather; person who takes the baths at a watering place; (slang) person who softsoaps another.

banho (m.) bath; bathing; (pl.) bath house, public baths; marriage banns.—alcalino, alkaline cleaning.—de ácido, acid bath.—de assento, a sitz bath.—de banheira, or de imersão, a tub bath.—de casamento, marriage banns. —de chumbo, lead coating.—de chuva, or de chuveiro, shower bath.—de estanho, tinning.—de mar, sea bathing.—de poeira, a spill (fall).—de zinco, zinc coating.— eletrolítico, electrolytic cleaning.—-maria, bain-marie; double-boiler.—parasiticida, cattle-dip; sheep-dip.— russo, steam bath. roupa de—, bathing suit.

baniano (m.) a banian or banya (Hindu trader); the banyan tree (*Ficus benghalensis*), c.a. FIGUEIRA-DE-BENGALA.

banimento (m.) banishment.

banir [25] (v.t.) to banish, expel, expatriate; to deport.

banível (adj.) deserving of banishment.

banja (f.) cheating at cards.

banjista (adj.) crooked; (m.) trickster, sharper.

banjo (m.) banjo.

banjoista (m.,f.) banjo player.

banqueiro (m.) banker; bank manager; dealer or banker (at gambling); (f.) bench.—de bicho, a bookmaker for the bicho game—see JÔGO DE BICHO.

banqueta [ê] (f.) a small desk or table; bench; footstool; banquette (firing step); the candles and crucifix on the altar; a small mining excavation.

banquete [ê] (m.) banquet, feast.

banqueteado -da (adj.) treated or honored with a banquet.

banqueteador -dora (adj.) banqueting; (m.,f.) banqueter.

banquetear (v.t.) to banquet, treat with a banquet or feast; (v.r.) to attend a banquet; to regale oneself with good food and drink.

banquisa (f.) ice-floe.

banto -ta (adj.; m.,f.) Bantu.

banza (f.), colloq.) fiddle; guitar.

banzado -da (adj.) startled, surprised.

banzar (v.t.) to startle, strike with wonder; (v.i.) to muse, ponder, reflect.

banzativo -va (adj.) pensive.

banzé (m., colloq.) tumult, affray, melee; row, rumpus; racket.—(de cuia) merrymaking, a noisy good time.

banzeiro -ra (adj.) somewhat disturbed (ref. to the sea); slow (ref. to a game such as poker); sad, blue; tipsy; (m.) a strong wind; turbulence; [GBAT: "a large wave or swell; undulatory motion in the water of a river, forming small waves; specifically, in Amazonas and Pará a wave stirred up by passage of the POROROCA."]

banzo -za (adj.) blue, low in spirits; (m.) the deep and sometimes fatal longing for their native land exhibited in the early days by the Negro slaves in Brazil; (pl.) handrails of a sedan chair or coffin; side rails of a bed or ladder.

baobá (m., Bot.) the baobab or monkey-bread-tree (*Adansonia digitata*).

baque (m.) a thud or thump; a fall; sudden disaster; misgiving; a flash or jiffy.—surdo, dull thud.

baquear (v.i.) to tumble, topple, plunk, plump, fall heavily; (v.t.) to convince; (v.r.) to prostrate oneself.

baqueano (m.) = TAPEJARA.

baquelita (f.), -te (m.) bakelite.

baquerubu [bú] (m.) = BACURUBU.

baqueta [ê] (f.) drumstick; umbrella rib.

baquetar, -tear (v.i.) to drum.

báquico -ca (adj.) bacchic.

baquiqui [kikí] (m.) a marine bivalve of southern Brazil— *Erodona mactroides* or *Azara labiata*.

baquista (m.,f.) bacchant.

baquité (m.) a kind of wicker basket carried on the back.

bar (m.) bar, barroom.

baraço (m.) cord, string; tie, lace; hangman's noose.

barafunda (f.) a noisy crowd; confusion, commotion, uproar; bedlam; clutter.

barafustar (v.i.) to struggle, flounder, writhe, twist.—por, to rush (dash) through (a door, etc.).

baralha (f.) the remainder of a deck after the first cards have been dealt; rack (gait of a horse).

baralhada (f.) confusion, uproar.

baralhador -dora (adj.) confusing; (m.,f.) shuffler (of cards); single-footer (horse).

baralhar (v.t.) to shuffle (cards); to jumble, clutter up, mix up; (v.i.) of a horse, to amble, pace; (v.r.) to get mixed up, become confused.

baralho (m.) a deck of cards.

barão (m.) baron. [Fem. BARONESA.]

barata (f.) see under BARATO.

baratão (m.) = BARBEIRO (insect).

baratar (v.t.) to cheapen.

barataria (f.) a giving with an eye to reward; a speculative or fraudulent enterprise; barter; barratry.

barateamento (m.) a dropping in price.

baratear (v.t.) to sell cheaper; to cut prices; to mis-prize, undervalue; (v.r.) to cheapen oneself.

barateiro –ra (adj.) cheap-selling; (m.,f.) a bargain-driver; (m.) a street vender of notions for dressmaking; the one who collects the "kitty" at a gambling establishment.

barateza [ê] (f.) cheapness.

baraticida (f.) cockroach poison.

baratinha (f.) a small roadster (automobile); (Bot.) a senna (Cassia fastuosa); (Zool.) a wood louse (Oniscus), c.a. TATUZINHO.

barato –ta (adj.) cheap, low-priced, inexpensive; by exten., easily had; (adv.) cheap(ly); (m.) the kitty or house percentage (at gambling); a boon; a concession. **dar de—**, to allow, admit, agree readily (without argument). **O—sai caro**, A cheap thing comes dear. (f.) any cockroach. [Of the approximately 100 species in Brazil, the most common are: Peri-planeta americana (a large flying species), Blatta orientalis (the so-called black beetle), and Blatella germanica (the Croton bug)]; a roadster; an old woman; a churn.—**-d'água**, any aquatic bug.—**de manteiga**, butter churn.—**-de-igreja** or—**-de-sacristia**, an inveterate church-goer, esp. an old woman.—**-descascada**, or—**-noiva**, a cockroach that is molting; as an epithet, an albino person.—**do-fígado**, a liver fluke (causing liver rot of cattle, sheep and swine).—**-do-mar**, a rock or water louse.—**-dos-coqueiros**, larva of a leaf beetle which infests coconut palms and injures their fruit. **ter sangue de—**, to be white-livered.

báratro (m.) bottomless pit, hell, abyss, depths.

baraúna (f., Bot.) the brauna, a prized Brazilian tree (Melanoxylon brauna—the only species—family Caesalpiniaceae) whose fine-grained, very hard wood is used for heavy-duty construction. Other common names are: BRAÚNA-PRETA, ÁRVORE-DA-CHUVA, GARAÚNA, GUARAÚNA, MUIRAÚNA, IBIRÁ-UNA, CANELA-AMARELA, MARIA-PRETA-DA-MATA, MARIA-PRETA-DO-CAMPO, PAROVAÚNA, RABO-DE-MACACO.

barba (f.) beard; (pl.) whiskers; baleen, whalebone; barbs of a feather.—**à americana**, old-fashioned under-chin whiskers (as formerly worn by New England fishermen).—**a barba (com)**, face to face (with).—**à inglêsa**, mutton chops (side whiskers).—**-azul**, (colloq.) a much-married man.—**cerrada**, a long thick beard.—**-de-barata**, the flowerforce poinciana (P. pulcherrima), c.a. BRIO-DE-ESTUDANTE, CHAGAS, CHAGUEIRA, FLÔR-DE-PAVÃO, FLÔR-DO-PARAÍSO.—**de bode**, a goat's beard, or one resembling it on a man.—**-de-bode**, any of various plants and grasses, such as: the queen-of-the-meadow (Filipendula ulmaria), c.a. ULMÁRIA, RAINHA-DOS-PRADOS; the creeping lovegrass (Eragrostis reptans); a flatsedge (Cyperus radiatus), c.a. CAPIM-CORTANTE, TIRIRICA-DO-CAMPO; a three-awn grass (Aristida pallens).—**-de-bode-de-vassoura** = CAPIM-RABO-DE-BURRO.—**de-cabra**, or **-de-paca**, the sylvan goatsbeard (ARUNCUS SYLVESTER), c.a. ARUNCO.—**-de-pau**, Spanish moss (Tillandsia usneoides), c.a.—**DE-VELHO**.—**de milho**, corn silk.—**de-surubim**, an orchid (Oncidium sprucei).—**de-velho**, a fennelflower (Nigella arvensis); the yellowsedge bluestem (Andropogon virginicus); a clematis (C. australis); Spanish moss, c.a.—**DE-PAU**, MUSGO-ESPANHOL.—**de-velho-verdadeira**, the bearded usnea (U. barbata).—**-jovis**, Jupiter's-beard anthyllis (A. barba-jovis), c.a. BARBAS-DE-JÚPITER.—**-ruiva**, in Brazilian folklore, a fantastic being resembling a tall white man with red hair and a red beard, who inhabits the waters of Paranaguá Lake in the State of Piauí, where he was cast as an infant by his mother. [He harms no one and does not speak but tries to kiss the women who come there to wash clothes.] **com a—por fazer**, needing a shave, unshaven. **fazer a—**, to shave or to get a shave. **fazer a—a** (or **em) um texto**, to polish a text. **ravalha de—**, razor. **pôr as—s de môlho**, to be on one's guard. **raspar a—**, to shave off one's beard. **um rapaz com—na cara**, a grown-

up boy. **ver-se à—com**, to be in difficulties with.

barbacã (f.) barbican, outpost; barbette.

barbaças (m.) full-bearded man; a graybeard.

barbada (f.) horse's lower lip; (slang) cinch, pushover.

barbadinho (m.) a (bearded) Capuchin monk; (Bot.) a tick-clover (Desmodium sp.)

barbado –da (adj.) bearded; (m.) a bearded man; a rooted cutting (for planting); a saki monkey, c.a. GUARIBA; a catfish (Pirinampus pirinampus);

barbalho (m.) a plant rootlet.

barbante (adj.) of poor quality; (m.) twine, string.

barbar (v.i.) to sprout (beard, rootlets).

Bárbara (f.) Barbara.

barbaria (f.) barbarousness.

barbaridade (f.) barbarity; cruelty, atrocity; crudity.

barbárie (f.) barbarism.

barbarismo (m.) in language, a barbarism.

barbarizar (v.t.) to barbarize; to corrupt (language).

bárbaro –ra (adj.) barbaric, barbarian; savage, cruel, inhuman; coarse, rude; (m.pl.) barbarians.

barbasco (m.) Webster: "any of various plants used by the Indians of Northern South America in making fish poison; also, the poison itself." Cf. VERBASCO, CALÇÃO-DE-VELHO.

barbatana (f.) fin of a fish; whalebone.

barbatimão (m.) the barbatimao alumbark tree (Stryphnodendron barbatimam).—**-de-fôlha-miúda** = FARINHA (a plant).

barbeação (f.) act of shaving.

barbear (v.t.,v.r.) to shave.

barbearia (f.) barber shop; barber's trade.

barbeiragem, –**beirice** (f.) wild or clumsy driving of an automobile, resulting in "close shaves".

barbeiro (m.) barber; a cold, cutting wind; an automobile driver who gives "close shaves" to pedestrians; (Zool.) the barber bug: a large, bloodsucking conenose bug (Conorhinus, syn. Triatoma, megistur) common in central Brazil. It transmits the trypanosome causing Chagas' disease. Some of many other common names are: BICHO-DE-PAREDE, BICHO-DE-CONCHA, BICHO-DO-MATO, GAUDÉRIO, FINCÃO, FURÃO, CHUPÃO, etc.

barbela (f.) dewlap; double chin; curb chain (of a bit); a barb.

barbete [ê] (m.) **barbeta** [ê] (f.) barbette.

barbiana (f.) a gangster's moll.

barbicacho (m.) a halter; a hindrance; chin strap.

barbicha (f.) a small, sparse, beard.

barbilhão (m.) wattle; barbel.

barbilho (m.) muzzle; impediment; fringe.

barbilongo –ga (adj.) long-bearded.

barbilouro –ra (adj.) yellow-bearded. Var. BARBILOIRO.

barbinegro –gra [ê] (adj.) blackbearded.

barbirrostro –tra [ó] (adj.) of birds, having bristles or hairs about the base of the bill.

barbirruivo –va (adj.) red-bearded; red-feathered.

barbiteso –sa [ê] (adj.) stiff-bearded; strong, stout.

barbitúrico –ca (adj., Chem.) barbituric.

barbo (m., Zool.) a barbel (Barbus sp.).

barbotina (f.) barbotine clay; slip.

barbudinho (m.) = RENDEIRA.

barbudo –da (adj.) heavily bearded.

barbula (f.) barbula (of a moss capsule); the genus Barbula of mosses; (pl.) barbules of a feather.

barbuzano (m.) ironwood.

barca (f.) bark, barge, lighter, ferry-boat.

barça (f.) a straw covering for packing glassware.

barcaça (f.) large barge; lighter; coastwise sailing vessel.

barcada (f.) a boatload.

barcagem (f.) a boatload; ferry fare.

barcarola (f.) barcarole.

barco (m.) any small open boat; any boat, vessel or ship. [GBAT: "A boat with an open hold, poop deck, two lateen sails, and a triangular foresail, used to ferry cattle to and from the Island of Marajó, with a carrying capacity of from fifty to a hundred head of cattle."].—**a motor**, motor boat.—**a vela**, sail boat.—**de remo**, row boat.—**salva-vidas**, lifeboat. **deixar correr o—**, to let things slide; to take things easy.

barda (f.) hedgerow; fence. **em—**, galore, in profusion.

bardana (f., Bot.) cotton burdock (Arctium tomentosum.]—**-maior**, the great burdock (Arctium lappa).—**-menor**, the smaller burdock, (Arctium minus), c.a. CARRAPICHO-GRANDE, PEGAMASSA, ERVA-DOS-PEGAMASSOS.

bardo (m.) bard; sheepfold; hedge; blockhead, booby.

barga (f.) straw hut; hammock; fishing net.

barganha (f.) barter, exchange; sharp bargain; a "deal," esp. a shady one; a swap. Var. BERGANHA.

barganhar (v.t.) to barter, trade, swap; to drive a shrewd bargain; to dicker. Var. BERGANHAR.

bargantaria (f.) crookedness; idleness.

bargante (m.) knave, rascal; a profligate.

bargantear (v.i.) to loaf; to live crookedly.

bária (f., Physics) bar.

baricêntrico -ca (adj.) barycentric.

baricentro (m.) barycenter, center of gravity.

bárico -ca (adj., Chem.) baric.

barifonia (f., Med.) baryphony.

barilito (m., Min.) barylite.

bário (m., Chem.) barium.

baririçó (m., Bot.) either of two spp. of Trimeza: T. juncifolia, c.a. BATATA-DE-PURGA, BATATINHA-DO-CAMPO, LÍRIO-ROXO-DO-CAMPO, RUIBARBO-DO-BREJO, or the Mexican trimeza (T. lurida) c.a. BATATINHA-AMARELA, MIRIRIÇÓ, CAPIM-REI.

barisfera (f., Geol.) barysphere.

barita (f., Chem.) baryta; (Min.) barite, heavy spar.

baritimia (f., Med.) barythymia, melancholia.

baritina, -tinita, -tita (f.) barite, heavy spar.

baritocalcito (m., Min.) barytocalcite.

barítono (m.) baritone (voice or singer).

barlaventear (v.i.) to sail against the wind.

barlaventejar (v.i.) to drift with the wind.

barlavento (m., Naut.) weather; windward side. a—, windward. [lee = SOTAVENTO.]

barnabita (m.) a Barnabite, member of an old religious order which has several educational institutions and seminaries in Brazil.

barociclonômetro (m., Meteorol.) barocyclonometer

barógrafo (m.) barograph.

barograma (m., Meteorol.) barogram.

barologia (f.) barology.

barométrico -ca (adj.) barometric.

barômetro (m.) barometer.—altimétrico, or orométrico, mountain barometer, orometer.—de sifão, siphon barometer.

baronato (m.) barony.

baronesa [ê] (f.) baroness; a water-lily, c.a. DAMA-DO-LAGO; (colloq.) = CACHAÇA; (pl.) lyre-shaped golden earrings.

baronete [ê] (m.) baronet.

baronia (f.) barony (domain of a baron).

baroscópio (m.) baroscope.

barotermógrafo (m.) barothermograph.

barquear (v.) = BARQUEJAR.

barqueiro (m.) boatman.

barquejar (v.i.) to steer a boat; to ride in one.

barquilha (f.) ship's log.

barquinha (f.) balloon basket; ship's log.

barquinho (m.) a small BARCO (boat).

barra (f.) bar (of iron, gold, soap, wood, etc.); a rod; a tiller; hem of a garment; a crude bedstead; bar of a harbor; sand bar; a band or stripe; (Heraldry) a diagonal band, crossing the field; gymnastic bar.—da saia, do vestido, hem of a skirt, of a dress.—de acoplamento, (Mach.) coupling rod.—de engate, or de tração, (R.R.) drawbar.—do tribunal, bar of the court.—fixa, horizontal bar (for gymnastics). ouro em—, gold ingot. uma—azul, a blue stripe or band. vir à—, to appear before the bar (of justice or of public opinion).

barraca (f.) tent; hut; shed; tool shed; a large shed or warehouse.—de feira, market stall.—de lona, canvas tent.—militar, Army tent. armar—s, to pitch tents. desarmar—s, to strike camp.

barracão (m.) a large shed or tent; an awning; a trading post. [GBAT: "(1) a large BARRACA; a bungalow of hardwood with tiles for door and window frames; (2) a tool shed; (3) a store in a sparsely settled locality; (4) an awning of sailcloth for protection from rain; (5) in Pará, a cottage or house thatched with straw; (6) on rubber plantations, the owner's house."]

barraco (m.) crude wooden hut.

barracuda (f.) = BICUDA.

barrado -da (adj.) mud-covered.

barra-fogo (m.) = CAGA-FOGO (a bee).

barragem (f.) a river barrier or dam; fish weir; any barrier; artillery barrage.

barranceira (f.) ravine.

barranco (m.) gully, ravine; steep bank; barricade, bar-

rier. [GBAT: "(1) a gully, steep river bank, or cliff; (2) the earthen facing of the wall of a dwelling; (3) an island composed of grass which floats down the rivers on the winter freshets."] aos trancos e—s, by fits and starts.

barrancoso -sa (adj.) full of gullies.

barranqueira (f.) = BARRANCEIRA.

barrão (m.) boar, esp. one selected for reproduction [= VARRÃO, VARRASCO].

barraquim (m.), -quinha (f.) a small tent or market stall.

barraquista (m.) rubber planter or trader.

barrar (v.t.) to bar, obstruct, shut out; to make into bars; to daub, cover, coat, spread, smear (as with plaster, mud, butter, etc.).

barrear (v.t.) to daub with BARRO (mud).

barregã (f.) kept woman.

barregana (f.) barracan (a coarse fabric).

barregão (m.) cohabiter with a mistress.

barregar (v.t.,v.i.) to shout.

barreira (f.) bar, barrier, barricade, stockade; obstacle, hindrance; hurdle; toll gate; clay pit; a large gully or ravine; an eroded river bank revealing varicolored strata; (pl.) caves and potholes along the seashore; water springs.—de calor, heat barrier (of jet flying). corrida de—s, hurdle race.

barreiro (m.) clay pit; natural salt lick.

barrela (f.) a solution of lye [= LIXÍVIA]; cleaning; hoax, deception.

barreleiro (m.) lye ashes.

barrenhão (m.) a large pan or basin.

barrento -ta (adj.) muddy; mud-colored.

barretada (f.) a lifting of one's cap or hat to another person.

barrete [ê] (m.) cap, skull cap, nightcap; a cleric's biretta; (Zool.) reticulum.—-de-padre, a bush pumpkin (Cucurbita pepo melopepo).

barretear (v.t.) to cast (metal) into ingots.

barretina (f.) a shako (military headdress).

barrica (f.) keg, small barrel.

barricada (f.) barricade.

barricar (v.t.) to barricade.

barriga (f.) belly, paunch, stomach, abdomen; a bulge or swelling; a sag; (slang) a news story which is published as a scoop but which turns out to be false.—cabeluda, the three-spot gourami (Trichogaster trichopterus) frequently seen in home aquaria.—d'água, abdominal dropsy.—da perna, calf of the leg. de—para o ar, belly-up. estar de—, (slang) to be big with child. fazer—, to bulge out.

barriga-verde (m.,f.) a nickname applied to natives of the State of Santa Catarina.

barrigada (f.) a bellyful; a litter (of pups, etc.); guts of slaughtered cattle.—s de riso, belly-laughs.

barriguda (f.) see BARRIGUDO.

barrigudinho (m.) any of numerous viviparous top minnows of the family Poeciliidae, including the guppy (Lesbistes) and the mosquito fish (Gambusia). Some other common names are: BOBÓ, BARRIGUDO, COSPE-COSPE, GARGAU, GUARU.

barrigudo -da (adj.) potbellied, paunchy; (colloq.) big with child; (f., Bot.) any of various floss-silktrees (esp. Chorisia insignis and C. ventricosa) whose big-bellied trunks give them the appearance of gigantic radishes; other names for them are: ÁRVORE-DE-LÃ, CASTANHA-DO-CEARÁ, PAINEIRA; (m.) any of various large woolly, fat-bellied, prehensile-tailed, easily-tamed monkeys, genus Lagothrix, of northern Brazil; also = BARRIGUDINHO (minnow).

barrigueira (f.) girth, cinch (of saddle or pack).

barril [-ris] (m.) barrel, cask, drum.

barrilete [ê] (m.) keg; carpenter's clamp; bench hook; (Zool.) any member of the genus Doliolum.

barrilha (f.) barilla (an impure sodium carbonate made from the ashes of the BARRILHEIRA).

barrilheira (f.) saltwort or Russian thistle (Salsola), used in the manufacture of barilla (soda ash).

barrir [25] (v.i.) to trumpet (as an elephant).

barro (m.) clay; clay mortar; mud; (pl.) facial pimples.

barroca (f.) gully, gorge; hole in the ground.

barroco -ca [rô] (adj.) baroque, rococo; grotesque, extravagant; (m.) an irregularly-shaped pearl; a work of art abounding in extremes or irregularities; a baroque style of architecture.

barroso -sa (adj.) clayey, muddy; pimply.

barrote (m.) a small piece of timber; a stud or scantling; a rafter.

baru [ú] (*m., Bot.*) a tonkabean (*Dipteryx sp.*).

barulhada, –lheira (*f.*) din, loud noise, confusion, uproar.

barulheiro –ra, –lhento –ta (*adj.*) noisy, vociferous, boisterous, clamorous; turbulent, obstreperous, factious; disorderly, rowdy; (*m.,f.*) such a person.

barulho (*m.*) noise, clamor, din, blare, hubbub, racket; brawl, quarrel, disturbance, row, rumpus. fazer—, to kick up a fuss; to make a noise.

barulhoso –sa (*adj.*) noisy.

basáltico –ca (*adj.*) basaltic.

basaltiforme (*adj.*) basaltiform, columnar.

basalto (*m., Petrog.*) basalt.

basanita (*f., Min.,*) touchstone; (*Petrog.*) basanite.

basbaque (*m.*) simpleton, nincompoop; "sucker".

basbaquice (*f.*) manners of a simpleton.

basco –ca (*adj.; m.,f.*) Basque [= VASCONÇO].

báscula (*f.*) steelyard, scale beam.

basculante (*m.*) dump truck.

basculhar (*v.*) & derivs. = VASCULHAR & derivs.

básculo (*m.*) a bascule bridge.

base (*f.*) base, basis, support, foundation.—de aviação, air base.—de operações, base of operations.—naval, naval base. de—, basic, fundamental.

baseado –da (*adj.*) based; firm, fixed; (*m.*) marihuana leaves [= DIAMBA].

basear (*v.t.*) to base (em, on, upon); to sustain, support; (*v.r.*) to base oneself (em, on, upon).

basicidade (*f., Chem.*) basicity.

básico –ca (*adj.*) basic; (*Chem., Metal., Petrog.*) basic.

basídio (*m., Bot.*) basidium.

basidiospório (*m., Bot.*) basidiospore,

basificação (*f., Chem.*) basification.

basificador –dora (*adj., Chem.*) base-forming.

basificar (*v.t., Chem.*) to basify.

basilar (*adj.*) basilar, basal, fundamental.

basílica (*f.*) basilica.

basilicão (*m., Pharm.*) basilicon (an ointment).

basílico –ca (*adj., Anat.*) veia—, basilic vein; (*m., Bot.*) basil; (*m.pl.*) the Greek Basilicae.—-grande = ALFAVACA CHEIROSA (sweet basil).

basilisco (*m.*) basilisk (fabled reptile); also, any tropical lizard of the genus Basiliscus.

basílise (*f., Med.*) basilysis, basiotripsy.

básio (*m., Craniol.*) basion.

basiótribo (*m., Med.*) basiotribe.

basiotripsia (*f., Med.*) basiotripsy.

basofilia (*f., Med.*) basophilia.

basófilo (*m., Biol.*) basophile.

basquetebol [-bóis] (*m.*) basketball [= CESTOBOL].

bassorina (*f., Chem.*) bassorin.

basta (*f.*) a tufting stitch (in mattress-making); (*interj.*) Stop! That's enough! Pooh! Fiddlesticks!—de tolices! Enough of nonsense!

bastamente (*adv.*) thickly; amply.

bastante (*adj.*) enough, sufficient, plenty, ample; (*adv.*) sufficiently, quite.

bastantíssimo –ma (*absol. superl. of* BASTANTE) greatly sufficient, more than enough.

bastão (*m.*) club; cane; baton; stick (of dynamite, candy, (etc.); (*Chem.*) glass rod.—-de-são-jorge = SANSEVIÉRIA. —-de-são-josé = PALMA-DE-SÃO-JOSÉ.

bastar (*v.i.*) to suffice, be enough.—-se a si próprio, to be self-sufficient. A bom entendedor meia palavra basta, A word to the wise is sufficient.

bastardão (*m.*) a bastard-cut file.

bastardia, –dice (*f.*) bastardy, illegitimacy.

bastardinha (*f.*) a second- or smooth-cut file.

bastardinho (*m.*) a certain cursive type face.

bastardo –da (*adj.; m.,f.*) bastard.

bastecer (*v.*) & derivs. = ABASTECER & derivs.

bastião (*m.*) bastion; also = TROPEIRO (a bird).

bastida (*f.*) palisade.

bastidão (*f.*) thickness, density.

bastidor [-es] (*m.*) an embroidery frame; (*pl.*) stage wings; inside information (about politics, etc.).

bastilha (*f.*) bastille.

basto –ta (*adj.*) thick, thickset; abundant, numerous.

bastonada (*f.*) bastinado, cudgeling, drubbing.

bastonete [nê] (*m.*) a small rod.

bata (*f.*) dressing gown, Mother Hubbard; duster; smock.

batalha (*f.*) battle, fight, struggle.—naval, naval battle. —perdida, a losing fight.—sêca, mock battle. campo de—, battlefield. cavalo-de—, the main argument.

batalhador –dora (*adj.*) battling, fighting; (*m.,f.*) battler, fighter.

batalhão (*m.*) battalion; (*colloq.*) a house-raising or other "bee".

batalhar (*v.i.*) to do battle, fight, struggle (contra, against); to argue, plead (com, with).

batata (*f.*) potato; an asininity; a solecism.—-brava = ABUTUA-DE-BATATA, ABUTUA-GRANDE.—da perna, calf of the leg [= PANTURRILHA].—-da-praia, the soilbind morning-glory (*Ipomoea pes-caprae*).—-de-purga, jalap (*Exogonium purga*), c.a. JALAPA-DE-LISBOA; also = BARI-RIÇÓ.—-doce, sweet potato (*Ipomoea batatas*), c.a. BATATA-DA-TERRA, JETICA, MUNHATA.—-do-inferno, tartago nettlespurge (*Jatropha podagrica*), c.a. BATATA-DE-MAR, a morning-glory (*Ipomoea maritima*), c.a. SALVA-DO-MAR. —-do-rio, Argentine Amazonvine (*Stigmaphylla littorale*). —-inglêsa, common white or Irish potoato (*Solanum tuberosum*), c.a. BATATINHA.—-ôvo, a dayflower (*Commerlina robusta*); (*Zool.*) either of two fishes closely related to the tilefish: *Lopholatilus villarii* and *Caulolatilus chrysops* (the blanquillo), c.a. BATATA-DA-PEDRA. Êle diz as coisas na—, (*slang*) He says what he means, calls a spade a spade. Êle é alí na—, (*slang*) He doesn't beat about the bush.

batatada (*f.*) a confection made from sweet potatoes; a string of solecisms.

batatal (*m.*) a potato field. É—! (*slang*) It can't miss!

batatão (*m.*) = BOITATÁ.

batatarana (*f.*) the seashore cowpea (*Vigna marina*).

bateira (*f.*) potato plant.

batateiral (*m.*) = BATATAL.

batateiro –ra (*adj.*) fond of potatoes; given to uttering solecisms; (*m.*) potato plant; potato plantar.

batatinha (*f.*) the common white potato.—-amarela = AÇAFRÃO-DA-ÍNDIA, BARIRIÇÓ.—-d'água, the Herbert cypella (*C. herberti*), c.a. BATATINHA-PURGATIVA, RUIBARBO-DO-CAMPO, VARETA; also = BARIRIÇÓ, CIPÓ-MIL-HOMENS.

batatudo –da (*adj.*) big and shaped like a potato (referring esp. to noses).

batavo –va [tá] (*adj.; m.,f.*) Batavian.

bateador (*m.*) one who pans for gold.

batear (*v.t.*) to pan sand and gravel for gold and diamonds.

bate-bate (*m.*) a striking or knocking together; beating, thrashing; (*slang*) a cocktail.

bate-bôca (*m.*) squabble, war of words.

bate-bola (*m., Soccer*) practice play.

bate-chinela (*m.*) shindig, breakdown, hoedown.

bate-cu [ú] (*m.*) a prat fall; a slap on the rump.

batecum (*m.*) = BATICUM.

batedeira (*f.*) beater; thresher; churn; hog cholera.—de ovos, egg beater.—elétrica, electric mixer.

batedela (*f.*) = BATEDURA.

batedor –dora (*adj.*) beating; (*m.*) beater; pulp beater; scout; outrider; (*m.pl.*) a mounted escort.—de carteira, pickpocket.—de estrada, military scout.

batedouro, –doiro (*m.*) a place at water's edge where clothes are washed and beaten on a rock.

batedura (*f.*) act of beating, striking, etc. See the verb BATER.

bateeiro [e-ei] (*m.*) a prospector who uses a BATEIA (pan) to wash sand and gravel for gold or diamonds.

bate-estacas (*m.*) pile driver.

bate-fôlha (*m.*) gold beater; tinsmith.

bátega (*f.*) sudden, heavy downpour.—de saraiva, hailstorm.

bateia (*f.*) a wooden trough or pan for washing gold- or diamond-bearing sand and gravel.

bateira (*f.*) a flat-bottomed boat.

batel [-téis] (*m.*) a small boat or canoe.

batelada (*f.*) a boatload; a batch.

batelão (*m.*) a heavy barge or lighter. [GBAT: "A large boat, displacing from three to ten tons, propelled by poles, oars or sails and often towed by motor launch."]

bateleiro (*m.*) bargeman.

batente (*adj.*) beating; knocking; (*m.*) doorpost, jamb; door knocker; one of the halves of a double door; bumper; batten of a loom; monkey of a pile driver; (*slang*) the job at which one earns a living.

bate-orelha (*m.*) donkey; by exten., stupid person.

bate-papo (*m.*) chat, friendly discourse.

bate-pé (*m.*) a country dance, hoedown, shindig.

bater (*v.t.*) to beat, strike, knock, hit, thump, bump, bang;

to whack, whip; to pound, batter, dash against; to defeat; (*v.i.*) to beat; to throb; to knock. (*v.r.*) to fight (**por**, for; **contra**, against).—**em**, to lay blows upon, to whip, strike.—**bôca**, to gab, chatter, jabber.—**a bota**, or **a caçoleta**, or **o trinta-e-um** (*all slang*) to kick the bucket (die).—**a estrada**, to beat the highways and byways; to search the countryside.—**a linda plumagem**, to fly away, disappear.—**a**, or **em, outra porta**, to turn elsewhere (for help).—**a porta**, to slam the door.—**à(s) porta(s) de**, to knock at the door of (charity, justice, etc.).—**a todas as portas**, to knock at every door (for help).—**a quilha**, to lay the keel of a vessel.—**as asas**, to fly away; to flee.—**bola**, (*Soccer*) to practice kicking the ball.—**carteira**, to pickpocket.—**com a cabeça pelas paredes**, to act crazily, as by striking one's head against the wall.—**com os costados no xadrez**, to land in the hoosegow.—**contra a parede**, to run into a wall.—**-de-asas**, (*noun*) wing-flapping.—**de chapa**, to strike full upon.—**em retirada**, to beat a retreat.—**horas**, (of a clock) to strike the hour.—**moeda**, to strike off coins.—**no peito**, to beat one's breast (in repentance).—**o compasso**, to beat time.—**o ferro enquanto está quente**, to strike while the iron is hot.—**o pé**, to stand pat, refuse to budge.—**o queixo**, or **os dentes**, to chatter with cold or fear.—**os calcanhares**, to click the heels.—**ovos**, to beat (whip) eggs.—**palmas**, to clap the hands.—**prego sem estôpa**, to take a leap in the dark.—**-se em duelo**, to fight a duel.—**-se para (algum lugar)**, to "beat it" (hurry) towards some place.—**sempre na mesma tecla**, to harp on the same string.—**uma chapa**, or **um flagrante**, (*colloq.*) to snap a picture.—**(um) papo**, to chew the fat. **Água mole em pedra dura tanto bate até que fura**, Constant dripping bores the stone. **Aí é que bate o ponto**, There's the rub.

bateria (*f.*) battery (of guns); electric battery; the percussion instruments in a band; the drummer himself. [*GBAT*: "A process of rubber extraction using an arrangement on each tree of multiple tin cups in which the latex is collected."]—**de acumuladores**, storage battery. —**de alta tensão**, high-tension battery.—**de cozinha**, a set of kitchenware.—**de longo alcance**, long-range battery.—**de pilhas sêcas**, dry battery. **assestar as—s**, to train guns on a target; fig., to lay one's plans.

bate-testa (*m.*) = CAMAPU.

batianestesia (*f.*, *Med.*) bathyanesthesia.

baticum (*m.*) the sound of handclapping and footstamping, as in a clog dance; any stamping, clattering, pounding noise; a pounding of the heart; an altercation.

batido –**da** (*adj.*) beaten; hackneyed, trite, "corny". **dar-se por**—, to admit defeat, quit, give up; (*f.*) act of beating; beat, rap; a beating of woods to flush game; a severe reprimand; a beaten path; a cocktail made of rum, lemon juice and sugar; (*Physics*, *Radio*) beat.— **das horas**, the striking of the hour.—**do relógio**, the striking of the clock. **dar uma—no mato**, to beat the woods. **de**—, hastily (retreating).

batimento (*m.*) beat; collision.—**cardíaco**, heartbeat.

batimetria (*f.*) = BATOMETRIA.

batina (*f.*) cassock; academic gown.

batisfera (*f.*) bathysphere.

batismal (*adj.*) baptismal. **pia**—, baptismal font.

batismo (*m.*) baptism; christening; (*colloq.*) watering of milk or wine.—**de fogo**, baptism of fire.—**de sangue**, blood bath.

batista (*adj.*; *m.*,*f.*) Baptist; (*f.*) batiste (delicate cotton fabric).

batistério (*m.*) baptistery.

batité (*m.*) = CATETE (corn.)

batizado –**da** (*adj.*) baptized, christened; (of wine or milk), diluted; (*m.*) a christening (-party).

batizando –**da** (*m.*,*f.*) the one to be (or being) baptized or christened.

batizar (*v.t.*) to baptize, christen; to water, dilute (wine, milk, etc.).

batimótropo –**pa** (*adj.*; *Physiol.*) bathmotropic.

batocar (*v.t.*) to plug (a hole) with a bung.

batocrômio (*m.*, *Chem.*, *Dyes*) bathochrome.

batólito (*m.*, *Geol.*) batholith.

batom (*m.*) lipstick.

batometria (*f.*) bathymetry.

batoque (*m.*) bung; bunghole; spigot; labret (savage lip ornament); earmark (of an animal); (*colloq.*) a squat person; (*pl.*) young fighting-cock's spurs. Cf. BOTOQUE.

batota (*f.*) act of cheating; fraud; skin game, swindle,

bunco, gyp; gambling.

batot[e]ar (*v.t.*) to cheat, defraud, swindle.

batoteiro –**ra** (*adj.*) crooked; (*m.*) cheat, sharper, gyp artist; cardsharp.

batracóide (*adj.*, *Zool.*) batrachoid.

batracoplastia (*f.*, *Surg.*) batrachoplasty.

batráquios (*m.pl.*) the Batrachia or Amphibia (frog, toads, salamanders, newts, etc.).

batucada (*f.*) the rhythm or chant of the BATUQUE.

batucador (*m.*) a poor piano player.

batucar (*v.i.*) to dance the BATUQUE; to hammer, make noise, beat time; to bang on the piano.

batuíra (*f.*) the common name for any of a number of shore birds, esp. the following: the American oyster catcher (*Haematopus ostralegus palliatus*), c.a. BATUÍRA-DO-MAR-GROSSO, BAIAGU, PIRU-PIRU; the upland plover (*Bartramia longicauda*), c.a. BATUÍRA-DO-CAMPO; the white-rumped sandpiper (*Erolia fuscicollis*), c.a. MAÇARI-QUINHO; the Paraguayan snipe (*Capella p. paraguaiae*), c.a. NARCEJA, NARCEJINHA.—**-do-campo**, the American golden plover (*Pluvialis p. dominica*), c.a. BATUIRUÇU, MAÇARICO.

batumado –**da** (*adj.*) kinky [hair].

batuque (*m.*) hammering, banging; a song-and-dance with stomping and hand-clapping; a hoedown.

batuqueiro (*m.*) a bird—the black-throated saltator (*Saltator atricollis*).

batuquira (*f.*) = JAPACANIM.

batuta (*f.*) baton (of an orchestra leader); wand; (*m.*) a person skilled at anything; (*adj.*) smart, clever.

baú (*m.*) an old-fashioned round-topped trunk; a species of box crab.—**de segredos**, a confidant.

bauínia (*f.*, *Bot.*) the genus Bauhinia. Cf. MORORÓ.

bauleiro [a–u] (*m.*) a maker of trunks.

baúna (*m.*) any of various fishes of the genus Serranus; the dog snapper (*Lutianus jocu*).

baunilha (*f.*) vanilla.—**-do-peru**, common heliotrope (*Heliotropium arborescens*), c.a. FLOR-DE-BAUNILHA, HELIOTRÓPIO.—**-falsa**, an orchid .(*Maxillaria picta*).

baunilhão (*m.*) an orchid (*Vanilla grandiflora*).

baunilhazinha (*f.*) either of two Brazilian orchids: *Sobralia pubescens* or *Selenipedium isabelianum*.

bauxita (*f.*) bauxite, aluminum ore.

bávaro –**ra** (*adj.*; *m.*,*f.*) Bavarian.

bazar (*m.*) bazaar; store.

bazófia (*f.*) vainglory; brag, swagger, "hot air".

bazofiador –**dora** (*adj.*) bragging, swaggering; (*m.*) braggart.

bazofiar (*v.i.*) to boast, brag; to show off; to blow one's own horn.

bazófio (*m.*) boaster.

bazuca (*f.*, *Milit.*) bazooka.

bazulaque (*m.*) a stew made of liver and lights; a short fat man; a Braz. sweet made of coconut and honey.

B.B. = BOMBORDO (larboard, port).

bdélio (*m.*) bdellium, a gum resin.

bê-a-bá (*m.*) the alphabet; the ABC's of anything.

beata (*f.*) a very devout woman; one who has been beatified; also, one who feigns devoutness, hypocrite.

beatão (*m.*, *colloq.*) a pious fraud [= SANTARRÃO].

beataria (*f.*), –**tério** (*m.*) bigots; bigotry; hypocrisy.

beatice (*f.*) bigotry; religious hypocrisy.

beatificação (*f.*) beatification.

beatificado –**da** (*adj.*) blissful; beatified.

beatificar (*v.t.*) to beatify.

beatífico –**ca** (*adj.*) beatific.

beatilha (*f.*) a nun's white veil, or the cloth from which it is made.

beatinha (*f.*) a scorpene (spiny-finned marine fish). c.a. MANGANGÁ, BEATRIZ.

beatitude (*f.*) beatitude; blessedness, bliss.

beato –**ta** (*adj.*) blissful; overly devout; sanctimonious; bigoted, fanatic; (*m.*) a very devout man; one who has been beatified; a loose thread. Cf. BEATA.

beatona (*f.*) a sanctimonious woman.

beatorro [tô] (*m.*) a pious fraud.

beatriz (*f.*) = BEATINHA (a fish); [*cap.*] Beatrice.

bebaça, –**ço** (*m.*) drunkard, tippler.

bêbado –**da** (*adj.*; *m.*,*f.*) = BÊBEDO.

bebê (*m.*) baby; doll.

bebedeira (*f.*) a drunken spree, binge. **caír na**—, to get drunk. **cozinhar a**—, to sober up after drinking. **estar de**—, to be drunk. **tomar uma**—, to go on a spree.

bebedice (*f.*) drunkenness.

bêbedo –da (adj.) drunk(en); (m.) drunkard, sot. Var. BÊBADO.

bebedor -dora (adj.) given to drink; (m.,f.) hard drinker.

bebedouro, -doiro (m.) drinking fountain; watering trough.

bebeeru [e-erú] (m.) = BEBERU.

beber (v.t.) to drink; imbibe; to drink in, absorb; to take a drink.—à saúde de, to drink to the health of.—como um gambá, to drink like a fish.—do fino, to be on the inside (in politics or important matters).—os ares, to drool over someone. Assinar e—não se faz sem ver, Look before you leap; Investigate before you invest. comer e—, to eat and drink. dar de—a, to give a drink (of water) to. dar para—, to take to drink.

beberagem (f.) medicinal brew or potion (c.a. MIXI-LANGA); unpleasant drink; bran mash for horses, etc.

bebêres (m.pl.) the drinks. Cf. BEBES.

bebericar (v.i.) to tipple.

beberrão -rona (adj.) hard-drinking; (m.) drunkard, sot, toper, tosspot, boozer; (f.) a hard-drinking woman.

beberraz (adj.) addicted to drink; hard-drinking.

bebericar (v.) = BEBERICAR.

beberu [ú] (m., Bot.) the bebeeru or greenheart ocotea (O. rodioei), an evergreen So. Amer. tree, whose hard durable wood is prized for shipbuilding and other heavy construction. Its bark yields bebeerine, a substitute for quinine. Other common names for the tree are: BEBEERU, BIBIRU, CANELA-LIMÃO, CORAÇÃO-VERDE, ITAÚBA-BRANCA.

bebes (m.pl.) the drinks, os comes e—, the eats and drinks. Cf. BEBERES.

bebida (f.) drink, beverage; drinking-place. dar-se, or entregar-se, à—, to take to drink.—gasosa, soda water, soft drink.

bebível (adj.) potable.

beca (f.) judge's robe; academic gown.

becabunga (f., Bot.) limewort (Veronica beccabunga).

bechamel (m.) béchamel sauce.

beco [ê] (m.) alley, side street.—sem saída, blind alley; fig., a tight spot, difficult situation, dilemma, deadlock, stalemate. desinfetar, or desocupar, o—, (colloq.) to die; to go away.

bedame (f.) sculptor's or stonecutter's chisel; turner's chisel; mortise chisel; cape chisel.

bedegüeba (m., colloq.) boss; chief.

bedel [déis] (m.) university beadle.

bedelhar (v.t.) to stick one's nose in, intrude; to chew the rag.

bedelho [ê] (m.) door bolt; a youngster. meter o—em negócios alheios, to stick one's nose into the affairs of others.

beduíno (m.) Bedouin.

bege (adj.) beige.

begônia (f., Bot.) the genus Begonia.—-de-fôlha-estreita is B. salicifolia.—-real, the rex or Assam king begonia (B. rex).—-sangue is B. sanguinea, c.a. ERVA-DE-SAPO-VERMELHA.

beguaba, -guava (f.) a wedge shell of So. Brazil (Donax hanleyanus), c.a. PEGUABA, PEGUAVA, PEGUIRA, BEGUIRA.

beguina (f., R.C.Ch.) a Beguine.

beguino (m., R.C.Ch.) a Beghard, mendicant friar.

behaviorismo (m., Psychol.) behaviorism.

bei (m.) bey.

beiçada (f.) thick lips; animal's lips.

beiçarrão (m.) big lip.

beicinho (m.) little lip; pout, pique. fazer—, to pout.

beiço (m.) lip.—-de-lebre, hare lip [= LÁBIO LEPORINO]. —-de-negra, (Bot.) a pipewort (Eriocaulon baginatum). —s de alguidar, very thick, out-turned lips. lamber os—s to lick one's lips (in anticipation). morder os—s, to bite one's lips (in chagrin). passar o—, (slang) to cheat, trick, swindle. trazer alguém pelo—, to lead someone by the nose.

beiçola (adj.) big-lipped; (m.) big lip; (m.,f.) big-lipped person.

beiçudo –da (adj.) thick-lipped.

beija (f.) the ceremony of kissing images in church.

beijado –da (adj.) kissed; spoiled with kisses. de mão—, gratuitously, for nothing.

beijador -dora (adj.) kissing; (m.,f.) kisser.

beija-flor [beija-flôres] (m.) any of numerous humming-birds, other common names for which are: COLIBRI, GUAINUMBI, PICA-FLOR, CHUPA-FLOR, CUITELO. The most common species are:—-besouro, amethyst humming-bird (Calliphlox amethystina).—-d'água is not a hum-

mingbird but the spot-tailed jacamar (Galbula rufo-viridis).—-de-bico-vermelho, the glittering emerald hummingbird (Chlorostilbon aureoventris) of southwestern Brazil; the taquara emerald (C. aureoventis egregius) of southern Brazil, and Pucheran's emerald (C. aureoventris pucherani) of eastern and central Brazil.—-de-chifre, the sun gem (Heliactin bilophum).—-de-coleira, the frilled coquette (Lophornis magnificus) and the festive coquette (L. chalybeus), both of southern Brazil; the tufted coquette (L. ornatus) of Amazon and Guiana; Gould's coquette (L. gouldi) of central and northeastern Brazil.—-de-penacho, Loddiges' plover-crest humming-bird (Stephanoxis loddigesi) of southern Brazil.—-de-rabo-branco, Petre's hermit (Phaethornis pretrii) and the Brazilian hermit (P. eurynome).—-do-papo-branco, the Brazilian white-throat (Leucochloris albicollis), very common in Rio de Janeiro.—-dourado, a sapphire (Hylocharis spp.).—-grande, a swallow-tail (Eupepto-mena macroura simone); also the black-breasted jacamar (Brachygalba melanosterna) which is not a hummingbird. —-prêto, the Brazilian swallow-tail (Eupeptomena m. macroura), c.a. BEIJA-FLOR-CAUDA-DE-ANDORINHA; also the dusky Jacobin (Melanotrochilus fuscus).—-vermelho, the widely distributed ruby-and-topaz hummingbird (Chrysolampis elatus), c.a. BEIJA-FLOR-CABEÇA-DE-FOGO. —-xerém, the tiny hairy hermit (Glaucis h. hirsuta), perhaps the smallest bird in the world.

beija-mão (m.) hand-kissing.

beija-pé (m.) foot-kissing (religious ceremony).

beijar (v.t.) to kiss; to touch with the lips· to touch (anything) lightly, gently.—o chão, to kiss the floor (fall down); (v.r.) to kiss one another.

beijinho (m.) a little kiss; the finest or choicest of any-thing.

beijo (m.) kiss.—-de-frade, the touch-me-not or garden balsam (Impatiens balsamina or I. noli-me-tangere), c.a. NÃO-ME-TOQUES, BALSAMO-DE-JARDIM.—de Judas, a Judas kiss.—-de-moça, candy kiss; (Bot.) the common cosmos (C. bipinnatus).—-de-palmas = CRISTA-DE-GALO. —-de-sinhá, a kind of small sweet cake.—s-de-freira, (Bot.) rose campion, mullein pink (Lychnis coronaria), c.a. CANDELÁRIA-DOS-JARDINS, ORELHA-DE-LEBRE. um—chocho, a perfunctory kiss.

beijoca (f.) a smack (loud kiss).

beijocar (v.t.) to kiss long, loud and often.

beijoqueiro -ra (adj.) fond of kissing

beiju [ú] (m.) a confection made of tapioca, c.a. MIAPATA, MAL-CASADO; a kind of wasp.

beijucaba (f.) = MARIMBONDO-DE-CHAPÉU.

beijupirá (m.) a sergeant fish (Rachycentron canadus). Var. BIJUPIRÁ.

beira (f.) edge, border, rim, brim, brink, margin.—do telhado, eaves. à—de, near, by, alongside of; on the verge of; at the edge of (a forest, the sea, etc.). à—do abismo, on the brink of ruin.

beirada (f.) edge, border, margin; eaves; environs.

beiradeiro (m.) a riverside dweller.

beirado, beiral (m.) roof-edge, eaves.

beira-mar (f.) seashore, seaside.

beirar (v.t.) to skirt; to lie or move along the edge of.—os quarenta, to be nearing forty (years of age).

beisbol (m.) baseball.

beiupirá (m.) = BIJUPIRÁ.

bejuco-amargo (m.) = ABUTUA.

bejupirá (m.) = BIJUPIRÁ.

B.el = BACHAREL (Bachelor).

bel, poetical form of belo.

bela (f.) a belle. A—Adormecida, Sleeping Beauty. A—e a Fera, Beauty and the Beast.

belacíssimo -ma (absol. superl. of BELICOSO) most war-iike.

belaco-caspi (m., Bot.) a frangipani (Plumeria floribunda).

beladona (f.) belladonna, the deadly nightshade (Atropa belladonna).—-dos-italianos, the queen's amaryllis (A. reginae).

beladônio (m.) belladonna extract.

bela-emília (f.) the Cape plumbago (P. capensis), c.a. DENTILÁRIA-DO-CABO, JASMIM-AZUL.

bela-luíza (f.) = LÚCIA-LIMA.

bela-luz (f.) mastic thyme (Thymus mastichina).

bela-margarida (f.) English daisy (Bellis perennis), c.a. BONINA, MÃE-DE-FAMÍLIA, MARGARITA.

bela-maria (f., Bot.) a plumbago (P. grandiflora).

belamente (adv.) beautifully; very well indeed; perfectly.

belas-artes (*f.pl.*) beaux-arts, fine arts.
belas-letras (*f.pl*). belles-lettres.
belbute (*m.*), **belbutina** (*f.*) cotton velvet, velveteen.
belchior [ór] (*m.*) junkman, second-hand dealer.
beldade (*f.*) a beauty, a belle.
beldosa [ó] (*f.*) floor tile.
beldroega (*f., Bot.*) the common purslane (*Portulaca oleracea*), c.a. BELDROEGA-PEQUENA, BELDROEGA-VERDADEIRA, CAAPONGA, ORA-PRO-NOBIS;—da-praia or—-miúda, the purslane sesuvium (*S. portulacastrum*).—-de-cuba, or—-do-inverno, miner's lettuce (*Claytonia perfoliata*), c.a. ESPINAFRE-DE-CUBA.—-de-fôlha-grande, or—-do-sul = ESPINAFRE-DA-NOVA-ZELÂNDIA (New Zealand spinach).—-grande, a flame flower (*Talinum racemosum*). (*m. colloq.*) [Also **beldroegas**, *s. & pl.*] dull, thick person.
beleguim (*m.*) bailiff; (*colloq.*) cop, flat-foot.
Belém (*m.*) Bethlehem.
beletrista (*m.,f.*) belletrist.
beleza [ê] (*f.*) beauty; a beautiful woman; a beautiful thing. **salão de**—, beauty parlor.
belfo –fa, –belfudo –da (*adj.*) thick-lipped, referring esp. to the lower lip.
belga (*adj.; m.,f.*) Belgian.
Bélgica (*f.*) Belgium.
belho [ê] (*m., colloq.*) door bolt, door latch [= BEDELHO].
beliche (*m.*) berth, bunk (on a ship).
bélico –ca (*adj.*) martial, warlike, military.
belicosidade (*f.*) bellicosity.
belicoso –sa (*adj.*) bellicose, warlike, pugnacious.
beligerância (*f.*) belligerence, belligerency.
beligerante (*adj.*) belligerent.
belígero –ra (*adj.*) belligerous.
beliquete [quê] (*m.*) a closet for storing old clothes and other useless things.
beliscadura (*f.*) nip, pinch.
beliscão (*m.*) a strong pinch, nip.
beliscar (*v.t.*) to pinch, nip; to nibble at (food); to nettle.
belisco (*m.*) pinch, nip; nibble.
belo –la (*adj.*) beautiful, handsome, fine, fair; (*m.*) that which is beautiful, the beautiful.
belo-horizontino –na (*adj.*) of or pertaining to the city of Belo Horizonte, in the State of Minas Gerais; (*m.,f.*) a native thereof.
belonave (*f.*) warship.
belonídeos (*m.pl.*) a family (*Belonidae*) of needlefishes.
bel-prazer (*m.*) will, choice. **a (seu)**—, as (he) sees fit [disregarding the convenience of others, or quite without warning].
Beltrano (*m.*) John Doe.
Beltrão (*m.*) Bertram, Bertrand.
beluga, beluca (*f.*) the beluga or white whale (*Delphinapterus leucas*).
beluíno –na (*adj.*) savage, brutal; coarse; (*m.*) a wild beast.
belveder, belvedere [dê], **belver** [vê] (*m.*) belvedere.
belverde [vê] (*m.*) = VALVERDE.
belzebu (*m.*) Beelzebub, head demon.
bem (*m.*) a good, that which is good; welfare; blessing; benefit, boon; goodness, righteousness; a beloved person; (*pl.*) goods, chattels, belongings, means, possessions. [See separate article under BENS.] (*adv.*) well, rightly, justly; much, very, highly, quite.—**bom, or—bonzinho,**. quite good, not bad at all. Cf. BEM-BOM below.—**bonito**, quite pretty, right pretty.—**cedinho**, real early.—**como**, also, as well.—**de família**, the family home property; an heirloom.—**frio**, quite cold,—**fundo na terra**, deep down in the earth.—**longe**, a long way off, quite distant.—**maior**, a good deal larger.—**melhor**, (very) much better.—**menor**, quite a bit smaller.—**pouco**, very little.—**que**, even though.—**que está doente!** He (she) certainly is ill!—**que lhe disse!** I told you (him, her) so! I warned you (him, her)!—**quente**, quite warm, hot.—**sucedido**, successful. [When **bem** is combined with other words to form attributive adjectives, nouns and verbs, the term is hyphened, as shown in the separate entries following this article.] **a—de**, for the sake of, in behalf of. **ainda**—! At least that! So much the better! That's better! What a relief! **até—pouco**, until quite recently. **É** (or **fica**)—**um quilômetro daqui**, It is a good kilometer from here. **Está muito**—, All right, Very well, O.K. **estar**—, to be well, comfortable, at ease; to be well-off. **estar—com (alguém)**, to be on good terms with (someone); to be in his (her) good graces. **estar—de vida**, or **de dinheiros**, to be well-off, in good circumstances. **estar—instalado na vida**, to be in clover, "sitting pretty".

Excesso de—**não faz mal a ninguém**, You can't have too much of a good thing. **Fazer o**—**sem olhar a quem**, Do good for its own sake. **gente**—, (*slang*) the "best" people. [A snobbish use of the word **bem**]. **homem de**—, a reputable man, a man of integrity. **ir**—, to be well, to go well. **Isso é**—**dêle!** That's just like him! **levar a**—, to take (something) in good part. **meu**—, my dear, my beloved. **Muito**—! Fine! Very well! O.K.! **Não há**—**que sempre dure, nem mal que por si perdure**, It's a long lane that has no turning. **Não tão**—**quanto você, mas . . .**, not as well as you (do, are), but . . . **nem**—**nem mal**, neither well nor badly, just so-so. **para o**, or **pelo**,—**de**, for the good of. **para o**—**e para o mal**, for good and for evil. **pois**—, very well; well then. **por—fazer, mal haver**, to receive evil for good. **por—ou por mal**, willy-nilly. **pôr-se, or ficar, de—com alguém**, to make up with, patch up a quarrel with, someone. **querer—a alguém**, to be very fond of someone; to wish someone well. **regularmente**—, fairly well. **sair(-se)**—, to come out well, succeed, end up successfully. **se—que**, although, even though. **sentir-se**—, to feel well. **tão—como qualquer outro**, as well as anyone (else). **tão—quanto possível**, as well as possible.
bem-acabado –da (*adj.*) well-finished.
bem-administrado –da (*adj.*) well-managed.
bem-afortunado –da (*adj.*) blessed, happy, fortunate.
bem-alimentado –da (*adj.*) well-fed, well-nourished.
bem-amado –da (*adj.*) beloved, well-loved; (*m.,f.*) the loved one.
bem-aparelhado –da (*adj.*) well-equipped, well-found, well furnished with supplies.
bem-aparentado –da (*adj.*) well-connected, well-related, having good family connections.
bem-apessoado –da (*adj.*) handsome, good-looking; well-groomed.
bem-aventurado –da (*adj.*) blessed; (*m.f.*) the blest; a saint.
bem-aventurança (*f.*) bliss, supreme blessedness, exalted happiness; (*pl.*) the Beatitudes.
bem-aventurar (*v.t.*) to bless.
bem-avisado –da (*adj.*) well-advised.
bem-bom (*m.*) comfort; pleasure.
bem-casado –da (*adj.*) well-married; (*m.*) a cupcake; (*m.pl.*) the Brazilian parrotfeather (*Myriophyllum brasiliense*), c.a. CAVALINHO-D'ÁGUA; the crown-of-thorns euphorbia (*E. mili*), c.a. DOIS-IRMÃOS.
bem-comportado –da (*adj.*) well-behaved.
bem-conservado –da (*adj.*) well-preserved.
bem-criado –da (*adj.*) well-bred, well-mannered; of animals, well-cared for, well-fed, fat, plump.
bem-descansado –da (*adj.*) well-rested; lackadaisical, unhurried, carefree.
bem-dirigido –da (*adj.*) well-conducted; well-managed.
bem-disposto –ta (*adj.*) hale-and-hearty, feeling well.
bem-ditoso –sa (*adj.*) fortunate.
bem-dormido –da (*adj.*) well-rested; said of one who has slept well.
bem-educado –da (*adj.*) well-trained; well-educated; well-mannered.
bem-encarado –da (*adj.*) pleasant-looking; personable; good-looking; well-appearing; affable.
bem-ensinado –da (*adj.*) well-taught; well-educated.
bem-entendido (*adv.*) certainly, naturally, of course, that is understood.—**que**, provided, with the understanding that.
bementita (*f., Min.*) bementite.
bem-equilibrado –da (*adj.*) well-balanced.
bem-estar (*m.*) well-being, welfare, comfort, health, happiness.
bem-fadado –da (*adj.*) fortunate, happy; born under a lucky star.
bem-falante (*adj.*) well-spoken; fluent; eloquent; [derogatory] fine-talking.
bem-fazer [47] (*v.i.*) to do good; (*m.*) good works.
bem-feito –ta (*adj.*) well-made; well-done; (*interj.*) Good! I'm glad! It serves you right!
bem-humorado –da (*adj.*) cheerful, in good spirits.
bem-intencionado –da (*adj.*) well-intentioned, well-meant; well-meaning.
bem-me-quer (*m.*) an ox-eye daisy (*Chrysanthemum leucanthemum*).
bem-merecer (*v.t.*) to well-deserve.
bem-merecido –da (*adj.*) well-deserved; worthy, deserving.

bem-nascido –da (*adj.*) well-born; born under a lucky star.

bemol (*m.*, *Music*) the flat sign [♭]; any flat note.

bem-ouvido –da (*adj.*) attentive, docile, submissive, obedient.

bem-parecido –da (*adj.*) well-favored, of pleasing appearance, handsome, good-looking. [**bem parecido com** (without hyphen) = having a strong resemblance to.]

bem-passado –da (*adj.*) well-done [steak, roast, etc.].

bem-pôsto –posta (*adj.*) graceful, polished, refined; well-groomed.

bem-provido –da (*adj.*) well-found, well-stocked, well-supplied.

bem-querer [24,68] (*v.t.*) to love, care very much for; (*v.r.*) to love one another; (*m.*) fondness, affection; the loved one.

bem-soante, bem-sonante (*adj.*) well-sounding, melodious.

bem-te-vi (*m.*) any of numerous widely-distributed Brazilian birds of the tyrant-flycatcher family, such as the bemtevi of Amazonia (*Pitangus s. sulphuratus*), c.a. TRISTE-VIDA, SIRIRICA; Maximilian's bemtevi of southern Brazil (*Pitangus sulphuratus maximiliani*); the Bolivian bemtevi (*Pitangus s. bolivianus*).—-**de-coroa** = SUIRIRI. —-**de-igreja,** (*colloq.*) a dandy who goes to church to see and be seen.—-**do-bico-chato,**—-**de-bico-largo,**—-**do-mato-virgem,**—-**gamela,** all = the boat-billed flycatcher (*Megarynchus p. pitangua*), c.a. PITAUÁ, PITANGAÇU, PITANGUÁ-AÇU, PITANGUÁ, NEINEI.—-**escuro,** the streaked flycatcher (*Myiodynastes m. maculatus*).—-**miúdo** = MARIA-É-DIA.—-**pequeno,** the vermillion-crowned flycatcher (*Myiozetetes s. similis*), c.a. BEM-TE-VIZINHO; the striped flycatcher (*Legatus l. leucophaius*); also = GUARA-CAVA, FILHO-DE-BEM-TE-VI.—-**prêto,** or—-**riscado,** the solitary flycatcher (*Myiodynastes solitarius*), c.a. SIRIRI-TINGA.

bem-te-vizinho (*m.*) the varied flycatcher (*Empidonomus v. varius*), c.a. PEITICA, MARIA-É-DIA; also = BEM-TE-VI-PEQUENO.

bem-vestir (*v.i.*) to dress well.

bem-vindo –da (*adj.*) welcome.

bênção [-ções] (*f.*) blessing.—-**de-Deus,** (*Bot.*) an abutilon (*A. esculentum*), c.a. CAMPAINHA.

bendé (*m.*) okra (*Hibiscus esculentus*) = QUIABO.

bendegó (*m.*) a five-ton meteorite found in the river of this name in the State of Bahia; by ext., any huge or uncommon thing.

bendenguê (*m.*) a Negro song and dance.

bendito –ta [bẽin] (*adj.*) blessed.—-**seja,** blessèd be.

bendizente [bẽin] (*adj.*) given to speaking well of others.

bendizer [bẽin . . . 41] (*v.t.*) to speak well of others; to bless, glorify, exalt, praise.

Benedita (*f.*) Benedicta.

beneditinas (*f.*,*pl.*) Benedictine nuns.

beneditino (*m.*) a Benedictine monk; by ext., a scholarly person; a liqueur.

benedito (*m.*) the yellow-fronted woodpecker (*Tripsurus flavifrons*), c.a. PICAPAU-DO-MATO-VIRGEM; [*cap.*] Benedict.

benefe (*f.*) the dog violet (*Viola canina*).

beneficiação (*f.*) improvement, betterment; processing (cleaning, grinding, etc.) of cotton, coffee, cereals, and so on.

beneficiado –da (*adj.*) benefited, bettered, improved, treated, processed; (*colloq.*) of animals, castrated, branded, or shod. algodão—, ginned cotton. **café**—, coffee beans that have been hulled, washed, dried, etc; (*m.*,*f.*) a beneficiary (of anything).

beneficiador –dora (*adj.*) beneficial; beneficent; (*m.*) a processor of coffee, rice, etc.; a benefactor; (*f.*) a machine for such processing; a benefactress.

beneficial (*adj.*) beneficial [but only as pert. to an ecclesiastical benefice. In the ordinary senses of advantageous, profitable, etc. the Port. equivalents of beneficial are BENÉFICO, PROVEITOSO, VANTAJOSO, SALUTAR].

beneficiamento (*m.*) = BENEFICIAÇÃO.

beneficiar (*v.t.*) to benefit; to better, improve; to process (coffee, rice, beans, cotton, etc.); to castrate (bullocks); to endow or invest with a benefice.

beneficiário –ria (*adj.*; *m.*,*f.*) beneficiary.

beneficiável (*adj.*) susceptible of being benefited or bettered.

benefício (*m.*) benefit; benefaction, beneficence, favor, good turn; advantage, profit, gain; an ecclesiastical benefice; a theatrical or other performance or game to raise money for a special cause or person(s); betterment, im-

provement. **em—de,** in favor (for the benefit) of; for; in behalf of.

benéfico –ca (*adj.*) benefic, beneficent, favorable, benign; salutary.

benemerência (*f.*) deservingness, worthiness; worthy cause.

benemerente (*adj.*) deserving of good.

benemérito –ta (*adj.*) worthy, deserving, meritorious; estimable; distinguished. **sócio**—, a most distinguished member (of a club or association).

beneplácito (*m.*) good pleasure (consent, sanction, approval); stamp of approval.

benesse [né] (*f.*) altar dues; emolument; benefit; benefice.

benevolência (*f.*) benevolence, kindliness; good will; affection.

benévolo –la, **benevolente** (*adj.*) benevolent, kind, charitable; well-wishing; humane; affable.

benfazejo –ja [bẽin . . . ê] (*adj.*) beneficent; charitable.

benfeitor –tora [bẽin . . . ô] (*adj.*) beneficent; (*m.*,*f.*) benefactor; well-doer, a doer of good deeds.

benfeitoria [bẽin] (*f.*) improvement (to property).

bengala (*f.*) cane, walking stick; Bengal cloth; (*Autom.*) rear shaft axle.—-**de estoque,** a walking stick with a concealed dagger.—-**de-fôlha-miúda** = CANAFLECHA. **fogos de—,** Bengal light, fireworks.

bengalada (*f.*) a caning; a whack with a cane.

bengaleiro (*m.*) a maker or seller of canes and umbrellas; an umbrella stand.

bengali [í] (*adj.*; *m.*,*f.*) Bengali.

bengalina (*f.*) common poinsettia (*Euphorbia pulcherrima*).

benguelas (*m.pl.*) a tribe of Portuguese West Africa, many of whose members were shipped to Brazil as slaves. Cf. BANGUELA.

benignidade (*f.*) benignity.

benigno –na (*adj.*) benign, kind(ly), benevolent, complaisant, gentle; benignant; (*Med.*) benign.

benjamim (*m.*) the family pet, usually the youngest child; the youngest member of a club or association; (*Elec.*) receptacle; double plug; [*cap.*] Benjamin.

benjoeiro (*m.*) Sumatra snowbell (*Sytrax benzoin*) and other shrubs and trees of this genus.

benjoim [o-ím] (*m.*) gum benzoin.

benquerença [bẽin] (*f.*) well-wishing; fondness, affection.

benquerente [bẽin] (*adj.*) well-wishing; (*m.*,*f.*) well-wisher.

benquistar [bẽin] (*v.t.*) to conciliate; to win over; (*v.r.*)to gain goodwill

benquisto –ta [bẽin] (*adj.*; *irreg. p.p. of* BEMQUERER) well-liked; generally esteemed; beloved.

bens [bẽins] (*m.pl.*) property, goods, riches, belongings, chattels. Some legal and descriptive terms:—**adquiridos,** acquired property.—**alodiais,** allodial (absolute) land or property.—**consumíveis,** or **de consumo,** consumer goods.—**da coroa,** crown goods.—**de capital,** capital goods.—**doados,** donated property.—**de mão morta,** property held in mortmain.—**de órfãos,** orphans property.—**de raíz,** fixed real property.—**do Estado,** government (State) property.—**dotais,** wife's dowry.—**hereditários,** hereditament.—**imóveis,** real estate; immovables. —**imprescritíveis,** property which is not usucaptable. —**móveis,** movables.—**particulares,** private property. —**pessoais,** personal effects.—**públicos,** public property. —**semoventes,** livestock, cattle ("self-movables").— **uxorianos,** wife's property.—**vacantes,** or **vagos,** unclaimed property or inheritance.

benteca (*f.*) = BONDARA.

bentererê (*m.*) = JOÃO-TENENÉM, JOÃO-TIRIRI.

bentevi [í] (*m.*) = BEM-TE-VI.

bentinhos (*m.pl.*) a scapular (religious amulet); (humorously) badges, decorations.

bento –ta (*adj.*; *irreg. p.p. of* BENZER) blessed, holy. **água**—, holy water; (*m.*) a Benedictine monk; (*m.pl.*) benthos.

bentonita (*f.*, *Petrog.*) bentonite.

benzaldeído (*m.*, *Chem.*) benzaldehyde.

benzamida (*f.*, *Chem.*) benzamide.

benzanilido (*m.*, *Chem.*) benzanilide, phenyl benzamide.

benzedeira (*f.*) woman healer; sorceress.

benzedeiro (*m.*) witch doctor; medicine man.

benzedor (*m.*) = BENZEDEIRO.

benzedura (*f.*) a superstitious blessing.

benzeno (*m.*, *Chem.*) benzene [= BENZOL].

benzer [24] (*v.t.*) to bless; to bestow a blessing on; to con-

secrate, hallow, sanctify; (v.r.) to cross oneself. **Benza-(-te) Deus,** God bless you.
benzidina (f., *Chem.*) benzidine.
benzilamino (m., *Chem.*) benzyl amine.
benzilo (m., *Chem.*) benzil, bibenzoyl, dibensoyl.
benzina (f.) benzine.
benzinho [bẽin] (m.) darling, honey, sweetie—(a term of endearment).
benzoato (m., *Chem.*) benzoate.
benzofenol (m., *Chem.*) phenol, carbolic acid, phenic acid.
benzofenona (f., *Chem.*) benzophenone, phenylketone.
benzóico -ca (adj., *Chem.*) **ácido**—, benzoid acid.
benzofla (f., *Chem.*) benzoyl.
benzoína (f.) gum benzoin.
benzol (m., *Chem.*) benzol, benzene.
benzonitrilo (m., *Chem.*) benzonitrile, benzene carbonitrile.
benzoquinona (f., *Chem.*) ordinary quinone.
beócio -cia (adj.) Boeotian; dull-witted; (m.) nitwit.
bequadro (m. *Music*) natural (♮).
beque (m.) beak (prow) of a vessel; (*colloq.*) a large nose; (*Soccer*) back, c.a. ZAGUEIRO.
bequilha (f., *Aeron.*) tail skid or wheel.
berbequim (m.) breast drill.
berbere [bére] (adj.; m.,f.) Berber.
berberidáceas (f.pl., *Bot.*) the barberry family (*Berberidaceae*).
berberina (f., *Chem.*) berberine.
bérberis (m.) the genus (*Berberis*) of barberries.
berbigão (m.) mussel or cockle (*Cardium edule*); also = MIJA-MIJA.
berbigueira (f.) = SAMBAQUI.
berçário (m.) nursery.
berço [ê] (m.) cradle; infancy; origin; place of birth, native land; seat, base, support (as for a motor); ways (for ship launching); ink pad; a cradle-like holder for blotting paper. **desde o**—, from the cradle.
bereba (f.) = PEREBA.
bereberé (m.) = JOÃO-NINGUÉM.
berenguendens (m.pl.) = BALANGANDÃS.
bereré (m.) hubbub, uproar, melee.
bergamota (f.) the bergamot orange (*Citrus bergamia*) from whose rind is extracted an essential oil used in perfumery; the name by which the tangerine is known in Rio Grande do Sul, and which in other parts of Brazil is called TANGERINA, LARANJA-CRAVO, MEXERICA, and in Portugal, MANDARINA; the bergamot mint (*Mentha citrata*); the wild bergamot beebalm (*Monarda fistulosa*); a minor variety of pear. Var. VERGAMOTA.
berganhar (v.) & derivs. = BARGANHAR & derivs.
bergantim (m.) small two-masted bark [= FRAGATIM].
beri [í] (m.) = BIRU-MANSO.
beriba (f.) = BIRIBA.
beribá (m.) a horse buyer [= BERIVÁ].
beribéri (m., *Med.*) beriberi.
beribérico -ca (adj.) beriberic; (m.,f.) one afflicted with beriberi.
berflia (f., *Chem.*) beryllium oxide.
berilino -na (adj.) beryline, beryl-blue in color.
berflio (m., *Chem.*) beryllium, glucinum.
berilo (m., *Min.*) beryl.
berilonita (f., *Min.*) berylonite.
berimbau (m.) jew's harp.
berinjela (f.) the garden eggplant (*Solanum melongena*), c.a. JILOEIRO; its fruit, c.a. JILÓ. Var. BRINJELA.
beririçô (m.) = BARIRIÇÔ.
berivá (m.) = BERIBÁ.
Berlim (m.) Berlin.
berlinda (f.) a berlin (large four-wheeled carriage); a horse-drawn litter for conveying religious images; a game of forfeits. **estar na**—, to be "it" in a game; of persons, to be the butt of critical comment, wit, sarcasm, etc.
berlinense, berlinês -nesa (adj.) of or pert. to Berlin; (m.,f.) a Berliner.
berliques e berloques (m.pl.) hocus-pocus; magicians' tricks.
berloque (m.) watch charm, trinket; (*pl.*) gewgaws, fripperies.
berma (f.) berm; narrow path along a ditch or canal; shoulder (of a road).
bermudas (f.pl.) Bermuda shorts.
bernarda (f., *colloq.*) popular uprising, revolt, riot.
bernardo (m.) a Bernardine monk; a glutton; [*cap.*]

Bernard; Barnard.
bernardo-eremita (m.) a hermit crab.
berne (adj.) designating a certain kind of red cloth used in drapes and religious garments; (m.) the larva of certain botflies (*Dermatobia*) which lives under the skin of domestic animals and sometimes of man, in tropical America.
bernear (v.i.) to suffer with BERNES.
bernento -ta (adj.) having BERNES.
bernês -nesa (adj.; m.,f.) Bernese.
bernicida (f.) a preparation for killing BERNES.
beroba (f.) mare.
beronha (f.) = BERUANHA.
berra (f.) rutting of deer. **andar na**—, (*colloq.*) to be on everyone's tongue, much discussed, very popular.
berrador -dora [ô] (adj.) bellowing; (m.,f.) bellower. **abrir o**—, to bawl (cry);—said of children.
berrante (adj.) loud, flashy, garish, gaudy; (m., *slang*) "gat" (revolver).
berrar (v.i.) to bellow, yell, howl; to roar (as a beast); to shout; to bawl; to have some Negro blood.
berraria (f.) = BERREIRO.
berregar (v.i.) shout, yell (frequently).
berreiro (m.) shouts, yells, bawling; shrieking. **abrir o**—, to cry out (shout) in protest.
berro (m.) bellow(ing), roar, shout; (*Bot.*) golden monkeyflower (*Mimulus luteus*); (*Zool.*) a botfly (*Dermatobia spp.*) whose larva is called berne.
Berta (f.) Bertha.
bertalha (f.) red vinespinach (*Basella ruba*).
bertéroa (f.) a false alyssum (*Berteroa sp.*)
Bertoldo (m.) Berthold.
bertrandita (f., *Min.*) bertrandite.
bertolécia (f.) the genus (*Bertholletia*) which comprises the Brazilnut (*B. excelsa*).
beruanha (f.) a blood-sucking stable fly (*Stomoxys calcitrans*), c.a. BERNANHA, BERONHA, BURNANHA, MURU-ANHA.
besoiro (m.) & derivs. = BESOURO & derivs.
besigue (m.) bezique (a card game like pinochle).
besouragem (f.) intrigue, plotting.
besourar (v.i.) to buzz.
besouro (m.) the common name for any beetle.—**-bicudo,** any snout beetle.—**-bicudo-do-coqueiro,** a palm weevil.—**-d'água,** water beetle.—**-da-batata,** potato bug.
bespa (f.) = VESPA.
besta [é] (f.) ancient crossbow or arbalest.
bêsta (adj.) stupid; (f.) beast, quadruped; a mare; fool, simpleton.—**de carga,** beast of burden; pack animal.—**de tiro,** draft animal.—**-fera,** wild beast.—**quadrada,** utter fool, complete ass, perfect jackass. **Deixe de ser**—, Don't be a fool; stop making an ass of yourself. **Ele é muito**—, He is quite conceited, cocky. **Você é uma**—! You're an ass!
bestagem (f.) = BESTEIRA.
bestalhão (m.), -lhona (f.) a very stupid or conceited person.
bestamente (adv.) stupidly.
bestar (v.i.) to say silly things; to act improperly; to be outside of a conversation; to wander about.
besteira (f.) asininity, stupidity; "baloney". **dizer**—s, to talk nonsense; to make an ass of oneself. **Lá vem**—! There he goes! (about to say something silly).
besteiro [bês] (m.) crossbowman.
bestial (adj.) bestial, beast-like, brutal; brutish, low.
bestialidade (f.) bestiality.
bestializar (v.) = BESTIFICAR.
bestialógico -ca (adj.) full of nonsense; (m.) asinine discourse.
bestice (f.) = BESTEIRA.
bestificar (v.t.) to dumfound; to flummox; to besot.
bestuntar (v.t.) to opine. [Derogatory]
bestuntaria (f.) dull-wittedness; mental deficiency.
bestunto (m., *colloq.*) the noodle (head); dull mind. **puxar pelo**—, to use one's noodle (brains).
besuntão (m.), -tona (f.) filthy, greasy person.
besuntar (v.t.) to grease; to smear, daub.
beta (f.) the genus (*Beta*) of beets.
bêta (f.) stripe or streak of color; metallic vein.
betacismo (m.) betacism.
betafita (f., *Min.*) betafite.
betaína (f., *Chem.*) betaine, lycine, oxyneurine, trimethyl glycocole.
betão (m.) concrete.

betar (*v.t.*) to streak or stripe with color.
betarda (*f.*) = ABETARDA.
betaru-amarelo (*m.*) = ESPINHO-DE-VINTÉM.
betatron, betatrônio (*m., Physics*) betatron.
bétele, betel (*m., Bot.*) betel (*Piper betle*).
beterraba (*f.*) beet. **açúcar de—,** beet sugar.
betesga [tê] (*f.*) narrow street or way; blind alley.
betilho (*m.*) a muzzle for oxen.
betonada (*f.*) one load of a concrete mixer.
betoneira (*f.*) concrete mixer.
betônica (*f., Bot.*) the genus (*Stachys*) of betonies or woundworts.—**brava,** a bushmint (*Hyptis multiflora*).—
-das-montanhas, mountain arnica (*A. montana*).—**de-água,** water figwort (*Scrophularia aquatica*).—**ver-dadeira,** common betony (*Stachys officinalis*).
betu [ú] (*m.*) olive shell; a beach snail (*Lintricula auri-cularia*), c.a. PACAVARÉ, LINGUARUDO, CALORIM.
bétula (*f., Bot.*) any birch (*Betula*), c.a. VIDOEIRO.
betuláceas, -líneas (*f. pl., Bot.*) the birch family.
betuláceo -cea, -líneo -nea (*adj.*) betulaceous.
betulina (*f., Chem.*) betulin(ol), birch camphor.
betumar (*v.t.*) to cover, treat or mix with any bitumen.
betume (*m.*) bitumen; asphalt; putty.
betuminizar (*v.t.*) to bituminize.
betuminoso -sa (*adj.*) bituminous.
bexiga (*f.*) bladder; a tube of paint.—**de fel,** gall bladder.
—**natatória,** the air or swim bladder of a fish; (*f.pl., Med.*) smallpox, variola; pock marks.—**s cristalinas,** or —**s doidas,** varicella, chicken pox, c.a. CATAPORAS.
bexigoso -sa, —guento -ta (*adj.*) pockmarked.
bexuanas (*m.pl.*) the Bechuanas (Negro peoples).
bezerra [zê] (*f.*) heifer.
bezerro [zê] (*m.*) calf, bullock; calfskin.
B.F. = BOAS-FESTAS (Merry Christmas).
biaba (*f.*) a severe beating.
biácido -da (*adj., Chem.*) diacid.
biacuminado -da (*adj., Bot.*) double acuminate.
bialado -da (*adj.*) having two wings.
biangulado -da (*adj.*) biangulate.
biangular (*adj.*) biangular.
biaribu [ú] (*m.*) Brazilian Indian method of roasting meat by wrapping it in leaves, covering it with dirt and build-ing a fire over it.
bias (*m., Elec.*) bias [In the ordinary senses, bias is VIÉS and PREVENÇÃO.]
biatatá (*m.*) = BIOTATÁ.
biatômico -ca (*adj., Chem.*) biatomic, diatomic.
biaxial [ks] (*adj.*) biaxial.
bibásico -ca (*adj., Chem.*) dibasic.
bibe [bíbe] (*m.*) a child's smock.
bibelô (*m.*) bibelot; knickknack.
biberão (*m.*) child's milk bottle.
bibi [bibí] (*m., Bot.*) a cypella (*C. plumbea*).
bibiano (*m.*) a small tin kerosene lamp [= FIFÓ, PERI-QUITO].
bibiru [ú] (*m.*) = BEBERU.
bibl. = BIBLIOGRAFIA (bibliography); BIBLIOGRÁFICO (bib-liographical); BIBLIOTECA (library).
Bíblia (*f.*) the Bible; [*not cap.*] (*m., colloq.*) a Protestant.
bíblico -ca (*adj.*) biblical.
biblioclasta (*m.,f.*) biblioclast.
biblioclepta (*m.,f.*) biblioklept, book thief.
bibliófago -ga (*adj., Chem.*) bibliophagic; (*m.,f.*) bibliophagist.
bibliofilia (*f.*) bibliophilism.
bibliófilo -la (*adj.*) bibliophilic; (*m.,f.*) book lover.
bibliofobia (*f.*) bibliophobia.
bibliogênese (*f.*) bibliogenesis, bibliogony.
bibliognosta (*m.,f.*) bibliognost.
bibliografia (*f.*) bibliography.
bibliográfico -ca (*adj.*) bibliographic.
bibliógrafo -fa (*m.,f.*) bibliographer.
bibliolatria (*f.*) bibliolatry.
bibliologia (*f.*) bibliology, booklore.
bibliomania (*f.*) bibliomania.
bibliomaníaco -ca (*adj.*) bibliomaniacal.
bibliômano -na (*m.,f.*) bibliomaniac.
bibliopola (*m.,f.*) bibliopole, bookseller.
bibliótafo -fa (*m.,f.*) bibliotaph.
biblioteca (*f.*) library.—**viva,** a walking encyclopedia (person who knows a great deal). **rato de—,** a book worm.
bibliotecário -ria (*m.,f.*) librarian.
biblismo (*m.*) Biblism.
biblista (*m.,f.*) Biblist; Biblicist.

biboca (*f.*) gully or gulch; straw hut.
bíbulo -la (*adj.*) bibulous; (*m.,f.*) nursing baby.
bica (*f.*) water spout, water faucet, spigot. [= TORNEIRA].
água da—, tap water. **estar na—,** to be about to happen.
bicada (*f.*) peck (with the beak); beakful. (*colloq.*) shot, slug (of liquor).
bicado -da (*adj.*) tipsy.
bicame (*m.*) a rustic or improvised wooden bridge across a small stream; roof gutter and downspout.
bicanca (*m.*) a huge nose; a stub-toed shoe for playing soccer; (*m.,f.*) a large-nosed person.
bicançudo (*m.*) bellows fish (*Macrorhamphosus scolopax*), c.a. CENTRISCO, PEIXE-TROMBETA.
bicapsular (*adj., Bot.*) bicapsular.
bicar (*v.t.*) to peck (at) with the beak.
bicarbonato (*m., Chem.*) bicarbonate.—**de potássio,** potas-sium acid carbonate.—**de sódio,** bicarbonate of soda.
bicarenado -da (*adj., Bot.*) bicarenate.
bicarrada (*f.*) bits of anything used by birds in building their nests.
bicaudado -da (*adj.*) having two tails, bicaudal, bi-caudate.
bicéfalo -la (*adj.*) bicephalous, having two heads.
bicelular (*adj., Biol.*) bicellular.
bicentenário -ria (*adj.; m.*) bicentennial.
bíceps (*m., Anat.*) biceps [= BICÍPITE].—**braquial,** biceps flexor cubiti.—**crural,** biceps flexor cruris.
bicha (*f.*) any long, worm-like creature; a leech; tape-worm; queue (long line of people); shrew, termagant, virago; a small revenue cutter; sleeve braid or insignia; a kind of firecracker; (*pl.*) earrings.—**amarela,** —**al-finete,**—**do-milho,** (*Zool.*) a wireworm (larva of the elat-er *Agriotes lineatus*), c.a. ALFINETE, AGUILHÃO, TRAVELA, GRAMIOLA, VERMIOLA.—**cadela,** an earwig (*Forficula*) c.a. RAPA.—**da consciência,** remorse.—**de rabear,** a squib (kind of firecracker).—**de sangrar,** leech. **entrar na—,** to stand in line. **fazer —,** to queue up.
bichado -da (*adj.*) wormy, buggy.
bichanar (*v.i.*) to talk in whispers.
bichano -na (*m.,f.*) a pet kitten.
bichão (*m.*) a large BICHO; a large man; (*colloq.*) a "shark" (person who excels at something).
bichar (*v.i.*) to get wormy (said of fruit, cheese, etc.).
bicharada (*f.*) a lot of BICHOS together.
bicharedo [ê] (*m.*) an infestation of vermin; also = BICHA-RADA.
bicharia (*f., colloq.*) a gathering of people; also = BICHA-RADA.
bicharoco [rô] (*m.*) a repulsive worm or other animal; a large, frightening animal; brute, beast.
bicharrão (*m.*) a big BICHO.
bicheira (*f.*) a maggot-filled sore on animals.
bicheiro (*m.*) a bookie of the BICHO game—see JÔGO DE BICHO.
bichento -ta (*adj.*) wormy.
bicho (*m.*) any unspecified animal, esp. bugs, insects and worms; an ugly or unsociable person; a new student; (*slang*) a shark (expert).—**barbeiro,**—**de-concha,**—**do-mato,**—**de-parede,** all common names for the barber bug—see under BARBEIRO.—**cabeludo,** any hairy caterpillar.—**careta,** a nobody.—**carpinteiro,** beetle, borer, wood weevil.—**da consciência,** remorse.—**da costa,** the Guinea worm (*Dracunculus medinensis*).—**da cozinha,** a kitchen drudge.—**da madeira,** termite.—**da-preguiça,** any hookworm.—**da-sêda,** silkworm.—**da toca,** (*colloq.*) a solitary, lone-wolf type of person.—**das-frutas,** fruit worm.—**das-verduras,** vegetable worm.—**-de-canastro,** or **-de-cêsto,** the larva of the bagworm moth.—**de-chifre,** the tobacco flea beetle (*Epitrix par-vula*).—**de-concha,** a mysterious, solitary person.—**de-conta,** pill bug, sow bug.—**de-conta-aquático,** a fresh-water isopod crustacean (*Asellus vulgaris*), c.a. ASELLO-DE-ÁGUA-DOCE. — **-de-frade** = BARBEIRO. — **-de-môsca,** maggot.—**-de-parede** = BARBEIRO.—**de-pau,** a stick in-sect, c.a. MANÉ-MAGRO.—**de-pé,** or **-de-porco,** the chigoe (*Tunga, syn. Sacropsylla, penetrans*), c.a. NÍGUA, TUNGA, PULGA PENETRANTE. [Not to be confused with the No. Amer. chigger, jigger or red bug].—**de pena,** any bird.—**-de-queijo,** cheese maggot.—**-de-sete-cabeças,** a Hydra-headed monster, hence, a persistent evil hard to overcome.—**do-mato,** a solitary person.—**escolástico,** a new student.—**gordo,** a grub.—**homem,** man as an animal.—**mineiro,** a leaf miner.—**mole,** tobacco worm, larva of a hawk moth (*Protoparce sp.*).—**papão** or—**-tatu,** bogey-man, bugbear, bugaboo, goblin.—**pau,** a

stick insect. **Êsse camarada é um**—! That fellow is a "shark"! **estar com o**, or **ter**,—**-carpinteiro (no corpo)**, to have "ants in the pants" (fidgets).

bichoco –**ca** (ôc) (adj.) wormy [fruit]; of horses, having swollen feet; (f., colloq.) an earthworm; a caterpillar; a child's penis; a small boil or felon.

bichoso –**sa** (adj.) wormy; buggy.

bicicleta [é] (f.) bicycle.—**de dois lugares**, tandem bicycle.

biciclista (m.,f.) bicyclist.

bicipital (adj., Anat.) bicipital.

bicípite (adj.) having two heads; (m.) biceps.

bicloreto (m., Chem.) bichloride, dichloride.—**de benzilo**, benzyl dichloride; benzyl chloride; benzyl chloride.—**de cobre**, hydrated copper chloride, copper dichloride.—**de mercúrio**, mercury chloride, corrosive sublimate.—**de platina**, platinum dichloride.

biclorobifluorometano (m., Chem.) Freon-12, dichlorodifluoro methane gas.

biclorotetrafluoretano (m., Chem.) Freon-114, dichlorotetrafluoro ethane.

bico (m.) beak; sharp point; pen point; (colloq.) a person's mouth; a sideline to one's regular occupation; lace edging; (pl.) chicken feed (change); (interj.) Quiet! Not another word!—**da mamadeira**, rubber nipple of a nursing bottle.—**da pena**, pen point.—**de acetileno**, acetylene torch.—**de Bunsen**, Bunsen burner.—**-de-brasa**, a nunbird (Monasa morpheous).—**-de-cegonha**, the robert geranium (G. robertianum), c.a. BICO-DE-GROU, PÉ-DE-POMBO. Also, alfeleria (Erodium cicutarium), c.a. MARIA-FIA. — **-de-cegonha-moscada** = AGULHEIRA-MOSCADA.—**-de-corvo** = BOI-GORDO, AMENDOEIRANA.—**-de-ferro**, a finch (Saltator similis).—**de gás**, gaslight jet.—**-de-grou**, musk heronbill (Erodium moschatum), c.a. AGULHEIRA-MOSCADA.—**-de-grou-robertino**, herb robert geranium (G. robertianum), c.a. BICO-DE-CEGONHA.—**-de-grou-sanguíneo**, bloodred geranium (G. sanguineum).—**-de-lacre**, the scarlet-cheeked weaver-bird (Estrilda m. melpoda), a native of Africa introduced in Brazil where it is quite at home.—**-de-latão**, a puffbird (Bucco collaris).—**-de-obra**, any difficult thing.—**-de-papagaio** (colloq.) hook-nose; (Bot.) a cactus (Rhipsalis salicornioides); an euphorbia (E. incarnata).—**-de-pato**, any duck-billed object; long-nose pliers.—**-de-pena**, a thumbnail sketch.—**-de-pomba-maior**, the longstalk geranium (G. columbinum).—**-de-pomba-menor**, the dovefoot geranium (G. molle).—**-de-veludo**, a brown-capped tanager (Schistochlamys ruficapillus), c.a. SANHAÇO-DE-COQUEIRO.—**-doce** = JACARÉ-PINIMA (a lizard).—**do peito**, or—**do seio**, breast nipple.—**dos pés**, tip-toes.—**-pimenta**, the black-throated grosbeak (Pitylus fuliginosus), c.a. BICUDO.—**-rasteiro**, the black skimmer (Rhynchops nigra), c.a. TALHA-MAR; Wilson's snipe (Capella delicata), c.a. NARCEJA.—**-vermelho** = CHORÃO (a bird). **calar o**—, (colloq.) to shut up, stop talking. **chá de**—, (colloq.) an enema. **desenho a—de pena**, a pen-and-ink sketch. **não abrir o**—, to keep mum, not let out a peep. **pau de dois**—**s**, evidence which supports either of two opposing opinions or statements.

bicô (adj.) tailless; bob-tailed [= SURU].

bicolor [lór] (adj.) bicolor.

bicôncavo –**va** (adj.) biconcave.

bicônico –**ca** (adj.) biconic.

biconjugado –**da** (adj., Bot.) biconjugate.

biconvexo –**xa** [ks] (adj.) biconvex.

bicorne (adj.) two-horned; crescentlike.

bicota (f.) a loud smack (kiss).

bicromato (m., Chem.) dichromate.—**de potássio**, potassium dichromate.—**de sódio**, sodium dichromate.—**de zinco**, zinc dichromate.

bicudinha (f.) = BICUDA-GUARANÁ.

bicudo –**da** (adj.) beaked; sharp, pointed; knotty, difficult; piqued; cross, grouchy; tight (drunk); (m.) any of several finches of the genus Oryzoborus; esp. Wied's rice grosbeak (Oryzoborus crassirostris maximiliani); also = CUITELÃO, CURIÓ, BICO-PIMENTA (birds); also, the 3-toed jacamar (Jacamaralcyon tridactyla); a sailfish (Istiophorus volador), c.a. AGULHÃO-BANDEIRA, PEIXE-VELA; a swordfish.—**-encarnado**, the red-and-black grosbeak (Periporphyrus erythromelas); (f.) a sharp-pointed knife; any barracuda (Sphyraena), esp. S. picudilla (a small slender species); S. barracuda (the great barracuda, c.a. BARRACUDA, BICUDA-DE-CORSO); S. sphyraena (the European barracuda, c.a. BICUDA-DA-LAMA), and S. branneri (c.a. BICUDA-GUARANÁ, BICU-

DINHA).

bicuíba (f.) any of various nutmegs (Myristica), c.a. BOCUBA, VICUÍBA, URUCUÍBA, BUCUUVA, BOCUUVA; also, the becuiba (Virola bicuhyba), a Brazilian timber tree whose nuts yield a wax.—**-redonda**, the Brazil nutmeg (Myristica officinalis), c.a. MOSCADEIRA-DO-BRAZIL, NOZ-MOSCADA-DO-BRASIL.

bicúspide (adj.) bicuspid.

bidê (m.) bidet (low washstand), a form of sitz bath; a night table.

bidentado –**da**, **bidênteo** –**tea** (adj.) bidentate.

bidigitado –**da** (adj.) bidigitate.

bíduo (m.) two days' time.

biela (f.) piston rod.

bienal (adj.) biennial.

biênio (m.) biennium.

bifar (v.t.) to pilfer, filch, swipe, steal.

bifásico –**ca** (adj., Elec.) two-phase.

bife (m.) beefsteak; a somewhat derogatory nickname for an Englishman; a blow with the fist; chopsticks (on the piano).—**a cavalo**, a beefsteak with fried eggs on top.—**à milanesa**, breaded cutlet.—**bem-passado**, a well-done steak.—**com batatas**, steak and French-fried potatoes.—**de lombinho**, porterhouse steak.—**mal-passado**, medium-rare steak;—**sangrento**, rare steak.

bifendido –**da** (adj.) bifid (cleft in two parts).

bifesteque (m.) beefsteak.

bifilar (adj.) two-threaded; (Elec.) two-wire.

bífido –**da** (adj.) bifid.

biflabelado –**da** (adj., Zool.) biflabellate.

biflexo –**xa** [ks] (adj.) biflected.

bifloro –**ra**, **biflor** [ô] (adj.) biflorate, bearing two flowers.

bifocal (adj.) bifocal.

bifoliado –**da**, **bifólio** –**lia** (adj., Bot.) bifoliate; diphyllous.

bifore (adj.) double-doored.

biforme (adj.) biform(ed).

bifronte (adj.) two-faced (lit. & fig.)

bifurcação (f.) bifurcation; a fork in the road; railroad junction.

bifurcado –**da** (adj.) forked.

bifurcar (v.i.) to bifurcate, fork, branch (in two);—**-se em**, to straddle; to sit astride (a horse, etc.).

bigamia (f.) bigamy.

bígamo –**ma** (adj.) bigamous; (m.,f.) bigamist.

bigêmeo –**mea**, **-geminado** –**da** (adj.; Bot.) bigeminate, biconjugate.

bigeminismo (m., Med.) bigeminal pulse.

biglanduloso –**sa** (adj.) biglandular.

bigle (m.) beagle (hound).

bignônia (f.) the genus (Bignonia) of trumpetvines.

bignoniáceo –**cea** (adj.) bignoniaceous; (f.pl.) the Bignoneaceae (trumpet creeper family).

bigode (m.) mustache; the white foam raised by the bow of a vessel cutting through the water; a kind of card game; a scolding; (Zool.) the lined seedeater (Sporophila lineola), c.a. PAPA-CAPIM, COLEIRINHA.—**-de-arame**, (slang) a man with pointed, up-turned mustaches. **dar um**—, to play a practical joke on; to shoot game missed by another hunter. **deixar crescer o**—, to raise a mustache. **raspar o**—, to shave off the mustache.

bigodear (v.t.) to trick, deceive.

bigodeira (f.) a large, heavy, untrimmed mustache; an animal's whiskers.

bigodudo –**da** (adj.) having a large mustache.

bigorna (f.) anvil; (Anat.) incus. **entre o martelo e a**—, between the devil and the deep blue sea.

bigorrilha (m.) a base, despicable man; rotter, "stinker," hangdog.

bigota (f., Naut.) deadeye.

bigotismo (m.) bigotry.

biguá (f., Zool.) a cormorant (Phalacrocorax) c.a. CORVO-MARINHO, PATA-D'ÁGUA.

biguane, **-guano** –**na** (adj.; colloq.) big.

biguatinga (m.) the American darter, snakebird or water-turkey (Anhinga anhinga).

bigúmeo –**mea** (adj.; Bot.) two-edged.

bijanilo (m., Bot.) a calathea (C. contamanensis).

biju [ú] (m.) = BEIJU.

bijugado –**da** (adj., Bot.) biconjugate.

bijupirá (m.) the cobia or crabeater, (Rachycentron canadus), a large voracious mackerel-like fish, c.a. BEJUPIRÁ, BEIUPIRÁ, CANADO, CAÇÃO-DE-ESCAMAS, CHANCARONA, PEIXE-REI, PIRABIJU, PARAMBIJU, PIRABEJU.

bijuteria (f.) costume jewelry; jewelry store.

bilabiado –da (*adj.*, *Bot.*) bilabiate.
bilabial (*adj.*, *Phonet.*) bilabial.
bilaminado –da, bilaminoso –sa (*adj.*) bilaminate.
bilaterado –da (*adj.*, *Bot.*) bisymmetrical.
bilateral (*adj.*) bilateral, two-sided.
bilbérgia (*f.*, *Bot.*) the genus (*Billbergia*) of airbroms.
bilboquê (*m.*) bilboquet, cup-and-ball game.
bile (*f.*) bile; gall; ill humor; hypochondria.
bilha (*f.*) jug; pitcher; a ball bearing; steel ball.
bilhão (*m.*) billion. Var. BILIÃO.
bilhar (*m.*) billiards; billiard table; billiard hall.—americano, pool.—chinês, a pin-ball game. salão de—es, billiard room.
bilhardar (*v.i.*) to play tipcat.
bilharista (*m.*,*f.*) billiard player.
bilh.e = BILHETE (ticket).
bilhete [lhê] (*m.*) note, short letter; ticket.—azul, a pink slip (notice of discharge from employment).—de entrada, admission ticket.—de ida, one-way ticket.—de ida e volta, round-trip ticket.—de loteria, lottery ticket. —(or cartão) postal, postal card.
bilheteira (*f.*) card tray; card case; the girl in a ticket booth; in Portugal, BILHETERIA.
bilheteiro (*m.*) ticket seller.
bilheteria (*f.*) ticket window; ticket booth; box office.
bilião (*m.*) = BILHÃO.
biliar, biliário –ria (*adj.*) biliary, vesícula biliar, gall bladder.
bilicianina (*f.*, *Biochem.*) bilicyanin, cholecyanin.
bilifucsina (*f.*, *Biochem.*) bilifucsin.
bilimbi [bí], –bim (*m.*, *Bot.*) the bilimbi (*Averrhoa bilimbi*), c.a. CARAMBOLEIRA-AMARELA, LIMÃO-DE-CAIENA; also, its very acid fruit, esteemed in India for a preserve or pickle.
bilíngüe (*adj.*) bilingual.
bilinguismo (*m.*) bilingualism.
bilionário –ria (*m.*,*f.*) billionaire.
bilioso –sa (*adj.*) bilious.
biliprasina (*f.*, *Biochem.*) biliprasin.
bilirrubina (*f.*, *Biochem.*) bilirubin.
bilirrubinúria (*f.*, *Med.*) bilirubinuria.
bílis (*f.*) = BILE.
biliteral (*adj.*) biliteral.
biliverdina (*f.*, *Biochem.*) biliverdin.
bilixantina (*f.*, *Biochem.*) choletelin.
bilobado –da (*adj.*) bilobate.
bilocular (*adj.*) bilocular.
bilontra (*m.*) a frequenter of brothels; keeper of bad company; rascal, scoundrel; lady-killer; idler.
bilontrar (*v.i.*) to behave as a BILONTRA.
bilrar (*v.t.*) to make bobbin lace.
bilreira (*f.*) = ATANGARATINGA, RENDEIRA.
bilreiro (*m.*) = CARRAPÊTA.
bilro (*m.*) a lace bobbin; a pin (at nine pins); a little boy's penis.
biltra (*f.*) a base woman.
biltre (*m.*) a despicable man; scoundrel, rotter, blackguard; coxcomb.
bimaculado –da (*adj.*) bimaculate.
bímano –na (*adj.*, *Zool.*) bimanous, two-handed.
bímare (*adj.*) between two seas.
bimarginado –da (*adj.*) bimarginate.
bimástico –ca (*adj.*, *Anat.*) bimastic.
bimba (*f.*) a little boy's penis.
bimbalhada (*f.*) a dingdong, jingling or chiming of bells.
bimbalhar (*v.t.*) to jingle (chime, play, toll) bells.
bimensal (*adj.*) twice-monthly, semi-monthly.
bimestral (*adj.*) bimonthly.
bimestre (*adj.*) bimestrial, lasting two months; (*m.*) a two-month period.
bimetalismo (*m.*) bimetalism.
bimetalista (*adj.*; *m.*,*f.*) bimetalist.
bimotor (*adj.*; *m.*) two-motor (plane).
binação (*f.*) = BINÁGIO.
binado –da (*adj.*, *Bot.*) binate, double.
binágio (*m.*) bination.
binar (*v.t.*) to do double duty; to say mass twice in one day.
binário –ria (*adj.*) binary; (*m.*) binary; (*Kinematics*) a pain.
binerval, –nérveo –vea (*adj.*) binervate.
binga (*f.*) horn; horn tobacco box, kerosene lamp; tinder rope fitted with flint and steel and used as a cigarette lighter.

binocular (*adj.*) binocular.
binóculo (*m.*) binoculars, opera glasses, field glasses.
binômio (*m.*, *Math.*) binomial.
binuclear (*adj.*) binucleate.
bioblasto (*m.*, *Biol.*) bioblast.
biocenose (*f.*, *Biol.*) biocenosis.
bioco [biô] (*m.*) head scarf; muffler; false modesty.
biodinâmica (*f.*) biodynamics.
bioelétrico –ca (*adj.*) bio-electric.
bioenergética, bioenergia (*f.*) bio-energetics.
biofagia (*f.*, *Biol.*) biophagy.
biofagismo (*m.*, *Biol.*) biophagism.
biófago –ga (*adj.*, *Biol.*) biophagous.
biofísica (*f.*) biophysics.
bióforo (*m.*, *Biol.*) biophore.
biogênese, biogenia (*f.*) biogenesis.
biogenésico –ca, biogenético –ca (*adj.*) biogenetic.
biógeno (*m.*) = BIÓFORO.
biogeografia (*f.*) biogeography.
biognose (*f.*, *Biol.*) biognosis.
biografar (*v.t.*) to write a biography of.
biografia (*f.*) biography.
biográfico –ca (*adj.*) biographic.
biógrafo –fa (*adj.*) biographer.
biólise (*f.*, *Biol.*) biolysis.
biólito (*m.*, *Petrog.*) biolith.
biologia (*f.*) biology.
biológico –ca (*adj.*) biologic.
biologista (*m.*,*f.*) biologist.
biólogo –ca (*m.*,*f.*) = BIOLOGISTA.
bioluminescência (*f.*, *Biol.*) bioluminescence.
biombo (*m.*) screen, partition.
biometria (*f.*) biometry.
bionomia (*f.*) bionomics, ecology.
bioplasma (*m.*, *Biol.*) bioplasm.
bioplástico –ca (*adj.*, *Biol.*) bioplastic, bioplasmic.
bioplasto (*m.*) = BIÓFORO.
biopse, biopsia (*f.*, *Med.*) biopsy.
bioquímica (*f.*) biochemistry.
bioquímico –ca (*adj.*) biochemical.
biorana (*f.*) = ABIORANA.
biose (*f.*, *Biol.*) biosis.
biosfera (*f.*) biosphere.
biotaxia [ks] (*f.*, *Biol.*) biotaxy, taxonomy.
biotecnia (*f.*) biotechnics.
biótico –ca (*adj.*, *Biol.*) biotic, biological.
biotita (*f.*, *Min.*) biotite.
biotomia (*f.*, *Med.*) vivisection.
bióxido [ks] (*m.*, *Chem.*) dioxide.—de carbono, carbon dioxide.—de chumbo, lead dioxide, brown lead oxide.—de enxôfre, sulfur dioxide.—de estanho, tin oxide, flowers of tin, tin anhydride.—de manganês, manganese dioxide, pyrolusite, manganese peroxide.—de nitrogênio, nitrogen dioxide, nitrogen peroxide. —de silício, silicon dioxide, cristobalite.
biparietal (*adj.*, *Craniol.*) biparietal.
bíparo –ra (*adj.*, *Zool.*, *Bot.*) biparous.
bipartição (*f.*) bipartition; bisection.
bipartidário –ria (*adj.*) bipartisan.
bipartido –da (*adj.*) bipartite; split in two.
bipartir (*v.t.*,*v.r.*) to divide into two parts.
bipartível (*adj.*) bipartible.
bipedal (*adj.*) bipedal.
bípede (*adj.*, *m.*) biped.
bipeltado –da (*adj.*, *Zool.*, *Bot.*) bipeltate.
bipenado –da (*adj.*) bipennate.
bipene (*adj.*) bipennate; (*m.*) a double-bitted hatchet.
bipétalo –la (*adj.*, *Bot.*) bipetalous.
bipinulado –da (*adj.*, *Bot.*) bipinnate.
bipiramidal (*adj.*, *Cryst.*) bipyramidal.
biplace (*adj.*, *m.*) two-seated (airplane).
biplano –na (*adj.*) biplanar; (*m.*) biplane.
biplume (*adj.*) = BIPENE.
bipolar (*adj.*) bipolar.
bipolaridade (*f.*) bipolarity.
biprisma (*f.*) biprism.—de Fresnel, Fresnel biprism.
biproduto (*m.*) = SUBPRODUTO.
biquadrado –da (*adj.*, *Math.*) biquadrate.
biquara (*f.*) a grunt called sailors' choice (*Haemulon parra*); also = CORCOROCA.
biquartzo (*m.*, *Min.*) biquartz.
biqueiro –ra (*adj.*) picky (as to food); of poor appetite; (*m.*) a shindig; (*f.*) water spout (extending from roof to

ground); ferrule of a cane or umbrella; toecap of a shoe or boot.
biquine (*m.*) a Bikini bathing suit.
biquintil (*adj.*, *Astrol.*) biquintile.
biraia (*f.*) drab; bitch.
biriba (*adj.*) suspicious; easily offended; (*f.*) club, stick; a young mare; (*m.*) a backwoodsman.
biribá (*f.*) the biriba ["A Brazilian tree (*Rollinia deliciosa*) whose fruit resembles the custard apple." *Webster*].
biriguí (*m.*) small bloodsucking sand fly (*Phletomus*).
Birmanês –**nesa** (*adj.*, *m.*,*f.*) Burmese.
Birmânia (*f.*) Burma.
birote (*m.*) topknot [= cocó].
birra (*f.*) aversion, antipathy; marihuana [= DIAMBA]. **de**—, for spite. **tomar**—**por**, to take a strong dislike to.
birrefração (*f.*, *Optics.*) double refraction.
birrefringência (*f.*, *Optics.*) birefringence.
birrefringente (*adj.*, *Optics.*) birefringent.
birreme (*f.*) bireme.
birrento –**ta** (*adj.*) sullen, sulky, pettish, cantankerous.
birretangular (*adj.*) having two right angles.
birrostrado –**da** (*adj.*) birostrate.
biru-manso (*m.*, *Bot.*) the edible canna (*C. edulis*), c.a. BERI, IMBIRI, MERU.
biru-listrada [ú] (*f.*) a non-poisonous colubrid arboreal Brazilian snake (*Eudryas boddaertii*), c.a. COBRA-CIPÓ.
biruta (*f.*) a wind or weather vane; (*Airport*) a wind sock; (*slang*) a person who is "nuts".
bis! encore!
bisagra (*f.*) hinge.
bisanual (*adj.*) biennial.
bisão (*m.*) the American bison.
bisar (*v.t.*) to encore; to repeat (a song, etc.).
bisavô (*m.*) great-grandfather.
bisavó (*f.*) great-grandmother.
bisbilhotar (*v.t.*) to meddle; to gossip; to tattle; to peer, pry, snoop.
bisbilhoteiro –**ra** (*m.*,*f.*) meddler, tattler, busybody, snooper.
bisbilhotice (*f.*) meddlesomeness.
bisbórria (*m.*) fool, jackass; scoundrel.
bisca (*f.*) a game played with a deck of 40 cards; the seven-spot; a cutting remark; rascal, scoundrel. **uma boa**—, a bad-tempered and insincere person.
biscaia (*f.*) a mare; a drab.
biscaio (*m.*) machete.
biscalongo (*m.*) a sandworm c.a. ARENÍCOLA.
biscar (*v.i.*) to play BISCA.
biscate (*m.*) a minor task or achievement; an odd job; a sideline.
biscatear (*v.t.*) to do odd jobs; to carry on a side line.
biscoitar, biscoutar (*v.*) = ABISCOITAR.
biscoitaria, biscoutaria (*f.*) cookie factory or store.
biscoiteira, biscouteira (*f.*) cookie jar.
biscoito, biscouto (*m.*) cookie, cracker, biscuit; (*colloq.*) a slap; one of the raised designs on the thread of a tire.
biscuit (*m.*, *Ceramics*) biscuit.
bisegre (*m.*) shoemaker's burnisher.
bisel [-séis] (*m.*) a bevel edge.
biselar (*v.t.*) to bevel.
bismita (*f.*, *Min.*) bismite, (hydrated) bismuth trioxide.
bismutal (*adj.*, *Chem.*) bismuthal.
bismútico –**ca** (*adj.*, *Chem.*) bismuthic.
bismutina (*f.*, *Min.*, *Chem.*) bismuthine, bismuth hydride.
bismutinita (*f.*, *Min.*) bismuthinite, bismuth sulfide, bismuth glance.
bismutita (*f.*, *Min.*) bismutite.
bismuto (*m.*, *Chem.*) bismuth.
bismutocre (*m.*, *Min.*) bismuth trioxide, bismuth yellow.
bisnaga (*f.*)·a collapsible tube (as for toothpaste); a small glass vial, equipped with a valve, and containing a highly volatile, aromatic, ether-like liquid under pressure, which persons squirt on each other at Carnival time; c.a. LANÇA-PERFUME.—**-das-searas**, (*Bot.*) the toothpick ammi (*A. visnaga*), c.a. PALITEIRA.—**-hortense**, the garden carrot (*Daucus carota sativa*), c.a. CENOURA.
bisnau (*m.*) a rascal, a "slicker".
bisneta (*f.*) great-granddaughter.
bisneto (*m.*) great-grandson.
bisonhice (*f.*) timidity; lack of experience.
bisonho –**nha** (*adj.*) inexperienced, green, unfledged; shy, timid; (*m.*) greenhorn; tyro, raw recruit, rookie.
bisoté (*adj.*) bevel-edged [glass].
bispado (*m.*) bishopric, diocese.

bispal (*adj.*) episcopal.
bispar (*v.t.*) to descry (espy) from a distance; (*v.r.*) to skedaddle.
bispo (*m.*) bishop.
bisseção, bissecção (*f.*) bisection.
bissegmentar (*v.t.*) to bisect.
bissemanal (*adj.*) twice-weekly.
bissetor –**toria**, **bissector** –**tora** (*adj.*) bisecting; (*m.*) bisector.
bissetriz, bissectriz (*f.*) bisectrix.
bissêxtil, bissexto –**ta** [ex = ês] (*adj.*) bissextile; (*m.*) bissext (the extra day which is added to February every fourth year). **ano**—, leap year.
bissexual, bissexo –**sexa** [ks] (*adj.*) bisexual.
bissexualidade [ks] (*f.*) bisexuality.
bissílabo –**ba** (*adj.*) = DISSÍLABO.
bissilicato (*m.*, *Mineral Chem.*) bisilicate.
bissimétrico –**ca** (*adj.*) bisymmetrical.
bissinuado –**da** (*adj.*) bisinuate.
bisso (*m.*, *Zool.*) byssus.
bissógeno –**na** (*adj.*, *Zool.*) byssogenous.
bissóide (*adj.*) byssoid, byssaceous; cottony, fiber-like.
bíssono –**na** (*adj.*) bisonant.
bissulcado –**da**, **bissulco** –**ca** (*adj.*) bisulcate, having two grooves.
bissulfato (*m.*, *Chem.*) disulphate.
bissulfito (*m.*, *Chem.*) disulphide.
bissulfureto [ê] (*m.*, *Chem.*) disulphuret.
bistorta (*f.*, *Bot.*) the European bistort (*Polygonum bistorta*).
bistre (*m.*, *Painting*) bister.
bisturi [rí] (*m.*) bistoury.—**-do-mato**, an orchid (*Cyrtopodium punctatum*), c.a. SUMARÉ, RABO-DE-TATU.
bitácula (*f.*) binnacle; (*colloq.*) the nose.
bitangente (*adj.*, *Math.*) bitangent.
bitartrato (*m.*, *Chem.*)—**de potássio**, potassium acid tartrate.
biternado –**da** (*adj.*, *Bot.*) biternate.
bitola (*f.*) gauge, standard measure; norm; pattern; railroad gauge (distance between rails).—**de arame**, a wire gauge.—**de um metro**, (*R.R.*) one-meter gauge. [Many if not most of the railroads in Brazil are of this gauge.]—**estreita**, (*R.R.*) narrow gauge (less than one meter).—**larga**, (*R.R.*) broad gauge (as the line which runs from São Paulo to Santos, and which is 5′4″, as compared to U.S.A. standard gauge of 4′8-1/2″.)
bitolar (*v.t.*) to gauge.
bitu [ú] (*m.*) ditty, popular song; bugbear, hobgoblin [= PAPÃO]; a male saúva ant [= SAVITU].
biurá [i-u] (*m.*) the grass Job's-tears (*Coix lacrymajobi*), c.a. LÁGRIMA-DE-NOSSA-SENHORA, CAPIM-DE-NOSSA-SE-NHORA, LÁGRIMA-DE-SANTA-MARIA. [The large white hard seeds can be strung like beads.]
biureto [i-urê] (*m.*, *Chem.*) biuret or allophanamide.
bivacar (*v.i.*) to bivouac.
bivalência (*f.*, *Chem.*) bivalence.
bivalente (*adj.*, *Chem.*) bivalent.
bivalve (*adj.*, *Zool.*, *Bot.*) bivalve, bivalvular.
bivaque (*m.*) bivouac.
biviário –**ria** (*adj.*) standing at a crossroads.
bixa [ks] (*f.*) = URUCUZEIRO.
bixáceas, bixíneas [ks] (*f.pl.*, *Bot.*) the Bixaceae.
bixáceo –**cea** [ks] (*adj.*, *Bot.*) bixaceous.
bixina [ks] (*f.*, *Chem.*) bixin.
bizantinismo (*m.*) hairsplitting.
bizantino –**na** (*adj.*; *m.*,*f.*) Byzantine; hairsplitting.
bizarrear (*v.t.*,*v.i.*) to boast (of).
bizarria (*f.*) gallantry, manliness; pomp.
bizarrice (*f.*) ostentation.
bizarro –**ra** (*adj.*) tall and handsome; well-groomed; noble, generous; gallant, brave. [But not bizarre in the French or Eng. sense of odd or freakish, which in Port. is CURIOSO, EXCÊNTRICO, ESQUISITO.]
bizigomático –**ca** (*adj.*, *Craniol.*) bizygomatic.
B/L = NOTA DE EMBARQUE (bill of lading).
blacaute (*m.*) black-out.
blague (*f.*) blah, rubbish.
blandície, blandícia (*f.*) blandishment, soft words, caress.
blandicioso –**sa** (*adj.*) bland, affable, suave.
blasfemador –**dora** [ô] (*adj.*) blaspheming; (*m.*,*f.*) blasphemer.
blasfemar (*v.t.*) to blaspheme, utter blasphemy (**contra**, against).
blasfematório –**ria** (*adj.*) blasphemous.

blasfêmia (*f.*) blasphemy.
blasfemo -ma [fê] (*adj.*) blasphemous; (*m.,f.*) blasphemer.
blasonador -dora (*adj.*) bragging, boasting; (*m.*) braggart, boaster.
blasonar (*v.t.*) to boast of; to vaunt; (*v.r.*) to sing one's own praises; to blow one's horn; to show off; to bluster; to brag, boast (**de**, of, about).
blastema (*m., Embryol.*) blastema.
blastídio (*m., Embryol.*) blastid.
blastocarpo -pa (*adj., Bot.*) blastocarpous.
blastocele (*m., Embryol.*) blastocoele.
blastócito (*m., Anat.*) blastocyte.
blastoderme (*m., Embryol.*) blastoderm.
blastóforo (*m., Zool.*) blastophore.
blastoftoria (*f., Med.*) blastopthoria.
blastogênese (*f., Biol.*) blastogenesis.
blastogenia (*f., Biol.*) blastogeny.
blastoma (*m., Med.*) blastoma, neoplasm.
blastomérico -ca (*adj., Embryol.*) blastometric,
blastomério, -tômero (*m., Embryol.*) blastomere.
blastomicete (*m., Bot.*) blastomycete.
blastomicose (*f., Med., Veter.*) blastomycosis.
blastóporo (*m., Embryol.*) blastopore.
blastoquilo (*m., Embryol.*) blastochyle.
blastosfera (*f., Embryol.*) blastosphere.
blástula (*f., Embryol.*) blastula.
blastulação (*f., Zool.*) blastulation.
blaterar (*v.t.*) to announce, proclaim; to berate.
blatóides (*m.pl., Zool.*) the Blattidae (cockroaches).
bledo (*m.*) = BREDO-VERDADEIRO.
blefador (*m.*) bluffer, four-flusher.
blefar (*v.i.*) to bluff (at poker, or otherwise).
blefarite (*f., Med.*) blepharitis.
blefe [é] (*m.*) a bluff (as at poker).
blefista (*m.*) bluffer.
bleima (*f., Veter.*) corn [= ESCARÇA].
blenda (*f., Min.*) blende.
blênio (*m.*), **blênia** (*f.*) a blenny (fish).
blindado -da (*adj.*) armored, ironclad, **carro**—, armored car. **divisão**—, (*Milit.*) armored division. **motor**—, (*Elec.*) shielded motor.
blindagem (*f.*) armor plating, or other shielding.—**electrostática**, electrostatic screening.
blindar (*v.t.*) to armor-plate, or to shield as with steel plates; to provide with a Faraday cage or other electrostatic screen.
blocausse (*m.*) blockhouse.
bloco (*m.*) a block of anything [but not a street block, which is QUARTEIRÃO]; a thick and heavy piece of wood, stone, etc.; a political bloc or coalition; a Carnival club. —**de cilindros**, motor block.—**de papel**, writing tablet. —**de vidro**, glass brick.—**errático**, boulder. **em**—, all together; wholesale.
bloquear (*v.t.*) to blockade; to jam; to block up.
bloqueio (*m.*) blockade.
blusa (*f.*) blouse.
blusão (*m.*) a single-breasted, semifitting jacket, such as worn by fliers.
bm. = BAIXA-MAR (low tide).
B.M.V. = BEATA MARIA VIRGEM (Holy Virgin Mary).
B.N. = BIBLIOTECA NACIONAL (National Library).
boa [ô] (*adj.*) fem. of BOM; (*f.*) boa (snake).
boá (*f.*) boa (scarf).
boa-fé (*f.*) good faith.
boa(s)-noite(s), boa(s)-noute(s) (*interj.*) Good night! Good evening! (*f.*) the large moonflower (*Calonyction acualeatum*, or *Ipomoea bona-nox*), c.a. CIPÓ-CAFÉ, COERANA, FLOR-DO-NORTE; (*pl.*) Madagascar periwinkle (*Lochnera rosea*), c.a. CONGORÇA; the common four-o'clock (*Mirabilis jalapa*), c.a. SUSPIROS.
boa-nova (*f.*) the Gospel; (*pl.*) good news, glad tidings.
boária (*f., Bot.*) the Chile boaria (*Maytenus boaria*).
Boas Festas, a phrase of greeting and well-wishing at Christmas, New Year's and Easter;—corresponds to Merry Christmas! Happy New Year! Happy Easter!
boas-vindas (*f.pl.*) welcome.
boa(s)-tarde(s) (*interj.*) Good afternoon! (*f.*) the bigleaf periwinkle (*Vinca major*); common evening primrose (*Oenothera biennis*), c.a. CÍRIO-DO-NORTE.
boataria (*f.*) rumors.
boateiro -ra (*adj.*) given to spreading rumors; (*m.,f.*) rumor-spreader, scandalmonger.
boato (*m.*) rumor, hearsay, report. **há**—s **de que**, "they say" that; there is a rumor that.

boava (*m.*) a somewhat derogatory term for a foreigner, esp. a Portuguese. Cf. EMBOABA.
boa-vida (*m.,f.*) one who seeks to live in clover with little work or none at all; idler.
boa-vontade (*f.*) goodwill. **de muita**—, very gladly.
bôba (*f.*) silly woman. Cf. BÔBO.
bobagem (*f.*) silliness, foolishness, folly, nonsense, puerility; drivel, baloney, applesauce, bunk, poppycock. **Deixe de**—! Nonsense! Don't be silly! **Não diga**—s, Stop talking nonsense.
bobalhão (*m.*), **-lhona** (*f.*) boob, laughing stock, nincompoop.
bobar, bobear (*v.i.*) to drivel, utter foolishness; to do something silly; to play the fool; to wait patiently for someone who doesn't come; to miss the point; to be had for a sucker; to wander aimlessly; to fool around (about).
bobeche [bé] (*m.*) bobèche.
bobete (*m.*) bobby pin.
bobice (*f.*) = BOBAGEM.
bobina (*f.*) bobbin, spool; coil; reel.—**blindada**, (*Elec.*) shielded coil.—**com núcleo de ferro**, (*Elec.*) iron-core coil.—**de acoplamento**, (*Elec.*) coupling coil.—**de antena**, (*Radio*) antenna coil.—**de arranque**, (*Elec.*) starter coil. —**de baixa perda**, (*Elec.*) low-loss coil.—**de campo**, (*Elec.*) field coil.—**de carga**, (*Elec.*) inductance coil.—**de excitação**, (*Elec.*) exciter coil.—**de exploração**, (*Elec.*) exploring coil.—**de fundo de cêsto**, (*Radio*) basket-weave coil.—**de ignição**, (*Elec.*) spark coil.—**de indução**, (*Elec.*) induction coil.—**de reação**, (*Elec.*) reactor.—**de reatância**, (*Elec.*) choke coil.—**de resistência**, (*Elec.*) resistor.—**"favo de mel"**, (*Elec.*) honeycomb coil.—**móvel**, (*Elec.*) moving coil.—**sintonizadora**, or **de sintonização**, (*Radio*) tuner.
bobinado (*m.*) the winding of an electric motor or generator.—**cilíndrico**, (*Elec.*) a solenoid.
bobinador (*m.*) reeler; winder; bobbin reeler.
bobinagem (*f.*) act of reeling or winding, as on a spool.
bobinar (*v.t.*) to wind on a bobbin, spool or reel.
bôbo -ba (*adj.*) simple, goofy, sappy, zany; (*m.*) court fool; buffoon; boob, dunce; (*Zool.*) a shearwater (*Puffinus*).—**alegre**, a simpleton. **fazer-se de**—, to play dumb; to play the fool.
bobó (*m.*) In Bahia, a dish consisting of mashed beans and bananas, mixed with DENDÊ palm oil and manioc meal; also = BÔBO (fool) and BARRIGUDINHO (a minnow).
boboca (*adj.; m.,f.*) very dumb or silly (person).
bóbonax [ks] (*m.*) = BOMBONAÇA.
bôca (*f.*) mouth (in any sense); muzzle; opening, entrance (as to a cave); (*Naut.*) beam; (*interj.*) Quiet! Shut up! —**da noite**, nightfall, dusk.—**da peça** (**canhão, cano**) muzzle of a gun.—**da serra**, mountain gap.—-**danada**, —-**de-inferno**, a maligner; one who is bitterly critical of others.—-**de-barro**, —-**de-sapo**, a stingless bee (*Melipona pallida*) which nests in termitaries; c.a. ABELHA-DE-CUPIM, CUPIRA, TIBUNA.—**de carga**, the charging door of a furnace.—-**de-cena**, the front part of a stage.—**de chupar ôvo**, a tiny mouth.—-**de-dragão**, an orchid (*Epidendrum sp.*).—-**de-fogo**, the yellow grunt (*Haemulon sciurus*), c.a. CORCOROCA; a canon.—**de forno**, a furnace or oven door.—**de incêndio**, fire hydrant.—**de jacaré**, a very large mouth.—-**de-leão**, common snapdragon (*Antirrhium majus*), c.a. BÔCA-DE-LÔBO.—-**de-lôbo**, drain pipe, culvert; also = BÔCA-DE-LEÃO.—-**de-ouro**, said of one who uses fine language.—-**de-praga**, said of one given to forecasting evil.—-**de-sapo**, a snake called JARARACA-PINTADA; a bee called BÔCA-DE-BARRO (see above); said also of a person having an unusually wide mouth.—**de sino**, mouth of a bell; said also of anything having a flared mouth, as a blunderbuss.—-**de-siri**, a tight-lipped person; keeping of a secret.—**do estômago**, pit of the stomach; **do porão**, (*Naut.*) hatchaway.—-**larga**, a mackerel (*Scomberomorus regalis*); a grunt (*Haemulon steindachneri*).—-**mole**, a drone (one who speaks monotonously, as with a drawl); a fish c.a. GUETE.—-**preta**, a squirrel monkey, c.a. MACACO-DE-CHEIRO.—-**suja**, a foul-mouthed person.—-**torta**, a fish c.a. GUETE; an anchovy c.a. MANJUBA; a person with a twisted mouth; a wasp (*Polybia occidentalis*). **à**—-**cheia**, [to speak] loudly, openly, freely. **à**—-**pequena**, [to speak] in whispers. **abrir a**—, to break the silence; to yawn; to grumble; to scold; to weep loudly. **andar**, or **estar**, **na**—**do povo**, or **nas**—**do mundo**, to be gossiped about; to be discussed by "everybody". **bater**—, (*slang*) to chat; to jaw, gab. **Cale a**—! Shut up! **céu da**—, roof of the

mouth, palate. **com o credo**, or **o coração, na—**, with one's heart in one's throat. **coser a—**, to seal the lips. **de—aberta**, open-mouthed, agape; thunderstruck. **Do prato à—perde-se a sopa**, There's many a slip twixt the cup and the lip. **duro de—** (or **de queixo**), hard-mouthed [horse]. **estar com a palavra na—**, to have a word or name on the tip of one's tongue. **pano de—**, stage curtain. **passar de—em—**, of news, to spread from one to another. **pôr**, or **botar, a—no mundo**, to yell, holler. **quebrado da—**, said of a horse having a very sensitive mouth.
bocaça (f.) a large mouth.
bocadinho (m.) a wee bit, mite.
bocado (m.) bite, mouthful; a bit or morsel of anything; a short time; a bridle bit.—**sem osso**, reward without effort.
bocagem (f.) foul language.
bocaina (f.) mountain gap; river mouth.
bocaiúva (f.) any of the tall, pinnate-leaved Acrocomia palms.
bocal (adj.) buccal; (m.) mouth of a jar, pitcher, etc; an opening; a socket; mouthpiece (of wind instrument or telephone); nozzle; bridle bit.
boçal (adj.) uncultured, uncouth; coarse, loutish; of slaves, newly-arrived from Africa.
boçalidade (f.) coarseness, loutishness.
bocar (v.) = ABOCAR.
bocarra (f.) a very large mouth.
bocaxim (m.) buckram.
bocejar (v.i.) to yawn, gape.
bocejo [ê] (m.) yawn. **disfarçar um—**, to stifle a yawn.
bocel [céis] m., Arch.) torus, large molding; fluted molding.
boceta [ê] (f.) jewel case; snuff box, tobacco pouch.—**-de-mula**, (Bot.) the Kuteeragum sterculia (S. urens).—**de Pandora**, Pandora's box.
boceteira (f.) a woman vender of dressmaker's notions.
bocha (m.) bowls; bowling ball.
bochecha [ê] (f.) cheek; (pl., colloq.) face. **dizer (alguma coisa) nas—s de alguém**, to tell someone something to his face.
bochechão (m.), **-chada** (f.) a slap in the face.
bochechar (v.t.) to swish water or other liquid about in the mouth, as when rinsing it; to gargle.
bochecho [ê] (m.) a mouthful of water, mouth-wash, etc.
bochechudo -da (adj.) fat-cheeked; heavy-jowled.
bochinchada (f.) making of trouble.
bochinche, -cho (m.) brawl, fracas, melee; rowdy dance, shindig.
bochincheiro -ra (adj.) trouble-making; (m.) brawler.
bochornal (adj.) sultry.
bochorno [chô] (m.) hot, sultry air or wind.
bociado -da (adj., Med.) goitrous.
bocim (m., Mach.) stuffing box [= CAIXA DE EMPANQUE].
bôcio (m.) goiter [= PAPEIRA].
bocó (adj.) simple, dull-witted; (m.) simpleton, boob, fool; dolt, dope, sap; a small, rawhide wallet.
bocônia (f.) the pink plumepoppy (Macleaya cordata).
bocório -ria (adj.) low, rascally; (m.) scoundrel; loud discussion.
boçoroca (f.) rain gully.
bocuba (f.) = BICUÍBA.
bocudo -da (adj.) big-mouthed; (f.) a heavy-gauge gun.
boda [ô] (f.) wedding; wedding feast; (pl.) wedding anniversary.—**de brilhante** or **de diamante**, diamond or 75th wedding anniversary.—**de coral**, coral or 35th w.a.—**de cristal**, crystal or 15th w.a.—**de esmeralda**, emerald or 40th w.a.—**de estanho**, tin or 10th w.a.—**de madeira**, wooden or 5th w.a.—**de ouro**, golden or 50th w.a.—**de pérola**, pearl or 30th w.a.—**de porcelana**, china or 20th w.a.—**de prata**, silver or 25th w.a.—**de rubi**, ruby or 45th w.a.
bode (m.) billy-goat; mulatto; half-breed; an ugly man; (colloq.) a Protestant; (sl.) ruckus, uproar, fracas; (pl.) face cards, esp. the jacks.—**expiatório**, scape goat.—**-prêto**, a Mason; the Devil. **estar de—amarrado**, to be angry.
bodeco (m.) a baby PIRARUCU.
bodega (f.) a (small, dirty) tavern or wineshop [= TABERNA]; filth; coarse food; (slang) any worthless thing ("piece of junk").
bodegão, -gueiro (m.) tavern-keeper; fig., a person of unclean habits.
bodeguice (f.) filthiness.

bodelha [ê] (f.) kelp, seaweed; (Bot.) the bladder rockweed (Fucus vesiculosus), c.a. ALGA-VESICULOSA, SARGAÇO-VESICULOSO, CARVALHO (or CARVALINHO)-DO-MAR, BOTILHÃO-VESICULOSO.
bodemeria (f., Marine Law) bottomry.
bodiame (m.) the bo or bodhi tree (Ficus religiosa), c.a. PIMPOL.
bodocada (f.) a shot with the BODOQUE; fig., a quick, cutting remark.
bodoque (m.) an Indian two-string bow, with a saddle in the middle, used for hurling small stones or hard clay pellets instead of arrows; also = ESTILINGUE.
bodoqueiro (m.) one who uses a BODOQUE.
bodoso -sa (adj.) filthy, evil-smelling.
bodum (m.) the rank smell of a BODE (billy-goat); fetid body odor; (Zool.) harvestman (daddy-long-legs), c.a. OPILIÃO.
boêmio -mia (adj.) Bohemian; vagabond; unconventional; free and easy; (m.) a Bohemian; person who lives in a free and easy, wild or unconventional way; playboy; a vagrant; (Chem.) = RÊNIO; (f.) Bohemia; unconventional mode of life; loose living. [In the latter senses, usually but erroneously pronounced: BOEMIA.]
bôer (adj.; m.,f.) Boer.
bofar (v.t.) to vomit, eject violently, discharge, spew; (v.i.) to gush out (as blood from the lungs).
bofe (m., colloq.) lung; nature (essential character) of a person; (pl.) lights and other animal viscera. **botar** or **pôr os—s pela bôca**, to be so tired that one's tongue hangs out.
bofé (adv.) in good faith, frankly, in truth, truly. [Contraction of **a+boa+fé**.]
bofetada (f.) a hard and insulting slap in the face; fig., an insult, affront, injury. **dar uma—com luvas de pelica**, to return good for evil, as to reply politely to a rude question.
bofetão (m.) a hard blow with the fist.
bofete [fê] (m., colloq.) a light tap or slap; buffet.
bofetear (v.) = ESBOFETAR.
boganga (f.) Malabar gourd (Cucurbita ficifolia).
bogari [rí] (m.) the Arabian jessamine (Jasmium sambac), or its flower.
bogui [í] bogie. [British].
boi (m.) ox, steer, head of cattle; (slang) prostitute, drab; (colloq.) menses.—**almiscarado**, musk ox (Ovibos moschatus).—**-bumbá** = BUMBA-MEU-BOI.—**cevado**, ox.—**-corneta**, one-horned steer; obstreperous person; black sheep (of a family).—**-de-cova**, a house-raising or other "bee".—**espaço**, wide-horned steer.—**-gordo**, a senna (Cassia rugosa), c.a. ALCAÇUZ-BRAVO, BICO-DE-CORVO, CABO-VERDE, BENDOBI-BRAVO, PARATUDO, RAIZ-DE-CORVO, RAIZ-PRETA, VOLÁCIO.—**marinho**, a seal (Phoca vitulinus).—**sonso**, a hypocrite.—**-surubi**, or **-surrubim**, = BUMBA-MEU-BOI.—**-vivo**, a stew of bull's testicles.
bóia (f.) buoy, float; ball-float (in a water tank); (slang) grub, chow, vittles, rations.—**de ancoragem**, mooring buoy.
boiaçu [bò-iaçú] (m.) "On the Rio Branco, a slight rising of the river level, elsewhere called REPIQUETE, which sets in November." [GBAT].
boiada (f.) herd of cattle.
boiadeiro (m.) cattle herder, cowhand, drover.
boiador [o], **-douro, -doiro** (m.) a body of quiet water in which turtles, manatees, etc., rise to the surface.
boiama = BOIADA.
boiante (adj.) floating.
boião (m.) a large-mouthed jar; small jar (for salve, cream, etc.); in the Amazon, a hearth and chimney for smoking latex.—**de farmácia**, gallipot.
boiar (v.i.) to float; (slang) to eat.
boicininga (f.) another name for CASCAVEL (rattlesnake.)
boicorá (f.) any of various false coral snakes (frequently mistaken for the poisonous ones), esp. Pseudoboa trigeminius and P. rhombifera, c.a. BACORÁ, and Erythrolamprus aesculapii. [The terms BOICORÁ and BACORÁ are also used to designate the true corals (Micrurus).]
boicotagem (f.) an act or instance of boycotting.
boicotar, boicotear (v.t.) to boycott.
boicote (m.) boycott.
boicotiara (f.) = COTIARA.
boieiro (m.) drover, cattle herder, cow puncher.
boina (f.) beret.
boipeba, boipeva (f.) either of two Braz. snakes: a small viper (Bothrops itapetiningae), c.a. COTIARINHA and

JARARACA-DO-CAMPO, or *Xenedon merremii*, a harmless member of the Colubridae, c.a. BOIPEBA, CAPITÃO-DO-MATO, PEPEVA, JARARACAMBEVA.

boipevaçu [ú] (*f.*) a harmless, semi-aquatic colubrid Brazilian snake (*Cyclagras gigas*), very similar to BOIPEVA, and c.a. SURUCUCU-DO-PANTANAL.

boiru [ú] (*f.*) = MUSSURANA.

boitatá (*m.*) will-o'-the-wisp; spirit protecting fields against would-be burners; bogeyman. Vars. BAITATÁ, BIATATÁ, BATATÃO.

boitiapóia (*f.*) = SUCURI.

boiubu [ú] (*m.*) a harmless green two-foot colubrine Brazilian snake (*Philodryas aestivus*).

boiúna (*f.*) = SUCURI.

bojador –dora [dô] (*adj.*) bulging, jutting, prominent. **cabo—**, an old name for the Cape of Good Hope.

bojamento (*m.*) bulge; flare.

bojante (*adj.*) = BOJADOR.

bojar (*v.i.*) to bulge, swell out, flare out.

bôjo (*m.*) bulge, belly, protuberance; capability.—**da mão**, hollow of the hand.

bojudo –da (*adj.*) big-bellied, pot-bellied.

bola (*f.*) ball, globe, sphere; any spherical body; (*colloq.*) the head; a bolus of poison; (*colloq.*) gag, wisecrack, joke; (*colloq.*) graft; (*pl.*) = BOLEADEIRAS; (*m.*) a milksop, a dull fellow; (*interj.*) (Ora)**—s!** Aw nuts! After all! Baloney! Hooey!**—s para**, to hell with, nuts to.**—ao cêsto**, basketball, c.a. BASQUETEBOL.**—de bilhar**, billiard ball.**—de futebol**, football.**—s de gude**, glass marbles.**—-de-neve**, the European cranberry bush viburnum (*V. opulus*), c.a. NOVÊLOS, SABUGUEIRO-DE-ÁGUA, SABUGUEIRO-DOS-PANTANOS.**—de sabão**, soap bubble.**—de tênis**, tennis ball.**—elástica**, rubber ball. **Boa—!** or **Que—!** That's a good one! What a gag! **bater—**, to kick a soccer ball (for fun or practice). **dar—**, (*slang*) to lead on (flirt); to pay attention; to bribe. **dar—a um cachorro**, to poison a dog. **dar tratos à—**, to rack (cudgel) one's brains. **Êle é um—s**, He is a weak sister. **Êle é uma—**, He is a funny guy. **Êle não regula bem da—**, He has a screw loose in his head. **não dar—**, to pay no attention to.

bolacha (*f.*) cracker, biscuit, cookie; (*colloq.*) a slap; a reprimand; a thin sheet of rubber; a sea urchin, c.a. CORRUPIO.**—quebrada**, a trifle.

bolacheiro –ra (*adj.*) large and flat (referring to a person's face); (*m.,f.*) cookie-maker or -seller.

bolada (*f.*) a big pot (at gambling); a pile of money; money loss; embezzlement.

bolandas (*f.pl.*) hurry, scurry. **andar em—**, to rush about.

bolandeira (*f.*) large cogwheel in a cane crusher; cotton gin.

bolão (*m.*) a ball-like mass of any substance; bowling game.

bolapé (*m.*) a deep ford (which a horse can barely cross without having to swim).

bolar (*v.t.*, *colloq.*) to perceive, catch on; to rack one's brains. **Estou bolando umas coisas**, I am mulling over some things. **Não bolei o que êle disse**, I didn't get what he said.

bolbo [ô] (*m.*) & derivs. = BULBO & derivs.

bolçar (*v.i.*) of babies, to spew up milk.

bolchevique (*adj.*; *m.,f.*) Bolshevik.

bolchevista (*adj.*; *m.,f.*) Bolshevist.

bolchevismo (*m.*) Bolshevism.

boldina (*f.*, *Chem.*) boldine.

boldo [bô] (*m.*, *Bot.*) boldutree (*Peumus boldus*).

boldrié (*m.*) baldric; shoulder belt; rifle sling.

boleadeiras (*f.pl.*) bolas. [A missile consisting of two or three leather-covered stones attached to the ends of a thong;—used by the GAÚCHOS of Rio Grande do Sul to hurl at and entangle the legs of cattle and horses which they wish to catch.]

boleado –da (*adj.*) rounded (like a ball); (*m.*) a round ear-mark on cattle.

boleador (*m.*) one who uses BOLEADEIRAS.

boleamento (*m.*) act of hurling BOLEADEIRAS.

bolear (*v.t.*) to make round as a ball; to round off; to hurl BOLEADEIRAS; to drive a coach.

boleeiro [e-ei] (*m.*) coachman, driver.

boléia (*f.*) driver's seat (on a carriage or wagon); coachman's box; whiffletree.

boleira (*f.*) woman who makes and/or sells cakes.

boleiro (*m.*) man who makes and/or sells cakes; a ball pitcher; (*colloq.*) a grafter.

bolero [é] (*m.*) a Spanish dance; a kind of short jacket.

boletim (*m.*) bulletin, (telegraphic) report, military communiqué; school report card; official periodical.—**financeiro**, financial report.—**meteorológico**, weather report.

boléto (*m.*, *Milit.*) billet; (*Bot.*) any fungus of the genus Boletus; (*Veter.*) fetlock joint.

boléu (*m.*) tumble, fall, thud, esp. of a lassoed horse.

bôlha (*f.*) blister; bubble.—**de ar**, air bubble.—**d'água**, water blister.—**de sabão**, soap bubble.

bolhar (*v.i.*) to bubble [= BORBULHAR].

boliche (*m.*) small, cheap, dirty store, esp. one where drinks are sold; bowling game.

bolicheiro (*m.*) keeper of a BOLICHE.

bólide (*f.*) bolide (flaming meteor).

bolina (*f.*) bowline; center board of a sail boat; (*colloq.*) the intentional nudging or rubbing, by a man, of the arm or leg of a woman seated next to him; (*m.*) a man who seeks such carnal contacts. **ir à—**, to luff. **navegar à—**, to sail close-hauled.

bolinar (*v.i.*) to sail close-hauled; to go obliquely; (*colloq.*) of a man, to rub or nudge (intentionally) the arm or leg of a woman seated next to him (on a streetcar, in a movie, etc.).

bolinete [nê] (*m.*) capstan; miner's pan.

bolita (*f.*) a marble.

bolívia (*f.*) the huanaco cocainetree (*Erythroxylon coca*), c.a. COCA, IPADU; [*cap.*] Bolivia.

boliviano– na (*adj.*; *m.,f.*) Bolivian.

bôlo (*m.*) cake; a smack in the palm of the hand with a ferule; the stake (kitty, pot) at gambling; a trick or catch; bolus.—**de noiva**, wedding cake.—**-de-rôlo**, roly-poly (pastry). **dar o—**, to fail to show up; to break an appointment. **levar o—**, to be stood up, wait in vain.

bolômetro (*m.*, *Physics*) bolometer.

Bolonha (*f.*) Bologna; Boulogne.

Bolonhês –nhesa, (*adj.*; *m.,f.*) Bolognese.

bolônio –nia (*adj.*) ignorant, simple, dull-witted.

bolor [lô] (*m.*) mold, mildew; fig., old age. **Pedra que rola não cria—**, A rolling stone gathers no moss.

bolorecer (*v.*) = ABOLORECER.

bolorento –ta (*adj.*) moldy, musty, stale. **Por fora, muita farofa; por dentro, pão—**, said of persons who make a great outward show of knowledge, money, etc., but who are in fact devoid of it.

bolota (*f.*) acorn; little ball; pendant, charm.

bolotal (*m.*) an oak grove abounding in acorns.

bôlsa (*f.*) purse, handbag, money pouch; any pouch or pouch-like object (*Anat.*, *Zool.*) pouch; (*pl.*) saddlebags; (*m.*) treasurer, cashier, purser.—**de estudos**, a scholarship.—**de imóveis**, real estate board.—**de-pastor**, (*Bot.*) shepherds-purse (*Capsella bursa-pastoris*), c.a. BUCHO-DE-BOI; also, species of *Calceolaria*.—**de valores**, stock market.—**do fel**, gall bladder [= VESÍCULA BILIAR].—**serosa**, (*Anat.*) a bursa or serous sac.—**sinovial** (*Anat.*) synovial capsule. **abrir a—(a alguém)**, to open one's pocketbook (to another). **afrouxar os cordões da—**, to loosen the pursestrings. **ter a—larga**, to be openhanded, generous.

bolsista (*m.,f.*) stock market speculator; the holder of a scholarship.

bôlso (*m.*) pocket.—**chapeado**, patch pocket.—**do colête**, vest pocket. **couraçado de—**, pocket battleship. **relógio de—**, pocket watch.

bom [bons; fem. boa(s)] (*adj.*) good (in all senses); (*m.*) good; (*interj.*) Good!—**de todo**, entirely well.—**êxito**, good result, success.—**homem**, a simple, good-natured man. **homem—**, a good man.—**para o fogo**, fit only to be burned.—**que dói!** so good it hurts!—**sujeito**, good fellow.—**tempo**, fine weather [Cf. BOM-TEMPO below]. **bons ares**, wholesome air. **achar—**, to consider desirable, good. **Acho—você ir já**, I think you'd better go now. **Ano—**, New Year. **bem—**, quite good, not bad at all; (*interj.*) Good! I'm glad! **Daí não vai sair nada de—**, No good will come of it. **de—grado**, gladly, willingly. **Dois é—, três é demais**, Two is company, three is a crowd. **Essa é boa!** That's a good one! **ficar—**, to get well. **Parecia—demais para acontecer**, It seemed too good to be true. **tão—quanto corajoso**, as good as he is brave **Você chegou no—momento**, You arrived in the nick of time. [See also the many compound words below.]

bomba (*f.*) pump; bomb; a small metal tube with a strainer on the end, used for sipping MATE tea from a gourd; bombshell (great surprise); wellhole of a stair; cream puff; failure in an examination.—**aspirante**, a lift or suction pump.—**atômica**, atomic bomb.—**centrífuga**, centrifugal pump.—**de água**, water pump.—**de ação direta**, direct-acting pump.—**de alimentação**, feed pump.—**de ar**, air pump.—**de bicicleta**, bicycle pump.—**de cisterna**, well pump.—**de combustível**, fuel pump.—**de compressão**, compressor pump.—**de demolição**, demolition bomb.—**de dinamite**, TNT bomb.—**de dois tempos**, or **de dupla ação**, double-acting pump.—**de efeito simples**, single-acting pump.—**de êmbolo**, piston pump.—**de escorva**, wobble pump.—**de fumaça**, or—**fumígena**, smoke bomb.—**de gasolina**, gas (filling) station.—**de hidrogênio**, hydrogen bomb.—**de incêndios**, fire engine; fire pump.—**de flit**, Flit gun.—**de lubrificação**, lubricating pump.—**de mão**, hand pump.—**de pressão**, pressure pump.—**de profundidade**, depth bomb.—**de urânio**, uranium bomb.—**de vácuo**, vacuum pump.—**de vapor**, steam pump.—**elevadora**, lift pump.—**enfeitada**, barely passing marks on an examination.—**falhada**, a dud (unexploded bomb).—**-foguete**, rocket bomb.—**hidráulica**, hydraulic pump.—**incendiária**, incendiary bomb.—**lacrimogênia**, tear-gas bomb.—**para ácidos**, acid pump.—**para pneu**, tire pump.—**pneumática**, air pump.—**premente**, force pump.—**real**, sky rocket.—**-relógio**, time bomb.—**rotatória**, rotary pump. **A notícia estourou como uma—**, The news burst like a bombshell. **à prova de—s**, bombproof. **alça de—s**, bomb sight. **cabide de—s**, bomb rack. **dar à—**, to pump. **levar**, or **tomar—**, to flunk an exam. **porta—s**, bomb rack.

bombacáceo **-cea** (*adj.*) bombacaceous; (*f.pl.*) the Bombacaceae (family of silk cotton trees).

bombachas (*f.pl.*) very wide, loose trousers, closely fitting around the waist and ankles, worn typically by the GAÚCHOS of southern Brazil.

bombada (*f.*) pumping action.

Bombaim [a-ím] (*m.*) Bombay.

bombão (*m.*) = MELANCIA-DA-PRAIA.

bombardão (*m., Music*) bass horn.

bombardeador (*m.*) bombardier; (*Physics*) cyclotron.

bombardeamento (*m.*) bombardment, shelling.

bombardear (*v.t.*) to bombard, shell.

bombardeio (*m.*) bombing, bombardment.—**aéreo**, air bombing.—**atômico**, atomic bombing. **avião de—**, bombing plane, bomber.

bombardeiro (*m.*) bombardier; bomber; bombing plane —**de mergulho**, dive bomber.

bombardino (*m., Music*) baritone horn.

bombástico **-ca** (*adj.*) bombastic, high-flown.

bômbax [ks] (*m., Bot.*) any silk-cotton tree of the genus Bombax.

bombazina (*f.*) bombazine, cotton twill.

bombeador **-dora** [dô] or **-deira** (*adj.*) said of a teacher who likes to give BOMBAS (flunking marks).

bombear (*v.t.*) to pump; to round off (the top of anything); to spy, watch; to flunk (pupils).—**água**, to pump water. **baú bombeado**, a trunk with a rounded lid.

bombeiro (*m.*) fireman; plumber; pumper, pump operator; spy; street peddler.—**-hidráulico**, plumber.—**voluntário**, volunteer fireman. **chamar os—s**, to call out the fireman. **chamar um—**, to call a plumber. **Corpo de—s**, Fire Department.

bômbix [ks], **bômbice** (*m.*) the genus (*Bombyx*) which comprises the common silkworm moth (*B. mori*).

bombista (*m.,f.*) maker of bombs; a criminal bomb-thrower.

bombo (*m.*) bass drum. Var. BUMBO.

bom-bocado (*m.*) a tidbit made with cheese, coconut milk, eggs and sugar. **O—não é para quem o faz, mas para quem o come**, Sometimes another reaps the reward of one's efforts.

bombom (*m.*) bonbon.

bombonaça (*f.*) the jipijapa, a palmlike plant known also as BOMBANASSA, or Panama-hat palm (*Carludovica palmata*), c.a. JIPIJAPÁ, LUCATIVA.

bombordo (*m.*) port, larboard (left side of a ship).

bom-calção (*m.*) a good horseman.

bom-copo (*m.*) one who holds his liquor well.

bom-dente (*m.*) a hearty eater.

bom-dia (*m.*) [also bons-dias] Good morning!

bom-garfo (*m.*) a good trencherman.

bom-gênio (*m.*) good nature.

bom-gôsto (*m.*) good taste.

bom-grado (*m.*) good will. **de—**, gladly.

bom-humor (*m.*) good humor.

bom-modo (*m.*) affable manner.

bom-nome (*m.*) good name, reputation.

bomôncia (*f., Bot.*) the Easter herald trumpet (*Beaumontia grandiflora*) having very large, showy, fragrant white flowers; also yields a pure white fiber.

bom-partido (*m.*) a good offer; good match (marriage).

bom-senso (*m.*) good sense, common sense.—**velho de guerra**, common horse sense.

bom-serás (*m., colloq.*) simpleton.

bom-sucesso (*m., colloq.*) normal childbirth.

bom-talher (*m., colloq.*) a good trencherman.

bom-tempo [also bons-tempos] (*m.*) the good old days.

bom-tom (*m.*) bon-ton.

bonachão **-chona**, **bonacheirão** **-rona** (*adj.*) good-hearted, kind, patient, simple; (*m.,f.*) that kind of person.

bonaerense (*adj.*) of or pert. to Buenos Aires; (*m.,f.*) a native of that city. [= BUENAIRENSE].

bonança (*adj.*) calm [sea, wind, weather]; (*f.*) fine weather; lull, calm; fig., peace, quiet, harmony. [But not bonanza, for which there is no single-word equivalent in Portuguese].

bonançoso **-sa** (*adj.*) quiet, serene.

bondade (*f.*) goodness, kindness, benevolence. **tenha a—(de)**, Please; if you please.

bondadoso **-sa** (*adj.*) = BONDOSO.

bondar (*v.i.*) to suffice. **Bonda!** That's enough!

bondara (*f., Bot.*) a crape myrtle (*Lagerstroemia microcarpa*), c.a. BENTECA.

bonde (*m.*) street-car, trolley car. [The name is derived from the English word "bonds" (securities), sold to finance the first construction of street-car lines in Brazil.] —**de burro**, horse car.—**elétrico**, trolley car.—**funicular**, cable car. **condutor de—**, street-car conductor. **ir de—**, to go by street-car. **motorneiro de—**, street-car motorman. **ponto** (or **parada**) **de—**, street-car stop.

bondoso **-sa** (*adj.*) good, kind(ly), benevolent.

bonduque (*m., Bot.*) the nickernut guilandia (*G. bonduc*), c.a. ÔLHO-DE-GATO.

boné (*m.*) a cap (for the head).—**de bispo**, (*Bot.*) the India Barringtonia (*B. speciosa*), c.a. BONÉ-QUADRADO.

boneca (*f.*) doll, dolly, doll-baby; puppet; a pretty but empty-headed woman; a sugar tit; corn tassel.—**de trapos**, rag doll.

bonecar (*v.i.*) of corn, etc., to tassel out.

boneco (*m.*) a male doll; manikin.—**de engonço**, puppet, marionette.

bongar (*v.t.*) to pick, cull.

Bonifácio (*m.*) Boniface.

bonificação (*f.*) bonus, allowance, gratuity.

bonificar (*v.t.*) to give a bonus or allowance to.

bonifrate (*m.*) marionette, puppet [= FANTOCHE]; jackanapes, whippersnapper, dandy.

bonina (*f., Bot.*) the common four-o'clock (*Mirabilis jalapa*), c.a. BOAS-NOITES, MARAVILHA, JALAPA-VERDADEIRA; also (in Portugal) the English daisy (*Bellis perennis*), c.a. BELA-MARGARIDA, MARGARIDA-DOS-PRADOS.

boníssimo **-ma** (*absol. superl. of* BOM) very kind.

bonitaço **-ça**, **bonitão** **-tona** (*adj., colloq.*) very pretty; good-looking.

bonitete [tête] (*adj.*) somewhat pretty; cute.

boniteza [ê] (*f.*) prettiness.

bonitinho **-nha** (*adj.*) cute. [dim. of BONITO].

bonito **-ta** (*adj.*) pretty, beautiful; handsome, attractive, fine, nice; natty; (*m.*) a child's "pretty-pretty" (toy); bonito (a marine food fish); (*Zool.*) a bird better known as GATURAMO (which see); (*exclam.*) Fine! [ironical].—**-cachorro**, the frigate mackerel (*Auxis thazard*).—**-debarriga-riscada**, the ocean bonito (*Gymnosarda pelamis*). —**-do-campo**, the blue-backed chlorophonia (*Chlorophonia c. cyanea*), c.a. GATURAMO (-VERDE).—**-pintado**, the false albacore (*Gymnosarda alleterata*), c.a. CURUATÁ-PINIMA; (*f.*) a cake called DOCE-DE-PIMENTA.

bonitete **-tota** (*adj.*) somewhat pretty.

bonomia (*f.*) bonhomie.

bons-dias (*m.pl., Bot.*) the common morning-glory (*Ipomoea purpurea*); the hedge glorybind (*Convolvulus sepium*). Cf. BOM-DIA.

bons-ofícios (*m.pl.*) good offices.

bônus (*m.,sing. & pl.*) bonus.

boquear (*v.i.*) to gasp, pant; to yawn.

boqueira (*f., Med.*) a form of stomatitis affecting the corners of the mouth [= SABIÁ].

boqueirão (*m.*) ravine, canyon, gap, mountain pass; river mouth.

boquejar (*v.i.*) to whisper (**sôbre**, about); to yawn.
boquiaberto –ta (*adj.*) open-mouthed (in wonder); gaping, agape; imbecile.
boquiabrir [26] (*v.t.*) to cause open-mouthed wonder; (*v.r.*) to be struck open-mouthed with wonder.
boquilha (*f.*) cigar or cigarette holder [= PITEIRA].
boquim (*m.*) mouthpiece of a musical instrument.
boquinha [dim. of boca] (*f.*) a little mouth; a kiss; a light meal, snack. **fazer—**, to pucker up; to pout.
boquirroto –ta (*adj.*) blabbing.
boquisseco –ca [ê] (*adj.*) closemouthed.
borá-boi, borá-cavalo (*m.*) = ARAMÁ.
borace (*m.*) = BÓRAX.
borácico –ca (*adj.*) boracic, boric.
boracífero –ra (*adj.*) boraciferous.
boracita (*f., Min.*) boracite.
boral (*m., Pharm.*) boral.
boraquira (*f.*) a partridgelike bird of the tinamou family (*Nothura minor*), c.a. CADORNA-MINEIRA.
borato (*m., Chem.*) borate.
bórax [ks] (*m.*) borax [= TRINCAL]. Var. BORACE.
borboleta [ê] (*f.*) butterfly; turnstile; a window catch; bow tie; the banded butterfly fish (*Chaetodon striatus*); c.a. FREIRE; (*Bot.*) butterfly flower (*Schizanthus spp.*); gingerlily (*Hedychium coronarium* and *H. flavescens*).— **-pintada**, the Amazon hatchet fish (*Carnegiella strigata*) sometimes seen in home aquaria.
borboletear (*v.i.*) to flit (**por**, about); to wander.
borborismo, borborigmo (*m., Med.*) borborygmus.
borbotão (*m.*) gush, rush (of liquids). **aos borbotões**, gushing, bubbling, gurgling.
borbotar (*v.i.*) to spout, spurt; to pour forth, gush out; to gurgle.
borbulha (*f.*) blister, boil; bubble; bud of a plant.
borbulhador (*m., Petrol.*) bubble cap.
borbulhamento (*m.*) bubbling. **bandeja**, or **prato, de—**, (*Petrol.*) bubble tray. **ponto de—**, bubbling point. **tôrre de—**, bubbling tower or column.
borbulhar (*v.i.*) to bubble up (**de**, from); to gurgle; to rush out, gush out; to bud, sprout; (*v.t.*) to cause to bud.
borbulhante (*adj.*) bubbling.
borbulho (*m.*) bubble.
borbulhoso –sa (*adj.*) bubbling.
borcar (*v.*) = EMBORCAR.
bôrco (*m.*) **de—**, face down, prone.
borda (*f.*) border, edge, rim; brim, brink, bank.—**da água**, water's edge.—**de ataque**, (*Aeron.*) leading edge (of a wing, etc.).—**de saída** or **de fuga**, (*Aeron.*) trailing edge (of a wing, etc.).—**do campo**, limit of the field.—**do mato**, edge of the woods.—**dum poço**, rim of a well.—**duma saia**, rim of a skirt. **à—de**, bordering; on the edge of. **dar—**, to keel almost over.
bordada (*f.*) tack (of a sailboat); broadside.
bordadeira (*f.*) embroideress.
bordado (*m.*) embroidery.—**de aplicação**, appliqué embroidery.
bordadura (*f.*) embroidery; border; enclosure.
bordalengo –ga (*adj.*) coarse, vulgar, ignorant.
bordalesa [ê] (*f.*) Bordeaux mixture (a fungicide).
bordão (*m.*) rod, staff; bass string of a musical instrument; help, support.—**de-velho**, (*Bot.*) the raintree saman (*Samanea saman*); also = AVAREMOTEMO.
bordar (*v.t.,v.i.*) to embroider; to border; (*v.t.*) to embellish, enhance (a statement or narrative).
bordejar, bordear (*v.i., Naut.*) to tack; to pursue a zigzag course; to stagger and reel (from drink).
bordel [-déis] (*m.*) bordel, brothel.
bordeleiro, bordelengo (*m.*) whoremonger.
bordelês, –lesa [ê] (*adj.; m.,f.*) Bordelais(e).
bordéus (*m.*) Bordeaux wine.
bordo (*m.*) board (side of a ship); broadside (of a ship); course of a ship; tacking (of a sailing vessel). **a—(de)**, aboard, on board. **aos—s**, reeling, staggering, lurching, zigzagging (as from drink). **de alto—**, of ships, having several decks; fig., of high rank. **descer de—**, to go ashore, get off the ship. **livro de—**, ship's logbook. **pôsto a—**, F.O.B. (free on board). **subir para—**, to go aboard.
bôrdo (*m., Bot.*) silver maple (*Acer saccharinum*).
bordoada (*f.*) blow with a stick; a drubbing.
bordoeira (*f.*) a trouncing.
boré (*m.*) Indian trumpet.
boreal (*adj.*) boreal, northern. **aurora—**, aurora borealis.
boreste (*m.*) starboard (right side of a ship); = ESTIBORDO.
borgonha (*m.*) Burgundy wine; (*f.*) [*cap.*] Burgundy.

borgonhês –nhesa [ê], **borguinhão** –nhona (*adj.; m.,f.*) Burgundian.
boricado –da (*adj., Chem.*) borated.
bórico –ca (*adj., Chem.*) boric. **ácido—**, boric acid.
borílio (*m., Chem.*) boryl.
borla (*f.*) tassel; doctor's cap; the degree of doctor. **doutor de—e capelo**, one who has received the highest academic degree.
bornal (*m.*) feed bag, nose bag; haversack.
borne (*m.*) an electrical terminal.
bornear (*v.t.*) to sight (a gun); to take a squint (at a line or surface to see if it is straight or level).
borneol [-óis] (*m., Chem.*) borneol, bornyl alcohol, camphol.
Bornéu (*m.*) Borneo.
bornita (*f., Min.*) bornite.
boro (*m., Chem.*) boron.
borô (*m.*) a species of sting ray.
borocalcita (*f., Min.*) calcium borate.
boronatrocalcita (*f.*) = ULEXITA.
bororé (*m.*) Indian arrow poison.
bororó (*m.*) a brocket (*Mazama rufina*), Brazil's smallest deer, c.a. CAMOCICA, GAPOROROCA, MÃO-CURTA, NHAMBI-BORORÓ, NHAMBIBOROROCA.
bororo [rôro] (*m.,f.*) an Indian of the Bororo, a once numerous and powerful, linguistically-independent tribe centering in Mato Grosso; c.a. COROADO (which see); (*adj.*) pert. to or designating the Bororo.
borossilicato (*m., Chem.*) borosilicate.
bôrra (*f.*) dregs, lees, sediment; sludge; trifles; fig., the dregs of society.—**de sêda**, silk floss.
borra-botas (*m.*) a rotter; a nobody.
borraceiro (*m.*) a drizzling rain.
borracha (*f.*) rubber; rubber bag; rubber eraser.—**butílica**, Butyl rubber.—**-chimarrona**, see under BORRAGEM.—**esponjosa**, sponge or foam rubber.—**-fraca**, a type of very weak rubber; see FINA-FRACA.—**-metílica**, Methyl rubber. **botas de—**, rubber boots. **capa de—**, rubber raincoat.
borrachão –chona (*m.*) sot.
borracheira (*f., slang*) drunkenness; a drunken spree, binge; a botch job; a mess.
borracheiro (*m.*) a gatherer of latex of the MANGABEIRA.
borrachífero –ra (*adj.*) rubber-producing.
borracho –cha (*adj.*) drunk; (*m.,f.*) drunkard, sot; (*m.*) a squab.
borrachudo –da (*adj.*) swollen up like a filled bag; (*m.*) a black fly or buffalo gnat (*Simulium pertinax*).
borradela (*f.*) blotch; blot.
borrado –da (*adj.*) blotched, blotted; badly painted.
borrador (*m.*) in bookkeeping, a day book; a dauber (bad painter); a scribbler (bad writer).
borradura (*f.*) = BORRADELA.
borragem (*f.*) common borage (*Borago officinalis*) and other plants of this genus; a viper's-bugloss (*Echium plantaginea*), c.a. BORRACHA-CHIMARRONA;—**-brava** and —**-do-campo**, are spp. of Heliotrope.
borragináceo –cea, **-gíneo** –nea (*adj., Bot.*) boraginaceous; (*f.pl.*) the Boraginaceae (borage family).
borralha (*f.*) = BORRALHO.
borralhara (*f., Zool.*) any of various ant shrikes, esp. Leach's ant shrike (*Mackenziaena leachii*), and the sooty ant shrike (*M. severa*), both of southeastern Brazil; c.a. BRUJAJARA, BRURAJARA, PAPA-ÔVO, PAPA-PINTO.—**-pintada** = CHOCÃO.
borralheira (*f.*) ash heap; a stay-at-home. **A Gata—**, Cinderella.
borralhento –ta (*adj.*) ashen, ash-colored.
borralho (*m.*) embers, hot ashes, cinders; hearth, fireplace.
borrão (*m.*) blot, ink stain; (*Printing*) blur, slur; a rough draft, sketch; day book.
borrar (*v.t.*) to blot, stain; to daub, blur; to erase.
borrasca (*f.*) storm, tempest, gale, squall; a sudden setback; towering rage. **Na hora da—não se muda o timoneiro**, Don't change horses in midstream.
borrascoso –sa (*adj.*) stormy. **tempo—**, foul weather.
borrazeira (*f.*) pussy willow (*Salix cinerea*).
borregã (*f.*) lamb's wool.
borregar (*v.i.*) to bleat (like a lamb).
borrêgo (*m.*) lamb. [More usual: CORDEIRO or CARNEIRI-NHO.]
borriçar (*v.*) = CHUVISCAR.
borrifador –dora (*adj.*) sprinkling; (*m.*) sprinkler.

borrifar (*v.t.*) to sprinkle, spray; to splatter, spatter.

borrifo (*m.*) a sprinkling; a spray; a spatter; (*pl.*) specks, spots.

bort (*m.*) bort; carbon diamond.

borzeguim (*m.*) a high lace shoe [= BOTINA]; buskin.

Bósforo (*m.*) Bosporus.

bosque (*m.*) boscage, grove, small woods, copse.

bosquejar (*v.t.*) to sketch, delineate, outline.

bosquejo [ê] (*m.*) sketch, rough draft, outline.

bosquete [ê] (*m.*) clump of trees.

bossa (*f.*) bump (swelling); a hump; hub; a tendency, bent, leaning; (*slang*) smooth talk. **ter—para a música,** to have a natural talent for music. **ter a—dos negócios,** to have a flair for business.

bossagem (*f., Arch.*) boss, knoblike projection.

bossoroca (*f.*) gully, gulch.

bosta (*f.*) dung.—**-de-barata,** name given by prospectors to certain types of pebbles found in diamantiferous gravel.

bosteiro (*m.*) dung beetle [= ESCARAVELHO].

bostela (*f.*) pustule, pimple.

bostelento **-ta, -loso, -sa** (*adj.*) pustular, -lous.

bóstrico (*m.*) a bostrychid beetle.

bota (*f.*) boot; a poor piece of artistic work.—**s de água,** hip boots.—**s de borracha,** rubber boots.—**s de cano alto,** high boots.—**s de montar(ia),** riding boots. **um par de—s,** (*colloq.*) a botched or bungled result.

bota-abaixo (*m.*) a razing, tearing down, destruction.

bota-fogo (*adj.*) fire-spitting; (*m.*) trouble-maker.

botafora (*m.*) a send-off; a good-by or bon voyage party; a ship's launching.

botaló (*m., Naut.*) spar, boom.

botânico **-ca** (*adj.*) botanic(al); (*m.,f.*) botanist; (*f.*) botany.

botanófilo (*m.*), **-la** (*f.*) botanophile.

botanologia (*f.*) botanology [= BOTÂNICA].

botão (*m.*) button; knob; push button; bud of a plant or flower; wart; wen.—**de alarme,** alarm button.—**de arranque,** (*Autom.*) starter button.—**-de-ouro,** yellow-eye grass (*Xyris sp.*), c.a. ERVA-DE-EMPIGEM; the tall buttercup (*Ranunculus acris*), c.a. RANÚNCULO-BRASILEIRO, RANÚNCULO-DOS-PRADOS; the creeping buttercup (*Ranunculus repens*), c.a. ERVA-BELIDA; also = AGRIÃO-DO-PARÁ, CELIDÔNIA-MENOR, FICÁRIA, JUPICAÍ, MAIACA. —**-de-prata,** the sneezewort yarrow (*Achillea ptarmica*). —**de rosa,** rosebud. **casa do—,** buttonhole. **falar com os seus botões,** to talk to oneself. **flor em—,** a budding flower. **pregar botões em,** to sew buttons on.

botar (*v.t.*) to put (on), place, lay. [Cf. PÔR].—**a bôca no mundo,** to raise a howl, yell.—**(a escrita) em dia,** to bring (the account books) up-to-date.—**a língua,** to stick out the tongue.—**a pique,** to send (a ship) to the bottom.—**as cartas,** to deal cards; to lay the cards (in fortune-telling). —**corpo** to put on weight; to round out (the body).—**fora,** to cast out, throw away.—**no chão,** to throw on the ground.—**o carro adiante dos bois,** to put the cart before the horse.—**o pé no mundo,** to hotfoot it away.—**poeira nos olhos,** to throw dust in the eyes.—**seus argumentos** (*colloq.*) of a beauty contestant, bathing beauty, sweater girl, etc., to display her charms, her good points.

botaréu (*m.*) buttress, abutment, pier.

bota-sela (*m.*) boots-and-saddles (cavalry bugle call).

bote (*m.*) a small boat; sword-thrust, stab with a knife; sudden leap, spring (of an animal).—**de remar,** rowboat. —**a vela,** sailboat.—**salva-vidas,** lifeboat. **dar um—,** to leap, spring.

boteco (*m.*) a small BOTEQUIM; (*colloq.*) eyeball.

botelha [ê] (*f.*) bottle, flask. [more usual: FRASCO, GARRAFA].

botelho [ê] (*m.*) = BODELHA.

botequim (*m.*) cheap saloon, tavern, bar, café, grogshop; small cheap coffee shop.

botequineiro **-ra** (*m.,f.*) keeper of a BOTEQUIM.

botica (*f.*) pharmacy.

boticão (*m.*) dentist's extracting forceps [= SACA-MOLAS].

boticário **-ria** (*m.,f.*) pharmacist, apothecary, druggist.

botija (*f.*) jug; flagon; terminal of undersea cables; fig., a jug-shaped person; buried treasure.—**de barro,** earthenware jug or bottle.

botilhão (*m.*) = ABUTILÃO.

botilhão-vesiculoso (*m.*) = BODELHA.

botina (*f.*) high lace shoe.

bôto **-ta** (*adj.*) dull, blunt; dull-witted, obtuse; of teeth, on edge; (*m.*) an Amazon porpoise.

botoado (*m.*) a dorad (So. Amer. catfish).

botoaria (*f.*) button factory.

botocudo **-da** (*adj.*) savage, uncivilized; uncultured; (*m.,f.*) an Indian of the BOTOCUDO (called also AIMORÉ), a linguistically-independent people of very low culture who occupied parts of what is now Espírito Santo, Minas Gerais and southern Bahia. They owe their name to the BOTOQUE (large cylindrical wooden plug) which men and women alike wore in their ear lobes and lower lip. Owing to the same custom, Indians of the unrelated Xocrém-Caingang of Santa Catarina are also called BOTOCUDO. The designation Botocudo is sometimes colloquially applied to the CAIPIRA; (*adj.*) pert. to or designating the BOTOCUDO.

botoeira (*f.*) buttonhole.

botoque (*m.*) labret, lip plug (as worn by certain Indians in Brazil, hence their name: Botocudo). Cf. BATOQUE.

botriocéfalo (*m.*) a genus (*Bothriocephalus*) of tapeworms.

botrióide (*adj.*) botryoid(al), botryose.

botriólita (*f., Min.*) botryolite.

botriomicose (*f., Veter.*) botryomycosis.

botrope (*m.*) a genus (*Bothrops*) of very venomous pit vipers, including the Braz. JARARACA.

botulismo (*m., Med., Veter.*) botulism.

bouba (*f., Med.*) bubo; yaws, frambesia.

bouçar, boiçar (*v.t.*) to clear land for planting.

bouganvílea (*f.*) = BUGANVÍLEA.

boulangerita (*f., Min.*) boulangerite.

bovarismo (*m.*) bovarysm ["domination by a romantic conception of oneself—from its protrayal in Madame Bovary." *Webster*].

bovídeos (*m.pl.*) the Bovidae (oxen, sheep, goats).

bovino **-na** (*adj.*) bovine.

bovista (*f.*) a genus (*Bovista*) of puffballs.

boxador [ks] (*m.*) boxer, prize-fighter.

boxe [ks] (*m.*) boxing, prize-fighting; brass knuckles.

boximane (*adj.; m.,f.*) Bushman.

boxista [ks] (*m.*) = BOXADOR.

bozó (*m.*) a Brazilian dice game.

br. = BROCHADO (paper-bound).

brabeza [ê] (*f.*) wildness, fierceness. Var. BRAVEZA.

brabo **-ba** (*adj.*) wild, untamed, savage, fierce; "sore": (*m.*) a new and inexperienced rubber gatherer; (*f., colloq*) malaria. Var. BRAVO.

braça (*f.*) fathom (6 ft.); also, an old lineal measure (2.2 mts., about 7.4 ft.) into which the sounding lines aboard the GAIOLAS of Amazonia are subdivided; in other areas—Mato Grosso, Sergipe, Alagôas—a land area of 3.052 square meters.

braçada (*f.*) an armful; overarm (swimming) stroke. **às —s,** by the armful; in profusion.

braçadeira (*f.*) a tieback for drapes and curtains; an arm strap (in a carriage or automobile); bracket; (*Bot.*) a rosewood (*Dalbergia variabilis*), c.a. CIPÓ-VIOLETA.

braçagem (*f.*) hand (manual) labor.

braçal (*adj.*) brachial; (*m.*) an arm band; an arm shield. **trabalhador—,** hand laborer. **serra-,** lumberman's two-handed saw; **trabalho—,** manual labor.

bracatinga (*f., Bot.*) a mimosa (*M. escabrella*).

bracear (*v.i.*) to swim with overarm strokes; to struggle; also = BRACEJAR.

bracejar (*v.i.*) to extend, lift up or wave the arms; to fling the arms about; to gesticulate; to struggle (with the arms); to bud, sprout.

bracelete [lê] (*m.*) bracelet [= PULSEIRA].

braço (*m.*) arm; upper arm; foreleg (of animals); a hand (worker, laborer); power might; neck plate of a violin; horizontal bar, bracket; (*pl.*) boughs.—**é—!** an interjection expressing the triumph of muscular strength; hence, any triumph after a struggle.—**de alavanca,** lever arm.—**-de-ferro,** strongarmed man.—**de mar,** arm of the sea; estuary.—**de movimento,** or—**de manivela,** crank arm.—**secular,** secular arm. **a—,** or **à força de—s,** by main strength. **a—s com,** at grips with. **abrir os—s,** to open the arms (in welcome). **cruzar os—s,** to fold the arms. **de—s dados,** arm-in-arm. **É o—dêle,** He is his righthand man. **estar a—s com,** to have one's hands full. **não dar o—a torcer,** not to display (one's) weakness, ignorance, or error. **sem dar o—a torcer,** without losing face. **receber de—s abertos,** to receive with open arms.

braçolas (*f.pl., Naut.*) coamings.

bráctea (*f., Bot.*) bract.

bracteado **-da** (*adj., Bot.*) bracteate.

bracteiforme (adj., Bot.) bracteiform.
bractéola (f., Bot.) bractlet, bracteole.
bracteolado –da (adj., Bot.) bracteolatè.
braçudo –da (adj.) having strong arms.
bradado (m.) = BRADO.
bradador –dora (adj.) shouting, yelling, bawling.
bradal (m.) bradawl.
bradar (v.t.,v.i.) to shout, exclaim, bawl, roar, yell; to cry out, call out.—aos céus, to cry out to heaven.—por socorro, to yell, cry out, for help.
bradejar (v.i.) to utter shouts, yells, cries.
bradípode (m., Zool.) bradypod, sloth [= PREGUIÇA].
bradipódidas (m.pl.) the family (Bradypodidae) of true sloths.
brado (m.) shout, roar, outcry, yell.
braga (f.) shackle, fetter; (pl.) breeches.
bragal (m.) household linen.
bragueiro (m.) a truss for hernias; a child's diaper.
braguilha (f.) fly (of a man's trousers).
brama (f.) rut, oestrus [= CIO].
brâmane (adj., m.,f.) Brahman.
bramanismo (m.) Brahmanism.
bramante (adj.) blatant; bellowing.
bramar (v.i.) to roar, bellow; to rut (as deer); to cry out (against).
bramido (m.) roar, bellow.
bramir [25] (v.i.) to roar, bellow (as a wild beast); to howl, rage; (v.t.) to shout (threats, insults).
branca (f.) see BRANCO.
brancacento –ta (adj.) whitish.
brancarão –rona (adj.; m.,f.) light-skinned (mulatto).
branco –ca (adj.) white; pale; blank; (m.) the color white; a white man; (f.) a white woman; white rum [= AGUARDENTE, CACHAÇA]; (f.) Blanch(e).—da Bahia, (colloq.) a mulatto.—de antimônio, antimony white; antimonous oxide.—de chumbo, white lead (pigment).—de marfim, ivory white.—de Neve e os Sete Anões, Snow White and the Seven Dwarfs.—de Paris, Paris white (prepared chalk).—de zinco, zinc oxide.—do ôlho, white of the eye.—do ôvo. white of egg.—-ursina, (Bot.) = CANABRÁS.
arma—, any blade (sword, dagger, etc.). assinar em—, to sign in blank. de ponto em—, with great care or accuracy. em—, in blank; fasting. manjar—, blancmange (a dessert). passar a vida em—, to go through life with no troubles, no sufferings. pôr o prêto no—, to set it down in black and white. roupa—, linen (garments). ter carta—, to have carte blanche. verso—, blank verse. vestido de—, dressed in white.
brancura (f.) whiteness.
brande (m.) brandy.
brandir [25] (v.t.) to brandish, flourish, wield (weapon, stick, etc.).
brando –da (adj.) soft, yielding; mild, gentle, bland, tender.
brandura (f.) kindliness, mildness, softness, gentleness; dew, drizzle; (pl.) caresses.
branqueação (f.) act or operation of whitening, bleaching.
branqueado –da (adj.) whitened; whitewashed.
branqueador –dora [ô] (adj.) whitening; (m.,f.) one who makes white; whitewasher.
branqueadura (f.), –queamento (m.) whitening.
branquear (v.t.) to whiten, blanch, bleach; to whitewash; (v.i.) to show white. (v.r.) to grow white.
branquejar (v.i.) to whiten; to turn white; to show white.
branquiado –da (adj., Zool.) branchiate.
branquial (adj., Zool.) branchial.
brânquias (f.pl., Zool.) branchiae (gills).
branquidão (f.) whiteness.
branquilho (m., Bot.) an apes-earring (Pithecellobium hassleri).
branquimento (m.) whitening; cleaning of silver objects.
branquinha (f., slang) sugarcane rum [= AGUARDENTE].
branquiobdélidas (m.pl.) a genus (Branchiobdella) of small annelid worms.
branquiômero (m., Anat.) branchiomere.
branquiópodes (m.pl.) a group (Branchiopoda) of aquatic crustaceans.
branquióstega (f.), –quiostégio (m., Zool.) branchiostegal ray (of a fish).
branquiostomídeos (m.pl., Zool.) the family (Branchiostomidae) typified by the lancelets.
branquir (v.t.) to clean gold and silver objects.
branquiúros (m.pl.) an order (Branchiura) of copepods, which includes the carp lice.

braquia (f.) a breve [curved mark (˘) used to indicate a short vowel].
braquial (adj.) brachial.
braquicataléctico –ca, –lecto –ta (adj., Pros.) brachycatalectic.
braquicefalia (f., Anthropom.) brachycephalism, brachycephaly.
braquicéfalo –la (adj.) brachycephalic.
braquícero –ra (adj.) short-horned; (m.pl.) a suborder (Brachycera) of flies, including horseflies, robber flies and the housefly.
braquidactilia (f., Anat., Zool.) brachydactyly.
braquidáctilo –la (adj.) brachydactylous.
braquidiagonal (adj., Cryst.) brachydiagonal.
braquignatia (f., Anthropol.) brachygnathia.
braquígnato –ta (adj., Anthropol.) brachygnathous
braquigrafia (f.) brachygraphy, shorthand.
braquígrafo –fa (m.,f.) brachygrapher, stenographer.
braquilogia (f.) brachylogy.
braquimetropia (f., Med.) brachymetropia.
braquiocefálico –ca (adj., Anat.) brachiocephalic.
braquiotomia (f., Surg.) brachiotomy.
braquipinacóide (m., Cryst.) brachypinacoid.
braquipnéia (f., Med.) brachypnea.
braquirrinia (f., Zool.) brachyrrhinia.
braquistégia (f.) the genus (Brachystegia) of barkcloth trees.
braquistocéfalo –la (adj., Craniom.) brachistocephalic.
braquistôcrona (f., Math.) brachistochrone.
braquiúros (m.pl.) the suborder (Brachyura) of crabs.
brasa (f.) ember, live coal; incandescence; passion; anxiety.—-viva, a lidflower (Calyptranthes grandifolia). estar em—, to be hot under the collar; to chafe at the bit. estar sôbre—s, to be on pins and needles, in a state of anxiety. ferro em—, red-hot iron. passar por (uma coisa) como gato por—s, to pass over a problem, a difficulty, like a cat over hot bricks. puxar a—para a sua sardinha, to draw water to one's mill; to bring grist to one's mill. tirar as—s, to rake the coals to one's pot.
brasão (m.) coat of arms; escutcheon; hatchment; (adj.) of cattle, reddish.
braseiro (m.) brazier; a heap of embers.
brasido (m.) a heap of live coals.
brasil (m.) a prickly tree of the senna family (Caesalpinia echinata), the principal source of PAU-BRASIL (brazilwood). Cf. BRASÍS.
brasilaçu [ú] (m.) another source of brazilwood (Caesalpinia brasiliensis), c.a. BRASILETE, BRASILETO, BRASILROSADO.
brasileirismo (m.) Brazilianism.
brasileiro –ra (adj.; m.,f.) Brazilian. à—, in the Brazilian manner.
brasilete, –leto [lê] (m.) brazilwood [= BRASILAÇU].
brasílico –ca (adj.) indigenous to Brazil.
brasilidade (f.) the essential nature or character of a Brazilian or of Brazil; love of Brazil; Brazilianism.
brasiliense (adj.) Brazilian.
brasilina (f., Chem.) brazilin.
brasílio –lia (adj.) Brazilian.
brasilita (f., Min.) brazilite.
brasilófilo –la (adj.) friendly to Brazil; liking Brazilians; (m.,f.) such a person.
brasilófobo –ba (adj.) unfriendly to Brazil; disliking Brazilians; (m.,f.) such a person.
brasilólogo (m.) ,–ga (f.) one who has much knowledge about Brazil.
brasil-rosado (m.) = BRASILAÇU.
brasis (m.pl.) the aborigines of Brazil, collectively; the Brazilians or their land.
brasonar (v.t.) to emblazon; to boast.
brassávola (f.) a genus (Brassavola) of orchids.
brássica (f.) a genus (Brassica) of cabbages or white mustards.
brassicáceas (f.pl.) the Brassicaceae (mustards, cresses, cabbages).
braúna (f.) a black steer; (Bot.) a red quebracho (Schinopsis brasiliensis).—-preta = BARAÚNA.
braúnea (f.) the glory flamebean (Brownea grandiceps).
brauniano –na (adj., Physics) Brownian [movement or motion].
braunita (f., Min.) braunite.
bravata (f.) bravado, boasting.
bravatear (v.i.) to boast, bluster, swagger.
bravejar (v.) = ESBRAVEJAR.

braveza [ê] (*f.*) = BRABEZA.
bravio -via (*adj.*) wild, rough, savage; rambunctious; (*m.*) untilled land.
bravo -va (*adj.*) brave, fearless, dauntless, plucky, valiant; wild, untamed; mad, furious; ill-tempered. Cf. BRABO; (*m.*) a brave man; a shout of applause; a worker new at rubber gathering; a greenhorn; (*interj.*) Bravo!
brávoa (*f.*) the Mexican twinbloom (*Bravoa geminiflora*), and other plants of this genus.
bravura (*f.*) bravery, boldness, prowess; valor; bravura.
breadura (*f.*) act of tarring.
brear (*v.t.*) to tar.
breca (*f.*) muscular cramp. Com a—!, Dammit! levado da—, devilish, mischievous.
brecar (*v.t.*) to apply the brakes; to bring (a vehicle) to a stop [= FREAR].
brecha (*f.*) breach, gap, rift; (*Petrog.*) breccia. abrir—, to force an opening. fazer uma—, to breach, break through.
brechiforme (*adj.*) breccial, brecciated.
bredo (*m.*, *Bot.*) princessfeather (*Amaranthus hypochondriacus*).—-caruru = CARURU-BRAVO.—-de-cabeça, the blite goosefoot (*Chenopodium capitatum*).—-de-espinho, or—-do-chile, spiny amaranth (*A. spinosus*), c.a. CRISTA-DE-GALO.—-de-muro = LÍNGUA-DE-SAPO.—-de-namorado = CRISTA-DE-GALO.—-de-porco, a spiderling (*Boerhaavia hirsuta*).—-fedorento, a spiderflower (*Cleome polygama*), c.a. MAÇAMBÊ-DE-TRÊS-FÔLHAS, PIMENTA-DE-MACACO.—-manjangome = MARIA-GOMES.—-verdadeiro, the tumbleweed amaranth (*A. graecizans*), c.a. BLEDO, CARURU-DE-PORCO.—-vermelho, or—-roxo, amaranth or love-lies-bleeding (*A. caudatus sanguineus*), c.a. CRISTA-DE-GALO.
bregma (*f.*, *Anat.*) bregma.
brejal (*m.*) the white-throated seed-eater (*Sporophila albogularis*), c.a. PAPA-CAPIM. also = COLEIRO-DO-BREJO.
brejaúva, brejaúba (*f.*) = AIRÍ.
brejeira (*f.*) see BREJEIRO.
brejeirice (*f.*) coarse talk or manners.
brejeiro -ra (*adj.*) impish, mischievous, wicked, naughty, coquettish, provocative; (*m.*) loafer; rascal; marshlander; (*f.*) a plug of chewing tobacco.
brejento -ta (*adj.*) marshy.
brejereba (*f.*) = PREJEREBA.
brejo (*m.*) bog, marsh, swamp, morass; "in Maranhão, any low place where rivers have their source; in northeastern Brazil, land with permanent watercourses, rendered fertile by the annual overflowing of the rivers." [GBAT]
brejoso -sa (*adj.*) marshy.
brenha (*f.*) thick woods; brambles; complication, confusion.
brenhoso -sa (*adj.*) brambly.
breque (*m.*) a wagonette (light, 4-wheeled wagon, with two longitudinal seats in back facing each other); a vehicular brake [= FREIO]; a brake shoe [= TAMANCO].
brequista (*m.*) railroad brakeman [= GUARDA-FREIOS].
Bretanha (*f.*) Brittany. [Britain = GRÃ-BRETANHA]
bretão -tã (*adj.*) British; Breton; (*m.*,*f.*) a Briton or Britisher; a Breton or the language of Brittany.
breu (*m.*) tar.—-branco, (*Bot.*) = ALMECEGUEIRA-MANSA.—-branco-verdadeiro = ALMECEGUEIRA-CHEIROSA. escuro como—, pitch-black.
breve (*adj.*) brief, short, slight, transitory, fleeting, momentary; concise, succinct, laconic, terse; (*m.*, *R.C.Ch.*) a brief (papal letter); a scapulary; (*f.*, *Mus.*) breve; (*adv.*) soon, shortly, presently, before long, pretty soon. até—, see you soon. dentro em—, before long, soon. em—, soon, shortly. o mais—possível, as soon as possible. para ser—, to be brief; in short. Seja—! be brief!
brevetado -da (*adj.*) commissioned (as an officer). ser—, to receive flying wings.
breviário (*m.*, *Eccl.*) breviary; an abridgment, a summary; (*Typog.*) brevier. ler pelo mesmo—, to be of the same mind (as another person).
brevidade (*f.*) brevity, briefness.
brevípede (*adj.*, *Zool.*) having short legs.
brevipenado -da, **brevipene** (*adj.*, *Zool.*) brevipennate, short-winged.
briáceas (*f.pl.*) a family (*Bryaceae*) of mosses.
briba (*f.*) = VÍBORA.
bricabraque (*m.*) bric-a-brac.
brida (*f.*) rein; (*Zool.*) lore. à tôda a—, at full tilt, headlong, at breakneck speed, hell-bent.
bridão (*m.*) bridoon (light snaffle bit).

bridar (*v.t.*) to restrain (as with a bit).
bridge (*m.*) bridge (card game).
briga (*f.*) fight, affray, hand-to-hand encounter; brawl, ruckus, scrap; quarrel, squabble, row, dispute, falling out, run-in.—de galo, cockfight [but bullfight is CORRIDA (not BRIGA) DE TOUROS]. comprar a—de alguém, to take on (fight) another's battle. Ela teve uma—com o namorado, She had a quarrel with her sweetheart. puxar—(com alguém), to pick a fight (with someone).
brigada (*f.*) brigade.—-de fogo, fire brigade.
brigadeiro (*m.*) brigadier (general).
brigado -da (*adj.*) at odds. Estão—s um com o outro, They are mad at each other.
brigalhão -lhona (*adj.*) given to brawling and fighting; (*m.*) brawler, bully, roughneck.
brigão -gona (*adj.*) quarrelsome, pugnacious.
brigar (*v.t.*) to fight, come to blows, engage in hand-to-hand combat (com, with); to quarrel, dispute, disagree (com, with).—por dá cá aquela palha, to quarrel about trifles, about nothing. Quando um não quer, dois não brigam, It takes two to make a fight.
Brígida (*f.*) Bridget, Brigid.
brigue (*m.*) brig.
briguento -ta (*adj.*) quarrelsome.
brilhante (*adj.*) brilliant, shining, bright; gorgeous; illustrious, famous; (*m.*) brilliant (cut diamond).
brilhantina (*f.*) brilliantine (hair dressing); (*Bot.*) roseroot sedum (*S. rosea*), c.a. ERVA-PINHEIRA-DE-ROSA, MILGRÃOS.—-brasileira, a clearweed (*Pilea hyalina*).
brilhantismo (*m.*) brilliance.
brilhar (*v.i.*) to shine, glitter, glisten, sparkle, gleam, glow; to be eminent, distinguished. brilhando como novo, shiny new. [The transitive verb, to shine, is LUSTRAR, POLIR, BRUNIR; FAZER BRILHAR. To shine shoes is ENGRAXAR SAPATOS.]
brilho (*m.*) brightness, brilliance; luster, shine, gloss; splendor, celebrity.
brim (*m.*) duck, canvas, sailcloth; linen.
brimbau (*m.*) = BERIMBAU.
brincadeira (*f.*) play, esp. of children; fun, amusement; lark; jest, joke; banter; pleasantry; prank. de, or por,—, for fun. Deixe-se de—s! That's enough now! Stop fooling! fora de—, all joking aside. Êle não é de—s, He won't stand for any foolishness. Não quero (não admito)—comigo! Don't try any foolishness with me! Don't try to get funny with me!
brincalhão -lhona (*adj.*) playful, prankish, frolicsome; fun-loving; facetious; (*m.*,*f.*) cutup, prankster, wag.
brincar (*v.i.*) to play, frolic, lark; to frisk, skip, cavort, romp; to amuse oneself; to make merry; to trifle, toy (com, with); to joke, tease, kid, make fun; to banter. [But to play cards is JOGAR (not BRINCAR) CARTAS, and to play the piano is TOCAR (not BRINCAR) piano.]—com fogo, to play with fire.—de esconder, or—de pique, to play hide-and-seek. Estou brincando, I'm just kidding; I didn't mean it. Percebeu que estavam brincando com êle, He saw that he was being trifled with. Você está brincando! You're kidding!
brinco (*m.*) earring; toy; play, fun, joke; elegant person or thing.—s-de-princesa, (*Bot.*) any fuchsia, esp. *F. integrifolia*, c.a. BRINCOS-DE-RAINHA, AGRADOS, LÁGRIMAS.—s-de-sagüim, an apes-earring (*Phithecellobium diversifolium*), c.a. FAVELA-BRANCA; also = ANGICO-VERDADEIRO.
brindar (*v.t.*) to drink to; to toast; to make a gift to; (*v.r.*) to drink to one another.
brinde (*m.*) a toast; a gift, present.
brinjela (*f.*) = BERINGELA.
brinquedo [ê] (*m.*) toy, plaything, de—, (*adj.*) toy. casa de—s, toy store.
brinquete [ête] (*m.*) a certain part of a manioc press.
brio (*m.*) self-respect, pride, dignity; mettle, spirit; vivacity.—-de-estudante = BARBA-DE-BARATA.
brioche (*f.*) bun, tea roll, muffin.
briofilo (*m.*, *Bot.*) a genus (*Kalanchoe*, syn. *Bryophyllum*) of succulents.
briófitos (*m.pl.*) the phyllum (*Bryophyta*) of mosses and liverworts.
briologia (*f.*) bryology.
briologista (*m.*,*f.*) bryologist.
briônia (*f.*, *Bot.*) the redberry bryony (*Bryonia dioica*), c.a. NORÇA-BRANCA.
brioso -sa (*adj.*) self-respecting; mettlesome; proud; brave; spunky; dignified; high-minded; open-handed. um cavalo—, a high-spirited horse.

briozoários (*m.pl., Zool.*) the class Bryozoa.
briquête (*m.*) coal briquette.
briquitar (*v.i.*) to drudge, slave.
brisa (*f.*) breeze.—**do mar,**—**marinha,** sea breeze. **viver de amor e**—**s,** to live on bread and cheese and kisses.
brita (*f.*) crushed rock (for road building).
britador –**deira** (*adj.*) crushing; (*m.*) rock crusher.
britamento (*m.*) crushing, esp. of rock.
britânia (*f.*) britannia metal.
britânico –**ca** (*adj.*) British, Britannic; (*m.,f.*) Britisher.
britanizar (*v.t.*) to Anglicize.
britano (*m.*), –**na** (*f.*) Briton, Britisher.
britar (*v.t.*) to crush (rock); to shatter.
brivana (*f.*) mare [= ÉGUA].
briza (*f.*) the genus (*Briza*) of quaking grasses.
broa [ô] (*f.*) corn bread; (*pl.*) gifts at Christmastime.
broca (*f.*) auger, drill, bit, brace-and-bit; dentist's drill; (*Zool.*) any of numerous plant or tree borers.—**de diamantes,** diamond drill.—**de expansão,** expanding drill.—**de milho,** corn borer.—**de rocha,** rock drill.
brocado (*m.*) brocade.
brocar (*v.t.*) to drill, bore. **máquina de**—, boring mill. Cf. PERFURAR.
brocardo (*m.*) saying, proverb.
brocha (*f.*) tack; axle pin. Cf. BROXA.
brochar (*v.t.*) to stitch (books); to tack on shoe soles and heels; to beat, trounce. Cf. BROXAR.
broche (*m.*) brooch or clasp.
brochura (*f.*) brochure, pamphlet, paper-covered book; the art of stitching books.
brôco –**ca** (*adj.*) said of a deer which has shed its antlers.
brócolos, brocos (*m.pl., Bot.*) broccoli (*Brassica oleracea botrytis*).
bródio (*m.*) banquet, party; merry feast; spree.
broinha [o-í] (*f.*) a kind of sweet cake.
broma (*f.*) joke, prank; (*m.,f.*) a stupid person; (*adj.*) stupid, awkward.
bromal (*m., Chem.*) bromal.
bromar (*v.t.*) to corrode; to spoil; (*v.i.*) to go bad.
bromargírio (*m.*), –**girita** (*f., Min.*) bromargyrite, bromyrite.
bromato (*m., Chem.*) bromate.
bromatologia (*f.*) the science of foods.
bromatólogo (*m.*), –**ga** (*f.*) food chemist.
bromatotoxicismo [ks] (*m.*) food poisoning.
bromélia (*f., Bot.*) any bromelia. Cf. ANANÁS.
bromeliáceo –**cea** (*adj., Bot.*) bromeliaceous; (*f.pl.*) the pineapple family.
bromelina (*f., Biochem.*) bromelin.
brometa (*m., Chem.*) bromide. Var. BROMURETO.
brômico –**ca** (*adj., Chem.*) bromic.
bromidrato (*m., Chem.*) bromohydrate, hydrobromide [= HIDROBROMATO].
bromidreto [ê] (*m., Chem.*) hydrogen bromide.
bromídrico –**ca** (*adj.*) hydrobromic [= HIDROBRÔMICO].
bromidrose (*f., Med.*) bromidrosis; osmidrosis.
bromina (*f., Chem.*) bromine.
bromirita (*f.*) = BROMARGIRITA.
brômio (*m.*) = BROMO.
bromismo (*m., Med.*) bromism.
bromo (*m., Chem.*) bromine.
bromoacetona (*f., Chem.*) bromo-acetone.
bromofórmio (*m., Chem.*) bromoform.
bromureto [ê] (*m.*) = BROMETO.
broncadenite (*f., Med.*) bronchodenitis.
bronco –**ca** (*adj.*) stupid, stolid, thick-skulled, "dumb"; rough, coarse, rude.
broncopneumonia (*f., Med.*) bronchopneumonia.
broncorragia (*f., Med.*) bronchorrhagy.
broncoscópio (*m., Med.*) bronchoscope.
bronquial (*adj.*) bronchial.
bronquice (*f.*) stupidity; the quality of BRONCO.
brônquico –**ca** (*adj.*) = BRONQUIAL.
brônquio (*m., Anat.*) bronchus, bronchial tube.
bronquiolite (*f., Med.*) bronchiolitis.
bronquíolo (*m., Anat.*) bronchiole.
bronquite (*f., Med.*) bronchitis.
brontofobia (*f.*) morbid fear of thunder.
brontômetro (*m., Meteorol.*) brontometer.
brontosáurio (*m.*) brontosaurus.
bronze (*m.*) bronze; crankshaft bearing; fig., toughness, insensibility.—**comercial,** commercial bronze.—**de alumínio,** aluminum bronze.—**de berílio,** beryllium bronze.—**de chumbo,** lead bronze.—**hidráulico,** hydraulic

bronze; composition brass; steam bronze.—-**manganês,** manganese bronze.—-**níquel,** nickel bronze; German silver; nickel silver.—-**silicioso,** silicon bronze; copper-silicon alloy.—**para sinos,** bell metal.
bronzeado –**da** (*adj.*) bronze; tanned.
bronzeador –**dora** (*adj.*) bronzing; (*m.,f.*) bronzer.
bronzeamento (*m.*) bronzing; (*Plant Pathol.*) bronzing.
bronzear (*v.t.*) to bronze; (*v.r.*) to tan.
bronzeo –**zea** (*adj.*) bronze.
bronzita (*f., Min.*) bronzite.
brooquita (*f.*) = BRUQUITA.
broquear (*v.*) = BROCAR.
broquel [-quéis] (*m.*) buckler; fig., shield, protection.
broquelar (*v.*) = ABROQUELAR.
broquento –**ta** (*adj.*) full of sores.
brosimo (*m.*) the cow breadnut tree (*Brosimum utile*), c.a. ÁRVORE-DA-VACA, and other species of this genus.
brossa (*f.*) a coarse brush.
brota (*f.*) spring (of water); also = ABRÓTEA.
brotação (*f.*), **brotamento** (*m.*) burgeoning.
brotar (*v.i.*) to sprout, bud, burgeon, shoot forth, burst (break) out, spurt.
brotinho (*m., slang*) bobby-soxer.
brôto (*m.*) bud, shoot, sprout; (*colloq.*) teenager, adolescent girl.—**de alface,** heart of lettuce.
brotoeja [ê] (*f.*) skin eruption, rash.
brótola (*f.*) = ABRÓTEA.
brotolândia (*f.*) children's world.
broxa (*f.*) a heavy paintbrush; a large brush for whitewashing; a shaving brush. Cf. BROCHA.
broxante (*m.*) painter's helper.
broxar (*v.t.*) to brush on (paint). Cf. BROCHAR.
bruaca (*f.*) saddlebag; hag, prostitute.
brucina (*f., Pharm.*) brucin(e).
brucita (*f., Min.*) brucite.
bruco (*m.*) = PIRETRO-DA-BEIRA.
bruços (*m.pl.*) **de**—, prone, face down, flat on the ground.
bruega (*f.*) fracas, row; drunkenness; light drizzle.
brujajara (*f.*) = BORRALHARA.
bruma (*f.*) fog, mist; hence, a hazy or mysterious matter.
brumaceiro –**ra** (*adj.*) foggy, misty, damp.
brumal (*adj.*) misty; winterlike.
brunela (*f., Bot.*) the genus (*Prunella*) of selfheals.
brunideira (*f.*) woman who gives starched clothes a high gloss with a sadiron.
brunido –**da** (*adj.*) glossy; shining; burnished.
brunidor [ô] (*m.*) burnisher, polisher.
brunidura (*f.*) act or result of burnishing.
brunir [25] (*v.t.*) to burnish, polish, shine.
bruquita (*f., Min.*) brookite (titanium dioxide).
brusco –**ca** (*adj.*) brusque, abrupt, sudden; gruff, blunt; dark and cloudy.
brusquidão (*f.*) brusqueness, abruptness.
bruta, used in the slang expression **à bruta,** brutally, roughly; wholesale, extensively.
brutal (*adj.*) brutal; surly.
brutalidade (*f.*) brutality.
brutalizar (*v.t.*) to brutalize; (*colloq.*) to maltreat, bully, use roughly.
brutamontes (*m.*) a brutal, coarse, loutish fellow; ruffian; a "gorilla".
brutesco –**ca** [ê] (*adj.*) rough, crude, coarse.
bruteza [ê] (*f.*) brutishness.
brutidade, brutidão (*f.*) = BRUTALIDADE.
brutificar (*v.t.*) to brutify, brutalize.
bruto –**ta** (*adj.*) coarse, rude, ill-mannered, impolite; rough, raw, crude; brutish; strong, strapping; huge, colossal, whopping; (*m.*) brute, wild beast, a stupid man. **em**—, unfinished [products], raw [materials]. **jôgo**—, rough play. **pêso**—, gross weight. **sorte**—, (*slang*) huge good luck. **sujeito**—, a coarse character. Cf. BRUTA.
bruxa (*f.*) witch; hag; harridan; rag doll; (*colloq.*) a large night moth.
bruxaria (*f.*), –**xedo** [ê] (*m.*) witchcraft, sorcery, hex.
Bruxelas (*f.*) Brussels.
bruxo (*m.*) medicine man, witch doctor, shaman, sorcerer, wizard.
bruxuleante (*adj.*) flickering.
bruxulear (*v.i.*) to flicker, glimmer, gleam.
buate (*f.*) nightclub [*Fr. boîte*].
búbalo (*m., Zool.*) bubalis.
bubão (*m., Med.*) bubo; a swollen gland, esp. in the groin.
bubonalgia (*f., Med.*) bubonalgia.
bubônico –**ca** (*adj.*) bubonic. **peste**—, bubonic plague.

bubonocele (*f.*, *Med.*) bubonocele, inguinal hernia.
bubuia (*f.*) floating, drifting. **de—**, floating downstream.
bubuiar (*v.i.*) to float downstream.
bucal (*adj.*) buccal, oral.
bucaneiros (*m.pl.*) buccaneers, freebooters, pirates.
bucardia (*f.*, *Zool.*) a cockle.
Bucareste (*m.*) Bucharest.
bucéfalo (*m.*) Bucephalus, the celebrated horse of Alexander the Great; hence, jocosely, any "fiery steed."
bucha (*f.*) wad, wadding; a dowel; a hunk of bread; food that is very filling; nuisance, annoyance, any bothersome thing; (*Mach.*) bushing, sleeve; (*Bot.*) the dishcloth or towel gourd (*Luffa spp.*).
buchada (*f.*) animal guts; a mouthful of food.
bucheiro (*m.*) = TRIPEIRO.
buchinha (*f.*, *Bot.*) a dishcloth or towel gourd (*Luffa operculata*), c.a. CABACINHA, PURGA-DE-JOÃO-PAIS, PURGA-DOS-PAULISTAS.
bucho (*m.*) crop, craw; stomach, belly, esp. of animals; (*slang*) harlot.**—-de-boi,** (*Bot.*) shepherds-purse (*Capsella bursa-pastoris*), c.a. BÔLSA-DE-PASTOR, MANDIO-QUINHA, MARFIM, VELAME-DO-MATO.**—-de-rã** = CAMAPU.
buchu [chú] (*m.*) to oval-leaf buchu (*Barosma crenulata*).
bucinador *–dora* (*adj.*; *m.*, *Anat*) buccinator (muscle).
bucinídeos (*m.pl.*) the family (*Buccinidae*) of whelks.
buço (*m.*) fuzz on the upper lip; down.
bucólico *–ca* (*adj.*) bucolic; (*f.*) bucolic; pastoral poem.
bucolista (*m.*,*f.*) bucoliast.
bucolizar (*v.i.*) to write bucolics.
buconídeos (*m.pl.*) the family (*Bucconidae*) of puffbirds.
bucrânio (*m.*, *Arch.*) bucranium.
buçu [çú] (*m.*) the bussu, troolie, or sleeve palm (*Manicaria saccifera*), whose enormous undivided leaves, resembling those of a banana tree, are used for thatching. Its fruit is often found floating in the sea, hence is known as sea apple or sea coconut.
bucurubu [rubú] (*m.*) a tropical tree (*Schizolobium parahybum*).
Buda (*m.*) Buddha.
Budapeste (*f.*) Budapest.
budião (*m.*) the red parrotfish (*Sparisoma abildgaardi*), c.a. GUDIÃO.**—-batata,** the scorched parrotfish (*Cryptotomus ustus*).
búdico *–ca* (*adj.*) Buddhic.
budismo (*m.*) Buddhism.
budista (*m.*,*f.*) Buddhist.
budístico *–ca* (*adj.*) Buddhistic.
budléia (*f.*) the genus (*Buddleia*) of butterfly bushes.
budoar (*m.*) boudoir.
budum (*m.*) = BODUM.
buduna (*f.*) a beating; a cudgel.
bueiro (*m.*) culvert; drainpipe; drain hole; chimney.
buena-dicha (*f.*) fortune, lot. **ler a—**, to read one's fortune.
buenairense (*adj.*; *m.*,*f.*) = BONAERENSE.
bufa-de-lôbo (*f.*, *Bot.*) a puffball.
bufador *–dora* (*adj.*) puffing, blowing; (*m.*) a blowhard; a whale's spout hole.
búfalo (*m.*) the Asiatic water buffalo. [The American buffalo—more properly bison—is BISÃO.]
bufante (*adj.*) puffed out, full, bulging. **manga—**, leg-of-mutton sleeve. **saia—**, a bouffant skirt.
bufão (*m.*) a blowhard, braggadocio; formerly, a buffoon; a fool.
bufar (*v.i.*) to puff and blow; to huff; to snort; (*v.r.*) to brag, swagger; to be a blowhard.
bufarinheiro (*m.*) hawker, peddler; faker.
bufete [fê] (*m.*) buffet, sideboard; a public refreshment counter or snack bar.
bufido (*m.*) a puff or pant.
bufo (*m.*) act of puffing; a snort; a blowhard; a buffoon, comic, jester.
bufonaria (*f.*) buffoonery; drollery.
bufonear (*v.i.*) to buffoon.
bufotalina (*f.*, *Biochem.*) bufotalin.
buftalmia (*f.*, *Med.*) buphthalmia.
buftalmo (*m.*, *Bot.*) the willowleaf oxeye (*Buphthalmum salicifolium*).
bugalho (*m.*) a gallnut.**—do ôlho,** (*colloq.*) the eyeball. **confundir alhos com—s,** to mistake one thing for another.
buganvília (*f.*, *Bot.*) the Brazil bougainvillea (*B. spectabilis*), c.a. PRIMAVERA, TRÊS-MARIAS.
bugia (*f.*) wax candle; small candlestick; female monkey; (*Med.*) bougie.
bugiar (*v.i.*) to cut up, behave like a BUGIO (monkey).

mandar—, to send to the devil (get rid of an annoying person).
bugiaria (*f.*) monkeyshines; trinket, trifle, bagatelle.
bugigangas (*f.pl.*) trinkets, gewgaws, fripperies, odds and ends.
bugio (*m.*) a person who mimics another; a piledriver; any howling monkey (genus *Alouatta*), esp. the following:—**-labareda,** a red howler (*A. seniculus*), c.a. GUARIBA-VERMELHO;**—-ruivo,** another red howler (*A. ursina* or *A. fusca*). Cf. GUARIBA.
buglossa (*f.*, *Bot.*) the common oxtongue or bugloss (*Anchusa officinalis*), c.a. LÍNGUA-DE-VACA.
bugra, fem. of BUGRE.
bugrada (*f.*) a group of BUGRES; a BUGRE-like action.
bugraria (*f.*) BUGRE-land; also = BUGRADA.
bugre (*m.*) a generic term for any Indian, wild or otherwise, esp. certain Caingang in Santa Catarina; by ext., a coarse or savage person, or a treacherous or suspicious one. (Fem. BUGRA.) [The term BUGRE is in general derogatory, and derives from French *bougre*.]
bugreiro (*m.*) a professional hunter of Indians.
bugrinho *–nha* (*m.*,*f.*) a little BUGRE; (*m.*) a plant called CHÁ-DE-BUGRE (*Cordia salicifolia*).
bugrismo (*m.*) lack of polish; vulgarity; gaucheness; denseness, stupidity; suspiciousness; awkwardness.
búgula (*f.*, *Bot.*) carpet bugle (*Ajuga reptens*), c.a. CONSOLDA-RÉGIA, ERVA-FÉRREA, ERVA-DE-SÃO-LOURENÇO, LÍNGUA-DE-BOI.
buir (*v.t.*) to polish by rubbing.
bujão (*m.*) wooden plug, peg or dowel; a threaded plug, cap or stopper.**—fusível,** a fusible plug (as of a boiler or overhead sprinkler system).
bujarrona (*f.*) jib sail.
bula (*f.*) bulla (ancient round leaden seal affixed to documents); a papal bull; directions for taking (on a bottle of medicine).
bulbar (*adj.*) bulbar; bulbous.
bulbilho (*m.*, *Bot.*) bulbil.
bulbo (*m.*) bulb (of a plant, but not light bulb, which is LÂMPADA ELÉTRICA, nor radio tube, which is VÁLVULA ELETRÔNICA).**—raqueano** or **—raquidiano,** (*Anat.*) bulb of the spinal cord or brain, medulla oblongata. Var. BOLBO.
bulboso *–sa* (*adj.*) bulbous.
bulbul (*m.*) bulbul (a bird).
búlbulo (*m.*) bulblet.
bulcão (*m.*) black cloud.
buldogue (*m.*) bulldog; a snub-nosed pistol.
buldozer (*m.*) bulldozer.
bule (*m.*).**—de café,** coffeepot.**—de chá,** teapot.
bulevar (*m.*) boulevard.
búlgaro *–ra* (*adj.*; *m.*,*f.*) Bulgarian.
bulha (*f.*) tumult, stir, noisy confusion, racket, din, uproar, turbulence; fuss, bustle; heated discussion.
bulhar (*v.i.*) to make an uproar, raise a row, = squabble.
bulhento *–ta* (*adj.*) rowdy; pugnacious.
bulício (*m.*) buzz(ing), rustling, restlessness; stir, tumult.
buliçoso *–sa* (*adj.*) stirring, active; unquiet, restless; sportive, frolicsome; boisterous.
bulimo (*m.*) a large edible tropical snail (*Strophocheilus ovatus*).
bulir [22] (*v.i.*) to stir, move; (*v.t.*) to touch; to disturb (move); to meddle with; to molest.**—com,** to banter, tease; to stir, arouse.**—em,** to monkey with. **Não bula nisso!** Don't touch that! Don't fiddle with it!
bum! Boom!
bumba! Bang! Boom! Wham!
bumba-meu-boi (*m.*) a traditional dance and pageant in northeastern Brazil, in which the townsfolk take part.
bumbo (*m.*) = BOMBO.
bumbum! Boom! Boom!
buna (*f.*) Buna (synthetic rubber).
bunda (*f.*) rump, buttock [vulgar].**—-de-mulata** = AMARE-LINHA.
bundo (*m.*) any of the Bunda languages (spoken by the Negroes imported into Brazil as slaves).
bunho (*m.*) the great bulrush (*Scirpus lacustris*).
bunsenita (*f.*, *Min.*) bunsenite.
bupreste [prés] (*m.*) a beetle of the genus Buprestis.
buque (*m.*) a dory or small fishing boat.
buquê (*m.*) bouquet.**—-de-noiva,** (*Bot.*) the germander spirea (*S. chamaedryfolia*), c.a. FLOR-DA-NOITE, FLOR-DE-NOIVA, DAMA-DA-NOITE.
buquinar (*v.i.*) to browse in a bookstore.
bur [-es] (*adj.*; *m.*) Boer.

búraca (*f.*) a game played with marbles [= GUDE].
buracada, -cama (*f.*) a lot of holes in the road; ground full of holes [= BURAQUEIRA].
buraçanga (*f.*) "a cylindrical piece of wood with which washer women beat out clothes; also used for separating the cotton husk from the boll." [*GBAT*].
buraco (*m.*) hole, aperture, perforation, opening, cavity; cave, hollow; gully, gorge, ravine.—**da fechadura,** keyhole. **Isso é um—!** (*colloq.*) That's a tough situation! **Oue—!** What a mess!
buranhém (*m., Bot.*) a So. Amer. tree (*Pradosia lactescens*) whose bark (monesia bark) yields monesia. Cf. MONÉSIA.
buraqueira (*f.*) ground full of holes [= BURACADA]; steep ground with many depressions; (*colloq.*) a tough spot, tight fix.
buraqueiro (*m.*) = BURACADA.
burburinhar (*v.i.*) to murmur, babble; to brawl.
burburinho (*m.*) babble; noise; tumult; a brawl.
burel [-réis] (*m.*) a coarse (usually brown) cotton cloth; a monk's or nun's outer garment.
bureta [ê] (*f.*) cruet; (*Chem.*) burette.
burgo (*m.*) burg, village, town; borough.
burguês -guesa [ê] (*adj.*) bourgeois; (*m.,f.*) burgher, burgess; bourgeois. **pequeno—,** petit bourgeois.
burguesia (*f.*) bourgeoisie, middle class.
buri [í] (*m.*) a Brazilian palm (*Polyandrococcos caudescens*), not to be confused with the buri palm of Ceylon, which is *Corypha utan*.—**da-praia,** a palm (*Diplothemium maritimum*), c.a. COQUEIRO-GURIRI, GURIRI, IMBURI, PIÇANDÓ.—**do-campo** = AIRI.
buril (*m.*) burin, graver; stone chisel; an engraver's manner or style of execution.
burilada (*f.*) a cut with a burin.
burilador -dora (*adj.*) engraving; (*m.,f.*) engraver.
burilar (*v.t.*) to engrave (with a burin); to polish, perfect (as, a text, a work of art).
buriti [tí] (*m.*) the wine mauritia or murity palm (*Mauritia vinifera*), c.a. CARANDÁ-GUAÇU, COQUEIRO-BURITI, MURITI.—**bravo,** another mauritia palm (*M. armata*), c.a. BURITI-MIRIM, BURITI-NANA, BURITIRANA.—**do-brejo,** the fiber mauritia or burity palm (*Mauritia flexuosa*), c.a. MURITI, MURITIZEIRO.—**mirim,** a mauritia palm (*M. pumila*), c.a. CARANAÍ-MIRIM; also = BURITI-BRAVO (above).—**palito,** the green Trithrinax palm (*T. acanthocoma*).)
buritirana (*f.*) a mauritia palm (*M. aculeata*), c.a. CARANÁ, CARANDAÍ; also = BURITI-BRAVO.
buritizada (*f.*) a sweet confection made from the fruit of the BURITI palm.
buritizal (*m.*) an area (usually low and damp), covered with BURITI palms.
buritizeiro (*m.*) = BURITI.
buritizinho (*m.*) a mauritia palm (*M. martiana*), c.a. CARANÁ, CARANAÍ, CARINÁ, CARANDAÌZINHO, RIPA.
burla (*f.*) trick, fraud, swindle, bunco game; hoax; collusion; deception; mockery.
burlador -dora (*adj.*) defrauding; mocking; (*m.,f.*) defrauder; gyp artist; swindler.
burlão (*m.*), **-lona** (*f.*) crook, shark, defrauder, trickster, humbug.
burlar (*v.t.*) to deceive, defraud, trick, cheat; to hoax; to hornswoggle, bamboozle; to circumvent; to ridicule, laugh at; to outwit, overreach, outsmart.—**a lei,** to circumvent the law.—**os incautos,** to cheat the unwary.
burlequear (*v.i.*) to roam about.
burlesco -ca [ê] (*adj.*) burlesque, incongruous; ludicrous.
burlesquear (*v.t.*) to burlesque.
burlingtônia (*f.*) a genus (*Burlingtonia*) of orchids.
burlista (*adj.; m.,f.*) = BURLADOR.
burocracia (*f.*) bureaucracy; officialdom; (*colloq.*) red tape.
burocrata (*m.,f.*) bureaucrat, government employee.
burocrático -ca (*adj.*) bureaucratic.
burocratizar (*v.t.*) to bureaucratize.
burra (*f.*) female donkey; iron chest, strong box [= COFRE].—**leiteira,** (*Bot.*) a sapium (*S. sceleratum*). **pagar na bôca da—**(or **do cofre**), to pay cash on the barrelhead.
burrada (*f.*) = BURRICADA.
burragem (*f.*) = BURRICE.
burrama (*f.*) a bunch of mules.
burrão (*m.*) a large donkey; sullenness; (*Bot.*) a windmill grass (*Chloris bahiensis*), c.a. CAPIM-BURRÃO, GRAMA (or GRAMINHA)-DE-JACOBINA.
burrego -ga [ê] (*adj.; m.,f.*) dull, stupid, "dumb" (person).
burrica (*f.*) a young or small jenny ass.

burricada (*f.*) a herd of mules or asses.
burrice (*f.*) asininity; sullenness.
burrico (*m.*) a young or small jackass.
burrificar (*v.*) = BESTIFICAR.
burrinho (*m.*) a small donkey; a small electric motor, air compressor, or pump; the common name for blister beetles.
burriquete [quê] (*m.*) a small burro; sawhorse; a drumfish (*Pogonias chromis*), c.a. MIRAGUAIA, PIRAÚNA.
burro (*m.*) burro, jackass, donkey; loosely, mule; sawhorse; dunce, blockhead; student's pony, crib; donkey motor; (*adj.*) stupid, dull, "dumb"; bullheaded.—**burreiro,** a jackass used for breeding with female asses.—**-chôro,** a jackass used for breeding with mares [= HECHOR]. **a lombo de—,** on muleback. **andar,** or **estar, com os—s,** to be out of sorts, crabbed, morose. **dar com os—s nágua,** (*colloq.*) to flop (fail); to be ruined. **Êle é um—** (or **um burrão**), He is a downright ass (fool). **Êle é um—chapado,** He is an arrant fool. **orelhas de—,** dunce's cap. **prá—,** (*slang*) lots, oodles, scads; like everything.
bursite (*f., Med.*) bursitis.
buruanha (*f.*) = BERUANHA.
burundunga (*f.*) confusion; mess; (*pl.*) trifles.
busano (*m.*) teredo, shipworm [= GUSANO].
busca (*f.*) quest, search, investigation. **à—de,** in search of. **dar uma—,** to make a search. **em—de,** in search of.
buscador -dora (*adj.*) searching, seeking; (*m.,f.*) searcher, seeker.
buscante (*adj.*) seeking, searching.
buscapé (*m.*) a squib (firecracker).
buscar (*v.t.*) to seek (for, after), search for, look for; to fetch, bring, get. **ir—,** to go and fetch. **mandar—,** to send for.
busílis (*m.*) rub (difficulty; crucial point; knotty problem). **Aí é que está o—!** There's the rub!
bússola (*f.*) mariner's compass, magnetic needle.—**de inclinação,** dip compass, inclinometer.
busto (*m.*) bust. **meio—,** a half-length portrait or sculptured bust.
butadieno (*m., Chem.*) butadiene.
butanal (*m., Chem.*) butanal, butyraldehyde, butyric aldehyde.
butano (*m., Chem.*) butane.
butanol (*m., Chem.*) butanol, butyl alcohol.
butargas (*f.pl.*) botargo (salted fish roes).
buteco (*m.*) a "joint," small night spot.
buteiro (*m.*) clothes mender.
butelo (*m., colloq.*) any large object; very tall man [= GALALAU]. Var. BITELO.
butiá (*f.*) Brazilian butia palm (*Butia capitata*), c.a. BUTIÁ-DE-VINAGRE, BUTIÁ-AZÊDO, COQUEIRO-CABEÇUDO; the woolly butia palm (*B. eirospatha*); the perfume butia palm (*B. capitata odorata*); the Argentine yatay (*Butia yatay*).
butileno (*m., Chem.*) butylene.
butílico -ca (*adj., Chem.*) butylic.
butilo (*m., Chem.*) butyl.
butiráceo -cea (*adj., Chem.*) butyraceous.
butírico -ca (*adj., Chem.*) butyric.
butirina (*f., Chem.*) butyrin.
butirinase (*f., Biochem.*) butyrinase.
butirômetro (*m.*) a butyrometer (instrument for measuring butter fat in milk).
butiroso -sa (*adj.*) butyrous, butyraceous.
bútomo (*m.*) flowering rush (*Butomus umbellatus*), c.a. JUNCO-FLORIDO.
butua (*f.*) = ABUTUA.
butuá-de-corvo (*m.*) a shellseed (*Cocklospermum insigne*), c.a. ALGODÃO-CRAVO, ALGODÃO-DO-MATO, ALGODOEIRO-DO-MATO, ALGODOEIRO-DO-CAMPO, PACOTÊ, PERIQUITEIRA-DO-CAMPO, RUIBARBO-DO-CAMPO, SUMAÚMA-DO-IGAPÓ.
butuca (*f.*) = MUTUCA.
butuinha [u-í] (*f.*) = CIPÓ-DE-COBRA.
buxáceo -cea [ks] (*adj., Bot.*) buxaceous; (*f.pl.*) the Buxaceae (box family).
buxina (*f., Chem.*) buxine.
buxo (*m., Bot.*) common box (*Buxus sempervirens*).
buzina (*f.*) automobile horn; trumpet; (*Naut.*) hawsehole.
buzinar (*v.t.*) to blow a trumpet; to honk (automobile horn).
buzinote (*m.*) drainpipe.
búzio (*m.*) conch; whelk; trumpet; deep-sea diver; a helmet shell (*Cassis tuberosa*).
B.V. = BARLAVENTO (windward).
B.V.M. = BEATA VIRGEM MARIA (Holy Virgin Mary).

C

C, the third letter of the Portuguese alphabet; as abbrev. = CALÇADA, (Walk—name of a side street); CARBONO, (carbon); COULOMB, (*Elec.*) coulomb.
c. = CANTO, (canto of a poem); CENA, (scene); CENTO, (hundred), CONTO, (1000 cruzeiros, formerly, 1000 milreis).
c/ = COM (with); CONTA (account).
ca = CENTIARE(s).
ca = CÁLCIO, (calcium).
C.A. = CORRENTE ALTERNADA, (alternating current).
cá (*adv.*) here, in this place; hither, to this place.'—**dentro,** here inside.—**fora,** here on the outside.—**-te-espero,** (*colloq.*) the cemetery; (lit., here I await you). **daí,** or **de então, para**—, since then; thereafter. **de lá prá**—, back and forth. **de uns tempos para**—, for some time now. **Eu—me entendo,** I know what I mean (even if you don't). **Eu—sou assim,** Me, that's the way I am. **lá e**—, there and here. **para**—, here, over here. **para—de,** this side of (a given place). **para—e para lá,** back and forth. **por**—, here, around here. **Venha (vem)**—! Come here! **Venha (vem) para**—! come over here!
cã (*f.*) see CÃS.
caá [ca-á] (*f.*) the Tupian word for plant; the mate tea plant (*Ilex paraguayensis*), better known as ERVA-MATE, or the tea drink itself, called CHÁ-MATE; a nightshade (*Solanum tabaciforme*).—**-açu,** (*Bot.*) a malpighia (*M. rosea*).—**-apia** = CAAPIÁ.—**-apoã,** a sweetleaf (*Simplocos celastrinea*).—**-ataia** = DOURADINHA.—**-bopoxi,** a morning-glory (*Ipomoea malvaoides*).—**-cambuí,** serpent euphorbia (*E. serpens*), c.a. ERVA-DE-COBRA.—**-có,** the sensitive plant (*Mimosa pudica*), better known as SENSITIVA.—**-guaçu,** a pipewort (*Eriocaulon sellowianum*).—**-ingá,** an apes-earring (*Pithecellobium sanguineum*).—**-membeca,** either of two polygalas: *P. paraensis* or *P. spectabilis*.—**-peba** = CAPEBA.—**-pomonga,** climbing plumbago (*P. scandens*), c.a. CAATAIA, ERVA-DO-DIABO, FÔLHAS-DE-LOUCO, JASMIM-AZUL, LOUCO.—**-xira,** an indigo (*Indigofera brasiliensis*).
caaetê [a-a] (*m.*) those portions of the Amazon forest which cover the rarely-flooded plains.
caajaçara (*f.*) = TAMEARAMA.
caapi [ca-api] (*f., Bot.*) caapi (*Banisteriopsis caapi*).
caapiá [a-a] (*m.*) = CAIAPIÁ.
caaponga [a-a] (*m.*) = CAPOTIRAGUÁ, ALECRIM-DE-SÃO-JOSÉ.
caataia [a-a] (*f.*) = CAA-POMONGA.
caataiá [a-a] (*f.*) = CAPITIÇOVA.
caatinga [a-a] (*f.*) = CATINGA.
caba (*f.*) any social wasp.—**-açu** = CABUÇU.—**-beiju-cega,** —**-de-ladrão** = MARIMBONDO-DE-CHAPÉU.—**-caçadeira,** any spider wasp.—**-da-igreja** = MARIMBONDO-CABOCLO.—**-mirim,** a tiny wasp of the genus Polybia.—**-tatu** = CABATATU.
cabaça (*f.*) a water dipper or other vessel made from the dried shell of a calabash or gourd; the gourd itself.—**-amargosa** or—**-purunga** = CABACEIRO-AMARGOSO. (*m.*) the second-born of twins.
cabaçada (*f.*) a gourdful.
cabaceira (*f.*) a gourd vine.
cabaceiro (*m.*) common calabashtree (*Crescentia cujete*), c.a. CUIEIRA, CUITIZEIRA.—**-amargoso,** calabash gourd (*Lagenaria siceraria*), c.a. CABAÇA (-AMARGOSA, -PURUNGA), CACOMBRO, TACUERA.
cabacinha (*f.*) a small gourd.—**-do-campo** the perado-campo (*Eugenia klotzschiana*), c.a. PEREIRA-DO-CAMPO; also, a gourd called BUCHINHA.—**-riscada** = ABÓBORA-OVOS.
cabacinho (*m.*) a tropical cucurbitaceous vine having a berrylike warty fruit (*Momordica bucha*); "a variety of cacao fruit, 11.5 by 8.5 centimeters, smooth and nearly round, containing an average of 36 small, bitter seeds." [GBAT].
cabaçu [ú] (*m.*) a social wasp, c.a. CABUÇU.
cabaíbas (*m.pl.*) an ancient Tupi tribe which once lived in the upper Tapajos River basin. They were destroyed by the fierce, head-hunting Mundurucu. Cf. CAVAÍBA.
cabal (*adj.*) complete, entire, full, perfect, full. **de maneira**—, in a conclusive manner. **prova**—, ample proof.
cabala (*f.*) cabal; clique; cabala.

cabalar (*v.i.*) to intrigue; to line up voters.
cabalístico -ca (*adj.*) cabalistic.
cabana (*f.*) cabin, hut, shack; (*Aeron.*) cabane.—**de colmo,** thatched hut.—**de palha,** grass shack.—**de toros,** log cabin.
cabaré (*m.*) cabaret, night club.
cabatatu [ú] (*m.*) a wasp (*Synoeca surinama*), c.a. TATU-CABA.
cabaú (*m.*) raw molasses.
cabaz (*m.*) hamper, large basket.
cabe (*m.*) a man's coat [= PALETÓ].
cabear (*v.i.*) of a horse, to switch his tail.
cabeça (*f.*) head; top; mind, intellect; wits; (*m.*) head, chief, leader.—**-branca,** (*Zool.*) a manakin (*Pipra leucocilla*), c.a. TANGARÁ.—**-chata,** a nickname applied to natives of Ceará and other parts of northern Brazil; c.a. ARATACA, NORTISTA.—**-d'água,** a freshet.—**-de-alhos,** a bulb of garlic.—**-de-boi,** an orchid (*Stanhopea insignis*), bearing large, fragrant flowers.—**-de casal,** (*Civil Law*) the surviving spouse who acts as administrator of the joint estate.—**-de-ferro** = ANUJÁ (a fish).—**-de gado,** head of cattle.—**-de-galinhola,** a mollusk (*Murex erinaceus*) which yields a purple dye, and other species of this genus.—**-de lança,** a spear head.—**-de-medusa,** (*Zool.*) a large stalked crinoid (*Pentacrinus caput medusae*), c.a. PALMEIRA-MARINHA.—**-de-padre,** violet melon cactus (*Melocactus violaceus*).—**-de-pau,** black-head.—**-de-pedra,** the wood ibis (*Mycteria americana*), c.a. CABEÇA-SÊCA, TUIUIU, PASSARÃO.—**-de ponte,** bridge-head.—**-de-porco,** (*slang*) rooming house; flop house; flea bag; slum.—**-de-prego,** tadpole; pimple.—**-de-turco,** (*Naut.*) bollard.—**-de-urubu,** a chocolate tree (*Theobroma obovatum*).—**-de-vento,** or—**-no-ar,** a giddy, frivolous person.—**-dura,** or—**-de-camarão,** chump, dullard.—**-encarnada,** (*Zool.*) a manakin (*Pipra rubrocapilla*).—**-inchada,** jealousy; chagrin.—**-ôca,** or—**-sem-miolos,** an empty-headed person.
cabeçada (*f.*) a butt with the head; a piece of stupidity; a blunder; head gear (of a harness). **dar uma**—, (*colloq.*) to bang one's head; to commit a faux pas.
cabeçalho (*m.*) shaft of a cart; title page of a book; mast-head of a newspaper; headline, caption.
cabeção (*m.*) the upper (usually embroidered) part of a woman's chemise; large collar (of a cloak or coat); vignette (of a book).
cabeçaria (*f.*) rough-hewn stones for foundation work.
cabecear (*v.i.*) to nod.
cabeceira (*f.*) head of a bed; pillow; head-rest; bedside; head of the table; spine of a book; the back of a building; high altar; head stone; "in northeastern Brazil, a cow-boy who goes at the head of the herd, immediately after the guide; on the island of Marajó, pasture land at some distance from the FAZENDA proper." [GBAT]; (*pl.*) head waters. **à—de,** at the bedside of. **mesa de**—, bed-side table.
cabecel [-céis] (*m.*) vignette at the top of a page.
cabeço (*m.*) knoll [= OUTEIRO].
cabeçote (*m.*) the head of a carpenter's bench; the head-stock of a lathe; a tadpole [= GIRINO].
cabeçudo -da (*adj.*) headstrong, pig-headed, stubborn, opinionated.—**como uma mula,** as stubborn as a mule; (*f.*) a fresh-water turtle (*Podocnemis dumeriliana*), c.a. ARARA-ACANGA-AÇU, TRACAJÁ; also = SAÚVA (an ant); (*m.*) = XARÉU (a fish), and COQUINHO-DO-CAMPO (a palm).
cabedal (*m.*) fund, capital; shoe leather; (*pl.*) means, resources; (*adj.*) copious, abundant.—**de (conhecimentos),** fund of (knowledge).
cabeira (*f.*) floor and ceiling corner or finish molding.
cabeleira (*f.*) head of hair; (*m.*) man with long hair; man of the old school; a bandit.—**-de-vênus,** (*Min.*) Venus's hairstone.—**postiça,** toupee, wig. **pau de**—, a chaperone; the butt of a joke.
cabeleireiro (*m.*) hairdresser; wigmaker.
cabelinho (*m.*) a small hair; (*Med.*) entropion.—**-de-jesus,** (*Bot.*) the tweed calliandra (*C. tweedii*).
cabelo (*m.*) hair, fur; a single strand of hair; hairspring (of a watch); (*pl.*) hair.—**à escovinha,** crew haircut.—**(en)cacheado,** naturally curly hair.—**carapinha,** kinky hair.—**castanho,** light brown hair.—**crespo,** curly hair.

—-de-negro, a cocaine tree (*Erythroxylum campestre*), c.a. COCA-DO-PARAGUAI, FRUTA-DE-TUCANO; also = GALINHA-CHOCA.—s-de-nossa-senhora = CUSCUTA.—s-de-vênus = NIGELA (fennel flower).—duro, stiff hair.—escuro, dark hair.—encarapinhado, kinky hair.—estrigado, thin hair.—grisalho, gray hair.—lambido, slicked-down hair. —liso (or corrido), straight hair.—louro, blond hair.— ondeado, or ondulado, wavy hair.—-vivo, a hairworm. arrancar os—s, to tear out one's hair. até a ponta (or a raiz) dos—s, up to one's neck; up to one's ears. corte de—, haircut. de arrepiar o—, or de se ficar com o—em pé, (adj.) hair-raising. em—, bareheaded. mulher de— (or de cabelinho) na venta, (*colloq.*) an energetic, mannish woman. tirar couro e—a (alguém), to scalp, cheat (someone). Vou cortar o—, I am going to get a haircut.

cabeludo -da (*adj.*) hairy; shaggy; complicated, intricate, involved; obscene; (*m.*) a saki monkey (*Pithecia leucocephale*) having a bushy non-prehensile tail, and long hair which usually forms a ruff around the face. couro—, the scalp; (*f., Bot.*) the cabelluda (*Eugenia tomentosa*).

caber [32] (*v.i.*) to be containable (em, in); to fit in or inside of; to go into; to be compatible with.—a, to be fitting to; to fall to one's lot; to befit, belong to.—em direito, (*Law*) to accrue.—por, to be passable through, as Essa mesa não cabe por aquela porta, That table won't go through that door.Cabe a você falar com êle, It is up to you to speak to him. cabe-me dizer que, it behooves me to say that. Coube-lhe a terça parte da herança, A third of the inheritance befell him. Êle não cabe em si de contente, He can hardly contain himself with joy. Não cabe aqui fazer comentários, This is not the time and place to comment (on that).

cabéua (*f.*) = PITIÚ.

cabide (*m.*) hatrack; coat-hanger.—de bombas, bomb rack.

cabidela (*f.*) chicken giblets, wings, neck, feet and blood, collectively; a stew made with these parts.

cabido -da (*adj.*) suitable, appropriate; valid; deserved; intrusive; (*m., Eccl.*) chapter.

cabimento (*m.*) fitness, pertinence, relevancy, suitableness. Isso não tem—! There is no reason for that, no room for it; it doesn't make sense.

cabina (*f.*) cabin, stateroom; compartment; cockpit (of an airplane); signal tower.—pressurizada, or—supercomprimida, (*Aeron.*) pressurized cabin.

cabineiro (*m.*) stateroom steward; sleeping car porter; elevator operator.

cabisbaixo -xa (*adj.*) with lowered head; crestfallen, downcast.

cabitu [ú] (*f.*) = SAÚVA.

cabiúna (*adj.*) negro; black; (*m.*) a Negro illegally brought into Brazil after the abolition of slavery; (*f., Bot.*) black rosewood (*Dalbergia nigra*), c.a. JACARANDÁ-CABIÚNA, JACARANDÁ-PRÊTO. Var. CAVIÚNA.

cabível (*adj.*) fitting, appropriate; admissible. uma expressão—, a fitting remark. medidas cabiveis, suitable measures.

cabixi [xí] (*m.,f.*) an Indian of the Cabishi, a subtribe of the Pareci; (*adj.*) pert. to or designating the Cabixi.

cablar (*v.i.*) to cable.

cabo (*m.*) handle; cable; hawser; electric cable; submarine cable; chief, commander; corporal; cape (point of land); end, terminal.—armado, armored cable.— bifilar, a two-conductor cable.—Bojador, an old name for the Cape of Good Hope.—coaxial, coaxial cable.— concêntrico, concentric cable.—da guarda, corporal of the guard.—de aço, steel cable.—de amarração, mooring rope.—de comando, (*Aeron.*) control cable.—de esquadra, squad leader.—de freio, braking cable.—de guerra, war chief; an old war horse.—de marinheiros, marine corporal.—de reboque, towline, towrope.—de suspensão, suspension cable.—de vassoura, broom handle, broomstick.—do mundo, ends of the earth.—eleitoral, ward boss.—flexível, flexible cable.—rígido, stiff cable.— submarino, submarine cable.—subterrâneo, underground cable.—verde = CABOVERDE. alma do—, cable core. ao—, at last, finally. ao—de, at the end of. ao—de dez dias, after ten days. ao—de tudo, after all, notwithstanding, in spite of. dar—de, to put an end to; to do away with; to destroy, ruin. de—a rabo, from head to tail; from stem to stern; from end to end. levar a—, to carry out, conclude, finish.

caboatã (*f.*) a guara tree (*Cupania vernalis*).

cabochão (*m.*) cabochon (gem).

cabocla [ô] (*f.*) see CABOCLO.

caboclinho (*m.*) the pinkish seed-eater (*Sporophila b. bouvreuil*), c.a. PAPA-CAPIM.—-do-norte, or—-da-bahia, the minute seed-eater (*Sporophila m. minuta*).

caboclo -cla [bô] (*adj.*) copper-colored; (*m.*) a civilized Brazilian Indian of pure blood; a Brazilian half-breed of white and Indian; a copper-colored mulatto with straight black hair; a backwoodsman.—-velho, (*Zool.*) a barbet (*Capito auratus*); (*f.*) a woman CABOCLO; (*Bot.*) the redstar zinnia.

cabograma (*m.*) cablegram.

caboje [ô] (*m.*) a section of sugar cane used for planting [= VIGÁRIO].

cabonegro (*m.*) = MARFIM-VEGETAL.

caboré (*m.*) = CABURÉ.

caborje (*m.*) witchcraft; voodooism; an amulet worn around the neck; a swamp fish.

cabotagem (*f.*) coastwise shipping.

cabotinagem (*f.*), -tinismo (*m.*) mode of living or behavior of a CABOTINO.

cabotino (*m.*) wandering minstrel; ham actor; vainglorious person.

caboucar (*v.t.*) = CAVOUCAR.

cabouco (*m.*) = CAVOUCO.

cabouqueiro (*m.*) = CAVOUQUEIRO.

caboverde (*f., Bot.*) a senna (*Cassia speciosa*), c.a. MANDUIRANA, PAU-FAVA; a shrub called BOIGORDO; (*Min.*) jewstone [= PEDRA-DE-JUDEU]; (*m.*) a half-breed [= CABORÉ].

caboverdeano -na (*adj.; m.,f.*) (a native or inhabitant) of Cape Verde.

cabra (*f.*) a she (nanny) goat; a water spider, c.a. ALFAIATE; a small tripod hoist; (*m*) bandit, ruffian; backwoods assassin; half-breed Negro—-cega, blindman's buff.—de sorte! lucky dog!—escovado (safado, sarado), (*slang*) slicker, rascal.—-loura, a stag beetle (*Lucanus cervus*).—-macho, a ruffian.—-montês, mountain goat.

cabrada (*f.*) herd of goats; zoom, pull-up (of an airplane in flight); = CABRAGEM, CABRÉ.

cabrão (*m.*) a tolerant cuckold.

cabrar (*v.i., Aeron.*) to zoom.

cábrea (*f.*) a tripod hoist; a derrick; a sort of hand winch; a hawser.

cabreiro -ra (*adj.*) goat-herding; made of goat's milk; sharp, sly; suspicious; (*m.,f.*) goatherd.

cabrestante (*m.*) capstan, windlass.

cabrestear (*v.i.*) to be easily led by, or as by, a halter.

cabresteiro -ra (*adj.*) easily led by, or as by, a halter; submissive, docile; (*m.,f.*) such a person.

cabrestilho (*m.*) a small halter; a spur strap.

cabresto [ê] (*m.*) halter; lead-ox; (*Naut.*) bobstay; (*Anat.*) frenum.

cabrião (*m.*) a chiton (coat-of-mail shell).

cabrilha (*f.*) shear legs, hoist.

cabrinha (*f.*) either of two sea robins. *Prinotus punctatus* (the spotted one) or *P. capella*.

cabrinha (*f.*) a young female goat; (*Zool.*) a gurnard or sea robin.

cabriola (*f.*) capriole, caper, antic.

cabriolar (*v.i.*) to caper, romp, gambol, cavort, frisk, prance, skip; to cut capers.

cabriolé (*m.*) cabriolet, gig.

cabrita (*f.*) a female kid goat; a fish called ALFINÊTE. às—s, upon the shoulders.

cabrit[e]ar (*v.i.*) to caper, jump, skip about.

cabrito (*m.*) kid goat; (*colloq.*) keeper of an unfaithful mistress.—montês, mountain goat.

cabríuva (*f.*) the Brazilian myrocarpus (*M. frondosus*) c.a. BÁLSAMO, CABRUÉ, ÓLEO-PARDO, PAU-BÁLSAMO, PAU-DE-ÓLEO-VERDADEIRO. [This tree yields one of the best Brazilian woods for shafts, beams, truck bodies and cabinet work. The wood is hard, strong, fragrantly scented and varies in color from reddish brown to purplish rose, and takes a high polish.]—-do-campo, a similar tree (*Myrocarpus fastigiatus*), c.a. BÁLSAMO, CABUREÍBA, ÓLEO-DE-MACACO, ÓLEO:PARDO, PAU-AMARELO.

cabrocha, cabroche (*f.*) a very dark mulatto girl; a dark-skinned half-breed woman; (*m.*) a young mulatto; a dark half-breed.

cabrochão)*m.*) a heavy-set mulatto.

cabroeira (*f.*), -ro (*m.*) gang of ruffians [= CABRAS].

cabrué (*m.*) = CABRIÚVA.

cabrum (*adj.*) caprine. gado—, goats.

cabuchão (m.) = CABOCHÃO.

cabucipe-vinhático (m.) an earpod tree (Enterolobium lutescens).

cabuçu (çú] (m.) a seagrape (Coccolobis martii), c.a. GUAJABARA, GUAJUVIRA; a social wasp, c.a. CABAÇU.

cabuim [u-ím] (m.) = MUNDAU.

cábula (m.) student who cuts classes; shirker; (f.) class cutting; shirking, malingering; bad luck; (adj.) unlucky; superstitious; given to shirking.

cabuloso –sa (adj.) unlucky; superstitious; pesky.

cabumbo-de-azeite (m.) a resin tree (Protium insigne) which yields acouchi resin. Cf. CARANÁ.

caburé (m.) any of various pygmy owls of genus Glaucidium, c.a. CABORÉ.—-de-orelha, Spix's screech owl (Otus choliba crucigerus).—-do-campo, = CORUJA-DO-CAMPO; the offspring of an Indian and Negro [= CAFUZO]; a backwoodsman [= CAIPIRA]; a tree, c.a. CABRIÚVA (which see).

cabureíba (f.) = CABRIÚVA-DO-CAMPO.

caç. = CAÇADOR (skirmisher).

caça (f.) hunt, hunting; game, quarry; chase, pursuit.— grossa (miúda), big (small) game. à—de, in pursuit of. cão de—, a hunting dog. dar—a, to chase, to hunt for. fazer boa—, to have a successful hunt. lugar de— abundante, a place where game is plentiful. Um dia da—, outro do caçador, Every dog has his day.

caçada (f.) hunting trip; game, prey.

caçador [ô] (m.) hunter, huntsman; (Mil.) rifleman, sniper, skirmisher.

caçadora (f.) huntress.

cacália-amarga (f.) = CARQUEJA.

caçamba (f.) any bucket; esp. for concrete handling; well bucket; 5-gallon can; a shoe-like stirrup; dump cart; (colloq.) an old tub (ship); a rattletrap vehicle.

caçambada (f.) a bucketful.

caça-minas (m.) mine sweeper.

caça-níqueis (m.) slot machine, c.a. CAÇA-TOSTÕES.

caçanje (m.) Afro-Portuguese dialect; broken Portuguese.

caçante (adj.) hunting.

cação (m.) a shark.—-anequim = TUBARÃO-ANEQUIM.— -angolista (or -torrador, or -fiuso) = SEBASTIÃO (a dogfish).—-anjo, the monkfish (Squatina squatina).—-bagre (or de-espinho, or -prego), a dogfish (Squalus fernandinus).—-de-areia = MANGANGÁ (a sand shark).—-de-escamas = BIJUPIRÁ.—-franço (or -alegrim, or -de-bicodoce), the sharp-nosed shark (Scoliodon terrae-novae), c.a. FRANGO, CUCURI.—-martelo = PEIXE-MARTELO, CHAPÉU-ARMADO (hammerhead sharks); also = PATA (bonnet-head shark).—-panã (or -rodela), a hammerhead shark (Sphyrna tiburo), c.a. PATA.—-pinto, a cat-shark or rousette (Scylliorhinus haecklii), c.a. PINTO, PINTA-DINHO, GATA.—-rapôsa (or -pena), the common thresher or fox-shark (Alopias vulpes).

cacaoal (m.) a grove of cacao trees.

caçapa (f.) billiards pocket.

caçapo (m.) young rabbit.

caçapó (m.) a saúva ant.

caçar (v.t.) to hunt, chase, pursue, catch. Quem não tem cão, caça com gato, One must make do with what one has.

cacaracá (f.) de—, (colloq.) of no account; insignificant.

cacarecos (m.pl.) pieces of old household goods.

cacarejar (v.i.) to cackle; to gabble, chatter; to laugh (with a cackling sound).—e não pôr ôvo, to make false promises.

cacarejo [ê] (m.) cackle; cackling.

cacaréus (m.pl.) = CACARECOS.

caçaroba (f.) a pigeon (Columba rufina), c.a. POMBA-LEGITIMA.

caçarola (f.) casserole, saucepan.

caça-submarino (m.) submarine chaser.

cacatua (f.) cockatoo.

caça-tostões (m.) = CAÇA-NÍQUEIS.

cacau (m.) cocoa bean; (Bot.) the cacao tree (Theobroma cacao) and others of this genus.—-de-mico, monkey chocolate tree (Theobroma angustifolia).—-do-peru, Nicaragua chocolate tree (Theobroma bicolor), c.a. MACAMBO.—-selvagem, the Trinidade pachira (P. insignis), c.a. CAROLINA, CASTANHEIRO-DAS-GUIANAS, CASTANHEIRO-DO-MARANHÃO, MAMORANA.

caçaú (m.) = ANGELICO and JARRINHA.

cacaual (m.) a planting of cacao trees.

cacaueiro, cacauzeiro (m., Bot.) cacão (Theobroma cacao).

caçava (f.), –ve (m.) = FARINHA-DE-MANDIOCA.

cacerenga (f.) = CAXIRENGUENGUE.

cacestesia (f., Med.) cacesthesia.

cacetada (f.) a cudgel-blow; a drubbing, beating (with a stick); bother, importunity. dar—s em, to hit or beat with a club. Que—! What a bore!

cacête (m.) a club or cudgel; a boring, annoying, tiresome person; (adj.) boring, boresome, dull, tiresome. dar de—, to beat (up) with a club. Não seja—, Don't be a nuisance. um velho—, an old fogy.

caceteação (f.) cudgeling; importunity.

caceteador –dora (adj.) boring, boresome; (m.,f.) such a person.

cacetear (v.t.) to cudgel; to pester, bore (another) "to death".

cachaça (f.) raw, white rum; booze, firewater, "chain lightning"; skimmings of boiling sugar cane juice; a craze (for something or someone); a hobby, foible; leaning, bent; (m.) a drunkard.

cachação (m.) a shove or blow on the back of the neck [= PESCOÇÃO].

cachaceiro –ra (adj.) given to boozing; (m.) boozer; (f.) crown of a bridle; drunkenness.

cachaço (m.) nape (of the neck); a boar.

cachalote (m.) sperm whale.

cachamorra (f.) bludgeon, club, cudgel.

cachão (m.) a bubbling, or boiling; a waterfall.

cachaporra (f.) = CACHAMORRA.

cacheado –da (adj.) in clusters; curly [= ONDULADO].

cachear (v.i.) of fruit, to form on the plant in clusters or bunches, as grapes; to curl.

cachecol [-cóis] [Fr. cache-col] (m.) neck scarf.

cacheira (f.) cudgel.

cachenê [Fr. cache-nez] (m.) muffler.

cachepô [Fr. cache-pot] (m.) ornamental vase to cover or hide flower-pot.

cachêta (f.) a trumpet tree (Tabebuia cassinoides), c.a. PAU-PARAÍBA, TAMANCÃO.

cachimã (f.) the bullockheart custardapple (Annona reticulata).

cachimbada (f.) a pipeful of tobacco; a puff on a pipe.

cachimbar (v.i.) to smoke a pipe.

cachimbo (m.) pipe (for smoking); socket (as of a candlestick); any of a number of plants, such as gloxinias, bearing tubular flowers; (Zool.) any pipefish (Syngnathus), c.a. AGULHA-DO-MAR, PEIXE-AGULHA; also = TICOTICO-DO-BIRI (a bird).

cachimônia (f. colloq.) noodle (head); brains; sense.

cachinar (v.i.) to cachinnate (laugh loudly, scoffingly).

cacho (m.) bunch (of grapes, bananas, etc.); cluster (of flowers); curl (of hair).—de marimbondo, hornet's nest.—vermelho (Bot.) an amasônia (A. punicea).

cachoeira (f.) waterfall. "A series of small drops in a section of a river; a cascade; a rapids." [GBAT]

cachola (f., colloq.) the noodle (head), = CACHIMÔNIA.

cacholeta [ê] (f.) a rap.

cachopa [ô] (f.) robust young wench (in Portugal).

cachopo [ô] [m.] underwater rock, sandbar, dangerous obstacle; in Portugal, a lad.

cachorra [ô] (f.) young bitch; female cub; slut.

cachorrada (f.) a pack of dogs; low behavior; dirty trick; canaille, rabble.

cachorrão (m.) a big dog; a big scoundrel.

cochorreiro (m.) dog breeder; dog trainer.

cachorrinho (m.) puppy, doggy; new-born calf.—-do-mato, the grison (Grison vittatus or G. vittata), closely related to the tayra (see under IRARA) which sometimes is also called cachorrinho-do-mato.

cachorro [ôr] (m.) dog, puppy; cub; (Arch.) bracket, corbel; stay, prop, shore in a drydock; a contemptible man.—de raça, pedigreed dog.—-de-padre = ANUJÁ (a fish).—doido, mad dog.—que late não morde, Barking dogs seldom bite.—quente, (slang) hot dog.—sem dono, or—viralata, stray dog, mongrel. estar no mato sem—, to be in a boat without a paddle (in a predicament).

cacife (m.) the ante (in poker).

cacif[r]o (m.) strongbox, safe; box; drawer; dark corner or nook.

cacimba (f.) a well or water hole [= POÇO].

cacique (m.) tribal chief; head man; political boss. Cf. MANDACHUVA.

caciquismo (m.) bossism.

caco (m.) fragment (of broken glass, china, etc.); shard,

potsherd; brick bat; (colloq.) an old person; the noodle (head);—-velho, broken-down old man.
caçoada (f.) mockery, jeering, raillery, banter [= TROÇA]. fazer—de, to make fun of.
caçoador -dora [dô] (adj.) jeering, jesting, bantering; (m.,f.) one who jeers, makes fun; teaser.
caçoar (v.t.,v.i.) to jeer, jest, banter; to make fun (de, com, of); to kid, tease, chaff.
cacodilo, cacodílio (m., Chem.) cacodyl.
cacoepia (f.) cacoepy.
cacoete [ê] (m.) cacoethes; an involuntary twitch of the face or screwing up of the mouth = TIQUE].
cacofonia (f.) cacophony.
cacografar (v.t.) to scrawl; to misprint; to misspell.
cacografia (f.) cacography.
caçoila (f.) earthen cooking vessel; incense burner. Var. CAÇOULA.
caçoísta (m.,f.) teaser.
caçoleta [ê] (f.) primer of a firearm; percussion cap; a goldsmith's or similar small crucible; a small frying pan.
cacologia (f.) cacology; solecism.
cacombro (m.) = CABACEIRO-AMARGOSO.
caçote (m.) = CABEÇOTE.
caçoula (f.) = CAÇOILA.
cactáceas (f.pl.) the Cactaceae (cactus family).
cacto (m.) any cactus.—-das-pedras or—-miúdo is Notocactus muricatus.—-rosa is Pereskia grandifolia, c.a. QUIABENTO.—-trepador is Leocereus melanurus, c.a. FLOR-DE-BAILE, SABUGO.
caçuá (m.) a pannier.
caçuiroba (f.) = POMBA-LEGÍTIMA.
caçuirova (f.) = POMBA-AMARGOSA.
caçula, caçulo (m.,f.) the youngest child in a family; the first-born of twins.
caculo (m.) = COGULO.
cacumbu [bú] (m.) a worn-out tool, knife, hoe, etc.
cacunda (f.) back, shoulders; hump. Var. CORCUNDA.
cacutu [tú] (m.) = MANDACHUVA.
cada (adj.) each, every.—cabeça,—sentença, Many men, many minds.—dia, every day.—louco com a sua mania, Each to his own taste.—macaco no seu galho, Everyone in his own place, job, etc.—(oito) dias, every (eight) days.—qual, each one, every one.—qual com o seu igual, Birds of a feather flock together.—qual tem os seus defeitos, Everyone has his faults.—um, each, each one.—um por si e Deus por todos, Each for himself and God for all.—vez, every time, each time.—vez mais, more and more (all the time).—vez mais rico, richer and richer.—vez melhor, better and better (all the time).—vez menos interessante, less and less interesting.—vez pior, worse and worse (all the time).—vez que, each (every) time that. a—hora, all the time, constantly. Êle faz—uma! He does the darndest things! No verão, cai—chuvarada! In the summer we get the biggest rainstorms (you ever saw)! Você tem—idéia! You get the queerest ideas!
cadafalso (m.) gallows, gibbet, scaffold.
cadarço (m.) floss silk; silk braid; binding tape; fringe, tassel.—de sapatos, shoestring.
cadaste (m., Naut.) sternpost.
cadastragem (f.) cadastramento (m.) the act or process of making a CADASTRO.
cadastral (adj.) cadastral.
cadastrar (v.t.) to make a CADASTRO.
cadastro (m.) cadastral map or survey; census; credit list; police record.
cadáver [-es] (m.) cadaver, corpse; carcass; (slang) creditor.
cadavérico -ca (adj.) cadaverous; ghastly, deathly pale. magreza—, extreme thinness. rigidez—, rigor mortis.
cadaverina (f., Chem.) cadaverine.
cade (m.) the prickly juniper (Juniperus oxycedrus).
cadê [corrup. of QUE É DE . . .] what's become of . . . ? where is . . . ?
cadeado (m.) padlock.
cadeia (f.) chain; handcuff; jail, prison; fig., enslavement. (Chem.) chain.—de agrimensor, surveyor's chain.—de estações de rádio, radio network.—de jornais, newspaper chain.—(or linha) de montagem, assembly line (in a factory).—de montanhas, mountain chain.—(or correia) sem fim, endless chain.—silogística, (Logic) sorites. ir para a—, to go to jail. ponto de—, chain stitch. uma—de acontecimentos, a chain of events.
cadeira (f.) chair, seat; stand (in a rolling mill); (pl.) buttocks, rump.—austríaca, reed-bottom chair.—de balanço, rocking chair.—de braços, armchair.—de palha or de palhinha, cane-bottom chair.—de platéia, orchestra seat (in a theater).—de rodas, wheelchair.—de teatro, theater seat.—espreguiçadeira, deck chair; lounge chair.—giratória, swivel chair.—portátil or dobradiça, folding chair. dôr nas—s, pain in the lower back. falar de—, to speak ex cathedra, with authority. mexer com as—s, to swing the hips.
cadeirinha (f.) a little chair.
cadeiruda (adj., fem. only) having large buttocks.
cadela (f.) bitch; slut.
cadência (f.) cadence, modulation; rate; rhythm; (Music) time. marchar em—, to keep step.
cadenciado -da (adj.) rhythmic.
cadente (adj.) falling; cadent. estrêla—, falling star.
cadernal (m.) pulley block.
caderneta (f.) note book.—de banco, bank book.—de campo, surveyor's field note book.—de cheques, check book.—de chofer, automobile driver's identification, record and license booklet.—de identidade, identification booklet (with picture, finger prints, etc.).—de reservista, military reservist's identification booklet.—de voô, flying logbook.
caderno (m.) note book, pad, tablet.
cadete [dê] (m.) army cadet.—naval, midshipman.
cadilho (m.) a small cup for catching the sap of rubber trees; (pl.) fringe of carpets, towels, etc.
cadimo -ma (adj.) dexterous; smart; every-day.
cadinhar (v.t.) to crucible.
cadinho (m.) crucible; (Metal.) hearth.—de raças, melting pot of races.—de recozer, annealing furnace.
cadiueus (m.pl.) remnants of the Guaycuru tribe, dwelling in Mato Grosso.
cádmio (m., Chem.) cadmium.
caduca (f.) see CADUCO.
caducante (adj.) falling away; decadent.
caducar (v.i.) to grow old, weak, decrepit; to become extinct; (Law) to lapse, expire.
caduceu (m.) caduceus.
caducidade (f.) caducity; decrepitude; expiration, forfeiture, lapse (of a license, patent, etc.).
caduco -ca (adj.) failing; decrepit; doting, weakminded (esp. from age); fleeting, transitory; null and void, lapsed; (f., Anat.) the decidua.
caduquice (f.) dotage [= CADUCIDADE].
caetê (m.) virgin woods; dense forest.
caetés (m.pl.) a once-large tribe on the coast of what is now the State of Pernambuco, and associated with the early history of that state.
cafajestada (f.) low behavior.
cafajeste (m.) a low (vulgar, offensive, dishonest) person.
cafanga (f.) insincere criticism or rejection of something which one in reality admires or desires. botar—em alguém, to impute defects in another.
café (m.) coffee (bean or beverage); coffee shop.—baixo, low-grade coffee.—caneca, a cheap coffee counter.—cantante, or—concêrto, a café offering musical entertainment.—-cereja, coffee berry.—com leite, coffee served with hot milk; (adj.) of the color cafe-au-lait.—comprido, or—de baile, weak coffee.—de chaleira, boiled coffee.—-do-mato is JASMIM-DE-CACHORRO.—mastigado,—com isca,—com mistura,—conosco,—de duas mãos,—gordo, all mean coffee served with cake, sandwiches, etc.—pequeno, any small, easily accomplished task; a trifling matter; (slang) a small potato (insignificant person); = CAFÈZINHO.—requentado, warmedover coffee; (slang) a sterile man.
cafedório (m., colloq.) weak coffee.
cafeeiral (m.) = CAFÈZAL.
cafeeiro -ra (ê-eiro) (adj.) of or pert. to coffee. esp. to the coffee industry; (m.) coffee tree; = CAFÈZEIRO.
cafeicultor [è-i] (m.) coffee grower.
cafeicultura [è-i] (f.) coffee growing.
cafeísmo (m., Med.) caffeinism.
cafelana (f.) large coffee plantation.
cafelista (m.,f.) = CAFÈZISTA.
cafeocracia [è-o] [f.) the class of wealthy coffee planters.
caferana (f., Bot.) the Guiana tachia (T. guianensis), c.a. JACARÉ-ARU, JACARUARU, QUASSIA-DO-PARÁ, QUINA-AMARGOSA, QUINA-CRUZEIRO, QUINA-DO-AMAZONAS, QUINA-DO-PARÁ, TINGUÁ-ABA, TINGUACIBA-DO-PARÁ, TUPARAPO, TUPAROBÁ, TUPURAPO.
cafetão (m., slang) = CÁFTEN.
cafeteira (f.) coffeepot.
cafeteiro (m.) proprietor of a coffee shop.

cafèzal (*m.*) coffee plantation.
cafèzeiro (*m.*) coffee planter; also = CAFEEIRO.
cafèzinho (*m.*) a small cup (demi-tasse) of black coffee; = CAFÈ PEQUENO; (*Zool.*) the middle American jacana (*J. spinosa*).
cafèzista (*m.,f.*) coffee-lover; coffee-planter, = CAFELISTA.
cafifa (*m.,f.*) jinx, hoodoo, Jonah.
cafife (*m.*) chicken mite.
cáfila (*f.*) a caravan, esp. of camels; fig., band, gang; pack of thieves, etc.
cafres (*m.pl.*) Kaffirs.
cáften (*m.*) pander, procurer, pimp.
caftina (*f.*) procuress.
caftinagem (*f.*) panderage.
caftinar, caftinizar (*v.i.*) to act the pimp; to pander.
caftinismo (*m.*) white slavery.
cafua (*f.*) den, cave; hideout; hut; dark closet.
cafuleta [ê] wooden chest; wooden vessel for rationing or keeping food.
cafundó (*m.*) a deep, narrow ravine, a faraway, out-of-the-way place.—-de-judas, jumping-off place, ends of the earth, sticks, backwoods.
cafuné (*m.*) a rubbing of a person's head (to soothe him or her); a scratching of a dog, cat, etc., behind the ears.
cafuz (*m.,f.*) cafuzo (*m.*) offspring of Indian and Negro, = CABURÉ. Var. CARAFUZ, CARAFUZO.
cagaço (*m.*) funk, fright, cowardice. [*Vulgar*].
cágado (*m.*) any of several semi-aquatic fresh-water turtles of family Chelydidae.—-de-pescoço-comprido, a South American snake-necked turtle (*Hydromedusa tectifera*, or *H. maximiliani*);—-do-amazonas = APEREMA; *fig.*, a slow-moving person.
caga-fogo (*m.*) firefly; (*colloq.*) a firearm; (*f.*) a black slender stingless bee (*Melipona tataira*), c.a. ABELHA-CAGA-FOGO, BARRA-FOGO, TATAÍRA.
caga-lume (*m.*) = VAGA-LUME.
caganitas (*f.,pl.*) droppings of goats, sheep, rabbits, rats, etc.
cagão (*m.*) poltroon. [*Vulgar*]
cagar (*v.i.*) to defecate. [*Vulgar*]
caga-sebinho (*m.*) any of several small tyrant birds, esp. *Mysiophobus fasciatus*, which feeds on mistletoe, and *Phyllomyias fasciatus brevirostris*, a short-billed tyrannulet common around Rio de Janeiro; c.a. CAGA-SEBO, CAGA-SEBITE, SEBITE, SEBITO.
caga-sebista (*m.*) used-books dealer.
caga-sebo (*m.*) the southern banded flycatcher (*Myiphobus fasciatus flammiceps*); also = CAGA-SEBINHO; the hang-nest tody-tyrant (*Euscarthmornis n. nidipendulus*); Temmnicks tyrannulet (*Camptostoma o. obsoletum*); also = CAMBACICA; second-hand book store [= SEBO].
cagosanga (*f.*) = IPECACUANHA.
caguete [êt] (*m.*, *slang*) stool pigeon.
caguincha (*adj.*) weak; fearful; cowardly; (*m.*) a weakling; a coward; the two of clubs.
caguira (*f.*) bad luck at gambling; abject fear; (*m.*) a good-for-nothing.
caiabi [bí] (*m.,f.*) one of the Cayabí, a virtually extinct Tupi-speaking tribe, dwelling on the São Manoel-Parantinga tributary of the Tapajós in Mato Grosso; (*adj.*) pert. to or designating the Caiabi.
caiação (*f.*) act of whitewashing.
caiador (*m.*) whitewasher.
caiadura, caiadela (*f.*) a coat of whitewash; act of whitewashing.
caiané (*m.*) = CAIAUÉ.
caiapiá (*m.*) any of several species of Dorstenia, tropical herbs of the mulberry family, called torus herbs, which yield medicinal roots, esp. *D. brasiliensis*, c.a. CAIAPIÁ-VERDADEIRO, CAAPIÁ, CHUPA-CHUPA, CONTA-DE-COBRA, CONTRA-ERVA, TAROPÉ, TIÚ, TEJÚ-AÇU.
caiapó (*m.,f.*) an Indian of the Cayapó, of the Ge linguistic family. The southern Cayapó, now extinct, occupied an immense region south and east of the upper Araguaya River. The Northern Cayapó are scattered to the north and east of the upper Xingu River. (*adj.*) pert. to or designating these tribes.
caiar (*v.t.*) to whitewash.
caiarara (*m.*) a capuchin monkey, = MICO.
caiaté (*m.*, *Bot.*) the Jamaica navelspurge (*Omphalea diandra*), c.a. CASTANHA-COMADRE-DE-AZEITE, CASTANHA-DE-CAIATÉ, CASTANHA-DE-CUTIA, CASTANHA-DE-PEIXE, CASTANHA-PURGATIVA COMADRE-DE-ZEITE.
caib+verb endings = irreg. forms of CABER 32].

caiaué (*m.*) American oilpalm (*Corozo oleifera*), c.a. CAIANÉ, CAIAUÁ, DENDÊZEIRO-DO-PARÁ.
cãibra (*f.*) cramp, kink, crick.—dos escrivães, writers' cramp. Var. CÃIMBRA.
caibrar (*v.t.*) to provide with, or support with, two-by-fours or similar pieces.
caibro (*m.*) scantling, a two-by-four or similar piece of lumber.
caiçaca (*f.*) the fer-de-lance (*Bothrops atrox*), a large and very venomous pit viper, allied to the rattlesnake but having no rattle. It is the most common of the Brazilian JARARACAS.
caiçara (*f.*) a fence of poles or stakes; a palisade fence, esp. around an Indian village; a chute at the river's edge for loading cattle onto barges; a hunter's blind made of tree branches; (*m.*) loafer, rascal; (*m.,f.*) a CAIPIRA dwelling on the seacoast of the States of Rio de Janeiro and São Paulo; also = SARDINHA-LAGE.
caiçuma (*f.*) a porridge of TUCUPI thickened with manioc, potato, etc.
caicumana (*m.*, *Bot.*) the murumuru astrocaryum palm (*A. murumuru*), c.a. MURUMURU.
caído -da (*adj.*) fallen; downcast; past-due [payments]; (*m.pl.*) past-due interest or earnings; (*f.*) fall, tumble; declivity; decline.—de caracol, (*Aeron.*) tailspin.
caieira (*f.*) lime kiln; lime pit; brick kiln; bonfire; in Pará, an oven in which material from a prehistoric shell mound [SAMBAQUI] is converted into lime; also = SAMBAQUI.
caieiro (*m.*) worker in a limekiln; whitewasher; mason's helper.
caim [a-ím] (*m.*) dog's mournful howl; Cain; (*adj.*) stingy.
caimão (*m.*, *Zool.*) cayman. Cf. JACARÉ.
cãimbra (*f.*) = CÃIBRA.
caimento [a-i] (*m.*) a fall or falling; ruin; decadence; slope (of a roof); (*Aeron.*, *Mach.*, *Naut.*) rake.
caimiteiro (*m.*) = ABIEIRO.
caimito (*m.*) the cainito starapple (*Chrysophyllum cainito*), c.a. ABIÚ-DO-PARÁ, CAINITI, MAÇÃ-ESTRELADA.
cainana (*f.*) = CANINANA.
cainca [a-ín] (*f.*) a milkberry (*Chiococca sp.*) from which is obtained the medicinal cahinca root; c.a. RAIZ-DE-FRADE, CIPÓ-CRUZ, FEDORENTA.
caingangue (*m.,f.*) an Indian of the Caingang, a non-Guarani but linguistically and culturally related group of tribes in the four southern states of Brazil, forming the southern branch of the Ge or so-called Tapuyan family; (*adj.*) pert. to or designating the Caingang. Cf. GUAIANÁ, XOCRÉM, BOTOCUDO.
cainguá (*m.,f.*) = CAIUÁ.
cainhar [a-i] (*v.i.*) to howl; to be a dog in the manger. [The noun is CAIM.]
cainheza [a-i . . . ê] (*f.*) stinginess.
cainho -nha [a-í] (*adj.*) doggish, canine; stingy; (*m.*) dog in the manger.
cainiti [tí], cainito (*m.*) = CAIMITO.
caiota (*f.*) = CHUCHU.
caipira (*m.*) backwoodsman, rustic; hayseed, hick, yokel; (*f.*) a woman of the backwoods.
caipirada (*f.*) a band or group of CAIPIRAS.
caipiragem, caipiricie (*f.*), caipirismo (*m.*) manners, habits, behavior, etc., typical of a CAIPIRA.
caipora (*adj.*) unlucky in everything; (*f.*) persistent bad luck in everything; (*m.,f.*) a victim of persistent bad luck; a jinx, Jonah, or hoodoo (person who gives bad luck to another); in Brazilian folklore, a certain hobgoblin.
caiporismo (*m.*) persistent bad luck.
caíque (*m.*) ketch, coastal fishing boat.
cair [75] (*v.i.*) to fall, drop (down), sink, topple, collapse, tumble.—a, or aos, pedaços, to fall apart, into pieces. —a sopa no mel, to happen just right (a stroke of luck.) —com os cobres, (*slang*) to come across with the dough (money).—como um pato, to be taken in (duped).—como uma bomba, to fall like a bombshell.—das mãos, to fall (drop) from the hands.—da memória, to fade from memory.—das nuvens, to arrive or to happen unexpectedly; to be astounded.—de cama, to fall sick abed. —de cavalo magro, to do something utterly clumsy and foolish.—de pé, to land on one's feet.—de quatro, to land on all fours.—do céu, to fall from the clouds, i.e., to happen unexpectedly.—em desgraça, to fall out of favor. —em desuso, to fall into disuse.—em êrro, to fall into error.—em esquecimento, to be forgotten.—em graças, or nas graças, de, to be well received, accepted.—em

ruínas, to fall into ruin.—**em si**, to come to one's senses.
—**em silêncio**, to fall silent.—**em tentação**, to fall into
temptation.—**fora**, (slang) to beat it (leave).—**na água**,
to jump into a pool, etc. (for a swim).—**na bebedeira**,
na chuva, na embriaguez, no porre, (all slang) to get
drunk.—**na bôca do mundo**, to get oneself talked about.
—**na esparrela (no laço, na ratoeira, na rêde)**, to fall into
a trap (net).—**na vida**, to sink into prostitution.—**nas
mãos (nas unhas) de**, to fall into the hands of.—**no desagrado de (alguém)**, to fall out of favor with (someone).
—**no jeito**, to fall into the habit, catch on, get the knack
(of).—**no mangue**, (slang) to scram, beat it.—**no mato**,
or **no mundo**, to run away, disappear.—**no ridículo**, to
make a fool of oneself.—**pela escada abaixo**, to tumble
downstairs.—**redondamente no chão**, to fall flat on the
ground. **ao—da noite**, at nightfall. **ao—da tarde**, at
twilight. **Caíu-lhe por sorte ganhar o prêmio**, It fell to
him to win the prize. **não ter onde—morto**, to be destitute [lit., to have no place to drop dead]. **O Natal que
vem, cai num domingo**, Next Christmas falls on a Sunday.
cairana (f.) welt, narrow border, trimming, ornamental
finish of a seam (as with braid); sewing tape; (Bot.) a
muskwood (Guarea rubicalyx).
cairé (m.) = SANHAÇO-FRADE.
cairiri (m.,f.) = CARIRI.
cairuçu [çú] (f.) a medicinal pennywort (Hydrocotyle
asialica), c.a. PATA-DE-CAVALO, PÉ-DE-CAVALO, CODAGEM.
—**-do-brejo**, floating pennywort (Hydrocotyle ranuncu-
loides).
cais (m. sing. & pl.) quay, wharf, dock, pier.
caité (m., Bot.) the scarlet canna (C. coccinea), c.a. CAITÉ-
VERMELHO, BANANEIRINHA-DO-MATO.—**açu**,—**do-mato**,
—**grande**, the broadleaf canna (C. latifolia), c.a. ERVA-
DOS-FERIDOS.—**imbiri** = COQUILHO.—**dos-jardins** = BA-
NANEIRINHA-DA-ÍNDIA.—**mirim** = BANANEIRA-DO-MATO.
caititu [tú] (m.) the wooden roller of a manioc grating
machine; (Zool.) a white-collared peccary (Pecari angu-
latus or P. tajacu), c.a. CAITETU, CATETE, CATETO, CANELA-
RUIVA, QUEIXO-BRANCO, COLEIRA-BRANCA, TAITETU,
TAJAÇU, TAIAÇU, PORCO-DO-MATO. Cf. QUEIXADA.
caiuá (m.,f.) an Indian of the Cainguá or modern Guarani
tribes; (adj.) pert. to or designating the Caiuá, called
also Cainguá. Cf. GUARANI.
caixa (f.) box, chest, case; safe; (m.) cashier; cash book;
cashier's booth or office.—**clara**, a snare drum.—**dágua**,
water tank or reservoir; (colloq.) a boozer.—**de amortização**, sinking fund.—**de compensação**, bank clearing
house.—**de cartão**, paper box.—**de corte**, (Carp.) miter
box.—**de descarga**, water closet box.—**de escada**, stair
well.—**de fusíveis**, fuse box.—**de gordura**, grease trap.—
de ligação, (Elec.) terminal box.—**de madeira**, wooden
box; packing case.—**de mudanças or—de velocidades**,
gear-shift case.—**de música**, music box.—**de plaina**, the
stock of a carpenter's plane.—**de rapé**, snuff box.—**de
ressonância**, soundbox (of stringed instruments).—**de
rufo**, parade snare drum.—**de segurança**, safe; safe-
deposit box.—**de transmissão**, transmission gear case.—
de vapor, steam chest.—**do correio**, mail box; postoffice
box.—**d'óculos**, (colloq.) a person who wears glasses.—**do
tímpano**, (Anat.) ear drum.—**econômica**, savings bank.
—**forte**, strongbox; also, a snare drum.—**postal**, postoffice box.—**registradora**, cash register.—**séptica**, septic
tank.—**torácica**, the thorax. **dinheiro em—**, cash on
hand. **livro—**, cash book. **pagar na—**, to pay the cashier.
caixão (m.) coffin, casket; caisson; any big box; trough in
a river's bed.
caixeira (f.) saleswoman.
caixeirada (f.) the class of salespeople—used disparagingly.
caixeiro (m.) salesclerk.—**de balcão**, salesperson who waits
on customers at a counter.—**viajante**, travelling salesman.
caixeta (f.) a little box; a trumpet tree (Tabebuia sp.).
caixilho (m.) window sash; picture frame; molding.
caixinha, caixola (f.) a little box.
caixotaria (f.) box factory.
caixote (m.) small wooden box (for packing).
caixoteiro (m.) box maker.
caixotim (m.) type case.
cajá (m.) the golden-yellow, plumlike fruit of the CAJÁZEI-
RA. [It has a sourish, aromatic flavor, and a faint smell
of turpentine.]—**manga**, the ambarella (Spondias
cytherea), c.a. ACAIA-AÇU, CAJARANA, CAJÀZEIRA-DE-

FRUTO-GRANDE,TAPERIBÁ-DO-SERTÃO.—**-mirim** = CAJÀZEI-
RA.
cajadada (f.) blow with a stick. **matar dois coelhos de
uma—só**, to kill two birds with one stone.
cajado (m.) shepherd's staff or crook. [**O teu—e o teu
bordão, êles me confortam**, Thy rod and thy staff, they
comfort me. (Ps. 23)]
cajaíba (f.) = CAJÀZEIRA.
cajaléu (m.) = VOADOR-CASCUDO.
cajàzeira (f.) the hog plum or yellow mombin (Spondias
lutea), c.a. ACAJÁ, ACAJAÍBA, ACAJÀZEIRA, CAJÁ-PEQUENA,
CAJÁ-MIRIM, CAJAÍBA, CAJÀZEIRO-MIUDO, TAPERIBÁ, IM-
BUZEIRO, MUNGUENGUE, AMBOLÓ.—**-de-fruto-grande**
= CAJÁ-MIRIM.
cajàzeiro (-miúdo) (m.) = CAJAZEIRA.
caju [ú] (m.) a time of year. **com sessenta e alguns—s**,
sixty-odd years old. **de—em—**, from year to year. (Bot.)
fruit of the CAJUEIRO.—**açu**,—**do-campo**,—**do-mato**,
are all species of cashew (Anacardium).—**manso**
= CAJUEIRO.—**japonês**, Japanese raisintree (Hovenia
dulcis).
cajuada (f.) a cooling drink, also a confection, made from
the ripe fresh fruit of the cashew tree.
cajueiro (m., Bot.) the common cashew (Anacardium occidentale), c.a. ACAJUÍBA, CAJU-MANSO.—**bravo** = CAU-
AÇU and CARVALHO-DO-BRASIL.—**do-campo** = CAJURANA.
cajurana (m., Bot.) a simaba (S. guayanensis), c.a.
PITOMBEIRA; a cashew (Anacardium nanum), c.a.
CAJUEIRO-DO-CAMPO.
cal (f.) lime; whitewash.—**apagada**,—**extinta**, slaked lime.
—**gorda**,—**rica**, fat (strong, rich) lime.—**magra**,—**pobre**,
(lean, weak, poor) lime.—**viva**,—**cáustica**,—**virgem**,—**não
apagada**, quick (unslaked) lime.
cala (f.) small cove or inlet; plug (as in a watermelon) for
testing ripeness; (m., Bot.) the common calla lily (Zantedeschia aethiopica), c.a. COPO-DE-LEITE.
calaba (f., Bot.) the calaba beautyleaf (Calophyllum
brasiliense antillanum).
calabaça (f.) = CABAÇA.
calaboca [ô] (m.) blackjack, club, billy; knife; gun.
calabouço,—**boiço** (m.) calaboose, jail, prison, dungeon.
calabre (m.) hawser.
calabrês,—**brêsa** (adj.; m.,f.) Calabrian.
calabroteado –**da** (adj.) hawser-laid, cable-laid (referring
to rope).
calabuco (m.) = CALAMBUCO.
calabura (f.) Jamaica cherry (Muntingia calabura), c.a.
PAU DE SÊDA. [The bark is used for making cordage.]
calaçaria (f.) laziness.
calacear (v.i.) to loaf, lounge.
calaceiro (m.) loafer.
calada (f.) silence, stillness, hush. **à—, or às—s**, stealthily.
na—da noite, in the dead of night.
caladão (m.) an unusually quiet, silent man.
caládio, caladião (m.) a genus (Caladium) of tropical
aroids.
calado –**da** (adj.) silent, quiet; mute, mum; tongue-tied;
reserved. **um homem—**, a man of few words; (m.) the
draft of a vessel. **alto—**, deep draft. **pequeno—**, shallow
draft.
calafate (m.) calker; (Bot.) the boxthorn barberry (Berberis lycium), c.a. CALAFATE-DE-PATAGONIA.
calafetador (m.) calking iron.
calafetagem (f.) **calafetamento** (m.) act of calking; oakum
or other material for calking.
calafetar (v.t.) to calk.
calafêto (m.) act of calking; weather-stripping.
calafrio (m.) chill, shiver, ague. **ter—s**, or **sentir um—**,
to feel chilly; to have a chill; to shiver. Var. CALEFRIO.
calagem (f.) liming (of soil).
calajar (m.) the nux vomica poison nut (Strychnos nuxvomica).
calalu [ú] (m., Bot.) the okra (Hibiscus esculentus), c.a.
QUINGOMBÔ, QUIABEIRO-CHIFRE-DE-VEADO. [The fruit is
called QUIABO.]
calamar (m., Zool.) a squid (Loligo brasiliensis), c.a.
CALMAR, CHÔCO, LULA, MÃE-DE-CAMARÃO.
calambuco (m.) the agalloch eaglewood
(Aquilaria agallocha) which yields agalloch or aloes wood,
burnt by Orientals as a perfume. It is the aloes of the
Bible. Cf. ALOÉS.
calamidade (f.) calamity, catastrophe; scourge.
calamina (f., Min.) calamine.—**nobre**, smithsonite.

calaminta (*f., Bot.*) any savory (*Satureia*), esp. *S. calamintha* and *S. nepeta*.

calamita (*f., Paleontol.*) calamite; (*Min.*) hemimorphite.

calamitoso -sa (*adj.*) calamitous, dire.

câlamo (*m.*) grass stem; quill; stylus; flute; (*Bot.*)—aromático, the drug sweetflag (*Acorus calamus*), c.a. ÁCORO.

calandra (*f.*) calender, roller, cylinder (for smoothing and giving a glossy finish to paper, cloth, etc.); a mangle; a corn weevil (*Calandra granaria*), c.a. GORGULHO; (*Zool.*) a calander (large European lark); also, a Brazilian mocking bird (*Mimus saturninus modulator*), c.a. SABIÁ-DO-CAMPO, SABIÁ-DO-SERTÃO. Cf. CALHANDRA. [A calendar is CALENDÁRIO.]

calandragem (*f.*) calendering.

calandrar (*v.t.*) to calender.

calandreiro (*m.*) -ra (*f.*) calenderer.

calandrínia (*f., Bot.*) the Peruvian purslane (*Calandrinia umbellata*); the Durban crowfoot grass (*Dactyloctenium aegyptium*), c.a. GRAMA, CAPIM-CALANDRINI, CAPIM-MIMOSO-DO-PIAUÍ, PÉ-DE-GALINHA-VERDADEIRO.

calango (*m.*) the sand-diver (*Synodus intermedius*), a lizard fish, c.a. LAGARTO-DO-MAR, TIRA-VIRA; also, any small lizard, esp. of the family Teiidae.

calangro (*m.*) = JACARÉ-PINIMA.

calão (*m.*) thieves' cant, argot; slang; also = CALEIRA.

calar (*v.i.*) to remain silent, not speak; (*v.t.*) to silence, still, hush; to plug (fruit); (*v.r.*) to fall silent, stop talking; to hold one's tongue, keep quiet.—baionêta, to fix bayonets.—o bico, or a bôca, (*colloq.*) to shut the mouth (stop talking).—um melão, to plug a melon. Cala (cale) a bôca! Shut up! Hold your tongue! Quem cala consente, Silence gives consent.

calástico -ca (*adj., Med.*) chalastic, laxative.

calátide (*f., Bot.*) capitulum; anthodium.

calatiforme (*adj., Bot.*) calathiform, cup-shaped.

calaverita (*f., Min.*) calaverite.

calaza (*f., Bot., Embryol.*) chalaza; (*Med.*) chalazion.

calazião, calázio (*m., Med.*) chalazion.

calazogamia (*f., Bot.*) chalazogamy.

calazógamo (*m., Bot.*) chalazogam.

Calç. = CALÇADA (Walk).

calça (*f.*) leg band (for pigeons, etc.); = CALÇAS.

calçada (*f.*) sidewalk; pavement; paved street; a steep street.

calcadeira (*f.*) foundryman's sand rammer.

calçadeira (*f.*) shoe horn.

calçado -da (*adj.*) shod; paved; (*m.*) footwear.

calcador (*m.*) rammer; ramrod; tamper.

calcadura (*f.*), **calcamento** (*m.*) ramming; tamping.

calçamento (*m.*) street paving.

calcâneo (*m., Anat.*) calcaneus.

calcanhar (*m.*) heel (of foot). [Heel of shoe is TACÃO or SALTO.]

calcanho (*m., slang*) foot.

calcantes (*m.pl., slang*) feet.

calcanita (*f., Min.*) chalcanthite; hydrated copper sulphate; bluestone.

calção (*m.*) shorts, trunks.—de banho, man's bathing trunks.—de futebol, a soccer player's shorts.—develho, (*Bot.*) a Brazilian butterfly bush (*Buddleia brasiliensis*), c.a. BARBASCO, CALÇAS-DE-VELHA, TINGUI-DA-PRAIA, VASSOURA, VASSOURINHA.

calcar (*v.t.*) to step on; to tread on; to crush under foot, trample on; to press (down) on.

calçar (*v.t.*) to put on (shoes, gloves, socks, etc.); to shoe; to block or scotch; to pave (a street); to underpin, underprop (a building); (*v.r.*) to put on one's shoes [but to put on one's trousers is PÔR, or ENFIAR, not CALÇAR, as CALÇAS.].—bem, of gloves, etc., to fit well. A designação lhe calça como uma luva, The name fits him like a glove.

calcário -ria (*adj.*) calcareous; (*m.*) limestone. pedra—, limestone.

calças (*f.pl.*) trousers; women's drawers.—bôca-de-sino, bell-bottom trousers.—de cuco, (*Bot.*) a gladiolus (*G. serotium*).—-de-velha = CALÇÃO-DE-VELHO. Cf. CALÇA.

calcedônio -nia (*adj.*) chalcedonic, chalcedonous; (*f., Min.*) chalcedony.

calceiforme (*adj., Bot.*) calceiform; calceolate.

calceolária (*f., Bot.*) any species of Calceolaria.

calcêta (*f.*) leg-iron, fetter; (*m.*) man condemned to forced labor.

calcetar (*v.t.*) to pave with stones.

calceteiro (*m.*) man who lays cobblestones.

cálcico -ca (*adj., Chem.*) calcic.

calcificação (*f.*) calcification.

calcificar (*v.t.,v.i.,v.r.*) to calcify.

calcífugo -ga (*adj., Bot.*) calcifugous.

calcímetro (*m., Chem.*) calcimeter.

calcinação (*f.*) calcination.

calcinador (*m.*) calciner.

calcinar (*v.t.*) to calcine; to oxidize; to roast; to scorch; to cauterize.

calcinável (*adj.*) calcinable.

calcinha (*f.*) panty.

câlcio (*m., Chem.*) calcium.

calcita (*f., Min.*) calcite; calcareous spar.

calcítrapa (*f.*) = ABRÔLHO.

calco (*m.*) a tracing (drawing).

calço (*m.*) chock, block, wedge; (*Print.*) overlay.

calcografar (*v.t.*) to engrave metal, esp. copper.

calcografia (*f.*) chalcography, engraving on brass or copper.

calcógrafo (*m.*) -fa (*f.*) chalcographer, copper engraver.

calçolas (*f.pl.*) women's drawers [= CALÇAS].

calcopirita (*f., Min.*) chalcopyrite.

calcocita, calcosina (*f., Min.*) chalcocite; copper glance.

calçudo -da (*adj.*) having feather-covered legs (as certain birds).

calculador -dora (*adj.*) calculating; (*m.,f.*) calculator (machine or person); a calculating person.—de deriva, (*Aeron.*) drift meter.

calcular (*v.t.*) to calculate, compute, reckon, estimate; to guess, conjecture; (*v.i.*) to make a computation. máquina de—, calculating machine.

calculável (*adj.*) calculable.

calculista (*m.,f.*) calculist, mathematician.

cálculo (*m.*) calculation, computation, reckoning; (*Math.*) calculus; (*Med.*) calculus, stone, gravel.—aproximado, rough estimate.—das probabilidades, (*Math.*) calculus of probabilities.—diferencial, (*Math.*) differential calculus of probabilities.—diferencial, (*Math.*) differential cal-—integral, (*Math.*) integral calculus.

Calcutá (*f.*) Calcutta.

calda (*f.*) syrup; fusing point (of iron); (*pl.*) hot springs.—bordalesa, Bordeaux mixture (a fungicide). pêssegos em—, canned peaches in syrup.

caldeação (*f.*), **caldeamento** (*m.*) welding; fusion; melting.—de raças, fusion of races.

caldear (*v.t.*) to weld by forging; to fuse, join together; of iron, to make hot and soft; to melt.

caldeira (*f.*) caldron, kettle; boiler. tubo de—, boiler tube.

caldeirada (*f.*) a kettleful of anything, but esp. of fish, such as a bouillabaisse.

caldeirão (*m.*) caldron, large kettle or boiler; pothole (in a riverbed); large hole in the road.

caldeiraria (*f.*) boiler factory.

caldeireiro (*m.*) boiler-maker; copper-smith.

caldeirinha (*f.*) a little kettle; tea kettle. entre a cruz e a—, between the devil and the deep blue sea.

caldo (*m.*) broth; juice; syrup; (*colloq.*) a "dunking" given by one person to another while at play in a pool or at the beach.—de cana de açúcar, sugar cane juice.—-de-feijão = APICUÍ (a bird).—entornado, spilled milk.—verde, "pot likker" (vegetable broth). entornar o—, to spill the beans; upset the apple cart.

caldoso -sa (*adj.*) syrupy; juicy; soupy.

caleche (*m.*) **caleça** (*f.*) a calash or calèche (kind of light carriage).

calefação (*f.*) = AQUECIMENTO.

calefaciente (*adj.*) calefacient.

calefator (*m.*) = AQUECEDOR.

calefrio (*m.*) = CALAFRIO.

caleidoscópio (*m.*) kaleidoscope.

caleira (*f.*) roof gutter [= CALÃO]; also = SAMBAQUI.

calejado -da (*adj.*) calloused; hard-boiled; hardy, hardened (by experience), used to.

calejar (*v.t.,v.i.*) to callous.

calembur[go] (*m.*) pun, play on words [= TROCADILHO].

calemburista (*m.,f.*) punster.

calendário (*m.*) calendar, almanack.

calendas (*f.pl.*) Calends.

calêndula (*f.*) the pot marigold (*Calendula officinalis*), c.a. MAL-ME-QUER.

calentura (*f., Med.*) calenture; high tropical fever; sunstroke.

calepino (*m.*) vocabulary; notebook.

calha (*f.*) trough, chute; channel; roof gutter.

calhamaço (*m.*) a big old book; a mass of written sheets.

calhambeque (*m.*) small coastwise vessel; a rattletrap vehicle, jalopy; any castoff article, esp. of old furniture.

calhambola, -bora (*m.,f.*) = CANHEMBORA.

calhandra (*f.*) the Old World skylark (*Alauda arvensis*), c.a. LAVERCA; also = SABIÁ-DO-CAMPO, a Brazilian mockingbird. Cf. CALANDRA.

calhandro (*m.*) slop bucket; chamber pot.

calhar (*v.i.*) of parts, to fit or fall together exactly; to coincide, square, tally; to happen, chance; to be fitting. **vir a—**, to happen at just the right moment.

calhau (*m.*) rock fragment, stone.

calheira (*f.*) flume.

calhorda (*m.,f., colloq.*) a low person; scoundrel.

cali (*m.*) potash.

calibita (*f., Min.*) siderite.

calibração, calibragem (*f.*) calibration.

calibrador (*m.*) calipers, gauge; calibrator.—**de pressão**, pressure gauge; —**micrométrico**, micrometer.

calibrar (*v.t.*) to calibrate; to gauge.—**os pneus**, to balance the air pressure in the tires of an automobile.

calibre (*m.*) caliber, bore, gauge; calipers.—**apalpador**, feeler gauge.—**de anel**, ring gauge.—**para rôscas**, thread gauge.

caliça (*f.*) fragments of dry mortar or plaster; debris.

cálice (*m.*) small wine glass; chalice; calyx of a flower.—**da amargura**, or—**de fel**, a bitter cup, a cup of gall.—**-de-vênus**, (*Bot.*) the angels-trumpet or floriopondio datura (*D. arborea*), c.a. TROMBETÃO-AZUL.

caliche (*m.*) caliche (the nitrate-bearing gravel or rock found in extensive surface deposits in Chile and Peru).

calicida (*f.*) a corn-cure.

caliciforme (*adj., Archaeol.*) caliciform.

calicô (*m.*) calico.

calicose (*f., Med.*) chalicosis.

calidez [ê] (*f.*) heat, warmth.

cálido -da (*adj.*) hot, burning; smart, clever.

calidoscópio (*m.*) = CALEIDOSCÓPIO.

califa (*m.*) caliph.

califado (*m.*) caliphate.

caligrafia (*f.*) calligraphy; handwriting; penmanship.

calígrafo -fa (*m.,f.*) a good penman; a teacher of penmanship.

calinada (*f.*) a ludicrous blunder; a "howler".

calinita (*f., Min.*) kalinite.

calino -na (*adj.*) stupid, dumb; (*m.,f.*) such a one.

calipígio -gia (*adj.*) callipygian, having shapely buttocks.

caliptra (*f., Bot.*) calyptra.

calista (*m.,f.*) chiropodist, pedicure, "corn doctor".

calistenia (*f.*) callisthenics.

calisto (*m.*) hoodoo, jinx, Jonah [= CAIPORA].

calitriquídeos (*m.pl.*) a family (*Callitrichidae*) of small South American monkeys comprising the tamarins and true marmosets.

cálix [x-s] (*m.*) = CÁLICE.

c.-alm. = CONTRA ALMIRANTE (rear admiral).

calma (*f.*) the warm(est) part of the day; lull; calm, calmness, quiet, poise; (*interj.*) Go easy! Take it easy! **levar tudo na—**, to take things easy. **perder a—**, to lose one's head or self-control.

calmante (*adj.*) soothing; (*m.*) a sedative, anodyne.

calmar (*v.*) = ACALMAR and CALAMAR.

calmaria (*f.*) calm, wind-lull; sultriness; (*pl.*) doldrums.

calmo -ma (*adj.*) calm, peaceful; sedate; becalmed; wàrm, hot, sultry.

calmoso -sa (*adj.*) calm; warm, sultry.

calo (*m.*) corn; callus.—**d'água**, water blister.

caloiro (*m.*) & derivs. = CALOURO & derivs.

calombo (*m.*) swelling, tumor, cyst.

calomelano, calomélane (*m.*) calomel.—**vegetal** (*Bot.*) the silver fern (*Pityrogramma calomelanos*). [The plural form —CALOMELANOS—is an erroneous variant.]

calopogônico (*m.*) any species of *Calopogonium* used as green manure.

calor [ô] (*m.*) heat, warmth; rut, oestrus [= CIO].—**animal**, animal heat.—**específico**, (*Physics*) specific heat.—**latente**, latent heat.—**livre**, sensible heat.—**nos olhos**, (*colloq.*) ophthalmia.—**obscuro**, dark heat.—**radiante**, radiant heat.—**sensível**, sensible heat. **estar com—**, to be warm, hot. **fazer—**, of weather, to be warm, hot.

calorão (*m.*) heat wave; a hot blush.

calorento -ta (*adj.*) hot.

calorescência (*f., Physics*) calorescence.

caloria (*f.*) calorie.

caloricidade (*f.*) caloricity.

calórico (*m.*) caloric.

calorífero -ra (*adj.*) calorific; (*m.*) heating apparatus, heater, furnace.

calorificação (*f.*) calorification.

calorificar (*v.t.*) to calorify.

calorífico -ca (*adj.*) calorific; (*m.*) heater.

calorígeno -na (*adj.*) calorigenic.

calorim (*f.*) = LINGUARUDO (snail).

calorimetria (*f., Physics*) calorimetry.

calorímetro (*m.*) calorimeter.

caloroso -sa (*adj.*) warm, ardent, fervid, glowing.

calosidade (*f.*) callosity, callus; callousness.

caloso -sa (*adj.*) calloused.

calota (*f.*) hub cap; skull cap; (*Geom.*) a cap (spherical segment); (*Anat.*) vertex of the skull; (*Arch.*) calotte. —**polar**, polar ice cap.

calote (*m.*) a bad debt, esp. one contracted without intention of repayment. **passar um—em**, to cheat, trick, gyp.

calotear (*v.t.,v.i.*) to defraud, swindle, cheat, bilk, gyp; to evade payment; to contract a debt with little or no expectation or possibility of repayment.

caloteiro (*m.*) swindler, cheat; unprincipled sponger; a deadbeat.

calotismo (*m.*) sponging; bilking.

calouro -ra (*m.,f.*) freshman, new pupil; tenderfoot; — (or peru) **enfeitado**, (jocosely) a sophomore.

calta (*f.*) the common marsh marigold (*Caltha palustris*).

caluda (*f.*) silence; (*interj.*) Quiet! Shut up!

calumba (*f., Bot.*) the calumba root (*Jateorhiza palmata*); also a simaba (*S. salubris*) called CALUNGA.

calumbé (*m.*) a type of bucket used by placer miners. Var. CARUMBÉ.

caluna (*f., Bot.*) heather (*Calluna sp.*).

calundu [dú] (*m.*) ill-humor, sullenness [= AMUO].

calunga (*m.*) a runt; a small rat; a heathen divinity; drayman's or trucker's helper; (*f., Bot.*) = CALUMBA and other species of *Simaba*.

calungo (*m.*) = CAMUNDONGO.

calúnia (*f.*) calumny, slander, malicious lying.

caluniador -dora (*adj.*) calumnious, slanderous; (*m.,f.*) calumniator, slanderer, maligner.

caluniar (*v.t.*) to calumniate, slander, malign, defame, traduce.

calunioso -sa (*adj.*) calumnious, slanderous.

calva (*f.*) baldness; bald pate; a clearing in the woods [= CLAREIRA].

Calvário (*m.*) Calvary.

calvície (*f.*) baldness.

calvinismo (*m.*) Calvinism.

calvinista (*m.,f.*) Calvinist.

calvinístico -ca (*adj.*) Calvinistic.

Calvino (*m.*) Calvin.

calvo -va (*adj.*) bald, hairless; bare, treeless; (*m.,f.*) a bald-headed person. **mentira—**, barefaced lie.

cama (*f.*) bed, resting-place; receptacle, underlayer; stratum; river-bed.—**de armação**, a tester bed.—**de casal**, a double bed.—, or **caminha, de gato**, cat's cradle (child's game played with a string).—**de penas**, feather bed.—**de solteiro**, single bed.—**de vento**, a canvas (folding) cot.—**e comida**, bed and board.—**s individuais** or **separadas**, twin beds. **abrir a—**, to turn back the bedclothes (prepare for the night). **cabeceira da—**, bedside, head of the bed. **cair de—**, to fall sick abed. **de—**, in bed; sick abed. **fazer a—**, to make the bed. **roupa de—**, bed clothes. **sofá—**, a studio couch.

camacã (*m.*) a tropical tree of the chocolate family (*Guazuma tomentosa*), c.a. PAU-DE-MOTAMBA. Cf. CAMBACÁ. Also, an Indian of the Camacan, a linguistically-independent people, small numbers of whom still exist in the state of Bahia; (*adj.*) pert. to or designating the Camacan.

camada (*f.*) layer, stratum, bed; coat (of paint).—**humífera**, forest litter.—**monomolecular**, (*Physical Chem.*) molecular film, monolayer, monofilm.—**social**, social stratum.

camafeu (*m.*) cameo.

camaíua (*m., Bot.*) the meadow rue paullinia (*P. thalictrifolia*), c.a. TIMBÓ.

camaiurá (*m.,f.*) an Indian of the Camayura, a Tupian tribe on the upper Xingu River in Mato Grosso.

camaleão (*m.*) any tropical chameleon of numerous species, esp. Anolis. [They are not true chameleons but iguanids.]; a small lizard, c.a. JACARÉ-PINIMA; a fickle, inconstant or hypocritical person; the hump between ruts on a dirt road [= CAMALHÃO]; a hillock on a plain.—**mineral**, chameleon mineral.

camalhão (*m.*) raised bed between plow furrows; the hump between ruts on a dirt road [= CAMALEÃO].

camalote (*m.*) in southern Brazil, a floating island of river plants, often sufficiently compact to support the weight of a man; in the Amazon region the same thing is called MATUPÁ.

camão (*m.*) = PORFIRIÃO.

camapu [ú] (*m.*, *Bot.*) groundcherry (*Physalis brasiliensis*); the cutleaf groundcherry (*P. angulata*), c.a. JUAPOCA, BUCHO-DE-RÃ, JUÁ-DE-CAPOTE, MATA-FOME; the downy groundcherry (*P. pubescens*), c.a. BALÃOZINHO, ALQUE-QUENJE-AMARELO, JUÁ-DE-CAPOTE; the Peruvian groundcherry or Cape gooseberry (*P. peruviana*), c.a. BATE-TESTA, ERVA-NOIVA-DO-PERU.

camapuã (*m.*) = CUMANÃ.

câmara (*f.*) chamber, room; stateroom; camera.—**alta**, House of Lords.—**ardente**, mourning chamber.—**baixa**, House of Commons.—**cinematográfica**, motion picture camera.—**da morte**, death chamber.—**de adaptação**, air lock; compression or decompression chamber.—**de admissão** or—**de adução**, intake chamber.—**de água**, water jacket.—**de ar**, inner tube.—**de comércio**, chamber of commerce.—**de combustão**, combustion chamber.—(or **caixa**) **de compensação**, bank clearing house.—**de compressão**, compression chamber.—**de explosão**, motor cylinder compression or combustion chamber.—**de vapor**, steam chest.—**escura**, (*Optics*) camera obscura; (*Photog.*) dark room.—**fotográfica**, camera.—**lenta**, slow motion picture.—**lúcida**, (*Optics*) camera lucida.—**municipal**, city council.—**real**, royal chamber.—**séptica**, septic tank.

camará (*m.*, *Bot.*) a lippia (*L. pseudo-thea*), c.a. CAPITÃO-DO-MATO, CHÁ-DE-FRADE, CHÁ-DE-PEDESTRE, CIDRILHA; a raphanea (*R. ferruginosa*), c.a. AZEITONA-DO-MATO.—-**bravo** = CAPITÃO-DA-SALA.—**de-bilro** or—-**do-mato**, a Braz. tree (*Geissospermum vellosii*), family Apocynaceae, which is the source of the medicinal pereira bark; c.a. PAU-PEREIRA or PAU-PEREIRO.—-**de-cavalo**, the rough heliopsis (*H. scabra*), c.a. ANDREQUICÉ, MALMEQUER-GRANDE. Cf. CAMBARÁ.

camarada (*m.*,*f.*) comrade, chum, companion, crony; colleague; roommate; (*m.*) pal, buddy; farm hand, hired hand; fellow, "customer"; (*slang*) cop; soldier; Communist (*adj.*) friendly; agreeable.

camaradagem (*f.*) camaraderie, comradeship, fellowship, companionship, friendliness.

camaradinha (*f.*, *Bot.*) a verbena (*V. chamaedryfolia*), c.a. FORMOSA-SEM-DOTE, JURUJUBA.

camarajuba (*f.*) = CAMBARÁ-DE-ESPINHO.

camarambaia (*f.*) a water primrose (*Jussiaea octonervia*), c.a. CRUZ DE MALTA.

camarão (*m.*) any shrimp or prawn, esp. *Penaeus brasiliensis*, *Palaemon potitinga*, and the fresh-water *Palaemon jamaicensis*.

camaratinga (*m.*) a half-climbing shrub of the vervain family (*Lantana brasiliensis*), c.a. CAMBARÁ-BRANCO.

camareira (*f.*) chambermaid; lady-in-waiting.

camareiro (*m.*) chamberlain; room servant (in a hotel); steward; groom.

camarilha (*f.*) camarilla, cabal, clique, inner circle.

camarim (*m.*) dressing room (in a theater).

camarinha (*f.*) a small bedroom; (*pl.*) crowberries or wolfberries; droplets; beads of sweat; (*Bot.*) a Brazilian eupatorium (*E. album*).

camarinheira (*f.*) a crowberry shrub (*Corema alba*), c.a. URZE-DAS-CAMARINHAS, CAMBROEIRA.

camaripu-guaçu (*m.*) = CAMORUPI.

camarista (*m.*) city councilman; chamberlain.

camaroeiro (*m.*) a shrimp net.

camarote (*m.*) theater box; stateroom, cabin.

camaroteiro (*m.*) room steward (on board ship); seller of tickets to theater boxes.

camartelo (*m.*) sledge hammer; bricklayer's hammer.

cambacá (*f.*) the bastard cedar (*Guazuma ulmifolia*), c.a. MUTAMBA, GUACIMA, GUAXUMA.

camatinga (*f.*) = AJURU-ETÊ.

camau (*m.*) = ALQUIMÃO.

camaxirra (*f.*) = CAMBAXIRRA.

camba (*f.*) felly.

cambacica (*f.*) a bird—the Brazilian bananaquit (*Coereba flaveola chloropyga*), c.a. MARIQUITA, CAGA-SEBO, GUARA-

TÃO.

cambado -**da** (*adj.*) bowlegged, bandy-legged; askew, twisted, lop-sided; of shoes, run-down-at-the heels; (*f.*) band (of people); gang (of lawbreakers); pack (of thieves); rabble, mob.

cambaí (*m.*) a swamp pea tree (*Sebania marginata*).

cambaio = (*adj.*) CAMBADO; (*m.*) BALANGANDÃ.

cambalacho (*m.*) a sharp trade; a "deal"; a tricky, shady piece of business.

cambaleante (*adj.*) staggering, reeling.

cambaleão-ferro (*m.*) = JACARÉ-PINIMA.

cambalear (*v.i.*) to stagger, totter, reel, sway, lurch.

cambaleio (*m.*) staggering, stumbling, lurch.

cambalhota (*f.*) somersault, flip-flop. **dar uma**—, to fall head over heels.

cambalhotar (*v.i.*) to somersault.

cambão (*m.*) shaft, tongue or pole of a wagon; a yoke of oxen; a heavy piece of wood hung on the neck of an animal to serve as a hamper. Cf. CAMBAU.

cambapé (*m.*) a trip (in wrestling); a pitfall.

cambar (*v.i.*) to twist and turn (while walking); to hobble along; to buckle; to tilt.

cambará (*m.*, *Bot.*) the common lantana (*L. camara*), c.a. CAMARÁ.—-**branco** or—-**tinga**, the yerba sagrada lantana (*L. brasiliensis*), c.a. CAMARATINGA.—-**de-espinho** or—-**juba**, spiny lantana (*L. aculeata*), c.a. CAMARAJUBA.—-**roxo** or—-**rosa**, lilac lantana (*L. lilacina*). Cf. CAMARÁ.

cambaràzinho (*m.*, *Bot.*) trailing lantana (*L. selloviana*).

cambau (*m.*) a triangular wooden frame placed around the necks of goats or other animals to prevent their passage through a fence. Cf. CAMBÃO.

cambaxirra (*f.*) the East Brazilian house wren (*Troglodytes m. musculus*), c.a. CORRUÍRA, CAMAXIBRA, CAMBALXIRA, CARRICINHA, CARRIÇA, GARRIÇA, GARRIXA, GARRIXO, GARRINCHA.

cambeba, cambeva (*f.*) = PEIXE-MARTELO.

cambêta (*adj.*) bandy-legged; lop-sided.

cambetear (*v.i.*) to limp, halt, hobble.

cambiador (*m.*) changer; exchanger.—**de discos**, record changer.—**de freqüência**, (*Elec.*) frequency converter.

cambial (*adj.*) pert. to money-changing; (*m. or f.*) a bill of exchange.

cambiante (*adj.*) changing; having a changeable luster or color, as shot silk. (*m.*) tint, tinge.

cambiar (*v.t.*) to change, exchange (**por**, for; **em**, into) referring esp. to foreign currency.—**dólares por cruzeiros**, to exchange dollars for cruzeiros.

câmbio (*m.*) foreign exchange (of currency, drafts, etc.); change; (*Bot.*) cambium.—**ao par**, exchange at par.—**livre**, free trade.—**negro**, black market. **letra de**—, a bank draft. **taxa de**—, rate of exchange.

cambira (*f.*) = TAINHA.

cambiro (*m.*) = CURIMÃ.

cambista (*m.*) money-changer; ticket scalper; lottery ticket vendor.

cambitar (*v.t.*) to load firewood, etc., on the backs of pack animals.

cambiteira (*f.*) small locomotive on a sugar-cane plantation.

cambiteiro (*m.*) a driver of pack animals.

cambito (*m.*) pig's shank; thin leg; wooden hanger.

comboa (*f.*) a weir on the seashore, for taking fish; a small seaside lake left by the receding tide [= GAMBOA].

camboatá (*m.*, *Bot.*) species of Cupania.—**da-bahia**, a bitterbush (*Picramnia bahiensis*).—-**mirim**, a bitterwood (*Trichilia pseudo-stipularis*).

camboatá (*m.*) any of several small Amazon catfishes; (*Bot.*) = CARRAPÊTA (a muskwood).—-**pequeno** = CAROBINHA.

cambota (*f.*) rim of a wheel; (*Arch.*) centering, falsework, frame; soffit scaffolding; piston rod [= BIELA].

camboté (*m.*) = CAROBINHA.

cambraia (*f.*) cambric; (*adj.*) of domestic animals, all-white.

cambraieta [ê] (*f.*) lawn (sheer linen or cotton cloth).

cambriano -**na** (*adj.*, *Geol.*) Cambrian.

cambroeira (*f.*) European wolfberry (*Lycium europaeum*); also = CAMARINHEIRA.

cambuba (*f.*) = COROCOROCA.

cambucá (*m.*) the sweet, yellow fruit, about the size of a plum, of the CAMBUCÀZEIRO.

cambucàzeiro (*m.*) a Brazilian tree myrtle (*Myrcia plicato-costata*).

cambueiras (*f.pl.*) in Brazil, heavy spring rains occurring in September; c.a. CHUVAS-DOS-IMBUS.

cambuí (*m.*) any of various myrtles of the genera Eugenia, Myrciaria and Myrtus, some of which yield building timber.—**-da-restinga** = COMANDAÍBA.

cambulhada, de—, helter-skelter.

cambuquira (*f.*) a stew of pumpkin-vine sprouts.

came (*f.*) cam (on a wheel or shaft).

camelão (*m.*) camel's-hair cloth; a Braz. vernal grass (*Anthoxanthum palmeira*), c.a. CAPIM-DE-CÔCO.

cameleão (*m.*) = CAMALEÃO.

cameleiro (*m.*) camel driver.

camélia (*f., Bot.*) spp. of Camellia.

camelo [ê] (*m.*) camel; fig., a stupid person.

camelô (*m.*) vender of small novelties on the street.

camelório (*m., colloq.*) dunderhead, dunce.

camerlengo (*m.*) camerlingo. [*Webster:* "The papal chamberlain; the cardinal who presides over the camera, or papal treasury."]

cametá, cametara (*m.*) Indian feather headdress.

cametaú (*m.*) = ANHUMA.

camião (*m.*) = CAMINHÃO.

caminhada (*f.*) walk, jaunt, stroll, hike; journey; a long road.

caminhador (*m.*), **-dora** (*f.*) rambler.

caminhante (*m.,f.*) walker, foot traveler, wayfarer; (*slang*) the foot.

caminhão (*m.*) truck, motor truck.—**basculante**, dump truck.—**de lixo**, garbage truck.—**de mudanças**, moving van.—**de socorro**, tow car. **chofer de**—, truck driver.

caminhar (*v.i.*) to walk, go on foot; to go, move, pass, travel; to advance, make headway (**a, para**, to, toward).

caminheiro (*m.*) a bird—the yellowish pipit (*Anthus l. lutescens*), c.a. FOGUETINHO; also, Natterer's pipit (*Anthus natteri*).

caminheta [ê] (*f.*) light truck; delivery truck.

caminho (*m.*) road, roadway, highway, path, pathway, trail, lane, way, route, course.—**batido**, beaten track.—**da roça**, a single file of pedestrians; Indian file.—**de cabras**, a steep, rough trail.—**de ferro**, railroad [= ESTRADA DE FERRO].—**de pé posto**, a well-trod path.—**de récua**, pack trail.—**direito**, the "straight and narrow path".—**estreito**, lane; narrow road.—**fundo**, a deeply rutted road.—**ingrato**, a very rough road.—**principal**, main highway.—**rural**, country road.—**trilhado**, beaten path.—**s cruzados**, crossroads. **a**—**(de)**, on the road to. **a meio**—, halfway, midway. **abrir**—, to pioneer; to clear the way. **atravessar-se no**—**de alguém**, to cross another's path (interfere in his affairs, with evil intent). **continuar o seu**—, to go (keep on) one's way. **cruzamento de**—**s**, crossroad. **de**—**para**, on the way to. **em**—, on the way. **errar o**—, to lose one's way. **no**—**de (Santos)**, on the way to (Santos). **pôr-se a**—, to start out, get going. **seguir o mesmo**—, to go the same way. **Todos os**—**s levam a Roma**, All roads lead to Rome. **um dia de**—, a day's journey.

camioneta [ê] (*f.*) a light truck; delivery truck; pickup truck; station wagon.

camiranga (*m.*) = URUBU-CAÇADOR.

camisa (*f.*) shirt; chemise; (*Mach.*) jacket.—**com colarinho pegado**, a shirt with collar attached.—**de água**, (*automobile motor*) water jacket.—**de dormir**, nightshirt.—**de fôrça**, straitjacket.—**de-onze-varas**, straits, predicament.—**de goma**, or **de peito engomado**, or **de rigor**, stiff (dress) shirt.—**de-Vênus**, a contraceptive or prophylactic rubber sheath.—**esporte**, sports shirt. **deixar alguém sem**, or **só**, **a**—**do corpo**, to take the shirt off another's back (impoverish him). **fralda de**—, shirttail. **mangas de**—, shirt sleeves. **meter-se em**—**de-onze-varas**, to put to sea without a compass; to go off the deep end. **plastrão**, or **peitilho, de**—, shirt front.

camisão de dormir (*m.*) nightgown, nightdress.

camisaria (*f.*) shirt shop or factory; haberdashery.

camiseta [ê] (*f.*) undershirt; shirt waist; chemisette; (*Zool.*) a damselfish (*Abudefduf saxatilis*), c.a. SABERÉ, QUERE-QUERÊ.

camisola (*f.*) nightgown, nightshirt.—**de-fôrça** = CAMISA-DE-FÔRÇA.

camixi [xí] (*m.*) = ANHUMA.

camoatim (*m.*) a social wasp (*Polybia scutellaris*).

camocica (*m.*) a small deer of the genus Mazama, c.a. BORORÓ, MÃO-CURTA.

camocim (*m.*) = CAMOTIM.

camões (*m., colloq.*) a one-eyed person (as was the great

Portuguese poet of that name).

camomila (*f., Bot.*) camomile (*Anthemis spp.*).—**-amarela**, yellow camomile (*A tinctoria*).—**-catinga**, the mayweed or stinking camomile (*A. cotula*), c.a. CAMOMILA-FÉTIDA, MACELA-FÉTIDA.—**-dos-alemães**, German camomile (*Matricaria chamomilla*).—**-romana**, Roman or English camomile (*A. nobilis*).

camondongo (*m.*) mouse.

camorim (*m.*) = ROBALO.—**-sovela**,—**-peba** = ROBALETE.

camorra [ô] (*f.*) a gang of lawbreakers.

camorupi [í] (*m.*) the common tarpon (*Tarpon atlanticus*), c.a. PIRAPEMA, CAMARIPU-GUAÇU; also, a thin old horse.

camote (*m.*) dalliance, courtship; sweetheart.

camotim (*m.*) a large, earthenware, Indian burial vase.

campa (*f.*) grave stone; a small hand bell.—**rasa**, plain, flat tombstone.

campainha [a-í] (*f.*) a small bell (for table, door, telephone, etc.). Cf. SINETA, SINO. (*Bot.*) any of numerous plants having bell flowers, such as morning-glory, campanula, convolvulus.—**-de-canudo** = ALGODÃO-BRAVO (a morning-glory).

campainhada [a-i] (*f.*) a ringing of a bell.

campana (*f., Arch.*) bell (of a capital); (*Mus.*) bell (of a wind instrument).

campanado -da (*adj.*) bell-shaped.

campanário (*m.*) campanile, bell-tower, belfry, steeple.

campanha (*f.*) campaign; wide plains, prairie; (*Metal.*) campaign or life, of an open hearth furnace. **canhão de**—, a field gun.

campaniforme (*adj.*) bell-shaped.

campanil (*m.*) bell metal.

campanudo -da (*adj.*) bell-shaped; tumid, pompous.

campânula (*f.*) bell jar, bell glass; (*Bot.*) any bellflower (*genus Campanula*).

campanuláceo -cea (*adj., Bot.*) campanulaceous; (*f.pl.*) the bellflower family.

campanulado -da (*adj.*) campanulate, bell-shaped.

campeador -dora (*adj.*) = CAMPEIRO.

campeão (*m.*) **-peã** (*f.*) champion.—**de pêso pesado**, heavyweight champion.

campear (*v.i.*) to camp; to campaign; to live in the country; to scour the countryside; to ride the range in search of cattle; to prevail, be predominant; of horses, to prance.—**sôbre**, to overlook, dominate.

campeche [pé] (*m.*) logwood (*Haematoxylon compechianum*).

campeiro -ra (*adj.*) rural, rustic; (*m.*) cowboy; wrangler; (*f.*) a kind of manioc.

campeonato (*m.*) championship.

campesinho -nha campesino -na, (*adj.*) = CAMPESTRE.

campestre (*adj.*) country; rural; rustic; (*m.*) a small high plain or meadow surrounded by forest; a large clearing in the forest.

campimetria (*f., Psychol.*) campimetry.

campímetro (*m., Psychol.*) campimeter.

campina (*f.*) prairie, plains, range; meadow; a natural pasture; typical Amazonian grassland with woody vegetation of some height.

campinarana (*f.*) an extensive open space in a forest but with many shrubs and some trees in a dense formation; "ground where scrub vegetation is interspersed with grass; a CAMPINA on which, through improvement in the condition of the land, trees are growing, and which as a result is changing from CAMPINA to CAMPO." [*GBAT*]

campineiro -ra (*adj.; m.,f.*) (a native) of Campinas, an important city in the state of São Paulo.

campista (*adj.; m.,f.*) (a native) of Campos, an important city in the state of Rio de Janeiro; (*m.*) a certain card game.

campo (*m.*) field, prairie; the country; grassland or savanna; a level open tract of grassland without forest cover, or having only scattered stunted trees or perennial herbs; an open square in a village; a camp or encampment; an arena or open space; a playing field; chance, opportunity; background (of a painting, or of a fabric).—**carbonífero**, coal field.—**cerrado**, a savanna with scattered thickets of deciduous scrub forest.—**de aviação**, airfield; flying field.—**de batalha**, battlefield.—**de corrida**, race track.—**de engorda**, fattening pasture.—**de futebol**, soccer field.—**de pouso**, airfield.—**dobrado**, hilly land.—**elétrico**, electro-magnetic field.—**s elísios**, Elysian fields.—**experimental**, experimental station.—**s gerais**, vast treeless plains between certain plateaux in Brazil; prairie lands.—**limpo**, a treeless savanna.—

magnético, magnetic field.—**nativo**, virgin prairie land. —**parelho**, flat prairie land.—**petrolífero**, oil field.—**raso**, a flat, level field.—**santo**, cemetery. **através do—**, cross-country. **abrir o—(a)**, to afford an opportunity (to). **Ajudante de—**, Aide-de-camp. **casa de—**, country house. **dar—a**, to give ground for (suspicion, etc.). **Há—para suspeitas**, There is ground for suspicion. **homem do—**, man from the country. **ir** (or **sair**) **a—**, to take to the field. **ir para o—**, to go to the country. **queimar—** to tell lies. **no—**, afield. **pôr em—**, to put or bring into play. **pôr fora de—**, to put out of business; render *hors de combat*. **vida do—**, country life.

camponês -nesa (*adj.*) rustic; country; (*m.,f.*) peasant.

campônio (*m.*) peasant, boor, bumpkin, yokel.

camuá (*f.*) a bramble palm (*Desmoncus nemorosus*).

camuengo (*m.*) a stingless bee (*Melipona schultzei*).

camuflagem (*f.*) camouflage.

camuflar (*v.t.*) to camouflage, disguise; to fake.

camumbembe (*m.*) loafer; beggar; guttersnipe.

camundongo (*m.*) = CAMONDONGO.

camunheca (*f., colloq.*) drunkenness.

camunhengue (*adj.*) = LEPROSO.

camurça (*adj.*) chamois-colored; (*f.*) chamois leather; suede.

camurim (*m., Zool.*) any of several snooks, genus Centro-pomis, esp. *C. pectinatus* and *C. parallelus*, c.a. CAMURIPEBA, CANGOROPEBA, and *C. undecimalis*, c.a. ROBALO.

camurupim (*m.*) the well-known tarpon (*Tarpon atlanticus*), c.a. PIRAPEMA.

cana (*f.*) cane, reed; sugar cane; the stem of various bamboo-like grasses; the upper end of a corn stalk; (*Anat.*) tibia or ulna; tiller (of a boat); (*colloq.*) rum; drunkenness; (*slang*) jug, cooler (jail). **aguardente de—**, "firewater" (white rum).—**brava**, the sugarcane plumegrass (*Erianthus giganteus*), c.a. CANA-DO-BREJO, MACEGA-BRAVA, PENACHINHO; also = CARDAMOMO-DA-TERRA.— -**da-Índia** = BANANEIRINHA-DA-ÍNDIA.—**-de-açúcar**, sugar cane (*Saccharum officinarum*).—**-de-frecha** = CANA-FRECHA.—**-de-jacaré**, a horsetail (*Equisetum*).—**-de-macaco**, a spiral flag (*Costus*), c.a.—BRANCA,—DO-BREJO,—DO-MATO,—ROXA, PACO-CATINGA, PERINÁ.— -**de-passarinho**, any of several species of tibisee grass (*Lasiacis*), c.a. ANDREQUICÉ, CAPIM-ANDREQUICÉ, CAPIM-GORDO, TABOQUINHA, TACUARINHA.—**-de-são-paulo** or -**de-víbora**, a chamaedorea palm (*C. concolor*).—**-de-vassoura**, common or ditch reed (*Phragmites communis*), c.a. JUNCO, CANIÇO-DE-ÁGUA.—**-do-brejo** = -BRAVA,—DE-MACACO; also a malanga (*Xanthosoma*) and the cardamon *Amomum*.—**-de-mato** = —DE-MACACO,—DA-TERRA,—DO-RIO (all spiral flags, *Costus*); also = CARDAMOMO-DA-TERRA.—**-do-reino**, the giant reed (*Arundo donax*), c.a. CANAMILHA, TAQUARA-DO-REINO, TAQUARÍ-UBÁ.—**-do-rio** = —DO-MATO.—**-marona**, a caladium.—**roxa** = —DE-MACACO.

Canaã (*f.*) Canaan.

canabina (*f.*) any hemp (*Canabis*).

canabíneas (*f.pl.*) the Cannabinaceae (hemp family).

canabismo (*m., Med.*) cannabism.

canabrás (*m.*) the hog weed cowparsnip (*Heracleum sphondylium*), c.a. BRANCA-URSINA.

canáceo -cea (*adj.*) cannaceous. (*f.pl.*) the Cannaceae (canna family).

canada [ná] (*f.*) a measure of capacity: in Brazil it is 2.77 liters or 2.52 dry qts; in Portugal, 1.40 liters or 1.47 liquid qts.

Canadá (*m.*) Canada.

canadense (*adj.; m.,f.*) Canadian.

canado (*m.*) = BIJUPIRÁ.

canadol (*m.*) canadol, petroleum ether, benzine.

canafístula (*f.*) any of several sennas, esp.—**verdadeira**, the goldenshower senna, or purging cassia, or drumstick tree (*Cassia fistula*), c.a. AMALTAS, CANAFRISTA, CHUVA-DE-OURO.

canaflecha (*f.*) a bamboo (*Chusquea pinifolia*), c.a. FÔLHA-MIÚDA, CHIBATA, TAQUARA-AÇU, TAQUARAÇU.

canafrecha (*f.*) uva grass (*Gynerium sagittatum*), c.a. CANA-DE-FRECHA, ARINÁ, UBÁ; the giant fennel (*Ferula communis*).

canafrista (*f*) = CANAFÍSTULA-VERDADEIRA.

canagra (*f., Bot.*) the canaigre (*Rumex hymenosepalus*).

canal (*m.*) canal, channel, duct, conduit, ditch; (*Radio*) channel.—**da Mancha**, English Channel.—**de derivação**, a canal leading from a river to a reservoir.—

deferente, (*Anat.*) vas deferens, seminal duct.—**de irrigação**, irrigation ditch.—**marítimo**, sea canal.—**medular**, (*Anat.*) medullary canal.—**raqueano**, or **vertebral**, (*Anat.*) spinal canal.—**torácico**, (*Anat.*) thoracic duct.

canalete (*m.*) a small canal or channel.

canalha (*f.*) canaille, rabble, dregs of society, scum of the earth; riff-raff; vulgar herd; mob; (*m.*) rascal, rapscallion, rogue, scoundrel, scalawag; wretch; (*adj.*) low, mean, base.

canalhada, -**lhice** (*f.*), -**lhismo** (*m.*) dirty trick; vile behavior.

canalícula (*f.*), -**lo** (*m.*) a small groove or channel, as have the leafstalks of most palms; (*Anat., Zool.*) canaliculus.

canaliculado -da (*adj.*) canaliculate.

canaliforme (*adj.*) canal-like.

canalização (*f.*) canalization; system of canals or of pipe-lines.

canalizar (*v.t.*) to canalize; to channel; to pipe.

canamilha (*f.*) = CANA-DO-REINO.

cânamo (*m.*) = CÂNHAMO.

cananga (*f.*) a nutmeg (*Myristica macrophylla*), c.a. UCUUBA.—**-do-Japão**, a resurrection lily (*Kaempferia sp.*).

canapaúba (*f.*) the false mangrove (*Laguncularia racemosa*), c.a. CANAPONGA, MANGUE-DE-CANA-POMBA, MANGUE-RASTEIRO.

canapé (*m.*) couch, sofa, chaise-longue, settee; canapé (appetizer).

canaponga (*f.*) = CANAPAÚBA.

canapu [ú] (*m.*) = TIMBÓ-DO-RIO-DE-JANEIRO.

canarana (*f.*) any of various grasses, esp.—**fina**, Egyptian panicum (*P. geminatum*), c.a. CAPIM-D'ÁGUA, CAPIM-FINO-DE-FÔLHA-COMPRIDA, TAQUARI-D'ÁGUA.—**-rasteira**, the horsetail paspalum grass (*P. repens*), c.a. MEMBECA, PIRIMEMBECA.—**-roxa**, a panicum or witch grass (*Panicum zizanioides*), c.a. CAPIM-ARROZ.—**-verdadeira** = CAPIM-DE-ANGOLA. [*GBAT*: "An aquatic grass (*Panicum spectabile*) which grows along the banks of rivers, IGARAPÉS and lakes, preferred above all other grasses by cattle; (since it is used as forage for cattle transported by GAIOLAS, these boats have to stop frequently to replenish their supply)."]

canária (*f.*) see CANÁRIO.

canaricultura (*f.*) canary raising.

canário -ria (*adj.*) Canary; canary; (*m.*) the ordinary canary bird (native of the Canary Islands), and c.a. —DO-REINO.—**baeta** = TIÉ-SANGUE (a tanager).—**-da-horta**, or—**-do-campo**, Pelzeln's yellow finch (*Sicalis flaveola pelzelni*).—**-da-terra**, or—**-do-ceará**, Holt's yellow finch (*Sicalis flaveola holti*). [The males are chiefly orange-yellow, with black wings and tails, and are noted for their amorous and pugnacious nature. **canário-da-terra** is also the common generic term for any canary-like finch, as opposed to **canário-do-reino**, native of the Canary Islands.]—**-do-brejo** = CURUTIÉ and PIA-COBRA. —**-do-campo**, the wedge-tailed ground finch (*Emberizoides h. herbicola*); also = —**-DA-HORTA**.—**-do-mato**, the saira tanager (*Piranga flava saira*), c.a. SANHAÇO-DE-FOGO, SAÍ-DE-FOGO, TIÉ-PIRANGA, SAÍRA-VERMELHA.— -**do-sapé** = PIA-COBRA.—**-pardo** = TICO-TICO.

canastra (*f.*) a shallow, open basket; a hamper; a wicker basket, or one made by plaiting thin wooden bands; (*slang*) a police raid [= CANOA]; (*m.*) a type of pig; a large armadillo.

canastrão (*m.*) hamper, large ·basket; ham actor; barn-stormer; a certain breed of Brazilian hogs.

canatinga (*f.*) = CAPIM-DOS-PAMPAS.

canavial (*m.*) cane brake.

canavieira (*f.*) sorghum (*Sorghum saccharatum*); a cane (*Arundinaria canavieira*).

cancã (*m.*) cancan (a dance); (*Zool.*) the black Braz. hawk (*Urubutinga u. urubutinga*), c.a. GAVIÃO-PRÊTO; also = CARACARÁ-PRÊTO and PATURI.

cancaborrada (*f.*) botch, mess.

can-can, cancão (*m.*) = QUENQUÉM.

canção (*f.*) chant, song, canticle; ballad.—**de ninar**, or —**de berço**, cradle song, lullaby.

cancela (*f.*) low, wooden gate; farm gate; barrier at a railroad crossing; wicket.

cancelamento (*m.*) cancellation; annulment; abrogation.

cancelar (*v.t.*) to cancel, cross out, wipe out; to quash; to annul, set aside, make void; to abrogate.

câncer (*m.*) cancer; (*Astrol., Geog.*) Cancer. Cf. CANCRO.

cancerar (v.t.,v.i.) to cancerate.
canceriforme (adj.) like a cancer.
cancerofobia (f.) morbid dread of cancer.
cancerologia (f., Med.) oncology.
canceroso -sa (adj.) cancerous; (m.,f.) one suffering from cancer.
cancha (f.) open enclosure such as race track, soccer field, handball court, brick yard, &c. abrir—, to open the way.
canchalágua (f.) a blue-eyed grass (Sisyrinchium vaginatum).
cancheada (f.) dried and crumbled MATE leaves ready for final processing.
canchear (v.t.) to crumble MATE leaves.
cancionerio (m.) song book.
cancionista (m.,f.) songster.
cançoneta (f.) popular song, ditty.
cançoneteiro (m.) writer of popular songs.
cançonetista (m.,f.) writer or singer of ballads.
cancra (f.) a heavy shower.
cancriforme (adj.) cancriform.
cancrinita (f., Min.) cancrinite.
cancrívoro -ra (adj.) cancrivorous.
cancrizante (adj., Music) cancrizans.
cancro (m.) cancer; canker; chancre, venereal ulcer; (Carp.) dog, cramp; (Med.)—duro, hard chancre.—mole, soft chancre.
cancróide (adj.) cancroid; (m.) a form of skin cancer.
cancroma (f.) = TAMATIÁ-AQUÁTICO-DO-PARÁ.
cande (m.) rock candy. [Ordinary candy is BALAS or BONBONS.]
candeeiro [e-ei] (m.) chandelier; kerosene lamp [= LAMPIÃO]; an ox-cart driver.
candeia (f.) a small hanging oil-lamp; a candle; (pl.) Candelmas [= CANDELÁRIA]; (pl., Bot.) = CAPUZ-DE-FRADINHO.
candeio (m.) torch.
candela (f.) = CANDEIA.
candelabro (m.) candelabrum; chandelier; (Bot.)—dos-jardins = BEIJOS-DE-FREIRA.
Candelária (f.) Candelmas (religious feast celebrated on February 2nd); also, the name of an old and fashionable church in Rio de Janeiro: Igreja da Candelária.
candelinha (f.) a small candle; (Med.) catheter [= ALGÁLIA].
candência (f.) candescence.
candente (adj.) candent, white-hot, glowing.
candidatar (v.t.) to present (-se, oneself) as a candidate (a, para, for).
candidato -ta (m.,f.) candidate.
candidatura (f.) candidacy, candidature.
candidez [ê] (f.) whiteness; purity.
cândido -da (adj.) white; naive; disarming; sincere, innocent. [But not candid in the sense of impartial, which is IMPARCIAL, nor in the sense of frank, which is FRANCO.]
candieiro (m.) = CANDEEIRO.
candiru [ú] (m.) a tiny, threadlike, bloodsucking catfish of the Amazon basin (Vandellia cirrhosa). [It is reputed to force its way into the urethra of bathers, and owing to the spines on the gill-covers cannot be extracted.]; (Bot.) = CUMANÃ.
candólea (f., Bot.) any stylewort (Stylidium).
candomblé (m.) voodoo rites [= MACUMBA].
candonga, candonguice (f.) false flattery.
candongueiro -ra (m.,f.) wheedler.
candor (m.), candura (f.) whiteness; innocence; naiveté. [But not candor, which is IMPARCIALIDADE and FRANQUEZA.]
caneca (f.) tin cup, mug. café—, cheap coffee shop.
canecada (f.) mugful.
caneco (m.) mug. pintar o—, to raise Cain.
canéfora (f., Arch.) canephoros.
caneiro (m.) small ditch; river channel.
canela (f.) cinnamon (spice, bark, tree); shin bone; bobbin; shuttle; any of numerous trees, esp. of Ocotea (syn. Nectandra), and others of the laurel family, some of which yield prized timber; (m.,f.) an Indian of the Canella, a tribe of the Ge family in the State of Maranhão; (adj.) pert. to or designating the Canella.—de-velho, common zinnia (Z. elegans).—-poca = CUIA-DO-BREJO.—-ruiva = CAITITU (a peccary). dar às—s, (slang) to run (away). esticar as—s, (slang) to kick the bucket (die). pôr sebo nas—s, (slang) to take to one's heels.
canelada (f.) a kick or blow on the shins.
canelar (v.t.) to groove or flute.

caneleira (f.) shinguard; (Bot.) cinnamon-bark tree; also = CANELEIRO (a bird).—-cravo = CRAVEIRO-DO-MARANHÃO (clovebark tree).—-da-índia, Ceylon cinnamon tree (Cinnamomum zeylanicum).
caneleirinho (m.) Vieillot's becard (Pachyramphus p. polychopterus) of northeastern Brazil, and the green-backed becard (P.v. viridis) of central and southern Brazil.
caneleiro (m.) the crested becard (Platypsaris r. rufus), c.a. CANELEIRA.
canêlo (m.) shin bone; a worn or broken horseshoe; an iron shoe for an ox.
canelura (f.) channeling, grooving, fluting.
caneta [ê] (f.) pen, penholder.—esferográfica, ball-point pen.—tinteiro, fountain pen.
canfeno (m., Chem.) camphene.
canfol (m., Chem.) camphol, borneol, bornyl alcohol.
cânfora (f.) camphor.
canforado -da (adj.) camphorated.
canforar (v.t.) to camphorate.
canforeira (f.), -ro (m.) the camphor tree (Cinnamomum camphora), c.a. ALCANFOREIRA, ÁRVORE-DA-CÂNFORA.
canfórico -ca (adj.) camphoric.
canga (f.) a yoke, esp. for oxen; oppression; a certain type of iron ore. sacudir a—, to throw off, the yoke. Cf. JUGO.
cangá (m.) a kind of saddlebag.
cangaçais (m.pl.) poor, cheap pieces of household goods.
cangaceiro (m.) bandit, outlaw; hired ruffian.
cangaço (m.) fruit skins and pulp (after squeezing); an outlaw's outfit of weapons; banditry.
cangalha (f.) a triangular yoke for small animals, such as goats or pigs, to prevent their passage through a fence; (pl.) sort of frame or saddle for supporting the load on each side of a pack animal; (colloq.) spectacles (m., colloq.) bowlegged man. de—, heels over head; upside down.
cangalhada (f.) a heap of junk.
cangalhão (m.) a piece of junk; fig., a man prematurely old.
cangalheiro (m.) driver of oxen or of pack animals; a funeral undertaker; (Bot.) a tree (Belangera tomentosa, family Cunoniaceae), c.a. AÇOITA-CAVALOS, CANGALHEIRA, GUARAPERÊ, GUARAPORÉ, SALGUEIRO-DO-MATO.
cangalheta (f.) a crude saddle.
cangalho (m.) a wooden yoke; an old, useless thing or person. Cf. CALHAMBEQUE.
cangambá (m.) any conepate or large badger-like skunk, esp. Conepatus suffocans, which eats venomous snakes, heedless of their bites; c.a. IRITACACA, IRITATACA, JAGUANÉ, JAGUARÉ, JAGUARECACA, JAGUARECAGUA, JAGUARITACA, JARATATACA, JARATICACA, JARITATACA, JERATICACA, JERITATACA, MARITACACA, MARITAFEDE, MARITATACA, TACACA, TICACA, ZORRILHO. [Do not confuse with GAMBÁ, which is an opossum.]
cangancha (f.) cheating, esp. at cards.
cangancheiro (m.) cheater, swindler.
cangoeira (f.) Indian flute made from human leg bone.
cangote (m.) nape, scruff [= CACHAÇO, CERVIZ].
canguçu [çú] (m.) = SUÇUARANA, ACANGUÇU.
canguinhas (m.) weakling; (m.,f.) miser.
canguinho -nha (adj.) miserly.
cangulo (m.) the common triggerfish (Balistes capriscus, syn. carolinensis), c.a. FANTASMA, MARACUGUARA, PIRÁ-AÇÁ, ACARÁ-MOCÓ.—rei, or—do-alto, the oldwife or queen triggerfish (Balistes vetula), c.a. CANGURRO, popular as a cheap and abundant food in northeastern Brazil; fig., (colloq.) a person with buck teeth.
canguru [rú] (m.) kangaroo.
canha (f.) the left hand. às—s, backwards.
canhada (f.) gorge, ravine.
cânhamo (m.) hemp; the hemp plant (Cannabis sativa), c.a.—-INDIANO,—-VERDADEIRO.—-americano, century plant (Agave americana).—-aquático, bur beggarticks (Bidens tripartita).—-brasileiro, the Kenaf hibiscus (H. cannabinus), cultivated for its hemplike fiber; c.a. PAPOULA-DE-SÃO-FRANCISCO, UMBARU.—-caloni, a nettle (Urtica tenacissima).—-da-nova-zelândia, New Zealand fiber lily (Phormium tenas).—-de-áfrica, Ceylon sansevieria (S. zeylanica), the sunn crotolaria (C. juncea).—-de-bombaim =—-BRASILEIRO.—-de-creta, the bastard hemp of western Asia (Datisca cannabina).—-de-manila (or manilha), the Manila hemp or abacá banana (Musa textilis), c.a. ABACÁ.—-do-canadá,

hemp dogbane (*Apocynum canabium*).—-do-japão, Japanese spiraea (*S. japonica*).

canhanha (*f.*) the brim (*Archosargus unimaculatus*), a fish, c.a. FRADE, GUATUCUPAJUBA, MERCADOR, SALEMA, SARGO.

canhão (*m.*) cannon, gun; canyon; sleeve cuff; (*slang*) ugly old hag.—**antitanque**, anti-tank gun.—**de campanha**, field gun. **alma do**—, bore of a cannon. **bucha** (or **carne**) **de**—, cannon fodder. **tiro de**—, cannon shot.

canhembora (*m.,f.*) runaway slave [= QUILOMBOLA].

canhengue (*adj.*) stingy, miserly.

canhenho (*m.*) note book, memorandum pad, diary.

canhestro —**tra** [ê] (*adj.*) left-handed; clumsy, awkward, stiff.

canhonaço (*m.*) cannon shot.

canhonear (*v.t.*) to fire cannon.

canhoneio (*m.*) cannonade, gunfire.

canhoneira (*f.*) gunboat; crenel (of a battlement).

canhota [ó] (*f.*) the left hand. **à**—, awkwardly.

canhoto [nhô] —**nhôta** (*adj.*) left(-handed); awkward, clumsy; (*m.,f.*) a left-handed person; (*m.*) the stub left in a checkbook, etc.; the devil.

canibal (*m.*) cannibal.

canibalesco —**ca** (*adj.*) cannibalistic.

canibalismo (*m.*) cannibalism.

caniçada (*f.*) lattice, trellis.

canicho (*m.*) puppy, small dog.

canície (*f.*) whiteness of hair; old age.

caniço (*m.*) reed; slender pole, fishing rod; (*Bot.*)—-**de-água**, common reed (*Phragmites communis*), c.a. JUNCO, CANA-DE-VASSOURA. **magro como um**—, as thin as a beanpole.

canícula (*f.*) dog days; sultry summer; (*Astron.*) the Dog Star, Sirius.

canicular (*adj.*) of or pert. to the canicular days; sultry.

canídeos (*m.pl.*) the Canidae (dogs, wolves, jackals and foxes).

canil (*m.*) kennel.

caninana (*f.*) a large but harmless black-and-yellow rat snake (*Spilotes pullatus*), c.a. CAINANA, IACANINÃ, ARABÓIA; also, a climbing shrub of the genus Securidaca, very beautiful in flower.

canindé (*m.*) the blue-and-yellow macaw (*Ara ararauna*), c.a. ARARA-AZUL, ARARI, ARARAÚNA.

caninha (*f.*) grog, rum; = CACHAÇA.—-**do-ó**, white rum.

canino —**na** (*adj.*) canine. **dente**—, eye tooth. **fome**—, ravenous appetite.

canitar (*m.*) Indian feather headdress; = ACANGUÇU.

canivete [vé] (*m.*) pocket knife, penknife. **fôlha de**—, knife blade. (*Bot.*) a scarlet-flowered coral tree (*Erythrina reticulata*).

canja (*f.*) chicken soup with rice; (*slang*) duck soup, cinch, snap, pushover (something sure and easy).

canjerana (*f., Bot.*) the canchara cabralea (*C. congerana*).—-**miúda** = CARRAPETA (muskwood).

canjica (*f.*) a traditional Brazilian dish made with grated green corn, coconut milk, sugar and cinnamon, variously called also CURAU, CORAL, PAPA DE MILHO, CANJIQUINHA, and JIMBELÊ; hominy served with milk, sugar and cinnamon, c.a. MUNGUNZÁ; a kind of snuff; coarse gravel mixed with sand, c.a. (CANJICA-) PIRURUCA, or PURURUCA; a cysticercus or pork measle, c.a. CANJIQUINHA; a bird called ARAPONGUIRA; a tree called CARVALHO-DO-BRASIL; (*pl., slang*) big white teeth.—**lustrosa**, (*Min.*) brown hematite in pebbly forms.

canjicada (*f.*) parties on St. John's and St. Peter's feast days (June 24th and June 29th), at which CANJICA is traditionally served.

canjiquinha (*f., Veter.*) cysticercosis, pork measles (*Taenia solium*).

canjirão (*m.*) a large jug or pitcher, esp. for wine.

cano (*m.*) pipe, large tube; conduit; main for water, gas or sewage; gun barrel; "a creek, canal, or small winding stream terminating in the great rivers; synonymous with IGARAPÉ, brook." [*GBAT*].—**da botina**, top of a high shoe.—**da chaminé**, chimney flue.—**da perna**, leg shank.—**de admissão**, intake pipe.—**de água**, water pipe.—**de algeroz**, downspout (from a roof gutter).—**de alumínio**, aluminum tube.—**de ar**, (compressed) air pipe.—**de descarga**, outlet or discharge pipe.—**de escapamento**, exhaust pipe.—**de gás**, gas pipe.—**do ar**, windpipe (trachea). **alma do**—, rifle bore. Cf. TUBO.

canoa [ô] (*f.*) canoe; (*colloq.*) bath tub; (*slang*) police raid.—**de embono**, outrigger boat.

canoagem (*f.*) canoeing.

canoeiro (*m.*) canoeman.

cânon, cânone (*m.*) canon, church decree; criterion; official list of books, saints, etc.; (*Print.*) 40-pt. type.

canonical (*adj.*) canonical.

canonicidade (*f.*) canonicity.

canônico —**ca** (*adj.*) canonic.

canonização (*f.*) canonization.

canonizar (*v.t.*) to canonize.

canopi [í] (*m., Bot.*) the mamoncillo genip or Spanish lime (*Melicocca bijuga*).

canópia (*f., Aeron.*) canopy.

canoro [nó] —**ra** (*adj.*) harmonious, melodius. **ave**—, song bird.

canoura (*f.*) a grain (or other) hopper.

cansaço (*m.*) fatigue, weariness. **morto de**—, dog-tired, tired to death.

cansado —**da** (*adj.*) tired; worn-out (referring esp. to land, printing type, and rubber trees).

cansanção (*m.*) the broadleaf scratchbush (*Urera baccifera*), c.a. URTIGA-BRAVA, URTIGA-FOGO, URTIGA-GRANDE, URTIGA-VERMELHA, URTIGÃO; a Chile nettle (*Loasa parviflora*), c.a. URTIGÃO; the flameberry scratchbush (*Urera caracasana*); c.a. CARACASANA, URTIGA-BRAVA; a nettlespure (*Jatropha vitifolia*); (*Zool.*) a small stinging jellyfish.—-**de-leite**, the drug treadsoftly (*Cnidoscolus urens*), c.a. ARRE-DIABO, PINHA-QUEIMADEIRA, URTIGA, URTIGA-DE-MAMÃO, URTIGA-CANSANÇÃO.

cansar (*v.t.*) to tire, fatigue, weary, jade; to irk, bore; (*v.i.*) to grow weary; (*v.r.*) to tire (**de, em**, of).

cansarina (*f.*) the lesser bougainvillea (*B. glabra*).

cansativo —**va** (*adj.*) tiring.

canseira (*f.*) fatigue; hard work, tiring work.

Cantabrígia (*f.*) Cambridge.

cantada (*f., colloq.*) seduction by flattery.

cantadeira (*f.*) a small wedge introduced between the hub and axle of an oxcart in order to make the big wheels "sing" (i.e. squeal) as they turn, failing which (it is claimed) the oxen will not work.

cantador —**dora** (*adj.*) singing; (*m.,f.*) singer, esp. of popular songs. Cf. CANTOR, CANTORA.

cantalupo (*m.*) cantaloup, muskmelon.

cantante (*adj.*) singing; (*m.*) crook, swindler, slicker.

cantão (*m.*) canton (Swiss state); Canton (China).

cantar (*v.i.*) to sing, chant, carol; to warble; to chirp (as a cricket); to crow; (*v.t.*) to seduce (inveigle) esp. by flattery.—**de galo**, to strut, swagger; to rule the roost.—**desafinado**, to sing off key.—**vitória**, to crow (exult). **ao**—**do galo**, at cockcrow (dawn).

cântara (*f.*) a wide-mouthed pitcher.

cantaria (*f.*) stonework, masonry; a stone building block, ashlar; ashlar masonry.

cantárida —**de** (*f.*) cantharis (Spanish fly; blister beetle).

cântaro (*m.*) water jug. **chover a**—**s**, to rain cats and dogs; to rain pitchforks.

cantarola (*f.*) humming, crooning.

cantarolar (*v.i.*) to hum, croon.

cantata (*f.*) cantata; (*slang*) smooth talk.

cantatriz (*f.*) cantatrice, professional female singer.

canteira (*f.*) rock quarry; open pit mine.

canteiro (*m.*) stone mason; flower bed.

cântico (*m.*) canticle, hymn.

cantiga (*f.*) ballad, popular song; (*slang*) a seductive "line".—**de ninar**, lullaby.

cantil (*m.*) rabbet plane; tonguing-and-grooving plane; match plane; stonecutter's chisel; canteen, flask.

cantilena (*f.*) ditty, carol; (*colloq.*) long-drawn-out story; hocus-pocus.

cantilever (*m.; adj.; Arch.; Engin.*) cantilever.

cantina (*f.*) canteen (at camp).

cantineiro (*m.*) proprietor of a canteen.

canto (*m.*) corner, angle, bend; nook, recess, niche; corner stone; canto; song, singing; (*Anat.*) canthus.—**s e recantos**, nooks and crannies.—**de sabiá**, or—**de bôca**, (*Med.*) a form of stomatitis affecting the corners of the mouth; thrush.—**do cisne**, swan song. **aos quatro**—**s**, to the four corners of the earth.

cantoeira (*f.*) angle iron; bracket.

cantoneira (*f.*) corner cupboard; angle iron; iron bracket.

cantoplastia (*f., Surg.*) canthoplasty.

cantor (*m.*), —**tora** (*f.*) singer Cf. CANTADOR.

cantoria (*f.*) singing; song feast.

cantorrafia (*f., Surg.*) canthorrhaphy.

Cantuária (*f.*) Canterbury.

canudeiro (*m.*) = CANUDO-DE-PITO.

canudo (*m.*) small tube; sheepskin (diploma); (*colloq.*)
a hoax.—**de palha,** sipping straw.—**amargoso** = PAU-
PEREIRA (a tree).—**de-pito,** a tall tree (*Carpotroche
brasiliensis*), family Flacourtiaceae), of central and
southern Brazil, the nut of which yields an oil used as
a substitute for chaulmoogra oil in the treatment of
leprosy; c.a. SAPUCAINHA, CANUDEIRO, FRUTA-DE-
BABADO, FRUTA-DE-LEPRA, FRUTEIRA-DE-CUTIA, MATA-
PIOLHO, PAPO-DE-ANJO, PAU-DE-ANJO, PAU-DE-LEPRA;
also, a senna (*Cassia laevigata*), and a euphorbiaceous
shrub of the genus Mabea.—**-de-purga,** a devil pepper
(*Rauwolfia blanchetti*).
cânula (*f., Surg.*) cannula.
canzá (*m.*) a native Brazilian musical instrument consisting of a length of bamboo with notches cut along the
side, over which a stick is rubbed to produce the sound;
c.a. QUEREQUERÊ, CARACAXA, RECO-RECO.
canzarrão (*m.*) a huge dog. [Augmentative of CÃO].
cão [cães] (*m.*) dog, hound; hammer of a gun. Cf. CACHOR-
RO.—**dalmata,** Dalmatian coach dog.—**danado,** mad dog.
—**de água,** water spaniel, poodle.—**de caça,** a hound,
beagle or other hunting dog.—**de chaminé,** or **de lareira,**
andiron.—**de fila,** bulldog; watchdog.—**de manga,** tiny
lap dog.—**de mostra,** pointer.—**de pastor,** shepherd
dog.—**esquimau do Alásca,** Eskimo dog.—**fraldeiro** or
fraldiqueiro, lapdog.—**perdigueiro,** pointer, setter.—
policial, police dog.—**que ladra não morde,** A barking
dog seldom bites.—**rasteiro** or **texugueiro,** dachshund.
—**tinhoso,** a cur; (*colloq.*) the Devil. **Quem não tem—
caça com gato,** One does with what one has.
caoba (*f.*) the West Indies mahogany (*Swietiana maho-
gani*).—**das planícies,** eucalyptus.
caolim (*m.*) kaolin.
caolho -**lha** [aô] (*adj.*) cross-eyed, cock-eyed, one-eyed.
caos [cá-us] (*m.*) chaos.
caótico -**ca** (*adj.*) chaotic.
cãozinho (*m.*) doggy, puppy. [Dim. of CÃO].
cap. = CAPÍTULO (chapter); CAPITÃO (captain).
capa (*f.*) cape, cloak, mantle; cover.—**de asperges,** cope
(ecclesiastical vestment).—**de borracha,** or **de chuva,**
raincoat.—**de santidade,** cloak of hypocrisy.—**de um
livro,** book cover.—**e espada,** cloak and dagger. **estar à—,**
to be on the lookout.
capação (*f.*) castration (of animals); pruning or disbudding
(of plants).
capacete [cê] (*m.*) helmet; steam dome of a locomotive.—
de aço, steel helmet.—**de cortiça,** pith helmet.—**de
gêlo,** ice bag.—**protetor,** crash helmet.
capachismo (*m.*) servility.
capacho (*m.*) door mat; fig., fawner, toady, lickspittle,
heeler, hanger-on; [In São Paulo, the term designates an
obliging, helpful person.] foot warmer.
capacidade (*f.*) capacity, extent of room or space; capability, ability, power, skill, competency.—**calorífica
específica,** thermal capacity.—**para combustível,** fuel
capacity.—**gerencial,** management ability. **de grande—,**
roomy, capacious.
capacitância (*f., Elec.*) capacitance.
capacitar (*v.t.*) to convince, persuade (**-se,** oneself).
capacitor [ô] (*m., Elec.*) capacitor, condenser.
capadete [dê] (*m.*) castrated young pig.
capadinho (*m.*) booklet. [*Pejorative*]
capado -**da** (*adj.*) castrated; (*m.*) a castrated ram, goat
or boar, esp. the latter.
capadócio (*m.*) rogue, impostor [= CAFAJESTE].
capador (*m.*) professional castrator, gelder.
capadura (*f.*) castration, gelding.
capa-homem (*m.*) a savannaflower (*Echites peltata*), c.a.
JOÃO-DA-COSTA, PAINA-DE-PENAS, CIPÓ-CAPADOR, ERVA-
SANTA; a dutchmanspipe (*Aristolochia cymbifera*); also
= ANGELICÓ, CIPÓ-CABOCLO, CIPÓ-MATA-COBRAS.
capanema (*f.*) a formicide.
capanga (*m.*) thug, ruffian; hoodlum; bully; hired assassin;
henchman; bodyguard; (*f.*) knapsack, money bag.
capangada (*f.*) band of CAPANGAS.
capangueiro (*m.*) diamond buyer.
capão (*m.*) capon; gelding; an isolated clump of trees in
an open plain; coppice, c.a. CAPUÃO (DE MATO); also
= PEIXE-GALO.
capar (*v.t.*) to castrate; to geld, spay; to prune. Cf.
CASTRAR.
caparidáceo -**cea, caparídeo** -**dea** (*adj., Bot.*) cappari-
daceous; (*f.pl.*) the caper family (*Capparidaceae*).
caparrosa (*f., Chem.*) any of various sulfates; (*Bot.*) an

evening primrose (*Oenothera mollissima*), c.a. MINUANA,
ERVA-MINUANA; also, a seedbox (*Ludwigia caparosa*).—
azul, bluestone (copper sulfate).—**branca,** zinc sulfate.—
do rosto, (*Med.*) acne rosacea.—**verde,** copperas (iron
sulfate).
capataz (*m.*) foreman, overseer.
capatazar (*v.t.*) to oversee.
capatazia (*f.*) foremanship; gang of workmen under a
foreman; wharfage.
capaz (*adj.*) capable, able.—**de,** capable of; able to; likely
to.
capcioso -**sa** (*adj.*) captious, insidious; specious; deceitful.
capeamento (*m., Arch.*) coping, crowning.
capear (*v.t.*) to cover, hide (com, with); to illude, deceive.
capeba (*f.*) a tropical American herb (*Pothomorphe
peltata*), of the pepper family, with aromatic medicinal
roots and oil-bearing, anise-scented fruits; c.a. PARI-
PAROBA; à pareira vine (*Cissampelos glaberrima*), of the
moonseed family, c.a. CIPÓ-DE-COBRA; (*m., colloq.*) friend,
pal, partner.
capeia (*f.*) coping stone.
capela (*f.*) chapel; altar; choir; funeral wreath; small
variety store.—**ardente,** mourning chamber.—**de-viúva,**
(*Bot.*) any of various species of climbing petrea, esp. *P.
volubilis,* the purple-wreath; other common names are:
FLOR-DE-VIÚVA, TOUCA-DE-VIÚVA, VIUVINHA, COROA-DE-
VIÚVA, GRINALDA-DE-VIÚVA, CIPÓ-AZUL.—**do ôlho,** eyelid.—**mor,** main altar, chancel.
capelão [-lães] (*m.*) chaplain; leader of a band of monkeys.
capelo [ê] (*m.*) monk's hood; coif; cardinal's hat; doctor's
cap; chimney pot or hood; cowl.
capenga (*adj.*) lame, crippled, halt; (*m.,f.*) a cripple.
capengar (*v.i.*) to limp, hobble.
capepena (*f.*) "A trail blazed through the forest by breaking off small branches by hand so as to leave trailmarks
to direct the returning hunters." [*GBAT*]
capericoba (*f., Bot.*) a goosefoot (*Chenopodium hircinum*).
—**branca** = QUINOA.
capeta [ê] (*m.*) imp.
capeticova (*f.*) = CAPITIÇOVA.
capetinha (*m.,f.*) little imp (mischievous child).
cap.frag. = CAPITÃO-DE-FRAGATA (Navy Commander).
capiau (*m.*) = CAIPIRA. [*fem* **capioa**]
capilar (*adj.*) capillary; hairlike; (*m.*) capillary tube or
vessel; (*Anat.*) capillary.
capilária (*f.*) maidenhair fern.—**do-canadá,** the American
maidenhair (*Adiantum pedatum*).—**do-méxico,** the fan
maidenhair (*A. tenerum*).
capilaridade (*f.*) capillarity.
capilé (*m.*) capillaire (a sweet syrup for mixing with
drinks).
capilício (*m., Bot.*) capillitium.
capiliforme (*adj.*) capilliform, hairlike.
capim (*m.*) grass, forage, hay, pasture; any of numerous
grasses, both wild and cultivated, whose vernacular
names more often than not apply to more than one
species of the same or different genus, and of which the
following is only a partial list.—**açu,** a bluestem
(*Andropogon*), c.a. CAPIM-COMPRIDO, CAPIM-DOIDO.—
-açu-da-bahia, the Bahia lovegrass (*Eragrostis bahiensis*).
—**agreste,** a flatsedge (*Cyperus diffusus*); also = CAPIM-
SAPÉ.—**alpiste,** canary grass (*Phalaris canariensis*).—
amarelo, the reed canary grass (*Phalaris arundinacea*),
c.a. ALPISTE-DOS-PRADOS.—**amargoso,** a balmscale
grass (*Elyonurus candidus*), c.a. CAPIM-LIMÃO, CAPIM-
MANGA, BARBA-DE-BODE; a dropseed grass (*Sporobolus
asperifolius*); also = CAPIM-CHEIROSO.—**amonjeaba,** a
cupscale grass (*Sacciolepis myuros*), c.a. AMONJEABA.—
amoroso, the dune sandbur (*Cenchrus tribuloides*).
—**andacaá,** a panic grass (*Panicum tricanthum*), c.a.
ANDACAÁ, CAPIM-MIMOSO, CAPIM-VINDECAÁ.—**andrequicé** = ANDREQUICÉ, ARROZ-BRAVO, CANA-DE-PASSARI-
NHO.—**apé,** West Indies bristlegrass (*Setaria setosa*).
—**azul,** a sedge (*Lagenocarpus velutinus*).—**balsa,** a
paspalum grass (*P. riparium*).—**bambu,** a leafstalk
grass (*Pharus glaber*), c.a. ARROZ-DE-CACHORRO, ES-
PARTO-DA-TERRA; an olyra grass (*O. floribunda*); a
senna shrub (*Cassia langsdorffii*). c.a. SENA.—**barba-
de-bode,** a flatsedge (*Cyperus compressus*); a dropseed
grass (*Sporobolus sprengelii*).—
-bobó, the pinhole bluestem grass (*Andropogon per-
foratus*); the silver bluestem (*Andropogon saccharoides*).
—**branco,** the manyspiked chloris (*C. polydactyla*);
the mourning lovegrass (*Eragrostis lugens*).—**cabaiu,**
the tropical carpetgrass (*Axonopus compressus*), c.a.

CAPIM-NÓ.—**camalote** (or **-dos-camalotes**), an itchgrass (*Rottboellia compressa*).—**canudinho**, a panic grass (*Panicum fistulosum*), c.a. CAPIM-DA-PRAIA.—**catingueiro**, a panic grass (*Panicum monstachyum*); also = CAPIM-GORDURA.—**cauda-de-rapôsa**, the meadow foxtail (*Alopecurus pratensis*), c.a. CAUDA-DE-RAPÔSA, RABO-DE-RAPÔSA.—**cebola**, the weeping chloris (*C. distichophylla*), c.a. CAPIM-BATATAL, CAPIM-COROROBÓ.—**cevadinha**, the smooth brome (*Bromus inermis*); the soft brome (*B. mollis*); the poverty brome (*B. sterilis*).—**cheiroso**, a bluestem (*Andropogon glaziovia*), c.a. CAPIM-AMARGOSO; a sedge (*Kyllinga brevifolia*); also = CAPIM-DE-CHEIRO, CAPIM-LIMÃO.—**cheiroso-da-índia**, the Iwarancusa grass (*Cymbopogon jawarancusa*).—**chorão**, the weeping lovegrass (*Eragrostis curvula*).—**cola-de-lagarto**, an itchgrass (*Rottboellia selloana*).—**colchão**, the brownseed paspalum (*P. plicatum*), c.a. CAPIM-COQUEIRINHO, CAPIM-MEMBECA.—**cololó**, India lovegrass (*Eragrostis pilosa*).—**comprido**, dallisgrass paspalum (*Paspalum dilatum*), c.a. GRAMA-COMPRIDA, MIUM.—**cortante**, a flatsedge (*Cyperus radiatus*).—**da-areia**, the sprawling panicum (*P. reptans*).—**da-colônia**, a paspalum grass (*P. densum*), c.a. MILHÃ-DA-COLÔNIA; the junglerice (*Echinochloa colonum*).—**da-praia**, the bentspike pennisetum (*P. nervosum*), c.a. GRAMA-DA-PRAIA.—**de-angola**, a cockspur grass (*Echinochloa polystachya*), c.a. CAPIM-DE-PERNAMBUCO, CAPIM-DE-FEIXE, CAPIM-NAVALHA, CANARANA-VERDADEIRA.—**de-bezerro**, a basketgrass (*Oplismenus compositus*), c.a. TAQUARI-DO-MATO.—**de-bota**, a beakrush (*Rhynccspora cephalotes*), c.a. PIRI.—**de-bucha**, the rough sprangletop (*Leptochloa scabra*).—**de-burro**, Bermuda grass (*Cynodon dactylon*), c.a. CAPIM-DA-CIDADE, CAPIM-SÊDA, GRAMA-COMUM, GRAMÃO, GRAMINHA-COMUM, ERVA-DAS-BERMUDAS, MATAI-ME-EMBORA, PÉ-DE-GALINHA.—**de-cabra**, the hooked bristlegrass (*Setaria verticillata*), c.a. CAPIM-GRAMA, MILHÃ, CAPITINGA.—**de-cheiro**, a sedge (*Kyllinga odorata*), c.a. CAPIM-BARATA, CAPIM-CHEIROSO, CAPIM-CIDREIRA, JAÇAPÉ; citronella grass (*Cymbopogon nardus*).—**de-esteira**, a bulrush (*Scirpus riparius*), c.a. ESTEIRA, ERVA-DE-ESTEIRA, PERI.—**de-flecha**, Uruguay needlegrass (*Stipa neesiana*).—**de-fogo**, the whirled dropseed (*Sporobolus pyramidatus*).—**de-fôlha-comprida**, a threeawn grass (*Aristida longifolia*).—**de-nossa-senhora**, the Job's-tears grass (*Coix lacrymajobi*), c.a. CAPIM-DE-CONTAS, CAPIM-MIÇANGA, CAPIM-ROSARIO, CONTAS-DE-NOSSA-SENHORA, LÁGRIMAS-DE-JÓ.—**de-raiz**, the showy chloris (*C. virgata*), c.a. MIMOSO-DE-CACHO, PÉ-DE-GALINHA.—**de-rodes**, Rhodes grass (*Chloris gayana*).—**de-rôla**, gophertail lovegrass (*Eragrostis ciliaris*), c.a. CAPIM-DE-BOSTA-DE-RÔLA.—**de-são-carlos**, the coconut paspalum (*P. laxum*), c.a. GRAMA-LARGA, GRAMA-DE-SÃO-CARLOS.—**de-venezuela**, the Mexican teosinte (*Euchlaena mexicana*), c.a. TEOSINTO-DE-GUATEMALA.—**do-campo**, Kentucky bluegrass (*Poa pratensis*), c.a. ERVA-DE-FEBRA.—**doce**, a canary grass (*Phalaris aquatica*), c.a. GRAMINHA-DOCE.—**do-colorado**, Texas panicum (*P. texanum*), c.a. CAPIM-DO-TEXAS.—**do-pará**, Pará grass (*Panicum purpurascens*), c.a. CAPIM-DA-COLÔNIA, CAPIM-DE-CORTE, CAPIM-FINO.—**do-prado**, meadow fescue (*Festuca elatior*).—**dos-pampas**, Selloa pampasgrass (*Cortaderia selloana*), c.a. CANA-DOS-PAMPAS, PALHA-DE-PENACHO, PENACHO-BRANCO, PLUMA-DE-CAPIM.—**do-sudão**, Sudan grass (*Sorghum vulgare sudanense*), c.a. ERVA-ELEFANTE.—**elefante**, Napier grass (*Pennisetum purpureum*), c.a. ERVA-ELEFANTE.—**elimo**, European dune wildrye (*Elymus arenarius*).—**espartilho**, a spikesedge (*Eleocharis capillacea*).—**estrêla**, a whitetop-sedge (*Dichromena ciliata*).—**flechinha**, a sprangletop (*Leptochloa mucronata*).—**gigante**, Eastern gamagrass (*Tripsacum dactyloides*).—**gomoso**, the creeping dayflower (*Commelina nudiflora*), c.a. GRAMA-DA-TERRA, MARIA-MOLE, MÀRIANINHA, TRAPOERABA-AZUL, TRAPOERABA-RANA.—**gordo**, sour paspalum (*P. conjugatum*), c.a. CAPIM-DE-MARRECA; also = CANA-DE-PASSARINHO, CAPIM-GORDURA.—**gordura**, Guinea grass (*Panicum maximum*), c.a. CAPIM-DE-CORTE, CAPIM-DE-FEIXE, CAPIM-MELADINHO, GRAMA-DA-GUINÉ, GUINÉ-LEGITIMO, ERVA-DA-GUINÉ, MILHÃ-DO-SERTÃO, MURUBU, PAINÇO-GRANDE, etc.—**japonês**, Morrow's sedge (*Carex morrowi*).—**jaraguá**, jaragua grass (*Hyparrhenia rufa*), c.a. CAPIM-PROVISÓRIO, CAPIM-VERMELHO, SAPÉ-GIGANTE.—**lanceta**, a skeleton grass (*Gymnopogon spicatus*), c.a. TAQUARI-NHA.—**lanudo**, common velvet grass (*Holcus lanatus*).

—**limão**, lemongrass (*Cymbopogon citratus*), c.a. CAPIM-CATINGA, CAPIM-CHEIROSO, CAPIM-CIDREIRA, CAPIM-DE-CHEIRO.—**maçambará**, Johnson grass (*Sorghum halepense*), c.a. CAPIM-AVEIA, CAPIM-CEVADA, CAPIM-DA-GUINÉ, CAPIM-DE-CUBA, CAPIM-DO-EGITO, CAPIM-MEXICANO, MILHO-BRAVO, SORGO-DE-ALEPO, PERIPOMONGA.—**marajó**, talquezal grass (*Paspalum virgatum*), c.a. TARIPICU-GRANDE.—**marmelada**, a signal grass (*Brachiaria plantaginea*), c.a. GRAMA-PAULISTA, MILHÃ-BRANCA.—**membeca**, yellowsedge bluestem (*Andropogon virginicus*), c.a. BARBA-DE-VELHO.—**milhã**, any of several paspalum grasses.—**milhã-roxo**, the browntop panicum (*P. fasciculatum*); the ribbed paspalum (*P. malacophyllum*).—**mimoso**, any of various grasses, esp. India lovegrass (*Eragrostis pilosa*); a skeleton grass (*Gymnopogon mollis*); a pitscale grass (*Hackelochloa granularis*).—**mimoso-do-agreste**, the slender fingergrass (*Digitaria filiformis*).—**mourão**, the West Indies smutgrass (*Sporobolus indicus*).—**naxenim**, the threespike goosegrass (*Eleusine tristachya*), c.a. CAPIM-PÉ-DE-PAPAGAIO, FENO-DOS-PERSAS.—**palmeira**, a panic grass (*Panicum sulcatum*), c.a. CAPIM-COQUEIRINHO, CAPIM-JERIVÁ, CAPIM-LEQUE, RABO-DE-RAPÔSA.—**panasco**, creeping bentgrass (*Paspalum distichum*), c.a. GRAMA-DOCE, PANACUÃ.—**paratará**, smooth cordgrass (*Spartina alterniflora*), c.a. CAPIM-DA-PRAIA, CAPIM-MARINHO.—**pé-de-galinha**, goosegrass (*Eleusine indica*), c.a. CAPIM-DA-CIDADE, GRAMA-DE-CORADOURO, PÉ-DE-PAPAGAIO; a panic grass (*Panicum sanguinale*), c.a. CAPIM-DA-ROÇA-VERDADEIRO, CEVADINHA-MIÚDA; annual bluegrass (*Poa annua*), c.a. PÉ-DE-GALINHA; orchard grass (*Dactylis glomerata*), c.a. CAPIM-DE-POMAR, PANASCO; a skeleton grass (*Gymnopogon radiatus*), c.a. FLOR-DE-GRAMA, GRAMINHA-DE-CAMPINAS; the red sprangletop (*Leptochloa filiformis*), c.a. CAPIM-MIMOSO; barnyard grass (*Echinochloa crusgalli*), c.a. CAPIM-DE-CAPIVARA, MILHÃ-MAIOR.—**peguento**, a sticky panic grass (*Panicum glutinosum*), c.a. GRAMINHA-DO-MATO; also = CANA-DE-PASSARINHO.—**piqui**, a whitetop sedge (*Dichromena repens*), c.a. PORORÓ, sourgrass (*Trichachne insularis*), c.a. MILHETE-GIGANTE.—**puba**, a bluestem (*Andropogon bicornis*), c.a. CAPIM-MOLE, CAPIM-DE-VASSOURA, CAPUPUBA, RABO-DE-RAPÔSA, SAPÉ, SUCAPÉ.—**puma**, silver bluestem (*Andropogon saccharoides*).—**rabo-de-boi** or —**rabo-de-burro**, a plumegrass (*Erianthus asper*): a bluestem (*Andropogon condensatus*), c.a. BARBA-DE-BODE, CAUDA-DE-RAPÔSA, RABO-DE-GUARAXAIM.—**rabo-de-cachorro**, a polypogon grass (*P. elongatus*), c.a. RABO-DE-CACHORRO.—**rabo-de-mucura**, West Indies pennisetum (*P. setosum*), c.a. TAQUARI-DE-CAVALO.—**rabo-de-rapôsa**, knotroot bristlegrass (*Setaria geniculata*), c.a. BAMBUZINHO, ESPARTILHO, ESPARTO-PEQUENO, PANASCO-DO-TABULEIRO; another bristlegrass (*Setaria scandens*), c.a. CAPIM-RABO-DE-RATO; the rabbitfoot polypogon (*P. monspeliensis*), c.a. RABO-DE-ZORRA-MACIO.—**rabo-de-rato**, timothy grass (*Phleum pratense*), c.a. PASTO-NATURAL, RABO-DE-GATO; also = CAPIM-MOURÃO, CAPIM-RABO-DE-RAPÔSA.—**relvão**, Teff grass (*Eragrostis abyssinica*), c.a. RELVÃO-DA-ABISSÍNIA.—**roseta**, any of various sandburs (*Cenchrus*), esp. the dune sandbur (*C. tribuloides*), c.a. CAPIM-DA-PRAIA, CARRAPICHO; also the big sandbur (*C. myosuroides*).—**salgado**, either of two cordgrasses: *Spartina ciliata* or *S. glabra*.—**sapé**, Brazil satintail (*Imperata brasiliensis*), c.a. AGRESTE, MASSAPÊ, JUÇAPÉ, SAPÉ.—**sempre-verde**, wood bluegrass (*Poa nemoralis*).—**setária**, knucklegrass or fall panicum (*P. dichotomiflorum*).—**trapoeraba**, a panic grass (*Panicum gladiatum*).—**trigo**, a quaking grass (*Briza calotheca*).—**turipucu**, talquezal grass (*Paspalum virgatum*).—**uamã**, Brazilian luziola (*L. bahiensis*).—**vassoura**, a saltgrass (*Distichlis scoparia*).—**verde**, the green bristlegrass (*Setaria viridis*), c.a. MILHÃ-VERDE, RABO-DE-RAPÔSA.—**vetiver**, the khuskhus vetiver (*Vetiveria zizanioides*), c.a. CAPIM-DE-CHEIRO, CAPIM-CHEIROSO, VETIVER.

capimpeba (*f.*) a vetiver grass (*Veteveria bicorne*).

capina, capinação (*f.*) weeding, hoeing [= CARPA, CARPIÇÃO]; a rebuke.

capinadeira (*f.*) weeding machine [= CARPIDEIRA].

capinador, capineiro (*m.*) hoer, weeder [= CARPIDOR].

capinar (*v.t.*) to weed, hoe [= CARPIR]; (*slang*) to speed.

capioa, fem. of CAPIAU.

capinzal (*m.*) pasture land; hay field.

capiscaba-mirim (*f.*, *Bot.*) a flatsedge (*Cyperus graci-*

lescens), c.a. JUNÇA-MIÚDA, JUNÇA-PEQUENA, JUNCO-MIÚDO, TIRIRICA.
capiscar (*v.t.*, *colloq.*) to catch on, understand.
capitação (*f.*) head tax; per capita tax.
capital (*adj.*) capital, head, chief, principal, leading, essential; (*m.*) capital; funds; stock; (*f.*) capital city; capital letter.—**circulante**, working capital; revolving fund.—**empatado**, frozen capital.—**fixo**, capital invested in fixed assets such as lands, buildings, etc.—**invertido**, or **investido**, invested capital.—**morto**, idle capital.—**privado**, private capital. **pena—**, capital punishment.
capitalismo (*m.*) capitalism.
capitalista (*m.*,*f.*) capitalist.
capitalização (*f.*) capitalization.
capitalizar (*v.t.*) to capitalize.
capitanear (*v.t.*,*v.i.*) to command, rule, govern; to head.
capitânia (*f.*) capital ship; flagship.
capitania (*f.*) captaincy; in colonial Brazil, a jurisdictional division corresponding to a province.—**do pôrto**, port captain; port authority.
capitão [-tães] (*m.*) captain, commander, chief; skipper, master. [In the Brazilian Navy,—**-de-mar-e-guerra** corresponds to Captain in the U. S. Navy;—**-de-fragata**= Commander;—**-de-corveta** = Lieutenant-Commander; —**-tenente**=Lieutenant.]; (*Zool.*) the scarlet-headed blackbird (*Amblyrhamphus holosericeus*), c.a. SOLDADO.—-chico, a breed of Brazilian hogs.—**-das-porcarias**, a small ovenbird (*Lochnias nematura*), common in southern Brazil and c.a. PRESIDENTE-DAS-PORCARIAS. [It derives its name from its habit of scavenging in filth for maggots.].—**-de-bigode**, any of various barbets or puffbirds [= DORMIÃO], whose bills are beset with bristles at the base (whence the name), esp. the black-spotted barbet (*Capito niger*).—**-de-pernambuco**, (*Bot.*) a pennywort (*Hydrocotyle pernambucensis*).—**-de-saíra**, a tyrant flycatcher (*Attila rufus*); also, an olive-green tanager (*Orthogonys chlorícterus*).—**-de-sala**, the blood-flower milkweed (*Asclepias curassavica*), c.a. ALGODÃOZINHO-DO-CAMPO, CAMARÁ-BRAVO, CAVALHEIRO-DA-SALA, CEGA-OLHOS, DONA-JOANA, FLOR-DE-SAPO, ERVA-DE-PAINA, MANÉ-MOLE, MARGARIDINHA, MATA-ÔLHO, OFICIAL-DA-SALA, PAINA-DE-SAPO, PAINA-DE-SÊDA.—**-do-mato**, in early times in Brazil, the leader of a band of men organized in each settlement to fight off attacks by the Indians; also, a man charged with catching runaway slaves; (*Zool.*) a trogon (*T. strigilatus*); a magnificent nymphalid butterfly (*Morpho achillaena*); a puffbird (*Bucco swainsoni*), c.a. JOÃO-BOBO; a cucurbitaceous plant (*Cayaponia glabosa*,), c.a. ANA-PINTA,'PURGA-DE-CABOCLO, PURGA-DE-CAIAPÓ, PURGA-DE-GENTIO; also, a lippia (*L. pseudothea*), c.a. CAMARÁ, CHÁ-DE-FRADE, CHÁ-DE-PEDESTRE, CIDRI-LHA.—**-do-pôrto**, port captain; harbor master.—**mercante**, captain of a merchant ship.—**-mor**, military officer who formerly commanded the local militia.
capitari [rí] (*m.*) a male turtle;= ZÉ-PREGOS.
capitel [-téis] (*m.*) fuze cap; head of a still ; (*Arch.*) capital (of a column).
capitiçoba, **-va** (*f.*) the bitter smartweed (*Polygonum acre*), c.a. ACATAIA, CAATAIÁ, CAPETIÇOBA, ERVA-DE-BICHO, PERSICÁRIA-DO-BRASIL.
capitinga (*f.*) = CAPIM-DE-CABRA.
capitiú (*m.*) = CARDAMOMO-DA-TERRA.
capitoa (*f.*) a woman captain.
capitólio (*m.*) glory, splendor; capitol.
capitoso **-sa** (*adj.*) headstrong; of wine, heady.
capitulação (*f.*) capitulation, surrender.
capitular (*v.i.*) to capitulate, surrender; (*adj.*, *Eccles.*) capitular, capitulary; (*f.*, *Print.*) display type face.
capítulo (*m.*) chapter; part, section (of a treatise, contract, etc.); (*Eccles.*) chapter; (*Bot.*) capitulum. **ter voz no—**, to have a voice in the matter.
capituva (*f.*, *Bot.*) a beakrush (*Rhynchospora aurea*).
capiuna (*f.*) = CORCOROCA.
capivara (*f.*) the capybara, carpincho or water cavy (*Hydrochoerus capybara*). [It is the largest living rodent, weighing about 100 pounds, and resembles a huge guinea pig, to which it is related. It has partly webbed feet, no tail, and rough coarse hair. It abounds in the rivers of Brazil, living generally in small colonies in the heavy vegetation on the banks. It is inoffensive and easily tamed. The flesh, though edible, is not much sought after, but the skin is used by saddlers.]; (*Bot.*) a dutchman's-pipe (*Aristolochia birostris*).
capixaba, **-va** (*adj.*; *m.*,*f.*) a nickname applied to the na-

tives of the State of Espírito Santo, and especially of its capital, Vitória.
cap.m.g. = CAPITÃO-DE-MAR-E-GUERRA (Navy captain).
capô (*m.*) hood, cowling (of a motor). [French *capot*.]
capoeira (*f.*) large cage or coop for domestic fowls or animals; hencoop; cut-over land; land covered by second growth; (*Zool.*) the capueira partridge (*Odontophorus capueira*), c.a. URU, CORCOVADO; a system of bodily assault practiced by ruffians in Brazil; (*m.*) a ruffian adept in this method of fighting; a highwayman, bandit.
—**branca**=COUVETINGA.
capoeiragem (*f.*) ruffianism, the CAPOEIRA system of fighting.
capoeiro (*m.*) chicken thief; (*Zool.*)=CATINGUEIRO (a deer).
capolim (*m.*) the capulin black cherry (*Prunus serotina salicifolia*).
caporal (*m.*) corporal. **fumo—**, a kind of strong, coarse tobacco.
capororoca (*f.*) the coscoroba swan (*Coscoroba coscoroba*). [Actually, not a true swan (*Cyginae*), but a shoal-water duck (*Anatinae*).]; (*Bot.*) any of various species of Rapanea.—**-picante** = CASA-DE-ANTA.
capororoquinha (*f.*, *Bot.*) any of various species of Ardisia.
capota (*f.*) bonnet; top of an automobile.—**de motor**, motor cowling.
capotagem (*f.*) capsizing; upset; ground loop (of an airplane).
capotar (*v.i.*) to capsize, overturn; to turn turtle.
capote (*m.*) overcoat, cape, cloak; also=GALINHA-D'ANGOLA (guinea hen).
capoteira (*f.*) cardboard file for papers.
capoteiro (*m.*) one who makes, sells, or repairs auto tops.
capotilho (*m.*) little cape.
capoxo (*m.*), **-xa** (*f.*) an Indian of the Caposhó, a tribe of the Maxacali in the State of Minas Gerais; (*adj.*) pert. to or designating this tribe.
caprato (*m.*, *Chem.*) caprate.
cápreo **-prea** (*adj.*)=CAPRINO.
capribarbudo **-da** (*adj.*) goat-bearded.
caprichar (*v.i.*) to take pride in (doing something).
capricho (*m.*) caprice, whim, vagary, fancy; craze, crotchet, oddity.—**da natureza**, a freak of nature. **a—**, meticulously. **ao—de**, at the whim of. **cheio de—s**, full of whims, capricious, fickle.
caprichoso **-sa** (*adj.*) capricious, whimsical, freakish, fickle; flighty; petulant; painstaking.
cáprico **-ca** (*adj.*, *Chem.*) **ácido—**, capric acid.
capricórnio (*m.*, *Astron.*) Capricorn; a capricorn beetle.
caprídeo **-dea** (*adj.*) caprid.
caprificar (*v.t.*) to caprificate (Smyrna figs).
caprifoliáceas (*f.pl.*) the Caprifoliaceae (honeysuckle family).
caprino **-na** (*adj.*) caprine, capric; of or like a goat.
caprizante (*adj.*) leaping—said of the pulse.
capróico **-ca** (*adj.*, *Chem.*) caproic, hexylic.
caprum (*adj.*)=CAPRINO.
capsela (*f.*) a small capsule; (*Bot.*) shepherdspurse (*Capsella bursa-pastoris*).
cápsico (*m.*, *Pharm.*) capsicum; (*Bot.*) the genus (*Capsicum*) of red peppers.
cápsula (*f.*) capsule; pod; fuze cap; cartridge shell; (*Chem.*) capsule.—**de algodão**, cotton boll.—**suprarrenal**, adrenal gland.—**espacial**, space capsule.
capsular (*adj.*) capsular.
capsulífero **-ra** (*adj.*) capsuliferous.
capsulite (*f.*, *Med.*) capsulitis.
captação (*f.*) captivation; impounding (of water).
captar (*v.t.*) to captivate, enthrall, hold spellbound; to impound (water).—**uma emissão**, to pick up a radio broadcast.
cap-ten. = CAPITÃO-TENENTE (Navy Lieutenant).
captor (-es) [ô] (*m.*), **-tora** [ô] (*f.*) capturer.
captura (*f.*) capture; apprehension.
capturador (*m.*), **-dora** (*f.*) capturer
capturar (*v.t.*) to capture, seize, arrest.
capuaba (*f.*) thatched hut; (*m.*) backwoodsman.
capuão (*m.*)=CAPÃO.
capucha (*f.*) hood, bonnet. **à—**, unpretentiously.
capuchinha (*f.*, *Bot.*) the five-finger nasturtium (*Tropaeolum pentaphyllum*) c.a. CHAGAS-DA-MIÚDA, CHAGAS-MIÚDAS, SAPATINHOS-DE-IAIA, SAPATINHOS-DO-DIABO; the shield nasturtium (*T. peltophorum*) c.a. CAPUCHINHO, CHAGAS.—**-de-três-côres**, the cornucopia nasturtium

(*T. tricolor*).—-do-Brasil, a Braz. nasturtium (*T. brasiliense*), c.a. CHAGAS-VERDES, CINCO-CHAGAS, CIPÓ-DE-CHAGAS, CIPÓ-DE-CINCO-FÔLHAS, FLOR-DE-CHAGAS.—-grande, the common nasturtium (*T. majus*), c.a. AGRIÃO-DO-MÉXICO, CHAGAS, COCLEÁRIA-DOS-JARDINS, FLOR-DE-SANGUE, MASTRUÇO-DO-PERU.—-pequena, the bush nasturtium (*T. minus*).—-tuberosa, the tuber nasturtium (*T. tuberosum*).—-viajante, the canary nasturtium (*T. peregrinum*).

capuchinho (*m.*) a small hood; a Capuchin monk; (*Bot.*) = CAPUCHINHA, CAPUCHINHA-VIAJANTE.

capucho (*m.*) black cotton seed.

capuco (*m.*) corncob.

capulho (*m., Bot.*) cupule, involucre; cotton boll.

capupuba (*m.*) = CAPIM-PUBA.

capuxu [xú] (*m.*) a social wasp (*Myschocyttarus ater.*)

capuz (*m.*) hood, bonnet, cowl.—-de-fradinho, (*Bot.*) common jack-in-the-pulpit (*Arisaema atrorubens*), c.a. CANDEIAS.

caquera (*f.*) a medicinal senna (*Cassia bicapsularis*), c.a. CARRUÍRA, DORMIDEIRA, FEDEGOSO, MATA-PASTO, PAU-DE-CACHIMBO, TAREOQUI.

caquético –ca (*adj.*) cachexic, in poor health. Var. CAQUÉCTICO.

caquexia [ks] (*f., Med.*) cachexia.

caqui [í] (*m.*) persimmon (fruit of the CAQUIZEIRO).

cáqui (*m.*) khaki; (*adj.*) khaki-colored.

caquibosa (*f., Bot.*) the cadillo (*Urena Lobata*).

caquidrose (*f.*) offensive perspiration.

caquizeiro (*m.*) the kaki (Japanese) persimmon tree (*Diospyros kaki*).

cara (*f.*) face, countenance; (*sl.*) mug; look, expression; boldness, brass; (*m.,sl.*) unfamiliar face; fellow, guy.—a —, face to face.—-branca, white-faced Hereford cattle, c.a. PAMPA.—-chupada, a drawn look or face.—-de-abobora, blockhead, dunce.—-de-anjinho, angel face.—-de-boneca, doll face.—-de-fome, a starved look.—-de-fuinha, (*colloq.*) a stingy person.—-de-herege, unpleasant face.—-de-juiz, stern face or look.—-de-mamão-macho, (*colloq.*) long, drawn face.—-de-nó-cego, (*colloq.*) disagreeable person.—-de-páscoa, smiling face.—-de-pau, wooden-faced person; deadpan.—-de-reu, scowling face.—-deslavada, or -estanhada, brazen-faced.—-fechada, cross look.—-inchada, (*Veter.*) bighead, osteoporosis.—-lisa, cynic.—-negra, black-faced cattle or sheep.—-ou coroa, heads or tails.—-suja, dirty face; also a kind of small parrot. **dar de—com,** to come face to face with, bump into. **de—fechada,** of forbidding look, unsmiling, scowling. **deixar alguém com—de besta,** (*slang*) to leave someone in the lurch, stand him up. **dar com a porta na—de alguém,** to slam the door in someone's face. **fazer—de dó,** to put on a pained expression. **fechar a—,** to frown, scowl. **ficar com a—no chão,** to be embarrassed to death. **meter a—,** (*slang*) to take the bull by the horns. **ter—de poucos amigos,** to have an evil look. **tirar—ou coroa,** to flip heads or tails.

cará (*m., Bot.*) kinds of yam (*Dioscorea spp.*).—-de-caboclo, a salsilla (*Bomarea salsilloides*) with edible tubers. —-inhame, —-branco, —-cultivado, —-da-guiné, —-de-angola, are all the winged yam (*Dioscorea alata*), c.a. INHAME-BRAVO, INHAME-DA-CHINA, INHAME-DA-ÍNDIA, INHAME-DE-CORIOLÁ.

carabina (*f.*) carbine, rifle.—-de ar comprimido, air rifle.—-de repetição, repeating rifle.

carabineiro (*m.*) rifleman.

cárabo (*m.*) a Carabus beetle.

caraca (*f.*) cork tissue; scab; dried nasal secretion.

caracará (*m., Zool.*) any caracara.—-prêto, the red-throated caracara (*Daptrius a. americanus*), c.a. CANCÃ, GRALHÃO.—-tinga, the chimachima caracara (*Milvago c. chimachima*), c.a. GAVIÃO-CARRAPATEIRO, CARAPINHÉ, GAVIÃO-PINHÉ, CARACARAÍ, CARACARÁ-BRANCO.

caracaraí (*m.*) = CARACARÁ-TINGA.

caracasana (*f.*) = CANSANÇÃO and URTIGA-BRAVA.

caracaxá (*m.*) = CANZÁ.

caracha (*f.*) a bamboo (*Chusquea jurgensii*).

caracínidas, caracinídeos (*m.pl.*) a family (*Characinidae*) of voracious fresh-water fishes, which includes the PIRANHA.

caracol [-cóis] (*m.*) caracole, spiral shell; any land snail; curl of hair; (*Bot.*) the corkscrew flower or snail bean (*Phaseolus caracalla*), c.a. CARACOLEIRO, TRIPA-DE-GALINHA. **caída de—,** tailspin (of an airplane). **escada de—,** spiral (winding) staircase. **Não vale um—,** It is not worth a tinker's dam (n).

caracolado –da (*adj.*) spiral; curled.

caracolar (*v.t.,v.i.*) to spiral; to twist and turn; to cork-screw; to curl; to twine.

caracoleiro (*m.*) = CARACOL (plant.)

carácter (*m.*) = CARÁTER.

caracteres (*m.pl.*) characters, graphic symbols; printing type; (*Bot., Zool.*) characters.

característico –ca (*adj.*) characteristic; (*f.*) trait; (*Math., Elec.*) characteristic.

caracterização (*f.*) characterization.

caracterizado –da (*adj.*) characterized; made-up (as an actor).

caracterizador –dora (*adj.*) characterizing; (*m.,f.*) character actor or actress).

caracterizante (*adj.*) characterizing.

caracterizar (*v.t.*) to characterize; to distinguish, mark; (*v.r.*) to dress and make-up (as an actor).

caracu [ú] (*m.*) a breed of native Brazilian cattle; bone marrow; (*colloq.*) "guts" (courage).

caradríidas [í-i] (*m.pl.*) the family of shore birds (*Charadriidae*) which includes the plovers, snipes and sandpipers.

caradura (*m.,f.*) a brazen-faced (brassy, cheeky) person; (*m.*) a second-class streetcar, or a front seat in a street-car, facing to the rear.

caradurismo (*m.*) effrontery; brazenness.

cafafuz, carafuzo = CAFUZ, CAFUZO.

caragana-arborescente (*f.*) the Siberian pea shrub (*Caragana asborescens*).

caraguatá (*m., Bot.*) any of various bromelias.—-acanga, the pinguin bromelia (*B. pinguin*), c.a. CURAUÁ, COROATÁ.—-falso, an eryngo (*Eryngium sp.*); c.a. COROATÁ-FALSO, GRAVATÁ-DO-CAMPO.

caraíba (*f., Bot.*) either of two cordias (*C. calocephala* and *C. insignis*), both c.a. GRÃO-DE-GALO; also = CAROBEIRA; (*m.,f.*) Carib Indian; (*adj.*) Cariban.

caraipé [a-i] (*m., Bot.*) any of various species of Licania.

carajá (*m.*) any howling monkey (*Alouatta*) of which the ursine howler of Brazil (*A. ursina*) is a well-known species; (*m.,f.*) an Indian of an independent linguistic family approaching extinction, who live in Goiás along the Araguaia River. Since pre-Columbian times they have held as the central portion of their territory the great inland island of Bananal, which is formed by a forking of the Araguaia river; (*adj.*) pert. to or designating the Carajá Indians.

carajuru [rú] (*m.*) a funnelvine (*Arrabidaea chica*), from whose leaves the Amazon Indians extract a red tattooing pigment, c.a. CHICA, CIPÓ-CRUZ, GUARAJURU(-PIRANGA); also, the pigment itself; the Brazilian alstroemeria (*A. brasiliensis*), c.a. CEBOLA.—-do-Pará, the Inca lily alstroemeria (*A. pelegrina*), c.a. LÍRIO-DOS-ÍNCAS.

caramanchão, caramanchel [-éis] (*m.*) arbor, bower, summer-house, pergola.

caramba! Good heavens! Dammit!

carambola (*f.*) in billiards, the red ball; a carom; a swindle; the fruit of the CARAMBOLEIRA.

carambolar (*v.t.*) to carambole, carom (in billiards); to trick, cheat.

caramboleiro –ra (*adj.*) deceiving, tricky; (*f.*) the carambola (*Averrhoa carambola*) sometimes called Chinese or coromandel gooseberry. It is widely cultivated in the tropics and yields an acid fruit called CARAMBOLA.—-amarela = BILIMBI (a tree).

carambolice (*f.*) trickery, deceit, fraud.

caramelo (*m.*) caramel candy; (*Bot.*) the balsam pear (*Momordica charantia*), c.a. BALSAMINA-LONGA.

caramemo (*m.*) a monkeypod tree (*Lecythis blanchetiana*).

cara-metade (*f., colloq.*) better half (wife).

carametara (*f.*) = PAPA-TERRA.

caraminguás (*m.pl.*) knickknacks; gewgaws; odds and ends; chicken feed (change).

caraminhola (*f.*) chignon (knot of hair); lie, trick.

caramujo (*m.*) any sea or fresh-water gastropod, esp. the periwinkles; a kind of cabbage; figurehead (on the bow of a vessel); (*fig.*), a clam (secretive person); an apple shell (*Ampullaria gigas*) considered a delicacy in Pará, where it is sold in straw-wrapped packages.—-cascudo, a chiton (coat-of-mail shell).—-do-banhado = ARUÁ (a snail).—-tijela, a limpet (*Acmaea subrugosa*).

caramuru [rú] (*m.*) the spotted moray (*Gymnothorax moringa*); also = PIRAMBÓIA (a fish).

caraná (*f.*) a palm (*Mauritia carana*), c.a. PALMEIRA-LEQUE-DO-RIO-NEGRO; also = CARANDAÍ, BURUTI-BRAVO, BURITIRANA, BURITIZINHO.—-branca, a resin tree

(*Protium altissimum*) which yields carana gum; c.a. CEDRO-BRANCO, PAU-ROSA-FÊMEA.—-**do-rio-negro**, a spiny clubpalm (*Bactris cuspidata*).

caranã (*f.*) = CARNAÚBA.

caranaí (*f.*) a palm (*Mauritia limnophila*); also = BURITIRANA, BURITIZINHO.—-**mirim** = buriti-mirim.

caranambu [bú] (*m.*) a yam (*Dioscorea trifoliata*), c.a. INHAME-NAMBU.

carananaí (*f.*) a palm (*Mauritia aculeata*).

carancho (*m., Zool.*) the southern caracara (*Caracara p. plancus*); (*colloq.*) a card-player standing around waiting for a chance to get in the game; a party-crasher.

caranda (*f.*) fruit of the CARANDEIRA.

carandá (*f.*) the caranda copernicia palm (*C. australis*), c.a. CARANDAÚ, CARANDÁ-UBA, COQUEIRO-CARANDÁ; also = CARANDAÍ. — -**guaçu** = BURITI. — -**muriti**, — -**piranga** = CARANDAÍ.

carandaí (*m.*) the Brazil trithrinax palm (*T. brasiliensis*), c.a. CARANÁ, CARANDÁ, CARANDÁ-MURITI, CARANDÁ-PIRANGA, CARANDÁ-UBA; also = BURITIRANA.—-**guaçu** = BURITI.

carandaizinho (*m.*) = CURITIZINHO.

carandaú (*f.*) = CARANDÁ.

carandaúba (*f.*) = CARANDÁ.

carandàzal (*m.*) a growth of CARANDÁ palms; high ground on which they grow and which is sought by cattle as a place of refuge from flood.

carandeira (*f.*) the karanda carissa hedgethorn (*Carissa carandas*).

carângidas, carangídeos, carangóides (*all m.pl.*) the *Carangidae* (pompanos, amberfishes, cavallas, etc.).

caranguda (*f., Bot.*) a caesalpinia (*C. acenaciformis*), c.a. CARRANCUDA.

carangueja [ê] (*f.*) mast for a large square sail; (*R.R.*) transfer table; also = CARANGUEJEIRA (plum) and CARANGUEJOLA (large crab).

caranguejal (*adj.*) crab.

caranguejar (*v.i., colloq.*) to sidle, move sideways (as a crab); to dawdle.

caranguejeira (*f.*) a large, hairy Braz. bird spider (*Avicularia avicularia*); a spiderlike person; (*Bot.*) a greengage plum, specif., the Reine Claude (= RAÍNHA CLÁUDIA).

caranguejeiro (*m.*) crabber.

caranguejo [ê] (*m.*) crab.—-**de-concha**, hermit crab.

cranguejola (*f.*) any large crab; any rickety framework, ramshackle building or unsteady pile; a rattletrap; a shaky enterprise.

caranha (*f.*) any of various snappers of genus Lutianus, esp. the gray snapper (*L. griseus*), c.a. CARANHA-DO-MANGUE (or -DE-VIVEIRO), CARANHO, CARANHOTA. Also = VERMELHO (red snapper).

caranho (*m.*) = CARANHA, CIOBA (-VERDADEIRA), CARANHO-VERDADEIRO, VERMELHO-HENRIQUE (all snappers).

caranhota (*f.*) = CARANHA.

carantonha (*f.*) ugly face; grimace.

carão (*m.*) large, ugly face; a bawling out (reprimand); (*Zool.*) the southern limpkin (*Aramus scolopaceus*), family Aramidae.

caraolho -lha [ô] (*adj.*) strabismic, cross-eyed [= VESGO].

carapaça (*f.*) carapace (of a turtle, crab, armadillo, etc.).

carapanã (*m.*) a large mosquito (*Culex quinquefasciatus*) which transmits filariasis.—-**ora**, an ichneumon fly.—-**pinima**, a mosquito (*Culex sp.*), c.a. PERERECA, MURIÇOCA, SOVELA.

carapanaúba (*f., Bot.*) a white quebracho (*Aspidosperma excelsum*), c.a. ARVORE-DE-MOSQUITO and SAPUPEMA.

caraparu [ú] (*m.*) a thalia (*T. geniculata*), sometimes confused with the Florida bananaleaf thalia (*T. divaricata*).

carapau (*m.*) = PALOMBETA, XIXARRO-CALABAR.—-**grande** = XIXARRO.

carapeba (*f., Zool.*) a mojarra (*Diapterus rhombeus*), c.a. ACARAPEBA.

carapela (*f.*) corn husk; scab (of a sore).

carapêta (*f.*) a small spinning top; a whirligig; a fib; knob; doorknob.

carapetão (*m.*) a whopper (big lie).

carapetar (*v.i.*) to tell whoppers.

carapeteiro -ra (*adj.*) given to telling whoppers; (*m.,f.*) a big liar.

carapiá (*f., Bot.*) a sida (*S. macrodon*); a torus herb (*Dorstenia multiforme*); (*Zool.*) = PEIXE-AGULHA (needlefish).

carapicu [ú] (*m.*) a malvaceous shrub (*Urena sinuata*), which furnishes a jute-like fiber; c.a. GUAXIMA-CÔR-DE-

ROSA, MALVAÍSCO-CÔR-DE-ROSA; (*Zool.*) the common mojarra or silver jenny (*Eucinostomus gula*).—-**açu**, a mojarra (*E. herengulus*), c.a. ESCRIVÃO, RISCADOR, CACUNDO.

carapina (*m., colloq.*) carpenter [= CARPINTEIRO].

carapinha (*f.*) kinky hair.

carapinhada (*f.*) a cold fruit drink, esp. one that is shaken until it is frothy.

carapinhé (*m.*) = CARACARÁ-TINGA.

carapirá (*f., Zool.*) a cormorant, c.a. CORMORÃO, TESOUREIRO.

carapitanga (*f.*) = MULATA, VERMELHO (fishes).

carapuça (*f.*) hood, stocking cap, knitted helmet; a liberty cap; calking mallet. **A Menina da—Vermelha**, Little Red Riding Hood. **fazer** (or **talhar**) **as—s**, to make cutting remarks. **Qual—**! Nothing of the kind!

caraputanga (*f.*) = VERMELHO (a fish).

carará (*m.*) = BIGUÁ, ANHINGA.

carássio (*m.*) goldfish [= PEIXE DOURADO].

caráter [pl. caracteres] (*m.*) character, quality, nature; moral qualities, personal traits; temperament; strong personality; mark, figure, sign, symbol; printing type. **em—oficioso**, of an informative or unauthorized nature; unofficial. Cf. CARACTERES.

caraterístico -ca (*adj.; f.*) = CARACTERÍSTICO.

caraterizar (*v.*) & derivs. = CARACTERIZAR & derivs.

caratinga (*m., Zool.*) a white-headed marmoset (*Hapale leucocephala*); a majorra (*Diapterus brasiliensis*, or possibly *D. plumieri*); (*Bot.*) kinds of yam (*Dioscorea spp.*).

carauá [a-u] (*m.*) = CARAGUATÁ-ACANGA, CAROÁ.

caraúba [a-u] (*f.*) = CAROBEIRA, CAROBA-DO-MATO.

caraubeira [a-u] (*f.*) = CAROBEIRA.

caraúna (*f.*) = GRAÚNA, GAROUPINHA.

caravana (*f.*) caravan.

caravaneiro (*m.*) caravaneer.

caravançarai, caravançará (*m.*) caravansary.

caravela (*f.*) caravel; (*Zool.*) the Portuguese Man-of-War (*Physalia arethusa*), c.a. FRAGATA-PORTUGUÊSA.

caraxixu [ú] (*m., Bot.*) black nightshade (*Solanum nigra*), c.a. ERVA-MOURA, ERVA-DE-BICHO, PIMENTA-DE-GALINHA.

caraxué (*m.*) the sabian thrush (*Turdus fumigatus*), c.a. SABIÁ-DE-CAPOEIRA; (*colloq.*) a pimp.

carbamato (*m., Chem.*) carbamate.

carbâmico -ca (*adj., Chem.*) carbamic.

carbamida (*f., Chem.*) carbamid(e), urea.

cárbaso (*m.*) carbasus (surgical gauze).

carbazol (*m., Chem.*) carbazole.

carbilamina (*f., Chem.*) carbylamine; isocyanide; isonitrile.

carbimida (*f., Chem.*) carbimide, isocyanic acid.

carbinol (*m., Chem.*) carbinol, methanol.

carbite (*m., Chem.*) carbide [= CARBONÊTO DE CÁLCIO].

carbodiamida (*f., Chem.*) carbamide, carbonyl diamide, urea.

carboídrato (*m., Chem.*) carbohydrate.

carbólico -ca (*adj.*) carbolic.

carbolíneo (*m., Chem.*) Carbolienum (a coal-tar preparation for preserving wood).

carbonação (*f., Chem.*) carbonation.

carbonáceo -cea (*adj.*) carbonaceous.

carbonado -da (*adj.*) containing carbon; (*m.*) a carbonado (black or carbon diamond).

carbonar (*v.t.*) to convert into a carbonate.

carbonatado -da (*adj.*) carbonated.

carbonatar (*v.t., Chem.*) to carbonate.

carbonato (*m., Chem.*) carbonate.—-**de amônio**, ammonium carbonate.—-**de cálcio**, calcium carbonate, limestone.—-**de chumbo**, lead carbonate, cerussite.—-**de cobre**, copper carbonate, artificial malachite.—-**de cobre hildratado**, malachite, green carbonate of copper.—-**de magnésio**, magnesium carbonate; magnesia; (*Min.*) magnesite.—-**de níquel**, nickel carbonate.—-**de potássio**, potassium carbonate, pearl ash, potash.—-**de sódio**, sodium carbonate.—-**de zinco**, zinc carbonate, smithsonite.

carbone (*m.*) = CARBÔNIO.

carbonemia (*f., Med.*) carbonemia.

carbôneo -nea (*adj.*) carbon.

carbonêto (*m.*) carbide —-**de cálcio**, calcium carbide.—-**de tungstênio**, or de volfrâmio, tungsten carbide.

carbônico -ca (*adj.*) carbonic.

carbonífero -ra (*adj.*) carboniferous.

carbonílio (*m., Chem.*) carbonyl.

carbônio (*m.*) carbon Vars. CARBONE, CARBONO.
carbonita (*f.*) carbonite (a mineral coke).
carbonização (*f.*) carbonization.
carbonizado –da (*adj.*) carbonized, charred.
carbonizador –dora [ô] (*adj.*) carbonizing; (*m.*) -izer.
carbonizante (*adj.*) carbonizing.
carbonizar (*v.t.*) to carbonize; to char. (*Metal.*) to add carbon to.
carbonizável (*adj.*) capable of being carbonized.
carbono (*m.*) carbon; carbon paper.
carbonometria (*f.*) carbonometry.
carbonoso –sa (*adj.*) carbonous.
carboretar (*v.*) = CARBONIZAR.
carborundo (*m.*) carborundum, silicon carbide.
carboxihemoglobina [ks] (*f.*, *Biochem.*) carboxyhemoglobin.
carboxilato [ks] (*m.*, *Chem.*) carboxylate.
carboxílico –ca [ks] (*adj.*, *Chem.*) carboxylic.
carboxílio, carboxilo [ks] (*m.*, *Chem.*) carboxyl group.
carbúnculo (*m.*) carbuncle, boil; cabochon.
carbunculoso –sa (*adj.*) carbuncular.
carburação (*f.*) carburetion.
carburador [ô] (*m.*) carburetor.
carbureto [ê] (*m.*) carbide [= CARBONÊTO].
carcaça (*f.*) carcass; skeleton; frame.—**do eixo de manivelas**, (*Autom.*) crankcase.
carcamano (*m.*) street peddler; shoeshine boy; an offensive name for Italians.
carcanel [-néis] (*m.*) calking iron.
carcará (*m.*) = CARACARÁ.
carcare(j)ar (*v.*) = CACAREJAR.
carcáricas, carcarídeos (*m.pl.*) the family (*Carchariidae*) of sharks.
carcarodonte (*m.*) the genus (*Carcharodon*) of man-eater sharks.
carcás (*m.*) = ALJAVA.
carcel [-céis] (*m.*) Carcel lamp; carcel (a light standard used in France).
carcela (*f.*) tape with button holes; bookbinder's tape.
carcergagem (*f.*) incarceration.
carcerar (*v.*) = ENCARCERAR.
cárcere (*m.*) dungeon, prison, jail.
carcereiro (*m.*) jail-keeper, jailer.
carchear (*v.t.*) to loot, pillage [= PILHAR].
carcinóide (*m.*, *Med.*) a non-malignant tumor.
carcinologia (*f.*, *Zool.*) carcinology.
carcinologista (*m.,f.*) carcinologist.
carcinoma (*m.*, *Med.*) carcinoma.
carcinomatoso –sa (*adj.*) cancerous, carcinomatous.
carcinose (*f.*, *Med.*) carcinosis.
carcoma (*f.*) woodworm; decay; that which eats away or destroys.
carcomer (*v.t.*) to eat away (as a woodworm); to erode; to undermine, ruin, destroy.
carcomido –da (*adj.*) worm-eaten; worn(-out), wasted, decayed.
carcunda (*adj.*; *m.,f.*) = CORCUNDA.
card. = CARDEAL (Cardinal).
carda (*f.*) a card (wire brush for carding wool, etc.); carding machine; hatchel, hackle, flax comb; act of carding; a fine small tack; mud and filth which have become matted in sheep's wool.
cardação (*f.*) carding.
cardadeira (*f.*) woman carder.
cardador –dora (*adj.*) carding; (*m.*) carder, flax hackler, wool-comber.
cardadura (*f.*) cleaned fiber, such as flax; carding [= CARDAÇÃO]; fleecing, extortion.
cardagem (*f.*) carding.
cardamina (*f.*, *Bot.*) cuckoo bittercress (*Cardamine pratensis*), c.a. AGRIÃO DOS PRADOS.
cardamomo (*m.*, *Bot.*) cardamon (*Elettaria cardamomum; Amomum cardamon*).—**-da-terra**, a tropical herb (*Renealmia occidentalis*) of the ginger family, c.a. CANA-BRAVA, CANA-DO-MATO, CAPITIÚ, CUITÉ-AÇU, PACO-SEROCA, PACOVA.
cardan (*adj.*, *Mach.*) having gimbals. **eixo**—, Cardan shaft. **junta**—, Cardan or universal joint. **suspensão**—, Cardanic, or Cardan's, suspension (on gimbals).
cardápio (*m.*) menu, bill of fare.
cardar (*v.t.*) to card (wool, flax, etc.); (*slang*) to fleece (extort).
cardeal (*adj.*) cardinal, chief, principal; (*m.*) a cardinal (of the R.C.Ch.); a cardinal bird, esp. the crested one

(*Paroaria coronata*); also = TICO-TICO-REI (a finch).—**-amarelo**, the yellow cardinal (*Gubernatrix cristata*), c.a. CARDEAL-DE-MONTEVIDEU; (*Bot.*) cardinal flower (*Lobelia cardinalis*).—**-do-brasil**, scarlet salvia (*S splendens*), c.a. PÉ-DE-CHUMBO; also, Texas salvia (*S. coccinea*). Cf. CARDIAL.
cardeiro (*m.*) = CARDO-DA-PRAIA.
cárdia (*m.*, *Anat.*) cardia.
cardíaca (*f.*, *Bot.*) common motherwort (Leonurus cardiaca), c.a. AGRIPALMA.
cardiáceos (*m.pl.*, *Zool.*) the family (*Cardiidae*) of cockles.
cardíaco –ca (*adj.*) cardiac(al); (*m.,f.*) a person with heart trouble. **colapso**—, heart failure; (*f.*, *Bot.*) see CARDÍACA above.
cardial (*adj.*, *Med.*) cardial. Cf. CARDEAL.
cardialgia (*f.*) severe pain in the chest; heartburn.
cardiastenia (*f.*, *Med.*) cardiasthenia.
cardiataxia [ks] (*f.*, *Med.*) cardiataxy.
cardido –da (*adj.*) water-rotted (said of wood).
cardife (*adj.*) from Cardiff—referring to coal.
cardigueira (*f.*) = POMBA-DE-BANDO.
cardina (*f.*) grime; drunkenness; a heart tonic.
cardinal (*adj.*) cardinal, principal. Cf. CARDEAL.
cardinalado –to (*m.*) cardinalate.
cardinheira (*f.*) = AVOANTE or POMBA-DE-BANDO.
cárdio –dia (*adj.*, *Anat.*) cardiac.
cardiografia (*f.*, *Med.*) cardiography.
cardiógrafo (*m.*, *Med.*) cardiograph.
cardiograma (*m.*, *Physiol.*) cardiogram.
cardiologia (*f.*) cardiology.
cardiologista (*m.,f.*) cardiologist.
cardite (*f.*, *Med.*) carditis, myocarditis.
cardo (*m.*, *Bot.*) the cardoon (*Cynara cardunculus*), c.a. ALCACHOFRA-BRAVA (wild artichoke); the Malta centaurea (*C. melitensis*); any of several thistles.—**-ananás**, the nightblooming cereus (*Hylocereus triangularis*).—**-asneiro**, the Scotch cottonthistle (*Onopordum acanthium*), c.a. CARDO-SELVAGEM.—**-azul**, the amethyst eryngo (*Eryngium amethystinum*).—**-bento** = CARDO-SANTO.—**-bosta**, a cereus (*Trichocereus macrogonous*).—**-corredor**, the snakeroot eryngo (*Eryngium campestre*).—**-da-praia**, a cereus (*C. variabilis*), c.a. CARDEIRO, CUMBEBA, JAMACARÚ, PITAIAIÁ.—**-de-ouro**, the goldenthistle or oyster plant (*Scolymus hispanicus*).—**-estrelado** = ABRÔLHO.—**-mariano** or—**-de-santa-maria**, the blessed milk thistle (*Silybum marianum*); also = CARDO-SANTO.—**-melão**, a cactus (*Notocactus ottonis*).—**-morto** = TASNEIRINHA.—**-negro**, the bull thistle (*Cirsium lanceolatum*).—**-penteador**, fuller's teasel (*Dipsacus fullonum*). c.a. DÍPSICO.—**-santo**, the Mexican pricklypoppy (*Argemone mexicana*), c.a.—**-MARIANO**, ERVA-DE-CARDO-AMARELO, PAPOULA-DE-ESPINHO, PAPOULA-DO-MÉXICO, PAPOULA-ESPINHOSA, FIGUEIRA-DO-INFERNO, ARGEMONA; also, the blessed thistle (*Cnicus benedictus*).
cardol (*m.*, *Chem.*) cardol.
carduáceo –cea (*adj.*, *Bot.*) carduaceous.
carduíneo –nea (*adj.*, *Bot.*) carduaceous.
cardume (*m.*) shoal (of fish); flock; throng.
careação (*f.*) = ACAREAÇÃO.
carear (*v.t.*) to win esteem, respect, admiration, etc.; also = ACAREAR.
careca (*adj.*) bald; (*m.,f.*) a bald person; (*f.*) baldness.
carecente (*adj.*) wanting; needy.
carecer (*v.t.*)—**de**, to want, lack, be without, be short of; to be in need of. **A notícia carece de fundamento**, The report is unfounded.
carecimento (*m.*) = CARÊNCIA.
carena (*f.*) keel [= QUERENA]; (*Bot.*) carina.
carenagem (*f.*) cowling; streamlining; act of careening.
carenar (*v.i.*) to careen [= QUERENAR]; (*v.t.*, *Aeron.*) to cowl; to streamline.
carência (*f.*) want, lack, dearth; need, privation.—**nutritiva**, food shortage.
carente (*adj.*) = CARECENTE.
carepa (*f.*) dandruff; scaly skin; fuzz on fruit; rough-hewn surface; sparks from an anvil; chimney soot; (*Metal.*) scale, mill scale.
carestia (*f.*) high prices, costliness; scarcity, dearth; **a**—**da vida**, the high cost of living.
careta [ê] (*f.*) wry face, grimace; mask.
caretear (*v.i.*) to grimace, make faces.
careteira (*f.*) = CARAMELO.
careza [ê] (*f.*) = CARESTIA.
carga (*f.*) cargo, load, burden; loading; encumbrance, op-

pression; charge, duty; onus; accusation; onset, onslaught; charge of gun powder; charge of electricity; charge of ore, etc., in a blast furnace; (*colloq.*) beating, trouncing; (*Mech.*) stress; load; (*Paper Mfg.*) loading, filler.—**axial**, axial load.—**admissível**, safe load.—**cerrada**, fusilade, volley.—**concentrada**, concentrated load.—**constante**, constant load or stress.—**d'água**, downpour of rain.—**de baioneta**, bayonet charge.—**de cauda**, (*Aeron.*) tail stress.—**de cavalaria**, cavalry charge.—**de cisalhamento**, shearing stress.—**de ossos**, bag of bones (very thin person).—**de pau** or—**de lenha**, (*colloq.*) a cudgelling.—**de ruptura**, (*Engin.*) breaking load.—**dinâmica**, (*Aeron.*) dynamic stress.—**elétrica**, electric charge.—**estática**, static load.—**excêntrica**, eccentric load.—**fixa**, fixed load.—**máxima**, top load.—**móvel**, moving load.—**permanente**, dead load.—**útil**, useful load.—**viva**, live load. **elevador de**—, freight elevator; hoist. **navio de**—, freighter. **pau de**—, derrick, boom. **voltar à**—, to return to the charge.
cargo (*m.*) charge, duty, office. **a**—**de**, in charge of; under the charge (responsibility) of.
cargueiro (*m.*) driver of pack animals.—**vagabundo**, tramp steamer. **navio**—, cargo boat, freighter.
cariacu [ú] (*m.*) a small, white-spotted deer (*Odocoileus suacuapara*), c.a. SUAÇUAPARA, VEADO-GALHEIRO.
cariado -**da** (*adj.*) carious.
cariar (*v.i.*) of teeth, bones, to decay, become carious.
cariátide (*f., Arch.*) caryatid.
cariba, **caribe** (*adj.*) Cariban; (*m.,f.*) Carib [=CARAÍBA].
caribé (*m.*) a dish prepared with avocado pulp; a cooling drink made with tapioca. [*GBAT*: "Thin saltless MINGAU of manioc flour, much used in the diet of convalescent CABOCLOS."]
cariboca (*m.,f.*) mestizo of white and Indian blood, c.a. CURIBOCA. [*GBAT*: "a dark-skinned person between a CABOCLO and a Negro in color."]
caribu [ú] (*m.*) caribou.
carica (*f., Bot.*) any papaya (*Carica*).
caricáceo -**cea** (*adj., Bot.*) caricaceous; (*f.pl.*) the Caricaceae (papaya family).
caricato -**ta** (*adj.*) caricatural; grotesque; (*m.,f.*) a satirical mimic, parodist or impersonator.
caricatura (*f.*) caricature; the art of caricature.
caricatural (*adj.*) caricatural.
caricaturar (*v.t.*) to caricature.
caricaturesco -**ca** [ê] (*adj.*) caricatural, grotesque.
caricaturista (*m.,f.*) caricaturist.
carícia (*f.*) caress, endearment.
cariciar (*v.*) = ACARICIAR.
cariciável (*adj.*) caressing; kindly.
caricioso -**sa** (*adj.*) caressing; endearing.
caridade (*f.*) charity, kindness; benefaction, alms. **Irmã de**—, Sister of Charity, nun.
caridoso -**sa** (*adj.*) charitable; kind, humane.
cárie(s) (*f.*) caries, decay of teeth or bones.—**do trigo**, wheat smut.
carijo (*m.*) rude wooden framework used for drying and toasting ERVA-MATE.
carijó (*adj.*) splotched white and black. **galinha**—, Plymouth Rock hen. (*m.*) half-breed Indian; (*pl.*) a formerly large tribe of Brazilian Indians [=GUARANI].
caril (*m.*) curry.
carimã (*f.*) sun-dried cakes of manioc paste; a loaf of manioc flour; fine dry manioc flour.
carimã (*f.*) fine manioc flour.
carimbação (*f.*) act of rubber-stamping.
carimbador (*m.*) mail canceller (in the postoffice).
carimbagem (*f.*) = CARIMBAÇÃO.
carimbar (*v.t.*) to rubber-stamp; to seal.
carimbo (*m.*) rubber stamp; seal.
carimbó (*m.*) hollow log drum.
carina (*f.*) = CARENA.
cariná (*m.*) = BURITIZINHO.
carinado -**da** (*adj.*) carinate.
carinão (*m.*) = CARÓ.
carinegro -**gra** [ê] (*adj.*) black-faced.
carinho (*m.*) affection, love, fondness; kindness, tenderness; endearment.
carinhoso -**sa** (*adj.*) affectionate, kind, tenderhearted.
carioca (*adj.*) of or pert. to the city of Rio de Janeiro; (*m.,f.*) a native of that city; (*f., slang*) strong coffee weakened with hot water.
cariocinese (*f., Biol.*) karyokinesis, mitosis.
cariocinético -**ca** (*adj.*) karyokinetic.

cariofiláceo -**cea** (*adj., Bot.*) caryophyllaceous; (*f.pl.*) the Caryophyllaceae (pink family).
cariofilada-maior (*f.*) = ERVA-BENTA.
cariogamia (*f., Biol.*) karyogamy.
cariólise (*f., Med.*) karyolysis.
cariomicrosomo (*m., Biol.*) karyomicrosome, nucleomicrosome.
cariomitomo (*m., Biol.*) karyomitome.
cariomitose (*f., Biol.*) karyomitosis.
cariopse (*f., Bot.*) caryopsis.
carioso -**sa** (*adj.*) carious.
cariota (*f.*) a fishtail palm (*Caryota sp.*).
caripé (*m., Bot.*) any of various species of Licania.
caripuna (*m.,f.*) "An Indian of a Panoan tribe on the borderland of Brazil and Bolivia." *Webster.*
cariri [irí] (*m.,f.*) an Indian of higher-than-average culture and of a distinct linguistic family who dwelled in the States of Piauí and Pernambuco; (*adj.*) pert. to or designating the Cariri. Var. CAIRIRI.
carisma (*f., Theol.*) charism.
carismático -**ca** (*adj.*) charismatic, divinely endowed.
caritativo -**va** (*adj.*) charitable [=CARIDOSO].
carixo (*m.*) = CHOPIM, VIRA-BOSTA.
cariz (*m.*) caraway seed; look, aspect; the looks of the weather.
carlequim (*m.*) jack (weight lifter).
carlina (*f.*) a bridge hoist; a genus of plants (*Carlina*).
carlinga (*f.*) cockpit (of an airplane); (*Naut.*) keelson.
Carlos (*m.*) Carlos; Charles; Carl.—**Magno**, Charlemagne.
Carlota (*f.*) Carlotta; Charlotte.
carludovica (*f.*) a genus of tropical American palmlike plants. The Panama-hat palm is *Carludovica palmata*. A Brazilian species is *C. chelidonura*.
carmear (*v.t.*) to disentangle (raw, dirty wool) preparatory to carding.
carmelita (*adj.; m.,f.*) Carmelite.
carmesim (*adj.; m.*) crimson.
carmim (*m.*) the color carmine; the cochineal from which it is made.
carmina (*f.*) carmine.
carminado -**da** (*adj.*) carmine.
carminar (*v.t.*) to carmine.
carminativo -**va** (*adj.*) carminative.
carmíneo -**nea** (*adj.*) carmine.
carmona (*f.*) a cremone bolt.
carnaça (*f.*) quantity of flesh; fleshy protuberance.
carnação (*f.*) flesh color.
carnadura (*f.*) fleshy part of the body; carnal nature.
carnagem (*f.*) slaughter (of cattle) for food; carnage.
carnaíba (*f.*) = CARNAÚBA.
carnaíbal (*m.*) = CARNAUBAL.
carnal (*adj.*) carnal; (*m.,pl.*) first cousins.
carnalidade (*f.*) carnality.
carnalita (*f., Min.*) carnallite.
carnaúba (*f.*) carnauba, a wax secreted by the CARNAUBEIRA, much used in the manufacture of floor wax, candles, shoe polish, etc.
carnaubal [a-u] (*m.*) a stand or grove of wax palms [=CARNAÍBAL].
carnaubeira [a-u] (*f.*) the wax palm (*Corpernicia cerifera*), source of carnaúba wax.
carnaval (*m.*) Carnival (the three days of merrymaking which precede Ash Wednesday).
carnavalesco -**ca** [ê] (*adj.*) Carnival; festive.
carnaz (*m.*) the rough (flesh) side of leather.
carne (*f.*) meat, flesh.—**assada**, roast meat; also (*colloq.*) a loafer, a good-for-nothing.—**de-anta**, (*Bot.*) a mayten (*Maytenus obtusifolia*), c.a. CONGONHA-BRAVA-DE-FÔLHA-MIÚDA, LENHA-BRANCA, LIMÃOZINHO.—**de boi**, beef.—**de canhão**, cannon fodder.—**de carneiro**, mutton.—**de fumeiro**, or **de fumo**, smoked meat.—**de galinha**, gooseflesh.—**de peito**, brisket.—**de porco**, pork.—**de sol** (**de vento, do Ceará, do sertão**), sun-dried meat [=CHARQUE].—**de vaca**, beef; (*Bot.*) a snow-bell (*Styrax acuminata*), c.a. ESTORAQUE-DO-CAMPO, PAU-DE-REMO, POROROCA; also = CARVALHO-DO-BRASIL.—**de vitela**, veal.—**do sul** or—**velha** = CHARQUE (jerky).—**em conserva** or **enlatada** canned meat.—**guisada**, beef stew.—**quebrada**, (*Med.*) myositis.—**salgada**, corned beef.—**sêca**, jerked meat [=CHARQUE].—**verde**, fresh meat.—**virada**, meat which has started to spoil.—**viva**, live flesh. **aguilhão da**—, carnal temptation. **andar como unha e**—**com alguém**, to be hand-and-glove with someone. **de côr de**—, flesh-

colored. **em**—**e osso**, in flesh and blood, in person. **nem**
—**nem peixe**, neither fish nor fowl.
carnear (*v.t.*) to slaughter and dress cattle; (*v.i.*) to engage
in the business of making jerked beef (CHARQUE).
carneira (*f.*) cured sheepskin; ewe; the leather sweat band
in a man's hat.
carneirada (*f.*) flock of sheep; malaria.
carneireiro (*m.*) sheep herder.
carneiro (*m.*) sheep, ram; burial niche, urn, grave; white
cap (wave).—**-castrado**, wether.—**-do-cabo** = ALBATROZ.
—**hidráulico**, hydraulic ram [= ARÍETE] **carne de**—,
mutton. **costeleta de**—, lamb (mutton) chop.
cárneo –**nea** (*adj.*) carneous; flesh-colored.
carnéola (*f., Min.*) carnelian.
carnerina (*f.*) sard (a variety of carnelian), c.a. SÁRDIO.
carniça (*f.*) carrion; animals slaughtered for food; edible
flesh; slaughter, massacre; butt of a joke; object of
ridicule or scorn. **pular**—, to play leapfrog.
carniçal (*adj.*) carnivorous.
carniçaria (*f.*) carnage; slaughter, butchery; butcher shop,
meat market.
carniceiro –**ra** (*adj.*) carnivorous; (*m.*) butcher; (*slang*)
a clumsy surgeon; (*Zool.*) a carnivore.
carnificação (*f., Med.*) carnification.
carnificar –**se** (*v.r.*) to carnify.
carnificina (*f.*) carnage, bloodshed.
carnívoro –**ra** (*adj.*) carnivorous, flesh-eating; (*m.pl.,
Zool.*) the Carnivora.
carnosidade (*f.*) fleshiness; abnormal fleshy excrescence;
tumor; polyp.
carnoso –**sa** (*adj.*) fleshy, plump.
carnotita (*f., Min.*) carnotite.
carnudo –**da** (*adj.*) fleshy, plump, fat, corpulent.
caro –**ra** (*adj.*) dear, costly, high-priced, expensive; beloved, highly esteemed.—**metade**, better half (wife);
(*adv.*) dearly, at great cost or sacrifice.
caró (*m.*) the nuxvomica poison nut (*Strychnos nuxvomica*), c.a. CARINÃO.
caroá (*m., Bot.*) caroa (*Neoglaziovia variegata*) whose
leaves yield a fiber substitute for hemp, jute, and flax,
used in making hammocks and cordage; c.a. CARAUÁ,
CARUÁ, COROÁ, CRAUÁ.
caroatá (*m.*) = CARAGUATÁ.
caroba (*f.*) any of various South American trees of the
genus *Jacaranda*. [Do not confuse with the carob tree
(*Ceratonia siliqua*) which is called ALFARROBEIRA.]—
-**branca**, a tree of the bignonia family (*Tecoma subvernicosa*—?), c.a. CAROBA-DE-FLOR-BRANCA, CINCO-CHAGAS,
CINCO-FÓLHAS, IPÊ-BATATA, IPÊ-BOIA, IPÊ-BRANCO.—
-**brava**, a ginseng (*Pentapanax angelicifolius*).—**da-
mata** = CAROBINHA. —**-de-flor-branca** = —BRANCA. —
-**de-flor-verde**, a plant of the bignonia family (*Cybistax
antisyphilitica*), the leaflets of which are used in Brazil
as an emetic, a cathartic and a remedy for syphilis; c.a.
CINCO-CHAGAS, IPÊ-BRANCO, IPÊ-DE-FLOR-VERDE, IPÊ-
MIRIM, IPÊ-PARDO. —**-de-folha-estreita** = —**-DE-SÃO-
PAULO**.—**-de-minas-gerais** is *Jacaranda endotricha*.—
-**de-são-paulo** is *Jacaranda oxyphylla*, c.a.—**-DE-FÓLHA-
ESTREITA**,—**-DO-CAMPO**, CAROBINHA-DO-CAMPO, JACA-
RANDÁ-DE-SÃO-PAULO.—**-do-campo**, any of three jaca-
randas: *J. paucifoliolata* (c.a. JACARANDÁ-DA-SERRA),
J. oxyphylla (c.a. CAROBA-DE-SÃO-PAULO) and *J. caroba*
(c.a. CAROBINHA).—**-do-carrasco** = CAROBINHA.—**-do-
mato**, the copaia jacaranda (*J. copaia*), c.a. CARAÚBA,
CAROBUÇU, MARUPÁ, PARAPARA(-PEUVA), SIMARUBA-
COPAIA, SIMARUBA-FALSA; also = various other species of
Jacaranda called CAROBINHA.—**-guaçú**, the sharpleaf
jacaranda (*J. acutifolia*), c.a. JACARANDÁ-CAROBA,
JACARANDÁ-MIMOSO, PALISSANDRA.—**-miúda**, any of
various spp. of Jacaranda, esp. *J. tomentosa*, *J. caroba*,
J. puberla (the latter two c.a. CAROBINHA), and *J. clausseniana* (c.a. CASCO-DE-CAVALO).—**-paulistana** = —**-DE-
SÃO-PAULO**.—**-preta**, either of two Jacarandas: *J. obovata*
and *J. subrhombea* (the latter c.a.—**-ROXA**, CAROBINHA-
DO-CAMPO).
carobeira (*f.*) a trumpet tree (*Tabebuia pentaphylla*—?)
of the bignonia family, c.a. CARAÍBA, CARAÚBA, CARAU-
BEIRA, CINCO-FÓLHAS-DO-CAMPO, PARA-TUDO, PAU-
D'ARCO-DO-CAMPO; also = CAROBINHA.
carobinha (*f., Bot.*) any of various species of Jacaranda,
esp. *J. caroba* (c.a. CAMBOATÁ-PEQUENO, CAMBOTÉ,
CAROBA-DO-CAMPO, CAROBA-DO-CARRASCO, CAROBA-
MIÚDA); *J. semiserrata* (c.a. CAROBEIRA, CAROBA-DO-
MATO, JACARANDÁ-CAROBA); *J. puberla* (c.a. CAROBA-

MIÚDA, CAROBEIRA); *J. rufa* (c.a. CAROBA-DO-CAMPO);
J. clausseniana (c.a. CASCO-DE-CAVALO).—**-do-campo**,
any of three species of Jacaranda: *J. ulei*, *J. oxphylla*
(c.a. CAROBA-DE-SÃO-PAULO), and *J. subrhombea* (c.a.
CAROBA-ROXA).—**-do-mato**, a jacaranda (*J. densicoma*).
carobuçu [cú] (*m.*) = CAROBA-DO-MATO.
carocha (*f.*) the European stag beetle (*Lucanus cervus*);
dunce's cap; (*pl.*) witches; lies, fibs.
carochinha (*f.*) **histórias da**—, fairy (nursery) tales.
caroço [rô; pl.: ró] (*m.*) fruit pit (stone, seed); core; lump;
a frog in the throat; lump in a gland; brain teaser; (*slang*)
dough (money).
carola (*adj.*) sanctimonious; very pious; (*m.,f.*) = PAPA-
MISSAS; (*m.*) a man with a bald spot at the rear top of
his head (in allusion to a priest's tonsure).
carolice (*f.*) sanctimoniousness.
carolina (*f.*) the sandal bead tree (*Adenanthera pavonina*)
whose bright-red, lens-shaped seeds (sometimes called
Circassian seeds) are used as beads; c.a. TENTO-CAROLINA;
[*cap.*] Carolina, Caroline, Carolyn.
carolismo (*m.*) sanctimoniousness.
carolo [rô] (*m.*) corn cob; a rap on the head.
carona (*m.*) a dead beat; gate crasher, deadhead; (*f.*) a
leather or rawhide sheet placed between the saddlecloth
and the saddle. **dar**—, to give (someone) a lift (free
ride). **entrada de**—, free ticket of admission. **levar**—, to
be taken (duped). **pedir**—, to hitch a ride. **pregar**—, to
dupe (someone).
carorocoatá (*f.*) = ALBACORA.
carótida, carotide (*f., Anat.*) carotid artery.
carotídeo –**dea** (*adj.*) carotid.
carotina (*f., Chem.*) carotene, carotin.
carpa (*f.*) a carp (fish); hoeing of weeds [= CAPINA].
carpal (*adj., Anat.*) carpal.
carpar (*v.t.*) to hoe weeds [= CAPINAR].
carpelo [é] (*m., Bot.*) carpel.
carpelar (*adj.*) carpellary.
carpeta [ê] (*f.*) the cloth which covers a card table; a
gambling house.
carpição (*f.*) = CAPINA.
carpideira (*f.*) a weeding machine [= CAPINADEIRA];
formerly, a professional mourner.
carpido –**da** (*adj.*) mournful; (*m.*) a wailing.
carpidor –**dora** (*adj.*) weed-hoeing; bemoaning, etc. See
the verb CARPIR; (*m.*) = CAPINADOR.
carpins (*m.pl.*) socks
carpintaria (*f.*) carpentry; carpenter's shop.
carpinteiração, carpinteiragem (*f.*) carpentry.
carpinteiro (*m.*) carpenter; stagehand; in southern Brazil,
a strong wind blowing in from the ocean; (*Zool.*) the
golden-green woodpecker (*Chloronerpes chrysochloros*).
carpintejar (*v.t.*) to saw and otherwise prepare lumber;
(*v.i.*) to work as a carpenter.
carpir [25] (*v.t.*) to hoe weeds [= CAPINAR]; to tear the
hair; to snatch, tear away; (*v.t.,v.i.*) to lament, bemoan,
bewail; (*v.i.*) to grieve.
carpite (*f., Veter.*) carpitis.
carpo (*m., Anat.*) carpus; (*Bot.*) fruit.
carpófago –**ga** (*adj.*) carpophagous, feeding on fruits.
carpofilo (*m., Bot.*) carpophyll, carpel.
carpóforo (*m., Bot.*) carpophore.
carpógono (*m., Bot.*) carpogone, carpogonium.
carpólito (*m.*) carpolite (fossil fruit, nut or seed).
carpologia (*f.*) carpology.
carpomania (*f., Bot.*) carpomania.
carpo-metacarpiano –**na** (*adj., Anat.*) carpometacarpal.
carqueja [ê] (*f., Zool.*) the red-gartered coot (*Fulica armillata*), c.a. MERGULHÃO; (*Bot.*) a woadwaxen (*Genista
tridentata*); a hydrolea (*H. spinosa*).—**-amargosa**, a
baccharis (*B. genistelloides*), c.a. CACÁLIA-AMARGA,
QUINA-DE-CONDAMINE, VASSOURA.
carquilha (*f.*) seam, crease, pleat.
carraca (*f.*) a tick [= CARRAPATO]; fig., a person who sticks
to another.
carrada (*f.*) cartload, wagon-load; a large quantity. **às**—**s**,
in great quantity.
carranca (*f.*) a stern, forbidding look; scowl, frown; gargoyle, grotesque carving; a catch for window shutters.
fechar a—, to scowl, glower.
carrança (*adj.*) hidebound; (*m.,f.*) old fogy.
carrancudo –**da** (*adj.*) cranky, cross, crabbed; surly, sullen; scowling, frowning; gruff; grim.
carranquear (*v.i.*) to scowl, frown.

carrão (m.) a large carriage; omnibus; the box car (double-six domino piece).

carrapata (f.) a bad sore.

carrapatal (m.) a place infested with ticks; a planting of castor oil plants.

carrapatar-se (v.r.) to cling tight (as a tick).

carrapatear (v.t.) to treat (animals) for ticks.

carrapateira(-branca) (f.) the castor oil plant (Ricinus communis), c.a. MAMONA.

carrapateiro (m.) a caracara or carrion hawk, c.a. CARA-CARÁ-TINGA, CARACARAÍ. [Its name is derived from its habit of jumping up from the ground to pick CARRA-PATOS (ticks) from the bellies and sides of grazing cattle.]

carrapaticida (f.) a parasiticide for destroying ticks on cattle.

carrapatinha (f.) a delicate and diminutive filmy fern (Trichomanes reptans), closely allied to the Irish or Killarney fern; c.a. MEIO-CHUMBO.

carrapato (m.) tick (blood-sucking parasite); an important-tunate person who sticks to another; castor bean [= MAMONA].—das galinhas, chicken tick (Argas persicus).—do boi, cattle tick (Margaropus spp.).—do chão, a tick (Ornithodoros spp.). —estrêla, the lone-star and other ticks of the genus Amblyomma, troublesome to man and beast; c.a. PICAÇO, RODELEIRO, RODOLEIRO, RODOLEGO.—de peixe, a carp louse (Argulus).—do mato = MUNDAÚ (a shrub).

carrapeta [ê] (f.) American muskwood (Guarea trichiloides), c.a. AÇAFROA, BILREIRO, CAMBOATÁ, CANJERANA-MIÚDA, CEDRÃO, CEDRO-BRANCO, CEDRORANA, JITÓ, GUARÉ, JATAÚBA(BRANCA), MACAQUEIRO, PAU-BOLA, PAU-DE-SABÃO, TAÚVA.

carrapichino (m.) a Brazilian malvaceous plant (Urena sinuata), c.a. QUIABO = BRAVO; also = CARRAPICHO-DE-BEIÇO-DE-BOI.

carrapicho (m.) a knot of hair on top of or on the back of the head; kinky hair; bur, cocklebur; (Bot.) any of numerous bur-bearing plants, esp. Demodium (syn. Meibomia).—de-agulha, a coreopsis (C. tricornea); a Spanish needles (Bidens pinnata).—de-beiço-de-boi, a tick clover (Desmodius adscendens), c.a. AMOR(ES)-DO-CAMPO, AMORZINHO-SÊCO, CARRAPICHINHO, MARMELADA-DE-CAVALO, PEGA-PEGA, TREVINHO-DO-CAMPO.—de-carneiro, the Oriental cocklebur (Xanthium orientale), c.a. ESPINHO-DE-CARNEIRO.—de-cavalo, a ratany (Krameria tomentosa).—de-duas-pontas = CUAMBU (a beggar-ticks). —de-santa-helena = ERVA-DE-CARNEIRO.—do-ceará = RATÂNIA. —do-grande = ESPINHO-DE-CAR-NEIRO.—grande, the smaller burdock (Arctium minus), c.a. BARDANA-MENOR, PEGA-PEGA; also = ESPINHO-DE-CARNEIRO.—rasteiro, Paraguay starbur (Acanthospermum australe), c.a. ESPINHO-DE-AGULHA, ESPINHO-DE-CARNEIRO, MATA-PASTO, PICÃO-DA-PRAIA, POEJO-DA-PRAIA; another starbur (A. hispidum), c.a. AMOR-DE-NEGRO, RETIRANTE; also = AMENDOEIRANA.

carrapito (m.) a young goat's spike.

carrasca (adj.) qualifying an inferior type of olive tree and its fruit.

carrascal (m.) a large area of poor, dry land covered with scrub, such as the chaparral of southwestern U.S.A.

carrascão (m.) strong, cheap wine; stunted vegetation.

carrasco (m.) hangman, executioner; a cruel person; rocky road; sparse, stunted vegetation; transition country between the CATINGAS and the CAMPOS, c.a. CARRASCAL, CARRASCÃO, CARRASQUEIRO, CARRASQUENHO.

carrascoso -sa (adj.) designating land of poor quality with sparse, stunted vegetation.

carraspana (f., slang) bender, drunken spree; a repri-mand.

carreador, carreadouro (m.) wagon trail.

carrear (v.t.) to cart, carry, haul; (v.i.) to drive wagons; to entail (expense, consequences); = ACARRETAR.

carrega-bêstas (f.) a type of large white grape, growing in heavy bunches.

carregação (f.) cargo; a load or act of loading; a lot of anything; (colloq.) sickness, disease, esp. an onslaught of venereal diseases, c.a. CARRÊGO, CARREGAMENTO.—do peito, bronchitis.—dos dentes, pyorrhea.—dos olhos, conjunctivitis. filme de—, inferior, shoddy. filme de—, a "quickie" (third-rate) motion picture. mercadoria de—, shoddy goods.

carregadeira (f.) any umbrella ant, of which the SAÚVA is the best-known in Brazil; a woman bearer (of loads); (Naut.) a clew line.

carregado -da (adj.) loaded; laden; of weather, threaten-ing; of color, dark, heavy; venereally infected; bad to eat. azul—, dark blue.

carregador (m.) loader, longshoreman; porter, bearer, carrier, conveyor.—de cartuchos, cartridge clip.—de baterias, battery charger.

carrega-madeira (m.) = JOÃO-DE-PAU.

carregamento (m.) load or act of loading; cargo, shipment; a consignment of goods; burden, weight; oppression; venereal disease [= CARREGAÇÃO].

carregão (m.) a jerk by a hooked fish.

carregar (v.t.) to load (ship, truck, gun, etc.); to carry, bear (a burden); (v.i.) to charge, attack; to become charged (as with power); (v.r.) to become dark, somber; to become sad.—a, to impute to.—a mão, to do some-thing with a heavy hand.—com, to endure, put up with; to carry off (away), purloin.—com a responsabilidade, to bear the responsibility.—de trabalho, to overburden with work.—em (sôbre), to lie (rest, weigh) heavily on; to press, bear down on; to emphasize (a point); to give weight (to an argument).—o povo, to oppress the people (de impostos, with taxes).—o preço, to up the price.—o sobrolho, to scowl.—para o sul, to bear south.—pedra enquanto descansa, to take a busman's holiday.—sôbre a esquerda, to bear (keep to) the left.—(sôbre) o inimigo, to charge (against) the enemy.—se (o tempo), to grow cloudy (the weather).—se (o aspecto, o rosto) to grow somber; of the face, to become clouded.—se de família, to raise a large family.—um acumulador, to charge a battery.—um navio, uma espingarda, to load a ship, a gun.—uma fornalha, to stoke a furnace.

carrêgo (m.) act of carrying; a bundle, box or other bur-den carried on the head or shoulders; a burden on the conscience; load of a cannon; a bad "dose" of gonorrhea, etc.; (colloq.) acute accent mark.

carregoso -sa (adj.) heavy, burdensome.

carreira (f.) course, route, track, road; race, run; rank, row; career, occupation, profession; general course of ac-tion or progress through life; hair part; course of bricks; river rapids [= CORREDEIRA]; a wagon-wide lane between plantings of corn, coffee, etc.; (pl.) ship ways; horse races. a tôda—, at top speed. às—s, headlong, hastily, hurried-ly. arrepiar—, to abandon one career in favor of another. avião de—, air liner. em—, in a row (rank, file). fazer—, to pursue a career.

carreiramento (m.) in southern Brazil, horse-racing on a flat field.

carreirista (m.,f.) a follower of horse races.

carreiro (m.) oxcart driver; coachman; path; narrow lane; track, trail; path followed by ants on the march; wild animal trail.—de-são-tiago, the Milky Way [= ESTRADA-DE-S.-TIAGO].

carrêta (f.) cart, wagon; oxcart; spool [= CARRETEL]; gun carriage [= REPARO].

carretagem (f.) cartage, trucking; carrying charge.

carretão (m.) a drayman; (R.R.) a transfer table; a primi-tive coffee shelling machine; (colloq.) the one who pays (for the drinks, etc.).

carretar (v.i.) = ACARRETAR.

carrête (m.) small cart; spool, reel.

carreteira (f.) wagon road.

carreteiro (m.) drayman; carter; (adj.) designating a barge used in lightering or loading ships.

carretel [-téis] (m.) spool, reel; small cart.—da barquinha (Naut.) log reel.

carreteleira (f.) a spool-making machine.

carretilha (f.) small spool; pastry cutter.

carretilhar (v.t., Mach.) to knurl.

carrêto (m.) carting; cartage; carrying charges; (Mach.) pinion.

carriça, carricinha (f.) = CAMBAXIRRA.

carriço (m., Bot.) a sedge (Carex ambigua).

carrieira (f.) an ant (Acromyrmex nigra).

carril (m.) rut, track; steel rail [= TRILHO].

carrilhador, carrilhanor (m.) carilloneur.

carrilhão (m.) carillon, set of bells; chimes clock.

carrilho (m.) corn cob.

carrinho (m.) small cart; play wagon; a spool of thread [= CARRETEL DE LINHA].—de criança, or—para bêbê, baby buggy.—de mão, wheelbarrow.

carro (m.) car, cart, carriage, coach, vehicle, van, wagon; automobile.—aéreo, aerial cable car.—anfíbio, (Milit.) amphibian car.—blindado, or—couraçado, armored car.—-correio, mail car.—de assalto,

(*Milit.*) armored car, tank.—**de bateria**, (*Aeron.*) starting-battery cart.—**de boi**, ox-cart.—**de bombeiro**, fire truck.—**de mão**, wheelbarrow, handcart.—**de rádio-patrulha**, radio patrol car, prowl car.—**dormitório**, sleeping car.—**elétrico**, street car [= BONDE].—**fúnebre**, hearse.—**-plataforma**, flat-car.—**-reboque**, trailer.—**-restaurante**, dining car.—**-tanque isotérmico**, double-walled tank truck (for transportation of chilled milk, etc.). **atulhamento**, or **bôlo**, **de—s**, traffic jam. **botar o—adiante dos bois**, to put the cart before the horse.
carroça (*f.*) wagon, cart.—**-báscula**, dump cart.
carroçada (*f.*) cartload, wagonload.
carroção (*m.*) large covered wagon or oxcart; in dominoes, the boxcar (double six); in students' slang, a long, complicated problem in math.
carroçaria, carroceria (*f.*) body (of an automobile, truck, bus, etc.).—**basulante**, dump-truck body.
carroceiro (*m.*) wagon driver, carter, drayman; teamster.
carrocim (*m.*) small cart, carriage or wagon.
carrocinha (*f.*) small dump cart; dog-catcher's cart.
carrossel [-éis] (*m.*) merry-go-round.
carrosseria (*f.*) = CARROCERIA.
carruageiro (*m.*) carriage maker.
carruagem (*f.*) carriage, coach.
carrufra (*f.*) = CAQUERA.
carstenito (*m., Min.*) anhydrite.
carta (*f.*) letter, missive; map, chart; diagram; charter; playing card; bill of fare.—**aberta**, an open letter (in the press).—**aérea**, airmail letter.—**branca**, carte blanche; full authority.—**celeste**, a map of the heavens.—**das Nações Unidas**, United Nations Charter.—**de alforria**, document granting freedom to a slave.—**de apresentação**, letter of introduction.—**de crédito**, letter of credit.—**de jogar**, playing card.—**de marear**, navigation chart.—**de naturalização**, certificate of naturalization.—**de prego**, sealed orders.—**de recomendação**, letter of recommendation.—**de saúde**, bill of health.—**de seguro**, a letter or pass of safe conduct.—**do Atlântico**, Atlantic Charter.—**de tempo**, weather map.—**expressa**, special delivery letter.—**falsa**, marked card.—**isobárica**, isobaric weather chart.—**partida**, charter party.—**patente**, letters-patent.—**registada**, registered letter.—**sinóptica**, synoptic weather chart. **botar—s**, to read cards (in fortune-telling). **botar as—s**, to act big; to be the boss. **dar—s**, to deal cards. **leitura da—**, map-reading. **partida de—s**, card game. **pôr as—s na mesa**, to lay one's cards on the table.
cartabuxa (*f.*) a small wire brush, such as used by printers and goldsmiths.
cartáceo -cea (*adj.*) chartaceous, papery.
cartada (*f.*) the playing of a card.
cartaginês -nesa [ê] (*adj.; m.,f.*) Carthaginian.
cartamina (*f., Chem.*) carthamin.
cártamo (*m.*) false saffron or safflower (*Carthamus tinctorius*), c.a. AÇAFRÃO-BASTARDO, AÇAFROA.
cartão (*m.*) card, cardboard, carton.—**de Boas Festas**, Christmas card.—**de visita**, calling card.—**postal**, postcard. **caixa de—**, paper box, carton.
cartapácio (*m.*) a large book; a big, old book, esp. one in bad repair; a stack of papers; a file of old newspapers.
cartaz (*m.*) poster, placard, billboard; fame, popularity (of a movie star, football player, etc.). **É proibido pregar—es**, Post no bills. **ganhar—**, to earn a reputation, make a name for oneself. **pregador de—es**, bill-poster. **ter**, or **ser, um ótimo—**, to be a drawing card.
cartear (*v.i.*) to plot (ship's course); to deal cards; (*v.t.*) to play cards.—**se (com alguém)**, to exchange letters with someone.
carteira (*f.*) billfold, wallet, pocket book, brief case; writing desk; department, section (as in a bank).—**de bôlso**, billfold.—**de chofer**, driver's license.—**de cigarros**, cigarette case.—**de identidade**, identification booklet. **batedor de—**, pickpocket.
carteiro (*m.*) postman, mailman, letter carrier.
cartel [-téis] (*m.*) challenge; cartel, pool; poster, label.
cárter (*m., Mach.*) gear housing.
cartesianismo (*m.*) Cartesianism.
cartesiano -na (*adj.*) Cartesian.
cartilagem (*f.*) cartilage, gristle.—**de Meckel**, (*Embryol., Zool.*) Meckelian cartilage.—**ensiforme**, (*Anat.*) the xiphoid process.—**tiroídea**, (*Anat.*) the thyroid cartilage.—**s semilunares**, (*Anat.*) the semilunar fibrocartilages.
cartilagíneo -nea (*adj.*) cartilaginous.

cartilaginoso -sa (*adj.*) cartilaginous.
cartilha (*f.*) primer, first reader.
cartista (*m.,f.*) Cartist. [*Webster*: "in Spain and Portugal, one who supports the Constitution."]
cartografia (*f.*) cartography, map-making.
cartógrafo -fa (*m.,f.*) cartographer, map-maker.
cartola (*f.*) topper, top hat.
cartolina (*f.*) thick, heavy paper; light cardboard.
cartomancia (*f.*) cartomancy, fortune-telling with playing cards.
cartonado -da (*adj.*) (of books) bound in boards.
cartonador (*m.*), **-dora** (*f.*) bookbinder.
cartonagem (*f.*) cardboard box, carton; manufacture of paper boxes, etc.; bookbinding.
cartonar (*v.t.*) to bind (books) in boards.
cartório (*m.*) archives; civil registry, notary's office.
cartucheira (*f.*) cartridge belt.
cartucho (*m.*) cartridge; paper or cardboard tube.—**de festim**, blank cartridge.—**de manejo** or—**de instrução**, dummy cartridge. **carregador**, or **pente, de—s**, cartridge clip. **papel—**, coarse wrapping paper. **queimar o seu último—**, to fire one's last shot.—**queimado**, empty cartridge.
cartusiano -na (*adj.*) Carthusian.
Cartuxa (*f.*) Chartreuse (Carthusian monastery).
cartuxo (*m.*) Carthusian monk.
caruã (*m.*) = CAROÁ.
caruana (*m.*) a good spirit invoked by Indian witch doctors.
caruara (*f.*) evil eye; rheumatic pain; paralysis of newborn calves, etc.
caruatá (*m.*) = CARAGUATÁ.
carueta [ê] (*f.*) coarse leavings of manioc after sifting; = CRUEIRA.
caruma (*f.*) pine leaf.
carumbé (*m.*) = CALUMBÉ.
carunchento -ta (*adj.*) = CARUNCHOSO.
caruncho (*m.*) a breed of small Brazilian pigs; dry rot; fig., old age; (*Zool.*) a plant or tree borer.—**-dos-cereais**, grain beetle.—**-do-mar**, a gribble (*Limnoria lignorum*).
carunchoso -sa (*adj.*) worm-eaten; old, broken.
carúncula (*f., Anat., Zool.*) caruncle, caruncula.
caruru [urú] (*m., Bot.*) any of various amaranths, esp. those used in cookery.—**açu** =—**BRAVO**.—**amarelo**, yellow amaranth (*A. flavus*), c.a. CARURU-CRISTA-DE-GALO, CRISTA-DE-GALO, CARURU-DO-MATO.—**amargoso**, American burnweed (*Erechtites hieracifolia*); another burnweed (*E. valerianaefolia*), c.a. CAPERIÇOBA-VERMELHA, MARIA-GOMES.—**azêdo**, the roselle (*Hibiscus sabdariffa*) whose fleshy calyxes are used for making an acid drink; also for making tarts and jellies. Other names are: AZEDINHA, CURURU-DA-GUINÉ, QUIABO-DE-ANGOLA, QUIABO-RÓSEO, QUIABO-ROXO, ROSELA, VINAGREIRA.—**bravo**, a pokeberry (*Phytolacca thyrsiflora*), c.a. BREDO-CARURU, CARURU-AÇU, CARURU-DE-PORCO, CARURU-SELVAGEM, CUPIEIRO; a groundsel (*Senecio crassiflorus*).—**da-mata**, Joseph's coat amaranth (*A. tricolor*).—**de-cacho**, a jute (*Corchorus aestuans*), c.a. CARURU-DA-BAÍA, CARURU-BRAVO, CARURU-GUAÇU, ERVA-DA-AMÉRICA, ERVA-DO-CANADÁ, ERVA-DOS-CACHOS-DA-ÍNDIA, MECHOAÇÃO-DO-CANADÁ, TIPI, TINTUREIRA-VULGAR.—**de-porco** = BREDO-VERDADEIRO, CARURU-VERDADEIRO.—**de-sapo**, the Martius oxalis (*O. martiana*); also = *O. palustris*.—**verdadeiro**, an amaranth (*A. blitum*), c.a. BREDO-VERDADEIRO, CARURU-DE-PORCO, CARURU-MIÚDO.—**verde**, green amaranth (*A. viridis*), c.a. AMARANTO-VERDE, CARURU-DE-SOLDADO, CARURU-MIÚDO.—**vermelho**, love-lies-bleeding (*Amaranthus caudatus*), c.a. BREDO-VERMELHO, CHORÃO, CRISTA-DE-GALO-CHORONA, VELUDO.
cárus (*m.*) a death-like sleep or coma.
caruto (*m., Bot.*) a Brazilian genip (*Genipa caruto*).
carvacrol (*m., Chem.*) carvacrol; cymo phenol.
carvalhal (*m.*) oak grove; (*adj.*) oak.
carvalheira (*f.*) oak tree; oak thicket.
carvalheiro (*m.*) young oak; oak club.
carvalhiça (*f.*) the Kermes oak (*Quercus coccifera*).
carvalinha (*f., Bot.*) the drug speedwell (*Veronica officinalis*); = TÊUCRIO.
carvalinho-do-mar (*m.*) = BODELHA.
carvalho (*m.*) oak tree; oak wood.—**alvarinho** or—**da-europa**, English oak (*Quercus robur*).—**da-américa** or—**dos-pântanos**, pin oak (*Quercus palustris*).—**das-antilhas** or—**-prêto**, the Haiti catalpa (*C. longissima*),

c.a. CATALPA.—**-do-brasil**, though it yields an oaklike timber, is not an oak at all (as *Quercus* does not occur in that country), but is any of several species of *Roupala*. (family Proteaceae), esp. *R. brasiliensis* (the Brazil roupala) and *R. complicata* (the Costa Rica roupala); c.a. CARVALHO-VERMELHO, CARNE-DE-VACA, CATUCANHÉ, GUAXICA, PAU-CONCHA, TUCAJÉ.

carvão (*m.*) charcoal; coal; charcoal sketch; wheat or other plant smut.—**animal**, animal charcoal.—**branco**, an immense Braz. tree (*Callisthene fasciculata*) with fetid resinous juice, c.a. CAPITÃO-DO-CAMPO.—**mineral** or—**de pedra**, anthracite coal, c.a. HULHA.—**vegetal** or—**de lenha**, or—**de madeira**, charcoal.

carvoaria (*f.*) charcoal kiln.

carvoeiro -ra (*adj.*) charcoal; coal; (*m.*) coal dealer; collier; (*m.,f.*) coal bin or bunker.

carvoejar (*v.t.*) to make and/or deal in charcoal.

carvoento -ta (*adj.*) coal-like.

cãs (*f.pl.*) white hair.

casa (*f.*) house, home, dwelling, abode, residence, domicile; building, edifice; household; room; commercial establishment.—**alugada**, a rented house; fig., a hermit crab, c.a. BERNARDO EREMITA.—**da misericórdia**, charity hospital.—**da moeda**, government mint.—**da sogra**, (*colloq.*) an unruly household.—**da tia**, (*colloq.*) an assignation house.—**das máquinas**, engine room.—**de abafo**, hot house.—**de asilo**, poor house.—**de bagaço**, bagasse dump in a sugar-cane mill.—**de barrotes**, thatched mud hut.—**de brinquedos**, toy shop.—**de câmbio**, money changer's establishment.—**de cômodos**, rooming house. —**de correção**, reformatory.—**de despejo**, a storeroom where old things are put.—**de detenção**, detention home (for minors); also, a temporary jail for other offenders and suspects.—**de dois pavimentos**, a two-story house.—**de flores**, flower shop.—**de jôgo**, gambling house.—**de modas**, dress shop.—**de móveis**, furniture store.—**de navegação**, (*Naut.*) chart-room.—**de negócio**, any business establishment, esp. a store.—**de orates**, madhouse; bedlam.—**de pasto**, eating place.—**de pau a pique**, a hut with walls of mud-covered wattle.—**de penhor**, or **de prego**, pawn shop.—**de rendezvous**, assignation house.—**de saúde**, private hospital; rest home—**de sobrado**, a house of two or more floors.—**de telha vã**, a house with tile roof but no ceiling.—**de um só andar**, one-story house.—**do botão**, buttonhole.—**editôra**, publishing house.—**forte**, a bank vault.—**grande**, the owner's house on a plantation.—**pia**, orphan asylum.— **senhorial**, manor house.—**térrea**, a one-story house. **A—é sua!** The house is yours! Make yourself at home! **a-pegada**, or **vizinha**, the house next door. **chegar em—**, to arrive home. **crise de—**, housing shortage. **dona de—**, housewife, lady of the house. **dono de—**, landlord. **em—**, at home. **em—dos Pereira**, at the Pereiras. **estar em—**, to be at home; in gambling, to be even with the board. **estar na—dos trinta, dos quarenta**, etc., to be thirtyish, fortyish, etc. **ficar em—**, to stay at home; to remain indoors. **sair de—**, to leave the house, go out of doors. **Santa—**, public charity hospital. **saudades de—**, homesickness. **voltar em—**, to return home.

Casabranca (*f.*) Casablanca.

casaca (*f.*) full dress coat, tails.—**-de-couro**, (*Zool.*) Pelzen's spine-tail (*Synallaxis f. frontalis*); also = JAPACANIM and GAVIÃO-CABOCLO.—**-de-ferro**, a circus roustabout. **virar**, or **voltar, a—**, to turncoat.

casação (*m.*) great coat, overcoat, top coat.

casaco (*m.*) coat; jacket.

casacudo (*m., colloq.*) a rich and important person; a rustic [= CAIPIRA].

casadeiro -ra (*adj.*) = CASADOURO.

casado -da (*adj.*) married; joined, matched, united; (*pl.*) man and wife.

casadouro -ra (*adj.*) marriageable; seeking marriage. Vars. CASADEIRO CASADOIRO.

casal (*m.*) married couple; any couple, as a cock and hen.

casalar (*v.*) = ACASALAR.

casalejo [ê] (*m.*) hamlet; hut.

casamata (*f.*) casemate, pillbox.

casamentear (*v.i.*) to engage in match-making.

casamenteiro -ra (*adj.*) match-making; (*m.,f.*) matchmaker.

casamento (*m.*) marriage, matrimony, wedlock; nuptials, wedding.—**civil**, civil wedding ceremony.—**de gambá**, or **de rapôsa**, or **de viúva**, rain and shine. [Sol e chuva, casamento de viúva.]—**de inclinação**, a love match.—**de

mão esquerda, marriage of a noble and a commoner.— **de razão**, a marriage of convenience.—**putativo**, (*Canon Law*) a putative marriage.—**religioso**, religious wedding ceremony. **compromisso de—**, wedding engagement. **participação de—**, wedding announcement.

casão (*m.*) a big house, esp. a rich one.

casaquinha (*f.*) woman's short jacket.

casar (*v.t.*) to marry; to match, mate; to give in marriage; to harmonize, unite.—**-se (com)**, to marry. **Antes que cases, olha o que fazes**, Look before you leap. **apalavrar para—**, to betroth. **Casou (-se) com a prima**, He married his cousin. **Quem pensa não casa, quem casa não pensa**, Think and marry not; think not and marry.

casarão (*m.*) a big house.

casaria (*f.*), **casario** (*m.*) a row or group of houses.

casca (*adj.*) tight, closefisted, stingy; (*m.,f.*) a stingy person; (*f.*) hull, husk, rind; peel, skin; bark; pod, capsule; shell, case, outer covering; fig., outward appearance. —**-de-anta**, the wintersbark drimys (*D. winteri*), an aromatic evergreen shrub of the magnolia family, which yields the medicinal Winter's bark; c.a. CATAIA, CANELA-AMARGA, CAPOROROCA-PICANTE, MELAMBO, PARATUDO, PAU-PARATUDO.—**de ôvo**, eggshell.—**-doce** = PAU-DOCE. —**-grossa**, a roughneck (coarse person); a wealthy but uncultured person.—**-preciosa**, an aniba (*A. canelilla*), c.a. CASCA-DO-MARANHÃO; an ocotea (*O. pretiosa*), c.a. CANELA-CHEIROSA, CANELA-SASSAFRAZ, SASSAFRAZ, LOURO-CHEIRO.—**-preta**, a tropical ironweed (*Vernonia diffusa*), c.a. PAU-CANDEIA.—**s-de-honduras**, the Jamaica bitterbush (*Picramnia antidesma*), which yields the medicinal cascara amarga or Honduras bark.

cascabulho (*m.*) husk, nut shell(s); pile of husks; a student engaged in preparatory work (premedical, etc.).

cascaburrento -ta (*adj.*) rough.

cascalhada (*f.*) loud laughter; gust of wind; gravel bed.

cascalhar (*v.i.*) to chortle, laugh.

cascalheira (*f.*) gravel bed; alluvial deposit; a rattling sound, as of gravel being poured; difficult and noisy breathing.

cascalhento -ta (*adj.*) gravelly.

cascalhinho (*m.*) fine crushed rock.

cascalho (*m.*) crushed rock; rock chips, pebbles, gravel; slag, dross; "A deposit of pebbles, gravel, and ferruginous sand, in which the Brazilian diamond is usually found." *Webster.*

cascalhoso -sa, cascalhudo -da (*adj.*) pebbly, gravelly.

cascão (*m.*) thick shell; crust; scab.

cascar (*v.t.*) to belabor, beat, drub; to peel [= DESCASCAR]. —**a**, to reply to bitterly.

cáscara (*f.*) crude copper.—**-amarga** = CASCAS-DE-HONDURAS.—**-sagrada**, (*Bot.*) the cascara buckthorn (*Rhamnus purshiana*) which yields the cathartic bark of the same name.

cascaria (*f.*) a quantity of wine casks; animals' hoofs, collectively; (*colloq.*) a worthless individual.

cascavel [-véis] (*m.*) rattle; rattlebrain; (*f.*) the tropical rattlesnake (*Crotalus terrificus*), c.a. MARACÁ, BOICININGA; a viper (malignant person); a gate in a corral, etc., formed by three or four horizontal sliding poles.

cascavilhar (*v.t.,v.i.*) to rummage, ransack.

casco (*m.*) skull; scalp; skin, hide; cask, barrel; animal's hoof; hull of a ship. [*GBAT*: "a small dugout canoe without seats, extremely uncomfortable and usually leaky."]—**-de-burro**, a mulefoot breed of hogs; a river pothole containing gold or diamond-bearing sand and gravel.—**-de-cavalo**, (*Bot.*) any of three species of JACARANDA: *J. clausseniana, J. tomentosa* (c.a. CAROBA-MIÚDA), and *J. caroba* (c.a. CAROBINHA).—**-de-peba**, a large hat made of straw or palm leaves, esp. one with trimmings.

cascoso -sa (*adj.*) thick-shelled, thick-skinned; pert. to animals' hoofs; having large hoofs.

cascudo -da (*adj.*) hard-shelled; thick-skinned; (*m.*) any hard-shelled beetle; a rap on the head [= COCOROTE]; a "flivver"; any mailed catfish (family *Loricariidae*); (*f.*) a certain ant; a certain cockroach.—**-espada** (or—**-viola**), any mailed catfish of the genus Loricaria.

caseação (*f.*) conversion of milk into cheese; act of working buttonholes.

caseadeira (*f.*) woman who works buttonholes.

casear (*v.t.*) to work (sew) buttonholes.

casease (*f., Biochem.*) casease.

casebre [sé] (*m.*) tumbledown shack, hovel; old country house.

caseificar [e-i] (*v.t.*) to make like cheese.
caseína (*f.*) casein.
caseinogênio (*m.*, *Chem.*) caseinogen.
caseiro –ra (*adj.*) home; domestic; home-made; fond of home; stay-at-home; simple, plain, homespun; (*m.*) tenant; farm manager; caretaker; (*f.*) a housekeeper; a kept woman; constipation; hemorrhoids; diarrhea. **afazeres**—s, household duties, chores. **de fabrico**—, home-made. **remédio**—, household remedy.
caseose (*f.*, *Biochem.*) caseose.
caseoso –sa (*adj.*) caseous; cheesy [= QUEIJOSO].
caserna (*f.*, *Milit.*) casernes, barracks.
casimira (*f.*) cashmere. worsted (cloth); men's suiting.
casinga (*f.*) = CIPÓ-CRUZ-VERDADEIRO.
casinha (*f.*) small house; out-house, privy.
casinhola –nhota (*f.*), –nholo, –nhoto (*m.*) small, poor house.
casino [ss] (*m.*) = CASSINO.
casmurrice (*f.*) obstinacy; somberness; self-absorption.
casmurro –ma (*adj.*) taciturn; gloomy; grumpy; sullen, morose; (*m.,f.*) one who is thus.
caso (*m.*) case, instance; circumstance, contingency. event; affair; adventure; condition, situation; esteem.—**chova**, in case it rains.—**de consciência**, matter of conscience.—**de força maior**, force majeure; unavoidable circumstance; act of God.—**haja (um)**, in case there is (one).—**imprevisto**, unforeseen circumstance.—**que**, if, in case.—**sentimental**, love affair. **conforme o**—, as the case may be; according to circumstances. **de**—**pensado**, purposely, deliberately. **em**—**de necessidade**, in case of need. **em qualquer**—, in any case; anyway. **em tal**—, in such a case. **em todo (o)**—, at all events; at any rate. **fazer**—**de**, to heed, pay attention to. **fazer pouco**—**de**, to make light of; to disregard. **não fazer**—**de**, to ignore, disregard, pay no attention to. **Não vem ao**—, It is beside the point. **naquele**—, in that case. **no**—**que**, in case that. **pouco**—, disregard. **Vamos ao**—, Let's get to the point; let's get down to business.
casoar (*m.*) = CASUAR.
casoarina (*f.*) cassowary tree: Australian she-oak or beefwood (*Casuarina spp.*).
casola (*f.*) a little house.
casório (*m.*, *slang*) a wedding.
casota (*f.*) a little house; dog house.
caspa (*f.*) dandruff.
caspacho (*m.*) = GASPACHO.
casposo –sa, **caspento** –ta (*adj.*) dandruffy.
casqueira (*f.*) strip of wood.
casqueiro (*m.*) a place where logs are stripped of bark; a hewer of logs; a kitchen midden [= SAMBAQUI]; in Bahia, a strong south wind; one who prepares horses' hoofs for shoeing.
casquejar (*v.i.*) to grow new skin; to heal over.
casquento –ta (*adj.*) having a tough shell or skin.
casquete (*m.*) a cap with a visor.
casquilharia, casquilhice (*f.*) dandyism.
casquilho –lha (*adj.*) foppish, dapper, garish; (*m.*) dandy, coxcomb, fop; (*Mach.*) metal sleeve or cap.
casquinada (*f.*) giggle, snicker.
casquinar (*v.i.*) to giggle, snicker, titter; to laugh scoffingly (at).
casquinha (*f.*) thin veneer; metal plating; skin-flint; ill-qualified teacher.—**de sorvete**, ice cream cone (the container). **tirar a sua**—, to have a finger in the pie.
cassa (*f.*) muslin.—**suissa**, dotted Swiss.
cassação (*f.*) cassation, abrogation, annulment.
cassaco (*m.*) opossum [= GAMBÁ]; railroad, sugar mill or bakery worker.
cassar (*v.t.*) to annul, cancel (license, permit, etc.); to countermand; to quash.
cassaú (*m.*) = CAÇAÚ.
cassetete [tét] (*m.*) policeman's billy.
cassia (*f.*, *Bot.*) kinds of senna (*Cassia spp.*).—**das-antilhas**, the partridge pea (*Chamaecrista fasciculata*).—**-fístula**, golden shower senna (*Cassia fistula*), c.a. CANA-FÍSTULA.
cassineta [ê] (*f.*) fine woolen dress goods.
cassino (*m.*) cassino (a card game); casino (for gambling, etc.).—**grande**, big cassino (the 10 of diamonds).—**pequeno**, little cassino (the 2 of clubs). Var. CASINO.
cassiterita (*f.*, *Min.*) black tin, tin ore, cassiterite.
cassoa (*f.*) = ALFAFA-DA-SUÉCIA.
casta (*f.*) caste; lineage, race, breed; kind, sort.
castanha (*f.*) chestnut; cashew nut; knot of hair; (*pl.*, *Radio*) antenna insulators; (*Naut.*) cleats; (*Mach.*)

shackles (for steel springs).—**comadre-de-azeite** = CAIATÉ.—**da-austrália**, the Moreton Bay chestnut (*Castanospermum australe*).—**da-vinhaça**, a tree (*Caryocar crenatum*) of the souari-nut family.—**de-arara**, a large and handsome Brazilian tree (*Joannesia heveoides*).—**d'água** = TRÍBULO-AQUÁTICO.—**de-caiaté** = CAIATÉ.—**de-caju**, common cashew nut.—**de-cutia** = CAIATÉ.—**de-macaco**, the Guiana cannonball tree (*Couroupita guianensis*), c.a. CASTANHA-DE-ANTA, ABRICÓ-DE-MACACO, AMÊMDOA-DOS-ANDES, CUIA-DE-MACACO.—**de-peixe** = CAIATÉ,—**do-maranhão**, a silk-cotton tree (*Bombax affine*) and also = CASTANHEIRO-DO-PARÁ.—**do-pará**, the well-known Brazil nut tree (*Bertholletia excelsa*), or its fruit.—**purgativa** = CAIATÉ.—**sapucaia** = FRUTA-DE-MACACO.
castanhal, castanhedo [ê] (*m.*) a grove of Brazil-nut trees, growing wild.
castanheira (*f.*) woman who sells roasted chestnuts.
castanheiro (*m.*) gatherer of Brazil nuts.—**da-europa**, common European or Spanish chestnut (*Castanea sativa*).—**da-índia**. common horse chestnut (*Aesculus hippocastanum*).—**das-guianas** = CACAU-SELVAGEM.—**do-maranhão**, the Guiana chestnut (*Pachira aquatica*), c.a. CACAU-SELVAGEM, EMBIRATANHA, MAMORANA, SAPOTE-GRANDE; the Brazil-nut tree (*Bertholletia excelsa*), c.a. and better known as CASTANHA (or CASTANHEIRO) -DO-PARÁ.—**do-pará**, the Brazil-nut tree (*Bertholletia excelsa*), the tallest and most impressive tree in the Amazon jungle; c.a. CASTANHA-DO-PARÁ, AMENDOEIRA-DA-AMÉRICA, CASTANHEIRO-DO-MARANHÃO.
castanheta [ê] (*f.*) a snap of the finger; (*pl.*) castanets [= CASTANHOLAS].
castanho –nha (*adj.*) chestnut brown; (*m.*) chestnut (wood or tree); (*f.*) see CASTANHA.
castanholar (*v.i.*) to play castanets.
castanholas (*f.pl.*) castanets.
castão (*m.*) head (knob) of a walking stick.
castelã (*f.*) chatelaine.
castelão (*m.*) castellan.
castelhano –na (*adj.*) Castilian; also, in southern Brazil, a native of Uruguay or Argentina.
castelo (*m.*) castle; fortress; whorehouse.—**de pôpa**, poop deck, quarterdeck.—**de proa**, forecastle.—**s de cartas**, house of cards.—**s no ar**, air castles, day dreams.
castiçal (*m.*) candlestick.
castiçar (*v.t.*) to purify; to mate (animals) for breeding purposes.
castiço –ça (*adj.*) genuine; pure; of good racial stock.
castidade (*f.*) chastity; continence; purity.
castigador –dora (*adj.*) punishing; (*m.,f.*) punisher.
castigar (*v.t.*) to castigate, chastise; to punish; to trounce.
castigável (*adj.*) punishable.
castigo (*m.*) castigation, chastisement, punishment.
castina (*f.*, *Metal.*) flux.
casto –ta (*adj.*) chaste; continent; pure, undefiled.
castor [ô] (*m.*) beaver; beaver hat.
castorina (*f.*, *Chem.*) castorin.
castração (*f.*) castration, gelding.
castrado –da (*adj.*) castrated, emasculated; spayed; **cavalo**—, a gelding.
castrador [ô] (*m.*) castrator.
castrar (*v.t.*) to castrate, geld, spay. Cf. CAPAR.
casual (*adj.*) casual, fortuitous.
casualidade (*f.*) casualty, chance, fortuity.
casuar (*m.*) cassowary.
casuarina (*f.*) any beefwood or Australian pine (*Casuarina spp.*).
casuísta (*m.,f.*) casuist.
casuístico –ca (*adj.*) casuistic; (*f.*) casuistry.
casula (*f.*, *Eccl.*) chasuble [= PLANETA].
casulo (*m.*) cocoon; seed capsule.
cat. = CATÁLOGO (catalogue).
cata (*f.*) search, hunt; culling (of coffee beans, etc.). **à**—**de**, in search of.
catabatista (*m.,f.*) catabaptist.
catabi [í] (*m.*) a bump in the road.
catabolismo (*m.*, *Biol. Physiol.*) catabolism [= DESASSIMILAÇÃO].
catacáustica (*f.*, *Optics*) catacaustic curve.
catacego –ga (*adj.*, *colloq.*) near-sighted; half-blind.
cataclísmico –ca (*adj.*) cataclismic.
cataclismo (*m.*) cataclism.
catacrese (*f.*, *Rhet.*) catachresis.
catacumbas (*f.pl.*) catacombs.

catacústica (f., *Physics*) catacoustics.
catadeira (f.) woman who culls coffee beans by hand.
catadicrotismo (m., *Physiol.*) catadicrotism.
catadióptrica (f., *Physics*) catadioptrics.
catador [ô] (m.) coffee-bean cleaner and separator (a machine).
catadupa (f.) waterfall, cataract.
catadura (f.) general appearance, aspect, esp. of persons. de má—, of evil aspect, tough-looking.
catafalco (m.) catafalque.
catáfora (f., *Med.*) cataphora.
cataforese (f., *Physical Chem., Med.*) cataphoresis.
catagênese (f., *Biol.*) catagenesis, retrogressive evolution.
cataglóssio (m., *Surg.*) tongue depressor.
catagmático -ca (adj., *Med.*) catagmatic.
cataguás (m.pl.) former tribe of fierce Brazilian Indians in the State of Mato Grosso.
cataia (f.) = CASCA-DE-ANTA, ERVA-DE-BICHO.
cataiguaçu [a-i . . . çú] (m., *Bot.*) the jaborandi pilocarpus (*P. jaborandi*), c.a. JABORANDI.
catalão -lã (adj.; m.,f.) Catalan, Catalonian.
catálase (f., *Chem.*) catalase.
cataléctico -ca (adj., *Pros.*) catalectic.
catalecto (m.) catalecta.
catalepsia (f., *Med., Psychiatry*) catalepsy.
cataléptico -ca (adj.) cataleptic; (m.,f.) one suffering from catalepsy.
catalisação (f., *Physical Chem.*) catalysis.
catalisador [ô] (m., *Physical Chem.*) catalyst, catalytic agent, catalyzer.
catálise (f., *Physical Chem.*) catalysis.
catalítico -ca (adj.) catalytic.
catalogação (f.) cataloguing.
catalogador -dora (m.,f.) cataloguer, -guist.
catalogar (v.t.) to catalogue.
catálogo (m.) catalogue; descriptive price list.—do telefone, telephone directory [= LISTA DE ASSINANTES].
catalpa (f., *Bot.*) a bignonia (*B. catalpa*); also = CARVALHO-DAS-ANTILHAS.
catamarã (m.) catamaran (raft.)
catambuera (f.) = GANGÃO.
catamênio (m., *Physiol.*) catamenia, menses.
catana (f.) Japanese sword; cutlass; sword-fish; (*Bot.*) large prop root; a palm spathe.
catanduba (f., *Bot.*) a piptadenia (*P. moniliformis*), c.a. ANGICO-SURUCUCU, RAMA-DE-BEZERRO, PAU-BRANCO, PAU-CARRASCO; also = CATANDUVA.
catanduva (f.) thorny, low-growing scrub on waste land, c.a. MATO-MAU; also, poor soil. Var. CATANDUBA.
catão (m.) an austere, or seemingly austere, man; a Catonian.
catapasmo (m., *Med.*) catapasm.
catapereiro (m.) the common pear (*Pyrus communis*).
catapétalo -la (adj., *Bot.*) catapetalous.
cata-piolho (m., *colloq.*) the index finger.
cataplasma (f.) poultice.
cataplexia [ks] (f., *Physiol.*) cataplexy.
catapora(s) (f.) varicella, chicken pox [= VARICELA].
catapu [ú] (m.) Peruvian groundcherry (*Physalis peruviana*).
catapulta (f.) catapult.
catapultar (v.t.) to catapult.
catar (v.t.) to search; to scrutinize; to cull, pick (out).—as letras, to pick out the letters (on a typewriter).—café, feijão, etc., to cull coffee, beans, etc., by hand.—piolho, to delouse (by picking out lice one by one).
cataraca (f.) = CARACA.
catarata (f.) cataract, waterfall; (*Med.*) cataract.
cataratado -da, -toso -sa (adj., *Med.*) cataractous.
Catarina (f.) Catherine, Catherina, Cathleen, Katherine, Katherina, Kathryn, Katrina; [*not cap.*] balance wheel of a timepiece.
catarinense (adj.; m.,f.) (a native) of the State of Santa Catarina.
catarineta [ê] (m.,f.) a nickname applied to natives of Santa Catarina.
catarral (adj.) catarrhal; (f.) acute bronchitis.
catarreira (f., *colloq.*) a cold; a running of the nose.
catarrento -ta (adj.) catarrhal.
catarro (m.) catarrh, cold.—pulmonar, (*colloq.*) bronchitis.
catarroso -sa (adj.) catarrhal.
catarse (f.) catharsis, purgation.
catártico -ca (adj.; m.,f.) cathartic.
catartina (f., *Chem.*) cathartin, cathartic acid.

catarto (m.) turkey buzzard (*Cathartes*); = URUBU.
catásseto (m., *Bot.*) any Catasetum orchid of tropical America.
catastáltico -ca (adj., *Med.*) catastaltic.
catástrofe (f.) catastrophe; calamity.
catastrófico -ca (adj.) catastrophic.
catatau (m., *colloq.*) a beating; tumult; a short person.
catatonia (f., *Psychiatry*) catatonia.
catau (m., *Naut.*) a sheepshank knot.
catavento (m.) weather vane; windmill; pinwheel.
catear (v.t.) to pan for gold, etc.
catecismo (m.) catechism (manual); by ext., any series of elementary questions and answers. Cf. CATEQUESE.
catecol (m., *Chem.*) catechol, pyrocatechol.
catecuamenato (m.) catechumentate.
catecúmeno -na (m.,f.) catechumen.
cátedra (f.) cathedra; professorial or episcopal chair. falar de—, to speak with authority; to know whereof one speaks.
catedral (adj.; f.) cathedral.
catedrático -ca (adj.) cathedratic, professorial, pedagogic; (m.,f.) college professor or high school teacher; (m., *slang*) a racetrack tout.
categoria (f.) category.
categôricamente [ê] (adv.) explicitly.
categórico -ca (adj.) categoric(al), absolute.
categute (m.) catgut.
catenação (f.) concatenation.
catenária (f., *Math.*) catenary.
catenóide (m., *Geom.*) catenoid.
catenula (f.) small chain.
catenulado -da (adj.) catenulate, having a chainlike form.
catequese (f.) catechism (oral religious instruction); indoctrination. Cf. CATECISMO.
catequético -ca (adj.) catechetical.
catequina (f., *Chem.*) catechol.
catequista (m.,f.) catechist.
catequização (f.) catechizing.
catequizador -dora [ô] (adj.) catechismal, catechistic; (m.,f.) catechist, catechizer.
catequizar (v.t.) to catechize.
cateretê (m.) a country dance, with handclapping and stomping of the feet, performed on dry cowhides laid on the ground.
caterina (f., *colloq.*) prostitute.
caterpilar (m., *Mach.*) caterpillar tread.
caterva (f.) mob, gang.
catesbéia (f.) the hedge lilythorn (*Catesbaea spinosa*).
catete [têtê] (m.) a variety of maize, c.a. CATÊTO and BATITÉ; a breed of Brazilian pigs; a wild pig called CAITITU.
cateter [tér] (m., *Med.*) catheter [= ALGÁLIA, CANDELINHA].
cateterismo (m., *Med.*) catheterism.
cateto (m.) vertical height; perpendicular line; (*Geom.*) cathetus.
catêto (m.) = CATETE.
catetômetro (m.) cathetometer.
catetu (m.) = CAITITU.
catião, cation, cationte (m., *Physical Chem.*) cation.
catilinária (f.) a severe accusation.
catimbau (m.) an exorcism [= CATIMBÓ]; a small, old pipe; a ridiculous man.
catimbauzeiro -ra, catimbôzeiro -ra (m.,f.) one who practices exorcism.
catimbó (m.) = CATIMBAU; also = CAIPIRA.
catimbueira (f.) a stunted ear of corn.
catimplora (f.) water-cooler; siphon; oil can; culvert; water sprinkler; ice cream freezer; high hat. Var. CANTIMPLORA.
catimpuera (f.) a fermented drink made from manioc and honey; c.a. QUITAMBUERA.
catinga (f.) rank smell; goaty smell; offensive body odor; a mean, stingy person; avariciousness; any region of stunted vegetation, esp. of type of stunted spare forest found in the drought areas of northeastern Brazil; (*Bot.*) a trumpet bush (*Tecoma ca'inga*); a purpleheart (*Peltogyne caiingae*); a caesalphina (*C. gardneriana*), c.a. CATINGUEIRA.—de-bode, the tropic ageratum (*A. conyzoides*), c.a. CATINGA-DE-BARRÃO, ERVA-DE-SÃO-JOÃO, MARIA-PRETA, MENTRASTO.—-de-macaca-brava, a velvetbean (*Stizolobium pungens*).—-de-mulata, the horseshoe pelargonium (*P. zonale*), c.a. GERÂNIO, MALVA-FLOR, PELARGÔNIO; the common tansy (*Tana-*

cetum vulgare), c.a. ERVA-CONTRA-VERMES, ANATÁSIA-DAS-BOTICAS.—**-de-negro** or—**-de-tatu**, the strong-smelling giant spiderflower (*Cleome gigantea*), c.a. MUCAMBÊ-CATINGA.—**-de-paca**, the thorny elaeagnus (*E. pungens*).—**-de-porco**, a mayten (*M. gonocladus*), c.a. CORAÇÃO-DE-NEGRO, SAPUVÃO, VERGA-VERGA; also any of various species of Caesalpinia.—**-de-prêto**, a cordia (*C. curassavica*), c.a. BALIEIRA, CATINGA-DE-BARRÃO, ERVA-BRASILEIRA, MARIA-PRETA, PIMENTEIRA.—**-de-tamanduá**, a mountain ebony tree (*Bauhinia rufa*), c.a. UNHA-DE-BOI-DO-CAMPO, UNHA-DE-VACA-ROXA.—**-de-urubu**, a poreleaf (*Porophyllum martii*).—**-manteiga**, a sea catfish; (*adj.*) miserly.

catingá (*m.*) = QUIRUÁ.

catingal (*m.*) a large area of stunted vegetation.

catingante (*adj.*) = CATINGOSO.

catingar (*v.i.*) to give off a rank smell; to stink; to be stingy.

catingoso –sa, catingudo –da (*adj.*) rank, strong-smelling.

catingueiro (*m.*), **-ra** (*f.*) inhabitant of the drought areas of northeastern Brazil; (*m.*) a brocket (*Mazama simplicicornis*), c.a. CAPUEIRO, GUAÇUBIRÁ, GUAÇUCATINGA, QUATRO-OLHOS, SUAÇA SUAÇUCATINGA, SUAÇUTINGA, VEADO-VIRÁ, VIRÁ, VIROTE; (*f.*, *Bot.*) either of two caesalpinias: *C. pyramidalis* (c.a. CATINGA-DE-PORCO, PAU-DE-FERRO, PAU-DE-RATO) or *C. gardneriana* (c.a. CATINGA, MARMELEIRO-BRANCO; (*m.*) molasses grass (*Melinis minutiflora*), c.a. CAPIM-GORDURA.—**-de-fôlha-miúda**, or—**-de-porco**, a caesalpinia (*C. microphylla*), c.a. CATINGA-DE-PORCO, ERVA-DE-RATO, PAU-DE-RATO.

catinguento –ta (*adj.*) = CATINGOSO-SA.

cationte, cation, cationio (*m.*, *Physical Chem.*) cation.

catira (*f.*) = CATERETÊ.

catita (*adj.*) spruce, dapper, elegant; nicely trimmed; (*m.,f.*) elegant, well-dressed person; (*f.*) small triangular sail; a mouse; (*colloq.*) jail.

catitice (*f.*), **catitismo** (*m.*) dressiness; dandyism.

catitu [ú] (*m.*) = CAITITU.

cativante (*adj.*) captivating, endearing, attractive, fascinating, prepossessing.

cativar (*v.t.*) to captivate, fascinate, charm; to capture, enslave.

cativeiro (*m.*) captivity, bondage; place of captivity.

cativo –va (*adj.*) captive; enslaved; (*m.*) war prisoner; (*m.,f.*) slave.—**de chumbo**, (*Min.*) anatase or octahedrite.—**de ferro**, a form of magnetite.

catléia (*f.*) any Cattleya orchid.

catoá (*m.*) = GAROUPINHA.

catódico –ca (*adj.*) cathodic(al). **raios—s**, cathode rays.

cátodo, catódio (*m.*, *Phys.*, *Chem.*) cathode.

catodofosforescência (*f.*, *Physics*, *Chem.*) cathodophosphorescence.

catodoluminesência (*f.*, *Physics*, *Chem.*) cathodoluminescence.

catojé (*m.*) = CIPÓ-DE-COBRA.

catolé (*m.*) a ladypalm (*Rhapis pyramidata*), or its fruit; a scheelea palm (*S. amylacea*), c.a. ANAJÁ; also = COCO-CATOLÉ, COCO-DE-QUARESMA, COQUEIRO-CATOLÉ.

catolicão (*m.*) a universal remedy.

catolicidade (*f.*) catholicity; catholicism.

catolicismo (*m.*) Catholicism.

católico –ca (*adj.*) [Roman] Catholic; catholic, universal; (*m.,f.*) a [Roman] Catholic.

católito (*m.*, *Physical Chem.*) catholyte.

catolizar (*v.t.*) to catholicize.

catóptrica (*f.*, *Optics*) catoptrics.

catóptrico –ca (*adj.*) catoptric—referring to reflected light.

catorra [ô] (*f.*) kind of parrot, c.a. CATURRITA.

catorrita (*f.*) the green paroquet (*Myopsitta monacha*), c.a. PERIQUITO-DO-PANTANAL.

catorze (*adj.*; *m.*) = QUATORZE.

catorzeno –na (*adj.*) = DÉCIMO-QUARTO and QUATORZENO.

catota [ô] (*f.*) dried nasal discharge.

catrabucha (*f.*) wire brush.

catraca (*f.*) ratchet.

catrafiar, catrafilar (*v.t.*, *colloq.*) to nab.

catraia (*f.*) a small one-man boat; a low prostitute.

catraieiro (*m.*) boatman.

catraio (*m.*) = LINGUADO.

catre (*m.*) rude bed; trundle bed; folding cot; bunk.

catuaba (*f.*) a goldentrumpet (*Anemopaegma glauca*); a leaf flower (*Phyllanthus nobilis*), c.a. PÉROLA-VEGETAL.—**-do-mato**, a holly (*Ilex conocarpa*).—**-verdadeira**, a

goldentrumpet (*Anemopaegma mirandum*), c.a. CATUÍBA.

catucação, catucada (*f.*) popular variants of CUTUCAÇÃO and CUTUCADA.

catucaém (*m.*) = CARVALHO-DO-BRASIL.

catuíba (*f.*) = CATUABA-VERDADEIRA.

catucão (*m.*) a dig with the elbow.

catucar (*v.*) = CUTUCAR.

cátulo (*m.*) a puppy.

catumbi [í] (*m.*) a certain dance; a certain game of chance.

catuqui [í], **catuquim** (*m.*) a gnat or midge.

caturra (*m.,f.*) a disputatious, pigheaded person who clings to out-moded ideas; fossil, old fogy; the castor-oil plant [= CARRAPATEIRA-BRANCA]; a certain small parrot, c.a. PERIQUITO-REI, TIUM.

caturrar (*v.i.*) to argue obstinately, pigheadedly; of a vessel, to pitch [sailor's slang].

caturreira, caturrice (*f.*) **caturrismo** (*m.*) obstinacy; pigheadedness; fogyism.

caturrita (*f.*) = CATORRA.

caturritar (*v.i.*) to gabble, chatter.

cauã (*f.*) = ACAUÃ.

cauaçu [çú] (*m.*, *Bot.*) a sea grape (*Coccolobis latifolia*), c.a. CAQUEIRO-BRAVO; a rubiaceous plant (*Exostemma australe*), closely related to the Caribbean princewood and c.a. QUINA-DE-SANTA-CATARINA, QUINA-DO-MATO, QUINA-DO-PARANÁ; a calathea (*C. lutea*), c.a. ARIÁ.

cauauã (*f.*) = JABURU-MOLEQUE.

caução (*f.*) surety bond; collateral security; a sum of money deposited as a guarantee. [But not caution, which is CAUTELA, PRECAUÇÃO.]. **prestar—**, to give bail or go bond. **sob—**, under bond.

caucasiano –na, caucásico –ca (*adj.*) Caucasian.

caucásio –sia (*adj.*; *m.,f.*) Caucasian.

cauchal (*m.*) an area abounding in gumtrees.

caucheiro (*m.*) a gatherer of caucho (wild rubber); owner of a stand of gumtrees.

caucho (*m.*) a gumtree (*Castilla ulei*) from which a wild rubber known commercially as caucho is obtained; this product.—**-macho**, a breadnut tree (*Brosimum amplicoma*).

caucionante (*adj.*; *m.,f.*) serving, or one who serves, as bond.

caucionar (*v.t.*) to give as bond; to guarantee.

caucionário –ria (*adj.*) bonding; (*m.*) bondsman, surety; (*f.*) bondswoman, surety.

cauda (*f.*) tail; tail-end, rear-end; any taillike appendage, as the tail of an airplane or the train of a gown.—**-de-andorinha**, dovetail.—**-s-de-cavalo**, (*Meteor.*) mare's-tail.—**-de-leão** = AGRIPALMA (a plant).—**-de-rapôsa** (*Bot.*) love-lies-bleeding (*Amaranthus caudatus*), other common names for which are: DISCIPLINAS-DE-FREIRA, RABO(S)-DE-RAPÔSA, VELUDO-DE-PENCA, RABO-DE-GATO, CHORÕES-DOS-JARDINS; the horseweed fleabane (*Erigeron canadensis*); either of two grasses called CAPIM-RABO-DE-BURRO and CAPIM-CAUDA-DE-RAPÔSA.—**-de-rato**, (*Veter.*) rattails.—**-de-são-francisco**, a clubmoss (*Phycopodium phlegmaria*).—**equina**, (*Anat.*) cauda equina.—**-de-zorro** = CAPIM-RABO-DE-BURRO.—**-vermelha**, the blood-fin (*Aphyocharax rubripinnis*), popular in home aquaria.

caudal (*adj.*) caudal; torrential; (*m.,f.*) torrent; waterfall; stream, current; flow or volume of a river; caudal fin.

caudaloso –sa (*adj.*) copious, plentiful, abundant; torrential; of rivers, carrying much water.

caudatário (*m.*) trainbearer; fig., subservient hanger-on; henchman.

caudato –ta (*adj.*) caudate, tailed.

caudel [-déis] (*m.*) = COUDEL.

caudelaria (*f.*) = COUDELARIA.

cáudex, cáudice (*m.*, *Bot.*) caudex.

caudículo (*m.*, *Bot.*) caudicle.

caudilhismo (*m.*) bossism; rule of a CAUDILHO.

caudilho (*m.*) caudillo, military chief or leader; head of a party; leader of a faction.

caudímano –na (*adj.*) having a prehensile tail.

cauim [au-ím] (*m.*) a native Brazilian drink prepared from fermented manioc, corn, etc.

cauixi [au-ixí] (*m.*) a caustic sponge-like matter which collects on the roots of trees on the banks of certain rivers in Amazonia. The ashes of this material are mixed with clay for making earthenware.

caule (*m.*) caulis, stalk, stem; trunk of a tree.

cauleoso –sa (*adj.*) = CAULESCENTE.

caulescente (*adj.*) caulescent [= CAULEOSO, CAULÍFERO].

caulícola (*adj.*) cauliculous; (*f.*) fungus or other parasitic growth on the stalk of a plant.
caulículo (*m.*, *Bot.*) caulicle; (*Arch.*) cauliculus.
caulífero –ra (*adj.*) = CAULESCENTE.
caulifloro –ra (*adj.*, *Bot.*) cauliflorous.
caulim (*m.*) kaolin, china clay [= CAULINO].
caulinita (*f.*) kaolinite.
caulocárpico –ca (*adj.*, *Bot.*) caulocarpic.
cauná (*m.*) a sweetleaf (*Symplocos uniflora*).
caúna (*f.*) kinds of holly (*Ilex spp.*).
cauré (*m.*) a bat falcon (*Falco albigularis*), c.a. TEMTEN-ZINHO, COL(H)EIRINHA; an aplomado falcon (*Falco fusco-caerulescens*).
cauri [í], **cauril**, **caurim** (*m.*) cowrie shell; (*colloq.*) a trick.
causa (*f.*) cause; reason, motive; final cause; (*Law*) cause, case, action.—**motora,** major cause. **em desespêro de**—, in despair of winning one's case. **falar com conhecimento de**—, to know what one is talking about; to speak advisedly. **por**—**de,** because of, on account of. **por sua**—, because of you (him, her, etc.). **ter ganho de**—, to gain one's point.
causação (*f.*) causation.
causador –dora (*adj.*) causing; (*m.,f.*) causer.
causal (*adj.*) causal; (*f.*) cause.
causalgia (*f.*, *Med.*) causalgia.
causalidade (*f.*) causality.
causante (*adj.*) causing; (*f.*) cause.
causar (*v.t.*) to cause, originate, bring into being; to effect, produce, occasion, give rise to.—**escândalo,** to give offence.—**espécie,** to raise eyebrows.—**mêdo,** to frighten.
causativo –va (*adj.*) causative.
causídico (*m.*) advocate, upholder, defender; lawyer (esp. for the defense).
causo (*m.*, *colloq.*) case; story.
cáustica (*f.*) see CÁUSTICO.
causticação (*f.*) cauterization; fig., harassment, importunity.
causticante (*adj.*) caustic.
causticar (*v.t.*) to sear with caustic; to harass.
causticidade (*f.*) causticity.
cáustico –ca (*adj.*) caustic (*adj.; m.*) caustic; (*f.*, *Optics*) caustic curve.
cautchu [ú] (*m.*) caoutchouc (pure rubber).—**sintético,** synthetic rubber.
cautela (*f.*) caution, care; discretion; precaution; ticket stub; temporary receipt.—**de penhor,** pawn ticket. **à**—, cautiously; as a precaution. Cf. CAUÇÃO.
cautelar (*v.*) = ACAUTELAR.
cauteloso –sa (*adj.*) cautious, careful; deliberate; chary; wary; prudent.
cautério (*m.*) cautery, caustic; fig., severe punishment.
cauterização (*f.*) cauterization.
cauterizar (*v.t.*) to cauterize; to sear; fig., to clean up a bad situation by taking strong measures.
cauto –ta (*adj.*) cautious, wary.
cava (*f.*) act of digging; hole, pit; armhole of a garment; cellar, basement; (*adj.*) hollow. **veia**—, (*Anat.*) vena cava.
cavação (*f.*) act or result of digging; (*colloq.*) a "good thing" (profitable job or business, esp. one obtained by pull).
cavaco (*m.*) chip, wood splinter; gossip, chat; kind of cruller; displeasure; either of two fishes c.a. GUAIVIRA and XARELETE.—**s do ofício,** the trials and tribulations inherent in any business or profession. **dar o**—, to hit the ceiling (display temper). **dar o**—**por,** to give anything for (be very fond of).
cavacué (*m.*) the diademed parrot (*Amazona diadema*) of north Brazil.
cavadeira (*f.*) a hoe or similar digging tool.
cavadela (*f.*) act of digging; a hoeing.
cavador –dora (*adj.*) hardworking, industrious, gogetting, hustling; (*m.*) digger (workman); (*colloq.*) a person who obtains an advantage by shrewd, sometimes unfair, means; (*f.*) a digging machine.
cavaíba (*m.,f.*) an Indian of the Tupi-Cawahib, living in Mato Grosso on the upper Gi-Paraná or Machado River. [They are an offshoot of the Cabaíba, which see.]; (*adj.*) pert. to or designating the Cavaíba.
cavala (*f.*) mackerel.—**africana** = ENXOVA-PRETA (oil-fish).—**branca** (or **-pintada,** or **-sardinheira**) the painted mackerel (*Scomberomorus regalis*).—**pintada** = SOROROCA (Spanish mackerel).—**verdadeira** (or **-preta**) the king mackerel (*Scomberomorus cavalla*).

cavalada (*f.*) asininity.
cavalagem (*f.*) stud service; stud fee.
cavalão (*m.*) a big horse; a kind of mackerel; fig., a person given to horseplay; an overgrown youth, esp. one who is not too bright.
cavalar (*adj.*) equine; horse; (*v.i.*) = CAVALOAR.
cavalaria (*f.*) herd of horses; band of horsemen; troop of cavalry; horsemanship.
cavalariano (*m.*) cavalryman.
cavalariça (*f.*) horse stall, stable. **moço de**—, groom, stableman.
cavalariço (*m.*) stableman.
cavaleiro –ra (*adj.*) of or pert. to horsemen, horsemanship and horseback riding; (*m.*) horseman, rider; trooper, cavalryman; cavalier; knight; a prawn (*Palaemon jamaicensis*) c.a. CUTIPACA; rider on a balance of precision; a high, strong wave; (*f.*) horsewoman. **a**—, atop, astraddle; in a prominent place.—**errante,** knight errant.
cavaleiroso –sa (*adj.*) chivalrous.
cavalete (*m.*) easel; sawhorse; trestle; work bench; bridge of violin; rack (torture).—**do telhado,** roof ridge. **nariz de**—, hooked nose.
cavalgação (*m.*) rut, oestrus [= CIO].
cavalgada (*f.*) cavalcade.
cavalgadura (*f.*) mount (horse, etc.); fig., dolt, numskull.
cavalgante (*adj.*) riding; (*m.*) horseman; (*f.*) horsewoman.
cavalgar [3] (*v.t.*) to mount (a horse); to leap over; (*v.i.*) to ride horseback; to sit astride, straddle.
cavalhada (*f.*) herd of horses; (*pl.*) joust.
cavalheiresco –ca [ês] (*adj.*) chivalrous.
cavalheirismo (*m.*) chivalrousness, gallantry.
cavalheiro –ra (*adj.*) gentlemanly, chivalrous, well-bred; (*m.*) gentleman; well-bred man; one of refined manners; lady's dancing partner.—**-da-sala** = CAPITÃO-DE-SALA (a plant).—**-das-onze-horas,** (*Bot.*) the common portulaca (*P. grandiflora*), c.a. AMOR-CRESCIDO, BELDROEGA-DE-FLOR-GRANDE, FLOR-DE-ONZE-HORAS, PEREXI.—**-de-indústria,** one who lives by his wits; swindler.
cavalheiroso –sa (*adj.*) chivalrous, gentlemanly, gallant, noble.
cavalinha (*f.*) a small mackerel, c.a. MUZUNDU; (*Bot.*) a horsetail or scouring rush (*Equisetum xylochoetum*), c.a. CAVALINHO, COLA-DE-CAVALO, RABO-DE-CAVALO, LIXA-VEGETAL, ERVA-CANUDO; (*Zool.*) = XIXARRO-CALABAR (a scad).
cavalinho (*m.*) a small horse; (*pl.*) incus; (*Bot.*) = CAVA-LINHA.—**-d'água,** the Brazilian parrotfeather (*Myrisphyllum brasiliensis*), c.a. BEM-CASADOS, PINHEIRINHO-D'ÁGUA, MIL-FÔLHAS-D'ÁGUA.—**-de-judeu,** a dragonfly.—**-do-mar,** a sea horse (*Hippocampus spp.*).
cavalo (*m.*) horse; root stock for grafting; syphilitic chancre; knight (chessman); jack (face card); H.P. (horsepower).—**aguado,** a foundered horse.—**baixeiro,** light-stepping, easy-riding horse.—**cambraia,** white horse.—**capado** or **castrado,** a gelding.—**castanho,** chestnut horse.—**com ferro,** branded horse.—**de-batalha,** charger; the main argument; major difficulty; one's forte.—**de campo,** cattle horse; cow pony.—**de corrida,** race horse.—**de lançamento,** stud horse.—**de pau,** (*Aeron.*) ground loop.—**de raça,** or—**de puro sangue,** thoroughbred horse.—**de sela,** saddle horse.—**de tiro,** draft horse.—**de um ano,** a one-year old.—**-de-cão,** any of numerous large spider wasps, esp. the great black *Pepsis albomaculata*, and the even larger *Pepsis pertys*; other common names are: MARIBONDO-CAÇADOR, VESPA-CAÇADORA, VESPÃO.—**ao freio,** actual or brake horse-power.—**de empuxo,** (*Aeron.*) thrust horsepower.—**desbocado,** or—**desenfreado,** runaway horse.—**-força** = CAVALO-VAPOR.—**garanhão,** or—**inteiro,** stallion.—**-judeu,** dragonfly.—**-marinho,** sea-horse; hippopotamus.—**para enxêrto,** a scion for grafting.—**selado de costas,** a saddle-backed horse.—**sem ferro,** unbranded horse.—**-vapor,** French, or metric, horsepower.—**(-vapor)-hora,** French horsepower-hour. **a**—, on horseback. **A**—**dado não se abre a bôca** (or, **não se olham os dentes**), One does not look a gift horse in the mouth. **corrida de**—s, horse race. **Êle é um**—, He is a downright ass. **montar,** or **andar, a**—, to ride horseback. **registo genealógico de**—s, studbook. **tirar o**—**da chuva,** (*slang*) to "cut out the bull".
cavaloar (*v.i.*) to cavort; to indulge in horseplay.
cavanhaque (*m.*) goatee.
cavaquear (*v.i.*) to chat, gossip.
cavaqueira (*f.*) intimate confab, chitchat.

cavaquinho (*m.*) ukelele (small guitar).
cavar (*v.t.*) to dig, excavate; to hollow out; to go after a thing, tooth and nail; to wangle; (*v.i.*) to burrow; (*slang*) to chisel.—**a vida**, to earn one's living.
cavatina (*f.*, *Music*) cavatina; simple air.
caveira (*f.*) death's head; skull.—**de burro**, bad luck.
caveiroso –**sa** (*adj.*) gaunt, haggard.
caverna (*f.*) cavern; (*Shipbuilding*) rib.
cavernal (*adj.*) cavernal.
cavername (*m.*, *Shipbuilding*) frame; (*colloq.*) skeleton.
cavernite (*f.*, *Med.*) cavernitis.
cavernoso –**sa** (*adj.*) cavernous; hollow.
caveto [ê] (*m.*, *Arch.*) cavetto.
cávia (*f.*) cavy, guinea pig [= COBAIA].
caviar (*m.*) caviar.
cavicórneo –**nea** (*adj.*) having hollow horns (as oxen, sheep, goats).
cavidade (*f.*) cavity.—**abdominal** (*Anat.*) abdominal cavity.—**bucal** (*Anat.*) buccal cavity.—**cariada** or **dentária**, tooth cavity.—**coronóide**, (*Anat.*) coronoid fossa.—**cotilóide**, (*Anat.*) cotyloid cavity.
cavilação (*f.*) quibbling, captiousness; quip.
calvilador –**dora** (*adj.*) caviling; (*m.*, *f.*) caviler.
cavilar (*v.i.*) to cavil, carp, quibble; to defraud, cheat.
cavilha (*f.*) peg, dowel, pin; cotter, key.—**J, J bolt.**—**U,** U bolt.—**de forquilha**, shackle bolt.
cavilhar (*v.t.*) to fasten with a peg, cotter or key.
caviloso –**sa** (*adj.*) tricky, fraudulent; deceitful; captious.
cavirão (*m.*) fid, marlinespike; shackle bolt.
cavitação (*f.*, *Mach.*) cavitation.
cavitar (*v.i.*) to cavitate.
caviúna (*f.*) = CABIÚNA.
cavo –**va** (*adj.*) hollow; cavernous.
cavoucar (*v.t.*) to dig into; to dig ditches; etc.; to grub. Var. CABOUCAR.
cavouco (*m.*) ditch, trench. Var. CABOUCO.
cavouqueiro (*m.*) ditch digger; quarryman. Var. CABOUQUEIRO.
Caxemira (*f.*) Kashmir, Cashmere.
caxeta (*f.*) the Ambay pumpwood (*Cecropia adenopus*).
caxicaém (*m.*) = CARVALHO-DO-BRASIL.
caxingar (*v.*) = COXEAR.
caxinguelê (*m.*) any member of the squirrel family [= SERELEPE and QUATIPURU].
caxirenguengue (*m.*) a useless old knife, esp. one without a handle, variously c.a. CAXERENGUENGUE, CAXERINGUENGUE, XERENGUE.
caxiri, caxirim (*m.*) a native beer made by fermenting manioc; a dish prepared with BEIJU soaked in water; also = CAXIRENGUENGUE.
caxixe (*m.*) = CHUCHU.
caxumba (*f.*, *Med.*) mumps [= TRASORELHO].
c/c = CONTA CORRENTE (current account).
CE = Ceará (State of).
cear (*v.i.*) to take supper. [noun: CEIA].
cearense (*adj.*; *m.,f.*) (person) of the State of Ceará.
cebídeos (*m.pl.*) the Cebidae (family of New World monkeys).
cebo [é] (*m.*) any cebid (monkey of the genus *Cebus*).
cebola [ô] (*f.*) onion (plant or bulb); any bulb; (*colloq.*) a large, old-fashioned pocket watch; (*Bot.*) the Braz. alstroemeria (*A. brasiliensis*), c.a. CARAJURU.—**berrante**, an alstroemeria (*A. isabellana*); the belladonna lily (*Amaryllis belladonna*) c.a. CEBOLA-CECEM.—**branca** = —BRAVA-DO-PARÁ—**brava**, an epiphytic tree, the Demerara waxflower (*Clusia insignis*) c.a. CEBOLA-GRANDE-DA-MATA; the greentube crinum (*C. scabrum*); also = CEBOLA-DO-MATO; also = CUPAÍ.—**brava-do-pará**, a pancratium (*P. guianensis*) c.a. AÇUCENA-D'ÁGUA CEBOLA-BRANCA, CILA-DA-TERRA.—**cecem**, the belladonna lily (*Amaryllis belladonna*) c.a. BELADONA-DOS-ITALIANOS, AÇUCENA-ENCARNADA, CEBOLA-BERRANTE—**de-cheiro**, Welsh onion (*Allium fistulosum*), c.a. CEBOLINHA, CEBOLA-DE-TODO-O-ANO.—**de-portugal**, or **de-são-tiago**, Portuguese onion (*Allium lusitanicum*).—**de-todo-o-ano** = CEBOLINHA.—**do-campo**, Barbados lily (*Amaryllis vittata*).—**do-mato**, the hyacinth griffinia (*G. hyacinthina*), c.a. CEBOLA-BRAVA.
cebolada (*f.*) onion stew or other dish made principally with onions.
cebolal (*m.*) onion field.
cebolão (*m.*, *colloq.*) large, old-fashioned pocket watch.
ceboletas-de-frança (*f.pl.*) chives (*Allium schoenoprasum*), c.a. CEBOLINHO.

cebolinha (*f.*) any small onion; pearl onion; Welsh onion (*Allium fistulosum*), c.a. CEBOLA-DE-CHEIRO, CEBOLA-DE-TODO-O-ANO.—**do-campo** = ALHO-DO-MATO.
cebolinho (*m.*) chive (*Allium schoenoprasum*), c.a. CEBOLETAS-DE-FRANÇA.—**branco**, Naples onion (*Allium neapolitanum*).—**cheiroso**, fragrant false garlic (*Nothoscordum fragrans*).
cecal (*adj.*, *Anat.*, *Zool.*) caecal.
cecê (*m.*) tsetse fly [= TSÉ-TSÉ]
ceceadura (*f.*) lisping.
cecear (*v.t.*,*v.i.*) to lisp. Cf. CICIAR.
cecectomia (*f.*, *Surg.*) caecectomy.
ceceio (*m.*) lisp; lisping.
cecidia (*f.*, *Bot.*, *Zool.*) cecidium, a gall.
cecília (*f.*) a wormlike burrowing amphibian of the genus Caecilia, c.a. MINHOCÃO; [*cap.*] Cecile, Cecilia, Cecily, Cicely.
Cecílio (*m.*) Cecil.
cecite (*f.*, *Med.*) caecitis.
ceco, cecum (*m.*, *Anat.*, *Zool.*) caecum.
cecografia (*f.*) Braille printing (for the blind).
cedência (*f.*) = CESSÃO.
cedente (*adj.*) yielding; assigning; (*m.,f.*) one who yields or assigns.
ceder (*v.t.*) to cede, yield, give up; to grant, convey; to assign; (*v.i.*) to yield, give in, give way; to sag;—**à evidência**, to concede, grant, admit to be true.—**o passo**, to step aside.—**terreno**, to give ground, give way.
cediço –**ça** (*adj.*) of news, information, etc., old, stale, hackneyed, trite, well-worn, "corny."
cedilha (*f.*) cedilla (mark under letter c—Ç).
cedilhar (*v.t.*) to mark with a cedilla.
cedimento (*m.*) = CESSÃO.
cedinho (*adv.*) quite early, pretty early. **bem—**, bright and early.
cedível (*adj.*) capable of being ceded or assigned.
cedo [ê] (*adj.*) early, soon, untimely, prematurely, too soon. **desde—**, early. **mais—ou menos trade**, sooner or later; eventually. **tão—quanto possível**, as soon as possible.
cedrão (*m.*) = CARRAPÊTA.
cedrela (*f.*) the cigarbox cedrela (*C. odorata*).
cedrilho (*m.*) a muskwood (*Guarea balansae*).
cedrinho (*m.*) = CEDRO-BATATA.
cedrino –**na** (*adj.*) cedar.
cedro (*m.*) cedar (*Cedrus*); cedrela (*Cedrela*); juniper (*Juniperus communis*), c.a. ZIMBRO; European larch (*Larix decidua*).—**batata**, a tree of the mahogany family (*Cedrela fissilis*), c.a. CEDRINHO, CEDRO-AMARELO (-BRANCO, -DA-VÁRZEA, -ROSA, -VERMELHO).—**canela**, an ocotea (*O. commutata*).—**cheiroso**, the Spanish cedar or cigarbox cedrela (*C. odorata*), c.a. CEDERLA, CEDRO-FÊMEA (-MOGNO, -VERMELHO), ACAJU.—**das-barbadas**, Bermuda red cedar (*Juniperus bermudiana*).—**da-virgínia**, Eastern red cedar (*Juniperus virginianum*).—**do-atlas**, Atlas cedar (*Cedrus atlantica*).—**do-bugaço**, Mexican cypress (*Cupressus lusitanica*), c.a. CEDRO-PORTUGUÊS, CIPRESTE, ÁRVORE-DA-VIDA.—**do-himalaia**, deodar cedar (*Cedrus deodara*).—**do-líbano**, Cedar-of-Lebanon (*Cedrus libani*).—**japonês**, Japanese cryptomeria (*C. japonica*), c.a. ARAUCÁRIA-DO-JAPÃO, ÁRVORE-DO-NATAL.—**vermelho**, a cedrela (*C. macrocarpa*), c.a. CEDRO-BRANCO; also = CEDRO-CHEIROSO; also = CEDRO-DA-VIRGÍNIA; also = CEDRO-BATATA.
cedrorana (*f.*) = CARRAPÊTA.
cédula (*f.*) any of various schedules or certificates, such as a written acknowledgement of public indebtedness; a ballot; a paper bill (currency); a policy; a slip of paper.
cefalado –**da** (*adj.*, *Zool.*) cephalate.
cefalagra (*f.*, *Med.*) cephalagra.
cefalalgia (*f.*, *Med.*) cephalalgia, headache.
cefalanto (*m.*) the common buttonbush (*Cephalanthus occidentalis*).
cefalária (*f.*, *Bot.*) the genus Cephalaria.
cefaléia (*f.*, *Med.*) chronic headache.
cefálico –**ca** (*adj.*) cephalic.
cefalina (*f.*, *Biochem.*) cephalin.
cefalômetro (*m.*) cephalometer.
cefalópodes (*m.pl.*) the Cephalopoda (octopuses, squids, cuttlefishes, etc.)
cefaloteca (*f.*, *Zool.*) cephalotheca.
cefalotomia (*f.*, *Surg.*) cephalotomy.
cefalotórax (*m.*, *Zool.*) cephalothorax.
cega (*f.*) a blind woman.

cegamento (*m.*) = CEGUEIRA.
cegante (*adj.*) blinding.
cega-ôlho (*m.*) kinds of milkweed (*Asclepias spp.*), c.a. CAMARÁ-BRAVO, CHIBANTE, SAUDADE-DE-CAMPINA, CAPI-TÃO-DA-SALA.
cegar (*v.t.*) to blind; to dazzle; to hoodwink; (*v.i.*) to go blind.
cega-rega (*f.*) a cicada [= CIGARRA]; a toy which imitates the shrill notes of the cicada; fig., a shrill-voiced insistent talker.
cego -ga (*adj.*) blind; dazzled; dark; of a knife, dull; (*m.*) blind man; blind gut (caecum). (*f.*) blind woman. **às—s,** blindly.
cegonha (*f.*) stork; a sweep, shadoof or picotah.
cegude (*f.*) = CICUTA-DA-EUROPA.
cegueira (*f.*) blindness; irrational enthusiasm; fanaticism.
ceia (*f.*) supper. [Verb: CEAR].—**do Senhor,** the Lord's Supper.
ceifa (*f.*) harvest, crop; harvest time.
ceifadeira (*f.*) reaper (machine).—**-debulhadora,** harvester combine.
ceifar (*v.t.*) to reap, harvest, mow.
ceifeiro -ra (*adj.*) reaping; harvesting; (*m.*) reaper; harvester; (*f.*) reaper; reaping machine; scythe
ceilonense (*adj.; m.,f.*) Ceylonese.
ceitil (*m.*) farthing, penny; trifle, mite.
C.el = CORONEL (colonel).
cela (*f.*) cell (in a prison, monastery, etc.). Cf. CÉLULA.
celação (*f.*) celation.
celadonita (*f.*) celadonite.
celagem (*f.*) cloud effect at sunset or sunrise.
celastro (*m., Bot.*) any bittersweet (*Celastrus*).
celastríneas (*f.,pl.*) the Celastraceae (stafftree family).
celebérrimo -ma (*absol. superl. of* CÉLEBRE) very famous, most famous.
celebração (*f.*) celebration, commemoration.
celebrado -da (*adj.*) celebrated, famous.
celebrador -dora (*m.,f.*) celebrator.
celebrante (*adj.; m.*) celebrant.
celebrar (*v.t.*) to celebrate, solemnize; to commemorate; to applaud.—**um acôrdo,** to conclude an agreement.
celebrável (*adj.*) worthy of celebration, praiseworthy.
célebre (*adj.*) famous, celebrated.
celebridade (*f.*) celebrity.
celebríssimo -ma (*adj.*) = CELEBÉRRIMO.
celebrizar (*v.t.*) to render famous; (*v.r.*) to become so.
celeiro (*m.*) granary, barn, storehouse.
celenterado (*m., Zool.*) a coelenterate.
celêntero (*m., Zool.*) coelenteron.
celerado -da (*adj*) villainous, vicious, criminal; (*m.*) miscreant, vile wretch, ruffian.
célere (*adj.*) swift, fleet.
celeridade (*f.*) celerity, swiftness.
celérrimo -ma, **celeríssimo** -ma (*absol. superl. of* CÉLERE) most swift.
celeste, celestial (*adj.*) celestial, heavenly, supernal, divine. **azul—,** sky-blue; (*f.*) a celesta (musical instrument).
celestial (*adj.*) celestial.
celestina (*f., Bot.*) Mexican ageratum (*A. houstonianum*); (*Min.*) coelestine, celestite, native stroutium sulphate, c.a. CELESTINITA, CELESTITA.
celestino (*m., Music*) celestina.
celestita (*f.*) = CELESTINA (mineral).
celeuma (*f.*) noisy clamor, esp. of men at work; uproar, hullabaloo, fuss, noise.
celga (*f.*) = AGELGA.
celhas [ê] (*f.,pl.*) eyelashes; (*Biol.*) cilia.
Célia (*f.*) Celia.
celíaco -ca (*adj., Anat.*) coeliac.
celialgia (*f., Med.*) coelialgia, bellyache.
celibatário -ria (*adj.*) celibate; (*m.*) celibate; bachelor.
celibatarismo (*m.*) celibacy.
celibato (*m.*) celibate.
celidografia (*f., Astron.*) celidography.
celidônia (*f.*) = QUELIDÔNIA.
celidonina (*f.*) = QUELIDONINA.
celobiose (*f., Chem.*) cellobiose, cellose.
celofane (*m.*) cellophane.
celoidina [o-i] (*f., Chem.*) celloidin, celluidine, photoxylin.
celoma (*m., Anat., Zool.*) coelom, -lome, -loma.
celose (*f., Chem.*) cellose, cellobiose.
celósia (*f., Bot.*) any cockscomb (*Celosia*).—**-branca,** the feather cockscomb (*Celosia argentea*), c.a. AMARANTO-

BRANCO, CRISTA-DE-GALO, VELUDO-BRANCO.
celotex (*m.*) Celotex.
celotomia (*f., Surg.*) celotomy.
celsitude (*f.*) exaltation.
célsius (*adj.*) Celsius, centigrade [thermometer].
celso -sa (*adj.*) noble, sublime. [*Poetical*]
celta (*adj.*) Celtic; (*m.,f.*) Celt.
celte (*m., Archaeol.*) celt.
céltico -ca (*adj.*) Celtic.
célula (*f.*) cell. Cf. CELA.—**-ôvo,** ovum.—**-electrolítica,** electrolytic cell.
celular (*adj.*) cellular.
celulase (*f., Biochem.*) cellulose.
celulífero -ra (*adj.*) celluliferous.
celulífugo -ga (*adj.*) cellulifugal.
celulípeto -ta (*adj.*) cellulipetal.
celulóide (*m.*) Celluloid.
celulose (*f., Chem.*) cellulose.
celulósico -ca (*adj.*) cellulosic.
celulosidade (*f.*) cellulosity.
celuloso -sa (*adj.*) cellulose.
celulótico -ca (*adj.*) = CELULÓSICO.
cem (*m.*) one hundred. Cf. CENTO.
cem-dobrado -da (*adj.*) centuplicate, hundredfold.
cem-dôbro (*m.*) centuplicate, hundredfold.
cementação (*f., Metal.*) cementation; casehardening. Cf. CIMENTAÇÃO.
cementar (*v.t.*) to cement (iron, steel). Cf. CIMENTAR.
cementita (*f., Metal.*) cementite.
cemento (*m., Anat.*) cementum; (*Metal.*) cement. Cf. CIMENTO.
cementoblasta (*m., Biol.*) cementoblast.
cem-fôlhas (*f.*) the cabbage rose (*Rosa centifolia*).
cemiterial (*adj.*) cemetery.
cemitério (*m.*) cemetery, burial ground.
cena (*f.*) scene (part of an act); stage scenery; stage; spectacle; scene of action, setting; an exhibition of strong feeling (between persons). **em—,** on the stage. **levar à—,** to stage (a play).
cenáculo (*m.*) coterie, circle, exclusive set; (in ancient Rome) supper room.
cenário (*m.*) stage; setting; stage scenery. [But not scenario which is SEQÜÊNCIA DAS CENAS.]
cenarista (*m.,f.*) a writer of scenarios.
cendrado -da (*adj.*) ash-colored.
cenestesia (*f., Psychol.*) coenesthesis; vital sense.
cenho (*m.*) scowl, frown; a disease of horses' hoofs.
cenhoso -sa (*adj.*) scowling, frowning.
cenóbio (*m.*) monastery; convent.
cenobita (*m.,f.*) cenobite.
cenógrafo -fa (*m.,f.*) scene painter; set designer.
cenosidade (*f.*) cenosity, filthiness.
cenoso -sa (*adj.*) filthy.
cenotáfio (*m.*) cenotaph.
cenoura (*f.*) carrot.
cenozóico -ca (*adj.*) Cenozoic.
censatário -ria, **censionário** -ria (*adj.*) census-paying; (*m.,f.*) one who pays a census (ground rent); also = CENSITÁRIO.
censitário -ria (*adj.*) of or pert. to a census; also = CENSATÁRIO.
censo (*m.*) census; quitrent; ground rent.
censor (*m.*), -sora (*f.*) [ô] censor.
censório -ria (*adj.*) censorial; censorious.
censura (*f.*) censure, reprimand; reproof; upbraiding; censorship.
censurador -dora (*adj.*) censuring; (*m.,f.*) censurer.
censurar (*v.t.*) to censure, reprove, reprehend, condemn; to accuse; to find fault with, disapprove of; to upbraid; to scold, chide; to nag.
censurável (*adj.*) censurable.
cent. = CENTAVO(s).
centafolho [ô] (*m.*) tripe [= LIVRO, FOLHOSO, FÔLHO].
centáurea (*f.*) any thistle of the genus Centaurea.—**-azul,** cornflower (*C. cyanus*), c.a. ESCOVINHA.—**-da-babilônia,** Syrian centaurea (*C. babylonica*).—**-do-jardim,** the plains coreopsis (*C. tinctoria*).—**-maior,** a medicinal thistle (*Centaurea centaurium*).—**-menor,** the drug centaury (*Centaurium umbellatum*), c.a. QUEBA-FEBRE.
centauro (*m.*) centaur.
centavo (*m.*) centavo (the hundredth part of a cruzeiro, peso or dollar).
centeio (*m.*) rye (*Secale cereale*); (*adj.*) rye.—**-espigado,** ergot of rye (*Claviceps purpurea*). **pão—,** rye bread.

centelha [ê] (*f.*) scintilla; spark; electric spark.
centelhador (*m.*, *Elec.*) spark gap, discharger.
centelhar (*v.i.*) to scintillate, sparkle; (*Elec.*) to spark.
centena (*f.*) a hundred. **às—s,** by (the) hundreds.
centenar (*m.*) = CENTENA.
centenário –ria (*adj.*) centennial; (*m.,f.*) centenarian; (*m.*) centennial; century.
centese (*f.*, *Surg.*) centesis, puncture.
centesimal (*adj.*) centesimal, hundredth.
centésimo –ma (*adj.*) hundredth.—**-primeiro, segundo,** etc., one hundred-first, second, etc. (*m.*) hundredth part; a small So. Amer. coin.
centiare (*m.*) a surface measurement equivalent to one square meter [1.196 sq. yds.]
centígrado –da (*adj.*) Centigrade, having one hundred degrees. **graus—s,** degrees Centigrade.
centigrama (*m.*) centigram = 1/100th gram = 0.15432 grain.
centilitro (*m.*) centiliter = 1/100th liter = 0.6102 cu. in. = 0.338 fl. oz.
centímetro (*m.*) centimeter = 1/100th meter = 0.3937 inch.
cêntimo (*m.*) centime [1/100th franc].
centípede (*adj.*) centipede. [The animal centipede is CENTOPEIA.]
cento (*m.*) a hundred. [Used instead of CEM for counting from 101 to 199: **cento e um, cento e dois, cento e três,** etc. 101, 102, 103, etc.] **aos—s,** by the hundreds. **por cento,** percent.
centopeia (*f.*) the centipede. Cf. CENTÍPEDE.
centragem (*f.*) centering.
central (*adj.*) central; (*f.*) telephone exchange; police headquarters.
centralista (*adj.; m.,f.*) centralist.
centralização (*f.*) centralization.
centralizado –da (*adj.*) centralized.
centralizador –dora (*adj.*) centralizing; (*m.,f.*) centralizer; centralist.
centralizar (*v.t.*) to centralize, concentrate.
centrar (*v.t.*) to center.
centricipital (*adj.*, *Anat.*) centricipital.
centricipúcio (*m.*, *Anat.*) centriciput.
centrífuga (*f.*) centrifuge; centrifugal machine.
centrifugação (*f.*) centrifugation.
centrifugar (*v.t.*) to centrifuge.
centrifugismo (*m.*) centrifugence.
centrífugo –ga (*adj.*) centrifugal; (*m.*) centrifugal machine.
centripetismo (*m.*) centripetence.
centrípeto –ta (*adj.*) centripetal.
centrisco (*m.*) bellows fish or trumpet fish (*Macrorhamphosus scolopax*), c.a. PEIXE-TROMBETA, BICANÇUDO.
centro (*m.*) center, middle; centrum; core, heart; point of assemblage.—**da cidade,** center of town; downtown.—**de colineação,** (*Math.*) perspective.—**de comunicação,** communications center.—**de diversões,** amusement center.—**de empuxo,** (*Aeron.*) center of thrust.—**de flutuação** (*Hydros.*) center of buoyancy; center of cavity or displacement.—**de gravidade,** or—**de atração,** center of gravity.—**morto,** (*Mach.*) dead center.—**de oscilação,** center of oscillation.—**de percussão,** center of percussion.—**de pressão,** (*Hydros.*) center of pressure; (*Aeron.*) center of pressure of an airfoil section.—**nervoso,** (*Physiol.*, *Anat.*) nerve center.
centro-avante (*m.*, *Soccer*) center forward.
centrobárico –ca (*adj.*) centrobaric.
centrodo (*m.*, *Kinematics*) centrode.
centróide (*m.*) centroid.
centrolécito –ta (*adj.; m.*, *Biol.*) centrolecithal (egg).
centro-médio (*m.*, *Soccer*) center halfback.
centrossemo (*m.*) the Brazil butterfly pea (*Centrosema brasilanum*).
centrossomo (*m.*, *Biol.*) centrosome.
centuplicado –da (*adj.*) centuplicate, hundredfold.
centuplicar (*v.t.*) to centuplicate.
cêntuplo –pla (*adj.*) centuple, hundredfold; (*m.*) hundredfold.
centurião (*m.*) centurion.
cenuro (*m.*, *Zool.*) coenurus (larva of a tapeworm).
cenurose (*f.*, *Veter.*) gid, water brain, staggers.
cepa (*f.*) onion [= CEBOLA].
cêpa (*f.*) a grapevine or its stock; heather.
cepáceo –cea (*adj.*, *Bot.*) cepaceous, onionlike.
cepilhar (*v.*) = ACEPILHAR.
cepilho (*m.*) small carpenter's plane; a fine metal file; pommel of a saddle.

cepo [ê] log; stump; butcher's block; wood block for an anvil; kind of trap for small game; wooden brake shoe [= TAMANCO]; kind of carpenter's plane; stocks [= TRONCO]; a dull or stupid person; plane stock; transverse stock of an anchor.—**de virus,** virus strain.
cepticismo (*m.*) skepticism. Var. CETICISMO.
céptico –ca (*adj.; m.,f.*) skeptic. Var. CÉTICO.
cêra (*f.*) wax; beeswax; (*Physiol.*) cerumen; (*Zool.*) cere. [Sealing wax is LACRE.]—**amarela,** yellow beeswax.—**de carnaúba,** canauba wax used in the mfr. of candles, shoe polish, floor wax, etc.—**do ouvido,** earwax.—**em rama,** crude wax.—**mineral,** mineral wax, ozocerite.—**parafinada,** paraffin wax.—**vegetal,** vegetable wax.—**virgem,** virgin wax. **fazer—,** to dawdle, make a pretense of working. **gastar—com mau defunto,** to pay for a dead horse; to send good money after bad; to play a game which is not worth the candle.
ceráceo –cea (*adj.*) ceraceous, like wax, waxy.
cerâmica (*f.*) ceramics (the art). [In the sense of articles formed of baked clay, the equivalent of ceramics is LOUÇA DE BARRO COZIDO.]
cerâmico –ca (*adj.*) ceramic; (*m.,f.*) ceramist.
ceramista (*adj.*) of or pert. to ceramics; (*m.,f.*) ceramist.
céramo (*m.*) a vessel of burnt clay.
ceramografia (*f.*) ceramography.
cerar (*v.t.*) to wax; to fill with wax.
cerargirita (*f.*, *Min.*) cerargyrite; native silver chloride; horn silver.
cerasina (*f.*, *Pharm.*) cerasein; (*Chem.*) cerasin.
ceraste (*m.*) horned viper (*Cerastes cornutus*).
ceratectomia (*f.*, *Surg.*) keratectomy.
ceratina (*f.*, *Biochem.*) keratin.
cerato (*m.*) = CEROTO.
ceratonia (*f.*) = ALFARROBEIRA.
ceratoplastia (*f.*, *Surg.*) keratoplasty.
ceráunia (*f.*, *Archaeol.*) keraunion; thunderbolt.
cérbero (*m.*) cerberus; fig., a surly gatekeeper or guardian.
cêrca (*f.*) fence, wall, hedge; enclosed piece of land; (*adv.*) —**de,** about, near(ly), almost, approximately.—**de arame farpado,** barbed-wire fence.—**de duas léguas,** a matter of two leagues (more or less).—**viva,** a hedge of living plants. **à—de,** about, in regard to, concerning. **por—de dois anos,** for about two years.
cercada (*f.*) fishgarth, fishpound, weir [= CURRAL-DE-PEIXE].
cercado (*m.*) fenced-in land; pound; enclosure.
cercadura (*f.*, *Print.*) panel.
cercanias (*f.pl.*) environs, outskirts, surroundings.
cercar (*v.t.*) to encircle, enclose, encompass, surround; to fence in; to beset; to besiege, beleaguer; (*Print.*) to provide with a panel.—**com corda,** to rope off.—**de (por) soldados,** to surround with soldiers.
cerce (*adv.*) at the base; at the bottom; short. **cotar—,** to cut off at the root; to cut short; to close-crop.
cércea (*f.*) template, gauge, pattern, mold; (*Founding*) sweep, strickle. Cf. GABARITO.
cerceamento (*m.*), **cerceadura** (*f.*), **cerceio** (*m.*) act of using a template or sweep; act of trimming or clipping; (*pl.*) shavings; clippings.
cercear (*v.t.*) to cut off at the root; to trim, clip, cut (esp. around the edges); to restrict, hinder; to retrench; (*Founding*) to sweep.
cerceativo –va (*adj.*) curtailing.
cercilho (*m.*) monk's tonsure.
cêrco (*m.*) encirclement; enclosure; military siege; fishweir; a certain type of fishnet; a partial dam (on one side only of a stream) made of rocks, logs, brush, etc. **apertar o—,** to tighten the ring, surround, close in on (wild animal, criminal, etc.). **pôr—,** to lay seige.
cerda [ê] (*f.*) bristle (esp. of a hog); coarse hair.
cerdear (*v.t.*) to clip, shear (an animal).
cerdo [ê] (*m.*) hog, boar [= PORCO].
cerdoso –sa (*adj.*) bristly.
cereal (*adj.; m.*) cereal; grain.
cerealina (*f.*, *Biochem.*) aleurone.
cerebelar, cerebeloso –sa (*adj.*) cerebellar.
cerebelo [bê] (*m.*, *Anat.*) cerebellum.
cerebração (*f.*) cerebration.
cerebral (*adj.*) cerebral.
cerébrico –ca (*adj.*) cerebric.
cerebriforme (*adj.*) cerebriform.
cerebrina (*f.*, *Biochem.*) cerebrin.
cerebrino –na (*adj.*) fanciful; fantastic.

cerebrite (*f., Med.*) cerebritis.

cérebro (*m.*) cerebrum; brain; mind.—**electrônico**, electronic brain, computer.—**espinhal** = CEREBROSPINAL.

cerebrospinal (*adj.*) cerebrospinal.

cerefolho [fô] **-fólio** (*m., Bot.*) salad chervil (*Anthriscus cerefolium*).

cereira-do-japão (*f.*) waxtree (*Toxicodendron succedaneum*).

cereja [rê] (*adj.*) cherry-colored; (*f.*) cherry; ripe coffee berry.—**-de-purga** = ABÓBORA-DO-MATO.

cerejal (*m.*) cherry orchard.

cerejeira (*f.*) cherry tree. cherry wood.—**-da-europa**, the Mazzard cherry (*Prunus avium*), c.a. CEREJA-DOS-PASSARINHOS, CEREJA-GALEGA; the sour cherry (*Prunus cerasus*), c.a. GINJEIRA.—**-das-antilhas**, or **-do-pará**, the holly malpighia (*M. coccigera*).—**-do-paraná**, a dimorphandra (*D. exaltata*), c.a. CEREJA-DA-TERRA (-DO-BRASIL, -DO-MATO).

céreo -rea (*adj.*) waxen, like wax. [*Poetical*]

ceresina (*f.*) ceresin(e).

cergir (*v.*) = CERZIR.

cérico -ca (*adj., Chem.*) ceric; (*f.*) a salve for chapped lips and hands.

cerífero -ra (*adj.*) ceriferous.

cerimônia (*f.*) ceremony, rite, solemnity; conventionality, formality, etiquette; excessive politeness. **fazer—**, to stand on ceremony. **sem—**, informal(ly); offhand.

cerimonial (*adj.; m.*) ceremonial.

cerimoniático -ca (*adj., colloq.*) ceremonious, full of ceremony.

cerimoniso -sa (*adj.*) ceremonious, formal, polite.

cerina (*f., Chem.*) cerin.

cerinto (*m., Bot.*) a honeywort (*Cerinthe sp.*).

cério (*m., Chem.*) cerium.

cerita (*f., Min.*) cerite.

cernambi (*m.*) sernamby; [*Webster*: "a poor grade of Pará rubber representing the remains of previous coagulations."]; also = SAMBAQUI; (*Zool.*) an edible bivalve marine mollusk (*Mesodesma mactroides*), c.a. AMÊIJOA.—**fino**, "a technical grade of commercial rubber: special, coarse, washed." [*GBAT*]. Var. SARNAMBI.

cerne (*m.*) duramen, heartwood; heart, essence.

cerneira (*f.*) the portion remaining of a fallen tree or branch after the bark and sapwood have rotted away; a board of heartwood.

cernelha (*f.*) withers (of a horse, etc.); a shock of grain.

cero (*m.*) cero (a large, mackerel-like fish, *Sierra cavalla*).

cerô (*m.*) earwax.

ceroferário (*m.*) a torchbearer or candlebearer in a religious procession.

cerografia (*f.*) cerography.

cerol [-róis] (*m.*) shoemaker's wax.

ceroma (*f.*) the cere of birds; cerumen.

ceroplastia, -plástica (*f.*) ceroplastics.

ceroso -sa (*adj.*) waxy.

cerótico -ca (*adj., Chem.*) cerotic.

ceroto [rô] (*m.*) salve, unguent.

ceroulas (*f.pl.*) men's drawers. Var. CEROILAS.

ceroxilina (*f.*) palm wax.

ceroxilo (*m.*) the So. Amer. wax palm (*Ceroxylon andicola*).

cerração (*f.*) fog, mist. "The smoke from large-scale burnings on the plains, especially in the eastern part of Amazonia, frequently so thick as to halt navigation at night; winter fogs produced by evaporation." [*GBAT*].—**da fala**, hoarseness.

cerradal (*m.*) stunted growth on the island of Marajó, in the Amazon estuary.

cerradão (*m.*) an extensive tract of waste land; a waterless area of scrub growth.

cerrado -da (*adj.*) thick; dense; close, tight; shut; locked; (*m.*) fenced-in land; a woods composed of stunted, twisted trees, growing on cattle-grazing land.—**fechado**, a dense such growth.—**ralo**, a scattered such growth which enables the cattle to move about with more ease.

cerradouro (*m.*) drawstring. Var. CERRADOIRO.

cerra-fila (*m., Milit.*) file closer; the last ship in a column.

cerramento (*m.*) act of closing, etc. See the verb CERRAR.

cerrar (*v.t.*) to close, shut; to conclude, bring to a close. Cf. ENCERRAR; (*v.r.*) to close in (referring to the weather); to grow dark.—**a noite**, of night, to fall.—**de cima** (*colloq.*) to be on top (running things).—**o namôro**, to fall deeper in love.—**o negócio**, to close a deal.—**o tempo**, to threaten rain (or a fight).—**o rodeio**, to close in on (a herd of cattle).—**os olhos à luz**, to close the eyes

---

(die); to close the mind to a fact.—**perna**, to ride horseback.

cerrito (*m.*) hillock; high rocky place.

cêrro (*m.*) small hill, esp. a craggy one.

certa (*f., colloq.*) a certainty. **na—**, **pela—**, certainly, surely.

certame, certámen (*m.*) contest, bout; show; affair, doings; debate, discussion; literary contest; industrial exposition; sporting event; public event.

certeiro -ra (*adj.*) well-aimed; well-managed.

certeza [tê] (*f.*) certainty; certitude; assurance, conviction.—**de mão**, surehandedness. **com—**, of course, certainly. **com tôda a—**, most certainly. **Tenho plena—**, I am quite sure.

certidão (*f.*) certificate; voucher.—**de casamento**, marriage certificate.—**de conclusão**, final certificate; certificate of completion.—**de idade** or **de nascimento**, birth certificate.—**de óbito**, death certificate.

certificado -da (*adj.*) certified; (*m.*) certificate.

certificador -dora, certificante (*adj.*) certifying; (*m.,f.*) certifier.

certificar (*v.t.*) to certify, attest, vouch for; to affirm; to make sure, ascertain; (*v.r.*) to be (make) sure; to find out.

certo -ta (*adj.*) certain, sure, correct, accurate, right, true; definite, particular; fixed, agreed upon; (*m.*) certainty; (*adv.*) certainly.—**dia** (on) a certain day.—**gente**, certain people.—**vez**, on a certain occasion. **ao—**, for certain, with certainty, exactly. **dar—**, to come out right; to fit. **dar por—**, to take for granted. **de—**, certain, sure, surely. **de—que**, certainly. **Está—!** Yes! O.K.! **estar—**, to feel certain, be sure, **por—**, surely, certainly. **ninguém sabe ao—**, no one knows for sure. **ser—**, to be correct. **ter por—que**, to be certain (sure) that. **um—quê**, a certain something.

ceruda (*f.*) = QUELIDÔNIA.

cerúleo -lea, cérulo -la (*adj.*) cerulean, sky-blue.

cerume, cerúmen (*m.*) cerumen, earwax.

ceruminoso -sa (*adj., Physiol.*) ceruminous.

cerusa (*f.*) ceruse, white lead [= ALVAIADE].

cerusita (*f.*) cerussite, native lead carbonate.

cerva (*f.*) doe (female deer).

cerval (*adj.*) deer.

cervantista (*m.,f.*) Cervantist.

cervantita (*f., Min.*) cervantite, antimony ochre.

cervato (*m.*) fawn.

cerveja (*f.*) beer, ale.—**de barbante**, a kind of beer made by Indians in northern Brazil. **fábrica de—**, brewery.

cervejada (*f.*) a glass of beer; a beer party.

cervejar (*v.i.*) to drink beer.

cervejaria (*f.*) beer hall, alehouse, beer garden; brewery.

cervejeiro (*m.*) brewer; beer merchant.

cervelha (*f.*) chuck (of beef).

cervical (*adj.*) cervical.

cervicite (*f., Med.*) cervicitis.

cervicodinia (*f., Med.*) cervicodynia.

cervicórneo -nea (*adj., Zool.*) cervicorn.

cervídeos (*m.pl.*) the Cervidae (family of deer, elk, moose, reindeer, etc.).

cervino -na (*adj.*) cervine.

cerviz (*f.*) cervix, neck; nape. **curvar a—**, to bow one's head (in resignation); to submit, knuckle under.

cervo (*m.*) any deer, esp. a certain swamp deer (*Blastoceros dichotomus*) having branched antlers. It is the largest of Brazilian if not South American deers, and is c.a. CERVO-DO-BANHADO, GUAÇUPUCU, SUAÇUPUCU, VEADO-GALHEIRO-GRANDE.

cerzedeira (*f.*) a woman who darns, patches, mends (clothes), or a shop where such work is done.

cerzidor -dora (*adj.*) mending, darning, patching; (*m.*) a writer whose work is mainly a patchwork of quotations from others.

cerzidura (*f.*), **cerzimento** (*m.*) act of darning, etc.; See the verb CERZIR.

cerzir [21b] (*v.t.*) to darn, patch. **agulha de—**, darning-needle.

cesalpíneas, -piniáceas (*f.pl., Bot.*) the Caesalpiniaceae (senna family).

cesalpíneo -nea, -piniáceo -cea (*adj., Bot.*) caesalpiniaceous.

cesalpínia (*f., Bot.*) any senna (*Caesalpinia sp.*)

César (*m.*) Caesar.

cesária (*f.*) bookbinder's shears.

cesariano -na (*adj., Surg.*) Caesarean.

césio (*m., Chem.*) cesium.

céspede (*m.*) piece of sod; divot.
cespitoso –sa (*adj., Bot.*) cespitose.
cessação (*f.*) cessation.
cessante (*adj.*) ceasing; inactive.
cessão (*f.*) cession; assignment. [Verb CEDER, not CESSAR.]
cessar (*v.i.*) to cease, come to an end; to stop, end.—**de chorar**, to stop crying.—**fogo** (*Milit.*) to cease fire. **sem**—, without letup.
cessionário –ria (*m.,f.*) assignee.
cessível (*adj.*) assignable [= CEDÍVEL].
cesta [ê] (*f.*) basket. Cf. CÊSTO.—**de costura**, sewing basket.—**de lixo** or **de papéis**, wastepaper basket.—**rôta**, blabbermouth.
cestada (*f.*) a basketful.
cestão (*m.*) large basket; river raft.
cestaria (*f.*) basket-making; basket shop.
cesteiro –ra (*adj.*) basket; (*m.,f.*) basket weaver; basket seller.
cêsto (*m.*) hamper, pannier; (*Zool.*) Venus's girdle (*Cestus veneris*), c.a. CINTO-DE-VENUS. Cf. CESTA.—**da gávea**, (*Naut.*) crow's nest.—**vindimo**, wicker basket.
cestobol (*m.*) basketball [= BASQUETE(BOL)].
cestóide (*adj., m., Zool.*) cestoid.
cestro (*m.*) the nightblooming jasmine (*Cestrum nocturnum*) or other plant of this genus; = BETÔNICA.
cesura (*f.*) a cutting or incision, as with a lancet; scar of an operation; (*Pros.*) caesura.
cesurar (*v.t.*) to lance, slash, cut.
cetáceo –cea (*adj.; m.,f.*) cetacean, whale.
ceteraque (*m.*) a medicinal spleenwort (*Asplenium ceterach*).
ceticismo (*m.*) skepticism. Var. CEPTICISMO.
cético –ca (*adj.; m.,f.*) skeptic(al). Var. CÉPTICO.
cetila (*f., Chem.*) cetyl, normal hexadecyl.
cetim (*m.*) satin. Var. SETIM.
cetina (*f.*) = ESPERMACETE.
cetíneo –nea (*adj.*) = CETINOSO, ACETINADO.
cetineta [ê] (*f.*) satinette.
cetinoso –sa (*adj.*) satiny, silky, smooth.
cetologia (*f., Zool.*) cetology.
cetose (*f., Med.*) ketosis.
cetraria (*f.*) falconry, hawking.
cetrária (*f.*) Iceland moss (*Cetraria islandica*), c.a. LÍQUEN-DA-ISLÂNDIA.
cetrino –na (*adj.*) red. [*Poetical*].
cetro (*m.*) scepter.
céu (*m.*) sky, heaven; roof of a furnace; (*pl., interj.*) Heavens! Good heavens!—**aberto**, open skies; a great good fortune.—**ardente**, or **de fogo**, burning sky.—**carregado**, overcast sky.—**da bôca**, roof of the mouth; palate.—**de chumbo**, leaden sky.—**limpo**, cloudless sky. **azul do**—, the color sky-blue. **uma coisa caída do**—, a windfall, godsend. **uma noite de**—**limpo**, a clear night.
ceva (*f.*) fattening (of animals, for market); feed for such purpose; bait, chum.
cevada (*f.*) barley (*Hordeum vulgare*).—**de-jardim**, foxtail barley (*Hordeum jubatum*). **grão de**—, barley corn.
cevadal (*m.*) barley field.
cevadeira (*f.*) feed bag, nose bag.
cevadeiro (*m.*) fattening pen.
cevadilha (*f., Bot.*) the drug salvadilla (*Schoenocaulon officinale*); common oleander (*Nerium oleander*), c.a. ESPIRRADEIRA, LOENDRO.
cevadina (*f., Chem.*) cevadine, veratrine.
cevadinha (*f.*) pearl barley; (*Bot.*) rescue brome grass (*Bromus catharticus*).—**miúda** = CAPIM-PÉ-DE-GALINHA, CAPIM-FLECHINHA.
cevado –da (*adj.*) fattened; (*m.*) a hog fattened for slaughter or for market; a very fat man.
cevador (*m.*) man who fattens animals; person who prepares and serves MATE tea to a group of people; worker who feeds sugar cane into the crusher.
cevadouro (*m.*) place where animals are fattened; place where birds are baited and trapped, where fish are chummed.
cevar (*v.t.*) to fatten; to bait; to chum (fish); to stimulate (as appetite); to feed or satisfy to the full (as an appetite or desire); to soak manioc until it begins to ferment; to place ground MATE leaves in the CUIA and mix with a little cold water before adding the boiling water; (*v.r.*) to satisfy one's desire; to grow rich.—**se em**, to batten on.
ceveiro (*m.*) place which is baited to attract animals or birds, or which is chummed to attract fish.

cevidina, cevina (*f., Chem.*) cevadine.
cêvo (*m.*) food; bait; chum.
CFF = CONSELHO FLORESTAL FEDERAL (Federal Forestry Council).
cg = CENTIGRAMA (centigram).
cgr. = CENTIGRADO (centigrade).
C.G.S. = CENTÍMETRO-GRAMA-SEGUNDO (centimeter-gram-second).
ch- [always now pronounced **sh**]. See under **X** and **QU** for certain words formerly spelled with **CH**; e.g., **chachim** = XAXIM; **chímica** = QUÍMICA; **máchina** = MÁQUINA.
chá (*m.*) tea (all senses); (*Bot.*) tea (*Thea sinensis*).—**da-campanha**, or—**mineiro**, a burhead (*Echinodorus pubescens*), c.a. CONGONHA-DO-BREJO.—**da-europa**, the drug speedwell (*Veronica officinalis*).—**da-índia**, common tea (*Thea sinensis*).—**dançante**, a tea dance.—**de-alecrim**, (*colloq.*) a hail of blows.—**de-bico** (*colloq.*) an enema; a kick in the rear.—**de-bugre**, a cordia (*C. salicifolia*); a casearia (*C. silvestris*).—**de-burro**, (*colloq.*) = MUNGUNZÁ.—**de-caboclo**, a seagrape (*Cocolobis argentinensis*).—**de-casca-de-vaca**, a rawhiding.—**de-frade** or—**de-pedestre** = CAPITÃO-DO-MATO (a plant).—**de-príncipe**, a bushmint (*Hyptis sp.*).—**do-méxico** = AMBRÓSIA.—**paulista**, an informal dance party which begins around tea time and lasts all evening.—**pomonga**, climbing plumbago (*P. scandens*).—**prêto**, black tea.—**verde**, green tea. **colhér de**—, teaspoon. **não ter tomado**—**em pequeno**, to be ill-bred.
chã (*adj., fem. of* CHÃO); (*f.*) plain, plateau; round of beef.—**de dentro**, top round (of beef), c.a. POJADOURO.—**de fora**, bottom round (of beef).
chabazita (*f., Min.*) chabazite.
chabouqueiro –ra (*adj.*) = CHAMBOQUEIRO.
chacal (*m.*) jackal; stool pigeon.
chácara (*f.*) a dwelling on the outskirts of a town, esp. one surrounded by an orchard; a house in the country, with fruit trees, chickens, etc. Var. CHACRA Cf. XÁCARA.
chacareiro (*m.*) overseer or proprietor of a CHÁCARA Var. CHACREIRO.
chacarola (*f.*) a small CHÁCARA.
chã-chão (*m.*) = PIXOXÓ.
chachim (*m.*) = XAXIM.
chacina (*f.*) slaughter; salt pork; cured meat.
chacinar (*v.t.*) to slaughter (animals); to put to the sword; to cure meat.
chacoalhar (*v.t.*) to shake up and down (as a bottle of medicine, a cocktail shaker, etc.); [= CHOCALHAR, VASCOLEJAR].
chacota (*f.*) banter; joke, jest; old folksong; satirical verse.
chacoteação (*f.*) jesting, banter.
chacoteador –dora (*m.,f.*) joker,· jester.
chacotear (*v.i.*) to sneer; to mock; to rib; to jest.
chacra (*f.*) = CHÁCARA.
chacreiro (*m.*) = CHACAREIRO.
chacrinha (*f.*) a little CHÁCARA.
chafariz (*m.*) public watering place, as a wall with projecting spouts for filling buckets; monumental public fountain.
chafurda (*f.*) pigsty; mud hole; filthy house; filth.
chafurdar (*v.i.*) to welter, wallow; to slosh; to splash, splatter; to get filthy; to become degraded.
chafurdeiro (*m.*) pigpen; one who soils or degrades himself.
chafurdice (*f.*) act of weltering or wallowing.
chaga (*f.*) open (running) sore; ulcer; affliction; (*pl., Bot.*) the flowerfence poinciana (*P. pulcherrima*), c.a. BARBA-DE-BARATA; the shield nasturtium (*Tropaeolum peltophorum*), c.a. CAPUCHINHO; the common nasturtium (*T. majus*), c.a. CAPUCHINHA-GRANDE.—**s-das-miúdas** or—**s-miúdas**, = CAPUCHINHA.—**s-de-são-sebastião**, a climber of the arum family (*Monstera pertusa*).
chagá (*m., Zool.*) the chaja or Southern screamer (*Chauna torquata*), c.a. TACHÃ.
chagado –da (*adj.*) sore-covered.
chaguento –ta (*adj.*) full of sores; ulcerated.
chaira (*f.*) a steel for sharpening knives.
chairar (*v.t.*) to sharpen (a knife) on a steel; to close-clip a horse's main.
chairel [-réis] (*m.*) saddlecloth [= SOBREANCA].
chalaça (*f.*) jest; crude or dirty joke; scurrility; jeer.
chalacear, chalaçar (*v.i.*) to joke.
chalaceador –dora (*m.,f.*) joker; (*adj.*) joking.
chalaza (*f., Zool.; Bot.*) chalaza.

chalé (*m.*) chalet, Swiss cottage.—**de bicho**, headquarters of a bookie for the BICHO game.

chaleira (*adj.*) flattering; (*f.*) tea kettle; (*m.*, *slang*) flatterer, fawner, adulator.

chaleiramento (*m.*) = CHALEIRISMO.

chaleirar (*v.t.*, *slang*) to flatter, fawn upon.

chaleirismo (*m.*, *slang*) flattery, adulation.

chaleirista (*adj.*; *slang*) flattering; (*m.*,*f.*, *slang*) flatterer.

chalibeado –da (*adj.*) chalybeate.

chalota (*f.*) shallot (a kind of small, mild onion).

chalrar (*v.i.*) to chatter, prattle, jabber.

chalreada (*f.*), **chalreio** (*m.*) a chatter(ing) esp. as of children or birds.

chalrear (*v.*) = CHALRAR.

chalreta (*f.*, *Zool.*) a tattler (*Totanus*).

chalrote (*m.*) pine bark.

chalupa (*f.*) a sloop, or shallop; (*slang*) a 500 or 1000 cruzeiros bill.

chama (*f.*) flame, blaze. **em—s**, ablaze, in flames; a call [= CHAMADA]; a lure; (*m.*) a bird placed in a trap to attract others.

chamada (*f.*) **–do** (*m.*) roll, roll call, muster; call; a bugle call; a catchword (printed at the top of a page, as in a dictionary); (*colloq.*) a call-down.—**telefônica**, telephone call. **fazer a—**, to call the roll.

chamador –dora (*m.*,*f.*) caller [but not in the sense of visitor, which is VISITA or VISITANTE]; (*m.*) one who rides in front of a herd [= PONTEIRO].

chamalote (*m.*) camlet, camel's-hair cloth.

chama-maré (*m.*) a fiddler crab (*Uca*).

chamamento (*m.*) act of calling; convocation [= CHAMADA].

chamar (*v.t.*) to call, summon (**a**, **para**, to); to send for; to convoke, call together; to designate, term, name, dub; (*v.r.*) to be called, named.—**a assistência**, to call the public ambulance.—**a atenção**, to attract attention.—**à autoria**, (*Law*) to call upon a person to defend his right of ownership.—**à baila**, to call up (a matter) for discussion.—**à contas**, to call to account.—**a Deus compadre**, to make vain boasts or claims.—**a juízo**, to summon to court.—**à lição**, to call on a student to recite the lesson.—**à ordem**, to call to order.—**(alguém) de burro**, to call (someone) stupid.—**a si**, to take on (responsibility for); to take over (control of).—**a terreiro**, to issue a challenge.—**as lágrimas aos olhos**, to bring tears to the eyes.—**nas canelas, or no pé**, to hotfoot it.—**nomes**, to call names.—**os bombeiros**, to call the firemen.—**um bombeiro**, to call a plumber. **Chama-se Paulo**, His name is Paul. **mandar—**, to send for. **Muitos são os—s e poucos os eleitos**, Many are called but few are chosen.

chamarisco (*m.*) decoy; lure; enticement.

chama-rita (*f.*) a form of song and dance, popular in the Açores and in Rio Grande do Sul, where it is called CHIMARRITA. Var. CHAMARRITA.

chamariz (*m.*) decoy, lure; birdcall.

chambão –bona (*adj.*) coarse, rude; inelegant; (*m.*) tough, stringy meat; (*f.*) a frump.

chamboqueiro –ra (*adj.*) coarse, rough; coarse-featured.

chambre (*m.*) house robe, bathrobe, dressing gown, negligee.

chambrié (*m.*) a long, slender whip used in horse-training.

chamego [ê] (*m.*) infatuation; sexual excitement; intimacy.

chamejamento (*m.*) act of flaming.

chamejante (*adj.*) flaming, glowing.

chamejar (*v.i.*) to blaze, flame, glow.

châmente (*adv.*) plainly, simply.

chamiço (*m.*) kindling, dry twigs.

chaminé (*f.*) chimney; stove pipe; chimney place; ship's funnel; smoke stack. **cão da—, and** andiron. **cano da—**, chimney flue. **prateleira da—**, mantel piece.

chamorro –ra (*adj.*) shorn (as a sheep); (*m.*) an offensive nickname formerly applied by Spaniards to Portuguese.

champa (*f.*) flat side of a sword blade. **de—**, flatwise.

champanha –nhe (*m.*) champagne.—**-da-terra**, (*colloq.*) white rum [= AGUARDENTE, CACHAÇA].

champô (*m.*, *Bot.*) the champac michelia (*M. champaca*).

champu (*m.*) shampoo [= XAMPU].

champunha (*f.*) handspring.

chamuscada (*f.*) a singe or singeing.

chamuscar (*v.t.*) to singe, scorch.

chamusco (*m.*) the smell of something burned or burning; act of singeing; a high plain; a skirmish; (*Bot.*) a gorse or furze (*Ulex genistoides*).

chanana (*f.*) = ALBINA.

chanca (*f.*, *slang*) clod-hopper (big foot); brogan.

chança (*f.*) jest; gibe.

chancarona (*f.*) = BIJUPIRÁ.

chance (*f.*) chance, opportunity.

chancear (*v.i.*) to gibe.

chancel. = CHANCELARIA (chancellery).

chancela (*f.*) a rubber stamp bearing a facsimile signature.

chancelaria (*f.*) chancellery, chancery.

chanceler [lê] (*m.*) chancellor; foreign minister.

chanchã (*m.*, *Zool.*) a flicker (*Colaptes campestris*), c.a. PICA-PAU-MALHADO, PICA-PAU-DO-CAMPO. Var: XANXÃ.

chanchada (*f.*) a slap-stick comedy; a second-rate play.

chaneco (*m.*) barren, infertile land.

cha[n]falho (*m.*) rusty old sword; out-of-tune instrument.

chanfrador (*m.*, *Carp.*) chamfer plane; any of various tools for chamfering or beveling; (*Print.*) miterer.

chanfradura (*f.*) chamfer, bevel.

chanfrar (*v.t.*) to chamfer, bevel, cant off.

chanfro (*m.*) chamfer; bevel; bevel square.

changa (*f.*) hand cartage; profit; a tip. **boa—**, a good piece of business.

changador (*m.*) a deliveryman; a baggage porter; an errand runner.

changar, changuear (*v.i.*) to work at making deliveries, running errands, etc.

changô (*m.*) = MANJUBÁ.

chaníssimo –ma (*absol. superl. of* CHÃO) most level; most open (frank).

chanqueta [ê] (*f.*) a slipper-like shoe.

chanta (*f.*) = CHANTÃO.

chantagem (*f.*) blackmail; extortion; exorbitance.

chantagista (*adj.*) blackmailing; (*m.*,*f.*) blackmailer; extortionist.

chantão (*m.*) a plant cutting [= CHANTA]. Var. TANCHÃO.

chantar (*v.t.*) to stick (something) in the ground; to plant a cutting.

chantre (*m.*, *Eccl.*) choir leader.

chão, chã [chãos, chãs] (*adj.*) level, smooth, flat; (*m.*) level ground, plateau; floor; background (of a painting); (*pl.*) lands. **de pé no—**, barefoot. **ficar com a cara no—**, to be embarrassed "to death".

chapa (*f.*) metal or plate; dental plate; automobile license plate; phonograph record; cliché (hackneyed phrase); slate of candidates.—**blindada**, armor plate.—**corrugada**, corrugated (steel) sheet.—**de aço**, steel plate.—**de alumínio**, aluminum sheet.—**de caldeira**, boiler plate.—**de enchimento**, filler plate.—**de identificação**, identification badge.—**de montagem**, mounting plate.—**eleitoral**, electoral slate, ballot. **bater uma—**, to snap a picture. **chassis de—s**, (*Photog.*) plate holder. **mudar a—** (*colloq.*) to change the subject; lit., to put on another record.

chapação (*f.*) first rough coat of plaster.

chapada (*f.*) plateau, plain; a clearing in the woods; (*Bot.*) a tree (*Sweetia dasycarpa*) of the pea family, c.a. PEROBINHA, UNHA-D'ANTA.

chapadão (*m.*) extensive plateau; tableland; prairie.

chapado –da (*adj.*) plated; (*slang*) complete, finished; downright. **Êle é um burro—**, He is a perfect ass, an arrant fool.

chapalheta (*f.*, *Zool.*) pewit, European blackheaded gull (*Larus ridibundus*), c.a. GAGOSA.

chapar (*v.t.*) to adorn (as a harness) with plate metal; to mint (coins); to beat (metal) into thin, flat pieces.

chaparia (*f.*) ornamental, thin, flat pieces of metal.

chaparral (*m.*) chaparral.

chape (*m.*) splash.

chapeado –da (*adj.*) plated (as with silver or gold); covered or lined with plates or sheets.—**de ouro**, gold-filled.

chapear (*v.t.*) to plate, overlay with gold, silver, etc., to laminate; to cover or line with plates or sheets.

chapelada (*f.*) a hatful.

chapelaria (*f.*) hattery; hat store; hat-making.

chapeleira (*f.*) milliner; hatbox.

chapeleiro (*m.*) hatter.

chapeleta [lê] (*f.*) a little hat; (*Mach.*) diaphragm valve.

chapelete [lê] **–linho** (*m.*) a little hat.

chapéu (*m.*) hat; toadstool.—**agaloado**, a hat cocked up in front.—**alto**, top hat.—**armado**, cocked hat; a hammerhead shark.—**das caldeiras**, steam dome of a boiler.—**-de-chuva**, umbrella [= GUARDA-CHUVA].—**-de-cobra**, chanterelle [*Webster:* "A widely distributed edible mushroom (*Cantharellus cibarius*), rich yellow in color, with a pleasant aroma."].—-de-côco, bowler hat.—-de-couro, (*Bot.*) a burhead (*Echinodorus macrophyllum*), c.a. CHÁ-DE-CAMPANHA, ERVA-DO-BREJO or -DO-PÂNTANO. —-de-ferro, (*Geol.*, *Mining*) gossan, iron hat.—-de fôrma, top hat.—-de-judeu = —-DE-COBRA.—de molas or de pasta, collapsible opera hat.—-de-napoleão, the luckynut thevetia (*T. nereifolia*).—de palha, straw hat [= PALHÊTA].—de sol, sunshade, parasol [= GUARDA-SOL]; (*Bot.*) = AMENDOEIRA-DA-ÍNDIA.—-de-sol-do-diabo, the common mushroom agaricus (*A. campestris*).—de três bicos or de três ventos, a tricorne or three-cornered hat.—-do-chile, a fine quality of Panama hat.—-do-panamá, Panama hat. cabide de—, hatrack. carneira de—, sweat band of a hat. fita de—, hatband.

chapèuzinho [í] (*m.*) a little hat; (*colloq.*) the circumflex accent mark.

chapim (*m.*) buskin; lady's slipper; base, pedestal; (*R.R.*) tie plate; the European blue titmouse (*Parus caeruleus*).

chapinhar (*v.t.*) to slosh water; to wade (paddle, dabble) in water; to splash water; to slap water with the hand.

chapitéu (*m.*, *Naut.*) forepeak or afterpeak.

chaplona (*j.*, *Mach.*) template, jig.

chapodar, chapotar (*v.t.*) to prune (plants).

chapuz (*m.*) wooden peg or wedge; dowel.

charabã (*m.*) charabanc.

charada (*f.*) charade.

charamela (*f.*) shawm (an early wood-wind instrument).

charanga (*f.*) small music band, composed mostly of wind instruments.

charão (*m.*) Chinese lacquer; Japanese waxtree (*Toxicodendron succedaneum*).

charco (*m.*) mud puddle; quagmire; swamp; morass; stagnant pool.

charcutaria, –teria (*f.*) meat shop; delicatessen store; sausage, salami, etc. [= SALSICHARIA].

charcuteiro (*m.*) pork-butcher; sausage-maker [= SALSICHEIRO].

charéu (*m.*, *Zool.*) the cavalla (*Caranx hippos*) [= XARÉU].

charivari (*m.*) charivari; bedlam; riot.

charla (*f.*) chatter, chit-chat.

charlador –dora (*m.*,*f.*) prattler.

charlar (*v.i.*) to chatter, chat, babble, prate.

charlatanice (*f.*), –tanismo (*m.*) charlatanism, buncombe, hokum.

charlatão [-tães, -tões] (*m.*) charlatan, faker, quack, impostor, humbug.

charneca (*f.*) tract of waste land; moor, heath; also = CORNICABRA (bush redpepper).

charneira (*f.*) hinge, joint; (*Anat.*) ginglymus.

charola (*f.*) a litter on which images are borne in a religious street procession; a niche; (*pl.*) stilts. levar em—, to carry (a hero) on the shoulders of a crowd.

charpa (*f.*) arm sling; scarf, sash.

charque (*m.*) jerked beef, c.a. CARNE-DO-CEARÁ, CARNE-DO-SUL, CARNE-SÊCA, CARNE-VELHA, JABÁ, IABÁ, SAMBAMBA, SUMACA.

charqueação (*f.*) jerking of beef.

charqueada (*f.*) place where beef is jerked (sun-dried).

charqueador (*m.*) maker of jerked beef.

charquear (*v.i.*) to make jerky.

charqueio (*m.*) = CHARQUEAÇÃO.

charqueiro (*m.*) = CHARCO.

charravascal (*m.*) an area overgrown with dense vegetation of medium height.

charro –ra (*adj.*) coarse, ill-bred.

charrua (*f.*) a moldboard or turn plow; (*Bot.*)—-grande, the bigleaf eupatorium (*E. macrophyllum*).

charruada (*f.*) plowed land.

charruar (*v.t.*) to plow.

charruás (*m.pl.*) a fierce tribe of Charruan Indians which dominated in Uruguay and adjacent parts of Brazil and Argentina. [*Webster*: "Uruguayans in large proportion are partly of Charruan descent."]

charutaria (*f.*) cigar store.

charutear (*v.i.*) to smoke a cigar.

charuteira (*f.*) cigar case.

charuteiro (*m.*) proprietor of a cigar store; cigar maker.

charuto (*m.*) cigar, cheroot.—-do-rei, (*Bot.*) the tree nicotiana (*N. glauca*).

chasco (*m.*) cutting remark, satirical jest; a sudden jerk on the reins.

ch_sque (*m.*) messenger.

chasqueador –dora (*adj.*) scoffing, teasing; (*m.*,*f.*) scof-fer, teaser.

chasquear (*v.t.*) to scoff; to banter, quiz; to make fun of; to tease, "kid".

chasqueiro –ra (*adj.*) hard-trotting [horse].

chassi [í] (*m.*, *Autom.*, *Radio*) chassis; (*Photog.*) frame.

chata(*f.*) flatboat, lighter. "Sternwheelers of the Amazon River Co. which sail on the upper Purus, the upper Juruá, and the Acre Rivers during the dry season; decked fore and aft, with their motors located well forward, they have a displacement of roughly 200 tons and draw about three feet of water." [*GBAT*]

chatada (*f.*) rebuke, reprimand; disagreeable remark.

chateação (*f.*, *slang*) act of boring, annoying. Que—! What a bore!

chatear (*v.t.*, *slang*) to bore someone "to death".

chateza [ê] chatice (*f.*) flatness; (*slang*) vulgarity; tediousness.

chatim (*m.*) a crooked merchant.

chatinar (*v.i.*) to deal crookedly.

chato –ta (*adj.*) flat, level, smooth; (*slang*) boresome, tiresome, dull, humdrum; (*m.*, *Zool.*) the common crablouse (*Phthirus pubis*), c.a. PIOLHO-DAS-VIRILHAS. Deixe de ser—! Don't be such a bore!

chatô (*m.*, *slang*) a bachelor's living quarters. [French *chateau*].

chauvinismo [au = ô] (*m.*) chauvinism, jingoism.

chauvinista [au = ô] (*adj.*; *m.*,*f.*) chauvinist, jingo.

chavão (*m.*) large key; cake mold; pattern; hackneyed phrase, cliché.

chavascal (*m.*) pigsty; infertile land; also = CHARRAVASCAL.

chave (*f.*) any key; door key; clock key; any wrench; electric switch; clue (key) to a situation (mystery, puzzle); symbol of authority; keystone; strategic military position; piston of a brass-wind musical instrument; (*Print.*) a brace; (*Zool.*) any cowrie-shell mollusk, esp. *Cypraea zebra*.—automática, (*Elec.*) circuit breaker.—curva, an S-wrench.—electromagnética, electromagnetic switch.—de abóbada, keystone of an arch.—de alarme, alarm switch.—de arranque, starter switch.—de bôca, open-end wrench.—de cabeça, headlock (in wrestling).—de caixa, socket wrench.—de canos, pipe wrench.—de catraca, or—a roquete, a wrench or screwdriver having a ratchet.—de corda, or—de relógio, clock-winding key.—de dois polos, (*Elec.*) a two-pole switch.—de emergência, emergency switch.—de fenda, or—de parafusos, screw driver.—de mancal, socket wrench.—de parada, stop switch.—de porca, nut wrench.—de trinco, latch key.—de tubos, pipe wrench.—do-inferno, (*Bot.*) a sac fungus (*Claviceps pallida*).—do pé, sole of the foot [= PLANTA DO PÉ].—em ângulo, offset wrench.—em cruz, cross lug wrench.—falsa, counterfeit key.—grifa, pipe wrench.—inglêsa, monkey wrench.—-mestra, master key.—Stillson, Stillson wrench.

chaveira (*f.*, *Veter.*) measles of swine and cattle.

chaveiro (*m.*) turnkey; keeper of the keys.

chaveirose (*f.*, *Veter.*) swine measles.

chavelha [ê] wooden pin; plow beam.

chavelho [ê] (*m.*) horn, feeler (of insects).

chávena (*f.*) cup, esp. a teacup.

chavêta (*f.*) axle pin; cotter pin; key; slot key; gib; hinge pin.—principal, kingbolt, kingpin.

chavetar (*v.t.*, *Mach.*) to key.

châzada (*f.*) a cup of tea; a medicinal tea or brew.

châzeiro –ra (*adj.*) tea-loving; (*m.*,*f.*) tea lover; (*m.*) = CHEDA.

châzista (*adj.*) tea-loving; (*m.*,*f.*) tea lover.

checoslovaco –ca (*adj.*; *m.*,*f.*) Czechoslovak(ian).

cheda [ê] (*f.*) the side rail of a truck or wagon in which stanchions are set.

chefão (*m.*) = MANDACHUVA.

chefatura (*f.*) police or other headquarters; chieftaincy [= CHEFIA].

chefe (*m.*,*f.*) chief, chieftain, leader, head, commander, master, boss; (*slang*) a familiar form of address to strangers: "Chief", "Doc", "Cap", "Boss".—da torcida, cheer leader.—de estação, station master.—de familia, family head; paterfamilias.—-de-obra, chef-d'oeuvre [= OBRA PRIMA].—de secção, department head.—de trem, train conductor.—do Estado, government head, Chief of State.—do Estado-Maior, Chief of Staff.

chefia (*f.*) chieftaincy, chieftainship, leadership.

chefiar (*v.t.*) to head, control, direct, lead, govern; (*v.i.*) to be the chief.

chega (*m.,f., colloq.*) rebuke, reprimand.

chegada (*f.*) see under CHEGADO.

chegadela (*f.*) arrival; a thrashing; rebuke, reprimand.

chegado –da (*adj.*) arrived; close, intimate. **parente—**, a close relative. (*f.*) arrival, advent; a coming or approach; also, a going to. **dar uma—a algum lugar**, to take a run over to (drop by) some place.

chega-e-vira (*f.*) a white-faced tree duck (*Dendrocygna viduata*), c.a. IRERÊ.

chegança (*f.*) formerly, a lascivious dance; in recent times, in Brazil, a folk play in the public square depicting a naval battle; (*pl.*) neighborhood visits by Christmas merrymakers.

chegaço (*m., colloq.*) a reprimand.

chegar (*v.i.*) to come, arrive (**de**, from; **a, até**, at); to reach (**a, até**, to); to suffice, be enough (**para**, for); (*v.t.*) to bring or carry near to; (*v.r.*) to come close, approach, draw near (**a, de, para**, to).—**a brasa à sua sardinha**, to draw water to one's mill.—**a mostarda ao nariz**, to irritate, upset, cause to lose patience.—**a ponto**, to come at the right time, in the nick of time.—**ao ponto de (fazer alguma coisa)**, to reach the point of (doing something).—**à razão**, to bring to reason.—**a ser**, to get to be; to become.—**a um acôrdo**, to reach an agreement.—**a tempo**, to arrive in time.—**a um têrmo**, to come to an end.—**a uma conclusão**, to reach a conclusion.—**ao vivo**, to touch (someone) to the quick.—**às vias de fato**, to come to blows.—**com atraso**, to arrive late.—**de imprevisto**, to show up unexpectedly, make a surprise visit.—**na hora**, to arrive on time. **Chega!** That's enough! That will do! Stop it! **Chegue uma cadeira**, Pull up a chair. **Cheguei no escritório às nove**, I got to the office at nine. **Não se chegue muito a mim**, Don't come too close to me. **A comida não chegou nem para dois dias**, The food didn't last even two days. **As ideias chegam-lhe mais depressa do que as palavras**, His mind works faster than his tongue. **Êles chegaram muito cedo**, They arrived too soon. **Chegou a crê-lo**, He came to believe it. **Em boa hora você chegou!** You couldn't have come at a worse time! **Você chegou no bom momento**, You arrived in the nick of time.

cheia (*f.*) see under CHEIO.

cheiinho –nha [ei-i] (*adj.*) chockful, quite full. [Dim. of CHEIO.]

cheio –a (*adj.; irreg. p.p. of* ENCHER) full, filled, replete; crammed, packed, crowded; complete; wealthy; stout; (*Print.*) unleaded; (*slang*) drunk; (*m.*) = DIAMBA; (*f.*) flood, overflow, freshet; full of the moon; abundance; excess.—**de admiração**, wonderstruck.—**de caprichos** or—**de veneta**, capricious.—**de besteira** (*de chove-e-não-molha, de luxo, de nove horas, de novidades*), all colloquialisms meaning finical, too particular or fussy; prissy; over-fastidious; affected.—**de corpo**, buxom, plump.—**de dedos**, all thumbs (awkward).—**de dias**, or **de anos**, full of years.—**de histórias**, fuss-budgety.—**de pontinhos**, punctilious.—**de nós pelas costas**, confused.—**de si**, stuck on oneself; smug; self-important. **à bôca—**, outspokenly. **acertar**, or **pegar, em—** to hit the bull's-eye. **em—**, fully, squarely, right, smack on. **lua—**, full moon. **maré—**, high tide. **O cinema está—**, The movie is crowded.

cheira-cheira (*m., slang*) a nosey person.

cheirar (*v.t.,v.i.*) to smell; to sniff; to smell out (a secret, etc.).—**a**, to smell of.—**a chamusco**, to smell scorched; to smell suspicious.—**a defunto**, of an impending conflict, to forebode grave consequences.—**bem (mal)**, to smell good (bad). **Isso está cheirando mal**, This bodes no good.

cheiro (*m.*) scent, fragrance, odor, smell; stench; (*pl.*) herbs for seasoning food.—**de santidade**, odor of sanctity.

cheiroso –sa (*adj.*) smelly, odorous; fragrant.

cheleme (*m.*) slam (at bridge or whist).

cheque (*m.*) bank check; a check at chess.—**cruzado**, (in Brazil) a bank check with two parallel lines drawn diagonally across its face, to indicate that it is payable only to a bank or only to the bank whose name is written within the lines.—**visado**, certified check. **receber um—**, to cash a check. Cf. XEQUE.

cherimólia (*f., Bot.*) the cherimoya (*Annona cherimolia*).

cherivia (*f.*) garden parsnip (*Pastinaca sativa*).

cherna(-preta) (*f.*) = CHERNE(-PINTADO).

cherne (*m., Zool.*) the snowy grouper (*Epinephelus niveatus*), c.a. CHERNE-PINTADO, CHERNETE, CHERNA(-PRETA), SERIGADO-CHERNE, SERIGADO-TAPOAN, MERO-PRÊTO.—

-vermelho = VERMELHO (snapper).

chernete, chernote (*m.*) = CHERNE (-PINTADO).

chessilita (*f., Min.*) chessylite, azurite.

cheviote (*m.*) cheviot.

chi! My! How awful!

chiada (*f.*) a shrilling, chirping, creaking, squeaking.

chiadeira (*f.*) strident noise; shrill voices or sounds.

chiado –da (*adj.*) squeaky; (*m.*) = CHIADA.

chiar (*v.i.*) to chirr or sing (as a cicada); to chirp (as a cricket); to squeak (as a rat, wagon wheel, pair of new shoes); to make a sizzling sound (as of frying); to make a hissing sound (as of escaping steam); to wheeze; to creak (as a door).

chiastolita (*f., Min.*) chiastolite.

chiba (*f.*) a young she-goat; a blister in the hand.

chibamba (*m.*) in Braz. folklore, a hobgoblin that grunts like a pig to frighten children.

chibanca (*f.*) a cutter mattock.

chibança, chibantaria (*f.*) foppishness; braggadocio.

chibante (*adj.*) vainglorious; foppish; pert; nifty, (*m., Zool.*) the shrike-like chatterer (*Laniisoma elegans*); also = ARAPONGUINHA and ASSOBIADOR.

chibantear, chibar (*v.i.*) to swagger, brag, strut.

chibantice (*f.*), **-tismo** (*m.*) = CHIBANÇA.

chibarrada (*f.*) a small herd of goats [= FATO].

chibarreira (*f.*), **-ro** (*m.*) goatherd.

chibarro (*m.*) a he-goat [= BODE].

chibata (*f.*) switch (slender whip); withe; (*Bot.*) = CANA-FLECHA (a bamboo).

chibatada (*f.*) blow(s) with a switch.

chibat(e)ar (*v.t.*) to switch (whip).

chibato (*m.*) a kid (goat) of from six to twelve months old. Cf. CHIBO.

chibé (*m.*) a cooling drink or mixture of manioc flour with water and sugar. When rum is added to it, it is called JACUBA, TIQUARA or SEBEREBA.

chibo (*m.*) a kid (goat) up to one year of age, esp. one not castrated. Cf. CHIBATO.

chica (*f.*) a wanton Negro dance; a certain alcoholic drink; a plant and dye called CARAJURU.

chicana (*f.*) chicane, chicanery; intrigue; pettifoggery; baffle plate.

chican(e)ar (*v.i.*) to engage in chicanery; to cavil.

chicaneiro –ra (*adj.*) pettifogging; (*m.*) trickster;·petti-fogger.

chicanice (*f.*) chicanery, pettifoggery.

chicanista (*adj.; m.*) = CHICANEIRO.

chicha (*f.*) in baby talk, food or meat; a sweetmeat; in students' slang, an interlinear translation; a fermented drink made with corn, fruit pits, etc.

chícharo (*m.*) the gram chickpea (*Cicer arietum*) or its edible seed; the flat peavine (*Lathyrus sylvestris*).—**s-miúdos** = CISIRÃO-BRANCO.

chichica (*f.*) = CUÍCA.

chichisbéu (*m.*) an importunate gallant or suitor. [Italian *cicisbeo*]

chicle (*m.*) chicle; chewing gum.

chico (*m.*) the usual pet name for a monkey; a pig; when capitalized: a nickname for FRANCISCO.—**-da-ronda**, or—**-puxado**, a sort of fandango.—**-lerê** = JOÃO-BÔBO (a bird).—**-prêto** = GRAÚNA (a bird).

chicória (*f.*) any chicory (*Cichorium*), esp. the endive (*C. endivia*).—**-amarga** or **-selvagem**, common chicory (*C. intybus*), c.a. ALMEIRÃO.—**-do-campo**, a cat's-ear (*Hypochoeris*).

chicoriáceo –cea (*adj., Bot.*) chichoriaceous; (*f.pl.*) the chicory family (*Chichoriaceae*).

chicotaço (*m.*), **chicotada** (*f.*) a whip lash(ing).

chicot(e)ar (*v.t.*) to lash, whip, scourge.

chicote (*m.*) whip, esp. one of rawhide; end of a rope.

chifra (*f.*) an iron scraper for hides.

chifraço (*m.*) **chifrada** (*f.*) a horn thrust [= CORNADA].

chifrar (*v.t.*) to gore with the horns.

chifre (*m.*) horn.—**-de-cabra**, a miserly person.—**-develado**, the yellow unicorn plant (*Ibicella lutea*), c.a. CORNOS-DO-DIABO; the common devil's-claws (*Proboscidea jussieui*), c.a. QUINGOMBÔ-DE-ESPINHO. **pegar o touro pelos—s**, to take the bull by the horns. **pôr os—s no marido**, to make a cuckold of the husband. Cf. CÔRNO.

chifrudo –da (*adj.*) having big horns; (*f.*) a hammerhead shark, c.a. CORNUDA.

chilca (*f., Bot.*) a eupatorium (*E. dendroides*), c.a. PERNA-DE-SARACURA, VASSOURA-DE-FERRO; the seep willow baccharis (*B. glutinosa*).

childrenita (f., Min.) childrenite.
chile (m.) = ESPINHO-DE-JERUSALEM.
chilenas (f.pl.) large spurs.
chileninha (f.) a commercial type of ERVA-MATE in very fine particles.
chileno –na (adj.; m.,f.) Chilean.
chilique (m.) faint, swoon, spell, attack, fit; conniption.
chilrada (f.) twittering of birds; chatter and laughter of children at play. Var. CHILREADA.
chilrar (v.i.) to twitter, chirp, chirrup, warble. Var. CHILREAR.
chilreante (adj.) twittering.
chilreio (m.) twitter(ing), chirp(ing), trill(ing), warble-(ing).
chilro (m.) chirp, twitter.
chim (adj.; m.) = CHINÊS.
chimango (m.) = XIMANGO.
chimarrão (m.) MATE, tea, coffee or other hot beverage served without sugar; wild stray cattle.
chimarrear, chimarronear (v.i.) to drink CHIMARRÃO.
chimarrita (f.) a popular song and dance [= CHAMARITA].
chimpanzé (m.) chimpanzee.
china (f.) prostitute; kept woman; a native Brazilian Indian woman.
chincada (f.) a coarse allusion.
chinchila (f.) chinchilla.
chincoã (m.) any of various birds of the cuckoo family, c.a. CUCU, ALMA-DE-GATO, PAPA-LAGARTAS.—-de-bico-vermelho, the black-bellied, red-beaked cuckoo (Piaya m. melanogaster).
chinela (f.), –lo (m.) house slipper; old shoe.
chinelada (f.) a paddling with a slipper.
chinês –nesa (adj.; m.,f.) Chinese.
chinesice (f.) Chinese trait; trifle; any object made by hand with great skill and patience.
chinfrim (adj.) petty; common; (m., colloq.) shindy, row, roughhouse; shindig, hoedown.
chinguiço (m.) a pad for the back of the neck and shoulders worn by porters when carrying burdens hanging from the ends of a pole. Cf. RODILHA.
chino –na (adj.; m.f.,) = CHINÊS.
chinó (m.) wig, toupee.
chinquilho (m.) game of quoits.
chio (m.) a squeak or squeaking sound; chirr (of a cicada); fuse (for fireworks). [Verb: CHIAR].
chipanzé (m.) = CHIMPANZÉ.
Chipre (m.) Cyprus. Var. CIPRO.
chique (adj.) chic, stylish, smart, dapper. nem—nem mique, nothing at all.
chiquê (m., slang) airs, pretension, affectation, a putting on.
chiqueira (f.) = QUERO-QUERO.
chiqueirador (m.) a riding crop.
chiqueirar (v.t.) to pen up (pigs, calves, etc.).
chiqueiro (m.) pigsty, pigpen; fig., a filthy house; part of a fish trap.
chiquismo (m.) chicness.
chirinola (f.) rigmarole.
chiripa (f.) fluke; lucky break.
chiripear (v.i.) to win by a fluke.
chiripento –ta (adj.) lucky at cards.
chiroquí (m.) Cherokee.
chirriar (v.i.) to hoot (as an owl).
chispa (f.) spark.
chispada (f., colloq.) a wild ride, a joy ride.
chispante (adj.) sparkling.
chispar (v.i.) to throw out sparks; to spit fire; to flare up (in anger); (slang) to burn up the road; to scram.
chispe (m.) pig's foot.
chispômetro (m., Elec.) sparker.
chiste (m.) witticism, jest, quip, flash of wit, drollery, pleasantry.
chistoso –sa (adj.) witty, waggish; facetious; sprightly, sparkling.
chita (f.) calico, chintz, cotton print; (Bot.) an Oncidium orchid.
chitado –da (adj.) speckled.
chitão (m.) chintz; (interj.) shut up! be quiet!
choca (f.) a kind of hockey stick; a kind of hockey ball; cowbell; a lead cow; (Zool.) any of several ant shrikes of genus Thamnophilus, esp. the bluish-gray (T. c. caerulescens), the rufous-capped (T. r. ruficapillus) and Swainson's spotted tailed (T. punctatus ambiguus), all of southern Brazil; (adj.) fem. of CHÔCO.

choça (f.) hut, hovel, cabin.—de palha, grass shack.
chocadeira (f.) incubator.—de crianças, baby incubator.
chocagem (f.) hatching of eggs.
chocalhado –da (adj.) shaken, agitated, rattled; (f.) a rattling, clanging, jingling (of small bells, rattles, etc.).
chocalhar (v.t.,v.i.) to rattle; to shake up and down (as a rattle); (v.i.) to blab; to shake with laughter.
chocalheiro –ra (adj.) rattling; chattering; (m.) rattler, senseless chatterer, blabbermouth; (f.) busybody, gossip; (Bot.) the big quaking grass (Briza maxima).
chocalhice (f.) tongue wagging, gabbling, blabbing.
chocalho (m.) cowbell; sleigh-bell; rattle; a rattling gourd used as a musical instrument [= MARACÁ].—-de-cascavel, (Bot.) a rattlebox (Crotolaria sp.).
chocante (adj.) shocking, frightful.
chocão (m., Zool.) Vieillot's ant shrike (Hypoedaleus guttatus) of southeastern Brazil, c.a. BORRALHARA-PINTADA.
chocar (v.t.) to bump, strike, collide with; to hatch (eggs, plot); to shock, offend; (v.i.) to brood, incubate; of food, to spoil, go bad; (v.r.) to collide against, bump into. O auto chocou-se com a árvore, The car ran into a tree.
chocarreiro –ra (adj.) waggish; zany; scurrilous; (m.) buffoon.
chocarrice (f.) coarse jest; crude remark; drollery.
chôcho –cha (adj.) empty, hollow; dry; dull, insipid; (m.) a smack (kiss).
chôco (m.) act of brooding; period of incubation; cuttle-fish; (adj., fem. CHOCA) addled, spoiled; vapid: água—, bad-smelling stagnant water. cerveja—, stale beer. galinha—, setting hen. ôvo—, egg being hatched.
chocolataria (f.) chocolate factory; chocolate shop.
chocolate (m.) chocolate.
chocolateira (f.) chocolate pot; (slang) "mug" (face).
chocolateiro (m.) chocolate manufacturer or dealer.
chofer (m.) chauffeur.—de caminhão, truck driver.
chôfre (m.) sudden blow or bump; a quick stroke (as of a billiard cue). de—, suddenly, abruptly, slapbang, slap-dash.
chopada (f., slang) a beer session (at a bar, beer garden, etc.).
chope [ô] (m.) draft beer.—duplo, a double-size glassful of such beer; (slang) a double-decker bus.
chopim (m.) any of various cowbirds of genus Molothrus, esp. the widely distributed shiny cowbird (M. b. bona-riensis) of southern Brazil, c.a. VIRA-BOSTA, AZULÃO, CARIXO, PÁSSARO-PRÊTO, PAPA-ARROZ, PARASITA, MARIA-PRETA, GAUDÉRIO, ENGANA-TICO(-TICO).—-do-brejo, the yellow-rumped marsh bird (Pseudoleistes guirahuro), c.a. MELRO-PINTADO-DO-BREJO; also = ARRANCA-MILHO (a grackle). Var. CHUPIM.
chopista (m.) beer-guzzler.
choque (m.) shock, collision, impact, jolt, clash; con-cussion; brunt; encounter, conflict; electric shock; (Med.) shock; (Elec.) choke coil.
choqueiro (m.) hen house.
choradeira (f.) a professional woman mourner; a spell of crying and whining, esp. by a child; (colloq.) a tearful request or plea.
choradinho (m.) a folksong for dancing, played on a fiddle; a mournful tune.
chorado –da (adj.) lamented; of tunes, folksongs, mourn-ful, blue; (m.) a sad folksong.
chora-lua (m.) a kind of goatsucker (nighthawk), c.a. URUTAU.
choramigar (v.) & derivs. = CHORAMINGAR & derivs.
choramingador –dora (m.,f.) whimperer, sniffler, whiner, blubberer. Var. CHORAMIGADOR.
choramingar (v.i.) to cry, whine, whimper, Var. CHORA-MIGAR.
choromingas (m.,f.) a whining (whimpering, sniveling, self-pitying) person; crybaby. Var. CHORAMIGAS.
choramingueiro –ra (adj.) whining, whimpering. Var. CHORAMIGUEIRO.
chorão –rona (adj.) whimpering, sniveling; maudlin; given to crying; (m.,f.) whimperer, sniveler; crybaby; (m.) any of various trees having pendulous branches, as the weeping willow; a fresh-water catfish called ANUJÁ; a bird—the white-winged seed-eater (Sporophila l. leucoptera)—c.a. PAPA-CAPIM, BICO-VERMELHO, CIGARRA; also, Pretre's parrot (Amazona pretrei) of southern Brazil, c.a. PAPAGAIO-DA-SERRA.—-salgueiro (Bot.), the

Babylon weeping willow (*Salix babylonica*), c.a. SAL-GUEIRO-CHORÃO, SALGUEIRO-DA-BABILÔNIA.

chorar (*v.i.*) to cry, weep, shed tears; to moan and sob; to wail, whimper; to sing the blues; (*v.t.*) to cry over; to bemoan, bewail; to lament, mourn over (about).—**a morte da bezerra**, to cry over spilled milk.—**a perda de**, to bewail the loss of.—**de alegria**, to cry for joy.—**de raiva**, to weep with rage.—**lágrimas de sangue**, to shed bitter tears.—**misérias**, to cry poor.—**por um ôlho só**, to shed crocodile tears.—**sôbre a sorte**, to bemoan one's luck.—**uma carta**, (*slang*) to squeeze one's cards (as at poker). **rebentar a**—, to burst out crying. **rir a**—, to shed tears from laughing.

choraria (*f.*) a crying spell (by a single person or by several persons together).

chôro (*m.*) act of weeping, crying, sobbing; an informal music fest at which a small orchestra plays popular songs and dances; also, the tunes so played.

chorona, fem. of CHORÃO.

chorões (*m.pl.*) the hottentot fig (*Mesembryanthemum edule*), c.a. FLOR-DO-MEIO-DIA.—**dos-jardins** = CAUDA-DE-RAPÔSA.

choroso -sa (*adj.*) tearful, weeping; maudlin; sad, moving.

chorrilho (*m.*) spate, rush; series, sequence; string, constant flow; a group of more or less similar persons or things.—**de pragas**, string of curses.

chorume (*m.*) fat; drippings, juice; abundance.

chorumela (*f.*) trifle, thing of little value [= NINHARIA].

choupa (*f.*) metal point of a spear or goad; sargo (a fish).

choupal (*m.*) a grove of poplars.

choupana (*f.*) thatched hut, grass shack.

choupaneiro (*m.*) hut-dweller.

choupo (*m.*, *Bot.*) poplar.—**-branco**, white poplar (*Populus alba*), c.a. ÁLAMO, FAIA-BRANCA.—**-do-canadá**, the Eastern poplar (*P. deltoides*).—**-negro** or **-prêto**, the black poplar (*P. nigra*), c.a. ÁLAMO-PRÊTO (or -NEGRO).—**-tremedor**, the European aspen (*P. tremula*), c.a. FAIA-PRETA.

chouriça (*f.*) an interlinear translation in a foreign language textbook. [*Students' slang*].

chouriceiro (*m.*), **-ra** (*f.*) sausage maker or merchant.

chouriço (*m.*) a kind of smoked sausage; a long, sausage-like bag, filled with sand or sawdust, for placing against door and window crevices to exclude drafts; a piece of cloth, twisted and rolled to form a head or shoulder pad. Cf. CHINGUIÇO, RODILHA; a rat (pad) for the hair; the padded part of a crupper.

choutador -dora, **choutão** -tona, **chouteiro** -ra (*adj.*) of a horse, hard-trotting, jogging.

choutar (*v.i.*) to jog along.

chouto (*m.*) jog, hard trot.

choutozinho (*m.*) slow, hard trot.

chovediço -da (*adj.*) rainy; threatening rain.

chove-não-molha (*m.*) anything which is at a standstill, which goes neither back nor ahead; a wishy-washy person.

chover (*v.i.*) to rain (**em**, **sôbre**, **on**).—**a cântaros**, to rain pitchforks; to rain cats and dogs.—**no molhado**, to expend time in useless effort. **chova ou faça sol**, rain or shine. **Continua a**—, It's still raining. **Quer chova, quer não chova**, rain or shine.

chucha (*f.*) act of sucking or suckling; sugar-tit.

chuchadeira (*f.*, *colloq.*) a "good thing"; also = CHUCHA.

chuchapitos (*m.*, *Bot.*) the spotted deadnettle (*Lamium maculatum*).

chuchar (*v.i.*) to suck, suckle.

chucho (*m.*) chills and fever

chuchu (*m.*) chayote (*Sechium edule*) a widely-cultivated, fast-growing, tendril-bearing tropical vine, c.a. MAXIXE-FRANCÊS, MACHUCHO, MACHUCHU, CAIOTA, CAXIXE; also, its fruit which is cooked and eaten as a vegetable;(*colloq.*) a person who falls in easily with another; also, a nickname applied to persons from Petropolis, Brazil. **p'ra**—(*slang*) much, heaps, lots, oodles, scads. **Ela é um**—, She's a honey.

chuchurreado -da (*adj.*) of kisses, long-drawn-out and loud.

chuchurrear (*v.i.*) to slurp (drink soup, etc., with sucking noises).

chuchuzeiro (*m.*) a CHUCHU vine.

chuco (*m.*) a rootspine palm (*Cryosophila sp.*).

chuço (*m.*) spear, harpoon; a goad.

chucrute (*m.*) sauerkraut.

chué (*adj.*) dejected, down-in-the-mouth, moping; trivial;

skinny; poorly-dressed; poor, insignificant, ordinary; insipid.

chufa (*f.*) jest, joke, gag (somewhat coarse); taunt; a confection somewhat like crystalized ginger; a beverage resembling ginger ale; (*Bot.*) the chufa flatsedge (*Cyperus esculentus*) on whose edible tubers hogs are fed.

chufar (*v.t.*) to make fun of.

chulé (*m.*) the filth between unwashed toes; the rank smell of sweaty feet.

chulear (*v.t.*) to overcast, whip, baste (sew): (*v.i.*) to root for (a team, etc.); to "pull" for something to come true.

chulice (*f.*), **-lismo** (*m.*) a coarse or spicy story; a crude or dirty expression; scurrility.

chulipa (*f.*) railroad crosstie [corrup. of sleeper]; (*colloq.*) a kick on the behind.

chulo -la (*adj.*) coarse, common, low, vulgar, dirty, indecent, scurrilous.

chumaçar (*v.t.*) to pad, stuff, wad.

chumaceira (*f.*) any sort of anti-friction bushing or bearing.—**de esferas**, ball bearing.—**de rôlos**, roller bearing.

chumaço (*m.*) padding, stuffing, wadding (of cotton, straw, feathers, etc.); in the interior of Brazil, the wooden axle-bearing of ox-carts. [The wood rubbing against wood as the wheels turn produces a loud squealing sound, which, it is said, the oxen enjoy and without which they will refuse to draw the cart.]

chumbado -da (*adj.*) filled (plugged) with lead or other metal; of a bolt, anchored in concrete; (*colloq.*) tipsy; in love; done for (very sick); stricken with syphilis, tuberculosis or other serious contagious disease; (*f.*) a load of buckshot; a slight gunshot wound; lead sinker (for fishing lines and nets).

chumbador (*m.*) an anchor bolt; person who anchors bolts, etc., with lead or concrete.

chumbagem (*f.*) plugging, as with lead; anchoring (as a bolt) in concrete.

chumbar (*v.t.*) to fasten (solder, weld, fill, plug, seal) with lead or other molten metal; to weight with lead; to wound with a shotgun; to anchor (a bolt, etc.) in concrete; to make drunk; to flunk a student.—**um dente**, to fill a tooth.—**uma rêde**, to weight a fish net.

chumbear (*v.t.*) to wound with a gunshot.

chumbeira (*f.*) a fish net weighted with lead sinkers; the sinkers themselves.

chumbeiro (*m.*) leather holder for shot; a lead pellet.

chumberga (*f.*) a young XARELETE.

chumbinho (*m.*) a belittling nickname applied to Portuguese persons in Minas Gerais; (*Bot.*) the showy heart-seed (*Cardiospermum grandiflora*), c.a. BALÃOZINHO, ENSACADINHA; a bean (*Phaseolus ellipticus*); a nickel coin; (*Fireworks*) a torpedo, c.a. TRAQUE-DE-CHUMBO; (*pl.*) printing type.—**amarelo** (*slang*) a gold sovereign.—**-roxo**, common lantana (*L. camara*).

chumbo (*m.*) lead; lead sinker; (*colloq.*) common sense; flunking of an exam.—**antimonial**, antimonial lead.—**electrolítico**, electrolytic lead.—**grosso**, buck shot.—**miúdo**, bird shot.—**químico**, chemical lead.—**tetraetílico**, tetraethyl lead.

chunga (*f.*) = SERIEMA.

chupa-caldo (*m.*) a sneak; flatterer.

chupa-chupa (*m.*) = CAIAPIÁ (an herb).

chupada, **chupadela** (*f.*) a suck or act of sucking.

chupa-dente (*m.*, *Zool.*) a pipit (*Conopophaga lineata*), c.a. CUSPIDOR (spitter).

chupado -da (*adj.*) sucked; (*colloq.*) very thin, skinny; drawn (in appearance).

chupador -dora (*adj.*) sucking; (*m.*,*f.*) sucker. [But only in the sense of one who or that which sucks. A sucker, in the sense of one who is easily duped, is a TROUXA.]—**-de-anta**, a salt lick.

chupadura (*f.*) = CHUPADELA.

chupa-ferro (*m.*, *Bot.*) a prickly ash (*Zanthoxylum pohlianum*), c.a. QUEBRA-MACHADO.

chupa-flor (*m.*) a humming bird. Other names are: CHUPA-MEL, BEIJA-FLOR, COLIBRI.

chupa-galhetas (*m.*, *colloq.*) acolyte; altar boy.

chupa-jantares (*m.*) = PAPA-JANTARES (sponge).

chupa-mel (*m.*) humming bird [= CHUPA-FLOR, BEIJA-FLOR, COLIBRI]; (*Bot.*) sweet honeysuckle (*Lonicera caprifolium*).

chupamento (*m.*) = CHUPADELA.

chupança (*f.*) = BARBEIRO (barber bug).

chupão -pona (*adj.*) sucking; (*m.*) a loud kiss; (*Zool.*) = BARBEIRO (barber bug).

chupa-ôvo (*m.*) = PAPA-ÔVO.
chupar (*v.t.*) to suck, imbibe, absorb; to sponge on; to drain of resources; (*v.i.*) to guzzle; (*v.r.*) to fade into the landscape (as game).—**os olhos da cara a,** to fleece (as by blackmail).
chupa-rôlha (*m.*) guzzler, tosspot.
chupa-sangue (*m.*) bloodsucker, human leech; a leech [= SANGUESSUGA].
chupeta [ê] (*f.*) rubber nipple, pacifier; a sipper (glass or rubber tube, straw, etc.); a pipette.
chupim (*m.*) a man who lets his wife support him, or who marries a rich woman with this end in view; a bird called CHOPIM.
chupista (*m.,f.*) tippler; sponger, cadger, hanger-on.
chupita (*f.*) a kind of caribe (cannibal fish).
chupitar (*v.i.*) to sip; (*colloq.*) to enjoy a sinecure.
churdo –**da** (*adj.*) of raw wool, dirty; sordid; (*m.,f.*) a sordid person.
churi [í] (*m.*) rhea (American ostrich) numerous in southern Brazil; = EMA.
churrascaria (*f.*) a restaurant which specializes in CHURRASCO.
churrasco (*m.*) a piece of meat broiled over live coals; an outdoor barbecue party.
churrasquear (*v.t.*) to barbecue and eat meat.
churro –**ra** (*adj.*) = CHURDO.
chusma (*f.*) crowd, throng, mob; heap, large quantity; a crew. **às**—**s,** in large quantities. **uma**—**de injúrias,** a volley of abuse.
chusmar (*v.t.*) to provide with a crew.
chutada (*f., Soccer*) a kick of the ball.
chutador (*m., Soccer*) a strong and accurate goal kicker.
chutar (*v.t.*) to kick the ball (in soccer).
chute (*m., Soccer*) a shot.—**livre,** free kick.
chuteira (*f.*) a heavy shoe (for kicking the ball in soccer).
chuva (*f.*) rain; downpour, shower; (*slang*) drunkenness; (*m., slang*) boozer.—**atômica,** atomic fall-out.—**criadeira,** a steady light rain which soaks the soil.—**de-caroço,** a hard, pelting rain.—**-de-pedra,** hailstorm.—**s -de-caju,** or—**s -de-rama,** in northern Brazil, the first showers of the rainy season, beginning usually in September or October; c.a. PIRAOBA. —**s-de-santa-luzia,** equinoctial rains.—**s-dos-cajueiros,** in Brazil, winter rains (July–August) which hasten the ripening of the fruit of the cashew trees.—**s-dos-imbus** = CAMBUEIRAS. —**de-ouro,** (*Bot.*) the golden shower senna (*Cassia fistula*), c.a. CANAFÍSTULA-VERDADEIRA; also, a butterfly orchid (*Oncidium flexuosum*). **à prova de**—, rainproof. **cair na**—, (*slang*) to get drunk. **Muito trovão é sinal de pouca**—, A barking dog seldom bites. **queda de**—, rainfall.
chuvada, chuvarada (*f.*), **chuvão** (*m.*) a heavy downpour.
chuveiro (*m.*) a shower-bathroom; a shower-bath nozzle; a sprinkler nozzle; a heavy shower; a spate (shower) of anything.—**de-são-josé,** (*Fireworks*) a shower of stars.
chuvinha (*f.*) sprinkle, light shower.
chuviscar (*v.i.*) to drizzle.
chuvisco, chuvisqueiro (*m.*) drizzle, light rain.
chuvoso –**sa** (*adj.*) rainy, wet.
cia. = COMPANHIA (Company).
ciamo (*m., Zool.*) a whale louse (*Cyamus spp.*); (*Bot.*) taro (*Colocasia antiquorum*). Cf. TAIOBA, INHAME.
cianamida (*f., Chem.*) cyanamide, amide cyanogen.
cianato (*m., Chem.*) cyanate.
cianemia (*f., Med.*) cyanemia.
cianetação (*f., Metal.*) cyanide process.
cianeto [ê] (*m.*) cyanide.—**de cobre,** copper cyanide.—**de hidrogênio,** hydrogen cyanide; hydrocyanic acid; formonitrile.—**de ouro e potássio,** gold potassium cyanide; potassium aurocyanide.—**de potássio,** potassium cyanide.—**de prata,** silver cyanide.—**de prata e potássio,** silver potassium cyanide; potassium argento-cyanide.—**de sódio,** sodium cyanide.—**de zinco,** zinc cyanide.
ciânico –**ca** (*adj., Chem.*) cyanic.
cianidreto (*m., Chem.*) hydrogen cyanide.
cianídrico –**ca** (*adj., Chem.*) hydrocyanic. **ácido**—, prussic acid.
cianina (*f., Biochem.*) cyanin.
cianita (*f., Min.*) cyanite, disthene [= DISTÊNIO].
ciano (*m.*) = ACIANO.
cianodermia (*f., Med.*) cyanoderma.
cianogênio (*m., Chem.*) cyanogen.
cianometria (*f.*) cyanometry.
cianômetro (*m.*) cyanometer.

cianopatia (*f., Med.*) cyanosis.
cianose (*f., Med.*) cyanosis; (*Min.*) cyanose, chalcanthite, bluestone.
cianótico –**ca** (*adj., Med.*) cyanotic.
cianuração (*f.*) = CIANETAÇÃO.
cianureto [ê] (*m.*) = CIANETO.
cianúrico –**ca** (*adj., Chem.*) cyanuric.
ciar (*v.i.*) to row backwards; to back water.
ciascopia (*f., Med.*) skiascopy.
ciático –**ca** (*adj., Med.*) sciatic. **dôr**—, sciatica. **nervo**—, sciatic nerve.
ciatiforme (*adj.*) cyathiform, shaped like a cup.
ciavogar (*v.t.*) to swing a boat around by rowing on one side and backing water on the other.
cibo (*m.*) food, esp. for birds.
cibório (*m., R.C.Ch.*) ciborium, pyx.
cica (*f.*) condition of astringency of the mouth as caused by tasting unripe fruit; (*Bot.*) a cycad.
cicadáceas, cicádeas (*f.pl., Bot.*) the family of cycads (*Cycadaceae*).
cicadárias (*f.pl., Zool.*) the family of cicadas (*Cicadidae*).
cicas (*m.*) a cycad (any plant of the genus *Cycas*).
cicatricial (*adj., Med.*) cicatricial.
cicatrícula (*f.*) small scar; cicatricle of an egg; hilum of a seed.
cicatriz (*f.*) cicatrix, scar, blemish; lasting effect on the memory of an insult suffered, of a wound to the feelings, etc.
cicatrização (*f.*) cicatrization, healing.
cicatrizado –**da** (*adj.*) healed (over); scarred.
cicatrizante (*adj.*) cicatrisive, cicatrizant.
cicatrizar (*v.t.,v.i.*) to heal (wound, sore); (*v.t.*) to scar.
cícero (*m., Print.*) em pica.
cicerone (*m.*) a tourist guide.
ciciar (*v.i.*) to rustle; to whisper, murmur; to lisp. Cf. CECEAR.
cicio (*m.*) a rustling sound; a whispering; a lisp.
cicioso –**sa** (*adj.*) rustling, whispering; lisping.
cíclame, ciclame (*m., Bot.*) cyclamen, c.a. ARTANITA, PÃO-PORCINO, PÃO-DE-PORCO; also, the color cyclamen.—**da-europa,** the European cyclamen (*C. europaeum*), c.a. VIOLETA-DOS-ALPES.—**da-pérsia,** the ivyleaf cyclamen (*C. indicum*).—**de-nápoles,** the Neapolitan cyclamen (*C. neapolitanum*). [Usually though wrongly pronounced CICLAME.]
ciclantáceas (*f.pl., Bot.*) the cyclanthus family (*Cyclanthaceae*).
ciclantáceo –**cea** (*adj., Bot.*) cyclanthaceous.
ciclanto (*m., Bot.*) a cyclanthus.
ciclartrose (*f., Anat.*) cyclarthrosis (a pivot joint).
ciclatão or –**ton** (*m.*) ciclatoun (a costly medieval fabric).
cíclico –**ca** (*adj.*) cyclic(al).
cíclidas, ciclídeos (*m.pl.*) the *Cichlidae* (large family of small, fresh-water, spiny-finned fishes).
ciclismo (*m.*) bicycling as a sport.
ciclista (*m.,f.*) cyclist, bicycle rider.
ciclite (*f., Med.*) cyclitis.
ciclizar (*v.i.*) to (bi)cycle.
ciclo (*m.*) cycle.
ciclohexanol [ks] (*m., Chem.*) cyclohexanol; hexalin.
cicloforia (*f., Med.*) cyclophoria.
cicloförmio (*m., Chem.*) Cycloform.
ciclógrafo (*m.*) cyclograph.
cicloidal (*adj.*) cycloidal.
ciclóide (*adj.; m.*) cycloid.
ciclometria (*f., Geom.*) cyclometry.
ciclômetro (*m.*) cyclometer.
ciclone, ciclônio (*m.*) cyclone.
ciclônico –**ca** (*adj.*) cyclonic.
ciclópeo –**pea, ciclópico** –**ca** (*adj., Arch.*) cyclopean.
ciclopes (*m., Myth.*) Cyclops; (*pl., Zool.*) water fleas.
cicloplegia (*f., Med.*) cycloplegia.
ciclóptero (*m.*) a lumpfish (*Cyclopterus sp.*).
ciclose (*f., Plant Physiol.*) cyclosis.
ciclóstomos (*m.pl., Zool.*) the Cyclostomata.
ciclotimia (*f., Psychiatry*) cyclothymia.
ciclótomo (*m., Surg.*) cyclotome.
cíclotron, ciclotrônio (*m., Physics*) cyclotron.
ciconídeas (*f.pl.*) the *Ciconidae* (stork family).
ciconiforme (*adj.*) ciconiform, like a stork.
cicuta (*f.*) the spotted water hemlock (*Cicuta maculata*).—**da-europa,** poison hemlock (*Conium maculatum*), c.a. FUNCHO-SELVAGEM, ANSARINHA-MALHADA, CEGUDE.
cidadã (*f.*) citizeness. [Fem. of CIDADÃO.]

cidadania (f.) citizenship.
cidadão [-dãos] (m.) citizen. [The fem. form is CIDADÃ].
cidade (f.) city, town.
cidadela (f.) citadel; (Soccer) goal [= ARCO].
cidadezinha (f.) small town.
cide (m.) the Cid.
cidra (f.) citron (the fruit); cider.
cidrada (f.) citron rind.
cidrão (m.) thick-skinned citron; citron rind; (Bot.) lemon-verbena lippia (L. citriodora), c.a. CIDRILHA, ERVA-CIDREIRA.
cidreira (f., Bot.) citron (Citrus medica).
cidrilha (f., Bot.) kinds of lippia, esp. creeping lippia (L. canescens) and lemon-verbena lippia (L. citriodora); also = CAMARÁ and CAPITÃO-DO-MATO.
cieiro (m.) a chapped or cracked condition of the skin of the lips or hands; fissured soil.
ciência (f.) science; knowledge.—do ser, science of being or reality, ontology.—s físicas, physical sciences.—s naturais, natural sciences.—social, social science. ter—de, to be aware of.
ciênidas, cienídeos (m.pl.) the Sciaenidae (roncadors, kingfishes, drumfishes, croakers, etc.).
ciente (adj.) aware, mindful, cognizant.
cientemente (adv.) consciously.
cientificar (v.t.) to inform, make known, make aware of. —se de, to inform oneself concerning.
científico -ca (adj.) scientific.
cientista (m.,f.) scientist.
C.I.F. or cif = CUSTO, SEGURO E FRETE (cost, insurance and freight).
cifoscoliose (f., Med.) kyphoscolisis.
cifose (f., Med.) kyphosis.
cifósidas, cifosídeos (m.pl.) a family (Kyphosidae) of basslike fishes.
cifótico -ca (adj.) kyphotic, humpbacked.
cifra (f.) cipher, naught, zero; number, figure, sum total; secret writing, code; key (cipher) of a code.
cifrado -da (adj.) written in code.
cifrão (m.) the sign [$] used as a symbol for the dollar, the CRUZEIRO or MIL-RÉIS of Brazil, the ESCUDO of Portugal, and the PESO of Argentine, Chile, etc.
cifrar (v.t.) to put in cipher; to summarize, condense.
cigana (f.) gypsy woman; (pl.) drop earrings; (f., Zool.) the hoatzin (Opisthocomus hoazin).
ciganada, ciganaria (f.) band of gypsies; gypsy behavior.
ciganear (v.i.) to lead a gypsy life.
ciganice (f.) gypsy trick, swindle.
cigano -na (adj.) gypsy; errant, vagabond, bohemian; sharp, tricky; (m.) gypsy man; by ext., an individual of unconventional, free-and-easy mode of living.
cigarra (f.) cicada, locust, harvest fly; (Elec.) buzzer; also = CHORÃO (a bird) and LAGOSTA-SAPATA (a crustacean).
cigarraria (f.) tobacco shop.
cigarrear (v.i.) to chirr (as a cicada).
cigarreira (f.) cigarette case [= PORTA-CIGARROS]; a woman worker in a cigarette factory.
cigarreiro (m.) worker in a cigarette factory; a certain type of tobacco.
cigarrilha (f.) cigarillo (a little cigar); an inhalator.
cigarrista (m.,f.) cigarette smoker.
cigarro (m.) cigarette. maço de—s, pack of cigarettes. ponta de—, cigarette butt.
ciguelina (f.) = CUPRITA.
cila (f., Bot.) a squill (Scilla sp.); the shore drugsquill (Urginea maritima); Scylla.—-brasileira,—-da-terra = CEBOLA-BRAVA-DO-PARÁ.
cilada (f.) ambush; trap, snare, noose; pitfall.
ciladear (v.t.) to lay a trap for.
cilha (f.) cinch, girth, bellyband.—mestra, surcingle.
cilhão -lhona (adj.) saddle-backed, sway-backed; (m.) a large girth or bellyband; a saddle-backed horse.
cilhar (v.t.) to cinch, girth tightly.
ciliado (m., Zool.) infusorian.
cilício (m.) cilice, hairshirt (worn as a penance).
ciliectomia (f., Surg.) ciliectomy.
ciliforme (adj.) ciliform.
cilindrada (f., Mach.) piston displacement.
cilindragem (f.) act of rolling (as with a steam roller); calendering (of paper. etc.).
cilindrar (v.t.) to press or level with a roller; to calender.
cilindrartrose (f., Anat.) cylindarthrosis.
cilindricidade (f.) quality or condition of being cylindri-

cal.
cilíndrico -ca (adj.) cylindrical. rolamento—, roller bearing.
cilindriforme (adj.) cylindriform.
cilindrita (f., Min.) cylindrite.
cilindro (m.) cylinder; roller. (Mach.) cylinder.—compressor a vapor, steam roller.—de impressão, printing roller.
cilindrocéfalo -la (adj., Anat.) cylindrocephalic.
cilindróide (adj.; m.) cylindroid(al).
cilindroma (m., Med.) cylindroma.
cilindro-ogival (adj.) cylindroogival.
cilindruria (f., Med.) cylindruria.
cílio (m.) eyelash; (pl., Biol., Bot., Zool.) cilia.
ciliógrado -da (adj., Zool.) ciliograde.
cilíolo (m., Biol.) ciliolum; (pl.) ciliola.
cilitina (f., Pharm.) scillitin(e).
cilose (f., Med.) cyllosis.
cima (f.) top, summit, apex; (Bot.) cyme. a parte de—, the upper part. ainda por—, moreover, in addition, to boot. de—, on top. de—de, from the top of, from above. de—para baixo, from top to bottom. em—, over, on, above. em—de, on top of, on, above. lá em—, up there; upstairs. lá por—, up over there, around up there. para—, upward, up. para—de, upwards of, more than, over. para—e para baixo, up and down. por—, overhead. por—de, over, above, on top of.
cimácio (m., Arch.) cymatium.
cimalha (f.) summit; (Arch.) cyma; (pl.) dieresis ['·].
cimarra (f.) a light cassock.
cimba (f.) a flatboat.
címbala (f., Music) cymbal (high-pitched mixture stop of an organ).
cimbalária (f.) the Kenilworth ivy (Cymbalaria muralis); the ivyleaf saxifrage (Saxifraga cymbalaria).
címbalos (m.pl.) cymbals [= PRATOS].
cimbídio (m.) any Cymbidium orchid.
cimbiforme (adj.) cymbiform, boat-shaped.
cimbocefalia (f., Craniol.) cymbocephaly.
cimbocéfalo -la (adj.) cymbocephalous, -phalic.
cimbre, címbrio (m., Arch.) soffit scaffolding, centering, falsework, frame; = CAMBOTA.
cimeiro -ra (adj.) top; (f.) helmet; crest of a helmet; top, crown, summit; (Her.) lion or other animal on a crest; (Bot.) cyme.
cimênio, cimeno (m., Chem.) cymene.
cimentação (f.) cementing; consolidation. Cf. CEMENTAÇÃO.
cimentar (v.t.) to cement; to unite, consolidate. Cf. CEMENTAR.
cimento (m.) cement.—de amianto or asbesto, asbestos cement.—armado, reinforced concrete; = CONCRETO ARMADO.—branco, white Portland cement.—de escória, slag concrete.—hidráulico, hydraulic cement.—Portland, Portland cement.—refratário, refractory cement. Cf. CEMENTO.
cimicífuga (f., Bot.) the black snakeroot or cohosh bugbane (Cimicifuga racemosa), c.a. ERVA-DE-SÃO-CRISTÓVÃO.
cimitarra (f.) scimitar.
cimo (m.) summit, top, crest. Cf. CIMA, CUME.
cimofânio (m.), cimófana (f., Min.) cymaphane. chrysoberyl.
cimogênio (m., Chem.) cymogene, rhigolene.
cimógrafo (m.) cymograph; kimograph.
cimol (m.) = CIMÊNIO.
cimólia, cimolítia (f., Min.) cimolite, a purified fuiler's earth.
cimoscópio (m., Elec.) cymoscope.
cinabre, cinábrio (m.) cinabrita (f., Min.) cinnabar; the color vermilion.
cinabrino -na (adj.) cinnabarine, cinnabaric.
cina-cina (f.) the Jerusalem thorn (Parkinsonia aculeata).
cinamato (m., Chem.) cinnamate.
cinâmico -ca (adj., Chem.) cinnamic; cinnamon-colored.
cinamomo (m.) the chinaberry, China tree, holy tree or bead tree (Melia azedarach), c.a. AMARGOSEIRA, ÁRVORE-SANTA, ÁRVORE-DO-ROSÁRIO, CONTEIRA, JASMIN-AZUL, JASMIN-DE-CAIENA, JASMIM-DE-SOLDADO, JASMIM-DA-TERRA, LILÁS-DA-ÍNDIA, LIÁS-DAS-ANTILHAS, LÍRIO-DA-ÍNDIA, SICÔMORO-BASTARDO. [The tree is cultivated in Brazil as a shade and timber tree. Do not confuse with cinramon, which is CANELA.]
cinância, cinanque (f., Med.) cynanche.

cinantropia (f., Med.) cynanthropy.
cínara (f.) the artichoke (Cynara scolymus), c.a. ALCACHO-
FRA-HORTENSE; the cardoon (Cynara cardunculus), c.a.
ALCACHOFRA-BRAVA, CARDO.
cináreas (f.pl.) the thistle family (Carduaceae).
cináreo –rea (adj., Bot.) cynareous, cynaraceous.
cinca, cincada (f.) mistake, blunder, bungle.
cincar (v.i.) to blunder, bungle, flounder.
cinceiro (m.) a thick fog.
cincerro [ê] (m.) a bell hung on the neck of a leading pack
animal.
cincha (f.) cinch, saddle-girth, bellyband.
cinchão (m.) an ornamental saddle-girth.
cinchar (v.t.) to cinch (up) a horse.
cincho (m.) cheese press; olive press.
cinchona (f.) any species of Cinchona, esp. C. officinalis,
whose bark yields quinine.
cinchonina (f., Chem.) cinchonine.
cincídeos (m., Pl.) the skinks (Scinidae), a family of small
lizards.
cincino (m., Bot.) a scorpioid cyme.
cinco (adj.; m.) five.
cinco-chagas (f.) = CAROBA-BRANCA, CAROBA-DE-FLOR-
VERDE, CAPUCHINHA-DO-BRASIL.
cinco-em-rama (m., Bot.) cinquefoil (Potentilla).
cinco-fôlhas (f.) = CAROBA-BRANCA.
cinco-fôlhas-do-campo (f.) = CAROBEIRA.
cindir (v.t.) to cut, split, sunder, sever, divide; to separate
(friends). [The noun is CISÃO.]
cine (m.) short for cinema.
cineasta (m.,f.) motion-picture technician, director or
producer.
cineastro (m.,f.) motion-picture star.
cine-jornal (m.) newsreel.
cinema (m.) cinema, motion-picture; motion-picture
theater; the movies.—falado, talking motion pictures.
—mudo, silent pictures.
cinemático –ca (adj.) kinematic; (f., Physics) kinematics.
cinematografar (v.t.) to show or to take motion pictures.
cinematografia (f.) cinematography.
cinematográfico –ca (adj.) cinematographic.
cinematógrafo (m.) motion-picture projector; motion-
picture theater.
cinemeiro –ra (m.,f.) assiduous movie-goer.
cineol (m., Chem.) cineole; eucalyptol.
cineração (f.) incineration, cremation.
cineral (m.) ash heap.
cinerar (v.t.) to incinerate, cremate [= INCINERAR].
cinerário –ria (adj.) cinerary; (m.) cinerary urn; (f.,
Bot.) cineraria (Senecio spp.).
cinéreo –rea (adj.) cinerous, ashen.
cinesalgia (f., Med.) kinesalgia.
cinesímetro (m., Physiol.) kinesimeter.
cine-teatro (m.) motion-picture theater.
cinético –ca (adj., Physics) kinetic; (f.) kinetics, dynamics.
cinetogênese (f., Biol.) kinetogenesis.
cinetógrafo (m.) kinetograph.
cinetoscópio (m.) kinetoscope.
cingalês –lesa (adj.; m.,f.) Singhalese, Ceylonese.
Cingapura (f.) Singapore.
cingel [-géis] (m.), cingelada (f.) a yoke of oxen.
cingeleiro (m.) one who owns, hires, or works, a yoke of
oxen.
cingento (m.) carpenter's clamp [= SARGENTO].
cingideira (f.) the middle claw of a hawk's, etc., foot.
cingidoiro, –douro (m.) belt, girdle.
tingir (v.t.) to gird (on); to encircle, surround, embrace,
encompass; to bind, confine, restrain, restrict; to tie,
bandage.—se a, to hold (restrict) oneself to.
cíngulo (m.) surcingle of a cassock.
cínico –ca (adj.) cynical; shameless, impudent; obscene;
(m.,f.) cynic.
cínipes (m.pl.) a genus (Cynips) of gallflilies.
cinismo (m.) cynicism; shamelessness, impudence; obscenity.
cinocéfalo (m.) a dog-headed ape.
cinófilo –la (adj.) cynophilic, dog-loving.
cinoglossa (f., Bot.) hound's-tongue (Cynoglossum spp.),
c.a. LÍNGUA-DE-CÃO.
cinorrexia [ks] (f., Med.) bulimia.
cinórrodo (m.) cynorrhodon (fruit of the dogrose).
cinosure (f.) Cynosure, the constellation in Ursa Minor
[but not cynosure in the sense of center of attraction,
which is ALVO, FOCO (DE INTERESSE, DE ATENÇÃO, DE
ATRAÇÃO, DE ADMIRAÇÃO, DE OLHARES).]; (Bot.) the

crested dog's-tail (Cynosurus cristatus).
cinqüenta (adj.) fifty.
cinqüentão –tona (adj.) fiftyish; (m.) a man in his fifties;
(f.) a woman in her fifties, referring esp. to an unmarried
woman.
cinqüentena (f.) a period of fifty years.
cinta (f.) girdle, band, belt; strap; sash, waistband;
waist; (Arch.) purlin. Cf. CINTO, CINTURAL. â—, fastened
to or hanging from the belt or waist.
cintado –da (adj.) belted; fitted to the waist; (m., Shipbldg.) strakes and wales, collectively.
cintar (v.t.) to belt, band, bind; to fit to the waist.
cinteiro (m.) bellyband; belt; hatband.
cintel [-téis] (m.) gin race or ring; trammel; beam compass.
Cíntia (f.) Cynthia.
cintilação (f.) scintillation, sparkling.
cintilante (adj.) glittering, sparkling.
cintilar (v.i.) to scintillate, sparkle, glitter, twinkle.
cintiloscópio (m., Physics.) scintilloscope.
cinto (m.) belt; shoulder strap; sash, waistband; money
belt; strip, zone, Cf. CINTA, CINTURA.—de cartuchos,
cartridge belt.—de-couro, a leather straitjacket used on
prisoners, c.a. COLÊTE-DE-COURO.—de-ne(p)tuno, the
sugar bladekelp (Laminaria saccharina).—de-segurança,
safety belt.—de-vênus, (Zool.) Venus's-Girdle (Cestus
veneris), c.a. CÊSTO.
cintradora (f.) a machine for bending rails, wagon-wheel
tires, etc. [= GIM].
cintura (f.) waist; waistline; waistband; belt; girdle.
—-de-vespa, wasp waist.
cinturão (m.) broad belt; money belt.—de-segurança,
safety belt.
cinza (f.) ash, cinder; (pl.) mortal remains.—vulcânica,
volcanic ash. Quartafeira de—s, Ash Wednesday. senda
de—s, cinder path.
cinzar (v.t.) to fool, take in, deceive; also = ACINZENTAR.
cinzeiro (m.) ash tray; ash heap; (Bot.) = CONGONHEIRO
cinzel [-zéis] (m.) sculptor's chisel; engraver's burin.
cinzelado –da (adj.) engraved, carved.
cinzelador (m.), –dora (f.) sculptor, engraver, chaser;
carver.
cinzeladura (f.) a carving or engraving.
cinzelamento (m.) act of carving or engraving.
cinzelar (v.t.) to chisel, engrave, carve.
cinzento –ta (adj.) ashen, gray.
cio (m.) rut, estrus, heat (of mammals).
cioba (f.) the muttonfish (Lutianus analis), c.a. CIOBA-
VERDADEIRA, SIOBA, CARANHO(-VERMELHO).—mulata
= RABO-ABERTO (the yellowtail).
ciografia (f., Arch.) skiagraph; vertical section; (Astron.)
skiagraphy.
cionectomia (f., Surg.) cionectomy.
cionite (f., Med.) cionitis.
cioso –sa (adj.) jealous; envious; zealous, solicitous.
ciótomo (m., Surg.) kiotome.
ciparoba (f.) = CIPÓ-DE-COBRA.
ciperáceo –cea (adj.) cyperaceous; (f.pl., Bot.) the sedge
family (Cyperaceae).
cípero (m.) = JUNÇA (a sedge).
cipo (m.) post, pillar; ancient landmark or milestone;
gravestone.
cipó (m.) any of numerous tropical plants, vines and
lianas, whose common names often apply to more than
one species, and of which the following is only a partial
list:—amarelo, a funnelweed (Cocculus dichroa).—azul
= CAPELA-DE-VIÚVA.—branco, a funnelvine (Arrabidaea
argentea).—branco-d'arco, a spiny shrub of the buckthorn family (Colletia sarmentosa).—branco-de-caboclo,
a woody vine (Bignonia prolixa).—branco-de-cêra, a
seagrape (Coccolobis sp.).—branco-de-rêgo, a woody
vine (Bignonia vulgaris).—cabeludo, a shrubby climber of the thistle family (Mikania hirsutissima) closely
related to the climbing hempweed (M. scandens); c.a.
ERVA-DUTRA.—caboclo (or -capa-homem, or -de-
caboclo, or -(de)-carijó, or -vermelho), a dilleniaceous
climber (Davilla rugosa), c.a. CAPA-HOMEM, FÔLHA-DE-
LIXA, MUIRAQUETECA, SAMBÁIBA, SAMBAIBINHA—sometimes used medicinally.—café= BOA-NOITE (a moonflower).—camarão, a woody vine (Bignonia eximia).
—capador (or -de-paina, or -santo), a savannaflower
(Echites peltata), c.a. CAPA-HOMEM, ERVA-SANTA, JOÃO-
DA-COSTA, PAINA-DE-PENAS.—carneiro, a savannaflower
(Echites suberosa).—catiguá, the catigua bitterwood

(*Trichilia catigua*).—-**catinga-de-paca**, a shrub of the oleaster family (*Elaeagnus trispermum*).—-**chumbo**, a dodder (*Cuscuta umbellata*), c.a. XIRIUBEIRA.—-**cravo** (or -**trinidade**), a medicinal plant of the bignonia family (*Tynnanthus sp.*).—-**cruapé-vermelho** = CURURU-APÉ.—-**cruz**, any of various crossvines (such as *Bignonia capreolata*) whose stems often show a conspicuous cross in a transverse section; a clematis (*C. dioica*); a funnelvine (*Arrabidaea chica*), c.a. CARAJURU.—-**cruz-verdadeiro**, a milkberry (*Chiococca brachiata*), c.a. CASINGA, CRUZEIRINHA, DAMBRÉ, PURGA-PRETA, QUINA-DE-RAIZ-PRETA.—-**cumuru-apé** = CURURU-APÉ.—-**cururu**, any of various plants of the dogbane family, esp. a shrub (*Anisolobus cururu*), c.a. CUCURU, CRUAPÉ.—-**da(s)-areia(s)**, a joint fir (*Ephedra triandra*), c.a. MORANGO-DO-CAMPO.—-**d'água**, a dilleniaceous climber (*Doliocarpus pubens*), c.a. MURIAQUETECA, CIPÓ-VERMELHO; a supplejack (*Serjania caracasana*), c.a. TIMBÓ-DO-CAMPO; also = CONDURANGO.—-**d'alho**, the garlic shrub (*Adenocalymna alliaceum*) the bruised foliage of which smells like garlic.—-**das-feridas**, a butterflypea (*Centrosema plumieri*).—-**de-beira-mar**, a tall tropical liana, the climbing entada or snuffbox bean (*Entada phaseoloides*), which bears very large swordlike pods, a foot or two long, and four or five inches wide, containing seeds two inches broad, which are often called mackay beans. —-**de-breu** = CUMANÃ.—-**de-cêsto-grande**, a burnet (*Poterium sarmentosum*).—-**de-chagas** (or -**de-cinco-fôlhas**) = CAPUCHINHA-DO-BRASIL.—-**de-coração**, either of two dutchman's-pipes: *Aristolochia tulliformis*, or *A. cordigera*, c.a. ANGELICÓ, GUACO-BRAVO.—-**de-corda** (or -**de-amarrar-caranguejo**, or -**de-cêsto**, or -**de-bamburral**) a bignoniaceous climber (*Cydista aequinoctialis*). —-**de-cobra**, a pareira vine (*Cissampelos glaberrima*) of the moonseed family, c.a. ABUTINA, ABÚTUA, BÚTUA, BUTUINHA, CAPEBA, CATOJÉ, CIPAROBA, ERVA-DE-NOSSA-SENHORA, PARREIRA-BRAVA-LISA, PARREIRA-CAPEBA; also, either of two dutchman's-pipes, *Aristolochia barbata* (c.a. JARRINHA) or *A. disticha*.—-**de-cunamã**, or -**de-cunanã** = CUMANÃ. —-**de-escada**, a bauhinia (*B. radiata*). —-**de-fogo**, a treebine (*Cissus erosa*), c.a. UVA-BRAVA. —-**de-gato** (or -**de-morcego**, or -**de-unha-de-gato**), a cat's-claw (*Batocydia unguis*), a bignoniaceous climbing shrub with hooked tendrils, c.a. UNHA-DE-GATO.—-**de-gota** (or -**da-gota**), a grape (*Vitis pulcherrima*).—-**de-imbé**, the twice-cut philodendron (*P. bipinnatifidum*), c.a. GUIMBÉ; also *Philodendron selloum*, c.a. GUEMBÉ, FRUTO-DE-IMBÉ, IMBÉ-DE-COMER.—-**de-leite**, either of two plants of the milkweed family: *Mesechites sulphurea* (c.a. MAQUINÉ-DO-MATO), or *Oxypetalum appendiculatum* (c.a. LEITE-DE-CACHORRO); also, a spurge called CUMANÃ (q.v.).—-**de-macaco**, the velvety Florida yellow trumpet (*Stenolobium velutinum*), c.a. TIMBÓ (or TINGUI)-DAS-PIRANHAS.—-**de-morcego**, the catclaw funnelcreeper (*Doxantha unguis-cati*); also = CIPÓ-DE-GATO.—-**de-paina**, any of several trigoniaceous woody vines, *Trigonia candida* (called CIPÓ-PAU); also = CIPÓ-CAPADOR.—-**de-penas**, a savannaflower (*Echites peltigera*), c.a. PAINEIRA-LOURA.—-**de-santa-isabel**, the Brazil stifftia (*S. chrysantha*).—-**de-são-joão** (or -**bela-flor**, or **pé-de-lagarto**), an ornamental bignonia (*Pyrostegia venusta*), c.a. FLOR-DE-SÃO-JOÃO, MARQUESA-DE-BELAS.—-**de-sapo** (or -**de-paque**, or -**ramo**, or -**sêda**), a bladderflower (*Araujia sericifera*), c.a. ANGÉLICA-DE-RAMA, CIPÒZINHO-DO-CAMPO, PAINA-DÊ-SEDA, PAINA-DO-CAMPO, SÊDA-VEGETAL, TIMBÓ.—-**de-timbó**, a supplejack (*Serjania erecta*), c.a. TIMBÓ-BRAVO, TURUVI.—-**de-tucunaré**, a rosewood (*Dalbergia inundata*), c.a. TIMBÓ.—-**do-imbé**, an arum (*A. arborescens*).—-**do-reino**, a climbing clematis (*C. campestris*), c.a. BARBA-DE-VELHO, VIDE-BRANCA.—-**em-pau-doce** = ALCAÇU-DA-TERRA.—-**escada**, any of several bauhinias, esp. *B. splendens* (c.a. CIPÓ-UNHA-DE-BOI, ESCADA-DE-JABUTI, MORORÓ-CIPÓ, UNHA-DE-BOI (or -DE-VACA). —-**gordo**, a treebine (*Cissus sp.*).—-**guaçu**, an Amazon-vine (*Stigmaphyllon jatrophaefolium*).—-**imbé**, any of various philodendrons.—-**mão-de-sapo**, a treebine (*Cissus coralinus*).—-**mata-cobras** (or -**paratudo**), a dutchman's-pipe (*Aristolochia cymbifera*), c.a. COIFA-DO-DIABO, JARRINHA, CAPA-HOMEM, PAPO-DE-GALO.—-**mil-homens**, any of several dutchman's-pipes, esp. *Aristolochia elegans* (the calico dutchman's-pipe, c.a. JARRINHA-PINTADA); *A. arcuata* (c.a. CIPÓ-JAᴿRINHA, JARRINHA-DOS-CAMPOS, JARRINHA-PRETA); *A. warmingii* (c.a. BATATINHA, FLOR-DE-SAPO, JARRINHA-BATATINHA, JAR-

RINHA-BICO-DE-PASSARINHO); *A. raja* (c.a. RAJA, JAR-RINHA-ARRAIA); *A. triangularis* (c.a. MIL-HOMENS-DO-RIO-GRANDE), and *A. allemanii* (c.a. MIL-HOMENS-DO-CEARÁ). —-**mole** = ESPORA-DE-GALO.—-**quina**, a green-brier (*Smilax oblongifolia*), c.a. TUIA.—-**rabo-de-timbu**, a heartseed (*Cardiospermum fragile*).—-**rêgo** (or -**de-rêgo**, or -**três-quinas**), a funnelvine (*Arrabidaea agnus-castus*). —-**sêco**, a stick insect, (ca. MANÉ-MAGRO.—-**suma**, the mercury anchietea (*A. salutaris*), c.a. SUMA, PARAGUAIA, PIRAGUARA, PIRIGUARA.—-**timbó**, any of various supple-jacks (some used as fish poison), esp. the rustywool supplejack (*Serjania fuscifolia*), c.a. MATA-PEIXE; the timbeehoney supplejack (*S. lethalis*), c.a. MATA-FOME; *S. acuminata*, c.a. TIMBÓ-DE-PEIXE, TIMBÓ-LEGÍTIMO; *S. ovalifolia*, c.a. TIMBÓ-AMARELO; *S. piscatoria*, c.a. TINGUI; also = CURURU-APÉ.—-**tinga**, a sea grape (*Coccolobis litoralis*).—-**tracuá**, an ant-harboring philodendron (*P. myrmecophilum*).—-**tripa-de-galinha**, the cow-itch dalechampia (*D. tiliaefolia*), c.a. TAMIARAMA, URTIGA-DE-CIPÓ, URTIGA-TAMIARAMA.—-**urtiguinha** (or -**de-leite**), a climbing plant of the spurge family (*Fragia volubilis*), c.a. URTIGUINHA-DE-CIPÓ.—-**violeta**, a rose-wood (*Dalbergia variabilis*), c.a. ASSAPUVA, BRAÇADEIRA, JACARANDÁ.

cipoal (*m.*) a tangled growth of lianas; fig., a difficulty in which one becomes entangled; a complicated problem.
cipolino (*m.*) cipolin (marble).
cipônima (*f.*) a sweetleaf (*Symplocos ciponima*).
cipotaia (*f.*) a medicinal caper (*Capparis urens*).
cipòzinho-do-campo (*m.*) = CIPÓ-DE-SAPO.
ciprestal (*m.*) a place abounding in cypress.
cipreste (*m.*) the pyramidal Italian cypress (*Cupressus sempervirens*, *var. pyramidalis*); the Easter arborvitae (*Thuja occidentalis*), c.a. PINHEIRO-DO-CANADÁ; the Oriental or Chinese arborvitae (*Thuja orientalis*); fig., death; mourning.—-**calvo** (or -**da-luisiana**, or -**do-brejo**), common bald cypress (*Taxodium distichum*), c.a. PINHEIRO-CALVO.—-**fúnebre**, the mourning cypress (*Cupressus funebris*).—-**comum** (or -**da-itália**, or -**piramidal**) Italian cypress (*C. sempervirens*).—-**do-japão**, the Sawara false cypress (*Chamaecyparis pisifera*).
ciprínidas (*f.pl.*), **ciprinídeos**, **ciprinóides** (*m.pl.*) the family (*Cyprinidae*) of soft-finned, fresh-water fishes which comprises the carps, barbels, breams, shiners, etc.
ciprino (*adj.*; *m.,f.*) = CÍPRIO.
ciprinodôntidas (*m.pl.*) a family (*Cyprinodontidae*) of small soft-finned fishes which comprises the killifishes and related minnows.
cíprio -**pria** (*adj.*; *m.,f.*) Cyprian.
cipriota (*adj.*; *m.,f.*) Cypriot(e).
cipripédio (*m.*, *Bot.*) ladyslipper (*Cypripedium*).
Cipro (*m.*) = CHIPRE.
cipsélidas (*m.pl.*, *Zool.*) the swifts (*Apodidae*, *syn. Cypselidae*)
ciranda (*f.*) a coarse screen for sand, grain, etc.; ring-around-a-rosy.
cirandagem (*f.*) act of screening; quantity (of anything) screened; chaff, dust; trifles.
cirandar (*v.t.*) to screen (grain, etc.), (*v.i.*) to dance ring-around-a-rosy.
circassiano -**na** (*adj.*; *m.,f.*) Circassian.
circense (*adj.*) circus; (*m.pl.*) circus performances.
circinado -**da**, **circinal** (*adj.*, *Bot.*) circinate, circinal.
circo (*m.*) circus; amphitheater.
circuitar (*v.i.*) to circle about; (*v.t.*) to make the circuit of; to circulate; to compass, enclose.
circuito (*m.*) circuit; circumference; compass, circular course.—-**aberto**, open circuit.—-**de palavras**, circumlocution.—-**elétrico**, electrical circuit.—-**em paralelo**, (*Elec.*) parallel circuit.—-**em série**, (*Elec.*) series circuit.—-**fechado**, closed circuit.—-**primário**, (*Elec.*) primary circuit.—-**ramificado**, (*Elec.*) divided circuit.—-**secundário**, (*Etec.*) secondary circuit. **curto**—, short circuit.
circulação'(*f.*) circulation.—-**forçada**, forced circulation.
circulante (*adj.*) circulating. **meio**—, currency.
circular (*v.i.*) to circulate, move in a circle; to have currency; (*v.t.*) to circulate; to surround, encirlce; (*adj.*) circular, round; (*f.*) circular letter.
circulatório -**ria** (*adj.*) circulatory.
círculo (*m.*) circle, hoop, loop, ring; compass, enclosure; coterie, set of people.—-**máximo**, great circle (of the sphere).—-**vicioso**, vicious circle.
circum-adjacente (*adj.*) circumjacent.
circum-ambiente (*adj.*) circumambient.

circumpatente (*adj.*) open all around.
circumpercorrer (*v.t.*) to travel around.
circumposto –ta (*adj.*) placed around.
circumurado –da [cū] (*adj.*) walled about.
circunavegação [cū] (*f.*) circumnavigation.
circunavegador [cū] (*m.*) circumnavigator.
circunavegar [cū] (*v.t.*) to circumnavigate.
circuncidado –da (*adj.*) circumcised; (*m.pl.*) the Jews.
circuncidar (*v.t.*) to circumcise.
circuncisão (*f.*) circumcision.
circunciso –sa (*adj.*) circumcised; (*m.*) a circumcised man.
circundante (*adj.*) surrounding, encircling.
circundar (*v.t.*) to surround, encircle.
circundução (*f.*) a turning about a center or axis; (*Physiol.*) circumduction.
circundutar (*v.t., Law*) to abrogate or annul.
circunferência (*f.*) circumference; circuit.
circunferente (*adj.*) encompassing, encircling.
circunflexão [ks] (*f.*) circumflexion.
circunflexo –xa [ks] (*adj.*) circumflex.
circunfluência (*f.*) circumfluence.
circunfluente (*adj.*) circumfluent, circumfluous.
circunfluir (*v.t.*) to flow around.
circunforâneo –nea (*adj.*) circumforaneous.
circunfundir (*v.t.*) to circumfuse.
circunfusão (*f.*) circumfusion.
circungirar (*v.t.,v.i.*) to circumgyrate.
circunjacente (*adj.*) circumjacent, surrounding.
circunjazer [54] (*v.i.*) to lie around, to border on every side, surround.
circunlóquio (*m.*), –locução (*f.*) circumlocution.
circunmeridiano –na (*adj.*) circummeridian.
circunutação (*f., Plant Physiol.*) circumnutation.
circunpolar (*adj.*) circumpolar.
circunrodar (*v.i.*) to turn around and around; to gyrate.
circunscrever [44] (*v.t.*) to circumscribe, confine, limit.
circunscrição (*f.*) circumscription.
circunscritivo –va (*adj.*) circumscriptive.
circunscrito –ta (*adj.*) circumscribed; circumscript.
circunsonar (*v.i.*) to sound on all sides.
circunspe(c)ção (*f.*) circumspection, caution, prudence, discretion.
circunspe(c)to –ta (*adj.*) circumspect, cautious, discreet; closemouthed.
circunstância (*f.*) circumstance, condition, state of affairs.
circunstanciado –da (*adj.*) circumstanced, detailed.
circunstancial (*adj.*) circumstantial.
circunstanciar (*v.t.*) to circumstantiate, detail.
circunstante (*adj.*) circumjacent, surrounding; (*m.,f.*) bystander, onlooker; (*pl.*) an audience.
circunstar (*v.t.,v.i.*) to lie around, surround; to be present or at hand.
circunvagar (*v.t.*) to walk around; to turn the eyes, look around; (*v.i.*) to move about.
circunvalação (*f., Fort.*) line, wall, etc. of circumvallation.
circunvalado –da (*adj.*) circumvallate, surrounded with a rampart.
circunvalar (*v.t.*) to circumvallate, surround with a wall, rampart, trenches, etc.
circunver [81] (*v.t.*) to see on all sides.
circunvizinhança (*f.*) neighborhood, vicinity; environs, suburbs.
circunvizinho –nha (*adj.*) neighboring, circumjacent, circumambient.
circunvoar (*v.t.,v.i.*) to fly around.
circunvolução (*f.*) circumvolution, rotation.
circunvolucionário –ria (*adj.*) circumvolutory.
circunvoluir (*v.i.*) to turn around and around.
circunvolver (*v.i.*) to circumvolve.
cirenaico –ca (*adj.; m.,f.*) Cyrenaic, Cyrenian.
cireneu –néia (*adj.; m.,f.*) Cyrenian.
cirial (*m.*) large candlestick (in a church).
cirieiro (*m.*) one who makes or deals in candles, esp. for religious purposes.
Cirilo (*m.*) Cyril.
círio (*m.*) large candle, esp. such as used in churches.
——**-de-nossa-senhora**, (*Bot.*) the moundlily yucca (*Y. gloriosa*).——**-do-norte**, common evening primrose (*Oenothera biennis*), c.a. BOA-TARDE, ERVA-DOS-BURROS.
——**-do-rei**, mullein (*Verbascum spp.*), c.a. VERBASCO.
ciriologia (*f.*) curiological writing.
ciriúba (*f., Bot.*) black mangrove (*Avicennia marina*). Cf. MANGUE.

Ciro (*m.*) Cyrus.
cirrífero –ra (*adj.*) cirriferous.
cirrípedes (*m.pl., Zool.*) the barnacles (*Cirripedia*).
cirro (*m., Bot., Zool.*) cirrus; (*pl.*) cirri; (*Meteor.*) cirrus cloud; (*Med.*) a scirrhous (indurated) cancer; death rattle.
cirrose (*f., Med.*) cirrhosis, esp. of the liver. Cf. ESCLEROSE
cirrosidade (*f., Med.*) scirrhosity.
cirroso –sa (*adj.*) cirrose; scirrhous.
cirsocele (*f., Med.*) cirsocele; varicocele.
cirsotomia (*f., Surg.*) cirsotomy.
cirtômetro (*m., Med.*) cyrtometer.
cirtopódio (*m.*) a genus (*Cyrtopodium*) of orchids.
cirtose (*f.*) = CIFOSE.
ciruíba (*f.*) = CIRIÚBA.
cirurgia (*f.*) surgery.
cirurgião [-giões, -giães] (*m.*) surgeon; a surgeonfish (*Acanthurus*), c.a. ACANTURO.——**-dentista**, dental surgeon. [Fem. CIRURGIÃ].
cirúrgico –ca (*adj.*) surgical.
cisa (*f.*) excise tax.
cisalha (*f.*) shear; (*pl.*) sheet-metal trimmings; metal shavings.
cisalhamento (*m.*) act of shearing; shearing stress; shearing strain.
cisalhar (*v.t.*) to shear.
cisalpino –na (*adj.*) cisalpine.
cisandino –na (*adj.*) cisandine.
cisão (*f.*) scission, division, split, fission; state of dissension in a group or union. [Verb: CINDIR.]
cisar (*v.t.*) to excise (tax).
cisatlântico –ca (*adj.*) cisatlantic.
ciscado (*m.*) a place which has been cleared of litter.
ciscador (*m.*) iron rake.
ciscalhada, -lhagem (*f.*) pile of trash.
ciscalho (*m.*) trash, rubbish, refuse.
ciscar (*v.t.*) to clean up trash; to pick and hunt in a pile of rubbish; to rake up trash; (*v.i.*) to scratch in litter (as do chickens); (*Aeron.*) to hedge-hop; (*v.r.*) to make oneself scarce.
cisco (*m.*) trash, refuse, rubbish, waste matter; sweepings; coom, coal dust.
cisirão (*m., Bot.*) bird vetch (*Vicia cracca*), c.a. ERVILHACA.——**-branco**, the flatpod peavine (*Lathyrus cicera*), c.a. CHICHAROS-MIÚDOS. Cf. CIZIRÃO.
cisma (*f.*) act of pondering, etc.;—see the verb CISMAR; musing, woolgathering; contemplation; misgiving, doubt, suspicion. **tirar a—de**, to take the wind out of (someone's) sails; (*m.*) schism, esp. in a religious body.
cismado –da (*adj.*) distrustful; suspicious; inclined to hypochondria.
cismar (*v.i.*) to think hard, ponder, meditate; to mull (over); to muse, brood over; to mistrust; to become obsessed with (a fear, a suspicion, a wish, etc.); (*v.t.*) to think hard about, dwell intently upon; to brood, ponder.
cismarento –ta (*adj.*) = CISMATIVO.
cismático –ca (*adj.; m.,f.*) schismatic (person); also = CISMATIVO.
cismativo –va (*adj.*) preoccupied, pensive, meditative; distrustful; full of misgivings about something; also = CISMARENTO, CISMÁTICO.
cismontano –na (*adj.*) cismontane, cisalpine.
cisne (*m.*) swan; the constellation Cygnus.——**-de-pescoço-prêto**, black-necked swan (*Cygnus melanochoryphus*), c.a. PATO-ARMINHO.——**-novo**, cygnet. **canto do—**, swan song. [Swan dive is SALTO-DE-ANJO].
cispadano –na (*adj.*) cispadane.
cisplatino –na (*adj.*) cisplatine, on this side of the Rio de la Plata.
cisqueiro (*m.*) trash pile, rubbish heap; garbage collector.
cisrenano –na (*adj.*) cisrhenane (on this side of the river Rhine).
cissão (*f.*) = CISÃO.
cissiparição, -paridade (*f., Biol.*) schizogenesis, fissiparism.
cissíparo –ra (*adj., Biol.*) schizogenous, fissiparous.
cisso (*m., Bot.*) the genus (*Cissus*) of treebines.
cissóide (*adj., Geom.*) cissoid.
cissura (*f.*) fissure, cleft; a breaking of friendly or of diplomatic relations; (*Anat.*) fissure; sulcus.
cistáceas (*f.pl.*) the rockrose family (*Cistaceae*).
cistalgia (*f., Med.*) cystalgia.
cistamina (*f., Chem.*) Cystamine; hexamethylene tetramine [= HEXAMINA].
cisteína (*f., Biochem.*) cysteine.

cisterna (*f.*) cistern, well [= POÇO].
cisticerco [ê] (*m., Zool.*) cysticercus, bladder worm, hydatid; pork measle; = HIDATÍGERO, HIDÁTULO.
cisticercose (*f., Med.*) cysticercosis; (*Veter.*) pork measles, c.a. CANJIQUINHA-DOS-PORCOS; also = CHAVEIRA.
cístico –ca (*adj.*) cystic.
cistídio (*m., Bot.*) cystidium.
cistífero –ra (*adj., Zool.*) cystiferous.
cistígero –ra (*adj.*) cystigerous.
cistina (*f., Biochem.*) cystine.
cistite (*f., Med.*) cystitis.
cistítomo (*m., Surg.*) cystitome.
cisto (*m., Med., Bot., Zool.*) cyst.—**hidático**, (*Zool., Med.*) hydatid cyst. (*Bot.*) any rockrose (*Cistus spp.*).
cistocele (*f., Med.*) cystocele.
cistogênio (*m.*) = HEXAMINA.
cistóide (*adj.*) cystoid, bladderlike; (*m.pl., Paleontol.*) the Cystoidea.
cistólito (*m., Med.*) cystolith, urinary calculus.
cistoscopia (*f., Med.*) cystoscopy.
cistotomia (*f., Surg.*) cystotomy.
cistótomo (*m., Surg.*) cystotome.
cit. = CITAÇÃO (citation); CITADO (cited).
cita (*f.*) citation, quotation; (*m.,f., pl.*) Scythians.
citação (*f.*) citation, quotation, excerpt; summons, subpoena.
citadino –na (*adj.*) urban; (*m.,f.*) city-dweller.
citado –da (*m.,f.*) one who has been subpoenaed.
citador –dora, **citante** (*adj.*) citing; summoning; (*m.,f.*) one who cites; one who summons.
citar (*v.t.*) to cite, summon, subpoena, order to appear (in court); to quote (verbatim); to name, mention, make reference to.—**na íntegra** or **por extenso**, to quote in full.
cítara (*f.*) cithara, cither, zither.
citável (*adj.*) citable, quotable.
citerior (*adj.*) hither, situated on this end.
citiso (*m., Bot.*) Easter broom (*Cytisus racemosus*).
citisina (*f., Chem.*) cytisine; laburnine; ulexine.
citissa (*f.*) a Scythian woman. Cf. CITA.
citoblasto (*m., Biol.*) cytoblast.
citoclase (*f., Biol.*) cytoclasis.
citoclástico –ca (*adj., Biol.*) cytoclastic.
citocromo (*m., Biochem., Anat.*) cytochrome.
citode (*m., Biol.*) cytode.
citodiagnóstico (*m., Med.*) cytodiagnosis.
citofagia (*f., Biol.*) cytophagia.
citófago –ga (*adj., Biol.*) cytophagous.
citofilático –ca (*adj., Immunol.*) cytophil.
citogênese, -genia (*f., Biol.*) cytogenesis.
citogenético –ca, –gênico –ca (*adj., Biol.*) cytogenetic.
citóide (*adj.*) cytoid, cell-like.
citole (*m., Bot.*) a heliconia (*H. stricta*).
citólise (*f., Physiol.*) cytolisis.
citolisina (*f., Biochem.*) cytolysin.
citolítico –ca (*adj., Biochem., Physiol.*) cytolytic.
citologia (*f., Biol.*) cytology.
citológico –ca (*adj., Biol.*) cytological.
citômetro (*m., Physiol.*) cytometer.
citomitoma (*f., Biol.*) cytoreticulum.
citoplasma (*m., Biol.*) cytoplasm.
citoplasto (*m., Biol.*) cytoplast.
citoquilema (*m., Biol.*) cytochylema, cytolymph.
citoquímica (*f.*) cytochemistry.
citorictes (*m., Biol., Med.*) cytoryctes.
citorretículo (*m., Biol.*) cytoreticulum.
citosina (*f., Biochem.*) cytosine.
citosomo (*m., Biol.*) cytosome.
citostoma (*f., Zool.*) cytostome.
citotaxia (*f., Physiol.*) cytotaxis.
citral (*m., Chem.*) citral.
citotropia (*f., Physiol.*) cytotropism.
citrato (*m., Chem.*) citrate.
cítreo –trea (*adj.*) citrus.
cítrico –ca (*adj.*) citric.
citrino –na (*adj.*) citron-colored; (*f.*) citrine. [*Webster:* "a semiprecious yellow stone resembling topaz but actually black quartz changed in color by heating."]
citronela (*f.*) any of a number of fragrant plants having a citronlike odor, esp. citronella grass (*Cymbopogon nardus*), common balm (*Melissa officinalis*) and lemon verbena (*Lippia citriodora*). Cf. ERVA-CIDREIRA.
cítula (*f., Zool.*) cytula.
ciumada, ciumagem, ciumaria [i-u] (*f.*) jealousy; jealous fit.

ciumar [i-u] (*v.i.*) to be jealous; to envy.
ciúme (*m.*) jealousy; envy. Cf. INVEJA. **ter—s de,** to be jealous (envious) of.
ciumeira [i-u] (*f., colloq.*) excessive jealousy.
ciumento –ta [i-u] (*adj.*) jealous, envious; (*m.,f.*) a jealous person.
ciurídeos (*m.pl.*) the Sciuridae (squirrel family).
cível (*adj., Law*), civil; (*m.*) civil jurisdiction. Cf. CIVIL.
civeta (*f.*) civet cat [= GATO-DE-ALGÁLIA].
cívico –ca (*adj.*) civic.
civil (*adj.*) civil; courteous; civilian; (*m.*) civil jurisdiction; a civilian. Cf. CÍVEL. **ano—,** calendar year. **Direito—,** Civil Law. **engenheiro—,** civil engineer.
civilidade (*f.*) civility; urbanity; good breeding.
civilização (*f.*) civilization.
civilizado –da (*adj.*) civilized; refined, cultured.
civilizador –dora (*adj.*) civilizing; (*m.,f.*) civilizer.
civilizar (*v.t.*) to civilize; to educate, enlighten.
civilizável (*adj.*) capable of being civilized.
civismo (*m.*) civic pride; patriotism.
cizânia (*f., Bot.*) tare, darnel (*Lolium temulentum*); disharmony, discord. **semear a—,** to sow discord. Var. ZIZÂNIA.
cizirão (*m.*) the perennial peavine (*Lathyrus latifolius*), c.a. LÁTIRO. Cf. CISIRÃO-BRANCO.
cl = CENTILITRO(S), (centiliter(s).
Cl. = CLÉRIGO (priest).
clã (*m.*) clan.
cladódio (*m., Bot.*) cladode, cladophyll.
cladófora (*f., Bot.*) a large genus (*Cladophora*) of green algae.
clamador –dora (*adj.*) clamoring; (*m.,f.*) clamorer.
clamante (*adj.*) clamoring.
clamar (*v.i.*) to clamor, shout; (*v.t.*) to cry out against; to implore, beseech.
clamor [ô] (*m.*) clamor, shout, outcry; hullabaloo, hue and cry, uproar; complaint.
clamoroso –sa (*adj.*) clamorous.
clandestino –na (*adj.*) clandestine; (*m., colloq.*) a stowaway.
clangor [ô] (*m.*) clangor, clang; blare (as of a trumpet).
clangorar, clangorejar (*v.i.*) to clang, resound.
clangoroso –sa (*adj.*) clangorous.
claque (*f.*) claque, paid applauders; a collapsible or crush opera hat.
clara (*f.*) white of egg; white of the eye; a clearing in the woods; Clara, Clare.—**s em neve,** beaten egg whites.
clarabóia (*f.*) skylight.
clarão (*m.*) flash of light or lightning; a clearing in the forest; clarion (organ stop).
clarear (*v.i.*) to grow light; to clear up; (*v.t.*) to light up.
clareira (*f.*) glade; a clearing in the woods.
clarete [rê] (*m.*) claret wine.
clareza [ê] (*f.*) clarity, clearness.
claridade (*f.*) clearness; light.
clarificação (*f.*) clarification.
clarificador –dora (*adj.*) clarifying; (*m.,f.*) clarifier.
clarificar (*v.t.*) to clarify, purify.
clarim (*m.*) clarion; bugle; bugler. **toque de—,** bugle call.
clarinada (*f.*) flourish (of horns).
clarinar (*v.i.*) to clarion.
clarineta [ê] (*f.*), –nete [nê] (*m.*) clarinet; clarinetist.
clarinetista (*m.,f.*) clarinetist.
Clarissa (*f.*) Clarissa.
Clarisse (*f.*) Clarice.
clarividente (*adj.*) clear-sighted, far-seeing, discerning.
claro –ra (*adj.*) clear, transparent, bright, light, limpid; cloudless, sunny; lucid, plain, unambiguous; overt; apparent, evident; light-colored; (*m.*) bright spot; clear space; blank space (in a form); (*adv.*) clearly, explicitly. —**como água,** crystal-clear; as clear as daylight.—**como dois e dois são quatro,** as plain as the nose on your face. —**que não,** of course not.—**que sim,** of course, why certainly. **às—s,** openly, publicly, above-board. **dizer as coisas às—s,** to say what one means; to call a spade a spade. **é—que,** it stands to reason that; it goes without saying that. **passar a noite em—,** to stay awake all night.
claro-escuro –ra (*m.*) chiaroscuro.
clasmatócito (*m., Biol.*) clasmatocyte.
clasmatocitose (*f., Biol.*) clasmatosis, fragmentation of cells.
classe (*f.*) class, category, group, division; pupil; rank, order; rating; social stratum.
classicismo (*m.*) classicism.

clássico –ca (*adj.*) classic(al); standard (in art and literature); pert. to Greek or Latin literature.

classificação (*f.*) classification, arrangement, assortment, grouping; rating; ranking.

classificador –dora (*adj.*) classifying; (*m.,f.*) classifier.

classificar (*v.t.*) to classify, class, arrange, assort.

classificável (*adj.*) classificable.

classismo (*m.*) = CLASSICISMO.

clástico –ca (*adj.*) clastic; (*f.*) clastic anatomy; (*pl.*, *Petrog.*) clastic rocks.

Claudia (*f.*) Claudia.

claudicação (*f.*) claudication, limp.

claudicante (*adj.*) limping, lame, hobbling, halt; ricketty; fig. wrong, twisted.

claudicar (*v.i.*) to limp, hobble; fig. to falter, waver; to err.

Claudio (*m.*) Claud(e), Claudius.

claustração (*f.*) claustration.

claustral (*adj.*) claustral; cloistral.

claustro (*m.*) cloister; monastery, convent.

claustrofobia (*f.*, *Med.*) claustrophobia.

cláusula (*f.*) clause, article, provision, condition, stipulation.

clausura (*f.*) closure, a shut-in place; confinement; reclusion.

clausurar (*v.t.*) to confine, as in a cloister.

clava (*f.*) club, cudgel.

clavária (*f.*, *Bot.*) a genus (*Clavaria*) of fleshy, mostly edible, club or coral fungi.

clave (*f.*, *Music*) clef.

clavicímbalo (*m.*) clavicymbal, harpsichord.

clavicórdio (*m.*) clavichord.

clavicórneos (*m.pl.*) the Clavicornia or Clavicornes—a large family of beetles which comprises the burying beetle, rove beetle, lady-bugs, etc.

clavícula (*f.*, *Anat.*) clavicle, collarbone.

claviculado –da (*adj.*, *Zool.*) claviculate.

clavicular (*adj.*) clavicular.

claviharpa (*f.*, *Music*) claviharp.

clavija (*f.*) coupling pin; wall peg.

clavina (*f.*) = CARABINA.

clavinote (*m.*) a small carbine.

clematite (*f.*, *Bot.*) clematis.

clemência (*f.*) clemency, lenience; mercy, forgivingness.

clemente (*adj.*) clement, merciful, kind-hearted, indulgent; (*m.*) Clement.

Clementina (*f.*) Clementina, Clementine.

cleptomania (*f.*) kleptomania.

cleptomaníaco –ca (*adj.*; *m.,f.*) kleptomaniac.

clerestório (*m.*, *Arch.*) clerestory.

clerezia (*f.*) clergy.

clerical (*adj.*) clerical (sacerdotal).

clericalismo (*m.*) clericalism.

clericato (*m.*) clericate.

clérigo (*m.*) cleric, clergyman, priest.

clero (*m.*) clergy; priesthood.

clerodendro (*m.*, *Bot.*) a glory bower (*Clerodendron*).

cletra (*f.*, *Bot.*) the genus (*Clethra*) of white alders.

cleveíte (*f.*, *Min.*) cleveite.

clianto (*m.*, *Bot.*) the glorypea parrotbeak (*Clianthus dampieri*).

clichagem (*f.*) = ESTEREOTIPIA.

clichê (*m.*) a stereotype printing-plate; a photo-engraving; a half-tone cut or illustration; a photographic negative; a cliché, trite expression, [= CHAPA, LUGAR-COMUM].—**de meio tom**, a half-tone photoengraving.—**de traços**, a line engraving.—**reticulado**, half-tone plate. **segundo**—, second edition (of a newspaper).

clicheria (*f.*) photoengraving shop; production of cuts.

cliente (*m.,f.*) client; patient; customer.

clientela (*f.*) clientele; patronage.

clima (*m.*) climate, usual weather.

climactérico –ca (*adj.*) climacteric(al).

climatérico (*adj.*) climatic.

climático –ca (*adj.*) climatic(al). [But not climactic, which is: RELATIVO A CLÍMAX.]

climatização (*f.*) = ACLIMAÇÃO.

climatizar (*v.*) = ACLIMAR.

climatologia (*f.*) climatology.

climatológico –ca (*adj.*) climatologic(al).

climatoterapia (*f.*, *Med.*) climatotherapy.

clímax [ks] (*f.*) climax; acme, apex, culmination.

clina (*f.*) = CRINA.

clinândrio (*m.*, *Bot.*) clinandrium, androclinium; = ROSTELO.

clinântio, clinanto (*m.*, *Bot.*) clinanthium.

clínica (*f.*) clinic; the practice of medicine; a doctor's clientele; a woman physician.

clinicar [2] (*v.i.*) to practice medicine.

clínico –ca (*adj.*) clinical; (*m.,f.*) a practicing physician; a clinician.

clinocefalia (*f.*, *Craniol.*) clinocephaly.

clinoclasito (*m.*, *Min.*) clinoclasite, c.a. ABICHITO, AFANESITO.

clinocloro (*m.*, *Min.*) clinochlore.

clinodiagonal (*adj.*, *Cryst.*) clinodiagonal.

clinodoma (*m.*, *Cryst.*) clinodome.

clinógrafo (*m.*) = CLINOGRAPH.

clinóide (*adj.*, *Anat.*) clinoid.

clinômetro (*m.*) clinometer.—**de esfera**, (*Aeron.*) ball-inclinometer.

clinopinacóide (*m.*, *Cryst.*) clinopinacoid.

clinopódio (*m.*) a genus (*Clinopodium*) of mints, closely related to *Satureia* (*syn. Calamintha*).

clínquer (*m.*, *Metal.*) clinker.

clipe (*m.*) clip.—**de fusível**, (*Elec.*) fuse clip.

clipeado –da (*adj.*) clypeate, scutate.

clipeiforme [e-i] (*adj.*) clypeiform, shield-shaped.

clípeo (*m.*) clipeus (ancient large, round shield); (*Zool.*) clypeus.

clíper (*m.*) clipper ship.

clique (*m.*) click (a sound)—but not clique, which is CAMARILHA or COMPADRIO.

clisma (*m.*, *Med.*) clysma, enema.

clister (*m.*, *Med.*) clyster, enema.

clitelo (*m.*, *Zool.*) clitellum.

clitória (*f.*, *Bot.*) Asian pigeonwings (*Clitoria ternatea*).

clitóride (*f.*) = CLITÓRIS.

clitoridectomia (*f.*, *Surg.*) clitoridectomy.

clitoridiano –na (*adj.*) clitoridean.

clitoridite (*f.*, *Med.*) clitoriditis.

clitoridotomia (*f.*, *Surg.*) clitoridotomy.

clitóris (*f.*, *Anat.*) clitoris.

clitorismia (*f.*) clitorism.

clitorismo (*m.*) Lesbianism.

clivagem (*f.*, *Cryst.*; *Geol.*) cleavage. [But not cleavage in the sense of splitting, separation, division, which is SEPARAÇÃO, DIVISÃO.].

clivar (*v.t.*,*v.i.*) to cleave, split (referring only to crystals).

clívia (*f.*) the scarlet kafirlily (*Clivia miniata*).

clivo (*m.*) slope; hill.

clivoso –sa (*adj.*) declivous.

cloaca (*f.*) sewer; (*Zool.*) cloaca.

cloacal (*adj.*) cloacal.

cloacite (*f.*) cloacitis (of fowls).

cloasma (*m.*, *Med.*) chloasma.

cloasonado –da (*adj.*) cloisonné.

Cloe (*f.*) Chloe.

clone (*m.*; *Biol.*, *Bot.*) clone.

clônico –ca (*adj.*, *Med.*) clonic.

clonismo (*m.*, *Med.*) clonism.

clono (*m.*, *Physiol.*; *Med.*) clonus.

cloração (*f.*) chlorination.

clorado –da (*adj.*) chlorinated.

cloral (*m.*, *Chem.*) chloral.

cloralismo (*m.*, *Med.*) chloralism.

cloralizar (*v.t.*) to chlorinate.

cloralose (*f.*, *Chem.*) chloralose.

cloramida (*f.*, *Chem.*) chloramide, chloral formamide.

cloranila (*f.*, *Chem.*) chloranil, tetrachloro quinone.

clorantia (*f.*, *Bot.*) chloranthy.

cloranto –ta (*adj.*) having green flowers.

clorar (*v.t.*) to chlorinate; to chlorodize.

clorargirita (*f.*, *Min.*) chlorargyrite.

cloremia (*f.*, *Med.*) chloremia, chlorosis.

clorato (*m.*, *Chem.*) chlorate.—**de alumínio**, aluminum chlorate.—**de bário**, barium chlorate.—**de potássio**, potassium chlorate, potassium oxymuriate.

cloreto [ê] (*m.*, *Chem.*) chloride.—**de acetilo**, acetyl chloride; ethanoyl chloride.—**de alumínio**, aluminum chloride.—**de amônio**, ammonium chloride; sal ammoniac; ammonium muriate.—**de antimônio**, antimony trichloride; butter of antimony.—**de arsênico**, arsenic chloride.—**áurico**, gold chloride.—**de bário**, barium chloride.—**de benzilo**, benzyl chloride.—**de benzoílo**, benzoyl chloride; benzene carbonyl chloride.—**de cádmio**, cadmium chloride.—**de cal** = DESCORANTE.—**de cálcio**, calcium chloride.—**de carbamilo**, carbamyl chloride; chloroform amide; urea chloride; carbamide chlo-

ride.—**de carbonilo**, phosgene.—**de césio**, cesium chloride. —**de chumbo**, lead chloride; cotunnite.—**de cianogênio**, cyanogen chloride; chlorine cyanide.—**de cobalto**, cobalt chloride.—**de cobre**, copper chloride.—**de estanho**, tin chloride.—**estânico**, stannic chloride.—**estanoso**, stannous chloride.—**de etilo**, ethyl chloride; chloro ethane; hypochloric ether; muriatic ether.—**de ferro**, iron chloride.—**de hidrogênio**, hydrogen chloride.—**isocrotilo**, isocrotyl chloride.—**de lítio**, lithium chloride.—**de magnésio**, magnesium chloride; chloromagnesite.—**de mercúrio**, mercury chloride; corrosive sublimate; mercury dichloride.—**mercuroso**, mercurous chloride.—**de metilo**, methyl chloride; chloro methane.—**de níquel**, nickel chloride.—**de ouro**=—ÁURICO.—**de potássio**, potassium chloride; sylvite.—**descorante**, calcium hypochlorite; bleaching powder.—**de sódio**, sodium chloride; common salt.—**de zinco**, zinc chloride.
clórico -ca (adj., Chem.) chloric.
cloridrato (m., Chem.) hydrochlorate [=HIDROCLORATO].
clorídrico -ca (adj., Chem.) hydrochloric.
clorino -na (adj.) of the color grass green; (f.) chlorine gas.
clorita (f., Min.) chlorite.
clorito (m., Chem.) chlorite.
cloritóide (m., Min.) chloritoid.
cloritoso -sa (adj.) chloritic.
cloritozar (v.t.) to chloritize.
cloro [ór] (m., Chem.) chlorine.
cloroacetona (f., Chem.) chloro acetone; chlorinated acetone.
cloroanemia (f., Med.) chloranemia, chlorosis.
clorococo (m.) a genus (Chlorococcum) of green algae.
cloroespinélio (m., Min.) chlorospinel.
clorofana (f., Min.) chlorophane.
clorofânio (m., Physiol.) chlorophane.
clorofenol (m., Chem.) chlorophenol.
clorofíceas (m.pl.) the family of green algae (Chlorophyceae).
clorofíceo -cea (adj., Bot.) chlorophyceous.
clorofila (f.) chlorophyll.
clorofilado -da (adj.) chlorophyllaceous, -llose.
clorofilana (f.) chlorophyllan.
clorofilase (f., Biochem.) chlorophyllase.
clorofórmico -ca (adj.) chloroformic.
clorofórmio (m.) chloroform.
cloroformização (f.) chloroformization.
cloroformizador -dora (m.,f.) chloroformist.
cloroformizar (v.t.) to chloroform.
cloroleucito (m., Bot.) chloroleucyte, chloroplast.
cloroma (f., Med.) chloroma.
clorometria (f.) chlorometry.
clorômetro (m.) chlorometer.
cloropicrina (f., Chem.) chloropicrin; nitro chloroform.
cloroplastídio, cloroplasto (m., Biol.) chloroplast; chloroplastid.
cloroplatinado (m., Chem.) chloroplatinate; platinichloride.
clorose (f., Med.) chlorosis, anemia; (Bot.) the yellows, peach yellows.
cloroso -sa (adj., Chem.) chlorous.
clorótico -ca (adj.) chlorotic, anemic.
clorureto (m.) = CLORETO.
cloróxido [ks] (m., Chem.) oxychloride.
Clotilde (f.) Clothilda, Clotilda.
cloveno (m., Chem.) clovene.
clube (m.) club; clubhouse.—**feminino**, women's club.
clubista (m.,f.) club member.
clúpeos (m.pl.) the family (Clupeidae) of herrings, sardines, shads, etc.
clúsia (f.) any plant of the genus Clusia.
clusiáceas (f.pl., Bot.) the Clusiaceae (clusia family).
clusiáceo -cea (adj., Bot.) clusiaceous.
cm = CENTÍMETRO (centimeter).
CNDE = CONSELHO NACIONAL DE DESENVOLVIMENTO ECONÔMICO (National Council on Economic Development).
cnico (m.) the blessed thistle (Cnicus benedictus), c.a. CARDO-BENTO.
cnidários (m.pl.) = CELENTERADOS.
cnidoblasto (m., Zool.) cnidoblast.
cnidose (f., Med.) urticaria.
cnute (m.) knout.
co', abbrev. of COM.
coa [qua] = COM A, with the.
côa (f.) = COAÇÃO.

coabitação (f.) cohabitation.
coabitar (v.i.) to cohabit, live together.
coação (f.) act of straining or filtering. [Verb: COAR]; coaction, compulsion, force. [Verb: COAGIR].
coacusada (f.) co-defendant [=CO-RÉ].
coacusado (m.) co-defendant [=CO-RÉU].
coada (f.) lye solution; strained vegetables.
coadeira (f.) = COADOR.
coadjutor -tora (m.,f.) co-worker; accomplice.
coadjuvação (f.) help, co-operation.
coadjuvante (adj.) helping, co-operating.
coadjuvar (v.t.) to help, work with.
coadministrar (v.t.) to coadminister.
coador (adj.) straining; (m.) colander, sieve, strainer; filter; cloth bag for percolating coffee. [Fem. COADEIRA]
coadquirir (v.t.) to acquire jointly.
coadunação (f.) coadunation.
coadunado -da (adj.) coadunate.
coadunar (v.t.) to coadunate, unite into one; to combine. —**se com**, to tie in with; to jibe, be in harmony or accord with.—**com**, to be in keeping with.
coadunável (adj.) capable of being united into one.
coadura (f.) passage of a liquid through a strainer; the strained liquid.
coagente (adj.) coactive, coercive.
coagir (v.t.) to coerce, compel, constrain, "bulldoze".
coaglutinação (f., Immunol.) group or cross agglutination.
coagulação (f.) coagulation.
coagulador -dora (adj.) coagulating; (m.) rennet; (Zool.) abomasum.
coagulante (adj.) coagulative; (m.) coagulant.
coagular (v.t.,v.i.,v.r.) to coagulate, clot, curdle. Var. COALHAR
coagulável (adj.) coagulable.
coágulo (m.) coagulum, lump, clot, curd. Var. COALHO
coajerucu (m., Bot.) the yellow-dye tree or related species of Xylopia (annona family), c.a. PIJERUCU, JEJERUCU, PAU-DE-EMBIRA, PINDAÍBA.
coajinduba (f.) a fig (Ficus anthelminthica), c.a. FIGUEIRA-DO-MATO (or -VERMELHA), GAMELEIRA-BRANCA (or -BRAVA, or -MANSA, or -ROXA), GUAXINDUBA-BRAVA, LOMBRIGUEIRA, RENACO.
coalescência (f.) coalescence.
coalescente (adj.) coalescent.
coalescer (v.i.) to coalesce, grow together.
coalhado -da (adj.) curdled; (f.) clabber.
coalha-leite (f., Bot.) the cardoon (Cyanara cardunculus), c.a. CARDO, ALCACHOFRA-BRAVA.
coalhamento (m.) curdling; coagulation.
coalhar (v.) = COAGULAR.
coalheira (f.) rennet; (Zool.) abomasum [=COAGULADAR]; horse collar [=COELHEIRA].
coalho (m.) coagulum; clot; curd [=COÁGULO]; rennet [=COALHEIRA]; (Bot.) cardoon.
coalização (f.) coalition.
coalizar-se (v.r.) to coalesce (unite, join) with.
côana (f.) = CÓANO.
coaltar (m.) coal tar.
coandu (m.) = OURIÇO-CACHEIRO.
côano (m., Anat., Zool.) choana.
coanóide (adj., Zool.) choanoid, funnel-shaped.
coaptação (f.) coaptation.
coar (v.t.) to strain, filter; to infiltrate; to percolate; to drip, drop; to pour (liquid metal); (v.i.,v.r.) to infiltrate.
coarador, -douro (m.) = QUARADOR.
coarar (v.) = QUARAR.
coar[c]tação (f.) a stricture or narrowing; (Med.) coarctation.
coar[c]tar (v.t.) to restrain, confine, restrict.
coatá (m.) any spider monkey (Ateles), c.a. MACACO-ARANHA, esp. the following:—**-branco**, a species which despite the name is mostly black (A. variegatus), c.a. MAGUÇAPÁ, MAQUIÇAPÁ.—**-da-cara-preta**, a black-faced species (A. longimembris).—**-da-testa-branca**, a species having a white forehead (A. marginatus).—**-prêto**, black with a reddish face (A. paniscus), c.a. MONO-AGARRADOR; MACACO-ARANHA-DE-CARA-VERMELHA.
coataquiçaua (f., Bot.) a purpleheart (Peltogyne paniculata).
coati (m.) = QUATI.
coativo -va (adj.) coactive, coercive.
coa[c]to -ta (adj.; irreg. p.p. of COAGIR) coerced, forced.
co-autor (m.) co-author; -**tora** (f.) co-authoress.
co-autoria (f.) co-authorship.

coaxação, coaxada (*f.*) croaking (of frogs).
coaxar (*v.i.*) to croak (as a frog).
coaxi (*m.*) silt deposited on vegetation during a flood and which later dries and blows away.
coaxial [ks] (*adj.*) coaxial.
coaxo (*m.*) = COAXAÇÃO.
cobaia (*f.*) guinea pig, commonly called PORQUINHO-DA-ÍNDIA.
cobaltífero -ra (*adj.*) cobaltiferous.
cobaltinita, -tita (*f., Min.*) cobaltite; cobaltine.
cobalto (*m., Chem.*) cobalt.—**oxidado negro** = ASBOLANA, a mineral. **azul**—, cobalt blue.
cobaltoso -sa (*adj., Chem.*) cobaltous.
cobarde (*m.*) coward, craven; traitor; (*adj.*) cowardly, pusillanimous, chickenhearted; dastardly; treacherous. Var. COVARDE.
cobardia, cobardice (*f.*) cowardice, timidity; treacherousness. Var. COVARDIA.
cobéia (*f., Bot.*) the purplebell cobaea (*C. scandens*).
coberto -ta (*adj.; irreg. p.p.* of COBRIR) covered, hidden; (*m.*) covered shed; (*f.*) bed cover, blanket, quilt; any cap, cover, or covering; covered deck; motor cowling, engine hood.
cobertor (*m.*) bed cover, blanket, quilt.
cobertura (*f.*) a covering or coating; cap; cover.
cobiça (*f.*) covetousness, avarice, cupidity, greed.
cobiçante (*adj.*) covetous.
cobiçar (*v.t.*) to covet, lust after; to long inordinately for.
cobiçável (*adj.*) sufficient to arouse covetousness; highly to be desired.
cobiçoso -sa (*adj.*) covetous, avid, greedy.
cobra (*f.*) snake, serpent, viper.—**capelo**, hooded cobra. —**cascavel**, rattlesnake.—**cega** or—**de-duas-cabeças**, any limbless lizard, popularly known as a two-headed snake.—**chupa-ôvo**, a kind of harmless chicken snake.—**-cipó**, any long, slender vine snake or tree snake.—**coral**, coral snake.—**de-asa** or **-do-ar**, a lantern fly (*Laternaria spp.*), c.a. JAQUIRANABOIA.—**de-cabelo**, hairworm.—**-de-veado**, boa constrictor.—**de-vidro**, glass snake (limbless lizard).—**papagaio**, a green arboreal pit viper (*Bothrops lineatus*).—**preta** = MUÇURANA.—**tapete** = JARARACUÇU. dizer—**s e lagartos de uma pessoa**, to malign another person. (*m.*) expert.
cobrador (*m.*), **dora** (*f.*) bill collector.
cobradoria (*f.*) collection agency.
cobrança (*f.*) collection (of bills).
cobrar (*v.t.*) to collect (bills); to charge (money) for; to regain (courage).—**a falta**, in sports, to inflict a penalty.—**ânimo**, to take heart; to rally; to cheer up.
cobrável (*adj.*) of bills, costs, taxes, etc., collectible.
cobre (*m.*) copper; copper coin; (*pl., colloq.*) money.—**amarelo**, brass [= LATÃO].
cobrejunta (*f., Carp.*) batten.
cobrelo [ê] (*m.*) a small snake; (*colloq.*) shingles, supposedly caused by contact with a COBRA (snake).
cobrição (*f.*) act of covering; copulation (of quadrupeds).
cobrimento (*m.*) act of covering; coverage.
cobril (*m.*) snake hatchery; serpentarium.
cobrir [33] (*v.t.*) to cover (com, de, with); to conceal, hide; to shield, shelter, protect; to envelop; to defray (expenses); (*v.r.*) to put on one's hat; to get under cover; to cover oneself (com, de, with).
côbro (*m.*) end, ending, close; (*Naut.*) coil of cable; (*Steam Engine*) lap. pôr—**a**, to put a stop to.
cobu [ú] (*m.*) a cornmeal cake baked on a banana leaf [= JOÃO-DEITADO].
coca [ó] (*f.*) kink (in a rope); (*Bot.*) a cocaine tree (*Erythroxylum coca*), c.a. BOLÍVIA.—**de-paraguai** = CABELO-DE-NEGRO. â—, on the lookout.
côca (*f.*) bogeyman, hobgoblin; head scarf.
coça (*f.*) a scratching (of oneself); (*colloq.*) a thrashing.
cocada (*f.*) coconut candy; a butt with the head; (*colloq.*) a person who serves as a go-between for lovers.
coçado -da (*adj.*) threadbare, worn thin.
coçadura (*f.*) act of scratching (oneself).
cocaína (*f.*) cocaine.
cocainismo [a-i] (*m., Med.*) cocainism.
cocainizar [a-i] (*v.t.*) to cocainize.
cocainomania [a-i] (*f., Med.*) cocainomania.
cocainômano -ma [a-i] (*m.,f., Med.*) cocainomaniac.
cocar (*v.i.*) to be on the lookout; (*m.*) cockade; crest.
coçar (*v.t.*) to scratch (with the nails); (*colloq.*) to thrash; (*v.r.*) to scratch oneself.
cocarada (*f.*) topknot; cockade.

côcaras, de—, squatting.
cocção (*f.*) cooking, stewing, boiling; digestion. [Verb: COZER].
cóccidas (*m.pl.*) the Coccidae (family of scale insects).
coccídeas (*f.pl.*) the Coccidia (an order of protozoans).
coccídio (*m., Zool.*) any coccidium, esp. of the genus Eimeria.
coccidiose (*f.*) coccidiosis.
coccígeo -gea, -giano -na (*adj., Anat.*) coccygeal.
coccigodinia (*f., Med.*) coccygodynia.
coccigomorfas (*f.pl.*) the Coccygomorphae, a superfamily of birds which includes the cuckoos, puffbirds, toucans, barbets, kingfishers, bee eaters, trogons, etc.
coccigotomia (*f., Surg.*) coccygotomy.
coccinela (*f.*) ladybug, ladybird [= JOANINHA].
coccinelídeo (*m.*) any coccinellid (ladybug).
cóccix [cocsis] (*m., Anat.*) coccyx. [Colloq. syns. MUCUMBU and OSSO-DO-PAI-JOÃO].
cócegas (*f.pl.*) ticklishness. fazer—, to tickle.
coceguenta -ta (*adj.*) ticklish.
coceira (*f.*) itch; itching.
côcha (*f.*) trough.
cochar (*v.t.*) to lay (rope); by exten., to tighten.
côche (*m.*) coach; carriage; hod.
cocheira (*f.*) carriage barn; stable.
cocheiro (*m.*) coachman; cab-driver.
cochichar (*v.t.,v.i.*) to whisper; to buzz.
cochicho (*m.*) a whisper; a skylark; a bird called the firewood gatherer (*Anumbius annumbi*).
cochilar (*v.i.*) to nap, nod, doze, snooze.
cochilo (*m.*) nap, forty winks, snooze; fig., an oversight, slip.
cochinada (*f.*) a herd of small pigs; fig., filth.
cochinar (*v.i.*) to grunt, as a pig.
cochinilha (*f.*) cochineal (dye stuff or insect). Var. COCHONILHA.
cochino -na (*adj.*) filthy; (*m.,f.*) an unfattened pig; fig., a filthy person.
côcho (*m.*) trough; hod; a coconut; a wooden mold in which latex is coagulated.
cochonilha (*f.*) = COCHINILHA.
cociente (*m.*) = QUOCIENTE.
cóclea (*f.*) caracol, spiral; Archimedean screw; (*Anat.*) cochlea.
cocleado -da coclear (*adj.*) spiral; (*Anat.*) cochlear.
cocleária (*f.*) common scurvyweed (*Cochlearia officinalis*). —**dos-jardins** = CAPUCHINHA-GRANDE.
cocleariforme (*adj.*) cochleariform.
cocleiforme (*adj.*) cochleiform.
coco [cóco] (*m., Bacteriol.*) coccus.
côco (*m.*) any of numerous palms or their nuts; a container or dipper made of coconut shell; (*colloq.*) head; bugaboo, hobgoblin.—**amargoso**, a palm (*Barbosa pseudococos*), c.a. CÔCO-VERDE, PALMITO-AMARGOSO; also = CÔCO-DE-QUARESMA.—**catolé**, a palm (*Attalea humilis*), c.a. CÔCO-DE-PINDOBA, CATOLÉ, ANAJÁ-MIRIM. —**da-bahia**, the common coconut (*Cocos nucifera*); also, its fruit.—**da-praia**, or—**de-guriri**, a palm (*Diplothemium maritimum*), c.a. ACUMÃ, Brazilian butia (*B. capitata*), c.a. ACUMÃ.—**de-catarro**, the mucaja acrocomia or macaw palm (*Acrocomia sclerocarpa*), c.a. BACAIUVA, CÔCO-BABOSA, CÔCO-DE-ESPINHOS, MACACAÚBA, MACAÍBA, MACAÚBA, MACAIBEIRA, MACAIUVEIRA, MACAJUBA, MOCAJÁ, MUCAJÁ, MUCAJUBA, MUCAÍA, MUCAJAZEIRO; also, its nut which yields a violet-scented oil used in perfumery.—**de-colher**, green coconut whose soft pulp may be eaten with a spoon.—**de-dendê** = DENDÊZEIRO.—**de-iri**, a palm (*Astrocaryum ayri*), c.a. AIRI.—**de-macaco** = BABAÇU.—**de-natal**, a spinyclubpalm (*Bactris setosa*).—**de-nazaré** = MANGARÁ.—**de-purga**, a palm (*Astrocaryum acu*), c.a. ANDÁ-AÇU.—**de-quaresma**, a syagrus palm (*S. picrophylla*), c.a. CÔCO-AMARGOSO, CATOLÉ; also = COQUEIRO-DO-CAMPO.—**de-vassoura**, a spinyclubpalm (*Bactris campestris*); also = AIRIRI.—**de-veado**, a bramblepalm (*Desmoncus inermis*).—**de-vinagre**, the beach spinyclubpalm (*Bactris major*).—**do-mar**, the double-coconut (*Lodoicea maldivica*). ["This palm bears probably the largest known seed." *Standardized Plant Names*.] —**indaiã** = ANAIÃ.
cocó (*m.*) a type of feminine hair-do; topknot [= COQUE, PIROTE, BIROTE, PITOTE, PERICOTE, PERIQUITO].
cocobacilo (*m., Biochem.*) coccobacillus.
coconote (*m.*) coconut.
cócoras = CÓCARAS.

cocoré (*m.*, *colloq.*) row, brawl [= RÔLO].
cocoricar, -ritar (*v.i.*) to crow (as a cock).
cocoricó or **-cô** (*m.*) cock's crow.
cocorobó (*m.*) = CAPIM-CEBOLA.
cocoroca (*f.*, *Zool.*) the yellow grunt (*Haemulon sciurus*).
cocorocó! cock-a-doodle-do!
cocorote (*m.*) a rap on the head with the knuckles [= CASCUDO, CAROLO, COCRE, CROQUE]
cocoruta (*f.*) **-to** (*m.*) topknot; crown of the head; hillock; the hump of zebu cattle; a swelling; crest, top.
cocote (*f.*) cocotte; (*Fireworks*) torpedo.
cocre (*m.*) = COCOROTE.
co-credor **-dora** (*m.,f.*) joint creditor.
coculo (*m.*) = COGULO.
cód. = CÓDICE (codex); CÓDIGO (code).
coda (*f.*, *Music*) coda.
codagem (*f.*) = CAIRUÇU.
codamina (*f.*, *Chem.*) codamine.
côdão (*m.*) frost; icicle. Var. CODO.
côdea (*f.*) crust of bread; scab; husk.
codeína (*f.*, *Chem.*) codeine.
co-delinqüência (*f.*) joint transgression.
co-delinqüente (*m.,f.*) cotransgressor.
co-demandante (*m.,f.*, *Law*) co-plaintiff.
codêsso (*m.*, *Bot.*) broom (*Cyticus sp.*).—**-alto**, a flatpod (*Adenocarpus hispanicus*).—**-bastardo** or **-dos-alpes**, goldenchain laburnum (*L. anagyroides*).
codetentor **-tora** (*m.,f.*) joint-holder, co-owner.
codeúdo **-da** (*adj.*) thick-skinned; having a thick crust.
co-devedor **-dora** (*m.,f.*) joint debtor.
códice (*m.*) codex.
codicilo (*m.*) codicil (of a will).
codificação (*f.*) codification.
codificador (*m.*), **-dora** (*f.*) codifier.
codificar (*v.t.*) to codify.
código (*m.*) code.
codilheira (*f.*, *Veter.*) capped elbow.
codilho (*m.*) codille. [*Webster*: "a term at omber used when the game is lost by the one challenging." (The Portuguese equivalent of omber is VOLTARETE).]; horse's knee; (*colloq.*) a hoax.
codimer (*m.*, *Chem.*) Codimer.
códio (*m.*) a genus (*Codium*) of green algae.
co-diretor (*m.*), **-triz** (*f.*) co-manager.
codo (*m.*) = = CÔDÃO.
codório (*m.*) a swig of liquor; a light snack.
codorna (*f.*, *Zool.*) any of several nothuras (tinamous), esp. the spotted nothura (*N. maculosa*), c.a. INHAMBU.—**-buraqueira**, the marbled nothura (*N. boraquira*); also, the dwarf tinamou (*Taoniscus nanus*).—**-mineira**, the least nothura (*N. minor*).
codorniz (*f.*) = CODORNA.
codornizão (*m.*, *Zool.*) a corn crake (*Crex pratensis*).
codorno (*m.*) a siesta; = SESTA.
codrá (*m.*, *Bot.*) India paspalum (*P. scrobiculatum*).
co-educação (*f.*) co-education.
co-educar (*v.t.*) to co-educate.
co-educativo **-va** (*adj.*) co-educational.
coeficiente (*m.*) coefficient; factor.—**de absorção**, (*Physics*) coefficient of absorption.—**de acoplamento**, (*Elec.*) coupling coefficient.—**de amplificação**, (*Elec.*) amplification factor.—**de atrito**, (*Mech.*) coefficient of friction.—**de atrito cinemático**, (*Mech.*) coefficient of sliding friction.—**de cisalhamento**, (*Mech.*) coefficient of rigidity.—**de compressibilidade**, (*Physical Chem.*) coefficient of compressibility.—**de contração**, (*Hydraul.*) coefficient of contraction.—**de depressão (do ponto de congelação)**, (*Physical Chem.*) coefficient of depression.—**de depressão molecular (do ponto de congelação)**, (*Physical Chem.*) coefficient of molecular depression.—**de deslocamento**, coefficient of displacement; block coefficient.—**de determinação**, (*Stat.*) path coefficient.—**de difusão**, (*Physical Chem.*) coefficient of diffusion.—**de dilatação**, (*Physics*) coefficient of expansion.—**de dilatação em volume**, (*Physics*) coefficient of cubical expansion.—**de dilatação linear**, (*Physics*) coefficient of linear expansion.—**de dilatação superficial**, (*Physics*) coefficient of superficial expansion.—**de dispersão**, (*Elec.*) coefficient of leakage.—**de escoamento**, (*Hydraul.*) coefficient of discharge; coefficient of efflux.—**de elasticidade**, (*Mech.*) coefficient of elasticity.—**de elasticidade transversal**, (*Mech.*) coefficient of rigidity.—**de escorregamento**, (*Physics*) coefficient of sliding friction.—**de finura**, (*Mech.*) coefficient of fineness.—**de fluidez**, (*Physics*) co-

efficient of fluidity.—**de histérese**, (*Magnetism*) coefficient of hysteresis.—**de impacto**, (*Physics*) coefficient of impact.—**de indução mútua**, (*Radio*) coefficient of mutual induction.—**de Peltier**, (*Elec.*) coefficient of Peltier's effect.—**de reflexão**, (*Physics*) coefficient of reflection.—**de regressão**, (*Stat.*) regression coefficient.—**de resistência**, (*Hydraul.*) coefficient of resistance.—**de restituição**, (*Mech.*) coefficient of restitution.—**de segurança**, safety factor.—**de self (autoindução)**, (*Elec.*) coefficient of self-induction.—**de vaporização**, coefficient of evaporation.—**de velocidade**, (*Hydraul.*) coefficient of velocity.—**de viscosidade**, (*Physics*) coefficient of viscosity.—**de viscosidade cinemática**, (*Physics*) coefficient of kinematic viscosity.—**higroscópica**, hygroscopic coefficient.
co'ela = COM ELA.
co'êle = COM ÊLE.
coelha (*f.*) doe rabbit. [The buck is COELHO.]
coelhal (*adj.*) rabbit.
coelheiro **-ra** (*adj.*) rabbit-hunting; (*m.,f.*) rabbit hunter; (*f.*) rabbit warren or hutch; collar of a harness [= COALHEIRA].
coelhinho (*m.*) bunny.
coelho [ê] (*m.*) rabbit. [Hare is LEBRE.]; (*slang.*) a ten-cruzeiro bill [ten being the rabbit's number in the BICHO game.]—**americano**, a paca (*Cuniculus sp.*). **matar dois —s de uma cajadada só**, to kill two birds with one stone.
coempção (*f.*, *Law*) joint purchase; reciprocal purchase.
coendu [ú] (*m.*) = OURIÇO-CACHEIRO.
coenha (*f.*, *Bot.*) the fiddleleaf dock (*Rumex pulcher*), c.a. LABAÇA.
coenito (*m.*, *Min.*) cohenite.
coentrilho (*m.*) a pricklyash (*Zanthoxylum sp.*).
coentro (*m.*, *Bot.*) coriander (*Coriandrum sativum*).—**-de-caboclo**,—**-bravo**,—**-da-colônia**, an eryngo (*Eryngium foetidum*).
coerana (*f.*) = COIRANA.
coerção (*f.*) coercion.
coercitivo **-va** (*adj.*) = COERCIVO.
coercível (*adj.*) coercible.
coercivo **-va** (*adj.*) coercive; stringent.
coerência (*f.*) coherence, consistency, harmony, unity.
coerente (*adj.*) coherent; consistent, logical.
coerir (*v.i.*) to cohere, stick together.
coesão (*f.*) cohesion; fig., harmony, unity.
coesivo **-va** (*adj.*) cohesive.
coeso **-sa** [é] (*adj.*) united, joined; coherent.
coessencial (*adj.*) coessential.
coestaduano **-na** (*adj.*) of the same state.
coetâneo **-nea** (*adj.*) coetaneous, contemporary [= COEVO].
coeterno **-na** (*adj.*) coeternal.
coevo **-va** [é] (*adj.*) coeval, contemporary.
coexistência [x = z] (*f.*) coexistence.
coexistir [x = z] (*v.i.*) to coexist.
coextensivo **-va** [x = z] (*adj.*) coextensive.
COFAP = COMMISSÃO FEDERAL DE ABASTECIMENTO E PREÇOS (Federal Commission on Supply and Prices).
co-fiador (*m.*), **-dora** (*f.*) joint warrantor.
cofiar (*v.t.*) to stroke (the beard, the hair).
cofo [ô] (*m.*) wicker creel [= SAMBURÁ]; "an oblong, narrow-mouthed, crudely woven, leaf-lined basket in which the CABOCLOS carry manioc flour and crabs." [*GBAT*]
cofose (*f.*, *Med.*) cophosis, deafness.
cofre (*m.*) chest, safe; (*Autom.*) motor hood; a trunk-fish (*Lactophrys*). **os —s públicos** or **do estado**, the public coffers. **pagar na bôca do—**(*colloq.*) to pay cash on the barrelhead.
cogitabundo **-da** (*adj.*) cogitative, meditative.
cogitação (*f.*) cogitation. **fora de—**, unthinkable.
cogitar (*v.i.*) to cogitate, think about; (*v.i.*) to think hard, ponder, meditate.—**de**, to consider.
cogitativo **-va** (*adj.*) cogitative, meditative.
cognação (*f.*) cognation.
cognato **-ta** (*adj.*; *m.*) cognate.
cognição (*f.*) cognition.
cógnito **-ta** (*irreg. p.p. of* CONHECER) cognized [= CONHECIDO].
cognome (*m.*) cognomen, surname; nickname.
cognominação (*f.*) cognomination.
cognominar (*v.t.*) to cognaminate; to nickname.
cognoscitivo **-va** (*adj.*) having the power of knowing.
cognoscível (*adj.*) cognizable, knowable.
cogote (*m.*) = CANGOTE.
cogotilho (*m.*) a short trim given to a horse's mane.
cogotudo **-da** (*adj.*) thick-necked.
cogula (*f.*) monk's hooded gown.

cogular (*v.*) = ACOGULAR.
cogulho (*m., Arch.*) rosette.
cogulo (*m.*) overmeasure, surplus, superabundance [= COCULO, CUCULO].
cogumelaria (*f.*) a mushroom nursery.
cogumelo (*m.*) mushroom; toadstool; any fungus.— **comestível**, the common, edible meadow mushroom (*Argaricus campestris*).—**-do-mar**, a sea kidney (*Renilla reniformis*).
cohabitação (*f.*) = COABITAÇÃO.
cohabitar (*v.i.*) = COABITAR.
co-herdar (*v.t.,v.i.*) to inherit jointly.
co-herdeiro -ra (*m.,f.*) joint heir.
coibição [o-i] (*f.*) cohibition, restraint, deterrence.
coibir [o-i] (*v.t.*) to cohibit, deter, restrain, stop, put a stop to.
coibitivo -va (*adj.*) deterrent.
coice (*m.*) a backward kick (as of a horse); recoil (of a gun); rear end (of anything); butt (of a gun); heel; door sill; a clothes moth [= TRAÇA].
coicear (*v.t.,v.i.*) to kick . Var. COUCEAR.
coiceiro -ra (*adj.*) kicking; of a horse, prone to kick; (*m.,f.*) kicker; (*f.*) jamb post; door sill; rough-hewn lumber. Var. COUCEIRO.
coifa (*f.*) coif (woman's headdress); hair net; kerchief; caul (membrane sometimes enclosing a child's head at birth); (*Bot.*) root cap; (*Artil.*) cap; (*Zool.*) reticulum [= BARRETE].—**do diabo**, = CIPÓ-MATA-COBRAS.
coima (*f.*) fine, penalty, esp. for damages; blame; ante (as in poker).
coimar (*v.t.*) to penalize, fine.
coimável (*adj.*) subject to fine or penalty.
coimbrão [brãos] **-brã** [-brãs] (*adj.; m.,f.*) (person) of Coimbra.
coincidência [o-in] (*f.*) coincidence.
coincidente [o-in] (*adj.*) coincident(al).
coincidir [o-in] (*v.i.*) to coincide (**com**, with).
coincidível [o-in] (*adj.*) capable of coinciding.
coió (*adj.*) ridiculous, fatuous; (*m.*) a ludicrous ladies' man; a boob; (*Zool.*) a flying gurnard (*Dactylopterus volitans*), c.a. CAJALÉU, PIRABEBE, VOADOR-CASCUDO, PEIXE-VOADAR.—**sem sorte**, (*slang*) unlucky suitor.
coiote (*m.*) coyote.
coiraça (*f.*) = COURAÇA.
coiraçar (*v.*) & derivs. = COURAÇAR & derivs.
coirama (*f.*) = COURAMA.
coirana (*f.*) any of various jessamines, esp. the night-blooming *Cestrum nocturnum;* a moonflower called BOA-NOITE.—**do-rio-grande-do-sul**, the Chilean cestrum (*C. parqui*). Var. COERANA.
coirear (*v.*) = COUREAR.
coireiro (*m.*) = COUREIRO.
coirela (*f.*) a long, narrow field; an old measure of land area: 100 BRAÇAS (722 ft.) long by 10 BRAÇAS (72.2 ft.) wide. Var. COURELA.
coirmão [o-ir; pl. -mãos] (*m.*), **-mã** [o-ir] (*f.*) first cousin.
coirinho (*m.*) = COURINHO.
coiro (*m.*) = COURO.
coisa (*f.*) thing, something, object, article; (*pl.*) matters, affairs. Var. COUSA.—**achada do vento**, something found of unknown ownership.—**alguma**, nothing [but **alguma coisa** is something, anything].—**à tôa**, trifling thing.—**da mão do homem**, man-made thing.—**da terra**, something made or used locally.—**de arromba**, something startling. —**de fora da terra**, something from another land or place. —**de mão de mestre**, masterpiece.—**de ouro**, something perfect.—**de preço**, something of great price.—**de respeito**, something worthy of respect.—**de vulto**, something big, important.—**s diferentes**, different things [but **diferentes coisas**, several things].—**s do arco da velha**, incredible happenings, unbelievable doings.—**em primeira mão**, something brand new.—**em que pensar**, food for thought.—**em segunda mão**, something secondhand. —**feita**, sorcery; hex; hocus-pocus; fracas.—**nenhuma**, nothing.—**que o valha** , something like it, what amounts to the same thing.—**ruim**, the Evil One. Aí há—! There's a nigger in the woodpile! I smell a rat! Aí vem—! This bodes no good! something's going to happen! **alguma**—, something. **dar pela**—, to catch on, perceive. **deixar as**—**s como são para ver como ficam**, to wait and see what happens. **dizer as**—**s como elas são**, to call a spade a spade. **Ela diz uma**—**e faz outra**, She says one thing and does another. **falar duma**—**e outra**, to talk of one thing and another. **há**—**de dois anos**, about two years ago. **Há qualquer**—, Something's brewing. **já que a**—**é assim**,

that being the case; since that is the way matters stand. **levar**, or **tomar, as**—**s a sério**, to take things seriously. **muita**—, much, many things. **outra**—, something else. **pôr as**—**s em pratos limpos**, to come clean, lay the cards on the table. **qualquer**—, something, anything, **uma**—, something. **uma**—**caída do céu**, a windfall, a godsend.
coisada (*f.*) a pile (heap, mess, bunch) of things. Var. COUSADA.
coisíssima, used in the expression: **coisíssima alguma** (or **nemhuma**), absolutely nothing.
coitadinho -nha (*m.,f.*) Poor little thing! (*m.*) a man whose wife has betrayed him.
coitado -da (*adj.*) poor, wretched, miserable. [Used as a term of pity.]—**dêle**, poor fellow!
coitar (*v.*) = COUTAR.
coiteiro (*m.*) = COUTEIRO.
coiteiro (*m.*) var. of COUTEIRO; in northeastern Brazil, one who protects or gives asylum to bandits.
coito (*m.*) coitus; also = COUTO.
coivara (*f.*) brush, branches, half-burned tree trunks, etc., gathered into a huge pile for final burning (to clear the land).
cola (*f.*) glue, mucilage; track, trail; tail; (*student slang*) trot, pony, crib; (*Bot.*) Sudan colanut (*Cola acuminata*). —**de-cavalo** = (*Bot.*) CAVALINHA.—**de-peixe**, fish glue; isinglass [= ICTIOCOLA].—**de-sapateiro**, a Catasetum orchid.—**de-zorro** = CAPIM-RABO DE BURRO.—**forte**, cobbler's glue; carpenter's glue.
colaboração (*f.*) collaboration, cooperation.
colaborador -dora (*adj.*) collaborating; (*m.,f.*) collaborator.
colaborar (*v.i.*) to collaborate, cooperate.
colação (*f.*) bestowal of a degree, benefice, etc.; collation (all senses).—**de grau**, bestowal of a college degree.
colacia (*f.*) status of foster brother or foster sister; intimate relationship.
colacionar (*v.t.*) to collate.
colaço -ça (*adj.*) friendly, intimate; (*m.*) foster brother; (*f.*) foster sister.
colada (*f.*) col, saddle, pass (between mountains).
colagem (*f.*) glueing; clarification of wine; collage.
colagogo (*adj.; m., Med.*) cholagogue.
colança (*f.*) cheating on exams.
colapso (*m.*) collapse.—**cardíaco**, heart failure.
colar (*v.t.*) to glue, fasten together with glue; to press together; to clarify (wine); to bestow (a degree, a benefice) upon; (*v.i.*, *slang*) to cheat in an exam; (*v.i.*) to stick close; (*v.r.*) to cling, to adhere, stick; (*m.*) collar, necklace.—**de afastamento**, a spacing ring or washer.—**grau**, to receive a (college) degree.
colarinho (*m.*) shirt collar; neck; (*slang*) head of foam on a glass of beer; (*Arch.*) necking or collarino.—**baixo**, turn-down collar.—**de bico**, wing collar.—**mole**, soft collar.
colatário (*m.*) **-ria** (*f.*) the one upon whom a benefice or degree is bestowed.
colateral (*adj.*) collateral.
colato (*m., Biochem.*) cholate.
colcha (*f.*) bed spread, counterpane, coverlet.—**de retalhos**, crazy quilt.
colchão (*m.*) mattress.—**de molas**, spring mattress.—**de noiva**, roly-poly (a pastry).
colcheia (*f., Music*) an 8th note. **semi**—, a 16th.
colcheiro -ra (*m.,f.*) maker and/or seller of bedspreads. Cf. COLCHOEIRO.
colchêta (*f.*) the eye of a hook-and-eye fastener.
colchête (*m.*) the hook of a hook-and-eye fastener; an S-shaped meat hook; a belt clamp; (*pl., Printing*) brackets, crotchets.—**de gancho**, hook-and-eye fastener. —**de pressão**, a snap fastener.
colchicina (*f., Chem.*) colchicine [= COLQUICINA].
colchoaria (*f.*) mattress and pillow shop.
colchoeiro (*m.*) mattress maker or dealer. Cf. COLCHEIRO.
colcotar (*m., Chem.*) colcothar.
coldre [ó] (*m.*) holster.
coleado -da (*adj.*) sinuous; winding.
colear (*v.i.*) to crawl, glide, slither (as a snake); to wind (as a river); to wriggle, wiggle; (*v.t.*) to throw (a steer) by twisting his tail.
coleção (*f.*) collection, accumulation.—**de amostras**, set of samples.—**de livros**, set of books.
colecionação (*f.*) collecting.
colecionador -dora (*m.,f.*) collector. Cf. COLETOR.
colecionar (*v.t.*) to collect, compile.

colecistectomia (f., Surg.) cholecystectomy, gall bladder removal.
colecistotomia (f., Surg.) cholecystotomy.
colega (m.,f.) colleague, fellow-member; classmate, schoolmate; chum, pal, crony.
colegiada (f.) student body; (Eccl.) college (chapter of canons); a collegiate church.
colegial (m.) schoolboy; (f.) schoolgirl; (pl.) school children; (adj.) collegial, collegiate.
colégio (m.) primary or secondary school; also college, but only in the sense of a society of person engaged in a common pursuit, as an electoral college, a society of scholars, a chapter of canons, etc. [The Port. equivalent of college, in the sense of institution of higher learning, is ESCOLA SUPERIOR or FACULDADE.]
coleguismo (m.) esprit de corps; loyalty to a colleague; cronyism.
coleira (f.) collar for dogs, etc.—branca, the white-collared peccary; = CAITITU.
coleirado –da (adj.) of dogs, etc., wearing a collar.
coleirinha (f.) = BIGODE (bird).
coleiro (m.) any of various seed-eating birds of genus Sporophila, all c.a. PAPA-CAPIM.—do-brejo,—de-sapé, the collared seed-eater (Sporophila c. collaris), c.a. BREJAL; Natterer's seed-eater (S. bouvreuil pilleata).—-virado, the screaming seed-eater (S. c. caerulescens).—-da-bahia,—da-serra, the yellow-bellied seed-eater (S. n. nigricollis), c.a. PAPA-CAPIM, GRAVATINHA.
colelitíase (f., Med.) cholelithiasis.
colélito (m.) gallstone; = CÁLCULO BILIAR.
colemanita (f., Min.) colemanite.
colemia (f., Med.) cholemia.
colendo –da (adj.) deserving respect; of court, venerable.
colênquima (f., Bot.) collenchyma.
cóleo (m., Bot.) the common coleus (C. blumei).
coleóptero –ra (adj., Zool.) coleopteral, coleopterous; (m.pl.) the Coleoptera.
coleorriza (f., Bot.) coleorhiza.
cólera (f.) choler, anger, rage, wrath, ire; (Med.; Veter.) cholera.—asiatica, Asiatic cholera.—infantil, cholera infantum.—-morbo, cholera morbus.—nostras, cholera morbus. acesso de—, fit of rage. verde de—, white with anger. onda de—, fit of anger.
colérico –ca (adj.) choleric, angry, enraged, wrathful; inflamed with anger.
coleriforme (adj.) choleriform, resembling cholera.
colerígeno –na (adj., Med.) cholerigenous.
colerina (f., Med.) cholerine.
colerofobia, coleromania (f., Med.) cholerophobia.
colesteatoma (m., Med.) cholesteatoma.
colesterato (m., Biochem.) cholesterate.
colestérico –ca (adj., Biochem.) cholesteric.
colesterina (f., Biochem.) cholesterin, cholesterol.
colesterinuria (f., Med.) cholesteroluria.
colesterol (m., Biochem.) cholesterol.
coleta (f.) assessment; church collection.
colêta (f.) bull-fighter's pigtail.
coletâneo –nea (adj.) of writings, excerpted, collected, compiled; (f.) collectanea.
coletar (v.t.) to assess; to collect.
coletário (m., Eccl.) a service book containing collects.
colête (m.) corset; vest.—de fôrças, straitjacket.—-de couro = CINTO-DE-COURO.
coletividade (f.) collectivity; collective body, assemblage, company, group; community.
coletivismo (m.) collectivism.
coletivista (adj.; m.,f.) collectivist.
coletivo –va (adj.) collective; (m., Gram.) collective noun.
coleto –ta (adj.) collected, gathered together; (m., Bot.) the point on a stem at which the roots begin.
coletor –tora (adj.) collecting; (m.,f.) tax collector; (m.) any device or receptacle in which something collects or is collected; (Elec.) collector.—de escapamento, exhaust manifold.—de pó, dust chamber. Cf. COLECIONADOR.
coletoria (f.) tax-collector's office.
colgadura (f.) wall hanging, drapery.
colgar (v.t.) to hang (draperies).
colha [ô] (f.) harvest of rubber latex.
colhedor –deira (adj.) gathering; (m.,f.) gatherer; (m.pl., Naut.) upper mast shrouds; (f.) harvester (machine).
colheireiro (m.) = AJAJÁ.
colheirinha (f.) = CAURÉ.
colheita (f.) harvest; harvesting; harvest time; crop.—de banana, banana crop.

colher [é] (f.) spoon; ladle; spoonful.—de café, small coffee spoon(ful).—de chá, teaspoon(ful).—de fundição, foundry ladle.—de pedreiro, mason's or bricklayer's trowel.—de sopa, soupspoon(ful).
colhêr (v.t.) to pick, pluck (flowers, fruit, etc.); to garner, gather; to furl (sails); to seize, take unawares.—de surpresa, to take by surprise.
colherada (f.) spoonful.
colherão (m.) ladle.
colhereiro (m.) = AJAJÁ and ARAPAPÁ.
colheril, colherim (m.) a stuccoer's pointing trowel.
colhimento (m.) gathering (garnering, picking, plucking) of fruit, flowers, etc.
coliambo (m., Pros.) choliamb.
colibacilo (m., Bacteriol.) coli.
colibacilose (f., Med.) colibacillosis.
colibri [brí] (m.) humming bird; c.a. BEIJA-FLOR, PICA-FLOR, CHUPA-MEL, CHUPA-FLOR.
cólico –ca (adj.) colonic; cholic; colic; (f.) colic.
colidir (v.i.) to collide, clash. [Noun: COLISÃO]
coligação (f.) coalition, alliance, confederation; conspiracy, plot.
coligar [3](v.t.) to bind together.
coligir (v.t.) to collect, compile.—dados, to gather data.
colimação (f.) collimation.
colimador (m., Optics) collimator.
colimar (v.t.) to envisage; (Astron., Physics) to collimate.
colímbidas (m.pl., Zool.) the grebe family (Colymbidae).
colimbo (m., Zool.) the typical family (Columbus) of grebes.
colimbriense (adj.; m.,f.) = COIMBRÃO, –BRÃ.
colina (f.) hill, foothill, mound; (Biochem.) choline.
colinoso –sa (adj.) hilly.
colinsônia (f., Bot.) the citranella horsebalm (Collinsonia canadensis).
coliquação (f., Med.) colliquation.
colírio (m., Med.) collyrium, eyewash, eye drops.
colisa (f., Zool.) the dwarf gouramie (Trichogaster lalia), popular in home aquaria.
colisão (f.) collision, crash. [Verb: COLIDIR]
coliseu (m.) coliseum, stadium.
colite (f., Med.) colitis.
colmado (m.) straw hut [= PALHOÇA].
colmar (v.t.) to thatch; to heighten, elevate, heap up.
colmatar (v.t.) to build up a lowland by flooding it with silt-laden water.
colmeagem (f.) hiving of bees.
colmeal (m.) apiary.
colmeeiro (m.) –ra (f.) beekeeper.
colmeia (f.) beehive; swarm of bees.
colmilho (m.) tusk; fang; claw; a horse's canine.
côlmo (m.) straw; (Bot.) culm. cabana de—, thatched hut.
Col.º = COLÉG.º (College; School).
colo (m.) neck; bosom; lap; gorge; (Anat.) colon [= CÓLON].—duma garrafa, neck of a bottle. ao—, in arms (ref. to an infant).
colóbio (m.) colobium; dalmatic.
coloboma (f., Med.) coloboma.
coloca (m., slang) a buyer of pawn tickets.
colocação (f.) act of placing; placement; position, job; place, standing (as of a soccer team).
colocar (v.t.) to place, put, set in place; to place in a job; (v.r.) to place oneself; to find a job.—(alguma coisa) nos eixos, to set (matters) right.
colocásia (f., Bot.) the elephant's-ear (Colocasia), esp. C. antiquorum (taro). Cf. TAIOBA and INHAME.
colocentese (f., Surg.) colocentesis.
colocíntida, colocíntide (f., Bot.) the colocynth (Citrullus colocynthis).
colóclise (f., Med.) cloclysis.
colódio (m., Chem.) colodion.
colofão (m., Chem.) colophon.
colofênio (m., Chem.) colophene.
cólofon (m.) = COLOFÃO.
colofônia (f.) colophony, rosin.
cologarítmo (m., Math.) cologarithm.
coloidal (adj.) colloidal.
colóide (m.) colloidal; (m., Physical Chem.) colloid.
coloma (m., Med.) colloid carcinoma.
Colômbia (f.) Colombia.
colombiano –na (adj.) Columbian; Colombian; (m.,f.) Colombian.
colômbio (m., Chem.) columbium, niobium.
colombita (f., Chem.) columbite, niobite.

colombofilia (*f.*) = COLUMBOFILIA.
colombófilo –la (*m.,f.*) = COLUMBÓFILO.
colomi [í] (*m.*) boy; Indian boy; servant.
cólon (*m.*, *Anat.*) colon [= COLO].
colonada (*f.*) a group of colonists. [But not colonnade, which is COLUNATA.]
colonato (*m.*) status or condition of a colonist.
colônia (*f.*) colony; [*cap.*] Cologne.
colonial (*adj.*) colonial.
colonialismo (*m.*) colonialism; the early colonial days (of Brazil).
colonião (*m.*) = CAPIM-DA-COLÔNIA.
colônico –ca (*adj.*) colony; colonist; colonial.
colonização (*f.*) colonization.
colonizador –dora (*adj.*) colonizing; (*m.,f.*) colonizer.
colonizar (*v.t.*) to colonize, settle.
colono –na (*m.,f.*) colonist, settler; (*m.*) tenant farmer.
colopatia (*f.*, *Med.*) colonopathy.
colopexia (*f.*, *Surg.*) colopexia, colonopexy.
coloquial (*adj.*) colloquial.
colóquio (*m.*) colloquy.
coloração (*f.*) coloration.
colorado –da (*adj.*) reddish, ruddy.
coloradoíta (*f.*, *Min.*) coloradoite; natural mercury telluride.
colorante (*adj.*) coloring.
colorar (*v.*) = COLORIR.
colorau (*m.*) red pepper powder.
colorear (*v.t.*) to color [= COLORIR]; to disguise; (*v.i.*) to show red.
colorido –da (*adj.*) bright-colored; (*m.*) color(ing); vivid coloring.
colorífico –ca (*adj.*) colorific.
colorimetria (*f.*) colorimetry.
colorímetro (*m.*) colorimeter.
colorir [25] (*v.t.*) to color; to brighten with color; to describe in bright colors.
colorista (*m.,f.*) colorist; a colorful writer.
colorização (*f.*) a showing or changing of color.
colorizar (*v.*) = COLORIR.
colossal (*adj.*) colossal.
colossalidade (*f.*) colossality.
colosso [lô] (*m.*) colossus; (*colloq.*) something good; lots of something.
colostomia (*f.*, *Surg.*) colostomy.
colostração (*f.*, *Med.*) colostration.
colostro (*m.*) colostrum.
colotifo (*m.*, *Med.*) colotyphoid.
colotomia (*f.*, *Surg.*) colotomy.
colpite (*f.*, *Med.*) colpitis.
colportagem (*f.*) colportage.
colportor (*m.*) colporteur.
colquicáceas (*f.pl.*, *Bot.*) = MELANTEÁCEAS.
colquicina (*f.*, *Chem.*) colchicine.
cólquico (*m.*) autumn crocus (*Colchicum*), c.a. DAMA-NUA, DEDO-DE-MERCÚRIO, LÍRIO-VERDE, NARCISO-DO-OUTONO, FALSO-AÇAFRÃO.
coltar (*m.*) coal tar.
colubreado –da (*adj.*) shaped like a snake.
colubre(j)ar (*v.i.*) to crawl or move like a snake.
colúbridas, colubrídeos (*m.pl.*) the Colubridae (largest family of snakes).
colubrino –na (*adj.*) colubrine, snakelike; (*f.*) culverin (ancient firearm); (*Bot.*) a genus (*Colubrina*) of tropical American shrubs of the buckthorn family.
columbário (*m.*) columbarium.
Colúmbia (*f.*) Columbia.
columbicultor –tora (*m.,f.*) pigeon fancier.
columbicultura (*f.*) pigeon-raising.
columbiformes (*m.pl.*) the Columbiformes (pigeons, doves, etc.)
columbino –na (*adj.*) of or pert. to the District of Columbia; columbine; of a dove; dovelike; (*m.pl.*, *Zool.*) the Columbidae (pigeon and dove family).
columbofilia (*f.*) raising of carrier pigeons. Var. COLOMBOFILIA.
columbófilo –la (*m.,f.*) pigeon fancier. Var. COLOMBÓFILO.
columela (*f.*, *Arch.*, *Anat.*, *Bacteriol.*, *Bot.*, *Zool.*) columella.
coluna (*f.*) column; pillar; military column; column of figures.**—de comando**, (*Aeron.*) control column.**—embutida**, (*Arch.*) pilaster.**—por um**, (*Mil.*) single file.**—por dois**, (*Mil.*) column of two, double file.**—vertebral**, spinal column. **quinta—**, fifth column.

colunar (*adj.*) columnar.
colunata (*f.*) colonnade.
colunelo (*m.*) –neta [ê] (*f.*) a small column.
coluria (*f.*, *Med.*) choluria.
coluro (*m.*, *Astron.*, *Geog.*) colure.
colusão (*f.*) collusion [= CONLUIO].
colútea (*f.*, *Bot.*) common bladder senna (*Colutea arborescens*), c.a. ESPANTA-LÔBOS.
colutório (*m.*, *Med.*) collutory, mouthwash.
coluvião (*m.*) = INUNDAÇÃO.
colza [ô] (*f.*, *Bot.*) rape (*Brassica napus* and *B. campestris*).
com. = COMANDANTE (commandant, commander); COMENDADOR (which see).
com (*prep.*) with.**—a bôca cheia de risos**, all smiles.**—a bôca na botija**, [caught] in the act.**—a cabeça no ar**, absent-mindedly.**—a condição que**, on condition that.**—ambas as mãos**, wholeheartedly.**—a orelha em pé**, or **—a pulga atrás da orelha**, on one's guard, suspicious.**—a redea na mão**, cautiously, wisely.**—as mãos vazias**, with empty hands.**—conhecimento de causa**, with full knowledge.**—desembaraço**, with ease, readily.**—dia**, before nightfall.**—efeito**, in effect,**—fé formada**, with full faith.**—freqüência**, frequently.**—igualdade**, equally.**—jeito**, skillfully, adroitly.**—mão intrépida**, fearlessly.**—mão larga**, generously.**—o ôlho aberto**, with eyes open.**—os olhos baixos**, with lowered eyes.**—os olhos fechados**, blindly.**—o suor do rosto**, by the sweat of one's brow.**—pés de ladrão**, stealthily.**—pouco**, soon, shortly.**—propósito**, purposefully.**—que**, so that; and so.**—razão**, truly.**—referência a**, with reference to, regarding.**—relevância a**, advantageously.**—respeito a**, with respect to.**—risco de**, at the risk of.**—segurança**, safely.**—tempo**, slowly.**—tôdas as letras**, literally, in full, with all details.**—todos os sacramentos**, (*colloq.*) with nothing wanting.**—vistas a**, with a view to.**—uma mão atrás e outra adiante**, with empty hands.**—uma mão sôbre a outra**, with folded hands.**—unhas e dentes**, with tooth and nail.**—vontade**, willingly.
coma (*f.*) head of hair; tuft; mane; coma, stupor; comma [more usual: VÍRGULA]; (*Music*) pause, rest; (*pl.*) quotation marks [more usual: ASPAS].
comadre (*f.*) a godmother [MADRINHA] in relation to her godchild's parents; a child's mother in relation to its godparents; crony; (*colloq.*) midwife; hot-water bottle; a bed pan [= APARADEIRA]; a gossip; (*pl.*) hemorrhoids. Cf. COMPADRE.**—-do-azeite**, (*Bot.*) the Jamaica navel spurge (*Omphalea diandra*), c.a. CAIATÉ.
comandá (*f.*) any of various pea vines.
comandaíba (*f.*, *Bot.*) a sophora (*S. tomentosa*), c.a. CAMBUÍ-DA-RESTINGA, FEIJÃO-DA-PRAIA.
comandância (*f.*) commandery.
comandanta (*f.*, *colloq.*) commander's wife.
comandante (*adj.*) commanding; (*m.*) commander; leader; captain of a ship; skipper; senior naval officer.**—-em-chefe**, commander-in-chief.
comandar (*v.t.*) to command; to direct; to rule; to dominate, overlook (as from a superior position).
comandita (*f.*) a partnership in which there are one or more silent partners who contribute funds but are liable only for the capital invested; a temporary joint-venture arrangement.
comanditar (*v.t.*) to furnish funds as a silent partner in a COMANDITA.
comanditário –ria (*m.,f.*) a silent partner who invests in a COMANDITA.
comando (*m.*) command, control.**—automático**, automatic control. **duplo—**, (*Aeron.*) dual control. **tomar o—**, to assume (take) control. **voz de—**, word of command.
comarca (*f.*) a judicial district presided over by a district judge.
cômaro (*m.*, *Bot.*) the marsh cinquefoil (*Potentilla palustris*).
comatoso –sa (*adj.*) comatose.
comátula (*f.*, *Zool.*) comatulid, feather star.
combalido –da (*adj.*) enfeebled, weakened; of fruit, over-ripe.
combalir [46] (*v.t.*) to weaken, sap, undermine, stagger.
combate (*m.*) combat, fight, battle, conflict; duel.**—de corpo a corpo**, hand to hand fighting. **fora de—**, *hors de combat;* out of the fight, disabled.
combatente (*adj.*) fighting; (*m.*) combatant, fighter. **não—**, noncombatant.
combater (*v.t.*) combat, oppose, struggle with; to fight, contend.

combatividade (*f.*) combativeness.
combativo –**va** (*adj.*) combative, pugnacious.
combinação (*f.*) combination, association; arrangement; agreement; slip (woman's undergarment); (*pl.*, *Math.*) combinations.
combinado –**da** (*adj.*) combined, joined, united; agreed; (*m.*) agreement; (*Chem.*) compound; (*Sports*) a scratch team; (*f.*, *Agric.*) combine, threshing machine.
combinador –**dora** (*adj.*) combining; (*m.,f.*) combiner.
combinar (*v.t.*) to combine, join together; to adjust, arrange, compose; to agree upon; to blend, compound.— **com,** to match, go well with; to agree with.
combinável (*adj.*) combinable.
comboiar (*v.t.*) to convoy.
comboieiro (*m.*) escort of a convoy.
comboio (*m.*) convoy, ships under escort; wagon train; pack train; (in Portugal) a railroad train;—-**correio,** mail train.
comborça [bó] (*f.*) a mistress in relation to her lover's wife or to another of his concubines.
comborço [bô] (*m.*) an illicit lover in relation to his mistress's husband or to another of her lovers.
combretáceas (*f.pl.*, *Bot.*) = MIRABOLÂNEAS.
combreto (*m.*, *Bot.*) the genus Combretum.
combro (*m.*) = CÔMORO.
combuca (*f.*) = CUIAMBUCA.
comburente (*adj.*) comburent, burning.
comburir (*v.t.*) to burn [= QUEIMAR].
combustão (*f.*) combustion.
combustar (*v.*) = QUEIMAR (burn).
combustibilidade (*f.*) combustibility.
combustível (*adj.*) combustible; (*m.*) fuel.—**antidetonante,** antiknock fuel.—**mineral,** coal. **indicador de—,** fuel gauge. **suprir-se de—,** to fuel or to refuel.
combustor [tôr] (*m.*) street-lamp, street light.
com.ᵉ = COMADRE.
come-aranha[s] (*f.*) any spider wasp or tarantula killer, esp. of the genus Pepsis.
começador –**dora** (*adj.*) beginning; (*m.,f.*) beginner.
comecante (*adj.*) commencing, incipient.
começar (*v.t.*) to commence, begin, start (**a,** to); to initiate; to originate.—**por,** to begin by. **Começa a chover,** It is beginning to rain.
começo (*m.*) commencement, beginning; onset. **dar—a,** to begin (something). **de—,** at the start. **ter—,** to begin, start.
comedão (*m.*, *Med.*) comedo, blackhead.
comedeira (*f.*) graft, peculation.
comedela (*f.*) victuals, rations; illicit gain, graft.
comedia (*f.*) pasture; feeding grounds; a place where wild animals find fallen fruit [= MESA].
comédia (*f.*) comedy, farce.—**de pastelão,** slapstick comedy.—**musicada,** musical comedy.
comediante (*m.,f.*) comedian, player.
comediar (*v.t.*) to turn into a comedy; to render comic.
comedido –**da** (*adj.*) moderate; temperate; respectful; unobtrusive.—**nos louvores,** sparing of praise.
comedimento (*m.*) moderation.
comediógrafo –**fa** (*m.,f.*) author of comedies; playwright.
comedir [25] (*v.t.*) to moderate, temper; to regulate, repress; (*v.r.*) to restrain oneself.
comedista (*m.,f.*) = COMEDIÓGRAFO.
comedor –**dora** (*adj.*) eating; (*m.,f.*) eater; glutton; wastrel; parasite.—**de formiga,** one who eats ants—a nickname applied by citizens of Santos to those of the city of S. Paulo.
comedoria(s) (*f.,pl.*) victuals, rations.
comedouro –**ra** (*adj.*) good to eat; (*m.*) feeding place; food trough, feed box. Var. COMEDOIRO.
comelina (*f.*) any dayflower (*Commelina*).
comelináceas, comelíneas (*f.pl.*) the spiderwort family (*Commelinaceae*).
côme-longe (*m.,f.*) geophagist, clay eater.
comemoração (*f.*) commemoration.
comemorar (*v.t.*) to commemorate, celebrate, solemnize.
comemorativo –**va** (*adj.*) commemorative.
comemorável (*adj.*) commemorable.
comenda (*f.*, *Eccl.*) commendam; a medieval commandery.
comendadeira, fem. of COMENDADOR.
comendador (*m.*) commander (a religio-military honorary title); (*Eccl.*) commendator.
comendativa –**va** (*adj.*) commendatory; laudatory.
comenos (*m.*) instant. **nesse—,** at that moment.
comensal (*m.,f.*) each of persons eating together; fellow-

boarder, messmate; table guest; (*Biol.*) commensal.
comensalismo (*m.*, *Biol.*) commensalism; symbiosis.
comensurável (*adj.*) commensurable.
comentação (*f.*) commentation.
comentado –**da** (*adj.*) commented upon; talked about, discussed (critically).
comentador –**dora** (*m.,f.*) commentator.
comentar (*v.t.*) to comment on or upon; to remark about; to discuss; to annotate; to animadvert upon, find fault with.
comentário (*m.*) comment, annotation; commentary; animadversion, aspersion.
comentarista (*m.,f.*) commentator; columnist.
comento (*m.*) commentary; a classical translation for school use.
comer (*v.t.*) to eat; to consume; to devour; to devastate; to corrode; to swallow (accept without question or suspicion); to jump (a man at checkers); (*v.i.*) to eat; to practice graft; (*v.r.*) to be consumed with anger; (*m.*) food.—**a abarrotar,** to eat to overfulness.—**a isca,** to take the bait (lit. & fig.).—**à farta,** to eat one's fill.—**bola,** (*slang*) to accept bribes or graft.—**com os olhos,** to gaze upon with lust or avarice.—**como um boi,** or **como um padre,** to eat hugely.—**de colhér,** to have things easy; to live on handouts.—**môsca,** to be taken in; to draw the wrong conclusions.—**o pão que o Diabo amassou** (or **que o Diabo enjeitou**), to have a hard time earning a living.— **os olhos a,** to extort money from.—**pela mão de,** to be under the thumb of.—**por uma perna,** to deceive, fool. —**uma pedra,** to jump a man (in checkers). **dar de—a,** to feed. **O gato comeu,** The cat got it (referring to the unexplained disappearance of something).
comercial (*adj.*) commercial. **direito—,** commercial law. **marca—,** trade mark.
comercialista (*adj.*) versed in commercial law; (*m.,f.*) one so versed.
comercializar (*v.t.*) to commercialize.
comerciante (*adj.*) trading; (*m.*) trader, tradesman, merchant, dealer, business man.
comerciar (*v.i.*) to trade, engage in business, have dealings with (someone).
comerciário –**ria** (*m.,f.*) anyone engaged in trade; commercial employee.
comerciável (*adj.*) marketable, negotiable.
comércio (*m.*) commerce, trade, business.—**exterior (interior),** foreign (domestic) commerce.
comes (*m.pl.*, *colloq.*) "eats", "vittles".—**e bebes,** food and drink.
comestível (*adj.*) edible, eatable; (*m.*) food; (*pl.*) comestibles, edibles.
cometa [ê] (*m.*) comet; drummer, traveling salesman.
cometedor –**dora** (*m.,f.*) perpetrator (of a crime).
cometer (*v.t.*) to commit, perpetrate.—**a,** to entrust to.
cometida (*f.*) an attack.
cometimento (*m.*) an undertaking; commitment.
comezaina (*f.*, *colloq.*) a big feed [= PAPAZANA].
comezinho –**nha** (*adj.*) simple, plain, every-day; good to eat.
comichão (*f.*) itch, itching; fig., burning desire.
comichar (*v.i.*) to itch; to feel ticklish.
comichoso –**sa** (*adj.*) itchy.
comicidade (*f.*) comicality.
comício (*m.*) meeting, assembly.—**monstro,** monster mass meeting.—**popular,** public rally.
cômico –**ca** (*adj.*) comic(al), droll, funny, ludicrous; clownish; (*m.*) comedian; (*f.*) comedienne.
comido –**da** (*adj.*) eaten, swallowed, consumed; (*f.*) food; meals; rations; board, fare. **dar—a,** to feed. **quarto e—,** room and board.
comigo (*pron.*) with me; to myself.—**mesmo,** with myself.
comilança, comilância (*f.*) much eating; (*colloq.*) graft.
comilão –**lona** (*adj.*) gluttonous; (*m.,f.*) glutton, gorger.
cominação (*f.*) commination.
cominador –**dora** (*adj.*) threatening; (*m.,f.*) one who threatens.
cominar (*v.t.*) to threaten punishment or vengeance.
cominativo –**va,** –**tório** –**ria** (*adj.*) comminatory.
cominho (*m.*, *Bot.*) cumin (*Cuminum cyminum*).— -**armênio,** common caper (*Capparis spinosa*).— -**prêto,** garden fennelflower (*Nigella sativa*).
cominuir (*v.t.*) to comminute; pulverize; triturate.
cominuto –**ta** (*adj.*) comminute.
comiseração (*f.*) commiseration, compassion, pity, sympathy.

comiserador –dora (*adj.*) commiserating.
comiserar (*v.t.*) to arouse pity in or for. (*v.r.*) to commiserate.—–**se de,** to pity, feel sorry for.
comiserativo –va (*adj.*) pitiable.
comissão (*f.*) committee; commission (all senses); commitment.
comissariado (*m.*) commissioner's office.
comissário (*m.*) commissioner, agent; ship's purser; steward.—**adjunto,** joint commissioner.—**de bordo,** ship's purser.—**de polícia,** police commissioner.
comissionar (*v.t.*) to commission.
comisso (*m.*) a fine or penalty for non-compliance with the law or with the terms of a contract.
comissura (*f.*) joint, seam, closure; cleft, juncture; (*Anat., Zool.*) commissure.—**das pálpebras,** corner of the eye where upper and lower eyelids meet.—**dos lábios,** corner of the mouth; angle of the lips.
comitê (*m.*) committee [= COMISSÃO]. **em**—, in private.
comitente (*adj.*) committing; constituent; (*m.,f.*) one who commits; consignor; constituent.
comitiva (*f.*) retinue, train, followers, escort.—**presidencial,** presidential party.
comível (*adj.*) eatable [= COMESTÍVEL].
como (*adv.*) how, by what means; in what way; to what degree; for what reason; in what condition; by what name; (*conj.*) as, like, similar to, in the same manner that; because, since, for the reason that; while, at the same time that.—**assim?** How so?—**é que,** how is it that.—**foi vendida a casa?** At what price was the house sold?—**não!** Why certainly! Of course! Why not!—**que,** like, as if; (*colloq.*) like nothing, like everything.—**quer,** probably, possibly.—**quer que seja,** howsoever, however it may be.—**se,** as if, as though.—**sempre,** as always, as usual.—**um só homem,** as one man, unanimously.—**vai você?** How are you? How do you do? **assim**—, as well as, also. **Não há**—**êle,** There is no one like him. **seja**—**fôr,** Be that as it may. **tal**—**deve ser,** just as it ought to be. **tão . . . como . . . , as . . . as . . .**
comoção (*f.*) commotion, agitation, disturbance; tumult; flurry; perturbation; shock; riot.
cômoda (*f.*) commode, chest of crawers; dresser.
comodante (*m.,f., Law*) one who makes a loan of commodatum.
comodatário –ria (*m.,f., Law*) commodatary.
comodato (*m., Law*) commodatum.
comodidade (*f.*) comfort, ease; coziness; convenience. [But not commodity, which is ARTIGO DE CONSUMO.]
comodismo (*m.*) self-seeking, selfishness, self-indulgence.
comodista (*adj.*) self-seeking, self-indulgent, selfish; (*m.,f.*) a self-seeking person.
cômodo –da (*adj.*) comfortable, convenient, cozy, handy, suitable; (*m.*) room, apartment.—**mobiliado,** furnished room.
comodoro [dó] (*m.*) commodore.
cômoro (*m.*) hillock, mound, knoll, hummock.
comovedor –dora, –vente (*adj.*) stirring, moving, affecting; impressive.
comover (*v.t.*) to disturb, agitate; to move, affect, touch, fill with emotion; (*v.r.*) to be moved.
comovido –da (*adj.*) moved, touched; overcome with emotion; excited.
comp. = COMPANHIA (company of soldiers); COMPOSTO (compound).
compadecer (*v.t.*) to pity; to deplore.—**se de,** to feel sorry for, take pity on: to relent; to condole with.—**se com,** to be compatible with.
compadecimento (*m.*) commiseration, condolence; concordance.
compadre (*m.*) a godfather [= PADRINHO] in relation to the godchild's parents; a child's father in relation to its godparents; intimate friend, crony, pal; each member of a scheme. Cf. COMADRE.
compadrice (*f.*), **compadrio** (*m.*) compaternity; excessive favoritism.
compadrismo (*m.*) political favoritism and patronage; cronyism.
compaginar (*v.t.*) to unite, knit or hold together.
compaixão (*f.*) compassion, pity, sympathy.
companheira (*f.*) female companion; wife, mate.
companheirão (*m.*) faithful (unfailing, understanding) friend.
companheirismo (*m.*) fellowship, comradeship, companionship.
companheiro –ra (*adj.*) companion, accompanying; (*m.*)

companion, comrade, mate; chum, pal, buddy.—**de chapa,** running mate.—**de trabalho,** fellow-worker.—**de viagem,** fellow-traveler, traveling companion.
companhia (*f.*) company; firm, concern; assemblage, gathering; companionship, fellowship. [But not company in the sense of visitors, which is VISITAS.] **fazer**—**com (alguém),** to keep (someone) company. **em**—**de,** accompanied by, in the company of.
cômpar [-es] (*adj.*) equal similar, or on a par with.
comparabilidade (*f.*) comparativeness.
comparação (*f.*) comparison.
comparador –dora (*adj.*) comparing; (*m.,f.*) comparer; (*m., Physics, Physical Chem., etc.*) comparator.
comparar (*v.t.*) to compare (com, with; a, to); (*v.r.*) to compare oneself with.
comparativo –va (*adj.*) comparative; (*m., Gram.*) comparative degree.
comparável (*adj.*) comparable.
comparecer (*v.i.*) to appear, attend, be present.—**em pêso,** to show up (attend) in a body.—**em pessoa,** to appear in person. **não**—, not show up, fail to appear.
comparecimento (*m.*) appearance, attendance. **não**—, non-appearance.
comparoquiano –na (*m.,f.*) fellow-parishioner.
comparsa (*m.,f.*) a stage super; a bit player; player of a minor role in anything; accomplice, partner.
comparsaria (*f.*) stage throng.
compartilhar (*v.t.*) to share with, partake of, participate in.—**de uma opinion,** to share another's opinion.
compartimento (*m.*) compartment; a room.—**estanque,** airtight compartment.
compartir (*v.t.*) to divide and share.
compáscuo (*m.*) common pasture.
compassado –da (*adj.*) slow; measured, unhurried.
compassageiro (*m.*) –ra (*f.*) fellow-passenger.
compassar (*v.t.*) to compass, measure; to space; to slow down; (*Music*) to beat time for.
compassivo –va (*adj.*) compassionate, sympathetic, tenderhearted, humane.
compasso (*m.*) compass, dividers; draftsman's compasses [but not a mariner's compass, which is BÚSSOLA]; (*Music*) time; measure, bar.—**de calibre,** inside calipers.—**de corrediça** slide caliper [= PAQUÍMETRO].—**de espessura,** outside calipers.—**de quadrante,** carpenter's quadrant compass.—**de redução,** proportional compass.—**simples,** dividers.—**tira-linhas,** a drawing compass. **bater o**—, to beat time. **em**—, or **dentro do**—, in step with, or in time with, the music.
compatibilidade (*f.*) compatibility.
compatível (*adj.*) compatible.
compatrício –cia (*m.*) fellow-countryman; (*f.*) fellow-countrywoman.
compatriota (*adj.*) compatriotic; (*m.,f.*) compatriot, fellow-citizen.
comp.ᵉ = COMPADRE.
compelação (*f., Law*) arraignment.
compelir [21a] (*v.t.*) to compel, force, oblige, constrain.
compendiar (*v.t.*) to sum up.
compêndio (*m.*) compendium, abridgment, summary; textbook.
compendioso –sa (*adj.*) compendious, brief.
compenetrado –da (*adj.*) inwardly convinced; (*colloq.*) smug.
compenetrar (*v.t.*) to convince (de, of);—**se de,** to penetrate, understand; to convince oneself that.
compensação (*f.*) compensation; indemnification; clearance (of checks). **em**—, on the other hand.
compensador –dora (*adj.*) compensating; (*m.,f.*) compensator.
compensar (*v.t.*) to compensate, indemnify; to recompense; to offset (losses); to counterbalance; to pay, be worthwhile.
compensativo –va (*adj.*) compensating.
compensatório –ria (*adj.*) compensatory.
compensável (*adj.*) compensable.
competência (*f.*) competence, capability, ability; competition; contest, conflict; (Law) competence.
competente (*adj.*) competent, able, capable, qualified; due, proper, suitable, fit.
competição (*f.*) competition, contest, rivalry.
competidor –dora (*adj.*) competing, competitive; (*m.,f.*) competitor, rival, antagonist.
competir [21a] (*v.i.*) to compete (**com,** with); to behoove; to be incumbent on.—**a,** to be due (belong to).

compilação (f.) compilation. Var. COPILAÇÃO.
compilador –**dora** (adj.) compiling; (m.,f.) compiler. Var. COPILADOR.
compilar (v.t.) to compile. Var. COPILAR.
compilatório –**ria** (adj.) compilatory. Var. COPILATÓRIO.
compita (f.) rivalry.
cômpito (m.) crossroads [= ENCRUZILHADA]; measure; pattern.
complacência (f.) complaisance, affability, desire to please. [But not complacence in the sense of self-satisfaction, which is SATISFAÇÃO DE SI MESMO.]
complacente (adj.) complaisant, affable, desirous of pleasing; accommodating; willing. [But not complacent in the sense of self-satisfied, which is CONVENCIDO, SATISFEITO.]
compleição (f.) build, physical make-up (of a person); temperament, disposition. [But not complexion in the sense of coloring of the face, which is O COLORIDO DA TEZ.] **de forte**—, stalwart, well-built.
complementar, –**tário**, –**ria** (adj.) complementary.
complemento (m.) complement.
completação (f.) completion.
completador –**dora** (adj.) completing; (m.,f.) completer.
completamente (adv.) completely, quite, wholly, entirely.
completamento (m.) completion; finishing.
completar (v.t.) to complete, finish; to accomplish; to fill. **Hoje completa vinte anos**, He is twenty today.
completo –**ta** (adj.) complete, completed, finished; perfect; entire, whole; all-round; (m.) the whole; (f.pl., Ecc.) Complin [= COMPLETÓRIO]. **por**—, completely.
complexão [ks] (m.) a combination or complex. [But not complexion in the sense of coloring, which is O COLORIDO DA TEZ.]
complexidade [ks] (f.) complexity.
complexo –**xa** [ks] (adj.) complex, manifold; complicated, intricate; (m.) a complex whole; a complex number; a psychological complex.—**cultural**, (Anthrop.) culture complex.—**brasileiro**, (Geol.) Brazilian complex.
complicação (f.) complication; obstacle, difficulty.
complicado –**da** (adj.) complicated, involved, entangled; intricate; complex; elaborate.
complicador –**dora** (adj.) complicating; (m.,f.) one who complicates matters.
complicar (v.t.) to complicate, render complex or intricate to tangle; (v.r.) to become complicated.
complô (m.) complot, scheme, conspiracy.
componedor (m.) a composing (printer's) stick; typesetter.
componente (adj.) component, composing; (m.) component, constituent, ingredient, component part.
componista (m.,f.) composer (of music).
compor [63] (v.t.) to compose, compound, frame, put together, make up; to set type; to write, create; to arrange, adjust, repair; to tranquilize, assuage, soothe. —**se de**, to consist of, be made up of, be composed of.
comporta (f.) canal lock; floodgate; (pl.) wiles.
comportamento (m.) deportment, conduct, behavior; demeanor, bearing, manners. **mau**—, bad behavior; misconduct.
comportar (v.t.) to bear, put up with, suffer; to hold, contain; to have room for; (v.r.) to behave, comport oneself; to comport, agree, accord with.
comportável (adj.) endurable, bearable.
composição (f.) composition (all senses); typesetting; the make-up of anything; a compromise with creditors; a railroad train, string of cars.
compositor –**tora** (m.,f.) composer; compositor, typesetter.
composto –**ta** (adj.) composed, composite, compound; sober, serious, staid; modest; (m.) a compound; (f.pl., Bot.) the Compositae (daisy family).—**de**, composed of, made up of. **juros**—**s**, compound interest.
compostura (f.) composure, sedateness; modesty; composition; imposture, sham; (pl.) cosmetics.
compota (f.) fruit preserves; compote.
compoteira (f.) compotier.
compra (f.) act of buying; a purchase; a drawing of cards (as in poker).—**e venda**, a buy-and-sell agreement. **fazer**—**s**, to go shopping.
compradiço –**ça** (adj.) easily bought (bribed).
comprador (m.) –**dora** (f.) buyer.
comprar (v.t.) to buy, purchase (**para**, **por**, for; **com**, with); to bribe (**com**, with); to draw cards (as in poker).—**a briga**, to take on (fight) another's battle.—**a crédito**, to buy on credit.—**a dinheiro**, to buy for cash.—**a prazo**, to buy on time.—**a prestações**, to buy on the instalment plan.—**a retalho**, to buy at retail.—**barato**

(**caro**) to buy cheaply (dearly).—**cartas**, to draw cards (as at poker).—**fiado**, to buy on credit.—**nabos em saco**, to buy a pig in a poke.—**por atacado**, to buy at wholesale.—**por preço vil**, to buy dirt-cheap.
compra-rixas (f.,m.) troublemaker.
comprável (adj.) purchasable; capable of being bought (bribed).
comprazedor –**dora** (adj.) complaisant. Cf. COMPLACENTE.
comprazente (adj.) = COMPLACENTE.
comprazer [54] (v.t.) to please, delight, gladden; (v.i.) to deign, be pleased to; (v.r.) to be pleased.—**se em** to take pleasure in.
comprazimento (m.) complaisance. Cf. COMPLACÊNCIA.
compreender (v.t.) to comprehend, comprise, include, take in; to apprehend, understand, grasp mentally.
compreendido –**da** (adj.) included; understood.
compreensão (f.) comprehension, inclusion; conception, understanding; awareness; (Logic) connotation.
compreensibilidade (f.) comprehensibility.
compreensível (adj.) comprehensible, understandable.
compreensivo –**va** (adj.) comprehensive; comprehensible; understanding.
compressa (f.) compress (pad, bandage).
compressão (f.) compression.
compressibilidade (f.) compressibility.
compressível (adj.) compressible.
compressivo –**va** (adj.) compressive; repressive.
compressor –**sora** (adj.) compressing; (m.) compressor (all senses); road roller; air compressor.
compridão –**dez** [ê] (f.) = COMPRIMENTO.
comprido –**da** (adj.) long, lengthy; (m.) length. **ao**—, lengthwise. **dez metros de**—, ten meters long.
comprimário (m.), –**ria** (f.) a bit player in a light-opera company.
comprimente (adj.) that compresses or represses.
comprimento (m.) length.—**de onda**, wave length. **salto em**—, broad jump (in athletics). [Do not confuse with CUMPRIMENTO.]
comprimido –**da** (adj.) compressed; (m.) medicine tablet.
comprimir (v.t.) to compress, squeeze; to press; to repress.
comprovação (f.) corroboration, confirmation.
comprovante (adj.) proving, confirming; (m.) = COMPROVANTE.
comprovativo –**va**, –**tório**, –**ria** (adj.) corroborative.
comprometedor –**dora** (adj.) compromising; jeopardizing; promising.
comprometer (v.t.) to promise, pledge; to compromise [but only in the sense of endangering life, reputation, dignity, etc. To compromise differences is RESOLVER (DISPUTA) POR MEIO DE CONCESSÕES MÚTUAS.];—**se a**, to undertake, promise to.—**a palavra**, to pledge one's word.—**o futuro**, to endanger the future.—**se com uma moça**, to promise marriage to a young lady.
comprometido –**da** (adj.) under obligation; in jeopardy; (colloq.) abashed, ashamed. **não**—, unaligned.
comprometimento (m.) compromising, discrediting; risking.
compromissão (f.) = COMPROMISSO.
compromisso (m.) promise, pledge; appointment, date, engagement; financial commitment; written agreement; obligation; compromise, settlement of differences; agreement to submit (a dispute) to arbitration.—**à Bandeira Nacional**, pledge to the flag.—**de casamento**, wedding engagement.—**de credores**, creditors' composition. **prestar**—**de posse**, to take oath of office. **sem**—, without obligation. **solver um**—, to meet an obligation, esp. a financial one.
compromitente (adj.) pledging, promising; (m.,f.) one who makes a commitment; one who agrees to refer matters in dispute to arbitrators.
compropriedade (f.) joint property.
comproprietário –**ria** (adj.) owning property jointly; (m.,f.) joint owner of property.
comprovação (f.) corroboration; documentary evidence (vouchers) of money spent.
comprovador –**dora** (adj.) corroborating; (m.,f.) corroborator.
comprovante (adj.) corroborative; (m.) voucher (of money spent); corroborant; exhibit.
comprovar (v.t.) to corroborate, substantiate, confirm, verify, prove; to re-check (printed copy).
comprovativo –**va** (adj.) corroborative, confirmatory.
compulsão (f.) compulsion, coercion, constraint.

compulsar (v.t.) to scan, scrutinize (printed matter); to search, consult (documents, a dictionary, etc.).

compulsivo –va (adj.) compulsive, coercive, compelling.

compulso –sa (irreg. p.p. of COMPELIR), compelled, forced.

compulsório –ria (adj.) compulsory; (f.) a decision of a superior court; compulsory retirement.

compunção (f.) –pungimento (m.) compunction, remorse, contrition.

compuncto –ta (adj.) contrite.

compungir [25] (v.t.) to move to compunction; (v.r.) to be contrite; to sympathize, feel compassion.

compurgação (f., Law) compurgation; formerly, trial by ordeal.

computação (f.) computation, reckoning, calculation.

computador –dora (adj.) computing, calculating; (m.) computer; calculating machine.

computar [34] (v.t.) to compute, reckon, calculate, estimate.

computável (adj.) computable, calculable.

cômputo (m.) computation, estimate.

comtismo (m.) Comtism, Positivism.

comtista (adj.) Comtian; (m.,f.) Comtist.

comua (f.) privy [= LATRINA].

comum (adj.) common, public, collective, common to all; usual, habitual, customary, every-day; trite; commonplace; vulgar, popular; (m.) the common people; the usual; the everyday; (pl.) the British Commons.—de-dois (Gram.) having the same form for both genders [= SOBRECOMUM]. de—acôrdo, by common consent. É—ouvir-se dizer que, One frequently hears it said that. em—com, in common with, together with.

comumente (adv.) commonly, generally; in common.

comuna (f.) commune; community.

comunal (adj.) communal; (m.,f.) member of a community.

comunalismo (m.) communalism.

comunalista (m.,f.) communalist.

comungante (m.,f.) communicant.

comungar (v.t., v.i.) to administer or to partake of, Holy Communion; to commune; to share (beliefs, opinions, etc.)

comungatório (m.) Communion rail or altar.

comunhão (f.) communion, participation; Holy Communion.—de bens, (Law) community property.—dos santos, (R.C.Ch.) communion of saints.—pascal, Easter Communion.

comunicação (f.) communication; message, information; connecting passage.

comunicado –da (adj.) communicated; (m.) private communication; official communiqué.

comunicador –dora (adj.) communicating; (m.,f.) communicator.

comunicante (adj.) communicating; communicant.

comunicar (v.t.) to communicate, transmit, impart (news, knowledge, disease, etc.); to disclose, reveal; (v.i.) to communicate with, have a connecting passage.—se com, to communicate with.

comunicativo –va (adj.) communicative, unreserved, free.

comunicável (adj.) communicable.

comunidade (f.) community; religious or civil community.

comunismo (m.) Communism.

comuníssimo –ma (absol. superl. of COMUM) most common.

comunista (adj.) communistic; (m.,f.) Communist.

comutação (f.) commutation, substitution.

comutador –dora (adj.) commuting; (m.) electric commutator.

comutar (v.t.) to commute, interchange, exchange; to reduce (a sentence); (Elec.) to commutate.

comutativo –va (adj.) commutative.

comutável (adj.) commutable.

côn. = CÔNEGO (canon of the Church).

conabi [í] (m.) a leafflower (Phyllanthus conami), c.a. TINGUI; also, "a small tree (Clibadium surinamense) whose leaves are used to poison fish." (GBAT]

conação (f., Psychol.) conation.

conambaia (f.) a Thipsalis cactus.

conarito (m., Min.) connarite.

conato –ta (adj.) connate, innate.

conatural (adj.) conatural; cognate; suitable; congenial.

conca (f.) quoit; (Anat.) concha (of the ear).

concameração (f., Arch.) concameration, vaulting.

concatenação (f.) concatenation.

concatenar (v.t.) to concatenate, link together.

concavar (v.t.) to render concave.

concavidade (f.) concavity.

côncavo –va (adj.) concave, hollow; (m.) concavity, hollowness.—côncavo, concavo-concave.—convexo, concavo-convex.—da mão, hollow of the hand.

conceber (v.t., v.i.) to conceive, imagine; to frame (plan, plot); to understand; (v.i.) to become pregnant.

concebimento (m.) conception; apprehension.

concebível (adj.) conceivable, imaginable.

concedente (adj.) conceding, granting.

conceder (v.t.) to concede, admit, grant; to award; to yield.

concedido –da (adj.) conceded, granted; permitted.

conceição (f., R.C.Ch.) the dogma of the Immaculate Conception.

conceito (m.) concept, idea, conception; mind; understanding; reputation; opinion; moral of a tale; a witty conceit [but not conceit in the sense of vanity, which is VAIDADE.]. enunciar um—, to put forward an idea. pessôa de—, estimable person.

conceituado –da (adj.) conceived; of good repute. muito—, highly regarded, highly esteemed, well thought of.

conceituar (v.t.) to form an opinion about; to conceive an idea; to look upon, regard as; to judge.

conceituoso –sa (adj.) witty, clever, spirited.

concelho [ê] (m.) council; municipality. Cf. CONSELHO.

concentração (f.) concentration; centralization; solitude; seclusion.

concentrado –da (adj.) concentrated; massed; secluded; (Chem.) concentrate—em si, lost in thought.

concentrador –dora (adj.) concentrating; (m.,f.) concentrator.

concentrar (v.t.) to concentrate, center, centralize; to condense, mass; to focus (thought, attention) on. (v.r.) to concentrate (em, on); to withdraw into oneself.

concentricidade (f.) concentricity.

concêntrico –ca (adj.) concentric.

concepção (f.) conception; pregnancy; conceiving; apprehension.

conceptáculo (m.) receptacle; (Bot.) conceptacle.

conceptível (adj.) = CONCEBÍVEL.

conceptual (adj.) conceptual.

conceptualismo (m., Philos.) conceptualism.

conceptualista (m.,f.) conceptualist.

concernente (adj.) concerning, regarding.

concernir [21a] (v.t.) to concern, affect, regard, relate to.

concertado –da (adj.) serene, composed; studied, affected; set in order.

concertador –dora (adj.) concerting; (m.,f.) harmonizer. —de casamentos, matchmaker. Cf. CONSERTADOR.

concertante (adj.; m., Music) concertante.

concertar (v.t.) to concert; to adjust, dispose, put (set) in order; (v.i.) to harmonize; to agree. Cf. CONSERTAR.

concertina (f.) concertina.

concertista (m.,f.) concert artist.

concêrto (m.) concert; (Music) concerto; consonance, harmony. Cf. CONSÊRTO.

concessão (f.) concession, compliance; compromise; grant; award; privilege.

concessionário –ria (adj.) concessionary; (m.,f.) concessionaire.

concessivo –va (adj.) concessive.

concessor –sora (m.,f.) concessor.

concessório –ria (adj.) = CONCESSIVO.

concha (f.) conch, shell; auricle of the ear; soup ladle; scalepan.—de-são-jaques, the great scallop (Pecten maximus).

conchado –da (adj.) shell-shaped.

conchal, concharia (f.) shell mound.

conchavado –da (adj.) in agreement; in collusion; (m.,f.) one who is in agreement with or in collusion with; (m.) peon, farm hand.

conchavar (v.t.) to close, conclude (a bargain); to contract the services of; (v.r.) to hire oneself out.—em, to insert, fit (something) in.—com, to conspire with (another or others); to reach agreement with.

conchavo (m.) collusion; conspiracy; domestic employment.

concheado –da (adj.) shaped like a shell.

conchegado –da (adj.) close to; sheltered; stocky, thickset.

conchegar (v.t.) to adjust, arrange, dispose; to bring close to; to cuddle; (v.r.) to approach, come close to.

conchego [ê] (m.) home comfort; snug place; a person who provides comfort to another.

concheira (f.) = SAMBAQUI.

conchelo (m., Bot.) the nodding navelwort (Umbilicus

pendulinus), c.a. COUCELO, COUXILGO, COUSSILHO, ARROZ-DE-TELHADO.
concidadão [-dãos] (*m.*), **-dã** [-dãs] (*f.*) fellow-citizen.
conciliábulo (*m., Eccl.*) conciliabulum.
conciliação (*f.*) conciliation; reconciliation; compromise.
conciliador –dora (*adj.*) conciliating; (*m.,f.*) conciliator.
conciliar (*v.t.*) to conciliate, reconcile; to adjust; to win over; (*v.r.*) to be in accord.
conciliatório –ria (*adj.*) conciliatory; disarming.
conciliável (*adj.*) reconcilable.
concílio (*m.*) council.
concisão (*f.*) conciseness, succinctness, brevity; precision.
conciso –sa (*adj.*) concise, brief, laconic, terse; precise.
concitação (*f.*) incitement; instigation.
concitador –dora (*adj.*) inciting, rousing; (*m.,f.*) incitor; instigator.
concitar (*v.t.*) to incite, rouse to action, arouse, urge, excite; stir up; to instigate.
conclamar (*v.i.*) to vociferate, clamor, shout; to acclaim, applaud.
conclave (*m.*) conclave.
concliz (*m.*) = SOFRÊ.
concludência (*f.*) conclusiveness.
concludente (*adj.*) concluding; conclusive.
concluído –da (*adj.*) concluded; finished, ended.
concluimento [u-i] (*m.*) conclusion.
concluinte [u-ín] (*m.,f.*) a senior student about to graduate.
concluir [24, 72] (*v.t.*) to conclude, end, finish, terminate; to accomplish; to infer, deduce.
conclusão (*f.*) conclusion, end, close; deduction, inference; decision. **chegar a uma—**, to arrive at a decision. **em—**, in conclusion. **tirar uma—**, to draw an inference.
conclusivo –va (*adj.*) conclusive.
concluso –sa (*irreg. and little used p.p. of* CONCLUIR) concluded (referring esp. to a court action ready for sentence).
concocção (*f.*) concoction (but only in the obsolete sense of digestion of food).
concoidal (*adj.*) conchoidal.
concóide (*adj.*) conchoidal; (*f., Math.*) conchoid.
concologia (*f.*) = CONQUILIOLOGIA.
concomitante (*adj.*) concomitant, concurrent, accessory.
concordância (*f.*) concordance, consonance, harmony.
concordante (*adj.*) concordant, accordant, harmonious.
concordar (*v.t.*) to reconcile, harmonize; to conform, adapt.—**com**, to concur with, agree with, acquiesce.—**em**, to agree to.—**em que**, to agree that. **Concordo!** I agree! **não—**, to disagree, disapprove.
concordata (*f.*) composition (of creditors); concordat (agreement between Church and State).
concordatário –ria (*m.,f.*) one who has entered into a composition with his or her creditors.
concordável (*adj.*) reconcilable.
concorde (*adj.*) concordant. **os médicos estão—s em que,** the doctors agree that.
concórdia (*f.*) concord, harmony, agreement.
concorrência (*f.*) concourse, a flocking together; crowd, throng; business competition; bidding. **acima de—**, in a class by itself, beyond compare, *hors concurs*.
concorrente (*adj.*) competing; bidding; (*m.,f.*) competitor; contestant; bidder. **linhas—**, intersecting lines.
concorrer (*v.i.*) to compete (**com**, with, against).—**a**, to throng, flock to.—**para**, to contribute to.
concorrido –da (*adj.*) crowded, well-attended.
concótomo (*m., Surg.*) conchotome.
concreção (*f.*) concretion; (*pl., Geol.*) concretions.
concrecionado –da (*adj.*) concretionary.
concrescência (*f.*) concrescence.
concretagem (*f.*) operation of pouring concrete.
concretação, –tização (*f.*) a becoming concrete; realization.
concretizar (*v.t.*) to render concrete; to make real.
concreto –ta (*adj.*) concrete, solid, compact; free from abstraction; (*m.*) concrete; concretion.—**armado**, reinforced concrete.
concriz (*m.*) = SOFRÊ.
concubina (*f.*) concubine.
concubinagem (*f.*) = CONCUBINATO.
concubinar-se (*v.r.*) to co-habit [= AMANCEBAR-SE].
concubinato (*m.*) concubinage.
concúbito (*m.*) concubitus, coitus.
conculcar (*v.t.*) to trample under foot.
concunhada (*f.*) brother-in-law's wife.

concunhado (*m.*) sister-in-law's husband.
concupiscência (*f.*) concupiscence, lust.
concupiscente (*adj.*) concupiscent.
concurso (*m.*) contest, competition; cooperation; concourse, throng, crowd.—**de habilitação**, competitive examination.
concussão (*f.*) concussion; public graft.
concussionário –ria (*adj.*) grafting; (*m.,f.*) grafter.
concutir (*v.i.*) to shake, tremble.
cond. = CONDUTOR (conductor); CONDICIONAL (conditional).
condado (*m.*) county; earldom.
condão (*m.*) privilege, prerogative; magic power. **varinha de—**, magic wand.
conde (*m.*) earl, count; jack, knave (card), c.a. VALETE.
condecoração (*f.*) decoration, medal, badge.
condecorado –da (*adj.*) decorated, honored; (*m.,f.*) one who has been decorated.
condecorar (*v.t.*) to decorate, bestow honors on.
condenação (*f.*) condemnation, conviction; doom; blame, censure, reproof; disapprobation, disapproval.
condenado –da (*adj.; m.,f.*) condemned.
condenador –dora (*adj.*) condemning, condemnatory; reproachful; (*m.,f.*) condemner.
condenar (*v.t.*) to condemn, sentence; to doom; to pronounce guilty; to blame, censure; to deplore; to disapprove (of), reprove; (*v.r.*) to blame oneself.
condenatório –ria (*adj.*) condemnatory.
condenável (*adj.*) blame-worthy, reprehensible.
condensabilidade (*f.*) condensability.
condensação (*f.*) condensation.
condensador –dora (*adj.*) condensing; (*m.,f.*) condenser (all senses).
condensar (*v.t.*) to condense, compress, consolidate; to contract, curtail.
condensável (*adj.*) condensable.
condescendência (*f.*) concession, complaisance, acquiescence, deference, assent [but not condescendence or condescension, in the sense of patronizing, for which there is no exact equivalent or short definition in Portuguese].
condescendente (*adj.*) complaisant, acquiescent, obliging, willing; deferential [but not condescending in the sense of patronizing—see notation under the previous entry word].
condescender (*v.i.*) to acquiesce, assent, give in [but not to condescend, in the sense of deigning or stooping, for which there is no exact equivalent or short definition in Portuguese].
condêssa (*f.*) countess.
condestável (*m.*) constable [but only in the medieval sense of high officer of the monarchy].
condição (*f.*) condition, situation, circumstances; proviso, stipulation; prerequisite; social status; (*pl.*) terms. **à—**, on condition that.—**com** (or **sob**) **a—de que**, on condition that; provided that. **em—s de**, in a position to; able; in condition to; fit (for work, duty, etc.). **em—s de navegabilidade**, seaworthy.
condicionado –da (*adj.*) conditioned on; in good (or bad) financial condition.
condicional (*adj.*) conditional, contingent.
condicionamento (*m.*)—**de ar**, air conditioning.
condicionar (*v.t.*) to subject to conditions; to make contingent on.
condigno –na (*adj.*) condign, deserved, merited.
condilartrose (*f., Anat.*) condylarthrosis.
côndilo (*m., Anat., Zool.*) condyle.
condilóide (*adj., Anat.*) condyloid.
condiloma (*f., Med.*) condyloma.
condimentação (*f.*) seasoning (of food).
condimentado –da (*adj.*) seasoned; spicy.
condimentar (*v.t.*) to season, spice, flavor.
condimento (*m.*) condiment, seasoning, spice, relish.
condiscípulo –la (*m.,f.*) classmate, fellow-student.
condizente (*adj.*) harmonious, consonant; suitable, accordant.—**com**, in keeping with.
condizer [41] (*v.i.*) to correspond, tally (**com**, with); to be proportionate; to suit, match; to go well together (as colors). **não—**, of dresses, colors, etc., to clash, jar, be discordant.
condoer [56] (*v.t.*) to arouse pity in.—**-se com**, to condole (commiserate, sympathize) with.
condoído –da (*adj.*) commiserating, pitying, sympathetic.
condoimento [o-i] (*m.*) = CONDOLÊNCIA.

condolência (*f.*) condolence, sympathy; (*pl.*) condolences, expressions of sympathy.
condolente (*adj.*) condolent.
condomínio (*m.*) joint domain, joint ownership.
condômino (*m.*) joint owner; joint ownership.
condor (*m.*) condor.
condoreiro –**ra** (*adj.*) high-flown (ref. esp. to a school of north Brazilian writers).
condralgia (*f., Med.*) chondralgia.
condrectomia (*f., Surg.*) chondrectomy.
condrificação (*f., Physiol.*) chondrification.
condrilha (*f.*) the rush skeletonweed (*Chondrilla juncea*).
condrina (*f., Biochem.*) chondrin.
condriosomo (*m., Biol.*) chondriosome.
condroma (*m., Med.*) chondroma.
condução (*f.*) conduction, transmission; transportation; (*colloq.*) a conveyance, carriage, vehicle; (*Physics*) conduction, as of heat.
conducente (*adj.*) conducent; conducive.
conduite (*m., Elec.*) conduit.—**subterraneo,** underground conduit.
conduplicação (*f.*) a doubling or duplication; (*Bot.*) conduplication.
conduplicado –**da** (*adj., Bot.*) conduplicate.
condurangina (*f., Chem.*) condurangin.
condurango (*m.*) condorvine (*Marsdenia cundurango*).
conduru [rú] (*m.*) a jacaranda (*J. filicifolia*); the Pará breadnut tree (*Brosimum paraense*), c.a. MUIRA-PIRANGA.
conduta (*f.*) conduct, deportment, behavior; conveying (of people). **mudar de—,** to turn over a new leaf.
condutância (*f., Elec.*) conductance.
condutibilidade (*f.*) conductibility; (*Physics, Elec.*) conductivity.
condutível (*adj.*) conductible.
condutividade (*f.*) conductivity.
condutivo –**va** (*adj.*) conductive.
conduto (*m.*) conduit, duct, channel, canal; chute.
condutômetro (*m., Physics*) conductometer.
condutor (*m.*) conductor, leader, guide, escort; conductor of heat, electricity, etc.; a streetcar conductor [but not a train conductor, which is CHEFE DO TREM.]—**sem corrente,** dead (electric) wire.
conduzir [36] (*v.t.*) to conduct, lead; to drive (an automobile, etc.); to transport, carry, convey; (*v.r.*) to conduct oneself, behave.
cone (*m.*) cone (all senses); taper.—**aluvial,**—**de dejeção,** alluvial fan or cone.—**de Seger,** (*Metal.*) pyrometric cone.—**de silêncio,** (*Radio*) cone of silence.—**vulcânico,** volcanic cone.
cônego (*m.*) canon (church dignitary).
conetivo –**va** (*adj.*) connective; connecting; (*m., Gram.*) a connective word or particle. **tecido—,** connective tissue. Var. CONECTIVO.
conetor (*m.*) electric plug; (*Autom.*) connecting rod. Var. CONECTOR.
conexão [ks] (*f.*) connection, union, junction; relationship; (*Mach., Elec.*) coupling.
conexidade [ks] (*f.*) connexity.
conexivo –**va** (*adj.*) connective, conjunctive.
conexo –**xa** [ks] (*adj.*) connected.
confabulação (*f.*) confabulation, familiar talk.
confabular (*v.i.*) to confabulate, chat, prattle.
confecção (*f.*) confection [but only in the sense of compounding, preparing or making. A sweet confection is BÔLO or DOCE.] Cf. CONFEIÇÃO, CONFEITO.
confeccionador –**dora** (*m.,f.*) confectioner [but only in the sense of one who puts ingredients together. A confectioner of sweets is: CONFEITEIRO.]
confeccionar (*v.t.*) to confect, mix, put together (ingredients); to make, finish (as, a garment); to compile (as, a dictionary). Cf. CONFEIÇOAR.
confederação (*f.*) confederation.
confederado –**da** (*adj.*) confederated; (*m.,f.*) confederate, ally.
confederar (*v.t., v.i.*) to confederate; (*v.r.*) to unite.
confederativo –**va** (*adj.*) confederative.
confeição (*f.*) confection, confect, sweet, sweetmeat. Cf. CONFECÇÃO, CONFEITO.
confeiçoar (*v.t.*) to mix drugs; to make confections (sweetmeats). Cf. CONFECCIONAR.
confeitar (*v.t.*) to sugar-coat (lit. and fig.).
confeitaria (*f.*) confectioner's store; sweet shop.
confeiteira (*f.*) a bonbon dish; a woman who makes and/or sells sweetmeats.
confeiteiro (*m.*) confectioner.
confeito (*m.*) comfit; sweetmeat, candy, pastry; sugar-coated almond.
conferência (*f.*) conference, parley; interview; meeting for consultation; public lecture, address, discourse, speech.
conferenciador –**dora** (*m.,f.*) = CONFERENCISTA.
conferencial (*adj.*) conferential.
conferenciar (*v.i.*) to confer, hold a conference; to give a public lecture.
conferencista (*m.,f.*) public speaker, platform lecturer.
conferente (*m.,f.*) conferee; checker; copy holder (assistant proofreader).
conferir [21-a] (*v.t.*) to compare, collate (**com,** with); to check, count, verify; to confer, bestow (**a,** on, upon); to vouchsafe (**a,** to); to confer (**com,** with); (*v.i.*) to tally, accord, agree.
conferva [é] (*f.*) any alga forming scum in ponds.
confessado –**da** (*adj.*) confessed; (*m.,f.*) confessant.
confessar (*v.t.*) to confess, acknowledge, own, admit; to concede, recognize; to disclose; to declare; to hear confession; (*v.r.*) to make confession (to a priest).—**se culpado,** to plead guilty. [The noun is CONFISSÃO.]
confessional (*adj.*) confessional.
confessionário (*m.*) confessional.
confêsso –**sa** (*adj.*) confessed; converted; (*m.*) a monk; confession to a priest.
confessor –**sora** (*m.*) father-confessor; (*m.,f.*) a professor of faith.
confessório –**ria** (*adj.*) confessory.
confete [éte] (*m.*) confetti.
confiadamente (*adv.*) confidently.
confiado –**da** (*adj.*) confident, self-confident; unsuspecting; (*colloq.*) bold, presumptuous.
confiança (*f.*) confidence, trust, faith; reliability, trustworthiness; familiarity, intimacy; impudence, "brass". [Confidence in the sense of boldness, assurance, courage, is FIRMEZA, INTREPIDEZ.] **abuso de—,** breach of trust. **dar—a (alguém),** to pay attention to (someone); to get personal or confidential with (someone); to encourage a flirtation. **de—,** trustworthy, reliable. **digno de—,** trustworthy. **em—,** in confidence, confidentially. **Êle não merece—,** He is not to be trusted.
confiante (*adj.*) unsuspecting; trustful.
confiar (*v.i.*) to confide in, trust in, rely on; to expect hope; (*v.t.*) to entrust to; (*v.r.*) to place one's trust in.—**em,** to depend on.
confidência (*f.*) a confidence, secret; confidential communication; confidence, trust, faith.
confidencial (*adj.*) confidential, secret; (*f.*) a confidential communication.
confidenciar (*v.t.*) to disclose something in confidence; (*v.r.*) to exchange confidences.
confidencioso –**sa** (*adj.*) confidential.
confidente (*m.*) confidant; (*f.*) confidante.
configuração (*f.*) configuration, form, figure, shape.
configurar (*v.t.*) to fashion, shape, form; to represent, portray, depict; (*v.r.*) to take shape.
confim (*adj.*) bounding, limiting; = CONFINANTE; (*m.pl.*) confines, boundaries, limits, frontiers.
confinante (*adj.*) confining, bounding, limiting; adjoining.
confinar (*v.t.*) to confine, limit, bound; to restrain, shut in.—**com,** to abut upon, adjoin, have a common boundary with.
confioso –**sa** (*adj.*) full of self-confidence.
confirmação (*f.*) confirmation, corroboration; (*Eccl.*) Confirmation.
confirmador –**dora** (*adj.*) confirming; (*m.,f.*) confirmer.
confirmante (*adj.*) confirming.
confirmar (*v.t.*) to confirm, ratify; to sanction; to corroborate, substantiate; to affirm, asseverate; (*v.r.*) to be confirmed; to receive Confirmation.
confirmativo –**va** (*adj.*) confirmative [= CONFIRMANTE].
confirmatório –**ria** (*adj.*) confirmatory, corroborative.
confiscação (*f.*) confiscation.
confiscador –**dora** (*adj.*) confiscating; (*m.,f.*) confiscator.
confiscar (*v.t.*) to confiscate; to commandeer; to seize.
confiscável (*adj.*) confiscable.
confisco (*m.*) confiscation [= CONFISCAÇÃO].
confissão (*f.*) confession, acknowledgement. [The verb is CONFESSAR.]—**auricular,** aural confession.—**de dívida,** written acknowledgement of debt.—**de fé,** profession of faith.—**do réu,** plea of guilty.

confitente (adj.) confessing; (m.,f.) confessant.
conflagração (f.) conflagration.
conflagrar (v.t.) to conflagrate.
conflito (m.) conflict, struggle; encounter, combat; clashing, disagreement, discord; ruckus, fray, brawl.
confluência (f.) confluence.
confluente (adj.) confluent; (m.) tributary.
confluir [72] (v.i.) to flow together.
conformação (f.) conformation, configuration; conformity, compliance; acquiescence.
conformador –dora (adj.) conforming; (m.,f.) conformer; conformator.
conformar (v.t.) to conform, adjust, adapt, (com, a, to). —se com, to adjust oneself to; to resign oneself to; to abide by; to accede to; to comply with.
conforme (adj.) conformable; resigned, acquiescent; agreeable to; pursuant to; (adv.) in conformity with; accordingly; (conj.) according to circumstances; how.
conformidade (f.) conformity, agreement, assent. de—com, in agreement with. em—com, in conformity with; according to. nesta—, in these circumstances.
conformismo (m.) compliance, acquiescence.
conformista (m.,f.) conformist.
confortado –da (adj.) comforted; strengthened.
confortador –dora (adj.) comforting; (m.,f.) comforter [but only in the sense of one who consoles. A comforter (quilted bedcover) is ALCOCHOADO; the Comforter is ESPÍRITO SANTO; comforter, in the British senses of a woolen tippet is MANTA DE LÃ PARA O PESCOÇO, and of a baby's pacifier is CHUPETA DE CRIANÇA.]
confortante (adj.) comforting; = CONFORTADOR.
confortar (v.t.) to comfort, console.
confortativo (m.) a cordial or tonic.
confortável (adj.) comfortable, snug.
confôrto (m.) comfort, ease; well-being; consolation.
confrade (m.) confrère, colleague.
confrangedor –dora (adj.) grievous, distressing, heartrending.
confranger (v.t.) to distress, afflict, torture; (v.r.) to suffer anguish.
confrangido –da (adj.) anguished; distressed; afflicted; tortured; oppressed.
confrangimento (m.) distress; affliction; oppression.
confraria (f.) brotherhood, fraternity.
confraternidade (f.) fraternal union.
confraternizar (v.t., v.i.) to fraternize.
confrontação (f.) confrontation; (pl.) distinguishing marks.
confrontar (v.t.) to confront (as witnesses); to compare; to collate. —se com, to face.
confronte (adj.) fronting, facing; (prep.) in front.
confronto (m.) confrontation; comparison.
confundas (f.pl.) the depths of hell.
confundido –da (adj.) confused, perplexed; abashed, disconcerted.
confundir (v.t.) to confuse; to confound; to jumble; to blend, merge, mix; to perplex, bewilder, baffle; to abash, disconcert; (v.r.) to become confused. —se com, to blend with, mingle with, become a part of. A sala confudia-se com a cozinha, The living room and kitchen were one.
confundível (adj.) confusable.
confusamente (adv.) pell-mell; indistinctly.
confusão (f.) confusion, disorder, muddle, disarray, jumble; mix-up, turmoil; commotion, stir; perplexity, embarrassment; abashment.
confuso –sa (adj.) confused; confounded; embarrassed; flurried, uncertain; topsy-turvy, helter-skelter, disorderly.
confutação (f.) confutation, refutation, disproof.
confutador –dora (m.,f.) one who confutes, refutes.
confutar (v.t.) to confute, disprove, refute; (v.r.) to confute one's own statements.
confutável (adj.) refutable.
conga (f.) conga (a dance).
congada (f.), –do (m.) among Negroes in Brazil, a dramatic song and dance depicting the crowning of a king in the Congo. Cf. CONGO.
congelação (f.) congealing, freezing, chilling.
congelado –da (adj.) congealed, frozen; (m.pl.) frozen assets. carne—, frozen beef.
congelador –dora (adj.) freezing; (m.) freezer; deep freezer.
congelar (v.t.) to freeze, congeal; to chill; (v.r.) to freeze.
congeminar (v.i.) to muse, ponder.
congênere (adj.) congeneric, congenerous; allied, akin,

kindred.
congeneridade (f.) congeneracy.
congenial (adj.) congenial.
congenialidade (f.) congeniality.
congênito –ta (adj.) congenital.
congérie (f.) congeries.
congestão (f.) congestion.
congestionado –da (adj.) congested; flushed (as with anger.
congestionar (v.t.) to congest; to choke (up); (v.r.) to suffer a congestion; to flush with anger.
congestivo –va (adj.) congestive.
congesto –ta (adj.) congested [= CONGESTIONADO].
conglobação (f.) conglobation.
conglobado –da (adj.) conglobate.
conglobar (v.t.) to conglobe, conglobate; to ball; to lump together.
conglomeração (f.) conglomeration.
conglomerado –da (adj.; m.) conglomerate.
conglomerar (v.t.) to conglomerate; to lump together.
conglomerato (m., Geol.) conglomerate.
conglutinação (f.) conglutination.
conglutinante (adj.) conglutinant.
conglutinar (v.t.) to glue together.
conglutinoso –sa (adj.) glutinous, sticky.
congo (m.) a Brazilian dance of African origin. Cf. CONGADA.
congonha (f.) any of various tropical holly and holly-like tropical plants, some of whose leaves serve as a substitute for ERVA-MATE. —brava-de-fôlha-miúda = CARNE-DE-ANTA. — -do-brejo = CHÁ-DA-CAMPANHA. —-do-campo = CONGONHEIRO.—-verdadeira, a tropical plant of the Icacinaceae family (Villaresia mucronata), c.a. CONGONHA-DO-SERTÃO.
congonhar (v.i.) to drink MATE or similar tea.
congonheiro (m.) a tree of the copaiyé family (Vochysia oppougnata), c.a. CINZEIRO, CONGONHA-DO-CAMPO, PAU-DE-BRINCOS, PAU-DE-CINZAS, PAU-DE-LÁGRIMA, RABO-DE-ARARA, RABO-DE-TUCANO, URURUCA.
congorsa (f.) periwinkle (Vinca major); the Madagascar periwinkle (Lochnera rosea), c.a. BOAS-NOITES.
congote (m.) = CANGOTE.
congraçador –dora (adj.) harmonizing, reconciling; (m.,f.) conciliator.
congraçamento (m.) reconciliation, harmonization.
congraçar (v.t.) to harmonize, attune, reconcile; (v.r.) to ingratiate oneself.
congratulação (f.) congratulation, felicitation.
congratulador –dora (adj.) congratulating; (m.,f.) congratulator.
congratulante (adj.) congratulating.
congratular (v.t.) to congratulate.—se com, to rejoice with.
congratulatório –ria (adj.) congratulatory.
congregação (f.) congregation; a gathering (of people).
congregacional (adj.) congregational.
congregacionalista (m.,f.) Congregationalist.
congregado –da (adj.) congregated; (m.,f.) member of a religious congregation.
congregante (adj.) congregating; (m.,f.) congregant.
congregar (v.t.) to congregate, assemble, convoke, bring together; (v.r.) to meet (gather, come, flock) together.
congressional (adj.) congressional.
congressista (adj.) congress; (m.,f.) member of a congress; (m.) congressman; (f.) congresswoman.
congresso (m.) congress, gathering, assembly; legislative body; international conference.
congro (m.) any unspecified conger eel, c.a. ENGUIA-DO-MAR.
côngrua (f.) ecclesiastical tithe. Cf. CÔNGRUO.
congruência (f.) congruence, congruity; (Math.) congruence.
congruente (adj.) congruent, congruous.
congruidade [u-i] (f.) congruity.
côngruo –grua (adj.) congruous. Cf. CÔNGRUA.
conhaque (m.) cognac, brandy.
conhecedor –dora (adj.) cognizant of, informed in, knowing, familiar with, conversant with; (m.,f.) connoisseur, expert judge.
conhecer (v.t.) to know, be aware of, cognizant of; to be familiar with, well-versed in; to have experience in; to recognize, distinguish. Cf. SABER. (v.r.) to know oneself. —de nome, de vista, to know by name, by sight.—os meios, to know the ropes. Conheci-o no Rio, I met him

in Rio. **dar a—**, to make known. **dar-se a—**, to make oneself known. **É na necessidade que se conhecem os amigos**, A friend in need is one indeed. **Que eu conheça, não**, Not to my knowledge; not that I know of.

conhecido –da (*adj.*) known, well-known; renowned; of one's acquaintanceship; (*m.,f.*) acquaintance, friend.— **por**, known as. **tornar-se—do público**, to come before the public eye.

conhecimento (*m.*) knowledge, cognizance; awareness; acquaintance, familiarity; acquaintanceship; bill of lading; (*pl.*) learning, lore. **falar com—de causa**, to know what one is talking about; to know whereof one speaks; to speak with authority, advisedly. **Não tenho—disso**, I have no knowledge of (know nothing about) it. **que seja do meu—**, to my knowledge. **sem o—de**, without the knowledge of. **tomar—de**, to take cognizance of; to notice, pay attention to; to look into; to inform oneself about.

conhecível (*adj.*) knowable, cognizable.
conicidade (*f.*) conicity.
conicina (*f.*, *Chem.*) conicine, coniine.
cônico –ca (*adj.*) conic.
conídio (*m.*, *Bot.*, *Bacteriol.*) conidium.
conidióforo (*m.*, *Bot.*) conidiophore.
conidiospório (*m.*) conidiospore, conidium.
coníferas (*f.pl.*, *Bot.*) conifers.
coniferina (*f.*, *Chem.*) coniferin.
conífero –ra (*adj.*) coniferous, cone-bearing.
coniforme (*adj.*) coniform, cone-shaped.
coniina [i-í] [*f.*, *Chem.*] coniine, cicutine.
conimbricense, –brigense (*adj.*; *m.,f.*) (a native) of Coimbra [= COIMBRÃO-BRÃ].
conirrostros (*m.pl.*) the Conirostres (finches, weaverbirds, tanagers).
conivência (*f.*) connivance, collusion.
conivente (*adj.*) conniving.
conjetura (*f.*) conjecture, supposition, surmise, guess.
conjeturador –dora (*adj.*) conjecturing; (*m.,f.*) conjecturer.
conjetural (*adj.*) conjectural.
conjeturar (*v.t.*) to conjecture, surmise, guess.
conjeturável (*adj.*) conjecturable.
conjugação (*f.*) conjugation.
conjugado –da (*adj.*) conjugate, joined together, coupled. **esforço—**, joint effort.
conjugal (*adj.*) conjugal, connubial.
conjugar (*v.t.*) to conjugate (a verb); to coordinate; to conjoin; (*v.r.*) to work together.
cônjuge (*m.,f.*) consort, spouse.
conjunção (*f.*) conjunction, union, conjoining; menstruation; (*Gram.*) conjunction.
conjunta (*f.*) a soft leather strap used for tying the yoke to the base of an ox's horns.
conjuntamente (*adv.*) together; jointly.
conjuntar (*v.t.*) to conjoin.
conjuntivite (*f.*, *Med.*) conjunctivitis.
conjuntivo –va (*adj.*) conjunctive, conjoining; (*m.*, *Gram.*) conjunctive mood; (*f.*, *Anat.*) conjunctiva.
conjunto –ta (*adj.*) conjoined; (*m.*) complex, assemblage of parts forming a whole; group, body; the whole; a set of things; a team of players. **declaração em—**, a joint statement. **de—**, in the aggregate; altogether. **em—**, in a body; together; as a whole; by and large.
conjuntura (*f.*) conjuncture; juncture, state of affairs; situation of the moment (economic, political, etc.). **ciclo da—**, business cycle. **previsão da—**, business forecast. **tendências da—**, business trends.
conjura (*f.*) = CONJURO.
conjuração (*f.*) conjuration, incantation; a conspiracy. **fomentar uma—**, to hatch a plot.
conjurado –da (*m.,f.*) conspirator.
conjurador –dora (*m.,f.*) conjurer.
conjurante (*adj.*) conjuring.
conjurar (*v.t.*) to conjure, exorcise, cast out (evil spirits); to beseech, implore; to conspire, plot, scheme; to swear together; to avert, ward off (war, danger, etc.).
conjuro (*m.*) conjuration, incantation, magic charm; exorcism.
conluiado –da (*adj.*) in collusion (with).
conluiar (*v.t.*) to unite (persons) in a collusion; to defraud; (*v.r.*) to enter into collusion with.
conluio (*m.*) conspiracy, plot, collusion, connivance; cahoots.
conocarpo (*m.*) a button tree (*Conocarpus*).

conoidal (*adj.*) conoidal, cone-shaped.
conóide (*adj.*) conoidal, cone-shaped; (*m.*) conoid.
conorrino (*m.*) a genus (*Conorhinus*) of bloodsucking bugs, which includes the BARBEIRO.
conosco [nô] (*pron.*) with us; to ourselves; regarding us; addressed to us.
conotação (*f.*) connotation.
conquanto (*conj.*) although, though.
conquém (*m.*) = GALINHA-D'ANGOLA.
conquífero –ra (*adj.*, *Zool.*) conchiferous.
conquiliologia (*f.*) conchology.
conquiliologista (*m.,f.*) conchologist.
conquista (*f.*) conquest, victory.
conquistado –da (*adj.*) conquered; won.
conquistador (*m.*) conqueror; (*colloq.*) lady-killer, heart-breaker, "wolf".
conquistar (*v.t.*) to conquer, vanquish; to gain by effort; to win (someone) over; to win another's love or liking.— **uma bôlsa**, to win a scholarship.
conquistável (*adj.*) conquerable; capable of being won.
cons. = CONSELHEIRO (counselor).
consagração (*f.*) consecration; dedication; fame, renown; praise, acclaim.
consagrado –da (*adj.*) established; recognized; acclaimed; renowned, famed; of long standing; devoted, dedicated; consecrated.—**ao problema**, dedicated to the problem. —**pelo uso**, of words, etc., approved (accepted, recognized) by usage.—**pela rotina**, established by routine.
consagrar (*v.t.*) to consecrate, dedicate, devote to; to enshrine; to sanction, authorize; to recognize; to acclaim. —**se a**, to devote oneself to (something); to dedicate oneself to (a profession, a task, etc.).
consangüíneo –nea (*adj.*) consanguineous; (*m.,f.*) a blood relation.
consangüinidade (*f.*) consanguinity, relationship by blood, esp. on the father's side.—**dirigida**, line breeding.
consciência (*f.*) consciousness, awareness; conscience; conscientiousness. **em—**, in (all) conscience. **estar em paz com a—**, to have a clear conscience. **examinar a—**, to search one's conscience. **pesar na—**, to weigh on the conscience. **por descarga de—**, for conscience's sake. **ter—de**, to be aware of. **ter—elástica**, to have an elastic conscience. **ter a—carregada**, to have a burden on one's conscience. **tomar—de**, to become aware of, to take note of (something).
consciencioso –sa (*adj.*) conscientious, scrupulous.
consciente (*adj.*) conscious; conscientious; aware; sentient.
cônscio –cia (*adj.*) fully aware (of one's duty, etc.).
conscrição (*f.*) conscription, draft.
conscrito –ta (*adj.*) drafted, recruited; (*m.*) conscript, draftee, recruit.
consecução (*f.*) = CONSEGUIMENTO.
consecutivo –va (*adj.*) consecutive.
conseguidor –dora (*m.,f.*) one who obtains, attains, achieves (desires, objectives, ends).
conseguimento (*m.*) accomplishment, attainment, achievement; getting, obtainment, acquirement.
conseguinte (*adj.*) consequent; consecutive; (*m.*) = CONSEQÜÊNCIA. **por—**, consequently, therefore.
conseguir [21a] (*v.t.*) to attain, obtain, get; to achieve, succeed in; to be able to (do something).
conseguível (*adj.*) attainable; obtainable.
conselheirice (*f.*) bombastic balderdash.
conselheirismo (*m.*) grave and pompous manner.
conselheiro (*m.*) counselor, adviser; mentor; privy councillor; an honorary title during the days of the Brazilian Empire.—**de embaixada**, an honorary title given to first secretaries of embassies.
conselho (*m.*) counsel, advice, admonition.—**de guerra**, council of war; courtmartial.—**de Segurança**, Security Council (in the U.N.) Cf. CONCELHO.
consenso (*m.*) consensus; consent.
consentâneo –nea (*adj.*) consentaneous, agreeable, suitable, accordant.
consentimento (*m.*) consent, assent; agreement, concensus; acquiescence, compliance.
consentir [21a] (*v.t.*) to consent, permit, assent, concur; to yield to, comply with, acquiesce in, accede to.—**em**, to agree (consent) to. **Quem cala consente**, Silence gives consent.
conseqüência (*f.*) consequence, result, effect; aftermath; conclusion, deduction, inference; importance; moment. **aceitar as—s**, to take the consequences. **em—**, consequently; accordingly. **em—disso**, by reason of that; on

that account; as a result of that. **graves—s,** serious results, grave consequences. **tirar (as)—s,** to draw inferences.
consequencial (*adj.*) consequential.
conseqüente (*adj., m.*) consequent.—**de,** due to.
conseqüentemente (*adv.*) consequently.
consertador (*m.*) mender, repairman, fixer.
consertar (*v.t.*) to repair, mend, patch, fix.—**o estômago,** to settle the stomach.
conserta-tudo (*m.*) repair shop.
consêrto (*m.*) repair, mending. **peça para—,** spare part. Cf. CONCÊRTO.
conserva (*f.*) conserve, preserve, pickle.—**s em latas,** canned goods. **fábrica de—s,** cannery.
conservação (*f.*) conservation, maintenance.
conservador –dora (*adj.*) conservative, conserving, conservatory; (*m.,f.*) conservator, preserver; curator; a conservative (in politics).
conservantismo (*m.*) conservatism.
conservantista (*adj.*) old-fogyish; (*m.*) mossback.
conservar (*v.t.*) to conserve; to preserve; to maintain, keep up; to retain; to remember, recollect; (*v.r.*) to remain, continue.—**se calado,** to remain silent, keep quiet.—**em latas,** to can (food). **Conserve sua direita,** Keep to the right.
conservativo –va (*adj.*) conservative, -tory.
conservatório (*m.*) conservatory.
conserveiro (*m.*) a canner, or a dealer in canned goods.
consideração (*f.*) consideration, attention, notice, heed; pondering, contemplation; (*pl.*) reasons, motives, grounds.
considerado –da (*adj.*) considered; considerate; esteemed.
considerando (*m.*) motive, reason; consideration.—**que,** whereas (used as the first word in paragraphs of formal preambles).
considerar (*v.t.*) to consider, ponder, weigh; to believe, deem; (*v.i.*) to reflect, meditate (**em, on**).—**a mal,** to think evil of.
considerável (*adj.*) considerable; worthy of consideration; a good deal of.
consignação (*f.*) consignment; sending, shipping.
consignador –dora (*m.,f.*) consignor; shipper.
consignante (*adj.*) consigning; (*m.,f.*) consignor.
consignar (*v.t.*) to consign; to ship (goods); to entrust, commit; to assign, appropriate (money); to record, register, chronicle.
consignatário –ria (*m.,f.*) consignee.
consignável (*adj.*) consignable, assignable.
consigo (*pron.*) with (to) himself (herself, itself, themselves).
consistência (*f.*) consistency, density; fig., stability, steadiness. [But not consistency in the sense of congruity, compatibility, which is CONCORDÂNCIA, HARMONIA, CONGRUÊNCIA.]
consistente (*adj.*) consisting (of); cohering; firm, stiff, solid, dense. [But not consistent in the sense of compatible, which is COMPATÍVEL, CONCILIÁVEL.]
consistir (*v.i.*) to consist (**em,** in, of); to lie in; to be made up of, constituted of.
consistorial (*adj.*) consistorial.
consistório (*m.*) consistory.
cons.º = CONSELHEIRO (counselor).
consoada (*f.*) light supper, snack, collation; a Christmas Eve party at home; a Christmas gift.
consoante (*adj.*) consonant(al), consonous; rhyming; (*f.*) a consonant (speech sound or letter); (*prep.*) consonant with or to.
consoar (*v.i.*) to consonate; to be consonant; (*v.t.*) to eat a light supper.
consociação (*f.*) consociation, association.
consociar (*v.i.*) to consociate, associate.
consócio –cia (*m.,f.*) associate, partner, colleague; member of a society.
consogra [só] (*f.*) a mother in relation to her son's or daughter's mother-in-law.
consogro [sô] (*m.*) a father in relation to his son's or daughter's father-in-law.
consola (*f., Arch.*) console.
consolação (*f.*) consolation, solace, comfort.
consolador –dora (*adj.*) consoling, solacing, comforting; (*m.,f.*) consoler, comforter; (*m.*) pacifier (for babies).
consolar (*v.t.*) to console, solace, comfort; to relieve from distress; (*v.r.*) to console oneself or be consoled.
consolatório –ria (*adj.*) consolatory.

consolável (*adj.*) consolable.
consolda, consólida (*f., Bot.*) common comfrey (*Symphytum officinale*).—**do-cáucaso,** Caucasian comfrey (*S. caucasicum*).—**espinhosa,** or **-peluda,** prickly comfrey (*S. asperum*).—**régia** = BÚGULA (*Ajuga reptans*).
consolidação (*f.*) consolidation, union, combination.
consolidar (*v.t.*) to consolidate, make firm; to fund (a debt); to ratify laws; (*v.i.*) to consolidate.
consôlo (*m.*) consolation [= CONSOLAÇÃO].
consolo (*m., Arch.*) console [= CONSOLA].
consoluto –da (*adj., Physical Chem.*) consolute.
consonância (*f.*) consonance, euphony; harmony; congruity; (*Physics*) consonance.
consonante (*adj.*) consonant. Cf. CONSOANTE.
consorciar (*v.t.*) to consort with, associate with; to join in marriage; (*v.r.*) to marry.
consórcio (*m.*) consortium; marriage.
consorte (*m.,f.*) consort, partner, associate; spouse.
conspicuidade [u-i] (*f.*) conspicuity, conspicuousness.
conspícuo –cua (*adj.*) prominent, distinguished, noteworthy [but not conspicuous in the sense of undesirably noticeable, which is ESPALHAFATOSO, nor in the sense of plainly visible, which is MUITO VISÍVEL].
conspiração (*f.*) conspiracy, plot.
conspirador –dora (*adj.*) conspiring; (*m.,f.*) conspirer, plotter.
conspirar (*v.t.*) to conspire, plot, scheme.
conspirativo –va (*adj.*) conspirative, conspiring.
conspiratório –ria (*adj.*) conspiratory; collusive.
conspurcar (*v.t.*) to soil, pollute, defile, smear.
consta (*f.*) rumor, report, hearsay.
constância (*f.*) constancy; permanence; stability, immutability; perseverance, steadfastness.
constante (*adj.*) constant; unchangeable, stable; steadfast; unremitting; (*f., Physics, etc.*) constant.—**de,** consisting of; included in.
constar (*v.i.*)—**de** or **em,** to consist of; to be recorded, appear in a record.—**que,** to be known (believed, accepted as fact) that. **consta-lhe que,** he is sure that. **consta que,** it is said that; it is believed that. **que me conste,** as far as I know.
constatação (*f.*) ascertaining, proving, authentication, verification.
constatar (*v.t.*) to ascertain, certify, verify; to prove; to record; to articulate. [A useful and much-used gallicism.]
constelação (*f.*) constellation.
constelado –da (*adj.*) starry, star-lit; star-shaped.
constelar (*v.t.*) to stud (adorn) with bright lights.
consternação (*f.*) consternation, alarm; dismay; fright, panic; depression, dejection.
consternado –da (*adj.*) prostrated, depressed, dejected; aghast.
consternador –dora (*adj.*) consternating, alarming; depressing.
consternar (*v.t.*) to consternate; to dismay; to prostrate.
constipação (*f.*) common cold [but not constipation, which is PRISÃO DE VENTRE.]
constipado –da (*adj.*) suffering from a cold [but not constipated, which is SOFRENDO DE PRISÃO DE VENTRE]; (*m.*) a common cold.
constipar-se (*v.r.*) to catch cold.
constitucional (*adj.*) constitutional; inherent.
constitucionalidade (*f.*) constitutionality.
constitucionalismo (*m.*) constitutionalism.
constitucionalista (*m.,f.*) constitutionalist.
constituição [u-i] (*f.*) constitution: formation, organization; temperament, characteristic; charter (as of a government, institution, etc.).
constituinte (*adj.*) constituent, component; (*m.,f.*) constituent; client; member of a constitutional assembly.
constituir [72] (*v.t.*) to constitute, to form, compose; to appoint, deputize; to elect to office; (*v.r.*) to constitute oneself, become, set oneself up as.
constrangedor –dora (*adj.*) constraining.
constranger (*v.t.*) to constrain, restrain; to cramp (someone's style); to compel, coerce.
constrangido –da (*adj.*) constrained, restrained; uncomfortable, ill at ease; stiff.
constrangimento (*m.*) constraint, restraint; compulsion, coercion.
constrição (*f.*) constriction, contraction.
constringente (*adj.*) constricting.
constringir (*v.t.*) to constrict, cramp, squeeze.
constritivo –va (*adj.*) constricting.

constritor –**tora** (*adj.*) constricting; (*m.*) constrictor (snake, muscle).

construção (*f.*) construction; act of building or building structure; syntax.—**naval**, shipbuilding.

construir [37] (*v.t.*) construct, build; (*Gram.*) to construe.

construtivo –**va** (*adj.*) constructive.

construtor –**tora** (*adj.*) constructing; (*m.,f.*) constructor. —**de imagens**, (*T.V.*) picture tube.

consubstanciação (*f., Theol.*) consubstantiation.

consubstanciar (*v.t.*) to consubstantiate.

consueto –**ta** (*adj.*) accustomed, usual.

consuetudinário –**ria** (*adj.*) usual, customary, common. **direito**—, unwritten (common) law.

cônsul (*m.*) consul.

consulado (*m.*) consulate; consulship.

consulagem (*f.*) consular fees.

consular (*adj.*) consular.

consulente (*adj.*) consultative; (*m.,f.*) consultant.

consulesa (*f.*) consul's wife; a woman consul.

consulta (*f.*) consultation; inquiry; conference, deliberation; interview. **marcar uma**—, to make an appointment for consultation (as with a doctor). **obra de**—, reference book.

consultador –**dora, consultante** (*adj.*) consulting; (*m.,f.*) consultant.

consultar (*v.t.*) to consult, ask the advice of; to consider, take into account; to confer with.—**a experiência**, to consult experience.—**o espelho**, to examine oneself in the mirror.—**o pais**, to hold elections for public office.— **o travesseiro**, (*colloq.*) to sleep on a matter.

consultivo –**va** (*adj.*) advisory.

consultor –**tora** (*m.,f.*) consultant.

consultório (*m.*) consultation room; doctor's office.

consumação (*f.*) consummation, completion, termination, fulfilment; drinks, refreshments.

consumado –**da** (*adj.*) consummate, unmitigated.

consumar (*v.t.*) to consummate: to complete; to accomplish; to perfect (to the highest degree).

consumição (*f.*) consumption; mortification, chagrin; source of worry.

consumidor –**dora** (*adj.*) consuming; (*m.,f.*) consumer.

consumir [22] (*v.t.*) to consume: to waste, destroy; to devour; to expend, use up, (*v.r.*) to fret, chafe; to pine away; to languish, waste away. **consumido de amor, de dôr**, consumed with love, with grief.

consumível (*adj.*) consumable.

consumo (*m.*) consumption, use, waste, expenditure. **artigos de**—, consumer goods.

consunção (*f., Med.*) consumption.

consuntível (*adj.*) consumable.

consuntivo –**va** (*adj.*) consumptive.

consútil (*adj.*) having a seam. [Seamless is SEM COSTURA or INCONSÚTIL.]

conta (*f.*) account, bill, statement, invoice; reckoning, count, score; (*pl.*) beads, rosary.—**aberta**, open account. —**corrente**, current account.—**s a pagar (a receber)**, bills payable (receivable). **à**—**de**, to (for) the account of. **acertar**—**s**, to balance (adjust) accounts. **afinal de**—**s**, after all (is said and done); taking all in all; to cut a long story short. **ajuste de**—**s**, settlement of accounts. **ao**, or **no, fim das**—**s**, after all. **arrumar as**—**s**, to keep books. **dar**—**de**, to account for; to destroy. **dar**—**do recado**, or **do negócio**, to do the job, deliver the goods, bring home the bacon. **Deixa isso por minha**—, Leave that to me. **deixar de levar em**—, to overlook, ignore. **fazer de** —**que**, to make believe (pretend) that. **Isso não é da sua**—, That is none of your business. **levar em**—, to take into account. **liquidar**—**s**, to settle accounts. **mais em**—, more reasonable, less expensive. **Não é de sua**—, It is not his responsibility. **no final das**—**s**, after all. **O resto fica por minha**—, Leave the rest to me. **pedir**—**s**, to demand an accounting (explanation). **por**—**de**, for the account of. **por**—**própria**, on his own account. **por fim de**—**s**, finally, eventually, at last. **pôr na**—, to charge (to one's account). **por sua**—**e risco**, on one's own account. **prestar**—**s**, to render an accounting. **prestar**—**s a**, to account to. **prestar**—**s de**, to account for. **revisor de**—**s**, accounts auditor. **sem**—, countless. **ser da**—**de**, to be the responsibility of. **ter em**—, to bear in mind. **ter em alta**—, to hold in high esteem. **tomar**—**de**, to take charge (care, control, possession) of; to care for. **tomar** **dum assunto**, to dwell at length upon a subject. **uma** —**com discriminação de verbas**, an itemized bill. **verificação de**—**s**, auditing of accounts.

contábil [-**beis**] (*adj.*) accounting, bookkeeping [procedures, principles]. **lançamentos**—**s**, bookkeeping entries; accounting records.

contabilidade (*f.*) accountancy; accounting; accounting department.

contabilista (*m.,f.*) accountant.

contacto (*m.*) = CONTATO.

contado –**da** (*adj.*) counted; recounted, related. **de**—, cash payment.

contador –**dora** (*m.,f.*) accountant, auditor; story teller; (*m.*) counter; meter (for gas, water, etc.).—**Geiger**, Geiger counter.—**de pó**, dust-counter (of air sample).— **de rotações**, speed counter; tachometer.

contadoria (*f.*) accounting department; auditing department.

conta-fios (*m.*) a thread counter (for textiles).

contagem (*f.*) count; counting; score.

contagiar (*v.t.*) to infect, contaminate.

contágio (*m.*) contagion, infection.

contagiosidade (*f.*) contagiousness.

contagioso –**sa** (*adj.*) contagious, infectious.

conta-giros (*m.*) speed counter, tachometer.

conta-gôtas (*m.*) medicine-dropper; eye-dropper.

contaminação (*f.*) contamination, pollution, infection.

contaminado –**da** (*adj.*) contaminated, defiled, polluted, infected.

contaminador –**dora** (*adj.*) contaminating; (*m.,f.*) contaminator.

contaminar (*v.t.*) to contaminate, defile, pollute, corrupt, infect.

contanto que (*conj.*) provided that, if, on condition that, with the understanding that.

conta-passos (*m.*) pedometer [= PEDÔMETRO].

conta-quilômetros (*m.*) speedometer.

contar (*v.t.*) to count; to recount, tell, relate; to number, enumerate, record, score; to calculate, compute, reckon; to expect; (*v.i.*) to count (calculate); (*v.r.*) to count (consider) oneself.—**com**, to count (depend) on.—**em**, to expect to.—**os passos**, to walk slowly.—**rodela**, to tell whoppers.—**uma boa**, to tell a good one.—**uma lorota**, to tell tales, pull someone's leg.—**vantagens**, (*slang*) to boast, brag. **a**—**de**, counting (dating) from. **Conta dois anos**, He is two years old. **conta-se que**, it is said that, they say that. **Conte comigo**, (you may) count (rely, depend) on me. **Conto com você**, I am depending on you. **Ela conta seus trinta anos**, She is about thirty. **Êle está com os dias contados**, His days are numbered. **Eu conto depois**, I'll tell you later. **Isso não conta!** That doesn't count! **Vá**—**isso a outro!** Don't tell *me* that!

contato (*m.*) contact, touch. **em**—**com**, in contact with; touching. **pôr-se em**—**com**, to get in touch with.

contável (*adj.*) countable; recountable.

conteira (*f.*) chape of a scabbard; ferrule of a cane; cascabel of a muzzle-loading cannon; (*Bot.*) bead tree or China tree [= CINAMOMO].

conteiro (*m.*) bead manufacturer or dealer.

contemplação (*f.*) contemplation; reflection, meditation, pondering; consideration, regard, deference.

contemplador –**dora** (*adj.*) contemplating; (*m.,f.*) contemplater.

contemplante (*adj.*) contemplative.

contemplar (*v.t.*) to' contemplate; to observe, gaze upon; (*v.i.*) to meditate; (*v.r.*) to contemplate oneself in a mirror.—**(alguém) com (alguma coisa)**, to bestow (something) upon (someone) as a gift, as a mark or esteem or of recognition.

contemplativa (*f.*) contemplation.

contemplativo –**va** (*adj.*) contemplative.

contemporaniedade (*f.*) contemporaneousness.

contemporâneo –**nea** (*adj.*) contemporary, contemporaneous; present-day; (*m.,f.*) contemporary.

contemporizar (*v.i.*) to temporize.

contemptível (*adj.*) contemptible.

contenção (*f.*) contention; strife; dispute; debate; containment.

contencioso –**sa** (*adj.*) contentious; (*m.*) any litigious matter.

contenda (*f.*) contention, wrangle, quarrel, squabble.

contendedor (*m.*), –**dora** (*f.*) contender.

contender (*v.i.*) to contend, strive, struggle; to debate, dispute, argue; to bicker, squabble; to compete.

contendor –**dora** (*adj.*) contending; (*m.,f.*) contender.

contensão (*f.*) struggle.

contentadiço –**ça** (*adj.*) easily satisfied.

contentamento (*m.*) contentment; satisfaction; pleasure; happiness.
contentar (*v.t.*) to content, satisfy.—**se de (em, com)**, to be content (satisfied) with. **difícil de—**, hard to please.
contentável (*adj.*) capable of being satisfied or pleased.
contente (*adj.*) content(ed), satisfied; glad, happy, pleased.
contento (*m.*) contentment. **a—**, to one's heart's content.
conter [78] (*v.t.*) to contain, hold; to comprise, embrace, include; to restrain, hold in check, hold back; (*v.r.*) to contain (restrain, control) oneself. **não se—de alegria**, to be beside oneself with joy.
contérmino –**na** (*adj.*) conterminous, adjoining; (*m.*) confine, boundary.
conterrâneo –**nea** (*adj.*) of or belonging to the same country; (*m.,f.*) fellow-countryman.
contestabilidade (*f.*) contestability.
contestação (*f.*) contention; controversy; answer, reply; attestation; denial; contradiction.
contestado –**da** (*adj.*) contested, disputed.
contestador –**dora**, **contestante** (*adj.*) contesting; (*m.,f.*) contester; contestant.
contestar (*v.t.*) to contest, dispute, controvert; to gainsay; to contradict; to talk back.—**o libelo**, (*Law*) to reply to charges.
contestável (*adj.*) contestable, questionable, disputable.
conteste (*adj.*) corroborative; confirmatory.
conteúdo (*m.*) contents.
contexto [ês] (*m.*) context; contexture.
contextura [ês] (*f.*) contexture, context; texture.
contido –**da** (*adj.*) contained, enclosed, held within; repressed, curbed.
contigo (*pron.*) with you; with thee.
contiguidade (*f.*) contiguity, juxtaposition, proximity.
contíguo –**gua** (*adj.*) contiguous, touching; adjoining; nearby.
continência (*f.*) continence, chastity; military salute.
continental (*adj.*) continental.
continente (*adj.*) continent, chaste; containing; (*m.*) continent, mainland; container.
contingência (*f.*) contingency; uncertainty.
contingente (*m.*) contingent, quota, share; (*adj.*) contingent, conditional, uncertain.
continuação (*f.*) continuation, continuance, sequel, succession, prolongation.
continuado –**da** (*adj.*) continued, continual, continuous.
continuador –**dora** (*adj.*) continuing; (*m.,f.*) continuer.
continuamente (*adv.*) continually; continuously.
continuar (*v.i.*) to continue (with), persist (in), persevere (in), go on (with); (*v.i.*) to continue, remain, endure, last; (*v.t.*) to continue, extend, prolong, protract.—**o seu caminho**, to keep on one's way. **Continua a chover**, It keeps on raining. **Continue!** Go ahead! Keep on! Go on!
continuidade [u-i] (*f.*) continuity.
contínuo –**nua** (*adj.*) continuous, continual; (*m.*) office boy, errand boy, door porter. **de—**, immediately; continually, continuously.
contismo (*m.*) Comtism, Positivism.
contista (*m.,f.*) story writer; teller of tales; Comtist, Positivist.
conto (*m.*) tale, (short) story, fable, yarn; one thousand CRUZEIROS [written thus: Crs. $1.000,00]; formerly, one thousand MIL-RÉIS [written thus: Rs. 1:000$000]; butt (of a lance).—**da carochinha**, fairy tale, nursery tale; cock-and-bull story.—**do-vigário**,—**do-paco**, confidence game, skin game, swindle, "pigeon drop". **um—de réis**, one thousand milreis.
contômetro (*m.*) comptometer.
contorção (*f.*) contortion, twist(ing).
contorcer (*v.t.*) to contort, twist; (*v.r.*) to writhe (as in pain); to squirm.
contorcionista, **contorcista** (*m.,f.*) contortionist.
contornar, **contornear** (*v.t.*) to contour; to surround, go around; to get around, avoid, by-pass (as, a difficulty).
contôrno (*m.*) contour, outline; pattern; circuit.
contra (*prep.*) counter to, against, opposed to, contrary to; facing, fronting, over against; in compensation for; (*adv.*) counter, contrariwise; (*m.*) rebuttal; counteraction.—**a mão**, on the wrong side of the street.—**a vontade**, unwillingly, reluctantly, grudgingly. **a—gôsto**, reluctantly. **a—pêlo** against the grain. **dar o—**, (*colloq.*) to oppose oneself to, go against (a proposal, an idea, etc.). **Êle é do—**, (*colloq.*) he is "agin" everything. **os prós e os**

—**s**, the pros and the cons.
contra-acusação (*f.*) countercharge.
contra-alíseos (*m.pl.*, *Meteor.*) the antitrades.
contra-almirante (*m.*) Rear Admiral.
contra-apêlo (*m.*) counterappeal.
contra-ataque (*m.*) counterattack.
contrabaixo (*m.*, *Music*) contrabass (voice or instrument).
contrabalançar (*v.t.*) to counterbalance, counterpoise; to compensate, countervail.
contrabalanço (*m.*) counterweight.
contrabandear (*v.t.*) to smuggle.
contrabandismo (*m.*) smuggling.
contrabandista (*m.,f.*) contrabandist, smuggler; (*colloq.*) peddler of supposedly smuggled goods.
contrabando (*m.*) contraband; smuggling; (*colloq.*) secret misconduct; low persons. **de—**, (*adj.*) bootleg.
contracampanha (*f.*) countercampaign.
contração (*f.*) contraction; shrinkage.
contracarril (*m.*, *R.R.*) guardrail.
contracena (*f.*) background action on a stage while the principal actors are talking or singing.
contrachaveta [ê] (*f.*, *Mach.*) cotter, key.
contrachoque (*m.*) countershock.
contracientífico –**ca** (*adj.*) unscientific.
contracifra (*f.*) key to a code or cipher.
contraclave (*f.*, *Arch.*) the voussoir next to a keystone.
contracorrente (*f.*) countercurrent, crosscurrent; (*Elec.*) back current.
contracosta (*f.*) the opposite shore.
contráctil (*adj.*) = CONTRÁTIL.
contractilidade (*f.*) = CONTRATILIDADE.
contractivo –**va** (*adj.*) = CONTRATIVO.
contracurva (*f.*) countercurve; a reverse curve.
contradança (*f.*) square dance, quadrille.
contradeclaração (*f.*) counterstatement.
contradição (*f.*) contradiction; disagreement; incongruity. **caír em—**, to contradict oneself. **sem—**, uncontradicted.
contradita (*f.*) denial, gainsaying.
contraditado –**da** (*adj.*) impugned.
contraditar (*v.t.*) to contradict, deny, gainsay; to oppose, impugn.
contraditável (*adj.*) contradictable, assailable.
contradito –**ta** (*adj.*) contradicted, denied.
contraditor –**tora** (*adj.*) contradicting; (*m.,f.*) contradicter.
contraditório –**ria** (*adj.*) contradicting; inconsistent; (*f.*) a contradicting or conflicting statement.
contradizer [41] (*v.t.*) to contradict, deny; to counter; to impugn. Cf. CONTRADITAR.
contra-empeno (*m.*) rafter strut.
contraente (*adj.*) contracting; (*m.,f.*) contracting party.
contra-erva (*f.*) = CAIAPIÁ.
contra-espionagem (*f.*) counterespionage.
contraestimular (*v.t.*) to counterstimulate.
contrafação (*f.*) counterfeiting; forgery; imitation; sham; constraint.
contrafator –**tora** (*m.,f.*) counterfeiter; forger.
contrafazedor –**dora** (*m.,f.*) counterfeiter; imitator.
contrafazer [47] (*v.t.*) to copy, imitate; to disguise; to counterfeit, forge; to constrain; (*v.r.*) to feign; to repress oneself.
contrafé (*f.*, *Law*) writ, subpoena.
contrafecho [ê] (*m.*, *Arch.*) the voussoir on either side of a keystone.
contrafeição (*f.*) = CONTRAFAÇÃO.
contrafeito –**ta** (*adj.*) constrained; uneasy; upset, put out; (*m.*) roof sill, eaves board.
contrafigura (*m.,f.*, *Theater*) double, stand-in; understudy.
contrafixa [ks] (*f.*, *Engin.*, *Arch.*) strut.
contrafixo [ks] (*m.*) pivot socket.
contraforte (*m.*) counterfort, buttress; strut; counter (of a shoe); spur (of a mountain).
contrafrechal (*m.*) pole plate of a roof truss.
contrafuga (*f.*, *Music*) counterfugue.
contragolpe (*m.*) counter blow, counterblast.
contragosto [gô] (*m.*) dislike, distaste. **a—**, reluctantly, unwillingly, against the grain.
contraído –**da** (*adj.*) tight, shrunken; contracted.
contra-indicação (*f.*) counterindication.
contra-informação (*f.*, *Milit.*) counterintelligence.
contrair [75] (*v.t.*) to contract; to constrict; to draw together; to catch (disease); to acquire (a habit); to incur (debt); (*v.r.*) to shrink, shrivel.
contra-irritante (*m.*) counterirritant.
contralto (*m.*) contralto (voice or singer).

contramalha (f.) double mesh.
contramandar (v.t.) to countermand.
contramarca (f.) countermark.
contramarchar (v.i.) to countermarch.
contramedida (f.) countermeasure.
contramestra (f.) sub-forewoman.
contramestre (m.) quartermaster; sub-foreman; overseer.
contramina (f.) countermine.
contramovimento (m.) countermovement.
contranatural (adj.) contranatural.
contra-ofensiva (f.) counteroffensive.
contra-ordem (f.) countermand.
contra-ordenar (v.t.) to countermand.
contrapancada (f.) counterblow.
contraparente (m.,f.) a distant relation.
contraparte (f.) counterpart.
contrapartida (f.) counterpart, complement; return, compensation, offset. em—, in rebuttal.
contrapeçonha (f., colloq.) counterpoison, antidote.
contrapelo [ê] (m.) the wrong way (of rubbing fur). a—, against the grain; the wrong way.
contrapesar (v.t.) to counterweigh.
contrapêso (m.) counterweight, counterbalance, offset.
contrapino (m.) cotterpin.
contraplaca (f.) anchor plate.
contrapontista (m.,f., Music) contrapuntist.
contrapontístico -ca (adj., Music) contrapuntal.
contraponto (m., Music) counterpoint; polyphony.
contrapor [63] (v.t.) to contrapose, set over against; to compare.
contraporca (f.) a lock nut.
contraposição (f.) contraposition; contradistinction.
contrapressão (f.) counterpressure; return pressure.
contraproducente (adj.) counterproductive; self-defeating.
contrapropaganda (f.) counterpropaganda.
contraproposta (f.) counterproposal.
contraprova (f., Print.) a revise (second proof).
contrapunçoar (v.t.) to countersink.
contra-reação (f.) counterreaction.
contra-regra (m., Theater) prompter.
contra-revolução (f.) counterrevolution.
contrariado -da (adj.) annoyed, upset, etc. See the verb CONTRARIAR.
contrariador -dora (adj.) contradicting; (m.,f.) contradicter.
contrariante (adj.) contradicting.
contrariar (v.t.) to contravene, oppose, contradict, counteract; to go against the will of; to thwart, hinder; to disappoint, balk, to refute, rebut; to annoy, displease; to spite; (v.r.) to contradict oneself.
contrariável (adj.) capable of being contravened.
contrariedade (f.) contrariety, opposition; obstruction; contretemps, setback; rebuff; disappointment; annoyance, unpleasantness.
contrário -ria (adj.) contrary, counter, adverse, opposed, opposite; dissenting; (m.,f.) adversary, opponent, rival. —a, against. ao—, on the contrary; unlike; in contrast to. bem ao—, quite the contrary. do—, otherwise; or else. em sentido—, in the opposite direction. pelo—, on the contrary.
contra-senha (f.) countersign; password; stub (of a ticket).
contra-senso (m.) nonsense, absurdity.
contra-soca (f.) fourth cutting of sugar cane.
contrastar (v.t.) to oppose; to assay (gold, etc.). [But not to contrast in the sense of comparing, which is PÔR EM CONTRASTE COM]; (v.i.) to contrast, form a contrast (com, with).
contrastaria (f.) assayer's office.
contraste (m.) contrast; assay. marca de—, hallmark.
contrastear (v.t.) to assay (gold, etc.).
contratador -dora (adj.) contracting; (m.,f.) contractor.
contratante (adj.) contracting; (m.,f.) contractant, contractor.
contratar (v.t.) to contract [but not in the sense of shrinking, which is CONTRAIR]; to engage; to covenant, bargain.
contratável (adj.) capable of being contracted.
contratempo (m.) contretemps, setback, reverse, mishap, snag; unpleasantness; disappointment. a—, untimely.
contrátil [-teis] (adj.) contractile.
contratilidade (f.) contractility.
contratista (m.) a share cropper on a cacao plantation.
contrativo -va (adj.) contractive.

contrato (m.) contract, covenant, bargain; pact, compact, agreement.—aleatório, (Law) aleatory contract.—de arras, marriage settlement.—de fretamento, (Maritime Law) charter party.
contratorpedeiro (m.) torpedo-boat, destroyer.
contratrilho (m.) inside rail or guardrail.
contratual (adj.) contractual.
contravapor [pôr] (m.) reverse steam pressure.
contraveio (m., Mach.) countershaft.
contravenção (f.) contravention, infringement, infraction, breach(ing), misdemeanor.—de apostas, illegal bookmaking.
contraveneno (m.) counterpoison, antidote.
contravento (m.) head wind; wind screen; outside window shutter.
contraventor -tora (m.,f.) contraventer, offender, transgressor (of laws), law-breaker.
contravertente (f.) an opposing slope.
contravigia (f.) a small fishing JANGADA.
contravir [82] (v.t.) to contravene, infringe, transgress, breach (laws); to retort.
contravolta (f.) counterturn.
contra-vontade (adv.) unwillingly.
contribuição [u-i] (f.) contribution; assessment, tax.
contribuinte [u-ín] (adj.) contributing; (m.,f.) contributor; taxpayer.
contribuir [72] (v.t.) to contribute, give, grant; to share; to pay taxes.
contribuitário -ria (adj.) contributory; (m.,f.) contributor; taxpayer.
contribuitivo -va (adj.) contributive.
contrição (f.) contrition. ato de—, Act (prayer) of Contrition. fazer ato de—, to profess repentance.
contristação (f.) saddening, sadness.
contristador -dora (adj.) saddening; distressing.
contristar (v.t.) to sadden; to afflict, distress; (v.r.) to grieve.
contrito -ta (adj.) contrite, penitent, sorrowful.
controlar (v.t.) to control, manage, direct, handle, regulate, supervise; to check, verify.
contrôle (m.) control, regulation, superintendence; verification, scrutiny; any mechanical controlling apparatus. —à distância, remote control.—do tom, (Radio) tone control.—do volume, (Radio) volume control.—duplo, dual control. manipular os—s, to handle the controls.
controvérsia (f.) controversy, discussion, dispute, debate; contention; war of words.
controversial (adj.) controversial, polemical. [But not in the sense of debatable, which is CONTROVERTÍVEL.]
controversista (m.,f.) controversialist.
controverso -sa (adj.) controversial.
controverter (v.t.) to controvert, dispute; to gainsay.
controvertível (adj.) controvertible; debatable, disputable.
contudo (conj.) nevertheless, for all that, notwithstanding, all the same.
contumácia (f.) contumacy; contempt of court; obstinacy, obduracy.
contumaz (adj.) contumacious; perverse; obstinate, refractory, obdurate.
contumélia (f.) contumely; insult, indignity; reproach.
contumelioso -sa (adj.) contumelious, abusive.
contundente (adj.) bruising, causing contusions; crushing.
contundir (v.t.) to bruise, batter, crush; to hurt.
conturbação (f.) disturbance.
conturbar (v.t.) to perturb, disturb (the peace).—idéias, to throw people's minds into confusion.
contusão (f.) contusion, bruise; hurt feelings.
contuso -sa (adj.) bruised, hurt.
conubial (adj.) connubial, conjugal, nuptial.
conúbio (m.) marriage, matrimony.
convalária (f.) lily-of-the-valley (Convallaria).
convalariáceas (f.pl., Bot.) the Convallariaceae.
convalarina (f., Chem.) convallarin.
convalescença (adj.) convalescence.
convalescente (adj.; m.,f.) convalescent.
convalescer (v.i.) to convalesce.
convecção (f., Physics) convection.
convém form of CONVIR [82].
convenção (f.) convention: agreement, compact, contract; conventional usage. [But not convention in the sense of a meeting or assembly, which is REUNIÃO, ASSEMBLÉIA].
convencer (v.t.) to convince, persuade; (v.r.) to be convinced.

convencido –da (*adj.*) convinced; (*colloq.*) conceited, stuck-up, smart alecky, cocksure; smug.

convencimento (*m.*) conviction, persuasion; (*colloq.*) conceit; smugness.

convencionado –da (*adj.*) agreed upon.

convencional (*adj.*) conventional; (*m.,f.*) party to a convention

convencionalismo (*m.*) conventionalism.

convencionalista (*adj.*) conventional; (*m.,f.*) conventionalist.

convencionar (*v.t.*) to agree upon; (*v.r.*) to agree.

convencível (*adj.*) capable of being convinced.

conveniência (*f.*) convenience, desirability; suitability; expediency; propriety, decorum; (*pl.*) social conventions. [But not *convenience*, in the sense of anything convenient, which is UTENSÍLIO, or APARELHO, ÚTIL.]

conveniente (*adj.*) fitting, appropriate; desirable; meet, proper; expedient; advantageous, useful. [But not *convenient* in the sense of at hand, easily accessible, which is A JEITO, DE FÁCIL ACESSO.]

convênio (*m.*) convention, agreement, contract; pact, compact; convenant.

conventículo (*m.*) conventicle; clique.

conventilho (*m., slang*) brothel.

convento (*m.*) convent, monastery.

Convêntria (*f.*) Coventry.

conventual (*adj.; m.,f.*) conventual.

convergência (*f.*) convergence.

convergente (*adj.*) convergent.

convergir [21a] (*v.i.*) to converge.

conversa (*f.*) conversation, talk; (*colloq.*) chatter.— **aborrecida**, boresome talk:—**fiada**, idle talk, poppycock. —**fiada**, (*m.,f.*) an idle talker, one who has no intention of living up to his promises; a gabbler.—**mole (p'ra boi dormir)**, (*slang*) idle chatter. **dois dedos de**—, brief chat. **ir na**—, (*slang*) to fall for (believe) something. **puxar**—, to strike up a conversation.

conversação (*f.*) conversation, familiar discourse.

conversador –dora (*m.,f.*) talker.

conversante (*adj.*) conversing, talking. [But not *conversant*, which is VERSADO, ENTENDIDO].

conversão (*f.*) conversion (all senses). Verb: CONVERTER.

conversar [17] (*v.i.*) to converse, talk, chat; to commune (with).

conversibilidade (*f.*) convertibility.

conversível (*ad;.*) convertible; exchangeable.

conversivo –va (*adj.*) converting.

converso –sa (*adj.*) converted.

conversor (*m., Elec., Steel Mfg.*) converter.

convertedor –dor (*adj.*) converting; (*m.,f.*) converter.

converter (*v.t.*) to convert, transform, change;—**se em**, to change into.

convertibilidade (*f.*) convertibility.

convertido –da (*adj.*) converted; (*m.,f.*) a convert.

convertimento (*m.*) conversion.

convertível (*adj.*) convertible.

convés (*m.*) (upper) deck; (*Naut.*) afterdeck.—**principal**, main deck.

convescote (*m.*) picnic [= PIQUE-NIQUE].

convexão [ks] (*f., Physics.*) convection.

convexidade [ks] (*f.*) convexity; camber.

convexo –**xa** [ks] (*adj.*) convex.

convexo-côncavo –va [ks] (*adj.*) convexo-concave.

convicção (*f.*) conviction. [But not *conviction* of a criminal, which is CONDENÇÃO DE UM RÉU.]

convício (*m.*) affront, insult, abuse.

convicto –ta (*irreg. p.p. of* CONVENCER) convinced. **réu**—, convicted criminal.

convidado –da (*adj.; m.,f.*) invited (guest).

convidador –dora (*m.,f.*) one who invites.

convidar (*v.t.*) to invite: to bid, ask; to allure, attract; (*v.r.*) to invite oneself.

convidativo –va (*adj.*) inviting; attractive.

convincente (*adj.*) convincing, persuasive, cogent.

convindo –da (*adj.*) suitable; acceptable.

convir [82] (*v.i.*) to suit (be suitable, be proper); to behoove; to befit, be in keeping with; to concur (in), agree (on). **convenhamos que**, let us agree that. **convém que**, it is meet that. **há-de—que**, must agree that. **Não me convém**, It doesn't suit me.

convite (*m.*) invitation.

conviva (*m.,f.*) fellow-banqueter; table companion; guest.

convival (*adj.*) convivial.

convivência (*f.*) a living together; familiarity, intimacy, close companionship.

convivente (*adj.*) familiar, intimate, close; (*m.,f.*) intimate friend; boon companion; sociable person.

conviver (*v.i.*) to live together; to be on intimate (familiar) terms with.

convívio (*m.*) banquet, feast; conviviality.

convocação (*f.*) convocation; military conscription; invitation.

convocado (*adj.*) summoned; invited; (*m.*) draftee.

convocador –dora (*adj.*) summoning; (*m.,f.*) summoner.

convocar (*v.t.*) to convoke, call together; to summon; (*Mil.*) to draft recruits.

convocatório –ria (*adj.*) convoking.

convolução (*f.*) convolution.

convoluto –ta (*adj.*) convolute, coiled.

convolvuláceas (*f.pl.*) the morning-glory family (*Convolvulaceae*).

convolvuláceo –cea (*adj., Bot.*) convolvulaceous.

convosco [vô] (*pron.*) with you (yourselves).

convulsão (*f.*) convulsion, spasm, cramp; violent disturbance, tumult, commotion.

convulsar, –sionar (*v.t.*) to convulse; (*v.i., v.r.*) to suffer a convulsion.

convulsivo –va (*adj.*) convulsive.

convulso –sa (*adj.*) convulsed.

coonestação (*f.*) whitewash, cover-up.

coonestar (*v.t.*) to extenuate, excuse, whitewash, cover up, gloss over.

cooperação (*f.*) co-operation.

cooperador –dora (*adj.*) co-operating; co-operative (*m.,f.*) co-operator.

cooperar (*v.i.*) to co-operate.

cooperativo –va (*adj.*) co-operative; (*f.*) a co-operative enterprise.

coordenação (*f.*) co-ordination.

coordenadas (*f.pl., Math.*) co-ordinates.

coordenado –da (*adj.*) co-ordinated.

coordenador –dora (*adj.*) co-ordinating; (*m.,f.*) co-ordinator.

coordenar (*v.t.*) to co-ordinate.

coorte (*f.*) cohort.

cop. = COPIADO (copied).

copa (*f.*) cupboard; pantry, butler's pantry; crown (of a tree or hat); (*pl.*) hearts (card suit). **fechar-se em—s** (*colloq.*) to keep mum.

copaço (*m.*) = COPÁZIO.

copado –da (*adj.*) rounded out, bulging; having a crown, shady [tree]; (*f.*) a glassful; (*Arch.*) torus.

copaíba (*f.*) a copal tree, or its timber; (*Pharm.*) copaiba balsam.—**verdadeira**, copaiba copal tree (*Copaifera officinalis*), c.a. JATOBÁ-MIRIM, ÓLEO-BRANCO, PAU-DE-ÓLEO.—**vermelha** or **-da-praia**, the balsam copal tree (*Copaifera langsdorfi*), c.a. COPAIBEIRA-DE-MINAS, ÓLEO-DE-COPAÍBA or -VERMELHO, PAU-DE-ÓLEO.

copaié (*m.*) a So. Amer. tree (*Vochysia guianensis*) from which is extracted copaiyé wood.

copal (*m.*) copal (used in varnish making).

copalina, copalita (*f., Min.*) copalite, copaline.

copalmo (*m.*) copalm, American storax balsam.

copar (*v.i., v.r.*) to branch out, develop crowns [trees]; (*v.t.*) to top (trees); to trim (hair).

coparrão (*m.*) = COPÁZIO.

co-participar (*v.i.*) to share jointly with.

copázio (*m.*) a large glass(ful). Vars. COPAÇO, COPARRÃO.

copé (*m.*) an Indian thatched hut.

copeira (*f.*) cupboard; pantry; waitress.

copeirar (*v.i.*) to work as a COPEIRO.

copeiro (*m.*) waiter, butler, pantryman.

copela (*f.*) cupel.

copelação (*f.*) cupellation.

copelar (*v.t.*) to cupel.

copépode (*m., Zool.*) copepod.

copeque (*m.*) kopeck (Russian coin).

cópia (*f.*) copy, reproduction, facsimile; imitation; copiousness, abundance.—**carbono**, carbon copy.—**figurada**, facsimile copy.

copiador –dora (*m.,f.*) copier, copyist, transcriber; (*m.*) copy-book; duplicating machine.

copiar (*v.t.*) to copy, transcribe; to imitate; (*m.*) shed, porch.

copilar (*v.*) & derivs. = COMPILAR & derivs.

copio (*m.*) small dragnet.

copiosidade (*f.*) copiousness, plenty.

copioso -sa (adj.) copious, abundant, plentiful, lavish, rich.
co-pilôto (m.) co-pilot, second pilot.
copirraite (m.) copyright.
copista (m.,f.) copyist; fig., plagiarist; (colloq.) a heavy drinker.
copla (f.) couplet.
copo (m.) glass, tumbler; (pl.) sword guard.—de graxa, grease cup.—de-leite, (Bot.) the Easter lily (Lilium longiflorum), c.a. LÍRIO-BRANCO, AÇUCENA-BRANCA, PALMA-DE-SÃO-JOSÉ; the wild calla (C. palustris); the common calla lily (Zantedeschia aethiopica).—de pé, stem goblet.—de roda, hub cap [= BUJÃO, CALOTA].
copofone (m.) musical glasses.
copolímero (m., Chem.) copolymer; heteropolymer.
copra [ó] (f.) copra (dried coconut meat).
copraol [-óis] (m.) copra (coconut) oil.
coproprietário -ria (m.,f.) co-proprietor, co-owner.
coprosterol (m., Chem.) coprosterol; coprostanol.
côptico -ca (adj.) Coptic.
copto [có] (m.) Coptic language; (pl.) Copts.
copudo -da (adj.) of trees, having a large crown.
cópula (f.) copula(tion); (Logic) copula; (Music) coupler.
copulação (f.) copulation.
copular (v.t., v.i.) to copulate; (v.t.) to couple.
copulativo -va (adj.) copulative.
coque (m.) coke; a rap on the head, esp. with the knuckles; topknot [= cocó]; cook.—metalúrgico, metallurgical coke.—de petróleo, petroleum coke.
coqueificação [e-i] (f.) process of changing coal into coke.
coqueificar [e-i] (v.t.) to coke.
coqueificável (adj.) of coal, etc., that can be coked.
coqueiral (m.) a grove of nut palmtrees.
coqueirinho (m.) any of various small palms.—do-campo = ACUMÃ.—de-vênus = COQUEIRO-DE-VÊNUS.
coqueiro (m.) any of numerous palms whose fruits are edible or employed in industry.—airi,—iri = AIRI.—amargoso, a syagrus palm (S. oleracea), c.a. GUARIROBA.—babunha = BABUNHA.—carandá = CARANDÁ.—cabeçudo, the Brazilian butia palm (Butia capitata), c.a. BUTIÁ-DE-VINAGRE.—catolé, a syagrus palm (S. comosa), c.a. CATOLÉ, PALMITO-AMARGOSO.—da-bahia, the common coconut (Cocos nucifera), c.a. INAJÁ-GUAÇU, INAIÁ-GUAÇU-IBA.—de-dendê = DENDÊZEIRO.—de-vênus, common dracena (Cordyline terminalis), c.a. COQUEIRINHO-DE-VÊNUS, PAPAGAIO, RAIZ-DE-CHÁ.—do-campo, the acuma syagrus palm (S. flexuosa), c.a. ARICURI, CÔCO-DE-QUARESMA, PALMITO-DO-CAMPO; also = COQUINHO-DO-CAMPO.—guriri = BURI-DA-PRAIA.—macho, a tree fern (Cyathea arborea).—marajabaíba = COQUINHO-BABÁ.—tucum = CUMARI.
coqueluche (m.) whooping cough [= TOSSE COMPRIDA]; (colloq.) fad, craze.
coquete (adj.) coquettish; (f.) coquette; flirt.
coquetel [-téis] (m.) cocktail; cocktail party.
coquetismo (m.) coquettishness.
coquilho (m.) copra; the extracted kernel or meat of palm nuts from which oil is expressed; (Bot.) a canna (C. glauca), c.a. ALBARÁ, BANANEIRO-DO-MATO, CAITÉ-IMBIRI, ERVA-DOS-FERIDOS, IMBIRI, MARACÁ, MURU.
coquinho (m.) a leafflower (Phyllanthus pendulus); a coco-palm (Arecastrum romanzoffiana), c.a. BABA-DE-BOI.—babá, a bramblepalm (Desmoncus setosus), c.a. COQUEIRO-MARAJAÍBA, TUCUM-DO-BREJO.—do-campo, a butiapalm (Butia leiospatha), c.a. CABEÇUDO, COQUEIRO-DO-CAMPO, MACUMÁ.
cor (adv.) de—, by heart.
côr [-es] (f.) color, hue, tint, dye; pigment; ruddiness (of complexion); redness; character; plea, pretext, guise; (pl.) colors (flag).—complementar, complementary color.—da noite, black.—de burro quando foge, (colloq.) a hard-to-describe color.—de fogo, flame-color.—de rosa, pink.—de granada, the color pomegranate.—de vinho, claret color.—es cruas, crude colors.—es elementares, elementary colors.—es inimigas, clashing colors.—fixa, fast color.—lisa, solid (plain) color.—local, local color.—neutra, neutral color.—primária or primitiva, primary color.—secundária, secondary color.—tirante a verde, azul, etc., a greenish, bluish, etc. tinge.—viva, bright (lively) color. ver tudo côr-de-rosa, to see everything through rose-colored glasses.
cora (f.) bleaching (of washed clothes).
coração (m.) heart; bosom, breast; courage; center, core; generosity; veranda; = MANGARÁ (f.) a blush or act of

blushing.—aberto, an open-hearted person.—da-índia, the balloonvine heartseed (Cardiospermum helicacabum), c.a. XEQUE-XEQUE, PARATUDO, PAÚNA; the soursop (Annona muricata), c.a. SAPE-SAPE.—de-boi = ARITICUM-DE-CHEIRO.—de-bugre = AROEIRA-DE-BUGRE.—de-estudante, a begonia (B. platanifolia), c.a. AZEDINHA-DO-BREJO, ERVA-DE-SAPO.—de-negro = CATINGA-DE-PORCO and ÉBANO-ORIENTAL.—de-ouro, person with a heart of gold.—de-pedra, or -de-rocha, person with a heart of flint.—de-rainha, (Bot.) the cherimoya (Annona cherimola).—magoado, the Herbst bloodleaf (Iresine herbsti), c.a. ORELHA-DE-PORCO.—verde = BEBERU. abrir o—a alguém, to unburden oneself to another. alargar o—, to take on new courage. com o— em festa, jubilant, joyful. de—, wholeheartedly. de todo o—, with all my heart. de cortar o—, heart-rending. fazer das tripas—, to display "guts". Longe dos olhos, longe do—, Out of sight, out of mind. O que os olhos não vêem, o—não sente, What you don't know won't hurt you.
coráceos (m.pl.) the crow family (Corvidae).
coracoidal (adj.) coracoidal.
coracóide, coracoídeo -dea (adj.; m., Anat., Zool.) coracoid.
coraçonada (f.) a sudden heartfelt impulse; a hunch.
corado -da (adj.) ruddy; rosy-cheeked; blushing.
coradouro (m.) a place where washed clothes are spread out to bleach in the sun; = QUARADOR.
coragem (f.) courage, bravery, boldness; valor, mettle; fortitude; act of coloring; bleaching (of washed clothes or fabrics).
corajoso -sa (adj.) courageous, valiant.
coral [-ais] (adj.) choral; (m.) chorale; coral; coral red; (f., Bot.) the mountainrose coralvine (Antigonon leptopus), c.a. AMOR-AGARRADO, AMOR-ENTRELAÇADO, AMORES-AGARRADINHOS, CORÁLIA, ENTRADA-DE-BAILE, GEORGINA, MIMO-DO-CÉU, ROSÁLIA, VIUVINHA; the Brazilian manettia vine (M. sp.), c.a. POAIA-DE-CIPÓ, POAIA-DE-MINAS, POAIA-DO-RIO, POEJO-DO-MATO; the coralplant (Russelia equisetiformis); (Zool.) a coral snake (Micrurus).—verdadeira, a coral snake (Micrurus marcgravii);—vermelha, a coral snake (Micrurus corallinus).
coraleiro -ra (adj.) coral-fishing; (m.) coral fisher (man or boat); a parrot (Amazona vinacea), c.a. JURUEBA, PEITO-ROXO; (f., Bot.) a wild ixora (Isertia).
corália (f.) = CORAL (vine).
coraliários (m.pl.) the group (Coralligena) consisting of the corals and their allies.
coralígeno -na (adj.; Zool.) coralligenous.
coralim (m.) a nonpoisonous Brazilian snake (Coluber formosus).
coralina (f.) coralline (a calcareous alga or seaweed of the genus Corallina); a Chamaedorea palm (C. corallina); corallin(e), a dye; (Min.) carnelian, c.a. CORNALINA.
coralináceo -cea (adj.; Bot.) corallinaceous; (f.pl.) a family (Corallinaceae) of red algae.
coralíneo -nea (adj.) coralline.
coralino -na (adj.) coral-red.
corana (f.) the orange jessamine (Cestrum aurantiacum).
corandel [-déis] (m., Printing) a runaround.
corango (m., Bot.) a globe amaranth (Gomphrena), c.a. CORONGO, PARATUDO.
corante (adj.) coloring, dyeing; (m.) dye, stain, coloring matter.
corar (v.t.) to color, tinge, dye; to bleach [= QUARAR]; to disguise, gloss over; (v.i.) to blush, flush, turn red.
corbelha [ê] (f.) a gift basket of fruit, flowers, etc.; (Arch.) corbeil.
corça [ô] (f.) female roe deer.
corcel [-céis] (m.) courser, charger (horse).
corcha [ô] (f.) tree bark; cork.
corço [ô] (m.) roebuck.
corcora (f.) = CORCOROCA.
côrcoro (m., Bot.) the potherb jute (Corchorus olitorius).
corcoroca (f.) any of various grunts of the genus Haemulon, esp. the blue-striped grunt (H. sciurus) and the white grunt (H. plumieri), both c.a. CORCORA-MULATA, NEGRA-MINA, BIQUARA, etc.—bôca-larga, a grunt (H. steindachneiri), c.a. FAROFA.—jurumiri(m), a pigfish (Orthopristis chrysopterus), c.a. CORCOROCA-VERDADEIRA.
corocotéu (m.) = COROTÉU.
corcova (f.) hunchback; hump; curvet, buck (of a horse).
corcovado -da (adj.) humped, hunchbacked; (m.) = URU

(a partridge); (m.) a butterfly (Morpho anaxibia) c.a. AZUL-SÊDA.

corcovar (v.i.) to curvet, leap, bound; to buck; (v.t.) to bend, arch; (v.r.) to curve, bend, stoop, hump over.

corcovear (v.i.) to curvet.

corcôvo (m.) curvet, buck (of a horse).

corcunda (adj.; m.,f.) hunchback. Var. CARCUNDA.

corda (f.) cord, rope; string, twine; string of musical instrument; spring of a timepiece; chord.—**bamba**, slack rope or wire (used by some acrobats instead of a tight-rope); (colloq.) precarious position.—**d'água**, heavy rain.—**de abacá**, manila rope.—**de arco**, bowstring.—**de cânhamo**, hemp rope.—**de juta**, jute rope.—**de nailon**, nylon cord.—**de pular**, jumping rope.—**reboque**, tow rope.—**de relógio**, mainspring of a timepiece.—**dorsal** (Anat., Zool.) chorda dorsalis, notochord.—**do tímpano**, (Anat.) chorda tympani.—**s da alma** or **do coração**, heartstrings.—**s vocais**, vocal cords.—**sensível**, the weak side or soft spot in a person's nature. **cercar com**—, to rope off. **dansar na**—**bamba**, to perform on the slack wire; fig., to waver with indecision. **com a**—**na garganta**, with a rope around one's neck, i.e., in a tight spot, hard-pressed (for money). **instrumento de cordas**, stringed instrument.

cordame (m.) ship's rigging; cordage.

cordão (m.) twine, string [= BARBANTE]; sanitary cordon; an organized group of Carnival merrymakers; sash bar [= PINÁSIO]; (Arch.) a small, circular molding of flowers, etc.—**de chapéu**, hat cord.—**de formigas**, a long line of ants on the march.—**-de-frade** or **-de-são-francisco**, (Bot.) a lion's-ear (Leonotis nepetaefolia), c.a. PAU-DE-PRAGA, RUBIM; also = AGRIPALMA.—**sanitário**, (Mil.) cordon.—**de sapato**, shoe string.—**umbilical**, navel cord.

cordato -ta (adj.) sagacious; sage, prudent, sensible, levelheaded; (m.pl., Zool.) the Chordata.

cordear (v.t.) to measure or align with a cord.

cordeira (f.) lambskin; a female lamb.

cordeirinho -nha (m.,f.) lambkin, baby lamb.

cordeiro (m.) lamb; fig., gentle person.

cordel [-déis] (m.) string, twine; chalk line. **literatura de**—, cheap pamphlets, magazines, etc., which are displayed hanging along a cord on the sides of a newsstand. **mexer os seus**—**inhos**, to pull strings.

cordial (adj.) cordial, affectionate; affable; sincere; cheerful; (m.) cordial, liqueur.

cordialidade (f.) cordiality, affection, sincerity.

cordierita (f., Min.) cordierite, iolite, dichroite.

cordiforme (adj.) heart-shaped.

cordilheira (f.) mountain chain; ridge.

cordoada (f.) a flogging with a piece of rope; cordage, ship's rigging.

cordoalha (f.) ship's rigging, tackle, gear.

cordoaria (f.) rope factory.

cordoeiro (m.) ropemaker.

cordovão (m.) cordovan leather.

cordoveia (f., colloq.) jugular vein.

cordura (f.) good sense; prudence.

coreano -na (adj.; m.,f.) Korean.

corê-corê (adj.) loquacious; (m.) a gabbler.

co-redator (m.) co-editor.

coregrafia (f.) choreography.

coregráfico -ca (adj.) choreographic.

corégrafo (m.), -fa (f.) choreographer.

coréia (f., Med.) chorea, St. Vitus's dance; (f.) Korea.

coreografia (f.) = COREGRAFIA.

coreográfico -ca (adj.) = COREGRÁFICO.

coreógrafo (m.), -fa (f.) = CORÉGRAFO, -FA.

coreopsis (m., Bot.) the genus Coreopsis.

coreotripanose (f., Med.) Chagas' disease, c.a. TRIPANOS-SOMÍASE AMERICANA.

corera [ê] (f.) = CRUEIRA.

coresma (f., colloq.) = QUARESMA.

coreto [ê] (m.) bandstand.

co-ré (f.), **co-réu** (m.) co-defendant.

coriáceo -cea (adj.) coriaceous, of or like leather, tough.

coriambo (m., Pros.) choriamb.

coriandro (m., Bot.) coriander (Coriandrum sativum), c.a. COENTRO.

coriária (f., Bot.) the genus Coriaria.

coriavo (m.) a nighthawk (Nyctidromus albicolis derbyanus). Cf. CURIANGO.

coribamba (f.) = XARÉU.

córico (m.) punching bag.

corículo (m.) strap, leather thong.

coridalina (f., Chem.) corydaline.

corídalo (m., Bot.) the genus Corydalis.

corifena (f.) common dolphin (Coryphaena hippurus); [= GOLFINHO, DELFIM].

corifeu (m.) the leader of a party, school of thought, etc.

corilina (f., Biochem.) corylin.

côrilo (m., Bot.) filbert or hazel (Corylus spp.)

corimbífero -ra (adj., Bot.) corymbiferous.

corimbo (m., Bot.) corymb.

corimbó-da-mata (m.) a ropevine (Tanaecium).

corincho (m.) braggadocio.

corindiba, corindiúba (f.) Brazilian hackberry (Celtis brasiliensis), c.a. QUATINDIBA.

corindo, corindon (m., Min.) corundum.

coringa (f.) small triangular sail; (m.) lighterman.

coríntio -tia (adj.; m.,f.) Corinthian.

cório (m.) = CÓRION.

coriocele (f., Med.) choriocele.

corióide (f., Anat.) choroid.

córion (m., Embryol., Zool.) chorion. Var. CÓRIO.

coriscação (f.) a flashing, sparkling, gleaming.

coriscado -da (adj.) struck by lightning; (f.) an electrical storm.

coriscante (adj.) flashing, gleaming.

coriscar (v.i.) to flash (as lightning); to gleam.

corisco (m.) flash (as of lightning); gleam.

corista (m.,f.) member of a chorus; chorister.

corixa (f.) outlet of a lake or marsh. Var. CORIXO.

corixo (m.) = CHUPIM (a bird), and CORIXA.

coriza (f., Med.) coryza, cold in the head.

corja (f.) rabble, mob, gang; pack (of thieves, etc.)

cornaca (m.) elephant keeper.

cornaço (m.), -**nada** (f.) a horn-thrust.

cornadura (f.) an animal's horns.

cornalheira (f., Bot.) the terebinth pistache (P. terebinthus).

cornalina (f., Min.) carnelian.

cornamusa (f.) bagpipe.

cornar (v.t.) to gore with the horns.

corne (m.) trumpet, horn.—**inglês**, English horn.

córnea (f., Anat., Zool.) cornea.—**opaca**, the sclerotic coat of the eye.

cornear (v.t.) to gore with the horns; (slang) to make a cuckold of (a husband).

Cornélia (f.) Cornelia.

Cornélio (m.) Cornelius.

córneo -nea (adj.) of or like horn; horny.

corneta [ê] (f.) cornet, trumpet, horn, bugle; auto horn; a wigwag flag; (m.) bugler, trumpeter.—**acústica**, ear trumpet; (adj.) having only one horn; nosey; awkward.

cornetada (f.) bugle call; a sounding of trumpets.

corneteiro (m.) bugler, trumpeter, cornet player.

cornetim (m.) French horn.—**de pistões**, cornet.

cornicabra (f.) bush redpepper (Capsicum frutescens), c.a. PIMENTÃO-LONGAL, CHARNECA.—**dos-algarvios**, the Medit. joint fir (Ephedra fragilis).

cornichão (m., Bot.) the birdsfoot deervetch (Lotus corniculatus).

corniche (m.) cornicle, a little horn; snail's feeler; insect's antenna.

cornicurto -ta (adj.) shorthorned.

cornífero -ra (adj.) having horns.

corniforme (adj.) shaped like a horn.

cornígero -ra (adj.) cornigerous.

cornija (f.) cornice.

cornilargo -ga (adj.) having widely spaced horns.

cornilhão (m., Bot.) a scorpiontail (Scorpiurus sulcata).

cornilongo -ga (adj.) longhorned.

corninho (m.) a little horn.

corniso (m.) the cornelian cherry dogwood (Cornus mas).

côrno [cornos] (m.) horn; insect feeler; hornlike process or object; (slang) cuckold.—**da abundância**, horn of plenty. —**godinho**, (Bot.) the European mountainash (Sorbus aucuparia), c.a. LAMA, GUEIRA, TRAMAGUEIRA.—**s-do-diabo** = CHIFRE-DE-VEADO. **aos**—**s da lua**, of praise, to the skies.

Cornualha (f.) Cornwall.

cornucópia (f.) cornucopia.

cornudo -da (adj.) having big horns; (f., Zool.) hammer-head shark (Sphyrna zygaena), c.a. CHIFRUDA, MARTELO, PEIXE-MARTELO.

cornuta (f.) a tobacco worm (Protoparce sp.).

cornutina (f., Chem.) cornutin(e).

cornuto -ta (*adj.*) bearing or having horns [= CORNÍFERO, CORNUDO]. **raciocínio**—, dilemma.

côro (*m.*) chorus (voices, stage, refrain); choir; choir loft; chancel. **menino de**—, choir boy.

coró (*m.*) dung beetle; maggot; also = RONCADOR (fish).

coroa [ôa] (*f.*) crown; wreath, garland; funeral wreath; royalty; top, summit; priest's tonsure; sun's corona; tuft, crest. "An isolated circular-shaped beach with light-coloured sand and no vegetation, which is the first land to appear as the waters recede." [GBAT]—**chinêsa** = COROA-IMPERIAL (a shell).—**de-cristo**, (*Bot.*) the Christthorn paliurus (*P. spina-christi*), c.a. ESPINHO-DE-CRISTO (or -de-JUDEU, or -ITALIANO); the crown-of-thorns euphorbia (*E. mili*), c.a. ÁRVORE-DE-SÃO-SEBAS-TIÃO, DOIS-IRMÃOS.—**de espinhos**, crown of thorns.—**de flores**, floral wreath.—**-de-frade**, Nery melon cactus (*Melocactus neryi*).—**de laranjeira**, bride's orange-blossom wreath.—**de louros**, laurel wreath.—**-de-mocambique**, scarlet bloodlily (*Haemanthus coccineus*). —**-de-nossa-senhora** = DOIS-IRMÃOS.—**de-rei**, a clover (*Trifolium melilotus segetalis*).—**-de-viúva** = CAPELA-DE-VIÚVA.—**do diferencial**, (*Autom.*) master gear of the differential.—**do pistão**, top surface of piston head.—**do-rei** = ANAFA (a clover).—**hereditária**, hereditary crown. —**imperial**, imperial frittilary (*Fritillaria imperialis*); (*Zool.*) a volute (*Voluta imperialis*).—**radial**, a glory around the head of images of saints.—**real**, yellow sweetclover (*Melilotus officinalis*).—**solar**, solar corona.

coroá (*m.*) = CAROÁ.

coroação (*f.*) crowning; coronation; deer's antlers.

coroado -da (*adj.*) crowned; royal; (*m.*) a tonsured priest; (*m.,f.*) an Indian of a virtually extinct tribe, originally one with the Puri, who dwelt in the mountainous region northeast of Rio de Janeiro. The name Coroado, which derives from COROA (crown), is descriptive of their circular monklike tonsure, and is used for the same reason to designate also the Bororo in Mato Grosso, and certain Caingang in southern Brazil who are not related to the Puri-Coroado; (*adj.*) pert. to or designating the Coroado or a Caingang.

coroamento (*m.*) crowning; finishing touch.

coroanha (*f.*, *Bot.*) a clusterpea (*Dioclea sp.*).

coroar (*v.t.*) to crown; to award a prize to; to complete, finish (something).

coroatá (*m.*) = CARAGUATÁ-ACANGA.

corobó (*m.*) = CAPIM-CEBOLA.

coroca (*adj.*) decrepit.

corocoroca (*f.*) = CORCOROCA.

corocotéu (*m.*) = COROTÉU, COROXÓ.

corocoturu (*m.*, *Zool.*) a caracara (*Ibycter ater*).

corografia (*f.*, *Geog.*) chorography.

coroia (*f.*) = ANUNGUAÇU.

coróide (*f.*, *Anat.*) chor(i)oid.

coroidite (*f.*, *Med.*) choroiditis.

coroinha (*m.*) altar boy [= CORINHA]; (*f.*) a little crown.

corola (*f.*, *Bot.*) corolla.

corolário (*m.*) corollary.

corolífero -ra (*adj.*, *Bot.*) corolliferous.

coroliforme (*adj.*, *Bot.*) corolliform.

corolítico -ca (*adj.*, *Arch.*) corollitic, carolitic.

coronal (*adj.*) coronal; (*m.*, *Anat.*) corona.

coronário -ria (*adj.*) coronary; (*f.*, *Anat.*) coronary artery.

coronel [-néis] (*m.*) colonel; (*colloq.*) a moneyed man (esp. an old one) who spends money freely (esp. on women).

coronelato (*m.*, *Mil.*) colonelcy.

corongo (*m.*) = CURANGO.

coronha (*f.*) butt, stock of a gun.

coronhada (*f.*) blow with a rifle butt.

coroniforme (*adj.*) crown-shaped.

coronilina (*f.*, *Chem.*) coronillin.

corônio (*m.*, *Astrophysics*) coronium.

coronóide, coronoídeo -dea (*adj.*) resembling the beak of a crow.

coropó (*m.,f.*) an Indian of the Coropó, related linguistically and culturally to the Puri; (*adj.*) pert. to or designating the Coropó.

coroque (*m.*) = RONCADOR.

cororô (*m.*) burned rice which sticks to the bottom of the pan.

cororó-coatá (*m.*) = ALBACORA.

corote (*m.*) water keg.

corotéu (*m.*) a bird—the hooded berry-eater (*Ampelion cucullatus*), c.a. COROCOXÓ, COROCOTÉU, ROCROROÉ, ROROCORÉ, CREJUÁ, CURUÁ; also = COROXÓ.

coroxó (*m.*) a bird—the black-headed berry-eater (*Ampelion melanocephalus*); also = COROTÉU.

corozo (*m.*) ivory nut; = MARFIM-VEGETAL.

corpanzil (*m.*, *colloq.*) a large-bodied person.

corpo [côr; pl.: córǀ (*m.*) body; corpus, mass, bulk; thickness, consistency, substance; corpse, carcass; bodice; military corps; corporation.—**a**—, hand-to-hand, body-against-body (contest, fight).—**atérmico**, (*Physics*) black body.—**cavernoso**, (*Anat.*) corpus cavernosum.—**celeste**, heavenly body.—**da guarda**, (*Milit.*) guard unit.— **da igreja**, body of the church.—**de aviação**, air corps.— **de baile**, corps de ballet.—**de bombeiros**, fire department.—**de delito**, corpus delicti.—**diplomático**, diplomatic corps.—**discente**, student body.—**docente**, teaching faculty.—**lenhoso**, (*Bot.*) xylem, woody tissue. —**tireoídeo**, (*Anat.*) thyroid gland or body.—**vítreo**, (*Anat.*) vitreous body. **botar**—, of the body, to fill out. **bem feito de**—, well-built. **cheio de**—, full-bodied, stout, buxom. **combate (embate, luta) de**—**a**—, hand-to-hand fighting. **de**—**e alma**, with body and soul. **fechar o**—, (*colloq.*) to render the body (through incantations, etc.) invulnerable to bullets, knives, snake bites, etc.; to take a drink on the pretext that it will ward off sickness. **mal feito de**—, ungainly, ill-shaped. **meio**—, the bust. **tirar o**—**fora**, to duck, dodge (work, trouble, responsibility).

corporação (*f.*) corporation, society, company. [But not corporation in the sense of a stock company, which is SOCIEDADE ANÔNIMA.]

corporal (*adj.*) corporal, corporeal; (*m.*, *Eccl.*) corporal, communion cloth. [The soldier corporal is CAPORAL.]

corporalidade (*f.*) corporality, corporeality.

corporalizar (*v.t.*) to corporealize.

corporativismo (*m.*) collectivism, communism.

corporativo -va (*adj.*) corporative.

corporeidade (*f.*) corporeity.

corpóreo -rea (*adj.*) corporeal.

corporificar (*v.t.*) to embody; (*v.r.*) to take form.

corpulência (*f.*) corpulence.

corpulento -ta (*adj.*) corpulent, stout.

corpuscular (*adj.*) corpuscular.

corpúsculo (*m.*, *Anat.*, *Bot.*) corpuscle.

correada (*f.*) a lashing, belting, strapping.

correagem (*f.*) **correame** (*m.*) leather belts and straps; harness.

correiaria (*f.*) leather-goods concern; saddlery.

corre-campo (*m.*) a colubrid snake (*Philodryas nattererei*).

correção (*f.*) correction, correcting; correctness; propriety; house of correction, reformatory. [The verb is CORRIGIR.] Cf. CORREIÇÃO.

correcional (*adj.*) correctional; (*m.*) lower criminal court.

corre-corre (*m.*) a scurrying, scampering; helter-skelter flight.

corredator (*m.*), **-tora** (*f.*) co-editor (of a periodical).

corredeira (*f.*) river rapids; a succession of small waterfalls; (*colloq.*) diarrhea.

corrediço -ça, **corredio** -dia (*adj.*) sliding, slipping, running; (*f.*) groove, slot, slide; stage curtain; draw curtain; slide valve. **porta**—, sliding door.

corredor -dora (*adj.*) fast-running, swift; (*m.*) corridor, runway, hallway, passageway; (*m.,f.*) runner, racer; (*f.*) portcullis.

corredouro (*m.*) a running; racetrack. Var. CORREDOIRO.

correeiro [re-ei] (*m.*) saddler; leather merchant.

correento -ta [re-en] (*adj.*) leathery.

corregedor (*m.*) corregidor (early-day magistrate).

córrego (*m.*) stream, brook, creek; ravine, gully.

correia (*f.*) leather strap; thong; belting; dog leash.— **compensada**, a belt made of two or more thicknesses of material.—**contínua**, —**sem fim**, endless belt.—**do ventilador**, fan belt.—**-vê**, a V-belt.

correição (*f.*) correction; correctness; house of correction; a stream or swarm of ants or other insects; a driver or legionary ant. Cf. CORREÇÃO.

correio (*m.*) post office; mail; mailbox; postman; courier; messenger.—**aéreo**, air mail. **pela volta do**—, by return mail. **pelo**—, by mail. **pombo**—, carrier (homing) pigeon.

correlação (*f.*) correlation.—**positiva (negativa, secundária, curvilínea)**, (*Statistics*) positive (negative, secondary, curvilinear) correlation.

correlacionar, correlatar (*v.t.*) to correlate.

correlativo -va (*adj.*) correlative.

correligionário (*m.*), **-ria** (*f.*) correligionist; fellow party member.

corrente (*adj.*) current, running; fluent, flowing; glib; rife, prevailing; common, popular; of common occurrence; (*adv.*) currently; (*f.*) current, stream; torrent; current of air; metal chain.—**anergética**, wattless current.—**alternada**, or —**alternativa**, alternating current.—**contínua**, direct current.—**de ar**, draft, current of air.—**de alta (baixa) freqüência**, high (low) frequency current.—**desvatada** = CORRENTE ANERGÉTICA.—**elétrica**, electric current.—**farádica**, (*Elec.*) induced current.—**parasita**, parasitic current. **condutor sem—**, dead wire. **conta—**, current account. **contra—**, cross current. **elo de—**, chain link. **estar ao—de**, a gallicism meaning to be *au courant*, well-informed, well-posted. [Better usage: **estar ao par de.**] **nadar contra a—**, to swim against the stream.
correnteza (*f.*) current, draft (of air); row (as of houses).
correntio -**tia** (*adj.*) current, generally received.
correntista (*m.,f.*) bookkeeper in charge of current accounts; person having a current bank account.
correntoso -**sa** (*adj.*) fast-running, fast-flowing.
correr (*v.i.*) to run, race, sprint; to hasten, hurry; to scamper, scurry; to pass, elapse [time]; to be spread [news, rumors]; to circulate [money]; to flow (as a river); to proceed, go on; to run across, extend from side to side; of interest, to accrue; (*v.t.*) to run after, pursue; to be exposed to risk; to run through, pierce; to run (the hand, the eyes) over; to run off, chase away; to draw (the curtain).—**a mesma sorte**, to run the same chance.—**a vista**, to run the eyes over.—**como nunca**, to run like everything.—**demais**, to run too fast.—**em árvore sêca**, (*Naut.*) to scud.—**mundo**, to rove, roam, see the world.—**parelhas**, to run neck-and-neck.— **ceca e meca**, to travel the world over. **ao—do martelo**, at the drop of the (auctioneer's) hammer. **deixar—(o marfim)**, to let things run to suit themselves; to be indifferent to what happens; to wait and see. **nos dias que correm**, nowadays, in these times.—**os olhos por**, to run the eyes over (scan) something. **pegar a—**, to start running. **porta de—**, a sliding door. **Quem corre, cansa; quem anda alcança**, Haste makes waste; make haste slowly.
correria (*f.*) a running about; raid, foray.
correspondência (*f.*) correspondence; letter-writing; intercourse, communication; concurrence, conformity; correlation.—**refugada** or **de refugo**, dead letters (in the postoffice). **em—a**, in response to; in accord with. **em —com**, in keeping with.
correspondente (*adj.*) correspondent; corresponding; (*m.,f.*) correspondent; letter-writer; corresponding word.
corresponder (*v.t.*) to correspond (to, with); to respond; to agree, tally; to answer letters; to requite, reciprocate. —**se com**, to correspond with.
corretagem (*f.*) brokerage; broker's fee.
corretar (*v.i.*) to function as a broker.
corretismo (*m.*) irreprehensible conduct.
corretivo -**va** (*adj.*) corrective; (*m.*) a corrective agent; correction, reprimand.
correto -**ta** (*adj. & irreg. p.p. of* CORRIGIR) correct, faultless; accurate, right; honorable, fair; correctly attired, trim.
corretor (*m.*) broker, commission agent.—**de amores**, pimp, pander.—**de apostas**, bookmaker, bookie.—**de câmbios**, exchange broker.—**de hotel**, tout.—**de imóveis**, real estate broker.
corrição (*f.*) coursing (hunting with dogs).
corrico (*m.*) **pescaria de—**, troll fishing.
corrido -**da** (*adj.*) abashed, confused; crestfallen; worn, wasted; driven out (off); (*f.*) race; a running; flight; rush; run (on the bank); stroke (of a piston); a pouring (of metal); a single or one-way trip (as of a taxi).—**com barreiras**, or —**de obstáculos**, hurdle race.—**de cavalos**, horse race; horse racing.—**de prova**, a test run.—**de revesamento**, relay race.—**de touros**, bullfight.—**de pedestre**, a foot race. **cavalo de—**, race horse.—**de vergonha**, embarrassed to death. **disputar—**, to run a race.
corrigenda (*f.*) corrigendum; errata (in printing).
corrigibilidade (*f.*) corrigibility.
corrigir [24] (*v.t.*) to correct, amend, rectify; to chastise. —**provas**, to read proof. [The noun is CORREÇÃO.]
corrigível (*adj.*) corrigible.
corrilho (*m.*) clandestine assembly; closed meeting; scheme, plot.
corrimaça (*f.*) hooting, jeering; clamorous pursuit; hue and cry.
corrimão [-mãos, -mões] (*m.*) handrail, guardrail.

corrimento (*m.*) running; noisy chase; (*Med.*) any morbid discharge; gleet.
corriola (*f.*) a kind of ribbon game; jeering; trick; (*Bot.*) European glorybind (*Convolvulus arvensis*) c.a. VERDESELHA.—**bastarda** = SANGUINÁRIA (plant).
corriqueirismo (*m.*) affectation, pretense.
corriqueiro -**ra** (*adj.*) commonplace, trite, hackneyed; everyday, routine; affected, conceited.
corrixo (*m.*) = CORIXO.
corroboração (*f.*) corroboration, confirmation; a strengthening.
corroborante, corroborativo -**va** (*adj.*) corroboratory.
corroborar (*v.t.*) to corroborate, confirm; (*v.r.*) to grow stronger.
corroer [56] (*v.t.*) to corrode, erode; to gnaw, eat away.
corroído -**da** (*adj.*) corroded; eroded; eaten away.
corrompedor -**dora** (*adj.*) corrupting; (*m.,f.*) corrupter.
corromper (*v.t.*) to corrupt, putrefy; to pollute, infect, spoil; to deprave, pervert; to adulterate; to taint.
corrompido -**da** (*adj.*) corrupted; corrupt; = CORRUTO.
corrompimento (*m.*) corruption; = CORRUÇÃO.
corrosão (*f.*) corrosion; erosion.—**eólica**, wind erosion (of rocks).—**electrolítica**, electrolytic corrosion.—**magmática**, (*Petrog.*) resorption borders.
corrosibilidade (*f.*) corrodibility.
corrosível (*adj.*) corrodible.
corrosividade (*f.*) corrosiveness.
corrosivo -**va** (*adj.; m.*) corrosive (agent).
corrubiana (*f.*) in the mountainous regions of Minas Gerais, a cold fog accompanied by a southeast wind. Var. CORRUPIANA.
corrução (*f.*) corruption; taint; also = MACULO.
corruchiar (*v.i.*) to sing in a low, quiet tone [canaries and other songsters].
corrugação (*f.*) corrugation.
corrugado -**da** (*adj.*) corrugated. **chapas—s**, corrugated steel sheets.
corrugar (*v.t.*) to corrugate; to wrinkle.
corruíra (*f.*) the Brazilian grass wren (*Cistothorus platensis polyglottus*), c.a. CUTIPURUÍ, ROUXINOL; also = CAMBAXIRRA.—**açu**, the Bahia long-billed wren (*Thryothorus longirostris bahiae*).—**do-brejo**, the southern yellow-throated spine-tail (*Certhiaxis cinnamonea, russeola*), c.a. CANÁRIO-DO-BREJO, MARREQUITO-DO-BREJO, CURUTIÉ, PEDREIRO-PEQUENO.
corrume (*m.*) groove, slide, slot.
corrupção (*f.*) = CORRUÇÃO.
corrupião (*m.*) the jamacai oriole (*Icterus j. jamacaii*), c.a. SOFRÊ, CONCRIS, JOÃO-PINTO.
corrupiar (*v.i.*) to whirl, spin around.
corrupiê, corrupié (*m.*) = CRUPIÊ.
corrupio (*m.*) a certain game for children; a toy windmill; pinwheel; (*colloq.*) hustle and bustle, flurry; whirlpool, whirlwind; a sea urchin, c.a. BALACHA.
corru[p]tela (*f.*) corruption, esp. of a word; corrupt practice, abuse.
corru[p]tibilidade (*f.*) corruptibility.
corru[p]tível, -tivo -**va** (*adj.*) corruptible.
corru[p]to -**ta** (*adj.*) corrupt, debased, perverted; (of language), corrupted.
corru[p]tor -**tora** (*adj.*) corrupting; (*m.,f.*) corrupter.
corsário (*m.*) corsair, privateer.
corselete [lê] (*m.*) corslet (all senses); thorax of an insect.
Córsega (*f.*) Corsica.
córsico -**ca** (*adj.; m.,f.*) Corsican.
corso (*m.*) piracy, privateering; a line of carriages or automobiles, as in a parade; a school of fish.
corta (*f.*) a cutting or pruning.
corta-água (*m.*, *Zool.*) the black skimmer (*Rhynchops nigra*), c.a. CORTA-MAR.
corta-arame (*m.*) a wire cutter.
corta-asma (*m.*) a wild coffee (*Psychotria involucrata*).
corta-chefe (*m.*) a drawknife.
corta-circuito (*m.*, *Elec.*) circuit breaker.
corta-dedos (*m.*) a large centipede.
cortada (*f.*) see CORTADO.
cortadeira (*f.*) pastry cutter.—**mansa** = CAPIM-DE-COLÔNIA.
cortadela (*f.*) = CORTADURA.
cortado -**da** (*adj.*) cut, slashed, etc. See the verb CORTAR. (*f.*) a cut; (*m.*) nagging; flurry. **trazer alguém num—**, to keep another under one's thumb.
cortador (*m.*) cutter; meat cutter; a cutting tool.—**chan-**

frador, (*Print.*) miterer.—**de frios,** a machine for slicing cold meats.

cortadura (*f.*) cut, incision; gap in the hills.

corta-ferro (*m.*) a chisel for cutting metals.

corta-frio (*m.*) cold chisel.

corta-garoupa (*m.*) a shark (*Carcharias limbatus*), c.a. SERRA-GAROUPA, SUCURI-DE-GALHA-PRÊTA.

corta-jaca (*f.*) a kind of tap dance or clog dance; (*m.,f., slang*) a soft-soaper.

corta-mão [-mãos] (*m.*) carpenter's square [= ESQUADRO].

corta-mar (*m.*) breakwater; (*Zool.*) the black skimmer (*Rhynchops nigra*), c.a. CORTA-ÁGUA, BICO-RASTEIRO, TALHA-MAR.

cortamento (*m.*) a cutting; amputation; = CORTE.

cortante (*adj.*) cutting, sharp; harrowing, heart-rending; freezing [wind].

corta-palha (*m.*) a straw chopper.

corta-papel (*m.*) paper cutter; paper knife.

cortar (*v.t.*) to cut (up, down, off, out, open, through); to sever, chop, incise, gash, cleave, slit, slice, trim; to interrupt, cut short; to intercept; to cross, intersect.—**a água,** to cut off the water; to divert a stream.—**a palavra a,** to cut (someone) short.—**as asas a,** to clip another's wings; to cramp his style.—**a vasa a,** to trump another's trick; to take the wind out of someone's sails.—**cerce** or **rente,** to cut off at the base, at the root, close to the ground.—**na casaca de,** to backbite.—**na pele dos outros,** to speak evil of others.—**o baralho** or **as cartas,** to cut the deck, the cards.—**o cabelo,** to get a haircut.—**pela raiz,** to cut off at the roots; to nip in the bud.—**por baixo,** to undercut.—**relações,** to sever relations. **de—o coração,** heart-rending.

corta-raízes (*m.*) root cutter.

corta-trapos (*m.*) rag shredder.

corta-tubos (*m.*) pipe cutter.

corta-vento (*m.*) = NARCEJA; windmill.

corta-vidro (*m.*) glass cutter.

corte (*m.*) cut, incision, slit; cutting edge; a cut of cloth sufficient for a garment; the cut (style) of a garment; a cutting down; sectional drawing; railroad cut.—**de cabelo,** haircut.—**transversal,** cross section.

côrte (*f.*) court (sovereign's residence, establishment, retinue); capital city; a houseraising or other bee; courtship; (*pl.*) legislative assembly; in olden times, the three estates of the Portuguese nation: the nobles, the commons and the clergy. **fazer a—,** to court, woo.

corteché (*m.*) a type of scraper plane; a drawknife.

cortejador **–dora** (*adj.*) overly courteous; (*m.,f.*) such a one.

cortejar (*v.t.*) to greet courteously; to flatter; to pay court to.

cortejo (*m.*) salutation, bow; cortège, retinue; procession.

cortês (*adj.*) courtly, courteous, polite, urbane, gracious, suave, well-bred, well-mannered, well-spoken.

cortesania (*f.*) courteous manners.

cortesanice (*f.*) hypocritical courtesy.

cortesão [-sãos, -sões] **cortesã** (*adj.*) courtly; (*m.*) courtier; flatterer; polite person; (*f.*) courtesan.

cortesia (*f.*) courtesy, civility, urbanity, affability, politeness.

córtex [ks] (*f.*) cortex; bark; (*Anat.*) cortex.

cortiça (*f.*) cork bark; (*Anat.*) cortex [= CÓRTEX]; (*pl.*) cork floats.—**brasileira,** (*Bot.*) a Brazilian begonia (*B. uliginosa*).—**do-brejo** = CORTICEIRA-DO-CAMPO.—**fêmea** or—**segundária,** second growth of cork bark.—**macha** or—**virgem,** the first growth of cork bark.

cortical (*adj.*) cortical.

córtice (*m.*) = CÓRTEX.

corticeira (*f.*) depôt for cork bark; the bark itself; (*Bot.*) a trumpet tree (*Tabebuia cassinoides*), c.a. CAIXETA; the cockspur coralbean (*Erythrina crista-galli*), c.a. FLOR-DE-CORAL, MULUNGU, CRISTA-DE-GALO, SANANDUVA, SUINÃ, SUMAUVEIRA, CORALEIRA-CRISTADA.—**do-campo,** the sensitive jointvetch (*Aeschynomene virginica*), c.a. CORTIÇA-DO-BREJO, PARICÁ, PARICÀZINHO, SENSITIVA-MANSA.

corticento **–ta** (*adj.*) corklike.

corticíceo **–cea** (*adj.*) corklike.

corticífero **–ra** (*adj.*) cork-yielding.

cortiço (*m.*) beehive; fig., a slum tenement [= CABEÇA-DE-PORCO]; a group of small houses built around a common courtyard.

corticoso **–sa** (*adj.*) thick-barked.

cortilha (*f.*) pastry or biscuit cutter.

cortina (*f.*) curtain, screen; low wall along the edge of a high road.—**de fumaça,** wire screen.—**de fumaça,** smoke screen. **correr as—s,** to draw the curtains. **por trás das—s,** behind curtains; underhandedly.

cortinado **–da** (*adj.*) having drapes and curtains; (*m.*) curtains, drapes.

cortinar (*v.t.*) to provide with curtains; to screen.

cortir (*v.*) = CURTIR.

corucão (*m.*) = BACURAU.

coruchéu (*m.*) spire; minaret; peaked roof; conical cap (as for dunces).

coruja (*f.*) owl; hag; —**das-torres,** the Brazilian barn owl (*Tyto alba tuidara*), c.a. CORUJA-DE-IGREJA, CORUJA-BRANCA, CORUJA-CATÓLICA, SUINDARA.—**do-campo,** the Brazilian burrowing owl (*Speotyto cunicularia grallaria*), c.a. CORUJA-BURAQUEIRA, CORUJA-MINEIRA, URUCURÉIA, URUCURIÁ, CABORÉ-DO-CAMPO.—**orelhuada** = MOCHO-ORELHUDO.—**pequena,** the Choliba screech owl (*Otus c. choliba*). Cf. CORUJÃO, MOCHO, CABORÉ.

corujão (*m.*) the spectacled owl (*Pulsatrix p. perspicillata*), c.a. MOCHO-MATEIRO, MOCHO-RASTEIRO, CORUJA-DO-MATO, MURUCUTUTU. Cf. CORUJA, CABORÉ, MOCHO.

corupiá (*f.*) a hackberry (*Celtis glycicarpa*), c.a. ESPORA-DE-GALO, FRUTA-DE-GALO, GURUPIÁ, JOÁ-GRANDE.

coruscação (*f.*) coruscation; a flash or flashing of light.

coruscante (*adj.*) flashing; sparkling.

coruscar (*v.i.*) to coruscate, sparkle, gleam.

coruta (*f.*) **-to** (*m.*) corn tassel; peak, pinnacle, summit; top of the head.

corvacho (*m.*) a small crow.

corvejamento (*m.*) cawing (of crows).

corvejar (*v.i.*) to caw (as a crow); to brood (mull) over (something).

corveta [ê] (*f.*) corvette; curvet. **capitão-de—,** (*Navy*) lieutenant-commander.

corvetear (*v.i.*) to curvet; to cavort.

corvídeo **–dea** (*adj.*) crow-like; (*m.pl.*) the crow family (*Corvidae*).

corvino **–na** (*adj.*) corvine, crow-like; (*f.*) any of various marine fishes, esp. the croaker.—**riscada,** the umbrina (*Umbrina coroides*), c.a. RONCADOR-TABOCA.

corvo [cô] (*m.*) crow. [A name sometimes wrongly applied in Brazil to the URUBU (turkey buzzard). The true crow (*Corvus*) does not occur in Brazil.]—**aquático** = ACALOTE.—**marinho,** a cormorant, c.a. BIGUÁ.—**noturno** = NOITIBÓ.

cos. = CO-SENO (cosine).

cós (*m.*) waistband.

COSB = COMISSÃO DE SIMPLIFICAÇÃO BUROCRÁTICA (Commission on Bureaucratic Simplification).

coscorão (*m.*) pancake, fritter; thick scab.

coscoro (*m.*) crust; wrinkling, crinkling.

coscoroba (*f.*) coscoroba [*Webster*: "A large swanlike So. Amer. bird (Coscoroba coscoroba) of the duck family."]

coscorrão (*m.*) a blow with the hand, esp. on the head.

co-secante (*adj.; f., Trig.*) cosecant.

cosedor (*m.*) a book-stitching machine.

cosedura (*f.*) sewing, stitching.

co-seno (*m., Trig.*) cosine.

co-senóide (*m.*) cosine curve.

coser (*v.t.*) to sew, stitch.—**a bôca,** to seal one's lips.—**a facadas,** to stab repeatedly.—**o ouvido com a porta,** to glue one's ear to the door.—**se com a parede,** to hug the wall. Cf. COZER.

cosmético **–ca** (*adj.; m.*) cosmetic.

cosmetologia (*f.*) cosmetology.

cósmico **–ca** (*adj.*) cosmic.

cosmo (*m.*) cosmos.

cosmogonia (*f.*) cosmogony.

cosmografia (*f.*) cosmography.

cosmolina (*f.*) cosmoline, petrolatum, petroleum jelly.

cosmologia (*f.*) cosmology.

cosmópole (*f.*) cosmopolis.

cosmopolita (*adj.*) cosmopolitan; (*m.,f.*) cosmopolite.

cosmos (*m., Bot.*) cosmos.

cospe-cospe (*m.*) = BARRIGUDINHO.

cosquento **–ta,** **–quilhento** **–ta,** **–quilhoso** **–sa** (*adj.*) ticklish [= COCEQUENTO].

cossacos (*m.pl.*) Cossacks.

cossinete (*m., Mach.*) bearing; brasses; bushing; screw die.

cosso (*m.*) chase; (*Bot.*) the kussotree (*Hagenia abyssinica*).

costa (*f.*) coast, shore; slope of a hill; reverse side of an object; (*Anat.*) costa; (*pl.*) back (of anything)—**abaixo,**

downhill.—-**acima**, uphill.—**brava**, a wild coast.—**s da mão**, back of the hand. **às—s**, on the back or shoulders. **dar à—**, to run ashore. **dar as—s a**, to turn one's back on (another). **de—s** backwards; on (one's) back. **de—a contra—**, from coast to coast. **estar com as—s quentes**, to have the backing of a powerful person. **estar de—s**, to have one's back turned. **Não há mouro na—**, The coast is clear. **pano da—**, striped cotton cloth. **voltar as—s**, to turn one's back.

costado (*m.*) back, shoulders; ribs (of a vessel); (*pl.*) grandparents.—**do navio**, broadside of a ship. **dar com os—s no chão**, to come a cropper. **de quatro—s**, dyed-in-the-wool.

costal (*adj.*) costal; (*m.*) a backload of anything.

costaneiro -ra (*adj.*) backing; (*m.*) back, loin; (*f.*) cheap, coarse paper; dust jacket of a book; a slab of lumber.

costão (*m.*) rough, wild coast.

costarriquenho –nha (*adj.; m.,f.*) Costa Rican.

costeagem (*f.*) coastwise shipping [=CABOTAGEM].

costear (*v.t.*) to follow (the coast); to curve around (a hill); to herd (cattle); to get even with (someone); (*v.i.*) to coast (sail close to) the shore.

costeio (*m.*) coasting; herding. **dar um—em alguém**, to bear down on someone.

costeiro -ra (*adj.*) of or pert. to the coast; coastwise (ships and shipping); (*m.*) coastwise sailor; (*f., Bot.*) the Wight chaulmoogra tree (*Hydnocarpus wightianus*).

costela (*f.*) rib.—**de Adão**, Adam's rib (the first woman). —**mindinha**, (*Anat.*) one of the false ribs.—**s abdominais**, or **asternais**, or **inferiores**, or **falsas**, (*Anat.*) the false ribs.—**s esternais** or **verdadeiras**, (*Anat.*) the true or vertebrosternal ribs.—**s flutuantes**, (*Anat.*) the floating or vertebral ribs.

costeleta [lê] (*f.*) chop, cutlet; (*pl.*) sideburns.—**s de porco**, pork chops.

costilhar (*m.*) the rib cage; ribs of beef, etc.

costo (*m., Bot.*) a spiralflag (*Costus arabicus*), c.a. PAUCATINGA.—**bastardo**, a parsnip (*Pastinaca opopanax*).

costumado -da (*adj.*) customary, habitual; accustomed; usual; (*m.*) custom.

costumar (*v.t.*) to accustom, habituate; (*v.r.*) to become accustomed to.

costumário -ria (*adj.*) customary.

costume (*m.*) custom, habit; addiction, usage, practice, rule; unwritten law; menstrual period; costume; man's suit; woman's tailored suit; (*pl.*) actions, behavior; social customs and habits. **como de—**, as usual. **de—**, customary, usual. **segundo o—**, according to custom. **ter o—de**, to have (be in) the habit of.

costumeiro -ra (*adj.*) accustomed, usual, habitual; (*f.*) usage; usual habit.

costura (*f.*) sewing; needlework; seam, stitch; splice; scar. **sem—**, seamless.

costuradeira (*f.*) book-stitching machine.

costuragem (*f.*) sewing of books.

costurar (*v.t.*) to sew [=COSER].

costureira (*f.*), **-ro** (*m.*) dressmaker; (*f.*) seamstress; sewing woman, needlewoman; (*m., Anat.*) sartorius [=SARTÓRIO].

cota (*f.*) quota, share; assessment; marginal annotation; cotta; the back of a knife or other cutting utensil; a letter or number placed on a paper to identify it; bench mark; (*Civ. Eng.*) datum point (line, level).—**de armas**, coat of arms.—**de malha**, coat of mail.—**parte**, assessed share, quota. Var. QUOTA.

cotação (*f.*) quotation (of prices); price-list; assessment; fig. the degree of esteem in which one person is held by another.

cotado -da (*adj.*) well-spoken of, well-thought of.

cotador –dora (*m.,f.*) marginal annotator.

cotamento (*m.*) labeling, marking or annotation of documents.

co-tangente (*m., Trig.*) cotangent.

cotanilho (*m.*) fine down or fuzz.

cotonilhoso –sa (*adj.*) fuzzy (as a peach).

cotanoso -sa (*adj.*) cottony, downy, nappy.

cotão (*f.*) fuzz, down, fluff; nap; lint; cotton.

cotar (*v.t.*) to mark, label, annotate (papers); to quote (prices); to assess, tax; to indicate the level of.

cotarnina (*f., Chem.*) cotarnin(e).

cote (*m.*) hone, whetstone; an everyday affair. **de—**, daily.

cotejador –dora (*adj.*) collating, checking; (*m.,f.*) collator, checker.

cotejar (*v.t.*) to collate, check, compare.

cotejo [ê] (*m.*) collation, comparison, esp. of something one by one, or side by side, as, for example, in parallel columns.

cotia (*f.*) = CUTIA.

cotiado -da (*adj.*) threadbare, frayed, worn.

cotiar (*v.t.*) to fray, render threadbare.

cotiara (*f.*) a lance-head type of pit viper of southern Brazil (*Bothrops cotiara*)—one of the JARARACAS—c.a. JARARACA-PRETA, BOICOTIARA; ALSO = URUTU.

cotiarinha (*f.*) a small, brown somewhat rare, lance-head-type pit viper of southern Brazil (*Bothrops itapetiningae*), c.a. JARARACA-DO-CAMPO, BOIPEVA. [The latter name is applied also to a harmless colubrine—see BOIPEVA.]

cotícula (*f.*) touchstone.

cotidiano -na (*adj.*) quotidian, daily, everyday; (*m.*) daily routine; everyday life. [= QUOTIDIANO.]

cótila (*f.*) = CÓTILO.

cotiledonário -ria (*adj.*) cotyledonary.

cotilédone (*m., Bot., Embryol.*) cotyledon.

cotilhão (*m.*) cotillion.

cótilo (*m., Anat.*) cotyla.

cotilóide, cotiloídeo –dea (*adj., Anat., Zool.*) cotyloid.

cotinga (*f.*) a blue, purple-breasted bird (*Cotinga coerula*); a fish—the yellow tomtate (*Bathystoma aurolineatum*), c.a. GARGANTA-DE-FERRO.

cotio (*m.*) daily use.

cotipo (*m., Bot., Zool.*) cotype.

cotista (*m.,f.*) shareholder.

cotização (*f.*) sharing, parceling out, assessment; quota.

cotizar (*v.t.*) to parcel out, distribute shares; (*v.r.*) to assess oneself.

côto (*m.*) butt, stub, stump; (*pl.*) knuckles.

cotó (*adj.*) peg-leg; bobtailed; (*m.*) stub; stump; a small, cheap knife.

cotoco [tô] (*m.*) stump, stub.

cotoína (*f., Chem.*) cotoin.

cotonária, –neira (*f.*) the cottonbatting cudweed (*Gnaphalium chilense*). c.a. GNAFÁLIO.

cotoníício (*m.*) cotton mill.

cotonoso -sa (*adj.*) cottony.

cotovelada (*f.*), **–lão** (*m.*) a dig (poke, nudge) with the elbow.

cotovelar (*v.*) = ACOTOVELAR.

cotoveleira (*f.*) cubitiere (elbow piece of a suit of armor).

cotovêlo (*m.*) elbow (all senses); a bend in the road or river. **apoiar-se sôbre os—s**, to lean on one's elbows. **falar pelos—s**, to talk a blue streak.

cotovia (*f.*) the Old World skylark (*Alauda arvensis*) which does not occur in Brazil, but the same name is used to designate its cousin, the pipit (genus *Anthus*), which does occur there. See SOMBRIO and CAMINHEIRO.

cotruco (*m.*) peddler of dress goods and notions; a long, thin dagger, c.a. LAMBEDEIRA.

cotucanhé (*m.*) = CARVALHO-DO-BRASIL.

cotula (*f., Bot.*) the genus Cotula (Brassbuttons).—**bastarda**, mayweed camomile (*Anthemis cotula*), c.a. CAMOMILA.

cotulo (*m.*) = COGULO.

coturno (*m.*) buskin; half-boot; sock.

coub+verb endings = irreg. forms of CABER [32].

couce (*m.*) & derivs. = COICE & derivs.

couceira (*f.*) stile of a door or sash.

coucelo (*m.*) conchelo (a plant).

couché (*adj.*) glazed [paper].

coudel [-déis] (*m.*) manager of a stud farm. Var. CAUDEL.

coudelaria (*f.*) stud farm; a horse-breeding establishment. Var. CAUDELARIA.

coulomb (*m., Physics.*) coulomb.

coulombmetro (*m., Elec.*) coulometer.

coumarina (*f.*) a tonkabean (*Dipteryx tetraphylla*), c.a. FAVA-TONCA.

coumarourama (*f.*) the British tonkabean (*Dipteryx oppositifolia*).

coupé (*m.*) = CUPÉ.

coupon (*m.*) = CUPÃO.

couraça (*f.*) cuirass, breastplate; armor; armor-plate. Var. COIRAÇA.

couraçado -da (*adj.*) cuirassed; armored, armor-plated, ironclad; (*m.*) battleship.—**de bôlso**, pocket battleship. **divisão de—s**, battle squadron. Var. COIRAÇADO.

couraçar (*v.t.*) to provide with a cuirass; to protect (ships, etc.) with armor plate; (*v.r.*) to become hardened, in-

sensible. Var. COIRAÇAR.
couraceiro (m.) cuirassier. Var. COIRACEIRO.
courama (f.) a pile of green hides; leather costume; (Bot.) the airplant (Kalanchoe pinnata), c.a. FÔLHA-DA-COSTA, FÔLHA-DE-FORTUNA, FÔLHA-DE-PIRARUCU, FORTUNA, RODA-DA-FORTUNA. Var. COIRAMA.
courear (v.t.) to skin (an animal).
coureiro (m.) dealer in hides or sheepskins.
courela (f.) = COIRELA.
courinho (m.) goatskin. Var. COIRINHO.
couro (m.) hide; leather; scalp.—artificial, imitation leather.—cabeludo, scalp.—cru, green hide; rawhide.—de bezerra, calfskin.—fresco, green hide.—nonato, the hide of an unborn animal.—verde, green hide. dar no— (slang) to show skill or aptitude for anything. ter o—grosso, to be thick-skinned. tira de—, leather strap. tirar o—e cabelo a alguém, to fleece someone.
cousa (f.) = COISA.
coussilho (m.) = CONCHELO.
coutada (f.) game preserve.
coutar (v.t.) to post land. Var. COITAR.
couteiro (m.) game keeper. Var. COITEIRO.
coutente (m.,f., Law) co-user.
couto (m.) posted land; refuge, asylum. Var. COITO.
couve (f.) kinds of kale, collards, cole, rape (Brasica spp.).—brócolos, broccoli.—chinêsa or -da-china, pakchoi (Chinese cabbage).—de-bruxelas, Brussels sprouts.—flor, cauliflower.—lombarda, kale.—nabo, turnip.—rábano or -rabão, kohlrabi.—repolho or -repolhuda, cabbage.
couvetinga (f., Bot.) violet nightshade (Solanum auriculatum), c.a. CAPUEIRA-BRANCA, FRUTA-DE-GUARÁ, FRUTA-DE-LÔBO, FUMO-BRAVO.
couxilgo (m.) = CONCHELO.
cova (f.) pit, cavity; hole in the ground; excavation; tooth socket; grave.—de ovos, hole in the sand in which turtles lay their eggs.—de rapôsa, foxhole. estar com um pé na—, to have one foot in the grave.
côvado (m.) an ell (old measure of length).
covagem (f.) the digging of a grave; the price for so doing.
coval (m.) burial ground; the price of a grave.
covarde (adj.; m.,f.) = COBARDE.
covardia (f.) = COBARDIA.
covardismo (m.) = COBARDIA.
covardo (m.) = COBARDE.
covato (m.) grave digging; place where graves are dug.
covear (v.t.) to dig holes (for planting young coffee trees).
coveiro (m.) grave digger.
covelita (f., Min.) covellite, covelline, indigo copper.
co-vendedor -dora (m.,f.) co-seller.
co-vibração (f., Physics) sympathetic vibration.
covil (m.) den, lair; bandit's hideout.
covilhão (m., Bot.) the twisted heath (Erica cinerea).
covilhete [ête] (m.) candy dish; small bowl; breast wheel.
covinha (f.) dimple.
covo [cô] (m.) wicker fish trap.
côvo -va (adj.) hollow; deep.
covolume (m., Physical Chem.) molecular covolume.
coxa (f.) thigh [but not coxa, which is QUADRIL (hip) or ARTICULAÇÃO COXO-FEMORAL (hip joint)].
coxal (adj.) of or pert. to the thigh [but not coxal]. osso—, thighbone.
coxalgia (f., Med.) coxalgia.
coxeadura (f.) lameness; a hobble or hobbling.
coxear (v.i.) to limp, hobble [=CAXINGUAR, MANCAR, CAPENGAR].
coxeira (f.) lameness of animals.
coxia (f.) aisle, gangway; stall; a folding seat; an orderly pile (as of bricks).
coxilha (f.) slope; knoll; rolling prairie land.
coxim (m.) cushion, pillow, pad; padded bench; seat of a saddle; rail clip; (Arch.) springer.
coximpim (m.) teeter-totter [= GANGORRA].
coxípede (adj.) lame.
coxite (f., Med.) coxitis.
coxo -xa [cô] (adj.) lame, crippled, hobbling; (m.,f.) a cripple. andar de pé—, to hop on one foot.
côxo-femoral (adj., Anat.) coxofemoral.
coxote (m.) cuisse (of a suit of armor).
cozedura (f.) cooking, boiling, baking.
cozer (v.t.) to cook, bake, boil (food).—a bebedeira or o vinho, to sleep off a drunken spree.—ao forno, to bake.—no bafo, to braise (meat). Cf. COZINHAR, COSER.
cozido -da (adj.) cooked; (m.) a boiled dinner.—a ponto,

done to a turn.
cozimento (m.) cooking.
cozinha (f.) kitchen; cooking, cookery.—de forno e fogão, all-around cooking.—trivial, light cooking. bateria de—, kitchen utensils. faxina de—, kitchen police. pia da—, kitchen sink.
cozinhado -da (adj.; m.,f.) cooked (food).
cozinhar (v.t.) to cook [= COZER].
cozinheira (f.), -ro (m.) cook.—de forno e fogão, all-round cook.
cp. = COMPARE (compare; Cf.).
Cr$ = CRUZEIRO.
cr.ª = CRIADA (maid servant).
craca (f.) barnacle; fluting on a column; wrinkles on the horns of old cattle; (Bot.) the bird vetch (Vicia cracca).
crachá (m.) medal, decoration, badge.
craguatá (f.) = CARAGUATÁ.
craião (m.) crayon.
crampa (f.) cramp, grip. [= CÃIBRA].
craniano -na (adj.) cranial.
craniectomia (f., Surg.) craniectomy.
crânio (m.) cranium, skull, brainpan; (slang) a "brain" (very smart person).
craniologia (f.) craniology.
craniologista, craniólogo -ga (m.,f.) craniologist.
craniomancia (f.) phrenology.
craniometria (f.) craniometry.
craniômetro (m.) craniometer.
cranioscopia (f.) cranioscopy.
craniostose (f., Anat.) craniostosis.
craniotabes (f., Med.) craniotabes.
craniotomia (f., Obstetrics, Surg.) craniotomy.
craniótomo (m., Surg.) craniotome.
cranque (m.) crank [= MANIVELA].
crápula (f.) debauchery; (m.) debauchee; low scoundrel.
crapuloso -sa (adj.) crapulous; debauched.
craque (interj.) Crack! (m.) a crackajack; one who is a crack at anything; a crack racing horse; financial crash.
craquear (v.t.) to crack (petroleum).
craqueamento (m.) cracking of oil.
craquento -ta (adj.) covered with CRACAS (barnacles); rough, cracked (hands, skin).
craquejar (v.t.) to click (grit, grind) the teeth.
crase (f., Gram.) crasis (contraction of two vowels).
craspedoto (adj., Zool.) craspedote.
crassidade, -sidão (f.) crassitude.
crassilíngue (adj.) crassilingual, thick-tongued.
crássula (f., Bot.) any succulent of the genus Crassula.
crassuláceo -cea (adj., Bot.) crassulaceous; (f.pl.) the Crassulaceae.
crasso -sa (adj.) crass, coarse; dense; thick. êrro—, a blunder.
crástino -na (adj.) of the morrow. [Poetical]
cratego (m.) the genus of hawthorns (Crataegus).
cratera (f.) crater.—lago, crater lake.
crateriforme (adj.) crateriform.
crauá (m.) = CAROÁ, CROÁ.
cravação (f.) setting of stones (as in a ring); a studding of nails; nailing.
cravado -da (adj.) driven in (as a nail); set in the ground (as a post); of gems, set in a ring; of eyes, staring, fixed.
cravador (m.) gem-setter; awl, punch; nailer.
cravadura (f.) = CRAVAÇÃO.
cravagem (f.) act of nailing; (Plant Pathol.) ergot, c.a. ESPORÃO, FUNGÃO, MORRÃO.—de centeio, rye ergot.
cravar (v.t.) to thrust (drive, stick, run, plunge) in (nail, spike, dagger, stake, etc.); to set gems; to stare at, fix the eyes on; (v.r.) to bury itself (as a bullet).
craveira (f.) measuring stick; shoemaker's compasses; hole for a horseshoe nail; one foot (12 inches) = PÉ.
craveiro (m.) the general term for carnations and clove pinks (genus Dianthus); any flower vase; maker of horseshoe nails.—da-índia, clovetree (Syzygium aromaticum), c.a. GIROFLEIRO.—do-campo = JAMBU.—do-maranhão, clovebark tree (Dicypellium caryophyllatum), c.a. CANELEIRA-CRAVO, CRAVO-DO-MATO, IBIRAQUIINHA, LOURO-CHEIROSO, LOURO-CRAVO, MUIRAQUIINHA, PAU-CRAVO.
cravejador (m.) gem-setter; nail driver; maker of horseshoe nails.
cravejamento (m.) gem-setting; nailing, spiking.
cravejar (v.t.) to set (gems); to spike; to stud with nails.
cravelha [ê] (f.) tuning peg (of violin, etc.).

cravelho [ê] (m.) wooden peg.

cravete [vê] (m.) tongue of a buckle.

cravina (f.) the grass pink (Dianthus plumarius), c.a. CRAVO-BORDADO.—-barbela, or—-dos-poetas, sweet william (Dianthus barbatus), c.a. CRAVINHO, CRAVO-DE-POETA, MAURITÂNIAS.—-da-arrabia, or—-da-china, Chinese pink (Dianthus chinensis).—-d'água or—-de lagartixa, the Brazilian water primrose (Jussiaea longifolia), c.a. PIMENTA-D'ÁGUA.—-da-sombra, the Corsican pearlwort (Sagina subulata).—-soberba, the lilac pink (Dianthus superbus).

cravinho (m.) small carnation, garden pink; a tack or small nail.—-de-defunto = CUARI-BRAVO (a marigold).—-de-lagartixa = CRAVINA-D'ÁGUA.

cravista (m.,f.) harpsichordist.

cravo (m.) horseshoe nail; spike; corn, callus; comedo (blackhead); spinet, harpsichord, clavichord; carnation, clove-pink. —-bordado = CRAVINA. —-da-carolina = ESPIGÉLIA-DE-MARYLAND.—-da-índia, clovetree (Syzygium aromaticum); also its dried flower buds (cloves).—-da-roça = CRAVORANA.—-de-amor, babysbreath (Gypsophila paniculata).—-de-defunto, kinds of marigold (genus Tagetes), c.a. CRAVO-DE-TUNES.—-de-montpelier, Montpelier pink (Dianthus monspessulanus).—-de-poeta = CRAVINA-DOS-POETAS.—-de-urubu, a heliotrope (H. indicum).—-do-maranhão or—-do-mato = CRAVEIRO-DO-MARANHÃO.—-franjado or—-renda = CRAVINA-SOBERBA.—-ordinario or—-saloio, common carnation or clove-pink (Dianthus caryophyllus).—-romano, the pinkball thrift (Armeria pseudoarmeria).

cravorana (f.) a ragweed (Ambrosia polystachya), c.a. ARTEMÍSIA-BRAVA, CRAVO-DA-ROÇA, PEITUDO, SALSA-DO-CAMPO.

cré (m.) chalk.—com—, lé com lé, Birds of a feather flock together.

crê, creais, creamos, forms of CRER [38].

creação (f.) = CRIAÇÃO.

crear (v.) = CRIAR.

creatina (f., Biochem.) creatine.

creatinina (f., Biochem.) creatinine.

creche (f.) crèche; day nursery.

crede, credes, forms of CRER [38].

credência (f.) credence table; sideboard.

credenciado –da (adj.) accredited (by).

credencial (adj.) credential; (f.pl.) credentials (of a diplomat, etc.).

crediário (m.) installment-payments plan.

credibilidade (f.) credibility.

creditar (v.t.) to credit (an account).

crédito (m.) credit; trust; good reputation; money due from others.—aberto, open credit.—público, public trust.—real, mortgage loan. a—, on credit. a—de, to the credit of. abrir—, to open a credit account.

creditório (adj.) of or pert. to credit.

credo (m.) credo; creed; (interj.) Goodness!

credor (m.), –ra (f.) creditor.

credulidade (f.) credulity.

crédulo –la (adj.) credulous, gullible, simple-minded; (m.,f.) an easily-duped person; a gull.

crêem, creia, creiam, creias, creio, forms of CRER [38].

crejuá (m.) = COROTÉU.

cremação (f.) cremation.

cremado –da (adj.) cremated; cream-colored.

cremador –dora (adj.) cremating; (m.,f.) cremator.

cremadouro (m.) crematory.

cremalheira (f.) cog rail; rack and pinion; a pothook and chain.

cremar (v.t.) to cremate.

cremaster (m., Anat.) cremaster.

crematista (m.,f.) cremationist.

crematística (f.) chrematistics.

crematório –ria (adj.; m.) crematory.

creme (m.) cream; cream sauce; the color of cream. —evanescente, vanishing cream.—de abacate, a dessert made of whipped avocado, lemon juice and sugar.—de barba, shaving cream.—de leite, cream custard.

cremocarpo (m., Bot.) cremocarp.

cremômetro (m.) creamometer.

cremona (f.) cremone bolt; cremona (violin).

cremor (m.) cremor.—de tártaro, cream of tartar.

cremos, form of CRER [38].

crena (f.) crena, notch, cleft; crenature; trough between gear teeth.

crenado –da (adj., Bot.) crenate.

crenadura (f.) = CRENATURA.

crenato (m., Chem.) crenate.

crenatura (f.) crenature; crenation.

crença (f.) belief, faith, credence; opinion.

crendeirice (f.) credulity, gullibility.

crendeiro –ra (adj.) credulous; (m.,f.) a credulous person.

crendice (f.) an absurd belief.

crendo, form of CRER [38].

crênico –ca (adj., Chem.) crenic.

crenífero –ra (adj.) crenulate.

crente (m.,f.) faithful, believing; (m.,f.) believer; (colloq.) a Protestant.

crênula (f.) crenula.

crenulado –da (adj.) crenulate.

creofagia (f.) creophagy.

creófago –ga (adj.) creophagous, carnivorous.

creolina (f.) almost any household deodorant or disinfectant smelling of phenol. [Originally, a trade-marked preparation (Creolin) containing creosol and resin soap.]

creosol (m., Chem.) creosol.

creosotar (v.t.) to creosote.

creosôto (m.) creosote.

crepe (m.) crepe, crape; black mourning crepe.

crepis (m., Bot.) the genus of hawk's-beards (Crepis).

crepitação (f.) crackling.

crepitante (adj.) crepitant, crackling.

crepitar (v.t.) to crackle (as fire in the fireplace).

crepitoso –sa (adj.) = CREPITANTE.

crepuscular (adj.) crepuscular, twilight.

crepúsculo (m.) twilight, dusk, gloaming; pre-dawn.

crer [38] (v.i.) to believe (em, in); to think, suppose; to have faith; (v.r.) to believe oneself to be (something). Creio que sim, I think so. Creio que não, I don't think so; I think not. fazer—, to cause to believe, convince. Quem haveria de—! Who would have thought it! Would you believe it! ver para—, seeing is believing.

crês, form of CRER [38].

cresamina (f., Pharm.) cresamine.

crescença (f.) growth.

crescendo (m.) gradual increase in force or loudness; (Music) crescendo.

crescente (adj.) growing, increasing; (m.) crescent; (f.) high tide.

crescer (v.i.) to increase, grow, augment; to grow up; to swell, expand; to wax, thrive, progress; to superabound.—para, to rise up against (an adversary); to assume a menacing attitude towards.

crescido –da (adj.) grown (up); enlarged; increased; developed. Seu filhinho está crescidinho, Your baby is getting big.

crescidote (adj., colloq.) almost grown (boy).

crescimento (m.) growth; increase.

crescimo (m.) surplus, remainder; leftovers.

cresilato (m., Chem.) cresylate.

cresílico –ca (adj., Chem.) cresylic.

Creso (m.) Croesus; by ext. a very rich man.

cresol (m., Chem.) cresol, phenol.

crespar (v.t.) to make crisp(y); (v.r.) to grow crisp.

crespidão (f.) crispness; roughness.

crespina (f., Zool.) reticulum [= BARRETE, COIFA].

crêspo –pa (adj.) crisp, coarse, rough; frizzled; angry.

cresta (f.) act of singeing, toasting, parching, scorching [= CRESTAMENTO].

crestadeira (f.) browning pan.

crestadura (f.) toasting, parching, scorching.

crestamento (m.) toasting; tanning, sunburning; scorching.

crestar (v.t.) to scorch, singe; to toast, parch; to tan.

crestomatia (f.) chrestomathy.

cretáceo –cea (adj.) cretaceous, chalky; (Geol.) Cretaceous.

cretinismo (m.) cretinism; idiocy.

cretino (m.), –na (f.) cretin; imbecile, idiot.

cretinoso –sa (adj.) cretinous.

cretone (m.) cretone.

cria (f.) the young of animals; colt, calf, kid; cattle; a child of poor parents brought up by well-to-do people as a member of their household.

criação (f.) raising, growing, propagation, breeding; rearing, upbringing; nursing, suckling; creation, invention; training, education; the stock of animals on a farm; (Masonry) fill-in.—de suínos, hog-raising.—miúda, domestic animals other than cows and horses. fazer—, to breed animals.

criada (*f.*) see under CRIADO.

criadagem (*f.*) servants of a household, collectively; the servant class.

criadeira (*f.*) brooder (for baby chicks); baby incubator; wet nurse; a prolonged drizzle (of the kind good for growing crops), c.a. CHUVA CRIADEIRA.

criado –**da** (*adj.*) created; grown, raised; educated, trained; (*m.,f.*) servant.—**particular**, a servant who attends a single person; (*m.*) man servant; waiter.—**de libré**, liveried footman.—**do paço**, palace servant.— -**mudo**, a night table. (*f.*) woman servant, maid, nurse. —**de quarto**, chambermaid.

criador –**dora** (*adj.*) creative; breeding; raising; (*m.*) breeder, esp. of cattle; The Creator; (*f.*) a day nurse for children of working mothers.

criadouro (*m.*) a plant nursery; a day nursery for children. Var. CRIADOIRO.

criança (*f.*) child; (*adj.*) childish.—**astrasada**, backward child.—**de colo** or **de peito**, infant in arms.—**exposta**, foundling.—**mimada** or **estragada**, spoiled child.

criançada (*f.*) group of children; childish behavior.

criancice (*f.*) childish action or remark.

criançola (*f.*) young boy, overgrown kid.

criar (*v.t.*) to create; to procreate; to rear, bring up, raise, educate, train, nurture (said esp. of children); to produce, yield, bear; to originate, invent; to breed, raise (animals); to grow, raise (plants); to develop, cause to grow; to constitute, appoint; (*v.r.*) to grow up.—**alma nova**, to renew courage, take heart.—**amizadas (inimigos)**, to create friendships (enemies).—**ao peito**, to suckle.—**banhas**, to grow fat, put on weight.—**bolor**, to grow moldy.—**coragem**, to take heart, buck up.—**forças**, to grow strong.—**gado, galinhas, pombos**, to raise cattle, chickens, pigeons.—**juízo**, to cut one's wisdom teeth, develop good sense.—**obstáculos a**, to handicap; to put obstacles in someone's way.—**raizes**, to take root.

criatura (*f.*) creature, being; man, person; tool, servile dependent.

cribelo (*m.*, *Zool.*) cribellum.

cribriforme (*adj.*) cribriform, sievelike.

criceto (*m.*, *Zool.*) hamster (*Cricetus cricetus*).

criciúma (*f.*) any bamboo of genus Chusquea.

cricóide (*adj.; f.*, *Anat.*) cricoid.

cricri, cricrido (*m.*) cricket's chirp.

cricrilar (*v.i.*) to chirp as a cricket.

crido –**da** (*p.p. of* CRER) believed [= ACREDITADO].

crila (*m.*) kid (child) [= MENINO.]

crilada (*f.*) bunch of kids.

crime (*m.*) crime.—**capital**, capital crime.—**contra a natureza**, crime against nature.—**de estado**, crime against the State.—**de lesa-majestade**, lese majesty.— **político**, political crime.

criminação (*f.*) (in)crimination.

criminador –**dora** (*m.,f.*) incriminator.

criminal (*adj.*) criminal; (*m.*) criminal court or trial.

criminalidade (*f.*) criminality; crime.

criminalista (*m.,f.*) criminal lawyer.

criminar (*v.t.*) to (in)criminate.

criminável (*adj.*) deserving of incrimination.

criminogêne (*f.*) criminogenesis.

criminologia (*f.*) criminology.

criminologista (*m.,f.*) criminologist.

criminoso –**sa** (*adj.; m.,f.*) criminal.

crina (*f.*) horsehair (mane, tail).

crindiúva, –diúba (*f.*) a tree of the elm family (*Trema micrantha*), c.a. CUATINDIVA (or -DIBA), CURINDIBA, GURINDIBA (or -DIVA), ORINDIÚVA, PAU-DE-PÓLVORA.

crineira (*f.*) mane.

crinito –**ta** (*adj.*) crinite.

crino (*m.*, *Bot.*) a crinum.

crinóide (*adj.*) crinoid(al); (*m.pl.*, *Zool.*) the Crinoidea.

crinolina (*f.*) crinoline.

criócelo (*m.*, *Zool.*) asparagus beetle (*Crioceris*).

crióforo (*m.*, *Physics*) cryophorous.

criogênico –**ca** (*adj.*) cryogenic.

criólita (*f.*, *Min.*) cryolite.

criolitionita (*f.*, *Min.*) cryolithionite.

criômetro (*m.*, *Physics*) cryometer.

crioscopia (*f.*) cryoscopy.

crioscópico –**ca** (*adj.*, *Physical Chem.*) cryoscopic. **metodo**—, cryoscopy.

crioscópio (*m.*, *Physical Chem.*) cryoscope.

criostato (*m.*, *Physical Chem.*) cryostat.

criouléu (*m.*) creole dance.

crioulo –**la** (*adj.*) creole; native; (*m.,f.*) creole; in Brazil, originally, a native-born Negro; nowadays, any Negro; in Rio Grande do Sul, any native of that State regardless of race. **cana**—, a sp. of native sugarcane. **cigarro**—, a cigarette made of coarse, black tobacco rolled in cornhusk instead of paper. **galinha**—, mongrel chicken.

cripta (*f.*) crypt, vault; (*Anat.*) crypt.

criptestesia (*f.*) clairvoyance.

críptico –**ca** (*adj.*) of or pert. to crypts [but not cryptic, which is SECRETO, OCULTO.]

criptobrânquio –**quia** (*adj.*, *Zool.*) cryptobranchiate.

criptocarpo –**pa** (*adj.*, *Bot.*) cryptocarpic.

criptocéfalo –**la** (*adj.*) cryptocephalous.

criptocristalino –**na** (*adj.*, *Petrog.*) cryptocrystalline.

criptógama, criptogâmica (*f.*, *Bot.*) cryptogam.

criptogâmico –**ca**, **criptógamo** –**ma** (*adj.*) cryptogamic.

criptografia (*f.*) cryptography.

criptograma (*m.*) cryptogram.

criptologia (*f.*) cryptology.

criptoméria (*f.*, *Bot.*) araucaria cryptomeria (*C. araucarioides*).

criptômetro (*m.*) cryptometer.

criptomnesia (*f.*, *Psychol.*) cryptomnesia.

criptônio (*m.*, *Chem.*) krypton.

criptopina (*f.*, *Chem.*) cryptopine.

criptorquidia (*f.*, *Med.*, *Veter.*) cryptorchidism.

críquete (*m.*) cricket (the game)—the insect is GRILO.

crisálida, –**de** (*f.*) chrysalis; cocoon.

crisântemo (*m.*) chrysanthemum.

crise (*f.*) crisis, turning point; crucial time, critical situation; economic depression; fit, spell.—**de casas**, acute housing shortage.—**de nervos**, nervous attack; hysterical outbreak.—**de trabalho**, widespread unemployment.

criselefantino –**na** (*adj.*) chryselephantine [Greek statues].

crisma (*m.* or *f.*, *Eccl.*) chrism; Confirmation.

crismar (*v.t.*) to anoint sacramentally; to confirm in the faith; to dub, term, call; (*v.r.*) to receive Confirmation; to call (name) oneself.

crisoberilo (*m.*, *Min.*) chrysoberyl.

crisobulo (*m.*) chrysobull.

crisocarpo –**pa** (*adj.*, *Bot.*) chrysocarpous, yellow-fruited.

crisocloro –**ra** (*adj.*) chrysochlorous, golden green.

crisocola (*f.*, *Min.*) chrysocolla.

crisofânico –**ca** (*adj.*, *Chem.*) chrysophanic.

crisofilo (*m.*) a starapple (*Chrysophyllum*).

crisografia (*f.*) chrysography.

crisoidina [o-i] (*f.*, *Chem.*, *Dye*) chrysoidine.

crisol [-sóis] (*m.*) crucible; fig. severe test or trial.

crisolita (*f.*, *Min.*) chrysolite, peridot.

crisomelo (*m.*), –**la** (*f.*) a leaf beetle (*Chrysomelid*).

crisópraso (*m.*, *Min.*) chrysoprase.

crisótilo (*m.*, *Min.*) chrysotile.

crispação (*f.*), **crispamento** (*m.*) crispation.

crispante (*adj.*) crisping.

crispar (*v.t.*) to crisp, crinkle, wrinkle, ripple; to wring (the hands).

crispim (*m.*) = SACI (a bird).

crista (*f.*) cock's comb; crest, ridge.—**de-galo**, (*Bot.*) Joseph's-coat amaranthus (*A. tricolor*), c.a. BREDO-VERMELHO, BREDO-ROXO, CARURU-DA-MATA (or -DO-MATO), CARURU-VERMELHO, CARURU-GRANDE; the common feather cock's-comb (*Celosia cristata*), c.a. BEIJO-DE-PALMAS, MARTINETES, BREDO-DE-NAMORADO, VELUDO, VELUDILHOS; the salt heliotrope (*H. curassavicum*); the Brazil dutchmanspipe (*Aristolochia brasiliensis*); also = CELÓSIA-BRANCA, BREDO-DE-ESPINHO.—**de-galo-chorona** = CARURU-VERMELHO.—**de-negra**, a pigeonwings (*Clitoria linearis*).—**de-peru**, the chenille copperleaf (*Acalypha hispida*), c.a. RABO-DE-MACACO.—**etmoidal**, (*Anat.*) ethmoidal crest. **abaixar a**—, to lower one's flag; to eat humble pie; to eat crow; to draw in one's horns. **levantar a**—, to stand up against, oppose.

cristado –**da** (*adj.*) crested.

cristal (*m.*) crystal.—**de rocha**, rock crystal, quartz.

cristaleira (*f.*) crystal or china closet; (*slang*) old-fashioned, high-bodied limousine.

cristaleiro (*m.*) prospector, explorer (of mineral deposits).

cristalífero –**ra** (*adj.*) crystalliferous.

cristalinidade (*f.*) crystallinity.

cristalino –**na** (*adj.*) crystalline; (*m.*, *Anat.*) crystalline lens; (*f.*, *Biochem.*) crystallin.

cristalito (*m.*, *Min.*) crystallite.

cristalização (*f.*) crystallization.

cristalizador (*m.*) crystallizer; a crystallizing vessel; a crystallizing tank (as for sugar).
cristalizar (*v.t.*, *v.i.*, *v.r.*) to crystallize.
cristalizável (*adj.*) crystallizable.
cristaloblástico –ca (*adj.*, *Petrog.*, *Min.*) crystalloblastic.
cristalofiliano –na (*adj.*, *Geol.*) crystallophyllian.
cristalogenia (*f.*) crystallogeny.
cristalografia (*f.*) crystallography.
cristalográfico –ca (*adj.*) crystallographic.
cristalógrafo –fa (*m.*,*f.*) crystallographer.
cristalóide (*adj.*) crystalloid; (*m.*, *Biol.*, *Physical Chem.*) crystalloid.
cristalologia (*f.*) crystallology.
cristalometria (*f.*) crystallometry.
cristãmente (*adv.*) Christianly.
cristandade (*f.*) Christendom; Christianity.
cristão [-tãos] –tã [-tãs] (*adj.*, *m.*,*f.*) Christian.
cristel [-téis] (*m.*) = CLISTER.
Cristiana (*f.*) Christiana.
cristianismo (*m.*) Christianism.
cristianização (*f.*) Christianization.
cristianizador –dora (*adj.*) Christianizing; (*m.*,*f.*) Christianizer.
cristianizar (*v.t.*) to Christianize.
Cristiano (*m.*) Christian (proper name).
Cristina (*f.*) Christina; Christine.
Cristo (*m.*) the Christ; (not capitalized) an innocent victim. ser—, (*colloq.*) to be the goat.
cristobalita (*f.*, *Min.*) cristobalite; silicon dioxide.
cristofle (*m.*) a silver-white alloy, similar to German silver, used for tableware.
cristologia (*f.*) Christology.
Cristóvão (*m.*) Christopher.
critério (*m.*) criterion, standard; discernment, perspicacity; judgment.
criterioso –sa (*adj.*) judicious, discerning –wise.
crítica (*f.*) critique, critical review; criticism; disparaging remarks; faultfinding.—especializada, the critics, as a class, of a given art (such as music). a—, the critics.
criticador –dora (*m.*,*f.*) critic; censurer; disparager.
criticar (*v.t.*) to criticize, judge, evaluate; to censure; to review (books).
criticastro (*m.*) criticaster.
criticável (*adj.*) deserving of criticism; censurable.
criticismo (*m.*) philosophical criticism.
crítico –ca (*adj.*) critical, crucial; acute; censorious; precarious; (*m.*,*f.*) critic.
critiqueiro (*m.*) criticaster.
critiquice (*f.*) a worthless review or criticism; frivolous objection; chronic petty faultfinding.
critmo (*m.*, *Bot.*) the samphire (*Crithmum maritimum*), c.a. EQUINÓFORA, FUNCHO-MARINHO.
criva (*f.*) a coarse sieve. Cf. CRIVO.
crivação (*f.*) sifting; riddling.
crivado –da (*adj.*) riddled, shot through; spotted.—de dívidas, debt-ridden.
crivar (*v.t.*) to sift, screen; to riddle (as with shot.)
crível (*adj.*) credible, believable.
crivo (*m.*) riddle, coarse sieve; strainer; colander; grate; drawn work embroidery.
cr.º = CRIADO (servant).
crô (*m.*) a card game.
croá (*m.*) = CURUÁ.
croaciano –na , croácio –cia (*adj.*; *m.*,*f.*) Croatian.
croata (*adj.*; *m.*,*f.*) Croat.
croatá (*m.*, *Bot.*) any of various bromelias.—falso = CARA-GUATÁ-FALSO.
króceo –cea (*adj.*) saffron, golden. [*Poetical*]
crochê, croché (*m.*) crochet.
crocidismo (*m.*, *Med.*) floccillation.
crocidólita (*f.*, *Min.*) crocidolite.
crocina (*f.*, *Chem.*) crocin.
crocitante (*adj.*) cawing, croaking.
crocitar (*v.i.*) to caw, croak.
crocito (*m.*) caw, croak.
croco (*m.*, *Bot.*) crocus [= AÇAFRÃO].
crocodiliano –na (*adj.*; *m.*).crocodilian.
crocodilo (*m.*) crocodile.
crocoíta (*f.*) crocoite, native lead chromate, red lead ore. Vars. CROCÍSA, CROCOISITA.
crocoroca (*f.*) = CORCOROCA.
croinha [o-i] (*m.*) altar boy; choir boy. Cf. COROINHA.
croma (*f.*) chroma, chromaticity, color quality.
cromado –da (*adj.*) chromium-plated.
cromascópio (*m.*) chromascope.

cromático –ca (*adj.*) cnromatic; (*f.*) chromatics.
cromatina (*f.*, *Biol.*) chromatin.
cromatismo (*m.*, *Bot.*, *Optics.*) chromatism.
cromato (*m.*, *Chem.*) chromate.—de chumbo, lead chromate, Paris yellow, chrome yellow.—de potássio, potassium chromate, tarapacaite.—de zinco, zinc chromate; zinc yellow.
cromatócito (*m.*, *Zool.*) chromatocyte.
cromatofilia (*f.*, *Biol.*) chromatophilia.
cromatófilo –la (*adj.*) = CROMÓFILO.
cromatóforo (*m.*, *Bot.*, *Zool.*) chromatophore.
cromatólise (*f.*, *Med.*) chromatolysis.
cromatômetro (*m.*) chromatometer.
cromatoplasma (*m.*) chromatoplasm.
cromatoscopia (*f.*, *Physics*) chromatoscopy.
cromatoscópio (*m.*, *Optics*, *Astron.*) chromatoscope.
cromatose (*f.*) chromatosis.
crômico –ca (*adj.*, *Chem.*) chromic.
cromídio (*m.*, *Biol.*) chromidium.
cromita (*f.*, *Min.*) chromite.
cromo (*m.*) chromo, colored lithograph; (*Chem.*) chrome.
cromoblasto (*m.*, *Biol.*) chromoblast.
cromócito (*m.*, *Anat.*) chromocyte.
cromófago (*m.*, *Anat.*) pigmentophage.
cromofânio (*m.*, *Physiol.*) chromophane.
cromófilo –la (*adj.*, *Biol.*) chromophilic, staining readily.
cromófobo –ba (*adj.*, *Micros.*) chromophobe, -bic, difficult to stain.
cromóforo –ra (*adj.*) chromophoric; (*m.*, *Chem.*) chromophore.
cromofotografia (*f.*) color photography; a color photograph.
cromogênese (*f.*) chromogenesis.
cromogênico –ca (*adj.*) chromogenic, -genetic.
cromogênio (*m.*) chromogen.
cromógeno –na (*adj.*) chromogenous.
cromograma (*m.*) a kromogram; (*Photog.*) chromogram.
cromogravura (*f.*) color printing.
cromoisomeria [o-i] (*f.*, *Chem.*) chromoisomerism.
cromoleucito (*m.*, *Bot.*) chromoleucyte, chromoplast.
cromólise (*f.*, *Med.*) chromatolysis.
cromolitografia (*f.*) chromolithography.
cromômeras (*m.pl.*, *Biol.*) chromomeres.
cromômetro (*m.*) chromometer, colorimeter.
cromóparo –ra (*adj.*, *Bacteriol.*) chromoparous.
cromoplasma (*m.*, *Biol.*) chromoplasm.
cromoplasto (*m.*, *Biol.*) chromoplast.
cromoscópio (*m.*) chromoscope.
cromóscopo (*m.*) a kromskop.
cromosfera (*f.*, *Astron.*) chromosphere.
cromossomo (*m.*, *Biol.*) chromosome.
cromoterapia (*f.*) chromotherapy.
cromotipia (*f.*) chromolithography.
cromotipografia (*f.*) chromotypography.
cromoxilografia (*f.*) chromoxylography.
crômula (*f.*) = CLOROFILA.
cronaxia [ks] (*f.*, *Physiol.*) chronaxie.
crônica (*f.*) chronicle; (*pl.*) annals.
cronicar (*v.t.*) to chronicle.
cronicidade (*f.*) chronicity.
crônico –ca (*adj.*) chronic; inveterate.
croniqueiro (*m.*, *colloq.*) newspaper writer of small local news items.
cronista (*m.*,*f.*) chronicler; columnist.—mundano, society editor.
cronofotografia (*f.*) chronophotograph.
cronografia (*f.*) = CRONOLOGIA.
cronógrafo (*m.*) chronograph.
cronologia (*f.*) chronology.
cronológico –ca (*adj.*) chronologic(al).
cronologista (*m.*,*f.*) chronologist.
cronometragem (*f.*) time-keeping (as at races)—de atividades industriais , time and motion study.
cronometrar (*v.t.*) to time, to clock.
cronometria (*f.*) chronometry.
cronometrista (*m.*,*f.*) timekeeper (at races, games).
cronômetro (*m.*) chronometer; stop watch; metronome.
cronoscopia (*f.*) chronoscopy.
cronoscópio (*m.*) chronoscope.
crookesita (*f.*, *Min.*) crookesite.
croque (*m.*) a boat hook; grapple; rap, light blow.
croquete (*f.*) croquette, meat ball.
croqui [i] (*m.*) sketch, rough drawing.
crossa (*f.*) crosier; (*Anat.*) arch of the aorta.

cróssima (f.) part of a railroad switch. [Corrup. of English *crossing*.]

crosta [ô] (f.) crust, scab.—**terrestre**, earth's crust.

crotafal, **-táfico** **-ca** (adj., Anat.) temporal.

crotafita, **-fito** (both m., Anat.) crotaphite.

crotalar (v.t.) to rattle (as a rattlesnake).

crotalária (f., Bot.) a crotalaria.

crotalídeo **-dea** (adj., Zool.) crotoline; (m.) a rattlesnake.

crótalo (m.) rattlesnake; crotalum.

crotalóide (adj., Zool.) crotaloid, crotaline.

crotão (m.) = CRÓTON.

crotina (f., Biochem.) crotin.

crotófaga (f., Zool.) an ani.

cróton (m., Bot.) the leaf croton (Codiaeum variegatum). Var. CROTÃO.

crotonaldeído (m., Chem.) croton aldehyde; propylene aldehyde.

crotônico **-ca** (adj., Chem.) crotonic.

crotonileno (m., Chem.) 2-butyne, dimethyl acetylene.

cru [fem. **crua**] (adj.) raw, unbaked, uncooked; cruel, hardhearted; crude (oil, language). **a verdade nua e crua**, the raw and naked truth. **couro—**, rawhide. **estar—**, to know nothing.

cruã (f., Bot.) the casabanana (Sicana odorifera), c.a. CURUÁ, CURUBÁ, CRAUÁ, CROÁ, MELÃO-CABOCLO.

cruamente (adv.) bluntly, crudely.

crubixá (m.) a black coral found at various points along the Brazilian coast.

cruciação (f.) torture.

crucial (adj.) cruciate, cross-shaped. [But not crucial, which is: CRÍTICO.]

crucianela (f., Bot.) a bedstraw (Galium cruciata).

cruciante (adj.) excruciating.

cruciar (v.t.) to torment, torture.

cruciferário (m., Eccl.) crucifer.

crucíferas (f.pl., Bot.) the Cruciferae (syn. Brassicaceae)—cabbage family.

crucífero **-ra** (adj.) bearing a cross; (Bot.) cruciferous; (m., Eccl.) crucifer.

crucificação (f.), **-ficamento** (m.) crucifixion.

crucificado **-da** (adj.) crucified; (m.) the Crucified One.

crucificador **-dora** (adj.) crucifying; (m.,f.) crucifier.

crucificar (v.t.) to crucify; fig. to torture.

crucifixão [ks] (f.) = CRUCIFICAÇÃO.

crucifixar [ks] (v.) = CRUCIFICAR.

crucifixo **-xa** [ks] (adj.) crucified; (m.) crucifix.

cruciforme (adj.) cruciform, cross-shaped.

crucígero **-ra** (adj.) bearing, or marked with, a cross.

crudelíssimo **-ma** (absol. superl. of CRUEL) most cruel.

crueira (f.) "(1) a tidal phenomenon characterized by flux and reflux of the tide at 15-minute intervals, beginning with the ebb tide. Var. CUIUÍRA; (2) the coarse part of the manioc flour which does not pass through the sieve in the sifting process." [GBAT.]

cruel (adj.) cruel, merciless, pitiless; harsh; grim, sanguinary; unfeeling.

crueldade (f.) cruelty, ruthlessness.

cruelíssimo **-ma** (adj.) = CRUDELÍSSIMO.

cruento **-ta** (adj.) bloody.

crueza [ê] (f.) rawness; crudeness; cruelty.

crume, **crúmen** (m., Zool.) crumen.

cruor (m., Physiol.) cruor, gore.

crupe (m., Med.) croup [= GARROTILHO].

crupiê (m.) croupier.

crusta (f.) crust [= CROSTA].

crustáceo **-cea** (adj.) crustaceous; (m.) crustacean; (pl., Zool.) the Crustacea.

crural (adj., Anat., Zool.) crural.

cruz (f.) cross; the Cross; Christianity; trial, affliction; (Printing) dagger (mark of reference); (interj.) Good heavens!—**de-jerusalem**, (Arch.) potent or Jerusalem cross; (Bot.) the Maltese-cross campion (Lychnis chalcedonia).—**de-lorena**, Loraine cross.—**de-malta**, Maltese cross; (Bot.) the creeping water primrose (Oussiaea repens), c.a. MURURÉ, and another sp. (J. pilosa) called MÃOS-DE-SAPO; also = CAMARAMBAIA.—**de-santo-andré**, St. Andrew's cross [X].—**do Sul** = CRUZEIRO DO SUL.—**gamada**, swastika.—**grega**, Greek cross [+].—**latina**, Latin cross.—**recruzetada**, (Arch.) crosslet; holly or German cross.—**Vermelha**, Red Cross. **assinar de—**, to sign by making a mark, such as a cross. **entre a—e a caldeirinha**, between the devil and the deep blue sea.

cruza (f.) cross (of breeds).

cruza-bico (m., Zool.) a crossbill (Loxia curvirostra) c.a.

LÓXIA, TRINCA-NOZES.

cruzado **-da** (adj.) crossed, crosswise. **caminhos—s** crossroads. **palavras—s**, crossword puzzle. (m.) an old Port. coin of gold and silver; in Bahia, forty centavos; a crusader; (f.) a crusade; a crossroads; crossing.

cruzador **-dora** (adj.) crossing; cruising; (m.) cruiser.—**couraçado** or **de combate**, battle cruiser.—**ligeiro** (**pesado**), light (heavy) cruiser.

cruzamento (m.) crossing; cross over.—**de caminhos**, road crossing.—**de estrada de ferro**, railroad crossing or junction.—**de raças**, cross-breeding; crossing of races.—**em dois níveis**, overhead crossing.—**recíproco**, (Genetics) reciprocal cross.

cruzar (v.t.) to cross; to traverse, intersect; to cruise over or about; to put (lay) across or athwart; to interbreed; to cross-fertilize (plants); (v.r.) to cross, lie across; to criss-cross; Cf. ATRAVESSAR.—**armas**, to cross swords.—**as raças**, to crossbreed.—**com (alguém)** to meet and pass by (someone).—**os braços**, to fold the arms. [To cross oneself is BENZER-SE.]

cruzeira (f.) = URUTU.

cruzeirinha (f.) = CIPO-CRUZ-VERDADEIRO.

cruzeiro (m.) a large cross erected in a square or other public place; a cruise; a cruiser; the Brazil money unit which replaced the MIL-RÉIS on Nov. 1, 1942; a snake called URUTU; (Arch.) transept; (Bot.) the Christmas-bush eupatorium (E. odoratum).—**do Sul**, the Southern Cross.

cruzeta [ê] (f.) a small cross; crosspiece; coat-hanger.

cruzilhada (f.) = ENCRUZILHADA.

cruzo (m.) crossroad.

C.ta = COMANDITA (silent partnership).

ctenóforo (m., Zool.) ctenophore.

ctenóide (adj., Zolol.) ctenoid.

ctetologia (f.) ctetology.

cuada (f., colloq.) a pratfall.

cuamanaxo **-xa** (m.,f.) an Indian of the Cumanshó, a tribe of the Maxacalí in Minas Gerais; (adj.) pert. to or designating this tribe.

cuambu (m., Bot.) a beggar-ticks (Bidens pilosa), c.a. GUAMBU, PICÃO-PRÊTO, PICÃO-DO-CAMPO, GARIOFILATA, CARRAPICHO-DE-DUAS-PONTAS, ERVA-PICÃO, PIOLHO-DE-PADRE, MACELA-DO-CAMPO.

cuandu (m.) = OURIÇO-CACHEIRO.

cuantindiba or **-diva** (f.) = CRINDIÚVA.

cuari-bravo (m.) a small marigold (Tagetes minuta), c.a. ALFINÊTE-DO-MATO, CRAVINHO (or CRAVO)-DE-DEFUNTO, ERVA-FEDORENTA, RABO-DE-ROJÃO, VARA-DE-FOGUETE, ROJÃO.

cuatá (m.) a spider monkey (Ateles paniscus).

cuatindiba (f., Bot.) a hackberry (Celtis sp.).

cuba (f.) vat, tub; bosh of a blast furnace.

cubagem (f.) cubature; cubic content.

cubano **-na** (adj.; m.,f.) Cuban.

cubar (v.t.) to cube (raise to the 3rd power); to ascertain the cubic content of; [= CUBICAR].

cubatão (m.) foothill.

cubatura (f.) cubature.

cube (m., Bot.) a lancepod (Lonchocarpus sp.).

cubeba [bé], **cubebeira** (f.) cubeb pepper (Piper cubeba).

cubeta (f.) sterilizing tray.

cubicar (v.) = CUBAR.

cúbico **-ca** (adj.) cubic(al).

cubículo (m.) cubicle; cubby-hole; school locker.—**do telefone**, telephone booth.

cúbio (m., Bot.) a nightshade (Solanum sessiliflorum).

cubismo (m.) cubism.

cubista (m.,f.) cubist.

cúbito (m., Anat.) the ulna.

cúbito-carpiano **-na** (adj., Anat.) cubitocarpal.

cúbito-cutâneo **-nea** (adj., Anat.) cubitocutaneous.

cúbito-digital (adj., Anat.) cubitodigital.

cúbito-palmar (adj., Anat.) cubitopalmar.

cúbito-radial (adj., Anat.) cubitoradial.

cubo (m.) cube; hexahedron; wheel hub.

cubóide (adj.; m., Anat.) cuboid (bone).

cuca (f.) bogyman, hobgoblin; hag; ugly old woman. **mestre—**, head cook.

cucamplê (m.) a certain card game—supposed to be a corruption of (any) "cook can play".

cucar (v.i.) to cuckoo.

cucharra (f.) horn spoon, wooden spoon; dipper.

cuco (m.) cuckoo; cuckoo clock; cuckold.

cucu (m.) = PAPA-LAGARTAS.

cucúlidas, cuculídeos (*m.pl.*, *Zool.*) the cuckoo family (*Cuculidae*).

cuculiforme (*adj.*) hood-shaped; cowl-like.

cuculo (*m.*) overplus, surplus, excess [= COGULO]; cucullus; hood, cowl.

cucúrbita (*f.*, *Chem.*) cucurbit; (*Bot.*) any plant of the genus Cucurbita.

cucurbitáceas (*f.*, *pl.*) the Cucurbitaceae (family of cucumbers, melons, squashes, gourds and pumpkins).

cucurbitáceo -cea (*adj.*, *Bot.*) cucurbitaceous.

cucurbitino -na (*adj.*) cucurbitine.

cucuri (*m.*) = CAÇÃO-FRANÇO.

cucuricar, cucuritar (*v.i.*) to crow (as a cock).

cu-de-ferro (*m.*, *slang*) a student who never cuts classes.

cudelume (*m.*, *colloq.*) firefly [= PIRILAMPO].

cuecas (*f.*, *pl.*) men's shorts (underdrawers).

cueira (*f.*) = CUIEIRA

cueiro (*m.*) swaddling band; diaper.

cuendu (*m.*) = OURIÇO-CACHEIRO.

cuera (*f.*) saddle gall [= UNHEIRA, TUBUNA].

cuerudo -da (*adj.*) having saddle sores.

cuguará (*m.*, *Zool.*) an anteater (*Myrmecophaga tetradactyla*).

cuí (*m.*) "(1) a very fine sifted flour free of lumps; (2) generically, anything which is very finely powdered, such as tobacco powder, etc." [GBAT]

cuia (*f.*) gourd; drinking cup or other vessel made from a gourd; postiche, chignon (for hair); (*colloq.*) prostitute. "A half-gourd (*Crescentia cujete*) used by the rubber tapper as a container for latex to be smoked; (2) polished, varnished, and artistically decorated gourd from the same plant." [GBAT]**—-de-macaco**, (*Bot.*) a cannonball tree (*Couroupita sp.*).**—-do-brejo**, a snowbell (*Styrax sp.*), c.a. ESTORAQUE-DA-AMÉRICA, ESTORAQUE-DO-CAMPO, FRUTA-DE-POMBA, PINDUÍBA.

cuiabano -na (*adj.*; *m.*,*f.*) of or pert. to, or a person of, Cuiabá, Brazil; (*f.*) a certain carpenter ant.

cuiada (*f.*) a gourdful, esp. of MATE tea.

cuiambuca (*f.*) a gourd water bottle. Vars. COMBUCA, CUMBUCA.

cuíca (*f.*) a Brazilian percussion instrument resembling a small keg; (*Zool.*) any of numerous mouse opossums (genus *Marmosa*), and other small marsupials of the same family, c.a. QUÍCA, GUAICUÍCA, GOIACUÍCA, CHICHICA, JUPITA.**—-cauda-de-rato**, any rat-tailed opossum of genus *Metachirus*, c.a. JUPATI.**—-d'água** or **—-pé-de-pato**, any yapok or water opossum (*Chironectes*).

cuidadeira (*f.*) a woman caretaker. [Masc. CUIDADOR.]

cuidado -da (*adj.*) imagined; foreseen; (*interj.*) Look out! Watch out!; (*m.*) care, caution, heed; anxiety, concern; object of concern or attention.**—com ela!** Watch out for her!**—com a cabeça!** Mind your head! **ao—de**, in care of. **com—**, carefully. **dar—**, to give cause for anxiety.

cuidador (*m.*) caretaker. [Fem. CUIDADEIRA].

cuidadoso -sa (*adj.*) careful, cautious; mindful; anxious, solicitous; minute, painstaking; deliberate.

cuidar (*v.t.*) to care (**de**, for), mind, take care (**de**, of), attend (**de**, to); to pay attention (**de**, to); to imagine, suppose, think, believe; to cogitate, consider; (*v.r.*) to take care of oneself; to judge oneself (to be something).**—da casa**, to take care of the house.**—de**, to treat of, deal with (a subject).**—dos doentes**, to care for the sick.**—da saúde**, to care for one's health. **Cuide de si**, Mind your own business. **Êle se cuida bem**, He takes good care of himself.

cuidaru (*m.*) a flat, wooden, swordlike Indian club, c.a. TAMARANA.

cuidoso -sa (*adj.*) = CUIDADOSO.

cuieira (*f.*) common calabashtree (*Crescentia cujete*), c.a. ÁRVORE-DE-CUIA, CABACEIRA, CUEIRA, CUIETÉ, CUITÉ, CUITEZEIRA, CUJETÉ.

cuim [u-ím] (*m.*) a hedgehog [= OURIÇO-CACHEIRO]; a pig's squeal.

cuinchar [u-in], **cuinhar** [u-i] (*u,i.*) to squeal (as a pig); = GUINCHAR.

cuipeúna (*f.*) a glorybush (*Tibouchina mutabilis*), c.a. FLOR-DE-MAIO, FLOR-DE-QUARESMA, JACATIRÃO-DE-CAPOTE, JAGUATIRÃO, PAU-DE-FLOR.

cuíra (*adj.*) fidgety, squirming, impatient.

cuité (*m.*) = CUIETÉ and CUIA (gourd).

cuitelão (*m.*, *Zool.*) the three-toed jacamar (*Jacamaralcyon tridactyla*), c.a. VIOLEIRO, BICUDO.

cuitelo (*m.*) = BEIJA-FLOR.

cuitezèira (*f.*) = CABACEIRO.

cuiú (*m.*) the red-capped parrot (*Pionopsitta pileata*).

cujara (*m.*) a rice rat (*Oryzomys leucogaster*).

cujo -ja (*adj.*; *rel. pron.*) whose, of whom, of which; (*m.*, *colloq.*) **o cujo**, the said person.

cujubi, cujubim (*m.*. *Zool.*) the Amazonian piping guan (*Pipile cujubi*) and the white-head piping guan (*P. cumanensis*).

culatra (*f.*) gun breech; head of an internal combustion motor; the curved portion of the core of an electromagnet which connects the two coils; (*slang*) the backside. **O tiro saiu pela—**, The charge (accusation) backfired. **tiro pela—**, backfire.

culatrear (*v.t.*) to drive (cattle) from behind; to pursue (a criminal, etc.).

cule (*m.*) coolie.

culicida (*f.*) culicide (mosquito poison).

culícidas, culicídeos (*m.pl.*) the mosquito family (*Culicidae*).

culinário -ria (*adj.*) culinary; (*f.*) culinary art.

culita (*f.*) the twinflower dolichos (*D. biflorus*).

culmífero -ra (*adj.*, *Bot.*) culmiferous.

culminação (*f.*) culmination, highest point, acme, zenith.

culminante (*adj.*) culminating, topmost. **ponto—**, highest point.

culminar (*v.i.*) to culminate, reach the highest point.

culote (*m.*) riding breeches.

culpa (*f.*) blame, fault; guilt. **Êle quer me pôr a—**, He is trying to put the blame on me. **ter—de**, to be to blame for. **tirar a—**, to remove the blame. **pôr a—por cima de outro**, to throw the blame on another.

culpabilidade (*f.*) culpability.

culpado -da (*adj.*) guilty; criminal; to blame.**—ou inocente?** guilty or not guilty? **Eu não sou—disto**, I am not to blame for this. (*m.*,*f.*) culprit; convicted criminal.

culpar (*v.t.*) to blame, accuse.

culpável (*adj.*) culpable, blameworthy.

culposo -sa (*adj.*) guilty.

cultamente (*adv.*) in a cultured (refined) manner.

culteranismo, cultismo (*m.*) "Gongorism as exaggerated by the 17th century Iberian writers." *Webster*.

cultivação (*f.*) cultivation; culture; refinement.

cultivar (*v.t.*) to cultivate, till; to improve, refine; (*v.r.*) to acquire culture.

cultivável (*adj.*) cultivable; arable.

cultivo (*m.*) cultivation; culture.

culto -ta (*adj.*) cultured, refined; civilized; (*m.*) cult, homage, worship.**—divino**, divine worship.

cultor (*m.*), **-tora** (*f.*) cultivator; grower; follower, adherent, partisan. **café—**, coffee grower.

cultriforme (*adj.*; *Bot.*, *Zool.*) cultrate.

cultrirrostros (*m.pl.*) the Cultirostres (storks, herons, cranes).

cultura (*f.*) culture, cultivation, tillage; education, enlightenment; refinement; civilization.**—alternada**, crop rotation.

cultural (*adj.*) cultural.

cumanã (*f.*, *Bot.*) an euphorbia (*E. phosphorea*), c.a. CAMAPUÃ, CANDOMBLÉ, CIPÓ-DE-BREU, CIPÓ-DE-CUNAMÃ, CIPÓ-DE-CUNANÃ, CIPÓ-DE-LEITE, PAU-DE-CUNANÃ.

cumandatiá (*f.*, *Bot.*) the hyacinth dolichos (*D. lablab*), c.a. LABE-LABE, FEIJÃO-DA-ÍNDIA, GUAR, MANGALÔ.

cumari, -rim (*m.*) an astrocaryum palm (*A. vulgare*), c.a. COQUEIRO-TUCUM, CURUÁ, TUCUM-BRAVO, TUCUM-DO-AMAZONAS, TUCUMÃ-PIRANGA; a bush pepper (*Capsicum frustescens*), c.a. PIMENTA-CUMARI.

cumarina (*f.*, *Chem.*) coumarin.

cumaru (*m.*) a tonkabean (*Dipteryx sp.*).**—-verdadeiro**, the Dutch tonkabean (*Dipteryx odorata*), c.a.**—AMARELO**,**—DO-AMAZONAS**, CUMARUZEIRO, PARU.

cumba (*adj.*, *slang*) strong, able.

cumbaca (*f.*) = ANAJÁ.

cumbé (*m.*) any soft and slimy creature, as a leech or slug.

cumbuca (*f.*) gourd bottle [= CUIAMBUCA]; a raffle; gambling den.

cume (*m.*) top, summit; apex; acme.

cumeada (*f.*) summit, ridge; roof ridge.

cumeeira (*f.*) top, summit; crest, ridgepole or ridgepiece of a gable roof.

cumerone (*m.*, *Chem.*) coumarone, benzofuran.

cumiada (*f.*) = CUMEEIRA.

cuminho (*m.*, *Bot.*) cumin (*Cuminum cyminum*); (*pl.*) cuminseed.

cumis (*m.*). kumiss.

cúmplice (*m.,f.*) accomplice, accessory; abettor.

cumpliciar-se (*v.r.*) to implicate oneself.

cumplicidade (*f.*) complicity.

cumpridor –**dora** (*adj.*) fulfilling; (*m.,f.*) executor (of a will).

cumprimentar (*v.t.*) to greet, speak to; to compliment, congratulate.

cumprimenteiro –**ra** (*adj.*) given to exaggerated compliments.

cumprimento (*m.*) accomplishment, fulfillment; compliance; salutation, greeting; compliment.—**s rasgados,** magniloquent greetings; exaggerated compliments. [Do not confuse with COMPRIMENTO].

cumprir [25] (*v.t.*) to fulfill, observe, obey, comply with; to discharge (duty); to accomplish, execute, bring to pass, carry out; to serve (a sentence); to behoove.—**a palavra,** to keep one's word.—**à risca (uma promessa, etc.),** to carry out (a promise, etc.) to the letter.—**com,** to comply with.—**instruções,** to obey (follow) instructions. **fazer**—, to enforce.

cump.to = CUMPRIMENTO (greeting).

cumulação (*f.*) accumulation.

cumular (*v.t.*) to heap (up) [= ACUMULAR].—**de gentilezas,** to overwhelm with kindnesses.

cumulativo –**va** (*adj.*) cumulative.

cumuliforme (*adj., Meteorol.*) cumuliform.

cúmulo (*m.*) heap, accumulation; acme, highest point; cumulus (cloud formation).—**nimbus,** (*Meteorol.*) cumulonimbus. **ao**—, to the highest degree. **É o**—! That's the limit! That takes the cake!

cumulus (*m., Meteorol.*) cumulus [= CÚMULO].

cumutanga (*f.*) = ACUMUTANGA.

cunanã (*m.*) = CUMANÃ.

cunapu(-guaçu) (*m.*) = MERO.

cunauarú (*m.*) a tree frog (*Hyla venulosa*).

cunca (*f.*) a thirst-quenching tubercle which develops on the roots of the mombin tree [UMBUZEIRO]; (*m.*) a kind of rummy (card game).

cuneano –**na** (*adj.*) wedge-shaped; (*Anat.*) cuneiform.

cuneiforme (*adj.*) cuneiform; (*m.pl.*) cuneiform characters; (*Anat.*) cuneiform bones.

cunha (*f.*) wedge; fig. one who arranges an entrée for another; (*Meteorol.*) wedge. **à**—, jammed, crowded; replete. **vértice da**—, spearhead.

cunhã (*f.*) an Indian or halfbreed girl; (*Bot.*) a butterfly pea (*Centrosema sp.*).

cunhado –**da** (*adj.*) coined; stamped out; (*m.*) brother-in-law; (*f.*) sister-in-law.

cunhador (*m.*) stamper, coiner.

cunhagem (*f.*) coinage; cold stamping.

cunhal (*m.*) corner, as of two walls.

cunhamucu (*m.*) "a kind of small turtle, roasted and eaten whole, after the viscera have been removed through a hole made in the bottom shell." [GBAT]

cunhar (*v.t.*) to coin, mint; to invent, create.

cunhete [ête] (*m.*) ammunition box.

cunho (*m.*) die; stamp; mark, seal.

cunicultura (*f.*) rabbit raising.

cupaí (*m., Bot.*) the copey clusia (*C. rosea*), c.a. CEBOLA-BRAVA, MATA-PAU.

cupão (*m.*) coupon [= CUPOM].

cupê (*m.*) coupé.

cupidez [ê] (*f.*) cupidity.

cupido (*m.*) Cupid, love; a vain, conceited man; also = CAPIVARA.

cúpido –**da** (*adj.*) covetous, greedy; displaying cupidity.

cupieiro = CARURU-BRAVO.

cupim (*m.*) termite, white ant [= FORMIGA BRANCA]; a termitary; a Negro's hair; the hump on the shoulder of zebu cattle; also = CUPINZEIRO.

cupincha (*m.,f.*) stooge.

cupineira (*f.*) termite nest.

cupinzeiro (*m.*) a dead tree or other habitation of termites.

cupira (*f.*) any of various small, stingless honeybees (*Melipona spp.*) which nest in termitaries—c.a. BÔCA-DE-BARRO.

cupiúba (*f., Bot.*) the kopie (*Goupia glabra*).

cupom (*m.*) = CUPÃO.

cupragol (*m.*) = CUPROL.

cupressíneas (*f.pl.*) the cypress family (*Cupressaceae*).

cupressíneo –**nea,** –**sino** –**na** (*adj., Bot.*) cupressineous.

cúprico –**ca** (*adj., Chem.*) cupric.

cuprífero –**ra** (*adj.*) cupriferous, copper-bearing.

cuprino –**na** (*adj.*) cupreous, coppery.

cuprita (*f., Min.*) cuprite, red copper oxide.

cupro-aço (*m.*) copper-steel alloy.

cuprobismutito (*m., Min.*) cuprobismutite.

cuprol (*m., Pharm.*) cuprol, copper nucleinate.

curpo-níquel (*m.*) copper-nickel alloy.

cuproso –**sa** (*adj., Chem.*) cuprous.

cupuaçu (*m.*) "A plant (*Theobroma grandiflorum,* Spreng.) very closely related to the cacao tree, whose pulp is used as a flavoring or as a preserve, with seeds yielding a white fat similar to cocoa butter." GBAT.

cupuaí (*m.*) a chocolate tree (*Theobroma sp.*)

cúpula (*f.*) cupola, dome; (*Bot.*) cup or cupule.

cupuláceas, –**líferas** (*f.pl., Bot.*) a group of trees (*Cupuliferae*) comprising the oaks, chestnuts, birches, etc.)

cupulado –**da** (*adj.*) domed; (*Bot.*) cupulate.

cupuliforme (*adj.*) cup-shaped; cupulate.

cura (*f.*) cure, healing; restoration, recovery; treatment; curing (of concrete); (*m.*) curate, rector, parish priest.

curabilidade (*f.*) curability.

curaca (*f.*) = MURUBIXABA, CACIQUE.

curação (*f.*) = BACURAU.

curaçau (*m.*) curaçao (a liqueur made from dried orange peel).

curaci (*f., Bot.*) the orange-gold chanconia (*Warzewiczia coccinea*), c.a. RABO-DE-ARARA.

curado –**da** (*adj.*) cured; healed; (*m.,f.*) a person who superstitiously believes that he has been rendered invulnerable to bullets, knife wounds, snake bites, etc., by the incantations of a medicine man.

curador (*m.*) curator, caretaker, custodian, trustee, guardian; witch doctor, herb doctor.

curadoria (*f.*) curatorship.

curanchim (*m., colloq.*) the tail bone (coccyx).

curandeirismo (*m.*) quackery, charlatanry; shamanism.

curandeiro (*m.*) quack, charlatan; medicine man, shaman, witch doctor.

curandice (*f.*) fake medical treatment; quackery.

curar (*v.t.*) to cure, heal; to practice a healing art; to treat; to dress a wound; to preserve (cure) by drying (meat, etc.); (*v.r.*) to heal oneself.

curare (*m.*) curare (a violent, paralyzing or stunning arrow poison used by some So. Amer. Indians). [It is extracted from the curare poisonnut vine (*Strychnos toxifera*) or related species.] Other names are: UIRARI, ICÓ, ERVADURA, ERVAGEM, TICUNA.

curarina (*f., Chem.*) curine or curarine (both are alkaloids of curare).

curarismo (*m.*) curare poisoning.

curarizar (*v.t.*) to poison with curare; fig. to stun or paralyze.

curatá (*f., Bot.*) a seagrape (*Coccolobis sp.*)

curativo –**va** (*adj.*) curative; (*m.*) remedy; dressing, treatment.

curato (*m.*) parsonage, rectory; parish.

curau (*m.*) a pap of grated green corn with sugar, milk and cinnamon [called CORAL or PAPA DE MILHO in Minas Gerais, and CANJIQUINHA in Rio]; in northern Brazil, a dish of ground salt meat mixed with manioc meal; a parrot (*Amazonia aestiva*); a rustic [CAIPIRA].

curauá (*m.*) a pineapple (*Ananas comosus*) having spineless leaves whose fiber is used for making hammocks and cordage.

curável (*adj.*) curable.

curculionídeos (*m.pl.*) the family of snout beetles (*Curculionidae*).

cúrcuma (*m., Bot.*) the common turmeric (*Curcuma longa*) or related species.

curcumina (*f., Chem.*) curcumin.

curêta (*f.*) curette.

curetagem (*f., Surg.*) curettage, curettement.

curetar (*v.t., Surg.*) to curette.

cúria (*f.*) curia; Curia, papal court.

curial (*adj.*) curial; fig. appropriate; (*m.*) an official of the Curia.

curiango (*m., Zool.*) the cuiejo or parauque (*Nyctidromus a. albicollis*), c.a. BACURAU, IBIIAÚ, MEDE-LÉGUAS.—**tesoura,** the ringed nighthawk (*Hydropsalis torquata*).

curiboca [ó] (*m.,f.*) = CARIBOCA.

curica (*m.*) any of various small parrots, esp. the orange-winged parrot (*Amazona a. amazonica*), c.a. CURUCA, AJURU-CURUCA, PAPAGAIO-DO-MANGUE, PAPAGAIO-POAIEIRO; Barraband's parrot (*Eucinetus barrabandi*), c.a. AJURU-CARAU.

curicaca (*f., Zool.*) an ibis.—**branca,** white-throated ibis

(*Theristicus c. caudatus*).—**parda**, the glossy ibis (*Plegadis falcinellus*), c.a. TAPICURU, MAÇARICO.

curimã (*f.*) the common striped mullet (*Mugil cephalus*).

curimba (*f., Bot.*) black mangrove (*Avicennia marina*) [=MANGUE].

curimbó, curimbu (*m.*) an Indian drum made from a piece of hollow log, c.a. TOBAQUE, TAMBAQUE.

curina (*f., Chem.*) curine.

curinga (*f.*) the joker in a deck of cards; the wild card in any game [=DUNGA].

curiango, curiangu (*m., Zool.*) a goatsucker or nighthawk.

curindiba (*f.*) =CRINDIÚVA.

curió (*m.*) any finch of the genus Oryzoborus; c.a. AVINHADO; (*m.*) the chestnut-bellied rice grosbeak (*Oryzoborus a. angolensis*); the large-billed rice grosbeak (*C. c. crassirostris*), c.a. BICUDO.

curiosidade (*f.*) curiosity, inquisitiveness; an oddity; a strange or rare object.

curioso –sa (*adj.*) curious, inquisitive; prying; odd, rare, strange, queer; interesting; (*m.*) a curious (inquisitive) man; snooper; bystander, onlooker; a curious thing; a Jack-of-all-trades.

curista (*m.,f.*) a person who is taking the cure at a spa.

curral (*m.*) corral, barnyard.—**de-peixe**, a fishgarth [=CERCADA].

curraleiro (*m.*) =PEITO-ROXO.

currículo (*m.*) curriculum.

curriqueiro (*m.*) the common miner bird (*Geositta c. cunicularia*), occurring mainly in southern Brazil.

curro (*m.*) bull pen; slave quarters.

currupira (*m.*) =CURUPIRA.

cursar (*v.t.*) to follow a course of study; to attend a university; to cross (the ocean).

cursista (*m.,f.*) one who follows a course of study.

cursivo –va (*adj.*) cursive; (*m.*) running style of handwriting.

curso (*m.*) course, running, race; route, way, track; round, orbit; direction, path; sequence; course of studies; career.—**ascendente**, (*Mach.*) upstroke (of a piston).—**de adestramento**, training course.—**de aperfeiçoamento** or **de pós-graduação**, postgraduate course.—**de êmbolo**, piston stroke.—**de férias**, summer (school) session.—**primário**, primary grade, elementary school.—**secundário**, secondary grades.—**vestibulo**, pre-college course. A nova lei terá—**a partir de primeiro de Janeiro**, The new law will become effective January first. **em**—, current.

cursor –sora (*adj.*) running alongside of, or along the length of; (*m.*) a sliding part, as the movable counterpoise of a scale beam.

cursoriamente (*adv.*) cursorily.

curtamão [-mãos] (*m.*) a mason's square.

curteza [ê] (*f.*) shortness; dullness (of mind); deficiency (of intellect); inadequacy (of education).

curtido –da (*adj.*) tanned; hard-boiled; tough.

curtidor (*m.*) tanner.

curtidura (*f.*), **curtimento** (*m.*) process of tanning.

curtir (*v.t.*) to tan (hides); to pickle; to harden, toughen, inure; (*v.i.*) to undergo, endure, suffer (hardship).—**as amarguras**, to swallow a bitter pill.

curto –ta (*adj.*) short; brief, curtailed; fig. mentally deficient.—**circuito**, (*Elec.*) short circuit.

curtume (*f.*) tannery; tanning. **fábrica de—s**, leather factory.

curuá (*m.*) any of various palms, esp. of Attalea; also =COROTÉU and ANAMBÉ-AZUL (birds). "(1) a widely distributed palm (*Attalea spectabilis*) bearing oil-producing seeds with two to six kernels which must be dried before shipping to prevent them from becoming rancid; (2) a palm (*A. monosperma*) whose leaves are used for thatch." [*GBAT*]

curuai, curuaia (*m.,f.*) one of the Curuaya, a practically extinct Tupian tribe which lived on the Curuá River, a tributary of the Iriri, in what is now the State of Pará; (*adj.*) pert. to or designating this tribe.

curuarana (*m.*) a Syagrus palm (*S. inajai*), c.a. JARÁ, JARARANA, JARAEUÁ, PUPUHARANA, IARARANA.

curuatá-pinima (*m.*) =BONITO-PINTADO.

curuba (*f.*) mange, itch.

curubá (*f.*) =CRUÁ.

curuca (*m.*) =CURICA.

curucuru (*m.*) the agua toad (*Bufo marinus*).

curuiri (*m., Bot.*) the pitomba (*Eugenia luschnathiana*), c.a. PITOMBA, PITOMBEIRA.

curul (*f.*) a curule chair.

curumba (*m.*) hobo, tramp; migrant worker; backwoodsman; rustic; (*f.*) an old woman.

curumi, –mim (*m.*) boy, urchin.

curupiá (*m.*) a hackberry (*Celtis sp.*)

curupira (*m.*) in Braz. folklore, a bogy-man whose feet point backwards. Var. CURRUPIRA.

curupitá (*m.*) =MURUPITA.

curuquerê (*m.*) larva of the cotton moth; bollworm.

cururá (*f.*) =ANAMBÉ-AZUL.

cururu (*m.*) the marine toad (*Bufo marinus*), c.a. SAPO-CURURU; a gopherlike rodent [=TUCO-TUCO]; (*pl.*) a former tribe of Indians in Minas Gerais who croaked like toads.—**apé**, (*m.*) an Amazonian woody vine (*Paullinia pinnata*) the bitter bark of which contains a fish poison; c.a. CIPÓ-CRUAPÉ-VERMELHO, CIPÓ-CUMARU-APÉ, CIPÓ-TIMBÓ, TIMBÓ-CIPÓ, MAFONE.—**pé-de-pato**. the Surinam toad (*Pipa pipa*), c.a. PIPA.

curutié (*m.*) any of numerous tree creepers of the genus Synallaxis esp. *S. ruficapilla*. [They are small birds (a few inches long) but they build huge coarse nests, sometimes two or three feet in diameter, or as large as a barrel, of sticks and twigs loosely thrown together, in the recesses of which they lay their eggs.] Other names for the various species are: JOÃO-TENENEM, TENENÉ, BENTERERÊ, PICHORORÉ, JOÃO-TIRIRI, TURUCUÉ, CORRUÍRA-DO-BREJO, CANÁRIO-DO-BREJO.

curva (*f.*) curve; bend; turn; arch; (*pl.*) ribs of a ship's hull.—**adiabática**, (*Thermodyn*) adiabatic curve or line.—**cabrada**, (*Aeron.*) a zooming up-curve.—**catenária**, (*Math.*) catenary.—**fechada**, sharp curve.—**francesa**, French (drawing) curve.—**de histérese**, (*Magnetism*) hysteresis loop or cycle.—**de nível**, (*Math.*) contour curve.—**normal**, (*Aeron.*) a one-minute turn.

curvado –da (*adj.*) curved, bent, arched; bowed down, bent over.

curvar (*v.t.*) to curve, bend, arch; to sag; to crook; to bend to one's will; (*v.i.*) to bend; to bow, stoop. (*v.r.*) to bow, bend over.—**a cerviz**, to bow in submission.—**os joelhos**, to bend the knees.—**se em vênia (diante de alguém)**, to bow in submission to (someone).

curvatão (*m., Naut.*) crosstree.

curvatura (*f.*) curvature; camber; sag.

curvejão (*m.*) hock (of a horse).

curveta [ê] (*f.*) curvet (of a horse); a small curve; a bend in the road.

curvetear (*v.i.*) to curvet; to cavort; to prance.

curvicaude (*adj., Zool.*) curvicaudate.

curvidentado –da (*adj., Zool.*) curvidentate.

curvifoliado –da (*adj., Bot.*) curvifoliate.

curvígrafo (*m.*) an arcograph.

curvilhão (*m.z*=CURVEJÃO.

curvilíneo –nea (*adj.*) curvilinear; curvaceous.

curvímetro (*m.*) curvometer.

curvirrostro –tra (*adj., Zool.*) curvirostral.

curvo –va (*adj.*) curved, bent, arched.

cusco (*m.*) small mongrel dog; small unimportant person [=GUAIPÉ, GUAIPECA, GUAIPEVA, GUAPEVA].

cuscuta (*f., Bot.*) a dodder (*Cuscuta europaea*), c.a. CABELOS-DE-NOSSA-SENHORA.

cuscuz (*m.*) a popular Brazilian dish made of steamed rice, manioc or corn meal. [It derives from the couscous of northeastern Africa.]

cuspada, cusparada (*f.*) copious spitting.

cuspária (*f.*) a So. Amer. tree (*Cusparia angostura*) which yields angostura bark.

cuspe, popular but erron. var. of CUSPO.

cuspidato –ta (*adj.*) cuspidate.

cúspide (*f.*) cusp, pointed end, sharp point.

cuspideira (*f.*) cuspidor, spittoon [=ESCARRADERIA].

cuspidiforme (*adj.*) cuspidal, peaked, pointed, sharp-ended.

cuspidor (*m.*) spitter; also=CHUPA-DENTE.

cuspidura (*f.*) spittle, spitting.

cuspilhar (*v.*) =CUSPINHAR.

cuspinhada (*f.*) =CUSPARADA.

cuspinhadura (*f.*) spittle.

cuspinhar (*v.i.*) to spit frequently.

cuspir (*v.i.*) to spit, expectorate; (*v.t.*) to spit insults.—**no prato em que se come**, to bite the hand that feeds one.

cuspo (*m.*) spit, spittle, saliva.—**de-cuco**, cuckoo spit, toad spittle, frog spit, c.a. LINHO-DE-CUCO.

cusso (*m.*) =COSSO.

custa (*f.*) cost, expense, charge; (*pl.*) court costs. **à— alheia**, at another's expense. **à—da vida**, at the cost of

one's life. **à—de**, at the expense of; by dint of. **à sua—**, at his (her, your) expense. **a tôda —**, at all costs.
custar (*v.i.*) to cost; to result in the loss of; to be difficult, painful, onerous.—**(a) fazer**, to be hard to do.—**barato**, to cost little, be cheap.—**caro**, to cost dear, be expensive. —**os olhos da cara** or—**um dinheirão**, to cost a mint of money. **Custa a crer**, It is hard to believe. **Custa-lhe (falar)**, It is hard for him (to speak). **custe o que—**, cost what it may. **Ganhei mas custou**, I won but it was hard.
custeamento (*m.*) defrayal; costs.
custear (*v.t.*) to defray (expenses).
custeio (*m.*) = CUSTEAMENTO.
custenau (*m.,f.*) an Indian of the Custenau, an Arawakan tribe on the upper Xingu River in Mato Grosso; (*adj.*) pert. to or designating this tribe.
custo (*m.*) cost, price; difficulty; effort.—**s fixos**, (*Econ.*) fixed overhead.—, **seguro e frete**, cost, insurance and freight [C.I.F.] **a—**, with difficulty. **a todo—**, at all costs; by all means
custódia (*f.*) see CUSTÓDIO.
custodiar (*v.t.*) to take or hold in custody; to safekeep, guard.
custódio –dia (*adj.*) custodial; (*f.*) custody; place of custody; (*R.C.Ch.*) a custodial; monstrance.
custoso –sa (*adj.*) costly; difficult; painful.
cutâneo –nea (*adj.*) cutaneous.
cutela (*f.*) meat cleaver, chopper.
cutelaria (*f.*) cutlery.
cuteleiro (*m.*) cutler.
cutelo (*m.*) cutlass; chopping knife, cleaver; studding sail, c.a. VARREDEIRA.
cúter (*m., Naut.*) cutter.
cutia (*f.*) the agouti (*S. Dasyprocta aguti*), a rodent about the size of a rabbit; (*Bot.*) a species of Pilocarpus.

cutícula (*f.*) cuticle.
cuticular (*adj.*) cuticular, epidermal.
cutículo (*m., Zool.*) cuticle.
cutilada (*f.*) a cut or slash, as with a knife or sabre.
cutimbóia (*f.*) = COBRA-CIPÓ.
cutina (*f., Biochem.*) cutin.
cutinizar (*v.t.,v.i.*) to cutinize.
cutipaca (*m.*) = CAVALEIRO.
cutipuruí (*m.*) = CORRUÍRA.
cutirreação (*f., Med.*) reaction to a skin test.
cútis (*f., Anat.*) cutis; skin, esp. of the face.
cutuba (*adj., slang*) nice; cute; swell; "tops"; splendid.
cutucação, cutucada (*f.*) a jogging, nudging, poking, as with the elbow.
cutucanhé (*m.*) = CARVALHO-DO-BRASIL.
cutucão (*m.*) a jab, poke or prod.
cutucar (*v.t.*) to nudge, jog, poke, dig, jab.
cutucurim (*m.*) the great crested harpy-eagle of South America (*Thrasyaetus harpyia*) one of the largest and most powerful of its kind; c.a. HARPIA, URAÇU, URUTAU-RANA, GAVIÃO-DE-PENACHO, GAVIÃO-REAL.
cuvu (*m.*) a type of fish trap, c.a. JUQUIÁ.
cuxiú (*m.*) any of several saki monkeys (*Pithecia*), esp.—-**judeu**, a bearded species (*P. chiropotes*) which cups its hand to drink water;—-**prêto**, a black species (*P. satanas*), and—-**prêto-de-nariz-branco** (*P. albinasa*) which has a white nose and is c.a. SAGUI-DE-NARIZ-BRANCO.
c.v. = CAVALO-VAPOR (horsepower).
Cx. or **cx.** = CAIXA (cashier).
czar (*m.*) czar
czarda (*f.*) = XARDA.
czarina (*f.*) czarina.
czarista (*m.,f.*) czarist.

D

D, d, the fourth letter of the Portuguese alphabet.
D. = DEVE (debit); DIGNO (worthy); DOM; DONA.
d = DINA (dyne).
d. = DINHEIRO (English penny).
d/ = DIAS (days).
da (*contraction of prep.* **de**+*art.* **a** *or dem. pron.* **a**) of the, of that, from the, from that. Cf. DE, DO.
dacito (*m., Petrog.*) dacite.
dáctila (*f., Bot.*) orchard grass (*Dactylis glomerata*).
dactílico –ca (*adj.*) dactylic.
dactilioglifo (*m.*) dactylioglyph.
dactilioteca (*f.*) dactyliotheca.
dá[c]tilo (*m., Pros.*) dactyl.
dactilografar (*v.t., v.i.*) to typewrite.
dactilografia (*f.*) typing, typewriting. [But not dactylography in the sense of dactylology, which is DACTILOLOGIA, nor in the sense of the scientific study of fingerprints as a means of identification, for which there is no exact equivalent or short definition in Portuguese.] Cf. DACTILOSCOPIA.
dactilógrafo –fa (*m.,f.*) typist; (*m.*) typewriter.
dactilologia (*f.*) dactylology.
dactilomegalia (*f., Med.*) dactylomegaly.
dactiloscopia (*f.*) dactyloscopy (identification by comparison of fingerprints). Cf. DACTILOGRAFIA.
dactiloscópico –ca (*adj.*) dactyloscopic.
dactiloscrito –ta (*adj.*) "dactyloscript" (typewritten) as opposed to manuscript (handwritten).
dactiloteca (*f., Zool.*) dactylotheca.
dada (*f.*) an act of giving; a raid on an Indian settlement.
dadeira (*f., colloq.*) a woman given to having fits.
dádiva (*f.*) donation, gift, present; boon.
dadivar (*v.t.*) to give to, present with, donate to.
dadivoso –sa (*adj.*) generous, open-handed.
dado –da (*adj.; p.p. of* DAR) given; affable, cordial, warm-hearted; (*m.*) die; datum; condition, proviso; the inherent nature of anything; (*Arch.*) dado, die; (*pl.*) dice; data.—**a**, fond of, given to (sports, drink, etc.).—**que**, provided that.—**s conhecidos**, known data.—**s falsos**, loaded dice. **aos tombos dos—s**, haphazardly (as the dice may fall). **em—momento**, at a given moment.
dador (*m.*), **-dora** (*f.*) donor, giver; dealer (at cards).

Dafne (*f.*) Daphne; (*Bot.*) the genus Daphne.
dáfnia (*f.*) Daphnia (water fleas).
dafnina (*f., Chem.*) daphnin.
dafnite (*f.*) = ESPIRRADEIRA.
dag = DECAGRAMA(S).
dágua, d'água, contraction of DA ÁGUA or DE ÁGUA (of water).
daguerreótipo (*m.*) daguerreotype.
daí [DE+AÍ] there, hence, from this, from thence, from that, after.—**a dias**, days later.—**a pouco**, a little later; shortly thereafter.—**avante,—em diante,—por diante**, from then on; ever since; ever after; thereafter. —**para cá**, since then; from then on; thereafter. **e—**? So what? Well?
dal = DECALITRO(S).
dala (*f.*) dale; trough; chute; slide; spout; (*Naut.*) scupper.
dalém [DE+ALÉM] from beyond.
dalfinho (*m.*) = DOURADO-DO-MAR.
dali [DE+ALI] from there, from that place; from then.—**a pouco**, a little later.—**mesmo**, from right there.—**por diante**, from then on; thereafter.
dália (*f.*) dahlia (plant of flower).
Dalila (*f.*) Delilah.
dalina (*f., Chem.*) inulin [= INULINA].
dálmata (*adj.; m.,f.*) Dalmation.
dalmática (*f.*) dalmatic (a church vestment); a colobium.
daltônico –ca (*adj.*) color-blind.
daltonismo (*m.*) Daltonism (congenital red-green color-blindness).
dam = DECÂMETRO(S).
dama (*f.*) dame, matron; lady; gentleman's dancing partner; the queen (at cards or chess); a king (at checkers); (*pl.*) the game of checkers; a king (at checkers); (*pl.*) the game of checkers; (*Engin.*) cones of earth left standing as datum points.—**de honor** or **de honra**, lady in waiting; maid of honor.—-**da-noite** = BUQUÊ-DE-NOIVA. —-**do-lago**, pickerelweed (*Pontederia*), c.a. BARONESA. —-**entre-verdes**, love-in-a-mist (*Nigella damascena*). —-**nua**, autumn crocus (*Colchium autumnale*), c.a. CÓLQUICO, NARCISO-DO-OUTONO.
damaísmo (*m.*) ladies in a group; ladies collectively; lady's manners.
dâmar (*m.*) dammar (resin).

dâmara (*f.*, *Bot.*) the genus Agathis of dammarpines.
damaria (*f.*) coquettishness; ladies' meeting or party; ladies' matters.
damascenina (*f.*, *Chem.*) damascenine.
damasceno –na (*adj.*; *m.*,*f.*) Damascene.
damasco (*m.*) apricot (the fruit); damask (the fabric); Damascus blade; (*cap.*) Damascus.
damasqueiro (*m.*) apricot tree (*Prunus armeniaca*).
damasquilho, –quim (*m.*) damask fabric.
damasquinado –da (*adj.*) damask; damascened.
damasquinagem, –quinaria (*f.*) damascene work.
damasquinar (*v.t.*) to damascene.
damasquino –na (*adj.*) damascene; damask.
dambrê (*f.*) = CIPÓ-CRUZ-VERDADEIRO.
damejar (*v.t.*) to court the ladies.
damiana (*f.*, *Bot.*) the damiana turnera (*T. diffusa*).
damice (*f.*) prudishness; affectation.
danação (*f.*) damnation; fury, rage; rabies.
danado –da (*adj.*) damned, cursed; mad; rabid; angry, wild, "sore"; clever, smart; (*m.*) madman.—**da vida**, furious. **alma—**, mean, evil, person.
danaida, danaíde (*f.*, *Mach.*) danaide (water wheel); (*Zool.*) a subfamily (*Danainae*) which comprises the monarch butterflies.
danamento (*m.*) = DANAÇÃO.
danar (*v.t.*) to anger; to damage, injure, hurt; to render rabid; (*v.r.*) to become exasperated, furious; to become rabid.—**do juízo**, to go mad.
danburita (*f.*, *Min.*) damburite.
dança (*f.*) dance; ball.—**-de-são-vito** or **-de-são-guido**, St. Vitus' dance. **salão de—**, ballroom; dance hall.
dançadeira (*f.*) dancer; ballerina.
dançador (*m.*) dancer; also = TANGARÁ (a bird).
dançante (*adj.*) dancing, **chá—**, a tea dance.
dançar (*v.i.*) to dance.
dançarina (*f.*) **-no** (*m.*) professional (stage) dancer; ballet dancer; (*m.*) = TANGARÁ (a bird).
dançata (*f.*) informal dance; country dance.
dandi (*m.*) dandy.
dandinar (*v.i.*) to walk in an ungainly manner.
dandinoso –sa (*adj.*) dandyish.
dandismo (*m.*) dandyism.
danês –nesa (*adj.*; *m.*,*f.*) = DIANAMARQUÊS -QUESA.
Daniel (*m.*) Daniel.
danificação (*f.*) damnification, damage, injury.
danificador –dora (*adj.*) damaging; (*m.*,*f.*) damager.
danificar (*v.t.*) to damnify, damage, injure, hurt.
danífico –ca (*adj.*) injurious.
daninhar (*v.t.*) to damage; (*v.i.*) of children, to be destructive; (of animals), to cause damage.
daninho –nha (*adj.*) damaging, injurious, **animais—s**, vermin. **ervas—s**, noxious weeds. **criança—**, destructive child.
danio-gigante (*m.*) the giant danio (*D. malabaricus*) seen in home aquaria.
dano (*m.*) damage, injury, detriment, impairment, loss; (*pl.*) Danes. Cf. DINAMARQUÊS.
danoso –sa (*adj.*) damaging, injurious; detrimental.
dantes [DE+ANTES] before, formerly.
dantesco –ca [ê] (*adj.*) Dantesque.
danubi[a]no –na (*adj.*) Danubian.
daquele [ê] [DE+AQUÊLE] of that (one), from that (one).
daqui [DE+AQUI] from here; from now; henceforth.—**a pouco (tempo)**, in a little while; in a few minutes; soon.—**a três dias**, three days from now.—**a um ano**, a year hence.—**até lá**, between now and then; from here to there.—**em diante**, from now on; henceforth.—**ou dali**, from here or from there.
daquilo [DE+AQUILO] of that, from that.
dar [39] (*v.t.*) to give, bestow; to present, proffer; to deliver, yield; to cause to be or have; to donate; to grant; to afford a view of; (*v.i.*) to give (presents, alms, etc.); to yield; (*v.r.*) to occur, take place.—**a (alguém) na cabeça (para fazer algo)**, to take it into one's head (to do something).—**a alma ao diabo**, to sell one's soul to the devil.—**a conhecer**, to make known.—**à costa**, to run ashore; to be washed ashore.—**a entender**, to give to understand.—**à língua**, to wag one's tongue.—**à luz**, to give birth to.—**a mão à palmatória**, to own up that one is wrong; to admit one's mistake.—**a mão em casamento**, to give (her) hand in marriage.—**a palavra (de honra)**, to give one's word (of honor).—**a palavra a**, to call on someone to speak; to yield the floor to another.—**a preferência a**, to give preference to.—**a última demão**

(or **mão**) **a**, to give the last coat (of paint, etc.) to; to put on the finishing touches.—**a vida**, to give one's life.—**a vida a**, to give life to.—**a vida por**, to give anything for (something or someone).—**alta**, of a doctor, to discharge (a patient).—**andamento a**, to get something going; to get a matter started, or on its way (through channels).—**ares de**, to resemble (another person).—**as boas vindas a**, to extend welcome to.—**as caras**, (*colloq.*) to show up, put in an appearance.—**as cartas**, to deal the cards; fig., to control matters.—**as entranhas por**, to sacrifice everything for.—**as mãos**, to join hands.—**atenção a**, to pay attention to.—**aula**, to teach; to tutor; to lecture (at a university).—**baixa**, to be mustered out (of military service).—**baixa ao hospital**, to be transferred from active duty to a hospital (for treatment).—**balanço**, to take a balance; to audit accounts.—**bola** (*slang*) to encourage amorous advances; to pay attention; to bribe, suborn.—**bôlo**, to correct (someone). Cf. DAR O BÔLO.—**busca a**, to make a search of or for.—**cabo de**, to put an end to; to do away with; to destroy, ruin; to finish up a job.—**caça a**, to give chase to; to hunt.—**(uma) carona**, (*slang*) to give (someone) a lift (free ride).—**certo**, to fit; to come out right; to end well (happily); of a trick, joke, experiment, etc., to succeed.—**com**, to come upon (meet); to encounter, run into (someone).—**com a cabeça na parede**, (*colloq.*) to strike one's head against the wall (lit. & fig.).—**com a janela na cara a**, to slam shut a window (with intentional rudeness) while someone is looking at it from the outside.—**com a língua nos dentes**, (*colloq.*) to let the cat out of the bag; to blab; to spill the beans.—**com a porta na cara de**, to slam the door (lit. & fig.) in someone's face.—**com o nariz na porta**, to find a door closed (to one); to go visiting and find no one at home.—**com o nariz no chão**, to fall on one's nose.—**com os burros n'água**, (*colloq.*) to founder (fail); to be ruined; to "goof" completely.—**com os olhos em**, to catch sight of.—**combate**, to give combat, fight.—**comida a**, to feed.—**confiança a**, to pay attention to (someone); to get personal with (someone); to encourage a flirtation, or any undue attentiveness from an actual or potential bore, borrower, etc.—**conta de**, to give an accounting of; to finish off, destroy.—**conta de si**, to give an accounting of oneself.—**conta do recado**, (*colloq.*) to do the job; deliver the goods; bring home the bacon.—**corda**, to wind (a watch, toy, etc.); to wind someone up (start him talking); to encourage amorous advances; to give (an animal) more rope; to let a fish run with the line; to blabber, chatter, gossip.—**corda ao relógio**, to wind (up) a timepiece.—**crédito a**, to believe in, credit. [But not to give someone credit *for*, which is RECONHECER O MÉRITO OU A BOA QUALIDADE DE ALGUÉM; nor to give credit *to* someone, which is CONCEDER A ALGUÉM UM CRÉDITO.]—**cria**, of domestic animals, to give birth to young.—**cumprimento a**, to comply with.—**de beber**, to give a drink of water to.—**de cara com**, (*colloq.*) to bump into someone.—**de comer**, to feed.—**de face com**, to meet with, bump into, someone.—**de graça**, to give away (gratis).—**de mamar**, to give suckle to.—**de ombros**, to shrug; to show indifference.—**de presente**, to bestow as a gift.—**de quebra**, to give (something) to boot.—**de si**, to give of oneself; to give way, start to fall; to sag.—**dois dedos de prosa com**, to have a brief chat with.—**em**, to hit, strike, beat.—**em droga**, to come to a bad end; come to nothing.—**em nada**, to come to nothing.—**em cima de**, to cajole, inveigle (someone into doing something); (*slang*) to make amorous advances.—**ensejo a**, to give opportunity to; to let, allow.—**entrada (saída) a**, to enter in a book, keep a record of, incoming (outgoing) items (of money, goods, documents, etc.).—**espetáculo**, to make a spectacle of oneself; to show off; to make a scene.—**escândalo**, to make a scandal; to cause repercussions; to behave publicly in a loud and vulgar manner.—**esperanças**, to give hope to; to give promise of.—**expansão a**, to give vent to (feelings, emotions) = EXPANDIR-SE.—**fé a**, to have faith in; to believe in.—**fé de**, to certify to (as a notary).—**fim a**, to put an end to; to dispose of, throw away.—**gôsto**, to be pleasing. [Dá gôsto vê-la tão sadia, It's wonderful to see you looking so well.]—**gôsto a**, to give pleasure to.—**horas**, to strike the hour.—**idéia de**, to give an idea of.—**importância a**, to attach importance to; to pay attention to.—**início a**, to begin something; to open (a meeting).—**jeito (de)**, to be possible, feasible. Cf. DAR UM JEITO.—**liberdade a**, to free; to give permission to.—**largas (or**

sôltas) **a,** to give free rein to; to give free expression to.
—**lição,** of a teacher, to hear a student's lesson; of a student, to recite his lesson. [dar lições, to give (private) lessons.]—**lugar,** to make way.—**lugar a,** to give place to; to give rise to (suspicions, etc.).—**mostras de,** to look as if (something is going to happen).—**motivo a,** to give rise to; to "ask for it".—(or **matar**) **na cabeça,** (*colloq.*) to hit the nail on the head (in an argument); to clinch an argument; to get the better of someone (in an argument).—**na trilha,** to hit upon another's intentions.—**na veneta a,** to be struck with (an idea); to have a whim, an impulse.—**no alvo,** to hit the mark (target, bull's-eye).—**na cabeça a,** to put the kibosh on.—**no couro,** (*slang*) to show skill and aptitude for something.—**no prêto para acertar no branco,** to proceed by indirection.—**no miolo,** to take it into one's head, be struck with an idea.—**no vivo,** to touch to the quick.—**nome a,** to give a name to; to bring renown to.—**nota,** to grade (school papers).—**o** (or **um**) **bôlo,** (*slang*) to stand (someone) up, not show up for an appointment. Cf. DAR BÔLO.—**o braço,** to offer one's arm.—**o braço a torcer,** to admit one's mistake or ignorance; to agree that one is wrong.—**o cavaco,** (*slang*) to hit the ceiling.—**o cavaco por,** (*slang*) to give anything for (something).—**o contra,** (*colloq.*) to be "agin," oppose (an idea, plan, etc.); to jilt (a suitor).—**o (devido) desconto,** to make allowances.—**o desespêro** (or **o estrilo**), (*slang*) to blow one's top, hit the ceiling.—**o dito por não dito,** to unsay (retract) something said.—**o exemplo,** to set the example.—**o fora,** (*slang*) to walk out on (one's job, sweetheart, etc.); to sneak out or away from (a party, an unpleasant scene, etc.).—**o fora a** (or **em**) (*slang*) to give (someone) the bounce.—**o prego,** (*colloq.*) to give out, poop out, be done in (in an athletic game or contest); fig., to give up before the end of a task, of a party, etc.—**o sim,** of a girl to a suitor, to say yes.—**o trôco,** to return change due for an amount; (*slang*) to give tit for tat; to pay back in the same coin.—**o último suspiro,** to draw one's last breath.—**origem a,** to give rise to.—**ouvidos a,** to give heed to.—**palmada,** to slap (someone); to spank (a child).—**palmas** (or **palminhas**) **a,** to clap hands, applaud.—**pancada** (**sova, surra, tunda**) **em,** to beat someone up.—**para,** to have or develop an aptitude, aptness, proneness for. [Examples: **dar para a pintura,** to have a talent for painting; **dar para os estudos,** to be studious by nature; **dar para ladrão,** to be a natural-born thief, (or, in past tense, he's been stealing lately); **dar para beber,** to take to drink; **dar para os negócios,** to have a flair for business.].—**para fora,** to look out on, afford a view of.—**para o gasto,** of goods or money, or, fig., intelligence, charm, etc., to be enough to get by on.—**para rir,** to give cause for laughter.—**para trás** (**num negócio, numa proposta, num acôrdo, etc.**), to set oneself against, obstruct, object strongly to (a business matter, a proposal, an agreement, etc.); of a job, undertaking, struggle, etc., to lose momentum; to slide backwards; to have setbacks.—**parabens,** to offer congratulations.—**parte de,** to inform, report; to impart, disclose.—**parte de fraco,** to reveal one's weakness or inability; to seem weak.—**passos por,** to take steps to (accomplish something).—**patada** (*slang*) to make an ass of oneself. Cf. DAR UMA PATADA.—**pela coisa,** to catch on to something.—**pela presença de alguém,** to be aware of another's presence.—**pontos,** to take stitches, sew.—**por bem empregado,** to be pleased with the results of money employed, time and effort spent, etc.—**por certo,** to take for granted.—**por concluido** (**acabado, terminado, encerrado**) **um negócio, um assunto,** to consider a matter closed, finished.—**por elas,** or **por isso,** to become aware of, catch on.—**por falta de,** to miss, become aware that something (or someone) is missing.—**por quites,** to call quits (release from further obligation). Cf. ESTAR QUITES COM.—**por si,** to come to one's senses.—(**um**) **pontapé em,** to kick; fig., to spurn.—**providências,** to take steps, measures.—**provimento a,** (Law) to admit, receive.—**pulos de contente,** to leap for joy.—**que falar,** to give rise to (scandalous) talk, gossip.—**que fazer,** to make trouble.—**queixa de** (**alguém**), to make a complaint against (someone).—**razão a,** to agree with; to support (defend) another's words and actions.—**razão de,** to give an accounting of.—**razão de si,** to give news of oneself; to justify one's behavior; to come alive.—**realce a,** to enhance (something).—**recados,** to deliver (convey) messages.—**rédeas,** to loosen the reins; fig., to remove all restraint.—**saída a,** to start something off, fire the open-

ing gun; to expedite (a slow case in court); to move (slow-moving merchandise); in bookkeeping, to record outgoing items of money, goods, etc.—**satisfações,** to explain oneself; to advise (one's superiors, spouse, etc.) of one's intentions; to apologize. Cf. DAR UMA SATISFAÇÃO.—**-se a conhecer,** to make oneself known.—**-se ares,** to put on airs.—**-se bem** (or **mal**) **em algum lugar,** to be well and happy (or the opposite) in a given place.—**-se bem** (or **mal**) **com alguém,** to get along (or not), be on good (or bad) terms with someone.—**-se conta de,** to be aware of.—**-se o luxo de,** to permit oneself a luxury.—**-se o trabalho,** to take the trouble.—**-se por batido** (**vencido**), to admit defeat, give in.—**-se por entendido,** to show that one understands or perceives a hidden meaning.—**-se por feliz,** to thank one's lucky stars.—**-se por satisfeito,** to acknowledge one's satisfaction.—**-se por sentido,** to show hurt feelings.—**-se por suspeito,** to disqualify oneself (as a judge or arbiter).—**sinal de,** to give the signal to begin; to give signs of, manifest.—**sinal de vida,** to show signs of life; to write, telephone, visit, or otherwise show that one is alive and interested.—**tempo ao tempo,** to bide one's time.—**tento de si,** to come to one's senses.—**testemunho de,** to give witness to.—**tratos à bola,** to rack (cudgel) one's brains.—**tréguas,** to declare a truce; fig., to afford a breathing spell.—**trela,** (*slang*) to give someone the green light; to encourage a flirtation or conversation.—**um ar de sua graça,** to drop in, put in an appearance, pay a visit; to grace an occasion with one's presence; also, ironically, to commit a faux pas.—**um ataque,** to suffer an attack, throw a fit.—**um baile em,** to give someone a bawling out; to boo, laugh at, ridicule.—**um espirro,** to sneeze.—**um jeito,** to fix something up, do something about it; to manage, arrange, find a way; also, to sprain (an ankle), wrench (one's back), etc. Cf. DAR JEITO.—**um passeio,** to go for a stroll; to go for a ride; to spend a time in outdoor leisure.—**um passo,** to take a step.—**um quinau em,** (*slang*) to give someone a tongue lashing; to get a better grade than one's schoolmate.—**um trote em,** to haze (a new student); to play a practical joke on someone.—**um grande pulo,** to take a big jump (in one's job); to move to a far place.—**um mau passo,** to take a bad step.—**um nó,** to tie, make a knot.—**um trambolhão,** to take a tumble.—**uma batida** (**em**), to beat about (try to find); of the police, to search (a neighborhood, etc.).—**uma descarga,** to fire a volley.—**uma facada em,** (*slang*) to touch (someone) for a loan.—**uma folga,** to slacken; to give one a break, a breathing spell.—**uma gafe,** or **uma rata,** to make a faux pas, commit a social error.—**uma lavagem,** to give (someone) an enema; to use a stomach pump on (someone); (*colloq.*) to whitewash (an opposing team).—**uma pancada em,** to hit, strike. [Dei uma pancada no braço I've bruised (hurt) my arm on something.].—**uma patada,** to do anything rude or coarse; to make a blunder, "pull a boner".—**uma prosa,** or **prosinha,** to hold a friendly chat.—**uma queda,** to take a tumble.—**uma surprêsa,** to spring a surprise.—**uma topada,** to stub one's toe (lit. & fig.).—**uma volta,** to go for a short walk, take a turn around the block. [When followed by **grande** or **enorme**=to detour, to stray.]—**uma satisfação,** to apologize; to offer an explanation (of one's irregular behavior); to make amends. Cf. DAR SATISFAÇOES.—**uma vista de olhos,** to glance at.—**vazão a,** to afford a way out; to give vent to; to decide matters; to keep (goods) flowing.—**volta,** to coil (a rope).—**volta à chave,** to turn a key in the lock.—**voltas,** to go 'round and 'round; to beat around the bush.—**voltas na cama,** to twist and turn in bed. **A cavalo dado não se olham os dentes,** One does not look a gift horse in the mouth. **A janela dá para o jardim,** The window looks out on, the garden. **Água mole em pedra dura, tanto dá até que, fura,** Constant dripping bores the stone. **ao Deus dará** aimlessly, unconcernedly. **Dá cá um beijinho,** Give me a little kiss. **Dá licença?** May I? **Dá muita gripe aqui,** There's lots of flu around here. **Dá para dois dias,** It is enough for two days. **Dá vontade de rir,** It makes one want to laugh. **Dá-se um jeito,** We'll fix it somehow; We'll find a way out. **dado que,** provided that. **de braços dados,** arm-in-arm. **de mãos dadas,** hand-in-hand. **Êste caminho dá no rio,** This road ends at the river. **Isso não dá,** It doesn't fit; It is too small; It is not sufficient. **Isso não vai—em nada,** Nothing will come of it. **Não dá para nada,** He (she, it) is good for nothing. **não—bola** (or **pelota**), to take no heed, pay no attention; to be happy-go-lucky. **não**—**por isso**, to pay little attention to. **não** —**uma palavra**, to say nothing, speak not a word. **não se**—**por achado**, to play dumb, not let on, pretend not to understand; to not turn a hair. **não se**—**o luxo de fazer algo**, to not be bothered to do something, or not be painstaking enough to; or, not to be so proud as to. **Não se deram**, They didn't hit it off (together). **O caso dá para pensar**, The matter calls for thought. **Para mim dá na mesma**, It's all the same to me. **Pouco se me dá**, I don't care; it's all one to me. **quando se der a ocasião**, when the opportunity presents itself. **Quem me dera!** I wish it were true! **quem me dera que**, would that I might; I wish I could; oh, if only. . . . **Tanto faz**—**na cabeça como na cabeça**—, It's six of one and half-a-dozen of the other. **Veremos em que vai**—**isso**, We shall see how things turn out.

dardar (*v.t.*) to pierce or transfix with a dart.
dardejante (*adj.*) darting.
dardejar (*v.t.*) to dart (angry glances) at; to shoot out (rays of heat or light); to throw darts at; to pierce with a dart or darts; (*v.i.*) to hurl, let fly (as a dart).
dardo (*m.*) dart, javelin, spear; shaft; insect's stinger; snake's tongue; (fig.) sarcastic or caustic remark.
dares e tomares (*m.pl.*) give-and-take disputes.
daroês (*m.*) dervish.
darto (*m., Anat.*) dartos; also = DARTRO.
dartrial (*m., Bot.*) ringworm senna (*Cassia alata*), c.a. MANJERIOBA-GRANDE, MARIA-PRETA, MATA-PASTO.
dartro (*m.*) tetter, eczema, herpes.
dartroso –**sa** (*adj.*) having tetter; tetterous.
darwiniano –**na** (*adj.*) Darwinian.
darwinismo (*m.*) Darwinism.
darwinista (*m.,f.*) Darwinist.
dasímetro (*m., Physics*) dasymeter.
dásipo (*m.*) a genus (*Dasypus*) of armadillos.
dasiúro (*m., Zool.*) a dasyure.
DASP = DEPARTAMENTO ADMINISTRATIVO DO SERVIÇO PÚBLICO (Public Service Administrative Dept.).
dast = DECASTÉREO(S).
data (*f.*) date; (*colloq.*) act of giving or the thing given; lot (parcel of land). **em**—**próxima**, at an early date; in the near future. **uma**—**de**, a lot of.
datador (*m.*) dater; date stamp.
datal (*adj.*) date.
dataria (*f., R.C.Ch.*) datary, dataria.
datil (*m.*) = TÂMARA.
datileira (*f.*) date palm (*Phoenix*).
dativo –**va** (*adj.*; *m., Gram.*) dative.
datolita (*f., Min.*) datolite.
datura (*f., Bot.*) the genus Datura.—**estramônio**, the jimsonweed or thorn apple (*Datura stramonium*).
davália (*f., Bot.*) the genus Davallia of ferns.
Davi, David (*m.*) David.
dávida (*f.*) = DÁDIVA.
davídico –**ca** (*adj.*) Davidic.
d.C. or **D.C.** = DEPOIS DE CRISTO (after Christ).
d/d = DIAS DE DATA (days from date).
DD. = DIGNÍSSIMO (Most Worthy).
de (*prep.*) of, from, for, by, than, with, in ,at, on, as.— **abalada**, headlong.—**acôrdo com**, in accordance with, in keeping with.—**afogadilho**, precipitately.—**agora em diante**, from here (now) on.—**alto a baixo**, from top to bottom.—**antemão**, previously, beforehand.—**arrancada**, suddenly, with a jerk.—**arrebate**, suddenly, unexpectedly.—**assentada**, at one sitting.—**atalaia**, on the lookout, on the alert.—**avessas**, at outs with.—**baque**, suddenly.—**barra a barra**, from one extreme to the other. —**boa fé**, in good faith.—**boa vontade**, with good grace; quite willingly.—**bôca**, orally, verbally.—**bôca aberta**, open-mouthed.—**bochecha**, for free, gratis.—**bom grado**, willingly, gladly.—**bom som**, in a clear voice.—**bôrco**, or —**bruços**, face down, flat on the ground.—**braços dados**, arm in arm.—**bubuia**, floating (down the river).—**cabelos louros**, fair-haired.—**cabo a cabo**, from beginning to end. —**cabo a rabo**, from stem to stern.—**cama**, sick abed. —**cambulhada**, helter-skelter.—**cambulhada com**, together with, mixed up with.—**cara a cara**, face to face. —**carona**, for free, for nothing.—**carregação**, shoddy, mass-produced.—**caso pensado**, purposely.—**certo**, certainly; probably.—**chapa**, squarely.—**chofre**, suddenly; abruptly.—**cima**, from above.—**comum acôrdo**, by mutual agreement; by common consent.—**conseguinte**, consequently.—**contínuo**, continually, constantly.—**cor**, by heart.—**de cor e salteado**, [to know something] for-

wards and backwards, perfectly memorized.—**corrida**, hurriedly, running.—**cutelo**, on edge, edgewise.—**dentro**, from inside, from within.—**dez em dez dias**, every ten days.—**dia**, by day; during the day.—**dia em dia**, day by day, from day to day.—**empreitada**, by the job (as opposed to pay by the hour).—**empréstimo**, by loan; on loan.—**encontro a**, counter to [often used wrongly to mean the opposite].—**enfiada**, one after another.— **esguelha**, obliquely.—**espaço em espaço**, here and there. —**face**, facing.—**fato**, really, in fact; actually; of course! —**feição que**, so that.—**fio a pavio**, from end to end; from cover to cover.—**fogo e sangue**, with sword and flame. —**foguete**, in a flash.—**fonte limpa**, from an official or reliable source.—**fora**, on the outside; from the outside; from abroad.—**fora de**, outside of.—**força**, by force.— **frente**, face to face; fearlessly; head-on.—**frente para**, facing (towards).—**fronte a fronte**, face to face.—**fugida**, in passing; briefly, hurriedly.—**futuro**, in the future.— **gatas**, or—**gatinhas**, crawling, on all fours.—**golpe**, suddenly.—**gôsto**, or **por gôsto**, because of liking to; for fun; as a hobby.—**graça**, gratis, for nothing.—**grau a** (or **em**) **grau**, by degrees.—**hoje em diante**, from today on, henceforth.—**hoje para amanhã**, from one minute to the next.—**homem para homem**, man to man.—**hora em hora**, minute by minute; (getting worse, etc.) by the hour.—**improviso**, suddenly; extemporaneously; impromptu; ad lib.—**jato**, straightway; (*Foundry*) en bloc (casting).—**joelhos**, kneeling.—**lado**, sideways; askew; crooked.—**lado a lado**, from one side to the other; all over.—**leve**, lightly.—**longe**, from afar; (to win, etc.) by far.—**longe a** (or **em**) **longe**, from time to time.—**luto**, in mourning.—**má fé**, in bad faith; insincerely.—**madrugada**, at dawn.—**mais a mais**, moreover.—**mal a pior**, from bad to worse.—**maneira que**, so that.—**manhã**, in the morning.—**manhã cedo**, early in the morning.— **mansinho**, quietly, softly.—**mão em mão**, from hand to hand.—**mão beijada**, gratuitously; as a gift.—**mão cheia**, excellently; also, as an adjective, excellent.—**mão na ilharga**, haughtily (with the hand on the hip); indolently. —**mãos dadas**, hand in hand, together.—**mar a mar**, from one end to the other.—**mau grado**, grudgingly.— **meio a meio**, from end to end.—**memória**, by heart; from memory.—**menos**, less. [**Isso é o de menos**, That isn't the worst; That's not all.].—**modo que**, so that, so. —**molde a**, in order to.—**momento**, offhand.—**momento a momento**, every minute.—**morte**, mortally. [**É de morte**, (*slang*), He (she, it) is unbearable.]—**moto próprio**, spontaneously.—**muito**, for a long time.— **nascimento**, by nature; from birth.—**noite**, at night; by night; in the evening.—**nome**, nominally. [**Conheço-o de nome**, I know him by name.].—**norte a sul**, from north to south; from one extreme to the other.—**novo**, anew; again.—**ôlho (em alguém, alguma coisa)**, (to have) one's eye on (someone, something). [**ficar de ôlho em**, to keep an eye on.].—**onde em onde**, now and then.—**ora avante**, or—**ora em diante**, henceforth, from now on.— **ordinário**, ordinarily.—**orelha em pé**; distrustfully; also, suddenly interested.—**ouvida** or **ouvido**, by hearsay. [**Tocar de ouvido**, to play by ear.].—**pagode**, (*colloq.*) in great quantity.—**pancada**, in one swoop.—**papo**, coldly, calmly.—**par em par**, wide open (doors, windows)—**parceria com**, in partnership with.—**parte**, aside; privately. —**parte a parte**, from one to the other, reciprocally.— **passagem**, in passing, incidentally.—**pé**, on foot; standing; up and about (convalescent); in force (an agreement, appointment, etc.).—**peito aberto**, outspokenly.—**peito a peito**, breast to breast.—**per si**, each in turn.—**perfil**, in profile; sideways.—**permeio**, intermixed.—**perto**, closely.—**pêso**, heavily, suddenly; also, as adjective, one of the best; good of its (his) kind.—**pólo a pólo**, from pole to pole.—**ponta a cordel**, (*Carp.*) diagonally.—**ponta a ponta**, from end to end.—**ponta cabeça**, head first.—**pôpa a proa**, from stem to stern; entirely; totally.—**porta em porta**, from door to door.— **portas a** (or **para**) **dentro**, indoors.—**potência a potência**, between equals.—**presente**, at present.—**prevenção**, forehandedly. [**Estar de prevenção com**, to be suspicious of (someone). **pôr de prevenção contra**, to warn against.] —**previsto**, previously.—**primeiro**, firstly; formerly.— **propósito**, purposely.—**quando em quando**, from time to time.—**quarentena**, in quarantine; under observation. —**raiz**, at the root.—**raspão**, lightly.—**rastos**, dragging, crawling.—**recuo**, backwards.—**regra**, as a rule. [**É de regra**, It's the custom.]—**relâmpago**, in a flash.—

relance, or **relanço,** in a glance; sideways. [**olhar de relance,** to look askance].—**repente,** suddenly.— **reserva,** in reserve.—**resguardo,** in reserve; at home (or taking it easy as a convalescent), on doctor's orders.—**ressaca,** [suffering] from a hangover.—**resto,** as to the rest; as a matter of fact.—**revés,** or **revesio,** obliquely.—**ricochete,** ricocheting; indirectly.—**rijo,** strongly; loudly.—**rojo,** crawling (on one's stomach).—**roldão** (or **rondão),** precipitately; helter-skelter.—**rompida,** quickly.—**rosto,** facing. [**Ela é bonita de rosto,** She has a pretty face.].—**rosto a rosto,** face to face.—**rosto descoberto,** with uncovered face; openly.—**rota batida,** quickly.—**salto,** in one jump.—**salto a salto,** by jumps.—**siso,** sensibly. [**dente de siso,** wisdom tooth.]—**sobejo,** perfectly well.—**sobra,** in excess, overmuch.—**sobresselente,** in reserve.—**sobremão,** carefully; plentifully.—**sobressalto,** by surprise.—**socapa,** furtively.—**sol a** (or **em) sol,** from sunrise to sunset.—**sopetão,** suddenly; unexpectedly.—**sorte que,** so that.—**telhas abaixo,** indoors.—**tempo(s) em tempo(s),** from time to time.—**todo,** wholly, entirely, altogether; absolutely.—**todo em todo,** completely.—**tombo em tombo,** tumbling.—**trainel,** sloping downward.—**través,** crosswise, athwart.—**tropel,** helter-skelter.—**um a outro pólo,** from one end to the other.—**um e outro lado,** from both sides; from one end to the other.—**um fôlego,** in one breath; without stopping.—**um ímpeto,** in one stroke.—**um jato,** in a single flash.—**um para outro lado,** from one side to the other.—**um pulo,** in one jump, quickly.—**uma assentada,** at one sitting.—**uma,** or **de certa, feita,** at one time.—**uma tirada,** at one time, without letup.—**uma vez para sempre,** once for all.—**vagar,** slowly.—**velha data,** of old.—**vento em pôpa,** prosperously; smoothly; swimmingly. [**A construção vai de vento em pôpa,** the job is progressing splendidly, hasn't hit a snag yet.]—**vez,** once for all; in good season.—**vez em quando,** once in a while.—**vez em vez,** from time to time.—**vez que,** considering (that).—**viés,** obliquely, on the bias.—**voga arrancada,** straining at the oars.—**volta,** back (returned).—**volta com,** intermixed with. **andar—bicicleta,** to ride a bicycle. **andar—gatinhas,** to go on all fours. **antes—,** before. **cavalo—raça,** a thoroughbred horse [but not race horse, which is CAVALO DE CORRIDA]. **doce—côco,** coconut candy; also a term of endearment, as: **Você é um doce de côco,** You're just as sweet as can be. **é—supor,** presumably; it is supposed that. **estar—férias,** to be on vacation. **forrar—papel,** to line with paper. **Há—tudo neste mundo,** There's a lot of strange things in this world; Anything can happen; It takes all kinds. **mais—,** more than. **sair—casa,** to go out of doors, leave the house. **vestir-se—prêto,** to dress in black.
deado (m.) deanery.
dealbar, dealvar (v.t.) to whiten; to light, brighten.
deambulação (f.) digression; promenade.
deambular (v.i.) to stroll.
deambulismo (m.) an habitual moving about from place to place, as by one constantly on the go.
deambulatório -ria (adj.) deambulatory, wandering.
deão [deãos, deães, deões] (m.) dean.
dearticular (v.t.) to articulate, enunciate.
deativação (f.) deactivation.
deativar (v.t.) to deactivate.
debacle (f.) debacle (military, financial).
debaixo (adv.) under; beneath something; in a lower place; in a lower degree, amount, etc.; in a subordinate position or condition.—**de,** (prep.) under; beneath and covered by; below the surface of; subject to.—**da telha,** (colloq.) indoors.—**da terra,** beneath the ground; in the grave.—**de armas,** under arms.—**de chave,** under lock and key.—**de forma,** in military formation.—**do braço,** under the arm.—**das mesmas telhas** or **do mesmo teto,** under the same roof.—**do pêso de,** under the weight of.
debalde (adv.) vainly, futilely.
debandada (f.) rout, stampede, disorderly flight.
debandar (v.t.) to disband, disperse; to rout, put to flight; (v.i.) to disband, disperse.
debate (m.) debate, discussion; argument.
debater (v.t.) to debate, discuss; to argue; (v.r.) to struggle (**com,** with; **contra,** against; **sob,** under); to beat against, thrash about.
debelação (f.) conquering, overwhelming.
debelador -dora (adj.) conquering, overpowering.
debelar (v.t.) to conquer, defeat, overthrow; to overcome

(as, an illness).
debelatório -ria (adj.) conquering.
debênture (f.) debenture bond.
debenturista (m.,f.) debenture bondholder.
debicador -dora (adj.) picking, pecking; nibbling; teasing, annoying.
debicar (v.i.) to pick, peck (**em,** at), esp. with the beak; to nibble (at food); to pick at or on (another person); (v.t.) to nibble.
débil [-beis] (adj.) weak, feeble; anemic; frail; flimsy; **um—mental,** a feebleminded person.
debilidade (f.) debility, weakness, feebleness.
debilitação (f.) debilitation.
debilitante (adj.) debilitating.
debilitar (v.t.) to debilitate, weaken, enfeeble; to sap; (v.r.) to lose strength, grow weak, grow feeble.
debique (m.) act of picking (on, at); a nibble; teasing, ridicule, mockery; banter.
debitar (v.t.) to debit; (v.r.) to become indebted.
débito (m.) debit; debt.
deblaterar (v.t.,v.i.) to rail (against); to vociferate; (v.r.) to struggle (physically).
debochado -da (adj.) debauched, dissolute; (m.) debauchee, rake, libertine.
debochador -dora (adj.) ridiculing, scoffing.
debochar (v.t.) to debauch, deprave; to taunt, deride; (v.r.) to become depraved.
debochativo -va (adj.) scoffing; depraved.
deboche (m.) debauchery; taunt, jeer, sneer.
Débora (f.) Deborah.
debrear (v.t., Autom.) to shift gears to neutral [= DESEMBREAR].
debruadeira (f.) hemming machine.
debruado -da (adj.) hemmed, edged.
debruar (v.t.) to hem, bind (edges).
debruçar (v.t.) to cause to bend over or lie down; (v.r.) to stoop, lean over (down, forward); to lean on the elbows.—**se para fora,** to lean far out.—**se na janela,** to lean out the window.
debrum (m.) hem, border, selvage; welt; binding (around the edge of a garment).
debulha (f.) threshing (of grain).
debulhador (m.) thresher, husker; shelling machine (for corn).
debulhadora (f.) grain-threshing machine.
debulhar (v.t.) to thresh (grain); to shell (corn); to husk, shuck (corn).—**se em pranto** or **em lágrimas,** to dissolve into tears; to cry one's eyes out.
debutante (f.) debutante.
debutar (v.i.) to make one's debut [= ESTREAR].
debute (m.) debut.
debuxar (v.t.) to sketch, draft, draw, outline.
debuxo (m.) rough draft, sketch; shape, outline.
dec. = DECRETO (decree).
década (f.) decade; set of ten.
decadência (f.) decadence, decadency, decline, fall, degeneracy.
decadente (adj.) decadent.
decaedro (m.) decahedron.
decafido -da (adj., Bot.) decemfid.
decagonal (adj.) decagonal.
decágono (m., Geom.) decagon.
decagrama (m.) decagram; 10 grams.
decaído -da (adj.) fallen; decayed; decrepit; (f.) a falling away; a fallen woman; (colloq.) hillside, slope.
decaidro-naftaleno [a-i] (m., Chem.) decahydro naphthalene, dekalin.
decaimento [a-i] (m.) a declining or falling; decadence; decaying.
decair [75] (v.i.) to fall (**de,** from); to sag; to decline; to pine, waste away; to droop; to decay; to lose caste.
decalagem (f., Aeron.) stagger.
decalcar (v.t.) to transfer (a picture, design, etc.,) by decalcomania; by ext. to copy slavishly.
decalco (m.) = DECALQUE.
decalcomania (f.) decalcomania.
decalescência (f., Metal.) decalescence.
decalina (f., Chem.) dekalen.
decalitro (m.) decaliter; 10 liters.
decalobado -da (adj., Bot.) decalobate.
decálogo (m.) the Decalogue, Ten Commandments.
decalque (m.) transference (of pictures, designs, etc.) by decalcomania; the pictures and designs so transferred; fig. a slavish copy; plagiarism.

decalvante (adj., Med.) decalvant.
decâmetro (m.) decameter; 10 meters.
decampar (v.i.) to decamp; to break camp.
decano [cã] (m.) dean; (Chem.) decane.
decantação (f.) decantation.
decantado –da (adj.) celebrated.
decantar (v.t.) to sing the praises of; to decant.
decapagem (f., Metal.) pickling.
decapar (v.t., Metal.) to pickle.
decapitação (f.) decapitation.
decapitar (v.t.) to decapitate.
decápode (adj.; m.) decapod; (m.pl., Zool.) the Decapoda.
decassílabo –ba (adj.) decasyllabic; (m.) decasyllable.
decastere, –stéreo (m.) decastere; 10 cu. mt.
decastilo (m., Arch.) decastyle.
decatlo (m., Athletics) decathlon.
decenal (adj.) decennial. plano—, ten-year plan.
decenário –ria (adj.) decennial; (m.) decennary.
decência (f.) decency; cleanliness, neatness; propriety, decorum.
decênio (m.) decennium; period of ten years.
decenlocular (adj., Bot.) decemlocular.
decente (adj.) decent, proper; becoming, suitable; cleanly.
decepamento (m.) act of cutting off, severing, mutilating.
decepar (v.t.) to cut (chop) off (as the head); to sever, amputate, mutilate; to interrupt, cut short.
decepção (f.) disappointment, disenchantment, let-down. [But not deception, which is ENGANO, LÔGRO, FRAUDE.]
decepcionante (adj.) disappointing.
decepcionar (v.t.) to disappoint.
decerto (adv.) surely.
decibel (m., Physics) decibel.
decidido –da (adj.) decided, determined, resolute, stanch, tenacious, unyielding; stalwart; forthright.
decidir (v.t.) to decide: to determine; to convince, persuade.—se (a), to make up one's mind (to).—de, to decide concerning (about); to determine.
decídua (f., Anat.) decidua.
decidual (adj., Anat.) decidual.
decíduo –da (adj.) deciduous.
decifração (f.) deciphering.
decifrador (m.), –dora (f.) decipherer.
decifrar (v.t.) to decipher.
decifrável (adj.) decipherable.
decigrama (f.) decigram, 1/10th gram.
decil (m., Stat.) decile.
decileno (m., Chem.) decylene.
decilitro (m.) deciliter, 1/10th liter.
décima (f.) a tenth part; a tithe.
decimal (adj.; f.) decimal (fraction).
decimar (v.) = DIZIMAR.
decímetro (m.) decimeter, 1/10th mt.
décimo –ma (adj.) tenth; (m.) a tenth part.—-primeiro or undécimo, eleventh.—-segundo or duodécimo, twelfth.—-terceiro, thirteenth.—-quarto, fourteenth.—-quinto, fifteenth.—-sexto, sixteenth.—-sétimo, seventeenth.—-oitavo, eighteenth.—-nono, nineteenth. em—lugar, in tenth place.
decisão (f.) decision, conclusion, determination; decree, sentence; resolution, firmness.
decisivo –va (adj.) decisive, conclusive, final.
decisório –ria (adj.) deciding.
decistere, decistéreo (m.) decistere = 1/10th cu. mt.
declamação (f.) declamation; recitation.
declamador –dora (m.,f.) declaimer.
declamante (adj.) declaiming; (m.,f.) declaimer.
declamar (v.i.) to declaim, harangue, rant; (v.t.) to recite.
declamatório –ria (adj.) declamatory.
declaração (f.) declaration, affirmation; statement, announcement; proclamation.—de amor, an avowal of love; a proposal.—de direitos, bill of rights.—jurada, sworn statement, affidavit.
declarado –da (adj.) declared; manifest, obvious.
declarador –dora, declarante (adj.) declaring; (m.,f.) declarer, declarant.
declarar (v.t.) to declare, affirm, assert, state, proclaim, announce, utter; (v.r.) to declare oneself.—sem rodeios, to speak out.—culpado, to declare guilty.
declarativo –va (adj.) declarative.
declaratório –ria (adj.) declaratory.
declinação (f.) declination, inclination, bending, sloping or moving downward; a swerving or deviating, as from a standard; (Astron.) declination; magnetic declension; (Gram.) declension, inflection.

declinador (m.) declinometer.
declinante (adj.) declining, sinking.
declinar (v.i.) to decline, sink; to sag; to decay; to wane; to incline; (v.t.) to decline, refuse; to shun; to mention (names); (Gram.) to inflect.—a, to sink to.—de, to turn away from; to refuse, decline to accept.—o (seu) nome, to give one's name.—para, to turn to; to incline to.—nomes, to name names. sem—nomes, without mentioning names.
declinatório –ria (adj.) declinatory; (f., Law) a declinatory plea; (Physics) a declination compass.
declinável (adj.) declinable.
declínio (m.) decline, deterioration, decadence.
declinômetro (m., Magnetism) declinometer.
declivar (v.i.,v.t.) to incline.
declive (m.) declivity, downgrade, incline, tilt, pitch; (adj.) declivous, sloping.
declividade (f.) declivity, down slope.
declivoso –sa (adj.) declivous, sloping downward.
decoada (f.) lye.
decocção (f.) decoction (process or result).
decocto (m.) decoction.
decoesor (m., Elec.) decoherer.
decolação (f., Med.) decollation, decapitation (of a fetus).
decolagem (f.) take off (of an airplane).
decolar (v.i., Aeron.) to take off.
decolorar (v.) = DESCOLORAR.
decomponente (adj.) decomposing.
decomponível (adj.) decomposable.
decompor [63] (v.t.,v.r.) to decompose (in any sense).
decomposição (f.) decomposition, disintegration; putrefaction.—da luz, decomposition of light.—electrolítica, electrolytic dissociation.
decompressão (f.) decompression.
decoração (f.) decoration, ornamentation.—interior, interior decoration.—teatral, stage setting, scenery.
decorado –da (adj.) memorized; decorated.
decorador –dora (adj.) decorating; memorizing; (m.,f.) decorator; one who learns de cor (by heart).
decorar (v.t.) to decorate, adorn, deck, ornament; to award a decoration or honor to; to learn by heart; to memorize.
decorativo –va (adj.) decorative, ornamental.
decôro (m.) decorum; decency; propriety; seemliness. faltar ao—, to offend against decorum.
decoroso –sa (adj.) decorous, decent, seemly, becoming, proper.
decorrente (adj.) running, flowing, current; (Bot.) decurrent.—de, arising out of.
decorrer (v.i.) of time, to elapse, pass by; of events, to occur, come to pass.
decorrido –da (adj.) elapsed; run out.
decorticação (f.) decortication.
decorticar (v.t.) to decorticate.
decotado –da (adj.) low-necked (dress); pruned; trimmed.
decotar (v.t.) to cut low (neckline of dress); to trim (shrubs), prune (trees); to cut out (off), excise; (v.r.)—to put on a low-cut gown.
decote (m.) décolletage; décolleté costume; neckline; pruning of trees and shrubs.
decremento (m., Math.) decrement.
decrepidez [ê] (f.) decrepitude.
decrepitar (v.t.) to decrepitate, roast, calcine (salt, etc.).
decrépito –ta (adj.) decrepit; ramshackle.
decrepitude (f.) decrepitude, infirm old age.
decrescendo (adv., m., Music) decrescendo.
decrescente (adj.) decreasing.
decrescer (v.i.) to decrease, diminish, dwindle, abate, grow less; to subside.
decrescimento, decréscimo (m.) decrease, diminution.
decretação (f.) decreeing; enactment.
decretado –da (adj.) decreed; (adv.) purposely, intentionally, deliberately.
decretal (adj., m., Eccl.) decretal.
decretalista (m., Theol.) decretalist; decretist.
decretar (v.t.) to decree, order, command, to enact; to adjudge.
decreto (m.) decree, edict, mandate, fiat. baixar um—, to hand down a decree. nem por um—, (colloq.) not on your life.—-lei, a law by decree, fiat.
decretório –ria (adj.) decretory.
decruar (v.t.) to break ground.
decúbito (m.) a lying position; (Med.) decubitus.
decúmano –na (adj.) decuman.

decumbente (*adj.*) decumbent; recumbent.

decuplar, decuplicar (*v.t.*) to multiply by ten; to increase tenfold.

décuplo –pla (*adj.*) decuple, tenfold; (*m.*) a number ten times repeated.

decúria (*f.*) decury; a group of students tutored by one of their number.

decurião (*m.*) decurion; a student selected to tutor a number of other students.

decursivo –va (*adj.*) decursive [= DECORRENTE].

decurso (*m.*) course, duration, passage (of time). **no—de**, in the course of.

decussação (*f.*, *Anat.*, *Biol.*) decussation, chiasma.

dedada (*f.*) finger mark; a quantity of something (as salve) taken with a finger.

dedais-de-dama (*m.pl.*, *Bot.*) the common allamanda (*A. cathartica*).

dedal (*m.*) thimble; also = DEDALEIRA.

dedaleira (*f.*, *Bot.*) the common foxglove (*Digitalis purpurea*), c.a. DIGITAL, ERVA-DEDAL, ABELOURA, TRÓCULOS, LUVAS-DE-NOSSA-SENHORA, LUVAS-DE-PASTÔRA, LUVAS-DE-SANTA-MARIA.

dédalo (*m.*) labyrinth, maze.

dedeira (*f.*) a covering or guard for the finger; plectrum.

dedetizar (*v.t.*) to spray DDT.

dedicação (*f.*) dedication, devotion; consecration.

dedicado –da (*adj.*) dedicated, devoted.

dedicador –dora (*m.*,*f.*) dedicator.

dedicar (*v.t.*) to dedicate, consecrate.—**-se a**, to apply oneself to; to sacrifice oneself to; to devote oneself to; to follow (the sea, the law, etc.).

dedicatória (*f.*) dedication, inscription.

dedignar-se (*v.r.*) to decline, refuse.

dedilhação (*f.*), **dedilhado, dedilhamento** (*m.*) fingering (of a musical instrument).

dedilhar (*v.t.*) to finger (a musical instrument); to strum; to finger mark (musical notes).

dedo⁰ = DEDICADO (devoted).

dedo [ê] (*m.*) finger; toe; a finger's length.—**anular**, ring finger.—**auricular**, little finger. [The term derives from the fact that the little finger is the one we generally employ to relieve an itching in the ear.].—**-de-mercúrio** = CÓLQUICO.—**do pé**, toe.—**duro**, stool pigeon.—**índice** or **indicador**, forefinger.—**máximo** or **médio**, middle finger.—**mínimo** or **mindinho**, little finger.—**polegar**, thumb. **como dois—s da mesma mão**, as alike as two peas in a pod. **conhecer nas pontas dos—s**, to have at one's finger-tips. **examiner a—**, to sift, examine critically. **juntas dos—s**, finger joints. **nós dos—s**, finger knuckles. **ter—para**, to be good at, excel in (something). **unhas dos—s**, finger nails.—**-de-dama**, ladyfinger grape.

dedução (*f.*) deduction; subtraction; abatement, allowance, rebate; inference, conclusion.

deducional (*adj.*) inferential.

dedutivo –va (*adj.*) deductive.

deduzir [36] (*v.i.*) to deduce, infer; (*v.t.*) to deduct, subtract.

defasado –da (*adj.*, *Elec.*) out of phase.

defasagem (*f.*, *Elec.*) difference in phase.

defasar (*v.t.*, *Elec.*) to dephase.

defecação (*f.*) defecation (all senses).

defecador (*m.*) defecator (for cane juice).

defecar (*v.t.*) to defecate, purify, refine; (*Sugar mfr.*) to clarify (juice); (*v.i.*) to defecate.

defecatório –ria (*adj.*) defecating.

defecção (*f.*) defection, desertion; apostasy, backsliding.

defectibilidade (*f.*) defectibility.

defectível (*adj.*) defectible.

defectivo –va (*adj.*) defective, deficient, imperfect, faulty [= DEFEITUOSO]; (*Gram.*) defective.

defeito (*m.*) defect, imperfection, blemish, flaw; fault, failing, foible, shortcoming. **pôr—s a (em)**, to find fault with; to impute faults to.

defeituar (*v.t.*) to find fault with.

defeituosidade (*f.*) defectiveness.

defeituoso –sa (*adj.*) defective; imperfect, faulty; marred.

defendente (*adj.*) defending; (*m.*,*f.*) defender [but not defendant at law, which is RÉU].

defender [24] (*v.t.*) to defend, shield, protect; to shelter, screen; to forbid, prohibit (esp. entry); to uphold, justify; (*v.r.*) to defend oneself; to stand up against attack; to get by; to live by one's wits; to wangle or chisel one's way.—**afirmativa**, to be for the affirmative.—**com unhas e dentes**, to fight tooth and nail.—**tese**, to main- tain or substantiate a thesis (for scholastic honors).

defendimento (*m.*) = DEFESA.

defendível (*adj.*) defensible [= DEFENSÍVEL].

defenestração (*f.*) defenestration.

defensa (*f.*) defense [= DEFESA]; (*pl.*) skids, cushions (to protect the sides of a ship while docking).

defensão (*f.*) = DEFESA.

defensável (*adj.*) defensible, defendable [= DEFENSÍVEL].

defensível (*adj.*) defensible [= DEFENDÍVEL].

defensivo –va (*adj.*) defensive; (*m.*) defense; preservative; (*f.*) defensive side.—**s agrícolas**, pesticides.

defensor –sora (*m.*,*f.*) defender; backer; upholder.

defensório –ria (*adj.*) defensory, defensive.

deferência (*f.*) deference, compliance; respect, esteem. **por—a** or **para com**, out of deference or respect to.

deferente (*adj.*) deferential; (*Anat.*) deferent.

deferido –da (*adj.*) granted; approved favorably.

deferimento (*m.*) act of granting (approving, deferring to).

deferir [21a] (*v.i.*) to defer to; (*v.t.*) to grant, yield, concede, approve. [But not to defer, which is DIFERIR.]

deferível (*adj.*) approvable.

defesa [ê] (*f.*) defense, protection, shield, bulwark; safeguard; justification, plea; attorney for the defense; prohibition, forbiddance, interdiction; the defensive players on a soccer team; (*pl.*) tusks, fangs, horns; (*colloq.*) wangling, scrounging.—**própria**, self-defense. **em legítima—**, in self-defense. **em—de**, in defense of. **sem—**, defenseless.

defeso –sa [fê] [*irreg. p.p. of* DEFENDER] forbidden, prohibited. [Used only in this sense.]. **A pesca por meio de explosivos foi—**, Fishing with dynamite was forbidden. (*m.*) closed season (hunting).

deficiência (*f.*) deficiency, want, lack, dearth; shortcoming.

deficiente (*adj.*) deficient, defective.

déficit (*m.*) deficit; shortage.

deficitário –ria (*adj.*) having a deficit.

definhado –da (*adj.*) emaciated, wasted; sickly.

definhamento (*m.*) emaciation, wasting away.

definhar (*v.i.*,*v.r.*) to emaciate; to waste away; to dwindle, pine away; to droop; to wither.

definibilidade (*f.*) definability.

definição (*f.*) definition; decision, determination (of a matter in doubt); (*TV*) definition, sharpness.

definido –da (*adj.*) defined, determined, fixed; distinct.

definidor –dora (*m.*,*f.*) definer.

definir (*v.t.*) to define, make definite; to explain; to determine.—**-se**, to take form.

definitivo –va (*adj.*) definitive, real.

definito –ta (*adj.*) definite, precise, exact; (*m.*, *Gram.*) definite noun.

definível (*adj.*) definable, determinable.

deflação (*f.*) deflation (of money); (*Phys. Geog.*) deflation. [Deflation of a balloon, tire, etc. is ESVAZIAMENTO.]

deflacionista (*adj.*) deflationary; (*m.*,*f.*) deflationist.

deflagração (*f.*) deflagration, conflagration.

deflagrador (*m.*, *Chem.*) deflagrator.

deflagrar (*v.t.*,*v.i.*) to deflagrate.; (*v.t.*) to set off (as mob violence, a strike, a fire, a raging epidemic).

deflegmação (*f.*) dephlegmation.

deflegmador (*m.*, *Petrol.*) dephlegmator, rectifier, fractionating column.

deflegmar (*v.t.*, *Chem.*) to dephlegmate, rectify by distillation.

defletor (*m.*) baffle plate.

deflexão [ks] (*f.*) deflection, deviation.

deflexionar [ks] (*v.t.*) to deflect.

defloração (*f.*) deflowering, ravishing; fading of flowers.

deflorador (*m.*) deflowerer, ravisher.

defloramento (*m.*) deflowering, ravishment.

deflorar (*v.t.*) to deflower; to ravish; to cull choice passages from a book.

defluente (*adj.*) flowing down; decurrent.

defluir [72] (*v.i.*) to flow down.

deflúvio (*m.*) a flowing.

defluxão [x = ss] (*f.*, *Med.*) defluxion.

defluxeira [x = ss] (*f.*, *colloq.*) a heavy cold.

defluxo [x = ss] (*m.*) head cold [= RESFRIADO].

deformação (*f.*) deformation, disfiguration; (*Optics*) distortion; (*Physics, etc.*) deformation.

deformador –dora (*adj.*) deforming; (*m.*,*f.*) deformer.

deformar (*v.t.*) to deform, disfigure, distort; to misrepresent; (*v.r.*) to become deformed.

deformatório –ria (*adj.*) deformative.

deforme (*adj.*) = DISFORME.

deformidade (f.) deformity, distortion, malformation.
deformômetro (m., *Civ. Engin.*) deformeter.
defraudação (f.) defraudation.
defraudador –dora (adj.) defrauding; (m.,f.) defrauder.
defraudar (v.t.) to defraud, cheat, rook, bilk, dupe, swindle, embezzle, "gyp".
defrontação (f.) act or state of facing (fronting).
defrontante (adj.) facing, fronting.
defrontar (v.t.) to face, front; to come face to face with; to confront.
defronte (adv.) facing, face to face, vis-a-vis.—**de**, in front of.
defumação (f.) smoke-curing (of rubber, etc.).
defumador –dora (adj.) smoke-curing; (m.) one who smoke-cures; an incense burner; a smoke-house for rubber.
defumadouro (m.) smoke-house; act of smoke-curing; incense burner.
defumar (v.t.) to smoke-cure (meat, fish, rubber, etc.); to fumigate; (v.r.) to perfume oneself.
defunção (f.) act of dying; death.
defuntar (v.i., *colloq.*) to die.
defuntear (v.t., *colloq.*) to kill, murder.
defunteiro –ra (adj.) funeral; (m.) undertaker.
defunto –ta (adj.) defunct, deceased, dead; (m.,f.) a dead person; a cadaver.—**sem chôro**, (*colloq.*) a luckless person with no one to share his woes. **cravo de**—, marigold. **gastar cêra com máu**—, to send good money after bad.
degas (m., *colloq.*) guy, fellow.
degelador (m., *Aeron.*) de-icer.
degelar (v.t.) to defrost, de-ice; (v.i.,v.r.) to thaw.
degêlo (m.) thaw(ing).
degeneração (f.) degeneration; (*Radio*) negative feedback.
degenerado –da (adj.; m.,f.) degenerate.
degenerar (v.i.) to degenerate, deteriorate.
degenerativo –va (adj.) degenerative.
degenerescência (f.) degeneration; degeneracy; a degenerate act; a freak of nature.
deglutição (f.) deglution, swallowing.
deglutir (v.t.,v.i.) to swallow.
degola, degolação (f.) decapitation, beheading; throat-cutting; wholesale demotion or firing of employees (esp. when a change of administration takes place).
degolador –dora (m.,f.) beheader; throatcutter, (*Smithing*) swage; cut-off tool.
degoladura (f.) = DEGOLAÇÃO.
degolar (v.t.) to decapitate, behead; to cut the throat of; (*Metal working*) to cut off; (v.r.) to cut one's throat.
degradação (f.) degradation, dishonor; demotion; deterioration, abasement; (*Phys. Geog.*) degradation, a wearing down by erosion; (*Chem.*) degradation.
degradador –dora (adj.) degrading; (m.,f.) degrader.
degradante (adj.) degrading; shameful.
degradar (v.t.) to degrade, dishonor, discredit; to depose; to demote; to debase, pervert; also = DEGREDAR (to exile); (v.r.) to demean oneself; to lose face.
degrau (m.) stair step; rung of a ladder; degree.
degredado –da (adj.) exiled, banished; (m.,f.) exile, outcast.
degredar (v.t.) to exile, banish.
degrêdo (m.) exile, banishment; place of exile.
degressivo –va (adj.) degressive.
degringolada (f.) debacle; downfall; tumble.
degringolar (v.i.) to topple.
degustação (f.) act of tasting.
degustar (v.t.) to taste.
deicida [e-i] (m.) deicide; (adj.) deicidal.
deidade (f.) deity.
deificação [e-i] (f.) deification.
deificador –dora [e-i] (adj.) deifying; (m.,f.) deifier.
deificar [e-i] (v.t.) to deify.
deífico –ca (adj.) deific.
deiscência [e-i] (f., *Bot.*) dehiscence.
deiscente [e-i] (adj., *Bot.*) dehiscent.
deísmo (m.) deism.
deísta (m.,f.) deist.
deístico –ca (adj.) deistic.
deitado –da (adj.) lying (down), stretched out; (f.) a lying down.
deitar (v.t.) to lay, put (down); to put to bed; to set, place, deposit (on); to cast, throw, fling (out, off, away); to pour, spill; (v.r.) to go to bed; lie down.—**a fugir**, to start running, take to one's heels.—**a língua de fora**, to stick

out the tongue.—**a mão a**, to lay hands on, seize.—**à margem**, to cast aside.—**a perder**, to cause the ruin of; to make a mess of.—**à terra**, or **por terra**, to raze, demolish; to strike to the ground.—**abaixo**, to raze.—**as linhas**, to lay plans for achieving something.—**as mãos**, or **os braços, de fora**, to become bold, no longer shy.—**as unhas**, to seize, grab.—**cartas**, to tell fortunes with cards.—**falação**, (*colloq.*) to make a speech.—**fora**, to throw out or away; to waste, squander.—**lenha no fogo**, to add fuel to the flames. —**poeira nos olhos de**, to throw dust in the eyes of.—**raizes**, to put forth roots.—**sangue**, to shed blood.—**-se com as galinhas**, to go to bed with the chickens.—**-se de fora**, to dodge blame or responsibility for.—**-se de ilharga**, to lie on one's side.—**sortes**, to tell fortunes.—**um véu sôbre**, to draw a veil over.—**uma criança**, to put a child to bed.—**uma galinha**, to set a hen.—**veneno em**, to put an evil interpretation on. Cf. PÔR.
deixa (f.) actor's cue; hint; (*Billiards*) position of balls as left for the next player.
deixar (v.t.) to leave, depart from; to abandon, forsake; to let, allow, permit; to renounce, lay aside; to leave (something) behind one.—**a vida**, to leave this life, die.—(**as coisas**) **como são para ver como ficam**, to leave things as they are; wait and see what happens.—**atrás**, to leave behind; to outrun.—**cair**, to let fall, drop.—**cair a máscara**, to drop one's mask.—**claro**, to make (it) clear.—**correr**, to let it be, pay no attention to.—**correr o barco**, to let things drift.—**crescer o bigode**, to raise a mustache.—**de**, to stop, cease from, refrain from, leave off, omit.—**de falar**, to stop talking.—**de fazer alguma coisa**, to avoid doing (fail to do) something.—**de fumar**, to stop smoking.—**de levar em conta**, to fail to take into account; to overlook.—**de ter esperanças**, to give up hope.—**em branco**, to leave in blank or open; to leave (someone) flat broke.—**em** (or **no**) **meio**, to leave (something) half-finished.—**em paz**, to let alone, in peace.—**murchar os louros**, to let a great reputation become tarnished; lit., to let one's laurels wither.—**o mundo**, to leave this world, die.—**para outro dia**, to put off to another day.—**passar**, to let (something) pass, overlook it; to let (someone) go through.—**perceber**, to give to understand; to lead to the belief.—**por fazer**, to leave undone.—**-se de**, to stop, leave off, quit.—**-se de histórias**, to stop beating about the bush, to quit lying, bragging, etc.—**-se levar pelo nariz**, to let oneself be led by the nose.—**uma porta aberta**, to leave the door open (lit. & fig.).—**ver**, to show, give to understand; to point out. **Deixa estar!** Just you wait and see! I'll get even! **Deixa de bobagens!** Stop the nonsense! Oh, cut it out! **Deixe de tolices!** Stop being silly! Don't be a sucker! **Deixa-o em paz!** Let him alone! Lay off! **Deixe isso comigo,** Leave it to me; that is my business. **Deixa muito a desejar,** It leaves much to be desired. **Deixou-se cair na cama,** He dropped on the bed. **não—de,** to not fail to, be sure to. **Não deixa de ser fácil,** It certainly is easy. **Não deixe de,** Don't fail to. **Não deixe de escrever,** Don't forget to write. **Não posso—de ir,** I must not fail to go. **Não posso deixar de** (**rir, pensar, etc.**), I can't help (laughing, thinking, etc.). **Vou—de,** I am going to stop (doing something).
dejarretar (v.t.) to hamstring.
dejeção (f., *Physiol.*) dejection, defecation; (pl.) dejecta. [But not dejection in the sense of depression of spirits, which is ABATIMENTO, DESÂNIMO.]
dejejua, dejua, dejuação (f.), **dejejuadouro** (m.) = DESJEJUA.
dejejuar (v.i.) to break fast.
dejetar (v.i., *Physiol.*) to defecate.
dejeto (m.) = DEJEÇÃO.
dejúrio (m.) solemn oath.
dela [DE+ELA] of her, from her (it); hers, its.
delação (f.) denunciation.
delamber-se (v.r.) to lick itself (cat, etc.); to purr with self-satisfaction.
delambido –da (adj.) prim, prissy, goody-goody; smug; weakly sentimental; (m.,f.) one given to affectations.
delatar (v.t.) to denounce; to inform against.
delator –tora (m.,f.) informer, accuser, denouncer; telltale, squealer, stool pigeon.
dêle [DE+ÊLE] of him, from him (it); his, its.
delegação (f.) delegation; delegating.
delegacia (f.) office or position of a delegate.—**de polícia**, police headquarters.

delegado (*m.*) delegate, deputy; commissioner.—**de polícia**, district chief of police.
delegante (*adj.*) delegating; (*m.,f.*) one who delegates.
delegar (*v.t.*) to delegate, deputize, commission.
delegatório –**ria** (*adj.*) delegatory.
deleitação (*f.*), –**tamento** (*m.*) delectation.
deleitante (*adj.*) enrapturing; delightful.
deleitar (*v.t.*) to delight, enrapture, transport; (*v.r.*) to rejoice, have great pleasure (**com, em, de,** in).
deleitável (*adj.*) delectable, delightful.
deleite (*m.*) delight; delectation; (*pl.*) amenities.
deleitoso –**sa** (*adj.*) delightful, delectable.
deletério –**ria** ʿ(*adj.*) deleterious, injurious, harmful, unwholesome.
deletrear (*v.t.*) to spell out; to read poorly.
delével (*adj.*) delible.
délfico –**ca** (*adj.*) Delphian.
delfim (*m.*) dolphin; dauphin; (in chess) the bishop.
Delfina (*f.*) Delphine.
delfínidas, –**finídeos** (*m.pl.*) the family of dolphins, porpoises, grampuses, etc. (*Delphinidae*).
delfinina (*f., Chem.*) delphinine.
delfínio (*m., Bot.*) any delphinium.
delfinóide (*adj., Zool.*) delphinoid.
delfinoidina (*f., Chem.*) delphinoidin(e).
delgadeza [dê] (*f.*) thinness; slimness.
delgado –**da** (*adj.*) thin, slender, slim; fine, tenuous; delicate.
Deli (*m.*) Delhi.
delibação (*f.*) a sip, taste.
Délia (*f.*) Delia.
delibar (*v.t.*) to take a little of, sip [= LIBAR].
deliberação (*f.*) deliberation; decision, resolution.
deliberado –**da** (*adj.*) deliberate, willful.
deliberante (*adj.*) deliberating; (*m.,f.*) deliberator.
deliberar (*v.t.*) to decide, resolve, determine; (*v.i.*) to deliberate, ponder, consider; (*v.r.*) to reach a decision.
deliberativo –**va** (*adj.*) deliberative.
delicada (*f.*) see under DELICADO.
delicadeza [ê] (*f.*) courtesy, politeness, urbanity; charm, attractiveness; attentiveness; niceness, daintiness; fragility.
delicado –**da** (*adj.*) polite, courteous, charming, suave, urbane; attentive; small, dainty; gentle; exquisite; delicate, fragile, frail; flimsy; ticklish, critical, risky. (*f., colloq.*) tuberculosis of the lungs.
delícia (*f.*) delight, joy, charm; any delightful thing.
deliciar (*v.t.*) to delight, enchant; (*v.r.*) to be delighted; to enjoy [= DELEITAR].
delicioso –**sa** (*adj.*) delightful, delicious, luscious; entrancing.
delimitação (*f.*) delimitation, demarcation.
delimitador –**dora** (*adj.*) delimiting; (*m.,f.*) delimiter.
delimitar (*v.t.*) to delimit; to bound, mark the limits.
delineação (*f.*), –**lineamento** (*m.*) delineation of.
delineador –**dora** (*m.,f.*) delineator.
delinear (*v.t.*) to delineate, design, sketch, outline; to plot (on a map); to lay out (a course of action); to portray.
delinqüência (*f.*) delinquency, transgression.—**juvenil**, juvenile delinquency.
delinqüente (*adj.*) delinquent; (*m.,f.*) delinquent, offender, miscreant, wrongdoer.
delinqüido –**da** (*adj., colloq.*) thin, sickly; fainted.
delinqüir [25] (*v.i.*) to transgress, be delinquent.
deliquar (*v.t.*) to distill.
deliqüescência (*f.*) deliquescence.
deliqüescente (*adj.*) deliquescent; diffluent.
delíquio (*m.*) deliquescence; a fainting away.
delir [25] (*v.t.*) to dissolve; to wipe out (spots); to expunge, blot out. ·
deliração (*f.*) = DELÍRIO.
delirado –**da** (*adj.*) delirious; mad.
deliramento (*m.*) a crazy fancy.
delirante (*adj.*) delirious, frenzied; (*colloq.*) overjoyed.
delirar (*v.i.*) to be delirious; to rave, rage, rant; to be overjoyed.
delírio (*m.*) delirium; raving; ecstasy, frenzy; enthusiasm; (*Psychiatry*) delusion.
delirioso –**sa** (*adj.*) delirious.
delito (*m.*) violation of law, offence, crime, trespass, misdemeanor; (*Law*) delict. **corpo de**—, corpus delicti.
delituoso –**sa** (*adj.*) involving crime.
delivramento (*m.*) the expulsion of the afterbirth [DEQUITAÇÃO, DEQUITADURA].

delomórfico –**ca,** –**morfo** –**fa** (*adj., Biol.*) delomorphous.
delonga (*f.*) delay, postponement, deferment. **sem mais** —**s**, without further delay.
delongar (*v.t.*) to prolong, postpone, defer.
delta (*f.*) delta (of a river).
deltaico –**ca** (*adj.*) deltaic.
deltóide (*adj.*) deltoid(al); (*m., Anat., Math.*) deltoid; (*Zool.*) a deltoid moth.
deltoídeo –**dea** (*adj.*) = DELTÓIDE.
deluzir-se (*v.r.*) to fade, grow dim.
demagogia (*f.*) demagogy.
demagógico –**ca** (*adj.*) demagogic.
demagogismo (*m.*) demagoguery.
demagogo [gô] (*m.*) demagogue, political agitator.
demais (*adv., adj.*) too, too much, overmuch; besides, moreover. **o**—, (*m.*) the rest (of it); **os**—**s**, the rest (of them). **Dois é bom, três é**—, Two is company, three is a crowd. **Isso tambem é**—! That's the limit! That takes the cake! **por**—, too much. **Já é**—! It is too much!
demanda (*f.*) lawsuit, plea, court action.—**por perdas e danos,** claim for damages. **em**—**de,** toward; in search of.
demandador –**dora** (*m.,f.*) pleader, plaintiff.
demandante (*m.,f., Law*) demandant, plaintiff; litigant; (*adj.*) pleading.
demandar (*v.t.*) to go in search of; to demand; to require; to sue at law; (*v.i.*) to question.
demão [-**mãos**] (*f.*) layer, coat (of paint, etc.). **última**—, final coat; finishing touch.
demarcação (*f.*) demarcation, boundary; location (ot land).
demarcador –**dora** (*adj.*) demarcating.
demarcar (*v.t.*) to demarcate, fix the boundaries of.
demasia (*f.*) excess, superabundance; surplus, remainder. **em**—, in excess.
demasiado –**da** (*adj.*) excessive, undue, too great, too much; (*adv.*) too.
demasiar-se (*v.r.*) to exceed oneself.
demência (*f.*) dementia; insanity; (*colloq.*) crazy behavior. —**precoce,** dementia praecox.
dementação (*f.*) = DEMÊNCIA.
dementado –**da** (*adj.; m.,f.*) = DEMENTE.
dementar (*v.t.*) to make insane.
demente (*adj.; m.,f.*) demented (person).
demerara (*m.*) Demerara (sugar) crystals.
demérito –**ta** (*adj.*) unworthy; (*m.*) demerit, unworthiness.
demilunar (*adj.*) shaped like a halfmoon.
demissão (*f.*) dismissal, removal (from office, job). **pedido de**—, formal resignation. **pedir**—, to submit one's resignation.
demissionário –**ria, demitente** (*adj.*) resigning; (*m.,f.*) one who has resigned or submitted a resignation.
demitir (*v.t.*) to discharge, dismiss, fire (from a job); to renounce (one's rights); (*v.r.*) to resign (**de,** from).
demiurgo [i-úr] (*m.*) demiurge.
demo (*m., colloq.*) demon.
democracia (*f.*) democracy.
democrata (*m.,f.*) democrat.
democrático –**ca** (*adj.*) democratic.
democratismo (*m.*) = DEMOCRACIA.
democratizar (*v.t.*) to democratize; to popularize.
demodulação (*f., Radio*) detection.
demodulador (*m., Radio*) demodulator, detector.
demodular (*v.t., Radio*) to detect, rectify.
demografia (*f.*) demography, vital statistics.
demográfico –**ca** (*adj.*) demographic.
demolição (*f.*) demolition.
demolidor –**dora** (*adj.*) demolishing; (*m.,f.*) demolisher.
demolir [25] (*v.t.*) to demolish, destroy, raze; to tear down (a building).
demonete [ête] (*m.*) imp.; impish child.
demonetizar (*v.t.*) to demonetize.
demoníaco –**ca** (*adj.*) demoniacal, diabolic.
demônio (*m.*) demon, devil; hobgoblin; wicked person.
demonismo (*m.*) demonism.
demonista (*m.,f.*) demonist.
demonólatra (*m.,f.*) a demon worshipper.
demonolatria (*f.*) demonolatry.
demonologia (*f.*) demonology.
demonstrabilidade (*f.*) demonstrability.
demonstração (*f.*) demonstration; proof; exhibition.
demonstrador –**dora** (*adj.*) demonstrating; (*m.,f.*) demonstrator.
demonstrante (*adj.*) demonstrating.

demonstrar (*v.t.*) to demonstrate, show, prove; to teach by demonstration.

demonstrativo **-va** (*adj.*) demonstrative; (*m., Gram.*) a demonstrative pronoun or adjective.

demonstrável (*adj.*) demonstrable.

demora (*f.*) delay, postponement; deferment; long wait; sojourn; lag.

demorado **-da** (*adj.*) slow, lingering; leisurely; long drawn-out; tardy; laggard; dilatory.

demorar (*v.t.*) to delay, retard, slow down; to defer; (*v.i.*) to dwell, tarry, abide; to stay; (*v.r.*) to linger, lag, delay. **—a partir**, to be long in leaving.—**em chegar**, to be long in arriving.

demos, form of DAR [39].

demostrar (*v.*) & derivs. = DEMONSTRAR (*v.*) & derivs.

demover (*v.t.*) to dissuade.

demudar (*v.t.*) to change, alter (look, face); (*v.r.*) to change (in appearance, character, etc.).

demulcente (*adj.; m.*) demulcent.

demultiplicador (*m., Mach.*) ratio gears.

dendê (*m.*) the African oilpalm (*Elaesis guineensis*) grown in Brazil, and from whose fruit is extracted DENDÊ oil, much used in cookery; c.a. DENDÊZEIRO, COQUEIRO-DE-DENDÊ.

dendêzeiro (*m., Bot.*) same as the preceding.—**-do-pará**, American oilpalm (*Corozo oleifera*), c.a. CAIAUÉ.

dendraxônio (*m., Anat.*) dendraxon.

dendriforme (*adj.*) dendriform.

dendrite (*m.*) = DENDRITO.

dendrítico **-ca** (*adj.*) dendritic.

dendrito (*m., Min., Anat., Physiol.*) dendrite.

dendróbio (*m.*) a large genus (*Dendrobium*) of orchids.

dendrografia (*f.*) dendrography.

dendróide, **-droídeo** **-dea** (*adj.*) dendroid(al).

dendrologia (*f.*) dendrology.

dendrômetro (*m.*) dendrometer.

denegação (*f.*) denial; disavowal; refusal.

denegar (*v.t.*) to deny; to refuse; to disallow.

denegrir [21b] (*v.t.*) to denigrate; to malign.

dengo (*m.*) = DENGUE.

dengoso **-sa** (*adj.*) prudish, prim, over-nice; goody-goody; coy; weakly sentimental; (*f.*) white rum.

dengue (*m.*) prudery, primness; affectation; (*f., Med.*) dengue, breakbone fever; (*adj.*) affected; effeminate.

denguice (*f.*) prudish affectation; effeminacy.

denier (*m.*) denier (unit of silk and rayon yarn size).

denodado **-da** (*adj.*) daring, intrepid, dauntless; plucky, valiant, stout.

denôdo (*m.*) courage, bravery, valor; pluck; high devotion to a cause.

denominação (*f.*) denomination, designation.

denominador **-dora** (*adj.*) denominating; (*m.,f.*) denominator.

denominar (*v.t.*) to denominate, name, call; (*v.r.*) to be called or nicknamed (something).

denominativo **-va** (*adj.*) denominative.

denotação (*f.*) denotation.

denotador **-dora** (*adj.*) denotative; (*m.,f.*) that which denotes.

denotar (*v.t.*) to denote, signify; to indicate , show.

densidade (*f.*) density;—**da corrente**, (*Elec.*) current density.—**demográfica**, density of population.—**dinâmica**, (*Sociol.*) dynamic density.—**estatística**, (*Sociol.*) the average number of persons per unit of area.—**magnética**, (*Elec.*) field strength.

densidão (*f.*) density [= DENSIDADE].

densificação (*f.*) densification.

densimetria (*f.*) densimetry.

densímetro (*m., Physical Chem.*) densimeter.

densitômetro (*m.*) densitometer.

denso **-sa** (*adj.*) dense, thick, condensed.

dentado **-da** (*adj.*) toothed; cogged; serrated; (*Bot.*) dentate; (*f.*) a bite; fig., a biting remark; (*slang*) a "bite" (request for a loan).

dentadura (*f.*) denture, set of teeth (natural or false).

dental (*adj.*) dental; (*Phonetics*) dental; (*f.*) a dental consonant.

dentálio (*m.*) a genus of tooth shells (*Dentalium*).

dentão (*m.*) = VERMELHO (red snapper).

dentar (*v.t.*) to bite [= MORDER]; to provide with teeth [= DENTEAR].

dentário **-ria** (*adj.*) dental; (*f., Bot.*) the genus of tooth-worts (*Dentaria*).

dente (*m.*) tooth, fang, tusk; gear tooth; cog of a wheel; prong, tine (of a fork); clove (of garlic).

—abalado, loose tooth.—**bicúspide**, a biscuspid or premolar.—**de coelho**, mystery, trick, scheme.—**de engrenagem**, gear tooth.—**de leite**, milk tooth, c.a. DENTE CADUCO, DENTE TEMPORÁRIO.—**de serra**, saw tooth.—**do siso**, wisdom tooth, c.a. DENTE CABEIRO, DENTE QUEIRO. —**incisivo**, incisor.—**molar**, a molar, c.a. DENTE QUEIXAL. —**por dente**, a tooth for a tooth; tit for tat.—**s enfrestados**, widely spaced teeth.—**s postiços**, false teeth.—**s substituintes**, those which replace the milk teeth.—**venenífero**, poison fang. **A cavalo dado não se olham os—s**, One does not look a gift horse in the mouth. **armado até os—s**, armed to the teeth. **arrancar um—**, to pull a tooth, or to have one pulled. **chumbar**, or **obturar**, **um—**, to fill a tooth, or to have one filled. **com unhas e —s**, tooth and nail. **dar com a língua nos—s**, to blab, let the cat out of the bag, spill the beans. **defender com unhas e—s**, to fight tooth and nail; to defend to the last ditch. **dôr de—s**, toothache. **falar entre os—s**, to mutter, mumble, growl. **mostrar os—s**, to bare the teeth (in a threatening manner). **ôlho por ôlho,—por—**, an eye for an eye, a tooth for a tooth; tit for tat. **ranger os—s**, to gnash (grind) the teeth.—**-de-cão**, a sharp fragment of quartz.—**-de-cavalo**, a type of corn.—**-de-cutia**, a type of chisel used in the pottery industry on the Island of Marajó.—**-de-elefante**, a tooth shell (*Dentalium*).—**-de-leão**, common dandelion (*Taraxacum officinale*), c.a. TARAXACO.—**-de-ôvo**, egg tooth.—**-de-velha** = GANGÃO.

denteação (*f.*) dentition.

dentear (*v.t.*) to provide with teeth; to cut gear teeth.

dentel [-téis] (*m., Carp.*) notch.

dentelete (*m., Arch.*) denticule.

dentelo (*m., Arch.*) dentil.

dentição (*f.*) dentition, teething.

denticulado **-da** (*adj.*) denticulate.

denticular (*adj.*) denticular.

dentículo (*m.*) denticle; (*Arch.*) dentil; (*Bot.*) dentate leaf margin.

dentificação (*f.*) dentification.

dentiforme (*adj.*) dentiform, tooth-shaped.

dentifrício (*m.*) dentifrice.

dentígero **-ra** (*adj.*) dentigerous.

dentilabial (*adj.; f.*) labiodental (consonant).

dentilária (*f., Bot.*) common plumbago (*P. europaea*).—**-da-china**, the blue ceratostigma (*C. plumbaginoides*).—**-da-índia**, the rose plumbago (*P. rosea*).—**-do-cabo**, the Cape plumbago (*P. capensis*), c.a. BELA-EMÍLIA, JAS-MIM-AZUL.

dentímetro (*m., Dentistry*) dentimeter.

dentina (*f., Anat.*) dentine; ivory.

dentirrostro **-tra** (*adj., Zool.*) dentirostral; (*m.pl.*) the Dentirostres.

dentista (*m.,f.*) dentist [= ODONTOLOGISTA]. **cirurgião—**, dental surgeon.

dentóide (*adj.*) dentoid, odontoid.

dentola (*m.*) a large tooth; (*m.,f.pl.*) person having large, ugly teeth.

dentolabial (*adj.*) = DENTILABIAL.

dentre [DE + ENTRE] (*prep.*) from among; in the midst of.

dentro (*adv.*) within, inwardly.—**de**, (*prep.*) inside of.—**de dez anos**, inside of ten years.—**em breve**, soon, presently, before long.—**em pouco**, soon, within a short time. **de—**, from within. **lá—**, inside there. **para—**, into, inward(s), inside. **por—(de)** inside, on the inside.

dentuça (*f.*) buck teeth.

dentuço **-ça**, **dentudo** **-da** (*adj.*) big-toothed.

denudação (*f.*) denudation.

denudar (*v.t.*) to denude.

denúncia (*f.*) denunciation, exposure, accusation; complaint; (*Law*) indictment [= PRONÚNCIA, ACUSAÇÃO].

denunciado **-da** (*m.,f.*) one who has been denounced or indicted; a defendant.

denunciador **-dora**, **denunciante** (*adj.*) denunciatory; (*m.,f.*) denouncer.

denunciar (*v.t.*) to denounce, inform against; (*Law*) to indict [= PRONUNCIAR.]; to divulge, reveal; to bring to light; to give notice of termination of (treaty, etc.); (*v.r.*) to betray (reveal) oneself.

denunciativo **-va** (*adj.*) denunciative.

denunciatório **-ria** (*adj.*) denunciatory.

deoperculado **-da** (*adj., Bot.*) deoperculate.

deparar (*v.t.*) to cause to appear (suddenly, unexpectedly); to find, come upon.—**-(se) com**, to come across, stumble upon; to encounter.—**-se a**, to appear (present itself) to; to come upon.

departamental (*adj.*) departmental.
departamento (*m.*) department.
departir (*v.t.*) to divide, distribute; to discern, distinguish; (*v.r.*) to leave, depart.
depauperação (*f.*) depauperation.
depauperador –dora (*adj.*) pauperizing, impoverishing.
depauperamento (*m.*) = DEPAUPERAÇÃO.
depauperar (*v.t.*) to pauperize, impoverish; to exhaust the strength or resources of; to deplete; (*v.r.*) to weaken oneself.
depenado –da (*adj.*) deprived of plumage; fig., picked clean (of money), flat broke.
depenar (*v.t.*) to pluck the feathers of; fig., to skin, fleece, strip (of money).
dependência (*f.*) dependence, subordination; dependency; subsidiary; annex (to a building).
dependente (*adj.*) dependent; (*m.*) hanger-on; dependent person.
depender (*v.i.*)—**de**, to depend on; to be dependent on.
dependura (*f.*) position of dangling or hanging down; a hanging object; (*colloq.*) a bad plight. **estar na**—, (*slang*) to be broke, on the rocks, in a tight spot; to lead a wretched life.
dependurado –da (*adj.*) suspended, hanging, dangling.
dependurar (*v.*) = PENDURAR.
depenicar (*v.t.*) to pick or pluck at with the fingers or with the beak; to preen (feathers); to nibble at.
deperecer (*v.i.*) to decline, fade away; to droop.
depilação (*f.*) depilation.
depilar (*v.t.*) to depilate, strip of hair.
depilatório –ria (*adj.; m.*) depilatory.
depleção (*f., Med.*) depletion. [But depletion in the ordinary sense of exhaustion is ESGOTAMENTO.]
depletivo –va (*adj.; m., Med.*) depletive.
deploração (*f.*) deploration, lamentation.
deplorador –dora (*adj.*) deploring; (*m.,f.*) deplorer.
deplorar (*v.t.*) to deplore, bewail; to rue, regret; (*v.r.*) to lament, bemoan.
deplorável (*adj.*) deplorable; pitiable; wretched.
deplumar (*v.*) = DESPLUMAR, DEPENAR.
depoente (*m.,f.*) deponent, affiant; (*adj., Gram.*) deponent.
depoimento [o-i] (*m.*) deposition, (written) testimony, esp. under oath; statement, declaration, affidavit. [Verb: DEPOR.]
depois (*adv.*) afterward(s), after, later, subsequently, then; besides, moreover.—**de**, (*prep.*) after, following, behind.—**disso**, after that.—**que**, (*conj.*) after, subsequent to.
depolarizar (*v.t.*) to depolarize.
depopular (*v.t.*) to depopulate [= DESPOVOAR].
depor [63] (*v.t.*) to depose; to set aside; to depone, depose, testify under oath (**contra**, against); to renounce, give up; to lay down (arms). [Nouns: DEPOSIÇÃO, DEPOIMENTO.]
deportação (*f.*) deportation, banishment.
deportado –da (*adj.*) deported, exiled; (*m.,f.*) deportee.
deportar (*v.t.*) to deport, banish, exile.
deposição (*f.*) act of deposing; overthrow. [Verb: DEPOR].
depositante (*adj.*) depositing; (*m.,f.*) depositor.
depositar (*v.t.*) to deposit; to lodge with, or entrust to, for safekeeping; (*v.r.*) to settle, be precipitated.—**confiança em**, to place confidence in.
depositário (*m.*) depository.
depósito (*m.*) deposit (act of depositing, the thing deposited or the depository); depot, warehouse, storehouse. —**a prazo**, (*Banking*) time deposit.—**de abastecimento**, supply dump.—**de água**, water reservoir.—**de óleo**, oil tank.—**de lixo**, garbage dump.—**eletrolítico**, electrolytic precipitation.
depravação (*f.*) depravity; turpitude; corruption.
depravado –da (*adj.*) depraved, degenerate.
depravador –dora (*adj.*) depraving, demoralizing; (*m.,f.*) depraver.
depravar (*v.t.*) to deprave, corrupt, pervert; (*v.r.*) to become depraved.
deprecação (*f.*) plea, prayer, petition.
deprecar (*v.t.*) to supplicate, beseech; to invoke. [But not to deprecate in the sense of expressing disapproval, which is REPROVAR, CONDENAR.]
depreciação (*f.*) depreciation; fig., disparagement.
depreciador –dora (*adj.*) depreciating; disparaging;(*m.,f.*) depreciator; disparager.
depreciar (*v.t.*) to depreciate, debase, lower in value; to

disparage; to underestimate; (*v.r.*) to lose prestige.
depreciativo –va (*adj.*) depreciative.
depreciável (*adj.*) depreciable.
depredação (*f.*) depredation.
depredador –dora (*adj.*) depredating; (*m.,f.*) depredator, spoiler.
depredar (*v.t.*) to depredate, plunder, pillage, spoil.
depredatório –ria (*adj.*) depredatory, plundering, predatory, rapacious.
depreender (*v.t.*) to gather, infer, deduce, conclude.
depressa [DE+PRESSA] (*adv.*) fast, swiftly, quickly, rapidly; hurriedly, hastily. **mais**—, faster. **o mais— possível**, the soonest (quickest) possible. **o mais—que puder**, the soonest you can, as soon as you can. **Vamos**—, Let's hurry.
depressão (*f.*) depression (all senses); a lowering or sinking; a hollow; reduction, diminution; dejection of spirit, the blues.—**barométrica**, a lowering of barometric pressure.
depressivo –va (*adj.*) depressive.
depressor –sora (*adj.*) depressing; (*m.,f.*) depressor.
deprimente (*adj.*) depressing; discouraging; degrading.
deprimido –da (*adj.*) depressed; dejected, downcast; heartsick.
deprimir (*v.t.*) to depress, lower; to debase; to depreciate, disparage.
dépside, depsídio (*m., Chem.*) depside.
depuração (*f.*) depuration, purification.
depurador –dora (*adj.*) purifying; (*m.,f.*) purifier.
depurante (*adj.*) depurant, purifying.
depurar (*v.t.*) to depurate, purify, cleanse; (*v.f.*) to purify (cleanse) oneself.
depurativo –va (*adj.; m., Med.*) depurative.
deputação (*f.*) deputation.
deputado –da (*m.,f.*) deputy, commissioner, agent; member of a legislative assembly. **Câmara dos—s**, Chamber of Deputies, House of Representatives.
deputar (*v.t.*) to depute, commission.
deque (*m.*) deck [= CONVÉS].
dequitação, dequitadura (*f.*) = DELIVRAMENTO.
dequitar-se (*v.r., Med.*) to expel the afterbirth.
der+verb endings are forms of DAR [39].
deriva (*f., Navigation*) drift, leeway; (*Artil.*) deflection; (*Aeron.*) drift angle. **medidor de**—, drift meter.
derivação (*f.*) derivation; shift; drift; deviation; fig., origin; (*Elec.*) a branch conductor.
derivada (*f., Math.*) derivative; differential coefficient or quotient.
derivado (*m., Gram.*) derivative.—**s de aço**, steel products.
derivante (*adj.*) derivational.
derivar (*v.t.*) to turn the course (as of a stream of water); to switch, shunt; to deflect, turn aside; (*v.i.*) to run, flow; to elapse; (*v.r.*) to originate from; to drift.—**com o movimento da maré**, to drift with the tide.—**de**, to derive from (as one word from another).
derivativo –va (*adj.*) derivative; (*m., Med.*) derivation.
derivável (*adj.*) derivable.
derma (*m.* or *f., Anat., Zool.*) derma.
dermatite (*f., Med.*) dermatitis.
dermatóbia (*f.*) a genus (*Dermatobia*) of botflies. Cf. BERNE.
dermatoblástio (*m., Anat., Zool.*) dermoblast.
dermatogênio (*m., Bot.*) dermatogen.
dermatóide (*adj.*) dermatoid.
dermatol (*m., Chem.*) Dermatol, bismuth subgallate.
dermatologia (*f.*) dermatology.
dermatologista (*m.,f.*) dermatologist.
dermatoplastia (*f., Surg.*) dermatoplasty.
derme (*v.*) = DERMA.
dermesto (*m.*) buffalo bug, tapestry beetle, carpet beetle, larder beetle.
dérmico –ca (*adj.*) dermic.
dermite (*v.*) = DERMATITE.
dermoblástio (*m.*) dermoblast.
dermóide (*adj.*) dermoid, dermatoid.
dermologia (*f.*) = DERMATOLOGIA.
derrabado –da (*adj.*) bobtailed.
derrabar (*v.t.*) to cut off the RABO (tail) of.
derradeiras (*f.pl., colloq.*) afterbirth [= PÁREAS].
derradeiro –ra (*adj.*) last, hindmost; final, ultimate.
derrama (*f.*) act of pruning branches; spilling, diffusion; levy, tax.
derramamento (*m.*) a spilling or pouring; dispersion

spreading, diffusion.—**cerebral,** brain hemorrhage.—**de sangue,** bloodshed.

derramar (*v.t.*) to spill, shed (water, tears, blood); to strew, sprinkle; to diffuse, disperse; to disseminate; to scatter; to pour, lavish; to prune (trees); to apportion a tax; (*v.r.*) to pour, flow, issue, spill, spread, diffuse.

derrame (*m.*) = DERRAMAMENTO.

derrancar (*v.t.*) to spoil, ruin; to taint; to corrupt; (*v.r.*) to turn rancid; to become depraved.

derrapagem (*f.*) skidding.

derrapar (*v.i.*) to skid.

derreado –**da** (*adj.*) bowed down (with fatigue, old age, adversity, etc.); worn out, done in; jaded; (*f., Bot.*) the tree heath (*Erica arborea*).

derrear (*v.t.*) to bend (the head, back or body) by, or as if by, a heavy weight or a beating; to jade; (*v,r.*) to bend down; to sag; to jade.

derredor [DE+REDOR] (*adv.*) around. **em—de** (*prep.*) around, about; encompassing.

derregar (*v.t.*) to dig drainage ditches.

derrelito –**ta** (*adj.*) derelict, abandoned.

derrengado –**da** (*adj.*) sway-backed, broken-down [horse].

derrengar (*v.t.*) to beat on the back; (*v.i.,v.r.*) to mince, simper.

derretedura (*f.*) act of melting; a molten something.

derreter (*v.t.*) to melt, liquefy, fuse; to make gentle, mollify; (*v.r.*) to melt; to become tenderhearted; to be overpolite; to "drool" (over someone); to melt away (disappear).

derretido –**da** (*adj.*) melted, molten.

derretimento (*m.*) a melting; (*colloq.*) affectation; tenderheartedness.

derribada (*f.*) = DERRUBADA.

derribadinha (*f.*) clearing of a small tract of land.

derribamento (*m.*) act of felling.

derribar (*v.t.*) to fell, strike down, cut down; (*v.r.*) to throw oneself on the ground. Cf. DERRUBAR.

derriça (*f., colloq.*) act of untangling, etc. See the verb DERRIÇAR.

derriçar (*v.t.*) to disentangle; to banter; to wrangle; (*colloq.*) to court; to flirt; to philander; to strip ripe coffee berries from the branches.

derriço (*m.*) courtship; love-making; flirtation; dalliance; sweetheart; banter; derision.

derrisão (*f.*) derision.

derriscar (*v.t.*) to scratch out (as, a name on a list).

derrisório –**ria** (*adj.*) derisory, derisive.

derrocado –**da** (*adj.*) overthrown; demolished; ruined; (*f.*) demolition, overthrow, ruin, downfall, debacle.

derrocador –**dora** (*adj.*) destructive; (*m.,f.*) destroyer, demolisher.

derrocar (*v.t.*) to destroy, demolish, overturn, raze; to overthrow; to humble, subdue; (*v.r.*) to cave in, fall down.

derrogação (*f.*) derogation [= DERROGAMENTO].

derrogador –**dora** (*adj.*) detracting; (*m.,f.*) detractor, derogator.

derrogamento (*m.*) = DERROGAÇÃO.

derrogante (*adj.*) derogative to or of.

derrogar (*v.t.*) to derogate. [But only in the sense of annuling or repealing in part (as, a law). To derogate from, detract from, disparage, depreciate, is DEPRECIAR, DETRAIR, DETRATAR.]

derrogatório –**ria** (*adj.*) derogatory.

derrota (*f.*) rout, defeat, overthrow, dispersion; ship's course; route; routine; rotation of stars; [*GBAT*: "a nautical term meaning detour, specifically applied in Pará to the course followed by ships in entering the Amazon River upon leaving the Atlantic Ocean, due to the fact that the old colonial channel between Chaves on the island of Marajó and Macapá has been lost, forcing ships to make this lengthy detour."].—**estimada,** (*Navig.*) dead reckoning.

derrotado –**da** (*adj.*) routed, defeated; down and out; downcast; of ships, off course.

derrotador –**dora** (*adj.*) defeating.

derrotar (*v.t.*) to put to rout, utterly defeat; to overthrow; to beat, outdo (in a contest); to exhaust, tire out; (*v.i.*) of ships, to be driven, or to go, off course; to follow a given course; (*v.r.*) to lose one's way.

derrotismo (*m.*) defeatism.

derrotista (*m.,f.*) defeatist.

derruba (*f.*) felling of trees (to clear the land); wholesale dismissal of public employees when a change of ad-

ministration takes place.

derrubado –**da** (*adj.*) overthrown, demolished; felled; (*f.*) = DERRUBA.

derrubamento (*m.*) act of overthrowing, etc. See the verb DERRUBAR.

derrubar (*v.t.*) to overthrow, overturn, prostrate, throw down; to unseat; to topple; to knock down.—**árvores,** to fell trees. Cf. DERRIBAR.

derrube (*m.*) = DERRUBA.

derruir (*v.t.*) to knock down; to destroy.

dervixe, derviz (*m.*) dervish, fakir [= DAROÊS].

dês = DESDE.

desabado –**da** (*adj.*) of a hat, having a wide or fallen brim; caved in. **chapéu—,** slouch hat; (*m.*) hillside, sloping ground.

desabafado –**da** (*adj.*) uncovered; unencumbered.

desabafamento (*m.*) = DESABAFO.

desabafar (*v.t.*) to free (from obstructions); to clear, loosen, disentangle; to give vent to (one's feelings); to get something off one's chest; to clear off (land); (*v.r.*) to express oneself freely.

desabafo (*m.*) act of freeing, releasing, disencumbering, etc.; free expression of one's feelings.

desabalado –**da** (*adj., colloq.*) headlong; immense.

desabamento (*m.*) cave-in; a crumbling or falling down.

desabar (*v.i.*) to cave in, crumble; to collapse, topple.

desabe (*m.*) a cave-in [= DESABAMENTO]; collapsed part of a building.

desabilidade (*f.*) want of ability [but not disability which is INCAPACIDADE, INABILIDADE.]

desabilitar (*v.t.*) to dishabilitate, incapacitate; (*colloq.*) to disqualify (in a competition).

desabitado –**da** (*adj.*) uninhabited; untenanted; unoccupied; deserted.

desabitar (*v.t.*) to disoccupy (a residence).

desabituar (*v.t.*) to disaccustom.—**de,** to cure of a habit. —**-se de,** to become disaccustomed to.—**-se de fumar,** to break the smoking habit.

desabocar (*v.i.*) to utter nonsense.

desabonado –**da** (*adj.*) discredited; moneyless; unsponsored.

desabonador –**dora** (*adj.*) discrediting; (*m.,f.*)depreciàtor.

desabonar (*v.t.*) to discredit, depreciate; (*v.r.*) to lose one's credit, prestige, reputation, etc.

desabonatório –**ria** (*adj.*) disreputable.

desabono (*m.*) discredit.

desabotinado –**da** (*adj.*) reckless, foolhardy; speedy.

desabotoar (*v.t.*) to unbutton; to unloosen; (*v.i.*) of flowers, to unfold; (*v.r.*) to loosen one's tongue.

desabrido –**da** (*adj.*) insolent, rude; brusque, gruff; disagreeable; unfriendly; harsh, severe, violent, ornery. **linguagem—,** unrestrained language.

desabrigado –**da** (*adj.*) unsheltered, exposed, open.

desabrigar (*v.t.*) to rob of shelter; to abandon, cast off; (*v.r.*) to leave one's shelter.

desabrigo (*m.*) want of shelter or protection.

desabrimento (*m.*) harshness, rudeness; acrimony; severity (of weather).

desabrir (*v.t.*) to let go of; (*v.r.*) to become irritable.

desabrochado –**da** (*adj.*) unclasped, unloosened.

desabrochar (*v.t.*) to unclasp, unbutton, unfasten; (*v.i.*) to burgeon; to bloom, flower; (*v.r.*) to free oneself.

desabrolhar (*v.i.*) of flowers, to unfold.

desabusado –**da** (*adj.*) free from prejudice or error; bold, impudent; unrestrained, rampant, unchecked.

desabusar (*v.t.*) to disabuse; to disillusion; (*v.r.*) to free oneself of error.

desabuso (*m.*) disabuse; disillusionment.

desaça(i)mar (*v.t.*) to unmuzzle.

desacampar (*v.i.*) to break camp.

desacanhado –**da** (*adj.*) bold, not shy; self-assured.

desacatado –**da** (*adj.*) not given due and proper respect; offended.

desacatamento (*m.*) disrespect.

desacatar (*v.t.*) to disrespect, disregard, slight; (*slang*) to knock one's eye out (with beauty, etc.).

desacato (*m.*) want of respect; irreverence; contempt (of authority).

desacautelado –**da** (*adj.*) careless, heedless; improvident.

desacautelar (*v.t.*) to be careless of; (*v.r.*) to be improvident, thoughtless, heedless.

desaceitar (*v.t.*) to reject, refuse to accept.

desaceito –**ta** (*adj.*) rejected, refused.

desaceleração (*f.*) deceleration.

desacelerar (*v.t.,v.i.*) to decelerate.
desacertado –**da** (*adj.*) ill-advised, imprudent; wrong.
desacertar (*v.t.*) to bungle; to do anything wrongly; (*v.r.*) to get out of whack.—**o passo,** to break step.
desacêrto (*m.*) blunder, fault, error, mistake.
desachegar (*v.t.*) to separate, disunite.
desacidificação (*f.*) deacidification.
desacidificar or **desacidular** (*v.t.*) to deacidify.
desacobardar (*v.t.*) to embolden; (*v.r.*) to grow bold.
desacochar (*v.i.*) to come down a peg, off one's high horse; to be at a loss, embarrassed.
desacoimar (*v.t.*) to absolve of blame; to relieve of a fine.
desacoitado –**da** (*adj.*) without refuge, shelterless.
desacoitar (*v.t.*) to unearth (a rabbit, etc.); to dislodge.
desacolchetar (*v.t.*) to unhook (a garment); to unclasp.
desacolher (*v.t.*) to not welcome, not receive.
desacolherar (*v.t.*) to unpen (animals).
desacolhimento (*m.*) refusal of welcome.
desacomodado –**da** (*adj.*) disarranged, disturbed.
desacomodar (*v.t.*) to discommode; to displace, disarrange, disturb.
desacompanhado –**da** (*adj.*) unaccompanied, unattended.
desacompanhar (*v.t.*) not to accompany.
desaconselhado –**da** (*adj.*) ill-advised; heedless.
desaconselhar (*v.t.*) to dissuade, divert (from a purpose); to advise against.
desaconselhável (*adj.*) inadvisable.
desacorçoar (*v.*) = DESCOROÇOAR.
desacoplar (*v.t.*, *Elec.*) to uncouple.
desacordado –**da** (*adj.*) unconscious.
desacordar (*v.t.*) to render discordant; (*v.i.*) to disagree; to be incoherent; to be discordant; to faint; (*v.r.*) to lose consciousness.—**se de,** to agree with no longer. Cf. DISCORDAR.
desacorde (*adj.*) discordant; dissonant; (*m., Music*) discord.
desacôrdo (*m.*) want of accord; disagreement; dissent; difference; unconformity; disharmony; loss of consciousness. Cf. DISCÓRDIA.
desacoroçoar (*v.*) = DESCOROÇOAR.
desacorrentar (*v.t.*) to unchain, unfetter.
desacostumado –**da** (*adj.*) unaccustomed, uncommon, non-habitual, unusual.
desacostumar (*v.t.*) to disaccustom; (*v.r.*) to break oneself of a habit.
desacreditado –**da** (*adj.*) discredited, disreputable.
desacreditador –**dora** (*adj.*) discrediting.
desacreditar (*v.t.*) to discredit, disparage, defame; to disbelieve; (*v.r.*) to lose face, prestige, reputation, etc.
desacumular (*v.t.*) to unpile; to unstack; to reduce the numbers or quantity of.
desadmoestar (*v.*) = DESACONSELHAR.
desadorar (*v.t.*) to detest; to disapprove of; to annoy; (*v.i.*) to suffer pain; to fly off the handle.
desadormecer, –**dormentar** (*v.t.*) to wake up.
desadornado –**da** (*adj.*) unornamented; untrimmed.
desadornar (*v.t.*) to divest of ornament.
desadôrno (*m.*) want of ornament; simplicity.
desadôro (*m.*) suffering of pain; annoyance.
desadvertido –**da** (*adj.*) inadvertent.
desafaimar (*v.t.*) to relieve the hunger of.
desafamar (*v.t.*) to defame.
desafazer (*v.t.*) to dishabituate (–**se,** oneself).
desafear (*v.t.*) to relieve the ugliness of.
desafeição (*f.*) disaffection; disinclination.
desafeiçoado –**da** (*adj.*) disaffected, disloyal.
desafeiçoar (*v.t.*) to disaffect, alienate, estrange; (*v.r.*) to lose one's affection for another.
desafeitar (*v.*) = DESENFEITAR.
desafeito –**ta** (*adj.*) unaccustomed.
desaferrar (*v.t.*) to unhook; to unloose; to weigh anchor. —**se de,** to free oneself of.
desaferrolhar (*v.t.*) to unbolt.
desafervoar (*v.t.*) to cool the fervor of.
desafetação (*f.*) unaffectedness.
desafetado –**da** (*adj.*) unsophisticated, unaffected.
desafeto –**ta** (*adj.*) disaffected; (*m.*) want of affection; disinclination; (*colloq.*) rival, enemy.
desafiado –**da** (*adj.*) blunt, dull; challenged; (*m.,f.*) person challenged.
desafiador –**dora, desafiante** (*adj.*) challenging; (*m.,f.*) challenger.
desafiar (*v.t.*) to challenge, defy; to baffle (description, pursuit); to dare, brave; to provoke; to blunt.

desafilhar (*v.t.*) to wean young animals; to separate them from their mothers.
desafinação (*f.*) dissonance.
desafinado –**da** (*adj.*) out of tune, dissonant, discordant.
desafinar (*v.t.*) to untune; (*v.i.*) to get out of tune; to play out of tune; (*v.r.*) to get out of sorts.
desafio (*m.*) challenge; defiance; (*colloq.*) a sort of musical duel between two singers of improvisations.
desafivelar (*v.t.*) to unbuckle, unclasp.
desafixar (*v.t.*) to unfix.
desafogado –**da** (*adj.*) relieved; unchoked, open, clear.
desafogar (*v.t.*) to unclutter, unchoke; to ease, relieve, disencumber; to free from pain, anxiety; to release from pressure, loosen; to give vent to feelings; (*v.r.*) to make oneself comfortable; to unburden oneself.
desafôgo (*m.*) alleviation, relief; respite.
desafoguear (*v.t.*) to cool (the face).
desaforado –**da** (*adj.*) rude, impudent, insolent, abusive.
desaforar (*v.t.*) to exempt from rent payment; to disfranchise; (*v.r.*) to relinquish a right or privilege; to become insolent, abusive.
desafôro (*m.*) outrage, affront, insult; effrontery, impudence; impertinence.
desafortunado –**da** (*adj.*) unhappy, unlucky.
desafreguesar (*v.t.*) to divert the customers of.—**se de,** to discontinue one's patronage of.
desafronta (*f.*) redress.
desafrontado –**da** (*adj.*) redressed; revenged.
desafrontar (*v.t.*) to redress; to avenge.
desagaloar (*v.t.*) to strip the gold braid from.
desagarrado –**da** (*adj.*) free, detached, unattached. Cf. DESGARRADO.
desagasalhado –**da** (*adj.*) unsheltered.
desagasalhar (*v.t.*) to deprive of shelter; (*v.r.*) to go without shelter.
desagasalho (*m.*) want of shelter, of clothing, of welcome.
desagastar (*v.t.*) to quiet down, appease; (*v.r.*) to cool down.
desaglomerar (*v.t.*) to de-agglomerate.
desagradado –**da** (*adj.*) displeased.
desagradar (*v.t.*) to displease, dissatisfy; to disgruntle.
desagradável (*adj.*) disagreeable, unpleasant; ungracious; pesky; grating [sound].—**ao gôsto,** unpalatable.
desagradecer (*v.t.*) not to thank, be ungrateful for.
desagradecido –**da** (*adj.*) ungrateful, thankless.
desagradecimento (*m.*) ingratitude, thanklessness.
desagrado (*m.*) displeasure; unpleasantness.
desagravar (*v.t.*) to redress (a wrong); to avenge; to make amends to.
desagravo (*m.*) redress, amends; satisfaction of a grievance.
desagregação (*f.*) disaggregation.
desagregado –**da** (*adj.*) disunited.
desagregante (*adj.*) disaggregating.
desagregar (*v.t.*) to disaggregate, separate; (*v.r.*) to crumble.
desagregável (*adj.*) separable.
desagrilhoar (*v.t.*) to unfetter.
desaguadouro (*m.*) drainage ditch; spillway.
desaguamento (*m.*) drainage.
desaguar [8] (*v.t.*) to drain, draw off.—**se em,** to flow, discharge, into.
desaguaxar (*v.t.*) to exercise a horse which has been permitted to grow fat and lazy.
desaguisado –**da** (*m.*) quarrel, clash, conflict.
desairado –**da** (*adj.*) = DESAIROSO.
desairar (*v.t.*) to render inelegant or uncouth; (*v.r.*) to become so.
desaire (*m.*) inelegance; gaucherie; want of distinction; uncouthness; snub; rebuff; reverse, ill luck.
desairoso –**sa** (*adj.*) inelegant; discreditable; gauche; undistinguished; uncouth; unlucky.
desajeitado –**da** (*adj.*) clumsy, awkward, unskillful, fumbling, maladroit; tactless; gawky, uncouth, loutish; cumbersome, ungainly.
desajoujar (*v.t.*) to unyoke , unharness (animals).
desajudado –**da** (*adj.*) helpless.
desajudar (*v.t.*) not to help.
desajuizado –**da** [u-i] (*adj.*) unwise, indiscreet; foolish.
desajuizar [u-i] (*v.t.*) to render foolish.
desajuntar (*v.t.*) to disjoin.
desajustamento (*m.*) disagreement [= DESAJUSTE]; ma adjustment.
desajustado –**da** (*adj.*) maladjusted.

desajustar (*v.t.*) to break an agreement; to disadjust, disarrange; to disunite, separate (partners, allies).
desajuste (*m.*) disagreement.
desalagar (*v.t.*) to drain (land).
desalastrar (*v.t.*) to remove the ballast from.
desalbardar (*v.t.*) to remove the pack saddle from.
desaleitar (*v.t.*) to wean [= DESMAMAR].
desalentado –da (*adj.*) dispirited, disheartened; dejected; heavyhearted, heartsick.
desalentador –dora (*adj.*) discouraging, depressing; gloomy.
desalentar (*v.t.*) to discourage, throw cold water on; to dismay; to depress, dishearten; (*v.r.*) to despond.
desalento (*m.*) discouragement, disheartening; dejection; despondency; the blues; hopelessness.
desalforjar (*v.t.*) to remove from the saddlebag or pocket.
desalgemar (*v.t.*) to unshackle, unfetter.
desalhear (*v.t.*) to alienate [= ALHEAR].
desaliar (*v.t.*) to disally, sunder; (*v.r.*) to dissassociate oneself.
desalijar (*v.t.*) to jettison.
desalinhado –da (*adj.*) out of line; disheveled, disorderly, unkempt, untidy, slovenly, slipshod, dowdy, frowzy.
desalinhar (*v.t.*) to put out of line; to disorder, disarrange; to dishevel.
desalinhavar (*v.t.*) to remove basting stitches from.
desalinho (*m.*) disarray; untidiness; unkemptness.
desalistar (*v.t.*) to take off the list; (*Mil.*) to muster out.
desalmado –da (*adj.*) inhuman, cruel, ruthless; unfeeling.
desalojamento (*m.*) dislodging, dislodgement.
desalojar (*v.t.*) to dislodge, oust (de, from).
desalterar (*v.t.*) to quench (thirst).
desalugado –da (*adj.*) unoccupied (not rented); untenanted.
desalumiado –da (*adj.*) without light; unenlightened.
desamabilidade (*f.*) discourtesy.
desamado –da (*adj.*) unloved.
desamalgamar (*v.t.*) to de-amalgamate.
desamamentar (*v.*) = DESMAMAR.
desamanhar (*v.t.*) to muss (the hair, the clothes).
desamar (*v.t.*) to cease to love; (*v.r.*) to hate oneself.
desamarrado –da (*adj.*) untied; adrift.
desamarrar (*v.t.*) to untie, unfasten; to untether; to separate, detach; to unmoor (a vessel).
desamarrotar (*v.t.*) to unwrinkle (cloth, paper).
desamassar (*v.t.*) to smooth out (something that has been crushed, as a hat or piece of tin).
desamável (*adj.*) unamiable, ungracious, unkind; uncomplimentary.
desambição (*f.*) want of ambition; unselfishness.
desambicioso –sa (*adj.*) unambitious; modest.
desambientado –da (*adj.*) out of one's natural element or surroundings, as a stranger in a foreign land.
desamigar (*v.t.*) to spoil the friendship of.
desamigo –ga (*adj.*) unfriendly.
desamizade (*adj.*) unfriendliness.
desamodorrar (*v.t.,v.i.*) to wake up, stir.
desamolgar (*v.*) = DESAMASSAR.
desamontoar (*v.t.*) to unpile, tear down (a pile).
desamor (*m.*) disaffection; want of love; disdain, unkindliness.
desamorável, desamoroso –sa (*adj.*) unloving, unkindly.
desamortalhar (*v.t.*) to unshroud.
desamortizar (*v.t.*) to convey (property) out of mortmain.
desamotinar (*v.t.*) to quell a riot.
desamparado –da (*adj.*) forsaken, abandoned; forlorn, solitary.
desamparar (*v.t.*) to forsake, abandon.
desamparo (*m.*) destitution, distress.
desamuar (*v.t.*) to put in good humor; (*v.r.*) to stop pouting, being sulky.
desancador –dora (*m.,f.*) one who beats (animals).
desancamento (*m.*) act of beating.
desancar (*v.t.*) to beat, drub, maul; to belabor; to lambaste.
desancorar (*v.t.,v.i.*) to weigh anchor.
desanda (*f.*) rebuke, reprimand, a dressing down.
desandar (*v.t.*) to turn back; to back up; to unscrew; to let loose (blows, laughter); (*v.i.*) to go back, retrocede; (*colloq.*) to go bad, spoil, worsen, deteriorate.—a chorar, to burst into tears.—a correr, to break into a run.
desando (*m.*) act of turning back, etc. See the verb DESANDAR; a worsening, deterioration.
desanelar (*v.t.*) to uncurl.

desanexação [ks] (*f.*) disjunction.
desanexar [ks] (*v.t.*) to disconnect.
desanexo –xa [ks] (*adj.*) disconnected, unattached.
desanichar (*v.t.*) to dislodge (as from a niche).
desanimação (*f.*) disanimation, depression.
desanimado –da (*adj.*) downhearted, depressed, dejected; downcast, discouraged; dispirited.
desanimar (*v.t.*) to discourage, depress; (*v.i.*) to despond, lose heart; to droop; to despair.
desânimo (*m.*) discouragement; dejection; despondency.
desaninhar (*v.t.*) to remove from the nest; to dislodge; (*v.r.*) to come out of hiding.
desanojar (*v.t.*) to condole with; to cheer; (*v.r.*) to cheer up.
desanuviado –da (*adj.*) unclouded. acordar com a cabeça—, to wake up with a clear head.
desanuviar (*v.t.,v.r.*) to uncloud; to clear up.
desapadrinhar (*v.t.*) to withdraw one's protection (of another) or one's sponsorship (of a cause or project).
desapagar (*v.t.*) to obliterate, blot out.
desapaixonado –da (*adj.*) dispassionate; impartial, unbiased; detached.
desapaixonar (*v.t.*) to calm, soothe (the feelings).
desaparafusar (*v.t.*) to unscrew; (*v.r.*) to come unscrewed.
desaparecer (*v.i.*) to disappear, vanish.—a olhos vistos, to disappear before one's very eyes.
desaparecido –da (*adj.*) disappeared, vanished, lost, missing; (*m.,f.*) missing person.
desaparecimento (*m.*) disappearance.
desaparelhado –da (*adj.*) unequipped; unprepared; unprovided with.
desaparelhar (*v.t.*) to strip, dismantle; to unrig (a ship); to disable; to disarm.
desaparição (*f.*) disappearance; fig., demise.
desapartar (*v.t.*) to part, separate [= APARTAR].
desapear (*v.*) = APEAR.
desapegado –da (*adj.*) detached, cool, indifferent.
desapegar (*v.*) = DESPEGAR.
desapêgo (*m.*) detachment, indifference, unconcern.
desaperceber (*v.t.*) to deprive, strip, of equipment, munitions, provisions, etc.
desapercebido –da (*adj.*) unequipped, unprovided with, unfurnished; deprived of. [Often erroneously used in place of DESPERCEBIDO, unperceived].
desaperrar (*v.t.*) to uncock (firearm).
desapertado –da (*adj.*) unloosened, unfastened.
desapertar (*v.t.*) to unloose, unfasten; (*v.r.*) to come loose; (*slang*) to get out of a tight spot.
desapêrto (*m.*) a loosening or unfastening; (*slang*) getting out of a tight spot.
desapiedado –da (*adj.*) ruthless, relentless, pitiless, uncompassionate, unmerciful.
desapiedar [29] (*v.t.*) to render cruel, pitiless.—-se de, to be insensible to the misfortunes of others.
desaplaudir (*v.t.*) to disapprove, not applaud.
desaplauso (*m.*) want of applause, disapproval.
desaplicar (*v.t.*) to divert the application of (capital, attention, etc.).
desapoderar (*v.t.*) to dispossess.—-se de, to divest oneself of (possessions).
desapoiar (*v.t.*) to deprive of APOIO (support, approval).
desapoio (*m.*) want of support or approval.
desapontado –da (*adj.*) disappointed.
desapontamento (*m.*) disappointment, letdown.
desapontar (*v.t.*) to disappoint. Cf. DESILUDIR.
desaponto (*m.*) = DESAPONTAMENTO.
desapoquentar (*v.t.*) to allay another's anger.
desaportuguesar (*v.t.*) to render unlike Portuguese.
desaposentar (*v.t.*) to deprive of lodging.
desapossar (*v.t.*) to dispossess, deprive (de, of).
desaprazer [30] (*v.t.*) to displease.
desaprazível (*adj.*) unpleasant, disagreeable.
desapreciar (*v.t.*) to disparage; to underrate.
desapreço [prê] (*m.*) disparagement.
desaprender (*v.t.*) to unlearn, forget.
desapressado –da (*adj.*) unhurried.
desapressar (*v.t.*) to relieve, release (de, from); (*v.r.*) to slow down; to free oneself of.
desapropositado –da (*adj.*) unsuitable; out of the question.
desapropriação (*f.*) expropriation.
desapropriar (*v.t.*) to expropriate.—de, to dispossess, deprive of.
desaprovação (*f.*) disapprobation; disallowance; dis-

pleasure; reproval. [But not disapproval, which is REPROVAÇÃO, CENSURA.]

desaprovador –**dora** (*adj.*) disapproving, reproving; (*m.,f.*) one who disapproves or reproves.

desaprovar (*v.t.*) to disapprove; to disallow; to reprove, condemn.

desaprovativo –**va** (*adj.*) disapprobative.

desaproveitado –**da** (*adj.*) squandered, wasted; not used to best advantage; unimproved [land].

desaproveitamento (*m.*) waste, squandering; want of progress in school work.

desaproveitar (*v.t.*) to waste, squander; to misuse.

desaprumado –**da** (*adj.*) out of plumb.

desaprumar (*v.t.*) to put out of plumb; (*v.r.*) to get out of plumb.

desaprumo (*m.*) want of plumbness; fig., misbehavior.

desapuro (*m.*) inelegance, unrefinement (of language); want of carefulness, neatness, correctness, etc. (in a piece of work).

desaquartelar (*v.t.*) to deprive of quarters.

desaquecer (*v.t.*) to cool.

desquinhoar (*v.t.*) to deprive of a share; (*v.r.*) to forego one's share.

desaranhar (*v.t.*) to rid of cobwebs; fig., to enlighten the understanding of.

desarborizar (*v.t.*) to remove the trees from.

desarcar (*v.t.*) to remove the hoops from barrels; (*v.r.*) to come apart.

desarear (*v.t.*) to remove the AREIA (sand) from. (Do not confuse with DESARREAR.]

desargentizar (*v.t.*) to desilverize.

desarmado –**da** (*adj.*) disarmed, unarmed; disassembled, unassembled; of deer, having no antlers.—**para a vida**, unprepared for life. **vista**—, unaided eye.

desarmamento (*m.*) disarmament.

desarmar (*v.t.*) to disarm; to deprive of armament; to disassemble, dismantle (clock, gun, ship, etc.).

desarmonia (*f.*) disharmony, discord; dissonance.

desarmônico –**ca** (*adj.*) inharmonious.

desarmonizar (*v.t.*) to disharmonize.

desaromar, **desaromatizar** (*v.t.*) to deodorize.

desarraigamento (*m.*) uprooting.

desarraigar (*v.t.*) to uproot, eradicate, extirpate.

desarrancar (*v.*) = ARRANCAR.

desarranchar (*v.t.*) to break up a RANCHO (mess); (*v.i.,v.r.*) to discontinue eating at the common mess.

desarranjado –**da** (*adj.*) out of order, out of kilter, on the blink.

desarranjar (*v.t.*) to disarrange, disturb, put out of order; to upset; (*v.r.*) to get out of order.

desarranjo (*m.*) disarrangement, disarray, disorder; upset; bother, annoyance, inconvenience; *(colloq.)* diarrhea.

desarrazoado –**da** (*adj.*) senseless, unreasonable, without rhyme or reason, absurd; perverse.

desarrazoamento (*m.*) unreasonable action.

desarrazoar (*v.i.*) to talk or act unreasonably, without sense.

desarrear (*v.t.*) to remove the ARREIOS (harness) from. [Do not confuse with DESAREAR.]

desarregaçar (*v.t.*) to turn down [sleeves, trouser legs].

desarreigar (*v.*) = DESARRAIGAR.

desarrimar (*v.t.*) to take away the ARIMO (support) of.

desarrimo (*m.*) want of support; non-support, abandonment of family.

desarriscar (*v.t.*) to scratch out; to check the name off a list; (*v.r.*) to fulfill one's Easter duty.

desarrochar (*v.t.*) to loosen (as the pack on an animal's back).

desarrolhar (*v.t.*) to uncork; to scatter (cattle).

desarroupado –**da** (*adj.*) unclothed; nude.

desarrufar (*v.r.*) to put in good humor with; (*v.r.*) to regain one's good feeling toward.

desarrufo (*m.*) reconciliation.

desarrugar (*v.*) = DESENRUGAR.

desarrumação (*f.*) confusion, disorder, disarray, muss, jumble; untidiness.

desarrumado –**da** (*adj.*) untidy, disordered; out of a job.

desarrumar (*v.t.*) to disarrange; to unpack (baggage).

desarticulação (*f.*) disarticulation.

desarticulado –**da** (*adj.*) out of joint.

desarticular (*v.t.*) to disarticulate, disjoint; to break up (a gang).

desartificioso –**sa** (*adj.*) guileless; simple.

desarvorado –**da** (*adj.*) dismasted; adrift; at large (having

fled); aimless, disorientated.

desarvorar (*v.t.*) to dismast, dismantle; (*v.i.*, *colloq.*) to bolt, run away.

desasa (*f.*) molt (of birds).

desasar (*v.t.*) to remove the ASAS (wings or handles) of; to beat up.

desasir (*v.t.*) to drop (from the hand).—**se de**, to rid oneself of.

desasnar (*v.t.*) to render less like an ASNO (ass), less ignorant.

desassanhar (*v.t.*) to placate.

desassazonado –**da** (*adj.*) out of season; inopportune; unripe.

desasseado –**da** (*adj.*) untidy, uncleanly, not neat, dirty.

desassear (*v.t.*) to destroy the ASSEIO (cleanliness, neatness) of; to make dirty, untidy.

desasseio (*m.*) want of ASSEIO (tidiness, cleanliness).

desassemelhar (*v.t.*) to render dissimilar.

desassestar (*v.t.*) to un-point (a gun); to un-train (binoculars).

desassimilação (*f.*, *Biol.*, *Physiol.*) catabolism [= CATABOLISMO].

desassimilar (*v.t.*) to unassimilate.

desassisado –**da** (*adj.*) wanting in good sense.

desassisar (*v.t.*) to make crazy; (*v.r.*) to lose one's good sense, go mad.

desassociar (*v.t.*) to dissociate, separate.

desassombrado –**da** (*adj.*) frank, open; fearless; not shady or shadowy.

desassombrar (*v.t.*) to render free of fear or of shadow; (*v.r.*) to become unafraid.

desassombro (*m.*) fearlessness, intrepidity, boldness, resoluteness; frankness.

desassorear (*v.t.*) to remove the silt or sand from (a harbor, river channel, etc.) by dredging.

desassossegado –**da** (*adj.*) unquiet, uneasy, restless; hectic.

desassossegar (*v.t.*) to disquiet, disturb.

desassossêgo (*m.*) uneasiness, unrest, disturbance; want of peace, quiet.

desassustar (*v.t.*) to allay the fright of; to tranquilize; (*v.r.*) to lose one's fright.

desastrado –**da** (*adj.*) disastrous, calamitous, hapless; awkward, bungling; clumsy; tactless.

desastre (*m.*) disaster, calamity; accident, misfortune; fatality.

desastroso –**sa** (*adj.*) disastrous; unhappy, unlucky.

desatacar (*v.t.*) to untie, unloose, unlatch, unlace, unbuckle.

desatado –**da** (*adj.*) untied; loose; free.

desatadura (*f.*), **desatamento** (*m.*) act of untying.

desatar (*v.t.*) to untie, unfasten, unlace, unbind; to untangle, unravel; to loose, release.—**a chorar**, to burst into tears.—**a língua**, to loose the tongue.—**a rir**, to break out laughing.

desatarraxar (*v.t.*) to unscrew, unbolt.

desatascar (*v.t.*) to pull (car, animal, person, etc.) out of a mudhole.

desataviado –**da** (*adj.*) simple, unadorned; ungarnished.

desataviar (*v.t.*) to strip of ornament; (*v.r.*) to strip, undress.

desatemorizar (*v.t.*) to remove the fear from; to embolden, reassure.

desatenção (*f.*) inattention; woolgathering; inconsiderateness; slight, disregard.

desatencioso –**sa** (*adj.*) inattentive; inconsiderate; disobliging; unmannerly.

desatender (*v.t.*) to disregard, neglect, pay no attention to, ignore; to turn a deaf ear to; to refuse, deny, turn down.

desatentar (*v.t.*) to pay no attention to.

desatento –**ta** (*adj.*) heedless, thoughtless; unmindful; absentminded; unobserving.

desaterrar (*v.t.*) to remove excess earth from; to tear down a hill. Cf. DESMONTAR.

desatêrro (*m.*) leveling of land; land that has been cleared and leveled. Cf. DESMONTE.

desatinado –**da** (*adj.*) crazy, cracked, nutty.—**de dor**, beside oneself with pain.

desatinar (*v.t.*) to render insane; (*v.i.*) to do or say crazy things.

desatino (*m.*) folly, madness. **praticar**—**s**, to do crazy things.

desatolar (*v.*) = DESATASCAR.

desatracar (*v.t.*) to unmoor; to pull apart (persons who are fighting).

desatravancar (*v.t.*) to clear of obstructions.—**a rua, a calçada,** to clear the street, the sidewalk.

desatrelar (*v.t.*) to unhitch, unharness (draft animals); to unleash.

desautorado –da (*adj.*) discredited, degraded.

desautorar (*v.t.*) to discredit, degrade; to take away the authority of; (*v.r.*) to lose one's prestige or authority.

desautorizado –da (*adj.*) stripped of authority, of prestige; unauthorized.

desautorizar (*v.t.*) to deprive of authority; to discredit; to disavow.

desauxiliar [x = ss] (*v.t.*) to withhold aid from, refuse to help.

desavença (*f.*) quarrel, falling out; dissension, disagreement, variance. **em**—, at loggerheads [Verb: DESAVIR].

desavergonhado –da (*adj.*) shameless, brazen(-faced), unblushing, impudent.

desavezar (*v.*) = DESACOSTUMAR.

desavindo –da (*adj.*) at outs with, in disagreement with, at variance with.

desavir [82] (*v.t.*) to set at variance; to estrange; to make inimical; (*v.r.*) to disagree, differ, dissent; to clash, fall out (**com,** with). [Noun: DESAVENÇA].

desavisado –da (*adj.*) unwise, foolish, ill-advised.

desavisar (*v.t.*) to revoke (a notice, an order, an invitation); to render foolish.

desaviso (*m.*) counter-notice; indiscretion, imprudence.

desazado –da (*adj.*) ungainly; awkward, clumsy.

desazo (*m.*) gaucherie, ineptness.

desbagoar (*v.t.*) to pick grapes from a bunch of them.

desbagulhar (*v.t.*) to pick out fruit seeds.

desbancar (*v.t.*) to break the bank; to supplant (a rival); to outclass.

desbandalhar (*v.*) = ESBANDALHAR.

desbandeirar (*v.t.*) to deprive of a flag or flags; to remove the tassels from corn plants.

desbaratado –da (*adj.*) defeated, routed, scattered.

desbaratamento (*m.*) defeat, rout; havoc; waste, squandering.

desbaratar (*v.t.*) to squander, waste; to rout, scatter; to defeat, upset, overthrow; to destroy, demolish, lay waste.

desbarate, desbarato (*m.*) = DESBARATAMENTO.

desbarbado –da (*adj.*) beardless.

desbarrancado (*m.*) steep bluff.

desbarrancar (*v.t.*) to make deep holes, remove much soil; to fill in gullies.

desbarrar (*v.t.*) to unbar (a door); to remove the mud from.

desbarretar (*v.t.*) to blow off or otherwise remove a cap or hat; (*v.r.*) to lift one's hat or cap in greeting.

desbarrigado –da (*adj., colloq.*) having a sunk-in belly, as a starving animal; having the lower part of the vest unbuttoned.

desbastador –dora (*adj.*) thinning; (*m., Carp.*) jack plane; (*Metal.*) roughing mill; clay modeling knife.

desbastamento (*m.*) a thinning out, thinning down, paring down [= DESBASTE].

desbastar (*v.t.*) to pare down (by cutting, grinding, chiseling, etc.); to rough hew; (*Metal.*) to rough roll; to thin out (plants).

desbaste (*m.*) a paring (hewing, grinding, chiseling, cutting, rolling) down; a thinning out (of plants).

desbastecer (*v.*) = DESBASTAR.

desbatizar (*v.t.*) to excommunicate; to change the name of; (*v.r.*) to lose or change one's baptismal name.

desbatocar (*v.t.*) to remove the bung (plug, stopper) from.

desbeiçar (*v.t.*) to break off the lip of a cup, the edge of a plate, etc.

desbloquear (*v.t.*) to lift the blockade of.

desbocado –da (*adj.*) foul-mouthed; of a horse, hard-mouthed.

desbocamento (*m.*) impudent language; rough talk.

desbocar (*v.t.*) to pour out (as water from a pitcher); to empty into the ocean (as a river); (*v.r.*) to utter obscenities; of a horse, to become hard-mouthed.

desbolado –da (*adj.*) wanting in good sense.

desboradar (*v.i.*) of a river, to overflow its banks.

desbotado –da (*adj.*) faded, lusterless.

desbotamento (*m.*) discoloration; fading.

desbotar (*v.t.*) to cause to fade; to discolor; (*v.i.,v.r.*) to fade.

desbragado –da (*adj.*) of language and behavior, indecent, indecorous, coarse, loose, shameless, immoderate.

desbragar (*v.t.*) to render dissolute.

desbravar (*v.t.*) to tame (animals); to cultivate (the wilderness).

desbravejado –da (*adj.*) of land, cleared of wild growth.

desbravejar (*v.i.*) to clear (land); to remove unburned stumps, etc.

desbriado –da (*adj.*) wanting in pride, self-respect, dignity; shameless.

desbriar (*v.t.*) to humble someone; (*v.r.*) to lose one's pride, self-esteem.

desbridar (*v.t.*) to unbridle.

desbrio (*m.*) want of BRIO (self-esteem, pride).

desbulhar (*v.*) = DEBULHAR.

desc. = DESCONTO (discount).

descabeçar (*v.t.*) to cut off the head of; to cut an end of; to remove stumps from a field; (*v.i.*) of the tide, to begin to fall.

descabelado –da (*adj.*) hairless; dishevelled; impetuous; "whopping".

descabelar (*v.t.*) to pull out the hair of; (*v.r.*) to pull out one's hair.

descaber [32] (*v.i.*) to not fit, not be suitable or proper.

descabido –da (*adj.*) improper, inappropriate, irrelevant, malapropos; foolish.

descabimento (*m.*) irrelevance, unfitness, unsuitability; impropriety.

descachaçar (*v.t.*) to skim (boiling cane juice).

descadeirado –da (*adj.*) felled, beaten; hipshot.

descadeirar (*v.t.*) to fell, knock down; to beat; to dislocate the hip; (*v.r.*) to rotate the hips while walking or dancing.

descaída (*f.*) a sloping down; a careless slip; chicken giblets.

descaidela (*f.*) an instance of carelessness or indiscretion.

descaído –da (*adj.*) fallen; sloping.

descaimento [a-i] (*m.*) a falling (down, off); decline; decadence.

descair [75] (*v.i.*) to drop; to sink, lower; to droop; to decline, fall; to drift; (*Naut.*) to sag, drift.

descalabro (*m.*) calamity, catastrophe, disaster.

descalçadeira (*f.*) bootjack; (*colloq.*) rebuke, reprimand; a dressing down.

descalçadela (*f.*) a bawling out, a dressing down.

descalçar (*v.t.*) to take off (boots, shoes, gloves) of; to remove a chock (from under a wheel); to remove the paving (from a street); to deprive (of help); (*v.r.*) to remove one's shoes.—**a bota,** to overcome a difficulty.

descalcificar (*v.t.*) to decalcify.

descalço –ça (*adj.*) barefoot; unshod; unpaved.

descalhoar (*v.t.*) to clear (land) of rocks.

descalicino –na (*adj., Bot.*) having no calyx.

descalvado –da (*adj.*) bald, bare [= ESCALVADO].

descamação (*f.*) act of scaling (a fish); (*Geol.*) exfoliation.

descamar (*v.*) = ESCAMAR.

descambada (*f.*) careless mistake; in Rio Grande do Sul, a rather steep hillside, c.a. **descambado** (*m.*).

descambar (*v.i.*) to swerve; to slide, slip, fall; to topple; to sink into error.

descaminhar (*v.*) = DESENCAMINHAR.

descamisado –da (*adj.*) shirtless; ragged; (*m.*) a shirtless one; a ragged fellow; (*f.*) corn-shucking [= DESFOLHADA].

descamisar (*v.t.*) to remove the shirt of; to shuck (corn) [= DESENCAMISAR, ESCAMISAR].

descampado –da (*adj.*) shelterless; uninhabited; (*m.*) wild prairie land; bleak desolate land; "wide open spaces" [= ESCAMPADO].

descampar (*v.i.*) to decamp, disappear; (*Naut.*) to put out to sea.

descansado –da (*adj.*) rested; calm, untroubled; deliberate, slow-going. **Você pode ficar**—, You may rest assured, don't worry about a thing.

descansar (*v.t.*) to give rest to; to put at rest; to lay, place, set, put (**em, in; sôbre,** on); (*v.i.*) to sleep, rest; to repose, confide (**em, in**); to lean ((**sôbre,** upon); to be at ease, tranquil.

descanso (*m.*) rest, repose, relaxation; calm, tranquility; relief; pause, respite; leisure; stay, brace, prop, support. **sem**—, without letup.

descantar (*v.t.,v.i.*) to sing; (*v.t.*) to speak ill of someone.

descapitalizar (*v.t.*) to liquidate capital.

descarado –da (*adj.*) bold, impudent, insolent, fresh, cheeky, nervy, brazen, barefaced, unblushing, shameless [= SEM-VERGONHA, DESAVERGONHADO].

descaramento (*m.*) effrontery, shamelessness; brass, cheek; insolence, impudence [= POUCA-VERGONHA].

descarar-se (*v.r.*) to become shameless, impudent.

descarbonizar (*v.t.*) to decarbonize.

descarboxilar (*v.t.*, *Chem.*) to decarboxylate.

descarga (*f.*) discharge, unloading; firing, gunfire; volley, broadside; (*Autom.*) exhaust; (*Med.*) excretion, evacuation. **dar uma—,** to fire a volley. [Verb: DESCARREGAR].

descargar (*v.*) = DESCARREGAR.

descaridoso –sa (*adj.*) uncharitable; unkindly.

descarinho (*m.*) want of love; unkindliness.

descarinhoso –sa (*adj.*) unkind, unloving.

descarnado –da (*adj.*) lean, lank, skinny, scrawny, gaunt, rawboned.

descarnar (*v.t.*) to strip the flesh off bones; to render thin; to emaciate; (*v.r.*) to grow thin.

descaro (*m.*) = DESCARAMENTO.

descaroável (*adj.*) ungracious, unkind, uncharitable.

descaroçador (*m.*) a machine for removing seeds.—**de algodão,** cotton gin.

descaroçamento (*m.*) removal of seeds or pits.

descaroçar (*v.t.*) to remove the seeds, esp. fruit pits, from; (*colloq.*) to tell one's beads.

descarregador –dora (*adj.*) unloading; discharging; (*m.,f.*) unloader; discharger; (*m.*, *Elec.*) discharger, spark gap.

descarregamento (*m.*) act of unloading; discharge.

descarregar (*v.t.*) to unload, discharge; to unburden; to fire a gun; to give vent to; to relieve, exonerate; to strike a blow; (*Med.*) to deplete. [Noun: DESCARGA].

descarreirar (*v.t.*) to put on the wrong road.

descarril(h)amento (*m.*) derailment.

descarril(h)ar (*v.t.*) to derail; (*v.r.*) to jump the track; to stray from the right road.

descartar (*v.t.*) to discard (cards).—**-se de,** to rid oneself of.

descarte (*m.*) discard; (*colloq.*) evasive reply [= EVASIVA].

descasar (*v.t.*) to unmarry; to mismatch or separate pairs of anything).

descascação (*f.*) process of hulling or peeling.

descascadeira (*f.*) hulling machine.

descascadinha (*f.*, *colloq.*) a fair-skinned woman.

descascador –dora (*adj.*) hulling; (*m.*) hulling machine. —**de frutas,** fruit peeler.

descascadura (*f.*) **descascamento** (*m.*) = DESCASCAÇÃO.

descascar (*v.t.*) to remove the CASCA (hull, shuck, peel, skin) from; (*colloq.*) to take the hide off; (*v.i.*) to shed hull, shell, peel, etc.

descaso (*m.*) neglect, carelessness, heedlessness; indifference; disregard.

descaspar (*v.t.*) to remove the dandruff from.

descasque (*m.*) = DESCASCADURA.

descativar (*v.t.*) to release, free from captivity.

descatolizar (*v.t.*) to decatholicize.

descaudado –da, **descaudato** –ta (*adj.*) tailless.

descaudar (*v.t.*) to crop a horse's tail.

descautela (*f.*) want of caution.

descautelado –da, –loso –sa (*adj.*) careless , not cautious.

descavalgar (*v.t.,v.i.*) to dismount, alight, from a horse.

descavalheiroso –sa (*adj.*) unchivalrous, ungentlemanly.

descavar (*v.*) = ESCAVAR.

descaveirado –da (*adj.*) = ESCAVEIRADO.

descaxelado –da (*adj.*) = DESQUEIXELADO.

descegar (*v.t.*) to cure the blindness of, restore sight to.

descendência (*f.*) descent, extraction, lineage; descendants, offspring. **ângulo de—,** (*Aeron.*) descending angle.

descendente (*adj.*) descendent, descending; (*f.*) a descent; (*m.,f.*) descendant, offspring; (*pl.*) descendants, lineage, progeny, breed.

descender (*v.i.*) to descend from, be derived from. [But not to descend, come or go down, which is DESCER.]

descendimento (*m.*) descent [= DESCIDA].

descensão (*f.*), **descenso** (*m.*) descent; a lowering.

descente (*adj.*) descending; (*f.*) descent [= DESCIDA].

descentralização (*f.*) decentralization.

descentralizador –dora (*adj.*) decentralizing; (*m.,f.*) one favoring decentralization.

descentralizar (*v.t.*) to decentralize.

descentrar (*v.t.*) to decenter.

descer (*v.i.*) to descend (**a,** to; **de,** from); to go down (**a, para,** to); to come down; to fall (**sôbre,** upon); to sink, drop; to dismount, alight, step down (**de,** from); to get down (**a;** to; **de,** from); to climb down (**de,** from); to get off of or out of a vehicle; (*v.t.*) to lower, let down, bring down (**de,** from).—**à sepultura, à terra, ao túmulo,** to go down into the grave.—**da burra,** (*colloq.*) to give in after an argument.—**do trono,** to step down from the throne. —**em vrille,** (*Aeron.*) to spin down. **sem—a pormenores,** without going into details. [Noun: DESCIDA].

descercar (*v.t.*) to unfence; to lift a siege.

descerebrar (*v.t.*) to render insane; (*Surg.*) to decerebrate; (*v.r.*) to become idiotic.

descerimônia (*f.*) informality.

descerimonioso –sa (*adj.*) unceremonious; informal; offhand.

descerrar (*v.t.*) to open (window, eyes, purse, etc.); to disclose (a secret).

deschapelar-se (*v.r.*) to remove or lift one's hat.

descida (*f.*) descent, fall, drop; down grade; (*Radio*) down-lead.—**picada,** (*Aeron.*) nose dive. [Verb: DESCER].

descimento (*m.*) descent; act of descending; in the early days, the bringing to the coast, as slaves, of Indians captured inland.

descingir (*v.t.*) to unbuckle, loosen.

descivilizar-se (*v.r.*) to become less civilized.

desclassificação (*f.*) disqualification.

desclassificado –da (*adj.*) disqualified; (*m.,f.*) a social outcast.

desclassificar (*v.t.*) to declass; to disqualify; to discredit.

descloretar (*v.t.*) to dechlore.

descoagular, descoalhar (*v.t.*) to decoagulate, melt, dissolve, liquefy.

descoberto –ta (*adj.*) discovered; uncovered, bare, naked, exposed; (*m.*) discovered mine; (*f.*) a discovery; disclosure; newly discovered land. **a—,** in the open. **sacar em—,** or **pôr (conta, crédito) em—,** to overdraw one's account.

descobridor –dora (*adj.*) discovering; (*m.,f.*) discoverer; explorer.

descobrimento (*m.*) discovery; discovering; uncovering; finding; disclosure; detection. Cf. DESCOBERTA.

descobrir [33] (*t.t.*) to discover, reveal, uncover, disclose, lay bare; to detect, unearth, find out; to discern; to impart, make known; (*v.r.*) to bare one's head; to disclose one's identity.—**a cara,** to show the face; to remove the mask (lit. & fig.).—**o campo,** to spy out the enemy.—**o coração,** or **o peito, a,** to bare one's heart to another.

descocado –da (*adj.*) wanting in sense; impudent.

descocar-se (*v.r.*) to act senselessly.

descochar (*v.t.*) to unravel (a rope).

descôco (*m.*) impudence, nerve, gall.

descodear (*v.t.*) to remove crust from (bread, etc.).

descoimar (*v.t.*) to relieve of a fine or penalty.

descoivarar (*v.t.*) to clear the land of heaps of burned trees.

descolar (*v.t.*) to unglue; (*v.i.*) of an airplane, to take off.

descoloração (*f.*) discoloration.

descolorar –rir [25] (*v.t.*) to discolor; (*v.i.*) to fade.

descolorido –da (*adj.*) faded, drab.

descomedido –da (*adj.*) immoderate; rude.

descomedimento (*m.*) insolence, rudeness, impudence; want of good manners.

descomedir-se [25] (*v.r.*) to speak (act, behave) in an unseemly, rude or rash manner.

descompadrar (*v.t.*) to set (friends) at variance.

descompaixão (*f.*) want of compassion.

descompassado –da (*adj.*) out of proportion; out of keeping with; out of step with.

descompassar-se (*v.r.*) to get out of step, not act in keeping with rules, principles, etc.

descomponenda (*f.*, *colloq.*) a bawling out, dressing down.

descompor [63] (*v.t.*) to discompose, disorder, derange; to disturb; to disconcert; to abuse; to flay; to lambaste; (*v.r.*) to get upset; to lose one's composure.

descomposto –ta (*adj.*) disarranged; indecorous.

descompostura (*f.*) discomposure; (*colloq.*) abuse, insult. **passar uma—em,** to give a tongue lashing to; to dress down, berate (someone).

descomprazer (*v.t.*) to displease, not comply with the wishes of.

descomprimir (*v.t.*) to decompress.

descomunal (*adj.*) uncommon, unusual; huge, colossal, outsize.

desconceito (*m.*) disrepute.

desconceituar (*v.t.*) to discredit, defame; (*v.r.*) to lose one's reputation.

desconcentrar (*v.*) = DECENTRALIZAR.

desconcertado –da (*adj.*) out of order; disarranged; in confusion; chagrined.

desconcertador **-dora, -certante** (adj.) disconcerting; baffling; discomposing; upsetting.
desconcertar (v.t.) to disconcert; to rattle; to squelch; to discompose, disarrange, disturb, put out of order; (v.r.) to lose one's composure.—**o estômago**, to upset the stomach.
desconcêrto (m.) disorder; derangement.
desconchavar (v.t.) to put out of gear; to disconnect; to set at variance; (v.i.) to behave erratically; (v.r.) to fall out with someone.
desconcordância (f.) discordance; discord.
desconcordante (adj.) discordant, not in harmony, not in agreement.
desconcordar (v.t.) to set at variance.—**de**, to disagree with.
descondensar (v.t.) to make less dense; to dissolve.
desconexão [ks] (f.) disconnection.
desconexo -xa [ks] (adj.) disconnected, unrelated; incoherent, rambling.
desconfessar (v.t.) to retract a confession.
desconfiado -da (adj.) distrustful, suspicious; skittish; (m.,f.) a suspicious person.
desconfiança (f.) distrust, suspicion, doubt, misgiving. **auto—**, self-doubt, diffidence.
desconfiante (adj.) suspicious, distrustful.
desconfiar (v.t.) to surmise, imagine; to distrust, suspect; (v.i.) to have doubts.—**de**, to suspect, distrust, mistrust, beware of.
desconforme (adj.) disagreeing, at variance; unconformable; disproportionate; prodigious.
desconformidade (f.) disconformity (with).
desconfortado -da (adj.) disconsolate, disheartened.
desconfortar (v.t.) to distress.
desconfôrto (m.) discomfort; disconsolateness.
descongelação (f.) thawing, melting.
descongelar (v.t.,v.r.) to thaw, melt.
descongestionar (v.t.) to rid of congestion; (Med.) to deplete.
desconhecedor -dora (adj.) ignorant, unknowing; ungrateful; (m.,f.) such a person.
desconhecer (v.t.) not to know; to be ignorant of; not to recognize; to ignore; to disown.
desconhecido -da (adj.) unheard of, unknown; unfamiliar; ignorant; (m.,f.) a stranger.
desconhecimento (m.) ignorance; ingratitude.
desconhecível (adj.) unknowable.
desconjuntado -da (adj.) disjointed, out of joint; loose-jointed; ramshackle.
desconjuntamento (m.) dislocation; disarticulation.
desconjuntar (v.t.) to disjoin, disunite; to disarticulate; to disjoint, dislocate; to wrench; to unhinge; to throw out of gear; (v.r.) to come apart.
desconjunto -ta (adj.) disjoined.
desconjuntura (f.) = DESCONJUNTAMENTO.
desconjurar (v.) = ESCONJURAR.
desconsagrar (v.t.) to desecrate.
desconselhar (v.) = DESACONSELHAR.
desconsentir (v.t.,v.i.) not to consent, disagree.
desconsideração (f.) disregard, disesteem, slight.
desconsiderar (v.t.) to disregard, slight, ignore.
desconsolação (f.) distress, suffering, sorrow; desolation.
desconsolado -da (adj.) disconsolate, desolate.
desconsolador -dora (adj.) saddening.
desconsolar (v.t.) to sadden, depress; (v.r.) to grieve.
desconsolável (adj.) = INCONSOLÁVEL.
desconsôlo (m.) = DESCONSOLAÇÃO.
descontar (v.t.) to discount (bills, notes, etc.); to leave out of account; to make light of; to make allowance for exaggeration.—**de**, to deduct from.
descontentadiço -ça (adj.) hard to please.
descontentamento (m.) discontent, dissatisfaction, displeasure; disaffection.
descontentar (v.t.) to discontent, dissatisfy, displease; to disaffect; to disgruntle.
descontente (adj.) discontented, dissatisfied, unsatisfied, malcontent; (m.) a "sorehead".
descontento (m.) = DESCONTENTAMENTO.
descontinuação (f.) discontinuation.
descontinuado -da (adj.) discontinued, interrupted.
descontinuar (v.t.) to discontinue, stop, interrupt.
descontinuidade [u-i] (f.) discontinuity.
descontínuo -nua (adj.) discontinuous.
desconto (m.) discount, rebate. **dar o—**, (colloq.) to discount (another's story).

descontratar (v.t.) to cancel a contract.
desconversar (v.t., v.i.) to change the subject of conversation.
desconvidar (v.t.) to withdraw an invitation.
desconvidativo -va (adj.) uninviting.
desconvir [82] (v.i.) to be inconvenient; to disagree.
descorado -da (adj.) discolored; colorless; pale, shallow.
descorajar (v.i.) to lose courage [but not to discourage, which is DESENCORAJAR, DESCOROÇOAR, DESANIMAR].
descoramento (m.) discoloring; a turning pale.
descorante (adj.) discoloring.
descorar (v.t.) to discolor; (v.i.,v.r.) to pale.
descorçoar (v.) = DESCOROÇOAR.
descornar (v.t.) to de-horn (cattle).
descoroar (v.t.) to uncrown.
descoroçoamento (m.) discouragement.
descoroçoado -da (adj.) disheartened; downcast; crestfallen, dejected, depressed; heartsick.
descoroçoar (v.t.) to discourage; (v.i.) to lose heart.
descortejar (v.t.) to be discourteous to.
descortês (adj.) discourteous, rude, inconsiderate, ungracious, disobliging.
descortesia (f.) discourtesy, impoliteness, rudeness; snub, slight.
descorticar (v.t.) to decorticate; to strip, peel.
descortinar (v.t.) to disclose to view (as a painting) by drawing back the curtain; to unveil, reveal, expose; to descry, discover; (v.r.) to come to light.
descortinável (adj.) discernible.
descortino (m.) unveiling, disclosure; foresight.
descoser (v.t.) to unstitch, rip out stitches; to take or rip apart (at the seams); (v.r.) to come unstitched.
descosido -da (adj.) loose or open at the seams; disconnected, incoherent.
descostumar (v.) = DESACOSTUMAR.
descravar (v.) = DESENCRAVAR.
descravejar (v.t.) to remove horseshoe nails; to remove a jewel from its setting.
descravizar (v.t. to) free from slavery.
descrédito (m.) discredit, disrepute, dishonor; reproach.
descremar (v.t.) to separate the cream from milk.
descrença (f.) disbelief; unbelief; incredulity.
descrente (adj.) unbelieving; (m.,f.) unbeliever.
descrer [38] (v.t.,v.i.) to disbelieve, not to believe.
descrever [44] (v.t.) to describe, portray, depict, detail; to delineate, trace, draw.
descrição (f.) description, representation, portrayal, depiction, narration.
descrido -da (adj.) unbelieving; (m.,f.) unbeliever.
descriminar (v.t.) to absolve of crime. [Do not confuse with DISCRIMINAR.]
descritível (adj.) describable.
descritivo -va (adj.) descriptive; (m.) description.
descruzar (v.t.) to uncross (as, the legs).
descuidado -da (adj.) careless, heedless, thoughtless; unmindful; forgetful, neglectful, negligent; listless; inattentive, absentminded; happy-go-lucky, carefree; unkempt; slovenly, untidy, sloppy, slipshod; (m.) carelessness, negligence.
descuidar (v.t.) to neglect, disregard; to overlook; (v.r.) to become careless (neglectful) of one's personal appearance, habits, health, etc.—**de**, to be forgetful, neglectful, of.
descuido (m.) negligence, carelessness, inattention, inadvertency; oversight, slip. **por—**, carelessly, through negligence.
descuidoso -sa (adj.) careless; care-free.
desculpa (f.) excuse, apology; extenuation, absolution; pretext, evasion. **apresentar—s**, to offer excuses (apologies). **arranjar uma—**, to find an excuse. **pedir—s**, to apologize, beg pardon.
desculpar (v.t.) to excuse, exculpate, pardon, forgive; to extenuate, justify, condone; (v.r.) to apologize; to excuse oneself.
desculpável (adj.) excusable.
descumprir (v.t.) not to comply with.
descurado -da (adj.) = DESCUIDOSO.
descurar (v.t.) to neglect, disregard; to overlook.
descuriosidade (f.) want of curiosity.
descurioso -sa (adj.) uncurious.
desdar [39] (v.t.) to take (something) back; to untie.
desde [ês] (prep.) from, since, after.—**agora**, henceforth. —**cedo**, early.—**então**, thenceforth, from that time, ever since.—**há muito**, for a long time past.—**já**, at once, immediately.—**logo**, at once.—**pequeno**, since childhood.

—que, ever since, from that moment; since, inasmuch as, seeing that; provided, so long as.—**quando?** since when?—**sempre,** since always.

desdém (*m.*) disdain, contempt, scorn; disregard. **com—,** disdainfully.

desdenhado -da (*adj.*) disdained, repudiated.

desdenhar (*v.t.*) to disdain, despise, look down upon, hold in contempt; to spurn; to scorn; to defy; to slight.

desdenhoso -sa (*adj.*) disdainful, supercilious, scornful, "snooty".

desdentado -da (*adj.*) toothless; (*m.pl.*, *Zool.*), the Edentata.

desdentar (*v.t.*) to remove the teeth of; (*v.r.*) to lose one's teeth.

desdentição (*f.*) falling out of teeth.

desdita (*f.*) misfortune, adversity, distress.

desditoso -sa (*adj.*) unfortunate, ill-fated, hapless, wretched.

desdizer [41] (*v.t.* to contradict, deny, gainsay; not to agree with, differ from; (*v.r.*) to retract, unsay, disavow.

desdobramento (*m.*) act of unfolding, expanding, etc.; breakdown. (*Chem.*) decomposition.

desdobrar (*v.t.*) to unfold (napkin, newspaper, etc.); to unbend; to disintegrate; to expand, extend; to redouble (efforts); to deploy (troops); (*v.r.*) to unfold before the eyes (as scenery); to deploy.

desdobre (*m.*) = DESDOBRAMENTO; development.

desdôbro (*m.*) log-sawing; cutting up of a log into heavy planks; a saw for this purpose.

desdormido -da (*adj.*) designating one who has not slept well and is yawning.

desdourar (*v.t.*) to tarnish; to slur; (*v.r.*) to become tarnished.

desdouro (*m.*) tarnish; stain, blot (on reputation); slur. Var. DESDOIRO.

deseclipsar (*v.t.*) to uncloud; to restore glory, fame, etc. to; (*v.r.*) to reappear; to shine again.

deseconômico -ca (*adj.*) uneconomical.

deseducado -da (*adj.*) untutored; ill-bred.

deseixar (*v.t.*) to remove (as a wheel) from its axle; (*v.r.*) to fall (as a wheel) off the axle.

desejar (*v.t.*) to desire, wish for, want.

desejável (*adj.*) desirable.

desejo [sê] (*m.*) desire, wish, aspiration, longing; appetite.

desejoso -sa (*adj.*) desirous, eager, avid.

deselegância (*f.*) inelegance.

deselegante (*adj.*) inelegant, ungainly; slouchy.

desemaçar (*v.t.*) to break up a package or bundle (as of bank notes).

desemaranhar (*v.t.*) to disentangle, unsnarl (hair, string, etc.); to unravel (a knotty problem).

desembaciar (*v.t.*) to untarnish (as, a mirror).

desembainhar [11] [a-i] (*v.t.*) to unsheathe.—**a espada,** to draw one's sword.—**a língua,** to loose one's tongue.

desembalar (*v.t.*) to unbale, unpack, unwrap; to remove the bullet from a cartridge.

desembandeirar (*v.t.*) to remove a flag or flags; (*v.i.*) to drop a flag or flags.

desembaraçado -da (*adj.*) unencumbered, untrammelled; unobstructed; adroit; free and easy, unconstrained, unrestrained, unreserved; jaunty.

desembaraçar (*v.t.*) to disembarrass, disengage, disentangle, rid, clear, set free; to expedite; (*v.r.*) to rid oneself of hindrances.

desembaraço (*m.*) ease, freedom, unconstraint, unrestraint, facility, readiness; liveliness, briskness; self-assurance.

desembaralhar (*v.t.*) to disentangle.

desembarcação (*f.*) = DESEMBARQUE.

desembarcadouro (*m.*) wharf, dock, landing place. Var. DESEMBARCADOIRO.

desembarcar (*v.i.*) to disembark, land, go ashore; (*v.t.*) to put on shore, send ashore; to unship, unload (goods).

desembargador (*m.*) a judge of the court of appeals.

desembargar (*v.t.*) to lift an embargo; to free, clear.

desembargo (*m.*) removal of embargo; replevin.

desembarque (*m.*) disembarkation; landing.

desembarrilar (*v.t.*) to take out of a barrel.

desembebedar (*v.t.,v.r.*) to sober up.

desembestado -da (*adj.*) unbridled; unrestrained; runaway (horse); (*f.*) a wild gallop.

desembestar (*v.i.*) to stampede; to run after; to lose one's temper; (*v.t.*) to hurl, let fly (arrow, etc.).

desembocadura (*f.*) mouth of a river.

desembocar (*v.i.*) to disembogue; to discharge at the mouth (as a river); to lead (as one street into another); to issue, flow out; to emerge.

desembolsar (*v.t.*) to disburse, expend.

desembôlso (*m.*) disbursement, outlay, expenditure.

desemboscar (*v.t.*) to drive out of the bushes (as game), or out of ambush; (*v.i.,v.r.*) to come out of ambush.

desembotar (*v.t.*) to make sharp again.

desembravecer (*v.t.*) to tame; (*v.i.*) to become tame.

desembrear (*v.t.*) to disengage the clutch (as of an automobile).

desembrenhar (*v.t.*) to drive out (game) from the woods. (*v.i.*) to get clear of the woods.

desembriagar (*v.t.*) to sober up.

desembrulhado -da (*adj.*) unwrapped, untangled; made clear.

desembrulhar (*v.t.*) to unwrap; to untangle; to unfold; to clear up (a matter).

desembruscar (*v.t.*) to sweep the clouds away.

desembrutecer (*v.t.*) to civilize.

desembruxar (*v.t.*) to free of witchcraft.

desembuçado -da (*adj.*) uncovered, plain, clear.

desembuçar (*v.t.*) to throw open or off (cloak, cape); to lower, take off (hood, veil); to reveal one's face thus.

desembuchar (*v.t.*) to unstop, free from obstruction; to utter freely, spill (secrets). **Desembuche!** (*colloq.*) Out with it!

desemburrar (*v.t.*) to render less ignorant; (*v.r.*) to become less ignorant; to get over being sulky [= DESAMUAR-SE].

desembutir (*v.t.*) to pry loose or out (as a tile or piece of inlay).

desemoldurar (*v.t.*) to remove (a picture) from its frame.

desempacar (*v.i.*) to stop balking.

desempachar (*v.t.*) to disencumber, rid of obstruction.

desempacho (*m.*) riddance; extrication.

desempacotar (*v.t.*) to unpack; to unwrap (a package).

desempalhar (*v.t.*) to remove the straw packing or straw stuffing from.

desempanar (*v.*) = DESEMBACIAR.

desemparelhar (*v.t.*) to separate a pair.

desempastar (*v.t.*) to untangle (as, sticky or matted hair).

desempatador (*m.*) umpire, referee, arbitrator.

desempatar (*v.t.*) to break a tie, cast the deciding vote (in a deadlock).—**cabedais,** to unfreeze capital.

desempate (*m.*) breaking of a tie. **partida de—,** a play-off game.

desempeçado -da (*adj.*) unobstructed.

desempeçar, -pecer (*v.t.*) to disencumber, disembarrass, disentangle; (*v.r.*) to rid oneself of hindrances.

desempecilhar (*v.t.*) to free oneself of hindrances.

desempedernir [46] (*v.t.*) to make less hard, soften.

desempedrar (*v.t.*) to remove the cobbles (from a street), stones (from a field).

desempenadeira (*f.*) mortar board; plasterer's float.

desempenado -da (*adj.*) straight, upright; flat (not warped or twisted); bold; quick.—**como um I,** stiff and straight as an arrow. **um andar—,** an erect gait. **uma pessoa—,** an upstanding person.

desempenar (*v.t.*) to unwarp, straighten; (*v.r.*) to straighten (oneself) up.

desempenhar (*v.t.*) to take out of pawn; to redeem (a pledged object at a pawn shop); to fulfill, discharge, make good (a promise, an obligation); to carry out, perform (the duties of); to free of debt; (*v.r.*) to acquit oneself.—**palavra,** to keep one's word.—**um papel,** to play a role, act a part.

desempenho (*m.*) fulfillment, execution (of a task); discharge (of an obligation, a duty); performance (of a role); redemption (from mortagage); indifference, unconcern.

desempeno (*m.*) an unwarping, a straightening up; upright carriage, graceful posture; carpenter's level; (*Mach.*) surface plate.

desemperrar (*v.t.*) to loosen (a stuck drawer, the tongue, etc.); (*v.i.*) to stop being sulky.

desempestar (*v.*) = DESINFECCIONAR.

desempilhar (*v.t.*) to unpile, unstack, disarrange.

desemplumar (*v.t.*) to pluck the feathers of.

desempoar (*v.t.*) to dust (-se, oneself) off.

desempobrecer (*v.t.*) to make rich; (*v.i.*) to get rich.

desempoladeira (*f.*) bricklayer's or plasterer's trowel; also, mortar board.

desempolar (*v.t.*) to smooth, level (as plaster).

desempossar (*v.t.*) to dispossess [= DESAPOSSAR].
desempregado –da (*adj.*) unemployed.
desempregar (*v.t.*) to dismiss from employment; (*v.r.*) to lose one's job.
desemprêgo (*m.*) unemployment. **indenização por—**, unemployment insurance; dole.
desemproar (*v.t.*) to take (someone) down a peg.
desempunhar (*v.t.*) to let go (release from the hand), as a sword.
desencabeçar (*v.t.*) to head (someone) the wrong way (lead him astray).—**de**, to dissuade from.
desencadear (*v.t.*) to unchain, unleash, unloose; to disconnect; (*v.i.*) to break loose (as a storm); to fall in torrents (rain).
desencadernado –da (*adj.*) unbound or with the covers missing [book].
desencaiporar (*v.i.*) to stop having bad luck.
desencaixar (*v.t.*) to disjoint, throw out of kilter; to oust, unseat; (*v.r.*) to come loose, get out of place.
desencaixilhar (*v.t.*) to remove (something) from its frame or molding.
desencaixotar (*v.t.*) to unbox, unpack.
desencalacrar (*v.t.*) to free of debt; (*v.r.*) to get out of debt.
desencalhar (*v.t.*) to set afloat (stranded vessel); to extricate; (*v.i.*) to get free.
desencalmar (*v.t.*) to cool, refresh (**-se**, oneself).
desencaminhado –da (*adj.*) astray, lost, perverted.
desencaminhar (*v.t.*) to mislead, misdirect; to lead astray, corrupt; to misappropriate (funds). (*v.r.*) to go astray.
desencamisar (*v.*) = DESCAMISAR.
desencantador –dora (*adj.*) disenchanting; disillusioning.
desencantamento (*m.*) disenchantment; disillusionment.
desencantar (*v.t.*) to disenchant; to disillusion; to unearth.
desencanto (*m.*) = DESENCANTAMENTO.
desencapar (*v.t.*) to unwrap.
desencapotar (*v.t.*) to uncloak; to reveal.
desencaracolar (*v.t.,v.r.*) to uncurl.
desencarapinhar (*v.t.*) to unkink (hair); to untangle (wool).
desencarcerar (*v.t.*) to release from prison.
desencardir (*v.t.*) to free from dirt and spots (clothing, etc.).
desencarecer (*v.t.*) to underestimate; to depreciate; (*v.i.*) to get cheaper.
desencarnar (*v.i.*) to leave the flesh (die).
desencarquilhar (*v.t.*) to unwrinkle.
desencarregar (*v.t.*) to relieve, exempt (from care, duties)
desencarril(h)ar (*v.*) = DESCARRIL(H)AR.
desencartar (*v.t.*) to oust from a job.
desencasar (*v.t.*) to remove (as, part of a machine) from its normal place.
desencavar (*v.t.*) to dig up.
desencerar (*v.t.*) to dewax.
desencerrar (*v.t.*) to release; to show, manifest; to uncover; (*v.r.*) to free oneself (as from jail).
desencharcar (*v.t.*) to drain, dry out (a piece of land).
desencher (*v.t.*) to empty.
desencilhar (*v.t.*) to unsaddle, unharness.
desencobrir [33] (*v.t.*) to uncover [= DESCOBRIR].
desencoivarar (*v.*) = DESCOIVARAR.
desencolerizar (*v.t.*) = to placate.
desencolher (*v.t.*) to stretch (legs, sails); (*v.r.*) to unshrink.
desencomendar (*v.t.*) to cancel an order (for goods).
desenconchar (*v.t.*) to remove from the shell, as oysters; to release (as from jail); to rout out (of bed, etc.); (*v.r.*) to come out of hiding.
desencontradiço –ça (*adj.*) hard to meet up with.
desencontrado –da (*adj.*) going in opposite directions; contrary; desultory. **notícias—s**, contradictory reports,
desencontrar (*v.t.*) to cause failure (of persons) to meet. (of things) to fit together; (*v.i.*) to go counter.—**se (em)**, to disagree, clash (as to ideas, opinions, interests, tastes, etc.).—**se de** (or **com**) **alguém**, to fail to meet (with) someone.
desencontro (*m.*) failure to meet; disagreement; clash (of ideas), conflict (of opinions).
desencorajar (*v.t.*) to discourage, throw cold water on.
desencordoar (*v.t.*) to unstring (guitar, tennis racket); (*v.r.*) to regain one's good humor.
desencorporar (*v.t.*) to detach (**-se**, oneself) from a corporation or body.
desencorrear (*v.t.*) to untie (as animals).

desencoscorar (*v.t.*) to remove crust from.
desencostar (*v.t.*) to take away the support of (something which is resting or leaning); (*v.r.*) to stop leaning against something, straighten up.
desencovar (*v.t.*) to ferret out.
desencovilar (*v.t.*) to rout out from a lair.
desencravado –da (*adj.*) pulled out, dug out; (*colloq.*) settled [difficult matter]; found at last.
desencravar (*v.t.*) to dig out, pull out (as nails).
desencravilhar (*v.t.*) to loosen (as a girth); to relieve (someone) of difficulties.
desencrencar (*v.t.*, *slang*) to straighten (matters) out.
desencrespar-se (*v.r.*) to uncurl.
desencruar (*v.t.*) to tenderize (meat); to make someone tenderhearted.
desencurralar (*v.t.*) to turn (animals) out of the corral.
desendemoninhar (*v.t.*) to cast demons out of.
desendeusar (*v.t.*) to undeify.
desendividar (*v.t.*) to free (**-se**, oneself) of debt.
desenegrecer (*v.t.*) to whiten (as teeth).
desenevoar (*v.t.*) to clear of clouds or fog.
desenfadar (*v.t.*) to amuse, entertain; to put in good humor.
desenfado (*m.*) amusement, relaxation.
desenfaixar (*v.t.*) to unswaddle.
desenfardar (*v.t.*) to unpack.
desenfastiar (*v.t.*) to whet the appetite; to amuse (**-se**, oneself).
desenfeitado –da (*adj.*) unadorned, simple, plain.
desenfeitar (*v.t.*) to strip of ornaments.
desenfeitiçar (*v.t.*) to disenchant; to free of a spell.
desenfeixar (*v.t.*) to unsheaf (as wheat.)
desenfermar (*v.i.*) to convalesce.
desenferrujar (*v.t.*) to free of rust.
desenfezar (*v.t.*) to free of dregs, lees, dross; to free the spirit of; to put in good humor.
desenfiar (*v.t.*) to unstring (beads); to unthread (a needle).
desenflorar (*v.t.*) to deprive or strip of flowers.
desenfornar (*v.t.*) to take (bread, etc.) out of the oven.
desenfreado –da (*adj.*) unbridled, uncurbed, unchecked, unrestrained; rampant; ungovernable; wanton.
desenfreamento (*m.*) unrestraint; immoderation.
desenfrear (*v.t.*) to unbridle, turn loose, free; (*v.r.*) to lose all restraint.
desenfronhar (*v.t.*) to remove (a pillow) from its case; to lay (a fact) bare; to utter (lies, etc.) freely.
desenfurecer (*v.t.*) to placate.
desengaiolar (*v.t.*) to uncage, remove from a cage; to release from jail.
desengajar (*v.t.*) to disengage, release (from employment).
desengalfinhar (*v.t.*) to separate (persons who are grappling with each other).
desenganado –da (*adj.*) undeceived; disillusioned; (*Med.*) given up (by the doctors).
desenganador –dora (*adj.*) disillusioning.
desenganar (*v.t.*) to undeceive, disabuse; to disappoint; to give up (someone) as incurable; (*v.r.*) to realize the truth (of something).
desenganchar (*v.t.*) to unhook.
desengano (*m.*) disillusionment; realization of the truth.
desengastar (*v.t.*) to remove (a jewel) from its setting.
desengatar (*v.t.*) to uncouple, disconnect.
desengatilhar (*v.t.*) to pull the GATILHO (trigger); to uncock (as a trigger); to trip (any device).
desengonçado –da (*adj.*) unhinged, loose, disjointed; ramshackle; ungainly; lanky; gangling.
desengonçar (*v.t.*) to unhinge; to disjoint, take apart; (*v.r.*) to fall apart.
desengordar (*v.i.*) to grow thin; (*v.t.*) to cause to grow thin.
desengordurar (*v.t.*) to degrease, remove the grease from.
desengorgitar (*v.t.*, *Med.*) to relieve an engorgement.
desengraçado –da (*adj.*) ungraceful; flat, insipid; dull.
desengraçar (*v.t.*) to render ungraceful.—**com**, to take a dislike to.
desengrandecer (*v.t.*) to belittle.
desengravecer (*v.t.*) to render less grave (as, an error).
desengraxar (*v.t.*) to remove the polish or shine of (as of shoes).
desengrenar (*v.t.*) to uncouple (gears).
desengrenhar (*v.*) = DESGRENHAR.

desengrossar (v.t.) to rough-hew, make less thick; (v.i.) to become less swollen.

desenguiçar (v.t.) to free from witchcraft, take off the "hex"; (v.r.) to free oneself of a spell.

desengulhar (v.t.) to relieve of nausea.

desenhador (m.) = DESENHISTA.

desenhar (v.t.) to design, draw, delineate; to depict; to show, reveal (in outline). (v.r.) to take form.

desenhista (m.,f.) designer; draftsman.

desenho (m.) drawing, sketch; draft, outline; pattern; plan, design.—**a carvão**, charcoal drawing.—**a mão livre**, freehand sketch(ing).—**animado**, animated cartoon.

desenjoar (v.t.) to relieve of nausea. (v.r.) to be thus relieved.—**se com**, to whet the appetite with.

desenjoativo -**va** (adj.) serving to relieve nausea or want of appetite; (m.) anything which so serves.

desenlaçar (v.t.) to unlace, loose; to untangle.

desenlace (m.) epilogue, outcome; dénouement; upshot, end.—**final,** death.

desenlamear (v.t.) to clean off the mud.

desenlapar (v.t.) to drive (as a rabbit) from a burrow or hiding place; (v.r.) to come out of hiding.

desenleado -**da** (adj.) expeditious; outspoken.

desenlear (v.t.) to untangle, unsnarl, unravel; to loose (the tongue); to free (someone) from entanglements.—**se de,** to free oneself from (entanglements).

desenleio (m.) disentanglement.

desenlevar (v.t.) to disenchant.

desenliçar (v.t.) to disentangle (**-se,** oneself).

desenlodar (v.t.) to remove mud from.

desenlouquecer (v.t.) to cure of insanity; (v.r.) to regain one's sanity.

desenlutar (v.t.) to relieve mourning; to console; (v.r.) to go out of mourning; to regain cheerfulness.

desenobrecer (v.t.) to deprive of titles of nobility; to degrade; (v.r.) to lose one's nobility; to degrade oneself.

desenodoar (v.t.) to remove stains.

desenojar (v.) = DESANOJAR.

desenovelar (v.t.,v.r.) to unravel, unwind (as a ball of yarn).

desenquadrar (v.) = DESMOLDURAR.

desenraivecer (v.t.) to placate the anger of; (v.r.) to lose one's anger.

desenraizar [a-i] (v.) = DESARRAIGAR.

desenramar (v.t.) to remove the branches of.

desenrascar (v.t.) to disentangle; free of difficulties; (v.r.) to so free oneself.

desenredar (v.t.) to disentangle; to unravel, explain (as a plot); (v.r.) to become clear; to get disentangled.

desenrêdo (m.) act of unravelling or untangling; deciphering; dénouement, outcome.

desenriçar (v.t.) to comb out, smoothe (the hair).

desenrijar (v.t.) to soften (as muscles); (v.r.) to soften (with age).

desenriquecer (v.t.) to deprive of riches; to impoverish; (v.r.) to become poor.

desenristar (v.t.) to remove (as a lance) from its rest.

desenrodilhar (v.t.) to uncoil (as a rope).

desenrolamento (m.) act of unrolling; development.

desenrolar (v.t.) to unroll; to unwind; to develop, unfold (story, plot); (v.i.) to unfold, come to pass (events); (v.r.) to uncoil (as a snake); to spread out; to unfold; to unwind.

desenroscar (v.t.) to uncoil, untwist; to disentwine; to unscrew; (v.r.) to uncoil (as a snake).

desenroupar (v.t.) to deprive of clothing.

desenrouquecer (v.t.) to relieve of hoarseness; (v.i.) to be so relieved.

desenrugar (v.t.) to unwrinkle, remove the wrinkles.

desensaboar (v.t.) to rinse of soap.

desensacar (v.t.) to unsack.

desensangüentar (v.t.) to dry (wipe, clean up) the blood.

desensarilhar (v.t.) to unstack (rifles).

desensebar (v.t.) to rid of grease spots.

desensinar (v.t.) to unteach.

desensoberbecer (v.t.) to humble (**-se,** oneself).

desensurdecer (v.t.) to relieve of deafness; (v.i.) to be so relieved.

desentaipar (v.t.) to unpen (a prisoner).

desentalar (v.t.) to remove from splints; to free from (trouble, difficulties, etc.); (v.r.) to get out of a tight spot, free of trouble.

desentender (v.t.) to misunderstand; to feign ignorance; (v.r.) to have a misunderstanding.

desentendido -**da** (adj.) without understanding; misunderstood. **fazer-se de**—, to make believe one does not understand; to turn a deaf ear to.

desentendimento (m.) misunderstanding, disagreement; unpleasantness; want of understanding, misconception.

desentenebrecer (v.t.) to scatter the darkness.

desenternecer (v.t.) to cause the loss of tenderness towards; (v.r.) to lose one's feelings of tenderness towards.

desenterrado -**da** (adj.) unearthed, exhumed; dug up.

desenterramento (m.) exhumation.

desenterrar (v.t.) to disinter, exhume; to unearth, dig up; to find, bring to light; to call up out of the past.

desentêrro (m.) exhumation.

desenterroar (v.t.) to break up clumps in the soil.

desentesar (v.t.) to render less taut, tense, stiff, firm; (v.i.,v.r.) to slacken.

desentesourar (v.t.) to remove (money) from the treasury; to dig up, discover (valuable knowledge).

desentoação (f.) dissonance.

desentoado -**da** (adj.) out of tune; discordant, dissonant, jarring.

desentoamento (m.) = DESENTOAÇÃO.

desentoar (v.i.,v.r.) to get out of tune; to sing off key; to speak or act in a discordant manner.

desentocar (v.t.) to unearth, rout out of hiding, ferret out.

desentolher (v.t.) to render less numb.

desentonar (v.t.) to take someone down a peg.

desentorpecer (v.t.) to remove the torpidity of, reanimate, wake up; (v.i.,v.r.) to wake up, come to life, regain vigor.

desentortar (v.t.) to untwist, unbend, straighten, make less crooked.

desentrançar (v.t.) to unplait (the hair).

desentranhar (v.t.) to draw from the bowels of the earth, from the depths of the soul; to disembowel, eviscerate; (v.r.) to commit harakiri; to sacrifice oneself (for another, for a cause).

desentravar (v.) = DESTRAVAR.

desentrelinhado -**da** (adj., Print.) unleaded.

desentrevar (v.t.) to relieve the paralysis of.

desentrincheirar (v.t.) to dislodge (the enemy) from the trenches.

desentristecer (v.t.) to take or drive away the sadness of; (v.r.) to cheer up.

desentronizar (v.) = DESTRONAR.

desentrouxar (v.t.) to undo a bundle of clothes; to untruss.

desentulhar (v.t.) to clear away impediments, rubbish, debris.

desentulho (m.) a clearing away of debris.

desentupimento (m.) an unstopping.

desentupir (v.t.) to unstop (as, the kitchen sink); to unclog, free of obstruction.

desenvasar (v.t.) to float (a vessel) which has got stuck in the mud.

desenvasilhar (v.t.) to pour (oil, milk, etc.) from a vessel.

desenvenenar (v.t.) to rid of poison; to administer an antidote against poison.

desenvencilhar (v.t.) to disentangle, disengage, untie, unknot; (v.r.) to free oneself (of obligations, duties, responsibilities, etc.).

desenvergar (v.t., Naut.) to unbend (sails); to remove (one's coat).

desenvincilhar (v.) = DESENVENCILBAR.

desenvolto -**ta** (adj.) unrestrained, uninhibited; self-assured; brazen; restless.

desenvoltura (f.) freedom from restraint; liveliness; brazenness, forwardness, boldness, lack of due modesty.

desenvolvente (adj.) developing.

desenvolver (v.t.) to develop, cause to grow, bring out; to expound; to unfold (an idea); (Mil.) to deploy; (Math.) to develop; (v.r.) to develop, grow, evolve; to unfold.

desenvolvimento (m.) development; (Mil.) deployment.

desenvolvível (adj.) developable.

desenxabidez (f.) insipidity; vapidity.

desenxabido -**da** (adj.) vapid, insipid; uninspired; humdrum; tame, flat; wishy-washy.

desenxabimento (m.) = DESENXABIDEZ.

desenxamear (v.t.) to disperse, break up a swarm of anything.

desenxovalhar (v.t.) to remove stains from (clothing, reputation).

desequilibrado -**da** (adj.) unbalanced.

desequilibrar (v.t.) to unbalance; (v.r.) to become unbalanced.

desequilíbrio (m.) disequilibrium, instability; imbalance.

deserção (*f.*) desertion.
deserdado –da (*adj.*) disinherited; ungifted, untalented.
deserdar (*v.t.*) to disinherit.
desertar (*v.t.*) to desert, leave, quit; to abandon one's post.
deserto –ta (*adj.*) deserted, forsaken; (*m.*) desert.
desertor (*m.*) deserter, runaway.
desesperação (*f.*) desperation; anger, fury [= DESESPÊRO].
desesperado –da (*adj.*) desperate, hopeless; dispairing; reckless; furious; (*m.,f.*) such a one.
desesperança (*f.*) despair, hopelessness.
desesperançado –da (*adj.*) hopeless, despairing.
desesperançar (*v.t.*) to dash or destroy the hopes of; to dishearten.—-se de, to despair of.
desesperar (*v.t.*) to drive to despair or to desperation; (*v.i.*) to despair, despond; to grow desperate; (*v.r.*) to rage, rave; to despair.
desespêro (*m.*) despair, loss of hope; desperation, rage, fury.—-dos-pintores, (*Bot.*) the Londonpride saxifrage (*S. umbrosa*). dar o—, to fly into a rage. em or com—, desperately; doggedly. em—de cause, in despair, in desperation, at wit's end, as a last resort.
desestima, –timação (*f.*) disesteem.
desestimar (*v.t.*) to disesteem; to undervalue; (*v.r.*) to be wanting in self-esteem.
desestorvar (*v.t.*) to remove the impediment from, to disimpede.
desestudado –da (*adj.*) unstudied.
desexcomunicar (*v.t.*) to disexcommunicate.
desfabricar (*v.t.*) to unmake, undo.
desfaçar-se (*v.r.*) to become insolent.
desfaçatez (*f.*) effrontery, impudence, brass, shamelessness.
desfadigar (*v.t.*) to take away the fatigue of, give rest to; (*v.r.*) to rest.
desfalcar (*v.t.*) to defalcate, embezzle; to reduce, curtail; to handicap.
desfalecente (*adj.*) faint, swooning; weakening.
desfalecer (*v.i.*) to faint, swoon; to droop; to sag; to weaken; to fade; (*v.t.*) to weaken.—de amor, to be lovesick.—no propósito, to waver in one's purpose.
desfalecido –da (*adj.*) faint; weakened; destitute.
desfalecimento (*m.*) weakness, faintness; exhaustion; momentary shock; wavering; slowing down.
desfalque (*m.*) defalcation, embezzlement; shortage.
desfastio (*m.*) cheerfulness.
desfavor (*m.*) disfavor, disregard, disesteem.
desfavorável (*adj.*) unfavorable, unpropitious, disadvantageous, adverse, contrary; uncomplimentary; unfriendly.
desfavorecer (*v.t.*) to disfavor, discountenance.
desfazedor –dora (*adj.*) undoing, unmaking, etc. See the verb DESFAZER; (*m.,f.*) one who unmakes, etc.; (*colloq.*) one who enviously tears down others.
desfazer [47] (*v.t.*) to unmake; to undo (a knot); to break up (a meeting); to destroy (a city); to annul (a contract); to dissolve (a lump of sugar); to scatter (clouds); to squander (a fortune); to dispel (doubts); to rip up (a garment); to give up (a project); to unpack (a trunk); (*v.r.*) to dissolve.—-se de, to rid oneself of; to sell, dispose of; to get rid of; to be shed of.—-se de um mau hábito, to get rid of a bad habit.—-se em pranto, to melt into tears.—um êrro, to undo a mistake. Desfaz na bôca, It melts in the mouth. Ela desfez o noivado, She broke up the engagement. Foi obrigado a—-se de tudo que possuia, He was forced to dispose of all his possessions. O homem faz e Deus desfaz, Man proposes and God disposes. O sorvete se desfez, The ice cream melted.
desfear (*v.*) = AFEAR.
desfechar (*v.t.*) to fire (a gun); to hurl (an insult); to let fly (blow, arrow); to break open (a seal); to unlock (a door); (*v.i.*) to break (storm, tragedy); (*v.r.*) to go off (gun). Cf. DESFERIR.
desfecho [ê] (*m.*) conclusion, outcome, upshot; dénouement.
desfeita (*f.*) affront, outrage, deliberate insult, slur, slight; an undoing.
desfeiteador –dora (*m.,f.*) insulter.
desfeitear (*v.t.*) to insult, offend, affront, slight, slur; to flout.
desfeito –ta (*p.p. of* DESFAZER) undone, etc. See the verb.
desferir [21a] (*v.t.*) to strike (strings of musical instrument); to emit (music, sound); to let fly (blow, arrow, kick).—a vôo da imaginação, to indulge a flight of fancy.

Cf. DESFECHAR.
desferrar (*v.t.*) to unshoe (a horse); to unfurl (sails); (*v.r.*) to cast a shoe (horse).
desfiado –da (*adj.*) unravelled, shredded, frayed; (*m.pl.*) stringy fringes (as of a carpet).
desfiador (*m.*) a shredding machine.
desfiar (*v.t.*) to ravel, fray out, separate into threads; to enumerate, relate in detail; (*v.i.*) to trickle, stream (tears); (*v.r.*) to become frayed.—o rosário de suas mágoas, to recount (one's) troubles one by one.
desfia-trapos (*m.*) rag shredder.
desfibrado –da (*adj.*) without moral fibre.
desfibrador (*m.*) cane shredder.
desfibrar (*v.t.*) to shred; to defiber.
desfibrinar (*v.t.*) to defibrinate (blood).
desfiguração (*f.*) disfigurement, defacement.
desfigurado –da (*adj.*) disfigured, marred; haggard.
desfigurar (*v.t.*) to disfigure, deface, mar; to distort.
desfilada (*f.*) parade, marching; wild flight. correr a—, to run like mad, at full speed.
desfiladeiro (*m.*) defile, gorge, ravine, col, narrow pass; bottleneck.
desfilar (*v.i.*) to march (by files); to file by; to parade past.
desfile (*m.*) parade, review, pageant, procession; a marching by.—de modas, fashion show.
desfilhar (*v.t.*) to disbud (plants); to take away the children of; to break up and separate a beehive.
desfitar (*v.t.*) to take the eyes off of, to divert the gaze.
desfivelar (*v.t.*) to undo the buckle, unbuckle.
desflorar (*v.t.*) to deflorate, strip of flowers; to deflower, ravish; to ruffle the surface of (water); to strip or despoil (anything) of its best. Cf. DEFLORAR.
desflorescer [7], **desflorir** (*v.i.*) to lose blossoms; to fade, wither.
desfocado –da (*adj.*) out of focus.
desfolha, –lhação (*f.*) shedding of leaves (as in the fall).
desfolhada (*f.*) shucking (of corn).
desfolhar (*v.t.*) to strip (a plant) of leaves; to pick (a flower) apart; to shuck (corn). (*v.r.*) to drop its leaves or petals.
desforçar (*v.t.*) to redress (a wrong).
desforforação (*f.*) dephosphorization.
desformar (*v.*) = DEFORMAR.
desforra [ó] (*f.*) redress, satisfaction; a getting even. tirar uma—, to get even.
desforrar (*v.t.*) to avenge (-se, oneself); to get even; to recoup (one's) losses.
desfôrro (*m.*) = DESFORRA.
desfortuna (*f.*) misfortune.
desfraldar (*v.t.*) to unfurl (flag, sails).
desfranzir (*v.t.*) to unwrinkle (brow, cloth).
desfrechar (*v.t.*) to shoot arrows. Cf. DESFERIR, DESFECHAR.
desfreqüentado –da (*adj.*) unfrequented.
desfruta (*f.*) gathering of coconuts.
desfrutação (*f.*) = DESFRUTE.
desfrutador –dora (*adj.*) having the use, possession or enjoyment of; (*m.,f.*) one having the right of using and enjoying the profits or fruits of something belonging to another; a sponge, parasite; (*colloq.*) teaser, joker.
desfrutar (*v.t.*) to enjoy the fruits or profits of; to relish; to gibe at, rib, make fun of.—alguém, to live at another's expense.
desfrutável (*adj.*) enjoyable; open to ridicule.
desfrute (*m.*) enjoyment of, delight in; ridicule, derision. dar-se ao—da, to lend oneself to ridicule.
desfundar (*v.t.*) to remove the bottom of (a barrel, etc.).
desgabar (*v.t.*) to depreciate, disparage, belittle.
desgadelhado –da (*adj.*) = DESGUEDELHADO.
desgalgar (*v.t.*) to hurl (rocks, etc.) down the mountainside; (*v.i.*) to hurtle (as a car) down an embankment.
desgarrado –da (*adj.*) straggling; gone astray; lost; off course; adrift. ovelha—, lost sheep, strayed from the fold. Cf. DESAGARRADO.
desgarrar (*v.i.*) to stray; to go off course (ship); (*v.t.*) to put off course.—-se de, to break away (from), to stray (from); to straggle.—-se a, to turn aside, diverge (from).
desgasificar, –gaseificar (*v.t.*) to degas, degasify.
desgastar (*v.t.,v.r.*) to abrade, rub or wear off (away, out) to erode; to fray.
desgaste, –to (*m.*) abrasion, wear, wear and tear.
desgasto –ta (*adj.*) worn (out, off, away).
desgelar (*v.*) = DEGELAR.
desgeneroso –sa (*adj.*) ungenerous, petty.

desgornir (*v.t.*, *Naut.*) to unreeve.
desgostar (*v.t.*) to displease, irritate, annoy, vex; to disgruntle; to grieve.—**de**, to dislike.—**se de**, to lose one's liking for.
desgôsto (*m.*) displeasure, dislike; disappointment; sorrow, grief. [But not disgust, which is REPUGNÂNCIA].
desgostoso –**sa** (*adj.*) sad, sorrowful; discontent.
desgovernado –**da** (*adj.*) misgoverned, disordered; out of control (ship, automobile, etc.); adrift; wasteful.
desgovernar (*v.t.*) to misgovern, mismanage; to squander; (*v.i.*) to get out of control; not to answer the helm; (*v.r.*) to lose self-control, behave badly.
desgovêrno (*m.*) misgovernment, mismanagement, want of control; wastefulness.
desgraça (*f.*) misfortune, calamity; adversity, trouble. [But not disgrace, which is VERGONHA, DESONRA.] **prevalecer-se da—alheia,** to take advantage of another's misfortune. **por—(minha),** unfortunately (for me).**Uma —nunca vem só,** Troubles never come singly; It never rains but it pours.
desgraçado –**da** (*adj.*) unfortunate, unlucky; accursed; miserable, wretched; unhappy; poor (deserving pity); disastrous; poverty-stricken; despicable; (*colloq.*) sharp, shrewd, clever; [But not disgraced, which is DESONRADO.]; (*m.,f.*) wretch; (*f.*) prostitute.
desgraçar (*v.t.*) to render unhappy, bring misfortune upon; (*colloq.*) to deflower, ravish. [But not to disgrace, which is DESONRAR, INFAMAR.]
desgracioso –**sa** (*adj.*) ungraceful, ungainly, gauche; stiff; clumsy.
desgraxar (*v.t.*) to degrease.
desgrenhado –**da** (*adj.*) disheveled, tousled, unkempt, frowzy; rambling (in speech).
desgrenhar (*v.t.*) to dishevel, tousle. Var. DESENGRENHAR.
desgrudar (*v.t.*) to unglue; (*v.r.*) to come unglued.
desguampar (*v.t.*) to dehorn (cattle).
desguaritar (*v.i.,v.r.*) to stray, wander, get lost.
desguarnecer (*v.t.*) to remove the garrisons from; to disarm; to strip (of ornaments, munitions, furniture, provisions, etc.).—**se de**, to deprive oneself of.
desguedelhado –**da** (*adj.*) disheveled. Vars. DESGADELHADO, ESGUEDELHADO, ESGADELHADO.
desiderato (*m.*) desideratum.
desídia (*f.*) laziness, inertness; negligence.
desidioso –**sa** (*adj.*) idle; negligent.
desidratação (*f.*) dehydration.
desidratar (*v.t.*) to dehydrate.
desidrogenar (*v.t.*) to dehydrogenate.
designação (*f.*) designation, indication; selection, appointment (to a position).
designar (*v.t.*) to designate, denote; to indicate, point out; to select; to fix, determine; to appoint (to office).
designativo –**va** (*adj.*) serving to designate or to indicate.
desígnio (*m.*) design, purpose, aim, intention.
desigual (*adj.*) unequal, uneven; unbalanced; ill-matched, disparate, rough, irregular, rugged.
desigualar (*v.t.*) to render (men) unequal to, or different from, one another.
desigualdade (*f.*) inequality, disparity; unevenness.
desiludido –**da** (*adj.*) disillusioned; disappointed; undeceived.
desiludir (*v.t.*) to disillusion; to disenchant; to disappoint; to disabuse; to undeceive; (*v.r.*) to lose one's illusions; to give up hope. Cf. DESAPONTAR.
desilusão (*f.*) disillusionment; disappointment.
desilusionante (*adj.*) disillusioning.
desimaginar (*v.t.*) to dissuade (**de**, from).—**se de**, to forget about, put out of mind.
desimaginoso –**sa** (*adj.*) unimaginative.
desimanizar, desimantar (*v.t.*) to demagnetize.
desimpedido –**da** (*adj.*) unimpeded, unobstructed.
desinchar (*v.t.*) to reduce a swelling; to deflate (a tire, self-esteem); (*v.i.*) to become unswollen; (*v.r.*) to lose one's vanity.
desinclinar (*v.t.*) to make something plumb.—**de**, to disincline.
desincompatibilizar-se (*v.r.*) to resign provisionally from one public office in order to campaign for election to another.
desincrustante (*m.*) scale remover.
desincumbir-se (*v.r.*) to discharge, carry out (one's duty, etc.) get a job done.

desinência (*f.*) termination; (*Gram.*) ending of a word, esp. an inflection.
desinfe(c)ção (*f.*) disinfection; decontamination.
desinfe(c)cionar (*v.*) = DESINFETAR.
desinfestar (*v.t.*) to disinfest. **sair desinfestado,** (*colloq.*) to rush out headlong.
desinfetador –**dora** (*adj.*) disinfecting; (*m.*) a disinfecting apparatus; an exterminator.
desinfetante (*adj.; m.*) disinfectant.
desinfetar (*v.t.*) to disinfect, decontaminate; to cleanse, purify; (*slang*) to make oneself scarce (clear out, disappear).
desinfetório (*m.*) a disinfecting station; a delousing post.
desinficionar (*v.*) = DESINFETAR.
desinflamar (*v.t.*) to reduce inflammation.
desinflação (*f.*) deflation (of currency).
desinflar (*v.t.*) to deflate currency. [But to deflate a balloon or a tire is ESVAZIAR or DESINCHAR.]
desinquietação (*f.*) act of disquieting, annoying, bothering, pestering, upsetting.
desinquietar (*v.t.*) to disquiet, upset, bother, annoy.
desinquieto –**ta** (*adj.*) unquiet; (*colloq.*) restless, fidgety.
desintegração (*f.*) disintegration; decomposition, break-up
desintegrar (*v.t.,v.r.*) to disintegrate.
desinteligência (*f.*) misunderstanding, disagreement, dissension.
desintencional (*adj.*) unintentional.
desinteressado –**da** (*adj.*) disinterested; detached, unconcerned; unbiased, impartial; unselfish.
desinteressante (*adj.*) uninteresting.
desinteressar (*v.t.*) to deprive of interest or profit (**de**, in). —**se**, to lose or give up interest in.
desinterêsse (*m.*) disinterest; unconcern; unselfishness.
desinteresseiro –**ra** (*adj.*) disinterested; unselfish.
desintri(n)car (*v.t.*) to untangle, make clear.
desinvejoso –**sa** (*adj.*) not jealous, not envious.
desinvernar (*v.i.*) of winter, to come to an end; of troops, to leave winter quarters.
desinvestir (*v.t.*) to divest (of office).
desirmanar (*v.t.*) to separate (a matched pair, as of gloves).
desistência (*f.*) act of desisting; a giving up (of a cause, job, etc.).
desistir (*v.i.*) to desist, cease (**de**, from); to give up (an idea, a trip, etc.); to leave off (doing something).—**de fumar,** to give up smoking.
desjeitoso –**sa** (*adj.*) awkward, clumsy [= DESAJEITADO].
desjejua (*f.*) breakfast.
desjejuar (*v.i.,v.r.*) to break fast.
desjejum (*m.*) = DESJEJUA.
desjuizar [u-i] (*v.*) = DESAJUIZAR.
desjungir [25] (*v.t.*) to unyoke (oxen).
deslaçar (*v.*) = DESENLAÇAR.
deslacrar (*v.t.*) to break the wax seal of (a letter, etc.).
desladrilhar (*v.t.*) to remove the tiles from.
deslajear (*v.t.*) to remove the flagstones or slabs from.
deslambido –**da** (*adj.*) = DELAMBIDO.
deslanar (*v.t.*) to shear (sheep), remove the wool from.
deslassar (*v.t.*) to render slack or loose.
deslastr(e)ar (*v.t.*) to remove the ballast from.
deslavado –**da** (*adj.*) brazen-faced, shameless; discolored.
deslavar (*v.t.*) to render faded or discolored; to render insipid; to render shameless; (*v.r.*) to become insipid; to become bold-faced.
desleal (*adj.*) disloyal, disaffected, unfaithful; underhanded.
deslealdade (*f.*) disloyalty, unfaithfulness, disaffection.
deslealdar (*v.t.*) to treat (someone) disloyally.
deslegitimar (*v.t.*) to delegalize.
desleitar (*v.t.*) to wean [= DESMAMAR].
desleixado –**da** (*adj.*) lax, negligent, careless, lazy, slovenly, unkempt, untidy, slipshod, sloppy.
desleixar (*v.t.*) to slight; (*v.r.*) to become lax.
desleixo (*m.*) laxity, carelessness, negligence, remissness, dereliction.
deslembrança (*f.*) forgetfulness.
deslembrar (*v.t.,v.r.*) to forget.
deslendear (*v.t.*) to remove nits (from the hair).
desliar (*v.*) = DESLIGAR.
desligado –**da** (*adj.*) disconnected; indifferent, detached.
desligadura (*f.*), **desligamento** (*m.*) disconnection, separation; detachment.
desligar (*v.t.*) to disconnect, uncouple; to unfasten, untie;

to free (**de**, from); to turn off (light, alarm clock, radio, etc.); to hang up (telephone).—-**se**, to detach, separate, oneself from.

deslindação (*f.*), **deslindamento** (*m.*) unravelling; explanation.

deslindar (*v.t.*) to unravel, clear up (**a** mystery, a plot); to demarcate.

deslinde (*m.*) = DESLINDAÇÃO.

deslizamento (*m.*) act of gliding, slipping, etc.

deslizar (*v.i.*) to glide, slip, slide, skid.

deslize (*m.*) act of gliding, sliding, slipping, etc.; misstep, lapse.

deslocação (*f.*) dislodgement; displacement; misplacement; dislocation (of arm, shoulder, etc.).

deslocado –**da** (*adj.*) displaced; misplaced; out of place; dislocated.—**de guerra**, displaced person.

deslocar (*v.t.*) to displace; to remove, transport, shift (from one place to another); to misplace; to dislocate (arm, leg, etc.).

deslodar (*v.t.*) to clean the mud from.

deslombar (*v.t.*) to beat up.

deslouvar (*v.t.*) to belittle.

deslumbrador –**dora** (*adj.*) dazzling.

deslumbramento (*m.*) a dazzling, dazing, blinding (by excess of light, by great beauty, etc.); fascination.

deslumbrante (*adj.*) dazzling, blinding; gorgeous.

deslumbrar (*v.t.*) to dazzle, blind (by excess of light); to astonish, overpower (by splendor); to hallucinate; (*v.i.*) to be dazzling; (*v.r.*) to be fascinated (**com**, by).

deslustrado –**da** (*adj.*) dull, tarnished.

deslustrar (*v.t.*) to tarnish; to dull; to sully; (*v.r.*) to become dull.

deslustre, –**tro** (*m.*) tarnishing (of reputation); dulling, dimming.

deslustroso –**sa** (*adj.*) lackluster; dull; tarnished.

desluzido –**da** (*adj.*) lusterless, dim.

desluzir (*v.t.*) to obscure; to darken; to tarnish; to discredit.

desmagnetizar (*v.t.*) to demagnetize.

desmaiado –**da** (*adj.*) unconscious; dull, dim, faded; slight; faint.

desmaiar (*v.i.,v.r.*) to faint, swoon; pass out; to turn pale; (*v.t.*) to discolor, cause to fade.

desmama, **desmamação** (*f.*), **desmamamento** (*m.*) weaning.

desmamar (*v.t.*) to wean.

desmanar (*v.t.*) to cause to stray from the herd or flock; (*v.r.*) to stray therefrom.

desmancha (*f.*) manufacture of manioc meal [= FARINHADA].

desmanchadão –**dona** (*adj.; m.,f.*) slovenly, slipshod (person).

desmanchadeira (*f., colloq.*) woman abortionist.

desmanchadela (*f.*) act of breaking up, undoing, etc. See the verb DESMANCHAR.

desmanchadiço –**ça** (*adj.*) easily broken up, undone, spoiled, etc.

desmancha-prazeres (*m.,f.*) kill-joy, wet blanket, dog in the manger.

desmanchar (*v.t.*) to rip up (as, a garment); to undo; to smash; to tear down; to take to pieces (as, a toy); to break up (a plot, a marriage engagement); to cancel (a contract); (*v.r.*) to come undone; to fall apart; to spoil (as, a cake).—**se em gargalhadas**, to double up in laughter.—**se em gentilezas, em desculpas**, to overdo oneself in politeness, in excuses. **Ela desmanchou o noivado**, She broke up her engagement.

desmancha-sambas (*m., slang*) hoodlum.

desmancho (*m.*) a breaking up, spoiling, undoing; (*colloq.*) abortion; miscarriage.

desmandado –**da** (*adj.*) countermanded, revoked; undisciplined.

desmandar (*v.t.*) to countermand, repeal, revoke; (*v.r.*) to go to extremes, commit excesses; to swerve from normal procedure.

desmandibular (*v.t.*) to cause someone to drop his jaw in amazement; (*v.r.*) to open wide one's mouth (in amazement).

desmando (*m.*) immoderation; want of discipline; flagrant disregard for rules, law and order; outrage.

desmanear (*v.t.*) to unfetter (an animal).

desmaninhar (*v.t.*) to bring wild land under cultivation.

desmantelado –**da** (*adj.*) dismantled; unrigged; broken up; run-down; tumble-down; demolished.

desmantelar (*v.t.*) to dismantle; to raze, demolish; to ruin;

(*v.r.*) to tumble, come down.

desmantêlo (*m.*) dismantlement; (*colloq.*) disorder; disrepair; unrepair.

desmarcado –**da** (*adj.*) outsize, huge.

desmarcar (*v.t.*) to remove the signs or marks; to render immoderate or excessive.

desmarear (*v.t.*) to remove stains (from); (*v.r.*) to go out of control.

desmascarar (*v.t.*) to unmask, expose, disclose; to debunk; (*v.r.*) to remove one's mask.

desmastr(e)ar (*v.t.*) to dismast; (*v.i.,v.r.*) of a ship, to lose its masts.

desmastreio (*m., colloq.*) "female trouble".

desmatar (*v.t.*) to deforest; to clear (land).

desmaterializar (*v.t.,v.r.*) to dematerialize.

desmazelado –**da** (*adj.*) careless, negligent; slovenly, untidy, slipshod.

desmazelar-se (*v.r.*) to become negligent, slipshod.

desmazêlo (*m.*) carelessness, negligence.

desmedidamente (*adv.*) unduly.

desmedido –**da** (*adj.*) immense, enormous; outsize; extraordinary (as, courage); inordinate (as ambition).

desmedir-se [60] (*v.r.*) = DESCOMEDIR-SE.

desmedrar (*v.t.*) to stunt, check (growth); (*v.i.*) to wilt, droop; to grow thin.

desmelindrar (*v.*) = DESAGRAVAR.

desmembramento (*m.*) dismemberment.

desmembrar (*v.t.*) to dismember.

desmemoriado –**da** (*adj.*) forgetful, unretentive; (*m.,f.*) one who has suffered a loss of memory; a victim of amnesia.

desmemoriar (*v.t.*) to cause forgetfulness of; (*v.r.*) to be forgetful of.

desmentido (*m.*) denial, contradiction, negation.

desmentir [21a] (*v.t.*) to give the lie to; to deny the truth of; to belie, refute, contradict; to deny, gainsay; (*v.r.*) to contradict oneself.

desmerecedor –**dora** (*adj.*) undeserving, unworthy.

desmerecer (*v.t.*) to undeserve, fail to deserve; to deprive of merit, detract from, disparage; (*v.i.*) to lose merit; to fade (as, cloth).—**de**, to be undeserving, unworthy, of. —**em**, to belittle.—**para com alguém**, to suffer the loss of another's regard.

desmerecido –**da** (*adj.*) unmerited, undeserved; faded.

desmerecimento (*m.*) demerit; unworthiness.

desmesurado –**da** (*adj.*) enormous; (of cost) inordinate.

desmesurar-se (*v.r.*) to go beyond the bounds of (propriety, etc.).

desmídio (*m., Bot.*) desmid.

desmilinguir-se (*v.r.*) to decrease, lessen, fall away, erode.

desmilitarizar (*v.t.*) to demilitarize.

desmiolado –**da** (*adj.*) lacking in brains; brainless, addlepated, rattle-brained; scatter-brained. [= ESMIOLADO, DESPARAFUSADO, "PANCADA".]

desmobilar (*v.t.*) to remove the furniture from (a house, apartment) etc. Var. DESMOBILIAR, DESMOBILHAR.

desmobilizar (*v.t.*) to demobilize.

desmochar (*v.t.*) to deprive of horns or limbs.

desmócito (*m.*) desmocyte.

desmoderar (*v.*) = DESCOMEDIR.

desmódio (*m.*) the genus (*Demodium, syn. Meibomia*) of tickclovers or tick trefoils.

desmodulador (*m., Radio*) detector.

desmodular (*v.t., Radio*) to detect, rectify.

desmografia (*f.*) desmography.

desmóide, **desmoídeo** –**dea** (*adj., Anat.*) desmoid, ligamentous, fibroid.

desmomiário (*m., Zool.*) any member of the suborder Hemimyaria [= SALPA].

desmonetizar (*v.t.*) to demonetize.

desmontado –**da** (*adj.*) dismounted (from a horse); dismantled [machinery]; (*f.*) act of dismounting.

desmontar (*v.t.*) to unhorse; to pull or bring down; to disassemble, dismantle (as, machinery); to raze (a hill); (*v.i.,v.r.*) to dismount (**de**, from).

desmontável (*adj.*) dismountable.

desmonte (*m.*) disassembly, dismantling; ore extraction; tearing down (of a hill), as by hydraulicking and sluicing.

desmoralização (*f.*) disparagement; demoralization.

desmoralizado –**da** (*adj.*) discredited; demoralized.

desmoralizador –**dora** (*adj.*) demoralizing.

desmoralizar (*v.t.*) to disparage, discredit; to down-grade; to demoralize; (*v.r.*) to become corrupt.

desmoronação (*f.*) = DESMORONAMENTO.

desmoronadiço -ça (*adj.*) shaky, apt to fall or crumble (as a wall, building, etc.).

desmoronamento (*m.*) collapse (as of a wall or building); cave-in (of a tunnel); landslide; washout (of a road).

desmoronar (*v.t.*) to demolish; (*v.r.*) to tumble down, collapse, cave-in, crumble, slide.

desmunhecar (*v.t.*) to cut off a limb.

desnacionalizar (*v.t.*) to denationalize.

desnatadeira (*f.*) cream separator (machine).

desnatar (*v.t.*) to separate (or skim) cream from milk.

desnaturado -da (*adj.*) unnatural, heartless; denatured [alcohol].

desnaturalizar (*v.t.*) to denaturalize.

desnaturante (*m.*) a denaturing agent, as for alcohol.

desnaturar (*v.t.*) to denature; to pervert; to misrepresent.

desnecessario -ria (*adj.*) unnecessary, needless, uncalled for.

desnecessitar (*v.t.*) not to have need of.

desnegociar (*v.t.*) to call off a deal.

desnervar (*v.*) = ENERVAR.

desniquelar (*v.t.*) to remove the nickel content of.

desnitrar (*v.t.*) to denitrate.

desnitrificar (*v.t.*) to denitrify.

desnível (*m.*) difference in levels.

desnivelar (*v.t.*) to render unlevel.

desnorteado -da (*adj.*) lost, off course; bewildered, muddled, confused; crazy; dizzy.

desnorteador -dora, **desnorteante** (*adj.*) bewildering, confusing.

desnortear (*v.t.*) to mislead, misguide; to throw off course; to bewilder; (*v.r.*) to lose one's bearings (lit. & fig.) Cf. DESORIENTAR.

desnudamento (*m.*) denudation.

desnudar (*v.t.*) to denude; (*Geol.*) to lay bare, as by erosion; (*v.r.*) to strip (undress).

desnudez (*f.*) nakedness [= NUDEZ].

desnudo -da (*adj.*) naked [= NU].

desnutrição (*f.*) malnutrition, undernourishment.

desnutrir (*v.t.*) to undernourish.

desobedecer (*v.t.*) to disobey.

desobediência (*f.*) disobedience; defiance.

desobediente (*adj.*) disobedient.

desobriga(ção) (*f.*) release from, or discharge of, an obligation.

desobrigado -da (*adj.*) unobligated, free, exempt of obligation.

desobrigar (*v.t.*) to exempt, free, release, exonerate (**de**, from, of) obligation; (*v.r.*) to discharge a duty, free oneself of obligation.

desobscurecer (*v.t.*) to enlighten (the understanding).

desobstrução (*f.*) unstopping, clearing, freeing of obstruction.

desobstruido -da (*adj.*) unobstructed.

desobstruir [72] (*v.t.*) to free of, or remove obstructions from.

desocupação (*f.*) unemployment; idleness.

desocupado -da (*adj.*) unoccupied; untenanted; vacant; unemployed; idle.

desocupar (*v.t.*) to disoccupy; vacate (a house); (*v.r.*) to become unoccupied, not busy.

desodor(iz)ante (*adj.*) deodorizing.

desodor(iz)ar (*v.t.*) to deodorize.

desofuscar (*v.t.*) to clear (the atmosphere); to enlighten (the mind); (*v.r.*) of the sky, to clear up.

desolação (*f.*) desolation, ruin, havoc; wretchedness, unhappiness; bereavement.

desolado -da (*adj.*) desolated, devastated; bleak; desolate, forlorn; disconsolate.

desolador -dora, **desolante** (*adj.*) desolating, devastating; dismal.

desolar (*v.t.*) to desolate, lay waste; to afflict, distress; to bereave.

desolhar (*v.t.*) to disbud (plants); to free (persons) from the evil eye.

desonerar (*v.t.*) to exonerate [= EXONERAR]; (*colloq.*) to degenerate.

desonestar (*v.*) = DESONRAR.

desonestidade (*f.*) dishonesty; indecency.

desonesto -ta (*adj.*) dishonest; crooked; indecent; unchaste.

desonra (*f.*) dishonor, disgrace, disrepute.

desonrado -da (*adj.*) dishonored, disgraced.

desonrar (*v.t.*) to dishonor, disgrace; to discredit; to sully; to deflower; to slander; (*v.r.*) to disgrace oneself.

desonroso -sa (*adj.*) dishonorable; disreputable; disgraceful; shameful.

desopilante (*adj.*) purgative; exhilarating; laugh-provoking.

desopilar (*v.t.*) to free of, or remove obstructions from; to exhilarate.—**o fígado**, (*colloq.*) to cheer up.

desoportuno -na (*adj.*) inopportune [= INOPORTUNO].

desoprimir (*v.t.*) to free (**-se**, oneself) of oppression.

desoras (*f.pl.*) **a**—, untimely; at a late hour of the night.

desordeiro -ra (*adj.*) disorderly; rowdy; unruly; (*m.*) rowdy, tough, plug-ugly, hoodlum, brawler, ruffian, roughneck, hooligan.

desordem (*f.*) disorder, confusion, disarray; turmoil, commotion; riot; tumult; uproar; shindy, ruckus, row, brawl, fracas. **em**—, pell-mell.

desordenado -da (*adj.*) disordered; topsy-turvy; disorderly; untidy; troublesome; inordinate.

desordenar (*v.t.*) to disorder, disturb, disarrange; (*v.r.*) to get out of hand.

desorganização (*f.*) disorganization, confusion, disorder.

desorganizador -dora (*adj.*) disorganizing.

desorganizar (*v.t.*) to disorganize, disorder, unsettle, disturb; to disarrange; to break up (an organization).

desorientação (*f.*) bewilderment; lack of judgment, foolishness.

desorientado -da (*adj.*) bewildered; at wit's end.

desorientar (*v.t.*) to throw off course, off the track; to cause to lose one's bearings; (*v.r.*) to become confused, bewildered, lost. Cf. DESNORTEAR.

desornar (*v.*) = DESENFEITAR.

desossar (*v.t.*) to bone (a turkey, etc.).

desova (*f.*), **desovamento** (*m.*) spawning, egg-laying (of fishes, etc.).

desovar (*v.i.*) of fishes, turtles, etc., to lay eggs; (*colloq.*) to come out with it (reveal something).

desoxidação [ks] (*f.*, *Chem.*) deoxidization.

desoxidante [ks] (*adj.*, *Chem.*) deoxidizing.

desoxidar [ks] (*v.t.*, *Chem.*) to deoxidize.

desoxigenação [ks] (*f.*, *Chem.*) deoxygenation.

desoxigenante [ks] (*adj.*, *Chem.*) deoxygenating.

desoxigenar [ks] (*v.t.*, *Chem.*) to deoxygenate.

desp. = DESPESA (expense).

despachado -da (*adj.*) dispatched, disposed of (referring esp. to official business); expeditious; outspoken; rough-and-ready; (*colloq.*) put to death. **negócio**—, finished business.

despachador -dora (*adj.*) expeditious; (*m.*,*f.*) dispatcher.

despachante (*m.*,*f.*) shipping clerk; forwarding agent.— **alfandegário**, customhouse broker.

despachar (*v.t.*) to dispatch, transact, dispose of, render decisions on (official business); to forward, express (goods); to hasten, expedite; to fill (a prescription).

despacho (*m.*) act of dispatching; transaction; an executive ruling or decision (as by a government official) consisting often of a few words written and initialed on a document; (*colloq.*) dispatch, diligence; a dressing down, rebuke; an object to conjure with.

despapar (*v.i.*,*v.r.*) of a horse, to hold the head high [= ESPAPAR].

desparafusar (*v.*) = DESAPARAFUSAR.

despargir, **desparzir** (*v.*) = ESPARGIR.

despatriota (*adj.*; *m.*,*f.*) = ANTIPATRIOTA.

despatriótico -ca (*adj.*) = ANTIPATRIÓTICO.

despatriotismo (*m.*) unpatriotism.

despautério (*m.*) absurdity, nonsense; crazy behavior.

despavorir [46] (*v.*) = ESPAVORIR.

despeado -da (*adj.*) untrammeled, unfettered.

despear (*v.t.*) to unfetter, unshackle; (*v.r.*) to free oneself.

despedaçador -dora (*adj.*) shattering.

despedaçamento (*m.*) act of shattering.

despedaçar (*v.t.*) to shatter, smash; to rend.

despedida (*f.*) leave-taking, farewell, departure; dismissal.—**-do-verão**, (*Bot.*) chrysanthemum.

despedir [60] (*v.t.*) to dismiss, send away; to fire (from a job); to oust; to emit; (*v.r.*) to say farewell, take one's leave.—**-se à francesa**, or **em latim**, to take French leave.

despegar (*v.t.*) to detach, unfix.

despêgo (*m.*) detachment, indifference, want of interest.

despeitado -da (*adj.*) resentful; piqued; spiteful, mean.

despeitar (*v.t.*) to pique, rile; (*v.r.*) to become riled, take umbrage.

despeito (*m.*) pique, resentment, umbrage; spite. **a**—**de**, in spite of, despite.

despejado -da (adj.) spilled, emptied; evicted; indecent, shameless.

despejadouro (m.) dumping place.

despejar (v.t.) to spill, pour out (as, wine from a bottle); to empty (as, the contents of a sack); to throw away or out (as, rubbish); to evict, dispossess, put out; to clear out; to vacate; (v.r.) to free oneself.

despejo [ê] (m.) act of spilling, pouring, emptying, or throwing out (of anything); eviction; garbage; slop; storage closet, catchall.

despelar (v.) = PELAR; DESCASCAR.

despenar (v.t.) to console, relieve of pain, sorrow, affliction; also = DEPENAR.

despencar (v.t.) to pick apart (as, a bunch of flowers, a bunch of grapes, etc.); (v.i.) to break off and fall (as, a rock from a mountainside); to topple (from a high place).

despender (v.t.) to spend (money); to expend (time, energy); to dissipate, squander (anything).

despendurar (v.t.) to take down something which is hanging.

despenhadeiro (m.) precipice, cliff, crag.

despenhar (v.t.) to precipitate, hurl headlong, cast down (from a high place or position); to bring low (in disgrace); (v.r.) to plunge (to ruin); to crash (to earth); to break (as a storm).

despensa (f.) larder, pantry.

despenseiro (m.) butler, steward, pantryman.

despenteado -da (adj.) uncombed, disheveled, unkempt.

despentear (v.t.) to dishevel, tousle.

desperceber (v.t.) not to perceive.

despercebido -da (adj.) unperceived, unnoticed, unobserved, unmarked; unseen; unfelt. Cf. DESAPERCEBIDO.

desperdiçado -da (adj.) wasted; wasteful, spendthrift.

desperdiçador -dora (m.,f.) spendthrift, wastrel.

desperdiçar (v.t.) to waste, squander, fritter away.

desperdício (m.) waste, squandering, loss; refuse.

desperfilar (v.t.) to disarrange (the alignment of); (v.r.) to get out of line.

despersonalizar (v.t.) to depersonalize; (v.r.) to be false, or act contrary, to one's nature or personality.

despersuadir (v.t.) to dissuade.—-se de, to change one's mind about (something).

despersuasão (f.) dissuasion.

despertador (m.) alarm clock.

despertar (v.i.) to rouse from sleep; (v.t.) to awake, arouse (appetite, suspicion); to wake; (v.r.) to awaken; to revive; (m.) an awakening.

desperto -ta (adj.) awake.

despesa [pê] (f.) expense, expenditure, outlay, cost, charge.—s de porte, carrying charges.—gerais, overhead expenses.—s miúdas, petty expenses.

despetalado -da (adj.) = APÉTALO.

despicar (v.t.) to avenge; (v.r.) to revenge oneself.

despiciendo -da (adj.) despicable.

despido -da (adj.) undressed, nude; bare [trees]; fig., free (from taint, vanity, etc.), stripped (of prejudice, etc.).

despiedade (f.) want of mercy, of pity; inhumanity.

despiedado -da (adj.) = DESAPIEDADO.

despiedar (v.) = DESAPIEDAR.

despiedoso -sa (adj.) pitiless, merciless.

despimento (m.) act of undressing.

despiolhar (v.) = ESPIOLHAR.

despique (m.) redress, satisfaction; revenge.

despir [21a] (v.t.) to strip, disrobe; to shed, throw off; to divest; dispossess (de, of); (v.r.) to strip, undress.—um santo para vestir outro, to rob Peter to pay Paul.

despistar (v.t.) to throw off the track, off the scent; to mislead.

desplantador (m.) gardener's trowel.

desplantar (v.t.) to strip of plants; to take up plants for transplanting.

desplante (m.) impudence, cheek; a lunge in fencing. dar-se ao—de, or ter o—de, to have the nerve (gall, brass) to (do something).

desplumar (v.t.) to pluck the feathers from [= DEPENAR].

despoetizar (v.t.) to make (life) dull, prosaic; (v.r.) to become so.

despois, vulgar form of DEPOIS.

despojar (v.t.) to despoil, rob, fleece, strip (of possessions); to deprive, divest.—-se de, to dispose of one's belongings (at a sacrifice).

despôjo [despojos (pó)] (m.) booty, loot; (pl.) scraps, leftovers.—s mortais, mortal remains.

despolarização (f., Elec.) depolarization.

despolarizante (m.) (m., Phys. Chem.) depolarizer.

depolarizar (v.t., Elec.) to depolarize.

despoliciado -da (adj.) unpoliced.

despolidez [ê] (f.) impoliteness.

despolir (v.t.) to render dull (unpolished).

despolpar (v.t.) to hull (coffee beans).

despontado -da (adj.) dull, blunt.

despontar (v.t.) to blunt; (v.i.) to appear, emerge, become visible; to sprout; to ebb; to come suddenly to mind; (v.r.) to be blunted.

desponte (m.) in Braz. agriculture, the practice of lopping off the tops of corn stalks to foster greater growth of the ears.

despopularizar (v.t.) to render unpopular; (v.r.) to become unpopular.

desporte, -to (m.) sport, game.

desportista (m.) sportsman; (f.) sportswoman.

desportivo -va (adj.) having to do with sports; sporting; sportive.

desposado -da (adj.) engaged; married; (f.) wife; bride.

desposar (v.t.) to marry; (v.r.) to get married.

desposável (adj.) marriageable.

despossar, despossuir [72] (v.) = DESAPOSSAR.

déspota (m.,f.) despot; (adj.) despotic.

despótico -ca (adj.) despotic; domineering, overbearing.

despotismo (m.) despotism, dictatorship, tyranny.

despotizar (v.t.,v.i.) to hold sway over, as a despot.

despovoação (f.), despovoamento (m.) depopulation.

despovoado -da (adj.) depopulated, deserted, uninhabited; (m.) a deserted place.

despovoar (v.t.) to depopulate, (v.r.) to become deserted.

despratear (v.t.) to desilverize.

desprazer [30] (v.t.,v.i.) to displease; (m.) displeasure.

desprazimento (m.) displeasure.

desprazível (adj.) unpleasant, disagreeable.

desprecatar-se (v.r.) = DESCUIDAR-SE.

desprecaver [65] (v.t.,v.r.) = DESACAUTELAR-SE.

despregado -da (adj.) loose, unfastened; smoothed out; unfurled; insolent. rir a bandeiras—s, to laugh uproariously.

despregar (v.t.) to unfix, take off (something which has been fastened or nailed on); to unpin; to remove (the nails from a board, etc., or the eyes from a scene or object); to smooth out, unwrinkle; to unfurl; (v.r.) to free oneself.

despreguiçar (v.) = ESPREGUIÇAR.

desprender (v.t.) to unfasten, release; to detach; to throw off (as heat); to loose.—-se (de), to come loose (from); to detach oneself (from); to issue (from).

desprendido -da (adj.) unselfish; unselfish.

desprendimento (m.) unselfishness; detachment; act of releasing.—de calor, a giving off of heat.

despreocupação (f.) unconcern, nonchalance.

despreocupado -da (adj.) unpreoccupied; unconcerned: nonchalant; happy-go-lucky; carefree.

despreocupar (v.t.) to relieve of concern or worry.

despreparo (m.) unpreparedness; ignorance.

desprestigiar (v.t.) to discredit, disparage, depreciate; to debunk; (v.r.) to lose one's prestige or standing.

desprestígio (m.) want of prestige; loss of prestige, authority, position, etc.

despretensão (f.) unpretentiousness, modesty.

despretensioso -sa (adj.) unpretentious, unassuming.

desprevenção (f.) improvidence.

desprevenido -da (adj.) unwarned; unwary, off-guard; not provided with, unprovided for; unprepared; (colloq.) having no money on one.

desprezador -dora (adj.) despising, disdainful of, neglectful of.

desprezar (v.t.) to slight; to scorn; to spurn; to disregard; to despise; to disdain; to neglect.

desprezível (adj.) despicable, contemptible; mean, paltry, worthless; negligible.

desprêzo (m.) scorn, contempt; disdain; defiance.

desprimor [ô] (m.) want of gentility (civility, courtesy, good manners).

desprimorar (v.t.) to tarnish (fame, reputation).

desprivilegiado -da (adj.) underprivileged.

despronúncia (f., Law) acquittal.

despronunciar (v.t., Law) to acquit.

desproporção (f.) disproportion, disparity.

desproporcionado -da, -cional (adj.) disproportionate; unequal, unbalanced; outsize.

despropositado -da (adj.) inopportune; preposterous: unreasonable; irrelevant; unconscionable.

despropositar (*v.t.*) to act or talk unreasonably, preposterously.

despropósito (*m.*) preposterousness; irrelevance; nonsense; extravagant amount of (money, goods).

desprotegido –**da** (*adj.*) unprotected, undefended, unarmed; exposed, unsheltered, uncovered.—**da fortuna,** underprivileged.

desproteger (*v.t.*) to deprive of or deny protection or shelter to.

desprovieto (*m.*) waste [= DESAPROVEITAMENTO].

desprover [66] (*v.t.*) to deprive of (provisions).

desprovido –**da** (*adj.*) unprovided with, destitute of, stripped of, lacking, without, devoid of.

desprovimento (*m.*) want of provision.

despudor (*m.*) impudence, shamelessness [= IMPUDOR].

despudorado –**da** (*adj.; m.,f.*) impudent, shameless (person).

desquadrar (*v.i.*)—**de**, not to square or tally with.

desqualificação (*f.*) disqualification.

desqualificado –**da** (*adj.; m.,f.*) disqualified (person).

desqualificador –**dora** (*adj.*) disqualifying; (*m.*) that which disqualifies.

desqualificar (*v.t.*) to disqualify.

desqualificativo –**va** (*adj.*) disqualifying.

desque = DESDE QUE.

desqueixar (*v.t.*) to break the jaw of.

desqueixelado –**da** (*adj.*) with mouth hanging open (in amazement).

desquerer [68] (*v.t.*) to leave off liking; to dislike.

desquerido –**da** (*adj.*) disliked; unloved.

desquiciar (*v.t.*) to unhinge.

desquietar (*v.*) = INQUIETAR.

desquieto –**ta** (*adj.*) restless.

desquitação (*f.*) = DESQUITE.

desquitar (*v.t., Law*) to divorce "a mensa et thoro".—**de**, to release from (an obligation); (*v.r.*) to separate legally (man and wife).—**se de**, to renounce, have done with; to quit, leave.

desquite (*m.*) a kind of divorce or legal separation which does not dissolve the marriage but discharges the parties from the duty of living together.—**amigável**, or—**por mútuo consentimento,** separation (of husband and wife) by mutual agreement.—**judicial**, or—**litigioso**, a legal separation.

desrabar (*v.*) = DERRABAR.

desraigar [a-i], **desraizar** [a-i] (*v.*) = DESARRAIGAR.

desrazoável (*adj.*) unreasonable.

desrecalcar (*v.t.*) to remove the inhibitions of.

desregrado –**da** (*adj.*) intemperate; unruly; disorderly; extravagant.

desregramento (*m.*) disorderliness; dissipation, intemperance, unrestraint.

desregrar (*v.t.*) to disrupt, disorder; (*v.r.*) to go astray; to dissipate.

desrespeitador –**dora** (*adj.*) disrespectful; (*m.,f.*) disrespecter.

desrespeitar (*v.t.*) to disrespect, disregard.

desrespeito (*m.*) disrespect; slight; defiance.

desrespeitoso –**sa** (*adj.*) disrespectful; flippant; "fresh".

desresponsabilizar (*v.t.*) to free (-**se**, oneself) of responsibility (**de**, for).

desrolhar (*v.*) = DESARROLHAR.

desroupar (*v.*) = DESPIR.

desrugar (*v.*) = DESENRUGAR.

dessa [DE + ESSA] of that, from that.

dessaber [74] (*v.t.*) to forget, unlearn.

dessaborido –**da**, **dessaboroso** –**sa** (*adj.*) unsavory; insipid.

dessagrar (*v.t.*) to desecrate.

dessalgar (*v.t.*) to desalt; to render tasteless; to remove the hex, spell (SALGAÇÃO) from.

dessangrar (*v.t.*) to bleed (lit. & fig.); (*v.r.*) to lose much blood.

dessaudar [a-u] (*v.t.*) not to greet.

desse, form of DAR [39].

dêsse [DE + ÊSSE], of that, from that.

dessecação (*f.*), **dessecamento** (*m.*) desiccation.

dessecador (*m., Chem., etc.*) a desiccator.

dessecante (*adj.*) desiccant, drying.

dessecar (*v.t.*) to desiccate, make dry.

dessicativo –**va** (*adj.*) desiccative, drying; (*m.*) a drying agent.

dessedentar (*v.t.*) to quench the thirst of; to water (animals); (*v.r.*) to quench one's thirst.

desseis, form of DAR [39].

desseivar (*v.t.*) to sap.

desselar (*v.t.*) to unsaddle.

dessem, form of DAR [39].

dessemelhança (*f.*) dissimilarity, dissimilitude, difference.

dessemelhante (*adj.*) dissimilar, different, unlike.

dessemelhar (*v.t.*) to make dissimilar; (*v.r.*) to differ.

déssemos, form of DAR [39].

dessensibilizar (*v.t.*) to desensitize.

dessentir [21a] (*v.t.*) not to feel.

dessepultar (*v.t.*) to exhume.

desserviçal (*adj.*) disobliging.

desserviço (*m.*) disservice.

desservir [21a] (*v.t.*) to disserve.

desses, form of DAR [39].

dessexualizar (*v.t.*) to unsex.

dessexuar [ks] (*v.t.*) to emasculate.

dessimetria (*f.*) dissymmetry, asymmetry.

dessimétrico –**ca** (*adj.*) dissymetric(al).

dessimpatizar (*v.r.*)—**com**, to have no liking for.

dessociável (*adj.*) unsociable.

dessocorrer (*v.t.*) not to give aid to.

dessolar (*v.t.*) to remove the soles from (shoes).

dessossegar (*v.*) = DESASSOSSEGAR.

dessoterrar (*v.*) = DESENTERRAR.

dessuar (*v.t.*) to wipe the sweat from; (*v.i.*) to stop sweating.

dessubjugar (*v.t.*) to free from subjugation.

dessubstanciar (*v.t.*) to deprive of substance.

dessuetude (*f.*) desuetude.

dessujar (*v.t.*) to remove the filth or dirt from.

dessulfuração (*f.*) desulfurization.

dessulfurar, dessulfurizar (*v.t.*) to desulfurize.

dessultório –**ria** (*adj.*) desultory.

desta [DE + ESTA] of this, from this.—**sorte**, thus; hence.—**vez**, this time; now.

destabocado –**da** (*adj.*) rough-spoken, outspoken, blunt, tactless, crude, cocky, "fresh," impudent.

destacado –**da** (*adj.*) outstanding.

destacamento (*m.*) detachment (of troops).

destacar (*v.t.*) to detach (troops); to cause to stand out in relief (as features of a sculpture); to staccato; (*v.i.*) to go as a member of a detachment (of troops); (*v.r.*) to stand out, be conspicuous; to distinguish oneself; to become detached; (*colloq.*) to die.—**de**, to detach from, separate from.—**para**, to cast (as a glance) towards.

destalingar (*v.t., Naut.*) to unbend (ropes).

destampado –**da** (*adj.*) uncovered (having no lid); boisterous.

destampar (*v.t.*) to uncover, remove the lid from; (*v.i.*) to cut loose (act wildly).

destampatório (*m.*), –**ria** (*f.*) uproar, fracas; loud argument.

destanizar (*v.t.*) to remove the tannin from.

destapar (*v.t.*) to open, uncover; to unstop.

destaque (*m.*) distinction, prominence, eminence. **pessôa de**—, person of note.

destarte [DE + ESTA + ARTE] thus, hence.

deste, destes, forms of DAR [39].

dêste [DE + ÊSTE] of this, from this.

destecer (*v.t.,v.r.*) to unravel.

destelar (*v.i.*) to fall to the ground [as ripe fruit].

destelhar (*v.t.*) to remove the roof tiles from.

destemer (*v.t.*) not to have fear of.

destemeroso –**sa** (*adj.*) unafraid.

destemidez [ê] (*f.*) intrepidity. Cf. DESTIMIDEZ.

destemido –**da** (*adj.*) fearless, dauntless, undaunted. Cf. DESTÍMIDO.

destemor [ô] (*m.*) fearlessness.

destêmpera (*f.*) annealing (of steel).

destemperado –**da** (*adj.*) intemperate; unruly; annealed [steel]; unseasoned, tasteless [food].

destemperança (*f.*) intemperance [= INTEMPERANÇA].

destemperar (*v.t.*) to dilute, weaken; to derange; to upset (the stomach); to untemper (anneal) steel [= RECOZER] (*v.i.*) to lose one's head; to speak or act insanely.

destempêro (*m.*) absurdity; fit of anger; (*colloq.*) gastrointestinal upset; tastelessness (of food).

desteridade (*f.*) = DESTREZA.

desterrado –**da** (*adj.*) exiled, banished; (*m.,f.*) an exile.

desterrar (*v.t.*) to exile, banish, expatriate; (*v.r.*) to emigrate.

destêrro (*m.*) exile, banishment; place of exile; wilderness.

desterroar (*v.t.*) to break up clods; to remove earth from.

destetar (*v.*) = DESMAMAR.

destilação (*f.*) distillation.—**destrutiva**, destructive distillation (of wood, coal, etc.).—**fracionada**, fractioned distillation (as of oil).—**primária**, straight-run distillation (of crude oil).—**sêca**, dry distillation.—**no vácuo**, vacuum distillation.

destilador –**dora** (*adj.*) distilling; (*m.*) still.

destilar (*v.t.*) to distill; to instill; (*v.i.*) to drip.

destilaria (*f.*) distillery.

destimidez [ê] (*f.*) boldness. Cf. DESTEMIDEZ.

destímido –**da** (*adj.*) bold, no longer timorous. Cf. DESTEMIDO.

destinação (*f.*) destination; fate.

destinar (*v.t.*) to destine, design; to predestine.—**-se a**, to dedicate oneself to (a given mode of life); to be intended for.

destinatário –**ria** (*m.,f.*) addressee, consignee.

destingir [24] (*v.t.,v.i.,v.r.*) to bleach; to fade.

destino (*m.*) destiny, fate; doom; destination; whereabouts; purpose, end. **com—a**, bound for.

destituição [u-i] (*f.*) dismissal from office. [But not destitution, which is MISÉRIA, DESAMPARO.]

destituído –**da** (*adj.*) deposed, dismissed; destitute; devoid of; deprived of.

destituir [72] (*v.t.*) to depose, dismiss, oust; to deprive of.

destoante (*adj.*) dissonant, discordant; harsh, jarring.

destoar (*v.i.*) to be discordant, jar, clash.

destocador (*m.*) stump puller.

destocamento (*m.*) operation of pulling stumps.

destocar (*v.t.*) to pull tree stumps from a field; to shave closely; to rout (animals) from their burrows or lairs.

destopetar (*v.t.*) to take (someone) down a peg; to trim a horse's forelock.

destorcedor (*m.*) small hand-operated sugar-cane crusher.

destorcer (*v.t.*) to untwist, untwine; to turn around (as, the head).—**caminho**, to retrace one's steps.

destorcido –**da** (*adj.*) active, quick; plucky.

destorroar (*v.t.*) to break up clumps of soil.

destoucar (*v.t.*) to remove the hood or bonnet from; to tousle the hair of.

destra (*f.*) the right hand. **à—**, on the right.

destramar (*v.t.*) to untangle; to unweave.

destrambelhar (*v.i.*) to get out of fix, go haywire.

destrancar (*v.t.*) to unbar, unbolt, unlock.

destrançar (*v.*) = DESENTRANÇAR.

destranque (*m.*) shindy, free-for-all; bad luck.

destratar (*v.t.*) to abuse, insult.

destravar (*v.t.*) to release the brake; to remove the shackles.

destrepar (*v.i.*)—**de**, to clamber down from.

destreza [ê] (*f.*) dexterity, skill. **com—**, adroitly.

destribar-se (*v.r.*) to lose one's stirrups or, fig., support.

destrilhar (*v.t.*) to throw off the track.

destrincar (*v.*) = ESTRINCAR.

destrinçar (*v.t.*) to particularize; to state or treat in detail; to untangle; to pick to pieces.

destrinchar (*v.t.*) to untangle.

destripar (*v.t.*) to gut (fish, etc.) [= ESTRIPAR].

destripular (*v.t., Naut.*) to unman (a vessel).

destro –**tra** (*adj.*) dexterous; deft, agile; clever.

destrocar (*v.t.*) to swap (something) back.

destroçar (*v.t.*) to shatter, wreck; to wreak havoc.

destrôço [destroços (ró)] (*m.*) destruction, havoc; (*pl.*) shattered remains, wreckage; debris.

destronar (*v.t.*) to dethrone; to take down, humble.

destroncado –**da** (*adj.*) dismembered, mutilated.

destroncar (*v.t.*) to dismember; to sprain (ankle, etc.).

destronizar (*v.*) = DESTRONAR.

destruição [u-i] (*f.*) destruction; havoc.

destruidor –**dora** [u-i] (*adj.*) destructive; (*m.,f.*) destroyer.

destruir [37] (*v.t.*) to destroy, demolish; to extinguish; to quell; to lay waste; (*v.r.*) to kill oneself.

destrunfar (*v.t.*) to force trumps (as in bridge).

destrutibilidade (*f.*) destructibility.

destrutível (*adj.*) destructible.

destrutivo –**va** (*adj.*) destructive.

destrutor –**tora** (*adj.; m.,f.*) = DESTRUIDOR.

desultrajar-se (*v.r.*) to get satisfaction, amends (for a wrong suffered).

desumanar (*v.t.*) to render inhuman; (*v.r.*) to become so.

desumanidade (*f.*) inhumanity.

desumanizar (*v.*) = DESHUMANAR.

desumano –**na** (*adj.*) inhuman; inhumane.

desunião (*f.*) disunion; breach, dissension.

desunir (*v.t.*) to disunite, disjoin; to set at variance.

desusado –**da** (*adj.*) disused, obsolete; unused, unaccustomed; unusual, uncommon.

desusar (*v.t.*) to discontinue the use of; (*v.r.*) to fall into disuse.

desuso (*m.*) disuse.

desutilidade (*f., Econ.*) disutility.

desvairado –**da** (*adj.*) crazy, crack-brained, wild, delirious, hallucinated, "off the beam". **de olhar—**, wild-eyed, frantic; (*m.,f.*) a lunatic.

desvairar (*v.t.*) to hallucinate, render crazy; to deceive, delude; (*v.r.*) to disagree (about); to stray; (*v.i.,v.r.*) to lose one's head; to wander.

desvaler [80] (*v.i.*) to lose value; (*v.t.*) to cause to lose value; not to help.

desvalia (*f.*) = DESVALIMENTO.

desvaliar (*v.t.*) to devalue; to undervalue, depreciate.

desvalidar (*v.*) = INVALIDAR.

desvalido –**da** (*adj.*) worthless; unlucky.

desvalimento (*m.*) worthlessness; disfavor.

desvalioso –**sa** (*adj.*) worthless.

desvalorização (*f.*) devaluation (of money, of the price of coffee, etc.); depreciation; loss of prestige.

desvalorizar (*v.t.*) to devaluate, depreciate (as, currency).

desvanecer (*v.t.*) to dispel (confusion, sorrow, etc.); to make vain, conceited; (*v.r.*) to evanesce, vanish.—**-se de**, to pride oneself on.—**qualquer dúvida**, to dispel all doubt.

desvanecido –**da** (*adj.*) dispelled; vain; grateful.

desvanecimento (*m.*) conceit, vanity; self-complacency, despondency; gratification; (*Radio*) fading.

desvantagem (*f.*) disadvantage; handicap.

desvantajoso –**sa** (*adj.*) disadvantageous.

desvão [-vãos] (*m.*) attic, garret; a hideout.

desvariado –**da** (*adj.*) beside oneself, delirious (with joy, pain, etc.). [= DESVAIRADO].

desvariar (*v.*) = DESVAIRAR.

desvaricado –**da** (*adj., Bot.*) divaricate.

desvario (*m.*) derangement, craziness; delirium; wildness, folly.

desvelado –**da** (*adj.*) unveiled; manifest; devoted, zealous.

desvelar (*v.t.*) to unveil; to keep awake; (*v.r.*) to be full of zeal (care, solicitude) for; to watch (by the bedside of).

desvêlo (*m.*) devotion, solicitude, zeal; diligence.

desvencilhar (*v.*) = DESENVENCILHAR.

desvendar (*v.t.*) to remove the blindfold from; to unveil, disclose, uncover.

desvenerar (*v.t.*) to disrespect.

desventura (*f.*) misfortune, misadventure, mishap; disaster; unhappiness.

desventurado –**da** (*adj.*) wretched; unhappy; unlucky; (*m.,f.*) a wretch.

desventurar (*v.t.*) to render unhappy, wretched.

desventuroso –**sa** (*adj.*) unhappy; unfortunate.

desvergonha (*f.*) shamelessness.

desvergonhado –**da** (*adj.*) shameless, unblushing; unscrupulous.

desvergonhamento (*m.*) = DESVERGONHA.

desvestir [21a] (*v.t.*) to undress (-se, oneself); [= DESPIR].

desvetar (*v.t.*) to unveto. [*A Brazilian neologism.*]

desviado –**da** (*adj.*) removed, distant, set aside, sidetracked.

desviar (*v.t.*) to divert, deflect, turn aside; to sidetrack, switch; to dissuade (**de**, from).—**-se de**, to avoid; to wander, stray, from; to keep clear of; to shun; to swerve.—**-se do assunto**, to digress.—**o olhar**, to look away.—**um golpe**, to parry a blow.

desvigorar, **desvigorizar** (*v.t.*) to deprive of vigor, render weak. (*v.r.*) to lose vigor.

desvigoroso –**sa** (*adj.*) weak, not vigorous.

desvincilhar (*v.*) = DESENVENCILHAR.

desvincular (*v.t.*) to free; to disentwine.—**-se de**, to disengage oneself from.—**bens de morgado**, (*Law*) to disentail an estate.

desvio (*m.*) deviation; deflection, diversion; detour, bypass; railroad switch or siding; evasion, subterfuge; sin of omission.—**padrão**, (*Stat.*) standard deviation. **no—**, (*colloq.*) sidetracked, jobless, idle.

desvirar (*v.t.*) to unturn or turn (something) back to a former position.

desvirginar, **desvirginizar** (*v.t.*) to deflower, deprive of virginity.

desvirilizar (*v.t.*) to destroy the virility of.

desvirtuar (*v.t.*) to disparage, minimize (the worth or

virtue of a thing or person); to misrepresent, misstate; to pervert.
desvirtude (*f.*) want of virtue.
desvirtuoso –**sa** (*adj.*) unvirtuous.
desvitalizar (*v.t.*) to devitalize; to sap.
detalhar (*v.t.*) to detail, particularize.
detalhe (*m.*) detail, particular.
detecção (*f., Radio*) detection, rectification. [But not detection in the sense of discovery, which is DESCOBERTA, REVELAÇÃO.]
dete[c]tive (*m.*) detective.
detector (*m., Radio*) detector. [But not one who detects, which is DESCOBRIDOR, REVELADOR.]
detença (*f.*) a detaining; a delay.
detenção (*f.*) detention; arrest, confinement. **casa de—,** temporary jail.
detento –**ta** (*m.,f.*) inmate of a jail or penitentiary.
detentor –**tora** (*m.,f.*) owner, holder; holder of an award, medal, etc.
deter [78] (*v.t.*) to detain, stop, hold back; to check, stem; to restrain; to retain in custody. [But not to deter, which is INTIMIDAR, COIBIR]; (*v.r.*) to tarry, linger; to stop, pause; to restrain oneself.
detergente (*adj.; m.*) detergent.
detergir [25] (*v.t.*) to deterge.
deterioração (*f.*) deterioration.
deteriorar (*v.t.*) to deteriorate; to damage; (*v.r.*) to deteriorate; to spoil.
deteriorável (*adj.*) capable of deterioration.
determinação (*f.*) determination, decision, resolution; instruction, order.
determinado –**da** (*adj.*) determinate; having definite limits; definitely settled; fixed; [But not determined, in the sense of resolute, which is DECIDIDO.] **em—dia,** on a given day.
determinador –**dora** (*adj.*) determining; (*m.,f.*) one who or that which determines, decides, etc. See the verb DETERMINAR.
determinante (*adj.; f., Math.*) determinant.
determinar (*v.t.*) to determine, ascertain; to cause, effect; to order, direct; to influence, impel; (*v.r.*) to decide (**a, em,** to); (*Med.*) to resolve (as a tumor).
determinativo –**va** (*adj.*) determinative.
determinável (*adj.*) determinable.
determinismo (*m.*) determinism.
determinista (*m.,f.*) determinist.
detersão (*f.*) detersion (of a sore).
detersivo –**va, detersório** –**ria** (*adj.*) detergent [=DETERGENTE].
detestação (*f.*) detestation, hatred.
detestar (*v.t.*) to detest, hate, abhor.
detestável (*adj.*) detestable, abdominable; mean; pesky.
detidamente (*adv.*) attentively, slowly; at length.
detido –**da** (*adj.*) detained; delayed; in custody; one held in custody. (*m.,f.*) = DETENTO.
detonação (*f.*) detonation.
detonador (*m.*) detonator; blasting cap; exploder.
detonante (*adj.*) detonating.
detonar (*v.i.*) to detonate; (*colloq.*) to fire (a gun).
detração (*f.*) detraction, disparagement.
detrair [75] (*v.t.*) to detract (**de,** from); to malign.
detrás (*adv.*) behind, back.—**de,** behind, back of. **por—(de),** from behind.
detratar (*v.t.*) to disparage, depreciate.
detrativo –**va** (*adj.*) detractive.
detrator –**tora** (*adj.*) detracting; (*m.,f.*) detractor, maligner.
detrimento (*m.*) detriment, injury, loss, damage. **em—de,** to the detriment of.
detrítico –**ca** (*adj.*) detrital.
detrito (*m.*) detritus, debris; chaff; (*Geol.*) debris.
detruncar (*v.*) = TRUNCAR.
deturbação (*f.*) perturbation.
deturbar (*v.t.*) to disturb, perturb [=PERTURBAR].
deturpação (*f.*) disfigurement, debasement; defilement, adulteration; perversion.
deturpar (*v.t.*) to disfigure, deform; to debase; to defile; to distort; to garble; to adulterate; to pervert.
deu, form of DAR [39].
deus (*m.*) god; (*cap.*) God.—**me livre!** God forbid!—**queira!** would to God!—**travêsso,** Cupid. **Graças a—!** Thank God! **meu—!** good Lord! **pelo amor de—,** for God's sake. **queira—,** or **se—quiser,** God willing. **um—nos-acuda,** an uproar.

deusa (*f.*) goddess.
deutério (*m., Chem.*) deuterium.
dêuteron (*m., Chem.*) deuteron; deuton; diplon.
deuterogamia (*f.*) deuterogamy.
deuterógamo –**ma** (*m.,f.*) deuterogamist.
deuteropatia (*f., Med.*) deuteropathy.
deuteroprisma (*m., Cryst.*) deuteroprism (a prism of the second order).
deuteroscopia (*f.*) deuteroscopy.
deutocloreto (*m., Chem.*) deutochloride.
deutoplasma (*m., Biol.*) deutoplasm.
déutzia (*f., Bot.*) the genus Deutzia.
devagar (*adv.*) slowly.—**-se-vai-ao-longe,** a game somewhat like parchisi.
devagar(z)inho (*adv.*) very slowly; slow and easy.
devaneador –**dora** (*m.,f.*) daydreamer; (*adj.*) daydreaming.
devanear (*v.i.*) to daydream, muse.
devaneio (*m.*) daydream, fancy, reverie; wool-gathering.
devassa (*f.*) official inquiry; exhaustive investigation, probe; dissolute woman. Cf. DEVASSO.
devassado –**da** (*adj.*) open to public view or access (said of private property).
devassador –**dora** (*m.,f.*) one who divulges or exposes (a secret or private matter).
devassamento (*m.*) exposure; invasion of privacy.
devassar (*v.t.*) to invade, penetrate, encroach upon (another's home, privacy, etc.); to overlook, afford a view over, look over, as from a higher position; to pry into, make inquiry about; to divulge, expose; to debauch; (*v.r.*) to become common knowledge; to become debauched.
devassidão (*f.*) licentiousness; lechery; debauchery; whoredom.
devasso –**sa** (*adj.*) wanton, dissolute, debauched; lecherous; (*m.*) libertine, rake, debauchee, lecher.
devastação (*f.*) devastation; havoc.
devastador –**dora** (*adj.*) devastating; (*m.*) ravager, plunderer, despoiler.
devastar (*v.t.*) to devastate, ravage, pillage, loot, plunder, lay waste.
deve (*m.*) debit item, debit column (in bookkeeping). —**e haver,** debit and credit.
devedor –**dora** (*adj.*) owing, in debt; (*m.,f.*) debtor.
dever (*m.*) duty, obligation; task; (*v.t.*) to owe (obedience, money, etc.) to. [dever+verb=should or ought to +verb, as: **Que devo fazer?** What shall I do? **Dever** is used also as an auxiliary impersonal verb, as: **Deve ser uma hora,** It must be one o'clock. **Tal como deve ser,** as it should be.] Other examples of **dever**: —**a Deus e todo mundo,** to owe money to everybody.—**a vida a,** to owe one's life to.—**de honra,** debt of honor.—**os cabelos da cabeça,** or **os olhos da cara,** to be head over heels in debt. **Como devo responder a esta carta?** How should I reply to this letter? **Ela não devia ter pago tanto,** She should not have paid so much. **Você devia ter falado antes,** You should have spoken sooner.
deveras (*adv.*) truly, indeed, in truth.
deverbal (*adj., Philol.*) postverbal [= POSVERBAL].
devidamente (*adv.*) duly.
devido –**da** (*adj.*) due, owed; proper, fit; (*m.*) due, right, just title, lawful claim.—**a,** owing to; due to; on account of.
devitrificar (*v.t.*) to devitrify.
dev.º = DEVOTADO (devoted).
devoção (*f.*) devotion (all senses).
devocionário (*m.*) prayer book.
devocionista (*m.,f.*) a religious devotee.
devolução (*f.*) devolution; return, restoration.
devoluto –**ta** (*adj.*) devolved; vacant (land); unoccupied, untenanted. **terras—s,** unoccupied government lands.
devolver (*v.t.*) to restore, give back [but not to restore health, or a building, which is RESTAURAR]; to send back, return; to put back; to devolve, transfer, pass on.
devoniano –**na** (*adj.; m., Geol.*) Devonian.
devorador –**dora** (*adj.*) devouring, ravenous; (*m.,f.*) one who devours.
devorante (*adj.*) devouring; greedy; avid.
devorar (*v.t.*) to devour, eat up, eat hungrily; to consume, destroy, waste.
devotação (*f.*) act of devoting, dedicating.
devotado –**da** (*adj.*) devoted; dedicated.
devotamento (*m.*) devoting; dedication.

devotar (*v.t.*) to devote, dedicate, consecrate.—**-se a,** to devote oneself to.

devoto -ta (*adj.*) devout, religious; (*m.,f.*) devotee, zealot.

dexteridade [ex=ês] (*f.*) = DESTREZA.

dextrimanismo [ex=ês] (*m.*) right-handedness, dextrality.

dextrímano -na [ex=ês] (*adj.*) dextromanual.

dextrina [ex=ês] (*f., Chem.*) dextrin.

dextrocardia [ex=ês] (*f., Anat.*) dextrocardia.

dextrocular [ex=ês] (*adj.*) dextrocular.

dextrodução [ex=ês] (*f.*) dextroduction.

dextrogiro -ra [ex=ês] (*adj.*) dextrogyrous, dextro-rotatory, clockwise.

dextrômano -na [ex=ês] (*adj.*) dextromanual, right-handed; (*m.,f.*) a right-handed person.

dextropedal [ex=ês] (*adj.*) dextropedal.

dextrorrotatório -ria [ex=ês] (*adj.*) dextrorotatory, clockwise.

dextrorso -sa [ex=ês] (*adj.*) dextrorse.

dextrose [ex=ês] (*f., Chem.*) dextrose, glucose, grape sugar.

dextrosuria [ex=ês] (*f., Med.*) dextrosuria, glycosuria.

dextrotorção [ex=ês] (*f.*) dextroversion.

dextrovolúvel [ex=ês] (*adj., Bot.*) dextrorse.

dez. = DEZEMBRO (December).

dez [é] (*adj.*) ten; (*m.*) ten; the 10-spot (card).

dezembro (*m.*) December.

dezena (*f.*) ten, half a score; ten days. **às—s,** by tens.

dezenove (*adj.; m.*) nineteen.

dezesseis (*adj.; m.*) sixteen.

dezessete (*adj.;m.*) seventeen.

dezincificar (*v.t.*) to dezincify.

dez.º = DEZEMBRO (December).

dezoito (*adj.; m.*) eighteen.

DF = DISTRITO FEDERAL (Federal District).

dg = DECIGRAMA(S).

dia (*f.*) day; daylight.—**a—,** day by day.—**após—,** day after day.—**artificial,** the hours from sunrise to sunset. —**da Árvore,** Arbor Day (observed in Brazil on September 22nd, the first day of Spring in the southern hemisphere).—**da semana,** day of the week.—**das almas** = DIA DE FINADOS.—**de abstinência,** or—**de jejum,** day of fasting.—**de Ano Bom,** New Year's day.—**de anos,** birthday, anniversary.—**de finados,** (R.C.Ch.) All Souls' Day (November 2nd).—**de folga,** a day of rest; a day off.—**de (grande) gala,** national holiday.—**de juízo,** Judgment Day, doomsday.—**de Natal,** Christmas Day. —**de pagamento,** payday.—**de Reis,** Epiphany.—**de rosas,** a clear, windless day.—**de Santo Antônio,** St. Anthony's day (June 13).—**de São João,** St. John's day (June 24).—**de São Nunca,** Greek calends (the time that never comes).—**de São Pedro,** and—**de São Paulo,** St. Peter's and St. Paul's day (June 29).—**de semana,** week day.—**de trabalho,** work day.—**dois, três, etc.,** the second, third, etc., of the month.—**do Senhor,** the Lord's Day, Sunday, the Sabbath.—**enforcado,** or—**imprensado,** a work day falling between two holidays, or between Sunday and a holiday.—**escolar,** school day.— **feriado,** legal holiday.—**legal,** from midnight to midnight.—**letivo,** school day.—**livre,** a free day, a day off. —**magro,** meatless day; a fruitless day (one of poor results).—**por—,** from day to day.—**primeiro,** the first of the month.—**santo,** religious feast day.—**santo de guarda** or **santificado,** holy day of obligation.—**semanal,** week day.—**sim,—não,** every other day.—**útil,** week day; work day.—**s a fio,** days on end.—**s de favor,** days of grace.—**s gordos,** the six days preceding Ash Wednesday. —**s obscuros,** the Dark Ages. **ajuntar,** or **juntar, o—com a noite,** to work day and night. **algum—,** some day. **ao romper do—,** at daybreak. **Bom—,** or **Bons—s,** Good morning! **botar a escrita em—,** to bring the records up to date. **com—,** with daylight left (before nightfall). **da noite para o—,** overnight. **daqui a três—s,** three days hence. **de—,** in the daytime; by day. **de—em—,** from day to day. **de dez em dez—s,** every ten days. **de uns—s a esta parte,** for the past few days. **dentro de cinco—s,** within five days. **dois—s antes,** two days before (earlier). **É—,** It is day. **em—,** up-to-date. **em—s que estão por vir,** in the days ahead, in days to come. **há—s,** a few days ago. **há dois—s,** two days ago. **hoje em—,** nowadays. **luz do—,** the light of day, daylight. **mais—, menos—,** sooner or later; some day. **marcar um—,** to set a day, agree on a date. **no outro—,** the next day. **nos—s que correm,** in these times. **o—de hoje,** today. **o—todo,** all

day long. **outro—,** the other day; recently. **por—,** per diem; by the day. **qualquer—,** some day; any day. **todo o—,** all day long. **todos os—s,** every day; daily. **todo santo—,** every blessed day. **um—,** one day, some day (indefinite occasion). **um—atrás do outro,** one day after another. **Um—da caça, outro do caçador,** Every dog has his day.

diaba (fem. of DIABO) a she-devil. Vars. DIÁBOA, DIABRA.

diábase (*f.*), **diabásio** (*m., Petrog.*) diabase, diorite.

diabásico -ca (*adj.*) diabasic.

diabete(s) (*m., Med.*) diabetes.

diabético -ca (*adj.*) diabetic.

diabetômetro (*m., Med.*) diabetometer.

diabinho (*m.*), **-nha** (*f.*) little devil, imp [= DIABRETE].

diabo (*m.*) devil, demon, fiend; (*interj.*) the devil!—**a quatro,** hubbub, hell-raising.—**-marinho,** an angler fish (*Lophis piscatorius,* or *L. gastrophysus*), c.a. PEIXE-DIABO, PEIXE-PESCADOR, TAMBORIL, XARROCO. **acender uma vela a Deus e outra ao—,** to engage in double-dealing. **alma do—,** fiendish person. **com os—s!** the devil! **como—?** how the devil? **como um—,** like the devil (with great energy, in large measure, etc.). **Disse o—,** He raised the devil. **dos—s,** fiendish, enquanto **o—esfrega um ôlho,** in two shakes of a dog's tail, in a jiffy. **fazer o—para,** to leave no stone unturned to (achieve something). **mandar ao,** or **para o,—,** to tell (someone) to go to the devil. **onde—?** where the devil? **pintar o—,** to raise the devil. **pobre—,** poor devil, poor wretch. **que—!** what the devil! **que—quer você?** What the devil do you want?

diabólico -ca (*adj.*) diabolical, devilish, fiendish.

diabolismo (*m.*) diabolism, deviltry.

diabolô (*m.*) diabolo (a toy).

diabrete [brê] (*m.*) imp, mischievous child; urchin; sprite; hobgoblin; a certain card game.

diabrótico -ca (*adj., Med.*) diabrotic, corrosive, ulcerative.

diabrura (*f.*) deviltry; mischief; prank; lark. **fazer—s,** to act up.

diacáustico -ca (*adj.*) diacaustic; (*m.*) a diacaustic lens.

diacético -ca (*adj.; Chem.*) diacetic.

diacetilmorfina (*f.*) diamorphine, heroin.

diacho, euphemism for DIABO; (*exclam.*) the deuce!

diacidrão (*m.*) candied citron rind.

diacinese (*f., Biol.*) diakinesis.

diáclase (*f., Geol.*) diaclase, joint, fracture.

diacódio (*m., Pharm.*) diacodion.

diaconado, -nato (*m.*) diaconate, deaconship.

diaconal (*adj.*) diaconal.

diacônico (*m., Eccl.*) diaconicon.

diaconisa (*f.*) deaconess.

diácono (*m.*) deacon.

diácope (*f., Surg.*) diacope; (*Gram.*) tmesis.

diacrítico -ca (*adj.*) diacritical; (*Med.*) diagnostic; (*m.*) diacritical mark or point.

diactínico -ca (*adj., Physics*) diactinic.

diactinismo (*m., Physics*) diactinism.

díade, díada (*f.*) dyad, couple, pair.

diadelfo -fa (*adj., Bot.*) diadelphous.

diadema (*m.*) diadem, crown.—**-real,** (*Bot.*) the Katherine bloodlily (*Haemanthus katharinae*).

diafaneidade [e-i] (*f.*) diaphaneity, transparency.

diáfano -na (*adj.*) diaphanous.

diafanometria (*f.*) diaphanometry.

diafanômetro (*m.*) diaphanometer.

diafisário -ria (*adj., Anat.*) diaphysial.

diáfise (*f., Anat.*) diaphysis.

diafonia (*f., Music*) diaphony.

diaforese (*f.*) diaphoresis (perspiration).

diaforético -ca (*adj.; m., Med.*) diaphoretic.

diafragma (*m.*) diaphragm (all senses).

diafragmar (*v.t.*) to stop down (camera).

diagênese (*f., Petrog.*) diagenesis.

diaglifo (*m.*) diaglyph, intaglio.

diagnose (*f.*) diagnosis.

diagnosticador -dora (*m.,f.*) diagnostician.

diagnosticar (*v.t.*) to diagnose.

diagnóstico -ca (*adj.*) diagnostic; (*m.*) diagnosis.

diagômetro (*m., Elec.*) diagometer.

diagonal (*adj.*) diagonal, oblique, (*f.*) a diagonal; oblique direction.

diagrafia (*f.*) diagraphics.

diágrafo (*m.*) diagraph.

diagrama (*m.*) diagram, graph, chart, sketch.—, or **gráfico, em setores,** (*Stat.*) a circle chart.—**de enrola-**

mento, (*Elec.*) winding chart.—**indicador,** indicator card or diagram (as of a steam engine or gasoline motor).

diagramático –ca (*adj.*) diagrammatic(al).

dial (*adj.*) daily [= DIÁRIO]; (*m., Radio*) dial; sun dial. [But not watch dial, which is MOSTRADOR DO RELÓGIO, nor telephone dial, which is DISCO DO TELEFONE.]

diálage, dialágico –ca (*adj., Min.*) diallagic.

diálágio (*m., Min.*) diallage.

dialagito (*m., Petrog.*) diallagite.

dialdeído (*m., Chem.*) dialdehyde.

dialetal (*adj.*) dialectal.

dialético –ca (*adj.*) dialectic; (*m.,f.*) dialectician; (*f.*) dialectics.

dialeto (*m.*) dialect.

dialetologia (*f., Philol.*) dialectology.

dialetólogo (*m.*), **–ga** (*f.*) dialectologist, dialectologer.

dialho, euphemism for DIABO.

dialicarpelar (*adj., Bot.*) dialycarpous.

dialipétalo –la (*adj., Bot.*) dialypetalous.

dialisador (*m., Physical Chem.*) dialyzer.

dialisar (*v.t., Physical Chem.*) to dialyze.

diálise (*f., Physical Chem.*) dialysis.

dialissépalo –la (*adj., Bot.*) dialysepalous.

dialistêmone (*adj., Bot.*) dialystaminous.

dialítico –ca (*adj.*) dialytic.

dialogado –da (*adj.*) expressed in dialogue.

dialogador –dora (*m.,f.*) dialoguer.

dialogal (*adj.*) dialogic.

dialogar (*v.t.,v.i.*) to dialogue; to converse, talk.

dialógico –ca (*adj.*) = DIALOGAL.

dialogismo (*m.*) dialogism.

dialogista (*m.,f.*) dialogist.

dialogístico –ca (*adj.*) = DIALOGAL.

dialogita (*f.*), **–to** (*m., Min.*) dialogite [= RODOCROSITO].

diálogo (*m.*) dialogue.

dialúrico –ca (*adj., Chem.*) dialuric.

diamagnético –ca (*adj.*) diamagnetic.

diamagnetismo (*m.*) diamagnetism.

diamantário –ria (*m.,f.*) diamond merchant.

diamante (*m.*) diamond. Cf. BRILHANTE.—**bruto,** rough diamond.—**de vidraceiro,** glazier's diamond.—**industrial,** industrial diamond.—**negro,** black diamond, carbon diamond, carbonado.—**-rosa,** a rose (-cut) diamond.

diamantífero –ra (*adj.*) diamond-bearing [soil].

diamantinense (*adj.*) of or pert. to the city of Diamantina, in Minas Gerais; (*m.,f.*) a native or inhabitant of that city.

diamantino –na (*adj.*) diamantine; diamond-hard; diamond-bright.

diamantista (*m.,f.*) diamond dealer.

diamantizar (*v.t.*) to diamondize.

diamontóide (*adj.*) diamantoid.

diamba (*f.*) marijuana, hemp (*Cannabis sativa*) whose dried leaves and flowers are smoked in cigarettes. Other common names are: ALIAMBA, BIRRA, DIRIGIO, DIRIJO, LIAMBA, MACONHA, PANGO, RIAMBA and SORUMA. The leaves are called also BASEADO, CHEIO and FININHO. [The name **diamba** is a variant of RIAMBA, the African Baluba word for hemp, and among the Bantu there is a secret society with a riamba-smoking cult.]

diametral (*adj.*) diametrical.

diâmetro (*m.*) diameter.

diamorfismo (*m.*) = ENDOMORFISMO.

Diana (*f.*) Diana.

diândrico –ca, diandro –dra (*adj., Bot.*) diandrous, having two stamens.

diangas, dianha, euphemisms for DIABO (devil).

dianito (*m., Min.*) dianite, a variety of columbite.

diante (*adv.*) before; in front.—**de,** (*prep.*) in front of. **dai,** or **dali, por—,** from then on; thereafter; thenceforth. **daquela dia em—,** from that day on. **de hoje em—,** from today on; from now on; after today; henceforth. **de trás para—,** backwards; reversely. **e assim por—,** and so on, and so forth. **em—,** forward, on(ward). **ir por—,** to go ahead; to keep on. **para—,** forward, onward. **por—,** ahead, in front. **tocar para—,** to go ahead, proceed, get on with.

dianteiro –ra (*adj.*) front, frontal, foremost; forward; (*m.*) front-line player (in soccer); (*f.*) front; forepart; vanguard; the front or forward line of soccer players. **ganhar a—de,** to get ahead of.

dianto (*m., Bot.*) the genus Dianthus (pinks and carnations).

diapalmo (*m., Pharm.*) diapalma.

diapasão (*m.*) diapason; tuning fork; level; tone, tune.

diapedese (*f., Physiol.*) diapedesis.

diapófise (*f., Anat., Zool.*) diapophysis.

diapositivo (*m.*) lantern slide; a transparency.

diaquilão (*m., Pharm.*) diachylon.

diário –ria (*adj.*); (*m.*) diary; daily newspaper; the journal (in bookkeeping).—**de bordo,** ship's log; (*f.*) daily wage; daily rate (as of a hotel); daily expense; per diem expense allowance.

diarista (*m.,f.*) a worker for daily wages; diarist.

diarréia (*f., Med.*) diarrhea.

diarréico –ca (*adj.*) diarrheal.

diartrodial (*adj., Anat.*) diarthrodial.

diartrose (*f., Anat.*) diarthrosis.

diaspório, diásporo (*m., Min.*) diaspore, aluminum hydroxide.

diásquise (*f., Physiol.*) diaschisis.

diástase (*f., Surg.*) diastasis; (*Biochem.*) diastase.

diastasemetria (*f., Biochem.*) diastasimetry.

diastasímetro (*m.*) = DIASTÍMETRO.

diastema (*f., Biol., Zool., Music*) diastema.

diáster (*f., Biol.*) diaster.

diástilo (*m., Arch.*) diastyle.

diastímetro (*m.*) diastimeter.

diastole (*f., Physiol., Pros.*) diastole.

diastólico –ca (*adj.*) diastolic.

diatermanismo (*m., Physics*) diathermancy.

diatérmano –na (*adj.*) diathermanous, diathermic.

diatermia (*f., Med.*) diathermy.

diatérmico –ca (*adj., Med.*) diathermic.

diatomáceas (*f.pl., Bot.*) the diatoms (*Diatomaceae*).

diatômico –ca (*adj., Chem.*) diatomic.

diatomito (*m.*) diatomite, infusorial earth, diatomaceous earth.

diatônico –ca (*adj., Music*) diatonic.

diatreme (*m., Petrog.*) diatreme.

diátribe (*f.*) diatribe.

dibranquiado –da (*adj., Zool.*) dibranchiate, having two gills; (*m.pl.*) = DIBRANQUIAIS.

dibranquiais (*m.pl., Zool.*) the Dibranchia (squids, octopuses).

dibrânquio –quia (*adj.*) = DIBRANQUIADO.

dibrânquios (*m.pl.*) = DIBRANQUIAIS.

dic. = DICIONÁRIO (dictionary).

dicaba (*f.*) = PALMEIRA-DE-LEQUE.

dicaz (*adj.*) sarcastic.

di(c)ção (*f.*) diction.

dicéfalo –la (*adj.*) dicephalous, two-headed.

dicentra (*f.*), **dicentro** (*m., Bot.*) the genus Dicentra (bleedingheart and dutchmans-breeches).

dicentrina (*f., Chem.*) dicentrine.

dicério (*m., Eastern Ch.*) dicerion (a two-branched candlestick).

dichote (*m.*) biting jest; wisecrack.

dichotesco –ca (*adj.*) wisecracking.

dicíclico –ca (*adj., Bot.*) dicyclic, having two whorls.

dicionário (*m.*) dictionary.

dicionarista (*m.,f.*) lexicographer.

diclínea (*adj., Bot.*) diclinous.

diclinismo (*m., Bot.*) diclinism.

dicloroetileno (*m., Chem.*) dichloroethylene.

dicogamia (*f., Bot.*) dichogamy.

dicógamo –ma (*adj., Bot.*) dichogamous.

dicogamia (*f., Bot.*) dichogamy.

diconroque (*m.*) = FEIJÃO-DOS-CABOCLOS.

dicórdio (*m., Music*) dichord.

dicotiledôneo –nea (*adj., Bot.*) dicotyledonous.

dicotilídeo (*m., Bot.*) dicotyledon.

dicotomia (*f.*) dichotomy (all senses).

dicotômico –ca, dicótomo –ma (*adj., Bot.*) dichotomous.

dicrano (*m., Bot.*) a genus (*Dicranum*) of mosses.

dicroísmo (*m., Cryst., Physics*) dichroism.

dicroíta (*f., Min.*) dichroite, iolite.

dicromático –ca (*adj.*) dichromatic.

dicromato (*m., Chem.*) dichromate.

dicrômico –ca (*adj.*) dichromic, dichromatic.

dicroscópico (*m., Physics*) dichroscope.

dicrotismo (*m., Physiol.*) dicrotism.

dicrótico –ca (*adj., Physiol.*) dicrotic.

dictiógeno –na (*adj., Bot.*) dictyogenous.

dictióide (*adj., Bot.*) muriform.

dictiosperma (*m., Bot.*) the genus (*Dictyosperma*) of princess palms.

dicumarina (*f., Chem.*) dicoumarin.

didáctilo **-la** (*adj.*, *Zool.*) didactyl.
didascálico **-ca** (*adj.*) didascalic, didactic.
didático **-ca** (*adj.*) didactic; (*m.*) didactics, pedagogy.
didélfio **-fia** (*adj.*, *Anat.*) didelphic; (*Zool.*) didelphian; (*m.pl.*) the Didelphidae (opossums).
didelfos (*m.pl.*) = DIDÉLFIOS.
didi-da-porteira (*f.*, *Bot.*) a dayflower (*Commelina*).
didímio (*m.*, *Chem.*) didymium.
didimite (*f.*, *Med.*) didymitis, orchitis.
dídimo **-ma** (*adj.*, *Bot.*, *Zool.*) didymous, paired, twin.
didínamo **-ma** (*adj.*, *Bot.*) didynamous.
didodecaedro **-dra** (*adj.*, *Cryst.*) didodecahedral.
diécico **-ca** (*adj.*, *Bot.*) dioecious.
diédrico **-ca** (*adj.*) dihedral.
diedro **-dra** (*adj.*) dihedral; (*m.*) a dihedral angle.
dielétrico **-ca** (*adj.*, *m.*) dieletric.
diélia (*f.*, *Astron.*) dihelios.
diérese (*f.*) dieresis.
diesel (*adj.*) Diesel.
dieta (*f.*) diet. —**láctea**, milk diet.
dietética (*f.*) dietetics.
dietético **-ca** (*adj.*) dietetic.
dietista (*m.*,*f.*) dietitian.
dietoterapia (*f.*) dietotherapy.
difamação (*f.*) defamation, calumny.
difamador **-dora** (*adj.*) defaming; (*m.*,*f.*) slanderer; maligner; scandalmonger.
difamante (*adj.*) defaming.
difamar (*v.t.*) to defame, malign, smear, sully.—**de**, to speak ill of.
difamatório **-ria** (*adj.*) defamatory.
difásico **-ca** (*adj.*, *Elec.*) diphase, diphasic.
difenilamina (*f.*, *Chem.*) diphenyl amine, anilino benzene.
difenilmetano (*m.*, *Chem.*) diphenyl methane; ditan.
difenilo (*m.*, *Chem.*) diphenyl.
diferença (*f.*) difference, dissimilarity, unlikeness, divergence; discrepancy; distinction; (*pl.*) disagreement, misunderstanding, dissension.—**de fase**, (*Elec.*) phase difference or displacement.—**-padrão**, (*Stat.*) standard difference.—**de potencial**, (*Elec.*) electric potential, or potential difference expressed in volts; voltage. **à—de**, unlike, differently from.
diferençar (*v.t.*) to differentiate (one from another); to distinguish (between); (*v.r.*) to differ (from).
diferençável (*adj.*) distinguishable.
diferenciação (*f.*) differentiation.
diferencial (*adj.*) differential; (*m.*, *Autom.*) differential; (*f.*, *Math.*) differential.
diferenciar (*v.t.*) to differentiate, discriminate.
diferente (*adj.*) different, unlike, unequal.—**com**, (*colloq.*) on the outs (at variance) with. **coisas—s**, different things.—**s coisas**, some (several) things.
diferimento (*m.*) delay, postponement.
diferir [21a] (*v.i.*) to differ (**de**, from); (*v.t.*) to defer, postpone.
difícil [-ceis] (*adj.*) difficult, hard, arduous, "tough"; obscure, intricate; exacting; "fussy".
dificílimo **-ma**, dificilíssimo **-ma** (*absol. superl. of* DIFÍCIL) most difficult.
dificilmente (*adv.*) with difficulty; scarcely, hardly.
dificuldade (*f.*) difficulty, obstacle, impediment, hindrance; arduousness.—**s sem conta**, no end of troubles.
dificultação (*f.*) act of making difficult.
dificultar (*v.t.*) to make difficult; to put difficulties in the way of; to hamper; to represent as difficult; (*v.r.*) to. become difficult.
dificultoso **-sa** (*adj.*) difficult.
difidência (*f.*) diffidence.
difidente (*adj.*) diffident.
dífilo **-la** (*adj.*, *Bot.*) diphyllous, having two leaves.
difiodonte (*adj.*, *Anat.*) diphyodont.
difluência (*f.*) diffluence.
difluente (*adj.*) diffluent.
difluir (*v.i.*) to flow away from or out of.
difosgênio (*m.*, *Chem.*) diphosgene.
difração (*f.*, *Physics*) diffraction.
difratar (*v.t.*) to diffract.
difrativo **-va** (*adj.*) diffractive.
difringente (*adj.*) diffractive.
difteria (*f.*, *Med.*) diphtheria.
diftérico **-ca** (*adj.*) diphtherial.
difundido **-da** (*adj.*) widespread.
difundir (*v.t.*,*v.r.*) to diffuse, scatter, spread; to suffuse; to divulge; to broadcast.

difusão (*f.*) diffusion, dispersion; suffusion; radio broadcasting.
difusibilidade (*f.*) diffusibility.
difusível (*adj.*) diffusible.
difusivo **-va** (*adj.*) diffusive.
difuso **-sa** (*adj.*) diffuse, prolix.
difusor (*m.*) diffuser (in any sense).
difusora (*f.*, *Radio*, *TV*) station.
diga, digais, digam, digamos, digas, foms of DIZER [41].
digástrico **-ca** (*adj.*; *m.*, *Anat.*) digastric (muscle).
digênese (*f.*, *Biol.*) digenesis.
digenético **-ca** (*adj.*, *Biol.*) digenetic.
digenismo (*m.*) digeny, sexual reproduction.
digerido **-da** (*adj.*) digested.
digerir [21a] (*v.t.*,*v.i.*) to digest.
digerível (*adj.*) digestible.
digestão (*f.*) digestion.
digestibilidade (*f.*) digestibility.
digestível (*adj.*) = DIGERÍVEL.
digestivo **-va** (*adj.*) digestive. **aparelho—**, digestive system.
digesto **-ta** (*irreg. p.p. of* DIGERIR) digested; (*m.*) a digest, a summary.
digestor (*m.*) digester (apparatus).
digitação (*f.*) digitation.
digitado **-da** (*adj.*) digitate.
digital (*adj.*) digital. **impressão—**, fingerprint. (*f.*, *Bot.*) common foxglove (*Digitalis*), c.a. DEDAL, DEDALEIRA.
digitalina (*f.*, *Chem.*) digitalin.
digitalismo (*m.*, *Med.*) digitalism.
digitígrado **-da** (*adj.*) digitigrade; (*m.pl.*, *Zool.*) the Digitigrada.
digitinervado **-da** (*adj.*, *Bot.*) digitinervate, palminerved.
digitipenado **-da** (*adj.*, *Bot.*) digitipinnate.
dígito **-ta** (*adj.*, *Math.*) digital; (*m.*, *Astron.*) digit or point. [But not a digit (number under ten) which is ALGARISMO or NÚMERO DÍGITO.]
digitonina (*f.*, *Chem.*) digitonin.
digitoxina [ks] (*f.*, *Chem.*) digitoxin.
digladiação (*f.*) fencing; fighting; wrangling; disputing.
digladiar (*v.i.*) to fight with swords; (*v.r.*) to fight; to wrangle.
diglifo (*m.*, *Arch.*) diglyph.
dignamente (*adj.*) worthily; appropriately; honorably.
dignar-se (*v.r.*) to deign, condescend, see fit (**a**, to).
dignidade (*f.*) dignity, worthiness, excellence; rank, eminence; dignified behavior; pride.
dignificação (*f.*) act of dignifying.
dignificante (*adj.*) dignifying.
dignificar (*v.t.*) to dignify, honor, exalt; to elevate, ennoble (**-se**, oneself).
dignitário (*m.*) dignitary.
digno **-na** (*adj.*) worthy, deserving, meritorious; upright, honorable.—**de confiança**, trustworthy; reliable.—**de louvor**, praiseworthy.
digo, form of DIZER [41].
dígono **-na** (*adj.*) digonous, having two angles.
digrama, dígrafo (*m.*) digraph.
digressão (*f.*) digression (all senses).
digressionar (*v.i.*) to digress (in discourse).
digressivo **-va** (*adj.*) digressive.
digresso (*m.*) = DIGRESSÃO.
diídrico **-ca** [i-í] (*adj.*, *Chem.*) dihydric.
diiodofórmio [i-i] (*m.*, *Pharm.*) diiodoform.
dijambo (*m.*, *Pros.*) diiamb.
dilação (*f.*) delay, postponement, a putting off. [But not dilation, which is DILATAÇÃO.
dilaceração (*f.*) laceration.
dilacerador **-dora** (*adj.*) lacerating.
dilacerante (*adj.*) harrowing.
dilacerar (*v.t.*) to lacerate, tear to pieces; to afflict, torment.
dilapidação (*f.*) act of dilapidating. [But not dilapidation (state of), which is ESTADO DE RUÍNA.]
dilapidador **-dora** (*adj.*) dilapidating.
dilapidar (*v.t.*) to dilapidate; to dissipate (fortune).
dilatabilidade (*f.*) dilatability.
dilatação (*f.*) dilation, expansion, enlargement, distension, stretching; delaying.—**do prazo de pagamento**, extension of the time for payment.
dilatado **-da** (*adj.*) dilated, expanded, wide, enlarged.
dilatador **-dora** (*adj.*) dilating; (*m.*) expander; (*Anat.*) dilator (muscle); (*Surg.*) dilator, dilatant.
dilatamento (*m.*) dilation.

dilatante (adj.) dilating, expanding.
dilatar (v.t.) to dilate, expand, enlarge, widen, stretch; to spread, diffuse; to delay, put off.
dilatável (adj.) dilatable; distensible.
dilatômetro (m., Physics.) dilatometer.
dilatório -ria (adj.) dilatory.
dileção (f.) deep affection.
dilema (m.) dilemma.
diletante (adj.; m.,f.) dilettante; amateur.
diletantismo (m.) dilettantism.
dileto -ta (adj.) dearly beloved. filho—, favorite child.
diligência (f.) diligence, assiduity, industry, activity; judicial proceeding; stagecoach.
diligenciar (v.t.) to exert (one's best) efforts.
diligente (adj.) diligent, assiduous, active, up and stirring.
dilucidar (v.) = ELUCIDAR.
dilúculo (m.) dawn. [Poetical]
diluente (adj.) diluent.
diluição [u-i] (f.), diluimento [u-i] (m.) dilution.
diluir [72] (v.t.) to dilute, thin (with water or other liquid); (v.r.) to dissolve.
diluto -ta (adj.) dilute.
diluviano -na, diluvial (adj.) diluvial.
diluvião (m., Geol.) diluvium.
dilúvio (m.) deluge, great flood, inundation; great abundance.
dimanação (f.) emanation.
dimanar (v.i.) to emanate, flow forth.—de, to spring or proceed from.
dimensão (f.) dimension, measure; measurement; (pl.) dimensions, size.
dimensional (adj.) dimensional.
dimensível (adj.) measurable [= MENSURÁVEL].
dimérico -ca (adj., Chem.) dimeric.
dímero -ra (adj., Biol., Bot.) dimerous.
dimetilbenzeno (m., Chem.) dimethylbenzene, xylene [= XILÊNIO].
dimétrico -ca (adj., Cryst.) dimetric, tetragonal.
dímetro (m., Pros.) dimeter.
diminuendo -da (adj., Music) diminuendo; (m., Math.) minuend.
diminuente (adj.) diminishing.
diminuição [u-i] (f.) diminution; reduction; cutback.
diminuidor -dora [u-i] (adj.) diminishing; (m., Math.) subtrahend.
diminuir [72] (v.t.) to diminish, reduce, make smaller; to lessen; to decrease; (v.i.) to diminish, dwindle, become less or smaller; (v.r.) to waste away.
diminutivo -va (adj., m.) diminutive.
diminuto -ta (adj.) minute, very small, tiny.
dimissórias (f.pl., R.C.Ch.) letters dimissory.
dimorfia (f.), dimorfismo (m.) dimorphism.
dimorfo -fa (adj.) dimorphous.
dimorfoteca (f.) cape marigold (Dimorphotheca).
dina (f., Physics) dyne.
Diná (f.) Dinah.
dinágrafo (m., R.R.) dynagraph.
Dinamarca (f.) Denmark.
dinamarquês -quesa (adj.) Danish; (m.,f.) a Dane; (m.) the Danish language; a Great Dane (dog).
dinâmetro (m., Optics.) dynameter.
dinâmico -ca (adj.) dynamic; (f.) dynamics.
dinamismo (m., Philos.) dynamism; "pep," energy.
dinamista (m.,f.) dynamist.
dinamitar (v.t.) to dynamite.
dinamitaria (f.) dynamite factory.
dinamite (f.) dynamite.
dinamiteiro -ra (adj.) dynamite; (m.) dynamiter (terrorist); one who makes or uses dynamite.
dinamizar (v.t.) to dynamize (drugs); to energize, invigorate.
dínamo (m., Elec.) dynamo.
dinamoelétrico -ca (adj.) dynamoelectric.
dinamogenia (f., Psychol.) dynamogenesis.
dinamometamorfismo (m., Geol.) dynamometamorphism.
dinamometria (f.) dynamometry.
dinamômetro (m.) dynamometer.—de absorção, absorption dynamometer.—elétrico, electrodynamometer.—de freio, Prony brake.
dinamotor (m., Elec.) dynamotor.
dinastia (f.) dynasty.
dinástico -ca (adj.) dynastic.
dínatron, dinatrônio (m., Elec.) dynatron.
dindinha (f.) pet name for godmother or grandmother.

dindinho (m.) pet name for gódfather or grandfather.
dinheirada (f.), dinheiral (m.), dinheirama (f.), dinheirame (m.), dinheirão (m.) a pot of money, lots of money, a pile of money.
dinheirento -ta (adj., colloq.) moneyed, well-to-do.
dinheiro (m.) money, currency, cash.—a juros, money at interest.—a rôdo, money to burn.—adiantado, money in advance.—apurado, money realized (as from a sale of something).—corrente, currency.—cunhado or amoedado, coined money.—de botija, hoarded money.—de contado, ready money, cash ("on the barrelhead").—de sardinhas, small payments on account.—deitado ao mar, money foolishly wasted.—em caixa, cash on hand.—empatado, money tied up (as in merchandise).—ganha—, money earns money.—líquido, cash on hand.—morto, idle money.—para os alfinetes, pin money. a—, for cash. andar mal de—s, to be hard up for money. andar sem—, to be broke. assunto, or negócio, de—, a money matter. empregar—, to employ (invest) money. estar bem de—s, to be well-off, well-fixed. fazer—de tudo, to turn everything to account. gastar—, to spend money. guardar—, to save money. jogar o—pela janela a fora, to throw money out the window. Quem—tiver, fará o que quiser, Money gives power to him who has it. valer o—empregado, to be worth the money spent. vender a—, to sell for cash.
dinheiroso -sa, dinheirudo -da (adj.)		neyed.
Dinis (m.) Denis; Dennis.
dinitronaftol (m., Chem.) Martius yellow.
dinitrotoluol (m., Chem.) dinitrotoluene.
dinossauro (m.) dinosaur.
dinotério (m., Paleontol.) dinothere.
dintel [-téis] (m.) lintel.
diocesano -na (adj.; m.) diocesan.
diocese (f.) diocese.
diódia (f., Bot.) the genus (Diodia) of buttonweeds.
díodo (m., Elec.) diode.
diodontídeos (m.pl.) the family (Diodontidae) of porcupine and related fishes.
diógenes (m.) the Diogenes hermit crab.
Diogo (m.) James.
dióico -ca (adj., Biol., Bot.) dioecious; (Bot.) dioicous.
dionéia (f., Bot.) Venusflytrap (Dionaea muscipula).
dionina (f., Chem.) dionin, ethyl morphine hydrochloride.
Dionísia (f.) Denise.
dionisíaco -ca (adj.) dionysian.
diopsídio (m., Min.) diopside.
dioptometria (f.) dioptometry.
dioptásio (m.), dioptasita (f., Min.) dioptase, dioptasite, hydrous copper silicate.
dioptria (f., Optics.) diopter.
dióptrica (f., Optics.) dioptrics.
diorama (m.) diorama.
diorito (m., Petrog.) diorite.
dióscorea (f.) the genus (Dioscorea) of yams, c.a. INHAME.
dioscoráceas (f.pl.) the family Dioscoreaceae (yams and related genera).
diósmea (f., Bot.) breath-of-heaven (Coleonema album).
diosmose (f.) diosmose, osmosis [= OSMOSE].
diospireiro (m.) = CAQUIZEIRO.
dióspiro (m.) any plant of the genus Dyospyros (persimmon and ebony); also its fruit.
dioxan [ks] (m., Chem.) dioxan.
dipenteno (m., Chem.) dipentene.
dipétalo -la (adj., Bot.) dipetalous.
dipirenado -da (adj., Bot.) dipyrenous.
dipiro (m., Min.) dipyre.
dipl., = DIPLOMA.
diplacusia (f., Psychol.) diplacusis.
dipladênia (f.) a genus (Dipladenia) of tropial So. Amer., woody vines. [D. splendens is the Brazil species.]
diplasismo (m.) diplasismus.
diplescópio (m., Astron.) dipleidoscope.
díploa (f.) = DIPLOE.
diplococo (m., Bacteriol.) diplococcus.
diplódoco (m., Paleontol.) diplodocus.
díploe (f., Anat.) diploe. Var. DÍPLOA.
diplogênese (f., Biol.) diplogenesis.
diplógrafo (m.) diplograph.
diplóide (adj., Biol.) diploid.
diploma (m.) diploma.
diplomação (f.) conferring of a diploma.
diplomacia (f.) diplomacy; tact; foreign service.

diplomaciar (*v.i.*) to practice diplomacy; to handle (someone) with tact.
diplomado –**da** (*adj.*) graduate, holding a diploma. **oficial**—, commissioned officer.
diplomar-se (*v.r.*) to graduate, receive a diploma.
diplomata (*m.,f.*) diplomat, diplomatist.
diplomático –**ca** (*adj.*) diplomatic; tactful. **corpo**—, diplomatic corps. (*f.*) diplomatics (a branch of paleography).
diplomatista (*m.,f.*) diplomatist.
díplon (*m.*, *Chem.*) diplon, deuteron.
diploneural (*adj.*, *Anat.*) diploneural.
diplopapa (*m.*) the genus (*Aplopappus*) of goldenweeds.
diplópode (*m.*, *Zool.*) diplopod, millipede; (*pl.*) the Diplopoda.
diplóstemo –**ma**, **diplostêmone** (*adj.*, *Bot.*) diplostemonous.
diplotaxis [ks] (*m.*, *Bot.*) the genus (*Diplotaxis*) of wall rockets.
dipneumônio –**nia** (*adj.*, *Zool.*) dipneumonous.
dipneusta (*m.*, *Zool.*) dipnoan.
dipnóico –**ca** (*adj.*, *Zool.*) dipnous; (*m.*) dipnoan.
dípode (*adj.*) = BÍPEDE.
dipodia (*f.*, *Pros.*) dipody.
dipsacáceas (*f.pl.*, *Bot.*) the Dipsacaceae (teasels).
dípsaco (*m.*, *Bot.*) fuller's teasel (*Dipsacus fullonum*), c.a. CARDO-PENTEADOR.
dipsético –**ca** (*adj.*) dipsetic, thirst-provoking.
dipsis (*f.*) the Madagascar butterfly palm (*Chrysalidocarpus madagascariensis*).
dipsomania (*f.*, *Med.*) dipsomania; alcoholism.
dipsomaníaco –**ca** (*adj.*) dipsomaniacal; (*m.,f.*) dipsomaniac.
diptérico –**ca** (*adj.*, *Bot.*, *Zool.*) dipterous.
díptero –**ra** (*adj.*, *Bot.*, *Zool.*) dipterous; (*m.*) a dipteron (fly, gnat, mosquito, etc.); (*pl.*) the Diptera.
dipterologia (*f.*) dipterology.
dipterólogo (*m.*), –**ga** (*f.*) dipterologist.
díptico (*m.*) diptych.
dique (*m.*) dike; dam; (*Geol.*) dike.—**isolante**, (*Dentistry*) rubber sheet.—**sêco**, dry dock.
dirã, dirão, dirás, forms of DIZER [41].
direção (*f.*) direction; management, control; directorship; course, bearing; street address. **em**—**a**, toward, in the direction of. **engrenagem de**—, steering gear. **volante de**—, steering wheel.
direi, direis, forms of DIZER [41].
direita (*f.*) see under DIREITO.
direiteza [tê] (*f.*) straightness; rightness; rectitude.
direitinho (*adv.*) right away; straight ahead; quite correct; just like; just right.
direitista (*adj.; m.,f.*) rightist.
direito –**ta** (*adj.*) right-hand; direct, straight; plumb; correct, right; honest, upright; (*adv.*) rightly; directly; (*m.*) uprightness; right, title, prerogative; law, jurisprudence; right side; royalty, fee; import duty or tax; (*f.*) right hand, right side.—**s alheios**, the rights of others.—**canônico**, canon law.—**s cívicos**, civil rights.—**civil**, civil law.—**comercial**, commercial law.—**comum**, common law.—**costumeiro** or **consuetudinário**, unwritten law.—**criminal**, criminal law.—**das gentes**, or **das nações**, international law.—**s de alfândega** or **de entrada**, customs duties.—**de asilo**, right of asylum.—**de passagem** or **de precedência**, right-of-way.—**de propriedade**, the right to hold property.—**de sucessão**, right of succession.—**diferencial**, (*Econ.*) differential tariff.—**divino**, divine law.—**eclesiástico**, canon law.—**escrito**, written law.—**inato** or **de primogenitura**, birthright.—**indiscutível**, unquestionable right.—**internacional**, international law.—**marítimo**, maritime law.—**mercantil**, mercantile law.—**não escrito**, unwritten law.—**natural**, natural right.—**penal**, penal law.—**s pessoais**, personal rights.—**s políticos**, political rights.—**público**, public law.—**social**, social right. **à**—, to the right, on the right. **a torto e a**—, blindly, indiscriminately; without thinking. **às**—**s**, honest, upright. **conserve**, or **guarde, a sua**—, keep to the right. **de**—, by rights. **declaração de**—**s**, bill of rights. **doutor em**—, doctor of law; lawyer. **juiz de**—, district judge. **livre de**—**s**, duty-free. **nulo de pleno**—, null and void. **rotação à**—, clockwise rotation. **sujeito a**—**s**, subject to duties. **vire à**—, turn to the right.
direitura (*f.*) = DIREITEZA.
diremos, form of DIZER [41].
diretivo –**va** (*adj.*) directive; (*f.*, *Geom.*) directrix.

direto –**ta** (*adj.*) direct; in a straight line; immediate; unambiguous; outspoken.
diretor –**triz** (*adj.*) directing, guiding, managing.
diretor (*m.*), –**tora** (*f.*) director, manager, administrator; guide.—**de consciência**, —**espiritual**, spiritual guide.—**de escola**, school principal.—**de orquestra**, orchestra leader.—**geral**, general manager.
diretorado (*m.*) office or tenure of a director.
diretoria (*f.*) management, administration; directorate, board of directors; office of director.
diretorial (*adj.*) directorial.
diretório (*m.*) directorate, executive committee; a directory.
diretriz (*f.*) directive; rule; policy; standard of behavior; (*Geom.*) directrix; line of direction; (*adj.*) directive.
diria, dirias, diríamos, diríeis, diriam, forms of DIZER [41].
dirigente (*adj.*) directing; (*m.,f.*) director.
dirigibilidade (*f.*) dirigibility.
dirígio (*m.*) = DIAMBA.
dirigir (*v.t.*) to direct, manage; to drive (an automobile); to pilot (an airplane); to address (remarks, insults, letters, etc.) to.—**-se a**, to address oneself to, speak to (someone).—**-se para**, to go towards a place or person. —**a palavra a**, to speak to.—**mal**, to misdirect; to steer badly; to drive (a car) pilot (a plane) badly.—**os olhos para**, to turn the eyes to, look at.—**os passos para**, to turn one's steps towards.—**um aeroplano**, to fly an airplane.—**um apêlo a**, to direct an appeal to.—**um automóvel**, to drive a car.—**uma carta a uma pessôa**, to address a letter to someone.—**uma carta para um lugar**, to send a letter to a place.—**uma oração a**, to address a prayer to. **Dirigiu-se em seguida para Londres**, He went next to London.
dirigível (*adj.; m.*) dirigible.
dirijo (*m.*) = DIAMBA.
dirimente (*adj.*, *Law*) diriment, nullifying.
dirimir (*v.t.*) to render null and void; to cancel out; to put an end to; to settle (questions).—**dúvidas**, to dispel doubts.
disacarídeo (*m.*) disaccharide (sucrose, lactose).
discar (*v.t.*) to dial (telephone numbers).
discente (*adj.*) learning. **corpo**—, student body; (*m.,f.*) a pupil.
discernente (*adj.*) discerning.
discernimento (*m.*) discernment; discretion.
discernir [21a] (*v.t.*) to discern; discriminate, distinguish; to perceive.
discernível (*adj.*) discernible.
disciforme (*adj.*) disciform, discoid.
disciplina (*f.*) discipline, control, order, regulations; branch of knowledge, course of study; (*pl.*) scourges.—**s-de-freira** = CAUDA-DE-RAPÔSA.
disciplinador –**dora** (*adj.; m.,f.*) disciplinarian.
disciplinante (*adj.*) disciplinary; (*m.,f.*) flagellant.
disciplinar (*v.t.*) to discipline, control; to punish; (*adj.*) disciplinary.
disciplinável (*adj.*) disciplinable.
discípulo (*m.*), –**la** (*f.*) student; disciple.
disco (*m.*) disk; any thin circular plate; discus; phonograph record.—**de embreagem**, automobile clutch disk. —**de longa duração**, long-play record.—**de telefone**, telephone dial.—**de tintagem**, (*Print.*) ink plate.—**divisor**, (*Mach.*) index plate.—**voador**, flying saucer. **arremêsso do**—, throwing of the discus. **mudar o**—, (*colloq.*) to change the subject.
discoblástula (*f.*, *Embryol.*) discoblastula.
discóbolo –**la** (*m.,f.*) discus thrower.
discóforos (*m.pl.*) the Discophora (group of jellyfishes).
discográstula (*f.*, *Embryol.*) discograstula.
discoidal, discóide, (*adj.*) discoid.
discoplacenta (*f.*, *Zool.*) discoplacenta.
discoplasma (*f.*, *Anat.*) discoplasm.
discordância (*f.*) discord(ance); unconformity; (*Geol.*) unconformity.
discordante (*adj.*) discordant; inconsistent; dissenting; jarring; unconformable; (*Geol.*) exhibiting unconformity; (*m.,f.*) one who or that which disagrees with or differs from.
discordar (*v.i.*) to disaccord, disagree, differ (**de**, with); to dissent, take exception (**de**, to).
discorde (*adj.*) discordant; disagreeing; incongruous.
discórdia (*f.*) discord, disagreement, wrangling. **pomo de**—, apple of discord, bone of contention.
discorrer (*v.i.*) to run to and fro; to go about; to reason.

—**acêrca de, a respeito de, sôbre,** to discourse on, about. —**em,** to meditate on.

discoteca (*f.*) a collection of phonograph records; record cabinet.

discrepância (*f.*) discrepancy, difference, disagreement, unconformity.

discrepante (*adj.*) discrepant, differing, disagreeing, dissenting; unconformable.

discrepar (*v.t.*) to differ, dissent, disagree.

discretear (*v.i.*) to chat (**com,** with).

discreto –**ta** (*adj.*) discreet; circumspect; wise; unobtrusive; discrete, distinct.

discrição (*f.*) discretion, circumspection; reserve. **à**—, at one's discretion.

discricionário –**ria** (*adj.*) discretionary, optional; arbitrary, capricious.

discriminação (*f.*) discrimination, distinction; discernment. **uma conta com**—**de verbas,** an itemized bill.

discriminador –**dora** (*adj.*) discriminating; (*m.,f.*) one who discriminates.

discriminar (*v.t.*) to discriminate (**entre,** between); to differentiate; to discern.

discriminável (*adj.*) discriminable; discernible.

discursador –**dora** (*adj.*) discoursing; (*m.,f.*) speaker, narrator.

discursar (*v.i.*) to discourse, hold forth.

discurseira (*f., colloq.*) speechification.

discursista (*adj.*) speechmaking; (*m.,f.*) speechmaker.

discursivo –**va** (*adj.*) characterized by reason or reasoning; rational; given to discourse. [But not discursive, which is DIGRESSIVO.]

discurso (*m.*) discourse, speech, lecture, address, oration.

discussão (*f.*) discussion, debating; disputation; controversy.

discutidor –**dora** (*adj.*) discussing; arguing; (*m.,f.*) discusser; arguer; "argufier".

discutir (*v.t., v.i.*) to discuss (**com,** with; **em, sôbre,** about); to debate; to argue, dispute.

discutível (*adj.*) disputable, debatable, moot.

disenteria (*f., Med.*) dysentery.—**amebiana,** amoebic or tropical dysentery.—**bacilar,** bacillary dysentery.

disentérico –**ca** (*adj.*) dysenteric; (*m.,f.*) person suffering from dysentery.

disfagia (*f., Med.*) dysphagia.

disfarçado –**da** (*adj.*) disguised; feigned; masked, in fancy dress.

disfarçar (*v.t.*) to disguise, conceal, cloak; to dissemble; to mask, hide; to feign.—**se (de),** to disguise oneself (as).—**um bocejo,** to stifle a yawn.

disfarce (*m.*) disguise; guise, pretense.

disfasia (*f., Med.*) dysphasia.

disfonia (*f., Med.*) dysphonia.

disforia (*f., Med.*) dysphoria.

disforme (*adj.*) misshapen, unshapely, monstrous, hideous.

disformidade (*f.*) deformity.

disga, disgra (*f., slang*) state of being flat (broke).

disgenesia (*f., Biol.*) dysgenesis.

disjunção (*f.*) disjunction.

disjungir [25] (*v.t.*) to disjoin; to unyoke.

disjuntivo –**va** (*adj.*) disjunctive.

disjunto –**ta** (*adj.*) disjunct, disjoined, disconnected.

disjuntor (*m., Elec.*) circuit breaker.

dislalia (*f.*) dyslalia.

dislate (*m.*) nonsense; absurdity; blunder; a "howler".

dislogia (*f.*) dyslogia.

díspar [-es] (*adj.*) disparate; dissimilar; unlike.

disparado –**da** (*adj.*) bold, daring; (*f.*) dash, plunge; stampede. **a**—, headlong, pell-mell.

disparador –**dora** (*adj., m.*) runaway or hard to catch (horse).

disparar (*v.t.*) to discharge, shoot, fire (a weapon); to let fly (as, a stone).—**contra,** to throw, hurl, against; (*v.i.*) to bolt, run away.—**atrás de,** to set out (rush) after; (*v.r.*) to go off (as a gun).

disparatado –**da** (*adj.*) absurd, preposterous.

disparatar (*v.i.*) to blurt out; to blunder; to rave, rant.

disparate (*m.*) absurdity, nonsense; piffle, flap-doodle, bosh; raving.

disparidade (*f.*) disparity, inequality.

disparo (*m.*) shot, discharge (of a gun); bolting (as of a horse).

dispartir (*v.t.*) to distribute; to dispense (**a,** to). (*v.r.*) to scatter.

dispêndio (*m.*) expense, expenditure; loss, sacrifice.

dispendioso –**sa** (*adj.*) expensive, costly.

dispensa (*f.*) dispensation, exemption; remission.

dispensabilidade (*f.*) dispensability.

dispensação (*f.*) dispensation.

dispensador (*m.*), –**dora** (*f.*) dispensator.

dispensar (*v.t.*) to exempt, release, excuse (**de,** from); to dismiss, discharge; to dispense, distribute, bestow; to dispense with, do without; to waive, forego.—**se de,** to excuse oneself (refrain) from.

dispensário (*m.*) dispensary.

dispensativo –**va** (*adj.*) dispensative, dispensatory.

dispensatório (*m.*) dispensary.

dispensável (*adj.*) dispensable, unnecessary, unessential, needless, superfluous.

dispepsia (*f., Med.*) dyspepsia, indigestion.

dispéptico –**ca** (*adj.; m.,f.*) dyspeptic.

dispermático –**ca, dispermo** –**ma** (*adj., Bot.*) dispermous, two-seeded.

dispermina (*f., Chem.*) dispermin, piperazine.

dispersador –**dora** (*adj.*) dispersing; (*m.,f.*) disperser.

dispersão (*f.*) dispersion, dispersal, breakup.

dispersar (*v.t.*) to disperse, scatter, dispel; (*v.r.*) to scatter, disband.

dispersivo –**va** (*adj.*) dispersive.

disperso –**sa** (*adj.*) dispersed, scattered.

dispersóide (*m., Physical Chem.*) dispersoid, colloid.

dispirema (*f., Biol.*) dispireme.

displasia (*f., Biol.*) maldevelopment.

displicência (*f.*) want of complaisance; disagreeableness; listlessness; remissness; indifference; carelessness; boredom.

displicente (*adj.*) uncomplaisant; disagreeable; remiss, careless; listless; lackadaisical; indifferent; bored.

dispnéia (*f., Med.*) dyspnea, labored breathing.

dispnéico –**ca** (*adj.*) dyspneal, dyspneic.

disponente (*adj.*) disposing; (*m.,f., Law*) one who disposes (of property) by living gifts or by will.

disponibilidade (*f.*) availability; (*pl.*) available funds (as in a budget). **suprimento em**—, available supply.

disponível (*adj.*) available; disposable; spare; unoccupied, disengaged.

dispor [63] (*v.t.*) to dispose, arrange, set in order; to prepare; to plan; to predispose.—**se a, para,** to be disposed to; to get ready to; to get set for; to decide to.—**de,** to dispose of, make free use of; to have available, at one's command, at one's disposal.—**de si,** to be free, disengaged.—**em pilhas,** to arrange in piles.—**por classes,** to classify—**se para o que der e vier,** to get set (ready) for anything that may happen. **ao**—**de,** at the disposal of. **O homem propõe e Deus dispõe,** Man proposes and God disposes.

disposição (*f.*) disposition; disposal, arrangement, layout; predisposition, proneness; temperament; willingness, inclination; proviso, clause (in a contract); condition, state (of health). **à**—**de,** at the disposal of.

dispositivo (*m.*) disposition, arrangement, layout (of parts or things); contrivance, device, "thingamajig," gadget; directive; stipulation, provision (of a law or contract). —**de proteção,** safety device.

disposto –**ta** (*adj.*) arranged, prepared; laid out; disposed, inclined, prone to; willing, eager; ready for anything. **bem**—, hale and hearty; feeling fine.

disprósio (*m., Chem.*) dysprosium.

disputa (*f.*) dispute, altercation, wrangle, clash, quarrel; disputation, squabble, controversy. **em**—, in dispute; at loggerheads.

disputado –**da** (*adj.*) disputed; sought after.—**pelos amigos,** eagerly sought by friends. **muito**—**na sociedade,** much sought after socially.

disputador –**dora** (*adj.*) disputatious; (*m.,f.*) disputer; debater.

disputante (*adj.*) disputant, disputing.

disputar (*v.t.*) to dispute, contend; to gainsay; to struggle (compete, contend) for; to try to win; to vie for something which is in great demand (as, tickets to the theater or to a soccer game); (*v.i.*) to debate, discuss; to squabble, bicker.—**corrida,** to run a race. **Todos lhe disputam a amizade,** Everyone seeks his friendship.

disputativo –**va** (*adj.*) disputatious.

disputável (*adj.*) disputable; debatable.

disquisição (*f.*) disquisition.

dissabor (*m.*) annoyance, vexation; grief; chagrin; contretemps; unsavoriness.

dissaborear (*v.t.*) to annoy, vex; to render insipid.

dissaborido –da, **dissaboroso** –sa (*adj.*) insipid; annoying; saddening.
disse, form of DIZER [41].
dissecação, dissecção (*f.*) dissection.
dissecar (*v.t.*) to dissect.
dissector (*m.*) dissector.
disseminação (*f.*) dissemination; diffusion.
disseminador –dora (*adj.*) disseminating; (*m.,f.*) disseminator; diffuser.
disseminar (*v.t.*) to disseminate, scatter, propagate, spread abroad; (*v.r.*) to diffuse.
dissemos, form of DIZER [41].
dissensão (*f.*) dissension, disagreement; difference; misunderstanding; [= DISSÍDIO].
dissentimento (*m.*) dissent, disagreement, dissidence.
dissentir [21a] (*v.i.*) to dissent (de, from).
dissépalo –la (*adj.*, *Bot.*) disepalous.
disser, dissera, disseram, disséramos, disseras, disserdes, disseres, dissereis, dissermos, all forms of DIZER [41].
dissertação (*f.*) dissertation, disquisition, treatise, essay, thesis.—**inaugural,** doctoral dissertation.
dissertador –dora (*m.,f.*) one who makes a dissertation, or who is given to long-drawn-out statements.
dissertar (*v.i.*) to give a dissertation; to discourse.
dissesse, disseste, dissestes, forms of DIZER [41].
dissidência (*f.*) dissidence, disagreement, dissent, unconformity.
dissidente (*adj.*) dissident, disagreeing; (*m.,f.*) dissident, non-conformist.
dissidiar (*v.i.*) to disagree with, dissent from, differ with.
dissídio (*m.*) dissension [= DISSENSÃO].
dissilábico –ca (*adj.*) dissyllabic.
dissílabo –ba (*adj.*) dissyllabic; (*m.*) dissyllable [= BISSÍLABO].
dissimetria (*f.*) dissymmetry.
dissimétrico –ca (*adj.*) dissymmetric(al), unsymmetrical.
dissímil (*adj.*) = DISSEMELHANTE.
dissimilação (*f.*, *Phonet.*) dissimilation.
dissimilar (*adj.*) dissimilar, unlike.
dissimulação (*f.*) dissimulation.
dissimuladamente (*adv.*) covertly.
dissimulado –da (*adj.*) sly, secretive; given to dissembling.
dissimulador –dora (*adj.*) dissimulating; (*m.,f.*) one who dissembles.
dissimular (*v.i.*) to dissimulate, dissemble, disguise, cloak; to pretend, feign.
dissimulável (*adj.*) susceptible of dissimulation.
dissipação (*f.*) dissipation, squandering, waste; dissoluteness; dispersion; dispelling.
dissipado –da (*adj.*) dissipated; dissolute, wasteful.
dissipador –dora (*adj.*) dissipating; (*m.,f.*) wastrel.
dissipar (*v.t.*) to dissipate, disperse; to dispel; to waste, squander, fritter away; (*v.r.*) to disappear, vanish.
dissipável (*adj.*) easily dissipated.
disso [DE + ISSO], of that. **depois**—, after that.
dissociação (*f.*, *Chem.*) dissociation.
dissociar (*v.t.*) to dissociate.
dissociativo –va (*adj.*) dissociative.
dissociável (*adj.*) dissociable.
dissolubilidade (*f.*) dissolubility.
dissolução (*f.*) dissolution, liquefaction; decomposition; breakup; dissoluteness.
dissolutivo –va (*adj.*) dissolutive.
dissoluto –ta (*adj.*) dissolute, debauched; bawdy; wanton; dissolved.
dissolúvel (*adj.*) dissoluble.
dissolvedor –dora (*adj.*) dissolving.
dissolvência (*f.*) = DISSOLUÇÃO.
dissolvente (*adj.; m.*) dissolvent, solvent.
dissolver (*v.t.*) to dissolve, melt; to put an end to; to break up; (*v.r.*) to melt, liquify; to dissolve.
dissonância (*f.*) dissonance, discord.
dissonante (*adj.*), **díssono** –na, **dissonoro** –ra, (*adj.*) dissonant; grating, harsh.
dissuadimento (*m.*) dissuasion.
dissuadir (*v.t.*) to dissuade; to deter.
dissuasão (*f.*) dissuasion [= DESPERSUASÃO].
dissuasivo –va, **dissuasório** –ria (*adj.*) dissuasive.
dissuasor –sora (*adj.*) dissuading; (*m.,f.*) dissuader.
distal (*adj.*) distal.
distância (*f.*) distance; interval; remoteness.—**focal,** (*Optics*) focal distance or length.—**de planeamento,** (*Aeron.*) gliding distance. **a**—, distantly; afar; aloof. **a**—**de,** far from. **a curta**—, a little ways off; a short dis-

tance away. **a pouca**—, at close range; a short distance. **contrôle a**—, remote control.
distanciado –da (*adj.*) placed at a distance; set at intervals.
distanciar (*v.t.*) to separate, place at a distance (de, from); to space, set at intervals; (*v.r.*) to withdraw (de, from); to move away (de, from).
distante (*adj.*) distant, far-away, remote; aloof.
distar (*v.i.*) to be distant (de, from); to differ (de, from).
disteleologia (*f.*) dysteleology.
distender (*v.t.*) to distend, dilate, swell; (*v.r.*) to stretch out; to relax (as nerves).
distênio (*m.*, *Min.*) disthene, cyanite [= CIANITA].
distensão (*f.*) distension; a sprain.
distenso –sa (*adj.*) sprained.
distensor –sora (*adj.*) distending.
disticado –da (*adj.*, *Nat. Hist.*) distichous, two-ranked.
dístico –ca (*adj.*, *Bot.*) distichous; (*m.*) distich, couplet; lettering, sign; label.
distinção (*f.*) distinction; discrimination; (characteristic) difference; urbanity, good-breeding; highest grade. (in an exam).
distinguir (*v.t.*) to distinguish; to discern; to differentiate (entre, between); to perceive (hear, see); to honor; (*v.r.*) to differ from; to distinguish oneself.
distinguível (*adj.*) distinguishable.
distintivo –va (*adj.*) distinctive. **caráter**—, distinctive feature, a characteristic. (*m.*) emblem, badge, symbol; (*pl.*) regalia.
distinto –ta (*adj.*) distinct; separate, different; well-defined; distinguished, eminent; conspicuous, outstanding.
disto [DE + ISTO], of this.
distoma (*m.*, *Zool.*) a fluke of Fasciola (syn. Distomum).
distomatose, distomíase (*f.*, *Med.*, *Veter.*) distomiasis, fascioliasis, fluke infestation.—**hepática das ovelhas,** liver rot of sheep.
dístomo –ma (*adj.*, *Zool.*) distomatous, having two mouths or suckers.
distorção (*f.*, *Physics*, *Optics*, *Acoustics*, *Radio*, *TV*) distortion.
distração (*f.*) distraction; inattention, absent-mindedness, woolgathering; thoughtlessness; (*pl.*) diversions, pastimes. **por**—, inadvertently. [Not an equivalent of distraction in the sense of frenzy or disturbance of the mind, which is PERTURBAÇÃO, FRENESI.]
distraído –da (*adj.*) absentminded, inattentive, thoughtless; unobservant. [But not distraught or distracted, which is TRESLOUCADO.]
distraimento [a–i] (*m.*) = DISTRAÇÃO.
distrair [75] (*v.t.*) to distract, divert (esp. the attention); to amuse, entertain; (*v.r.*) to amuse oneself, have a good time.
distratar (*v.t.*) to cancel a contract or agreement.
distrato, distrate (*m.*) undoing or nullification of a contract.
distrativo –va (*adj.*) distractive.
distribuição [u–i] (*f.*) distribution (all senses).—**retangular,** (*Stat.*) rectangular distribution. **engrenagem de**—, timing gear (of an automobile motor).
distribuidor –dora [u-i] (*adj.*) distributing; (*m.,f.*) distributor; (*m.*) mail carrier [= CARTEIRO].—**de ignição,** timer (of automobile motor).
distribuir [72] (*v.t.*) to distribute (entre, por, among); to apportion, allocate (a, to); to partition (entre, among); to classify, dispose.
distributivo –va (*adj.*) distributive.
distrital (*adj.*) district.
distrito (*m.*) district.
distrofia (*f.*, *Med.*, *Biol.*) dystrophy.
distrófico –ca (*adj.*) dystrophic.
disturbar (*v.t.*) to disturb [= PERTURBAR].
distúrbio (*m.*) disturbance, disorder; affray, riot.
disúria, disuria (*f.*, *Med.*) dysuria.
dita (*f.*) good fortune.
ditado –da (*adj.*) dictated; inspired by; (*m.*) dictation; saying, proverb.
ditador (*m.*) dictator.
ditadura (*f.*) dictatorship.
ditafone (*m.*) Dictaphone.
ditame (*m.*) dictate (of conscience, of reason); precept, maxim.
ditamno (*m.*, *Bot.*) dittany (Dictamnus spp.).
ditar (*v.t.*) to dictate (matter to be written down); to decree, prescribe; to suggest, inspire.

ditatorial, ditatório -ria (*adj.*) dictatorial.
diteísmo (*m.*) ditheism.
diteque (*m.*) the anatto tree (*Bixa orellana*), c.a. QUISAFÚ.
ditirâmbico -ca (*adj.*) dithyrambic.
ditirambo (*m.*) dithyramb.
dito -ta (*adj.; irreg. p.p. of* DIZER) said; aforesaid; (*m.*) saying; witticism.—**agudo**, sharp and witty saying or remark.—**e feito**, no sooner said than done.—**pesado**, coarse saying.—**sentencioso**, dictum.
ditografia (*f.*) dittograph.
ditongal (*adj.*) diphthongal.
ditongar (*v.t.*) to diphthongize.
ditongo (*m.*) diphthong.—**crescente (decrescente)**, rising (falling) diphthong.
ditono (*m., Music*) ditone.
ditoso -sa (*adj.*) fortunate, lucky.
ditríglifo (*m., Arch.*) ditriglyph.
diurese [i-u] (*f., Med.*) diuresis.
diurético -ca [i-u] (*adj.; m.,f.*) diuretic.
diurnal [i-ur] (*adj.*) diurnal, daily; (*m., Eccl.*) diurnal.
diúrno -na [i-úr] (*adj.*) diurnal, daily; (*m.*) a day train.
diuturnidade [i-u] (*f.*) diuternity.
diuturno -na [i-u] (*adj.*) diuturnal, of long continuance.
div. = DIVISÃO, -SÕES (division[s]).
diva (*f.*) diva; goddess.
divã (*m.*) divan; lounge.
divagação (*f.*) divagation, digression; a wandering (from the subject).
divagador -dora (*adj.*) discursive; (*m.,f.*) one given to rambling in conversation.
divagante (*adj.*) rambling; discursive; digressive.
divagar (*v.i.*) to divagate, ramble, wander, stray; to gad about; to digress.
divaricado -da (*adj.*) divaricate, divergent.
divergência (*f.*) divergence; deviation; disagreement; unconformity.
divergente (*adj.*) divergent, differing, disagreeing.
divergir [21a] (*v.i.*) to diverge; to disagree; to differ, disaccord.
diversamente (*adv.*) diversely.
diversão (*f.*) diversion, amusement, entertainment; sport; deflection.
diversicolor (*adj.*) diversicolored.
diversidade (*f.*) diversity; variety; dissimilarity; difference.
diversificação (*f.*) diversification.
diversificante (*adj.*) diversifying.
diversificar (*v.t.,v.i.*) to diversify; to vary.
diversificável (*adj.*) diversifiable.
diversifloro -ra (*adj.*) diversiflorous.
diversivo -va (*adj.*) divertive.
diverso -sa (*adj.*) diverse, different, unlike, varying; (*pl.*) divers, several, sundry, various.
diversório -ria, (*adj.*) = DIVERSIVO; (*m.*) = DIVERSÃO.
divertículo (*m., Anat.*) diverticulum.
divertido -da (*adj.*) amusing, diverting, entertaining; funny, laughable; fun-loving, merry, jolly.
divertimento (*m.*) amusement, diversion, divertissement; merrymaking, frolic; lark; fun; sport; (*Music*) episode.
divertir [21a] (*v.t.*) to divert (the attention), change (the intention); to entertain, amuse, beguile, (*v.r.*) to enjoy oneself; to have fun; to have a good time; to make merry; to be amused.—**-se a valer**, to have a high old time.—**-se com**, to tease, kid. **Divirta-se!** Have fun! Enjoy yourself!
dívida (*f.*) debt; obligation; duty.—**de honra**, debt of honor.—**flutuante**, floating debt, unfunded debt.—**fundada**, funded debt.—**pública**, public debt. **contrair—s**, to run into debt. **crivado de—s**, debt-ridden. **em—**, in debt.
dividendo (*m.*) dividend; bonus; (*Math.*) dividend.
dividir (*v.t.*) to divide, sever, disunite; to separate; to rend, dismember; to set at variance; to demarcate; to distribute; (*v.r.*) to become divided.—**as despesas**, to share expenses.
dividivi (*m., Bot.*) divi-divi (*Caesalpinia coriaria* and *C. tinctoria*).
dividundo -da, divíduo -dua (*adj.*) dividual.
divinação (*f.*) divination [= ADIVINHAÇÃO].
divinador -dora (*m.,f.*) diviner [= ADIVINHADOR].
divinal (*adj.*) = DIVINO.
divindade (*f.*) divinity.
divinhar (*v.*) = ADIVINHAR.
divinização (*f.*) deification, divinization.
divinizador -dora, divinizante (*adj.*) deifying.

divinizar (*v.t.*) to divinize, deify; (*v.r.*) to become "high and mighty".
divino -na (*adj.*) divine, godlike; sublime. **ofícios—s**, divine services; (*m.,f.*) divine being.
divisa (*f.*) device, emblem; badge; motto, slogan; stripe (on a uniform); dividing line; cattle brand; (*pl.*) foreign exchange credits.
divisão (*f.*) division, separation; section, compartment; dividing line; portion; classification, distribution, partition; (*Mil., Math.*) division; (*Mach.*) indexing.
divisar (*v.t.*) to descry, perceive, behold.
divisibilidade (*f.*) divisibility.
divisionário -ria (*adj.*) divisional. **moedas—s**, divisional coins.
divisível (*adj.*) divisible.
diviso -sa (*adj.*) divided [= DIVIDIDO].
divisor -sora (*adj.*) dividing; (*m., Math.*) divisor.—**comum**, common divisor.
divisório -ria (*adj.*) dividing; divisory; (*f.*) dividing line, fence, screen, wall or partition.
divorciar (*v.t.*) to divorce, separate, sunder; (*v.r.*) to get divorced.
divórcio (*m.*) divorce. Cf. DESQUITE.
divorcista (*adj.; m.,f.*) (person) favoring divorce.
divulgação (*f.*) act of divulging, disclosure.
divulgador -dora (*adj.*) divulging; (*m.,f.*) divulger.
divulgar (*v.t.*) to divulge, disclose, reveal, make public, (*v.r.*) to become known.
dixe (*m.*) gold trinket.
dixe-me-dixe-me (*m.*) gossip.
díz. = DÍZIMO(S) = tenth(s), tithe(s).
diz, dize, forms of DIZER [41].
dizedor -dora (*adj.*) saying, telling, etc.;—see the verb DIZER; (*m.,f.*) talker.
dizer [41] (*v.t.*) to say, tell, speak, express, utter, declare, pronounce, assert; to recount, relate, recite; (*v.i.*) to say, speak; (*v.r.*) to proclaim oneself to be (something); to hold oneself out as; (*m.*) a saying; manner of speech.—**adeus (a)**, to say goodby (to); to take one's leave (of).—**amem a tudo**, to say yes (agree) to everything.—**as coisas como elas são**, to call a spade a spade.—**bem de**, to speak well of.—**besteiras**, to talk nonsense; to talk gibberish. —**cobras e lagartos de**, to say nothing but the worst about (someone); to criticize unreservedly (an establishment, a book, etc.).—**coisa com coisa**, (usually in the negative) to make sense; to be intelligible.—**com**, to jibe with; to go well with.—**com os seus botões**, or **consigo**, to say to oneself.—**com todos os ff e rr**, to enunciate (words) with great precision; to say it all too clearly, unequivocally.—**duas palavras**, to say a few words.—**e fazer**, to suit the action to the word.—**extravagâncias**, to make wild statements.—**mal de**, to speak ill of [more commonly, **falar mal de**].—**maravilhas de**, to say wonderful things about (something or someone).—**missa**, to celebrate mass.—**que sim (não)**, to say yes (no).—**o que pensa**, to speak one's mind.—**respeito a**, to make reference to; to be part of, or to be about, something; to concern. [**No que diz respeito à Rússia . . .** where Russia is concerned . . . .]—**versos**, to recite poetry. **a bem—**, to tell the truth; so to speak. **a** (or **para**)—(or **falar**) **a verdade**, to tell the truth; properly speaking. **Agora me diga!** Now I ask you! **dar o dito por não dito**, to call off the deal; to cancel an agreement. **Dito e feito**, No sooner said than done; Sure enough! It was just as I said! **Diz bem**, He is right. **Dize-me com quem andas e dir-te-ei quem és**, A man is known by the company he keeps. **dizem que**, they say that . . . ; it has been said that . . . **dizendo-se profeta**, claiming to be a prophet. **É fácil—, mas . . .** , That is all very well (easy to say), but . . . **E—que**, and to think that . . . **Ela nega haver dito isso**, She denies having said that. **Êle diz as coisas às claras**, He does not beat about the bush. **Êle diz as coisas na batata**, or, **o que êle diz é na batata mesmo (no duro)**, You can rely on what he says; He comes right out with it. [*Slang*]. **Êle diz as coisas pela metade**, He minces his words; does not tell the full story. **Êle diz uma coisa e faz outra**, He says one thing and does another. **Escusado é dizê-lo**, or **escusado é dizer que**, (it is) needless to say; suffice it to say that. **Eu não disse!** or **Não lhe disse?** I told you so! Didn't I tell you? **Isso não se diz em português**, One doesn't say that in Portuguese; You can't say that in Portuguese. **Lindas coisas me disseram a seu respeito**, I've been hearing fine things about

you. **mandar—que,** to send word that. **mais fácil (de)— que (de) fazer,** easier said than done. **Não diga mais (nada)!** Say no more! **Não é preciso—,** It goes without saying. [**Não preciso te—que,** I don't have to tell you that . . . .] **Não me diga!** You don't say so! **não ter que—,** or **não ter nada a (que)—,** to have nothing to say. **no que me diz respeito,** as far as I am concerned. **ouvir—que,** to hear it said that; to be told that. **para—a verdade,** to tell the truth. **por assim—,** so to speak; virtually; hardly ever; hardly at all. [**Eu, por assim—, não saio de casa,** I hardly ever go outside.] **Pròpriamente dito,** strictly speaking; proper. [**Em São Francisco pròpriamente dito (dita),** in San Francisco proper . . .]. **Que é que você está dizendo?** What are you talking about? What are you saying? **Que me diz!** You don't say so! **Que quer— isto?** What does this mean? **quer—,** that is to say; in other words; it means. [**Bem, quer—,** (*colloq.*), Well, not quite!] **Quero—,** I mean to say. **saber o que está dizendo,** to know what one is talking about. **Se bem o disse, melhor o fez,** no sooner said than done. **Tenho dito,** I have spoken. **Todo o mundo diz que . . .´,** everybody says (is saying) that . . . .

dize-tu-direi-eu (*m.*) heated discussion, loud argument.

dízima (*f.*) tithe, one tenth.—**periódica,** (*Math.*) periodic decimal.

dizimação (*f.*) decimation.

dizimador –**dora** (*adj.*) decimating; (*m.,f.*) decimator.

dizimar (*v.t.*) to decimate.

dízimo (*m.*) tenth; tithe.

dizível (*adj.*) that may be said or spoken.

diz-que, diz-que-diz, diz-que-diz-que (*m.*, *colloq.*) "they say that" (gossip, rumor).

djim (*m.*) a jinni.

d°=DECILITRO(S).

dm=DECÍMETRO(S).

DNC=DEPARTAMENTO NACIONAL DO CAFÉ (National Coffee Department).

D.N.S.=DEUS NOSSO SENHOR (God Our Lord).

d°=DITO (said).

do [DE+O] of the. Cf. DE, DA.—**contrário,** on the contrary. —**lado de,** on the side of; in favor of.—**pé para a mão,** hurriedly.—**peito,** heartfelt.—**que,** than. [**mais do que—,** more than].—**seu próprio movimento,** spontaneously. —**s pés à cabeça,** from head to foot.

dó (*m.*) pity, mercy; mourning; (*Music*) do.

doação (*f.*) donation, gift, grant.—**causa mortis** or—**por morte,** a bequest.—**entre vivos,** or **inter vivos,** an inter vivos gift.

doado –**da** (*adj.*) donated; (*m.*) donation, gift.

doador –**dora** (*m.,f.*) donor.

doar (*v.t.*) to donate (**a,** to), give (**a,** to), bestow (**a,** upon).

dobadeira (*f.*) woman yarn winder.

dobadoura (*f.*) reel (for winding yarn, etc.); (*colloq.*) flurry, bustle. Var. DOBADOIRA.

dobagem (*f.*) act or place of winding (yarn, etc.).

dobar (*v.t.*) to wind; to reel; (*v.i.*) to reel.

doble (*adj.*) double [=DOBRO]; two-faced; double-six (domino).

doblete [lê] (*m.*) doublet (counterfeit gem).

doblez [ê] (*f.*)=DOBREZ.

dobra (*f.*) fold; pleat; act of doubling or folding; doubloon; (*Geol.*) fold.

dobração (*f.*) act of doubling or folding; on Marajó Island, cattle roundup.

dobrada (*f.*) see under DOBRADO.

dobradeira (*f.*) bookbinder's folding machine.

dobradiço –**ça** (*adj.*) flexible, supple, easily bent; folding; (*f.*) hinge [=CHARNEIRA]. **canoa—,** collapsible canoe.

dobradinha (*f.*) tripe stew; tripe [=DOBRADA, FOLHOSO].

dobrado –**da** (*adj.*) folded; double; (*colloq.*) robust; (*m.*) a military march; hilly land; (*f.*) tripe [=DOBRADINHA, FOLHOSO, LIVRO]; tripe stew; the top of a hill as it starts down; an ondulation in the terrain.

dobrador –**dora** (*m.,f.*) folder.

dobradura (*f.*) act of doubling or folding; a fold.

dobramento (*m.*) act of folding; (*Geol.*) fold.

dobrão (*m.*) doubloon.

dobrar (*v.t.*) to double; to increase manyfold; to fold; to bend; to double, sail (around a cape); to double, go around (a corner); (*v.i.*) to double; to bend; of a bell, to toll; (*v.r.*) to bow, stoop; to bend; to sag; to yield; to multiply.—**a cerviz,** to bow one's head (in submission). —**a esquina,** to turn the corner.—**a língua,** to hold one's tongue; to keep a civil tongue in one's head.—**a parada,**

to double the bet.—**o joelho,** to bend the knee (in submission); to knuckle under.—**o passo,** to quicken one's step.—**o sino,** to toll a bell. ["**Por Quem os Sinos Dobram**", For Whom the Bell Tolls]. **ao—deste século,** at the turn of this century.

dobrável (*adj.*) foldable, bendable.

dobre (*m.*) knell; (*adj.*) double; double-dealing.

dobrez [ê] double dealing; duplicity.

dôbro (*m.*) double.

dobrum (*m.*)=DEBRUM.

doc(s).=DOCUMENTO(S).

doca (*f.*) dock, quay.—**de querena,** dry dock.—*flutuante,* floating dock. (*adj., colloq.*) one-eyed [=CAOLHO].

docar (*m.*) dogcart.

doçaria (*f.*) cake and pastry shop; sweet shop.

doce (*adj.*) sweet, sugary; soft, gentle; mild; affectionate; benign; (*colloq.*) smooth-working; (*m.*) tart, sweet pastry, sweetmeat, piece of candy.—**de bôca,** having a sensitive mouth [horse].—**de-pimenta,** a cake made with manioc flour, sugar and black pepper, c.a. BONITA, FRUITA.— **de tijolo,** guava or other paste in tablets. **água—,** fresh water.

doce-amargo –**ga** (*adj.*) bitter-sweet; (*f.*)=DULCÂMARA.

doceiro –**ra** (*m.,f.*) confectioner, candy-maker, candy seller; (*f.*) woman who makes or sells sweets; any sugar-loving ant.

docência (*f.*) the teaching profession.

docente (*adj.*) teaching. **corpo—,** teaching body. (*m.,f.*) teacher.

dócil [-ceis] (*adj.*) docile, pliant; gentle; willing.

docilidade (*f.*) docility, tractableness.—**ao commando,** ease of handling (as, of an airplane).

docílimo –**ma, docilíssimo** –**ma** (*absol. superls. of* DÓCIL) very docile, most docile.

docilizar (*v.t.*) to soften, render docile; (*v.r.*) to be docile, submissive.

docimasia (*f.*) docimasy.

docíssimo –**ma,** pop. var. of DULCÍSSIMO.

docmíase, docmiose (*f.*) hookworm disease [=ANCILO-STOMOSE].

documentação (*f.*) documentation.

documentado –**da** (*adj.*) supported by documents.

documental (*adj.*) documentary.

documentar (*v.t.*) to document; to substantiate.

documentário –**ria** (*adj.*) documentary.

documento (*m.*) document; proof; orders, instructions.

doçura (*f.*) sweetness; gentleness.

dodecaedro (*m.*) dodecahedron.

dodecágono (*m.*) dodecagon.

dodói (*m.*) hurty-hurt (baby talk).

dodonéia (*f.*) the genus (*Dodonaea*) of hopseed bushes.

doença (*f.*) illness, sickness; disease, ailment, malady, complaint.—**aftosa,** hoof-and-mouth disease.—**aguda,** acute illness.—**crônica,** chronic disease.—**de Barlow,** Barlow's disease (infantile scurvy).—**de Basedow** or **de Graves,** exophthalmic or hyplastic goiter.—**de Chagas,** Chagas' disease: a form of trypanosomiasis in Brazil.— **de Corrigan,** water-hammer pulse.—**de cuidado,** serious illness.—**de Parkinson,** Parkinson's disease.—**de São Vito,** chorea.—**do ar,** apoplexy.—**do soro,** serum sickness. —**estival,** summer complaint.—**do peito,** pulmonary tuberculosis.—**do sono,** sleeping sickness.—**ruim,** serious or incurable disease.—**simulada,** feigned illness.— **tropical,** tropical disease.—**venérea,** venereal disease.— **zimótica,** zymotic disease.

doente (*adj.*) sick, ill; diseased, unhealthy, ailing; (*m.,f.*) a sick person, patient.—**do peito,** (person) having pulmonary tuberculosis.

doentio –**tia** (*adj.*) sickly; unwholesome; morbid.

doer [56] (*v.i.,v.r.*) to ache, feel hurt, suffer pain; to feel distressed.

doestador –**dora** (*adj.*) affronting; (*m.,f.*) affronter.

doestar (*v.t.*) to insult, affront, revile.

doesto [é] (*m.*) injury, insult, indignity, affront; vituperation.

doge (*m.*) doge.

dogma (*m.*) dogma.

dogmático –**ca** (*adj.*) dogmatic(al), opinionated; cocksure; (*m.,f.*) dogmatist.

dogmatismo (*m.*) dogmatism.

dogmatista (*m.,f.*) dogmatist; (*adj.*) dogmatic.

dogmatizador –**dora, dogmatizante** (*adj.*) dogmatic; (*m.,f.*) dogmatizer.

dogmatizar (*v.i.,v.t.*) to dogmatize.

dogre (*m.*) dogger (Dutch fishing vessel).
dogue (*m.*) pug dog.
doida (*f.*) see under DOIDO.
doidamente (*adv.*) crazily. Var. DOUDAMENTE.
doidarrão –rona (*adj.*) very foolish or stupid; (*m.,f.*) big fool. Vars. DOUDARRÃO.
doidejante (*adj.*) crazy-acting. Var. DOUDEJANTE.
doidejar (*v.i.*) to cut up, act crazily. Var. DOUDEJAR.
doidice (*f.*) madness, craziness, folly; foolishness. Var. DOUDICE.
doidinho –nha (*adj.*) quite crazy; crazily in love. Var. DOUDINHO.
doidivanas (*adj.*) rattlebrained; (*m.*, *colloq.*) a screwball; (*f.*) a madcap. Var. DOUDIVANAS.
doido –da (*adj.*) mad, crazy, insane; wild, extravagant; enthusiastic, impassioned; (*m.,f.*) a demented person; a crackpot.—**de atar**, "fit to be tied," raving mad.—**manso**, a harmless lunatic.—**por**, crazy about.—**varrido**, —**de pedras**, downright fool; utter madman. Var. DOUDO.
doído –da (*adj.*) hurt, aching, bruised.
doirar (*v.*) & derivs. = DOURAR & derivs.
dois [fem. DUAS] (*adj.*) two; (*m.*) two; two-spot (card, die, domino); the second one; the second day of the month.— **a dois**, by twos, two by two.—**de paus**, the deuce of clubs; (*slang*) a worthless person.—**é bom, três é demais**, Two is company, three is a crowd. **os**—, both (of the), the two. **Quando um não quer,—não brigam**, It takes two to make a quarrel.
dois-amores (*m.*) the redbird slipperflower (*Pedilanthus tithymaloides*), c.a. DOIS-IRMÃOS, SAPATINHO-DE-JUDEU or -DO-DIABO or -DOS-JARDINS, PICÃO.
dois-irmãos (*m.*) the crown-of-thorns euphorbia (*E. mili*), c.a. ÁRVORE-DE-SÃO-SEBASTOÃO, BEM-CASADOS, COROA-DE-CRISTO, COROA-DE-NOSSA-SENHORA, DUAS-AMIGAS, MARTÍRIOS; also = DOIS-AMORES.
dois-pontos (*m.*) colon [:].
dolabriforme (*adj., Bot.*) dolabriform.
dólar (*m.*) dollar.
doldrames (*m.pl.*) doldrums.
dolência (*f.*) dolor, sorrow, grief.
dolente (*adj.*) dolorous, sorrowful; grievous, painful.
dolerite (*f., Petrog.*) dolerite.
dólico (*m.*) the genus Dolichos, which includes the hyacinth bean (*D. lablab*), called LABE-LABE in Brazil, where it is grown as green manure.
dolicocefalia (*f.*) dolichoecphalism, -phaly.
dolicocéfalo –la (*adj.*) dolichocephalic.
dólmã (*m.*) jacket of a uniform.
dólmen (*m.*) dolmen, cromlech.
dolo (*m.*) fraud, deceit, deception [= LOGRO]; foul dealing; (*Law*) malice.
dolomia, dolomita (*f., Min., Petrog.*) dolomite.
Dolores (*f.*) Dolores.
dolorido –da (*adj.*) aching; sore; dolorous.
doloroso –sa (*adj.*) dolorous; painful; sore; grievous, harrowing; (*f., slang*) the "bad news" (bill at a restaurant, etc.).
doloso –sa (*adj.*) fraudulent, crooked; deliberately misleading.
dom (*m.*) gift, present; talent, knack. **o—da palavra**, the "gift of gab," a talent for speech. Also, a title (corresponding to Spanish Don) prefixed to Christian names of the royal family, church hierarchy, etc., as, Dom Pedro II, last emperor of Brazil.
doma (*f., Cryst.*) dome.
domador (*m.*) animal trainer; horse breaker.
domar (*v.t.*) to break in, tame (animals); to overcome, subdue; (*v.r.*) to hold oneself in check.
domatofobia (*f.*) domatophobia, claustrophobia.
domável (*adj.*) tameable.
dom-bernardo (*m.*) a wild coffee (*Psychotria tetraphylla*).
domesticação (*f.*) domestication.
domesticado –da (*adj.*) domesticated; housebroken.
domesticador –dora (*adj.*) domesticating; (*m.,f.*) one who domesticates.
domesticar (*v.t.*) to domesticate.
domesticável (*adj.*) capable of domestication.
domesticidade (*f.*) domesticity.
doméstico –ca (*adj.*) domestic; household; (*m.,f.*) domestic, house servant.
dom-fafe (*m., Zool.*) a bullfinch (*Pyrrhula sp.*) c.a. PISCO-CHILREIRO.
domiciliar (*v.t.*) to domicile, domiciliate.—**-se em**, to

settle in, take up residence in.
domiciliário –ria (*adj.*) domiciliary.
domicílio (*m.*) domicile, residence, abode.—**legal**, legal residence.
dominação (*f.*) domination, dominance.
dominador –dora (*adj.*) dominating, ruling, commanding; domineering; (*m.,f.*) dominator, ruler.
dominância (*f.*) dominance.
dominante (*adj.*) dominant, predominant; ruling, commanding; (*f., Biol. Music*) dominant.
dominar (*v.t.*) to dominate, reign over; to sway, control; to overcome, subdue; to overlook (as from a superior position); to predominate; (*v.r.*) to control oneself.
dominável (*adj.*) that can be dominated; controllable.
domingar (*v.i.*) to dress up on Sunday.
domingo (*m.*) Sunday.—**da Paixão**, Passion Sunday.— **da Rosa**, Rose Sunday.—**de Páscoa**, Easter Sunday.—**de Ramos**, Palm Sunday.—**gordo**, the last Sunday before Lent (Shrove or Quinquagesima Sunday). **aos—s**, on Sundays.
Domingos (*m.*) Dominic.
domingueiro –ra (*adj.*) Sunday; worn on Sunday. **traje—**, Sunday best.
dominguinha (*f.*) a jessamine (*Cestrum levigatum*).
dominical (*adj.*) dominical. **escola—**, Sunday School.
dominicano –na (*adj.; m.,f.*) Dominican.
domínio (*m.*) domain, rule, control, authority; upper hand; tenure; domain; field of action.—**público**, public domain. **Não é dos meus—s**, It is not in my field. **sob o seu—**, under his thumb.
dominó (*m.*) domino: a masquerade costume consisting of a robe, hood and half mask; a masquerader wearing such a costume; one of the dotted pieces used in playing dominoes.
dom-joão (*m.*) a Don Juan, seducer of women.
dom-juanismo (*m.*) Don Juanism.
domo (*m.*) dome.—**salino,** (*Petrol.*) salt dome.
dom-quixotismo (*m.*) Quixotism.
dona (*f.*) lady, mistress, matron, madam; wife. Also, a title equivalent to Miss or Mrs., prefixed to the Christian name, as Dona Maria, Miss Mary.—**branca**, (*colloq.*) white rum; white frost, hoarfrost.—**da casa**, lady of the house.—**de casa**, housewife.—**-joana** = CAPITÃO-DE-SALA (a plant). Cf. DONO.
donaire (*f.*) gentility; elegance; gracefulness; comeliness; adornment; witticism; pleasantry.
donairoso –sa (*adj.*) genteel; debonair.
donatário (*m.*), **-ria** (*f.*) donee.
donativo (*m.*) donation, gift.
donde [DE+ONDE], whence, from where, from which.
dongri (*m.*) dungaree.
doninha (*f.*) a kind of polecat (*Putorius paraensis*); also, a dolphin.
donjuanismo (*m.*) Don Juanism.
dono (*m.*) owner, proprietor; master, boss.—**da casa**, head of the house; landlord. **sem—**, unowned. Cf. DONA.
donoso –sa (*adj.*) graceful; witty.
donzel [-zéis] (*adj.*) unsophisticated; (*m.*) squire (aspirant to knighthood).
donzela (*f.*) damsel; virgin.
donzelinha (*f.*) a little girl; a dragonfly [= LIBELINHA, LIBÉLULA, LAVADEIRA].
donzelona (*f., colloq.*) old maid.
dopado –da (*adj.*) doped [racehorse].
dopar (*v.t.*) to dope (a racehorse).
doqueiro (*m.*) a dock worker, longshoreman.
Dor = DOUTOR (Doctor).
dor (*f.*) pain, ache; suffering; sorrow, grief; (*pl.*) labor pains.—**cansada**, dull ache.—**ciática**, sciatica.—**d'alma**, heartache.—**de barriga**, bellyache.—**de cabeça**, headache.—**de cadeiras**, lower backache.—**-de-canela,**—**-de-côrno,**—**-de-cotovêlo**, (*all slang*) love jealousy.—**de dentes**, toothache.—**de jeito**, a crick.—**de pedra**, renal colic.—**de peito**, pain in the chest.—**-de-tortos**, uterine colic following parturition.—**de viúva**, pain caused by striking the funny bone.—**do coração**, heartache.— **d'olhos**, (*colloq.*) trachoma.—**nos rins**, (*colloq.*) lumbago. —**tenebrante**, piercing pain.
doradídeos (*m.pl., Zool.*) the dorad family (*Doradidae*).
doravante [DE+ORA+AVANTE] from now on; henceforth.
dore (*m.*) dory.
dórico –ca (*adj.; m.*) Doric (order, dialect).
doridamente (*adv.*) painfully.

dorido –da (*adj.*) painful, sore, aching; grieved; sorrowful; (*m.,f.*) a recently bereaved person.

dório –ria (*adj.*) = DÓRICO; (*m.pl.*) the Dorians.

Doris (*f.*) Doris.

dorme-dorme (*m.*) = DORMINHOCO (bird), DORMIDEIRA (snake).

dorme-maria (*f.*) = DORMIDEIRA (plant).

dormência (*f.*) dormancy; torpidity.

dormente (*adj.*) dormant, sleeping; quiescent, lethargic; torpid. **água**—, still water. (*m.*) a floor beam; a railroad crosstie (sleeper) = CHULIPA, SULIPA.

dormião (*m.*) = JOÃO-BOBO.

dormida (*f.*) a night's lodging; a period of sleep.

dormideira (*f.*) somnolence; a narcotic; (*Bot.*) opium poppy (*Papaver somniferum*); a senna (*Cassia bicapsularis*), c.a. CAQUERA; the sensitive plant (*Mimosa pudica*), c.a. INQUIRI, JUQUIRI, MALÍCIA-DAS-MULHERES, MALÍCIA-DE-MULHER, MORRE-JOÃO, VERGONHA, SENSITIVA; (*Zool.*) any of several small harmless snakes(*Dipsas* and *Sibynomorphus*) which sleep by day, c.a. DORMINHOCA, DORME-DORME, JARARACA-PREGUIÇOSA (the latter being a misnomer, since the JARARACA is highly dangerous).

dorminhoco –ca (*adj.*) fond of sleep, given to much sleeping; (*m.,f.*) sleepy-head; (*m.*) a night heron (*Nycticorax*); a puffbird (*Bucco*); also = SOCOÍ and MATIRÃO (herons); (*f.*) an innocuous, tree-climbing serpent (*Dipsas indica*).

dormir [21a] (*v.i.*) to sleep, slumber; to rest, repose; to be still, motionless; (*m.*) sleep.—**à cabeceira de**, to sleep at the bedside of.—**a fome**, to quiet hunger.—**a sesta**, to take a siesta.—**a sono sôlto**, to sleep soundly.—**ao relento**, to sleep out of doors.—**chiqueirado**, to sleep apart from one's wife.—**com um ôlho aberto e outro fechado**, to feign sleep; to sleep lightly or unsoundly.—**como uma pedra**, to sleep like a log.—**e acordar com alguém**, to be with someone day and night.—**em Deus**, to be dead. —**fora**, to sleep out (away from home).—**mais cedo**, to die in infancy.—**nas palhas**, to sleep on the ground.—**o sono da inocência**, to sleep the sleep of the innocent.—**o sono do esquecimento**, to be dead.—**o sono eterno**, to sleep the eternal sleep.—**sôbre o caso**, to sleep on a matter.—**sôbre os louros**, to rest on one's laurels. **a bom**—, sound asleep. **a hora de**—, bedtime. **quarto de**—, bedroom.

dormitar (*v.i.*) to doze, drowse, nap, "snooze".

dormitoreiro (*m.*) sleeping-car porter.

dormitório (*m.*) dormitory; bedroom; a set of bedroom furniture. **carro**—, sleeping car.

dorna (*f.*) huge tub for pressing grapes; vat.

dornada (*f.*) a tubful.

dorneira (*f.*) grain hopper [= TREMONHA].

dorônico (*m.*, *Bot.*) plantain leopardbane (*Doronicum plantagineum*).

Dorotéia (*f.*) Dorothea; Dorothy.

dorremifassolar (*v.i.*) to play scales (on the piano).

dorsal (*adj.*) dorsal; (*f.*, *Zool.*) dorsal fin.

dorsalgia (*f.*) backache.

dorsífero –ra (*adj.*, *Bot.*, *Zool.*) dorsiferous.

dorsifixo –xa [ks] (*adj.*) attached by the back.

dorsiflexão [ks] (*f.*) dorsiflexion.

dorsiventral (*adj.*, *Bot.*) dorsiventral; (*Zool.*) dorsoventral.

dorso [ô] (*m.*) back (side); (*Anat.*, *Zool.*) dorsum.

dosagem (*f.*) dosing; dosage.

dosar (*v.t.*) to dose.

dose (*f.*) dose, potion; portion.

doseamento (*m.*) = DOSAGEM.

dosear (*v.*) = DOSAR.

dosificar (*v.t.*) to divide into doses.

dosimetria (*f.*) dosimetry.

dosimétrico –ca (*adj.*) dosimetric.

dosologia (*f.*) dosology, posology.

dossel [-séis] (*m.*) tester, canopy.

dossiê (*m.*) dossier.

dotação (*f.*) endowment; allotment.

dotado –da (*adj.*) gifted, talented; accomplished; endowed; equipped (de, with).

dotal, dotalício –cia (*adj.*) having to do with a dowry or endowment. **bens dotais**, dowry.

dotar (*v.t.*) to endow (de, with); to give as a dowry.

dote (*m.*) dowry; talent, natural gift, accomplishment.

dotienenteria (*f.*, *Med.*) typhoid fever.

dou, form of DAR [38].

doudejar (*v.*) & derivs. = DOIDEJAR & DERIVS.

doudo (*adj.*) & derivs. = DOIDO & DERIVS.

douração (*f.*) act of gilding; act of gold-lettering. Var. DOIRAÇÃO.

dourada (*f.*) a kind of catfish; (*Bot.*) = DOURADÃO.

douradão (*m.*, *Bot.*) a wild coffee (*Psychotria rigida*) c.a. BATEDEIRA, CONGONHA-DO-GENTIO, DOURADA, DOURADINHA-GRANDE, DOURADINHA-DO-CAMPO, GONGO-DO-CAMPO, GRITADEIRA-DO-MATO, GRITADEIRA-DOS-TABULEIROS, ERVA-GRITADEIRA, TANGARACA-AÇU.

douradinha (*f.*) a golden plover (*Pluvialis apricaris apricarius*) c.a. TARAMBOLA; (*Bot.*) common polypody, (*Polypodium vulgare*); a groundsel (*Senecio incrassatus*); a false pimpernel (*Lindernia diffusa*) c.a. COÁ-ATAIA, ORELHA-DE-RATO, PAPATERRA, PURGA-DE-JOÃO-PAIS; a spleenwort (*Asplenium auritum*), c.a. SAMAMBAIA-DOURADINHA.—**-do-campo**, a false pimpernel (*Lindernia crustacea*), c.a. DOURADINHA-DO-PARÁ, MATA-CANA, MATUCANA, ORELHA-DE-RATO; also = DOURADÃO.—**-falsa**, a tree of the Barbados-cherry family (*Byrsonima verbascifolia*), c.a. MURICI-AÇU.—**-grande** = DOURADÃO.—**-verdadeira**, a wild coffee (*Psychotria xanthophylla*).

dourado –da (*adj.*) golden; gilded; (*m.*) gold leaf.—**-domar**, the common dolphin or dorado (*Coryphaena hippurus*) c.a. DALFINHO, GRASSAPÉ, GUARAÇAPEMA, MACACO. [Not a porpoise.] Var. DOIRADO.

dourador –dora (*adj.*) gilding; (*m.,f.*) gilder. Var. DOIRADOR.

douradura (*f.*) gold leaf; gilding. Var. DOIRADURA.

douramento (*m.*) act of gilding. Var. DOIRAMENTO.

dourar (*v.t.*) to gild; to cover with gold leaf; to provide with gold letters; to make lustrous; to brighten.—**a pílula**, to sugarcoat the bitter pill. Var. DOIRAR.

douro (*m.*) dory [= DORE].

dous = DOIS.

douto –ta (*adj.*) learned, erudite.

doutor (*m.*) –tôra (*f.*) doctor; (*Zool.*) = GALO (moonfish).—**-da-mula-ruça**, (*colloq.*) a quack.—**de borla e capelo**, one who has received the highest degree conferred by a university or college.—**-de-raiz**, a "herb doctor" [= RAIZEIRO].—**in honoris causa**, an honorary degree of doctor.

doutoraço (*m.*) a would-be doctor.

doutorado –da (*adj.*) having a doctor's degree; (*m.*) doctorate, doctor's degree.

doutoral (*adj.*) doctoral.

doutorando –da (*m.,f.*) an aspirant to a doctor's degree.

doutorar (*v.t.*) to confer a doctor's degree upon; (*v.r.*) to receive a doctor's degree.

doutorato (*m.*) = DOUTORADO.

doutoria (*f.*) doctorship.

doutrina (*f.*) doctrine.

doutrinação (*f.*) indoctrination.

doutrinal (*adj.*) doctrinal.

doutrinamento (*m.*) = DOUTRINAÇÃO.

doutrinar (*v.t.*) to (in)doctrinate.

doutrinário –ria (*adj.*) doctrinal; (*m.,f.*) doctrinaire.

doutrinável (*adj.*) teachable.

doutrineiro (*m.*) doctrinaire. [Derogatory]

doutro –tra [DE+OUTRO –TRA] of (from) the other.

doxologia [ks] (*f.*) doxology.

doze [ô] (*adj.*) twelfth; (*m.*) twelve; the twelfth. [Dozen is DÚZIA.]

DPN = DEPARTAMENTO DE PORTOS E NAVEGAÇÃO.

Dr(s) = DOUTOR(ES).

Dr.ª = DOUTORA (Doctor).

dracena (*f.*) dragon's-blood resin [= DRACINA]; (*Bot.*) dracena (*Cordyline*); dracaena (*Dracaena*).

dracma (*f.*) drachma; dram.

dracocéfalo (*m.*, *Bot.*) the Ruyschianum dragonhead mint (*Dracocephalum ruyschianum*).

dracogrifo (*m.*) the dragon of heraldry.

draconiano –na (*adj.*) Draconian; fig. barbarously severe; harsh; cruel.

dracunculose (*f.*, *Med.*) a diseased condition resulting from infestation with the Guinea worm (*Dracunculus medinensis*).

draga (*f.*) dredge.—**de nora**, bucket dredge. (*pl.*) shores (of a ship in dry dock).

dragador (*m.*) dredger.

dragagem (*f.*) act of dredging; a dredging operation.

dragão (*m.*) dragon; dragoon; the brown-rumped marsh bird (*Pseudoleistes virescens*).—**-fedorento**, (*Bot.*) a monstera (*M. adansonii*), c.a. FÔLHA-FURADA, FÔLHA-RÔTA, IMBÊ-FURADO, IMBÊ-SÃO-PEDRO, TIMBÓ-MANSO.—**-marinho** or—**-do-mar**, (*Zool.*) the greater weever (*Trachinus draco*), c.a. VÍBORA.

dragar (v.t.) to dredge; to drag or sweep (bottom of a harbor, etc.).

dragoeiro (m.) = ÁRVORE-DO-DRAGÃO.

dragomano (m.) dragoman.

dragona (f.) = ENCONTRO (a bird).

dragonas (f.pl.) epaulettes.

dragoneiro (m.) = ÁRVORE-DO-DRAGÃO.

dragontéia (f.) = SERPENTÁRIA.

drainar (v.) & derivs. = DRENAR & DERIVS.

drama (m.) drama; series of events; dram (weight).

dramalhão (m.) melodrama.

dramaticidade (f.) dramatic Quality.

dramático -ca (adj.) dramatic.

dramatista (m.,f.) = DRAMATURGO.

dramatização (f.) dramatization.

dramatizar (v.t.) to dramatize.

dramaturgo -ga (m.,f.) dramaturge, dramatist, playwright.

drapejamento (m.) drapery.

drapejar (v.t.) to drape; (v.i.) to wave (flags).

drástico -ca (adj.) drastic; (m.) a drastic laxative.

dravidianos (m.pl.) Dravidians.

dreifusista (m.,f.) Dreyfusard.

drenagem (f.) drainage.

drenar (v.t.) to drain.

dreno (m.) drain, drain pipe, drainage ditch, culvert; (Surg.) drain.

drepânio (m., Bot.) drepanium.

dresina (f.) a small, motor-driven four-wheel car for running on railroad tracks [So called in Paraná; elsewhere: TROLE.]

dríade, dríada (f.) dryad.

driça (f.) = ADRIÇA.

dril (m.) drill (fabric).

dringo (m., Bot.) the drug sweetflag (Acorus calamus), c.a. CÁLAMO-AROMÁTICO, CANA-CHEIROSA.

dro = DINHEIRO (money).

droga (f.) drug; ingredient; (colloq.) any worthless thing; cheap article; junk, trash.—entorpecente, narcotic drug. dar em—, to come to naught; to "flop".

drogaria (f.) a drugstore in which drugs and medicines are sold, but in which no compounding or dispensing is done. Cf. BOTICA, FARMÁCIA.

drogomano (m.) dragoman.

droguista (m.,f.) druggist.

dromedário (m.) dromedary.

dromógrafo (m.) dromograph.

dromomania (f., Psychopathol.) dromomania.

dromômetro (m.) dromometer.

drósera (f.) a genus (Drosera) of insectivorous herbs—the sundews.

drosômetro (m.) drosometer.

druída (m.) druid.

drupa (f., Bot.) drupe (peach, plum, etc.).

drupáceo -cea (adj., Bot.) drupaceous; (f.pl.) = AMIGDALÁCEAS.

drupéola (f., Bot.) druplet, drupeol.

drusa (f., Min.) druse.

D.ˢ = DEUS (God).

dual (adj.) dual.

dualidade (f.) duality.

dualismo (m.) dualism.

dualista (adj.) dualistic; (m.,f.) dualist.

dualístico -ca (adj.) dualistic.

duas, fem. of DOIS (two).

dubiedade (f.) dubiety.

dúbio -bia (adj.) dubious, doubtful, uncertain, hesitant; ambiguous; nondescript.

dubitativo -va (adj.) doubtful.

Dublim (m.) Dublin.

duboisina (f., Pharm.) duboisine.

ducado (m.) dukedom; ducat.

ducal (adj.) ducal.

ducentésimo -ma (adj.; m.) two-hundredth.

ducha (f.) shower bath; external douche; damper (on the spirits); a call-down; (pl.) a public bathhouse.

duchar (v.t.) to douse; to douche.

ducina (f., Arch.) cyma.—direita, cyma recta.—reversa, cyma reversa.

dúctil [-teis] (adj.) ductile; docile; flexible, elastic.

ductilidade (f.) ductility; flexibility.

ductilímetro (m.) ductilimeter.

ductílimo —ma, ductilíssimo -ma (absol. superls. of DUCTIL) most ductile; most docile.

ducto (m., Anat.) duct.—s seminíferos, seminiferous tubules.

duelar (v.t.,v.i.) to duel; (adj.) dueling.

duelista (m.,f.) duelist.

duelo (m.) duel.

duende (m.) goblin, hobgoblin; sprite; pixy.

duenha (f.) duenna, chaperon.

duetista (m.,f.) duetist.

dueto [ê] (m.) duet, duo.

dugão, dugongo (m., Zool.) dugong.

dulcamara (f., Bot.) the false bittersweet (Solanum dulcamara), c.a. DOCE-AMARGA, UVA-DE-CÃO.

dulcido -da (adj.) dulcet.

dulcificar (v.t.) to sweeten; to dulcify, mollify.

dulcífloquo -qua (adj.) sweet-talking.

dulcinéia (f., colloq.) sweetheart; (f.) Dulcinea [Don Quixote's ladylove].

dulcíssimo -ma (absol. superl. of DOCE) most sweet.

dulcissonante, dulcíssono -na (adj.) dulcet, melodious. [Poetical]

dulia (f., R.C.Ch.) dulia.

dum(a) [DE+UM(A)], of a, from a. duma vezada, at one stroke; at one time.

dumortierita (f., Min.) dumortierite.

duna (f.) dune.

dundum (f.) dumdum bullet.

dunga (m.) headman; bully; the joker or deuce of clubs; battery charger; (adj.) exceptional, incomparable.

dunguinha (f.) kind, helpful friend; the two of clubs; an insignificant person.

dunito (m., Petrog.) dunite.

duns [DE+UNS] of about, of some.—três metros de altura, about three meters high.

duo (m.) duo, duet.

duodecimal (adj.) duodecimal.

duodécimo -ma (adj.; m.) twelfth (part); (f., Music) duodecimo.

duodécuplo -pla (adj.) duodecuple.

duodenal (adj., Anat.) duodenal.

duodenite (f., Med.) duodenitis.

duodeno (m., Anat.) duodenum.

dúplex [ks] (adj.) duplex [= DÚPLICE].

duplicação (f.) duplication.

duplicado -da (adj.; m.) duplicate.

duplicador -dora (adj.) duplicating; (m.,f.) duplicator.

duplicar (v.t.) to duplicate; to repeat; to double.

duplicata (f.) a duplicate copy; a counterpart. [In Brazil, a certified and negotiable copy of an invoice.]—aceita, a trade acceptance.

duplicatura (f.) duplicature.

duplicável (adj.) duplicable.

dúplice (adj.) duplex, double [= DÚPLEX]; double-dealing, two-faced.

duplicidade (f.) duplicity, double-dealing.

duplo -pla (adj.) double, duplex, twofold, dual; (m.,f.) a double; a pair.—comando, (Aeron.) dual control.—refração, (Optics.) double refraction.

duque (m.) duke; deuce (cards, dice); a two-piece man's suit.

duquesa [ê] (f.) duchess.

durabilidade (f.) durability.

duração (f.) duration. de pouca—, short-lived.

duraculi (m.) a night ape (Aotus infulatus).

duradouro -ra (adj.) enduring, durable, lasting, abiding. Var. DURADOIRO.

dural, duralumínio (m.) duralumin (alloy).

dura-máter (f., Anat.) dura mater.

durame, durâmen (m., Bot.) duramen, heartwood.

duramente (adv.) harshly, unkindly, severely.

durante (prep.) during, while.

duraque (m.) a strong, serge-like fabric formerly used in making shoes for women.

durar (v.i.) to endure, last; to be durable, wear. [But not endure in the sense of to bear or to suffer which is SUPORTAR, SOFRER.] Não há bem que sempre dure, nem mal que por si perdure, It's a long lane that has no turning.

durasno (m.) peach [= PÊSSEGO].

durável (adj.) durable.

dureza [ê] (f.) hardness, compactness; toughness; harshness, severity.—Brinell, (Metal.) Brinell hardness number.—esclerometrica, (Min.) sclerometric surface hardness.—Shore, (Metal.) Shore or Scleroscope hardness number.

durião (m., Bot.) the civet durian (Durio zibethinus).

durindana (*f.*, *colloq.*) sword, dagger.
durma, durmo, forms of DORMIR [21a].
duro -ra (*adj.*) hard, firm, solid, compact, impenetrable; tough; stiff; difficult; obdurate; unfeeling; mean; grim; harsh; stubborn; "hard-boiled"; (*m.*) a Spanish peso; a hard (syphillitic) chancre.—**a fogo,** (*m.*) an inferior, poor-burning grade of tobacco; a hard-boiled individual.—**de bôca** (or **de queixo**), hard-mouthed [horse].—**de cabeça,** hardheaded.—**de ouvido,** hard of hearing.—**de roer** (or **de pelar**), hard to take, hard to swallow. **no—,** (*colloq.*) sure as fate; really. **pão—,** stale bread; (*colloq.*) a miser.
durômetro (*m.*) durometer.
durra (*f.*, *Bot.*) a bluestem grass (*Andropogon saccharatus*) c.a. MILHO-DAS-VASSOURAS, SORGO-DE-AÇÚCAR.
duunvirado [u-u] (*m.*) duumvirate.
duúnviro [u-ú] (*m.*) duumvir.
dúvida (*f.*) doubt, uncertainty; qualm, misgiving; dis-

trust; suspicion, mistrust; skepticism; hesitation. **fora de—,** beyond doubt; doubtless; indubitable. **não resta—,** there is no doubt (about it). **pôr em—,** to doubt. **pôr—s,** to raise doubts. **sem—,** doubtless, no doubt. **sem— nenhuma,** without the slightest doubt. **ter—sôbre,** to have doubt about.
duvidador -dora (*m.,f.*) doubter.
duvidar (*v.t.*) to doubt, question; (*v.i.*) to hesitate, waver. **—de,** to have doubts about; to distrust.
duvidoso -sa (*adj.*) doubtful, undecided; dubious; questionable; suspicious.
duzentos -tas (*adj.; m.*) two hundred.
dúzia (*f.*) dozen. [Twelve is DOZE.]—**de frade,** baker's dozen (13). **à—,** by the dozen. **às—s,** by dozens.
d/v = DIAS DE VISTA (days from sight, as for payment of a note).
dz. = DÚZIA(S), dozen(s).

E

E, e, the fifth letter of the Portuguese alphabet.
e (*conj.*) and; yet, but.
E. = EDITOR (publisher); ESTE (east); ESQUERDA (left).
é, form of SER [76].
E.B. = ESTIBORDO (starboard).
ebanáceas (*f.pl.*, *Bot.*) the Ebanaceae (ebony family).
ebâneo -nea (*adj.*) ebony.
ébano (*m.*) ebony (plant, wood, color).—**-da-austrália,** (*Bot.*) the blackwood acacia (*A. melanoxylon*), c.a MADEIRA-PRÊTA, MÓGNO-DA-AUSTRÁLIA.—**-verdadeiro,** the ebony persimmon (*Diospyros ebenum*), c.a.—**DA-ÍNDIA,**—**-oriental,** the lebbek albizzia (*A. kalkora*), c.a. CORAÇÃO-DE-NEGRO.
EBAP = ESCOLA BRASILEIRA DE ADMINISTRAÇÃO PÚBLICA (Brazilian School of Public Administration).
ebó (*m.*) voodoo rites [= DESPACHO].
ebonista (*m.,f.*) ebonist.
ebonite (*f.*) ebonite.
ebriedade (*f.*) inebriety, drunkenness [= EMBRIAGUEZ].
ébrio -ria (*adj.*) inebriated, drunk; (*m.*) sot, drunkard.
ebulição (*f.*) ebullience; ebullition, **ponto de—,** boiling point.
ebuliente (*adj.*) ebullient, boiling over.
ebuliômetro (*m.*) ebulliometer.
ebulioscopia (*f.*) ebullioscopy.
ebulioscópio (*m.*) ebullioscope.
ébulo (*m.*) = ACTÉIA.
eburina (*f.*) eburine.
eburnação (*f.*, *Med.*) eburnation.
ebúrneo -nea (*adj.*) eburnean, ivory. **dentes—s,** ivory teeth.
e.c. = ERA CRISTÃ (Christian Era).
ecbálio (*m.*) the squirting cucumber (*Ecballium elaterium*), the source of elaterium.
ecdise (*f.*, *Zool.*) ecdysis, molting.
écfora (*f.*, *Arch.*) ecphora.
ecgonina (*f.*, *Chem.*) ecgonine.
echalota (*f.*, *Bot.*) shallot (*Allium ascalonicum*).
echarpe (*f.*) scarf.
echevéria (*f.*, *Bot.*) a genus (*Echeveria*) of succulents.
eciano -na (*adj.*) pert. to or characteristic of the Port. writer Eça de Queirós, or his writings [= QUEIROSIANO].
écl. = ÉCLOGA(S) = eclogue(s).
eclampsia (*f.*, *Med.*) eclampsia.
eclesiástico -ca (*adj.; m.*) ecclesiastic.
eclético -ca (*adj.; m.,f.*) eclectic.
ecletismo (*m.*) eclectism.
eclipsar (*v.t.*) to eclipse; to shroud, hide; to overshadow; to outdo, outsmart; (*v.r.*) to disappear.
eclipse (*m.*) eclipse.—**anular do sol,** annular eclipse.—**de lua,** eclipse of the moon.—**do sol,** eclipse of the sun.—**parcial,** partial eclipse.—**total,** total eclipse.
eclíptico -ca (*adj.*) ecliptic. (*f.*, *Astron.*) ecliptic.
eclodir (*v.i.*) to hatch; to emerge; to burst forth, erupt.
écloga (*f.*) eclogue.
eclosão (*f.*) emergence, appearance, unfoldment; (*Zool.*) eclosion; hatching (of eggs); eruption (of an oil well).

eclusa (*f.*) dam [= REPRÊSA].
eco (*m.*) echo; *fig.* one who parrots another.
ecô (*interj.*) sick 'im! (to dogs); get along! (to cattle).
ecoante (*adj.*) echoing.
ecoar (*v.i.*) to echo, re-echo, reverberate; (*v.t.*) to repeat; to resound.
ecologia (*f.*, *Biol.*) ecology, bionomics.
economato (*m.*) office of steward.
economia (*f.*) economy; thrift; organization, system, (*pl.*) savings, nest egg.—**dirigida,** a managed economy.—**doméstica,** household management.—**política,** social, political, economy. **fazer—s,** to put by (for future use). **fazer—s de palitos,** to be penny-wise and pound-foolish.
econômico -ca (*adj.*) economic(al); thrifty, frugal; relating to economics. **caixa—,** public savings bank.
economista (*m.*) economist.
economizador -dora (*adj.*) economizing; thrifty.
economizar (*v.t.*) to economize; to save, husband; to manage frugally; (*v.i.*) to be frugal; to avoid waste; to stint.
ecônomo (*m.*) steward (of a household); butler.
ectima (*m.*, *Med.*) ecthyma.
éctipo (*m.*) ectype.
ectipografia (*f.*) ectypography.
ectlipse (*f.*, *Latin. Pros.*) ecthlipsis.
ectoblasto (*m.*, *Biol.*) ectoblast, epiblast.
ectocárpaceas (*f.pl.*) a family (*Ectocarpaceae*) of marine brown algae.
ectocisto (*m.*, *Zool.*) ectocyst.
ectocôndilo (*m.*, *Anat.*) ectocondyle.
ectocórnea (*f.*, *Anat.*) ectocornea.
ectoderma (*m.*, *Embryol.*) ectoderm.
ectodérmico -ca (*adj.*) ectodermic.
ectófito (*m.*, *Zool.*) ectophyte.
ectolecítico -ca (*adj.*, *Embryol.*) ectolecithal.
ectômera (*f.*, *Embryol.*) ectomere.
ectoparasito (*m.*, *Zool.*) ectoparasite.
ectoplacenta (*f.*, *Embryol.*, *Zool.*) ectoplacenta, chorion.
ectoplasma (*m.*, *Biol.*, *Phot.*, *Spiritualism*) ectoplasm.
ectostose (*f.*, *Anat.*) ectostosis.
ectoteca (*f.*, *Zool.*) ectotheca.
ectozoários (*m.pl.*) ectozoa.
ectrodactilia (*f.*) ectrodactylia.
ectrogenia (*f.*) ectrogeny.
ectromelia (*f.*) ectromelia.
ectrópio (*m.*, *Med.*) ectropion.
ecúleo (*m.*) rack (instrument of torture); *fig.* torment.
ecumênico -ca (*adj.*) ecumenical, universal.
eczema (*m.*, *Med.*) eczema.
eczomatoso -sa (*adj.*) eczematous.
ed. = EDIÇÃO (edition).
E.D. = ESPERA DEFERIMENTO (awaiting approval).
edacíssimo -ma (*absol. superl.* of EDAZ) most voracious.
edafologia (*f.*) pedology, soil science.
edaz (*adj.*) edacious, voracious.
edelvais (*m.*, *Bot.*) edelweiss (*Leontopodium*),.
edema (*m.*, *Med.*) edema, dropsy.

edematoso –sa (*adj.*) edematous.

Éden (*m.*) Eden.

edentado –da (*adj.*) edentate; toothless; (*m.pl.*) = DESDENTADOS.

Edgar (*m.*) Edgar.

edição (*f.*) publication (of a book, etc.); edition.—**príncipe**, first edition.

edictal (*adj.*) edictal.

edificação (*f.*) edification, moral uplift; construction, erection.

edificador –dora (*adj.*) edifying; (*m.*) edifier.

edificamento (*m.*) = EDIFICAÇÃO.

edificante (*adj.*) edifying; (*m.,f.*) edifier.

edificar (*v.t.*) to build, construct, erect; to edify.

edificativo –va (*adj.*) = EDIFICANTE.

edifício (*m.*) edifice, building, structure.—**público**, public building.

edil (*m.*) aedile.

Edimburgo (*m.*) Edinburgh.

Édipo (*m.*) Oedipus.

edital (*m.*) edict; bill, poster, placard; (*adj.*) edictal.

editar (*v.t.*) to publish (books, etc.) [To edit, in the sense of to revise and correct, is EMENDAR, REVER.]

Edite (*f.*) Edith.

édito (*m.*) public (published) legal notice, proclamation, or court order.

edito (*m.*) edict, decree.

editor –tôra (*adj.*) pertaining to publishing. **casa**—, publishing house; (*m.*) publisher. [But not editor, which is REDATOR.]

editorial (*adj.*) pertaining to publishing; (*m.*) newspaper editorial; (*f.*) publishing house.

Edmundo (*m.*) Edmund.

edredão (*m.*) eider down; down comforter.

Eduardo (*m.*) Edward.

educabilidade (*f.*) teachability.

educação (*f.*) education, teaching, instruction; training, upbringing, breeding, culture; good manners.

educacional (*adj.*) educational.

educador –dora (*adj.*) educating; (*m.,f.*) educator, teacher.

educandário (*m.*) a teaching establishment.

educando –da (*m.,f.*) pupil, student.

edução (*f.*) education; deduction.

educar (*v.t.*) to educate, teach, instruct; to raise, train, bring up; to discipline.

educativo –va (*adj.*) educative; educational.

educável (*adj.*) teachable.

edulcoração (*f.*) edulcoration.

edulcorar (*v.t.*) to render sweet.

edulcorado –da (*adj.*) sweet, sugary.

édulo –la (*adj.*) edible [= COMESTÍVEL].

eduzir (*v.t.*) to educe.

EE. = EDITÔRES (publishers).

E.F.C.B. = Estrada de Ferro Central do Brasil (Brazil Central Railway).

efebo [fê] (*m.*) ephebus (Greek youth).

éfedra (*f., Bot.*) the jointfir ephedra (*E. distachya*).

efedrina (*f., Pharm.*) ephedrine.

efeito (*m.*) effect, result, outcome; fulfilment; efficacy. **com**—, in effect; in fact; indeed; as a matter of fact.

efeituar (*v.*) = EFETUAR.

efélide (*f.*) ephelis, freckle [= SARDA].

efemérida (*f.*) ephemerid, May fly.

efemérides (*f.pl.*) ephemerides; daily news items.

efêmero –ra (*adj.*) ephemeral, short-lived, transitory, fleeting; (*m.pl.*) the Ephemeridae (family of May flies).

efeminação (*f.*) effeminacy.

efeminado –da (*adj.*) effeminate, womanish, timorous, unmanly, prissy.

efeminar (*v.t.*) to render effeminate; (*v.r.*) to become effeminate.

efêndi (*m.*) effendi.

eferente (*adj.*) efferent.

efervescência (*f.*) effervescence; ebullience; excitement.

efervescente (*adv.*) effervescent; ebullient; irascible.

efervescer (*v.i.*) to effervesce.

efes-e-erres (*m.pl., colloq.*) F's and R's (all the details).

efetivação (*f.*) act of rendering effective.

efetivamente (*adv.*) really, in reality, in fact, in effect.

efetivar (*v.t.*) to put in (into) effect.

efetível (*adj.*) effectible.

efetividade (*f.*) effectiveness.—**do serviço**, term of office, of military service, etc.

efetivo –va (*adj.*) real, actual, positive: in office; in power.

[But not effective, which is: EFICIENTE, EFICAZ, EFETUOSO]; (*m.*) that which actually exists; a regular, permanent employee; (*Mil.*) an effective.—**humano**, manpower.

efetuação (*f.*) effectuation; accomplishment, achievement, fulfilment.

efetuar (*v.t.*) to effectuate, bring to pass; to cause; to achieve, accomplish; to transact; (*v.r.*) to occur, take place, result in.

efetuoso –sa (*adj.*) effective.

eficácia (*f.*) efficacy, effectiveness.

eficacíssimo –ma (*absol. superl. of* EFICAZ) most effective.

eficaz (*adj.*) efficacious, effective.

eficiência (*f.*) efficiency.

eficiente (*adj.*) efficient, effective.

efigiar (*v.t.*) to represent in, or as in, effigy.

efígie (*f.*) effigy, image.

eflorescência (*f.*) efflorescence.

eflorescente (*adj.*) efflorescent.

eflorescer (*v.i.*) to effloresce.

efluência (*f.*) effluence.

efluente (*adj.*) effluent.

efluir [72] (*v.i.*) to issue as an effluvium.

eflúvio (*m.*) effluvium, exhalation; aroma.

efluviografia (*f.*) effluviography.

efluvioso –sa (*adj.*) issuing as an effluvium.

efluxo (*m.*) efflux, effusion, outflow.

E.F.M. = ESTRADA DE FERRO MOGIANA (Mogyana Railway).

efó (*m.*) Brazilian dish made with shrimps, greens, pepper and DENDÊ palm oil.

E.F.P. = ESTRADA DE FERRO PAULISTA (Paulista Railway); ESTRADA DE FERRO DO PARANÁ (Paraná Railway).

E.F.R.G.S. = ESTRADA DE FERRO RIO GRANDE DO SUL (Rio Grande do Sul Railway).

E.F.S. = ESTRADA DE FERRO SOROCABANA (Sorocabana Railway).

efundir (*v.t.,v.r.*) to effuse.

efusão (*f*) effusion; effusiveness.—**de sangue**, shedding of blood.

efusiômetro (*m.*) effusiometer.

efusivo –sa (*adj.*) effusive.

efuso –sa (*adj.*) effuse.

egesta (*f., Physiol.*) egesta.

egestivo –va (*adj., Physiol.*) egestive.

egeu (*m.*) Aegean.

égide (*f.*) aegis, sponsorship, protection; shield.

egipã, egipano (*m.*) Aegipan, Pan.

egipcíaco –ca (*adj.*) Egyptian.

egipcianismo (*m.*) Egyptianism.

egipcianista (*m.,f.*) = EGIPTÓLOGO.

egípcio –cia (*adj.; m.,f.*) Egyptian.

egiptologia (*f.*) Egyptology.

egiptólogo –ga (*m.,f.*) Egyptologist.

Egito (*m.*) Egypt.

égloga (*f.*) = ÉCLOGA.

ego (*m.*) ego.

egocêntrico –ca (*adj.*) egocentric.

egoísmo (*m.*) egoism; extravagant self-love; selfishness.

egoísta (*adj.*) egoistic; selfish; conceited; (*m.,f.*) egoist.

egoístico –ca (*adj.*) egoistic.

ególatra (*m.,f.*) self-worshipper.

egolatria (*f.*) worship of self.

egomania (*f.*) egomania.

egomaníaco –ca (*adj.*) egomanic(al).

egotismo (*m.*) egotism; extravagant self-love.

egotista (*adj.*) egotistic(al), conceited; selfish; (*m.,f.*) egotist, egoist.

egrégio –gia (*adj.*) distinguished, illustrious, notable. [But not egregious, in the modern sense of flagrant, shocking, which is FLAGRANTE, CHOCANTE.]

egressão (*f.*) egression.

egresso –sa (*adj.*) egressed; (*m.*) egress, departure; a former inmate or patient, or civil servant.

egreta (*f.*) the plume of an egret.

égrio (*m., Bot.*) a nasturtium (*Tropaeolum pumilum*).

égua (*f.*) mare. [*Horse* = CAVALO] (*vulgar*) prostitute;—**madrinha**, bell mare.—**parida**, brood mare.

eguada (*f.*) a herd of mares.

eguariço –ça (*adj.*) mare; mule; (*m.*) hostler.

eh! ei! Hey!

eia! Come on! Get up! (to animals).

eiã, eiã (*m.*) a night ape (*Aotus vociferans*).

eido (*m.*) patio; yard.

ei-lo(s), ei-la(s) [contr. of **eis-lo(s), eis-la(s)**] here (there) you have it (him, her, them); here (there) it (he, she) is, here they are.

eira (*f.*) threshing floor; (*m.*) the eyra (*Felis eyra*, or *Herpailurus eyra*), a wildcat closely resembling the tayra [= IRARA], a weasel with which it is sometimes confused. Cf. JAGUARUNDI. **sem—nem beira,** down and out.

eirado –**da** (*adj., colloq.*) ready for fattening [pig]; (*m.*) terrace; roof terrace.

eiró (*m.*) an eel.

eis (*interj.*) here is, here are, this is, these are; here it is; behold.—**aí o problema,** There you have the problem. —**aqui,** Here you have it.—**porque,** that is why, here's why.—**que,** behold.—**senão quando,** suddenly.—**tudo,** That is all.

eita-pau (*exclam.*) Hot diggity! Cf. ETA.

eito (*m.*) succession, sequence; hoeing of land by a gang of slaves; a piece of land so cleared. **a—,** one after another.

eiva (*f.*) flaw, crack; blemish; (in fruit) rotten spot.

eivar (*v.t.*) to contaminate; (*v.r.*) to go bad; of glass, to crack. **eivado de falhas,** shot through with mistakes.

eixo (*m.*) axle, axle-shaft, axletree; **axis.—da hélice,** propeller shaft.—**da roda,** axletree.—**das abscissas,** (*Geom.*) axis of abscissas.—**de manivela,** crankshaft.—**de perspectiva,** (*Math.*) axis of perspective.—**de ressaltos,** camshaft.—**de simetria,** axis of symmetry.—**dianteiro,** front axle.—**motor** or **motriz,** driving shaft.—**propulsor,** driving axle.—**transmissor,** or **de transmissão,** drive shaft.—**transverso da hipérbole,** (*Math.*) transverse axis of a conic.—**traseiro,** rear axle.—**visual,** visual axis, line of vision. **espaço entre—s,** wheel base.

eixo-badeixo (*m.*) leapfrog [= CARNIÇA].

eixú (*m.*) devil (in voodoo rites). Cf. EXÚ.

ejaculação (*f.*) ejaculation, discharge; exclamation.

ejaculador –**dora** (*adj.*) ejaculating; (*m.,f.*) ejaculator.

ejacular (*v.t.*) to ejaculate, eject, discharge; to utter suddenly and briefly, exclaim.

ejaculatório –**ria** (*adj.*) ejaculatory.

ejeção (*f.*) ejection [= DEJEÇÃO].

ejectar (*v.t.*) to eject.

ejeto, ejetamento (*m.*) ejecta, ejectamenta (of a volcano).

ejetor (*m.*) ejector; jet pump.

ela (*3rd pers. fem. pron.*) she, it; (*pl.*) they; (with prep., her, them).—**por ela,** one or the other, it's all the same. —**s por elas,** an eye for an eye, a tooth for a tooth.

elaboração (*f.*) elaboration.—**de um projeto,** the working up of a project. **em—,** (something) in the making.

elaborar (*v.t.*) to elaborate, draw up or work out in detail; to organize, perfect (a project).

elágico –**ca** (*adj., Chem.*) ellagic.

elanguescência (*f.*) languishing, lassitude.

elanguescente (*adj.*) languishing, languid.

elanguescer (*v.i.,v.r.*) to languish, droop [= ENLANGUESCER].

elasmobrânquio (*m., Zool.*) elasmobranch (shark, ray).

elastância (*f., Elec.*) elastance.

elastério (*m.*) elasticity [= ELASTICIDADE]; fig., reaction.

elasticidade (*f.*) elasticity, resiliency; reaction; moral laxness.

elasticina (*f.*) = ELASTINA.

elástico –**ca** (*adj.; m.*) elastic.

elastina (*f., Biochem.*) elastin.

elastômetro (*m.*) elastometer.

elaterídeo (*m.*) elaterid, click beetle.

elaterina (*f., Chem.*) elaterine.

elatério (*m., Pharm.*) elaterium; (*Bot.*) the squirting cucumber; elater.

elaterita (*f., Min.*) elaterite.

elatina (*f., Bot.*) waterwort (*Elatine sp.*).

ele [éle] (*m.*) the letter L.

êle (*3rd pers. masc. pron.*) he; it; (*pl.*) they. [With prep., him, them].—**mesmo,** he himself.—**s mesmos,** they themselves.

eleágneas (*f.pl., Bot.*) the oleaster family (*Elaeagnaceae*).

electr–, in the following words, the first C may be omitted, but it is preferable to leave it in; however, see also words under **eletr**–, in which the first C is never included.

electracústico –**ca** (*adj.*) electroacoustic.

eléctrio (*m.*) electron. Var. ELÉCTRON.

electro (*m., Metal.*) electrum.

electroanálise (*f., Chem.*) electroanalysis.

electrocapilaridade (*f., Physics*) electrocapillarity.

electrocardiógrafo (*m.*) electrocardiograph.

electrocardiograma (*m.*) electrocardiogram.

electrocatálise (*f.*) electrocatalysis.

electrocatalítico –**ca** (*adj.*) electrocatalytic.

electrocautério (*m.*) electrocautery, electrocauterization.

electrocinética (*f.*) electrokinetics.

electrocronógrafo (*m.*) electrochronograph.

electrodeposição (*f.*) electrodeposition.

electrodiálise (*f., Phys. Chem.*) electrodialysis.

electrodinâminco –**ca** (*adj.*) electrodynamic; (*f.*) electrodynamics.

electrodinamômetro (*m., Electrometry*) electrodynamometer.

electródio, eléctrodo (*m.*) electrode.—**negativo,** cathode. —**positivo,** anode.

electroduto (*m.*) electrical conduit.

electroencefalógrafo (*m., Med.*) electroencephalograph.

electroextração (*f.*) electroextraction.

electrofisiologia (*f., Physiol.*) electrophysiology.

electrofone (*m., Physics*) electrophone.

electroforese (*f., Phys. Chem.*) electrophoresis, cataphoresis.

electróforo (*m., Physics*) electrophorus.

electrofotômetro (*m.*) electrophotometer.

electrogalvânico –**ca** (*adj.*) electrogalvanic.

electrogalvanização (*f.*) electroplating with zinc.

electrogalvanizar (*v.t.*) to electroplate with zinc.

electrogêneo –**nea** (*adj.*) electrogenetic.

electrografia (*f.*) electrography.

electrógrafo (*m.*) electrograph.

electrogravar (*v.t.*) to electroengrave.

electrogravura (*f.*) an electroengraving.

electroidráulico –**ca** (*adj.*) electrohydraulic.

electroímã (*m.*) electromagnet.

electrolítico –**ca** (*adj.*) electrolytic.

electrólito (*m.*) electrolite.

electroluminescência (*f.*) electroluminescence.

electromagnético –**ca** (*adj.*) electromagnetic.

electromagnetismo (*m.*) electromagnetism.

electromecânico –**ca** (*adj.*) electromechanical; (*f., Physics, Elec.*) electromechanics.

electrometalizar (*v.t.*) to electroplate.

electrometalurgia (*f.*) electrometallurgy.

electrometria (*f.*) electrometry.

electrômetro (*m.*) electrometer.

eléctron (*m., Physics*) electron. Vars. ELÉCTRIO, ELECTRÔNIO.

electrônico –**ca** (*adj.*) electronic; (*f.*) electronics.

electrônio (*m.*) = ELÉCTRON.

eléctron-volt (*m., Physics*) electron volt.

electro-óptica (*f., Physics*) electrooptics.

electro-osmose (*f., Phys. Chem.*) electroosmosis.

electropirômetro (*m.*) electropyrometer.

electropneumático –**ca** (*adj.*) electropneumatic.

electroprateação (*f.*) electroplating with silver.

electroquímico –**ca** (*adj.*) electrochemical; (*f.*) electrochemistry.

electrorrefinação (*f.*) electrolytic refining (of metal).

electroscópico –**ca** (*adj., Physics*) electroscopic.

electroscópio (*m., Physics*) electroscope.—**de fôlhas de ouro,** gold-leaf electroscope.

electrossiderurgia (*f.*) electrical smelting and refining of iron.

electrossíntese (*f., Chem.*) electrosynthesis.

electrossoldadura (*f.*) electrical welding.

electrostático –**ca** (*adj.*) electrostatic; (*f.*) electrostatics.

electrostenólise (*f., Chem.*) electrostenolysis.

electrostrição (*f.*) electrostriction.

electrotecnia (*f.*) electrotechnics.

electrotécnico –**ca** (*adj.*) electrotechnic(al).

electrotecnologia (*f.*) electrotechnology.

electrotelegrafia (*f.*) electrotelegraphy.

electrotelurógrafo (*m., Elec.*) electrotellurograph.

electroterapeuta (*m.,f.*) electrotherapist.

electroterapia (*f.*) electrotherapy, electrotherapeutics.

electrotermia (*f.*) electrothermics.

electrotérmico –**ca** (*adj.*) electrothermal.

electrotipia (*f.*) electrotypy.

electrótipo (*m.*) electrotype.

electrótonus (*m., Physiol.*) electrotonus.

electrotropismo (*m., Biol.*) electrotropism.

elefante (*m.*), –**ta** (*f.*) elephant.—**do mar,** elephant seal. —**marinho,** walrus (*Odobenus rosmarus*).

elefantíase (*f., Med.*) elephantiasis.—**dos árabes,** filariasis.—**dos gregos,** leprosy.

elefântico –ca, elefantino –na (adj.) elephantine.
elegância (f.) elegance, grace, polish (of speech, dress, manners); gentility, refinement.
elegante (adj.) elegant, graceful; handsome; well-built; jaunty; well-dressed, dapper, smart, spruce, trim, natty; fashionable; polished, refined. (m.,f.) such a person.
eleger (v.t.) to elect (by votes); to choose, select.— (de) entre, to choose between, from among.
elegia (f.) elegy.
elegíaco –ca (adj.) elegiac.
elegibilidade (f.) eligibility.
elegível (adj.) eligible.
eleição (f.) election (by votes); choice, selection.
eleiçoeiro –ra (adj.) = ELEITOREIRO-RA
eleito –ta (adj.; irreg. p.p. of ELEGER) elected (by votes); chosen, selected; (m.,f.) one chosen or elected (to office).
eleitor –tora (m.,f.) elector, voter, constituent.
eleitorado (m.) electorate.
eleitoral (adj.) electoral, voting. urna—, ballot box.
eleitoreiro –ra (adj., derog.) said of actions or statements of an officeholder seeking re-election.
elemental, elementar, elementário –ria (adj.) elemental; elementary, simple; rudimentary; essential; fundamental, basic.
elemento (m.) element; constituent, ingredient, component (part); natural medium; proper sphere.—de bateria elétrica, battery cell; (pl.) rudiments, first steps or principles.
elemi (m.) elemi oleoresin; (Bot.) the Brazil resintree (Protium heptaphyllum).
elenco (m.) list, index; cast (of actors).
eleólita (f., Min.) eleolite.
eleômetro (m.) oleometer.
eletividade (f.) electivity.
eletivo –va (adj.) elective.
eletr–, see also under electr–.
eletricidade (f.) electricity.—estática, static electricity.
eletricista (m.,f.) electrician.
elétrico –ca (adj.) electric.
eletrificação (f.) electrification.
eletrificar (v.t.) to electrify.
eletrificável (adj.) electrifiable.
eletrizador –dora (adj.) electrizing; (m.) electrizer.
eletrizante (adj.) electrifying; thrilling.
eletrizar (v.t.) to electrize; to electrify, excite, thrill.
eletrocultura (f.) electroculture.
eletrocussão (f.) electrocution.
eletrocutar (v.t.) to electrocute.
eletrocutor (m.) electrocutioner.
eletrolisação (f.) = ELETRÓLISE.
eletrolisar (v.t.) to electrolyze.
eletrolisável (adj.) electrolyzable.
eletrólise (f.) electrolysis.
eletromotor (m.) electromotor.
eletronegativo –va (adj., Physics, Chem.) electronegative.
eletropositivo –va (adj., Physics, Chem.) electropositive.
eletuário (m., Pharm.) electuary.
elevação (f.) elevation; promotion; height; altitude; eminence; flat drawing of the front or side of a building; act of heightening or raising.
elevado –da (adj.) elevated; high, lofty.
elevador –dora (adj.) elevating, lifting; (m.) elevator, lift; checkrein (of a bridle); elevator muscle.—de carga, freight elevator.—de passageiros, passenger elevator. —de serviço, service elevator,—de tensão, (Elec.) step-up transformer.
elevar (v.t.) to elevate, raise, lift (up); to exalt, aggrandize, promote; (v.r.) to mount; to tower; to rise.—às nuvens, to praise to the skies.
elevatório –ria (adj.) elevatory.
elfo (m.) elf.
Elias (m.) Elias, Elijah, Ellis.
elidir (v.t.) to elide; to suppress; to eliminate.
elidível (adj.) elidible.
eliminação (f.) elimination.
eliminador –dora (adj.) eliminating; (m.,f.) eliminator.
eliminar (v.t.) to eliminate, get rid of; (Alg., Physiol.) to eliminate.
eliminatório –ria (adj.) eliminatory; (f. Sports) play-off; final.
elipse (f. Gram.) ellipsis; (Geom.) ellipse. [But not ellipses (printing marks), which are RETICÊNCIAS.]
elipsiógrafo (m.) ellipsograph, elliptic compass.
elipsóide, elipsoidal (adj.) ellipsoidal; (m.) ellipsoid.—de revolução, (Math.) ellipsoid of revolution; a spheroid.

elipticidade (f.) ellipticity.
elí[p]tico –ca (adj.) elliptic(al).
Elisa (f.) Eliza, Elizabeth, Elisabeth. Cf. ISABEL.
elisão (f., Gram.) elision.
Eliseu (m.) Elysium; Elisha.
elísio –sia (adj.) blissful, delightful. campos—s, Elysian fields.
elite (f.) elite.
élitro (m., Zool.) elytron.
elixar (v.t.) to make an elixir of.
elixir (m., Pharm.) elixir.—da longa vida, elixir of life.— dentifrício, mouth wash.
elmo [é] (m.) helmet.
elo [é] (m.) link.
elocução (f.) elocution.
eloendro (m.) = ESPIRRADEIRA (a plant).
elogiador –dora (adj.) eulogizing. (m.,f.) eulogizer, eulogist.
elogiante (adj.) eulogizing.
elogiar (v.t.) to eulogize, extol; to praise; to boost.—-se a si proprio, to sing one's own praises; to blow one's own horn.
elogio (m.) eulogy, praise; compliment.—fúnebre, eulogy of a deceased person. um côro de—s, a chorus of praise.
elongação (f., Astron.) elongation. Cf. ALONGAMENTO.
eloqüência (f.) eloquence.
eloqüente (adj.) eloquent; persuasive.
Elsa (f.) Elsa.
elucidação (f.) elucidation, explanation.
elucidar (v.t.) to elucidate, explain, clarify.
elucidativo –va (adj.) elucidative, explanatory.
elucubrar (v.) = LUCUBRAR.
elutriação (f.) elutriation, decantation.
elutriador (m.) elutriator.
elutriar (v.t.) to elutriate.
eludir (v.t.) to elude.
Elvira (f.) Elvira.
elzevir (adj.; m., Bibliog., Printing) Elzevir.
E.M. = EM MÃO (at hand, in hand); estado maior (general staff).
em (prep.) in, on, at, into, by. [Contracts with the articles A(S) and O(S) to form NA(S) and NO(S).]—aberto, open, not concluded.—alto grau, in high degree.—aparência, apparently.—artigo de morte, on the point of death. —atenção a, in view of, in consideration of.—ato contínuo, then, next.—atropêlo, confusedly.—baixo, down, under.—balanço, in the balance, uncertainly.—barda, in abundance.—bloco, in a block, wholesale.—boa hora, at a good time, just right.—boa hora você chegou! (ironically) You couldn't have come at a worse time!—boa me meti eu! I've got myself in a fine mess.—boas mãos, in good hands.—branco, in blank.—breve, soon, briefly. —breves termos, briefly and to the point.—bruto, in the rough.—busca de, in search of.—carne e osso, in flesh and blood, in person.—casa, at home.—chefe, in chief. —cima (de), on top (of).—claro, in blank; without sleep. —compensação, on the other hand.—competência, in competition.—côro, in a chorus.—couro, in the nude.— demanda de, in search of.—demasia, in excess.—derredor (de), around (about).—desabano de, to the discredit of.—descanso, unhurriedly.—devida forma, in due form.—diante, ahead; in the future.—dias alternados, on alternate days.—direção a, in the direction of. —direitura a, straight on the way to.—dois pulos, in two jumps.—duplicado, in duplicate.—dúvida, doubtfully, hesitantly.—especial, especially.—esquadria, squarely, on a right angle.—esqueleto, in skeleton form.—estado de, in condition to, capable of.—estado normal, as usual. —evidência, clearly, patently.—excesso, excessively.— exercício, in the exercise of (an office).—face de, in the face of.—falso, vainly.—falta de, for want of.—família, en famille, at home.—favor de, in favor of.—fim, finally. —flagrante, in the very act.—folio, in folio.—força, in force.—forma, in due form; formally; in good form.— —frente de, in front of; fronting.—funeral, in mourning. —geral, in general; generally.—globo, wholly, as a whole.—grande escala, on a large scale.—grosso, on a large scale.—grupo, in a group.—guerra aberta, in open warfare.—honra de, in honor of.—imaginação, in imagination.—jejum, in complete ignorance of.—lanço, at auction.—liberdade, freely.—linha, in line.—lugar de, in place of.—má hora, at a bad time.—mangas de camisa, in shirt sleeves.—mão própria, for personal delivery.—massa, en masse, in a body.—maus lençóis, in

a jam, in a bad fix, in hot water.—**meio de**, in the midst of; between.—**menos de**, in less than.—**mente**, in mind. —**mentes**, meanwhile.—**mim**, in me.—**moço**, when young; as a young man.—**montão**, in confusion.—**movimento**, in motion.—**nome de**, in the name of.—**novo**, new, first-hand.—**ôlho**, under observation.—**oposição a**, against.—**palpos de aranha**, in a fluster; in a pickle.—**parte**, partly.—**particular**, privately.—**pé**, upright, standing (up).—**pé de guerra**, on a war footing.—**peça**, by the (whole) piece.—**pêlo** or **pelota**, in the nude, naked. —**penca**, in heaps, much, "lots," "oodles".—**pequeno**, in childhood, as a child.—**perspectiva**, in the foreseeable future.—**pêso**, fully, wholly; in full force.—**pés de lã**, on tiptoes.—**pessoa**, in person.—**petição de miséria**, in the depths of penury.—**pilha**, in a pile.—**pinha**, jammed together.—**pirâmide**, in a pyramid.—**ponto**, exactly, on the dot.—**pôs de**, after.—**poucas palavras**, laconically.—**poucos minutos**, shortly.—**presença de**, in view of. —**primeiro lugar**, firstly, in the first place.—**pról de**, in behalf of.—**proporção**, porportionately.—**proporção de**, at the rate of.—**proveito de**, to the profit of; for the benefit of.—**punho**, (held) in the closed hand, in the fist. —**pura perda**, entirely in vain; completely useless.—**quantidade**, in quantity, in abundance.—**quanto**, while. —**que pese a**, in spite of.—**razão de**, in view of, for the reason that.—**realidade**, in reality, really.—**recurso extremo**, as a last resort.—**redondo**, round about.—**redor (de)**, around.—**referência a**, in reference to,—**regra**, as a rule.—**remate**, in conclusion.—**respeito de**, in respect of. —**resumo**, in summary.—**riba**, on top; furthermore.—**rigor**, strictly.—**risco de**, at the risk of.—**roda (de)**, around (about).—**salvo**, safely.—**sangue**, bleeding. —**sêco**, dry, out of water, on dry land.—**segrêdo**, secretly.—**seguida**; afterwards; right away; next; then; following.—**segundo lugar**, in second place, secondly. —**seguro**, safely, in a safe place.—**sentido oposto a**, against.—**separado**, separately.—**ser**, in being, in existence; on hand.—**si**, in itself, of itself.—**silêncio**, silently. —**sobressalto**, in a state of terror.—**sociedade**; socially; in a group, together with.—**socorro**, in aid.—**sonho**, in a dream.—**subido grau**, in high degree.—**substância**, in substance.—**suma**, in a word.—**surdina**, mutedly.—**tal maneira**, in such a manner, to such a degree, so excessively.—**tempo**, in time, opportunely; in other times, formerly.—**términos**, almost, about.—**termos gerais**, in general terms.—**termos hábeis**, in proper or reasonable terms, circumspectly.—**tese**, in theory; generally.—**tôda a extensão da palavra**, in the fullest sense of the word. —**tôda a parte**, everywhere.—**todo caso**, in any case.—**todos os termos**, in fullest terms.—**todos os tons**, in every way.—**tôrno (de)**, around, roundabout, surrounding.—**tôsco**, in the rough.—**través**, crosswise.—**três tempos**, in three seconds.—**triunfo**, triumphantly.—**trôco de**, in exchange for.—**tropel**, helterskelter.—**tudo**, entirely, in everything.—**tudo e por tudo**, in any and all circumstances.—**tumulto**, tumultuously.—**turbilhões**, in a whirlwind.—**última análise**, in the last analysis.—**última instância**, as a last resort.—**último lugar**, in the last place, finally.—**último recurso**, as a last resort.—**uma palavra**, in a word.—**um instante**, in an instant.—**um minuto**, in a minute.—**uníssono**, in unison.—**vão**, in vain.—**verdade**, truly, in truth.—**verde**, prematurely, ahead of time.—**vez de**, instead of.—**vida**, during life.—**virtude de**, by virtue of.—**vista de**, in view of.—**vista do que**, in view of which.—**volta (de)**, around (about).

Em.ª = EMINÊNCIA (*Eminence*).

ema (f.) rhea, the 3-toed American ostrich, c.a. AVESTRUZ, XURI. [Not to be confused with the Australian emu.]

emaçar (*v.t.*) to assemble in a bundle or package.

emaciação (f.) emaciation.

emaciado –**da** (*adj.*) gaunt, rawboned.

emaciar (*v.t.,v.i.*) to emaciate.

emadeiramento (*m.*) woodwork or wood frame (of a building).

emadurecer (*v.*) = AMADURECER.

emagrecer (*v.i.*) to grow thin, emaciate. **regime para**—, reducing diet.

emagrecimento (*m.*) a growing thin or weak.

emalar (*v.t.*) to put in a trunk.

emalhar (*v.t.*) to net (as, fish).

emalhetar (*v.t.*) to mortise.

emanação (f.) emanation; aura.

emanar (*v.i.*) to emanate, come forth (sounds, odors).

emancipação (f.) emancipation; liberation (esp. of slaves).

emancipacionista (*adj.*) emancipationist.

emancipador –**dora** (*adj.*) emancipating; (*m.,f.*) emancipator.

emancipar (*v.t.*) to emancipate, set free.

Emanuel (*m.*) Immanuel.

emaranhado –**da** (*adj.*) tangled; confused; involved.

emaranhamento (*m.*) entanglement; confusion.

emaranhar (*v.t.*) to snarl, tangle; to entangle, complicate; (*v.r.*) to become entangled (**em**, in); to snarl, tangle.

emarelecer (*v.t.*) to make yellow; (*v.i.*) to grow yellow; = AMARELECER.

emascular (*v.t.*) to emasculate; (*v.r.*) to lose virility or vigor.

emassilhar (*v.t.*) to putty (window panes).

emb. = EMBALAGEM (packing).

embaçadela (f.) embarrassment; trickery.

embaçado –**da** (*adj.*) pale (as from fright); dull (sound, surface); disappointed.

embaçar (*v.t.*) to blur, obscure, dim (as a window with mist); to obfuscate; to hoodwink; (*v.i.*) to lose the power of speech; (*v.r.*) to fool oneself.

embaciado –**da** (*adj.*) dull, dim, lackluster.

embaciar (*v.t.*) to tarnish, dim, dull; (*v.i.,v.r.*) to grow dull, lusterless.

embaiás (*m.pl.*) the Mbaya or Guaycuru Indians of S. A.

embaíba (f.) = UMBAÚBA.

embaidor –**dora** [a-i] (*adj.*) deceiving; (*m.,f.*) deceiver.

embaimento [a-i] (*m.*) deception.

embainhar [11] (*v.t.*) to sheath (a sword); to hem, border, edge (a garment or piece of cloth); (*v.i.*) to make hems in sewing.

embair [42] (*v.t.*) to hoodwink, hoax, deceive; to wheedle.

embaixada (f.) embassy.

embaixador [ô] (*m.*) ambassador.

embaixadora (f.) ambassadress (woman ambassador). Cf. EMBAIXATRIZ.

embaixatriz (f.) ambassadress (wife of an ambassador). Cf. EMBAIXADORA.

embaixo (*adv.*) down, under.

embaladeira (f.) rocker (of a chair or cradle).

embalado –**da** (*adj.*) loaded (with bullets).

embalagem (f.) baling, boxing, packaging (of goods).

embalar (*v.t.*) to bale, pack, wrap (goods); to rock (a child) to sleep; to lull, soothe; to load (a gun); to delude; to accelerate.

embalete [lê] (*m.*) pump handle.

embalo (*m.*) act of rocking (to sleep); shift, change.

embalsamento (*m.*), **embalsamação** (f.) act of embalming.

embalsamador –**dora** (*adj.*) embalming; (*m.*) embalmer.

embalsamar (*v.t.*) to embalm (a corpse); to endue with fragrance.

embandeirado –**da** (*adj.*) flag-bedecked; of a person, decked out, dressed up.

embandeirar (*v.t.*) to deck with flags; (*v.r.*) to deck oneself out.

embaraçado –**da** (*adj.*) embarrassed; tangled; involved; confused; encumbered.

embaraçador –**dora** (*adj.*) embarrassing, hindering, etc. See the verb EMBARAÇAR.

embaraçar (*v.t.*) to embarrass, hinder; to cramp; to encumber, handicap; to disturb; to perplex; to complicate; mix up; to entangle; (*v.r.*) to become embarrassed.

embaraço (*m.*) embarrassment, impediment, encumbrance; difficulty; perplexity; confusion; financial embarrassment; functional difficulty.—**gástrico**, gastric upset.

embaraçoso –**sa** (*adj.*) embarrassing, troublesome; cumbersome.

embarafustar (*v.i.*) to rush headlong; to dive into (a house, etc.) in a rude or disorderly manner.

embaralhar (*v.t.*) to shuffle (cards, etc.); to mix, jumble [= BARALHAR].

embarbascar (*v.t.*) to stupefy (fish) with poison.

embarcação (f.) embarkation; vessel, craft; boat; shipping bottom, cargo-carrier.

embarcadiço –**ça** (*adj.*; *m.*) seafaring (man).

embarcador –**dora** (*adj.*) embarking; loading; shipping; (*m.*) embarker; shipper.

embarcadouro (*m.*) wharf, pier, quay. Var. -DOIRO.

embarcamento (*m.*) = EMBARQUE.

embarcar (*v.t.*) to load, put on board; (*v.i.*) to board (ship, train, plane, etc.).—**para**, to embark, leave (for a given place).—**em canoa furada**, to embark on a risky enterprise; to play the sucker.

embargado –da (adj.) hindered; held up, stopped.
embargador –dora (adj.) hindering, impeding; (m.) one who issues a legal injunction.
embargar (v.t.) to embargo; to stay (as the execution of a sentence); to hinder, impede; to restrain; (Law) to attach.
embargo (m.) embargo, hindrance, impediment; (Law) attachment. sem—, nevertheless, notwithstanding, yet, just the same.
embarque (m.) embarkation; shipment.
embarrar (v.t.) to daub (wattles) with clay.
embarricar, embarrilar (v.t.) to barrel.
embasamento (m., Archit.) base or lower part; (Const.) foundation.
embasbacado –da (adj.) agape. Cf. BOQUIABERTO.
embasbascar (v.i.) to gape, stare (as in wonder); (v.t.) to amaze, flabbergast.
embastecer (v.t.) to thicken (as soup); to make dense.
embate (m.) collision, impact; a dashing together; opposition, resistance; sudden onset; (pl.) reverses of fortune. —de ideologias, clash of ideologies.
embater (v.i.) —em, to dash against; to collide with; (v.r.) to clash.
embatocar (v.t.) to stop with a bung; = EMBATUCAR.
embatucar (v.t.) to silence; to nonplus, flabbergast, dumfound; (v.i.) to fall silent; to be stopped (by a question).
embaúba (f.) = UMBAÚBA.
embaucar [a-u] (v.t.) to beguile, inveigle, lure, entice.
embaular [a-u] (v.t.) to pack away (hide) in a trunk.
embebedar (v.t.) to intoxicate, inebriate, make drunk; (v.r.) to get drunk.
embeber (v.t.) to imbibe, absorb; to drench, soak (em, in; de, with); to plunge (a dagger, etc.) in. (v.r.) to become absorbed (em, in).
embeberar (v.t.) to water (animals); to soak (something) in (something).—se em, to soak up (knowledge, etc.).
embebido –da (adj.) drenched, soaked; fig., rapt, absorbed.
embeiçado –da (adj.) dominated by; infatuated with, "stuck on" (someone).
embeiçamento (m.) amorous infatuation.
embeiçar-se (v.r.) to fall madly in love.
embelecar (v.t.) to entice, beguile; to wheedle; (v.r.) to "fall for" (something or someone).
embelecer (v.t.) to beautify, embellish.
embelêco (m.) lure, bait; fraud.
embelezador –dora (adj.) embellishing; beautifying.
embelezamento (m.) embellishment.
embelezar (v.t.) to embellish, beautify (-se, oneself).
embestar (v.i.) to be obstinate, pigheaded; to persist in.
embevecedor –dora, –vecente (adj.) ravishing.
embevecer (v.t.) to enrapture; (v.r.) to be enraptured.
embevecido –da (adj.) rapt.
embevecimento (m.) rapture, ravishment.
embezerrado –da (adj., colloq.) sulky, grouchy.
embezerrar (v.i.,v.r.) to sulk or be grouchy.
embiara (f.) game; Indian war booty.
embicado –da (adj.) beaked, peaked.
embicadura (f.) heading (of a ship) into port.
embicar (v.t.) to give (something) the shape of a beak or peak; (v.i.) to become confused; to trip, stumble; to heave to; to run ashore.—em, to touch upon.—com, to have a quarrel with.—para, to head towards.
embigo (m.) = UMBIGO.
embiocar-se (v.r.) to muffle oneself up; to hide oneself.
embira (f). any of various trees which yield a bast fiber (also called embira) used for cordage and net-making; (colloq.) critical situation, hot spot; bag of game or mess of fish.—da-mata-branca, a screwtree (Helicteres baruensis).—do-mangue, the linden hibiscus (H. tiliaceus).
embiratanha (f.) = CASTANHEIRO-DO-MARANHÃO.
embirra, embirração (f.) pig-headedness; aversion; grouchiness; tiff.
embirrado –da (adj.) sullen.
embirrante (adj.) obstinate, pig-headed.
embirrar (v.i.) to sulk.—em, to persist obstinately (in doing something).—com, to take a strong dislike to.
embiru (m.) = MUTAMBA.
emblema (m.) emblem, symbol, badge.
emblemar (v.t.) to emblem, emblematize.
emblemático –ca (adj.) emblematic.
emboaba, emboava (m.,f.) a scornful nickname applied by the Brazilian colonists to newly-arrived Portuguese who came in search of gold and precious stones.

emboca (m.) party crasher [= PENETRA].
embocadura (f.) mouthpiece of a musical instrument; bit of a bridle; mouth of a river; mouthpiece of a bridle.
emboçamento (m.) rough-plastering.
embocar (v.t.) to apply the mouth to (a musical instrument); to bring (something) to the mouth; to place the bit in a horse's mouth.—por, to enter through or into.
emboçar (v.t.) to rough-plaster (a wall, etc.).
embôço (m.) first or rough coat of stucco or plaster.
embodegar (v.t.) to make filthy.
embófia (f.) = EMPÁFIA.
embolar-se (v.r.) to roll over and over (as a wrestler).
embolia (f., Med.) embolism.
embolismo (m.) intercalation of a day in a year; (Med.) embolism.
embolorado –da (adj.) musty.
êmbolo (m.) piston; (Med.) embolus. curso de—, piston stroke. segmento de—, piston ring.
embolsar (v.t.) to pocket; to pay, reimburse.
embôlso (m.) payment, reimbursement.
embonar (v.t.) to sheathe the hull of a vessel.
embonecar (v.t.,v.r.) to dress like a doll.
embora (adv.) even so, even thus; (conj.) though, although, even though; (interj.) Be it so! Begone! Be off!; (m.pl.) congratulations [= PARABENS]. ir (-se)—, to go away. muito—, despite.
emborcação (f.) act of turning (a glass, etc.) bottom up; upset; act of gulping down; embrocation.
emborcado –da (adj.) upside down (referring to a cup, glass, etc.).
emborcar (v.t.) to turn (a glass, etc.) upside down; to swig, gulp (down) liquids; to overturn (a bottle, etc.); (v.i.) to fall prone.
embornal (m.) feed bag; (pl., Naut.) scuppers.
emborrachar (v.t.) to make drunk; (v.r.) to get drunk.
emborrascar (v.t.) to trouble, agitate, disturb; (v.r.) to cloud up.
emboscado –da (adj.) ambushed; (m.) evader of military service,·slacker: (f.) ambuscade; ambush.
emboscar (v.t.) to ambush; (v.r.) to lurk.
embotado –da (adj.) blunt, dull; numb, torpid.
embotar (v.t.) to blunt, make dull; to benumb; to enervate; (v.r.) to grow dull; to grow weak.
embotelhar (v.t.) to bottle.
embraçadeira (f.) = BRAÇADEIRA.
embrace (m.) a curtain clasp.
embraiagem (f.) = EMBREAGEM.
embranquecer (v.t.) to bleach, make white; (v.i.) to whiten, grow white.
embranquecido –da (adj.) grown white (as hair).
embravecer (v.t.) to enrage; (v.i.,v.r.) to rage.
embravecido –da (adj.) raging.
embravecimento (m.) act of raging.
embreagem (f.) automobile clutch.·
embrear (v.t.) to operate the clutch of an automobile; to cover with tar.
embrechar (v.t.) to adorn (a wall, etc.) with shells, pebbles, bits of glass, etc.
embrenhar (v.t.) to hide in the woods; to penetrate deep into; (v.r.) to hide away.—se no mato, to hide or disappear in the woods.
embriagado –da (adj.) drunk; intoxicated (excited).
embriagador –dora, embriagante (adj.) intoxicating.
embriagar (v.t.) to inebriate, intoxicate; to enrapture; (v.r.) to get drunk.
embriaguez [ê] (f.) drunkenness; intoxication, rapture.
embrião (m.) embryo.
embriogenia (f., Biol.) embryogeny.
embriografia (f.) embryography.
embriologia (f., Biol.) embryology.
embrionado –da (adj.) having an embryo.
embrionário –ria, embryonic.
embrionífero –ra (adj.) bearing an embryo.
embrioniforme (adj.) embryoniform.
embrioscópio (m.) embryoscope.
embriossaco (m.) embryo sac.
embrocação (f.) embrocation.
embroma, embromação (f.) humbug, hoax, sham, fake, hocus-pocus.
embromador (m.) cheat, imposter, swindler.
embromar (v.i.) to cheat, defraud; to sham.
embrulhado –da (adj.) wrapped up; confused, tangled, mixed up; (f.) imbroglio, embroilment, complication, entanglement, mix-up, jumble, muddle. uma—do diabo, a devil of a mess.

embrulhador –dora (*adj.*) wrapping; (*m.,f.*) wrapper.
embrulhamento (*m.*) act of wrapping; also = EMBRU-
LHADA.—**de estômago,** stomach upset.
embrulhar (*v.t.*) to wrap (up); to confuse, complicate,
tangle; to embroil; to deceive, fool, cheat; (*v.r.*) to
wrap oneself up (in a coat).—**o estômago,** to upset the
stomach.
embrulho (*m.*) bundle, parcel, package [= PACOTE]; a
jumble; trick, imposture, hocus-pocus. **levar no—,** to
gyp.
embrutecer (*v.t.*) to brutalize; to besot.
embrutecido –da (*adj.*) brutish, coarse, stupid.
embrutecimento (*n.*) act of brutalizing.
embruxar (*v.t.*) to "hex".
embuá (*m.*) a millipede, myriapod [= GONGOLÔ].
embuçado –da (*adj.*) cloaked, hooded, disguised.
embuçar (*v.t.*) to cloak, mask, veil; to dissemble; (*v.r.*) to
muffle up, wrap oneself up (in a cape or cloak).
embuchar (*v.t.*) to stuff (stomach, craw); (*Mach.*) to
provide with a bushing or bushings; (*v.i.*) to be unable
or unwilling to speak out.
embuço (*m.*) hood, veil, muffler.
embude (*m., Bot.*) the nodding navelwort (*Umbilicus
pendulinus*); a kind of fish poison; a funnel.
embuia (*f.*) *Webster:* "Any of several Brazilian trees
(genus *Nectandra*) whose wood is used for fine cabinet
work and construction."
emburacar-se (*v.r.*) to hole up.
emburana (*f., Bot.*) a bursera (*B. leptophleos*), c.a.
UMBURANA.
emburi (*m.*) = ARIRI.
emburrado –da (*adj.*) sulky, morose, out of humor, annoyed [= ZANGADO]; (*m.*) an area covered with rounded
stones.
emburrar (*v.i.*) to sulk, act stubbornly.
emburricado –da (*adj.*) spellbound.
embuste (*m.*) trick, deceit; fraud; snare; hoax; humbug,
flimflam.
embustear (*v.t.*) to trick, cheat, deceive.
embusteiro (*m.*), –ra (*f.*) cheater, imposter; liar; humbug; four-flusher; adventurer.
embutido –da (*adj.*) forced in; inlaid, imbedded. **armário
—,** a built-in closet; (*m.*) inlay work, mosaic.
embutidor (*m.*) inlayer.
embutir (*v.t.*) to inlay, imbed; to place or set in a recess.
emedar (*v.t.*) to stack (as grain).
emelar (*v.t.*) to sweeten with, or as with, honey; (*v.r.*) to
become smeared with honey (as beekeepers).
emenda (*f.*) emendation, correction; amendment; mending; patch(ing); proofreader's corrections.
emendar (*v.t.*) to emend, amend, correct, rectify; to
mend; to patch on; (*v.r.*) to mend one's ways.
emendável (*adj.*) emendable.
ementa (*f.*) list; note; memorandum; summary.
ementário (*m.*) list; notebook.
emergência (*f.*) emergence; emergency.
emergente (*adj.*) emergent.
emergir [24, 25] (*v.i.*) to emerge (de, from); to rise out of.
emérito –ta (*adj.*) emeritus; distinguished, noted.
emersão (*f.*) emersion, emergence.
emerso (*adj.; irreg. p.p. of* EMERGIR) emersed, emerged.
emético –ca (*adj.; m.*) emetic.
emigração (*f.*) emigration, migration.
emigrado –da, **emigrante** (*adj.; m.,f.*) emigrant.
emigrar (*v.i.*) to emigrate, migrate.
Emília (*f.*) Emily, Emilie.
Emílio (*m.*) Emil.
eminência (*f.*) eminence; prominence; elevated ground.
eminente (*adj.*) eminent, lofty; prominent.
eminentíssimo –ma (*absol. superl. of* EMINENTE) most
eminent.
emir (*m.*) Emir.
emissão (*f.*) emission; radio broadcast; issue of paper
currency.
emissário –ria (*adj.*) emissary; (*m.,f.*) emissary; secret
agent.
emissionismo (*m.*) governmental policy of emission of
paper currency.
emissionista (*adj.*) committed to the policy of EMIS-
SIONISMO.
emissividade (*f., Physics., Metal.*) emissivity.
emissivo –va (*adj.*) emissive.
emissor –sora (*adj.*) issuing bank; (*m.*) emitter, sender;
radio transmitter; (*f.*) radio broadcasting station.

emitir (*v.t.*) to emit, throw out (light, sparks); to issue
(paper currency); to utter (an opinion); to broadcast
(on the radio).
Em.mo = EMINENTÍSSIMO (Most Eminent).
emoção (*f.*) emotion, feeling; thrill.
emocional (*adj.*) emotional.
emocionante (*adj.*) moving, impressive; thrilling; exciting; hectic.
emocionar (*v.t.*) to excite emotion in; to move; impress;
to thrill; (*v.r.*) to be moved, feel emotion.
emocionável (*adj.*) impressionable.
emodina (*f., Chem.*) emodin.
emol. = EMOLUMENTOS (emoluments).
emoldurar (*v.t.*) to frame.
emoliente (*adj.; m., Med.*) emollient.
emolir [46] (*v.t., Med.*) to soften.
emolumento (*m.*) emolument, prerequisite, extra fees;
(*pl.*) profits.
emotismo (*m.*) emotiveness.
emotivo –va (*adj.*) emotive.
E.M.P. = EM MÃO PRÓPRIA (into the hand of—referring to
the delivery of a letter, etc.).
empa (*f.*) act of tying, staking, propping (grape vines).
empacador –dora (*adj.*) balky; recalcitrant.
empacar (*v.i.*) to balk, stop short.
empachado –da (*adj.*) overfull; big-bellied.
empachar (*v.t.*) to encumber; to stuff; to clog; to overload (the stomach); (*v.r.*) to be embarrassed.
empacotador –dora (*adj.*) packing, baling; (*m.,f.*) packer,
baler; (*f.*) binder, baling maching.
empacotamento (*m.*) act of packing, binding, baling.
empacotar (*v.t.*) to pack, bale, bind (into bundles).
empada (*f.*) patty, little meat or shrimp pie; (*colloq.*)
pest, bore.
empáfia (*f.*) conceit, self-esteem; haughtiness; (*m.,f.*)
person exhibiting such.
empafiado –da (*adj.; m.,f.*) "snooty" (person); self-important (person).
empalação (*f.*) impalement (form of torture).
empalar (*v.t.*) to torture by impalement.
empalhação (*f.*) act of stuffing, etc.;—see the verb EM-
PALHAR.
empalhador (*m.*) one who stuffs animals, who packs in
straw, etc.;—see verb EMPALHAR.
empalhamento (*m.*) = EMPALHAÇÃO.
empalhar, to stuff (animals, birds, etc.); to pack (dishes,
etc.) in straw; to provide (a chair) with a cane bottom;
to stow hay; to cover (bottles) with straw; (*colloq.*) to
kid (someone) along.
empaliar (*v.*) = PALIAR.
empalidecer (*v.i.*) to pale; to blanch.
empalmar (*v.t.*) to palm, conceal in the hand; to filch.
empanado –da (*adj.*) dim; lusterless; wrapped in cloth;
dressed up; (*f.*) window blind; awning; large EMPADA.
empanar (*v.t.*) to dim, tarnish, dull; to sully; to blot out
(light); (*v.r.*) to discolor; to blur.
empancar (*v.t.*) to hold back; to dam.
empanque (*m.*) gasket; any material for stuffing or
packing joints to make them steamtight, watertight,
etc.
empanturrado –da (*adj.*) replete, overfull.
empanturrar (*v.t.*) to cram, overfeed, gorge (-se, oneself).
empanzinado –da (*adj.*) = EMPANTURRADO.
empanzinamento (*m.*) glut, repletion, surfeit.
empanzinar (*v.t.*) to glut, gorge, surfeit.
empapado –da (*adj.*) soggy.
empapar (*v.t.*) to steep, soak; to drench; to fill the craw;
to swell, puff out.
empapelar (*v.t.*) to wrap in paper; to put (something)
away carefully.
empapuçado –da (*adj.*) pouchy, bloated, puffy. **olhos—s,**
puffy eyes.
empar (*v.t.*) to tie up, stake, prop (grape vines, etc.).
emparceirar (*v.t.*) to match up.
emparedar (*v.t.*) to wall in, immure.
emparelhado –da (*adj.*) paired with; yoked together;
matched.
emparelhar (*v.t.*) to pair off; to yoke together; (*v.r.*) to
equal, match.—**com,** to match; to come up to; to vie
with.
empastado –da (*adj.*) thickened (as paste); plastered
down (as wet hair).
empastar (*v.t.*) to paste, plaster; to impaste, decorate by
impasto; (*v.r.*) to turn to paste.

empastelamento (*m.*) destructive raid on a newspaper office.

empastelar (*v.t.*) to pie (type); to raid a newspaper office.

empata (*m.*, *colloq.*) a third wheel (unwelcome third person); a dog in the manger.

empatar (*v.t.*) to stalemate; to cramp (another's) style; to tie (a score, etc.); to tie up (money) in an investment.

empate (*m.*) draw, tie; stalemate; deadlock.

empavesar-se (*v.r.*) to deck oneself out.

empavonar (*v.i.*) to fill (-se, oneself) with pride (as a peacock).

empeçar (*v.t.*) to tangle; to confuse; to obstruct; to start.

empecer (*v.t.*) to hinder, hamper; to damage.

empecilho (*m.*) impediment, difficulty, stumbling-block, cumbrance, drawback.

empêço (*m.*) delay; obstacle; a beginning.

empeçonhar (*v.t.*) to poison.

empedernido –da (*adj.*) hardened; petrified; impassive, unfeeling; inflexible, stiff; de coração—, hardhearted.

empedernir [46] (*v.t.*) to petrify; to harden; (*v.r.*) to become hardhearted.

empedrado –da (*adj.*; *m.*) rock-paved (road).

empedrar (*v.t.*) to pave or cover with stone; to render hard as a rock; (*v.i.*,*v.r.*) to turn hard.

empelicar (*v.t.*) to make (hides) into kid leather; to cover with kid leather.

empena (*f.*) the upper expanse of a gable wall; roof rafter; warping of wood.

empenado –da (*adj.*) warped.

empenagem (*f.*, *Aeron.*) tail assembly.

empenamento (*m.*) act or effect of curving, twisting, warping.

empenar (*v.t.*) to warp, twist out of shape, spring; to feather (airplane propeller); (*v.i.*,*v.r.*) to warp.

empenhado –da (*adj.*) pledged; pawned; wagered; committed; bent upon.

empenhar (*v.t.*) to pledge, pawn, "hock"; to mortgage; to lay under obligation, bind; (*Milit.*) to engage (the enemy); (*v.r.*) to bind oneself; to strive diligently, exert oneself, fight, struggle (em, para, por, to, for); to pledge oneself (para, to; por, a favor de, in behalf of).—-se contra, to strive against.—a palavra, to pledge one's word.

empenho (*m.*) pledge; promise; assiduity, diligence; zeal; backing (support of another). com—, earnestly, diligently. pôr—em, to make a point of.

empeno (*m.*) a warping; (*colloq.*) mistake; hindrance.

emperramento (*m.*) act of balking; act of sticking, jamming.

emperrado –da (*adj.*) stuck, jammed; stubborn; stiff.

emperrar (*v.i.*) to balk (refuse to go); to stick, jam; (*v.t.*) to make obstinate.

empêrro (*m.*) stubbornness.

empertigado –da (*adj.*) upright, erect; haughty, proud; prim; perky.

empertigar-se (*v.r.*) to stiffen, stand up straight; to bridle; to become haughty; to perk up.

empestado –da (*adj.*) pestilential, pestiferous; (*m.*,*f.*) person suffering from bubonic plague.

empestar (*v.t.*) to contaminate (esp. the air); to infect with the plague.

empiêma (*f.*, *Med.*) empyema.

empilhado –da (*adj.*) piled (up), stacked (up), heaped (up).

empilhamento (*m.*) act of piling, heaping, stacking (up).

empilhar (*v.t.*) to pile, heap up; to amass; to stack.

empinado –da (*adj.*) steep, sheer; upright, on end; haughty; rearing up on hind legs (as a horse); (*m.*) steep mountainside.

empinar (*v.t.*) to uplift, upraise; (*v.r.*) to prance, rear up (as a horse).—papagaio, to fly kites.

empipocar (*v.i.*) to pop (as corn); to break out in pustules.

empíreo –rea (*adj.*) empyreal.

empireuma (*f.*, *Chem.*) empyreuma.

empírico –ca (*adj.*) empiric(al); (*m.*) quack, empiric.

empirismo (*m.*) empiricism.

empistolado –da (*adj.*) strongly sponsored (for appointment to office) by an influential person; (*m.*) protégé; (*f.*) protégée.

emplasmado –da (*adj.*) bandaged up, covered with plasters; sickly; full of sores.

emplastrar (*v.t.*) to cover with plaster; to apply like a plaster.

emplastro (*m.*) medicinal plaster.

emplumado –da (*adj.*) plumed, feathered.

empoado –da (*adj.*) dust-covered, powdered.

empoar (*v.t.*) to powder (a wig); to cover with dust.

empobrecer (*v.t.*) to impoverish; to deplete; (*v.t.*) to grow poor; (*v.r.*) to become impoverished.

empobrecimento (*m.*) impoverishment.

empoçamento (*m.*) stagnation.

empoçar (*v.t.*) to store up (as, water in a pool); to form a pool or puddle.

empoeirar (*v.t.*) to cover with dust; (*v.r.*) to become dust-covered.

empôla (*f.*) blister; bubble; ampoule [= AMPOLA].

empolado –da (*adj.*) swollen; hilly; of style, stilted, "high-falutin," bombastic.

empolar (*v.t.*) to blister; (*v.r.*) to blister; to swell; to become puffed up.

empoleirado –da (*adj.*) perched (high); (*colloq.*) in a position of authority.

empoleirar (*v.t.*) to set on a perch; (*v.r.*) to perch; to roost; to reach a high office.

empolgante (*adj.*) gripping, arresting, absorbing, thrilling.

empolgar (*v.t.*) to grip, grasp, clutch, snatch, take firm hold of, seize forcibly; to arrest, excite, engage, engross, absorb (the attention), to grip (the mind, attention, interest).—as massas, to grip the masses.

empopar (*v.i.*) of a vessel, to be overladen in the stern.

emporcalhar (*v.t.*) to soil, foul, dirty, defile (-se, oneself); = SUJAR, BORRAR.

empório (*m.*) emporium, center of trade; grocery store.

empossado –da (*adj.*) installed (in office).

empossar (*v.t.*) to give possession to; to install in office. —-se de, to take possession of; to assume office.

emposta (*f.*, *Arch.*) impost.

empostar (*v.t.*) to pitch (the voice).

emprazar (*v.t.*) to (invite) summon (witnesses, etc.) to appear at a given time and place; (*v.r.*) to agree (with someone) on a time and place of meeting.

empreendedor –dora (*adj.*) enterprising, active, bold, venturesome; (*m.*) entrepreneur.

empreender (*v.t.*) to undertake, attempt (a difficult task); to embark upon (a venturesome enterprise, etc.).

empreendimento (*m.*) undertaking, enterprise, venture. livre—, free enterprise.

empregado –da (*adj.*) employed; (*m.*,*f.*) employee, store clerk; servant; (*f.*) maid, domestic servant.

empregador –dora (*m.*,*f.*) employer.

empregar (*v.t.*) to employ, make use of; to hire; to exert; (*v.r.*) to get a job.—-se em, to busy oneself at.—dinheiro, to invest money.

emprêgo (*m.*) employment, occupation; job, position; use, application.

empreguismo (*m.*) job handouts; political appointments.

empreitada (*f.*) contract work or job; piece-work; (*colloq.*) a tough assignment.

empreitar (*v.t.*) to give or take a contract for work.

empreiteiro (*m.*) contractor; entrepreneur.—de obras, building contractor.

emprenhar (*v.t.*) to impregnate, make pregnant; (*v.i.*) to become pregnant.

emprêsa (*f.*) enterprise, undertaking; concern, business.— funerária, undertaking concern.

empresário (*m.*) entrepreneur; contractor; theatrical empresario.

emprestado –da (*adj.*) loaned; borrowed. tomar or pedir—, to borrow.

emprestar (*v.t.*) to lend, loan; to impart, communicate.— a, to lend to.—de, to borrow from.

empréstimo (*m.*) act of lending or borrowing; a loan.— hipotecário, a mortgage loan.—pignorático, collateral loan.—sem juro, interest-free loan.—sob chamada, call loan. arrendamento e—, lend-lease. de—, borrowed; on loan.

emproado –da (*adj.*) headed for; haughty.

emproar (*v.t.*) to head for, steer towards; (*v.r.*) to become haughty; to swagger; to prance.

empubescer (*v.i.*,*v.r.*) to reach puberty; to become covered with hair; to grow.

empulhação (*f.*) gag (horseplay).

empulhar (*v.t.*) to make a fool of (someone).

empunhadura (*f.*) hilt (of a sword), handle (of a dagger), butt (of a pistol).

empunhar (*v.t.*) to grasp or hold by the handle (as, a sword).—o cetro, to wield the scepter.

empurra (*f.*) act of pushing. jôgo de—, buck passing (shifting of responsibility to someone else).

empurrão (m.) shove, push, jostle, poke.
empurrar (v.t.) to push; to press; to shove; to jostle; to thrust aside.
empurro (m.) shove, push.
empuxão (m.) shove; jerk; tug.
empuxar (v.t.) to push, shove, thrust.
empuxo (m.) push, shove; (Arch.) thrust; (Physics.) upward thrust through the center of buoyancy of a floating object.—dinâmico, (Aeron.). effective propeller thrust.—estático, (Aeron.). static propeller thrust.—final, (Mech.) end thrust (of an axle).—da hélice, (Aeron.) propeller thrust.
emudecer (v.i.) to grow mute, speechless, silent; (v.t.) to silence.
emulação (f.) emulation; competition; rivalry.
emular (v.t.) to emulate; to compete with.
emulgente (adj.) emulgent.
êmulo –la (adj.) emulative; emulous; (m.,f.) emulator.
emulsão (f.) emulsion.
emulsificar (v.t.) to emulsify.
emulsionar (v.t.) to emulsionize, emulsify.
emulsivo –va (adj.) emulsive.
emunctório –ria (adj.; m., Physiol.) emunctory.
emurchecer (v.i.,v.r.) to wilt.
enálage (f., Gram.) enallage.
enaltecedor –dora (adj.) exalting.
enaltecer (v.t.) to exalt.
enaltecimento (m.) exaltation.
enamorado –da (adj.) enamored, infatuated.—de, enamored of, in love with.
enamorar (v.t.) to enamor, charm; (v.r.) to become enamored (de, of); to fall in love (de, with).
enantal (m., Chem.) enanthal; enanthaldehyde; heptanal.
enantiotropia (f., Physical Chem.) enantiotropy.
enargita (f., Min.) enargite; clairite; luzonite.
enartrose (f., Anat.) enarthrosis, ball-and-socket joint.
enastrar (v.t.) to adorn with ribbons.
enateirar (v.t.) to warp, cover with mud or silt.
enc. = ENCADERNADO (bound in boards).
encabadouro (m.) the eye (hole) of an axe, hammer or other tool, in which the handle is inserted.
encabar (v.t.) to provide (an axe, etc.) with a handle.
encabeçado –da (adj.)—por, headed (up) by.
encabeçamento (m.) heading.
encabeçar (v.t.) to head, lead; to put a head on; to put at the head of; to initiate, start.—uma rebelião, to lead a rebellion.
encabeira (f., Carp.) header.
encabelado –da (adj.) hair-covered.
encabelar (v.i.) to grow hair.
encabrestar (v.t.) to put a halter on (a horse).
encabritar-se (v.r.) to rear up (as a goat); to clamber.
encabruado –da (adj.) pigheaded.
encabulação (f.) abashment.
encabulado –da (adj.) bashful, ill at ease, embarrassed.
encabular (v.t.) to abash; (v.i.) to turn bashful.
encaçapar (v.t.) to pocket (a billiard ball).
encachar-se (v.r.) to cover the lower half of the body, as with a towel, sarong, loin cloth, etc.
encacho (m.) loincloth [= TANGA].
encachoeirado –da (adj.) having, or resembling, a waterfall.
encadeação (f.), encadeamento (m.) act of chaining up, linking together; an interlocking; string, series; concatenation.
encadear (v.t.) to enchain, fetter; to attract and hold fast, (v.r.) to form a chain (as mountains).
encadernação (f.) bookbinding; book cover.
encadernador (m.) bookbinder.
encadernado –da (adj.) bound [book].
encadernar (v.t.) to bind (books).
encafifado –da (adj.) abashed; peeved.
encafuar, encafurnar (v.t.) to shut or hide in, or as in, a cave or grotto; (v.r.) to hide, shut, oneself up.
encaiporar (v.t.) to bring or cause bad luck to; (v.i.) to become unlucky.
encaixado –da (adj.) boxed; incased; telescoped.
encaixamento (m.) act of boxing, etc.;—see the verb ENCAIXAR.
encaixante (adj.) enclosing, surrounding, incasing.
encaixar (v.t.) to box; to fit or set (one part into another); to mortise; to rabbet; to inlay, imbed; to incase; (v.i.)

to fall easily into place; to fit perfectly.
encaixe, encaixo (m.) rabbet, groove, socket, mortise; dovetailing; a setting or fitting of one thing into another; cash on hand; bank deposit.
encaixilhar (v.t.) to frame; to provide with a sash.
encaixotado –da (adj.) boxed.
encaixotador –dora (m.,f.) packer (of goods) in boxes.
encaixotamento (m.) act of packing in boxes.
encaixotar (v.t.) to pack (goods) in boxes.
encalacração (f.) pickle, mess, fix; indebtedness.
encalacrado –da (adj.) in a pickle; head over heels in debt.
encalacrar-se (v.r.) to get into trouble or into debt.
encalamistrar (v.t.) to curl (mustache, hair).
encalcadeira (f.) calking tool; fullering tool.
encalcar (v.t.) to calk.
encalçar (v.t.) to follow close on the heels of.
encalço (m.) close pursuit. ao—de, on the track of; on the heels of.
encaldeirar (v.t.) to dig a water pan around trees.
encalecer (v.i.) to grow corns.
encalecido –da (adj.) having corns; caloused.
encalhação (f.) = ENCALHE.
encalhado –da (adj.) aground, stranded, high and dry. mercadoria—, goods that have got stuck on the shelves.
encalhamento (m.) = ENCALHE.
encalhar (v.t.,v.i.) to run aground; (v.i.) to bog down; to get stuck (in the mud); to stall.
encalhe (m.) a running aground, a bogging down; burden, obstacle; unsold or unsalable merchandise.
encalho (m.) place where ships run aground.
encalir (v.t.) to sear or braise (meat).
encalistar (v.t.) to hoodoo (bring or cause bad luck to).
encalistrar (v.t.) to abash; (v.i.) to become peeved.
encalmar (v.t.) to heat; to anger; (v.i.) to feel hot; to grow calm.
encalombado –da (adj.) swollen.
encalvecer (v.i.) to grow bald.
encamaçar (v.t.) to stack a deck of cards.
encamar (v.t.) to pack or place (something) in layers; to put to bed; (v.i.) to fall sick abed.
encambar (v.t.) to string (fish, peppers, etc.).
encambulhar (v.t.) to tie together, join together.
encameração (f.) seizure of church property by the State.
encaminhador –dora (adj.) guiding, directing; (m.,f.) guide, conductor.
encaminhar (v.t.) to direct, show the way, put upon the right track; to guide, conduct; (v.r.) to direct one's steps (para, to); to make one's way (para, to, toward).
encamisada (f.) a group of revelers wearing hooded gowns; originally, a night attack by soldiers wearing shirts; a difficulty; an entanglement.
encamisado (m.) reveler wearing hooded gown.
encamisar (v.t.) to cover (a kiln) with straw and mud to keep in the heat; to provide (a cylinder, etc.) with a jacket.
encampação (f.) expropriation; recapture of property.
encampador –dora (adj.) expropriating; (m.,f.) expropriator.
encampanado –da (adj.) campanulate, bell-shaped.
encampar (v.t.) to expropriate, take over (properties, utilities, etc.) esp. for public use; to cancel a lease, rescind a contract (by legal means).
encanação (f.) act of providing with pipes; channeling.
encanado –da (adj.) piped; set in a splint (broken bone); (slang) in the hoosegow (jail).
encanador (m.) plumber [= BOMBEIRO].
encanamento (m.) piping, plumbing; gas and water mains.
encanar (v.t.) to channel; to pipe; to flute, furrow, groove; to set (broken bones); (sl.) to arrest.
encanastrado (m.) plaid or basket-weave cloth.
encanastrar (v.t.) to put in plaited baskets; to plait (as a basket).
encandear (v.t.) to daze; to dazzle; (v.r.) to shine.
encandecer (v.t.,v.i.) to incandesce [= INCANDESCER].
encandilar (v.t.,v.r.) to candy.
encanecer (v.t.,v.i.,v.r.) to turn gray.
encanecido –da (adj.) hoary, white-haired.
encangalhar (v.t.) to strap panniers on to the backs of pack animals; (v.r.) to become involved with another person.
encanoado –da (adj.) of a board, curled.
encantação (f.) = ENCANTAMENTO.

encantado –da (adj.) enchanted, charmed, delighted.

encantador –dora (adj.) enchanting, charming, delightful, lovely; captivating, bewitching, ravishing; (m.,f.) enchanter, charmer; sorcerer.

encantamento (m.) enchantment, sorcery; a wonder, marvel.

encantar (v.t.) to enchant, conjure, bewitch; to delight; to charm, fascinate; (v.r.) to become charmed (de, com, by).

encanto (m.) enchantment; charm; "hex"; delight. tomar-se de—s por alguém, to be enchanted by, fall in love with, someone.

encantoar (v.t.) to put or drive into a corner; (v.r.) to bury oneself (hide away).

encanudado –da (adj.) tubelike.

encanzinar-se, encanzoar-se (v.r.) to insist upon; to persist stubbornly in; to rage.

encapado –da (adj.) covered, wrapped up, cloaked; (m.) a package done up in burlap (for shipment).

encapar (v.t.) to wrap up (in a cape); to cover (with burlap).

encapelado –da (adj.) rough, choppy, white-capped [sea].

encapelar (v.i.,v.r.) of waves, to rise, become rough.

encapoeirar (v.t.) to put in a pen or large cage.

encapotar (v.t.) to cover with a cape or cloak; to disguise, hide, conceal; (v.i.,v.r.) to become dark and cloudy; (v.i.) to turn bashful; of a horse, to prance with his neck bowed.

encaracolado –da (adj.) curly, curled [hair]; spiraled.

encaracolar (v.t.) to spiral; to curl; (v.i.,v.r.) to curl.

encarado –da (adj.) bem—, of pleasing appearance; well-appearing, pleasant-looking. mal—, cross-looking, disagreeable-looking.

encarangado –da (adj.) stiff (with cold, age, rheumatism).

encarangar, encaranguejar (v.i.,v.r.) to grow stiff with cold, age, or rheumatism; to become sickly.

encarapelar (v.) = ENCAPELAR, ENCARAPINHAR.

encarapinhado –da (adj.) frizzly, curly, crimpy, kinky.

encarapinhar (v.t.) to frizz, curl (the hair); to congeal; (v.i.) to begin to freeze; (v.r.) to curl.

encarapitar-se (v.r.) to climb to the top.

encarar (v.t.) to look (at) upon, view, regard; to face (a problem, question, etc.); to look straight at; (v.r.) to face boldly.

encarceramento (m.) incarceration.

encarcerar (v.t.) to incarcerate, imprison; (v.r.) to shut oneself up.

encardido –da (adj.) soiled, stained; dull, dingy, grimy.

encardimento (m.) grime; dinginess.

encardir (v.t.) to soil, stain, make dingy.

encarecer (v.t.) to raise the price of; to exalt; to stress; to exaggerate; (v.i.) to increase in price.

encarecido –da (adj.) grown high-priced; over-praised; given to over-praising.

encarecimento (m.) raising (of prices); insistence upon (something).

encargo (m.) charge, duty; task; assessment, tax.

encarnação (f.) incarnation.

encarnado –da (adj.) red, incarnadine; incarnate; (m.) the color red, scarlet.

encarnar (v.t.) to make (images) flesh-colored; (v.i.) to become incarnate; to embody, to live a part (on the stage).

encarneirar (v.i.,v.r.) of the sea, to become white-capped; of the sky, to become cloud-flecked.

encarniçado –da (adj.) bloodthirsty, cruel. luta—, bloody battle.

encarniçamento (m.) ferocity, savage cruelty; fury.

encaroçado –da (adj.) lumpy; (f.) a type of lumpy red soil in southern Brazil.

encarquilhado –da (adj.) wrinkled; dry, wilted.

encarquilhar (v.t.) to wrinkle; (v.r.) to become wrinkled.

encarregado –da (adj.) charged with, in charge of, entrusted with; (m.,f.) person in charge;—de negócios, chargé d'affaires.

encarregar (v.t.) to charge, entrust (de, with).—-se de, to take charge of; to take (something) upon oneself.

encarreirar (v.t.) to direct, steer, guide (another's course or actions).

encarrilar (v.) = ENCARRILHAR.

encarrilhador (m.) a device for rerailing cars and engines.

encarrilhamento (m.) act of rerailing (railroad cars and engines).

encarrilhar (v.t.) to rerail, replace on the rails, as a car or engine; to put (something or someone) on the right road; (v.i.) to follow the right road; to get things straight.

encartar (v.t.) to invest with office; to insert, intercalate; (v.i.) to take a trick (at cards).

encarte (m.) act of winning a trick (at cards).

encartuchar (v.t.) to load cartridges.

encarvoar (v.t.) to soil or blacken with coal dust.

encasacar-se (v.r.) to put on a frock coat; dress formally.

encasar (v.t.) to fit or set (something) in its proper place. —-se em, to fit in; to engage (as gears).—-se com, to harmonize with.

encascar (v.t.) to put (wine) in casks; to rough-coat (a wall) with plaster; (v.i.) of trees, to grow bark; of soil, to crust over.

encasquetar (v.t.) to put (something, as an idea or a hat) in or on the head of.—-se, to cover one's head.—-se em (or com), to become obsessed with.

encasquilhar (v.r.) to dress like a dandy.

encastelado –da (adj.) castellated; hoofbound [horse].

encastelamento (m., Veter.) the condition of being hoofbound.

encastelar (v.t.) to castellate; to heap up; —-se to withdraw to a castle or other fortified place; to pile up (as clouds, rocks).

encastoar (v.t.) to enchase, mount, place (as gems) in a setting.

encatarroar-se (v.r.) to catch catarrh.

encauchar (v.t.) to rubberize (cloth).

encáustico –ca (adj.) encaustic; (f.) encaustic; floor or furniture wax.

encausto (m.) encaustic painting.

encavacar-se (v.r.) to pout; to fly off the handle.

encavalgar (v.t.) to mount a horse [= CAVALGAR].

encavilhar (v.t.) to fasten with pegs [= CAVILHAR].

encefálico –ca (adj.) encephalic.

encefalite (f., Med.) encephalitis.—letárgica, sleeping sickness.

encéfalo (m., Anat.) encephalon, brain.

encefalomielite (f., Med.) encephalomyelitis.

enceguecer (v.i.) to become blind.

encegueirado –da (adj., colloq.) blindly in love; obsessed.

enceleirar (v.t.) to store (up, away).

encélia (f.) a brittlebush or other plant of Encelia.

encenação (f.) staging (of a play); (colloq.) showing off.

encenador –dora (m.,f.) producer of a play.

encenar (v.t.) to stage (a play).

encendrar (v.) = ACENDRAR.

enceradeira (f.) floor-waxing machine.

encerado –da (adj.) waxed; (m.) oilcloth; tarpaulin.

encerador –dora (m.,f.) floor waxer.

enceradura (f.), enceramento (m.) act of waxing.

encerar (v.t.) to wax.

encerra (f.) an enclosure for holding animals.

encerrado –da (adj.) enclosed, shut in, locked up; closed, ended [a meeting, a matter].

encerrador –dora (adj.) enclosing; closing; (m.,f.) closer; encloser.

encerramento (m.) act of closing or enclosing.

encerrar (v.t.) to enclose, encompass; to adjourn (a meeting); to close, bring to a conclusion (as, an investigation); to lock up (em, in); to confine (em, in); to contain, comprise (em, in); (v.r.) to come to a close.—-se em casa, to shut oneself up at home.—a sessão, to close a meeting.

encêrro (m.) act of closing, enclosing or confining; place where someone is confined.

encestar (v.t.) to put in baskets.

encetar (v.t.) to enter upon, begin, start.—assunto, to broach a subject; (v.r.) to do something for the first time.

enchafurdar-se (v.r.) to wallow (in the mud); = CHAFURDAR.

enchamboado –da (adj.) squat; ungainly; poorly dressed.

enchança (f.) favorable chance or circumstance.

enchapelado –da (adj.) covered with a hat.

encharcadiço –ça (adj.) swampy.

encharcado –da (adj.) swampy; flooded; waterlogged; soggy; soaked to the skin, sopping wet, dripping wet; swamped.—pela luz, flooded with light.

encharcar (v.t.) to flood, inundate; to drench; (v.r.) to get soaking wet.

enchavetar (v.t.) to fix in place with a key or cotter.

enchedeira (f.) a funnel for filling sausages.

enchedela (f.) act of filling; bellyful.

enchedor –dora (adj.) filling; (m.,f.) filler (as of bottles).

enche-mão (*adj.*) **de—,** topnotch, first-rate.

enchente (*f.*) flood, inundation, deluge; overflow; freshet; a full house; (*adj.*) filling.—**da lua,** full of the moon.—**do mar,** flood tide.

encher [24] (*v.t.*) to fill, fill up (**com, de,** with); to satiate; to stuff; (*v.r.*) to become full.—**a abarrotar,** to fill to overflowing.—**as medidas,** to satisfy the need; to exhaust another's patience.—**linguiça,** to dawdle.

enchia (*f.*) the wave which runs the farthest up the beach.

enchimento (*m.*) act of filling; inflation (of a tire).

enchiqueirar (*v.t.*) to pen (animals).

enchova (*f.*) anchovy [= ANCHOVA, MANJUBA]; the blue-fish (*Pomatomus saltatrix*).—**-baeta,** a young bluefish.

enchovinha (*f.*) a young ENCHOVA.

enchumaçar (*v.t.*) to pad (with cotton, etc.).

enciclia (*f.*) rings formed on the surface of water by an object dropped therein.

encíclico -ca (*adj.; f.*) encyclical (letter).

enciclopédia (*f.*) encyclopedia.

enciclopédico -ca (*adj.*) encyclopedic.

enciclopedista (*m.,f.*) encyclopedist.

encilhada (*f.*) act of saddling and mounting.

encilhadela (*f.*) act of cinching or saddling; quantity of MATE leaves added to that which is already in the CUIA or pot.

encilhado -da (*adj.*) saddle-backed.

encilhamento (*m.*) a period of wild speculation in the early days of the Brazilian Republic, from 1890–1892.

encilhar (*v.t.*) to cinch; to fasten the girth; to saddle; to add MATE tea leaves to the brew.

encimado -da (*adj.*) placed on high or on top of; topped by (something); crowned.

encistar (*v.i.*) to encyst.

enciumar-se (*v.r.*) to become jealous.

enclaustrado -da (*adj.*) cloistered.

enclaustramento (*m.*) act of cloistering.

enclaustrar (*v.t.*) to cloister.

enclausurado -da (*adj.*) enclosed, shut up, cloistered.

enclausurar-se (*v.r.*) to become a recluse.

enclavinhar (*v.t.*) to entwine; to clasp (the hands).

ênclise (*f.*) enclisis.

enclítico -ca (*adj.; f., Gram.*) enclitic (word or particle).

encoberta (*f.*) shelter; pretext.

encobertar (*v.*) = ACOBERTAR.

encoberto -ta (*adj.; p.p. of* ENCOBRIR) covered, concealed; **céu—,** overcast sky.

encobridor -dora (*m.,f.*) concealer; fence (receiver of stolen goods).

encobrimento (*m.*) act of covering or concealing.

encobrir [33] (*v.t.*) to cover (up), conceal, hide.—**o pensamento,** to hide one's thoughts.

encoimar (*v.*) = ACOIMAR.

encoivarar (*v.t.*) to pile up and burn branches, etc., left over when clearing the land.

encoleirar (*v.t.*) to put a collar on (an animal).

encolerizar (*v.t.*) to make angry; (*v.r.*) to flare up, fly off the handle.

encolher (*v.t.*) to contract, draw up or together; to cramp, confine, restrict; (*v.i.*) to shrink; (*v.r.*) to cringe, crouch, cower; to wince, flinch; to huddle; to bend over.—**as velas,** to take in sail.—**os ombros,** to shrug the shoulders.

encolhido -da (*adj.*) shrunken, shriveled; shy, fearful.

encolhimento (*m.*) shrinkage, contraction; shyness.

encólpio (*m., Eccl.*) encolpion.

encomenda (*f.*) an order (for goods); an article that is ordered; charge, commission.—**postal,** parcel post. **feito de—,** made to order.

encomendação (*f.*) act of ordering (goods); recommendation; (*Eccl.*) commendation.

encomendar (*v.t.*) to order (something to be made or sent); to commend, recommend (**a,** to); to commit, entrust (**a,** to).—(**alguma coisa**) **a** (**alguém**), to place an order (for something) with (someone).—**à memória,** to commit to memory.

encomiar (*v.t.*) to eulogize.

encomiasta (*m.,f.*) encomiast, eulogist.

encomiástico -ca (*adj.*) eulogistic.

encômio (*m.*) encomium, high praise.

encompridar (*v.t.*) to make longer; to lengthen.

enconcar (*v.t.,v.i.*) of boards, etc., to warp.

enconchar-se (*v.r.*) to withdraw into, or as into, a shell.

encondroma (*f., Med.*) enchondroma.

encontrada (*f.*) = ENCONTRÃO.

encontradiço -ça (*adj.*) frequently or easily encountered

(met with, come upon, run across, found).

encontrão (*m.*) collision; shove, jostle.

encontrar (*v.t.*) to encounter, meet; to find, run across, light upon.—**com,** to come upon; to meet up with; to bump into; (*v.r.*) to be, find oneself (in a given place or condition).—**-se com,** to meet up with; to collide with.—**-se de chofre,** to bump hard into.

encontro (*m.*) encounter, meeting; find, discovery; clash, collision, bump; engagement, skirmish; elbow of a bird's wing; conjunction; (*Zool.*) the chestnut-shouldered oriole (*Icterus cayanensis pyrrhopterus*), c.a. SOLDADO-DO-BICO-PRÊTO, NHAPIM, DRAGONA, GORRIXO, XEXÉU-DE-BANANEIRA, PÊGA; also the Cayenne oriole (*Icterus c. cayanensis*), c.a. PÊGA, ROUXINOL; (*Veter.*) counter (breast of a horse); (*pl.*) shoulder blades; bridge abutments.—**d'água,** "in Pará, a point where the currents of the Amazonas Sea and the estuary of the Pará River mingle (these zones are more or less extensive because of the variable level of the waters)." [*GBAT*]—**marcado,** a set engagement, date.—**s verdes** = AJURÚ-CURAU (a parrot). **de—a,** against; in opposition to. **ir ao—de,** to go to meet; to meet halfway. **marcar—com,** to make a date with. **marcar um—,** to make an appointment to meet. **vir ao—dos desejos de,** to meet the wishes of.

encorajar (*v.t.*) to encourage, hearten.

encordoamento (*m.*) the strings of, or act of stringing (a musical instrument, tennis racket, etc.); rigging (of a vessel).

encordoador (*m.*) stringer.

encordoar [12] (*v.t.*) to string (tennis racket, guitar, etc.); to rig (a vessel); (*v.r.*) of animals, to string out one behind another.

encorpado -da (*adj.*) full-bodied; firm, thick, solid; close-woven [cloth].

encorpar (*v.t.*) to increase the body or consistency of; (*v.i.,v.r.*) to grow, take on weight.

encorreado -da (*adj.*) leathery.

encorrear (*v.t.*) to bind with leather straps; (*v.i.,v.r.*) to become leathery.

encorujar-se (*v.r.*) to hide oneself away (as an owl); to become sad and lonely.

encoscorado -da (*adj.*) wrinkled, crinkled; crusty; incrusted.

encoscorar (*v.t.,v.i.,v.r.*) to crinkle, wrinkle; to make, or become, hard, crusty; to shrivel.

encôspias (*f.pl.*) shoe trees.

encosta (*f.*) slope, acclivity, declivity; hillside, mountain side [= VERTENTE].

encostadela (*f., slang*) act of importuning for favors or money.

encostado -da (*adj.*) leaning, propped up; pestered (by demands for money); unemployed; (*colloq.*) lazy; (*m.*) dependent, hanger-on, protégé; retainer.

encostar (*v.t.*) to prop, lean (**a, em, sôbre,** on, against).—**a** (or **em**), to place against (as, a watch against one's ear); (*v.r.*) to lean back, recline.—**-se a uma árvore,** to lean against a tree.—**alguém à parede,** to drive someone to the wall (in an argument).

encoste (*m.*) a mating (of animals); a matching (of contestants); (*pl.*) abutments.

encôsto (*m.*) stay, prop, support; back (of a chair, etc.); fig., protection; a narrow stretch of open land surrounded on three sides by woods or swampland.

encouraçado -da (*adj.*) steel-armored; (*m.*) a dreadnought.

encouraçar (*v.t.*) to provide with armor plate.

encourar (*v.t.*) to line or cover with leather or hides; to flog; (*v.i.,v.r.*) to heal, form scar tissue. Var. ENCOIRAR.

encovado -da (*adj.*) hidden, sunken, deep-set. **faces—s,** hollow cheeks. **olhos—s,** hollow eyes.

encovar (*v.t.*) to bury, hide (as in a den).

encravado -da (*adj.*) stuck (in); embedded (in). **unha—,** ingrowing toenail.

encravar (*v.t.*) to nail; to drive in (a nail); to fix (the eyes) on something; to spike (a cannon); (*v.r.*) to become stuck in, imbedded in.

encrenca (*f., slang*) difficulty, knotty problem, hard nut to crack, hitch.

encrencado -da (*adj., slang*) difficult, complicated, knotty.

encrencar (*v.t., slang*) to render (a situation) difficult; to complicate (matters); (*v.r.*) to hit a snag.

encrenqueiro -ra (*adj., slang*) said of one who creates difficulties, who "throws a monkey wrench in the works".

encrespado -da (*adj.*) of hair, frizzled, fuzzy; of sea, showing white caps.

encrespador (*m.*) curling iron (for the hair).
encrespar (*v.t.*) to frizzle (the hair); to curl (the lips); (*v.r.*) to become roiled; to bristle.
encruado **–da** (*adj.*) half-cooked, raw; doughy, soggy (cake); hard to digest; of steel, hardened, toughened. **negócio—**, a piece of business that went sour.
encruar (*v.t.*) to make hard, tough; to make difficult; (*v.i.*) to retrogress; to become hard, tough; (*v.r.*) to grow cruel.
encruzar (*v.t.*) to cross ((arms, legs); (*v.r.*) to sit cross-legged.
encruzilhada (*f.*) crossroads.
encubar (*v.t.*) to put (wine) in vats.
encueirar (*v.t.*) to swaddle (infants).
encurralado **–da** (*adj.*) corraled; hemmed in, shut in, cooped up.
encurralamento (*m.*) act of corraling.
encurralar (*v.t.*) to corral; to fence in, hem in.
encurtar (*v.t.*) to curtail, cut short; to shorten, diminish. **—razões**, to be brief. **Encurte isso!** Cut it short!
encurvação, encurvadura (*f.*), **encurvamento** (*m.*) act or effect of curving, bending, arching; curvature.
encurvar (*v.t.,v.i.*) to curve, bend; (*v.r.*) to bow, stoop, bend.
endecha [dê] (*f.*) threnody, dirge.
endedar (*v.t.*) to "put the finger on."
endefluxar-se [x = ss] (*v.r.*) to catch cold.
endemia (*f.*) endemic disease.
endemicidade (*f.*) endemism.
endêmico **–ca** (*adj.*) endemic.
endemoniado **–da, endemoninhado** **–da** (*adj.*) possessed of the devil; demoniac.
endentar (*v.t.*) to mesh (gears).
endentecer (*v.i.*) to teethe.
endereçar (*v.t.*) to address, direct (words, letters, etc.) to. **—se a**, to address oneself to.
endereço (*m.*) address (place, direction).
endérmico **–ca** (*adj., Med.*) endermic.
endeusado **–da** (*adj.*) deified.
endeusamento (*m.*) deification.
endeusar (*v.t.*) to deify; to praise to the skies.
endez [dêz] (*m.*) = INDEZ.
endiabrado **–da** (*adj.*) devilish, cruel, wicked; impish, mischievous.
endinheirado **–da** (*adj.*) moneyed, rich.
endireita (*m.*) bonesetter [= ALGEBRISTA].
endireitado **–da** (*adj.*) straightened out (up).
endireitar (*v.t.*) to straighten; to rectify; to repair; (*v.r.*) to become straight; to straighten up (out). **—as coisas**, to straighten things out. **Pau que nasce torto, tarde ou nunca se endireita**, Just as the twig is bent the tree's inclined.
endiva, endívia (*f., Bot.*) endive (*Cichorium endivia*).
endividar (*v.t.*) to put another in one's debt or under obligation; (*v.r.*) to go into debt.
endoartéria (*f., Anat.*) endarterium.
endobiótico **–ca** (*adj., Biol.*) endobiotic.
endoblasto (*m., Biol.*) endoblast, hypoblast.
endocanibalismo (*m., Anthropol.*) endophagy.
endocárdia, endocárdio (*f.*) endocardium.
endocardite (*f., Med.*) endocarditis.
endocárpio, endocarpo (*m., Bot.*) endocarp.
endocraniano **–na** (*adj.*) endocranial.
endocrânio (*m., Anat.*) endocranium.
endócrino **–na** (*adj., Anat.*) endocrinous.
endocrinologia (*f.*) endocrinology.
endocromo (*m., Biol., Bot.*) endochrome.
endoderma (*f., Zool.*) endoderm; (*Bot.*) endodermis.
endoenças (*f.pl.*) church rites on Maundy Thursday.
endófito **–ta** (*adj., Zool.*) endophytous; (*m., Bot.*) endophyte.
endogamia (*f.*) endogamy.
endógamo **–ma** (*adj.*) endogamous.
endógenas (*f.pl., Bot.*) the Monocotyledones.
endógeno **–na** (*adj.*) endogenous.
endognátio (*m., Anat., Zool.*) endognathion.
endoidecer, endoidar (*v.t.*) to make crazy; (*v.r.*) to go crazy. Vars. ENDOUDAR, ENDOUDECER.
endolinfa (*f., Anat.*) endolymph.
endomicose (*f., Med.*) small white patches occurring in the mouths and fauces of infants and young children, characteristic of thrush [= SAPINHOS].
endomingado **–da** (*adj.*) dressed up in one's Sunday best.
endomingar-se (*v.r.*) to dress up for Sunday.

endomísio (*m., Anat.*) endomysium.
endomorfismo (*m., Petrog.*) endomorphism.
endonéurio (*m., Anat.*) endoneurium.
endoparasito (*m., Zool.*) endoparasite.
endoperídio (*m., Bot.*) endoperidium.
endoplasma (*m., Biol.*) endoplasm.
endopleura (*f., Bot.*) endopleura, tegmen.
endorraque (*f., Anat.*) endorachis.
endoscópio (*m., Med.*) endoscope.
endosmômetro (*m., Physics*) endosmometer.
endosmose (*f., Physical Chem., Physiol.*) endosmosis.
endosperma, endospermo (*m., Bot.*) endosperm.
endósporo (*m., Bot.*) endospore.
endossado **–da** (*adj.*) endorsed; (*m.,f.*) endorsee (of a note).
endossador **–dora, endossante** (*adj.*) endorsing; (*m.,f.*) endorser.
endossamento (*m.*) act of endorsement.
endossar (*v.t.*) to endorse; to sanction.
endossatário **–ria** (*m.,f.*) endorsee [= ENDOSSADO].
endosse (*m.*) = ENDÔSSO.
endossepsia (*f., Plant Pathol.*) endosepsis.
endôsso (*m.*) act of, or an, endorsement.
endóstoma (*f., Bot.*) endostome.
endoteca, endotécia (*f., Bot.*) endothecium.
endotelial (*adj., Anat.*) endothelial.
endotélio (*m., Anat.*) endothelium.
endotelioma (*m., Med.*) endothelioma.
endotérmico **–ca** (*adj., Chem.*) endothermic.
endótrix (*m., Bot.*) *endothrix* (a ringworm fungus).
endotrófico **–ca** (*adj., Bot.*) endotrophic.
endoudecer (*v.*) = ENDOIDECER.
endoutrinar (*v.*) = DOUTRINAR.
endovenoso **–sa** (*adj., Anat.*) endovenous [= INTRA-VENOSO].
endozóico **–ca** (*adj.*) entozoic.
endrão (*m., Bot.*) a hogfennel (*Peucedanum graveolens*), c.a. FUNCHO-BASTARDO.
endro (*m., Bot.*) dill (*Anethum graveolens*).
End. tel. = ENDERÊÇO TELEGRÁFICO (telegraphic address; cable address).
enduração (*f.*) induration, hardening; obduracy; (*Med.*) induration [= INDURAÇÃO].
endurado **–da** (*adj.*) hardened [= ENDURECIDO]; obdurate.
endurar, endurecer (*v.t.,v.i.*) to harden; (*v.r.*) to become hard-hearted, callous.
endurecido **–da** (*adj.*) hardened; unfeeling.
endurecimento (*m.*) act or result of hardening.
E.N.E. = ÉS-NORDESTE (east-northeast).
eneágono (*m., Geom.*) nonagon.
enegrecedor **–dora** (*adj.*) blackening; (*m.,f.*) one who or that which blackens.
enegrecer (*v.t.*) to blacken, darken; to defame; (*v.i.,v.r.*) to turn black.
enegrecimento (*m.*) a darkening; blackening (of character).
enema (*f.*) enema [= CLISTER].
êneo **–nea** (*adj.*) bronze, brazen. [*Poetical.*]
energia (*f.*) energy, power; spirit, vigor, vim, pep.—**atômica**, atomic energy.—**calorífica**, or **térmica**, heat energy.—**elétrica**, electric energy.—**química**, chemical energy. **com—**, energetically.
enérgico **–ca** (*adj.*) energetic, active, vigorous, forceful, strenuous.
enérgide (*f., Biol.*) energid.
energúmeno (*m.*) energumen; demoniac; fanatical enthusiast.
enervação (*f.*) enervation; nervation.
enervado **–da** (*adj.*) enervate.
enervante (*adj.*) enervating.
enervar (*v.*) & derivs. = INERVAR & derivs.
enevoar (*v.t.*) to cloud, fog, darken, dim, blur.
enf. = ENFERMEIRO, ENFERMEIRA (nurse).
enfadadiço **–ça** (*adj.*) easily tired or bored; peevish; touchy.
enfadar (*v.t.*) to tire, irk, bore; to rile; to bother, annoy; to disgust; (*v.r.*) to become tired (**de**, of); "fed up" (**com**, with); annoyed (**com**, with); riled (**com**, at).
enfado (*m.*) unpleasant feeling of annoyance, displeasure, disgust, etc.
enfadonho **–nha, enfadoso** **–sa** (*adj.*) tiresome, tedious, boring, stuffy, stodgy, vapid, humdrum; annoying.
enfaixar (*v.t.*) to swathe, bind, bandage.
enfarar (*v.t.*) to loathe, detest; to nauseate, pall, sicken.

enfardadeira (f.) hay baling machine.
enfardador –dora (m.,f.) bundler, baler, binder.
enfardamento (m.) act of bundling, baling, binding.
enfardar (v.t.) to bundle, bale, bind.
enfarinhar (v.t.) to cover with flour; to powder; to turn into dust.
enfaro (m.) loathing, disgust, nausea, repugnance.
enfarpelar-se (v.r.) to dress up in new or "Sunday-go-to-meeting" clothes.
enfarruscado –da (adj.) grimy, smutty.
enfarruscar (v.t.) to smudge; to become dark, cloudy; to become morose.
enfartado –da (adj.) gorged, filled to repletion; turgid.
enfartamento (m.) glut, surfeit, repletion.—de glândulas, (Med.) infarct [= ENFARTE].
enfartar (v.t.) to gorge, glut, stuff.
enfarte (m., Med.) infarct.
ênfase (f.) emphasis; bombast; exaggerated, (affected, pompous) manner of writing or speaking.
enfastiadiço –ça (adj.) tiresome, irksome.
enfastiado –da (adj.) fed up; squeamish.
enfastiamento (m.) act of tiring, boring.
enfastiar (v.t.) to tire, weary; to irk, bore; to pall.—-se (de, com), to grow tired (of), bored (with).
enfático –ca (adj.) bombastic, pompous; emphatic.
enfatiotar-se (v.r.) to dress up.
enfatuação (f.) enfatuamento (m.) act of making, or state of being, foolishly vain. [Not an equivalent of infatuation, in the sense of foolish love, which is paixão ridícula.]
enfatuado –da (adj.) vain, self-satisfied, smug.
enfatuar (v.t.) to make vain; to make fatuous; (v.r.) to become vain;—-se de, to pride oneself on, boast of.
enfear (v.) = AFEAR.
enfeitar (v.t.) to adorn, decorate, trim; to disguise; (v.r.) to beautify oneself; to dare; to presume above one's station.—-se para, to aspire to, aim at.
enfeite (m.) ornament, trimming; (pl.) fripperies.
enfeitiçado –da (adj.) spellbound.
enfeitiçamento (m.) witchery; fascination.
enfeitiçar (v.t.) to bewitch, conjure; to "hex"; to seduce, allure; (v.r.) to be fascinated (de, by).
enfeixar (v.t.) to tie together in bundles (as sticks of wood); to make into a fagot, sheaf, etc.
enfermagem (f.) nursing, care of the sick.
enfermar (v.i.) to become sick.
enfermaria (f.) infirmary, hospital ward.
enfermeira (f.) nurse (of the sick).
enfermeiro (m.) male nurse; hospital orderly.
enfermiço –ça (adj.) sickly, unhealthy.
enfermidade (f.) infirmity, ailment, complaint; sickness, illness, disease; foible, failing.
enfêrmo –ma (adj.) infirm, ailing, sick, ill, diseased; (m.,f.) a sick person; patient.
enferrujar (v.i.,v.r.) to rust.
enfestação (f.) act of cheating on one's score in a game.
enfestador –dora (m.,f.) one who habitually cheats in a game.
enfestar (v.t.) to fold (a piece of cloth) lengthwise; to pad (an account, a score, etc.); to cheat (in a game).
enfêsto –ta (adj.) steep [= ÍNGREME].
enfezado –da (adj.) rachitic; stunted; wizened; puny; grouchy, peevish; "fed up".
enfezamento (m.) act or result of stunting; peevishness.
enfezar (v.t.) to stunt, dwarf; to peeve; to rile; (v.r.) to decay, wither; to become peeved, riled.
enfiação (f.) running of wires through an electrical conduit.
enfiada (f.) string, file, series (of things, happenings, etc.). de—, at a stretch; without interruption.
enfiadeira (f.) bodkin.
enfiamento (m.), enfiadura (f.) act of threading, stringing (needles, beads, fish, etc.).
enfiar (v.t.) to thread (a needle); to string (beads); to resume the thread (of a story, etc.); to slip on (trousers, shoes, a dress, etc.); to run (a person) through (as with a sword); to pass, go through (a street); to traverse (the length of a road); (Mil.) to enfilade; (Elec.) to run wires through a conduit; (v.i.) to pale; to faint; to be ashamed; (v.i.,v.r.) to sneak in; to be furious, hit the ceiling.—em, to insert in.—por, to slip through.—-se na cama, to slip into bed.
enfileiramento (m.) alignment.
enfileirar (v.t.) to range, align, set in a row, in files; (v.r.) to line up, get in line; to align oneself with.

enfim (adv.) finally, at last, in short, after all. até que—, at last, finally.
enfincar (v.) = FINCAR.
enfisema (m., Med.) emphysema.
enfistular (v.t., Med.) to fistulize; (v.i.,v.r.) to become fistulous.
enfitadora (f., Elec.) a taping machine.
enfiteuse (f., Civil Law) emphyteusis.
enfiteuta (m.,f., Civil Law) emphyteuta.
enfixar [ks] (v.t.) to splice rail ends with a fishplate.
enflechamento (m., Aeron.) sweepback.
enflorar (v.t.,v.i.,v.r.) to flower.
enfocação (f.) act of focusing.
enfocar (v.t.) to put in focus.
enfolhar (v.i.,v.r.) to grow leaves, become leaf-covered; (v.t.) to cover with leaves.
enforcado –da (adj.; m.,f.) hanged (person).
enforcamento (m.) act of hanging (by the neck).
enforcar (v.t.) to hang (by the neck); to squander; to sell dirt-cheap; (v.r.) to hang oneself.
enfranque (m.) shank of a shoe; waistline of a garment.
enfraquecer (v.i.,v.r.) to grow weak, feeble; to decline; (v.t.) to weaken, undermine.
enfraquecido –da (adj.) weak, run-down, enfeebled.
enfraquecimento (m.) weakness, enfeeblement.
enfrascar (v.t.) to put in flasks, bottles; (v.r.) to fill oneself (with beer, perfume, poetry, etc.).
enfraxia [ks] (f., Med.) emphraxis, obstruction.
enfreamento (m.) act of curbing, braking, repressing.
enfrear (v.t.) to bridle, curb, refrain; to apply the brakes; of horses, to toss the head; (v.r.) to hold oneself down.
enfrechadura (f.), enfrechate (m., Naut.) ratline.
enfrechar (v.t., Naut.) to rattle down.
enfrentar (v.t.) to meet face to face; to confront, face; to brave, dare; to take on (an adversary).
enfronhado –da (adj.) covered with a pillowcase; well-versed in a subject.
enfronhar (v.t.) to put a case on a pillow; to slip on (coat, gloves, etc.).—-se em, to become versed in, conversant with, (a subject).
enfueirar (v.t.) to provide (a cart, etc.) with stakes; to load (a cart, etc.) to the top of or above the stakes.
enfumaçado –da (adj.) smoky, sooty; dingy.
enfumaçar, enfumar, enfumarar (v.t.) to fill or cover with smoke; to becloud.
enfunar (v.t.) to puff out; to swell; to fill (as sails); (v.r.) to swell out; to become puffed up.
enfunilar (v.t.) to funnel [= AFUNILAR].
enfurecer (v.t.) to infuriate, enrage; to provoke; (v.r.) to become furious; to lose one's temper; to "fly off the handle"; to rage, storm.
enfurecido –da (adj.) furious, enraged.
enfuriar (v.) = ENFURECER.
enfurnar (v.t.) to hide (-se, oneself) in a grotto [= ENCAFUAR].
eng. = ENGENHARIA (engineering).
engabelação (f.) act of duping, etc. See the verb ENGABELAR. Vars. ENGAMBELAÇÃO, ENGRAMBELAÇÃO, ENGABÊLO, ENGAMBÊLO, ENGRAMBÊLO.
engabelar (v.t.) to dupe, lure, inveigle, wheedle (with blandishments); to soft-soap. Vars. ENGAMBELAR, ENGRAMBELAR.
engabêlo (m.) = ENGABELAÇÃO.
engachetamento (m., Mach.) stuffing box [= CAIXA DE EMPANQUE].
engadanhado –da (adj.) numb, stiff with cold.
engaifonar (v.i.) to make faces [= GAIFONAR].
engaiolar (v.t.) to cage; to imprison; (v.r.) to live in solitude.
engajado –da (adj.; m.,f.) (one who has been) engaged for work, esp. manual labor.
engajamento (m.) engagement (for work); military enlistment.
engajar (v.t.) to engage (workmen); (v.r.) to engage oneself (take employment); to enlist (for military service).
engalanar (v.t.) to deck, decorate, adorn; (v.r.) to put on gala dress.
engalfinhar-se (v.r.) to grapple, struggle, tangle (with another person).
engalinhar (v.t.) to give bad luck to.
engambelar (v.) & derivs. = ENGABELAR & derivs.
engambitar (v.t.) to jump or step across (a ditch, etc.).
enganadiço –ça (adj.) easily deceived.
enganado –da (adj.) mistaken, wrong, in error; deceived; betrayed.

enganador –dora (*adj.*) deceiving, deceptive, deceitful; specious; (*m.,f.*) deceiver; four-flusher; cheat.

enganar (*v.t.*) to deceive, delude; to hoodwink; to dupe; to bamboozle; to victimize; to seduce; to mislead; (*v.r.*) to be mistaken; to deceive oneself.

engana-tico = CHOPIM.

engana-vista (*m.*) trompe-l'oeil (deceptive painting of still life).

engana-tolo (*m.*) a large, brightly colored butterfly (*Victorino steneles*).

enganchar (*v.t.*) to hook (on); to hitch on.

enganjento –ta (*adj.*) silly; vain; presumptuous [= GAN-JENTO].

engano (*m.*) error, mistake; oversight; misapprehension; fallacy; deception, fraud; guile; deceit.

enganoso –sa (*adj.*) deceiving; deceitful.

engarrafadeira (*f.*) bottling machine.

engarrafado (*adj.*) bottled, in bottles; bottled up.

engarrafador –dora (*adj.*) bottling; (*m.,f.*) bottler; bottling machine.

engarrafamento (*m.*), **engarrafagem** (*f.*) act or process of bottling; (*m.*) bottleneck, traffic jam.

engarrafar (*v.t.*) to bottle (up).

engasgado –da (*adj.*) choked (up).

engasgalhar-se (*v.r.*) to choke; (*colloq.*) to grapple.

engasgamento (*m.*) act of choking, straggling, gagging.

engasgar (*v.t.,v.i.,v.r.*) to choke, strangle, gag.

engasgo (*m.*) act of choking; gag; obstruction in the throat; (*colloq.*) difficulty in swallowing.

engastar (*v.t.*) to set (precious stones).

engaste (*m.*) a setting (of gold, etc.) for precious stones.

engatar (*v.t.*) to fasten together (with a clamp); to couple together (as railroad cars); to hitch up (horses).

engate (*m.*) a clamp; a railroad car coupling.

engatilhado –da (*adj.*) cocked [trigger]; by ext., ready. **sempre de resposta**—, always ready with an answer, with a snappy comeback.

engatilhar (*v.t.*) to cock (a firearm).

engatinhar (*v.i.*) to crawl (on hands and knees).

engavetar (*v.t.*) to put in a drawer; to pigeon-hole; (*v.r.*) to telescope (vehicles, in an accident).

engazopador –dora (*m.,f.*) trickster, sharper.

engazopar (*v.t.*) to fool, deceive, dupe; to hoodwink; to clap into jail. Var. ENGAZUPAR.

engelhado –da (*adj.*) wrinkled, dry, shriveled.

engelhar (*v.t.,v.i.,v.r.*) to wrinkle, shrivel.

engendrar (*v.t.*) to engender, beget; to invent, make up; to cook up (a scheme); to hatch (a plot).

engenhar (*v.t.*) to engineer, maneuver, contrive; to invent, devise; to hatch, concoct.

engenharia (*f.*) engineering; corps of engineers.—civil, civil engineering.—elétrica, electrical engineering.—hidraúlica, hydraulic engineering.—militar, military engineering.

engenheirando –da (*m.,f.*) a senior student of engineering.

engenheiro (*m.*) engineer (civil, electrical, etc.); [But not an engineer who operates an engine, which is MAQUI-NISTA]; owner of an ENGENHO (sugar mill).

engenho (*m.*) ingenuity, inventiveness; wit; skill; machine; mill, manufactory.—de açúcar, sugar mill and plantation complex.—de serra, sawmill.

engenhoca (*f.*) any simple contrivance or mechanical apparatus; gadget; contraption.

engenhoso –sa (*adj.*) ingenious, inventive; artful; resourceful; shrewd, sharp; smart, clever; adroit.

engessar (*v.t.*) to cover with plaster; to put (broken arm, leg) in a plaster cast; (*slang*) to put the finger on.

englobadamente (*adv.*) as a whole, as a group.

englobar (*v.t.*) to gather into a whole; to conglomerate; to embody; to comprise.

eng.º = ENGENHEIRO (engineer).

engodar (*v.t.*) to lure, inveigle, entice, esp. with false promises.

engôdo (*m.*) lure, bait, decoy; allurement; blandishment.

engole-vento (*m.*) nighthawk, goatsucker [= CURIANGO].

engolfar (*v.t.*) to engulf; (*v.r.*) to be plunged (em, in).

engolir [21a] (*v.t.*) to swallow; to absorb; to gulp down (at a swallow).—a pílula, (*colloq.*) to swallow an insult, a reprimand, etc.—araras or—maranhão, (*colloq.*) to swallow lies.—a saliva, not dare to speak.—em sêco, to bite one's tongue, remain silent.—gato por lebre, to buy a pig in a poke.—uma afronta, to put one's pride in one's pocket.

engomadeira (*f.*) a woman whose work it is to starch and iron (but not wash) clothes. [The latter is a LAVADEIRA.]

Also, a sizing machine.

engomadela (*f.*) = ENGOMADURA.

engomado –da (*adj.*) starched and ironed; stiff in demeanor; (*m.*) clothes that have been starched and/or ironed; (*m.,f.*) a stiff person.

engomadura, **engomagem** (*f.*) act of starching and ironing clothes.

engomar (*v.t.*) to starch and iron clothes; to be employed as an ENGOMADEIRA.

engonçar (*v.t.*) to provide with a hinge or joint.

engonço (*m.*) hinge; joint.

engorda (*f.*) fattening (of animals); pasture for fattening.

engordar (*v.t.*) to fatten (animals); (*v.i.*) to grow fat, gain weight.

engordurar (*v.t.*) to smear with grease.

engorgitamento (*m.*) swelling (as of glands in the neck).

engorgitar (*v.t.,v.i.*) to gorge (-se, oneself); to fill, choke up (as a vein with blood).

engos (*m.*, *Bot.*) the Medit. herb elder (*Sambucus edulus*), c.a. SABUGUEIRINHO.

engoteirado –da (*adj.*) leaky [roof].

engraçadinho –nha (*adj.*) cute, cunning; (*m.*) = PIABINHA-BRANCA.

engraçado –da (*adj.*) amusing, droll, witty, comical, funny; jolly; queer; ridiculous. **fazer-se de**—, to be funny.

engraçar (*v.t.*) to grace, adorn, embellish; (*v.r.*) to engratiate oneself (with another).

engradado –da (*adj.*) enclosed with a grating; crated; (*m.*) a shipping crate.

engradamento (*m.*) grating, railing; crating.

engradar (*v.t.*) to provide with a grating or railing; to enclose in a crate.

engrambelar (*v.*) & derivs. = ENGABELAR & derivs.

engrandecer (*v.t.*) to enlarge; to aggrandize; (*v.i.*)—em, to increase (in power, riches, etc.); (*v.r.*) to become greater, richer, more powerful, etc.

engrandecimento (*m.*) enlargement; aggrandizement.

engranzagem (*f.*), **engranzamento** (*m.*) act of meshing (as gears); dental occlusion.

engranzar (*v.t.*) to string (beads); to connect (links of a chain); to mesh (gears) [= ENGRENAR].

engravecer (*v.i.,v.r.*) of a situation, to grow grave, precarious; (*v.t.*) to aggravate (an evil).

engraxadela (*f.*) a shining (of shoes).

engraxador (*m.*) bootblack.

engraxar (*v.t.*) to shine (shoes); to smear (with grease, wax).

engraxateria, **–taria** (*f.*) shoeshine stand or parlor.

engraxate (*m.*) shoe shiner, bootblack.

engraxar (*v.*) = ENGRANZAR.

engrenagem (*f.*) gear, gearing, set of gears.—acionadora (motriz, principal, tocadora, or de arrasto), main gear, drive gear, motor gear.—anular, ring gear.—de avanço, feed gear.—cônica, miter gear; bevel gear.—diferencial, differential gearing.—de direção, steering gear.—de distribuição, timing gear.—interna, internal gear.—louca, idle gear.—planetária, planetary gear.—redutora, reduction gear. **razão das**—**s**, gear ratio.

engrenamento (*m.*) meshing of gears.

engrenar (*v.t.*) to gear, mesh [= ENGRANZAR].

engrimanço (*m.*) rigmarole.

engrimpar-se, **engrimpinar-se**, **engrimponar-se** (*v.r.*) to clamber to the top (of a tree, rocks, etc.); fig., to become haughty.

engrinaldar (*v.t.*) to adorn with garlands, wreaths, chaplets, crowns of flowers, etc.

engrolado –da (*adj.*) half raw, badly cooked; botched; half studied.

engrolar (*v.t.*) to undercook; to botch, bungle; (*v.i.*) to mutter, sputter; to gabble.

engrossador –dora (*m.,f.*, *slang*) self-seeking flatterer, adulator, sycophant [= BAJULADOR].

engrossamento (*m.*) enlargement, thickening; (*slang*) cajolery; flattery [= ADULAÇÃO, BAJULAÇÃO].

engrossar (*v.t.*) to thicken; to swell, enlarge; (*slang*) to cajole; (*v.i.,v.r.*) to become thick(er), large(r); to become deeper [the voice].

engrouvinhado –da (*adj.*) tall and thin.

enguia (*f.*) eel.—-do-mar = CONGRO (conger eel).

enguiçado –da (*adj.*) hexed, bewitched; puny, wizened; stalled; out of order.

enguiçar (*v.t.*) to hex, bewitch; (*v.i.*) to stall, break down, get out of fix, conk out.

enguiço (m.) evil eye; bad luck; snag, hitch; mishap.
enguirlandar (v.t.) to deck with garlands.
engulhar (v.t.) to nauseate; (v.i.) to be nauseated.
engulho (m.) nausea; queasy feeling; disgust.
enho (m.) fawn.
enidros (m., Min.) enhydros.
enigma (m.) enigma, riddle, puzzle, conundrum.
enigmático –ca (adj.) enigmatic(al), obscure, mysterious, puzzling.
enjambrar (v.i.,v.r.) of lumber, to wrap, curl, twist.
enjaular (v.t.) to cage.
enjeitado –da (adj.) rejected; (m.,f.) a foundling.
enjeitar (v.t.) to reject, refuse, repudiate; to abandon, cast away (a newborn child).
enjoadiço –ça (adj.) queasy, squeamish.
enjoado –da (adj.) seasick, car sick, nauseated; nauseating; distasteful; insufferable.
enjoamento (m.) nausea [= ENJÔO].
enjoar (v.t.) to nauseate, turn one's stomach; to revolt, disgust; to cloy; (v.i.) to feel nausea, disgust; to pall. Cf. ANOJAR, ENOJAR.
enjoativo –va (adj.) nauseous; mawkish.
enjôo (m.) nausea, seasickness, travel sickness, inclination to vomit; surfeit.
enlaçar (v.t.) to bind, tie, fasten; to link, join; to entwine; to interlace; to splice; (v.r.) to twist together; to be bound (de, por, by).
enlace (m.) union; marriage; splice.
enlambuzar (v.t.) to smear [= LAMBUZAR].
enlameado –da (adj.) muddied; sullied.
enlamear (v.t.) to spatter (splash) with mud; to besmirch (another's name, reputation); (v.r.) to get dirty, muddy.
enlanguescer (v.i.,v.r.) to languish, droop, waste away.
enlapar (v.t.,v.r.) to hide in a cave or den.
enlatamento (m.) canning (of fruits, etc.).
enlatar (v.t.) to can (food); to train (vines) on a trellis.
enleado –da (adj.) enmeshed, entangled; perplexed.
enleamento (m.) entanglement; embarrassment [= ENLEIO].
enlear (v.t.) to tie, bind, fasten; to tangle; to perplex; (v.r.) to become entangled (em, in); to flounder.
enleio (m.) entanglement; embarrassment; perplexity.
enlevado –da (adj.) rapt.
enlevar (v.t.) to enrapture, enchant, ravish, transport.
enlêvo (m.) rapture, ecstasy; delight.
enlodar (v.t.) to muddy; to besmirch; (v.r.) to get soiled.
enlouquecedor –dora (adj.) maddening.
enlouquecer (v.t.) to make mad, crazy; to infatuate; (v.i.) to become insane, to go mad.
enlouquecimento (m.) act or effect of going mad.
enluarado –da (adj.) moonlit.
enlurar (v.t.) to hide in a burrow; (v.r.) to hole up; to wallow (in mud).
enlutar (v.t.) to drape in mourning; to plunge into mourning; to darken; (v.r.) to go into mourning.
enluvado –da (adj.) wearing gloves.
enobrecedor –dora (adj.) ennobling.
enobrecer (v.t.) to ennoble, glorify; to exalt, dignify.
enobrecimento (m.) ennoblement; fame.
enocarpo (m.) a genus (Oenocarpus) of So. Amer. palms. Cf. BACABA.
enodar (v.t.) to knot.
enodoar (v.t.) to spot, soil; to sully.
enófilo –la (adj.) wine-loving; (m.,f.) oenophilist (wine lover).
enófobo –ba (m.,f.) oenophobist (one who has an aversion for wine).
enoftalmia (f., Med.) enophthalmos.
enoitecer (v.) = ANOITECER.
enojado –da (adj.) disgusted; nauseated.
enojador –dora (adj.) disgusting; nauseating.
enojamento (m.) = ENÔJO.
enojar (v.t.) to disgust, nauseate; (v.r.) to become disgusted. Cf. ANOJAR, ENJOAR.
enôjo (m.) disgust; nausea; mourning. Cf. NOJO.
enojoso –sa (adj.) nauseating; disgusting; tedious.
enol (m., Chem.) enol.
enolina (f., Chem.) oenolin.
enologia (f.) oenology.
enologista (m.,f.), enólogo –ga (m.,f.) oenologist.
enomania (f.) dipsomania.
enômetro (m.) oenometer.
Enoque (m.) Enoch.
enorme (adj.) enormous, huge; inordinate.

enormidade (f.) enormity; atrociousness; hugeness.
enosteose (f., Med.) enostosis.
enoveladeira (f.) winding or reeling machine.
enovelar (v.t.) to wind (yarn, etc.) into a ball; to coil; (v.r.) to curl, twist.
enquadramento (m.) act of framing or fitting.
enquadrar (v.t.) to frame (as a picture); to fit in (com, with); (Mil. sl.) to punish; (v.r.) to square, harmonize.
enquadrilhar (v.t.) to round up (cattle); (v.r.) of people, to gather.
enquanto (conj.) while; as long as.—isso, meanwhile, in the meantime.—que, while. por—, for the time being; for the present.
enquilema (m., Biol.) enchylema, hyaloplasm.
enquistado –da (adj.) enclosed in a cyst or sac.
enquistamento (m.) encystment.
enquistar (v.i.,v.r.) to encyst.
enrabar (v.t.) to seize by the tail; to tie to the tail of; to tail (follow) another person.
enrabichar (v.t.) to tie (the hair) in a pigtail; to infatuate.
—se com, to become infatuated with, taken with.
enraiar (v.t.) to provide (a wheel) with spokes.
enraivar, enraivecer (v.t.) to enrage; (v.i.,v.r.) to become enraged, furious.
enraizar [a-i] (v.i.) to take root.
enramalhar (v.t.) to ornament (as an altar) with branches.
enramalhetar (v.t.) to gather (flowers) into sprays or bunches; to ornament with flowers and branches.
enramar (v.t.) to cover, hide, shelter or ornament with branches; to join with.
enramilhetar (v.) = ENRAMALHETAR.
enrascada (f.) predicament, "jam".
enrascar (v.t.) to net (fish, etc.); to trap; to entangle; to frame (a person); (v.r.) to become entangled, get into trouble.
enredadeira (f.) a busybody.
enredado –da (adj.) tangled, snarled.
enredador (m.) mischief-maker; talebearer.
enredar (v.t.) to net; to entangle; to foul (a line); to embroil; (v.r.) to become tangled.—se em, to become entangled.
enrêdo (m.) entanglement; intrigue; meddling; story, plot.
enregelado –da (adj.) freezing; frozen.
enregelamento (m.) freezing, chilling.
enregelar (v.t.) to freeze; to chill; (v.i.) to congeal; (v.r.) to become frozen.
enrijar, enrijecer (v.t.,v.i.,v.r.) to harden, toughen, stiffen.
enriquecer (v.t.) to enrich; to adorn, embellish; (v.i.,v.r.) to grow rich.
enristar (v.t.) to couch (a lance).—com, to tilt with.
enrocado –da (adj.) rocky; craggy.
enrocamento (m.) a mass of large rocks, used as a break-water or seawall.
enrocar (v.t.) to fix (a bunch of flax, tow or wool) on the distaff; to provide (a garment) with ornamental slits; (v.i.) to castle (at chess); (v.r.) to become caught (as net or fishing line) on rocks.
enrodilhar (v.t.) to twine, wind around, twist; (v.r.) to curl.
enrola-cabelo (m.) = TORCE-CABELO.
enrolado –da (adj.) rolled, coiled; wrapped up.
enrolamento (m.) act of coiling or winding; (Elec.) winding.—de campo, field winding.—compound, compound winding.—em derivação, shunt winding.—diferencial, differential winding.—do filamento, filament winding.—do induzido, armature winding.—em série, series winding.—em tambor, drum winding.
enrolar (v.t.) to roll (up); to wind, twist, coil, curl; to wrap up; (v.r.) to roll; to curl.
enroscado –da (adj.) rolled, twisted, coiled, spiraled.
enroscar (v.t.) to coil, twist; to twine, wind around; (v.r.) to wind, coil; to snuggle, curl up (in bed).—se em tôrno de, to wind around something.
enroupado –da (adj.) clothed; (colloq.) having a good wardrobe.
enroupar (v.t.) to clothe (com, de, with; em, in); to provide with clothing; (v.r.) to clothe oneself.
enrouquecer (v.t.) to make (the voice) hoarse; (v.i.,v.r.) to become hoarse.
enrouquecimento (m.) hoarseness.
enrubescer (v.t.) to redden; (v.i.,v.r.) to blush, color, become red.
enrufar-se (v.r.) to become ruffled, vexed.
enrugar (v.t.) to wrinkle, crease, furrow, crimp.

ensaboadela (*f.*) a soaping; (*colloq.*) a dressing down, reprimand.

ensaboar (*v.t.*) to soap, lather; to reprimand.

ensacadinha (*f.*, *Bot.*) the showy heartseed (*Cardiospermum grandiflorum*), c.a. BALÃOZINHO, CHUMBINHO.

ensacador –**dora** (*m.*,*f.*) a sacker; a wholesale merchant or exporter of green coffee in bags.

ensacamento (*m.*), **ensacagem** (*f.*) act of bagging (grain, coffee, etc.).

ensacar (*v.t.*) to bag, sack (coffee, beans, etc.).

ensaiador –**dora** (*m.*,*f.*) assayer; tester; rehearser.

ensaiar (*v.t.*) to test, try; to assay; to essay, attempt; to rehearse; (*v.r.*) to make ready, prepare oneself (**para**, to); to rehearse, practice.

ensaio (*m.*) test, trial; practice, rehearsal; attempt; an essay.—**de carga dinâmica**, live-load test.—**de cisalhamento**, shear test.—**de compressão**, compressive test.—**de dureza**, hardness test.—**de esmagamento**, crushing test.—**de fadiga**, fatigue test.—**hidráulico**, hydraulic test.—**hidrostático**, hydrostatic test.—**de impacto**, impact test.—**de torção**, torsional test.—**de tração**, tensile test. **balão de**—, trial balloon.

ensaísta (*m.*,*f.*) essayist.

ensalmo (*m.*) superstitious healing jargon; spell; witchcraft.

ensalmourar (*v.t.*) to place in brine.

ensamambaiado –**da** (*adj.*) overgrown with SAMAMBAIAS (bracken).

ensamblador (*m.*) joiner, carpenter.

ensambladura, –**blagem** (*f.*), –**blamento** (*m.*, *Carp.*) joinery; a joint.

ensamblar (*v.t.*, *Carp.*) to join, fit together (by rabbets, etc.); to scarf.

ensancha (*f.*) wide hem; surplus width; freedom; (*pl.*) opportunity.

ensanchar (*v.t.*) to expand, widen.

ensandecer (*v.t.*) to go insane; (*v.t.*) to make insane; to infatuate.

ensangüentado –**da** (*adj.*) bloody, gory.

ensangüentar (*v.t.*) to bloody; (*v.r.*) to become bloodstained or bloodthirsty.

ensapèzado –**da** (*adj.*) overgrown with SAPÉ (satin-tail or sape grass).

ensaque (*m.*) = ENSACAMENTO.

ensarilhar (*v.t.*) to wind on a reel; to stack (arms); (*v.i.*) to pace up and down.

enseada (*f.*) bay, cove, inlet; [*GBAT*: "A small bay; a wide curve along the bank of a river; in Marajó, an area of open land between two IGARAPÉS or at the bend of a river."]

ensebado –**da** (*adj.*) grease-covered; greasy; dirty.

ensebar [17a] (*v.t.*) to grease; to make greasy.

ensecadeira (*f.*) cofferdam; caisson

ensecar (*v.t.*) to drain dry; to run or pull (boats) up on dry land; to investigate.

ensejar (*v.t.*) to occasion, cause; to await an opportunity; (*v.r.*) of an opportunity, to arise, present itself.—**a**, to give an opportunity to.

ensejo [sê] (*m.*) opportunity; fitting occasion. **dar**—**a**, to let, allow.

enselado –**da** (*adj.*) sway-backed.

ensiforme (*adj.*) ensiform, sword-shaped.

ensilagem (*f.*) ensilage.

ensilar (*v.t.*) to silo (fodder, etc.).

ensimesmado –**da** (*adj.*; *m.*,*f.*) self-engrossed; reserved; introverted (person).

ensimesmamento (*m.*) self-absorption.

ensimesmar-se (*v.r.*) to become self-absorbed.

ensinadela (*f.*, *colloq.*) costly lesson; a dressing down.

ensinamento (*m.*) teaching; lesson.

ensinar (*v.t.*) to teach (**a**, to; **sôbre**, about); to train (animals); to instruct, inform.

ensino (*m.*) teaching, instruction, education; training.—**superior**, higher education. **estabelecimento de**—, a school (of any kind).

ensisterno (*m.*, *Anat.*) xiphisternum.

enslênia (*f.*) Enslen's vine, sand vine (*Gonolobus laevis*).

ensoalhado –**da** (*adj.*) sun-drenched.

ensoamento (*m.*) a wilting; also = INSOLAÇÃO.

ensoar (*v.i.*,*v.r.*) to wither, wilt, droop.

ensoberbecer (*v.t.*) to make proud, haughty; (*v.r.*) to become so.

ensolarado –**da** (*adj.*) sun-drenched.

ensombrar (*v.t.*) to shadow, shade; to obscure; to make somber, sad; (*v.r.*) to grow dark.

ensopado –**da** (*adj.*) sopping wet, wringing wet; soggy; stewed; (*m.*) a stew of meat or fish.

ensopar (*v.t.*) to drench; to soak (**em**, in); to make into a stew; (*v.r.*) to get sopping wet.

enstatita (*f.*, *Min.*) enstatite.

ensurdecedor –**dora** (*adj.*) deafening.

ensurdecer (*v.t.*) to deafen; to deaden (sound); to stun; (*v.i.*) to grow deaf; to turn a deaf ear to.

ensurdecimento (*m.*) a deafening; deafness.

entablamento (*m.*, *Arch.*) entablature.

entabuado –**da** (*adj.*) boarded (up); hard as a board.

entabuamento (*m.*) act of boarding up.

entabuar (*v.t.*) to board up; (*v.r.*) to grow hard as a board.

entabular (*v.t.*) to open, begin, enter upon, initiate.—**assunto**, to broach a subject.—**conversa**, to strike up a conversation.—**negociações**, to start negotiations.

entaipar (*v.t.*) to screen, wall off or in, with wattles or stud-and-mud; to tamp, (as, concrete in a form).—**-se em**, to seclude oneself in (a cloister, etc.).

entalação, **entaladela** (*f.*) tight squeeze, tight spot, pinch, difficulties, straits, fix, dilemma.

entalado –**da** (*adj.*) squeezed, tightened, pinched, cramped; in splints; in a predicament, "up against it"; (*f.*) tight corner, tight squeeze, predicament.

entalar (*v.t.*) to put between splints; to put in a tight spot, in a difficult situation.

entalha (*f.*) cut, groove, notch, etc., (in wood).

entalhador –**dora** (*m.*,*f.*) wood carver.

entalhadura, –**lhamento** (*m.*) wood carving.

entalhar (*v.t.*) to carve (wood).

entalhe (*m.*) notch, cut, groove.

entalho (*m.*) intaglio carving; notch; mortise.

entaliscar (*v.t.*) to force (something) into a crack or crevice; (*Carp.*) to join boards with a spline; (*v.r.*) to squeeze or crawl into a crevice.

entanguido –**da** (*adj.*) stunted, wizened; stiff with cold.

entanha (*f.*) a large frog.

entanto (*adv.*; *m.*) meanwhile, meantime. **no**—, nevertheless, however, yet; in the meantime.

então (*adv.*) then, at that time; in that case; (*m.*) then, that time; (*exclam.*), Well then? Well? How about it? **até**—, up to that time. **desde**—, ever since.

entaramelar (*v.t.*) to tongue-tie; (*v.r.*) to stutter.

entardecer (*v.i.*) to draw on [nightfall]; to grow late, dark.

entarraxar (*v.t.*) to fasten with screws [= ATARRAXAR].

entase (*f.*, *Arch.*) entasis.

ente (*m.*) a being, living thing, creature.—**de Deus**, a creature of God.—**de razão** or—**imaginário**, a creature of the imagination.—**humano**, human being.—**pensante**, a thinker, man.—**supremo**, Supreme Being.

enteada (*f.*) stepdaughter.

enteado (*m.*) stepson.

entediar (*v.t.*) to weary; (*v.r.*) to become weary.

entejo [tê] (*m.*) tedium.

enteléquia (*f.*, *Philos.*) entelechy.

entelhar (*v.*) = IMBRICAR.

entendedor –**dora** (*adj.*) understanding, knowing; (*m.*,*f.*) one who knows, understands. **A bom**—**meia palavra basta**, A word to the wise is sufficient.

entender (*v.t.*) to understand, apprehend; to perceive, know; to comprehend, catch; (*v.r.*) to understand each other.—**-se com**, to come to an understanding with.—**como ninguém (de alguma coisa)**, to know all about something (how it works, how to do it, etc.) better than anybody.—**de música**, to understand music.—**do assunto** or **do riscado**, to be well-versed in a matter. **dar a**—, to give to understand. **não**—**nem uma palavra de**, to know nothing whatever about (a subject). **no meu**—, according to my understanding; in my opinion. **Os que se entendem andam juntos**, Birds of a feather flock together.

entendido –**da** (*adj.*) understood; knowing, expert. **bem**—, certainly, of course; that is understood.

entendimento (*m.*) understanding; reason; apprehension, perception; agreement, accord.

entenebrecer (*v.t.*,*v.i.*,*v.r.*) to darken.

entenebrecido –**da** (*adj.*) dark, cloudy; gloomy.

entenrecer (*v.t.*) to soften; to make tender; (*v.i.*) to grow tender.

entérico –**ca** (*adj.*) enteric, intestinal.

enterite (*f.*, *Med.*) enteritis.

enternecer (*v.t.*) to move to compassion, tenderness. (*v.r.*) to relent, to feel sorry; to be moved.

enternecimento (*m.*) tenderness, pity.

enterocinese (f., Biochem.) enterokinase.
enterose (f.) a generic term for intestinal disease.
enterozoário (m., Zool.) entozoon; (pl.) entozoa.
enterramento (m.) burial.
enterrar (v.t.) to inter, bury; to hide, conceal; to plunge, drive in (as a dagger).—-se em, to bury oneself in.
entêrro (m.) interment, burial; funeral procession.
entesado –da (adj.) taut, tight, stretched.
entesar (v.t.) to stretch, make taut; (v.r.) to stiffen.
entesourar (v.t.) to lay up treasure; to hoard; to enshrine. Var. ENTESOIRAR.
entestar (v.i.) —com, to border (touch) upon; to stand opposite to; to come abreast of.
entibiamento (m.) = TIBIEZA.
entibiar (v.t.) to cool (the ardor of); (v.i.,v.r.) to grow luke-warm, indifferent.
entica (f.) provocation.
enticador –dora, enticante (adj.) provoking, exasperating.
enticar (v.i.)—com, to pick on, provoke, exasperate; to quarrel with.
entidade (f.) entity, being; existence; body (collective group).—privada, private group.
entisicar (v.t.) to cause to suffer phthisis; (v.i.) to become consumptive, thin, weak.
entoação (f.) entoamento (m.) intonation; (Photog.) development.
entoar (v.t.) to intone; to chant; to tune; (Photog.) to de-velop.—com, to be in tune with.
entocar (v.t.,v.r.) to hide in a hole; (v.r.) to burrow.
entoderme (m., Zool.) entoderm, endoderm; hypoblast; (Bot.) endodermis.
entófito (m., Bot.) entophyte.
entojado –da (adj.) disgusted, nauseated; puffed up, conceited.
entojar (v.t.) to disgust, nauseate; (v.i.) to feel disgust.
entôjo (m.) nausea or bizarre desires caused by pregnancy.
entom. = ENTOMOLOGIA (Entomology).
entomério (m., Embryol.) entomere.
entômico –ca (adj.) entomic(al).
entomófago –ga (adj., Zool.) entomophagous, insecti-vorous.
entomófilo –la (adj., Bot.) entomophilous; (m.,f.) collector of insects.
entomógeno –na (adj., Bot.) entomogenous.
entomologia (f.) entomology.
entomológico –ca (adj.) entomologic(al).
entomologista (m.,f.) entomologist.
entomostráceo (m.) any entomostracan crustacean.
entonação (f.) entonation [= ENTOAÇÃO].
entonar (v.t.) to lift (the head) haughtily; (v.r.) to rise haughtily. [But not to intone, which is ENTOAR.]
entono (m.) pride, haughtiness, swagger.
entontecedor –dora (adj.) dizzying.
entontecer (v.t.) to make dizzy; to fluster; (v.i.,v.r.) to grow dizzy.
entontecimento (m.) dizziness; dizzying.
entoparasito (m., Biol.) endoparasite.
entóptico –ca (adj., Optics) entoptical.
entoptoscópio (m.) entoptoscope.
entornar (v.t.) to overturn; to spill, shed; to pour out.—o caldo, to upset the applecart, spill the beans.
entorpecedor –dora (adj.) deadening, numbing, stupe-fying.
entorpecente (adj.; m.) narcotic.
entorpecer (v.t.) to make torpid, benumb; (v.i.,v.r.) to grow numb.
entorpecido –da (adj.) numb, stiff; sluggish; torpid.
entorpecimento (m.) torpor, numbness; sluggishness.
entorretina (f., Anat.) entoretina.
entorse (f.) severe strain or wrench of a ligament.
entortar (v.t.) to make crooked, twist, bend; (v.r.) to be-come twisted, crooked; to intort.—os olhos, to squint.
entótico –ca (adj., Anat.) entotic.
entozoários (m.pl.) entozoa, intestinal worms.
entrabrir (v.) = ENTREABRIR.
entrada (f.) entrance, ingress; entry, access; inlet; open-ing; vestibule; passage, doorway; beginning; a down payment; entrance fee; ticket of admission; (Elec.) inlet; (pl.) entrées; total paid admissions; raids; excursions;—de baile = CORAL (coral vine).—de carona, free admis-sion to a show.—franca, free entry, free admission.—pessoal, a non-transferable ticket of free admission to all public places, held by a government official. meia—, half-price ticket of admission.

entrado –da (adj.) entered; forward, presumptuous.—em anos, advanced in years.
entrajar (v.t.) to clothe; (v.i.,v.r.) to dress.
entralhada (f.) entanglement, tangled web.
entralhar (v.t.) to weave (a net); to ensnare in a net; to entangle; (v.i.,v.r.) to become entangled.
entrançado –da (adj.) braided, twisted; interlaced; (m.) interlacing.
entrançar (v.t.) to interlace; to braid, twist.
entranha (f.) any of the viscera; (pl.) entrails, bowels.
entranhado –da (adj.) deeply rooted or imbedded; in-grained; deep-seated; profound.
entranhar (v.t.) to drive (sword, spear) deeply into.—em, to cause to penetrate; (v.r.) to penetrate, enter deeply (em, a, para, into).
entranhável (adj.) deep, penetrating, profound.
entrante (adj.) entering; beginning.
entrar (v.i.) to enter, go in (to), come in (to); to begin (a, to); to join (become a member).—a falar, to begin to speak.—com o pé direito, to start off on the right foot.—de carona, to crash the gate.—em, to enter in or into.—em conta, to be taken into account.—em contato com, to get in touch with.—em funcionamento, to begin to function.—em moda, to come into vogue.—em vigor, to become effective.—em um assunto, to start on a subject.—em uma carreira, to embark on a career.—na faca, to be operated on.—na forma, (Mil.) to fall in line.—na linha, to fall into line.—nos cobres. (colloq.) to come into money.—nos eixos, to get going.—para, to enter.—por um ouvido e sair pelo outro, to go in one ear and out the other.
entravar (v.t.) to trammel, hamper, cramp, cumber; to hold in check; to stymie.
entrave (m.) shackle, clog, restraint.
entre (prep.) between; among, amid, in the midst of.—a bigorna e o malho (or o martelo),—a cruz e a caldeirinha (or a água benta),—a espada e a parede, are all equiva-lents of "between the devil and deep blue sea".—a vida e a morte, between life and death.—Cila e Caribde, be-tween Scylla and Charybdis.—lôbo e cão, between sun-set and darkness.—os presentes, among those present.—si, among themselves.—zangado e sorridente, half-angry, half-smiling. aqui—nós, just between ourselves. por—, among, between.
entreaberto –ta (adj.) ajar, half-open; (f.) an opening in the clouds; interval.
entreabrir [26] (v.t.) to half-open (as the eyes); to set ajar (as a door); (v.r.) to open (as a flower).
entreamar-se (v.r.) to love one another.
entreaparecer (v.i.) to appear between.
entreato (m.) entr'acte; intermission.
entrebater-se (v.r.) to clash.
entrebranco –ca (adj.) whitish.
entrecana (f., Arch.) arris.
entrecasca (f.) inner bark, bast tissue.
entrecena (f.) interval between acts.
entrecerrar (v.t.) to half-close.
entrechar (v.t.) to weave a plot (of a story or play).
entrecho (m.) plot of a drama; weave.
entrechocar-se (v.r.) to collide with, crash together; to clash, be at variance with.
entrecoberta (f., Naut.) between-decks.
entreconhecer (v.t.) to recognize (perceive) vaguely; (v.r.) to recognize one another.
entrecoro [cô] (m.) chancel.
entrecorrer (v.t.) to criss-cross; (v.i.) to occur in the mean-time.
entrecortar (v.t.) to intersect; to interrupt (from time to time); (v.r.) to cross, intersect.
entrecosto [cô] (m.) ribs of beef.
entrecruzar-se (v.r.) to cross, mix, blend (as colors, sounds).
entrededo [dê] (m.) space between fingers or toes.
entredente (m.) indentation, notch.
entredevorar-se (v.r.) to devour one another.
entredilacerar-se (v.r.) to lacerate one another.
entredizer [41] (v.t.,v.r.) to say to oneself or to one another.
entredizimar-se (v.r.) to decimate one another.
entredormido –da (adj.) half-asleep.
entrefalar (v.) = ENTREDIZER.
entrefechar (v.t.) to close slightly.
entreferro (m., Physics) air gap; clearance.
entrefigurar-se (v.r.) to seem to one.

entrefino -na (adj.) middling; intermediate; half and half; (m.) "washed medium fine, a technical grade of commercial rubber." [GBAT].

entrefôlha (f.) interleaf.

entrefolhar (v.t.) to interleave.

entreforro [ô] (m.) inner lining; ceiling.

entrega (f.) delivery; handing over, transmission; surrender.—a domicílio, home delivery.—urgente, special delivery (of mail, etc.). pagamento na—, C.O.D.

entregador -dora (adj.) delivering; traitorous; (m.) betrayer, traitor; deliverer of newspapers.

entregar [24] (v.t.) to deliver, hand over (a, to); to give up; to give back; to entrust (a, to); (v.r.) to give oneself up, surrender.—se a, to devote (addict) oneself to (study, vice, etc.); to abandon oneself to (despair, drink, etc.). —a alma a Deus, to yield up one's soul (die).—a rapadura, to throw in the sponge.—os pontos, to throw in the sponge, quit, give up. Quase entregou os pontos, He almost cashed in his chips (died).

entregue (adj.; irreg. p,p. of ENTREGAR) delivered; dedicated; busy, absorbed.—aos seus próprios recursos, left to (his, her) their own devices.

entreguismo (m.) sellout of a nation's natural resources. [A derogatory epithet applied to the policy of Brazilian statesmen and others who favor admitting foreign capital for the development of oil, etc.]

entrelaçado -da (adj.) interlaced, interwoven.

entrelaçamento (m.) act of interlacing; an interlacement; a splice.

entrelaçar (v.t.) to interlace, interweave, intertwine; to braid, plait.

entrelace (m., Biol.) a crossing over.

entrelinha (f.) space between lines; interlineation; (Printing) slug. ler nas—, to read between the lines.

entrelinhar (v.t.) to interline; (Printing) to lead.

entrelinhista (m.,f.) interliner.

entrelopo [lô] (m.) smuggler; interloper [but only in the original sense of an unlawful trader. In the modern meaning of intruder, the equivalent is INTRUSO.]

entreluzir [36] (v.i.) to glimmer; to shine through.

entremanhã (f.) dawn.

entrematar-se (v.r.) to kill one another.

entremear (v.t.) to intermingle, mix; to interlard; to intersperse (com, de, with).

entremeio (m.) interim, meantime; interval (of space); a lace insert.

entrementes (adv.; m., colloq.) meanwhile.

entremeter (v.t.) to interpose, put in or between; (v.r.) to intervene, intermeddle; to intrude oneself.

entremetimento (m.) act of interposing, etc. See the verb ENTREMETER.

entremez [mêz] (m.) intermezzo, short farce; ridiculous person or thing.

entremisturar (v.t.) to intermix.

entremontano -na (adj.) intermontane, between mountains.

entremostrar (v.t.) to afford a glimpse of, show; (v.r.) to appear.

entre-nó (m.) internode.

entreolhar-se (v.r.) to eye one another; to exchange glances.

entreouvir [58] (v.t.) to hear indistinctly; to overhear.

entrepano (m.) riser (between shelves); space between columns.

entreparar (v.i.) to pause for a moment.

entrepausa (f.) an intermission.

entrepelado -da (adj.) of mixed colors [horse]; (m.,f.) person of indefinite or contradictory ideas.

entrepernas (adv.) between the legs.

entrepilastras (m., Arch.) space between pilasters.

entrepor [63] (v.) = INTERPOR.

entreposto [pô], entrepósito (m.) entrepôt, large warehouse, supply station.

entrequerer-se [68] (v.r.) to care (have affection) for one another.

entrescolher (v.t.) to choose at random.

entresilhado -da (adj.) skinny, skin-and-bones.

entressachar (v.t.) to intersperse, interlard; to interlace, interweave; (v.r.) to mix in (com, with).

entresseio (m.) dip, hollow.

entressemear (v.t.) to sow in the midst of.—de, to intersperse with.

entressola (f.) inner sole of a shoe.

entressôlho (m., Arch.) entresol, mezzanine.

entressonhar (v.t.) to glimpse in a dream; (v.i.) to daydream.

entretalhadura (f.), entretalho (m.) bas-relief.

entretanto (adv.) meanwhile, in the meantime.—que, while; (conj.) however, on the other hand; (m.) the interim.

entretecer (v.t.) to interweave, intertwine.

entretela (f.) interlining (of a garment).

entretelar (v.t.) to interline.

entretempo (m.) interim. nesse—, meanwhile.

entretenimento (m.) entertainment, amusement, pastime; sport.

entreter [78] (v.t.) to detain, delay (as with promises); to maintain, carry on, keep up; to entertain, harbor (hopes, etc.); to divert, amuse; (v.r.) to amuse, occupy, oneself.

entretimento (m.) = ENTRETENIMENTO.

entretom (m.) tint.

entretrópico -ca (adj.) intertropical.

entrevação (f.) paralysis, a crippling.

entrevado -da (adj.) paralyzed; (m.,f.) a paralytic.

entrevar (v.t.) to paralyze, cripple.

entrever [81] (v.t.) to glimpse, catch sight of; to descry, perceive. [Often confused with INTERVIR.]

entrevêro (m.) melée, free-for-all, fracas.

entrevia (f.) railroad gauge (distance between rails).

entreviga (f.) space between beams.

entrevinda (f.) unexpected arrival.

entrevista (f.) interview; meeting, conference; appointment.—coletiva, press conference.

entrevistar (v.t.) to interview.

entre-vivos (adv., Law) inter vivos, between living persons.

entrilhar (v.t.,v.i.) to run (automobile) on the streetcar tracks.

entrincheiramento (m.) entrenchment.

entrincheirar (v.t.) to entrench; (v.r.) to become entrenched; to dig in; to stand fast.

entristecedor -dora (adj.) saddening.

entristecer (v.t.) to sadden, grieve; (v.i.,v.r.) to grow sad.

entristecimento (m.) saddening; sadness.

entronar (v.) = ENTRONIZAR.

entroncado -da (adj.) big, broad-shouldered, well-built.

entroncamento (m.) road junction; railroad junction.

entroncar (v.i.,v.t.) to join, connect (a, to; em, com, with).

entronização (f.) enthronement.

entronizar (v.t.) to enthrone; to exalt.

entropia (f., Thermodyn.) entropy.—específica, heat weight.

entrópio, entrópion (m., Med.) entropion.

entrós (m.), entrosa (f.), cogwheel; gear; distance between gear teeth.

entrosagem (f.) meshing of gears.

entrosar (v.t.) to put in gear; to organize; (v.i.) to mesh; to dovetail.

entrouxar (v.t.) to make a bundle of (clothes, etc.).

entrudar (v.i.) to make merry at carnival time, esp. by playing tricks and practical jokes.

entrudo (m.) carnival sport, revelry.

entuchar (v.i.) to swallow, put up with (indignities).

entufado -da (adj.) puffed up, arrogant; angry.

entulhar (v.t.) to heap up; to choke, fill full; to fill with rubble.

entulho (m.) rubble, debris; (colloq.) roast turkey stuffing.

entupido -da (adj.) stopped up, clogged; (colloq.) struck dumb.

entupigaitação (f., colloq.) muddle, confusion; speechlessness.

entupigaitar (v.t., colloq.) to fuddle, muddle; (v.i.) to fall silent.

entupimento (m.) stoppage, jam, a clogging.

entupir (v.t.) to stop up, clog, choke; (v.i.) to choke.

enturvar (v.t.) to cloud; to disturb; to sadden; (v.r.) to become turbid.

entusiasmado -da (adj.) full of enthusiasm; elated; (colloq.) stuck up.

entusiasmar (v.t.) to fill with enthusiasm; (v.i.) to enthuse, thrill; (v.r.) to become enthusiastic.

entusiasmo (m.) enthusiasm, eagerness, fervor; rapture; verve; boisterousness.

entusiasta (m.,f.) enthusiast; (adj.) enthusiastic.

entusiástico -ca (adj.) enthusiastic; rapturous.

enublar (v.t.) to cloud [= ANUVIAR].

enuclear (v.t.) to enucleate; to pit (fruit); to explain.

ênula-campana (f., Bot.) elecampane (Inula helenium).

enumeração (*f.*) enumeration; computation; specification.

enumerador –**dora** (*adj.*) enumerative; (*m.,f.*) enumerator.

enumerar (*v.t.*) to enumerate (one by one); to number, recount, specify.

enumerável (*adj.*) that can be enumerated.

enunciação (*f.*) enunciation.

enunciado –**da** (*adj.*) stated, declared; (*m.*) enunciation, definite statement, announcement.

enunciar (*v.t.*) to enunciate, proclaim, declare.

enunciativo –**va** (*adj.*) enunciative.

enurese, enuresia (*f., Med.*) enuresis; bed-wetting.

enuviar (*v.*) = ANUVIAR.

envaginado –**da** (*adj.*) invaginate.

envaidar, envaidecer [7,19] (*v.t.*) to puff up with pride; (*v.r.*) to become conceited, vain.

envaidecedor –**dora** (*adj.*) flattering.

envasamento (*m., Arch.*) base of a column.

envasar (*v.t.*) to bottle (wine, etc.); to plant (flowers, etc.) in pots; to run (a ship) into the mud.

envasilhamento (*m.*) act of bottling, etc.;—see the verb ENVASILHAR.

envasilhar (*v.t.*) to bottle; to barrel.

envelhecer (*v.i.*) to age; to become old, grow older.

envelhecimento (*m.*) aging.

envelope (*m.*) envelope; boiler jacket.

envenenado –**da** (*adj.*) poisoned.

envenenador –**dora** (*adj.*) poisonous; poisoning; (*m.,f.*) poisoner.

envenenamento (*m.*) poisoning.

envenenar (*v.t.*) to poison; to taint, contaminate; to envenom; (*v.r.*) to take poison.

enverdecer, enverdejar (*v.t.*) to make green; (*v.i.,v.r.*) to grow green.

enveredar (*v.i.*) to head for, set out for, direct one's course toward a given place or along a given road; to enter, go in.—**por um caminho**, to follow a road.

envergadura (*f.*) spread (of a sail, of a bird's wings); span (of an airplane wing); scope, extent.—**moral**, moral character. **um ataque de grande**—, a full-scale attack.

envergar (*v.t.*) to fasten (sails) to the yards; to bend, curve; to put on (a coat, etc.).—**uma camisa nova**, to put on a new shirt.

envergonhado –**da** (*adj.*) ashamed; shamefaced.

envergonhar (*v.t.*) to shame; to disgrace; (*v.r.*) to be ashamed; to blush.

envermelhar, envermelhecer (*v.t.*) to make red; (*v.r.*) to redden.

envernizado –**da** (*adj.*) varnished.

envernizador (*m.*) varnisher.

envernizar (*v.t.*) to varnish.

enverrugar (*v.t.*) to wrinkle; (*v.i.,v.r.*) to grow warty or wrinkled; to grow wormy [fruit].

envesgar (*v.t.,v.i.*) to squint.

envessar (*v.t.*) to turn (garment, etc.) inside out; to reverse the order of.

enviado –**da** (*adj.*) sent; (*m.,f.*) envoy, messenger.

enviar (*v.t.*) to send, dispatch; to ship.

envidar (*v.t.*) to raise another player's bet; to invite.—**de falso**, to make a pretense of offering something, as a mere courtesy.—**esforços**, to exert, put forth, one's best efforts.

envide (*f.*) a bet or act of betting, esp. at poker.

envidraçado –**da** (*adj.*) glazed; glass-inclosed; glassy.

envidraçamento (*m.*) act of glazing.

envidraçar (*v.t.*) to glaze; (*v.r.*) to become glassy.

enviés (*m.*) = VIÉS.

enviesado –**da** (*adj.*) aslant; (cut) on the bias.

enviesar (*v.t.*) to slant, slope, tilt, to set awry; to cut on the bias; (*v.r.*) to slant.

envigamento (*m.*) beamwork.

envigotar (*v.t.*) to provide with floor beams.

envilecer (*v.t.*) to debase; to vilify; (*v.r.*) to degrade oneself.

envilecimento (*m.*) abasement [= AVILTAMENTO].

envinagrado –**da** (*adj.*) vinegary.

envinagrar (*v.t.*) to mix with vinegar; to make sour.

envio (*m.*) act of sending, dispatching, shipping, etc.; envoy of a ballade, sestina, etc. Cf. OFERTA, REMATE, TORNADA.

envira (*f.*) any of several annonaceous trees, esp. of *Xylopia* and *Guateria*, yielding bast fibers and medicinal seeds; [*GBAT*: "Strips of the bark of the ENVIREIRA used as cordage; in a generalized sense, any textile fiber used as thread, line or rope."]

envireira (*f.*) any of various annonaceous trees.—**do-campo**, a whiptree (*Luhea paniculata*), c.a. AÇOITA-CAVALO.

envite (*m.*) raising of another player's bet; an offer of something as mere courtesy. **de**—, as a challenge.

enviuvar [i-u] (*v.i.*) to become a widow or widower; (*v.t.*) to make a widow or widower of.

envolto –**ta** (*adj.*) enveloped, wrapped; involved.

envoltório (*m.*) wrapper, covering.

envoltura (*f.*) envelopment; baby's blanket.

envolvente (*adj.*) involving, enveloping.

envolver [24] (*v.t.*) to involve, envelop, wrap (up); to include, embrace; to cover, hide.—**se em**, to involve oneself in (affairs); to wrap oneself up in (a coat, etc.).

envolvimento (*m.*) envelopment; involvement.

enxabidez (*f.*), –**bimento** (*m.*) = DESENXABIDEZ.

enxabido –**da** (*adj.*) = DESENXABIDO.

enxada (*f.*) hoe; the spade fish (*Chaetodipterus faber*).—**do arado**, plowshare.

enxadada (*f.*) a stroke or blow with a hoe.

enxadão (*m.*) mattock [= ALVIÃO].

enxadeiro (*m.*) hoer.

enxadrezado –**da** (*adj.*) checkered.

enxadrezar (*v.t.*) to checker.

enxadrista (*m.,f.*) chess player [= XADREZISTA].

enxaguar [8] (*v.t.*) to rinse (clothes, dishes).

enxaimel [-méis] (*m.*) upright pole or stick used in the framework of a mud hut.

enxama (*f.*) oarlock.

enxambrado –**da** (*adj.*) damp.

enxambrar (*v.t.*) to damp-dry (clothes) preparatory to ironing; (*v.i.,v.r.*) to dry (oneself) incompletely.

enxame (*m.*) a swarm of bees; a teeming multitude.

enxamear (*v.i.,v.r.*) to swarm; (*v.t.*) to hive bees.

enxaqueca [êc] (*f.*) migraine.

enxárcia (*f.*) shrouds and stays of a vessel.

enxarciar (*v.t.*) to rig (a ship).

enxercar (*v.t.*) to put out (meat) to dry.

enxêrco (*m.*) = ERVA-DE-PASSARINHO.

enxêrga (*f.*) pallet; poor bed.

enxergão (*m.*) mattress; wire mattress; saddle blanket.—**de molas**, spring mattress.

enxergar (*v.t.*) to discern, perceive, descry, behold; to sense; (*colloq.*) to comprehend or understand.

enxerir-se (*v.r.*) to intrude, butt in.

enxertadeira (*f.*) grafting knife.

enxertador –**dora** (*adj.*) grafting; (*m.,f.*) grafter; grafting tool.

enxertadura (*f.*) act of grafting (plants).

enxertar (*v.t.*) to do grafting on (trees, etc.).

enxêrto (*m.*) grafting of plants; the graft itself.—**de-passarinho**, mistletoe.—**de pele**, skin graft.

enxó (*f.*) adze.

enxofradeira (*f.*) apparatus for dusting (plants) with sulfur.

enxofrar (*v.t.*) to sulfur.

enxôfre (*m.*) sulfur, brimstone.

enxota-cães (*m., colloq.*) doorman, gatekeeper.

enxota-diabos (*m., colloq.*) exorcist.

enxota-môscas (*m.*) fly whisk; fly swatter.

enxotar (*v.t.*) to scare or drive away; to oust.—**da cása**, to drive out of the house.—**môscas**, to shoo flies.

enxoval (*m.*) trousseau; layette; boarding school student's outfit of clothing and personal effects.

enxovalhado –**da** (*adj.*) soiled; crumpled; smeared, defiled.

enxovalhar (*v.t.*) to crumple; to soil (clothing); to smear, sully, defile.—**a honra de (alguém)**, to sully, blacken (someone's) reputation.

enxova-preta (*f.*) the escolar or oilfish (*Ruvettus pretiousus*), c.a. CAVALA-AFRICANA, PEIXE-ESCOBAR, PEIXE-ESCOLAR, PEIXE-PREGO, PESCADA-DE-ANGOLA. [The oil is highly purgative.]

enxovia (*f.*) dark, dank dungeon.

enxu (*f.*) a social wasp (*Nectarina lecheguana*), or its nest.

enxuga (*f.*) an ironweed (*Vernonia scorpioides*).

enxugador (*m.*) clothes' wringer; clothes' drier; bath towel.

enxugadouro (*m.*) drying place. Var. ENXUGADOIRO.

enxugar [24] (*v.t.*) to dry; to wipe dry; to drink, drain.

enxugo (*m.*) act of drying; drying place.

enxuí (*m.*) a social wasp (*Polybia sedula*), c.a. SIÇUÍRA.

enxúndia (*f.*) pork fat; chicken fat; fat flesh.

enxundioso –sa (*adj.*) very fat.
enxurdar-se (*v.r.*) to wallow in mud.
enxurdeiro (*m.*) mudhole; pigsty.
enxurrada (*f.*), **enxurro** (*m.*) spate, freshet; torrent; fig., abundance.
enuxurrar (*v.t.,v.i.*) to flood.
enxuto –ta (*adj.; irreg. p.p. of* ENUXUGAR) dried; dry; slim, trim; (*m.*) dry place; safe place.
enzenza (*f.*) the roots of a tropical woody vine (*Paullinia pinnata*) used for basketry.
enzima (*f.*) enzyme.
enzimólise (*f., Biochem.*) zymolysis.
enzinha (*f.*) = AZINHA.
enzinheira (*f.*) = AZINHEIRA.
enzootia (*f.*) an enzootic disease (of animals).
enzoótico –ca (*adj.*) enzootic.
eoceno –na (*adj., Geol.*) Eocene.
eocênio (*m.*) Eocene epoch.
eólico –ca (*adj.*) Aeolian; aeolian, wind-borne, wind-deposited [sand].
eólio –lia (*adj.*) Aeolian; aeolian. **harpa**—, aeolian harp or lyre. **motor**—, wind-driven motor. **rochas**—s, (*Geol.*) aeolian rocks; (*m.,f.*) Aeolian.
éolo (*m.*) strong wind; Aeolus.
eolotropia (*f., Physics.*) aelotropy.
eolotrópico –ca (*adj.*) aelotropic.
eosina (*f., Chem.*) eosin.
eosinofilia (*f., Med.*) eosinophilia.
eosinófilo –la (*adj., Biol.*) eosinophile.
epacta (*f., Chron.*) epact.
epactal (*adj., Anat.*) epactal.
epagoge (*f., Logic.*) epagoge.
epanadiplose (*f., Rhet.*) epanadiplosis.
epanáfora (*f., Rhet.*) anaphora.
epanalepse (*f., Rhet.*) epanalepsis, repetition, echo.
epanástrofe (*f., Rhet.*) anadiplosis.
epânodo (*m., Rhet.*) epanodos.
epanortose (*f., Rhet.*) epanorthosis.
epêndima (*m., Anat.*) ependyma.
epêntese (*f., Phonet.*) epenthesis.
eperua (*f.*) = ESPADEIRA.
epexegese (*f.*) epexegesis.
eph-, look under **ef-**.
epiblasto (*m., Biol., Bot.*) epiblast.
epiblema (*m., Bot.*) epiblema.
epicanto (*m., Anat.*) epicanthus.
epicardia (*f., Anat.*) epicardia.
epicárpio (*m., Bot.*) epicarp.
epicédio (*m.*) epicedium, dirge, elegy.
epiceno –na (*adj.*) epicene.
epicentro (*m., Seismol.*) epicenter.
epicíclo (*m., Astron.*) epicycle.
epiciclóide (*f., Geom.*) epicycloid.
epícito (*m., Biol.*) epicyte.
épico –ca (*adj.*) epic, heroic; (*m.*) an epic poet.
epicôndilo (*m., Anat.*) epicondyle.
epicório (*m., Anat.*) epichorion.
epicrânio –nia (*adj., Anat., Zool.*) epicranial; (*m.*) epicranium.
epicureu –réia (*adj.; m.*) Epicurean; epicurean.
epicurismo (*m.*) Epicureanism; epicureanism.
epicurista (*m.,f.*) epicure.
epidemia (*f.*) epidemic.
epidêmico –ca (*adj.*) epidemic.
epidemiologia (*f.*) epidemiology.
epidemiologista, epidemiólogo –ga (*m.,f.*) epidemiologist.
epidendro –dra (*adj., Bot.*) epidendric; (*m.*) a genus (*Epidendrum*) of orchids.
epiderme (*f., Anat.*) epidermis.
epidérmico –ca (*adj.*) epidermal, epidermic; skin-deep, superficial (of feelings).
epidermóide (*adj.*) epidermoid.
epidiascópio (*m.*) epidiascope.
epidíctico –ca (*adj.*) epideictic, ostentatious (oratory).
epidídimo (*m., Anat.*) epididymis.
epididimodeferencial (*adj., Anat.*) epididymodeferential.
epídoto (*m., Min.*) epidote.
Epifania (*f., Eccl.*) Epiphany.
epifaringe (*f., Zool.*) epipharynx.
epifenomenalismo (*m., Philos.*) epiphenominalism, automatism.
epifenômeno (*m., Med.*) epiphenomenon.
epifilo –la (*adj., Bot.*) epigenous.
epifisário –ria (*adj., Anat., Zool.*) epiphyseal.

epífise (*f., Anat.*) epiphysis; pineal body of the brain.
epifitia (*f., Bot.*) an epiphytotic disease.
epífito –ta (*adj., Bot.*) epiphytic; (*m.*) epiphyte.
epifitotia (*f.*) = EPIFITIA.
epifleose (*f., Bot.*) periderm.
epifonema (*m., Rhet.*) epiphonema.
epifragma (*m., Zool., Bot.*) epiphragm.
epigástrico –ca (*adj.*) epigastric.
epigástrio (*m., Anat.*) epigastrium.
epigéia (*f., Bot.*) trailing arbutus (*Epigaea spp.*).
epigéico –ca (*adj., Geol.*) epigene.
epigenesia (*f., Biol.*) epigenesis.
epigenia (*f., Geol.*) epigenesis.
epígeno –na (*adj., Bot.*) epigenous.
epigeu –géia (*adj., Bot.*) epigeous.
epiginia (*f., Bot.*) epigyny.
epígino –na (*adj., Bot.*) epigynous.
epiglote (*f., Anat.*) epiglottis.
epignato –ta (*adj., Zool.*) epignathous; hook-billed.
epigônio (*m., Bot.*) epigonium.
epígono –na (*m.,f.*) epigonus, descendant; successor.
epígrafe (*f.*) epigraph, inscription.
epigrafia (*f.*) epigraphy.
epigráfico –ca (*adj.*) epigraphic(al).
epigrafista (*m.,f.*) epigraphist, epigrapher.
epigrama (*m.*) epigram.
epigramar, –maticar (*v.t.*) to epigrammatize.
epigramático –ca (*adj.*) epigrammatic.
epigramatista (*m.,f.*) epigrammatist.
epigramatizar (*v.t.*) to epigrammatize.
epilação (*f.*) depilation.
epilatório –ria (*adj.; m.*) depilatory [= DEPILATÓRIO].
epilepsia (*f., Med.*) epilepsy.
epiléptico –ca, **epilético** –ca (*adj.; m.,f.*) epileptic.
epilóbio (*m.*) the genus (*Epilobium*) of willow weeds.
epilogação (*f.*) a final summing up.
epilogador –dora (*m.,f.*) epilogist.
epilogar (*v.t.*) to epilogize.
epílogo (*m.*) epilogue.
epimédio (*m.*) a genus (*Epimedium*) of woody herbs, c.a. ERVA-DE-BESTEIROS.
epimísio (*m., Anat.*) epimysium.
epimítio (*m.*) epimyth, moral.
epinastia (*f., Plant Physiol.*) epinasty.
epinefrina (*f.*) epinephrine, adrenaline.
epineural (*adj., Anat.*) epineural.
epinêurio (*m., Anat.*) epineurium.
epiótico –ca (*adj., Anat., Zool.*) epiotic.
epipétalo –la (*adj., Bot.*) epipetalous.
epipial (*adj., Anat.*) epipial.
epiplasma (*m., Bot.*) epiplasm.
epíploo, epíploon (*m., Anat.*) epiploon, the great omentum, caul.
epípode, epipódio (*m., Bot., Zool.*) epipodium.
epipterado –da (*adj., Bot.*) epipterous.
epiquirema (*m., Logic.*) epicheirema.
epirrizo –za (*adj., Bot.*) epirhizous.
episcopado (*m.*) episcopate; episcopacy.
episcopal (*adj.*) episcopal.
episódico –ca (*adj.*) episodic(al).
episódio (*m.*) episode.
epispástico –ca (*adj., Med.*) epispastic; (*m.*) a blistering agent.
epispermo (*m., Bot.*) testa, episperm.
episporo (*m., Bot.*) epispore.
epissépalo –la (*adj., Bot.*) episepalous.
epissilogismo (*m., Logic.*) episyllogism.
epíst. = EPÍSTOLA(S) = epistle(s).
epistasia (*f., Biol.*) epistasis.
epistaxe [ks] (*f., Med.*) epistaxis, nosebleed.
epistemologia (*f.*) epistemology.
episternal (*adj.*) episternal.
episterno (*m., Zool.*) episternum.
epistilbita (*f., Min.*) epistilbite.
epistílio (*m., Arch.*) epistyle, architrave [= ARQUITRAVE].
epístola (*f.*) epistle, letter; (*Eccl.*) Epistle.
epistolar (*adj.*) epistolary.
epistolário –ria (*adj.; m.*) epistolary.
epistolografia (*f.*) epistolography, letter writing.
epistológrafo –fa (*m.,f.*) epistolographer, letter writer.
epístoma, epistômio (*m., Zool.*) epistome.
epístrofe (*f., Rhet.*) epistrophe.
epistrofeu (*m., Anat.*) epistropheus.
epitáfio (*m.*) epitaph.

epitalâmio (m.) epithalamium (nuptial song or poem).
epítase (f.) epitasis (of a play).
epitelial (adj.) epithelial.
epitélio (m., Anat., Biol.) epithelium.
epitelióide (adj.) epithelioid.
epitelioma (m., Med.) epithelioma.—pavimentoso, (Med.) a cancroid.
epiteliomatoso -sa (adj.) epitheliomatous.
epitetar (v.t.) to epithet.
epitético -ca (adj.) epithetic.
epíteto (m.) epithet.
epitomar (v.t.) to epitomize.
epítome (m.) epitome. em—, in a nutshell.
epitróclea (f., Anat.) epitrochlea.
epítrope (f., Rhet.) epitrope.
epíxilo -la [x = ks] (adj., Bot.) epixylous.
epizeuxe [x = ks] (f., Rhet.) epizeuxis.
epizoário -ria (adj., Zool.) epizoic; (m.) epizoon.
epizootia (f.) epizooty, an epizootic disease.
epizoótico -ca (adj.) epizootic.
época (f.) epoch, age; term, length of time, period during which.—das colheitas, harvest time.—de viração, the turtle-hunting season.—teatral, theatrical season. na-quela—, then, at that period (time). nesta—do ano, at this time of year.
eponímia (f.) eponym.
eponíquio (m., Anat.) eponychium.
epoóforo (m., Anat.) epoophoron.
epopéia (f.) epopée, epic poem.
epsilão, epsilo (m.) epsilon.
epsomita (f., Min.) epsomite.
épura (f., Arch.) épure.
equabilidade (f.) equability.
equação (f.) equation.
equacionar (v.t.) to equate; to solve (a problem).
equador (m.) equator. (cap.) Ecuador.
equânime (adj.) equanimous, self-possessed; impartial.
equanimidade (f.) equanimity, calmness. composure, self-possession.
equatorial (adj.) equatorial.
equatoriano -na (adj.; m.,f.) Ecuadorian.
equável (adj.) equable.
eqüestre (adj.) equestrian. [But not an equestrian, which is EQUITADOR.]
eqüevo -va (adj.) equaeval, coeval.
eqüiângulo -la (adj.) equiangular.
eqüidade (f.) equity.
eqüídeos (m.pl.) the Equidae (horses, asses, zebras).
eqüidiferente (adj.) equidifferent.
eqüidistância (f.) equidistance, equal distance.
eqüidistante (adj.) equidistant.
eqüidistar (v.i.)—de, to be equidistant from.
eqüidna (m., Zool.) echidna, porcupine anteater.
eqüilateral, eqüilátero -ra (adj.) equilateral.
equilibração (f.) equilibration.
equilibrado -da (adj.) level-headed; well-balanced; even; evenly-matched.
equilibrador -dora (adj.) equilibratory.
equilibrante (adj.) equilibrative.
equilibrar (v.t.) to equilibrate, balance.—o orçamento, to balance the budget.
equilíbrio (m.) equilibrium, equipoise.—do ânimo, impartial judgment.—estável (indiferente, instável), stable (neutral, unstable) equilibrium.
equilibrista (m.,f.) equilibrist, acrobat, tight-rope walker.
equimolecular (adj., Chem.) equimolecular.
equimosar (v.t., Med.) to ecchymose; (v.r.) to turn black-and-blue.
equimose (f., Med.) ecchymosis (black-and-blue mark).
eqüimultíplice, eqüimúltiplo -pla (adj.) equimultiple.
equino (m., Arch.) echinus.
eqüino -na (adj.) equine.
equinocial (adj.) equinoctial.
equinócio (m.) equinox.
equinociste (f.) wild mock cucumber (Echinocystis lobata).
equinococo (m., Zool.) echinococcus.
equinodermo (m., Zool.) echinoderm (sea urchin, star-fish).
equinóide (m.) echinoid, sea urchin.
equipagem (f.) ship's crew; outfit, equipment, furnishings, supplies.
equipamento (m.) equipment, accoutrement; gear, outfit.
equipar (v.t.) to equip, rig, fit out, furnish with all that is needed.

equiparado -da (adj.) on a par with. escola—, an accredited school.
equiparar (v.t.) to put on a par with; to put on the same footing with; to equate with.
equipe (f.) a football or other team.
eqüipendência (f.) equilibrium.
eqüipendente (adj.) of equal weight; in balance.
eqüipolência (f.) equipollence.
eqüipolente (adj.) equipollent, equivalent.
eqüiponderar (v.t.) to counterbalance; (v.i.,v.r.) to be of equal weight.
equipotencial (adj.) equipotential.
eqüissetáceas (f.pl., Bot.) the Equisetaceae (horsetails).
eqüisseto (m., Bot.) any horsetail (genus Equisetum), c.a. CAVALINHA.
eqüissonante (adj.) equisonant.
equitação (f.) equitation, horseback riding, horsemanship.
equitador (m.) equestrian, horseman.
eqüitativo -va (adj.) equitable.
equivalência (f.) equivalence, parity.
equivalente (adj.; m.) equivalent.—electroquímico, electrochemical equivalent.—mecânico, mechanical equivalent (of heat).
equivaler [80] (v.i.) to be equivalent (a, to).
equivocação (f.) a mistaking of one thing for another. [But not equivocation, in the sense of prevarication, which is USO DE EXPRESSÕES AMBÍGUAS PARA INDUZIR OUTRÉM EM ÊRRO].
equivocado -da (adj.) mistaken.
equivocar (v.t.) to mistake one thing for another; (v.r.) to be mistaken; to make a wrong statement. [But not to equivocate, in the sense of prevaricate, which is USAR INTENCIONALMENTE DE EXPRESSÕES AMBÍGUAS PARA ENGANAR OUTRA PESSOA; SOFISMAR; MENTIR.]
equívoco -ca (adj.) equivocal, dubious, suspicious; (m.) mistake (in meaning); oversight; ambiguity; quibble; pun.
E.R. = ESPERA RESPOSTA (answer awaited).
era (f.) era, epoch, period, age.
era, eram, éramos, eras, éreis, forms of verb SER [76].
erado -da (adj.) fully grown [animal]; ready for the butcher [cattle].
erar (v.t.) to buy up and raise yearlings for later resale.
erário (m.) exchequer, state treasury, public funds.
eratataca (f.) = MANACÁ.
erbina (f., Chem.) erbia, erbium oxide.
érbio (m., Chem.) erbium.
Érebo (m.) Erebus.
ereção (f.) erection.
eremacause (f.) eremacausis. [Webster: "Gradual oxidation of organic matter from exposure to air and moisture."]
eremita (m.,f.) eremite; hermit.—-bernardo, hermit crab.
eremitério (m.) hermitage.
eremófita (f., Phytogeog.) eremophyte, desert plant.
erepsina (f., Biochem.) erepsin.
erétil [-teis] (adj.) erectile. Var. ERÉCTIL.
eretilidade (f.) erectility. Var. ERECTILIDADE.
eretismo (m., Physiol.) erethism.
ereto -ta (adj.; irreg. p.p. of EREGIR) erect, upright, uplifted. Var. ERECTO.
eretor -triz (adj.) erecting; (m.,f.) erector, Vars. ERECTOR, ERECTRIZ.
erg (m., Physics.) erg.
ergástulo (m.) cell, dungeon.
ergmetro (m., Physics.) ergmeter.
ergofobia (f.) ergophobia.
ergógrafo (m., Psychol.) ergograph.
ergograma (m., Psychol.) ergogram.
ergômetro (m., Physics.) ergometer.
ergônio (m., Physics.) ergon.
ergotina (f., Pharm.) ergotin(e).
ergotinina (f., Chem.) ergotinin(e).
ergotismo (m.) sophistical reasoning; (Med.) ergotism.
ergotoxina [ks] (f., Chem.) ergotoxine.
erguer [5] (v.t.) to raise (up), lift, uplift; to erect, rear; (v.r.) to get up, arise (de, from).—a voz, to lift the voice.
erguido -da (adj.) lifted up, raised up.
erguimento (m.) act of lifting or raising.
erica (f., Bot.) heath.
Érica (f.) Erica.
Érico (m.) Eric.

ericáceo –cea (*adj.*, *Bot.*) ericaceous; (*f.pl.*) the heath family (*Ericaceae*).

eriçado –da (*adj.*) bristly; standing on end [hair]; bristling.

eriçar (*v.t.*) to bristle; to stand (hair) on end; (*v.r.*) to bristle.

erigir [24] (*v.t.*) to erect, raise, rear; to build.

érina (*f.*) surgeon's pincers.

erináceo –cea (*adj.*, *Zool.*) erinaceous; (*Bot.*) bristly.

erinacídeos (*m.pl.*) hedgehog family (*Erinaceidae*).

erinite (*f.*, *Min.*) erinite.

erinose (*f.*, *Plant Pathol.*) erinose.

eriômetro (*m.*, *Optics.*) eriometer.

erísimo (*m.*, *Bot.*) the Afghan erysimum (*E. perofskianum*).

erisipela (*f.*, *Med.*) erysipelas.

erisipeloso –sa (*adj.*) erysipelatous.

eritema (*m.*, *Med.*) erythema.

eritematoso –sa (*adj.*, *Med.*) erythematous. **lupo—**, lupus erythematosus.

eritreno (*m.*, *Chem.*) erythrene, 1,3-butadiene.

eritrina (*f.*, *Chem.*) erythrin; (*Bot.*) the genus (*Erythrina*) of coral beans.

eritrismo (*m.*) erythrism.

eritrite (*f.*, *Min.*) erythrite, cobalt bloom.

eritroblasto (*m.*, *Med.*, *Anat.*) erythroblast.

eritrocarpo –pa (*adj.*, *Bot.*) erythrocarpous, red-fruited.

eritrocatálise (*f.*) erythrocatalysis.

eritrócite (*m.*, *Anat.*) erythrocyte, red corpuscle.

eritrocitólise (*f.*) erythrocytolysis.

eritrocitômetro (*m.*) erythrocytometer.

eritrodextrina (*f.*, *Chem.*) erythrodextrin.

eritrófago –ga (*adj.*) erythrophagous.

eritrófilo –la (*adj.*, *Biol.*) erythrophilous.

eritrofleína (*f.*, *Chem.*) erythrophleine.

eritroglicínio (*m.*, *Chem.*) erythroglucin, erythritol.

eritróide (*adj.*) erythroid, reddish.

eritrol (*m.*, *Chem.*) erythritol.

eritrose (*f.*, *Chem.*) erythrose.

eritroxiláceas [ks] (*f.pl.*, *Bot.*) the coca family (*Erythroxylaceae*).

eritróxilo –la [ks] (adj.) having red wood; (*m.*, *Bot.*) the genus (*Erythroxylum* or *-xylon*) of cocaine trees.

E.R.M. = ESPERA RECEBER MERCÊ (praying your indulgence).

ermar (*v.t.*) to depopulate, desolate; (*v.i.*) to live like a hermit; (*v.r.*) to become like a desert.

ermida (*f.*) small chapel in the country.

ermita (*m.*) = EREMITA.

ermitão [-tãos, -tães, -tões] (*m.*) hermit; anchorite.

êrmo –ma (*adj.*) solitary, uninhabited; secluded; desolate; devoid of; (*m.*) wilderness, desert.

Ernestina (*f.*) Ernestine.

Ernesto (*m.*) Ernest.

eroder (*v.t.*) to erode.

erodido –da (*adj.*) eroded; water-worn.

eródio (*m.*, *Bot.*) the genus (*Erodium*) of heronbills.

erosão (*f.*) erosion, corrosion.

erosivo –va (*adj.*) erosive.

erótico –ca (*adj.*) erotic.

erotismo (*m.*) eroticism.

erotóforo –ra, **erotogêneo** –nea (*adj.*) erogenous.

erotomania (*f.*, *Psychopathol.*) erotomania.

erotomaníaco –ca, **erotômano** –na (*m.,f.*, *Psychopathol.*) erotomaniac.

erpe (*m.*) self-praising [= GABOLAS].

errada (*f.*) straying; error; wrong road.

erradicação (*f.*) eradication.

erradicante, **-cativo**, **-va** (*adj.*) eradicative.

erradicar (*v.t.*) to eradicate, root up [= DESARRAIGAR].

erradio –dia (*adj.*) errant, wandering; vagrant, strayed, lost.

errado –da (*adj.*) erroneous, wrong; (*m.*) a ne'er-do-well.

errante (*adj.*) erring; wayward; errant; vagrant; roving.

errar (*v.t.*) to miss, muff, fail in; to make a mistake; (*v.i.*) to stray, wander; to roam; to stroll; to err, be wrong.—**a êsmo**, to roam, ramble.—**o alvo**, to miss the target.—**o golpe**, to miss a stroke.—**o caminho**, to lose one's way; to go astray. **Errei todas as palavras**, I got all the words wrong.

errata (*f.*) errata; erratum.

errático –ca (*adj.*) erratic. **rocha—**, **bloco—**, (*Geol.*) an erratic boulder or block or rock.

erre [ér] (*m.*) the letter R.

errino –na (*adj.*, *Med.*) errhine, sternutative.

êrro (*m.*) error, mistake; bungle; sin, wrong-doing.—**de amostra**, (*Stat.*) sampling error.—**crasso**, blunder.—**de palmatória**, inexcusable mistake.—**palmar**, big mistake, gross blunder.—**padrão**, (*Stat.*) standard error.—**provável**, (*Stat.*) probable error or deviation.—**subjetivo**, (*Stat.*) subjective error. **sem temor de—**, without fear of contradiction. **salvo—ou omissão**, errors and omissions excepted.

errôneo –nea (*adj.*) erroneous, wrong, mistaken.

erubescita (*f.*, *Min.*) erubescite, bornite, purple copper ore.

eruca (*f.*, *Bot.*) rocket salad (*Eruca sativa*), c.a. FEDORENTA.

eruciforme (*adj.*) eruciform, like a caterpillar.

eructação (*f.*) eructation, belching.

eructar (*v.t.,v.i.*) to eruct, belch.

erudição (*f.*) erudition.

eruditismo (*m.*) eruditeness.

erudito –ta (*adj.*) erudite, learned, scholarly; (*m.,f.*) scholar, savant.

erupção (*f.*) eruption; skin eruption, rash.

eruptivo –va (*adj.*) eruptive.

erva (*f.*) any herb or weed; a locoweed; (*pl.*) garden greens. [Used in compound words to designate numerous plants, ranging from herbs and grasses to vines and trees, of which the following is a partial list. Many of the vernacular names apply to other species in addition to those listed.]—**abelha** = ABELHA-FLOR (an orchid).—**agulheira**, the Venus comb shepherdsneedle (*Scandix pecten-veneris*), c.a. AGULHA-DE-PASTOR.—**alheira** = ALIÁRIA.—**almiscarada**, muskroot (*Adoxa moschatellina*) c.a. ADOXA.—**almiscareira** = AGULHEIRA-MOSCADA.—**andorinha**, the pillpod euphorbia (*E. pilulifera*); the Brazilian euphorbia (*E. brasiliensis*), c.a. ERVA-DE-SANTA-LUZIA.—**aranha**, an orchid (*Listera arachnites*).—**armoles**, the garden orach (*Atriplex hortensis*).—**azêda**, Brazil begonia (*B. brasiliensis*).—**babosa** = ALOÉS.—**belida**, the creeping buttercup (*Ranunculus repens*) c.a. BOTÃO-DE-OURO.—**benta**, the common avens (*Geum urbanum*), c.a. SANAMUNDA, CARIOFILADA-MAIOR.—**besteira**, the fetid or bearsfoot hellebore (*Helleborus foetidus*), c.a. HELÉBORO-FÉTIDO.—**bezerra**, common snapdragon (*Antirrhinum majus*), c.a. BÔCA-DE-DRAGÃO, BÔCA-DE-LEÃO.—**borboleta** = ABELHA-FLOR (an orchid).—**brasileira** = CATINGA-DE-PRÊTO.—**canuda**, the field horsetail (*Equisetum arvense*).—**canudo** = CAVALINHA.—**carneira**, meadow fescue (*Festuca elatior*).—**castelhana**, Italian ryegrass (*Lolium multiflorum*).—**cicutária**, the bur beakchervil (*Anthriscus vulgaris*).—**cidreira**, the common balm (*Melissa officinalis*); the lemonverbena (*Lippia critriodora*).—**coalheira**, the yellow bedstraw (*Galium verum*).—**coentrinha**, wild carrot (*Daucus carota*); also = CENOURA.—**colégio** (or **-do-diabo**), an elephantsfoot (*Elephantopus tomentosus*).—**confeiteira**, a bedstraw (*Galium valantia*).—**contraveneno**, the white swallowwort (*Cynanchum vincetoxicum*).—**contra-vermes** = CATINGA-DE-MULATA.—**cruz**, West Indian spigelia (*S. anthelmia*), c.a. LOMBRIGUEIRA.—**da-américa** (or **-do-canadá**, or **-dos-cachos-da-índia**) = CARURU-DE-CACHO.—**da-costa** = FÔLHA-DA-FORTUNA.—**da-guiné** = CAPIM-GUINÉ.—**da-lua** = LUNÁRIA.—**da-muda**, prostrate knotweed (*Polygonum aviculare*).—**das-azeitonas** = NÊVEDA.—**das-bermudas**, Bermuda grass (*Cynodon dactylon*), c.a. CAPIM-DE-BURRO.—**das-crianças** = ABECEDÁRIA (Pará cress).—**das-escaldadelas**, a figwort (*Scrophularia auriculata-aquatica*).—**das-sete-sangrias** = SARGAÇA-HÍSPIDA or SARGACINHA.—**das-verrugas** = CELIDÔNIA.—**de-besteiros** = EPIMÉDIO, ERVA-BESTEIRA.—**de-bicho**, the bitter smartweed (*Polygonum acre*), c.a. PIMENTA-D'ÁGUA, CATAIA.—**de-bugre** (or **-de-tiú**), a Brazilian tree (*Casearia sylvestris*) of the Indian-plum family, whose leaves and bark are medicinal.—**de-cabrita** = AMARELINHA.—**de-cardo-amarelo** = CARDO-SANTO.—**de-chumbo**, the woevine (*Cassytha americana*).—**de-cobra** = CAÁ-CAMBUÍ.—**de-empigem**, a yelloweyegrass (*Xyris laxifolia*), c.a. BOTÃO-DE-OURO.—**de-esteira** = CAPIM-DE-ESTEIRA (a bulrush).—**de-febra** = CAPIM-DO-CAMPO (Kentucky bluegrass).—**de-gêlo** = FÔLHA-DE-GÊLO.—**de-gota**, a buttonbush (*Cephalotus strigosus*).—**de-lagarto**, a tournefortia (*T. laevigata*), c.a. LÍNGUA-DE-TEJÚ.—**de-louco**, the climbing plumbago (*P. scandens*).—**de-maleitas** = ÉSULA.—**de-nossa-senhora** = CIPÓ-DE-

COBRA.—**-de-paina**=CAPITÃO-DE-SALA.—**-de-pântano**, a waterplantain (*Alisma floribundum*); an arrowhead (*Sagittaria brasiliensis*).—**-de-passarinho**, mistletoe.— **-de-rato** = CATINGUEIRO-DE-FÔLHA-MIÚDA.—**-de-santa-bárbara**, a nightshade (*Solanum argentum*); bitter wintercress (*Barbarea vulgaris*).—**-de-santa-catarina** (or **-não-me-toques**), a touchmenot or snapweed (*Impatiens noli-tangere*).—**-de-santa-lúcia**, a dayflower (*Commelina sulcata*).—**-de-santa-luzia**, the Brazil euphorbia (*E. brasiliensis*), c.a. ERVA-ANDORINHA.—**-de-santa-maria**, the wormseed goosefoot (*Chenopodium ambrosioides*).—**-de-santana**, an ironweed called FÔLHA-DE-SANTANA (q.v.), a kuhnia (*K. arguta*); also = FURA-PAREDE.—**-de-são-cristóvão**=CIMICÍFUGA, ACTÉIA.—**-de-são-joão**, common St. Johnswort (*Hypericum perforatum*), c.a. MILFURADA; the tropic ageratum (*A. conyzoides*), c.a. CATINGA-DE-BODE; the mugwort wormwood (*Artemesia vulgaris*), c.a. ARTEMÍSIA; the sweet yarrow (*Achillea ageratum*), c.a. AGERATO.—**-de-são-lourenço** = ERVA-FÉRREA.—**-de-sapo** = CORAÇÃO-DE-ESTUDANTE (a begonia). —**-de-sapo-vermelha** = BEGONIA-SANGUE.—**-de-saracura**, a begonia (*B. brasila*).—**-de-veado** = FAXINA-VERMELHA.—**-de-vidro** = LÍNGUA-DE-SAPO.—**-dedal** = DEDALEIRA (foxglove).—**-diurética**, common pipissewa or princespine (*Chimaphila umbellata*).—**-do-amor**, clover [= TREVO].—**-do-bicho** = ACATAIA.—**-do-brejo** (or **-do-pântano**) = CHAPÉU-DE-COURO.—**-do-capitão**, the largeleaf pennywort (*Hydrocotyle bonariensis*), c.a. ACARI-ÇOBA, CAIRUÇU.—**-do-cardeal**, prickly comfrey (*Symphytum asperum*), c.a. CONSÓLIDA.—**-do-chá**, the broomjute sida (*S. rhombifolia*).—**-do-diabo** = CAÁ-POMONGA; also = ERVA-COLÉGIO.—**-do-fígado**, the sowthistle tasselflower (*Emilia sonchifolia*).—**-do-orvalho** = ORVALHO-DA-AURORA (iceplant).—**-do-pará** = CAPIM-DO-PARÁ.—**-do-sabão**, a castorbean (*Ricinus saponarius*).—**-doce**, the anise (*Pimpinella anisum*).—**-dos-besteiros** = ERVA-BESTEIRA.—**-dos-burros** = CÍRIO-DO-NORTE (evening primrose).—**-do-bicho** = FAVÁRIA.—**-dos-cancros** (or **-dos-cachos-da-índia**), common pokeberry (*Phytolacca americana*), c.a. GAIA-MOÇA, TINTUREIRA.—**-dos-feridos**, broadleaf canna (*C. latifolia*), c.a. CAETÊ-GRANDE, COQUILHO.—**-dos-gatos**, catnip (*Nepeta cataria*), c.a. GATÁRIA, ERVA-GATO.—**-dos-golpes**, common yarrow (*Achillea millefolium*), c.a. MIL-FÔLHAS, MILEFÓLIO.— **-dos-pegamassos** = BARDANA-MENOR (a burdock).—**-dutra** = CIPÓ-CABELUDO.—**-elefante** = CAPIM-ELEFANTE.— **-espirradeira**, the sneezewort yarrow (*Achillea ptarmica*).—**-fedegosa**, sickle senna (*Cassia tora*), c.a FEDEGOSA.—**-fedorenta** = CUARI-BRAVO (a marigold).— **-férrea**, common selfheal (*Prunella vulgaris*); carpet bugle (*Ajuga reptans*).—**-fome**, the pepperweed whitetop (*Cardaria draba*).—**-formigueira** = AMBRÓSIA.—**-gigante** = ACANTO-MOLE.—**-gritadeira** = DOURADÃO.—**-gorda** = FÔLHA-GORDA.—**-grossa**, an elephantsfoot (*Elephantopus scaber*).—**-impigem**, bloodroot or puccoon (*Sanguinaria canadensis*).—**-lanar**, common velvetgrass (*Holcus lanatus*). —**-lombrigueira** = ABRÓTONO-MACHO. —**-luiza** = LÚCIA-LIMA.—**-macaé** (or **-santos-filho**), the Siberian motherwort (*Leonurus sibiricus*), c.a. MARROIO.—**-maleiteira**, the sun euphorbia (*E. helioscopia*).—**-mata-pulgas**, the branching canaryclover (*Corycnium suffruticosum*).— **-mate**, Paraguay tea (*Ilex paraguariensis*), c.a. MATE. —**-minuana** = CAPARROSA (primrose).—**-molar**, German velvetgrass (*Holcus mollis*).—**-moleirinha** = FUMÁRIA.— **-moura**, the black nightshade (*Solanum nigra*), c.a. ERVA-DE-BICHO, PIMENTA-D'ÁGUA.—**-noiva** = ALQUE-QUENJE.—**-noiva-de-perú** = CAMAPU.—**-passarinheira**, a hemiparasitic tropical plant (*Loranthus engenioides*) which infests orange trees.—**-pessegueira**, spotted ladysthumb (*Polygonum persicaria*), c.a. PERSICÁRIA, PESSE-GUELHA.—**-picão**, the railway beggarticks (*Bidens pilosa*), c.a. CUAMBU.—**-pimenteira**, a pepperweed (*Lepidium latifolium*), c.a. LEPÍDIO.—**-pinheira-de-rosa** = BRILHANTINA.—**-piolheira** = ESTAFISÁGRIA (larkspur). —**-pipi** = GUINÉ.—**-pombinha**, common columbine (*Aquilegia vulgaris*), c.a. ANCÓLIA; the flyroost leafflower (*Phyllanthus niruri*), c.a. ARREBENTA-PEDRA.—**-preá**, an ironweed (*Vernonia scorpioides*).—**-prego**, a nailwort (*Paronychia echinata*).—**-pulgueira**, the marshpepper smartweed (*Polygonum hydropiper*).—**-real** = ALFAVACA-CHEIROSA (sweet basil).—**-roberta**, the herbrobert geranium (*G. robertianum*).—**-saboeira**, bouncingbet (*Saponaria officinalis*), c.a. SABOEIRA, SABONEIRA.— **-sangue** (or **-do-fígado**), Italian bugloss (*Anchusa*

azurea), c.a. LÍNGUA-DE-VACA.—**-santa**, tobacco plant; also = CIPÓ-CAPADOR.—**-silvina**, a polypody (*Polypodium vaccinifolium*).—**-sofia**, flixweed tansymustard (*Descurainia sophia*).—**-tostonera**, a maidenhair fern (*Adiantum reniforme*).—**-traqueira**, the bladder silene (*S. cucubalus*).—**-turca**, the common burstwort (*Herniaria glabra*), c.a. HERNÍOLA.—**-ulmeira**, the queen-of-the-meadow or European meadowsweet (*Filipendula ulmaria*), c.a. ULMÁRIA, BARBA-DE-BODE.

ervaçal (*m.*) grass-covered area; weeds.
ervado **-da** (*adj.*) grassy; poisoned [arrow]; of an animal, poisoned by some weed; (*slang*) loaded (with money).
ervadura (*f.*) = CURARE.
ervagem (*f.*) herbage; pasture land; greens, curare (poison).
erval (*m.*) an area abounding in ERVA-MATE trees or shrubs.
ervanaria (*f.*) medicinal herbs store.
ervanário (*m.*) = HERBANÁRIO.
ervanço (*m.*, *Bot.*) chickpea (*Cicer arietinum*); also = PERPÉTUA-DA-MATA.
ervar (*v.t.*) to poison (arrows, etc.); (*v.r.*) to suffer poisoning from some herb.
ervário (*m.*) = HERBÁRIO.
ervatão (*m.*, *Bot.*) a parsley (*Petroselium macedonium*).
ervatário **-ria** (*m.,f.*) person who gathers and sells medicinal herbs.
ervateiro (*m.*) dealer in ERVA-MATE; man who gathers and prepares MATE leaves.
ervilha (*f.*) garden pea (*Pisum sativum*), or its seed.—**-de-angola** = GUANDU.—**-de-cheiro**, sweetpea (*Lathyrus odoratus*).—**-de-pombo** = ÓROBO.—**-de-sete-anos** = GUANDU. —**-de-vaca** = FEIJÃO-DE-VACA.—**-do-congo** = GUANDU.— **-forrageira** (—**-da-primavera**, —**-de-lebre**, —**-do-campo**, —**-miúda**), are all the field pea (*Pisum arvense*).
ervilhaca (*f.*, *Bot.*) the common or fodder vetch (*Vicia sativa*); bird vetch (*V. cracca*), c.a. CISIRÃO.—**-da-primavera** = ERVILHA-FORRAGEIRA.—**-de-narbona**, the Narbone or French vetch (*Vicia narbonensis*).—**-peluda** (—**-das-areias**), the hairy or Russian vetch (*Vicia villosa*).
ervinha (*f.*, *Bot.*) the litmus roccella (*R. tinctoria*); also = ALFAVACA.—**-de-parida**, a woodruff (*Asperula cyanea*).
ervoeira (*f.*, *colloq.*) prostitute.
ervoso **-sa** (*adj.*) herbous.
es-, look also under **ex-** and **ez-**.
ES = ESPÍRITO SANTO (State of).
és, form of SER [76].
esbaforido **-da** (*adj.*) breathless; blown, puffing and blowing; winded; worn out.
esbaforir-se (*v.r.*) to get out of breath; to wear oneself out.
esbagaçar (*v.t.*) to break into pieces.
esbagachar (*v.t.*) to bare the chest.
esbagoar (*v.t.*) to remove seeds from (fruit); to pick fruit from (a bunch); (*v.i.,v.r.*) to drop seeds.
esbaldar-se (*v.r.*, *slang*) to enjoy oneself rowdily, let oneself go.
esbandalhado **-da** (*adj.*) strayed; shattered; ragged.
esbandalhar (*v.t.*) to break up, shatter, destroy; (*v.r.*) to scatter.
esbanjador **-dora** (*adj.*) squandering, dissipated, prodigal; (*m.,f.*) squanderer, spendthrift; wastrel.
esbanjamento (*m.*) squandering, waste.
esbanjar (*v.t.*) to squander, waste, dissipate.
esbarrada (*f.*) a scuffle, skidding halt (as by a horse).
esbarrancada (*f.*), **-do** (*m.*) a gully, washout or cave-in.
esbarrão (*m.*) collision, bump.
esbarrar (*v.i.*)—**com**, to run into, crash into, collide with, bump into.—**contra**, to knock against, strike against. —**em**, to run into, bump into.—**em um obstáculo**, to come up against (be stopped by) an obstacle.
esbarro (*m.*) bump, jostle; (*Mach.*) stop; (*colloq.*) reprimand.
esbarrondar (*v.t.*) to tear down; to cause to cave in; (*v.i.,v.r.*) to crumble, fall away.
esbater (*v.t.*) to cause to stand out (in relief); to shade from one color into another; to attenuate (colors).
esbeiçar (*v.t.*) to break the edge or lip (as of a teacup); to thrust out the lips; (*v.i.*) to hang over the edge of.—**com**, to touch the edge of, border on.
esbelteza(a) [tê] (*f.*) elegance, gracefulness; slenderness.
esbelto **-ta** (*adj.*) elegant, graceful; handsome; well-proportioned; svelte, slender, tall, willowy, lithsome.
esbirro (*m.*) bailiff, myrmidon; a piece of timber used as a temporary prop under a building, etc.

esboçado -da (adj.) sketched (out), outlined.
esboçar (v.t.) to sketch, outline to design; to delineate; (v.r.) to appear in outline.
esboceto [cê] (m.) small sketch.
esbôço (m.) rough sketch, outline.
esbodegado -da (adj.) slack, lax; dirty; drunk; careless; dog-tired.
esbodegar (v.t.) to waste, squander; (v.r.) to become ESBODEGADO.
esbofar (v.t.) to jade, exhaust, wear out; (v.r.) to knock oneself out.
esbofetear (v.t.) to strike another person in the face with the hand or fist; to buffet.
esborcinar (v.t.) to chip, break off pieces of (a statue, etc.).
esbordoar (v.t.) to bludgeon.
esbórnia (f.) drunken bout; spree.
esboroamento (m.) crumbling (of a wall, etc.).
esboroar (v.t.) to reduce to dust, efface, destroy; (v.r.) to crumble into dust.
esboroável (adj.) friable.
esborrachado -da (adj.) squashed, crushed.
esborrachar (v.t.) to squash, crush, flatten; (v.r.) to be squashed (by falling, as a ripe tomato).
esborrar (v.i.) to spill over; (v.t.) to skim (boiling cane sirup).
esborrifar (v.t.) to spatter, splash [= BORRIFAR].
esbranquiçado -da (adj.) whitish, whitened; hoary.
esbrasear (v.t.) to burn (as does the sun); to make red (the face); to inflame (the temper, spirit, etc.); (v.i.,v.r.) to become fiery red; to become inflamed.
esbravear, esbravecer, esbravejar (v.i.) to shout angrily; to become angry; to rave; to bluster.—contra, to cry out against.
esbregue (m., slang) fracas, shindy; reprimand, dressing down.
esbrugar (v.) = ESBURGAR.
esbugalhado -da (adj.) pop-eyed.
esbugalhar (v.t.) to bug out (the eyes).
esbulhado -da (adj.) despoiled, robbed, plundered.
esbulhar (v.t.) to fleece, rob; to usurp; to deprive (another) of rights, possessions, etc.; to despoil; to "gyp," do (someone) out of something.
esbulho (m.) robbery; plunder; dispossession, usurpation.
esburacado -da (adj.) full of holes.
esburacar (v.t.) to fill with holes, ref. esp. to streets or buildings.
esburgar (v.t.) to remove the peel or husk of; to pick bones. Var. ESBRUGAR.
esburnir (v.t.) to give (something) grudgingly.
esc. = ESCUDO(S)—(a Port. coin).
Esc. = ESCOLA (School, College).
escabeche (m. Cookery) marinade; (fig.) disguise.
escabelado -da (adj.) = DESCABELADO.
escabelar (v.t.) to loose, ruffle or dishevel the hair: to pull out the hair of; (v.r.) to muss one's hair.
escabêlo (m.) footstool [= ESCANO].
escabichar (v.t.) to examine closely; to pick (teeth, nose, nails).
escabiosa (f., Bot.) scabious (Scabiosa).—-dos-jardins, sweet scabiosa (S. atropurpurea), c.a. SUSPIRO-DOS-JARDINS.
escabiose (f.) scabies, itch [= BOSTELA].
escabioso -sa (adj.) having the itch, mangy.
escabreado -da (adj.) distrustful; exasperated; repentant.
escabrear (v.t.) to annoy; to infuriate; (v.i.,v.r.) to become furious; to rear up (as a goat); to clamber.
escabrosidade (f.) roughness; difficulty.
escabroso -sa (adj.) scabrous, rough; harsh, beset with difficulties; improper, indecorous.
escabujar (v.i.) to squirm, struggle.
escabulhar (v.t.) to remove the peel or husk of [= ES-BURGAR].
escachar (v.t.) to split, cleave; to spread apart; to squelch.
escachoar (v.i.) to boil, foam, bubble; to fall (as a waterfall).
escacholar (v.t., colloq.) to break the head of.
escachôo (m.) act of falling (as a waterfall).
escada (f.) stairs, ladder; steps; fig., a means of ascending; (colloq.) whale's belly.—de bombeiro, fire-truck ladder. —de caracol,—de parafuso,—em espiral,—torcida, spiral stairs.—de incêndio, or de socorro, fire escape.—-de-jabuti, a bauhinia (B. alata or B. rutilans).—-de-jacó, Jacob's ladder; (Bot.) Greek valerian polemonium (P. caeruleum).—de mão, stepladder.—de pedreiro,

mason's ladder.—de pintor, painter's ladder.—de tesoura, a double (hinged) ladder.—-do-céu, a Brazilian fern (Blechnum brasiliense).—portátil, portable stepladder.—rolante, escalator.
escadaria (f.) stairway, staircase; flight of stairs; steps.
escadear (v.t.) to provide with steps; to give a stepped appearance to (a haircut).
escadeirar (v.t.) to fell (with blows); to cut open (slaughtered cattle). Cf. DESCADEIRAR.
escadelecer (v.i.) to snooze [= COCHILAR].
escadinha (f.) a little ladder.—-do-céu, a fern (Polypodium loriceum).
escadote (m.) a small four-legged stepladder.
escafa (f., Anat.) scapha.
escafandrar (v.t.) to delve deeply into (a matter).
escafandrista (m.,f.) deep-sea diver.
escafandro (m.) diving suit.
escafeder-se (v.r.) to bolt, run away, skedaddle, take to one's heels.
escafocefalia (f.) scaphocephaly.
escafocéfalo -la (adj.) scaphocephalous.
escafóide (adj.; m., Anat.) scaphoid.
escaiola (f.) scagliola, imitation marble.
escala (f.) scale (for measuring but not for weighing, which is BALANÇA); relative dimensions; degree; gradation; ladder; port of call; (Mus.) gamut.—cromática, (Music) chromatic scale.—de dureza, Mohs' scale (of hardness).—diatônica, (Music) diatonic scale. em grande—, on a grand (great, large) scale. sem—, nonstop (as an airplane flight).
escalabro (m.) squandering; ruin.
escalada (f.) act of scaling, etc. See ESCALAR; escalation.
escalador -dora (adj.) scaling; (m.,f.) scaler; fish scaler.
escalafrio (m.) = CALAFRIO.
escalamento (m.) = ESCALADA.
escalão (m.) stair step. em—, in echelon.
escalar (v.t.) to scale, climb; to assault, assail, storm; to assign (persons) to duty; to scale (fish).
escalavrar (v.t.) to scarify, scratch, scar, batter.
escalda (f.) a hot sauce; act of scalding.
escaldadela (f.) a scalding; a bitter lesson [= ESCALDA-DURA].
escaldadiço -ça (adj.) easily burned or scalded; fig., very impressionable.
escaldador -dora (adj.) scalding; (m.,f.) scalder.
escaldadouro (m.) a vessel for scalding.
escaldadura (f.) = ESCALDÃO; (Plant Pathol.) scald.
escalda-mar (f.) young sororoca (Spanish mackerel).
escalda-mão (f.) the common ginger lily (Hedychium coronarium).
escaldante (adj.) scalding, burning.
escaldão (m.) act or result of scalding; a scald; a rebuke.
escalda-pés (m.) a hot footbath.
escaldar (v.t.,v.i.) to scald, burn; (v.r.) to burn oneself. Gato escaldado tem medo de água fria, A scalded cat dreads cold water; Once bitten, twice shy.
escalda-rabo (m., colloq.) a hot rebuke.
escaldo (m.) plant scald.
escaleno -na (adj., Geom., Anat.) scalene; (m., Anat.) scalenus.
escaler [lér] (m.) gig, small boat.
escalfar (v.t.) to poach (eggs) in hot water.
escalheiro (m.) English hawthorn (Crataegus oxycantha), c.a. ESPINHEIRO-ALVAR-DE-CASCA-VERDE, ESPINHEIRO-ORDINÁRIO, PILRITEIRO, PIRLITEIRO.
escalinata (f.) a flight of stairs.
escalonado -da (adj.) staggered. polia—, stepped pulley.
escalonar (v.t.) to stagger (form into an echelon).
escalpar (v.t.) to scalp.
escalpelar, escalpelizar (v.t.) to dissect (with a scalpel); to examine carefully part by part.
escalpêlo (m.) scalpel.
escalpo (m.) scalp.
escalracho (m.) torpedo grass (Panicum repens).
escalrichado -da (adj.) insipid.
escalvado -da (adj.) bald, hairless; bare, treeless [= DES-CALVADO].
escalvar (v.t.) to render bald or bare [= DESCALVAR].
escama (f.) scale (of fish, reptiles, skin, plants, etc.).
escamar (v.t.) to scale (fish, etc.).
escambar (v.) = TROCAR.
escambroeiro (m.) the common buckthorn (Rhammus cathartica).
escameado -da (adj.) covered with scales.

escamento –ta (*adj.*) = ESCAMOSO.
escamônea (*f.*) scammony glorybind (*Convolvulus scammonia*).—de-montpellier, (*Pharm.*) cynanchum.
escamonina (*f., Chem.*) jalapin.
escamoso –sa (*adj.*) scaly; flaky.
escamotar (*v.i.*) to conjure, perform tricks; (*v.t.*) to swipe, snatch, pinch; (*v.r.*) to make one's getaway.
escamoteção (*f.*) magic trick, palming, conjuring; sleight of hand; swiping, snatching, pilfering.
escamotear (*v.*) = ESCAMOTAR.
escamoteável (*adj.*) retractable (as the landing gear of an airplane); that can be hidden away (as a folding bed hinged to the back of a closet door).
escampado –da (*adj.*) = DESCAMPADO.
escampar (*v.*) = ESTIAR.
escanção (*m.*) cupbearer.
escâncara (*f.*) quality of being manifest, clear, patent. às—s, wide-openly, publicly.
escancarado –da (*adj.*) wide-open (as doors).
escancarar (*v.t.*) to fling open; to open wide.
escancelar (*v.t.*) to open wide (the eyes or mouth).
escanchado –da (*adj.*) straddling, astride.
escanchar (*v.t.*) to spread, open wide; (*v.r.*) to straddle.
escandalizador –dora (*adj.*) scandalizing; (*m.,f.*) scandalizer.
escandalizar (*v.t.*) to scandalize, offend; (*v.r.*) to take offense.
escândalo (*m.*) scandal; bad example; uproar, commotion; outrage. abafar um—, to hush up a scandal. dar or fazer—, to cause tongues to wag. fazer um—, to kick up a row, make a scene, raise a scandal. pedra de—, stumbling block.
escandaloso –sa (*adj.*) scandalous, disgraceful, shameful; shocking; unseemly.
escandescência (*f.*) state of being aglow.
escandescente (*adj.*) glowing.
escandescer (*v.t.*) to set aglow; to excite, inflame; (*v.i.,v.r.*) to glow.
Escandinávia (*f.*) Scandinavia.
escandinavo –va (*adj.; m.,f.*) Scandinavian.
escândio (*m., Chem.*) scandium.
escandir (*v.t.*) to scan (verse); to enunciate clearly; to scan, scrutinize.
escanelado –da (*adj.*) slim-legged; straight-limbed.
escangalhado –da (*adj.*) broken up, smashed, out of order, "busted."
escangalhar (*v.t.*) to break (up), shatter, smash (up), ruin; (*v.r.*) to get broken, out of order.
escangalho (*m.*) a steep retaining wall.
escangotar (*v.t., colloq.*) to seize and shake by the scruff.
escanhoar-se (*v.t.,v.r.*) to shave closely.
escanifrado –da (*adj.*) scrawny, skinny, raw-boned.
escanifrar (*v.t.*) to make thin or scrawny.
escaninho (*m.*) pigeonhole (in a desk); hiding place, cubbyhole.
escano (*m.*) footstool [= ESCABÊLO].
escansão (*f., Pros.*) scansion.
escanteio (*m.*) corner (in soccer).
escantilhado –da (*adj.*) bevelled.
escantilhão (*m.*) a standard gauge for sizes, weights, measures, etc. de—, headlong, hastily.
escantilhar (*v.t., Carp.*) to bevel edges.
escanzelado –da (*adj.*) thin as a starving dog; skinny.
escapada, escapadela (*f.*) escapade.
escapamento (*m.*) escapement (of a timepiece or typewriter); exhaust (of an automobile); leakage (of gas, etc.).
escapar (*v.i.*) to escape (a, de, from); to slip, be omitted; (*v.r.*) to bolt, flee (de, from; para, to).—de boa, to have a narrow escape. Escapou por pouco, or por um triz, He had a close shave, hair-breadth escape.
escapatória (*f.*) loophole, "out," pretext, subterfuge.
escape (*adj.; m.*) = ESCAPO.
escapelada (*f.*) shucking (of corn).
escapelar (*v.t.*) to shuck (corn).
escapo –pa (*adj.*) escaped, free, safe; (*m.*) escapement (of a watch or typewriter); shaft of a feather; (*Arch.*) fillet.
escapula (*f.*) escape; pretext, an "out" [= ESCAPADELA; ESCAPATÓRIA].
escápula, tenterhook; wall hook; hammock hook; screw hook; brace, stay.
escapulal, escapular (*adj.*) scapular.
escapulário (*m., Eccl., Surg.*) a scapular.
escapulida (*f.*) escapade, runaway.

escapulir (*v.i.*) to escape (de, from); to bolt, run away; (*v.r.*) to effect one's escape, skip out, slink off (away).—se de, to give the slip to.
escaquear (*v.t.*) to checker.
escaques (*m.pl.*) squares (of a checkered pattern or checkerboard).
escara (*f.*) scab.—de decúbito, bedsore.
escarabeu (*m.*) scarab, beetle [= ESCARAVELHO].
escarabídeo –dea (*adj.; m., Zool.*) scarabaeid, scarabaean.
escarabocho [bô] (*m.*) crude drawing; scrawl.
escarafunchar (*v.t.*) to dig at, pick at; to investigate.
escarambar-se (*v.r.*) to dry up and crack (as the soil); to wrinkle (as the skin).
escaramuça (*f.*) skirmish.
escaramuçar (*v.i.*) to skirmish.
escarapelar (*v.t.,v.i.,v.r.*) to scratch with the nails.
escaravelhar (*v.i.*) to walk or move like a beetle.
escaravelho [ê] (*m.*) scarab, dung beetle, tumble bug [= BOSTEIRO, ESCARABEU].
escarça (*f., Veter.*) corn [= BLEIMA].
escarçar (*v.t.*) to remove honeycombs from beehives; (*v.r., Veter.*) to suffer from corn.
escarcear (*v.i.*) of waves, to pitch and toss; of a horse, to toss the head.
escarcela (*f.*) leather pouch.
escarcéu (*m.*) billow, wave; row, riot, hullabaloo; exaggeration. fazer grandes—s, to make much ado about nothing.
escarcha (*f.*) hoarfrost.
escarchar (*v.t.*) to cover with rime; to make rough.
escardilho (*m.*) a weeding hoe.
escareador (*m.*) reamer; a countersink (tool).
escarear (*v.t.*) to countersink; to ream.
escarificação (*f.*) scarifying.
escarificador (*m.*) scarifier; scarificator.
escarificar (*v.t.*) to scarify; to cultivate (the soil).
escarioso –sa (*adj., Bot.*) scarious.
escarlate (*adj.; m.*) scarlet, bright red (color, cloth).
escarlatina (*f., Med.*) scarlet fever.
escarmentado –da (*adj.*) bitterly disillusioned; wise through costly experience; burned, punished.
escarmentar (*v.t.*) to punish severely; to reprimand harshly; (*v.r.*) to take heed, be warned by experience; to burn one's fingers.
escarmento (*m.*) rebuke, reproof; punishment; painful lesson, costly experience; disappointment.
escarnar (*v.t.*) to strip (a bone) of its flesh; to scrape (hides).
escarnecedor –dora (*adj.*) derisive, mocking, contemptuous; (*m.,f.*) scoffer, scorner.
escarnecer (*v.t.*) to scoff, jeer, sneer (de, at); to deride, mock, taunt; to rail (de, at or against).
escarnecido –da (*adj.*) scoffed at, mocked.
escarnecimento (*m.*) derision, mockery.
escarnecível (*adj.*) deserving of contempt.
escarninho –nha (*adj.*) scornful, derisive, mocking, contemptuous.
escárnio (*m.*) scorn, sneer, derision, mockery. gesto de—, a taunting gesture.
escarola (*f.*) escarole, endive.
escarpa (*f.*) scarp, cliff, steep slope.
escarpado –da (*adj.*) steep, bluff.
escarpadura (*f.*), escarpamento (*m.*) escarpment.
escarpar (*v.t.*) to scarp, slope (a bank).
escarpim (*m.*) pump (low shoe with no fasteners); dancing shoe.
escarradeira (*f.*) cuspidor, spittoon.
escarrado –da (*adj.*) hawked up, expectorated.
escarranchado –da (*adj.*) astride, straddled.
escarranchar-se (*v.r.*) to straddle, bestride; to sprawl.
escarrapachar (*v.t.*) to straddle; to spread the legs; (*v.r.*) to sprawl.
escarrar (*v.i.*) to expectorate, hawk up, spit out.
escarro (*m.*) phlegm, mucus.
escarva (*f., Carp.*) scarf joint.
escarvar (*v.t.*) to paw the ground (as a horse); (*Carp.*) to scarf.
escassamente (*adv.*) scarcely, barely.
escassear (*v.i.*) to grow scarce or less frequent; (*v.t.*) to withhold, curtail.
escassez [sêz] (*f.*) scarcity, lack, dearth.
escasso –sa (*adj.*) scarce, rare; scanty, sparse, thin.
escatel (*m., Mach.*) keyway; splineway.
escatelador (*m., Mach.*) slotter.

escatelar (*v.t.*, *Mach.*) to slot; to spline.
escatimar (*v.t.*) to grudge.
escatologia (*f.*) scatology; (*Theol.*) eschatology.
escavação (*f.*) excavation.
escavadeira (*f.*) mechanical digger or shovel.
escavacar (*v.t.*) to excavate, dig [=CAVAR]; to hew, chip, split (wood, etc.); to shatter, shiver; to destroy.
escavador –dora (*adj.*) excavating, digging; (*m.,f.*) excavator, digger; fig., one who digs up information; (*f.*) steam shovel.
escavar (*v.t.*) to excavate, dig (up, out); to hollow out (as a log); fig., to dig up clues, information, etc.; (*v.r.*) to become hollow.
escaveirado –da (*adj.*) skeleton-thin, skinny, emaciated.
escaveirar (*v.t.*) to render very thin.
escirpo (*m.*) bulrush (*Scirpus*); = JUNCO.
esclarecer (*v.t.*) to light, illumine, give light to; to enlighten, inform; to clarify, explain, clear up; (*v.r.*) to be enlightened.
esclarecido –da (*adj.*) light; enlightened; illustrious.
esclarecimento (*m.*) elucidation, clearing up; enlightenment.
esclareia (*f.*, *Bot.*) clary sage (*Salvia sclarea*).
escleral (*f.*, *Biol.*) scleroid, hard, indurated; fibrous.
esclerênquima (*m.*, *Bot.*) sclerenchyma.
esclereritrina (*f.*, *Chem.*) sclererythrin.
escléria (*f.*, *Bot.*) the genus (*Scleria*) of razor sedges.
esclerismo (*m.*, *Med.*) induration of an organ.
esclerite (*f.*, *Med.*) scleritis.
esclerodermia (*f.*, *Med.*) scleroderma.
escleroma (*m.*, *Med.*) scleroma.
escleromério (*m.*, *Anat.*, *Zool.*) scleromere.
esclerômetro (*m.*, *Min.*) sclerometer.
escleropatia (*f.*) = ESCLEROSE.
escleroproteína (*f.*) = PROTEÍNA.
esclerosado –da (*adj.*, *Med.*) sclerosed.
escleroscópio (*m.*, *Metal.*) scleroscope.
esclerose (*f.*, *Med.*) sclerosis.
escleroso –sa (*adj.*) sclerous, hard, indurated.
esclerótica (*f.*, *Anat.*) sclera.
esclerotomia (*f.*, *Surg.*) sclerotomy.
esclerotinia (*f.*, *Plant Pathol.*) sclerotiniose.
esclerotite (*f.*, *Med.*) sclerotitis, scleritis.
esclusa (*f.*) canal lock.—**de ar**, air lock.
escoação (*f.*) drainage; flowage.
escoadeira (*f.*) drain pipe.
escoadouro (*m.*) drain, sewer, gutter; outlet; drain pipe.
escoamento (*m.*) draining, drainage, flowage; watershed; outlet.
escoar (*v.t.*) to drain (off); to discharge; (*v.i.*) to flow off or away; to slip away or by; to ooze, seep, trickle (away); (*v.r.*) to ooze out, leak away; to slip out or away.
escocês –sa (*adj.*) Scotch, Scottish; (*m.*) Scot, Scotchman; plaid cloth; (*f.*) Scotchwoman; Scottish reel.
escócia (*f.*, *Arch.*) scotia; Scotland.
escoda (*f.*) stone-cutter's hammer, having an indented face.
escodar (*v.t.*) to dress (stone, skins, lumber).
escogitar (*v.*) = EXCOGITAR.
escoicear (*v.t.*) to kick; to insult, mistreat; (*v.i.*) to kick. Var. ESCOUCEAR.
escoimar (*v.t.*) to absolve (of blame, censure); to free (of impurities).—**-se de**, to be free of.
escol [-cóis] (*m.*) the choice, the pick, the best of anything.
escola (*f.*) school, college; student body; faculty; teaching method; school of thought.—**de aprendizagem**, training school, esp. in manual arts.—**de enfermagem**, school of nursing.—**dominical**, Sunday School.—**de esgrima**, fencing school.—**equiparada**, an accredited State or Federal District school.—**normal**, normal taechers' college.—**particular**, private school.—**primária**, elementary school.—**profissional**, manual arts training school.—**rural**, agricultural college.—**secundária**, secondary school.—**superior**, university college.—**veterinária**, veterinary college.
escolado –da (*adj.*) schooled, wise, sharp.
escolar (*adj.*) scholastic; (*m.,f.*) scholar, student [= ALUNO, ESTUDANTE].
escolástico –ca (*adj.*; *m.*) scholastic; (*f.*) scholasticism.
escolecita (*f.*, *Min.*) scolecite.
escolecite (*f.*) = APENDICITE.
escolecófago –ga (*adj.*, *Zool.*) feeding on worms.
escolecospório (*m.*, *Bot.*) scolecospore.
escólex [ks], **escolece** (*m.*, *Zool.*) scolex.

escolha [ô] (*f.*) choice, selection, option; an inferior grade of coffee, beans, rice, etc. à—, with freedom of choice.
escolhedeira (*f.*) a wool carding machine.
escolhedor –dora (*adj.*) choosing; (*m.,f.*) chooser.
escolher (*v.t.*) to choose, pick out, select.—**a dedo**, to pick and choose with care.—**por alto**, to choose at random.
escolhido –da (*adj.*) choice; selected; chosen.
escolhimento (*m.*) act of choosing [= ESCOLHA].
escolho [cô] (*m.*) reef, shelf; fig., dangerous obstacle.
escoliador, **escoliasta**, **escoliaste**, **escoliastes** (*m.*) scholiast.
escólio (*m.*) scholium.
escoliocifose (*f.*, *Med.*) scoliokyphosis.
escoliômetro (*m.*) scoliometer.
escoliose (*f.*, *Med.*) scoliosis.
escolopendra (*f.*, *Zool.*) scolopendrid; centipede.
escolopêndrio (*m.*) hartstongue fern (*Phyllitis scolopendrium*), c.a. LÍNGUA-DE-BOI, LÍNGUA-CERVINA.
escolta (*f.*) escort, convoy; bodyguard.
escoltar (*v.t.*) to escort, convoy.
escombroscídeos (*m.pl.*) a family (*Scombresocidae*) comprising the sauries, halfbeaks and flying fishes.
escômbridas, **escombróides** (*m.pl.*) the mackerel family (*Scombridae*).
escombrídeo –dea (*adj.*) scombroid; (*m.*) a mackerel or related scombroid fish.
escombro (*m.*) the genus (*Scomber*) of common mackerels; (*pl.*) ruins, debris.
escomunal (*adj.*) uncommon [= DESCOMUNAL].
escondedoiro, **escondedouro** (*m.*) = ESCONDERIJO.
escondedor –dora (*m.,f.*) hider.
escondedura (*f.*) act of hiding.
esconde-esconde (*m.*) hide-and-seek.
esconder (*v.t.*) to hide, conceal; to cloak, veil; (*v.r.*) to abscond; to hide (a, de, from; em, in).—**o jôgo**, to cover up (dissimulate). **brincar de—**, to play hide-and-seek.
esconderijo (*m.*) hiding place, hideout [= ESCONDEDOURO].
escondido –da (*adj.*) hidden; secret. **às escondidas**, furtively, without the knowledge of; secretly; on the sly. (*m.*, *Geol.*) limestone sinkhole [= ITARARÉ].
escondimento (*m.*) act of hiding.
esconjuração (*f.*) = ESCONJURO.
esconjurar (*v.t.*) to conjure, adjure; to exorcise.
esconjuro (*m.*) conjuration, adjuration; exorcism.
esconso –sa (*adj.*) sloping; (*m.*) shelter; corner, angle.
escopária (*f.*) Scotch broom (*Cytisus scoparius*), c.a. GIESTEIRA-DAS-VASSOURAS.
escopo [cô] (*m.*) purpose, aim, end, intention, object. [But not scope, which is CAMPO DE AÇÃO, RAIO DE OBSERVAÇÃO.]
escopolamina (*f.*, *Chem.*) scopolomin(e).
escopoleína (*f.*, *Chem.*) scopolein(e).
escopoletina (*f.*, *Chem.*) scopoletin.
escopolina (*f.*, *Chem.*) scopolin(e).
escoprear (*v.t.*) to mark (lines on a piece of work) with a steel chisel.
escopro [cô] (*m.*) steel chisel.
escora (*f.*) prop, stay, brace, support; strut; stanchion; chock, scotch.
escorador –dora (*adj.*) bracing, staying, supporting; (*m.*) one who stands up against his adversary.
escoramento (*m.*) act of propping, shoring, etc. See the verb ESCORAR.
escorar (*v.t.*) to prop (up), shore up; to underpin; to bolster, brace; to stand up and fight; (*v.r.*) to lean upon; to rely upon.
escórbutico –ca (*adj.*, *Med.*) scorbutic.
escorbuto (*m.*, *Med.*) scurvy.
escorçar (*v.t.*, *Fine Arts*) to foreshorten.
escorchado –da (*adj.*) stripped, peeled; flayed; fleeced.
escorchador –dora (*adj.*; *m.,f.*) that, or one who, strips, etc. See the verb ESCORCHAR.
escorchante (*adj.*) that flays; that despoils. **impostos—s**, ruinous taxes.
escorchar (*v.t.*) to strip, denude, peel; to skin, flay; to fleece, despoil; fig., to scalp, gouge (on prices); to singe (beehives).
escorcioneira (*f.*) the blacksalsify serpent-root (*Scorzonera hispanica*), c.a. SALSIFI-NEGRO, SALSIFI-PETRO.
escôrço (*m.*) foreshortening (of perspective); mental view; a miniature; a summary.
escórdio (*m.*) the wood germander (*Teucrium scorodona*), c.a. SALVA-BASTARDA, SALVA-BRAVA, SEIXEBRA; the water germander (*Teucrium scordium*).

escore (*m.*) score (in a game).
escória (*f.*) scoria, slag; dross, scum; clinkers. a—da humanidade or da sociedade, the dregs of humanity (of society), scum of the earth.
escoriação (*f.*) excoriation; abrasion.
escoriar (*v.t.*) to excoriate, flay, chafe, abrade [but not to excoriate in the sense of flaying verbally, which is DESCOMPOR]; (*Metal.*) to remove the scoria from.
escorificar (*v.t.*) to scorify.
escorificatório -ria (*adj.*) scorifying; (*m.*) scorifier.
escorjar (*v.t.*) to contort; to twist out of shape; (*v.r.*) to writhe.
escorlo (*m., Min.*) schorl, black tourmaline.
escornado -da (*adj., slang*) tired out.
escornar (*v.t.*) to gore.
escorodita (*f., Min.*) scorodite.
escorpena (*f.*) the hogfish (*Scorpaena scrofa*).
escorpião (*m.*) scorpion;—-d'água, water bug.
escorpióide (*adj.*) scorpioid(al).
escorpionídeo -dea (*adj.; m.*) scorpionid.
escorraçado -da (*adj.*) driven out (away).
escorraçar (*v.t.*) to expel, oust; to drive out; to reject; to send (someone) packing.
escorralhas (*f.pl.*), escorralho (*m.*) dregs.
escorregadela (*f.*) slip; mistake, fault [= ESCORREGADURA, ESCORREGAMENTO, ESCORREGÃO, ESCORRÊGO].
escorregadiço -ça, escorregadio -dia (*adj.*) slippery.
escorregadouro (*m.*) slippery place.
escorregar (*v.i.*) to slip, slide, glide; to fall into error.
escorreito -ta (*adj.*) impeccable, faultless; sound, healthy.
escorrer (*v.t.,v.i.*) to trickle, dribble, drip; to drop.—em suor, to drip sweat.—sangue, to bleed.
escorrido -da (*adj.*) exhausted; tight-fitting; smooth, flat.
escorrimento (*m.*) running (as of a sore); dripping; oozing; separation of butter from milk.
escorropicha-galhetas (*m., colloq.*) sexton.
escorropichar, escorrupichar (*v.t., colloq.*) to drain, drink dry (bottoms up); to "come across" (with money).
escorva (*f.*) primer (of pump, etc.).
escorvar (*v.t.*) to prime (a pump, etc.).
escota (*f., Naut.*) sheet.
escote (*m.*) quota; share; amount subscribed.
escoteira (*f., Naut.*) cleat.
escoteirismo (*m.*) Boy Scouting.
escoteiro (*m.*) a scout; a Boy Scout.
escotilha (*f., Naut.*) scuttle, hatchway; cockpit (of an airplane).—de pôpa, (*Naut.*) afterhatch.
escotismo (*m.*) = ESCOTEIRISMO.
escotoma (*m., Med.*) scotoma, blind spot.
escoucear (*v.*) = ESCOICEAR.
escova (*f.*) = ESCOVADELA.
escôva (*f.*) brush; (*colloq.*) reprimand; annoying person.—de cabelo, hairbrush.—de cobre, (*Elec.*) copper brush.—de dentes, toothbrush.—de pintar, paintbrush.—de roupa, clothes brush.
escova-botas (*m.,f.*) bootlicker.
escovação, escovadela, a brushing; (*colloq.*) a bawling out.
escovado -da (*adj.*) sharp, shrewd; brushed.
escovador -dora (*adj.*) brushing; (*m.,f.*) brusher; scrubber; wheat cleaning machine.
escovar (*v.t.*) to brush, scrub.
escovém (*m., Naut.*) hawsehole.
escovilhão (*m., Ordn.*) sponge, swab.
escovinha (*f.*) a little brush. à—, of hair, close-cropped, crew-cut; (*Bot.*) the cornflower or bluebottle (*Centaurea cyanus*).
escravatura (*f.*) slave trade; slavery.
escravidão (*f.*) slavery, serfdom, bondage.
escravização (*f.*) enslavement.
escravizar (*v.t.*) to enslave; (*v.r.*) to subjugate oneself.
escravo -va (*m.,f.*) slave, serf, vassal; (*adj.*) slavish; captive.
escrevedor -dora (*m.,f.*) writer; scribbler.
escrevedura (*f., colloq.*) a piece of poor writing.
escrevente (*m.,f.*) scribe, clerk, amanuensis.
escrever [44] (*v.t.,v.i.*) to write (a, para, to; sôbre, on, about).—à máquina, to typewrite.
escrevinhador -dora (*m.,f.*) scribbler.
escrevinhar (*v.t.,v.i.*) to scribble; to "doodle".
escriba (*m.*) scribe; (*colloq.*) scribbler.
escrínio (*m.*) small writing desk; small safe.
escrita (*f.*) writing; handwriting.
escritinho -nha (*adv.*) just so.
escrito -ta (*adj.; irreg. p.p. of* ESCREVER) written; in

writing; (*m.*) a piece of writing.—à mão, handwritten. pôr por—, to put in writing.
escritor -tora (*m.,f.*) writer, author.
escritório (*m.*) office, study.
escritura (*f.*) a writ, legal document; deed; handwriting.—sagrada, Holy Writ. as—s, the Scriptures.
escrituração (*f.*) bookkeeping, accounting.—por partidas dobradas (simples), double-entry (single-entry) bookkeeping.
escriturar (*v.t.*) to keep books; to write up (a document); (*v.t.,v.r.*) to sign up (under a contract).
escriturário -ria (*m.,f.*) bookkeeper, accountant; scribe, clerk.
escrivã (*f.*) clerk in a convent.
escrivaninha (*f.*) writing desk, secretary.—de tampo corrediço, rolltop desk.
escrivão [-vães] (*m.*) scribe, notary, clerk; (*Zool.*) = CARAPICU (a fish).
escrobiculado -da (*adj., Bot., Zool.*) scrobiculate, pitted.
escrobículo (*m., Zool.*) scrobicula; (*Anat., Med.*) scrobiculus.
escrófula (*f., Med.*) scrofula.
escrofulária (*f.*) the water figwort (*Scrophularia aquatica*).
escrofulariáceo -cea (*adj.*) scrophulariaceous; (*f.pl., Bot.*) the figwort family (*Scrophulariaceae*).
escrofuloso -sa (*adj.*) scrofulous; (*m.,f.*) one suffering from scrofulosis.
escrópulo (*m.*) unit of weight for precious stones (1.125 grams).
escroque (*m.*) swindler, crook, cheat.
escrotal (*adj., Anat.*) scrotal.
escroto -ta (*adj., slang*) bad, low, ordinary; (*m., Anat.*) scrotum; (*pl., colloq.*) testicles.
estrotocele (*f., Med.*) scrotal hernia.
escrunchante (*m., slang*) housebreaker, porch-climber.
escrupulizar (*v.i.,v.t.*) to have scruples (em, de, about).
escrúpulo (*m.*) scruple, hesitation, qualm; nicety, delicacy.
escrupuloso -sa (*adj.*) scrupulous, careful; punctilious; circumspect.
escrutador -dora (*adj.*) scrutinizing; (*m.,f.*) one who scrutinizes.
escrutar (*v.t.*) to scrutinize, search, canvass, scan.
escrutável (*adj.*) scrutable.
escrutinador -dora (*m.,f.*) vote counter.
escrutinar (*v.i.*) to check and count votes; to scrutinize.
escrutínio (*m.*) scrutiny; balloting, voting; counting of ballots; ballot box.—secreto, secret ballot.
escudar (*v.t.*) to shield (-se, oneself; com, with; contra, against).
escudeiro (*m.*) shield-bearer; squire, equerry.
escudela (*f.*) wooden scoop.
escudete [dê] (*m.*) escutcheon (of a keyhole).
escudinha (*f.*) = AÇAFATE-DE-PRATA.
escudo (*m.*) escutcheon; shield; Portuguese coin.—de armas, coat of arms.
esculápio (*m., colloq.*) physician.
esculento -ta (*adj.*) esculent, edible.
esculetina (*f., Chem.*) esculetin.
esculhambar (*v.t.*) to ridicule; to shatter; to "raise hell". [*Inelegant slang.*]
esculina (*f., Chem.*) esculin.
ésculo (*m.*) buckeye; horse chestnut (*Aesculus*).
esculpido -da (*adj.*) sculptured. É parecido com o pai,—e encarnado [wrongly: "cuspido e escarrado"], He is the spit and image of his father.
esculpir [25] (*v.t.*) to sculpture, carve, chisel.
escultor -tora (*m.*) sculptor; (*f.*) sculptress.
escultura (*f.*) sculpture.
escultural (*adj.*) sculptural.
esculturar (*v.t.,v.i.*) to sculpture.
escuma (*f.*) foam, froth; spume; scum. Cf. ESPUMA.—-de-sangue, red coral.—-do-mar, meerschaum.
escumadeira (*f.*) skimmer (for liquids).
escumalha (*f.*) riff-raff, scum of society.
escumalho (*m.*) slag; dross, scruff, scum.
escumana (*f.*) a male SAÚVA ant [= BITU].
escumante (*adj.*) foaming. Cf. ESPUMANTE.
escumar (*v.t.*) to skim; (*v.i.*) to froth.—de raiva, to foam at the mouth with rage.
escumilha (*f.*) birdshot; (*Bot.*) the common crapemyrtle (*Lagerstroemia indica*), c.a. EXTREMOSA, MIMOSA-DOS-JARDINS, NORMA, LAGERSTRÊMIA.
escumoso -sa (*adj.*) foamy.
escuna (*f.*) schooner.
escuras (*f.pl.*) darkness. às—s, in the dark; occultly.

escurecedor –**dora** (*adj.*) darkening; (*m.,f.*) darkener.
escurecer (*v.t.*) to darken, obscure, cloud; (*v.r.*) to grow dark. **ao**—, at dusk.
escurejar (*v.i.*) to grow dark.
escureza (*f.*) darkness [= ESCURIDÃO].
escuridade (*f.*) obscurity; darkness.
escuridão (*f.*) darkness, obscurity; ignorance.
escuro –**ra** (*adj.*) dark; dim; obscure; somber; gloomy; overcast; swarthy; (*m.*) darkness.—**como breu**, pitch-black. **no**—, in the dark. **às escuras**, blindly.
escusa (*f.*) excuse, pardon; release.
escusado –**da** (*adj.*) unnecessary, unneeded, useless.—**é dizê-lo**, (it is) needless to say.
escusar (*v.t.*) to excuse, forgive; to justify, warrant; to dispense, exempt (**de**, from); to have no need of; (*v.r.*) to excuse oneself (**de**, from).—**-se de fazer alguma coisa**, to refuse to do a thing or to avoid doing it.
escusável (*adj.*) excusable; dispensable, needless.
escuso –**sa** (*adj.*) excused; dispensed with; dark, hidden.
escuta (*f.*) act of listening; listener; spy.
escutador –**dora** (*adj.*) listening; (*m.,f.*) listener.
escutar (*v.t.,v.i.*) to listen (to); to hear. Cf. OUVIR.
escutelária (*f., Bot.*) the genus (*Scutellaria*) of skullcaps.
escutelarina (*f., Pharm.*) scutellarin.
escutelo (*m., Bot., Zool.*) scutellum.
escutiforme (*adj.*) scutiform, shield-shaped.
Esdras (*m.*) Ezra.
esdrúxulo –**la** (*adj.*) accented or stressed on the antepenult (as is this word); (*colloq.*) whimsical; odd, strange. **verso**—, verse ending in a dactyl.
E.S.E. = ÉS-SUESTE (east-southeast).
esfacelado –**da** (*adj.*) broken up; destroyed; decadent; cut up, mangled (in an accident); (*Med.*) sphacelate.
esfacelar (*v.t.*) to destroy, spoil, ruin; (*v.r.*) to waste away; to deteriorate; (*Med.*) to sphacelate.
esfácelo (*m., Med., Pathol.*) sphacelus, gangrene.
esfacêlo (*m.*) mortification (of tissues); ruin, destruction.
esfaceloderme (*f., Med.*) sphaceloderma.
esfacelotoxina [ks] (*f., Chem.*) sphacelotoxin.
esfaimado –**da** (*adj.; m.,f.*) famished, starving (person); = FAMINTO.
esfaimar (*v.t.*) to starve [= ESFOMEAR].
esfalerita (*f., Min.*) sphalerite, blende, zinc blende, false galena.
esfalfado –**da** (*adj.*) dog-tired, beat out, worn out.
esfalfamento (*m.*) great fatigue, exhaustion.
esfalfar (*v.t.*) to tire out, fag, jade; (*v.r.*) to tire oneself out.
esfanicar (*v.t.*) to break to pieces.
esfaqueado –**da** (*adj.*) stabbed, knifed.
esfaquemento (*m.*) knifing, stabbing.
esfaquear (*v.t.*) to knife, stab.
esfarelado –**da** (*adj.*) powdery, crumbly.
esfarelar (*v.t.*) to crumble, crush; to bolt (cornmeal); (*v.r.*) to crumble.
esfarinhar (*v.t.*) to reduce to meal or flour; to crumble; (*v.r.*) to crumble into dust.
esfarpado –**da** (*adj.*) ragged, in shreds.
esfarpar (*v.t.*) to tear, shred.
esfarrapadeira (*f.*) devil (shredding machine).
esfarrapado –**da** (*adj.*) ragged, in tatters, shabby. **Ri-se o rôto do**—, The pot calls the kettle black.
esfarrapar (*v.t.*) to shred, tear apart, reduce to tatters, destroy.
esfarripado –**da** (*adj.*) sparse, thin, wispy (said esp. of hair).
esfênio, esfeno (*m., Min.*) sphene, titanite.
esfenobasilar (*adj., Anat.*) sphenobasilar.
esfenocefalia (*f., Craniol.*) sphenocephaly.
esfenoidal (*adj.*) sphenoidal.
esfenóide (*m., Anat., Zool.*) the sphenoid bone.
esfenoidite (*f., Med.*) sphenoiditis.
esfenótribo (*m., Surg.*) sphenotribe.
esfenotripsia (*f., Obstetrics*) sphenotripsy.
esfenozigomático –**ca** (*adj., Anat.*) sphenozygomatic.
esfera (*f.*) sphere, globe, ball; scope.—**armilar**, armillary or skeleton sphere.—**celeste**, (*Astron.*) celestial sphere.—**de ação or de atividade**, sphere or range of action.—**oblíqua**, (*Astron., Geog.*) oblique sphere.—**paralela**, (*Astron., Geog.*) parallel sphere.—**reta**, right sphere.—**terráquea or terrestre**, terrestrial sphere, earth. **rolamento de**—**s**, ball bearing.
esfericidade (*f.*) sphericity, roundness.
esférico –**ca** (*adj.*) spherical, globular.

esferográfica (*f.*) ball-point pen.
esferoidal (*adj.*) spheroidal.
esferóide (*m.*) spheroid.
esferômetro (*m.*) spherometer.
esférula (*f.*) spherule.
esfervilhar (*v.i.*) to seethe; to scurry.
esfiapar (*v.t.*) to shred (fiber, etc.); to fray.
esfiar (*v.*) = DESFIAR.
esfigmógrafo (*m., Physiol.*) sphygmograph.
esfigmologia (*f., Physiol.*) sphygmology.
esfigmomanômetro (*m., Physiol.*) sphygmomanometer.
esfigmômetro (*m., Physiol.*) sphygmometer.
esfíncter, esfincter [tér] (*m., Anat., Zool.*) sphincter.
esfinge (*f.*) sphinx; a hawk moth.
esfingético –**ca** (*adj.*) sphinxlike.
esfíngidas, esfingídeos, esfingíneos (*m.pl.*) the family (*Sphingidae*) constituted by the hawk moths.
esfirena (*f., Zool.*) barracuda (*Sphyraena spp.*); = BICUDA.
esfírnidas, esfírnídeos (*m.pl.*) the *Sphyrnidae* (family of hammerhead sharks).
esflorar (*v.t.*) to run over lightly (as the keys of a piano); to ruffle the surface (of water, etc.); to leaf through (a book).
esfogueado –**da** (*adj.*) flushed, red-faced; eager for.
esfogueteado –**da** (*adj.*) wild, reckless.
esfoguetear (*v.t.*) to celebrate with fireworks; to fire a gun; to reprimand severely; to drive away; (*v.i.*) to set off sky-rockets.
esfola, esfoladela, –ladura (*f.*), **-lamento** (*m.*) a scratch or abrasion of the skin; a flaying or skinning (of animals).
esfolar (*v.t.*) to flay, skin; to abrade, rub, graze, chafe, scratch (the skin); to fleece (customers); (*v.r.*) to suffer a scratch or abrasion.
esfolegar (*v.*) = RESFOLEGAR.
esfolhar (*v.*) = DESFOLHAR.
esfolhear (*v.t.*) to leaf (books).
esfolhoso –**sa** (*adj.*) leafless.
esfoliação (*f.*) exfoliation.
esfoliar (*v.t.,v.r.*) to exfoliate.
esfomeação (*f.*) starvation.
esfomeado –**da** (*adj.*) famished, starved, hungry.
esfomear (*v.t.*) to starve.
esforçado –**da** (*adj.*) energetic; strenuous; strong; bold.
esforçar (*v.t.*) to strengthen; to encourage; (*v.i.*) to gain strength or courage; (*v.r.*) to strive, exert oneself, struggle, strain (to do something).
esfôrço [esforços (fó)] (*m.*) effort, endeavor, exertion, attempt, struggle; stress.—**axial**, longitudinal stress.—**Cristão**, Christian Endeavor (Young People's Society of).—**conjugado or conjunto**, joint effort.—**de cisalhamento**, shearing stress.—**de compressão**, compressive stress.—**de curvatura**, bending stress.—**lateral**, side stress.—**de ruptura**, breaking stress; ultimate or rupture strength.—**unitário**, unit stress.
esfrangalhar (*v.t.*) to rend, tear to shreds; to shatter.
esfrega (*f.*) a rubbing or scrubbing; a scolding; (*colloq.*) a drubbing, thrashing [= SURRA].
esfregação, -gadela, -gadura (*f.*) act of scrubbing or scouring.
esfregador –**dora** (*adj.*) rubbing; scrubbing; (*m.*) scrubbing brush; scrub cloth.
esfregão (*m.*) scrub cloth, dish rag, mop; (*Bot.*) the suakwa vegetable sponge or dishcloth gourd (*Luffa cylindrica*).
esfregar (*v.t.*) to rub; to scratch; to scrub, scour; to fray. **enquanto o diabo esfrega um olha**, in two shakes of a dog's tail.
esfriamento (*m.*) act of cooling.
esfria (*m.*) in newspaper slang, an informant who insists on seeing the editor personally instead of talking to a reporter; a kill-joy, wet blanket; also = ESFRIA-VERRUMA.
esfriar (*v.t.*) to cool, chill; (*v.i.,v.r.*) to grow cold; to lose ardor or enthusiasm.
esfria-verruma (*m., colloq.*) attendant, helper; hanger-on, esp. one who performs minor tasks in a servile or flattering sort of way.
esfulinhar (*v.t.*) to sweep away soot and cobwebs.
esfumado –**da** (*adj.*) shaded (drawing); smoky; hazy (ideas).
esfumar (*v.t.*) to draw with crayon; to shade, soften, tone down; to darken with smoke; (*v.r.*) to go up in smoke; to vanish in thin air.
esfuminho (*m.*) a stump (for shading and softening crayon drawings).

esfuracar (*v.t.*) to bore into.
esfuziante (*adj.*) whizzing, whistling; rippling, bubbling, sparkling, lively.
esfuziar (*v.i.*) to whiz, whine, (as a bullet); to whistle (as the wind); to break out (as laughter).
esfuziote (*m.*) reprimand.
esgadanhar (*v.t.*) to scratch, claw.
esgadelhado –da (*adj.*) = ESGUEDELHADO.
esgalgado –da (*adj.*) lanky; gangling; thin.
esgalhar (*v.t.*) to strip of branches, prune; (*v.i.*) to branch out.
esganação (*f.*) strangulation; greediness.
esganado –da (*adj.*) starving; eager, avid; greedy, grasping; (*m.,f.*) such a person.
esgana-gata (*f.*) stickleback (fish).
esganar (*v.t.*) to strangle, choke, stifle; (*v.r.*) to hang oneself; to grow green with envy.
esganiçado –da (*adj.*) shrill, piercing.
esganiçar (*v.t.,v.r.*) to yell, shriek, screech, yelp.
esgar (*m.*) grimace, scowl, frown.
esgarapatana (*f.*) = ESGARAVATANA.
esgaratujar (*v.t.,v.i.*) to scribble [= GARATUJAR].
esgaravatana (*f.*) Indian blow gun [= ESGARAPATANA, ZARABATANA].
esgaravatar (*v.t.*) to scratch (with the nails); to pick (teeth, nose); to rake over (coals); to dig (inquire) into; to ransack; to delve in, probe into.
esgaravatil (*m.*) tool for making mortises or sockets in wood.
esgarçar (*v.t.*) to rend, tear, fray (cloth); (*v.i.*) to wear thin; (*v.r.*) to dissolve, fade, melt away.
esgardunhar (*v.*) = ESGADANHAR.
esgargalar (*v.t.*) to bare the throat, neck or chest.
esgargalhar-se (*v.r.*) to laugh aloud.
esgarrar (*v.i.,v.r.*) to stray.—-se da razão, to depart from reason.
esgazeado –da (*adj.*) blanched, pallid; of eyes, wild, staring.
esgoelar (*v.t.,v.i.,v.r.*) to shout, yell; (*v.t.*) to choke, strangle.
esgotado –da (*adj.*) exhausted, depleted.
esgotamento (*m.*) exhaustion; depletion; draining.— nervoso, nervous breakdown.
esgotar (*v.t.*) to drain (to the last drop); to sap; to empty, exhaust; to deplete; (*v.r.*) to become exhausted; to peter out.
esgotável (*adj.*) exhaustible.
esgôto (*m.*) drain; sewer.
esgravat[e]ar (*v.*) = ESGARAVATAR.
esgrima (*f.*) act or art of fencing.
esgrimidor –dora (*adj.*) fencing; (*m.,f.*) fencer.
esgrimir (*v.t.*) to brandish (weapons); (*v.i.*) to fence; to bicker.
esgrimista (*m.,f.*) fencer.
esgrouviado –da, esgrouvinhado –da (*adj.*) lank, lean; gangling; dishevelled.
esguedelhado –da (*adj.*) rumpled; disheveled [= DESGUEDELHADO].
esguedelhar (*v.t.*) to muss, rumple (the hair); (*v.r.*) to become disheveled.
esgueirar (*v.t.*) —a, to steal (a glance) at; to steal from; (*v.r.*) to steal away, slink away, slip away, sneak off (out, away).
esguelha [guê] (*f.*) slant, bias, diagonal. de—, obliquely, askew. olhar de—, to look askance at, out of the corner of one's eye. andar de—, to sidle.
esguelhado –da (*adj.*) oblique, sideways.
esguelhar (*v.t.*) to place obliquely or sideways; to cut on the bias.
esguichar (*v.t.*) to squirt (water, etc.); (*v.i.*) to spurt, gush (out).
esguicho (*m.*) squirt, jet; squirter.
esguio –guia (*adj.*) tall and slender; willowy; long and slim; lanky.
esipra (*f., colloq.*) erysipelas [= ERISIPELA].
eslabão (*m., Veter.*) spavin.
esladroar (*v.i.*) to disbud or sucker (plants).
eslávico –ca (*adj.*) Slavic.
eslavo –va (*adj.; m.,f.*) Slav.
eslinga (*f.*) sling (for loading or unloading ships).
eslingar (*v.t.*) to hoist goods in a sling.
eslote (*m., Aeron.*) slot.
eslovaco –ca (*adj.; m.,f.*) Slovak.
esloveno –na (*adj.; m.,f.*) Slovene.

esmaecer (*v.i.*) to fade; to grow faint.
esmaecimento (*m.*) fading; fainting.
esmagação (*f.*) act or result of smashing, crushing.
esmagador –dora (*adj.*) crushing, smashing; overwhelming; (*m.*) sugar cane crusher.
esmagadura (*f.*), esmagamento (*m.*) act of crushing, etc. See the verb ESMAGAR.
esmagar (*v.t.*) to crush, squash; to smash; to overpower, subdue; (*v.r.*) to be crushed.
esmaiar (*v.*) = DESMAIAR.
esmaltado –da (*adj.*) enamelled; ornate.
esmaltador –dora (*adj.*) enamelling; (*m.,f.*) enameller.
esmaltagem (*f.*) enamelling; enamel.
esmaltar (*v.t.*) to enamel; to polish, embellish.
esmalte (*m.*) enamel; tooth enamel; brilliancy, splendor. —de unhas, nail polish.
esmaltina, esmaltinita (*f., Min.*) smaltite, smaltine.
esmar (*v.t.*) to estimate; to guess.
esmarelido –da (*adj.*) yellowish.
esmegma (*m., Physiol.*) smegma.
esmerado –da (*adj.*) done with great care, skill and neatness; trim; perfect, finished; refined, accomplished; natty.
esmeralda (*f.*) emerald.—-do-brasil, Brazilian emerald, green tourmaline.
esmeraldino –na (*adj.*) emerald, deep-green.
esmerar (*v.t.*) to perfect, finish, elaborate; (*v.r.*) to take great care with; to take pride in doing a thing well.
esmeril (*m.*) emery, corundum, aluminum oxide, etc.; emery wheel.
esmerilador –dora (*m.,f.*) grinder, polisher.
esmerilamento (*m.*) act of grinding or polishing (metal).
esmerilar, esmerilhar (*v.t.*) to rub, polish, grind (with emery); to perfect; to scrutinize, probe, investigate; (*v.r.*) to groom oneself.—as válvulas, to grind the valves (of a motor).
esmêro (*m.*) diligence; carefulness; nicety, fastidiousness; perfection.
esmigalhar (*v.t.*) to shatter; to crumble; (*v.r.*) to crumble.
esmilácea (*f., Bot.*) greenbrier (*Smilax*).
esmilacáceo –cea (*adj., Bot.*) smilacaceous; (*f.pl.*) the smilax or greenbrier family (*Smilacaceae*).
esmiolado –da (*adj.*) brainless [= DESMIOLADO].
Esmirna (*f.*) Smyrna.
esmirrado –da (*adj.*) stunted, wizened [= MIRRADO].
esmitsonita (*f., Min.*) smithsonite, c.a. CALAMINA NOBRE.
esmiuçado –da [i-u] (*adj.*) crumbled, in small pieces; very detailed.
esmiuçador –dora [i-u] (*adj.; m.,f.*) (person) given to minute inquiry or exposition.
esmiuçar [i-u] (*v.t.*) to crumble, crush into pieces; to explain in detail; to thrash out (a question); to investigate in great detail.
êsmo (*m.*) estimate; guess. a—, at random. andar a—, to wander about.
esmocar (*v.t.*) to drub.
esmoer [56] (*v.t.*) to grind with the teeth; to munch; to digest.
esmola (*f.*) alms; (*colloq.*) a thrashing, beating [= SURRA].
esmolambado –da (*adj.*) ragged, in tatters; shabby.
esmolambar (*v.i.*) to go about in rags.
esmolar (*v.t.,v.i.*) to beg; (*v.t.*) to give alms to.
esmoler (*m.*) almoner, almsgiver; (*colloq.*) beggar; (*adj.*) kind, charitable; almsgiving; (*colloq.*) given to begging.
esmoncar (*v.t.,v.r.*) to blow the nose.
esmorecer (*v.t.*) to discourage; to throw cold water on; (*v.i.*) to despond, despair, lose heart, become fainthearted; to droop; to become faint.
esmorecido –da (*adj.*) discouraged, despondent.
esmorecimento (*m.*) faintness; faint-heartedness.
esmurrar (*v.t.*) to buffet, cuff, beat, sock, slug, pommel. um ôlho esmurrado, a black eye.
és-não-és (*m.*) trifle, speck; (*adv.*) nearly, almost, within a little.
esnobe (*m.*) snob; (*adj.*) stuck-up, high-hat.
esnobismo (*m.*) snobbishness.
esnobístico –ca (*adj.*) snobbish.
ésoces, esócidas (*m.pl.*) the family (*Esocidae*) which comprises the pikes, pickerels and muskellunges.
esofagiano –na, esofágico –ca (*adj.*) esophageal.
esôfago (*m.*) esophagus, gullet [= GOLELHA].
esópico –ca (*adj.*) Aesopian.
Esopo (*m.*) Aesop.

esotérico –ca (*adj.*) esoteric.
espaçadamente (*adv.*) from time to time; at intervals.
espaçado –da (*adj.*) spaced; unhurried.
espaçamento (*m.*) spacing; postponement.
espaçar (*v.t.*) to space; to postpone.
espacejamento (*m.*, *Print.*) spacing.
espacejar (*v.t.*, *Print.*) to space.
espacial (*adj.*) spatial.
espácio (*adj.*; *m.*) wide-horned (steer).
espaciosidade (*f.*) spaciousness.
espacioso –sa (*adj.*) = ESPAÇOSO.
espaço (*m.*) space; interval; duration; (*Print.*) space.— cósmico, outer space.—**entre eixos**, wheel base.—**livre**, (*Mach.*) clearance; free space; gap—**para estacionar carros**, parking space. **a—s**, from time to time.
espaçosamente (*adv.*) spaciously.
espaçoso –sa (*adj.*) spacious, extensive, vast; roomy, capacious; ample, broad.
espada (*f.*) sword; (*pl.*) spades (at cards). [But not a spade, which is: PÁ DE CAVAR A TERRA]; (*m.*) matador. —**-de-são-jorge** = SANSEVIERIA (a plant).
espadachim (*m.*) swashbuckler.
espadana (*f.*) jet, spout; spray; ribbon (of blood, water, etc.); comet's tail; fin of a fish; scutcher; (*Bot.*) an arrowhead (*Sagittaria acutifolia*); Spanish iris (*I. xiphium*). —**-d'água**, a bur reed (*Sparganium erectum*).—**-das-searas**, the cornflag gladiolus (*G. segetum*).—**-dos-montes**, common gladiolus (*G. communis*).
espadanar (*v.i.*) to gush (out); to spout, spurt [blood, water]; to splash; to flop about (as a fish out of water); to seethe, foam, froth; (*v.t.*) throw to up spray (as a speedboat.)
espadarte (*m.*) the common swordfish or broadbill (*Xiphias gladius*), c.a. PEIXE-ESPADA; a dolphin (*Phocaena orca*).
espadaúdo –da (*adj.*) broad shouldered; stout.
espadeira (*f.*) the soft wallabatree (*Eperua falcata*), c.a. APÁ, APÀZEIRO, EPERU, EPERUA, VOUAPA.
espadeirada (*f.*) blow with a sword.
espadeirar (*v.t.*) to hit or wound with a sword; to beat on the back of (a person).
espadeiro (*m.*) swordmaker; swordsman.
espadela (*f.*) swingle, scutcher; large steering oar.
espadelar (*v.t.*) to swingle, scutch (flax or hemp).
espadice (*f.*, *Bot.*) spadix.
espadilha (*f.*) the ace of spades; (*m.*) fig., head man, chief.
espadim (*m.*) rapier.
espadongado –da (*adj.*) = ESPANDONGADO.
espádua (*f.*) shoulder; shoulder blade.
espaduar (*v.t.*,*v.i.*,*v.r.*) to sprain or dislocate the shoulder.
espaguete (*m.*) spaghetti.
espairecer (*v.t.*) to amuse, divert, relax (**-se**, oneself).
espairecimento (*m.*) amusement, recreation.
espalda (*f.*) = ESPÁDUA, ESPALDAR.
espaldar (*m.*) chair back.
espaldeira (*f.*) antimacassar, tidy; epaulière (of a suit of armor); (*Hort.*) espalier.
espaleiro (*m.*, *Hort.*) espalier.
espalha-brasas (*m.*, *colloq.*) a hothead.
espalhadeira (*f.*) pitchfork [= FORCADO].
espalhado –da (*adj.*) scattered, spread; diffuse.
espalhafato (*m.*) noise, commotion, confusion, fuss.
espalhafatoso –sa (*adj.*) conspicuous, showy; gaudy, over-dressed; garish, tawdry; loud, noisy, blatant.
espalhamento (*m.*) act of scattering or spreading.
espalhante (*adj.*) scattering, spreading; (*m.*) wetting agent (for fungicides).
espalhar (*v.t.*) to scatter, strew; to disseminate; to broadcast; to spread around (about); to dispel; (*v.r.*) to spread, be scattered. **O boato logo se espalhou**, The rumor soon spread.
espalmado –da (*adj.*) flattened out, spread out; splayed.
espalmar (*v.t.*) to flatten, spread (as, the hand); to splay; to make flat and smooth (with the palm); (*v.r.*) to spread, become flat and smooth.
espanador (*m.*) duster, dust broom, dust cloth, feather duster.
espanar (*v.t.*) to dust; to sweep, brush away; to strip (a screw thread).
espanca-diabos (*m.*) exorcist; lit. devil beater.
espancador (*m.*) bully, ruffian.
espancamento (*m.*) beating, drubbing.
espancar (*v.t.*) to belabor, drub, whack, buffet, bludgeon, maul, pommel, cudgel; to disperse, drive away.

espandongado –da (*adj.*) of persons, slack, careless, esp. as to personal appearance; slouching; tattered; gawky; blustering.
espanejar (*v.t.*) to dust (**-se**, oneself).
Espanha (*f.*) Spain.
espanhol –la (*adj.*) Spanish; (*m.*,*f.*) a Spaniard; (*f.*) the Spanish language; (*colloq.*) the Spanish flu (of 1918).
espanholada (*f.*, *colloq.*) exaggeration, gasconade.
espanta-boiada (*m.*, *Zool.*) a lapwing, c.a. QUERO-QUERO.
espanta-coió (*m.*) firecracker.
espantadiço –ça (*adj.*) timid, easily frightened, skittish.
espantado –da (*adj.*) startled, aghast, amazed, astonished; scared, frightened.
espantalho (*m.*) scarecrow; bogy, bug-bear, bugaboo.
espanta-lôbos (*m.*,*f.*) a very talkative person; (*m.*, *Bot.*) common bladder senna (*Colutea arborescens*), c.a. COLÚTEA, SENE-DA-EUROPA, SENE-FALSO, SENE-VESICULOSO.
espantar (*v.t.*) to frighten (away), scare; to chase away; to startle; to astonish, amaze; (*v.i.*) to be astonishing; (*v.r.*) to be amazed; (de, at); to be startled.
espantável (*adj.*) capable of being frightened, etc.;—see the verb ESPANTAR.
espanto (*m.*) fright, alarm; surprise; amazement, astonishment.
espantoso –sa (*adj.*) frightening, appalling, dreadful; awful; startling; astounding.
espapaçado –da (*adj.*) pappy.
espapar (*v.r.*) to lie face down, on one's elbows (as on the grass); (*v.i.*) = DESPAPAR.
esparadrapo (*m.*) adhesive tape, sticking plaster.
esparavão (*m.*, *Veter.*) spavin.—**caloso** or **ósseo**, bone spavin.
esparavel [-véis] (*m.*) fish net; fringe; canopy; plasterer's trowel; mason's float [= TALOCHA].
espardeque (*m.*, *Naut.*) spar deck.
esparganiáceas (*f.pl.*) a family (*Sparganiaceae*) of marsh or aquatic herbs—the bur reeds.
espargir [24] (*v.t.*) to scatter, spread; to strew; to spray, sprinkle.
espargo (*m.*) asparagus.—**-de-jardim**, Sprenger asparagus (*A. sprengeri*).—**-hortense**, garden asparagus (*A. officinalis*).
esparguta (*f.*) the corn spurry (*Spergula arvensis*).
esparóides (*m.pl.*, *Zool.*) the sea breams (*Sparidae*).
esparramado –da (*adj.*) scattered, spread about; scatter-brained.
esparramar (*v.t.*) to scatter, strew, throw about loosely; (*v.r.*) to spread, scatter; to sprawl; to splash.
esparrame, –mo (*m.*) scattering, dispersion; ostentation; brawl, shindy.
esparrar-se (*v.r.*) to fall flat; to talk nonsense.
esparrela (*f.*) snare; pitfall; trap; hoax; swindle.
esparrinhar (*v.i.*,*v.r.*) to slosh (as water); splash, splatter.
esparso –sa (*adj.*; *irreg. p.p.* of ESPARGIR) sparse, scattered; dispersed.
espartano –na (*adj.*; *m.*,*f.*) Spartan.
esparteína (*f.*, *Pharm.*) sparteine.
espartilhado –da (*adj.*) corseted; fig. fashionable.
espartilho (*m.*) corset, bodice, stays; (*Bot.*) = CAPIM-RABO-DE-RAPÔSA.
esparto (*m.*) esparto needlegrass (*Stipa tenacissima*).—**-da-terra** = CAPIM-BAMBU.—**-pequeno** = CAPIM-RABO-DE-RAPÔSA.
esparzeta [ê] (*f.*, *Bot.*) the common sainfoin (*Onobrychis viciaefolia*), c.a. SANFENO.
esparzir (*v.*) = ESPARGIR.
espasmar (*v.t.*) to cause a spasm; (*v.i.*,*v.r.*) to suffer a spasm.
espasmo (*m.*) spasm, cramp, convulsion.
espasmódico –ca (*adj.*) spasmodic.
espasmotina (*f.*, *Chem.*) sphacelotoxin.
espasmotoxina [ks] (*f.*, *Biochem.*) spasmotoxin(e).
espata (*f.*, *Bot.*) spathe.
espatela (*f.*) small wooden spatula used for depressing the tongue.
espatélia (*f.*, *Bot.*) glume.
espático –ca (*adj.*) spathic, like spar.
espatifado –da (*adj.*) smashed to pieces; squandered.
espatifar (*v.t.*) to smash to smithereens; to tear to pieces; to dissipate, squander.
espato (*m.*, *Min.*) spar.—**adamantino**, adamantine spar, corundum.—**calcário**, calc-spar.—**da-islândia**, Iceland spar.—**flúor**, fluor-spar.—**pesado**, heavy spar, barite.

espatódea (*f.*) bell flambeautree (*Spathodea campanulata*), c.a. TULIPA-DA-ÁFRICA.

espátula (*f.*) spatula; paper knife.

espatulado -da (*adj.*) spatulate.

espaventar (*v.t.*) to frighten; (*v.r.*) to become frightened; to become haughty.

espavento (*m.*) fright; pomp.

espaventoso -sa (*adj.*) frightening; lurid; tawdry; pompous; haughty.

espavorecer (*v.*) = ESPAVORIR.

espavorido -da (*adj.*) terrified.

espavorir [46] (*v.t.*) to frighten, appall, terrify.

especar (*v.t.*) to prop (up); to underpin; (*v.i.*) to balk; (*v.r.*) to lean on something.

especial (*adj.*) special, especial, particular. **em**—, especially.

especialidade (*f.*) specialty, particularity. **Não é da minha**—, It is not in my line.

especialista (*m.,f.*) specialist, expert, technician.

especialização (*f.*) specialization.

especializar (*v.t.*) to specialize, particularize; to singularize; (*v.r.*) to specialize (em, in).

especiarias (*f.*) spices.

espécie (*f.*) species; kind, sort; specie, coined money. **as santas**—**s**, (*R.C.Ch.*) the consecrated elements. **causar**—, to cause surprise. **de todas as**—**s**, of all kinds. **fazer**—, to raise a doubt.

especieiro (*m.*) a dealer in spices.

especificação (*f.*) specification.

especificado -da (*adj.*) specified; itemized.

especificador -dora (*adj.*) specifying; (*m.,f.*) specifier.

especificar (*v.t.*) to specify, name with precision, particularize, itemize.

especificativo -va (*adj.*) specificative.

específico -ca (*adj.*) specific, particular; (*m.*) specific remedy.

especilho (*m.*, *Surg.*) probe.

espécime, espécimen (*m.*) specimen, sample.

especiosidade (*f.*) speciosity.

especioso -sa (*adj.*) specious.

espectador -dora (*m.,f.*) spectator, onlooker.

espectral (*adj.*) spectral.

espectro (*m.*) specter; spectrum.—**de absorção**, absorption spectrum.—**aerodinâmico**, streamlines.—**de centelha**, spark spectrum.—**contínuo**, continuous spectrum. —**cromático**, color spectrum.—**descontínuo**, discontinuous spectrum.—**de difração**, diffraction spectrum.—**de emissão**, emission spectrum.—**magnético**, (*Physics*) magnetic spectrum.—**de massa**, mass spectrum.— **prismático**, prismatic spectrum.—**solar**, solar spectrum.

espectrobolômetro (*m.*, *Physics*) spectrobolometer.

espectrocolorimetria (*f.*, *Physics*) spectrocolorimetry.

espectrocomparador (*m.*, *Astrophysics*) spectrocomparator.

espectroeliógrafo (*m.*, *Astrophysics*) spectroheliographer.

espectroeliograma (*m.*, *Astrophysics*) spectroheliogram.

espectroelioscópio (*m.*, *Astrophysics*) spectrohelioscope.

espectrofotoelétrico -ca (*adj.*, *Physics*) spectrophotoelectric.

espectrofotometria (*f.*) spectrophotometry.

espectrofotômetro (*m.*, *Optics*) spectrophotometer.

espectrografia (*f.*, *Physics*) photograph of a spectrum.

espectrógrafo (*m.*, *Physics*) spectrograph.—**de massa**, mass spectrograph.

espectrograma (*m.*, *Physics*) spectrogram.

espectrologia (*f.*) spectrology.

espectrometria (*f.*, *Physics*) spectrometry.

espectrômetro (*m.*, *Physics*) spectrometer.

espectropireliômetro (*m.*, *Physics*) spectropyrheliometer.

espectrorradiômetro (*m.*, *Physics*) spectroradiometer.

espectropolarímetro (*m.*, *Optics*) spectropolarimeter.

espectroscopia (*f.*) spectroscopy.

espectroscópico -ca (*adj.*) spectroscopic(al).

espectroscópio (*m.*, *Physics*) spectroscope.

especulação (*f.*) speculation, conjecture; a risky business transaction.

especulador -dora (*m.,f.*) speculator, adventurer; (*colloq.*) snooper.

especular (*adj.*) specular; (*v.i.*) to speculate on, ponder, contemplate, theorize; to speculate (in business); (*colloq.*) to snoop.

especulativo -va (*adj.*) speculative; theoretical.

espéculo (*m.*, *Med.*, *Surg.*) speculum.

espedaçar (*v.*) = DESPEDAÇAR.

espeleologia (*f.*) speleology.

espeleologista, espeleólogo -ga (*m.,f.*) speleologist.

espelhamento (*m.*), **espelhação** (*f.*) act of polishing, shining; reflection.

espelhado -da (*adj.*) bright, shining, smooth (as a mirror).

espelhante (*adj.*) that mirrors.

espelhar (*v.t.*) to give a high polish to; to mirror, reflect; (*v.r.*) to be reflected; to behold oneself in a mirror.

espelhento -ta (*adj.*) like a mirror.

espelho [pê] (*m.*) mirror, looking-glass; riser (of a step); escutcheon (of a keyhole); (*Elec.*) switch plate.—**ardente** or **ustório**, burning mirror.—**do alvo**, bull's-eye of a target.—**retrovisor** or—**de retrovisão**, (*Autom.*) rear-view mirror.—**de-vênus**, (*Bot.*) Venus' looking glass (*Specularia speculum-veneris*).

espelina (*f.*) a tropical cucurbitaceous plant (*Cayaponia espelina*), c.a. CARIJÓ, DISCIPLINA, FEL-DE-GENTIO, FEL-DE-CARIJÓ, TOMBA.—**falsa**, a pigeonwings (*Clitoria guianensis*), c.a. FALSA-ESPELINA.

espeloteado -da (*adj.*; *m.,f.*) foolish, hare-brained (person).

espeloteamento (*m.*) craziness, wildness.

espelotear (*v.i.*) to behave in a senseless manner; to act crazily.

espeloteio (*m.*) = ESPELOTEAMENTO.

espelta (*f.*) spelt (wheat) (*Triticum spelta*), c.a. ÁLICA.

espelunca (*f.*) den, low dive; joint, dump; hovel; gambling hell; flophouse.

espenda (*f.*) saddle seat.

espenejar (*v.t.*) to dust; (*v.r.*) to dust (brush) oneself off.

espenicar (*v.t.*) to pluck the feathers of; to pick (a person) to pieces; (*v.r.*) to preen.

espeque (*m.*) prop, strut, support, underpinning; post.

espera (*f.*) expectation; a wait, stay, delay; ambush; toolpost of a lathe; (*exclam.*) Wait! **à**—, waiting (de, for). **à sua**—, waiting for him (her, you). **sala de**—, waiting room.

esperado -da (*adj.*) awaited, hoped for, expected. **não**—, unlooked-for, unexpected.

esperadouro (*m.*) waiting place. Var. ESPERADOIRO.

esperança (*f.*) hope; expectancy.—**ilusória**, pipe dream. **Que**—! Not a chance!

esperançado -da (*adj.*) hopeful.

esperançar (*v.t.*) to give hope to; (*v.r.*) to have hope (de, of; em, in).

esperançoso -sa (*adj.*) hopeful, promising.

esperanto (*m.*) Esperanto.

esperar (*v.t.*) to expect, await; to wait for; to anticipate, look for; to hope for.—**pela pancada**, to wait for something to happen, for the blow to fall. **Espera aí!** Wait! Hold on! **Espero que sim!** I hope so. **estar esperando filho**, to be "expectant" (pregnant). **fazer-se**—, to keep people waiting. **O melhor da festa é**—**por ela**, Expectation is better than realization. **Quem espera sempre alcança**, Everything comes to him who waits.

esperdiçador -dora (*adj.*; *m.,f.*) prodigal.

esperdiçar (*v.t.*) to waste [= DESPERDIÇAR].

esperdício (*m.*) waste [= DESPERDÍCIO].

espérgula (*f.*, *Bot.*) spurry (*Spergula*).

esperlina (*f.*) a wild bean (*Phaseolus prostratus*), c.a. FEIJÃO-DO-MATO.

esperma (*m.*, *Biol.*) sperm, semen.

espermacete (*m.*) spermaceti.

espermático -ca (*adj.*, *Anat.*, *Zool.*) spermatic.

espermatite (*f.*, *Med.*) spermatitis.

espermatizar (*v.t.*) to spermatize.

espermatocele (*f.*, *Med.*) spermatocele.

espermatócito (*m.*, *Biol.*) spermatocyte.

espermatófago -ga (*adj.*) seed-eating.

espermatófito (*m.*, *Bot.*) spermatophyte.

espermatóforo (*m.*, *Zool.*) spermatophore.

espermatogênese (*f.*, *Biol.*) spermatolysis.

espermatolítico -ca (*adj.*) spermatolytic.

espermatose (*f.*, *Biol.*) spermatogenesis.

espermatozóide (*m.*, *Biol.*) spermatozoon; (*Bot.*) spermatozoid.

espermina (*f.*, *Biochem.*) spermin(e).

espermocentro (*m.*, *Biol.*) sperm center.

espermogônio (*m.*, *Bot.*) spermogonium.

espermotoxina [ks] (*f.*, *Biochem.*) spermotoxin.

espernear (*v.i.*) to kick one's legs; to kick (complain).

esperrilita (*f.*, *Min.*) sperrylite, platinum arsenide.

espertalhão -lhona (*m.,f.*) rascal, scoundrel, crook, sharper, slicker.

espertar (*v.t.*) to quicken, kindle, incite; to arouse, awaken.

esperteza [tê] (*f.*) sharpness, shrewdness, quickness; sharp dealing.

esperto -ta (*adj.*) alert, active, smart; lively, alive, quick; nimble; dexterous; clever, crafty; foxy, bright, intelligent; sharp, keen-witted. [But not expert, which is: PERITO, EXPERIMENTADO, SABEDOR.] estudante—, smart student. ladrão—, clever thief.

espescoçar-se (*v.r.*) to stretch one's neck.

espessamento (*m.*) a thickening.

espessar (*v.t.*) to render dense or thick; (*v.r.*) to grow thick (fog, soup, woods, etc.).

espessartina (*f., Min.*) spessartite, manganese aluminum garnet.

espêsso -sa (*adj.*) thick; dense.

espessor (*m.*) = ESPESSURA.

espessura (*f.*) thickness; density.

espeta-caju (*m.,f.*) an Indian or half-breed having stiff, bristly hair.

espetacular (*adj.*) spectacular.

espetáculo (*m.*) spectacle, show, display.—em benefíco, benefit show. dar—, to make a spectacle of oneself; to show off.

espetaculoso -sa (*adj.*) showy, ostentatious, blatant.

espetada, espetadela (*f.*) prick, jab (with a sharp point). —de alfinete, a pinprick.

espetado -da (*adj.*) on a spit; impaled; run through; stiff, upright; stuck (with something).

espetar (*v.t.*) to impale (as on a spit); to prick, pierce, stick, stab; to prod, poke (as with a stick).

espêto (*m.*) roasting spit; sharp stick, prod; spike; broach; (*slang*) difficulty; nuisance.

espetro (*m.*) & derivs. = ESPECTRO & derivs.

espevitadeira (*f.*) candle snuffers.

espevitado -da (*adj.*) lively, spirited, vivacious, full of "pep"; trim; voluble; pretentious, affected; petulant, forward, immodest.

espevitar (*v.t.*) to snuff (trim wick of lamp or candle); to stimulate, rouse; (*v.r.*) to put on airs.

espezinhado -da (*adj.*) humiliated, scorned.

espezinhar (*v.t.*) to trample, tramp on; to treat harshly, scornfully.

espia (*m.,f.*) spy; lookout; peeper, prying person; (*f.*) hawser; guy rope, guy wire.

espiã (*f.*) fem. of ESPIÃO.

espiada (*f.*) a peep or quick glance.

espia-maré (*m.*) a sprite (*Ocypode*)—small, swift-running beach crab.

espião (*m.*) spy, undercover agent, secret agent.

espiar (*v.t.*) to spy (on, out); to watch secretly; to take a peep at; to lie in wait (for an opportunity); to warp (a ship); (*v.i.*) to peep.

espicaçar (*v.t.*) to peck (with the beak); to prick, sting; to "needle"; to spur, goad; to incite, impel, spur on.— a curiosidade, to prick one's curiosity.

espicanardo (*m., Bot.*) spikenard.

espicha (*f.*) string of fish; (*colloq.*) fiasco; (*Naut.*) marlinespike, fid.

espichar (*v.t.*) to stretch out, stick out (as the neck); to stretch (hides); to broach, tap (kegs); to string (fish) by the gills; to stop (another person)) cold (in a discussion); to fluster (a pupil); (*v.i.,v.r., colloq.*) to stretch out and die; (*v.r.*) to stretch oneself out (as on a sofa); to flop, fall down (fail).—a canela, (*slang*) to croak, kick the bucket.—os cobres, (*slang*) to come across with the dough (pay). Cf. ESTICAR.

espiche (*m.*) spigot, plug; (*colloq.*) fizzle, fiasco, esp. of a student in an exam; a speech.

espicho, spigot, plug; (*colloq.*) bean pole, spindlelegs (tall thin person); fiasco.

espiciforme (*adj., Bot.*) spiciform.

espícula (*f.*) spicule; spikelet.

espiculado -da (*adj.*) spiculate; spiciform.

espículo (*m.*) spicule, spine.

espiga (*f.*) spike, ear (of corn, wheat, etc.); a flower spike; (*Bot.*) spadix; a tenon or other pluglike piece; a hangnail; a nuisance, annoyance, bore; trick, deception.— -céltica, (*Bot.*) Celtic nard (*Valeriana celtica*).—da-virgem, (*Astron.*) the star Spica in Virgo.—de-água, floating pondweed (*Potamogeton natans*).—de-ferrugem, a pinefern (*Anemia*).—de-leite, (*Bot.*) a Star-of-Bethle-

hem (*Ornithogallum pyrenaicum*), c.a. LÚPULO-DO-MONTE. —-de-sangue, a balanophoraceous root parasite (*Helosis ginanensis*).—florida, (*Bot.*) mouse-ear betony (*Stachys germanica*). Que—! What a nuisance!

espigado -da (*adj.*) of grain, flowers, bearing spikes; fig. grown tall; (*colloq.*) stuck, cheated.

espigaitado -da (*adj.; slang*) stiff, upright; tipsy.

espigão (*m.*) a large spike; large nail; tenon; pointed peg; sharp point; crest, mountain ridge; hip; roof ridge.

espigar (*v.i.*) to develop ears (of grain); of children, to "shoot up".

espigélia (*f., Bot.*) any spigelia, esp. the pinkroot (*S. Marilandica*), c.a. ESPIGÉLIA-DO-MARYLAND, CRAVO-DA-CAROLINA.

espigo (*m.*) spike (of wood or iron).

espigoso -sa (*adj.*) spiky.

espigueiro (*m.*) corn crib; granary.

espigueta [guê] (*f.*) spikelet.

espiguilha (*f.*) lace edging, purl; spikelet.

espiloma (*m.*) spiloma, nevus, birthmark.

espim (*adj.*) spiny [= ESPINHOSO].

espinafrar (*v.t.*) to ridicule, make a butt of; to ridicule; to dress down.

espinafre (*m.*) spinach;—da-guiana, the eightstamen pokeberry (*Phytolacca octandra*).—da-nova-zelândia, New Zealand spinach (*Tetragonia expansa*), c.a. BELDROEGA-DO-SUL, BELDROEGA-DE-FÔLHA-GRANDE.—de-cuba = BELDROEGA-DE-CUBA.

espinal (*adj.*) spinal.

espinel [-néis] (*m.*) = ESPINHEL.

espinélio (*m., Min.*) spinel.

espíneo -nea (*adj.*) spiny, thorny.

espinescente (*adj.*) spinescent, spinulose.

espineta [nê] (*f.*) spinet.

espingarda (*f.*) shotgun, rifle, musket.—de brinquedo, toy gun.—pneumática or—de pressão, air rifle.

espingardada (*f.*) gunshot.

espingardaria (*f.*) a body of musketeers; fusillade.

espingardear (*v.t.*) to shoot, wound or kill with a shotgun or rifle.

espingardeira (*f., Mil.*) loophole.

espingardeiro (*m.*) gunsmith.

espinha (*f.*) spine, spinal column; fishbone; pimple, blackhead; (*pl.*) acne.—cervina or—de-veado, (*Bot.*) common buckthorn (*Thamnus cathartica*).—de-carneiro, (*Bot.*) sheep bur (*Xanthium macrocarpum*).—de-peixe, herringbone stitch.—dorsal, backbone.—sempre-verde, English holly (*Ilex aquifolium*).

espinhaço (*m., colloq.*) backbone, spinal column; back; mountain ridge; place on which the saddle rests on a horse's back.

espinhado -da (*adj.*) pricked (with thorns); nettled.

espinhal (*m.*) brier patch; (*adj.*) spinal.

espinhar (*v.t.*) to prick, irritate, nettle; (*v.r.*) to be vexed, offended; to flare up.

espinheiral (*m.*) bramble patch.

espinheiro (*m.*) bramble.—alvar, European wolfberry (*Lycium europaeum*).—alvar-de-casca-verde = ESCALHEIRO.—ardente, the scarlet firethorn (*Pyracantha coccinea*), c.a. SARÇA-DE-MOISÉS.—da-virgínia, the common honey locust (*Gleditsia triacanthos*), c.a. ACÁCIA-MELEIRA, ESPINHO-DE-CRISTO, FAVEIRA.—de-ameixa = AMEIXEIRA-DO-BRASIL. —de-cêrca = ESPINHO-DE-MARICÁ.—de-cristo, Christ-thorn paliurus (*P. spina-cristi*), c.a. PALIÚRO.—prêto = VIBURNO.

espinhel [-éis] (*m., Fishing*) trotline [= ESPINEL].

espinhela (*f.*) a popular term for the lower part of the breastbone (xiphisternum).—caída, (*colloq.*) any of various ailments or pains in the chest popularly supposed to be caused by a falling of the breastbone.

espinhento -ta (*adj.*) = ESPINHOSO.

espinho (*m.*) thorn; spine; prickle; porcupine quill; fig. thorny problem; (*Bot.*)—amarelo, a senna (*Cassia aculeata*).—de-agulha, a starbur (*Canthospermum*).— -de-carneiro, southern sandbur (*Cenchrus echinatus*); a species of cocklebur (*Xanthium*) called CARRAPICHO.— -de-cêrca, the Mysore thorn (*Caesalpinia sepiara*).—de-cristo, the Christ-thorn paliurus (*P. spina-cristi*), c.a. COROA-DE-CRISTO; also = ESPINHEIRO-DA-VIRGÍNIA (honey locust); also = ESPINHO-DE-jerusalém, the Jerusalem thorn (*Parkinsonia aculeata*), c.a. ROSA-DA-TURQUIA, TURCO, CHILE.—de-judeu, a balm tree (*Myroxylon salzmanni*), c.a. QUAIAPÁ, QUARENTA-FERIDAS, SESSENTA-FERIDAS; also = COROA-DE-CRISTO.—

-de-ladrão, Asian toddalia (*T. asiatica*).—-de-maricá, a mimosa (*M. sepiara*), c.a. ESPINHEIRO-DE-CÊRCA, UNHA-DE-GATO.—-de-são-joão, a barberry (*Berberis laurina*), c.a. QUINA-CRUZEIRO, UVA-DE-ESPINHO.—-de-vintém, a prickly ash (*Zanthoxylum rhoifolium*), c.a. BETARU-AMARELO, LARANJINHA, MAMICA-DE-CACHORRA (or -DE-CADELA or -DE-PORCA), TAMBATARUGA, TAMAN-QUEIRA, TINGUACIBA.—-italiano = COROA-DE-CRISTO.—-rosa = BUGUENVÍLEA.

espinhoso -sa (*adj.*) spiny, thorny, prickly; troublesome, difficult; pernickety, finical.

espinicar-se (*v.r.*) to preen oneself.

espiniforme (*adj.*) spiniform.

espinilho (*m., Bot.*) the amorpha honey locust (*Gleditsia amorphoides*), c.a. ESPINHO-DE-CRISTO.

espinoteado -da (*adj.*) flighty, giddy.

espinotear (*v.i.*) to rear and plunge (as a horse); to writhe in anger.

espintariscópio, espinteroscópio (*m., Physics*) spinthariscope.

espinterismo (*m.*) spintherism.

espiolhar (*v.t.*) to delouse; to investigate (something) in great detail.

espionagem (*f.*) spying, espionage. contra—, counter-espionage.

espionar (*v.t.*) to spy out; (*v.i.*) to snoop.

espipar (*v.i., v.r.*) to squirt out; to burst (as a balloon).

espipocar (*v.*) = PIPOCAR.

espique (*m.*) trunk of palm tree.

espira (*f.*) spire (coil); thread of a screw; turn of a spiral.

espiráculo (*m.*) spiracle, breathing hole, air vent.

espiral (*adj.*) spiral; (*f.*) spiral; hairspring.—de Arquimedes, Archimedean screw.—hiperbólica, hyperbolic spiral.—logarítmica, equiangular spiral.

espiralado -da (*adj.*) spiralled.

espiralar (*v.t., v.r.*) to spiral.

espirálico -ca (*adj.*) spiral.

espirante (*adj.*) breathing; living.

espirar (*v.t.*) to breathe out, emit, exhale (breath, odor); (*v.i.*) to be alive.

espiréia (*f., Bot.*) the genus (*Spiraea*) of spireas.

espirema (*m., Biol.*) spireme.

espirícula (*f., Bot.*) spiricle.

espirífero -ra (*adj., Zool.*) spiriferous.

espiriláceas (*f.pl.*) a family (*Spirillaceae*) of bacteria.

espírilo (*m., Bacteriol.*) spirillum.

espirilose (*f.*) spirillosis (a disease of fowls), c.a. PESTE-DAS-GALINHAS.

espírita (*m.,f.*) spiritualist; (*adj.*) spiritualistic.

espiritar (*v.t.*) to spiritize; to possess with the devil; to excite.

espiritismo (*m.*) spiritualism; spiritism.

espiritista (*adj., m.,f.*) spiritualist.

espiritístico -ca (*adj.*) spiritistic.

espírito (*m.*) spirit, soul, person; life; ghost; spirits, alcohol; vivacity, vim; wit, humor.—crédulo, superstitious person.—de amoníaco, spirits of ammonia.—de madeira, wood spirit, wood naphtha.—de nitro, spirit of niter.—de sal, hydrochloric acid.—de vinho, spirits of wine.—de vitríolo, dilute sulfuric acid.—divino, divine spirit.—do mundo, worldly spirit.—forte, freethinker.—fraco, a weakling.—santo, Holy Ghost. dar o—a (alguém), to enlighten (another person). de—abatido, low in spirits. de—tacanho, narrow-minded. de—vivo, quick-witted, wide-awake. presença de—, presence of mind. uma frase de—, a witty remark.

espírito-santense (*adj.*) of the state of Espírito Santo; (*m.,f.*) a native thereof.

espiritual (*adj.*) spiritual.

espiritualidade (*f.*) spirituality.

espiritualismo (*m.*) spiritualism.

espiritualista (*adj.; m.,f.*) spiritualist.

espiritualização (*f.*) spiritualization.

espiritualizar (*v.t.*) to spiritualize.

espirituosidade (*f.*) spirituosity.

espirituoso -sa (*adj.*) witty, clever; spirituous.

espiro (*m.*) zephyr.

espirófero (*m.*) pulmotor.

espirógrafo (*m., Physiol.*) spirograph.

espiróide (*adj.*) spiroid.

espirômetro (*m.*) spirometer.

espiroqueta, espiroqueto [quê] (*m., Bacteriol.*) spirochete.

espiroquetose (*f., Med., Veter.*) spirochetosis.

espiroscópio (*m., Physiol.*) spiroscope, spirometer.

espirra-canivetes (*m., colloq.*) a hothead; spitfire.

espirradeira (*f., Bot.*) the common oleander (*Nerium oleander*), c.a. ADELFA, ALOENDRO, ELOENDRO, LOENDRO, OLEANDRO, CEVADILHA.—do-campo, the Brazil dipladenia (*D. splendens*), a woody vine (of the dogbane family) having large varicolored racemose flowers.

espirrador -dora (*adj.*) sneezing; (*m.,f.*) sneezer.

espirrar (*v.i.*) to sneeze; to burst forth or let out (as laughter); to squirt out (as blood).

espirro (*m.*) sneeze.

esplanada (*f.*) esplanade.

esplâncnico -ca (*adj., Anat.*) splanchnic, visceral.

esplendecência (*f.*) resplendency.

esplendente (*adj.*) resplendent.

esplender (*v.*) = RESPLENDER.

esplendidez [dêz] (*f.*) splendidness; splendor.

esplêndido -da (*adj.*) splendid, magnificent, rich.

esplendidíssimo -ma, **esplendíssimo** -ma (*absol. superl. of* ESPLÊNDIDO) most splendid.

esplendor [ô] (*m.*) splendor, brilliance, magnificence, pomp.

esplendoroso -sa (*adj.*) splendid, splendiferous.

esplenectomia (*f., Surg.*) splenectomy.

esplenético -ca (*adj.*) splenetic.

esplênico -ca (*adj.*) splenic.

esplenite (*f., Med.*) splenitis.

esplim (*m.*) spleen (ill humor; melancholy).

espoar (*v.t.*) to resift; to dust (off).

espocar (*v.i.*) to explode (as fire, rockets, laughter); (*v.t.*) to pop.

espôco (*m.*) pop; explosion.

espodumênio (*m., Min.*) spodumene; hiddenite; kunzite.

espojar-se (*v.r.*) to roll or stretch out on the ground; to wallow; to flounder.

espoldrar (*v.t.*) to prune (grapevines).

espolêta (*f.*) cap, fuse; detonator; (*colloq.*) unscrupulous henchman; bodyguard, "trigger-man".—de percussão, percussion cap.—de tempo, time fuse.

espoliação (*f.*) spoliation, robbery, plundering.

espoliado -da (*adj.*) plundered [= ESBULHADO].

espoliador -dora, **espoliante** (*adj.*) plundering; (*m.,f.*) plunderer.

espoliar (*v.t.*) to despoil, rob, plunder; to strip of possessions; to swindle.

espolinhar-se (*v.r.*) = ESPOJAR-SE.

espólio (*m.*) mortal remains; estate, earthly possessions (of a deceased person); spoils, booty, loot.

espolpar (*v.t.*) to remove the pulp from.

espondaico -ca (*adj., Pros.*) spondaic, spondean.

espondeu (*m., Pros.*) spondee.

espondílico -ca (*adj.*) spondylic.

espondilite (*f., Med.*) spondylitis.

espôndilo (*m.*) vertebra [= VÉRTEBRA].

espongiários (*m.pl., Zool.*) the Porifera (sponges).

espongiforme (*adj.*) spongiform.

esponja (*f.*) sponge; sponger, parasite; a "soak" (drunkard); (*Bot.*) the sweet acacia (*A. farnesiana*), c.a. ESPONJEIRA; (*Veter.*) an epizootic disease.—artificial (or sintética), artificial or synthetic sponge.—de cobre, copper sponge (for bearings).—de platina, platinum sponge; platinum black; platinum mohr.—de-raiz, a balanophoraceous root parasite (*Scybalium fungiforme*). —do-mato, (*Bot.*) any of various species of Escallonia. passar a—em (or sôbre), to wipe out (forgive, forget).

esponjar (*v.t.*) to sponge out (erase); to sponge up (absorb).

esponjeira (*f.*) sponge-holder; (*Bot.*) the sweet acacia (*A. farnesiana*), c.a. COROA-CRISTI; a nittatree (*Parkia ulei*).—-do-japão, Japanese kerria (*K. japonica*).

esponjosidade (*f.*) sponginess.

esponjoso -sa (*adj.*) spongy.

esponsais, esponsálias (*f.pl.*) espousals, marriage vows, betrothal.

esponsal, esponsalício -cia (*adj.*) spousal.

esponta (*f., Agric.*) topping (of plants).

espontaneidade (*f.*) spontaneity.

espontâneo -nea (*adj.*) spontaneous, voluntary; off hand.

espontar (*v.t.*) to trim (hair, beard); to clip, top (plants).

espora (*f.*) spur, rowel; incentive, goad; (*Bot.*) larkspur (*Delphinium*); (*adj., colloq.*) no-good.—-de-galo, (*Bot.*) devilsclaw pisonia (*P. aculeata*), c.a. CIPÓ-MOLE, TAPA-CIRIBA; also = CORUPIÁ.

esporada (*f.*) a spur-dig; fig. incitement; severe rebuke.

esporadicidade (*f.*) sporadicalness.

esporádico –**ca** (*adj.*) sporadic, scattered; infrequent.

esporângio (*m.*, *Bot.*) sporangium, spore case.

esporão (*m.*, *Bot.*, *Zool.*) spur; (*Arch.*) spur, buttress; (*Plant Pathol.*) ergot [=CRAVAGEM]; (*Naut.*) forepeak; (*Bot.*)—**-de-galo** = ESPORA-DE-GALO.

esporar, esporear (*v.t.*) to spur; to spur on, urge on.

esporídio (*m.*, *Bot.*) sporidium.

esporidíolo (*m.*, *Bot.*) sporidiole, sporidiolum.

esporífero –**ra** (*adj.*, *Bot.*) sporiferous.

esporim (*m.*) a spur without a rowel.

esporinha (*f.*, *Bot.*) larkspur (*Delphinium*).

espório (*m.*) spore.

esporocárpio (*m.*, *Bot.*) sporocarp.

esporocnáceas (*f.pl.*, *Bot.*) a family (*Sporochnaceae*) of brown algae.

esporodóquio (*m.*, *Bot.*) sporodochium.

esporóforo –**ra** (*adj.*, *Bot.*) sporophorous; (*m.*) sporophore.

esporogênese (*f.*, *Biol.*) sporogenesis.

esporógeno –**na** (*adj.*, *Bot.*, *Zool.*) sporogenous.

esporogonia (*f.*, *Biol.*) sporogony.

esporogônio (*m.*, *Bot.*) sporogonium.

esporozoários (*m.pl.*, *Zool.*) the Sporozoa.

esporozoíta (*m.*, *Zool.*) sporozoite.

espórro (*m.*, *slang*) brawl; a dressing down.

esporte (*m.*) sports, athletics.

esportismo (*m.*) fondness for sports; sportsmanship.

esportista (*m.,f.*) sports-lover; (*m.*) sportsman; (*f.*) sportswoman.

esportivo –**va** (*adj.*) pertaining to sports. [But not sportive, which is BRINCALHÃO, ALEGRE.]

espórtula (*f.*) tip, gratuity.

esporulação (*f.*, *Biol.*) sporulation.

espórulo (*m.*, *Biol.*) sporule.

espôsa (*f.*) wife, spouse; bride.—**de Jesus Cristo**, the Church.—**s do Senhor**, nuns.

esposado –**da** (*adj.*) married [=DESPOSADO, CASADO].

esposar (*v.t.*) to marry; to espouse, support (a cause).—**-se com**, to marry.

espôso (*m.*) spouse, husband; (*pl.*) man and wife.

esposório (*m.*) espousals; marriage feast, wedding party.

espostejar (*v.t.*) to slice, cut into pieces (meat, etc.).

espoucar (*v.*) = ESPOCAR.

espouco (*m.*) sound of bursting, popping, cracking.

espraiado –**da** (*adj.*) cast up (on the beach); spread (out); splayed; (*m.*) part of beach showing at low tide.

espraiar (*v.t.*) to cast or wash ashore; (*v.i.*) to extend along the shore; to spread, shed, diffuse; to range the eyes (over a scene); to expatiate; to ebb; (*v.r.*) to spread out (as a river); to expand (one's thoughts); to outdo oneself; to sprawl.

espreguiçadeira (*f.*), **espreguiçador** (*m.*) lounge chair, deck chair, couch, chaise longue, cot, couch.

espreguiçamento (*m.*) stretching (of arms and legs); lounging.

espreguiçar (*v.t.*) to stretch (arms, legs); (*v.r.*) to stretch out (as in an easy chair); to lounge; to yawn.

espreita (*f.*) a peep, sly look, hidden glance; a spying out. **à—**, on the lookout (de, for); lurking.

espreitadeira (*adj.*) designating a woman who spies on her neighbors; (*f.*) a peephole.

espreitadela (*f.*) a spying (out).

espreitador –**dora**, **espreitante** (*adj.*) spying; (*m.,f.*) hidden observer.

espreitar (*v.t.*) to spy (out); to pry into; (*v.i.*) to observe, watch (in secret); to pry; to peer.

espremedor –**dora** (*adj.*) squeezing; (*m.,f.*) squeezer.

espremedura (*f.*) act of squeezing.

espremer (*v.t.*) to express, squeeze; to compress; to wring out; (*v.r.*) to press together; to strain, try hard.

espremido –**da** (*adj.*) squeezed.

espresso –**sa** (*adj.*) expressed, squeezed out.

espruce (*m.*) spruce (tree).

espuir (*v.t.,v.i.*) to spew, spit.

espulgar (*v.t.*) to rid (-se, oneself) of fleas.

espuma (*f.*) spume, foam, froth, spray.—**-do-mar**, meerschaum, sepiolite. Cf. ESCUMA.

espumadeira (*f.*) skimmer (utensil).

espumante (*adj.*) foamy, frothy. **vinho—**, sparkling wine.

espumar (*v.i.*) to foam, froth, spume; (*v.t.*) to skim; = ESCUMAR.

espumarada (*f.*) much foam or foaming.

espumosidade (*f.*) frothiness.

espumoso –**sa** (*adj.*) spumous, frothy, foamy; foaming;

= ESPUMENTO, ESPUMÍGERO.

espurcícia (*f.*) filth.

espurco –**ca** (*adj.*) filthy; sordid.

espuriedade (*f.*) spuriousness.

espúrio –**ria** (*adj.*) spurious, bastard; counterfeit, sham, bogus.

esputar (*v.i.*) to spit, drivel, drool.

esputo (*m.*) sputum.

esquadra (*f.*) naval squadron; a squad of infantry.

esquadrão (*m.*) a squadron (of cavalry).

esquadrar (*v.t.*) to square; to cut square.

esquadrejar (*v.t.*) to cut square; to square.

esquadria (*f.*) a right angle; a square (instrument for making or testing right angles); a T-square; a stone block; (in construction work) door and window frames, sashes, etc.

esquadrilha (*f.*) a flotilla; a squadron of airplanes.

esquadrinhador –**dora** (*m.,f.*) investigator, minute observer.

esquadrinhadura (*f.*) **-nhamento** (*m.*) investigation, minute inquiry.

esquadrinhar (*v.t.*) to search, scrutinize, scan, sift, pry into, ferret (out), probe, ransack.

esquadro (*m.*) square (an L-shaped or T-shaped instrument for testing angles).—**em T**, T-square.

esquálidas, esqualídeos (*m.pl.*) the Squalidae (family of sharks comprising the spiny dogfishes).

esqualidez [dêz] (*f.*) squalidness.

esquálido –**da** (*adj.*) very pale and weak; squalid.

esqualo (*m.*) dogfish, small shark (genus *Squalus*).

esquarroso –**sa** (*adj.*, *Biol.*) squarrose.

esquartejar (*v.t.*) to quarter; to rend or tear apart.

esquatina (*f.*, *Zool.*) the genus (*Squatina*) of angelfishes.

esquecer (*v.t.*) to forget; to overlook; to slight, neglect; (*v.r.*) to forget (de, to).—**-se de si**, to forget oneself.

esquecidiço –**ça** (*adj.*) forgetful.

esquecido –**da** (*adj.*) forgotten; forgetful; (*colloq.*) having a paralyzed limb; of horses, having no canine teeth; of cocks, having no spurs; (*m.,f.*) a forgetful person.

esquecimento (*m.*) forgetfulness; inattention, heedlessness; oversight.

esquecível (*adj.*) that may be forgotten.

esqueletal (*adj.*) skeletal.

esquelético –**ca** (*adj.*) skeletal; very thin.

esqueleto [lê] (*m.*) skeleton; framework; outline, rough draft.—**ambulante**, a bag of bones; walking skeleton.

esquema (*m.*) scheme, diagram, arrangement; schematic drawing. [But not scheme in the sense of plot or conspiracy, which is CONLUIO, INTRIGA.]

esquemático –**ca** (*adj.*) schematic.

esquentação (*f.*) act of heating or of getting hot; great heat; heated discussion.

esquentadiço –**ça** (*adj.*) hotheaded.

esquentado –**da** (*adj.*) heated; angry, "het up"; hotheaded; (*f.*) warmest part of the day.

esquentador –**dora** (*adj.*) heating; (*m.*) heater; bedwarming pan.

esquentamento (*m.*) heating; (*colloq.*) gonorrhea.

esquentar (*v.t.*) to warm, heat (up); to incense; (*v.r.*) to become warm; to become excited, "het up". **Não se esquente!** Keep your shirt on! Cf. AQUECER, AQUENTAR.

esquerda [êr] (*f.*) see under ESQUERDO.

esquerdismo (*m.*) the left (political position or party); leftist attitudes; the leftists, collectively.

esquerdista (*adj.; m.,f.*) leftist (in politics).

esquerdo –**da** [quê] (*adj.*) left, leftward; lefthanded; awkward.—**de um ôlho**, cockeyed; (*m.*) left side; left foot; (*f.*) the left (side, hand); the left. **à—**, to the left; on the left; counter-clockwise.

esqui (*m.*) ski.

esquiação (*f.*) skiing.

esquiâmetro (*m.*) skiameter.

esquiar (*v.t.*) to ski.

esquiça (*f.*) spigot, plug.

esquife (*m.*) casket, coffin; a skiff.

esquila (*f.*, *Bot.*) squill (*Scilla*); (*Zool.*) a squilla or mantis crab, c.a. TAMARUTACA.

esquilar (*v.*) = TOSQUIAR.

esquiliano –**na** (*adj.*) Aeschylean.

esquilo (*m.*) squirrel.

esquimó, esquimau (*m.,f.*) Eskimo.

esquina (*f.*) corner, street corner. **dobrar a—**, to turn the corner.

esquinado –**da** (*adj.*) having a corner or angle.

esquinar (*v.t.*) to furnish with corners; to cut on an angle, bevel; to cut (gems); (*v.r.*) to get tipsy.

esquinência (*f.*, *Med.*) quinsy.

esquipação (*f.*) equipment of, or act of equipping, a vessel.

esquipado -da (*adj.*, *Naut.*) equipped, rigged; (*m.*) amble (horse's gait).

esquipamento (*m.*) = ESQUIPAÇÃO.

esquipar (*v.t.*) to equip, outfit; (*v.i.*) to speed; of a horse, to amble.

esquipático -ca (*adj.*) queer.

esquírola (*f.*) bone splinter; hard chip.

esquiroloso -sa (*adj.*) flaky, splintery.

esquisitão -tona (*m.,f.*) a queer (odd, peculiar) person.

esquisitice (*f.*) queerness, oddness, excentricity, oddity.

esquisito -ta (*adj.*) odd, queer, freakish, "funny"; peculiar, strange; ugly; outlandish; finicky; exquisite, rare; (*m.*) a deserted place; a steep, narrow path.

esquisto (*m.*) = XISTO.

esquiva (*f.*) a dodging, ducking or sidestepping.

esquivança (*f.*) disdain; avoidance; unsociability.

esquivar (*v.t.*) to dodge, shun, avoid; to treat with aloofness; (*v.r.*) to dodge, sidestep; to shun; to slink off (away).—**se a,** to shun, shirk.—**se de,** to keep away from, keep clear of, fight shy of, shy away from.—**se de responder,** to avoid answering.

esquivo -va, **esquivoso** -sa (*adj.*) cantankerous; sulky; scornful; chary, shy, coy, elusive, hard to get, hard to find; rare, exceptional, few and far between.

esquizocarpo (*m.*, *Bot.*) schizocarp.

esquizófito -ta (*adj.*, *Bot.*) schizophytic; (*m.*) schizophyte.

esquizofrenia (*f.*, *Psychiatry*) schizophrenia.

esquizofrênico -ca (*adj.*) schizophrenic.

esquizóide (*adj.; m.,f.*, *Psychiatry*) schizoid.

esquizomicete, -ceto (*m.*, *Bot.*) schizomycete, bacterium.

esquizonte (*m.*, *Zool.*) schizont.

esquizotimia (*f.*, *Psychiatry*) schizothymia.

esquizotriquia (*f.*, *Med.*) schizotrichia.

esquizotímico -ca (*adj.*) schizothymic.

essa (*f.*) bier, catafalque, cenotaph; (*adj.; pron.*) fem. of ÊSSE.

essaísta (*m.,f.*) essayist.

esse (*m.*) ess, S; something shaped like an S.

êsse (*adj.; pron.*) that, that one; (*pl.*) those.—**outro,** that other one. [fem. ESSA].

essência (*f.*) essence, nature, substance; existence; essential oil; kind, species (of trees).—**de amêndoas amargas,** oil of bitter almonds.—**de banana,** banana oil; isoamyl acetate.—**de pérolas** (or **do oriente**), essence d'orient, pearl essence.—**de Portugal,** orange-peel oil.—**de terebentina,** I-pinene, terebenthene.—**resinosa,** essence of resin; rosin spirit.

essencial (*adj.*) essential, vital, indispensable; (*m.*) the essential point or thing.

essencialidade (*f.*) essentiality.

essênios (*m.pl.*) the Essenes.

essoutro -tra [ÊSSE+OUTRO] that other one.

és-sudeste, és-sueste (*m.*) east-southeast [= LÊS-SUESTE].

est. = ESTANCIA (stanza); ESTROFE (strophe).

Est. = ESTRADA (Road, as a name).

esta [*fem. of* ÊSTE]—é (muito) boa! (ironically) That's a good one! Don't make me laugh!—**gente,** these people.—**noite,** last night; tonight.—**outra,** this other one [= ESTOUTRA].

estabanado -da (*adj.*) harum-scarum, crazy, nutty, screwball; devil-may-care.

estabelecedor -dora (*adj.*) establishing; (*m.,f.*) one who establishes, etc. See the verb ESTABELECER.

estabelecer (*v.t.*) to establish, secure; to found, institute; to decree, ordain; to fix, settle; (*v.r.*) to settle or establish oneself.

estabelecido -da (*adj.*) having an establishment; established; of long standing.

estabelecimento (*m.*) establishment; institution; business house, shop; settlement.—**do pôrto,** (*Naut.*) establishment (of the tide).—**s pios,** charitable institutions.—**s públicos,** public institutions.

estabilidade (*f.*) stability, firmness, steadiness; (*Mech.*, *Aeron.*)—**automática,** automatic stability.—**direcional,** directional stability.—**dinâmica,** dynamic stability.—**estática,** static stability.—**inerente,** inherent stability.—**lateral,** lateral stability.—**longitudinal,** longitudinal stability.

estabilização (*f.*) stabilization.

estabilizador (*m.*) stabilizer (in any sense).

estabilizar (*v.t.*) to stabilize; (*v.r.*) to become stable.

estabular (*v.t.*) to stable; (*adj.*) stable.

estábulo (*m.*) stable; cow barn.

estaca (*f.*) stake, picket, post; pile;—**zero,** (*fig.*) starting point.

estacada (*f.*) stockade.

estação (*f.*) station; post, stand; season, term; season of the year; stay, sojourn; telephone exchange.—**balneária,** seaside resort.—**calmosa,** warm season.—**das chuvas,** rainy season.—**das rosas,** springtime.—**de águas,** watering place (resort).—**de batalha,** battle station.—**de cura,** health resort.—**de força motriz,** power station.—**de monta,** stud farm.—**de pagamento de peagem,** toll gate.—**de veraneio,** summer resort.—**do prazer** (or **dos amôres**), youth; springtime.—**ferroviária,** railway station.—**formosa** (or **nova**), springtime.—**intermediária,** way station.—**meteorológica,** weather station.—**telegráfica,** telegraph office.—**transmissora** or—**de radiodifusão,** broadcasting station.

estacar (*v.t.,v.i.*) to halt, stop short; (*v.i.*) to pull up, come to a sudden stop; to stand still (in bewilderment); (*v.t.*) to prop up (with stakes).

estacaria (*f.*) piling; stockade.

estacional (*adj.*) seasonal; stationary.

estacionamento (*m.*) parking; parking place.—**particular,** private parking place.

estacionar (*v.i.*) to remain stationed (stationary, motionless); to come to a stop.—**em,** to spend much time at or in (a given place); to park (automobiles).

estacionário -ria (*adj.*) stationary, motionless; (*m.,f.*) person in charge of a (weather) station.

estada (*f.*) stay, sojourn.

estadão (*m.*) pomp, splendor, display, luxury.

estadear (*v.t.*) to flaunt, parade; (*v.r.*) to show off, be ostentatious; to become vain.

estadia (*f.*) lay days (of a ship in port); stay, delay.

estádia (*f.*, *Surv.*) stadia.

estádio (*m.*) stadium; phase; epoch; season.

estadismo (*m.*) statism.

estadista (*m.*) statesman; politician; (*f.*) stateswoman.

estadística (*f.*) statesmanship; statistics.

estado (*m.*) state, condition, status; situation, position; commonwealth; pomp, splendor.—**bruto,** rough state.—**civil,** civil status.—**civilizado** (or **da sociedade**), civilized state.—**comum** (geral, raso), common state (not of the nobility).—**crepuscular,** sleepy condition.—**da atmosféra,** weather condition.—**da natureza,** state of nature.—**da temperatura,** temperature of the weather.—**de casado,** married status.—**de graça,** state of grace.—**de guerra,** state of war.—**de inocência,** state of innocence.—**de paz,** state of peace.—**desesperado,** desperate condition.—**de sítio,** state of seige.—**de solteiro,** bachelorhood.—**de viúva,** widowhood.—**do céu,** looks of the weather.—**do meio,** middle class.—**do tempo,** state of the weather.—**esferoidal** (or **vesicular**), (*Physics*) spheroidal state.—**gasoso,** gaseous state.—**s gerais,** States-General (in France).—**fantoche,** puppet state.—**higrométrico do ar,** humidity of the air.—**humilde,** humble condition.—**interessante,** enceinte, "expecting" (pregnant).—**líquido,** liquid state.—**livre,** free state.—**maior,** general staff.—**nascente,** nascent state.—**nativo** (or **natural**), native or natural state.—**sólido,** solid state.—**tampão,** buffer state.—**tifóide** (or **tifoso**), (*Med.*) typhoid state. **chefe de**—, chief of state; statesman. **em**—**de novo,** as good as new. **mudar de**—, to change one's civil status (e.g., to marry). **tomar**—, to marry, settle down; of race horses, fighting cocks, etc., to get into shape (to run, fight, etc.).

estadual (*adj.*) of or pert. to a state; statewide.

estadunidense (*adj.*) of or pert. to the U.S.A.; (*m.,f.*) an inhabitant of the U.S.A. Cf. NORTE-AMERICANO.

estafa (*f.*) labor, toil; fatigue.

estafado -da (*adj.*) fatigued, tired out, jaded.

estafamento (*m.*) toil; weariness [= ESTAFA].

estafante (*adj.*) toilsome; wearisome.—**s responsabilidades,** wearying responsibilities.

estafar (*v.t.,v.i.,v.r.*) to tire (out); to overdo; to jade.

estafermo [fêr] (*m.*) scarecrow; a dull, stupid fellow; a worthless fellow.

estafêta (*m.*) dispatch rider, courier, messenger; mail carrier, postman; deliverer of telegrams.

estafilococo (*m.*, *Bacteriol.*) staphylococcus.

estafiloma (*m.*, *Med.*) staphyloma.

estafiloplastia (*f.*, *Surg.*) staphyloplasty.
estafilorrafia (*f.*, *Surg.*) staphylorrhaphy.
estafiságria (*f.*) stavesacre larkspur (*Delphinium staphis-agria*), c.a. PAPARRAZ, ERVA-PIOLHEIRA. [The ripe seeds are used to kill head lice.]
estagiário **-ria** (*adj.*) probationary; (*m.,f.*) probationer (student nurse, intern, student teacher, etc.).
estágio (*m.*) apprenticeship; internship; a period of practical professional training; stage [= ETAPA].
estagnação (*f.*) stagnation; inertia.
estagnado **-da** (*adj.*) stagnant.
estagnar (*v.t.,v.r.*) to stagnate.
estai (*m.*) stay, guy rope.—**de arame**, guy wire.—**de traquete**, (*Naut.*) forestay.—**principal**, (*Naut.*) mainstay.
estala (*f.*) stall, stable [= ESTÁBULO].
estalactite (*f.*, *Geol.*) stalactite.
estalada (*f.*) sound of snapping or cracking; noise, clatter; (*colloq.*) a roof thatching "bee".
estalageiro (*m.*) = ESTALAJADEIRO.
estalagem (*f.*) inn, hostelry; group of small houses around a common court; bosh (of a blast furnace), c.a. ETALAGE, RAMPA.
estalagmite (*f.*, *Geol.*) stalagmite.
estalagmômetro (*m.*) stalagmometer, stactometer.
estalajadeiro (*m.*) **-ra** (*f.*) innkeeper.
estalante (*adj.*) snapping, cracking, popping.
estalão (*m.*) measuring rod; gauge; pattern; standard.
estalar (*v.t.,v.i.*) to crack, split, burst; (*v.i.*) to break, snap; to crackle, pop; to break out suddenly (as hand clapping or a revolution); to explode (as firecrackers).—**a paciência**, to lose patience.—**de (fome, sêde, etc.)**, to be dying of (hunger, thirst, etc.).—**de raiva**, to burst with anger.—**por casar**, to be dying to get married.—**pipoca**, to pop corn. **estar a**—**de dôr de cabeça**, to have a splitting headache.
estaleiro (*m.*) shipyard; dry dock.—**naval**, navy yard. **no**—, on the ways; fig. in process of completion.
estalejar (*v.i.*) to crackle, snap; (*v.t.*) to snap.
estalia (*f.*, *Law*) lay days (of a ship in port); = ESTADIA.
estalicar (*v.i.*) to snap the fingers; (*colloq.*) to grow thin.
estalicídio (*m.*) = ESTILICÍDIO.
estalidante (*adj.*) cracking, snapping.
estalidar (*v.i.*) to crackle.
estalido (*m.*) a click; cracking, snapping, popping.—**com os dedos**, a snap of the fingers.
estalo (*m.*) a sharp noise; a burst of sound; crackling, cracking; (fireworks) a torpedo, c.a. CHUMBINHO, TRAQUE DE CHUMBO; (*colloq.*) brain wave.
estambre (*m.*) wool or silk yarn.
estame (*m.*) weaving yarn; thread of life; (*Bot.*) stamen.
estamenha (*f.*) estamene (a coarse woolen cloth used esp. for undergarments); bunting.
estaminado **-da** (*adj.*, *Bot.*) staminate.
estaminífero **-ra** (*adj.*, *Bot.*) staminiferous.
estaminódio (*m.*, *Bot.*) staminodium.
estampa (*f.*) a printed picture; a print.—**dos pés**, footprints. **dar à**—, to send to press.
estampado **-da** (*adj.*) printed, imprinted; die forged; die stamped; (*m.*) printed cloth.
estampagem (*f.*) cold stamping (of metal).
estampar (*v.t.*) to print, imprint; to press, stamp; to cold stamp (metal).
estamparia (*f.*) print shop; metalworking shop.
estampido (*m.*) crack, clap, report, explosion, detonation.
estampilha (*f.*) revenue stamp.
estampilhado **-da** (*adj.*) of documents, bearing a revenue stamp.
estampilhar (*v.t.*) to affix revenue stamps (on documents).
estanato (*m.*, *Chem.*) stannate.
estancamento (*m.*) a stanching, checking, stopping (of a flow of anything).
estancar (*v.t.*) to stanch, stop the flow of (blood, tears, etc.); to check, stay, stop; to put an end to; to bring to a halt; to cause to stagnate; to make waterproof; (*v.i.,v.r.*) to run dry, stop running.
estanceiro **-ra** (*m.,f.*) owner of a lumber yard.
estância (*f.*) stock farm; cattle ranch; abode; station; watering place; country estate; lumber yard; coal yard; wood yard; stanza, verse.—**balnear**, bathing beach.
estanciar (*v.i.*) to abide, stay, sojourn, rest.
estancieiro **-ra** (*m.,f.*) cattle raiser; owner of a lumber yard.
estandardização (*f.*) standardization.
estandarte (*m.*) standard, banner. [But not standard in the sense of model or criterion, which is PADRÃO or NORMA.]
estande (*m.*) stand (stall, booth).
estanhado **-da** (*adj.*) tin-coated.
estanhador (*m.*) tinner.
estanhadura, estanhagem (*f.*) tin-coating.
estanhar (*v.t.*) to coat with tin.
estanho (*m.*) tin.—**cinzento**, gray tin.—**de soldar**, soldering tin.
estânico **-ca** (*adj.*) stannic.
estanífero **-ra** (*adj.*) stanniferous; stannic.
estanita (*m.,f.*, *Min.*) stannite; tin pyrites.
estanque (*adj.*) hermetic, tight, impervious; stagnant; (*m.*) stoppage (of flow), stanching; corner (monopoly); tobacco, cigar store.
estante (*f.*) bookcase; music stand; lectern, desk.
estapafúrdio **-dia** (*adj.*) queer, eccentric, odd; preposterous; harebrained.
estape (*m.*, *Bot.*) a jacaranda (*J. intermedia*).
estapédio (*m.*, *Anat.*) the stirrup bone.
estapélia (*f.*) an evil-smelling carrion flower (*Stapelia variegata*).
estaquear (*v.t.*) to stretch and peg down (hides) to dry; to erect stakes (as for a fence); to beat with a stick.
estáquida-do-japão (*f.*) Japanese artichoke or betony (*Stachys sieboldi*).
estar [45] (*v.i.*) to be; to be in. [In contrast with SER (to be) which denotes an inherent quality or permanency of state or condition, estar denotes the opposite, as illustrated in the examples to follow]; (*v.aux*) **estar**+p.pr. (gerund), or **estar a**+inf., describes a continuing action: **está dormindo**, she is sleeping; **esteve a conversar com ela**, he was talking with her. **estar a** (or **para**)+inf. also denotes proximity in time: **o mês de Março estava a** (or **para**) **expirar**, the month of March was about to expire; (*m.*) state of being. **bem**—, well-being; welfare. **mal**—, general discomfort, malaise; embarrassment. Cf. FICAR.—**a braços com**, to have one's hands full; to be grappling with.—**a pique de**, to be about to (happen); to be tempted to.—**a ponto de**, to be on the verge of.—**às môscas**, left to the flies (said of a theater, place of business, etc., devoid of customers).—**às portas da morte**, to be at death's door.—**bem**, to be all right; to look healthy; to look one's best.—**(de) bem com**, to be on good terms with.—**bem consigo mesmo**, to have a clear conscience.—**bem de vida**, to be well-off.—**com (alguém)**, to agree with (someone).—**com (fome, sêde, mêdo, ciumes, etc.)**, to be hungry, thirsty, afraid, jealous, etc.—**com a faca e o queijo na mão**, to be sitting in the driver's seat (in power, in control).—**com a palavra na bôca**, to have a word or name on the tip of one's tongue.—**com uma pedra no sapato**, to bear a suspicion.—**com a pulga atrás da orelha**, to have a flea in one's ear (be suspicious).—**com dor de cabeça**, to have a headache.—**com o pé no estribo**, to be about to depart; lit., to have one foot in the stirrup.—**com os olhos em**, to have one's eyes on. [Cf.—**de ôlho em**.]—**com os pés na cova**, or **com um pé na sepultura**, to have one foot in the grave.—**com pressa**, to be in a hurry.—**com (or em) sorte**, to be in luck.—**com vontade de**, to feel like, have a notion to, have a mind to.—**de acôrdo**, to be agreed, in accord, in agreement.—**de caminho**, to be about to depart; to be on the way.—**de crista caída**, to be crestfallen, dismayed, disappointed, depressed.—**de faxina**, to be on K.P. duty.—**de férias**, to be on vacation.,—**de licença**, to be on leave (of absence).—**de mal com (alguém)**, to be on bad terms with (someone).—**de boa maré**, to be well-disposed toward something.—**de môlho**, (*colloq.*) to be soaking (in the bathtub); to be in bed; to be idle.—**de ôlho em**, with an eye on; watching (a test tube in the lab, a pot on the stove, etc., i.e., warily). [Cf.—**com os olhos em**].—**de passagem**, to be passing through.—**de plantão**, to be on duty; to be on call; to be open for business (ref. esp. to drugstores that stay open late at night); to be ready for emergency calls.—**de prevenção com (alguém)**, to be prejudiced against (someone); to have become suspicious of (someone).—**de quarentena**, to be in quarantine.—**de ressaca**, (*slang*) to be "hung over".—**de sentinela**, to be on guard duty; to be on the lookout.—**de serviço**, to be on duty.—**de viagem**, to be on a trip; to be getting ready for a trip.—**de visita**, to be on a visit.—**de volta**, to be back (returned).—**em bom ponto**, to measure up, be just right. [Cf. **estar no ponto**].—**em brasa**, to be on fire; (*colloq.*) to be hot under the collar.

—**em dia com,** to be up-to-date (caught up) with (one's correspondence, bills, etc.).—**em dívida,** to be in debt.—**em dúvida,** to be in doubt.—**em maus lençóis,** to be in hot water.—**em pano verde,** to have lost all one's money at the gaming table.—**em paz com a conciência,** to have a clear conscience.—**em pecado,** to be in condemnation (for sin).—**em perigo de vida,** to be in danger of losing one's life.—**em regra,** to be in keeping with (laws, rules, customs, etc.). [Cf.—**no regulamento**].—**em si,** to be in one's right mind.—**em tempo,** to be on time; to be in season.—**frito,** (*slang*) to be sunk (done for).—**intrigado com (alguém),** to be baffled by, disappointed in, unfavorably surprised at (someone).—**limpo com (alguém),** to be on the best of terms with (someone); to have vindicated oneself before (someone).—**liso,** (*slang*) to be broke.—**mal,** to be in a bad way; to be seriously ill.—**mal de,** to be short of (money, etc.).—**mal de vida,** (*slang*) to be in trouble.—**mal visto,** to be looked upon unfavorably (by someone).—**meio cá, meio lá,** (*slang*) to be half-drunk or half-dead; (*colloq.*) to be pretty close to a climax (as a woman about to give birth).—**na berlinda,** of persons, to be the subject of either praise or criticism, censure, etc., i.e., to be in the spotlight.—**na bica,** (*slang*) to be on the verge of.—**na bôca do povo,** to be talked (gossiped) about.—**na cana,** (*slang*) to be in the jug (jail).—**na moda,** to be in vogue.—**na ordem do dia,** (*colloq.*) to come in for public praise or censure; to be the most-talked-about subject.—**na sombra,** to be unnoticed; lit., in the shade or shadow.—**nas últimas,** to be about to die; to be near a breakdown; of an object, to be on its last legs.—**no desvio,** to be on the sidetrack (idle, jobless).—**no estaleiro,** to be on the ways; fig., in process of completion.—**no fim do mundo,** to be at the ends of the earth.—**no mato sem cachorro,** to be in a boat without a paddle (in a predicament).—**no mundo da lua,** to be woolgathering, daydreaming, miles away.—**no ponto,** to have come to a head (as a boil or any infection); to be ready to explode; to be done (ready to take off the stove or out of the oven). [Cf.—**em bom ponto.**]—**no prego,** (*slang*) to be pooped (tired out); of an object, to be in hock.—**no regulamento,** to be in the rules and regulations. [Cf.—**em regra.**]—**no sereno,** to work, roam, or just loaf in the streets at night.—**para**+inf., to be about to. [—**para chegar,** about to arrive.]—**para cada hora,** to be on the verge of happening (at any moment).—**pela hora da morte,** to be exorbitant in price.—**por,** to be for, in favor of.—**por**+inf., still (yet) to be +p.p. [A casa está **por alugar,** the house has yet to be rented. O trabalho está **por fazer,** the work remains to be done.]—**por tudo,** to agree with everyone and everything.—**por um fio,** to be hanging by a thread, i.e., about to happen, nearly ready; about to die; of a light, etc., to be dying out.—**pronto,** to be ready; also (*slang*) to be broke.—**que,** to be of the belief (opinion) that.—**quites (com),** to be "even" (with someone).—**sôbre brasas,** to be on pins and needles (in a state of anxiety). **Aí está,** That's how it is; There you have it; That's how matters stand. **Está (em casa)?** Is he (she) in (at home)? **Está bem,** All right, very well, O.K. **Está bom,** He is well; It is good. **Está certo,** Yes, O.K. **Está claro,** Of course. **Está na hora!** It's time (de, for, to). **Está para crer,** I still don't believe (something is possible). **Está para ver,** It remains to be seen; I've never seen one yet. **ir**—**com alguém,** to go to meet (be with) someone. **Se eu estivesse no seu lugar, não faria isso,** If I were in your place, I would not do that.

estardalhaço (*m.*) din, uproar; clatter; noisy show, fanfare, hullabaloo; splurge.

estardiota (*f.*) = ESTRADIOTA.

estarrecer (*v.t.*) to appall; (*v.i.,v.r.*) to be filled with dismay.

estarrecimento (*m.*) consternation, dismay.

estase (*f., Physiol.*) stasis.

estatal (*adj.*) pert. to the state. **monopólio**—, state monopoly.

estatelado –**da** (*adj.*) stock still; stretched out (on the ground).

estatelamento (*m.*) a throwing or falling to the ground; a dumfounding.

estatelar (*v.t.*) to throw or lay on the ground; to dumfound (with astonishment); (*v.r.*) to fall sprawling; to fall flat on the ground.

estático –**ca** (*adj.*) static, at rest, standing still; (*f.*) statics; (*Radio*) static.

estatístico –**ca** (*adj.*) statistical; (*m.,f.*) statistician; (*f.*) statistics.

estatômetro (*m., Med.*) statometer.

estator (*m., Elec.*) stator.

estatoscópio (*m., Physics*) statoscope.

estatua (*f.*) statue.

estatuar (*v.t.*) to erect a statue to; to make a statue of.

estatuaria (*f.*) statuary.

estatuário –**ria** (*adj.*) statuary; (*m.*) sculptor; (*f.*) sculpture; sculptress.

estatueta [ê] (*f.*) statuette, figurine.

estatuir [72] (*v.t.*) to establish, decree, ordain.

estatura (*f.*) stature.

estatutário –**ria** (*adj.*) statutory.

estatuto (*m.*) statute, ordinance; (*pl.*) by-laws.

estaurolita (*f., Min.*) staurolite.

estauroscópio (*m., Cryst.*) stauroscope.

estavanado –**da** (*adj.*) = ESTABANADO.

estável (*adj.*) stable, fixed, firm; enduring; steady.

êste (*adj.; masc. pron.*) this, this one, the latter; (*pl.*) these.—**outro,** this other one [= ESTOUTRO].

este (*m.*) east [= LESTE].

estear (*v.t.*) to prop, support.

estearato (*m., Chem.*) stearate.—**de bário,** barium stearate.—**de cálcio,** calcium stearate.—**de níquel,** nickel stearate.—**de zinco,** zinc stearate.

esteárico –**ca** (*adj., Chem.*) stearic.

estearina (*f., Chem.*) stearin; stearic acid.

esteatita (*f., m., Min.*) steatite, soapstone.

esteatocele (*f., Med.*) steatocele.

esteatólise (*f., Chem.*) steatolysis.

esteatoma (*m., Med.*) steatoma, lipoma; sebaceous cyst.

esteatopigia (*f., Anthropol.*) steatopygia.

esteatose (*f., Med.*) steatosis.

estefânia (*f., Bot.*) the purplebell cobaea (*C. scandens*).

estefanita (*f., Min.*) stephanite.

estefânio (*m., Craniol.*) stephanion.

estefanote (*f., Bot.*) the Madagascar jasmine (*Stephanotis floribunda*).

estégano –**na** (*adj.*) having webbed feet.

estegnose (*f., Med.*) stegnosis.

estegomia (*m.*) yellow-fever mosquito (*Aedes aegypti*).

esteio (*m.*) stay, prop; strut; support.

esteira (*f.*) a mat woven of straw, rushes, fibers, etc.; direction, course; trace, vestige; norm, standard; wake of a ship; slipstream of an airplane; a bulrush, c.a. CAPIM-DE-ESTEIRA.—**sem-fim,** endless belt. **trator de**—**s,** caterpillar tractor.

esteirar (*v.t.*) to cover with, or as with, a mat or carpet; (*v.i., Naut.*) to follow a course.

esteiro (*m.*) estuary; inlet.

estej– +personal verb endings = forms of ESTAR [45].

estela (*f.*) stele, pillar; (*cap.*) Stella, Estelle.

estelar (*adj.*) stellar.

estelária (*f., Bot.*) a starwort (*Stellaria*), c.a. ALSINA ORELHA-DE-TOUPEIRA.

estelionatário –**ria** (*m.,f.*) fraud, swindler.

estelionato (*m.*) a swindle (esp. one such as selling the same property to different persons).

estelo (*m., Bot.*) stele. Cf. ESTELA.

estema (*m.*) garland; family tree; (*Zool.*) stemma.

estêncil (*m.*) stencil.

estendedouro (*m.*) place where something is laid out to dry. Var. ESTENDEDOIRO.

estender (*v.t.*) to extend, stretch out; to floor (someone) in an argument; to expand; to unfold; prolong; to spread; to enlarge, amplify; to lengthen, draw out; to spread abroad; (*v.r.*) to spread, stretch, extend (itself); to sprawl; to expatiate, dilate.—**a mão,** to put out one's hand.—**a mesa,** to spread (set) the table. Cf. ESTICAR, ESTIRAR.

estenderete [rê] (*f.*) sorry figure; boner, fiasco.

estenia (*f., Med.*) sthenia, strength, vigor.

estênico –**ca** (*adj., Med., Psychol.*) sthenic.

estenodactilógrafo –**fa** (*m.,f.*) steno-typist.

estenografar (*v.t.*) to write shorthand [= TAQUIGRAFAR].

estenografia (*f.*) stenography, shorthand [= TAQUIGRAFIA].

estenográfico –**ca** (*adj.*) stenographic.

estenógrafo –**fa** (*m.,f.*) stenographer.

estenose (*f., Med.*) stenosis.

estentóreo –**rea, estentórico** –**ca** (*adj.*) stentorian, loud-voiced.

estepe (*f.*) steppe.

Ester (*f.*) Esther; Hester.
éster (*m.*, *Chem.*) ester.
estercar (*v.t.*) to manure.
estêrco (*m.*) manure, dung.
estercoral, estercorário −ria (*adj.*) stercoral.
estercoremia (*f.*, *Med.*) stercoremia.
esterculiáceo −cea (*adj.*, *Bot.*) sterculiaceous; (*f.pl.*) the chocolate family (*Sterculiaceae*).
estéreo, estere (*m.*) stere (cubic meter), used to measure cordwood.
estereóbata (*m.*, *Arch.*) stereobate.
estereocromia (*f.*) stereochromy.
estereografia (*f.*) stereography.
estereográfico −ca (*adj.*) stereographic(al).
estereógrafo (*m.*) stereograph.
estereograma (*m.*) stereogram.
estereoisomérico −ca (*adj.*, *Chem.*) stereoisomeric(al).
estereoisomerismo (*m.*, *Chem.*) stereoisomerism.
estereometria (*f.*) stereometry.
estereômetro (*m.*, *Physics*) stereometer.
estereoquímica (*f.*) sterochemistry.
estereoscopia (*f.*) stereoscopy.
estereoscópico −ca (*adj.*) stereoscopic(al).
esteroscópio (*m.*) stereoscope.
estereostática (*f.*, *Physics*) stereostatics.
estereotipar (*v.t.*) to stereotype.
estereotipia (*f.*) stereotypy.
estereótipo (*m.*) stereotype.
estereotipografia (*f.*) stereotypography.
estereotomia (*f.*, *Bot.*) stereotomy.
esterigma (*m.*, *Bot.*) sterigma.
estéril [-téreis] (*adj.*) sterile; barren; (*m.*, *Mining*) burden.
esterilidade (*f.*) sterility; barrenness.
esterilização (*f.*) sterilization.
esterilizado −da (*adj.*) sterilized.
esterilizador −dora (*adj.*) sterilizing; (*m.*) sterilizer.
esterilizante (*adj.*) sterilizing.
esterilizar (*v.t.*) to sterilize; (*v.r.*) to become barren.
esterlicado −da (*adj.*) tight-fitting (gloves, garments, shoes, etc.).
esterlino −na (*adj.*) sterling; (*m.*) pound sterling.
esternal (*adj.*) sternal.
estérnebra (*f.*, *Anat.*) sternebra.
esterno (*m.*) sternum, breastbone.
esternoclidomastoídeo −dea (*adj.*, *Anat.*) sternocl(e)ido-mastoid.
esterno-maxilar (*adj.*) sternomaxillary.
esternutação (*f.*) sneeze; sneezing.
esternutatório −ria (*adj.*) provocative of sneezing.
estero [tê] (*m.*) marsh land, bottom land [on Brazil's southwestern frontier].
esterqueira (*f.*), **esterqueiro, esterquilínio** (*m.*) manure pile, dunghill; hotbed.
esterroar (*v.t.*) to break up clods (with a harrow).
estertor (*m.*) stertor; labored, noisy breathing; death rattle.
estertoroso −sa (*adj.*) stertorous.
estese, estesia (*f.*) esthesia, esthesis.
estesiologia (*f.*) esthesiology.
estesiometria (*f.*) esthesiometry.
estesiômetro (*m.*) esthesiometer.
estesioneurose (*f.*) esthesioneurosis.
estesourar (*v.t.*) to cut with a TESOURA (scissors).
esteta (*m.*, *f.*) aesthete.
estético −ca (*adj.*) aesthetic; (*f.*) aesthetics.
estetismo (*m.*) aestheticism.
estetoscópio (*m.*) stethoscope.
estêva (*f.*) plow handle; (*Bot.*) the gum rockrose (*Cistus ladaniferus*).
estevão (*m.*) the poplar leaf rockrose (*Cistus populifolius*).
esteve, form of ESTAR [45].
estevia (*f.*, *Bot.*) the purple stevia (*S. purpurea*).
estiada (*f.*) a dry spell; lull.
estiagem (*f.*) drought, lack of rain, dry weather; low water mark.
estiar (*v.i.*) of weather, to dry up; to stop raining; of flood, to go down.
estibamina (*f.*, *Chem.*) antimony hydride, stibine.
estibiado −da (*adj.*, *Chem.*) stibiated.
estibial (*adj.*, *Chem.*) stibial, antimonial.
estibina (*f.*, *Min.*) stibnite, antimonite.
estíbio (*m.*, *Min.*) stibium; (*Chem.*) antimony.
estibordo (*m.*) starboard.

estica (*f.*) thinness; thin person; ill health; pusillanimity. **estar na—,** (*colloq.*) to be well-dressed.
esticador −dora (*adj.*) stretching; (*m.*) stretcher.
esticar (*v.t.*) to stretch (out); to stretch tight (as a rope); to pull, draw, tug; (*v.i.*, *colloq.*) to "croak" (die); (*v.r.*) stretch out.—**as canelas,** (*slang*) to kick the bucket (die); lit., to stretch one's shinbones. [Cf. ESTENDER, ESTIRAR, ESPICHAR].
estictáceas (*f.pl.*) a family (*Stictaceae*) of common foliaceous lichens.
estígio −gia, estigial (*adj.*) Stygian.
estigma (*m.*) stigma; scar; brand; stain, slur; (*Bot.*, *Zool.*) stigma; (*pl.*) stigmata.
estigmar, estigmatizar (*v.t.*) to stigmatize; to brand.
estilação (*f.*) dripping, trickling.
estilar (*v.t.*) to distill; to shed tears; (*v.i.*) to drip; to trickle; (*v.r.*) to waste away.
estilbito (*m.*, *Min.*) stilbite.
estilete [lê] (*m.*) stiletto; (*Surg.*) probe; (*Bot.*) style.
estilha (*f.*) chip; splinter, sliver.
estilhaçar (*v.t.*) to splinter, shatter (to bits).
estilhaço (*m.*) fragment, splinter; (*pl.*) shrapnel.
estilhar (*v.t.*) to shatter.
estilhial (*m.*, *Zool.*) stylohyal.
estilicídio (*m.*) a dripping (as of rain water from the eaves); fig. a running of the nose.
estilidiáceas (*f.pl.*, *Bot.*) the styleworts or stylidium family (*Stylidiaceae*).
estilidiáceo −a (*adj.*, *Bot.*) stylidiaceous.
estiliforme (*adj.*) styliform.
estilingue (*m.*) slingshot.
estilismo (*m.*) exaggerated nicety of speech or dress.
estilista (*m.*, *f.*) stylist.
estilístico −ca (*adj.*) stylistic.
estilita (*m.*) stylite, pillar saint; (*adj.*) stylitic.
estilização (*f.*) stylization.
estilizar (*v.t.*) to stylize.
estilo (*m.*) style, mode of expression; fashion, vogue; a stylus.—**antigo,** old-fashioned style. **de—,** customary.
estilobata, estilóbata (*m.*, *Arch.*) stylobate.
estilofaríngeo −gea (*adj.*, *Anat.*) stylopharyngeal.
estiloglosso −sa [glô] (*adj.*, *Anat.*) styloglossal.
estilógrafo (*m.*) stylograph.
estilóide, estiloídeo −dea (*adj.*) styloid.
estilômetro (*m.*) stylometer.
estima (*f.*) esteem, respect, high regard; liking, affection.
estimação (*f.*) esteem, regard; estimation, computation. **animal de—,** pet animal. **objeto de—,** prized possession.
estimar (*v.t.*) to esteem, prize, value; to like, admire; to estimate, appraise, value (**em,** at); to rejoice, be glad (**que,** that); (*v.r.*) to esteem one another; to have high regard for oneself; to deem (hold) oneself to be (something).—**em nada,** or **em pouco,** to have little or no regard for.
estimativo −va (*adj.*) estimative; (*f.*) estimation, appraisement; calculation, reckoning.
estimável (*adj.*) estimable, computable; worthy of esteem.
estimulação (*f.*) stimulation.
estimulador −dora (*adj.*) stimulating; (*m.*, *f.*) one who, or that which, stimulates.
estimulante (*adj.*) stimulating; (*m.*) stimulant.
estimular (*v.t.*) to stimulate, incite, rouse, stir up.
estimulativo −va (*adj.*) stimulative.
estímulo (*m.*) stimulus; incentive; provocation.—**da consciência,** remorse.—**de honra,** point of honor.
estio (*m.*) summer; (*adj.*) estival.
estiolar (*v.t.*) to etiolate; to weaken; (*v.i.*, *v.r.*) to grow weak.
estipa (*f.*) the genus (*Stipa*) of needlegrasses and feathergrasses.
estipe (*m.*, *Bot.*) stipe.
estipela (*f.*, *Bot.*) stipel.
estipendiar (*v.t.*) to pay a stipend to.
estipendiário −ria (*adj.*) stipendiary.
estipêndio (*m.*) stipend, allowance.
estipitado −da (*adj.*, *Bot.*) stipitate.
estípite (*m.*, *Zool.*) stipes, stalk, stem, peduncle; (*Law*) stipes, stock, ancestor.
estipticidade (*f.*) stypticity, astringency.
estíptico −ca (*adj.*) styptic, astringent; very thin; mean, miserly.
estípula (*f.*, *Bot.*) stipule.
estipulação (*f.*) stipulation; clause, condition.

estipulado –da (*adj.*) stipulated; conventional; (*Bot.*) stipulate.

estipulador –dora (*adj.*) stipulatory; (*m.,f.*) stipulator.

estipulante (*m.,f.*) party to a stipulation; (*adj.*) stipulating.

estipular (*v.t.*) to stipulate, agree upon; to require as a condition; (*adj., Bot.*) stipular.

estiracáceo –cea (*adj., Bot.*) styracaceous; (*f.pl.*) the storax family (*Styracaceae*).

estiraçar (*v.t.*) to stretch; to spread on the ground; (*v.r.*) to stretch oneself.

estirada (*f.*), **estirão** (*m.*) a long journey; a long pull; a weary trudge or tramp; a stretch of river.

estirado –da (*adj.*) stretched (out); long-drawn-out; of wire, etc., drawn.—**na areia**, stretched out on the sand.

estirar (*v.t.*) to stretch (out), pull; to draw out, lengthen out; to draw, beat out or roll (metal); (*v.r.*) to stretch out. Cf. ESTENDER, ESTICAR.—**as pernas**, to stretch one's legs.—**no chão**, to stretch out on the ground.

estirene (*m., Chem.*) styrene; vinylbenzene.

estirpe (*f.*) stirps, stock, strain; breed; ancestry, pedigree, race.

estirpicultura (*f.*) stirpiculture.

estiv-+personal verb endings = forms of ESTAR [45].

estiva (*f.*) ship's hold; stowage; heavy cargo which is stowed first; ship's ballast; wooden grating; footbridge; staple goods.

estivação (*f.*) stowage.

estivado –da (*adj.*) of a vessel, loaded and trimmed; full, replete.

estivador –dora (*adj.*) stevedoring; (*m.*) stevedore, long-shoreman.

estivagem (*f.*) stevedoring, loading and unloading of ships.

estival (*adj.*) summer, estival.

estivar (*v.t.*) to stow cargo; to load and unload ships.

estivo –va (*adj.*) estival, summer [= ESTIO, ESTIVAL].

esto (*m.*) intense heat; ardor, frenzy; roaring of waves.

estocada (*f.*) stab, jab, lunge, thrust (as with a dagger); unpleasant surprise.

estôfa (*f.*) stuff (woven material or fabric); fig. inward character, qualities.

estofado –da (*adj.*) upholstered; padded.

estofador –dora (*m.,f.*) upholsterer.

estofar (*v.t.*) to upholster; to pad.

estôfo –fa (*adj.*) slack [tide]; (*m.*) woven fabric; inter-lining; padding; stuffing; (*pl.*) upholstered furniture.

estoicidade (*f.*) stoical quality.

estoicismo (*m.*) stoicism, impassivity; indifference (to pleasure and pain).

estóico –ca (*adj.*) stoic(al), impassive.

estoirar (*v.*) = ESTOURAR.

estôjo (*m.*) kit, case; set.—**de campanha**, field kit.—**de costura**, sewing kit.—**de desenho**, drawing set.—**medular**, (*Bot.*) medullary sheath.

estol [ó] (*m.*) stall (of an airplane).

estola (*f.*) stole.

estolar (*v.i., Aeron.*) to stall.

estolho [tô] (*m., Bot.*) stolon.

estolhoso –sa (*adj., Bot.*) stolonate.

estolidez (*f.*) stolidity; stupidity.

estólido –da (*adj.*) stupid, dull, stolid.

estolonífero –ra (*adj., Bot.*) stoloniferous.

estoma (*m., Bot.*) stoma [= ESTÔMATO].

estomacal (*adj.*) stomachic.

estomagado –da (*adj.*) irritated; vexed, annoyed; angered, upset; resentful.

estomagar (*v.t.*) to anger; to offend, vex; (*v.r.*) to resent; to take offense at.

estômago (*m.*) stomach; appetite, inclination; disposition.

estomápode (*adj., Zool.*) stomatopod; (*m.pl.*) = ESTOMATÓPODES.

estomáquico –ca (*adj.*) stomachic(al) [= ESTOMACAL].

estomatite (*f., Med.*) stomatitis.

estômato (*m., Bot.*) stoma [= ESTOMA].

estomatomicose (*f., Med.*) stomatomycosis [= SAPINHOS].

estomatoplastia (*f., Surg.*) stomatoplasty.

estomatópode (*adj., Zool.*) stomatopod; (*m.pl.*) the Stomatopoda.

estomentar (*v.t.*) to dress, scutch, swingle, hatchel (flax, hemp, jute).

estomódio (*m., Embryol., Zool.*) stomodaeum.

estomoxo [ks] (*m.*) the blood-sucking stable fly (*Stomoxys calcitrans*) and others of this genus.

estonar (*v.t.*) to peel; to skin.

estoniano –na, **estônio** –nia (*adj.; m.,f.*) Esthonian.

estonteado –da (*adj.*) stunned; bewildered, dazed; mud-dleheaded.

estonteante (*adj.*) stunning, bewildering; dazzling.

estontear (*v.t.*) to stun, daze, bewilder, fuddle, muddle.

estôpa (*f.*) cotton waste; oakum, tow; coconut fiber.

estopada (*f.*) wad; padding; oakum; (*colloq.*) annoyance; boring talk; a grind (long, tiresome work); a blunder.

estopador –dora, **estopante** (*adj.*) importunate; annoying.

estopar (*v.t.*) to calk with oakum; (*colloq.*) to bore, annoy.

estopetar (*v.t.*) to muss, rumple (the hair).

estopim (*m.*) fuse.

estoque (*m.*) stock of goods; rapier.—**d'água**, "a point at which conflicting currents cause a stream to shift in an oblique direction." [*GBAT*].

estoquear (*v.t.*) to wound with a rapier; to prod.

estoquésia (*f., Bot.*) stokesia (*S. leavis*).

estoquista (*m.*) one who stocks merchandise; stock clerk.

estoraque (*m.*) storax (resin, tree).—**-da-america,—-do-campo** = CUIA-DO-BREJO. — **-do-campo,** — **-do-mato,** — **-liso** = CARNE-DE-VACA.

estorcegar (*v.t.*) to twist; to pinch, tweak; (*v.r.*) to writhe.

estorcer (*v.t.*) to twist; (*v.r.*) to squirm; to twist and turn; to writhe (in pain).

estore (*m.*) window shade; blind.

estória (*f.*) anecdote, story, tale.

estornar (*v.t.*) to transfer from debit to credit and vice-versa; to cancel a marine insurance contract.

estornicado –da (*adj.*) tight-fitting [garment].

estorninho –nha (*adj.*) of horses, solid-colored with small white patches; (*m.*) a starling.

estôrno (*m.*) a cross-entry (in bookkeeping); cancellation of an insurance contract.

estorrador (*m.*) harrow.

estorricado –da (*adj.*) parched; of soil, hard and dry.

estorricar (*v.t.*) to scorch, parch.

estorroar (*v.*) = ESTERROAR.

estortegar (*v.t.*) to twist; to tweak; (*v.r.*) to writhe.

estorturar-se (*v.r.*) to writhe in agony.

estorva (*f.*) hindrance; (*pl.*) seams (in a ship's hull).

estorvador –dora (*adj.*) hindering, impeding; (*m.,f.*) one who hinders.

estorvamento (*m.*) = ESTÔRVO.

estorvante (*adj.*) hindering, impeding.

estorvar (*v.t.*) to hinder, hamper, impede, obstruct, en-cumber; to disturb.

estorvilho (*m.*) slight obstacle.

estôrvo (*m.*) hindrance, obstaclè, cumbrance, difficulty.

estou-fraca (*f.*) guinea fowl. [This is the onomatopoeic name. Other common names are: GALINHA-DA-ANGOLA, GALINHA-DA-GUINÉ, GALINHA-DA-NUMÍDIA, MELEAGRIS, PINTADA.]

estourado –da (*adj.*) burst, exploded; of persons, wanton, unrestrained, unconventional, boisterous; (*m.,f.*) such a person; (*f.*) sound of explosions; (*colloq.*) an explosion of anger; a brawl.

estourar (*v.i.*) to burst; to explode, blow up; of a tire, to blow out; to "blow up" in anger; of cattle, to stampede; (*v.t.*) to burst, explode.—**a banca**, to "bust" the bank. —**de riso**, to burst laughing.—**os miolos**, to blow out (one's or another's) brains.

estoura-vèrgas (*m.*) a hothead. Var. ESTOIRA-VÊRGAS.

estouro (*m.*) blast, burst, explosion; fig. a bombshell (surprise).—**da boiada**, stampede of cattle.

estoutra = ESTA OUTRA.

estoutro = ÊSTE OUTRO.

estouvado –da (*adj.*) brash, rash, foolhardy, rattlebrained, harumscarum; hotheaded; devil-may-care.

estouvamento (*m.*) wildness, rashness, foolhardiness.

estrábico –ca (*adj.*) strabismic, cross-eyed.

estrabismo (*m.*) strabismus, squint, cross-eye.

estrabo (*m.*) dung.

estrabômetro (*m., Med.*) strabismometer.

estrabotomia (*f., Surg.*) strabotomy.

estrabulega(s) (*m.*) hothead, foolhardy fellow.

estraçalhar (*v.t.*) to tear to pieces, to shreds.

estracinhar, estraçoar (*v.t.*) to shatter; to smash, to shred.

estrada (*f.*) road, highway; "the circular path followed by the SERINGUEIRO in the bleeding of his rubber trees." [*GBAT*].—**abaúlada**, crowned road.—**de duas mãos**, two-way road.—**de ferro**, railroad.—**de rodagem**, high-way.—**de uma só mão**, one-way road.—**mestra (or real)**

main road.—**nacional**, government highway. **à beira da—**, at the side of the road.

estradal (*adj.*) of or pert. to roads (a Brazilian neologism).

estradar (*v.t.*) to build roads.

estradear-se (*v.r.*) to go (travel) over a road.

estradeiro –ra (*adj.*) of horses, having a good stride; of persons, given to leaving home and taking to the road; rascally; crooked.

estradiota (*f.*) a stiff-legged style of horseback riding.

estradivário (*m.*) a Stradivarius (violin).

estrado (*m.*) platform; dais; broad bench; bed frame; automobile chassis.

estrafegar (*v.t.*) to tear to pieces.

estraga-albardas (*m.*) wastrel; foolhardy person.

estragado –da (*adj.*) spoiled; damaged, in need of repairs, run down. **Criança mimada, criança—**, Spare the rod and spoil the child.

estragador –dora (*adj.; m.,f.*) that, or one who spoils, etc. See the verb ESTRAGAR.

estraga-festas (*m.,f.*) kill-joy, wet blanket.

estragão (*m., Bot.*) tarragon (*Artemesia dracunculus*).

estragar (*v.t.*) to spoil, injure, mar, blemish, damage; to bungle; to ruin, destroy; to corrupt; (*v.r.*) to become spoiled or damaged; to deteriorate.

estrago (*m.*) damage, harm; deterioration; ruination; waste, destruction; (*pl.*) spoilage, havoc.

estragol (*m., Chem.*) estragol(e).

estragoso –sa (*adj.*) = ESTRAGADOR.

estralada (*f.*) a brawl.

estralar (*v.t.,v.i.*) to burst [= ESTALAR].

estralejar (*v.i.*) to bang; to resound; to crack, snap (as a whip).

estralheira (*f.*) ship's hoist.

estrambótico –ca (*adj.*) odd, ridiculous, queer.

estramíneo –nea (*adj.*) stramineous, straw-colored.

estramônio (*m.*) the jimsonweed datura (*D. stramonium*), c.a. FIGUEIRA-DO-DIABO, FIGUEIRA-DO-INFERNO, FIGUEIRA-BRAVA, ZABUMBA.

estrangeirado –da (*adj.*) imitative of foreigners; (*f.*) a horde of foreigners. [*Derogatory*]

estrangeirice (*f.*) foreign ways; fondness for foreigners.

estrangeirismo (*m.*) foreign word or expression.

estrangeiro –ra (*adj.*) foreign, alien; (*m.,f.*) foreigner; foreign lands. **do—**, from abroad. **no—**, abroad.

estrangulação (*f.*) strangulation.

estrangulador –dora (*adj.*) strangling; (*m.,f.*) strangler; (*m.*) choke (of a carburetor).

estrangulamento (*m.*) strangulation; choking; constriction; (*Med.*) strangulation. **ponto de—**, bottleneck.

estrangular (*v.t.*) to strangle, choke, throttle, suffocate; (*v.r.*) to hang oneself.

estranguria (*f., Med.*) strangury.

estranhado –da (*adj.*) shy, ill-at-ease.

estranhão –nhona (*adj.; m.,f.*) shy, timorous (person).

estranhar (*v.t.*) to find strange, odd, reprehensible; to wonder at; to feel ill at ease with (strangers); (*v.r.*) to have a falling out (of persons).

estranhável (*adj.*) to be wondered at.

estranheza [êz] (*f.*) strangeness; oddity; wonder, surprise.

estranho –nha (ɐad·.) strange, foreign, alien, outlandish; extraneous; odd, queer, peculiar; unfamiliar, unknown. **um sujeito—**, a queer fellow; (*m.,f.*) stranger, outsider.

estranja (*m.,f.*) foreigner, stranger; (*f.*) foreign lands.

estrapada (*f.*) strappado (form of torture).

estratagema (*m.*) stratagem, device, artifice, ruse.

estratégia (*f.*) strategy; strategics.

estratégico –ca (*adj.*) strategic; (*m.*) strategist.

estrategista (*m.,f.*) strategist.

estratificação (*f.*) stratification.

estratificar (*v.t.,v.r.*) to stratify.

estratiforme (*adj.*) stratiform.

estratigrafia (*f.*) stratigraphy.

estratigráfico –ca (*adj.*) stratigraphic(al).

estrato (*m.*) stratum; stratus.—**-cúmulo**, strato-cumulus.

estratocracia (*f.*) stratocracy.

estratocrata (*m.*) stratocrat, military governor.

estratosfera (*f.*) stratosphere.

estratosférico –ca (*adj.*) stratospheric.

estreante (*adj.*) appearing in public, or trying out, for the first time; (*m.,f.*) one making his or her first public or professional appearance; beginner.

estrear [14] (*v.t.*) to try out (or use, or do a thing) for the first time; to make a first public or professional appearance (as an actor, writer, etc.); (*v.r.*) to make one's debut.

estrebaria (*f.*) stable.

estrebuchamento (*m.*) tossing about of arms and legs, floundering.

estrebuchar (*v.i.*) to struggle, flounder, toss (about); to writhe, twist (as in pain); (*v.r.*) to toss convulsively.

estréia (*f.*) debut, first appearance, coming out; theatrical first night or première; an author's first book.

estreitamento (*m.*) constriction, tightening, narrowing; (*Med.*) stricture.

estreitar (*v.t.*) to straiten, narrow; to tighten, confine, limit; to constrict, constrain; to diminish; to shorten; (*v.i.,v.r.*) to narrow.

estreiteza [tê] (*f.*) narrowness; tightness; tightfistedness; (*pl.*) straits.

estreito –ta (*adj.*) strait, narrow, close; narrow-minded; (*m.*) a strait; an inlet.

estreitura (*f.*) = ESTREITAMENTO, ESTREITEZA.

estrêla (*f.*) star.—**cadente**, falling star.—**-d'alva** or **da manhã**, morning star.—**da tarde,**—**do pastor,**—**Vésper,**—**vespertina**, evening star.—**-de-Jerusalem**, (*Bot.*) snow-in-summer (*Cerastium tomentosum*).—**-de-ouro**, (*Bot.*) the corn marigold (*Chrysanthemum segetum*), c.a. PAMPILHO-DAS-SEARAS.—**-de-rabo**, (*colloq.*) comet.—**-do-mar**, starfish.—**-do-norte**, (*Bot.*) a box brier (*Randia*).—**polar**, polestar. **ver—s ao meio dia**, to see stars (be stunned).

estreladeira (*f.*) frying pan for eggs.

estrelado –da (*adj.*) starry, star-studded; of eggs, fried; of animals, having a blaze.

estrelante (*adj.*) star-studded; shining, scintillating.

estrelar (*v.t.*) to set or adorn with stars; to bespangle.—**ovos**, to fry eggs.

estrelário –ria (*adj.*) star-shaped.

estrelato (*m.*) stardom.

estrelejar (*v.i.*) of the sky, to fill with stars.

estrelinha (*f.*) asterisk; star-shaped bits of noodle paste (for soup); a sparkler (kind of fireworks).

estrelítzia (*f.*) bird-of-paradise flower (*Strelitzia sp.*).

estrêlo –la (*adj.*) of animals, blazed; of persons, having a white forelock.

estrema (*f.*) line of demarcation; boundary line; landmark.

estremadura (*f.*) frontier, boundary line.

estremar (*v.t.*) to demarcate; to separate; to distinguish.—**o bem do mal**, to distinguish between good and evil.

estreme (*adj.*) unmixed, undiluted, pure.

estremecer (*v.t.*) to shake, convulse, stagger; to daunt; (*v.i.*) to tremble, shiver, quiver; to shudder; to start, wince; to love to extremes.

estremecido –da (*adj.*) shaken; frightened; dearly loved.

estremecimento (*m.*) shaking, shuddering, shivering; quiver; a thrill.

estremunhado –da (*adj.*) startled from sleep, half-awake, drowsy, heavy-lidded.

estremunhar (*v.t.,v.i.*) to startle, arouse suddenly (from sleep); (*v.r.*) to start up half-asleep.

estrênuo –nua (*adj.*) strenuous.

estrepar-se (*v.r.*) to wound oneself (as on a jagged piece of glass or other sharp point); (*colloq.*) to come a cropper (fall).

estrepe (*m.*) thorn, sharp point; (*Mil.*) caltrop; (*pl.*) pieces of broken glass imbedded in the mortar along the top of a wall to discourage trespassers; (*colloq.*) thin, ugly woman; busybody.

estrepitante (*adj.*) strepitant, loud, noisy, clamorous, boisterous.

estrepitar (*v.t.,v.i.*) to make a loud noise; to crack (as a whip).

estrépito (*m.*) noise, din, rachet, clatter, rattle.

estrepitoso –sa (*adj.*) strepitous, noisy, loud, clamorous.

estrepolia (*f.*) tumult; hubbub; prank; shindy, fracas.

estreptococo (*m., Bacteriol.*) streptococcus.

estria (*f.*) groove, channel; score; fluting; rifling (of a gun); a stripe or streak (color or texture); (*Arch.*) stria.

estriamento (*m.*) striation.

estriar (*v.t.*) to channel, groove; to score; to rifle (a gun); to stripe or streak; (*Arch.*) to flute.

estribado –da (*adj.*) with foot in stirrup; fig. firmly based, well-grounded.

estribar (*v.t.*) to rest, base (**em, sôbre**, on, upon).—**uma opinão**, to back up an opinion; (*v.r.*) to place one's foot in the stirrup; to base oneself on.

estribeira (*f.*) stirrup; step. **perder as—s**, (*colloq.*) to lose one's head.

estribeiro (m.) stableman.
estribilho (m.) refrain, chorus; catchword, pet expression.
estribo (m.) stirrup; hanger; (Autom.) running board; any boarding step or platform; (Anat.) stapes, stirrup bone. com o pé no—, fig,. about to depart (on a journey).
estricnina (f., Chem.) strychnine.
estricnismo (m., Med.) strychninism.
estricno (m.) a genus (Strychnos) of poison nuts.
estridência (f.) stridency.
estridente (adj.) strident, shrill; noisy; jarring; raucous; grating.
estridor (m.) harsh, grating sound; stridor.
estridulação (f.) stridulation (of crickets, etc.).
estridulante (adj.) stridulous.
estridular (v.i.) to stridulate; to shrill; to chirr (as a cicada).
estrídulo –la, estriduloso –sa (adj.) strident, stridulous.
estriga (f.) a combed bunch of flax, tow or wool tied on the distaff; a lock of hair; pure white hair.
estrige (f.) vampire; ghoul; witch; owl.
estrilar (v.i., colloq.) to blow up in anger; to shout in protest.
estrilo (m., colloq.) a fit of rage; a squawk (protest, complaint). dar o—, to "blow one's top"; to have a conniption.
estrincar (v.t.)-to crack one's knuckles; to crack with the teeth.
estrinçar (v.) = DESTRINÇAR.
estringir (v.t.) to draw or bind tight.
estripado –da (adj.) disemboweled, gutted.
estripar (v.t.) to disembowel; to gut.
estrito –ta (adj.) strict, exact, precise; severe, rigorous, stringent.
estritura (f.) stricture.
estro (m.) oestrus, esp. in the sense of passionate, creative impulse; poetic inspiration; gadfly.
estrobilante (m., Bot.) Burma conehead (Strobilanthes dyerianus).
estróbilo (m., Bot.) strobile, cone.—de pinheiro, pine cone.
estroboscopia (f.) stroboscopy.
estroboscópio (m.) stroboscope.
estrôço (m.) swarm of bees.
estrofantina (f., Pharm.) strophanthin.
estrofanto (m., Bot.) the Transvaal strophanthus (S. hispidus).
estrofe (f.) strophe, stanza.
estrófulo (m., Med.) strophulus.
estrôina (adj.) wild, dissipated; harum-scarum; hotheaded; (m.) such a fellow; playboy.
estroinar (v.i.) to lead a wild, fast life, sow one's wild oats; to squander.
estroinice (f.) extravagance; folly; wildness; a spree.
estroma (m., Anat., Bot.) stroma.
estromania (f.) = NINFOMANIA.
estromaníaco (m.) = NINFOMANÍACO.
estromateídeos (m.pl.) a family (Stromateidae) of spiny-finned fishes, such as the GORDINHO (which see).
estrombo (m.) a conch shell of the genus Strombus.
estrompa (adj.; m.) rough, coarse (person).
estrompado –da (adj.) worn out; tired out; stupid.
estrompar (v.t.) to wear out (as shoes); (v.r.) to tire out.
estronca (f.) shore, prop, strut.
estroncar (v.t.) to dismember; to mutilate.
estrôncia, estronciana (f., Chem.) strontia, strontium oxide.
estroncianita (f., Chem.) strontianite.
estrôncio (m., Chem.) strontium.
estrondeante (adj.) roaring, rumbling, etc.;—see the verb ESTRONDEAR.
estrondear (v.i.) to roar, boom, resound; to rumble; to bluster; to be notorious. Var. ESTRONDAR.
estrondo (m.) roar; peal, blare; rattle, racket, din; rumble; bluster; notoriety.—sônico, sonic boom.
estrondoso –sa (adj.) noisy; thunderous; blatant. sucesso—, a resounding success.
estrôngilo (m., Zool.) strongle (roundworm of Strongylus).
estropalho (m.) dish rag.
estropeada (f., colloq.) tumult; sound of trampling feet.
estropelia (f.) tumult.
estropiado –da (adj.) maimed, crippled; lame.
estropiar (v.t.) to maim, cripple, disable; to mutilate; to bungle.
estropício (m.) damage; evil.

estropo [trô] strap; razor strop; (m., Naut.) strap; (Locom.) eccentric strap.
estrotejar (v.i.) to trot.
estrovenga (f.) gear; gadget; thingumbob.
estrugir (v.i.) to resound; to crackle; to clatter; to burst forth (as applause); to thunder; (v.t.) to braise.
estruir (v.) = DESTRUIR.
estruma (f.) scrofula; goiter.
estrumar (v.t.) to manure.
estrume (m.) manure, dung; any fertilizer.—de curral, barnyard manure.
estrumeira (f.) manure pile; compost heap.
estrumoso –sa (adj., Med.) strumous.
estrupada (f.) gust; skirmish.
estrupício (m., colloq.) riot, hubbub, fracas; a lot of something; a huge something; an instance of stupidity.
estrupido (m.) clatter (of horses' hoofs); stamping (of feet); tumult.
estrutura (f.) structure; frame.—atômica, atomic structure.—colunar, (Geol.) columnar structure.—cristalina, crystalline system.—molecular, molecular structure.—social, social structure.—zonada or zonar, (Cryst.) zonal structure.
estrutural (adj.) structural.
estuação (f.) glow; great heat; nausea.
estuante (adj.) seething, boiling; burning. mocidade—, fiery youth.
estuar (v.i.) to burn, glow; to boil, seethe.
estuário (m.) estuary.
estucador (m.) stuccoer, plasterer.
estucar (v.t.) to stucco; to plaster.
estucha (f.) wedge, spike, peg.
estuchar (v.t.) to drive in (a wedge, spike, etc.).
estudado –da (adj.) studied; affected.
estudantaço (m.) –ça (f., colloq.) quite a student, a "brain".
estudantada (f.) a crowd of students; a students' prank.
estudantão –tona (m.,f.) = ESTUDANTAÇO –ÇA.
estudante (m.,f.) student.
estudantesco –ca (adj.) student.
estudantil (adj.) of or pert. to students.
estudantina (f.) students' glee club.
estudar (v.t.,v.i.) to study, learn; to analyze, scrutinize; (v.r.) to analyze oneself.
estúdio (m.) studio.
estudioso –sa (adj.) studious.
estudo (m.) study; research; survey; (pl.) course of study.
estufa (f.) stove, heater; hot house; sterilizer (in a laboratory); kiln.
estufadeira (f.) covered stew-pan.
estufado –da (adj.) stewed; placed in a hot house; sterilized; (m.) a stew.
estufar (v.t.) to place in a hot house; to stew, braise (meat); to sterilize (surgical instruments).
estufim (m.) bell jar or small glass case for plants; hot frame.
estugar (v.t.) to quicken one's step; to urge on.
estultícia (f.) doltishness; folly.
estultificar (v.t.) to stultify.
estulto –ta (adj.) doltish, stupid, foolish.
estumar (v.t.) to egg on, incite.
estupefação (f.) stupefaction, numbness; astonishment.
estupefaciente, estupefactivo –va (adj.; m.) stupefacient, narcotic.
estupefato –ta (adj.) stupefied, numb; dumfounded, amazed, aghast.
estupefazer, estupeficar (v.t.) to stupefy; to flabbergast.
estupefeito –ta (adj.) = ESTUPEFATO.
estupendo –da (adj.) stupendous, wonderful; huge.
estupidarrão –rona (adj.) very stupid.
estupidez [dêz] (f.) stupidity, dullness; boorishness; rough, impolite manners.
estupidificar (v.t.) to fuddle, muddle, confuse, (v.r.) to become muddled.
estúpido –da (adj.) stupid; "dumb," dense; ill-mannered, uncouth; (m.,f.) blockhead, dunce, numskull.
estupor [-es] [ô] (m.) stupor; lethargy; trance; (colloq.) a very bad or ugly person; rotter.
estuporado –da (adj.) seized with stupor; evil, ugly.
estuprador (m.) rapist, ravisher.
estuprar (v.t.) to rape, ravish, outrage.
estupro (m.) rape, ravishment.
estuque (m.) stucco.
estúrdia (f.) prank, frolic.

esturdiar (*v.i.*) to frolic, play pranks.
esturjão (*m.*) sturgeon.
esturrado –**da** (*adj.*) scorched, nearly burned; fiery, excited; having antiquated notions; (*m.,f.*) dyed-in-the-wool partisan, fanatic.
esturrar (*v.t.*) to scorch; (*v.i.,v.r.*) to almost burn; to get hot under the collar.
esturricar (*v.*) = ESTORRICAR.
ésula (*f.*) leafy euphorbia (*E. esula*), c.a. ERVA-DE-MALEITAS.—**pequena**, small euphorbia (*E. peplus*).
esvaecer (*v.t.*) to dissipate, disperse; to efface; (*v.i.*) to faint; (*v.r.*) to weaken; to vanish.
esvaecido –**da** (*adj.*) dispersed, dissipated; weakened.
esvaecimento (*m.*) fainting; act of weakening; discouragement; confusion; vanity.
esvaimento [a-i] (*m.*) evaporation, dissipation; fainting.—**de cabeça**, dizziness.—**de sangue**, loss of blood.
esvair-se [75] (*v.r.*) to evanesce, vanish; to fade, pass away.—**em sangue**, to bleed to death.
esvanecente (*adj.*) evanescent.
esvanecer (*v.i.*) evanesce.
esvaziamento (*m.*) emptying, draining; deflation (of a balloon, tire, etc., but not of currency, which is DE-FLAÇÃO).
esvaziar (*v.t.*) to empty, drain, deplete; to deflate (as a tire or balloon, but not currency, which is DESINFLAR).
esverdeado –**da** (*adj.*) greenish.
esverdear (*v.t.*) to make green; (*v.r.*) to turn green.
esverdinhado –**da** (*adj.*) light green; greenish.
esverdinhar (*v.t.*) to make light green; (*v.i.,v.r.*) to turn so.
esviscerado –**da** (*adj.*) disemboweled; fig. ruthless.
esviscerar (*v.t.*) to eviscerate.
esvoaçar (*v.i.*) to fly, flit, flutter.
esvurmar (*v.t.*) to squeeze out the pus (from a sore); fig. to lay bare (ugly facts); to give vent to (hate, etc.).
êta! êta-ferro! êta-mundo! êta-pau! hot dog! hotdiggity!
étagère (*f.*) an open-shelved cabinet for china and silver; a whatnot for bric-a-brac. [French].
etal (*m., Chem.*) ethal, cetyl alcohol.
etalage (*f.*) bosh (of a blast furnace), c.a. RAMPA.
etanadióico (*m., Chem.*) oxalic acid; ethane dioic acid.
etanal (*m., Chem.*) acetaldehyde.
etano (*m., Chem.*) ethane.
etanóico (*m., Chem.*) ethanoic acid, acetic acid.
etanol (*m., Chem.*) ethanol, ethyl alcohol.
etapa (*f.*) a day's rations; a day's march; halting place; stage (of growth, of progress); (*Radio*) stage.
etena (*f., Chem.*) ethylene.
éter (*m.*) ether.—**aceto-acético**, ethyl-aceto acetate; diacetic ether.—**dicloroetilo**, dichloro ethyl ether.—**difenilo**, phenyl ether; diphenyl ether.—**etílico**, ethyl ether; ethyl oxide.—**metílico**, methyl ether; dimethyl ether.
eterato (*m., Chem.*) etherate.
etéreo –**rea** (*adj.*) ethereal.
eterificar (*v.t., Chem.*) to etherify.
eterizar (*v.t.*) to etherize.
eternal (*adj.*) eternal. [Poetic form of ETERNO.]
eternar (*v.*) = ETERNIZAR.
eternidade (*f.*) eternity.
eternizar (*v.t.*) to make eternal, immortalize; (*v.r.*) to become immortal.
eterno –**na** (*adj.*) eternal, everlasting; immortal; unchanging; (*m.*) the Eternal (God).
eterolato (*m., Chem.*) etherolate.
ético –**ca** (*adj.*) ethical, moral; (*f.*) ethics.
etilamina (*f., Chem.*) ethylamin(e).
etilar (*v.t., Chem.*) to ethylate.
etil-celulose (*f., Chem.*) ethyl cellulose; cellulose ether.
etilênico –**ca** (*adj.*) ethylenic.
etílico –**ca** (*adj., Chem.*) ethylic.
etilismo (*m.*) = ACOOLISMO.
etilista (*m.,f.*) = ALCOOLATRA.
etilmorfina (*f., Chem.*) ethylmorphine.
etilo (*m., Chem.*) ethyl; tetraethyl lead; lead tetraethide.
etilsulfúrico –**ca** (*adj., Chem.*) ethylsulfuric.
étimo (*m.*) a primitive or root word.
etimologia (*f.*) etymology.
etimológico –**ca** (*adj.*) etymological.
etimologismo (*m.*) etymologization.
etimologista (*m.,f.*) etymologist.
etimologizar (*v.t.*) to etymologize.
etimólogo –**ga** (*m.,f.*) etymologist.
etiogênico –**ca** (*adj.*) etiogenic.

etiologia (*f.*) etiology.
etiônico –**ca** (*adj., Chem.*) **ácido**—, ethionic acid.
etíope, etiópico –**ca** (*adj.; m.*) Ethiopian.
etiopisa (*f.*) an Ethiopian woman.
etiquêta (*f.*) etiquette; tag, label, sticker.
etiquetar (*v.t.*) to label, put stickers on.
etmoidal (*adj., Anat., Zool.*) ethmoid(al).
etmóide (*m., Anat., Zool.*) ethmoid (bone).
etmoídeo –**da** (*adj.*) ethmoidal.
étnico –**ca** (*adj.*) ethnic(al). **grupo**—, ethnic group. (*m.,f.*) heathen, pagan.
etnocentrismo (*m.*) ethnocentrism.
etnogenia (*f.*) ethnogeny.
etnografia (*f.*) ethnography.
etnográfico –**ca** (*adj.*) ethnographic.
etnógrafo –**fa** (*m.,f.*) ethnographer.
etnologia (*f.*) ethnology.
etnológico –**ca** (*adj.*) ethnologic(al).
etnólogo –**ga** (*m.,f.*) ethnologist.
etografia (*f.*) ethography.
etologia (*f.*) ethology.
etopéia (*f., Rhet.*) ethopoeia.
etrusco –**ca** (*adj.; m.,f.*) Etruscan.
eu (pron.) I.—**mesmo**, I myself. **como**—, as I; like me.
E.U.A. = ESTADOS UNIDOS DA AMÉRICA (United States of America).
E.U.B. = ESTADOS UNIDOS DO BRASIL (United States of Brazil).
eucaína (*f., Pharm., Chem.*) eucaine.
eucaliptal (*m.*) a grove of eucalyptus.
eucalipteol (*m., Pharm.*) euclypteol.
eucalipto (*m., Bot.*) the genus Eucalyptus; a eucalypt.—**gigante**, the delegate eucalyptus (*E. gigantea*).—**limão**, the lemon eucalyptus (*E. citriodora*).—**pimenta**, the Sydney peppermint eucalyptus (*E. piperita*).—**vermelho**, the Kino eucalyptus (*E. resinifera*).
eucaliptol (*m.*) eucalyptus oil.
eucarídio (*m., Bot.*) a clarkia (*C. breweri*).
Eucaristia (*f.*) Eucharist; Holy Communion; Lord's Supper.
eucarístico –**ca** (*adj.*) Eucharistic.
euclidiano –**na** (*adj.*) Euclidean; also, of or pert. to Euclides da Cunha (Brazilian author).
Euclides (*m.*) Euclid.
euclorina (*f., Chem.*) euchlorine.
eucólogo (*m.*) euchology, prayer book.
eudemonismo (*m.*) eudaemonism.
eudiômetro (*m., Chem.*) eudiometer.
eufêmico –**ca** (*adj.*) euphemistic.
eufemismo (*m.*) euphemism.
eufonia (*f.*) euphony.
eufônico –**ca** (*adj.*) euphonic.
êufono –**na** (*adj.*) euphonious; (*m.*) a tanager.
euforbiáceo –**cea** (*adj., Bot.*) euphorbiaceous; (*f.pl.*) the succulents (*Euphorbiaceae*).
euforbina (*f., Pharm.*) euphorbium.
eufórbio (*m., Bot.*) the genus Euphorbium.
euforia (*f.*) euphoria, sense of well-being.
eufórico –**ca** (*adj.*) hale, in good spirits.
eufrásia (*f., Bot.*) the genus (*Euphrasia*) of eyebrights.
eufuísmo (*m.*) euphuism.
eufuístico –**ca** (*adj.*) euphuistic(al).
eugenia (*f.*) eugenics.
eugênia (*f., Bot.*) the genus Eugenia.—**uvalha**, the pitanga (*Eugenia uniflora*).
eugênico –**ca** (*adj.*) eugenic.
Eugênio (*m.*) Eugene.
eugenismo (*m.*) eugenism.
eugenista (*m.,f.*) eugenist.
eugenol (*m., Chem.*) eugenol; caryophyllic acid.
eulalia (*f.*) fair speech.
eulália (*f.*) Chinese silvergrass (*Miscanthus sinensis*).
eulóbio (*m., Bot.*) the genus (*Oenothera*) of evening primroses or sundrops.
eumorfo –**fa** (*adj.*) well-formed.
eunecto (*m., Zool.*) the genus Eunectes which includes the anaconda.
Eunice (*f.*) Eunice.
eunuco (*m.*) eunuch.
eunucóide (*adj., Med.*) eunuchoid.
eupatia (*f.*) eupathy, right feeling.
eupatorina (*f., Pharm.*) eupatorine.
eupatório (*m., Bot.*) the genus Eupatorium.—**comum**, —**de-avicena**, the hemp eupatorium (*E. cannabium*),

c.a. TREVO-CERVINO, TREVO-DE-SEARA.—-de-merué, sweet yarrow (*Achillea ageratum*), c.a. MACELA-DE-SÃO-JOÃO.—-dos-antigos (or -dos-gregos), common agrimony (*Agrimonia eupatoria*), c.a. AGRIMÔNIA.
eupepsia (*f.*) eupepsia, good digestion.
euplástico –ca (*adj.*, *Physiol.*) euplastic.
eupnéia (*f.*, *Physiol.*) eupnea.
eupódio (*m.*, *Bot.*) a fern (*Marattia alata*).
euquinina (*f.*, *Chem.*) quinine ethyl carbonate; Euquinine.
eurasiano –na (*adj.*; *m.*,*f.*) Eurasian.
Eureka! Eureka!
eurialino –na (*adj.*, *Biol.*) euryhaline.
euricéfalo –la (*adj.*) eurycephlic, having a wide head.
eurignato –ta (*adj.*) eurygnathic, having a wide jaw.
êurio (*m.*, *Craniol.*) euryon.
euripo (*m.*) strait, frith.
eurístomo –ma (*adj.*) eurystomatous, broad-mouthed.
euritérmico –ca (*adj.*, *Zool.*) eurythermal.
europeanismo (*m.*) European influence.
europeísmo (*m.*) admiration of Europe.
europeísta (*m.*,*f.*) admirer of Europe.
europeização [e-i] (*f.*) Europeanization.
europeizar [e-i] (*v.t.*) to Europeanize; (*v.r.*) to become European.
europeu –péia (*adj.*; *m.*,*f.*) European.
európio (*m.*, *Chem.*) europium.
eurritmia (*f.*) eurythmy.
Eustáquio (*m.*) Eustace.
eustático –ca (*adj.*, *Geol.*, *Physical Geog.*) eustatic.
eustilo (*m.*, *Arch.*) eustyle.
eutanásia (*f.*) euthanasia.
eutaxia [ks] eutaxy.
eutéctico –ca (*adj.*) eutectic [alloy, solution].
eutenia (*f.*) euthenics.
eutérios (*m.pl.*) the Eutheria (all mammals but the monotremes).
euterpe (*f.*, *Bot.*) "A small genus of graceful tropical American pinnate-leaved palms (family *Arecaceae*)." [*Webster*]
eutoca (*f.*) the sticky placelia (*Eutoca viscida*) and other plants of this genus.
eutrofia (*f.*) *Med.*) eutrophy, healthy, nutrition.
eutrópico –ca (*adj.*, *Chem.*) eutropic.
euxantona (*f.*, *Chem.*) euxanthone.
Eva (*f.*) Eva, Eve.
evacuação (*f.*) evacuation; excretion.
evacuar (*v.t.*) to evacuate, quit, withdraw from; to excrete; (*v.r.*) to leave, withdraw.
evadir (*v.t.*) to evade, elude, escape from; to dodge, duck; (*v.r.*) to escape, get away (**a**, **de**, from); to abscond.
evanescente (*adj.*) evanescent; elusive.
evangelho (*m.*) evangel, the Gospel. **tomar uma coisa por palavra do—**, to take a thing for gospel truth.
evangélico –ca (*adj.*) Evangelical.
Evangelina (*f.*) Evangeline.
evangelismo (*m.*) evangelism.
evangelista (*m.*) an Evangel; an evangelist; (*m.*,*f.*) a preacher; (*colloq.*) a Protestant.
evangelização (*f.*) evangelization.
evangelizador –dora (*adj.*) evangelizing; (*m.*,*f.*) evangelist.
evangelizante (*adj.*) evangelizing.
evangelizar (*v.t.*) to evangelize.
evaporação (*f.*) evaporation.
evaporadeira (*f.*) cane sirup evaporator.
evaporado –da (*adj.*) evaporated, vaporized.
evaporador (*m.*) evaporator.
evaporar (*v.t.*,*v.i.*) to evaporate, vaporize; to exhale; to volatilize; (*v.r.*) to evaporate; to vanish.
evaporativo –va (*adj.*) evaporative.
evaporável (*adj.*) evaporable.
evaporizar (*v.*) = EVAPORAR.
evasão (*f.*) flight, escape; (*fig.*) evasion.—**de talentos**, "brain drain."
evasivo –va (*adj.*) evasive, misleading; (*f.*) evasion, subterfuge, dodge, "double talk".
Evelina (*f.*) Evelina, Eveline, Evelyn.
evento (*m.*) event, happening.
eventual (*adj.*) fortuitous, casual, contingent. [But not eventual in the sense of ultimate, which is FINAL.]
eventualidade (*f.*) eventuality, chance happening, possible outcome; contingency. **nessa—**, in case that should happen.
evicção (*f.*) eviction.
evictor (*m.*) evictor.

evidência (*f.*) evidence. [But not in the legal sense of proof, which is PROVA.]; prominence, eminence.
evidenciar (*v.t.*) to evince, manifest, make evident, make clear; (*v.r.*) to become evident.
evidente (*adj.*) evident, plain, clear, obvious, unmistakable. **É—**, It goes without saying.
evisceração (*f.*) evisceration.
eviscerar (*v.t.*) to eviscerate, disembowel.
evitação (*f.*), evitamento (*m.*) avoidance.
evitar (*v.t.*) to avoid, shun, elude, dodge, keep away from; to forestall; to duck (a blow.)
evitável (*adj.*) avoidable.
evocação (*f.*) evocation, a calling up (of memories, etc.).
evocar (*v.t.*) to evoke, call forth; to conjure up.
evocativo –va (*adj.*) evocative.
evocatório –ria (*adj.*) evocatory.
evocável (*adj.*) evocable.
evoé! (*interj.*) evoe!
evolar-se (*v.r.*) to fly away, disappear.
evolução (*f.*) evolution; evolvement; maneuver.
evolucionar (*v.i.*,*v.t.*) to evolutionize.
evolucionismo (*m.*) the doctrine or science of evolution.
evolucionista (*adj.*; *m.*,*f.*) evolutionist.
evoluir (*v.i.*) to evolve, develop; to maneuver, perform evolutions [= EVOLVER, EVOLUCIONAR].
evoluta (*f.*, *Geom.*) evolute.
evolutivo –va (*adj.*) evolutional.
evolvente (*f.*, *Geom.*) involute.
evolver (*v.i.*) to evolve [= EVOLUCIONAR, EVOLUIR].
evônimo (*m.*, *Bot.*) the eastern wahoo (*Eunoymus atropurpureus*).—-**da-america**, the brook euonymus (*E. americanus*).—-**da-europa**, the European euonymus (*E. europaeus*).—-**do-japão**, the evergreen euonymus (*E. japonicus*).
evulsão (*f.*) evulsion, forcible extraction.
ex-, see also es-.
ex. = EXEMPLO (example); EXEMPLAR (copy).
ex.ª = EXCELÊNCIA (Excellency).
exabundante (*adj.*) most abundant.
exação (*f.*) exaction.
exacerbação (*f.*) exacerbation.
exacerbar (*v.t.*) to exacerbate, embitter, irritate, ramble, exasperate; (*v.r.*) to become aggravated, heightened.
exact-, see under exat-.
exageração (*f.*) exaggeration; overstatement.
exagerado –da (*adj.*) exaggerated; undue; immoderate; (*m.*,*f.*) one given to exaggeration.
exagerador –dora (*adj.*) exaggerating; (*m.*,*f.*) exaggerator.
exagerar (*v.t.*) to exaggerate, overstate, magnify; (*v.i.*) to use exaggeration, overdo.
exagêro (*m.*) exaggeration, overstatement.
exalação (*f.*) exhalation.
exalante (*adj.*) exhaling.
exalar (*v.t.*) to exhale, emit; (*v.r.*) to be exhaled (**de**, from); to evaporate.
exaltação (*f.*) exaltation; excitation; delirium.
exaltado –da (*adj.*) overexcited, delirious, heated, fanatical; hot-tempered; (*m.*,*f.*) a fanatic, a radical.
exaltar (*v.t.*) to exalt, ennoble; to elevate, heighten; to elate; to excite; to irritate; to extol, praise highly; (*v.r.*) to become enhanced or intensified; to get excited; to become irritated, to fly off the handle; to exalt oneself; to become elated.
exame (*m.*) examination; questioning; test, review; inquiry, scrutiny.—**de admissão**, entrance examination.—**de madureza**, (or de maturidade), final exams in high school.—**médico**, medical examination.—**s parciais**, interim school exams.—**vestibular**, university entrance examination. **após cuidadoso—**, after careful review. **fazer um—**, to take an exam (in school). **livre—**, free thought, free inquiry.
examinador –dora (*adj.*) examining; (*m.*,*f.*) examiner.
examinando –da (*m.*,*f.*) examinee.
examinar (*v.t.*) to examine, put questions to; to look into; (*v.r.*) to examine one's conscience.—**a dedo**, to examine critically, carefully.
examinável (*adj.*) examinable.
exangue (*adj.*) bloodless, anemic; feeble, debilitated.
exânime (*adj.*) inanimate, lifeless. [*Poetical*].
exantema (*m.*, *Med.*, *Plant Pathol.*) exanthema.
exantemático –ca (*adj.*) exanthematic.
exantematoso –sa (*adj.*) exanthematous.
exarar (*v.t.*) to engrave; to set down in writing, make a written notation of.

exarticulação (*f.*) = DESARTICULAÇÃO.
exasperação (*f.*) exasperation, irritation.
exasperador –**dora** (*adj.*) exasperating.
exasperar (*v.t.*) to exasperate, irritate, chafe, ramble, nettle; to provoke; to exarcebate; (*v.r.*) to become exasperated, infuriated, "sore".
exatidão (*f.*) exactness, accuracy, precision.
exato –**ta** (*adj.*) exact, accurate, precise.
exator –**tora** (*m.,f.*) tax collector.
exaurir [24, 25] (*v.t.*) to exhaust, drain; to deplete; to impoverish; (*v.r.*) to become exhausted.
exaurível (*adj.*) exhaustible.
exaustão (*m.*) exhaustion.
exaustar (*v.*) = EXAURIR.
exaustivo –**va** (*adj.*) exhaustive.
exausto –**ta** (*adj.*; *irreg. p.p. of* EXAURIR) exhausted; spent, jaded.
exaustor (*m.*) exhaust (for air, gas, etc.).
exautorar (*v.t.*) to deprive (divest) of honors, authority, privilege, etc.
exceção (*f.*) exception. **A—confirma a regra,** The exception proves the rule. **à—de,** except(ing), excluding, save, leaving out, with the exception of. **Não há regra sem—,** There is an exception to every rule.
excedente (*adj.; m.*) surplus.
exceder (*v.t.* to exceed, transcend, surpass; to overreach; to overstep; to excel, outdo, outstrip; (*v.r.*) to overdo; to go to excess; to forget oneself, esp. in anger.
excedível (*adj.*) surpassable.
excelência (*f.*) excellence, superiority. **por—,** par excellence, preeminently. **Vossa—,** Your Excellency.
excelente (*adj.*) excellent, superior.
excelentíssimo –**ma** (*absol. superl. of* EXCELENTE) most excellent.
exceler, excelir (*v.*) = EXCEDER.
excelso –**sa** (*adj.*) exalted, sublime; eminent.
excentricidade (*f.*) eccentricity; vagary.
excêntrico –**ca** (*adj.*) eccentric; peculiar, freakish, queer, odd; (*m.,f.*) a "screwball".
exce(p)cional (*adj.*) exceptional, uncommon, peculiar, anomalous.
exce(p)cionar (*v.t.*) to take exception to; (*Law*) to interpose an objection to.
exce(p)tiva (*f.*) an exceptive clause or condition.
exce(p)tivo –**va** (*adj.*) exceptive.
excerto (*m.*) excerpt.
excessivo –**va** (*adj.*) excessive; undue; immoderate.
excesso (*m.*) excess, surplus, remainder; superabundance; redundance; immoderation, overdoing; outrage.—**de pêso,** overweight. **em—,** in excess, extra, too much.
exceto (*prep.*) except(ing), excluding, save.
excetuado –**da** (*adj.*) excepted; exempted.
excetuar (*v.t.*) to except, exclude; to exempt (**de,** from); (*v.i., Law*) to take exception to; (*v.r.*) to make an exception of oneself.
excipiente (*m.*, *Pharm.*) excipient.
excisão (*f.*) excision.
excisar (*v.t.*) to excise.
excitabilidade (*f.*) excitability.
excitação (*f.*) excitation, excitement; thrill; flurry; agitation; irritation; (*Elec.*) excitation.
excitador –**dora** (*adj.*) exciting; (*m.,f.*) exciter; (*m., Elec.*) exciter.
excitamento (*m.*) = EXCITAÇÃO.
excitante (*adj.*) exciting, thrilling; (*m.*, *Physiol., Elec.*) excitant.
excitar (*v.t.*) to excite, arouse, stimulate, animate, incite; to thrill; to irritate, provoke; (*v.r.*) to become excited, aroused, angry.
excitável (*adj.*) excitable.
exclamação (*f.*) exclamation, outcry. **ponto de—,** exclamation point [!].
exclamar (*v.t.,v.i.*) to exclaim, shout, cry out.
exclamativo –**va, exclamatório** –**ria** (*adj.*) exclamatory.
excluir [72] (*v.t.*) to exclude (**de,** from); to preclude; to eliminate; (*v.r.*) to eliminate oneself.
exclusão (*f.*) exclusion, elimination; exception.
exclusiva (*f.*) = EXCLUSÃO.
exclusive (*adv.*) exclusive of.
exclusividade (*f.*) exclusiveness.
exclusivismo (*m.*) exclusionism.
exclusivista (*m.,f.*) exclusionist; (*adj.*) intransigent; intolerant.
exclusivo –**va** (*adj.*) exclusive; (*m.*) exclusive right; (*f.*) exclusion.

excluso –**sa** (*adj.*) excluded.
excogitar (*v.t.*) to excogitate; to devise; (*v.i.*) to cogitate.
excomungado –**da** (*adj.*) excommunicated; (*m.,f.*) an excommunicated person; (*colloq.*) a scapegrace.
excomungar (*v.t.*) to excommunicate.
excomunhão (*f.*) excommunication.
excreção (*f.*) excretion; excreta.
excrementício –**cia** (*adj.*) excrementitious.
excremento (*m.*) excrement; excreta.
excrescência (*f.*) excrescence.
excrescente (*adj.*) excrescent.
excrescer (*v.i.*) to grow abnormally.
excretar (*v.t.*) to excrete.
excreto –**ta** (*adj.*) excreted; (*m.*) excretion; (*f.*) excreta.
excretor –**tora** (*adj.*) excreting.
excretório (*adj.*) excretory.
excruciante (*adj.*) excruciating.
excruciar (*v.t.*) to excruciate.
exculpar (*v.t.*) to acquit, excuse [= DESCULPAR].
excursão (*f.*) excursion, trip, tour, jaunt, ramble, outing; sally, sortie, foray, raid; digression.—**de experiência,** trial run.
excursionista (*m.,f.*) excursionist; hiker.
excutir (*v.t., Law*) to attach (seize) property.
execração (*f.*) execration, abhorrence, loathing, detestation.
execrado –**da** (*adj.*) accursed.
execrando –**da** (*adj.*) execrable.
execrar (*v.t.*) to execrate, detest; to curse.
execrável (*adj.*) execrable.
execução (*f.*) execution, performance; accomplishment; transaction; skill in performing music; capital punishment; (*Law*) foreclosure.
executado –**da** (*adj.*) executed, put to death; (*m.,f.*) one who has been executed; (*Law*) one whose property is under foreclosure.
executante (*adj.*) executing; (*m.,f.*) one who executes a piece of music; (*Law*) one who seeks foreclosure of a mortgage.
executar (*v.t.*) to execute, accomplish, carry out; to perform; to discharge (duties); to play (music or a part); to put to death; (*Law*) to foreclose (a mortgage, etc.).
executável (*adj.*) executable; achievable.
executivo –**va** (*adj.; m.,f.*) executive.
executor (*m.*) executor; executioner.—**testamenteiro,** (*Law*) executor of a will.
exegese (*f.*) exegesis.
exegeta (*m.,f.*) exegete.
exegética (*f.*) exegetics.
exemplar (*m.*) specimen, model, copy; (*adj.*) exemplary; (*v.t.*) to punish, esp. by spanking; to make an example of.
exemplificação (*f.*) exemplification.
exemplificar (*v.t.*) to exemplify.
exemplo (*m.*) example, model; instance. **a—de,** following the example of; as in the case of; in imitation of; as. **por—,** for example, for instance. **sem—,** without equal, unexampled. **um—disso,** an example of that; a case in point. **trazer uma pessoa como—,** to cite or point to someone as an example.
exeqüente (*adj.; m.,f., Law*) designating the plaintiff, or the plaintiff himself, in a suit for attachment.
exéquias (*f.pl.*) exequies, obsequies.
exeqüibilidade (*f.*) workability; feasibility, practicability.
exeqüível (*adj.*) executable; achievable; feasible, practicable; workable. **tornar—,** to render possible.
exercer (*v.t.*) to exercise, carry out in action, perform (functions, duties of office); to exert; to practice. Cf. EXERCITAR.
exercício (*m.*) exercise; exertion; term of office; fiscal year; period of time covered by a budget; practice of a profession; military drill.—**de ginástica,** calisthenics.—**de redação,** a written exercise. **em—,** acting (in office). **fazer—,** to take exercise; to drill.
exercitação (*f.*) exercise; practice; training.
exercitar (*v.t.*) to exercise, practice; pursue; to discipline, train, drill.—**se em,** to practice, drill oneself in. Cf. EXERCER.
exército (*m.*) army.—**da Salvação,** Salvation Army.
exerdar (*v.*) = DESERDAR.
exergo (*m.*, *Numismatics*) exergue.
exfetação (*f.*, *Med.*) extrauterine pregnancy.
exfoliar (*v.*) & derivs. = ESFOLIAR & derivs.
exibição (*f.*) exhibition, display.
exibicionismo (*m.*) exhibitionism.

exibicionista (*adj.; m.,f.*) exhibitionist.

exibir (*v.t.*) to exhibit, show, display, manifest; (*v.r.*) to flaunt.

exido [xi = chí] (*m.*) public land, common.

exigência (*f.*) exigency, demand, exaction; extortion.—s burocráticas, bureaucratic red tape.

exigente (*adj.*) exigent; exigeant, demanding, exacting; fussy, hard to please, finical, difficult.

exigir (*v.t.*) to demand, require, exact, rightfully claim.

exigível (*adj.*) exigible; demandable; requirable.

exigüidade (*f.*) exiguity, scantiness.

exíguo -gua (*adj.*) exiguous, scanty, small.

exilado -da (*adj.*) exiled; (*m.,f.*) an exile.

exilar (*v.t.*) to exile, banish; (*v.r.*) to go into exile.

exílio (*m.*) exile, banishment, expatriation.

exímio -mia (*adj.*) extraordinary, excellent, choice, select.

eximir (*v.t.*) to exempt, free, release (**a**, **de**, from).—**se a** or **de**, to shun, evade (an unpleasant task); to shirk. Cf. ISENTAR.

exinanição (*f.*) exhaustion, prostration.

exinanir-se [46] (*v.r.*) to become debilitated.

existência (*f.*) existence, life, being; stock of goods on hand.

existencial (*adj.*) existential.

existencialismo (*m., Philos.*) existentialism.

existente (*adj.*) existing; (*m.,f.*) an existing person.

existir (*v.i.*) to exist, be; to last, endure.

êxito (*m.*) issue, result, success. [But not exit, which is SAÍDA; LUGAR POR ONDE SE SAI.]—**de bilheteria**, box office success. **lograr**—, to meet with success. **não lograr** (or **ter máu**)—, to fail, be unsuccessful. **o segredo do**—, the secret of success. **ter**—**na vida**, to get on in the world. Cf. SUCESSO.

Ex.ᵐᵒ = EXCELENTÍSSIMO (Most Excellent).

exoceto (*m., Zool.*) the genus (*Exocoetus*) of flying fishes.

exoderme (*f., Bot.*) exodermis; (*Zool.*) ectoderm.

êxodo (*m.*) exodus.

exodontia (*f., Dentistry*) exodontia, extraction of teeth.

exoforia (*f., Med.*) exophoria.

exoftalmia (*f.*), exoftalmo (*m., Med.*) exophthalmos, proptosis; (*colloq.*) = ÔLHO-DE-BOI, ÔLHO-DE-SAPO.

exoftálmico -ca (*adj., Med.*) exophthalmic.

exogamia (*f.*) exogamy.

exógamo -ma (*adj.*) exogamous.

exógeno -na (*adj.*) exogenous.

exognátio (*m., Anat.*) exognathion.

exografia (*f.*) exograph, radiograph.

exomorfico -ca (*adj., Petrog.*) exomorphic.

exoneração (*f.*) exoneration, release, relief, discharge. **pedido de**—, resignation (of public office).

exonerar (*v.t.*) to exonerate, release, let off; to dismiss, discharge (from office); (*v.r.*) to resign (from office).—**de culpa**, to free from blame.

exorador -dora (*adj.*) entreating, pleading.

exorar (*v.t.*) to beg, entreat, plead.

exorativo -va (*adj.*) = EXORADOR.

exorável (*adj.*) exorable, capable of being moved by entreaty.

exorbitância (*f.*) exorbitance; excessive price.

exorbitante (*adj.*) exorbitant, inordinate, excessive, unreasonable, unconscionable.

exorbitar (*v.t.*) to exorbitate; to transcend, exceed, transgress, overstep, go beyond.

exorcismar (*v.t.*) to exorcise.

exorcismo (*m.*) exorcism.

exorcista (*m.,f.*) exorcist.

exorcizar (*v.*) = EXORCISMAR.

exórdio (*m.*) exordium, preamble; introductory part of a speech.

exornar (*v.t.*) to embellish.

exortação (*f.*) exhortation.

exortador -dora (*m.,f.*) one who exhorts.

exortar (*v.t.*) to exhort, urge, incite; to advise, caution, warn, admonish.

exortativo -va (*adj.*) exhortative.

exortatório -ria (*adj.*) exhortatory; (*f.*) exhortation.

exosmose (*f., Physical Chem., Physiol.*) exosmosis.

exosmótico -ca (*adj.*) exosmotic.

exosporo (*m., Bot.*) exospore.

exostema (*m.*) Caribbean princewood (*Exostemma caribaeum*).

exóstoma (*m., Bot.*) exostome.

exostose (*f., Med., Bot.*) exostosis.

exotérico -ca (*adj.*) exoteric.

exotérmico -ca (*adj., Chem.*) exothermic.

exótico -ca (*adj.*) exotic, not native; odd, queer, strange.

exotismo (*m.*) exoticism.

expandir (*v.t.*) to expand, spread, unfold; (*v.r.*) to dilate, enlarge, be expanded; to be expansive; to expatiate.

expansão (*f.*) expansion, dilation; effusiveness, expansiveness, geniality. **dar**—**a**, to give vent to (an emotion).

expansibilidade (*f.*) expansibility.

expansionismo (*m.*) expansionism.

expansionista (*adj.; m.,f.*) expansionist.

expansível (*adj.*) expansible.

expansivo -va (*adj.*) expansive; genial, enthusiastic; bluff, boisterous.

expansor (*m., Mach.*) boiler tube expander.

expatriação (*f.*) expatriation, banishment; emigration.

expatriado -da (*adj.; m.,f.*) expatriate.

expatriar (*v.t.*) to expatriate, banish, exile; (*v.r.*) to go into exile.

expectação (*f.*) expectation. Var. EXPETAÇÃO.

expectador -dora (*m.,f.*) one who has expectations. Var. EXPETADOR.

expectante (*adj.*) expectant. Var. EXPETANTE.

expectar (*v.t.*) to expect, anticipate.

expectativa (*f.*) expectation, prospect, anticipation, presumption. **contra tôda a**—, contrary to all expectations. **corresponder à**—, to come up to expectations. Var. EXPETATIVA.

expectável (*adj.*) expectable; probable. Var. EXPETÁVEL.

expectoração (*f.*) expectoration. Var. EXPETORAÇÃO.

expectorante (*adj.; m.*) expectorant. Var. EXPETORANTE.

expectorar (*v.t.*) to expectorate. Var. EXPETORAR.

expedição (*f.*) dispatching, shipment, of goods; a military expedition; dispatch, promptness.

expedicionário -ria (*adj.*) expeditionary; (*m.,f.*) member of an expedition.

expedidor -dora (*adj.*) shipping, forwarding; (*m.,f.*) shipper, forwarder.

expediência (*f.*) expeditiousness. [But not expediency, which is UTILIDADE, CONVENIÊNCIA.]

expediente (*m.*) business hours and routine work of an office or government department; office hours; expedient, resource. **viver de**—**s**, to live by one's wits; (*adj.*) expeditious; resourceful. [But not expedient, which is CONVENIENTE, ÚTIL, PRÁTICO.]

expedir [60] (*v.t.*) to ship (goods); to send out (letters, etc.); to expedite, push forward.

expedito -ta (*adj.*) expedite.

expelir [24, 21a] (*v.t.*) to expel, eject, drive out; to spit out.

expender (*v.t.*) to expound; to expend.

expensas (*f.pl.*) **a**—**de**, at the expense of.

experiência (*f.*) experience; experiment, trial, test.

experiente (*m.,f.*) an adept, expert; (*adj.*) experienced, skilled, versed.

experimentação (*f.*) experimentation.

experimentado -da (*adj.*) tried; tested.

experimentador -dora (*adj.*) experimenting; (*m.,f.*) experimenter.

experimenta-genros (*f.*) a peavine (*Lathyrus heterophyllus*).

experimental (*adj.*) experimental.

experimentar (*v.t.*) to make experiment of, try, test; to taste; to try on (as shoes); to attempt, essay; to experience, undergo.—**a sorte**, to try one's luck.

experimento (*m.*) experiment; experience.

experto -ta (*adj.; m.,f.*) expert. [But the word commonly used is PERITO.]

expetar (*v.*) & derivs. = EXPECTAR & derivs.

expetorar (*v.*) & derivs. = EXPECTORAR & derivs.

expiação (*f.*) expiation, atonement.

expiar (*v.t.*) to expiate, atone for.

expiatório -ria (*adj.*) expiatory.

expiável (*adj.*) expiable.

expiração (*f.*) expiration, exhalation; termination, cessation.

expirar (*v.t.*) to exhale; (*v.i.*) to expire, come to an end; to die.

explanação (*f.*) explanation, elucidation.

explanador -dora (*adj.*) explaining; (*m.,f.*) explainer, expositor.

explanar (*v.t.*) to explain, make plain, elucidate. Cf. EXPLICAR.

explanatório -ria (*adj.*) explanatory.

expletivo -va (*adj.; f.*) expletive.

explicação (*f.*) explication, explanation; apology; solution, key.

explicador –dora (adj.) explaining; (m.,f.) expositor; coach, tutor.

explicar (v.t.) to explain, elucidate; to account for; (v.r.) to explain oneself; to make one's meaning clear. Cf. EXPLANAR.

explicativo –va (adj.) explanatory.

explicável (adj.) explicable.

explícito –ta (adj.) explicit, clear, positive.

explodir [25] (v.t.,v.i.) to explode, burst.

exploração (f.) exploration, search; exploitation; (TV) scanning.

explorador –dora (adj.) exploring, exploiting; (m.,f.) explorer; prospector; exploiter.

explorar (v.t.) to explore; to ransack; to inquire into; to exploit, utilize to one's own ends.

exploratório –ria (adj.) exploratory; (m., Surg.) sound.

explorável (adj.) exploitable.

explosão (f.) explosion, blast; outburst.

explosível (adj.) explodable.

explosivo –va (adj.; m.) explosive.

expoente (m.) exponent.—máximo, greatest exponent.

exponencial (adj., Alg.) exponential.

expor [63] (v.t.) to expose, exhibit; to bare; to subject; to endanger; to disclose; to expound, make plain; (v.r.) to expose oneself.

exportação (f.) export, exportation.

exportador –dora (m.,f.) exporter; (adj.) exporting.

exportar (v.t.) to export.

exportável (adj.) exportable.

exposição (f.) exposition, exhibition, display; explanation; exposure (to light).—demasiada, (Photog.) over-exposure.—insuficiente, (Photog.) underexposure.

expositivo –va (adj.) expository.

expositor –tora (m.,f.) expositor; exhibitor.

exposto –ta (m.,f.) a foundling; an abandoned child; (adj.) exposed; open, apparent.

expostulação (f.) expostulation.

expressão (f.) expression; phrase, saying; expressiveness. —familiar, a colloquial or idiomatic expression. reduzir à—mais simples, to reduce to the lowest common denominator.

expressar (v.) = EXPRIMIR.

expressionismo (m.) expressionism (in art).

expressionista (adj.; m.,f.) expressionist.

expressividade (f.) expressiveness.

expressivo –va (adj.) expressive, significant, revealing.

expresso –sa (m.) express train; (adj.; irreg. p.p. of EXPRIMIR) express, explicit, definite. carta—, special delivery letter.

exprimir [24] (v.t.) to express, utter, manifest; to reveal, show, indicate; (v.r.) to express oneself.

exprimível (adj.) expressible.

exprobação (f.) an upbraiding; rebuke, reprimand.

exprobar (v.t.) to upbraid, reproach, scold.

exprobatório –ria (adj.) reproachful.

expropriação (f.) expropriation.

expropriador –dora (adj.) expropriating; (m.,f.) expropriator.

expropriar (v.t.) to expropriate, dispossess.

expugnar (v.t.) to attack and conquer (by force of arms).

expugnável (adj.) expugnable.

expulsão (f.) expulsion; ejection; excretion.

expulsar [24] (v.t.) to expulse, expel, eject, evict, oust.

expulsivo –va (adj.) expulsive.

expulso –sa (adj.; irreg. p.p. of EXPULSAR) expulsed, expelled, ousted.

expulsor (adj.) expelling; (m.) one who expels.

expultriz, fem. of EXPULSOR.

expunção (f.) expunction, deletion, erasure.

expungir [25] (v.t.) to expunge, delete, plot out.

expurgação (f.) expurgation.

expurgado –da (adj.) purged, cleansed.

expurgar (v.t.) to expurgate, purge, cleanse.

expurgatório –ria (adj.) expurgatory; (m., R.C.Ch.) Expurgatory Index.

expurgo (m.) expurgation; a political purge.

exsicação (f.) exsiccation, dehydration.

exsicador (m.) drier; dehydrator; (Chem.) dessicator.

exsicante (adj.) drying; dehydrating.

exsicar (v.t.) to exsiccate.

exsicata (f.) a dried herbarium specimen.

exsicativo –va (adj.) exsiccative.

exsuar (v.) = EXSUDAR.

exsudação (f.) exudation.

exsudar (v.t.,v.i.) to exude.

exsudato (m.) exuded matter.

êxtase (m.) ecstasy, delight; trance; (Med.) ecstasy.

extasiante (adj.) entrancing.

extasiado –da (adj.) rapt, enraptured, ecstatic.

extasiar (v.t.) to enrapture, entrance; (v.r.) to become enchanted, delighted; (Med.) to go into ecstasy.

extático –ca (adj.) ecstatic, delirious, rapturous.

extemporaneidade (f.) extemporaneousness; untimeliness.

extemporâneo –nea (adj.) extemporaneous; untimely, inopportune.

extensão (f.) extension, expansion; expanse, area, extent, length, breadth; bulk; full meaning of a term.—de água, a stretch of water. salto de—, in sports, a broad jump.

extensibilidade (f.) extensibility.

extensível (adj.) extensible.

extensivo –va (adj.) extensive, comprehensive.—a, applicable to.

extenso –sa (adj.) extensive, wide, large, vast; ample. por—, at length, in full.

extensômetro (m.) extensometer.

extensor (m., Anat.) extensor.

extenuação (f.) prostration, weakness, debility. [But not extenuation, which is PALIAÇÃO, MITIGAÇÃO.]

extenuado –da (adj.) exhausted, tired out; run down; weakened; "bushed".

extenuador –dora, extenuante, extenuativo –va (adj.) debilitating, exhausting.

extenuar (v.t.) to exhaust, debilitate; to overdo. [But not to extenuate, which is ATENUAR.]

exterior (adj.) exterior, external, outward, outside, outer; on the surface; (m.) the outside, exterior; foreign lands. do—, from abroad.

exterioridade (f.) outwardness; (pl.) outward appearances.

exteriorização (f.) outward expression.

exteriorizar (v.t.) to give outward expression to thought.

exterminação (f.) extermination.

exterminador –dora (adj.) exterminating; (m.,f.) exterminator.

exterminar (v.t.) to exterminate, annihilate.

extermínio (m.) extermination, annihilation; destruction, ruin.

externar (v.t.) to express, give utterance to.—gratidão, to express thanks.—pùblicamente, to declare publicly.— uma opinião, to voice an opinion; (v.r.) to express oneself; to speak out.

externato (m.) day school. [A boarding school is INTERNATO.]

externo –na (adj.) external, outside. aluno—, day pupil.

extraterritorialidade (f.) extraterritoriality.

extinção (f.) extinction, destruction, extermination.

extinguir [24] (v.t.) to extinguish, quench, put out; to suppress; to obliterate; (v.r.) to be extinguished; to go out (as a light); to die out.

extinguível (adj.) extinguishable.

extinto –ta (adj.; irreg. p.p. of EXTINGUIR) extinct; ended; dead; (m.,f.) a dead person.

extintor –tora (adj.) extinguishing; (m.) fire extinguisher.

extirpação (f.) extirpation.

extirpador –dora (adj.) extirpating; (m.,) a weed puller.

extirpar (v.t.) to extirpate, root out.

extirpável (adj.) capable of being extirpated.

extorquir [25] (v.t.) to extort, exact; to wring from (by intimidation or terrorism).

extorsão (f.) extortion; blackmail; shakedown, "racket".

extorsionário –ria (adj.) extortionate; exorbitant; exacting; (m.,f.) extortioner.

extorsivo–va (adj.) extortionate; exorbitant; exacting.

extorso [tô] (m.) = EXTORSÃO.

extra (m.,f.) an extra (person, edition); (adj.) extraordinary; extrafine.

extrabranquial (adj., Anat.) extrabranchial.

extrabronquial (adj., Anat.) extrabronchial.

extrabucal (adj., Anat.) extrabuccal.

extração (f.) extraction; that which is extracted; drawing of lottery numbers; (Math.) determination of a root.

extracapsular (adj., Anat., Zool.) extracapsular.

extracelular (adj.) extracellular.

extracerebral (adj., Anat.) extracerebral.

extracostal (adj.) extracostal.

extracraniano –na (adj., Anat.) extracranial.

extracurrículo (m.) extracurricular activities.

extracutâneo –nea (*adj.*) extracutaneous.
extradição (*f.*) extradition.
extraditar (*v.t.*) to extradite.
extraditável (*adj.*) extraditable.
extradorso (*m., Arch.*) extrados.
extraentérico –ca (*adj., Zool.*) extraenteric.
extraepifisário –ria (*adj., Anat., Zool.*) extraepiphyseal.
extrafino –na (*adj.*) extrafine.
extrafísico –ca (*adj.*) extraphysical.
extrafoliáceo –cea (*adj., Bot.*) extrafoliaceous.
extra-humano –na (*adj.*) = SÔBRE-HUMANO.
extraidor –dora (*m.,f.*) extractor.
extrair [75] (*v.t.*) to extract (**de**, from), draw out, pull out; to remove, withdraw; to make an extract of.
extraível (*adj.*) extractable.
extrajudicial (*adj.*) extrajudicial.
extralegal (*adj.*) extralegal.
extramarginal (*adj., Psychol.*) extramarginal, subconscious.
extramedular (*adj.*) extramedullary.
extramolecular (*adj., Chem.*) extramolecular.
extramural (*adj.*) extramural.
extranatural (*adj.*) extranatural; supernatural.
extraordinário –ria (*adj.*) extraordinary, uncommon, rare, singular, abnormal, extra. **lucros—s**, excess profits; (*m.*) an extra expense; an unusual thing.
extrapassar (*v.t.*) to surpass, exceed [= ULTRAPASSAR].
extraplacental (*adj.*) extraplacental.
extrapolação (*f., Math.*) extrapolation.
extrapolar (*v.t., Math.*) to extrapolate.
extraprograma (*adj.*) not on the program.
extrarrenal (*adj., Anat., Zool.*) extrarenal.
extrasseroso –sa (*adj., Anat.*) extraserous.
extrassístole (*f., Med.*) extrasystole.
extratar (*v.t.*) to extract; to make excerpts of.
extraterreno –na (*adj.*) extraterrestrial; unworldly.
extraterrestre (*adj.*) extraterrestrial.
extraterritorial (*adj.*) extraterritorial.
extraterritorialidade (*f.*) extraterritoriality.
extratimpânico –ca (*adj., Anat.*) extratympanic.
extrativo –va (*adj.; m.*) extractive.
extrato (*m.*) extract; excerpt, quotation; abstract.
extrator (*m.*) extractor.
extratorácico –ca (*adj., Anat.*) extrathoracic.
extratraqueal (*adj., Anat.*) extratracheal.
extratubal (*adj., Anat.*) extratubal.
extra-uterino –na (*adj., Anat.*) extrauterine.
extravagância (*f.*) extravagance; wildness, folly, excess; whim, fancy; oddity; wild prank; (*pl.*) wild oats.
extravagranciar (*v.t.*) to waste, dissipate extravagantly; (*v.i.*) to live, behave or speak wantonly.
extravagante (*adj.*) extravagant, irregular, wild, wanton; (*m.*) wastrel, spendthrift; "cutup," "playboy".
extravagar (*v.i.*) to be outside of bounds or limits; to rove; to divagate, digress.
extravaginal (*adj., Anat., Bot.*) extravaginal.

extravasamento (*m.*) extravasation (as of blood); effusion.
extravasar (*v.t.,v.i.*) to extravasate.
extravascular (*adj., Anat.*) extravascular.
extraviado –da (*adj.*) strayed, missing, lost; perverted.
extraviador –dora (*adj.*) misleading; (*m.,f.*) one who leads astray; seducer.
extraviar (*v.t.*) to lead or send astray; to mislay; to embezzle; (*v.r.*) to go astray, get lost; miscarry.
extravio (*m.*) a going or sending astray; loss, disappearance; embezzlement.
extrema-direita (*f., Politics*) the extreme right; (*Soccer*) right-end position; (*m.*) right-end soccer player.
extremado –da (*adj.*) distinguished; extraordinary.
extrema-esquerda (*f., Politics*) the extreme left; (*Soccer*) left-end position; (*m.*) left-end soccer player.
extremar (*v.t.*) to exalt, extol; (*v.r.*) to distinguish oneself (**em**, **in**).
extrema-unção (*f.*) extreme unction.
extremidade (*f.*) extremity, end, tip, edge; last resource; utmost distress. **à ultima—**, down to the last penny.
extremismo (*m.*) extremism.
extremista (*adj.; m.,f.*) extremist.
extremo –ma (*adj.*) extreme, most distant; last, final; highest; (*m.*) extreme, extremity, highest degree; limit; last resource; (*pl.*) excessive fondness. **à—s**, extremely; to extremes. **ao—**, to the extreme. **Está reduzido ao—**, He is down to his last penny.
extremo-oriente (*m.*) Far East.
extremoso –sa (*adj.*) extremely fond, excessively tender, overly-affectionate, doting, loving, devoted; (*f., Bot.*) the common crapemyrtle (*Lagerstroemia indica*), c.a. ESCUMILHA, LOUCURA, MINERVA-DOS-JARDINS, NORMA.
extrínseco –ca (*adj.*) extrinsic; extraneous.
extrorso –sa (*adj., Bot.*) extrorse.
extrusão (*f.*) extrusion, expulsion; (*Metal.*) extrusion.
extrusivo –va (*adj.*) extrusive; (*f.*) extrusive rock.
exu (*m.*) evil spirit feared and worshipped in voodoo rites.
exuberância (*f.*) exuberance.
exuberante (*adj.*) exuberant, over-abundant; abounding; overflowing; lush.
exuberar (*v.i.*) to abound, superabound.
exúbere (*adj.*) weaned [= DESMAMADO].
exular (*v.i.*) to go into exile; to expatriate oneself.
exulcerar (*v.t.*) to ulcerate; to fret, chafe.
êxule (*adj.*) in exile; (*m.,f.*) an exile.
exultação (*f.*) exultation, great rejoicing; glee.
exultante (*adj.*) exultant, elated; gleeful.
exultar (*v.i.*) to exult, rejoice; to gloat.
exumação (*f.*) exhumation.
exumar (*v.t.*) to exhume.
exutório (*m., Med.*) an artificial ulcer for the discharge pus.
exúvias (*f.pl.*) exuviae (cast skins, shells, etc. of snakes, etc.).
ex-voto (*m.*) a votive offering.

F

F, f, the 6th letter of the Portuguese alphabet.
F = FÁRADE (*Elec.*) farad.
F. = FULANO (John Doe); FRENTE, FUNDO (front, back—stage directions).
f. = FEMININO (feminine); FORMA (form); FÔLHA (sheet, page).
fã (*m.,f.*) fan (fanatical devotee).—**do cinema**, movie fan.
F.A.B. = FÔRÇA AÉREA BRASILEIRA (Brazilian Air Force).
fabagela (*f.*) Syrian beancaper (*Zygophyllum fabago*), c.a. FALSO-ALCAPARREIRO.
fabela (*f., Anat.*) fabella.
fabiana (*f.*) Peru falseheath (*Fabiana imbricata*).
fabiforme (*adj.*) fabiform, bean-shaped.
Fábio (*m.*) Fabius.
fábrica (*f.*) factory, mill, workshop; fabric; building construction; ingenious mechanism. [But only in the sense of structure or composition. Fabric as cloth is TECIDO, PANO.]—**de cerveja**, brewery.—**de conservas**, cannery. —**de papel**, paper mill. **marca de—**, trade mark.

fabricação (*f.*) fabrication; manufacture, production.
fabricante (*m.,f.*) manufacturer, producer; factory-owner; factory worker.
fabricar (*v.t.*) to fabricate; to manufacture, ʌnake; to operate a factory.
fabricável (*adj.*) capable of being manufactured.
fabrico (*m.*) manufacture; product of a factory; (*Naut.*) ship repairs.
fabril (*adj.*) factory. **equipamento—**, plant equipment.
fabriqueiro (*m.*) churchwarden.
fabroniáceas (*f.pl.*) a family (*Fabroniaceae*) of tropical tree mosses.
fábula (*f.*) fable; myth; falsehood.
fabulação (*f.*) fiction; story; falsehood; moral of a story.
fabular (*v.i.*) to write or tell fa les; to lie; (*adj.*) fabular.
fabulista (*m.,f.*) fabulist.
fabulizar (*v.*) = FABULAR.
fabuloso –sa (*adj.*) fabulous, fictitious; marvelous.
Fac. = FACULDADE (Faculty).

faça, façais, façam, façamos, faças, forms of FAZER [47].
faca (*f.*) knife; hackney horse.—**de papel,** paper knife.—
de trinchar, carving knife.—**inglêsa,** drawknife [= CORTA-
CHEFE]. **à ponta de—,** sternly, inflexibly. **com a—e o
queijo na mão,** fig., in full control, having complete
authority. **entrar na—,** (*colloq.*) to be operated on. **fôlha
de—,** knife blade.
facada (*f.*) stab; (*colloq.*) a touch (for a loan or gift of
money); a shakedown.
facadista (*m.,f., slang*) a confirmed sponger, parasite,
dead beat.
facalhão, facalhaz (*m.*) large knife.
façalvo –va (*adj.*) of horse, white-faced, having a blaze.
façanha (*f.*) feat; deed, exploit; achievement; prowess;
perversity.
façanheiro –ra (*adj.*) given to boasting of personal prowess; (*m.,f.*) braggart.
façanhoso –sa, façanhudo –da (*adj.*) given to stunts and
feats; hell-bent.
facão (*m.*) a large knife; worker who cuts up whales; a hog-
backed road.
facção (*f.*) faction, clique; a feat at arms. Var. FAÇÃO.
faccionar (*v.t.*) to gather into factions. Var. FACIONAR.
faccionário –ria (*adj.*) factional, partisan; (*m.,f.*) faction-
ary, partisan. Var. FACIONÁRIO.
facciosidade (*f.*), **facciosismo** (*m.*) factionism, partisanship. Vars. FACIOSIDADE, FACIOSISMO.
faccioso –sa (*adj.*) factious, cliquish. Var. FACIOSO.
face (*f.*) face of anything; visage; cheek; facet; heads (of
a coin); the right side of a piece of cloth.—**a—,** face to
face. **à—de,** in front of. **em—de,** in view of; before, con-
fronted by. **fazer—a,** to confront; to meet, offset.
facear (*v.t.*) to face [But only in the sense of making flat
or smooth the face of; to face (confront) is ENCARAR,
ENFRENTAR.]
facécia (*f.*) jest, quip, witticism; wisecrack; pleasantry;
facetiousness.
facecioso –sa (*adj.*) = FACÊTO.
faceira (*f.*) see FACEIRO.
faceirar (*v.i.*) to show off (in dress and manners).
faceirice (*f.*) coquetry; feminine vanity; self-display.
faceiro –ra (*adj.*) given to self-display; of horses, proud,
prancing; (*m.*) fop, coxcomb; funster; simpleton; (*f.*)
cheekpiece of a bridle; jowl; a woman given to affectation.
facêta (*f.*) facet.
facetar (*v.t.*) to facet. Var. FACETEAR.
facetear (*v.i.*) to jest, banter; also = FACETAR.
facêto –ta (*adj.*) facetious; witty; droll, jolly, playful.
fachada (*f.*) façade; title page of a book [= ROSTO, FRON-
TISPÍCIO or PÁGINA DE ROSTO]; (*colloq.*) mug (face);
(*colloq.*) sham. Cf. FRONTISPÍCIO.
facheada (*f.*) night fishing by torchlight.
facheador (*m.*) torcher (in night fishing).
fachear (*v.i.*) to fish at night by torchlight.
facheiro (*m.*) torchbearer; torch holder; kind of torch-
wood; (*Bot.*) any of various cacti of genera Cereus,
Pilocereus and Zehntmerella.
fachís (*m.pl.*) chopsticks.
facho (*m.*) torch, flambeau; firebrand; bright light.
fachudo –da (*adj.*) handsome.
facial (*adj.*) facial.
fácies (*m.*) general aspect; (*Geol.*) facies.
fácil [-ceis] (*adj.*) easy; natural, smooth; facile, mild,
affable; compliant; of easy virtue; (*adv.*) easily.—**de se
fazer,** easy to make, easy to do.
facilidade (*f.*) facility, ease; dexterity; easy manners, informality; (*pl.*) facilities, advantages, opportunities
(though in referring to physical facilities perhaps INS-
TALAÇÕES may be preferable to FACILIDADES).
facílimo –ma (*absol. superl. of* FÁCIL) very easy.
facilíssimo –ma (*absol. superl. of* FÁCIL) very, very easy;
most easy.
facilitação (*f.*) facilitation.
facilitar (*v.t.*) to facilitate, make easy; to expedite; (*v.i.*)
expose oneself to, be unmindful of, danger; (*v.r.*) to become skillful.
facilitário (*m.*) installment-payments plan [= AUXILIÁRIO,
CREDIÁRIO].
facínora (*m.*) criminal, felon, malefactor, thug; ruffian;
desperado.
facinoroso –sa (*adj.*) atrociously wicked.
faço, form of FAZER [47].
facóide (*adj.*) phacoid, lens-shaped.
façoila (*f., colloq.*) large, coarse face.

facólito (*m., Min.*) phacolite; (*Geol.*) phacolith.
facômetro (*m.*) phacometer.
facoscópio (*m.*) phacoscope.
fac-similado –da (*adj.*) facsimile.
fac-similar (*adj.*) facsimile; (*v.t.*) to make a facsimile of.
fac-símile (*f.*) facsimile.
factício –cia (*adj.*) factitious, artificial. Var. FATÍCIO.
factível (*adj.*) possible, feasible. Var. FATÍVEL.
factótum (*m.*) factotum.
façudo –da (*adj.*) broad-faced, fat-faced.
fácula (*f., Astron.*) facula.
faculdade (*f.*) faculty, capability, ability; mental power;
authorization; permission; a learned profession (medicine, law, etc.); faculty of teachers; a university school.
—**de direito,** law school.—**de medicina,** medical school.
facultar (*v.t.*) to facilitate; to allow, permit.—**a,** to present
to.
facultativo –va (*m.,f.*) physician; (*adj.*) elective, optional.
ponto—, optional work day.
facultoso –sa (*adj.*) well-to-do.
facúndia (*f.*) eloquence, fluency; glibness.
facundo –da (*adj.*) eloquent, fluent; glib.
fada (*f.*) fairy; enchantress; a fascinating woman. **história
de—s,** fairy tale. **mãos de—,** a woman highly skilled
with her hands.
fadado –da (*adj.*) fated, predestined. **bem-—,** fortunate,
lucky.
fadar (*v.t.*) to destine, determine the fate of; to presage,
foretell; to endow, enrich. **bem-—,** to wish or prognosticate good fortune (for someone).
fadário (*m.*) fate, destiny; a hard life.
fadejar (*v.i.*) to carry out one's destiny; meet one's fate;
(*v.t.*) to sing or play a FADO.
fadiga (*f.*) fatigue; toil.
fadigar (*v.t.*) to fatigue [= FATIGAR].
fadigoso –sa (*adj.*) fatiguing.
fading (*m., Radio*) fading.
fadista (*m.,f.*) a singer or player of FADOS; (*m.*) ruffian; (*f.*)
prostitute.
fado (*m.*) fate, destiny; popular (usually plaintive) song
or melody. **Os—s estão contra êle,** The fates, or odds,
are against him. **os maus—s,** adversity, ill-luck. **Bons—s
o levem!** Good luck to you!.
fadômetro (*m.*) fadometer (device for testing colors for
fastness to light).
faéton, faetonte (*m.*) phaeton.
fagáceo –cea (*adj., Bot.*) fagaceous; (*f.pl.*) the family
(*Fagaceae*) of oaks, beeches, chestnuts.
fagedênico –ca (*adj.*) gangrenous. **úlcera—,** a phagedena
(eating ulcer).
fagócito (*m., Biol., Med.*) phagocyte.
fogocitose (*f.*) phagocytosis.
fagópiro (*m.*) buckwheat (*Fagopyrum*), c.a. TRIGO-MOURO,
TRIGO-SARRACENO.
fagote (*m.*) a bassoon. [Fagot is FEIXE.]
fagotista (*m.,f.*) bassoon player.
fagueiro –ra (*adj.*) caressing; kind, loving; pleased with
oneself.
fagulha (*f.*) spark; (*m.*) a "live wire" (hustler).
fagulhar (*v.i.*) to throw off sparks.
fagulheiro (*m.*) spark arrester [= PÁRA-CHISPAŚ].
fagulhento –ta (*adj.*) that sends out sparks; fig. lively,
restless.
faia (*f.*) any beech (*Fagus*) especially the European beech
(*F. sylvatica*), or its wood. Also, a Brazilian species of
Cordia (family *Ehretiaceae*).—**branca,** white poplar
(*Populus alba*), better known as CHOUPO-BRANCO.—
preta, the European aspen (*Populus tremula*), better
known as CHOUPO-TREMEDOR.
faial (*m.*) a beech grove.
faialita (*f., Min.*) fayalite.
faiança, faiença (*f.*) faience.
faina (*f.*) work on board ship; any tedious chore or task.
faisande (*adj.*) of game, fowl, etc., high, slightly tainted.
faisão [-sães or -sões] (*m.*) pheasant cock. [The hen is
FAISOA.]
faísca (*f.*) spark, flash; a speck of gold dust; (*adj.*) ardent,
fiery.
faiscação [a-i] (*f.*) sparking, flashing.
faiscador (*m.*) prospector.
faiscante [a-i] (*adj.*) sparkling.
faiscar [a-i] (*v.i.*) to sparkle, glitter, flash; to prospect for
gold or diamonds; (*v.t.*) to throw out (off) sparks.
faisqueira [a-i] (*f.*) gold diggings.

faisqueiro [a-i] (*m.*) gold prospector.

faixa (*f.*) strip, band, belt; swaddling band; strap; scarf; strip of land (*Arch.*) fascia.—**s de absorção**, absorption bands (in a spectrum).—**de planagem**, (*Aeron.*) glide path.—**etária**, age group.

fala (*f.*) speech, talk; discourse; language; voice; power of speech.—**arrastada**, drawl. **um homem de poucas—s**, a man of few words. **chamar à—**, to call (someone) to account.

falaça (*f.*) whipping post.

falação (*f., colloq.*) talk. **deitar—**, to make a speech.

falácia (*f.*) fallaciousness; sound of voices.

falacioso –sa (*adj.*) fallacious.

falacíssimo –ma (*absol. superl. of* FALAZ) most fallacious.

falaço (*m., colloq.*) hearsay.

falada (*f.*) sound of voices, murmuring; rumor, gossip.

faladeira (*f.*) a talkative woman.

falado –da (*adj.*) much spoken of; highly touted; famous; (*f.*) talk, sound of voices; rumor.

falador –dora (*adj.*) very talkative; (*m.,f.*) gabbler, prater. —**da vida alheia**, scandalmonger.

falalgia (*f., Med.*) phallalgia.

falange (*f.*) phalanx; (*Anat., Zool.*) phalanx.

falangeal (*adj.*) phalangeal.

falangeta [ê] (*f., Anat.*) third or terminal phalanx.

falanginha (*f., Anat.*) second or middle phalanx.

falante (*adj.*) speaking, talking. **alto—**, (*Radio*) loudspeaker. **bem—**, fluent, eloquent; well-spoken; fine-talking [*Derogatory*]; (*m., slang*) mouthpiece (lawyer).

falar (*v.t.,v.i.*) to speak, talk (**a**, to; **de**, of; **em**, **sôbre**, of, on, about; **com**, with, to); (*v.r.*) to be on speaking (friendly) terms with; (*m.*) manner of speaking. Cf. DIZER.—**a êsmo**, to talk at random.—**a favor de**, to speak in favor of.—**a torto e a direito**, to gabble, talk nonsense. —**alto**, to speak out, frankly, clearly.—**ao coração**, to speak to the heart.—**às massas**, to speak to the people. —**bem (mal) de**, to speak well (ill) of.—**claro**, to speak clearly, frankly.—**com acêrto**, to speak with assurance. —**com conhecimento de causa**, to know whereof one speaks.—**com desprêzo**, to scoff.—**com o coração nas mãos**, to speak frankly, sincerely, from the heart.—**com os olhos**, to speak with the eyes.—**com os seus botões**, to talk to oneself.—**com sete pedras na mão**, (*colloq.*) to speak rudely, angrily; to talk back, reply in kind.—**com têrmos a**, to speak politely to.—**como um livro**, to talk like a book.—**como um oráculo**, to speak like an oracle. —**da vida alheia**, to talk about others, gossip.—**de cadeira**, or **de cátedra**, to speak with authority.—**de farto**, to talk as though one had no need of anything.— **de papo**, to speak coldly, calmly, haughtily; to speak with special knowledge.—**de papo cheio**, to speak full of self-importance.—**de poleiro**, to speak dictatorially.—**de vento**, to talk through one's hat.—**desentoadamente**, (*colloq.*) to shout, yell, talk loudly.—**difícil**, to indulge in highfalutin (pretentious) speech.—**duma coisa e outra**, to talk of one thing and another.—**em bons têrmos**, to address another in a proper manner.—**em bons (maus) têrmos de**, to refer in good (bad) terms to.—**entre os dentes**, to mutter between one's teeth.—**francês**, (*slang*) to have money.—**grosso**, (*slang*) to talk big, with authority.—**mal de**, to knock (disparage) someone.—**na pele de**, to talk about someone.—**no ar**, to talk without purpose.—**no deserto**, to talk without being heeded.—**para dentro**, to mutter to oneself.—**pela mesma toada**, to parrot another's words.—**pelo nariz**, to talk through one's nose.—**pelos cotovêlos**, or **pelas tripas de Judas**, to talk a blue streak; to talk the hind leg off a mule.—**por falar**, to talk to be talking.—**por si mesmo**, to speak for itself.—**pouco e bem**, to speak briefly and to the point. —**rasgado**, to speak out fearlessly.—**sem parar**, to talk unceasingly.—**sem rebuços**, to speak right out.—**sem rodeios**, to get right to the point.—**que falar**, to give rise to talk; to get oneself talked about. **Êle pode—que não adianta nada**, It's no use for him to talk. **Êles não se falam**, They don't speak to each other. **falando a sério**, all joking aside. **Fale sem rodeios!** Speak up! **Não se fala mais nisso**, There is no more talk of it. **não se—**, to not be on speaking terms (with someone). **ouvir—de**, to hear tell of; to hear about. **para—a verdade**, to tell the truth. **por—em**, by the way; speaking of.

falastrão –trona (*adj.; m.,f.*) talkative (person).

falatório (*m.*) babbling, gabbling; hum of voices.

fala-verdade (*m., colloq.*) any weapon carried in self-defense.

falaz (*adj.*) fallacious, deceptive, misleading, false.

falca (*f.*) a square-hewn log.

falcaçar (*v.t., Naut.*) to whip the end of a rope or cord to keep it from unravelling.

falcado –da (*adj.*) falcate, hooked; curved like a sickle.

falcão (*m.*) falcon; hawk [= GAVIÃO].

falcato –ta (*adj.*) = FALCADO.

falcatrua (*f.*) trick, swindle, fraud.

falcatruar (*v.t.*) to cheat, swindle, defraud.

falciforme (*adj.*) falciform, sickle-shaped [= FALCADO].

falcoar (*v.i.*) to hunt with falcons.

falcoaria (*f.*) falconry.

falcoeira (*f.*) a herring gull (*Larus argentatus*).

falcoeiro (*m.*) falconer.

falconídeo –dea (*adj.*) falconine; (*m.pl.*) the Falconidae (hawks, falcons, eagles, kites, etc.).

falcula (*f., Anat.*) falcula, falx cerebelli.

falda (*f.*) foothill.

faldistório (*m.*) faldstool.

falecer (*v.i.*) to die; to lack; to grow scarce.—**a** or **de**, to be lacking in (authority, age, money, etc.).—**de**, to die of (tuberculosis, etc.).

falecido –da (*adj.*) deceased; lacking, wanting; (*m.,f.*) deceased person.

falecimento (*m.*) death, demise; dearth; privation.

falena (*f.*) a night moth.

falência (*f.*) commercial failure, bankruptcy; want, lack; omission. **abrir—**, to take bankruptcy.

falésia (*f.*) high and rugged cliff or crags; sea cliff.

falha (*f.*) see FALHO.

falhadão (*m.*) a place on a coffee FAZENDA where a number of the trees have died.

falhado –da (*adj.*) having a flaw; cracked; failed.

falhar (*v.i.*) to fail, fall short; to miss, miscarry; to misfire.

falho –lha (*adj.*) faulty, defective; short, wanting; that failed or miscarried; (*f.*) flaw, defect; blemish; shortcoming; gap, omission; crack, fissure; chip, fragment; (*Geol.*) fault; (*Metal.*) blowhole.—**do motor**, a missing in a motor.

falhudo –da (*adj.*) = FALHADO.

falibilidade (*f.*) fallibility.

falicismo (*m.*) phallicism.

fálico –ca (*adj.*) phallic.

falido –da (*adj.*) that failed; faulty; bankrupt; (*m.,f.*) a bankrupt.

falimento (*m.*) failure (in business).

falir [46] (*v.i.*) to fail (in business); to go bankrupt.

falite (*f., Med.*) phallitis.

falível (*adj.*) fallible.

falo (*m.*) phallus.

falquear, falquejar (*v.t.*) to rough-hew (a log).

falquejo [ê] (*m.*) square hewing of logs.

falripas (*f.pl.*) = FARRIPAS.

falsa (*f.*) see FALSO.

falsa-braga (*f.*) barbican.

falsa-cainca [a-ín] (*f.*) David's milkberry (*Chiococca alba*).

falsa-camomila (*f.*) field camomile (*Anthemis arvensis*).

falsa-caribéia (*f.*) a shrub of the madder family (*Exostema longiflorum*), closely related to the Caribbean princewood.

falsa-erva-mate (*f.*) a shrub of the theophrasta family (*Rapanea matensis*) used as an adulterant of the genuine ERVA-MATE (*Ilex paraguaiensis*).

falsa-ervilha (*f.*) the hedge or bush vetch (*Vicia sepium*).

falsa-espelina (*f.*) = ESPELINA-FALSA.

falsa-gameleira (*f.*) a fig (*Ficus vermifuga*), c.a. FIGUEIRA-DE-LOMBRIGUEIRA.

falsa-glicínia (*f.*) a celery (*Apium tuberosum*).

falsa-ipeca (*f.*) the minnieroot ruellia (*R. tuberosa*).

falsa-laranja (*f.*) the Dudaim melo (*Cucumis melo dudaim*).

falsa-membrana (*f., Med.*) false membrane.

falsa-posição (*f.*) = REGRA DE FALSA POSIÇÃO.

falsa-quilha (*f., Naut.*) false keel.

falsa-quina (*f., Bot.*) a medicinal poison nut (*Strychnos pseudo-quina*) whose bark is used as a substitute for quinine; c.a. QUINA-BRANCA, QUINA-DA-CHAPADA, QUINA-DE-MATO-GROSSO, QUINA-DE-PERIQUITO, QUINA-DO-CERRADO, QUINA-DO-CAMPO.

falsar (*v.t.*) to falsify; to forge; to cheat; to frustrate; (*v.i.*) to lie; to give way, fail.

falsário –ria (*m.,f.*) forger, counterfeiter; perjurer.

falsas-costelas (*f.pl.*, *Anat.*) floating ribs.
falsa-tiririca (*f.*) gold star grass (*Hypoxis*), c.a. MARIRIÇÔ-BRAVO, TIRIRICA-FALSA.
falsa-verônica (*f.*) the roundleaf fluvellin (*Kickxia spuria*).
falseamento (*m.*) misrepresentation, distortion, frustration.
falsear (*v.t.*) to play false to; to represent falsely; to pervert; to distort; (*v.i.*) to get out of tune; to miss a step.
falsete [sê] (*m.*) falsetto voice.
falsetear (*v.t.*) to speak or sing falsetto.
falsidade (*f.*) falsity, falseness; guile; imposture, deception.
falsídico –ca (*adj.*) deceitful, lying.
falsificação (*f.*) falsifying, falsification; forgery, adulteration.
falsificador –dora (*adj.*) falsifying; (*m.,f.*) falsifier; counterfeiter, forger; faker.
falsificar (*v.t.*) to falsify, adulterate, forge, counterfeit, "doctor," "fake".
falsificável (*adj.*) falsifiable.
falsinérveo –vea (*adj.*, *Bot.*) false-nerved.
falso –sa (*adj.*) false, untrue; wrong, erroneous; fallacious; dishonest; crooked; deceitful; deceptive; faithless; fictitious; bogus, fake. em—, vainly, ineffectually; (*f.*, *Music*) false note.
falso-açafrão (*m.*) = CÓLQUICO.
falso-alcaparreiro (*m.*) = FABAGELA.
falso-anil (*m.*) common goatsrue (*Galega officinalis*).
falso-arroz (*m.*) rice cutgrass (*Leersia oryzoides*).
falso-benjoim (*m.*, *Bot.*) a terminalia (*T. angustifolia*).
falso-crupe (*m.*, *Med.*) false croup.
falso-ébano (*m.*, *Bot.*) goldenchain laburnum (*L. anagyroides*).
falso-oró (*m.*, *Bot.*) a calopogonium (*C. mucunoides*).
falso-parasito –ta (*adj.*, *Bot.*) epiphytic.
falso-pinho (*m.*, *Bot.*) Norway spruce (*Picea abies*).
falso-plátano (*m.*) = FALSO-SICÔMORO.
falso-sene (*m.*, *Bot.*) common bladdersenna (*Colutea arborescens*).
falso-sicômoro (*m.*) Norway maple (*Acer platanoides*).
falso-testemunho (*m.*) false witness.
falso-topázio (*m.*) false topaz, citrine.
falta (*f.*) see FALTO.
faltar (*v.i.*) to want, lack, be lacking; to fail, fall short.—a, to be absent from (fail to appear); to default.—à classe, to cut a class.—à palavra, to go back on one's word.—ao respeito a, to be wanting in respect for.—com a verdade, to fail to tell the truth.—pouco para, to be almost, nearly. Era o que faltava! That is the last straw! Faltam vinte para as treze, It is 20 minutes to one P.M. Não me faltava mais nada! That's all I needed! It's the last straw! Falta-lhe dinheiro, He lacks money. Falta pouco para o trem chegar, It won't be long before the train arrives.
falto –ta (*adj.*) deficient; devoid; wanting.—de, short of, destitute of.—de juízo, lacking in good sense.—de piedade, wanting in mercy; (*f.*) lack, wanting, need; default; shortcoming; blame; fault; defect; misdeed; trespass; (in sports), a foul.—de ar, shortness of breath.—de atenção, heedlessness.—de palavra, broken promise.—primitiva, original sin. à (or na)—de, for want (lack) of; in the absence of. Achamos muita—dela, We miss her very much. cobrar a—, (in sports) to impose a penalty. cometer uma—, to commit a wrong. Ela me faz—, I miss her. estar em—, to be in default. por—de, for want of. sem—, without fail. sentir—de, to miss, feel the want of. ter—de, to require, need, want.
falua (*f.*) small sailboat.
faluca (*f.*), **falucho** (*m.*) felucca.
falupa (*f.*) a silkworm cocoon in which the pupa has died.
fálus (*m.*) = FALO.
fama (*f.*) fame, reputation; renown; rumor, report; (*m.*) famous man. Êle tem—de ser rico, He is reputed to be rich. ma—, ill-fame. pessôa de—, famous person.
famatinita (*f.*, *Min.*) famatinite.
famélico –ca (*adj.*) famished, starved.
famigerado –da, **famígero** –ra (*adj.*) famous (generally with a connotation of notorious).
família (*f.*) family (all senses).—humana, mankind.—real, royal family. ar de—, family likeness. chefe de—, head of a family, of a household. Santa—, the Holy Family. uma—de recursos, a well-to-do-family.
familial (*adj.*) familial.

familiar (*m.*) a member of the household; (*adj.*) familiar, domestic; intimate; well-known, common. [But not familiar in the sense of too free, presumptuous, which is ATREVIDO, CONFIADO.] expressão—, a colloquialism. no meio—, in the family circle.
familiaridade (*f.*) familiarity, intimacy. [But not in the sense of over-freedom, which is ATREVIMENTO.] evitar—s, to keep one's distance.
familiarizar (*v.t.*) to familiarize, accustom.—se com, to acquaint oneself (thoroughly) with.
faminto –ta (*adj.*) famished, ravenous.
famoso –sa (*adj.*) famous, renowned, notable.
fâmula (*f.*) female servant.
famulagem (*f.*) servants collectively.
famulatício –cia (*adj.*) servant.
famulato (*m.*) servant's work.
famulatório –ria (*adj.*) servant.
famulento –ta (*adj.*) famished; voracious.
fâmulo (*m.*) servant, attendant, esp. of a high officer of the church.
fanal (*m.*) lighthouse; guiding light, beacon.
fanar-se (*v.r.*) to wilt, fade.
fanático –ca (*adj.*) fanatic, rabid, bigoted; (*m.,f.*) fanatic, zealot, bigot, devotee; "screwball".
fanatismo (*m.*) fanaticism, bigotry.
fanatizador –dora (*adj.; m.,f.*) that, or one who, inspires fanaticism.
fanatizar (*v.t.*) to make fanatic; to inspire fanaticism in; (*v.r.*) to become fanatic.
fanca (*f.*) stock of dry goods for sale.
fancaria (*f.*) dry goods business.
fanchone (*m.*) dolly, low truck.
fandangaçu (*m.*, *slang*) a noisy, lively, rock-and-roll type of carnival dance.
fandango (*m.*) fandango (dance); (*colloq.*) shindy, fracas.
fandangueiro –ra, **fandanguista**, (*adj.*) fond of dancing the fandango; (*m.,f.*) fandango-dancer.
faneco –ca (*adj.*) dried, wilted; thin; (*m.*) piece (as of bread). pintar o—, (*colloq.*) to raise Cain; (*f.*) a codfish; a soft chestnut; piece of bread.
fânega (*f.*) a measure of dry weight equivalent to 100 kilos, used in Rio Grande do Sul.
fanerógamo (*m.*, *Bot.*) phanerogam; (*pl.*) the Phanerogamia.
fanfã (*m.*) the fork leaf hibiscus (*H. bifurcatus*), c.a. ALGODÃO-DO-BREJO, CARURU-AZÊDO, MAJORANA, VINAGREIRA.
fanfarra (*f.*) brass band; fanfare.
fanfarrada (*f.*) fanfanrice.
fanfarrão –rona (*adj.*) blustering, swaggering; swashbuckling; (*m.*) a fanfaron, blusterer, swaggerer, bully, boaster, braggart, ruffian.
fanfarrear (*v.i.*) to bluster, swagger, boast.
fanfarria (*f.*) = FANFARRICE.
fanfarrice (*f.*) boasting, swaggering, bluster, bravado, braggadocio.
fanfarronada (*f.*) fanfaronade, bluster, bravado [= FANFARRICE].
fanfarronar (*v.i.*) to bluster, swagger, bully [= FANFARREAR].
fanfarronice (*f.*) = FANFARRICE.
fanfreluche (*f.*) bauble; light dress ornaments, finery. [*French*].
fanga (*f.*) fanga (an old measure for grain, equivalent to 4.12 bu. in Brazil and to 1.57 bu. in Portugal); market place for staple goods at wholesale.
fanhosear (*v.t.,v.i.*) to speak with a nasal twang.
fanhoso –sa (*adj.*) nasal, twangy.
fanico (*m.*) a fainting fit; crumb, tiny bit; small profit.
faniquito (*m.*, *colloq.*) a conniption (fit) [= CHILIQUE].
fanisco (*m.*) small, thin man.
fanqueiro (*m.*) small dry goods merchant.
fantã (*m.*) fan-tan (Chinese gambling game).
fantasia (*f.*) fantasy, fancy, imagination; vagary; caprice, whim; illusion; fancy dress; (*Music*) fantasia.
fantasiador –dora (*adj.*) fancying; daydreaming; (*m.,f.*) daydreamer.
fantasiar (*v.t.*) to fancy, imagine; (*v.i.*) to daydream.—se de, to dress up as.
fantasioso –sa (*adj.*) fanciful; fantastic.
fantasista (*adj.; m.,f.*) imaginative (person).
fantasma (*m.*) phantasm, ghost, spectre, spook; a trigger fish [= CANGULO].
fantasmagoria (*f.*) phantasmagoria.

fantasmagórico –ca (adj.) phantasmagoric.
fantástico –ca (adj.) fantastic, fanciful, imaginary; uncanny; whimsical; (m.) fantasy.
fantastiquice (f.) extravagant tastes or appetites.
fantil (adj.) of good size and quality [horse, mare].
fantochada (f.) puppetry; fig. ridiculous behavior.
fantoche (m.) puppet, marionette; tool, catspaw.
faquear (v.t.) to knife [= ESFAQUEAR]; to make a touch for a loan.
faqueiro (m.) knife case; a cutler.
faquinha (f.) a small knife; (m.) worker who cuts up into small pieces the large pieces of a whale cut by the FACÃO.
faquir (m.) fakir.
faquista (m.,f.) cut-throat; (colloq.) a dead beat.
fará, farão, farás, forms of FAZER [47].
farad (m., Elec.) farad.
farádico –ca (adj.) faradic.
faradímetro (m., Elec.) faradmeter.
faradismo (m., Med.) faradism.
faradizar (v.t., Med.) to faradize.
farândola (f.) farandole; (colloq.) gang of ragamuffins; quantity of rags.
farandolar (v.i.) to dance a farandole; to go about in rags.
faraó (m.) pharaoh.
farauta (f.) an old ewe [= FAROTA].
farcino (m., Veter.) farcy.
farda (f.) uniform; livery.
fardalhão (m.) fancy uniform.
fardamenta (f.), **-to** (m.) uniform; style of uniform.
fardão (m.) richly ornamented uniform, esp. such as worn by members of the Brazilian Academy of Letters.
fardar (v.t.) to furnish with or put into uniform: (v.r.) to put on a uniform.
fardel [-éis] (m.) = FARNEL.
fardeta [ê] (f., Mil.) fatigue uniform.
fardo (m.) bale, bundle, pack, package; burden.—**de algodão,** bale of cotton.—**intolerável,** unbearable burden.
farei, fareis, forms of FAZER [47].
farejar (v.t.) to smell, scent; to follow the scent of; to smell out; (v.i.) to sniff.
farejo [ê] (m.) sniffing, smelling.
fareláceo –cea (adj.) like bran; mealy.
farelada (f.) a ration of bran; bran slops for hogs.
farelagem (f.) quantity of bran; chaff.
farelento –ta (adj.) of meal, coarse, full of bran.
farelhão (m.) small headland; steep-sided islet.
farelice (f.) = FANFARRICE.
farelo (m.) wheat middlings; bran; chaff; sawdust; fig. trifle; (Med.) scurf.
faremos, form of FAZER [47].
farelório (m.) trifle; empty words.
fáretra (f.) = ALJAVA.
farfalha (f.) rustle; bluster; (pl.) filings, shavings; fig. trifles.
farfalhada (f.) rustling, swishing (sounds); bluster.
farfalhador –dora (m.,f.) big talker.
farfalhante (adj.) rustling; talkative.
farfalhão –lhona (m.,f.) big talker.
farfalhar (v.i.) to rustle; to boast.
farfalharia (f.) = FARFALHADA.
farfalheiro –ra (adj.) gabby; (f.) = FARFALHADA.
farfalhento –ta (adj.) = FARFALHANTE.
farfalhice (f.) ostentatiousness; also = FANFARRICE.
farfalho (m.) rustling; idle talk.
farfalhoso –sa, **farfalhudo** –da (adj.) showy; gaudy; ornate; boastful.
farfância (f.) = FANFARRICE.
farfante (adj.; m.,f.) = FANFARRÃO.
faria, fariam, faríamos, farias, faríeis, forms of FAZER [47].
farináceo –cea (adj.) farinaceous.
farinar (v.t.) to convert into meal or flour.
faringe (f., Anat.) pharynx.
faríngeo –gea (adj.) pharyngeal.
faringite (f., Med.) pharyngitis.
faringologia (f.) pharyngology.
farinha (f.) flour, meal, farina; manioc meal; (Bot.) a dimorphandra (D. mollis), c.a. BARBATIMÃO-DE-FÔLHA-MIÚDA.—**-d'água,** a type of coarse manioc meal.—**de mandioca,** manioc meal (a nutritious starch obtained from the bitter cassava, Manihot esculenta).—**de milho,** corn meal,—**de osso,** bone meal.—**-de-pau,** a type of manioc meal.—**de-raspa,** manioc meal.—**de sangue,** blood meal.—**de trigo** or—**-do-reino,** wheat flour.—**-sêca,** any of various trees and plants.—**de trigo integral,**

wholewheat flour.—**do mesmo saco,** tarred with the same brush.—**-sêca** = TAMBORIL-BRAVO.
farinhada (f.) manufacture of manioc meal [= DESMAN-CHA].
farinheiro –ra (adj.) mealy [potatoes]; meal-like; (m.) dealer in manioc meal; (f.) a dish for serving manioc meal at table.
farinhento –ta (adj.) mealy; floury; flour-covered.
farinhoso –sa, **farinhudo** –da (adj.) mealy, floury.
farisaico –ca (adj.) pharisaical, self-righteous, hypocritical.
fariscar (v.t.,v.i.) to sniff [= FAREJAR].
fariseu (m.) pharisee; hypocrite.
farm. = FARMACÊUTICO (pharmicist; pharmaceutical); FARMÁCIA (pharmacy).
farmacêutico –ca (adj.) pharmaceutical; (m.,f.) pharmacist, apothecary, druggist.
farmácia (f.) pharmacy (art, profession, shop).
farmacodinâmica (f.) pharmacodynamics.
farmacognosia (f.) pharmacognosy.
farmacolando –da (m.,f.) a graduate in pharmacy.
farmacologia (f.) pharmacology.
farmacopéia (f.) pharmacopoeia.
farmacopola (m.) jokingly, a druggist; charlatan.
farnel [-éis] (m.) provisions, esp. for a journey.
faro (m.) an animal's sense of smell; scent, smell; an inkling; lighthouse.
faroeste (m.) Far West.
farofa (f.) a popular Braz. dish made of manioc meal browned in a frying pan with grease or butter; sometimes mixed with bits of meat, crisp fat, chopped eggs, etc. It is much used as a stuffing for roast turkey; also (colloq.) pretentiousness; idle chatter.—**-bôca-larga** = CORCOROCA (a fish).—**-de-casco** "a dish prepared in the following manner: a turtle is split open, the eggs, viscera, filet, etc., are taken out and the shell (which is apparently now clean) is placed in the oven with salt and lemon; upon being heated the shell yields a copious amount of oil, and this mixed with manioc flour, is known as FAROFA DE CASCO, a dish which is eaten in the shell and is used as bread." [GBAT]
farofada (f.) = FANFARRICE.
farofeiro –ra (adj.) boastful, pretentious; (m.,f.) boaster.
farofento –ta (adj.) boastful; blustering.
farófia (f.) pretentiousness [= FAROFA].
farol [-óis] (m.) lighthouse; beacon; fig. guidance; ship's lantern; headlight of an automobile or locomotive. In colloq. usage: a large diamond set in a ring, a shillaber; hokum, buncombe.—**de aeroporto,** (Aeron.) airport beacon.—**de aterragem,** (Aeron.) landing light.—**de neblina,** (Autom.) fog headlight. **fazer—,** to show off, boast, brag; to put oneself in the limelight. **rádio—,** radio beam.
farolagem (f.) claptrap, mere show.
faroleiro (m.) lighthouse-keeper; (colloq.) braggart, show-off; idle talker.
farolete [lê] (m., Autom.) parking or tail light; flashlight.
farota (f.) = FARAUTA.
farpa (f.) barb; a barbed dart employed by the banderilla in bullfighting; sliver, splinter.
farpado –da (adj.) barbed. **arame—,** barbed-wire.
farpante (adj.) harpooning.
farpão (m.) harpoon; javelin; fig. aggression.
farpar (v.t.) to harpoon; to furnish with barbs.
farpear (v.t.) to strike with a dart or harpoon.
farpela (f.) the hook of a crochet hook; (colloq.) a suit of clothes.
farra (f.) fun, frolic, good time, spree; revelry, carousal, binge, bender; a salmon (Salmo lavaretus).
farracho (m.) a kind of dull sword used to kill fish in night fishing.
farrancho (m.) group of persons who go on a junket or pilgrimage together.
farrapo (m.) rag, tatter; ragamuffin, tatterdemalion.—**de papel,** scrap of paper. **em—s,** in rags.
farrear (v.i.) to revel, carouse, make merry.
farripas (f.pl.) wisps of hair on the head.
farrista (m.,f.) reveller, carouser, merrymaker.
farroupa, farroupilha (m.,f.) tatterdemalion.
farrusco –ca (adj.) smutty, grimy; black; (m.) smut, grime.
farsa (f.) farce, burlesque; slapstick comedy; ridiculous action.
farsante (m.,f.) low comedian; coarse jester; a farceur.

farsista (*m.,f.*) player in a farce; buffoon; joker, wag; (*adj.*) given to coarse jokes.
farsola (*m.,f.*) wag, joker, cutup.
fartadela (*f.*) a bellyful.
fartar [24] (*v.t.*) to satiate, satisfy (**de**, with); to surfeit; to cloy; to irk.—**-se**, to indulge in (anything) to excess; to become fed-up; to get enough of. **a—**, to repletion.
farto -ta (*adj.; irreg. p.p. of* FARTAR) full, sated, glutted; satisfied; rich; abundant.—**de**, fed up with, sick of.
fartote (*m., colloq.*) blowout, big feed; bellyful.
fartum (*m.*) foul smell [= FORTUM].
fartura (*f.*) repletion, satiety; affluence; abundance. **com—**, in abundance, galore.
fas (*m.*) that which is right and proper. **por—ou por nefas**, rightly or wrongly; by hook or by crook.
fasc. = FASCÍCULO (fascicle).
fascal (*m.*) shock of grain.
fasces (*m.pl.*) fasces.
fasciação (*f., Bot.*) fasciation.
fasciculado -da (*adj.*) fasciculate.
fascicular (*adj.*) fascicular.
fascículo (*m.*) fascicle.
fascinação (*f.*) fascination, enchantment, charm; lure.
fascinado -da (*adj.*) fascinated, enchanted.
fascinador -dora (*adj.*) fascinating, enchanting, bewitching, alluring, charming; (*m.,f.*) fascinator, charmer.
fascinante (*adj.*) fascinating; entrancing.
fascinar (*v.t.*) to fascinate, charm; to bewitch, spellbind; to dazzle.
fascínio (*m.*) evil eye; enchantment; fascination.
fascíola (*f.*) a liver fluke or other two-suckered trematode worm of Fasciola (Syn. Distomum).
fasciolose (*f., Med., Veter.*) fascioliasis, distomiasis.—**hepática**, liver rot, esp. of sheep.
fascismo (*m.*) Fascism.
fascista (*adj.; m.,f.*) Fascist.
fase (*f.*) phase (all senses); aspect, state.
faseado -da (*adj., Elec.*) in phase.
faseolar (*adj.*) bean-shaped; kidney-shaped.
faseolina (*f., Biochem.*) phaseolin.
fasímetro (*m., Elec.*) phasemeter.
fasmóide (*m.*) any stick insect.
fasquia (*f.*) a thin strip of wood, used for various purposes; lath, batten.
fastidioso -sa (*adj.*) tedious, irksome, dull, boring; disgusting, annoying. [But not fastidious in the sense of squeamish, hard to please, which is DIFÍCIL DE CONTENTAR].
fastiento -ta (*adj.*) = FASTIDIOSO.
fastigiado -da (*adj.*) of trees, lofty; (*Bot.*) fastigiate.
fastígio (*m.*) fastigium; apex, summit.
fastigioso -sa (*adj.*) at the very top; prominent.
fastio (*m.*) tedium, ennui; disgust; dislike; want of appetite.
fasto -ta (*adj.*) happy; fortunate; (*m.*) ostentation; (*pl.*) annals.
fastoso -sa, fastuoso -sa (*adj.*) ostentatious; pompous.
fatacaz (*f.*) a large slice or piece.
fatal (*adj.*) fated, foredoomed; inescapable; fatal, deadly; calamitous.
fatalidade (*f.*) fate, fatality, destiny; a fatal accident; calamity, disaster.
fatalismo (*m.*) fatalism.
fatalista (*adj.; m.,f.*) fatalist.
fatalmente (*adv.*) surely, infallibly, undoubtedly; fatally.
fateiro (*m.*) seller of tripe and other animal viscera [= BUCHEIRO, TRIPEIRO].
fateixa (*f.*) grapnel; grappling hook; meat hook; a heavy stone used as an anchor for a small boat.
fatia (*f.*) slice (of bread, cheese etc.); (*colloq.*) "rake-off".—**dourada** or **—de-parida**, French toast [= RABANADA].
fatiar (*v.t.*) to cut into slices.
fatídico -ca (*adj.*) fateful, portentous, ominous.
fatigador -dora, fatigante (*adj.*) fatiguing, wearying, tiring.
fatigamento (*m.*) fatigue [= FADIGA].
fatigar (*v.t.*) to fatigue, tire; to fag, jade; to irk, bother; to harass; (*v.r.*) to tire oneself out (**de, com**, with); to get tired.
fatigoso -sa (*adj.*) = FATIGANTE.
fatiota (*f.*) a suit or outfit of clothes.
fatitivo -va (*adj., Gram.*) factitive.
fato (*m.*) fact, event, occurrence; deed, act, thing done; man's suit; small herd of goats; animal viscera.—**à**

paisana, civilian clothes.—**consumado**, fait accompli. **de—**, in fact, really, actually. **estar ao—**, to be au fait (familiar with the facts of). **o—é que**, the fact (of the matter) is that. **restringir-se aos—s**, to stick to the facts.
fator [-es] (*m.*) factor; coefficient; agent.—**de acoplamento**, (*Elec.*) coupling coefficient.—**de amplificação**, (*Elec.*) amplification factor.—**de carga**, (*Elec., Aeron.*) load factor.—**de filtro**, (*Photog.*) filter factor.—**de forma**, (*Elec.*) form factor.—**de impedância**, (*Elec.*) impedance factor.—**de potência**, (*Elec.*) power factor.—**de reflexão**, (*Physics*) coefficient of reflection.—**de segurança**, safety factor.
fatorial (*m., Math.*) factorial.
fatual (*adj.*) factual.
fatuidade [u-i] (*f.*) fatuity; vainglory; self-complacency.
fátuo -tua (*adj.*) fatuous, witless, foolish; smug; vainglorious. **fogo—**, ignis fatuus; will-o'-the-wisp.
fatura (*f.*) invoice, bill of goods.—**consular**, consular invoice. **tirar uma—**, to make out an invoice.
faturar (*v.t.*) to invoice, bill.
faturista (*m.,f.*) bill clerk.
fauce (*f.*) gullet, throat; (*Anat., Bot.*) fauces.
faúla (*f.*) = FAGULHA.
faular [a-u] (*v.t.*) to emit sparks; (*v.i.*) to spark.
faúlha (*f.*) spark [= FAGULHA]; flour dust.
faulhento -ta (*adj.*) that throws off sparks; that raises dust.
fauna (*f.*) fauna.
fauno (*m., Myth.*) faun.—**-dos-bosques**, monkey.
faunologia (*f.*) faunology, zoogeography.
faúnula (*f., Paleontol., Zool.*) faunule.
fausto -ta (*adj.*) lucky, prosperous, propitious, happy; (*m.*) pageantry, pomp.
faustoso -sa (*adj.*) pompous, showy, ostentatious.
fauteuil (*m.*) arm chair. [*French*].
fautor -triz (*adj.*) aiding, abetting; (*m.,f.*) abettor.
fautorizar (*v.t.*) to favor, aid, abet
fava (*f.*) bean; bean pod; broad bean, horse bean (*Vicia faba*). **— -branca, — -contra-o-máu-olhado, — -de-quebranto**, common jackbean (*Canavalia ensiformis*) better known as FEIJÃO-DE-PORCO.—**café,—coceira**, cowage velvetbean (*Stizolobium prutitum*).—**s contadas**, sure thing, dead certainty.—**contra**, sword jackbean (*Canavalia gladiata*).—**de-besouro**, a senna (*Cassia xinguensis*).—**de-bolota**, a nittatree (*Parkia*).—**de-calabar**, the deadly Calabar bean (*Physostigma venenosum*).—**de-cavalo**, small horsebean (*Vicia faba minor*).—**de-chapa**, the poonga oil pongamia (*Pongamia pinnata*).—**de-cheiro,—da-índia**, the Dutch tonkabean (*Dipteryx odorata*).—**s-de-engenho**, the Bengal kimo (*Butea monosperma*).—**s-de-lázaro**, the fragrant albizzia (*A. odoratissima*).—**de-malaca**, cashew markingnut (*Semecarpus anacardium*).—**de-rama**, a jackbean (*Canavalia*).—**de-rôsca**, an earpod tree (*Enterolobium schomburgkii* whose wood is used in construction and for railroad ties; c.a. TIMBÓ-DA-MATA, TIMBORANA, TIMBAÚBA.—**de-santo-inácio**, St. Ignatius poison nut (*Strychnos ignati*).—**de-sucupira**, the fuzzy faveiro (*Pterodon pubescens*).—**preta**, blackball (adverse vote). **mandar à(s)—(s)**, to send (someone) to the devil.
favar (*v.i.*) to fail of success.
favária (*f., Bot.*) the live-forever sedum (*S. telephium purpureum*), c.a. ERVA-DOS-CALOS; FAVÁRIA-MAIOR, FAVÁRIA-VULGAR.
faveira (*f.*) any of various leguminous trees or their timber.
faveiro (*m., Bot.*) the fuzzy faveiro (*Pterdon pubescens*); an apes-earring (*Pithecellobium*) *multiflorum*).
favela (*f.*) slum, shantytown.—**branca**, (*Bot.*) an apesearring (*Pithecellobium diversifolium*), c.a. BRINCOS-DE-SAGÜIM; an earpod tree (*Enterolobium ellipticum*), c.a. ORELHA-DE-NEGRO, VINHÁTICO-DO-CAMPO.
favelado -da (*m.,f.*) shantytown dweller.
faveleiro (*m., Bot.*) a nettlespurge (*Jatropha phyllacantha*), c.a. MANDIOCA-BRAVA.
faveolado-da (*adj.*) faveolate; alveolate.
faviforme (*adj.*) faviform, resembling a honeycomb.
favinha (*f., Bot.*)—**brava**, a rhynchosia (*R. lobata*), c.a. FEIJÃO-DO-MATO, ÔLHO-DE-CABRA-MIÚDO.—**do-campo**, the crabseye rhynchosia (*R. phaseoloides*), c.a. FEIJÃO-BRAVO.—**de-capoeira** = AMENDOIM-DE-VEADO.
favo (*m.*) honeycomb.
favônio -nia (*adj.*) pertaining to the west wind; mild; favoring; (*m.*) gentle, favorable west wind.

favor [ô] (*m.*) favor, kindness, benefit; patronage. **a—de**, in behalf of; for the benefit of. **a (seu)—**, in (his) favor. **a—dêle**, to his advantage. **em—de**, in favor of, in behalf of. **em—dêle**, in his favor. **faça o—de**, please; be so kind as to. **por—**, please. **ter a seu—**, to have to one's credit.
favorável (*adj.*) favorable (**a**, to); propitious, auspicious.
favorecedor –dora (*adj.*) favoring; (*m.,f.*) one who favors.
favorecer (*v.t.*) to favor, assist; to support, aid; to represent in a (more) favorable light.
favorecido –da (*adj.*) favored.
favoritismo (*m.*) favoritism.
favorito –ta (*adj.; m.,f.*) favorite.
favoso –sa (*adj.*) favose; (*f., Med., Veter.*) favus, tinea favosa.
faxina (*f.*) fascine; fagot; kitchen or fatigue duty (in the Army); havoc. **fazer—**, to do K.P. or similar duty at a hotel, restaurant, etc.—**vermelha**, (*Bot.*) the clammy hopseed bush (*Dodonaea viscosa*), c.a. ERVA-DE-VEADO, VASSOURA-VERMELHA, VASSOURA-DO-CAMPO, VASSOURI-NHA-DO-MATO.
faxinar (*v.t.*) to cover, protect, or strengthen with fascines; to cause havoc.
faxineiro (*m.*) a soldier on K.P.; dishwasher; hotel porter.
faz, faze, forms of FAZER [47].
faz-de-conta (*m., colloq.*) cuckold [= CÔRNO].
fazedor (*m.*) doer; maker.
fazenda (*f.*) a plantation, esp. a coffee plantation or cattle ranch; estate, property, possessions; the public treasury; fabric, cloth, material.—**de algodão**, cotton cloth.—**de café**, coffee plantation.—**nacional**, national treasury; exchequer.—**pública**, the public treasury.—**s estampadas**, printed (cloth) goods. **loja de—s**, drygoods store. **Ministro da—**, Minister of the Treasury. **tratador de—**, a ranch hand.
fazendeiro –ra (*m.,f.*) planter, farmer, rancher (on a large scale); owner of a FAZENDA; (*m., Bot.*) the little-flower quickweed (*Galinsoga parviflora*), c.a. PICÃO-BRANCO.
fazendola (*f.*) a small FAZENDA.
fazer [47] (*v.t.*) to make (things); to produce by an action or causitive agency (noise, music, etc.); to cause to be or become; to render (e.g., **fazer das tripas coração**—see below); to bring into proper condition for use (**fazer a cama**); to cause, induce or compel (someone to do something); to produce, earn or win for oneself (**fazer fortuna**); to compose (**fazer versos**); to do, perform, execute; to put forth, exert (**fazer esforços**); to be the cause of; bring about; effect (**fazer bem, mal, justiça, injustiça**, etc.); (*v.r.*) to become (turn, grow into) something.—**a barba**, to shave oneself; to get a shave (at the barbershop). [**Êle está fazendo a barba no banheiro**, He's shaving in the bathroom. **Êle saiu para fazer a barba**, He's gone out to get a shave.]—**a côrte a**, to woo, pay court to.—**a chamada**, to call the roll.—**as vontades de**, to do the will of, give in to, comply with the wishes of (usually without moderation); to spoil, esp. a child. [**Ela sempre fez as vontades daquele menino**, She always gave in to whatever that child wanted.]—**abstração de si**, to exclude oneself; to be self-effacing; to sacrifice oneself. —**água**, to spring a leak.—**(alguém) andar com a cabeça à roda**, to turn a person's head.—**alto**, to come to a halt. —**anos**, to have a birthday; to reach, or turn, a certain age. [**Eu fiz 30 anos ontem**, I was (turned)) 30 yesterday. **Ela vai fazer dois anos**, She's not yet two years old.]—**as malas**, to pack up one's bags.—**as pazes**, to make up (patch up a quarrel); to bury the hatchet.—**as refeições no hotel**, to take one's meals at the hotel.—**as vezes de**, to take the place of, substitute for; to act as or for.—**ato de presença**, to put in an appearance.—**badernas**, to raise Cain.—**barulho** (esbregue, espôrro), to kick up a row, raise hell.—**beiço** (beicinho, biquinho), to pout.— **bem**, to do good (right); to be good for; to agree with (speaking of climate, foods, drugs, etc.). [**O ar livre faz bem à saúde**, Fresh air is good for you. **Sardinha não me faz bem**, Sardines don't agree with me. **Este regime vai te fazer bem**, This diet will do you good.]—**caretas**, to make faces.—**carreira**, to get on in the world.—**caso de**, to pay attention to; to insist on, be particular about. [**Êle faz muito caso dessas coisas**, He always insists on things like that. **Êle não faz caso de comida**, He's not particular about food, or food is a matter of indifference to him.]—**cêra**, to dawdle, make a pretense of working; to "goldbrick"; to stall, linger too long.—**cerimônia**, to

stand on ceremony, be stiff, formal.—**cocégas**, to tickle (someone).—**com que (alguém) faça (alguma coisa)**, to make (someone) do (something).—**com que (algo) aconteça**, to cause (something) to happen; to bring (something) to pass.—**comentários sôbre**, to comment on, make remarks about, chat about, discuss.—**companhia a (alguém)**, to keep (someone) company; to stay with (someone).—**compras**, to go shopping.—**continência**, to salute (in a military sense only).—**cumprir (uma lei)**, to enforce (a law).—**curso de**, to take a course in.— **das tripas coração**, to turn one's fears into courage, take heart, pull oneself together.—**de conta que**, to make believe that, pretend that.—**diabruras**, to act up; to cut up.—**dieta**, to diet, go on a diet.—**e acontecer**, to make threats; to do exactly as one wishes.—**economia de palitos**, to be penny-wise and pound-foolish.—**economias**, to put by, save for the future.—**em pedaços**, to smash to pieces.—**entrar**, to show (someone) in.—**escândalo**, to give rise to scandal, cause tongues to wag; to make a scene. [**Ela faz escândalo por qualquer coisa**, She'll make a scene at the slightest provocation.]—**esmolas**, to give alms.—**espécie**, to raise a doubt.—**exercício** (or **ginástica**), to take exercise.—**exercícios**, to do homework; to drill (in the Army).—**face a**, to confront.—**falta**, to be needed, wanting, lacking.—**farol (farolagem)**, (*slang*) to put oneself in the limelight; to show off, brag; to splurge. —**feio**, to behave badly.—**festas a**, to make a fuss over; to pet affectionately; to show affection; to welcome gleefully. [**Quando eu entrei, o cachorrinho me fez muita(s) festa(s)**, When I came in, the little dog jumped all over me happily. **O povo americano fez muita festa à Rainha da Inglaterra**, The American people gave the Queen of England a warm welcome.]—**finca-pé**, to put one's foot down.—**fita**, (*slang*) to show off; to put on airs; to be coy, coquettish; to play hard-to-get; to fuss excessively over something (usually something unpleasant). [**Na presença de um rapaz bonito ela sempre faz fita**, She's always coy (coquettish) when there's a handsome fellow around. **Ela não veio, ficou fazendo fita**, She didn't come; she was playing hard-to-get. **Êste menino faz uma fita para tomar remédio!** This boy makes an awful fuss over taking medicine.]—**fogo**, to open fire.—**fogo emboscado**, to snipe.—**força**; to exert force; to make an effort.—**fortuna**, to make one's fortune, get rich.—**frente a**, to face. [**fazer frente a uma dificuldade**, to take the bull by the horns.]—**furor**, to make a hit.—**gafe**, to put one's foot in one's mouth.—**gazêta**, to cut classes, play hookey.— **gestos**, to gesticulate.—**gôsto**, to please, be pleasing, be a pleasure.—**greve**, to strike, go on strike.—**guerra**, to wage war.—**hora(s)**, to kill time.—**incursão**, to go on a raid.—**leilão**, to sell at auction.—**macaquices**, to cut up, caper.—**mal**, to do evil, wrong; to do harm; of foods, etc., to disagree with. [**Os seus conselhos fizeram mal a ela**, Your advice did her harm. **Vinho me faz mal**, Wine doesn't agree with me.]—**mêdo**, to frighten, cause fright. —**milagre**, to pass a miracle (do wonders).—**o melhor que se pode**, to do one's best.—**notar**, to call attention to, cause to be noted.—**o mesmo**, to do the same (likewise).—**o papel de**, to play the part of.—**o percurso entre**, to run a course (go the distance) between.—**o possível**, to do one's utmost.—**ouvidos moucos**, or **ouvidos de mercador**, to turn a deaf ear.—**papel triste**, to act foolishly; to make a fool of oneself; to cut miserably and publicly; to do something shameful or embarrassing in public.—**parede**, to picket, form a picket line.— **parte de**, to be a part of; to belong to (a club, etc.). —**passar gato por lebre**, to sell gold bricks; to sell a pig in a poke.—**patrulha**, to patrol, go on patrol.—**pena**, to cause pity.—**perguntas**, to ask questions.—**ponto**, to frequent, hang out at (a particular place).—**por**, to strive (to do something).—**por fazer**, to do to be doing; to act to no purpose.—**por onde**, to find a way (of doing something); to give rise to, cause for.—**pouco de**, to belittle, look down on; to deride.—**pouco caso de**, to pay scant attention to; to fail to appreciate; to disregard; to snub; to ignore; to underestimate; to make fun of (someone, usually superciliously).—**propaganda**, to advertise; also, to engage in propaganda (in the political sense, esp. in wartime).—**que**, to make, cause, oblige (someone) to (do something); to pretend, make out that.—**questão de**, to insist on; to make a point of; to put one's foot down.—**regime**, to be on a diet; to go on a diet.—**roda**, to form a circle; to hold hands in a circle.—**rodeios**, to beat about the bush.—**saber**, to cause or to let (some-

one) know.—**sair**, to eject.—**saltar (uma ponte)**, to blow up (a bridge).—**saltar os miolos**, to blow out one's brains.—**se ao mar**, to put out to sea.—**se de**, to pretend to be, act the part of.—**se de bôbo**, to play dumb.—**se esperar**, to keep someone waiting.—**se de tolo**, to act the fool.—**se médico, advogado, etc.**, to become a doctor, lawyer, etc.—**se rogado**, to seek to be coaxed; to play hard-to-get.—**sinal**, to signal, make signals.—**tromba**, (colloq.) to thrust out the lips (in a pout).—**um passeio**, to take a stroll, go for a walk; to go for a ride; to take a pleasure trip.—**uma viagem**, to take a trip, go on a journey.—**uma visita**, to pay a call, make a visit.—**versos**, to write poetry. **A ocasião faz o ladrão**, Opportunity makes the thief. **com a barba por—**, needing a shave. **deixar por—**, to leave undone; to leave to be done. **faça (o) favor de**, please (do me the favor of). **Faça você mesmo**, Do it yourself. **Farei o possível para você**, I'll do my best for you. **Faz bem**, He is right; He does right. **Faz bom (mau) tempo**, The weather is good (bad). **Faz dois anos que não o vejo**, I haven't seen him for two years. **Faz-me bem**, It does me good. **Faz mêdo**, It is frightening. **Faz pena**, It is distressing. **Faz uma semana**, A week ago. **faz-se mister**, it becomes necessary. **Faz-se tarde**, It is getting late. **Fez menção de sair**, He prepared to leave. **Fez-se um silêncio**, There was a silence. **feito um bôbo**, like a dope, like a fool. **mais fácil de dizer que de fazer**, easier said than done. **mandar fazer**, to order (something) to be made or done. **Não faz mais do que estudar**, All he does is study. **Não faz mal**, No matter; Never mind; That's all right. **Não faz outra coisa senão queixar-se**, He does nothing but complain. **não—caso de**, to ignore, pay no attention to, disregard. **não saber que—**, to be at a loss as to what to do. **Nunca faria isso**, (I, she, he) would never do such a thing. **O homem faz e Deus desfaz**, Man proposes but God disposes. **Para mim, tanto faz**, To me it's all the same. **passar a—**, to proceed to do. **Que faço?** What am I to do? **Que é (or que foi) feito dêle?** What has become of him? **Quer chova, quer faça sol**, Rain or shine. **Roma não se fez num dia**, Rome was not made in a day. **tanto faz que**, it makes no difference whether. **ter muito que—**, to have much to do; to be very busy. **tornar a—(alguma coisa)**, to do something again; to repeat (an action).
fazimento (m.) the doing of a thing.
fazível (adj.) = FACTÍVEL.
faz-tudo (m.) a Jack-of-all-trades.
fé [ê] (f.) faith, creed; belief, credence, confidence; fidelity, faithfulness; legal certification (of documents, etc.).—**conjugal**, conjugal fidelity.—**de ofício**, certificate of record; testimonial of work completed.—**do carvoeiro**, blind faith.—**púnica**, punic faith, i.e., faithlessness, treacherousness. **à—**, truly. **à—de quem sou**, on my word of honor. **artigo de—**, article of faith (religion). **dar—a**, (colloq.) to put faith in, take stock in (a person or thing); to certify to (as a notary). **dar—de**, to take notice of, perceive. **de boa—**, in good faith; bona fide. **em—do que**, in witness whereof. **fazer—**, to be trustworthy; to believe. **má—**, faithlessness, dishonesty. **portar por—**, to certify. **ter—em**, to trust, have faith in.
fealdade (f.) ugliness, outrage.
fearrão (m.) very ugly man.
fearrona (f.) very ugly woman.
Feba (f.) Phebe, Phoebe.
febo (m.) the sun. [Poetical].
febra [ê] (f.) edible meat without bone or fat; fibre, muscle; (Bot.) hair root; strength, energy.
febre (f.) fever; excitement, desire; (m.) light weight (coins).—**aftosa**, aphthous fever (hoof-and-mouth disease).—**amarela**, yellow fever, yellow jack.—**de-caroço**, bubonic plague;—**de feno**, hay fever, c.a. POLINOSE.—**de Malta** or **de Mediterrâneo**, c.a. undulant or Malta fever (brucellosis).—**de Oroya**, Oroya fever, verruga peruana.—**do Texas**, Texas (cattle) fever, c.a. FERRUJÃO, TRISTEZA.—**erratica**, intermittent fever.—**intermitente**, intermittent fever, malaria.—**láctea**, or **do leite**, milk fever.—**miliar**, miliaria.—**palustre**, malaria.—**puerperal**, puerperal fever.—**tifóide**, typhoid fever.
febrento -ta (adj.) feverish.
febricitante (adj.) feverish.
febricitar (v.i.) to be feverish.
febricula (f., Med.) febricula, light fever.
febrífugo -ga (adj.; m.) febrifuge.
febril (adj.) febrile, feverish.
fecal (adj.) fecal.

fecha [ê] (m.) tumult, riot.
fechado -da (adj.) closed, enclosed; unopened. **ter o corpo—**, to be immune to bullets and other dangers by reason of amulets. **curva—**, sharp curve; (m.) "a passageway of water arched by canopies of impenetrable low-growing vegetation which impedes navigation." [GBAT]
fechadura (f.) lock (of door, drawer, etc.).
fecha-fecha (m.) panicky closing up of stores and business houses during a riot or other public disorder.
fechamento (m.) a closing; (Mach.) a cut-off; (Arch.) keystone.
fechar (v.t.) to close (up, in, down); to shut (up, in, down); to lock (up, in); to conclude, finish; (v.r.) to close (in); to become dark.—**a bôca**, to force another to stop talking.—**a cadeado**, to padlock.—**a cara** or **a carranca**, to frown, scowl.—**à chave**, to lock with a key.—**a sete chaves**, to lock up securely; to put under lock and key.—**com chave de ouro**, to finish well.—**com ferrôlho**, to secure with a slide bolt.—**com tranca**, to bar (the door)—**a loja**, to close up a shop (for good).—**a mala**, to close the mail.—**a mão**, to clench the fist.—**a porta a**, to close the door to; to shut out.—**a raia**, to be last in a race.—**o corpo**, to render the body immune to disease, bullets, snake bite, etc., by means of witchcraft.—**os olhos**, to close the eyes; fig., to die.—**os olhos a (alguma coisa)**, to wink, connive at (something).—**os ouvidos**, to turn a deaf ear.—**se a noite**, to grow dark.—**se em casa**, to close oneself up at home.—**se em copas**, to be wary, clam up, keep mum.—**um negócio**, to close a deal; to strike a bargain. **num abrir e—d'olhos**, in the twinkling of an eye.
fecharia (f.) firing mechanism.
fecho [ê] (m.) latch, bolt, lock; any fastening device; keystone; finish, close (of a letter); upshot, conclusion.—**éclair**, a slide fastener (zipper).—**de segurança**, safety catch. **arruela de—**, a lock washer (for bolts and nuts).
fécula (f.) fecula, starch (of plants).
feculência (f.) feculence.
feculento -ta, **feculoso** -sa (adj.) starchy; feculent.
fecundação (f.) fecundation.
fecundador -dora (m.,f.; adj.) one who, or that, fecundates.
fecundante (adj.) that fecundates.
fecundar (v.t.) to fecundate, impregnate, fertilize; to make fruitful; (v.r.) to become fecund.
fecundativo -va (adj.) fecundative.
fecundez, fecúndia (f.) = FECUNDIDADE.
fecundidade (f.) fecundity, fertility, fruitfulness.
fecundo -da (adj.) fecund, fruitful, fertile, prolific; rich [soil].
fedegoso -sa (adj.) evil-smelling, fetid, stinking; (f., Bot.) the sickle senna (Cassia tora); (m.) a combining term for many other species of Cassia, some of which are:—**de-fôlha-torta**, flowery senna (Cassia corymbosa), c.a. MANJERIOBA.—**grande**, ringworm senna (C. alata).—**verdadeiro**, coffee senna (C. occidentalis), c.a. FÔLHA-DE-PAJÉ, IBIXUNA, LAVA-PRATOS, MAN(J)ERIOBA, MA-MANGÁ, MATA-PASTO, PAJAMARIOBA, TARARUCU.
fedelho [dê] (m.) child, brat.
fedentina (f.) foul odor.
feder [48] (v.i.) to stink, smell bad.
federação (f.) federation.
federado -da (adj.) federated.
federal (adj.) federal.
federalismo (m.) federalism.
federalista (adj.; m.,f.) federalist.
federar (v.t.) to federate.
federativo -va (adj.) federative.
fedido -da (adj.) fetid.
fedor (m.) stink, stench [= MAU CHEIRO].
fedorentina (f.) foul smell.
fedorento -ta (adj.) fetid, stinking; (f.) = CAINCA and ERUCA (plants).
feérico -ca (adj.) fairy, fairy-like.
feianchão -chona (adj.; m.,f.) very ugly (man, woman).
feição (f.) fashion, form, figure, shape; countenance, aspect, look; good disposition; (pl.) facial features. **à—de**, in the manner of.
feiíssimo -ma [ei-í] (absol. superl. of FEIO) most ugly.
feijão (m.) bean, bean pod; cooked beans; a type of pebble found in diamantiferous gravel; (Bot.) any of many kinds of beans, esp. the edible sorts of Phasseolus.—**anão**, a dwarf variety of kidney bean.—**andu** = GUANDU.—**baru**, a tonka bean (Dipteryx sp.).—**boi-de-capueira**,

a caper (*Capparis sp.*).—**-bravo,** any of numerous uncultivated tropical plants, shrubs and trees of the pea family (*Fabaceae*).—**-bravo-amarelo,** a senna (*Cassia hirsuta*).—**-cabeludo-da-índia** = FEIJÃO-DA-FLÓRIDA.—**-careta (-carita, -carito)** = FEIJÃO-FRADINHO.—**catinga-de-macaco,** jicama (*Colopogonium coeruleum*).—**-chicote,** the yardlong cowpea (*Vigna sesquipedalis*), c.a. FEIJÃO-ESPARGO.—**-chinês,** a cowpea (*Vigna catjang*); the soybean (*Glycine soja*), c.a. FEIJÃO-SOJA.—**-côco,** a tonka bean (*Dipteryx*).—**-colubrino** = FEIJÃO-DA-ÍNDIA.—**-comum,** common kidney bean (*Phaseolus vulgaris*).—**-corda** = FEIJÃO-DE-FRADE.—**-cru,** the raintree saman (*Samanea saman*); also = MENDUBI-DE-VEADO.—**-cutelinho,** the hyacinth bean (*Dolichos lablab*), c.a. LABE-LABE, FEIJÃO-DA-ÍNDIA, CUMANDATIÁ.—**-da-china,** a cowpea (*Vigna catjang*), c.a. FEIJÃO-CHINÊS.—**-da-flórida,** the Deering or Florida velvetbean (*Stizolobium deeringianum*), c.a. FEIJÃO-CABELUDO-DA-ÍNDIA, MUCUNA-VILOSA, FEIJÃO-DO-GADO, FEIJÃO-MUCUANA, FEIJAO-VELU-DO.—**-da-índia,** the hyacinth bean (*Dolichos lablab*), c.a. LABE-LABE, CUMANDATIÁ, FEIJÃO-CUTELINHO; the mungo bean (*Phaseolus mungo*).—**-da-praia,** a seashore sophora (*S. littoralis*); the ground jackbean (*Canavalia obtusifolia*); the seashore cowpea (*Vigna marina*).—**-de-árvore,** a shrub of genus *Sesbania* (*syn. Agati*), c.a. DORMIDEIRA; also = GUANDU.—**-de-boi,** the dog caper (*Capparis flexuosa*), c.a. MUÇAMBÊ-INDECENTE, SAPOTAIA; a clusterpea (*Dioclea rostrata*); a tickclover (*Desmodium pabularis*); the catjang cowpea (*Vigna catjang*), c.a. FEIJÃO-DE-VACA, FEIJÃO-CHINÊS.—**-de-cavalo,** small horsebean (*Vicia faba minor*), c.a. FEIJÃO-DE-PORCO, FEIJÃO-MIÚDO, FEIJÃO-FORRAGEIRO.—**-de-cobra,** common jackbean (*Canavalia ensiformis*), c.a. FEIJÃO-DE-PORCO, FEIJÃO-HOLANDÊS.—**-de-espanha,** scarlet runner bean (*Phaseolus coccineus*).—**-de-frade,** a variety of common cowpea (*Vigna sinensis*), c.a. FEIJÃO-FRADINHO.—**-de-guizos,** a rattlebox (*Crotolaria sp.*).—**-de-lima,** lima bean (*Phaseolus limensis*), c.a. FAVA-BRANCA, sieva bean (*Phaseolus lunatus*).—**-de-metro** = FEIJÃO-DE-CHICOTE.—**-de-pombinha** = FEIJÃO-DE-RÔLA.—**-de porco,** common jackbean (*Canavalia ensiformis*), c.a. FEIJÃO-DE-COBRA; the small horsebean (*Vicia faba minor*), c.a. FEIJÃO-DE-CAVALO.—**-de-rôla,** a bean (*Phaseolus lathyroides*), cultivated as a green manure; c.a. FEIJÃO-DE-POMBINHA.—**-de-vaca,** a cowpea (*Vigna sp.*), c.a. FEIJÃO-DE-BOI.—**-do-gado** = FEIJÃO-DA-FLÓRIDA.—**-do-mato,** coastal butterfly pea (*Centrosema virginianum*); the crabseye rhychosia (*R. phaseoloides*); kinds of bean (*Phaseolus*); also = ESPERLINA.—**-dos-caboclos,** a tropical tree of the mulberry family (*Trophis brasiliensis*), bearing a round, thin-fleshed fruit with a single, rather large seed; the bark yields tannin and the wood is used in joinery; c.a. DICONROQUE.—**-espada,** common jackbean (*Canavalia ensiformis*), c.a. FEIJÃO-DE-COBRA, FEIJÃO-DE-PORCO.—**-esparto** = FEIJÃO-CHICOTE.—**-farinha** = FEIJÃO-DE-PORCO.—**-fava-bravo,** a jackbean (*Canavalia sp.*).—**-flor,** scarlet runner (*Phaseolus coccineus*).—**-forrageiro** = FEIJÃO-DE-CAVALO.—**-fradinho** = FEIJÃO-DE-FRADE.—**-grande,** a trumpet-creeper (*Adenocalymma*).—**-guandu** = GUANDU.—**holandês,** common jackbean (*Canavalia ensiformis*), c.a. FEIJÃO-DE-COBRA.—**-lablab,** the hyacinth bean (*Dolichos lablab*), c.a. LABE-LABE.—**-manteiga,** kinds of butter beans or wax beans.—**-miúdo,** small horsebean (*Vicia faba minor*), c.a. FEIJÃO-DE-CAVALO.—**-mucuna** = FEIJÃO-DA-FLÓRIDA.—**-mulatinho,** a variety of kidney bean (*Phaseolus sp.*).—**-mungo,** the mung bean (*Phaseolus aureus*).—**-oró,** a cover crop and forage bean plant (*Phaseolus panduratus*).—**-prêto,** kind kidney bean (*Phaseolus vulgaris*); a rounded pebble of black jasper or tourmaline.—**-soya** (or **-soja**), soybean (*Glycine soja*), c.a. FEIJÃO-CHINÊS.—**-veludo** = FEIJÃO-DA-FLÓRIDA.—**-verde,** string beans.—**-virado,** a dish of beans mixed with manioc meal.

feijoada (*f.*) a popular Braz. dish made of black beans boiled with bits of pork, sausage, jerky, etc., seasoned with pepper sauce and served with rice and manioc meal.

feijoal (*m.*) bean field.

feijoeiro (*m.*) bean plant.

feila (*f.*) flour dust.

feio -a (*adj.*) ugly, unsightly, homely; forbidding; grim; unseemly; disreputable; (*m.*) ugly person; ugliness; discreditable situation. **fazer**—, to behave badly. **Quem a —ama, bonito lhe parece,** Love is blind.

feioso -sa (*adj.*) somewhat ugly.

feira (*f.*) fair, open-air (public) market; sale at reduced prices.—**livre,** free market.

feirante (*m.,f.*) buyer or seller at a market; fair-goer.

feirar (*v.i.,v.t.*) to buy and sell at a fair.

feita (*f.*) act, deed; time, occasion. **certa—,** on a certain occasion. **de outra—,** another time; on another occasion. **de uma—,** once upon a time. **desta—,** this time; in this case. Cf. FEITO.

feital (*m.*) exhausted land.

feitiar (*v.t.*) to fashion something.

feitiçaria (*f.*) witchcraft, sorcery, voodoo.

feiticeiro -ra (*adj.*) bewitching, charming, alluring; (*m.*) sorcerer, witch doctor, wizard, shaman; (*f.*) witch, sorceress, hag.

feiticismo (*m.*) = FETICHISMO.

feiticista (*adj.; m.,f.*) = FETICHISTA.

feitiço (*m.*) magic spell, jinx, hex; fetish; mumbo-jumbo. **virar o—contra o feiticeiro,** to turn the tables, have the last laugh.

feitio (*m.*) pattern, figure, shape, design; mettle; workmanship.

feito -ta (*adj.; irreg. p.p. of* FAZER) made, done; finished, accomplished; skilled; grown, adult; used to, accustomed, mature; settled; ready; (*m.*) feat, act, deed; fact; exploit, achievement; purpose; (*pl.*) legal processes; (*conj.*) like, as, in the same manner as.—**à máquina,** machine-made.—**cachorro,** like a dog.—**de armas,** feat of arms.—**de encomenda,** made to order.—**louco,** like a crazy man.—**(uma) criança,** like a child. **bem—,** well done; (as an exclam.) It serves you right! **de—,** in fact. **dito e—,** no sooner said than done. **frase—,** set phrase. **homem—,** grown man. **já—,** ready-made. **mal—,** badly done; ill-shaped. **meio—, meio por fazer,** half-finished. Cf. FEITA.

feitor (*m.*) administrator; steward; manager; superintendent; foreman; overseer; manufacturer.

feitorar (*v.t.*) to oversee, boss, superintend.

feitoria (*f.*) stewardship; foremanship; wine-making; trading post (in early Brazil); in the Amazon, a camping spot; river settlement or village; place where fish are salted.

feitoriar, feitorizar (*v.*) = FEITORAR.

feitura (*f.*) making, production; work; workmanship.

feiúme (*f.*) ugliness; something ugly.

feiúra (*f.*) ugliness.

feixas-fradinho (*m.*) the Cape pigeon (*Daption capensis*), c.a. POMBA-DO-CABO.

feixe (*m.*) bundle; sheaf; cluster.—**de lenha,** fagot.—**direcional,** radio beam.—**luminoso,** beam of light.

fel [féis, feles] (*m.*) bile; gall; gall bladder; fig. bitterness, rancor; (*Bot.*)—**-da-terra,** the drug fumatory (*Fumaria officinalis*), c.a. FUMÁRIA, ERVA-MOLEIRINHA; also = AMOR-DE-NEGRO, CENTÁUREA-MENOR.—**-de-carijó** or **-de-gentio** = ESPELINA.

felá (*m.*) fellah. [Fem. **felaína**].

felandrina (*f., Chem.*) phellandrene.

felândrio (*m.*) fennel leaf waterdropwort or water fennel (*Oenanthe phellandrium*).

feldmarechal (*m.*) field marshal.

feldspático -ca (*adj., Petrog.*) feldspathic.

feldspato (*m., Min.*) feldspar.—**adulária,** moonstone.—**albita,** sodium feldspar, albite.—**anortita,** anorthite, lime feldspar.

feldspatóide (*m., Petrog.*) feldspathoid.

féleo -lea (*adj., Biochem.*) fellic.

felga (*f.*) clod.

felícia (*f., colloq.*) = FELICIDADE.

felicidade (*f.*) felicity, happiness; good fortune, success.

felicíssimo -ma (*absol. superl. of* FELIZ) most happy.

felicitação (*f.*) felicitation, congratulations.

felicitar (*v.t.*) to felicitate, congratulate; to make happy; (*v.r.*) to congratulate oneself.

felídeo -dea (*adj.*) feline; (*m.*) one of the Felidae (cat family).

felino -na (*adj.*) feline, catlike; stealthy; (*m.pl.*) the Felinae.

Félix (*m.*) Felix.

feliz (*adj.*) happy, lucky, fortunate, prosperous; felicitous. **dar-se-por—,** to consider oneself lucky; to thank one's lucky stars. **Seja—!** Good luck to you!

felizão -zona (*adj.; m.,f., colloq.*) very fortunate or happy (person).

felizardo (*m.*) lucky dog (fellow).

felizmente (*adv.*) fortunately.

feliz-meu-bem (*m.*) a sort of fandango.
felô (*m.*) chew candy.
felôgeno (*m., Bot.*) phellogen, cork cambium.
felonia (*f.*) rebellion by a vassal; treachery. [But not felony in the modern sense of a serious crime which is DELITO GRAVE.]
feloplástica (*f.*) phelloplastics, modeling in cork.
fêlpa (*f.*), **fêlpo** (*m.*) nap (of fabrics), down (of birds), fuzz (on peaches).
felpado –da (*adj.*) = FELPUDO.
felpar (*v.t.*) to put a nap on.
felpudo –da (*adj.*) nappy, shaggy, downy, fuzzy.
felsítico –ca (*adj., Petrog.*) felsitic.
felsito (*m., Petrog.*) felsite.
feltradeira (*f.*) felter (woman, machine).
feltragem (*f.*) process of making felt.
feltrar (*v.t.,v.i.*) to felt.
fêltro (*m.*) felt; (*pl.*) boiler lining.
felugem (*f.*) = FULIGEM.
F.E.M. = FORÇA ELETROMOTRIZ (electromotive force).
fêmea (*f.*) see FÊMEO.
femeaço (*m., colloq.*) a gathering of low women.
femeal (*adj.*) female.
femeeiro –ra [e-ei] (*adj.*) given to woman-chasing; designating a bull or stud horse whose offspring are mostly female; (*m.*) woman chaser; whoremonger; a group of prostitutes.
fementido –da (*adj.*) perfidious; perjured.
fêmeo –mea (*adj.*) female; feminine; (*Mach.*) designating a hollow part, tool, etc., into which is inserted a corresponding, or male, part; (*f.*) female animal; (*colloq.*) kept woman; prostitute; groove of tongue-and-groove boards; eye of a hook-and-eye fastener; (*Naut.*) gudgeon. **macho e fêmea**, male and female.
feminal, femíneo –nea (*adj.*) = FEMINIL.
feminidade (*f.*) femaleness; femininity.
feminil (*adj.*) feminine.
feminilidade (*f.*) femininity, womanliness.
feminino –na (*adj.*) feminine; female.
feminismo (*m.*) feminism.
feminista (*adj.; m.,f.*) feminist.
feminizar (*v.t.*) to feminize; (*v.r.*) to become effeminate.
femoral (*adj., Anat., Zool.*) femoral.
fêmur (*m., Anat., Zool.*) femur, thighbone.
fenação (*f.*) haymaking.
fenacetina (*f., Pharm.*) phenacetin.
fenacita (*f., Chem.*) phenacite.
fenar (*v.i.*) to grow.
fenazina (*f., Chem.*) phenazine.
fenda (*f.*) slit, split, rent, crack, fissure; crevice, chink; slot.—**palatina**, cleft palate.
fendedor –dora (*m.,f.; adj.*) one who, or that, splits or cracks (something).
fendeleira (*f.*) iron wedge for splitting rocks, logs, etc.
fendente (*adj.*) serving to crack or split.
fender (*v.t.*) to slit, rend, split; (*v.r.*) to crack.—**-se ao meio,** to split in half.
fendimento (*m.*), **fendidura** (*f.*) cleavage.
fenecer (*v.i.*) to finish, end, die; to wither.
fenecimento (*m.*) finish, end; death; withering.
fenestrado –da (*adj.*) fenestrated, having windows; (*Anat., Bot., Zool.*) fenestrate.
fenestral (*adj.; m., Arch.*) fenestral.
fenetidina (*f., Chem.*) phenetidine.
fenetol (*m., Chem.*) phenetole.
fenfém (*m.*) striped cuckoo (*Tapera naevia*), c.a. SACI.
feniano –na (*adj.; m.,f.*) Fenian.
fenicio –cia (*adj.; m.,f.*) Phoenician.
fênico –ca (*adj., Chem.*) ácido—, phenol, carbolic acid.
fenígeno –na (*adj.*) haylike.
fenilacético –ca (*adj., Chem.*) phenyl acetic [acid].
fenilamina (*f., Chem.*) phenylamine.
fenílio (*m., Chem.*,) phenyl.
fênix (*f.*) phoenix; fig. nonesuch, paragon.
feno (*m.*) hay; grass.—**-de-cheiro**, sweet vernal grass (*Anthoxanthum odoratum*), c.a. ANTOXANTO, FLAVA.—**-de-cheiro-amargoso** = LESTAS.—**-dos-persas**, = CAPIM-NAXENIM.—**-grego**, fenugreek trigonella (*T. foenum-graecum*).—**-do-mar** = FITA-DO-MAR (eel grass). **febre de—**, hay fever. **segundo—**, after-crop, aftermath.
fenocristal (*m., Petrog.*) phenocryst.
fenol (*m., Chem.*) phenol, carbolic acid.
fenolaldeído (*m., Chem.*) phenol-aldehyde resin, phenolic resin.

fenolftaleína (*f., Chem.*) phenolphthalein.
fenólico –ca (*adj., Chem.*) phenolic.
fenologia (*f., Biol.*) phenology.
fenológico –ca (*adj.*) phenologic.
fenologista (*m.,f.*) phenologist.
fenomenal (*adj.*) phenomenal; extraordinary, remarkable, amazing.
fenômeno (*m.*) phenomenon; prodigy, wonder.—**alotrópico,** (*Chem.*) allotropy.
fenomenologia (*f.*) phenomenology.
fenotípico –ca (*adj.*) phenotypic(al).
fenótipo (*m., Biol.*) phenotype.
fenózigo –ca (*adj., Craniol.*) phenozygous.
fera (*f.*) see FERO.
feracidade (*f.*) feracity, fertility, fruitfulness.
feracíssimo –ma (*absol. superl. of* FERAZ) most fertile.
feral (*adj.*) funereal; deadly. [But not feral, which is FERINO, FEROZ, BRAVIO.]
feraz (*adj.*) feracious, fruitful, fertile.
ferberita (*f., Min.*) ferberite.
fere-fôlha (*m.,f.*) busybody, mischief-maker.
fere-lume (*m.*) firefly [= PIRILAMPO].
féretro (*m.*) bier.
fereza [rê] (*f.*) ferociousness, fierceness.
fergusonita (*f., Min.*) fergusonite; bragite; tyrite.
féria (*f.*) weekday, workday; daily or weekly wage; the money intake (daily, weekly, etc.) of a business; (*pl.*) holidays, vacation, days off.—**do dia,** the day's receipts. **em gôzo de—s,** on vacation.
feriado (*m.*) holiday; feast day.
ferial (*adj.*) of or pert. to a holiday or to vacations; of or pert. to a weekday.
feriar (*v.i.*) to take a day off (from work); to be (go) on vacation; to have a holiday; (*v.t.*) to give a vacation to.
ferida (*f.*) see FERIDO.
feridade (*f.*) = FEREZA.
feridagem (*f.*) a breaking out in sores.
feridento –ta (*adj.*) covered with sores.
ferido –da (*adj.*) wounded.—**de morte,** fatally wounded. **mal—,** badly wounded; (*m.,f.*) wounded person; (*f.*) sore; wound; injury, offense; grievance.—**braba,** an ulcer or malignant sore.—**incisa,** a cut.—**ruim,** gangrene. —**velha,** chronic ulcer.
feridor –dora (*adj.; m.,f.*) that, or one who, wounds.
ferimento (*m.*) wound, injury.—**de bala,** bullet wound.
ferino –na (*adj.*) feral, brutal, savage.
ferir [21-a] (*v.t.*) to wound, hurt, injure, harm; to pain, pierce; to strike, to wound the feelings of; (*v.r.*) to get hurt; to hurt oneself.—**a batalha,** to join battle.—**as cordas,** to strike (pluck) the strings (of a musical instrument).—**melindres,** to hurt (someone's feelings).—**o alvo,** to hit the target.—**o amor-próprio (de alguém),** to wound (another's) feelings, hurt his pride,—**os ouvidos,** to grate upon the ear.—**um pleito,** to join battle, engage in a contest.—**um problema,** to tackle a problem.—**um princípio,** to go against a principle.—**um tema,** to touch upon a subject.—**um regulamento,** to break a rule. **Quem com ferro fere, com ferro será ferido,** He who lives by the sword, shall die by the sword.
fermata (*f., Music*) hold, pause.
fermentáceo –cea, fermentante (*adj.*) fermentative; fermenting.
fermentação (*f.*) fermentation.
fermentar (*v.t., v.i.*) to ferment; (*v.t.*) to foment.
fermentativo –va (*adj.*) fermentative.
fermentável (*adj.*) fermentable.
fermentescente (*adj.*) fermenting; fermentescible; beginning to ferment.
fermentescível (*adj.*) fermentescible.
fermento (*m.*) ferment, yeast, leaven.—**em pó,** baking powder.—**figurado,** or **organizado,** formed or organized ferment.—**solúvel,** diastase.—**solúvel, não figurado,** unformed ferment.
fermentoso –sa (*adj., fig.*) that agitates, excites, enlivens, stirs up.
Fernando (*m.*) Ferdinand.
fero –ra (*adj.*) ferocious; wild, savage; strong, robust; (*f.*) wild animal; beast; fig. blood-thirsty person; a spitfire.
ferocidade (*f.*) ferocity, fierceness.
ferocíssimo –ma (*absol. superl. of* FEROZ) most ferocious.
feroz (*adj.*) ferocious, fierce, feral, cruel, savage.
Ferr.ᵃ = FERREIRA (proper name).

ferra (f.) fireman's shovel; act of branding; cattle-branding season.
ferrã (f.) green fodder [=FERREJO].
ferrabras (adj.) bragging, blustering; (m.,f.) braggart, bully, blusterer.
ferrado -da (adj.) ironbound, ironclad; of a horse, shod; fig. ironwilled.—no sono, fast asleep.
ferrador (m.) farrier, horseshoer; the bellbird, better known as ARAPONGA.
ferradura (f.) horseshoe.
ferrageiro, ferragista (m.) hardware dealer; ironmonger.
ferragem (f.) hardware; iron fittings; set of horseshoes; common name for rutile, found in diamond beds, c.a. AGULHA, FUNDINHO. ferragens grossas, heavy hardware. loja de ferragens, hardware store.
ferrajão (m.) kinds of pebbles found in diamantiferous gravel [=INFORMAÇÃO].
ferramenta (f.) a workman's tool; set of tools; cowboy's spurs.—de estamparia, tool die.—de tôrno, lathe tool. —manual, hand tool.—mecânica, machine tool.
ferramentaria (f.) tool shop.
ferramenteiro (m.) toolmaker; toolsmith; die maker.
ferrão (m.) goad, prick; stinger (of a bee or other insect).
ferrar (v.t.) to shoe (a horse); to bind with iron; to mark with a branding iron; to furl (a sail).—a or em, to inflict (a lesson, blows, wounds, etc.) upon.—com, (em, de), to grapple with.—-se em (a), to seize upon.—no sono, to fall sound asleep.
ferraria (f.) hardware factory; blacksmith's shop; ironmonger's shop; a heap of iron.
ferratina (f., Biochem.) ferratin.
ferrato (m., Chem.) ferrate.
ferregial (m.) a field of green fodder.
ferreirinho (m.) =TEQUE-TEQUE.
ferreiro -ra (adj.) iron-gray; (m.) blacksmith; ironmonger; the bellbird (see ARAPONGA); a large tree frog (Hyla faber), c.a. SAPO-FERREIRO, JUIPONGA; a tern [=GAIVÃO]; a fish called RONCADOR. Em casa de—, espêto de pau, The cobbler's children have no shoes.
ferrejar (v.t.) to harvest green fodder.
ferrejo [rê] (m.) green fodder [=FERRÃ].
ferrenho -nha (adj.) iron-like; hard as iron, inflexible; iron-willed; relentless, intransigent; stubborn, headstrong.
férreo -rea (adj.) made of iron; ferric; ferrous; hard and strong as iron; hard-hearted; unflagging.
ferrêta (f.) small iron point, as of a top.
ferretar, ferretear (v.t.) to brand (with a hot iron); to stigmatize.
ferrête (m.) branding iron; fig., brand, stigma. azul—, navy blue, dark blue.
ferretoada (f.) =FERROADA.
ferretoar (v.t.) to sting (as a bee); to cut to the quick.
ferricianeto (m., Chem.) ferricyanide.
férrico -ca (adj., Chem.) ferric.
ferrífero -ra (adj.) ferriferous.
ferrinhos (m.pl., Music) triangle and rod [=TRIÂNGULO].
ferrita (f., Chem.) ferrite.
ferro (m.) iron; loosely, soft steel; iron tool or weapon; envy; anger, vexation; (pl.) shackles.—alfa, alpha iron. —batido, wrought iron.—branco, white cast iron.—corrugado, corrugated sheet iron.—de engomar, or de passar, flat iron, sadiron.—de frizar, curling iron.—de fundição, foundry pig.—de soldar, soldering iron.—de verruma, brace bit.—doce, soft iron.—electrolítico, electrolytic iron.—em barras, iron bars.—em brasa, red-hot iron.—em lingotes, ingot iron.—esmaltado, enamelware.—especular, specular iron ore.—esponjoso, sponge iron.—forjado, wrought iron.—fundido, cast iron.—galvanizado, galvanized iron.—-gusa, pig iron.—inoxidável, rustproof iron alloy.—laminado, rolled iron.—magnético, magnetic iron.—maleável, malleable cast iron.—meia-cana, half-round iron bars.—nativo, native iron.—niquelado, nickel-coated iron.—para marcar gado, branding iron.—pedrês, brittle iron.—perfilado, rolled iron (or mild steel) shapes (angles, tees, etc.).—pudlado, puddled iron.—redondo, round iron (or mild steel) bars.—-velho, junkman; junk shop. a—e a fogo, at all costs. alma de—, iron will. estrada de—, railroad. levantar—, to weigh anchor. malhar o—enquanto está quente, to strike while the iron is hot. passar a—, to iron (clothes). pôr a—s, to put in irons. Quando o—está acendido, então há de ser batido, Strike while the iron is hot; Make hay while the sun

shines. Quem com—fere, com—será ferido, He who lives by the sword shall die by the sword. sucata de—, scrap iron.
ferroada (f.) prick, sting; fig., a stinging rebuke.—de abelha, bee sting [=FERRETOADA].
ferroar (v.) =FERRETOAR.
ferroboro (m.) ferroboron alloy.
ferrocianeto (m., Chem.) ferrocyanide.—de potássio, potassium ferrocyanide.—de sódio, sodium ferrocyanide.
ferrociânico -ca (adj., Chem.) hydroferrocyanic [acid].
ferrocobalto (m.) ferrocobalt alloy.
ferrocolômbio (m.) ferrocolumbium alloy.
ferroconcreto (m.) ferroconcrete, reinforced concrete.
ferrocromo (m.) ferrochromium alloy.
ferrofósforo (m.) ferrophosphorous alloy; iron phosphide.
ferrolhar (v.) =AFERROLHAR.
ferrôlho (m.) sliding door bolt; latch; window bolt.
ferromagnético -ca (adj.) ferromagnetic.
ferromanganês (m.) ferromanganese alloy.
ferromolibdênio (m.) ferromolybdenum alloy.
ferroníquel (m.) ferronickel alloy.
ferropear (v.t.) to fetter.
ferropéia (f.) fetter, shackle [=GRILHÃO, PEIA].
ferroprussiato (m.) ferroprussiate; potassium ferrocyanide.
ferroso -sa (adj., Chem.) ferrous.
ferrosselênio (m.) ferroselenium alloy.
ferrossílico (m.) ferrosilicon alloy.
ferrotitânio (m.) ferrotitanium alloy.
ferrotungstênio (m.) ferrotungsten alloy.
ferrourânio (m.) ferrouranium alloy.
ferrovanádio (m.) ferrovanadium alloy.
ferrovia (f.) railroad, railway [=VIA FÉRREA, ESTRADA DE FERRO].
ferroviário -ria (adj.) of or pert. to railroads; (m.,f.) a railroad employee.
ferrovolfrâmio (m.) =FERROTUNGSTÊNIO.
ferrozircônio (m.) ferrozirconium alloy.
ferrugem (f.) rust; common name for hematite in small pieces.—do trigo, wheat rust. vermelho de—, rusty-red.
ferrugento -ta (adj.) rusty [=ENFERRUJADO, RUBIGINOSO].
ferrugíneo -nea (adj.) rust-colored.
ferruginoso -sa (adj.) ferruginous.
ferruncho (m., colloq.) spite; jealousy.
fértil [-teis] (adj.) fertile, prolific, fecund, fruitful; rich [soil].
fertilidade (f.) fertility, fecundity; fruitfulness.
fertilização (f.) fertilization.
fertilizador -dora (adj.) fertilizing; (m.) fertilizer.
fertilizante (adj.) fertilizing; (m.) fertilizer.
fertilizar (v.t.) to fertilize; (v.i.) to become fertile.
fertilizável (adj.) fertilizable.
férula (f.) ferule; (Bot.) giant fennel (Ferula).
fervedouro (m.) a boiling or seething; agitation; a crowd of people.
ferventar (v.) =AFERVENTAR.
fervente (adj.) boiling; fervent; tempestuous. água—, boiling water.
ferver (v.t.,v.i.) to boil, bubble; (v.i.) to seethe, rage; (v.t.) to cook by boiling.—a fogo lento, to boil gently, simmer. A coisa está fervendo! (colloq.) Things are beginning to pop! Isso faz—o sangue, That makes one's blood boil.
fervescente (adj.) =FERVENTE.
férvido -da (adj.) fervid, hot, boiling; ardent, eager.
fervilha (m., colloq.) live-wire, go-getter.
fervilhar (v.t.) to boil, bubble; to seethe.
fervo [ê] (m.) tumult.
fervor [ô] (m.) fervor, fervency; ardor, eagerness; zeal; act of boiling.—de sangue (colloq.) itch, rash, hives.
fervoroso -sa (adj.) fervent, ardent, impassioned, vehement.
fervura (f.) boiling, seething; commotion, excitement. lançar água na—, to pour oil on troubled waters.
fescenino -na (adj.) obscene, scurrilous.
festa (f.) feast, festive celebration; entertainment, party, banquet; (pl.) caresses; gifts.—das candeias, Candelmas [=CANDELÁRIA].—de formatura, graduation exercises. —s juinas, celebrations during the month of June honoring Saints Anthony (on the 13th), John (on the 24th), Peter and Paul (on the 29th).—pirotécnica, fire works display. Boas—s! Merry Christmas! Happy New Year! dar uma—, to give a party. dia de—, feast day, holiday. fazer—s a, to make a fuss over, fondle, caress,

show affection for. **O melhor da—é esperar por ela,** Anticipation is better than realization. **no melhor da—,** when least expected.

festança (*f.*) revelry, festivity; merrymaking; feast.

festão (*m.*) festoon, wreath; (*colloq.*) big party, merrymaking.

festar (*v.i.*) to make merry, dance, have a good time.

festarola (*f., colloq.*) party, fun, frolic.

festeiro -ra (*adj.*) party-going, merrymaking; caressing, petting; (*m.,f.*) party-giver; party-goer.

festejador -dora (*adj.*) feasting, celebrating; (*m.,f.*) feaster, celebrant.

festejar (*v.t.*) to celebrate (with a feast or party); to praise, applaud; to caress, make a fuss over.

festejo [ê] (*m.*) celebration, festivity; merrymaking; a fussing over (someone) by petting or caressing.

festim (*m.*) party, junket, feast; home party.

festival (*adj.*) festive; (*m.*) festival, gala day, jubilee.

festividade (*f.*) religious feast; festivity.

festivo -va (*adj.*) festive, joyous, merry.

festo (*m.*) party; dance; spree. Cf. FESTA.

fêsto (*m.*) width of a piece of cloth; crease down the middle of a length of cloth. **subir a—,** to go straight up (as a hill).

festoar, festonar (*v.t.*) to festoon.

festonadas (*f.pl., Arch., Sculp.*) festoons.

fetação (*f., Embryol.*) fetation, gestation.

fetal (*adj., Embryol.*) fetal; (*m.*) a place abounding in ferns.

fetiche (*m.*) fetish; mumbo jumbo.

fetíchico -ca (*adj.*) fetishistic.

fetichismo (*m.*) fetishism, fetish-worship.

fetichista (*adj.*) fetishistic; (*m.,f.*) fetishist.

feticida (*m.,f.*) one who commits feticide.

feticídio (*m.*) feticide.

fetidez (*f.*) fetidness.

fétido -da (*adj.*) fetid; (*m.*) stench.

feto (*m.*) fetus; embryo; (*Bot.*) any fern or brake of the polypody family. Cf. SAMAMBAIA, AVENCA, AVENCÃO,— **-aquilino,** western bracken (*Pteridium aquilinum pubescens*), c.a. FETO-FÊMEA-DAS-BOTICAS.—**-arborescente,** a tree fern (*Hemitelia multiflora*).—**-fêmea-dos-italianos,** ladyfern (*Athyrium filixfemina*).—**-grande,** a tropical fern (*Acrostichum aureum*), c.a. AVENCÃO.—**-macho** = FETO-MACHO-VERDADEIRO.—**-macho-de-goiás,** a woodfern (*Dryopteris triste*).—**-macho-de-minas,** the nipple polypody (*Polypodium percussum*), c.a. SILVINA-DE-FÔLHA-GRANDE.—**-macho-do-brasil,** a polypody (*P. instans*).—**-macho-do-pará,** a spleenwort (*Asplenium serratum*), c.a. RABO-DE-ARANATA.—**-macho-do-rio-grande,** a polypody (*Polypodium lepidopteris*).—**-macho-verdadeiro,** the malefern (*Dryopteris filixmas*).—**-real,** the common royal fern (*Osmunda regalis*).

feudal (*adj.*) feudal.

feudalismo (*m.*) feudalism.

feudalista (*m.,f.*) feudalist; (*adj.*) feudalistic.

feudatário -ria (*adj.*) feudal; (*m.,f.*) vassal, feudal tenant.

feudo (*m.*) feud, fief; personal estate.

fev., fev.º = FEVEREIRO (February).

fêvera (*f.*) = FEVRA.

fevereiro (*m.*) February; (*Zool.*) a barbet or puffbird, c.a. JOÃO-BOBO.

fevra (*f.*) fiber; filament; mineral vein [= FÊVERA].

fêz, form of FAZER [47].

fêz (*m.*) fez.

fezes (*f.pl.*) lees, dregs, offscourings; dross; feces, excrement; fig. the scum of the earth, dregs of society.

ff = FORTÍSSIMO (*Music*).

F.I. = FREQUÊNCIA INTERMÉDIA (intermediate frequency).

fiação (*f.*) spinning; spinning mill.—**e tecelagem,** spinning and weaving.

fiacre (*m.*) fiacre, hackney coach.

fiada (*f.*) course, range, (of stones, brick, or the like, in a wall, face of a building, etc.); line, file.

fiadeira (*f.*), **fiadeiro** (*m.*) spinner.

fiadilho (*m.*) floss silk.

fiado -da (*adj.*) spun; drawn out; trusting, trustful; sold on credit; (*adv.*) on credit; (*m.*) yarn, spun thread. **comprar—,** to buy on credit. **conversa—,** insincere statements. **vender—,** to sell on credit.

fiador -dora (*m.,f.*) surety, warrantor; (*m.*) bondsman, bailsman; safety chain.—**bastante,** a surety with ample means to make good any default in payment.

fiadoria (*f.*) surety, guaranty.

fiadura (*f.*) = FIAÇÃO.

fiambre (*m.*) cold meats, esp. ham; delicatessen.

fiambreria (*f.*) delicatessen store.

fiança (*f.*) bond, bail, security; amount deposited as a guarantee.—**de licitação,** a bid bond.

fiandeira (*f.*) woman who spins cotton, wool, etc., into thread; a spider's spinneret.

fiandeiro (*m.*) a spinner of cotton, etc.

fiango (*m.*) a small traveling hammock.

fiapo (*m.*) a slender thread. **tirar um—,** (*slang*) to take a peep at; to look over.

fiar (*v.t.*) to spin (cotton, wool, etc.); to weave; to draw (wire); to saw (wood) into narrow strips; to trust, believe; (*v.t.,v.i.*) to sell on credit (a, to).—**a,** to entrust to. —**de (em),** to trust in, rely on.—**-se de (em),** to have faith in.—**fino,** to be wary, cautious; **tôrno de—,** spinning wheel.

fiasco (*m.*) fiasco, ignominious failure, flop.

fiável (*adj.*) capable of being spun, etc.;—see the verb FIAR.

fibra (*f., Anat., Zool.*) fiber; thread, filament; moral fiber. —**sintética,** synthetic fiber.

fibrila, fibrilha (*f.*) fibril, fine fiber; (*Bot.*) fibril.

fibrilar (*adj.*) fibrillar.

fibriloso -sa (*adj.*) fibrillous.

fibrino -na (*adj.*) fibrine; (*f., Biochem.*) fibrin.—**muscular,** myosin fibrin.—**vegetal,** plant or vegetable fibrin, gluten.

fibrinofermento (*m., Biochem.*) thrombin (thrombase, fibrin ferment).

fibrinogênio (*m., Biochem.*) fibrinogen.

fibrinoso -sa (*adj.*) fibrinous.

fibroblasto (*m., Biol.*) fibroblast.

fibrocartilagem (*f., Anat.*) fibrocartilage.

fibrocelular (*adj.*) fibrocellular.

fibroferrito (*m., Min.*) fibroferrite.

fibróide (*adj.*) fibroid.

fibroína (*f., Biochem.*) fibroin.

fibrolita (*f., Min.*) fibrolite.

fibroma (*m., Med.*) fibroma.

fibromucoso -sa (*adj.*) fibromucous.

fibrose (*f., Med.*) fibrosis.

fibroso -sa (*adj.*) fibrous; fibroid; stringy.

fibroseroso -sa (*adj.*) fibroserous.

fibrovascular (*adj., Bot.*) fibrovascular.

fíbula (*f., Anat.*) fibula [= PERÔNIO].

ficáceo -cea (*adj., Bot.*) ficoid.

ficada (*f.*) a remaining, an abiding; (*colloq.*) in billiards, a difficult "leaving" (position left by one player for the next).

ficar [2] (*v.i.*) to stay, remain (in a place, situation, etc.); to contiuue to be (as specified) as to condition, etc.; to hold out, endure; to stop or halt; to pause, wait, linger, tarry; to remain for (a meal, performance, etc.); to remain through or during (a period of time); to be left after the removal, loss, etc., of something or someone; to be left to be done, told, etc.; to continue, last; to be; to become; to be situated at (on, in, by).—**à mercê de,** to be left at another's mercy or disposal.—**à mostra,** to be left showing, exposed.—**a nu,** to be left bare, exposed, nude.—**a par de,** to become au courant, learn about, acquainted with.—**a (trabalhar),** to keep on (working).—**a ver navios,** to be left holding the bag; to be disappointed.—**aborrecido,** to become annoyed, cross, peevish, bored.—**até o fim (de),** to stay to the end (of).—**atrás,** to be left behind.—**atrasado,** to lag behind.—**bem,** to be well-suited, becoming. [**Fica-lhe bem o chapéu,** The hat is very becoming to her.]—**besta,** (*slang*), to be astonished, amazed, incredulous.—**bom,** to get well [= SARAR-SE, CURAR-SE].—**coçando,** to be left rubbing one's chin (or scratching one's head) in puzzlement.—**com (alguém),** to keep (someone) company. [Eu fico com as crianças enquanto você sai, I'll stay with the children while you go out.]; to be the guest of (someone) overnight. [Quando estive no Rio, fiquei com a família de minha mulher, When I was in Rio I was a guest of my wife's family.]; to keep (a child, after parents are divorced; a maid, after former employers have no further need for her; a relative who has nowhere else to go). [Depois do divórcio, o pai ficou com as crianças, After the divorce, the father kept the children. Or, conversely, as crianças ficaram com o pai, the children stayed with their father.].—**com (alguma coisa),** to acquire (through an inheritance, etc.). [As meninas herdaram o dinheiro e êle ficou com a casa, The girls got the money and he inherited the house.]; to take (one thing in preference to another). [Eu fico com êste, I'll take this one.]; to develop (a symptom, an illness). [Quando fumam muito perto de mim, eu fico com dor de cabeça, When people are smoking a lot around me, I get a headache.]; to feel (cold, hunger). [Ela ficou com frio e fechou a janela, She felt cold and closed the window.]; to get (angry, frightened). [A criança ficou com mêdo, The child was frightened.]; to be stuck with (an obligation, a chore). [Ela ficou com a obrigação de cozinhar para tôda a família, She got stuck with the job of cooking for the whole family.]; to turn (from one condition to another. [Ela estava passando bem, mas quando o navio jogou, ficou com a cara verde, She was doing all right, but when the ship started rolling, she turned green.].—com a cara à banda (or com cara d'asno, or com cara de pau), to be made to look silly; to be crestfallen.—com a cara no chão, to be embarrassed to death.—com a pulga atrás da orelha, to become suspicious; (lit., to have a flea behind one's ear).—com os olhos abertos, to keep one's eyes open.—com Deus, to be left in God's keeping.— com nariz de palmo e meio, to be left sadly (keenly, completely) disappointed.—com pena de, to feel sorry for, take pity on.—contente, to be pleased, glad, happy, satisfied.—debaixo, to come out loser.—debaixo da mesa, to fall under the table (drunk).—de barriga, (colloq.) to become big with child.—de bem, to make up (make peace, bury the hatchet).—de bôca aberta (or ficar boquiaberto), to gape, stare with open mouth, as in wonder.—de cama, to stay in bed; to fall sick abed.— de castigo, to be]kept in after school.—de cima, to come out on top (winner); to put on airs.—de fora, to be left out, excluded.—de gêlo, to grow cold, lose interest.—de nariz torcido, to become angry and spiteful.—de orelha murcha, to get less than one had hoped for.—de papo p'ro ar, to indulge in idleness; to relax deliberately (as on a vacation, etc.).—de pé, to remain standing (in force); to subsist.—de pés juntos, (colloq.) to turn up one's toes (die).—de poita, to remain anchored.—de queixo na mão, to gape in wonderment.—de reserva, to have a mental reservation (about what someone has said); to wait and see what is going to happen.—de resguardo, to be careful (while convalescing).—de tanga, (slang) to lose one's shirt.—em, to remain in, stay at.—em branco, to remain blank (as to what was said).—em casa, to stay at home; to come out even with the board (in gambling).— em concertos, to be getting things ready.—em jejum, to fast (for religious or medical reasons); (colloq.) to remain wholly ignorant of (fail to understand) something.—em, or pelo, meio, to remain half-finished.—em palpos de aranha, or em panos quentes, to find oneself in a jam, in trouble.—em pano verde, to lose one's last chip (at the gaming table).—em paz, to remain quiet, at peace.—emocionado, to be touched or moved.—encrencado, or enguiçado, to hit a snag, get out of kilter, break down.—engasgado, to become confused, disturbed, choked up, unable to speak, forget what one had to say. —entalado, to choke; to be unable to swallow; to get stuck with an insoluble problem; to bog down; to fall for a hoax or swindle.—entre, to be or to remain between.—espantado, to be astonished.—fiel, to remain faithful (a, to).—firme, to sit tight.—fula (de raiva), (colloq.) to fly into a rage, blow one's top, hit the ceiling. —fora de si, to be beside oneself.—limpo, to be cleaned out, left penniless.—mais barato (caro, bonito, etc.)+infinitive=to be cheaper (dearer, prettier, etc.). [Fica mais barato comprar na cidade, It is cheaper to buy in the city.].—na cidade, to stay in town.—na mão, to be cheated, lose everything.—na rua, to sleep in the streets (unable to find a dwelling place).—no campo da batalha, to fall on the field of battle.—no chôco, (colloq.) to lie abed.—no mato (or na várzea) sem cachorro, to be up the creek without a paddle.—no papel, to not get beyond the planning stage.—no porco, (colloq.) to lie chagrined.—no tinteiro, to remain forgotten (unsaid or unwritten).—noivo, to become engaged.—para além de, to lie beyond.—para a retaguarda, to fall behind.—para galo de São Roque, to become an old maid.—para o dia seguinte, to be left (held over, postponed) to the next day.—para semente, to be kept (held back) for seed; (colloq.) to be left behind (as an old maid after her contemporaries are all married).—para sempre, to remain (abide) forever.—para tia, to become an old maid.— para trás, to be left behind.—penhorado, to become extremely grateful, obligated (to someone).—por fazer, to remain to be done.—pronto, (colloq.) to go broke.— quente, to get warm or hot. [Você está ficando quente, You're getting warm (in the search for something)].— quieto, to stay quiet.—reduzido à miséria, to be reduced to poverty, lose everything.—reduzido a zero, to be reduced to zero, to abject poverty; to come to naught; to become worthless.—responsável, to become responsible, obligate oneself.—sem (alguma coisa), to run out of, become short of (something).—sem jeito, to feel awkward, embarrassed.—sem mel nem cabaça, to risk one thing to win another, and lose both.—senhor do campo, to be victor on the field of battle; to be in complete control (master) of the situation.—sensibilizado, to become extremely grateful (to someone), touched by his generosity, kindness, etc.—sujo, to suffer in one's reputation; to drop in another's esteem.—têso, to be cleaned out (at gambling).—todo bêsta (or muito bêsta), to put on airs, become unbearably conceited; also, to become thoroughly confused. Êle ficou danado comigo, He was sore at me. Está ficando bom, He is getting well. Ficaram de voltar, They were supposed to return. Fique descansado, Rest easy, don't worry. Fique entre nós, Let's keep this to ourselves. Fique tranquila, Don't worry, you have nothing to fear. Fique você sabendo que não foi assim, não! I'll have you know it wasn't that way at all! Não fica bem, It is not proper, it won't look right. Não fica nada, There is nothing left. Não posso ficar, I can't stay. Não me fica nenhuma esperança, I haven't a single hope left. Onde fica o correio? Where is the postoffice? O resto fica por minha conta, Leave the rest to me. O serviço ficou por fazer, The work was left undone.

ficária (f.) the figroot buttercup (Ranunculus ficaria), c.a. BOTÃO-DE-OURO.

ficção (f.) fiction, fancy, imagination; novel, work of fiction.

ficcionista (m.,f.) a writer of fiction.

ficha (f.) (poker, roulette) chip; index card, file card.— **antropométrica**, or **de identidade**, identification card.— **de consolação**, consolation prize; a sop.

fichar (v.t.) to record (list) on index cards.

fichário (m.) card-index. c.a. FICHEIRO.

ficheiro (m.) a Brazilian leguminous tree (Schizolobium parahybum); = FICHÁRIO.

fichu [ú] (m.) fichu.

ficiforme (adj.) ficiform, fig-shaped.

fico (m.) an early form of printed I.O.U. beginning with the words: FICO DEVEDOR.

ficociano (m.) phycocyanin (pigment).

ficóide (adj.) like seaweed; fig-shaped; (f., Bot.)—**tricolor**, tricolor mesembryanthemum (M. gramineum).

ficologia (f., Bot.) phycology, algology.

ficológico –ca (adj.) phycological.

ficologista (m.,f.) phycologist.

ficomicetos (m.pl.) the Phycomycetes (alga-like fungi).

fictício –cia (adj.) fictitious, imaginary; false, artificial; bogus.

ficto –ta (adj.) feigned; supposed.

ficus (m.) the genus (Ficus) of figs.

fidagal, corruption of FIGADAL and FIDALGAL.

fidalgal (adj.) of the nobility.

fidalgaria (f.) the nobility, or their ways.

fidalgo –ga (adj.) of or pert. to the nobility; noble; magnanimous; (m.) nobleman, lord, grandee; (colloq.) man of leisure; (f.) noblewoman.

fidalgote (m.) lordling.

fidalguia (f.) nobleness; a noble deed; the nobility.

fidalguice (f.) affectedly lordly manner; ostentatiousness.

fidedignidade (f.) trustworthiness.

fidedigno –na (adj.) trustworthy; credible; dependable.

fideicomissário –ria (adj.; m.,f., Civil Law) fideicommisary.

fideicomisso (m., Civil Law) fideicommissum.

fideísmo (m.) fideism (exclusive reliance upon faith).

fideísta (m.,f.) fideist (one who places faith ahead of reason).

fidejussório –ria (adj., Civil Law) fidejussory; (m.) fidejussion, contract of suretyship.

fidelidade (f.) fidelity, faithfulness, devotion, loyalty; accuracy.

fidelíssimo –ma (absol. superl. of FIEL) most faithful.

fidéus (*m.pl.*) vermicelli.
fidúcia (*f.*) confidence, trust; (*colloq.*) brazenness, insolence.
fiducial (*adj.*) fiducial.
fiduciário –ria (*adj.; m.,f.*) fiduciary.
fieira (*f.*) drawplate; wire gauge; sheetmetal gauge; line, row; string (of things tied together); spinaret; vein (of ore); fishing line.
fiel [fiéis] (*adj.*) faithful, loyal, true, steadfast; trustworthy; exact, accurate; (*m.*) an assistant cashier; storekeeper; pointer of a scale. Os fiéis, the faithful.
fieldade, pop. form of FIDELIDADE.
fifia (*f.*) a shrill, disonant voice or sound.
fifó (*m.*) small, tin kerosene lamp [= PERIQUITO, BIBIANO].
fig. = FIGURA (figure).
figa (*f.*) an amulet of wood, stone, etc., in the shape of a clenched fist with the thumb clasped between the fore and middle fingers; also, a gesture with the fist so clenched to ward off evil eye, witchcraft, etc. fazer—, to tease, make fun of, (someone). sujeito duma—! darn fellow!
figadal (*adj.*) of or pert. to the liver; fig. profound, intimate, deep-seated.
figadalmente (*adv.*) profoundly, intensely.
figadeira (*f.*) liver disease of animals; (*colloq.*) hepatitis.
fígado (*m.*) liver; fig. courage, "guts". desopilar o—, to cheer up. pessoa de maus—s, vindictive person.
fígaro (*m., colloq.*) barber.
figle (*m.*) ophicleide (a brass-wind instrument).
figo (*m.*) fig.—do-inferno, Barbados nut (*Jatropha curcas*).
figueira (*f.*) fig tree, esp. the common fig (*Ficus carica*).—branca, a strangler tree (*Ficuas doliaria*), c.a. MATAPAU.—chinêsa, the fiddleleaf fig (*Ficus pandurata*).—da-barbaria, the India fig prickly pear (*Opuntia ficus-indica*), c.a. FIGUEIRA-DA-ÍNDIA, which is also the name for the Roxburgh fig (*Ficus roxburghii*).—da-polinésia, the mosaic fig (*Ficus parcelli*).—de-bengala, the banyan fig (*Ficus benghalensis*), c.a. BANIANO.—de-lombrigueira = FALSA-GAMELEIRA, QUAXINDUBA-PRETA.—de-surinã, the shieldleaf pumpwood (*Cecropia peltata*).—do-inferno, the jimsonweed datura (*D. stramonium*), c.a. ESTRAMÔNIO.—do-mato, or—vermelha = COAJINDUBA.—dos-pagodes, the botree (*Ficus religiosa*).
figueiral, figueiredo [rê] (*m.*) an area abounding in fig trees.
figulino –na (*adj.*) figuline, fuctile, made of clay; (*f.*) piece of pottery esp. a statuette.
figura (*f.*) figure, form, shape; person; image, likeness; appearance; design, pattern; picture; member of a cast; trope, figure of speech; dancing steps or positions; a face card. [But not figure in the sense of number which is NÚMERO, CIFRA.]—de proa, a figurehead. fazer—, to cut a fine figure.
figuração (*f.*) figuration.
figurado –da (*adj.*) figurative, symbolic, metaphorical. no—, figuratively.
figural (*adj.*) figural.
figurante (*m.,f.*) an accessory character on the stage, with no speaking part; a figurant.
figurão (*m.*) bigwig, big shot; ostentation.
figurar (*v.i.*) to figure, appear; to be conspicuous; (*v.t.*) to make a drawing or other representation of; to symbolize, typify; to imagine, conceive; to picture. [To figure, in the sense of calculate, is COMPUTAR.].—de, to seem, have the appearance of.—em, to take a part in.
figurativo –va (*adj.*) figurative.
figurável (*adj.*) figurable.
figurina (*f.*) figurine.
figurino (*m.*) fashion plate; fashion magazine; pattern; person dressed in the height of fashion; model.
figuro (*m., colloq.*) big shot [= FIGURÃO]; a doubtful character.
fila (*f.*) file, row, rank, tier, line; queue; (*slang*) "mug" (face).—por um, (*Milit.*) single file. cão de—, mastiff. em—, in a row. fazer—, to stand in line (in a queue). primeira—, front rank. última—, rear rank.
filaça (*f.*) coarse thread.
filactério (*m.*) phylactery.
Filadélfia (*f.*) Philadelphia.
filagrana (*f.*) = FILIGRANA.
filamentar (*adj.*) filamentary.
filamento (*m.*) filament, fiber.

filamentoso –sa (*adj.*) filamentous, stringy, fibrous.
Filandro (*m.*) Philander.
filante (*adj.; m.,f.*) sponging, cadging (person); a moocher.
filanto (*m.*) leaf flower (*Phyllanthus*).
filantropia (*f.*) philanthropy.
filantrópico –ca (*adj.*) philanthropic.
filantropo –pa [trô] (*m.,f.*) philanthropist.
filão (*m.*) vein (of ore), lode; spring; (*colloq.*) long loaf of bread.
filar (*v.t.*) to catch, lay hold of; to seize with the teeth; to sic on (dog); (*slang*) to cadge, sponge, mooch; to kibitz; to "squeeze" one's cards in poker; (*v.i.*) to cheat in an exam.—se a, to lay hold of.
filargíria (*f.*) miserliness [= AVAREZA].
filária (*f., Zool., Med.*) the genus (*Filaria*) of nematode parasitic worms, a species of which (*F. bancrofti*) causes elephantiasis.—de Guiné, or de Medina, the Guinea worm (*Dracunculus medinensis*).
filariose (*f., Med.*) filariasis, elephantiasis.
filarmônico –ca (*adj.*) philharmonic; (*f.*) philharmonic society; music band [= BANDA DE MÚSICA].
filástica (*f.*) oakum, rope yarn.
filatelia (*f.*) philately.
filatélico –ca (*adj.*) philatelic.
filatelista (*m.,f.*) philatelist, stamp collector.
filatório –ria (*adj.; m.*) spinning (machine).
filáucia (*f.*) self-love, self-esteem, conceit.
filé (*m.*) fillet of beef, fish, etc.; tenderloin; filet lace.
fileira (*f.*) rank, row, line, tier; (*pl.*) military service. abandonar as—s, to desert the ranks. entrar para as—s de, to join the ranks of. primeira—, front rank.
filetar (*v.t.*) to fillet.
filête (*m., Arch., Anat.*) fillet; thread of a screw.
filha (*f.*) daughter.
filhação (*f.*) = FILIAÇÃO.
filhar (*v.t.*) to adopt as a child [= PERFILHAR]; to seize by force [= FILAR]; (*v.i.*) to burgeon [= BROTAR].
filharada (*f.*) large family, spawn, brood.
filharar (*v.i.*) to burgeon.
filheiro –ra (*adj.*) prolific; very fond of own children.
filhento –ta (*adj.*) prolific.
filho (*m.*) son; child; scion, descendant; sprout, shoot.—adotivo, adopted son (or child).—adulterino, adulterine son (or child).—bastardo, bastard son (or child).—s da Candinha, (*colloq.*) the common people.—das ervas, a waif.—de-bem-te-vi, the lictor flycatcher (*Pitangus l. lictor*), c.a. BEM-TE-VI-PEQUENO.—de leite, foster son (or child).—de peixe, peixinho é, or—de peixe sabe nadar, Like father, like son.—de-saí, the hooded tanager (*Nemosia p. pileata*).—s de um ventre, twins.—do vento, a child without a family.—espúrio, spurious child.—famílias, a minor child living with its parents.—ilegítimo, illegitimate child.—legitimado, a legitimated child.—mais velho, the oldest son; the first-born child.—natural, natural child.—póstumo, posthumous child.—putativo, putative child.—único, only son (or child).—varão, male child. Tal pai, tal—, Like father, like son. Êle tem—s homens, He has grown sons.
filhó, filhós (*m.,f.*) fritter.
filhotão (*m.*) an almost full-grown animal or plant.
filhote (*m.*) young son; the young of birds and animals, as a cub, pup, whelp, nestling, etc.; a political pet or favorite; (*pl.*) brood.
filhotismo (*m.*) political or other favoritism; nepotism.
filiação (*f.*) filiation; affiliation; relationship, connection.
filial (*f.*) branch office, branch store; (*adj.*) filial.
filiar (*v.t.*) to adopt (a child).—a, to relate (tie) to.—se a, to join, affiliate with.—se em, to originate in, descend from; to associate with.
filicida (*m.,f.*) a filicide.
filicídio (*m.*) filicide.
filifôlha (*f.*) fern [= FETO].
filiforme (*adj.*) filiform, threadlike.
filigrana (*f.*) filigree; watermark.
filigranar (*v.t.*) to filigree.
Filipa (*f.*) Philippa.
Filipe (*m.*) Philip.
filípica (*f.*) phillipic, bitter denunciation.
filipino –na (*adj.*) Philippine; (*m.,f.*) a Filipino; (*f.*) philopena (a game of forfeits); (*f.pl.*) the Philippines.
Fílis (*f.*) Phyllis.
filisteu –téia (*m.,f.*) Philistine; by ext. an uncultured person.
filite, filito (*m., Min.*) phyllite.

filmagem (*f.*) filming of pictures.
filmar (*v.t.*) to film pictures.
filme (*m.*) photographic film; moving picture reel.—**de atualidades**, newsreel.—**de faroeste**, cowboy movie.
filmoteca (*f.*) film collection; microfilm section of a library.
filo (*Bot.*) phylum.
filó (*m.*) netting, esp. mosquito netting; tulle.
filocládio (*m.*, *Bot.*) phylloclade.
filode (*f.*), **filódio** (*m.*, *Bot.*) phyllode.
filodendro (*m.*, *Bot.*) philodendron.
filófago –**ga** (*adj.*) phyllophagous (feeding on leaves); (*m.pl.*) June beetle and others of genus Phyllophaga.
filogênese (*f.*) = FILOGENIA.
filogenesia (*f.*) phylogenesis.
filogenia (*f.*) phylogeny.
filógeno –**na** (*adj.*) growing or produced on leaves.
filogínia (*f.*) philogyny, fondness for women.
filógino –**na** (*adj.*) philogynous, fond of women; (*m.*) a lover of women; woman chaser.
filoheleno –**na** (*m.,f.*) philhellenist.
filóide (*adj.*) phylloid, resembling a leaf.
filologia (*f.*) philology.
filológico –**ca** (*adj.*) philological.
filologista, filólogo –**ga** (*m.,f.*) philologist.
filomela (*f.*) philomel, nightingale. [*Poetical*].
filosela (*f.*) filoselle (a kind of floss).
filosofal (*adj.*) philosophical. **pedra**—, philosophers' stone; fig. something hard to find.
filosofar (*v.i.*) to philosophize.
filosofastro (*m.*) a dabbler in philosophy.
filosofia (*f.*) philosophy.
filosófico –**ca** (*adj.*) philosophic(al).
filosofismo (*m.*) philosophism.
filósofo –**fa** (*m.,f.*) philosopher; a philosophical person.
filotaxia [ks] (*f.*, *Bot.*) phyllotaxy.
filotécnico –**na** (*adj.*) philotechnic(al).
filoxantina [ks] (*f.*) phylloxanthin, xanthophyll (pigment).
filoxera [ks] (*f.*) a plant louse of the genus Phylloxera.
filtração, filtragem (*f.*), **filtramento** (*m.*) filtration; filtering.
filtrar (*v.t.*) to filter, strain; (*v.i.,v.r.*) to infiltrate.
filtrável (*adj.*) filterable.
filtreiro (*m.*) = FILTRO.
filtro (*m.*) filter, strainer; philter, magic potion.—**de ar**, air filter.—**de areia**, sand filter.—**de alta (baixa) passagem**, (*Elec.*) high (low) -pass filter.—**de coque**, coke filter.—**de passagem**, (*Elec.*) a band, or band-pass, filter.
filustria (*f.*, *colloq.*) stunt.
fim (*m.*) end, close, finish; terminus; upshot; aim, purpose. —**-de-século**, (*adj.*) fin de siècle, characteristic of the close of the 19th century.—**de semana**, week end. **a**—**de**, in order to, so as to. **a**—**de que**, so that; in order that. **ao**—, at the last. **ao** (**no**)—**de**, at the end of. **ao**—**de contas**, after all (is said and done). **com o**—**de**, for the purpose of; in order to. **em**—**s de Abril**, toward the end of April. **no**—, finally. **no**—**de**, at the end of. **O**—**justifica os meios**, The end justifies the means. **por**—, at last, finally; in conclusion. **por**—**de contas**, after all. **Que levou** (**êle**)? What ever happened to (him)? **sem**—, endless, never-ending. **ter por**—, to have as a purpose.
fímbria (*f.*) fringe; hem.
fimbriado –**da** (*adj.*) having a fringe.
fimbriar (*v.t.*) to fringe; to hem.
fimícola (*adj.*, *Biol.*) fimicolous.
fimose (*f.*, *Med.*) phimosis.
fina-acre (*f.*) "washed Acre, a technical grade of commercial rubber." [*GBAT*]
finado –**da** (*adj.; m.,f.*) deceased (person). **Dia de**—**s**, All Souls Day (Nov. 2). **dobre de**—**s**, knell.
fina-fraca (*f.*) "washed weak fine, a technical grade of commercial rubber." [*GBAT*]
final (*adj.*) final, last, eventual. **ponto**—, stopping point; last stop; a period [.]; (*m.*) end, ending, last part, finale. **no**—**das contas**, after all (is said and done).
finalidade (*f.*) purpose, end, aim, object; finality; end result. **com a**—**de**, with a view to. **sem**—, aimlessly. **sem**—**lucrativa**, non-profit.
finalista (*adj.*) finalist; (*m.,f.*, *Philos.*, *Sports*) finalist.
finalista (*m.,f.*) finalist.
finalização (*f.*) conclusion.
finalizar (*v.t.,v.i.,v.r.*) to end, conclude.
finamento (*m.*) act of dying; death.
finanças (*f.pl.*) finances; public funds.
financeiro –**ra** (*adj.*) financial; (*m.,f.*) financier, capitalist.

financiador –**dora** (*m.,f.*) financial backer.
financial (*adj.*) = FINANCEIRO.
financiamento (*m.*) financing.
financiar (*v.t.*) to finance.
financista (*m.,f.*) financial expert.
fina-pará (*f.*) "up-river fine Pará, a technical grade of commercial rubber." [*GBAT*]
finar (*v.i.*) to end; (*v.r.*) to pine, waste away; to faint away; to pass away (die); to long for something.
finca (*f.*) stake, prop.
fincão (*m.*) = BARBEIRO (bug).
finca-pé (*m.*) a putting down of one's foot (in opposition to or in insistence upon a thing).
fincar (*v.t.*) to stick (**em**, **in**) as a pin in the flesh; to drive (**em**, **in**) as a stake in the ground; to dig (**em**, **in**) as spurs in the side of a horse; to poke in.—**se em**, to stand one's ground; to stick by one's belief; to stand pat on one's position.
fincudo (*m.*) = BARBEIRO (bug).
findar [24] (*v.t.*) to put an end to; (*v.t.,v.i.*) to end, finish.
findável (*adj.*) endable, terminable.
findo –**da** (*irreg. p.p. of findar*) ended; finished.
finês –**sa** (*adj.*) Finnish; (*m.,f.*) Finn.
fineza [ê] (*f.*) fineness; politeness, courtesy; refinement; favor, kindness. **fazer uma**—, to perform a kindness, a courtesy.
finfim (*m.*) bedbug [= PERCEVEJO].
fingido –**da** (*adj.*) feigned, sham; hypocritical; deceptive; make-believe; (*m.*) sly dog.
fingidor –**dora** (*m.,f.*) feigner, imitator; simulator.
fingimento (*m.*) feigning, simulation, pretense, make-believe, affectation.
fingir (*v.t.,v.i.*) to feign, pretend, make-believe, put on, sham.—**se de**, to pretend to be.—**se de morto**, to play dead.
finidade (*f.*) finiteness.
fininha (*f.*, *colloq.*) tuberculosis.
fininho (*m.*) = DIAMBA.
finito –**ta** (*adj.*) finite, transitory; (*m.*) the finite.
finlandês –**dêsa** (*adj.*) Finnish; (*m.,f.*) Finlander; the Finnic language.
fino –**na** (*adj.*) fine, slender, thin; delicate; elegant, refined, polite; exquisite; choice, superior; shrewd, sharp, canny; quick, clever, keen; shrill; (*m.*) fine thing.
finório –**ria** (*adj.; m.,f.*) sharp-witted, sly, shrewd, cunning, cagey, foxy (person).
finta (*f.*) feint; dodge; tax, assessment; in soccer, a dribbling.
fintador (*m.*) dead beat, sponger.
fintar (*v.i.*) to feint, dodge; to trick; in soccer, to dribble; (*v.t.*) to tax, assess (-**se**, oneself); to sponge on.
finura (*f.*) fineness, thinness; fineness, acuteness, wit, tact; delicacy.
fio (*m.*) thread; filament, fiber; wire; string, slender cord; a fine thread of any liquid; keen edge (as of a knife); (*pl.*) means, methods.—**a**—, thread by thread.—**de linha**, sewing thread.—**de marca**, cross-stitch.—**de ouro**, **de prata**, etc., gold wire, silver wire, etc.—**de pedra**, (*Geol.*) line of cleavage.—**de pérolas**, string of pearls. —**de prumo**, plumb line.—**de sêda**, silk thread.—**elétrico com cavilha**, a plug cord.—**flexível**, an electric extension cord.—**nu**, (*Elec.*) bare conductor.—**quente**, (*Elec.*) hot wire.—**de solda**, soldering wire.—**-terra**, ground wire. **a**—, strung out; one after another; uninterruptedly; at a stretch. **achar o**—**da meada**, to find a clue. **de**—**a pavio**, from stem to stern; from beginning to end; from start to finish; from A to Z. **dias a**—, days on end. **estar no**—, to be threadbare. **estar por um**—, to hang by a thread. **horas a**—, hours at a stretch. **meio**—, curbstone. **perder o**—, to lose the thread (of conversation). **reduzir a**—, to pick to threads.
fiorde (*m.*) fjord.
fiorita (*f.*, *Min.*) fiorite.
fiota, fiote (*adj.*, *colloq.*) foppish, dressy.
fique (*f.*, *Bot.*) a portulacca (*P. pusilla*); (*v.*) a form of FICAR [2].
firma (*f.*) signature; firm, commercial house.—**reconhecida**, notarized signature.
firmação (*f.*) act of signing.
firmador –**dora** (*m.,f.*) signer.
firmal (*m.*) ancient brooch; seal bearing a signature; reliquary.
firmamento (*m.*) firmament, sky; foundation; prop.
firmar (*v.t.*) to make firm, stable, steady, secure; to sign

(a contract, etc.); to subscribe, endorse; to base, rest
(**em**, on, upon); (*v.r.*) to sign one's name.—**-se em**, to
lean upon; to rely on.

firme (*adj.*) firm, fast, stable, secure; resolute; sturdy;
steady, steadfast, unfaltering, unbending; (*m.*) a patch of
high ground in a flooded area. **a pé—**, resolutely. **cor—**,
a fast color. **mal—**, unsteady. **terra—**, terra firma, solid
earth, dry land.

firmeza [ê] (*f.*) firmness, solidity; stability; steadfastness,
resoluteness; assurance, aplomb.—**-dos-homens**, cottonrose hibiscus (*H. mutabilis*).

firo (*m.*) a kind of checker game.

firro (*m.*) marbles.

fisália (*f.*, *Zool.*) Portuguese man-of-war or other member
of genus Physalia.

fisalita (*f.*) physalite (a coarse variety of topaz).

fiscal (*m.*) checker; controller; customs inspector; revenue
agent; inspector; supervisor; (*adj.*) fiscal.

fiscalização (*f.*) supervision, checking, inspection, control.

fiscalizar (*v.t.*) to fiscalize; to inspect, examine; to supervise.

fiscela (*f.*) muzzle [= AÇAIMO].

fisco (*m.*) exchequer, national treasury; department of
tax collection.

fisetério (*m.*) a sperm whale (*Physeter*).

fisga (*f.*) fish gig, gaff, small harpoon; chink, narrow opening.

fisgada (*f.*) pang, sudden pain, sharp twinge.

fisgador **-dora** (*adj.*) gigging, gaffing; (*m.,f.*) gigger,
gaffer.

fisgar (*v.t.*) to gig, gaff, spear, hook (fish); to catch on
(understand) quickly.

fisgo (*m.*) barb, hook.

FISI = FUNDO INTERNACIONAL DE SOCORRO À INFÂNCIA
(International Fund for Aid to Children).

física (*f.*) see FÍSICO.

fisicismo (*m.*) physicism.

fisicista (*m.,f.*) physicist.

físico **-ca** (*adj.*) physical, material; (*m.*) physiognomy;
physique; (*m.,f.*) physicist; (*f.*) physics.—**nuclear**, nuclear physics.

fisicoterapia (*f.*) physicotherapy.

fisiogenia (*f.*) physiogeny.

fisiografia (*f.*) physiography, physical geography.

fisiográfico **-ca** (*adj.*) physiographic.

fisiógrafo **-fa** (*m.,f.*) physiographer.

fisiologia (*f.*) physiology.

fisiológico **-ca** (*adj.*) physiologic(al).

fisiologista, **fisiólogo** **-ga** (*m.,f.*) physiologist.

fisionomia (*f.*) physiognomy, face, visage, countenance,
appearance, expression.

fisionômico **-ca** (*adj.*) physiognomic(al).

fisionomista (*m.,f.*) physiognomist.

fisioterapia (*f.*) physiotherapy.

fisioterápico **-ca** (*adj.*) physiotherapic.

fisocarpo **-pa** (*adj.*, *Bot.*) physocarpous.

fisogastria (*f.*, *Zool.*) physogastry.

fisostigma (*f.*) the deadly calabar bean (*Physostigma
venenosum*), c.a. FAVA-DE-CALABAR.

fisostigmina (*f.*, *Chem.*) physostigmine.

fissidentáceas (*f.pl.*) a small family (*Fissidentaceae*) of
mosses.

físsil [físseis] (*adj.*) fissile, cleavable, fissionable.

fissilíngüe (*adj.*, *Zool.*) fissilingual.

fissiparidade (*f.*, *Biol.*) fissiparism, schizogenesis.

fissíparo **-ra** (*adj.*, *Biol.*) fissiparous.

fissípede (*adj.*, *Zool.*) fissiped.

fissirrostro **-tra** (*adj.*, *Zool.*) fissirostral [birds].

fissura (*f.*) fissure, cleft, crack, split; (*Med.*) fissure; anal
fistula.

fissuração (*f.*) fissuration.

fístula (*f.*, *Med.*) fistula.

fistulado **-da** (*adj.*) fistulous; fistular.

fistular (*adj.*) fistular; (*v.i.*) to develop a fistula.

fistuloso **-sa** (*adj.*) fistulous, ulcerated; tubelike.

fita (*f.*) see under FITO.

fitar (*v.t.*) to fix (eyes, attention) on; to look fixedly at,
stare at.—**as orelhas**, to cock the ears.

fiteiro **-ra** (*adj.*) that shows off, pretends, feigns, bluffs;
(*m.*) a show-off; bluffer, pretender; (*f.*) a woman who
puts on airs.

fitilho (*m.*) narrow ribbon, tape.

fitina (*f.*, *Biochem.*, *Pharm.*) phytin.

fitinha (*f.*, *colloq.*) a ribbon (decoration).

fito **-ta** (*adj.*) fixed, fast. **com os olhos—s em**, with eyes
fixed on. (*m.*) mark, aim; intent, purpose. **com o—de**,
with a view to; for the purpose of; **pôr o—em**, to aim at;
(*f.*) ribbon, tape, band; strip; moving-picture reel;
magnetic recording tape; (*colloq.*) false display, showing
off, pretense, swank.—**de chapéu**, hatband.—**de celulose**
or **—gomada**, Scotch tape.—**de cinema**, movie reel.—
-do-mar, (*Bot.*) common eel grass (*Zostera marina*), c.a.
ALGA-DAS-LAGOAS, FENO-DO-MAR.—**isolante**, electrical
tape.—**métrica**, measuring tape. **fazer—**, to show off,
pretend, put on airs.

fitobiologia (*f.*) phytobiology.

fitófago **-ga** (*adj.*, *Zool.*) phytophagous.

fitogêneo **-nea** (*adj.*) phytogeneous.

fitogenia (*f.*) phytogenesis.

fitogênico **-ca** (*adj.*) phytogenic.

fitogeografia (*f.*) phytogeography.

fitografia (*f.*) phytography.

fitógrafo **-fa** (*m.,f.*) phytographer.

fitóide (*adj.*) phytoid.

fitolaca (*f.*) the genus (*Phytolacca*) of pokeberries, which
comprises the ombu tree (*P. dioica*), called UMBUZEIRO
or IMBUZEIRO.

fitolacáceo **-cea** (*adj.*, *Bot.*) phytolaccaceous; (*f.pl.*) the
pokeweed family (*Phytolaccaceae*).

fitólito (*m.*) a fossil plant.

fitologia (*f.*) phytology, botany.

fitônia (*f.*, *Bot.*) any Fittonia, esp. *F. argyroneura*, the
silvernerve.

fitonomia (*f.*) phytonomy.

fitoparasito (*m.*) phytoparasite, vegetable parasite.

fitopatologia (*f.*) phytopathology, plant pathology.

fitopatológico **-ca** (*adj.*) phytopathologic(al).

fitopatologista (*m.,f.*) phytopathologist.

fitoplancto (*m.*, *Biol.*) phytoplankton.

fitoquímico **-ca** (*adj.*) phytochemical.

fitosterol (*m.*, *Chem.*) phytosterol.

fitotomia (*f.*) phytotomy, vegetable anatomy.

fitozoário (*m.*, *Zool.*) a zoophyte.

fiúza (*f.*) trust; hope.

fivela (*f.*) buckle.

fixa [ks] (*f.*) surveyor's leveling rod; the stationary half of
a door hinge; a fish plate (for connecting rails).

fixação [ks] (*f.*) fixation; fastening.—**de nitrogênio** (*Chem.*)
nitrogen fixation.

fixador (*m.*, *Photog.*) fixer.

fixar [ks] (*v.t.*) to fix, fasten, secure (in place); to establish;
to locate; to settle, decide; to eye fixedly, stare at; (*v.r.*)
to become fixed.—**na memória**, to fix in memory. [But
not to fix, in the sense of repair, which is CONSERTAR.]

fixativo [ks] (*m.*, *Photog.*) hypo; a fixative solution (for
pastels).

fixe [sh] (*adj.*, *colloq.*) firm, steady; ready-made (cigarettes).

fixidade, **fixidez** (*f.*) fixity.

fixo **-xa** [ks] (*adj.*) firm, fixed; steady, stable; settled, determined upon; of color, fast; (*m.*) fixture. **preço—**, set
price (no reductions).

fiz+personal verb endings = forms of FAZER [47].

F.J. = FAÇA-SE JUSTIÇA (may justice prevail—added as a
formal close to a petition).

fl. = FÔLHA (page); FLORIM (florin).

flabelação (*f.*) flabellation, act of fanning.

flabelado **-da** (*adj.*) flabellate, fan-shaped.

flabelar (*adj.*) fan-shaped; (*v.t.,v.i.*) to fan.

flabelifoliado **-da** (*adj.*, *Bot.*) flabellifoliate.

flabeliforme (*adj.*) fan-shaped, flabelliform.

flabelo (*m.*) fan; (*Eccl.*) flabellum.

flacidez [ê] (*f.*) flaccidity, laxity, flabbiness.

flácido **-da** (*adj.*) flaccid, drooping, lax, flabby, limp.

flaco **-ca** (*adj.*) = FRACO.

flacúrtia (*f.*) any plant of the genus Flacourtia.

flacurtiáceo **-cea** (*adj.*, *Bot.*) flacourtiaceous. (*f.pl.*) the
Flacourtiaceae (Indian plum family.)

flagelação (*f.*) flagellation, scourging.

flagelado (*m.*) = MASTIGÓFORO.

flagelador **-dora** (*adj.*) scourging; (*m.,f.*) scourger.

flagelante (*adj.*) flagellant.

flagelar (*v.t.*) to flagellate, scourge, whip, lash, flog.

flagelativo **-va** (*adj.*) flagellatory.

flagelífero **-ra** (*adj.*, *Bot.*) flagelliferous.

flageliforme (*adj.*) flagelliform.

flagelo (*m.*) scourge, whip; punishment, curse; (*Biol.*)
flagellum.

flagício (m.) flagitiousness.
flagicioso –sa (adj.) flagitious, infamous.
flagrância (f.) flagrancy.
flagrante (adj.) flagrant, glaring; flaming, glowing; (m., colloq.) a candid photo, an action snapshot. **em—(delito)**, in the very act. **Pegaram-no em—**, They caught him red-handed.
flagrar (v.i.) to flame, burn.
flajolé (m.) flageolet.
flama (f.) flame, blaze; ardor.
flamância (f.) flaming; blazing; idleness.
flamante (adj.) flaming.
flambar (v.i.) to buckle, bend; (v.t.) to sterilize by flame.
flamboyant (m., Bot.) royal poinciana (Delonix regia).
flamejante (adj.) flaming; flamboyant.
flamejar (v.i.) to flame, blaze.
flamengo –ga (adj.) Flemish; (m.,f.) a Fleming; the Flemish language; (m.) the roseate flamingo (Phoenicopterus ruber), c.a. GANSO-DO-NORTE, GANSO-CÔR-DE-ROSA, GUARÁ, MARANHÃO.
flâmeo –mea (adj.) flaming.
flamífero –ra, flamígero –ra (adj.) producing flame.
flamingo (m.) = FLAMENGO.
flamívolo –la (adj.) vomiting flames.
flâmula (f.) pennant, streamer; a small flame.
flanador (m.) stroller; loiterer. [French: flaneur].
flanar (v.i.) to loiter, saunter, walk up and down; stroll; to idle, loaf. [French: flâner].
flanco (m.) flank, side.
flandeiro (m.) tinsmith [= FUNILEIRO].
flandre(s) (m.) tin can; tinplate [= FÔLHA-DE-FLANDRES].
flanela (f.) flannel.
flange (m.) flange of a car wheel; coupling flange for pipes.
flanquear (v.t.) to flank.
flaqueirão –rona, flaquito –ta (adj.) somewhat thin and weak, referring esp. to horses.
flato (m.) flatus, gas in the stomach or bowels.
flatulência (f.) flatulence.
flatulento –ta (adj.) flatulent.
flatuloso –sa, flatuoso –sa (adj.) flatulent.
flatuosidade (f.) = FLATULÊNCIA.
flauta (f.) flute; (colloq.) idle living; raillery. **levar tudo na—**, to take nothing seriously. **tocar—**, to play the flute.
flautar (v.) = AFLAUTAR.
flautear (v.i.) to play the flute; to idle, loiter; to duck responsibility; to cut classes; (v.t.) to hoodwink, trick; (colloq.) to make fun of.
flauteio (m.) fun, jollity.
flauteiro –ra (m.,f.) = FLAUTISTA.
flautim (m.) piccolo.
flautista (m.,f.) flutist.
flavescent (adj.) flavescent.
flavescer (v.i.) to turn yellow.
flavo –va (adj.) golden-yellow; (f.) = FENO-DE-CHEIRO.
flébil [-beis] (adj.) mournful, weeping.
flebite (f., Med.) phlebitis.
flebosclerose (f. Med.) phlebosclerosis.
flebotomia (f., Med.) phlebotomy, blood-letting, bleeding.
flecha (f.) arrow, dart; flection, bend, sag; deflection; rise of an arch; spire; (Bot.) arrowhead (Sagittaria); terminal bud or inflorescence. **arco e—**, bow and arrow.
flechaço (m.), **flechada** (f.) an arrow wound.
flecha-peixe (m.) a kingfisher [= MARTIN-PESCADOR].
flechar (v.t.) to pierce with an arrow; to wound the feelings of; to go and come like an arrow. Var. FRECHAR.
flecheiro (m.) bowman, archer [= FRECHEIRO].
flechilha (f.) Uruguay needlegrass (Stipa neesiana).
flechinha (f.) tanglehead grass (Heteropogon contortus); a ricegrass (Piptochaetium).
flectir (v.t.) to deflect, flex, bend. Var. FLETIR.
flegma (f.) = FLEUMA.
flegmão, fleimão (m.) an inflammatory tumor; boil, felon, etc.; (Med.) phlegmon, Var. FREIMÃO.
flegmático –ca (adj.) = FLEUMÁTICO.
fleima (f.) phlegm, apathy; coolness.
flertar (v.i.) to flirt, dally.
flêrte (m.) a flirtation, dalliance.
flete (m.) fine-looking, well-saddled horse.
fleuma (m.,f.) phlegm, sluggishness, apathy; equanimity, coolness; (in old physiology) one of the four humors. [Phlegm, in the sense of mucus, is MUCO].
fleumático –ca (adj.) phlegmatic, sluggish; cool, self-possessed; unemotional. Var. FLEGMÁTICO.

flexão [ks] (f.) flection, flexure; deflection; sag; (Gram.) inflection.
flexibilidade [ks] (f.) flexibility, pliability; pliancy, yielding disposition.
flexibilizar [ks] (v.t.) to make flexible.
flexional [ks] (adj., Gram.) inflectional.
flexionar [ks] (v.t.) to inflect.
flexível [ks] (adj.) flexible, pliable, supple; yielding, complaisant, docile.
flexor –xora [ks] (adj.) flexing; (m., Anat.) flexor.
flexório [ks] (m., Anat.) flexor.
flexuosidade [ks] (f.) flexuosity.
flexuoso –sa [ks] (adj.) flexuous.
flexura [ks] (f., Anat.) flexion.
flibusteiro (m.) filibuster, pirate, buccaneer.
flintglass (m.) flint glass; crystal glass.
flocado –da (adj.) flaky.
floco (m.) snowflake; fluff, flock, tuft of wool; lint.
flocoso –sa (adj.) flocculent; flaky.
flóculo (m.) floccule.
floema (m., Bot.) phloem.
flogístico –ca (adj., Med.) phlogistic.
flogopita (f., Min.) phlogopite; magnesium mica.
floorrizina [o-o] (f., Chem.) phlorizin.
flor (f.) flower, bloom, blossom; the flower (of youth, of society, etc.); the cream, the choicest, the fairest, the élite, the pick (of anything); the prime of life.—**boreal**, the pagoda collinsia (C. bicolor).—**cheirosa** = FLOR-DA-NOITE.—**d'água**, water lettuce (Pistia stratioites), c.a. ALFACE-D'ÁGUA, GÔLFO, LENTILHA-D'ÁGUA, MURURÉ-PAJÉ.—**da-imperatriz**, the tall amaryllis (A. procera), c.a. AÇUCENA.—**da-lua**, the large moonflower (Calonyction aculeatum).—**da-noite**, the queenofthenight (Selenicereus grandiflorus), c.a. FLOR-CHEIROSA, FLOR-DE-BAILE, FLOR-DE-SÊDA; also = BUQUÊ-DE-NOIVA and PRINCESA-DA-NOITE.—**da-paixão**, passionflower; = MARACUJÁ.—**da-páscoa**, European pasqueflower (Anemone pulsatilla).—**da-quaresma**, a glorybush (Tibouchina mutabilis).—**da-resurreição**, the roundleaf resurrecⁱᵒnlily (Kaempferia rotunda).—**da-verdade**, the white false hellebore (Veratrum album), c.a. HELÉBORO-BRANCO.—**de-abril**, the India dillenia (D. indica), c.a. FRUTA-ESTRELADA.—**de-amor** (or —**de-amôres**, or —**dos-amôres**), the babyblue-eyes nemophila (N. menziesi); the spotted nemophila (N. maculata).—**de-baunilha** = BAUNILHA-DO-PERU.—**de-baile** = FLOR-DA-NOITE, PRINCESA-DA-NOITE, CACTO-TREPADOR.—**de-cachimbo**, common dutchmanspipe (Aristolochia durior).—**de-carnaval**, the Anderson habranthus (H. andersonianus).—**de-cêra**, the wax plant (Hoya carnosa).—**de-cetim**, the mangles sunray (Helipterum mangles), c.a. SEMPRE-VIVA.—**de-chagas** = CAPUCHINCA-DO-BRASIL.—**de-contas**, Arabian star-of-Bethlehem (Ornithogalum arabicum).—**de-coral**, the coral plant (Russelia equisetiformis); the coralplant nettlespurge (Jatropha multifida), c.a. FLOR-DE-SANGUE; the common coralbean (Erythrina corallodendrum); the cockspur coralbean (Erythrina crista-galli); the Java glorybower (Clerodendron speciossissimum); the jungleflame (Ixora coccinea).—**de-cuco**, ragged robin (Lychnis floscuculi).—**de-duas-esporas**, the rose twinspur (Diascia barberae).—**de-enxofre**, flowers of sulphur.—**de-gêlo** = FÔLHA-DE-GÊLO.—**de-grama** = CAPIM-PÉ-DE-GALINHA.—**de-índio**, the paradise poinciana (Poinciana gilliesi), c.a. FLOR-DO-PARAÍSO.—**de-jesus**, an orchid (Laeliocattleya elegans).—**de-jupiter**, flowerofjove (Lychnis flosjovis).—**de-lis**, fleur-de-lis.—**de-maio**, the broadleaf epiphyllum (E. oxypetalum), c.a. FLOR-DE-SÊDA; lilyofthevalley (Convallaria majalis); also = CUIPEÚNA.—**de-mel**, globe butterflybush (Buddleia globosa).—**de-merenda**, common four-o'clock (Mirabilis jalapa), c.a. BOAS-NOITES, SUSPIROS.—**de-mico** = AÇUCENA-DO-MATO.—**de-noiva**, the germander spirea (S. chamaedryfolia), c.a. BUQUÊ-DE-NOIVA.—**de-onze-horas** = CAVALHEIRO-DAS-ONZE-HORAS.—**de-palha**, strawflower (Helichrysum bracteatum).—**de-papagaio** = FÔLHA-DE-SANGUE.—**de-paraíso**, the flowerfence poinciana (P. pulcherrima)—the official flower of the State of Rio de Janeiro.—**de-pavão**, peacock-flower, flamboyant, royal poinciana (Delonix regia), c.a. FLOR-DO-PARAÍSO.—**de-quaresma** = CUIPEÚNA.—**de-sangue** = CAPUCHINHA-GRANDE; also the coral nettlespurge (Jatropha multifida), c.a. FLOR-DE-CORAL.—**de-santo-antônio** = FÔLHA-DE-SANGUE.—**de-são-bento**, the Chile avens (Geum chiloense).—**de-são-joão**, either of two

orchids: *Phajus grandifolius* or *P. wallichi;* also = CIPÓ-DE-SÃO-JOÃO. —-de-são-miguel = FLOR-DE-VIÚVA. —-de-sapo = CIPÓ-MIL-HOMENS and CAPITÃO-DE-SALA.—-de-sêda = FLOR-DE-MAIO and FLOR-DA-NOITE.—-de-trombeta, the scalloped salpiglossis (*S. sinuata*).—-de-um-dia, the Virginia spiderwort (*Tradescantia virginiana*). —-de-vaca, an orchid (*Stanhopea sp.*).—-de-viúva, the purplewreath petrea (*P. volubilis*), c.a. CAPELA-DE-VIÚVA; the jasmin nightshade (*Solanum jasminoides*); the common throatwort (*Trachelium caeruleum*).—-do-cardeal, the cardinal starglory (*Quamoclit sloteri*); the cypressvine starglory (*Quamoclit pennata*), c.a. PRIMAVERA, BOA-TARDE. —-do-céu = QUEBRA-FOICE. —-do-espírito-santo, an orchid (*Oncidium sp.*).—-do-general, cape-jasmine (*Gardenia jasminoides*).—-do-imperador, the sweet osmanthus (*O. fragrans*), c.a. JASMIM-DO-IMPERADOR.—-do-natal, an orchid (*Cattleya guttata*).—-do-norte = BOA-NOITE.—-do-paraíso, bird-of-paradise flower, paradise poinciana (*P. gilliesi*), c.a. FLOR-DE-ÍNDIO; also = FLOR-DE-PAVÃO.—dobrada, any double flower.—dos anos, the flower of youth; the prime of life.—-dos-tintureiros, common woadwaxen or dyers greenweed (*Genista tinctoria*).—es de zinco, flowers of zinc; zinc oxide; zinc white.—-tigre, common tigerflower (*Trigridia pavonia*).—-trombeta, cape-honeysuckle (*Tecomaria capensis*). à—-de, on the surface of (water, soil). fina—, the choicest, the cream (of anything).
flora (*f.*) flora.
floração (*f.*) flowering, blooming, blossoming.
floral (*adj.*) floral.
florão (*m., Arch.*) a ceiling floral piece.
florar (*v.i.*) to flower.
floreado -da (*adj.*) flowered, flowery; (*m., Music.*) flourish.
florear (*v.t.,v.i.*) to flower; (*v.t.*) to flourish; to brandish.
floreio (*m.*) a flourish or flourishing.
floreira (*f.*) flower vase.
florejar (*v.t.,v.i.*) to flower; (*v.t.*) to adorn with flowers; to flourish.
Florença (*f.*) Florence (name of city).
Florência (*f.*) Florence (name of person).
florente (*adj.*) in flower.
florentino -na, **florentim** (*adj.; m.,f.*) Florentine.
flóreo -rea (*adj.*) florescent; flowery.
florescência (*f.*) florescence.
florescente (*adj.*) florescent; flourishing.
florescer (*v.t.,v.i.*) to flower; (*v.i.*) to flourish, thrive, prosper.
floresta (*f.*) forest.
florestal (*adj.*) forest; sylvan.
floreta [ê] (*f.*) floret.
florete [rê] fleuret, fencing foil; also = BABOSA (a fish).
florianapolitano -na (*adj.; m.,f.*) of or pert. to, or a native or inhabitant of, Florianopolis.
floricultor -tora (*m.,f.*) floriculturist.
floricultura (*f.*) floriculture.
floricoroado -da (*adj.*) flower-crowned.
florido -da (*adj.*) in flower; florescent; ornate.
flórido -da (*adj.*) florid, flowery. água—, rose water.
florífero -ra, **florígero** -ra, (*adj.*) floriferous.
floriforme (*adj.*) floriform.
florilégio (*m.*) an anthology.
florim (*m.*) florin (coin).
floríparo -ra (*adj.*) producing flowers.
florir [46] (*v.i.*) to flower, bloom; (*v.t.*) to embellish, as with flowers; to flourish, thrive.
florista (*m.,f.*) florist; a maker of artificial flowers.
florístico -ca (*adj.*) floristic.
floritura (*f., Music.*) ornament.
floromania (*f.*) a passion for flowers.
flórula (*f., Bot.*) florula.
flósculo (*m.*) floweret; floret.
flosculoso -sa (*adj., Bot.*) flosculous, discoid.
flotilha (*f.*) flotilla.
flox [ks] (*m., Bot.*) phlox.
floxo -xa [flô] (*adj.*) var. of FROUXO.
fluência (*f.*) fluency.
fluente (*adj.*) fluent, flowing; glib.
fluidal (*adj.*) fluidal.
fluidez [u-i] (*f.*) fluidity.
fluidificação [u-i] (*f.*) fluidification.
fluidificar [u-i] (*v.t.*) to fluidify, fluidize; (*v.r.*) to become fluid.
fluido -da (*adj.; m.*) fluid, liquid; (*m.*) aura.

fluir [72] (*v.i.*) to flow.
flume, flúmen (*m.*) river. [*Poetical*].
fluminense (*adj.*) fluvial; of or pert. to the State of Rio de Janeiro; (*m.,f.*) a native of the same.
flumíneo -nea (*adj.*) = FLUVIAL.
fluobórico -ca (*adj., Chem.*) fluoboric [acid].
flúor (*m., Chem.*) fluorine.
fluoreno (*m., Chem.*) fluorene.
fluoresceína (*f., Chem.*) fluorescein; resorcinol phthalein.
fluorescência (*f.*) fluorescence.
fluorescente (*adj.*) fluorescent.
fluoreto [ê] (*m., Chem.*) fluoride.—de cálcio, calcium fluoride; fluorite; fluorspar.—de cromo, chromium fluoride.—de hidrogênio, hydrogen fluoride; fluorhydric acid.—de silício, silicon tetrafluoride.
fluorídrico -ca (*adj., Chem.*) hydrofluoric [acid].
fluorita, fluorina (*f.*), **fluorito** (*m., Min.*) fluorite.
fluorítico -ca (*adj., Chem.*) fluoric.
fluoróforo (*m., Chem.*) fluorophor.
fluorofórmio (*m., Chem.*) fluoroform.
fluorogênio (*m., Chem.*) fluorogen.
fluorômetro (*m., Physics*) fluorometer.
fluoroscopia (*f.*) fluoroscopy.
fluoroscópio (*m.*) fluoroscope.
fluossilicato (*m., Chem.*) fluosilicate.
fluotantálico -ca (*adj., Chem.*) fluotantalic.
fluotitânico -ca (*adj., Chem.*) fluotitanic.
flutuabilidade (*f.*) buoyancy.
flutuação (*f.*) fluctuation; floating; vacillation; (*Ore dressing*) flotation.
flutuador (*m.*) a float, pontoon, esp. of hydroplane; floating platform; carburetor float; (*Aeron.*) float.
flutuante (*adj.*) floating, afloat; buoyant; fluctuating; unfunded (debit).
flutuar (*v.i.*) to float; to fluctuate, vacillate, waver.
flutuável (*adj.*) floatable; buoyant; navigable.
flutuosidade (*f.*) buoyancy.
flutuoso -sa (*adj.*) floating; buoyant.
fluvial, fluviátil [-teis] (*adj.*) fluvial.
fluviógrafo (*m.*) fluviograph.
fluviômetro (*m.*) fluviometer.
flux [x = s] (*m.*) = FLUXO.
fluxão [ks] (*f.*) fluxion.
fluxibilidade [ks] (*f.*) fluxibility.
fluxímetro [ks] (*m., Elec.*) fluxmeter. Var. FLUXÔMETRO.
fluxionário -ria [ks] (*adj.*) fluxionary, fluxional.
fluxível [ks] (*adj.*) fluxible.
fluxo -xa [ks] (*adj.*) fluxional, fluid, transitory; (*m.*) tide, flood; flux, flow; a fusing agent.—branco, (*Med.*) leucorrhea.—da bôca, salivation.—de riso, a flood of laughter.—de sangue, (*Med.*) bloody dysentery.—de ventre, diarrhea.—e refluxo da sorte, the ups and downs of fortune.—luminoso, (*Physics*) luminous flux or power. —magnético, (*Physics*) magnetic flux.
F.M.M. = FÔRÇA MAGNETOMOTRIZ (magnetomotive force).
f.° = FÓLIO (folio).
F.° = FILHO (Son).
F.O.B. or **FOB** = FRANCO A BORDO, or PÔSTO A BORDO (free on board).
foba (*adj.; m.,f., colloq.*) timid; lazy (person).
fobar (*v.t.*) to win all of another player's money; to lose money at gambling.
fobia (*f.*) phobia.
fobô (*adj., colloq.*) low, common; (*m.*) a person of little importance, having no means.
foboca (*f., Zool.*) a brocket (*Mazama rondoni*), c.a. VEADO-NEGRO, VEADO-ROXO, GARAPU, GUARAPU.
fobofobia (*f.*) = NOSOFOBIA.
foca (*f.*) seal; sea lion; (*m.*) miser, stingy person; (*slang*) cub reporter; (*adj.*) raw, green, inexpert.
focagem (*f.*) act of focusing.
focal (*adj.*) focal.
focalização (*f.*) focalizing; focusing.
focalizar (*v.t.*) to focalize, focus.
focar (*v.t.*) to focus, focalize.
focena (*f.*) the genus (*Phocaena*) of porpoises.
focenato (*m., Chem.*) phocenate.
focenina (*f., Chem.*) phocenin.
focinegro -gra (*adj.*) blackfaced [bull].
focinhada (*f.*) a blow with the muzzle, snout or trunk.
focinhar (*v.*) = AFOCINHAR.
focinheira (*f.*) a pig's snout; a muzzle or muzzler; noseband (of a bridle).
focinho (*m.*) muzzle, snout; (*colloq.*) "mug" (face).—-de-

burro, (*Bot.*) common snapdragon. **dar de—com alguém,** to bump into another person (face to face). **ir de—ao chão,** to fall flat on one's face.

focinhudo –da (*adj.*) having a big FOCINHO (in any sense); snooty; sullen, sulky.

foco (*m.*) focus; focal point, center.

focômetro (*m., Optics.*) focimeter.

fofice (*f.*) fluffiness.

fôfo –fa (*adj.*) fluffy, soft; puffy; spongy; light and hollow; puffed up, vain.

fofoca (*f.*) gossip.

fogaça (*f.*) a large cake or loaf.

fogacho (*m.*) a small flame; a powder blast; a hot flush; a flash of anger.

fogagem (*f.*) common term for any of various skin eruptions; plant blisters; flash of anger.

fogaleira (*f.*) fireman's shovel.

fogão (*m.*) stove; heater; hearth; an area abounding in ipecac plants; a barbecue pit; a piece of land more suitable for farming than the surrounding area.—**sem fogo,** fireless cooker.

fogareiro (*m.*) a small portable heater; a brazier.—**elétrico,** an electric hot plate or heater.

fogo [fô] (*m.*) fire; combustion; firing; blaze; heat; ardor, mettle; fireplace; (*interj.*) Fire!—**apagou,** the scaled dove (*Scafardella squammata*), c.a. RÔLA-CASCAVEL, POMBA-CASCAVEL, POMBINHA-CASCAVEL, PICUIPIÚMA.—**central,** a certain type of double-barreled pistol.—**cruzado,** crossfire.—**de artifício,** fireworks display, c.a. FOGO DE VISTA.—**de-bengala,** Roman candle.—**de bilbode,** volley.—**de boitatá,** jack-o'lantern.—**de monturo,** a smoldering fire (as in a garbage dump).—**de palha,** flash in the pan; love at first sight.—**de revérbero,** reverberatory flame.—**de-santelmo,** St. Elmo's light.—**de-santo-antão,** St. Anthony's fire (any of various skin eruptions, esp. erysipelas and ergotism).—**s de São João,** fire works in celebration of St. John's day.—**do céu,** lightning.—**-fátuo,** ignis fatuus, will-o'-the-wisp.—**-grego,** or **-grégués,** Greek fire.—**latente,** latent heat; fig., predisposition.—**-selvagem,** pemphigus; shingles. **a—lento,** slowly, gradually, little by little. **abrir—,** to open fire. **abrir—a queima-roupa,** to fire point-blank. **a ferro e a—,** tooth-and-nail; at all costs. **à prova de—,** fireproof. **atiçar o—,** to poke the fire. **brigada de—,** fire brigade. **céu de—,** burning sky. **côr de—,** flame-colored. **de—morto,** of mills, shut-down; of persons, broken down. **deitar—a,** to set fire to. **em—,** afire, ablaze, burning. **errar—,** to misfire. **fazer—,** to shoot, open fire. **fazer—emboscado,** to snipe. **ferver a—lento,** to cause to simmer. **fogão sem—,** fireless cooker. **lançar—,** to spit fire, throw out sparks. **mentir,** or **negar,—,** to misfire. **Não há—sem fumo,** Where there's smoke, there's fire. **olhos de—,** fiery eyes. **pegar—,** to catch fire. **pegar—em,** to set fire to. **pôr a mão no—,** to swear on a stack of Bibles. **potencial de—,** fire power. **puxar—,** (*slang*) to get drunk. **seguro contra—,** fire insurance. **tição de—,** firebrand. **tocar—na canjica,** to build a fire under something (get it started).

fogosidade (*f.*) fieriness.

fogoso –sa (*adj.*) fiery, glowing, flaming; ardent, fervent; hot-headed; impetuous; of a horse, spirited, mettlesome.

foguear (*v.t.*) to burn [= QUEIMAR].

fogueira (*f.*) flame; bonfire, camp fire; (*R.R.*) trestlework, c.a. GAIOLA; (*Zool.*) the candil or Frère Jacques (*Myripristis jacobus*), a bright-colored little tropical marine fish closely related to JAGUARUÇÁ (squirrel fish), c.a. ÔLHO-DE-VIDRO, PIRANEMA, ARABAIANA.

fogueiro (*m.*) = FOGUISTA.

foguetada (*f.*) noisy fireworks display; scolding, rebuke.

foguetão (*m.*) rope-carrying rocket.

foguete [guê] (*m.*) skyrocket; firecracker; space rocket; (*colloq.*) a lively person; a coquettish young woman; an upbraiding; (*adj.*) lively; fiery.—**de assobio,** whistling skyrocket.

foguetear (*v.i.*) to set off fireworks.

fogueteiro (*m.*) maker of fireworks.

foguetinho (*m.*) dragonfly [= LIBÉLULA]; also = CAMINHEIRO (a bird).

foguista (*m.*) fireman, stoker.

foi, form of IR [53] and SER [76].

foiçada (*f.*) a blow with a FOICE. Var. FOUÇADA.

foiçar (*v.t.*) to scythe. Var. FOUÇAR.

foice (*f.*) scythe.—**roçadeira** or **de roçar,** brush hook, bush hook. **a talho de—,** just right. Var. FOUCE.

foiciforme (*adj.*) = FALCIFORME.

foicinha (*f.*), **–nho** (*m.*) sickle. Vars. FOUCINHA, –NHO.

foiteza (*f.*) = AFOITEZA.

foito –ta (*adj.*) = AFOITO.

fojo [fô] (*m.*) pitfall; trap, cave.

fôl. = FÔLHA (page; sheet).

fola [ó] (*f.*) roar of surf.

folacho –cha (*m.,f., colloq.*) a mild, sickly person.

folada (*f.*) piddock (*Pholas*), a burrowing clam, c.a. MARISCO-TATU.

folar (*m.*) Easter-gift; cake, bun.

folastria (*f.*) wild rejoicing.

folclore [lô] (*m.*) folklore.

folclórico –ca (*adj.*) folkloric.

folclorista (*m.,f.*) folklorist.

fole (*m.*) bellows; small leather bag; (*colloq.*) stomach.

folecha (*f.*), **folecho** (*m.*) water blister.

fôlego (*m.*) breath; wind; breathing spell.—**de gato,** robust health. **perder o—,** to get out of breath. **sem—,** breathless. **ter sete—s (como os gatos),** to have as many lives as a cat.

folga (*f.*) breathing-spell, rest, respite; relaxation; leisure time; (*Mach.*) clearance; play, backlash. **dar—,** to slacken. **dia de—,** a day off.

folgado –da (*adj.*) loose, slack, loose-fitting; unhampered; easygoing.

folgador –dora (*adj.*) = FOLGAZÃO.

folgança (*f.*) mirth, frolic.

folgar (*v.t.*) to rest; to let out, loosen; to free (**de,** of); (*v.i.*) to rejoice (**de, em, com, por,** in); to rest; to make merry; to be free, loose; (*m.*) frolic.

folgazão –zona, folgaz (*adj.*) waggish, frolicsome; playful; fun-loving; genial, jovial, jolly, merry, prankish; jaunty.

folgazar (*v.*) = FOLGAR.

fôlgo (*m.*) = FÔLEGO.

folguedo [ê] (*m.*) fun, frolic, prank; revelry, merrymaking.

folh. = FOLHETO (leaflet).

fôlha (*f.*) leaf; folio; sheet; blade; lamina, layer; log, register; roster; door or table leaf.—**corrida,** a running record of a person's experience, conduct, etc.; dossier; police record.—**da-costa** = FÔLHA-DA-FORTUNA and COURAMA.—**da-fonte,** heartleaf philodendron (*P. cordatum*), c.a. GUIMBERANA.—**da-fortuna,** a life plant or airplant (*Kalanchoe pinnata*), the several leaves of which develop new plants whose greater or lesser numbers are said to foretell one's fortune.—**da-independência,** an acanthus (*Sanchezia nobilis*).—**de-bôlo** = FÔLHA-REDONDA.—**decanivete,** blade of a pocketknife.—**de estanho,** tinfoil.—**de faca,** knife blade.—**decorrente,** a decurrent leaf.—**de-flandres,** tinplate.—**de-gêlo,** the iceplant mesembryanthemum (*M. crystallinum*), c.a. ERVA-DE-GÊLO, FLOR-DE-GÊLO, PLANTA-DE-NEVE.—**de-hera,** ivyleaf pelargonium (*P. lateripes*).—**de-lixa** = CIPÓ-CABOCLO.—**de ouro,** gold leaf.—**de-ouro,** a chrysanthemum (*C. praealtum*); a myrtle (*Myrcia chrysophylla*), c.a. FÔLHA-DOURADA.—**de pagamento,** payroll.—**de-pajé** = FEDEGOSO-VERDADEIRO.—**de-papagaio,** leafcroton (*Codiaeum variegatum*), c.a. CRÓTON.—**de pirarucu** = COURAMA.—**de rosto,** title page.—**de-sangue,** the common poinsettia (*Euphorbia pulcherrima*), c.a. ASA-DE-PAPAGAIO, PAPAGAIO, PAPAGAIEIRA, POINSETIA, PARECE-MAS-NÃO-É, FLOR-DE-PAPAGAIO, FLOR-DE-SANTO-ANTÔNIO.—**de-sant'ana,** an ironweed (*Vernonia macrophylla*), c.a. ERVA-DE-SANT'-ANA.—**de serviço,** service record.—**de serviços prestados,** record of services rendered.—**de vencimentos,** payroll.—**de zinco,** galvanized steel sheet.—**dourada** = FÔLHA-DE-OURO; also, gold leaf; also, the cainito starapple (*Chrysophyllum cainito*).—**furada** = DRAGÃO-FEDORENTO.—**gorda,** the artillery clearweed (*Pilea microphylla*), c.a. ERVA-GORDA, URTIGA.—**grande,** a scratchbush (*Urera armigera*).—**grossa** = FÔLHA-DA-FORTUNA.—**linear,** a linear leaf.—**livre,** a lippia (*L. urticoides*).—**morta,** (*Aeron.*) falling leaf, c.a. FÔLHA-SÊCA.—**mucronada,** a mucronate leaf.—**redonda,** a Christmasbush (*Alchornea iricurana*), c.a. FÔLHA-DE-BÔLO, IRICURANA, MARIA-MOLE, TAPIÁ-GUAÇU.—**rôta** = DRAGÃO-FEDORENTO.—**santa,** a savannaflower (*Echites macrocalyx*); also = MALVA-DO-CAMPO.—**sêca,** butterflies of the genus Zaretes; also = FÔLHA-MORTA.—**s-da-china** = CRÓTON.—**de-louco** = CAÁ-POMONGA.—**sôlta,** a handbill.

folhado –da (*adj.*) leaf-covered; foliate; covered with a layer of gold, etc.; veneered; (*m.*) thin pastry dough; leafage; fallen leaves; (*Bot.*) the Laurestinus viburnum (*V. tinus*); (*f.*) thick carpet of leaves; forest litter; foliage.

folhagem (*f.*) foliage, leafage; foliation; ornamental foliage.

folhame (*m.*) = FOLHAGEM.

folhar (*v.t.*) to foliate; to ornament with leaves; to foil; (*v.i.,v.r.*) to be leaf-covered.

folharada (*f.*) a lot of leaves.

folharia (*f.*) = FOLHAGEM.

folhato (*m.*) = FOLHELHO.

folheação (*f.*) foliation.

folheado –da (*adj.*) foliate; veneered; (*Geol.*) schistose.—**a ouro**, gold-plated; (*m.*) veneer; foil.

folhear (*v.t.*) to leaf (thumb) through (the pages of a book); to foil; to veneer; (*adj.*) foliar.

folheatura (*f.*) foliation; (*Bot.*) vernation.

folhedo [ê] (*m.*) quantity of fallen leaves; leafage.

folheio (*m.*) act of thumbing (leafing) through a book.

folheiro –ra (*adj.*) cheerful; jaunty; (*m.*) tinsmith [= FUNILEIRO]; sheet metal worker.

folhelho [ê] (*m.*) husk, pod, skin [= FOLHATO]; (*Geol.*) schist.

folhento –ta (*adj.*) leafy.

folheoso –sa (*adj.*) foliaceous.

folheta [ê] (*f.*) leaflet; jewelers' foil.

folhetaria (*f.*) ornamental leafage.

folhetear (*v.t.*) to back or cover with foil; to veneer.

folhetim (*m.*) daily chapter of a newspaper serial.

folhetinista (*m.,f.*) a writer of FOLHETINS.

folhetista (*m.,f.*) pamphleteer.

folheto [ê] (*m.*) leaflet, pamphlet.

folhinha (*f.*) calendar, almanack.

fôlho [folhos (fó)] (*m.*) ruffles, flounce; tripe [= FOLHOSO]. —**s-de-sinhá**, a kind of pastry.

folhoso –sa (*adj.*) leafy, foliose; (*m.*) tripe [= CENTAFOLHO, FÔLHO, DOBRADINHA]; (*Zool.*) manyplies, omasum.

folhudo –da (*adj.*) leafy, foliose.

folia (*f.*) merrymaking, frolic, lark, "highjinks".

foliação (*f.*) foliation.

foliáceo –cea (*adj.*) foliaceous.

foliado –da (*adj.*) foliate; veneered.

foliador –dora (*m.,f.*) reveler.

folião –liona (*m.,f.*) buffoon; cutup; merrymaker.

foliar (*adj.*) foliar; (*v.i.*) to revel, make merry.

folicular (*adj.*) follicular.

foliculário (*m.*) cheap pamphleteer; hack journalist.

foliculite (*f., Med.*) folliculitis.

folículo (*m.*) leaflet; follicle; (*Anat.*) follicle, crypt.

foliculose (*f., Med.*) folliculosis.

foliculoso –sa (*adj.*) folliculous, folliculose.

folidoto –ta (*adj.*) scaly.

folífago –ga (*adj.*) leaf-eating.

folífero –ra (*adj.*) foliferous.

foliforme (*adj.*) leaf-shaped; bellows-shaped.

fólio (*m.*) folio.

foliolado –da (*adj.*) having leaflets.

folíolo (*m.*) leaflet.

foliona, fem. of FOLIÃO.

folipa (*f.*), **folipo** (*m.*) blister.

foma (*f.*) a form genus (*Phoma*) of imperfect fungi.

fome (*f.*) hunger; appetite; famine.—**canina**, ravenous hunger. **com—**, hungry. **estar com**, or **ter,—**, to be hungry. **matar a—**, to satisfy hunger. **matar à—**, to kill by starvation. **morrer de—**, to die of hunger. **unha de—**, miserly, stingy, niggardly.

fomentação (*f.*) fomentation, stirring up, encouragement; embrocation.

fomentador –dora (*adj.; m.,f.*) that, or one who, foments, etc.;—see the verb FOMENTAR.

fomentar (*v.t.*) to foment, promote, encourage, foster, stimulate; to embrocate.

fomento (*m.*) fomentation; fostering; embrocation; patronage; encouragement; stimulation.

fomitura (*f.*) hunger; poverty.

fomo (*m.*) shallow vessel for drying and toasting manioc.

fomos, form of SER [76] and IR [53].

fona (*m.*) effeminate man; (*m.,f.*) miserly person; (*f.*) spark; flurry.

fonação (*f.*) phonation.

fonador –dora (*adj.*) phonatory.

fonascia, fonástica (*f.*) voice exercise.

fonautógrafo (*m., Physics*) phonautograph.

fone (*m.*) telephone receiver; earphone; earpiece.

fonema (*m., Phonet.*) phoneme.

fonendoscópio (*m.*) phonendoscope.

fonética (*f.*) see FONÉTICO.

foneticismo (*m.*) phoneticism.

foneticista (*m.,f.*) phonetist.

fonético –ca (*adj.*) phonetic; (*f.*) phonetics.

fônico –ca (*adj.*) phonic.

fono (*m.*) = FONE.

fonocâmptico –ca (*adj.*) sound-reflecting.

fonofilme (*m.*) sound film.

fonóforo (*m.*) phonophore.

fonografia (*f.*) phonography.

fonógrafo (*m.*) phonograph.

fonólito (*m., Petrog.*) phonolite, clinkstone.

fonologia (*f.*) phonology.

fonológico –ca (*adj.*) phonologic(al).

fonometria (*f., Physics*) phonometry.

fonômetro (*m., Physics*) phonometer.

fonomímico (*adj.*) phonomimic (system of teaching the deaf to read).

fonoplex [ks] (*adj.*) phonoplex [telegraph].

fonoscópio (*m., Physics*) phonoscope.

fontainha [a-i] (*f.*) a little fountain. [dim. of FONTE.]

fontal (*adj.*) original, primary.

fontanela (*f., Anat.*) fontanel.—**anterior** or **bregmática**, bregmatic fontanel.

fonte (*f.*) fountain, fount, spring; source, origin, fountainhead; temple (side of forehead).—**da cabeça**, (*Anat.*) temple [= TÊMPORA].—**de riquezas**, source of wealth.—**fidedigna**, reliable source.—**limpa**, reliable source (of information).—**oficiosa**, an unofficial but government-inspired source.

fontícula (*f.*) a small spring.

footing (*m.*) promenade, stroll, saunter.

fôr, fôra, forms of IR [53] and SER [76].

fora (*adv.*) out, on the outside, without, outdoors, outwards, abroad, away, (*prep.*) except(ing), save, excluding; (*interj.*) Out! Begone! Get out!—**de**, outside of; foreign to; with the exception of.—**de casa**, out of doors. —**de dúvida**, beyond doubt.—**de horas**, out of hours; at an unreasonable hour.—**de mão**, not at hand; at a distance.—**de moda**, out of fashion; outmoded.—**de propósito**, out of reason; preposterous.—**de serviço**, out of service, out of order, not running (e.g., the elevator). —**de si**, beside oneself; out of one's mind.—**do comum**, uncommon.—**do natural**, unnatural. **abrir** (or **dar**) **para—**, to open out on, look out on (as a window). **cá por—**, here on the outside. **Cai—**! (*slang*) Scram! Beat it! **Dá o—**! (*slang*) Get out! Begone! **dar o—** (*slang*) to walk out on (one's job, sweetheart, etc.); to sneak away from (a party, etc.). **dar o—a** (or **em**) (*slang*) to give someone the bounce. **Deu o—no namorado** (*slang*) She gave her sweetheart the gate. **de—**, (on the) outside; from outside. **do lado de—**, on the outside. **jogar—**, to throw out (away). **lá—**, outside there. **o mundo lá de—**, the outside world. **para—**, outward(s) (to the) outside, out. **para—de**, out of, outside. **pelo mundo a—**, throughout the (wide) world. **por—**, outside, on the outside. **sair—de si**, to lose control of oneself; to go out of one's mind.

foragido –da (*adj.*) expatriated; wandering; runaway, fugitive; at large; (*m.,f.*) expatriate; wanderer; an outlaw, fugitive from justice; absconder.

foragir-se (*v.r.*) to flee, abscond (from persecution, from justice).

foral (*m.*) charter.

foram, fôramos, fôras, forms of IR [53] and SER [76].

forame, forâmen [-es] (*m.*) foramen.

foraminífero –ra (*adj.*) foraminiferous; (*m.pl., Zool.*) the Foraminifera.

foraminoso –sa (*adj.*) foraminous.

forâneo –nea (*adj.*) foreign.

foranto (*m., Bot.*) clinanthium.

forasteiro –ra (*adj.*) strange, foreign; (*m.,f.*) stranger, foreigner, outsider.

fôrca (*f.*) gallows, gibbet.

fôrça (*f.*) force, strength, power, might; vigor, vim, energy; impelling motive; compulsion; troops; (*interj.*) Pull! Push! Buck up!—**aceleratriz**, accelerative force.— **ascensional**, lifting force.—**centrífuga**, centrifugal force. —**centrípeta**, centripetal force.—**coercitiva**, (*Magnetism*) coercive force.—**contra-eletromotriz**, (*Elec.*) back electromotive force.—**de ânimo**, strength of spirit.—**de inércia**, inertia.—**de vontade**, will power.—**elástica**, (*Mech.*) elastic limit or strength.—**elétrica**, electric power.—**eletromotriz**, electromotive force.—**eletromotriz de contato**, contact electricity.—**hidráulica**, hydraulic power.—**magnetomotriz**, (*Elec.*) magneto-motive force.—**maior**, force majeure, so-called "act of God".—**motriz**, motive power.—**pública**, police force.—**tênsil**, (*Physics*) tensile strength.—**termoeletromotriz**, (*Elec.*) thermoelectromotive force. **à**—, by force; forcibly. **à**—**bruta**, by brute force. **à**—**de**, by dint of. **a bem ou à**—, willy-nilly. **à fina**—, by force, regardless of reason. **à meia**—, at half speed. **à viva**—, by main strength. **camisa de**—, straitjacket. **com**—, vigorously. **com todas as**—**s (a mais não poder)**, with might and main. **desta**—, of this size; of this kind. **é**—**que**, it is unavoidable that. **fazer (uma)**—, (*slang*) to try hard, make an effort. **por**—, perforce, of necessity. **por**—**de**, because of.

forcada (*f.*) fork (of a tree, road, etc.).
forcado (*m.*) pitchfork; torero.
forçado **-da** (*adj.*) forced; unnatural; strained, far fetched; (*m.*) a criminal condemned to hard labor; galley slave.
forçador (*m.*), **-dora** (*f.*) forcer.
forcadura (*f.*) space between the tines of a pitchfork.
forçamento (*m.*) forcing; violation.
forçante (*adj.*) forcing.
forçar (*v.t.*) to force, compel; to strain; to force open; to ravish; to twist (the meaning of); (*v.r.*) to force (compel) oneself.—**a**, to compel ·to.—**a porta**, to force the door.
forcejar (*v.t.,v.i.*) to struggle, strive (**em, para, por**, to; **com**, with; **contra**, against); (*v.r.*) to exert (force) oneself (**em**, to).
forcejo [ê] effort, exertion, struggle.
fórceps, fórcipe (*m.*) forceps.
forçoso **-sa** (*adj.*) forcible; forceful; compulsory; vehement. **é**—**reconhecer que**, one must recognize that.
forçudo **-da** (*adj.; colloq.*) strong, "hefty".
fordes, fôreis, forem, fores, forms of IR [53] SER [76].
foreiro **-ra** (*adj.*) pert. to a building lease; rent-paying; (*m.,f.*) lessee of a building.
forense (*adj.*) forensic, judiciary.
fórfex [ks], **fórfice** (*m.*) surgeon's scissors.
forficulídeo (*m., Zool.*) an earwig (*Forficula*).
forja (*f.*) blacksmith's forge and anvil; furnace; iron worker's shop; foundry; a trap or pitfall [= FORJE].—**de rebites**, riveting forge.
forjador **-dora** (*adj.*) forging; (*m.*) forger (of metals); a falsifier.
forjadura (*f.*), **-amento** (*m.*) forging.
forjar (*v.t.*) to forge (metal); to fabricate (fashion, devise, invent); to falsify, "fake". **ferro forjado**, wrought iron.
forje (*m.*) = FORJA (trap).
forjicar (*v.t.*) to frame, trump up.
forma [ó] (*f.*) form, shape, figure; outward appearance; athletic form; mode, method, manner.—**corrente**, current (standard) form. **da mesma**—, likewise. **de**—**alguma**, by no means; under no circumstances. **de**—**que**, so that. **debaixo de**—, under command. **de qualquer**—, anyway, in any case. **dessa**—, at that rate. **desta**—, in this way. **de tal**—**que**, in such a way that. **em**—, in good shape, in proper form. **entrar na**—, to fall in (ranks). **por esta**—, by this means.
fôrma (*f.*) shoe last, shoetree; mold, matrix; foundry mold; pattern; hat block; cake or jelly mold; printer's type case.—**de bôlo**, cake pan.
formação (*f.*) formation; act of forming; (*Geol., Milit.*) formation.—**climática**, (*Plant Ecology*) climatic association.—**edáfica**, (*Plant Ecology*) edaphic association.
formado **-da** (*adj.*) formed; graduated (from college); (*m.,f.*) a college graduate; holder of a degree.
formador **-dora** (*adj.*) forming, shaping; (*m.,f.*) former, shaper.
formadura (*f.*) forming.
formal (*adj.*) formal, express, explicit, definite; peremptory; (*Metaph.*) formal, essential. [But not formal in the sense of ceremonious, which is CEREMONIOSO, nor perfunctory, which is PERFUNCTÓRIO.]
formaldeído (*m., Chem.*) formaldehyde.
formaldicloroetilo (*m., Chem.*) dicholoro-ethyl formal.
formalidade (*f.*) formality, custom; ceremony, conventionality; formula.
formalina (*f.*) formalin.
formalismo (*m.*) formalism.
formalista (*m.,f.*) formalist; (*adj.*) ceremonious; stiff, stuffy.
formalizado **-da** (*adj.*) formalized; (*colloq.*) piqued, offended; in formal attire.
formalizar (*v.t.*) to formalize, make formal; (*v.r., colloq.*)

to take offense, be scandalized; to put on formal attire.
foramida (*f., Chem.*) formamid(e).
formão (*m.*) carpenter's chisel.
formar (*v.t.*) to form, fashion, shape, mold; to make, create; to constitute, make up; to arrange, dispose; to educate; (*v.r.*) to form; to graduate (with a college degree).—**se em direito, em medicina**, etc., to graduate in law, medicine, etc.
formaria (*f.*) set of hatter's blocks, of shoemaker's lasts, etc.
formativo **-va** (*adj.*) formative.
formato (*m.*) format, shape, size.
formatura (*f.*) forming, formation; troop muster; parade; graduation from college.
formeiro (*m.*) maker of shoe lasts.
formeno (*m., Chem.*) formene, methane [= METANA].
formiato (*m., Chem.*) formiate, formate.
formicação (*f.*) an itching sensation as of ants crawling on the skin [= FORMIGUEIRO].
formicante (*adj., Med.*) formicative.
formicário **-ria** (*adj., Zool.*) formicarian; (*m.pl.*) ant birds.
formicida (*m.*) formicide, ant poison.
formícidas (*m.pl., Zool.*) the Formicidae (ant family).
formicídio (*m.*) the destruction of ants.
formicívoro **-ra** (*adj., Zool.*) feeding on ants.
fórmico **-ca** (*adj., Chem.*) formic [acid].
formicular (*adj.*) resembling ants.
formidando **-da** (*adj.*) dreadful, fearful, terrible.
formidável (*adj.*) formidable, dreadful, fearful; tremendous; (*colloq.*) amazing, wonderful, "swell".
formidoloso **-sa** (*adj.*) frightening.
formiga (*f.*) any ant; fig., a thrifty person; (*colloq.*) a person having a sweet tooth.—**açucareira**, any of numerous sweet-loving small ants, some of which constitute household pests, such as the little black *Monomorium minimum* and the red *M. pharaonis;* c.a. FORMIGA-DOCEIRA.—**aguilhoada**, stinging ants of the genus Ponera.—**argentina**, the Argentine ant (*Iridomyrmex humilis*).—**branca**, any white ant or termite [= CUPIM].—**carregadeira**,—**cortadeira**, an umbrella ant [= SAÚVA].—**chiadeira**, the velvet ant (a parasitic wasp having wingless females resembling ants, family Mutillidae), c.a. FORMIGA-FEITICEIRA, ONCINHA.—**da-roça** = SAÚVA.—**de-correição**, a legionary ant.—**de-cupim**, a termite (*Camponotus termitarius*).—**de-fogo**, a fire ant (*Solenopsis geminata*), c.a. LAVA-PÉS.—**de-mandioca** = SAÚVA.—**de-novato**, a venomous ant which inhabits the hollow stems of the ant tree, c.a. TAXI, NOVATO.—**doceira** = —**açucareira**.—**feiticeira** = —**CHIADEIRA**.—**lavapés** = LAVAPÉS.—**leão**, the ant lion (*Myrmeleon spp.*).
formigamento (*m.*) an itching, burning, or tingling sensation of the skin; act of swarming.
formigante (*adj.*) teeming, swarming.
formigão (*m.*) a large ant; coarse or heavy mortar; seminarist; a bird called JURUVA.—**de pólvora**, powder fuse.—**hidráulico**, hydraulic concrete.
formigar (*v.i.*) to itch, burn, tingle; to teem, abound, swarm; to scurry about (like ants) in search of a living.
formigueira (*f.*) an ant tree (*Triplaris*), c.a. PAU-DE-FORMIGA, PAU-DE-NOVATO.
formigueiro (*m.*) formicary, ants' nest, ant hill; pruritus, tingling, itching; fidgetiness; a mass of people milling about.
formiguejar (*v.i.*) to mill about (like ants); to itch.
formiguilho (*m., Veter.*) thrush.
formilho, formilho (*m.*) hatter's block.
formol (*m.*) = ALDEÍDO FÓRMICO.
formos, form of IR [53] and SER [76].
formosa-sem-dote (*f.*) = CAMARADINHA (a plant).
formosano **-na** (*adj.; m.,f.*) Formosan.
formose (*f., Chem.*) formose.
formosear (*v.*) = AFORMOSEAR.
formoso **-sa** (*adj.*) beautiful, handsome.
formosura (*f.*) beauty, attractiveness; a belle, a beauty.
fórmula (*f.*) formula, form; recipe; prescription; blank form.—**bruta**, or **empírica**, (*Chem.*) empirical, minimum, or composition formula.—**de constituição**, or **de estrutura**, (*Chem.*) constitutional or structural formula.—**eletrônica**, (*Chem.*) electronic formula.—**estereoquímica**, or **no espaço**, (*Chem.*) stereometric, configurational, or space formula.—**geral**, (*Chem.*) general formula.—**gráfica**, (*Chem.*) graphic formula.—**molecular**, (*Chem.*) molecular formula.—**química**, chemical formula.—

racional, (*Chem.*) rational formula. **sagrada**—, (*Eccl.*) Host.

formulação (*f.*) formulation.

formular (*v.t.*) to formulate; to give form or expression to; to prescribe (a recipe); (*v.r.*) to appear, manifest itself.

formulário (*m.*) blank form, application blank, questionnaire; formulary.

fornaça (*f.*) furnace, oven [=FORNALHA].

fornada (*f.*) a batch (of anything). **às**—**s**, in batches.

fornalha (*f.*) furnace, firebox; oven.—**de cadinhos,** crucible furnace.

fornalheiro (*m.*) stoker, fireman [=FOGUISTA].

fornecedor –**dora** (*m.,f.*) supplier; (*adj.*) supplying.

fornecer (*v.t.*) to furnish, supply (**a,** to; **de,** with); to provide (**de,** with); to purvey; (*v.r.*) to supply oneself.

fornecimento (*m.*) supply(ing), provision(ing).—**de guerra,** war matériel.

forneiro (*m.*) ovenman; an ovenbird [=JOÃO-DE-BARRO].

fórnice (*m.*) archway; (*Anat.*) fornix.

fornido –**da** (*adj.*) supplied; robust.—**de carnes,** plump.

fornilho (*m.*) small oven; bowl of a pipe.

fornir [46] (*v.t.*) to furnish, provide (**de,** with); to make firm, solid.

forno [fôr; *pl.*: fór] (*m.*) oven; kiln; furnace.—**d'água,** (*Bot.*) the Victoria regia, c.a. FORNO-DE-JAÇANA, FORNO-DE-JACARÉ, MORÍNQUA, MURURÉ.—**de arco,** (*Metal.*) electric-arc furnace.—**de cal,** lime kiln.—**de calcinação,** calcining furnace.—**de carvão,** coal furnace.—**de coque,** coke furnace.—**de cuba,** shaft furnace.—**de gás,** gas furnace.—**de indução,** induction furnace.—**de lenha,** wood-burning furnace.—**de pudlar,** puddling hearth.—**de recozer,** annealing furnace.—**de revérbero,** open-hearth furnace.—**elétrico,** electric furnace. **alto**—, blast furnace. **cozer ao**—, to bake, roast.

foro [fó] (*m.*) forum.

fôro [foros (fó)] (*m.*) the courts (of law); customary or legal rights, immunities and prerogatives; rent money; use and occupancy of a building.—**s de verdade, de autenticidade, de legitimidade, de civilização,** etc., claims (appearance, attributes, prestige, authority) of truth, authenticity, legitimacy, civilization, etc.

foronomia (*f.*) kinematics.

forqueadura (*f.*) bifurcation [=BIFURCAÇÃO].

forquear (*v.t.*) to bifurcate [=BIFURCAR].

forqueta [ê] (*f.*) forked stick or tree; fork of a river; crotch; oarlock.

forquilha (*f.*) small three-pronged pitchfork; forked stick; fork; oarlock; earmark; crotch; wishbone; clevis; (*Bot.*) species of paspalum grass; (*Zool.*) gapeworm (*Syngamus trachealis*), c.a. SÍNGAMO.

forquilhar (*v.t.*) to fork; to branch.

forra [fó] (*f., colloq.*) =DESFORRA.

fôrra (*f.*) see FÔRRO.

forração (*f.*) act of providing with a lining, etc.; see FÔRRO.

forra-gaitas (*m.,f.*) a stingy person [=AVARO].

forrageador –**dora** (*adj.*) foraging; (*m.,f.*) forager.

forragear (*v.t.*) to forage; to glean; (*v.i.*) to cut fodder.

forragem (*f.*) forage, fodder, feed.

forramento (*m.*) =FORRAÇÃO.

forrar (*v.t.*) to line the inside of (**com, de,** with) as, a coat with silk; to cover, overlay (**com, de,** with) as, a wall with paper, a table top with veneer, a floor with carpets, etc.; to emancipate (slaves); to save (money, time, etc.); (*v.r.*) to bundle oneself up against the cold; to retrieve one's losses; to avoid, shun; to avenge oneself.

forreta [ê] (*m.,f.*) skinflint, pinchpenny.

fôrro –**ra** (*adj.*) freed; emancipated; (*m.*) padding, stuffing; lining; sheathing; ceiling; attic.—**de macho e fêmea,** tongue-and-groove ceiling.—**de saia e camisa,** a ceiling of boards and battens; (*f.*) a facing or veneer of stone, marble, etc.

forró, forrobodó (*m., slang*) shindig; noisy party; hubbub [=ARRASTA-PÉ].

forsterita (*f., Min.*) forsterite.

fortalecedor –**dora** (*adj.*) fortifying, bracing; (*m.,f.*) fortifier.

fortalecer (*v.t.*) to fortify, strengthen, encourage; to corroborate; (*v.r.*) to grow strong.

fortalecimento (*m.*) act of fortifying, strengthening.

fortaleza [ê] (*f.*) fortress, stronghold; fortitude, courageous endurance.

forte (*adj.*) strong, sturdy, robust, stout, husky; powerful; strong-flavored; (*adv., Music*) forte; (*m.*) fort, strong-

hold; one's forte.

forteza [ê] (*f., colloq.*) strength.

fortidão (*f.*) strength, solidity.

fortificação (*f.*) fortification.

fortificado –**da** (*adj.*) fortified, defended.

fortificador –**dora** (*adj.*) fortifying; (*m.,f.*) fortifier.

fortificante (*adj.*) fortifying; (*m.*) a tonic medicine.

fortificar (*v.t.*) to fortify, strengthen; (*v.r.*) to grow strong.

fortim (*m.*) blockhouse, small fort.

fortíssimo –**ma** (*adj., adv., Music*) fortissimo.

fortuito –**ta** (*adj.*) fortuitous.

fortuna (*f.*) fortune, riches; chance, luck; fate, lot; (*Bot.*) =COURAMA. **fazer**—, to get rich.

fortunoso –**sa** (*adj.*) =AFORTUNADO.

forum [ó] (*m.*) =FORO.

fosca [ó] =FOSQUINHA.

fôsco –**ca** (*adj.*) dull, dim,'lackluster; dingy.

fosfagênio (*m., Biochem.*) phosphagen.

fosfamina (*f., Chem.*) phosphine; hydrogen phosphide.

fosfatado –**da** (*adj.*) phosphated.

fosfático –**ca** (*adj.*) phosphatic.

fosfátides (*m.pl., Biochem.*) phosphatides.

fosfato (*m.*) phosphate.—**bissódico,** dibasic sodium orthophosphate.—**de amônio,** ammonium phosphate.—**de cresilo,** tolyl phosphate.—**de cromo,** chromium orthophosphate; Plessy's green; Arnaudon's green.

fosfatúria (*f., Med.*) phosphaturia.

fosfeno (*m., Physiol.*) phosphene.

fosfinas (*f.pl., Chem.*) phosphines.

fosfeto =PHOSPHURETO.

fosfito (*m.*) phosphite.

fosfoglicerato (*m., Chem.*) a glycerophosphate.

fosfomolibdato (*m., Chem.*) phosphomolybdate.

fosfônio (*m., Chem.*) phosphonium.

fosforado –**da** (*adj.*) phosphorated.

fosforar (*v.t.*) to phosphorate.

fosforear (*v.i.*) to burn brightly, as phosphorus.

fosforeira (*f.*) matchbox.

fosforeiro (*m.*) worker in a match factory.

fosforejante (*adj.*) brightly burning.

fosforejar (*v.*) =FOSFOREAR.

fosfóreo –**rea** (*adj.*) phosphoric.

fosforescência (*f.*) phosphorescence.

fosforescente (*adj.*) phosphorescent.

fosforescer (*v.i.*) to phosphoresce.

fosfórico –**ca** (*adj.*) phosphoric; (*colloq.*) ignorant; cheap, of poor quality.

fosforífero –**ra** (*adj.*) phosphoriferous.

fosforizar (*v.t.*) to phosphorate.

fósforo (*m.*) phosphorus; a (sulfur) match; (*colloq.*) an ignorant or insignificant person; intruder.—**branco,** or **hialino,** or **ordinário,** ordinary yellow or white phosphorus.—**de segurança,** safety match.—**queimado,** burnt match; (*colloq.*) an impotent man.—**rubro** or **vermelho,** red phosphorus.—**violeta,** violet (metallic) phosphorus. **riscar um**—, to strike a match.

fosforogênico –**ca** (*adj., Physics*) phosphorogenic.

fosforógrafo (*m., Physics*) phosphorograph.

fosforoscópio (*m., Physics*) phosphoroscope.

fosforoso –**sa** (*adj.*) phosphorous.

fosfureto (*m., Chem.*) phosphide.

fosforia (*f.*) =FOSFATURIA.

fosgênio (*m., Chem.*) phosgene.

fosgenita (*f., Min.*) phosgenite; cromfordite.

fôsmeo –**mea** (*adj.; f.*) vague, confused, abstruse, indefinable (idea).

fosquinha (*f.*) gesture; disguise; grimace; (*pl.*) pettings, caresses.

fossa (*f.*) pit; cesspool; dimple (on chin or cheek); (*Anat.*) fossa.—**canina,** (*Anat.*) fossa canina.—**nasal,** (*Anat.*) nasal fossa.—**orbitária,** (*Anat.*) orbital fossa.—**pituitária,** (*Anat.*) fossa hypophyseos.—**pterigoídea,** (*Anat.*) pterigoid fossa.—**séptica,** septic tank.—**zigomática,** (*Anat.*) zygomatic fossa.

fossado (*m.*) trench, ditch; foray.

fossar (*v.t.,v.i.*) to root (as a pig); to dig; to nose about.

fossário (*m.*) gravedigger; cemetery.

fosse, fôsseis, fossem, fôssemos, fosses, forms of IR [53] and SER [76].

fosseta [ê] (*f.*) a small FOSSA.

fossete [ê] (*m.*) a small FOSSO.

fóssil [-seis] (*adj.; m.*) fossil.

fossilífero –**ra** (*adj.*) fossiliferous.

fossilismo (*m.*) fondness for antiquities; fogyism.

fossilização (*f.*) fossilization.
fossilizar (*v.t.,v.r.*) to fossilize.
fossiloligia (*f.*) = PALEONTOLOGIA.
fôsso [fossos (fó)] (*m.*) trench, ditch; pit; gutter; moat.
foste, fostes, forms of IR [53] and SER [76].
fot. = FOTÓGRAFO (photographer).
fota (*f.*) turban.
fotelétrico –ca (*adj., Physics*) photoelectric.
fótico –ca (*adj.*) photic.
foto (*f.*) photo.—**fixa,** still shot.
fotoactínico –ca (*adj.*) photoactinic.
fotoanisotropia (*f.*) photoanisotropy.
fotoativo –va (*adj.*) photoactive.
fotobactéria (*f.*) photobacterium.
fotobático –ca (*adj.*) photobathic.
fotocarta (*f.*) air map.
fotocatálise (*f., Physical Chem.*) photocatalysis.
fotocela, fotocélula (*f., Physics.*) photoelectric cell.
fotocinesia (*f., Physiol.*) photokinesis.
fotocinético –ca (*adj.*) photokinetic.
fotocomposição (*f., Print.*) photocomposition.
fotocondutibilidade (*f,. Elec.*) photoconductivity.
fotocópia (*f.*) photocopy.
fotocromático –ca (*adj.*) photochromatic.
fotocromia (*f.*) photochromy, color photography.
fotocronógrafo (*m., Physics.*) photocronograph.
fotodesintegração (*f., Phys. Chem.*) photodecomposition.
fotodinâmica (*f., Physiol.*) photodynamics.
fotodisforia (*f., Med.*) photophobia.
fotodissociação (*f., Physical Chem.*) photo-dissociation.
fotoelétrico –ca (*adj.*) = FOTELÉTRICO.
fotoelétron (*m., Physical Chem.*) photoelectron.
fotoemissão (*f., Physics*) photoelectric emission.
fotofobia (*f., Med.*) photophobia.
fotófobo –ba (*adj.; m.,f.*) photophobe.
fotoforese (*f., Physical Chem.*) photophoresis.
fotogalvanografia (*f.*) photogalvanography.
fotogênico –ca (*adj.*) photogenic.
fotogênio (*m.*) photogen (a light oil).
fotografar (*v.t.*) to photograph.
fotografia (*f.*) photography; a photograph.—**aérea,** aerial photograph.—**estática,** a still photograph.
fotográfico –ca (*adj.*) photographic.
fotógrafo –fa (*m.,f.*) photographer.
fotogrametria (*f.*) photogrammetry.
fotogravura (*f.*) photogravure; photoengraving.
fotoheliógrafo (*m., Astron.*) photoheliograph.
fotoionização (*f., Physical Chem.*) photoionization.
fotólise (*f.*) photolysis.
fotolítico –ca (*adj.*) photolytic.
fotolitografar (*v.t.*) to photolithograph.
fotolitografia (*f.*) photolithography.
fotologia (*f.*) photology, optics, photics.
fotoluminescência (*f., Physics*) photoluminescence.
fotomecânico –ca (*adj.*) photomechanical.
fotometria (*f.*) photometry.
fotômetro (*m., Physics*) photometer.
fotomicrografia (*f.*) photomicrography.
fóton (*m., Optics*) photon.
fotonêutron (*m., Physical Chem.*) photoneutron.
fotoquímico –ca (*adj.*) photochemical; (*f.*) photochemistry.
fotorradiograma (*m.*) photoradiogram.
fotoscópio (*m., Physics*) photoscope.
fotosfera (*f., Astron.*) photosphere.
fotossensibilidade (*f., Physics*) photosensitivity.
fotossensível (*adj., Physics*) photosensitive.
fotossíntese (*f., Chem., Physiol., Plant Physiol.*) photosynthesis.
fotostático –ca (*adj.*) photostatic.
fotóstato (*m.*) photostat.
fototaxia [ks] (*f., Biol.*) phototaxis.
fototelegrafia (*f.*) phototelegraphy.
fototerapia (*f.*) phototherapy.
fototérmico –ca (*adj.*) photothermic.
fototipia (*f.*) phototypy.
fotótipo (*m.*) cut, printing plate.
fototipografia (*f.*) phototypography.
fototopografia (*f.*) phototopography, photogrammetry.
fototropia (*f., Physical Chem.*) phototropism.
fototropismo (*m., Biol.*) phototropism.
fotovoltaico –ca (*adj.*) photovoltaic; photoelectric.
fotozincografia (*f.*) photozincography.
fouce (*f.*) & derivs. = FOICE & derivs.
fouveiro –ra (*adj.*) of horses, chestnut.

fóvea (*f.*) pit, fossa; (*Bot., Anat.*) fovea.
fovéola (*f., Bot.*) foveola.
foveolado –da, **foveolar** (*adj., Bot., Zool.*) foveolate.
fox [ks] (*m.*) fox terrier; fox trot.
foxtrote [ks] (*m.*) fox trot.
foz (*f.*) mouth of a river.
Fr. = FREI (Fra).
fracalhão –lhona (*adj.*) weakly, cowardly, (*m.,f.*) weakling, milksop, coward.
fração (*f.*) fraction; fracture, breaking.
fraca-roupa (*m.,f., colloq.*) a shabby or shabby-genteel person.
fracassado –da (*m.*) a failure; ruined man (*adj.*) unsuccessful.
fracassar (*v.i.*) to collapse, fail utterly; to miscarry; to crash; (*v.t.*) to shatter, smash.
fracasso (*m.*) failure, collapse; ruin; crash; "flop".
fracatear (*v.i.*) to let down, weaken.
fracativo –va (*adj., slang*) puny; miserable; pitifully small or ridiculous.
fracionamento (*m.*) a breaking up; (*Chem.*) fractionation.
fracionar (*v.t.,v.r.*) to break up (into pieces); to divide into fractions; (*Chem.*) to fractionate.
fracionário –ria (*adj.*) fractional.
fraco –ca (*adj.*) weak, feeble; frail; faint; defenseless; weak-kneed; thin, watery.—**de memória,** forgetful.—**do peito,** predisposed to tuberculosis of the lungs; (*m.,f.*) weakling; (*m.*) weakness, foible. **Êle tem um—para bebida,** He has a weakness for drink.
fradaço, fradalhão (*m.*) fat friar. [*Derogatory.*]
fradalhada, fradaria (*f.*) monks collectively. [*Derogatory.*]
fradar-se (*v.r.*) to become a monk or nun.
frade (*m.*) friar, monk; stone post; a mole cricket; (*Zool.*) an avocet (*Recurvirostra avosetta*); another bird called ALFAIATE; a black angelfish (*Pomocanthus*); other fishes c.a. PARU, CANHANHA.—**carmelita,** a Carmelite.—**fedorento,** harvestman (daddy longlegs).—**leigo,** lay brother. —**s menores,** Franciscans.—**s prêtos,** Benedictines.
fradesco –ca [ê] (*adj.*) monklike.
fradice (*f.*) monk's speech or behavior.
fradinho (*m.*) kind of edible bean; a macruran crustacean (*Scyllarus sp.*).—**de-mão-furada,** imp, hobgoblin.
fraga (*f.*) crag, rock; bluff; rocky road.
fragal (*adj.*) craggy, rocky; (*m.*) crags.
fragalheiro (*m.*) rag picker.
fragalhotear (*v.i.*) to make merry, play.
fragária (*f.*) strawberry plant.
fragata (*f.*) frigate; frigate bird, c.a. ALCATRAZ; a sailfish (*Istiophorus volador*), c.a. AGULHÃO-BANDEIRA, PEIXE-VELA.—**portuguêsa,** (*Zool.*) Portuguese Man-of-War (*Physalia arethusa*), c.a. CARAVELA.
fragateiro –ra (*adj.*) licentious; (*m.*) bargeman.
fragatim (*m.*) brigantine [= BERGANTIM].
frágil [-geis] (*adj.*) fragile, brittle; delicate; flimsy; frail, weak.
fragilidade (*f.*) fragility, brittleness; frailty.
fragilíssimo –ma, **fragílimo** –ma (*absol. superl. of* FRÁGIL) most fragile.
fragmentação (*f.*) fragmentation; splintering; breakage.
fragmentar (*v.t.*) to break into fragments, shatter; (*v.r.*) to crumble.
fragmentário –ria (*adj.*) fragmentary, piecemeal.
fragmite (*m., Bot.*) common reed (*Phragmites communis*).
fragmento (*m.*) fragment, scrap, splinter, part broken off; fraction.
fragmose (*f., Zool.*) phragmosis.
frago (*m.*) dung or other spoor of wild animals.
fragoído (*m.*) noise, din.
fragor [ô] (*m.*) loud crashing noise, din.
fragoroso –sa (*adj.*) loud, noisy.
fragosidade (*f.*) abruptness, ruggedness, cragginess.
fragoso –sa (*adj.*) craggy; rugged.
fragrância (*f.*) fragrance, perfume, aroma.
fragrante (*adj.*) fragrant, aromatic.
frágua (*f.*) furnace, forge; great heat; sorrow, bitterness.
fraguar (*v.*) = FORJAR.
fraguedo [ê] (*m.*) crags.
fragueiro –ra (*adj.*) rugged, hardy; coarse, rude; independent; hardworking; (*m.*) woodcutter; quarryman; riverboat pilot; (*Bot.*) a buttonweed (*Diodia prostrata*).
fragura (*f.*) ruggedness, cragginess [= FRAGOSIDADE].
frajola (*adj., slang*) swell (stylish).
fralda (*f.*) shirttail; diaper; skirt; flap.—**do mar,** beach. —**do monte,** foothill.—**rota** = GALO (moonfish).

fraldear (v.t.) to skirt (a hill, a marsh, etc.).
fraldeiro –ra (adj.) = FRALDIQUEIRO.
fraldilha (f.) leather apron.
fraldi[s]queiro –ra (adj.) effeminate. **cão—**, lap dog.
framboesa [ê] (f.) raspberry (fruit).
framboeseira (f.), **framboseiro** (m.) raspberry (plant).
framboesia (f., Med.) yaws, frambesia.
frança (f.) coquette, flirt; (m.) coxcomb; (pl.) tree branches; (adj.) foppish; [cap.] (f.) France.
francalete [lê] (m.) strap with buckle.
francatripa (f.) puppet.
francear (v.t.) to trim tree branches.
francelho –lha [ê] (m.) cheese mold; prattler; (m.,f.) one having an exaggerated fondness for France or who makes excessive use of gallicisms; (m., Zool.) a kestrel (Falco tinnunculus).
francês –cêsa (adj.) French; (m.) a Frenchman; the F. language; (f.) French woman.
francesia (f.) Frenchiness.
francesiar (v.i.) to speak French badly.
francesismo (m.) gallicism; Frenchism; Frenchiness.
franchinote (m.) jackanapes, whippersnapper.
Francisca (f.) Frances.
Francisco (m.) Francis.
franciscano –na (adj.; m.) Franciscan; (f.) the Order of St. Francis.
Franc.º = FRANCISCO (Francis).
franco –ca (adj.) frank (para com, towards; em, in); free, sincere, guileless; candid, outspoken, forthright; straightforward, aboveboard; overt; (m.) franc.—**a bordo**, free on board, F.O.B.—**de porte**, postpaid. **entrada—**, free admission. **porto—**, free port.
franco-atirador (m.) sniper; by ext. a lone wolf.
francófilo –la (adj.; m.,f.) francophile.
francófobo (adj.; m.,f.) francophobe.
franco-maçom (m.) freemason.
franco-maçonaria (f.) freemasonry.
frandulagem (f.) gang of ragamuffins; junk.
franduno –na (adj.) affectedly foreign in manner.
franga (m.) pullet.—**do-rio** = RABILA (a gallinule).
frangainha [a-i] (f.) young pullet.
frangainho [a-i] (m.) young cockerel.
frangalheiro –ra (adj.) ragged, tattered; (m.,f.) ragamuffin.
frangalho (m.) rag, tatter.
frangalhona (f.) slattern.
frangalhote (m.) cockerel; (colloq.) a stripling; whippersnapper.
franganito, franganote (m.) young cockerel; fig. young whippersnapper.
frângão, frangão [-gãos] (m.) young domestic cock.
frangelha [ê] (f.) cheese hoop.
franger, frangir (v.) = FRANZIR.
frangibilidade (f.) frangibility, brittleness.
frangipana (f.) frangipani (perfume); frangipane (pastry).
frangível (adj.) frangible, breakable, brittle.
frango (m.) cockerel, young chicken, fryer; a dry ear of corn or one which has been roasted; in soccer, an easy shot which the goalkeeper fails to stop; (Zool.) = CAÇÃO-FRANÇO (a shark).—**d'água**, any of numerous rails, crakes and gallinules, esp. the white-throated rail (Porzana albicollis), c.a. SANÃ, SARACURA; the Brazilian crake (Laterallus melanophaius), c.a. AÇANÃ, PINTO-D'ÁGUA; the red-and-white crake (Laterallus leucopyrrhus), c.a. PINTO-D'ÁGUA; the purple gallinule (Porphyrula martinica), c.a. SARACURA-DA-CANARANA, FRANGO-D'ÁGUA-AZUL; the Brazilian gallinule (Gallinula chloropus galeata), c.a. RABILA; the red-gartered coot (Fulica armillata), c.a. CARQUEJA, MERGULHÃO.—**de-botica**, young blade, young buck, "drugstore cowboy".
frangote (m.) young cockerel; (colloq.) growing boy.
franguinha (f.) pullet; (colloq.) flapper, teenager.
frângula (f.) frangula, the glossy buckthorn (Rhamnus frangula).
frangulina (f., Chem.) frangulin.
franja (f.) fringe; tassels; bang (hair on the forehead).
franjado –da (adj.) fringed; overdressed.
franjar (v.t.) to provide with a fringe; to overdress.
frankeniácea (f., Bot.) a sea heath (Frankenia sp.).
franklinita (f., Min.) franklinite.
franquear (v.t.) to frank, exempt from duties, carrying charges, postage, etc.; to facilitate the passage of; to enable to pass freely (as through a port).—**as dificuldades** or **o campo**, to clear away obstacles and difficulties.
franqueável (adj.) frankable.

franqueio (m.) franking (of mail).
franqueira (f.) a certain type of pointed knife made in Franca (State of São Paulo).
franqueiro (m.) a type of full-bodied cattle with large horns; (colloq.) a man whose wife is unfaithful. Cf. CÔRNO.
franqueza [ê] (f.) frankness, sincerity.
franquia (f.) exemption, immunity; free entry; franchise; postage.—**democrática**, democratic freedom.
franzimento (m.) wrinkling; pleating; shirring.
franzino –na (adj.) slender, thin; frail; puny.—**de corpo**, slight of build.
franzir (v.t.) to wrinkle, furrow; to fold, pleat; to crimp, (Sewing) to shirr.—**a testa**, to wrinkle the forehead; to raise the eyebrows; to scowl.—**as sobrancelhas** or **o(s) sobrolho(s)**, to frown, scowl.
fraque (m.) cutaway (coat).
fraquear, fraquejar, to grow weak; to lose vigor; to flag; to give up; to sag.
fraquete [êt] (adj.) somewhat weak.
fraqueza [ê] (f.) weakness; frailty; foible; shortcoming; faintness; helplessness.—**do peito**, predisposition to tuberculosis of the lungs.—**no sangue**, (colloq.) anemia. **dar na—**, to grow weak, languid.
frasca (f.) dishes; kitchen utensils; provisions.
frascaria (f.) dissoluteness.
frascário –ria (adj., colloq.) dissolute, licentious, lewd.
frasco (m.) vial, perfume or medicine bottle; flask.—**lavador**, (Chem.) wash bottle.
frase (f.) phrase, sentence or expression.—**feita**, an idiom or colloquialism; stock phrase; cliché. **fazer—s**, to indulge in highfalutin language. **uma—de espírito**, a witty remark. **uma—redonda**, a well-turned, polished, sentence.
fraseado –da (adj.) phrased; (m.) a phrase; (Music) phrasing.
fraseador –dora (adj.) phrasing; (m.,f.) phraser.
frasear (v.t.,v.i.) to phrase.
fraseologia (f.) phraseology.
frasqueiro –ra (adj.) licentious; of gowns, very low-cut; (f.) cellaret.
fraterna (f.) see FRATERNO.
fraternal (adj.) fraternal; affectionate.
fraternidade (f.) fraternity, brotherhood, brotherliness, brotherly-love. [But not fraternity in the sense of club, society, etc., which is ASSOCIAÇÃO, CONFRARIA, GRÊMIO.]
fraternização (f.) fraternization, fraternizing.
fraternizar (v.t.,v.i.,v.r.) to fraternize (com, with).
fraterno –na (adj.) fraternal, brotherly; (f.) friendly reprimand.
fratricida (adj.) fratricidal; (m.,f.) a fratricide.
fratricídio (m.) fratricide; by ext., civil war.
fratura (f.) fracture; (Geol.) fault.—**cominutiva**, (Surg.) comminuted fracture.—**complicada**, (Surg.) complicated fracture.—**composta**, (Surg.) compound fracture.
fraturar (v.t.) to fracture.
fraudação (f.) defraudation.
fraudador –dora (adj.) defrauding; (m.,f.) defrauder; smuggler.
fraudar (v.t.) to defraud, cheat, dupe; to smuggle.
fraudatário –ria (adj.) fraudulent.
fraude (m.) fraud, deception, imposture, trick, cheat; fake.
fraudulento –ta, fraudento –ta, frauduloso –sa (adj.) fraudulent, crooked, dishonest.
frauta (f.) = FLAUTA.
frauteiro –ra (m.,f.) = FLAUTISTA.
fraxetina [ks] (f., Chem.) fraxetin.
fraxina [ks] (f., Chem.) fraxin.
fraxinela [ks] (f.) the fraxinella or gas plant (Dictamnus albus).
frear (v.t.) to brake; to slow down; to restrain, curb. Cf. ENFREAR, FRENAR, REFREAR.
frecha, frechada (f.) = FLECHA, FLECHADA.
frechal (m., Const.) wall plate.
frecha-peixe (m.) = MARTIM-PESCADOR.
frechar (v.) = FLECHAR.
frecheira (f.) loophole (in a wall) = SETEIRA. [A loophole in the sense of means of escape or evasion is ESCAPATÓRIA, SAÍDA.]; (Zool.) a stingless bee (Melipona timida), c.a. LAMBE-OLHOS.
frecheiro (m.) = FLECHEIRO.
Frederica (f.) Frederica.
Frederico (m.) Frederic(k).

frega (*f., colloq.*) prostitute.

frege (*m.*) fracas, brawl.—-môscas, a "greasy spoon" (dirty eating place).

fregereba (*f.*) the tripletail or flasher (*Lobotes surinamensis*)—a large edible marine fish.

fregista (*m.*) proprietor of a dirty tavern; a waiter in the same.

fregona (*f.*) kitchen drudge.

freguês (*m.*), **-guêsa** (*f.*) customer, client; patron(ess); a person to whom one sells, or one from whom one buys, regularly; a parishioner; any "party" (person). à vontade do—, just as the customer wishes. Que—besta! What a stupid "character"!

freguesia (*f.*) parish; customers (collectively); patronage.

frei (*m.*) fra (Brother).—-bode, (*colloq.*) a Protestant.

freibergita (*f., Min.*) freibergite.

freijó, frei-jorge (*m.*) the Goeldi cordia (*C. goeldiana*), which yields a strong, light wood (known commercially as cordia or jenny wood), used in airplane propellers and fine interior cabinet work and furniture. Other names are FREJÓ, QUIRI, QUIRIM.

freima (*f.*) impatience, impetuosity, eagerness.

freimão (*m.*) = FLEGMÃO, FLEIMÃO.

freio (*m.*) brake; bit (of a bridle); check, curb; (*Anat.*) frenum.—aerodinâmico,—de ar, (*Aeron.*) air brake.—de ar comprimido,—pneumático, (*Mach.*) air brake.—de mão, hand brake.—de pé, foot brake.—de emergência or de socorro, emergency brake.—de Prony, Prony brake.—electromagnético, electromagnetic brake.—de vácuo, vacuum brake.

freira (*f.*) nun, sister.

freirático –ca, **freiral** (*adj.*) monastic, monasterial.

freirar (*v.i.*) to live as a monk or nun; (*v.r.*) to become a monk or nun.

freire (*m.*) friar, monk, brother; a butterfly fish called BORBOLETA.

freiria (*f.*) convent of nuns.

freirinha (*f.*) novice nun; a box crab (*Calappa sp.*).

freixal, freixial (*m.*) grove of ash trees.

freixo (*m., Bot.*) ash (*Fraxinus*).

fremente (*adj.*) roaring, booming; quivering, trembling; rustling, fluttering.

fremir [25] (*v.i.*) to roar; to flutter, rustle; to tremble, quiver.

frêmito (*m.*) roar(ing); resonance; fluttering; quivering; thrill; (*Med.*) fremitus.

frenação, frenagem (*f.*) act of braking.

frenar (*v.t.*) to brake, Cf. FREAR, ENFREAR.

frender (*v.i.*) to gnash (grind) the teeth.

frenesi [í] (*m.*) frenzy, madness; delirium; transport, rapture. Var. FRENESIM.

frenético –ca (*adj.*) phrenetic, splenetic; frantic; delirious, raving; excited.

frênico –ca (*adj.*) phrenic, diaphragmatic.

frenologia (*f.*) phrenology.

frenologista (*m.,f.*) phrenologist.

frenopatia (*f.*) mental disease.

frente (*f.*) front, face, frontage; façade.—a—, face to face.—fria (quente), (*Meteor.*) cold (hot) front. à—, ahead, in front, at the front, forward, toward the front. à (sua)—, in front of (him). de—, in front of. de—para, facing (towards). de—para trás, from front to rear (back). em—a (de), in front of, facing. fazer—a, to face, withstand. fazer—a uma dificuldade, to take the bull by the horns. na—, ahead, in front, out in front. na (sua)—, in front of (him). na—de, in front of. olhar (alguém) de—, to look directly at (someone). para (a)—, onward, forward. pela—, in front. sala da—, front room.

freon (*m., Chem.*) freon.

freqüência (*f.*) frequency; attendance (persons present). —da classe, (*Stat.*) class frequency.—de batida, (*Radio*) beat frequency.—relativa, (*Stat.*) relative frequency.—ultra alta, (*Elec.*) U.H. frequency.—alta, (*Radio*) high frequency. com—, frequently, often.

freqüencímetro (*m., Elec.*) frequency meter.

freqüentação (*f.*) frequenting.

freqüentador –dora (*adj.*) frequenting; (*m.,f.*) frequenter. —assíduo dos cinemas, a steady moviegoer.

freqüentar (*v.t.*) to frequent, visit often, attend regularly.

freqüente (*adj.*) frequent; common; habitual; constant.

fresa (*f., Mach.*) milling machine; milling cutter.—angular, angle milling cutter.—de duplo ângulo, double-angle milling cutter.—helicoidal, spiral milling cutter.—

de ranhuras, grooving mill.

fresador (*m.*) operator of a metal milling machine.

fresadora (*f.*) a metal milling machine [= FRESA].

fresagem (*f.*) milling (of metals).

fresar (*v.t.*) to mill (metal); to remove metal by milling.

fresca [ê] (*f.*) see FRESCO.

frescal (*adj.*) fresh; youthful.

frescalhão –lhona (*adj.*) very fresh; well-preserved, sprightly.

fresco –ca [ê] (*adj.*) cool, chilly; fresh, refreshing; unfaded; vigorous; not stale, sweet; (*m.*) fresh air; a fresco (painting). ao—, in the open (air). de—, recently, freshly. ir tomar—, to go for an airing. pôr-se ao—, to take to one's heels. tinta—, wet paint; (*f.*) cool evening breeze. à—, coolly dressed.

frescor [ô] (*m.*) freshness; fresh wind.

frescura (*f.*) freshness, coolness.

frese (*f.*) = FRESA.

frésia (*f., Bot.*) common freesia (*F. refracta*).

fresquidão (*f.*) freshness, coolness [= FRESCOR].

fressura (*f.*) lights and other animal viscera (when used as food).

fresta (*f.*) loophole, vent, small window; gap, aperture.

frestão (*m.*) an ogival window.

fretado –da (*adj.*) hired, chartered.

fretador [ô] (*m.*) freighter (person).

fretagem (*f.*) freightage.

fretamento (*m.*) charter party (shipping indenture); freightage.

fretar (*v.t.*) to freight, charter, let or hire for transportation.

frete (*m.*) freight, freightage; cargo; lading.

fretenir (*v.i.*) to chirr (as a cicada); = ZIZIAR.

frevo [ê] (*m.*) shindig, wild dance, esp. at carnival time; rumpus; brawl. (The word derives from FERVER, to boil.]

friabilidade (*f.*) friability.

friacho –cha (*adj.*) somewhat chilly.

friagem (*f.*) cold spell; cold-damage to plants.

frialdade (*f.*) coldness; low temperature; cold weather; frigidity; insensibility.

friável (*adj.*) friable, crumbly.

fricandó (*m.*) fricandeau.

fricassé (*m.*) fricassée.

fricativo –va (*adj., Phonet.*) fricative.

fricção (*f.*) rubbing, massaging.—de álcool. an alcohol rub. [But not friction, in the sense of attrition, which is ATRITO.]

friccionar (*v.t.*) to rub, massage.

frieira (*f.*) chilblain; cold spell; (*slang*) intense hunger.

frieirão –rona (*adj.*) dull, insipid; (*m.,f.*) dull, timid person.

friento –ta (*adj.*) = FRIORENTO.

frieza [ê] (*f.*) coldness, chilliness; frigidness; indifference, coolness.—de ânimo, coldbloodedness.

frigideira (*f.*) frying pan; (*m.*) a show-off.

frigidez [ê] (*f.*) frigidity.

frigidíssimo –ma (*absol. superl. of* FRIO) most cold.

frígido –da (*adj.*) frigid, cold.

frígio –gia (*adj.; m.,f.*) Phrygian.

frigir [24, 49] (*v.t.*) to fry; to pester; (*v.i.*) to show off.

frigorífero –ra (*adj.*) frigorific; (*m.*) a freezing mixture; a freezer; cold storage plant.

frigorificar (*v.t.*) to chill, freeze (meat, etc.).

frigorífico (*m.*) cold storage plant; freezer; refrigerator. [*Webster:* "A South American slaughtering establishment primarily for the exportation of frozen meat."]

friíssimo –ma [i-í] (*absol. superl. of* FRIO) most cold.

frincha (*f.*) crack, chink.

fringilídeo –dea (*adj., Zool.*) fringilline, finchlike; (*m.pl.*) the Fringillidae (finches and sparrows).

frinina (*f., Chem.*) phrynin.

frio –ria (*adj.*) cold; frigid; stiff, standoffish; unemotional; lifeless. bem—, quite cold; (*m.*) cold; coldness, frigidity; (*pl.*) cold cuts (of meat).

frioleira (*f.*) silk tuft or tassel; trifle; bagatelle, bauble.

friorento –ta (*adj.*) very sensitive to cold [= FRIENTO.]

frisa (*f.*) frieze (cloth); theater box (on the main floor).

frisado –da (*adj.*) frizzled, crisp, curly, fuzzy; (*Arch.*) having a frieze or friezes; (*m.*) frizzled hair.

frisador (*m.*) curling iron.

frisagem (*f.*) curling, frizzling.

frisante (*adj.*) emphatic, significant, telling. um exêmplo—, a striking example.

frisão (*adj.; m.*) Frisian.

frisar (*v.t.*) to frizzle, curl, crisp; to stress, emphasize; to underscore.—**com**, to jibe with.

friso (*m.*) crease (as of trousers); (*Arch.*) frieze.

frita (*f.*) fried food; (*Ceramics*) frit.

fritada (*f.*) a dish of eggs scrambled with shrimp, or chopped meat or vegetables; a batch of anything fried.

fritalhada, fritangada (*f.*) a large quantity of poorly fried food.

fritar (*v.t.*) to fry [= FRIGIR].

frito –**ta** (*adj.; irreg. p.p. of* FRIGIR) fried; (*slang*) broke. **estar**—, to be sunk (done for); to be in a mess (fine fix); (*m.*) fritter.

fritura (*f.*) fritter; any fried dish.

friúra (*f.*) coldness.

frivolidade, frivoleza (*f.*) frivolity.

frívolo –**la** (*adj.*) frivolous, trifling, trivial; flippant; light, giddy; sportive.

froco (*m.*) snow flake; chenille.—**rasteiro**, (*Bot.*) a clubmoss (*Lycopodium*).

frolo (*m.*) a rustling of silk, froufrou.

FRONAPE = FROTA NACIONAL DE PETROLEIROS [National Fleet of Oil Tankers].

frondar (*v.i.*) to form fronds, develop leafy foliage.

fronde (*f.*) frond, esp. of palms and ferns; leafy foliage.

fronde[j]ar (*v.i.*) to frondesce.

frondente, frondeo –**dea** (*adj.*) having fronds.

frondescência (*f.*) frondescence.

frondícola (*adj.*) living in trees.

frondífero –**ra** (*adj.*) frondiferous.

frondiforme (*adj.*) frondiform.

frondoso –**sa** (*adj.*) frondose, leafy.

fronha (*f.*) pillowcase; pillow.

frontaberto –**ta** (*adj.*) white-faced [horse].

frontal (*adj.*) frontal; (*m.*) frontlet; phylactery; front (of a bridle). **parede de**—, partition wall.

frontaleira (*f.*) front altar cloth.

frontão (*m.*) a pediment; a court surrounded by high walls in which the game of PELOTA (jai alai) is played.

frontaria (*f.*) façade; front; frontispiece (of a building).

fronte (*f.*) forehead; front.

frontear (*v.t.,v.i.*) to front [= DEFRONTAR].

fronteira (*f.*) see FRONTEIRO.

fronteiriço –**ça** (*adj.*) frontier; borderline; (*m.*) frontiersman.

fronteiro –**ra** (*adj.*) fronting, facing; frontier; white-faced [cattle].—**a**, facing; in front of; (*f.*) frontier, border.

frontino –**na** (*adj.*) having a white blaze [horse].

frontispício (*m., Arch.*) façade, frontispiece; title page of a book [but not its frontispiece, which is ANTE-ROSTO.]; (*colloq.*) mug (face). Cf. FACHADA.

frontonasal (*adj., Zool., Anat.*) frontonasal.

frontoparietal (*adj., Zool. , Anat.*) frontoparietal.

frota (*f.*) fleet.

frouva (*f., Zool.*) rook (*Corvus frugilegus*), ca. GRALHA-CALVA.

frouxel (*m.*) down, fluff, soft plumage; fuzz.

frouxelado –**da** (*adj.*) downy, fluffy; fuzzy.

frouxidão, frouxeza [ê], **frouxidade, frouxura** (*f.*) looseness, slackness; sluggishness.

frouxo –**xa** (*adj.*) loose, slack; dull, inactive; limp, limber; flabby; cowardly; (*colloq.*) impotent. **parafuso**—, loose screw (in the head); (*m.*) flux.—**de riso**, a fit of laughter. —**de sangue**, hemorrhage.

frufru (*m.*) froufrou, a rustling (as of silk skirts).

frufrulhar, frufrutar (*v.i.*) to rustle (as silk or leaves).

frugal (*adj.*) frugal.

frugalidade (*f.*) frugality.

frugífero –**ra** (*adj.*) frugiferous.

frugívoro –**ra** (*adj., Zool.*) frugivorous, feeding on fruit; (*m. pl.*) the Frugivora (fruit bats).

fruição [u-i] (*f.*) fruition.

fruir [25] (*v.i.*) to enjoy, have fruition of, profit from.

fruíta (*f.*) the fruit of the JABUTICABEIRA; a kind of manioc flour and pepper cake, c.a. DOCE-DE-PIMENTA.

fruiteira (*f.*) = JABUTICABEIRA.

fruitivo –**va** (*adj.*) fruitive, enjoying, possessing; fruitful.

fruito (*m.*) = FRUTO.

frumental, frumentáceo –**cea, frumentício** –**cia** (*adj.*) frumentaceous.

frumento (*m.*) any grain, esp. wheat.

frumentoso –**sa** (*adj.*) fruitful in grain.

fruncho, frunco, frúnculo, popular forms of FURÚNCULO.

frusto –**ta** (*adj.*) worn [coin]; weather-beaten [sculpture]; rough; (*Med.*) benign.

frustração (*f.*) frustration; defeat.

frustrado –**da** (*adj.*) frustrated, unsuccessful.

frustrador –**dora** (*adj.*) frustrating; baffling.

frustrar (*v.t.*) to frustrate, disappoint, thwart, bring to naught; to defeat, baffle, foil; (*v.r.*) to fail, miscarry, come to nothing.

frustratório –**ria** (*adj.*) frustrating; illusory, fallacious.

fruta (*f.*) any edible fruit; also, a combining term for many kinds of plants. Cf. FRUTO.—**bôlsa**, balloonvine· heart-seed (*Cardiospermum halicacabum*).—**cota**, suakwa vegetablesponge (*Luffa cylindrica*).—**de-arara** = ANDÁ-AÇU.—**de-babado** = CANUDO-DE-PITO.—**de-burro**, an annonaceous tree (*Xylopia xylopioides*) which yields a light and durable timber and aromatic medicinal berries, c.a. PIMENTA-DE-BUGRE, PIMENTA-DE-MACACO, PIMENTEIRA-DA-TERRA, PIMENTEIRA-DO-SERTÃO.—**de-conde**, the fruit of the sweetsop or sugar apple (*Annona squamosa*), c.a. ATA, PINHA.—**de-condêssa**, the biriba (*Rollinia deliciosa*); also its fruit.—**de-conta** = JEQUIRITI.—**de-galo** = CORU-PIÁ.—**de-guará** = COUVETINGA.—**de-jacu**, the creeping sky-flower (*Duranta repens*), c.a. FRUTEIRA-DE-JACU, VIO-LETEIRA.—**de-jacu-fêmea**, a persimmon (*Diospyros hispida*).—**de-jacu-macho**, an ebony (*Maba inconstans*), c.a. FRUTO-DE-JACU-MACHO, FRUTO-DE-JACU-DO-MATO, MARIA-PRETA.—**de-lôbo**, kinds of nightshade, esp. *Solanum lycocarpum;* also = COUVETINGA.—**de-macaco**, a monkeypot tree (*Lecythis pisonis*) which yields valuable timber and edible sapucaia nuts; c.a. CASTANHA-SAPUCAIA, JAÇAPUCAIA, SAPUCAIA, SAPUCAIA-AÇU, SAPU-CAIA-DE-CASTANHA; another timber tree (*Posoqueria acutifolia*—family Rubiaceae), c.a. PAU-DE-MACACO, BACUPARI-MIÚDO.—**de-pomba** = CUIA-DO-BREJO.—**de-pombo** = GALINHA-CHOCA.—**de-sabiá**, tree which yield tobacco (*Acnistus arborescens*), c.a. MARIANA, MARIANEIRA.—**de-tatu**, the redrodwood eugenia (*E. supraaxillaris*).—**de-tucano** = CABELO-DE-NEGRO.—**de-paraíso**, the yellow-sweet tabernaemontana (*T. grandiflora*).—**estrelada** = FLOR-DE-ABRIL.—**pão**, breadfruit (*Artocarpus altilis*).—**pão-de-macaco**, baobab (*Andansonia digitata*).—**trilha** = ALPÃO.

frutar (*v.t.*) to fruit; to give rise to.

frutear (*v.i.*) to bear fruit.

fruteiro –**ra** (*adj.*) fruitful; fond of fruit; (*m.,f.*) fruit dish, basket or holder; fruit vender; (*f.*) fruit tree.—**de-cutia** or —**de-macaco** = CANUDO-DE-PITO.—**de-jacu** = FRUTA-DE-JACU.—**do-pão**, breadfruit (*Artocarpus altilis*) c.a. ÁRVORE-DO-PÃO.

frutescência (*f.*) the period of maturing of fruit.

frutescente (*adj.*) fruit-bearing.

frútice (*m.*) small shrub.

frutíceto (*m.*) fruit orchard.

fruticoso –**sa** (*adj., Bot.*) fruticose.

fruticuloso –**sa** (*adj., Bot.*) fruticulose.

fruticultor –**tora** (*m.,f.*) fruit grower.

fruticultura (*f.*) fruit-growing.

frutífero –**ra** (*adj.*) fruit-bearing; fruitful.

fruitificação (*f.*) fructification.

frutificar (*v.i.*) to bear fruit, be fruitful.

frutiforme (*adj.*) fructiform.

frutígero –**ra** (*adj.*) = FRUTÍFERO.

frutilha (*f.*) strawberry [= MORANGO].

frutívoro –**ra** (*adj.*) = FRUGÍVORO.

fruto (*m.*) fruit (in all senses). Cf. FRUTA.—**carnudo**, fleshy fruit (tomato, orange, apple, etc.).—**composto**, collective fruit (mulberry, fig, pineapple, etc.).—**de-imbê** = CIPÓ-DE-IMBÊ. —**de-jacu-do-mato**, —**de-jacu-macho** = FRUTA-DE-JACU-MACHO.—**deiscente**, dry-dehiscent fruit.—**de-morcêgo**, a pepper (*Piper geniculatum*), c.a. PIMENTA-DO-MATO, PIMENTA-DOS-ÍNDIOS.—**de-sabia**, the Brazil peppertree (*Schinus terebinthifolia*), c.a. AROEIRA-VERMELHA.—**desassazonado**, unripe fruit.—**encandilado**, candied or crystallized fruit.—**indeiscente**, dry-indehiscent fruit.—**proibido**, forbidden fruit. O—**proibido é o mais gostoso**, Stolen fruits are sweetest.

frutose (*f., Chem.*) d-fructose, levulose, fruit sugar.

frutuoso –**sa** (*adj.*) fruitful; prolific; productive.

fruxu (*f.*) a bird—the smoky-fronted tody-tyrant (*Todirostrum f. fumifrons*) c.a. TRUXU, TAXURI.

fs. = FAC-SÍMILE (facsimile).

ftalameto (*m., Chem.*) phthalamide.

ftalato (*m., Chem.*) phthalate.

ftaleína (*f., Chem.*) phthalein.

ftálico -ca (*adj.*, *Chem.*) phthalic.
ftalina (*f.*, *Chem.*) phthalin.
ftanito (*m.*, *Petrog.*) phthanite.
fuá (*adj.*) skittish [horse]; suspicious; (*m.*) gossip; dandruff.
fuão [fuãos, fuões] **fuã** [fuãs] (*m.,f.*) short for FULANO, -NA.
fubá (*m.*) cornmeal; (*colloq.*) fracas, brawl.—**de arroz**, rice flour.—**mimoso**, fine cornmeal.
fubana (*f.*, *colloq.*) prostitute.
fubeca (*f.*, *slang*) beating, defeat, trouncing (as of the opponent in a soccer or other game).
fubecar (*v.t.*) to trounce.
fubica (*m.*) a small, insignificant person.
fuça (*f.*) snout, muzzle, "mug". **irem-se às—**, (*slang*) to come to blows.
fucáceas (*f.pl.*) the Fucaceae (family of rockweeds and gulfweeds).
fucívoro -ra (*adj.*, *Zool.*) eating seaweeds.
fuco (*m.*) a genus (*Fucus*) of rockweeds.
fucóide (*adj.*, *Bot.*) fucoid.
fucose (*f.*, *Chem.*) fucose.
fucoxantina (*f.*, *Biochem.*) fucoxanthin.
fúcsia (*f.*, *Bot.*) any fuchsia, c.a. BRINCOS-DE-PRINCÊSA (princess' earrings), LÁGRIMAS-DE-JÓ (Job's tears).
fucsina (*f.*) fuchsine, fuchsin dye.
fucsita (*f.*, *Chem.*) fuchsite.
fueirada (*f.*) a blow with a stanchion.
fueiro (*m.*) car stake, stanchion; the rear half of a horse's belly.
fúfio -fia (*adj.*) common, ordinary; (*m.,f.*) a person who achieves greatness more by chance than by merit; (*f.*) conceit; pretentious woman; dance; party; revelry.
fuga (*f.*) flight, escape; hegira; (*Music*) fugue; (*Elec.*) leak.—**precipitada**, headlong flight, stampede, rout.
fugace (*adj.*) fugacious, fleeting; (*Bot.*) fugacious.
fugacidade (*f.*) fugacity.
fugalaça (*f.*) rope of a harpoon, or other long line for hunting or fishing; a postponement.
fugaz (*adj.*) fugacious, transitory; short-lived; brief, fleeting.
fugente (*adj.*) fleeing.
fugida (*f.*) = FUGA.
fugidiço -ca, fugidio -dia (*adj.*) fugitive; fleeting.
fugir [22] (*v.i.*) to flee, fly, escape, run away (**a, de,** from); to shun.—**ao assunto**, to digress.—**com o corpo**, to dodge. —**o mundo**, to flee the world.
fugitivo -va (*adj.*: *m.,f.*) fugitive, runaway.
fui, form of IR [53] and of SER [76].
fuinha [u-í] (*f.*) stone marten (*Mustela foina*), c.a. GAR-DUNHO; (*m.,f.*) pinchpenny; skinflint; gossiper; busy-body; hatchet-faced person.
fuinho [u-í] (*m.*) a kind of woodpecker called PICA-PAU-CINZENTO.
fujão -jona (*adj.*) scary, inclined to run away; (*m.,f.*) a runaway.
fujicar (*v.t.*) to mend or patch (old clothes).
fula (*adj.*) furious; mulatto; (*f.*) haste; blister; chop (oral cavity); large quantity; fulling of felt for hats; calender, roller; (*m.,f.*) a Sudanese Fulah, c.a. FULÁ.—**de raiva**, wild with rage. **à—**, in great haste.
Fulana (*f.*) Jane Doe.
Fulano (*m.*) John Doe.—, **Beltrano e Sicrano**, Tom, Dick and Harry.
fular (*m.*) foulard.
fulcro (*m.*) fulcrum; prop, support; oarlock.
fulgência (*f.*) effulgence.
fulgente (*adj.*) effulgent, resplendent.
fulgentear (*v.t.*) to cause to shine forth.
fúlgido -da (*adj.*) = FULGENTE.
fulgir [50] (*v.i.*) to shine; to be bright, brilliant; to be eminent, distinguished, conspicuous; to excel; (*v.t.*) to cause to radiate.
fulgor [ô] (*m.*) dazzling brightness; flash; glare; splendor.
fulguração (*f.*) a flashing of light or lightning.
fulgural (*adj.*) pert. to lightning.
fulgurância (*f.*) refulgence.
fulgurante (*adj.*) fulgurant, flashing, resplendent; (*Med.*) fulgurating.
fulgurar (*v.i.*) to fulgurate, flash (as lightning); to glare; to glisten, scintillate.
fulgurito (*m.*, *Geol.*) fulgurite.
fulguroso -sa (*adj.*) fulgurous, flashing.
fulheiro -ra (*adj.*) cheating; crooked, esp. at gambling;

(*m.,f.*) cheat, crook, sharper.
fuligem (*f.*) soot, grime, smut.—**de combustível**, fuel soot.
fuliginosidade (*f.*) sootiness.
fuliginoso -sa (*adj.*) fuliginous, sooty, smoky.
fulista (*m.,f.*) fuller (of felt for hats).
fulminação (*f.*) fulmination, detonation.
fulminado -da (*adj.*) blasted; stricken (as by lightning).
fulminador -dora (*adj.*) fulminating; (*m.,f.*) fulminator.
fulminante (*adj.*) fulminating; (*m.*) primer; fuse.
fulminar (*v.t.*) to fulminate, hurl threats, etc. (**contra**, against); to stun, blast, lay low.
fulminatório -ria (*adj.*) fulminating.
fulmíneo -nea (*adj.*) fulminous.
fulmínico -ca (*adj.*, *Chem.*) fulminic.
fulminoso -sa (*adj.*) fulminous.
fúlvido -da (*adj.*) fulvous.
fulvo -va (*adj.*) fulvous, tawny.
fumaça (*f.*) smoke; (*pl.*) airs (haughty manner); (*adj.*) smoke-colored. **cortina de—**, smoke screen. **sem—**, smokeless.
fumaceira (*f.*) a cloud of smoke.
fumada (*f.*) smoke; smoke signal; puff of smoke.
fumador -dora (*m.,f.*) smoker; (*m.*) a rubber tapper's smoking hut.
fumagem (*f.*) act of smoking; curing (of meats) by smoking.
fumagina (*f.*, *Plant Pathol.*) fumagine.
fumal (*m.*) tobacco field.
fumante (*adj.*) smoking; (*m.,f.*) a (tobacco) smoker.
fumar (*v.t.*) to smoke (tobacco); to cure by smoking; (*v.i.*) to emit smoke, steam; to fume, rage.
fumaraça, fumarada (*f.*) a quantity of smoke.
fumarar (*v.t.,v.i.*) to smoke.
fumarento -ta (*adj.*) smoky.
fumária (*f.*, *Bot.*) the drug fumitory (*Fumaria officinalis*), c.a. ERVA-MOLEIRINHA, FUMO-DA-TERRA, FEL-DA-TERRA.
fumárico -ca (*adj.*, *Chem.*) fumaric.
fumarina (*f.*, *Chem.*, *Pharm.*) fumarine, protopine.
fumarola (*f.*) fumarole.
fumável (*adj.*) suitable for smoking.
fumear (*v.*) = FUMEGAR.
fumega (*m.*) a small, unimportant person.
fumegante (*adj.*) smoking, steaming.
fumegar (*v.i.*) to emit smoke, steam.
fumeira (*f.*) tobacco pouch.
fumeiro (*m.*) chimney; smoky corner over an open fire; (*Zool.*) a grunt (*Anisotremus bicolor*), c.a. PIRAZUMBI. **carne de—**, smoked meat.
fúmeo -mea, fúmido -da, fumífero -ra, fumífico -ca (*adj.*) = FUMOSO.
fumigação (*f.*) fumigation.
fumigatório -ria (*adj.*) fumigating; (*m.*) fumigation.
fumígeno (*m.*) smudge pot.
fumista (*m.,f.*) smoker (of tobacco).
fumo (*m.*) smoke; vapor; tobacco; tobacco plant; vain airs; black mourning crepe.—**agreste**, Aztec tobacco (*Nicotiana rustica*), c.a. FUMO-BRASILEIRO, FUMO-DE-PAISANO.—**bravo** = COUVETINGA.—**bravo-de-per-nambuco**, a crownbeard (*Verbesina sp.*).—**bravo-do-amazonas**, a knotweed (*Polygonum hispidum*), c.a. TABACARANA.—**da-terra** = FUMÁRIA.—**de-angola** = DIAMBA.—**de-jardim**, winged tobacco (*Nicotiana alata*).—**de-palha**, a trifling matter; high-sounding but empty words.—**do-mato**,—**selvagem** = DIAMBA.—**em rama**, leaf tobacco.
fumosidade (*f.*) smokiness.
fumoso -sa (*adj.*) smoky; vain.
funambulesco -ca (*adj.*) fantastic, queer, exotic.
funâmbulo (*m.*) tightrope walker; by ext., a weathercock (fickle person).
funca (*m.,f.*) trifling thing or person; (*adj.*) bad.
funçanada, -nata (*f.*) big party or merry-making.
funçanista (*m.,f.*) merrymaker.
função (*f.*) function, performance; role, office, duty; party, ceremony. **em—de**, functioning as; in keeping with; in terms of.
funcho (*m.*, *Bot.*) common fennel (*Foeniculum vulgare*).— **anual**, the toothpick ammi (*A. visnaga*).—**bastardo** = ENDRÃO.—**da-china** = BADIANA.—**de-porco**, common hogfennel (*Peucedanum officinale*).—**doce**, Florence fennel (*Foeniculum dulce*).—**marinho**, the samphire (*Crithmum maritimum*), c.a. CRITMO, PERREXIL-DO-MAR. —**selvagem** = CICUTA-DA-EUROPA.
funcional (*adj.*) functional.

funcionalismo (m.) governmental bureaucracy; public servants (as a class).

funcionamento (m.) functioning, performance, operation.

funcionar (v.i.) to function, perform, operate; to run.

funcionário -ria (m.,f.) functionary, officeholder.—de banco, bank clerk.—público, government employee, civil servant, public officer, officeholder.

funçonata (f.) = FUNÇANATA.

funda (f.) sling (for hurling stones); truss (for hernias).

fundação (f.) foundation, base; donation, endowment; an endowed institution.

fundado -da (adj.) well-founded.

fundador -dora (adj.) founding; (m.,f.) founder.

fundagem (f.) sediment, residue.

fundamentado -da (adj.) well-founded, well-grounded, resting on facts, reasons, etc.

fundamental (adj.) fundamental, basic, essential.

fundamentar (v.t.) to lay a foundation for; to substantiate; to prove.—-se em, to base oneself on (facts, etc.).

fundamento (m.) basis, foundation, groundwork; reason, motive.

fundão (m.) whirlpool; deep bottom; faraway place.

fundar (v.t.) to found, build; to lay a foundation; to establish, institute; to endow; to fund (a debt); to make deeper; (v.r.) to base oneself (em, on).

fundeado -da (adj.) at anchor.

fundeadouro, fundeadoiro (m.) anchorage.

fundear (v.t.) to cast anchor.

fundeiro -ra (adj.) at or on the bottom; deep.

fundente (adj.) molten; fused; that promotes fusion; (m., Metal.) flux.

fundiário -ria (adj.) pert. to land.

fundição (f.) melting, fusion; iron, steel or other foundry. —em matrizes, die casting.

fundido -da (adj.) cast (iron, steel); molten.

fundidor (m.) founder, caster; foundryman.

fundilho (m.) seat (of trousers).

fundinho (m.) common name for rutile found in diamond beds [= AGULHA, FERRAGEM].

fundir [25] (v.t.) to cast (metal); to smelt; to melt, fuse; to amalgamate, blend; to merge; (v.r.) to fuse, melt.

fundível (adj.) fusible.

fundo -da (adj.) deep; profound; (slang) awkward; "dumb," dense; (m.) bottom; the depths; deepest part or place; scenic backdrop; background; profundity; fund, capital; back of a violin.—da agulha, eye of a needle.— de cêsto, (Radio) basket-weave coil.—-de-lima, a red-pepper (Capsicum umbilicatum).—de reserva, reserve fund.—de saco, (Anat.) fundus.—s públicos, public funds. a—, deeply, intimately; fully, thoroughly. ao—, at the end, in or to the bottom, at the back, in the rear. ao (no)—de, inside of, at the end of, at the bottom of. artigo de—, principal editorial or leading article in a newspaper. dar—, to cast anchor. do—da alma, from the bottom of the heart. marchar a um de—, to march in single file. no—, deep-set; at heart; at bottom; in-trinsically. nos—s da casa, in the back part of the house. prometer mundos e—s, to promise the moon. sem—, bottomless.

fundura (f.) depth (as of a well); (slang) ignorance.

fúnebre (adj.) funereal; lugubrious.

funeral (adj.) funereal; (m. pl.) funeral.

funerário -ria (adj.) funerary.

funéreo -rea (adj.) funereal.

funestar (v.t.) to render FUNESTO.

funesto -ta (adj.) bringing or portending death or evil; fatal; doleful; dire.

funfungagá (m.) = FUNGAGÁ.

funga (f.) dog distemper.

fungadela (f.) snuffle, sniff.

fungagá, fungangá (m., colloq.) corny (second-rate) band or orchestra.

fungão -gona (adj.) sniffling, snuffling; (m.,f.) snuffer; sniveller; snuff-taker; (m., colloq.) nose; snivelling child; mushroom, toadstool (mostly poisonous); fungus; (Plant Pathol.) ergot [= CRAVAGEM].

fungar (v.t.,v.i.) to sniff, snuff; (v.i.) to snore; to snort; to sniffle, snivel; to mutter, mumble.

fungicida (m.) fungicide.

fungívoro -ra (adj.) fungivorous.

fungo (m.) fungus; mushroom, toadstool; act of sniffing, smelling.

fungologista (m.,f.) fungologist, mycologist [= MICOLO-GISTA].

fungosidade (f.) fungosity.

fungoso -sa (adj.) fungous.

fungu (m.) voodooism, witchcraft.

funicular (adj.) funicular; (m.) funicular railway; cable car.

funículo (m., Bot.) funicle; (Anat.) funiculus.

funiforme (adj.) funiform, resembling a cord or rope.

funil (m.) funnel.—de decantação, or de separação, separatory funnel.

funilaria (f.) tinsmith's shop.

funileiro (m.) tinker; tinsmith.

fúnquia (f.) the genus of plantain lilies (Hosta, syn. Funkia).

fura (f.) a large hole made with bit or chisel.

fura-bôlo (m., colloq.) the index finger; a prying, meddle-some person.

fura-buxo (m.) a shearwater (Puffinus) or a petrel (Pterodroma).

furacão (m.) hurricane, tornado, cyclone, typhoon; whirl-wind, windstorm.

fura-capa (m., Bot.) a beggar's-tick (Bidens).

furacar (v.) = ESBURACAR.

furadeira (f.) boring machine.

furado -da (adj.) pierced through, perforated, punctured; worn through (as the sole of a shoe); bankrupt.

furador -dora (adj.) boring, perforating, piercing; (m.) awl, punch, perforator; bodkin.

fura-greve (m.) strikebreaker, "scab," "fink".

fura-mato (m.) a paroquet, c.a. TIRIBA.

furão (m.) a ferret; fig. a nosy, prying person; a go-getter, hustler; same as BARBEIRO (bug); (adj.) pushing, resource-ful, "go-getting".

fura-paredes (m.,f.) active, wide-awake person; "live wire"; (m., Bot.) the wall pellitory (Parietaria officinalis), c.a. ERVA-DE-SANT'ANNA, QUEBRA-PAREDE.

furar (v.t.) to pierce, perforate, drill, bore; to puncture; to penetrate; to defeat, thwart.—uma greve, to pass through a picket line. Água mole em pedra dura tanto bate até que fura, Constant dripping bores the stone.

fura-vidas (m.,f.) live wire, go-getter, hustler.

furbesco -ca [ê] (adj.) rascally, cunning.

furcífero -ra (adj., Zool.) furciferous.

furco (m.) the distance between the tips of the spread and extended thumb and forefinger.

fúrcula (f., Anat., Zool.) furculum, wishbone.

furdunçar (v.i.) to go on a spree; to raise hell.

furdunceiro -ra (adj.) hell-raising.

furdúncio, furdunço (m., colloq.) boisterous party; shindy, free-for-all, uproar.

furfuráceo -cea (adj.) furfuraceous, scurfy.

furfuramido (m., Chem.) furfuramid(e).

furfúreo -rea (adj.) = FURFURÁCEO.

furfurina (f., Chem.) furfurine.

furfurol (m., Chem.) furfural.

furgão (m.) baggage car; van.

fúria (f.) fury, furor, rage; impetuosity, fierceness; a spit-fire; a hag; (pl.) the Furies.

furibundo -da (adj.) full of fury, raging.

furiosidade (f.) furiousness.

furioso -sa (adj.) furious, infuriated; raving; fierce, ardent.

furna (f.) cave, cavern, den.

furo (m.) hole, perforation; a news scoop; "a natural channel of communication between two rivers or be-tween a river and a lake." [GBAT]

furoar (v.t.) to ferret out (facts, etc.).

furor [ô] (m.) furor, fury, rage; frenzy, excitement.— uterino, nymphomania. fazer—, to make a hit, be the rage.

furriel (m.) the Brazilian green grosbeak (Caryothraustes canadensis brasiliensis).

furrundu [dú], furrundum (m.) a sweet confection made of citron and ginger; a kind of country dance.

furta-côr (adj.) having a changeable luster or color, as of shot silk; (m.) changeable color; a snake called COTI-ARINHA.

furtadela (f.) act of sneaking, hiding or stealing away. às—s, furtively.

furta-fogo (m.) dark lantern.

furta-moça (adj.) unshod [horse].

furta-passo (m.) pace, rack or amble (gait of a horse). a—, stealthily.

furtar (v.t.,v.i.) to steal (a, de, from); to cheat.—-se a, to avoid, escape; to side-step; to shirk; to steal away from.

—se a questões, to dodge questions.**—se ao dever,** to shirk one's duty.**—o corpo,** to shun, avoid, escape (blame, responsibility); to balk at (a question or proposition).**—o corpo ao golpe,** or **à pancada,** to dodge a blow.**—os olhos,** to look away from.
furto (*m.*) a theft.
furufuru [rú . . . rú] (*m.*) the foam of boiling molasses.
furuncular (*adj.*) furuncular.
furúnculo (*m., Med.*) furuncle, boil.
furunculose (*f., Med.*) furunculosis.
furunculoso **-sa** (*adj.*) furunculous.
fusada (*f.*) a spindleful; a blow with a spindle.
fusão (*f.*) fusion, melting; amalgamation, blending; coalition, merger.
fuscina (*f., Biochem.*) fuscin.
fusco **-ca** (*adj.*) dark, dusky; of sky, overcast; fig. melancholy; of cattle, black.
fusco-fusco (*m.*) dusk [= LUSCO-FUSCO].
fuselado **-da** (*adj.*) fusiform, spindle-shaped; streamlined.
fuselagem (*f.*) fuselage (of an airplane).
fuselar (*v.t.*) to streamline.
fusibilidade (*f.*) fusibility.
fusiforme (*adj.*) fusiform, spindle-shaped.
fúsil [-seis] (*adj.*) fusible; fused, molten.
fusionar (*v.t.*) to fuse.
fusionista (*adj., m.,f., Politics*) fusionist.
fusível (*adj.*) fusible; (*m.*) an electric fuse.
fuso (*m.*) spindle; (*Geog.*) surface of terrestrial globe included between adjoining meridians.**—do relógio,** fusee of a watch.**—horário,** time zone.
fusta (*f.*) pinnace.
fustão (*m.*) fustian, corduroy, velveteen, dimity.
fuste (*m.*) a cudgel; wooden shaft (as of a spear); rod, staff; wand; switch; (*Bot.*) main stem; (*Arch.*) shaft.
fustete [êt] (*m., Bot.*) sumac (*Rhus spp.*)
fustigação (*f.*) cudgelling, drubbing, thrashing, flogging.
fustigar (*v.t.*) to cudgel; to drub, whack, thrash, beat, flog.
fustigo (*m.*) a blow with a cudgel or shaft.
futebol (*m.*) association football, soccer.
futicar (*v.t.*) to pester.

fútil [-teis] (*adj.*) futile, trivial, petty.
futilidade (*f.*) futility.
futilizar (*v.i.*) to deal with or utter futilities; (*v.t.*) to render futile.
futre (*m.*) cad; rotter; miser.
futrica (*f.*) small tavern; unsteady framework; heap of junk; (*m.*) a cheap individual; trouble-maker; intrigue.
futricada, futricagem (*f., colloq.*) dirty trick; low behavior; junk.
futricar (*v.t.*) to deal crookedly with; to meddle; to intrigue; to joke.
futriquice (*f.*) low behavior.
futura (*f.*) see FUTURO.
futuração (*f.*) conjecture, prediction.
futurar (*v.t.*) to foretell; to foresee; (*v.i.*) to conjecture.
futuridade (*f.*) futurity.
futurismo (*m.*) futurism.
futurista (*adj.*) futuristic; (*m.,f.*) futurist.
futuro **-ra** (*adj.; m.*) future. **em—próximo,** in the near future; (*f., colloq.*) bride-to-be, fiancée.
futuroso **-sa** (*adj.*) auspicious, promising.
fuxicada (*f.*) scheming, machinations.
fuxicar (*v.t.,v.i.*) to meddle (in); to gossip (about).
fuxico (*m.*) gossip; political intrigue.
fuxiqueiro **-ra** (*m.,f.*) busybody, gossip, mischief-maker.
fuzil (*m.*) a soldier's rifle (formerly, a fusil, flintlock musket); a piece of steel for striking fire with flint; iron link; flash of lightning.
fuzilação (*f.*) flash.
fuzilada (*f.*) fusillade.
fuzilado **-da** (*adj.*) shot (executed).
fuzilador (*m.*) fusillier.
fuzilamento (*m.*) shooting (execution).
fuzilante (*adj.*) flashing.
fuzilar (*v.t.*) to execute by shooting; (*v.i.*) to flash (as lightning); to sparkle, gleam, shine.
fuzilaria (*f.*) fusillade, volley.
fuzileiro (*m.*) rifleman (formerly, a fusilier).
fuzuê (*m.*) shindy, brawl, ruckus; uproar; noisy party.

G

G, g, the 7th letter of the Portuguese alphabet. (For words not listed under **G,** try **J**).
g = GRAMA(S) = gram(s).
g. = GRAU(S) = degree(s).
ga = GÁLIO (gallium).
gabação, gabadela (*f.*), **gabamento** (*m.*) praise, praising.
gabador **-dora** (*adj.*) praising; (*m.,f.*) praiser.
gabão **-bona** (*m.,f.*) praiser; (*m.*) a cloak with hood and cape [= GARNACHO].
gabar (*v.t.*) to praise, extol, laud; to boost; (*v.r.*) to boast, brag (**de,** of, about); to pride oneself (**de,** on).
gabardina (*f.*) gabardine (cloth); a gabardine raincoat or overcoat.
gabardo (*m.*) a hooded cloak [= GABINARDO].
gabarito, gabari (*m.*) gauge, pattern, jig, template; specifically, a gauge for measuring the distance between rails, or between the curbing of a street, etc., and for testing the clearance for cars, as in tunnels; (*fig.*) caliber, capacity. Cf. CÉRCEA.
gabarola(s) (*m.,f.*) self-praiser, boaster, braggart [= GA-BOLA(S)].
gabarolice (*f.*) braggadocio, boasting, swank; "apple-sauce," "bunk," "baloney" [= GABOLICE].
gabarra (*f.*) flatboat; dragnet.
gabião (*m.*) gabion.
gabinardo (*m.*) = GABARDO.
gabinete [nê] (*m.*) cabinet, private office, study room, laboratory; ministry, council, cabinet.
gabiroba, gabirobeira (*f.*) = GUABIROBEIRA.
gabiru [rú] (*m.*) common rat [= GUABIRU]; (*slang*) an awkward fellow.
gabo (*m.*) praise; boasting.
gabola(s) (*m.,f.*) = GABAROLA(S).
gabolice (*f.*) = GABAROLICE.
Gabriel (*m.*) Gabriel.

Gabriela (*f.*) Gabriella, Gabrielle.
gaçaba (*f.*) = IGAÇABA.
gadanha (*f.*) soup ladle; a type of broad-bladed scythe, used especially in cutting the grass on lawns; claw.
gadanhar (*v.t.*) to reap with a scythe; to seize with the claw; fig., to grasp greedily.
gadanheira (*f.*) reaping machine.
gadanho (*m.*) claw, talon; hay rake.
gadão (*m.*) fine cattle.
gadaria (*f.*) cattle; herd of cattle.
gademar (*m.*) a hybrid variety of Brazilian cattle; c.a. GADEMÃ, GUADEMÃO.
gadídeo **-dea** (*adj., Zool.*) gadid; (*m.pl.*) the Gadidae (cods, haddocks, tomcods, etc.).
gaditano **-na** (*adj.; m.,f.*) of or pert. to, or an inhabitant of, Cádiz, in Spain.
gado (*m.*) cattle, livestock, herd; (*vulgar*) prostitutes.**—asinino,** mules and donkeys.**—bovino,** oxen, steers.**—bravo,** wild cattle.**—caprino,** goats.**—cavalar,** horses.**—cornilongo,** longhorn cattle.**—de bico,** (*colloq.*) domestic fowls.**—de cria,** breeding cattle.**—de curral,** milch cows and their calves.**—de engorda,** or **de sôlta,** cattle on pasture.**—grosso,** cows, bulls, steers, horses and mules (collectively).**—lanífero** or **ovino,** sheep.**—leiteiro,** milk cattle.**—miúdo,** sheep, goats and swine (collectively).**—muar,** mules.**—para o corte,** beef cattle.**—suíno** or **porcino,** swine.**—tresmalhado,** stray cattle.**—vacum,** cows, steers, calves. **cabeça de—,** a head of cattle. **criar—,** to raise cattle. **ferro do—,** cattle branding. **ferro para marcar—,** branding iron.
gadóides = GADÍDEOS.
gadolínio (*m., Chem.*) gadolinium.
gadolinita (*f., Min.*) gadolinite.
gaduína (*f., Biochem.*) gaduin.

gadunhar (v.) = GATUN(H)AR.

gaélico -ca (adj., m.) Gaelic.

gafa (f.) mange; leprosy.

gafanhão (m.) large cricket or grasshopper.

gafanhoto [ôt] (m.) any of numerous leaping insects (grasshoppers, crickets, etc.); spring of a trigger; (Bot.) a nettlespurge (Jatropha officinalis) c.a. MEDICINEIRO; (slang) minimum lottery ticket [= GASPARINHO].—-de-jurema or -de-marmeleiro, any stick insect, c.a. JOÃO-MAGRO.

gafar (v.t.) to infect with mange or leprosy; (v.i.,v.r.) to become so infected; (v.i.) to commit a GAFE.

gafe (f.) blunder, bloomer, gaucherie [French: gaffe]. cometer (dar, fazer) uma—, to commit a faux-pas; to put one's foot in one's mouth.

gafeira (f.) dog mange; a certain eye disease of cattle; formerly, leprosy.

gafeirento -ta, gafeiroso -sa, gafento -ta (adj.) having GAFEIRA.

gafeira (f., slang) a cheap dance; shindig; lowest class of people.

gafo -fa (adj.) having GAFEIRA; corrupted, contaminated; (m.) = GAFEIRA.

gaforina, gaforinha (f.) mop or shock of hair; Negro's bushy head of hair.

gagá (adj.) decrepit, doting.

gagata (f.) pitch coal [= AZEVICHE].

gagino (m.) a rooster with hen-like plumage.

gago -ga (adj.) stuttering, stammering; (m.,f.) stutterer, stammerer.

gagosa (f.) black-headed gull (Larus ridibundus) c.a. CHAPALHETA; (adv.) à—, free-for-all; on the sly; at will.

gaguejante (adj.) stuttering; faltering.

gagueira (f.) = GAGUEZ.

gaguejar (v.t.,v.i.) to stammer, stutter, falter; (v.i.) to "hem and haw".

gaguejo [ê] (m.) act of stammering.

gaguez, gaguice (f.) stuttering, stammering [= GAGUEIRA].

gaiaco, gaiacol (m.) = GUAIACO, GUAIACOL.

gaia-moça = ERVA-DOS-CANCROS.

gaias (m.pl.) swirls and eddies in the hair on a horse's chest.

gaiatada (f.) gang of urchins; prank, escapade.

gaiatar (v.i.) to play tricks.

gaiatice (f.) playfulness, mischievousness.

gaiato -ta (adj.) roguish, playfully mischievous; waggish; urchinlike; (m.) mischievous youngster; urchin; wag, joker. ar—, roguish air.

gaifona, gaifonice (f.) face, grimace, antic.

gaifonar (v.i.) to make faces [= ENGAIFONAR].

gailárdia (f.,.Bot.) the painted gaillardia (G. picta), c.a. LAÇOS-ESPANHÓIS.

gainambé (m.) = ARAPONGA.

gaio -aia (adj.) gay, jovial. verde—, light green; (m.) the European jay (Garrulus glandarious).

gaiola (f.) cage; prison; frame of a building; wood crate; (R.R.) trestlework, c.a. FOGUEIRA; an Amazon River steamboat having a single stack and either stern or side paddles, or one or two propellers. They displace up to 600 tons and have long been an important mode of transport and travel on that river. Cf. VATICANO.

gaioleiro (m.) maker or seller of bird cages.

gaiolim (m.) a small cage.

gaipapo (m.) a bird—the green-throated euphonia (Tanagra chalybea).

gaipara (f.) = GATURAMO.

gaita (f.) fife; a tin or bamboo flute; prop root of a man-grove; (colloq.) any worthless thing; (slang) money; an accordion [= HARMÔNICA, SANFONA]; (pl.) lamprey's gill pouches.—de bôca, harmonica, mouth organ.—de capador, panpipe.—de foles, or —galega, bagpipe [= CORNAMUSA]. Salta a—! (slang) Come across with the dough!

gaitada (f., colloq.) rebuke, upbraiding.

gaitear (v.i.) to play a GAITA.

gaiteiro -ra (adj.) playful, lively; (m.,f.) harmonica or ac-cordion player.

gaivagem (f.) drainage ditch.

gaivão (m., Zool.) a tern (Sterna hirundo), c.a. GUINDRO, ANDORINHÃO, FERREIRO, ZIRRO; a conical fishing net.

gaivar (v.t.) to provide with drainage ditches.

gaivel [-véis] (m.) a wall whose thickness diminishes with its height.

gaivin[h]a (f.) a tern (Sterna minuta), c.a. ANDORINHA-DO-MAR.

gaivota (f.) any gull (Larus).—-preta, a ploverlike shore bird.—-rapineira, the great skua gull (Catharacta skua) and the parasitic jaeger (Stercorarius parasiticus).

gaivotão (m.) a large gull.

gaivotinha (f., Bot.) a croton.

gajão (m.) used by gypsies as an equivalent of SENHOR.

gajeiro (m., Naut.) topman.

gajeru, gajiru, gajuru (m.) = GUAJERU.

gajo (m.) fellow, guy, "gink".

gala (f.) formal dress, gala dress; gala-day; pomp, ostenta-tion; treadle (of an egg); sperm, semen.

galã (m.) the leading man in a romantic play; gallant, beau, suitor.

Galaaz (m.) Galahad.

galação (f.) = GALADURA.

galacrista (f., Bot.) cockscomb.

galactagogo -ga (adj.; m., Veter., Med.) galactagogue.

galactanas (f.pl., Chem.) galactans.

galáctase (f., Biochem.) galactase.

galáctico -ca (adj.) galactic [= LÁCTICO].

galactite (f., Min.) galactite.

galactófaco, galactófago -ga (adj.) galactophagous.

galactóforo -ra (adj., Anat.) galactophorous.

galatóide (adj.) galactoid, like milk.

galactometria (f.) galactometry.

galactômetro (m.) galactometer, lactodensimeter.

galactônico -ca (adj., Chem.) galactonic.

galactopiria (f., Med., Veter.) galactopyra, milk fever.

galactorréia (f.) galactorrhea, excessive flow of milk.

galactoscópio (m.) galactoscope.

galactose (f., Chem.) galactose; (Physiol.) galactosis.

galadura (f.) the act (by a male bird) of treading the hen; treadle (of an egg).

galalau (m.) tall man [= VARAPAU, COMPRIDÃO]; large object [= BUTELO].

galamatias (f.pl.) = GALIMATIAS.

galane (adj.) = GALANTE.

galanear (v.t.,v.i.) to dress richly.

galanga (f., Bot.) the lesser galangal (Alpinia officinarum).

galangina (f., Chem.) galangin.

galanice (f.) gallantry.

galantaria (f.) gallantry, politeness.

galante (adj.) gallant, chivalrous, courtly, polite, compli-mentary; (m.) a gallant.

galanteador -dora (adj.) gallant, complimentary, (m.) a ladies' man; philanderer.

galantear (v.t.) to court, woo; (v.i.) to dally; to pay com-pliments; to act the gallant.

galanteio (m.) courtship, gallantry; flirtation; dalliance; attentiveness (to the ladies); flattering remark.

galanteria (f.) = GALANTARIA.

galantina (f.) galantine (of chicken, veal, etc.).

galanto (m., Bot.) the genus (Galanthus) of snowdrops.

galão (m.) galloon, braid, trimming; gold stripe (on uni-forms); a gallon; (slang) the head on a glass of beer.—americano, the U.S. gallon (4 quarts = 3.7853 liters).—imperial, the imperial or British gallon (= 1.20094 U.S. gals. = 4.546 liters); spring (buck) of a horse.

Galaor (m.) Galahad.

galápago (m., Veter.) scratches, mud fever.

galapo (m.) saddle pad; bandage.

galar (v.t.) to tread—(said of male birds).

galardão (m.) reward, prize.

galardoador -dora (adj.) rewarding; (m.,f.) rewarder.

galardoar (v.t.) to reward, recompense (com, by, with).

galarim (m.) doubling of a gambling bet; highest point, top.

galáxia [ks] (f.) galaxy.

gálbano (m., Bot.) galbanum giant fennel (Ferula galvani-flua); galbanum resin.

gálbulo (m., Bot.) galbulus (cypress cone).

galdrope (m.) tiller rope [= GUALDROPE].

galé (f.) galley (oared ship); printer's galley; (m.) galley slave; (pl.) forced labor.

gálea (f.) helmet.

galeaça (f.) galleass (a large galley).

galeado -da (adj.) helmeted.

galeandra (f., Bot.) a genus (Galeandra) of orchids.

galeão (m.) galleon; printer's galley; purse seine.

galear (v.i.) to dress ostentatiously; of a boat, to rock; of a horse, to buck.

galeato -ta (adj.) having or wearing a helmet.

galega [ê] (f., Bot.) common European goat's-rue (Galega officinalis); a pigeon (Columba rufina).

galegada (f.) act or remark of a GALEGO; a number of GALEGOS; the Portuguese in Brazil, collectively. [Derogatory].

galego –ga [ê] (adj.; m.,f.) Spanish Galician; in Brazil, a deprecatory epithet applied to the Portuguese there. Cf. GALICIANO.

galeídeos (m.pl., Zool.) the Galeidae (syn. Carcharidae)—large family of sharks.

galeiforme (adj.) helmet-shaped.

galeína (f., Chem.) gallein.

galeio (m.) a sudden dodge, twist or swerve of the body.

galena, galenita (f., Min.) galena (native lead sulfide).

galeno (m., colloq.) a physician.

galenobismutito (m., Min.) galenobismutite.

galeonete [nê] (m.) fishing dory.

galeopiteco (m.) the genus (Cynocephalus, syn. Galeopithecus) of flying lemurs.

galeota (f.) galiot (small galley); a type of Amazon watercraft resembling a large canoe and displacing two to four tons. It has an awning and closed compartment in the stern, is manned by two oarsmen, and is used principally by itinerant river peddlers. [It is larger than an IGARITÉ.]

galeote (m.) galley slave.

galera (f.) galley (oared ship); fire wagon; foundry furnace.

galerão (m.) large man [= GALALAU, BUTELO].

galeria (f.) gallery, arcade, colonnade; corridor, hall; a collection of works of art; gallery in a theater, etc.; covered porch; (pl.) the spectators in a gallery. dirigir-se à—, to play to the gallery.

galeriano (m.) galley slave.

galês –sa (adj.) Welsh; (m.) a Welshman; the Welsh language; (f.) a Welsh woman.

galezia (f., colloq.) rascality; cheat.

galga (f.) see GALGO.

galgação (f.) planing of a board or piece of wood.

galgar (v.t.) to reach the top of (stairs, wall, tree, etc.) by springing up; to reach by climbing to (mountain top, etc.); to leap over (obstacles); to leave behind (by running); to gain (attain) rapidly (high office, throne, etc.); to reach, arrive at (a given age); to stride rapidly (over a distance).

galgaz (adj.) lean as a greyhound.

galgo –ga (adj.) hungry as a dog; avid, keenly desirous of (something); (m.) greyhound.—russo, Russian wolfhound; (f.) a female greyhound; a small anchor; mill stone in an olive oil press; (colloq.) cock-and-bull story.

galguincho –cha (adj.; colloq.) skinny; starving.

galha (f.) gall; gallnut.

galhada, galhadura (f.) antlers; branches.

galhardear (v.t.) to show off, exhibit; (v.i.) to shine, excel (em, in; como, as).

galhardete [dê] (m.) pennant, streamer.

galhardia (f.) gallantry, bravery, chivalry.

galhardo –da (adj.) gallant, chivalrous.

galhas (f.pl.) antlers, horns.

galheiro (m.) a large deer (Odocoileus dichotomus) having branched antlers; (colloq.) a cuckold [= CÔRNO].

galheta [ê] (f.) cruet, vial.

galheteiro (m.) a cruet stand.

galho (m.) branch (of a tree); antler; quarrel; (colloq.) side line, part-time job.

galhofa (f.) merriment, antics; fun; taunt; persiflage.

galhofada, galhofaria (f.) much fun-making and skylarking.

galhof[e]ar (v.i.) to joke, jest; to skylark.—de, to make fun of.

galhofeiro –ra (adj.) jovial, jocular, merry; playful; waggish; (m.,f.) merrymaker, funster, wag.

galhudo –da (adj.) having many branches; having large horns or antlers; (m., Zool.) the palometa (Trachinotus glaucus), a fish, c.a. ARATABOIA, PAMPANO, PAMPO, PAMPO-ARACANGUIRA, PAMPO-DE-ESPINHA-MOLE, PAMPO-GALHUDO, PAMPO-RISCADO, SARGENTO, VERMELHO.

Gália (f.) Gaul.

galiciano –na (adj.; m.,f.) [Polish] Galician. Cf. GALEGO and GALIZIANO.

galicínio (m.) cockcrow, early morning, dawn.

galiciparla (m.,f.) a person of Frenchified speech.

galicismo (m.) gallicism.

galicista (m.,f.) a person who indulges in gallicisms.

gálico –ca (adj.) Gallic; (Chem.) gallic [acid]; (m.) mal—, (colloq.) syphilis.

galícola (adj., Zool.) gallicolous; gallicole.

galileu –léia (adj.; m.,f.) Galilean.

galimatias (m.pl.) confused talk; gibberish.

galináceo –cea (adj.) gallinaceous; (m.,f.) a gallinacean; (f.pl.) the Gallinaceae (domestic fowls and pheasants).

galinha (f.) hen, chicken; chicken-hearted person; (colloq.) loose woman.—carijó, Plymouth Rock hen.—-choca, setting hen; (colloq.) a restless person; (Bot.) either of two cocaine trees, Erythroxylum suberosum or E. tortuosum, c.a. AZOUGUE-DO-CAMPO, CABELO-DE-NEGRO, FRUTA-DE-POMBO, JACARÉ-DO-CAMPO, MERCUREIRO, MERCÚRIO-DO-CAMPO, SESSENTA-E-DOIS.—-d'água, a finfoot (Helicornis fulica), c.a. IPEQUI, MERGULHÃO, PATINHO-D'ÁGUA; also = RABILA (a gallinule).—-d'angola, the Guinea fowl (Numida meleagris), known also by many other names: GALINHA-DA-ÍNDIA, GALINHA-DA-NUMÍDIA, GALINHA-DA-GUINÉ, GUINÉ, CONQUEM, ANGOLINHA, ANGOLISTA, GALINHOLA, CAPOTE, COCAR, ESTOU-FRACA, PICOTA, PINTADA, etc.—-do-mato, the chestnut-capped antthrush (Formicarius r. ruficeps), c.a. PINTO-DO-MATO; the imperial antpitta (Grallaria varia imperator), c.a. PERNA-LAVADA, TOVACUÇU.—-morta, (slang) a sure thing, cinch, "pushover"; something sold dirt-cheap; a chicken-hearted person.—poedeira, laying hen. A galinha do vizinho é sempre mais gorda, The grass is always greener on the other side of the fence. cabeça de—, a weakminded person. De grão em grão, a—enche o papo, Little and often fills the purse. matar a—dos ovos de ouro, to kill the hen that lays the golden eggs. pele de—, goose-flesh.

galinheiro (m.) chicken yard, chicken coop, hen house; poultry dealer; (colloq.) buzzards' roost, peanut gallery (in a theater).

galinho (m.) = GALO (moonfish).

galinhola (f.) the Brazilian giant snipe (Capella undulata gigantea), c.a. NARCEJÃO, ÁGUA-SÓ; also, the guinea fowl [= GALINHA D'ANGOLA].

galinicultor (m.), –tora (f.) chicken-raiser.

galinicultura (f.) chicken-raising.

gálio (m., Chem.) gallium; (Bot.) bedstraw (Galium spp.).

galipão (m., slang) jalopy.

galiparla, garliparlista (m.,f.) = GALICIPARLA.

galípea (f.) Angostura barktree (Galipea officinalis).

galipódio, galipó, galipote (m.) galipot (a kind of turpentine).

galispo (m.) cockalorum, a little cock.

galista (m.) breeder and handler of gamecocks.

galito (m.) a bird—the cock-tailed tyrant (Alectrurus tricolor), c.a. TESOURA.

galivar (v.t.) to shape (a piece of wood).

galizia (f., colloq.) obstacle, difficulty, question; vanity.

galiziano –na (adj.) [Portuguese] Galician. Cf. GALICIANO.

galo (m.) cock, rooster; a lump on the head; (Zool.) the moonfish (Vomer setapinnis), c.a. GALO-BRANCO, GALO-DE-REBANHO, GALO-DA-COSTA, GALO-DO-MORRO, ARACORAM, DOUTOR, FRALDA-ROTA, GALINHO, ZABUCAÍ.—-bandeira, the look-down (Selene vomer), c.a. GALO-DE-PENACHO, PEIXE-GALO.—-da-rocha, cock-of-the-rock (Rupicola rupicola), c.a. GALO-DA-SERRA, GALO-DO-PARÁ.—de briga, or de rinha, gamecock; fig., a quarrelsome person.—-de-campina, the black-throated cardinal (Paroaria g. gularis), c.a. TANGARÁ.—do-campo, a mockingbird, c.a. SABIÁ-DO-CAMPO.—do-mato = TICO-TICO-REI (a finch).—do seu terreiro, cock of the walk.—-fita, a threadfish [= ARACANGUIRA].—novinho, cockerel. ao cantar do—, at cockcrow, at dawn. briga de—, cockfight. cabeça de—, weakmindedness. cantar de—em casa, to be the master in one's own household. crista de—, cock's comb; also, a garden plant. missa do—, Christmas night mass (at midnight). Se êles fizessem isso, outro—nos cantaria, If they would do that, things would be different.

galocha (f., Bot.) terminal bud or inflorescence; (Naut.) open snatch-block; (pl.) galoshes, rubber overshoes.

galocrista (f.) = GALACRISTA.

galofobia (f.) Gallophobia.

galomania (f.) excessive Gallophilism.

galonar (v.) = AGALONAR.

galopada (f.) a galloping run.

galopador –dora (adj.) galloping; (m.,f.) galloper.

galopante (adj.) galloping. tísica—, galloping consumption.

galopar (v.t.,v.i.) to gallop.
galope (m.) gallop; (colloq.) rebuke. a—, at a gallop, galloping. a todo o—, at full gallop. meio—, a canter.
galopeação –peada (f.) = GALOPADA.
galopeado –da (adj.) said of a horse being trained to race.
galopeador (m.), –dora (f.) galloper.
galopeadura (f.) exercising of a race horse.
galopear (v.i.) to gallop; (v.t.) to train a horse to run.
galopim (m.) errand boy; whippersnapper.—de chefe político, ward heeler.—eleitoral, election tout; canvasser for votes.
galopinar (v.i.) to tout (for votes).
galpão (m.) shed (for wagons, animals, etc.).
galrão –rona (adj.) gabbling; (m.,f.) gabbler.
galrar (v.i.) to prate; to bluster.
galreador –dora (adj.) prattling; (m.,f.) prattler.
galrear (v.i.) to babble, prattle. Var. GALREJAR.
galucho (m.) rookie, raw recruit.
galvânico –ca (adj.) galvanic.
galvanismo (m.) galvanism.
galvanização (f.) galvanization.
galvanizado –da (adj.) galvanized.
galvanizador –dora (adj.) galvanizing.
galvanizar (v.t.) to galvanize; to plate; to excite, electrify.
galvanografia (f.) galvanography.
galvanômetro (m.) galvanometer.—astático, astatic galvanometer.—balístico, ballistic galvanometer.—de bobina móvel, moving-coil galvanometer.—de espelho, or de reflexão, reflecting galvanometer.
galvanoplastia, -plástica (f.) galvanoplastics; electrotypy; electroplating.
galvanoscópio (m.) galvanoscope.
galvanostegia (f.) electroplating.
galvanotaxia [ks] (f.) galvanotaxis.
galvanoterapia (f.) galvanotherapy.
galvanotropismo (m.) galvanotropism.
gama (f.) gamut, scale; range (of sizes, etc.). raios—, gamma rays.
gamacismo (m.) gammacism, guttural stammering.
gamado –da (adj.) formed of gammas. cruz—, a gammadion or swastika.
gamão (m.) backgammon.
gâmaro (m.) any water flea of the genus Gammarus.
gamarra (f.) martingale; checkrein.
gamarrilha (f.) pole strap (of a harness).
gambá (m.) any opossum of genus Didelphys, c.a. CASSACO, MICURÊ, MUCURA, SARIGUÊ, SARIGUÉIA, SARUÊ, TIMBU; (colloq.) a sot, tosspot, boozer; a bad-smelling person.—de galinheiro, chicken thief. beber como um—, to drink like a fish. comer—errado, to buy a pig in a poke.
gambarra (f.) a large two-master, employed in the region of Marajó Island in the transport of cattle.
gambêlo (m.) something which is good, sweet or pleasant.
gambérria (f.) a tripping up (of another person); trick, fraud; quarrel.
gambeta [ê] (f.) a dodge or dodging movement.
gambetear (v.i.) to dodge, duck.
gâmbia (f., colloq.) leg.
gambiarras (f.pl.) stage lights.
gambito (m.) gambit.
gamboa (f.) quince (fruit); small seaside lake left by the receding tide [= CAMBOA]; a lakelike spot in a river; "an enclosure or trap of wooden slats, or sometimes of stone, used to catch fish along the beaches". [GBAT]
gamboeiro (m.) a variety of the common quince (Cydonia oblonga britannica).
gamboína (f., colloq.) cheating at cards.
gambota (f.) centering (falsework over which an arch is formed).
gamela (f.) wooden trough or vessel; small antelope; (colloq.) fib, lie; a practical (non-graduate) engineer.
gamelada (f.) a troughful.
gamelão (m.) a large trough.
gameleira (f.) any of several figs (Ficus).—branca (-brava, -mansa, -roxa) = COAJINDUBA.
gamelo (m.) trough; a type of paper kite.
gamenho (m.) a fop.
gameta (m., Biol.) gamete.
gametócito (m., Biol.) gametocyte.
gametófito (m., Bot.) gametophyte.
gametogênese (f., Biol.) gametogenesis.
gâmico –ca (adj., Biol.) gamic.
gamo (m.) fallow deer (Dama dama); stag, buck.

gamóbio (m., Zool.) gomobium.
gamofilo –la (adj., Bot.) gamophyllous.
gamogênese (f., Biol.) gamogenesis.
gamomania (f.) gamomania.
gamopétalo –la (adj., Bot.) gamopetalous.
gamossépalo –la (adj., Bot.) gamosepalous.
gamostilo (m., Bot.) gamostele.
gamote (m.) a vessel for bailing water out of a boat.
gana (f.) a craving or hungering; a "yen"; hate, ill will; (cap.) Ghana.
ganacha (f.) lower jaw of a horse.
ganância (f.) greed for gain; usury; greediness.
ganancioso –sa (adj.) greedy, grasping, avaricious; (m.,f.) such a person.
ganchar (v.t.) to hook [= ENGANCHAR].
gancheado –da (adj.) hook-shaped.
gancho (m.) any kind of hook; hairpin [= GRAMPO]; (colloq.) a part-time job or side line [= BICO].—de esquerda (direita), left (right) hook (in boxing).
ganchorra (f.) a big hook.
ganchoso –sa (adj.) hooked.
gandaia (f.) rag-picking; loafing; loose living. andar na—, to lead an idle or dissolute life.
gandaiar (v.i.) to loaf; to bum; to gad about.
gandaieiro –ra (adj.) bumming; (m.,f.) bum, loafer.
gândara (f.) wasteland.
gandular (v.i.) to bum, sponge.
gandulo –la (adj.) parasitic, sponging; (m.,f.) parasite, sponger.
ganga (f.) nankeen; (Min.) gangue; a brownish-yellow species of cotton (Gossypium religiosum); (slang) liquor.—azul, denim.
gangão (m.) a dwarfed and sparsely filled ear of corn, c.a. CATAMBUERA, TATAMBUERA, DENTE-DE-VELHA, XERÉM; (adv.) de—, without stopping.
gangarina (f., slang) church.
gangarreão (m.) a severe lowering of one's state of health.
gangliectomia (f., Surg.) ganglionectomy.
gangliforme (adj.) gangliform.
gangliite [i-í] (f.) = ADENITE.
gânglio (m.) ganglion.
ganglionar (adj.) ganglionic.
gangolina (f.) shindy, brawl.
gangolino (m.) a deadbeat, scoundrel.
gangonçu (m.) cohune palm (Orbignya speciosa).
gangorra [ô] (f.) seesaw; crude cane crusher; bicycle; animal trap.
gangorrear (v.i.) to seesaw, teeter.
gangrena (f., Med.) gangrene.—sêca, dry gangrene or mummification.—úmida, moist gangrene.
gangrenado –da (adj.) affected by gangrene.
gangrenar (v.t.,v.i.,v.r.) to gangrenate.
gangrenoso –sa (adj.) gangrenous.
ganguê (m.) "misery" (vague indisposition or ailment).
ganhadeiro –ra (adj.) earning; (m.,f.) wage earner, worker.
ganha-dinheiro (m.) worker, laborer, wage earner.
ganhado –da, the regular but little-used p.p. of GANHAR. It has been replaced almost entirely by the irreg. form, GANHO. Vintem poupado, vintem—, Penny saved, penny earned.
ganhador –dora (adj.) gaining, winning; (m.,f.) gainer, winner; wage earner; in Bahia, a porter [= CARREGADOR].
ganhão (m.) wage earner.
ganha-pão (m.) breadwinner; means of livelihood.
ganha-perde (m.) = PERDE-GANHA.
ganhar [24] (v.t.) to earn, gain, get, win, acquire; to reach, arrive at (a given place); (v.i.) to win.—a dianteira, to forge ahead of.—a palma, to win a victory.—a partida, to win the game (lit. & fig.).—a rua, to gain the street.—a vida, to earn a living.—ânimo, to gain courage.—caminho, to get ahead.—juízo, to get sense.—mundos e fundos, to acquire great wealth.—o jôgo, to win the game.—o mundo, to wander from place to place.—o prêmio, to take the prize.—pé, to touch bottom (in water).—tempo, to gain time; to stall for time.—tento, to regain one's calm or composure.—terra, to make land.—terra com, to make headway with.—terreno, to gain ground.—uma aposta, to win a bet.—um presente, to receive a gift. Aí você ganha de mim, That's where you have me. Que é que se ganha com isso? What's in it for people like us?
ganha-saia (m., Bot.) either of two plants: Hybanthus (syn. Ionidium) atropurpureus, c.a. APANHASAIA, PURGA-

DE-VEADO, or *Centropogon surinamensis*, c.a. CRISTA-
DE-PERU.

ganhável (*adj.*) gainable, winnable.

ganho –nha (*irreg. p.p. of* GANHAR) gained, won, earned; (*m.*) gain, profit, earning.—s e perdas, profit and loss.—s eventuais, uncertain profits. Cf. GANHADO.

ganhoso –sa (*adj.*) profitable; greedy for gain.

ganhuça (*f., colloq.*) gain, profit.

ganiçar (*v.*) = GANIR.

ganido (*m.*) howl(ing), yelp(ing).

ganir [25] (*v.i.*) to howl, yelp, bark.

ganita (*f., Min.*) gahnite.

ganja (*f.*) conceit; presumption; (*adj.*) vain; forward; presumptuous.

ganjento –ta (*adj.*) vain, presumptuous [= ENGANJENTO].

ganoídeo –dea, **ganóide** (*adj., Zool.*) ganoid; (*m.pl.*) the Ganoidei.

ganoína (*f., Zool.*) ganoin.

ganomalito (*m., Min.*) ganomalite.

gansão (*m.*) flamingo [= FLAMENGO].

ganso (*m.*) gander, goose; (*colloq.*) drunkenness; rump of beef.—côr-de-rosa,—do-norte, a flamingo.—novo, gosling.

ganzá (*m.*) a rattlebox [= RECO-RECO].

ganzepe (*m., Carp.*) splice joint.

gape (*m.*) the gapes (a disease of poultry and other birds, caused by the gapeworm); c.a. SINGAMOSE.

gapinar (*v.i.*) to fish [= PESCAR].

gapira (*f.*) = GUAPIRA.

gapó (*m.*) = IGAPÓ.

gaponga (*f., Angling*) a ball made of manatee bone and used to attract fish by bobbing it in the water.

gapororoca (*f.*) = BORORÓ or MÃO-CURTA (a deer).

gapuiar (*v.i.*) to fish haphazardly in shallow water with bow and arrow or harpoon; to net shrimp with small baskets; to look for something haphazardly.

garabebel (*m.*) = SERNAMBIGUARA.

garabu (*m.*) = GUARABU.

garabulha (*f.*) brawl, turmoil; scrawl; (*m.*) intriguer.

garabulhar (*v.*) = GARATUJAR.

garabulhento –ta (*adj.*) rough; in turmoil.

garabulho (*m.*) roughness; turmoil.

garafunhas –nhos (*f.,m.pl.*) = GARATUJAS.

garage(m) (*f.*) garage.

garagista (*m.*) garageman.

garajau (*m.*) an oblong, cylindrical basket for carrying chickens, etc. to market; (*Zool.*) a tern (*Sterna fluviatilis*).

garança (*adj.; f.*) madder red; (*f., Bot.*) the common madder (*Rubia tinctorum*), c.a. GRANZA, RUIVA.

garançar (*v.t.*) to madder.

garanceira (*f.*) madder field.

garancena (*f.*) garanceux (inferior garancine).

garancina (*f.*) garancine (madder dye).

garanço (*m.*) madder red.

garanhão (*m.*) stallion; stud horse; fig. woman chaser.

garanjão (*m.*) a big man.

garante (*m.,f.*) warrantor.

garantia (*f.*) guaranty, surety, bond; assurance; deposit (collateral security).—s constitucionais, constitutional rights and privileges.—pignoratícia, collateral security.

garantidor –dora (*adj.*) guaranteeing; (*m.,f.*) one who guarantees.

garantir (*v.t.*) to guarantee, warrant; to vouch for; to avow. sentir-se garantido, to feel secure.

garapa (*f.*) fresh sugar cane juice; any sweet, cooling drink, esp. when made with fruit juice; any liquid set aside to ferment prior to distillation; something good and easily obtained; a Braz. leguminous tree (*Apuleia praecox*) which yields construction timber, c.a. GARAPA-AMARELA, GARAPIAPUNHA, GRAPIAPUNHA-BRANCA.

garapeira (*f.*) a roadside shed selling GARAPA, as well as fodder for pack animals.

garapu [ú] (*m.*) = FOBOCA, GUARAPU.

garatéia (*f.*) a fishing line having two or more hooks; a stone used as an anchor for a fishing boat.

garatuja (*f.*) scrawls, scribbles; a grimace.

garatujar (*v.i.*) to scrawl, scribble; to doodle; to make faces.

garaúna (*f.*) = BARAÚNA.

garavato (*m.*) a pole with a hook on one end, used for picking fruit. Var. GRAVATO.

garavêto (*m.*) kindling wood, chips, tinder.

garavunha (*f.*) = GARATUJA.

garbo (*m.*) elegance; gallantry; distinction.

garboso –sa (*adj.*) elegant; gallant; distinguished.

garça (*f.*) a heron.—azul, the little blue heron (*Florida caerula*), c.a. GARÇA-MORENA.—branca-grande, the American egret (*Casmerodius albus egretta*), c.a. GARÇA-GRANDE, GARÇA-REAL, GUIRATINGA, ACARÁ, ACARATINGA.—branca-pequena, the small snowy egret (*Leucophoyx* [or *Egretta*] *thula thula*).—cinzenta = SOCOÍ.—de-guiana, the agami heron (*Agamia agami*), c.a. SOCÓ-AZUL, SOCÓ-BEIJA-FLOR.—real, the capped heron (*Philerodius pileatus*), c.a. GARÇA-DE-CABEÇA-PRETA; also = GARÇA-BRANCA-GRANDE.—vermelha, the southern least bittern (*Ixobrynchus exilis erythromelas*), c.a. SOCOÍ-VERMELHO.

garção (*m.*) a waiter. [French *garçon*.]

garço –ça (*adj.*) greenish; bluish-green.

garçotas (*f.pl.*) egret feathers; an aigrette (plume, tuft) for the head.

gardênia (*f.*) gardenia, cape jasmine, c.a. JASMIM-DO-CABO.

gardunho (*m.*) = FUINHA.

gare (*f.*) a railroad station.

garfada (*f.*) a forkful.

garfar (*v.t.*) to fork over; to make a saddle graft (of plants).

garfo (*m.*) fork; pitchfork; a saddle graft (of plants); um bom—, a hearty eater.

gargaçalada (*f.*) a pouring out of something (as from a bottle) with a gurgling sound.

gargalaçar (*v.t.*) to drink from the bottle.

gargajola (*m.*) a gangling youth.

gargaleira (*f.*) bung hole.

gargalhada (*f.*) burst of laughter, horselaugh, guffaws.

gargalhadear, gargalhar (*v.i.*) to guffaw.

gargalheira (*f.*) spiked dog collar; chain, fetter; fig., tyranny, oppression.

gargalho (*m.*) phlegm.

gargalo (*m.*) bottleneck.

garganta (*f.*) throat, gullet; gorge, defile, ravine; col; any strait or narrow passage; a blowhard, braggart; groove or swallow of a sheave; (*Zool.*)—de-ferro, the caesar (*Bathystoma rimator*)—a fish c.a. SAPURUNA; also = COTINGA(-CHIRRA) and TRINCA-FERRO.—inflamada, sore throat. estar com a corda na—, to be hard-pressed for money. estar com alguém pela—, to be thoroughly fed up with someone. molhar a—, to wet one's whistle. ter alguma coisa atravessada na—, to have something stick in one's craw.

gargantão –tona (*adj.*) gluttonous; (*m.,f.*) glutton.

garganteação (*f.*) warbling, trilling.

garganteado –da (*adj.*) trilled; (*m.*) a trilling or warbling.

garganteador –dora (*adj.*) trilling; (*m.,f.*) one who trills.

gargantear (*v.t.*) to quaver; (*v.i.*) to trill; (*colloq.*) to brag, boast, bluster.

garganteio (*m.*) trill.

gargantilho –lha (*adj.*) of dogs, having a white neck; (*f.*) choker (necklace).

gargântua (*m.*) a Gargantuan eater.

gargarejar (*v.t.,v.i.*) to gargle.

gargarejo [ê] (*m.*) a gargle or gargling; (*Bot.*) a calliandra (*C. santosiana*).

gargau (*m.*) = BARRIGUDINHO.

gárgula (*f.*) gargoyle, waterspout.

gari (*m.*) street sweeper.

garimpagem (*f.*) prospecting for gold, etc.

garimpar (*v.i.*) to prospect for diamonds, gold, etc.; (*colloq.*) to pick one's nose.

garimpeiro (*m.*) prospector for gold, diamonds, etc. [= FAISCADOR].

garimpo (*m.*) diamond beds; gold fields.

gariofilata (*f.*) = CUAMBU.

garlopa (*f.*) jointer plane, jack plane.

garnacha (*f.*) robe or gown (of judge, priest, etc.); (*m.*) one wearing a robe or gown.

garnacho (*m.*) = GABÃO (cloak).

garnear (*v.t.*) to burnish (leather).

garnierita (*f., Min.*) garnierite; noumeite.

garnimento (*m.*) garnishment.

garnisé (*adj.*) bantam [chicken].

garoa (*f.*) fog; fine drizzle.

garoar (*v.i.*) to drizzle; to fog.

garoento –ta (*adj.*) foggy; drizzly.

garóta (*f.*) see GARÔTO.

garotada, garotagem (*f.*) a group of youngsters.—da vizinhança, the neighborhood kids.

garotar (v.i.) to behave like an urchin; to loaf.
garôto –ta (m.,f.) youngster, kid, teen-ager; an urchin; (f.) attractive young woman; (adj.) mischievous, roguish, childish.
garoupa (f.) any of several groupers, esp. the red grouper or mero (Epinephelus morio), c.a. GAROUPA-DE-SÃO-TOMÉ (or -BICHADA, or -DE-SEGUNDA, or -VERMELHA-DE-ABROLHOS, or -VERDADEIRA), PIRAGAIA; another grouper (E. gigas) c.a. GAROUPA-VERDADEIRA (or -PRETA, or -CRIOULA), PIRACUCA.—-chita = GAROUPINHA.—-pintada = BADEJO-PINTADO.
garoupeira (f.) a certain type of fishing boat.
garoupinha (f.) the coney (Cephalopholis fulvus), c.a. CATOÁ, GAROUPA-CHITA, CARAÚNA, PIRAÚNA.
garra (f.) claw, talon; (pl.) fingers, nails, hands; long hairs of a horse's fetlocks; worn-out pieces of harness. à—, adrift.
garrafa (f.) bottle.—térmica, thermos bottle.—de Leyden, (Elec.) Leyden jar.
garrafada (f.) a bottleful.
garrafal (adj.) bottleshaped; big, well-rounded.
garrafão (m.) demijohn, carboy; jug.—empalhado, a demijohn cased in wickerwork.
garrafaria (f.) a lot of bottles; wine cellar.
garrafeira (f.) wine cellar.
garrafeiro (m.) buyer of old bottles.
garraio –raia (adj.) poor [horse]; (m.) young unfought bull; fig., beginner, amateur.
garrana (f.) small but sturdy mare.
garranchada (f.) a pile of brush.
garrancho (m.) a twig or slender branch; a crooked branch; bad handwriting, scrawl, scribble.
garranchoso –sa (adj.) twisted, crooked (as a branch).
garrano (m.) a sturdy pony; a rogue.
garrão (m.) hamstring. afrouxar o—, to weaken in the legs; to turn coward.
garrar (v.i.) to drag the anchor; to drift.
garrear (v.t.) to trim a horse's fetlocks; to clip the wool remaining on the lower legs of sheared sheep.
garreio (m.) act of clipping or trimming (horse, sheep).
garriça, garricha (f.) = CAMBAXIRRA.
garrida (f.) see GARRIDO.
garridice (f.), garridismo (m.) foppishness.
garrido –da (adj.) chic, elegant; natty, dapper; bright-colored, gay; (f.) a little bell; a roller for moving heavy rocks.
garril (m.) a tree laid across a road to block it.
garrincha (f.) = CAMBAXIRRA.
garrinchão (m.) a spotted cactus wren (Heleodytes t. turdinus), and the Amazonian spotted cactus wren (H. turdinus hyposticus).
garrir [46] (v.i.) to tinkle; to chirp; to chatter; (v.r.) to dress up.
garrixa (f.), garrixo (m.) = CAMBAXIRRA.
garrocha (f.) a goad stick.
garrochada (f.) a jab with a goad stick.
garrochar (v.t.) to goad (bulls).
garrota (f.) a young cow.
garrotar (v.t.) to garrote. Var. GARROTEAR.
garrote (m.) garrote; act of garroting; a young bull.
garrotear (v.t.) to soften hides by beating; also = GARRO-TAR.
garrotilho (m., Med.) croup; (Veter.) colt distemper or strangles.
garrucha (f.) a cudgel for twisting the cord about a pack; a pulley for torturing; a muzzle-loading pistol; a cautious card player; (pl., Naut.) cringles.
garruchar (v.i.) to gamble with caution (in order to hold on to previous winnings).
garruchismo (m., slang) tightfistedness.
garrular (v.i.) to gabble, prattle.
garrulice (f.) garrulity, loquacity; prattle.
gârrulo –la (adj.) garrulous; (m.,f.) garrulous person; chatterbox.
garua (f.), garuar (v.) = GAROA, GAROAR.
garupa (f.) crupper, hindquarters (of a horse); saddle pack. dar a—, to give (someone) a lift on horseback. tirar na—, (colloq.) to rescue (someone) from danger or trouble.
garupada (f.) a buck with the hindquarters [horse].
gás (m.) gas.—carbônico, carbonic-acid gas.—de água, water gas.—de ar, air gas.—de iluminação, illuminating gas.—de óleo or—rico, oil gas.—dos pântanos, marsh gas, firedamp.—fétido or hepático, foul gas (sulfureted

hydrogen).—hélio, helium gas.—hilariante, laughing gas.—lacrimogênio, tear gas.—mostarda, mustard gas.—pobre, producer gas.—sulfídrico, hydrogen sulfide. à prova de—, gasproof. bico de—, gas jet. fábrica de—, gas works.
gasalhado (m.) clothing; bed clothes; shelter; welcome; lodging.
gasalhar (v.) = AGASALHAR.
gasalho (m.) shelter [= AGASALHO].
gasalhoso –sa (adj.) welcoming; hospitable.
gascão (adj.; m.) Gascon; (m.) a gascon, boaster, swashbuckler.
gasconada (f.) gasconade, bravado [= FANFARRICE].
gasear (v.t.) to gas.
gaseificação [e-i] (f.) gasification.
gaseificar [e-i] (v.t.) to gasify.
gaseificável [e-i] (adj.) gasifiable.
gaseiforme [e-i] (adj.) gasiform.
gasganete [nê], gasnate, gasnete [nê] (m.) gullet, throat; neck.
gasista (m.) gas fitter; street lamplighter.
gasogênio (m.) apparatus for producing gas, esp. as a substitute for gasoline.
gasógeno –na (adj.) gasogenic; (m.) = GASOGÊNIO.
gasolina (f.) gasoline; motor boat.—anti-detonante, anti-knock gasoline.—de alta prova, high-test gasoline.—de aviação, aviation gasoline.—etílica, ethyl gasoline.—sintética, synthetic gasoline.
gasometria (f.) gasometry.
gasômetro (m.) gas meter; gas tank; gas works.
gasoso –sa (adj.) gaseous; (f.) soda pop.
gaspacho (m.) panada (dish made of bread boiled and flavored).
Gaspar (m.) Caspar, Casper.
gasparin[h]o (m.) the minimum-size lottery ticket [= GAFANHOTO].
gáspea (f.) vamp (of a shoe).
gaspear (v.t.) to provide (shoes) with vamps.
gastador –dora (adj.) wasteful; consuming; thriftless; (m.,f.) spendthrift, squanderer, wastrel.
gastalho (m.) clamp, cramp.
Gastão (m.) Gaston.
gastar [24] (v.t.,v.i.) to wear out, consume; to expend; to waste, spend, use up; (v.r.) to wear (oneself) out; to deteriorate.—à toa, to fritter (something) away.—cera com mau defunto, to send good money after bad; to pay for a dead horse.—dinheiro, to spend money.—palavras, to waste words.—tempo, to waste time. [To spend time is PASSAR TEMPO.]
gastável (adj.) spendable; expendable.
gasteromiceto (m., Bot.) gasteromycete.
gasterópodes (m.pl., Zool.) the Gast(e)ropoda.
gasterosteídeos (m.pl., Zool.) the family (Gasterosteidae) of sticklebacks.
gasterósteos (m.pl., Zool.) the typical genus (Gasterosteus) of sticklebacks.
gasto –ta (adj.; irreg. p.p. of GASTAR) spent, worn (out), wasted, exhausted.—até à trama, worn threadbare. (m.) expenditure; waste; outlay. dar para o—, to be enough to get along (get by) with.
gastralgia (f., Med.) gastralgia.
gastrectomia (f., Surg.) gastrectomy.
gástrico –ca (adj.) gastric. indisposição—, gastric upset. suco—, gastric juice.
gastrite (f., Med.) gastritis.
gastroentérico –ca (adj., Anat., Med.) gastroenteric, gastrointestinal.
gastroenterite (f., Med.) gastroenteritis.
gastroenterostomia (f., Surg.) gastroenterostomy.
gastrolito (m., Zool.) gastrolith.
gastrologia (f.) culinary art.
gastronomia (f.) gastronomy, epicurism.
gastronômico –ca (adj.) gastronomic.
gastrônomo (m.) gourmet, gourmand, epicure.
gastrópode (m., Zool.) gastropod; (pl.) the Gastropoda (snails, slugs, etc.).
gastroscopia (f., Med.) gastroscopy.
gastroscópio (m., Med.) gastroscope.
gastrostomia (f., Surg.) gastrostomy.
gastroteca (f., Zool.) gastrotheca.
gastrotomia (f., Surg.) gastromy.
gastrovascular (adj., Zool.) gastrovascular.
gastrozóide (m., Zool.) gastrozooid; hydranth.
gástrula (f., Embryol.) gastrula.

gastrulação (*f.*, *Embryol.*) gastrulation.
gastura (*f.*) a disagreeable sensation, resulting in a shiver, gooseflesh, teeth on edge, etc., such as caused by a squeaky piece of chalk, by cutting a cork with a dull knife, etc. [=ARREPIO]; boredom, ennui.
gata (*f.*) a she-cat, pussycat; (*Naut.*) mizzen topmast; (*colloq.*) drunkenness.—**borralheira**, Cinderella; a stay-at-home.—**-parida**, a pushing and squeezing game played by school boys seated on a bench, accompanied by yowls like a cat in distress.
gatafunhar (*v.t.*) to scribble, scrawl; to doodle.
gatafunhos (*m.pl.*) scrawls, scribblings.
gatão -tona (*m.,f.*) a big cat.
gataria (*f.*) cats (collectively).
gatária (*f.*) catnip, c.a. ERVA-DOS-GATOS.
gatázio (*m.*) claw, nail.
gateado -da (*adj.*) greenish-yellow (as the eyes of a cat); reddish-yellow [horse].
gateador (*m.*) stalker of game; a stealthy thief.
gatear (*v.t.*) to fasten with metal clamps; to stalk (creep up on) game.
gateio (*m.*) stalking of game.
gateiro -ra (*adj.*) fond of cats; (*m.,f.*) cat-lover; (*f.*) a hole cut in a door for the convenience of cats; vent, outlet; skylight.
gaticida (*f.,m.*) cat-killer.
gaticídio (*m.*) killing of cats.
gatilho (*m.*) trigger.
gatimanhos (*m.pl.*), **-mônias** (*f.pl.*) grimaces; waving about of the hands; children's cutting-up; scrawls.
gatinha (*f.*) kitten. **andar de—s**, to creep, crawl (on hands and knees).
gato (*m.*) cat; a nimble, quick-witted person; a slip or oversight; a misprint; rebuke; sneak thief; carpenter's or other clamp.—**açu**, a wildcat.—**com** (or **-de**) **-botas**, Puss-in-Boots; by ext., a teller of tall tales.—**de-algália**, civet cat, c.a. CIVETA.—**do-mar**, a chimaera (fish).—**do-mato**, the margay or spotted cat (*Felis tigrina*), resembling the ocelot.—**do-mato-grande** = JA-GUATIRICA.—**do-mato-pintado**, any of three small wildcats: *Noctifelis pardinoides*, c.a. MARACAJÁ-MIRIM; *Margay tigrina*, c.a. MARACAJÁ-PINTADO; and *Oncifelis geoffroyi*.—**escaldado de água fria tem mêdo**, A scalded cat dreads cold water; Once bitten, twice shy.—**escondido com o rabo de fora**, something intended to be hidden but which inadvertently betrays itself.—**-maltês**, Maltese cat.—**mansinho**, a fish (*Chimaera arctica*).—**-marinho**, a wolf fish (*Anarhichas lupus*), c.a. LÔBO-DO-MAR.—**montês**, mountain lion.—**mourisco**, a wildcat (*Herpailurus jaguarundi*), c.a. JAGUARUNDI.—**-pingado**, a humorous term applied to members of a sparse audience; (*slang*) guy, bozo, gink; formerly, a pallbearer or torchbearer in a funeral procession.—**prêto**, (*colloq.*) the Devil.—**-sapato**, a trifle; blind-man's buff.—**-tigre**, any wildcat. **alma-de—**, robust health. **comer** (or **comprar**)—**por lebre**, to buy a pig in a poke. **fazer passar—por lebre**, to sell gold bricks. **levar um—**, to receive a call-down. **O—comeu**, The cat got it (referring to the unexplained disappearance of something). **Quem não tem cão, caça com—**, Half a loaf is better than none. **Viver como cão e—**, to fight like cats and dogs.
gatorro (*m.*), **-ra** (*f.*) a big cat.
gatunagem (*f.*) thievery; thieves, collectively.
gatunar (*v.t.,v.i.*) to steal, pilfer.
gatunice (*f.*) theft.
gatuno -na (*adj.*) thieving; (*m.,f.*) thief, pilferer.—**de golpe**, purse snatcher; pickpocket.—**de môsco**, housebreaker.
gaturamo (*m.*) a common generic name for any euphonia (a bird of genus *Tanagra*), c.a. GATURAMA, GUTURAMO, GORINHATÃ, GURIANTÃ, TEM-TEM, TENTEM, TEI-TEI, TIETÊ-I, VEM-VEM, VIM-VIM, BONITO.—**miudinho**, the greater purple-throated euphonia (*Tanagra chlorotica serrirostris*), c.a. PUVI, or the purple-throated euphonia (*T. c. chlorotica*).—**rei**, the southern blackthroated euphonia (*T. musica aureata*), c.a. TERENO.
gauchaço [a-u] (*m.*) an able horseman; a man of courage; a real GAÚCHO.
gauchada [a-u] (*f.*) a number of GAÚCHOS together; typical GAÚCHO behavior.
gauchagem, gaucharia, gaucheria [a-u] (*f.*) any deed or feat worthy of a GAÚCHO; braggadocio.
gauchar, -cherear [a-u] (*v.i.*) to live like a GAÚCHO; to

wander about; to idle.
gauchesco -ca [a-u] (*adj.*) having to do with GAÚCHOS.
gauchismo [a-u] (*m.*) custom, habit, expression, mode of speech, etc., typical of a GAÚCHO.
gauchito -ta, dim. of GAÚCHO.
gaúcho -cha (*adj.*) of or pert. to Rio Grande do Sul; (*m.,f.*) a native of Rio Grande do Sul and of parts of Uruguay and Argentina; (*m.*) formerly, a plainsman.
gauda (*f.*, *Bot.*) a mignonette (*Reseda sp.*).
gauderiar (*v.i.*) to stray from place to place; to look on hopefully while others eat.
gaudério (*m.*) merrymaking, fun; loafer; sponger, parasite; stray dog; a cowbird (*Molothrus bonariensis*), c.a. CHOPIM, VIRA-BOSTA; also = BARBEIRO, the bug which transmits Chagas' disease.
gáudio (*m.*) rejoicing, merrymaking, fun.
gaulês (*adj.*) Gaulish; (*m.,f.*) a Gaul; (*m.*) Gaulish.
gavarro (*m.*) hangnail; (*Veter.*) quittor, whitlow.
gávea (*f.*) a platform around and midway up a ship's mast; a topsail.—**do traquete**, (*Naut.*) foretop. **cêsto de—**, crow's-nest.
gavela (*f.*) sheaf (of grain).
gaveta [ê] (*f.*) drawer (of desk, table, etc.); steam chest, valve chest; wild horse.—**de sapateiro**, a cobbler's bench; by ext., a clutter of any sort.
gaveteiro (*m.*), **-ra** (*f.*) hoarder.
gavião (*adj.*) of horses, wild, hard to catch; (*m.*) any hawk or falcon; the last tooth on each side of a horse's upper jaw; a sharp-witted person; a "wolf" ("ladies' man).—**-belo**, the black-collared hawk (*Busarellus nigricollis*), c.a. GAVIÃO-PADRE, GAVIÃO-VELHO.—**caboclo**, the savanna hawk (*Heterospizias meridionalis*), c.a. GAVIÃO-PUVA, GAVIÃO-TINGA, CASACA-DE-COURO.—**caburé** = GAVIÃO-MATEIRO. — **-caipira** = GAVIÃO-PESCADOR. —**caramujeiro**, the southern everglade kite (*Rostrhamus s. sociabilis*), c.a. GAVIÃO-DE-URUÁ.—**carijó**, a large-billed hawk (*Buteo magnirostris*), c.a. GAVIÃO-PEGA-PINTO, INDAIÉ.—**carrapateiro**, either of two caracaras or carrion hawks: *Milvago chimachima* or *M. chimanga*.—**(de)-coleira**, the small plumbeous or femoral hawk (*Falco fusco-coerulescens* or *F. femoralis*).—**de-penacho** = GAVIÃO-REAL.—**de-uruá** = GAVIÃO-CARAMUJEIRO.—**-mateiro**, a harrier-hawk (*Micrastur ruficollis*), c.a. GAVIÃO-CABURÉ.—**padre** = GAVIÃO-BELO.—**papa-peixe** = GAVIÃO-PESCADOR.—**papa-pinto**, the red-thighed hawk (*Accipiter e. erythronemius*).—**pato**, the black-and-white crested eagle (*Spizastur melanoleucus*).—**pega** (or **-papa**)**-formiga** = GAVIÃO-POMBO.—**pega-macaco**, the tyrant hawk-eagle (*Spizaëtus tyranus*), said to live chiefly on monkeys; c.a. PEGA-MACACO, APACANIM, PAPA-MICO, UIRUUCUTIM.—**pega-pinto** = GAVIÃO-CARIJÓ.—**-pescador**, the osprey or fish hawk (*Pandion haliaëtus carolinensis*), c.a. GAVIÃO-PAPA-PEIXE.—**pinhé** = CARA-CARA-TINGA.—**pombo**, any of several small Brazilian hawks of genus Leucopternis, esp. *L. polionata* and *L. lacernulata*; the plumbeous kite (*Ictinia plumbae*), closely related to the common Mississippi kite and c.a. SOVI, GAVIÃO-SAUVEIRO, GAVIÃO-PEGA-FORMIGA.—**prêto** = CANCÃ.—**puva** = GAVIÃO-CABOCLO.—**quiriquiri**, or—**rapina**, a very small sparrow-hawk (*Falco sparverius*).—**-real**, the harpy eagle (*Harpia harpyja*); the Guianan crested eagle (*Morphus guianensis*), both c.a. GAVIÃO-DE-PENACHO.—**sauveiro** = GAVIÃO-POMBO.—**tesoura**, the southern swallow-tailed kite (*Elanoides forficatus yetapa*), c.a. ITAPEMA, TAPEMA, TESOURÃO.—**tinga** = GAVIÃO-CABOCLO.—**velho** = GAVIÃO-BELO.
gaviãozinho (*m.*) a small kite of Brazil (*Gampsonyx swainsoni*)—the only species.
gavinha (*f.*) tendril.
gavinhoso -sa (*adj.*) having tendrils.
gavota (*f.*) gavotte (dance).
gaxeta [ê] (*f.*) gasket, packing.
gaza, gaze (*f.*) gauze, chiffon; tissue.—**de cobre**, copper wire netting.
gazão (*m.*) garden lawn.
gazeador -dora (*m.*, *adj.*) truant.
gazeamento (*m.*) truancy.
gazear (*v.i.*) to play truant (hooky); to twitter.
gazeio (*m.*) truancy; twitter.
gazela (*f.*) gazelle.
gazeta [ê] (*f.*) newspaper; truancy. **fazer—**, to cut classes; to play truant (hooky).
gazetal (*adj.*) gazette.
gazetear (*v.i.*) to cut school, play truant [=GAZEAR].

gazeteiro (*m.*) newspaper hack; newsboy, newsmonger; truant.
gazetilha (*f.*) section of a newspaper giving personal news items, births, marriages, etc.
gazetilhista (*m.,f.*) writer of local news items.
gazetismo (*m.*) newspaper influence.
gazua, (*f.*) picklock's tool.
g.de = GRANDE (big, large).
gê (*m.,f.*) = JÊ.
geada (*f.*) frost.
gear (*v.i.*) to freeze, frost.
gêba (*f.*) see GÊBO.
gebar (*v.t.*) to crush with blows.
gêbo –ba (*adj.*) humped; poorly dressed; (*m.*) tatter-demalion; a zebu steer; (*f.*) a hump on the back [= GIBA].
Gedeão (*m.*) Gideon.
gedrito (*m.*, *Min.*) gedrite.
Geena (*f.*) Gehenna.
geento –ta (*adj.*) frost-covered, freezing.
geio (*m.*) frost.
gêiser (*m.*) geyser.
gel (*m.*, *Chem.*) gel.
gelada (*f.*) see GELADO.
geladeira (*f.*) refrigerator, icebox.
gelado –da (*adj.*) frozen, ice-cold. **bem**—, well-iced; (*m.*) ice cream, sherbet; a cold drink; (*f.*) iceplant [= OR-VALHO-DA-AURORA]; frost; an iced drink.
gelador –dora (*adj.*) freezing; (*m.*) freezer.
geladura (*f.*) frost damage (to plants).
gelar (*v.t.*) to freeze; to chill; to paralyze (with fear); (*v.i.,v.r.*) to become frozen, chilled; to grow numb.
gelatina (*f.*) gelatine.
gelatiniforme (*adj.*) gelatiniform.
gelatinoide (*adj.*) gelatinoid.
gelatinoso –sa (*adj.*) gelatinous.
geléia (*f.*) jelly.—**de mocotó**, calf's foot jelly.
geleira (*f.*) glacier; ice cream freezer.
geleiro (*m.*) ice manufacturer; iceman.
gelha [ê] (*f.*) wrinkle.
gelidez [dèz] (*f.*) gelidity.
gélido –da (*adj.*) gelid, icy, frozen.
gelignite (*f.*) gelignite (a gelatin dynamite).
gêlo (*m.*) ice; fig., frigidity; indifference.—**-sêco**, dry ice.
gelose (*f.*, *Chem.*) gelose.
gelsemínico –ca (*adj.*, *Chem.*) **ácido**—, gelseminic acid, scopoletin.
gelosia (*f.*) lattice, trellis, grating; lattice window; window blinds, venetian blind.
gelsêmio (*m.*, *Bot.*) the carolina or yellow jessamine (*Gelsemium sempervirens*), c.a. JASMIN-AMARELO, JASMIN-DA-VIRGÍNIA.
gema (*f.*) egg-yolk; gem, jewel; central or vital part, essence. **da**—, genuine, through-and-through.
emação (*f.*, *Biol.*, *Bot.*) gemmation.
gemado –da (*adj.*) having buds; of color of egg yolk; (*f.*) eggnog.
gemagem (*f.*) operation of extracting exudates (turpentine, latex, etc.) from trees.
gemante (*adj.*) shining like gems.
gemar (*v.i.*) to put forth buds; (*v.t.*) to prepare with egg yolk; (*Hort.*) to bud, graft.
gemebundo –da (*adj.*) full of groans and moans; whining, complaining.
gemedor –dora (*adj.*) groaning; (*m.,f.*) groaner.
gemelhicar (*v.*) = GEMICAR.
gemente (*adj.*) groaning.
gêmeo –mea (*adj.*) twin, double; alike, identical; (*m.,f.*) twin; span (of the thumb and forefinger); (*pl.*) twins; the Gemini. **três**—**s**, triplets. **quatro**—**s**, quadruplets. **cinco**—**s**, quintuplets.
gemer (*v.i.*) to groan, moan; to wail, lament; to sob and sigh (as the wind); to creak (as a door); to utter plaintive notes (as a mourning dove); (*slang*) to pay out money or to lend it.
gemicar (*v.i.*) to groan or moan softly but continuously.
gemido (*m.*) moan, groan; mournful sigh; lamentation, wail.
gemífero –ra (*adj.*) producing, or containing, gems; (*Bot.*, *Zool.*) gemmiferous.
gemiforme (*adj.*, *Bot.*) gemmiform.
geminação (*f.*) gemination, coupling, pairing.
geminado –da (*adj.*) geminate, in pairs, coupled.
geminar (*v.t.*) to geminate, couple; to double (consonants).
gêmino –na (*adj.*) = GEMINADO.

gemiparidade (*f.*, *Biol.*) gemmiparity.
gemíparo –ra (*adj.*, *Biol.*) gemmiparous.
gêmula (*f.*, *Biol.*, *Bot.*) gemmule.
gemulação (*f.*, *Biol.*) gemmulation.
gen. = GENERAL.
genal (*adj.*, *Zool.*) genal.
genciana (*f.*, *Bot.*) any species of Gentiana, esp. the following: —**-amarela**, the yellow gentian (*G. lutea*), c.a. GENCIANA-DA-EUROPA.—**-brasileira** or—**-do-brasil**, a prairie gentian (*Eustoma*), c.a. RAIZ-AMARGA.—**-da-terra**, the common name for numerous unspecified varieties.—**-dos-jardins**, the stemless gentian (*G. acaulis*).
gencianáceo –cea (*adj.*) gentianaceous; (*f.pl.*, *Bot.*) the gentian family (*Gentianaceae*).
gencianela (*f.*, *Bot.*) yellow gentian.
gendarmaria (*f.*) gendarmerie.
gendarme (*f.,m.*) gendarme.
gene (*m.*, *Biol.*) gene.
genealogia (*f.*) genealogy, pedigree.
genealógico –ca (*adj.*) genealogical.
genealogista (*m.,f.*) genealogist [= LINHAGISTA].
genebra (*f.*) gin (alcoholic beverage); [*cap.*] Geneva; Geneva; Guinevere.
genebrada (*f.*) gin fizz.
genebrês –brêsa, genebrino –na (*adj.; m.,f.*) Genevan.
general (*m.*) general.—**de Brigada**, Brigadier General.—**de Divisão**, Major General. [The equivalent of general, as an adjective, is GERAL.]
generala (*f.*) a drum or bugle call to general quarters; a general's wife.
generalado, –to (*m.*) generalship.
generalidade (*f.*) generality, universality; the greater part, main body; (*pl.*) rudiments, first principles. Cf. GENERALIZAÇÃO.
generalíssimo –ma (*absol. superl. of* GERAL) most general; (*m.*, *Mil.*) generalissimo.
generalização (*f.*) generalization; general idea, statement, etc.—**lata**, broad generality.
generalizar (*v.t.*) to generalize; (*v.r.*) to become generalized.
generante (*adj.*) generating.
generativo –va (*adj.*) generative.
generatriz (*adj.; f.*) = GERATRIZ.
genérico –ca (*adj.*) generic. **em têrmos**—**s**, in general terms.
gênero (*m.*) genus; gender; genre; kind, sort; (*pl.*) provisions, produce.—**s alimentícios**, foodstuffs. **quadro de**—, genre painting. **único no**—, unique, sui generis.
generosidade (*f.*) generosity; generous deed.
generoso –sa (*adj.*) generous, noble, liberal; (*m.*, *Folklore*, *Spiritism*) poltergeist, a noisy imp or ghost.
gênese, gênesis (*f.*) genesis, origin; (*m.*) Book of Genesis.
genesíaco –ca, genésico –ca (*adj.*) = GENÉTICO.
genetlíaco –ca (*adj.*) pertaining to nativities or birthdays; (*m.,f.*, *Astrol.*) a nativity or calculator of nativities.
genetliologia (*f.*) astrology.
genético –ca (*adj.*) genetic; (*f.*) genetics.
genetriz (*f.*) mother. [*Poetical*]
gengibirra (*f.*) = JINJIBIRRA.
gengibre (*m.*, *Bot.*) common ginger (*Zingiber officinalis*), c.a. MANGARATAIA; also = ITAPITANGA (a rockweed).—**-da-terra**, India gingerlily (*Hedychium gardnerianum*), c.a. LÍRIO-AMARELO-DO-BREJO.—**-dourado**,—**-de-dourar** = AÇAFRÃO-DA-ÍNDIA.
Gengiscão (*m.*) Genghis Khan.
gengiva (*f.*) gum (of the teeth).
gengival (*adj.*) gingival.
gengivite (*f.*, *Med.*) gingivitis.
genial (*adj.*) that shows genius; genial, cordial.
geniculado –da (*adj.*) geniculate
gênio (*m.*) genius; talent, gift; creative power; temperament, disposition; (*colloq.*) irascibility. **de**—**áspero**, ill-natured, irritable. **de bom**—, good-natured.
genioglosso –sa (*adj.*, *Anat.*) genioglossal.
geniohioideu –déia (*adj.*, *Anat.*) geniohyoid.
genioso –sa (*adj.*) ill-tempered.
genístea, genista (*f.*) = GIESTA.
genital (*adj.*) genital.
genitivo –va (*adj.*, *Gram.*) genitive.
genito-crural (*adj.*, *Anat.*) genitofemoral.
genitor –tora (*m.*) progenitor, father; (*f.*) mother.
genitura (*f.*) generation; race, origin.
geniturinário –ria (*adj.*, *Anat.*) genitourinary.
genótipo (*m.*, *Biol.*) genotype.

Gênova (*f.*) Genoa.
genovês –vêsa (*adj.; m.,f.*) Genoese.
Genoveva (*f.*) Genevieve.
genrear (*v.i., slang*) to live on one's parents-in-law.
genro (*m.*) son-in-law. [Daughter-in-law is NORA.]
gentaça, gentalha (*f.*) mob, riff-raff [=RALÉ].
gentama, gentarada (*f., colloq.*) crowd, mass of people.
gente (*f.*) people, persons, mankind, family; personnel,
staff.—da mesma laia, birds of a feather.—de alto
coturno, people in high places.—de côr, colored people.—
-de-fora-já-chegou, the East Brazilian pepper shrike
(*Cyclarhis gujanensis cearensis*).—de nação, descendants
of Jews.—grande, grown-ups. a—, any person, esp. the
speaker—corresponds to French *on*. a—diz que, they
say that. minha—, my folks, tôda (a)—, everybody.
gentil (*adj.*) courteous; kind; thoughtful, gracious;
genteel, refined; noble.
gentileza [ê] (*f.*) politeness, courtesy; gracefulness; good
breeding; kindness, favor; graciousness. cumular de—s,
to overwhelm with kindnesses.
gentil-homem (*m.*) gentleman, nobleman.
gentílico –ca, gentilício –cia (*adj.*) gentile.
gentilidade (*f.*), gentilismo (*m.*) paganism; the Gentiles.
[But not gentility, which is DISTINÇÃO; NOBREZA.]
gentilizar (*v.t.,v.i.*) to gentilize.
gentinha (*f.*) the common people; small fry; riffraff;
meddlesome people.
gentio –tia (*adj.; m.,f.*) heathen; (*colloq.*) populace; gentile; savage.
gentísico –ca (*adj., Chem.*) ácido—, gentisic acid.
gentisina (*f., Chem.*) gentisin.
gentuça (*f.*) riffraff [=RALÉ].
genuflectir (*v.t.,v.i.*) to bend the knee. Var. GENUFLETIR.
genuflector –tora (*adj.*) genuflecting. Var. GENUFLETOR.
genuflexão [ks] (*f.*) genuflection.
genuflexo –xa [ks] (*adj.*) on bended knees.
genuflexório [ks] (*m.*) kneeling-desk.
genuinidade [u-i] (*f.*) genuineness.
genuíno –na (*adj.*) genuine.
geoanticlinal (*m., Geol.*) geanticline.
geobiologia (*f.*) geobiology.
geobotânica (*f.*) phyto-geography.
geocárpico –ca (*adj., Bot.*) geocarpic.
geocêntrico –ca (*adj.*) geocentric.
geocerina (*f., Min.*) geocerite.
geocíclico –ca (*adj., Astron.*) geocyclic.
geocrático –ca (*adj., Geol.*) geocratic.
geodo (*m., Geol.*) geode.
geodésia, geodesia (*f., Math.*) geodesy.
geodético –ca, geodésico –ca (*adj.*) geodetic, geodesic.
geodinâmico –ca (*adj.*) geodynamic; (*f.*) geodynamics.
geofagia (*f.*) geophagy.
geofísico –ca (*adj.*) geophysical; (*m.,f.*) geophysicist;
(*f.*) geophysics.
geófito –ta (*adj., Phytogeog.*) geophytic.
geognosia (*f.*) geognosy.
geognóstico –ca (*adj.*) geognostic.
geografar (*v.t.*) to geographize.
geografia (*f.*) geography.—biológica, biogeoraphy.—botân-
ica, phytogeography.—econômica, commercial geography.—física, physical geography.—humana, anthropogeography.—matemática, mathematical geography.—
política, political geography.—zoológica, zoogeography.
geográfico –ca (*adj.*) geographic(al). acidente—, geo-
graphic feature.
geógrafo (*m.*), -fa (*f.*) geographer.
geóide (*m.*) geoid.
geologia (*f.*) geology.
geológico –ca (*adj.*) geologic(al).
geólogo (*m.*) -ga (*f.*) geologist.
geômetra (*m.,f.*) one versed in geometry.
geometral (*adj., Design*) geometric; (*m., Perspective*)
ground plane.
geometria (*f.*) geometry.—analítica, analytic geometry.
—das linhas, line geometry.—descritiva, descriptive
geometry.—hiperbólica, hyperbolic geometry.—eucli-
diana, Euclidean geometry.—no espaço, space geometry.
geométrico –ca (*adj.*) geometric(al).
geoquímica (*f.*) geochemistry.
georama (*m.*) georama.
georgiano –na (*adj.*) Georgian.
Georgina (*f.*) Georgiana; Georgina; also=CORAL, AMOR-
AGARRADO.
geoscopia (*f.*) geoscopy.

geosfera (*f.*) geosphere.
geoso –sa (*adj.*) frosty.
geossinclinal (*m., Geol.*) geosyncline.
geostática (*f., Physics*) geostatics.
geotaxia [ks] (*f., Biol.*) geotaxis.
geotecnia (*f.*) geotechnics.
geotectônica (*f.*) geotectonics, structural geology.
geotermal (*adj., Geol.*) geothermal.
geotermia (*f.*) the heat of the earth's interior.
geotérmico –ca (*adj., Geol.*) geothermal.
geotermômetro (*m., Physics*) geothermometer.
geotrópico –ca (*adj., Geol., Bot.*) geotropic.
geotropismo (*m., Biol.*) geotropism.
geração (*f.*) generation (in any sense); origination, production, formation.
gerador –triz (*adj.*) generating; (*m.,f.*) generator (in any
sense); (*f., Geom.*) generatrix; (*Elec.*) dynamo.
geral [-ais] (*adj.*) general, generic, universal; (*m.*) the
common run; the greater part; the chief of a religious
order; (*f.*) bleacher, gallery; (*m.pl.*) plains, prairies;
distant uninhabited places. campos gerais, the central
upland plains of Brazil.
Geraldina (*f.*) Geraldine.
Geraldo (*m.*) Gerald.
geralista (*m.,f.*) a native or inhabitant of the State of
Minas Gerais [=MINEIRO]; (*m.*) plainsman; (*f.*) plains-
woman.
geraniáceo –cea (*adj., Bot.*) geraniaceous; (*f.pl.*) the
geranium family (*Geraniaceae*).
gerânio (*m., Bot.*) geranium; the sticky pelargonium
(*P. inquinans*).—brasileiro, a heronbill (*Erodium
geoides*).—rosa, the rosecrescent pelargonium (*P. capitatum*).—sanguíneo, the bloodred geranium (*G. sanguineum*).
geraniol (*m., Chem.*) geraniol.
gerar (*v.t.*) to generate; to procreate; to create (complica-
tions, a new idea, etc.); (*v.r.*) to be born, take form.
geratriz (*adj.; f.*) see GERADOR.
gerbão (*m.*) =GERVÃO.
gérbera (*f., Bot.*) the flame ray gerbera (*G. jamesoni*).)
gerência (*f.*) management, administration.
gerenciar (*v.t.*) to manage.
gerente (*m.,f.*) manager; (*adj.*) managing.
gergelim (*m.*) sesame (plant or seed).
geriatria (*f.*) geriatrics.
gerifalte (*m., Zool.*) gyrfalcon [=GIROFALCO].
geringonça (*f.*) jargon; slang; contraption, rattletrap.
Var. GERIGONÇA.
gerir [21a] (*v.t.*) to manage, run, administer, direct.
germânico –ca (*adj.; n.*) Germanic.
germânio (*m., Chem.*) germanium.
germanismo –mo (*m.*) Germanism.
germanista (*m.,f.*) Germanist.
germanita (*f., Min.*) germanite.
germanizar (*v.t.*) to Germanize.
germano –na (*adj.*) german. irmão—, brother-german;
(*adj.; m.*) German [=ALEMÃO]; [*cap.*] (*f.*) Germaine.
germanófilo –la (*adj.; m.,f.*) Germanophile.
germanofobo –ba (*adj.; f.*) Germanophobe.
germão (*m., Zool.*) germon, albacore (*Germo alalunga*),
c.a. ALBACORA, ATUMBRANCO.
germe, gérmen (*m.*) germ, embryo; microbe; origin.
germicida (*adj.; m.*) germicide.
germinação (*f.*) germination.
germinador (*m.*) germinator (a device for testing the
germinating capacity of seeds).
germinal (*adj.*) germinal.
germinante (*adj.*) germinant; germinative.
germinar (*v.i.*) to germinate, sprout, burgeon; (*v.t.*) to engender, generate.
germinativo –va (*adj.*) germinative.
germinogonia (*f., Biol.*) germinogony.
gêro (*m.*) =ÓROBO.
gerontocracia (*f.*) gerontocracy.
gerontologia (*f.*) gerontology.
gertrudes (*f.*) a species of celery (*Apium ammi*), c.a.
MASTRUÇO; [*cap.*] Gertrude.
gerúndio (*m., Gram.*) gerund.
gervão (*m., Bot.*) a false valerian (*Stachytarpheta*).
gerzelim (*m.*) =GERGELIM.
gesnéria (*f., Bot.*) any of numerous gesneriaceous plants,
especially of the genera Achimenes, Alloplectus, Corytholoma and Naegelia.

gesneriáceo –cea (*adj.*, *Bot.*) gesneriaceous; (*f.pl.*) the Gesneriaceae (gesneria family).

gessal (*m.*) gypsum pit.

gessar (*v.t.*) to cover (a wall, etc.) with gesso for painting; to stucco.

gesseira (*f.*) = GESSAL.

gêsso (*m.*) gypsum; plaster of Paris; gesso; a plaster model. aparelho, or revestimento, de—, plaster cast.

gestação (*f.*) gestation, prègnancy; development.

gestante (*adj.*; *f.*) pregnant (woman).

gestão (*f.*) management, administration; diplomatic representation; (*pl.*) negotiations.

gestatório –ria (*adj.*) gestatory.

gesticulação (*f.*) gesticulation.

gesticulado (*m.*) a gesture.

gesticulador –dora (*adj.*) gesticulating, gesturing; (*m.,f.*) gesticulator.

gesticular (*v.i.,v.t.*) to gesticulate, gesture.

gesto (*m.*) gesture, motion, signal; aspect.—de escárneo, a taunting gesture. fazer—s, to gesticulate, motion. ter um—, to display a feeling or attitude (as of forgiveness, anger, repentance, etc.).

gestor (*m.*) manager [= GERENTE]; attorney in fact.

gia (*f.*) a common collective term for the larger frogs.

giba (*f.*) humpback [= CORCUNDA]; jib sail.

gibão (*m.*) kind of overall; leather jacket; doublet; gibbon.

gibelino –na (*adj.*; *m.,f.*) Ghibelline.

gibi (*m.*) pickaninny; comic book.

gibosidade (*f.*) gibbosity.

giboso –sa (*adj.*) gibbous, humpbacked.

gibista (*f.*, *Min.*) gibbsite, hydrargillite.

gicleur (*m.*) jet (of a carburetor). [*French*]

giesta (*f.*, *Bot.*) woadwaxen (*Genista tinctoria*).

giesteira (*f.*, *Bot.*) genista, broom.—-das-vassouras, Scotch broom (*Cytisus scoparius*), c.a. ESCOPÁRIA.

giga (*f.*) large wooden tub; low basket.

giganta (*f.*) giantess.

gigante (*m.*) giant; buttress; (*adj.*) gigantic, colossal. a passo de—, with giant strides.

gigânteo –tea, gigantesco –ca [ê] (*adj.*) giant, gigantic.

gigantismo (*m.*, *Biol.*, *Med.*) gigantism.

gigantócito (*m.*, *Anat.*) gigantocyte.

gigantólito (*m.*, *Min.*) gigantolite.

gigantologia (*f.*) gigantology.

gígia (*f.*, *Bot.*) a tree (*Parinarium capense*) related to the gingerbread tree.

gigo (*m.*) pannier; wicker basket; large woven crate for shipping china and glassware packed in straw.

gigô, gigote (*m.*) a meat stew.

gigóia = AGUAPÉ. (waterlily).

gigolô (*m.*) gigolo [but only in the sense of a young man who lives on the gains of a prostitute, or who is kept by an older man's mistress].

Gil (*m.*) Giles.

gilbarbeira (*f.*, *Bot.*) butcher's-broom (*Ruscus aculeatus*), c.a. RUSCO.

Gilberto (*m.*) Gilbert.

gilete [lé] (*f.*) safety razor.

gília (*f.*, *Bot.*) bird's-eye gilia (*G. tricolor*).

gilsonita (*f.*, *Min.*) gilsonite, uintaite.

gilvaz (*m.*) cut (gash, slash, scar) on the face.

gim (*m.*) gin (alcoholic drink); jim-crow (a machine for bending or straightening rails).

gimnanto –ta (*adj.*, *Bot.*) gymnanthous, achlamydeous.

gimnêmico –ca (*adj.*) gymnemic [acid].

gimnito (*m.*, *Min.*) gymnite, Deweylite.

gimnoblasto –ta (*adj.*, *Zool.*) gymnoblastic.

gimnocarpo –pa (*adj.*, *Bot.*) gymnocarpous.

gimnóclado (*m.*, *Bot.*) the genus which includes the Kentucky coffee tree (*Gymnocladus dioicus*) whose seeds are sometimes used as a substitute for coffee. [No relation to Coffea, the real coffee tree].

gimnodonte (*adj.*, *Zool.*) gymnodont.

gimnógino –na (*adj.*, *Bot.*) gymnogynous.

gimnosperma (*f.*, *Bot.*) a gymnosperm.

gimnospérmico –ca, gimnospermo –ma (*adj.*, *Bot.*) gymnospermous.

gimnospório (*m.*, *Bot.*) gymnospore.

gimnóstomo –ma (*adj.*, *Bot.*) gymostomous.

gimnoto (*m.*, *Zool.*) a genus (*Gymnotus*, syn. *Electrophorus*) of So. Amer. eellike fishes allied to the electric eel.

ginandrismo (*m.*) gynandrism; hermaphroditism.

ginandro –dra (*adj.*, *Bot.*) gynandrous.

ginandromorfo –fa (*adj.*, *Zool.*) gynandromorphous.

ginasial (*adj.*) gymnasial; of, or pert. to, GINÁSIO.

ginasiano (*m.*), –na (*f.*) student at a GINÁSIO.

ginásio (*m.*) gymnasium; lower secondary school (upper secondary school is COLÉGIO).

ginasta (*m.,f.*) gymnast.

ginástica (*f.*) gymnastics, exercise; physical education.—sueca, calisthenics.

gincana (*f.*) gymkhana.

ginceu (*m.*, *Bot.*) gynoeceum.

ginecóforo (*m.*, *Zool.*) gynecophore.

gineocologia (*f.*) gynecology.

ginecológico –ca (*adj.*) gynecological.

ginecologista (*m.,f.*) gynecologist.

ginério (*m.*) uva grass (*Gynerium sagittatum*).

gineta (*f.*) style of riding with stirrups high and knees bent; (*Zool.*) genet (*Genetta genetta*).

ginete [nê] (*m.*) jennet; a fine, small horse; skilled horseman.

ginetear (*v.i.*) to ride well, esp. on a wild or frisky horse.

ginga (*f.*) sculling oar.

gingação (*f.*) swaying, swinging, rocking.

gingar (*v.i.*) to sway from side to side while walking; to waddle (as a very fat person); to scull.

ginge (*m.*, *colloq.*) chill, thrill.

gingerlina (*f.*) a camel's hair wool.

gínglimo (*m.*, *Anat.*) ginglymus, hinge-joint.

ginja (*f.*) morello cherry (fruit); (*m.*) old fogy; miser.

ginjeira (*f.*, *Bot.*) morello (sour) cherry (*Prunus cerasus*, var. *austera*), c.a. CEREJEIRA-DA-EUROPA.—-da-terra, the myrtle laurelcherry (*Prunus myrtifolia*), c.a. IBIRÓ, JUÁ-AÇU, MARMELO-BRAVO, GINJEIRA-BRAVA, PESSE-GUEIRO-BRAVO, PESSEGUEIRO-DO-MATO, SUPAVA; Jerusalem cherry (*Solanum pseudocapsicum*), c.a. GINJEIRA-DO-BRASIL, PIMENTÃO-DOCE.

ginjinha (*f.*) cherry brandy.

gino-, see also under gimno-.

ginobásico –ca (*adj.*, *Bot.*) gynobasic.

ginodióico –ca (*adj.*, *Bot.*) gynodioecious.

ginóforo (*m.*, *Bot.*) gynophore.

ginogênese (*f.*, *Biol.*) gynogenesis.

ginomonóico –ca (*adj.*, *Bot.*) gynomonoecious.

ginostégio (*m.*, *Bot.*) gynostegium.

ginostêmio (*m.*, *Bot.*) gynostemium.

ginsão, ginsém (*m.*, *Bot.*) ginseng (*Panax*).

gio (*m.*, *Shipbldg.*) transom.

giobertita (*f.*, *Min.*) geobertite; breunnerite; messitite.

gípseo –sea (*adj.*) gypseous.

gipsífero –ra (*adj.*) gypsiferous.

gipsita (*f.*), gipsito (*m.*, *Min.*) gypsum.

gipso (*m.*) gypsum, plaster of Paris [= GÊSSO DE PARIS].

gipsófila (*f.*, *Bot.*) gypsophila [= CRAVO-DE-AMOR].

gipsografia (*f.*) gypsography.

gira (*f.*) gyration; (*m.*, *f.*, *colloq.*) lunatic; (*adj.*, *colloq.*) crazy; "nuts".

giração (*f.*) gyration.

girador –dora (*adj.*) gyrating, turning, whirling; (*m.*) turner; turntable.

girafa (*f.*) giraffe; (*m.,f.*, *colloq.*) a long-necked person.

girame (*m.*) popular name of geranium [= GERÂNIO].

girândola (*f.*) girandole (firework).

girante (*adj.*) gyrating.

girar (*v.i.*) to gyrate, revolve, turn (around); to whirl, spin; to circulate; (*colloq.*) to go crazy; (*v.t.,v.i.*) to rotate. —sôbre si mesmo, to turn on one's heels.

girassol [-ssóis] (*m.*) sunflower; (*Min.*) girasol opal.—-batateiro,—-de-batatas, Jerusalem artichoke sunflower (*Helianthus tuberosus*), c.a. TUPINAMBO.—-do-mato, a gumweed (*Grindelia discoidea*), c.a. MAL-ME-QUER-DO-RIO-GRANDE.—-miúdo, a sunrose (*Helianthemum nummularium*).

girassolina (*f.*) silverleaf sunflower (*Helianthus argophyllus*).

girata (*f.*, *colloq.*) turn (short walk).

giratório –ra (*adj.*) gyratory, rotary, revolving, whirling [= CIRCULATÓRIO].

gíria (*f.*) slang; jargon; cant.

girice (*f.*) lunacy.

girino (*m.*) tadpole; a whirligig beetle (*Gyrinus*).

gírio –ria (*adj.*) slangy.

giro (*m.*) gyration, whirl(ing), rotation; a circumlocution; trade circle; a turn (at work, at a game, etc.); a short excursion, stroll; hinge. dar um—, to go for a turn.

girofleiro (*m.*) = CRAVEIRO-DA-ÍNDIA.

giróforo (m.) a genus (Gyrophora) of lichens.
girógrafo (m.) gyrograph.
giro-horizonte (m., Aeron.) gyro horizon.
girolas (m.,f.) giddy-brained person.
girolito (m., Min.) gyrolite.
girómetro (m.) gyrometer.
giropilôto (m., Aeron.) gyro (automatic) pilot.
giroscópio (m.) gyroscope.
girosela (f., Bot.) shooting star, cowslip (Dodecatheon meadia).
girostático –ca (adj.) gyrostatic; (f.) gyrostatics.
giróstato (m.) gyrostat.
gismondina (f., Min.) gismondite.
gitano (m.) = CIGANO.
gito (m., Founding) gate.
giz (m.) chalk.
gizar (v.t.) to chalk; to chalk out, delineate.
glabela (f., Anat.) glabella.
glabrescente (adj., Bot.) glabrescent.
glabro –bra (adj.) smooth, clean-shaven, hairless; (Bot.) glabrous.
glacê (m.) glossy silk; (adj.) glacé; glossy; glazed; of dry fruit, candied.
glaciação (f.) glaciation.
glacial (adj.) glacial; cold-mannered.
glaciar (m.) glacier [= GELEIRA].
glaciário –ria (adj.) glacial. período—, glacial epoch.
glaciarista (m.,f.) glaciologist.
gladiado –da (adj., Bot.) gladiate; ensiform.
gladiador (m.) gladiator.
gladiar (v.) = DIGLADIAR.
gladiatório –ria (adj.) gladiatorial.
gládio (m.) two-edged sword; dagger; fig., strength, power.
gladíolo (m.) gladiolus, c.a. PALMA-DE-SANTA-RITA.
glamuroso –sa (adj.) glamorous. [Brazilian neologism.]
glande (f.) acorn [= BOLOTA], or acorn-shaped object; (Anat.) glans.
glandífero –ra (adj.) acorn-bearing.
glandiforme (adj.) acorn-shaped.
glândula (f., Anat., Bot.) gland.—s corticais, (Bot.) stomata.—s nectaríferas or ovarianas, (Bot.) nectary. —pineal, pineal body, epiphysis.—pituitária, pituitary gland, hypophysis.—s salivares, salivary glands.—s sebáceas, sebaceous glands.—s sudoríparas, sweat glands.—veneípara, poison sac (of a snake).—vesicular, (Bot.) vesicular gland.
glandular (adj.) glandular.
glandulífero –ra (adj.) glanduliferous, bearing small glands.
glanduliforme (adj.) glanduliform, acorn-shaped; gland-like.
glanduloso –sa (adj.) glandulous, glandular.
glarímetro (m.) glarimeter.
glaserita (f., Min.) glaserite; arcanite; aphthitalite.
Glásgua (f.) Glasgow.
glauberita (f., Chem.) glauberite.
glaucescente (adj., Bot.) glaucescent.
glaucia (f., Bot.) horn poppy (Glaucium).
glaucina (f., Chem.) glaucine.
glauco –ca (adj.) glaucous, bluish-green, greenish-blue.
glaucodote (m., Min.) glaucodote.
glaucofânio (m., Chem.) glaucophane; glaucophanite.
glaucófilo –la (adj., Bot.) glaucophyllous.
glaucoma (m., Med.) glaucoma.
glaucomatoso –sa (adj.) glaucomatous.
glauconífero –ra (adj.) glauconiferous.
glauconita (f., Min.) glauconite.
gleba (f.) glebe, soil, field, piece of (farming) land.
glena (f., Anat.) glenoid cavity.
glenoidal, glenóide, glenoídeo –dea (adj., Anat.) glenoid.
glia (f., Anat.) neuroglia.
gliadina (f., Biochem.) gliadin.
glicemia (f., Med.) glucemia.
glicéreo –rea, glicérico –ca (adj., Chem.) glyceric.
glicéria (f.) water manna grass or floating fescue (Glyceria fluitans).
glicéride (f., Chem.) glyceride.
glicerina (f.) glycerin.
glicerofosfato (m., Chem.) glycerophosphate.
glicerofosfórico –ca (adj.) glycerophosphoric.
glicerol [-óis] (m.) glycerol, glycerin.
glicerôleo (m., Pharm.) glycerite.
glicerose (f., Chem.) glycerose.

glicerriza (f., Bot.) licorice (Glycyrrhiza).
glicina (f., Chem.) glycine; glucina, beryllia.
glicínia (f., Bot.) Chinese wistaria (W. sinensis).
glicirrizina (f., Chem.) glycyrrhizin.
glicocola (f., Chem.) glycoll, glycine.
glicocolato (m., Biochem.) glycocholate.
glicocólico –ca (adj., Chem.) glycocholic [acid].
glicogênese, glicogenia (f., Biochem.) glycogenesis.
glicogênico –ca (adj., Biochem.) glycogenic.
glicogênio (m., Biochem.) glycogen.
glicógeno –na (adj., Biochem.) glycogenous, glycogenic.
glicol [-cóis] (m., Chem.) glycol.
glicólise (f., Biochem.) glicolysis.
glicolítico –ca (adj.) glycolytic.
glicômetro (m.) glucometer.
glicosana (f., Chem.) glucosan(e).
glicose (f.) glucose, dextrose, grape sugar.
glicosido (m., Chem.) glucosid(e).
glicosina (f., Chem.) glycosin(e).
glicosúria, glicosuria (f., Med.) glycosuria.
glifo (m., Arch.) glyph.
glioma (m., Med.) glioma.
gliose (f., Anat.) gliosa.
glioxal [ks] (m., Chem.) glyoxal.
glíptica, gliptografia (f.) glyptography.
gliquemia (f., Med.) glucemia.
glissada, glissagem (f.) glissade; sideslip (of an airplane).
glissar (v.i.) to perform a glissade; of an airplane, to sideslip.
global (adj.) global; whole; over-all.
globicéfalos (m.pl.) a genus of cetaceans (Globicephala) which includes the blackfish (G. mela).
globo (m.) globe, ball; earth.—ocular, eyeball.—do-sol, California poppy (Eschscholzia california), c.a. PAPOULA-DA-CALIFÓRNIA. em—, as a whole; all together.
globóide (adj.; m.) globoid.
globosidade (f.) globosity.
globoso –sa (adj.) globous, globose.
globular (adj.) globular.
globulária (f.) globe daisy (Globularia).
globulífero –ra (adj.) globuliferous.
globulímetro (m., Physiol.) globulimeter.
globulina (f., Biochem.) globulin.
globulito (m., Min.) globulite.
glóbulo (m.) globule; blood corpuscle.
globuloso –sa (adj.) globulous; globulose.
glomerar (v.) = AGLOMERAR.
glomérula (f., Bot.) glomerule.
glomerulado –da (adj., Bot.) glomerulate.
glomérulo (m., Bot.) glomerule; (Anat.) glomerulus.
glomo (m., Veter.) glome.
glonoína (f.) glonoin(e), nitroglycerin.
gloquidiado –da (adj., Bot.) glochidiate.
gloquídio (m., Bot., Zool.) glochidium.
glória (f.) glory; fame; splendor; gloriousness; halo; boast.—celeste,—da-manhã, (Bot.) common morning glory (Ipomoea). levar a banca à—, to break the bank (at gambling). ir à—, to go to pot.
gloriar (v.t.) to glorify.—se-de, to glory in.
glorificação (f.) glorification.
glorificador –dora (adj.) glorifying; (m.,f.) glorifier.
glorificante (adj.) glorifying.
glorificar (v.t.) to glorify, extol, exalt.
gloríola (f.) gloriole; (colloq.) a bit of fame or glory; unmerited good reputation.
glorioso –sa (adj.) glorious, renowned; splendid; exalted; (f.)—dos-jardins, glory lily (Gloriosa superba).
glosa (f.) gloss, comment, annotation; footnote.
glosador –dora (m.,f.) commentator.
glosar (v.t.) to gloss, explain, comment on; (v.i.) to improvise verses.
glossantraz (m., Veter.) glossanthrax.
glossário (m.) glossary.
glossarista (m.,f.) glossarist.
glossectomia (f., Surg.) glossectomy.
glossiano –na, glóssico –ca (adj.) glossal, lingual.
glossifônia (f.) a genus (Glossiphonia, syn. Clepsine) of fresh-water leeches.
glossímetro (m.) glossmeter.
glossógrafo (m., Physiol.) glossograph.
glossina (f.) the genus (Glossina) containing the tsetse fly.
glossite (f., Med.) glossítis.
glossofitia (f., Med., Veter.) blacktongue.

glossografia (f.) glossography.
glossógrafo (m.), **-fa** (f.) glossographer; (m., Physiol.) glossograph.
glossoial (m., Anat.) glossohyal.
glossóide (adj.) glossoid, tonguelike.
glossolalia (f.) glossolalia, gift of tongues.
glossologia (f.) glossology.
glossologista, glossólogo –ga (m.,f.) glossologist.
glossopatia (f., Med.) glossopathy.
glote (f., Anat.) glottis.
glótico –ca (adj.) glottic; (f.) linguistics.
glotologia (f.) glossology; linguistics.
glotologista, glotólogo –ga (m.,f.) glottologist, linguist.
gloxínia [ks] (f., Bot.) gloxinia (Sinningia speciosa).
G.L.P.= GÁSES LIQUEFEITOS DE PETRÓLEO (liquified petroleum gas).
glúcico –ca (adj., Chem.) glucic [acid].
glucina (f.) = GLICINA.
glucínio (m., Chem.) glucinum, beryllium.
glucose (f.) = GLICOSE.
gluglu (m.) gobble-gobble (of a turkey); gurgle-gurgle (of liquid pouring from a bottle). [Onomatopoeic]
gluma (f., Bot.) glume.
glumáceo –cea (adj., Bot.) glumaceous.
glutâmico –ca (adj., Chem.) glutamic.
glutamina (f., Chem.) glutamin(e).
glutão –tona (m., f.) glutton; (adj.) gluttonish, greedy.
glúten, glute (m.) gluten.
glúteo –tea (adj., Anat.) gluteal.
glutina (f., Biochem.) glutin.
glutinar (v.t.) to glue [= AGLUTINAR, CONGLUTINAR].
glutinina (f., Biochem.) glutenin.
glutinosidade (f.) glutinosity.
glutinoso –sa (adj.) glutinous; gluey; adhesive.
glutonaria, glutoneria, glutonia (f.) gluttony.
gnafálio (m.) = COTONÁRIA.
gnaisse (m., Petrog.) gneiss.
gnássico –ca (adj.) gneissic.
gnoma (f.) gnome, aphorism, saw.
gnômo (m.) gnome, goblin.
gnomologia (f.) gnomology.
gnômon, gnômone (m.) gnomon.
gnomoniáceas (f.pl., Bot.) a family (Gnomoniaceae) of fungi.
gnomônico –ca (adj.) gnomonic; (f.) gnomonics.
gnose (f., Metaph.) gnosis.
gnosiologia (f.) gnosiology; epistemology.
gnosticismo (m.) Gnosticism.
gnóstico –ca (adj.; m.,f.) gnostic.
gnu (m., Zool.) gnu.
GO = GOIÁS (State of).
gobelino (m.) Gobelin tapestry.
gobião (m.) goby (a fish).
gobíidas, [i-i] **gobiídeos** [i-í] (m.pl., Zool.) the family (Gobiidae) consisting of the gobies.
gobo [gô] (m.) paving stone.
godé (m.) small pan of water color; godet (of a skirt).
godeme (m.) a fist-blow in the face; an epithet for an Englishman. (Corrup. of goddam.]
goderar (v.t.) to sponge, cadge; to watch hungrily while another eats [= GAUDERIAR].
godes (adv., colloq.) gratis.
godilhão (m.) knot; lump.
gôdo –da (adj.) Gothic (m.,f.) Goth.
Godofredo (m.) Godfrey.
goela (f.) gullet, gorge, throat; (Metal.) throat of a blast furnace; (m.) a greedy, unscrupulous person; one who accepts bribes; gabbler.
goelar (v.i.) to shout, yell; to talk a lot.
goense, goês –êsa (adj.; m.,f.) Goanese, Goan.
goete [ête] (m.) = GUETE.
gôgo (m.) = GOSMA.
gogó (m.) Adam's apple [= POMO-DE-ADÃO].
gogoroba (m.) boozer.
gogoso –sa, goguento –ta (adj.) = GOSMENTO.
goiaba (f.) guava (fruit). Var. GUAIAABA.
goiabada (f.) guava paste. Var. GUAIAABADA.
goiabeira (f., Bot.) guava tree (Psidium guajava). Var. GUAIAABEIRA.
goiaca (f.) = GUAIACA.
goiacuíca (f.) = CUÍCA.
goiamu(m) (m.) = GUAIAMU(M).
goiano –na (adj.) of or pert. to the Brazilian state of Goiás; (m.,f.) a native of that state.

goianzeiro (m.) grassland; dense woods.
goitacá (m.,f.) an Indian of a nearly extinct tribe, remnants of which dwell in Espírito Santo, Brazil; (adj.) pert. to or designating this tribe.
goiva (f.) carpenter's gouge.
goivadura (f.) groove made by a gouge.
goivar (v.t.) to groove with a gouge.
goiveiro (m.) any wallflower (Cheiranthus).—**-branco,** white stock (Mathiola albiflora).—**-das-damas,** dames rocket (Hesperis matronalis).
goivete [vê] (m.) grooving plane.
goivira (f.) = GUAIVIRA.
goivo (m.) any gillyflower, such as stock, wallflower, etc.
gol [ô; pl.: goles ou gois(ô)] (m.) goal (in soccer).
gola (f.) collar, neckband; neck; groove (of a sheave); (Arch.) cyma.—**direta,** cyma recta.—**reversa,** cyma reversa; (Fort.) gorge of a bastion.
golada (f.) = GOLE.
golconda (f.) golconda, lit. & fig.
gole (m.) gulp, swallow, swig [= GOLADA, GOLETA].
golear (v.i.) to score a goal (in soccer).
goleiro (m.) goalkeeper.
golelha [ê] (f.) gullet, esophagus [= ESÔFAGO].
goleta [ê] (f.) inlet; small schooner; also = GOLE.
golfada (f.) a gushing, spouting or spewing; all that is vomited at one time.—**de vento,** a gust of wind. **a—s,** in gushes, in spurts.
gôlfão [-ãos] (m.) = AGUAPÉ (waterlily).
golfar (v.t.) to spout, spew, vomit; (v.i.) to spurt, gush.
gôlfe (m.) golf. **taco de—,** golf stick.
golfinho (m.) dolphin, porpoise; miniature golf.
golfista (m.,f.) golfer.
gôlfo (m.) gulf; (Bot.) the Rudge waterlily (Nymphaea rudgeana), c.a. ÁGUA-PÉ, LÍRIO-D'ÁGUA; waterpoppy (Hydrocleis nymphoides); yellow velvetleaf (Limnocharis flava).
Gólgota (m.) Golgotha, Calvary; a place of martyrdom.
Golias (m.) Goliath.
golilha, golinha (f.) an iron collar by which a criminal is held against a post; a starched ruff.
golpada (f.) a heavy blow.
golpe (m.) blow, hit, stroke, lunge, slash, gash.—**de estado,** coup d'état.—**de mão,** coup de main, surprise attack.—**de mestre,** master stroke.—**de misericórdia,** coup de grâce, finishing stroke.—**de morte,** death blow. —**de vento,** gust of wind.—**de vista,** coup d'oeil, quick glance.—**por—,** blow for blow; tit for tat.—**reverso,** backhand stroke (in tennis). **a—s,** with blows, **de—,** suddenly. **de um—só,** at one stroke. **errar o—,** to miss the mark. **uma chusma de—s,** a shower of blows.
golpeado –da (adj.) hit, struck; slashed. **manga—,** slashed sleeve.
golpeão (m.) crosscut saw.
golpear (v.t.) to strike, beat, hit, slug; to slash, cut, stab; fig., to grieve, afflict.
golpelha [ê] (f.) a large wicker basket.
goma (f.) gum; starch (for linen); tapioca; (Med.) gumma; (Bot.) gummosis.—**amoníaca,** gum ammoniac.—**-arábica,** gum arabic.—**-arábica-de-lagoa-santa** = GOMEIRA. —**-copal,** copal.—**-de-mascar,** chewing gum.—**-de-peixe,** isinglass.—**-elástica,** rubber plant (Fiscus elastica). —**-guta,** gamboge.—**-laca,** shellac. **camisa de—,** stiff shirt.
gomar (v.i.) to sprout, put out buds; (v.t.) = ENGOMAR; also, to smear or treat with gum.
gomável (m.) = GONÇALO-ALVES.
gombô (m.) gumbo (okra).
gomeira (f.) either of two tropical trees of the copaiyé family: Vochysia gummifera, c.a. PELADO, or V. thyrsoidea, c.a. GOMA-ARÁBICA-DE-LAGOA-SANTA, PAU-D'ÁGUA, VINHEIRO-DO-CAMPO, GOMEIRO-DE-MINAS.
gomeiro (m.) dealer in starch (for linen).—**azul,** blue gum tree (Eucalyptus globulus).—**-de-minas** = GOMEIRA.
gomeleira (f.) a plant sucker.
gomeza (f.) an orchid (Gomesa crispa).
gomil (m.) a tall, narrow-mouthed jug or pitcher with handle. Old variants: AGOMIL, AGOMIA.
gomo [gô] (m.) bud, sprout, burgeon; a gore; pulpy segment of citrus fruits; (Veter.) glome.—**de alho,** a clove of garlic.—**principal,** terminal bud.
gomose (f., Bot.) gummosis.
gomosidade (f.) gumminess.
gomoso –sa (adj.) gummy.
gomuto (m.) the gomuti sugarpalm (Arenga pinnata or

A. saccharifera); it yields a sweet sap from which jaggery and palm wine are made; the pith yields a kind of sago and the fiber is made into rope.

gonadia (*f.*, *Anat.*, *Zool.*) gonad.

gonaduto (*m.*, *Zool.*) gonaduct.

gonçalo-alves (*m.*) ashleaf startree (*Astronium fraxinifolium* or *A. graveolens*), c.a. ADERNO-PRÊTO, GOMÁVEL, GONÇALOURO, JEJUÍRA, PAU-GONÇALO, QUEBRA-MACHADO, UBATÃ. [This is one of the most beautiful woods in Brazil, with rose-yellowish undulating grain. It is very resistant to the elements and is unrivalled for fine cabinet work, furniture, pianos, veneers, interior trim and Pullman-car finish; also used for railroad ties and shipbuilding.]

gonçaluro (*m.*) = GONÇALO-ALVES.

gonda (*f.*) the weld mignonette (*Reseda luteola*).

gôndola (*f.*) gondola; (*colloq.*) watch chain; (*Aeron.*) gondola; (*R.R.*) a gondola car.

gondoleiro (*m.*) gondolier.

gonete [nê] (*m.*) gimlet, drill.

gonfalão (*m.*) gonfalon.

gonfose (*f.*, *Anat.*) gomphosis.

gonfrena (*f.*) globe amaranth (*Gomphrena globosa*).

gongo (*m.*) gong; a boat hook.—**do-campo**, a wild coffee (*Psychotria rigida*), c.a. DOURADÃO.

gongolô (*m.*) a millipede [= EMBUÁ].

gongorar (*v.*) = GODERAR.

gongorismo (*m.*) Gongorism.

gonídia (*f.*, *Bot.*) gonidium.

gônio (*m.*, *Anat.*) gonion.

goniometria (*f.*, *Math.*) goniometry.

goniômetro, goniometer; radiogoniometer.—**de contacto**, contact goniometer.—**de reflexão**, reflecting goniometer.

gonioteca (*f.*, *Bot.*) megasporangium.

gônis (*m.*, *Zool.*) gonys.

gonócito (*m.* *Zool.*) gonocyte.

gonococo (*m.*) gonococcus.

gonocorismo (*m.*, *Biol.*) gonochorism.

gonóforo (*m.*, *Bot.*) gonophore.

gonorréia (*f.*, *Med.*) gonorrhea.

gonorréico –ca (*adj.*) gonorrheal.

gonosoma (*m.*, *Zool.*) gonosome.

gonozoário (*m.*, *Zool.*) gonozooid.

gonzo (*m.*) hinge, movable joint [= CHARNEIRA].

gorar (*v.i.*) to addle, become spoiled [egg]; to miscarry [plans]; (*v.t.*) to frustrate.

gordacho –cha, **gordaço** –ça, **gordalhaço** –ça, **gordalhão** –lhona, **gordalhudo** –da, **gordalhufo** –fa, **gordanchudo** –da, **gordão** –dona (*adj.*) very fat, plump, roly-poly, obese, portly, paunchy.

gordinho (*m.*) harvest fish (*Peprilus paru*), c.a. PARU.

górdio –**dia** (*adj.*) Gordian. **nó**—, Gordian knot.

gordo –da [gôr] (*adj.*) fat; fatty, oily, greasy; fleshy, corpulent, obese; fertile, fruitful. **à**—, plenteously, lavishly. **dias**—s, the six days preceding Ash Wednesday. **uma**—**recompensa**, a fat reward.

gorducho –cha (*adj.*) = GORDACHO.

gordura (*f.*) fat, grease, shortening; fatness, stoutness.— **animal (vegetal)**, animal (vegetable) fat.—**de-porco**, an Amazon vine (*Stigmaphyllon fulgens*).

gordural (*m.*) an area planted with molasses grass.

gordurento –ta, **gorduroso** –sa (*adj.*) greasy, fatty.

gorete(-de-pedra) (*m.*) = GUETE.

gorga (*f.*) corn spurry (*Spergula arvensis*).

gorgolhão (*m.*) gush; stream.

gorgolhar (*v.i.*) to gush (out).

gorgolejante (*adj.*) gurgling.

gorgolejar (*v.i.*) to gurgle.

gorgolejo [lê] (*m.*) a gurgling.

gorgomilo(s) (*m.*, *colloq.*) gullet.

górgone, **górgona** (*f.*) Gorgon; a terrible or repulsive woman.

gorgonzola (*f.*) Gorgonzola cheese.

gorgorão (*m.*) grosgrain (silk and wool fabric).

gorgorejo [ê] (*m.*) gurgle.

gorgulho (*m.*) curculio, snout beetle; corn or granary weevil; "a short rapids, in which water flows over rocks in the stream bed with a rush, creating air bubbles; to be distinguished from CACHOEIRA, CORREDEIRA and PANCADA." [*GBAT*]

goril[h]a (*m.*) gorilla.

gorinhatã (*m.*) = GATURAMO.

gorja (*f.*) gorge, throat.

gorjal (*m.*) gorget.

gorjear (*v.i.*) to warble, trill, sing; to chirrup.

gorjeio (*m.*) a warbling or chirping.

gorjeira (*f.*) lace or muslin tucker; high net collar.

gorjeta [ê] (*f.*) tip (gratuity).

gorne (*m.*) groove or swallow of a sheave.

gornir (*v.t.*) to reeve (a rope).

gôro –ra (*adj.*) addled; spoiled.

gororoba (*f.*) sluggard; weakling; grub (poor food); (*Bot.*) the Pará porcupine podtree (*Centrolobium paraense*).

gorovinhas (*f.pl.*) pleats; wrinkles.

gorrixo (*m.*) = ENCONTRO (a bird).

gorra (*f.*) a "liberty cap".

gôrro (*m.*) cap, beret; (*slang*) a jockey.

gorutubano –na (*m.,f.*) a half-breed.

goslarita (*f.*, *Min.*) goslarite; zinc vitriol.

gosma (*f.*) chicken pip; horse distemper, strangles; phlegm, mucus; goo.

gosmar (*v.t.,v.i.*) to hawk up (phlegm).

gosmento –ta (*adj.*) of poultry, having the pip; of horses, having distemper; of persons, given to much spitting or hawking up of phlegm; sickly, feeble; gooey.

gostar (*v.t.*) to like, enjoy, relish; to taste.—**de (beber)**, to like to (drink).—**de (música)**, to like (music).— **muito**, to like very much, love.—**um do outro**, to like each other. **não**—**de**, to dislike. **Quem**—**de mim, tem que**—**dos meus**, Love me, love my dog.

gostável (*adj.*) likeable, delectable.

gôsto (*m.*) sense of taste; taste, flavor, savor; relish; discrimination, culture; elegance; manner, style; liking; joy, delight, pleasure. **a**—, at ease. **Esteja a**—, Make yourself at home. **ao**—**de**, in keeping with; in the manner of. **com todo o**—, gladly. **desagradável ao**—, unpleasant to the taste, unpalatable. **fazer**—, to please, be a pleasure. **Sôbre**—**s não se discute**, There's no accounting for tastes.

gostosão (*m.*, *slang*) a "big hunk of man"; playboy; big shot; philanderer; a "character" who considers himself irresistible.

gostoso –sa (*adj.*) tasteful, toothsome, delicious; pleasing, delightful. **O fruto proíbido é o mais**—, Stolen fruits are sweetest.

gostosura (*f.*) intense pleasure; something delightful.

gôta (*f.*) drop, droplet; tear; dewdrop; (*Arch.*) gutta; (*Med.*) gout; (*colloq.*) epilepsy.—**s-de-sangue**, (*Bot.*) summer adonis (*A. aestivalis*).—**serena**, the "drop serene" of Milton (*amaurosis*). **a**—**d'água que faz transbordar o copo**, the straw that breaks the camel's back. **conta**—**s**, medicine dropper. **Parecem-se como duas**—**s d'água**, They are as like as two peas in a pod. **uma**—**d'água no meio do mar**, a drop in the bucket.

goteira (*f.*) roof gutter; down spout; a leak in the roof.

gotejamento (*m.*) a dripping.

gotejante (*adj.*) dripping.

gotejar (*v.t.,v.i.*) to drip, trickle, dribble.

gótico –ca (*adj.*) Gothic.

goto (*m.*) glottis. **cair** or **dar no**—, to go down (the throat) the wrong way; also, of things, to become popular.

gotoso –sa (*adj.*) gouty; (*m.,f.*) a sufferer from gout.

gougre (*adj.*) inelegant; tasteless in dress.

governação (*f.*) governing; government [= GOVÊRNO].

governadeira (*adj.; f.*) thrifty (housewife).

governado –da (*adj.*) governed; self-controlled; frugal.

governador –**dora** (*adj.*) governing; (*m.*) governor; (*f.*) governor's wife; woman governor.

governamental (*adj.*) governmental.

governança (*f.*) the government. [*Derogatory*]

governanta (*f.*) governess; housekeeper.

governante (*adj.*) governing; (*m.*) governor; (*f.*) governess [= GOVERNANTA].

governar (*v.t.*) to govern, rule; to sway; to guide, steer, direct; (*v.r.*) to manage oneself.—**bem o seu barco**, to manage well one's affaris.

governativo –va (*adj.*) governmental.

governatriz (*f.*) a woman who governs, manages or directs; (*adj.*) governing.

governável (*adj.*) governable.

governicho, governículo (*m.*) the government. [*Derogatory*]

governismo (*m.*) governance; dictatorial government.

governista (*m.,f.*) a partisan or supporter of the government; (*adj.*) government-supporting.

govêrno (*m.*) government, administration, regime; reign; governance, rule, control, command; steering.—**dis-**

cricionário, autocratic government.—**fantoche,** puppet government.

gozado –**da** (*adj., slang*) funny; "swell". **O**—**do troço é que . . . ,** The best part of the joke is that. . . . **um camarada**—, a queer guy.

gozador (*m.*) one who enjoys life (doesn't worry, crosses bridges when he comes to them); a "sport".

gozar (*v.t.*) to enjoy, have the use of (advantages, etc.); (*v.i.*) to enjoy (life, etc.), experience pleasure; (*v.r.*) to rejoice in, delight in.—**a vida,** to have one's fling.—**saúde,** to enjoy good health.

gôzo (*m.*) enjoyment, delight; possession, use, fruition; cause for laughter; little dog. **em**—**de férias,** on vacation.

gozoso –**sa** (*adj.*) joyous.

G/P = GANHOS E PERDAS (profit and loss).

gr. = GRÃO (grain of weight); GRÁTIS (free); GREGO (Greek); GRAU (degree); GROSA (gross).

grã (*f.*) grain of wood; (*adj.*) short for grande. Cf. GRÃO.

Grã-bretanha (*f.*) Great Britain.

graça (*f.*) grace, kindness; forgiveness; mercy; gracefulness, comeliness; charm; wit; drollery; divine favor; baptismal name; (*pl.*) thanks.—**s a,** thanks to.—**s a Deus!** Thank God!—**pesada,** a coarse joke. **a**—**da história foi que . . . ,** the joke of the matter was that. . . . **Acho nisso,** I think that's funny. **dar**—**s,** to give thanks. **dar de**—, to give away (free of charge). **dar um ar de sua**—, to show up, put in an appearance. **de**—, gratis (free). **estado de**—, a state of grace. **estar nas**—**s de alguém,** to be in another's good graces. **Qual a sua**—? Your name, please? **sem**—, insipid, tasteless; spiritless, unamusing; ungraceful. **ter**—, to be funny, amusing.

gracejador –**dora** (*adj.*) bantering; (*m.,f.*) jester, joker.

gracejar (*v.i.*) to jest, joke, banter.

gracejo [ê] (*m.*) pleasantry, quip, witticism, jest, joke, raillery, wisecrack. **por**—, for fun; in fun.

grácil [-ceis] (*adj.*) gracile; slender, thin.

gracilidade (*f.*) graceful slenderness.

gracíola (*f.*) the drug hedgehyssop (*Gratiola officinalis*).

graciolina (*f., Chem.*) gratiolin.

graciosidade (*f.*) graciousness; gracefulness; facetiousness.

gracioso –**sa** (*adj.*) graceful; gracious; dainty; comely; "cute"; witty, facetious; gratuitous; (*m.,f.*) jester, buffoon; comedian in a play.

graçola (*f.*) a joke in poor taste; wisecrack; (*m.,f.*) a coarse jester.

graçolar (*v.i.*) to indulge in coarse jokes.

grã-cruz (*f.*) grand cross (decoration); (*m.*) a person wearing it.

gradação (*f.*) graduation; (*Rhet.*) climax.

gradador (*m.*) harrow; harrower; grader.

gradadura, gradagem (*f.*) harrowing; grading.

gradar (*v.t.*) to harrow; to grade (the soil); (*v.i.*) to grow, swell (as grain, fruit).

gradaria (*f.*) grating; paling.

gradativo –**va** (*adj.*) gradual.

grade (*f.*) grating, bars, latticework, grille, railing; a harrow; currycomb; (*Elec.*) grid; (*pl., colloq.*) jail.—**de discos,** disk harrow.

gradear (*v.t.*) to rail in; to fence off; to provide with bars (as a window); to harrow.

gradiente (*m.*) gradient.

gradil (*m.*) low fence or railing.

gradim (*m.*) sculptor's finishing chisel.

gradiômetro (*m.*) gradiometer.

grado –**da** (*adj.*) filled-out, well-developed (as, an ear of corn); big, important (said of persons); (*m.*) will; intent. **ajudar de bom**—, to lend a willing hand. **de bom**—, willingly. **de bom ou de mau**—, willy-nilly. **de mau**—, unwillingly. **mau**—, in spite of.

gradômetro (*m.*) gradometer.

graduação (*f.*) graduation (of a scale), degree; rank.—**universitária,** graduation at a university [= FORMATURA].

graduado –**da** (*adj.*) graduated, graded; graduate. **mais**—, higher-ranking.

graduador –**dora** (*adj.*) grading; (*m.,f.*) grader.

gradual (*adj.*) gradual; (*m., Eccl.*) Gradual.

graduamento (*m.*) = GRADUAÇÃO.

graduando –**da** (*m.,f.*) a senior student who is about to graduate.

graduar (*v.t.*) to graduate (mark with degrees); to grade, classify; to give a diploma to; (*v.r.*) to graduate (at college) [= FORMAR-SE].—**se em medicina,** to graduate in medicine.

graduável (*adj.*) adjustable.

grã-ducado (*m.*) = GRÃO-DUCADO.

grã-duque (*m.*) = GRÃO-DUQUE.

grã-duquesa (*f.*) Grand Duchess.

graeiro (*m.*) a lead pellet; a grain (of wheat, etc.).

grafar (*v.t.*) to write (a word).

grafia (*f.*) orthography; spelling.

gráfico –**ca** (*adj.*) graphic (referring to the graphic arts or methods but not to language); (*m.*) a graph; chart;—(or **diagrama**) **em setores,** (*Stat.*) a circle chart. (*m.,f.*) one who is employed in the graphic arts; (*f.*) writing; spelling.

grã-finismo (*m.*) status, manners, dress, etc. of a GRÃ-FINO; the class of GRÃ-FINOS.

grã-fino –**na** (*m.,f., slang*) uppercruster, swell, socialite; (*pl.*) the "400," the "smart set"; (*m.*) a certain grade of sugar; (*adj.*) swanky, "swell".

grafista (*m., slang*) an untrained draftsman.

grafita (*f.*) graphite.—**coloidal,** colloidal graphite.

grafítico –**ca** (*adj.*) graphitic.

grafito (*m.*) graffito.

grafologia (*f.*) graphology.

grafólogo –**ga, grafologista** (*m.,f.*) graphologist, handwriting expert.

grafômetro (*m.*) graphometer.

grafoscópio (*m.*) graphoscope.

grafostático –**ca** (*adj.*) graphostatic; (*f.*) graphostatics.

grahamita (*f., Min.*) grahamite.

grainha [a-í] (*f.*) pip, grape seed.

gral (*m.*) mortar (bowl-shaped vessel); Holy Grail.

gralha (*f.*) a misprint; a garrulous woman; a magpie; in Brazil, any of various jays, esp. of genus Cyanocorax. [In Portugal, the term refers to rooks and jackdaws, which do not occur in Brazil, as do not either the common blue jays of North America (genus Cyanocitta).] The principal Brazilian jays are: Diesing's jay (*Cyanocorax chrysops diesingii*) and Heilprin's jay (*C. heilprini*), both of the Amazon region; the blue-headed jay (*Cyanocorax cyanopogon*), c.a. QUEM-QUEM; the Cayenne jay (*Cyanocorax cayanus*); the black-headed jay (*Cyanocorax cyanomelas*) of southern Brazil.—**azul,** the azure jay (*Cyanocorax caerulus*).—**do-campo,** the pega jay (*Uroleuca cristatella*), c.a. GRALHA-DE-PEITO-BRANCO.—**do-mato,** the urraca jay (*Cyanocorax c. chrysops*).

gralhada (*f.*) chattering of birds; a hubbub.

gralhão (*m.*) = CARACARÁ-PRÊTO, QUEM-QUEM.

gralhar (*v.i.*) to caw, croak; to chatter.

grama (*f.*) a gram, the 1000th part of a kilogram.—**-átomo,** (*Chem.*) gram-atom, gram-atomic weight.—**-caloria,** (*Physics*) gram (small) calorie.—**-massa,** (*Physics*) the gram as a unit of mass in the C.G.S. system.—**-molécula,** (*Chem.*) gram-molecular weight; gram-mol; mole. Any of numerous grasses, esp. the following:—**branca,** redtop grass (*Agrostis alba*).—**-cheirosa** = CAPIM-VETIVER.—**comprida** = CAPIM-COMPRIDO.—**comum,** Bermuda grass (*Cynodon dactylon*), c.a. CAPIM-DE-BURRO; also the Bahiagrass paspalum (*P. notatum*).—**da-guiné,** Guinea grass, c.a. CAPIM-GUINÉ.—**da-praia,** the seashore dropseed (*Sporobolus virginianus*).—**da-terra** = CAPIM-GOMOSO.—**de-coradouro** = CAPIM-PÉ-DE-GALINHA.—**de-forquilha** = CAPIM-PANCUÃ.—**de-jacobina** = BURRÃO.—**de-jardim,** St. Augustine grass (*Stenotaphrum secundatum*).—**de-ponta,** quackgrass (*Agropyron repens*).—**do-maranhão** = CAPIM-GOMOSO.—**doce,** the brook paspalum (*P. acuminatum*).—**italiana,** the pink reineckia (*R. carnea*)—not a grass.—**larga** = CAPIM-DE-SÃO-CARLOS.—**paulista** = CAPIM-MARMELADA.—**pêlo-de-urso,** the dwarf lilyturf (*Mondo japonicum*)—not a grass.—**pesada,** heavy turf (at the racetrack).

gramadeira (*f.*) a swingle for beating flax.

gramado (*m.*) lawn, grassplot, turf; grass-covered soccer field.

gramão (*m.*) Bermuda grass (*Cynodon dactylon*), c.a. GRAMA-COMUM, CAPIM-DE-BURRO.

gramar (*v.t.*) to swingle, scutch (flax, hemp, etc.); to swallow, gobble; to undergo, be subjected to; to trudge, tramp, plod; to cover with turf or grass.—**uma espiga,** to be fooled.—**uma sova,** to catch a "licking"

gramática (*f.*) see under GRAMÁTICO.

gramatical (*adj.*) grammatic(al).

gramaticalismo (*m.*) pedantic devotion to grammar.

gramaticão (*m.*), –**cona** (*f.*) a grammatical pedant or pretender.

gramaticar (*v.i.*) to discuss points of grammar; to teach grammar.

gramaticista (*m.,f.*) grammatist.

gramático –ca (*adj.*) grammatical; (*m.,f.*) grammarian; (*f.*) grammar.

gramatiqueiro (*m.*), –ra (*f.*) a pedantic grammarian.

gramatiquice (*f.*) pedantic emphasis on correct diction.

gramatista (*m.,f.*) gramatist; pedantic grammarian.

gramatita (*f., Min.*) tremolite; grammatite.

grameal (*m.*) shrubby vegetation.

gramíneo –nea (*adj.*) gramineous, grass-like; (*f.*) any member of the grass family.

graminha (*f.*) roughstalk bluegrass (*Poa trivialis*).— –comum, — -da-cidade, — -de-raiz, — -do-mato, — -fina = CAPIM-DE-BURRO (Bermuda grass).—-de-araquara = CAPIM-CEBOLA. — -de-campinas = CAPIM-PÉ-DE-GALI-NHA. — -de-jacobina = BURRÃO.—-doce = CAPIM-DOCE.— -nativa, the Bahiagrass paspalum (*P. notatum*), c.a. GRAMA-COMUM, GRAMA-DE-FÔLHA-LARGA, GRAMA-NATIVA. —-sêda, the fringed chloris (*C. ciliata*).

graminho (*m.*) carpenter's marking gauge; mortise gauge; scriber, scribe awl.

graminícola (*adj., Zool.*) graminicolous.

graminifólio –lia (*adj., Bot.*) graminifolious.

graminiforme (*adj., Bot.*) graminiform.

graminoso –sa (*adj.*) grassy.

gramíola (*f.*) = BICHA-AMARELA.

gramofone (*m.*) gramophone.

grampeador (*m.*) stapler.

grampear (*v.t.*) to staple.

grampo (*m.*) cleat; clamp; cotter pin; hairpin; staple, fencing staple.

granada (*f.*) grenade, bomb, shell; (*Min.*) garnet.—de mão, hand grenade.

granadeiro (*m.*) grenadier, bomber.

granadilha (*f.*) the wingstem passionflower (*Passiflora alata*) or its fruit, c.a. MARACUJÁ-AÇU, MARACUJÁ-DE-CAIENA.

granadilho (*m.*) a macawood c.a. MACACAÚBA.

granadino –na (*adj.*) of the color of grenadine (syrup); garnet-red; (*f.*) grenadine (fabric).

granal (*adj.*) grain.

granalha (*f.*) granulated metal; shot.

granar (*v.t.*) to granulate; (*v.i.*) to form grains.

grandalhão –lhona, grandão –dona (*adj.*) very large, huge, outsize.

grande (*adj.*) large, big, great; vast, of great size; broad, wide; long, tall; grown-up; grand; (*m.*) a bigwig; a grandee. à—, grandly, on a grand scale. um—homem, a great man. um homem—, a big man.

grande-mundo (*m.*) grand monde, high society.

grande-senhor (*m.*) grand seigneur.

grandes-labios (*m.pl., Anat.*) labia majora pudendi.

grandessíssimo –ma (*adj., colloq.*) = GRANDÍSSIMO.

grandeza [ê] (*f.*) largeness, bigness, size; greatness, magnitude; grandeur, magnanimity.

grandinho –nha (*adj.*) biggish.

grandiloqüência (*f.*) grandiloquence, bombast.

grandíloquo –qua (*adj.*) grandiloquent, bombastic, high-sounding.

grandiosidade (*f.*) grandeur, magnificence.

grandioso –sa (*adj.*) grandiose; grand; gorgeous.

grandíssimo –ma (*absol. superl. of* GRANDE) most large.

grandote (*adj.*) biggish.

grandura (*f., colloq.*) = GRANDEZA.

granear (*v.i.*) to grain (form grains), as corn.

granel [-néis] (*m.*) granary; heap of grain; printer's composing stick [= PAQUÊ]. a—, in bulk; loose.

granido –da (*adj.*) stippled; (*m.*) stipple.

granfino –na (*adj.; m.,f.*) = GRÃ-FINO.

granífero –ra (*adj.*) grain-bearing.

graniforme (*adj.*) graniform.

granir (*v.t.*) to stipple.

granita (*f.*) soft pellet, as of goat droppings; pip, grape seed.

granítico –ca (*adj.*) granitic.

granitito (*m., Petrog.*) granitite.

granito (*m.*) a small grain; granite; hot weather after a rainy spell.

granitófiro (*m., Petrog.*) granite porphyry.

granitóide (*adj., Petrog.*) granitoid.

granitoso –sa (*adj.*) = GRANÍTICO.

granívoro –ra (*adj.*) granivorous.

granizada (*f.*) hail storm.

granizar (*v.i.*) to hail; (*v.t.*) to shower as hail; to granulate.

granizo (*m.*) hail.—miúdo, sleet.

granja (*f.*) grange; farm.—avícola, poultry farm.— leiteira, dairy farm.

granjeador (*m.*) tiller (of the soil).

granjear (*v.t.*) to till (the soil); to gain, achieve; to obtain; to win, attract.

granjeio (*m.*) tillage; harvest.

granjeiro (*m.*) granger, farmer.

granjola (*adj.*) corpulent; (*m.*) overgrown boy.

granodiorito (*m., Petrog.*) granodiorite.

granoso –sa (*adj.*) grainy.

grânula (*f., Med.*) granulitis, miliary tuberculosis.

granulação, granulagem (*f.*) granulation.

granulado –da (*adj.*) granulated.

granular (*adj.*) granular; (*v.t.*) to granulate.

granuliforme (*adj.*) granuliform.

granulítico –ca (*adj., Petrog.*) granulitic.

granulito (*m., Petrog.*) granulite.

grânulo (*m.*) granule.

granulócito (*m., Anat.*) granulocyte.

grânulo-gorduroso –sa (*adj., Anat.*) granuloadipose, granulofatty.

granulóide (*adj.*) granular.

granuloma (*m., Med.*) granuloma.

granulosidade (*f.*) grain-like character.

granuloso –sa (*adj.*) granular.

granza (*f., Bot.*) a madder (*Rubia splendens*), c.a. RUIVA, GARANÇA.—brava, Levant madder (*R. peregrina*), c.a. RASPA-LINGUA.—-da-praia, a crosswort (*Crucianella maritima*).

grão [-ãos] (*m.*) grain, seed, kernel; grain of a material; round particle; a measure of weight equivalent to 0.77 grains or 0.05 grams; (*adj.; m.*) short for GRANDE. Cf. GRÃ.—-de-bico, chickpea, c.a. GRAVANÇO.—-de-bode, a swartzpea tree (*Swartzia*).—-de-cevado, barleycorn. —-de-galo, a hackleberry (*Celtis iguaneus*), c.a. JUÁ-MIÚDO, VURAPIÁ; a cordia (*C. magnoliaefolia*), c.a. JAGUARAMURU; a jujube (*Zizyphus undulata*), c.a. JUÁ-MIRIM, JUÀZEIRO, MAMINHA-DE-CABRA; also = GRÃO-DE-PORCO.—-de-galo-miúdo = GRÃOZINHO-DE-GALO.— -de-ouriço, (*Zool.*) echinococcus.—-de-porco, the big-flower cordia (*C. grandiflora*), c.a. GRÃO-DE-GALO, JAGUARAMURU, RAMELA-DE-CACHORRO.—-de-pulha, the mungo bean (*Phaseolus mungo*).—-gnídio, the fruit of the spurgeflax daphne (*D. gnidium*).—-s de chumbo, small young coffee berries. De—em—a galinha enche o papo, Little and often fills the purse; Little strokes fell great oaks; Many a little makes a mickle.

grão-ducado (*m.*) grand duchy.

grão-duque (*m.*) grand duke.

grão-lama (*m.*) Grand Lama.

grão-mal (*m., Med.*) grand mal, epilepsy.

grão-mestre (*m.*) grand master.

grão-rabino (*m.*) a chief or high priest of the Jews.

grão-sacerdote (*m.*) Supreme Pontiff.

grão-senhor, grão-turco (*m.*) Grand Seignior (former sultan of Turkey).

grão-tinhoso (*m., colloq.*) the Devil.

grão-vizir (*m.*) grand vizier.

grãozinho (*m.*) small pebble of ilmenite found in diamond beds.—-de-galo, a hackberry (*Celtis spinosissima*), c.a. GRÃO-DE-GALO-MIÚDO.

grapa (*f., Veter.*) scratches.

grapelim (*m.*) grappling iron, grapnel.

grapiapunha(-branca) (*f.*) a caesalpiniaceous tree (*Apuleia praecox*) which yields timber for heavy outdoor construction, posts, railroad ties, beams, etc.; also a medicinal bark and tannin. Other common names are: GARAPA, GARAPA-AMARELA, GUARAPIAPUNHA, GUARETÃ, IBIRÁ-PERÊ, MULATA, MULATEIRA.

grapibu [ú] (*m.*) a tropical leguminous tree (*Schizolobium parahybum*).

grapirá (*m.*) frigate bird [= ALCATRAZ].

grapiúna (*m.*) a derogatory epithet applied by the inlanders of the State of Bahia to persons dwelling on the coast.

grapso (*m.*) a genus (*Grapsus*) of crabs.

grapsóide (*adj., Zool.*) grapsoid.

grasnada, grasnadela (*f.*) a cawing, croaking or quacking.

grasnador –dora, grasnante (*adj.*) cawing, quacking, croaking.

grasnar (*v.i.*) to caw (as a crow), to screech (as a parrot); to quack (as a duck); to croak (as a frog); (*v.t.*) to croak.

grasneiro –ra (*adj.*) = GRASNADOR.
grasnido, grasno (*m.*) a loud cawing, quacking, croaking.
grasnir (*v.*) = GRASNAR.
grassapé (*m.*) = DOURADO-DO-MAR.
grassar [51] (*v.i.*) to spread (as news); to rage (as an epidemic).
grassento –ta (*adj.*) greasy, fat.
grassitar (*v.i.*) to quack (as a duck).
gratamente (*adv.*) gˌatefully; agreeably.
gratéia (*f.*) a river-bottom drag; a grappling iron.
gratidão (*f.*) gratitude.
gratificação (*f.*) gratuity, bounty, bonus, fee, tip.
gratificador –dora (*adj.*) rewarding, remunerating; (*m.,f.*) rewarder.
gratificar (*v.t.*) to reward, remunerate, recompense. [But not to gratify, in the sense of pleasing or indulging, which is SATISFAZER, AGRADAR.]
gratífico –ca (*adj.*) grateful.
grátis (*adv.*) gratis, for nothing, free.
grato –ta (*adj.; irreg. p.p. of* AGRADAR *and of* AGRADECER) grateful (**a,** to); gratifying; pleasing.
gratuidade [u–i], **gratuitidade** (*f.*) gratuitousness.
gratuitamente (*adv.*) gratuitously.
gratuito –ta [túi] (*adj.*) gratuitous, voluntary; free, without recompense; uncalled for, wanton. **acusação—,** an unfounded accusation.
gratulação (*f.*) congratulation.
gratular (*v.t.*) to congratulate.
gratulatório –ria (*adj.*) congratulatory.
grau (*m.*) degree, step; grade, rank, order; station, standing; university degree; unit of measurement; division (as, on a scale, of a circle, etc.); a remove in the line of descent; an exponent (algebraic symbol).—**adiantado,** advanced stage.—**de parentesco,** degree of kinship.—**s centígrados,** degrees centigrade. **alto—,** high degree, intensity. **ao sumo—,** in the highest degree. **em alto—,** in high degree.
graúdo –da (*adj.*) big, fully developed; whopping; (*m.pl.*) bigwigs, big shots.
graúlho (*m.*) grape seed; pip.
graúna (*f., Zool.*) the rice grackle (*Psomocolax o. oryzivorus*), c.a. CHICO-PRÊTO, IRAÚNA, MELRO, MELRÃO, CARAÚNA, REXENXÃO, VIRABOSTA-MAU.—**-de-bico-branco,** Azara's black cacique (*Archiplanus solitarius*), c.a. IRAÚNA-DE-BICO-BRANCO; (*Bot.*) = BARAÚNA.
gravação (*f.*) engraving; carving; phonograph recording or radio transcription (on a disc); tape recording; grievance.
gravado –da (*adj.*) engraved; burdened down.
gravador –dora (*adj.*) engraving; carving; recording; (*m.,f.*) engraver; carver; recording artist; (*m.*) a radio recording device.—**magnético,** magnetic (wire, tape) recorder.
gravame (*m.*) grievance; hardship; heavy tax; (*Law*) gravamen.
gravancelo (*m.*) = ESPARAVÃO.
gravanço (*m.*) = GRÃO-DE-BICO.
gravar (*v.t.*) to engrave, emboss, etch, chisel, carve; to imprint, stamp; to fix (in the memory); to burden, oppress; to record (phonograph record or tape).
gravata (*f.*) cravat, necktie; a strangle hold (in wrestling). —**-borboleta,** bow tie.
gravatá (*m.*) any of numerous bromeliads (plants of the pineapple family). Cf. CARAGUATÁ, CARUÁ, CARUATÁ and CRAUÁ.—**-açu,** a bromelia (*B. karatas*), c.a. CARAGUATÁ, PITEIRA.—**-branco,** an eryngo (*Eryngium pandanifolium*).—**-bravo,** a bromelia (*B. mucilaginea*).—**-da-índia,** a hardy terrestrial orchid (*Listera mullicaule*).—**-da-pedra,** an aechmea (*A. nudicaulis*), c.a. GRAVATÁ-DO-CAMPO; also = CARAGUATÁ-FALSO.—**-das-rãs,** an aechmea (*A. legrelliana*).—**-de-agulha,** a bromelia (*B. muricata*), c.a. ANANÁS-DE-AGULHA.—**-de-árvore,** the Sander airbrom (*Billbergia sanderiana*).—**-de-flor-verde,** an airbrom (*Billbergia ensifolia*).—**-de-gancho,** a bromelia (*B. fastuosa*), c.a. GRAVATÁ-DA-PRAIA, MANÁ-DE-RAPÔSA.—**-de-muqueca,** an aechmea (*A. dealbata*).—**-de-rapôsa** = GRAVATÁ-AÇU.—**-de-tingir,** an airbrom (*Billbergia tinctoria*).—**-do-ar,** a tillandsia (*T. linearis*).—**-do-mato,** a bromelia (*B. binoti*); an eryngo (*Eryngium glaziovianum*).—**-falso,** an eryngo (*Eryngium elegans*).—**-vermelho,** an aechmea (*A. miniata*).—**-zebra,** the zebra airbrom (*Billbergia zebrina*); the flaming vriesia (*V. speciosa*).
gravataria (*f.*) necktie shop or factory.
gravatàzal (*m.*) an area abounding in GRAVATÁS.

gravatàzinho (*m., Bot.*) an eryngo (*Eryngium nudicaule*)
gravatear (*v.t., colloq.*) to behead.
gravateiro (*m.*) dealer in neckties; (*colloq.*) a criminal strangler.
gravatinha (*f.*) = COLEIRO-DA-BAHIA.
gravato (*m.*) = GARAVATO.
grave (*adj.*) grave, weighty; serious, momentous; sober, dignified; grievous; (of sound) low, deep; (of accent) grave.
gravela (*f.*) pressed grape husks; wine lees.
gravéola (*f., Bot.*) the cherimoya (*Annona cherimola*), c.a. GRAVIOLA.
graveolência (*f.*) bad smell.
graveolente, graveolento –ta (*adj.*) strong-smelling; bad-smelling.
gravêta (*f.*) grapnel.
gravêto (*m.*) = GARAVÊTO.
gravidade (*f.*) gravity, seriousness; dignity; importance, weightiness; gravitation; (*Physics*) gravity.—**específica,** specific gravity.
gravidar (*v.t.*) to render pregnant.
gravidez [ê] (*f.*) pregnancy.
grávido –da (*adj.*) gravid, pregnant.
gravígrado –da (*adj.*) heavy-footed; (*m.pl., Paleontol.*) the Gravigrada (ground sloths).
gravimetria (*f.*) gravimetry.
gravimétrico –ca (*adj., Chem.*) gravimetric.
gravímetro (*m.*) gravimeter.
graviola (*f.*) the cherimoya (*Annona cherimola*) tree or fruit; c.a. GRAVÉOLA; (shipbuilding) cradle.
gravitação (*f.*) gravitation.
gravitante (*adj.*) gravitating, tending.
gravitar (*v.i.*) to gravitate, tend, incline (**para,** toward).
gravoso –sa (*adj.*) grievous, onerous, troublesome. **produtos—s,** products which are overpriced and unable to compete in foreign markets.
gravotear (*v.t., Carp.*) to mark the line to be cut.
gravura (*f.*) an engraving; picture, illustration.—**a água forte,** etching.
graxa (*f.*) grease; shoe polish; (*Bot.*) Chinese hibiscus (*H. rosa-simensis*), c.a. GRAXA-DE-ESTUDANTE, MIMO-DE-VÊNUS.
graxeira (*f.*) boiler for rendering fat.
graxeiro (*m.*) oiler (as of railroad switches); greaser.
graxento –ta (*adj.*) greasy; fat.
graxo –xa (*adj.*) greasy, oily, fatty.
graxudo –da (*adj.*) of animals, fat, sleek.
grazina (*m.,f.; adj.*) (person) given to much and loud talking.
grazinada (*f.*) hubbub.
grazinador –dora (*adj.*) = GRAZINA.
grazinar (*v.i.*) to talk much and loudly; to grumble, complain.
grecânico –ca, **greciano** –na (*adj.; m.,f.*) Greek [= GREGO].
Grécia (*f.*) Greece.
grecismo (*m.*) Grecism, Hellenism.
greco-Latino –na (*adj.*) Greco-Latin.
grecomania (*f.*) Grecomania.
greco-romano –na (*adj.*) Greco-Roman.
greda [ê] (*f.*) chalk.
gredoso –sa (*adj.*) chalky; marly.
greenockita (*f., Min.*) greenockite; cadmium sulfide.
grega (*f.*) see GREGO.
gregal (*adj.*) Greek; gregal.
gregalada (*f.*) gregale (a Mediterranean wind).
gregalóide (*adj., Zool.*) gregaloid.
gregário –ria (*adj.*) gregarious.
gregarismo (*m.*) gregarianism.
grego –ga (*adj.*) Grecian, Greek; fig. unintelligible. **Isto para mim é—,** It's Greek to me; (*m.,f.*) Greek; (*f., Arch.*) Greek fretwork; (*m., slang*) a crook.
gregoriano –na (*adj.*) Gregorian.
Gregório (*m.*) Gregory.
gregotins (*m.pl.*) grimaces; scribbles [= GARATUJAS].
greguejar (*v.i., colloq.*) to speak Greek.
grei (*f.*) flock, herd; congregation; followers, people; party, coterie.
grelação (*f., slang*) ogling.
grelado –da (*ad*) having buds or sprouts.
grelador –dora (*adj.*) ogling; (*m.*) ogler.
grelar (*v.i.*) to bud, sprout; to swell, grow in size; to grow by leaps and bounds; (*v.t., slang*) to ogle; to stare at.

grelha [é] (*f.*) grill, grid, gridiron, grating; (*slang*) an old plug (horse); (*Elec.*) grid [= GRADE].
grelhar (*v.t.*) to grill, broil.
grêlo (*m.*) seed germ; bud, sprout.
grêmio (*m.*) body, society, coterie; literary guild.
grenho –**nha** (*adj.*) of hair, unruly, disheveled; (*f.*) mop of hair; lion's mane.
grenhudo –**da** (*adj.*) having a mop of hair.
grés (*m.*) sandstone [= ARENITO]; sandy clay.
grêta (*f.*) crack (in the soil, in a wall, in the ceiling, in a painting, etc.); rift.
gretado –**da** (*adj.*) cracked.
gretadura (*f.*) a chap (crack in the skin.)
gretar (*v.t.,v.i.,v.r.*) to crack.
grevas [é] (*f.pl.*) jambeau (of a suit of armor).
greve (*f.*) strike (work stoppage).—**de fome**, hunger strike. **fazer—**, to strike (cease work).
grevílea (*f., Bot.*) silkoak grevillea (*G. robusta*).
grevista (*m.,f.*) striker.
grifa (*f.*) see GRIFO.
grifar (*v.t.*) to italicize; to underscore, underline; to emphasize.
grifo –**fa** (*adj.*) sloping to the right; underlined, underscored; italic; (*m.*) enigma; griffin; italic letter; (*f.*) a pipe wrench.
grigri (*m.*) greegree (African charm, amulet or fetish).
grilagem (*f.*) land grabbing.
grileiro (*m.*) claim jumper; land grabber.
grilento –**ta** (*adj.*) said of land held under fake title.
grilhagem (*f.*) iron chain.
grilhão (*m.*) chain; watch chain; (*pl.*) fetters.
grilheta [é] (*f.*) shackle, fetter; (*m.*) a criminal condemned to hard labor.
grilo (*m.*) a cricket; (*colloq.*) a squeak in the body of an automobile; (*slang*) a traffic cop or his whistle; (*slang*) a pocket watch; a piece of land held under fake title; a squatter.—**noturno**, (*colloq.*) night watchman.—**toupeira**, a mole cricket, c.a. PAQUINHA.
grimaça (*f.*) grimace.
grimiáceas (*f.pl.*) a large family (*Grimmiaceae*) of rock mosses.
grimpa (*f.*) weathervane; cockscomb, crest; top, summit. **abaixar a—**, to draw in one's horns, lower one's flag. **levantar a—**, to bristle, bridle; to get one's dander up.
grimpado –**da** (*adj.*) at the very top.
grimpante (*adj.*) climbing [plants].
grimpar (*v.i.*) to talk back rudely; to come to grips (with another person); to clamber (as a cat up a tree).
grinalda (*f.*) garland, wreath, chaplet; anthology.—**de-noiva**, (*Bot.*) bridal wreath (*Spiraea prunifolia*).—**de-viuva** = CAPELA-DE-VIUVA.
grindélia (*f.*) the field gumweed (*Grindelia camporum*), c.a. MALMEQUER-DO-CAMPO.
grinfar (*v.i.*) to twitter [= TRISSAR].
gringada, gringalhada (*f.*) gringos (collectively).
gringo—ga (*m.,f.*) gringo; any foreigner, esp. a blond one. [*Depreciative*]; peddler [= MASCATE].
gripado –**da** (*adj.*) suffering from the grippe.
gripagem (*f.*) = GRIPAMENTO.
gripal (*adj.*) pert. to the grippe.
gripamento (*m., Mach.*) gripping, jamming or sticking, as from want of lubrication.
gripar (*v.r.*) to come down with the grippe; (*v.i., Mach.*) to stick, jam or grip (as from want of lubrication).
gripe (*f.*) grippe, bad cold, influenza.—**espanhola**, the Spanish flu of 1918.—**asiática**, Asiatic flu (1957).
gris (*adj.*) gray; brown.
grisalhar (*v.i.*) to turn gray.
grisalho –**lha** (*adj.*) grizzly; gray-headed; gray-bearded; hoary; brown.
griseta [é] (*f.*) wickholder (of a lamp).
grisete (*f.*) grisette. [French working girl.]
griséu (*adj.*) grayish.
grisu [ú] (*m.*) methane, firedamp (in mines).
grita, gritada (*f.*) = GRITARIA.
gritadeira (*f.*) loudmouthed woman; shouting, clamor; (*Bot.*) wild coffee (*Psychotria*), c.a. DOURADÃO.
gritador –**dora** (*adj.*) shouting, yelling; (*m.,f.*) loudmouthed person, shouter.
gritalhão (*m.*), —**lhona** (*f.*) shouter, yeller.
gritar (*v.i.*) to shout, yell, "holler"; to clamor, cry out (**contra**, against); to shriek; to scream; to bawl; to rail at. **Não me grite!** Don't shout at me!

gritaria (*f.*) hullabaloo, clamor, outcry, shouting, hue and cry, uproar, din.
grito (*m.*) shout, cry, yell; a scream, shriek.—**de aviso** a cry of warning.—**de guerra**, war cry. **dar um—**, to cry out.
grizandra (*f., Bot.*) a wall rocket (*Diplotaxis catholica*).
Groenlândia (*f.*) Greenland.
groenlandês –**dêsa** (*adj.*) Greenlandic; (*m.,f.*) Greenlander; the language of the Greenlanders.
grogojó (*m.*), **grogotuba** (*f., Bot.*) a gourd (*Cucurbita ovoide*).
grogotó (*exclam.*) All is finished! It's too late!
grogue (*m.*) grog; (*adj.*) groggy.
groló (*m., Zool.*) an ani (*Crotophoga major*), c.a. ANU(N)-GUAÇU, ANUM-PEIXE.
gronga (*f.*) a ramshackle thing; drunken witchcraft; a drink made with rum and lemon juice.
grosa (*f.*) gross, twelve dozen; rasp (coarse file).
grosar (*v.t.*) to rasp (wood).
groselha (*f.*) currant, gooseberry; gooseberry syrup (for mixing drinks); (*adj.*) currant-red.
groselheira (*f.*) any currant or gooseberry plant.—**da-índia**, the otaheite-gooseberry leaf-flower (*Phyllanthus acidus*).—**espinhosa**, or -**grossa**, European gooseberry (*Ribes uva-crispa*).—**preta**, European black currant (*Ribes nigrum*).—**vermelha**, Northern red currant (*Ribes rubrum*).
grossa-aventura (*f., Maritime Law*) gross adventure.
grossagrã, grossagrana (*f.*) grosgrain.
grossaria (*f.*) thick cotton or linen cloth; also = GROSSERIA.
grosseirão –**rona** (*adj.*) common, inferior; lowbred; boorish; gruff; very thick-brained; (*m.*) boor, churl; cad; roughneck.
grosseirismo (*m.*) coarseness; uncouthness; incivility.
grosseiro –**ra** (*adj.*) coarse, rough, crude; uncouth, rude, uncivil, surly; gross, vulgar; scurrilous; (*m.,f.*) skin eruption.
grosseria (*f.*) coarseness, rudeness; disrespect; a crude or vulgar expression, scurrility.
grossista (*adj.*) wholesale; (*m.,f.*) wholesaler [= ATA-CADISTA].
grosso –**sa** (*adj.*) thick (not thin); bulky, solid; voluminous; abundant; gross, coarse; stiff. (*m.*) mass, bulk, largest part. **a—**, in bulk. **o—de**, the bulk of.
grossulária (*f.*) the gooseberries (*Grossularia, syn. Ribes*). Cf. GROSELHEIRA.
grossularita (*f., Min.*) grossularite.
grossura (*f.*) grossness; thickness.
grota (*f.*) hole in a river bank; deep, dark valley. Cf. GRUTA.
grotão (*m.*) deep, narrow valley.
groteiro (*m.*) backwoodsman [= CAIPIRA].
grotesco –**ca** [ê] (*adj.*) grotesque, ridiculous, preposterous; (*m.,f.*) a grotesque person. Cf. GRUTESCO.
grou (*m.*), **grua** (*f.*) any crane of the genus Grus; (*f.*) crane (derrick); (*R.R.*) water crane.
grudado –**da** (*adj.*) glued together.
grudador –**dora** (*adj.*) glueing; (*m.,f.*) gluer.
grudadura (*f.*) glueing, pasting.
grudar (*v.t.*) to glue, stick, fasten tightly (as with glue); (*v.i.,v.r.*) to cling, stick, adhere (**a, com**, to).
grude (*m.*) glue; paste; (*colloq.*) grub (food); (*colloq.*) dalliance; (*colloq.*) shindy.—**de peixe**, fish glue.
grudento –**ta** (*adj.*) gluey, sticky.
grugulejar (*v.i.*) to gobble (as a turkey).
grugulhar (*v.i.*) to boil, bubble; also = GRUGULEJAR.
grugunzar (*v.i.*) to meditate, ponder; to rack one's brains.
grulha (*m.,f.*) chatterer; (*m.*) daredevil.
grulhada (*f.*) din, clamor; blather.
grulhar (*v.i.*) to prate, prattle, chatter.
grumar (*v.t.,v.i.,v.r.*) to clump or clot.
grumecência (*f.*) state of coagulation.
grumecer (*v.*) = GRUMAR.
grumete [mé] (*m.*) ordinary seaman; cabin boy.
grumixama (*f.*) fruit of the
grumixameira (*f.*) grumichama or Brazilian cherry (*Eugenia dombeyi*, not *E. brasiliensis*) having edible fruit and medicinal bark and leaves; c.a. IBAPOROTI, GURUMIXAMEIRA.
grumo (*m.*) small clot or cluster, clump, lump.
grumoso –**sa** (*adj.*) grumous, thick, clotted; grumose.
grúmulo (*m.*) a small grume or clot.
gruna (*f.*) deep hole in a river bank; hole made by digger for diamonds.

grunado (*m.*, *Geol.*) sinkhole [=ITARARÉ].
grunhidela (*f.*), **grunhido** (*m.*) grunt.
grunhidor –**deira** (*adj.*) grunting; (*m.*,*f.*) grunter.
grunhir [25] (*v.i.*) to grunt (as a pig); to grumble.
grupal (*adj.*) group.
grupamento (*m.*) grouping.
grupar (*v.t.*) to group [=AGROUPAR].
grupelho [ê] (*m.*) a small and insignificant group or party. [*Derogatory.*]
grupo (*m.*) group, assemblage, body; cluster.—**minoritário**, minority group.—**social**, social group.
gruta (*f.*) grotto, cave, den. Cf. GROTA.
grutescos [ê] (*m.pl.*) grotesques, arabesques. Cf. GROTESCO.
guabiju [ú] (*m.*) fruit of the
guabijueiro (*m.*, *Bot.*) an eugenia (*E. pungens*) c.a. QUABIJUZEIRO, GUABIROBA-AÇU, IBABIU.
guabirabeira (*f.*)=GUABIROBA.
guabiroba (*f.*) any of various myrtaceous trees and shrubs (esp. of genus Campomanesia), or their fruit; c.a. GABIROBA, GABIROBEIRA, GUABIRABA, GUABIRABEIRA. —**açu**=GUABIJUEIRO.—**brava**, a chaste tree (*Vitex mullinervis*), c.a. MARIA-PRETA, IPÊ-DO-CÓRREGO, TARUMÃ.—**de-minas**, the guabiroba (*Abbevillea fenzliana*).
guabirobeira (*f.*)=GUABIROBA.
guabiru [ú] (*m.*) common rat (*Mus decumanus*).
guaçatonga (*f.*) any of several trees of the Indian-plum family, genus Casearia.
guachamaca (*f.*) a So. Amer. tree (*Malouetia nitida*) of the dogbane family; also its bark which contains a violent narcotic poison.
guache (*m.*) gouache (painting).
guacima (*f.*)=CAMBACÁ.
guacina (*f.*) a resin extracted from guaco.
guaco (*m.*) guaco, a tropical American vine (*Mikania guaco*); the climbing hempweed (*Mikania scandens*).—-**bravo**=CIPÓ-DE-CORAÇÃO, ANGELICÓ.
guaçu [çú] (*adj.*) the Tupian word for big—used alone or in combination; (*m.*) the cohune palm (*Orbignya cohune*), c.a. AGUAÇU.
guaçubirá (*m.*)=CATINGUEIRO (a deer).
guaçuboi (*m.*) the rainbow or ringed boa (*Epicrates cenchris*).
guaçucatinga (*m.*)=CATINGUEIRO (a deer).
guaçucuia (*m.*)=PEIXE-MORCEGO.
guaçuetê (*m.*)=VEADO-MATEIRO.
guaçupita (*m.*)=VEADO-MATEIRO.
guaçupucu (*m.*)=CERVO (a deer).
guacuri (*m.*) a palm (*Scheelea princeps*), c.a. NAIÁ, RUCURI, UACURI.
guacuru (*m.*)=SOCOÍ.
guaçuti (*m.*)=VEADO-CAMPEIRO.
guademã (*f.*), **guademão** (*m.*)=GADEMAR.
guaiaba (*f.*)=GOIABA.
guiabeira (*f.*)=GOIABEIRA.
guaiabada (*f.*)=GOIABADA.
guaiaca (*f.*) a soft leather belt for carrying money or weapons [=GOIACA].
guáiaco (*m.*, *Bot.*) the common lignumvitae (*Guajacum officinale*) and the holywood lignumvitae (*G. sanctum*), c.a. PAU-SANTO, LENHO-SANTO; also, the resin guaiacum.
guaiacol (*m.*, *Chem.*) guaiacol.
guaiá-das-pedras (*m.*) any of various rock crabs.
guaiamu(m) (*m.*) any of various land crabs, c.a. GOIAMU(M).
guaianá (*m.*,*f.*) an Indian of the Guayaná, an ancient tribe of Caingang Indians who lived in what is now the State of São Paulo, and who were associated with the early history of that state. [The public square in the City of São Paulo called Praça Princêsa Isabel used to be called Largo dos Guayanazes.]; (*adj.*) of or pert. to the Guayaná.
guaiar (*v.i.*) to wail, moan.
guaiara (*f.*) a wide, ornamented, shiny leather belt (for money, weapons, tobacco, etc.).
guaíba (*f.*) a deep swamp; (*m.pl.*) an Indian tribe which dwelt on the São Francisco River in Brazil.
guaibira (*f.*)=GUAIVIRA.
guaicanãs (*m.pl.*) an aboriginal tribe of São Paulo.
guaicuru [rú] (*m.*) the indigenous language of Paraguay; (*pl.*) the Guaycuru tribe, remnants of which, called Cadiueus, dwell in southern Mato Grosso; (*Bot.*) Brazil sea lavender (*Limonium brasiliense*).—-**de-campo**, a button plant (*Spermacoce centranthoides*), c.a. SABUGUEIRO-DO-CAMPO.

guaimbé (*m.*, *Bot.*) a medicinal philodendron (*P. squamiferum*).
guainumbi (*m.*) any hummingbird [=BEIJA-FLÔR].
guaipé, guaipeca, guaipeva (*m.*)=CUSCO.
guajuru [rú] (*m.*)=GUARAJURU-PIRANGA.
guaiule (*m.*, *Bot.*) the guayule parthenium (*P. argentatum*).
guaiuvira (*f.*, *Bot.*) a viraru (*Ruprechtia salicifolia*), c.a. IBIRARO, IVIRARO; also=GUAJUVIRA-BRANCA.
guaivira (*m.*) the leather-jacket (*Oligoplites saurus*), a small fish c.a. GOIVIRA, GUAIBIRA, CAVACO, TÁBUA, TIBURO, SOLTEIRA, PAMPARRONA.
guajabara (*f.*)=CABUÇU.
guajajara (*m.*,*f.*) an Indian of a small Tupi-Guarani-speaking group in the State of Maranhão, closely related to the Tembé in the adjoining State of Pará, together with whom they form the Tenetehara; (*adj.*) pert. to or designating the Guajajara.
guajará (*m.*, *Bot.*) a star apple (*Chrysophyllum*).
guajuru, guajeru, guajiru, [rú] (*m.*) the icaco cocoplum (*Chrysobalanus icaco*), c.a. GAJERU, UAJERU, UAJURU.
guajuvira (*f.*, *Bot.*)=CABUÇU.—-**branca**, a Patagonia tree (*Patagonula americana*), whose brown to blackish purple wood is well-known for its elasticity and flexibility; used for tool handles, railroad ties, barrel hoops and cabinet work; c.a. GUAIUVIRA, GUARAJUVIRA, IPÊ-BRANCO.
gualdra (*f.*) drawer knob or handle.
gualdrapa (*f.*) saddlecloth.
gualdripar (*v.t.*) to steal.
gualdrope (*m.*) tiller rope.
guambu (*m.*)=CUAMBU.
guamirim (*m.*) a bitterwood (*Trichilia claussenii*) c.a. VAMIRIM.
guamixinga (*f.*) angostura barktree (*Galipea officinalis*) c.a. JASMIM-DO-MATO, QUINA-DAS-TRÊS-FÔLHAS, QUINA-FALSA, QUINA-QUINA, TICORÓ, TRÊS-FOLHAS-DO-MATO.
guampa (*f.*) horn; drinking horn.
guampear (*v.t.*) to lasso (a steer) by the horns.
guampo (*m.*)=GUAMPA.
guampudo –**da** (*adj.*) big-horned.
guanabano (*m.*, *Bot.*) sour sop (*Annona muricata*).
guanacaste (*m.*, *Bot.*) an earpodtree (*Enterolobium cyclocarpum*).
guanaco (*m.*, *Zool.*) the largest species of wild llama, (*Auchenia huanaco*).
guanambi (*m.*) hummingbird [=BEIJA-FLORES].
guanandi (*m.*) Brazil beautyleaf (*Calophyllum brasiliense*) whose wood is used as building timber; c.a. JACAREÚBA, LANDIM, LANTIM, OLANDI.
guanás, guanases (*m.pl.*) an aboriginal tribe of Mato Grosso.
guandeiro (*m.*)=GUANDU.
guandira (*m.*) a bat [=ANDIRÁ].
guando, guandu [dú] (*m.*) the pigeonpea (*Cajanus cajan*), c.a. ANDU, ERVILHA-DE-ANGOLA, ERVILHA-DE-SETE-ANOS, ERVILHA-DO-CONGO, FEIJÃO-ANDU, FEIJÃO-GUANDU, FEIJÃO-DE-ÁRVORE, GUANDEIRO.
guango (*m.*) the raintree saman (*Samanea saman*).
guanidina (*f.*, *Chem.*) guanidin(e).
guanina (*f.*, *Chem.*) guanin(e).
guano (*m.*) guano.—**artificial**, chemical fertilizer.—
guante (*m.*) iron gauntlet.
guanxuma (*f.*)=GUAXIMA.
guaparaíba (*m.*, *Bot.*) American mangrove (*Rhizophora mangle*).
guapear (*v.i.*) to be valorous, stalwart [=GUAPETONEAR]; to endure.
guaperuvu [vú] (*m.*)=GRAPIBU.
guaperva (*f.*) a frogfish (*Antennarius scaber*), c.a. PEIXE-SAPO, ANTENÁRIO.
guapetaço –**ça**, **guapetão** –**tona** (*adj.*) valiant.
guapetonagem (*f.*)=GUAPEZA.
guapetonear (*v.i.*)=GUAPEAR.
guapeva (*adj.*; *m.*) short-legged (dog);=CUSCO.
guapeza, guapice (*f.*) manliness; handsomeness; spruceness.
guapira (*f.*) head of a valley; headwaters. Var. GAPIRA.
guapirá (*m.*, *Bot.*) black mangrove (*Avicennia marina*).
guapiruvu [vú] (*m.*)=BACURUBU.
guapo –**pa** (*adj.*) stalwart, manly; handsome; smart, elegant, dapper, spruce, trim, nifty, natty.
guapô (*m.*, *colloq.*) steam locomotive.
guapurubu [bú] (*m.*)=BACURUBU.
guaqui (*m.*) an opossum (*Didelphys*).

guaquica (*f.*, *Bot.*) an eugenia (*E. guaquica*).

guar (*m.*) = CUMANDATIÁ.

guará (*m.*) the scarlet ibis (*Guara rubra*); the flamengo (*Phoenicopterus ruber*), c.a. GANSO-DO-NORTE; the agouara (a wild dog), c.a. AGUARÁ.

guarabu [bú] (*m.*) any of several Brazilian timber trees of the genus Peltogyne (the purplehearts), c.a. JIGAÍ, JUTAIRANA, PAU-ROXO, ROXINHO, QUARIBU.——prêto, a startree (*Astronium concinnum*), c.a. ADENO-PRÊTO.

guaraçapema (*m.*) = DOURADO-DO-MAR.

guaracava (*f.*) any of various flycatchers or tyrant birds of genus Elaenia, c.a. GURACAVA, BEM-TE-VI-PEQUENO.

guaracavuçu (*f.*) the dusky flycatcher (*Cnemotriccus f. fuscatus*).

guaraguá (*m.*, *Zool.*) the manatee (*Trichechus manatus* or *T. inunguis*), c.a. PEIXE-BOI.

guarã-guarã (*m.*, *Bot.*) the Florida yellowtrumpet (*Stenolobrium stans*).

guaraipo (*m.*) a bee c.a. URUÇU, GUARAPU; a sly, rascally person.

guarajau (*m.*) an oblong basket for carrying chickens, etc., to market.

guarajuba (*f.*) (*Bot.*) the guarabu terminalia (*T. acuminata*), c.a. GUARAJUBEIRA; (*Zool.*) the horse-eye jack (*Caranx latus*); also, a paroquet called GUARUBA.

guarajuru-piranga [rú] (*m.*) a funnelvine (*Arrabidaea chica*), c.a. CARAJURU, GUAJURU.

guaraná (*f.*) the guarana paullinia (*P. cupana*), a Brazilian climbing shrub, from the pounded seeds of which is prepared a dried paste for medicinal use and also for flavoring a stimulating and refreshing drink. Other names for the shrub are: NARANAZEIRO, NARANÁ.

guaranázeiro (*m.*) the shrub GUARANÁ, or one who gathers its seeds.

guarandi [í] (*m.*) the greater white-shouldered tanager (*Tachyphonus rufus*), c.a. TIÉ-PRÊTO, TACHÁ, MACHO-DE-JOÃO-GOMES.——-azul = SANHAÇO-FRADE (a tanager) and AZULÃO (a grosbeak).——prêto = TIÉ-PRÊTO (a tanager).

guaranhém (*m.*) a starapple (*Chrysophyllum flexuosum*).——do-campo, either of two eugenias (*E. pseudo-verticilliflora* or *E. riedeliana*).

guarani [í] (*m.*) *Webster*: "(a) An Indian of a group of Tupian tribes, formerly occupying most of the valleys of the Paraguay, Paraná and Uruguay rivers between the Tropic of Capricorn and northern Uruguay. Most of them were Christianized by the Jesuits in the early 17th century, and gathered into settlements or reductions, called the Paraguay Missions, which prospered until the expulsion of the Jesuits in 1767. (b). The language of the Guarani, called also ABAÑEÊME, developed from the Southern Tupian dialects under the influence of the Jesuits"; (*adj.*) pert. to or designating the Guarani or their language.

guaranina (*f.*, *Chem.*) guaranin(e).

guaranítico -ca (*adj.*) Guaranian, Guarani.

guarantã (*f.*, *Bot.*) the guarantan gasparillo (*Esenbeckia leiocarpa*); a cupania (*C. xanthoxyloides*); a caesalpinia (*C. ferrea*), c.a. GURATÃ, PAU-FERRO.

guarapará (*m.*) = VEADO-MATEIRO.

guarapariba (*f.*) a trumpet tree (*Tabebuia aquatilis*), c.a. GUARAPARAÍBA, TATAJUPOCA.

guaraperê, guaraporê (*m.*) = CANGALHEIRO.

guarapiapunha (*f.*) = GRAPIAPUNHA-BRANCA.

guarapu [pú] (*m.*) a brocket (*Mazama rondoni*), c.a. FOBOCA, GARAPU; a stingless, tropical honeybee (*Melipona nigra*), c.a. GUARUPU, GUARAÍPO, URUÇU.——miúdo, a small melipona (*M. marginata*), c.a. MANDURIM, TAIPEIRA, URUÇU-MIRIM.

guarapuvira (*f.*) = GUAJUVIRA-BRANCA.

guaratã (*f.*) = CAMBACICA.

guaraxaim [a-í], guaraxim (*m.*) = AGUARAXAIM.

guarda (*f.*) guard, defense, protection; care, watchfulness; safeguard; flyleaf; guardrail; scion, twig, cutting; (*m.*) watch, watchman, guardian, warden, keeper, sentry; sleeping-car porter. anjo da—, guardian angel. casa da—, guardhouse. cabo da—, corporal of the guard.

guarda-arnês (*m.*) harness room.

guarda-barreira (*m.*) tollkeeper; customhouse guard.

guarda-braço (*m.*) brassard.

guarda-calhas (*m.*) cow-catcher [= LIMPA-TRILHOS].

guarda-cancela (*m.*) flagman at a R.R. crossing.

guarda-chapim (*m.*) a low wall supporting an iron fence; a sloping wall alongside masonry steps.

guardachaves (*m.*) R.R. switchman.

guarda-chuva (*m.*) umbrella.

guarda-comida (*m.*) food cupboard; (*slang*) belly.

guarda-costas (*m.*) a coastguard cutter; a bodyguard.

guardado(s) (*m.*) one's (small) personal belongings; keepsake.

guardador -dora (*adj.*) keeping; careful in observing (a law, rule, custom, etc.); (*m.,f.*) keeper, guardian.

guarda-fato (*m.*) wardrobe.

guarda-fio(s) (*m.*) a telephone or telegraph lineman.

guarda-florestal (*m.*) forester.

guarda-fogo (*m.*) fire screen; fire wall.

guarda-freio(s) (*m.*) railroad brakeman.

guarda-jóias (*m.*) jewel case.

guarda-lama (*m.*) mud guard; automobile fender.

guarda-linha (*m.*) railroad track walker.

guarda-livros (*m.,f.*) bookkeeper.

guarda-louça (*m.*) glass cupboard, china closet.

guarda-mão (*m.*) guard of sword handle.

guarda-marinha (*m.*) midshipman, ensign.

guarda-mato (*m.*) trigger-guard.

guardamento (*m.*) guarding; keeping; guard.

guarda-meta (*m.*) goalkeeper [= ARQUEIRO].

guarda-mor (*m.*) chief customs officer.

guardamoria (*f.*) department of customs inspection.

guarda-móveis (*m.*) furniture warehouse.

guardanapo (*m.*) table napkin.

guarda-noturno (*m.*) night watchman.

guarda-peito (*m.*) a leather chest protector worn by cowboys.

guarda-pó (*m.*) a duster (overgarment).

guarda-portão (*m.*) gatekeeper [= PORTEIRO].

guarda-pratas (*m.*) silver closet.

guardar (*v.t.*) to guard, protect, defend, shield; to watch, safeguard; to keep, retain; to put away (for safekeeping); to preserve; to observe (as a holiday); to save, lay away.——(a) fé, to keep the faith.——a palavra, to keep one's word.——à vista, to keep sight of.——as conveniências, to observe decorum.——as distâncias, to keep one's distance.——as leis, to observe the laws.——debaixo de chave, to keep under lock and key.——domingos e dias santos, to observe Sundays and holidays.——o leito, to keep to one's bed.——o passo, to stand pat.——os prisioneiros, to guard the prisoners.——para amanhã, to put off (something) until tomorrow.——silêncio, to keep silent.——suas distâncias, to keep one's distance.

guarda-rêde (*m.*) goalkeeper [= ARQUEIRO].

guarda-roupa (*m.*) wardrobe, clothes closet, clothes press; in a theater, the person entrusted with care of the wardrobe.

guarda-sol (*m.*) sunshade, parasol; (*Bot.*) tropical-almond terminalia (*T. catappa*), c.a. AMENDOEIRA-DA-ÍNDIA.

guarda-soleiro (*m.*) umbrella manufacturer.

guarda-vala (*m.*) goalkeeper [= ARQUEIRO].

guarda-vassouras (*m.*) baseboard (of a wall); = RODAPÉ.

guarda-vento (*m.*) wind screen.

guarda-vestidos (*m.*) wardrobe, clothes closet.

guarda-vista (*m.*) eye shade.

guarda-voz (*m.*) sounding board (over a pulpit).

guardear (*v.t.*) to provide with guardrails.

guardião [-diães, -diões] (*m.*) caretaker.——dos dinheiros, holder of the purse-strings; (*Soccer*) goalkeeper [= ARQUEIRO]; (*Bot.*) = ABÓBORA-DO-MATO.

guaré (*m.*) a muskwood (*Guarea pohlii*); also = CARRAPETA.

guaretã (*m.*) = GRAPIAPUNHA-BRANCA.

guariare (*m.*, *Bot.*) a caper (*Capparis tenuisiliqua*).

guariba (*m.* or *f.*) any howling monkey of the genus Alouatta (syn. Mycetes), esp. *A. ursina*, the ursine howler of Brazil, c.a. BUGIO, BARBADO.——da-mão-ruiva, the rufous-handed howler (*Alouatta b. belzebul*).——negra, the black howler (*A. nigerrima*).——prêto, another black howler (*A. caraya*),——ruiva (or -vermelho), the red howler (*A. seniculus*), c.a. BUGIO-LABAREDA.

guaricanga (*f.*) any of various shadowpalms (*Geonoma*).——de-fôlha-miúda, aricanga shadowpalm (*Geonoma schottiana*).

guarida (*f.*) den; place of refuge. dar—, to give shelter.

guariroba (*f.*) = COQUEIRO-AMARGOSO.

guarita (*f.*) sentry box; lookout.

guarnecer (*v.t.*) to garrison; to provide with troops, munitions, etc.; to garnish, adorn, trim; to furnish.

guarnecimento (*m.*) garrisoning; garnishing; furnishing, provisioning.

guarnição (*f.*) garrison; crew; hilt (of a sword); metal trim; trimming (of a dress).

guaruba (*m.*) the golden paroquet (*Eupsittula guarouba*) of northeastern Brazil, c.a. ARAJUBA, ARARAJUBA, AJURUJUBA, GUARAJUBA, TANAJUBA, PAPAGAIO-IMPERIAL.

guarucaia (*f.*) = LEPRA.

guaru-guaru [rú] (*m.*) = BARRIGUDINHO.

guaruma (*f.*, *Bot.*) a calathea (*C. juncea*).

guarumbe (*m.*) a butterflypea (*Centrosema plumieri*) c.a. FEIJÃO-BRAVO, JEQUIRANA, MARMELADA.

guarumina (*f.*, *Bot.*) a supplejack (*Serjania cuspidata*) used as a fish poison; c.a. TIMBÓ-CABELUDO, TIMBÓ-DE-PEIXE.

guarupema (*f.*) = URUPEMA.

guarupu [pú] (*m.*) = GUARAPU.

guasca (*f.*) leather thong or strap; (*m.*,*f.*) a native of Rio Grande do Sul.

guascada (*f.*) a lash with a GUASCA.

guasquear (*v.t.*) to lash with a GUASCA.

guatambu [bú] (*m.*) any of several Braz. timber trees of the genus Aspidosperma c.a. PAU-PEREIRA, PEREIRO, PEROBA-SETIM, PAU-SETIM, PEQUIÁ, JIPIO.

guatapará (*m.*) = VEADO-MATEIRO, GUAÇUETÊ.

guatemalense (*adj.*; *m.*,*f.*) Guatemalan.

guatemaleco -ca (*adj.*; *m.*,*f.*) Guatemalecan, Guatemalan.

guató (*m.*,*f.*) an Indian of the Guató, a virtually extinct tribe in the region of Lake Uberaba in Mato Grosso; (*adj.*) pert. to or designating this tribe.

guatucupajuba (*f.*) = CANHANHA.

guaxe (*m.*) the Brazilian red-rumped cacique (*Cacicus haemorrhus affinis*), c.a. JAPIRÁ, JAPÚ-IRÁ, GUAXE-DO-COQUEIRO, JOÃO-CONGUINHO.

guaxica (*f.*) = CARVALHO-DO-BRASIL.

guaxima (*f.*, *Bot.*) any of several malvaceous plants yielding a jute-like fiber; a species of screwtree (*Helicteres*) c.a. IMBIRA-BRAVA, IMBIRA-DO-MATO, SACA-RÔLHAS; the broomjute sida (*S. rhombifolia*), c.a. RELÓGIO, MALVA-RELÓGIO-GRANDE, MALVA-DA-PRAIA, MALVA-PRETA, UACIMA-DA-PRAIA, TUPITIXA, VASSOURA, VASSOURINHA, ZANZO.—-côr-de-rosa, a malvaceous shrub (*Urena sinuata*) which yields a useful fiber; c.a. CARAPICU.—-roxa, the cadillo (*Urena lobata*) which furnishes a useful fiber comparable to jute; c.a. GUAXUMA, GUAXIÚMA, GUAN-XUMA, IBAXAMA, MALVA-ROXA-RECORTADA, MALVAÍSCO, RABO-DE-FOGUETE, UAICIMA, UACIMA, UAIXIMA.

guaxinduba (*f.*) = CUAXINGUBA.

guaxinim (*m.*,*f.*) a crab-eating raccoon (*Procyon cancrivorous*), c.a. MÃO-PELADA.

guaxuma (*f.*) = GUAXIMA-ROXA.

guaxo -xa (*adj.*) motherless; (*m.*) young plants of ERVA-MATE; a child or young animal raised on milk other than its mother's.

gude (*m.*) a game played with marbles [= BÚRACA].

gudião (*m.*) parrotfish, c.a. BUDIÃO.

gudunho (*m.*) a filefish (*Alutera monoceros*).

guebuçu [çú] (*m.*) a sailfish (*Istiophorus nigricans*), c.a. BICUDO, QUEBUÇU, AGULHÃO-BANDEIRA, PEIXE-VELA.

guedelha [dê] (*f.*), -lho [dê] (*m.*) long, dishevelled hair; mop of hair. Vars. GADELHA, GADELHO.

guedelhudo -da (*adj.*) having long dishevelled hair. Var. GADELHUDO.

guegue (*m.*, *Bot.*) the yellow mombin (*Spondias mombin*).

gueijo (*m.*) a railroad track gauge.

gueixa (*f.*) Japanese geisha.

guelra (*f.*) fish gill.

guembê (*m.*) = CIPO-DE-IMBÉ.

guenilha (*f.*) fast, rough trot.

gueriri (*m.*) = OSTRA-AMERICANA.

guerra (*f.*) war, warfare.—aberta, open warfare.—civil, civil war.—santa, holy war.—relâmpago, blitzkrieg. após—, postwar. conselho de—, court martial. em pé de—, on a war footing. fazer—, to wage war. Ministério de—, War Department. neurose de—, shell shock.

guerreador -dora (*adj.*) warring; (*m.*) warrior.

guerrear (*v.t.*,*v.i.*) to wage war (a, against).

guerreiro -ra (*adj.*) warlike; (*m.*) warrior; (*f.*) an ant—see CORREIÇÃO.

guerrilha (*f.*) guerrilla band; gang of thieves; motley political faction.

guerrilhar (*v.i.*) to fight as a guerrilla.

guerrilheiro (*m.*,*f.*, *adj.*) guerrilla.

gueta [ê] (*f.*) trifle.

guete [guê] (*m.*) a croaker (*Archoscion petranus* family

Sciaenidae), c.a. GORETE (-DE-PEDRA), GOETE, PESCADINHA-BRANCA, PESCADINHA-GOETE, BÔCA-MOLE, BÔCA-TORTA, PIRAMEMBECA,

gueto [ê] (*m.*) ghetto.

guexa [ê] (*f.*) a female mule.

guia (*f.*) a guiding or guidance; bill of lading, way bill; shipping permit; rein; jig, template; (*pl.*) ends of a mustache; (*m.*) guide, leader; mentor; guidebook, directory, manual;—de bagagem, baggage check.—do passeio, street curbing.

guiador -dora (*adj.*) guiding; (*m.*) guide.

guiamento (*m.*) guiding.

guiará (*m.*) = XARÉU.

guião [guiães, guiões] (*m.*) banner, standard; guidon; standard-bearer.

guiar (*v.t.*) to guide, lead; to direct, control; to steer, pilot. —um carro, to drive an automobile.

guichê (*m.*) ticket window; bank teller's window.

guidão, guidom (*m.*) handlebar of a bicycle.

guido (*m.*) guy.

guieiro -ra (*adj.*) leading, guiding; (*m.*) cowherd.

guiga (*f.*, *Naut.*) gig.

guigó (*m.*, *Zool.*) a marmoset (*Callithrix melanchir*), or titi monkey (*Callicebus*).

guildas (*f.pl.*) the medieval guilds.

guilhada (*f.*) = AGUILHADA.

guilherme (*m.*) a tonguing and grooving plane; (*m.*) [*cap.*] William.

guilhochês (*m.pl.*, *Arch.*) guilloches.

guilhotina (*f.*) guillotine; a window with vertical sliding sashes; a bookbinder's shear; paper cutter.

guilhotinar (*v.t.*) to guillotine, behead.

guimbé (*m.*) = CIPÓ-DE-IMBÉ.

guimberana (*f.*) = FÔLHA-DA-FONTE.

guinada (*f.*) a shift, switch, change of course; a sudden twist, swerve or lurch; a sharp, sudden pain; (*Naut.*, *Aeron.*) a yaw(ing).

guinar (*v.i.*) to yaw, tack; to lurch; to twist, swerve; to fishtail.

guincha (*f.*) mare; filly.

guinchada (*f.*), **guinchado** (*m.*) a squealing.

guinchante (*adj.*) squealing.

guinchar (*v.i.*) to squeal (as a pig or as car brakes); to shrill; to shriek.

guincho (*m.*) a squeal; a shriek; a winch or windlass.

guinda (*f.*) a hoisting rope.

guindagem (*f.*) hoisting.

guindaleta (*f.*) -lete [lê] (*m.*) a hoisting cable.

guindamento (*m.*) hoisting.

guindar (*v.t.*) to hoist, raise (with a GUINDASTE); to lift, raise (to a high position).—-se a, to raise oneself to.

guindaste (*m.*) a derrick, crane, hoist, winch, windlass; jack.—corrente sôbre pontilhão, a traveling crane.—de cavalete or—sôbre pontilhão, a gantry crane.

guindola (*f.*) boatswain's chair, hanging scaffold.

guindro (*m.*) = GAIVÃO.

guiné (*f.*) guinea fowl [= GALINHA-D'ANGOLA]; a guineahen weed (*Petiveria hexaglochin*), c.a. ERVAPIPI, MUCURA-CAÁ; a paspalum grass (*P. paniculatum*), c.a. CAPIM-GRAMA-DA-GUINÉ.—legítimo = CAPIM-GUINÉ (Guinea grass).

guinéu (*m.*) an English guinea (21 shillings).

guingão (*m.*) gingham.

guio (*m.*) iron wedge used in splitting rocks.

guipura (*f.*) guipure (lace).

guirá (*f.*) = IRUÇU-DO-CHÃO.

guiraponga (*f.*) = ARAPONGA.

guirarepoti [tí] (*f.*) mistletoe.

guiratangueima (*f.*) = XEXÉU.

guiratinga (*f.*, *Zool.*) American great white egret (*Casmerodius albus egretta*), c.a. GARÇA-GRANDE.

guirlanda (*f.*) garland.

guiruçu [çú] (*m.*) a stingless bee (*Melipona quadriculata*), c.a. ABELHA-MULATA, PAPA-TERRA.

guisa (*f.*) à—de, like, by way of; in the guise of.

guisado (*m.*) stew, ragout, fricassee.

guisar (*v.t.*) to stew.

guita (*f.*) twine; money; (*m.*, *colloq.*) a cop.

guitarra (*f.*) guitar; a guitar fish, c.a. (ARRAIA-)VIOLA; (*slang*) a fake money-making machine.

guitarrear [13] (*v.i.*) to play the guitar.

guitarrista (*m.*,*f.*) a guitar player; (*m.*, *slang*) a crook who employs a fake money-machine to "take" his victims.

guizalhar (*v.t.*,*v.i.*) to jingle.

guizo (m.) sleigh bell.—de-cascavel, (Bot.) a rattlebox (Crotalaria brachystachya).
gula (f.) greediness; gluttony.
guleima (m.) glutton.
gulodice (f.) greediness; tidbit, dainty, goody.
guloseima, gulosice (f.) tidbit, choice morsel.
guloso –sa (adj.) greedy; gluttonous.—de, greedy for; (m.,f.) greedy person.
gume (m.) cutting edge; sharpness, acuteness. de dois—s, two-edged.
gumífero –ra (adj.) gummiferous.
gunga, gunga-muxique (m.) head man, chief [= MANDACHUVA].
gunite (f., Civ. Engin.) gunite.
gupiara (f.) shallow gold-bearing gravel.
guracava (f.) = GUARACAVA.
guratã (m.) = GUARANTÃ.
gureri [rí] (m.) a kind of oyster.
guri [í] (m.) child, youngster, kid.—guaçu, a large catfish.
guria (f.) young girl.
guria(n)tã (m.) = GATURAMO.
gurindiba, –diva (f.) = CRINDIÚVA.
guriri (m.) = ACUMÃ-RASTEIRO, BURI-DA-PRAIA.
guriri-do-campo (m.) = ARIRI.
gurizada (f.) kids, boys (collectively).
gurumixama (f.) = GRUMIXAMA.

gurumixameira (f.) = GRUMIXAMEIRA.
gurundi (m.) = AZULÃO.
gurupés (m.) bowsprit.
gurupi (m.) a shill (accomplice of an auctioneer who starts the bidding to encourage others).
gurupiá (f.) = CORUPIÁ.
gusa (f.) pig iron; (Naut.) ballast.—Bessemer, acid or bessemer pig.—branca, white pig iron.—ao carvão vegetal, charcoal pig.—ao coque, coke pig.—para conversor Thomas, basic pig for open hearth.—para moldagem, foundry pig.—de primeira fusão, all-mine pig; virgin iron.—de segunda fusão, re-cast pig iron.—sintética, pig iron from scrap.
gusano (m.) teredo, shipworm; any grub; horsefly.
gustação (f.) gustation, tasting.
gustativo –va (adj.) gustatory.
Gustavo (m.) Gustavus.
guta (f.) gutta, latex.—-percha, gutta-percha.
gutação (f., Plant Physiol.) guttation.
guteiro (f., Bot.) a garcinia (G. cambogia).
gutiferáceo –cea, gutífero –ra (adj., Bot.) guttiferous, yielding gum or resinous substances; clusiasceous; (f.pl.) the Clusiaceae.
gutural (adj.) guttural.
guturalizar (v.t.) to gutturalize.
guturamo (m.) = GATURAMO.

H

H, h, the eighth letter of the Portuguese alphabet.
H = HENRY (Elec., henry).
H. = HAVER (credit; asset.)
h = HORA (hour).
ha = HECTARE.
há, there is; there are; ago. [Impersonal use of third pers. sing. pres. ind. of HAVER [52], which see. The shortened form á is used in forming the future of all verbs: voltará, virá, terá, etc.]. Não há dúvida, there is no doubt. Há cinco anos atrás, five years ago. Há-de, to be obliged or necessary. Há-de voltar, He (she, it) shall (certainly) return. Cf. HÃO, HÃO-DE, HEI.
habanera (f.) habanera (Cuban dance).
habênula (f., Anat.) habenula.
hábil [-beis] (adj.) able, clever, adroit, dexterous; capable; legally competent.
habilidade (f.) ability, skill, dexterity; cleverness, ingenuity; stunt; (pl.) skillful gymnastics; stunts; accomplishments.
habilidoso –sa (adj.) dexterous, skillful; clever with one's hands.
habilititação (f.) qualification, eligibility; concurso de—, competitive examination.; (pl.) legal formalities to establish a right; body of proofs; documentary evidences.
habilitado –da (adj.) capable, qualified; able, competent; fullfledged; (m.) a processor of MATE leaves.
habilitador –dora (adj.) qualifying, enabling; (m.,f.) qualifier.
habilitanço (m.) sum of money loaned by one player to another.
habilitando –da (m.,f.) one who is seeking to prepare or qualify himself.
habilitante (m.,f.) a petitioner at law.
habilitar (v.t.) to enable, qualify, capacitate; to qualify oneself (como, as; para, to); to prepare, equip, oneself (para, as, for).
hàbilmente (adv.) ably.
habitação (f.) habitation, abode, dwelling, place of residence; habitat.
habitador –dora, habitante (adj.) inhabiting; (m.,f.) inhabitant, dweller.
habitar (v.t.) to inhabit, live in.
habitável (adj.) habitable.
hábito (m.) habit, usage, wont, custom; addiction; habiliment, dress, garb.
habituação (f.) habituation.
habituado –da (adj.) in the habit of; used to.
habitual (adj.) habitual, usual, customary, routine.

habituar (v.t.) to habituate, accustom.—-se a, to get accustomed to; to become addicted to.
hacanéia (f.) hackney horse.
hadroma (m., Bot.) hadrome.
hadromicose (f., Plant Pathol.) hadromycosis.
háfnio (m., Chem.) hafnium.
hagiografia (f.) hagiography, hagiology.
hagiógrafo (m.) hagiographer.
hagiologia (f.) hagiology.
haia (f.) The Hague.
haitiano –na (adj.; m.,f.) Haitian.
haj + personal endings = forms of HAVER [52].
hálito (m.) breath; exhalation. mau—, offensive breath.
halita (f.), halito (m.) halite, native salt.
halitose (f., Med.) halitosis.
halo (m.) halo; aura; areola.
haldcromia (f., Chem.) halochromic effect.
halófilo –la (adj., Biol.) halophilous.
halófito –ta (adj., Bot.) halophytic.
halogenação (f., Chem.) halogenation.
halogêneo –nea, halógeno –na (adj., Chem.) halogenous; (m.) halogen.
halóide (adj.; m., Chem.) haloid.
halômetro (m.) halometer.
haloscópio (m.) haloscope.
halotriquita (f., Min.) halotrichite.
haltere (m.) dumbbell; balancer (of flies).
halterofilismo (m.) weight-lifting.
halurgia (f.) salt working.
halux (m., Anat., Zool.) hallux.
hamadríade, hamadríada (f.) hamadryad.
hamamelidáceo –cea (adj., Bot.) hamamelidaceous; (f.pl.) the Hamamelidaceae (witch hazel family).
hamamélis (f.) common witch hazel (Hamamelis virginiana).
hamburguês –guêsa (adj.) of or pert. to Hamburg; (m.,f.) a native of that city.
hamítico –ca (adj.) Hamitic.
hâmulo (m., Anat., Zool.) hamulus.
hanemaniano –na (adj.) Hahnemannian.
hanemanismo (m.) Hahnemannism.
hangar (m.) hangar.
hansa (f.) hanse, medieval guild.
hanseático –ca (adj.) Hanseatic.
hanseniano –na (adj.) = LEPROSO.
hão [archaic and literary form of HAVER [52], largely replaced by TER. The shortened form ão is used in forming the future indicative of all verbs, as voltarão. darão,

escreverão, etc.] **hão-de**, to be obliged or necessary. Hão-de me pagar, they shall pay me (I'll get even). Cf. HÁ, HÁ-DE, HEI.

hapalídeos (*m.pl.*) a family (*Callitrichidae*) of monkeys.

hapaxântico –ca (*adj.*) hapaxanthous, monocarpic.

haploclamídeo –dea (*adj.*, *Bot.*) haplochlamydeous.

haplodonte (*adj.*, *Zool.*) haplodont.

haplografia (*f.*) haplography.

haplóide (*adj.*; *m.*, *Biol.*) haploid.

haplologia (*f.*, *Philol.*) haplology.

haplopétalo –la (*adj.*, *Bot.*) haplopetalous.

haploscópio (*m.*, *Psychol.*) haploscope.

haptero (*m.*, *Bot.*) hapteron.

háptico –ca (*adj.*, *Psychol.*) haptic.

haptóforo –ra (*adj.*, *Immunol.*) haptophorous.

haptotropismo (*m.*, *Biol.*) haptotropism.

harangan(e)ar (*v.i.*) of horses, to run wild; fig., to loaf.

harangano –na (*adj.*) of horses, hard to catch; fig., rascally; indolent.

haraquiri (*m.*) hara-kiri.

haras (*m.*) horse breeding farm.

harda (*f.*) a squirrel (*Sciurus bicolor*).

harém (*m.*) harem.

harmala (*f.*, *Bot.*) harmel (*Peganum harmala*).

harmalina (*f.*, *Chem.*) harmaline.

harmatão (*m.*) harmatan. [*Webster:* "A dry, dust-laden wind blowing from the interior on the Atlantic coast of Africa in certain seasons."]

harmonia (*f.*) harmony; concord, accord; congruity; peace, friendship.

harmônico –ca (*adj.*) harmonic, harmonious; (*f.*) any of various old-time musical instruments. [Although the term is applicable also to the modern harmonica (i.e., mouth organ) or accordion, the former is better known as GAITA (DE BÔCA) and the latter as ACORDEÃO or SANFONA.]

harmônio (*m.*) harmonium.

harmonioso –sa (*adj.*) harmonious; melodious.

harmonista (*m.,f.*, *Music*) harmonist.

harmonização (*f.*) harmonization.

harmonizador –dora (*adj.*) harmonizing; (*m.,f.*) harmonizer.

harmonizar (*v.t.*) to harmonize, attune, reconcile, adjust, suit (one thing to another); (*v.i.*) to accord, be harmonious.

harmonômetro (*m.*) harmonometer.

harmotômio (*m.*, *Min.*) harmotome.

harmotomita (*f.*, *Min.*) harmotomite.

Haroldo (*m.*) Harold.

harpa (*f.*) harp.—**eólia**, aeolian harp or lyre.

harpagão (*m.*) a usurious miser.

harpar, harpejar (*v.t.,v.i.*) to play the harp.

harpia (*f.*, *Myth.*) Harpy; harpy; (*Zool.*) the So. Amer. harpy eagle (*Harpia harpyja*), c.a. URUÇU, UIRAÇU, GAVIÃO-DE-PENACHO, GAVIÃO-REAL, CUTUCURIM, APACANIM.

harpista (*m.,f.*) harpist.

harrisito (*m.*, *Petrog.*) harrisite.

hasta (*f.*) spear, pike; auction.—**pública**, a public sale by court order.

haste, hástea (*f.*) rod, shaft, staff; flagpole; stem or trunk (of a tree); pointed horn.

hastear (*v.t.*) to hoist, raise to the top (as a flag).

hastil (*m.*) shaft of a lance.

hastim (*m.*) long, narrow field.

hatchetita (*f.*, *Min.*) hatchettite; hatchetin; adipocerite.

hauerita (*f.*, *Min.*) hauerite, manganese sulfide.

hauinita (*f.*, *Min.*) haüynite.

haurir [25].(*v.t.*) to inhale; to suck up (as a plant sucks up moisture from the soil); to draw out; to exhaust.

haurível (*adj.*) exhaustible.

hausmanita (*f.*, *Min.*) hausmannite.

hausto (*m.*) gulp, swallow.

haustório (*m.*, *Bot.*) haustorium; sucker.

Havaí (*m.*) Hawaii.

havaiano –na (*adj.*; *n.*) Hawaiian.

havanês –nêsa (*adj.*; *m.,f.*) Havanese.

havano –na (*adj.*) light brown; (*m.,f.*) Havana cigar.

haver [52] (*v.t.*) to have, possess; to obtain, get; to feel, experience; to handle (comport) oneself. [This verb is becoming archaic and in everyday speech is nearly always replaced by TER and, in reference to time, by FAZER, as illustrated in the examples to follow. When used impersonally, **haver** = there to be. As an auxiliary

verb, **haver** = to have.]; (*m.*) in bookkeeping, a credit entry; (*pl.*, -es), goods, wealth, possessions, assets, personal effects.—**-de** (or **ter que**), to be bound to; to have to; to be obliged to; to be necessary; must.—**-de** + infinitive = must or will + future tense, as: Havemos-de vencer, We will (certainly) win. Havemos-de morrer, We will (must) (all) die (some day).—**por bem**, to deem advisable.—**mister de**, to have need (want) of.—**-se bem**, to handle (acquit) oneself well.—**-se com alguém**, to deal (discuss, talk) with someone. **caso haja um**, in case there is one. Estão aqui de há muito, They have been here a long time. Estão aqui há uma semana, They have been here (for) a week. Estava aqui havia uma semana, He had been here (for) a week. de há muito, for a long time (now). **deve**—, there should be; there must be. Ela há-de vir hoje, She will probably come today. Êle ha-de me pagar, He'll pay me for this; I'll get even with him. Êle há-de vencer, He is bound to win. **há**, there is; there are; ago. Há-de—um ano, It must be about a year ago. **há** (or **faz**) dias, a few days ago; Há (or faz) dez dias que êle esteve aqui, It is ten days since he was here. Há (or faz) dois dias que não durmo, I haven't slept for two days. Há (or tem) muita gente aqui, There are many people here. Há (or tem) jôgo hoje, There is a game today. **há** (or **faz**) um mês, a month ago. Há (or faz) um mês que êle está aqui, He has been here (for) a month. Há (or tem) de tudo, There is some of everything. Há (or faz) cinco dias que me acho aqui, I have been here (for) five days. Há (or faz) dois anos que não o vejo, I haven't seen him for two years; or, it is two years since I last saw him. **há** (or **faz**) **muito**, long ago. Há (or tem) muito que fazer, There is much to be done. há (or faz) muito tempo, a long time ago. há (or faz) muitos meses, many months ago. Há tanto a (or que) fazer, There is so much to be done. Há (or faz) um mês que êle morreu, It is a month since he died. Haja o que houver, Come what may. **haja vista**, bear in mind; refer to; witness. Haverá jôgo amanhã, There will be a game tomorrow. haveria, there would be. **havia**, there was; there were. **havia** (or **fazia**) dois dias, two days earlier. Havia (or fazia) dois anos que êles moravam no Rio, They had been living in Rio (for) two years. havia pouco, a short time ago. Havia (or fazia) um mês que êle estava (or que estivera) aqui, He had been here for a month. **Hei-de fazer isso!** I will do it! (emphatic). **houve**, there was; there were. **houve por bem**, he thought it advisable to. houve tempo em que, there was a time when. **Houvesse o que houvesse**, No matter what. **não há**, there is not. Não há de quê, You're welcome; don't mention it. **Não há** (or **não tem**) **remédio**, It can't be helped. não haverá, there will not be. o que ela havia (or devia) ter feito, what she ought to (should) have done. **pode**—, there can be; there may be. Quando haverá? When will there be? Que Deus o haja, God rest his soul. **Que é** (or **que foi**) **que houve?** What happened? **se houver**, if there is; if there are. **tem havido**, there have (has) been. tempos houve em que, there was a time when. **Que há** (or **que é que há**) **com êle?** What's the matter with him? Que há de novo? What's new? Que há-de ser de mim? What's to become of me? Vai—uma festa (uma briga, o diabo), There is going to be a party (a fight, the devil to pay).

haveis, havemos, forms of HAVER [52].

haxixe (*m.*) hashish.

hebdómada (*f.*) hebdomad; seven days, weeks or years.

hebdomadário –ria (*adj.*) weekly; (*m.*) a weekly publication.

hebecarpo –pa (*adj.*, *Bot.*) hebecarpous.

hebefrenia (*f.*, *Psychiatry*) hebephrenia, dementia praecox.

hebepétalo –la (*adj.*, *Bot.*) hebepetalous.

hebetar (*v.t.,v.r.*) to hebetate, dull, blunt.

hebético –ca (*adj.*) hebetic, pubertal.

hebetismo (*m.*) hebetude.

hebetude (*f.*) hebetude, dullness, stupidity.

hebr. = HEBRAICO.

hebraico –ca (*adj.*) Hebraic; (*m.,f.*) Hebrew.

hebraísmo (*m.*) Hebraism.

hebraísta (*m.,f.*) Hebraist.

hebraizar [a-i] (*v.i.*) to Hebraize.

hebreu –bréia (*adj.*; *m.,f.*) Hebrew.

hecatombe (*f.*) hecatomb. Var. HECATOMBA.

hecatostilo, hecatônstilo (*m.*, *Arch.*) hecatonstylon.

hechor [ô] (*m.*) a jackass used for breeding with mares [= BURRO-CHÔRO].

hectare (*m.*) hectare = 10,000 sq. mts. = 2.471 acres.
héctico –ca (*adj.*) hectic, consumptive. [Not employed in the English colloq. sense of excited, feverish]; (*m.,f.*) a hectic patient; (*f.*) hectic fever, consumption.
hectógrafo (*m.*) hectograph.
hectograma (*m.*) hectogram, 100 grams.
hectolitro (*m.*) hectoliter, 100 liters.
hectômetro (*m.*) hectometer, 100 meters.
hectostéreo, hectostere (*m.*) hectostere, 100 cu. mts.
hedenbergita (*f.*, *Min.*) hedenbergite.
hédera (*f.*) = HERA.
hederáceo –cea (*adj.*) hederaceous.
hederiforme (*adj.*) hederiform.
hederina (*f.*, *Chem.*) hederin.
hediondez(a) [dê] (*f.*) hideousness.
hediondo –da (*adj.*) hideous; vile; revolting.
hedônico –ca (*adj.*) hedonic.
hedonismo (*m.*) hedonism.
hedonista (*adj.*; *m.,f.*) hedonist.
hedrocele (*f.*, *Med.*) hedrocele.
hedrumito (*m.*, *Petrog.*) hedrumite.
hegelianismo (*m.*) Hegelianism.
hegeliano –na (*adj.*; *m.,f.*) Hegelian.
hegemonia (*f.*) hegemony.
hei, an archaic and literary form of HAVER [52], largely replaced by TER. The shortened form ei is used in forming the fut. indic. of all verbs: terei, voltarei, comprarei, etc. hei-de, to be obliged or necessary. Hei-de vê-la, I must (will, shall certainly) see her. Cf. HÁ, HÁ-DE, HÃO.
hein? What? What say? Hm? Huh? Isn't it so?
Heitor (*m.*) Hector.
héjira (*f.*) hegira.
helcoídeo –dea (*adj.*) helcoid, like an ulcer.
heleborinha (*f.*) an orchid (*Epidendrum elongatum*).
heléboro (*m.*, *Bot.*) hellebore (*Helleborus*) and false hellebore (*Veratrum*).—-americano, or -verde, American false hellebore (*Veratrum viride*).—-branco, white false hellebore (*V. album*).—-fétido, fetid or bearsfoot hellebore (*Helleborus foetidus*), c.a. ERVA-DOS-BESTEIROS.—-negro, black hellebore or Christmas rose (*H. nigrum*).—-prêto, blackfoot (*Melanpodium*), c.a. MELAMPÓDIO.
Helena (*f.*) Helen, Helena, Eileen, Elena, Ellen.
helênico –ca (*adj.*) Hellenic.
helênio (*m.*) the genus (*Helenium*) of sneezeweeds.
helenismo (*m.*) Hellenism.
helenista (*m.,f.*) Hellenist.
helenístico –ca (*adj.*) Hellenistic(al).
helenização (*f.*) Hellenization.
helenizar (*v.t.*) to Hellenize.
heleno –na (*adj.*; *m.,f.*) Hellene, Greek.
helíaco –ca (*adj.*, *Astron.*) heliacal.
heliântemo (*m.*) the sunrose (*Helianthemum*).
heliânteo –tea (*adj.*, *Bot.*) helianthaceous.
helianto (*m.*) the sunflower (*Helianthus*), c.a. GIRASSOL.
hélice (*f.,m.*) helix; any spiral; a genus of land snails; (*Anat.*) helix; ship or airplane propeller.—de passo variável, (*Aeron.*) variable-pitch propeller. eixo da—, propeller shaft. pá da—, propeller blade.
helicídios (*m.pl.*) the Helicidae (family of land snails).
heliciforme (*adj.*) heliciform, spiral.
helicina (*f.*, *Chem.*) helicin.
helicógrafo (*m.*) helicograph.
helicoidal (*adj.*) helicoidal.
helicóide (*adj.*; *m.,f.*) helicoid.
helicometria (*f.*) helicometry.
hélicon (*m.*, *Music*) helicon, large bass tuba.
helicônia (*f.*, *Bot.*) the genus Heliconia, which includes the Carib heliconia or wild plantain (*H. bihai*); (*Zool.*) a large genus (*Heliconius*) of butterflies.
helicóptero (*m.*) helicopter.
helicorrubina (*f.*, *Biochem.*) helicorubin.
helicotrema (*m.*, *Anat.*) helicotreme.
helicriso (*m.*, *Bot.*) the everlasting (*Helichrysum*), c.a. PERPÉTUA-AMARELA.
hélio (*m.*, *Chem.*) helium.
heliocêntrico –ca (*adj.*) heliocentric.
heliocromia (*f.*) heliochromy, color photography.
heliocromo (*m.*) a color photograph.
heliocromoscópio (*m.*) heliochromoscope.
heliodoro (*m.*, *Min.*) heliodor.
heliófilo –la (*adj.*) heliophilous.
heliografia (*f.*) heliography.
heliógrafo (*m.*) heliograph.
heliograma (*m.*) heliogram.

heliogravura (*f.*, *Photog.*) heliogravure.
helióide (*adj.*) helioid, resembling the sun.
heliolatria (*f.*) heliolatry, sun worship.
heliologia (*f.*, *Astron.*) heliology.
heliometria (*f.*) heliometry.
heliômetro (*m.*, *Astron.*) heliometer.
helionose (*f.*, *Plant Pathol.*) sunburn.
heliopse (*f.*, *Bot.*) the genus Heliopsis.
helioscopia (*f.*, *Astron.*) helioscopy.
helioscópio (*m.*, *Astron.*) helioscope.
heliose (*f.*, *Bot.*) heliosis, sunburn; (*Med.*) heliotherapy; sunstroke.
helióstato (*m.*) heliostat.
helioterapia (*f.*, *Med.*) heliotherapy.
heliotermômetro (*m.*, *Astrophysics*) heliothermometer.
heliótipo (*m.*, *Photog.*) heliotype.
heliotipografia (*f.*, *Photog.*) heliotypography.
heliotropia (*f.*, *Biol.*) heliotropism.
heliotrópico –ca (*adj.*, *Biol.*) heliotropic.
heliotropina (*f.*, *Chem.*) heliotropin(e).
heliotrópio (*m.*, *Bot.*) the common heliotrope (*Heliotropium arborescens*); any plant which turns toward the sun; (*Min.*) bloodstone; heliotrope (instrument used in geodetic surveying).
heliotropismo (*m.*) heliotropism.
hélix [ks] (*m.*, *Anat.*) helix [= HÉLICE].
helmintíase (*f.*, *Med.*) helminthiasis.
helmíntico –ca (*adj.*) helminthic.
helminto, helminte (*m.*) helminth, parasitic worm.
helmintocladiáceas (*f.*) a family (*Helminthocladiaceae*) of red algae.
helmintóide (*adj.*) helminthoide, wormlike.
helmintologia (*f.*) helminthology.
helobiáceo –cea (*adj.*) helobious.
Heloísa (*f.*) Heloise; Eloise.
helvécio –cia (*adj.*; *m.,f.*) Helvetian, Swiss.
helvético –ca (*adj.*) Helvetic.
hem? = HEIN?
hemácia (*f.*) red blood cell. Var. HEMÁTIA.
hemameba (*f.*, *Med.*, *Zool.*) hemamoeba; (*Med.*, *Biol.*) a leucocyte.
hemadromômetro (*m.*) hemadromometer.
hemafeína (*f.*, *Biochem.*) hemaphein [= HEMOFEÍNA].
hemapófise (*f.*, *Zool.*) hemapophysis.
hêmase (*f.*, *Biochem.*) hemase.
hemateína (*f.*, *Chem.*) hematein.
hematia (*f.*) = HEMÁCIA.
hemático –ca (*adj.*) hematic, sanguineous.
hematímetro (*m.*, *Physiol.*) hematimeter, hemocytometer.
hematina (*f.*, *Biochem.*) hematin.
hematita (*f.*, *Min.*) hematite, iron oxide.—parda, limonite.
hematóbio –bia (*adj.*, *Biol.*) hematobic; (*m.*) hematobium.
hematoblasta (*m.*, *Anat.*) hematoblast.
hematocele (*f.*, *Med.*) hematocele.
hematócito (*m.*) hematocyte, hemocyte, blood corpuscle [= HEMÓCITO].
hematócrito (*m.*, *Physiol.*) hematocrit.
hematodinamômetro (*m.*, *Physiol.*) hematodynamometer.
hematode (*adj.*, *Physiol.*) hematoid, resembling blood.
hematogênese (*f.*) homogenesis.
hematóide (*adj.*, *Physiol.*) hematoid, resembling blood.
hematoidina (*f.*, *Biochem.*) hematoidin.
hematólise (*f.*, *Physiol.*) hemolysis [= HEMÓLISE].
hematologia (*f.*) hematology.
hematoma (*f.*, *Med.*) hematoma.
hematopoese (*f.*) hematopoiesis [= HEMOPOESE].
hematoporfirina (*f.*, *Biochem.*) hematoporphyrin.
hematoscopia (*f.*, *Physiol.*) hemoscopy.
hematoscópio (*m.*, *Physiol.*) hemoscope.
hematose (*f.*, *Physiol.*) hematosis.
hematosina (*f.*, *Chem.*) the hematin from blood.
hematospectroscópio (*m.*, *Physiol.*) hematospectroscope.
hematoxilina [ks] (*f.*, *Chem.*) haematoxylin.
hematôxilo [ks] (*m.*) the Brazil bloodwood tree (*Haematoxylon brasiletto*), or the logwood (*B. campechianum*), c.a. CAMPECHE.
hematozoário (*m.*, *Zool.*) hematozoon.
hematúria, hematuria (*f.*, *Med.*) hematuria.
hemeralopia (*f.*, *Med.*) hemeralopia.
hemeróbio (*m.*) a genus (*Hemerobius*) of lace-winged flies.
hemerocale (*f.*) a day lily (*Hemerocallis*).
hemialgia (*f.*, *Med.*) hemialgia.
hemianestesia (*f.*) hemianesthesia.
hemicarpo (*m.*, *Bot.*) mericarp.

hemicíclico -ca (adj., Bot.) hemicyclic.
hemiciclo (m.) hemicycle, semicircle.
hemicilíndrico -ca (adj.) hemicylindrical.
hemicilíndro (m.) half a cylinder axially divided.
hemicrânia (f., Med.) hemicrania.
hemiedria (f., Cryst.) hemihedrism.
hemiédrico -ca (adj., Cryst.) hemihedral.
hemiedro (m., Cryst.) hemihedron.
hemiélitro (m., Zool.) hemelytron.
hemimorfita (f., Min.) hemimorphite; calamine.
hemina (f., Chem.) hemin.
hemiprisma (m., Cryst.) hemiprism.
hemiparasita (f., Biol., Bot.) hemiparasite.
hemipínico -ca (adj., Chem.) hemipic, heminipic.
hemipirâmide (f., Cryst.) hemipyramid.
hemiplegia (f., Med.) hemiplegia.
hemiplégico -ca (adj., Med.) hemiplegic; (m.,f.) one affected with hemiplegia.
hemiplexia [ks] (f.) = HEMIPLEGIA.
hemiprismático -ca (adj., Cryst.) hemiprismatic.
hemíptero -ra (adj., Zool.) hemipterous; (m.pl.) the Hemiptera.
hemirranfídeos (m.pl.) the Hemiramphidae (family of halfbeaks).
hemisférico -ca (adj.) hemispheric(al).
hemisfério (m.) hemisphere.
hemisferoidal (adj.) hemispheroidal.
hemisferóide (adj.) hemispheroidal; (m.) hemispheroid.
hemissaprófito -ta (adj., Biol., Bot.) hemisaprophytic.
hemiteria (f.) hemiteria, congenital malformation.
hemitropia (f., Cryst.) hemitropism.
hemítropo -pa (adj., Cryst.) hemitrope, twinned.
hemocianina (f., Biochem.) hemocyanin.
hemócito (m.) hemocyte, blood corpuscle [= HEMATOCITO].
hemocitômetro (m.) hemocytometer.
hemocroína (f.) = HEMATOSINA.
hemocrômio (m., Biochem.) hemachrome, hematin.
hemocromogênio (m.) hemochromogen.
hemocromometria (f.) hemochromometry.
hemocromômetro (m.) hemochromometer, hemoglobinometer.
hemocultura (f.) hemoculture.
hemodia (f.) the condition of having one's teeth set on edge.
hemodromômetro (m.) hemadromometer.
hemofagócito (m., Physiol., Med.) hemophagocyte, hemophage.
hemofeína (f.) = HEMAFEÍNA.
hemofilia (f., Med.) hemophilia.
hemofílico -ca (adj., Med.) hemophilic.
hemófilo -la (m.,f., Med.) a hemophiliac.
hemoglobina (f., Biochem.) hemoglobin.
hemoglobinemia (f., Med.) hemoglobinemia.
hemoglobinômetro (m.) hemoglobinometer.
hemóide (adj., Physiol.) hemoid, resembling blood.
hemólise (f., Immunol.) hemolysis [= HEMATÓLISE].
hemolisina (f., Biochem.) hemolysin [= ISOLISINA].
hemolítico -ca (adj.) hemolytic.
hemômetro (m.) hemometer.
hemopatologia (f.) hemopathology.
hemopirrol (m., Chem.) hemopyrrol(e).
hemoplástico -ca (adj.) hemoplastic.
hemopoese (f.) hematopoiesis [= HEMATOPOESE].
hemoptise (f., Med.) hemoptysis.
hemorragia (f., Med.) hemorrhage.—cerebral, cerebral hemorrhage.—nasal, nosebleed [= EPISTAXE].
hemorrágico -ca (adj.) hemorrhagic.
hemorrinia (f.) nosebleed [= EPISTAXE].
hemorroidal (adj., Med.) hemorrhoidal.
hemorroidaria (f., colloq.) an attack of piles.
hemorroidário -ria (adj.) hemorrhoidal; (m.,f.) one suffering from hemorrhoids.
hemorróidas (f.), -des (m., Med.) hemorrhoids.
hemorroidectomia (f., Surg.) hemorrhoidectomy.
hemorroidoso -sa (adj.) = HEMORROIDÁRIO.
hemos, an archaic and literary form of HAVER [52] largely replaced by TER. The shortened form emos is used in forming the fut. indic. of all verbs: mandaremos, voltaremos, viremos, etc. Cf. HÁ, HÃO, HEI.
hemoscopia (f., Physiol.) hemoscopy.
hemoscópio (m., Physiol.) hemoscope.
hemospasto (m.) cupping glass [= VENTOSA].
hemosporídio (m., Zool.) haemosporid.
hemostático -ca (adj., Med.) hemostatic; (m.) hemostat.

hemotacômetro (m., Physiol.) hemotachometer.
hemotoxia [ks] (f.) blood poisoning.
hena (f., Bot.) henna (Lawsonia inermis).
hendecagonal (adj.) hendecagonal.
hendecágono (m.) hendecagon.
henequém (m., Bot.) the agave which yields henequen fiber (Agave fourcroydes).
Henrique (m.) Henry.
Henriqueta (f.) Henrietta.
henry [ê] (m., Elec.) henry.
hep! giddap!
hepático -ca (adj.) hepatic; (f., Bot.) the common liverwort (Marchantia polymorpha); an anemone (A. triloba); (pl.) the liverworts (Hepaticae).
hepatita (f., Min.) hepatite.
hepatite (f., Med.) hepatitis.
hepatização (f., Med.) hepatization.
hepatocístico -ca (adj., Anat.) hepatocystic.
hepatogástrico -ca (adj., Anat.) hepatogastric.
hepatografia (f.) hepatography.
hepato-intestinal (adj., Anat.) hepatointestinal.
hepíalo (m.) a swift or ghost moth (Hepialus).
heptacosana (f., Chem.) heptacosane.
heptacordo -da (adj., Music) having seven strings; (m.) a heptachord.
heptaédrico -ca (adj.) heptahedrical.
heptaedro (m.) heptahedron.
heptafilo -la (adj., Bot.) heptaphyllous.
heptágino -na (adj., Bot.) heptagynous.
heptagonal (adj.) heptagonal.
heptágono -na (adj.) heptagonal; (m.) heptagon.
heptâmero (m.) heptameride.
heptâmetro -tra (adj.) heptametrical; (m.) heptameter.
heptandro -dra (adj., Bot.) heptandrous.
heptano (m., Chem.) heptane.
heptapétalo -la (adj., Bot.) heptapetalous.
heptassépalo -la (adj.) heptasepalous.
heptateuco (m.) Heptateuch.
heptavalente (adj., Chem.) heptavalent.
heptílico -ca (adj., Chem.) heptylic.
héptodo (m., Elec.) heptode.
heptose (f., Chem.) heptose.
H.er = HAVER (credit; asset).
hera (f., Bot.) ivy (Hedera).—do-verão, climbing hempweed (Mikania scandens).—hélix, English ivy (Hedera helix).—terrestre, common ground ivy (Glecoma hederacea).
heráldico -ca (adj.) heraldic; (f.) heraldry.
herança (f.) heritage, inheritance; heredity.—jacente (Law), hereditas jacens.—vinculada ao sexo, (Biol.) crisscross inheritance. Cf. HEREDITARIEDADE.
herbáceo -cea (adj.) herbaceous.
herbanário (m.) a dealer in medicinal herbs [= ERVANÁRIO].
herbário (m.) herbarium.
Herberto (m.) Herbert.
herbífero -ra (adj.) herbiferous.
herbívoro -ra (adj., m.) herbivorous (animal).
herbolário (m.) herbalist, herb collector.
herborista (m.,f.) a dealer in medicinal herbs.
herborização (f.) herborization.
herborizar (v.i.) to herbalize, esp. to collect medicinal herbs.
herboso -sa (adj.) herbose, herbous [= ERVOSO].
hercogamia (f., Bot.) hercogamy.
herculano -na, hercúleo -lea (adj.) herculean; mighty.
herdade (f.) large country estate; inheritance.
herdar (v.t.) to inherit (de, from); to bequeath (a, to). Cf. LEGAR.
herdeira (f.) heiress.
herdeiro (m.) heir.—fiduciário, fiduciary legatee.—presuntivo, heir presumptive.—universal, residuary legatee.
hereditariedade (f.) heredity.—em mosaico, (Biol.) mosaic inheritance or heredity. Cf. HERANÇA.
hereditário -ria (adj.) hereditary; ancestral.
herege (m.,f.) heretic; (adj.) heretical.
heresia (f.) heresy.
heresiógrafo -fa (m.,f.) heresiologist.
heresiologia (f.) heresiology.
heresiólogo -ga (m.,f.) heresiologist.
hereticidade (f.) hereticalness.
herético -ca (adj.) heretical; (m.,f.) heretic [= HEREGE].
herma (f., Greek Antiq.) herma.

hermafrodito –ta (*adj.*, *Biol.*) hermaphroditic; (*m.*,*f.*) hermaphrodite.
hermafroditismo (*m.*, *Biol.*) hermaphroditism.
Hermano (*m.*) Herman.
hermeneuta (*m.*,*f.*) a hermeneutic scholar.
hermenêutico –ca (*adj.*) hermeneutic, interpretive; (*f.*) hermeutics.
Hermengarda (*f.*) Ermengarde.
hermeticidade (*f.*) airtightness.
hermético –ca (*adj.*) hermetic, airtight.
Hermínia (*f.*) Erminia, Ermina, Erminie.
hermodáctilo (*m.*, *Bot.*) hermodactyle.
hernandia (*f.*, *Bot.*) the genus (*Hernandia*) which typifies the jack-in-a-box family.
hérnia (*f.*, *Med.*) hernia, rupture.—**estrangulada**, strangulated hernia.
herniado –da (*adj.*) herniated.
hernial, herniário –ria, **hérnico** –ca (*adj.*) hernial.
herníola (*f.*, *Bot.*) common burstwort (*Herniaria glabra*), c.a. ERVA-TURCA.
herniorrafia, (*f.*, *Surg.*) herniorrhaphy.
hernioso –sa (*m.*,*f.*; *adj.*) (one) suffering from hernia.
herniotomia (*f.*, *Surg.*) herniotomy.
herói (*m.*) hero.
heroicidade (*f.*) heroicity [= HEROÍSMO].
heróico –ca (*adj.*) heroic; valiant; epic.
herói-cômico –ca (*adj.*) mock-heroic.
heroína (*f.*) heroine; (*Pharm.*) heroin.
heroísmo (*m.*) heroism.
herpes (*m.*, *Med.*) herpes.—**-zóster**, herpes zoster (shingles).
herpetografia (*f.*, *Zool.*) herpetography.
herpetologia (*f.*, *Zool.*) herpetology; (*Med.*) herpetography.
herpetologista, herpetólogo –ga (*m.*,*f.*) herpetologist.
hertziano –na (*adj.*) hertzian. **ondulação**—, hertzian wave.
herva (*f.*) = ERVA.
hesitação (*f.*) hesitation, hesitancy, indecision; diffidence.
hesitante (*adj.*) hesitant, undecided; unsure; diffident.
hesitar (*v.i.*) to hesitate (**em**, to; **entre**, between); to be undecided (**sôbre**, about); to demur.
hespéria (*f.*) a skipper butterfly.
hespéridas (*f.pl.*, *Zool.*) the Hesperiidae (family of skipper butterflies).
hesperídio –dia (*adj.*, *Bot.*) hesperideous.
hesperidina (*f.*, *Chem.*) hesperidin.
hespério –ria (*adj.*) Hesperian (western, occidental). [*Poetical*].
hesperis (*f.*, *Bot.*) the genus (*Hesperis*) of rockets, which includes the damewort (*H. matronalis*), c.a. JULIANA.
hessita (*f.*, *Min.*) hessite.
hessocênico –ca (*adj.*, *Geol.*) Tertiary.
hessonita (*f.*, *Min.*) hessonite; grossularite.
hetera (*f.*) hetaera. Var. HETAIRA.
heterandro –dra (*adj.*, *Bot.*) heterandrous.
heterécio –cia (*adj.*, *Biol.*) heteroecious; (*Bot.*) heteroicous; (*f.*) heteroecism.
heteroblástico –ca (*adj.*, *Biol.*) heteroblastic.
heterocarpo –pa (*adj.*, *Bot.*) heterocarpous.
heterocerca (*adj.*, *Zool.*) heterocercal.
heteróceros (*m.pl.*, *Zool.*) the Heterocera (moths).
heteróclito –ta (*adj.*) heteroclite; irregular; anomalous; abnormal.
heterocromático –ca, **heterocrômico** –ca (*adj.*) heterochromous.
heterocromia (*f.*, *Anat.*) heterochromia.
heterocromosomo (*m.*, *Biol.*) heterochromosome.
heterocronia (*f.*, *Biol.*, *Physiol.*) heterochronia.
heterocrono –na (*adj.*) heterochronous.
heterodáctilo –la (*adj.*, *Zool.*) heterodactylous; (*m.pl.*) the *Trogonidae*.
heteródino –na (*adj.*, *Radio*) heterodyne.
heterodonte (*m.*) the genus (*Heterodon*) of hognose snakes.
heterodoxia [ks] (*f.*) heterodoxy.
heterodoxo –**xa** [ks] (*adj.*) heterodox, unorthodox, heretical.
heterodromia (*f.*, *Bot.*) heterodromy.
heterofilo –la (*adj.*, *Bot.*) heterophyllous.
heterogâmeto (*m.*, *Biol.*) heterogamete.
heterogamia (*f.*) heterogamy.
heterogâmico –ca, **heterógamo** –ma (*adj.*) heterogamous.
heterogeneidade (*f.*) heterogeneity.
heterogêneo –nea (*adj.*) heterogeneous.

heterogenesia (*f.*, *Biol.*) heterogenesis.
heterógino –na (*adj.*, *Zool.*) heterogynous.
heterogonia (*f.*, *Biol.*) heterogony.
heteróico –ca (*adj.*, *Bot.*) heteroicous.
heterologia (*f.*) heterology.
heterômero –ra (*adj.*, *Anat.*) heteromeric; (*Bot.*) heteromerous.
heteromorfia (*f.*), **heteromorfismo** (*m.*) heteromorphism.
heteromorfo –fa (*adj.*) heteromorphous.
heteromorfose (*f.*, *Biol.*) heteromorphosis.
heteronímia (*f.*) heteronymy.
heterônimo –ma (*adj.*) heteronymous.
heteronomia (*f.*) heteronomy.
heteropatia (*f.*) heteropathy, allopathy.
heteropático –ca (*adj.*) allopathic.
heteropétalo –la (*adj.*) *Bot.*) heteropetalous.
heteroplasia (*f.*, *Biol.*, *Med.*) heteroplasia.
heteroplasma (*m.*) heteroplasm.
heteroplastia (*f.*, *Biol.*, *Surg.*) heteroplasty.
heteroplástico –ca (*adj.*) heteroplastic.
heteroploidia (*f.*, *Biol.*) heteroploidy.
heteroquiro –ra (*adj.*, *Physics*) heterochiral.
heterose (*f.*, *Biol.*) heterosis.
heteróside (*f.*, *Chem.*) glucide.
heterósporo –ra (*adj.*, *Bot.*) heterosporous.
heterossexual (*adj.*) heterosexual.
heterostêmone (*adj.*., *Bot.*) having dissimilar stamens.
heterostilia (*f.*, *Bot.*) heterostylism, heterogony.
heterostrofia (*f.*, *Zool.*) heterostrophy.
heterotaxia [ks] (*f.*) heterotaxis.
heterotérmico –ca (*adj.*, *Physiol.*, *Zool.*) poikilothermic.
heterotípico –ca (*adj.*, *Biol.*) heterotypic.
heterotopia (*f.*, *Biol.*, *Med.*) heterotopia.
heterótrico –ca (*adj.*, *Zool.*) heterotrichous.
heterotrofia (*f.*, *Physiol.*) heterotrophy.
heterotrófico –ca (*adj.*, *Physiol.*) heterotrophic.
heterótropo –pa (*adj.*, *Bot.*) amphitropous.
heteroxênio –nia [ks] (*adj.*, *Biol.*) heteroxenous.
heterozigoto (*m.*, *Biol.*) heterozygote.
hético –ca (*adj.*; *m.*,*f.*) = HÉCTICO.
heulandita (*f.*, *Min.*) heulandite.
heureca! Eureka!
heurético –ca (*adj.*) heuristic.
heurística (*f.*) heuretic; heuristic.
hévea (*f.*) the genus (*Hevea*) of rubber trees, of which *H. brasiliensis* is the principal source of Pará rubber.
hewetita (*f.*, *Min.*) hewettite.
hexacanto –ta [ks] (*adj.*, *Zool.*) hexacanth(ous).
hexacordo [ks] (*m.*, *Music*) hexachord.
hexadá[c]tilo –la [ks] (*adj.*) hexadactyle.
hexaedro [ks] (*m.*) hexahedron.
hexafilo –la [ks] (*adj.*, *Bot.*) hexaphyllous.
hexágino –na [ks] (*adj.*) having six pistils.
hexagonal [ks] (*adj.*) hexagonal.
hexágono [ks] (*m.*) hexagon.
hexagrama [ks] (*m.*) hexagram.
hexalina [ks] (*f.*, *Chem.*) hexalin, cyclohexanol.
hexâmero –ra [ks] (*adj.*, *Bot.*, *Zool.*) hexamerous.
hexâmetro [ks] (*m.*) hexameter.
hexamina [ks] (*f.*, *Chem.*) hexamethylene tetramine.
hexandro –dra [ks] (*adj.*, *Bot.*) hexandrous.
hexano [ks] (*m.*, *Chem.*) hexane.
hexaoctaedro [ks] (*m.*, *Cryst.*) hexoctahedron.
hexapétalo –la [ks] (*adj.*, *Bot.*) hexapetalous.
hexápode [ks] (*m.*) hexapod; (*pl.*) the Hexapoda (6-legged insects); (*adj.*) hexapodous, six-footed.
hexáptero –ra [ks] (*adj.*, *Bot.*) hexapterous.
hexaspermo –ma [ks] (*adj.*, *Bot.*) hexaspermous.
hexassépalo –la [ks] (*adj.*, *Bot.*) hexasepalous.
hexassílabo –ba [ks] (*adj.*) hexasyllabic.
hexastêmone [ks] (*adj.*, *Bot.*) hexastemonous.
hexastilo [ks] (*m.*, *Arch.*) hexastylos.
hexatlo [ks] (*m.*, *Sports*) hexathlon.
hexavalente [ks] (*adj.*, *Chem.*) hexavalent.
hexileno [ks] (*m.*, *Chem.*) hexylene, hexene.
hexílico –ca [ks] (*adj.*, *Chem.*) hexylic, caproic.
hexilo [ks] (*m.*, *Chem.*) hexil, hexite.
hexosana [ks] (*f.*, *Chem.*) hexosan.
hexose [ks] (*f.*, *Chem.*) hexose.
hg = HECTOGRAMA(S).
hia, hias, híamos, híeis, hiam, archaic and literary imperf. indic. forms of HAVER [52] largely replaced by TER. The endings **ia, ias**, etc. are used in forming the cond. of all verbs: **deveria, poderíamos, pagariam**, etc.

hiacintino –na (*adj.*) hyacinthine.
hiacinto (*m.*, *Bot.*, *Min.*) hyacinth [= JACINTO].
híades (*f.pl.*, *Astron.*) Hyades.
hial (*adj.*, *Anat.*, *Zool.*) hyoid.
hiálico –ca (*adj.*) glassy.
hialino –na (*adj.*) hyaline, glassy, crystalline; (*m.*, *Biochem.*) hyalin(e).
hialita (*f.*, *Min.*) hyalite.
hialobasalto (*m.*, *Petrog.*) basalt glass.
hialofânio (*m.*, *Min.*) hyalophane.
hialógrafo (*m.*) hyalograph.
hialóide (*adj.*; *m.*, *Anat.*) hyaloid.
hialoídeo –dea (*adj.*, *Anat.*) pert. to the hyaloid.
hialoplasma (*m.*, *Biol.*) hyaloplasm.
hialossiderito (*m.*, *Min.*) hyalosiderite.
hiante (*adj.*) gaping. **sepultura**—, gaping tomb. [*Poetical.*]
hiato (*m.*) hiatus; gap; lacuna.
hibernação (*f.*) hibernation.
hibernal (*adj.*) hibernal, wintry.
hibernante (*adj.*) hibernating.
hibernar (*v.i.*) to hibernate.
hibérnico –ca (*adj.*) Hibernian, Irish; (*m.*) Irish language, Gaelic.
hibisco (*m.*, *Bot.*) hibiscus.
hibridação (*f.*) hybridization.
hibridez [ê] (*f.*) hybridity.
hibridismo (*m.*) hybridism; a hybrid word.
híbrido –da (*adj.*; *m.*) hybrid; mongrel.—**inter-específico**, (*Genetics*) species hybrid.—**s recíprocos**, (*Genetics*) reciprocal hybrids.
hidantoína (*f.*, *Chem.*) hydantoin.
hidátide (*f.*, *Med.*, *Zool.*) hydatid.
hidatiforme (*adj.*) hydatiform.
hidatígero –ra (*adj.*) hydatigenous; (*m.*) = CISTICERCO.
hidatopirogênico –ca (*adj.*, *Petrog.*) hydatopyrogenic, aqueoigneous.
hidatopneumatolítico –ca (*adj.*, *Geol.*) hydatopneumatolytic.
hidátulo (*m.*) = CISTICERCO.
hidnáceas (*f.pl.*, *Bot.*) the tooth fungi (*Hydnaceae*).
hidra (*f.*, *Myth.*, *Astron.*) Hydra; (*Zool.*) hydra; a multifarious evil.—**-d'água**, a dogfish (*Squalus hydra*).
hidracetina (*f.*, *Chem.*) hydracetin, acetylphenylhydrazine [= PIRODINA].
hidrácido (*m.*, *Chem.*) hydracid.
hidrângea (*f.*, *Bot.*) hydrangea [= HORTÊNSIA].
hidrante (*m.*) hydrant.
hidrargilito (*m.*, *Min.*) hydrargillite; gibbsite.
hidrargírico –ca (*adj.*, *Chem.*) hydrargyric; mercuric.
hidrargiria (*f.*, *Med.*) hydrargyria, mercurialism.
hidrargírio (*m.*, *Chem.*) hydrargyrum, mercury.
hidrargirismo (*m.*, *Med.*) hydrargyrism, chronic mercurial poisoning.
hidraste (*f.*, *Bot.*) goldenseal (*Hydrastis canadensis*).
hidrastina (*f.*, *Chem.*) hydrastine.
hidratação (*f.*, *Chem.*) hydration.
hidratado –da (*adj.*, *Chem.*) hydrated.
hidratar (*v.t.*, *Chem.*) to hydrate.
hidrato (*m.*, *Chem.*) hydrate.—**de alumínio**, aluminum trihydroxide.—**de cálcio**, calcium hydroxide; slaked lime.—**de cloral**, chloral hydrate; knockout drops.—**de magnésio**, magnesium hydroxide.—**de potássio**, potassium hydroxide; lye; caustic potash.—**de sódio**, sodium hydroxide; caustic soda.
hidráulica (*f.*) see HIDRÁULICO.
hidraulicidade (*f.*) hydraulicity (of cements).
hidráulico –ca (*adj.*) hydraulic; (*m.*) hydraulic engineer; (*f.*) hydraulics.
hidravião (*m.*) hydroplane.
hidrazina (*f.*, *Chem.*) hydrazin(e).
hidrazona (*f.*, *Chem.*) hydrazone.
hidrelétrico –ca (*adj.*) hydroelectric.
hidreto [ê] (*m.*, *Chem.*) hydride.—**de bismuto**, bismuth hydride; bismuthine.—**de cálcio**, calcium hydride; hydrolith.—**de lítio**, lithium hydride.—**de potássio**, potassium hydride.
hidrextrator (*m.*) hydroextractor.
hídrico –ca (*adj.*, *Chem.*) hydric.
hidriódico –ca (*adj.*, *Chem.*) hydroiodic [acid].
hidroautomático –ca (*adj.*) hydromatic.
hidroavião (*m.*) = HIDRAVIÃO.
hidrobrânquio –quia (*adj.*, *Zool.*) hydrobranchiate.
hidrobromato (*m.*, *Chem.*) hydrobromate, hydrobromide [= BROMIDRATO].

hidrobrômico –ca (*adj.*, *Chem.*) hydrobromic [= BROMÍDRICO].
hidrocarbonato (*m.*, *Chem.*) hydrocarbonate.—**de chumbo**, basic lead carbonate; white lead; ceruse.
hidrocarboneto (*m.*, *Chem.*) hydrocarbon.
hidrócaria (*m.*, *Bot.*) frogbit (*Hydrocharis morsus-ranae*).
hidrocefalia (*f.*, *Med.*) hydrocephalus, c.a. CABEÇA-D'ÁGUA.
hidrocéfalo –la (*adj.*, *Med.*) hydrocephalic; (*m.,f.*) one suffering from hydrocephalus.
hidrocefalóide (*adj.*) hydrocephaloid.
hidrocele (*f.*, *Med.*) hydrocele.
hidrocelulose (*f.*, *Chem.*) hydrocellulosis.
hidrocerusita (*f.*, *Chem.*) hydrocerussite, basic lead carbonate.
hidrocianato (*m.*, *Chem.*) hydrocyanate.
hidrociânico –ca (*adj.*, *Chem.*) hydrocyanic [= CIANÍDRICO].
hidrocinética (*f.*) hydrokinetics.
hidroclorato (*m.*, *Chem.*) hydrochlorate [= CLORIDRATO].
hidroclórico –ca (*adj.*, *Chem.*) = CLORÍDRICO.
hidrocótila (*f.*, *Bot.*) the genus of march pennyworts (*Hydrocotyle*).
hidrodictiáceas (*f.pl.*) a family (*Hydrodictyaceae*) of green algae.
hidrodinâmico –ca (*adj.*) hydrodynamic; (*f.*) hydrodynamics.
hidroelétrico –ca (*adj.*) = HIDRELÉTRICO.
hidroextrator (*m.*) = HIDREXTRATOR.
hidrófano –na (*adj.*, *Min.*) hydrophanous; (*f.*) hydrophane.
hidrófido (*m.*) a sea snake (*Hydrophis*).
hidrofiláceo –cea (*adj.*, *Bot.*) hydrophyllaceous; (*f.pl.*) the waterleaf family (*Hydrophyllaceae*).
hidrofilia (*f.*, *Bot.*) hydrophily.
hidrófilo –la (*adj.*, *Physical Chem.*) hydrophile. **algodão**—, absorbent cotton; (*Bot.*) hydrophilous.
hidrófito –ta (*adj.*, *Biogeog.*) hydrophytic; (*m.*) hydrophyte.
hidrofluórico –ca (*adj.*, *Chem.*) = FLUORÍDRICO.
hidrofobia (*f.*, *Med.*) hydrophobia; rabies.
hidrofóbico –ca (*adj.*, *Chem.*) hydrophobic.
hidrófobo –ba (*adj.*) hydrophobic; (*m.,f.*) hydrophobe.
hidrofone (*m.*) hydrophone.
hidrofráctico –ca (*adj.*) waterproof.
hidrófugo –ga (*adj.*) hydrofuge, shedding water or moisture.
hidrogel (*m.*, *Min.*) hydrogel.
hidrogenação (*f.*, *Chem.*) hydrogenation.
hidrogenar (*v.t.*, *Chem.*) to hydrogenate.
hidrogênio (*m.*, *Chem.*) hydrogen.—**atômico** or **nascente**, atomic hydrogen [welding].—**pesado**, deuterium.
hidrogênion (*m.*, *Chem.*) hydrogenion.
hidrogenita (*f.*, *Chem.*) hydrogenite; aluminum amalgam.
hidrogeologia (*f.*) hydrogeology.
hidrognosia (*f.*) hydrognosy.
Hidrogr. = HIDROGRAFIA (Hydrography).
hidrografia (*f.*) hydrography.
hidrográfico –ca (*adj.*) hydrographic.
hidrógrafo (*m.*) hydrographer.
hidróide (*m.*, *Zool.*) hydroid, hydrozoan.
hidrólise (*f.*, *Chem.*) hydrolysis.
hidrólita (*f.*, *Chem.*) hydrolith; calcium hydride.
hidrolítico –ca (*adj.*, *Chem.*) hydrolytic.
hidrologia (*f.*) hydrology.
hidrológico –ca (*adj.*) hydrologic.
hidrólogo (*m.*) hydrologist.
hidromagnesita (*f.*, *Chem.*) hydromagnesite; basic magnesium carbonate.
hidromania (*f.*) hydromania.
hidromático –ca (*adj.*) hydromatic.
hidromecânico –ca (*adj.*) hydromechanical; (*f.*) hydromechanics.
hidromedusa (*f.*, *Zool.*) hydromedusa, jellyfish; c.a. POLIPOMEDUSA; (*pl.*) the *Hydromedusae* or *Hydrozoa*.
hidromel [-méis] (*m.*) hydromel, mead.
hidrometalurgia (*f.*) hydrometallurgy.
hidrometeoro (*m.*) hydrometeor.
hidrometeorologia (*f.*) hydrometeorology.
hidrometria (*f.*) hydrometry; (*Med.*) hydrometra.
hidrômetro (*m.*) hydrometer; water meter.
hidromotor (*m.*) hydromotor; jet propeller.
hidrópata (*m.,f.*) hydropath(ist).
hidropatia (*f.*) hydropathy, the water cure.

hidrópico –ca (*adj.*, *Med.*) dropsical; (*m.,f.*) a person having the dropsy.
hidropisia (*f.*, *Med.*) hydrops(y); dropsy.
hidroplano (*m.*) hydroplane, seaplane, flying boat.
hidropneumático –ca (*adj.*) hydropneumatic.
hidrópota (*m.,f.*) hydropot, water drinker.
hidroquinona (*f.*, *Chem.*) hydroquinone, hydroquinol.
hidróscopo (*m.*) hydroscopist (dowser).
hidrosfera (*f.*) hydrosphere.
hidrossilicato (*m.*, *Chem.*) hydrosilicate.
hidrossol (*m.*, *Chem.*) hydrosol.
hidrossolúvel (*adj.*) water-soluble.
hidrossulfato (*m.*, *Chem.*) hydrosulfate.
hidrossulfito (*m.*, *Chem.*) hydrosulfide.
hidrossulfúrico –ca (*adj.*, *Chem.*).) = SULFÍDRICO.
hidrossulfuroso –sa (*adj.*, *Chem.*) hydrosulfurous.
hidrostático –ca (*adj.*) hydrostatic; (*f.*) hydrostatics.
hidróstato (*m.*) hydrostat.
hidrotecnia (*f.*) hydrotechny.
hidrotécnico –ca (*adj.*) hydrotechnic; (*f.*) hydrotechny.
hidroterapêutico (*f.*, *Med.*) hydrotherapeutics.
hidroterapia (*f.*) hydrotherapy.
hidrotérmico –ca (*adj.*) hydrothermal.
hidrotímetro (*m.*) hydrotimeter.
hidrotipia (*f.*, *Photog.*) hydrotype.
hidrotomia (*f.*, *Anat.*) hydrotomy.
hidrotórax [ks] (*m.*, *Med.*) hydrothorax.
hidrotrópico –ca (*adj.*, *Biol.*) hydrotropic.
hidrotropismo (*m.*, *Biol.*) hydrotropism.
hidrovia (*f.*) waterway.
hidroxiamoníaco [ks] (*m.*) = HIDROXILAMINA.
hidróxido [ks] (*m.*, *Chem.*) hydroxide.—de alumínio, aluminum tri-hydroxide.—de amônio, ammonium hydroxide.—de potássio, potassium hydroxide; lye; caustic potash.—de sódio, sodium hydroxide; caustic soda.
hidroxilamina [ks] (*f.*, *Chem.*) hydroxylamine.
hidroxilo [ks] (*m.*, *Chem.*) hydroxyl [= OXIDRILO].
hidrozincita (*f.*, *Min.*) hydrozincite, zinc bloom.
hidrozoário –ria (*adj.; m.*, *Zool.*) hydrozoan.
hiena (*f.*) hyena.
hieranose (*f.*, *Pathol.*) epilepsy [= EPILEPSIA].
hierarca (*f.*) hierarch.
hierarquia (*f.*) hierarchy.
hierárquico –ca (*adj.*) hierarchic(al).
hierático –ca (*adj.*) hieratic, sacred.
hierocracia (*f.*) hierocracy.
hierofante (*m.*) hierophant. Var. HIEROFANTA.
hieróglifo, hieroglifo (*m.*) hieroglyph; fig., unintelligible or illegible writing [= JEROGLIFO].
hierografia (*f.*) hierography.
hierógrafo –fa (*m.,f.*) hierographer.
hierograma (*f.*) hierogram.
hierologia (*f.*) hierology.
hierólogo –ga (*m.,f.*) hierologist.
hierosolimita, hierosolimitano –na (*adj.*) of or pert. to the city of Jerusalem; (*m.,f.*) a native of Jerusalem. Vars. JEROSOLIMITA, JEROSOLIMITANO.
hietógrafo (*m.*) hyetograph.
hietologia (*f.*) hyetology.
hietômetro (*m.*) hyetometer, a rain gauge.
hifa (*f.*, *Bot.*) hypha.
hífen [-ens, -enes] (*m.*) hyphen [= TRAÇO-DE-UNIÃO].
hifenizar (*v.t.*) to hyphen (-ate, -ize).
hígido –da (*adj.*) healthy, healthful.
higiene (*f.*) hygiene, hygienics; sanitation; diet.
higiênico –ca (*adj.*) hygienic; sanitary.
higienista (*m.,f.*) hygienist.
higienizar (*v.t.*) to hygienize.
higrina (*f.*, *Chem.*) hygrin(e).
higrófano –na (*adj.*) hygrophanous.
higrófilo –la (*adj.*, *Bot.*) hygrophilous.
higrófito (*m.*, *Biogeog.*) hygrophyte.
higrofobia (*f.*, *Med.*) hygrophobia.
higroftálmico –ca (*adj.*, *Anat.*) hygrophthalmic.
higrógrafo (*m.*) hygrograph.
higrologia (*f.*) hygrology.
higroma (*m.*, *Med.*, *Veter.*) hygroma.
higrometria (*f.*) hygrometry.
higrômetro (*m.*) hygrometer.
higroscopia (*f.*) = HIGROMETRIA.
higroscopicidade (*f.*) hygroscopicity.
higroscópico –ca (*adj.*) hygroscopic.
higroscópio (*m.*) hygroscope.
higróstato (*m.*) hygrostat.

higrotermógrafo (*m.*, *Meteorol.*) hygrothermograph.
hílare (*adj.*) hilarious.
hilariante (*adj.*) exhilarating, cheering, enlivening, elating. gás—, laughing gas.
hilaridade (*f.*) hilarity, mirth, glee.
Hilário (*m.*) Hilary.
Hildegarda (*f.*) Hildegarde.
hiléia (*f.*) Amazon rain forest.
hilídeos (*m.pl.*) a family (*Hylidae*) of tree toads.
hilo (*m.*, *Bot.*, *Anat.*, *Zool.*) hilum.
hilozoísmo (*m.*) hylozoism.
hímen [-ens, -enes] (*m.*) hymen.
himeneu (*m.*) marriage; wedding feast.
himênio (*m.*, *Bot.*) hymenium.
himenofiláceas (*f.pl.*) a family (*Hymenophyllaceae*) of filmy ferns.
himenóforo (*m.*, *Bot.*) hymenophore.
himenogastráceas (*f.pl.*) a family (*Hymenogastraceae*) of false truffles.
himenomiceto (*m.*, *Bot.*) hymenomycete.
himenóptero –ra (*adj.*, *Zool.*) hymenopterous; (*m.*) hymenopteron; (*m.pl.*) the Hymenoptera (bees, wasps, ants).
himenopterologia (*f.*) hymenopterology.
himenotomia (*f.*, *Surg.*, *Anat.*) hymenotomy.
hinário (*m.*) hymnal, hymnbook.
hindu (*adj.; m.,f.*) Hindu; Indian.
hinista (*m.,f.*) hymnist.
hino (*m.*) hymn. —nacional, national anthem.
hinografia (*f.*) hymnography.
hinógrafo –fa (*m.,f.*) hymnographer.
hinologia (*f.*) hymnology.
hinologista (*m.,f.*) panegyrist.
hinólogo –ga (*m.,f.*) = HINISTA.
hinterlândia (*f.*) hinterland.
hiocólico –ca (*adj.*, *Biochem.*) hyodeoxycholic [acid].
hioglosso [glô] (*m.*, *Anat.*) hyoglossus.
hióide (*m.*, *Anat.*, *Zool.*) hyoid bone.
hióideo –dea (*adj.*) hyoid.
hioscíamo (*m.*, *Bot.*) henbane (*Hyoscyamus*), c.a. MEIMENDRO.
hiosciamina (*f.*, *Chem.*) hyosciamine.
hioscina (*f.*, *Chem.*) hyoscine.
hiosternal (*adj.*, *Anat.*, *Zool.*) hyosternal.
hipálage (*f.*, *Gram.*, *Rhet.*) hypallage.
hipalgesia (*f.*) hypalgia.
hipanto (*m.*, *Bot.*) hypanthium.
hipantôdio (*m.*, *Bot.*) syconium [= SICÔNIO].
hiperacidez (*f.*) hyperacidity.
hiperácido –da (*adj.*) hyperacid.
hiperacusia (*f.*, *Med.*) hyperacusia.
hiperalgesia, hiperalgia (*f.*, *Med.*) hyperalgesia.
hipérbato (*m.*) hyperbaton. Var. HIPÉRBATON.
hipérbole (*f.*, *Rhet.*) hyperbole; (*Geom.*) hyperbola.
hiperbólico –ca (*adj.*) hyperbolic.
hiperbolismo (*m.*) hyperbolism.
hiperbolizar (*v.i.*) to hyperbolize.
hiperbolóide (*adj.; m.*, *Geom.*) hyperboloid.
hiperbóreo –rea (*adj.*) of the far north; (*m.pl.*) the Arctic peoples.
hiperbulia (*f.*) hyperbulia.
hipercardia (*f.*, *Med.*) enlargement of the heart.
hipercinese, hipercinesia (*f.*, *Med.*) hyperkinesia.
hipercrítico –ca (*adj.*) hypercritical; (*m.,f.*) hypercritic.
hiperdulia (*f.*, *R.C.Ch.*) hyperdulia.
hiperelíptico –ca (*adj.*, *Math.*) hyperelliptic.
hiperemia (*f.*, *Med.*, *Physiol.*) hyperemia.
hiperestesia (*f.*) hyperesthesia.
hipereutético –ca (*adj.*, *Physics*, *Metal.*, *Chem.*) hypereutectic.
hipereutectóide (*adj.*, *Physics*, *Metal.*, *Chem.*) hypereuctectoid.
hiperfocal (*adj.*, *Photog.*) hyperfocal.
hiperfísico –ca (*adj.*) hyperphysical.
hipericão (*m.*, *Bot.*) St. John's wort (*Hypericum*).
hiperite (*f.*, *Petrog.*) hyperite.
hipermetamorfose (*f.*, *Zool.*) hypermetamorphosis.
hipermetropia (*f.*, *Med.*) hypermetropia, hyperopia.
hipermnésia, hipermnesia (*f.*) hypermnesia.
hiperopia (*f.*, *Med.*) hyperopia [= HIPERMETROPIA].
hiperostose (*f.*, *Med.*) hyperostosis.
hiperpiesia (*f.*, *Med.*) hyperpiesia.
hiperpirexia [ks] (*f.*, *Med.*) hyperpyrexia.
hiperpituitarismo (*m.*, *Med.*, *Psychol.*) hyperpituitarism.

hiperplasia (*f., Med., Biol.*) hyperplasia.
hiperplóide (*adj., Biol.*) hyperploid.
hiperploidia (*adj., Biol.*) hyperploidy.
hiperpnéia (*f., Physiol.*) hyperpnea.
hiperprodução (*f.*) hyperproduction.
hiperprosexia [ks] (*f., Psychol.*) hyperprosexia.
hipersensível (*adj.*) hypersensitive.
hipérstena (*f., Min.*) hypersthene.
hiperstênio (*m., Petrog.*) hypersthenite.
hipertensão (*f., Med.*) hypertension, high blood pressure [=HIPERPIESIA].
hipértese (*f., Philol.*) hyperthesis.
hipertiroidismo (*m., Med.*) hyperthyroidism.
hipertonia (*f., Physiol.*) hypertonia.
hipertônico –ca (*adj., Physiol.*) hypertonic.
hipertricose (*f.*) hypertrichosis.
hipertrofia (*f., Med., Biol.*) hypertrophy.
hipertrofiar (*v.i., Med., Biol.*) to hypertrophy.
hipervaidade (*f.*) excessive vanity.
hipervaidoso –sa (*adj.*) excessively vain.
hipestesia (*f., Med.*) hypesthesia.
hipetro –tra (*adj., Class. Arch.*) hypaethral, open to the sky, not roofed over.
hipiatria (*f.*) hippiatry.
hipiatro (*m.*) hippiater, horse doctor.
hípico –ca (*adj.*) of or pert. to horses.
hipidiomórfico –ca (*adj., Petrog.*) hypidiomorphic.
hipismo (*m.*) horse racing.
hipnáceas (*f.pl.*) a large family (*Hypnaceae*) of pleurocarpous mosses.
hipnagógico –ca (*adj., Psychol.*) hypnagogic.
hipnestesia (*f.*) hypnesthesis, dulled sensibility.
hipnógeno –na (*adj.*) hypnogenetic.
hipnóide (*adj., Psychol.*) hypnoid.
hipnologia (*f.*) hypnology.
hipnona (*f., Chem.*) hypnone, acetophenone.
hipnose (*f.*) hypnosis.
hipnósporo (*m., Bot.*) hypnospore.
hipnoterapia (*f.*) hypnotherapy.
hipnótico –ca (*adj.; m.,f.*) hypnotic.
hipnotismo (*m.*) hypnotism.
hipnotista (*m.,f.*) hypnotist.
hipnotização (*f.*) hypnotization.
hipnotizador –dora (*adj.*) hypnotizing; (*m.,f.*) hypnotizer.
hipnotizar (*v.t.*) to hypnotize.
hipnotizável (*adj.*) capable of being hypnotized.
hipnotoxina [x=ks] (*f.*) hypnotoxin.
hipo (*m., Photog.*) hypo.
hipoblasto (*m., Embryol., Zool.*) hypoblast.
hipobrânquio –quia (*adj., Zool.*) hypobranchial.
hipocampo (*m.*) sea horse (*Hippocampus*).
hipocárpio (*m., Bot.*) hypocarp.
hipocastanáceas (*f.pl.*) the horse-chestnut family (*Aesculaceae*).
hipocilóide (*f., Geom.*) hypocycloid.
hipociste (*f.*) an herb (*Cytinus hypocistis*) which is parasitic on the roots of the cistus, and whose fruit yields hypocist—an astringent juice.
hipoclórico –ca (*adj., Chem.*) hypochloric.
hipoclorina (*f.*) =LÍQUIDO DE DAKIN.
hipoclorito (*m., Chem.*) hypochlorite.—de cálcio, calcium hypochlorite; bleaching powder.—de sódio, sodium hypochlorite.
hipocloroso –sa (*adj., Chem.*) hypochlorous.
hipocondria (*f., Med.*) hypochondria.
hipocondríaco –ca (*adj.; m.,f.*) hypochondriac.
hipocôndrio (*m., Anat.*) hypochondrium.
hipocorístico –ca (*adj.*) hypocoristic; (*m.*) an endearing pet name, as Billy, Mama, etc.
hipocótilo (*m., Bot.*) hypocotyle.
hipocrático –ca (*adj.*) Hippocratic. juramento—, H. oath.
hipocrepiforme (*adj.*) hippocrepiform (horseshoe-shaped).
hipocrisia (*f.*) hypocrisy; deceit, pretence.
hipocristalino –na (*adj., Petrog.*) hypocrystalline, hemicrystalline.
hipócrita (*adj.*) hypocritical; (*m.,f.*) hypocrite.
hipodáctilo (*m., Zool.*) hypodactylum.
hipoderme (*m., Zool.*) hypodermis.
hipodérmico –ca (*adj.*) hypodermic.
hipódromo (*m.*) hippodrome, race track.
hipoeutectóide (*adj., Physics, Metal., Chem.*) hypoeutectoid.
hipofagia (*f.*) hippophagy (eating of horseflesh).
hipófago –ga (*adj.*) hippophagous; (*m.,f.*) an eater of horseflesh.

hipofaringe (*f., Zool.*) hypopharynx.
hipofilo –la (*adj., Bot.*) hypophyllous.
hipofisário –ria (*adj., Anat.*) hypophyseal.
hipófise (*f., Anat.*) hypophysis, pituitary body.
hipofosfato (*m., Chem.*) hypophosphate.
hipofosfito (*m., Chem.*) hypophosphite.
hipofosfórico –ca (*adj., Chem.*) hypophosphoric.
hipofosforoso –sa (*adj., Chem.*) hypophosphorous.
hipofrenia (*f.*) hypophrenia, feeble-mindedness.
hipofrênico –ca (*adj.*) hypophrenic, feeble-minded.
hipogástrico –ca (*adj., Anat.*) hypogastric.
hipogástrio (*m., Anat.*) hypogastrium.
hipogeu (*m., Arch.*) hypogeum.
hipoginia (*f., Bot.*) hypogyny.
hipógino –na (*adj., Bot.*) hypogynous.
hipoglosso –sa (*adj.; m., Anat.*) hypoglossal; (*m., Zool.*) the halibut (*Hippoglossus hippoglossus*).
hipógnato –ta (*adj.*) hypognathous; undershot.
hipogrifo (*m.*) hippogriff.
hipohialino –na (*adj., Petrog.*) hypohyaline, partly glassy.
hipologia (*f.*) hippology.
hipômetro (*m.*) hippometer.
hipomnesia (*f.*) hypomnesis, weak memory.
hiponiquial (*adj., Anat.*) hyponychial.
hiponíquio (*m., Anat.*) hyponychium.
hipopatologia (*f.*) hippopathology.
hipopíese (*f., Med.*) low blood pressure.
hipopígio (*m., Zool.*) hypopygium.
hipópio (*m., Med.*) hypopyon.
hipoplancto (*m., Biol.*) hypoplankton.
hipoplasia (*f., Med.*) hypoplasia.
hipoplástico –ca (*adj., Med.*) hypoplastic.
hipopotâmico –ca (*adj.*) hippopotamic; fig., obese.
hipopótamo (*m.*) hippopotamus.
hipoprosexia [ks] (*f., Psychol.*) hypoprosexia.
hipossulfito (*m., Chem.*) hyposulfite.—de soda, hyposulfite of soda; sodium thiosulfate.—de sódio, sodium hyposulfite.
hipossulfuroso –sa (*adj., Chem.*) hyposulphurous.
hipóstase (*f., Med., Eccl., Hist.*) hypostasis.
hipostático –ca (*adj.*) hypostatic.
hipostilo –la (*adj., Arch.*) hypostyle.
hipostoma (*m., Zool.*) hypostome.
hipoteca (*f.*) mortgage; lien; pledge.
hipotecar (*v.t.*) to hypothecate, mortgage, pledge.
hipotecário –ria (*adj.*) hypothecary.
hipotécio (*m., Bot.*) hypothecium.
hipotênar, hipótenar (*adj., Anat.*) hypothenar.
hipotensão (*f., Med.*) hypotension.
hipotenusa (*f., Geom.*) hypotenuse.
hipotermal (*adj.*) hypothermal, tepid.
hipótese (*f.*) hypothesis, theory, assumption.—de ausência, (*Stat.*) null hypothesis. aventurar uma—, to put forward a theory, venture a supposition. em—alguma, under no circumstances. no melhor das—s, at best. no pior das—s, if the worst comes to the worst. tomar por—, to take for granted, assume, suppose.
hipotético –ca (*adj.*) hypothetical, conjectural.
hipotipose (*f., Rhet.*) hypotyposis.
hipotireoidismo (*m., Med.*) hypothyroidism.
hipotomia (*f.*) hippotomy.
hipotônico –ca (*adj., Physiol.*) hypotonic.
hipotraquelio (*m., Arch.*) hypotrachelium, gorgerin, necking.
hipotrofia (*f., Biol., Bot.*) hypotrophy, atrophy.
hipoxantina [ks] (*f., Biochem.*) hypoxanthin(e).
hipoxis [ks] (*f.*) the goldstar grasses (genus *Hypoxis*) of amaryllis family.
hipsocefalia (*f., Craniol.*) hypsicephaly.
hipsocefalo –la (*adj., Craniol.*) hypsicephalic.
hipsocromo –ma (*adj., Chem.*) hypsochromic.
hipsografia (*f., Geog.*) hypsography.
hipsometria (*f., Geog.*) hypsometry.
hipsômetro (*m.*) hypsometer.
hipurato (*m., Chem.*) hippurate.
hipúrico –ca (*adj., Chem.*) hippuric.
hipuridáceas (*f.pl.*) a family of aquatic herbs typified by the marestail (*Hippuris vulgaris*).
Hirão (*m.*) Hiram.
hircino –na (*adj.*) hircine, goatish.
hircismo (*m.*) goatish odor.
hircoso –sa (*adj.*) strong-smelling [plants].
hirsutez [ê] (*f.*) hirsuteness.

hirsuto –ta (*adj.*) hirsute, hairy; rough, bristly.
hirteza [ê] (*f.*) stiffness; erectness; hirsuteness.
hirto –ta (*adj.*) stiff, rigid; tough; hispid.—**de frio**, stiff with cold.—**de medo**, rigid with fright.
hirudíneos (*m.pl.*, *Zool.*) the leeches (*Hirundinea*).
hirundinídeos (*m.pl.*, *Zool.*) the family of swallows and martins (*Hirundinidae*).
hirundino –na (*adj.*, *Zool.*) hirundine.
hispânico –ca (*adj.*) Hispanic, Spanish.
hispanismo (*m.*) Hispanicism.
hispanista (*m.,f.*) Hispanist.
hispanizar (*v.t.*) to Hispaniolize.
hispano-americano –na (*adj.*; *m.,f.*) Spanish-American.
hispar-se, hispidar-se (*v.r.*) to bristle.
hispidez [ê] (*f.*) hispidity.
híspido –da (*adj.*) hispid, bristly.
hispiduloso –sa (*adj.*, *Bot.*, *Zool.*) hispidulous.
hissopada (*f.*, *Eccl.*) act of sprinkling.
hissopar (*v.t.*, *Eccl.*) to sprinkle with holy water.
hissope [ó] (*m.*, *Eccl.*) aspergillum.
hissôpo (*m.*, *Bot.*) hyssop (*Hyssopus officinalis*).
histeranto –ta (*adj.*, *Bot.*) hysteranthous.
histerectomia (*f.*, *Surg.*) hysterectomy.
histerese (*f.*, *Physics*, *Elec.*) hysteresis.
histeresímetro (*m.*, *Elec.*) hysteresis meter.
histerético –ca (*adj.*, *Elec.*) hysteretic.
histeria (*f.*, *Med.*) hysteria.
histérico –ca (*adj.*) hysterical; (*m.,f.*) one subject to hysteria.
histerotomia (*f.*, *Surg.*) hysterotomy.
histerótomo (*m.*, *Surg.*) hysterotome.
histoblasto (*m.*, *Anat.*, *Zool.*) histoblast.
histogênese (*f.*, *Biol.*) histogenesis.
histogenia (*f.*, *Biol.*) histogeny.
histogênico –ca (*adj.*, *Biol.*) histogenic.
histogênio (*m.*, *Bot.*) histogen.
histografia (*f.*) histography.
histograma (*m.*, *Statistics*) histogram; block diagram.
histólise (*f.*, *Biol.*, *Zool.*) histolysis.
histologia (*f.*) histology; microscopic anatomy.
histológico –ca (*adj.*) histologic(al).
histologista (*m.,f.*) histologist.
histone (*f.*, *Biochem.*) histone.
histonomia (*f.*) histonomy.
histoquímica (*f.*) histochemistry.
história (*f.*) history; story, tale; fable; fib; poppycock; (*pl.*) fiddlesticks! pooh!—**antiga**, ancient history.—**da carochinha** or **de fadas**, nursery tale, fairy tale.—**de sempre**, same old story.—**em quadrinhos**, comic strip, the funnies.—**moderna**, modern history.—**natural**, natural history.—**profana**, profane history.—**sacra**, sacred history.—**seriada**, a serial. **cheio de—s**, fussy. **Que—é essa?** What are you talking about? What do you mean?
historiada (*f.*) long, complicated story.
historiador –dora (*m.,f.*) historian; story-writer.
historiar (*v.t.*) to write or tell the history of.
historicidade (*f.*) historicity.
histórico –ca (*adj.*) historical.
historiento –ta (*adj.*, *colloq.*) fussy, demanding.
historiografia (*f.*) historiography.
historieta [ê] (*f.*) historiette, short story; anecdote; novelette.
historiógrafo –fa (*m.,f.*) historiographer.
historizar (*v.t.,v.i.*) to historize.
histotomia (*f.*, *Anat.*) histotomy.
histozima (*f.*, *Biochem.*) histozyme.
histrião (*m.*) clown, buffoon.
histrionia, histrionice (*f.*) clowning, buffoonery.
hititas (*m.pl.*) the Hittites.
hitlerismo (*m.*) Hitlerism.
hizone (*m.*, *Chem.*) hyzone, tritium.
hl = HECTOLITRO(S).
hm = HECTÔMETRO(S).
hoazim (*f.*, *Zool.*) hoatzin, stinkbird (*Opisthocomos cristatus*).
hodiernamente (*adv.*) nowadays; today.
hodierno –na (*adj.*) present-day, modern-day.
hodômetro (*m.*) odometer.
hoje [ô] (*adv.*; *m.*) today.—**à tarde**, this afternoon.—**à noite**, this evening, tonight.—**de manhã**, this morning.—**de noite**, tonight.—**em dia**, nowadays.—**mesmo**, this very day.—**não**, not today.—**ou amanhã**, soon, sooner or later. **de—a um mez**, a month from today. **de—em**

diante, from today on, henceforth. **de—para amanhã**, at any moment, from one day to the next.
holanda (*f.*) holland (a fine linen fabric, first made in Holland).
holandês –dêsa (*adj.*) Dutch; (*m.,f.*) a Hollander; the Dutch language.
hólmio (*m.*, *Chem.*) holmium.
holoblástico –ca (*adj.*, *Embryol.*) holoblastic.
holocarpo –pa (*adj.*, *Bot.*) holocarpic.
holocausto (*m.*) holocaust; by ext., self-sacrifice.
holocentrídeos (*m.pl.*) the Holocentridae (squirrelfishes.)
holócrino –na (*adj.*, *Anat.*) holocrine.
holocristalino –na (*adj.*, *Petrog.*) holocrystalline.
holoédrico –ca (*adj.*, *Cryst.*) holohedral.
holoedro (*m.*, *Cryst.*) holohedron.
holófito –ta (*adj.*) holophytic.
holofote (*m.*) holophote; searchlight.
holófrase (*f.*) holophrase, holophrasis.
holofrástico –ca (*adj.*) holophrastic.
hológrafo –fa (*adj.*) holograph(ic).
holohialino –na (*adj.*, *Petrog.*) holohyaline.
holometabólico –ca (*adj.*, *Zool.*) holometabolic.
holômetro (*m.*) holometer, pantometer.
holomórfico –ca (*adj.*, *Cryst.*) holomorphic.
holomorfose (*f.*, *Biol.*) holomorphosis.
holoparasito (*m.*, *Biol.*) holoparasite.
holoplancto (*m.*, *Biol.*) holoplankton.
holotônico –ca (*adj.*, *Med.*) holotonic.
holotúria (*f.*) holothurian (sea cucumber).
homatômico –ca (*adj.*, *Chem.*) homatomic.
homaxial [ks] (*adj.*, *Biol.*) homaxial.
hombridade (*f.*) manliness; masculinity; loftiness of purpose, magnanimity.
homem (*m.*) man; mankind; workman.—**ao mar!** Man overboard!—**apagado**, a dimwit.—**às direitas**, an inflexibly upright man.—**à-toa**, a no-good.—**cosmopolita**, man of the world.—**de bem**, reputable man.—**de confiança**, trustworthy man.—**de côr**, a colored man.—**de Deus!** My dear fellow! Man alive!—**de idade**, elderly man.—**de letras**, man of letters.—**de negócios**, business man.—**de palavra**, man of his word.—**de palha**, straw man, puppet, dummy,—**de pena**, a writer.—**de poucas palavras**, a man of few words.—**direito**, upright man.—**do mundo**, man of the world.—**do povo**, a man of the people.—**feito**, grown man.—**grande**, large man.—**grande—**, great man.—**interior**, the inner man.—**pobre**, a poor man. **pobre—**, Poor man!—**marginal**, (*Sociol.*) marginal man.—**-peixe** = DUGONGO.—**público**, public man.—**-rã**, frogman.—**reto**, an upright man.—**-sanduíche**, sandwich man.—**sêco**, man of few words.—**simples**, a simple man. **um simples—**, a mere man. **a massa dos homens**, the bulk of mankind. **bonito—[not —bonito]**, a fine figure of a man. **Êle tem filhos homens**, He has grown sons. **O—faz e Deus desfaz**, Man proposes but God disposes. **ser—dos sete intrumentos**, to have several irons in the fire; to have more than one string to one's bow. **Um—e tanto!** Quite a man!
homenageado –da (*adj.*) honored; (*m.,f.*) one who is being or has been honored.
homenagear (*v.t.*) to pay homage to, do honor to.
homenagem (*f.*) homage; honor; respects. **em—a**, in honor of.
homenzarrão (*m.*) huge man.
homenzinho (*m.*) small man; midget; a youth; a nonentity.
homeomorfismo (*m.*, *Cryst.*) homeomorphism.
homeopata (*adj.*; *m.,f.*) homeopath(ic).
homeopatia (*f.*) homeopathy.
homeopático –ca (*adj.*) homeopathic.
homérico –ca (*adj.*) Homeric; heroic, epic.
Homéro (*m.*) Homer.
homessa! (*interj.*) Man alive! For Pete's sake!
homicida (*adj.*) homicidal; (*m.,f.*) manslayer.
homicidiar (*v.t.*) to commit homicide.
homicídio (*m.*) homicide; murder.—**culposo**, or **involuntário**, manslaughter.
homilética (*f.*) homiletics.
homilia or **homília** (*f.*) homily.
homiliar (*v.i.*) to preach.
homiliasta (*m.,f.*) homilist.
hominal (*adj.*) hominal.
hominalidade (*f.*) man's nature.
hominho (*m.*, *colloq.*) little man.
homínido –da (*adj.*) hominoid, manlike.

homiziado –da (*adj.*) in hiding; (*m.,f.*) a fugitive from justice.

homiziar (*v.t.*) to conceal, hide (as, a fugitive); to give sanctuary to; (*v.r.*) to abscond, go into hiding; to take refuge.

homizio (*m.*) protection, refuge, sanctuary.

homoblásteo –tea (*adj., Bot.*) homotropous.

homocêntrico –ca (*adj.*) homocentric(al).

homocerca (*adj.; f., Zool.*) homocercal (tail fin).

homocíclico –ca (*adj., Chem.*) homocyclic, isocyclic.

homoclamídeo –dea (*adj., Bot.*) homochlamydeous.

homocromático –ca, **homocrômico** –ca (*adj.*) homochromous.

homocromia (*f.*) homochromatism.

homócrono –na (*adj., Biol.*) homeochronous.

homodinâmica (*f., Biol.*) homodynamy.

homodianâmico –ca (*adj., Biol.*) homodynamous.

homodromia (*f., Bot.*) homodromy.

homódromo –ma (*adj., Bot., Mech.*) homodromous.

homoédrico –ca (*adj.*) homohedral.

homofilo –la (*adj., Bot.*) homophyllous.

homofonia (*f.*) homophony.

homofônico –ca (*adj.*) homophonous; homophonic.

homófono (*m.*) homophone.

homogamia (*f., Bot.*) homogamy.

homógamo –ma (*adj., Bot.*) homogamous.

homogeneidade (*f.*) homogeneity.

homogeneização (*f.*) homogenization.

homogeneizadeira (*f.*) homogenizer.

homogeneizar (*v.t.*) to homogenize.

homogêneo –nea (*adj.*) homogenous.

homogenesia (*f., Biol.*) homogenesis.

homogenia (*f.*) homogeneity; (*Biol.*) homogeny.

homogenizar (*v.t.*) to homogenize.

homogonia (*f., Bot.*) homogony.

homografia (*f.*) homographic spelling; (*Geom.*) homography.

homógrafo –fa (*adj.*) homographic; (*m.*) homograph.

homolateral (*adj.*) homolateral.

homologação (*f.*) homologation, approval, ratification; acceptance.

homologar (*v.t.*) to homologate, approve, ratify.

homologia (*f.*) homology.

homólogo –ga (*adj.*) homologous.

homômero –ra (*adj.*) homomeral, homomerous.

homométrico –ca (*adj.*) homometrical.

homomorfia (*f.*) homomorphy .

homomorfismo (*m.*) homomorphism.

homomorfo –fa (*adj.*) homomorphous.

homonímia (*f.*) homonymy.

homonímico –ca (*adj.*) homonymic; (*m.,f.*) a namesake.

homônimo –ma (*adj.*) homonymous; (*m.*) homonym; (*m.,f.*) a namesake.

homonomia (*f., Biol.*) homonomy.

homópata & derivs. = HOMEÓPATA & derivs.

homopétalo –la (*adj., Bot.*) homopetalous.

homoplasia (*f., Biol.*) homoplasy; (*Med.*) homeoplasia.

homoplástico –ca (*adj., Biol.*) homoplastic.

homopolar (*adj.*) homopolar, unipolar.

homóptero (*m., Zool.*) a homopteron; (*pl.*) the order Homoptera (cicadas, lantern flies, leaf hoppers, plant lice, etc.).

homorgânico –ca (*adj.*) homorganic.

homosistes (*f.pl.*) coseismal lines.

homossexual (*adj.*) homosexual.

homossexualismo (*m.*) homosexuality, homosexualism.

homotaxes [ks] (*f.pl., Geol.*) homotaxic formations.

homotermal, homotérmico –ca (*adj., Physiol., Zool.*) homoiothermal, homoiothermic.

homotesia, homotetia (*f., Math.*) homothety.

homotético –ca (*adj., Math.*) homothetic.

homotipia (*f., Biol.*) homotypy.

homotípico –ca (*adj.*) homotypic(al).

homótipo (*m., Biol.*) homotype.

homótono –na (*adj.*) homotonous.

homotópico –ca (*adj., Biol.*) homotopic.

homótropo –pa (*adj., Bot.*) homotropous.

homúnculo (*m.*) homunculus, dwarf, manikin.

hon. = HONORÁRIO (honorary).

honestar (*v.t.*) to make honest, or honorable; to honor.

honestidade (*f.*) honesty, honor; chastity, virtue.

honesto –ta (*adj.*) honest, honorable; trustworthy; above-board, suitable, proper; chaste, virtuous.

honorabilidade (*f.*) honorableness, uprightness, probity.

honorário –ria (*adj.*) honorary; honorific (*m.pl.*) honorarium, fees.

honorífico –ca (*adj.*) honorific: honorable; honorary.

honra (*f.*) honor, honesty, probity; esteem, respect, homage; dignity, distinction; reputation, fame, glory; chastity, virginity.—**s militares**, military honors.

honradez [ê] (*f.*) honesty, integrity; morality.

honrado –da (*adj.*) honorable; honest, virtuous; (*m.,f.*) one whose draft is honored by someone other than the drawee.

honrar (*v.t.*) to honor, dignify; to glorify; to venerate, respect; to celebrate.

honraria (*f.*) honor, rank, distinction.

honroso –sa (*adj.*) honorable; illustrious, noble.

hopeíta (*f., Min.*) hopeite.

hóquei (*m.*) hockey.

hora, hour; time of day; opportune moment.—**avançada,** late hour.—**das refeições,** mealtime.—**de jantar,** dinner-time.—**de verão,** daylight saving time.—**do almoço,** lunch time.—**do recreio,** recess time (at school).—**H,** zero hour.—**s a fio,** or—**s esquecidas,** hours on end; hour after hour.—**s de lazer,** or—**s vagas,** leisure hours.—**s do expediente,** official business hours.—**s extraordinárias,** overtime.—**s mortas,** dead of night. **à** —, at the moment; just in time; punctually; by the hour. **à boa**—, in good time, opportunely. **a cada**—, every little while. **a esta(s)** —(**s**), at this time of day; now; at this moment; presently. **A que**—**s**? When? At what time? **a tantas**—**s**, at such and such a time. **a tôda**—, at all hours; continually; at any time. **à última**—, at the last minute; lately, recently. **às sete**—**s em ponto,** at seven o'clock on the dot (sharp). **às tantas**—**s,** late (at night). **até altas**—**s da noite,** far into the night; till all hours of the night. **cada**—, every hour. **chegar na**—, to arrive on time. **com o estômago a dar**—**s,** faint with hunger. **daqui a doze**—**s,** twelve hours from now. **dar**—**s,** to strike the hour. **de**—**em**—, every hour. **de duas em duas**—**s,** every two hours. **de última**—, last-minute. **de uma**—**para outra,** suddenly, from one hour to the next. **dentro de uma**—, within an hour. **está na**—**de,** it is time to (for). **Está quase na**—, It is almost time. **fazer**—**s,** to kill time. **fora de**—**s,** after hours, late, at the wrong time. **há uma**—, an hour ago. **havia uma**—, an hour earlier. **mais**—**menos**—, sonner or later, eventually. **marcar**—, to set a time. **na**—**H,** in the nick of time. **na mesma**—, at the same moment. **o adiantado da**—, the lateness of the hour. **pela**—**da morte,** (of prices) sky-high. **quarto de**—, quarter hour. **Que**—**s são?** What time is it? **São**—**s de ir,** It is time to go. **São quinze**—**s,** it is 15 o'clock (3:00 p.m.). **treze**—**s,** one p.m. **uma**—, one a.m.

Horácio (*m.*) Horace, Horatio.

horal (*adj.*) hour; (*m.*) time schedule.

horário –ria (*adj.*) hour; hourly; (*m.*) timetable, schedule; office hours.

horda (*f.*) horde; mob; gang.

hordeáceo –cea (*adj., Bot.*) hordaceous.

hordeína (*f., Biochem.*) hordein.

hordenina (*f., Chem.*) hordenine.

horista (*m.,f.*) hourly-wage worker.

horizontal (*adj.; f.*) horizontal.

horizontalidade (*f.*) horizontality.

horizonte (*m.*) horizon.—**artificial,** (*Astron.*) artificial or false horizon.—**visual,** visible horizon.

hormogônio (*m. Bot.*) hormogonium.

hormônio (*m., Physiol.*) hormone.

hornblenda (*f., Min.*) hornblende.

hornblendito (*m., Petrog.*) hornblendite.

horografia (*f.*) horography.

horologia (*f.*) horology.

horologial (*adj.*) horologic(al).

horometria (*f.*) horometry.

horóptero (*m., Physical Optics*) horopter.

horoscópio, horóscopo (*m.*) horoscope.

horoscopista (*m.,f.*) horoscopist.

horrendo –da, **horrente, hórrido** –da, **horrífero** –fa, **horrífico** –ca (*adj.*) horrendous, horrible, horrid, horrifying, ghastly, terrible, grim.

horripilacão (*f.*) horripilation, goose flesh.

horripilante, horrípilo –a (*adj.*) horrifying.

horripilar (*v.t.*) to horrify; to make one's flesh creep; to make one's hair stand on end; (*v.r.*) to be horrified.

horrível (*adj.*) horrible; awful, hideous; ghastly.

horror (*m.*) horror, terror; aversion, loathing. **Que—! How awful! ter—de,** to dread.

horrorizado –da (*adj.*) horrified, aghast.

horrorizar (*v.t.*) to horrify, terrify.

horroroso –sa (*adj.*) horrific, horrifying, appalling.

horta (*f.*) vegetable garden, truck farm.

hortaliça (*f.*) vegetable; (*pl.*) greens.

hortar (*v.t.*) to make into a vegetable garden; (*v.i.*) to grow vegetables.

hortativo –va (*adj.*) hortative, hortatory.

hortelã (*f.*) any of various mints (family *Lamiaceae*).— **-comum,** or **-verde,** spearmint (*Mentha spicata*).—**-de-cheiro,** crispleaf mint (*Mentha crispa*).—**-doce,** field mint (*Mentha arvensis*).—**-de-fôlha-larga,** or **-do-maranhão,** summer savory (*Satureia hortensis*), c.a. SEGURELHA.—**-francesa,** costmary chrysanthemum (*C. majus*).—**-pimenta,** peppermint (*Mentha piperita*). —**-silvestre,** horsemint (*Mentha longifolia*).

hortelão –loa (*m.,f.*) a truck gardener.

hortense (*adj.*) pert. to or grown in a truck garden; (*f., Bot.*) the small burnet (*Sanguisorba minor*).

hortênsia (*f., Bot.*) hydrangea [= HIDRÂNGLA, NOVELOS]; [*cap.*] Hortense.

horticultor –tora (*m.,f.*) horticulturist.

horticultura (*f.*) horticulture.

hôrto (*m.*) small flower or vegetable garden; horticultural nursery.—**-da-beira,** kale (*Brassica oleracea acephala*), c.a. TRONCHUDA-MAIOR.—**florestal,** tree nursery.

hortulana (*f.*) ortolan (a European bunting).

hosana (*m.*) hosanna.

hóspeda (*f.*) woman guest; landlady.

hospedador (*m.*) host.

hospedagem (*f.*) hospitality; lodging.

hospedar (*v.t.*) to receive as a guest; to give lodging to. —**se no hotel,** to put up at the hotel.

hospedaria (*f.*) inn, hotel.

hóspede (*m.*) guest; lodger; host; (*adj.*) foreign.

hospedeiro –ra (*adj.*) hospitable; (*m.*) host; innkeeper; (*f., Bot.*) a host plant; hostess.

hospício (*m.*) an asylum (usually free) for the poor, sick or insane; an animal shelter.

hospital (*m.*) hospital.—**de pronto socorro,** emergency hospital.—**de sangue,** field hospital.

hospitalar (*adj.*) of or pert. to a hospital.

hospitaleiro –ra (*adj.*) hospitable; (*m.*) host; hospitable or charitable person; a hospitaler; (*f.*) member of a religious order devoted to the care of the sick or needy in hospitals.

hospitalidade (*f.*) hospitality.

hospitalização (*f.*) hospitalization.

hospitalizar (*v.t.*) to hospitalize.

hoste (*f.*) host, army, legion; (*pl.*) rank and file; troops.

hóstia (*f., Eccl.*) Host, consecrated wafer; a sacrificial victim.

hostil (*adj.*) hostile, inimical; adverse, contrary.

hostilidade (*f.*) hostility, enmity; opposition.

hostilizar (*v.t.*) to display hostility towards; to wage war against; (*Milit.*) to harass; (*v.r.*) to fight one another.

hotel [-éis] (*m.*) hotel.

hoteleiro (*m.*) hotelman, innkeeper, landlord.

houlétia (*f.*) a genus (*Houlletia*) of orchids.

hudsônia (*f.*) the genus (*Hudsonia*) of beach heathers.

houv+verb endings = forms of HAVER [52].

hubnerita (*f., Min.*) hübnerite.

hudo (*m.*) = JURUVA.

Hugo (*m.*) Hugh.

huguenote (*m.*) Huguenot.

hulha (*f.*) coal.—**antracitosa,** anthracite, hard coal.— **branca,** white coal (meaning the waterfalls of Brazil as sources of electrical energy).—**betuminosa,** bituminous coal, soft coal.—**gorda (magra),** fat (lean) coal. **alcatrão de—,** coal-tar.

hulheira (*f.*) coal mine or pit.

humanar (*v.t.*) to humanize.

humanidade (*f.*) humanity; human nature; mankind; humaneness; (*pl.*) the humanities.

humanismo (*m.*) humanism.

humanista (*adj.*) humanistic; (*m.,f.*) humanist.

humanitário –ria (*adj.; m.,f.*) humanitarian.

humanitarianismo (*m.*) humanitarianism.

humanização (*f.*) humanizing.

humanizar (*v.t.*) to humanize, make humane; to civilize.

humano –na (*adj.*) human; humane. **efetivo** or **potencial—,** manpower; (*m.pl.*) humans, humanity, mankind.

Humberto (*m.*) Humbert.

humboldtita (*f., Min.*) humboldtite.

humificação (*f.*) humification.

humildade (*f.*) humility, meekness; diffidence; humbleness.

humildar (*v.t.*) to humble.

humilde (*adj.*) humble, meek; modest, unassuming; low, mean, plain.

húmile (*adj.*) poetical form of HUMILDE.

humilhação (*f.*) humiliation, humbling, abashment.

humilhante (*adj.*) humiliating, mortifying.

humilhar (*v.t.*) to humble, humiliate; to depress; to snub, rebuff; to browbeat; (*v.r.*) to demean oneself; to eat humble pie.

humite (*f., Min.*) humite.

humo (*m.*) humus.

humor (*m.*) humor, temper, disposition; mood; sense of humor; humidity; fluid (of animal bodies).—**aquoso,** aqueous humor (of the eye).—**vítreo,** vitreous humor (of the eyeball). **de mau—,** out of humor.

humorado –da (*adj.*) full of humors. **bem—,** good-humored. **mal—,** ill-humored.

humoral (*adj.*) humoral.

humorismo (*m.*) humoralism; humorousness.

humorista (*m.,f.*) humorist.

humorístico –ca (*adj.*) humoristic, witty.

humoroso –sa (*adj.*) full of humors; humid.

humoso –sa (*adj.*) rich in humus.

húmulo (*m., Bot.*) hop (*Humulus*); = LÚPULO.

húmus (*m.*) = HUMO.

húngaro –ra, hungarês, –resa (*adj.; m.,f.*) Hungarian.

Hungria (*f.*) Hungary.

hunos (*m.pl.*) Huns.

huri (*f.*) houri.

huroniano –na (*adj., Geol.*) Huronian.

hurra! Hurrah!

husa (*f., Bot.*) the roselle (*Hibiscus sabdariffa*).

hússar, hussardo (*m.*) hussar.

hutchinsonita (*f., Min.*) hutchinsonite.

I

I, i, the ninth letter of the Portuguese alphabet. [Pronounced ee.]

ia, form of IR [53].

iabá (*m.*) jerked beef [= JABÁ, CHARQUE].

iaburu (*m.*) = JABURU.

iaca (*f.*) = INHACA.

iaçanã (*f.*) = JAÇANÃ.

iacaninã (*f.*) = CANINANA.

iacitarapui (*m.*) a bramblepalm (*Desmoncus pumilus*).

iacuruaru (*m.*) = JACURUARU.

iaía (*f.*) = PAPAGAIO-DE-COLEIRA.

iaiá (*f.*) a familiar term, in the days of slavery in Brazil, used as the equivalent of "missy"; when capitalized, a nickname for Laura; cotton print (cloth).

iam, íamos, forms of IR [53].

iambo (*m., Pros.*) iamb.

ianque (*adj.; m.,f.*) Yankee.

iantino –na (*adj.*) ianthine, violet-colored.

iapa (*f.*) = INHAPA.

iapoque (*m.*) the yapok or water opossum (*Chironectes minimus*).

iaque (*m., Zool.*) the yak of Tibet.

iara (*f.*) a river siren [= MÃE-D'ÁGUA].

iará (*f.*) a piassava palm (*Leopoldinia pulchra*).

iararana (f.) = CURUARANA.
iatá (f.) a syagrus palm (S. cocoides), c.a. JATÁ, PIRINA, PIRIRIMA.
iate (m.) yacht.
iatroquímica (f.) iatrochemistry.
iauácano (m.) the wallaba (Eperua), a valuable timber tree of northern Brazil.
ibabiu (m.) = GUABIJUEIRO.
ibairiba (f.) an angelin tree (Andira).
IBAM = INSTITUTO BRASILEIRO DE ADMINISTRAÇÃO MUNICIPAL (Brazilian Institute of Municipal Administration).
ibapocaba (f., Bot.) an allamanda (A. doniana).
ibá-poó (m.) a honeyberry (Melicocca lepido-petala).
ibaporoti (m.) = GRUMIXAMEIRA.
ibarô (m.) the southern soapberry (Sapindus saponaria).
ibaxama (f.) = GUAXIMA-ROXA.
IBC = INSTITUTO BRASILEIRO DO CAFÉ (Brazilian Coffee Institute).
IBECC = INSTITUTO BRASILEIRO DE EDUAÇÃO, CIÊNCIA E CULTURA (Brazilian Institute of Education, Science and Culture.
ibérico -ca (adj.; m.,f.) Iberian.
ibérida (f., Bot.) a candytuft (Iberis linifolia).
ibero -ra [é] (adj.; m.,f.) Iberian.
IBGE = INSTITUTO BRASILEIRO DE GEOGRAFIA E ESTATÍSTICA (Brazilian Institute of Geography and Statistics).
ibídidas, ibidídeos (m.pl.) the Threskiornithidae (family of ibises and spoonbills).
ibipitanga (f.) = PITANGUEIRA.
ibiraiú (m., Bot.) an apes-earring (Pithecellobium hassleri).
ibirá-perê (m.) = GRAPIAPUNHA-BRANCA.
ibirapitanga (f.) = PAU-BRASIL.
ibiraqüiinha (f.) = CRAVEIRO-DO-MARANHÃO.
ibiraro (m.) = GUAIUVIRA.
ibirataí (m.), ibirataíba (f., Bot.) the spike pilocarpus (P. pennatifolius).
ibirauna (f.) [a-u] (f.) = BARAUNA.
ibirô (m.) = GINJEIRA-DA-TERRA.
íbis (m.,f.) ibis.—-branca, or -sagrada, the sacred ibis.
ibixuna (f.) = FEDEGOSO-VERDADEIRO.
icã (m.) the Weddell syagrus palm (S. weddelliana).
içá (f.) a winged femal SAÚVA ant.
içabitu (m.) = SABITU.
icacináceo -cea (adj., Bot.) icacinaceous.
icaco (m.) the icaco cocoplum (Chrysobalanus icaco).
icaçu (m.) a syagrus palm (S. insignis).
içar (v.t.) to hoist, lift, raise.
Ícaro (m.) Icarus; fig., one who has suffered a downfall in his high-flown ambitions.
icéria (f.) cottony-cushion scale insect (Icerya purchasi).
icica (f.) a resintree (Protium icicariba).—-açu = ALMECE-GUEIRA-CHEIROSA.
icnêumon(e) (m.) ichneumon, mongoose; ichneumon fly.
icnografia (f., Drawing) ichnography, ground plan.
ícone (m.) icon.
iconoclasmo (m.) iconoclasm.
iconoclasta (m.,f.) iconoclast; (adj.) iconoclastic.
iconografia (f.) iconography.
iconolatria (f.) iconolatry, image worship.
iconologia (f.) iconology.
iconomania (f.) iconomania.
iconometria (f.) iconometry.
iconômetro (m.) iconometer.
iconoscópio (m., Photog.) iconoscope, view finder.
icor (m., Med.) ichor, sanies.
icoroso -sa (adj.) ichorous, sanious.
icosaedro (m., Geom.) icosahedron.
icterícia (f., Med.) jaundice; of animals, the yellows.
ictérico -ca (adj.) jaundiced; (m.,f.) a person affected with jaundice.
icterídeos (m.pl.) the orioles, etc. (family Icteriade).
icteróide (adj.) icteroid.
ictíico -ca [í-i] (adj., Zool.) ichthyic.
ictiocola (f.) isinglass; fish glue.
ictiodonte (m., Paleontol.) ichthyodont.
ictiodorolite (m., Paleontol.) ichthyodorulite.
ictiofagia (f.) ichthyophagy.
ictiófago -ga (adj.) ichthyophagous; (m.,f.) ichthyophagist.
ictiofobia (f.) ichthyophobia.
ictiografia (f.) ichthyography.
ictiógrafo -fa (m.,f.) ichthyographer.
ictióide, ictioídeo -dea (adj.) fishlike.

ictiol (m., Pharm.) Ichthyol.
ictiólito (m., Paleontol.) ichthyolite.
ictiologia (f.) ichthyology.
ictiólogo -ga (m.,f.) ichthyologist.
ictiomorfo -fa (adj.) fish-shaped.
ictiose (f., Med.) ichthyosis.
ictiosismo (m., Veter.) ichthyosism.
ictiossauro (m., Paleontol.) ichthyossaur.
icto (m., Pros., Med.) ictus.
id (m., Psychoanalysis) id.
ida (f.) departure, a going, a leaving; Ida.—e volta, round trip.—s e vindas, goings and comings.—por vinda, a quick round trip. Na—jogamos pôquer, On the way there we played poker.
idade (f.) age, time of life; period, epoch; old age; time. —áurea, golden age.—antiga, period of ancient history. —contemporânea, a period of contemporary history.—crítica, critical period of life.—da pedra, Stone Age.—da pedra polida, Neolithic Era.—da pedra talhada, Paleolithic Era.—da razão, age (years) of discretion.—de bronze, Bronze Age.—de ferro, Iron Age.—de inocência, Age of Innocence (childhood).—de ouro, Golden Era.—média, Middle Ages.—moderna, modern age.—Vitoriana, Victorian age. a—ingrata, the awkward age. certidão de—, birth certificate. de—avançada, of advanced years. de meia—, middle age. de—madura, middle-aged. de menor—, under-age. flor da—, prime of life. na—de, at the age of. Que —tem você? How old are you?.
ide, form of IR [53].
ideação (f.) ideation.
ideador -dora (m.,f.) imaginer.
ideal (adj.) ideal, mental; imaginary; (m.) the ideal.
idealidade (f.) ideality.
idealismo (m.) idealism.
idealista (adj.) idealistic; (m.,f.) idealist.
idealístico -ca (adj.) idealistic.
idealização (f.) idealization.
idealizador -dora (adj.) idealizing; (m.,f.) one who idealizes.
idealizar (v.t.) to idealize.
idear [14] (v.t.) to ideate; think; to devise, frame, design.
ideável (adj.) imaginable.
idéia (f.) idea; thought; opinion, belief; notion.—esfumada, hazy idea.—fixa, a fixed idea; associação de—s, association of ideas. aventar uma—, to put forward an idea. fazer—, to imagine. obcecado por uma—, haunted by an idea. teve a—de, he took a notion to (do something).
idem (pron., adj.) the same; ditto.
idêntico -ca (adj.) identical, exactly the same.
identidade (f.) identity.
identificação (f.) identification. letras de—, (Radio) call letters. placa de—, identification tag.
identificar (v.t.) to identify (com, with); to make identical; to regard as one.—-se com, to identify oneself with.
identificável (adj.) identifiable.
ideogenia (f.) ideogeny.
ideografia (f.) ideography.
ideograma (m.) ideogram, ideograph.
ideologia (f.) ideology.
ideológico -ca (adj.) ideological.
ideomoção (f.) ideomotion.
ideomotor (adj.) ideomotor.
ideoplastia (f.) ideoplasty.
ides, form of IR [53].
idielétrico -ca (adj., Physics) idioelectric.
idílico -ca (adj.) idyllic.
idílio (m.) idyl.
idilista (m.,f.) idylist.
idioblasto (m., Biol., Bot., Petrog.) idoblast.
idiocrasia (f.) idocrasy [= IDIOSINCRASIA].
idiocromático -ca (adj.) idochromatic.
idioelétrico -ca (adj.) = IDIELÉTRICO.
idiolatria (f.) idolatry, self-worship.
idioma (m.) idiom, tongue, language. [But not idiom in the sense of an idiomatic expression, which is IDIOTISMO or EXPRESSÃO IDIOMÁTICA.]
idiomático -ca (adj.) idiomatic.
idiomografia (f.) idiomography.
idiomórfico -ca (adj., Cryst.) idiomorphic.
idiomorfo -fa (adj.) idiomorphous.
idiomuscular (adj., Physiol.) idiomuscular.
idiopatia (f.) idiopathy.
idioplasma (m., Biol.) idioplasm, germ plasm.

idiopsicológico –ca (*adj.*) idiopsychological.
idiosomo (*m., Biol.*) idiosome, idioblast.
idiossincrasia (*f.*) idiosyncrasy, peculiarity, eccentricity [= IDIOCRASIA].
idiossíncrise (*f.*) idiosyncrasy.
idiostático –ca (*adj., Élec.*) idiostatic.
idiota (*m. f.*) idiot, fool; dunce, blockhead; (*adj.*) idiotic.
idiotálamo (*m., Bot.*) idiothalamus.
idiotar (*v.i.,v.r.*) to become idiotic.
idiotez [ê] (*f.*) idiotism.
idiotia (*f.*) idiocy.
idiotice (*f.*) idiotism; foolish or senseless act, statement, etc.
idiótico –ca (*adj.*) idiotic.
idiotificar (*v.t.*) to make a fool of.
idiotismo (*m.*) idiotism, idiocy; (*Gram.*) idiom, idiomatic expression.
idiotizar (*v.t.*) to render idiotic.
ido, past part. of IR [53].
idocrásio (*m., Min.*) idocrase, vesuvianite.
idólatra (*adj.*) idolatrous; (*m.,f.*) idolater.
idolatrar (*v.t.*) to idolize; (*v.i.*) to practice idolatry.
idolatria (*f.*) idolatry.
ídolo (*m.*) idol; adored person.
idoneidade (*f.*) appropriateness, suitableness, fitness, aptness; competence.
idôneo –nea (*adj.*) capable (**para**, of); qualified (**para**, to); suited, fitted; able; apt.
idos (*m.pl.*) the ides (of March, etc.).
idoso –sa (*adj.*) aged, old, elderly.
idouro –ra (*adj.*) transient, evanescent.
idrialina (*f., Chem.*) idrialin.
idrialite, idriatina (*f., Min.*) idrialite.
IEA = INSTITUTO DE ENERGIA ATÔMIA (Atomic Energy Institute).
iébaro (*m.*) a wallabatree (*Eperua purpurea*), c.a. COPAIBARANA.
ieis, form of IR [53].
iene (*m.*) a Japanese yen.
iérico (*m., Bot.*) a selaginella (*S. convolvulata*).
igaçaba (*f.*) earthen pot or jar; Indian burial urn [= GAÇABA, QUIÇABA].
igapó (*m., Phytogeog.*) *Webster* (under GAPÓ): "A forest bordering a river which is subject to such fluctuations of water level that for months the trees are partly inundated." *GBAT*: "(1) an aquatic jungle; (2) a marshy forest; (3) a pool in which aquatic plants grow; (4) a lake of dark and transparent water overhung with trees; (5) the lowest portion of the river bank, a few feet above the level of the river."
igapòzal (*m.*) a stretch of IGAPÓS.
igara (*f.*) dugout canoe.
igarapé (*m.*) "A waterway in a forest passable by the native canoes." [*Webster*] "a narrow natural channel between two islands or between an island and the mainland; a canoe passage." [*GBAT*]; bayou.
igaratim (*m.*) the canoe of an Indian chief.
igaripitá (*m., Bot.*) a cedrela (*C. fissilis*).
igarité (*f.*) "a small vessel with a single mast; a large canoe, smaller than a GALEOTA but larger than a MONTARIA; a large canoe with a span of 2 to 3 meters amidships, propelled by a trapezoidal sail or paddles and usually decked over in the stern, forming a cabin, generally used for short voyages and carrying little baggage." [*GBAT*]
igariteiro (*m.*) canoeman.
igaruçu (*m.*) a large Indian canoe.
ignaro –ra (*adj.*) ignorant, unlearned, unenlightened; stupid.
ignavo –va (*adj.*) idle, slothful; weak; cowardly.
ígneo –nea (*adj.*) igneous, fiery.
ignescente (*adj.*) ignescent, emitting sparks.
ignição (*f.*) ignition; state of being ignited.—**adiantada**, or **avançada**, advanced ignition (advancing the spark).—**dual**, dual ignition. **vela de**—, spark plug.
ignícolo –la (*adj.*) fire-worshiping; (*m.,f.*) ignicolist, fire worshipper.
ignífero –ra (*adj.*) igniferous.
ignificar (*v.t.*) to ignify, set on fire.
ignívomo –ma (*adj.*) ignivomous, vomiting fire.
ignívoro –ra (*adj.*) fire-eating.
ignóbil [beis] (*adj.*) ignoble, mean, infamous.
ignobilidade (*f.*) ignobility.
ignomínia (*f.*) ignominy, dishonor, infamy.

ignominioso –sa (*adj.*) ignominious, shameful.
ignorado –da (*adj.*) unknown, obscure.
ignorância (*f.*) ignorance.
ignorantão –tona (*m.,f.*) ignoramus.
ignorante (*adj.*) ignorant, unlearned; (*m.,f.*) an ignorant person; dunce, ignoramus.
ignorantismo (*m.*) ignorantism, obscurantism.
ignorantista (*m.,f.*) ignorantist, obscurantist.
ignorar (*v.t.*) to be ignorant (unaware) of. [But not to ignore, in the sense of disregard, which is DESPREZAR, DESCONSIDERAR.]
ignoto –ta (*adj.*) unknown, obscure.
igoga (*f.*) the dotleaf waterlily (*Nymphaea ampla*).
igreja [ê] (*f.*) church, temple; the church.—**do ocidente**, Western Church.—**do oriente**, Eastern Church.—**estacional**, (*R.C.Ch.*) station church.—**grega**, Greek (Orthodox) Church.—**latina**, Latin Church.—**-matriz**, mother-church.—**militante**, church militant.—**ortodoxa**, (Greek) Orthodox Church.—**primitiva**, primitive (Christian) Church.—**protestante**, Protestant Church.—**reformada**, Reformed Church.—**s suburbicárias**, (*R.C.Ch.*) suburbicarian churches (of Rome).—**triunfante**, church triumphant.
igrejeiro –ra (*adj., colloq.*) of or pert. to churches; churchgoing; sanctimonious.
igrejica (*f.*) a little church.
igrejinha (*f.*) a small church; (*colloq.*) a group of plotters or intriguers, clique; "mutual admiration society."
igual (*adj.*) equal, like, identical; even, uniform; even-tempered; (*m.,f.*) an equal, peer. **Cada qual com seu**—, Like with like; Birds of a feather flock together. **Êle encontrou um**—, He met his match. **sem**—, unequalled, unmatched. **por**—, equally, also. **Nunca vi coisa**—, I never saw the like. **tratar de**—**para**—, to treat, deal with, (one another) as equals.
igualação (*f.*) equalizing.
igualador –dora (*adj.*) equalizing, levelling; (*m.,f.*) equalizer, leveller.
igualamento (*m.*) equaling, equalizing, equating; equality.
igualar (*v.t.*) to equal, equalize, equate (**com**, with); to match; to level, make even; to come up to the level of; (*v.r.*) to match; to liken oneself to another.
igualável (*adj.*) that can be equaled.
igualdade (*f.*) equality; uniformity.
igualha (*f.*) social equality.
igualhar, pop. form of IGUALAR.
igualitário –ria (*adj.; m.,f.*) equalitarian.
igualitarismo (*m.*) equalitarianism.
igualização (*f.*) equalization.
igualmente (*adv.*) likewise, also; equally.
igualzinho –nha (*adj.*) exactly like; just like.
iguano (*m.*) iguana, large lizard.
iguânidas, iguanídeos (*m.pl.*) the Iguanidae (family of lizards).
iguarapé (*m.*) = IGARAPÉ.
iguaria (*f.*) a dainty dish; appetizing food; a table delicacy.
ih! My! my, my! My word! Oh!
IHGB = INSTITUTO HISTÓRICO E GEOGRÁFICO BRASILEIRO (Brazilian Historical and Geographical Institute).
iídiche [i-í] (*adj.; m.*) Yiddish.
ijolito (*m., Petrog.*) ijolite.
ilação (*f.*) illation, inference, conclusion, deduction.
ilangue-ilangue (*m., Bot.*) ylangylang (*Cananga odorata*).
ilaquear (*v.t.*) to ensnare, entrap, catch (lit. & fig.).
ilativo –va (*adj.*) illative, inferential.
Ilda (*f.*) Hilda.
ileal (*adj.*) unloyal.
ilectomia (*f., Surg.*) ilectomy.
ilegal (*adj.*) illegal, unlawful.
ilegalidade (*f.*) illegality, unlawfulness, illicitness.
ilegibilidade (*f.*) illegibility.
ilegitimidade (*f.*) illegitimacy.
ilegítimo –ma (*adj.*) illegitimate, spurious; bastard.
ilegível (*adj.*) illegible, undecipherable.
ileíte (*f., Med.*) ileitis.
íleo (*Anat., Entom.*) ileum; (*Med.*) ileus.
íleo-cecal (*adj., Anat.*) ileocaecal.
íleo-cólico –ca (*adj., Anat.*) ileocolic.
ileostomia (*f., Surg.*) ileostomy.
ileso –sa (*adj.*) unhurt, unharmed, uninjured, unscratched, unscathed, safe (and sound).
iletrado –da (*adj.*) illiterate, unlettered, unlearned.
ilha (*f.*) island, isle.

ilhal (*m.*) flank (of an animal).
ilhar (*v.t.*) to isolate.
ilharga (*f.*) flank, side (of a body); (*pl.*) confidants, counsellors. **de—**, sideways. **deitar-se de—**, to lie on one's side.
ilhéu (*m.*) an islander; specif. an Azorian.
ilhó, ilhós (*m.,f.*) eyelet, grommet.
ilhoa, fem. of ILHÉU.
ilhota (*f.*) islet.
ilíaco –ca (*adj., Anat.*) iliac; (*m.*) ilium.
ilíada (*f.*) the Iliad; an epic.
ilibado –da (*adj.*) unsullied, spotless, unblemished.
ilibar (*v.t.*) to cleanse.
iliberal (*adj.*) illiberal, stingy, miserly; not of liberal principles.
iliberalidade (*f.*) illiberality.
iliberalismo (*m.*) illiberalism.
ilíceas (*f., Bot.*) the Ilicaceae (holly family).
ilicina (*f., Chem.*) ilicin.
ilicíneo –nea (*adj., Bot.*) ilicic.
ilícito –ta (*adj.*) illicit, unlawful, illegal; bootleg; improper.
ilimitado –da (*adj.*) unlimited, limitless, unbounded; vast, endless.
ilimitável (*adj.*) illimitable.
ilínio (*m., Chem.*) illinium.
ílio (*m., Anat.*) ilium.
ílio-costal (*adj., Anat.*) iliocostalis.
ílio-femoral (*adj., Anat.*) iliofemoral.
ílio-hipogástrico –ca (*adj., Anat.*) iliohypogastric.
ílio-inguinal (*adj., Anat.*) ilioinguinal.
ílio-lombar (*adj., Anat.*) iliolumbar.
ílio-pectíneo –nea (*adj.*) iliopectineal.
ílio-púbico –ca (*adj., Anat.*) iliopubic.
ílio-sacro –cra, ílio-sagrado –da (*adj., Anat.*) iliosacral.
ílio-trocanteriano –na (*adj., Anat.*) iliotrochanteric.
iliquidez (*f.*) illiquidity.
ilíquido –da (*adj.*) illiquid, not liquid; gross (not net).
ilírio –ria (*adj.; m.,f.*) Illyrian.
iliterato –ta (*adj.; m.,f.*) illiterate [= ILETRADO].
Il.ᵐᵒ = ILUSTRÍSSIMO (Most Illustrious).
ilmenita (*f., Min.*) ilmenite.
ilogia (*f.*) illogicality.
ilógico –ca (*adj.*) illogical, absurd, fallacious; far-fetched.
ilogismo (*m.*) want of logic.
ilota (*m.*) helot, serf.
ilotismo (*m.*) helotism, serfdom.
iludente (*adj.*) illusioning.
iludido –da (*adj.*) deluded, deceived.
iludimento (*m.*) delusion.
iludir (*v.t.*) to delude; to deceive; to elude, evade. (*v.r.*) to fool oneself.
iludível (*adj.*) capable of being deluded; illusory.
iluminação (*f.*) illumination, lighting, lights; enlightenment. **poste de—**, lamppost.
iluminado –da (*adj.*) illuminated, alight, lit up; enlightened; (*m.*) an illuminato.
iluminador –dora (*adj.*) illuminating; (*m.*) illuminator.
iluminante (*adj.*) illuminating; enlightening.
iluminar (*v.t.*) to illuminate, light up; to decorate a building, etc., with lights; to illumine, enlighten; to decorate (manuscripts, books) with gold, colors, etc.
iluminativo –va (*adj.*) illuminative.
iluminismo (*m.*) illuminism; the Enlightenment (18th cent.).
iluminista (*m.,f.*) Illuminist.
iluminômetro (*m., Photog.*) illuminometer.
iluminura (*f.*) illumination of books, letters, etc., with gold and colors.
ilusão (*f.*) illusion, delusion, error, fallacy.
ilusionismo (*m.*) conjuring, magic, prestidigitation.
ilusionista (*m.,f.*) illusionist, conjurer, prestidigitator.
ilusivo –va (*adj.*) = ILUSÓRIO.
ilusor –sora (*m.,f.*) one who deludes; (*adj.*) illusory.
ilusório –ria (*adj.*) illusory, illusive, deceptive, deceitful, specious.
ilustração (*f.*) illustration; an illustrative picture; a picture magazine; knowledge, learning, attainments.—**divina**, divine inspiration.
ilustrado –da (*adj.*) erudite, learned; illustrated.
ilustrador –dora (*adj.*) illustrating, elucidating; (*m.,f.*) illustrator.
ilustrante (*adj.*) = ILUSTRADOR.
ilustrar (*v.t.*) to render illustrious; to enlighten (the mind); to elucidate; to illustrate with pictures; (*v.r.*) to become illustrious, distinguished; to instruct oneself.

ilustrativo –va (*adj.*) illustrative.
ilustre (*adj.*) illustrious, noted, conspicuous, eminent, honorable.
ilustríssimo –ma (*absol. superl. of* ILUSTRE) most illustrious.
ilutação (*f.*) mud bath.
ilvaíta (*f., Min.*) ilvaite.
imã (*m.*) Moslem imam.
ímã (*m.*) magnet.—**de campo**, field magnet.—**de ferradura**, horseshoe magnet.
imaculabilidade (*f.*) immaculateness.
imaculado –da (*adj.*) immaculate, spotless; unblemished; innocent, pure, undefiled, sinless, stainless.—**conceição**, Immaculate Conception; (*f.*) a brand of rum.
imaculável (*adj.*) incapable of being sin-stained.
imagem (*f.*) image, likeness, figure, picture; reflection; statue; idol. **à—de**, in the likeness of.
imaginação (*f.*) imagination; mental image, conception, notion; fantasy; fanciful belief. **dar asas**, or **rêdeas soltas, à—**, to give wings, or free rein, to the imagination.
imaginador –dora (*adj.*) imagining; (*m.,f.*) imaginer.
imaginar (*v.t.*) to imagine, devise, frame; to conceive, picture; to suppose, assume, opine; (*v.r.*) to picture oneself as.
imaginário –ria (*adj.*) imaginary, fancied, unreal.
imaginativo –va (*adj.*) imaginative; (*f.*) the imaginative faculty.
imaginável (*adj.*) imaginable.
imaginoso –sa (*adj.*) imaginative.
imago (*m., Entom.*) imago.
imaleável (*adj.*) non-malleable.
imame (*m.*) imam [= IMÃ].
imanar (*v.*) = IMANIZAR.
imanência (*f.*) immanence; inherence.
imanente (*adj.*) immanent, intrinsic, inherent.
imanização (*f.*) magnetization.
imanizar (*v.t.*) to magnetize [= IMANAR, IMANTAR].
imantação (*f.*) = IMANIZAÇÃO.
imantar (*v.*) = IMANIZAR.
imarescível (*adj.*) fadeless; unfading; imperishable; incorruptible.
imarginado –da (*adj.*) immarginate.
imatéria (*f.*) non-matter.
imaterial (*adj.*) immaterial (in the sense of incorporeal, but not in the sense of unimportant, which is DE POUCA IMPORTÂNCIA]; (*m.*) non-matter.
imaterialidade (*f.*) immateriality.
imaterialismo (*m., Philos.*) immaterialism.
imaterialista (*m.,f., Philos.*) immaterialist.
imaterializar (*v.t.*) to immaterialize; (*v.r.*) to become immaterial.
imaturidade (*f.*) immaturity.
imaturo –ra (*adj.*) immature, premature.
imbaíba, imbaúba, imbaúva (*f.*) = UMBAÚBA.
imbê (*m., Bot.*) any of various aroids, esp. *Philodendron imbe*, which yields a cordage fiber.—**da-praia** = ANINGAÚBA.—**de-comer** = CIPÓ-DE-IMBÉ.—**furado** or—**são-pedro** = DRAGÃO-FEDORENTO.
imbecil [cíl] (*adj.*) imbecilic, feeble-minded; (*m.,f.*) imbecile, half-wit, nitwit.
imbecilidade (*f.*) imbecility.
imbele (*adj.*) unwarlike; pusillanimous.
imberana (*f.*) = ANINGAÚBA.
imberbe (*adj.*) beardless; youthful.
imbicar (*v.*) = ABICAR.
imbira-brava, imbira-do-mato (*f.*) = GUAXIMA.
imbiri (*m.*) = BIRU-MANSO, COQUILHO.
imbiriçu, imburuçu (*m.*) a timber tree (*Bombax hexaphyllum*), the pods of which yield a kapoklike brownish fiber.
imbocaiá (*m.*) the totaí palm (*Acrocomia totai*).
imbondeiro (*m.*) = ADANSÔNIA.
imbretada (*f.*) = ENCRENCA.
imbricação (*f.*) imbrication, an overlapping (as of shingles).
imbricado –da (*adj.*) overlapped, overlapping.
imbricante (*adj.*) imbricate.
imbricar (*v.t.*) to imbricate, overlap (as shingles).
imbróglio (*m.*) imbroglio.
imbu (*m.*) a hog plum (fruit of the IMBUZEIRO); also, the tree itself. Var. UMBU.
imbuia (*f.*) the imbuya phoebe (*P. porosa*)—the premier cabinet wood of Brazil, frequently mis-named Brazilian walnut; it has a rich brown color and is finely figured in veneer cuttings; c.a. UMBUIA.

imbuir [72] (*v.t.*) to imbue, soak (as in blood); to imbue, saturate; to impregnate, permeate.—**-se em,** to be imbued with, impressed by.—**-se de,** to become imbued with (sentiments, ideas, etc.).
imburana (*f.*) a valuable timber tree (*Bursera leptophleos*), c.a. UMBURANA.
imburi (*m.*) = BURI-DA-PRAIA, PATIOBA.
imburi-de-cachorro (*m.*) = JERIVÁ.
imbuzada (*f.*) a dish made with cooked and strained hog plums, milk and sugar. Var. UMBUZADA.
imbuzeiro (*m.*) any mombin or hog plum, esp. *Spondias tuberosa* and *S. purpurea*, c.a. JIQUE; also, the ombutree pokeberry (*Phytolacca dioica*). Var. UMBUZEIRO.
imediação (*f.*) immediacy; (*pl.*) environs, neighborhood.
imediatamente (*adv.*) at once, right away.
imediatar (*v.i.*) to ship as first mate.
imediato **-ta** (*adj.*) immediate, near; instantaneous; next, following; contiguous, adjoining. (*m.*) the second in command; the next in line; first mate; first assistant. **o—,** the next one.
imemorado **-da** (*adj.*) unremembered.
imemorável (*adj.*) immemorable.
imensidade, imensidão (*f.*) immensity, boundless space; infinitude; wilderness.
imenso **-sa** (*adj.*) immense, illimitable, measureless, infinite.
imensurabilidade (*f.*) immeasurability.
imensurável (*adj.*) immeasurable.
imerecido **-da** (*adj.*) unmerited, undeserved.
imergente (*adj.*) immerging.
imergir [19, 24, 25] (*v.t.*) **—em,** to immerge, immerse, plunge into; (*v.i.*,*v.r.*)**—em,** to plunge into, sink, disappear (as in a fluid).
imérito **-ta** (*adj.*) undeserved, unmerited.
imersão (*f.*) immersion. **sino de—,** diving bell.
imerso **-sa** (*adj.*; *irreg. p.p. of* IMERGIR) immersed, plunged, dipped, sunk.
imida (*f.*, *Chem.*) imide.
imidogênio (*m.*, *Chem.*) imidogen; the imido or imino group.
imigo **-ga** (*adj.*; *m.*,*f.*) poetical form of INIMIGO.
imigração (*f.*) immigration.
imigrado **-da** (*adj.*) immigrated; (*m.*,*f.*) one who has immigrated.
imigrante (*m.*,*f.*) immigrant, migrant; (*adj.*) migrating.
imigrar (*v.i.*) to immigrate.
imigratório **-ria** (*adj.*) migratory.
imina (*f.*, *Chem.*) imine.
iminência (*f.*) imminence. **na—de,** about to (happen), on the verge of.
iminente (*adj.*) imminent, impending; threatening.
imisção (*f.*) a mixing in or meddling with; interference. [verb: IMISCUIR-SE.]
imiscibilidade (*f.*) immiscibility.
imiscível (*adj.*) immiscible.
imiscuir-se (*v.r.*)**—em,** to thrust oneself into; to mix in with; to interfere (meddle) with.
imissão (*f.*) immission.
imitação (*f.*) imitation; copy.
imitador **-dora** (*adj.*) imitating; mimetic; (*m.*,*f.*) imitator; copycat.
imitante (*adj.*) imitating, imitative.
imitar (*v.t.*) to imitate, copy, reproduce; to counterfeit; to mimic, ape.
imitativo **-va** (*adj.*) imitative.
imitável (*adj.*) imitable; worthy of imitation.
imo **-ma** (*adj.*) innermost; intimate.
imobiliário **-ria** (*adj.*) of property, immovable, fixed; (*m.*) an immovable piece of property (as a building, land, etc.). **bens—s,** real estate, the improvements thereon, etc. Cf. IMÓVEL.
imobilidade (*f.*) immobility, fixedness.
imobilismo (*m.*) fogyism, overconservatism, opposition to change.
imobilização (*f.*) immobilization.
imobilizador **-dora** (*adj.*) immobilizing; (*m.*,*f.*) one who or that which immobilizes.
imobilizar (*v.t.*) to immobilize; (*v.r.*) to become immobile.
imoderação (*f.*) immoderation.
imoderado **-da** (*adj.*) immoderate, inordinate, unrestrained, wanton; undue, unreasonable.
imodéstia (*f.*) immodesty.
imodesto **-ta** (*adj.*) immodest; brazen, forward.
imodicidade (*f.*) exorbitancy.

imódico **-ca** (*adj.*) exorbitant; excessive, esp. as to price.
imodificável (*adj.*) unmodifiable.
imolação (*f.*) immolation.
imolado **-da** (*adj.*) sacrificed.
imolador **-dora** (*adj.*) immolating; (*m.*,*f.*) immolator.
imolante (*adj.*) immolating [*Poetical*].
imolar (*v.t.*) to immolate, sacrifice (**-se,** oneself).
imoral (*adj.*) immoral, wicked; licentious.
imoralidade (*f.*) immorality; vice.
imorigerado **-da** (*adj.*) dissolute, unrestrained.
imorredouro **-ra** (*adj.*) undying, immortal, imperishable. Var. IMORREDOIRO.
imortal (*adj.*) immortal, deathless; (*m.*) a member of the French Academy or of the Brazilian Academy of Letters; (*pl.*, *Gk. and Rom. Myth*) the gods.
imortalidade (*f.*) immortality, deathlessness.
imortalização (*f.*) immortalization.
imortalizador **-dora** (*adj.*) immortalizing; (*m.*,*f.*) immortalizer.
imortalizar (*v.t.*) to immortalize; to perpetuate in memory; (*v.r.*) to gain immortal fame.
imoto **-ta** (*adj.*) = IMÓVEL.
imóvel (*adj.*) immovable, immobile; motionless, still; (*m.*) a piece of real property (land, houses, etc.). Cf. IMOBILIÁRIO.
impaciência (*f.*) impatience, impetuosity; want of patience, irritability; petulance.
impacientar (*v.t.*) to provoke, exasperate, make impatient; (*v.r.*) to lose one's patience; grow impatient; to fret.
impaciente (*adj.*) impatient (**com,** with); impetuous, eager; restless; petulant, pettish.
impacto **-ta** (*adj.*) impacted; (*m.*) impact; shock; a hit by a bomb.
impagável (*adj.*) priceless; absurd. **Isso é—!** That's rich!
impalpabilidade (*f.*) impalpability.
impalpável (*adj.*) impalpable, intangible.
impaludação (*f.*) infection with malaria.
impaludar (*v.t.*) to infect with malaria.
impaludismo (*m.*) malaria.
impante (*adj.*) haughty, stuck-up.
impar (*v.i.*) to pant, puff; to swell with pride; to become stuffed with food; (*v.t.*) to choke.
ímpar (*adj.*) odd (not even); one of a pair. **número—,** odd number. **par ou—,** even or odd.
imparcial (*adj.*) impartial, unprejudiced, unbiased.
imparcialidade (*f.*) impartiality.
imparidade (*f.*) oddness, unevenness (of a number).
imparipenado **-da** (*adj.*, *Bot.*) imparipinnate.
imparissílabo **-ba** (*adj.*, *Gram.*) imparissyllabic.
impartilhável (*adj.*) unsharable.
impartível (*adj.*) indivisible.
impassável (*adj.*) impassable.
impasse (*m.*) an impasse; stalemate; deadlock. **levar a um—,** to drive into a corner.
impassibilidade (*f.*) impassiveness, impassivity.
impassível (*adj.*) impassive, impassible, insensitive to pain; expressionless; undisturbed, unconcerned.
impatriótico **-ca** (*adj.*) unpatriotic.
impavidez [ê] (*f.*) intrepidity, dauntlessness.
impávido **-da** (*adj.*) dauntless; undismayed; intrepid.
impecabilidade (*f.*) impeccability.
impecável, impeccable; faultless.
impecunioso **-sa** (*adj.*) impecunious.
impedância (*f.*, *Elec.*, *Acoustics*) impedance.
impedição (*f.*) impediment; prohibition.
impedido **-da** (*adj.*) impeded, hindered, thwarted; (*Soccer*) offside; (*m.*) an officer's personal attendant.
impedidor **-dora** (*adj.*) impeding; (*m.*,*f.*) impeder.
impediente (*adj.*) impedient.
impedimenta (*f.*, *Milit.*) supply trains [= IMPEDIMENTOS].
impedimento (*m.*) impediment; stumbling-block, encumbrance; (*Soccer*) offside.—**dirimente,** (*Law*) diriment impediment.—**impediente** or **proibitivo,** (*Law*) prohibitive impediment.
impedir [60] (*v.t.*) to impede, hinder, obstruct; to keep back, restrain; to balk, thwart; to preclude, prevent (**de,** from).
impelente, impelidor **-dora** (*adj.*) impelling.
impelir [21a] (*v.t.*) to impel, push; to incite, stir up.
impendente (*adj.*) imminent.
impender (*v.i.*) to impend.
impene (*adj.*) featherless.
impenetrabilidade (*f.*) impenetrability.
impenetrado **-da** (*adj.*) unpenetrated.

impenetrável (*adj.*) impenetrable; insensible; reticent, reserved.
impenhorável (*adj.*) that cannot be pledged or mortgaged.
impenitência (*f.*) impenitence.
impenitente (*adj.*) impenitent, unrepentant; stubborn.
impensado –**da** (*adj.*) thoughtless; inconsiderate; unpremeditated.
impensável (*adj.*) unthinkable.
imperador (*m.*) emperor; (*Zool.*) a big-eye or catalufa (*Priacanthus cruentatus*); also = ÔLHO-DE-CÃO.
imperante (*adj.*) ruling, reigning; (*m.,f.*) ruler, sovereign.
imperar (*v.t.,v.i.*) to reign, rule (**sôbre**, over); (*v.r.*) to prevail.
imperativo –**va** (*adj.*) imperious; peremptory, imperative; (*m.*) imperative verb form.
imperatório –**ria** (*adj.*) imperial; imperative; (*f.*, *Bot.*) the masterwort hogfennel (*Peucedanum ostruthium*).
imperatriz (*f.*) empress.
impercebido –**da** (*adj.*) unperceived.
imperceptibilidade (*f.*) imperceptibility.
imperceptível (*adj.*) imperceptible; minute, very small.
imperdível (*adj.*) unlosable.
imperdoável (*adj.*) unpardonable, unforgivable.
imperdurável (*adj.*) unenduring.
imperecedouro –**ra**, **imperecível** (*adj.*) imperishable, undying. Var. IMPERECEDOIRO.
imperfectibilidade (*f.*) imperfectibility.
imperfectível (*adj.*) imperfectible.
imperfeição (*f.*) imperfection, defectiveness; deflect, flaw, blemish.
imperfeiçoado –**da** (*adj.*) unperfected; imperfect.
imperfeiçoar (*v.t.*) to render imperfect.
imperfeito –**ta** (*adj.*) imperfect; defective; (*m.*) imperfect verb tense.
imperfuração (*f.*) imperforation.
imperfurado –**da** (*adj.*) imperforate, unperforated.
imperfurável (*adj.*) imperforable.
imperial (*adj.*) imperial, imperious; (*f.*) upper deck of a bus; a card game similar to piquet.
imperialismo (*m.*) imperialism, imperial rule.
imperialista (*adj.; m.,f.*) imperialist.
imperialístico –**ca** (*adj.*) imperialistic.
imperiante (*adj.*) imperious, arrogant.
imperiosamente (*adv.*) imperiously.
imperícia (*f.*) inexpertness, unskillfulness.
império (*m.*) empire, domain; imperium, rule, sway; control.—**da morte** or **dos mortos**, the grave.
imperiosidade (*f.*) imperiousness.
imperioso –**sa** (*adj.*) imperious; imperative. **motivos**—**s**, compelling reasons.
imperito –**ta** (*adj.*) inexpert, unskilled, unskillful.
impermanência (*f.*) impermanence, -cy.
impermanente (*adj.*) impermanent.
impermeabilidade (*f.*) impermeability; impermeableness.
impermeabilização (*f.*) waterproofing, impermeabilization.
impermeabilizante (*m.*) waterproofing material.
impermeabilizar, impermear (*v.t.*) to waterproof, impermeabilize.
impermeável (*adj.*) impermeable, impervious, impassable; waterproof.—**ao ar**, airtight; (*m.*) a raincoat.
impermisto –**ta** (*adj.*) unmixed.
impermutável (*adj.*) impermutable, not subject to permutation.
imperscrutável (*adj.*) inscrutable.
impersistente (*adj.*) not persistent; inconstant.
impersistir (*v.i.*) to nòt persist.
impersonalidade (*f.*) impersonality.
impersonificar (*v.*) = IMPESSOALIZAR.
imperspicaz (*adj.*) not perspicacious.
impertérrito –**ta** (*adj.*) imperturbable; dauntless; undismayed.
impertinência (*f.*) impertinence, insolence; a piece of impertinence; petulance, peevishness; irrelevance.
impertinente (*adj.*) impertinent, rude, uncivil; brash; flippant; "fresh," petulant; pernickety; crusty; not pertinent, irrelevant.
imperturbabilidade (*f.*) imperturbability, nonchalance, aplomb.
imperturbado –**da** (*adj.*) unperturbed, undisturbed, unruffled, unmoved.
imperturbável (*adj.*) imperturbable, cool, calm, nonchalant.

impérvio –**via** (*adj.*) impervious, impenetrable; (*m.*) an inaccessible place.
impessoal (*adj.*) impersonal.
impessoalidade (*f.*) impersonality.
impessoalizar (*v.t.*) to impersonalize.
impetigem (*f.*), **impetigo** (*m.*, *Med.*) impetigo.
impetiginoso –**sa** (*adj.*) impetiginous.
ímpeto (*m.*) impetus, impelling force; urge; impulse; thrust; sudden rush; impetuosity; snap; vehemence, excitement; flight (of imagination).
impetra (*f.*) petition.
impetração (*f.*) entreaty, pleading, petitioning.
impetrante (*adj.*) pleading; (*m.,f.*) petitioner; one who has obtained an injunction against another.
impetrar (*v.t.*) to plead, entreat, petition; to enter a plea (in court).—**contra**, to seek a court injunction against.
impetrativo –**va**, **impetratório** –**ria** (*adj.*) impetrative.
impetuosidade (*f.*) impetuosity, vehemence.
impetuoso –**sa** (*adj.*) impetuous, passionate, headlong, rash, hotheaded, brash, boisterous.
impiedade (*f.*) impiety, irreverence; ungodliness; an impious act; cruelty, ruthlessness.
impiedoso –**sa** (*adj.*) impious; pitiless, merciless, ruthless, grim, harsh.
impigem (*f.*) the common name for almost any skin disease or blemish; tetter; popular term for impetigo.
impinge-araras (*m.*, *colloq.*) liar.
impingir [25] (*v.t.*)—**a**, to impose (a hoax) upon; to deal (a blow) to; to inflict (something unpleasant) upon; to palm off, foist (a worthless object) on.—**em**, to saddle (another) with something disadvantageous.—**por**, to pass off (one thing for another). [Not equivalent of impinge, which is COLIDIR; INFRINGIR.].—**gato por lebre**, to sell a gold brick to.
impio –**pia** (*adj.*) pitiless, unmerciful; (*m.,f.*) such a one.
ímpio –**pia** (*adj.*) impious, ungodly, unholy; (*m.,f.*) such a one.
implacabilidade (*f.*) implacability.
implacável (*adj.*) implacable, relentless, inexorable; unforgiving; ruthless, merciless, pitiless, grim.
implacentários (*m.pl.*, *Zool.*) the Implacentalia (marsupials and monotremes).
implacidez (*f.*) want of placidity.
implantação (*f.*) implantation.
implantar (*v.t.*) to implant, insert (**em**, in); to introduce (**em**, in); to plant, set, fix (as a flagpole in the ground); (*v.r.*) to become implanted (imbedded, established) (**em**, in).
implante (*m.*) = IMPLANTAÇÃO.
implausível (*adj.*) implausible.
implemento (*m.*) implement, instrument, tool.
implicação (*f.*) implication, entanglement; connotation; ill-will.
implicado –**da** (*adj.*) implicate, intertwined, entangled; involved. (*m.,f.*) one who is implicated (as in a crime).
implicador –**dora** (*adj.*) implicating; (*m.,f.*) one who, or that which, implicates.
implicância (*f.*) ill will, ill nature, grudge; implication.
implicante (*adj.*) implicating; cantankerous; (*m.,f.*) bickerer, troublemaker.
implicar (*v.t.*) to implicate, involve, entangle (**em**, in); to imply, import; to bring about (result, consequences); to connote; presuppose; to clash, conflict (**com**, with).—**-se em**, to become involved in.—**-se com (alguém)**, to pick on (someone); to have it in for (someone).
implicativo –**va**, **implicatório** –**ria** (*adj.*) implicative; implicatory.
implícito –**ta** (*adj.*) implicit, implied, tacit.
imploração (*f.*) imploration, imploring.
implorador –**dora**, **implorante** (*adj.*) imploring; (*m.,f.*) implorer.
implorar (*v.t.*) to implore, beseech, supplicate.
implorativo –**va** (*adj.*) imploring.
implorável (*adj.*) implorable.
implume (*adj.*) unfeathered, featherless, unfledged.
impolidez [ê] (*f.*) impoliteness, rudeness.
impolido –**da** (*adj.*) impolite, rude; uncouth.
impolítico –**ca** (*adj.*) impolitic; tactless; (*f.*) want of tact.
impoluído –**da** (*adj.*) = IMPOLUTO.
impoluível (*adj.*) that cannot be polluted.
impoluto –**ta** (*adj.*) unsullied, unpolluted, undefiled, unspotted, unstained.
imponderabilidade (*f.*) imponderability; weightlessness.
imponderado –**da** (*adj.*) ill-pondered; thoughtless.

imponderável [-veis] (*adj.*) imponderable; (*m.pl.*, *Physics*) imponderables.

imponência (*f.*) splendor, magnificence; impressiveness.

imponente (*adj.*) imposing, impressive; grand.

impontual (*adj.*) unpunctual.

impontualidade (*f.*) unpunctuality.

impopular (*adj.*) unpopular.

impopularidade (*f.*) unpopularity.

impopularizar (*v.t.*) to make unpopular; (*v.r.*) to become unpopular.

impor [63] (*v.t.*) to impose (laws, etc.); to pass off deceptively; (*Printing*) to impose (lay, arrange) type; (*v.r.*) to obtrude; to impose one's authority, prestige, influence; to prevail.—**a**, to lay on (taxes, etc.); to enjoin (silence, etc.) on; to inflict (penalty) on; to impute (a crime) to.—**respeito**, to command respect.

importação (*f.*) importation; merchandise imported.

importador –dora (*adj.*) importing; (*m.,f.*) importer.

importância (*f.*) importance, import, significance, consequence; sum of money; cost. **até a**—**de cem contos**, up to one hundred CONTOS [Cr$100.000,00]. **dar**—**a**, to give consideration, or attach importance, to. **não dar**—**a**, to attach no importance to; to take no notice of, pay no heed to. **Não tem**—, It is of no importance; it doesn't matter.

importante (*adj.*) important, momentous, significant; (*m.*) that which is essential, of moment. **O**—**é (saber)**, The important thing is (to know). **os**—**s**, (*colloq.*) big shots, bigwigs.

importar (*v.t.*) to import, bring in from abroad; (*v.i.*) to matter (be important).—**a**, to be of importance (consequence, concern) to.—**em**, to amount to (in money); to result in.—**se com**, to care about, bother with. **A conta importa em mil cruzeiros**, The bill amounts to 1,000 cruzeiros. **a única coisa que importava**, the only thing that mattered. **Não importa!** Never mind! No matter! **Não me importa**, I don't care. **Não se importa com coisa alguma**, He pays attention to nothing. **Pouco me importa!** I should worry! That's the least of my worries! It's all the same to me! I don't care a rap! I don't give a damn (about it)! **Que importa?** What of it? What does it matter? What's the difference? **Que me importa?** What's that to me?

importável (*adj.*) importable.

importe (*m.*) amount, sum; cost.—**total**, gross amount.—**líquido**, net amount.

importunação (*f.*) importunity; molestation.

importunador –dora (*adj.*) importuning; (*m.,f.*) importuner.

importunar (*v.t.*) to importune, entreat; to annoy, pester; to nag; to disturb, incommode.

importunidade (*f.*) importunity; annoyance.

importuno –na (*adj.*) importunate; troublesome, annoying; impertinent; inopportune; (*m.,f.*) an annoying person.

imposição (*f.*) imposition, an imposing upon, a laying on (of something); (*Print.*) imposition.

impositivo –va (*adj.*) not positive; imposing.

impossança (*f.*) impotence.

impossibilidade (*f.*) impossibility.

impossibilitar (*v.t.*) to render impossible; to preclude; to disable, incapacitate; to make unable (**de**, **para**, to).—**se para**, to be unable to; to be deprived of the means of. **ver-se impossibilitado** (or **na impossibilidade**) **de (fazer alguma coisa)** to find oneself unable (to do something).

impossível (*adj.*) impossible; unthinkable; insufferable; (*m.*) the impossible.

impôsto –ta (*adj.*) imposed; (*m.*) impost, tax, duty; (*f.*, *Arch.*) impost.—**de consumo**, consumer or excise tax.—**de renda**, income tax.—**de sêlo**, stamp tax.—**de viação**, road tax.—**proporcional**, apportioned tax.

impostor –tora (*adj.*) deceptive, illusory; (*m.*) an impostor; fourflusher, cheat, faker, humbug.

impostura (*f.*) imposture, hoax, fraud, hokum, buncombe, humbug.

impotável (*adj.*) undrinkable.

impotência (*f.*) impotence.

impotente (*adj.*) impotent, powerless (**para**, to; **contra**, against); (*m.*) impotent man.

impracticabilidade (*f.*) impracticability.

impraticável (*adj.*) impracticable, unfeasible; of roads, impassable.

imprecação (*f.*) imprecation, curse, malediction.

imprecar (*v.i.*) to imprecate, call down a curse upon.

imprecatado –da (*adj.*) unwary, incautious.

imprecativo –va (*adj.*) imprecating.

imprecatório –ria (*adj.*) imprecatory.

imprecaução (*f.*) unwariness.

imprecisão (*f.*) imprecision, inaccuracy.

impremeditação (*f.*) want of premeditation.

impreciso –sa (*adj.*) imprecise, inaccurate; vague, indefinite.

impreenchível [e-en] (*adj.*) unfillable.

impregnação (*f.*) impregnation.

impregnar (*v.t.*) to impregnate, saturate, fill, permeate (**de**, with).

impregnável (*adj.*) impregnable [but only in the sense of capable of being impregnated. In the more usual sense of unconquerable, the Port. equivalent of impregnable is INCONQUISTÁVEL, INEXPUGNÁVEL.]

impremediatação (*f.*) unpremeditation.

impremiditado –da (*adj.*) unpremeditated, unwitting.

imprensa (*f.*) a printing press; printing plant; the art or business of printing; the daily press; journalism; newspapers and periodicals, collectively.—**periódica**, periodicals, collectively. **segundo a**—, according to the press.

imprensado –da (*adj.*) pressed between (referring to a work day which falls between a Sunday and a holiday, or vice-versa).

imprensador (*m.*) pressman.

imprensadura (*f.*) pressing; printing.

imprensar (*v.t.*) to press; to print.

impresciência (*f.*) imprescience.

imprescindível (*adj.*) indispensable.

imprescritível (*adj.*, *Law*) imprescriptible, not subject to prescription. **bens imprescritíveis**, property which is not usucaptable.

impressão (*f.*) impression; printing, stamping; edition; mark, stamp, brand; effect produced on the mind.—**cerebral**, (*Anat.*) digital impression.—**digital**, fingerprint.—**em côres**, color printing.

impressionabilidade (*f.*) impressionability.

impressionante (*adj.*) impressive; stirring; thrilling; startling.

impressionar (*v.t.*) to impress, move, affect deeply; to create an impression upon; to thrill; (*v.r.*) to be impressed (**com**, by). **Não se impressione!** Don't get excited!

impressionável (*adj.*) impressionable.

impressionismo (*m.*) impressionism.

impressionista (*adj.*; *m.,f.*) impressionist.

impressivo –va (*adj.*) impressive.

impresso –sa (*irreg. p.p. of* IMPRIMIR) printed; (*m.*) a printed leaflet, circular, pamphlet; (*pl.*) printed matter in general.

impressor –sora (*adj.*) printing; (*m.*) printer, pressman (*f.*) printing press.

impressório (*m.*, *Photog.*) printing frame.

imprestabilidade (*f.*) inutility.

imprestabilizar (*v.t.*) to render useless.

imprestável [-veis] (*adj.*) useless; unserviceable; (*m.,f.*, *colloq.*) a person of no account.

impreterível (*adj.*) unavoidable, inevitable, indispensable.

imprevidência (*f.*) want of foresight.

imprevidente (*adj.*) without foresight.

imprevisão (*f.*) carelessness, heedlessness (of the future).

imprevisível (*adj.*) unforeseeable.

imprevisto –ta (*adj.*) unforeseen, unlooked for; sudden, unexpected. **chegar de**—, to show up suddenly, make a surprise visit. **ser tomado de**—, to be taken unawares; (*m.,f.*) one heedless of the future; something unexpected.

imprimação, imprimadura (*f.*) priming (of a surface).

imprimar (*v.t.*) to prime (a surface) preparatory to painting.

imprimir [24] (*v.t.*) to impress, imprint; to stamp; to print; to publish.—**em**, to leave an imprint upon; to mold, fashion; to inculcate.—**a**, to impart (life) to, give impetus to.—**maior velocidade a**, to speed up .—**se em**, to be impressed upon, fixed upon (in).

improbabilidade (*f.*) improbability, unlikelihood.

improbidade (*f.*) improbity, dishonesty.

improbo –ba (*adj.*) without probity, dishonest; unfair; toilsome, arduous.

improcedência (*f.*) want of justification, of fundamental basis.

improcedente (*adj.*) unfounded, baseless, groundless, not justified; inconsequent.

improdutível (*adj.*) non-productive.

improdutividade (f.) non-productiveness.
improdutivo –va (adj.) unproductive.
improferível (adj.) unutterable; unpronounceable.
improficiente (adj.) not proficient.
improficuidade [u-i] (f.) futility, fruitlessness.
improfícuo –cua (adj.) futile, bootless, unavailing, fruitless.
improfundo –da (adj.) unprofound.
improgressivo –va (adj.) unprogressive.
improlífero –ra (adj.) unproliferous.
improlífico –ca (adj.) unprolific.
impronunciável (adj.) unpronounceable.
improperar (v.t.) to vituperate.
impropério (m.) an upbraiding; a coarse or insulting word or act; scurrility.
impropício –ca (adj.) unpropitious.
improporção (f.) disproportion.
improporcionado –da, improporcional (adj.) disproportionate.
improporcionalidade (f.) disproportionality.
impropriar (v.t.) to render unfit, improper.
impropriedade (f.) impropriety, unseemliness; unsuitableness; inaccuracy.
impróprio –pria (adj.) improper, unsuited; unfit; inept; unbecoming, unseemly; wrong, amiss; risqué; (f., Math.) improper fraction.
improrrogável (adj.) that cannot be deferred or postponed.
impróspero –ra (adj.) inauspicious; unprosperous.
improtelável (adj.) that cannot be delayed or put off.
improvável (adj.) improbable, unlikely.
improvidência (f.,) improvidence.
improvidente, impróvido –da (adj.) improvident, imprudent, shiftless; happy-go-lucky.
improvisação (f.) improvisation.
improvisado –da (adj.) improvised, makeshift, impromptu offhand, extempore.
improvisador –dora (adj.) improvising; (m.,f.) improvisor.
improvisar (v.t.) to improvise; extemporize; to ad-lib; to invent or provide offhand.—-se em, to set oneself up (falsely) as; to pass oneself off as.
improviso –sa (adj.) unlooked for, sudden; impromptu. de—, unexpectedly; on the spur of the moment; offhand; (m.) extemporaneous remark, verse, composition, etc.
imprudência (f.) imprudence, rashness, recklessness, heedlessness; improvidence.
imprudente (adj.) imprudent, injudicious, ill-advised; careless, reckless; rash; foolhardy; improvident.
impuberdade, impubescência (f.) impuberty.
impúbere, impubescente (adj.) impubic, impurberal, impuberate.
impudência (f.) shamelessness, indecency; impudence, insolence; effrontery.
impudente (adj.) shameless; impudent; bold-faced, unblushing.
impudicícia (f.) lewdness; shamelessness.
impúdico –ca (adj.) lewd; shameless; wanton.
impudor (m.) lewdness; shamelessness; impudence.
impueira (f.) = IPUEIRA.
impugnação (f.) impugnation, impugning.
impugnador –dora (adj.) impugning; (m.,f.) impugner.
impugnar (v.t.) to impugn, oppose, resist, contradict, gainsay.
impugnável (adj.) impugnable.
impulsionar (v.t.) to impel, stimulate; to drive foward.
impulsividade (f.) impulsiveness.
impulsivo –va (adj.) impulsive; propulsive; (m.,f.) an impulsive person.
impulso (m.) impulse, impetus, push, thrust; incitement, urge. tomar—, to gather way; to dart forward.
impulsor –sora (adj.) impelling; (m.) driver, starter, mover; impeller.
impune (adj.) unpunished.
impunidade (f.) impunity.
impunível (adj.) unpunishable.
impureira (f.) = IPUEIRA.
impureza [ê] (f.) impurity; unchastity, lewdness.
impuro –ra (adj.) impure foul, unclean; unchaste, lewd, indecent, obscene.
imputabilidade (f.) imputability.
imputação (f.) imputation; blame.
imputador –dora (adj.) imputing.
imputar (v.t.) to impute to, ascribe to, blame for.

imputável (adj.) imputable.
imudável (adj.) immutable.
imundícia (f.) filth, dirt; grime; squalor; vermin; (colloq.) oodles of little things.
imundície (f.) small fur-bearing game; also = IMUNDÍCIA.
imundo –da (adj.) foul, filthy, unclean, nasty, dirty; squalid; obscene.
imune (adj.) immune.
imunidade (f.) immunity, exemption; prerogative.
imunização (f.) immunization.
imunizador –dora (adj.) immunizing.
imunizar (v.t.) to immunize (contra, against).
imutabilidade (f.) immutability, unchangeability, invariableness.
imutável (adj.) immutable, unalterable, unchangeable.
in-, look also under en-.
inabalável (adj.) unshakeable; immovable, steadfast; unflinching; inexorable.
inábil [-beis] (adj.) wanting in ability, inapt, inexpert, unskillful; clumsy; maladroit, tactless.
inabilidade (f.) inability, incompetence, incapacity; unskilfulness, clumsiness.
inabilitação (f.) want of qualifications; disqualification.
inabilitado –da (adj.) unfit.
inabilitar (v.t.) to disqualify (as, a student in an examination); to render unable (to do something).
inabitado –da (adj.) uninhabited.
inabitável (adj.) uninhabitable; unfit to live in.
inabordável (adj.) unapproachable.
inacabado –da (adj.) unfinished.
incabável (adj.) unending; that cannot be finished.
inação (f.) inaction, inactivity, inertness; indolence.
inaceitável (adj.) unacceptable; inadmissible.
inacessibilidade (f.) inaccessibility.
inacessível (adj.) inaccessible; unapproachable.
Inácio (m.) Ignatius.
inacreditável (adj.) incredible, unbelievable.
inacusável (adj.) unblamable.
inadaptação (f.) inadaptation.
inadaptado –da (adj.) unadapted.
inadaptável (adj.) unadaptable.
inadequado –da (adj.) inadequate; unsuited; unfit; inept.
inaderente (adj.) unadherent.
inadestrado –da (adj.) untrained; unschooled.
inadiável (adj.) not postponable; urgent, pressing.
inadimplemento (m.) nonfulfillment of contract; noncompliance with its terms.
inadmissão (f.) non-admission.
inadmissibilidade (f.) inadmissibility.
inadmissível (adj.) inadmissible.
inadmitido –da (adj.) not admitted.
inadquirível (adj.) not acquirable.
inadvertência (f.) inadvertence; oversight. por—, inadvertently.
inadvertidamente (adv.) inadvertently, unwittingly.
inadvertido –da (adj.) inadvertent, unintentional.
inafiançável (adj.) unbailable [crime, offense].
inaiá-guaçu-iba (m.) = COQUEIRO-DA-BAHIA.
inajá (m.) the Regal Maximiliana (M. regia) a tall, pinnate-leaved palm having immense prickle-tipped spathes used in basketry; c.a. ANAJÁ, MARIPÁ, NAJÁ.
inajustável (adj.) unadjustable.
inalação (f.) inhalation.
inalado –da (adj.) wingless.
inalador –dora (adj.) inhaling; (m.) inhaler.
inalante (adj.) inhaling.
inalar (v.t.) to inhale.
inalbuminado –da (adj.) having no albumin; (Bot.) having no endosperm.
inalcançável (adj.) unattainable.
inaliável (adj.) incapable of being allied or alloyed.
inalienabilidade (f.) inalienability.
inalienado –da (adj.) not alienated.
inalienável (adj.) inalienable.
inalterabilidade (f.) inalterability.
inalterado –da (adj.) unaltered, unchanged, unmodified. unimpaired.
inalterável (adj.) unalterable.
inamável (adj.) unamiable.
inambu [ú] (m.) = INHAMBU.
inambuquiá, inambu-sujo (m.) = INHAMBUCUÁ.
inamovível (adj.) unremovable (from office); unshakeable.
inamu [ú] (m.) = INHAMBU.
inamuí (m.) = LOURO-INHAMUÍ.

inane (*adj.*) inane, empty, void; worthless.
inanição (*f.*) inanition, emptiness; exhaustion from hunger, starvation.
inanidade (*f.*) inanity.
inanimado –da, inânime (*adj.*) inanimate, inert, lifeless.
inantéreo –rea (*adj.; Bot.*) inantherate.
inapagável (*adj.*) unerasable.
inaparente (*adj.*) unapparent.
inapelável (*adj.*) unappealable; inescapable.
inapetência (*f.*) inappetence, lack of appetite.
inapetente (*adj.*) inappetent.
inaplicabilidade (*f.*) inapplicability.
inaplicado –da (*adj.*) inattentive.
inaplicável (*adj.*) inapplicable; inapposite.
inapreciável (*adj.*) inappreciable, tiny; inestimable.
inapreensível [e-e] (*adj.*) inapprehensible.
inapresentável (*adj.*) unpresentable.
inaproveitado –da (*adj.*) unused; unworked.
inaproveitável (*adj.*) inapproveitável.
inaptidão (*f.*) inaptitude, inability, disability.
inapto –ta (*adj.*) inapt; inept; unfit.
inarmonia (*f.*) inharmony.
inarmônico –ca, inarmonioso –sa (*adj.*) inharmonious, discordant.
inarrável (*adj.*) indescribable; unspeakable.
inarticulado –da (*adj.*) inarticulate; not jointed or articulated.
inarticulável (*adj.*) that cannot be articulated.
inartificial (*adj.*) inartificial.
inartístico –ca (*adj.*) inartistic, unartistic.
inassíduo –dua (*adj.*) unassiduous.
inassimilável (*adj.*) not assimilable.
inassinável (*adj.*) unsignable.
inatacável (*adj.*) unassailable; unimpeachable.
inatenção (*f.*) inattention.
inatendível (*adj.*) unworthy of attention.
inatento –ta (*adj.*) inattentive.
inatingido –da (*adj.*) unattained.
inatingível (*adj.*) unattainable; untouchable; (*m.,f.*) an untouchable (East Indian).
inatividade (*f.*) inactivity, inertness; unemployment.
inativo –va (*adj.*) inactive, inert; on the retired or inactive list.
inato –ta (*adj.*) innate, inborn, inbred; unborn.
inatravessável (*adj.*) uncrossable.
inatural (*adj.*) unnatural.
inaturável (*adj.*) unbearable, insufferable.
inaudito –ta (*adj.*) unheard of, unexampled, unprecedented; inconceivable.
inaudível (*adj.*) inaudible.
inauferível (adj.) that may not be taken away (from someone).
inaufragável (*adj.*) unsinkable.
inauguração (*f.*) inauguration.
inaugurador –dora (*adj.*) inaugurating; (*m.,f.*) inaugurator.
inaugural (*adj.*) inaugural.
inaugurar (*v.t.*) to inaugurate; to initiate.
inautencidade (*f.*) want of authenticity.
inautêntico –ca (*adj.*) unauthentic.
inavegável (*adj.*) not navigable.
inaveriguável (*adj.*) unverifiable.
inaxônio [ks] (*m., Anat.*) inaxon.
inca (*adj.; m.,f.*) Inca.
incabi [bí] (*f.*) a rubber tree (*Hevea lutea*).
incabível (*adj.*) inadmissible, unacceptable.
inçado –da (*adj.*) teeming; alive with (flees, bedbugs, ants, etc.); overrun.
incalcinável (*adj.*) not calcinable.
incalculado –da (*adj.*) unexpected, unforeseen.
incalculável (*adj.*) incalculable.
incameração (*f., R.C.Ch.*) incameration.
incandescência (*f.*) incandescence.
incandescente (*adj.*) incandescent; fiery.
incandescer (*v.t.,v.i.*) to incandesce.
incansável (*adj.*) indefatigable, untiring; unremitting
incapacidade (*f.*) incapacity, incompetence, inability; disability.
incapacitar (*v.t.*) to incapacitate, disable; to hamstring.
incapaz (*adj.*) incapable (**de**, of); unable (**de**, to); incompetent (**para**, for); unequal (**para**, to); unfit.
inçar (*v.t.*) to infest, overrun, beset (said esp. of vermin).
incara[c]terístico –ca (*adj.*) uncharacteristic.
incaridoso –sa (*adj.*) uncharitable.

incarnar (*v.*) = ENCARNAR.
incasto –ta (*adj.*) unchaste.
incauteza (*f.*) incautiousness, unwariness.
incauto –ta (*adj.*) incautious, unwary; rash, reckless; unsuspecting; (*m.,f.*) dupe.
incender (*v.t.*) to fire, ignite; to inflame, excite; (*v.r.*) to catch fire.
incendiado –da (*adj.*) burned (up, down); (*m.,f.*) one whose property has burned.
incendiar [16] (*v.t.*) to set afire to; to burn (up, down); to inflame; (*v.r.*) to burn.
incendiário –ria (*adj.*) incendiary; inflammatory; (*m.,f.*) incendiary, arsonist; firebrand, political agitator.
incêndio (*m.*) fire, conflagration. **aparelho contra—**, fire apparatus. **avisador de—**, fire alarm. **bôca de—**, fire hydrant, fire plug. **bomba de—**, fire pump; fire engine. **extintor de—**, fire extinguisher.
incensador –dora (*adj.*) flattering; (*m.,f.*) flatterer, adulator.
incensar (*v.t.*) to perfume with incense; to flatter, puff up, overpraise.
incenso (*m.*) incense; flattery; (*Bot.*) the orange-berry pittosporum (*P. undulatum*).
incensório, incensário (*m.*) censer.
incensurável (*adj.*) uncensurable.
incentivador (*m.*) inciter, instigator; booster.
incentivar (*v.t.*) to stimulate, give incentive to, boost.
incentivo –va (*adj.*) incentive, stimulative; (*m.*) incentive, stimulus.
incentor –tora (*m.,f.*) inciter.
incerimonioso –sa (*adj.*) unceremonious; abrupt.
incerteza [tê] (*f.*) uncertainty, incertitude, doubt(fulness); ambiguity, obscurity; indecision; aimlessness.
incerto –ta (*adj.*) uncertain (**de**, of), doubtful, dubious; desultory, fitful; (*m.*) an uncertainty, unknown quantity.
incessância (*f.*) incessantness.
incessante, incessável (*adj.*) incessant, ceaseless, unremitting (**em**, in), continual.
incessível (*adj.*) that may not be ceded.
incestar (*v.i.*) to commit incest; (*v.t.*) to subject to incest.
incesto (*m.*) incest.
incestuoso –sa (*adj.*) incestuous.
inchação (*f.*), **inchamento** (*m.*) act of swelling; a lump or swelling; dropsy, c.a. INCHAÇO, INCHUME; (*colloq.*) swell-headedness.
inchado –da (*adj.*) swollen; (*colloq.*) swell-headed.
inchar (*v.t.*) to swell, bloat, dilate, distend, inflate; to puff up, make arrogant; (*v.r.*) to swell up; to become puffed up.
incidência (*f.*) incidence; (*Geom., Physics*) incidence.
incidentado –da (*adj.*) full of incidents.
incidental (*adj.*) incidental.
incidente (*adj.*) incident; (*m.*) an incident, event.
incidir (*v.i.*) to happen, chance, befall, occur.—**com**, to coincide with.—**em**, to fall into (**êrro**, error).—**sôbre**, to rest on, fall on, be based on.
incineração (*f.*) incineration.
incinerador (*m.*) incinerator.
incinerar (*v.t.*) to incinerate, cremate.
incinerável (*adj.*) that may be incinerated.
incipiente (*adj.*) incipient, inchoate.
incircunciso –sa (*adj.*) uncircumcised.
incircunscrito –ta (*adj.*) not circumscribed.
incisamente, incisivamente (*adv.*) incisively.
incisão (*f.*) incision [= INCISURA].
incisar (*v.t.*) to incise.
incisivo –va (*adj.*) incisive, cutting; trenchant, penetrating; (*m.*) an incisor (cutting tooth).
inciso –sa (*adj.*) incised, cut.
incisor –sora, incisório –ria (*adj.*) incisive, incisory.
incisura (*f.*) = INCISÃO.
incitabilidade (*f.*) incitability.
incitação (*f.*), **incitamento** (*m.*) incitement, provocation.
incitador –dora (*adj.*) inciting; (*m.,f.*) inciter, rouser.
incitante (*adj.*) inciting.
incitar (*v.t.*) to incite (**a**, to), rouse to action; to instigate; to egg on.
incivil (*adj.*) uncivil, discourteous, rude, ungentlemanly, boorish.
incivilidade (*f.*) incivility, discourtesy; impertinence; ill manners.
incivilizado –da (*adj.*) uncivilized; barbarian.
incivilizável (*adj.*) uncivilizable.

incivismo (*m.*) incivism, want of patriotism.
inclassificado –da (*adj.*) unclassified.
inclassificável (*adj.*) unclassifiable.
inclemência (*f.*) inclemency.
inclemente (*adj.*) inclement, severe; unmerciful, harsh.
inclinação (*f.*) inclination, incline, slope, dip, gradient, pitch, cant, tilt; leaning, tendency, penchant, bent; liking.—**lateral aguda**, (*Aeron.*) a steep bank.—**magnética**, magnetic dip.—**suave**, a gentle slope.
inclinado –da (*adj.*) inclined, slanting, sloping, tilted; bent, bowed down; predisposed, prone to; willing.
inclinar (*v.t.*) to incline, bend; to predispose (**para**, to); to turn (**para**, toward); (*v.i.*) to lean, slope, tilt, slant; to have a propensity (**a, para**, for); (*v.r.*) to be inclined, tilt (**a**, toward); to bow (**diante de**, before); to stoop.
inclinvael (*adj.*) inclinable.
inclinômetro (*m.*) inclinometer.
ínclito –ta (*adj.*) distinguished, illustrious.
incluir [72] (*v.t.*) to include, embrace, embody, take in; to contain; to enclose (**em, dentro de,** in).
inclusa (*f.*) = ESCLUSA.
inclusão (*f.*) inclusion.
inclusive, inclusivamente (*adv.*) inclusively.
inclusivo –va (*adj.*) inclusive, including.
incluso –sa (*adj.*) included; enclosed.
inço (*m.*) weeds; (in Portugal) plants left standing to produce seed.
incoação (*f.*) inchoation, inception.
incoado –da (*adj.*) inchoate.
incoadunável (*adj.*) uncombinable.
incoagulável (*adj.*) that is not coagulable.
incoar (*v.t.,v.i.*) to begin [= COMEÇAR].
incoativo –va (*adj.*) inchoative, inceptive.
incobrável (*adj.*) unrecoverable; that cannot be charged or collected.
incoercível (*adj.*) incoercible; irrepressible, uncontrollable; uncontainable; overwhelming.
incoerência (*f.*) incoherence, incongruity.
incoerente (*adj.*) incoherent; inconsistent, disconnected; irrational, rambling.
incoesão (*f.*) want of cohesion.
incogitado –da (*adj.*) not thought of (ahead of time).
incogitável (*adj.*) inconceivable, unimaginable, unthinkable.
incógnito –ta (*adj.; adv.; m.,f.*) incognito; (*f., Math.*) unknown quantity or factor.
incognoscível (*adj.*) unknowable, not cognizable; (*m:,f.*) one who or that which is unknowable.
íncola (*m.,f.*) dweller. [*Poetical*]
incolor (*adj.*) colorless; wavering, uncertain.
incólume (*adj.*) unscathed, unharmed, unhurt, safe and sound.
incolumidade (*f.*) invulnerability.
incombinável (*adj.*) uncombinable.
incombustível (*adj.*) incombustible.
incombusto –ta (*adj.*) unburned.
incomensurável (*adj.*) incommensurable; immeasurable.
incomerciável (*adj.*) non-negotiable.
incomível (*adj.*) uneatable.
incomodado –da (*adj.*) indisposed; upset; annoyed.
incomodador –dora (*adj.*) troublesome, annoying, vexatious; irksome; importunate; (*m.,f.*) importuner.
incomodante (*adj.*) disturbing; bothersome; annoying.
incomodar (*v.t.*) to incommode, annoy, disturb; to molest, vex, bother; to nag; to spite; to inconvenience; (*v.r.*) to trouble oneself; to bother; to become put out (upset); to worry. **Não se incomode!** Never mind! Don't bother!
incomodativo –va (*adj.*) incommoding; annoying.
incomodidade (*f.*) incommodiousness.
incômodo –da (*adj.*) unhandy; cumbersome; incommodious; annoying; irksome; pesky; (*m.*) slight illness; (*colloq.*) menses; nuisance; annoyance; inconvenience; hardship.
incomovido –da (*adj.*) unmoved.
incomovível (*adj.*) unshakeable, unmovable.
incomparabilidade (*f.*) incomparability.
incomparável (*adj.*) incomparable, unrivalled, matchless, peerless, unique.
incompassível (*adj.*) pitiless; implacable.
incompatibilidade (*f.*) incompatibility.
incompatibilizar (*v.t.*) to make incompatible; (*v.r.*) to become incompatible.
incompatível (*adj.*) incompatible (**com**, with), inharmonious, uncongenial; inconsistent, irreconcilable; un-

conformable; unsuited.
incompensado –da (*adj.*) not compensated.
incompensável (*adj.*) that cannot be compensated.
incompetência (*f.*) incompetence, inability.
incompetente (*adj.*) incompetent, incapable, unfitted.
incompleto –ta (*adj.*) incomplete, uncompleted, unfinished; imperfect, defective.
incomplexo –plexa [ks] (*adj.*) not complex, uncomplicated.
incomponível (*adj.*) irreconcilable.
incomportável (*adj.*) intolerable, unbearable.
incompossível (*adj.*) incompatible.
incompreendente [e-e] (*adj.*) uncomprehending.
incompreendido –da [e-e] (*adj.*) misunderstood.
incompreensão [e-e] (*f.*) want of comprehension.
incompreensibilidade [e-e] (*f.*) incomprehensibility.
incompreensível [e-e] (*adj.*) incomprehensible; unintelligible.
incompressível (*adj.*) incompressible.
incomprimido –da (*adj.*) not compressed.
incomprovado –da (*adj.*) unproved.
incompto –ta (*adj.*) plain (not ornate); rudely wrought.
incomputável (*adj.*) incomputable.
incomum (*adj.*) uncommon, unusual.
incomunicabilidade (*f.*) incommunicability.
incomunicação (*f.*) lack of communication.
incomunicante (*adj.*) not communicating.
incomunicável (*adj.*) incommunicable; not communicating; fig., unsociable, aloof.
incomutabilidade (*f.*) incommutability.
incomutável (*adj.*) incommutable.
inconcebível (*adj.*) inconceivable; incredible.
inconcertável (*adj.*) that cannot be harmonized.
inconcessível (*adj.*) that cannot or should not be granted.
inconcesso –sa (*adj.*) not granted.
inconciliabilidade (*f.*) irreconcilability.
inconciliável (*adj.*) irreconcilable; inconsistent.
inconcludente (*adj.*) inconclusive.
inconcluso –sa (*adj.*) unfinished, incomplete.
inconcordável (*adj.*) irreconcilable.
inconcusso –sa (*adj.*) unshakable; incontestable; incorruptible.
incondicional (*adj.*) unconditional.
incôndito –ta (*adj.*) disordered; ill-constructed; crude.
inconexão [ks] (*f.*) lack of connection.
inconexo –nexa [ks] (*adj.*) unconnected.
inconfessado –da (*adj.*) unconfessed.
inconfessável (*adj.*) not confessable.
inconfesso –sa (*adj.*) unconfessed.
inconfidência (*f.*) unfaithfulness; disloyalty; abuse of confidence.
inconfidente (*adj.*) unfaithful, disloyal.
inconfinado –da (*adj.*) unconfined.
inconformidade (*f.*) inconformity; nonconformity; (*Geol.*) unconformity.
inconfortável (*adj.*) uncomfortable.
inconfundível (*adj.*) unmistakable; distinct.
incongelado –da (*adj.*) uncongealed.
incongelável (*adj.*) uncongealable.
incongênere (*adj.*) not of the same kind.
incongruência (*f.*) incongruence.
incongruente (*adj.*) incongruent; incongruous; unconformable.
incongruidade [u-i] (*f.*) incongruity.
incôngruo –grua (*adj.*) incongruous.
inconhecível (*adj.*) not knowable.
inconjugável (*adj.*) that cannot be conjugated.
inconquistado –da (*adj.*) unconquered; untamed.
inconquistável (*adj.*) unconquerable.
inconsciência (*f.*) unconsciousness; want of conscience.
inconsciencioso –sa (*adj.*) unconscientious; lacking in conscience.
inconsciente (*adj.*) unconscious; unaware; unwitting; (*m.*) the unconscious; the subconscious; (*m.,f.*) an unthinking person.
inconscio –scia (*adj.*) unconscious; unconscientious.
inconseqüência (*f.*) inconsequence; irrelevance.
inconseqüente (*adj.*) inconsequent, illogical, irrelevant; inconsistent.
inconsideração (*f.*) want of consideration; inconsiderateness.
inconsiderado –da (*adj.*) inconsiderate, thoughtless, imprudent, rash.
inconsistência (*f.*) inconsistency.

inconsistente (*adj.*) inconsistent, inconstant; incoherent; flimsy.
inconsolado -da (*adj.*) unconsoled.
inconsolativo -va (*adj.*) unconsolatory.
inconsolável (*adj.*) inconsolable, disconsolate.
inconsonância (*f.*) inconsonance.
inconsonante (*adj.*) inconsonant.
inconspurcado -da (*adj.*) undefiled.
inconstância (*f.*) inconstancy, fickleness.
inconstante (*adj.*) inconstant, changeable, fickle, unsteadfast, unsteady.
inconstante-amante (*f.*) = ROSA-DA-CHINA.
inconstelado -da (*adj.*) without stars, dark [sky].
inconstitucional (*adj.*) unconstitutional.
inconstitucionalidade (*f.*) unconstitutionality.
inconsulto -ta (*adj.*) unconsulted; thoughtless.
inconsumível, inconsuntível (*adj.*) unconsumable.
inconsumpto -ta, inconsunto -ta (*adj.*) unconsumed.
inconsútil [-teis] (*adj.*) seamless; weldless.
incontaminado -da (*adj.*) uncontaminated.
incontável (*adj.*) countless.
incontendível (*adj.*) incontestable.
incontentado -da (*adj.*) discontented; hard to please.
incontentamento (*m.*) discontentedness.
incontentável (*adj.*) hard to please, difficult.
incontestabilidade (*f.*) incontestability.
incontestado -da (*adj.*) undisputed, uncontested.
incontestável (*adj.*) incontestable, indisputable, unquestionable, undeniable.
inconteste (*adj.*) undoubted, undisputed, unquestioned.
incontido -da (*adj.*) unchecked unrestrained, uncurbed.
incontinência (*f.*) incontinence, want of self-restraint; (*Med.*) incontinence.
incontinente (*adj.*) incontinent, unrestrained; licentious; (*m.,f.*) such a one.
incontinenti (*adv.*) immediately, forthwith, at once, instantly.
incontingente (*adj.*) not contigent.
incontinuidade [u-i] (*f.*) incontinuity.
incontínuo -nua (*adj.*) not continuous.
incontraditável (*adj.*) uncontradictable.
incontrastado -da (*adj.*) unopposed.
incontrastável (*adj.*) unopposable; irrevocable.
incontrito -ta (*adj.*) uncontrite.
incontrolável (*adj.*) uncontrollable, unmanageable, ungovernable.
incontrovertível (*adj.*) incontrovertible, indisputable.
incontroverso -sa, incontrovertido -da (*adj.*) unquestioned, undisputed.
inconveniência (*f.*) impropriety, unseemliness; rudeness, impoliteness. [But not inconvenience, which is INCOMODIDADE.]
inconveniente (*adj.*) improper, unseemly; unbecoming; inappropriate, inopportune; rude. [But not inconvenient, which is INCÔMODO]; (*m.*) an inconvenience; handicap, hindrance, drawback; nuisance.
inconversável (*adj.*) undiscussable.
inconversibilidade (*f.*) unconvertibility.
inconversível, inconvertível (*adj.*) unconvertible.
inconverso -sa (*adj.*) unconverted.
inconvicto -ta (*adj.*) unconvinced.
incoordenação [o-o] (*f.*) incoordination.—dos movimentos, (*Physiol.*) incoordination of muscular movement.
incorporação (*f.*) incorporation.
incorporalidade (*f.*) incorporality.
incorporar (*v.t.*) to incorporate, unite, blend, merge; to embody; to form into a corporation; (*v.r.*) to become part of, join, take part in.—uma coisa a (em, com) outra, to incorporate one thing with another. irem (pessoas) incorporadas, of persons, to go in a body.
incorporeidade (*f.*) incorporeity.
incorpóreo -rea (*adj.*) incorporeal, bodiless.
incorreção (*f.*) incorrectness, impropriety.
incorrer [24] (*v.i.*) to incur, bring on oneself.—no desagrado de (alguém), to incur (another's) displeasure; to be in (his) bad graces.
incorreto -ta (*adj.*) incorrect, improper.
incorrigível (*adj.*) incorrigible.
incorrosível (*adj.*) non-corrosible, rustproof.
incorrução (*f.*) incorruption.
incorru[p]tibilidade (*f.*) incorruptibility.
incorru[p]tível (*adj.*) incorruptible.
incorru[p]to -ta (*adj.*) uncorrupted, undefiled.

incredibilidade (*f.*) incredibility.
incredulidade (*f.*) incredulity, unbelief, skepticism.
incrédulo -la (*adj.*) incredulous; (*m.,f.*) unbeliever.
incrementar (*v.t.*) to increase, augment.
incremento (*m.*) increment, increase, enlargement.
increpação (*f.*) increpamento (*m.*) chiding; rebuke; reproof.
increpante (*adj.*) rebuking.
increpar (*v.t.*) to rebuke; to inveigh against; to twist.
incréu (*m.*), -creia (*f.*) unbeliever [= INCRÉDULO].
incriado -da (*adj.*) uncreated.
incriminação (*f.*) incrimination.
incriminar (*v.t.*) to incriminate, accuse.
incristalizável (*adj.*) uncrystallizable.
incriterioso -sa (*adj.*) without criterion.
incriticável (*adj.*) above criticism.
incrível (*adj.*) incredible, unbelievable.
incruento -ta (*adj.*) bloodless.
incrustação (*f.*) incrustation; scale.—a ouro, gold inlay.
incrustador -dora (*adj.*) incrusting; (*m.,f.*) one who incrusts.
incrustante (*adj.*) incrusting; scale-forming.
incrustar (*v.t.*) to incrust, coat over.
incubação (*f.*) incubation.
incubador -dora (*adj.*) incubating; (*m.,f.*) incubator.
incubar (*v.t.*) to incubate, hatch; to premeditate, plan.
íncubo -ba (*adj.*) incubent, lying; (*m.*) incubus; nightmare.
incude (*f.*) anvil [= BIGORNA]; (*Anat.*) incus.
incudectomia (*f., Surg.*) incudectomy.
incúdico -ca (*adj., Anat.*) incudal.
incudomáleo -lea (*adj., Anat.*) incudomalleal.
incudostapédico -ca (*adj., Anat.*) incudostapedial.
incuidoso -sa (*adj.*) carefree.
inculca (*f.*) inculcation; suggestion; (*m.*) search; (*f.pl.*) verifications.
inculcador -deira (*adj.*) inculcating; (*m.,f.*) inculator; (*f.*) gossip, busybody.
inculcante (*m.*) impostor.
inculcar (*v.t.*) to point out; to show, make clear; to inculcate (in), impress (upon);—a, to urge upon. (*v.r.*) to insinuate oneself; to show oneself (to be something).
inculpabilidade (*f.*) non-culpability.
inculpação (*f.*) inculpation.
inculpado -da (*adj.*) inculpable, blameless; (*m.,f.*) culprit.
inculpar (*v.t.*) to inculpate, incriminate, blame (-se, oneself).
inculpável (*adj.*) inculpable, blameless, innocent.
inculpe, inculposo -sa (*adj.*) blameless.
incultivável (*adj.*) uncultivable.
inculto -ta (*adj.*) uncultivated; desert [land]; uncultured; unenlightened; uncouth; unkempt.
incultura (*f.*) want of culture.
incumbência (*f.*) incumbency; charge, mission.
incumbir (*v.t.*) to commit, assign, entrust (a, to); to put in charge (de, of); (*v.i.*) to devolve upon, be the duty of. —se de, to take upon oneself; to undertake to.
incunábulo --la (*adj.*) incunabular; (*m.*) incunabulum.
incurabilidade (*f.*) incurability.
incurável (*adj.*) incurable; irremediable; (*m.,f.*) confirmed invalid.
incúria (*f.*) carelessness, neglect.
incuriosidade (*f.*) incuriosity.
incurioso -sa (*adj.*) incurious.
incursão (*f.*) incursion, foray, raid; inroad.
incurso -sa (*adj.; irreg. p.p. of* INCORRER) incurred; liable to; (*m.*) incursion.
incurvado -da (*adj.*) curved inward.
incutir (*v.t.*) to instill, inspire (in), impress (on, upon), inculcate (in, upon).
ind.= ÍNDICE (index).
inda (*adv.*) popular form of AINDA.
indagação (*f.*) search, quest, examination, inquiry.
indagador -dora (*adj.*) inquiring; (*m.,f.*) inquirer questioner.
indagar (*v.t.*) to ask, question; to search into, investigate, inquire into.
indá-guaçu (*m.*) = ANDÁ-AÇU.
indaiá (*f.*) any of several palms, c.a. ANAJÁ.—rasteiro or—-do-campo = ACUMÃ-RASTEIRO.
indaié (*f.*) = GAVIÃO-CARIJÓ.
indébito -ta (*adj.*) not owing; not deserved; undue.
indecência (*f.*) indecency, offensiveness; obscenity.
indecente (*adj.*) indecent, offensive, obscene, lewd; scurrilous; shameful; unseemly; risqué.

indecidido –da (adj.) undecided; unsettled; undetermined.
indecifrável (adj.) undecipherable.
indecisão (f.) indecision; hesitation.
indeciso –sa (adj.) undecided, irresolute; hesitant.
indeclarável (adj.) undeclarable.
indeclinável (adj.) undeclinable.
indecoro [cô] (m.) indecorum.
indecoroso –sa (adj.) indecorous, unseemly, indecent, shameful.
indefectibilidade (f.) indefectibility.
indefectível (adj.) indefectible.
indefensável, indefensível (adj.) indefensible, untenable.
indefenso –sa (adj.) defenseless, weak, helpless.
indeferido –da (adj.) denied, not granted.
indeferimento (m.) disallowance, denial, refusal.
indeferir (v.t.) to deny, disallow, refuse to grant (a petition).
indeferível (adj.) not allowable; that cannot be granted.
indefeso –sa [fê] (adj.) undefended.
indefesso –sa [fé] (adj.) indefatigable, unwearied.
indefinido –da (adj.) indefinite, vague; undefined; nondescript; (Bot.) of an inflorescence, indeterminate.
indefinível (adj.) indefinable, vague; nondescript.
indeiscência [e-i] (f., Bot.) indehiscence.
indeiscente [e-i] (adj., Bot.) indehiscent.
indelebilidade (f.) indelibility.
indelével (adj.) indelible.
indeliberação (f.) indecision.
indeliberado –da (adj.) unpremeditated, unintentional, not deliberate.
indelicadeza [êz] (f.) discourtesy, incivility, rudeness.
indelicado –da (adj.) discourteous, impolite, ill-mannered; tactless; brusque; inconsiderate; coarse, indelicate.
indelineável (adj.) indistinct, that cannot be delineated.
indemarcado –da (adj.) not demarcated.
indemonstrável (adj.) undemonstrable.
indene (adj.) undamaged, unscathed, uninjured, unhurt; (m., Chem.) indene.
indenidade (f.) indemnity.
indenização (f.) indemnification; indemnity, reimbursement; amends.—por desemprêgo, unemployment compensation; dole.
indenizador –dora (adj.) indemnifying; (m.,f.) indemnifier.
indenizar (v.t.) to indemnify, reimburse, make amends to.
indenizável (adj.) indemnifiable.
independência (f.) independence, freedom, liberty.
independente (adj.) independent, free, autonomous. por razões—s de nossa vontade, for reasons beyond our control.
independer (v.i.) to not depend on.
inderrotável (adj.) undefeatable.
indesconfiável (adj.) unsuspecting.
indescritível (adj.) indescribable.
indesculpável (adj.) inexcusable.
indesejável (adj.) undesirable; (m.,f.) an undesirable alien.
indestronável, indestronizável (adj.) undethronable.
indestrutibilidade (f.) indestructibility.
indestrutível (adj.) indestructible.
indestruto –ta (adj.) undestroyed.
indesunível (adj.) that cannot be disunited.
indesvendado –da (adj.) unrevealed.
indeterminabilidade (f.) indeterminableness.
indeterminação (f.) indetermination.
indeterminado –da (adj.) indeterminate, indefinite; nondescript; irresolute; (Bot.) of an inflorescence, indeterminate.
indeterminável (adj.) indeterminable; indecisive.
indeterminismo (m., Philos.) indeterminism.
indeterminista (adj.; m.,f.) indeterminist.
indeturpável (adj.) undefilable.
indevassável (adj.) unfathomable.
indevidamente (adv.) unduly.
indevido –da (adj.) undue, improper, unsuitable.
indevoto –ta (adj.) undevout.
índex [ks] (adj.) indicial. dedo—, index finger; (m.) index; pointer, indicator; nest egg; (R.C.Ch.) Prohibitory Index (of books).—purgatório, (R.C.Ch.) Index Purgatorius. pôr no—, fig., to point out (something or someone) as dangerous. Cf. ÍNDICE.
indexteridade (f.) = INDESTREZA.
indez [ê] (m.) nest egg [= ENDEZ]; (colloq.) a very sensitive

person; a whining child.
indiada (f.) Indians collectively; also = GAUCHADA.
indianismo (m.) Indianism.
indianista (adj.; m.,f.) Indianist.
indianita (f., Min.) indianite.
indianizar (v.t.) to Indianize.
indiano –na (adj.; m.,f.) East-Indian. Cf. ÍNDIO.
indicã (f.) = INDICÂNIO.
indicação (f.) indication; hint, clue; appointment to office.
indicador –dora (adj.) indicating; (m.) indicator; any gauge or dial for measuring or testing; the index finger; a guide or hand book; a directory; an usher; (Chem.) indicator.—da velocidade do ar, (Aeron.) air-speed indicator.—de ascenção, (Aeron.) climb indicator.—de combustível, fuel gauge.—de fases, (Elec.) phasemeter.—de fuga, (Elec.) leakage detector.—de passo, (Aeron.) pitch, or pitching, indicator, c.a. INDICADOR DE AFASTAMENTO.—de potencial, (Elec.) voltmeter.—de temperatura, thermometer.—de velocidade, speedometer.—do nível do oleo, oil gauge.
indicana (f., Chem.) indican.
indicânio (m., Biochem.) indican.
indicante (adj.) indicating.
indicanuria (f., Med.) indicanuria.
indicar (v.t.) to indicate, show, denote; to manifest, exhibit; to point out, designate; to suggest, imply; to sketch briefly; to appoint to office; to betray ("put the finger on").
indicativo –va (adj.) indicative; (m.) an indication; (Gram.) indicative mood.
indicatório –ria (adj.) indicatory.
indicatriz (f.) = INDICADORA.
índice (m.) index; table of contents; needle, pointer; indicator; (Craniom.) index.—octana, (Chem.) octane number; antiknock value.—de mortes, death rate.—de preços, price index.—de refração, (Optics) index of refraction.—de saponificação, (Chem.) saponification number.—remissivo, cross index. Cf. ÍNDEX.
indiciado –da (adj.) indicted; (m.,f.) indictee.
indiciador –dora (adj.) indicting; (m.,f.) indicter.
indiciar (v.t.) to indict, charge, accuse; to give indications of.
indício (m.) indication, token, mark, sign; clue; trace, vestige; (pl.) indicia.
índico –ca (adj.) = INDIANO.
indicolito (m., Min.) indicolite.
indículo (m.) a small index; a brief indication.
indiferença (f.) indifference, unconcern, apathy; disinterestedness; aloofness; nonchalance.
indiferente (adj.) indifferent (a, to), disinterested; neutral; listless; nonchalant; unconcerned, uninterested; fair, so-so; (m.,f.) a person who is indifferent to, or who has lost interest in, something or someone; (m.pl.) slight acquaintances.
indiferentemente (adv.) indifferently, without distinction.
indiferentismo (m.) indifferentism, esp. regarding religion and politics.
indiferentista (adj.; m.,f.) indifferentist.
indígena (m.,f.) a native; (adj.) native, indigenous, aboriginal.
indigência (f.) indigence, destitution, pauperism.
indigente (adj.) indigent, destitute, needy; (m.,f.) an indigent person; a pauper.
indigerido –da (adj.) undigested.
indigerível (adj.) indigestible.
indigestão (f.) indigestion.
indigestar (v.i.,v.r.) to suffer an attack of indigestion.
indigestibilidade (f.) indigestibility.
indigesto –ta (adj.) indigestible; undigested; dull, heavy; (slang) of study-matter, hard to digest.
indigitação (f.) a pointing out.
indigitado –da (adj.) indicated, pointed out; (m.,f.) one pointed out as culprit.
indigitar (v.t.) to point out, point to.
indignação (f.) indignation, anger, resentment.
indignado –da (adj.) indignant, incensed.
indignar (v.t.) to anger, provoke, incense; to become indignant, get one's dander up.—-se com, to resent.
indignidade (f.) an indignity, affront, outrage; unworthiness.
indigno –na (adj.) undeserving, unworthy (de, of); base, low, despicable; shameful; (m.,f.) such a person.
índigo (m.) indigo (dye or plant).

indigófera (f., Bot.) indigo (Indigofera) esp. I. suffructicosa; also I. sumatrana and I. hirsuta used as green manure.
indigóide (adj.) indigoid [dye].
indigoteiro (m.) = INDIGUEIRO.
indigotina (f., Chem.) indigotin.
indigueiro (m., Bot.) the anil indigo (Indigofera suffructicosa).
indiligência (f.) want of diligence.
indiligente (adj.) not diligent, slothful.
indiminuto –ta (adj.) undiminished.
índio –dia (adj.) Indian; (m.,f.) an East Indian; an Indian of No. or So. America; (Chem.) the element indium.
indireto –ta (adj.) indirect; circuitous, roundabout; of speech, veiled; (f., colloq.) a sly dig; a cutting remark; allusion; innuendo.
indirigível (adj.) ungovernable.
indirrubina (f., Chem.) indirubin(e).
indiscernível (adj.) indiscernible.
indisciplina (f.) indiscipline, insubordination.
indisciplinado –da (adj.) undisciplined, disobedient, unruly, rambunctious; unschooled.
indisciplinar (v.t.) to make unruly, rebellious; (v.r.) to become rebellious, undisciplined.
indisciplinável (adj.) that cannot be disciplined, insubmissive.
indiscreto –ta (adj.) indiscreet, imprudent, foolish; tactless; given to idle talk; (m.,f.) an indiscreet person; a tattler, blabber.
indiscrição (f.) indiscretion; blunder, misstep.
indiscriminado –da (adj.) indiscriminate; not detailed; nondescript.
indiscriminável (adj.) undistinguishable.
indiscutível (adj.) unquestionable; undeniable; unimpeachable; not to be discussed.
indisfarçado –da (adj.) undisguised.
indisfarçável (adj.) undisguisable.
indispensabilidade (f.) indispensability.
indispensável (adj.) indispensable; (f.) lady's handbag; (m.) something indispensable.
indisponível (adj.) not subject to disposal; inalienable.
indispor [63] (v.t.) to indispose, disarrange, disorder; to upset, unsettle (the stomach); to irritate, nettle, "rile"; —contra, to indispose, disaffect, render averse; (v.r.) to become ruffled, exasperated.
indisposição (f.) indisposition, ill-health; disturbance; dissension, breach of friendship.—gástrica, a stomach upset.
indisposto –ta (adj.) indisposed; seedy; out of sorts; loath, averse.
indisputabilidade (f.) indisputability.
indisputado –da (adj.) undisputed, undoubted, unquestioned.
indisputável (adj.) indisputable.
indissimulado –da (adj.) overt, unfeigned.
indissumalável (adj.) that cannot be dissembled.
indissolubilidade (f.) indissolubility.
indissolúvel (adj.) indissoluble.
indistinção (f.) indistinctness.
indistinguível (adj.) undistinguishable.
indistintamente (adv.) indiscriminately; indistinctly.
indistinto –ta (adj.) indistinct, ill-defined; vague, hazy, dim.
inditoso –sa (adj.) ill-fated, unlucky [= DESDITOSO].
índium (m., Chem.) indium [= ÍNDIO].
indívidua (f.) see under INDIVÍDUO.
individual (adj.) individual. [An individual is INDIVÍDUO.]
individualidade (f.) individuality.
individualismo (m.) individualism.
individualista (adj.; m.,f.) individualist.
individualização (f.) individualization.
individualizante (adj.) individualizing.
individualizar (v.t.) to individualize.
individuar (v.t.) to individuate, specify, particularize, name with precision; to single out.
indivíduo –dua (adj.) undivided; (m.,f.) an individual, person, fellow. Cf. INDIVIDUAL.
indivisão (f.) indivision, oneness.
indivisibilidade (f.) indivisibility.
indivisível (adj.) indivisible; (m.) an indivisable entity; formerly, the atom.
indiviso –sa (adj.) undivided.
indivorciável (adj.) inseparable.
indizível (adj.) unspeakable; indescribable; (m., colloq.) a tiny bit of something.

indo, pres. part. (gerund) of IR (to go) [53].
indo-africano –na (adj.; m.,f.) Indo-African.
indo-árabe (adj.; m.,f.) Indo-Arabian.
indo-britânico –ca (adj.) Indo-British; (m.,f.) Indo-Briton.
indobrável (adj.) inflexible, unbending.
indo-céltico –ca (adj.; m.,f.) Indo-Celtic [= INDO-EUROPÉU-PÉIA.]
indo-chim –china (adj.) = INDO-CHINÊS.
indócil [-ceis] (adj.) indocile, unmanageable; intractable; difficult, ornery.
indocilidade (f.) indocility.
indocumentado –da (adj.) undocumented.
indo-espanhol –la (adj.) Indo-Spanish; (m.,f.) Indo-Spaniard.
indo-européu –péia (adj.; m.,f.) Indo-European.
indofenina (f., Chem.) indophenin.
indo-francês –cêsa (adj.) Indo-French; (m.) Indo-Frenchman; (f.) Indo-Frenchwoman.
indo-germânico –ca (adj.; m.,f.) Indo-German.
indo-helênico –ca (adj.) Indo-Hellenistic; (m.,f.) Indo-Greek.
indo-holandês –dêsa (adj.) Indo-Dutch (m.,f.) Indo-Hollander.
indol (m., Chem.) indole.
índole (f.) natural disposition or quality; temperament, mettle; propensity, bent. de boa—, good-natured.
indolência (f.) indolence, laziness, sloth.
indolente (adj.) indolent; sluggish; easy-going; insensible to pain.
indolina (f., Chem.) indolin(e).
indologia (f.) Indology.
indólogo –ga (m.,f.) Indologist, Indologue.
indolóide (adj., Chem.) indoloid.
indolor [lôr] (adj.) painless.
indomado –da (adj.) untamed, unconquered, unsubdued.
indo-malaio –laia (adj.) Indo-Malayan; (m.,f.) Indo-Malay.
indomável (adj.) indomitable; untamable; unconquerable; unruly, headstrong, rambunctious.
indomesticado –da (adj.) undomesticated, wild.
indomesticável (adj.) that cannot be domesticated.
indoméstico –ca (adj.) wild; savage.
indominado –da (adj.) = INDOMADO.
indominável (adj.) = INDOMÁVEL.
indômito –ta (adj.) untamed, unconquered; fig., unbowed; undaunted; haughty, proud.
indonésio –sia (adj.; m.,f.) Indonesian.
indo-persa (adj.; m.,f.) Indo-Iranian.
indo-português –guêsa (adj.; m.,f.) Indo-Portuguese.
indormido –da (adj.) unsleeping, unremitting, unflagging.
indo-russo –sa (adj.; m.,f.) Indo-Russian.
indostânico –ca (adj.) Hindustani.
indostano (m.) Hindustani.
Indostão (m.) Hindustan.
indoutamente (adv.) ignorantly.
indouto –ta (adj.) unlearned.
indrí (m., Zool.) the indri (Indris brevicaudatus).
indú –dua (adj.; m.,f.) Hindu.
indubitabilidade (f.) indubitableness.
indubitado –da (adj.) undoubted.
indubitável (adj.) indubitable, unquestionable, indisputable.
indução (f.) inducement; induction, inference, conclusion; (Elec., Magnetism) induction.—heterógena, (Plant Physiol.) heterogenetic induction.—isógena, (Plant Physiol.) isogenetic induction.
indúcias (f.pl., Com.) indulgence (an extension, through favor, of time for payment). Cf. INDULGÊNCIA.
indúctil [-teis] (adj.) inductile.
inductilidade (f.) inductility.
induísmo (m.) Hinduism.
indulgência (f.) indulgence, lenience; kindness; remission, forgiveness; tolerance. Cf. INDÚCIAS.
indulgente (adj.) indulgent, lenient, mild, forbearing.
indultado –da (adj.) exempted; (m.,f.) one to whom an indulgence has been granted (by the R.C.Church); one who has received a special privilege, exemption or pardon.
indultar (v.t.) to furnish with an indulgence; to grant an indult to.
indultário –ria (adj.) that enjoys special privilege.
indulto (m.) indult, grant, privilege, favor.

indumentário -ria (*adj.*) of or pert. to raiment; (*f.*) dress, apparel, raiment; the art and history of dress.
indumento (*m.*) raiment; covering; (*Bot., Zool.*) indumentum.
induplicado -da (*adj., Bot.*) induplicate.
induplicativa (*f., Bot.*) induplication.
indúsia (*f., Bot.*) indusium.
indústria (*f.*) industry, trade; skill; cleverness.—**conserveira**, canning industry.—**correlata**, allied trade.—**petrolífera**, oil industry. **de**—, purposely. **cavalheiro de**—, a sharper. **sócio de**—, a working partner: one who furnishes none of the capital.
industrial (*adj.*) industrial; (*m.,f.*) an industrialist; manufacturer.
industrialismo (*m.*) industrialism.
industrialista (*adj.; m.,f.*) industrialist.
industrialização (*f.*) industrialization.
industrializar (*v.t.*) to industrialize.
industriar (*v.i.*) to work skillfully, artfully.—**a, em**, to teach (how) to.—**alguém**, to coach a person (as to how he shall act, what he shall say, etc.).—**alguma coisa**, to find ways and means of achieving something.—**para**, to coach (prepare) for.
industriário (*m.*), -ria (*f.*) industrial worker or employer.
industrioso -sa (*adj.*) industrious, laborious; skillful, clever.
indutância (*f., Elec.*) inductance.
indutivo -va (*adj.*) inductive.
induto -ta (*adj.*) induced; (*m.*) = INDUMENTO.
indutômetro (*m., Elec.*) induction meter.
indutor -tora (*adj.*) inducing; (*m.*) inducer; (*Elec.*) induction coil; stator.
indúvia (*f., Bot.*) induviae.
induviado -da (*adj., Bot.*) induviate.
induvial (*adj., Bot.*) induvial.
induzido -da (*adj.*) induced; (*Elec.*) armature.—**cerrado**, (*Elec.*) closed-coil armature.—**de anel**, (*Elec.*) ring armature; gramme ring.—**de disco**, (*Elec.*) disk armature.—**de tambor** (*Elec.*) drum armature.
induzidor -dora (*adj.*) inducing; (*m.,f.*) inducer, instigator.
induzimento (*m.*) inducement.
induzir [36] (*v.t.*) to induce, influence, prevail upon; to instigate, prompt; to cause, provoke, occasion; to lead (into error).
inebriamento (*m.*) inebriation.
inebriante (*adj.*) inebriating; (*m.*) an intoxicant.
inebriar (*v.t.*) to inebriate, intoxicate.
inédito -ta (*adj.*) inedited, unpublished; original; novel; unprecedented; unexampled; (*m.*) an unpublished work.
inefabilidade (*f.*) ineffability.
inefável (*adj.*) ineffable, inexpressible, indescribable.
ineficácia (*f.*) inefficacy.
ineficaz (*adj.*) inefficacious, unavailing.
ineficiente (*adj.*) inefficient.
inegável (*adj.*) undeniable, incontrovertible, irrefutable.
inegociável (*adj.*) non-negotiable; unmarketable.
inegualável (*adj.*) matchless.
inelasticidade (*f.*) inelasticity.
inelástico -ca (*adj.*) inelastic.
inelegância (*f.*) inelegance.
inelegante (*adj.*) inelegant.
inelegibilidade (*f.*) inelegibility.
inelegível (*adj.*) ineligible.
ineloqüente (*adj.*) ineloquent.
inelutável (*adj.*) ineluctable, irresistible, inevitable.
inenarrável (*adj.*) inenarrable [= INARRÁVEL].
INEP = INSTITUTO NACIONAL DE ESTUDOS PEDAGÓGICOS (National Institute of Pedagogical Studies).
inépcia, ineptidão (*f.*) ineptitude; foolishness; gaucherie.
inepto -ta (*adj.*) inept, unfit; clumsy; foolish, nonsensical.
ineqüiângulo -la (*adj., Geom.*) inequiangular.
ineqüigranular (*adj., Petrol.*) inequigranular.
ineqüilateral (*adj.*) inequilateral.
ineqüivalve (*adj., Zool.*) inequivalve.
inequivocável (*adj.*) unmistakable.
inequívoco -ca (*adj.*) unequivocal, clear, definite; unmistakable.
inércia (*f.*) inertia; inertness, sluggishness, lethargy; (*Physics*) inertia.
inerência (*f.*) inherence.
inerente (*adj.*) inherent.
inerir (*v.i.*) to inhere.
inerme (*adj.*) unarmed, defenseless.

inerradicável (*adj.*) ineradicable.
inerrante (*adj.*) inerrant.
inerrável (*adj.*) infallible.
inerte (*adj.*) inert; inactive; torpid.
inervação (*f.*) innervation.
inervar (*v.t.*) to innervate.
Inês (*f.*) Agnes; Inez.
inescrito -ta (*adj.*) not written.
inescrupuloso -sa (*adj.*) unscrupulous, unprincipled; unconscientious.
inescrutabilidade (*f.*) inscrutability.
inescrutável (*adv.*) inscrutable, unsearchable.
inescurecível (*adj.*) unforgettable.
inescusável (*adj.*) inexcusable; indispensable.
inesgotabilidade (*adj.*) inexhaustibility.
inesgotável (*adj.*) inexhaustible.
inesperadamente (*adv.*) unexpectedly, unawares.
inesperado -da (*adj.*) unexpected, unlooked-for, unhoped for.
inesquecível (*adj.*) unforgettable.
inestético -ca (*adj.*) inaesthetic.
inestimado -da (*adj.*) unesteemed.
inestimável (*adj.*) inestimable, priceless.
inevidência (*f.*) lack of evidence.
inevitabilidade (*f.*) inevitability.
inexaminável [x = z] (*adj.*) unexaminable.
inexatidão [x = z] (*f.*) inexactitude, inaccuracy.
inexato -ta [x = z] (*adj.*) inexact, inaccurate.
inexaurível [x = z] (*adj.*) inexhaustible.
inexausto -ta [x = z] (*adj.*) unexhausted.
inexcedível [x = s] (*adj.*) unexceedable.
inexcitável [x = s] (*adj.*) unexcitable.
inexecução [x = z] (*f.*) inexecution, nonperformance.
inexecutável [x = z], **inexeqüível** [x = z] (*adj.*) impracticable, unfeasible, unworkable.
inexigível [x = z] (*adj.*) that cannot be required or demanded.
inexistência [x = z] (*f.*) inexistence; lack, deficiency.
inexistente [x = z] (*adj.*) inexistent.
inexorabilidade [x = z] (*f.*) inexorability.
inexorado -da [x = z] (*adj.*) unentreated.
inexorável [x = z] (*adj.*) inexorable, unrelenting, implacable; unforgiving; stern, severe.
inexpansivo -va (*adj.*) inexpansive, restrained.
inexperiência (*f.*) inexperience.
inexperiente (*adj.*) unexperienced; callow, green, raw, unfledged.
inexperimentado -da (*adj.*) untasted, unexperienced.
inexpiado -da (*adj.*) unatoned for.
inexpiável (*adj.*) inexpiable.
inexplicabilidade (*f.*) inexplicability.
inexplicável (*adj.*) inexplicable, unaccountable.
inexplícito -ta (*adj.*) unexplicit.
inexplorado -da (*adj.*) unexplored.
inexplorável (*adj.*) unexplorable.
inexplosível (*adj.*) unexplosive.
inexpressável (*adj.*) inexpressible [= INEXPRIMÍVEL].
inexpressivo -va (*adj.*) inexpressive.
inexprimível (*adj.*) inexpressible.
inexpugnabilidade (*f.*) inexpugnability.
inexpugnado -da (*adj.*) unconquered.
inexpugnável (*adj.*) inexpugnable, impregnable; invincible, unassailable.
inextensível (*adj.*) inextensible; not applicable in all cases.
inextenso -sa (*adj.*) unextended.
inexterminável (*adj.*) incapable of extermination.
inextinguibilidade (*f.*) inextinguishableness.
inextinguível (*adj.*) inextinguishable, unquenchable.
inextinto -ta (*adj.*) not extinct.
inextirpável (*adj.*) inextirpable.
inextricabilidade (*f.*) inextricability.
inextricável (*adj.*) inextricable, intricate. Var. INEXTRINCÁVEL.
inf. = INFANTARIA (infantry); INFINITIVO (infinitive); INFINITO (infinite).
infa[c]tível (*adj.*) unrealizable.
infacundo -da (*adj.*) ineloquent.
infalibilidade (*f.*) infallibility.
infalibilismo (*m.*) infallibilism.
infalibilista (*m.,f.*) infallibilist.
infalível (*adj.*) infallible, unerring; unfailing; "sure-fire"; (*f., Bot.*) a globe amaranth (*Gomphrena pohlii*).
infalsificável (*adj.*) unfalsifiable.

infamação (f.) defamation, slander.
infamador –dora (adj.) slanderous, defamatory; (m.,f.) defamer, slanderer.
infamante, infamatório –ria (adj.) defaming.
infamar (v.t.) to defame, malign, blacken.
infame (adj.) infamous, vile, nefarious; (m.,f.) an infamous person.
infâmia (f.) infamy.
infância (f.) infancy, childhood, boyhood, girlhood.
infantaria, infanteria (f.) infantry.—marinha, Marine Corps. soldado de—, infantryman, foot soldier.
infante (adj.) infant(ile); (m.) infant; infantryman; infante.
infanticida (adj.) infanticidal; (m.,f.) infanticide (the criminal).
infanticídio (m.) infanticide (the crime).
infantil (adj.) infantile, childish.
infantilidade (f.) childishness.
infantilismo (m.) infantilism.
infatigabilidade (f.) indefatigability.
infatigável (adj.) indefatigable, tireless, unflagging.
infausto –ta (adj.) inauspicious; ill-fated, unlucky, unhappy, unfortunate.
infe[c]ção (f.) infection, contagion, contamination.
infe[c]cionado –da (adj.) infected, polluted.
infe[c]cionar (v.t.) to infect, contaminate, defile.
infe[c]cioso –sa (adj.) infectious.
infe[c]tante (adj.) infecting.
infe[c]tar (v.t.) to infect, pollute, contaminate.
infe[c]to –ta (adj.) infected; pestilential; evil-smelling; loathsome; abhorrent.
infe[c]tuoso –sa (adj.) infectious.
infecundidade (f.) infecundity, unfruitfulness.
infecundo –da (adj.) infecund, infertile, sterile, barren.
infelicidade (f.) infelicity, unhappiness, wretchedness; ill-luck, misfortune.
infelicitar (v.t.) to render unhappy (unfortunate).
infeliz (adj.) unhappy, unfortunate, unlucky; wretched; unsuccessful; (m.,f.) such a one.
infenso –sa (adj.) inimical, unfriendly.—a, hostile toward, averse to, opposed to.
inferaxilar [ks] (adj., Bot.) infra-axillary.
inferência (f.) inference, conclusion, consequence; induction.
inferior [ô] (adj.) inferior, lower, nether; subordinate; poor, shabby.—a, less than. leito—, lower berth (in a sleeping car); (m.) a subordinate; a noncommissioned officer.
inferioridade (f.) inferiority.
inferiorizar (v.t.) to make inferior, lower.
inferir [21a] (v.t.) to infer, deduce, conclude (de, from).
infermentescibilidade (f.) unfermentableness.
infermentescível (adj.) unfermentable.
infernação (f.) annoyance.
infernado –da (adj.) worried; upset.
infernal (adj.) infernal, hellish; atrocious, nefarious.
infernalidade (f.) infernality.
infernar (v.t.) to condemn to hell; to bedevil; (v.r.) to afflict oneself.
inferneira (f.) an infernal lot of noise (din, racket).
infernizar (v.t.) to torment [= INFERNAR].
inferno (m.) inferno, hell, torment, remorse.
infero –ra (adj.; m.) lower (place or part).
infero-axilar [ks] (adj.; Bot.) infra-axillary.
infero-exterior (adj.) inferoexterior.
ínfero-frontal (adj.) inferofrontal.
ínfero-interior (adj.) inferointerior.
ínfero-lateral (adj.) inferolateral.
ínfero-posterior (adj.) inferoposterior.
infértil [-teis] (adj.) infertile, unfruitful.
infertilidade (f.) infertility, barrenness.
infertilizar (v.t.) to render infertile; to sterilize.
infestação (f.) infestation.
infestador –dora (adj.) infesting; (m.,f.) infester.
infestante (adj.) infesting.
infestar (v.t.) to infest, overrun (de, with); to plague, torment.
infesto –ta (adj.) hostile; harmful.
infetar (v.t.) to infect.
infe[c]to –ta (adj.) infected; pestilential.
infe[c]tuoso –sa (adj.) infectious.
infibulação (f.) infibulation.
infibular (v.t.) to infibulate.
infidelidade (f.) infidelity, faithlessness; treachery, dis-

loyalty.
infido –da (adj.) unfaithful. [Poetical]
infiel [-fiéis] (adj.) unfaithful, disloyal [a, to]; (m.,f.) faithless person; an infidel.
infiltração (f.) infiltration; seepage.
infiltrar (v.t.) to infiltrate; to ooze; seep.
ínfimo –ma [superl. of BAIXO] lowest, basest, meanest, vilest.
infin[d]amente (adv.) infinitely.
infindável (adj.) unending, never-ending.
infindo –da (adj.) infinite.
infinidade (f.) infinity, infinitude.
infinitesimal (adj.) infinitesimal.
infinitésimo –ma (adj.; m.) infinitesimal; (f., Math.) infinitesimal quantity.
infinitivo –va (adj.; m.) infinitive.
infinito –ta (adj.) infinite; (adj.; m.) infinitive.
infirme (adj.) unfirm.
inflação (f.) inflation; swelling; inflated opinion of oneself.
inflacionismo (m.) inflationism.
inflacionista (adj.; m.,f.) inflationist.
inflacioso –sa (adj.) inflationary.
inflado –da (adj.) inflated; swollen; puffed up.
inflamabilidade (f.) inflammability.
inflamação (f.) inflammation, conflagration; swelling (of tissues). sistema de—, (Autom.) ignition system.
inflamado –da (adj.) inflamed, swollen; sore; ablaze, afire, aglow.
inflamador –dora (adj.) inflaming; inflammatory.
inflamar (v.t.) to inflame, excite, stimulate; to set afire; (v.r.) to become inflamed.
inflamativo –va, inflamatório –ria (adj.) inflammatory.
inflamável (adj.) inflammable.
inflar (v.t.) to inflate, sufflate, blow up; to puff up, make conceited.—o peito, to swell the chest.
inflativo –va (adj.) inducing inflation.
inflatório –ria (adj.) inflationary.
infle[c]tir [21a] (v.t.) inflect, curve, bend; to incline; (Gram.) to inflect.—à direita, to bear right.
inflexão [ks] (f.) inflection, curvature, bend; (Gram.) inflection.
inflexibilidade [ks] (f.) inflexibility.
inflexível [ks] (adj.) inflexible; stiff; unflinching; adamant, inexorable.
inflexivo –va [ks] (adj., Gram.) without inflection.
inflexo –xa [ks] (adj.) inflected.
inflição (f.) infliction.
infligir [4] (v.t.) to inflict, impose (punishment).
inflorescência (f.) inflorescence.
inflorescente (adj.) inflorescent.
influência (f.) influence.
influencial (adj.) influential.
influenciar (v.t.) to influence.
influente (adj.) influential; (m.,f.) influential person.
influenza (f.) influenza, grippe, "flu".
influição [u-i] (f.) inducing, inspiring; influence.
influidor –dora [u-i] (adj.) influencing; (m.,f.) influencer.
influir [72] (v.t.) to induce, infuse, inspire.—em, (para, sôbre), to influence, have influence on; to sway, affect.
influxo [ks] (m.) influx; affluence; high-tide.
infolhescência (f.) foliation; foliage.
infólio (adj.; m.) folio (book).
informação (f.) act of informing; (piece of) information; account, report; evidence of the existence of diamonds or other precious stones in alluvial deposits and stream beds, as revealed by the presence of certain minerals or kinds of pebbles; (Milit.) intelligence; (pl.) facts, data. informações de última hora, last-minute news. pedir informações, to make inquiries.
informante, informador –dora (adj.) informative; (m.,f.) informant; informer.
informar [18] (v.t.) to inform (de, sôbre, about; de que, that); to advertise, apprise; to tell, acquaint.—se de, to inform oneself about; to inquire about.
informativo –va (adj.) informative.
informe (m.) information; (adj.) unformed, formless, shapeless, rough.
infortificável (adj.) unfortifiable.
infortuna (f.) ill fortune.
infortunado –da (adj.) unfortunate, unlucky; wretched.
infortunar (v.t.) to cause ill fortune to.
infortúnio (m.) misfortune, adversity; mischance; mishap; misadventure; set-back.
infortunoso –sa (adj.) unfortunate, hapless, unlucky.

infra-axilar [ks] (adj., Bot.) infra-axillary.
infra[c]ção (f.) infraction, infringement, breach.
infra-escrito -ta (adj.) written below, underwritten.
infra-estrutura (f.) substructure; understructure; (R.R.) undercarriage.
infra-excavação (f.) an undercutting (as of a bridge pier) by running water.
infraliásico -ca (adj., Geol.) Rhaetic.
inframedíocre (adj.) less than mediocre.
infrangibilidade (f.) infrangibility.
infrangível (adj.) infrangible, unbreakable.
infra[c]tor -tora (m.,f.) infringer.
infra-vermelho -lha (adj., Physics) infrared.
infrene (adj.) unbridled, unrestrained.
infreqüência (f.) infrequency.
infreqüentado -da (adj.) unfrequented.
infreqüente (adj.) infrequent.
infringência (f.) infringement.
infringente (adj.) infringing.
infringir [4] (v.t.) to infringe, break, transgress, overstep.
infringível (adj.) that cannot be infringed.
infrutífero -ra (adj.) infructiferous, not bearing fruit; unsuccessful.
infrutuoso -sa (adj.) infructuose, fruitless; profitless.
infuca (f.) intrigue, plot.
infumável (adj.) of tobacco, not fit to smoke.
infumígeno -na (adj.) smokeless [powder].
infundado -da (adj.) unfounded, groundless.
infundibuliforme (adj., Bot.) funnel-shaped.
infundíbulo (m.) funnel [= FUNIL].
infundir (v.t.) to infuse instill, inculcate.
infusão (f.) infusing, steeping; infusion, brew. pôr de—, to steep, soak.
infusibilidade (f.) infusibility.
infusível (adj.) infusible.
infuso -sa (adj.) steeped; of natural virtues, ingrained, inbred; (m.) a medicinal brew or infusion.
infusório -ria (adj., Zool.) infusorial; (m.) infusorian; (pl.) the Infusoria. terra de—s, tripoli, rottenstone, infusorial earth.
ingá (m.), ingàzeira (f.), ingàzeiro (m., Bot.) any of several species of Inga (mimosa family) some of which yield useful timber and edible fruit.
ingalgável (adj.) that cannot be climbed up or over.
inganhável (adj.) that cannot be gained or won.
ingarana (f., Bot.) any of a number of apes-earrings (genus Pithecellobium, mimosa family); also = ARARANDÉUA.
ingàzinho (m.) = ARARANDÉUA.
ingênito -ta (adj.) inborn, innate, congenital, ingrained.
ingente (adj.) enormous, vast, immense.—s sacrifícios, great sacrifices. esforço—, huge effort. batalha—, tremendous battle. [Poetical]
ingenuidade [u-i] (f.) ingenuousness, candor, artlessness, naïveté. [Not an equivalent of ingenuity in the sense of ingeniousness, which is ENGENHO, INVENTIVA.]
ingênuo -nua (adj.) ingenuous, artless, candid, guileless, simple-minded; unsophisticated, naïf; (m.) such a person; a dupe, gull; (f.) an ingenue (actress or part). [Not an equivalent of ingenious, which is ENGENHOSO.]
ingerência (f.) intermeddling, interference; influence, strong suggestion; ingestion.
ingerimento (m.) = INGESTÃO.
ingerido -da (adj.) meddlesome.
ingerir [21a] (v.t.) to ingest, swallow.—em, to introduce in (into).—se em, to inject oneself into (a discussion, etc.); to interfere, meddle.
ingerminável (adj.) ungerminative [seed].
ingesta (f., Physiol.) ingesta.
ingestão (f.) ingestion; swallowing.
Inglaterra (f.) England.
inglês -sa (adj.) English; (m.) an Englishman; the English language; (f.) an Englishwoman.
inglesada (f.) a gathering of Englishmen. [Somewhat derogatory.]
inglesar (v.t.) to render English; (v.r.) to turn English.
inglesismo (m.) = ANGLICISMO.
inglório -ria, inglorioso -sa (adj.) inglorious [in the sense of not famous but not of ignominious].
ingluvial (adj., Zool.) ingluvial.
inglúvio (m.) crop (craw) of birds.
ingovernável (adj.) ungovernable, unruly, uncontrollable, unmanageable.
ingratão, ingratatão (m.) ingratona, ingratatona (f.) very ungrateful person.

ingratidão (f.) ingratitude.
ingrato -ta (adj.) ungrateful; thankless. unpleasant; ungracious; bootless, to no advantage; (m.,f.) an ingrate.
ingrediente (adj.; m.) ingredient, constituent, component.
íngreme (adj.) steep, sheer; arduous.
ingremidade, ingremidez (f.) steepness; arduousness.
ingresia (f.) hubbub, babel.
ingressar (v.i.) to enter (em, in); to join (as a member).
ingresso (m.) ingress, entry, access, entrance (para, to); debut, beginning; an admission ticket.
íngua (f., Med.) bubo.
inguinal (adj., Anat., Med.) inguinal.
ingurgitação (f.), –amento (m.) ingurgitation; swelling, distension (as of the bowels).
ingurgitar (v.t.) to ingurgitate, swallow greedily, gulp down; (v.i.) to become swollen (distended, obstructed) as an intestine; (v.r.) to gorge oneself.
inhab-, see under inab-.
inhaca (f.) unpleasant body odor; (slang) bad luck at poker.
inhambu [ú] (m.) any of a number of partridge-like birds —the tinamous—esp. of the genera Tinamus, Crypturellus and Nothura. Other names are: INAMU, INAMBU, NAMBU, NHAMBU, PORANGO, MACUCO, SURURINA.— -açu, the great gray tinamou (Tinamus tao tao).— -anhanga = INHAMBU-SARACUÍRA.—-carapé, the dwarf tinamou (Taoniscus nanus), c.a. CODORNA-BURAQUEIRA, PERDIGÃO, INHAMBUÍ.—-galinha, the white-throated tinamou (Tinamus guttalus).—-grande = MACUCO-DO-PANTANAL.—-guaçu, the brown tinamou (Crypturellus o. obsoletus).—-peauí = INHAMBU-RELÓGIO.—-pixura, the cinereous tinamou (Crypturellus cinereus), c.a. INHAMBU-SUJO, INHAMBUCUÁ, INAMBUQUIÁ.—-relógio, the Brazilian tinamou (Crypturellus strigulosus).—-saracuíra, the variegated tinamou (Crypturellus v. variegatus). —-xoxorô, the small-billed tinamou (Crypturellus parvirostris).
inhambucuá (m.) = INHAMBU-PIXURA.
inhambuí (m.) the dwarf tinamou (Taoniscus nanus), c.a. INHAMBÚ-CARAPÉ; the spotted nothura (N. maculosa).
inhame (m., Bot.) any of various yams and aroids.— -branco,—-da-costa,—-taioba, the ornamental elephantsear or edible taro (Colocasia antiquorum), c.a. TARO. —-bravo, —-da-china, —-da-índia, —-de-cariolá, are all the winged yam (Dioscorea alata).—-de-são-tomé, giant alocasia (A. macrorhiza).—-nambu = CARA-NAMBU.
inhapa (f.) lagniappe (something given to boot or for good measure); trifling present given to customers; = ANHAPA, JAPA, MOTA; tip, gratuity.
inhar-, see inar-.
inhenho –nha (adj.) dull, slow-witted, "dumb"; shy; (m.,f.) such a one; a "dumbbell".
inho, a diminutive suffix.
inhosp-, see inosp-.
inhuma (f.) = ANHUMA.
inhuman-, see inuman-.
inia (f.) = CASTANHEIRO-DO-PARÁ.
inibição (f.) inhibition, restraint; prohibition.
inibidor –dora (adj.) inhibiting.
inibir (v.t.) to inhibit, hinder; to forbid.
inibitivo –va (adj.) = INIBITÓRIO.
inibitório –ria (adj.) inhibitory; deterrent; (f.) a hindrance.
INIC = INSTITUTO NACIONAL DE IMIGRAÇÃO E COLONIZAÇÃO (National Institute for Immigration and Colonization).
iniciação (f.) initiation, beginning; admission; indoctrination.
iniciado –da (m.,f.) an initiate.
iniciador –dora (adj.) initiatory; (m.,f.) initiator, starter.
inicial (adj.) initial, initiatory; first, at the beginning; (f.) an initial letter.
iniciar (v.t.) to initiate, begin; to indoctrinate; to introduce.—em, to initiate in; (v.r.) to begin.—-se em, to be initiated in.
iniciativo –va (adj.) initial; (f.) initiative, enterprise; energy. por sua própria—, on one's own initiative.
iniciatório –ria (adj.) initiatory.
início (m.) initiation, beginning. de—, at first, at the start, in the beginning, to begin with. desde o—, from the first. ter—, to start, get started.
inidentificável (adj.) unidentifiable.

inidôneo -nea (*adj.*) unfit; unsuited; not qualified (for a given job).
inigualável (*adj.*) that cannot be equalled; unique.
iniludível (*adj.*) unmistakable; ineludible.
inimaginável (*adj.*) unimaginable, unthinkable.
inimbô (*m., Bot.*) = ÔLHO-DE-GATO.
inimicícia (*f.*) enmity [= INIMIZADE].
inimicíssimo -ma (*absol. superl. of* INIMIGO) most inimical.
inimigo -ga (*adj.*) inimical; unfriendly; (*m.,f.*) enemy, foe, adversary.—**jurado**, sworn enemy. **A pressa é—da perfeição**, Haste makes waste.
inimistar (*v.*) = INIMIZAR.
inimitável (*adj.*) inimitable; unique.
inimizade (*f.*) enmity, animosity, hostility, aversion, rancor, ill will.
inimizar (*v.t.*) to render inimical; to arouse enmity; (*v.r.*) to become inimical.
ininflexo -xa [ks] (*adj.*) uninflected.
inintelectual (*adj.*) unintellectual.
ininteligência (*f.*) unintelligence.
ininteligente (*adj.*) unintelligent.
ininteligível (*adj.*) unintelligible.
ininterrompido -da (*adj.*) uninterrupted [= ININTERRUP-TO].
ininterrupção (*f.*) uninterruption; continuity.
ininterrupto -ta (*adj.*) uninterrupted; continuous; unremitting.
ínio(n) (*m., Craniol.*) inion.
iniqüidade (*f.*) inequity; iniquity, wickedness.
iníquo -qua (*adj.*) inequitable; unfair; iniquitous.
injeção (*f.*) injection; a "shot" (of liquid medicine); (*slang*) tedious discourse; importunity.—**endovenosa** or **intravenosa**, (*Med.*) intravenous injection.—**hipodérmica**, (*Med.*) hypodermic injection.—**intramuscular**, (*Med.*) intramuscular injection.
injetado -da (*adj.*) injected; bloodshot [eyes].
injetar (*v.t.*) to inject (fluids) (**em**, into); (*slang*) to annoy.—**se (de sangue)**, to become bloodshot.
injetor -tora (*adj.*) injecting; (*m.*) injector, specif., of feed water into a boiler.
injucundo -da (*adj.*) of persons, disagreeable, unpleasant.
injudicioso -sa (*adj.*) injudicious.
injulgado -da (*adj.*) unjudged.
injunção (*f.*) injunction, mandate.
injungir [25] (*v.t.*) to enjoin.
injuntivo -va (*adj.*) injunctive, enjoining.
injúria (*f.*) injury, wrong, injustice; grievance; abuse, insult, slander. [Not an equivalent of injury in the sense of bodily hurt or harm, which is FERIMENTO.] **as—s do tempo**, the ravages of time. **uma chusma de—s**, a volley of abuse.
injuriado -da (*adj.*) abused, insulted.
injuriador -dora (*adj.*) abusive, insulting; injurious; (*m.,f.*) insulter.
injuriante (*adj.*) injurious.
injuriar (*v.t.*) to abuse, revile, defame, slander, insult; to rail against (at); to injure.
injurídico -ca (*adj.*) non-juridical.
injurioso -sa (*adj.*) offensive, abusive, insulting; injurious [but only in the sense of calumnious].
injustiça (*f.*) injustice, wrong, injury, grievance.
injustiçoso -sa (*adj.*) inequitable, iniquitous.
injustificadamente (*adv.*) unjustifiably, unduly.
injustificável (*adj.*) unjustifiable, untenable.
injusto -ta (*adj.*) unjust, unfair; unwarranted; (*m.,f.*) unjust person.—**possuidor**, unlawful possessor.
inobediência (*f.*) disobedience [= DESOBEDIÊNCIA].
inobediente (*adj.*) disobedient [= DESOBEDIENTE].
inobliterável (*adj.*) ineffaceable, indelible.
inobscurecível (*adj.*) inobscurable.
inobservado -da (*adj.*) not observed (not complied with); unmarked, unseen, unobserved (unnoticed).
inobservância (*f.*) non-observance; non-compliance.
inobservante (*adj.*) inobservant, unseeing.
inobservável (*adj.*) that cannot be observed or complied with.
inobstável (*adj.*) unpreventable.
inocarpo (*m., Bot.*) the Polynesian chestnut (*Inocarpus edulis*).
inocência (*f.*) innocence, guiltlessness; innocuousness; chastity; simplicity.
inocentação (*f.*) declaration of another's innocence.
inocentador -dora (*adj.*) that declares innocence.

inocentar (*v.t.*) to declare innocent, acquit; to whitewash; (*v.r.*) to pretend innocence, play innocent.
inocente (*adj.*) innocent (**de**, of); harmless; blameless, guileless, artless, simple; (*m.,f.*) a young child. **fazer-se de—**, to play the innocent.
inocuidade [u-i] (*f.*) innocuousness.
inoculação (*f.*) inoculation.
inoculador -dora (*adj.*) inoculating; (*m.,f.*) inoculator.
inocular (*v.t.*) to inoculate.
inoculável (*adj.*) inoculable.
inocultável (*adj.*) that cannot be hidden.
inócuo -cua (*adj.*) innocuous, harmless.
inodoro -ra [dó] (*adj.*) inodorous, odorless, scentless.
inofensibilidade (*f.*) inoffensiveness.
inofensivo -va (*adj.*) inoffensive, harmless, unoffending, innocent.
inoficioso -sa (*adj., Civil Law*) inofficious [testament].
inolente (*adj.*) odorless.
inolvidado -da (*adj.*) unforgotten.
inolvidável (*adj.*) unforgettable.
inominado -da (*adj.*) unnamed, innominate.
inominável (*adj.*) not nameable; unspeakably bad.
inoperabilidade (*f., Surg.*) inoperativeness.
inoperante (*adj.*) inoperative.
inoperável (*adj., Surg.*) inoperable.
inoperosidade (*f.*) inactivity.
inópia (*f.*) poverty.
inopinado -da (*adj.*) unexpected, unlooked for, unforeseen.
inopinadamente (*adv.*) unawares.
inopinável (*adj.*) unforeseeable; unappreciable.
inopino -na (*adj.*) unexpected [= INOPINADO]. **de—**, unawares.
inopioso -sa (*adj.*) poor.
inoportunidade (*f.*) want of opportunity; untimeliness; irrelevance; unfitness.
inoportuno -na (*adj.*) inopportune, unseasonable; untimely; inept.
inoprimido -da (*adj.*) unoppressed.
inosculação (*f., Surg.*) inosculation.
inose, inosite (*f., Chem.*) inositol, inosite, muscle sugar.
inorgânico -ca (*adj.*) inorganic.
inorganizado -da (*adj.*) unorganized; inorganic.
inosite (*f., Chem.*) inosite; inositol.
inospitaleiro -ra (*adj.*) inhospitable.
inospitalidade (*f.*) inhospitality.
inóspito -ta (*adj.*) inhospitable, forbidding; uninhabitable; barren, wild.
inótropo -pa (*adj., Physiol., Med.*) inotropic.
inovação (*f.*) innovation.
inovador -dora (*adj.*) innovatory; (*m.,f.*) innovator.
inovar (*v.t.*) to innovate; to renovate.
inoxidável [ks] (*adj.*) inoxidizable; rustproof. **aço—**, stainless steel.
inóxio -a [ks] (*adj.*) innocuous [= INÓCUO].
inqualificável (*adj.*) unqualifiable; unspeakably bad.
inquebrantável (*adj.*) unbreakable; adamant; unfailing; unflagging.
inquebrável (*adj.*) unbreakable.
inquérito (*m.*) inquest; judicial inquiry, probe. **instaurar—**, to hold an inquest.
inquestionável (*adj.*) unquestionable; unimpeachable.
inquietação (*f.*) disquiet, uneasiness, anxiety; unrest; disturbance; perturbation; turmoil.
inquietador -dora (*adj.*) disquieting, disturbing; (*m.,f.*) disturber.
inquietamento (*m.*) = INQUIETAÇÃO.
inquietante (*adj.*) disquieting, disturbing, alarming.
inquietar (*v.t.*) to disquiet, trouble, disturb; to agitate; to harass; (*v.r.*) to become worried; to fuss.
inquieto -ta (*adj.*) unquiet, restless, fidgety; uneasy, anxious.
inquietude (*f.*) = INQUIETAÇÃO.
inquilinato (*m.*) tenancy.
inquilinismo (*m., Zool.*) inquilinism, epiphytic existence.
inquilino (*m.*), **-na** (*f.*) tenant, renter.
inquinar (*v.t.*) to defile, pollute, corrupt, stain, blot.
inquiri [rí] (*m.*) = DORMIDEIRA (sensitive plant).
inquirição (*f.*) inquiry, interrogatory [= INQUÉRITO].
inquiridor -dora (*adj.*) inquiring; (*m.,f.*) inquirer, examiner.
inquirimento (*m.*) = INQUIRIÇÃO.
inquirir (*v.t.*) to inquire, ask (**sôbre**, about); to query, interrogate.

inquisição (*f.*) inquisition, official inquiry.
inquisidor –**dora** (*m.,f.*) inquisitor.
inquisitivo –**va** (*adj.*) inquisitive.
inquisitorial, inquisitório –**ria** (*adj.*) inquisitorial.
inrestaurável (*adj.*) unrestorable.
insaciabilidade (*f.*) insatiability; greediness.
insaciado –**da** (*adj.*) unsatiated, unsated.
insaciável (*adj.*) insatiable; greedy, rapacious.
insaciedade (*f.*) insatiety.
insalivação (*f.*, *Physiol.*) insalivation.
insalivar (*v.t.*, *Physiol.*) to insalivate.
insalubérrimo –**ma** (*absol. superl. of* INSALUBRE) most unhealthful.
insalubre (*adj.*) insalubrious, unhealthful, unsanitary, unwholesome; unhealthy, sickly.
insalubridade (*f.*) insalubrity, unhealthfulness.
insanabilidade (*f.*) incurability.
insanável (*adj.*) incurable; irremediable.
insânia (*f.*) insanity, lunacy, craziness, dementia, madness.
insanidade (*f.*) insanity.
insano –**na** (*adj.*) insane, mad, demented, crazy; senseless.
insaponificável (*adj.*) unsaponifiable
insarável (*adj.*) incurable.
insatisfação (*f.*) unsatisfaction.
insatisfatório –**ria** (*adj.*) unsatisfactory.
insatisfeito –**ta** (*adj.*) unsatisfied; discontent; dissatisfied.
insaturável (*adj.*) not saturable; insatiable.
insciência (*f.*) inscience, nescience, ignorance.
insciente (*adj.*) inscient, nescient, ignorant.
inscrever [44] (*v.t.*) to inscribe, engrave; to enroll, register, (*v.r.*) to sign up, enlist.
inscrição (*f.*) inscription; registration, signing up (to join something).
inscritível (*adj.*) inscribable.
inscrito –**ta** (*adj.*) inscribed; enrolled.
insculpir [25] (*v.t.*) to engrave, carve.
insecável (*adj.*) that cannot be dried (up); inexhaustible.
insect-, see **inset-**.
inseduzível (*adj.*) unseducible.
insegurança, inseguridade (*f.*) insecurity; instability.
inseguro –**ra** (*adj.*) insecure.
insensatez [têz] (*f.*) foolishness, nonsense; folly.
insensato –**ta** (*adj.*) insane; delirious; without sense; unreasonable. [But not insensate, which is INSENSÍVEL.]
insensibilidade (*f.*) insensibility.
insensibilizar (*v.t.*) to insensibilize.
insensível (*adj.*) insensible (**a, to**); impassive, unfeeling; cold-blooded; insensate; unresponsive; not perceptible to senses. **crescimento**—, imperceptible growth.
inseparabilidade (*f.*) inseparability.
inseparável (*adj.*) inseparable (**de,** from).
insepulto –**ta** (*adj.*) unburied.
inserção (*f.*) insertion (the act or process of inserting but not an insert); (*Bot.*, *Zool.*, *Anat.*) insertion.
inserir [24, 21a] (*v.t.*) to insert, introduce.
inserto –**ta** (*irreg. p.p. of* INSERIR) inserted.
inservível (*adj.*) unserviceable, useless.
insetarrão (*m.*) a huge insect. [Augmentative of INSETO].
inseticida (*adj.; m.*) insecticide (spray, powder, etc.).
inseticídio (*m.*) killing of insects.
insetífero –**ra** (*adj.*) insectiferous.
insetiforme (*adj.*) insectiform.
insetífugo –**ga** (*adj.*) insectifuge.
insetívoro –**ra** (*adj.*) insectivorous; (*m.pl.*) the Insectivora (moles, hedgehogs, etc.).
inseto (*m.*) insect.
insetologia (*f.*) entomology.
insetologista (*m.,f.*) entomologist.
insexuado –**da** (*adj.*) [ks] sexless.
insídia (*f.*) ambush; snare; treachery.
insidiador –**dora** (*adj.*) guileful, treacherous; (*m.,f.*) an insidious person; one who lies in wait.
insidiar (*v.t.*) to lie in wait for, ambush, waylay; to plot against.
insidioso –**sa** (*adj.*) insidious; deceitful, designing.
insigne (*adj.*) distinguished, noted, eminent; marked, conspicuous.
insígnia (*f.*) badge, emblem; banner; (*pl.*) insignia, regalia.
insignificância (*f.*) insignificance, unimportance, triviality; a trifle.
insignificante (*adj.*) insignificant, unimportant, trifling, paltry, piddling, petty; (*m.,f.*) a person of no importance.

insignificativo –**va** (*adj.*) not significant; unmeaning.
insinceridade (*f.*) insincerity.
insincero –**ra** (*adj.*) insincere; slippery.
insinuação (*f.*) insinuation, hint, cue, suggestion, lead, intimation; innuendo.
insinuador –**dora** (*adj.*) insinuating; (*m.,f.*) insinuator.
insinuante (*adj.*) insinuative, ingratiating; winsome; tactful. **maneiras**—**s**, engaging manners.
insinuar (*v.t.*) to insinuate; to insert, introduce.—**se na graça de alguém,** to insinuate oneself into the favor (good graces) of another.—**se na confiança de alguém,** to worm oneself into another's confidence.
insinuativo –**va** (*adj.*) = INSINUANTE.
insipidez [ê] (*f.*) insipidity; staleness; dullness.
insípido –**da** (*adj.*) insipid, tasteless, stale, flat; uninspired, uninteresting; drab, dull, monotonous; wishy-washy.
insipiência (*f.*) insipience, want of intelligence.
insipiente (*adj.*) insipient, stupid, foolish.
insistemático –**ca** (*adj.*) unsystematic.
insistência (*f.*) insistence; persistence; importunity.
insistente (*adj.*) insistent; persistent; obstinate; importunate.
insistir (*v.i.,v.t.*) to insist (**em, por, sôbre,** on); to persist (**em,** in); to urge (**com,** upon); to (re)iterate; **Não adianta**—, It's no use insisting.
insobriedade (*f.*) insobriety.
insóbrio –**bria** (*adj.*) intemperate.
insociabilidade (*f.*) unsociability; aloofness.
insocial (*adj.*) unsocial.
insociável (*adj.*) unsociable; sullen, morose; aloof, unapproachable, standoffish.
insofismável (*adj.*) indubitable, unquestionable, unmistakable, undeniable.
insofrido –**da** (*adj.*) impatient, restless; testy, fretful.
insofrível (*adj.*) insufferable, unbearable.
insolação (*f.*) sunstroke; treatment of disease by sun baths; insolation (in any sense).
insolar (*v.t.*) to sun; to cause to suffer sunstroke.
insoldável (*adj.*) unweldable.
insolência (*f.*) insolence, rudeness; pride; impertinence.
insolente (*adj.*) insolent, overbearing, insulting; impertinent; scurrilous; (*m.,f.*) such a one.
insolaridade (*f.*) want of solidarity.
insólito –**ta** (*adj.*) unusual; uncommon; irregular; unaccustomed, strange; extraordinary.
insolubilidade (*f.*) insolubility.
insolúvel (*adj.*) insoluble.
insolvabilidade (*f.*) state of (financial) insolvency.
insolvável (*adj.*) insolvent.
insolvência (*f.*) insolvency.
insolvente (*adj.; m.,f.*) insolvent (person).
insolvível (*adj.*) that cannot be paid.
insondado –**da** (*adj.*) unplumbed, unfathomed.
insondável (*adj.*) fathomless; unfathomable, incomprehensible.
insone (*adj.*) unsleeping.
insonhado –**da** (*adj.*) undreamed (of).
insonhável (*adj.*) unimaginable.
insônia (*f.*) insomnia, sleeplessness.
insonioso –**sa** (*adj.*) sleepless.
insonolência (*f.*) insomnolence, sleeplessness.
insonoro –**ra** [nó] (*adj.*) dissonant; soundless; (*Phonet.*) surd, voiceless.
insopitável (*adj.*) irrepressible, unquenchable; that cannot be lulled (allayed, relieved, downed).—**desespêro,** unconquerable despair.
insôsso –**sa** (*adj.*) saltless; flat, tasteless; of masonry, dry.
inspeção (*f.*) inspection, examination; review, check-up.
inspecionar (*v.t.*) to inspect, examine, scrutinize; to oversee.
inspetar (*v.t.*) to inspect.
inspetor –**tora** (*adj.*) inspecting; (*m.,f.*) inspector, supervisor, overseer.
inspetoria (*f.*) inspectorship; inspector's department.
inspiração (*f.*) inspiration, inhalation; exaltation, enthusiasm.
inspirador –**dora** (*adj.*) inspiring; (*m.*) inspirer [*fem.* INSPIRATRIZ].
inspirar (*v.t.*) to inspire, infuse, instil, exalt; to inhale.
inspirativo –**va** (*adj.*) inspirative.
inspiratório –**ria** (*adj.*) inspiratory.
inspiratriz, *fem. of* INSPIRADOR.
inspirável (*adj.*) inspirable.
inspirômetro (*m.*, *Physiol.*) inspirometer.

inspissação (f.) inspissamento (m.) inspissation.
inspissar (v.t.) to inspissate, thicken.
instabilidade (f.) instability.
instalacão (f.) installation; plant; equipment (of a plant, hospital, school, etc.)—de fios, electrical wiring.—elétrica, electric plant.—hidráulica, hydraulic plant.
instalador –dora (adj.) installing; (m.,f.) installer.
instalar (v.t.) to install, introduce (into office); to locate; to set up, establish; (v.r.) to lodge oneself.—-se num assunto, to dwell at length upon a subject. bem instalado, well-fixed, in clover.
instaminado –da (adj., Bot.) without stamens.
instância (f.) instance, urging; insistent request; entreaty; the successive steps in a legal action; court; jurisdiction. [Not an equivalent of instance, in the sense of example, which is EXÉMPLO or CASO ILUSTRATIVO.] tribunal de primeira—, a lower court. em última—, as a last resort.
instantaneidade (f.) instantaneousness.
instantâneo –nea (adj.) instantaneous; (m.) instant, flash; a snapshot.
instante (adj.) instant, urgent, pressing; current, present; (m.) an instant, moment. a cada—, every minute, continually, all the time. a todo o—, at any moment. de—a—, from moment to moment. de um—para outro, from one moment to the next. neste—, just a moment ago. no mesmo—, at that (very) moment. por um—, for a moment. um—, awhile.
instar (v.t.,v.i.) to insist (com, with; em, por, upon) to press, urge (a, upon); to request with insistence; to entreat.—com, to persuade.—contra, to argue insistently against.
instauração (f.) institution or establishment (of something); restoration.
instaurador –dora (adj.) founding, establishing; (m.,f.) founder.
instaurar (v.t.) to institute, establish; to renew, repair, restore.
instável (adj.) unstable; changeable, unsteady; fickle.
instigação (f.) instigation, incitement, provocation.
instigador –dora (adj.) instigating; (m.,f.) instigator, abettor.
instigar (v.t.) to instigate, incite; to provoke, prompt; to encourage; to stir up, spur on, egg on.
instilação (f.) instillation.
instilar (v.t.) to instill.
instintivo –va (adj.) instinctive, natural, spontaneous.
instinto (m.) instinct; blind or natural impulse.
institor (m., Law) instry, agent.
institucional (adj.) institutional.
instituição [u-i] (f.) institution; institute.
instituidor –dora [u-i] (adj.) instituting; (m.,f.) institutor.
instituir [72] (v.t.) to institute, found, establish; to constitute, appoint, ordain.
instituto (m.) institute; institution.—de beleza, beauty parlor.
instrucão (f.) instruction; teaching, education, schooling; training, drill.
instruído –da (adj.) learned; instructed.
instruir [72] (v.t.) to instruct, teach, educate; to train, coach; (v.r.) to acquire learning or information.—um processo (uma causa), to prepare a suit or action for hearing.
instrumentação (f.) instrumentation.
instrumental (adj.) instrumental; (m.) the instruments of an orchestra collectively.
instrumentalista (m.,f.) instrumentalist.
instrumentar (v.t., Music) to instrumentate.
instrumentário –ria (adj.) instrumentary (witness).
instrumentista (m.,f.) instrumentalist.
instrumento (m.) instrument, tool, utensil; musical instrument; document, deed.—agrário, farming implement, farm tool.—de cobre, brass instrument.—de cordas, string instrument.—de incorporação, articles of incorporation.—de palheta, reed instrument.—de pancada or de percussão, percussion instrument.—de sôpro, wind instrument.—de teclado, keyboard instrument.
instrutivo –va (adj.) instructive.
instrutor –tora (adj.) that instructs; (m.,f.) instructor, teacher, coach.
ínsua (f.) river island.
insubmergível, insubmersível (adj.) non-submersible, unsinkable.
insubmissão (f.) want of submission.

insubmisso –sa (adj.) unsubmissive; unconformable; (m.) draft-dodger.
insubordinação (f.) insubordination, mutiny, revolt.
insubordinado –da (adj.) insubordinate; (m.,f.) insubordinate person.
insubordinar (v.t.) to render insubordinate; to cause to revolt; (v.r.) to become insubordinate.
insubordinável (adj.) incorrigible, rebellious.
insubornável (adj.) not to be bribed, incorruptible.
insubstancial (adj.) unsubstantial.
insubstancialidade (f.) unsubstantiality.
insubstituível (adj.) that cannot be substituted.
insucesso (m.) ill success, failure, unsuccess.
insueto –ta (adj.) of words and expressions, disused.
insuficiência (f.) insufficiency, inadequateness; incompetence; (Med.) insufficiency.
insuficiente (adj.) insufficient; incompetent.
insuflação (f.) insufflation.
insuflador –dora (adj.) insufflating; (m.) insufflator.
insuflar (v.t.) to insufflate; to blow (air) into; to blow up (with air); to breathe (life) into; to incite, provoke, instigate.
ínsula (f.) island [= ILHA].
insulamento (m.), insulação (f.) insulation; seclusion.
insulador –dora (adj.) insulating; (m.) insulator.
insulano –na (adj.) insular; (m.,f.) islander.
insulante (adj.) insulating.
insular (m.,f.) islander; (v.t.) to insulate; to isolate; to seclude.
insularidade (f.) insularity.
insulcado –da (adj.) unplowed, unfurrowed.
insulina (f.) insulin.
insulsaria, insulsez, insulsice, insulsidade (f.) insipidity.
insulso –sa (adj.) unsalted, insipid, savorless; flat, prosaic. Cf. INSÔSSO.
insultador –dora, insultante (adj.) insulting; (m.,f.) insulter.
insultar (v.t.) to insult, affront; to taunt (with insults); to outrage; (v.r.) to insult one another.
insulto (m.) insult, affront, taunt, outrage.—cardíaco, heart attack. levar um—para casa, to swallow an insult.
insultuoso –sa (adj.) insulting, scurrilous, provocative, provoking.
insuperável (adj.) insuperable; unsurmountable.
insuportável (adj.) insupportable, unbearable, unendurable, intolerable, insufferable; nerve-racking.
insuprível (adj.) that cannot be supplied.
insurdescência (f.) deafness [= SURDEZ].
insurgência (f.) insurgency.
insurgente (adj.) insurgent, rebellious; (m.,f.) insurgent, rebel.
insurgir-se [4] (v.r.) to revolt, rebel, rise up (contra, against).
insurrecionado –da (adj.; m.,f.) insurgent.
insurrecional (adj.) insurrectional, rebellious.
insurrecionar (v.) = INSURGIR.
insurrecionário –ria, insurrecionista (adj.; m.,f.) insurrectionary, insurrectionist, insurgent.
insurreição (f.) insurrection, rebellion, uprising.
insurreto –ta (adj.; m.,f.) insurgent.
insuspeição (f.) want of suspicion.
insuspeito –ta (adj.) unsuspected; not suspect.
insustentável (adj.) untenable, insupportable.
intá[c]til [-teis] (adj.) intactile, impalpable.
inta[c]tilidade (f.) intangibility.
inta[c]to –ta (adj.) intact, untouched, uninjured; undefiled; unimpaired.
intangibilidade (f.) intangibility.
intangido –da (adj.) untouched; uninjured.
intangível (adj.) intangible.
intanha (f.) any of several tropical toads of family Cystignathidae, esp. Ceratophrys ornata, having a horn-like process over the eye; c.a. UNTANHA, SAPO-INTANHA, SAPO-BOI, SAPO-DE-CHIFRE. [No relation whatever to the horned toad of western U.S.A. and Mexico, which is a lizard.]
intátil [-teis] (adj.) intactile, impalpable [= INTANGÍVEL]. Var. INTÁCTIL.
intato –ta (adj.) intact. Var. INTACTO.
intê, illiterate form of ATÉ.
integérrimo –ma (absol. superl. of ÍNTEGRO) most upright.
íntegra (f.) an integral, specif., a complete text. na—, wholly; word for word; in full.
integração (f.) integration.

integrador (*m.*) integrator.
integral (*adj.*) integral, whole, complete, entire. **cálculo—,** integral calculus; (*f., Math.*) an integral.
integralidade (*f.*) integrality.
integralizar (*v.t.*) to integrate.
integrante (*adj.*) integrating; integrant, constituent; (*m.,f.*) an integral part; member of a group.
integrar (*v.t.*) to integrate, make entire, complete.
integrável (*adj.*) that can be integrated.
integridade (*f.*) integrity, entirety, wholeness; moral uprightness.
integrifólio –lia (*adj., Bot.*) integrifolious.
íntegro –gra (*adj.*) entire, whole; righteous, upright.
inteirado –da (*adj.*) aware, informed.
inteiramente (*adv.*) entirely, wholly; quite, completely; altogether.
inteirar (*v.t.*) to make entire; to complete; to fulfill, accomplish.**—de,** to make known (entirely); to inform completely; (*v.r.*) to become whole.**—-se de,** to inform oneself completely about.
inteireza (*f.*) entireness; moral integrity.
inteiriçar (*v.t.*) to stiffen (the body); (*v.r.*) to become stiff, rigid.
inteiriço –ça (*adj.*) of one piece, whole; stiff, rigid; inflexible.
inteirinho –nha (*adj.*) every bit, all of it.
inteiro –ra (*adj.*) entire, whole, unbroken; full, complete; uncastrated; upright, incorruptible; (*Math.*) integral; (*m.*) integer, whole number.
intelecção (*f.*) exercise of the intellect.
intelectivo –va (*adj.*) having intellectual power.
intelecto (*m.*) intellect.
intelectual (*adj.; m.,f.*) intellectual; "highbrow".
intelectualidade (*f.*) intellectuality.
intelectualismo (*m.*) intellectualism.
intelectualista (*adj.*) intellectualistic; (*m.,f.*) intellectualist.
intelectualizar (*v.t.*) to intellectualize.
inteligência (*f.*) intelligence; mind, intellect; acumen, quickness, brightness; an intelligent person; news, tidings. **falto de—,** doltish, stupid.
inteligente (*adj.*) intelligent, acute, bright, quick, clever. **pouco—,** unintelligent.
intelegibilidade (*f.*) intelligibility.
intelegível (*adj.*) intelligible, understandable.
intemente (*adj.*) fearless.
intemerato –ta (*adj.*) undefiled, unsullied; spotless; inviolate. [Do not cofnuse with INTIMORATO, fearless.]
intemperado –da (*adj.*) intemperate.
intemperança (*f.*) intemperance.
intemperante (*adj.*) intemperate.
intempérie (*f.*) bad weather.
intempestividade (*f.*) untimeliness.
intempestivo –va (*adj.*) untimely, ill-timed, unseasonable.
intenção (*f.*) intention, intent, design, purpose. **segundas —s,** ulterior motives. Cf. INTENSÃO.
intencionado –da (*adj.*) intentional, deliberate. **bem-—,** well-meaning. **mal-—,** ill-meaning.
intencional (*adj.*) intentional, willful, intended, designed, deliberate.
intencionar (*v.*) = TENCIONAR.
intencionável (*adj.*) = INTENCIONAL.
intendência (*f.*) intendancy; an administrative department or headquarters; quartermaster's depot.
intendente (*m.,f.*) an intendant, superintendent, manager, person in charge; a steward; a city councilman.
intender (*v.t.*) to superintend [but not to intend, which is TENCIONAR, INTENTAR, PRETENDER.]
intensão (*f.*) intenseness, vehemence. Cf. INTENÇÃO.
intensar (*v.t.*) to intensify.
intensidade (*f.*) intensity (in any sense).
intensificação (*f.*) intensification.
intensificar (*v.t.*) to intensify, aggravate.
intensivar (*v.*) = INTENSAR.
intensivo –va (*adj.*) intensive, intense.
intenso –sa (*adj.*) intense, vigorous, energetic; strenuous; acute.
intentar (*v.t.*) to intend, aim at; to attempt, undertake. **—um processo,** or **uma ação, contra alguém,** to prefer charges, or to bring a lawsuit, against someone. Cf. INTENDER.
intento –ta (*adj.*) intent, earnest; bent, set; (*m.*) intent, intention, design, purpose.
intentona (*f.*) mad scheme; wild plan; subversive conspiracy; revolutionary plot.

interacadêmico –ca (*adj.*) interacademic.
interação (*f.*) interaction.
interacionismo (*m., Philos*) interactionism.
interacionista (*adj.; m.,f.*) interactionist.
interaçoreano –na (*adj.*) inter-Azorean.
interafricano –na (*adj.*) inter-African.
interalveolar (*adj., Anat.*) interalveolar.
interamericanismo (*m.*) inter-Americanism.
interamericano –na (*adj.*) inter-American.
interantenário –ria (*adj., Zool.*) interantennary.
interarticular (*adj., Anat., Zool.*) interarticular.
interasiático –ca (*adj.*) inter-Asiatic.
interbranquial (*adj., Zool.*) interbranchial.
intercadência (*f.*) irregular rhythm; (*Med.*) intercadence.
intercadente (*adj.*) intermittent, irregular (in rhythm); of the pulse, showing intercadence.
intercalação (*f.*) intercalation.
intercalar (*v.t.*) to intercalate, insert between, interpolate; (*adj.*) intercalary.
intercâmbio (*m.*) interchange; give and take.
intercedente (*adj.*) interceding, intervening.
interceder (*v.i.*) to intercede, plead (in behalf of another).
intercelular (*adj.*) intercellular.
intercep(ta)ção (*f.*) interception.
interceptar (*v.t.*) to intercept, stop on the way; to interrupt; to obstruct; to cut off.
intercepto –ta (*adj.*) intercepted.
interceptor –tora (*adj.*) intercepting; (*m.,f.*) interceptor.
intercervical (*adj., Anat.*) intercervical.
intercessão (*f.*) intercession, pleading.
intercessor –sora (*adj.*) intercessory; (*m.,f.*) intercessor, interceder.
intercílio (*m., Anat.*) intercilium, glabella.
intercisão (*f.*) interruption.
interclavicular (*adj., Anat.*) interclavicular.
interclubista (*adj.*) interclub [match].
intercolegial (*adj.*) interschool.
intercolonial (*adj.*) intercolonial.
intercolunar (*adj., Arch.*) intercolumnar.
intercolúnio (*m., Arch.*) intercolumniation.
intercomunicação (*f.*) intercommunication.
intercomunicador (*m.*) intercommunicator.
intercondral (*adj., Anat.*) interchondral.
intercontinental (*adj.*) intercontinental.
intercorrente (*adj.*) intercurrent.
intercorrer (*v.i.*) to run or come between (as, a river).
intercostal (*adj., Anat.*) intercostal.
intercultura (*f.*) interculture.
intercurso (*m.*) intercourse.
intercutâneo –nea (*adj.*) subcutaneous.
interdentário –ria (*adj.*) interdental.
interdependência (*f.*) interdependence.
interdepender (*v.i.*) to interdepend.
interdição (*f.*) interdiction; ban, proscription; a judicial restraining order or injunction.
interdigital (*adj.*) interdigital.
interditar (*v.t.*) to interdict, forbid; to proscribe. **Os aeroportos estavam interditados por causa do mau tempo,** The airports were closed down by the bad weather.
interdito –ta (*adj.*) interdicted; forbidden; restrained; (*m.*) interdiction, prohibition, ban; a person who has been judicially restrained; (*Law*) interdict; injunction.
interdizer [41] (*v.t.*) to interdict, forbid; to restrain (by court order).
interessado –da (*adj.*) interested; having an interest; selfseeking; (*m.,f.*) a profit-sharing employee, one having an interest in the firm.
interessante (*adj.*) interesting; attractive, pleasing. **em estado—,** enceinte, pregnant.
interessar (*v.t.*) to interest (**em, in**); to engage the attention of; to affect, concern; to give an interest (share) in; (*v.r.*) to take an interest, show interest (**em, por, in**).**—de perto,** to be keenly interested in or affected by.
interêsse (*m.*) interest, benefit, profit, advantage; concern regard; sympathy; self-interest.**—amoroso,** a flirtation. **—de lucro,** profit motive. **sem—,** uninterested. [Interest on capital is **juros** or **rendimento.**]
interesseiro –ra (*adj.*) self-seeking.
interestadual (*adj.*) interstate.
interestelar (*adj.*) interstellar [space].
interestratificado –da (*adj.*) interstratified.
intereuropeu –péia (*adj.*) inter-European.
interfalangeano –na (*adj., Anat.*) interphalangeal.

interferência (*f.*) interference, intervention; (*Physics, Radio*) interference.
interferente (*adj.*) interferent.
interferir [21a] (*v.t.*) to interfere, intervene.
interferômetro (*m., Physics*) interferometer.
interfibrilar (*adj., Anat.*) interfibrilar.
interfoliáceo –cea (*adj., Bot.*) interfoliaceous.
interfixo –fixa [ks] (*adj.*) of levers, having the fulcrum between the weight and the power.
interfone (*m.*) interphone.
interfrontal (*adj., Anat.*) interfrontal.
interglaciário –ria (*adj., Geol.*) interglacial.
interglobular (*adj., Anat.*) interglobular.
intergovernamental (*adj.*) intergovernmental.
ínterim (*m.*) interim, interval. **nesse**—, meanwhile, meantime.
interinado (*m.*) temporary holding of office.
interinamente (*adv.*) provisionally.
interindependência (*f.*) interindependence.
interinfluência (*f.*) interinfluence.
interinidade (*f.*) provisionality.
interino –na (*adj.*) interim, provisional, temporary; acting, in charge.
interinsular (*adj.*) interisland.
interior (*adj.*) interior, internal, inner; inland; (*m.*) interior, inside; inland; inner nature; hinterland.
interioridade (*f.*) interiority.
interjacente (*adj.*) interjacent; interposed.
interjecional (*adj.*) interjectional.
interjeição (*f.*) interjection, exclamation.
interjetivo –va (*adj.*) interjectional; ejaculatory.
interligação (*f.*) interconnection; interlocking.
interlínea (*f.*) = ENTRELINHA.
interlinear (*adj.*) interlinear.
interlobular (*adj.*) interlobular.
interlocução (*f.*) interlocution, colloquy; interpellation.
interlocutor –tora (*m.,f.*) interlocutor.
interlocutório –ria (*adj.; f.*) interlocutory (court order).
interlope (*m.*) = ENTRELOPO.
interlúdio (*m.*) interlude.
interlunar (*adj.*) interlunar.
interlúnio (*m.*) interlunar period.
intermaxilar [ks] (*adj.*) intermaxillary.
intermediar [16] (*v.t.*) to intermingle, intermix; to intermediate.
intermediário –ria (*adj.*) intermediate; (*m.,f.*) intermediary, mediator, go-between; middleman.
intermédio –dia (*adj.*) intermediate; interposed; (*m.*) intermediary, mediator; intervention, interlude. **por**—**de**, by means of; through the medium of.
intermeter (*v.t.*) to insert between or among.
intermezzo (*m.*) intermezzo.
interminável, intérmino –na (*adj.*) interminable; immeasurable, limitless, infinite; long-drawn out.
intermissão (*f.*) intermission, interval, interruption.
intermisturar (*v.t.*) to intermix.
intermitência (*f.*) intermittence, -cy.
intermitente (*adj.*) intermittent; alternating; recurrent.
intermitir (*v.i.*) to intermit, cease for a time.
intermundial (*adj.*) intermundane; world-wide.
intermunicipal (*adj.; m.*) intermunicipal, intercity (match).
intermural (*adj.*) intermural.
intermuscular (*adj.*) intermuscular.
internação (*f.*) internment (in a camp, insane asylum, hospital, etc.); placement (in a boarding school.)
internacional (*adj.*) international. **política**—, foreign policy.
internacionalidade (*f.*) internationality.
internacionalismo (*m.*) internationalism.
internacionalista (*adj.; m.,f.*) internationalist.
internacionalizar (*v.t.*) to internationalize.
internado –da (*adj.*) interned; (*m.,f*) internee; inmate.
internamento (*m.*) internment.
internar (*v.t.*) to intern; to place in a boarding school. —**se em**, to bury oneself in; to enter (deeply) into.
internato (*m.*) boarding school; orphanage.
interno –na (*adj.*) inside; internal; inner; of pupils, resident, boarding; (*m.,f.*) hospital interne; resident student.
internodial (*adj.*) internodal.
internódio (*m.*) internode.
internúncio (*m.*) internuncio.
interoceânico –ca (*adj.*) interocean(ic).
interocular (*adj.*) between the eyes.

interósseo –sea (*adj., Anat.*) interosseous.
interparietal (*adj., Anat., Zool.*) interparietal.
interparlamentar (*adj.*) interparliamentary.
interpeciolar (*adj., Bot.*) interpetiolar(y).
interpelação (*f.*) interpellation; formal questioning; inquiry; official summons or citation.
interpelador –dora, **interpelante** (*adj.; m.,f.*) interpellant.
interpelar (*v.t.*) to interpellate, question formally; to summon, cite; to interrupt.
interpenetração (*f.*) interpenetration.
interpenetrar (*v.t.*) to interpenetrate.
interplanetário –ria (*adj.*) interplanetary.
interpolação (*f.*) interpolation.
interpolado –da (*adj.*) interpolated.
interpolador –dora (*adj.*) interpolating; (*m.,f.*) interpolator.
interpolamento (*m.*) = INTERPOLAÇÃO.
interpolar (*v.t.*) to interpolate, insert (foreign matter in a text); to interlard; to interrupt; (*adj.*) interpolar.
interpontuação (*f.*) ellipses [dots . . .].
interpor [63] (*v.t.*) to interpose, place between; to obstruct, hinder.—**agravo** or **recurso**, (*Law*) to lodge an appeal.
interporto [pôr] (*m.*) intermediate port.
interposição (*f.*) an in-between position; fig., intervention; interruption; intrusion.
interposto –ta (*adj.*) interposed; interposing; intermediate; (*m.*) store; depot; bonded warehouse; entrepôt.
interpotente (*adj.*) of levers, having the power between the weight and the fulcrum.
interpretação (*f.*) interpretation, version, explication, elucidation; translation.
interpretador –dora, **interpretante** (*adj.*) interpreting; (*m.,f.*) interpreter.
interpretar (*v.t.*) to interpret, translate, render; to explain, expound, make clear.
interpretativo –va (*adj.*) interpretative.
interpretável (*adj.*) interpretable.
intérprete (*m.,f.*) interpreter.
interproximal (*adj.*) interproximal [space between adjacent teeth].
interregional (*adj.*) interregional.
interregno (*m.*) interregnum.
inter-resistente (*adj.*) of levers, having the weight between the fulcrum and the power.
interrogação (*f.*) interrogation; question, query; **ponto de**—, question mark [?].
interrogado –da (*adj.; m.,f.*) (person) questioned.
interrogador –dora (*adj.*) interrogating; (*m.,f.*) interrogator.
interrogamento (*m.*) = INTERROGAÇÃO.
interrogante (*adj.*) interrogating; (*m.,f.*) interrogant.
interrogar (*v.t.*) to interrogate, question, put questions to (acêrca de, about).
interrogativo –va (*adj.*) interrogative.
interrogatório –ria (*adj.; m.*) interrogatory.—**cerrado**, a close grilling.
interromper (*v.t.*) to interrupt; to stop, break; to break in upon; (*v.r.*) to leave off, cease for a time.
interrompido –da (*adj.*) interrupted; suspended.
interrupção (*f.*) interruption, stop; break; suspension.
interrupto –ta (*adj.*) interrupted; discontinued [= INTERROMPIDO].
interruptor –tora (*adj.*) interrupting; (*m.*) interruptor; electric switch.
interse[c]ção (*f.*) intersection.
interse[c]cional (*adj.*) intersectional.
interserir [24] (*v.t.*) to insert.
intersexualidade [ks] (*f., Biol.*) intersexuality.
intersideral (*adj.*) intersidereal, interstellar.
intersocial (*adj.*) intermember.
interspinoso –sa (*adj.; Anat., Zool.*) interspinal.
interstelar (*adj.*) interstellar.
intersticial (*adj.*) interstitial.
interstício (*m.*) interstice; chink, crack, crevice; interval.
Intertipo (*m., Print.*) Intertype.
intertransversário –ria (*adj., Anat.*) intertransverse.
intertrigem (*f.*), **intertrigo** (*m., Med.*) intertrigo.
intertropical (*adj.*) intertropical.
interuniversitário –ria (*adj.*) interuniversity.
interurbano –na (*adj.*) interurban; (*m.*) long distance telephone.

intervalado –da (*adj.*) intervaled, spaced at intervals.
intervalar (*v.t.*) to space, place at intervals (as fence posts, printing type, etc.); to interpose, inlard.
intervalo (*m.*) interval, gap; interlude, pause, intervening time; intermission.—**de classe**, (*Stat.*) class interval.— **quartil (quintil)**, (*Stat.*) quartile (quintile) range or interval.
intervenção (*f.*) intervention, interference; intercession, mediation.—**cirúrgica**, surgical operation.
intervencionismo (*m.*) interventionism.
intervencionista (*m.,f.*) interventionist.
interveniente (*adj.*) intervening; (*m.,f.*) endorser of a bill of exchange; a mediator; go-between.
interventivo –va (*adj.*) interventive.
interventor –tora (*adj.*) intervening; (*m.*) interventor—a temporary governor of a state appointed by the dictator-president as his direct agent.
interventricular (*adj., Anat.*) interventricular.
interversão (*f.*) inversion; interversion.
intervertebral (*adj., Anat., Zool.*) intervertebral.
intervertebrocostal (*adj., Anat., Zool.*) intervertebrocostal.
interverter (*v.t.*) to intervert; to invert.
intervir [82] (*v.t.*) to intervene, interpose, come between; to meddle; to mediate; to occur, befall; to participate (in); to be present (at).
intervocálico –ca (*adj., Phonet.*) intervocal(ic).
intestado –da (*adj.*) intestate.
intestável (*adj.*) having testamentary incapacity.
intestinal (*adj.*) intestinal. **lavagem**—, enema. **oclusão**—, (*Med.*) intestinal obstruction.
intestino –na (*adj.*) intestine; (*m.*) intestine, gut.—**delgado (grosso)**, small (large) intestine.—**reto**, rectum.
intimação (*f.*) notification, announcement; authoritative admonishment; summons, injunction. [Not an equivalent of intimation, in the sense of hint, which is ALUSÃO, SUGESTÃO.] (*slang*) swank.
intimar (*v.t.*) to enjoin; to order, require; to notify; to urge, admonish; to "summons"; to taunt. [Not an equiv. of intimate, in the sense of hint, which is SUGERIR, INSINUAR.]
intimativo –va (*adj.*) declaratory; forceful, authoritative; (*f.*) a forceful (overbearing, domineering) statement, admonishment, or notification.
intimidação (*f.*) intimidation.
intimidade (*f.*) intimacy, familiarity, closeness, friendship; privacy.
intimidador –dora (*adj.*) intimidating; (*m.,f.*) intimidator.
intimidar (*v.t.*) to intimidate, frighten, overawe, cow, bully, bulldoze, browbeat; (*v.r.*) to quail, lose heart.
intimidativo –va (*adj.*) = INTIMIDADOR.
intimismo (*m.*) = INTIMIDADE.
íntimo –ma (*adj.*) intimate, deep-seated, innermost; very dear, close; (*m.,f.*) a bosom friend; (*m.*) the inner soul. **no**—, at heart; in one's heart.
intimorato –ta (*adj.*) fearless. [Do not confuse with INTEMERATO.]
intin[c]ção (*f., Eccl.*) intinction.
intitulação (*f.*), **intitulamento** (*m.*) titling.
intitular (*v.t.*) to entitle, give a title to; (*v.r.*) to entitle (call) oneself. [Not employed as an equiv. of entitle, in the sense of giving a right or legal title to, which is DAR DIREITO A.]
intocável (*adj.; m.,f.*) untouchable (East Indian).
intolerância (*f.*) intolerance, bigotry.
intolerante (*adj.*) intolerant (**com**, of; **para com**, towards); overbearing; bigoted; narrow-minded; (*m.,f.*) intolerant person; bigot.
intolerantismo (*m.*) intolerance, narrowness, dogmatism.
intolerável ·(*adj.*) intolerable, unbearable, unsufferable; plaguy.
intonso –sa (*adj.*) hirsute, shaggy.
intorção (*f., Bot.*) intorsion.
intorso –sa (*adj.*) winding, twisted.
intoxicação [ks] (*f.*) intoxication [but only in the medical sense of poisoning, not drunkenness, which is EMBRIAGUEZ, INEBRIAMENTO].
intoxicante [ks] (*adj.*) poisonous [but not intoxicating, which is INEBRIANTE].
intoxicar [ks] (*v.tt*) to intoxicate [but only in the medical sense, and not to inebriate, which is INEBRIAR, EMBRIAGAR].
intra-atômico –ca (*adj.*) intra-atomic.
ıntra-auricular (*adj., Anat.*) intra-auricular.

intrabalhado –da (*adj.*) unworked.
intracraniano –na (*adj., Anat.*) intracranial.
intradérmico –ca (*adj., Anat.*) intradermic.
intradorso [dôr] (*m., Arch.*) intrados.
intradutibilidade (*f.*) untranslatability.
intraduzível (*adj.*) untranslatable; inexpressible.
intrafegável (*adj.*) impassable, untraversable.
intragável (*adj.*) that cannot be swallowed; unpalatable; unreadable.
intra-hepático –ca (*adj., Anat.*) intrahepatic.
intramedular (*adj., Anat.*) intramedullary.
intramuscular (*adj., Anat.*) intramuscular.
intranqüilidade (*f.*) disquiet, uneasiness.
intranqüilizar (*v.t.*) to disquiet, make uneasy, disturb.
intranqüilo –na (*adj.*) intranquil, perturbed, disturbed, restless, unsettled.
intransferível (*adj.*) non-transferable.
intransigência (*f.*) intransigency.
intransigente (*adj.*) intransigent, uncompromising; intolerant.
intransitado –da (*adj.*) untraveled [road].
intransitável (*adj.*) impassable [road, street], intransitable.
intransitivo –va (*adj., Gram.*) intransitive.
intransmissível (*adj.*) non-transmissible; non-transferable
intransplantável (*adj.*) not transplantable.
intransponível (*adj.*) that cannot be passed, overtaken or transposed; insurmountable.
intransportável (*adj.*) not transportable.
intra-ocular (*adj., Anat.*) intraocular.
intrapulmonar (*adj., Anat.*) intrapulmonary.
intratado –da (*adj.*) of illness or injury, not treated; of matters, not dealt with, untried.
intratável (*adj.*) intractable; stubborn, unmanageable, difficult, mulish; sulky, sullen, unsociable, standoffish; gruff; churlish.
intratelúrico –ca (*adj., Petrol., Geol.*) intratelluric.
intratômico –ca (*adj.*) = INTRA-ATÔMICO.
intratorácico –ca (*adj., Anat.*) intrathoracic.
intrauterino –na (*adj., Anat.*) intra-uterine.
intravascular (*adj., Anat.*) intravascular.
intravenoso –sa (*adj., Anat.*) intravenous.
intrêmulo –la (*adj.*) unshaking; fig., fearless.
intrepidez [dêz] (*f.*) intrepidity, boldness, dauntlessness, prowess.
intrépido –da (*adj.*) intrepid, bold, fearless, daring; undismayed, undaunted.
intricado –da (*adj.*) intricate; abstruse.
intricar (*v.t.*) to render intricate (entangled, involved); to perplex, confuse.
intriga (*f.*) intrigue, plot, scheme, wile, ruse.—**amorosa**, a love affair.—**s de bastidores**, backstage schemings and bickerings. **fomentar uma**—, to hatch a plot.
intrigado –da (*adj.*) intrigued; piqued.—**com alguém**, at outs with someone; (*m.,f.*) personal enemy.
intrigalhada (*f.*) intriguery.
intragalhar (*v.i.*) to engage in low scheming.
intrigante, intriguista (*adj.*) intriguing; designing; (*m.,f.*) intrigant, intriguer; troublemaker; talebearer.
intrigar (*v.t.*) to hatch plots; to stir up trouble; to embroil; to intrigue, pique the curiosity; to puzzle; (*v.i.*) to scheme, devise, intrigue.
intrincado –da (*adj.*) = INTRICADO,
intrincar (*v.*) = INTRICAR.
intrínseco –ca (*adj.*) intrinsic, inherent, ingrained.
introdução (*f.*) introduction; ushering in; importation; insertion; presentation; preface; foreword; a preliminary step.
introdutivo –va (*adj.*) introductive.
introdutor –tora (*adj.*) introductory; (*m.,f.*) introducer.
introdutório –ria (*adj.*) introductory.
introduzir [36] (*v.t.*) to introduce, usher in; to insert; to bring in, import; to bring into use; to start; (*v.r.*) to penetrate, invade; to enter in. [Not employed in the sense of introducing one person to another, which is APRESENTAR UMA PESSÔA À OUTRA.]
introflexão [ks] (*f.*) introflexion.
intróito (*m.*) first part, beginning; (*Eccl.*) Introit.
intrometer (*v.t.*)—**em**, to insert, put in.—**-se em**, to intrude, interfere in; to meddle; to inject oneself (into the affairs of others); to "butt in," pry into.
intrometido –da (*adj.*) intrusive, meddlesome; "nosey"; impertinent, "fresh"; (*m.,f.*) meddler, intruder; interloper.
intrometimento (*m.*) act of intruding, meddling.

intromissão (f.) intromission.
introrso –sa (adj., Bot.) introrse.
introspe[c]ção (f.) introspection, self-contemplation.
introspe[c]tivo –va (adj.) introspective.
introversão (f.) introversion.
introvertido –da (adj.) introverted.
introverter (v.t.) to introvert.
intrujão, –jona (m.,f.) impostor, swindler; fence (receiver of stolen goods).
intrujar (v.t.) to hoodwink, take in, dupe; to bamboozle; to inveigle; to spoof; (v.i.) to tell tall tales; (v.r.) to kid oneself or one another.
intrujice (f.) hoax, imposture, big lie.
intrujir (v.i., colloq.) to catch on (perceive).
intrusão (f.) intrusion; encroachment, infringement, trespass.
intrusivo –va (adj., Petrog.) intrusive.
intruso –sa (adj.) intrusive. ser—, to intrude; (m.,f.) intruder, interloper, trespasser; outsider; "gatecrasher"; meddler.
intubação, intubagem, (f., Med.) intubation.
intuição [u-i] (f.) intuition, insight; presentiment.
intuitivismo [u-i] (m., Ethics) intuitionism.
intuitivo –va [u-i] (adj.) intuitive, instinctive.
intuito (m.) intent, design, purpose.
intumescência (f.) intumescence.
intumescente (adj.) intumescent, swollen.
intumescer (v.i.) to intumesce, swell up.
inturgescência (f.) turgescence, turgidity, distention.
inturgescente (adj.) turgescent.
inturgescer (v.i.) to become turgid.
intussuscepção (f., Med., Biol.) intussusception.
inúbia (f.) Indian war trumpet. [Poetical]
inúbil [-beis] (adj.) not nubile.
inúbilo –la (adj.) cloudless.
inubo –ba (adj.) = INUPTO.
inúlase (f., Biochem.) inulase.
inulificável (adj.) not nullifiable.
inulina (f., Chem.) inulin [= DALINA].
inulto –ta (adj.) unsatisfied, unavenged [insult, etc.].
inultrapassável (adj.) unsurpassable.
inumação (f.) inhumation, burial, interment.
inumanidade (f.) inhumanity [= DESUMANIDADE].
inumano –na (adj.) inhuman; inhumane [= DESUMANO].
inumar (v.t.) to inhume, bury.
inumerabilidade (f.) innumerability.
inumerável, inúmero –ra (adj.) innumerable, numberless.
inundação (f.) inundation, flood, deluge; a horde (of invaders).
inundado –da (adj.) flooded; (m.,f.) a flood victim.
inundante (adj.) inundating.
inundar (v.t.) to inundate, flood, deluge; to glut; to invade, overrun.
inundável (adj.) that can be flooded.
inupto –ta (adj.) unmarried.
inusitado –da (adj.) unaccustomed, unusual; strange, new.
inútil [-teis] (adj.) useless, worthless, needless, unserviceable, of no use; unavailing.
inutilidade (f.) inutility; uselessness.
inutilizar (v.t.) to render useless; to incapacitate, disable; (v.r.) to become useless (unfit).
inutilizável (adj.) that cannot be utilized.
invadeável (adj.) unfordable, impassable.
invadir (v.t.) to invade; to trespass; to encroach on; to overrun, spread over; to usurp.
invaginação (f.) invagination; (Med.) intussusception.
invaginado –da (adj.) invaginate.
invaginante (adj.) invaginating.
invaginar (v.t.) to invaginate; (v.r.) to suffer an intussusception.
invalidação (f.) invalidation; (Law) defeasance.
invalidade (f.) invalidity.
invalidar (v.t.) to invalidate, nullify, annul, quash.
invalidável (adj., Law) defeasible.
invalidez [ê] (f.) invalidity; disability.
inválido –da (adj.) physically or mentally disabled. [But not invalid in the sense of null or void, which is NULO, NÃO VÁLIDO]; (m.,f.) a disabled person.—s de guerra, war-disabled persons. [But not an invalid (sick person), which is ENFERMO.]
invar (m.) Invar (a nickel steel alloy).
invariabilidade (f.) invariability, unchangeableness.
invariável (adj.) invariable, changeless, constant.

invasão (f.) invasion, incursion.
invasivo –va (adj.) invasive.
invasor –sora (adj.) invading; (m.,f.) invader.
invectiva (f.) see under INVECTIVO.
invectivador –dora (adj.) vituperative; (m.,f.) vituperator, inveigher.
invectivar (v.i.) to inveigh against, rail at, vituperate, "bawl out".
invectivo –va (adj.) invective, abusive; (f.) invective; diatribe; tirade.
inveja (f.) envy, jealousy. com—, enviously. Cf. CIUME.
invejar [17a] (v.t.) to envy, covet; to grudge, begrudge.
invejável (adj.) enviable.
invejoso –sa (adj.; m.,f.) envious, grudging (person).
invenção (f.) invention; creation, discovery; device, contrivance; falsehood, fabrication.
invencibilidade (f.) invincibility.
invencionar (v.t.) to ornament artfully.
invencioneiro –ra (adj.) given to fabrication (of lies); affected; sly; (m.,f.) such a person.
invencionice (f.) fabrication, falsehood, figment, make-believe.
invencível (adj.) invincible, unconquerable.
invendável, invendível (adj.) unsalable, unmarketable.
inventar (v.t.) to invent, contrive, devise; to create, originate; to fabricate, forge.
inventariação (f.) inventorying.
inventariante (m.,f.) one who makes an inventory (esp. of a decedent's estate); (adj.) inventorying.
inventariar (v.t.) to inventory.
inventário –ria (adj.) inventory (esp. of a decedent's estate).
inventividade (f.) inventiveness.
inventivo –va (adj.) inventive, ingenious, creative; (f.) inventiveness, ingeniousness.
invento (m.) an invention; gadget; [= INVENÇAO].
inventor –triz (adj.) inventive; (m.) inventor; (f.) inventress.
inverídico –ca (adj.) untrue; untruthful.
inverificado –da (adj.) unverified.
inverificável (adj.) unverifiable.
inverna (f.) = INVERNADA.
invernação (f.) wintering (of cattle).
invernáculo –la (adj.) not vernacular.
invernada (f.) hard winter; cold rainy season; winter pasture.
invernador (m.) one who provides winter pasturage.
invernadouro (m.) wintering place; winter pasture; hot house (for plants).
invernagem (f.) wintering (of cattle).
invernal (adj.) wintry, hibernal.
invernar (v.i.) to winter; to hibernate; (v.t.) to move (cattle) to winter pasture.
invernia, inverneira (f.) a hard winter.
invernista (m.,f.) = INVERNADOR.
inverno (m.) winter. [In the southern hemisphere, from June 21 to September 22]; the rainy season [in Brazil]. **no mais forte do**—, in the depth (dead) of winter.
invernoso –sa (adj.) wintry; cold and wet.
inverossímil [-meis] (adj.) unlikely, improbable, implausible, hard to believe, that doesn't ring true.
inverossimilhança (f.) inverisimilitude, unlikelihood, improbability.
inversa (f.) see INVERSO.
inversamente (adv.) contrariwise.
inversão (f.) inversion, reversal; homosexuality.—**de capital**, investment of capital.
inversionista (m.,f.) investor.
inversivo –va (adj.) inversive.
inverso –sa (adj.; m.) inverse; (f.) an inverse proposition. **ao**—, inversely; in reverse. **ao**—**de**, contrary to.
inversor –sora (adj.) inverting; (m.,f.) inverter.
invertebrado –da (adj.; m.) invertebrate.
inverter (v.t.) to invert, reverse, turn about; to invest (capital).
invertido –da (adj.) inverted; topsy-turvy; (m.) an invert, passive pederast.
invertina (f., Biochem.) invertase.
invés (m.) the wrong side (as of a garment); the opposite. **ao**—, on the contrary. **ao**—**de**, contrary to; opposite to; instead of. Cf. AVÉSSO.
investida (f.) charge, onslaught, lunge, thrust.
investidura (f.) investiture.
investigação (f.) investigation, examination, scrutiny.

investigador –**dora** (*adj.*) investigating, scrutinizing; (*m.,f.*) investigator; detective.
investigante (*adj.*) investigating.
investigar (*v.t.*) to investigate, examine, scrutinize, inquire into.
investigativo –**va** (*adj.*) investigative.
investigável (*adj.*) investigable.
investimento (*m.*) investing; investment; investiture.
investir [21a] (*v.t.*) to attack, storm; to clothe (with power, authority, etc.); to invest (money).—**com, sôbre,** to fall upon, set upon.—**contra, para,** to rush at, fly at, lunge at.—**de, em,** to invest with power; to install in office.—**de vento em pôpa,** to sail into.—**para, por,** to rush out or through.
inveterado –**da** (*adj.*,) inveterate, confirmed, deep-seated, deep-rooted, long-established.
inveterar (*v.t.*) to make inveterate; (*v.r.*) to become chronic.
inviável (*adj.*) impassable [road, street].
invicto –**ta** (*adj.*) unconquered, unconquerable; unbeaten.
invídia, poetical form of INVEJA.
ínvido –**da** (*adj.*) invidious (but only in the obsolete sense of envious); = INVEJOSO.
invigilância (*f.*) want of vigilance.
invigilante (*adj.*) not vigilant.
ínvio –**via** (*adj.*) of waste or forest, trackless; of roads, impassable.
inviolabilidade (*f.*) inviolability.
inviolado –**da** (*adj.*) inviolate, unbroken.
inviolável (*adj.*) inviolable.
inviolentado –**da** (*adj.*) uncompelled, unforced.
inviscerar (*v.*) = ENTRANHAR.
invisibilidade (*f.*) invisibility.
invisível (*adj.*) invisible; (*m.*) the unseen; (*f.*) a lady's hair net; a fine hairpin.
inviso –**sa** (*adj.*) unseen; envied; hated. [*Poetical*]
invitar (*v.*) & derivs. = CONVIDAR & derivs.
invitatório –**ria** (*adj.*) invitational; inviting; invitatory [psalm].
invite (*m.*) invitation [= CONVITE]; doubling of gambling stakes.
invito –**ta** (*adj.*) involuntary, unwilling.
invitrescível (*adj.*) invitrescible, invitrifiable.
invocação (*f.*) invocation, invoking.
invocador –**dora** (*adj.*) invoking; (*m.,f.*) invoker.
invocar (*v.t.*) to invoke, call upon; (*sl.*) to nag.
invocativo –**va** (*adj.*) invocative.
invocatório –**ria** (*adj.*) invocatory; (*f.*) invocation.
invocável (*adj.*) invocable.
involução (*f.*, *Biol.*) involution, degeneration.
involucelo (*m.*, *Bot.*) involucel.
involucrado –**da** (*adj.*, *Bot.*) involucrate.
involucral (*adj.*, *Bot.*) involucral.
involucriforme (*adj.*, *Bot.*) involucriform.
invólucro (*m.*) outer covering, envelope, wrapper; (*Bot.*) involucre.
involuntário –**ria** (*adj.*) involuntary, unintentional, unintended; unwilling.
involuto –**ta** (*adj.*, *Bot.*) involute.
involutório (*m.*) = ENVOLTÓRIO.
invulgar (*adj.*) uncommon, unusual, unwonted, out of the ordinary.
invulnerabilidade (*f.*) invulnerability.
invulnerado –**da** (*adj.*) unharmed.
invulnerável (*adj.*) invulnerable.
Iocoama (*f.*) Yokohama.
iocroma (*f.*, *Bot.*) the violetbush (genus *Lochroma*).
iodar (*v.t.*) to iodize.
iodargirita (*f.*, *Chem.*) iodargyrite: iodyrite.
iodato (*m.*, *Chem.*) iodate.
iodeto [ê] (*m.*, *Chem.*) iodide.
iódico –**ca** (*adj.*, *Chem.*) iodic.
iodídrico –**ca** (*adj.*, *Chem.*) hydriodic [acid].
iodidrina (*f.*, *Chem.*) iodohydrin.
iodífero –**ra** (*adj.*) iodiferous.
iodina (*f.*) = IODO.
iodirita (*f.*, *Chem.*) iodyrite; silver iodide.
iodismo (*m.*, *Med.*) iodism.
iodite (*f.*, *Min.*) iodyrite.
iôdo (*m.*) iodine.
iodobromite (*f.*, *Min.*) iodobromite.
iodocloreto [ê] (*m.*, *Chem.*) iodochloride.
iodofórmio (*m.*, *Chem.*) iodoform.
iodol (*m.*, *Chem.*) iodol.

iodometria (*f.*, *Chem.*) iodometry.
iodoterapia (*f.*, *Med.*) iodotherapy.
iodureto (*m.*) = IODETO.
ioga (*f.*) yoga.
iogue (*m.*) yogi.
ioiô (*m.*) yo-yo (toy); Negro slaves' corruption of SENHOR, equivalent in use and meaning to "massa" (master). Cf. NHONHÔ.
iole (*m.*) shell (light racing boat).
iôlito (*m.*, *Min.*) iolite.
íon, iônio, ionte (*m.*, *Phys.*, *Chem.*) ion.
iônico –**ca** (*adj.*) ionic; Ionic [= JÔNICO].
iônio –**nia** (*adj.*) Ionian [= JÔNIO]; (*m.*, *Chem.*) ionium; ion [= ÍON].
ionização (*f.*) ionization.
ionizar (*v.t.*) to ionize.
ionona (*f.*, *Chem.*) ionone, irone.
ionosfera (*f.*) ionosphere, Heaviside layer.
ionte (*m.*) = ÍON.
iontoforese (*f.*, *Physical Chem.*) iontophoresis, cataphoresis [= CATAFORESE].
Iorque (*m.*) York.
iota (*m.*) iota.
iotacismo (*m.*) iotacism.
iotização (*f.*, *Phonet.*) iotization.
iotizar (*v.t.*, *Phonet.*) to iotize.
ipadu [ú] (*m.*) the coca plant (*Erythroxylum coca*), c.a. COCA, BOLÍVIA, IPADU-VERDADEIRO.—**mirim** is *E. cataracta*. [The leaves of these plants are chewed (with alkali) by a large section of the Indian population and CABOCLOS, to ward off hunger and impart endurance.]
IPASE = INSTITUTO DE PENSÕES E APOSENTADORIA DOS SERVIDORES DO ESTADO (Institute for Pensions and Retirement of State Servants).
ipê (*m.*) a building timber; a combining form for the common names of many Brazilian trees and plants of the mimosa, bignonia and borage families, and for which there are no common equivalents in English.—**-amarelo,** a tecoma (*T. chrysostricha*), c.a. IPÊ-DO-BREJO or PAU-DE-OURO, whose yellow flower is the national flower of Brazil.—**batata** = CAROBA-BRANCA.—**bóia,** a tecoma (*T. subvernicosa*).—**branco,** a tecoma (*T. odontodiscus*); also = CAROBA-BRANCA, CAROBA-DE-FLOR-VERDE, GUAJUVIRA-BRANCA.—**-de-flor-verde,** —**mirim,** —**pardo,** all = CAROBA-DE-FLOR-VERDE.—**do-córrego** = GUABIROBA-BRAVA, TARUMÃ.
ipecaconha (*f.*) a ruellia (*R. geminoflora*).—**de-flor-branca,** a violaceous plant (*Ionidium ipecacuanha*), c.a. IPECA-BRANCA, IPECA-DO-MARAJÓ, PIRAIA, POAIA-BRANCA, POAIA-DA-PRAIA, POAIA-DO-CAMPO, PURGA-DA-PRAIA.
ipecacuanha (*f.*) a tropical creeping plant with drooping flowers (*Cephaelis ipecacuanha*), c.a. POAIA, CAGOSANGA. [It is the source of Rio or Brazilian ipecac.]—**dos-alemães,** white swallow-wort (*Cynanchum vincetoxicum*).—**estriada** or —**preta,** a wild coffee (*Psychotria emetica*).—**falsa,** a spiderling (*Boehaavia diffusa*).—**-rubra,** the yellow palicourea (*P. croces*), c.a. POAIA-VERMELHA.
ipecuacamirá (*f.*) the lineated woodpecker (*Coephoeus l. lineatus*).
ipecuati (*m.*) = PICAPAU-DE-CABEÇA-AMARELA.
ipecumirim (*m.*) the little black woodpecker (*Melanerpes cruentatus*). Cf. PICA-PAU.
ipecupará (*m.*) Wagler's eastern woodpecker (*Veniliornis spilogaster*). Cf. PICA-PAU.
ipecupinima (*m.*) the waved woodpecker (*Celeus u. undatus*). Cf. PICA-PAU.
ipecutauá (*m.*) = PICAPAU-AMARELO.
ipequi [í] (*m.*, *Zool.*) the sun grebe (*Heliornis fulica*), c.a. PATINHO-D'ÁGUA, MERGULHÃO, PICAPARRA, PECAPARRA, GALINHA-D'ÁGUA, PEQUI, PATINHO-DE-IGAPÓ.
iph-, see under **if-.**
ipoméia (*f.*, *Bot.*) morning-glory (*Ipomoea*).
ipu [ú] (*m.*) a tract of low moist land fed by mountain streams; (*Angling*) wire leader; a certain ground-nesting bee.
ipuaça (*f.*) an extensive tract of marshy meadowland.
ipuada (*f.*) a thatched hut.
ipue[i]ra (*f.*) a small pond left by receding flood waters.
ir [53] (*v.i.*) to go; to move, proceed; to travel, journey; of time, to go by; to fare; (*v.r.*) to go away. [As an auxiliary verb, **ir** followed by an infinitive expresses futurity. **Vou comprar um livro,** I am going to buy a book. When followed by a present participle, **ir** expresses

continuity of a state or action. **Como eu ia dizendo**, as I was saying. Or, it may indicate something about to occur. **Ia morrendo**, He (she) was dying (about to die)]. —**a**, to go to. [Cf. IR PARA].—**à bolina**, to luff.—**a caminho de**, to go in the direction of; to be on the way to.—**a campo**, to take to the field.—**a cavalo**, to go on horseback; to ride a horse.—**à cena**, of a play, to be staged. —**à cidade**, to go downtown; or, to go into town (from a suburb or from the country).—**à costa**, of a ship, to run ashore.—**à deriva**, to drift; to flounder; to go astray. —**a êsmo**, to go (act, move, run) haphazardly.—**à francêsa**, to take French leave; to sneak out.—**a leilão**, to be put up at auction.—**a um leilão**, to go to an auction. —**à orça**, to luff.—**à parede**, to hit the ceiling.—**a pé**, to go afoot, walk.—**à pele de (alguém)**, to go after (someone's) hide.—**a pique** or **ao fundo**, to founder, sink, go to the bottom.—**à praça**, to be put up for public sale. —**a processo** or **à justiça**, to go to law, to court.—**a Pindamonhangaba**, to go to P. (for a short time). [Cf. IR PARA].—**a Roma e não ver o Papa**, to seek but not see (something) after it is found; lit., to go to Rome and not see the Pope; to miss the best of a place, etc.; to waste one's time.—**à rua**, to go out (into the street).—**à terra**, to land; to fall to the ground; of an enterprise, to fail.—**à vela (com vento fresco)**, to go under full sail (with a favorable wind); to go fast and well. —**abaixo**, to come (fall) down; to crumble; to fail.—**adiante**, to go ahead (**de**, of); to succeed; fig., to go through; to go further; to amount to something.—**além**, to go beyond; to exceed expectations.—**andando**, to keep going; to keep moving; to be so-so (in health).—**ao chão**, to fall to the ground; to take a tumble.—**ao encontro de**, to go to meet; to meet halfway. [Cf. IR DE ENCONTRO A.]—**ao lado de**, to go alongside of.—**ao mar buscar laranjas**, to go after horse feathers (waste time and effort).—**ao pau**, to flunk (an exam).—**aos ares**, to blow up; to hit the ceiling. [Cf. IR PELOS ARES].—**às carreiras**, to rush headlong.—**às vias de fato**, to come to blows.—**atento a** (or **em**), to give attention to, take care with.—**atrás de**, to follow, go after, keep after (someone or something); to believe in. [Eu não vou atrás disso! I won't go for that!]—**avante**, to go ahead.—**bater em (algum lugar)**, to end up at or in (some place); to resort to.—**bem**, to go well; of a person, business, etc., to be all right.—**bem de saúde**, to be well, in good health.—**buscar**, to go fetch. —**buscar lã e sair tosquiado**, to go after wool and be shorn as a sheep.—**com a cara de**, (slang) to hate (his) guts; to hate without cause.—**com Deus**, to go in peace. —**com o tempo**, to temporize, humor, yield (to current opinion, circumstances, etc.).—**com pressa**, to go in a hurry.—**contra**, to go counter to (oppose).—**contra a corrente**, to swim against the tide; to go against popular opinions, etc.—**contra o vento e contra a maré**, to go against wind and tide; to forge ahead despite all obstacles.—**de**, to go (dressed); as; to wear. [Eu fui de capa e chapéu, I wore a hat and coat.]—**de avião**, to go by plane.—**de bonde**, to go by streetcar.—**de carro**, to drive, go by car.—**de encontro a**, to collide with, run into. [Cf. IR AO ENCONTRO DE].—**de fugida**, to bolt, run away.—**de garupa**, to ride (a horse) behind the saddle. —**de mal a pior**, to go from bad to worse.—**de pés juntos**, to turn up one's toes (die).—**de vento em popa**, to be favored by circumstances.—**de vez**, to go (away) for good.—**de volta**, to make a return trip; to be on one's way back.—**desta para melhor**, to leave this world for a better one (die).—**direito a**, to go straight to.—**direito como um fuso**, to go straight as an arrow.—**em debandada**, of a crowd, herd, pack, to flee headlong.—**em decadência**, to become decadent, grow old.—**em diminuição**, to wane. [Vá diminuindo o volume, Keep on turning the volume down.]—**em progressão**, to progress step by step.—**em progresso** or **em aumento**, to wax, thrive.—**em (or de) retirada**, to beat a retreat. —**embora**, to go away; to leave [for a while or for good]. —**estar com (alguém)**, to go (be) with (someone); to keep (someone) company.—**informar-se**, to go to make inquiries; to look into; to consult.—**junto**, to go together (**com**, with).—**longe**, to go far (lit. & fig.).—**mal**, to go badly.—**mal de saúde**, to be in poor health.—**muito longe**, to exaggerate; to carry (something) too far.—**na esteira de (alguém)**, to follow (another's) footsteps.—**na onda**, or **nas águas**, to follow along with others, make no resistance; to be fooled (taken in).—**nas pegadas de**, to follow in another's footsteps; to track, pursue (some-

one).—**no arrastão**, to be taken in (played for a sucker). —**no embrulho**, to be taken in, fooled; to be jailed.—**no encalço de**, to go after, pursue (someone).—**num pé e vir noutro**, to go and come without delay.—**para**, to go to (a place, with the intention of staying there). [Cf. IR A].—**para casa**, to go home.—**para o céu**, to go to heaven (die).—**para o céu das formigas**, (colloq.) to go to hell.—**para o (seu, meu) quarto**, to retire to (one's) room.—**para pior**, to worsen.—**pelos ares**, to be blown sky high. [Cf. IR AOS ARES].—**por água abaixo**, to go downstream; fig., to go downhill, deteriorate; of plans, intentions, etc., to fall through.—**por diante**, to keep on, continue, go ahead with.—**por partes**, to proceed by steps.—**primeiro**, to go first.—**respirar o ar pátrio**, to return to one's birthplace.—**se**, to be on one's way, be off, depart.—**se andando**, to start leaving.—**se com Deus**, to leave in peace.—**se com o tempo**, to temporize, go along with the times.—**se como um passarinho**, to die quietly and peacefully.—**se de**, to depart from.—**se embora**, to go away; fig., to die; to run out. [O dinheiro foi-se embora, the money ran out.]—**se para**, to (travel) to (some place, with the idea of staying there). —**se para o céu**, to go to heaven.—**ter com (alguém)**, to call on (someone); to seek (someone) out.—**tomar ares**, to have a change of scenery, move to the country, etc., for health reasons. **Água vem, água vai,** Easy come, easy go. **Como vai indo?** How are you making out? **Como vai você?** How are you? How do you do? **Daí não vai sair nada de bom**, No good will come of it. **Devagar se vai ao longe**, Easy does it; Haste makes waste. **Éle foi p'ro Exército,** He's in the Army [usually in the sense: He's enlisted in the Army]. **Éle vai melhor,** He is feeling better. **Eu vou mas é dormir,** Enough of this—*I'm* going to bed. **Foi-se,** It's gone; He has left (died). **Foi-se para casa,** He went (has gone) home. **Ja se foi o tempo!** That was in the old days! [implying a permanent loss of something.] **Já vou!** I'm coming! [Cf. VOU JÁ, JÁ.] **Lá se vão êles,** There they go. **Meu tio vai já nos oitenta anos,** My uncle is going on eighty. **Não vá isso explodir!** What if it explodes? **Não vá lá fora!** Don't you go outside! **Não vá se esquecer,** Don't you forget (it)! **Não vão bem um com o outro,** They don't get along well together. **Não vou bem,** I am not well; I'm not doing so well. **Não vou nisso,** I don't go for that. **O dinheiro foi-se todo,** The money all went. **O vestido vai-lhe bem,** The dress fits her well. **Onde você vai agora?** Where are you going now? **Ora, vamos!** for Pete's sake! Oh, come on, let's hurry! **Ora, vamos e venhamos!** Well, after all! That's carrying things a bit too far! Let's be sensible about this. **Parece que vai chover,** It looks like rain. **Posso—sem gravata?** Do I have to wear a tie? **Quem quer, vai, quem não quer, manda,** If you want a thing done, do it yourself. **São horas de —,** It is time to go (leave). **Sem dizer "água vai,"** without warning. **Um—e vir de gente,** a stream of people coming and going. **Vá às favas! Vá bugiar! Vá pentear macacos! Vá plantar batatas!** All mean: Scram! Don't bother me! Go to the devil! **Vá (-se) embora!** Beat it! Go away! **Vá lá!** Oh, all right! **Vá ser imbecil no inferno!** Gee, how dumb can you get! **Vá ver,** Go see. **Vai acontecer uma coisa boa,** Something good is going to happen. **Vai andando,** It keeps moving; He is walking. **Vai (-te) embora!** Get along with you! **Vai (-se) embora,** He goes away; He is leaving. **Vai para cinco anos que estou aqui,** I have been here going on five years. **Vai para dois anos que êle se foi,** He left about two years ago. **Vai-se fazendo tarde,** It's getting late. **Vai-se o tempo,** Time is running short. **Vai sem chapéu?** Aren't you going to wear a hat? **Vai com Deus,** Peace be with you. **Vai ter!** There's going to be trouble! **Vai ver que o avião está atrasado,** I wouldn't be surprised if the plane were late. **Vai um ano que não o vejo,** It's a whole year since I last saw him (you). **Vamos!** Come on! Let's go! Okay, let's do it! **Vamos andando (caminhando, tocando),** Let's be on our way. **Vamos ao caso,** Let's get to the point. **Vamos ao que importa,** Let's get down to business. **Vamos de-pressa!** Let's hurry! **Vamos embora,** Let's leave; We are leaving; Come on! Hurry up! **Vamos indo?** Shall we get started? **Vamos lá!** Let's get going! Also, Okay, I'm willing to try it (in connection with a game, experiment, etc.). **Vamos, não chore mais,** Come now, stop crying. **Vamos parar com isso!** Cut it out! Lay off! Stop it! Keep quiet! **Vamos ver,** We shall see; Let's go see. **Vamos ver com quantos paus se faz uma canoa!** We'll see about that! I'll show you (him, them,

etc.)! **Você vai ver**, you'll see. **Vou ao Rio**, I am going to Rio (expecting to return). **Vou para o Rio**, I am going to Rio (expecting to remain there). **Vou indo**, I'm leaving. **Vou indo bem**, I'm getting on well. **Vou já, já**, I'll be right there (in a minute). [Cf. **já vou**.] **Vou puxando**, I'm leaving now. **Vou-me embora**, I am leaving, going away (**agora mesmo**, right now). **Vou ter com êle**, I am going to meet him.
ira (*f.*) ire, fury, anger, rage, wrath.
Irã, Irão (*m.*) Iran.
irá (*m.*) a ground-nesting bee.
iracúndia (*f.*) irefulness.
iracundo -da (*adj.*) iracund; irascible.
irado -da (*adj.*) irate, mad, indignant.
iraí = CASTANHEIRO-DO-PARÁ., CANAFRECHA.
iraniano -na, irânico -va (*adj.;.m.,f.*) Iranian.
irapuá (*m.*) = ABELHA-DE-CACHORRO.
irapuã (*m.*) = TORCE-CABELO.
irapuru [rú] (*m.*) the orange-bellied manakin (*Pipra a. aureola*); also = UIRAPURU.—**-verdadeiro**, the western red-fronted hylophilus (*Hylophilus ochraceiceps lutescens*).
Iraque (*m.*) Iraq.
irar (*v.t.*) to anger; (*v.r.*) to get angry.
irara (*f.*) the tayra (*Tayra barbara* or *Galictis barbara*), a weasel closely allied to the grison [= CACHORRINHO-DO-MATO]; c.a. JAGUAPÉ, PAPA-MEL. [It is sometimes mistaken for the JAGUARUNDI.]
irascibilidade (*f.*) irascibility.
irascível (*adj.*) irascible; touchy.
iratauá (*m.*) the yellow-headed marsh bird (*Agelaius icterocephalus*) of northern Brazil in the Amazon region.
iratim (*m.*) = IRAXIM.
iraúna (*f.*) = GRAÚNA.—**-de-bico-branco** = GRAÚNA-DE-BICO-BRANCO.
iraxim (*m.*) a stingless bee (*Melipona limão*), c.a. IRATIM, ARANCIM, ABELHA-LIMÃO, LIMÃO, LIMÃO-CANUDO.
Irene (*f.*) Irene.
irerê (*m.*) white faced tree-duck (*Dendrocygna viduata*), c.a. MARRECA-DO-PARÁ, MARRECA-VIÚVA, MARRECA-PIADEIRA, MARRECA-APAÍ, APAÍ, CHEGA-E-VIRA.
iri (*f.*) = AIRI.
iriante (*adj.*) iridescent.
iriar (*v.t.*) to make iridescent.
iribiru-bixá (*m.*) = URUBU-REI.
iricurana (*f.*, *Bot.*) a Christmasbush (*Alchornea*), c.a. FÔLHA-REDONDA.
iricuri (*m.*) = ARICURI.
iridáceo -cea (*adj.*, *Bot.*) iridaceous; (*f.*) an iris; (*pl.*) the *Iridaceae* (iris family).
iridescência (*f.*) iridescence.
iridescente (*adj.*) iridescent.
irídico -ca (*adj.*, *Chem.*) iridic.
iridina (*f.*, *Chem.*) iridin.
irídio (*m.*, *Chem.*) iridium.
iridite (*f.*) = IRITE.
iridosmina (*f.*, *Chem.*) iridosmine; osmiridium.
irimirim (*f.*, *Bot.*) a spiny palm, *Astrocaryum vulgare*.
iribá (*m.*) = ARARIBÁ-AMARELO.
iribá-rosa (*m.*) = ARARIBÁ-ROSA.
íris (*m.,f.*) rainbow; solar spectrum; any rainbowlike play of colors; (*Anat.*, *Bot.*, *Min.*, *Zool.*) iris.
irisação (*f.*) irisation.
irisar (*v.*) = IRIAR.
iritacaca, iritataca (*f.*) = CANGAMBÁ.
irite (*f.*, *Med.*) iritis.
iritinga (*f.*) a sea catfish.
irlandês -dêsa (*adj.*) Irish; (*m.*) an Irishman; the Irish language; (*f.*) Irish woman.
irmã (*adj.*; *f.*) sister.—**de caridade**, Sister of Charity. Cf. IRMÃO.
irmanar (*v.t.*) to couple, join, link together, pair.
irmandade (*f.*) fraternity (brotherly relation); brotherhood, association; confraternity.
irmão [-ãos] (*m.*) brother; half-brother; fellow-member; lay brother; member of a religious order; brother-mason; (*pl.*) brothers; brother(s) and sister(s); (*adj.*) alike, selfsame, of a piece.—**adotivo**, brother by adoption.—**carnal**, brother-german.—**-da-opa**, (*slang*) a drunkard.—**de mãe**, half-brother on the mother's side.—**de pai**, half-brother on the father's side.—**por afinidade**, half-brother.—**s carnais**, brothers-german.—**s colaços** or—**s de leite**, foster brothers.—**s consangüíneos**, children born of different mothers by the same father.—**s de armas**,

brothers at arms.—**s em armas**, brothers-in-arms.—**s gemeos**, twin brothers.—**s siameses**, Siamese twins.—**s uterinos**, uterine brothers (same mother, different fathers). **meio**—, half-brother.
irmãozinho (*m.*) baby brother.
irmãzinha (*f.*) baby sister.
irona (*f.*, *Chem.*) irone.
ironia (*f.*) irony, mockery, sarcasm.
irônico -ca (*adj.*) ironic(al), sarcastic, mocking.
ironizar (*v.t.*) to deride, ridicule.
iroquês (*adj.*; *m.*) Iroquois.
iroso -sa (*adj.*) irascible, angry.
irra! (*interj.*) the devil! (or other mild oath expressing disgust or annoyance).
irracional (*adj.*) irrational, unreasoning, unreasonable, without reason; of animals, nonhuman; (*Math.*) surd; (*m.,f.*) an irrational being; brute, dumb animal.
irracionalidade (*f.*) irrationality.
irracionalismo (*m.*) irrationalism.
irracionalizar (*v.t.*) to irrationalize.
irracionável (*adj.*) irrational.
irradiação (*f.*) irradiation; radiation; radio broadcast(ing).
irradiador -dora (*adj.*) radiating; (*m.*) radiator; broadcaster; (*f.*) broadcasting station.
irradiante (*adj.*) radiating: broadcasting; beaming.
irradiar (*v.t.*) to radiate; to irradiate; to beam; to radio-broadcast.
irré (*m.*) = PAPA-MÔSCA(S).
irreal (*adj.*) unreal.
irrealidade (*f.*) unreality.
irrealizável (*adj.*) unrealizable, unfeasible, impracticable.
irreclamável (*adj.*) irreclaimable.
irreconciliado -da (*adj.*) irreconciled.
irreconciliável (*adj.*) irreconcilable.
irreconhecível (*adj.*) unrecognizable.
irrecorrível (*adj.*) unavoidable, inescapable; (*Law*) unappealable.
irrecuperável (*adj.*) irrecoverable, irretrievable.
irrecusável (*adj.*) that cannot be refused; irrefragable.
irredentismo (*m.*) Irredentism.
irredentista (*m.,f.*) Irredentist.
irredento -ta (*adj.*) unredeemed.
irredimível (*adj.*) unredeemable.
irredutível (*adj.*) irreducible; tough, tenacious.
irreduzível (*adj.*) irreducible; invincible.
irreelegível (*adj.*) that cannot be reelected.
irrefletido -da (*adj.*) thoughtless; unreasoning, unthinking; inconsiderate; rash.
irreflexão [ks] (*f.*) thoughtlessness. **num momento de**—, in an unguarded moment.
irreflexivo -va [ks] (*adj.*) thoughtless; rash.
irreflexo -flexa [ks] (*adj.*) not reflexive; also = IRREFLETIDO.
irreformável (*adj.*) irreformable.
irrefragável (*adj.*) irrefragable.
irrefrangível (*adj.*) irrefrangible.
irrefreável (*adj.*) unrestrainable.
irrefutabilidade (*f.*) irrefutability.
irrefutado -da (*adj.*) not refuted.
irrefutável (*adj.*) irrefutable.
irregenerado -da (*adj.*) unregenerate.
irregressível (*adj.*) from which there is no turning back.
irregular (*adj.*) irregular.
irregularidade (*f.*) irregularity.
irrelegião (*f.*) irreligion.
irreligiosidade (*f.*) irreligiousness.
irreligiosismo (*m.*) irreligion.
irrelegioso -sa (*adj.*) irreligious.
irremediável (*adj.*) irremediable, past mending.
irremissível (*adj.*) unpardonable; obligatory; incurable; unfailing.
irremitente (*adj.*) unremitting.
irremível (*adj.*) unredeemable.
irremovível (*adj.*) irremovable; unavoidable.
irremunerado -da (*adj.*) unremunerative; unremunerated.
irreparabilidade (*f.*) irreparability.
irreparável (*adj.*) irreparable.
irrepartível (*adj.*) that cannot be divided up.
irreplicável (*adj.*) to which reply cannot be made.
irrepreensibilidade [e-e] (*f.*) irreprehensibleness.
irrepreensível [e-e] (*adj.*) irreprehensible, irreproachable blameless, faultless.

irreprimível (*adj.*) irrepressible.
irreprochável (*adj.*) irreproachable.
irrequietação (*f.*) restlessness.
irrequieto -ta (*adj.*) unquiet, restless, turbulent, fidgety, fussy.
irresgatável (*adj.*) unredeemable.
irresistência (*f.*) non-resistance.
irresistente (*adj.*) unresisting.
irresistibilidade (*f.*) irresistibility.
irresistível (*adj.*) irresistible, resistless.
irresolução (*f.*) irresolution, indecision.
irresoluto -ta (*adj.*) irresolute, vacillating, unsure, hesitant, undecided.
irresolúvel (*adj.*) insoluble.
irresolvido -da (*adj.*) unresolved; undecided.
irrespirável (*adj.*) irrespirable.
irrespondível (*adj.*) unanswerable, irrefutable.
irresponsabilidade (*f.*) irresponsibility.
irresponsável (*adj.*) irresponsible, unaccountable.
irrestringível (*adj.*) unrestrainable.
irrestrito -ta (*adj.*) unrestricted; unconditional.
irretorquível (*adj.*) irrefutable.
irretratável (*adj.*) irreversible, irrevocable.
irreverência (*f.*) irreverence.
irreverencioso -sa, irreverente (*adj.*) irreverent, disrespectful, flip(pant).
irrevogabilidade (*f.*) irrevocability.
irrevogável (*adj.*) irrevocable.
irrigação (*f.*) irrigation.
irrigador -dora (*adj.*) irrigational; (*m.*) irrigator; water sprinkler.
irrigar (*v.t.*) to irrigate.
irrigatório -ria (*adj.*) irrigational.
irrigável (*adj.*) irrigable.
irrisão (*f.*) derision, scorn, contempt; sneer.
irrisório -ria (*adj.*) derisive, scornful; ludicrous; petty, picayunish.
irritabilidade (*f.*) irritability; petulance.
irritação (*f.*) irritation, exasperation; itching, burning (of the skin).
irritadiço -ça (*adj.*) cranky, crabby, grumpy; petulant; peevish.
irritado -da (*adj.*) irritated; exasperated, annoyed, resentful, sore.
irritador -dora (*adj.*) irritating; (*m.,f.*) irritator.
irritamento (*m.*) = IRRITAÇÃO.
irritante (*adj.*) irritating; provoking; galling; nerveracking; (*m.,f.*) an irritant.
irritar, to irritate, provoke, exasperate; to tease, annoy; to inflame; to rankle; (*v.r.*) to chafe; to become irritated.
irritativo -va (*adj.*) = IRRITANTE.
irritável (*adj.*) irritable, irascible, touchy.
irrivalizado -da (*adj.*) unrivaled.
irrogar (*v.t.*) to impose against, inflict upon.
irromper (*v.i.*) to irrupt; to burst forth; to break out (as an epidemic, a fire, a revolution, etc.).—em, break into, burst into.
irrorar (*v.t.*) to bedew, moisten.
irrupção (*f.*) irruption; incursion, inroad.
irruptivo -va (*adj.*) irruptive.
iruçu-do-chão, iruçu-mineiro (*m.*) a stingless bee (*Melipona subterranea*), c.a. GUIRÁ.
isabel [-béis] (*adj.*) light tan, yellowish, cream-colored; (*f.*) the color Isabella; Isabel; Isabella; Elizabeth; Elisabeth.
isadelfo -fa (*adj.*, *Bot.*) isadelphous.
Isaías (*m.*) Isaiah; Isaias.
isalóbara (*f.*, *Meteorol.*) isallobar.
isalotérmico -ca (*adj.*, *Meteorol.*) isalothermic (line).
isandro -dra (*adj.*, *Bot.*) isandrous.
isanômalo -la (*adj.*, *Meteorol.*) isanomalous.
isanto -ta (*adj.*, *Bot.*) isanthous.
isapostólico -ca (*adj.*) isapostolic.
ísate, ísatis (*f.*, *Bot.*) dyer's woad (*Isatis tinctoria*).
isatina (*f.*, *Chem.*) isatin.
isca (*f.*) bait; lure; tinder; a piece of fried liver or codfish; bit, morsel.
iscar (*v.t.*) to bait; to sick on (dogs).
isenção (*f.*) exemption; impartiality, disinterestedness.
isentar [24] (*v.t.*) to exempt (de, from), free, let off.
isento -ta (*adj.*; *irreg. p.p. of* ISENTAR) exempt, free, not liable.—de direitos, free of customs duties.
isentrópico -ca (*adj.*, *Physics*) isentropic.
Isidora (*f.*) Isidora.
Isidoro (*m.*) Isidore, Isador(e).

isipeptesial (*adj.*, *Zool.*) isipeptesial.
iserina (*f.*, *Min.*) iserine.
Islã, Islame (*m.*) Islam.
islamismo (*m.*) Islamism, Mohammedanism.
islamita (*m.,f.*) Mohammedan.
islandês -dêsa (*adj.*) Icelandic; (*m.,f.*) Icelander; (*m.*) Icelandic language.
Islândia (*f.*) Iceland.
islão (*m.*) = ISLAME.
ismênia (*f.*, *Bot.*) Peruvian daffodil (*Ismene*).
isnárdia (*f.*, *Bot.*) the seedbox (*Ludwigia*).
isoaglutinação (*f.*, *Med.*) isoagglutination.
isoaglutinina (*f.*, *Immunol.*) isoagglutinin.
isóbare, isobárico -ca (*adj.*) isobaric.
isóbaro (*m.*, *Chem.*) isobar(e).
isobático -ca (*adj.*) isobath(ic).
isobatitérmico -ca (*adj.*, *Phys. Geog.*) isobathythermal.
isobiogenético -ca (*adj.*) isobiogenetic.
isoborneol (*m.*, *Chem.*) isoborneol.
isobutano (*m.*, *Chem.*) isobutane.
isocarpo -pa (*adj.*, *Bot.*) isocarpous.
isocefálico -ca (*adj.*, *Art.*) isocephalic.
isoclásio (*m.*), isoclasite (*f.*, *Min.*) isoclasite.
isoclinal, isóclino -na (*adj.*) isoclinal.
isocrimal (*adj.*) isocrymal.
isocromático -ca, isocrômico -ca (*adj.*) isochromatic.
isocrônico -ca, isócrono -na (*adj.*) isochronous.
isocronismo (*m.*) isochronism.
isodá[c]tilo -la (*adj. Zool.*) isodactylous.
isodiabático -ca (*adj.*, *Physics*) isodiabatic.
isodiametral (*adj.*) isodiametric(al).
isodimorfismo (*m.*, *Min.*) isodimorphism.
isodinâmico -ca (*adj.*) isodynamic.
isodonte (*adj.*, *Zool.*) isodont(ous).
isodulcita (*f.*) = RAMNOSE.
isoelétrico -ca (*adj.*) isoelectric.
isoenergético -ca (*adj.*) = ISODINÂMICO.
isoetáceo -cea (*adj.*, *Bot.*) isoetaceous; (*f.pl.*) the quillworts (*Isoetaceae*).
isofâneo -nea, isofano -na (*adj.*, *Biol.*) isophane.
isofenomenal (*adj.*) isophenomenal.
isofíleo -lea, isofilo -la (*adj.*, *Bot.*) isophyllous.
isoforia (*f.*, *Med.*) isophoria.
isogamético -ca (*adj.*, *Biol.*) isogametic.
isogâmetos (*m.pl.*, *Biol.*) isogametes.
isogamia (*f.*, *Biol.*) isogamy.
isógamo -ma (*adj.*, *Biol.*) isogamous.
isogênese (*f.*) isogenesis.
isogenético -ca (*adj.*) isogenetic.
isógeno -na (*adj.*) isogenous.
isogeotérmico -ca, isogeotermo -ma (*adj.*, *Geol.*) isogeothermic [line].
isógino -na (*adj.*, *Bot.*) isogynous.
isoglossa (*f.*) isogloss.
isoglóssico -ca (*adj.*) isoglossal.
isognatismo (*m.*, *Zool.*) isognathism.
isógnato -ta (*adj.*, *Zool.*) isognathous.
isógono -na (*adj.*) isogonic.
isografia (*f.*) isography.
isográfico -ca (*adj.*) isographic; homolographic.
isógrafo (*m.*) isograph.
isoietal (*adj.*, *Meteorol.*) isohyetal [line].
isolação (*f.*) isolation [= ISOLAMENTO].
isolacionismo (*m.*) isolationism.
isolacionista (*adj.*; *m.,f.*) isolationist.
isoladamente (*adv.*) singly.
isolado -da (*adj.*) isolated; lone, sole, single; detached, solitary; insulated.
isolador -dora (*adj.*) insulating; isolating; (*m.*) insulator.
—acústico, acoustic plaster, tile, etc.—de estribo, a shackle or strain insulator.
isolamento (*m.*) isolation; insulation.
isolante (*adj.*) insulating; isolating; (*m.*, *Elec.*) insulating material (rubber, etc.).
isolar (*v.t.*) to isolate, detach; to insulate; (*colloq.*) to "knock on wood"; (*v.r.*) to isolate oneself.
isolépide (*f.*, *Bot.*) bulrush (genus *Scirpus*). Var. ISÓLEPIS.
isoliquenina (*f.*, *Chem.*) isolechinin.
isólise (*f.*, *Biochem.*) isolysis.
isolisina (*f.*) = HEMOLISINA.
isologia (*f.*, *Chem.*) isology.
isólogo -ga (*adj.*, *Chem.*) isologous.
isomagnético -ca (*adj.*) isomagnetic.
isômere (*adj.*) isomerous; (*m.,f.*) isomer.

isomeria (f., Chem.) isomerism.
isomérico -ca (adj.) isomeric.
isomerismo (m., Chem.) isomerism.
isométrico -ca (adj.) isometric(al).
isometrógrafo (m.) isometrograph.
isometropia (f.) isometropia.
isomorfia (f.) = ISOMORFISMO.
isomórfico -ca (adj.) isomorphic.
isomorfismo (m.) isomorphism.
isomorfo -fa (adj.) isomorphous.
isonefélico -ca (adj., Meteorol.) isonephelic.
isonimia (f.) isonymy.
isônimo (m.) isonym, paronym [= PARÔNIMO].
isonitrila (f., Chem.) isonitrile; carbylamine.
isonomia (f.) isonomy.
isônomo -ma (adj.) isonomous.
iso-octano (m., Chem.) isooctane.
isópaco -ca (adj.) isopachous.
isópago (m., Meteorol.) isopag.
isopéctico -ca (adj., Meteorol.) isopectic.
isoperimétrico -ca (adj., Geom.) isoperimetric.
isoperímetros (m.pl., Geom.) isoperimeters.
isopétalo -la (adj., Bot.) isopetalous.
isopínico -ca (adj., Physics) isopycnic.
isopiésico -ca (adj., Thermodyn.) isopiestic.
isopírio (m., Min.) isopyre.
isópiro (m., Bot.) the genus Isopyrum.
isópode (m.; adj., Zool.) isopod; (m.pl.) the Isopoda.
isopreno (m., Chem.) isoprene.
isopropanol (m., Chem.) isopropanol, isopropyl alcohol.
isóptero -ra (adj., Zool.) isopterous; (m.pl.) the Isoptera
(termites).
isoquímeno -na (adj., Phys. Geog.) isocheimal.
isóscele[s] (adj., Geom.) isosceles.
isosmótico -ca (adj.) isosmotic.
isosporado -da (adj., Bot.) isosporous.
isossísmico -ca (adj.) isoseismic.
isóstase (f., Geol.) isostasy.
isostático -ca (adj., Physics, Geol.) isostatic.
isostêmone (adj., Bot.) isostemonous.
isotérico -ca (adj.) = ISÓTERO.
isotérmico -ca (adj.) isothermal.
isótero -ra (adj., Phys. Geog.) isotheral.
isotípico -ca (adj., Biol.) isotypical.
isótipo (m., Biol.) isotype.
isotonia (f., Biochem.) isotonia.
isotônico -ca (adj.) isotonic.
isotopia (f., Physical Chem.) isotopy.
isótopo -pa (adj.) isotopic; (m.pl.) isotopes.
isotropia (f.) isotropy.
isotrópico -ca, isótropo -pa (adj.) isotropic.
isozoóide (m., Zool.) isozooid.
isqueiro (m.) cigarette lighter; tinderbox.
isquemia (f., Med.) ischemia.
isquêmico -ca (adj., Med.) ischemic.
isquiádico -ca (adj.) = ISQUIÁTICO.
isquial (adj., Anat.) ischial.
isquianal (adj.) = ÍSQUIO-ANAL.
isquiático -ca (adj., Anat.) ischial.
isquidrose (f.) ischidrosis.
isquio[n] (m., Anat.) the ischium.
isquio-anal (adj., Anat.) ischioanal.
isquiococcígeo -gea (adj., Anat.) ischiococcygeal.
isquio-femoral (adj., Anat.) ischiofemoral.
isquio-perineal (adj., Anat.) ischioperineal.
israelita (adj.; m.,f.) Israelite.
isso (neuter dem. pron.) it, this, that, those; (scornfully)
that thing.—mesmo, That's it; That's right; Exactly.
—não me interessa, That doesn't concern me.—não tem
importância, That doesn't matter. É—, That's right.
nem por—, not even so. por—, therefore, that's why.
por—mesmo, for that very reason. por tudo—, on account of all that. sem—, but for that; without that.
Só—? Is that all?
ístmico -ca (adj.) isthmian.

istmo (m.) isthmus.
isto (neuter dem. pron.), it, this, that, those.—é, that is
(to say). por—, therefore, that's why. Que é—? What's
this?
isuretina (f., Chem.) isuretine.
itã (f.) ornate stone artefacts found in funeral urns; a
certain shell called LINGUEIRÃO.
itá (f.) a Tupi-Guarani word meaning rock or metal, used
in forming a number of Brazilian Portuguese words—
see below.
itabirito (m., Min.) itabirite.
itacolumito (m., Petrog.) itacolumite.
itacuruba (f.) = TACURUBA.
itaimbé (m.) peak; steep hill; precipice.
itaipava (f.) rock forming a waterfall; a reef extending
across a river, making it fordable.
italianada (f.) a derogatory term for a group of Italians.
italianidade (f.) Italianity.
italianismo (m.) Italianism.
italianizar (v.t.) to Italianize.
italiano -na (adj.; m.,f.) Italian.
italianófilo -la (adj.; m.,f.) Italophile.
italianomania (f.) Italomania.
itálico -ca (adj.) Italic; (Print.) italic.
ítalo -la (adj.; m.,f.) Italian.
italófilo -la (adj.) = ITALIANÓFILO.
italomania (f.) = ITALIANOMANIA.
itambé (m.) = ITAIMBÉ.
itaoca (f.) rock cave.
itapeba, itapeva (f.) "a rock shelf running parallel to the
river bank." [GBAT]
itapecerica (f.) a smooth granite mountain.
itapema (f.) = GAVIÃO-TESOURA.
itapiri [rí] (m.) = TAPIRI.
itapitanga (f.) a rockweed, c.a. GENGIBRE.
itararé (m., Geol.) limestone sinkhole [= SUMIDOURO,
ESCONDIDO, GRUNADO].
itauá (m., Bot.) a jointfir (Gnetum nodiflorum).
itaúba (f., Bot.) ita-uba (Endiandra ita-uba); also, a
species of Ocotea.—branca or -vermelha = BEBERU or
BIBIRU.—preta, a tree yielding very durable wood
(Mezilaurus itauba), c.a. CEDRO-PARDO.
ite (m., slang) "it" (sex appeal).
ité (adj.) insipid; tasteless.
item (adv.) also; likewise; (m.) item.
iteração (f.) iteration.
iterar (v.t.) to iterate, repeat.
iterativo -va (adj.) iterative.
itérbia (f., Chem.) ytterbia, ytterbium oxide.
itérbio (m., Chem.) ytterbium.
iterícia (f.) = ICTERÍCIA.
itérico -ca (adj.) = ICTÉRICO.
itinerante (adj.; m.) itinerant.
itinerário (adj.; n.) itinerary.
ítria (f., Chem.) yttria, yttrium oxide.
ítrio (m., Chem.) yttrium.
itu [ú] (m.) = JUTAIPEBA.
ituá (m.) = ITAUÁ.
ituá-açu [çú] (m.) a jointfir (Gnetum urens).
ituí (m.) an eel-like fish (Sternopygus carapus), allied to
the electric eel but having no electric organs.
ituituí (m.) = MAÇARICO-DE-COLEIRA.
itupava, itupeba, itupeva (f.) a small waterfall or river
rapids.
iúca (f., Bot.) yucca.
Iucão (m.) Yukon.
Iucatão (m.) Yucatan.
Iugoslávia (f.) Jugoslavia, Yugoslavia.
iugoslavo -va (adj.; m.,f.) Yugoslav.
ivantiji [jí] (m.) = AÇOITA-CAVALO.
iviraro (m.) = GUAIUVIRA.
ivitinga (f.) = AÇOITA-CAVALO.
Ivone (f.) Yvonne.
ixódidas [ks] (m.pl., Zool.) the Ixodidae (family of ticks).
ixômetro [ks] (m., Chem.) viscosimeter.

J

J, j (*m.*) the tenth letter of the alphabet. [For words not listed under **J**, try **G**.]

já (*adv.*) already; now, at once.—**já**, right now, immediately.—**e já**, right now, at once.—**agora**, just now. **agora**—, at once, now.—**não**, no longer.—**não existe mais**, It no longer exists.—**que**, inasmuch as, since, seeing that.—**se vê**, of course; to be sure.—**vou!** I'm coming! **desde já**, immediately, from right now.

jabá (*m.*) jerked beef [= IABÁ, CHARQUE].

jabebireta (*f.*), **jabebiretê** (*m., Zool.*) a sting ray (*Dasyatis gymnura*), c.a. RAIA-LIXA.

jabiraca (*f.*) a fury; virago; old or ill-fitting clothes.

jabiru [ú] (*m.*) = JABURU.

jaborandi [í] (*m., Bot.*) the jaborandi pilocarpus (*Pilocarpus jaborandi*), whose dried leaflets yield pilocarpine. Also, the jaborandi pepper (*Piper jaborandi*), possessing similar properties.—**-do-ceará**, the spike pilocarpus (*P. pennatifolius*).—**-do-pará** is *Monniera trifolia*, c.a. ALFAVACA-DE-COBRA.

jaborina (*f., Pharm.*) jaborin(e).

jaboticaba (*f.*) = JABUTICABA.

jaburu [rú] (*m.*) the jabiru stork (*Jabiru mycteria*), c.a. JABIRU, TAPUCAJA; fig., an unkempt, ungainly, person. —**-moleque**, the American stork (*Euxenura maguari* or *E. galeata*), c.a. MANGUARI, BAGUARI, CEGONHA, CAUAUÁ.

jabuti [í] (*m.*) a fruit-eating Brazilian land turtle (*Testudo tabulata*) which lives chiefly in the forests; a primitive cotton gin.—**-aperema**, a terrestrial turtle (*Niconia punctulata*), c.a. APEREMA, PITIÚ.—**-da-várzea**, a medium-sized tree (*Erisma uncinatum*), of the copaifé family, "the seeds of which contain 50 percent of a white fat analogous to that from the jabuti turtle (hence the name of the plant). Fat used in frying, cooking, etc." [*GUAF*]—**-machado**, a fresh-water turtle (*Podocnemis platycephala*), c.a. MACHADINHA.

jabuticaba (*f.*) the round, blue-black, pulpy fruit of the JABUTICABEIRA.—**-de-cipó** = ABUTUA-GRANDE.

jabuticabeira (*f., Bot.*) the jaboticaba (*Myciaria cauliflora*).

jaca (*m.*) jack, the fruit of a large tree (see JAQUEIRA) closely allied to the breadfruit, often weighing forty pounds or more. The pulp is insipid but the seeds are eaten, roasted or otherwise.—**-do-pará**, a soursop (*Annona muricata*).

jacá (*m.*) a wicker hamper, esp. for transporting chickens, pigs, farm produce, etc.

jaça (*f.*) flaw, fault, imperfection, esp. in precious stones; (*colloq.*) calaboose. **sem**—, flawless, perfect.

jacaçu [ú] (*m.*) = POMBA-TROCAZ.

jacaió (*m., Zool.*) the common jacamar (*Galbula galbula*).

jacamacira (*m.*) the spot-tailed jacamar (*Galbula rufoviridis*).

jacamaici [cí] (*m.*) the paradise jacamar (*Urogalba dea dea*).

jacamim (*m.*) the agami or trumpeter (*Psophia crepitans*), and other birds of this genus. [It is a very large, long-legged, long-necked, easily domesticated bird, and, in Brazil, is often kept to protect poultry. Its cry is loud, clear, and prolonged.] Other names are: AGAMI, TROMBETEIRO, TROMBONE, PÁSSARO-TROMBETA.—**-copejuba**, or **-das-costas-amarelas**, the ochre-winged trumpeter (*Psophia leucoptera ochroptera*).—**-copetinga**, or **-de-costas-brancas**, the white-winged trumpeter (*Psophia l. leucoptera*).—**-prêto**, or **-das-costas-pretas**, the dusky trumpeter (*Psophia viridis obscura*), c.a. JACAMIM-UNA, JACAMIÚNA.

jacamincá (*f.*) a dayflower (*Commelina*).

jaçanã (*f.*) the common jacana (*Jacana spinosa*). [Their feet are equipped with extremely long toes which enable them to run about on lily pads and other floating vegetation.]

jaçapé (*m., Bot.*) a sedge (*Kyllinga odorata*), c.a. CAPIM-DE-CHEIRO.

jacapucaia (*f.*) = FRUTA-DE-MACACO.

jacaranda (*m.*) any of the tall pinnate-leaved tropical trees of the genus *Jacaranda* (family *Bignoniaceae*), esp. the Brazil jacaranda (*J. brasiliensis*); the sharpleaf jacaranda (*J. acutifolia* or *J. mimosaefolia*), c.a. CAROBAGUAÇU, PALISSANDRA, common in Florida and southern California where it is prized for its showy paniculate blue flowers; the copaia jacaranda (*J. copaia*), c.a. CARAÚBA; the toothleaf jacaranda (*J. cuspidifolia*). [Do not confuse **jacaranda** with JACARANDÁ.]

jacarandá (*m.*) any of several tropical leguminous trees, family *Fabaceae*, or their heavy dark wood, usually called rosewood. (The black or Brazilian rosewood of commerce is *Dalbergia nigra*, and is c.a. CABIÚNA, JACARANDÁ-CABIÚNA, JACARANDÁ-PRÊTO.) [Do not confuse **jacarandá** with JACARANDA.]

jacaré (*m.*) any alligator or cayman; frog of a railroad switch; a pointing trowel; a squeezing device used in pharmacies to soften dry corks [from its resemblance to the jaws of an alligator]; a large heavy knife used by the backwoodsmen of Bahia; an earpodtree (*Enterolobium monjolo*), c.a. MONJOLO; "the commonest variety of cacao tree, with an elongated pod sometimes curved at the end, and always a noticeable narrowing near the base, which is itself hooked." [*GBAT*]; (*slang*) a young man who loiters near the church entrance awaiting his inamorata.—**-açu**, the large black Amazon cayman (*Melanosuchus niger*), said to attain a length of 20 feet. —**-bicudo**, an alligator (*A. lucius*).—**-copaíba**, a wallabatree (*Eperua oleifera*).—**-coroa**, or—**-curuá**, the smooth-fronted cayman (*Paleosuchus trigonatus*), c.a. CURULANA. —**-de-lunetas**, or—**-de-óculos**, the spectacled cayman (*Caiman scleros*), c.a. JACARETINGA.—**-de-papo-amarelo**, the broad-nosed cayman (*Caiman latirostris*).—**-do-campo** = GALINHA-CHOCA (a tree).—**-pinima**, a teiid lizard (*Ameiva ameiva*), c.a. CALANGO, CALANGRO, CAMALEÃO, CAMBALEÃO-FERRO, BICO-DOCE.—**-una** = JACARÉ-AÇU.

jacarerana (*m.*) a forked-tongued lizard (*Crocodilurus lacertilus*).

jacaretinga (*m.*) an alligator (*A. palpebrosus*); the Paraguay cayman (*Caiman yacare*); also = JACARÉ-DE-ÓCULOS.

jacareúba, jacareúva (*f., Bot.*) the Brazil beautyleaf (*Calophyllum brasiliense*), c.a. GUANANDI.

jacarina (*f.*) = SERRA-SERRA.

jacaruaru [arú] (*m.*) = CAFERANA.

jacaruba (*f., Bot.*) an apes-earring (*Pithecellobium latifolium*).

jacatirão (*m., Bot.*) a meadow beauty (*Miconia prasina*). —**-de-capote** = CUIPEÚNA.

jacatirica (*f.*) = JAGUATIRICA.

jacatupé (*m., Bot.*) West Indies yambean (*Pachyrhizus tuberosus*), c.a. JOCOTUPÉ.

jacàzinho (*m.*) a small woven basket in which coffee seedlings are first started, the whole later being planted where the tree is to grow.

jacente (*adj.*) recumbent, lying; (*m.*) a bridge girder.

jacina (*f.*) kinds of dragonflies, c.a. LAVA(N)DEIRA, PITO.

Jacinta (*f.*) Hyacinth.

jacinto (*m. Min.*) jacinth, jargon, hyacinth, zircon; (*Bot.*) hyacinth.—**-das-searas**, the tassel grapehyacinth (*Muscari comosum*).—**-do-oriente**, common hyacinth (*Hyacinthus orientalis*).—**-serôdio**, a plant of the lily family (*Dipcadi serotina*).

jacitara (*f.*) any Brazilian bramble palm of the genus *Desmoncus*.

Jacó (*m.*) Jacob; James.

jacobéia (*f., Bot.*) the ragwort groundsel (*Senecio jacobaea*).

jacobinismo (*m.*) Jacobinism; jingoism.

jacobino (*m.*) a Jacobin; an extreme nationalist.

jacobita (*adj.; m.*) Jacobite.

jacobitismo (*m.*) Jacobitism.

jacobsita (*f., Min.*) jacobsite.

já-começa (*f., colloq.*) an itch(ing).

jacruaru [arú] (*m.*) the yellow-banded tegu (*Tupinambis nigro-punctatus*), a large and vicious lizard, c.a. IACURUARÚ, JACRUARÚ, JACUARÚ; also = TEIUAÇU (another tegu).

ja[c]tância (*f.*) boasting; braggadocio; vainglory; vanity, self-conceit.

ja[c]tancioso -sa (*adj.*) proud, haughty; boastful; vainglorious.

ja[c]tar-se (v.t.) to boast (de, of), brag (de, about); to bluster; to talk big.

ja[c]to (m.) jet, stream, gush, spurt.—da hélice, slipstream, backwash (of a propeller).—de areia, sand blast.—de luz, a sudden beam of light. aos—s, in spurts. propulsão a—, jet propulsion.

jacu [ú] (m., Zool.) any guan (Penelope), esp. Spix's guan (P. superciliaris).—molambo, a ground cuckoo (Neomorphus geoffroyi dulcis), c.a. JACU-PORCO.—do-norte, the white-headed guan (P. pileata), c.a. JACUAÇU, JACU-VERMELHO.—velho jacupeba.

jacuapeti [i] (m.) = JACUTINGA.

jacuaru [rú] (m.) = JACRUARU.

jacuba (f.) = CHIBÉ.

jacucaca (m., Zool.) the brown guan (Penelope jacu-caca).

jacuguaçu [çú] (m., Zool.) the large bronze-green guan (Penelope obscura bronzina).

jaculatório -ria (adj.) jaculatory; (f.) ejaculatory prayer.

jacumã (m.) "a steering sweep." [GBAT]

jacumaíba jacumaúba (m.) "(1) one who works the JACUMÃ; (2) the pilot of a small boat." [GBAT]

jacundá (m., Bot.) bigleaf calathea (C. ornata); also any of various cichloid fishes, genus Crenicichla.

jacupará (m.) = JACUTINGA.

jacupeba, jacupem[b]a (m., Zool.) the superciliated guan (Penelope superciliaris), c.a. JACU, JACU-VELHO.

jacupói (m., Zool.) Sclater's guan (Penelope sclateri).

jacuruaru [arú] (m.) = JACRUARU.

jacurutu [tú] (m., Zool.) Magellan's great horned owl (Buco virginianus magellanicus), c.a. JUCURUTU.

jacuruxi [í] (m.) the caiman lizard (Dracaena guianensis).

jacutaquara (m.) = JURUVA.

jacutinga (m., Zool.) the black-fronted piping guan (Pipile jacutinga), c.a. PERU-DO-MATO, JACUAPETI, JACU-PARÁ; (Geol.) a variety of hematitic iron ore occurring in the State of Rio de Janeiro.

jacutupé (m.) = JACATUPÉ.

jade (m.) jade.

jadeíta (f., Min.) jadeite.

jaez [ê] (m.) harness, trappings; ilk, kind, sort; quality, nature.

jaezar (v.) = AJAEZAR.

jaguacatiguaçu [çú] (m.) = ARIRAMBA-GRANDE.

jaguapé (m.) = IRARA.

jaguar (m.) the jaguar (Felis onca), better known as ONÇA-PINTADA.

jaguaramuru [rú] (m., Bot.) the bigflower cordia (C. grandiflora), c.a. JARAGUAMURU.

jaguaré, jaguarecaca, jaguarecagua (m.) = CANGAMBÁ.

jaguareçá (m.) a squirrelfish (Holocentrus ascencionis), c.a. JAGUARIÇÁ, JAGUARUÇÁ.

jaguaripe (m., Bot.) the catclaw mimosa (M. biuncifera), c.a. UNHA-DE-GATO.

jaguaritaca (m.) = GAMBÁ.

jaguaruçá (m.) squirrel fish (Holocentrus ascencionis), c.a. JAGUARIÇÁ, JAGUAREÇÁ, JOÃO-CACHAÇA.

jaguarundi[í] (m., Zool.) the yaguarundi. [Webster: "A grayish unspotted wildcat (Herpailurus jaguarundi), ranging from Paraguay to southern Texas, by some considered a color variety of the eyra."]; c.a. GATO-MOURISCO.

jaguatirão (m.) = CUIPEÚNA.

jaguatirica (f.) a spotted leopard-cat (Leopardus pardalis chibiguazu), c.a. JACATIRICA, GATO-DO-MATO-GRANDE, MARACAJÁ.

jagunçada, jagunçaria (f.) a gang of ruffians.

jagunço (m.) hired assassin; ruffian, hoodlum; thug.

jaibradeira (f.) = JAVRADEIRA.

jaibro (m.) = JAVRE.

Jaime (m.) James.

jalão (m.) leveling rod; also = (Bot.) JAMELÃO.

jalapa (f., Bot.) jalap (Exogonium purga) which yields a purgative tuberous root.—de-lisboa = BATATA-DE-PURGA.—verdadeira, the common four-o'clock (Mirabilis jalapa), c.a. BONINA.

jalapão (m., Bot.) a nettlespurge Jatropla elliptica; c.a. TIÚ.

jalapina (f., Chem.) jalapin.

jalapinha (f.) the Trinidad morning-glory (Ipomoea sinuata); the Brazil dipladenia (D. splendens), c.a. ESPIR-RADEIRA-DO-CAMPO.

jalde (adj.) = JALNE.

jaleca (f.) = JAQUETA.

jaleco (m.) jacket; also = TAMANDUÁ-MIRIM; GALEGO.

jalne (adj.) bright golden yellow.

jamacaru [ú] (m.) = PRINCÊSA-DA-NOITE; CARDO-DA-PRAIA.

jamaiquinho (m.) bantam domestic fowl.

jamais (adv.) never; at no time.

jamanta (f.) devilfish, gigantic ray (Manta birostris), c.a. MORCÊGO-DO-MAR, PEIXE-DIABO; (m.) an unkempt person.

jamaru [ú] (m., Bot.) a cucurbit whose large gourds are used as feeding troughs, dippers, etc.

jamba (f.) door jamb.

jambeiro (m., Bot.) any of several myrtles of the genus Syzygium.

jâmbico -ca (adj.) iambic; satirical.

jambo (m.) iamb [= IAMBO].—rosa, the rose apple (Syzygium jambos).—vermelho, the ohia or Malay apple (Syzygium malaccense).

jambolão (m.) = JAMELÃO.

jambu [ú] (m., Bot.) the Paracress spotflower (Spilanthes oleracea), c.a. ABECEDÁRIA, JAMBUAÇU; a composite (Wulffia stenoglossa), c.a. CRAVEIRO-DO-CAMPO, JAM-BURANA.

jamburana (f.) a pepper plant (Piper tuberculatum); also = JAMBU.

jamegão (m., colloq.) "John Hancock" (one's signature).

jamelão (m., Bot.) the jambolan (Syzygium cumini), c.a. JALÃO, JAMBOLÃO.

jamesonita (f., Min.) jamesonite.

jan. = JANEIRO (January).

janatuba (f., Bot.) a muskwood (Guarea pendula).

janaúba (Bot.) a frangipani (Plumeria drastica).

jandaia (f.) the yellow-headed paroquet of eastern Brazil (Eupsitula jendaya), c.a. NANDAIA, NHANDAIA. [This, it is believed, is the bird immortalized in Alencar's classic, "Iracema."] Also, the golden-fronted paroquet (Eupsitula auricapillus aurifrons), c.a. PERIQUITO-REI.

jandaíra (f.) a kind of bee.

jandiá (m.) any freshwater catfish.

jandiparana (m.) = JENIPAPARANA.

jandiroba (f.) = ANDIROBA.

janeireiro -ra (adj.) of January; born in or occurring in January.

janeiro (m.) January; (pl.) years of age.

janela (f.) window; a slit or other opening; (Geol.) erosion thrust.—arcada, arched window.—de correr, sliding window.—de guilhotina, or de suspender, a window with vertical sliding sashes.

janelar (v.i.) to spend much time at the front window.

janeleiro -ra (adj.) said of one who spends much time at the front window, esp. a young woman engaged in furtive love-making or coquetry.

jangada (f.) a raft, esp. a very seaworthy kind of catamaran used by fishermen off the coast of northeastern Brazil. [The typical jangada consists of five extraordinarily light tibourbou (Apeiba) logs lashed together. It is 20 to 25 feet long and 6 to 7 feet wide, has a single mast, and is manned by three men who frequently stay out days at a time.]—brava, a tree of the linden family (Heliocarpus americanus).

jangadeira (f.) a tree of the linden family (Apeiba tibourbou) whose light wood is used in raft-making; c.a. PAU-DE-JANGADA, PAU-FÔFO.

jangadeiro (m.) the owner of a JANGADA.

jângal, jângala (m.) jungle.

jangalamarte (m.) see-saw.

janipaba, janipabeiro, janipapeiro (m.) = JENIPAPEIRO.

janipapo (m.) = JENIPAPO.

janiparandiba, janiparanduba (f.) = JENIPAPARANA.

janistroques (m., colloq.) a nobody.

janízaro (m.) janizary.

jano = JANEIRO (January).

janota (adj.) foppish, dandyish, dapper; (m.) fop, dandy, coxcomb, dude.

janotar (v.i.) to play the dude.

janotice (f.), janotismo (m.) foppery.

janta (f., colloq.) dinner.

jantar (m.) dinner; (v.i.) to dine; to eat dinner.—fora de casa, to dine out.—mal, to dine poorly. a hora de—, dinner-time. filante de—es, a sponger of meals. sala de—, dining room.

jantarão (m.) a fine dinner, a banquet.

jaó (m., Zool.) either the banded tinamou (Crypturellus u. undulatus) or the zabele red-footed tinamou (Crypturellus noctivagus zabele).

jap. = JAPONÊS(A) (Japanese).

japa (*f.*) = INHAPA; GORGETA.

japá (*m.*) a mat woven from palm leaves (esp. of the pindova palm, *Attalea humilis*) and used extensively in Amazonas as awnings on small river boats, and for thatching or screening.

japacanim (*m.*, *Zool.*) the black-capped mocking-thrush (*Donacobius a. atricapillus*), c.a. SABIÁ-GUAÇU, SABIÁ-DO-BREJO, CASACA-DE-COURO, VIOLA, PINTASSILGO-DO-BREJO, BATUQUIRA, ANGU, PÁSSARO-ANGU, ARREBITA-RABO.

japaconina (*f.*, *Chem.*) japaconin(e).

japaconitina (*f.*, *Chem.*) japaconitin(e).

japani[m] (*m.*, *Bot.*) a nitta tree (*Parkia oppositifolia*).

Japão (*m.*) Japan.

japaranduba (*f.*) = JENIPAPARANA.

japecanga (*f.*, *Bot.*) a sarsaparilla (*Smilax japicanga*).

japeraçaba (*f.*, *Bot.*) the piassava attalea palm (*A. funifera*).

japiaçoca (*f.*) = JAÇANÃ.

japim (*m.*) a common Brazilian oriole—the yellow-rumped cacique (*Cacicus c. cela*), c.a. XEXÉU, JOÃO-CONGUINHO. [It is black and golden-yellow and a great mimic of other birds.]—**-de-costa-vermelha** (or **-de-mata-encarnado**) the red-rumped cacique (*Cacicus h. haemorrhous*).

japira (*m.*) = GUAXE.

japona (*f.*) a short jacket; also = GALEGO.

japonês –nêsa (*adj.; m.,f.*) Japanese.

japonesismo (*m.*) Japanism.

japonista (*m.,f.*) Japanologist.

japonizar (*v.t.*) to Japonize.

japu (ú) (*m.*) a large and well-known Brazilian bird of the oriole family: the pied crested oropendola (*Xanthornus decumanus maculosus*), c.a. JAPU-GUAÇU, JOÃO-CONGO, RUBIXÁ. [It is mostly black, with a yellow bill which mounts on the forehead, forming a frontal shield. The occiput is crested. The **japu** build their nests in large colonies, and have voracious appetites].—**-açu** is Spix's oropendola (*Gymnostinops bifasciatus*).—**-irá** = GUAXE. —**-verde**, the green oropendola (*Xanthornus v. viridis*).

japuaranduba (*f.*) = JENIPAPARANA.

japuçá (*m.*) titi (any small reddish or grayish monkey of the genus *Callicebus*).

japuruca (*f.*) a centipede (*Scolopendra marsitani*).

jaque (*m.*) union jack (signal flag).

jaqueira (*f.*) the jakfruit (*Artocarpus heterophyllus*).

jaqueta [ê] (*f.*) a short jacket; (*m.*) an old fogy.

jaquetão (*m.*) a double-breasted coat.

jaquiranabóia (*f.*) a large lantern fly (*Fulgora laternaria* or *F. lucifera*) whose bite is erroneously believed to be harmful; c.a. JEQUITIRANABOIA, TIRAMBÓIA, COBRA-DE-ASA, COBRA-DO-AR.

jará (*f.*, *Bot.*) a piassava palm (*Leopoldinia pulchra*), c.a. JARAIÚBA, JARAIÚVA; also = CURUARANA.

jarabandaia (*m.*) = MANDACHUVA.

jaracatiá (*m.*, *Bot.*) a close relative of the common papaya, c.a. MAMOEIRO-DO-MATO.

jaraguá (*m.*, *Bot.*) a tall forage grass (*Hyparrhenia rufa*) of Brazil, c.a. PROVISÓRIO.

jaraguamuru [rú] (*m.*) = JAGUARAMURU.

jaraiúba, jaraiúva (*f.*) = JARÁ.

jarandeua (*f.*, *Bot.*) an apes-earring (*Pithecellobium latifolium*).

jaranganha (*f.*, *Bot.*) the edible bomarea (*B. edulis*).

jarara (*f.*) = COBRA-DE-CAPIM or COBRA-DE-LIXO.

jararaca (*f.*, *Bot.*) the Brazil dragon aroid (*Dracontium asperum*); (*colloq.*) a harridan; a common collective term for the highly dangerous pit vipers of the lance-head type (*Bothrops*) frequent throughout Brazil, esp. *B. jararaca*, c.a. JARARACA-DO-CAMPO (or -DO-CERRADO, or -DA-MATA).—**-ilhoa**, a three-foot species (*B. insularis*) confined to an island off the coast of southern Brazil.—**-pintada** (or **-de-rabo-branco**), one of the most widespread of the Brazilian pit vipers (*B. neuweidii*), c.a. BÔCA-DE-SAPO, URUTÚ, TIRA-PEIA.—**-preta** = COTIARA.—**-verde** = SURUCUCU-DE-PATIOBA. [The term **jararaca** is used also to designate various harmless snakes, such as:—**-da-praia**, the harmless COBRA-NARIGUDA;—**-preguiçosa**, the harmless DORMIDEIRA;—**-de-barriga-vermelha**, the timid and quite harmless little JARARAQUINHA-DO-CAMPO;—**-do-banhado**, the harmless COBRA-NOVA, c.a. JARA-RACUÇU-DO-BREJO.]

jararacambeva (*f.*) = BOIPEVA.

jararacuçu [çú] (*m.*) an extremely dangerous Brazilian pit viper (*Bothrops jararacussu*), allied to but larger than the fer-de-lance, c.a. JARARACUÇU-VERDADEIRO, JARARACUÇU-MALHA-DE-SAPO, JARARACUÇU-CABEÇA-DE-SAPO, JARARACUÇU-TAPETE, PATRONA, SURUCUCU-DOU-RADO, SURUCUCU-TAPÊTE, URUTU-DOURADO, URUTU-ESTRÊLA.—**-do-brejo**, the harmless COBRA-NOVA.

jararaquinha-do-campo (*f.*) a harmless two-foot colubrine Brazilian snake (*Leimadophis almadensis*), c.a. JARA-RACA-DE-BARRIGA-VERMELHA, COBRA-ESPADA.

jaratataca, jaraticaca jaratitaca (*f.*) = CANGAMBÁ.

jarázal (*m.*) a tract abounding in JARÁS (piassava palms).

jarda (*f.*) a yard (36 inches); = 0.9144 mt.

jardim (*m.*) garden; flower-garden.—**-da-infância**, kinder-ga:ten.—**público**, public park.—**zoológico**, a zoo.

jardinagem (*f.*) gardening; selective logging.

jardinar (*v.i.*) to garden.

jardineira (*f.*) a jardiniere; an ornamental stand or small table; a woman gardener; a preparation of mixed vegetables; (*colloq.*) a small passenger bus.

jardineiro (*m.*) a man gardener.

jardinista (*m.,f.*) a garden enthusiast.

jarerê (*m.*) a hand net for catching shrimp and small fish; c.a. JERERÊ, PUÇÁ, LANDUÁ.

jareuá (*f.*) = CURUARANA.

jargão (*m.*) jargon; slang; (*Min.*) jacinth (reddish-orange zircon).

jarina (*Bot.*) the common ivorypalm (*Phytelephas macrocarpa*), c.a. MARFIM-VEGETAL. [This species is the source of the vegetable-ivory of commerce. Not to be confused with Metroxylon, the ivory-nutpalm.]

jaritacaca, jaritataca (*f.*) = CANGAMBÁ.

jarivá (*f.*) an astrocaryum palm (*A. acaule*).

jaroba (*f.*, *Bot.*) the Trinidad ropevine (*Tanaecium jaroba*).

jarosite (*f.*, *Min.*) jarosite.

jarra (*f.*) jar, vase, esp. for flowers; (*Naut.*) water keg, cask or butt. Cf. JARRO.

jarretar (*v.t.*) to hamstring; to cripple or disable.

jarrête (*m.*) hock (of a horse); hamstring.

jarreteira (*f.*) garter; the Order of the Garter.

jarrinha (*f.*, *Bot.*) any of several species of *Aristolochia* (dutchmanspipe) of the birthwort family, esp. *A. brasiliensis*, c.a. ANGELICÓ, CAÇAÚ.—**-de-franja**, the Argentine dutchmanspipe (*A. frimbriata*).—**-pintada**, the calico dutchmanspipe (*A. elegans*), c.a. CIPÓ-MIL-HOMENS.

jarro (*m.*) water pitcher; jug; (*Bot.*) any of various aroids, such as TAIOBA. Cf. JARRA.

jarruva (*f.*, *Bot.*) a prickly ash (*Zanthoxylum praecox*).

jarumá (*m.,f.*) an Indian of the Yarumá, a Cariban tribe on the upper Xingu River; (*adj.*) pert. to or designating this tribe.

jaruva (*f.*) the amorpha honeylocust (*Gleditsia amorphoides*), c.a. ESPINHILHO, ESPINHO-DE-CRISTO.

jasmim (*m.*) jasmine; also a combining name for a number of unrelated plants.—**-amarelo**, the yellow or Carolina jessamine (*Gelsemium sempervirens*), c.a. GELSÊMIO; the Italian jasmine (*Jasminum humile*).—**-azul**,—**-da-terra**, —**-de-soldado**,—**-de-caiena**, are all names for the china-berry (*Melia azederach*); also = CAÁ-POMONGA and BELA-EMÍLIA.—**-cambraia**, an oleander (*Nerium ochrolenum*). —**-catavento** and—**-pipoca** are the palovivara taber-naemontana (*T. australis*).—**-da-áfrica**, a wolf-berry (*Lycium afrum*).—**-da-arábia**, an night jasmine (*Nyc-thanthes*), c.a. NICTANTO.—**-da-virgínia** = GELSÊMIO.— **-de-cachorro** or —**-de-leite**, a tabernaemontana (*T. laeta*), c.a. CAFÉ-DO-MATO.—**-de-veneza**, the common trumpetcreeper (*Campsis radicans*).—**-do-cabo**, Cape jasmine (*Gardenia jasminoides*).—**-do-imperador**, sweet osmanthus (*O. fragrans*), c.a. FLOR-DO-IMPERADOR.— **-do-mato**, the orange-leaf tabernaemontana (*T. citri-folia*); also = BACUPARI-AÇU, JASMIM-MANGA-DA-ÍNDIA.— **-do-mato-do-pará**, the red jasmine or nosegay frangipani (*Plumeria rubra*), c.a. JASMIM-DE-SÃO-JOSÉ, JASMIM-VAPOR.—**-dos-açores**, the Azores jasmine (*J. azoricum*). —**-laranja**, the Chinabox jasminorange (*Murraya exotica*).—**-manga**, a frangipani (*Plumeria tricolor*).— **-manga-da-índia**, a cerberus tree (*Cerbera mangas*).— **-porcelana**, the crape jasmine tabernaemontana (*T. coronaria*).—**-verde**, the nightblooming jessamine (*Cestrum nocturnum*).

jasmineiro (*m.*) a jasmine shrub.

Jasão (*m.*) Jason.

jaspe (*m.*) jasper.—**-prêto** or **-negro**, touchstone.

jatá (*f.*) = IATÁ.

jataí (*m.*, *Bot.*) the courbaril tree (*Hymenaea courbaril*), c.a. JATOBÁ, JATUBÁ, PÃO-DE-LÓ-DE-MICO.—**-mindé**, a purpleheart tree (*Peltogyne discolor*).—**-mosquito,**—**-preta** = ABELHA-MIRIM.
jatância (*f.*) = JACTÂNCIA.
jatancioso **-sa** (*adj.*) = JACTANCIOSO.
jatar-se (*v.*) = JACTAR-SE.
jataúba (*f.*) = CARRAPETA-VERDADEIRA.
jati [í] (*f.*) = ABELHA-MIRIM.
jaticá (*m.*) a long harpoon employed along the Amazon for catching turtles.
jato (*m.*) = JACTO.
jatobá (*m.*) = JATAÍ.—**-do-campo**, a senna (*Cassia*).—**-mirim**, the copaiba copaltree (*Copaifera officinalis*), c.a. COPAÍBA-VERDADEIRA.
jatuamba (*f.*) = CARRAPETA-VERDADEIRA.
jatuarana (*f.*, *Bot.*) a bitterwood (*Trichilia singularis*); (*Zool.*) a characinid (*Hemiodus microcephalus*).
jatuaúba-branca (*f.*) = CARRAPETA-VERDADEIRA; PAU-BALA.
jatuaúba-preta (*f.*, *Bot.*) black muskwood (*Guarea thompsoni*).
jatubá (*m.*) = JATAÍ.
jaú (*m.*) a very large Amazon catfish (*Paulicea lutkeni*); a suspended scaffold (as used by painters, etc.).
jauá (*m.*) the red-browed parrot (*Amazona rhodocorytha*) of S. E. Brazil.
jauari [a-u-arí] (*m.*) an astrocaryum palm (*A. jauary*), "common along the low alluvial banks of the Amazonian rivers; . . . trunk from 10 to 15 meters high, armed with black thorns 3 to 5 cms. long; leaves 3 meters long; . . . the nut is hard and contains 21 per cent fatty matter; . . . folioles yield very strong fibers; when split the folioles may be used in the manufacture of straw hats; the split epidermis of the petiole is raw material for woven mats and TIPITIS; fruit pulp contains an edible oil." [*GUAF*]
jaula (*f.*) a cage, esp. for wild animals.
jaulapiti [tí] (*m.*,*f.*) an Indian of the Yaulapiti, an Arawakan tribe of the upper Xingu River in Mato Grosso; (*adj.*) pert. to or designating this tribe.
javaé (*m.*,*f.*) a member of a fast-disappearing group of the CARAJÁ (which see); (*adj.*) pert. to or designating the Javaé. Var. XAVAÉ.
javali [í] (*m.*) the European wild boar (*Sus scrofa*), c.a. PORCO-BRAVO, PORCO-MONTÊS; also, sometimes, the South American peccary. [Fem. **javalina** and **gironda**.]
javradeira (*f.*) croze (cooper's tool).
javre (*m.*) croze (groove near either end of a barrel stave).
jazer [54] (*v.i.*) to lie (at rest, in the grave, etc.); to be situated, located. **Aqui jaz (fulano)**, Here lies (so and so).
jazida (*f.*) bed or layer of ore; a mine; act of lying or resting; a resting place, bed or couch.
jazigo (*m.*) grave, tomb; burial monument; ore deposit, mine; resting place or shelter.
J.C. = JESUS CRISTO (Jesus Christ).
J.ᵉ = JOSÉ (Joseph).
jê or **jé** (*m.*,*f.*) a Ge or Gesan, or so-called Tapuyan—an Indian of the Ge linguistic family comprising many South American tribes. Var. GÊ.
jebaru [ú] (*m.*) a wallabatree (*Eperua purpurea*), c.a. JEBARO, JEBARA.
jeca (*m.*) backwoodsman, rustic, hayseed, rube.—**-tatu**, a fictitious name for the typical CAIPIRA.
jecoral (*adj.*, *Anat.*) jecoral.
jecorina (*f.*, *Biochem.*) jecorin.
jecuíba (*f.*, *Bot.*) a Brazilian cariniana (*C. brasiliensis*), c.a. JEQUITIBÁ.
jecuiriti [tí] (*m.*) = JEQUIRITI.
jefersite (*f.*, *Min.*) jeffersite.
jefersônia (*f.*, *Bot.*) the twinleaf (*Jeffersonia spp.*).
jeira (*f.*) a yoke of land (an old land measure based originally on the amount of plowing done in one day by a plowman and his yoke of oxen); a day's work; a day's wages. **à—**, by the day. Var. GEIRA.
jeitão (*m.*) a person's characteristic aspect, trait, habit or manner.
jeito (*m.*) way, manner; tact; air, appearance; knack, adroitness, aptitude; dexterity. **ao—de**, in the manner of. **com—**, adroitly; properly; tactfully. **com—de**, having the manner and appearance of. **dar (um)—**, to find a way (of doing something); to fix things; to manage, arrange; also, to sprain (an ankle), wrench (one's back, etc.). **Dá-se um—**, We'll fix it somehow. **de qualquer—**, by hook or by crook; in some way or other. **de todo o—**, of

all kinds. **desse (deste)—**, in that (this) way; by that (this) means. **falta de—**, clumsiness. **fazer força contra o—**, to go against nature. **ficar sem—**, to be ill at ease, awkward, embarrassed. **nao ter—para**, to have no knack or talent for something; to be no good at something. **Não tem—mesmo**, It's hopeless, no use trying. **pelo—**, from the looks of things. **sem—**, clumsy, awkward, all thumbs; bungling. **Tem—de estrangeiro**, He looks like a foreigner.
jeitoso **-sa** (*adj.*) adroit, dexterous, deft; tactful; handsome; appropriate.
jejá (*f.*) a certain ant (*Camponotus abdominalis*), c.a. TABOCA.
jejerecu, jejerucu [cú] (*m.*) = COAJERUCU.
jejuador **-dora** (*adj.*) fasting; (*m.*,*f.*) one who fasts.
jejuar (*v.i.*) to fast.
jejuíra (*f.*) = GONÇALO-ALVES.
jejum (*m.*) fasting, fast. **em—**, fasting. **quebrar o—**, to break fast.
jejuno **-na** (*adj.*) in a period of fasting; (*m.*, *Anat.*) jejunum. [But not jejune, which is ESCASSO, ÁRIDO, INSÍPIDO.]
jeneúna (*f.*) = CANAFISTULA.
jenipá (*m.*) = JENIPAPEIRO.
jenipapada (*f.*) a dessert made of sliced genipap and sugar; a refreshing drink made from the genipap.
jenipaparana (*f.*) a tropical tree (*Gustavia augusta*) of the sapucaia-nut family (*Lecythidaceae*), c.a. JANIPARANDIBA, JANIPARANDUBA, JAPARANDUBA, JENIPARANA, JAPUARANDUBA, JANDIPARANA, PAU-FEDORENTO. [It is "a small tree with white flexible timber which gives off a fetid odor when wet or burned; the bark contains tannin; the flowers are large, white or rose-colored. Timber used for ornamental purposes and for furniture manufacture." *GUAF*]; —**-da-mata**, a similar tree, is *Gustavia pterocarpa*. Cf. JENIPARANA.
jenipapo (*m.*) = JENIPAPO-BRAVO.
jenipapeiro (*m.*, *Bot.*) the marmaladebox genip (*Genipa americana*) whose elastic and flexible wood is used for carriage wheels, rims and spokes, boat ribs, tennis rackets, barrel hoops, tool handles, etc. The bark yields tannin and the orange-sized fruit is edible. Other names are: JENIPÁ, JENIPAPINHO, JANIPABA, JANIPABEIRO, JANIPAPO, JANIPAPEIRO.
jenipapinho (*m.*) = JENIPAPEIRO.
jenipapo (*m.*) genipap (the edible orange-sized fruit of the JENIPAPEIRO); also, the tree itself.—**-bravo,**—**-do-campo**, a rubiaceous shrub (*Tocoyena formosa*) with beautiful flowers and edible fruit which tastes something like PURUÍ; c.a. JENIPAPIM, PAU-DE-CERA, PURUÍ-DA-COSTA.
jeniparana (*f.*) any of various tropical trees of the sapucaia-nut family (*Lecythidaceae*), esp. of the genus *Gustavia*.—**-da-mata** is *Gustavia fastuosa*. Cf. JENIPAPARANA.
Jeová (*m.*) Jehovah.
jequi (*m.*) "a funnel-shaped device of woven splints used to catch fish." [*GBAT*]
jequirana = GUARUMBÉ; AMENDOIM-DE-VEADO.
jequiriti [tí] (*m.*, *Bot.*) the jequirity rosary pea or Indian licorice (*Abrus precatorius*) whose scarlet-and-black seeds are used by people in tropical regions as beads in rosaries and necklaces; c.a. FRUTA-DE-CONTA, ÔLHO-DE-POMBO, ÔLHO-DE-CABRA, ARVOEIRO, ASSACÚ-MIRIM.
jequitá (*m.*) a bramble palm (*Desmoncus rudentum*).
jequitibá (*m.*) any tree of the genus *Cariniana*, (esp. *C. domestica* or *C. brasiliensis*), a small but important genus of large So. Amer. timber trees of the sapucaia-nut family.—**-vermelho**, the giant cariniana (*C. excelsa*), c.a. TAUARI.
jequitiguaçu [çú] (*m.*, *Bot.*) the southern soapberry (*Sapindus saponaria*).
jequitirana (*f.*) the coastal butterfly pea (*Centrosema virginianum*).
jequitiranabóia (*f.*) = JAQUIRANABÓIA.
jeratataca (*f.*) = MANACÁ.
jereba (*m.*) broken-down nag; harness; clumsy or messy person; (*f.*) a turkey buzzard; prostitute; mange.
jeremataia (*f.*) a chastetree (*Vitex gardneriana*), c.a. JIRIMATE.
jeremiada (*f.*) jeremiad.
jeremiar (*v.i.*) to whine, complain; to indulge in tales of woe.
Jeremias (*m.*) Jeremias; Jeremiah.

jereré (*m.*) a hoop net with a long handle, used for scooping up shrimp and small fish; c.a. JARERÉ, PUÇÁ, LANDUÁ; also = JÁ-COMEÇA and XIXIXI.
jeribá (*m.*) = BABA-DE-BOI, JERIVÁ.
jericada (*f.*) a herd of asses.
jerico (*m.*) donkey [= JUMENTO].
jericó (*m., Bot.*) the resurrection plant (*Selaginella lepidophylla*).
jerimu[m] (*m.*) pumpkin [= ABOBORA];—com leite, (*colloq.*) everyday routine.
jerimu[n]zeiro (*m.*) pumpkin vine.
jeritacaca, jeritataca (*f.*) = CANGAMBÁ.
jerivá (*m.*) the queenpalm (*Arecastrum romanzoffianum*), c.a. BABA-DE-BOI, JERIBÁ, JIRIBÁ, JIRUBÁ, JIRUVÁ, IMBURI-DE-CACHORRO, JUREVA, PALMITO-AMARGOSO, PATÍ, PINDOBA-DO-SUL, TÂMARA-DA-TERRA; also its fruit; (*colloq.*) a tall, thin person, c.a. JERIVÁ-SEM-FÔLHA.
jerivázal (*m.*) a tract abounding in JERIVÁS.
jerivàzeiro (*m.*) = JERIVÁ (the tree.)
jeriza (*f.*) rage; hate.
jero (*m.*) = ÓROBO.
jeróglifo (*m.*) = HIERÓGLIFO.
Jerônimo (*m.*) Jerome.
jeropiga (*f.*) a strong, cheap wine.
jerosolimita, jerosolimitano -na (*adj.; m.,f.*) = HIEROSO-LIMITA, HIEROSOLIMITANO.
jerra (*f.*) an outdoor barbecue or picnic.
jérsei (*m.*) jersey (sweater or knitted fabric).
jeruti [í] (*f.*) = JURITI.
jeruva (*f.*) = JURUVA.
Jessé (*m.*) Jesse.
jesuíta (*m.*) a Jesuit; (*adj.*) fig., hypocritical; shrewd.
jesuítico -ca (*adj.*) jesuitic(al); fig., crafty.
jesuitismo (*m.*) Jesuitism; fig., casuistry; fanaticism.
jesus-meu-deus (*m.*) the half-collared sparrow (*Arremon taciturnus*), c.a. TICO-TICO-DO-MATO.
jetaicica (*f.*) copal.
jetatura (*f.*) evil eye, bad luck. [from Italian *iettatura*.]
jetica (*f.*) = BATATA-DOCE.
jeticuçu [çú] (*m.*) the ivyleaf morning-glory (*Ipomoea hederacea*), c.a. JETUÇU.
jetirana (*f.*) the scarlet starglory (*Quamoclit coccinea*), c.a. PRIMAVERA-DE-CAIENA.
jetuçu [çú] = JETICUÇU.
jia (*f.*) a bullfrog (*Rana edulis*).
jibóia (*f.*) the boa (*Constrictor constrictor*).—-vermelha (or -parda, or -furta-côr) the rainbow, or ringed, boa (*Epicrates cenchris*), c.a. SALAMANTA.
jiboiar (*v.i., colloq.*) to sleep off a heavy meal.
jiçara (*f.*) = AÇAÌZEIRO.
jiló (*m.*) fruit of the egg-plant.
jiloeiro (*m.*) = BERINJELA.
jimbelê (*m.*) = CANJICA.
jimbula (*f.*) = RÃ-PIMENTA.
jingoísmo (*m.*) jingoism.
jingoísta (*m.,f.*) jingoist.
jinjibirra (*f.*) ginger beer. Var. GENGIBIRRA.
jinriquixá (*m.*) jinrikisha.
jinsão (*m.*) American ginseng (*Panax quinquefolium*).
jinsonje (*m.*) the pigeon pea (*Cajanus cajan*).
jipe (*m.*) jeep.
jipijapá (*m.*) the Panamá hatpalm (*Carludovica palmata*), c.a. BOMBONAÇA.
jipio (*m.*) a white quebracho (*Aspidosperma olivaceum*), c.a. QUATAMBU.
jipoúba (*m.*) a nitta tree (*Parkia discolor*), c.a. MANOPÉ-DA-PRAIA, SIPOÚBA.
jique (*m.*) = UMBUZEIRO.
jiquirioba (*f.*) = JUCIRI-DE-COMER.
jiquitaia (*f.*) hot pepper sauce; powdered red pepper.
jirau (*m.*) any rude wooden frame, bunk, platform or indoor balcony raised above the ground (on stilts or suspended from the rafters)—variously used for sleeping, for holding cooking utensils, for spreading clothes to dry, etc.; a food cage suspended from the ceiling.
jiriba (*f.*) = JERUVA.
jiribá (*m.*) = JERIVÁ.
jiribanda (*f., colloq.*) a scolding; a "bawling out".
jirimate (*m.*) = JEREMATAIA.
jirimu[m] (*m.*) = JERIMU[M].
jirimuzeiro (*m.*) = JERIMU[M]ZEIRO.
jirivá, jirubá, jiruvá (*m.*) = JERIVÁ.
jitaí (*m.*) = GUARABU.
jitirana (*f.*) scarlet starglory (*Quamoclit coccinea*), c.a.

JETIRANA.
jitiranabóia (*f.*) = JAQUIRANABÓIA.
jito (*m., Metal.*) sow.
jitó (*m.*) a muskwood (*Guarea tuberculata*).
jiu-jitsu (*m.*) jujitsu.
jívaro -ra (*adj.; m.,f.*) Jivaro (Indian of Peru and Equador).
J.M.J. = JESUS, MARIA, JOSÉ (Jesus, Mary and Joseph).
J.º = JOÃO (John).
joá (*m.*) = JUÁ.
joalharia, jolheria (*f.*) jewelry store.
joalheiro (*m.*) jeweller.
Joana (*f.*) Joan; Joanna; Johanna; Jean; Jeanne; Jane.
joanete [nê] (*m.*) bunion; (*Naut.*) topsail.
joaninha (*f.*) any ladybird (beetle), c.a. COCCINELA; a safety pin; a sunfish.
joanino -na (*adj.*) of or pert. to the Portuguese influence in Brazil during the reign of John III.
João (*m.*) John; Ian; Jean.
joão-barbudo (*m., Zool.*) the striped malacoptila (*M. striata*) c.a. JOÃO-DOIDO.
joão-barreiro (*m.*) = JOÃO-DE-BARRO.
joão-bôbo (*m.*) the white-eared puff-bird (*Ecchaunornis chacuru*), c.a. JOÃO-DOIDO, JOÃO-TOLO, CAPITÃO-DO-MATO, DORMIÃO, FEVEREIRO, PAULO-PIRES, MACURU, SUCURU, CHACURU, TAMATIÃO.
joão-caçador (*m.*) a large spider wasp or tarantula killer of the genus *Pepsis*.
joão-cachaça (*m.*) = JAGUARUÇÁ.
joão-congo (*m.*) = JAPÚ.
joão-conguinho (*m.*) = GUAXE; JAPIM.
joão-da-costa (*m.*) = CAPA-HOMEM; CIPÓ-CAPADOR.
joão-de-barro (*m.*) any of several oven-birds, esp. the red or white-throated oven-bird (*Furnarius r. rufus*), c.a. FORNEIRO, AMASSA-BARRO, JOÃO-BARREIRO, BARREIRO, MARIA-DE-BARRO; Commerson's oven-bird (*F. r. commersoni*); the white-throated oven-bird (*F. r. badius*).
joão-de-cristo (*m.*) = TEQUE-TEQUE.
joão-de-pau (*m.*) the red-fronted thorn-bird (*Phacelodomus f. rufifrons*) whose enormous nest is a veritable fagot; c.a. CARREGA-MADEIRA.
joão-deitado (*m.*) = COBU.
joão-dias (*m.*) = SEBASTIÃO (a dogfish).
joão-doido (*m., Zool.*) the striped malacoptila (*M. torquata torquata*), c.a. JOÃO-BARBUDO; also = JOÃO-BÔBO.
joão-do-mato (*m.*) Swainson's puff-bird (*Notharchus swainsoni*), c.a. CAPITÃO-DE-BIGODES, CAPITÃO-DO-MATO.
joão-fernandes (*m.*) a nobody; a fandango.
joão-galamarte (*m.*) see-saw [= GANGORRA].
joão-gomes (*m.*) = MARIA-GOMES.
joão-grande (*m.*) = ALCATRAZ (frigate bird); socoí (a heron).
joão-magro (*m.*) any stick insect, c.a. GAFANHOTO-DE-JUREMA (or -DE-MARMELEIRO).
joão-ninguém (*m.*) a nobody.
joão-pinto (*m.*) = CORRUPIÃO.
joão-pobre (*m.*) a bird—the blackish serpophaga (*Serpophaga nigricans*).
joão-teneném (*m., Zool.*) the rufous-capped spine-tail (*Synallaxis ruficapilla*), c.a. TENENÉ, BENTERERÉ, JOÃO-TIRIRI, PICHORORÉ, TIRIRI, CURUTIÉ.
joão-tiriri (*m., Zool.*) Spix's spine-tail (*Synallaxis s. spixi*), c.a. JOÃO-TENENÉM, BENTERERÉ.
joão-velho (*m.*) the Brazilian yellow woodpecker (*Celeus flavescens flavescens*), c.a. PICAPAU-DE-CABEÇA-AMARELA.
joàzeiro (*m.*) = JUÀZEIRO.
joça (*f., slang*) thingumajig, thingumbob, jigger, contraption.
jocosidade (*f.*) jocularity, jocoseness, facetiousness, waggery; a quip.
jocoso -sa (*adj.*) jocose, jocular, facetious, droll, funny, playful.
jocotupé (*m.*) = JACATUPÉ.
joeira (*f.*) screen, sieve, riddle.
joeiramento (*m.*) act of screening (grain).
joeirar (*v.t.*) to screen, sift; to separate the wheat from the chaff, lit. & fig.
joeireiro -ra (*m.,f.*) screener.
joelhada (*f.*) a blow with the knee.
joelheiro -ra (*adj.*) knee-deep; knee-high; (*f.*) knee-pad; kneepiece; baggy knees (of trousers).
joelho [ê] (*m.*) knee. de—s para dentro, knock-kneed. de—s, on bended knees; kneeling. pôr-se de—s, to kneel down.

joelhudo –da (*adj.*) big-kneed.
jogada (*f.*) act of playing or gaming; a move (in a game); a play (for stakes); a throw, cast, fling (as of a ball, rock, etc.).
jogador –dora (*adj.*) playing; (*m.,f.*) player; gambler; (*colloq.*) wishbone.—**viciado,** a confirmed gambler.
joga-pau (*m.*) a horsefly [=MUTUCA].
jogar (*v.t.*) to throw, fling, cast; to play (a game, a card); to gamble; to risk, stake; of a vehicle, to jounce; of a ship, to toss.—**água na fervura,** to pour oil on troubled waters.—**a última carta,** to play one's last card.—**água no mar,** to carry coals to Newcastle.—**às deveras,** to play for keeps.—**com,** to go along with (agree).—**com pau de dois bicos,** to double-cross; to betray by double dealing; to play both ends against the middle; to straddle the fence.—**com todo o baralho,** to play every card in the deck.—**fora,** to throw out; to scrap.—**jôgo franco,** to play square; to deal above-board.—**o dinheiro pelas janelas,** to spend money like water. [It resembles the numbers game in Harlem.]—**pela certa,** to play a sure thing.—**por tabela,** to use indirection (roundabout means); to "work the angles"; to make an oblique reference.—**porrinha,** (*slang*) to match coins.—**p'rás arquibancadas,** to play to the gallery. **É a vez dêle—,** It is his turn to play.
jogata (*f.*) a game of cards.
jogatina (*f.*) gambling.
jôgo [jogos(jó)] (*m.*) game, play; amusement, pastime; sport; gamble; gambling; set or collection (of tools, etc.); movement, backlash; tossing, pitching (of vehicles, vessels).—**da amarelinha,—da sapata,—da macaca,** hopscotch.—**da bola,** bowling.—**da velha,—das cruzes e dos pontos,** ticktacktoe.—**das escondidas,** hide-and-seek.—**da vermelinha,** 3-card monte.—**de arquibancada,** grandstand play.—**de azar,** game of chance.—**de cabra-cega,** blindman's buff.—**de cartas,** card game.—**de damas,** checkers.—**de empurra,** (*colloq.*) passing the buck; letting George do it.—**de contas,** juggling of accounts.—**de malha,** quoits; horseshoes.—**de palavras,** play upon words.—**de prendas,** forfeits.—**de sala de jantar,** a diningroom set (of furniture).—**de salão,** parlor game, indoor game.—**de trinchar,** carving set.—**de vocábulo,** play on words.—**do bicho,** an illegal but national pastime in Brazil, related to the lottery. [It resembles the numbers game in Harlem.]—**franco,** aboveboard dealing.—**s olímpicos,** Olympic games. **abrir o—,** to open the pot (as in poker). **esconder o—,** to dissemble. **achar-se,** or **estar, em—,** to be at stake. **ao—,** at gambling. **casa de—,** gambling-house. **em—,** under consideration; involved. **pôr em—,** to stake. **viciado no—,** addicted to gambling.
jogral (*adj.; m.*) buffoon.
jogralidade (*f.*) buffoonery.
joguête (*m.*) toy, plaything; butt, laughing stock; dupe; fool.
joguetear (*v.i.*) to joke and play.
jóia (*f.*) gem, jewel; piece of jewelry; initiation fee; entrance fee.—**s de fantasia,** costume jewelry.
jóina (*f., Bot.*) a restharrow (*Ononis hispanica*).
joio (*m., Bot.*) darnel (*Lolium temulentum*). **separar o—do trigo,** to separate the wheat from the tares.—**venenoso,** common corncockle (*Agrostemma githago*).
Jônatas (*m.*) Jonathan.
Jonas (*m.*) Jonah; Jonas.
jônico –ca, jônio –nia (*adj.*) Ionic [=IÔNICO, IÔNIO].
joque, jóquei (*m.*) jockey.
Jordânia (*f.*) Jordan (country).
Jordão (*m.*) Jordan (River).
jorna (*f., colloq.*) spree, bender.
jornada (*f.*) journey, short trip; a day's march or travel. **por—,** by the day.
jornadeante (*adj.*) wayfaring.
jornadear (*v.i.*) to journey; to take a day's journey.
jornal (*m.*) journal, daily newspaper; day book; diary; daily wage.—**cinematográfico** or **falado,** newsreel. **banca de jornais,** newsstand. **recorte de—,** newspaper clipping.
jornaleco (*m.*) a "rag" (shabby newspaper).
jornaleiro –ra (*adj.*) daily; (*m.*) journeyman (worker by the day); newsboy; newspaper carrier.
jornalismo (*m.*) journalism; the press.
jornalista (*m.,f.*) journalist; news editor; newspaper publisher; newspaper man or woman.
jornalístico –ca (*adj.*) journalistic.
jôrra (*f.*) dross (of metals).
jorrão (*m.*) a low truck for heavy hauling; a sledge for hauling rocks; a harrow.

jorrar (*v.i.*) to spurt, spout, gush, pour. **O sol jorrava pelas janelas,** The sun poured in at the windows.
jôrro (*m.*) spate, rush, torrent.—**jôrro,** the luckynut thevetia or yellow oleander (*Thevetia nereifolia*), c.a. CHAPÉU-DE-NAPOLEÃO.
José (*m.*) Joseph.
Josefa (*f.*) Josepha.
Josefina (*f.*) Josephine.
josefinite (*f., Min.*) josephinite.
joseíto (*m., Min.*) joseite.
Josué (*m.*) Joshua.
jota (*m.*) the letter J; (*f.*) the jota (Spanish dance); (*m.*) jot, tittle, iota.
jovem (*adj.*) young, youthful; (*m.,f.*) a young person.
jovial (*adj.*) jovial, jolly, joyful, jocund; cheerful; jaunty.
jovialidade (*f.*) joviality; cheerfulness, good humor; facetiousness.
jovializar (*v.t.,v.i.*) to make, or to be, jovial.
J.r = JÚNIOR (Junior).
juá (*m., Bot.*) a nightshade (*Solanum paniculatum*), c.a. JUREPEBA, JURIPEBA; a jujube (fruit of the JUÀZEIRO).—**açú** = GINGEIRA-DA-TERRA.—**amarelo,** a nightshade (*Solanum ambrosiacum*).—**de-capote** = ALQUEQUENJE-AMARELO, CAMAPU.—**de-comer,** a nightshade (*Solanum balbisii*), or its edible fruit.—**grande** = CORUPIÁ.—**mirim,** a jujube (*Zizyphus undulata*), c.a. GRÃO-DE-GALO.—**miúdo,** a hackberry (*Celtis iguaneous*), c.a. GRÃO DE GALO.—**uvá,** the myrtle laurelcherry (*Prunus myrtifolia*), c.a. GINGEIRA-BRAVA, GINGEIRA-DA-TERRA.
juapoca (*m.*) = CAMAPU.
juar (*m.*) sorghum (*S. vulgare*).
juaz (*m.*) fruit of the JUÀZEIRO.
juàzeiro (*m., Bot.*) a jujube (*Zizyphus undulata*), c.a. JUÁ-MIRIM, GRÃO-DE-GALO.
juàzinho-amarelo (*m.*) a nightshade (*Solanum toxinorium*).
juba (*f.*) lion's mane.
jubaí (*m.*) = TAMARINDO, TAMARINHEIRO.
jubarte (*f.*) a humpback whale (*Megaptera*).
jubati [í] (*m.*) = JUPATI.
jubeba (*f.*) = JURUBEBA-GRANDE.
jubilação (*f.*) jubilation, rejoicing; retirement of a teacher on a pension.
jubilar (*v.t.,v.i.*) to rejoice; (**com,** at; **em,** in); to grant retirement (to a teacher); (*v.r.*) to retire from teaching; (*adj.*) of or pert. to a jubilee.
jubiléu (*m.*) jubilee.—**de ouro,** golden jubilee.
júbilo (*m.*) exultation, elation, joy; mirth; glee.
jubiloso –sa (*adj.*) jubilant, elated.
jucá (*m.*) a tree of Caesalpinia (*C. ferrea*), c.a. PAU-FERRO.
juçá (*m.*) an itch(ing).
juçana (*f.*) a bird trap.
juçapé (*m.*) the satintail or sapegrass (*Imperata brasiliensis*), c.a. CAPIM-SAPÉ.
juçara (*f.*) the assai euterpe palm (*E. oleracea*), c.a. AÇAIZEIRO, the young unexpanded leaves of which (called PALMITO) are used as a vegetable.
juciri [rí] (*m.*) a nightshade (*Solanum juciri*), c.a. JIQUIRIOBA, CARURU-DE-ESPINHO.
jucundidade (*f.*) jocundity.
jucundo –da (*adj.*) jocund, merry.
jucurutu [tú] (*m.*) = JACURUTU.
judaico –ca (*adj.*) Judaic.
judaísmo (*m.*) Judaism.
judaísta (*m.,f.*) Judaist.
judas (*m.*) traitor; false friend; person dressed in rags; (*cap.*) Judas.
judengo –ga (*adj.*) Jewish.
judeu –dia (*adj.*) Jewish; (*m.*) a Jew; (*f.*) a Jewess.
judiação (*f.*) mistreatment, abuse, cruelty.
judiar (*v.i.*) —**com** or—**de,** to ridicule, make fun of; to mistreat.
judiaria (*f.*) ghetto; mockery; cruelty, mistreatment.
judicativo –va (*adj.*) judicative.
judicatório –ria (*adj.*) judicatory.
judicatura (*f.*) judicature; judiciary; jurisdiction; judgeship.
judicial (*adj.*) judicial, juridical, judiciary.
judiciar (*v.i.*) to adjudicate; to pass judgment.
judiciário –ria (*adj.*) juridical, judicial, judiciary.
judicioso –sa (*adj.*) judicious, sensible, wise, discreet.
judô (*m.*) judo, jujitsu.
jugada (*f.*) = JEIRA (a yoke of land).
juglandáceas (*f.pl.*) the *Juglandaceae* (walnut family).

juglandina (f., *Pharm.*) juglandin.
jugo (m.) yoke; a yoke of oxen; bondage, servitude.
jugoslavo -va (adj.; m.,f.) Jugoslav.
jugular (adj.) jugular; (f.) a chinstrap; jugular vein; (v.t.) to strangle.
juiporga (f.) = FERREIRO.
juiz [-es] (m.) judge, magistrate; referee, umpire; arbitrator. [Fem. juíza].—de direito, a district judge—one who presides over a COMARCA.—-de-fora, in Brazil, in colonial days, a sort of circuit judge; lit., a judge from the outside.—de linha, (*Soccer*) linesman [= BANDEIRINHA].—de paz, justice of the peace.—de primeira instância, a judge of a lower court.—de segunda instância, a superior-court judge.—do-mato, the white-breasted nun bird (*Monasa m. morphoeus*), c.a. BICO-DE-BRASA, TANGURU-PARÁ, SAUNÍ, BICO-DE-CRAVO.
juizado (m.) judgeship.
juiz-forano -na (adj.) of or pert. to Juiz de Fora (Minas Gerais); (m.,f.) a native of that city.
juízo (m.) judgment, decision; opinion; intelligence, common sense; discretion; wits; trial court.—a quo, lower court.—de Deus, trial by ordeal.—perfeito, sound mind.—de Salomão, Solomonic decision. ao—de, in the judgment of. chamar a—, to summon to court. criar—, to cut one's wisdom teeth. dar volta ao—, to go crazy. dia de—, judgment day. Êle não tem migalha de—, He hasn't a grain of sense. perder o—, to lose one's mind. sem—, addle-pated, sappy, foolish. ter—, to use good sense. ter o—perfeito, to be sane. tomar—, to develop good sense. varrido de—, stark mad.
jujuba (f.) the common jujube (*Zizyphus jujuba*), or its fruit; c.a. MACIEIRA-DE-ANÁFEGA.
jul. = JULHO (July).
julavento (m.) = SOTAVENTO.
julgado -da (adj.) judged; sentenced; (m.) a judicial district.
julgador -dora (adj.) judging; (m.,f.) one who judges.
julgamento (m.) trial, judgment.—à revelia, judgment by default.
julgar (v.t.) to judge, try, sentence; to render judgment; to deem, suppose; to consider, regard; to form an opinion about; to adjudge.—a mal, to think evil of.—outros por si, to judge others by oneself.
julho (m.) July.
Júlia (f.) Julia; Julie.
juliana (f.) julienne (soup); (*Bot.*) = HÉSPERIS.
Juliano (m.) Julian.
Júlio (m.) Jules; Julius.
jumbeba (f., *Bot.*) either of two cacti: *Cereus variabilis* or *Pereskia aculeata*, the latter c.a. ROSA-MADEIRA, ORA-PRO-NOBIS.
jumenta (f.) jenny-ass.
jumento (m.) ass, donkey.
jun. = JUNHO (June).
junça (f., *Bot.*) the chufa flatsedge (*Cyperus esculentus*).—-de-conta = JUNCINHA.—-miúda or -pequena = CAPIS-CABA-MIRIM (a sedge).
juncáceo -cea (adj., *Bot.*) juncaceous; (f.pl.) the *Juncaceae* (rush family).
juncada (f.) a quantity of rushes; the same when strewn in streets and churches on festive days.
juncal, junçal (m.) a tract abounding in sedges and rushes.
junção (f.) junction, conjunction.
juncar (v.t.) to cover (the ground) with leaves or flowers; to strew, litter, scatter; to clutter up.
juncinha (f.) the nutgrass flatsedge (*Cyperus rotundus*), c.a. JUNÇA-MIÚDA, JUNÇA-PEQUENA.
junco (m.) a Chinese junk; (*Bot.*) any of a number of sedges and rushes.—-agreste,—-ananico,—-manso,—-popoca, are all spike sedges (*Eleocharis*).—-bravo,—-da-praia,—-miudo, are all flat sedges (*Cyperus*).—-florido, a flowering rush (*Butomus umbellatus*).—-de-banhado, a rush (*Juncus*).—-de-três-quinas, a beak rush (*Rhyncospora*).
juncoso -sa, junçoso -sa (adj.) abounding in sedges and rushes.
jundiá (m.) any unspecified catfish.
jungermaniáceas (f.pl.) the *Jungermanniaceae* (a family of liverworts).
jungir [25] (v.t.) to yoke, couple.
junho (m.) June.
junino -na (adj.) June.
Júnio (m.) Junius.

júnior (adj.) junior.
junípero (m., *Bot.*) juniper (*Juniperus*), c.a. ZIMBRO.
junquilho (m., *Bot.*) jonquil (*Narcissus jonquilla*).
junta (f.) joint, union; coupling; pair, couple, brace; team (of animals); board, council; (*colloq.*) a house-raising or other "bee"; (*Anat.*) articulation.—administrativa, administrative council.—de bois, yoke of oxen.—de expansão, expanding joint.—de meia esquadria, miter joint.—estanque or hermética, hermetic joint.—universal, universal joint.
juntamente (adv.) jointly, together (com, with).
juntamento (m.) = AJUNTAMENTO.
juntar [24] (v.t.) to join (together), connect, couple; to amass, collect, pile up; to annex, append, adjoin, subjoin; (v.r.) to come together; to assemble; to adhere.—-se a, to unite with; to join.—o dia come a noite, to work day and night.—os pés, (*colloq.*) to turn up one's toes (die). Cf. AJUNTAR.
junteira (f.) joiner's plane.
juntinho -nha (adj.) very close (together), quite close (to).
junto -ta (adj.; irreg. p.p. of JUNTAR) joined together; adjoining, near, close; (adv.) jointly, together.—a, attached to; against; next to; near, beside; close to.—com, together with.—de, near, next to, beside. para—de, close to, toward. por—, all told.
juntoura (f.) joiner's plane; (*Const.*) header. Var. JUNTOIRA.
juntura (f.) juncture, junction, union.
juó (m., *Zool.*) the banded tinamou (*Crypturellus u. undulatus*).
jupará (m.) the kinkajou (*Potos flavus*), c.a. JAPURÁ, JURU-PARÁ, MACACO-ADUFEIRO, MACACO-DA-MEIA-NOITE.
juparaba (f.) the yellow-winged paroquet (*Tirica virescens*), c.a. PERIQUITO-DA-CAMPINA.
jupati [í] (m.) the jupati or Brazilian raffia palm (*Raphia faedigera*) "common in the flooded forest and in the swampy lowlands of the Amazon estuary. Very short thick trunk; enormous erect leaves; ovoid fruit 7 cms. by 3 to 4 cms., which grows in bunches weighing more than 50 kilos; fruit about the size of an egg, reddish and shiny; fruit pulp is oleaginous, reddish, astringent and bitter and yields a red oil; harvest season from February to May. Leaf petioles yield long, thick, light, blonde cylindrical fibres suitable for the manufacture of hats and small baskets." [GUAF]; also = CUÍCA.
jupiá (m.) whirlpool.
jupicaí (m.) a yellow-eye grass (*Xyris laxifolia*), c.a. BOTÃO-DE-OURO.
jupindá (m.) a spiderflower (*Cleome*).
jupiteriano -na (adj.) Jupiter-like; by ext., lordly, domineering.
juqueiraçu [çú] (m.) a bead tree (*Adenanthera thyrsosa*).
juquiá (m.) = CUVU.
juquiri [rí] (m.) any of various leguminous plants and trees, esp. of the genera *Mimosa* and *Machaerium*.—-carrasco, a sensitivebrier (*Schrankia leptocarpa*).—-manso, a neptunia (*N. oleracea*).—-rasteiro, the sensitiveplant (*Mimosa pudica*), c.a. SENSITIVA, DORMIDEIRA, MALÍCIA-DE-MULHER.
Jur. = JURISPRUDÊNCIA (Jurisprudence).
jura (f.) oath, vow; imprecation, curse.
jurado -da (m.,f.) juror; (adj.) sworn (under oath); (*colloq.*) threatened. inimigo—, sworn enemy.
jurador -dora (adj.) swearing; (m.,f.) swearer.
juramentar (v.t.) to swear an oath [= AJURAMENTAR].
juramento (m.) an oath, vow; curse.—hipocrático, Hippocratic oath. prestar—, to take an oath; to swear allegiance.
jurão (m.) a house built on stilts, in flood areas.
jurar (v.t.,v.i.) to swear, take an oath; to vow, promise; to curse.—falso, to swear falsely.—pelos santos evangelhos, to swear on the Bible.—que sim (não), to swear it is true (untrue).
jurará (m.) = MUÇUÃ.
jurássico -ca (adj., *Geol.*) Jurassic.
jurema (f., *Bot.*) an acacia (*A. jurema*).—branca, an apes-earring (*Pithecellobium diversifolium*).—marginada, a mimosa (*M. burgonia*).—preta, a mimosa (*M. nigra*).
jureminha (f., *Bot.*) a mimosa (*M. malacocentra*).
jureva (f.) = JERIVÁ.
júri (m.) jury.
juricana (f.) = SURUCUCU-DE-PATIOBA.
jurídico -ca (adj.) juridical, forensic, legal.
jurimágua (m.,f.) a member of a formerly important

Tupian tribe at the headwaters of the Amazon; (*adj.*) of or pert. to these people.
juripeba (*f.*) a nightshade (*Solanum paniculatum*), c.a. JURUBEBA.
jurisconsulto -ta (*m.,f.*) jurist, legal counsellor.
jurisdição (*f.*) jurisdiction.
jurisdicional (*adj.*) jurisdictional.
jurisdicionar (*v.t.*) to exercise jurisdiction over.
jurisprudência (*f.*) jurisprudence.
jurisprudencial (*adj.*) jurisprudential.
jurisprudente (*m.*) jurisprudent, jurist.
jurista (*m.,f.*) jurist, legal counsellor; money lender; bondholder.
jurístico -ca (*adj.*) = JURÍDICO.
juriti [tí] (*f.*) any of various doves (c.a. JERUTI and JURUTI) such as Reichenbach's gray-fronted dove (*Leptoptila rufaxilla reichenbachii*) and the cinnamon-winged white-fronted dove (*Leptoptila verreauxi decipiens*).—-**azul**, the cinereous dove (*Claravis pretiosa*).—-**carregadeira** = POMBA-DE-BANDO.—**piranga**, the ruddy quail-dove (*Oreopeleia m. montana*) and the violaceous quail-dove (*Oreopeleia v. violacea*).
juritiubim [i-u] (*m.*) a shadow palm (*Geonoma camana*).
juro (*m.*) interest (on money loaned).—**s acrescidos**, added or accrued interest.—**s capitalizados** or **compostos**, compound interest.—**s de mora**, delay interest.—**s simples**, simple interest.—**s sôbre** —**s**, compound interest.
juruaçu [çú] (*m.*) the mealy parrot (*Amazona f. farinosa*), c.a. MOLEIRO.
jurubeba (*f.*) a nightshade (*Solanum paniculatum*), c.a. JURIPEBA, JURUBEBA-GRANDE.
jurucuá (*f.*) = TARTARUGA-VERDE.
jurueba (*f.*) the vinaceous parrot (*Amazona vinacea*), c.a. CORALEIRO.
jurujuba (*f.*) = CAMARADINHA.
juruma (*f.*) = UBARANA-MIRIM.
jurumbeba (*f.*) a prickly pear (*Opuntia brasiliensis*).
juruna (*m.,f.*) one of the Juruna, a Tupian tribe which lived on the middle Xingu River; (*adj.*) pert. to or designating this tribe.
jurupará (*m.*) = JUPARÁ.
jurupema (*f.*) = URUPEMA.
jurupixuna (*m.*) a squirrel monkey, c.a. MACACO-DE-CHEIRO.
jururu [urú] (*adj.*) dejected, glum, gloomy, mopish, in the dumps.
juruti [tí] (*f.*) = JURITI.
jurutipiranga (*f.*) ruddy quail-dove (*Oreopeleia m. montana*).
juruva (*f., Zool.*) any of various motmots, esp. the following: the common motmot (*Momotus m. momota*) of northern Brazil; the Pará motmot (*M. m. parensis*) of northeastern Brazil; and the rufous-headed motmot (*Baryphthengus ruficapillus*); other common names for any of these are: JERUVA, URITUTU, JACU-TAQUARA, TUTU, TAQUARA, UDU, UAU, FORMIGÃO, JIRIBA, HUDU, SIRIÚVA, SIRIÚ, PIRAPUIA, PURURU.

juruviara (*f.*) a bird—the chivi vireo (*Vireo virescens chivi*).
jus (*m.*) justice. **fazer—a**, to deserve, or strive to deserve (something).
jusante (*f.*) ebbtide, low tide. **a—**, downstream.
justa (*f.*) joust, tilt.
justador -dora (*adj.*) jousting, tilting; (*m.*) jouster, tilter.
justafluvial (*adj.*) riparian.
justalinear (*adj.*) interlinear or side-by-side [translation].
justamente (*adv.*) precisely, exactly.
justapor [63] (*v.t.*) to juxtapose.
justaposição (*f.*) juxtaposition.
justaposto -ta (*adj.*) juxtaposed, in juxtaposition with.
justar (*v.i.*) to joust, tilt (at); also (*colloq.*) = AJUSTAR.
justeza [ê] (*f.*) exactness, precision, correctness.
justiça (*f.*) justice, justness, right, equity, fairness; judiciary, the bar; the magistrates; the court. **administrar—**, to dispense justice. **ir à—**, to go to court. **oficial de—**, a court employee.
justiçado -da (*adj.*) executed; (*m.,f.*) one who has been executed.
justiçar (*v.t.*) to execute (a sentence of death).
justiceiro -ra, justiçoso -sa (*adj.*) just, righteous.
justificação (*f.*) justification, warrant, excuse; apology.
justificado -da (*adj.*) justified; absolved.
justificador -dora (*adj.*) justifying; (*m.,f.*) justifier.
justificante (*adj.*) justifying; (*m.*) voucher; warrant.
justificar (*v.t.*) to justify, vindicate, uphold; to exonerate, absolve, acquit; (*Printing*) to adjust; (*v.r.*) to clear oneself. **O fim justifica os meios**, The end justifies the means.
justificativo -va (*adj.*) justifying, explanatory; (*f.*) justification, defense, excuse.
justificável (*adj.*) justifiable, defensible, warrantable.
justilho (*m.*) bodice.
Justino (*m.*) Justin.
justo -ta (*adj.*) just, fair, impartial; reasonable; exact, accurate; legally right; upright, righteous; tight, close-fitting. **a—título**, deservedly. **ao—**, exactly, precisely; **calças—s**, tight pants.
justura (*f.*) adjustment.
juta (*f.*) jute; (*Bot.*) roundpod jute (*Corchorus capsularis*).—-**paulista**, a sp. of Hibiscus.
jutaí (*m.*) any of a number of tropical timber trees of the genus Hymenaea (family Caesalpiniaceae), all of which yield copal.—-**açu**, the courbaril (*Hymenaea courbaril*); yields a very hard tough wood used in construction.
jutairana (*f.*) = GUARABU.
jutuaúba (*f.*) a muskwood (*Guarea pendula*).
juúna (*f.*) = JURIPEBA.
juva (*m.*) = PALOMBETA.
juvenê, juvevê (*m.*) a pricklyash (*Zanthoxylum*).
juvenil (*adj.*) juvenile, youthful.
juvenília (*m.pl.*) juvenilia.
juvenilidade (*f.*) juvenility.
juvenilismo (*m., Med.*) juvenilism.
juventude (*f.*) youth; boyhood, girlhood; boys and girls, young people.
juvira (*f.*) swordfish [= PEIXE-ESPADA].

K

K, k, This letter is no longer a part of the official Brazilian alphabet. It still is used, however, in proper names and as a part of internationally-recognized symbols and abbreviations. For Port. words formerly spelled K-, see under **QU-** and **C-**.
kc = QUILOCICLO (kilocycle).

kg = QUILOGRAMA (kilogram).
kl = QUILOLITRO (kiloliter).
km = QUILÔMETRO (kilometer).
K.O. = NOCAUTE (knockout).
kw = QUILOWATT (kilowatt).

L

L, l, the 11th letter of the Portuguese alphabet.
l = LITRO (liter).
l. = LETRA (promissory note); LINHA (line); LIVRO (book).
la(s), form of direct object fem. pers. pron. used instead of **a(s)** when attached to verb forms ending in **r, s,** or **z,** to indirect object pronouns **nos** and **vos,** and to adverb **eis,** which forms, in turn, drop their last letters. Examples: **manda-la, vimo-la, fi-la** instead of **mandar-a, vimos-a, fiz-a; no-la, vo-la** instead of **nos-a, vos-a;** and **ei-la** instead of **eis-a.**
lá (adv.) there, in that place; yonder; thither.—**adiante,** ahead there, yonder, over there.—**dentro,** inside there, in there, within.—**em baixo,** down there; downstairs. —**em cima,** up there; upstairs.—**fora,** out(side) there. —**longe,** way off there, far away.—**mesmo,** right there. —**onde,** there where.—**para dentro,** inside (there).—**por,** around (there), along about.—**por baixo (cima),** down (up) over (around) there.—**se foi,** There it (he, she) went.—**se vai,** There it (he, she) goes. **daqui até—,** between now and then; from here there. **de—,** thence. **de—prá cá,** back and forth. **Eu sei—,** I haven't any idea. **o mundo—de fora,** the outside world. **para—,** thither; there; over there. **para—e para cá,** back and forth. **por—,** that way; over there **Toma—!** Take that!
lã (f.) wool; woolen cloth.—**de trapo,** shoddy.—**de vidro,** glass wool.—**fóssil,** asbestos [= AMIANTO].—**meirinha,** wool from merino sheep.—**vegetal,** the silverleaf pumpwood (*Cecropia palmata*), c.a. UMBAÚBA.
labaça (f., Bot.) patience dock (*Rumex patientia*), c.a. PACIÊNCIA.—**-aguda,** pond dock (*R. aquaticus*).—**-crêspa,** curly dock (*R. crispus*).—**-obtusa,** bitter dock (*R. obtusifolius*), c.a. LABAÇAL.—**-sinuada,** fiddleleaf dock (*R. pulcher*), c.a. COENHA.
labareda (f.) flame, blaze; ardor, enthusiasm. Var. LAVAREDA.
lábaro (m.) labarum (banner).
labdano (m.) = LÁDANO.
labe-labe (f., Bot.) the hyacinth bean (*Dolichos lablab*).
labelado -da (adj., Bot., Zool.) labellate.
labelo (Bot., Zool.) labellum.
labéu (m.) blot, stain, dishonor, disgrace; slur.
lábia (f.) smooth (wily) talk; fine words; guile, cunning. **ter—,** to have the gift of gab.
labiado -da (adj.) labiate; (f.) a plant of the mint family; (pl.) the Labiateae or Lamiaceae (mint family).
labial (adj.) labial; (f., Phonet.) a labial consonant.
labializar (v.t., Phonet.) to labialize.
labidóforo -ra (adj., Zool.) labidophorous.
lábil [-beis] (adj., Chem., Physics) labile.
lábio (m.) lip.—**leporino** (or—**rachado de nascimento**), harelip.
labiodental (adj., Phonet.) labiodental.
labiógrafo (m.) labiograph.
labionasal (adj., Phonet.) labionasal.
labioso -sa (adj.) big-lipped.
labiovelar (adj., Phonet.) labiovelar.
labioversão (f., Dentistry) labioversion.
labiríntico -ca (adj.) labyrinthine.
labirintiforme (adj.) labyrinthiform.
labirintite (f., Med.) labyrinthitis.
labirinto (m.) labyrinth, maze; tangled affairs; (Anat., Zool.) the internal ear.
lablab (f.) = LABE-LABE.
labor (m.) labor, toil [= LAVOR, TRABALHO]; task.
laboração (f.) laboring.
laborar (v.i.) to work, labor, toil [= TRABALHAR, LABUTAR, LIDAR].
laboratório (m.) laboratory.
laboratorista (m.,f.) laboratory worker or technician.
laboriosidade (f.) laboriousness.
laborioso -sa (adj.) hard-working, industrious, diligent; arduous, laborious.
laborista (adj.; m.,f.) Laborite.
labradorita (f., Min.) labradorite.
labrego -ga [ê] (adj.) rustic; coarse, uncouth; (m.) boor, lout, bumpkin, clodhopper, yokel.
lábridas, labrídeos, labróides (m.pl., Zool.) the wrasse family of fishes (*Labridae*).
labro (m., Zool.) labrum.

labroso -sa (adj.) labrose, having thick lips.
laburno (m., Bot.) the golden chain laburnum (*L. anagyroides*).
labuta, labutação (f.) hard work, drudgery; daily toil.
labutar (v.t.) to work hard; to work long hours; to plod, grub.
laca (f.) lac; lacquer; shellac.
laçada (f.) bow-knot, slip-knot. **bainha de—,** hemstitch.
laçador (m.) lassoer.
lacaico -ca (adj., Chem.) laccaic [acid].
lacaiesco -ca [ê] (adj.) lackey-like.
lacaio (m.) lackey, footman, flunky.
laçar (v.t.) to lasso, catch, snare; to lace (shoes).
laçaria (f., Arch.) tracery, swags, festoons, garland, etc.
laçarotes (m.pl.) bows, furbelows.
lácase (f., Biochem.) laccase.
laceração (f.) laceration.
lacerador -dora (adj.) lacerating.
lacerante (adj.) lacerating [= DILACERANTE].
lacerar (v.t.) to lacerate [= DILACERAR].
lacértidas, lacertídeos (m.pl.) a family (*Lacertidae*) of lizards.
lacertiforme (adj., Zool.) lacertiform.
lacertílio (m.) a lacertilian reptile (lizard); (pl.) the Lacertilia.
lacerto (m., Anat.) lacertus fibrosus.
lacete [cê] (m.) a small lace bow; an S-curve in a road; rock surfacing of a road.
lacínia (f., Bot.) lacinia.
laciniado -da (adj., Bot.) laciniate.
laciniforme (adj.) laciniform, fringe-like.
lacínula (f., Bot.) lacinula.
lacinulado -da (adj., Bot.) lacinulate.
laço (m.) bow, knot; tie, bond; noose, slip-knot, lasso; trap, snare; trick.—**de chegada** (Athletics) finishing-line tape.—**s de sangue,** blood ties.—**s-espanhóis,** (Bot.) the painted gaillardia (*G. picta*). **apanhar no—,** to ensnare. **armar um—,** to set a trap; fig., to lure, decoy.
lacol (m., Chem.) laccol.
lacolito (m., Geol.) laccolith.
lacônico -ca (adj.) laconic, terse, succinct.
laconismo (m.) laconism.
lacraia (f.) any millipede, centipede, earwig or small scorpion.
lacrainha [a-í] (f.) earwig.
lacrar (v.t.) to seal with wax.
lacrau (m.) any scorpion.
lacre (m.) sealing-wax; (Bot.) bloodwood (*Vismia spp.*).
lacreada (f.) lacework.
lacrimação (f.) secretion of tears.
lacrimal (adj.; m.) lachrymal (bone).
lacrimante (adj.) lachrymose.
lacrimatório -ria (adj.; m.) lachrymatory.
lacrimejar (v.) = LAGRIMEJAR.
lacrimogêneo -nea (adj.) tear-provoking. **gás—,** tear gas.
lacrimoso -sa (adj.) tearful.
lactação (f.) lactation.
lactalbumina (f.) lactalbumin.
lactame (m., Chem.) lactam.
lactamida (f., Chem.) lactamide.
lactante (adj.) milk-producing; milk-giving.
lactar (v.t.) to lactate, to secrete milk; to suckle young; (v.i.) to suck.
lactário -ria (adj.) secreting a milky juice or fluid; lactary; (m.) a milk dispensary for infants.
láctase (f., Chem.) lactase.
lactato (m., Chem.) lactate.
lactéia (f.) fish milt [= LEITA].
lacteína (f., Biochem.) lactenin.
lactente (adj.; m.) suckling (child).
lá[c]teo -tea (adj.) lacteal, milky.
la[c]tescência (f.) lactescence, milkiness.
la[c]tescente (adj.) lactescent.
la[c]ticínio (m.) any food consisting of, or prepared from, milk; (pl.) dairy products.
la[c]ticinoso -sa (adj.) = LACTESCENTE; LÁCTEO.
lá[c]tico -ca (adj.) lactic [acid].
lacticolor (adj.) of the color of milk.
láctide (f., Chem.) lactid(e).

lactífero -ra (*adj.*) lactiferous.
lactiforme (*adj.*) lactiform, milklike.
lactífugo -ga (*adj.*) lactifuge.
lactígeno -na (*adj.*) lactigenic.
lactobutirômetro (*m.*) lactobutyrometer.
lactocitrato (*m., Pharm.*) lactocitrate.
lactodensímetro (*m.*) lactodensimeter.
lactofosfato (*m., Pharm.*) lactophosphate.
lactoglobulina (*f.*) lactoglobulin.
lactômetro (*m.*) lactometer.
lactona (*f., Chem.*) lactone.
lactoproteína (*f., Biochem.*) lactoprotein.
lactoscópio (*m.*) lactoscope.
lactose (*f.*) lactose, sugar of milk.
lactosuria (*f., Med.*) lactosuria.
lactotoxina [ks] (*f., Biochem.*) lactotoxin.
lactovegetariano -na (*adj.; m.,f.*) lactovegetarian.
lacuna (*f.*) lacuna, hiatus, gap, space; an omission.
lacunar (*adj.*) lacunary.
lacunário (*m., Arch.*) lacunar.
lacunoso -sa (*adj.*) having, or full of, lacunae.
lacustre (*adj.*) lacustrine; (*m.*) lake dweller.
ladainha [a-í] (*f.*) litany; fig., tiresome recital; rigmarole.
ladanífero -ra (*adj.*) ladanigerous.
ládano (*m.*) labdanum, ladanum; (*Bot.*) the gum rockrose (*Cistus landaniferus*), and others of this genus, c.a. ESTEVÃO, LADÃO.
ladear (*v.t.*) to flank, lie or stand alongside of; to accompany, escort; to attack on the side; to dodge, evade; to sidestep; to get around (avoid), by-pass; (*v.r.*) of a horse, to sidestep.—**a questão**, to dodge the issue.
ladeira (*f.*) see under LADEIRO.
ladeirento -ta (*adj.*) steep, sloping, acclivitous, declivitous.
ladeiro -ra (*adj.*) side, sideways; (*f.*) a steep street; slope, hillside, acclivity, declivity; "in Amazonas, a small pool of wet clay several meters long, which occurs along trails, making it difficult for pedestrians and animals to pass." [*GBAT*].—**abaixo**, downhill. **na metade da—**, half-way up (or down) the slope.
ladeiroso -sa (*adj.*) = LADEIRENTO.
ladineza, ladinice (*f.*) smartness, cleverness, adroitness.
ladino -na (*adj.*) smart, keen-witted; crafty, cunning, wily; adroit.
lado (*m.*) side, flank; direction.—**a—**, side by side; neck and neck.—**de laçar**, the lasso (right) side of a saddle.—**de montar**, the mounting (left) side of the saddle.—**direito**, righthand side.—**do coração**, left side.—**esquerdo**, lefthand side.—**fraco**, foible.—**occidental**, west side.—**oriental**, east side.—**vulnerável**, weak point. **a um—**, aside, to one side. **ao—**, to one side. **ao—de**, beside, near, close to; against; at the side of . **de—**, aside, to one side; sideways. **de cada—**, on each side. **de um—**, on one side. **do—de**, from the direction of; toward. **do—de fora**, on the outside. **do—esquerdo (direito)**, on the left (right) side. **dum—e de outro**, on both sides. **dum—para outro**, from side to side; back and forth. **no outro—de**, across.—**máu do negócio**, the short end of the stick. **para o—**, aside. **para o—de**, toward, near. **pôr de—**, to put by, put aside (save). **por outro—**, on the other hand. **por todos os—s**, on all sides, everywhere. **por um—**, on (the) one hand. **por um—e outro**, from one place to another.
ladrão [fem. LADRA, LADROA, LADRONA] (*adj.*) thieving, thievish; (*m.*) thief, burglar, robber; housebreaker, hold-up man; sucker (of a plant); spillway; overflow pipe (of a water tank).—**de estrada**, highwayman.—**formigueiro**, petty thief.
ladrar (*v.i.*) to bark, bay; to vociferate.—**à lua**, to bark at the moon. **Cão que ladra não morde**, A barking dog seldom bites.
ladriço (*m.*) fetter (for a horse).
ladrido (*m.*) bark, barking [= LATIDO].
ladrilhado -da (*adj.*) tiled; (*m.*) a tiled area.
ladrilhador (*m.*) a tile setter.
ladrilhar (*v.t.*) to tile; (*v.i.*) to work as a tilesetter.
ladrilheiro (*m.*) tile-maker.
ladrilho (*m.*) floor or wall tile; brick.—**de cortiça**, cork tile.—**vidrado**, glazed tile.
ladro -dra (*adj.; m.,f.*) = LADRÃO.
ladroagem (*m.*) thievery, robbery, burglary; thieves collectively.
ladroar (*v.t.*) to rob [= ROUBAR].
ladroeira (*f.*) robbery; extortion; swindle.

ladroeiro (*m.*) sucker (of a plant).
ladroíce (*f.*) = LADROEIRA.
ladrona, fem. of **ladrão**.
ladronaça (*m.*) = LADRÃO.
lagalhé (*m.*) blackguard; a nobody. Var. LEGUELHÉ.
lagamar (*m.*) lagoon.
lagar (*m.*) wine press; olive press.
lagaragem (*f.*) wine pressing; olive pressing.
lagareiro -ra (*m.,f.*) wine presser; olive presser.
lagarta (*f.*) caterpillar.—**aranha**, a small, sluglike caterpillar.—**de-fogo**, caterpillar of the flannel moth, c.a. BICHO-CABELUDO, TATURANA.—**rosada**, pink bollworm (*Pectinophora*, syn. *Gelechia, gossypiela*).
lagartear (*v.i.*) to bask in the sun.
lagartixa (*f.*) any of numerous small lizards, esp. the geckos; a small lizard (*Hemidactylus mabouia*) which came to Brazil with the slaves from Africa, and is now widespread in town and country. After dark, it is commonly seen on walls and ceilings. [The term **lagartixa** is applied also to some iguanids, better known as PAPAVENTO or CALANGO.] (*slang*) hiker, mountain climber; (*colloq.*) a slender, supple woman.—**d'água**, a newt, eft or triton.—**das-dunas**, a South American iguanid (*Liolaemus occipitalis*); a tegu called TÉIU.
lagarto (*m.*) any lizard except the small ones (which are called LAGARTIXAS) but esp. the TEJU, which grows to about three feet and whose flesh is eaten as a delicacy; fig., the biceps; a certain cut of beef; a small hand press for softening corks [used in drugstores].—**do-mar**, the sand-diver (*Synodus intermedius*), a lizard fish c.a. PEIXE-LAGARTO, TIRAVIRA, CALANGO.—**verde**, a teiid lizard called TÉIU. **dizer cobras e—s de uma pessoa**, to greatly malign another person.
lagena (*f.*) an eared earthen vessel; slender-necked bottle or flask.
lageniforme (*adj.*) flask-shaped.
lagênula (*f.*) small flask.
lagerstrêmia (*f., Bot.*) the queen crapemyrtle (*Lagerstroemia speciosa*), c.a. ESCUMILHA.
lago (*m.*) lake; pond.
lagoa (*f.*) lagoon, pool, pond; moor.
lagoacho (*m.*) a small lake.
lagoão (*m.*) large, deep lake.
lagoeiro (*m.*) rain pond.
lagomia (*m., Zool.*) a pika (*Ochotona sp.*), c.a. PICA.
lagópode (*adj., Bot.*) having hairy rhizomes suggestive of the foot of the hare; (*m., Zool.*) ptarmigan or red grouse (*Lagopus sp.*).
lagoquilia (*f.*) harelip [= LÁBIO LEPORINO].
lagosta (*f.*) a spiny lobster or sea crayfish, genus *Palinurus*. [The large American or European lobster of genus Homarus is called LAVAGANTE.]; (*colloq.*) a red-faced person.—**comum** is the common European species of Palinurus (*P. vulgaris*)—the langouste of French menus.—**de-espinho** is the large species (*P. argus*) common in Bermuda.—**gafanhoto**, a mantis shrimp (*Squilla sp.*).—**sapata**, or **-sapateira**, a locust lobster (*Scyllarus sp.*), c.a. CIGARRA.
lagosteiro -ra (*adj.*) lobster-fishing; (*f.*) lobster boat.
lagostim (*m.*) any small lobster; a locust lobster (*Scyllarus*); a crawfish; the Norway lobster (*Nephrops norwegicus*).
lagostomia (*f., Med.*) lagostoma (harelip).
lágrima (*f.*) tear; drop.—**de-moça**, the common ginger lily (*Hedychium coronarium*), c.a. LÍRIO-DO-BREJO.—**s da aurora** or **da manhã**, dewdrops. [*Poetical*].—**s-de-napoleão** = RAIOS-DE-JÚPITER (a spiderlily).—**s-de-nossa-senhora** or **-de-santa-maria** = CAPIM-DE-NOSSA-SENHORA.—**s de aguardente**, beads formed by shaking spirituous liquors.—**s de crocodilo**, crocodile tears.—**s-de-jó** = FUCSIA; CAPIM-DE-NOSSA-SENHORA.
lagrimal (*adj.*) lachrymal [= LACRIMAL].
lagrimejar (*v.i.*) to shed a few tears; of eyes, to water.
lagrimoso -sa (*adj.*) lachrymous, tearful [= LACRIMOSO].
laguna (*f.*) lagoon, basin.
lai (*m.*) lay (song, poem, ballad).
laia (*f.*) kind, sort. **à—de**, as a kind of. **gente da mesma—**, birds of a feather.
laicalidade (*f.*) laicality.
laicidade (*f.*) laicity.
laicificar, laicizar (*v.t.*) to laicize.
laico -ca (*adj.*) lay, secular.
lais [-es] (*m., Naut.*) yardarm.
laivar (*v.t.*) to spot, stain, soil.

laivo (m.) spot, stain; tinge; a trickle of blood, as from the corner of the mouth; (pl.) slight or superficial ideas; a smattering of something.

lajão (m.) a huge stone slab.

laje (f.) flagstone; flagging; pavestone; cement slab; stone slab; any large, flat rock. Vars. LAJA, LÁJEA.

lajeado –da (adj.) paved, flagged; (m.) a courtyard or other area paved with flagstones; a bed of rocks (as of a dry creek).

lajeador (m.) paver (man).

lajeamento (m.) paving with stones or slabs; paved area.

lajear (v.t.) to pave with stones.

lajedo [ê] (m.) a flagged area; a large, flat rock.

lajeiro (m.) a large flat rock surface.

lajota (f.) a small concrete paving block or tile; a small flagstone.

lalação (f.) lallation, infantile utterance.

lama (f.) mud, mire, sludge. arrastar na—, lit., to drag in the mud; fig., to besmirch. saír da—e meter-se no atoleiro, to jump out of the frying pan into the fire; (m.) llama (camel-like animal of Peru); (m.) lama (Buddhist priest).

lamaçal (m.), lamaceira (f.) slough, quagmire, mud hole.

lamacento –ta (adj.) muddy, miry, slimy.

lamaísmo (m.) Lamaism.

lamaísta (m.,f.) Lamaist.

lama[n]gueira (f.) = CORNO-GODINHO.

lamantim (m.) = MANATI.

lamarão (m.) mud flat.

lamarquia (f.) goldentop grass (Lamarckia aurea).

lamarquismo (m.) Lamarckism.

lambada (f.) beating, lashing; a strip of something; a bawling out, dressing down; a swig (of liquor).

lambaio (m.) mop; scullion.

lambança (f.) an eatable; a goody; vanity; wrangling; falsehood; cheating; crooked scheme; laziness; blarney.

lambão –bona (adj.) greedy, gluttonous; sloppy, slobbery; (m.,f.) glutton.

lambarão –rona (adj.) = LAMBUZÃO.

lambareiro –ra (adj.) greedy; sweet-toothed; gossiping; (m.,f.) gossip; (m.) anchor cable.

lambari [í] (m.) minnow.

lambarice (f.) sweetmeat; greediness.

lambaz (m.) mop; (adj.) greedy.

lambazar (v.t.) to mop (deck or floor).

lambdacismo (m.) lambdacism.

lambedor—deira (adj.) licking; lambent; (m.,f.) licker; lickspittle; (f.) long, thin knife, c.a. BICUDA, COTRUCO, ESPINHO, LAPIANA, PAJEÚ, PERNAMBUCANA, TIJUBINA.

lambedura (f.) = LAMBIDELA.

lambe-esporas (m.,f.) lickspittle, bootlicker, toady.

lambeiro –ra (adj.) that licks; (m.,f.) licker.

lambe-lambe (m.) itinerant photographer.

lambe-olhos (m.) a stingless bee (Melipona timida), c.a. FRECHEIRA.

lambe-pratos (m.,f., colloq.) glutton; lit., plate-licker.

lamber (v.t.) to lick; to touch lightly; to lick up, devour. —a poeira, to bite the dust (fall).—os dedos, os beiços, to lick one's fingers, one's lips (in anticipation).—embira, to go through hard times.—os pés a alguém, to be a bootlicker.—-se de contentamento, to bubble over with joy.

lambeta (adj.) flattering; (m.,f.) adulator, flatterer; bootlicker.

lambeteiro –ra (adj.) flattering; (m.,f.) flatterer.

lambição (f.) servile adulation.

lambidela (f.) a lick; act of licking; adulation; bargain; tip.

lambido –da (adj.) of poetry, works of art, etc., over-refined. cabelo—, slicked-down hair; (f.) = LAMBIDELA.

lambiscador –dora (adj.; m.,f.) fond of, or one who is fond of, nibbling dainties.

lambiscar (v.t.,v.i.) to nibble, pick at (food).

lambiscaria (f.) dainty, tidbit.

lambisco (m.) morsel, tidbit.

lambisgóia (f.) prude; busybody; dull person.

lambona, fem. of lambão.

lamborada (f.) = LAMBADA.

lambrequim (m.) lambrequin; (Arch.) label.

lambril, lambrim (m.) wainscot(ing).

lambrisar (v.t.) to wainscot.

lambujeiro –ra (adj.) lickerish.

lambujem (f.) tidbit, dainty; boot, gain; odds, handicap. dar (uma)—a, to give odds or an advantage to another,

with a handicap to oneself. de—, to boot, in addition, over and above.

lambuzada, lambuzadela (f.) smear, stain; fig., thin coat of paint.

lambuzão –zona (adj.) unclean, greasy, messy, untidy, sloppy.

lambuzar (v.t.) to daub, smear, soil, stain; (v.r.) to soil one's clothes with food stains; to smear one's face while eating.

lamecha (adj.) infatuated.

lameira (f.), –ro (m.) quagmire, marshland; (slang) a mudder (race horse).

lameirão (m.) mud flat(s).

lamela (f., Anat., Zool., Bot.) lamella.

lamelação (f.) lamellation.

lamelado –da (adj.) lamellate.

lamelar (adj.) lamellar.

lamelária (f., Zool.) a genus (Lamellaria) of marine gastropod mollusks.

lamelibrânquio –quia (adj.; m., Zool.) lamellibranch.

lamelífero –ra (adj.) lamelliferous.

lameliforme (adj.) lamelliform.

lamelirrostro –tra (adj.) lamellirostral; (m.pl.) the Lamellirostres (ducks, geese, swans).

lameloso –sa (adj.) lamellose, lamellate.

lamentação (f.) lamentation; wail; plaint.

lamentador –dora (adj.) lamenting; (m.,f.) lamenter.

lamentar (v.t.) to lament, mourn; to bewail, bemoan; to regret, deplore; to rue; (v.r.) to wail, moan, cry, sob; to grieve; to complain; to feel sorry (de, for, about).

lamentável (adj.) lamentable; pitiful, pitiable; deplorable; wretched.

lamento (m.) lament(ation); dirge; wail; moan(ing); plaint; complaint.

lamentoso –sa (adj.) mournful; whining; lamentable, deplorable.

lâmia (f.) lamia, vampire.

lamigueiro (m., Bot.) the European hackberry (Celtis australis).

lâmina (f.) lamina, thin plate, scale; blade; (Bot.) lamina. —de serra, saw blade.

laminação, laminagem (f.) lamination; rolling (of steel, etc.).

laminado –da (adj.) laminate; laminated; of steel shapes, plates, etc., rolled.

laminador (m.) one who laminates; a rolling-mill (for steel, etc.).

laminar (adj.) laminar; (v.t.) to laminate; to roll (steel, etc.).—a frio, to cold-roll.—a quente, to hot-roll.

lamináría (f.) a genus (Laminaria) of kelps.

laminectomia (f., Surg.) laminectomy.

laminite (f., Veter.) laminitis, founder.

laminoso –sa (adj.) laminose.

lamínula (f.) a little lamina; glass slide (for microscopy).

lâmio-branco (m., Bot.) the white deadnettle (Lamium album), c.a. URTIGA-BRANCA, URTIGA-MORTA.

lamiré (m.) tuning fork; fig., a starting signal; (colloq.) a bawling out, rebuke, reprimand.

lâmpada (f.) lamp; light bulb.—a neon, neon light.—de álcool, alcohol lamp.—de arco, arc light.—de quartzo, quartz light.—de querosene, kerosene lamp.—de rádio, radio tube.—de mesa, table lamp.—de pé, floor lamp. —de segurança, a miner's safety lamp.—de soldar, a blowtorch.—de vapor de mercúrio, mercury-vapor light. —de vapor de sódio, sodium-vapor light.—elétrica, electric light bulb.—elétrica de mão, an electric flashlight.—-pilôto, pilot light.—ultravioleta, ultraviolet lamp.

lampadário (m.) candelabrum; chandelier.

lampadite (f., Min.) lampadite.

lamparina (f.) small night lamp, consisting of a string wick inserted through a cork disk floating in a dish of oil; (colloq.) cuff, box, slap.

lampeiro –ra (adj.) lively, nimble, quick; forward, pushing; premature.

lampejador (m.) blinker (signal).

lampejante (adj.) flashing.

lampejar (v.i.) to flash, shine, sparkle.

lampejo [ê] (m.) sudden flash of light.

lampianista (m.,f.) lamplighter.

lampião (m.) a large lamp; a street lamp.

lampíride (f.), lampírio, lampiro (m.) a firefly.

lampo –pa (adj.) soon-ripe; early, premature.

lampreeiro [e-ei] (m.) eel fisherman.

lampreia (*f.*) lamprey eel, sea lamprey (*Petromyzon marinus*).—**-dos-rios**, fresh-water lamprey (*Petromyzon fluvialis*).

lampsana (*f., Bot.*) common nipplewort (*Lapsana communis*).

lamúria (*f.*) lamentation; wail; complaint; whining.

lamuriante (*adj.*) complaining, whining, crying.

lamuriar (*v.i.*) to lament; to wail, to complain; to whine, whimper, cry; (*v.r.*) to snivel.

lamuriento –ta, lamurioso –sa (*adj.*) whining, maudlin, sniveling.

lana-caprina (*f.*) trifle, thing of no consequence. **questão de—**, a trifling matter.

lanada (*f., Ordn.*) sponge, swab.

lanar (*adj.*) wool.

lanarquita (*f., Min.*) lanarkite.

lança (*f.*) lance, spear; javelin; carriage or wagon shaft; boom of a crane. **à ponta de—**, to the utmost; lit., at spear-point. **cabeça de—**, spearhead. **meter uma—em África**, to perform a very difficult task. **quebrar—s por alguém**, to take up the cudgels in behalf of another.

lança-bombas (*m.*) bomb-thrower.

lança-chamas (*m.*) flame-thrower.

lançada (*f.*), **lançaço** (*m.*) a spear thrust.

lançadeira (*f.*) shuttle; fig., a restless person.

lançador –dora (*m.,f.*) thrower; bidder; (*adj.*) that throws; bidding.

lançamento (*m.*) cast, throw; bid; act of casting, etc.—see the verb LANÇAR; a bookkeeping entry; launching (of a ship); shoot (of a plant).—**de concreto**, pouring of concrete.

lança-minas (*m.*) mine layer.

lança-perfume (*m.*) perfume squirter. [A small glass ampoule containing perfumed ether under pressure which the merrymakers at carnival-time (in Brazil) squirt on each other.]

lançar (*v.t.*) to cast, throw, hurl, fling; to launch; to project, throw out, eject; to utter; to vomit, throw up, cast up; (*v.r.*) to throw oneself; to rush.—**à água**, to launch (a vessel).—**à conta de**, to impute to; to charge to.—**a luva a**, to fling down the gauntlet, challenge, defy.—**à margem**, or **à monte**, to cast aside, abandon.—**à praia**, to cast up on the beach.—**a responsabilidade sôbre outrém**, to impute the blame to another; to pass the buck.—**água no mar**, to carry coals to Newcastle.—**ao chão**, to hurl to the ground.—**aos pés de**, to cast at the feet of.—**de si**, to hurl from oneself.—**em**, to cast into; to inject; to bid on.—**em conta**, to enter in an account.—**em ferros**, to throw in irons.—**em terra**, to put ashore.—**em rosto a**, to twit, taunt, fling at.—**ferro**, to cast anchor.—**fora**, to throw out; to vomit.—**luz sôbre**, to shed light on.—**mão de**, to seize upon; to take hold of; to resort to; to avail oneself of.—**no mercado**, to introduce in the market.—**o repto**, to hurl a challenge.—**os alicerces de**, to lay the foundations of.—**os olhos para**, to dart the eyes toward.—**poeira aos olhos de**, to throw dust in the eyes of, mislead, deceive.—**por terra**, to throw to the ground.—**raízes**, to strike root.—**rebentos**, to burgeon.—**-se aos pés de**, to throw oneself at the feet of.—**-se de cabeça em**, to throw oneself headlong into.—**-se nos braços de**, to throw oneself in the arms of.—**suspeitas sôbre**, to cast suspicion on.—**uma sombra sôbre**, to cast a shadow over.—**um teoria**, to put forward a theory.—**um livro**, to publish a book.—**um navio ao mar**, to launch a ship.—**uma pedra fundamental**, to lay a cornerstone. **A sorte está lançada**, The die is cast.

lança-torpedos (*m.*) torpedo tube.

lance (*m.*) throw, cast; predicament; emergency; climax; incident, event; play (in a game); stroke; bid (at auction).—**cômico**, point of a joke.—**de olhos**, a quick glance.—**forçoso**, a fortuitous occurrence. **de um—**, all at once, in one stroke. **do primeiro—**, from the first onset.

lancear (*v.t.*) to spear; to wound with a lance; fig., to pierce the heart; to fish with a casting net.

lanceiro (*m.*) lancer; (*pl.*) lancers (a set of quadrilles).

lanceolado –da, lanceolar (*adj.*) lanceolate.

lancêta (*f.*) surgeon's lancet; (*Bot.*) goldenrod (*Solidago*).

lancetada (*f.*) a lancet-cut.

lancetar (*v.t.*) to lance.

lancha (*f.*) launch, motor boat; "a very specialized type of craft averaging 80 feet long, having powerful single screw engines, and constructed of hardwood, used on the lower Amazon for towing BATELÕES loaded with cattle." [*GBAT*]; (*pl., slang*) clodhoppers, gunboats (big shoes);

big feet.

lanchada (*f.*) launchful.

lanchão (*m.*) large launch; barge, lighter.

lanchar (*v.i.*) to eat a light lunch or snack.

lancha-torpedeira (*f.*) motor torpedo-boat.

lanche (*m.*) afternoon snack [but not lunch, which is ALMOÇO].

lancheria (*f.*) lunchroom.

lancheta (*f.*) a small launch.

lanchonete (*f.*) lunch counter.

lancil (*m.*) a piece of hewn stone suitable as an edgestone, a window sill, etc.

lancinante (*adj.*) shooting, stabbing [pain]; poignant, harrowing, heart-rending.

lancinar (*v.t.*) to pierce, prick, sting; to torment.

lanço (*m.*) a cast, throw or fling; act of casting, throwing or flinging; a bound or rebound; the fish caught in a cast of the net; a stretch (as of road, wall, river, etc.); a bid (at auction).—**de dados**, a throw of the dice.—**de escadas**, a flight of stairs.—**de olhos**, a glance.—**de política**, a political stroke.—**de rêde**, a cast of the net. **a—s**, in spurts. **num só—**, at one fell stroke. **cobrir—o**, to cover a bid.

lancoa [ô] (*f., Bot.*) a galangal (*Alpinia galanga*).

landau, landô (*m.*) landau.

lande (*f.*) acorn; (*m.*) wasteland.

landim (*m.*) = GUANANDI.

landuá (*f.*) a false report; a hand fishnet [= JERERÉ].

langanho (*m.*) jellyfish; by ext., any soft, repugnant mass.

langite (*f., Min.*) langite.

langor [ô] (*m.*) languor.

langoroso –sa (*adj.*) languorous, languid.

langua [ú] (*f.*) a low-lying coastal plain.

langue, languente (*adj.*) languid.

languento –ta (*adj.*) ailing, sickly.

languescer (*v.i.*) to languish, droop, pine [= ELANGUESCER].

languidez[a] (*f.*) languidness, listlessness, weakness.

lânguido –da, lângüido –da (*adj.*) languid, languishing, drooping, listless.

languir [25] (*v.i.*) to languish [= ELANGUESCER].

lanhar (*v.t.*) to tear to pieces (as with the teeth); to rip open, slash, gash; to gut (fish); to butcher (language).

lanho (*m.*) a cut, slash, gash (with a knife); a slice of meat.

laníadas, laniádeas (*f.pl., Zool.*) the Laniidae (family of shrikes).

lanífero –ra (*adj.*) laniferous; fur-bearing.

lanifício (*m.*) anything made of wool; woolen cloth; the spinning of wool.

lanígero –ra (*adj.*) lanigerous; lanuginous.

lanolina (*f., Pharm.*) lanolin(e).

lanosidade (*f.*) woolliness, lanosity.

lanoso –sa (*adj.*) lanose, woolly.

lansquenê (*f.*) lansquenet (a gambling game at cards), c.a. MERERÉ.

lantana (*f., Bot.*) common lantana (*L. camara*).

lantânio (*m., Chem.*) lanthanum.

lantanite (*f., Min.*) lanthanite.

lantejoula, lantejoila (*f.*) = LENTEJOULA.

lanterna (*f.*) lantern.—**-de-aristóteles**, (*Zool.*) Aristotle's lantern (of sea urchins).—**elétrica de mão**, flashlight.—**furta-fogo**, dark lantern.—**mágica**, magic lantern.—**traseira**, tail-light.

lanternária (*f.*) a lantern fly (*Lanternaria sp.*)

lanterneiro (*m.*) maker of lanterns; light-keeper; lantern bearer; man who does automobile fender and body work.

lanternim (*m.*) lantern wheel; (*Arch.*) lantern; clerestory.

lanterninha (*f.*) tail-light.

lanternista (*m.,f.*) member of a certain political faction in Brazil which bitterly opposed President Getúlio Vargas before his suicide in 1955.

lantim (*m.*) the Brazil beautyleaf (*Calophyllum brasiliense*), c.a. LANDIM, GUANANDI, OLANDI, PAU-AZEITE, PAU-DE-SANTA-MARIA.

lantopina (*f., Chem.*) lanthopin(e).

lanudo –da (*adj.*) woolly [= LANOSO].

lanugem (*f.*) lanugo; down, fluff; fuzz (on peaches, etc.).

lanugento –ta, lanuginoso –sa (*adj.*) lanuginous, downy, woolly.

lanzinha (*f.*) bunting, thin woolen fabric.

lanzudo –da (*adj.*) woolly [= LANUDO]; coarse, ill-mannered.

lapa (*f.*) rock cave or den; a limpet; the floor of a mine gallery.

lapáceo –cea (*adj.*, *Bot.*) lappaceous; echinate.

lapacho (*m.*) a tropical American timber tree (*Tecoma caraiba*).

lapão (*adj.; m.*) Lapp.

laparão (*m.*, *Med.*) gland enlargement of person suffering from glanders [=MORMO]; scrofula; (*Zool.*) a limpet [=LAPA].

láparo (*m.*) baby rabbit.

lapela (*f.*) coat lapel.

lapidação (*f.*) cutting of precious stones; polishing, refining; lapidation, stoning (to death).

lapidar (*v.t.*) to lapidate, stone; to cut (polish, engrave) precious stones; to shape, mould, fashion; (*adj.*) lapidary; of speech or writing, crystal-clear, well-expressed; terse.

lapidaria (*f.*) the art of cutting stones; lapidary's shop.

lapidário –ria (*adj.; m.*) lapidary; (*f.*) deciphering of stone inscriptions.

lápide (*m.*) a tombstone or other engraved stone.

lapídeo –dea (*adj.*) stony.

lapidícola (*adj.*, *Zool.*) lapidicolous.

lapidificar (*v.t.*) to petrify.

lapíli (*m.pl.*, *Geol.*) lapilli.

lápis (*m.*) pencil—-**tinta**, indelible pencil.

lapisada (*f.*) pencil stroke.

lapiseira (*f.*), **-ro** (*m.*) pencil box; pencil sharpener.

lápis-lazúli (*m.*) lapis lazuli [=LAZULITE].

lapo (*m.*) rawhide snapper on the end of a whip; strip, slice; slash.

lapônio –nia (*adj.*) =LAPUZ; (*cap.*, *f.*) Lapland.

lapso –sa (*adj.*) delinquent, in default, erring; (*m.*) lapse of time; slip, fault, oversight.

lapuz (*adj.*) rude, coarse; (*m.*) yokel, boor.

laquear (*v.t.*) to tie off (a severed blood vessel); to paint with lacquer; (*m.*) tester, canopy.

lar [-es] (*m.*) fireside, hearth; home.

laracha (*f.*) jest; (*m.*) jester, wit.

laranja (*f.*) orange; (*slang*) a simpleton; (*adj.*) orange-colored.—-**amarga**,—-**azêda**,—-**da-terra**, all varieties of the sour or Seville orange (*Citrus aurantium*).—-**cravo**, king orange (*Citrus nobilis*), the fruit of which is called MEXERICA or TANGERINA.—-**da-baía**, the navel orange, a variety of sweet orange (*Citrus sinensis*) developed in Brazil and much grown in California. [The original plant brought from Brazil is preserved at Riverside, California.].—-**da-china**, the sweet orange (*Citrus sinensis*).—-**de-cafre**, the kafirorange poisonnut (*Strychnos spinosa*).—-**de-umbigo**, navel orange.—-**do-mato** = LA-RANJARANA.—-**mimosa** = TANGERINA; TANGERINEIRA.—-**pêra**, a small, smoothskinned, oblongish variety of sweet orange (*Citrus sinensis*).—-**seleta**, a variety of sweet orange.—-**turan ja** = CIDRA.

laranjado –da (*adj.*) orange-colored [= ALARANJADO]; (*f.*) orangeade.

laranjal (*m.*) orange grove.

laranjarana (*f.*) a mangrove (*Cassipourea guianensis sp.*), c.a. LARANJA-DO-MATO, MANGUE-DE-ÁGUA-DOCE.

laranjeira (*f.*) any orange tree.

laranjeiro (*m.*) orange grower or dealer.

laranjinha (*f.*) any small orange; sugar-cane rum flavored with orange peel; also = LIMA-DE-CHEIRO; ESPINHO-DE-VINTEM.—-**do-mato**, a pricklyash (*Zanthoxylum*).—-**do-campo** = BABARÉ, BAMBORÉ.

larapiar (*v.t.*) to filch, pilfer.

larápio –pia (*m.,f.*) filcher, pilferer, sneak thief.

lardear (*v.t.*) to lard; to interlard.

lardiforme (*adj.*) lardiform, lardaceous.

lardo (*m.*) fat or bacon, esp. in strips.

lardose (*f.*, *Med.*) fatty degeneration.

laré (*m.*) a word used in the expression **andar ao laré**, meaning: to idle; to lead a precarious life.

lareiro –ra (*adj.*) of or pert. to the hearth or home; (*f.*) fireplace, hearth. **parapeito da—**, mantelpiece.

larga (*f.*) a loosing or releasing; largess; looseness; wide open spaces. **à—**, with a free hand; generously, lavishly. **dar—s a**, to give free rein to.

largado –da (*adj.*) loosed; abandoned; (*f.*) act of releasing; a wisecrack; a stunt or deed; start (as of a race).

largamente (*adv.*) liberally, generously.

largar (*v.t.*) to let go, let loose, let fly, release, set free; to put down; to put aside; to cast off; to unfurl (sails).—-**se a**, to give oneself over to.—-**se de**, to escape from.—**a**,

to release to.—**a máscara**, to drop (one's) mask.—**a(s) rédea(s) a**, to give free rein to.—**da costa**, to sail away from land.—**da pena**, to drop one's pen (stop writing). —**de**, to set sail from.—**de** (**fumar**), to leave off (smoking).—**de mão**, to take hands off; to abandon.—**mão de**, to desist from.—**o couro**, (*colloq.*) to work hard, exert oneself.—**para**, to depart for. **Largou tudo**, He gave up everything.

largata (*f.*) = LAGARTA.

largo –ga (*adj.*) broad, wide; large, ample; spacious; liberal; **—s anos**, long (many) years; (*adv.*) largely; (*Mus.*) largo; (*m.*) public square, plaza. **ao—**, afar; in the offing; offshore. **ao—de**, far from.

larguear (*v.t.*) to give or spend freely.

largueto (*adv.; m.*, *Music*) larghetto.

largueza [ê] (*f.*) width; largess, liberality; spaciousness.

largura (*f.*) width, breadth.

lariço (*m.*) = PINHEIRO-LARÍCIO.

laridão (*m.*) baying of hounds in the hunt.

larídeo –dea (*adj.*, *Zool.*) laridine; (*m.*) larid, gull [= GAI-VOTA]; (*m.pl.*) the *Laridae* (family of gulls, terns and jaegers).

laringe (*m.,f.*, *Anat.*, *Zool.*) larynx.

laríngeo –gea, laringiano –na (*adj.*) laryngeal.

laringite (*f.*, *Med.*) laryngitis.

laringografia (*f.*) laryngography.

laringologista (*m.,f.*) laryngologist.

laringoscópio (*m.*) laryngoscope.

laroz (*m.*) jack rafter.

larva (*f.*) larva; jack rafter; specter.—-**mineira**, a plant rust of the genus *Hemileia*.

larval (*adj.*) larval.

larvicida (*adj.*) larvicidal.

larvícola (*adj.*) larvicolous.

larviforme (*adj.*) larviform.

larvíparo –ra (*adj.*) larviparous.

larvívora –ra (*adj.*) larvivorous.

lasanha (*f.*) lasagna (wide Italian noodle).

lasca (*f.*) chip, fragment, piece; chunk; splinter, sliver.

lascar (*v.t.*) to splinter, sliver; to chip off; (*v.i.*) to split; to chip; to whip.

lascívia (*f.*) lasciviousness, wantonness.

lascivo –va (*adj.*) lascivious; bawdy, lewd, wanton; frolicsome.

lasiocampo (*m.*, *Zool.*) a genus (*Lasiocampa*) of moths.

lassidão, lassitude (*f.*) lassitude, weariness.

lasso –sa (*adj.*) weary, worn out; lax; loose, slack, limp, flabby.

lástima (*f.*) compassion, pity; heartache; moan, lament. **Que—**! What a pity!

lastimadura (*f.*) bruise, contusion.

lastimar (*v.t.*) to deplore, lament; to grieve at; to feel sorry for; to wound; (*v.r.*) to regret; to wail; to complain.

lastimável (*adj.*) lamentable, deplorable, pitiable.

lastimoso –sa (*adj.*) pitiful; direful; mournful.

lastração, lastragem (*f.*), **lastr[e]amento** (*m.*) act or operation of ballasting.

lastrar (*v.t.*) to ballast; to fill in (railroad bed) with ballast.

lastro (*m.*) ballast; (*fin.*) gold reserve (for currency); (*colloq.*) appetizers; switch engine.

lat. = LATIM; LATINO (Latin); LATITUDE (latitude).

lata (*f.*) tin can; tin plate; wood lath or strip; (*slang*) "mug" (face).—**de lixo**, garbage pail.—**velha**, (*slang*) a jalopy. **conservas em—s**, canned goods. **pôr em—s**, to can (food). **Ela deu a—no namorado**, She canned (discarded) her lover.

latada (*f.*) trellis; trellised vine; arbor; palm-thatched shed; nuptial charivari.

latagão (*m.*) a strapping big fellow.

latagona (*f.*) a large, robust woman.

latânia (*f.*) the red latania palm (*Latania commersoni*).

latão (*m.*) brass; a large can.—**de leite**, milk can.

lategada (*f.*) a lash with a whip.

lategar (*v.t.*) to whip.

látego (*m.*) scourge or whip, esp. of rawhide; a rawhide strap.

latejante (*adj.*) throbbing, beating.

latejar (*v.i.*) to throb, beat, pulsate.

latejo [ê] (*m.*) beat, pulsation, throb.

latência (*f.*) latency.

latente (*adj.*) latent, occult, veiled; in abeyance.

lateral (*adj.*) lateral, side.

lateralidade (*f.*) state of being sideways.

laterifólio –lia (adj., Bot.) axillary.
laterígrado –da (adj., Zool.) laterigrade, running sidewise.
laterita (f., Geol.) laterite.
látex [ks], **látice** (m.) latex.
laticar (v.t.) to extract latex from.
laticífero –ra (adj.) laticiferous.
laticolo –la (adj.) broad-necked.
laticórneo –nea (adj.) wide-horned.
latido (m.) bark, yelp, bay [=LADRIDO].
latifloro –ra (adj.) having broad flowers.
latifólio –lia (adj.) having broad leaves.
latifundiário (m.), –ria (f.) large landowner.
latifúndio (m.) a large landed estate.
latilabro –bra (adj.) thick-lipped.
latim (m.) Latin. **perder o—**, to waste one's breath.
latímano –na (adj.) having broad hands.
latinada (f.) a mistake in Latin; a speech in Latin.
latinar (v.i.) to speak or write in Latin.
latinidade (f.) Latinity.
latinismo (m.) Latinism.
latinista (m.,f.) Latinist.
latinizar (v.t.) to Latinize.
latino –na (adj.) Latin; lateen; (m.,f.) a Latin.
latino-americano –na (adj.) Latin-American.
latinório (m.) bad Latin; (colloq.) flowery speech.
latípede (adj.,Zool.) having broad feet.
latipene (adj., Zool.) latipennate, broad-winged.
latir [25] (v.i.) to bark, bay, yelp.
látire, latfride (m.) = TARTAGO.
latirismo (m., Med.) lathyrism.
látiro (m.) = CIZIRÃO.
latirrostro –tra (adj., Zool.) latirostral; (m.pl.) the Latirostres (swallows).
latitude (f.) latitude; scope, range.—**meridional** or **sul**, latitude south (of the equator).—**norte** or **setentrional**, latitude north (of the equator.).
latitudinário –ria (adj.) latitudinous; latidudinarian.
latitudinarismo (m.) latitudinarianism.
latitudinarista (m.,f.) a latitudinarian.
lato –ta (adj.) broad, wide, ample. **em sentido—**, in a broad sense.
latoaria (f.) tinsmith's shop [=FUNILARIA].
latoeiro (m.) tinsmith; brazier; = FUNILEIRO.
Latrão (m.) Lateran.
latria (f., R.C.Ch.) latria.
latrina (f.) latrine, privy; water-closet.
latrocinar (v.t.) to commit armed robbery.
latrocínio (m.) armed robbery; a hold-up.
latrodecto (m.) a genus (Latrodectus) of venomous spiders which includes the black widow (L. mactans).
lauda (f.) page (of a book); one side of a sheet of paper.
laudabilidade (f.) laudability, laudableness.
laudânico –ca (adj.) soporific; narcotic.
laudanina (f., Chem.) laudanin(e).
laudanizado –da (adj.) containing laudanum; narcotized.
laudanizar (v.t.) to narcotize.
láudano (m.) laudanum, tincture of opium.
laudanosina (f., Chem.) laudanosin(e).
laudatício –cia, –tivo –va, –tório –ria (adj.) laudatory, laudative.
laudável (adj.) laudable, praiseworthy, commendable.
laúde (m.) catboat.
laudes (m.pl., Eccl.) lauds.
laudo (m.) findings, report (as of a board of inquiry); expert's report.—**arbitral**, arbiter's award.
laumon[t]ite (f., Min.) laumon(t)ite.
laura (f., Bot.) the polyanthus Narcissus (N. tazetta.)
lauráceo –cea (adj., Bot.) lauraceous; (f.pl.) the laurel family (Lauraceae).
láurea (f.) a crown of laurel; honor, distinction.
laureado –da (adj.; m.,f.) laureate.
laurear (v.t.) to laureate.
laureio (m.) a crowning with laurel.
laurel [-éis] (m.) a crown of laurel; honor, homage.
laurentino –na (adj., Geol.) Laurentian.
lauréola (f.) a wreath of laurel.—**-fêmea**, (Bot.) the mezereon or February daphne (D. mezereum), c.a. MEZEREÃO. —**-macha**, (Bot.) the spurge laurel (Daphne laureola), c.a. MEZERÉU-MENOR.
láurico –ca (adj., Chem.) lauric [acid].
laurionite (f., Min.) laurionite.
laurite (f., Min.) laurite; ruthenium sulfide.
lautarita (f., Min.) lautarite.
lauto –ta (adj.) sumptuous, lavish; plentiful.

lava (f.) lava; also = LAVAGEM.
lavabo (m.) small wash basin; finger bowl; (Eccles.) Lavabo.
lava-bunda (m.) a dragon fly.
lavação (f.) wash; washing.
lavadaria (f.) = LAVANDERIA.
lavadeira (f.) washerwoman, laundress; washing machine; (Zool.) the courier water-tyrant (Fluvicola c. climazura), c.a. LAVANDEIRA, LAVADEIRA-DE-NOSSA-SENHORA; also = VIUVINHA, POMBINHA-DAS-ALMAS.
lavadela (f.) a light washing or rinsing.
lavado –da (adj.) washed; bathed; washed-out [color].— **em lágrimas**, bathed in tears.
lavadouro (m.) a clothes-washing place (as by the side of a stream); a wash tub. Var. LAVADOIRO.
lavadura (f.) wash; washing.
lavagante (m.) the American lobster (Homarus americanus). Cf. LAGOSTA.
lavagem (f.) act or operation of washing; wash; hogwash, swill; enema; (slang) a bawling out; a whitewashing (of an opposing team).—**cerebral**, brain washing.—**química**, dry cleaning.
lava-louças (m.) in Portugal, kitchen sink. [In Brazil it is PIA or LAVATÓRIO DE COZINHA].
lavamento (m.) washing.
lavanda (f., Bot.) lavender (Lavandula officinalis).
lavandaria (f.) = LAVANDERIA.
lavandeira (f.) washerwoman; kinds of dragonflies, c.a. JACINA, PITO.
lavanderia (f.) laundry. Vars. LAVANDARIA, LAVADARIA.
lava-pé (m., Bot.) the blueweed or common viper bugloss (Echium vulgare), c.a. VIPERINA, VIOMAL; a centaure (C. sempervirens), c.a. VIOMAL; (pl.) foot washing (a religious ceremony); kinds of small stinging ants, esp. the fire ant (Solenopsis geminata), c.a. FORMIGA-DE-FOGO, FORMIGA-MALAGUETA, FORMIGA-LAVA-PÉS.
lava-pratos (m.) coffee senna (Cassia occidentalis), c.a. FEDEGOSO-VERDADEIRO; another senna (Cassia quin quangulata), c.a. FEDEGOSO-GRANDE. Both are c.a. MAMANGÁ.
lavar (v.t.) to wash, bathe (-se, oneself); to cleanse, purify (-se, oneself).—**a sêco**, to dry-clean.—**as mãos de (como Pilatos)**, to wash one's hands of something (as did Pilate).—**-se em água de rosas**, to rejoice, esp. in another's discomfiture.
lavatório (m.) lavatory, wash basin, washstand.
laverca (f., Zool.) the Old World skylark (Alauda arvensis), c.a. CALHANDRA.
lavoira (f.) = LAVOURA.
lavoirar (v.) = LAVOURAR.
lavor [-es] (m.) labor; handiwork; fancy needlework; ornate carving.
lavorar (v.t.) to decorate by embroidering, carving, chiseling, etc.
lavoso –sa (adj.) lavalike.
lavoura (f.) field work, plowing, tillage; farming, agriculture.
lavourar (v.t.) to till the soil [=LAVRAR].
lavra (f.) work; tillage; mining; production.
lavradeiro –ra (adj.) farmwork [animals]; (f.) a woman farm worker; peasant woman; needlewoman.
lavradio –dia (adj.) tillable; (f.) tillage.
lavrado –da (adj.) wrought, worked; carved; embroidered, chased; tilled; of documents, executed; (m.) fancy needlework; tilled land; (pl.) gold and silver ornaments.
lavrador (m.) farmer, farm hand, agricultural worker; peasant.
lavragem (f.) work; plowing, tillage; woodworking.
lavrante (m.) goldsmith, silversmith.
lavrar (v.t.) to plow, till; to work, plane, chisel, carve (wood, etc.); to cut, carve, polish (stones); to chase (metal); to engrave; to embroider; to draw up (a document); (v.i.) to develop, grow, increase; to spread.
lavrita (f.) black diamond, carbon diamond; c.a. DIA MANTE NEGRO.
laxação (f.) laxation.
laxante (adj.; m.) laxative.
laxar (v.t.) to slacken; to unstop, open; to loosen; fig., to alleviate.
laxativo –va (adj.) laxative [= LAXANTE].
laxidão (f.) = LASSIDÃO.
laxo –xa (adj.) lax, slack; loose.
lazão (adj.) = ALAZÃO. [Fem. LAZÃ].
lazarar (v.t.) to infect with a repellent disease, as leprosy;

lazarento –ta (adj.) leprous; full of sores; (colloq.) famished; (m.,f.) a leper; a lazar.

lazareto [ê] (m.) a building for detention in quarantine; formerly, a lazaretto (pesthouse).

lazarina (f.) an old-fashioned fowling piece [= PICA-PAU].

lázaro –ra (m.,f.) a lazar; a leper.

lazarone (m.) Neapolitan beggar; by ext., any beggar.

lazeira (f.) poverty; (colloq.) hunger.

lazeirento –ta (adj.) destitute; (colloq.) starving.

lazer [ê] (m.) leisure [= ÓCIO].

lazulita (f., Min.) lazulite; lapis lazuli.

lazurita (f., Min.) lazurite.

lb.= LIBRA (pound).

L.da, L.do = LICENCIADA, LICENDIADO (Licentiate).

lê, leais, leamos, forms of LER [38].

lé (m.) a word used in the expression lé com lé, cré com cré, birds of a feather flock together; like with like.

leadilite (f.) = LEDILITE.

leal (adj.) loyal, faithful (a, to).

lealdação (f.) legalization; customhouse inspection.

lealdade (f.) loyalty, fidelity, allegiance.

lealdado –da (adj.) very clean [sugar].

lealdamento (m.) = LEALDAÇÃO.

lealdar (v.t.) to legalize; to submit to customs inspection.

leão [fem. LEOA] (m.) lion; social lion; Leo.—de chácara, (colloq.) watch dog; a bouncer.—do mar, an old sea dog (sailor).—dragonado, (Heraldry) lion dragonné.—-marinho, sea lion.—rompente, (Heraldry) lion rampant.

lebracho (m.) bunny.

lebrada (f.) rabbit stew.

lebrão (m.) a buck hare or rabbit.

lebre (f.) a doe hare or rabbit. comer (or comprar) gato por—, to buy a pig in a poke. fazer passar gato por—, to sell a gold brick.

lebré (m.) mastiff.

lebreiro –ra (adj.) hare-hunting.

lebreu, lebrel (m.) harrier; greyhound.

lecheguana (f.) a social wasp (Nectarina lecheguana), c.a. ENXU. tirar—, to be cold at night for lack of covers.

lechia (f.) the litchi tree (Litchi chinensis), or its fruit.

lecionando –da (adj.; m.,f.) pupil.

lecionar (v.t.) to teach, lecture.

lecionário (m., Eccl.) lectionary.

lecionista (m.,f.) teacher, esp. a private one.

lecitidáceo –cea (adj., Bot.) lecythidaceous; (f.pl.) the Lecythidaceae (sapucaia-nut family).

lecitina (f., Biochem.) lecithin.

lécito (m.) lecythus (ancient jug or vase).

lecitol (m.) = LECITINA.

lecontite (f., Min.) lecontite.

lecre (m., Zool.) the royal flycatcher (Onychorhynchus c. coronatus).

lede, ledes, forms of LER [38].

ledice (f.) joyfulness, gaiety; (pl.) quips.

ledilite (f., Min.) leadhillite.

ledo –da [ê] (adj.) gay, smiling, joyful.—engano, happy illusion.

ledor –dora (adj.) reading; (m.,f.) reader [= LEITOR].

lêem, form of LER [38].

leérsia (f., Bot.) the genus (Leersia) of cutgrasses.

lég.= LÉGUA (league).

lega (f.) a device for extracting latex.

legação (f.) legation; (Bot.) the Eurasian greenbrier (Smilax aspera).

legacia (f.) legateship.

legado (m.) ambassador, envoy; legate; legacy.

legal (adj.) legal, lawful; (colloq.) correct, regular, in order.

legalidade (f.) legality.

legalismo (m.) legalism.

legalista (adj.) legalistic; (m.,f.) legalist, loyalist.

legalização (f.) legalization.

legalizar (v.t.) to legalize; to authenticate, certify, countersign.

legar (v.t.) to bequeath, devise, will; to delegate.

legatário –ria (m.,f.) legatee; devisee.

legatorio –ria (adj.) legatorial.

legenda (f.) lettering, inscription; caption, heading; label; legend; legenda.

legendário –ria (adj.) legendary; (m.,f.) legendarian; legendary (writer or book).

legião (f.) legion; multitude. [cap.] —de Honra, Legion of Honor.

legionário –ria (adj.; m.) legionary.

legislação (f.) legislation.—tributária, tax legislation.

legislador –dora (m.) legislator; (f.) legislatress; (adj.) legislating.

legislar (v.t.,v.i.) to legislate.

legislativo –va, legislatório –ria (adj.) legislative.

legislatura (f.) legislature.

legislável (adj.) that can be enacted into law.

legisperito (m.), –ta (f.) legal expert; jurist.

legista (m.,f.) one skilled in the law [= LEGISPERITO].

legítima (f.) an heir's legal portion.

legitimação (f.) legitimation.

legitimado –da (adj.; m.,f.) legitimized (child).

legitimador –dora (adj.; m.,f.) that, or one who, legitimates.

legitimar (v.t.) to legitimate.

legitimidade (f.) lawfulness; legitimacy; genuineness.

legitimismo (m.) legitimism.

legitimista (adj.; m.,f.) legitimist.

legítimo –ma (adj.) legitimate, rightful; legal, lawful; real, valid; genuine, authentic; lawfully begotten.

legível (adj.) legible, readable.

legra (f.) a surgeon's bone scraper; a half-round chisel or gouge; a mason's jointer or pointing trowel.

legração, legradura (f.) bone-scraping.

legrar (v.t.) to scrape or trim a bone. Cf. ALEGRAR.

legre (m.) horseshoer's knife.

légua (f.) league (a unit of distance) varying in Brazil from 6,000 meters [3.72 mi.] to 6,600 meters [4.10 mi.].—marítima, marine league, 5555.55 meters [3.45 mi.].—quadrada brasileira, Brazilian square league (called also SESMARIA DO CAMPO), 43.57 sq. kms. [16.8 sq. mi.].

leguelhé (m.) = LAGALHÉ.

leguleio (m.) a legalistic stickler; pettifogger; shyster lawyer.

legume (m.) legume, pea, bean; (pl.) vegetables.

legumeiro –ra (adj.) leguminous; (m.) a vegetable dish.

legumina (f., Biochem.) legumin.

leguminiforme (adj.) leguminiform.

leguminoso –sa (adj.) leguminous; (f.pl., Bot.) the Leguminosae.

lei (f.) law, statute, rule.—agrária, agrarian law.—civil, civil law.—criminal, criminal law.—da guerra, rules of war.—da necessidade, law of necessity.—das médias, law of averages.—das nações, law of nations.—das rôlhas, gag law.—de arrôcho, gag law.—de Lynch, lynch law.—de meios, budgetary law.—de oferta e procura, law of supply and demand.—de talião, retaliation, an eye for an eye, a tooth for a tooth.—divina, divine law.—marcial, martial law.—militar, military law.—moral, moral law.—-mordaça, gag law.—s da natureza, laws of nature.—s de repressão, repressive laws.—rôlha, gag law. à—de, in keeping with the rule or custom. madeira de—, hardwood. ouro de—, solid gold. prata de—, sterling silver. previsto pela—, statutory. projeto de—, a proposed bill (in the legislature).

leia, leiam, leias, leio, forms of LER [38].

leicenço (m.) boil, felon, etc. [= FLEGMÃO].

leigal (adj.) laical.

leigo –ga (adj.) lay, secular; non-professional, not expert; (m.) layman, one of the laity; outsider.

leilão (m.) auction. pôr em—, to put up at auction.

leiloamento (m.) auctioning.

leiloar (v.t.) to auction.

leiloeiro (m.), –ra (f.) auctioneer.

leira (f.) furrow; raised bed in a garden; ridge of dirt between furrows.

leita (f.) fish milt [= LACTÉIA].

leitão [fem. LEITOA] (m.) suckling pig.

leitar (v.i.) to lactate; (adj.) milky.

leitaria (f.) = LEITERIA.

leite (m.) milk; milky juice (of some plants); a sea catfish.—-de-cachorro = CIPÓ-DE-LEITE (a milkweed).—de cal, limewater; useless thing or effort.—de creme, cream.—-de-galinha, (Bot.) the common star-of-Bethlehem (Ornithogalum umbellatum).—de pato, a no-stakes game; a no-pay job.—magro, skim milk.—talhado, sour milk. arroz de—, rice pudding. dente de—, milk tooth. irmão de—, foster brother. sapinhos de—, small white patches occurring in the mouth and fauces, esp. of young children, characteristic of thrush. tirar—de vaca morta, to cry over spilled milk.

leitegada (f., colloq.) a litter of pigs.

leiteiro –ra (adj.) milk-yielding; (m.) milkman; (Bot.) a tree of the dogbane family (Tabernaemontana sp.); (f.) milk-woman; milk pitcher or jug; (Bot.) birdlime

sapium (*S. laurocerasus*); an ant (*Crematogaster quadri-jormis*).
leitelho [ê] (*m.*) buttermilk; powdered milk.
leitento –**ta** (*adj.*) lacteous, milky; milk-yielding.
leiteria (*f.*) a dairy or creamery.
leito (*m.*) bedstead; couch, berth, cot, bunk; bed.—**da morte,** the grave [*Poetical*].—**de estrada,** roadbed.—**de Procrusto,** Procrustean bed.—**de rio,** river bed.—**inferior (superior),** lower (upper) berth. **guardar o—,** to keep to one's bed.
leitoa, fem. of LEITÃO.
leitoado –**da** (*adj.*) fat as a pig; (*f.*) a litter of pigs; a feast of roast suckling pig.
leitor –**tora** (*adj.*) reading; (*m.,f.*) reader.
leitorado (*m.*) lectureship.
leitoso –**sa** (*adj.*) milky; lactescent.
leituga (*f.*, *Bot.*) a composite (*Tolpis barbata*), c.a. ÔLHO-DE-MÔCHO.
leitura (*f.*) reading, perusal; reading matter.—**da ata,** reading of the minutes.—**da carta,** map reading.
leiva (*f.*) plowed land; field; furrow; strip of soil between furrows.
Lélia (*f.*) Lelia.
lema (*m.*) lemma, premise of a proposition; motto, saying.
lembradiço –**ça** (*adj.; m.,f.*) (one) having a good memory.
lembrado –**da** (*adj.*) remembered; memorable; mindful.
lembrador –**dora** (*adj.*) remindful, awakening memories; (*m.*) reminder.
lembrança (*f.*) remembrance, recollection; memory; reminder; memento, souvenir; gift, keepsake; (*pl.*) greetings, compliments.—**s à família!** Remember me to the folks!
lembrar (*v.t.*) to recall (to mind); to remind, suggest, prompt; to admonish.—**se de,** to think of, remember. **lembro-me de,** or **lembra-me, ter visto,** I remember having seen. **Não me lembro de mais nada,** I don't remember anything more.
lembrete [ê] (*m.*) memorandum, note; reprimand, reproof, remonstrance.
leme (*m.*) rudder; helm; direction, control.—**de profundidade,** elevator (of an airplane). **perder o—,** to be at one's wit's end. **ter o—,** to have control.
lemingue (*m., Zool.*) lemming.
lemna (*f., Bot.*) any duckweed (*Lemna*), c.a. LENTILHA-D'ÁGUA.
lemnáceo –**cea** (*adj.*) like a lentil; (*Bot.*) lemnaceous; (*f.pl.*) the Lemnaceae (duckweed family).
lemniscata (*f., Geom.*) lemniscate.
lemnisco (*m., Anat., Math., Zool.*) lemniscus.
lêmos, form of LER [38].
lêmure (*m., Zool.*) lemur.
lençalho (*m.*) a large, cheap handkerchief.
lençaria (*f.*) linen store or factory; white goods.
lenço (*m.*) handkerchief, neckerchief, kerchief.
lençol [–çóis] (*m.*) sheet.—**d'água** or—**freático,** water table. **em maus lençóis,** in hot water, in a bad fix, in a pickle, in a mess.
lenda (*f.*) legend; fable, myth; fig., a made-up story (lie); a long-drawn-out (boresome) account.
lendário –**ria** (*adj.*) legendary.
lêndea (*f.*) nit (egg of a louse).
lendeoso –**sa** (*adj.*) infested with nits.
lendo, pres. part. of LER [38].
lengalenga (*f.*) prolix discourse; tiresome recital; rigmarole, balderdash.
lengalengar (*v.i.*) to drone; to speak monotonously and endlessly.
lengue (*m.*) = ABELHEIRO (bird).
lenha (*f.*) firewood; (*colloq.*) blows with a stick.—**-branca,** (*Bot.*) a member of the staff-tree family (*Maytenus sp.*).
lenhador (*m.*) woodcutter.
lenhar (*v.i.*) to cut firewood.
lenheira (*f.*) a woods from which firewood is taken.
lenheiro (*m.*) woodcutter; dealer in firewood; woodpile.
lenho (*m.*) xylem; wood; tree trunk.—**-álpe(s),** aloeswood or agalloch—the soft, resinous wood of an East Indian tree (*Aquilaria agallocha*) burnt by Orientals as a perfume. [It is the aloes of the Bible.]—**da cruz,** the cross of Jesus.—**-santo** = GUÁIACO. **santo—,** Holy Cross.
lenhose (*f., Bot., Chem.*) lignin.
lenhoso –**sa** (*adj.*) ligneous, woody.
lenidade, leniência (*f.*) lenity, lenience, leniency.
leniente (*adj.*) lenient; lenitive.
lenir [46] (*v.t.*) to assuage, mitigate.

lenimento (*m.*) liniment.
lenitivo –**va** (*adj.*) palliative; (*m.*) lentive; liniment; relief.
lenocínio (*m.*) pandering, white slavery.
lentar (*v.t.*) to moisten; (*v.i.*) to become moist.
lente (*f.*) lens.—**acromática,** achromatic lens.—**bifocal,** bifocal lens.—**de aumento,** magnifying glass. (*m.*) high school teacher; college professor; (*adj.*) reading.
lentejar (*v.i.*) to ooze moisture; (*v.t.*) to moisten.
lentejoula (*f.*) spangle, sequin.
lentejoular (*v.t.*) to bespangle.
lentescente (*adj.*) sticky; moist.
lentescer (*v.*) = LENTAR.
lenteza (*f.*) = LENTIDÃO.
lenticela (*f., Bot.*) lentical.
lentícula (*adj.; f.*) a lens of small size.
lenticular (*adj.*) lenticular.
lentidão (*f.*) slowness; sluggishness; moisture.—**de jabuti,** snail's pace; turtle slowness.
lentiforme (*adj.*) lentiform, lenticular.
lentigem (*f.*), **lentigo** (*m.*) freckle; (*Med.*) lentigo.
lentiginoso –**sa** (*adj.*) freckly.
lentilha (*f.*) lentil seed; (*Bot.*) lentil (*Lens culinaris*); carbuncle (boil); (*Geol.*) lentil.—**brava,** (*Bot.*) a lentil (*Ervum nigricans*).—**-d'água,** swollen duckweed (*Lemna gibba*); Brazilian jointvetch (*Aeschynomene brasiliana*); a water lettuce (*Pistia occidentalis*).—**-do-campo,** jointvetch (*Aeschynomene hystrix*).
lentiprisma (*f.*) a prismatic lens.
lentisco (*m., Bot.*) the lentisk pistache (*Pistacia lentiscus*), c.a. ALMECEGUEIRA; the pinkberry pepper tree (*Schinus lentiscifolia*).
lento –**ta** (*adj.*) slow (**em,** to); dilatory; slack; sluggish; laggard; lazy; flabby; moist; sticky; (*adv., Music*) slowly.—**de percepção,** dull-witted. **a fogo—,** on a slow fire.
lentor (*m.*) slowness; humidity [= LENTIDÃO].
lentura (*f.*) slowness; slight moisture; dew; (*colloq.*) sweat.
leoa (fem. of LEÃO) lioness.
Leonardo (*m.*) Leonard.
leônculo (*m.*) lion cub.
leoneira (*f.*) lion's den; lion cage.
Leonel (*m.*) Lionel.
leonino –**na** (*adj.*) leonine.
leonita (*f., Min.*) leonite.
Leonor (*f.*) Eleanor; Eleanora; Elinor; Lenore; Leonora.
leontodonte (*m., Bot.*) the genus (*Leontodon*) of hawkbits.
leontopódio (*m., Bot.*) common edelweiss (*Leontopodius alpinum*).
leopardado –**da** (*adj.*) spotted like a leopard.
leopardo (*m.*) leopard; a small tropical catfish—the leopard cat (*Corydoras julii*)—seen in home aquaria.
leopoldínia (*f.*) the genus (*Leopoldinia*) of piassava palms.
Leopoldo (*m.*) Leopold.
lepádidas, lepadídeos (*m.pl.*) the family (*Lepadidae*) containing the goose barnacles.
lepas (*m.*) a goose barnacle (*Lepas sp.*).
lepideno (*m., Chem.*) lepidene.
lepidina (*f., Chem.*) lepidine.
lepídio (*m.*) a pepperweed (*Lepidium latifolium*), c.a. ERVA-PIMENTEIRA.
lépido –**da** (*adj.*) pleasant, cheerful, gay; jaunty; jocose; charming; sprightly; lively, nimble, spry.
lepidólita (*f., Min.*) lepidolite.
lepidomelânio (*m., Min.*) lepidomelane.
lepidopterologia (*f.*) lepidopterology.
lepidopterologista (*m.,f.*) lepidopterologist.
lepidóptero (*m.*) any lepidopteron (butterfly or moth); (*pl.*) the Lepidoptera.
lepidosperma (*f., Bot.*) a genus (*Lepidosperma*) of sedges.
lepidossirene (*m.*) the lepidosiren (*L. paradoxa*), an eel-shaped fish, c.a. CARAMURU.
lepóride (*m.*) Belgian hare.
leporídeo (*m.*) any hare or rabbit; (*pl.*) the Leporidae.
leporino –**na** (*adj.*) leporine. **lábio—,** harelip.
lepra (*f.*) leprosy, some common names for which are MORFÉIA, GUARUCAIA, MACOTA, MACUTENA. [Others are listed under MAL.]; dog mange; fig., moral corruption (*colloq.*) a no-good, evil person.—**italiana,** pellagra.—**tuberculosa** or —**dos hebreus,** tubercular leprosy.
leprologia (*f.*) leprology.
leprosaria (*f.*) leprosarium.
leprose (*f., Med.*) leprosy; (*Plant Pathol.*) leprosis, scaly bark, nailhead rust.
leproso –**sa** (*adj.*) leprous; loathsome. (*m.,f.*) leper.

leptidas, leptídeos (*m.pl.*, *Zool.*) the family (*Rhagionidae*, *syn. Leptidae*) consisting of the snipe flies.

leptinite (*f.*, *Petrog.*) leptinolite.

leptinotarsa (*f.*, *Zool.*) the Colorado potato beetle (*Leptinotarsa sp.*).

leptocefalia (*f.*, *Craniol.*) leptocephalia.

leptocéfalo –**la** (*adj.*) leptocephalous; (*m.*, *Med.*) a leptocephalus; (*Zool.*) a leptocephalus (larval eel); a conger eel.

leptocêntrico –**ca** (*adj.*, *Bot.*) leptocentric.

leptoclase (*f.*, *Geol.*) a minute crack or fracture in rock.

leptoclorite (*f.*, *Min.*) leptochlorite.

leptocúrtico –**ca** (*adj.*, *Statistics*) leptokurtic, less flat-topped than the Gaussian curve.

leptodáctilo (*m.*, *Zool.*) an arciferous frog (*Leptodactylus sp.*).

leptodérmico –**ca** (*adj.*, *Bot.*) leptodermous, thin-skinned.

leptofilo –**la** (*adj.*, *Bot.*) having slender leaves.

leptoma (*f.*, *Bot.*) leptome.

leptomeninge (*f.*, *Anat.*) leptomeninges.

leptoprosopo –**pa** (*adj.*, *Anthropom.*) leptoprosopic.

leptorrino –**na** (*adj.*, *Anthropom.*) leptorrhinian.

leptosperma (*f.*, *Bot.*) a genus (*Leptospermum*) of tea trees.

leptosporangiado –**da** (*adj.*, *Bot.*) leptosporangiate.

leptótrix [ks] (*f.*, *Bacteriol.*) a genus (*Leptothrix*) of bacteria.

leque (*m.*) fan; fanlike curve in a staircase; any fanlike object; (*Zool.*) the knobbed scallop (*Lyropecten nodosus*).

lequéssia (*f.*) drunkenness; idleness.

ler [38] (*v.t.,v.i.*) to read, peruse; to perceive, discern; to decipher, unravel; to lecture (in class).—**a buena-dicha**, to tell fortune.—**a sorte de**, to read the fortune of.—**de cadeira**, to speak with authority (on a subject).—**música**, to read music.—**nas entrelinhas**, to read between the lines.—**pelo mesmo breviário** or **pela mesma cartilha**, to be of the same mind.

lerca (*f.*) a very thin cow; (*pl.*) hanging folds of skin.

lerdaço –**ça** (*adj.*) dim-witted.

lerdeador –**dora** (*adj.*) slow, sluggish—said of one who dillydallies.

lerdear (*v.i.*) to loiter, lag, dillydally.

lerdeza [ê], **lerdice** (*f.*) slowness, sluggishness, slothfulness.

lerdo –**da** (*adj.*) dull, stupid, slow; doltish; boorish.

leréia (*f.*) idle talk.

léria (*f.*) twaddle, poppycock, idle talk, hooey.

leriaçu (*m.*) = OSTRA-AMERICANA.

lero-lero (*m.*, *slang*) chit-chat, twaddle.

lês, form of LER [38].

lesa (*m.*, *slang*) poor soccer player, poor kicker.

lesado –**da** (*adj.*) injured, hurt, damaged; (*colloq.*) touched (in the head).

lesa-majestade (*f.*) lese majesty.

lesante (*adj.*) damaging, detrimental, hurtful; (*m.,f.*) one who hurts, injures or damages another.

lesão (*f.*) lesion, hurt, injury; wrong, grievance.

lesar (*v.t.*) to hurt, injure; to wrong; to aggrieve; to cheat, rook, bilk. **Êle me lesou em 100 contos**, He cheated me out of 100 CONTOS.

lesbianismo (*m.*) Lesbianism.

lesbiano –**na**, **lésbico** –**ca** (*adj.*) Lesbian.

leseira (*f.*) idiocy; idiotic behavior; (*m.,f.*) idiot, fool.

lesivo –**va** (*adj.*) hurtful, prejudicial.

lêsma (*f.*) slug, snail; by ext., sluggard.—**-de-coqueiro**, larva of a leaf beetle.—**-do-mar**, a sea cucumber. **passo de**—, snail's pace.

lesmar (*v.i.*) to dawdle.

lesmento –**ta** (*adj.*) slow, indolent.

lés-nordeste (*m.*) east-northeast wind or bearing.

leso –**sa** (*adj.*) hurt, injured; disabled; palsied; paralytic; foolish, crazy.

lés-oeste (*m.*) east-west wind or bearing.

lesse, lesses, lêssemes, lesseis, lessem, forms of LER [38].

lés-sueste (*m.*) east-southeast wind or bearing.

lestas (*f.*) a vernal grass (*Anthoxanthum amarum*), c.a. FENO-DE-CHEIRO-AMARGOSO, LESTRAS.

leste (*m.*) east; eastward, east wind.—**quarta a nordeste**, east by north.—**quarta a sudeste**, east by south. (*adv.*) **a**—, **para**—, easterly, eastwardly; eastward(s); (*adj.*) **de**—, eastern; oriental; eastwardly. Cf. LÉS, ESTE.

lêste, form of LER [38].

lesto –**ta** (*adj.*) sprightly, brisk, nimble, spry, quick, alert.

letal (*adj.*) lethal, deadly, mortal.

letalidade (*f.*) lethality.

letão, –**tona** (*m.,f.*) Lett; (*m.*) Latvian (Lettish) language; (*adj.*) Lettish.

letargia (*f.*) lethargy, stupor, torpor; apathy.

letárgico –**ca** (*adj.*) lethargic; torpid. **encefalite**—, sleeping sickness.

letargo (*m.*) letargia.

letícia (*f.*) Letitia.

lético –**ca** (*adj.*) Lettish; (*m.*) Latvian (Lettish) language.

letífero –**ra** (*adj.*) lethiferous, deadly.

letífico –**ca** (*adj.*) lethal; gladsome.

letivo –**va** (*adj.*) of or pert. to lessons. **ano**—, school year.

letra [ê] (*f.*) letter (of the alphabet); handwriting; printing type; promissory note; (*pl.*) letters, literature; lyrics (of a song).—**a**—, literally, word for word.—**à ordem**, a note payable to bearer.—**à vista**, a note payable on sight.—**composta**, a digraph.—**consonante**, a consonant.—**cursiva**, running hand.—**de câmbio**, bill of exchange.—**de fôrma**, round hand.—**de mão**, handwriting.—**dobrada**, double letters.—**dominical**, red letter day (on the calendar).—**gótica**, Gothic type.—**inicial**, initial letter.—**maiúscula**, capital letter.—**minúscula**, lowercase letter.—**morta**, dead letter (of the law).—**muda**, silent letter.—**negociável**, a negotiable note.—**s apostólicas**, papal bulls.—**s de identificação**, call letters.—**vogal**, vowel. **à**—, literally, exactly. **ao pé da**—, literally. **belas**—**s**, belles-lettres. **de**—**s gordas**, unlearned, uneducated. **homem de**—**s**, man of letters. **reformar uma**—, to renew a note (at the bank). **ter boa**—, to have a good handwriting.

letrado –**da** (*adj.*) lettered, literate, educated, learned; (*m.*) man of letters; learned man.

letreiro (*m.*) lettering; label; inscription; sign; poster.

leu, form of LER [38].

léu (*m.*) chance; idleness. **ao**—, aimlessly. **ao**—**da vida**, at the whim of fate.

leucântimo (*m.*) ox-eye daisy (*Chrysanthemum leucanthemum*).

leucanto –**ta** (*adj.*; *Bot.*) having or bearing white flowers.

leucagite (*f.*), –**to** (*m.*, *Min.*) leucaugite.

leucana (*f.*, *Bot.*) the white popinac leadtree (*Leucaena glauca*).

leucina (*f.*, *Biochem.*) leucine.

leucita (*f.*, *Min.*) leucite.

leucito (*m.*, *Min.*) leucite; (*Bot.*) a leucoplast.

leucitófiro (*m.*, *Petrog.*) leucitophyre.

leucobase (*f.*, *Chem.*) leuco base.

leucoblasto (*m.*, *Anat.*) leucoblast.

leucobriáceas (*f.pl.*, *Bot.*) a family (*Leucobryaceae*) of tufted mosses.

leucocalcite (*f.*, *Min.*) leucochalcite.

leucocarpo –**pa** (*adj.*, *Bot.*) leucocarpous.

leucocitemia (*f.*, *Med.*) leucocythemia, leukemia.

leucócito (*m.*, *Anat.*) leucocyte.

leucomaína (*f.*, *Biochem.*) leucomaine.

leucopenia (*f.*, *Med.*) leucopenia.

leucopirita (*f.*, *Min.*) leucopyrite.

leucorréia (*f.*, *Med.*) leucorrhea.

leucosfenite (*f.*, *Min.*) leucosphenite.

leucospermo –**ma** (*adj.*, *Bot.*) leucospermous.

leucoxênio [ks] (*m.*, *Min.*) leucoxene.

leuquemia (*f.*, *Med.*) leukemia.

leva (*f.*) weighing of anchor; mustering of troops; a levy (of troops, prisoners, etc.)

levada (*f.*) see under LEVADO..

levadente (*f.*) rebuke, reprimand.

levadiço –**ça** (*adj.*) movable, portable; easily lifted; (*f.*) drawbridge.

levado –**da** (*adj.*) mischievous, impish [child]; undisciplined, unruly.—**da breca**, "full of the Old Nick".—**do diabo**, furious; (*m.*, *slang*) a lookout for a gambling joint; (*f.*) mill stream; sluice, millrace; an elevation (hill); a carrying (off, away).

levador –**dora** (*adj.*) carrying; transporting; (*m.*) transporter; carrier.

leva-e-traz (*m.,f.*) tale bearer.

levantado –**da** (*adj.*) lifted; arisen; high; elevated; noble; rough [sea]; uprisen, insurgent; (*f.*) act of lifting or of rising.

levantador –**dora** (*adj.*) lifting, raising; that stirs up rebellion; (*m.*) a lifting muscle; an elevator (surgical instrument).

levantamento (*m.*) lifting, raising; an uprising; a survey; investigation, inquiry.

levantar (*v.t.*) to raise (up); to lift (up); to elevate, hoist, erect; to uplift, exalt; to heighten; to excite. stir up; to levy; to remove; to suspend, discontinue (a session, a meeting, etc.); (*v.r.*) to rise, arise; to stand up; to get up; to rebel; (*m.*) a raising; an arising.—**à altura de**, to raise to the level of.—**a bitola**, to increase the demands.—**a cabeça**, to raise (one's) head; to regain (one's) lost fortune or position.—**a caça**, to startle (raise) game.—**a crista**, to get one's dander up.—**a luva**, to accept a challenge.—**a mão contra**, to raise (one's) hand against.—**a mesa**, to clear the table (after a meal).—**âncora**, to weigh anchor.—**a sessão**, to adjourn the meeting.—**a voz**, to raise the voice.—**auto**, to prepare the papers in a court case.—**dificuldades**, to raise obstacles, doubts, etc.—**estátua a**, to raise a statue to.—**ferro**, to weigh anchor.—**fervura**, to start to boil.—**mão**, to desist.—**o encampamento**, to break camp.—**o estandarte**, to raise a standard to.—**o lanço**, to raise the bid.—**o sítio**, to raise the seige.—**os espíritos**, to raise (one's) spirits.—**os olhos ao céu**, to raise (one's) eyes to heaven.—**os ombros**, to shrug the shoulders.—**poeira**, to kick up the dust.—**se com as estrelas**, to get up with the chickens.—**se com o pé esquerdo**, to get up on the wrong side of the bed (in a bad humor).—**se contra**, to rise up against.—**um brinde**, to raise (propose) a toast.—**um inventário, um mapa, etc.**, to draw up an inventory, a map, etc.—**vôo**, to take wing; of an airplane, to take off. **ao**—**do sol**, at sunrise.

levante (*m.*) east, orient; the Levant; act of raising (something); an uprising; (*Bot.*) horsemint (*Mentha longifolia*). **de**—, unsettled; uneasy; about to leave.

levar (*v.t.*) to take (away), carry (off); to conduct, lead; to bear, convey; to steal; to require, need (time); to gain, win; to endure, undergo; to wear (on the person). —**a**, to induce to.—**a banca à glória**, to break the bank (at gambling). —**a bem**, to take in good part.—**a bom têrmo**, to carry (something) to a successful conclusion. —**a cabo**, to carry out, accomplish, finish (something). —**à cena**, to enact, perform (a play).—**adiante (avante)**, to carry forward.—**a efeito**, to carry out (an undertaking); to bring (a thing) to pass.—**à força**, to take by force.—**à frente**, to push a thing ahead; go ahead with it. —**a'** (or **em**) **mal**, to take amiss; to take offense.—**à mão**, to carry by hand.—**a melhor**, to get the better of; to gain the upper hand.—**a** (or **em**) **paciência**, to tolerate, accept (a situation) patiently.—**a palma**, to carry the day; to take the cake, win the prize; run away with the show; to outrival.—**a pior**, to get the worst of.—**à sepultura**, to lead to the grave, bring about the death of.— **(alguém ou alguma coisa) a sério**, to take (someone or something) seriously.—**a sua avante**, to gain one's ends. —**a um impasse**, to drive into a corner.—**a vida na maciota**, to take things easy, not work too hard.—**ao cabo (ao fim, ao têrmo)**, to carry (something) to conclusion.—**ao crime**, to conduce to crime.—**as lampas a**, to get ahead of.—**avante**, to carry forward, go ahead with.—**boa vida**, to lead an easy life.—**bomba**, or **pau**, to flunk (an exam).—**com a porta na cara**, to have the door slammed in one's face; fig., to get turned down.—**de assalto**, to take by assault.—**de chalaça, de galhofa, de mangação, de risota**, to make fun of; not to take seriously.—**(alguma coisa) em conta**, to take (something) into account.—**na cabeça**, (*colloq.*) to get it in the neck.— **no embrulho**, to gyp (someone).—**o diabo**, to disappear. —**para diante**, to carry forward, advance.—**para o seu tabaco**, to take a beating.—**se da breca**, or **do diabo**, to blow one's top.—**tempo**, to spend (take) time.—**um gato**, to receive a call-down.—**um insulto para casa**, to swallow an insult.—**um prejuizo**, to suffer a loss or damage.— **uma vida desordenada**, to lead a wild life.—**vantagem a**, to have the advantage over.—**deixar de**—**em conta**, to overlook, leave out of account. **Não leva a coisa nemhuma**, It leads to nothing. **Que fim levou (êle)?** What has become of (him)? What ever happened to (him)? **Que fita estão levando hoje no Bijou?** What picture is showing at the Bijou today? **Que os leve o diabo**, The devil take them. **Todos os caminhos levam a Roma**, All roads lead to Rome.

leve (*adj.*) light (not heavy); slight; **de**—, lightly, softly, gently. **nem de**—, not even slightly. **o mais**—, the slightest. **tocar de**—, to touch lightly.

levedação (*f.*) leavening.

levedar (*v.t.*) to leaven; (*v.i.*) to rise (as dough).

lêvedo –**da** (*adj.*) leavened; (*m.*) a yeast of the genus *Saccharomyces*.

levedura (*f.*) yeast, leaven [= FERMENTO].

leveza [vê] (*f.*) lightness; levity.

leviandade (*f.*) levity; frivolity folly; carelessness.

leviano –**na** (*adj.*) frivolous, flippant; fickle; flighty; thoughtless; rattlebrained; (*colloq.*) light (not fully loaded).

leviatã (*m.*) leviathan.

levidade (*f.*) = LEVEZA.

levigação (*f.*) levigation.

levigar (*v.t.*) to levigate.

levirato (*m., Anthropol.*) levirate.

levitação (*f.*) levitation.

levodução (*f.*) levoduction.

levogiro –**ra** (*adj.*) counter-clockwise; levorotatory.

levulina (*f., Chem.*) levulin.

levulose (*f.*) levulose, fructose, fruit sugar.

levulosuria (*f., Med.*) levulosuria.

lewisita (*f., Min.*) lewisite.

lexical [ks] (*adj.*) lexical.

léxico [ks] (*m.*) lexicon, dictionary.

lexicografia [ks] (*f.*) lexicography.

lexicógrafo (*m.*) –**fa** (*f.*) [ks] lexicographer.

lexicologia [ks] (*f.*) lexicology.

léxicon (*m.*) = LÉXICO.

leziria (*f.*) river meadowland.

lha(s), fem. form of LHO(S).

lhama (*f.*) lamé (rich metallic fabric); llama (woolly Andean ruminant).

lhaneza (*f.*) sincerity, frankness; unaffectedness; affability; smoothness.

lhano –**na** (*adj.*) sincere, open, frank; affable; kind; (*m.pl.*) llanos (great open plains).

lhanura (*f.*) = LHANEZA.

lhe(s) (*pers. pron.*) to or for him (her, it, you); (*pl.*) to or for them (you).

lho(s) (*pers. pron.*) it to him (to her, to you); (*pl.*) it to them (to you). [Contraction of indirect obj. pron. LHE & direct obj. O(S).]

li, lia, liam, líamos, forms of LER [38].

lia (*f.*) lees, dregs.

liaça (*f.*) packing straw.

liação (*f.*) act of tying, or binding, or bonding.

liadouro (*m.*) bondstone.

liamba (*f.*) = DIAMBA.

liame (*m.*) tie; bond; connection; ship's rigging.

liana (*f., Bot.*) woody liana [= CIPÓ].

Lião (*m.*) Lyons (France).

liar (*v.t.*) to tie, bind, bond.

lias (*m., Geol.*) Lias.

libação (*f.*) libation.

libar (*v.t.*) to sip; (*v.i.*) to libate.

libelar (*v.t., Law*) to proceed against by filing a libel. [But not to libel in the sense of defame, which is CALUNIAR, DIFAMAR.]

libelinha (*f.*) dragonfly [= LIBÉLULA].

libelista (*m.,f.*) libelant. [But not a libeler, which is DIFAMADOR.]

libelo [bé] (*m., Law*) formal charge; bill of indictment; a small book.—**infamatório**, lampoon, pasquinade. [But not libel, in the sense of defamation, which is DIFAMAÇÃO.]

libélula (*f.*) dragonfly, c.a. LIBELINHA, CAVALO-JUDEU, DONZELINHA.

líber (*m., Bot.*) liber, phloem.

liberação (*f.*) liquidation, settlement (of debt). [But not liberation, which is LIBERTAÇÃO.]

liberado –**da** (*m.,f.*) one who is free on parole.

liberal (*adj.*) liberal, generous, openhearted; munificent; unbigoted, broadminded; befitting a free man; (*m.,f.*) a liberal(ist).

liberalidade (*f.*) liberality, generosity.

liberalismo (*m.*) liberalism.

liberalista (*adj.; m.,f.*) liberalist.

liberalizar (*v.t.*) to give liberally; to liberalize.

liberar (*v.t.*) to release; to free (from obligation); to settle (a debt); to decontrol (prices). [But not to liberate, which is LIBERTAR.]

liberativo –**va** (*adj.*) that frees (from obligation).

liberatório –**ria** (*adj.*) suitable as legal tender.

liberdade (*f.*) liberty, freedom; freewill; (*pl.*) liberties, immunities, privileges; undue familiarity, unwarrantable freedom.—**civil**, civil liberty.—**de associação**, freedom of association.—**de comércio,** freedom of trade.—**de consciência,** freedom of conscience.—**de cultos,** freedom of religion.—**de ensino,** freedom of education.—**de imprensa,** freedom of the press.—**de indiferença,** freedom of choice.—**de pensamento,** freedom of expression. —**de pensar,** freedom of thought.—**dos mares,** freedom of the seas.—**do ventre,** freedom from slavery granted by law to the children of slaves [in Brazil].—**individual,** individual freedom.—**natural,** natural freedom.—**poética,** poetical license.—**política,** political freedom. **em**—, at liberty; at large. **pôr em**—, to set free.

liberiano –**na** (*adj.; m.,f.*) Liberian.

libérrimo –**ma** (*absol. superl. of* LIVRE) most free.

libertação (*f.*) liberation; deliverance; discharge, acquittal.

libertador –**dora** (*adj.*) liberating; (*m.,f.*) liberator.

libertar (*v.t.*) to liberate, release, unfetter; set free; (*v.r.*) to free oneself; to escape (**de,** from).

libertário –**ria** (*adj.; m.,f.*) libertarian.

liberticida (*adj.*) destructive of liberty; (*m.,f.*) destroyer of liberty.

liberticídio (*m.*) destruction of liberty.

libertinagem (*f.*) libertinism, debauchery, lewdness, lechery.

libertino –**na** (*adj.*) dissolute, licentious; (*m.*) libertine, rake, lecher.

libertista (*adj.; m.,f.*) libertarian.

liberto –**ta** (*adj.*) free, at liberty; (*m.*) freedman; (*f.*) freedwoman.

libetenita (*f., Min.*) libethenite.

líbico –**ca** (*adj.*) = LÍBIO.

libidibi (*m., Bot.*) the dividivi (*Caesalpinia coriaria*).

libidinagem (*f.*) libidinousness, lechery.

libidinoso –**sa** (*adj.*) libidinous, lascivious, lecherous, lustful, lewd, (*m.*) lecher, debauchee.

libido [bí] (*m.*) the libido.

líbio –**bia** (*adj.; m.,f.*) Libyan.

libra (*f.*) pound (16 ozs.).—**esterlina,** pound sterling.

libração (*f.*) libration.

librar (*v.t.*) to balance; weigh; cause to librate; (*v.i.*) to librate, be poised.

libratório –**ria** (*adj.*) libratory.

libré (*f.*) livery.

libretista (*m.,f.*) librettist.

libreto (*m.*) libretto (of an opera).

libriforme (*adj., Bot.*) libriform.

librinar (*v.i., colloq.*) to drizzle; to be foggy; = NEBLINAR.

liça (*f.*) a tilting field or other arena; fig., a contest; the heddle of a loom. **abandonar a**—, to retire from the lists.

licanço (*m.*) the four of spades; (*Zool.*) a worm lizard (*Amphisbaena cinerea*).

licantropia (*f.*) lycanthropy.

lição (*f.*) lesson, school exercise; reading, lecture; precept; reproof, scolding.

lice (*f.*) = LIÇA.

liceidade (*f.*) licitness.

licença (*f.*) license, permission, leave; right, authorization; leave of absence, furlough; a permit; excessive liberty; licentiousness.—**de motorista,** driver's license.—**de tráfego,** driving license. **ausência sem**—, A.W.O.L. **Com**—, By your leave; With your permission; Excuse me; Allow me. **Dá**—? May I? Excuse me. **dar**—, to permit, allow; to excuse. **dar**—**para ausentar-se,** to grant a leave of absence. **de** or **em**—, on leave.

licenciado –**da** (*adj.*) discharged, mustered out; on leave of absence; permitted; licensed; (*m.,f.*) a licentiate (one holding a university degree between that of bachelor and that of doctor).

licenciamento (*m.*) licensing; mustering out.—**honrável,** honorable discharge.

licenciar (*v.t.*) to license, allow; to grant permission to; to grant leave of absence to; to dismiss (from service) temporarily; to discharge, muster out; (*v.r.*) to obtain permission (**para,** to); to take liberties.—**se em medicina,** to obtain a license to practice medicine.

licenciatura (*f.*) licentiate (a university degree between that of bachelor and that of doctor); act of licensing.

licenciosidade (*f.*) licentiousness.

licencioso –**sa** (*adj.*) licentious, dissolute, lewd, wanton.

liceu (*m.*) lycée, secondary school.

lichi (*f.*) = LECHIA.

Lícia (*f.*) Lycia.

liciatório (*m.*) reed of a loom.

licitação (*f.*) selling or bidding at auction; **fiança de**—, bid bond.

licitador –**dora** (*adj.; m.,f.*) = LICITANTE.

licitante (*adj.*) that bids or sells at auction; (*m.,f.*) bidder or seller at auction.

licitar (*v.i.,v.t.*) to bid or sell at auction.

lícito –**ta** (*adj.*) licit, lawful; (*m.*) that which is licit. **É**— **esperar que,** one may rightfully expect that.

lícnico (*m., Eastern Ch.*) Lychnic; vespers.

liço (*m.*) wire of a weaving heddle.

licoperdáceas (*f.pl., Bot.*) the puffballs (*Lycoperdaceae*).

licoperdo (*m.*) any fungus of the genus *Lycoperdon*.

licopérsico (*m.*) any tomato plant (*Lycopersicon*).

licopo (*m.*) any bugleweed (*Lycopus*), c.a. MAROIO-AQUÁTICO, PÉ-DE-LÔBO.

licopodiáceo –**cea** (*adj., Bot.*) lycopodiaceous; (*f.pl.*) the clubmoss family (*Lycopodiaceae*).

licopódio (*m.*) lycopodium powder; (*Bot.*) any clubmoss (*Lycopodium*).

licopse (*f.*) any plant of the genus *Lycopsis*, especially *L. arvensis*, the wild bugloss.

licópside (*f.*) the Lycopsida (plant group comprising the club mosses, horsetails and allied forms).

licor (*m.*) liqueur, cordial; liquor (in the sense of any liquid or fluid, but not of strong distilled alcoholic beverage, which is BEBIDA ALCOÓLICA).—**de ferro,** or—**negro,** (*Chem.*) iron acetate liquor; black liquor; black mordant.

licoreiro (*m.*) **licoreira** (*f.*) a set of bottles and small glasses for serving liqueurs.

licorista (*m.,f.*) maker or seller of liqueurs.

licorne (*m.*) unicorn.—**do-mar,** the narwhal [= NARVAL].

licoroso –**sa** (*adj.*) strong and sweetish [wines].

licose (*f.*) the European wolf spider or true tarantula (*Lycosa tarentula*), c.a. TARÂNTULA.

licranço (*m.*) a limbless lizard (*Amphisbaena sp.*).

li[c]tor (*m.*) lictor.

licuri [rí] (*m.*) = ALICURI.

lida (*f.*) drudgery; chore.

lidador –**dora** (*adj.*) struggling, striving, toiling; (*m.,f.*) struggler, toiler, fighter.

lidar (*v.i.*) to struggle, strive, toil; to drudge; to fight (**com,** with; **contra,** against, **para, por,** to).—**com,** to cope with; to deal with.

lide (*f.*) struggle, fight; toil, fatigue; contest, combat.

líder [-es] (*m.*) leader.—**sindical,** union leader.

liderança (*f.*) leadership.

liderar (*v.t.*) to lead; to head up as a leader.

Lídia (*f.*) Lydia.

lidimar (*v.*) = LEGITIMAR.

lídimo –**ma** (*adj.*) authentic, legitimate.

lídio –**dia** (*adj.; m.,f.*) Lydian.

lido –**da** (*adj.; p.p. of* LER) read; well-read, literate; erudite, learned.

lieis, form of LER [38].

lienal (*adj., Anat.*) lineal, splenic.

lienteria (*f., Med.*) lientery.

lierne (*m., Arch.*) lierne.

liga (*f.*) league, alliance, coalition; garter; alloy (of metals).—**metálica,** metallic alloy.

ligação (*f.*) joining, splicing; union, connection; liaison; coherency.—**Cardan,** universal joint.—**elétrica,** electrical connection.—**em cascata,** (*Elec.*) cascade connection.

ligadura (*f.*) ligature, bandage; bond; (*Music*) tie, slur.

ligal (*m.*) a hide used to cover goods transported by pack animals.

ligame, ligâmen (*m.*) connection; union; an obstacle to marriage.

ligamento (*m.*) tie, bond, union; a ligament.

ligamentoso –**sa** (*adj.*) ligamentous; fibrous.

ligar (*v.t.*) to tie, fasten, bind; to link, connect; to join, unite; to alloy, amalgamate; (*Music*) to slur.—**a,** to mind, pay attention to; to attach importance to.—**se a,** to join.—**se com,** to become intimately associated with.—**o gás, a luz, o rádio,** etc., to turn on the gas, the light, the radio, etc.—**para,** to telephone to. **não**—**importância a,** to attach no importance to, be indifferent to. **Não ligo,** I don't care a rap.

ligário (*m.*) a calf's hide used as a saddle blanket.

ligatura (*f.*) ligature [= LIGADURA].

ligeira (*f.*) lightness; agility. **à**—, quickly.

ligeireza, ligeirice (*f.*) quickness; promptness; agility;

lightness; levity; (colloq.) trickery.—de **mãos**, legerdemain.

ligeiro –ra (adj.) light, not heavy; slight, thin, slender; quick, agile, nimble; swift, fast; flighty; slippery, dishonest; (adv.) quickly.—**s melhoras**, slight improvement (in health).

lígio –gia (adj.; m.) liege.

lígneo –nea (adj.) ligneous, woody.

lignícolo –la (adj.) lignicolous.

lignificação (f.) lignification.

lignificar-se (v.r.) to lignify, become woody.

lignina (f. Bot., Chem.) lignin.

lignite (f.), –to (m., Min.) lignite, brown coal, wood coal.

lignívoro –ra (adj.) lignivorous, that gnaws or eats wood; (m.pl.) the Tylophaga (a division of weevils), c.a. XILÓFAGOS.

lignocelulose (f., Bot., Chem.) lignocellulose.

lígula (f., Bot., Anat., Zool.) ligula.

ligulado –da (adj.) ligulate.

liguifloro –ra (adj., Bot.) liguliflorous.

liguiforme (adj.) liguliform.

lígulo (m., Bot.) ligule.

ligurite (f., Min.) ligurite.

lilás (m.) lilac (flower, color, scent); (adj.) lilac.—**da-índia**, or—**das-antilhas**, pride of India, or China, tree (Melia azederach), c.a. CINAMOMO.

liliáceo –cea (adj., Bot.) liliaceous; lilylike; (f.pl.) the lily family (Liliaceae).

lilianite (f., Min.) lillianite.

liliforme (adj.) liliform.

liliputiano –na (adj.; m.) Lilliputian.

lima (f.) steel file; a variety of sweet lime.—**agulha**, needle file.—**bastarda**, bastard-cut file.—**de cheiro**, a hollow sphere, about the size of a small orange, made of paraffin and filled with perfumed water. In former times, in Brazil, these served as missiles with which the merrymakers at Carnival-time pelted each other.—**lanceteira**, rattail file.—**meia-cana**, half-round file.—**murça**, smoothcut file.—**oval**, oval file.—**paralela**, parallel or blunt file. —**redonda**, round file.—**triangular**, triangular file.

limação (f.) = LIMADURA.

limacídeo –dea (adj., Zool.) limaceous, limacine; (m.pl.) the Limacidae (family of slugs).

limado –da (adj.) filed; finished, polished, perfected; worn.

limador –dora (adj.) filing; (m.) filer.

limadura, limagem (f.) act or operation of filing (metal); finishing.

limalha (f.) filings, shavings.

limão (m.) lemon (fruit).—**canudo** = IRAXIM (a bee).—**cravo**, lemon tree (Citrus limon).—**de-caiena** = BILIMBI. —**de-cheiro** = LIMA-DE-CHEIRO.—**do-campo**, frangipani (Plumeria warmingo).—**doce**, a variety of sweet lime. —**do-mato** = BACUPARI-AÇU.—**francês**, the limeberry (Triphasia trifolia).—**galêgo**, citron (Citrus medica).— **pimentoso**, a pricklyash (Zanthoxylum rhetsa).

limãorana (f.) the fustic (Chlorophora tinctoria), a common tropical American tree of the mulberry family, c.a. TATAJUBA-DE-ESPINHO. "The wood . . . yields a lightyellow dye much used in the arts." [Webster]—**da-terra-firme**, a small tree (Basanacantha spinosa) of the Rubiaceae, c.a. PAPA-TERRA. It has "white hard wood which splinters easily; on distillation the leaves yield an essential oil used in the perfume industry." [GUAF]— **da-varzea** = PAPA-TERRA.

limãozinho (m.) = CARNE-DE-ANTA (a plant).

limar (v.t.) to file, smooth, polish; to wear down.

limatão (m.) round file.

limbo (m.) limbo; (Bot., Zool.) limbus; the circular edge of a protractor.

limeira (f.) a sweet variety of lime (Citrus limetta var.).

limetina (f., Chem.) limettin, citropten.

limiar (m.) threshold, doorstep, doorsill; fig., entrance, beginning.—**da vida**, threshold of life.

limícolo –la (adj.) limicolous; limicoline.

liminar (adj.) at the threshold; preliminary; (Psychology) liminal.

limitação (f.) limitation, restriction.—**de natalidade**, birth control.

limitador –dora (adj.) limiting; (m.) limiter.—**de corrente**, (Elec.) current limiter.

limitar (v.t.) to limit, restrict.—**se a**, to limit or confine oneself to.—**com**, to be bound by; to adjoin.

limitativo –va (adj.) limiting.

limite (m.) limit, boundary, border; (Math.) limit.—**de**

carga, load limit.—**s de classe**, (Stat.) class boundary; class range.—**elástico**, elastic limit. **passar dos**—**s**, to go too far.

limítrofe (adj.) limitrophe, bordering (upon), adjoining.

limívoro –ra (adj., Zool.) limivorous.

limnantáceo –cea (adj., Bot.) limnanthaceous; (f.pl.) the Limnanthaceae (family of the meadowfoam or falsemermaid aquatic herbs).

limnanto (m., Bot.) the genus (Limanthes) of meadowfoam.

limnímetro (m.) limnometer.

limnite (f.), –to (m., Min.) limnite, bog iron ore.

limnóbio (m., Biol.) limnobios.

limnobiologia (f.) limnobiology.

limnofílidas (m.pl., Zool.) the Limnophilidae (family of caddis flies).

limnófilo –la (adj., Zool.) limnophilous.

limnologia (f.) limnology.

limnologista, limnólogo –ga (m.,f.) limnologista.

limnômetro (m.) limnometer.

limnoplancto (m., Bot.) limnoplankton.

limnória (f., Zool.) the genus (Limnoria) which contains the gribble.

limo (m.) pond scum; slime; ooze; slimy clay.—**do rio**, a rockweed (Fucus communis).—**mestre**, a widgeonweed (Ruppia spiralis).

limoado –da (adj.) lemon-colored; lemon-yellow.

limoal (m.) lemon orchard.

limoeiro (m.) lemon tree (Citrus limon); a bluebells (Mertensia utilis).

limoento –ta (adj.) muddy [= LODOSO].

limonada (f.) lemonade.—**gasosa**, lemon soda water.— **purgativa**, citrate of magnesia employed as a laxative.

limoneno (m., Chem.) limonene.

limonete (m.) = LÚCIA-LIMA.

limonina (f., Chem.) limonin.

limônio (m., Bot.) sea-lavender, marsh rosemary (Limonium), c.a. ACELGA-BRAVA.

limonito (m., Min.) limonite, brown hematite.

limosela (f., Bot.) the genus (Limosella) of mudworts.

limosidade (f.) sliminess; muddiness.

limosina (f.) limousine.

limoso –sa (adj.) slimy, muddy, miry.

limote (m.) a three-square (triangular) file.

limpa (f.) a cleaning; (slang) a political purge or housecleaning.

limpa-campo (m.) = MUSSURANA.

limpação, limpadela (f.) a cleaning (up).

limpado (m.) a cleared piece of land.

limpador –dora (adj.) cleaning, cleansing; (m.,f.) cleaner, wiper.—**de parabrisa**, windshield wiper.

limpadura (f.) a cleaning (up); (pl.) table scraps.

limpamento (m.) = LIMPEZA.

limpa-penas (m.) pen wiper.

limpa-pés (m.) door mat; foot scraper.

limpa-planta (m.) a small tropical mailed catfish (Plecostomus commersoni) seen in home aquaria.

limpa-pratos (m., colloq.) a plate "cleaner-upper" (glutton).

limpar [24] (v.t.) to clean (up); to wash, scour, sweep, wipe; to cleanse, purify; (Milit.) to mop up.

limpa-trilhos (m.) cowcatcher (locomotive pilot).

limpa-vidro (m.) a small tropical mailed catfish (Otocinclus vittatus) seen in home aquaria.

limpeza [ê] (f.) cleaning; cleanliness; neatness.—**eletrolítica**, (Metal.) electrolytic cleaning.

limpidez [ê] (f.) limpidity.

límpido –da (adj.) limpid, clear, transparent.

limpo –pa (adj.; irreg. p.p. of LIMPAR) clean, cleanly; neat, trim, tidy; clear, bright; bare; aboveboard; (colloq.) "broke," "clean"; (m.) a strip of bare land.—**como Deus quer as almas**, flat broke. **a**—, in the open. **céu**—, clear sky. **pôr as coisas em pratos**—**s**, to lay the cards on the table. **passar a**—, to make a clean copy of. **tirar a**—, to get at the bottom of a matter.

limurito (m., Petrog.) limurite.

limusine (f.) limousine.

lináceas (f.pl., Bot.) the Linaceae (flax family).

linalol (m., Chem.) linaloöl.

lináceo (adj.) linen; flaxen; (Bot.) linaceous.

linária (f., Bot.) the genus (Linaria) of toadflaxes.— **cimbalária**, the Kenilworth ivy (Cymbalaria muralis). —**comum**, the butter-and-eggs toadflax (Linaria vulgaris), c.a. VALVERDE.

linarita (*f., Min.*) linarite.
lince (*m.*) lynx; sharp-eyed, perspicacious person.
linchador –dora (*adj.*) lynching; (*m.,f.*) lyncher.
linchamento (*m.*) linchagem (*f.*) lynching.
linchar (*v.t.*) to lynch.
linda (*f.*) see under LINDO.
lindaflor (*f., Bot.*) the plains coreopsis (*C. tinctoria*).
lindaquerite (*f., Min.*) lindackerite.
lindar (*v.t.*) to bound, delimit.—com, to border upon.
lindeira (*f.*) head jamb or yoke of a door or window frame.
lindeza [ê] (*f.*) beauty, loveliness, grace.
lindo –da (*adj.*) beautiful, pretty, lovely, handsome, elegant, pleasing; (*f.*) limit, boundary; landmark.
lindo-azul (*m.*) = SANHAÇO-FRADE.
lindote (*adj.*) somewhat pretty.
lindura (*f.*) = LINDEZA.
lineado –da (*adj.*) lineate.
lineal (*adj.*) = LINEAR.
lineamento (*m.*) outline; (*pl.*) lineaments.
linear (*adj.*) lineal, linear.
linearidade (*f.*) linearity.
linéia (*f.*) twinflower (*Linnaea*).
líneo –nea (*adj.*) linen.
lineolar (*adj.*) lineolate.
Lineu (*m.*) Linnaeus.
linfa (*f.*) lymph.
linfadenite (*f. Med.*) lymphadenitis.
linfangite (*f., Med., Veter.*) lymphangiitis.
linfático –ca (*adj.*) lymphatic; sluggish, phlegmatic.
linfócito (*m., Anat.*) lymphocyte.
linfóide (*adj., Anat.*) lymphoid.
linga (*f.*) a sling (for hoisting); linga (phallic symbol); also = ANINGAÇU.
lingada (*f.*) a slingful (of cargo).
lingaísmo, lingalismo (*m.*) the phallicist aspect of Sivaism.
lingar (*v.t.*) to hoist (cargo) in a sling.
lingavá (*m.*) = LINGA (phallus).
lingote (*m.*) ingot; pig iron; (*Printing*) slug. **metal em—s**, ingot metal.
lingoteira (*f.*) ingot mold.
língua (*f.*) tongue; language, idiom; (*m.*) interpreter.
—afiada, sharp tongue.—cervina,—cipo-de-escada,—-de-boi, all names for the hart's-tongue fern [= ESCOLOPÊNDRIO].—comprida, slanderer.—crioula, "a creole dialect; variously applied to corrupt or hybrid Portuguese colonial dialects in general, and esp. to the negro dialects of Brazil and those spoken in the Cape Verde Islands and other parts of Portuguese Africa." [*Webster*]—danada = LÍNGUA VIPERINA.—das ondas, or de água, ocean surf.—de areia, sand spit.—de-cão, (*Bot.*) hound's-tongue (*Cynoglossum sp.*), c.a. CINOGLOSSA.—-de-cobra, (*Bot.*) adder's-tongue (*Ophioglossum sp.*).—de fogo, a tongue of flame, as of a blowtorch; a vituperator.—de-mulata, a sole or tongue fish (*Symphurus plagiusa*); c.a. SÔLHA, TAPA.—de oc, langue d'oc: "the Romance dialects of the southerly provinces of France." [*Webster*]—de-ovelha, (*Bot.*) sheep fescue (*Festuca ovina*).—de-palmo, slanderer.—de palmo e meio, long-winded talker.—depravada, or de praga, slanderer.—-de-sapo, (*Bot.*) a pepper (*Piper transparens*), c.a. BREDO-DE-MURO, ERVA-DE-VIDRO.—-de-serpente = LÍNGUA-DE-COBRA.—de-sogra, slander.—de-teju, (*Bot.*) a tournefortia (borage family), and a casearia (Indianplum family).—de terra, a point or spit of land.—detiú, (*Bot.*) a lantana (*L. pseudothea*), c.a. CHÁ-DE-FRADE.—de trapos, a babbling child; stammerer; a "blabbermouth."—de-tucano, (*Bot.*) an eryngo (*Eryngium sp.*).—de-vaca, (*Bot.*) a bugloss (*Anchusa indica*), c.a. BUGLOSA; also = MARIA-GOMES.—de-víbora, (*Bot.*) an adderstongue fern (*Ophioglossum palmatum*).—dos caluniadores, or dos maldizentes, slander, calumny.—expedita, a fast talker.—extinta, an extinct language.—farpada, a forked tongue (as of a snake).—franca, lingua franca; " . . . any hybrid or other language used over a wide area as a common or commercial tongue among peoples of different speech. . . ." [*Webster*]—geral, lingua geral; "literally, a general, common, or universal, language; a lingua franca; specif., an uninflected language, based on Tupi, used as a lingua franca in Brazil by Indians, negroes and whites." [*Webster*]—impura, a foul-mouthed person.—mãe, or —materna, mother tongue.—morta, dead language.—românica, romance language.—saburosa, coated tongue.

—viperina, slanderer.—viva, living language.—vulgar, common speech; popular language. [But not vulgar language, in the ordinary sense, which is LINGUAGEM BAIXA (GROSSEIRA, CHULA).] bater, or dar, com a—nos dentes, to let the cat out of the bag; to spill the beans. dar à (or de)—, to wag one's tongue; to blab. dobrar a—, to correct oneself; to keep a civil tongue in one's head. saber, or ter, na ponta da—, to have (something) on the tip of one's tongue. trocar—, to chat.
linguado (*m.*) a long blade; a strip of copy paper; any flounder, esp. the large *Paralichthys brasiliensis*, c.a. RODOVALHO, CATRAIO.—-da-areia, a small flounder (*Syacium papillosum*), c.a. ARAMAÇA.—lixa, a sand dab or other small flatfish, c.a. TAPA.
linguagem (*f.*) language, speech, tongue.
linguacista (*m.,f.*) linguist.
linguajar (*v.i.*) to blab; to chatter; (*m.*) mode of speech.
lingual (*adj.*) lingual; (*f.*) a lingual sound or letter.
lingual-alveolar (*adj., Phonet.*) alveololingual.
lingual-dental (*adj., Phonet.*) dentilingual.
lingual-gutural (*adj., Phonet.*) guttarolingual.
lingual-palatal (*adj., Phonet.*) linguopalatal.
linguará, linguaral (*m.*) an interpreter between whites and Indians in Brazil.
linguarão –rona, linguaraz, linguareiro –ra (*adj.*) talkative, windy, gossipy; shrewish; (*m.,f.*) windbag; gossip; busybody; shrew; blabbermouth; tattletale.
linguarudo –da (*adj.; m.,f.*) = LINGUARÃO, -RONA; (*m.*) a small beach snail (*Lintricula auricularia*), c.a. PACAVARÉ, CALORIM, BETU.
linguátulo (*m., Zool.*) a genus (*Pentastomum, syn. Linguatula*) of parasitic, worm-like arthropods.
lingüeirão (*m.*) a big tongue; (*Zool.*) a discinoid shell (*Orabiculoidea lamellosa*) c.a. ITÃ, LONGUEIRÃO, NAVALHA, UNHA-DE-VELHO; a razor clam.
lingüeta (*f.*) a small tongue; languet; languette; tongue of a shoe; bolt or a lock or latch; the index needle of a scale; a tongue of land; a pawl.
lingüiça (*f.*) kind of thin sausage; padding, spacefillers (newspaper slang).
lingüiforme (*adj.*) linguiform, tongue-shaped.
lingüipalatal = LINGUAL-PALATAL.
lingüista (*m.,f.*) linguist.
lingüístico –ca (*adj.*) linguistic; (*f.*) linguistics.
lingulado –da (*adj.*) lingulate.
línguo-alveolar = LINGUAL-ALVEOLAR.
línguo-dental = LINGUAL-DENTAL.
linguo-gutural = LINGUAL-GUTURAL.
línguo-palatal = LINGUAL-PALATAL.
linha (*f.*) line; streak, stripe; sewing thread; cord, string; row, rank, file; fishing line; mark, limit; lineage; telephone or telegraph line; transport line; correct demeanor; tie beam of a roof truss.—aclínica, aclinic line; magnetic equator.—aérea, airline; air route.—agônica, (*Physics*) agonic line.—conjunta, telephone party line.—de água, watermark; water line.—de bonde, streetcar line.—de bordar, embroidery thread.—de corso, trolling line.—de empuxo, (*Aeron.*) thrust line.—de flutuação, line of flotation; ship's water line.—de força, (*Physics*) line of force; line of induction.—de halves, (*Soccer*) line of halfbacks.—de montagem, assembly line.—de pescar, fishing line.—de prumo, plumb line; sounding line.—de tiro, civilian military training.—de transmissão, power line.—dianteira, (*Soccer*) forward line.—férrea, railway line.—geodésica, (*Math.*) geodesic line.—isobárica, (*Meteor.*) isobar.—isoclina, isoclinal line.—isodinâmica, isodynamic line.—isogônica, (*Magnetism*) isogonic line.—isotérmica (*Phys. Geog.*) isotherm.—loxodrômica, (*Naut.*) rhumb line.—média, (*Soccer*) line of halfbacks.—pontilhada, dotted line.—quebrada, broken line.—reta, straight line.—tronco, main line; trunk line. entrar na—, to fall into line; to toe the mark. navio de—, a ship of the line. perder a—, or sair da—, to get out of line, lose one's decorum. por uma—, by a hair; within a little; all but. salgar a—de pesca, to give jerks on one's fishing line. tirar uma—, to make eyes at someone. tropas de—, line troops.
linhaça (*f.*) linseed, flaxseed.
linhada (*f.*) fishline; a cast of a fishline; a peep, a peering; flirtation from a distance.
linhagem (*f.*) sackcloth; lineage, genealogy, descent; pedigree; strain.
linhagista (*m.,f.*) = GENEALOGISTA.
linheiro –ra (*adj.*) slender, upright; (*m.,f.*) one who pre-

pares flax for spinning; one who deals in threads and linens. **madeira**—, straight-grained wood.
linhita (*f.*) lignite [= LIGNITOL.
linho (*m.*) linen; (*Bot.*) flax (*Linum*).—**cânhamo**, hemp (*Cannabis sativa*).—**da-nova-zelândia**, New Zealand fiberlily (*Phormium tenax*), c.a. SÊDA-VEGETAL.—**de-cuco**, cuckoo spit [= CUSPO-DE-CUCO].—**do-rio-grande**, a flax (*Linum salaginoides*).—**galego-bravo**, common flax (*Linum usitatissimum*).—**purgante**, purging flax (*Linum catharticum*). **fio de**—, sewing thread.
linhol [-óis] (*m.*) waxed thread (used by cobblers and sail-makers).
linhoso –**sa** (*adj.*) linen-like; flaxen.
linhote (*m.*) joist, beam.
liniffcio (*m.*) linen industry.
linimento (*m.*) liniment.
linina (*f., Chem., Biol.*) linin.
Lino (*m.*) Linus.
linoleato (*m., Chem.*) linolate.
linoléico –**ca** (*adj., Chem.*) linoleic.
linoleína (*f., Chem.*) linolein.
linóleo (*m.*) linoleum.
linoleogravura (*f.*) linoleum-block print(ing).
linólico –**ca** (*adj.*) = LINOLÉICO.
linômetro (*m.*) linometer.
linotipar (*v.i.*) to linotype.
linotipista (*m.,f.*) linotypist.
linotipo, linótipo (*m.*) a linotype machine.
linotipógrafo (*m.*), –**fa** (*f.*) an operator of any typecasting machine.
lintel (*m.*) = DINTEL.
línter (*m.*) linters.
liocéfalo –**la** (*adj.*) leiocephalous.
liócomo –**ma** (*adj.*) = LIÓTRICO.
liofilo –**la** (*adj., Bot.*) leiophyllous.
liólise (*f., Chem.*) lyolysis; solvolysis.
liomioma (*m., Med.*) leiomyoma.
lionês –**nesa** (*adj.; m.,f.*) Lyonese.
Liorne (*m.*) Leghorn (Italy).
liótrico –**ca** (*adj.*) leiotrichous (having straight hair).
lioz (*f.*) kind of limestone.
lipáridas (*m.pl.*) the family (*Lymantriidae, syn. Liparidae*) consisting of the tussock moths.
liparito (*m., Petrog.*) rhyolite.
liparóleo (*m.*) = POMADA.
lípase (*f., Biochem.*) lipase.
lipocroma (*m., Biochem.*) lipochrome.
lipogênese (*f., Physiol.*) lipogenesis.
lipogenético –**ca** (*adj., Physiol.*) lipogenetic.
lipograma (*m.*) lipogram.
lipóide (*adj.*) lipoid, fatty.
lipólise (*f.*) lipolysis, decomposition of fat.
lipolítico –**ca** (*adj.*) lipolytic.
lipoma (*m., Med.*) lipoma.
liposo –**sa** (*adj.*) bleary.
lipossolúvel (*adj.*) fat-soluble.
lipotimia (*f.*) lipothymia, swooning.
liquação (*f.*) liquation.
liquefação (*f.*) liquefaction.
liquefativo –**va** (*adj.*) liquefactive.
liquefato –**ta** (*adj.*) = LIQUEFEITO.
liquefazer [47] (*v.t.,v.r.*) to liquefy.
liquefeito –**ta** (*adj.*) liquefied.
líquen (*m.*) lichen.—**da-islândia**, Iceland moss (*Cetraria islandica*), c.a. CETRÁRIA.—**facultativo**, (*Bot.*) lichenism.
liquenáceo –**cea** (*adj.*) lichenaceous.
liquêneas (*f.pl., Bot.*) the division (*Lichenes*) consisting of the lichens.
liquênico –**ca** (*adj., Chem.*) lichenic.
liquenícolo –**la** (*adj., Zool.*) lichenicolous.
liqueniforme (*adj.*) licheniform.
liquenina (*f., Chem.*) lichenin.
liquenografia (*f.*) lichenography.
liquenóide (*adj.; Bot., Med.*) lichenoid.
liques (*m.*) the five of diamonds.
liquescente (*adj.*) liquescent.
liquescer (*v.i.*) to become liquid; (*v.t.*) to liquefy.
liquidação, liqüidação (*f.*) liquidation; settling of ac-counts; closing out of a business; a special sale of merchandise.—**de saldos**, a clearance sale.
liquidado –**da** (*adj.*) liquidated; (*colloq.*) down-and-out.
liquidador –**dora** (*adj.*) liquidating; (*m.,f.*) liquidator.
liquidâmbar (*m., Bot.*) the American sweetgum (*Liquid-*

ambar styraciflua); also copalm, the fragrant balsam which it yields.
liquidando –**da** (*adj.*) to be liquidated.
liquidante (*m.,f.*) liquidator (of a business concern).
liquidar, liqüidar (*v.t.*) to liquidate, settle, adjust; to sell out, close out, wind up (a business); to finish off (kill); (*v.i.*) to liquidate.—**contas**, to settle accounts.—**o as-sunto**, to settle a matter.—**uma conta**, to pay (up) a bill.
liquidatário –**ria** (*m.,f.*) liquidator (of a business); (*adj.*) of or pert. to the winding up of a business.
liquidável (*adj.*) that can be liquidated.
liquidez [ê] (*f.*) liquidity.
liquidificação (*f.*) liquefying.
liquidificador –**dora** (*adj.*) liquefying; (*m.*) liquifier; blender (machine).
liquidificante (*adj.*) liquefying.
liquidificar (*v.t.*) to liquefy [= LIQUEFAZER].
liquidificável (*adj.*) capable of being melted or liquefied.
líquido –**da**, **líqüido** –**da** (*adj.*) liquid, fluid; net [assets, profits, weights, prices, etc.]; (*m.*) liquid; fluid; solution, liquor.—**de Dakin**, (*Pharm.*) Dakin's solution.—**fisio-lógico**, (*Biochem.*) physiological salt solution.—**sobressa-turado**, (*Chem.*) supersaturated solution.
lira (*f.*) lyre; lyre bird; the Italian lira.
lirial (*adj.*) lilylike; (*m.*) lily field.
lírico –**ca** (*adj.*) lyric(al). **temporada**—, the opera season; (*m.*) a lyric poet; (*f.*) lyric poetry or poems.
liriforme (*adj.*) lyriform, lyre-shaped.
lírio (*m.*) any lily, esp. the madonna lily (*Lilium candi-dum*).—**ácoro-bastardo**, or—**amarelo-dos-charcos**, the yellowflag iris (*I. pseudacorus*), c.a. ÁCORO-FALSO.—**amarelo-do-brejo** = GENGIBRE-DA-TERRA (gingerlily).—**branco**, the Easter lily (*Lilium grandiflorum*), c.a. AÇUCENA-BRANCA, COPO-DE-LEITE, PALMA-DE-SÃO-JOSÉ; the Barbados lily (*Amaryllis vittata*).—**convale**, lily-of-the-valley (*Convallaria majalis*), c.a. CONVALÁRIA, LÍRIO-DO-VALE.—**cravinho**, the scorpion iris (*I. alata*).—**d'água**, waterlily; = GÔLFO.—**da-índia**, pride of India or China tree (*Melia azedarach*), c.a. CINAMOMO.—**da-pérsia**, Persian iris (*I. persica*).—**de-petrópolis** = LÍRIO-DO-BREJO.—**do-amazonas**, the Amazonlily eucharis (*E. grandiflora*).—**do-brejo**, common gingerlily (*Hedy-chium coronarium*).—**dos-incas** = CARAJURU-DO-PARÁ.—**dos-tintureiros**, the weld mignonette (*Reseda luteola*).—**fétido**, the Gladwin iris (*I. foetidissima*).—**martagão**, the martagon lily (*Lilium martagon*); c.a. LÍRIO-TURCO.—**roxo**, the Portugal iris (*I. subbiflora*).—**roxo-do-campo** = BARIRIÇÓ.—**roxo-dos-montes**, the German iris (*I. germanica*), c.a. CINAMOMO.—**triste**, the mourning iris (*I. susiana*).—**turco**, Turk's-cap lily (*Lilium martagon*); c.a., LÍRIO-MARTAGÃO.—**verde** = CÓLQUICO.—**vermelho**, the tawny daylily (*Hemerocallis fulva*).
liriodendro (*m.*) the tuliptree (*Liriodendron tulipifera*), or the Chinese tuliptree (*L. chinense*).
lirismo (*m.*) lyricism.
lirista (*m.,f.*) lyrist.
liroconite (*f., Min.*) liroconite.
Lisandro (*m.*) Lysander.
Lisboa (*f.*) Lisbon.
lisboeta [ê] (*adj.*) of or pert. to Lisbon; (*m.,f.*) a native of Lisbon. Vars. LISBOANO, LISBOÉS, LISBONENSE, LISBONÊS, LISBONINO.
lisidina (*f., Chem.*) lysidin(e).
lisígeno –**na** (*adj., Bot.*) lysigenous.
lisim (*m.*) vein or crack in rock or marble.
lisimáquia (*f., Bot.*) golden loosestrife (*Lysimachia vulg.*).
lisímetro (*m.*) lysimeter.
lisina (*f., Biochem.*) lysin(e).
lísio (*m., Biochem.*) lysis, cell destruction.
liso –**sa** (*adj.*) smooth, even, flat; (*slang*) flat broke. **cabelo**—, straight hair.
lisol (*m.*) lysol.
lisonja (*f.*) flattery, blandishment, blarney. **comprar pela**—, to win with flattery.
lisonjaria (*f.*) flattery.
lisonjeador –**dora** (*adj.*) flattering; (*m.,f.*) flatterer.
lisonjear (*v.t.*) to flatter, cajole, wheedle; to softsoap; to please, satisfy; (*v.r.*) to be pleased (**de, com**, at, with).—**com servilismo**, to fawn upon.
lisonjeiro –**ra** (*adj.*) flattering, complimentary, courtly; pleasing; satisfying; (*m.,f.*) flatterer.
lissofobia (*f., Med.*) lyssophobia.
lissótrico –**ca** (*adj., Anthropol.*) lissotrichous, having straight, lank hair.

lista (*f.*) list; roll, roster; directory; catalogue; stripe; streak; a strip (of cloth, paper, etc.); a bill of fare.—**negra**, black list.—**telefônica**, telephone book.
listão (*m.*) broad stripe, band; carpenter's rule; ship's wake.
listel [-téis] (*m.*) listel, fillet.
listerina (*f.*) Listerine.
listra (*f.*) a stripe (in cloth).
listrado –**da** (*adj.*) striped, streaked.
listrão (*m.*) a wide stripe.
listrar (*v.t.*) to stripe.
lisura (*f.*) smoothness; softness; fig., sincerity, guilelessness, good faith.
Lit. = LITERATURA (Literature).
litania (*f.*) littany [= LADAINHA].
litargírio, litargo (*m.*) litharge, lead monoxide.
liteira (*f.*) litter, palanquin, sedan.
literal (*adj.*) literal.
literalidade (*f.*) literality; literal interpretation.
literalismo (*m.*) literalism.
literalista (*adj.; m.,f.*) literalist.
literário –**ria** (*adj.*) literary.
literata (*f.*) authoress; bluestocking.
literataço, literateiro, literatelho, literatiço, literatiqueiro (*m.*) all derogatory terms for a mediocre or pretentious man of letters.
literatice (*f.*) trashy literature; an inordinate fondness for literature.
literato (*m.*) man of letters.
literatura (*f.*) literature, learning, letters; literary works. —**de cordel**, cheap reading matter.—**de ficção**, fiction, novels.—**de vanguarda**, "avantgarde" literature.
lítia (*f., Chem.*) lithia; lithium oxide.
lítico –**ca** (*adj.*) lithic.
litigação (*f.*) litigation.
litigante (*adj.; m.,f.*) litigant.
litigar (*v.t.,v.i.*) to litigate.
litigável (*adj.*) litigious, disputable.
litígio (*m.*) litigation, lawsuit; a dispute.
litigioso –**sa** (*adj.*) litigious, disputable.
lítio (*m., Chem.*) lithium.
litobíidas (*m.pl.*) a family (*Lithobiidae*) of myriapods.
litóclase (*f., Geol.*) lithoclase.
litoclasia (*f.*) = LITOTRÍCIA.
litoclasto (*m.*) = LITOTRITOR.
litocromia (*f.*) chromolithography.
litódomo (*m.*) a genus (*Lithodomus*) of rock-burrowing bivalves.
lifófago –**ga** (*adj., Zool.*) lithophagous.
litofélico –**ca, litofélnico** –**ca** (*adj., Biochem.*) lithofellic or lithofellinic [acid].
litofilo (*m.*) lithophyl.
litófilo –**la** (*adj., Bot., Zool.*) lithophilous.
litófito –**ta** (*adj., Phytogeog.*) lithophytous.
litofone (*m.*) = LITOPONE.
litogenesia (*f., Petrog.*) lithogenesis, petrogenesis.
litoglifia (*f.*) the art of engraving on stone, esp. on a gem.
litóglifo (*m.*) lithoglypher.
litografar (*v.t.*) to lithograph.
litografia (*f.*) lithography; a lithograph; lithographer's shop.
litográfico –**ca** (*adj.*) lithographic.
litógrafo (*m.*) lithographer.
litóide (*adj.*) lithoid, stonelike.
litologia (*f.*) lithology.
litologista, litólogo –**ga** (*m.,f.*) lithologist.
litomarga (*f., Min.*) lithomarge.
litômetro (*m.*) lithometer.
litondo (*m., Bot.*) the India rubber fig (*Ficus indica*).
litopone (*m.*) lithopone.
litoral (*adj.*) littoral, coastal; (*m.*) seaboard, coastline.
litorâneo –**nea** (*adj.*) littoral [= LITORAL].
litóreo –**rea** (*adj.*) poetical form of LITORAL.
litorina (*f.*) a motor-driven railroad car [= AUTOMOTRIZ].
litosfera (*f.*) lithosphere.
litospermo –**ma** (*adj., Bot.*) lithospermous; (*m.*) a gromwell (*Lithospermum sp.*).
litotomia (*f., Surg.*) lithotomy.
litotrese (*f., Surg.*) lithotresis.
litotrícia, litotripsia (*f., Surg.*) lithotrity.
litotritor (*m., Surg.*) lithotrite, lithotritor.
litóxilo [ks] (*m.*) lithoxyl, petrified wood.
litráceas (*f.pl., Bot.*) the family (*Lythraceae*) of loose-strifes.

litragem (*f.*) quantity expressed in liters.
litro (*m.*) liter; a one-liter bottle; (*Bot.*) any plant of the genus *Lythrum*, esp. the purple lythrum (*L. salicaria*), called SALGUEIRINHA.
Lituânia (*f.*) Lithuania.
lituano –**na** (*adj.; m.,f.*) Lithuanian.
Liturg. = LITURGIA (Liturgy).
liturgia (*f.*) liturgy.
litúrgico –**ca** (*adj.*) liturgical.
liturgista (*m.,f.*) liturgist.
liv. = LIVRO (book).
livel [é] (*m.*) level [= NÍVEL]; (*Const.*) strut of a rafter.
livelar (*v.*) = NIVELAR.
Liverpul (*m.*) Liverpool.
lividez [ê] (*f.*) lividness.
lívido –**da** (*adj.*) livid.
livingstonita (*f., Min.*) livingstonite.
livra! Heaven forbid!
livrador –**dora** (*adj.*) liberating, freeing. (*m.,f.*) liberator.
livralhada (*f., colloq.*) a pile of books.
livramento (*m.*) liberation, release, deliverance.—**condicional**, release on parole.
livrança (*f.*) a written order for payment; also = LIVRA-MENTO.
livrar (*v.t.*) to liberate, set free, release; to save, deliver (**de**, from).—**se de**, to escape from, be free from, be free of, free oneself of. **Deus me livre!** Heaven forbid!
livraria (*f.*) bookstore; library.
livre (*adj.*) free, independent; released, liberated; exempt, clear; disengaged, unoccupied; loose, unimpeded; unconstrained, unrestrained; (*adv.*) freely.—**a bordo**, free-on-board, FOB.—**comércio**, tree trade. **ao ar**—, out of doors, in the open. **luta**—, catch-as-catch-can. **tradução**—, free translation. **verso**—, free verse.
livre-arbítrio (*m.*) free will.
livre-câmbio (*m.*) free trade [= LIVRE-TROCA].
livre-cambista (*m.,f.*) free trader.
livreco (*m.*) trashy book.
livre-cultismo (*m.*) free worship.
livre-exame (*m.*) free thought.
livreiro (*m.*) bookseller.
livre-pensador (*m.*) freethinker.
livre-pensamento (*m.*) free thought; freethinking.
livre-rodagem (*f.*) free-wheeling.
livresco –**ca** [ê] (*adj.*) pert. to books.
livrete (*m.*), –**ta** (*f.*) a small book; a note book.
livre-troca (*f.*) free trade [= LIVRE-CÂMBIO].
livro (*m.*) book; tripe [= FOLHOSO, DOBRIADINHA].—**branco**, a diplomatic white paper.—**caixa**, cash book. —**de bordo**, (*Naut.*) logbook.—**de cabeceira**, bedside book.—**de mortalhas**, a packet of cigarette papers.—**-diário**, a day book, journal.—**em oitavo**, an octavo book.—**em quarto**, a quarto book.—**-mestre**, ledger.—**negro**, black book.—**-razão**, ledger.—**s Sagrados**, Holy Scriptures. **arrumar os**—**s**, to keep books.
livrório (*m.*) a big but valueless old book, esp. one in bad repair.
lixa (*f.*) sandpaper; a dogfish or its rough skin; angelfish (*Squatina*).—**vegetal** = CAVALINHA.
lixação (*f.*) act or operation of sandpapering.
lixadeira (*f.*) sanding machine.
lixador –**dora** (*adj.*) sanding; (*m.*) sander (man or machine).
lixar (*v.t.*) to sandpaper; to sand; to smooth, polish.
lixeiro (*m.*) garbage-collector.
lixívia (*f.*) lye; scouring powder.
lixiviação (*f.*) lixiviation.
lixiviar (*v.t.*) to lixiviate, leach.
lixo (*m.*) trash, litter, garbage; (*colloq.*) dregs of society.
l.º = LIVRO (book).
lo(s) form of direct object masc. pers. pron. used instead of **o(s)** when attached to verb forms ending in **r, s** or **z**, to indirect object pronouns **nos** and **vos**, and to adverb **eis**, which forms, in turn, drop their last letters. Examples: **manda-lo, vimo-lo, fi-lo** instead of **mandar-o, vimos-o, fiz-o; no-lo, vo-lo**, instead of **nos-o, vos-o**, and **ei-lo** instead of **eis-o**.
ló (*m.*) yellow gauze; (*Naut.*) luff.
loa (*f.*) prologue; (*pl.*) carols; praises; fibs.
loando, loango (*m.*) a fish called SURUBIM (*q.v.*); also, in Bahia, a breed of pigs.
loasáceas (*f.pl., Bot.*) the family Loasaceae.
lôba (*f.*) she-wolf; cassock [= BATINA].
lobacho (*m.*) wolf cub.

lobado –da (*adj.*) lobed, lobate.
lobal (*adj.*) wolfish, wolflike.
lobaz (*m.*) big wolf.
lobeiro –ra (*adj.*) wolf-hunting; wolflike; (*m.*) wolf hunter.
lobélia (*f., Bot.*) any species of Lobelia, especially *L. inflata* (the Indian tobacco lobelia) and *L. siphilitica* (the big blue lobelia).
lobeliáceo –cea(*adj., Bot.*) lobeliaceous; (*f.pl.*) the Lobeliaceae (lobelia family).
lobelina (*f., Pharm.*) lobeline.
lobinho (*m.*) wolf cub; Cub Scout; wen, sebaceous cyst.
lobishomem (*m.*) werewolf.
lobo (*m.*) lobe.
lôbo (*m.*) wolf; fig., bloodthirsty man.—**com pele de ovelha**, a wolf in sheep's clothing.—**do-mar**, a seal; an old sea dog.—**-marinho**, sea lion; the sea wolf or wolf fish (*Anarchichas lupus*), c.a. ARRINCO, GATO-MARINHO. **cair na goela do—**, to put one's head into the lion's mouth. **entre o—e o cão**, at twilight. **Falai no—**, **ver-lhe-eis a pele**, Speak of the devil and he will appear.
lôbrego –ga (*adj.*) dark, gloomy; dismal, depressing; frightful.
lobrigar (*v.t.*) to descry, discern (indistinctly), perceive (with difficulty); to catch a glimpse of; to see in the distance.
lobulado –da (*adj.*) lobulate [= LOBADO].
lobular (*adj.*) lobular.
lobulária (*f., Bot.*) sweet alyssum (*Lobularia maritima*).
lôbulo (*m.*) lobule; lobe.—**da orelha**, ear lobe.
lobuloso –sa (*adj.*) lobulose.
loca (*f.*) a small grotto; an underwater cave; a fish's hiding place.
locação (*f.*) letting, leasing; location (of roads); a locating or staking (of limits or boundaries); a staked area. [But not location in the sense of locality, which is LOCAL or LOCALIDADE.]
locador –dora (*m.,f.*) lessor. [Lessee is LOCATÁRIO].
local (*adj.*) local; (*m.*) locality, place, site; (*f.*) local news item in the paper.
localidade (*f.*) locality, location, place; a small village; reserved seat (for a performance).
localista (*m.,f.*) local news editor.
localização (*f.*) localization, location.
localizador (*m.*) localizer; (*Mach.*) jig, holder, clamp.—**submarino**, submarine detector.
localizar (*v.t.*) to localize, locate.
locanda (*f.*) low tavern; cheap eating place; [= TABERNA].
locandeiro –ra (*m.,f.*) innkeeper; shopkeeper.
loção (*f.*) lotion, wash; hair lotion.—**antissolar**, sunburn preventive.
locar (*v.t.*) to let, lesse; to locate, mark out; to localize.
locatário –ria (*m.,f.*) leasee, lesseholder; tenant. [Lessor is LOCADOR].
locativo –va (*adj.*) locative.
locomobilidade (*f.*) locomobility.
locomoção (*f.*) locomotion.
locomotivo –va (*adj.*) locomotive; (*f.*) locomotive, train engine.—**de vapor**, steam engine.—**Diesel**, Diesel engine. —**Diesel-elétrica**, Diesel-electric engine.—**elétrica**, electric engine.—**pilôto**, pilot-engine.
locomotor –triz (*adj.*) locomotor.
locomóvel (*adj.*) self-propelling; (*f.*) locomotive.
locomover-se (*v.r.*) to move about.
locução (*f.*) locution, phrase; idiomatic expression.
locular (*adj., Bot., Zool.*) locular.
loculicida (*adj., Bot.*) loculicidal.
lóculo (*Bot.*) loculus.
locupletar (*v.t.*) to enrich; (*v.r.*) to get rich; to feather one's nest, fill one's pockets; to get one's fill.
locutor (*m.*) radio announcer.
locutório (*m.*) the visiting room in a monastery, convent or prison.
lodaçal (*m.*) mudhole, sea of mud; fig., a dissolute life; a den of vice.
lodacento –ta (*adj.*) muddy [= LODOSO].
lodeira (*f.*) mudhole, bog, mire.
lôdo (*m.*) mud, mire, sludge; clay; silt; fig., degradation. **arrastar no—**, to besmirch, befoul.
lodoso –sa (*adj.*) muddy; turbid.
loendro (*m.*) = ESPIRRADEIRA (plant).
Loengrim (*m.*) Lohengrin.
loess (*m., Geol.*) loess.

lôfio (*m.*) angler fish (*Lophius gastrophysus* or *L. piscatorius*), c.a. PEIXE-PESCADOR.
lofobrânquios (*m.pl.*) a suborder (*Lophobranchii*) which includes the pipefishes and sea horses.
lofornis (*m.*) the genus (*Lophornis*) of coquette humming-birds.
lofospermo (*m., Bot.*) the plumeseed maurandia (*M. lophospermum*).
lofótrico –ca (*adj., Biol., Bacteriol.*) lophotrichous.
log. = LOGARÍTMO (logarithm).
loganiáceo –cea (*adj., Bot.*) loganiaceous; (*f.pl.*) the Loganiaceae.
loganina (*f., Chem.*) loganin.
logarítmico –ca (*adj.*) logarithmic.
logaritmo (*m.*) logarithm.
logia (*f., Arch.*) loggia.
lógico –ca (*adj.*) logical; (*m.,f.*) logician; (*f.*) logic; reasoning; dialectics.
logo (*adv.*) at once, right away, immediately; soon, shortly, before long, pretty soon, by and by; (*conj.*) so, therefore, hence, ergo.—**de saída**, right from the start.—**depois**, soon after, right after.—**em seguida**, right after. —**logo**, at once.—**mais**, later (on).—**no comêço**, right at the start.—**que**, as soon as. **Até—**! So long! Goodby! See you soon! **desde—**, ever since then; at once. **ir—ao assunto**, to go straight to the point.
logografia (*f.*) logography.
logogrifo (*m.*) logogriph; fig., puzzle.
logomaquia (*f.*) logomachy; war of words.
logorréia (*f.*) excessive talkativeness.
logotecnia (*f.*) science of the use and meaning of words.
logótipo (*m., Printing*) logotype.
logração (*f.*) enjoyment, possession; artifice, fraud.
logradeira (*f.*) woman cheat or crook.
logrador –dora (*adj.*) cheating, cozening; (*m.*) crook, cheat.
logradouro (*m.*) public park or playground. Var. LOGRADOIRO.
logrão (*m.*) swindler, cheat; greedy person.
lograr (*v.t.*) to enjoy, profit from (the possession of something); to attain, win, achieve; to succeed in; to trick, cheat, deceive, bamboozle, victimize, dupe, gyp, hoodwink, hornswoggle; to double-cross; to outsmart, outwit; to make a fool of.—**êxito**, to meet with (enjoy) success. **não—êxito**, to come off badly, fail.
lôgro (*m.*) fraud, swindle, trick; humbug; hoax; prank, profit, fruition; success; possession, enjoyment.
loiça (*f.*) = LOUÇA.
Lóide (*m.*) Lloyd.
loiro –ra (*adj.; m.,f.*) = LOURO.
loja (*f.*) shop, store; masonic lodge.—**americana**, 5-and-10 store.—**de artigos para homem**, haberdashery.—**de ferragens**, hardware store.—**de miudezas**, notions shop. —**de modas**, dress shop.—**de prego**, pawnshop.—**de sêcos e molhados**, grocery store.—**de varejo**, retail store.—**maçônica**, masonic lodge.
lojista (*m.,f.*) shopkeeper.
loligídeos (*m.pl.*) a family (*Loliginidae*) of squids.
loligopse (*m.*) a genus (*Loligo*) of squids.
lolingita (*f., Min.*) löllingite, leucopyrite.
lólio (*m.*) darnel ryegrass (*Lolium temulentum*), c.a. JOIO.
lomba (*f.*) ridge, crest; brow of a hill; high plain; rising ground; laziness.
lombada (*f.*) long ridge; spine of a book; back of a steer.
lombar (*adj.*) lumbar.
lombear (*v.t.*) to gall (the back of a horse); (*v.r.*) to twist and turn; to writhe; to dillydally, put off, procrastinate.
lombeira (*f.*) laziness; listlessness.
lombilho (*m.*) a type of Brazilian saddle with high bow and cantle; tenderloin.
lombinho (*m.*) tenderloin.
lombo (*m.*) back (of an animal); loin of beef or pork; a book-cover; any rounded ridge. **a**(or **em**)—**de burro**, on muleback.
lombo-abdominal (*adj.*) lumbo-abdominal.
lombo-costal (*adj.*) lumbo-costal.
lombo-sagrado –da (*adj.*) lumbosacral.
lombrical (*adj., Anat.*) lumbrical; (*Zool.*) lumbricoid.
lombricídeos (*m.pl.*) a family (*Lumbricidae*) of earthworms.
lombriciforme (*adj.*) lumbriciform; vermiform.
lombricóide (*adj.; m.*) lumbricoid.
lombriga (*f.*) the common roundworm (*Ascaris lumbri-*

coides) parasitic in human intestines; a genus (*Lumbricus*) of earthworms.

lombrigueira (*f., Bot.*) West Indian spigelia (*S. anthelmia*) c.a. ERVA-CRUZ; also = COAJINGUBA.

lombrigueiro (*m.*) a vermicide; anthelmintic.

lombudo –da (*adj.*) strong-backed.

lomentáceo –cea (*adj., Bot.*) lomentaceous.

lomento (*m., Bot.*) loment.

lona (*f.*) canvas, sail cloth.—**encerada,** tarpaulin.—**do freio,** brake lining.

lonca (*f.*) half of a horse's hide; (*pl.*) narrow strips of rawhide.

Londres (*f.*) London.

londrino –na (*adj.*) of or pert. to London; (*m.,f.*) a Londoner.

longamente (*adj.*) for a long time; extensively.

longana (*f.*) the longan (*Euphoria longan*), or its fruits.

longânime, longânimo –ma (*adj.*) forbearing, tolerant.

longarina (*f.*), –no (*m.*) a stringer (long, horizontal piece such as a bridge beam or girder); one of the long members of an automobile chassis or locomotive frame; longéron or spar (of an airplane).

longe (*adv.*) far, far off, afar; (*adj.*) far, remote, distant; (*m.pl.*) background (of a painting); great distance; remote past; traces, vestiges; suspicion; foreboding. —**daqui,** a long way from here.—**de,** far from.—**disso,** far from it, "not by a long shot."—**dos olhos, longe do coracão,** Out of sight, out of mind. **ao—**, far off, in the distance, far away, afar. **bem—**, a good (long) way off. **de—**, from afar, from a distance. **De vagar se vai ao—**, Make haste slowly. **ir—**, to go far, make much progress; to be a long time since. **ir muito—**, to go too far. **mais—**, farther (on), later (on). **muito—**, very far away. **muito ao —**, far afield. **para—**, far away.

longerão (*m.*) the side member of a locomotive's frame; longéron of an airplane. Cf. LONGARINA.

longevidade (*f.*) longevity.

longevo –va (*adj.*) long-lived; enduring; very old.

longicórneo –nea (*adj.; m.*) longicorn (beetle).

longínquo –qua (*adj.*) distant, remote, far away.

longipene (*adj., Zool.*) longipennate.

longitude (*f.*) longitude; distance.

longitudinal (*adj.*) longitudinal.

longo –ga (*adj.*) long, lengthy; drawn out, protracted. **ao—de,** alongside (of), beside, along.

longrina (*f.*) = LONGARINA.

longueirão (*m.*) razor clam [= LINGUEIRÃO].

longuidão (*f.*) length [= COMPRIMENTO].

longulito (*m., Min.*) longulite.

lonicera (*f.*) the genus (*Lonicera*) of honeysuckles [= MADRESSILVA].

longura (*f.*) length; delay.

lonjura (*f., colloq.*) a long distance.

lonquear (*v.t.*) to scrape and otherwise prepare a hide.

lontra (*f.*) any otter, esp. *Lutra platensis;* sometimes confused with the much larger ARIRANHA.—**-do-mar,** sea otter (*Enhydralutis*).

loquacidade (*f.*) loquacity, talkativeness, garrulity.

loquaz (*adj.*) loquacious, talkative, garrulous, glib.

loqüela (*f.*) fluency, glibness; verbosity.

lóquios (*m.pl., Med., Veter.*) lochia.

loran (*m., Aeron.*) loran ("Long Range Navigation").

lorantáceo –cea (*adj., Bot.*) loranthaceous; (*f.pl.*) the Loranthaceae (mistletoe family).

loranto (*m., Bot.*) any plant of the genus Loranthus.

lorde (*m.*) an English lord; a member of the House of Lords; (*colloq.*) one who lives or dresses like a lord; (*adj.*) lordly.

lordeza (*f.*) lordliness.

lordose (*f., Med.*) lordosis.

lorica (*f., Zool.*) lorica; (*Bot.*) testa.

loricado –da (*adj., Zool.*) loricate.

loriga (*f.*) a cuirass protected by plates.

lornhão (*m.*) lorgnette.

loro (*m.*) stirrup strap; any strap; (*Zool.*) lore.

lorota (*f., colloq.*) fib, tall tale; nonsense; twaddle, bunk, "baloney," "applesauce".

lorotar (*v.i.*) to lie; to gabble.

loroteiro –ra (*adj.*) lying; (*m.,f.*) liar.

lorpa [ô] (*adj.*) imbecile, silly, foolish; boorish, coarse; (*m.,f.*) imbecile; fool; boor.

losângico –ca (*adj.*) lozenge-shaped; diamond-shaped.

losango (*m.*) lozenge; diamond; rhomb.

losanjas (*f.pl., Pharm.*) medicated lozenges.

losna (*f.*) sagebrush; wormwood.—**-do-algarve,** or—**-menor,** shrubby wormwood (*Artemisia arborescens*). —**-maior,** common wormwood (*Artemisia absinthimum*), c.a. ABSÍNTIO.

lossenite (*f., Min.*) lossenite.

lotação (*f.*) holding capacity; tonnage (of a ship); estimated returns; blending of wines; (*m.*) omnibus, jitney bus.

lotado –da (*adj.*) filled to capacity; chock full.

lotar (*v.t.*) to allot; to divide into lots; to blend wine.

lotaria (*f.*) = LOTERIA.

lote (*m.*) lot, allotment, portion; batch; a building lot, parcel of land; a shipment (of goods).

lotear (*v.t.*) to subdivide real estate into building lots.

loteria (*f.*) lottery.

lotérico –ca (*adj.*) of or pert. to lottery.

loto (*m.*) lotus flower; the Hindu lotus (*Nelumbium nelumbo*).—**-sagrado-do-egito,** white Egyptian lotus (*Nymphaea lotus*).

lôto (*m.*) lotto, keno, bingo.

louça (*f.*) dishware, chinaware; earthenware; bathroom fixtures; dishes collectively.—**esmaltada,** graniteware. Var. LOIÇA.

louçainha [a-í] (*f.*) finery.

loução [-çãos] –çã (*adj.*) gaily dressed; dapper; smartly dressed; fine, elegant; goodlooking.

louçaria (*f.*) chinaware shop. Var. LOIÇARIA.

louceiro (*m.*) chinaware manufacturer or dealer; china closet.

louco –ca (*adj.*) crazy, mad, insane; frenzied; delirious; rash, reckless; wild, impetuous; (*m.,f.*) such a person; (*m., Bot.*) climbing plumbago (*P. scandens*), c.a. CAÁ-POMONGA.—**de atar,** raving mad, "fit to be tied".—**rematado,** a completely mad person.—**varrido,** stark crazy. **cada—com sua mania,** each to his own taste.

loucura (*f.*) insanity, dementia, madness; delirium; folly, crazy action, crazy idea; foolishness; also ESTREMOSA (a plant).

louquejar (*v.i.*) to act crazily or foolishly.

louquice (*f.*) = LOUCURA.

loura (*f.*) see under LOURO

louraça (*m.,f.*) a person with faded blond hair. Var. LOIRAÇA.

loureira (*f.*) wanton woman; seductress; prostitute. Var. LOIREIRA.

loureiro (*m., Bot.*) the Grecian laurel or true bay (*Laurus nobilis*), c.a. LOUREIRO-DE-APOLO.—**cereja,** common laurelcherry (*Prunus laurocerasus*).—**-de-portugal,** the Portuguese laurelcherry (*Prunus lusitanica*).—**-rosa** = ESPIRRADEIRA.—**tim,** the Laurestinus vibernum (*V. tinus*), c.a. FOLHADO. Var. LOIREIRO.

lourejar (*v.i.*) to turn yellow (as grain, fruit).

Lourenço (*m.*) Lawrence; Laurence; Lorenzo.

louro –ra [var. LOIRO -RA] (*adj.*) yellow, golden; blond; (*f.*) a blonde. [LOURA PLATINADA, platinum blonde]; a burrow [= LURA]; a parrot [PAPAGAIO-LOURO]; (*m.*) bay leaf; (*Bot.*) any laurel; any sweetwood (tropical American tree of the genera *Ocotea* or *Nectandra*).—**amarelo,** the onion cordia (*C. alliodora*).—**branco,** the whitelaurel ocotea (*O. strumosa*).—**cereja,** common laurelcherry (*Prunus laurocerasus*).—**cravo,** clovebark tree (*Dicypellium caryophyllatum*), c.a. PAU-CRAVO, CRAVEIRO-DO-MARANHÃO.—**cheiroso** = CASCA-PRECIOSA; CRAVEIRO-DO-MARANHÃO.—**inhamuí,** a laurel (*Nectandra elaeophora*), c.a. LOURO-MAMORIM, LOURO-NHAMUÍ, INAMUÍ, PAU-DE-GASOLINA, QUEROSENE.—**vermelho,** red ocotea (*O. rubra*).

lousa (*f.*) slate; gravestone; flagstone; writing slate.

louseira (*f.*) slate quarry.

louva-a-deus (*m., Zool.*) praying mantis, c.a. PÕE-MESA.

louvação (*f.*) laudation, praise.

louvado –da (*adj.*) praised.—**em,** of opinions, based on, supported by. (*m.*) arbiter, judge, expert, appraiser.

louvador –dora (*adj.*) laudatory; (*m.,f.*) praiser.

louvamento (*m.*) = LOUVAÇÃO.

louvaminha (*f.*) flattery, adulation.

louvaminhar (*v.t.*) to flatter.

louvaminheiro –ra (*adj.*) flattering; (*m.,f.*) flatterer.

louvar (*v.t.*) to laud, praise, extol; to applaud, commend; to appraise; (*v.r.*) to boast.—**se em,** or **na opinião de, alguém,** to base one's own opinion on that of another.

louvável (*adj.*) laudable, praiseworthy; honorable.

louvor (*m.*) laudation, praise, eulogy.

lóxia [ks] (*f.*) = CRUZA-BICO.

loxoclásio [ks] (*m.*, *Petrog.*) loxoclase.
loxodromia [ks] (*f.*) loxodrome, a rhumb line; loxodromics.
Lt.da = LIMITADA (Ltd., Limited.)
lua (*f.*) moon; (*colloq.*) menses.—**cheia**, full moon.— **-crescente**, the northern cliff swallow (*Petrochelidon p. pyrrhonota*).—**de mel**, honeymoon.—**nova**, new moon. **aos cornos da—**, of praise, to the skies. **meia—**, half-moon.
luar (*m.*) moonlight.
luarento -ta (*adj.*) moonlit.
lubricidade (*f.*) lubricity, slipperiness; lasciviousness; lechery.
lúbrico -ca (*adj.*) lubric, slippery; lascivious, lewd, lecherous; wanton.
lubrificação (*f.*) lubrication.
lubrificador -dora (*adj.*) lubricating; (*m.,f.*) lubricator.
lubrificante (*adj.*) lubricating; (*m.*) lubricant.—**de corte**, coolant, cutting oil.
lubrificar (*v.t.*) to lubricate, oil, grease.
lucanário (*m.*) space between beams.
lucarna (*f.*, *Arch.*) lucarne, dormer window.
Lucas (*m.*) Luke.
lucerna (*f.*) lucerne (a small lamp).
Lúcia (*f.*) Lucia; Lucy.
lúcia-lima (*f.*, *Bot.*) the lemon-verbena lippia (*L. citriodora*), c.a. LIMONETE, BELA-LUÍSA, ERVA-LUÍSA, VERBENA.
Luciano (*m.*) Lucian.
lucidar (*v.t.*) to trace (a design).
lucidez [ê] (*f.*) lucidity, brightness, clearness; clearheadedness, perspicuity.
lúcido -da (*adj.*) lucid, bright; clear, pellucid; intelligible, rational; sane; clearheaded.
luciferino -na (*adj.*) Luciferian; diabolical.
lucífero -ra (*adj.*) luciferous.
lucífugo -ga (*adj.*, *Biol.*) lucifugous.
Lucila (*f.*) Lucile; Lucille [= LUCÍLIA].
lucilação (*f.*) glimmering.
lucilante (*adj.*) glimmering, gleaming, flickering.
lucilar (*v.i.*) to glimmer, gleam, flicker.
Lucília (*f.*, *Zool.*) a genus (*Lucilia*) of green-bottle flies; Lucile; Lucille [= LUCILA].
lucímetro (*m.*) lucimeter; photometer.
luciluzir (*v.i.*) to flicker, twinkle, glimmer.
lucina (*f.*) the moon. [*Poetical*]
lúcio (*m.*, *Zool.*) an Old World pike (*Esox lucius*); [*cap.*] Lucius.—**-marinho**, a barracuda.
lucrar (*v.i.*) to gain, reap; to profit (**de**, from; **com**, by); (*v.t.*) to benefit, await.
lucrativo -va (*adj.*) lucrative, gainful, profitable, advantageous.
Lucrécia (*f.*) Lucretia.
lucro (*m.*) profit, gain, advantage.—**s e perdas**, profits and losses.—**s extraordinários**, excess profits.—**s ilícitos**, ill-got gains. **participação nos—s**, profit-sharing.
lucubração (*f.*) lucubration, laborious study, esp. one carried on at night.
lucubrar (*v.i.*) to lucubrate, "burn the midnight oil"
luculiano -na (*adj.*) Lucullean.
luculita (*f.*, *Min.*) lucullite.
ludar (*m.*, *Bot.*) the lodebark sweetleaf (*Symplocos racemosa*).
ludibriante (*adj.*) ridiculing, derisive; mock, sham.
ludibriar (*v.t.*) to illude, cheat, dupe; to outwit; to mock, deride, ridicule; to treat with scorn.
ludíbrio (*m.*) mockery, scorn; laughingstock, subject of ridicule; fool.
ludibrioso -sa (*adj.*) mocking.
ludo (*m.*) parchesi (a game played on a board with dice and disks).
lues [lú-ès] (*f.*, *Med.*) lues, syphilis.
luético -ca (*adj.*, *Med.*) luetic, syphilitic.
lufa (*f.*) wind, gust; fig., flurry, ado.
lufada (*f.*) flurry, gust of wind. **às—s**, by fits and starts.
lufa-lufa (*f.*) hurry, flurry, bustle, hurry-skurry, hurly-burly. **à—**, in great haste.
lufar (*v.i.*) to blow hard, puff.
lugar (*m.*) place, room; seat (as in a theater); position, employment; locality; spot, site; opportunity, occasion. —**aparente**, (*Astron.*) apparent place.—**comum** commonplace, cliché, trite figure [= CHAPA, CHAVÃO, CLICHÊ]. —**defeso**, forbidden territory.—**de honra**, place of honor.—**es santos**, holy places.—**heliocêntrico**, (*Astron.*) heliocentric place, latitude, longitude, etc. (of a celestial body).—**público**, public place.—**-tenente**, locum tenens:

" . . . one filling an office for a time or temporarily taking the place of another . . . " [*Webster*]. **dar—a**, to give rise to. **em—algum**, nowhere. **em—de**, in place of, instead of. **em—nenhum**, anywhere. **em nenhum—**, nowhere. **em primeiro—**, in (the) first place; firstly. **em qualquer—**, anywhere. **em todo—**, everywhere. **Este—já tem dono**, This seat is already taken. **marcar—e hora**, to indicate (agree on) time and place. **ter—**, to take place (**em**, in, at). **um—abrigado**, a sheltered place.
lugarejo (*m.*) hamlet, small village.
lugre (*m.*) lugger (small sailing vessel); also = PINTASSILGO-VERDE.
lúgubre (*adj.*) lugubrious, mournful; sad, gloomy; dismal; doleful.
lugubridade (*f.*) lugubriousness.
luís (*m.*) a French louis d'or; [*cap.*] Louis.
luís-cacheiro, **luíz-caixeiro** (*m.*) = OURIÇO-CACHEIRO.
Luísa (*f.*) Louisa.
Luisiana (*f.*) Louisiana.
lula (*f.*) cuttlefish; squid [= CALAMAR].
lulu (*m.*) Pomeranian (lap dog).—**gigante**, a chow dog.
lumaquela (*f.*) lumachel(la). [*Webster:* "A grayish-brown limestone, containing fossil shells, which reflect a beautiful play of colors."]
lumbagem (*f.*) = LUMBAGO.
lumbágico -ca (*adj.*) lumbaginous.
lumbago (*m.*) lumbago.
lumbrical, lumbricário -ria (*adj.*) = LOMBRICAL.
lumbricida (*adj.*; *f.*, *Med.*) vermicide, anthelmintic.
lume (*m.*) fire, bonfire; light; candle; insight, comprehension.—**de água**, surface of water.—**de vista**, light of the eyes.—**es-prontos** or—**es de pau**, sulfur matches. **dar a—**, to publish. **ter—de alguma coisa**, to have a smattering of knowledge about something.
lumeeira [e-ei] (*f.*) torch; candlestick; skylight; bright light; fire; firefly.
lumeira (*f.*) transom.
lúmen (*m.*) lumen (a unit of light); (*Anat.*, *Zool.*, *Bot.*) lumen.
luminar (*adj.*) light-giving; (*m.*) luminary, leading light.
lumināria (*f.*) light; small lantern; luminaire; luminary; (*pl.*) outdoor illuminations.
luminescência (*f.*) luminescence.
luminescente (*adj.*) luminescent.
luminífero -ra (*adj.*) luminiferous.
luminista (*m.,f.*) luminarist. [*Webster:* "An artist skillful in light and shade."]
luminosidade (*f.*) luminosity, brilliance; value (of colors).
luminoso -sa (*adj.*) luminous, bright; clear, brilliant; keen, discerning.
lunação (*f.*) lunation; lunar month, synodical month.
lunado -da (*adj.*) lunate, crescent-shaped.
lunar (*adj.*) lunar; (*m.*) birthmark; mole.
lunária (*f.*) the perennial honesty (*Lunaria rediviva*), or the dollarplant (*L. annua*), c.a. ERVA-DA-LUA.
lunático -ca (*adj.*) moonstruck, lunatic; (*m.,f.*) a lunatic.
lundu[m] (*m.*) primitive lascivious dance; comic song.
luneta [ê] (*f.*) eyeglass, pincenez; the hole in a guillotine for the victim's neck; in church rites, the crystal case used to hold the Host; a small oval or round window or wall-opening; a circular gauge.—**telescópica**, telescopic sight.
lunetaria (*f.*) optician's shop.
lunícola (*m.,f.*) an inhabitant of the moon; a selenite.
luniforme (*adj.*) luniform.
lunissolar (*adj.*) lunisolar.
lúnula (*f.*, *Astron.*) a satellite; (*Geom.*) a crescent-shaped figure; [*Anat.*, *Zool.*] lunule.
lunulado -da, lunular (*adj.*) lunulate.
lunulite (*f.*, *Paleontol.*, *Zool.*) lunulite.
lupa (*f.*) magnifying glass; (*Veter.*) capped knee; (*Metal.*) bloom.
lupanar (*m.*) brothel, bawdyhouse.
lupinastro (*m.*) a Siberian species of clover (*Trifolium lupinaster*).
lupinina (*f.*, *Chem.*) lupinin(e).
lupino -na (*adj.*) lupine, wolfish.
lupinose (*f.*, *Med.*, *Veter.*) lupinosis.
lupo (*m.*, *Med.*) lupus.—**eritematoso**, lupus erythematosus.—**vulgar**, lupus vulgaris.
luposo -sa (*adj.*, *Med.*) lupous.
lupulina (*f.*, *Bot.*) the black medic (*Medicago lupulina*).
lupulino (*m.*, *Bot.*) lupulin.

lúpulo (*m.*) hop (*Humulus lupulus*), c.a. PÉ-DE-GALO.—-do-monte = ESPIGA-DE-LEITE.
lúpus (*m.*) = LUPO.
lura (*f.*) burrow. Var. LOURA.
lúrido –**da** (*adj.*) lurid.
lusco –**ca** (*adj.*) one-eyed; cross-eyed; (*m.*) dawn or dusk.
lusco-fusco (*m.*) dusk, nightfall; dawn, daybreak; (*colloq.*) a mulatto.
lusíada (*adj.; m.,f.*) Lusitanian, Portuguese; (*cap.*, *m.pl.*) the Lusiads (Camoens' epic poem).
lusismo (*m.*) a Lusitanism (a word or expression peculiar to the Portuguese language).
lusitânico –**ca**, **lusitano** –**na** (*adj.; m.,f.*) Lusitanian, Portuguese.
lusitanismo (*m.*) the quality of being Portuguese; a word or idiom peculiarly Portuguese.
lusitanizar (*v.t.*) to render Portuguese; (*v.r.*) to become Portuguese.
lusitanofilia (*f.*) fondness for, or admiration of, Portugal or the Portuguese.
lusitanófilo –**la**, **lusófilo** –**la** (*m.,f.*) one who admires or favors Portugal and things Portuguese.
lusofobia (*f.*) dread of, or aversion to, Portugal or the Portuguese.
lusófobo –**ba** (*m.,f.*) one who is averse to Portugal and things Portuguese.
lustração (*f.*) act or operation of polishing.
lustradela (*f.*) a glossing, shining or polishing.
lustrador –**dora** (*adj.*) glossing, polishing; (*m.,f.*) glosser, shiner, polisher; floor waxer.
lustrar (*v.t.*) to polish; to gloss, shine; to purify.
lustre (*m.*) luster, brightness, sheen, gloss; renown, repute; splendor, glory; a chandelier; lighting fixture.
lustrina (*f.*) a lustrous fabric used for lining.
lustro (*m.*) luster, shine; lustrum (period of five years).
lustroso –**sa** (*adj.*) lustrous, bright, shining.
luta, fight, contest, struggle; fray.—**livre**, free-style wrestling.—**romana**, wrestling.—**sem quartel**, a fight with no quarters. **em**—, struggling.
lutador –**dora** (*adj.*) fighting, struggling; (*m.,f.*) fighter, wrestler; contender.
lutar (*v.i.*) to fight (**contra**, against); to contend, cope (**com**, with); to strive, struggle; to wrestle; (*v.t.*) to lute; cover, close or seal (as, a joint) with lute.—**pela vida**, to work hard for a living.
lutécio (*m.*, *Chem.*) lutecium.
luteína (*f.*, *Biochem.*) lutein, lipochrome, chromolipoid.
luteolado –**da** (*adj.*) slightly yellow; yellowish.
luteolina (*f.*, *Chem.*) luteolin.
luterano –**na** (*adj.; m.,f.*) Lutheran.
Lutero (*m.*) Luther.
luto (*m.*) bereavement; mourning, sorrow, grief; mourning garments or symbols; lute (a cement for sealing).—**aliviado**, half mourning.—**fechado**, or **rigoroso**, deep or full mourning.—**oficial**, official mourning. **de**—, in mourning.
lutuoso –**sa** (*adj.*) mournful.
luva (*f.*) glove; pipe coupling or sleeve; (*pl.*) a gratuity or reward; a premium paid as "key money" by a lessee to the lessor, or his agent, at the time of signing the contract; a brokerage fee; a bribe.—**s-de-nossa-senhora**, or -de-pastôra, or -de-santa-maria = DEDALEIRA (foxglove). **apanhar** (or **levantar**) **a**—, to take up the gauntlet (accept a challenge). **atirar a**—, to fling down the gauntlet; to issue a challenge; to raise a challenging question. **dar com**—**de pelica**, to turn the other cheek. **escrever com**—**branca**, to write in polite terms.
luvaria (*f.*) glove shop or factory.
luveiro –**ra**, **luvista** (*m.,f.*) glovemaker; glove merchant.
luxação (*f.*) luxation, dislocation; wrench, sprain.
luxar (*v.t.*) to luxate, dislocate, put out of joint; to wrench, sprain; (*v.i.*) to parade, show off, display wealth, luxury, etc.; to decline something (as an offer of food or drink) through mere formality.
luxento –**ta** (*adj.*) fussy, overnice, too particular.
luxo (*m.*) luxury, magnificence; extravagance, excess; luxuriousness; airs, false formality, mock refusal. **artigos de**—, luxury items of merchandise. **cheio de**—, fussy, demanding, pretentious. **dar-se o**—**de**, to permit oneself the luxury of. **de**—, de luxe. **deixar-se de**—, to stop being formal. **não dar-se o**—**de (fazer algo)**, to not be bothered to (do something).
luxuliana (*f.*, *Petrog.*) luxulianite.
luxuosidade (*f.*) luxuriousness.
luxuoso –**sa** (*adj.*) luxurious, sumptuous; de luxe.
luxúria (*f.*) luxuriance, lushness (in growth of plants); lasciviousness, lechery; lust.
luxuriância (*f.*) luxuriance.
luxuriante (*adj.*) luxuriant, lush, rank; lascivious.
luxuriar (*v.i.*) to luxuriate; to indulge in lust.
luxurioso –**sa** (*adj.*) luxuriant; lustful, lewd.
luz [-es] (*f.*) light; brightness; that which furnishes light, as a candle, lamp, etc.; publicity; elucidation; (*pl.*) knowledge, education.—**artificial**, artificial light.—**baça**, dim light.—**de arco**, arc light.—**de arterissagem**, landing light.—**de bengala**, Bengal light.—**de tráfego**, traffic light.—**difusa**, diffused light.—**do dia**, daylight.—**do sol**, sunlight.—**elétrica**, electric light.—**es da balizagem**, (*Avn.*) landing lights.—**es da ribalta**, footlights.—**infra-vermelha**, infrared light.—**negra**, black light.—**ultra-violeta**, ultraviolet light. **à**—**de**, in the light of; in view of. **à meia**—, darkly, dimly. **dar à**—, to give birth to; to publish. **vir à**—, to come to light.
luzeiro (*m.*) a light-producing object (torch, etc.); a bright light; a lighthouse; a bright star; a luminary (illustrious personage); (*pl.*, *colloq.*) the eyes.
luze-luze (*m.*, *colloq.*) firefly; glow worm [= PIRILAMPO].
luzente (*adj.*) shiny, shining, bright.
luzerna (*f.*) bright light; skylight; (*Bot.*) alfalfa (*Medicago sativa*), c.a. ALFAFA-VERDADEIRA.—-**amarela** = ALFAFA-DE-FLOR-AMARELA.—-**arborescente**, the tree medic (*Medicago arborea*).—-**de-sequeiro** = ALFAFA-DA-SUÉCIA.—-**entretecida**, interlaced medic (*Medicago intertexta*).—-**lupulina** = ALFAFA-DE-FLOR-AMARELA.
luzernal, **luzerneira** (*f.*) alfalfa field.
luzidio –**dia** (*adj.*) shiny, glossy, sleek.
luzido –**da** (*adj.*) showy, sumptuous, dazzling.
luziluzir (*v.i.*) to twinkle, blink, glimmer.
luzimento (*m.*) splendor, brilliance; magnificence.
luzir [36] (*v.i.*) to shine, glitter, sparkle; to brighten. **Nem tudo que luz é ouro**, All is not gold that glitters.
Lx.ª (*f.*) = LISBOA.

M

M, m, the twelfth letter of the Portuguese alphabet.
m. = MÊS, MESES (month, months).
m = METRO(S)—meter(s).
m/ = MEU, MINHA (my).
m/a = MEU ACEITE (my acceptance—endorsed on a draft)
m.ª = MESMA (same); MINHA (my).
M.ª = MARIA (Mary).
MA = MARANHÃO (State of).
má, (*adj.*, *fem. of* MAU)—**hora**, a bad time; a bad hour.—**língua**, an evil tongue.—**vida**, a hard life.—**vontade**, ill will.
ma (*pers. pron.*) it to me; (*pl.*) them to me. [Contraction of indirect object pron. **me**+direct object **a**.]

maatma (*m.*) mahatma.
mabaça (*m.,f.*) a twin brother or sister [= BABAÇA].
mabala (*f.*, *Bot.*) a Goabean (*Psophocarpus longipedunculatus*).
mabolo (*m.*) mabola persimmon (*Diospyros discolor*).
mabu (*f.*) papyrus (*Cyperus papyrus*).
maca (*f.*) sailor's hammock; litter, stretcher.
maça (*f.*) mace; club, bat; tamper (for paving blocks).
maçã (*f.*) apple.—**do rosto**, cheek.—-**de-adão**, Adam's apple.—-**do-mato**, a mountain ash (*Sorbus brasiliensis*).—**do peito**, brisket (of beef).—**estrelada** = CAIMITO.
macaá (*m.*) = ACAUÃ.

macabro –bra (*adj.*) macabre, gruesome.

macaca (*f.*) a female monkey; an ugly woman; bad luck; hopscotch; the flu; short-handled whip. **estar de—**, to be down on one's luck.

macacaacá, macacacacau (*f.*) monkey chocolate tree (*Theobroma angustifolia*), c.a. CACAURANA.

macacada (*f.*) a band of monkeys.

macacal (*adj.*) simian.

macacalhada (*f.*) a band of monkeys.

macacão (*m.*) a smooth, clever person; workman's overalls; dungarees; a man of grotesque, apelike appearance.

macacapuranga (*f.*) a small tree of the laurel family (*Aniba fragrans*). "The entire plant is aromatic, giving off a very delicate rose odor. The powdered wood is used to perfume wardrobes and bureau drawers." [*GUAF*]

macacar (*v.*) = MACAQUEAR.

macacaria (*f.*) a band of monkeys; mimicry.

macacaúba (*f.*) either of two leguminous trees: *Platymiscium duckei*, c.a. MACACAÚBA-DA-TERRA-FIRME, and *P. ulei*, c.a. MACACAÚBA-DA-VÁRZEA; both yield timber (maca wood) for fine furniture and inlay work; also, a macaw palm (*Acrocomia sclerocarpa*), c.a. CÔCO-DE-CATARRO, MACAJÁ.

macaco (*m.*) monkey, ape, simian; jack (lifting tool); ram of a pile driver; granite paving block.**—adufeiro**, or**—-da-meia-noite**, a kinkajou (*Potus flavus*), c.a. JUPARÁ. [This is not a monkey at all but of the same family as the raccoon.]**—-aranha**, any spider monkey (*Ateles*), c.a. COATÁ. **—-aranha-de-cara-vermelha** = COATÁ-PRÊTO. **—-barrigudo**, any of the large big-bellied woolly monkeys of genus *Lagothrix***—-cabeludo**, the hairy saki or foxtailed monkey (*Pithecia monacha*), c.a. PARAUAÇU, PARAUACU, PARAGUAÇU, UAPUÇÁ, UAIAPUÇÁ; also = MACACO-PREGUIÇA.**—-da-noite** (or**—-dorminhoco**, or**—-do-diabo**) any night ape (*Aotus*) having large eyes and a long non-prehensile tail.**—-de-bando**, any capuchin monkey (*Cebus*).**—-de-cheiro** (or**—-esquilo**), a squirrel monkey (*Saïmiri sciurus*), c.a. SAÍ-MIRIM, BÔCA-PRETA, JURUPIXUNA.**—-cotó** (or**—-mal-acabado**) = UACARI-DE-CABEÇA-PRETA.**—-hidráulico**, hydraulic jack.**—-inglês**, an ouakari monkey (*Cacajao rubicundus*) having a bright red face; c.a. ACARI, UACARI-VERMELHO.**—-leão** = ACARIMA.**—-prego** (or**—-itapuá**) any capuchin monkey (*Cebus*), c.a. MICO-(DE-TOPÊTE), CAIARARA.**—-preguiça**, a hairy saki monkey (*Pithecia albicans*).**—-vermelho**, a spider monkey (*Eriodes arachnoides*), c.a. MURIQUI.

macacoa (*f.*) the flu or other minor illness.

maçada (*f.*) irksome task; tedious talk; nuisance; a bludgeoning; cheating at cards. **Que—!** What a nuisance!

macadame (*m.*) macadam (system of road surfacing).

macadamizar (*v.t.*) to macadamize a roadway.

maçador –dora (*adj.*) tedious, boring; pestiferous; (*m.,f.*) a bore, pest.

maçadura (*f.*) bruise.

maçagem (*f.*) = MASSAGEM.

macaíba (*f.*) = MACAJÁ.

macaíra (*m.*) a marlin (*Makaira sp.*); a sailfish, c.a. AGULHÃO-BANDEIRA.

macajá (*f.*) a tall pinnate-leaved macaw palm, the mucaja acromia (*A. sclerocarpa*), c.a. MACACAÚBA, MACAÚBA, MACAÍBA, MACAJUBA, MACAJUBEIRA, MUCAJÁ, BOCAIUVA, CÔCO-DE-CATARRO. "Wood of the trunk used to make lathing; oil from the nuts edible and suitable for soapmaking; the young leaves yield fine, white, silky fibers; fruit pulp is edible and the grease which it contains is also edible." [*GUAF*]

maçal (*m.*) whey, milk serum.

macamã (*m.*) runaway slave.

maçambará (*m.*) Johnson grass (*Sorghum halepense*) c.a. CAPIM-MAÇAMBARÁ, ARROZ-BRAVO, SORGO-DE-ALEPO, PERIPOMONGA.**—-do-piauí**, a bluestem forage grass (*Andropogon avenaceus*).

maçambé-catinga (*f.*) a spiderflower (*Cleome polygama*).

macambira (*f., Bot.*) a common bromeliad of northeastern Brazil (*Bromelia laciniosa*).**—-de-pedra**, or**—-de-serrote**, a bromeliad of the genus *Vriesia*.

macambo (*f.*) = CACAU-DO-PERU.

macambúzio –zia (*adj.*) glum, sullen; moody.

macaná (*m.*) "A wooden weapon widely employed by Indians of South America and the Antilles, generally of swordlike form, but also having the shape of an ax, or a club, sometimes headed with stone." [*Webster*]

maçanêta (*f.*) knob of a lock, door or drawer; any knoblike ornament or handle; pommel of a saddle.

maçante (*adj.*) = MAÇADOR.

macanudo –da (*adj.*) strong, fine, superior, "tops".

mação (*m.*) a Freemason; a large mallet.

maçapão [-pães] (*m.*) marzipan.

macaqueação (*f.*) mimicking; mimicry; monkeyshines.

macaqueador –dora (*adj.*) mimicking; (*m.,f.*) a mimic; one who apes.

macaquear (*v.t.*) to ape, mimic [= MACACAR].

macaqueiro –ra (*adj.*) monkey, simian; (*m.*) a cutter of stone paving blocks; (*Bot.*) a muskwood (*Guarea sp.*); = CARRAPÊTA.

macaquice (*f.*) mimicry; monkeyshines. **fazer—s**, to cut up, show off, play tricks.

macaquinho (*m.*) a little monkey. **Êle tem—s no sótão,** He has bats in his belfry.**—-de-bambá**, a dragonfly.

maçar (*v.t.*) to pound, as with a club or mallet; hence, fig., to bore, weary, by tedious repetition; to importune.

maçaranduba, –duva (*f.*) any of several milk or cow trees, of *Mimusops* and *Lucuma*, esp. *M. elata*, *M. excelsa*, *L. procera*.**—-do-pará**, or**—-verdadeira**, is *M. huberi*, c.a. ÁRVORE-DA-VACA. It is a very large tree, having hard, dark-red, fine-grained wood, which is moist-resistant and suitable for many industrial uses. They all have abundant latex, in some instances drinkable.

macaréu (*m.*) tidal bore [= PORORÓCA].

maçaricão (*m., Zool.*) the So. Amer. stilt (*Himantopus h. melanurus*), c.a. PERNA-DE-PAU, PERNILONGO; also = MAÇARICO-DE-BICO-TORTO (a curlew).

maçarico (*m.*) blowtorch; blowpipe; (*Zool.*) the common name for any of a number of shore birds, esp. the ruddy turnstone (*Arenaris interterpres morinella*), c.a. AGACHADEIRA; the American golden plover (*Pluvialis d. dominica*), c.a. BATUÍRA-DO-CAMPO, BATUIRUÇU; the sanderling (*Crocethia alba*); the Hudsonian godwit (*Limosa haemastica*).**—-agachadeira** = BATUÍRA.**—-de-coleira**, Azara's collared plover (*Charadrius collaris*), c.a. AGACHADEIRA, ITUÍ-TUÍ.**—-de-bico-torto**, Hudsonian curlew (*Numenius phaeopus hudsonicus*) and the Eskimo curlew (*Numenius borealis*), both c.a. MAÇARICÃO.**—-grande-da-praia**, the greater yellow-legs (*Tringa melanoleuca*).**—-real**, the plumbeous ibis (*Harpiprion caerulescens*).**—-oxiacetilê-nico**, oxyacetylene blowpipe or torch.**—-oxídrico** or**—de oxidrogênio**, oxyhydrogen blowpipe or torch.

maçariquinho (*m.*) = BATUÍRA.

maçaroca (*f.*) a spindleful of thread; tangled mass of hair; a sheaf; an ear of corn.

maçaroco [rô] (*m.*) a curl of hair; (*Bot.*) the Madeira viper bugloss (*Echium candicans*).

maçaroqueiro (*m.*), **–ra** (*f., Textiles*) a rover (machine or operator); (*f., Bot.*) Brazil satintail or sapegrass (*Imperata brasiliensis*), c.a. SAPÉ.

maçaroquinha (*f.*) cotton waste.

macarrão (*m.*) macaroni; (*slang*) a weak sister; (*Elec.*) spaghetti.

macarronada (*f.*) a dish made with macaroni.

macarrone (*m.*) a derogatory epithet for Italians in Brazil.

macarrônea (*f.*) a macaronic composition.

macarroneiro (*m.*) macaroni manufacturer.

macarrônico –ca (*adj.*) macaronic(al).

macarronismo (*m.*) macaronic style of writing.

macarronista (*m.,f.*) macaronic writer.

macassa (*f.*) = CORCOROCA.

macau (*m.*) a certain breed of Brazilian pigs; also = ARARACANGA (a macaw).

macauã, macaguã (*m.*) = ACAUÃ.

macaúba (*f.*) = MACAJÁ.

macavana (*f.*) = AJURU-CATINGA.

macaxe[i]ra (*f.*) = AIPIM.

maçãzeira (*f.*) = MACIEIRA.

macedônio –nia (*adj.; m.,f.*) Macedonian; (*f.*) a macedoine of fruits or vegetables.

macega (*f.*) weeds; high, dry grass; scrub growth.**—-brava** = CANA-BRAVA.

macegal (*m.*) scrub-covered land.

macegoso –sa, **maceguento** –ta (*adj.*) scrubby land.

maceioense [ô] (*adj.*) of or pert. to the State of Maceió; (*m.,f.*) a native or inhabitant of that State.

maceiro (*m.*) mace-bearer [= PORTA-MAÇA].

macela (*f.*) camomile (*Anthemis*).**—-de-são-joão**, sweet yarrow (*Achillea ageratum*), c.a. EUPATÓRIO-DE-MERUÉ, AGERATO, MACELA-FRANCÊSA.**—-do-brasil**, a mayweed (*Magricaria americana*).**—-do-campo**; a plant of the thistle family (*Achryocline satureioides*), whose dried flowers provide an aromatic stuffing for pillows and mattresses; also = CUAMBU.—**-do-mato,** a tropical herb of the amaranth family (*Alternanthera ramosissima*), c.a. MACELA (-DO-MATO), PERPÉTUA-DO-MATO.—**-fedegosa** or **-fétida** = CAMOMILA-CATINGA.—**-galega,** an herb of the thistle family (*Anacyclus aureus*), c.a. AMARANTO, MACELÃO.

macerá (*m.*) a kind of fish trap.

maceração (*f.*) maceration; steeping, soaking; mortification (of carnal desire).

macerar (*v.t.*) to macerate, steep, soak; to mortify (the flesh).

macéria (*f.*) rough dry masonry.

macêta (*f.*) a stonecutter's mallet; a muller (for grinding pigments); (*adj.*) having swollen fetlock joints.

macetação (*f.*) pounding (of vegetable fibers).

macetar (*v.t.*) to maul, pound (as with a mallet); of a horse, to develop swollen fetlock joints.

macête (*m.*) a small maul; a carpenter's or carver's mallet.

macetudo –**da** (*adj.*) of a horse, having enlarged fetlock joints; of a horse or person, old, useless.

machacaz (*adj.; m.*) sly, cunning (man); (*m.*) slow, ponderous man.

machada (*f.*) hatchet.

machadada (*f.*) hatchetblow; axblow.

machadar (*v.t.*) to wield an ax or hatchet.

machadeiro (*m.*) one who fells trees with an ax; wood chopper.

machadiano –**na** (*adj.*) of or pert. to the Brazilian writer Machado de Assis (1839–1908); (*m.,f.*) an admirer of, or an authority on, his works.

machadinha (*f.*) small hatchet; butcher's cleaver; also = JABOTI-MACHADO (a turtle).—**de tanoeiro,** cooper's adz.

machadinho (*m.*) small ax; rubber tapper [= SERINGUEIRO]; a certain brand stamped on the ears of cattle.

machado (*m.*) ax.

machador (*m.*) cleaver of carcasses (in a slaughter house).

macha-fêmea (*f.*) hood-and-eye hinge; hermaphrodite; (*adj.*) hermaphroditic.

machão (*m.*) manlike woman; also, a "he man".

macheado (*f.*) box pleating.

machear (*v.t.*) to form box pleats; (*Carp.*) to form a mortise-and-tenon joint.

macheiro –**ra** (*adj.*) designating a bull or stallion whose offspring are predominantly male also; (*m.*) a young cork tree; a misshapen tree fit only for firewood.

machetada (*f.*) a blow with a machete.

machete [chê] (*m.*) machete; saber; small guitar.

machial (*m.*) barren land.

machinho (*m.*) fetlock joint [= BOLÊTO]; a small guitar; a young donkey.

machio (*m.*) of animals, act of mating.

máchio –**chia** (*adj.*) withered, shriveled, stunted [trees].

macho (*m.*) any male animal; a mule; a box pleat; any piece or part that fits into another, as the pintle of a hinge or rudder, the male end of a section of pipe, etc.; a canoe adz; foundry molding core; a large eel; (*adj.*) masculine; (*colloq.*) manly, virile.—**e fêmea,** male and female.—**de-joão-gomes** = GUARANDI (a bird).—**de parada,** a goat trained to lead cattle. **Êle é—!** he is a "he-man"!

machoa, machona (*f.*) = MACHÃO.

macho-fêmea (*m.*) a tonguing and grooving plane.

machorra (*adj.*) barren [animal].

machuca, machucação (*f.*) = MACHUCADURA.

machucador –**dora** (*adj.*) mashing, bruising, crushing, grinding; (*m.*) masher, bruiser, crusher, grinder.

machucadura (*f.*) act or operation of mashing, crushing, pounding, threshing.

machucar (*v.t.*) to hurt; to mash, bruise, batter, crush.

machuca-rolhas (*m.*) a hand device for squeezing and softening corks. [Formerly used in pharmacies.]

machucheiro (*m.*) = CHUCHUZEIRO.

machucho –**cha** (*adj.*) influential; rich; shrewd; big, heavy; (*m.*) = MACHACAZ; CHUCHU.

maciço –**ça** (*adj.*) massive; dense, solid. **ouro—,** solid gold. **hemorragia—,** severe hemorrage; (*m.*) a dense clump of trees; a massive piece of construction; (*Geol.*) massif.

macieira (*f.*) any apple or crabapple tree.—**com-fôlhas-de-ameixeira,** the pearleaf crabapple (*Malus prunifolia*).—**da-china,** the Chinese flowering crabapple (*Malus spectabilis*).—**de-anáfega,** the common jujube

or Chinese date (*Zizyphus jujuba*).—**de-boi,** the bull apple or jungle plum (*Sideroxylon rugosum*).—**de-coroa,** the wild sweet crabapple (*Malus coronaria*).—**-ordinária,** the common apple (*Malus pumila*, syn. *Pyrus malus*).

maciez[a] (*f.*) softness.

macilência (*f.*) emaciation, gauntness.

macilento –**ta** (*adj.*) emaciated, gaunt; haggard.

macio –**cia** (*adj.*) soft, smooth (to the touch).

maciota (*f.*) ease. **levar a vida na—,** to take things easy. **na—,** smoothly, slowly.

macis (*m.*) mace (spice).

mackenzista (*m.,f.*) an alumnus of Instituto Mackenzie or Universidade Mackenzie in São Paulo.

macla (*f., Min.*) macle, twin crystal.

macleia (*f., Bot.*) the genus (*Macleaya*) of plume poppies.

maço (*m.*) a packet (as of cigarettes); a bundle (as of letters); a stacked deck of cards; a wooden mallet, maul or gavel; a pile or stack (of papers).

maçoca (*f.*) manioc paste which has been expressed in the TIPITI.

macóia (*f.*) = CÔCO-DE-CATARRO.

maçom (*m.*) = MAÇÃO.

maçonaria (*f.*) Freemasonry. [Masonry in the sense of work or art of a mason is OBRA DE PEDREIRO.]

maconha (*f.*) Indian hemp; marijuana [= DIAMBA].

maçônico –**ca** (*adj.*) Masonic; (*m., colloq.*) a Mason.

macorongo (*m.*) a pimp.

macota (*m.*) big shot, big wig [= MACOTEIRO]; (*f.*) bad luck; also = LEPRA; (*adj.*) big, powerful, rich; goodlooking; "tops".

macotena (*adj.*) = LEPROSO.

macouba (*f.*) maccaboy (a kind of snuff made in Macouba, Martinique).

macradênia (*f.*) an orchid (*Macradenia brassovolae*).

macramé (*m.*) macramé (lace, cord).

macrencefálico –**ca** (*adj.*) macrencephalic.

má-criação (*f.*) illbreeding; rudeness.

macrobia (*f.*) macrobiosis, longevity.

macróbio –**bia** (*adj.*) macrobian, of advanced age; long-lived; (*m.,f.*) macrobiote, one that is long-lived; an old person.

macrobiota (*m., Zool.*) a bear animalcule or water bear—one of the Tardigrada.

macrocisto (*m.*) macrocyst.

macrócito (*m., Med.*) macrocyte.

macrocosmo (*m.*) mocrocosm, the universe.

macrocristalino –**na** (*adj.; Petrog.*) macrocrystalline.

macrodactilia (*f.*) macrodactylia.

macrodáctilo –**la** (*adj.*) macrodactylous.

macrodiagonal (*adj.; Cryst.*) macrodiagonal.

macrodoma (*f., Cryst.*) macrodome.

macrodonte (*adj.*) macrodont.

macrodontia (*f.*) macrodontia, macrodontism

macrófago (*m., Anat.*) macrophage.

macrofilo –**la** (*adj.; Bot.*) macrophyllous.

macrofotografia (*f.*) macrophotography.

macrogâmeta (*m., Biol.*) macrogamete.

mácron (*m.*) macron.

macropétalo –**la** (*adj.; Bot.*) macropetalous.

macropia (*f.*) = MACROPSIA.

macropinacóide (*m., Cryst.*) macropinacoid.

macrorranfosídeos (*m.pl.*) the family (*Macrorhamphosidae*) consisting of the bellowfishes.

macrorrino (*m.*) the elephant seal (*Mirounga*, syn. *Macrorhinus*.

macróscio –**scia** (*adj.*) macroscian (casting a long shadow).

macroscópico –**ca** (*adj.*) macroscopic.

macrospermo –**ma** (*adj.; Bot.*) having large seeds.

macrosporângio (*m., Bot.*) megasporangium.

macrospório, macrósporo (*m., Bot.*) macrospore.

macrossomático –**ca** (*adj.*) macrosomatous.

macrostilo –**la** (*adj.; Bot.*) macrostylous.

macrostomia (*f.*) macrostomia.

macrozoospório [o-o] (*m., Bot.*) macrozoospore.

macruro –**ra** (*adj.; Zool.*) macruran, macrurous, long-tailed; (*m.*) a macruran crustacean (lobster, shrimp, prawn, etc.).

macucar (*v.i.*) to mutter to oneself.

macucau (*m., Zool.*) the yapurá banded tinamou (*Crypturellus undulatus yapura*).

macuco (*m., Zool.*) the solitary tinamou (*Tinamus solitarius*).—**do-pantanal,** the Rio Negro tinamou (*Tinamus major serratus*), c.a. INHAMBU-GRANDE.

macucu [ucú] (*m.*) any of several rosaceous and leguminous tropical trees.—**-verdadeiro,** a large tree of the holly family (*Ilex macoucoua*).
maçudo **-da** (*adj.*) bulky; hulking; of discourse, dull, heavy; humdrum.
macujá (*m.*) a queenpalm (*Arecastrum romanzoffianum botryophorum*).
mácula (*f.*) macula, blotch, stain; hence, dishonor, blemish.
maculado **-da** (*adj.*) maculate, blotched, stained, soiled, spotted.
maculador **-dora** (*adj.*) staining, sullying.
macular (*v.t.*) to maculate, stain, spot, soil, sully, defile.
maculícola (*adj.; Bot.*) maculicole, maculicolous.
maculífero **-ra** (*adj.*) maculiferous, spotted.
maculo (*m.*) at the peak of slavery in Brazil, a form of dysentery which attacked new arrivals from Africa; c.a. CORRUÇÃO, MAL-DE-BICHO.
maculoso **-sa** (*adj.*) maculose, spotted [= MACULADO].
macuma (*f.*) = MUCAMA.
macumã (*f.*) = COQUINHO-DO-CAMPO.
macumba (*f.*) a Brazilian variant of voodooism or fetishism; a song and dance of this ceremony. Cf. CANDOMBLÉ.
macumbeiro (*m.*), **-ra** (*f.*) a devotee of MACUMBA.
macuni [í] (*m.,f.*) an Indian of the Macuni, a tribe of the Maxacalí in the State of Minas Gerais; (*adj.*) pert. to or designating the Macuni.
macuquinho (*m., Zool.*) the sharp-tailed creeper (*Lochmias n. nematura,* family *Furnariidae*), c.a. CAPITÃO-DA-PORCARIA, PRESIDENTE-DA-PORCARIA, TRIDI.
macuracaá (*f.*) garlic guineahenweed (*Petiveria alliacea*).
macura-chicha (*f.*) a woolly opossum (*Philander*).
macuru [rú] (*m.*) a puffbird [= JOÃO-BÔBO].
macutena (*f.*) = LEPRA.
Madalena (*f.*) Madelline; Madeline; Magdalen; Magdalene.
madama (*f.*) mistress, lady of the house; a "madam"; (*colloq.*) "the missus"; a seamstress; a midwife.
madapolã (*m.*) madapollam (cotton cloth originally made in India); = MORIM.
madarose (*f., Med.*) madarosis; ptilosis.
madeficar (*v.t.*) to wet, moisten.
madeira (*f.*) wood, lumber, timber; rubber tree; Madeira wine.—**branca,** softwood.—**compensada,** plywood.—**de lei** or—**dura,** hardwood.—**-preta** = ÉBANO-DA-AUSTRÁLIA. —**ventada,** wind-shaken timber.
madeiramento (*m.*) the wooden framework of a house; timberwork.
madeirar (*v.t.*) to erect a wooden frame ; (*v.i.*) to do woodwork.
madeireiro (*m.*) lumber dealer; woodworker; lumberjack.
madeirense (*adj.*) of or pert. to Madeira; (*m.,f.*) a native or inhabitant of Madeira.
madeiro (*m.*) log, beam, timber.
madeixa (*f.*) lock of hair; curl, tress, ringlet; skein.
mádido **-da** (*adj.*) moistened; soaked.
Madona (*f.*) Madonna.
madorna, **madôrra** (*f.*) = MODÔRRA.
madorrento **-ta** (*adj.*) = MODORRENTO.
madraçaria, **madracice** (*f.*) sloth.
madracear (*v.i.*) to loiter, idle, loaf.
madraceirão (*m.*) a big loafer.
madraceiro **-ra** (*adj.*) loitering, loafing; (*m.,f.*) = MADRAÇO.
madraço **-ça** (*adj.*) lazy; (*m.,f.*) idler, loafer, sluggard [= MANDRIÃO].
madrasta (*f.*) stepmother; [*cap.*] Madras (*India*).
madrasto (*m.*) madras, white cotton cloth [= MORIM].
madre (*f.*) nun; mother superior; matrix (womb); river channel; (*Const.*) purlin; mother of vinegar.—**caída,**—**saída,**—**de fora,**—**emborcada,** all popular terms for prolapse of the uterus.—**caprina,** sweet honeysuckle (*Lonicera caprifolium*), c.a. MADRESSILVA.—**das-boticas,** woodbine honeysuckle (*Lonicera periclymenum*).—**de metais,** gangue.
madrepérola (*f.*) mother-of-pearl.
madrépora (*f., Zool.*) madrepore.
madreporário (*m., Zool.*) madreporarian.
madreporite (*f., Zool.*) madreporite.
madressilva (*f., Bot.*) honeysuckle (*Lonicera*).—**-da-terra,** —**-terrestre,** Brazilian alstroemeria (*A. brasiliensis*).—**-dos-jardins,** Japanese honeysuckle (*Lonicera japonica*)
Madri (*f.*) Madrid.
madria (*f.*) whitecaps (waves).
madrigal (*m.*) madrigal.

madrigalista (*m.,f.*) madrigalist.
madrigaz (*m.*) gaunt man.
madrileno **-na,** **madrilense,** **madrilês** **-lêsa** (*adj.*) of or pert. to Madrid; (*m.,f.*) native or inhabitant of Madrid. Var. MATRITENSE.
madrinha (*f.*) godmother; sponsor, patroness; the lead mare in a band of mules or horses.
madrugada (*f.*) dawn, daybreak; early rising; fig., unusually early development. **ao romper da**—, at break of day. **de**—, at dawn; in the early morning; **lá pelas duas da**—, around two o'clock in the morning. **pela**—, in the early morning.
madrugador **-dora** (*adj.*) early-rising; (*m.,f.*) early riser; early bird; one who gets a head start (in anything).
madrugar (*v.i.*) to rise early; to get an early start; to be ahead of time. **Deus ajuda a quem cedo madruga,** God helps him who helps himself.
maduração (*f.*) maturation, ripening; suppuration.
madurar (*v.i.*) to ripen; to mature; (*colloq.*) to suppurate.
madureza (*f.*) ripeness; maturity (of judgment).
maduro **-ra** (*adj.*) ripe; mature, fully developed; mellow; judicious.
mãe (*f.*) mother; fig., source, origin.—**-benta,** a kind of cupcake.—**-boa,** (*Bot.*) a treebine (*Cissus*).—**-d'água,** source of water; water sprite.—**-da-lua,** (*Zool.*) a nighthawk (*Nyctibus*), c.a. URUTAU.—**-da-mata,** a wood spirit. —**-da-taoca,** any of various ant birds, esp. the blackspotted bare-eye (*Phlegopsis nigromaculata*).—**-das-boubas,** (*colloq.*) the initial tumor of yaws (frambesia). —**de criação,** in slave days, the "Black Mammy" of the household.—**de família,** mother of a family; the English daisy [= BELA-MARGARIDA].—**-de-porco,** (*Zool.*) a ground cuckoo (*Neomorphus geoffroyi*), c.a. TAJAÇU-IRA,—**-de-saúva,** a limbless lizard.—**-de-torá** = PAPA-FORMIGAS (ant bird).—**-do-camarão,** a mantis shrimp (*Squilla*), c.a. TAMARUTACA.—**-do-corpo,** (*colloq.*) the uterus.—**-do-fogo,** a smoldering tree trunk.—**-do-rio,** flooded river bottom.—**-do-santo,** fetishistic sorceress. —**-do-sol,** a buprestid beetle (*Euchroma gigantea*); also the vermillion flycatcher (*Pyrocephalus rubineus*), c.a. VERÃO.—**-pátria,** motherland.—**-preta,** "black mammy".
maestria (*f.*) = MESTRIA.
maestrino (*m.*), **-na** (*f.*) a composer of light music; (*f.*) a woman conductor.
maestro (*m.*) maestro, conductor, composer.
má-fé (*f.*) bad faith.
Mafoma (*f.*) Mahomet; Mohammed; Muhammad; [= MAOMÉ].
mafome (*m.*) = CURURU-APÉ.
mafuá (*m.*) amusement park.
maga (*f.*) witch, sorceress.
Magalhães (*m.*) Magellan.
maganão (*m.*) a cutup; a rascal.
magano **-na** (*adj.*) roguish; jovial; wanton; (*m.*) rogue; wag; slave dealer; (*f.*) loose woman.
magarefe (*m.*) a butcher [in a slaughterhouse but not in a meat shop, which is AÇOUGUEIRO]; (*colloq.*) a clumsy surgeon.
magazine (*m.*) department store; magazine (*periodical*); magazine of a typesetting machine.
magenta (*f.*) magenta.
magérrimo **-ma** (*adj.; absol. superl. of* MAGRO) most thin.
magia (*f.*) magic; witchery, charm.—**negra,** black magic.
magiar (*adj.; m.,f.*) Magyar, Hungarian.
mágico **-ca** (*adj.*) magic(al); enchanting; (*m.*) magician. **truque de**—, magician's trick or feat; (*f.*) magic; enchantment.—**de salão,** parlor magic. **passe de**—, sleight-of-hand trick.
maginação (*f., colloq.*) = IMAGINAÇÃO.
maginar (*v., colloq.*) = IMAGINAR.
magíster (*m., colloq.*) magister, master; a "solemn-as-a-judge" sententious person.
magistério (*m.*) the office, duties or position of a teacher; the teaching profession; teachers collectively.—**público,** public school teachers as a class. **trinta anos de**—, thirty years as a teacher.
magistrado (*m.*) magistrate, judge.
magistral (*adj.*) magisterial; masterly; fig., excellent, perfect, exemplary [speech, performance, etc.].
magistralidade (*f.*) magisterial manner; commanding tone; pedantry.
magistratura (*f.*) magistracy.
magma (*f., Geol.*) magma.
magmático **-ca** (*adj.*) magmatic. **corrosão**—, (*Petrog.*)

resorption borders. **diferenciação—**, (*Petrog.*) magmatic segregation.
Magna-carta (*f.*) Magna Charta.
magnanimidade (*f.*) magnanimity, generosity.
magnânimo -ma (*adj.*) magnanimous, noble; generous.
magnata, -te (*m.*) magnate; tycoon; distinguished person; also = MANDACHUVA.
magneferrite (*f.*, *Min.*) magnesioferrite.
magnésia (*f.*, *Chem.*) magnesia (magnesium oxide).— **branca,** (*Pharm.*) magnesia alba.—**usta,** (*Chem.*) magnesia usta; calcined magnesia.
magnesiano -na, magnésico -ca (*adj.*) magnesian.
magnésio (*m.*, *Chem.*) magnesium.
magnesioferrite (*f.*) = MAGNEFERRITE.
magnesita (*f.*, *Min.*) magnesite.
magnete (*m.*) magnetite, loadstone; an iron or steel magnet.
magnetelétrico -ca (*adj.*) magnetoelectric(al).
magnético -ca (*adj.*) magnetic; attractive.
magnetismo (*m.*) magnetism; attractiveness.
magnetita (*f.*) magnetite, loadstone.
magnetização (*f.*) magnetization.
magnetizador -dora (*adj.*) magnetizing; (*m.*) magnetizer.
magnetizar (*v.t.*) to magnetize; fig., to influence, control; to attract, captivate.
magnetizável (*adj.*) magnetizable.
magneto (*m.*, *Elec.*) magneto.
magnetofônio (*m.*, *Physics*) magnetophone.
magnetogerador (*m.*) magnetogenerator.
magnetógrafo (*m.*, *Physics*) magnetograph.
magnetograma (*m.*, *Physics*) magnetogram.
magnetóide (*adj.*) magnetoid.
magnetologia (*f.*) the study of magnetism.
magnetometria (*f.*, *Physics*) magnetometry.
magnetômetro (*m.*, *Physics*) magnetometer.
magnéton (*m.*, *Physics*) magneton.
magneto-óptica (*f.*) magnetooptics.
magnetopirite (*f.*, *Min.*) magnetic pyrrites, pyrrhotite.
magnetoplumbite (*f.*, *Min.*) magnetoplumbite.
magnetoquímica (*f.*) magnetochemistry.
magnetoscópio (*m.*, *Physics*) magnetoscope.
magnetostrição (*f.*, *Physics*) magnetostriction.
magnetron (*m.*) magnetron.
magnicaudado -da (*adj.*; *Zool.*) magnicaudate.
magnificação (*f.*) magnification; laudation, exaltation.
magnificar (*v.t.*) to magnify, extol, praise.
magnificatório -ria (*adj.*) tending to magnify.
magnificência (*f.*) magnificence, splendor, pomp.
magnificente (*adj.*) magnificent, grand, imposing; magnanimous.
magnífico -ca (*adj.*) magnificent; grand, splendid, excellent; fine, beautiful; gorgeous.
magniloqüência (*f.*) magniloquence.
magniloqüente (*adj.*) magniloquent.
magnífloquo [quo = co] (*adj.*) eloquent.
magnitude (*f.*) magnitude, greatness; importance, consequence.
magno -na (*adj.*) great, important.
magnólia (*f.*, *Bot.*) any magnolia, esp. *M. coco* and *M. grandiflora* (the southern magnolia).—**-iulã**, the ulan magnolia (*M. denudata*).—**branca** = PINHO-DO-BREJO.
magnoliáceo -cea (*adj.*; *Bot.*) magnoliaceous; (*f.*,*pl.*) the Magnoliaceae (magnolia family).
mago -ga (*adj.*) magical; charming; (*m.*) one of the Magi; one of the Three Wise Men from the East; a magician, wizard, sorcerer.
mágoa (*f.*) bruise, black-and-blue mark; fig., grief, sorrow, heartbreak; regret; envy, jealousy, spite.
magoado -da (*adj.*) hurt; aggrieved; heartsick; regretful.
magoar (*v.t.*) to bruise; to afflict, hurt, offend; to aggrieve; to wound the feelings of; (*v.r.*) to hurt oneself.
magoativo -va (*adj.*) afflictive; hurtful; vexing.
magonga (*f.*) var. of MANGONGA.
magorim (*m.*) the Arabian jasmine (*Jasminum sambac*).
magote (*m.*) a crowd of people; a heap of things.
magra (*f.*) see under MAGRO.
magrelo -la (*adj.*; *m.*,*f.*) = MAGRICELA.
magrém (*f.*) thinness [= MAGREZA].
magrete [grê] (*adj.*) somewhat thin.
magreza [ê] (*f.*) thinness, leanness.
magricela (*adj.*) thin, skinny; scrawny; lanky; (*m.*,*f.*) such a person.
magrinha (*f.*, *colloq.*) small-bore gun.
magriz -za (*adj.*) skinny; (*m.*,*f.*) skinny person.

magrizela (*m.*,*f.*) = MAGRICELA.
magro -gra (*adj.*) thin, lean; meagre.—**como um caniço**, slender as a beanpole; (*f.*, *colloq.*) tuberculosis; death.
magruço -ça (*adj.*) = MAGRICELA.
maguari [í] (*m.*) the American stork (*Euxenura moguari*), c.a. JABURU-MOLEQUE; the cocoi heron (*Ardea cocoi*), c.a. BAGUARI, SOCOÍ.
maguei (*f.*, *Bot.*) maguey (*Agave atrovirens*) which yields pulque.
maguiçapá (*m.*) = COATÁ-BRANCO.
maiá (*m.*) Mayathan (language of the Mayas).
maiaca (*f.*) a yellow-eye grass (*Xyris pallida*), c.a. BOTÃO-DE-OURO.
maiêutica (*f.*) maieutics (Socratic method).
mainça [a-ím] (*f.*) handful [= MÃO-CHEIA].
mainel [-néis] (*m.*) handrail [= CORRIMÃO].
mainumbi (*m.*) a hummingbird [= GUAINUMBI].
maio (*m.*) the month of May; (*pl.*, *Bot.*) the Tangiers iris (*I. tingitana*).—**s pequenos**, the Moraea iris (*I. sisyrinchium*).
maiô (*m.*) a woman's bathing suit; a pair of tights. [Fr. *maillot*].
maiólica (*f.*) majolica, faience.
maionese (*f.*) mayonnaise.
maior (*adj.*; *comparative of* GRANDE) larger, greater, bigger; of age, adult; (*m.*,*f.*) an adult.—**(do) que**, greater (bigger) than.—**de vinte-e-um anos**, over 21.—**-de-todos**, (*colloq.*) the middle finger.—**divisor comum**, greatest common divisor.—**número**, majority. **a—parte**, the majority; the greater, or greatest, part; the most. **bem—**, quite a bit (a good deal) larger. **de—idade**, of age. **É o—!** (*slang*) He is the most! **força—**, superior or irresistible force; so-called act of God. [Fr. *force majeure*]. **modo—**, (*Music*) major mode. **premissa—**, (*Logic*) major premise.
maioral (*m.*) the head man; ranch foreman; big shot; also = MANDACHUVA.
maioranta (*f.*) = FANFÃ (a plant).
Maiorca (*f.*) Majorca.
maioria (*f.*) majority, greater number.
maioridade (*f.*) majority, full legal age. **atingir a—**, to come of age.
maioríssimo -ma (*adj.*) greatest of all.
maiormente (*adv.*) = MORMENTE.
maipoca (*f.*) replanting of a field of manioc.
maipuré (*m.*, *Zool.*) the black-headed caique (*Pionites melanocephala*), c.a. PERIQUITO-DE-CABEÇA-PRETA.
mais (*adv.*) more, moreover, besides; (*m.*) the rest; (*adj.*) more.—**a tempo**, sooner.—**adiante**, further on.—**as vozes do que as nozes**, more shadow than substance; stuff and nonsense.—**cedo ou—tarde**, sooner or later, eventually. —**de (que)**, more than.—**de uma vez**, more than once.— **dia, menos dia**, some day; sooner or later.—**e mais**, more and more.—**essa!** and now this!—**hoje, mais amanhã**, any day (now).—**logo**, later.—**nada**, nothing more, anything else.—**ou menos**, more or less, about.—**por aqui, mais por ali**, more or less.—**(de) que**, more than.—**que muito**, in the highest degree.—**-que-perfeito**, (*Gram.*) pluperfect.—**que tudo**, more than all else.—**tarde**, later. —**um**, one more, another.—**um pouquinho**, a little bit more.—**uma vez**, once more. **a—**, too much, in excess; besides, additional. **a—e melhor**, more and better. **ainda—**, all the more, still better. **ao—**, at most; moreover. **as—das vezes**, almost always, more often than not. **até—não poder**, to the limit, to the utmost. **cada vez—**, more all the time. **de—a mais**, more and more; besides. **É o—que posso fazer**, It is the most I can do. **quanto ao—**, as for the rest. **gostar—**, to like better or best; to prefer. **Gostaria—de ficar aqui**, I'd rather stay here. **logo—**, a little later (on). **Não existe—**, It no longer exists. **não—**, no more, no longer, not again. **não—que**, not more than, only. **Não posso—!** I can't stand it any longer! **Não posso esperar muito—**, I cannot wait much longer. **Não quero—nada**, I want nothing more. **nunca—**, never more, never again. **o—**, the rest. **o—tardar**, at the latest. **os—dos homens**, most men. **outro tanto—**, as much again. **para—de**, upwards of. **por—que**, however much. **por—que custe**, whatever the price (cost). **pouco —ou menos**, almost, nearly, more or less. **Quanto—(ganhava), tanto—(gastava)**, The more (he earned), the more (he spent). **sem—nem menos**, without more ado; without warning; for no reason.
Maisena (*f.*) brand name of a corn starch.
maisquerer [68] (*v.t.*) to like better, prefer.

mais-valia (f.) an increase in value (of goods).
maitaca (f.) any of various parrots of the genus *Pionus*, esp. *P. menstruus* (the blue-headed parrot), *P. m. maximiliana* (Maximilian's parrot), and *P. fuscus* (the dusky parrot, c.a. MAITACA-PARDA, PARANÁ-I, PAPAGAINHO-ROXO).—-cabeça-de-côco = PERIQUITO-REI.—-de-cabeça-vermelha, the red-capped parrot of southeastern Brazil (*Pionopsittacus pileata*). Cf. PAPAGAIO; PERIQUITO.
maiúsculo -la (adj.) upper-case, capital; (f.) capital letter.
majestade (f.) majesty, grandeur, dignity; magnificence.
majestoso -sa (adj.) majestic, august; grand, sublime.
majólica (f.) = MAIÓLICA.
maj. = MAJOR (major).
major (m.) major (army officer).
majoração (f.) increase.—de preço, price increase.—do custo de vida, increase in the cost of living.
majorana (f.) = FANFÃ; ALGODÃO-DO-BREJO.
majorar (v.t.) to augment, increase.
majoria (f.) the office or rank of a major.
majoritário -ria (adj.) of the majority. partido—, majority party.
mal [-es] (m.) evil, wrong; injury, harm; wickedness; woe, grief; illness; disease; misfortune; (adv.) scarcely, hardly, barely; but just; no sooner had; badly, poorly.—-americano, syphilis, c.a. MAL-CANADENSE, MAL-CÉLTICO, MAL-DA-BAÍA-DE-SÃO-PAULO, MAL-DE-FIÚME, MAL-DE-FRANGA (or FRENGA), MAL-DE-SANTA-EUFÊMIA, MAL-DE-SÃO-JÓ, MAL-DE-SÃO-MÉVIO (or NÉVIO), MAL-DE-SÃO-SEMENTO, MAL-DOS-CRISTÃOS, MAL-ESCOCÊS, MAL-FRANCÊS, MAL-GALÍCO, MAL-GERMÂNICO, MAL-ILÍRICO, MAL-NAPOLITANO, MAL-POLACO, MAL TURCO.—-caduco, epilepsy, c.a. MAL-DE-GÔTA, MAL-DE-TERRA.—-da-ave-maria, paralysis.—-da-terra, hookworm disease.—-das-ensecadeiras, the bends, caisson disease, c.a. MAL-DOS-MERGULHADORES.—-das-montanhas, mountain sickness.—-de-amôres, (*colloq.*) venereal disease.—-de-bicho = MACULO.—-de-bright, Bright's disease.—-de-cernelha, saddle gall, c.a. MAL-DO-DORSO.—-de-escancha = QUEBRA-BUNDA, a horse disease, c.a. MAL-DAS-ANCAS, MAL-DE-CADEIRAS, MAL-DOS-QUARTOS.—-de-garapa, (*Veter.*) a trypanosomiasis.—-de-lázaro, leprosy, c.a. LEPRA, MORFÉIA, MAL-BRUTO, MAL-DE-CUIA, MAL-DE-FÍGADO, MAL-DE-HANSEN, MAL-DE-SÃO-LÁZARO, MAL-MORFÉTICO.—-de-luanda (or loanda), scurvy.—-de muitos consôlo é, Misery loves company.—-de-panamá, a fungus (genus *Fusarium*) which attacks banana plants.—-de-pott, Pott's disease (caries of the vertebrae).—-de-sangria, (*Med.*) a thrombosis or thrombus.—-de-secar, tuberculosis.—-de-vaso, (*Veter.*) sore coronet, c.a. MAL-DOS-CASCOS.—-do-baço, any disease of the spleen.—-do-bicho, intestinal worms.—-do-veado, tetanus.—-elefantino, elephantiasis.—-dos-aviadores, airsickness.—sabe ler, He can scarcely read.—tinha chegado, he had no sooner arrived.—-triste, Texas (tick) fever.—virei as costas, just as soon as my back was turned. a—de seu grado, not to one's liking; to one's sorrow. de—a pior, from bad to worse. estar—, to be in a bad way; to be sick. estar—de, to be short of (money, etc.). estar—com alguém, to be on bad terms (at outs) with someone. estar bem—, to be quite ill. fazer—a, to harm; to ravish. ir—de saúde, to be in poor health. menos—, not so bad. Não faz—, No matter; Never mind. Não há bem que sempre dure, nem—que por si perdure, It's a long lane that has no turning. O menor de dois—es, the lesser of two evils. por bem ou por—, for good or for ill; for better or for worse; willy-nilly. sair—, to turn out badly. sentir-se—, to feel bad. tomar (or levar) a—, to take (something) amiss, take offense. [See also the many hyphenated words below which begin with the adverb mal-.]
mala (f.) trunk, traveling bag; (*pl.*) baggage, luggage.—armârio, wardrobe trunk.—de mão, handbag, valise, suitcase.—postal, mailbag. fazer as—s, to pack one's bags.
malabarismo (m.) juggling.
malabarista (m.,f.) juggler.
mal-acabado -da (adj.) poorly finished; queer-looking.
malacacheta [ê] (f.) = MICA.
malacão (m., Min.) malacon(e).
malacara (adj.; m.) white-faced (horse); evil-looking (man).
malacate (m.) a whim gin (hoisting device).
malacodermo -ma (adj., Zool.) malacodermous, soft-skinned.

malacófilo -la (adj., Bot.) malacophilous.
malacofono -na (adj.) malacophonous (having a soft voice).
malacólito (m., Min.) malacolite.
malacologia (f., Zool.) malacology.
mal-acondicionado -da (adj.) in poor condition; badly packed.
mal-aconselhado -da (adj.) ill-advised.
malacossoma (f.) a tent caterpillar.
malacostracologia (f.) malacostracology; carcinology.
maláctico -ca (adj.) malactic, emollient.
mal-adaptação (f.) poor adaptation.
mal-adaptado -da (adj.) ill-adapted.
maladia (f.) malady [Archaic]—see DOENÇA.
maladrito (m., Min.) malladrite.
mal-afeiçoado -da (adj.) not good-looking; evilly inclined.
mal-afortunado -da (adj.) ill-starred.
málaga (f.) Malaga wine.
malagma (m.) malagma, an emollient poultice.
mal-agradecido -da (adj.) ungrateful; (m.,f.) an ingrate.
malaguenho -nha (adj.; m.,f.) of or pert. to, or a native or inhabitant of, Malaga; (f.) malaguena (Spanish song and dance).
malagueta [ê] (f.) bush redpepper (*Capsicum frutescens*).
malaico (m.) Malay (language).
malaio -laia (adj.; m.,f.) Malayan; (cap., f.) Malaya.
mal-ajambrado -da (adj.) unattractive [person]; ungainly; queer-looking; shabbily dressed.
mal-ajeitado -da (adj.) ungainly, awkward.
mal-amanhado -da (adj.) unkempt; untidy; clumsy; poorly arranged.
malandra (f.) low woman.
malandragem (f.) gang of rascals; rascality; vagabondage.
malandr[e]ar (v.i.) to loaf; ; to live by one's wits.
malandres (m.pl., Veter.) malanders, sallenders.
malandrice (f.) loafing; rascality.
malandrim (m., colloq.) a bum; a thief.
malandrino -na (adj.) that loafs; thievish; (m.) = MALANDRIM.
malandro (m.) loafer, bum, good-for-nothing; vagabond; rascal, sharper.
mala-posta (f.) mail coach.
Malaquias (m.) Malachi; Malachias.
malaquita (f., Min.) malachite.
malar (m.) malar bone, cheekbone.
malaria (f.) a pile of trunks.
malária (f.) malaria.
malárico -ca (adj.) malarial.
malarina (f., Pharm.) malarin.
malarioso -sa (adj.) malarial.
mal-arrumado -da (adj.) badly arranged; poorly packed; untidy [room, drawer, etc.]; (m.) rock-strewn ground.
mal-asado -da (adj.) ungainly; unlucky, ill-starred.
malasarte (adj.; m.) awkward (fellow).
Malásia (f.) Malaysia.
mal-assada (f.) scrambled eggs; a kind of poultice.
mal-assimilação (f., Med.) malassimilation.
mal-assombrado -da (adj.) haunted; (m.) a ghost.
mal-assombramento, mal-assombro (m.) apparition; haunting.
malato (m., Chem.) malate.
mal-aventurado -da (adj.) unlucky, ill-starred.
mal-avindo -da (adj.) at variance [= DESAVINDO].
malaxação [ks] (f.) malaxation, softening; a form of massage.
malaxadeira [ks] (f.), **malaxador** [ks] (m.) a machine for grinding, kneading, stirring (clay, etc.); a pugmill.
malaxar [ks] (v.t.) to soften by kneading, stirring, mixing (clay, butter, etc.).
malbarat[e]ar (v.t.) to sell at a loss; to squander, to fritter away; to abuse.
malbarato (m.) a cheap sale; wasteful expenditure; disparagement.
malcasado -da (adj.) unhappily married; ill-mated; (m.) = BEIJU (a confection).
malcheiroso -sa (r 'j.) malodorous, ill-smelling; unsavory.
malcomido -da (adj.) undernourished, thin.
malcondizer [41] (v.i.) to be not in accord with.
malconfiar-se (v.r.) to have doubts about.
malconformação (f.) malconformation.
malcontentadiço -ça (adj.) hard to please.
malcontente (adj.) malcontent.
malcriado -da (adj.) ill-bred, rude, ill-behaved, ill-mannered, badly brought up.

maldade (*f.*) evil, wrong, badness; misdeed; iniquity; unfairness.
maldadoso –sa (*adj.*) maleficent.
maldar (*v.i.*) to think evil of.
maldelazento –ta (*adj.*) leprous.
maldição (*f.*) curse, malediction.
maldiçoar (*v.*) = AMALDIÇOAR.
maldito –ta (*adj.*) accursed, damned; damnable; (*f.*, *colloq.*) persistent tetter; carbuncle; erysipelas.
maldizente (*adj.*) slandering; evil-speaking; (*m.,f.*) slanderer; scandalmonger.
maldizer [41] (*v.t.,v.i.*) to curse; to slander; to malign.
maldoente (*adj.*) very sick.
maldonite (*f.*, *Min.*) maldonite.
maldoso –sa (*adj.*) bad, evil; mean, malicious; unkind.
maleabilidade (*f.*) malleability, ductility.
maleador –dora (*adj.*) hammering; (*m.,f.*) hammerer.
malear (*v.t.*) to hammer (metal) into sheets.
maleável (*adj.*) malleable.
maledicência (*f.*) slander, "dirt," vilification.
mal-educado –da (*adj.*) ill-bred; lowbred; uncivil.
maleficência (*f.*) maleficence.
maleficiar (*v.t.*) to do harm or evil to.
malefício (*m.*) evil deed; evil spell.
maléfico –ca (*adj.*) maleficent; malefic; malign.
maleico –ca (*adj.*, *Chem.*) maleic [acid].
maleiforme (*adj.*) malleiform, hammer-shaped.
maleína (*f.*, *Veter.*) mallein.
maleinação (*f.*, *Veter.*) malleinization.
maleinizar (*v.t.*, *Veter.*) to malleinize.
maleita(s) (*f.*) malaria.
maleiteira (*f.*, *Bot.*) euphorbia, spurge.
maleitoso –sa (*adj.*) suffering from malaria; malarial.
mal-e-mal (*adv.*) more or less; barely; scarcely.
mal-empregado –da (*adj.*) poorly or improperly used or employed.
mal-empregar (*v.t.*) to use or employ poorly.
mal-encarado –da (*adj.*) cross-looking; evil-looking.
mal-enganado –da (*adj.*) badly mistaken.
mal-engraçado –da (*adj.*) not funny; uncivil.
mal-enjorcado –da (*adj.*) awkward; improperly dressed.
mal-entendido –da (*adj.*) misunderstood; that understands poorly; (*m.*) a misunderstanding, misapprehension.
mal-entrouxado –da (*adj.*) sloppily dressed.
maléolo (*m.*, *Anat.*) malleolus.
maleolar (*adj.*, *Anat.*) malleolar.
mal-estar (*m.*) indisposition; discomfort; uneasiness.
mal-estreado –da (*adj.*) that failed at the start; disastrous; unlucky.
maleta [ê] (*f.*) handbag, suitcase.—**de mão**, grip.
maleva (*adj.*; *colloq.*) malevolent; perverse; of a horse, mean; (*m.*) evildoer; bandit. Vars. MALEVO, MALEBRA.
malevolência (*f.*) malevolence; malignity; spite.
malevolente, malévolo –la (*adj.*) malevolent; malign, malignant; spiteful.
malfadado –da (*adj.*; *m.,f.*) ill-fated, ill-starred, unlucky (person).
malfadar (*v.t.*) to predict bad luck for; to foredoom.
malfalante (*adj.*) = MALDIZENTE.
malfamado –da (*adj.*) ill-famed.
malfazejo –ja, **malfazente** (*adj.*) evil-doing, harmful; baleful.
malfazer [47] (*v.t.*) to harm; (*v.i.*) to do evil.
malfeito –ta (*adj.*) ill-formed; poorly made; (*m.*) hex, witchcraft.
malfeitor (*m.*) malefactor, criminal, evildoer; desperado; gangster.
malfeitoria (*f.*) evil deed.
malferir [21a] (*v.t.*) to wound badly.
malformação (*f.*) malformation.
malformado –da (*adj.*) malformed.
malfurada (*f.*, *Bot.*) a globe daisy (*Globularia salicida*).
malgalante (*adj.*) unchivalrous, discourteous.
malgastar (*v.t.*) to squander.
malgaxe (*adj.*; *m.,f.*) Madagascan.
malgovernado –da (*adj.*) spendthrift, wastrel.
malgovernar (*v.t.*) to govern (manage) poorly.
malgradado –da (*adj.*) displeased.
malgrado (*prep.*) despite, notwithstanding; (*m.*) spite; ill will.
malha (*f.*) mesh; network; mail (of armor); mottle, blotch, spot; quoit; a beating.

malhação (*f.*) a beating; mauling or flailing; a "knocking" (criticism).
malhada (*f.*) see under MALHADO.
malhadeiro –ra (*adj.*) stupid, dull; (*m.*) flail; maul; whipping boy.
malhado –da (*adj.*) piebald, mottled, brindled, spotted. **cavalo**—, pinto horse; dappled horse; (*f.*) a mauling; shepherd's hut; sheepfold; cattle pen; "(1) a place where cattle, to be used as work animals, are herded; (2) a place where the cattle or packtrain sleeps; (3) in northeast Brazil, where the cattle can be sheltered from hot sun by the shadow of large trees." [*GBAT*]
malhador (*m.*) thresher.
malhadouro (*m.*) threshing floor. Var. MALHADOIRO.
malhar (*v.t.*) to hammer, beat; to flail (grain); to batter; to maul, cudgel; to mottle.—**em ferro frio,** to strive fruitlessly; to work to no avail.—**o ferro enquanto está quente,** to strike while the iron is hot.
malhetar (*v.t.*) to mortise.
malhête (*m.*) mortise joint; mallet.
malho (*m.*) maul, mallet, hammer; sledge hammer.—**de polo,** polo mallet.
mal-humorado –da (*adj.*) ill-humored; gruff; sullen; sulky; grumpy; disagreeable; petulant; peevish.
malícia (*f.*) malice, ill will, evil intent, spitefulness; cattiness; sarcastic humor; humorous finesse; the ability to spot double meanings and expose them to ridicule; tongue-in-cheek humor; slyness, cunning; mischievousness; misconstruction.—**d'água,** (*Bot.*) sensitive brier (*Neptunia*).—**de-mulher,** (*Bot.*) the sensitive plant (*Mimosa pudica*), c.a. SENSITIVA, DORME-MARIA, DORMIDEIRA, JUQUIRIRASTEIRO.
maliciador –dora (*adj.*; *m.,f.*) malicious (person).
maliciar (*v.t.*) to misconstrue, take amiss (remarks, intent, meaning).
malicioso –sa (*adj.*) malicious, spiteful; catty; cunning; foxy; mischievous, prankish; tongue-in-cheek; good at spotting double meanings, etc.
málico –ca (*adj.*; *Chem.*) malic [acid].
malicório (*m.*) malicorium.
malífero –ra (*adj.*) maliferous, harmful; unhealthful, as a climate.
maliforme (*adj.*) shaped like an apple.
maligna (*f.*) see under MALIGNO.
malignância (*f.*) malignancy.
malignar (*v.t.*) to render evil or malign; (*v.i.*) to grow worse. [But not to malign, which is MALDIZER DE, DIFAMAR, CALUNIAR.]
malignidade (*f.*) malignity; spite.
maligno –na (*adj.*) malign; malignant; spiteful; **espírito**—, evil spirit, devil; (*f.*) malignant fever; malaria; any bad disease.
má-língua (*f.*) slander; backbiting; (*m.,f.*) slanderer, backbiter.
mal-intencionado –da (*adj.*) of evil intentions.
malíssimo –ma (*absol. superl. of* MAU) very bad; most evil.
mal-jeitoso –sa (*adj.*) awkward, clumsy.
mal-limpo –pa (*adj.*) filthy.
malmente (*adv.*) = MAL.
malmequer (*m.*, *Bot.*) pot marigold (*Calendula officinalis*). —**-da-sécia,** common china-aster (*Callistephus chinensis*), c.a. SÉCIA.—**-de-buenos-aires,** a gumweed (*Grindelia sconzonerfolia*).—**-do-campo,** field gumweed (*G. camporum*), c.a. GRINDÉLIA.—**-grande,** the rough heliopsis (*H. scabra*), c.a. CAMARÁ-DE-CAVALO.
malmequerzinho (*m.*, *Bot.*) a terrestrial orchid (*Epipactics campinaria*).
mal-montado –da (*adj.*) that rides (horseback) awkwardly.
malnascido –da (*adj.*) ill-starred; low-born.
malo –la (*adj.*) bad; mean [= MAU].
maloca (*f.*) a large hut housing more than one Indian family; an Indian camp or village; herd of cattle; a band of dubious-looking people (as of gypsies).
malocado –da (*adj.*; *m.,f.*) (an Indian) settled in a village.
malocar (*v.t.*) to settle (Indians) in villages.
maloclusão (*f.*, *Dent.*) malocclusion.
malogrado –da (*adj.*) unlucky; unsuccessful.
malograr (*v.t.*) to spoil, wreck; to thwart; to disappoint; (*v.r.*) to fail, come to naught, miscarry, come to grief.
malôgro (*m.*) failure, defeat, ill success; disappointment; miscarriage; bad luck.
mal-olhado –da (*adj.*) looked-upon with hate.
malonato (*m.*, *Chem.*) malonate.

malônico –ca (*adj.; Chem.*) malonic [acid].
maloqueiro (*m.*) street urchin.
malossísmico –ca (*adj.*) malloseismic.
malotão (*m.*) a large trunk, or bundle.
malote (*m.*) a small trunk.
mal-ouvido –da (*adj.*) heedless; disobedient.
malparado –da (*adj.*) in a perilous state; in a precarious situation.
malparição (*f.*) an induced abortion.
malparir (*v.i.*) to abort, suffer a miscarriage.
mal-passado –da (*adj.*) rare, underdone.
malpíguia (*f., Bot.*) any plant of the genus *Malpighia*.
malpiguiáceo –cea (*adj.; Bot.*) malpighiaceous; (*f.,pl.*) the Malpichiaceae (Barbados cherry family).
malposição (*f.*) malposition, misplacement.
malpropício –cia (*adj.*) unsuitable.
malquerença (*f.*) ill will.
malquerente (*adj.*) ill-disposed (towards others); malevolent.
malquerer [24; 68] (*v.t.*) to hate; to wish ill to.
malquistar (*v.t.*) to render ill-disposed or inimical (toward others); to disaffect; to set at variance.—-se com, to incur another's ill-will or enmity.
malquisto –ta (*adj.*) hated, disliked; unpopular.
malregido –da (*adj.*) unruly.
malsadio –dia (*adj.*) unhealthy.
malroupido –da (*adj.*) shabbily clothed [= MALTRAPILHO].
malsão [-sãos] –sã (*adj.*) sickly, unhealthy, unwholesome.
malservido –da (*adj.*) badly served; not satisfied.
malsim (*m.*) customhouse inspector; bailiff; informer, stool pigeon; (*adj.*) that brings to light something one sought to hide.
malsinar (*v.t.*) to denounce, inform against; to misconstrue, misjudge; to censure; to bring misfortune to; to slander, defame, malign.
malsoante (*adj.*) dissonant, jarring, harsh [sounds, words]. Var. MALSONANTE.
malsofrido –da (*adj.*) impatient, testy.
malsorteado –da (*adj.*) unfortunate, unlucky, ill-fated.
malta (*f.*) gang, mob; band of migrant workers; loose living; maltha, mineral tar. [*cap.*] Malta.—de desordeiros, gang of rowdies. andar à—, to loaf.
maltar (*v.t.*) to malt (barley).
maltase (*f., Biochem.*) maltase.
malte (*m.*) malt.
maltês –tesa (*adj.; m.,f.*) Maltese; (*m.*) migrant farm worker.
maltose (*f., Chem.*) maltose.
maltoso –sa (*adj.*) malty.
maltrapilho –lha (*adj.*) ragged, in tatters; (*m.,f.*) ragamuffin. Var. MALTRAPIDO.
maltratar (*v.t.*) to mistreat; to maltreat; to outrage; to mishandle; to injure, hurt; to victimize.
malucagem (*f.*) = MALUQUICE.
malucar (*v.i.*) to act crazily; to rave.
maluco –ca (*adj.*) crazy, insane; screwy, "batty".—de atar, raving mad ("fit to be tied"). pôr—, to run crazy; (*m.*) madman; crackpot; screwball; (*f.*) madwoman.
malungo (*m.*) pal; foster brother; fellow-slave who came (to Brazil) in the same ship.
maluquear (*v.i.*) to say or do crazy things.
maluqueira (*f.*) madness, insanity; insane behavior; crazy idea.
maluquice (*f.*) insane or foolish behavior or utterance [= MALUCAGEM].
malva (*f.*) a hibiscus or rosemallow; also, used as a combining term for numerous plants of the mallow family, esp. of the genera *Althaea, Abutilon, Malva, Pavonia, Sida, Wissadula, Waltheria;* (*colloq.*) an umbrella; a floppy hat (in allusion to the shape of the typical mallow flower).—-branca, a tropical weed (*Sida carpinifolia*).—-branca-do-salgado = PACO-PACO.—-cajuçara, a screwtree (*Helicteres pentandra*), c.a. SACA-TRAPO, UAICIMA.—-de-pendão = PACO-PACO.—-do-campo, any of various small resinous shrubs (genus *Kielmeyera*), all native to Brazil, with flowers resembling mallows or camellias; c.a. FÔLHA-SANTA, PAU-SANTO, PAU-DE-CORTIÇA (from the corky bark).—-flor = CATINGA-DE-MULATA.—-rosa, hollyhock (*Althaea rosea*).—-roxa-recortada = GUAXIMA-ROXA.—-relógio-grande, the broomjute sida (*S. rhombifolia*), c.a. MALVA-DA-PRAIA, MALVA-PRETA, UACIMA-DA-PRAIA, VASSOURA, VASSOURINHA.—-silvestre, the high mallow (*Malva sylvestris*).—-simples, the running mallow (*Malva rotundifolia*).

malváceo –cea (*adj., Bot.*) malvaceous; (*f.pl.*) the *Malvaceae* (mallow family).
malvadez[a] (*f.*) cruelty, meanness.
malvado –da (*adj.*) cruel, mean, wicked; (*m.,f.*) such a one; (*m.*) ruffian.
malvaísco (*m., Bot.*) marshmallow (*Althaea officinalis*); also = GUAXIMA-ROXA.—-côr-de-rosa = CARAPICU.—-do-rio-grande-do-sul, the brick goldmallow (*Sphaeralcea cisplatina*).
malvasia (*f.*) a sweet grape from which malmsey or Madeira wine is made.
malvavisco (*m., Bot.*) a waxmallow (*Malvaviscus mollis*).
mal-usar (*v.t.*) to misuse.
malventuroso –sa (*adj.*) unlucky [= MAL-AVENTURADO].
malversação (*f.*) improper or corrupt behavior in office, esp. in the handling of money.
malversar (*v.t.*) to mismanage (funds, an estate, etc.).
malvisto –ta (*adj.*) looked-upon with dislike or suspicion; ill-regarded.
mamã (*f.*) mamma, mother; wet-nurse.
mama (*f.*) breast, teat, dug; (*Anat., Zool.*) mamma; (*colloq.*) mother's milk; suckling age.
mamada (*f.*) = MAMADURA.
mamadeira (*f.*) baby's milk bottle; a snake (*Pseudoboa cloelia*), c.a. LIMPA-CAMPO; also = MUÇURANA.
mamãe (*f.*) mamma, mother.
mama-em-onça (*m.*) self-seeker; fortune hunter (through marriage); very daring man.
mamaiacu [ú] (*m.*) a species of globefish.
mamalgia (*f., Med.*) mammalgia.
mamalogia (*f., Zool.*) mammalogy.
mamalogista (*m.,f.*) mammalogist.
mamaluco (*m.*) = MAMELUCO.
mamangá (*m.,f., Bot.*) a senna (*Cassia*), c.a. FEDEGOSO-VERDADEIRO.
mamangaba, –gava (*f.*) a bumblebee, c.a. MANGANGÁ.
mamão (*m.*) the well-known tropical fruit of the papaya tree (*Carica papaya*), or the tree itself; plant sucker; young donkey; unweaned calf; (*adj.*) unweaned.
mamãozeiro (*m.*) = MAMOEIRO.
mamãozinho (*m.*) the oakleaf papaya (*Carica quercifolia*).
mamar (*v.i.*) to suckle; to take the breast; to suck (as on a cigar); (*colloq.*) to drink; (*colloq.*) to enjoy illicit gains; (*slang*) to ride the gravy train.—em onça, (*colloq.*) to be very daring; lit., to suckle on a wildcat. dar de—, to nurse (breastfeed).
mamareis (*m., Zool.*) a common silverside (*Menidia brasiliensis*).
mamário –ria (*adj.*) mammary.
mamarracho (*m.*) dauber (unskillful painter).
mamarrote (*adj.*) tippling; (*m.*) tippler.
mamata (*f.*) public graft; a profitable sinecure.
mambembe (*adj.*) cheap, second or third-rate (hotel, show, etc.).
mamelão (*m.*) rounded protuberance; hillock, mound; nipple of the breast.
mameluco (*m.*) mameluke; in Brazil, offspring of white and Indian. Var. MAMALUCO.
mamica (*f.*) little nipple; the spot ball (in billiards).
mamífero –ra, mammiferous; mammalian; (*m.,f.*) a mammal.
mamiforme (*adj.*) mammiform; mammillary.
mamila (*f.*) nipple of the breast; (*Anat.*) mammilla.
mamilão (*m.*) = MAMELÃO.
mamilar (*m.*) brassière; (*adj.*) mammillary.
mamilária (*f.*) a genus (*Mammillaria*) of cacti.
mamilo (*m.*) = MAMILA.
maminha (*f.*) breast nipple.—-de-cabra = GRÃO-DE-GALO (a plant).—-de-cadela,—-de-porca, = ESPINHO-DE-VINTEM (a tree).
mamoa (*f.*) = MAMÃO (fruit); a mound or hillock.
mamoeiro (*m.*) the common papaya (*Carica papaya*), c.a. PAPAEIRA, PAPAIA, PINOGUAÇU. [The fruit is called MAMÃO.]; (*colloq.*) a tippler, guzzler.—-do-mato = JARACATIÁ.
mamona, mamoneira (*f.*), mamoneiro (*m.*) the castorbean or castor-oil plant (*Ricinus communis*), c.a. CARRAPATEIRA, or its fruit.
mamoninho-bravo (*m.*) the jimsonweed datura (*D. stramonium*), c.a. MAMONINHO-DE-CARNEIRO, ESTRAMÔNIO, FIGUEIRA-DO-INFERNO, ZABUMBA.
mamorana (*f.*) = CASTANHEIRO-DO-MARANHÃO, CACAU-SELVAGEM.

mamote (*m.*) a child or animal which continues to suckle though old enough to be weaned.
mamparra (*f.*) dawdling; petty theft; (*pl.*) quibbles.
mamparrear (*v.i.*) to dawdle; to quibble.
mamparreiro –ra (*adj.*) dawdling; (*m.,f.*) dawdler.
mamudo –da (*adj.*) having large breasts.
mamujar (*v.i.*) to suckle intermittently (not being hungry).
mamulengos (*m.pl.*) puppet show.
mamute (*m.*) mammoth.
mana (*f.*) short for IRMÃ (sister).
maná (*m.*) manna; (*Bot.*) flowering ash (*Fraxinus ornus*).
manacá (*m., Bot.*) the manaca raintree (*Brunfelsia hopeana*), c.a. MANAJÁ, ERATATACA, JERATATACA.
manaçaia (*f.*) = MANDAÇAIA.
manaíba (*f.*) a cutting of taro or manioc (for planting).
manada (*f.*) drove, herd.
manajá (*f.*) = MANACÁ.
manajó (*m.*) variant of AMANAJÉ.
manalvo –va (*adj.*) having white forefeet [horse].
manampança (*f.*) a kind of sweet made with manioc meal and flavored with anise.
manancial (*m.*) fountain, spring, source; (*adj.*) flowing.
mananga (*m.*) medicine man [= PAJÉ].
manante (*adj.*) emanant, issuing, flowing forth.
manaquim (*m.*) manakin (bird). Cf. MANEQUIM.
manar (*v.i.*) to emanate, flow (out), run (out), issue; to ooze; (*v.t.*) to send out, emit; to pour out, shed.
manata (*m.*) rascal; dude; big shot [= MANDACHUVA]; magnate.
manati[m] (*m., Zool.*) manatee (better known as PEIXE-BOI).
manau (*m.,f.*) an Indian of the Manao, a now extinct but once famous Arawakan tribe which lived in the region south of the Rio Negro and north of the Amazon; (*adj.*) pert. to or designating the Manao.
manauense (*adj.*) of or pert. to the city of Manaus, capital of Amazonas state; (*m.,f.*) a native or inhabitant of that city.
mancada (*f.*) gross error; faux pas.
mancador –dora (*adj.; m.*) lame (horse).
mancal (*m.*) bearing, journal; door hinge.—**de empuxo**, thrust bearing.—**de esferas**, ball bearing.—**de roletes**, roller bearing.
mancar (*v.t.*) to lame; (*v.i.*) to limp, hobble; to want, lack; to fail to keep a promise or obligation; (*v.r.*) to go lame; (*slang*) to goof.
manceba (*f.*) concubine, mistress, paramour.
mancebia (*f.*) concubinage.
mancebo (*m.*) lad, youth; man servant; clothes tree.
mancenilha (*f.*) manzanilla olive; also = MANCENILHEIRA. Var. MANCINELA.
mancenilheira (*f.*) the manchineel (*Hippomane mancinella*), "a poisonous tropical American tree, having a blistering milky juice, and apple-shaped fruit." [*Webster*]
mancha (*f.*) spot, blot; blotch, splotch; blemish, stain (on reputation).—**de-ferro**, a sphere fungus (*Mycosphaerella coffeicola*), damaging to coffee trees.—**solar**, sunspot.
manchado –da (*adj.*) spotted; stained; of cattle, mottled.
manchar (*v.t.*) to spot; to stain, sully; to tarnish (reputation).
manche (*m., Aeron.*) control stick.
manchear (*v.t.*) to induce the fermentation of (cacao beans).
mancheia (*f.*) handful [= MÃO-CHEIA]. **a—s**, by the handful; prodigally. **de—**, tops, excellent.
manchete (*f.*) newspaper headline.
manchil (*m.*) butcher's cleaver.
mancinela (*f.*) = MANCENILHA.
mancinismo (*m.*) left-handedness. [More usual: CANHOTISMO].
manco –ca (*adj.*) lame, maimed, crippled; hobbling; wanting, lacking, missing (a part); (*m.,f.*) a cripple.
mancomunação (*f.*) collusion.
mancomunar (*v.i.*) to collude.—**se com**, to make common cause with.
manda (*f.*) reference mark; also = MANDACHUVA.
mandaçaia (*f.*) a stingless honeybee (*Melipona anthioides* or *M. quadrifasciata*), c.a. AMANAÇAIA, MANAÇAIA.—**do-chão** is *Melipona santhilarii*.
mandacaru, –curu [rú] (*m., Bot.*) the Peru cereus (*C. peruvianus*), c.a. JAMACARU, PRINCÊSA-DA-NOITE.
mandachuva (*m.*) big shot, bigwig; political boss, esp. in

country districts; c.a. CACIQUE, CHEFÃO, MAIORAL, PAREDRO.
mandada (*f.*) see under MANDADO.
mandadeiro (*m.*) order-taker, errand runner.
mandado –da (*adj.*) said of one who has been sent or ordered (to do something); (*f.*) act of dealing cards; (*m.*) mandate, order, command; judicial writ.—**-de-deus**, bolt of lightning.—**de penhora**, writ of attachment.—**de prisão**, warrant for arrest.—**de segurança**, a court injunction. **ao (por)—de**, by order of.
mandaguari [í] (*f.*) either or two stingless bees: *Melipona postica* or *Trigona bipunctata*, the latter c.a. TUBUNA.
manda-lua (*f.*) = URUTAU.
mandamento (*m.*) order, command; an ordering or commanding; divine commandment.—**s da lei de Deus**, the Ten Commandments.—**s da Santa Madre Igreja**, (*R.C.Ch.*) the commandments of the Church.
mandante (*adj.*) ordering, commanding; (*m.,f.*) one who orders (directs, commands); mastermind (of a plot).
mandão –dona (*adj.*) bossy; (*m.,f.*) a domineering person; despot, tyrant.
mandar (*v.t.*) to send; to ship; to command, order, direct; to require (enjoin).—**a (para)**, to send (dispatch) to.—**à imprensa**, to send to press.—**ao diabo**, or—**às favas**, or—**bugiar**, to send to the devil; to snub.—**aviar uma receita**, to have a prescription filled.—**buscar**, to send for (have something fetched).—**chamar (o médico)**, to call, send for (the doctor).—**dizer**, to send word.—**em**, to hold sway over (rule, govern).—**fazer (alguma coisa)**, to have (something) made to order.—**levar**, to send (have something taken). **Aqui quem manda sou eu**, I'm the boss around here. **Êle mandou uma direita à cara do outro**, He hit the other guy with an upper right. **Mande o tintureiro passar esta calça a ferro de novo**, Have the cleaners press these trousers again. **Mandei lembranças para todos**, I sent (my) regards to everyone. **Mandei pedir desculpas a êle**, I had someone deliver (offer) my apologies to him. **O senhor aqui não pede, manda**, Your requests are orders around here. **Que é que você manda?** How can I help you? **Quem mandou ser tão teimoso?** I told you so, but you're so stubborn. **Quem mandou você fazer isso?** Who told you to do that? **Quem quer vai, quem não quer manda**, If you want something done, do it yourself.
mandaravé (*f., Bot.*) a calliandra (*C. tweedi*), c.a. QUEBRA-FOICE.
mandarim (*m.*) Chinese mandarin; Mandarin (dialect).
mandarina (*f.*) mandarin orange (*Citrus reticulata*), c.a. TANGERINA.
mandatário (*m.*) mandatary; agent, attorney, proxy.—**apostólico**, (*R.C.Ch.*) apostolic delegate.—**do povo**, one to whom a mandate has been given by the people; a congressman.
mandato (*m.*) mandate, charge, commission.—**apostólico**, (*R.C.Ch.*) apostolic brief.
manda-tudo (*m.*) = MANDACHUVA.
mandélico –ca (*adj.; Chem.*) mandelic [acid].
mandi [í] (*m.*) a combining term for any of numerous fresh-water catfishes.—**chorão** = ANUJÁ.
mandíbula (*f.*) mandible; lower jawbone.
mandibular (*adj.*) mandibular; (*v.t.,v.i., colloq.*) to chew [= MASTIGAR].
mandibuliforme (*adj.; Zool.*) mandibuliform.
mandíbulo-auricular (*m., Anat.*) mandibulo-auricularis.
mandíbulo-maxilar [ks] (*adj.; Zool.*) mandibulo-maxillary.
mandigüera (*m.*) runt (esp. pig).
mandil (*m.*) kind of coarse cloth for cleaning or wiping; cook's apron.
mandinga (*f.*) magic, sorcery, witchcraft; (*m.,f.*) a Mandingo or Mandinga (tall Negro of western Sudan, often having non-Negro features, and reputed to possess magical powers); (*adj.*) Mandingan.
mandingar (*v.t.*) to practice witchcraft on.
mandingaria (*f.*) witchcraft, sorcery.
mandingueiro –ra, mandinguento –ta (*m.,f.*) witch, sorcerer.
mandioca (*f., Bot.*) the common or bitter cassava (*Manihot esculenta*), of great economic importance in Brazil. [The food staple FARINHA DE MANDIOCA (manioc meal) is made from this species, the tubers of which must first be roasted to expel the poisonous hydrocyanic acid. It is also the source of tapioca].—**doce**, c.a. MACAXEIRA, is the sweet or aipi cassava (*Manihot aipi*). [Its long, non-

poisonous tubers are boiled and eaten like potatoes].—
-brava = FAVELEIRO.
mandiocal (m.) MANDIOCA field.
mandioqueira (f., Bot.) matchwood (Didymopanax morototoni).
mandioqueiro (m.) a small planter of MANDIOCA.
mando (m.) power, authority; command. **a—de**, by order of.
mandolim (m.), **mandolina** (f.) mandolin.
mandolinista (m.,f.) mandolin player.
mandonismo (m.) despotism, authoritativeness, bossiness, bullying.
mandraca (f.) sorcery, witchcraft; magic potion.
mandraco (m.) charm, good-luck piece, "rabbit's foot".
mandrágora (f., Bot.) mandrake (Mandragora officinarum).
mandrana (m.,f.) lazy person.
mandranice (f.) laziness.
mandraqueiro -ra (adj.; m.,f.) = FEITICEIRO.
mandraquice (f.) sorcery, witchcraft.
mândria (f.) laziness, sloth.
mandrião (adj.) lazy; (m.) lazy person, idler, loafer, slouch, sluggard; (m.) scalawag. [Fem. MANDRIONA]
mandriar (v.i.) to idle, loaf, loiter, lounge; to dally; to dawdle.
mandriice [i-í] (f.) = MÂNDRIA.
mandril (f., Mach.) chuck of a lathe; mandrel; broach, reamer; (m.) mandrill, baboon.—**magnético**, magnetic chuck.—**universal**, universal chuck.
mandrilar (v.t.) to broach, ream.
mandriona, fem. of MANDRIÃO.
mandubi [í] (m.) peanut (Arachis), c.a. MENDUBI.
mandubiguaçu [ú] (m.) Barbados nut (Jatropha curca).
mandubirana (f.) = AMENDOEIRANA.
manducar (v.t.,v.i., colloq.) to chew [= MASTIGAR].
manducuru [rú] (m.) the saguaro or giant cactus (Cereus giganteus).
manduirana [u-i] (f.) = CABO-VERDE.
manduri[m] (f.) a stingless bee (Melipona marginata), c.a. TAIPEIRA, URUÇU-MIRIM, GUARAPU-MIÚDA.
manduricão (m.) a large stingless bee (Melipona interrupta).
manduvira (f., Bot.) a crotalaria.
mané (m.) a lazy, inept, slack, worthless sort of fellow; a half-wit.—**côco**, idiot, fool.—**do-jacá**, fool, half-wit.—**gostoso**, puppet; a person on stilts, esp. one of the characters in BUMBA-MEU-BOI (which see).—**magro**, a stick insect, c.a. MANUEL-MAGRO, BICHO-DE-PAU.—**mole** = CAPITÃO-DE-SALA (a plant).
manear (v.t.) to handle, manipulate; to manage [= MANEJAR]; to fetter, hobble (a horse).
maneia (f.) fetter, shackle; hobble (for a horse).
maneio (m.) manipulation, handling; hand work; management.
maneira (f.) manner, method, way; mode, form, style; custom, habit, practice; placket (of a garment); (pl.) manners, behavior, deportment.—**de pensar**, way of thinking.—**de se comportar**, way to behave.—**de ver**, way of looking (at something).—**s desafogadas**, free and easy manners. **à—de**, like; in the manner of; after the fashion of; of; as; by way of. **à—que**, as, while, at the same time that. **da mesma—**, in the same manner. **de—a**, in a way to. **de—alguma**, not at all, in no wise, by no manner of means. **de—nenhuma**, by no means. **de—que**, so that. **de qualquer—**, in any case; in one way or another. **desta—**, (in) this way.
maneirismo (m.) mannerism.
maneirista (m.,f.) mannerist (in art); a person of studied, affected, manners.
maneiro -ra (adj.) light, easy to handle; agile; portable.
maneiroso -sa (adj.) mannerly; courteous, polite; tactful.
manejador -dora (m.,f.) handler [but not manager, which is GERENTE].
manejar (v.t.) to handle, wield; to manage.
manejável (adj.) manageable, easy to handle.
manejo [ê] (m.) handling, wielding; management; manège; (pl.) wiles, tricks; military maneuvers.
manelo [è] (m.) a small handful of something.
manequim (m.) mannequin, model.
maneta [ê] (adj.; m.,f.) one-armed (person).
manga (f.) sleeve (of a garment); any of various sleeve-like objects; glass chimney (for a lamp); glass bell; glass funnel; water spout; detachment of troops; gang; cattle

chute; mango (the fruit); (Mach.) journal of a car axle; a bushing or long thimble; a pipe sleeve.—**da-praia**, a tropical aromatic tree (Clusia fluminensis), c.a. ABANO, ABANEIRO, MANGUE-BRAVO.—**de-água**, water spout; cloud burst [= TROMBA-DE-ÁGUA].—**de-alpaca**, (m.) a public functionary (in allusion to the formerly worn black alpaca office coats).—**de colete**, (colloq.) nothing; lit., sleeve of a vest.—**de incandescência**, the Welsbach or similar mantle for placing over a light-giving flame.—**perdida**, wide unfitted, uncuffed sleeve.—**s-de-veludo**, wandering albatross (Diomedea exulans).—**de vidro**, glass chimney for a lamp. **em—s de camisa**, in shirt sleeves. **Isto é outro par de—s**, That's quite a different thing; That's a horse of another color.
mangaba (f.) fruit of the MANGABEIRA.
mangabarana (f.) a jungleplum (Sideroxylon sp.).
mangabeira (f.) a small Brazilian tree (Hancornia speciosa) with reddish, hard wood; the latex produces an inferior grade of rubber; the plum-sized pleasant-tasting fruit is used to flavor sweets and sherbets; when fermented it produces a valuable wine; the timber is used for wheels, pulleys and furniture manufacture.
mangabeiro (m.) one who gathers the latex of the MANGABEIRA.
mangação (f.) mockery, derision, jesting.
mangador -dora (adj.) derisive; (m.,f.) scoffer, mocker.
mangagá (adj.) huge.
mangal (m.) an area covered with mangroves.
mangalaça (f.) idling, sloth.
mangalho (m.) large penis; (pl.) products of domestic industry sold at country markets.
mangalô (m.) = CUMANDATIÁ.
manganapite (f., Min.) manganapatite.
manganato (m., Chem.) mangante.—**de bário**, barium manganate, manganese green, Cassel's green.
manganês (m.) manganese (metal or ore).—**alumínio**, manganese-aluminum alloy.—**bronze**, manganese bronze.
manganesiato (m.) = MANGANATO.
manganésico -ca (adj.) = MANGÂNICO.
manganesífero -ra (adj.) = MANGANÍFERO.
manganésio (m.) = MANGANÊS.
manganesito (m.) = MANGANITA.
mangangá (adj.) huge; (m.) any bumblebee (Bombus), c.a. ABELHÃO, MANGANGABA, MANGANGAVA, MANANGAVA, MAMANGAIA; (colloq.) bigwig, "big shot"; any of various scorpion fishes, esp. the Brazilian scorpene (Scorpaena brasiliensis), the West Indian scorpene (S. plumieri), and the lionfish (S. grandicornis), all c.a. BEATINHA, BEATRIZ, NINQUIN-DE-PEDRA.—**liso**, a toad-fish (Nautopaedium porossissimum), c.a. BACALHAU (cod) —a quite inappropriate term for this unrelated fish.
mangânico -ca (adj.; Chem.) manganic.
manganífero -ra (adj.) manganiferous.
manganilha (f.) trick; sleight of hand.
manganina (f.) Manganin (a copper-base alloy).
manganita (f., Min.) manganite [= ACERDÉSIO].
manganocalcite (f., Min.) manganocalcite.
manganofilite (f., Min.) manganophyllite.
manganopectólito (m., Min.) manganpectolite.
manganosita (f., Min.) manganosite.
manganoso -sa (adj.; Chem.) manganous.—**mangânico**, manganomanganic [oxide].
manganossiderito (m., Min.) manganosiderite.
manganostibite (f., Min.) manganostibite.
manganotantalite (f., Min.) manganotantalite.
mangão (adj.) given to making fun, joking, bantering. [Fem. MANGONA] (m.) wide sleeve.
mangar (v.i.) to make fun (**de**, **em**, **com**, of); to razz; poke fun at; to joke; to banter; to dawle.
mangará (m., Bot.) common caladium (C. bicolor), the yautia malanga (Xanthosoma sagittaefolium); the inflorescence at the end of a banana stalk, c.a. CORAÇÃO.—**mirim** = MANGARITO.
mangaraí (m., Bot.) Desfontaine's taro (Colocasia fontanesi).
mangarataia (f.) = GENGIBRE; AÇAFRÃO-DA-INDIA.
mangarataua (f.) saffron crocus (C. sativus).
mangarito (m.) primrose malanga (Xanthosoma violaceum), c.a. MANGARÁ-MIRIM.
mangarobeira (f., Bot.) a garcinia (G. mangle), c.a. MANGUE-DE-SAPATEIRO.
mangaua (m.,f.) a godchild in relation to its godparents' own children; foster-brother.

mangífera (*f.*, *Bot.*) the genus (*Mangifera*) which includes the common mango (*M. indica*).

mango (*m.*) the handle of a flail; a whip with a wooden handle and a rawhide lash. [The fruit mango is MANGA.]

mangona (*f.*) sloth, indolence; also = MANGONA; (*m.*) lazy man. (*adj.*) = MANGÃO.

mangon[e]ar (*v.i.*) to laze.

mangonga (*m.*) a large sand shark (*Carcharias taurus*), c.a. MAGONGA, MANGONA, CAÇÃO-DE-AREIA; (*colloq.*) a huge man.

mangorra (*f.*) the blues.

mangostão (*m.*) mangosteen (*Garcinia mangostana*), or its fruit; (*Pharm.*) the pericarp of this fruit used as an astringent; c.a. MANGUSTO.

mangote (*m.*) small fishnet; short length of hose.

mangra (*f.*) plant blight.

mangrar (*v.t.*) to blight.

mangual (*m.*) flail; whip.

manguara (*f.*) stick, staff, pole, cudgel, club.

manguarão (*m.*) bean pole (tall, thin man).

manguari [i] (*m.*) a tall, thin man; also = MAGUARI.

mangue (*m.*) mangrove; mangrove swamp; mud flat.—-amarelo, black mangrove (*Avicennia marina*), c.a. MANGUE-CIRIÚBA, MANGUE-GUAPIRÁ.—-branco, a terminalia (*T. aggregata*), c.a. MANGUE-CANOÉ, MANGUE-DE-BOTÃO, MANGUE-SEREÍBA; also = MANGUE-CANAPOMBA.—-bravo = ABANEIRO.—-canapomba, the white buttonwood or falsemangrove (*Laguncularia racemosa*—the only species), c.a. MANGUE-RASTEIRO, MANGUE-BRANCO, CANAPAÚBA.—-da-praia = MANGA-DA-PRAIA.—-de-água-doce = LARANJARANA.—-de-espêto, a garcina (*G. minifolia*), c.a. MANGUE-GAITEIRO.—-de-sapateiro = MANGAROBEIRA.—-do-brejo, an eugenia (*E. nitida*).—-vermelho, the true American (common, red) mangrove (*Rhizophora mangle*), c.a. MANGUE-DE-PENDÃO, MANGUE-NEGRO, MANGUE-SAPATEIRO, MANGUE-VERDADEIRO, MANGUE-PRÊTO, GUAPARAÍBA, MAPAREÚBA, MANGUEIRO. ["There are large areas of mangrove swamps in the Amazon estuary, but despite the wood's fuel value and the high tannin content of the bark, it is not utilized excessively for either purpose." *GBAT*]

mangueira (*f.*) rubber or canvas hose; cattle chute; (*Bot.*) the common mango (*Mangifera indica*) whose fruit is called MANGA.

mangueiral, manguezal (*m.*) an area abounding in mangroves.

mangueiro (*m.*) = MANGUE-VERMELHO.

manguito (*m.*) mitten; muff; obscene gesture [= BANANA].

mangusto (*m.*, *Zool.*) mongoose or ichneumon (*Herpestes sp.*), c.a. SACA-RABO; (*Bot.*) = MANGOSTÃO.

manha (*f.*) cleverness; skill; craftiness; guile; ruse; cunning; wile; whim, crochet; whining of children; complaining.

manhã (*f.*) morning, forenoon. à—, in the morning [but AMANHÃ = tomorrow]. **alta**—, mid morning. **amanhã de**—, tomorrow morning. **até de**—, until morning. **de**—, in the morning. **de**—**até a noite**, from morning till night. É **de**—, it is morning. **hoje de**—, this morning. **pela**—, in the morning. **tôdas as**—**s**, every morning.

manhãzinha (*f.*) early morning.

manheirar (*v.i.*) to be crotchety; to dawdle; to play sick; of cattle, to be ornery.

manheiro -ra, **manhento** -ta (*adj.*) ornery; given to malingering; of a matter, tough, complicated.

manhoso -sa (*adj.*) clever; smart; wily; guileful; crafty, cunning, sharp, sly; ornery; of children, whining.

mania (*f.*) mania, madness; hobby; fad; craze; obsession.

maníaco -ca (*adj.*) maniacal; (*m.,f.*) maniac; crank.

maniatar (*v.t.*) to manacle; to restrain.

maniçoba (*f.*) "(1) a dish made from the leaves of the manioc plant ground up in a mortar and cooked up with a fish or meat mixture; the people of Amazonia usually use MOCOTÓ, salt tongue, tripe or pig's head when preparing this dish; (in order sufficiently to soften the manioc leaves they must be boiled for at least 24 hours); (2) a manioc plant (*Manihot glaziovii*) which yields Ceará rubber." [*GBAT*]

manicômio (*m.*) insane asylum.

manicórdio (*m.*) clavichord.

manícula (*f.*) animal's front paw; crank handle [= MANIVELA].

manicura (*f.*) manicure; manicurist.

manidestro -tra (*adj.*) of persons, right-handed.

manietar (*v.*) = MANIATAR.

manifestação (*f.*) manifestation; display; disclosure.

manifestado -da (*adj.*) manifested; (*m.,f.*) one who is honored by a public manifestation.

manifestante (*adj.*) manifesting; (*m.,f.*) demonstrator; demonstrant; manifester.

manifestar (*v.t.*) to manifest, display, evince; to reveal, make known; to declare (in a custom's manifest); (*v.r.*) to appear, manifest itself.

manifesto -ta (*adj.*) manifest, open, clear, obvious; (*m.*) manifest; manifesto.

maniforme (*adj.*) shaped like a hand.

manigância (*f.*, *colloq.*) sleight-of-hand; tricks; underhanded dealing.

maniguete [ête] (*m.*) seed of the paradise melegueta pepper (*Aframomum grana-paradisi*), c.a. SEMENTE-DO-PARAÍSO.

manijuba (*f.*) a small tropical catfish (*Pimelodus clarias*) sometimes seen in home aquaria.

manilha (*f.*) bracelet, armlet; shackle, manacle; clevis; link; a certain card game; a length of terra cotta pipe.

manilhar (*v.t.*) to shackle, manacle.

manimbé (*m.*) a grasshopper sparrow (*Myospiza humeralis*), c.a. TICO-TICO-DO-CAMPO.

manina (*adj.*) of cows, sterile.

maninhez (*f.*) sterility, barrenness.

maninho -nha (*adj.*; *m.*) sterile, barren (land); (*m.pl.*) worldly goods of a childless decedent.

maniota (*f.*) shackle, fetter; hobble (for a horse).

manipanso (*m.*) fetish; mumbo jumbo; (*colloq.*) obese person.

manipresto -ta (*adj.*) clever with the hands.

manipueira, -puera (*f.*) the milky, poisonous juice of grated manioc. [After heating (to remove the poison) the juice serves as a food condiment.] Cf. TUCUPI.

manípula (*f.*) handle.

manipulação (*f.*) manipulation.

manipulador (*m.*) manipulator; handler; telegraph key.

manipular (*v.t.*) to manipulate, handle; to prepare with the hands.

manípulo (*m.*) a handful; a body of soldiers; (*Eccl.*) maniple.

maniqueísmo (*m.*) Manichaeism.

manirroto -ta (*adj.*) spendthrift.

manita (*adj.*; *m.,f.*) = MANETA; (*f.*) a little hand [= MÃOZINHA]; (*Chem.*) mannite, mannitol.

manitana (*f.*, *Chem.*) mannitan.

manitol (*m.*, *Chem.*) mannitol.

manitsauá (*m.,f.*) an Indian of the Manitsaua, a Tupian tribe on the Manitsáuamirim River, a left tributary of the upper Xingu River in Mato Grosso; (*adj.*) pert. to or designating this tribe.

maniva (*f.*, *Bot.*) the common cassava (*Manihot esculenta*), or a cutting of it for planting; c.a. MANIVEIRA.

manivela (*f.*) handle; crank.

manivelar (*v.i.*) to crank.

manja (*f.*) act of eating; eats; hide-and-seek.

manjadoura (*f.*) = MANJEDOURA.

manjaléu (*m.*) bogy, bugbear, hobgoblin.

manjangom[b]e (*m.*) = MARIA-GOMES.

manjar (*v.t.*) to eat [= COMER]; (*m.*) food; tidbit, delicacy.—-branco, blancmange.

manjedoura (*f.*) manger, trough. Var. MANJEDOIRA.

manjericão (*m.*, *Bot.*) basil (*Ocimum*).—-de-ceilão, East Indies basil (*O. gratissimum*).—-de-môlho, sweet basil (*O. basilicum*) c.a. MANJERICÃO-GRANDE, MANJERICÃO-DOS-COZINHEIROS, ALFAVACA-CHEIROSA.—-maior-anisado, a variety of sweet basil (*O. basilicum anisatum*).—-menor, or—-ordinário, the least basil (*O. minimum*).

manjerioba (*m.*) the coffee senna (*Cassia occidentalis*), c.a. FEDEGOSO-VERDADEIRO.—-grande = DARTRIAL.

manjerona (*f.*, *Bot.*) sweet marjoram (*Marjorana hortensis*).

manjuba (*f.*) food; (*slang*) salary; tip; school of small fish; a sand smelt (*Menidia brasiliensis*), c.a. ALETRIA, PITITINGA, PIPITINGA.

mano -na (*adj.*) of friends, intimate, inseparable; (*m.*, *colloq.*) short for IRMÃO (brother); pal; also = MÃO.

manobra (*f.*) maneuver; handling; ruse; switching (of railroad cars).—-protelatória, a delaying tactic.

manobrador (*m.*) handler.

manobrar (*v.t.*) to maneuver; to handle; to manipulate; to manage; to contrive; to wangle; to scheme; to switch (cars, railroad engines).

manobreiro (*m.*) maneuverer; one who manipulates (handles, manages); railroad switchman.
manoca (*f.*) a hand (bundle) of tobacco leaves tied together.
manógrafo (*m., Engin.*) manograph.
manômetro (*m.*) pressure gauge, manometer.—**metálico de Bourdon**, Bourdon gauge.
manopé-da-praia (*m.*) a nitta tree (*Parkia discolor*), c.a. JIPOÚBA.
manopla (*f.*) steel gauntlet; coachman's whip; (*colloq.*) huge hand.
manose (*f., Chem.*) mannose.
manotaço (*m.*) a slap; pawing (by a horse).
manotear (*v.t.,v.i.*) to grab (something); of a horse, to paw.
manquecer (*v.i.*) to grow lame.
manqueira (*f.*) lameness; limping; limp, hobble.
manquejante (*adj.*) hobbling.
manquejar (*v.i.*) to limp, hobble; to falter.
manquetear, manquitar (*v.*) = COXEAR.
manquitô, manquitola (*adj.; m.,f., colloq.*) lame (person); = COXO.
mansão (*m.*) mansion.
mansarda (*f.*) mansard roof, curb roof.
mansarrão -rona (*adj.; m.,f.*) meek, mild (person).
mansidão (*m.*) tameness; meekness, mildness, gentleness.
mansinho (*adv.*) de—, quietly, softly, gently.
manso -sa (*adj.*) tame, gentle; docile, domesticated; meek, mild; (*m.*) a slow-moving stretch of river; a greenhorn rubber tapper; (*adv.*) quietly, slowly.—**de palavras**, soft-spoken.—**e manso**, slowly, little by little. **de**—, quietly, gently.
mansozinho (*adv.*) very quietly; very softly.
mansuetude (*f.*) = MANSIDÃO.
manta (*f.*) manta; cloak, wrap; blanket; neckerchief; saddle blanket; a furrow for planting cuttings; forest litter; school of fish; a slab of meat, esp. sun-dried.—**de retalhos**, patch quilt.—**de toucinho**, a flitch (slab) of bacon.—**espanhola**, or **alentejana**, a poncho. **pintar a**—, to raise Cain. **tomar uma**—, to get "taken" in a deal.
mantear (*v.t.*) to toss (someone) in a blanket; to trick, cheat someone (in a deal); to cut up (a beef steer); (*v.i.*) to make furrows for plant cuttings.
manteiga (*f.*) butter; in Amazonia, any edible oil or fat; a kind of bean; (*colloq.*) flattery; (*slang*) handicap given in a contest.—**de cacau**, cacao, or cocoa, butter.—**de porco**, lard.—**derretida**, a cry baby.—**de tartaruga**, an oily paste made from the yolks of turtle eggs (in the Amazon region).—**de zinco**, zinc chloride, butter of zinc.—**fresca**, sweet (saltless) butter.—**em venta de gato**, or **em focinho de cachorro**, (*colloq.*) fig., something evanescent.
manteigaria (*f.*) butter store or factory.
manteigoso -sa (*adj.*) buttery; butterlike.
manteigueiro -ra (*adj.*) fond of butter; (*m.*) butter manufacturer; (*f.*) butter dish.
manteiguento -ta (*adj.*) = MANTEIGOSO.
mantel [-téis] (*m.*) altar cloth; table cloth.
mantelete [lê] (*m.*) mantelet; (*Milit.*) manta; (*R.C.Ch.*) mantelletta.
mantém (*m.*) tablecloth [= TOALHA DE MESA].
mantença (*f.*) maintenance.
mantenedor -dora (*adj.*) maintaining, sustaining, supporting; (*m.,f.*) maintainer, supporter; defender; champion.
manter [78] (*v.t.*) to maintain, sustain, support; to uphold; to keep up; to provide food for; to hold, keep.—**em vigor**, to keep in force.—**palavra**, to keep one's word.—**pé firme**, to stand fast; to stand one's ground.—**segrêdo**, to keep a secret.—**-se afastado**, to stand aloof.—**-se de esperanças**, to live on hopes.—**-se firme**, to stand firm.
mantéu (*m.*) monk's cloak; neck ruff; underskirt.
manteúdo -da (*adj.*) maintained; well-preserved. **amante teúda e**—, a kept mistress.
mantídeos (*m.pl.*) a family (*Mantidae*) of carnivorous insects, typified by the praying mantis.
mantilha (*f.*) mantilla, head scarf.
mantimento (*m.*) maintenance, support; sustenance; food; (*pl.*) groceries; victuals.—**de-araponga**, (*Bot.*) an eugenia (*E. adstringens*).
mantissa (*f., Math.*) mantissa.
manto (*m.*) mantle; cloak; veil; mantle of a bird; mantle of a mollusk.—**do-diabo**, kind of wild lily.
mantô (*m.*) manteau, mantle, cloak.

manual (*adj.*) manual; (*m.*) manual, handbook.
manúbrio (*m., Anat.*) manubrium.
Manuel (*m.*) Manuel; Emanuel; Emmanuel. [*not cap.*]— **-de-abreu**, or **-de-breu**, a kind of bee.—**magro**, a stick insect, c.a. MANÉ-MAGRO.
manuelino -na (*adj.*) designating a style of architecture which flourished in Portugal during the reign of D. Manuel I (1495–1521).
manufator -tora (*m.,f.*) manufacturer; (*adj.*) of or pert. to manufacturing.
manufatura (*f.*) manufacture; manufactory.
manufaturar (*v.t.*) to manufacture.
manufatureiro -ra (*adj.*) of or pert. to manufacture.
manuleio (*m., colloq.*) a political deal.
manumissão (*f.*) manumission.
manumisso (*m.*), **-sa** (*f.*) a freed slave.
manumissor -sora (*m.,f.*) manumitter.
manumitir (*v.t.*) to manumit, free (a slave).
manuscrever [44] (*v.t.*) to write by hand.
manuscrito -ta (*adj.*) handwritten; (*m.*) a manuscript.
manuseação (*f.*) **manuseamento, manuseio** (*m.*) handling, touching; thumbing, leafing (of the pages of a book). **de fácil manuseio**, easy to handle.
manusear (*v.t.*) to handle; to leaf through (a book).
manutenção (*f.*) maintenance, support; upkeep.
manutenível (*adj.*) maintainable.
manutérgio (*m., Eccl.*) a towel or napkin.
manzanilha (*f.*) = MANCENILHA.
manzanzar (*v.i.*) = MAZANZAR.
manzorra [ô] (*f.*) huge hand.
mão [*pl.* **mãos**] (*f.*) hand; paw; forefoot; claw; fig., power, control; first hand (in a game); coat (of paint, etc.); round (of cards); a handful (of something); right or left side (of a street); pestle; fig., help, a helping hand; handle (of a tool); fig., skill, execution.—**aberta**, (*m.,f.*) openhanded person; spendthrift; friendly hand.—**amiga**, friendly hand.—**certa**, or **certeira**, sure hand.—**cheia**, a handful (of anything). [**de mão-cheia**, crackerjack, tops, first-rate. **a mãos-cheias**, by the handful.]—**curta**, a brocket or small deer (*Mazama rufina*), c.a. BORORÓ, CAMOCICA.—**de almofariz**, pestle.—**de-branco**, a herblily (*Alstroemeria amazonica*).—**de-cabelo**, a hobgoblin whose hands are made of long hair.—**de ferro**, iron hand, iron fist.—**definado**, miser, closefisted person, c.a. MÃO-DE-LEITÃO.—**-de-gato**, zebrawood (*Connarus erinthus*).—**de linho**, a bundle of twelve bunches of flax ready for spinning.—**-de-manteiga**, butterfingers.—**de mestre**, master hand.—**de-obra**, hand labor; labor cost; handiwork; workmanship.—**de-onça**, an epiphytic woody vine of genus *Marcgravia*.—**de-padre**, an idler.—**de papel**, a quire of paper.—**de pilão**, pestle.—**de regador**, rose of a water sprinkler.—**-de-sêda**, or—**de-veludo**, a careful hand; a gentle hand, as of a pilot skilled in take-offs and landings.—**firme**, a firm hand; a steady hand.—**francêsa**, bracket, angle brace.—**furada**, a spendthrift.—**morta**, (*Law*) mortmain, inalienable ownership (of lands, etc.).—**pelada**, a crab-eating raccoon (*Procyon cancrivorous*).—**pendente**, a bribe.—**posta**, prejudice; something set aside for a proper occasion; a handshake in agreement on something. Cf. MÃOS POSTAS.—**quadra**, an open or extended hand.—**s à obra!** Let's get to work!—**s ao alto!** Hands up!—**s-atadas**, a helpless person.—**s de anéis**, dainty hands.—**s de fada**, fairy (clever) hands (as of an expert seamstress).—**s-de-sapo**, clammy hands; (*Bot.*) a water primrose, c.a. CRUZ-DE-MALTA.—**s-largas**, a generous, openhanded person.—**s limpas**, clean hands (lit. & fig.).—**s postas**, hands raised in supplication or prayer. Cf. MÃO-POSTA.—**s-rotas**, a spendthrift.—**tenente**, or—**tente**, used in the expression: **à mão-tenente**: pointblank; forcefully.—**travessa**, the width of a hand (used as a measure). **a**—, or **à**—, by hand; handy; at hand; near by. **a—armada**, by armed force. **à-direita** (esquerda), on the right (left) [hand]. **abrir—de**, to release, forego, let go; to desist; to relinquish (a privilege or right). **abrir as—s**, to be open-handed; to accept a bribe. **acertar a**—, (*slang*) to make a killing (at gambling); to hit the jackpot. **andar com as—s** (or **de—s**) **nos bolsos**, to have idle hands. **andar nas**, or **passar pelas,—s de todo o mundo**, of a woman, to be promiscuous. **apêrto de**—, hand clasp, handshake. **às—s cheias**, prodigally. **assentar a**—, to gain skill. **assentar a—em alguém**, to strike someone with the fist. **boa—**, handiness, deftness. **bôjo da**—, hollow of the hand. **com a faca e o queijo na**—, in complete control; in a position to help (oneself

or others). **com a**—na consciência, with a clear conscience. **com ambas as**—s, with both hands. **com as**—s abanando, empty-handed. **com a(s)**—(s) na massa, actively engaged in the task of the moment; (lit., kneading dough); red-handed (caught in the act). **com**—de gato, underhandedly. Da—à bôca se perde a sopa, There's many a slip twixt the cup and the lip. **dar a**—, to put out one's hand; to offer a helping hand. **dar a**—à palmatória, to admit one's mistake; to eat crow. **dar de**—, to reject out of hand; to forsake. **dar u'a**—, to lend a hand. **de**—beijada, gratuitously, free for nothing, on a silver platter. **de**—cheia, of the best, top-flight, first-rate, crackerjack. **de**—s dadas, hand-in-hand; holding hands. **de**—em—, from hand to hand; from one to another. **de chapéu na**—, with hat in hand. **de**, or **em**, **primeira**—, first hand, new. [Comprei meu carro em primeira mão, I was the first owner of this car.] **de**, or **em**, **segunda**—, secondhand. **em**—s, in one's possession. [Em mãos a sua carta de 2 dêste mês, Your letter of the 2nd is at hand.] **em suas**—s, in your hands. **entregar a** (or à)—, to deliver by hand. **Está em boas**—s, He (she, it) is in good hands. **estender a**—, to put out one's hand. **feito a**—, handmade. **feito por**—de mestre, made (done) by a master-hand. **ir contra a**—, to go against the traffic (on the wrong side of the street). [Estar na contra—, to be on the wrong side of the street.] **ir na** (or pela)—, to stay on the right side, keep to the right. **lançar**—de, to lay hold of. **lavar as**—s de, or **lavar as**—s como Pilatos, to wash one's hands (of a matter). **levar pela**—, to lead (take) by the hand. **limpo de**—s, honorable, upright. **Mais vale um pássaro na**—que dois voando, A bird in the hand is worth two in the bush. **meter a**—em cumbuca, to fall for a gag or swindle. **meter os pés pelas**—s, to get mixed up in one's remarks; to put one's foot in one's mouth. **não ter**—s a medir, to have one's hands full. **nem à**—de Deus Padre, under no conditions whatever; absolutely not. **passar a**—em, to lift (steal) something; to run one's hand over something; to rub something. **passar a**—pela cabeça de alguém, to condone another's fault. **pedir a**—de, to ask the hand of (in marriage). **pôr a**—no fogo por alguém, to vouch for someone, swear to his integrity. **pôr as**—s em, to lay (violent) hands on. **pôr**, (or **meter**)—s à obra, to set to work (with a will). **rua de**—única, a one-way street. **ter**—leve, to be light-fingered; to be quick to raise one's hand (in anger). **ter**—mole (or, **estar de mão mole**, or **estar com a mão mole**), to be clumsy; to drop things easily. **ter entre**—s, to be working on (something), to have (something) in hand. **ter na**—, to have (something) in possession, in one's hand. **vir às**—s de, to fall into (someone's) hands.

Maomé (m.) Mahomet; Mohammed; Muhammad; [= Mafoma].

maometano -na (adj.; m.,f.) Mohammedan.

mãozada (f.) tight hand clasp; a handful (of anything).

mãozinha (f.) a small hand.—-preta, a hobgoblin.

mãozudo -da (adj.) big-handed.

mapa (m.) map, chart.—-múndi, a world map.

mapá, mapão (m., Bot.) a manchineel (Hippomane brasiliensis).

mapará (m., Zool.) a caribe (Serrasalmo denticulatus).

maparajura (f.) a bulletwood (Mimusops).

mapareíba (f.) = MANGUE-VERMELHO.

mapiação, mapiagem (f.) idle talk.

mapiar (v.i.) to chatter, talk at random.

mapinguari [rí] (m.) a legendary giant of Amazon folklore who wears an armor of turtle shells.

mapixi [xí] (m.) a myrtle of genus Myrcia.

mapoão (m.) a plant used by Indians to poison arrows.

mapoteca (f.) a map collection.

mapuá (m., Bot.) a cyclanthus (C. bipartitus).

mapurá (m.) = MAPARÁ.

maq. = MAQUINISTA (locomotive engineer; steamship engineer).

maqueira (f.) a sleeping hammock made from tucum fiber.

maqueiro (m.) a litter-bearer.

maqueta [ê] (f.) in sculpture, small rough model; mock-up.

maquia (f.) miller's toll; (colloq.) money; profit.

maquiavélico -ca (adj.) Machiavellian; wily, astute.

maquiçapa (m.) = COATÁ-BRANCO.

maquil[h]agem (f.) facial makeup. (French maquillage)

maquil[h]ar-se (v.r.) to put on make-up; to paint the face. [French se maquiller].

máquina (f.) machine; engine; mill; machine tool; puppet; (colloq.) automobile.—a vapor, steam engine.—aritmética, calculating machine.—caça-níqueis, slot machine.—centrífuga, a centrifuge.—composta, a composite machine.—de alta pressão, high-pressure steam engine.—de Atwood, (Physics) Atwood's machine.—de baixa pressão, low-pressure steam engine.—de Brinell, Brinell (hardness testing) machine.—de brocar, drilling mill.—de calcular, calculating machine.—de cereais, grain mill.—de cilíndro, cylinder (printing) press.—de compor, typesetting machine.—de compressão, compressor.—de comutação, (Elec.) commutator.—de contabilidade, bookkeeping machine; calculating machine.—de corrente alternada, (Elec.) alternator; a machine using A.C.—de corrente contínua, (Elec.) a machine using direct current.—de corrugar, a corrugator (for steel sheets).—de cortar cabelo, hair clippers.—de costura, sewing machine.—de endereçar, addressing machine.—de envelopes, an envelope-making machine.—de escrever, typewriter.—de furar, boring mill.—de gêlo, ice-making machine.—de limar, grinder.—de picotar, paper perforator,—de platina, platen (printing) press.—de rebitar, rivetting machine.—de solda elétrica, electric welder.—de soldar, welding machine.—de somar, adding machine.—de vapor, steam engine.—de vender, vending machine.—do estado, the machinery of government.—duplicadora, duplicator.—elétrica, electric motor, dynamo.—elevatória, a hoist, crane, or other lifting device.—endiabrada, or infernal, infernal machine.—ferramenta, machine tool.—fotográfica, or de retratos, camera.—Fourdrinier, a Fourdrinier (papermaking) machine.—hectográfica, a hectograph.—hidráulica, any hydraulic machine.—horizontal, horizontal motor.—Jordan, a Jordan (pulp-refining) machine.—pneumática, pneumatic pump; any machine operated by compressed air.—rotativa, rotary (printing) press.—síncrona, (Elec.) synchronous machine.—térmica, a thermotor; a heat engine. escrever à—, to typewrite. feito à (or a)—, machine-made.

maquinação (f.) machination; collusion.

maquinador -dora (adj.; m.,f.) plotting, scheming, designing (person).

maquinal (adj.) pert. to machinery; mechanical, automatic; perfunctory.

maquinar (v.t.) to machinate, contrive, scheme, plot (contra, against); to concoct, hatch (a plot).

maquinaria (f.) machinery; machines collectively.—de agricultura, farm machinery.

maquiné-do-mato (m.) = CIPÓ-DE-LEITE.

maquineta [ê] (f.) small glass frame or case for displaying holy objects.

maquinismo (m.) machinery, mechanism; stage apparatus.

maquinista (m.,f.) machinist; engine driver; locomotive engineer; machine-tool operator; stage engineer.

mar (m.) sea, ocean; fig., vast expanse.—alto, or largo, high seas, open sea.—banzeiro, an ocean with lazy swells.—cavado, or encapelado, or encrespado, a choppy sea, with white caps.—chão, or—de leite, smooth sea.—crêspo, or levantado, or picado, choppy, rough sea.—de Sargaço, Sargasso Sea.—de rosas, smooth sea; easy sailing.—interior, inland sea.—roleiro, a sea with rolling waves.—travêsso, cross sea. água do—, sea (salt) water. banho de—, sea-bathing. caír no—, to fall overboard. braço de—, arm of the sea. de—, totally. em alto (pleno)—, on the high seas. estrêla-do—, starfish. fazer muito—, to run high [the waves]. fazer-se ao—, to put out to sea. homem ao—! man overboard! homem do—, seafaring man. lançar (deitar, jogar) água no—, to carry coals to Newcastle. largar para o—, to put out to sea. lobo do—, sea dog, old salt. no fundo do—, at the bottom of the ocean. ouriço do—, sea urchin. por—e por terra, by sea and by land. pôrto de—, sea port.

mará (f.) a pole, one used to propel a boat; (Zool.) the Patagonian cavy (Dolichotys patagonica).

marabá (m.) offspring of a white man and Indian woman; waif; child of unknown parentage.

marabu [ú] (m.) a marabou stork of the genus Leptoptilus, esp. the African species (L. crumeniferus); also a stork of the genus Ciconia; a Marabout (Mohammedan hermit) or his mosque, c.a. MARABUTO; (pl.) the soft under-tail and under-wing coverts of the stork, used in millinery.

marabumbo (m.) the saury, a slender long-beaked fish (Scombresox saurus) related to the flying fishes.

marabuto (*m.*) = MARABU (hermit).
maracá (*m.*) a gourd rattle; (*Bot.*) = COQUILHO (a canna); (*f.*) rattlesnake [= CASCAVEL].
maracajá (*m.*) a wild cat (*Felis pardalis*), c.a. JAGUARTI-RICA.—**-mirim** or —**-pintado** = GATO-DO-MATO-PINTADO.
maracanã (*f.*, *Zool.*) any of various small macaws (c.a. ARARINHA), esp. the noble macaw (*Diopsittaca nobilis*) and the red-and-blue macaw (*Ara maracana*).—**-açu**, the Brazilian macaw (*Ara severa*), and the red-bellied macaw (*Orthopsittaca manilata*).—**-guaçu** = ANACÃ.
maracatu [ú] (*m.*) a Brazilian dance of African origin; in Pernambuco, a group of street-dancing merrymakers at Carnival time.
maracauim (*m.*) a fiddler crab (*Uca*), c.a. CHAMA-MARÉ.
maracotão (*m.*) = MELOCOTÃO.
maracuguara (*m.*) = CANGULO.
maracujá (*m.*) any of various passionflowers (*Passiflora*), or their fruit.—**-açu**,—**-de-caiena**,—**-mamão**,—**-melão**, are all the giant granadilla (*Passiflora quandrangularis*), c.a. GRANADILHA.—**-amarelo**, or—**-grande**, the wingstem passionflower (*P. alata*).—**-branco**, white passionflower (*P. alba*, *P. capsularis*).—**-de-alho**, or—**-de-cobra**, garlic passionflower (*P. alliacea*).—**-de-estalo**, or—**-de-mochila**, maypop passionflower (*P. incarnata*, *P. involucrata*).—**-de-estrada**, the Tagua passionflower (*P. foetida*).—**-poranga**, scarlet passionflower (*P. coccinea*). —**-prêto**,—**-mirim**,—**-de-garapa**,—**-suspiro**,—**-de-três-pernas**, are all the purple granadilla or passionfruit (*P. edulis*).—**-vermelho**, red passionflower (*P. rubra*).
maracujàzeiro (*m.*) any passionflower vine.
marafona (*f.*) rag doll; harridan, wench, hussy, prostitute.
maragota (*f.*, *Zool.*) the European wrasse (*Labrus sp.*), c.a. MARGOTA.
marajá (*m.*) maharaja; (*f.*) any spiny-club palm (*Bactris*).
marajoara (*adj.*) of or pert. to the Brazilian island of Marajó; designating a certain style of art and architecture typical of that island; (*m.,f.*) a native of the same; (*m.*) a northeast wind.
marambaia (*m.*, *slang*) dry-land sailor.
maranha (*f.*) tangled skein; snarl; fig., plot, scheme.
maranhão (*m.*) = FLAMENGO.
maranhense (*adj.*) of or pert. to the Brazilian state of Maranhão; (*m.,f.*) a native or inhabitant thereof.
maranta (*f.*) the arrowroot (*Maranta*).
marantáceo -cea (*adj.; Bot.*) marantaceous; (*f.,pl.*) the Marantaceae (arrowroot family).
marapajuba (*f.*) a bullet wood (*Mimusops*).
marapuã (*m.*, *Bot.*) the Orinoco simaruba (*Simaruba amara*), c.a. MARUPÁ.
marasca (*f.*) marasca sour cherry (*Prunus cerasus marasca*) [from which maraschino is made].
marasmático (*adj.; Med.*) marasmic.
marasmo (*m.*, *Med.*) marasmus, a wasting away; fig., apathy, melancholy.
marasquino (*m.*) maraschino.
maratiáceo -cea (*adj.; Bot.*) marattiaceous; (*f.*, *pl.*) the Marattiaceae (giant ferns).
maratona (*f.*) marathon race.
maratro (*m. Bot.*) fennel [= FUNCHO].
marau (*m.*) wretch, rascal.
maravalhas (*f.*, *pl.*) wood chips, shavings; fig., trifles.
maravilha (*f.*) marvel, wonder; kind of small meat pie. **às mil—s**, wonderfully, marvelously; (*Bot.*) the common four-o'clock (*Mirabilis jalapa*), c.a. BONINA, BOAS-NOITES.
maravilhar (*v.t.*) to amaze, astonish, dazzle; (*v.r.*) to marvel, wonder (**de**, **at**).
maravilhoso -sa (*adj.*) marvellous, wonderful, amazing; (*m.*) something marvellous.
marca (*f.*) mark; make (brand); stamp, brand; sign, token; label, badge; trace; eminence, distinction; score; blaze (on a tree).—**barbante**, cheap, of poor quality, referring esp. to beer.—**comercial** (or—**de fábrica**), trade mark.—**d'água**, watermark [= FILIGRANA].—**de contraste**, hallmark. **de—maior**, outsized; uncommon.
marcação (*f.*) marking; demarcation; scoring; cattle branding; action on stage.
marcado -da (*adj.*) marked; distinct; labeled; tagged.
marcador -dora (*adj.*) marking; (*m.*) marker; scoreboard; a piece of cross-stitch canvas (on which to embroider a sampler).
marca-grande (*m.*) wealthy plantation owner.
marçano (*m.*) apprentice store clerk; by ext., any beginner.

marcante (*adj.*) marking; remarkable; outstanding.
marca-pés (*m.*) kind of earth employed in the defecation of sugar.
marcar (*v.t.*) to mark, label, earmark; to stamp, brand; to indicate, point out; to keep an eye on (someone); to register; to cross stitch.—**a fogo**, to brand with a hot iron.—**dia**, to agree on (set) a date.—**encontro** (or—**lugar e hora**), to agree to meet at a certain time and place.—**o compasso**, to keep score.—**passo**, to mark time.—**um ponto**, to score a point.—**uma consulta**, to make an appointment (with the doctor).—**uma entrevista**, to make an appointment for interview.
marcassita (*f.*, *Min.*) marcasite, white iron pyrites.
marcela (*f.*) = MACELA.
marcenaria (*f.*) cabinetmaking; a cabinetmaker's shop or his handiwork.
marceneiro (*m.*) a cabinetmaker or joiner.
marcescente (*adj.*) that withers; (*Bot.*) marcescent.
marcha (*f.*) march; gait, pace, step; advance, course, progression; (*Music*) military march.—**à-ré**, march to the rear; (*Autom.*) reverse gear.—**forçada**, forced march.—**fúnebre**, funeral march.—**normal**, cruising speed.—**surda**, muffled steps. **abrir a—**, to lead the way. **em—**, on the march. **pôr-se em—**, to start off.
marchadeira, fem. of MARCHADOR.
marchador (*adj.*) marching; light-stepping [horse]; (*m.*, colloq.) person who pays the expenses, who picks up the tab.
marchantaria, -teria (*f.*) beef or cattle business.
marchante (*m.*) supplier of beef cattle; butcher; (*slang*) angel (person of wealth who is easily fleeced); keeper of a mistress who is unfaithful to him.
marchântia (*f.*, *Bot.*) the common liverwort (*Marchantia polymorpha*).
marchantiáceas (*f.,pl.*, *Bot.*) a family (*Marchantiaceae*) of liverworts and hepatics.
marchar (*v.i.*) to march, step, tramp, walk; to move forward, go ahead; (*colloq.*) to pay the bill for others. —**sem cadência**, to break step.
marche-marche (*m.*, *Milit.*) quick step.
marchetado -da (*adj.*) inlaid; mottled; (*m.*) inlay work.
marchetar (*v.t.*) to inlay; to insert; to dot, stud (with color, gold, ornaments, etc.).
marchetaria (*f.*) the art or process of marquetry; an example of such work; parquetry.
marchête (*m.*) a piece of material (wood, ivory, etc.) to be inlaid.
marcheteiro (*m.*) one skilled in marquetry or inlay work; inlayer.
marchinha (*f.*) a lively carnival tune and dance.
Márcia (*f.*) Marcia.
marcial (*adj.*) martial, warlike.
marciano -na, marciático -ca (*adj.*) Martian.
márcio -cia (*adj.*) = MARCIAL.
marco (*m.*) boundary mark; landmark; window frame, door frame; mark (coin); [*cap.*] Mark.—**fontenário**, drinking fountain.—**miliário**, a milliary column (in ancient Rome); fig., a milestone in history.—**quilométrico**, a post marking distance in kilometers.—**zero**, or—**número um**, starting point.
março (*m.*) month of March.
Marcos (*m.*) Marcus.
Mardoqueu (*m.*) Mordecai.
maré (*f.*) tide; course of events; opportunity.—**alta**, or **cheia**, high tide.—**baixa**, or **vazia**, low tide.—**de quadratura**, or **de quarto**, neap tide.—**de rosas**, a tide of good fortune.—**de sizígia**, spring tide.—**descendente**, a dropping tide.—**de sorte**, a wave of good fortune; a bonanza. —**me-leva**,—**me-traz**, a wishy-washy person.—**montante**, rising tide. **aproveitar a—**, to ride the tide; to seize the opportunity. **derivar com o movimento da—**, to drift with the tide. **estar de (boa)—**, to be well-disposed (toward doing something). **ir**, or **recuar, contra a—**, to go against the tide.
mareado -da (*adj.*) seasick; (*colloq.*) tipsy.
mareagem (*f.*) navigation; ship's course.
mareante (*adj.*) navigating; (*m.*) mariner.
marear (*v.t.*) to sail, steer; to rig sails; to make seasick; to tarnish; (*v.i.*) to become seasick; to sail; to navigate; (*v.r.*) to become tarnished; to steer one's course (**por**, by). **agulha de—**, compass. **carta de—**, marine map.
marechal (*m.*) marshal.—**de campo**, field marshal.
marégrafo (*m.*) = MAREÓGRAFO.
mareiro -ra (*adj.*) of wind, from the ocean; of weather,

good for sailing; (*m.*) an ocean wind.

marejada (*f.*) surging, billowing (of waves).

marejamento (*m.*) suffusion.

marejar (*v.t.*) to exude; (*v.i.*) to flow out; to ooze out; (*v.r.*) of eyes, to become tear-filled. **olhos marejados,** eyes brimming with tears.

maremático –ca (*adj.*) maremmatic, miasmatic.

marêmetro (*m.*) = MAREÔMETRO.

maremoto (*m.*) submarine earthquake.

marenina (*f.*) marennin. [*Webster:* "A light-blue or greenish pigment found sometimes in oysters, etc."]

mareógrafo, mareômetro (*m.*) tide gauge.

maresia (*f.*) the strong sea-smell when the tide is out; "(1) a small river wave; (2) slightly troubled waters; (3) ripples in the current." [*GBAT*]

mareta [ê] (*f.*) a small wave.

marfar (*v.t.*) to annoy; to infuriate; to offend; to bore.

marfim (*m.*) ivory.——**vegetal,** the So. Amer. ivory palm (*Phytelephas macrocarpa*), c.a. JARINA, CABONEGRO, TAGUÁ. [This species is the source of the ivory nut of commerce (= COROZO), and should not be confused with the Polynesian ivorynut palm (*Metroxylon amicarum*) which is the source of Tahiti nuts.] **deixar correr o——,** to be unconcerned, unworried (about things as they are or may be).

marga (*f.*) marl; loam.

margagem, margação (*f.*) operation of fertilizing or dressing (the soil) with marl.

marganheira (*f.*) the moleplant or caper euphorbia (*E. lathyrus*).

margarato (*m., Chem.*) margarate [acid].

margárico –ca (*adj.; Chem.*) margaric.

margar (*v.t.*) to marl (the soil).

margarida (*f.*) marguerite, daisy; [*cap.*] Margaret; Margueritte.——**amarela,** crown daisy (*Chrysanthemum coronarium*).——**anual,** or——**do-campo,** Spanish daisy (*Bellis annua*).——**dos-campos,** ox-eye daisy (*Chrysanthemum leucanthemum*),——**rasteira,** English daisy (*Bellis perennis*), c.a. BELA-MARGARIDA.

margaridinha (*f.*) = CAPITÃO-DE-SALA (plant); BELA-MARGARIDA (English daisy).

margarina (*f.*) margarine, oleomargarine; (*Chem.*) margarin.

margarita (*f.*) a pearl; a pearl oyster; (*Min.*) margarite, calcium mica; (*Bot.*) a daisy.

margaritáceo –cea (*adj.*) margaritaceous, pearly.

margarite (*f., Min.*) margarite.

margaritífero –ra (*adj.*) pearl-bearing.

margarodite (*f., Min.*) margarodite.

margeante (*adj.*) bordering (on).

margear (*v.t.,v.i.*) to border (on); to follow the border of; to run alongside of; to skirt.

margem (*f.*) margin, border, edge; brink; shore, river bank. **à——,** to one side, aside. **à——de,** alongside (of), near. **dar——,** to afford opportunity for. **deitar,** or **lançar, à——,** to cast aside.

marginado –da (*adj.*) marginate.

marginador (*m.*) feeder (printing press).

marginal (*adj.*) marginal.

marginar (*v.i.*) to skirt, border; to make marginal notes.

marginela (*f.*) a genus (*Marginella*) of small marine snails.

margoso –sa (*adj.*) marly, marlaceous; loamy.

margota (*f.*) = MARAGOTA.

margueira (*f.*) marl bed, loam bed.

mari [í] (*m.*) = ANGELIM-DE-ESPINHO.

Maria (*f.*) Maria; Mary; Marie.

maria-branca (*f.*) = POMBINHA-DAS-ALMAS.

maria-caraíba (*f.*) = ALMA-DE-GATO.

maria-cavalheira (*f.*) the fierce or southern flycatcher (*Myiarchus f. ferox*).

maria-com-a-vovó (*f.*) a bird—the Pará spine-tail (*Synallaxis rutilans omissa*).

maria-congueira (*f.*) hide-and-seek (game).

maria-da-toca (*f.*) = BABOSA.

maria-de-barro (*f.*) = AMASSA-BARRO; JOÃO-DE-BARRO.

maria-é-dia (*f.*) a bird—yellow-bellied elaenia (*Elaenia·f. flavogaster*), c.a. MARIA-JÁ-É-DIA, MAREDEDIA, MARIDO-É-DIA, BEM-TE-VI-MIÚDO, TOPETUDA; the varied flycatcher (*Empidonomus v. varius*), c.a. PEITICA, BEM-TE-VIZINHO; also = POMBINHA-DAS-ALMAS; the rufous-bellied wren (*Thryothorus leucotis rufiventris*), c.a. MARIA-JÁ-É-DIA.

maria-faceira (*f.*) the whistling heron (*Syrigma sibilatrix*).

maria-fede (*f.*) = MARITACACA.

maria-fia (*f.*) = BICO-DE-CEGONHA.

maria-gomes (*f.*) the panicled fameflower (*Talinum paniculatum*), c.a. JOÃO-GOMES, BREDO-MANJANGOME, MANJANGOMBE, MARIA[N]GOMBE, LÍNGUA-DE-VACA.

maria-já-é-dia (*f.*) = MARIA-É-DIA; POMBINHA-DAS-ALMAS.

maria-judia (*f.*) = TICO-TICO.

marial (*adj.*) Marian (of or pert. to the Virgin Mary).

marialita (*f., Min.*) marialite.

maria-macumbé (*f.*) hide-and-seek game [= MARIA-CONGUEIRA].

maria-mole (*f.*) any of various fishes; also = CAPIM-GOMOSO (a dayflower); also = SOCÔZINHO and ALCARAVÃO (herons); also = FÔLHA-REDONDA (a tree).

maria-mucanguê (*f.*) = MARIA-MACUMBÉ.

maria-mulata (*f.*) a bird—Vieillot's black tyrant (*Knipolegus nigerrimus*).

mariana (*f.*) see under MARIANO.

maria-nagô (*f.*) a ribbonfish (*Eques lanceolatus*); the cubbyu (*Eques acuminatus*).

marianeiro (*m.*) a nightshade (*Solanum fasciculatum*).

maria[n]gombe (*f.*) = MARIA-GOMES.

marianinha (*f.*) the white-bellied caique (*Pionites leucogaster*), c.a. PERIQUITO-D'ANTA; (*Bot.*) = ANDACA (a spiderwort) and CAPIM-GOMOSO (a dayflower).

marianismo (*m.*) Mariolatry.

mariano -na (*adj.*) Marian; (*cap., f.*) Marianna; Marianne; Marian; also [*not cap.*] a plant called MARIANEIRA or FRUTA-DE-SABIÁ.

maria-peidorreira (*f.*) = AÇUCENA-DO-MATO.

maria-pereira (*f.*) a rubiaceous tree (*Posoqueria macrocarpus*).

maria-preta (*f.*) a chastetree (*Vitex polygana* or *V. multinervis*), the latter c.a. GUABIROBA-BRAVA; the tropic ageratum (*A. conyzoides*), c.a. CATINGA-DE-BODE; a cordia (*C. curassavica*), c.a. CATINGA-DE-PRÊTO; the ringworm senna (*Cassia alata*), c.a. DARTRIAL; an ebony (*Maba inconstans*), c.a. FRUTA-DE-JACU-MACHO; a bird—the crested black tyrant (*Knipolegus lophotes*); also = CHOPIM, a cowbird.

maria-rita (*f.*) either of two social wasps: *Polistes versicolor* and *P. canadensis*, the latter c.a. MARIMBONDO-CABOCLO.

maria-rosa (*f.*) a syagrus palm (*S. macrocarpa*).

maria-sêca (*f.*) a stick insect, c.a. MANÉ-MAGRO.

mariato (*m., Naut.*) signalling flags (collectively).

maria-vai-com-as-outras (*m.,f.*) wishy-washy person.

maribondo (*m.*) = MARIMBONDO.

maricá (*m., Bot.*) a mamosa (*M. sepiaria*), c.a. ESPINHO-DE-MARICÁ.

maricas, maricão (*m.*) milksop, sissy, pantywaist, mollycoddle; effeminate man.

maricaua (*f., Bot.*) a nightshade (*Datura insignis*), c.a. TOÉ.

maridagem, maridança (*f.*) marriage; married life; harmony between two or more things.

maridar (*v.t.*) to marry (a woman to a man); (*v.r.*) to take a husband; to cling, twine (as a vine).

marididia (*f.*) = MARIA-É-DIA.

marido (*m.*) husband.——**é-dia** = MARIA-É-DIA (a bird).

Marieta (*f.*) Marietta.

Marilândia (*f.*) Maryland.

marimacho (*m.*) mannish-mannered woman; tomboy; a virago.

marimari [í] (*m., Bot.*) the pinkshower senna (*Cassia grandis*).

marimba (*f.*) marimba; (*slang*) an old, out-of-tune piano.

marimbá (*m.*) the silvery porgy (*Diplodus argenteus*), c.a. PINTO-NO-CABO.

marimbar (*v.i.*) to play the marimba; to win at MARIMBO; to trick, cheat.——**sem trunfo,** to be smart, clever.

marimbo (*m.*) a certain card game.

marimbondo (*m.*) a common collective term for the wasps.——**amoroso,** a social wasp (*Polybia occidentalis*) which works in bad weather.——**caboclo,** a social wasp (*Polistes canadensis*), c.a. MARIA-RITA, CABA-DA-IGREJA.——**caçador,** any of various spider wasps, such as the tarantula killer; c.a. VESPÃO, CAVALO-DO-CÃO.——**de-chapéu,** a paper wasp (*Aploica pallida*) whose nest resembles a hat, whence the name; c.a. BEIJUCABA, CABA-CEGA, BEIJUCABA, CABA-DE-LADRÃO, CABA-BEIJU.——**mangangá,** any bumblebee [= MANGANGÁ]. **mexer em cacho de——,** to stir up a hornet's nest. **Não mexa em casa** (or **ninho**) **de——,** Let sleeping dogs lie.

marimbu [ú] (*m.*) river marshland; mud flat.

marimonda (*m.*) a spider monkey (*Ateles*).

marinaresca (*f.*) sailors' chantey.
maringá (*adj.*) having black spots [cows, goats].
marinas (*f. pl.*) marine plants.
marinha (*f.*) see under MARINHO.
marinhagem (*f.*) ship's crew; seamanship.
marinhar (*v.t.*) to sail (a ship); (*v.i.*) to climb or clamber (as a sailor).
marinharia (*f.*) sailor's lore, sailing as a tradition, etc. **têrmo de—**, nautical term.
marinheiro **-ra** (*adj.*) of or pert. to the sea and ships; seafaring; fond of the sea and of sailing; seaworthy; (*m.*) mariner; sailor, seaman; member of a crew; man in the navy; kind of small crabs having a squarish carapace; (*Bot.*) American muskwood (*Guarea trichilioides*), c.a. CARRAPETA.—**de água doce**, fresh-water sailor, landlubber.—**de primeira viagem**, tyro.
marinhista (*m.,f.*) seascapist.
marinho **-nha** (*adj.*) marine; (*f.*) marine; navy; naval service; salt bed; seashore; seascape.—**de guerra**, navy. **—mercante**, merchant marine. **arsenal de—**, navy yard. **guarda—**, midshipman.
Mário (*m.*) Marius.
mariola (*m.*) messenger, servant; scoundrel; a small block of sweet (candied) banana paste; (*adj.*) rascally.
mariolão (*m.*) an outright scoundrel.
mariólatra (*m.,f.*) mariolater.
mariolatria (*f.*) Mariolatry.
marionete (*f.*) marionette, puppet.
maripá (*m.*) = INAJÁ.
maripôsa (*f.*) moth or butterfly; (*Civil Eng.*) a horse-drawn earth scraper.
mariquice (*f.*) act or condition of a MARICAS.
mariquina (*f.*) = ACARIMA; MONO.
mariquinha (*f.*) a kitchen trivet; a fib; also = MONO.
mariquita (*f.*) trivet made of three sticks; the olive-backed warbler (*Compsothlypis p. pitiayumi*); also = CAMBACICA; a butterfly (*Heliconius eucrates*).
mariricó (*m.*, *Bot.*) Mexican trimeza (*T. lurida*), c.a. BARIRICÓ.—**bravo** = FALSO-TIRIRICA (a grass).
mariroba (*f.*, *Bot.*) a palm (*Syagrus macrocarpa*).
mariscadeira (*f.*) a woman vender of shellfish.
mariscador (*m.*) gatherer of shellfish; clam digger; "an experienced hunter or fisherman, attached in a professional capacity to BARRACÕES so as to insure a supply of fresh meat and fish." [*GBAT*]
mariscar (*v.t.,v.i.*) to gather shellfish; of birds, to hunt for worms and insects; of taxis, to cruise the streets, on the lookout for passengers; of a diamond prospector, to pick over abandoned gravel beds.—**no sêco**, to hunt (game) on dry land.
marisco (*m.*) any edible shellfish, esp. clams and mussels; a barnacle; a special tool for scooping out the meat of coconuts.—**faca**, a razor clam (*Solem ensis*).—**pedra**, a cockle (*Cardium edule*).—**tatu**, a piddock (burrowing clam).
marisqueiro **-ra** (*m.,f.*) one who gathers and/or sells shellfish; (*m.*) a kingfisher.
maritacaca, maritafede, maritataca (*f.*) = JARITACACA; CANGAMBÁ.
marital (*adj.*) marital.
mariticida (*f.*) mariticide (a woman who kills her husband).
mariticídio (*m.*) mariticide (the murder of a husband by his wife).
marítimo **-ma** (*adj.*) maritime, marine, naval; (*m.*) seafaring man; maritime worker. **rotas—s**, sea lanes.
marlota (*f.*) Moorish gown with hood.
marma (*f.*) marver (used in rolling or shaping hot glass).
marmanjo (*m.*) lubber; big, clumsy young man; a big boy; a grown man; a rascal.
marmatita (*f.*, *Min.*) marmatite.
marmelada (*f.*) quince marmalade; (*slang*) a snap, something "pretty soft"; a rake-off; a rigged contest; (*Bot.*) = GUARUMBÉ.—**de-cavalo**, a tickclover (*Desmodium*), c.a. CARRAPICHO.
marmeleiral (*f.*) quince orchard.
marmeleiro (*m.*, *Bot.*) quince (*Cydonia oblonga*).—**da-china**, Chinese flowering quince (*Chaenomeles sinensis*). —**dos-marmelos-molares**, Portuguese quince (*Cydonia oblonga lusitanica*), c.a. GAMBOEIRO.
marmelo (*m.*) fruit of the quince tree.—**bravo**, myrtle laurelcherry (*Prunus myrtifolia*), c.a. GINGEIRA-DA-TERRA.
marmita (*f.*) deep metal pot with lid; soldier's messkit;

lunch pail.—**de-gigante**, pothole (in river bed).—**de Papin**, a type of autoclave or pressure cooker.—**dos pensamentos**, (*colloq.*) one's noodle (head).
marmiteiro (*m.*, *colloq.*) a workman who carries a lunch pail; [in Brazil it implies an unskilled, low-wage worker].
marmolite (*f.*, *Min.*) marmolite.
marmoraria (*f.*) marble works.
marmorário **-ria** (*adj.*) marmoreal; (*m.*) marbler.
mármore (*m.*) marble; marblelike insensibility, indifference, coldness, etc.
marmorear (*v.t.*) to marbleize.
marmoreira (*f.*) marble quarry.
marmoreiro (*m.*) marble cutter.
marmóreo **-rea** (*adj.*) marblelike, marmoreal.
marmorista (*m.*) marbler [= MARMOREIRO].
marmorização (*f.*) marbleization.
marmorizar (*v.t.*) to marbleize.
marmota (*f.*) marmot, groundhog, woodchuck.
marmulano (*m.*) a jungleplum (*Sideroxylon marmulano*).
marna (*f.*) marl, loam [= MARGA].
marnoso **-sa** (*adj.*) marly [= MARGOSO].
marnota (*f.*) salt marsh; salt pan.
marnotagem (*f.*) salt industry.
marnoteiro, marnoto (*m.*) a worker in salt beds.
maro (*m.*, *Bot.*) cat-thyme germander (*Teucrium marum*).
maroma (*f.*) hawser; tight rope; house built on stilts (on a river bank).
maromba (*f.*) balancing pole; fig., precarious situation; fence-straddling; ferry cable; cattle raft; bunch of cattle; brick-making machine; "a substantial platform of logs or squared wood connected with the ground by an inclined plane on which flood-driven cattle can climb." [*GBAT*]
marombar (*v.i.*) to teeter-totter (as on a tightrope); to shirk, malinger; to waver, be undecided; to fence-straddle; to hinder or upset a deal for selfish reasons.
marombeiro **-ra** (*adj.*) cleverly flattering.
marombista (*adj.; m.,f.*) opportunist.
marosca (*f.*) trick, fraud, hoax.
marotagem (*f.*) rascality, scurrility; rabble.
marotear (*v.i.*) to lead a rascally life.
marotice (*f.*) a rascally act; rascality.
maroto **-ta** (*adj.*) rascally, knavish; naughty; lewd; (*m.,f.*) rascal, scoundrel, rogue.
marouço (*m.*) heavy sea; billow; (*pl.*) big waves, breakers.
marqueiro (*m.*) cattle brander.
marquês (*m.*) marquis.
marquesa [ê] (*f.*) marquise, marchioness; cane-bottomed settee; marquee (canopy); a glassed-in porch or sun-room.—**de-belas** = CIPÓ-DE-SAO-JOÃO (a plant).
marquesado (*m.*) marquisate.
marquesinha (*f.*) lady's sunshade; officer's field tent; a marquise or canopy extending over a station platform.
marquesota (*f.*, *Bot.*) the winged yam (*Dioscorea alata*).
marquise (*f.*, *Arch.*) marquise; marquee.
marra (*f.*) weeding hoe; sledge hammer; roadside ditch; tag (game); gap in a row of trees.
marrã (*f.*) young sow; fresh pork.
marrada (*f.*) butt (as of a goat).
marrafa (*f.*) curled forelock; lovelock; each side of the hair-parting line; side comb; flounce.
marralhar (*v.i.*) to insist obstinately (**com**, with; **em**, upon).
marralheiro **-ra** (*adj.*) insistent, obstinate.
marrano **-na** (*adj.*) excommunicated; unclean.
marrão (*m.*) weaned pig; sledge hammer; wild cattle.
marrar (*v.i.*) to butt (as a goat); to buck (as a horse); to strike with a sledge hammer.—**com**, to bump into, collide with.
marraxo (*m.*) playful old cat; large shark; fish peddler.
marreca (*f.*) the common name for any of numerous wild ducks, esp. of Nettion and Querquedula (teals) and Dendrocygna (tree ducks).—**apaí**, or—**do-pará** or —**piadeira**, or—**viúva** = IRERÊ (a tree duck).—**ananaí**, or—**dos-pés-encarnados** = ANANAÍ (a teal).—**assobiadeira**, or **-assoviadeira**, a whistling teal (*Nettion flavirostre*).—**cabocla**, or—**grande-do-marajó**, a black-bellied tree duck (*Dendrocygna autumnalis*).—**peba**, or —**caneleira**, the fulvous tree-duck (*Dendrocygna bicolor*).—**toucinho**, the Bahaman pintail (*Dafila b. bahamensis*).
marrecão (*m.*) the Orinoco goose (*Neochen jubata*); also, the rosy-billed duck (*Metopiana peposaca*).

marreco (*m.*) the European teal (*Nettion c. crecca*).—do-pará = IRERÊ (a tree duck).

marrequinha (*f.*) the masked duck (*Nomonyx dominicus*).

marrequinho (*m.*) the sun grebe (*Heliornis fulica*), c.a. IPEQUI.—do-campo, the gray teal (*Punanetta v. versicolor*).

marrequito-do-brejo (*m.*) = CORRUÍRA-DO-BREJO.

marrêta (*f.*) small sledge hammer, spalling hammer; a heavy club; a powerful kick of a soccer ball; fake smuggled goods; fake bindle of dope; crooked gambling game.

marretada (*f.*) blow with a MARRÊTA.

marretar (*v.t.*) to hammer, beat; to cudgel.

marreteiro (*m.*) rock driller (one who uses bit and hammer).

marroada (*f.*) herd of young pigs; blow with a sledge hammer.

marroio (*m., Bot.*) the Siberian motherwort (*Leontopodium sibiricum*), c.a. ERVA-MACAÉ.—branco, common horehound (*Marrubium vulgare*).—do-brasil, Brazilian horehound (*M. americanum*).—negro, black horehound (*Ballota nigra*).

marrom (*adj.*) marron, brown, chestnut. [Fr. *marron*].

marroquim (*m.*) morocco leather.

marroquino –na (*adj.; m.,f.*) Moroccan.

marrote (*m.*) shoat.

marruá (*m.*) wild yearling; gullible person, "sucker".

marruco (*m.*) breeding bull.

marrueiro (*m.*) one who breaks (tames) yearlings.

Marselha (*f.*) Marseilles.

marselhês –sa (*adj.; m.,f.*) Marseillais(e); (*f.*) the Marseillaise (French national song).

marsília (*f.*) the genus (*Marsilea*) of pepperworts or clover ferns.

marsiliáceo –a (*adj.; Bot.*) marsileaceous; (*f.pl.*) the family of pepperworts (*Marsileaceae*).

marsipobrânquios (*m.pl.*) = CICLÓSTOMOS.

marsopa (*f.*) a harbor porpoise (*Phocaena phocaena*), c.a. TONINHA.

marsuíno (*m.*) porpoise.

marsupiais (*m.pl.*) the order Marsupiala (kangaroos, opossums, etc.).

marsupial (*adj.; m.*) marsupial.

marsúpio (*m., Zool.*) marsupial pouch.

marta (*f.*) sable, marten; [*cap.*] Martha.

martagão (*m., Bot.*) martagon or Turk's-cap lily (*Lilium martagon*), c.a. LÍRIO-TURCO.

Marte (*m.*) Mars; [*not cap.*] war; warrior.

martelada (*f.*) hammer blow.

martelador (*m.*) hammerer.

martelagem (*f.*) hammering.

martelar (*v.t.,v.i.*) to hammer; to beat; to hammer away (on a subject).

marteleiro (*m.*) hammerhead shark.

martelete [lê] (*m.*) small hammer.

martelo (*m.*) hammer; mallet; gavel; a person who harps on, or hammers away at, something; (*Anat.*) maleus of the ear; (*Zool.*) wriggler (larva of mosquito); hammerhead shark (*Sphyrna zygaena*), c.a. CORNUDA, PEIXE-MARTELO.—de-unha, claw hammer.—frontal or—de-retouça, trip hammer.—pilão, steam hammer.

martensita (*f., Metal.*) martensite.

martim-pescador (*m.*) any of various kingfishers, c.a. ARIRAMBA.—grande, the great ringed kingfisher (*Streptoceryle t. torquata*), c.a. MATRACA, MARTIM-GRANDE, MARTIM-CACHÁ, MARTIM-CACHAÇA, JAGUACATIGUAÇU, ARIRAMBA-GRANDE.—miudinho, the least green kingfisher (*Chloroceryle a. aena*), c.a. ARIRAMBA-MIUDINHO.—pequeno, the green kingfisher (*Chloroceryle a americana*), c.a. ARIRAMBA-PEQUENO.—pintado, the green and rufous kingfisher (*Chloroceryle inda*), c.a. ARIRAMBA-PINTADO.—verde, the Amazon kingfisher (*Chloroceryle amazona*), c.a. ARIRAMBA-VERDE.

martinete [nê] (*m.*) steam hammer; pile driver; piano hammer; gnomon of a sundial; martin, swift; head plumage of a heron; (*Bot.*) princessfeather (*Amaranthus hybridus var.*); feather cockscomb (*Clelosia cristata*), c.a. CRISTA-DE-GALO.—pescador = ACALOTE.

martiniáceo –cea (*adj.; Bot.*) martyniaceous; (*f.pl.*) the Martyniaceae (unicorn plant family).

mártir (*m.*) martyr.

martírio (*m.*) martyrdom, affliction, torment, suffering; (*Bot.*) the bluecrown passionflower (*Passiflora caerulea*);

(*pl.*) crown-of-thorns euphorbia (*E. mili*); c.a. DOIS-IRMÃOS.

martirizar (*v.t.*) to martyrize; to torment; (*v.r.*) to fret, worry.

martirológio (*m., R.C.Ch.*) martyrology.

martirologista (*m.,f.*) martyrologist.

martita (*f., Min.*) martite.

marufle (*m.*) painter's glue; lining paste. [French *maroufle*]

maruim, maruí (*m., Zool.*) punkie or biting midge, of family Chironomidae, which appear in immense swarms in north Brazil; c.a. MERUIM, MIRUIM, MURUIM.

marujada (*f.*) seafaring people (collectively); a crowd of sailors.

marujo (*m.*) sailor, seaman [= MARINHEIRO].

marulhado –da (*adj.*) sea-tossed; (*f.*) = MARULHO.

marulhante (*adj.*) tossing, seething. um regato—, a tumbling brook.

marulhar (*v.i.*) of the sea, to toss, seethe; to roar (as the surf).

marulho (*m.*) tossing of the sea; pounding surf; fig., agitation, tumult; [= MARULHADA].

marupá (*m., Bot.*) the Orinoco simaruba (*S. amara*), c.a. MARAPUÁ, MARUPAÚBA, SIMARUBA-AMARGA.

maruparana (*m.*) = MOROTUTÓ.

marxismo [ks] (*m.*) Marxism.

marxista [ks] (*adj.; m.,f.*) Marxist.

marzoco [zô] (*m.*) buffoon, fool.

mas (*conj.*) but, yet, still, however, nevertheless.—também, but also.—enfim, but finally; (*m.*) snag, hindrance. Há um—na questão, There's a catch in it. nem—nem meio mas, no ifs, ands or buts.

mas [*contraction of* ME + AS]. them to me. Êle—deu, He gave them to me.

más (*adj.; fem., pl. of* MAU) bad.

mascador –dora (*adj.*) chewing; (*m.,f.*) chewer.

mascar (*v.t.,v.i.*) to chew without swallowing (as gum, tobacco); fig., to chew the cud (ruminate, plan, meditate); to mutter, mumble. Cf. MASTIGAR.

máscara (*f.*) mask; face guard; disguise; mascara; (*m.,f.*) masked person.—de beleza, beauty mask.—de gás, gas mask.

mascarado –da (*adj.*) masked, disguised; camouflaged; of cattle or horses, white-faced; (*m.*) masquerader, masker; (*slang*) a poor but popular soccer player; (*f.*) masquerade.

mascarão (*m., Arch.*) mascaron.

mascarar (*v.t.*) to mask, disguise; (*v.r.*) to put on a mask; to disguise oneself.

mascarilha (*f.*) a half mask.

mascarino –na (*adj.; Bot.*) masked, personate; also = PERSONADO.

mascarra (*f.*) a smudge; an ink spot; fig., stigma.

mascarrar (*v.t.*) to spot, stain; to daub, begrime, soil.

mascataria (*f.*) peddling (as an occupation).

mascate (*m.*) hawker (street peddler) of small wares. [Better known nowadays as TURCO DA PRESTAÇÃO.]

mascateação, mascateagem (*f.*) street peddling.

mascatear (*v.t.,v.i.*) to peddle.

mascavado –da (*adj.*) impure, unrefined. açúcar—, raw sugar.

mascavar (*v.t.*) to separate raw sugar (from the molasses); to adulterate; to use poor language.

mascavinho (*m.*) brown sugar.

mascavo –va (*adj.*) = MASCAVADO.

mascotar (*v.t.*) to stamp, pound, crush; to chew, crunch.

mascote (*f.*) mascot.

mascoto [ô] (*m.*) a heavy hammer, stamp or pestle.

masculinidade (*f.*) masculinity; virility.

masculinizar (*v.t.*) to render masculine; (*v.r.*) become masculine in manners or appearance.

masculino –na (*adj.*) masculine; male; virile.

másculo –la (*adj.*) masculine; virile; manly.

masdevália (*f.*) a genus (*Masdevallia*) of Brazilian orchids.

masmorra [ô] (*f.*) dungeon.

masoquismo (*m.*) masochism.

masoquista (*m.,f.*) masochist.

massa (*f.*) dough; paste; mortar; lump; bulk; mass, whole, body; mortar; a cake or mass of grated and pressed manioc ready for roasting; (*Elec.*) ground; ground connection; (*sl.*) money, dough; (*pl.*) the masses. —de vidraceiro, putty. em—, en masse, wholesale.

massacrar (*v.t.*) to massacre.

massacre (*m.*) massacre.

massagada (*f., colloq.*) mixture, jumble.

massagem (*f.*) massage.

massagista (*m.*) masseur; (*f.*) masseuse.
massame (*m.*) ship's rigging (cordage); stone lining in a well; mortar bed for tiles.
massapê, massapé (*m.*) a type of black, fertile, clayey soil found in northeastern Brazil, and especially suitable for growing sugar cane; also = CAPIM-SAPÉ (a grass).
massaroco [rô] (*m.*) yeast; (*Bot.*) the Madeira viper bugloss (*Echium candicans*).
masseira (*f.*) kneading-trough; water trough (as at a well); sluice of a water wheel; part of a manioc press.
masseiro (*m.*) one who kneads dough (in a bakery).
masseter [tér] (*m., Anat.*) masseter.
massicote (*m.*) massicot (unfused lead oxide).
massudo –da (*adj.*) massy, bulky; hulking.
mastaréu (*m.*) small mast; upper mast.
mastectomia (*f., Surg.*) mastectomy.
mástica (*f.*) = MÁSTIQUE.
masticatório (*m.*) masticatory.
mastigação (*f.*) mastication.
mastigado –da (*adj.*) masticated; well-planned.
mastigar (*v.t.,v.i.*) to masticate, chew; to chew the cud (think, plan); to clip one's words; to mutter, mumble. Cf. MASCAR.
mastim (*m.*) mastiff; watch dog; by ext., a detective or policeman.
mástique (*m.*) mastic resin.—**asfáltico**, asphalt mastic.
mastite (*f., Med.*) mastitis.—**bovina**, or—**das vacas**, (*Veter.*) garget.
mastodonte (*m.*) mastodon.
mastóide, mastoídeo –dea (*adj.; Anat., Zool.*) mastoid. **apófise—**, the mastoid process.
mastoidite (*f., Med.*) mastoiditis.
mastreação (*f.*) masting.
mastrear (*v.t.*) to mast.
mastro (*m.*) mast; staff.—**da mezena**, mizzenmast.—**de amarração**, mooring mast.—**de bandeira**, flagpole.—**grande**, mainmast. **a meio—**, at halfmast.
mastruço, mastruz (*m., Bot.*) the wormseed goosefoot (*Chenopodium ambrosioides*); a celery (*Apium amni*), c.a. GERTRUDES; a paracress spotflower (*Spilanthes*), c.a. AGRIÃO-DO-PARÁ.—**da-américa**, a swine cress (*Coronopus*) and a pepperweed (*Lepidium*).—**de-buenos-aires**, a pepperweed (*Lepidium*).—**do-brasil**, a swine cress (*Coronopus*).—**dos-rios**, watercress (*Rorippa*), c.a. AGRIÃO.—**do-peru**, common nasturtium (*Tropaeolum majus*), c.a. CAPUCHINHA-GRANDE.—**ordinário**, garden-cress pepperweed (*Lepidium sativum*).
masturbação (*f.*) masturbation.
masturbar-se (*v.r.*) to masturbate.
mata (*f.*) woods, forest, jungle; thicket, coppice.—**virgem**, virgin forest. Cf. MATO.
mata-baiano (*m.*) a cold westerly winter wind in southern Brazil.
mata-baleia (*m.*) a killer whale.
mata-baratas (*m.*) = ANGELIM-DOCE.
mata-bicho (*m., slang*) a shot (dram) of liquor; a tip, gratuity.
mata-borrão (*m.*) blotting paper; fig., (*slang*) a sponge, sot.
mata-burro (*m.*) a cattle guard, as at railroad crossings.
mata-cabras (*m.*) = ALGODÃO-BRAVO (a morning-glory).
mata-cachorro (*m.*) a zebrawood (*Connarus*); (*colloq.*) cop, flatfoot; a circus roustabout.
mata-cana (*f.*) = DOURADINHA-DO-CAMPO.
matacão (*m.*) boulder; cobblestone; also, a small stone.
mata-cão (*m., Bot.*) aconite monkshood (*Aconitum napellus*).
mata-cavalo (*m., Bot.*) a nightshade (*Solanum ciliatum*); also = CAVALO-DE-CÃO (a spider wasp).
mataco (*m.*) rump.
mata-cobra (*f.*) a ponerine stinging ant (*Euponia marginata*); a club (lit., a snake killer).
matado –da (*adj.*) badly made; poorly finished; a fruit, picked green and artificially ripened; galled, chafed. [Not the p.p. of MATAR, which is MORTO.]
matador –dora (*adj.*) murderous, deadly; (*m.,f.*) killer, murderer; a matador (bullfighter); a bore; a ladykiller; (*pl.*) the winning cards; (*f.*) femme fatale.
matadouro (*m.*) slaughterhouse.
matadura (*f.*) gall (harness or saddle sore); moral defect.
mata-feijão (*m.*) "an unexpected rise of the river level which occurs at the beginning of the VAZANTE on the upper tributaries of the Amazon and the Solimões,

often destroying the crops planted on the flats exposed during the low-water season." [GBAT]
mata-fome (*f.*) any of various vines or shrubs of genus Paullinia; also = CAMAPU; CIPÓ-TIMBÓ.
matagado (*m., Bot.*) a cordia (*C. sellowiana*); the American false hellebore (*Veratrum viride*).
matagal (*m.*) dense thicket, bushes, grove, forest, woods.
matagoso –sa (*adj.*) woody [land].
matai-me-embora (*m.*) = CAPIM-DE-BURRO.
mata-junta (*m., Carp.*) batten.
matalotagem (*f.*) food, provisions (on board ship); a jumble of things; "(1) food supply in general; (2) food supplies carried while traveling; (3) fish or meat roasted with manioc flour which is kept in a cloth bag within a knapsack as food supply for several days to be spent in clearing land or on fishing expeditions." [GBAT]
matalote (*m.*) sailor; shipmate.
matamatá (*m.*) the matamata (*Chelys fimbriata*), an Amazon fresh-water turtle of fantastic appearance. It attains a length of three feet and is remarkable for its rough shell and long neck; a medium-sized tree (*Eschweilera matamata*), having chestnut-colored hard, heavy wood, not attacked by insects.
matambre (*m.*) rib beef.
matame (*m.*) scalloped edging; flesh which adheres to a hide after skinning.
mata-mosquito (*m.*) a public servant employed in mosquito control.
mata-mouros (*m.*) braggadocio, bully, "giant killer".
matança (*f.*) slaughter, killing, butchery, carnage; slaughtering of cattle; (*colloq.*) fuss, bustle; in soccer, rough play.
matão (*m.*) a jockey who crowds the others against the fence.
mata-ôlho (*m.*) = CAPITÃO-DA-SALA.
mata-pasto (*m., Bot.*) a senna (*Cassia bicapsularis*) whose bark is used in medicine; c.a. CAQUERA, TAREROQUI; also = CARRAPICHO; DARTRIAL; FEDEGOSO-VERDADEIRO.
mata-pau (*m.*) any of numerous strangler trees or epiphytic plants, esp. of the fig family; also = CUPAÍ. Cf. MULEMBÁ.
mata-peixe (*m.*) = CIPÓ-TIMBÓ.
mata-pinto (*m.*) = ALGODÃO-BRAVO.
mata-piolhos (*m., colloq.*) "louse killer" (the thumb); also = CANUDO-DE-PITO (a plant).
matar [24] (*v.t.*) to kill, slay; to murder, assassinate; to slaughter (cattle); to quench (thirst); to satisfy (hunger); to perform (work, etc.) in a hasty or careless manner; (*slang*) to cut classes; in soccer, to play rough; (*v.r.*) to commit suicide.—**a fome**, to satisfy hunger.—**à fome**, to kill by starvation.—**as saudades**, to satisfy one's yearnings or longings for someone or something.—**de inveja**, to arouse great jealousy in.—**de vez o assunto**, to settle the matter once and for all.—**dois coelhos duma cajadada só**, to kill two birds with one stone.—**o bicho**, (*colloq.*) to take a drink.—**o tempo**, to kill time. **Êle não se mata**, He doesn't kill himself (takes things easy). **estar**, or **ficar, a—**, to suit to perfection.
mata-rato[s] (*m.*) rat poison; (*colloq.*) cheap wine; strong cheap cigar or cigarettes.
mataria (*f.*) an extensive forest.
mata-sano[s] (*m., colloq.*) quack doctor.
matassa (*f.*) raw silk.
matataúba (*f.*) the silverleaf pumpwood (*Cecropia palmata*), c.a. SAMBACUIM.
mate (*m.*) maté or mate (Paraguay tea (*Ilex paraguayensis*), c.a. ERVA-MATE, or the brew made from its dried leaves).—**chimarrão**, maté tea without sugar.—**de armada curta**, maté tea served boiling hot; (*adj.*) mat, dull; lackluster.
mateador –dora (*m.,f.*) lover of MATE (tea).
matear (*v.i.*) to drink MATE; to spend time in the MATO (woods).
mateiro (*m.*) forester, woodsman, bushwhacker; an expert rubber tapper; backwoodsman; kind of deer (*Cervus rufus*); dealer in ERVA-MATE (Paraguay tea).
matejar (*v.i.*) to cut firewood.
matemático –ca (*adj.*) mathematical; exact; (*m.,f.*) mathematician; (*f.*) mathematics.
matéria (*f.*) matter, substance; subject matter; topic; school subject; pus.—**julgada**, foregone conclusion. **em—de**, in the field of, regarding.—**prima**, raw material.
material (*adj.*) material, physical; crass; (*m.*) material goods; material equipment, apparatus.—**bélico**, ord-

nance.—**humano,** manpower.—**para construção,** building material.—**rodante,** railway rolling stock.
materialidade (*f.*) materiality.
materialismo (*m.*) materialism.
materialista (*adj.*) materialistic; (*m.,f.*) materialist; (*colloq.*) a dealer in building materials.
materialização (*f.*) materialization.
materializar (*v.t.*) to materialize; (*v.r.*) of spirits, to assume visible form.
maternal (*adj.*) maternal [=MATERNO].
maternidade (*f.*) maternity; a maternity or lying-in hospital.
materno -na (*adj.*) maternal; motherly. **avó—,** maternal grandmother. **língua—,** mother tongue.
Mateus (*m.*) Matthew. **Mateus, primeiro os teus,** Charity begins at home.
maticar (*v.i.*) of hunting dogs, to bay.
mático (*m., Bot.*) matico pepper (*Piper angustifolium*).
Matilde (*f.*) Matilda; Mathilda.
matilha (*f.*) a pack of hounds; fig., canaille, rabble; a gang (of evildoers).
matimpererê (*m.*) = SACI (bird).
matina (*f.*) early rising; early morning; dawn; (*pl.*) matins.
matinada (*f.*) dawn, daybreak; matins; an early rising; a matinée; early morning clatter.
matinal (*adj.*) matutinal; early-rising.
matinar (*v.t.,v.i.*) to awaken early; (*v.i.*) to rise early; (*v.t.*) to train, teach.
matinê (*f.*) matinée; negligee, dressing gown.
matinho (*m.*) underbrush.
matintapere[i]ra (*m.*) the striped cuckoo (*Tapera m. naevia*), c.a. SACI.
matirão (*m.*) the Guianan yellow-crowned night-heron (*Nyctanassa violacea cayennensis*), c.a. SOCÓ, SABACU, SAVACU-DE-COROA, DORMINHOCO.
matista (*m.,f.*) lover of MATE (tea).
matitaperê (*m.*) = SACI (bird).
matiz (*m.*) a blend of colors; complexion; shade, hue, tint, tinge; fig., political hue or leanings.
matização (*f.*) blending of colors, tinting, tinging, shading.
matizado -da (*adj.*) motley, parti-colored.
matizar (*v.t.*) to blend colors; to tinge, color, tint, shade.
mato (*m.*) woods, forest, jungle; brush, wild growth; the country as opposed to the city; (*slang*) lots of anything.
—**bom,** luxuriant woods revealing fertile soil.—**a dentro,** deep in the woods.—**-mau** = CATANDUVA. **botar no—,** to throw (something) out. **cair no—,** to run away. **no—sem cachorro,** in a boat without a paddle (in a predicament). Cf. MATA.
mato-grossense (*adj.*) of or pert. to the State of Mato Grosso; (*m.,f.*) a native or inhabitant of the same.
matoso -sa (*adj.*) woody; covered with wild growth.
matraca (*f.*) a rattle; a noisemaker; fig., clatter, racket; (*Zool.*) the cinerous bush shrike (*Batara c. cinerea*) of southeastern Brazil, c.a. PAPA-OVA, RAJADÃO; also a kingfisher called ARIRAMBA-GRANDE.—**-da-quaresma,** (*m., colloq.*) rattler (talker).
matracar (*v.t.,v.i.*) to harp (upon), hammer.
matracolejar (*v.i.*) to rattle; to clatter; to rouse, stir up.
matraqueado -da (*adj.*) experienced, old at it, trained.
matraquear (*v.i.*) to rattle, clatter; (*v.t.*) to jeer at, hoot at; to break in, teach the ropes to.
matraz (*m.*) matrass, flask (in a laboratory).
matreiro -ra (*adj.*) knowing, shrewd, sharp, sly, crafty; wily, foxy; sneaky; of cattle, wild.
matriarca (*f.*) matriarch.
matriárcado (*m.*) matriarchy.
matriarcal (*adj.*) matriarchal.
matricária (*f.*) feverfew chrysanthemum (*C. parthenium*). —**-camomila,** German-camomile (*Matricaria chamomilla*).
matricida (*m.,f.*) matricide (person).
matricídio (*m.*) matricide (crime).
matrícula (*f.*) matriculation; enrollment, registration; matriculation or registration fee; roster, register.
matriculado -da (*adj.*) matriculated; (*colloq.*) wise, on to the ropes.
matricular (*v.t.,v.r.*) to matriculate.
matrimonial (*adj.*) matrimonial, marital.
matrimoniar (*v.t.,v.r.*) to marry [= CASAR].
matrimônio (*m.*) matrimony, marriage.—**clandestino,** clandestine marriage.—**consumado,** consummated matrimony.—**de consciência,** a marriage without benefit of

state or clergy.—**de-joão-das-vinhas,** fake marriage.—**espiritual,** spiritual marriage.—**putativo,** putative marriage.—**rato,** a legal but unconsummated marriage.—**secreto,** secret marriage.
mátrio -tria (*adj.*) mother.
matritense (*adj.*; *m.,f.*) = MADRILENO.
matriz (*f.*) matrix (womb); mother church (cathedral); source; (*Math., Type Founding*) matrix; (*Mach.*) die; (*adj.*) mother, originating; primordial.—**de cortar** or **de recortar,** blanking die.—**de cunhar,** coining die.—**de curvar** or **de dobrar,** bending die.—**de enrolar** or **de revirar,** curling die.—**de estampar,** blanking die; coining die.—**de perfurar,** piercing or perforating die.—**múltipla,** combination, compound or gang die.
matroca (*f.*) **à—,** aimlessly, haphazardly. **ir** or **andar à—,** to live or behave aimlessly or negligently.
matrona (*f.*) a matron, an elderly married woman; (*colloq.*) a virago.
matronaça (*f.*) big, fat woman.
matronal (*adj.*) matronly, matronal.
matrucar (*v.t.*) to quarter slain beef cattle.
matruco (*m.*) a quarter of beef.
matruqueiro (*m.*) butcher in a slaughterhouse.
matucana (*f.*) = DOURADINBA-DO-CAMPO.
matula (*f.*) mob, gang of rowdies; victuals, esp. for a journey.
mátula (*f.*) = URINOL.
matulagem (*f.*) bums collectively.
matungo (*m.*) plug, nag; any horse.
matupá (*m.*) in the Amazon region, a large floating island of matted vegetation; c.a. PARIATÁ, PERIANTÁ.
maturação (*f.*) maturation.
maturar (*v.t.,v.i.*) to mature, ripen; (*v.i.,v.r.*) to grow wise.
maturidade (*f.*) maturity.
maturrango (*m.*) poor horseman; greenhorn on a ranch.
maturrão (*m.*) worthless old horse.
Matusalém (*m.*) Methuselah; (*colloq., fig.*) a very old person.
matutar (*v.i.*) to ponder, meditate, reflect (upon); (*v.t.*) to purpose, intend.
matutice (*f.*) behavior or appearance of a MATUTO.
matutinal (*adj.*) matutinal, morning.
matutino -na (*adj.*) matutinal, morning; early-rising; (*m.*) a morning newspaper.
matuto -ta (*adj.*) said of backwoodsmen; shy; suspicious; pondering, meditative; (*colloq.*) sly, scheming; (*m.*) backwoodsman, esp. a shy and clumsy one; a simple-minded person, esp. one from the country.
mau [fem. **má**] (*adj.*) bad, evil; pernicious; detrimental; unwholesome; mean; wicked; vile; poor; inferior; naughty; (*m.*) evil, badness.—**ar,** impure air.—**comportamento,** misconduct, bad behavior.—**coração,** bad heart.—**de contentar,** hard to please.—**estado,** bad condition.—**exemplo,** bad example.—**gênio,** irascibility.—**grado,** unwillingly.—**humor,** bad humor.—**jôgo,** unfair play; dirty trick.—**modo,** ill manners.—**-olhado,** evil eye. —**pagador,** a dead beat.—**passo,** evil step.—**serviço,** disservice.—**tempo,** bad weather. **de—s fígados,** vindictive.
maú (*m.*) the capuchin bird (*Perissocephalus tricolor*), c.a. URUTAÍ.
maué (*m.,f.*) one of the Maué, a civilized Tupian tribe of which remnants remain in the region west of the lower Tapajós River; (*adj.*) pert. to or designating the Maué.
maueza [ê] (*f., colloq.*) badness [= MALDADE].
Maurício (*m.*) Maurice; Morris; Mauritius.
mauritânia (*f.*) sweet william (*Dianthus barbatus*), c.a. CRAVINA-DOS-POETAS.
mausoléu (*m.*) mausoleum.
maviosidade (*f.*) sweetness, gentleness, tenderness.
mavioso -sa (*adj.*) tenderhearted, affectionate; compassionate. **som—,** sweet sound.
maxacali [í] (*f.*) the Mashacalí, a linguistic family and one of its tribes which lived in Bahia and Minas Gerais; (*adj.*) pert. to or designating these people.
maxambomba (*f.*) a rattletrap vehicle. [Originally, a double-decker railroad car.] (*slang*) the human body.
maxicote (*m.*) a mortar of dirt, sand, lime and water.
maxila [ks] (*adj.*; *m.*) maxillary (bone).—**inferior,** lower jawbone.—**superior,** upper jawbone.
máxima [x = ss] (*f.*) see under MÁXIMO.
màximamente [x = ss] (*adv.*) principally.
máxime [ks] (*adv.*) principally, especially, above all.
máximo -ma [x = ss] (*adj.*; *superl.* of GRANDE) maximum; greatest.—**divisor comum,** greatest common divisor; (*m.*)

the maximum. **no—**, at most; at the outside; (*f.*) maxim, proverb.—**de almanaque**, trite maxim.

maxixar (*m.*) to dance the MAXIXE.

maxixe (*m.*) a one-time popular Brazilian round dance; a gherkin.

maxixeiro (*m.*) West Indian gherkin (*Cucumis anguria*); one who dances the MAXIXE.

mazagrã (*m.*) cold weak coffee, served in a glass or mug.

mazama (*m., Zool.*) any brocket (*Mazama sp.*).

mazanza (*adj.; m.,f.*) slow, lazy (person). Var. MANZANZA.

mazanzar (*v.i.*) to dawdle. Var. MANZANZAR.

mazela (*f.*) gall or sore spot; (*colloq.*) any ailment; blot, blemish (on reputation).

mazelento -ta (*adj.*) full of sores; sickly.

mazorca (*f.*) disturbance, commotion; riot.

mazorqueiro (*m.*) rabble-rouser.

mazorro -ra [zô] (*adj.*) coarse; rude; lazy; glum.

mazurca (*f.*) mazurka.

mbacaiá (*m., Bot.*) a spiral flag (*Costus spicatus*).

mbuí (*m., Bot.*) a golden rod (*Solidago*).

Mc = MEGACÍCLO (megacycle).

m/c = MINHA CARTA (my letter); MINHA CONTA (my account).

m.ᶜᵒ = MARÇO (March).

m/d = MESES DE DATA (months' date—term of a note).

m.d. = MUITO DIGNO (Worthy—form of address—but not doctor of medicine).

M.ᵉ = MADRE (Mother Superior).

me (*pers. pron. dir. obj.*) to me, to myself; (*indirect obj.*) me, myself.

meã, fem. of MEÃO.

meacão (*f.*) a halving; a half.

meado -da (*adj.; m.*) middle; (*f.*) skein or hank (of yarn, thread, etc.); fig., intrigue, plot. **achar o fio da—**, to find a clue to the puzzle.

mealha (*f.*) mite; bit, morsel.

mealheiro -ra (*adj.*) meager; poor; (*m.*) savings, nest egg; piggy bank; the poor box in a church.

meâmente (*adv.*) middling.

meandrar (*v.i.*) to meander.

meandrina (*f.*) the genus (*Maeandra*) of reef-building corals.

meandro (*m.*) meander(ing); fig., tergiversation; intrigue.

meante (*adj.*) divided in half; half gone, half over.

meão [pl. meãos] (*adj.*) middling; mean, intermediate; average; mediocre; (*m.*) hub of a wagon wheel. [Fem. MEÃ]

mear (*v.t.*) to halve; (*v.i.,v.r.*) to arrive at the middle.

meato (*m., Anat.*) meatus.—**acústico** or **auditivo**, auditory meatus.—**do nariz**, meatus of the nose.—**intercelular**, (*Biol.*) intercellular space.—**urinário**, meatus urinarius.

meça, meças, forms of MEDIR [60].

mecânico -ca (*adj.*) mechanical; (*m.*) a mechanic or machinist; (*f.*) mechanics.—**analítica**, analytic, or theoretical, mechanics.—**aplicada**, applied mechanics.—**pura**, or **racional**, pure, or rational, mechanics.

mecanismo (*m.*) mechanism.—**acionador** or **motor**, drive mechanism.—**de avanço**, (*Mach.*) feed mechanism.

mecanização (*f.*) mechanization.

mecanizar (*v.t.*) to mechanize.

mecanologia (*f.*) mechanology.

mecanoterapia (*f., Med.*) mechanotherapy, esp. massage and exercise.

mecê (*pers. pron.*) you. [Short for VOSSEMECÊ].

Mecenas (*m.*) Maecenas; fig., a patron of the arts.

mecha (*f.*) fuse; wick; (*Carp.*) tenon, tongue.

mechar (*v.t.*) to fumigate (wine barrels) with sulfur; (*Carp.*) to join with mortise and tenon.

mechoacão-do-canadá (*m.*) = CARURU-DE-CACHO.

meco (*m., colloq.*) fellow, guy; a loose character.

mecônico -ca (*adj., Chem.*) meconic [acid].

meconídio (*m., Zool.*) meconidium.

meconina (*f., Chem.*) meconin.

meço, form of MEDIR [60].

méd. = MÉDICO (physician).

meda (*f.*) shock (sheaves of grain piled up); hay stack; pile, heap.

medalha (*f.*) medal.

medalhão (*m.*) medallion; locket; (*colloq.*) a "big shot," a "stuffed shirt," figurehead.

medalhar (*v.t.*) to commemorate with a medal.

medalhário, medalheiro (*m.*) a set of medals.

medalhista (*m.,f.*) medalist [but not in the sense of one

who has gained a medal, which is PESSOA AGRACIADA COM UMA MEDALHA.]

médão [médãos] (*m.*) sand dune.

medeixes (*m.pl., colloq.*) a leave-me-alone attitude; mock disdain.

mede-léguas (*m.*) = CURIANGO.

mede-palmos (*m.*) a looper (measuring worm).

média (*f.*) mean, average; median; large cup of *café au lait* (hot milk and coffee).—**aritmética**, arithmetical mean.—**de posição**, (*Stat.*) position average.—**geométrica**, geometric mean.—**harmônica**, harmonic mean.—**ponderada**, (*Stat.*) weighted average.—**proporcional**, mean term of a proportion, when the second and third terms are equal to each other. **a—dos homens**, the average man. **achar a—**, to find the average. **em—**, on the average. **lei das—s**, law of averages. Cf. MÉDIO.

mediação (*f.*) mediation; intervention.

mediador [fem. **mediatriz**] (*adj.*) mediating; (*m.,f.*) mediator, arbitrator; go-between, peacemaker.

medial (*adj.*) medial, median.

medianeiro (*m.*) = MEDIADOR.

mediania (*f.*) mediocrity; half-wayness.

mediano-na (*adj.*) medium; median; (*f.*) a median (line, number); (*Stat.*) median.

mediante (*adj.*) intervening, intermediate; (*prep.*) for, by, by means of, through, in view of; (*m.*) interim.

mediar [16] (*v.t.*) to divide in the middle; to mediate; (*v.i.*) to fall or lie between two extremes; to happen in the meantime.

mediastino (*m., Anat.*) mediastinum.—**anterior (médio, posterior, superior)**, anterior (middle, posterior, superior) mediastinum.

mediatamente (*adv.*) mediately.

mediatário -ria (*adj.; m.,f.*) = MEDIADOR.

mediato -ta (*adj.*) mediate.

mediatriz, fem. of MEDIADOR.

médica (*f.*) a woman physician; medic, alfalfa.

medicação (*f.*) medication.

medical (*adj.*) medical.

medicamentação (*f.*) medication.

medicamentar (*v.t.*) to medicate.

medicamento (*m.*) medicament, medicine.—**registrado**, patent medicine.

medicamentoso -sa (*adj.*) medicamental, medicinal.

medição (*f.*) measurement, measuring.

medicar (*v.t.*) to medicate, treat with medicine; (*v.r.*) to take medicine.

medicastro (*m.*) quack doctor.

medicativo -va (*adj.*) medicative, medicinal.

medicável (*adj.*) medicable.

medicina (*f.*) medical science; the practice of medicine; medicine.—**-legal**, legal medicine.

medicinal (*adj.*) medicinal.

medicinar (*v.*) = MEDICAR.

medicineiro (*m.*) a nettlespurge (*Jatropha elliptica*), c.a. GAFANHOTO, PINHÃO-DE-PURGA.

médico (*m.*), **-ca** (*f.*) doctor, physician.—**assistente**, attending physician.—**-cirurgião**, or—**-operador**, surgeon; (*adj.*) medicinal.

medida (*f.*) measure, gauge, rule, yardstick; measurement; (*pl.*) steps, means to an end.—**de capacidade**, dry or liquid measure.—**de comprimento**, linear measure.—**de superfície**, square measure.—**legislativa**, legislative measure.—**rasa**, or **rodada**, struck measure. **à—que**, as, while, at the same time that, according as. **à—que o tempo passa**, while time goes by. **contra—**, countermeasure. **encher as—s**, to fill the bill; to come up to expectations. **feito sob—**, made to measure (as a suit of clothes). **passar das—s**, to carry things too far; to forget oneself. **tomar—s**, to take steps.

medidor -dora (*adj.*) measuring; (*m.*) measurer; gauge; meter.—**de deriva**, (*Aeron.*) drift meter.—**de eletricidade**, electric meter.—**de exposição**, (*Photog.*) exposure meter.—**de gás**, gas meter.—**de gasolina**, gasoline gauge.—**de marés**, tide gauge.—**de pressão**, pressure gauge.—**de resistência elétrica**, ohmmeter.—**de tempo de estacionamento**, parking meter.

medieval, mediévico -ca, medievo -va (*adj.*) medieval.

medievalista (*m.,f.*) medievalist.

médio -dia (*adj.*) medium, mean, middling; intermediate, middle; average; (*f.*) see MÉDIA; (*m., Soccer*) a half-back.

medíocre (*adj.*) mediocre, medium, average, fair.

mediocridade (*f.*) mediocrity; a mediocre person.

medir [60] (*v.t.*) to measure; to gauge; to take the measure

of; to size up (another person); to weigh (one's words or acts).—-se com, to vie with.—a espada, or as armas, com, to measure swords with.—as palavras, to weigh one's words. não ter mãos a—, to have one's hands full.
meditabundo -da (adj.) meditative, contemplative.
meditação (f.) meditation, contemplation, musing.
meditador -dora (adj.) meditating; (m.,f.) one who meditates.
meditar (v.t.,v.i.) to meditate, play, scheme; to contemplate, study; to muse, ponder.—em, sôbre, think on, about.
meditativo -ta (adj.) = MEDITABUNDO.
meditável (adj.) worthy of meditation.
mediterrâneo -nea (adj.) mediterranean; [cap., m.] Mediterranean sea.
mediterrânico -ca (adj.) Mediterranean.
médium [-uns] (m.) a spiritualistic medium.
mediúnico -ca (adj.) mediumistic.
medo [é] (m.) sand dune [= MÉDÃO]; (adj.) Median.
mêdo (m.) fear, dread, fright. a—, fearfully, timidly. aniquilado pelo—, prostrated by fear. com—, afraid. com—que, lest, for fear that. Ela está de dar—, She is a fright. fazer—, to frighten. Gato escaldado tem—até de água fria, Once bitten, twice shy. morrer de—, to die of fright. não ter—, to have no fear. ter—da própria sombra, to be afraid of one's own shadow. ter—de, to be afraid of (to).
medonho -nha (adj.) frightful, terrible; ghastly, grim, formidable, menacing. Estou num espêto—, I'm in an awful fix.
medra, medrança (f.) growth, development.
medrar (v.i.) to grow, thrive, flourish.
medrica (m.,f., colloq.) 'fraid cat.
medronheiro (m.) strawberry madrone (Arbutus unedo).
medroso -sa (adj.) fearful; timid; fainthearted.
medula (f., Bot.) medulla, pith; fig., essence, heart, core; (Anat.) medulla.—espinhal, spinal cord.—óssea, bone marrow.—supra-renal, suprarenal medulla.
medular (adj.) medullary; essential.
medulite (f., Med.) medullitis.
meduloso -sa (adj.) medullose; pithlike.
medusa (f.) jellyfish; fig., an ugly woman.
medusiforme (adj., Zool.) medusiform.
medusóide (adj., Zool.) medusoid.
méd. vet. = MÉDICO VETERINÁRIO (veterinarian).
meeiro -ra [e-ei] (adj.) of shares, divisible, or to be divided, in halves; (m.) a half-owner; a share-cropper; (f.) second picking of cotton.
mefistofélico -ca (adj.) Mephistophelean, diabolic.
mefítico -ca (adj.) mephitic; noxious; pestilential.
mefitismo (m.) mephitis; mephitism.
megacefálico -ca (adj., Craniom.) megacephalic.
megacíclo (m., Radio) megacycle.
megadina (m.) megadyne.
megadonte (adj.) megadont.
megafone (m.) megaphone.
megafotografia (f.) megaphotography.
megagâmeta (m., Biol.) megagamyte, macrogamete [= MACROGÂMETA].
megajúlio (m.) megajoule.
megálito (m., Archaeol.) megalith.
megalocarpo -pa (adj., Bot.) megalocarpous.
megalocefalia (f., Med.) megalocephalia, megalocephaly.
megalocéfalo -la (adj., Craniom.) megacephalous.
megalomania (f.) megalomania.
megalomaníaco -ca, **megalômano** -na (adj.; m.,f.) megalomaniac.
megalopo (m., Zool.) megalops (larval crab); Megalops (genus of fishes).
megalossauro (m., Paleontol.) megalosaur.
meganha (m., slang) flat-foot, cop.
megápode (adj.) megapod, large-footed; (m.) a megapode, jungle fowl, or mound bird, genus Megapodius.
megáptero (m.) the genus (Megaptera) consisting of the humpbacked whales.
megasporângio (m., Bot.) megasporangium.
megásporo (m., Bot.) megaspore.
megasporofilo (m., Bot.) megasporophyll.
megassemo -ma (adj., Craniom.) megaseme.
megassismo (m.) megaseism, violent earthquake.
megatério (m., Paleontol.) megathere.
megatermo (m., Bot.) megatherm.
megera (f.) fierce or cruel woman; virago, shrew.
meia (f.) see under MEIO.

meia-água (f.) a single or pitched roof; shed roof.
meia-cana (f.) fluting, channel; half-round file. ferro—, half-round iron or steel bars.
meia-cara (m.,f.) contraband or bootleg slave. de—, free of charge (said of admission to a show, ride on a public conveyance, etc.).
meia-colher (m.) bricklayer's helper.
meia-coroa (f.) half-crown (coin).
meia-direita (m., Soccer) inside right (player or his position).
meia-esquadria (f.) line bisecting a right angle; a 45° miter joint; (Carp.) miter; bevel square.
meia-esquerda (m., Soccer) inside left (player or his position).
meia-idade (f.) middle age; the Middle Ages.
meia-laranja (f.) a domelike hill.
meia-lona (f.) coarse linen cloth.
meia-lua (f.) half moon.
meia-luz (f.) half light, dusk.
meia-murça (f.) a second-cut file.
meia-nau (f.) line extending amidships.
meia-noite (f.) midnight. à—, at midnight.
meia-pataca (f.) = ALMA-DE-GATO; also = MEIA-TIGELA.
meia-pausa (f., Music) a half rest or minim.
meia-porção (f.) half portion.
meia-praça (m.) a prospector who has been grubstaked and who works on half-shares.
meia-rotunda (f., Arch.) semidome.
meias (f.pl.) halves; half-shares.
meias-palavras (f.pl.) subterfuges, evasions.
meias-partidas (f.pl.) the four intermediate points of the compass: NE, SE, SW, NW.
meias-razões (f.pl.) half reasons [= MEIAS-PALAVRAS].
meia-tigela (f.) a trifle; a person of little or no importance.
meia-tinta (f.) tint, half tint, halftone.
meia-volta (f.) half-turn, about face.—volver! About face! (military command).
meia-voz (f.) undertone.
meigo -ga (adj.) mild, gentle; kind, tender; sweet, affectionate.
meiguice (f.) meekness, mildness, gentleness; tenderness; (pl.) kind words; endearments; caresses.
meijoada (f.) night work.
meimendro (m., Bot.) henbane (Hyoscyamus)—-branco, roundleaf henbane (H. albus).—-negro, black henbane (H. niger).
meiminho (m.) the little finger [= MINDINHO].
meinâcu (m.,f.) an Indian of the Mehinacu, an Arawakan tribe dwelling on the upper Xingu River in Mato Grosso; (adj.) pert. to or designating this tribe.
meio [fem. meia] (adj.) half; middle; semi, demi; (m.) middle; center; midst; medium; milieu, environment; expedient, device, resource; way; (Math.) mean; (pl.) means, resources, wealth; ways and means; (f.) sock; stocking; —artificial, (Biol.) artificial (culture) medium. —cá—lá, (colloq.) half drunk.—de cultura, (Biol.) culture medium.—de vida, (colloq.) means of livelihood. —extremo, extreme measure.—feito, half-finished.— morto, half-dead, tired out.—natural, natural habitat; (Biol.) natural medium.—prático, expedient, device.—s de transporte, means of transportation.—sintético, (Biol.) synthetic medium.—social, social environment. a—, half-and-half. a—caminho, half-way. A bom entendedor meia palavra basta, A word to the wise is sufficient. ao—, in or through the middle (de, of); between; in half, in two. conhecer os—s, to know the ropes. cortar (or dividir) pelo—, to bisect; to cut (divide) in half. em meio a (or de), in the midst of. lei de—s, law of ways and means. no—de, amid, among; in the middle of. Para velhaco, velhaco e—, Set a thief to catch a thief. pelo—, in (through) the middle. por—de, by means of.
meio-busto (m., Sculpture, Painting) head, half-bust.
meio-chumbo (m.) a filmy fern (Trichomanes) c.a. CAR-RAPATINHA.
meio-copeiro (m.) an undershot waterwheel.
meio-corpo (m.) half-length portrait or sculpture.
meio-dia (m.) midday.
meio-fio (m.) curb line of a sidewalk; (Arch.) bead; (Naut.) a fore-and-aft partition in the hold of a ship.
meio-galope (m.) canter.
meio-irmão (m.) half-brother.
meio-médio (m.) welterweight (boxer).
meionita (f., Min.) meionite.
meio-quadratim (Printing) en quad.

meio-relêvo (*m.*, *Sculp.*) alto-relievo.
meio-rufo (*m.*) halfway-cut file.
meiose (*f.*, *Biol.*) meiosis.
meio-sangue (*m.*) half-blooded horse.
meio-soprano (*m.*) mezzo-soprano voice; (*f.*) mezzo-soprano singer.
meio-têrmo, midway point; fig., avoidance of extremes; middle of the road; (*pl.*) half measures.
meio-tom (*m.*, *Music*) semitone.
meirinho –nha (*adj.*) of sheep or wool, merino; (*m.*) kinds of small jumping spiders; a bailiff.
meizinha (*f.*) = MEZINHA.
M.ᵉˡ = MANUEL (proper name).
melaconita (*f.*, *Min.*) melaconite.
melamina (*f.*, *Chem.*) melamin(e).
Melânia (*f.*) Melanie.
melanita (*f.*, *Min.*) melanite.
mel [meles or méis] (*m.*) honey; sirup; sweetness.—**-cabaú**, —de furo, or—de tanque, molasses [= MELAÇO, MELADO].—**-de-anta**, a stingless bee (*Melipona flavipennis*).—de engenho, boiled cane-sugar sirup.—**-de-pau**, any of numerous bees that nest in tree hollows.—**-de-sapo**, a stingless bee (*Melipona fuscipennis*).—silvestre, wild honey.—virgem, virgin honey. favo de—, honeycomb. lua de—, honeymoon.
mela (*f.*) plant blight; sickness; partial baldness; (*colloq.*) drunkenness; beating, trouncing.
melaço (*m.*) molasses.
melaconite (*f.*, *Min.*) melaconite.
melado –da (*adj.*) honey-colored; sweet as honey; of plants, blighted; (*m.*) molasses; (*slang*) blood.
meláfiro (*m.*, *Petrog.*) melaphyre.
melaína (*f.*) = MELANINA.
melambo (*m.*, *Bot.*) wintersbark drimys (*D. winteri*), c.a. CASCA-DE-ANTA.
melamina (*f.*, *Chem.*) melamine, cyanuro triamide.
melampirina (*f.*, *Chem.*) melampyritol, dulcitol.
melâmpiro (*m.*) the genus (*Melampyrum*) consisting of the cowwheats.
melampódio (*m.*, *Bot.*) blackfoot (*Melampodium*) c.a. HELÉBORO-PRÊTO.
melancia (*f.*) watermelon vine (*Citrullus vulgaris*), or its fruit.—**-da-praia**, a nightshade (*Solanum agrarium*), c.a. ARREBENTA-CAVALO, BABÁ, BOMBÃO.
melancial (*m.*) watermelon patch.
melancieira (*f.*) watermelon vine; a woman who sells melons.
melancolia (*f.*) melancholy, dejection, gloominess; the "blues".
melancólico –ca (*adj.*) melancholic, depressed, unhappy, "blue"; doleful, gloomy, dismal; causing melancholy. andar (or estar)—, to be blue, in the dumps.
melanismo (*m.*, *Physiol.*, *Zool.*) melanism.
melanésio –sia (*adj.*; *m.*,*f.*) Melanesian.
melanina (*f.*, *Biochem.*) melanin [= MELAÍNA].
melanita (*f.*, *Min.*) melanite.
melanoblasto (*m.*, *Biol.*) melanoblast.
melanocerite (*m.*, *Min.*) melanocerite.
melanócito (*m.*, *Biol.*) melanocyte.
melancroíta (*f.*, *Min.*) melanochroite, phoenicochroite.
melanóforo (*m.*, *Biol.*) melanophore.
melanógeno (*m.*, *Biochem.*) melanogen.
melanoma (*m.*, *Med.*) melanoma.
melanose (*f.*, *Plant Pathol.*) melanose; (*Med.*) melanosis.
melanospermo –ma (*adj.*, *Bot.*) melanospermous.
melanterita (*f.*, *Min.*) melanterite, native copperas.
melão (*m.*) muskmelon (*Cucumis melo*), or its fruit.—**-caboclo**, casabanana (*Sicana odorifera*), c.a. CRUÁ.—**-de-morcego** = ABÓBORA-DO-MATO.—**-de-são-caetano**, fruit of the balsampear (*Mormodica charantia*), c.a. SABÃO-DE-SOLDADO.—**-de-soldado**, a vinespinach (*Basella saponaria*).
mela-pinto (*m.*, *Bot.*) a starwort (*Stellaria fornisata*).
melar (*v.t.*) to sweeten with honey or syrup; to smear with honey; to blast (plants); (*v.i.*) to hunt wild honey; of sugar, to melt; (*v.i.*,*v.r.*) to become blighted.
melastomo (*m.*, *Bot.*) any plant of the genus Melastoma.
melátopo (*m.*, *Optic.*, *Mineral.*) melatope.
melcatrefe (*m.*) = MEQUETREFE.
melê (*m.*) joker (card); [= CURINGA].
melê (*m.*) a carbon diamond of poor quality [= TORRA].
meleagris (*f.*) = GALINHA-DA-ANGOLA.
meleca (*f.*) dried nasal secretion.
melena (*f.*) long hair; long lock; mop, shock (of hair).—s

brancas, long white hair; (*Med.*) melena.
meleta (*f.*) = TAMANDUÁ-MIRIM.
melga (*f.*) crane fly, daddy-long-legs.—**-dos-prados**, alfalfa (*Medicago sativa*), c.a. ALFAFA.
melgueira (*f.*) bee hive; fig., a hoard of money.
melharuco (*m.*) = ABELHEIRO.
melhor (*adj.*; *comp.* & *superl.* of BOM) better, best; (*adv.*; *comp. superl.* of BEM) better, best; (*m.*,*f.*) the better; the best. ainda—, better still, better yet.—que nunca, better than ever.—seria, it would be better (if). beber do—, to drink of the best. bem—, very much better. cada vez—, better and better; better all the time. Era o—que tinhamos a fazer, It was the best we could do. Êste é o—, This is the best (or better) one. levar a—, to best, get the better of, outdo. mudar para—, to change for the better. no —da festa, when least expected. o—, the best, the pick of. o—da história, the best part of the story; the joke of the matter. quanto mais—, the more the better. Seria—você ficar em casa, You had better stay home. tanto—, so much the better.
melhora (*f.*) betterment; improvement.
melhorado –da (*adj.*) bettered; improved.
melhoramento (*m.*) betterment, amelioration; improvement.
melhorar (*v.t.*) to ameliorate, make better; (*v.t.*,*v.i.*) to improve; (*v.i.*) to become (grow, get) better.—de saúde, to improve in health, get better.—de vida, de situação, to better oneself, one's position.
melhoria (*f.*) betterment, improvement.—de vencimentos, a raise in salary.
melia (*f.*, *Bot.*) Chinaberry (*Melia sp.*).
meliáceo –cea (*adj.*, *Bot.*) meliaceous; (*f.pl.*) the Meliaceae (mahogany family).
meliano (*m.*, *Bot.*) a white quebracho (*Aspidosperma platyphyllum*).
meliantáceo –cea (*adj.*, *Bot.*) melianthaceous.
meliante (*m.*) miscreant; rascal; loafer; a good-for-nothing; a plug-ugly.
melianto (*m.*) any honeybush (*Melianthus*).
mélico –ca (*adj.*) honey; sweet; (*Chem.*) mellitic [acid]; (*f.*, *Bot.*) melic or oniongrass (*Melica*).
meleiro –ra (*adj.*) endearing by use of honeyed words.
melífago –ga (*adj.*) meliphagous; (*m.*) a honey eater (bird).
melifanito (*m.*, *Min.*) meliphanite.
melífero –ra (*adj.*) melliferous.
melificar (*v.i.*) to make honey; (*v.t.*) to convert into honey; to sweeten.
melífico –ca (*adj.*) = MELÍFERO.
melifluidade [u-i] (*f.*) mellifluence.
melífluo –flua (*adj.*) mellifluous; mellow, euphonious; suave.
melílito (*m.*, *Min.*) melilite.
meliloto (*m.*) sweet clover [= ANAFA].
melindrar (*v.t.*) to offend, pique, hurt (pride, feelings); (*v.r.*) to take offense (easily).—**-se com**, to resent.
melindre (*m.*) sensitivity, fastidiousness; delicacy; squeamishness; touchiness; (*Bot.*) garden asparagus.
melindrice (*f.*), **melindrismo** (*m.*) pettishness, touchiness; prudishness.
melindroso –sa (*adj.*) touchy; ticklish; finical; coy; namby-pamby; precarious, risky; (*f.*) an affected young woman.
melinita (*f.*) melinite (an explosive).
meliorativo –va (*adj.*) meliorative.
melipona (*f.*) a genus (*Melipona*) of small, stingless bees.
melissa (*f.*, *Bot.*) common balm (*Melissa officinalis*), c.a. ERVA-CIDREIRA.
melíssono –na (*adj.*) melisonant, sweet-sounding.
melissugo –ga (*adj.*) mellisugent, honey-sucking.
melítico –ca (*adj.*, *Chem.*) mellitic [acid].
melito (*m.*, *Min.*, *Pharm.*) mellite.
melitose (*f.*, *Chem.*) raffinose [= RAFINOSE].
melívoro –ra (*adj.*) mellivorous; eating, or living on, honey.
meloal (*m.*) melon field.
melocacto (*m.*) the genus (*Melocactus*) consisting of the melon cacti.
melocatão (*m.*) a peach grafted on a quince [= MARA-COTÃO].
melodia (*f.*) melody.
melodiar (*v.t.*) to make melodious; (*v.i.*) to make melody.
melódico –ca (*adj.*) melodic, melodious; (*f.*) a music box; melodics.

melodioso –sa (*adj.*) melodious.
melodista (*m.,f.*) melodist.
melodizar (*v.t.,v.i.*) to melodize.
melodrama (*m.*) melodrama.
melodramar, melodramatizar (*v.t.*) to melodramatize.
melodramático –ca (*adj.*) melodramatic.
meloeiro (*m.*) muskmelon vine (*Cucumis melo*).—-de-são-caetano, the balsampear (*Momordica charantia*).—-de-soldado = MELÃO-DE-SOLDADO.
melolonta (*f., Zool.*) the common cockchafer (*Melolontha vulgaris*).
melomania (*f.*) a craze for music.
melomaníaco –ca, melômano –na (*adj.*) mad about music; (*m.,f.*) music-mad person.
melonídeo –dea (*adj., Bot.*) fleshy and full of seeds; melonlike [= PEPONÍDEO].
meloniforme (*adj.*) melon-shaped.
melonita (*f., Min.*) melonite.
meloso –sa (*adj.*) sweet (as honey); sticky; of music, "corny".
melrão (*m.*) = GRAÚNA.
melro (*m.*) the merle, common European blackbird (*Turdus merula*); also, in Brazil, any of a number of orioles, c.a. SOLDADO, GRAÚNA; fig., slicker, smart fellow.—-pintado,—-do-brejo, = CHOPIM-DO-BREJO.
melúria (*f.*) whining, wheedling; (*m.,f.*) a slippery person.
membeca (*adj.*) mild, tender; (*f., Bot.*) horsetail paspalm (*P. repens*), c.a. CANARANA-RASTEIRA.
membrana (*f.*) membrane; film.—fibrosa, (*Anat.*) fibrous (connective) tissue.—mucosa, (*Anat.*) mucous membrane.—própria, (*Anat.*) basement membrane.—serosa, (*Anat.*) serous membrane.—sinovial, (*Anat.*) synovial membrane.—vitelina, (*Embryol.*) vitelline membrane.
membranoso –sa (*adj.*) membranous.
membro (*m.*) member; component part; limb (of the body); (*pl.*) arms and legs.
membrudo –da (*adj.*) big-limbed, robust.
membura (*f.*) side member of a JANGADA.
memento (*m.*) memento; reminder; memorandum; note book; (*R.C.Ch.*) Memento.
memorando –da (*adj.*) memorable; (*m.*) memorandum; note; note book.
memorar (*v.t.*) to remember, remind; to commemorate.
memorativo –va (*adj.*) commemorative.
memorável (*adj.*) memorable ,signal, notable.
memória (*f.*) memory, remembrance, reminiscence; fame, renown; memorial, monument; memorandum; (*pl.*) memoirs. à—de, in memory of. de—, by heart. fraco de—, having a weak memory.
memorial (*m.*) memorandum book; a memorial, petition (to the government); (*adj.*) memorable.
memorialista (*m.,f.*) author of memoirs.
memorizar (*v.t.*) to memorize, learn by heart; to recall to memory.
menacanita (*f., Min.*) menaccanite, titanic iron ore.
menagem (*f.*) confinement to quarters, house arrest.
menção (*f.*) mention, citation, notice; gesture, indication. fazer—de (sacar da faca), to start (to pull out a knife). Fez—de sair, He made as if to leave.
mencionar (*v.t.*) to mention, speak of.
mencionável (*adj.*) mentionable.
mendace (*adj.*) = MENDAZ.
mendacíssimo –ma (*absol. superl.* of MENDAZ) most mendacious.
mendacidade (*f.*) mendacity.
mendáculo (*m.*) moral defect.
mendaz (*adj.*) mendacious; lying, untruthful.
medicância (*f.*) medicancy.
mendicante (*adj.; m.,f.*) mendicant.
mendicidade (*f.*) mendicity, begging; pauperism; beggars collectively.
mendigação (*f.*) begging.
mendigagem (*f.*) begging; beggars collectively.
mendigar (*v.t.*) to beg (alms); (*v.i.*) to panhandle; to ask humbly; to live by begging.
mendigo –ga (*m.,f.*) beggar; pauper.
mendipita (*f., Min.*) mendipite.
mendozita (*f., Min.*) mendozite, solium alum.
mendubi, mendubim, menduí (*m.*) peanut [= AMENDOIM].
—-bravo = BOI-GORDO (a shrub).—-de-veado, the rain-tree saman (*Samanea saman*), c.a. FEIJÃO-CRU.
meneador –dora (*adj.*) shaking, wagging; (*m.,f.*) shaker; wagger; nodder; wielder.

meneamento (*m.*) a shaking or swaying; a nodding or wagging; a wielding.
menear (*v.t.*) to shake, wag (head, tail, finger); to brandish, flourish (as a sword); to wield (as a pen); to manage; (*v.r.*) to move, wave, shake (oneself); to sway; to waggle, wiggle.
meneável (*adj.*) that can be shaken (wielded); fig., flexible.
meneio (*m.*) shaking, swaying (of the body or of a part of it); wiggle wriggle; artful management; mode of life.
menequi [í] (*m., Bot.*) the Malay glycosmis (*G. pentaphylla*).
menestrel [-tréis] (*m.*) minstrel, troubadour.
Mênfis (*m.*) Memphis.
menhã, old form of MANHÃ.
meniantes (*m., Bot.*) the common bogbean (*Menyanthes trifoliata*).
menilita (*f., Min.*) menilite.
menina (*f.*) (young) girl; lass, maiden; daughter; young woman; dear.—-de-cinco-olhos, a ferule.—do ôlho, pupil of the eye.—dos olhos, apple of the eye (something very dear).
meninada (*f.*) a group of children.
menineiro –ra (*adj.*) boyish, childish; fond of children.
meninez (*f.*) = MENINICE.
meninge (*f., Anat.*) meninx; (*pl.*) meninges.
meníngeo –gea (*adj.*) meningeal.
meningite (*f., Med.*) meningitis.
meninice (*f.*) infancy, early childhood, boyhood, girlhood, youth; puerility.
menino (*m.*) (young) boy; lad; son; (*colloq.*) old fellow, old boy.—de côro, choir boy.
meninório (*m.*) overgrown boy.
meninota (*f.*) teenage girl.
menir (*m.*) menhir, monolith.
menisco (*m.*) meniscus (in any sense).
meniscóide, meniscoídeo –dea (*adj.*) meniscoid(al).
menispermáceo –cea (*adj., Bot.*) menispermaceous; (*f.pl.*) the Menispermaceae (moonseed family).
menispérmea (*f., Bot.*) a menisperm.
menispermo (*m., Bot.*) moonseed (*Menispermum*).
menofania (*f., Physiol.*) menophania.
menológio (*m.*) menology.
menopausa (*f., Physiol.*) menopause, change of life.
menopoma (*m., Zool.*) the hellbender (*Cryptobranchus alleganiensis*).
menor (*adj.; comp. & superl.* of PEQUENO) smaller, smallest; littler, littlest; lesser, least; younger, youngest; under age; (*m.,f.*) a minor; (*m., Logic*) the minor term; (*m.pl.*) details.—múltiplo comum, (*Math.*) least common multiple. bem—, quite a bit smaller. frade—, = MENO-RITA. trajes—es, underclothes.
menoridade (*f.*) minority, nonage; fig., a minority.
menorita (*f.*) a Minorite (Franciscan friar); = FRADE MENOR.
menorragia (*f., Med.*) menorrhagia.
menorréia (*f.*) menstrual flow, menses.
menorzinho –nha (*adj.*) a little smaller.
menos (*adj.; comp. & superl.* of POUCO; *indef. pron.*) less, least; fewer, fewest; minus; wanting, lacking; (*adv.*) less, not so much, in a less degree; least; (*prep.*) except, excepting, save; (*m.*) the least.—aos domingos, except on Sundays.—de, less than; under.—(do) que, less than.—mal, not so badly.—que nunca, less than ever. a—que, unless. a—que haja, except there be (is). a—que seja, unless it be (is). ao—, at least. em—de, in less than. mais dia,—dia, some day; sooner or later. mais ou—, more or less. Não era para—, It is not to be wondered at. não—que, not less than. nem mais nem—, neither more nor less; just so. pelo—, at least. por—que, no matter how little. pouco mais ou—, just about; pretty near. quando—, when least; at least. quanto—, let alone. sem mais nem—, just like that; without further ado; without so much as by your leave. tudo (todos)—, everything (everyone) but.
menoscabador –dora (*adj.*) belittling, detracting; (*m.,f.*) disparager, detractor, belittler.
menoscabar (*v.t.*) to detract from; to belittle; to underestimate.
menoscabo (*m.*) undervaluation, disparagement, belittling, detraction.
menosprezar (*v.t.*) to misprize, underrate; to belittle; to depreciate, disparage; to slight, disregard, disdain.
menosprezível (*adj.*) despicable.
menosprêzo (*m.*) contempt, scorn, disdain, disregard.

mensageiro –ra (*adj.*) message-bearing; annunciative; (*m.,f.*) messenger; (*m.*) courier, runner.—**de más novas**, a spreader of bad news.

mensagem (*f.*) message, communication.—**cifrada**, code message.—**verbal**, oral message.

mensal (*adj.*) monthly.

mensalidade (*f.*) monthly payment; monthly dues.

mensalmente (*adv.*) monthly.

mensário –ria (*adj.*) of, pertaining to, or used at the table; (*m.*) a monthly (publication).

menstruação (*f.*) menstruation.

menstruada (*adj.*) menstruant.

menstrual (*adj.*) menstrual.

menstruar (*v.i.*) to menstruate.

mênstruo (*m.*) the menses; (*Chem.*) menstrum, solvent.

mensual (*adj.; colloq.*) monthly; (*m.,f.*) salaried employee.

mensurabilidade (*f.*) mensurability.

mensuração (*f.*) mensuration, measuring.

mensurador –dora (*adj.*) measuring; (*m.,f.*) measurer.

mensurar (*v.t.,v.i.*) to measure [= MEDIR].

mensurável (*adj.*) measurable.

menta (*f., Bot.*) kinds of mint.

mental (*adj.*) mental, intellectual.

mentalidade (*f.*) mentality.

mentana (*f., Chem.*) menthane.

mentastro, mentastre (*m., Bot.*) apple mint (*Mentha rotundifolia*), c.a. MENTRASTE, MENTRASTO; also = CATINGA-DE-BODE (an ageratum).

-mente, a suffix which added to a fem. adj. produces the adverb; e.g., ABERTA, ABERTAMENTE (open, openly); SINCERA, SINCERAMENTE (sincere, sincerely).

mente (*f.*) mind, soul, spirit; intellect; inclination, disposition. **de boa**—, quite willingly. **de má**—, unwillingly, grudgingly. **ter em**—, to bear in mind.

mentecapto –ta (*adj.*) out of one's mind, demented; crackbrained.

mentênio, menteno (*m., Chem.*) menthene.

mentido –da (*adj.*) false; illusory.

mentilo (*m., Chem.*) menthyl.

mentir [21a] (*v.t.,v.i.*) to lie, prevaricate, falsify, deceive. —**como um espanhol**, to lie like a trooper.—**pela gorja**, to tell bald-faced lies.

mentira (*f.*) lie, falsehood.—**de rabo e cabeça**, a whopper. —**inocente**, innocent lie.—**oficiosa**, a lie told to help out another person.

mentirada, mentiralha (*f.*) = MENTIROLA.

mentiraria (*f.*) a pack of lies.

mentirola (*f.*) a harmless fib, white lie.

mentiroso –sa (*adj.*) mendacious, untruthful; (*m.,f.*) liar.

mento (*m.*) chin.

mentol (*m., Chem.*) menthol, peppermint camphor.

mentolado –da (*adj.*) mentholated.

mentona (*f., Chem.*) menthone.

mentoniano –na (*adj., Anat.*) pert. to the chin.

mentor –tora (*m.,f.*) mentor, counselor, adviser.

mentraste, mentrasto (*m.*) = MENTASTRE.

mentruz (*m.*) = MASTRUÇO.

mentzélia (*f., Bot.*) the genus (*Mentzelia*) which comprises the mentzelias and blazing stars.

menu (*m.*) menu, bill of fare [= CARDÁPIO].

menziézia (*f.*) the genus (*Menziesia*) of skunk-bushes.

mequetrefe (*m.*) busybody, meddler; a nobody [= MELCATREFE].

merca (*f., colloq.*) a purchase (act or goods).

mercadejar (*v.i.*) to trade, traffic, buy and sell.

mercadinho (*m.*) small market; small food store; neighborhood market; = QUITANDA.

mercado (*m.*) market; market place; commerce.—**a têrmo**, futures market.—**cambial**, foreign exchange market.—**de físicos**, spot market.—**de valores**, stock market.—**varejista**, retail market.

mercadologia (*f.*) marketing; merchandising. [*A neologism*].

mercador (*m.*) retail merchant, tradesman, dealer; (*Zool.*) = CANHANHA. **fazer ouvidos de**—, to turn a deaf ear.

mercadoria (*f.*) merchandise; (*pl.*) goods, wares, commodities.—**s de consumo**, consumer goods.

mercancia [cía] (*f.*) merchandise; act of trading.

mercanciar (*v.*) = MERCADEJAR.

mercante (*adj.*) merchandizing; commercial; (*m.,f.*) merchant.

mercantil (*adj.*) mercantile, commercial; fig., self-seeking.

mercantilismo (*m.*), **mercantilagem** (*f.*) mercantilism, commercialism (in a bad sense).

mercaptan, mercaptã (*m., Chem.*) mercaptan.

mercar (*v.t.*) to buy and sell, trade.

mercatório –ria (*adj.*) mercantile.

merca-tudo (*m.*) secondhand dealer.

mercável (*adj.*) marketable.

mercê (*f.*) grace, favor; mercy; benefice; reward.—**de**, thanks to, owing to. **à**—**de**, at the mercy of.

mercearia (*f.*) grocery store; (*pl.*) groceries.

merceeiro –ra [e-ei] (*m.,f.*) grocer; beadsman.

mercenário –ria (*adj.; m.,f.*) mercenary, hireling.

mercenarismo (*m.*) mercenariness.

merceologia (*f.*) trade, buying and selling.

mercerizar (*v.t.*) to mercerize (cotton fiber or fabrics).

mercureiro (*m.*) = GALINHA-CHOCA.

mercurial (*adj.; m.*) mercurial; (*f., Bot.*) herbmercury (*Mercurialis annua*); (*m., colloq.*) a call-down.

mercurialismo (*m., Med.*) mercurialism.

mercuriato (*m., Chem.*) mercuriate.

mercúrico –ca (*adj.*) mercuric.

mercúrio (*m.*) mercury, quicksilver.—**-do-campo** = GALINHA-CHOCA (plant).—**-doce**, (*Chem.*) calomel.

mercurioso –sa (*adj.*) mercurous.

merda (*f.*) = French *merde*.

merecedor –dora (*adj.*) meretorious, worthy, deserving.

merecer (*v.t.*) to merit, deserve; to earn, be entitled to. **Não merece confiança**, He is not trustworthy. **Êle nos merece muito**, He is worthy of our highest praise; We have the highest regard for him.

merecido –da (*adj.*) deserved; earned.

merecimento (*m.*) merit, worth, worthiness.

merencório –ria (*adj.*) melancholic.

merenda (*f.*) afternoon snack; light lunch; school lunch.

merendar (*v.t.,v.i.*) to eat a light lunch.

merendeiro –ra (*m.,f.*) roll (of bread); (*m.*) lunch box or basket; (*adj.*) intended for lunch.

merendiba (*f., Bot.*) Brazilian terminalia (*T. brasiliensis*).

merengue, merenque (*m.*) meringue; frosting.

merenquima (*f., Bot.*) merenchyma.

merequém (*m., Zool.*) the cactus paroquet of southeastern Brazil (*Aratinga c. cactorum*), c.a. TIRIBA. Cf. PERIQUITO.

mereré (*m.*) a certain card game [= LANSQUENÊ]; the disk fish [= PEIXE-DISCO].

meretriciar-se (*v.r.*) to prostitute oneself.

meretrício –cia (*adj.*) meretricious (but only in the archaic sense of pertaining to or characteristic of a prostitute); (*m.*) prostitution, harlotry. **zona de**—, red light district.

meretriz (*f.*) prostitute.

merganso (*m., Zool.*) the red-breasted merganser (*Mergus serrator*).

mergulhador –dora (*adj.*) diving; (*m.,f.*) diver; (*m.*) deep-sea diver; pearl diver; (*Zool.*) a merganser (*Mergus*).

mergulhante (*adj.*) diving.

mergulhão (*m.*) high dive; (*Hort.*) plant layer; (*Zool.*) any of various diving birds, such as: the white-bellied booby (*Sula leucogaster*), c.a. ATOBA; the sun grebe (*Heliornis fulica*), c.a. IPEQUI; the red-gartered coot (*Fulica armillata*), c.a. CARQUEJA.—**-caçador**, the dabchick or pied-billed grebe (*Podilymbus podiceps*).—**-grande**, a large grebe (*Aechmorphus major*).—**-pequeno**, the least grebe (*Colymbus dominicus*).

mergulhar (*v.t.,v.i.*) to plunge, immerse, submerge, dip; (*v.i.*) to dive. **sino de**—, diving bell.

mergulhia (*f., Hort.*) layerage; layering.

mergulho (*m.*) plunge, dive; (*Geol.*) dip.

meridiano –na (*adj.*) meridian; (*colloq.*) clear as day; (*f.*) intersection of a meridional plane with the horizontal or other plane; sun dial; (*colloq.*) siesta; (*m.*) meridian, great circle.—**magnético**, magnetic meridian.—**primo**, prime meridian.

merídio –dia (*adj.*) midday; meridional.

meridional (*adj.*) meridional, southern, southerly; (*m.,f.*) an inhabitant of the south.

meriedria (*f., Cryst.*) merohedrism.

meriédrico –ca (*adj.*) merohedral; merohedric.

merinaque (*m.*) hoop skirt [= SAIA-BALÃO].

merino –na, **merinó** (*adj.; m.*) Merino (sheep, yarn, fabric).

merisma (*m., Rhet., Biol.*) merism.

merismático –ca (*adj., Bot., Zool.*) merismatic.

meristema (*m., Bot.*) meristem.

merístico –ca (*adj., Biol.*) meristic.

meriti [tí] (*m., Bot.*) the fiber mauritian or burity palm (*Mauritia flexuosa*).

meritíssimo –ma (adj.) most worthy [corresponds to "Your Honor" in addressing a judge].
mérito (m.) merit, worth, worthiness.
meritório –ria (adj.) meritorious; honorable.
merlão (m.) merlon (of a battlement).
merlim (m., Naut.) marline; buckram, crinoline; axe.
merluza (f.) the silver hake (Merluccius bilinearis).
merma (f.) breakage; shrinkage (in weight); outage; leakage.
mermar (v.t.,v.i.) to decrease (in value, weight, etc.).
mermítidas (m.pl.) a family (Mermithidae) of very slender nematode worms.
mero –ra (adj.) mere, sheer, unmixed; (m.) the huge spotted jewfish (Promicrops itaiara), c.a. CUNAPU (-GUAÇU).—prêto = CHERNE (-PINTADO).
meroblástico –ca (adj., Embryol.) meroblastic.
merogonia (f., Embryol.) merogony.
meroxênio [ks] (m., Min.) meroxene.
merozoíta (m.) merozoite.
meru (m., Bot.) edible canna (C. edulis), c.a. BIRU-MANSO.
merua (f.) a buttonplant (Spermacoce longifolia).
meruçoca (f.) var. of MURIÇOCA.
meruí, meruim (m.) vars. of MARUÍ, MARUIM.
meruquiá (f.) a lovegrass (Eragrostis vahlii).
mês (m.) month; a month's wage.—corrente, current month.—da aparição, lunar month.—de cortesia, a month's grace.—legal, legal month; thirty days.—lunar, lunar month.—lunar anomalístico, anomalistic month.—lunar periódico, tropical month.—lunar sinódico, synodical month.—solar, solar month. daqui a seis—es, six m. from now. de dois em dois—es, every two m. dentro de três—es, within three m. faz um—, a month ago. há dois—es, two m. ago. havia dois—es, two m. earlier (prior). no—passado, (during) last month. no—que vem, (during) next month. o—passado, last m. o—proximo, next month. o—que vem, the coming m. o—seguinte, the following m. todos os—es, every m. uns quantos—es, several m.
mesa [ê] (f.) table; board.—da comunhão, communion rail.—de cabeceira, a night table.—de jôgo, card table.—de obragem, work bench or table.—de toilete, vanity, dressing table.—de trinchar, side table, buffet.—elástica, extension table.—telefônica, switchboard.—travessa, head table. à—, at table. levantar-se da—, to get up from the table. pôr a—, to set the table. pôr-se à—, to sit down at table. servir à—, to wait on table. tirar a—, to clear the table.
mesada (f.) monthly allowance, monthly pay, monthly dues.
mescal (m., Bot.) the mescalbutton peyote (Lophophora williamsi).
mescla (f.) mixture, medley, jumble (esp. of colors); cloth of mixed colors; a resintree (Protium icicariba).
mesclado –da (adj.) variegated; motley; blended, mixed; jumbled.
mesclador (m., Radio) mixer.
mescladora (f., Radio) mixer tube.
mesclar (v.t.) to mix, mingle, blend.—-se (a, em), to mix (with, in).
mesembriântemo (m.) the genus (Mesembryanthemum) which consists of the fig marigolds.
mesencéfalo (m., Anat.) mesencephalon, midbrain.
mesênquima (m., Embryol.) mesemchyme.
mesentérico –ca (adj., Anat.) mesenteric(al).
mesentério (m., Anat.) mesentery.
mesenterite (f., Med.) mesenteritis.
meseta [sê] (f.) small plateau.
mesial (adj.) mesial; middle; median.
mesinha (f.) a small table.—de cabeceira, night table.
mesitileno (m., Chem.) mesitylene.
mesitina, mesitita (f.) mesitine (spar), mesitita.
mesma (f.) see under MESMO.
mesmice (f.) sameness.
mesmíssimo –ma (adj.; absol. superl. of MESMO) exactly the same, the very same, the self same.
mesmo –ma (adj.) same; self-same; identical; unchanged; (pron.) the same (person or thing). [êle mesmo, he himself]; (adv.) the same (with the same manner); indeed; even [Eu mesmo não posso, Even I can't]; very, quite; truly, really. [Ela está doente mesmo! She is really sick!]; (f.) the same (state of affairs or condition).—assim, even so; nevertheless.—que, even if. agora—, right now. at this very moment. ainda—que, even though (if). ao—tempo, at the same time. aqui—, right here. assim—,

just so; just the same. **Continua na—,** She is just the same. **dar na—(coisa),** to result in the same thing. **do—modo,** in the same way. **É—,** That's true; That's so. **É isso—!** That's just it! **eu—,** myself. **hoje—,** (on) this very day. **na—noite** (on) that same night. **naquele dia—,** (on) that very day. **nem—,** not even. **no—ato,** simultaneously. **no—instante,** at that instant. **no—momento,** at the same moment. **o—,** the same. **Para mim é o—,** It's all the same to me. **por isso—,** for that very reason. **por si—,** for or by himself (itself, herself). **quando—,** even when. **só—,** just. **vós—s,** you yourselves.
mesoblasto (m., Embryol., Zool.) mesoblast.
mesocarpo (m., Bot.) mesocarp.
mesocefálico –ca (adj., Anat.) mesocephalic.
mesocéfalo –la (adj., Anat.) mesocephalic, mesocranial; (m.) the midbrain.
mesocúrtico –ca (adj., Statistics) mesokurtic, equally flat-topped with the Gaussian curve.
mesoderma (f., Embryol., Zool.) mesoderm.
mesodesmo (m., Zool.) a genus (Mesodesma) of marine bivalves.
mesofilo (m., Bot.) mesophyll(um).
mesogástrio, mesogastro (m., Anat.) mesogastrium.
mesognátio (m., Anat., Zool.) mesognathion.
mesólito (m., Min.) mesolite.
mesomorfo –fa (adj., Physical Chem.) mesomorphic.
meson (m., Physics) meson.
mesópodo (m., Bot.) mesopodium.
mesoquílio (m., Bot.) mesochilium.
mesorrino –na (adj., Anthropom.) mesorrhinial.
mesospermo (m., Bot.) secundine.
mesóstomo (m., Zool.) a genus (Mesostoma) typifying a family (Mesostomatidae) of small fresh-water turbellarian worms.
mesotélio (m., Embryol., Anat.) mesothelium.
mesotórax (m., Zool.) mesothorax (of an insect).
mesotório (m., Chem.) mesothorium.
mesotron (m., Physics) mesotron.
mesoxálico –ca [ks] (adj., Chem.) mesoxalic [acid].
mesozóico –ca (adj.; m., Geol.) Mesozoic.
mesquinhar (v.t.) to grudge, give unwillingly; (v.i.) to dodge, be evasive; (v.r.) to be stingy.
mesquinharia, –nhez (f.) pettiness, stinginess, paltriness.
mesquinho –nha (adj.) stingy, niggardly; closefisted; mean; piddling, trifling, petty; paltry; spare, scanty; meager; puny; narrow, illiberal; (m.,f.) such a person.
mesquita (f.) mosque.
messageiro (m.) var. of MENSAGEIRO.
messalina (f.) a profligate woman, prostitute [but not messaline, a soft silk fabric].
messar (v.t.) to strip bark from cork trees.
messe (f.) field ready for reaping; harvest.
messiânico –ca (adj.) Messianic.
Messias (m.) the Messiah; [not cap.] fig., a social reformer.
mestiçagem (f.), **mestiçamento** (m.) miscegenation; cross-breeding.
mestiçar-se (v.r.) to interbreed; to crossbreed.
mestiço –ça (adj.) half-blooded; of mixed blood; (m.,f.) mestizo; half-breed; hybrid; mongrel.
mestra (adj.; f.) see under MESTRE.
mestraço (m.) past master, master hand.
mestrado (m.) mastership.
mestrança (f.) arsenal; navy yard; (colloq.) masters or experts as a class.
mestrão (m., colloq.) a master (expert); also = MESTRAÇO.
mestre –tra (adj.) master, main; (m.) schoolmaster, teacher, professor, instructor; a master of art, music, etc.; a master hand at anything; the master of a small vessel; a boatswain; a master Mason; (f.) school mistress, woman teacher; forewoman; fig., master; (Building) ground.—-cuco or -cuca, (colloq.) head cook.—-de-armas, fencing master.—de cerimônias, master of ceremonies; "emcee".—-de-obras, construction foreman.—-escola, schoolmaster.—-sala, master of ceremonies; grandmaster of a ball. estrada—, main highway. livro—, ledger. O uso faz—, Practice makes perfect.
mestria (f.) mastery, supreme skill or knowledge.
mesura (f.) bow, obeisance.
mesurado –da (adj.) moderate; judicious; courtly.
mesurar (v.i.) to address, speak to, bow to; (v.r.) to act with moderation.
mesureiro –ra (adj.) obsequious; servile.
mesurice (f.) obsequiousness; servility.

meta (f.) mete, boundary (stone); end, aim, purpose; (*Soccer*) goal.
meta-antimoniato (*m.*, *Chem.*) meta-antimoniate.
metabiótico –ca (*adj.*, *Biol.*) metabiotic.
metabólico –ca (*adj.*, *Biol.*, *Physiol.*, *Zool.*) metabolic.
metabolismo (*m.*, *Biol.*, *Physiol.*, *Zool.*) metabolism. —basal, or básico, basal metabolism.
metaborato (*m.*, *Chem.*) metaborate.
metacarpo (*m.*, *Anat.*, *Zool.*) metacarpus.
metacêntrico –ca (*adj.*) metacentric, metacentral.
metacentro (*m.*, *Hydros.*, *Shipbldg.*) metacenter.
metacinabarita (*f.*, *Min.*) metacinnabarite.
metacis uo (*m.*) metacism.
metacone (*f.*, *Zool.*) metacone.
metacromático –ca (*adj.*, *Physiol.*) metachromatic.
metacromatismo (*m.*, *Physical Chem.*) metachromatism.
metade (*f.*) half; middle. cara—, "better half" (wife). pela—, in half; half and half.
metáfase (*f.*, *Biol.*) metaphase.
metafísico –ca (*adj.*) metaphysical; (*m.*,*f.*) metaphysician; (*f.*) metaphysics.
metafloema (*m.*, *Bot.*) metaphloem.
metafonia (*f.*, *Phonet*) metaphony, umlaut.
metáfora (*f.*) metaphor, trope, figure of speech.
metafórico –ca (*adj.*) metaphorical.
metaforista (*m.*,*f.*) metaphorist.
metafosfato (*m.*, *Chem.*) metaphosphate.
metáfrase (*f.*) metaphrase.
metagénese (*f.*, *Biol.*) metagenesis.
metagenético –ca (*adj.*, *Biol.*) metagenetic.
metal [-tais] (*m.*) metal; ore; coin; (*pl.*) brass instruments; kitchen utensils.—amarelo, brass.—amorfo, amorphous (non-crystalline) metal.—Babbitt, babbitt (bearing alloy).—branco, white metal.—da voz, timbre of the voice.—de antifricção, Babbitt metal.—de contatos, electrical contact metal.—duplex, duplex (laminated) metal.—em lingotes, pig metal.—espalmado, laminated metal.—incorrosível, rustproof, stainless, metal.—monel, Monel metal.—Muntz, muntz metal, c.a. METAL PATENTE.—sonante, coined money, hard cash.—virgem, metal ore.
metalbumina (*f.*, *Biochem.*) pseudomucin.
metaldeído (*m.*, *Chem.*) metaldehyde.
metalicidade (*f.*) metallicity.
metálico –ca (*adj.*) metallic.
metalífero –ra (*adj.*) metalliferous.
metaliforme (*adj.*) metalliform.
metalino –na (*adj.*) metalline.
metalista (*m.*) metalist; metallurgist; mining engineer.
metalização (*f.*) metallizing; metal spraying.
metalizar (*v.t.*) to metallize.
metalocromia (*f.*) metallochromy.
metalografia (*f.*) metallography.
metalóide (*adj.*; *m.*) metalloid.
metaloscópio (*m.*) metaloscope.
metaloterapia (*f.*, *Med.*) metallotherapy.
metalurgia (*f.*) metallurgy.
metalúrgico –ca (*adj.*) metallurgic(al); (*m.*,*f.*) metal worker.
metalurgista (*m.*,*f.*) metallurgist.
metameria (*f.*, *Zool.*, *Chem.*) metamerism.
metamerização (*f.*, *Zool.*) metamerization.
metâmero (*m.*, *Chem.*) metamer; (*Zool.*) metamere.
metamórfico –ca (*adj.*) metamorphic.
metamorfismo (*m.*) metamorphism.
metamorfose (*f.*) metamorphosis.
metamorfosear (*v.t.*) to metamorphose, transform; (*v.i.*) to undergo metamorphosis.
metano (*m.*) methane gas, marsh gas, c.a. GÁS DOS PÂNTANOS, GÁS DAS MINAS, GRISU.
metanal (*m.*, *Chem.*) methanal, formaldehyde [= FORMOL].
metanol (*m.*, *Chem.*) methyl alcohol, wood alcohol.
metanômetro (*m.*) methanometer.
metaplasia (*f.*, *Physiol.*) metaplasia.
metaplasmo (*m.*, *Biol.*, *Gram.*) metaplasm.
metaplástico –ca (*adj.*) metaplastic.
metaquímico –ca (*adj.*) metachemic(al).
metara (*f.*) = TEMBETÁ.
metassomatose (*f.*, *Geol.*) metasomatosis.
metástase (*f.*, *Biol.*, *Med.*, *Petrog.*, *Rhet.*) metastasis.
metastático –ca (*adj.*) metastatic.
metastável (*adj.*, *Chem.*) metastable [equilibrium].
metasterno (*m.*, *Anat.*, *Zool.*) metasternum.

metastibnite (*f.*, *Min.*) metastibnite.
metatarso (*m.*, *Anat.*) metatarsus.
metátese (*f.*, *Gram.*) metathesis.
metatórax [ks] (*m.*, *Zool.*) metathorax.
metatrófico –ca (*adj.*, *Biol.*) metatrophic, saprophytic.
metaxilema (*m.*, *Bot.*) metaxylem.
metaxita (*f.*) *Min.*) metaxite.
metazoário –ria (*adj.*, *Zool.*) metazoan; (*m.pl.*) Metazoa.
metazóico –ca (*adj.*) metazoic, metazoan.
meteco (*m.*) resident foreigner.
metediço –ça (*adj.*) meddlesome, intrusive. pessoa—, a busybody.
metempsicose (*f.*) metempsychosis.
meteórico –ca (*adj.*) meteoric.
meteorite (*f.*), –to (*m.*) meteorite.
meteorizar (*v.t.*) to vaporize; (*Med.*) to meteorize.
meteoro (*m.*) any atmospheric phenomenon; meteor, shooting star.
meteorógrafo (*m.*) meteorograph.
meteorólito (*m.*) meteorite, aerolite.
meteorologia (*f.*) meteorology.
meteorológico –ca (*adj.*) meteorologic. boletim—, weather report.
meteorologista (*m.*,*f.*) meteorologist.
meter (*v.t.*) to insert, introduce, stick, thrust, put, set in. Cf. BOTAR, FINCAR, PÔR.—a cara, (*slang*) to intrude, butt in.—(alguém) em boa, to put (someone) in a pickle. —a ferro, to put to the sword.—a mão em cumbuca, (*colloq.*) to get oneself into trouble; lit., to put one's hand in a trap.—a mão no fogo por (alguém), to swear by (someone).—a pique, to send (a ship) to the bottom. —mãos à obra, to set to work, get busy.—mêdo a (or em), to inspire fear in, frighten (someone).—na cabeça, to put (an idea) into someone's head; to learn something by heart.—o bedelho (or o nariz, or o bico), to stick one's nose in.—o pau em, (*slang*) to give hell to; to criticize pitilessly; to "pan"; lit., to belabor with a stick.—ombros a, to put one's shoulder to the wheel.—os pés pelas mãos, to become flustered, confused.—raiva a (or em), to enrage.—se a, to set oneself up as; to undertake something for which one is not fully qualified.—se a caminho, to get started, on the way.—se com alguém, to take up with someone; to get involved (mixed up) with someone; to pick a quarrel with someone.—se consigo mesmo, to mind one's own business; to keep to oneself.—se em alguma coisa até à ponta dos cabelos, to get involved in something up to one's ears.—se em (algum lugar), to hide oneself (somewhere).—se em apuros, or em maus lençóis, to get oneself into trouble. —se em camisa de onze varas, to get into a peck of trouble.—se em casa, to bury oneself indoors. Em boa me meti eu! I've got myself into a fine mess! Meta isso na cabeça, Get that into your head. Meta-se com sua vida, Mind your own business. Meteu-se na cama, He got into bed. Não se meta na vida dos outros, Don't meddle in other people's affairs. Não te metas com êle, Leave him alone; don't get mixed up with him. Não sabe onde se meter, He doesn't know where to turn (to escape embarrassment).
metição (*f.*) act of inserting (something).
meticulosidade (*f.*) meticulosity; meticulousness.
meticuloso –sa (*adj.*) meticulous; punctilious; finical; timid, fearful.
metido –da (*adj.*) intrusive; brassy; "nosey".
metilado –da (*adj.*, *Chem.*) methylated.
metilal (*m.*, *Chem.*) methylal.
metilamina (*f.*, *Chem.*) methylamine.
metilarsina (*f.*, *Chem.*) methyl arsine.
metilato (*m.*, *Chem.*) methylate.
metil-benzeno (*m.*, *Chem.*) methyl benzene, toluene.
metileno (*m.*, *Chem.*) methylene.
metílico –ca (*adj.*, *Chem.*) methylic.
metilo (*m.*, *Chem.*) methyl.
metilorange (*m.*, *Chem.*) methyl orange (dye).
metilose (*f.*, *Geol.*) metasomatosis.
metilpropanol (*m.*, *Chem.*) 2-methyl-1-propanol.
metódico –ca (*adj.*) methodic; orderly.
metodismo (*m.*) Methodism.
metodista (*adj.*) Methodist; orderly, methodic; (*m.*,*f.*) a Methodist; a methodical person.
metodizar (*v.t.*) to methodize.
método (*m.*) method, mode, manner, way, procedure.—crioscópico, (*Physical Chem.*) cryoscopy.—ebulioscópico,

(*Physical Chem.*) ebullioscopic determination of atomic weights.—**zetético,** zetetic investigation.
metodologia (*f.*) methodology.
metodologista (*m.,f.*) methodologist.
metonímia (*f., Rhet.*) metonymy.
metonímico –ca (*adj.*) metonymic(al).
métopa, métope (*f., Arch.*) metope.
metópico –ca (*adj., Anat.*) metopic.
metragem (*f.*) length or extent in meters; yardage in meters.
metralgia (*f., Med.*) metralgia.
metralha (*f.*) shrapnel; fig., rubble.
metralhada (*f.*) a shot of shrapnel.
metralhador –dora (*adj.*) machine-gunning; (*m.,f.*) machine gunner; (*f.*) machine gun.
metralhar (*v.t.*) to shell or bombard fiercely; to "strafe"; to machine-gun.
metrar (*v.t.*) to measure in meters.
métrico –ca (*adj.*) metric(al); (*f.*) metrics.
metrificar (*v.t.,v.i.*) to metrify; to versify.
metrite (*f., Med.*) metritis.
metro (*m.*) meter [= 39.37 inches = 3.2808 ft.]; verse meter.—**cúbico,** cubic meter.—**quadrado,** square meter.
metrô (*m.*) subway. [From the French.]
metrofotografia (*f.*) metrophotography; photogrammetry.
metrologia (*f.*) metrology.
metrônomo (*m.*) metronome.
metrópole (*f.*) metropolis.
metropolita (*m., Eccl.*) metropolite.
metropolitano –na (*adj.*) metropolitan; (*m.*) a metropolitan bishop; an underground railway (subway).
metrorragia (*f., Med.*) metrorrhagia.
metrossídero (*m.*) the genus (*Metrosideros*) consisting of the irontrees.
metroxilo [ks] (*m.*) the genus (*Metroxylon*) which includes the sagopalms and the ivorynut palms.
meu [fem. **minha**] (*poss. adj.*) my; (*pron.*) mine. **a**—**ver,** in my opinion; as I see it. **Êle é muito**—**amigo,** He is very much my friend. **os**—**s,** my folks. **um amigo**—, a friend of mine.
mexediço –ça (*adj.*) restless, squirming, fidgety.
mexedor –dora (*adj.*) stirring; mixing; (*m.,f.*) stirrer; mixer; meddler.
mexedura (*f.*) mixing; stirring; mixture.
mexe-que-mexe (*m.*) stir, confusion.
mexe-mexe (*m.*) scrabble (the game).
mexer (*v.t.*) to stir, move; to mix by stirring; to agitate, disturb; (*v.r.*) to budge; to stir; to get a move on; to make haste; to wriggle, fidget.—**a cauda,** to wag the tail.—**a treta,** to stir up trouble.—**céus e terra,** to move heaven and earth; to leave no stone unturned.—**com,** to molest; to fool with; to tease, devil, needle.—**em,** to touch, disturb, disarrange.—**em cacho de marimbondo,** to stir up a hornet's nest.—**os seus cordelinhos,** or **os pausinhos,** to pull strings. **Essa música mexe com a gente!** That music gets one stirred up! **Mexa-se!** Get a move on! Get going! Snap out of it! **Panela que muitos mexem, ou sai salgada ou sai insôssa,** Too many cooks spoil the broth.
mexerica (*f.*) tangerine, mandarin [= TANGERINA; LARANJA-CRAVO].
mexericar (*v.i.*) to carry tales; to tittle-tattle; to gossip.
mexerico (*m.*) malicious gossip, tittle-tattle, meddling, mischief-making.
mexeriqueiro –ra (*m.*) scandalmonger, telltale, tale-bearer, tattler, tattletale, mischief-maker, busybody, newsmonger; (*f.*) = TANGERINEIRA; (*adj.*) gossiping; mischiefmaking; talebearing.
mexerucar (*v.t.*) to be always fiddling with (touching, moving, disturbing) something.
mexerufada (*f.*) swill, hogwash; clutter; jumble.
mexicano –na (*adj.; m.,f.*) Mexican.
mexido –da (*adj.*) mixed, stirred; restless. **ovos**—**s,** scrambled eggs; (*m.*) a Christmas pudding; a shaking of the hips; a bit of malicious gossip or meddling; (*f.*) mess, hodgepodge, disorder, clutter; turmoil.
mexilhão –lhona (*adj.*) mischievous, meddlesome; (*m.*) in Portugal, the edible mussel (*Mytilus edulis*). In Brazil, any of several species of *Mytilus* and *Modiola*; (*m.,f.*) a meddlesome, mischievous person.
mexinflório (*m.*) trifle; mishmash, disarray; tangle; plot.
mezanelo (*m.*) paving brick.
mezanino (*m.*) mezzanine floor or window; a basement window.

mezena (*f., Naut.*) mizzen sail.
mezereão (*m., Bot.*) the mezereon or February daphne (*D. mezereum*), c.a. LAURÉOLO-FÊMEA; the spurgeflax daphne (*D. gnidium*).
mezeréu-menor (*m., Bot.*) the spurge laurel (*Daphne laureola*), c.a. LAURÉOLA-MACHA.
mezinha (*f.*) household remedy; physic.
mezinheiro –ra (*m.,f.*) quack; a person who practices frequent self-medication.
MG = MINAS GERAIS (State of).
mg = MILIGRAMA(S) = milligram(s).
mgr = miligrado(s) = milligrade(s).
mi = MILHA MARÍTIMA INTERNACIONAL (international nautical mile).
miada (*f.*) noise of cats' miaowing.
miadela (*f.*) a miaowing.
miado (*m.*) a cat's miaow.
miador –dora (*adj.*) mewing; (*m.,f.*) a mewing cat.
mialgia (*f., Med.*) myalgia; muscular rheumatism.
miar (*v.i.*) to mew (as a cat.)
miargirite (*f., Min.*) miargyrite.
miarolítico –ca (*adj., Petrog.*) miarolytic.
miasma (*f.*) miasma, bad air.
miasmático –ca (*adj.*) miasmatic, noxious.
miascito (*m., Petrog.*) miaskite.
miastenia (*f., Med.*) myasthenia.
miau (*m.*) miaow (of a cat.)
mica (*f.*) mica, isinglass; crumb, grain, particle.—**de cálcio,** or—**nacarda,** (*Min.*) margarite.—**dos pintores,** lapislazuli.—**magnesiana,** magnesia mica, phlogopite.—**monoclínica,** or—**potássica,** common or potash mica, muscovite.—**verde,** uranium oxide, pitchblende.
micáceo –cea (*adj.*) micaceous.
Micado (*m.*) the Japanese Mikado.
micajem (*m.*) funny face; grimace.
miçanga (*f.*) glass beads; trifle; 4½- or 5-point type.
micaxisto (*m., Petrog.*) mica schist.—**de anfibólio,** hornblende schist.—**de biotita,** biotitic schist.—**de piroxênio,** pyroxenic schist. Var. MICASQUISTO.
micção (*f.*) urination.
micélico –ca (*adj., Bot.*) mycelial.
micélio (*m., Bot.*) mycelium.
micetismo (*m., Med.*) mycetism, mushroom poisoning.
micetogênese (*f., Bot., Med.*) mycetogenesis.
mico (*m.*) any capuchin monkey (*Cebus*), c.a. MICO-DE-TOPÊTE; old maid (card game).
micoderma (*f.*) mother of wine, vinegar, etc.; mycoderma.
micologia (*f.*) mycology.
micólogo –ga (*m.,f.*) mycologist.
micorriza (*f., Bot.*) micorhiza.
micose (*f., Med.*) mycosis; athlete's foot.
micótrofo –fa (*adj., Bot.*) mycotrophic.
micracústico –ca (*adj.*) micracoustic.
micrampère (*m.*) = MICROAMPÈRE.
micro (*m.*) micron [= MÍCRON].
microaerófilo –la (*adj., Biol.*) micro-aerophilic.
microampère (*m., Elec.*) microampere.
microamperímetro (*m., Elec.*) microammeter.
microanálise (*f., Chem.*) microanalysis.
microbalança (*f., Physics*) microbalance.
microbar (*m., Physics*) microbar.
microbarógrafo (*m., Meteorol.*) microbarograph.
microbial, microbiano –na (*adj.*) microbial, microbic.
microbicida (*adj.*) microbicidal, germicidal; (*m.*) microbicide, germicide.
micróbio (*m.*) microbe, germ.
microcaloria (*f., Physics*) microcalorie.
microcefalia (*f.*) microcephaly; idiotism.
microcefálico –ca (*adj.*) microcephalic.
microcéfalo –la (*adj.*) microcephalous; (*m.,f.*) a microcephal; a microcephalic idiot.
micrócero –ra (*adj., Zool.*) microceratous.
microcinematógrafo (*m.*) microcinematograph, a motion photomicrograph.
micrócito (*m., Anat.*) microcyte.
microclina (*f.*), **microclínio** (*m., Min.*) microcline.
micrococos, micrococos (*m.pl., Bacteriol.*) micrococci.
microcósmico –ca (*adj.*) microcosmic.
microcosmo (*m.*) microcosm.
microcoulomb (*m., Elec.*) microcoulomb.
microcristalino –na (*adj., Pegrog.*) microcrystalline.
microdina (*f., Physics*) microdyne.
microdonte (*adj.*) microdontous.
microestrutura (*f.*) microstructure.

microfárad (*m.*, *Elec.*) microfarad.
microfilo –la (*adj.*, *Bot.*) microphyllous, small-leaved.
microfísica (*f.*) microphysics.
micrófita (*f.*), -to (*m.*, *Bot.*) microphyte.
microfone, –no (*m.*) microphone.
microfônico –ca (*adj.*) microphonic.
microfonismo (*m.*, *Radio*) blasting.
microfot (*m.*, *Photom.*) microphot.
microfotografia (*f.*) microphotography.
microfotográfico –ca (*adj.*) microphotographic.
microfotômetro (*m.*, *Optics*) microphotometer.
microgâmeta (*m.*, *Biol.*) microgamete.
microgametócito (*m.*, *Biol.*) microgametocyte.
microgilbert (*m.*, *Elec.*) microgilbert.
micrografia (*f.*) micrography.
micrógrafo (*m.*) micrograph; micrographer.
micrograma (*m.*) microgram(me).
microgranito (*m.*, *Petrog.*) microgranite.
microhenry (*m.*, *Elec.*) microhenry.
microhme (*m.*, *Elec.*) microhm.
microjoule (*m.*, *Physics.*, *Elec.*) microjoule.
micrólito (*m.*, *Petrog.*, *Min.*) microlite.
microlitro (*m.*) microliter.
micrologia (*f.*) micrology.
microlux (*m.*, *Photom.*) microlux.
micromanômetro (*m.*) micromanometer.
microméria (*f.*, *Bot.*) the genus (*Micromeria*) which includes the yerba buena (*M. chamissonis*).
micrometria (*f.*) micrometry.
micrômetro (*m.*) micrometer.
micromicete (*m.*) a yeast plant or cell.
micromilímetro (*m.*) micromillimeter; millimicron.
mícron (*m.*) = MICRO.
micronésio –sia (*adj.*; *m.*,*f.*) Micronesian.
microômetro (*m.*, *Elec.*) microhmmeter.
micro-ondas (*f.pl.*, *Radio*) microwaves.
micro-organismo (*m.*, *Biol.*) microorganism.
micropegmatito (*m.*, *Petrog.*) micropegmatite.
micropertito (*m.*, *Petrog.*) microperthite.
micrópila (*f.*), -lo (*m.*, *Bot.*) micropyle.
micropirômetro (*m.*, *Physics*) micropyrometer.
microplancto (*m.*, *Biol.*) microplankton.
micropolegada (*f.*) microinch.
microquímica (*f.*) microchemistry.
microrradiômetro (*m.*, *Physics*) radiomicrometer.
microscopar (*v.t.*) to microscope.
microscopia (*f.*) microscopy.
microscópico –ca (*adj.*) microscopic.
microscópio (*m.*) microscope.
microscopista (*m.*,*f.*) microscopist.
microsfera (*m.*, *Bot.*) a genus (*Microsphaera*) of powdery mildews.
microspectroscópio (*m.*, *Physics*) microspectroscope.
microsporângio (*m.*, *Bot.*) microsporangium.
microspório –ria (*adj.*, *Bot.*, *Zool.*) microsporous; (*m.*) microspore.
microssegundo (*m.*) microsecond.
microssismo (*m.*) microseism.
microssulco (*m.*) microgroove (of a phonograph record).
microtasímetro (*m.*, *Physics*) microtasimeter.
microtelefone (*m.*) microtelephone.
microtermo (*m.*, *Bot.*) microtherm.
micrótomo (*m.*) microtome.
microvolt (*m.*, *Elec.*) microvolt.
microwatt (*m.*, *Elec.*) microwatt.
microzoários (*m.pl.*, *Zool.*) microzoa, microzoaria.
mictéria (*f.*, *Zool.*) the American wood ibis (*Mycteria americana*).
micterismo (*m.*) sneering derision.
mictório (*adj.*) diuretic; (*m.*) a public urinal.
micturição (*f.*) micturition.
micuim [u-ím] (*m.*) chigger, red bug, mite, small tick.
micurê (*m.*) = GAMBÁ.
mida (*f.*) spindletree (*Fusanus sp.*).
midaleína (*f.*, *Biochem.*) mydaleine.
midríase (*f.*, *Physiol.*, *Med.*) mydriasis.
midriático –ca (*adj.*) mydriatic.
mielencéfalo (*m.*, *Anat.*, *Embryol.*) myelencephalon.
mielina (*f.*, *Biochem.*) myelin(e).
mielite (*f.*, *Med.*) myelitis.
mielítico –ca (*adj.*, *Med.*) myelitic.
mielóide (*adj.*, *Anat.*) myeloid.
miersite (*f.*, *Min.*) miersite.
miga (*f.*) crumb; (*pl.*) panada.

migado –da (*adj.*) chopped (cut, crumbled) to bits.
mígala (*f.*) the bird spider (*Avincularia avincularia*).
migalha (*f.*) crumb, bit, particle, morsel; (*pl.*) table scraps.—de gente, a tiny person. às—s, bit by bit. não tem—de juizo, (he) hasn't a grain of sense.
migalhar (*v.*) = ESMIGALHAR.
migalheiro –ra (*adj.*) overly concerned with details; miserly; (*m.*,*f.*) a miserly person.
migalhice (*f.*) a trifle [= NINHARIA].
migálidas (*m.*, *Zool.*) a family (*Avinculariidae*) of spiders.
migar (*v.t.*) to crumble (bread).
migração (*f.*) migration.
migrador –dora (*adj.*) migrating [birds].
migrante (*adj.*) migrant.
migratório –ria (*adj.*) migratory.
Miguel (*m.*) Michael.
miguim (*m.*) = VERÃO (a bird).
mijacão (*m.*) toadstool.
mijada (*f.*) the quantity of urine passed at one time.
mijadeiro, mijadouro (*m.*) urinal.
mijadela (*f.*) stream of urine; urine stain.
mija-mija (*m.*) a cockle or heart shell (*Trachycardium muricatum*), c.a. BERBIGÃO, RALA-CÔCO, TAMATI.
mijão, –jona (*m.*,*f.*) person (esp. a child) who frequently wets himself; a bed-wetter; fig., a coward.
mijar (*v.i.*) to urinate; (*v.r.*) to wet oneself.
mija-vinagre (*m.*, *Zool.*) a Portuguese man-of-war (*Physalia pelagica*).
mijo (*m.*, *colloq.*) urine.
mil. = MILHA (mile); MILICIANO (militiaman).
mil (*adj.*; *m.*) thousand; mil (1/1000 inch).—circular, circular mil.—vezes, a thousand times. um em—, one in a thousand. Cf. MILHAR, MILHEIRO.
milagre (*m.*) miracle; marvel; also, in Brazil, a waxen or wooden reproduction of some formerly diseased member of the body which is placed on display in the church as a votive offering of gratitude for miraculous cure obtained; or, a pictorial representation of the event. Santo de casa não faz—, A prophet is not without honor savè in his own country.
milagreiro –ra (*adj.*) gullible, credulous; (*m.*,*f.*) a miracleworker.
milagroso –sa (*adj.*) miraculous; wonderful; (*f.*) a kind of manioc.
milanês –nêsa (*adj.*; *m.*,*f.*) Milanese.
Milão (*m.*) Milan.
milarite (*f.*, *Min.*) milarite.
mil-covas (*f.*) a land measure in north Brazil corresponding to 3,025 square meters.
míldio (*m.*) plant mildew.
mildiosado –da (*adj.*) mildewed.
mileáceo –cea (*adj.*) pert. to maize; maize-like.
milefólio (*m.*, *Bot.*) the yarrow (*Achillea millefolium*), c.a. MIL-EM-RAMA, MIL-FÔLHAS, MIL-FOLHADA, ERVA-DOS-GOLPES.
milenário –ria (*adj.*) millennial; age-old; (*m.*) = MILÊNIO.
milênio (*m.*) millennium.
milépora (*f.*) a genus (*Millepora*) of reef-building corals.
milerite (*f.*, *Min.*) millerite.
milésimo –ma (*adj.*) millesimal, thousandth; (*m.*,*f.*) the thousandth one; a thousandth part.
mil-flores (*m.*) millefleurs (a kind of perfume).
milfolhada, mil-fôlhas (*f.*) = MILEFÓLIO.
mil-fôlhas-da-água (*f.*) = CAVALINHO-D'ÁGUA.
milfurada (*f.*, *Bot.*) St. Johnswort (*Hypericum*), c.a. HIPERICÃO.
milgrada, milgranada (*f.*) pomegranate [= ROMÃ].
mil-grãos (*m.*) = BRILHANTINA (a plant).
milha (*f.*) mile.—inglêsa, a statute mile.—marítima, or náutica, a nautical or sea mile.—quadrada, square mile.
milhã (*f.*) a panic grass (*Panicum sanguinale*); also = CAPIM-DE-CABRA. —branca = CAPIM-PAULISTA. —da-colônia = CAPIM-DA-COLÔNIA.—de-pendão, hairy crabgrass (*Digitaria sanguinalis*).—do-sertão, or—gigante, or—verde = CAPIM-GUINÉ (Guinea grass).—garça, or -glauca, a bristlegrass (*Setaria glauca*).—maior or—pé-de-galo, a basketgrass (*Oplismenus crusgalli*), c.a. CAPIM-PÉ-DE-GALINHA. —verde = CAPIM-VERDE. —verticilada, the hooked bristlegrass (*Setaria verticillata*).
milhado –da (*adj.*, *colloq.*) drunk; corn-fed, fat.
milhafre (*m.*) the common European kite or glede (*Milvus ictinus*), c.a. MILHANO, MILVIO.
milhagem (*f.*) mileage.
milhal (*m.*) cornfield.

milhão (*m.*) a million [expressed in Brazil as 1.000.000 instead of 1,000,000 as in U.S.A.].

milhar (*m.*) a thousand(th). aos –es, by (the) thousand(s). Cf. MIL, MILHEIRO.

milharada (*f.*) a large pile of corn; a cornfield.

milharal (*m.*) cornfield.

milharas (*f.pl.*) fig seeds; fish roe.

milhardário (*m.*) millionaire [= MILIONÁRIO].

milharoz (*m.*) = ABELHEIRO.

milheiral (*m.*) cornfield.

milheiro (*m.*) a thousand [usually applied only to concrete objects]. Cf. MIL, MILHEIRO.

milhete [ê] (*m.*) millet.—-gigante = CAPIM-PORORÓ (sourgrass).

milho (*m.*, *Bot.*) maize, Indian corn (*Zea mays*), plant or grain; (*slang*) money.—-bravo = CAPIM-MAÇAMBARÁ.—-cozido, an apes-earring (*Pithecellobium pubescens*).—-d'água, the edible seeds of the giant Amazon water lily.—-da-guiné, sorghum; guinea grass, Johnson grass.—-da-itália, Italian millet (*Setaria italica*).—-das-vassouras, broom grass.—embandeirado, tasseled corn plants.—-miúdo, or—-painço, millet.—-pipoca, popcorn.—-sorgo, or—-zaburro, sorghum.

mil-homens (*m.*) = JARRINHA; CIPÓ-MIL-HOMENS.

miliampère (*m.*, *Elec.*) milliamp(ere).

miliamperômetro, miliamperímetro (*m.*, *Elec.*) milliammeter.

miliar (*adj.*) miliary. febre—, (*Med.*) miliaria, miliary fever; (*m.*) billion, milliard.

miliare (*m.*) milliarie [0.001 are = 1.076 sq. ft.].

miliário –ria (*adj.*) milliary. marco—, milestone; (*f.*, *Med.*) miliaria.

milibar (*m.*, *Physics*) millibar.

milícia (*f.*) militia, soldiery.

miliciano (*m.*) militiaman.

miligrama (*m.*) milligram [0.001 gram = 0.0154 grain].

milihenry (*m.*, *Elec.*) millihenry.

mililambert (*m.*, *Photom.*) millilambert.

mililitro (*m.*) millileter [0.001 liter = 0.061 cu. in.].

mililux (*m.*, *Photom.*) millilux.

milímetro (*m.*) millimeter [0.001 meter = 0.03937 inch].

milimicro, milimícron (*m.*) millimicron.

miliobatídeos (*m.pl.*) the family (*Aetobatidae*, *syn. Myliobatidae*) consisting of the eagle rays.

milfolo (*m.*, *Zool.*) a genus (*Miliola*) of Foraminifera.

milionário –ria (*adj.*; *m.,f.*) millionaire.

milionésimo –ma (*adj.*; *m.,f.*) millionth.

milípede (*adj.*) myriapodous [but not a millipede, which is EMBUÁ].

militança (*f.*) the military.

militante (*adj.*) militant; that militates.

militar (*adj.*) military. área—, military reservation. (*m.*) a military man, soldier.—de alta patente, a high-ranking officer; (*v.i.*) to serve as a soldier; to militate (against).

militarão (*m.*, *colloq.*) a high-handed military man.

militarismo (*m.*) militarism.

militarista (*adj.*) militaristic; (*m.,f.*) militarist.

militarização (*f.*) militarization.

militarizar (*v.t.*) to militarize.

milivolt (*m.*, *Elec.*) millivolt.

milivoltômetro, milivoltímetro (*m.*, *Elec.*) millivoltmeter.

miliwatt (*m.*, *Elec.*) milliwatt.

milola (*f.*) the linden hibiscus (*H. tiliaceus*).

milolô (*m.*) bullocksheart custardapple (*Annona reticulata*).

milonga (*f.*) a kind of sad or mournful folksong of Uruguay and Argentina; witchcraft (in Africa); (*pl.*) in Brazil, gossiping; airs; lame excuses.

milorde (*m.*) milord, my lord; by ext., a wealthy or prominent person, or one who so appears.

mil-réis (*m.*) former Brazilian money, replaced in 1942 by the CRUZEIRO. [One mil-réis is written 1$000.]

miltônia (*f.*) the genus (*Miltonia*) consisting of the pansy orchids.

mílvio (*m.*) kite, glede. [*Poetical.*]

mim (*pers. pron.*) me. a—mesmo, to myself. Para—dá no mesmo, or para—tanto faz, It's all the same to me. por—, for my part. quanto a—, as for me.

mima (*f.*) a woman mime.

mimaça (*f.*) excessive pampering of children.

mimado –da (*adj.*) petted, spoiled, pampered. Criança—, criança estragada, Spare the rod and spoil the child.

mimalho, mimanço (*m.*) a mollycoddle.

mimar (*v.t.*) to pet, stroke, fondle; to pamper; to make a fuss over; to mimic.

mimeografagem (*f.*) mimeographing.

mimeografar (*v.t.*) to mimeograph.

mimeógrafo (*m.*) mimeograph machine.

mimese (*f.*, *Biol.*, *Med.*, *Rhet.*) mimesis; mimicry.

mimetita, mimetesita (*f.*, *Min.*) mimetesite, mimetite.

mimetismo (*m.*) mimicry; protective coloration, etc. (of animals).

mimi (*f.*) kitty, pussycat.

mimicar (*v.t.,v.i.*) to mimic.

mímico –ca (*adj.*) mimetic, imitative; (*m.,f.*) mimic; (*f.*) mimicry.

mimo (*m.*) dainty gift; a caress; petting, fondling; mime (farce, player).—-de-vênus, Chinese hibiscus (*H. rosa-sinensis*), c.a. ROSA-DA-CHINA, GRAXA, GRAXA-DE-ESTUDANTE.—-do-céu = AMOR-AGARRADO.

mimosa (*f.*) see under MIMOSO.

mimosáceo –cea (*adj.*, *Bot.*) mimosaceous; (*f.pl.*) the Mimosaceae (mimosa family).

mimosear (*v.t.*) to pet, pamper.—com, to present with (a gift). mimosearem-se mútuamente com injúrias, to trade insults.

mimoso –sa (*adj.*) sweet, darling; cute; delicate, dainty, exquisite; natty. fubá—, very fine cornmeal. (*m.,f.*) the favorite or favored one, the pet; (*f.*) any plant of the genus *Mimosa*; also certain species of *Acacia*, as *A. decurrens*.—-carmezim, a species of *Inga* (mimosa family).—-de-vereda is *Mimosa ursinoides*.—-dos-jardins, crapemyrtle (*Lagerstroemia*), c.a. ESCUMILHA, EXTREMOSA.

mina (*f.*) a mine; an explosive charge; (*slang*) bonanza.—de ouro, gold mine.—de saber, a fountain of knowledge.—de cernambi = SAMBAQUI; (*m.,f.*) the name applied to Senegalese Negroes brought to Brazil as slaves.

minador –dora (*adj.*) mining; (*m.*) miner.

minadouro (*m.*) spring (of water). Var. MINADOIRO.

minar (*v.t.*) to mine, burrow, dig into; to sap, undermine, dig under; to ruin, destroy (secretly).

minarete [rê] (*m.*) minaret.

mindinho (*m.*) the little finger [= MINGUINHO].

mineiro –ra (*adj.*) of or pert. to mines, or to the State of Minas Gerais; (*m.*) a miner; (*m.,f.*) a native or inhabitant of Minas Gerais; (*f.*) land rich in ores.

mineração (*f.*) mining.

minerador (*m.*) miner.

mineral [-rais] (*adj.,m.*) mineral.

mineralizar (*v.t.*) to mineralize.

mineralogia (*f.*) mineralogy.

mineralógico –ca (*adj.*) mineralogical.

mineralogista (*m.,f.*) mineralogist.

minerar (*v.t.,v.i.*) to mine.

minério (*m.*) mineral, ore.

minerva (*f.*) a small job printing press.—-dos-jardins = EXTREMOSA (a plant).

minestra (*f.*) dodge, expedient, artifice.

minestre (*m.*) person who employs artful devices to get his way.

mingacho (*m.*) a large gourd in which fish are kept alive after catching.

mingau (*m.*) pap, soft food, mush, porridge, gruel.

mingolas (*m.,f.*, *colloq.*) stingy person [= AVARO].

míngua (*f.*) want, lack, dearth, scarcity. à—de, for want of.

minguado –da (*adj.*) wanting, lacking, scanty.—de juízo, wanting in good sense.

minguante (*adj.*) waning; (*m.*) wane, diminution, decline. lua—, decrescent moon. quarto—, the fourth quarter of the moon.

minguar [8] (*v.i.*) to wane, grow less, abate, ebb.

minguinho (*m.*) = MINDINHO.

minha, fem. of MEU (my, mine).

minhoca (*f.*) earthworm, angleworm.

minhocaçu [ú] (*m.*) a huge (3-foot) earthworm, of genus *Glossocolex*.

minhocão (*m.*) any blind, wormlike, burrowing amphibian of the family Caeciliidae, c.a. CECÍLIA, COBRA-CEGA, COBRA-DE-DUAS-CABEÇAS, COBRA-PILÃO, MÃE-DE-SAÚVA, INDOÁ-MBOI; (*colloq.*) a huge earthworm; in Brazilian folklore, a monstrous serpentlike creature with supernatural powers; c.a. MINHOCAÇU.

minhonete (*f.*, *Bot.*) common mignonette (*Reseda odorata*).

minhoteira (*f.*) footbridge.

minhoto [nhô] (*m.*, *Carp.*) dovetail joint; (*adj.*; *m.,f.*) (person) from the Port. province of Minho.

miniano –na (*adj.*) vermillion, miniaceous.

minianto (*m.*) a clover (*Trifolium fibrinum*).
miniatura (*f.*) miniature.
miniaturista (*m.,f.*) miniaturist.
minigâncias (*f.pl.*) trifles.
mínimo **-ma** (*adj.; superl. of* PEQUENO), least, smallest, slightest; (*m.*) the minimum.—**múltiplo comum**, least common multiple. **ao** (**no**)—, at least, in the least. **dedo**—, the little finger.
mínio (*m.*) minium, red lead.
ministerial (*adj.*) ministerial.
ministério (*m.*) ministry; cabinet, body of ministers; a branch of government.—**da Guerra**, War Department. —**do Exterior**, State Department (Foreign Office).—**de Fazenda**, Treasury Department.—**do Interior**, Department of the Interior.—**da Marinha**, Navy Department.
ministra (*f.*) minestrone (soup); a woman minister.
ministrador (*adj.; m.,f.*) ministrant.
ministral (*adj.*) ministerial.
ministrante (*adj.; m.,f.*) ministrant.
ministrar (*v.t.*) to minister, furnish, supply, give (**a**, to); to administer.
ministro (*m.*) minister, government official; magistrate; judge.—**da religião**, or—**do altar**, or—**do Senhor**, a priest.—**de estado**, minister of state.—**do Evangelho**, a preacher of the Gospel.—**plenipotenciário**, minister plenipotentiary.—**sem pasta**, minister without portfolio.
minjolinho (*m.*) = NARCEJA.
minoração (*f.*) diminishing, curtailment, attenuation.
minorar (*v.t.*) to diminish, lessen, reduce.
minorativo **-va** (*adj.*) diminishing; gentle, soothing.
minoria (*f.*) minority (less than half).
minoritário **-ria** (*adj.*) of the minority. **grupo**—, minority group.
minuana (*f., Bot.*) evening primrose or sundrops (*Oenothera*), c.a. CAPARROSA.
minuano (*m.*) in southern Brazil, a cold, dry winter wind which blows from the southwest.—**sujo**, a very disagreeable cold wind in wet weather.
minúcia (*f.*) minor detail; (*pl.*) minutiae, particulars. **em**—, minutely, in detail.
minucioso **-sa** (*adj.*) minute, detailed; particular, precise.
minudência (*f.*) detail, minute particular.
minudencioso **-sa, minudente** (*adj.*) minute, detailed, particular, precise, thorough.
minuendo (*m., Arith.*) minuend.
minuete, minueto [ê] (*m.*) minuet.
minúsculo **-la** (*adj.*) minuscule. **letra**—, small (lower-case) letter.
minuta (*f.*) see under MINUTO.
minutador **-dora** (*m.,f.*) one who draws up the minutes or details.
minutar (*v.t.*) to write, draw up, the minutes or details.
minuteria (*f.*) the works of a timepiece.
minuto **-ta** (*adj.*) minute; (*m.*) a minute (60 seconds); a moment; (*f.*) note, memorandum; rough draft or sketch; in a restaurant, any dish cooked to order.
mio (*m.*) a cat's miaow.
miocárdio (*m., Anat.*) myocardium.
miocardite (*f., Med.*) myocarditis.
mioceno **-na** (*adj.; m., Geol.*) Miocene.
miócito (*m., Anat., Zool.*) myocyte.
miocoma (*f., Zool.*) myocomma.
miofibrilha (*f., Anat., Zool.*) myofibril.
miografia (*f., Anat., Physiol.*) myography.
miógrafo (*m., Physiol.*) myograph.
miolada (*f.*) brains; a dish made with brains.
mioleira (*f., colloq.*) brains; sense.
miolema (*f., Anat.*) miolemma.
miolinho (*m.*) = TATERA.
miolo [miô] (*m.*) the "insides" of a loaf of bread; core, kernel, pith; the brain; fig., sense. **não tem**—, (he) hasn't an ounce of brains, a grain of sense.
miologia (*f.*) myology.
mioloso **-sa** [lô], **mioludo** **-da** (*adj.*) pithy [stem, fruit]; pulpy.
mioma (*f., Med.*) myoma.
miomério, miômero (*m., Embryol., Zool.*) myomere.
miômetro (*m., Anat.*) myometrium.
mio-mio (*m., Bot.*) the miomio baccharis (*B. cordifolia*).
míope (*adj.*) myopic, nearsighted, shortsighted; (*m.,f.*) such a person; by ext., one who is purblind, dull, obtuse.
miopia (*f.*) myopia; shortsightedness, lit. & fig.
mioplasma (*m., Physiol., Anat.*) myoplasm.
mióporo (*m.*) the windstaybush (*Myoporum acuminatum*);

the bastard sandalwood (*M. tenuifolium*).
miopótamo (*f.*) the coypu (*Myocastor coypus*). [Its fur is known in the trade as nutria.]
miose (*f., Med.*) myosis.
miosina (*f., Biochem.*) myosin, paramyosinogen.
miosótis (*f., Bot.*) myosotis, forget-me-not (*Myosotis*), c.a. NÃO-TE-ESQUEÇAS-DE-MIM.
miosuro (*m., Bot.*) the mousetail (*Myosurus*).
miótico **-ca** (*adj., Med.*) myotic.
miqueado **-da** (*adj., old slang*) broke, strapped (financially); = PRONTO.
miquear (*v.t., slang*) to ruin, impoverish.
Miquéias (*m.*) Micah; Micheas.
mira (*f.*) a gun sight; aim, intent, view; goal, object; sighting; (*Zool.*) = BADEJO-MIRA, a fish.—**de bombardeio**, or—**de lança-bombas**, bomb sight.—**falante**, surveyor's leveling rod. **à**—, on the lookout. **ter em**—, to aim at, have in view.
mirabela (*f., Bot.*) a goosefoot (*Chenopodium*).
mirabolâneas (*f.pl.*) = MIROBALÂNEAS.
mirabólano (*m.*) = MIROBÂLANO.
mirabolante (*adj.*) showy, gaudy, "loud"; dazzling.
miracéu (*m.*) = TANDUJU.
miraculoso **-sa** (*adj.*) miraculous [= MILAGROSO].
miradouro, miradoiro (*m.*) = MIRANTE.
miragaia (*f.*) a drumfish (*Pogonias chromis*), c.a. VACA-BURRIQUETE, PIRAÚNA. Var. MIRAGUAIA.
miragem (*f.*) mirage; an illusion.
miramar (*m.*) a belvedere overlooking the sea.
mirante (*m.*) an open pavilion or terrace on a high point, commanding a fine prospect; a belvedere; c.a. MIRADOIRO, MIRADOURO.
mirão (*m.*) = MIRONE.
mira-ôlho (*adj.*) eye-filling.
mirar (*v.t.*) to look (closely) at; to fix the gaze upon; to aim at, lit. & fig.; (*v.r.*) to look at oneself (in the mirror).
miri, mirim (*m., Bot.*) a bumelia of Brazil (*Bumelia nigra*).
miriacanto **-ta** (*adj., Bot., Zool.*) myriacanthous.
miríade, miríada (*f.*) myriad; the number of ten thousand.
miriagrama (*m.*) myriagram [10,000 grams].
mirialitro (*m.*) myrialiter [10,000 liters].
miriâmetro (*m.*) myriameter [10,000 meters].
miriápode, var. of MIRIÓPODE.
miriare (*m.*) myriare [10,000 ares].
mírica (*m., Bot.*) the wax myrtle or bayberry (*Myrica*).
miricáceo **-cea** (*adj., Bot.*) myricaceous; (*f.pl.*) the Myricaceae (bayberry family).
mirífico **-ca** (*adj.*) marvelous, wonderful.
mirim (*adj.*) a Tupian word meaning small—used alone or in combination. [Antons.: AÇU and GUAÇU]; (*f.*) a common collective term for any of numerous tiny stingless bees of *Melipona* and *Trigona*.
mirimbiba (*f., Bot.*) a Brazilian terminalia (*T. lucida*).
mirindiba (*f.*) any of several Amazonian trees, esp. *Buchenavia grandis* (family *Terminalaceae*), c.a. CUIARANA.
miriofilo (*m., Bot.*) water milfoil (*Myriophyllum*).
miriópode (*adj.; m.*) myriapod; (*m.pl.*) the Myriapoda.
miriquiná (*m.*) a night ape of the genus Aotus (syn. Nyctipithecus), ranging from Nicaragua to Argentina.
miristicáceo **-cea** (*adj., Bot.*) myristicaceous; (*f.pl.*) the Myristicaceae (nutmeg family).
miritizeiro (*m.*) the fiber mauritia palm (*M. flexuosa*), c.a. BURITI-DO-BREJO.
mírmeces (*m.pl.*) the genus of ants (*Myrmecia*) containing the bulldog ant.
mirmecóbio (*m.*) a genus of insectivorous marsupials (*Myrmecobius*) comprising the banded ant-eater of Australia (*M. fasciatus*).
mirmecófago **-ga** (*adj., Zool.*) myrmecophagous, feeding on ants.
mirmecófilo **-la** (*adj., Zool.*) myrmecophilous; (*Bot.*) myrmecophytic.
mirmecófito **-ta** (*adj., Bot.*) myrmecophytic.
mirmecofóbico **-ca** (*adj., Bot.*) myrmecophobic.
mirmecologia (*f., Zool.*) myrmecology.
mirmecológico **-ca** (*adj., Zool.*) myrmecological.
mirmeleão (*m.*) an ant lion (*Myrmeleon*).
mirmidão (*m.*) myrmidon; (*colloq.*) scullion; cook's helper.
mirobâlano (*m.*) myrobalan (dried astringent fruit of East Indian terminalias).
mirobalâneas (*f.pl., Bot.*) the myrobalan family (*Terminalaceae*), c.a. MIRABOLÂNEAS and COMBRETEÁCEAS.
mirone (*m., colloq.*) kibitzer, onlooker [= MIRÃO].

mironga (*f., colloq.*) a misunderstanding, a falling-out.
mirônico –ca (*adj., Chem.*) myronic [acid].
mirosina (*f., Biochem.*) myrosin.
miróxilo [ks] (*m., Bot.*) the tolu tree of northern South America (*Myroxylon balsamum*) which yields tolu balsam.
mirra (*f.*) myrrh; (*Bot.*) myrrhtree (*Commiphora*); (*m.,f.*) scrawny person; skinflint.
mirrado –da (*adj.*) dried up, withered; shrivelled; wizened.
mirrar (*v.t.*) to parch, dry up; (*v.i.,v.r.*) to wither, shrivel; to waste away; to fade away.
mirsifilo (*m., Bot.*) any plant of the genus Asparagus (syn. Myrsiphyllum).
mirsina (*f., Bot.*) any plant of the genus Myrsine.
mirsináceo –cea (*adj., Bot.*) myrsinaceous; (*f.pl.*) the Myrsinaceae.
mirtáceo –cea (*adj., Bot.*) myrtaceous; (*f.pl.*) the Myrtaceae (myrtle family).
mirtiforme (*adj., Bot.*) myrtiform.
mírtil (*m.*) a satyr butterfly.
mirtilo (*m.*) the myrtle whortleberry (*Vaccinium myrtillus*).
mirtíneas (*f.pl.*) = MIRTÁCEAS.
mirto (*m.*) = MURTA.
mirtol (*m.*) myrtol (myrtle oil).
miruim (*m.*) var. of MARUIM.
misandria (*f.*) misandry (dislike of man by woman).
misantropia (*f.*) misanthropy.
misantrópico –ca (*adj.*) misanthropic; unsociable.
misantropo –pa [trô] (*m.,f.*) misanthrope; (*adj.*) unsociable.
míscaro (*m.*) edible milk mushroom (*Lactarius deliciosus*).
miscelânea (*f.*) a literary miscellany; by ext., odds and ends, sundries, hodgepodge.
miscibilidade (*f.*) miscibility.
miscigenação (*f.*) miscegenation.
miscível (*adj.*) miscible [= MISTURÁVEL].
misenite (*f., Min.*) misenite.
miserabilíssimo –ma (*adj.; absol. superl.* of MISERÁVEL) most unhappy.
miseração (*f.*) commiseration.
miserando –da (*adj.*) lamentable; deplorable.
miserar (*v.t.*) to render miserable, unhappy.
miserável (*adj.*) miserable, wretched, pitiable; deplorable; miserly; destitute, needy; paltry; despicable, mean; crummy; (*m.,f.*) a wretched person; a beggar; a mean person; a scoundrel, miscreant.
miserê (*m.,sl.*) extreme MISÉRIA.
miséria (*f.*) misery, distress, wretchedness; destitution, stark poverty, acute need; squalor; avarice; meanness; a pittance. **cair na**—, to become poverty-stricken. **o aguilhão da**—, the goad of poverty.
misericórdia (*f.*) mercy, compassion, pity; an almshouse; (*exclam.*) Have mercy!—**divina**, divine mercy.
misericordioso –sa (*adj.*) merciful, compassionate (**com, para com**, toward).
mísero –ra (*adj.*) unfortunate, unlucky; unhappy; miserable, wretched; miserly, stingy.
misis (*f.*) the genus (*Mysis*) of opossum shrimps.
misogamia (*f.*) misogamy, hatred of marriage.
misógamo –ma (*adj.*) misogamic; (*m.,f.*) misogamist.
misoginia (*f.*) misogyny, hatred of women.
misógino –na (*adj.*) misogynous; (*m.*) misogynist, woman hater.
misologia (*f.*) misology, hatred of discussion or of enlightenment.
misoneísmo (*m.*) misoneism; intolerance of anything new.
misoneísta (*adj.; m.,f.*) misoneist.
misopedia (*f.*) misopedia, dislike of children, esp. one's own.
misosofia (*f.*) misosophy, hatred of wisdom.
mispíquel (*m., Min.*) mispickel, arsenopyrite.
missa (*f.*) Mass, the Eucharistic rite of the Roman Catholic Church; (*Music*) the setting of certain portions of the Mass considered as a musical composition.—**do galo**, midnight mass at Christmas. **ajudar à**—, to serve at mass. **dizer**—, to celebrate mass. **não ir à**—**com alguém**, (*colloq.*) not to be attracted to another person. **não saber da**—**a metade**, not to know the half of it. **ouvir**—, to attend mass.
missagra (*f.*) hinge, joint [= BISAGRA].
missal (*m.*) missal.
missão (*f.*) mission, charge; commission, a delegation.

misseiro –ra (*adj.*) zealous in attending mass.
míssil [-sseis] (*adj.*) missile, capable of being thrown, hurled, etc.; (*m.*) missile.
missionar (*v.t.,v.i.*) to preach the faith.
missionário (*m.*) missionary.
missivista (*m.,f.*) a person who writes or bears missives.
missivo –va (*adj.*) missive; missile; (*f.*) missive, letter.
Missuri (*m.*) Missouri.
missurite (*f., Min.*) missourite.
mister [tér] (*m.*) want, need; trade, occupation. **é (de)**—, it is necessary. **faz-se**—, it becomes necessary. **haver**—**de**, to be in need of.
mistério (*m.*) mystery, enigma, riddle.
misterioso –sa (*adj.*) mysterious, enigmatical; secretive.
misticidade (*f.*), **misticismo** (*m.*) mysticism.
místico –ca (*adj.*) mystic(al); (*m.,f.*) a mystic.
mistificação (*f.*) deception, hoax, shenanigan, humbug. [Not mystification in the sense of puzzlement, which is PERPLEXIDADE.]
mistificador –dora (*adj.*) mystifying; (*m.,f.*) mystifier.
mistificar (*v.t.*) to hoodwink; to bamboozle; to "kid".
mistifório (*m.*) jumble, hodge-podge.
misto –ta (*adj.*) mixed, mingled; jumbled; (*m.*) a mixture, compound. **colégio**—, a coeducational school. **trem**—, a train made up of both freight and passenger cars.
mistol (*m., Bot.*) the Argentine jujube (*Zizyphus mistol.*)
mistral (*m.*) mistral (cold, dry, northerly wind common in southern France).
mistura (*f.*) mixture, blend; compound.—**abrasiva**, abrasive compound.—**coloidal**, colloidal mixture.—**explosiva**, (*Autom.*) fuel mixture.—**pobre**, lean (fuel) mixture.—**rica**, rich (fuel) mixture. **de**—, pell-mell. **sem**—, perfectly; completely.
misturado –da (*adj.*) mixed, blended; joined, associated; (*f.*) a jumble, hodgepodge.
misturador (*m.*) mixer; concrete mixer [= BETONEIRA].
misturadora (*f., Radio*) mixer [= MESCLADORA.]
misturar (*v.t.*) to mix, mingle, blend, compound; to cross (breeds). —**se (com)**, to mix, mingle (with).
misturável (*adj.*) miscible [= MISCÍVEL].
mísula (*f., Archit.*) bracket, corbel.
mitene (*f.*) mitten [= PUNHETE].
mítico –ca (*adj.*) mythical.
mitigação (*f.*) mitigation, alleviation, relief.
mitigador –dora (*m.,f.*) mitigator; (*adj.*) mitigating.
mitigar (*v.t.*) to mitigate, ease; to quiet, allay, quell.
mitigativo –va (*adj.*) mitigative.
mitigável (*adj.*) that can be mitigated.
mitilotoxina [ks] (*f., Chem.*) mytilotoxine.
mito (*m.*) myth.
mitologia (*f.*) mythology.
mitológico –ca (*adj.*) mythological.
mitose (*f., Biol.*) mitosis, karyokinesis [= CARIOCINESE].
mitossomo (*m., Biol.*) mitosome.
mitótico –ca (*adj., Biol.*) mitotic, karyokinetic.
mitra (*f.*) miter; (*Zool.*) miter shell; (*colloq.*) Pope's nose (uropygium of cooked chicken, etc.).
mitral (*adj.*) mitral; (*Anat.*) mitral [valve].
mitridatismo (*m., Med.*) mithridatism.
mitrídeos (*m.pl.*) the family (*Mitridae*) which comprises the miter shells (genus *Mitra*).
mitriforme (*adj.*) miter-shaped.
mitu, mitua (*m.*) = MUTUM.
miúça (*f.*) bit, fragment, small piece; small domestic animals (sheep, goats, etc. = MIUNÇA); (*pl.*) church tithes paid in kind.
miúçalhas [i-u] (*f.pl.*) trifles.
miudagem [i-u] (*f.*) odds and ends; leftover goods; small livestock; small fry (children).
miudeza [i-u . . . ê] (*f.*) minuteness; precision; parsimony; (*pl.*) details; trifles; gewgaws. **loja de**—s, a shop selling toys, notions, small odds and ends.
miúdo –da (*adj.*) minute, slender, very small, tiny; fine; frequent; particular, precise; mean, small, stingy; (*m.pl.*) small change; giblets, pluck. **chumbo**—, bird shot. **despezas**—s, petty expenses.
mium (*m.*) = CAPIM-COMPRIDO.
miunça [i-ú] (*f.*) = MIÚÇA.
mixameba (*f., Bot., Zool.*) myxamoeba.
mixe (*adj.*) punk (inferior); picayunish; of a party, dull.
mixedema [ks] (*f., Med.*) myxedema.
mixila (*f.*) = TAMANDUÁ-MIRIM.
mixita [ks] (*f., Min.*) mixite.

mixobacteriáceas [ks] (*f.pl.*) the Myxobacteriaceae (family of bacteria or slime molds).

mixole (*m.*) a serrano (*Diplectrum radiale*), c.a. MARGARIDA.—**-da-areia**, the sand fish (*Diplectrum formosum*), also called MARGARIDA.

mixomicete [ks] (*m.*) myxomycete (a slime mold).

mixórdia (*f.*) mixture, medley; jumble, confusion; rigmarole; a mixed-up situation.

mizonite (*f.*, *Min.*) mizzonite.

mizóstomo (*m.*, *Zool.*) a genus (*Myzostoma*) of parasitic marine animals.

ml = MILILITRO(s) = milliliter(s).

m/l = MINHA LETRA (my [promissory] note).

mm = MILÍMETRO(s) = millimeter(s).

MM. = MERITÍSSIMO (Most Worthy).

m/min = METROS POR MINUTO (meters per minute).

mnemônico –ca (*adj.*) mnemonic; (*f.*) mnemonics.

m.º = MESMO (same); MAIO (May).

m/o = MINHA ORDEM (my order—business term).

mo (*pers. pron.*) it to me; (*pl.*) them to me. [*Contraction of indirect obj. pron.* ME + *direct obj.* o(s)].

mó (*f.*) millstone; grindstone; crowd, large number.

moafa (*f.*, *slang*) drunkenness.

moageiro (*m.*) miller [= MOLEIRO].

moagem (*f.*) grinding, milling [= MOEDURA].

Moâmede (*m.*) Mohammed; Muhammad.

móbil [-beis] (*adj.*) mobile, movable [= MÓVEL]; (*m.*) motive, prime mover.

mobilador –dora (*adj.*) furnishing; (*m.,f.*) supplier of furniture.

mobilar, mobilhar, mobiliar [55] (*v.t.*) to provide with furniture.

mobília (*f.*) household furniture.

mobiliaria (*f.*) furniture store or factory; a set of furniture.

mobiliário –ria (*adj.*) pert. or relating to furniture or to movables; (*m.*) the furniture of a house (apartment, room) as a whole.

mobilidade (*f.*) mobility; changeableness, fickleness; (*Sociol.*) mobility.

mobilização (*f.*) mobilization.

mobilizar (*v.t.*) to mobilize (troops); to put (money) into movement or circulation.

mobilizável (*adj.*) that can be mobilized.

mobúlidas, mobulídeos (*m.pl.*, *Zool.*) a family (*Mobulidae*) of large rays.

moca (*f.*) club, bat, cudgel, bludgeon; mockery; (*m.*) Mocha coffee.

môça (*f.*) girl, young woman; (*colloq.*) mistress.—**-branca**, a stingless bee (*Melipona varia*); also = ABREU.—**do fado**, prostitute.—**-donzela**, maiden.—**-e-velha**, Japanese glorybower (*Clerodendron japonicum*); (*pl.*) zinnia.—**-vagalume**, usherette equipped with a flashlight.

mocada (*f.*) a blow with a club.

moçada (*f.*) a group of young women or of young men.

mocajá (*m.*) = CÔCO-DE-CATARRO.

mocamau (*m.*) = QUILOMBOLA.

mocambeiro –ra (*adj.*) runaway [cattle]; fugitive [slave]; (*m.*) in Brazil's early days, a runaway slave, or lawbreaker, who hid and lived with others of his kind in a MOCAMBO.

mocambinho (*m.*) thatched hut.

mocambo (*m.*) a hiding-place in the jungle, sought by lawbreakers and runaway slaves [= QUILOMBO]; also, a shack or hut in the woods; a thicket in which grazing cattle are hidden from sight.

moçame (*f.*) group of girls.

mocanquice (*f.*) var. of MOGANGUICE.

moção (*f.*) motion, movement; deliberative proposal (for action to be taken). —**de ordem**, point of order.

mocetão (*m.*) a strapping fellow.

mocetona (*f.*) a buxom young woman.

môcha, fem. of MÔCHO.

mochar (*v.t.*) to dehorn; to maim; (*colloq.*) to deceive; to hide; to go back on one's word.

mocheta [ê] (*f.*, *Arch.*) listel, fillet; beading.

mochila (*f.*) knapsack, haversack, rucksack; a saddle cloth; fig., humpback.

môcho –cha (*adj.*) hornless; polled [cattle]; of firearms, hammerless; (*m.*) any of various owls, c.a. CORUJA; fig., a misanthropist; backless bench, stool.—**de três pernas**, three-legged stool.—**-diabo**, the stygian owl (*Asio stygius*).—**-masteiro**, or—**-rasteiro** = CORUJÃO.—**-negro**, the dark wood owl (*Ciccaba huhula*).—**-orelhudo**, the striped owl (*Rhinotynx clamator*). Cf. CORUJA, CORUJÃO, CABORÉ.

mocidade (*f.*) youth; youthfulness; young people.

mocinha (*f.*; *dim. of* MOÇA) young girl.—**-branca** = POMBINHA-DAS-ALMAS (a bird).

mocinho (*m.*; *dim. of* MOÇO) very young man; hero or "good guy" in an adventure movie.

mocitaíba (*f.*, *Bot.*) a swartzpea (*Swartzia crocea*).

mocô (*m.*) sorcery, witchcraft; amulet.

mocó (*m.*) a kind of guinea pig; a musette bag; a variety of long-staple Braz. cotton; an amulet; a fetish.

môço –ça (*adj.*) young, youthful; immature; (*m.*) lad, boy, young man.—**de cavalariça**, horse groom.—**de recados**, messenger.—**dos programas**, theater usher. **em**—, while young. **mais**—, younger, junior. Cf. MÔÇA.

moçoila (*f.*) young girl. [*Dim.* of MOÇA.]

mocorongo (*m.*) backwoodsman [= CAIPIRA].

mocotó (*m.*) feet of calves and oxen used as food. **geleia de**—, calf's-foot jelly.

moda (*f.*) mode, manner, way; vogue, fashion, style; a piece of popular music; (*pl.*) articles of women's wear. **à—antiga**, in the old-fashioned way. **à—de**, in the manner of, like. [French *à la mode*]. **casa de—s**, dress shop. **da**—, popular, fashionable. **fora da**—, old-fashioned, out-of-style. **na**—, in style, in vogue, fashionable, up-to-date.

modal (*adj.*) modal.

modalidade (*f.*) modality; mode; kind; aspect; feature.

modelação (*f.*) modeling.

modelador –dora (*m.,f.*) modeler.

modelagem (*f.*) modeling.

modelar (*v.t.*) to model, shape, mold; (*adj.*) model.

modêlo (*m.*) model, pattern, mold; a store dummy; type, design; gauge, standard; an artist's model; a fashion model; a model person; a model hat, gown, etc.

moderação (*f.*) moderation, temperance; equanimity; diminution, slackening.

moderado –da (*adj.*) moderate, mediocre, limited; temperate; judicious; frugal; unobtrusive.

moderador –dora (*adj.*) moderating, restraining; (*m.,f.*) moderator, regulator.

moderante (*adj.*) moderating.

moderar (*v.t.*) to moderate, temper; to control, regulate; to allay; to diminish, slacken; (*v.r.*) to control oneself; to be temperate.

modernice (*f.*) ultra-modernism.

modernidade (*f.*) modernity.

modernismo (*m.*) modernism.

modernista (*adj.*) modernist; newfangled; (*m.,f.*) modernist; fadist.

modernização (*f.*) modernization.

modernizar (*v.t.*) to modernize. (*v.r.*) to adjust oneself to modern things, become up-to-date.

moderno –na (*adj.*) modern, recent, present, up-to-date; (*m.,f.*) a modern (person).

modéstia (*f.*) modesty, freedom from presumption; moderation; bashfulness, diffidence.

modesto –ta (*adj.*) modest, unassuming; diffident; unobtrusive; moderate.

modicar (*v.t.*) to moderate.

modicidade (*f.*) moderateness, smallness.

módico –ca (*adj.*) moderate, modest, small.

modificação (*f.*) modification, alteration.

modificador –dora (*adj.*) modifying; (*m.*) modifier.

modificar (*v.t.*) to modify, change, alter; to moderate; (*v.r.*) to change.

modilhão (*m.*, *Arch.*) modillion.

modinha [mó] (*f.*) a sad or sentimental folk song; a ditty.

modíola (*f.*) a horse mussel (genus *Modiolus*).

modismo (*m.*) idiom, colloquialism.

modista (*f.*) modiste, dressmaker; (*m.,f.*) a singer of MODAS and MODINHAS.

modo [mó] (*m.*) mode, way, method, manner, means; (*pl.*) deportment; (*Gram.*) mood; (*Music*) mode.—**de falar**, way of speaking.—**de pensar**, way of thinking; point of view.—**de se comportar**, way to behave.—**de ser**, a way to be; manner of existence.—**de vida**, mode of living or of earning a living.—**maior**, (*Music*) major mode.—**prático**, a practical means, way or method.—**s amolecados**, coarse manners, low behavior.—**s cativantes**, engaging manners.—**s definidos**, personal behavior. **a**—, handily, dextrously. **a—que**, (*colloq.*) seems like. **de—a**, in a way to. **de—algum**, absolutely not; not at all; on no account. **de—geral**, by and large. **de—que**, so that. **de nenhum**—, on no account; by no manner of means. **de tal**—, so much so (**que**, that). **dêste**—, in this way. **do**

mesmo—, in the same way. **Tenha—s!** Behave yourself!
ter bons—s, to have good manners.
modôrra (*f.*) drowsiness; sluggishness; torpor; apathy; (*Veter.*) staggers, gid, water brain, sturdy (of sheep, etc.).
modorrar (*v.t.*) to make drowsy; (*v.i.*) to drowse, doze.
modorrento –ta (*adj.*) drowsy; sluggish; stupid.
modulação (*f.*) modulation.—**de alta freqüência,** (*Radio*) HF modulation.—**de amplitude,** (*Radio*) AM.—**de fre-qüência,** (*Radio*) FM.
modulador –dora (*adj.*) modulating; (*m.,f.*) modulator; (*m., Radio*) modulator tube.
modular (*v.t.,v.i.*) to modulate, sing, intone; to play or sing with modulation; (*Elec., Radio*) to modulate (frequency); (*adj.*) modular.
módulo (*m.*) module; modulus.—**de elasticidade,** (*Physics*) modulus of elasticity.—**de ruptura,** (*Civ. Engin.*) modulus of rupture.
moeda (*f.*) coin, specie, money.—**corrente,** currency.—**de cálculo,** or—**imaginária,** an imaginary unit of money, as the mill.—**divisionária,** divisional coins; small change. —**falsa,** counterfeit money.—**fiduciária,** bank notes. —**sonante,** hard cash. **casa da—,** the mint. **pagar na mesma—,** to return tit for tat.
moedagem (*f.*) coinage, mintage.
moedeira (*f., colloq.*) weariness; tiring work; dull, pro-longed pain.
moedeiro (*m.*) minter, coiner.—**falso,** counterfeiter.
moedela (*f.*) a beating, cudgeling.
moedor –dora (*adj.*) grinding; (*m.,f.*) grinder.—**de tintas,** ink, or paint, grinder.
moedura (*f.*) act or operation of grinding.
moega (*f.*) grain hopper [=TREMONHA].
moela (*f.*) bird's ventriculus, gizzard.
moenda (*f.*) any sort of mill, grinder or crusher; cane crusher; a grist mill; grindstone, millstone; act of grinding.
moendeiro (*m.*) miller; man who feeds the sugar cane into the crusher.
moente (*adj.*) grinding; (*m., Mach.*) trunnion.
moer [56] (*v.t.*) to grind, crush, crunch; to batter, bruise; to harass; (*v.i.*) to mull over in the mind; (*v.r.*) to tire oneself out.—**(alguém) de pancadas,** to thrash (one) within an inch of his life. **pedra de—,** millstone.
mofa (*f.*) mockery, derision, scorn.
mofado –da (*adj.*) musty, moldy.
mofador –dora (*adj.*) mocking; (*m.,f.*) mocker.
mofar (*v.i.*) to mold; to grow musty or moldy.—**de,** to mock at, deride, sneer at.
mofatra (*f.*) fake, fraud [=LÔGRO].
mofento –ta (*adj.*) musty, moldy; baleful.
mofeta [ê] (*f., Geol.*) mofette.
mofino –na (*adj.*) unlucky; mean, miserable; sickly; cowardly; wretched; (*m.,f.*) such a person; (*f.*) unhappi-ness; stinginess; a paid, anonymous newspaper attack; (*colloq.*) hookworm disease.
môfo (*m.*) mold, mustiness; mildew.
mofoso –sa (*adj.*) = MOFENTO.
moganga, moganguice (*f.*) mimicry, faces, grimaces; blandishments.
mogno, mógono (*m.*) mahogany (*Sweetenia mahagoni*), known in the trade as West Indies mahogany.—**-branco,** eucalyptus.—**-da-austrália,** blackwood acacia (*A. melan-oxylon*), c.a. ÉBANO-DA-AUSTRÁLIA.—**-da-colômbia,** the albarco cariniana (*C. pyriformis*) erroneously called Colombian mahogany, to which it is not related.—**-do-peru,** Peru mahogany (*Swietenia tessmanni*).
moi–, look under mou– for words which cannot be found under moi–.
moído –da (*adj.*) crushed, ground; tired, worn out; of meat and fish, tainted, "high".
moinante [o-i] (*adj.; m.,f.*) fun-loving; indolent (person).
moinha [o-í] (*f.*) chaff.
moinho [o-í] (*m.*) mill, grinder.—**de água,** waterwheel.—**de vento,** windmill.
moirão, var. of MOURÃO.
moiro (*m.*) & derivs. = MOURO & derivs.
moisaico –ca (*adj.*) Mosaic.
Moisés (*m.*) Moses.
moita (*f.*) thicket; dense underbrush; (*interj.*) Not a word! **moitão** (*m.*) sheave, pulley block. Var. MOUTÃO.
mol (*m., Chem.*) mole, gram-molecule.
mola (*f.*) steel spring; fig., a motive or source of action; (*Med.*) a blood or carneous mole.—**hidatiforme,** hydati-form mole.—**vesicular,** (*Veter.*) vesicular mole. [An ordi-

nary skin mole is SINAL, MANCHA NA PELE, or NEVO.]; (*Zool.*) a sunfish (*Mola* or *Ranzania*), c.a. PEIXE-LUA.—**de segmento,** piston rings.—**mestra** or **real,** main spring.
molambento –ta, molambudo –da (*adj.*) in rags; (*m.,f.*) ragamuffin, tatterdemalion.
molambo (*m.*) a rag; a dirty, ragged garment; a weakling.
molancas (*m.,f.*), **molangueiro** (*m.*) slouch, slow poke.
molar (*adj.*) molar, adapted for grinding (as teeth); (*Chem.*) molar; molal; (*m.*) molar tooth.
molariforme (*adj.*) molariform.
molarinha (*f., Bot.*) drug fumitory (*Fumaria officinalis*).
molassa (*f.*) wood grinder (for pulp-making).
molasso (*m., Geol.*) molasse.
moldação (*f.*) molding; casting.
moldado (*m.*) a molding or casting.
moldador (*m.*) molder; a gouge (woodworking chisel).
moldagem (*f.*) molding; casting; wood carving; fossil impressions in rocks.
moldar (*v.t.*) to mold, shape, form; to cast (iron, etc.).
moldavite (*f., Petrog.*) moldavite.
molde (*m.*) mold, form, shape; template, pattern; type matrix.—**para vestidos,** dress pattern.
moldeira (*f.*) a casting frame or box.
moldura (*f.*) molding; picture frame.
moldurar (*v.t.*) to frame.
moldureiro (*m.*) maker of frames (as for pictures).
mole (*adj.*) soft, yielding; limp; flabby; tender; easy-going; listless, lackadaisical; (*f.*) huge bulk, large mass; a massive structure (as a mole); (*m.*) the lily leek (*Allium moly*).
molear (*v.i.*) to go limp; to droop.
moleca (*f.*) young negro girl.
molecada (*f.*) a group of MOLEQUES.
molecagem (*f.*) knavery; low behavior.
molecão, molecote (*m.*) a strapping young urchin.
molecar (*v.i.*) to behave as a MOLEQUE [=MOLEQUEAR].
molecoreba (*f.*), **molecório** (*m.*) a gang of street urchins [=MOLEQUES].
molécula (*f., Chem., Physics*) molecule.—**-grama,** gram-molecule.
molecular (*adj.*) molecular. **pêso—,** molecular weight.
moleira (*f.*) the miller's wife; (*Anat.*) fontanel.
moleirão –rona (*adj.*) lazy; (*m.,f.*) a lazy person; a softy.
moleiro (*m.*) a miller; also = AJURU-AÇU (a parrot).
moleja (*f.*) dewlap; bird droppings.
molejo (*m.*) springiness; the springs of a vehicle collec-tively.
molenga (*adj.*) lazy, slothful; (*m.,f.*) such a person; a lazybones; a milksop.
molengão, –gona (*m.,f.*) a very lazy person; a slob; lag-gard, loiterer.
molengar (*v.i.*) to saunter lazily; to dawdle.
molengo, molengue, vars. of MOLENGA.
moleque (*m.*) urchin; ragamuffin; scamp, rascal; in slave days, a black boy. **pé-de—,** peanut brittle (candy).
molequear (*v.*) = MOLECAR.
molequeira, molequice (*f.*) = MOLECAGEM.
molesquim (*m.*) moleskin (fabric).
molestador –dora (*adj.*) molesting; (*m.,f.*) molester.
molestamento (*m.*) molesting; molestation.
molestar (*v.t.*) to molest, annoy; to discommode, trouble, put to inconvenience; to disturb, disquiet; to harass; to aggrieve.
moléstia (*f.*) sickness, disease; discomfort; uneasiness.—**de Chagas,** Chagas' disease.—**de encommenda,** a feigned illness.—**do estanho,** (*Metal.*) tin disease, tin pest.—**magra,** (*colloq.*) pulmonary tuberculosis.—**-negra,** (*Bot.*) bitter rot, ripe rot, anthracnosis, c.a. ANTRACNOSE. **quarta—,** German measles.
molesto –ta (*adj.*) annoying; tiresome; laborious, difficult; harmful.
moleza [ê] (*f.*) lassitude, languor, weakness; sluggishness; indolence; dawdling.
molhadela, molha (*f.*) wetting; (*colloq.*) bath; tip, gratuity.
molhado –da (*adj.*) wet, moist, damp; (*m.*) a damp or wet place; (*m.pl.*) liquid food products and beverages. **armazem de sêcos e—s,** a grocery store.
molhar (*v.t.*) to wet, soak, moisten, dampen.—**a garanta,** to wet one's whistle.
molhe (*m.*) mole, pier, wharf, jetty, c.a. MOLHE-CAIS.
molheira (*f.*) gravy boat, sauce dish.
molhe-molhe (*m.*) drizzle [=CHUVISCO].
molho [mó] (*m.*) a bunch of something (as carrots, keys,

etc.); a bundle or sheaf (as of wheat).—**de nervos**, a bundle of nerves (referring to a person).

môlho (*m.*) sauce, gravy.—**branco**, white sauce.—**de salada**, salad dressing.—**holandês**, Hollandaise sauce. **de—**, (*colloq.*) soaking; idle; in bed; in the bath tub.

moliana (*f.*) a scolding, rebuke, reprimand.

molibdato (*m., Chem.*) molybdate.—**de cálcio**, calcium molybdate, powellite.

molibdênio, molibdeno (*m., Chem.*) molybdenum.

molibdenita (*f., Min.*) molybdenite, molybdenum glance.

molibdenocre (*m.*) = MOLIBDITA.

molíbdico –ca (*adj., Chem.*) molybdic [acid].

molibdita (*f., Min.*) iron molibdate; molybdic ocher.

molibdomenite (*f., Min.*) molybdomenite.

molição (*f.*) strong effort or endeavor to achieve something.

molície, molícia (*f.*) listlessness; idleness [= MOLEZA].

mólidas, molídeos (*m.pl.*) the family (*Molidae*) which comprises the sunfishes (*Mola* and *Ranzania*).

molienésia (*f.*) any "molly" (*Mollienisia*)—a popular aquarium fish.

molificação (*f.*) mollifying; mollification.

molificante (*adj.*) mollifying.

molificar (*v.t.*) to mollify.

molificativo –va (*adj.*) = EMOLIENTE.

molime, molímen (*m.*) effort; endeavor; (*Physiol.*) molimen; (*Mech.*) impulsive power.

molinete [nê] (*m.*) windlass; turnstile; flourish (of a weapon); wind gauge.

molinha (*f.*) fine drizzle [= MOLHE-MOLHE].

molinhar (*v.t.*) to grind; (*v.i.*) of a mill, to turn; to drizzle.

molínia (*f.*) the genus Molinia of moorgrasses.

molinilho (*m.*) hand mill (such as a coffee grinder).

molinote (*m.*) sugar-cane crusher.

molisite (*f., Min.*) molysite.

molosso (*m.*) mastiff, large hound.

molugem (*f.*) white bedstraw (*Gallium mollugo*), c.a. SOLDA.

molúria (*f.*) softness; heavy dew; (*m.*) timid man.

molusco (*m.*) mollusk; (*pl.*) the Mollusca.

momentâneo (*adj.*) momentary, instantaneous.

momento (*m.*) moment, instant; (*Mech.*) moment. [But not momentum, which is QUANTIDADE DE MOVIMENTO.] —**de arranque**, starting torque.—**flector**, moment of flexure, bending moment.—**de inércia**, moment of inertia.—**de torção**, torque. **a cada** (or **a todo**)—, every minute, constantly. **de um—para outro**, suddenly, from one minute to the next. **naquele—**, at that moment.— **magnético**, magnetic moment.

momentoso –sa (*adj.*) momentous, weighty, of importance.

momices (*f.pl.*) faces, grimaces [= CARETAS].

momo (*m.*) mummery; mummer; mimicry; king of carnival; also = MOMICES.

momórdica (*f.*) a genus (*Momordica*) of balsamapples.

momota (*f., Zool.*) a motmot.

momotídeos (*m.pl., Zool.*) the Momotidae (family of motmots).

mona (*f.*) female monkey; (*slang*) bender (drunken spree).

monacal (*adj.*) monachal; monastic.

monacântidas, monacantídeos (*m.pl.*) a family of fishes (*Monacanthidae*) which includes the filefishes.

monacato (*m.,f.*) monachate.

monacetina (*f., Chem.*) monoacetin.

monactino –na (*adj., Zool.*) monactine, single-rayed.

monada (*f.*) monkeyshines, didos [= MONICES]; a band of monkeys.

mônade, mônada (*f., Philos., Biol., Zool., Chem.*) monad.

monadelfo –fa (*adj., Bot.*) monadelphous.

monândrico –ca, monandro –dra (*adj., Bot.*) monandrous.

monanto –ta (*adj., Bot.*) monanthous, one-flowered.

monarca (*m.f.*) monarch.

monarda (*f., Bot.*) the wild bergamot beebalm (*Monarda fistulosa*).

monaria (*f.*) a band of monkeys.

monarquia (*f.*) monarchy.

monárquico –ca (*adj.*) monarchic; (*m.,f.*) monarchist.

monarquismo (*m.*) monarchism.

monarquista (*m.,f.*) monarchist.

monáster (*m., Biol.*) monaster.

monástico –ca (*adj.*) monastic(al).

monasticismo (*m.*) monasticism.

monatômico –ca (*adj., Chem.*) monatomic.

monaxônico –ca [ks] (*adj.*) monaxonic.

monazita (*f., Min.*) monazite.

monção (*f.*) monsoon; trade wind; a favorable wind; opportunity. In Brazil, in the early days, a band of explorers called BANDEIRANTES.

moncar (*v.i.*) to blow one's nose [= ASSOAR-SE].

monco (*m.*) nasal mucus; (*colloq. and vulgar*) snot.—**de peru**, turkey's wattle; (*Bot.*) love-lies-bleeding (*Amaranthus caudatus*), c.a. VELUDO-DE-PENCA, CAUDA-DE-RAPÔSA, RABO-DE-RATO; the common feather cockscomb, (*Celosia cristata*), c.a. VELUDILHO; a polygon grass (*P. orientale*).

moncoso –sa (*adj.*) snotty, sniveling.

monda (*f.*) weeding; weeding-time.

mondadeira (*f.*), **–ro** (*m.*) weeder, hoer.

mondador –dora (*adj.*) weeding; (*m.*) weeder; hoe.

mondar (*v.t.*) to weed, hoe; to grub up; to trim, prune; by ext., to expurgate.

mondego (*m.*) = PARATI (a mullet).

mondonga (*f.*) slattern.

mondongo (*m.*) tripe, pluck (of animals killed for food); slovenly person; Amazon swampland.

mondongueiro (*m.*) one who deals in animal pluck.

monecia (*f., Bot.*) monoecism.

monel (*m.*) Monel metal.

monembrionia (*f., Bot., Embryol.*) monembryony.

monera (*f., Zool.*) a moneran.

monésia (*f.*) monesia bark; (*Bot.*) the monesia-bark tree (*Pradosia lactescens*). Cf. BURANHÉM.

monesina (*f., Pharm.*) monesia.

monetário –ria (*adj.*) monetary; (*m.*) a coin collection.

monetite (*f., Min.*) monetite.

monetizar (*v.t.*) to monetize [= AMOEDAR].

monge (*m.*) monk; an ascetic man.

mongil (*adj.*) monkish; (*m.*) nun's garb; mourning garb.

mongol (*adj.; m.,f.*) Mongol(ian).

mongólico –ca (*adj.*) Mongolian.

mongolóide (*adj.*) Mongoloid.

monguba, mongubeira (*f.*) a silk-cotton tree (*Bombax monguba*).

Mônica (*f.*) Monica.

monices (*f.pl.*) monkeyshines, antics [= MONADA].

monilicorne (*adj., Zool.*) monilicorn.

moniliforme (*adj., Bot., Zool.*) moniliform.

monimiáceo –cea (*adj., Bot.*) monimiaceous; (*f.pl.*) the Monimiaceae (boldo family).

monimolite (*f., Min.*) monimolite.

monir [25] (*v.t.*) to admonish [= ADMOESTAR].

monismo (*m., Philos.*) monism.

monista (*adj.*) monistic; (*m.,f.*) monist.

monístico –ca (*adj.*) monistic.

monitor (*m.*) monitor, adviser, mentor.

monitória (*f.*) admonition, warning; rebuke, reprimand; a summons to appear.

monja (*f.*) nun. [Fem. of MONGE.]

monjolo [jô] (*m.*) a primitive water-driven device used in the interior of Brazil for pounding grain;= JACARÉ (tree); Negro slave from Port. East Africa.

mono (*m.*) any large monkey, esp. a spider monkey, c.a. MURIQUI; fig., an apelike man; also = RENDEIRA (bird). **—agarrador** = COATÁ-PRÊTO (a spider monkey).—**tigre**, a night ape (*Aotus trivirgatus*).

monoamida (*f., Chem.*) monoamide [= AMIDA PRIMÁRIA].

monoamina (*f., Chem.*) monoamine [= AMINA PRIMÁRIA].

monobacilar (*adj., Med.*) monobacillary.

monobásico –ca (*adj., Chem.*) monobasic.

monoblástico –ca (*adj., Zool.*) monoblastic.

monobromado –da (*adj., Pharm., Chem.*) monobromated.

monocarpelar (*adj., Bot.*) monocarpellary.

monocarpiano –na, monocárpico –ca (*adj., Bot.*) monocarpic.

monocarril (*adj.*) monorail.

monocásio (*m., Bot.*) monochasium.

monocéfalo –la (*adj., Bot.*) monocephalous.

monocelular (*adj., Bot., Zool.*) unicellular.

monoceronte (*m.*) = UNICÓRNIO.

monocíclico –ca (*adj., Bot., Zool., Chem., Physics*) monocyclic.

monoclínico –ca (*adj., Cryst.*) monoclinic; (*Geol.*) monoclinal.

monoclino –na (*adj., Bot.*) monoclinous.

monoclorado –da (*adj., Chem.*) monochlorinated.

monocórdio (*m.*) monochord; (*adj.*) monotonous.

monocotiledônea (*f., Bot.*) monocotyledon.

monocrômico –ca, **monocromático** –ca (*adj.*) monochromatic.

monocromo –ma (*adj.*) monochromic.

monocrotismo (*m., Physiol.*) monocrotism.

monocroto –ta (*adj., Physiol.*) monocratic [pulse].

monóculo –la (*adj.*) monocular, one-eyed; (*m.*) monocle.

monocultura (*f., Agric.*) monoculture, one-crop farming.

monodactilar, monodáctilo –la (*adj.*) monodactylous.

monodelfo –fa (*adj., Zool.*) monodelphous, monodelphic.

monodérmico –ca (*adj., Anat.*) monodermic.

monodimétrico –ca (*adj., Cryst.*) monodimetric, tetragonal.

monodonte (*adj.*) one-toothed.

monódromo –ma (*adj., Math.*) monodromic, one-valued.

monofilo –la (*adj., Bot.*) monophylous.

monofobia (*f., Med.*) monophobia.

monofoto (*m., Elec.*) monophote.

monogamia (*f.*) monogamy.

monogamista (*adj.; m.,f.*) monogamist.

monógamo –ma (*adj.*) monogamous; (*m.,f.*) monogamist.

monogênese (*f., Biol.*) monogenesis.

monogenia (*f.*) monogeny.

monogenismo (*m.*) monogenism.

monógino –na (*adj.; Bot.*) monogynous.

monogonia (*f., Biol.*) monogony.

monografia (*f.*) monograph, treatise.

monográfico –ca (*adj.*) monographic.

monógrafo –fa (*m.,f.*) monographer.

monograma (*m.*) monogram.

monohíbrido (*m., Biol.*) monohybrid.

monohidrato (*m., Chem.*) monohydrate.

monohídrico –ca (*adj., Chem.*) monohydric.

monóico –ca (*adj., Bot.*) monoecious.

monolítico –ca (*adj.*) monolithic.

monólito –ta (*adj.*) monolithic; (*m.*) monolith.

monologar (*v.i.*) to soliloquize.

monólogo (*m.*) monologue.

monomania (*f.*) monomania.

monomaníaco –ca (*adj.*) monomaniacal; (*m.,f.*) monomaniac.

monometálico –ca (*adj.*) monometallic.

monomolecular (*adj., Chem.*) monomolecular.

monomorfo –fa (*adj.*) monomorphic.

monomotor (*m.*) a single-motor plane.

monometalismo (*m.*) monometallism.

monômio (*m., Alg.*) monomial expression of quantity.

monônimo –ma (*adj.*) mononymic.

monopétalo –la (*adj., Bot.*) monopetalous, gamopetalous.

monopireno –na (*adj., Bot.*) monopyrenous.

monoplace (*adj.*) single-seated [airplane].

monoplano (*m.*) monoplane.

monoplástico –ca (*adj., Biol.*) monoplastic.

monoplatídeo (*m., Biol.*) a monoplast.

monópode (*adj.*) monopode.

monopódio (*m.*) a pedestal table; (*Bot.*) monopodium.

monopolar (*adj.*) monopolar, unipolar.

monopólio (*m.*) monopoly.

monopolista (*m.,f.*) monopolist.

monopolização (*f.*) monopolizing.

monopolizador –dora (*adj.*) monopolistic; (*m.,f.*) monopolist.

monopolizar (*v.t.*) to monopolize.

monopse (*adj.*) monoptic, one-eyed.

monóptero –ra (*adj., Zool., Arch.*) monopteral.

monose (*f., Chem.*) monose.

monospermo –ma (*adj., Bot.*) monospermous, one-seeded.

monosporângio (*m., Bot.*) monosporangium.

monósporo (*m., Bot.*) monospore.

monossépalo (*adj., Bot.*) monosepalous, gamosepalous.

monossilábico –ca (*adj.*) monosyllabic.

monossílabo –ba (*adj.*) monosyllabic; (*m.*) monosyllable.

monossulfureto [ê] (*m., Chem.*) monosulfide.

monóstico –ca (*adj., Bot., Zool.*) monostichous.

monostilo –la (*adj., Bot.*) monostylous.

monóstomo –ma (*adj., Zool.*) monostomous; (*m.*) a genus (*Monostomum*) of trematode worms.

monóstrofe (*m.*) monostrophe.

monóstrofo –fa (*adj.*) monostrophic.

monotálamo –ma (*adj., Bot., Zool.*) monothalmous.

monoteísmo (*m.*) monotheism.

monoteísta (*adj.*) monotheistic; (*m.,f.*) monotheist.

monótipo –pa (*adj., Print.*) monotypic.

monotipo (*m.*) a monotype (typesetting machine).

monotonia (*f.*) monotony; sameness.

monótono –na (*adj.*) monotonous, unvaried; drab; humdrum; tiresome.

monotremo (*m., Zool.*) monotreme.

monótrico –ca (*adj., Biol.*) monotrichous.

monotriglifo (*m., Arch.*) monotriglyph.

monótropa (*f., Bot.*) an Indian pipe (*Monotropa sp.*).

monotropáceo –cea (*m., Bot.*) monotropaceous; (*f.pl.*) Indian pipe family (*Monotropaceae*).

monotropia (*f., Physical Chem.*) monotropy.

monotrópico –ca (*adj., Physical Chem.*) monotropic.

monovalente (*adj., Chem.*) monovalent, univalent.

monóxido [ks] (*m., Chem.*) monoxide.—**de carbono**, carbon monoxide.—**de chumbo**, lead monoxide; litharge. —**de lítio**, lithium monoxide; lithia.

monóxilo –la [ks] (*adj.*) made of wood in one piece; (*m.*) dugout canoe, pirogue.

monoxó (*m.,f.*) an Indian of the Monoshó, a tribe of the Maxacalí in Mato Grosso; (*adj.*) pert. to or designating this tribe.

monozócio –cia (*adj., Zool.*) monozoic.

Monrói (*m.*) Monroe.

monroísmo (*m.*) Monroeism.

monroísta (*m.,f.*) Monroeist.

monrolite (*f., Min.*) monrolite.

Mons. = MONSENHOR (Monsignor).

Monsenhor (*m.*) Monsignor; (*not cap., Bot.*) chrysanthemum.—**-amarelo**, the Caucasian pyrethrum (*Chrysanthemum marschalli*), c.a. PIRETRO-DO-CAUCASO, MATRICÁRIA.

monstera (*f., Bot.*) ceriman (*Monstera deliciosa*).

monstrengo (*m.*) var. of MOSTRENGO.

monstro (*m.*) monster (all senses).

monstruosidade (*f.*) monstrosity; freak.

monstruoso –sa (*adj.*) monstrous; prodigious; hideous.

monta (*f.*) sum, amount; cost, price. **pôsto**, or **estação, de—**, breeding station, stud farm.

monta-cargas (*m.*) freight elevator; a hoist; a lift truck.

montado –da (*adj.*) mounted; sitting astride; equipped; (*m.*) oak grove; (*f.*) mounting; a mount (horse).

montador –dora (*m.*) assembler (of parts); erector.

montagem (*f.*) mounting; assembly (of parts); erection, setting-up; stage setting, scenery. **linha**, or **cadeia, de—**, assembly line. **usina de—**, assembly plant.

montanha (*f.*) mountain.—**-russa**, roller coaster. [*cap.*] —**s Rochosas**, Rocky Mountains.

montanhês –nhêsa (*adj.*) mountain; (*m.,f.*) mountaineer.

montanhoso –sa (*adj.*) mountainous.

montanite (*f., Min.*) montanite.

montano –na (*adj.*) montane.

montante (*m.*) amount, sum, total; strut (of an airplane); an upright; broadsword. **a—**, upstream; (*adj.*) mounting; rising; climbing.

montão (*m.*) heap, pile, stack; clutter.

montar (*v.t.*) to mount (a horse); to set up, assemble, put together; to set (a diamond in a mount); (*v.i.*) to ride horseback; to ascend, climb, rise. (*v.r.*) to mount, straddle, bestride.—**a**, or—**em**, to amount to.—**à amazona**, to ride sidesaddle.—**a cavalo**, to ride horseback.—**banca de advogado**, to hang out one's shingle (as a lawyer).—**em (cima de)**, to get up on.—**em osso**, or **em pêlo**, to ride bareback.—**escarranchado**, to sit (ride) astride.—**guarda**, to mount guard.—**sôbre**, to place on top of.— **uma loja**, to set up shop.—**uma máquina**, to set up (assemble the parts of) a machine.—**uma peça**, to stage a play.

montaria (*f.*) mount, saddle horse; sidesaddle; woman's riding skirt; big game hunting; a dugout canoe in the Amazon region.

monte (*m.*) hill, mountain; mound; heap, pile; (*pl.*) oodles.—**de piedade**, or **de socorro**, public pawnshop.— **de Vênus**, (*Anat.*) mons Veneris.—**escarpado**, a bluff or cliff. **aos—s**, in great profusion.

montear (*v.t.*) to pile up, heap up; to hunt in the mountains; (*v.i.*) to ride horseback.

montebrasita (*f., Min.*) amblygonite.

montéia (*f.*) sketch of a building or floor plan.

montepio (*m.*) a mutual insurance or pension society.

montês –têsa (*adj.*) mountain; wild. **cabra—**, mountain goat.

montesinho –nha, **montesino** –na (*adj.*) mountain; rough; wild.

monticelite (*f., Min.*) monticellite.

montícola (*adj.*) monticoline; (*m.,f.*) mountain-dweller.

montículo (*m.*) knoll, hillock, mound.

montmorilonita (*f.*, *Min.*) montmorillonite.
montoeira (*f.*) heaps of stones and gravel left by diamond searchers.
montra (*f.*) showcase.
montuoso -sa (*adj.*) mountainous, hilly.
montureiro -ra (*m.*,*f.*) ragpicker.
monturo (*m.*) garbage dump; dunghill.
monumental (*adj.*) monumental; huge; magnificent; extraordinary.
monumento (*m.*) monument; memorial; cenotaph.
moquear (*v.t.*) to prepare meat on the MOQUÉM.
moqueca (*f.*) a kind of fish stew; a string of fish; a string of peppers.
moquém (*m.*) a framework of sticks on which meat is spread for roasting or drying; c.a. MOQUETEIRO.
moquenca (*f.*) a kind of beef stew.
moqueta [ê] (*m.*,*f.*) = CAIPIRA.
moqueteiro (*m.*) = MOQUÉM.
moquiço (*m.*) thatched hut [= CABANA].
m.ᵒʳ = MORADOR (resident).
mor (*adj.*) short and poetic form of MAIOR.
mora (*f.*) delay, postponement [= DEMORA]; default; respite; extension of time for payment or delivery of something; (*Bot.*) a tree (*Mora excelsa*, family *Caesalpiniaceae*) whose tough wood is much esteemed for shipbuilding and fine cabinetwork; (*colloq.*) = AMORA (mulberry).
moráceo -cea (*adj.*, *Bot.*) moraceous; (*f.pl.*) the Moraceae [family comprising the fig (*Fiscus*), the mulberry (*Morus*), the breadfruit (*Artocarpus*) and the breadnut (*Brosimum*), etc.].
morada (*f.*) dwelling(-place), abode, home, living quarters. última—, final resting place (the grave).
moradia (*f.*) dwelling, domicile.
morador -dora (*adj.*) dwelling; (*m.*,*f.*) dweller, inhabitant; tenant; neighbor; farm hand; poor sharecropper.
moral (*f.*) morals, ethics; the moral of a story; (*m.*) morality; morale; (*adj.*) moral, ethical.
moralidade (*f.*) morality; the moral (of a tale, fable, etc.).
moralista (*adj.*) moralistic; (*m.*,*f.*) moralist.
moralização (*f.*) moralization.
moralizador -dora (*adj.*) moralizing; (*m.*,*f.*) moralizer.
moralizar (*v.t.*) to moralize.
moranga (*f.*) winter squash (*Cucurbita maxima*).
morangal (*m.*) strawberry field.
morango (*m.*) strawberry.—-bravo, India wild strawberry (*Duchesnea indica*).—-do-campo = CIPÓ-AREIA.
morangueiro (*m.*) strawberry plant (*Fragaria*).—-do-chile, chiloe strawberry (*Fragaria chiloensis*).
morar (*v.i.*) to dwell, reside, abide, inhabit.—à (or na) rua tal-e-tal, to reside on such-and-such a street.—à (or sôbre a) beira do rio, to live on the bank of a river.—entre, to live among.—na cidade, to live in the city.—porta com porta, or—paredes-meias com, to live next-door to.
moratório -ria (*adj.*) dilatory; moratory; (*m.*) moratorium.
morbidez[a] (*f.*) morbidity.
mórbido -da (*adj.*) morbid, sick, unhealthy.
morbífico -ca, morbígeno -na, morbígero -ra, morbíparo -ra (*adj.*) morbific(al), causing disease.
morbiliforme (*adj.*, *Med.*) morbiliform, resembling measles.
morbo (*m.*) disease; pathology.
morboso -sa (*adj.*) = MÓRBIDO.
morcêgo (*m.*) a bat (winged quadruped); (*colloq.*) an urchin who steals rides on a street car; a batfish (*Ogcocephalus vespertilio*), c.a. PEIXE-MORCÊGO.—-do-mar = JAMANTA (the manta).—-orelhudo, big-eared bat (*Corynorhinus sp.*).
morcegueira (*f.*) cabbage angelin tree (*Andira inermis*).
morcela, morcilha (*f.*) blood sausage.
mordaça (*f.*) a gag; fig., any restraint on freedom of speech or of the press; a muzzle.
mordacidade (*f.*) mordance; causticity; piquancy; acrimony.
mordaz (*adj.*) mordant, biting, cutting; caustic; sarcastic; acrimonious.
mordedela (*f.*) = MORDEDURA.
mordedor -dora (*adj.*) biting; (*m.*) biter; sponger, dead beat.
mordedura (*f.*) bite; teeth marks.
morde-e-assopra (*m.*,*f.*) two-faced person.
mordelídeos (*m.*,*pl.*) the Mordellidae (family of beetles).
mordenite (*f.*, *Min.*) mordenite.

mordentagem (*f.*) dyeing with a mordant.
mordente (*adj.*) mordant, caustic, sarcastic; (*m.*) (*Dyeing*) mordant; (*Music*) mordent; (*Mach.*) chuck jaw; a lead liner for the jaws of a vise.
morder (*v.t.*,*v.i.*) to bite; (*v.t.*) to bite into; to corrode; to sting; (*slang*) to put the "bite" on (someone).—a língua, to bite the tongue (to restrain oneself from speaking).—o pó, to bite the dust.—os beiços, to bite one's lips (in chagrin).—-se de inveja, to grow green with envy. Cachorro que late não morde, Barking dogs seldom bite.
mordicação (*f.*) nibbling, gnawing; stinging, smarting.
mordicante (*adj.*) gnawing; stinging.
mordicar (*v.t.*) to nibble; to nip; to sting.
mordida, mordidela (*f.*) = MORDEDURA.
mordimento (*m.*) biting; bite; teeth marks; fig., remorse.
mordiscar (*v.*) var. of MORDICAR.
mordomo (*m.*) majordomo; butler; steward.
moréia (*f.*) moray eel (*Muraena*); stacked sheaves of grain; hay stack; also = BABOSA (a fish).
moreiatim (*m.*) a poison toadfish (*Thalassophryne branneri*), c.a. NIQUIM-DA-AREIA, NIQUIM-DO-MAR.
moreno -na (*adj.*) dark-complexioned; (*m.*) brunet; (*f.*) brunette; a paca (spotted cavy); a partridge; (*Geol.*) moraine.
morerê (*m.*) a disk fish (*Symphysodon discus*).
morféia (*f.*) morphea; leprosy.
morfema (*f.*, *Gram.*) morpheme.
morfético -ca (*adj.*) Morphean; leprous.
morfina (*f.*) morphine.
morfinismo (*m.*, *Med.*) morphinism.
morfinomania (*f.*) addiction to morphine.
morfinômano -na (*m.*,*f.*) morphine addict.
morfogenia (*f.*, *Embryol.*) morphogenesis.
morfogênico -ca (*adj.*, *Embryol.*) morphogenic.
morfologia (*f.*, *Biol.*, *Gram.*) morphology.
morfológico -ca (*adj.*) morphologic(al).
morfologista, morfólogo -ga (*m.*,*f.*) morphologist.
morfometria (*f.*) morphometry.
morfoplasma (*m.*, *Biol.*) morphoplasm.
morfose (*f.*, *Biol.*) morphosis.
morfotropia (*f.*, *Chem.*) morphotropy, morphotropism.
morgado (*m.*) the first-born or eldest son; the one next in line as heir to an entailed estate; such an estate.
morganático -ca (*adj.*) morganatic.
morganita (*f.*) morganite [a rose-colored semiprecious variety of beryl].
morgue (*f.*) morgue [= NECROTÉRIO].
moribundo -da (*adj.*) moribund; (*m.*,*f.*) a dying person.
morigeração (*f.*) moderation; good behavior.
morigerado -da (*adj.*) upright, well-behaved; temperate.
morigerar (*v.t.*) to teach, train (morally); (*v.r.*) to mend one's ways.
morim (*m.*) madras, white cotton cloth, c.a. MADAPOLÃO, MADRASTO, PANO PATENTE.
morina (*f.*, *Chem.*) morin.
morindina (*f.*, *Chem.*) morindin.
morindona (*f.*, *Chem.*) morindone.
morinda (*f.*) Indian mulberry (*Morinda citrifolia*).
moringa (*f.*) a water jug made of porous clay (which permits cooling by evaporation); c.a. MORINGUE; (*Bot.*) the horseradish tree (*Moringa oleifera*).
morínqua (*f.*) = FORNO-D'ÁGUA.
moririçó (*m.*) a blue-eyedgrass (*Sisyrinchium galaxoides*).
morisqueta [ê] (*f.*) funny faces [= CARETAS].
moriti (*m.*) = BURITI.
mormaceira (*f.*) sultry weather.
mormacento -ta (*adj.*) sultry, sweltering, muggy [weather].
mormaço (*m.*) sultry weather; (*colloq.*) dalliance, courtship.
mormente (*adv.*) chiefly, principally.
mormo [mô̂r] (*m.*, *Veter.*) glanders.
mórmon (*m.*) Mormon.
mormoso -sa (*adj.*) of horses, etc., glandered.
mornidão (*m.*) lukewarmness.
môrno -na (*adj.*) warm; lukewarm, tepid; listless, unconcerned.
moroçoca (*f.*) "The commonest of the Anopheles mosquitoes in Amazonia (*Anopheles argyrotarsis*)." [GBAT]
mororó (*m.*, *Bot.*) any sp. of Bauhinia, esp. the bell bauhinia (*B. forficata*) c.a. PÉ-DE-BOI, UNHA-DE-BOI (or -DE-VACA), PATA-DE-VACA.
morosidade (*f.*) slowness, tardiness, slackness. [Not an equivalent of moroseness, which is RABUGEM, MAU HUMOR.]

moroso –sa (*adj.*) slow, deliberate; dilatory; sluggish; delayed, lingering. [Not an equivalent of morose, in the sense of sullen or ill-natured, which is RABUGENTO, CASMURRO.]

morotó (*m.*) maggot; (*Bot.*) a bluestem grass (*Andropogon glaucescens*).

morototó (*m.*) the matchwood (*Didymopanax morototoni*), c.a. MARUPAÚBA-FALSA, PARÁ-PARÁ.

Morra! (*exclam.*) Down with it (him, etc.)!

morraca (*f.*) tinder.

morrão (*m.*) fuse; wick; snuff (charred part of candlewick); ergot.

morrediço –ça (*adj.*) dying; perishable.

morredouro –ra (*adj.*) perishable, frail; mortal; (*m.*) a place with a high death rate. Var. MORREDOIRO.

morre-joão (*m.*) = DORMIDEIRA (sensitive plant).

morremorrer [24] (*v.i.*) to die slowly.

morre-não-morre (*m., colloq.*) a moribund person.

morrente (*adj.*) moribund.

morrer [24] (*v.i.*) to die; to wither, perish; to cease, vanish; to subside, disappear.—**à nascença**, to die aborning.—**a rir**, or—**de riso**, to die laughing.—**da mão de**, to die by the hand of.—**de (sêde, fome, frio, mêdo, etc.)** to die of (thirst, hunger, cold, fright, etc.).—**de amores por alguém**, to be dying-in-love for ("crazy about") someone.—**de morte desastrada**, to die in an accident, wreck or disaster.—**de morte macaca**, to die a violent death.—**de morte natural**, to die a natural death.—**de sucesso**, (*colloq.*) to die suddenly.—**de velho**, to die of old age.—**por**, to be inordinately desirous of, "crazy" about or for, something or someone.—**santo**, to die in the faith.—**sem dizer ai Jesus**, (*colloq.*) to die suddenly.—**sem sentir**, to die an easy death. **ajudar a bem—**, to comfort a dying person. **O seguro morreu de velho**, Better safe than sorry. **rir a—**, to nearly die laughing.

morrião (*m.*) morion; scarlet pimpernel (*Anagallis arvensis*), c.a. ANAGALIS.—**d'água**, a brookweed (*Samolus*).—**dos-passarinhos**, chickweed (*Stellaria media*).

morrinha (*f.*) murrain (infectious disease of cattle); any slight ailment; offensive body odor; the blues, the dumps; languor, lassitude.

morrinhento –ta (*adj.*) affected with MORRINHA.

morro [mô] (*m.*) hill, hillock, mound.—**abaixo**, downhill.

morrote (*m.*) small hill.

morruína (*f., Biochem.*) morrhuin(e).

morsa (*f.*) walrus, c.a. VACA-MARINHA; a bench vise.

morsegão (*m.*) a piece bitten off; a pinch.

morsegar (*v.t.*) to bite off.

morta-côr (*f.*) var. of MORTE-CÔR.

mortadela (*f.*) Bologna sausage.

mortagem (*f.*) mortise.

mortal (*adj.*) mortal; deadly; dying (*m.*) mortal, human being; (*pl.*) mankind, humanity.

mortalha (*f.*) shroud, winding sheet; grave clothes; a cigarette paper.

mortalidade (*f.*) mortality.

mortandade (*f.*) mortality; slaughter, carnage.

morte (*f.*) death.—**do diabo**, (*Bot.*) the meadow succisa (*S. pratensis*).—**macaca**, disastrous death.—**súbita**, sudden death.—**violenta**, violent death. **às portas da—**, at death's door. **de—**, mortally. **de má—**, vile, evil. **estar pela hora da—**, to be very high-priced. **estar com a—no coração**, to be grieved to death. **ter uma bela—**, to die a peaceful death.

morte-côr (*f.*) ground colors (of a painting).

morteiro (*m.*) mortar (short cannon; also vessel in which drugs are pounded with a pestle); binnacle.

morte-luz (*f.*) = MORTE-CÔR.

morticínio (*m.*) slaughter, massacre. Cf. MORTANDADE, MATANÇA.

mortiço –ça (*adj.*) dying; dimming; spiritless.

mortífero –ra (*adj.*) deadly, mortal.

mortificação (*f.*) mortification, gangrene; penitential self-discipline. [But not mortification in the sense of humiliation which is HUMILHAÇÃO, VEXAME.]

mortificante, mortificador –dora, mortificativo –va (*adj.*) that mortifies, deadens; irksome; galling.

mortificar (*v.t.*) to mortify, deaden (a part of the body); to curb (the appetites); to subdue, repress; to spite; to harass, annoy, irk; to "gripe"; (*v.r.*) to practice self-mortification; to torment oneself; to grieve. [Not employed in Port. as equivalent of mortify in the sense of shaming or abashing which is ENVERGONHAR, HUMILHAR.]

morto –ta (*adj.; irreg. p.p. of* MORRER *and* MATAR) dead, lifeless, deceased; killed; inert; gone and forgotten; useless; (*m.,f.*) a dead person; a dummy (at bridge).—**de cansaço**, tired to death, dogtired.—**em ação**, killed in action. **Está—**, He is dead. **Foi—**, He was killed. **mais—que vivo**, more dead than alive. **meio—**, half-dead, tired-out. **não ter onde cair—**, to have no place to lay one's head (destitute). **Rei—, rei pôsto**, The king is dead, long live the king.

mortório (*m.*) funeral; death; oblivion.

mortualha (*f.*) pile of corpses.

mortuário –ria (*adj.*) mortuary.

morubixaba (*m.*) tribal chief; political boss. Vars. MURUMUXAUA, MURUXAUA.

morula (*f.*) slight delay; (*Embryol.*) morula.

mos [me+os] (*pers. pron.*) them to me.

Mosa (*f.*) Meuse (French river).

mosaicista (*adj.*) mosaic; (*m.,f.*) designer of or worker in mosaics. Var. MOSAÍSTA.

mosaico –ca (*adj.*) Mosaic; (*m.*) mosaic; mosaic plant disease.

mosaísta, var. of MOSAICISTA.

mosandrite (*f., Min.*) mosandrite.

môsca (*f.*) a housefly or other similar two-winged insect; fig., an annoying person; a small tuft of hair grown just below the lower lip; a beauty-spot; bull's-eye (of a target).—**-aranha**, or—**-dos-cavalos**, a certain fly (*Hippobosca*) called a horse tick but not related to the true ticks.—**-brava**, or—**-de-bagaço**, the stable fly (*Stomoxys calcitrans*).—**-das-frutas**, fruit fly.—**-de-elefante**, or—**-piroga**, tsetse fly (*Glossina morsitans*), c.a. CECÉ.—**-de-fogo**, firefly.—**-de-ura**, a botfly (*Dermatobia cyaniventris*).—**-do-mediterrâneo**, Mediterranean fruit fly.—**-dourada**, green-bottle fly.—**-morta**, a seemingly innocuous person; a slow poke.—**-de-espanha**, or—**-s-de-milão**, (*Pharm.*) cantharides [powdered Spanish flies (*Lyttia vesicatoria*) or blister beetles].—**-varejeira**, gadfly, blowfly. **às—s**, empty, deserted (no customers); idle. **comer—**, to be fooled; not to catch on.

moscadeira (*f., Bot.*) nutmeg (*Myristica fragrans*), c.a. NOZ-MOSCADA; —**-do-brasil** = BICUÍBA-REDONDA (nutmeg tree).

moscadeiro (*m.*) a fly whisk.

moscado –da (*adj.*) musky.

moscão (*m.*) a large fly; fig., a dull-witted person.

moscar [57] (*v.i.,v.r.*) to escape, run away, disappear; to take to one's heels.

moscardo (*m.*) horsefly, gadfly.

moscaria (*f.*) swarm of flies.

moscatel [-téis] (*adj.; m.*) muscatel (grapes, wine).

moscatelina (*f., Bot.*) muskroot (*Adoxa moschatellina*).

môsco (*m.*) little fly; mosquito; musk deer (*Moschus moschiferus*).

moscóvia (*f.*) Russia leather; [*cap.*] Moscow.

moscovita (*adj.; m.,f.*) Muscovite.

moslim (*adj.; m.*) Moslem.

mosqueado –da (*adj.*) spotted (as a leopard); speckled; flecked.

mosquear (*v.t.*) to spot, speckle; of cattle and horses, to switch the tail; (*v.i.*) of a cab-driver, to cruise.

mosquedo [ê] (*m.*) swarm of flies; fly-infested place.

mosqueiro (*m.*) fly trap (lit. & fig.).

mosqueta [ê] (*f.*) Arabian jasmine (*Jasminum sambac*), c.a. BOGARI; the musk rose (*Rosa moschata*); the evergreen rose (*Rosa sempervirens*).

mosquetaço (*m.*) musket shot.

mosquetada (*f.*) musket shot; wound caused by the same.

mosquetão (*m.*) a snap hook; musket.

mosquetaria (*f.*) musketry.

mosquete [quê] (*m.*) large, old-fashioned musket.

mosqueteiro (*m.*) musketeer.

mosquitada (*f.*) swarm of mosquitoes.

mosquitador (*m.*) dealer in diamond chips.

mosquiteiro (*m.*) mosquito net.

mosquito (*m.*) mosquito; gnat; (*colloq.*) tiny rough diamond.—**-berne**, crane fly, daddy-long-legs.—**do-mangue**, a punkie or biting midge.—**-palha**, or—**-polvora**, small bloodsucking sand fly.—**-trombeteiro**, or—**-zumbidor**, common house mosquito (*Culex pipiens*).

mossa (*f.*) dent; indentation; nick, notch; a disagreeable impression or emotion.

mostarda (*f.*) mustard (seed, powder, condiment); (*m.*) fine bird shot.—**-branca**, white mustard (*Brassica hirta*).—**-da-china**, pakchoi or Chinese cabbage (*B. chinensis*).—**-da-índia**, India mustard (*B. juncea*).—

-dos-campos, charlock (*B. kaber*).—**-ordinária,** or—**-preta,** black mustard (*B. nigra*). **subir a—ao nariz,** to flare up in anger.

mostardeira (*f.*) mustard pot; (*Bot.*) mustard plant.

mostardeiro (*m.*) mustard dealer; mustard pot.

mostardinha-do-mar (*f., Bot.*) a searocket (*Cakile lanceolata*).

mosteiro (*m.*) monastery.

mosto (*m.*) must, grape or other fruit juice, new wine.

mostra (*f.*) a showing; sign, token, indication; exhibit, display; (*pl.*) gestures; outward appearances. **pôr à—,** to place on display.

mostrador –dora (*adj.*) showing, indicating; (*m.*) dial (of a timepiece, radio, etc.); a show window; a glass counter. **dar a volta ao—,** to sleep around the clock.

mostrar (*v.t.*) to show, display, exhibit; to indicate, point out; to manifest; to disclose; (*v.r.*) to show oneself; to appear; to show off.—**as costas a,** to turn one's back and flee.—**as ferraduras,** to show one's heels.—**com quantos paus se faz uma canôa,** to teach (someone) a lesson.—**má cara a,** to show displeasure.—**os ventos que traz,** to show one's intentions.—**que sabe perder,** to show (oneself) to be a good loser.—**os dentes,** to bare the teeth (in a threatening manner).—**-se superior a,** to rise above something, be superior to it.

mostrengo (*m.*) lubber, lout, slob.

mostruário (*m.*) sample case or book; showcase; market stand.

mota (*f.*) dike, embankment; mound of earth; something given for good measure or to boot.

motacilídeos (*m.pl., Zool.*) the Motacillidae (wagtails and pipits).

motacu [ú] (*f.*) a palm (*Scheelea princeps*).

mote (*m.*) motto; burden (of a song, etc.).

motejador –dora (*adj.*) mocking, jeering, taunting; (*m.,f.*) scoffer, jester, taunter.

motejar (*v.i.*) to mock, scoff, jeer (**de,** at); (*v.t.*) to taunt.

motejo [ê] (*m.*) mockery, derision; raillery; a jest.

motete [tête] (*m.*) mot, witty remark; (*Music*) motet.

motevo (*m., colloq.*) a screwball.

motilidade (*f.*) motility.

motim (*m.*) mutiny, riot, tumult, revolt; rumpus, row.

motinar (*v.*) = AMOTINAR.

motineiro (*m.*) rioter; mutineer.

motinoso –sa (*adj.*) riotous; mutinous.

motivação (*f.*) motivation.

motivado –da (*adj.*) motivated, impelled (**por,** by).

motivador –dora (*adj.*) motivating, impelling.

motivar (*v.t.*) to motivate, impel, induce; to expound the reasons or motives.

motivo –va (*adj.*) motive, motor; moving; (*m.*) motive, cause; provocation; reason, ground; (*Music*) motif, theme.—**por que,** for which reason; by reason of which. **dar—s,** to give rise to. **por—de,** on account of, by reason of.

moto (*m.*) motion. **de—próprio,** of one's own free will; of one's own accord.

motocicleta (*f.*), **motocíclo** (*m.*) motorcycle.

motociclista (*m.,f.*) motorcyclist.

motociclismo (*m.*) motorcycle riding.

motogodile (*f.*) boat with an outboard motor.

motopatinete (*m.*) motor scooter.

motor –tora (*adj.*) motor, motive; (*m.*) motor, engine; motive.—**axial,** axial motor.—**bicilíndrico,** two-cylinder motor.—**compound,** (*Elec.*) compound motor.—**de arranque,** or **de arranco,** or **de partida,** starter; starting motor.—**de combustão interna,** internal combustion engine.—**de X cavalos,** X-horsepower motor.—**de corrente alternada,** (*Elec.*) A.C. motor.—**de corrente contínua,** (*Elec.*) D.C. motor.—**de dupla ação,** double-acting motor.—**de êmbolos,** piston engine.—**de explosão,** internal combustion engine.—**de gás,** gas engine.—**de guindaste,** crane motor.—**de pôpa,** outboard motor.—**em V,** V-type motor.—**polifásico,** (*Elec.*) polyphase motor.—**radial,** radial engine. —**sincrônico,** synchronous motor.—**semidiesel,** semi-Diesel motor. **eixo—,** driving shaft. Cf. MOTRIZ.

motor-gerador (*m.*) generator.

motoreiro (*m.*) = MOTORNEIRO.

motorista (*m.*) motorist, driver, chauffeur. **licença de—,** driver's license.

motorneiro (*m.*) streetcar motorman.

motoro (*m.*) a stingray.

motramite (*f., Min.*) mottramite.

motricidade (*f.*) motricity, motor function.

motriz [fem. of MOTOR] (*adj.*) motive, moving, driving. **força—,** motive power.

motu-próprio (*adv.*) motu proprio; (*m.*) spontaneousness; one's own free will.

mou-, look under **moi-** for words which cannot be found beginning with **mou-.**

moucarrão –rona (*adj.*) stone deaf.

mouco –ca (*adj.*) deaf, hard of hearing. **fazer ouvidos—s a,** to turn a deaf ear to; (*m.,f.*) deaf person.

mouquice, mouquidão (*f.*) deafness [= SURDEZ].

moura (*f.*) see under MOURO.

mourão (*m.*) stake, post.—**de cêrca,** fence post.

mouraria (*f.*) Moorish quarter.

mourejado –da (*adj.*) won or obtained after much work or great effort. Var. MOIREJADO.

mourejar (*v.i.*) to work like a trojan; to slave, drudge, plod, grub. Var. MOIREJAR.

mourejo [ê] (*m.*) hard, unremitting toil. Var. MOIREJO.

mouresco –ca (*adj.*) Moorish. Var. MOIRESCO.

mouriscado –da (*adj.*) laid with mortar [Spanish roof tiles].

mourisco –ca (*adj.*) moorish; (*m.pl.*) articles of jewelry.

mouro –ra (*adj.*) Moorish; (*m.*) Moor; infidel; hard worker.—**s na costa,** "nigger in the woodpile" [suspicious signs, peculiar circumstances, concealed motives, etc.]; (*f.*) Moorish woman.—**-encantada,** in Portuguese folklore, a river siren.—**-torta,** in Portuguese folklore, a witch. Var. MOIRO.

mouta (*f.*) var. of MOITA.

moutão (*m.*) var. of MOITÃO.

movediço –ça (*adj.*) mobile, movable; fickle. **areia—,** quicksand.

movedor –dora (*adj.*) moving; (*m.,f.*) mover.

móvel [-veis] (*adj.*) movable; (*m.*) motive, cause; an article of furniture; (*pl.*) furniture; chattels. Cf. MOBILIA.

movente (*adj.*) moving, shifting.

mover (*v.t.*) to move, shift; to propel, drive; to rouse; to provoke; to affect, touch; to prevail upon; (*v.r.*) to move, stir, budge.—**uma ação,** to start a lawsuit.

movimentação (*f.*) moving, movement.

movimentado –da (*adj.*) active. **rua—,** busy street.

movimentar (*v.t.*) to give movement to; to set in motion; (*v.r.*) to move.

movimento (*m.*) movement, motion; moving; ado, bustle; lively trade; a drive, crusade; (*Music*) movement, tempo.—**acelerado,** accelerated motion.—**amebóide,** (*Biol.*) amoeboid motion.—**angular,** angular motion.—**aperiódico,** (*Physics, Elec.*) aperiodic (deadbeat) motion.—**brauniano,** (*Physics*) Brownian movement or motion.—**composto,** (*Physics, Math.*) compound (harmonic) motion.—**contínuo,** or—**perpétuo,** perpetual motion.—**curvilíneo,** a curving motion.—**de restituição,** (*Mech.*) resilience, work of recovery.—**de tenazes,** (*Milit.*) pincers movement.—**de terra,** moving of earth (as in road building).—**de translação,** (*Mech.*) translation.—**de vaivem,** reciprocating motion, as of a piston.—**diferencial,** (*Mach.*) differential motion.—**diurno,** (*Astron.*) diurnal motion.—**s fotohélicos,** or—**s nictinásticos,** (*Plant Physiol.*) nyctitropism.—**ondulatório,** (*Physics*) wave motion.—**oscilatório,** (*Physics*) oscillation.—**s paratônicos,** (*Plant Physiol.*) paratonic movements.—**perdido,** lost motion.—**retardado,** deceleration, negative acceleration.—**retilíneo,** rectilinear motion. **em—,** astir; in motion. **pôr em—,** to set going.'

móvito (*m.*) premature birth; abortion.

movível (*adj.*) movable.

moxamar (*v.t.*) to smoke-dry (fish).

moxinifada (*f.*) hodgepodge.

moxubiá (*m., Bot.*) a mombin (*Spondias myrabolanus*).

m/p = MESES DE PRAZO (months' time—for payment).

M.R.P.M. = MUITO REVERENDO PADRE-MESTRE (Very Reverend Father-Teacher).

ms. = MANUSCRITO (manuscript).

m.ˢ = MAIS (more).

m/s = METROS POR SEGUNDO (meters per second).

m.ᵗᵃ, m.ᵗᵒ = MUITA, MUITO (much; many).

mu (*m.*) a mule [= MULO]; (*Elec.*) mu.

muamba (*f.*) knapsack; warehouse robbery; smuggling; shady business; a kind of magic spell or somewhat mysterious charm.

muambeiro (*m.*) rascal; swindler; a "fence".

muar (*adj.; m.,f.*) mule. **gado—,** mules.

muavé (*m.*) sassy or sassywood (*Erythropholeum guineense*) whose poisonous bark is used as an ordeal poison; c.a. PAU-DOS-FEITICEIROS.

mucajá (*f.*) = MACAJÁ.
mucama, mucamba (*f.*) In old Brazil, a favorite young woman slave employed as housemaid, nurse, or lady's companion; a "mammy".
muçambê, muçambê (*m.*) a spiderflower (*Cleome heptaphylla*).—**-catinga** = CATINGA-DE-NEGRO.—**côr-de-rosa**, a pink spiderflower (*Cleome rosa*).—**-de-três-fôlhas** = BREDO-FEDORENTO.—**-indecente**, the dog caper (*Capparis flexuosa*), c.a. FEIJÃO-DE-BOI.
muçarete (*m.*) a marine snail of Purpura (syn. Thais), c.a. SAGUARITÁ.
mucedinácea, mucedínea (*f.*) mucedine, a mold fungus.
mucica (*f.*) twitch; jerk; pull, yank (as on a fishing line).
múcico –ca (*adj.; Chem.*) mucic.
mucilagem (*f., Bot., Pharm.*) mucilage [but not in the ordinary sense of gum or glue, which is COLA.]
mucilaginoso –sa (*adj.*) mucilaginous.
mucina (*f., Biochem.*) mucin.
mucíparo –ra (*adj.; Bot.*) muciparous.
mucívoro –ra (*adj.; Zool.*) mucivorous.
muco (*m.*) mucus.
mucomembranoso –sa (*adj.; Anat.*) mucomembranous.
mucor (*m.*) a genus (*Mucor*) of common molds (such as found on bread).
mucosa (*f., Anat.*) mucosa, mucous membrane.
mucosidade (*f.*) mucosity.
mucoso –sa (*adj.*) mucous, viscous.
mucro, múcron (*m., Anat., Zool.*) xiphisternum; (*Bot., Zool.*) mucro.
mucronado –da (*adj.*) mucronate.
mucronífero –ra (*adj.*) mucroniferous, mucronate.
mucronulado –da (*adj.*) mucronulate.
muçu [çú] (*m.*) = MUÇUM.
muçuã (*m.*) a small Amazon mud turtle (*Kinosternon scorpioides*) prized as food; c.a. JURARÁ.
mucuaxeiro (*m.*) cattle thief.
mucudo –da (*adj.; slang*) big-muscled.
mucuim [u-ím] (*m.*) chigger, red bug; "an almost microscopic red tick (*Tetranchus molestissimus*) which lives in the CAPIM during the winter season, disappearing at the height of the summer; its sting produces a terrible itching." [*GBAT*]
muçulmano –na (*adj.; m.,f.*) Mohammedan.
muçum (*m.*)—**do-mar**, an eellike teleost tropical fish (*Symbranchus marmoratus*), common in Brazil where it is considered a delicacy.—**-de-rio**, a snake eel (*Ophichthis gonesii*).—**-de-orelhas** = PORAQUÊ (electric eel).
mucumbagem (*f.*) worthless odds and ends; junk.
mucumbu [bú] (*m., colloq.*) the coccyx; also = CACARÉUS.
mucunã, mucuna (*f.*) any of several leguminous plants of Mucuna, Stizolobium (velvetbean), Dolichos, and Dioclea (clusterpea), esp. the cowage mucuna (*M. urens*) and the cowage velvetbean (*Stizolobium pruritium*), the hairs on whose pods cause an intense itching.—**-do-mato**, the giant hyacinth bean (*Dolichos giganteus*), c.a. ÔLHO-DE-BOI.—**-do-norte**, beaked velvetbean (*Stizolobium rostratum*).—**-preta**, the Bengal velvetbean (*Stizolobium aterrinum*).—**-rajada** or—**-vilosa**, the Deering or Florida velvetbean (*Stizolobium deeringianum*), c.a. FEIJÃO-DA-FLÓRIDA. Cf. LABE-LABE.
muçunga, muçungão (*m.*) a pinch [= BELISCÃO].
mucungo (*m.*) = MUTAMBA.
mucuoca (*f.*) a fishing dam made by Indians with poles and brush.
mucura (*f.,m.*) an opossum [= GAMBÁ].—**-xixica**, a small opossum (*Philander*).
mucuracaá (*f.*) the garlic guineahenweed (*Petiveria alliacea*); also = ERVA-PIPI.
mucurana (*m.,f.*) var. of MUQUIRANA.
muçurana (*f.*) this is the noted large, blue-black snake, *Pseudoboa cloelia*, reputed harmless to man, and immune to the bites of the highly venomous snakes not much smaller than itself, such as the deadly JARARACA, which it subdues by constriction and swallows whole; c.a. LIMPA-CAMPO, LIMPA-MATO, LIMPA-PASTO, COBRA-PRETA, MAMADEIRA, BOIRÚ, BAIRÚ. Also, a rope used by Indians to tie up prisoners.
muçurango (*m.*) a goby (fish).
muçurungo (*m.*) = BABOSA (fish).
mucuta (*f.*) musette bag or knapsack [= EMBORNAL].
muda (*f.*) see under MUDO.
mudadiço –ça (*adj.*) movable [= MUDÁVEL].
mudado –da (*adj.*) changed, different; removed; displaced.

mudador –dora (*adj.*) removing; changing; (*m.,f.*) remover; changer.
mudamente (*adv.*) mutely; quietly; silently.
mudança (*f.*) removal; transference; departure; change; alteration, shift, deviation; (*Mach.*) gear box.—**de temperatura**, change of weather.—**eutéctica**, (*Metal.*) eutectic change (freezing or melting). **alavanca de**—, (*Autom.*) gear-shift lever. **em**—, changing, shifting.
mudar (*v.t.*) to remove, move, displace, dislodge; to change, alter; of birds and animals, to shed, molt; (*Bot.*) the mudar or Akund calotrope (*Calotropis gigantea*); (*v.r.*) to change (oneself); to move (away).—**a chapa** or **o disco**, (*slang*) to change the subject.—**de casa**, to change one's residence.—**de conduta**, to turn over a new leaf.—**de conversa**, or **de conversação**, to change the conversation.—**de côr**, to change color.—**de estado**, to change one's status (i.e., to marry).—**de galho**, to switch (political) parties; to switch sides.—**de opinião**, to change one's mind.—**de roupa**, to change clothes.—**de tecla**, (*slang*) to harp on another string.—**de vida**, to change one's mode of life; to turn over a new leaf.—**para melhor**, to change for the better.
mudável (*adj.*) mutable, changeable; inconstant.
mudez[a] (*f.*) muteness; silence.
mudo –da (*adj.*) mute, dumb; tongue-tied; silent; taciturn; (*m.,f.*) a mute person. **surdo**—, a deafmute; (*f.*) removal, change, shift; a relay (of horses); molt (of birds, reptiles, etc.); a plant cutting; a seedling (for transplanting); a change of clothing.
muezim (*f.*) muezzin [= ALMUADEM].
mufla (*f.*) muffile (of a kiln or furnace).
mufti [í] (*m.*) Mohammedan mufti.
mugeira (*f.*) a net, or a boat, for mullet fishing.
mugem (*f.*) a striped mullet (*Mugil cephalus*).
mugido (*m.*) low, moo, bellow, roar.
múgil (*m.*) the genus (*Mugil*) of gray mullets.
mugílidas, mugilídeos (*m.pl.*) the family (*Mugilidae*) consisting of the gray mullets.
mugir (*v.i.*) to moo, low; to bellow; to roar. **sem tugir nem**—, without a peep, without protest, without a whimper.
mui [short form of MUITO] (*adv.*) very.
muiana (*f.*) = MUIÚNA.
muirá (*m.*) an Indian word for wood or stick.—**-gonçalo**, a euphorbiaceous tree (*Hieronyma alcorneoides*), c.a. URUCURANA.
muiracutaca (*f.*) a swartzpea (*Swartzia acuminata*), c.a. PITAICA.
muirajuba (*f.*) a very large Amazonian leguminous tree (*Apuleia molaris*).
muirajuçara (*f., Bot.*) a devil pepper (*Rauwolfia pentaphylla*),—**-verdadeira**, a white quebracho (*Aspidosperma duckei*).
muirapara (*f.*) bow (for shooting arrows) = ARCO.
muirapaxiúba (*f., Bot.*) a senna (*Cassia adiantifolia*).
muirapinima (*f., Bot.*) a snakewood (*Piratinera guianensis*, or *Brosimum guianense*).
muirapiranga (*f.*) brazilwood (*Caesalpinia brasiliensis*) c.a. PAU-BRASIL; a wallabatree (*Eperua*); the Pará breadnut tree (*Brosimum paraense*), c.a. CONDURU-DE-SANGUE.
muiraquatiara (*f.*) a large star tree (*Astronium lecointei*), one of the most beautifully colored woods of Amazonia; also = PAU-RAINHA.
muiraqueteca (*f.*) = CIPÓ-CABOCLO; CIPÓ-D'ÁGUA.
muiraquila, muiraquiinha = CRAVEIRO-DO-MARANHÃO (the clovebark tree).
muiraquitã (*m.*) figure of a snake, turtle, alligator, etc., carved from certain greenish, jade-like minerals, and worn by Amazon Indians as a talisman or good-luck charm; c.a. PEDRA-VERDE, PEDRA-DAS-AMAZONAS.
muitíssimo –ma [*absol. superl.* of MUITO] very, very much; (*pl.*) very, very many.
muito –ta [uin] (*adj.*) much, plenteous, considerable, a lot (of), a great deal (of); (*pl.*) many (a), numerous. [The singular form is frequently used in a plural sense, as in the examples below.] (*adv.*) much, greatly; very; too, overmuch.—**abaixo**, far below (beneath).—**bem**, very well.—**bom**, very good.—**cedo**, too soon.—**embora**, even though, although.—**melhor**, much better.—**obrigado**, much obliged.—**tempo**, a long time.—**coisa**, very much; many things.—**gente**, many people.—**(s) vez(es)**, often, many times. **Conheço-o e**—, I know him very well. **de**, or **desde há**,—, for a long time (past); long since. **há**—

tempo, a long time ago. **mais que—,** far too much. **por—que,** however much; no matter how much. **quando—,** at most.

muiúna (*m.*) Amazon whirlpool.

mujangüê, mujanguê (*m.*) in Amazonas, a dish of raw turtle eggs mixed with manioc meal and sugar.

mujolo (*m.*) var. of MONJOLO.

mula (*f.*) a she-mule; (*Med.*) a bubo.

mulada (*f.*) a drove of mules.

muladeiro (*m.*) muleteer.

mulata (*f.*) a mulatto woman; a kind of baking potato; (*Zool.*) the vermilion snapper (*Rhomboplites aurorubens*), c.a. VERMELHO-PARAMIRIM, REALITO, CARAPITANGA.

mulateira (*f.*) jennet (female donkey); (*Bot.*) = GRAPIUNHA-BRANCA.

mulateiro (*m.*) jackass.

mulatinha (*f.*) a small stingless bee (*Melipona basalis*), c.a. ABELHA-DO-CHÃO, MUMBUCA-LOURA; also = a small mulatto girl or woman.

mulatinho (*m.*) a small mulatto; a kind of small edible bean.

mulato (*m.*) a mulatto.—**-velho,** dried and salted catfish [= PATUREBA].

muleiro (*m., slang*) short-change artist.

mulembá (*m.*) a strangler fig (*Ficus doliaria*).

muleta (*f.*) crutch (*lit.&fig.*); matador's staff; Port. fishing vessel.

muletada (*f.*) herd of mules; a whack with a crutch.

muleteiro (*m.*) mule driver.

mulher (*f.*) woman; wife.—**à-toa,** wench, trollop—**da comédia,**—**da rótula,**—**da rua** (streetwalker),—**da vida,**—**-dama,**—**de má nota,**—**de ponta de rua,**—**do fado,**—**do fandango,**—**do mundo,**—**do pala aberto,**—**errada** (strayed woman),—**perdida** (lost woman),—**pública,**—**vadia:** all are euphemisms for prostitute.—**da verônica,** the woman who takes the part of Veronica in religious street processions.—**de casa,** housewife,—**durazia,** (*colloq.*) a well-preserved middle-aged woman.—**pobre,** (*Bot.*) the toothleaf jacaranda (*H. cuspidifolia*).—**sapeca,** a forward woman.

mulheraça (*f.*) **mulherão** (*m.*) big, strong woman.

mulherada (*f.*), **mulherame** (*m.*) = MULHERIO.

mulherengo –**ga** (*adj.*) womanish, effeminate, sissy; (*m.*) mollycoddle; milksop; woman chaser.

mulherico –**ca** (*adj.*) womanish; weak.

mulherigo (*m.*) effeminate man; a sissy.

mulheril (*adj.*) womanly; womanish.

mulherinha (*f.*) a little woman; a common woman; busybody.

mulherio (*m.*) a large number of women; womenfolk; womankind; = MULHERADA, MULHERAME.

mulherona (*f.*) big, strong woman [= MULHERAÇA, MULHERÃO].

muliado –**da** (*adj.*) unnatural; hybrid.

múlidas (*m.pl.*) the Mullidae (family of red mullets, or surmullets).

mulita (*f.*) the mule armadillo (*Dasypus septemcinctus*); trick, deception; (*Min.*) mullite, aluminum silicate.

mulo (*m.*) mule [= MU].

mulso (*m.*) mead [= HIDROMEL].

multa (*f.*) fine, penalty.

multangular (*adj.*) = MULTIANGULAR.

multar (*v.t.*) to impose a fine on; fig., to condemn.

multiacoplador (*m.*) multiple coupler.

multiangular (*adj.*) multiangular.

multiarticulado –**da** (*adj.*) multiarticulate(d).

multiaxífero –**ra** [ks] (*adj.*) multiaxial.

multicapsular (*adj., Bot.*) multicapsular.

multicelular (*adj.*) multicellular.

multiciente, multício –**cia** (*adj.*) having extensive knowledge of many subjects.

multicoco –**ca** (*adj., Bot.*) multicoccus.

multicilíndrico –**ca** (*adj.*) multicylinder.

multicolor, multicor (*adj.*) multicolored; motley, pied.

multicuspidado –**da, multicúspide** (*adj., Anat., Zool.*) multicuspidate.

multidão (*f.*) multitude, throng, crowd; the populace; mob; a great number.

multidentado –**da** (*adj., Bot., Zool.*) multidentate.

multidigitado –**da** (*adj.*) multidigitate.

multiface (*adj.*) multifaced; multifaceted.

multifário –**ria** (*adj.*) multifarious.

multífido –**da** (*adj., Bot.*) multifid.

multifilar (*adj.*) made of two or more conductors [electric cable].

multifloro –**ra** (*adj., Bot.*) multiflorous.

multifoliado –**da** (*adj., Bot.*) multifoliate.

multiforme (*adj.*) multiform, diverse.

multiformidade (*f.*) multiformity.

multiganglionar (*adj.*) multiganglionic.

multígeno –**na** (*adj.*) comprising more than one genus or species.

multijugado –**da** (*adj., Bot.*) multijugate.

multilátero –**ra** (*adj.*) multilateral, many-sided.

multilinear (*adj.*) multilineal.

multilíngue (*adj.*) multilingual.

multilith (*m.*) a Multilith machine.

multilobado –**da, multilobular** (*adj.*) multilobular, multilobate.

multilocular (*adj.*) multilocular.

multíloquo –**qua** [quo = co] (*adj.*) loquacious.

multilustroso –**sa** (*adj.*) very bright.

multimâmio –**mia** (*adj., Zool.*) multimammate.

multimilionário –**ria** (*adj.; m.,f.*) multimillionaire.

multímodo –**da** (*adj.*) multimodal.

multimotor (*m.*) multimotor airplane.

multinérveo –**vea** (*adj., Bot.*) multinervate.

multiocular (*adj.*) multiocular.

multiovulado –**da** (*adj.*) multiovulate.

multiparidade (*f., Biol., Med.*) multiparity.

multíparo –**ra** (*adj.*) multiparous.

multipartido –**da** (*adj., Bot.*) multipartite.

multípede (*adj., Zool.*) multiped(e).

multiplex [ks] (*m.*) multiplex telegraph transmitter.

multiplicação (*f.*) multiplication.

multiplicador –**dora** (*adj.*) multiplying; (*m.,f.*) multiplier.

multiplicando (*m.*) multiplicand.

multiplicar (*v.t., v.i.*) to multiply, increase.

multiplicativo –**va** (*adj.*) multiplicative.

multipolar (*adj., Elec.*) multipolar.

multiplicável (*adj.*) multipliable.

multíplice (*adj.*) multiplex.

multiplicidade (*f.*) multiplicity.

múltiplo –**pla** (*adj.*) multiple; manifold; (*m.*) multiple.

multipotente (*adj.*) multipotent.

multisseriado –**da** (*adj.*) multiseriate.

multíssono –**na** (*adj.*) multisonous.

multistriado –**da** (*adj.*) multistriate.

multituberculoso –**sa** (*adj.*) multituberculate.

multitubular (*adj.*) multitubular [boiler].

multívago –**ga** (*adj.*) wandering.

multivalente (*adj., Chem.*) multivalent.

multivalve (*adj.; m.*) multivalve (shellfish).

multivalvular (*adj.*) multivalvular.

multívoco –**ca** (*adj.*) multivocal, equivocal.

mulundu [dú] (*m.*) a Negro dance.

mulungu [gú] (*m.*) the common coralbean (*Erythrina corallodendron*), c.a. SAPATINHO-DE-JUDEU.—**-crista-de-galo,** the cockspur coralbean (*Erythrina cristagalli*), c.a. CORTICEIRA, SANANDUVA, CORALEIRA-CRISTADA.

mumbaca (*f.*) an astrocaryum palm (*A. mumbaca*).

mumbanda (*f.*) favorite slave girl [= MUCAMA].

mumbava (*m.*) creature; hanger-on; protégé; henchman.

mumbavo (*m.*) an animal raised as a pet [= XERIMBABO].

mumbica (*adj.*) punk; skinny.

mumbuca (*f.*) a stingless bee (*Melipona capitata*), c.a. PAPA-TERRA.—**-loura** is *Melipona basalis*, c.a. MULATINHA.

múmia (*f.*) mummy; fig., person who is described as "mere skin and bone".

mumificação (*f.*) mummification.

mumificador –**dora** (*adj.*) mummifying; (*m.,f.*) mummifier.

mumificar (*v.t.*) to mummify.

mumuca (*m.,f.*) bogy, bugbear, hobgoblin.

munã (*f.*) mare [= ÉGUA].

mundana (*f.*) see under MUNDANO.

mundanal (*adj.*) mundane [= MUNDANO].

mundanalidade (*f.*), **mundanismo** (*m.*) worldliness.

mundano –**na** (*adj.*) mundane, worldly; (*f.*) a demimondaine.

mundão, mundaréu (*m.*) a "world" of things or people; vast extent of land; faraway place.

mundaú (*m.*) a leafflower (*Phyllanthus inflata*), c.a. CABUIM, CARRAPATO-DO-MATO.

mundeiro (*m.*) strolling; rambling; (*m.*) rambler; tramp.

mundéu, mundé (*m.*) trap, pitfall; any ramshackle structure.

mundial (*adj.*) world-wide; worldly.
mundiça (*f.*) chicken mite; rabble, mob; large family.
mundícia, mundície (*f.*) cleanliness.
mundificação (*f.*) mundification, cleansing.
mundificador -dora (*adj.*) mundifying; (*m.,f.*) mundifier.
mundificante (*adj.*) serving to cleanse and heal; (*m.*) a mundificant oil or plaster.
mundificar (*v.t.*) to mundify, cleanse, deterge.
mundificativo -va (*adj.*) = MUNDIFICANTE.
mundo -da (*adj.*) cleansed, pure; (*m.*) world, universe; earth, globe; planet; life, human affairs; mankind; infinite number.—**aberto sem porteira**, (*colloq.*) wide open spaces.—**desportivo**, sporting world.—**elegante**, high society.—**literário**, literary world. **alma do outro—**, ghost, "spook". **coisa do outro—**, something "out of this world". **correr—**, to "see the world". **enfiar a cara no—**, to run away. **na bôca do—**, on everyone's tongue. **o outro—**, the next world. **o—lá de fora**, the big outside world. **pelo—a fora**, throughout the (wide) world. **pôr a bôca no—**, to yell, "holler". **prometer—s e fundos**, to promise the moon. **todo o—**, everybody [Fr. *tout le monde*]. **um—de gente**, a world of people.
mundrunga (*f.*) sorcery, witchcraft [= BRUXARIA].
mundurucu [cú] (*m.,f.*) one of the Mundurucu, a Tupi-speaking people in the southwestern portion of Pará and southeastern corner of Amazonas. Acculturated remnants of this once fierce, headhunting tribe are settled along the middle Tapajós River; (*adj.*) pert. to or designating this tribe.
munefe (*m.*) the sylvan violet (*Viola sylvestris*).
mungida, mungidura (*f.*) milking (of cows, goats); quantity of milk extracted.
mungir [25] (*v.t.*) to milk (a cow, etc.); to bleed (extort money from).
munguba, mungubarana, mungubeira (*f.*) silk-cotton trees (*Bombax*).
munguengue (*m., Bot.*) the yellow mombin (*Spondias mombin*), c.a. CAJÀZEIRA.
mungu[n]zá (*m.*) a dish of hominy with milk, sugar and cinnamon; c.a. CHÁ-DE-BURRO. [In São Paulo = CANJICA.]
munhão (*m.*) trunnion; gudgeon.
munhata (*f.*) = BATATA-DOCE.
munheca (*f.*) wrist; (*Bot.*) crosier (circinate young frond of a fern).—**-de-cutia**, (*f.*) crop (short whip) made from the leg of an agouti.—**-de-samambaia**, tightfisted person.
munhoneira (*f.*) bearing of a trunnion.
munição (*f.*) munition; ammunition; military supplies; bird shot. **depósito de munições**, ammunition dump.
munício (*m.*) coarse bread; army's herd of cattle; herder's grub.
municionar (*v.t.*) to munition.
municipal (*adj.*) municipal; (*m.*) municipal theater or opera house.
municipalidade (*f.*) municipality; township; local government, city council.
munícipe (*adj.*) municipal; (*m.,f.*) townsman, townswoman, local citizen.
município (*m.*) in Brazil, a division of local government corresponding roughly to a county.
munificência (*f.*) munificence, liberality, generosity.
munificente, munífico -ca (*adj.*) munificent, liberal, generous.
Munique, Muníquia (*f.*) Munich.
munir (*v.t.*) to provide, supply, furnish (**de**, with).
munjolo (*m.*) = MONJOLO.
muque (*m., slang*) biceps. **a—**, by main force.
muquinhar (*v.i., colloq.*) to loaf.
muquirana (*f.*) body louse; (*m.,f.*) a pinchpenny.
mura (*m.,f.*) one of the Mura, a once large and savage tribe living on the Madeira River below the Falls; (*adj.*) pert. to or designating this tribe.
murador -dora (*adj.; m.,f.*) rat-catching (cat).
mural (*adj.*) mural.
muralha (*f.*) rampart; wall.
muralhado -da (*adj.*) immured, walled in.
muralhar (*v.t.*) to immure, wall in.
murapiranga (*f.*) var. of MUIRAPIRANGA.
murar (*v.t.*) to wall (in); to fortify; to chase rats.
murça (*f., Eccl.*) pallium; a smooth-cut file.
murcha (*f.*) wilt (plant disease).
murchar (*v.i.*) to wither, shrivel, wilt.
murchidão (*f.*) wilt.
murcho -cha (*adj.*) withered, wilted, faded; puckered, wrinkled (as a prune); fig., droopy.

mureia (*f.*) moray (eel), genus Muraena.
mureira (*f.*) dunghill near a wall [= ESTRUMEIRA].
murênidas (*f.pl.*) the Muraenidae (family of morays).
mureru [rú] (*m.*) tropical fanwort (*Calbomba aqualica*), c.a. MURURÉ-REDONDINHO; common water hyacinth (*Eichhornea crassipes*).
murexide [ks] (*f., Chem.*) murexid(e).
murganho (*m.*) a kind of small brown rat.
murianha (*f.*) the stable fly (*Stomoxys calcitrans*), c.a. MÔSCA-BRAVA, MÔSCA-DE-BAGAÇO. Var. MURIANHA.
muriático -ca (*adj.*) muriatic [acid].
muribixaba (*m.*) = MORUBIXABA.
muricado -da (*adj.*) muricate; prickly.
múrice (*m.*) any murex shell.
murici [cí] (*m.*) any of several trees of genus Byrsonima (Barbados cherry family), or their fruit.
muricida (*adj.*) rat-killing.
muricidas, muricídeos (*m.pl., Zool.*) the family (*Muricidae*) of marine gastropods, typified by *Murex*.
muriçoca (*f.*) = see CARAPANÃ-PINIMA.
murídeo -dea (*adj.; Zool.*) murine; (*m.pl.*) the Muridae (rats and mice).
murinhanha (*f.*) var. of MURIANHA.
murino -na (*adj.*) = MURÍDEO.
muriqui [quí] (*m.*) a spider monkey (*Eriodes arachnoides*), c.a. MACACO-VERMELHO, MONO.
muriquina (*f.*) a night ape (*Aotus, syn. Nyctipithecus, azare*).
muriti, muritim, muritizeiro (*m.*) see BURUTI(-DO-BREJO).
murixaba (*f.*) prostitute. Var. MURUXABA.
murmulhante (*adj.*) rustling.
murmulhar (*v.i.*) to rustle, swish.
murmulho (*m.*) rustling (of leaves); rippling (of waves).
múrmur (*m.*) murmuring, rippling, swishing.
murmuração (*f.*) murmuring; muttering.
murmurador -dora (*adj.*) murmuring; backbiting.
murmurante (*adj.*) murmuring; muttering.
murmurar (*v.i.*) to murmur, whisper; to babble; to mutter, grumble, complain; to backbite.
murmurejar (*v.i.*) to murmur, mutter.
murmurinho (*m.*) murmuring, rustling, purling, swishing.
murmúrio (*m.*) murmur, hum, undertone; rustling, swishing.
murmuroso -sa (*adj.*) murmurous.
muro (*m.*) a brick or other strong outside wall; a retaining wall; a garden wall.—**das lamentações**, wailing wall.—**de chicana**, baffle wall. [An inside wall is PAREDE.]
muromontite (*f., Min.*) muromontite.
murrão (*m., Plant Pathol.*) ergot [= CRAVAGEM].
murro (*m.*) sock, slug, blow with the fist. **dar—s em faca de ponta**, to act in a foolhardy manner. **dar um—na mesa**, to bang the table with one's fist.
murta, murteira (*f., Bot.*) myrtle (*Myrtus*), c.a. MIRTO.—**-de-cheiro**, the chinabox jasminorange (*Murraya exotica*).—**-do-mato**, a bitter-barked rubiaceous plant (*Coutarea hexandra*) used as a substitute for quinine; c.a. QUINA, QUINAQUINA, QUINQUINA, QUINA-DE-PERNAMBUCO.
murtinho (*m.*) myrtle berry; (*Bot.*) any Eugenia.
muru [rú] (*m.*) = COQUILHO.
muruanha (*f.*) var. of MURIANHA.
murubu [bú] (*m.*) = CAPIM-GUINÉ.
muruci [í] (*m.*) var. of MURICI.
murubixaba (*m.*) var. of MORUBIXABA.
muruçoca (*f.*) var. of MURIÇOCA.
murucututu [tutú] (*m.*) = CORUJÃO.
murugem (*f.*) field forget-me-not (*Myosotis arvensis*).
murui, muruim (*m.*) var. of MARUIM.
murumuru [murú] (*m.*) murumuru astrocaryum palm (*A. murumuru*), c.a. CAICUMANÁ.
murumuxaua (*m.*) = MORUBIXABA.
murungu [gú] (*m.*) var. of MULUNGU.
murupita (*f.*) the Brazil sapium (*S. biglandulosum*) which yields rubber latex; c.a. PAU-DE-BICHO, SERINGARANA, TAPURU, CURUPITÃ.
mururé (*m.*) a large mass of floating river vegetation; (*Bot.*) the European waterlily (*Nymphaea alba*); a pickerelweed (*Pontederia cordata*); also = FORNO-D'ÁGUA (a waterlily) and CRUZ-DE-MALTA (a water primrose).—**-carrapatinho**, a salvinia fern (*S. auriculata*).—**-redondinho** = MURERU.—**-rendado**, mosquito fern (*Azolla caroliniana*).
mururu [rurú] (*m.*) aches and pains.
muruti [í], **murutizeiro** (*m.*), see BURUTI.
muruxaba (*f.*) var. of MURIXABA.

murumuxaua (*m.*) = MORUBIXABA.
muruxi [í] (*m.*) a tree of the Barbados-cherry family, *Byrsonima sericea*.
musa (*f.*) muse; (*Bot.*) the genus (*Musa*) comprising the common banana.
musáceo –**cea** (*adj.*; *Bot.*) musaceous; (*f.pl.*) the family Musaceae.
muscadínea (*f.*) muscadine grape (*Vitis rotundifolia*).
muscari [í] (*m.*) grape hyacinth (*Muscari*).
muscarina (*f.*, *Chem.*) muscarin(e).
muscicápidas, muscicapídeos (*m.pl.*, *Zool.*) the family Muscicapidae of O.W. or true flycatchers [= PAPA-MÔSCAS].
muscícola (*adj.*; *Zool.*) muscicolous.
múscidas, muscídeos (*m.pl.*) the family Muscidae, of which the common housefly is the type.
musciforme (*adj.*) fly-shaped.
muscíneas (*f.pl.*) the Musci (class of mosses).
muscívoro –**ra** (*adj.*) fly-eating.
muscóide (*adj.*) muscoid, mosslike.
muscovita (*f.*) muscovite mica; Muscovy glass [= VIDRO DE MOSCÓVIA].
musculação (*f.*) muscular exercise; the muscles collectively.
musculado –**da** (*adj.*) muscled.
muscular (*adj.*) muscular.
musculatura (*f.*) musculature; muscularity.
musculina (*f.*, *Biochem.*) musculin.
músculo (*m.*) muscle.
musculosidade (*f.*) muscularity.
musculoso –**sa** (*adj.*) muscular, sinewy, brawny, stalwart.
museu (*m.*) museum.
musgo (*m.*) moss.—**acrocárpico**, acrocarpous moss.—**aquático**, aquatic moss.—**islândico**, or—**-da-islândia**, Icelandmoss (*Cetraria islandica*).—**pleurocárpico**, pleurocarpous moss.—**terrestre**, clubmoss (*Lycopodium*).
musgoso –**sa**, **musguento** –**ta** (*adj.*) mossy.
música (*f.*) see under MÚSICO.
musical (*adj.*) musical.
musicar (*v.t.*,*v.i.*) to make music; to set (a poem, etc.) to music.
musicata (*f.*, *colloq.*) playing of music; musicale.
musicista (*m.*,*f.*) music-lover, musician.
músico –**ca** (*adj.*) musical; (*m.*,*f.*) musician, composer, player, singer; member of a band or orchestra; (*m.*) = UIRAPURU (a wren); (*f.*) music; musical composition; band, orchestra.—**caipira**, hill-billy music.—**de câmara**, chamber music.
musicólogo –**ga** (*m.*,*f.*) musicologist.
musicomania (*f.*) music madness.
musicômano –**na** (*adj.*) mad about music; (*m.*,*f.*) one who is music-mad.
musiqueta [ê] (*f.*) a bit of music; poor music.
musiquim (*m.*) second-rate musician.
musselina (*f.*) muslin.
mussitar (*v.i.*) to mutter; to whisper.
mussiú (*m.*, *slang*) a Frenchman. [Corrup. of MONSIEUR].
musteldeo –**dea** (*adj.*) musteline; (*m.*) a weasel or weasel-like animal.
mutá, mutã (*m.*) "a kind of crude ladder used by the SERINGUEIROS to tap the rubber trees; an elevated platform on a tree trunk (concealed by foliage) in the forest or at the edge of the water, where the hunter awaits his game or fish." [GBAT]
mutabilidade (*f.*) mutability; fickleness.

mutação (*f.*) mutation, change, alteration; fickleness; change of stage scenery; plant or animal mutation.
mutacismo (*m.*) mytacism.
mutamba (*f.*), –**bo** (*m.*) the bastard cedar (*Guazuma ulmifolia*), c.a. CAMBACA, IBIXUNA, MUCUNGO, GUAXIMA, EMBIRU.—**preta** = AÇOITA-CAVALO.
mutarrotação (*f.*, *Physics*, *Chem.*) mutarotation.
mútase (*f.*, *Biochem.*) mutase.
mutatório –**ria** (*adj.*) mutatory.
mutável (*adj.*) mutable [= MUDÁVEL].
mútico –**ca** (*adj.*; *Bot.*, *Zool.*) mutic.
mutila (*f.*) velvet ant (*Mutilla sp.*)—in reality a solitary, fossorial, parasitic, wingless wasp.
mutilação (*f.*) mutilation.
mutilado –**da** (*adj.*) mutilated, maimed; (*m.*,*f.*) an amputee.
mutilador –**dora** (*adj.*) mutilating; (*m.*,*f.*) mutilator.
mutilar (*v.t.*) to mutilate, maim, amputate; to mar, deface; to garble.
mutílidas, mutilídeos (*m.pl.*) the Mutillidae (family of parasitic wasps). Cf. MUTILA.
mutirão, mutirom, mutirum (*m.*) vars. of MUXIRÃO.
mutismo (*m.*) muteness, dumbness; silence.
mútua (*f.*) see under MÚTUO.
mutuação (*f.*) exchange, interchange.
mutualidade (*f.*) mutuality.
mutualismo (*m.*, *Ethics*, *Biol.*, *Social*) mutualism.
mutualista (*m.*,*f.*) member of a mutual benefit society or insurance company.
mutuante (*m.*,*f.*) a lender; (*adj.*) lending.
mutuar (*v.tt*) to exchange mutually; to lend or borrow.
mutuário –**ria** (*m.*,*f.*) borrower.
mutuca (*f.*) motuca fly; "A large Brazilian biting fly (*Lepislaga lepidota*) of the family Tabanidae." [*Webster*]; also (*slang*) = MACONHA.
mútulo (*m.*, *Arch.*) mutule.
mutum (*m.*, *Zool.*) any curassow (family Cracidae).—**açu**, or—**vulgar**, Blumenbach's curassow (*Crax blumenbachii*).—**cavalo**, razor-billed curassow (*Mitu mitu*), c.a. MUTUM-DA-VÁRZEA, MUTUM-ETÊ.—**de-assobio**, the globose or wattled curassow (*Crax globulosa*).—**pinima**, Natterer's curassow (*Crax pinima*).—**paranga**, crested curassow (*Crax nigra*).
mútuo –**tua** (*adj.*) mutual, reciprocal; (*m.*) loan; exchange; reciprocity; (*f.*) a mutual aid society.
muti [í] (*m.*, *Bot.*) padauk (*Pterocarpus*).
mututi [tí] (*m.*) any of several leguminous trees, esp. the dragonsblood padauk (*Pterocarpus draco*), c.a. CORTI-CEIRA, TINTEIRA.—**da-margem-da-terra-firme**, a leguminous-papillonaceous tree (*Etaballia guinanensis*), having beautiful wavy wood.—**da-várzea**, a padauk (*Pterocarpus amazonicus*).
muxiba (*f.*) lean dog meat; hanging folds of skin; hag.
muxinga (*f.*) whip [= CHICOTE]; beating, cudgeling [= SURRA].
muxirão (*m.*), **muxirã** (*f.*) a house-raising or other "bee". [The word has many variants and synonyms.]
muxôxo (*m.*) smack (kiss); a disdainful or contemptuous *tchu* or *tck* (sound made with the tongue) accompanied by a toss of the head and turning up of the nose.
muxurundar (*v.t.*, *slang*) to beat, trounce [= SURRAR].
muzundu [dú] (*m.*) the chub mackerel (*Pneumatophorus colias*), c.a. CAVALINHA.
mV, milivolt (millivolt).

N

N, n, the 13th letter of the Port. alphabet.
n. = NOME (name).
N. = NORTE (north).
na [em + a] in the, at the, on the, into the, by the, with the; (*dir. obj. pers. pron. fem.*) her (it, you). [Used instead of 3rd pers. **a** when attached to verb forms with a nasal ending: MANDARAM-NA instead of MANDARAM-A.] Cf. NO.
nababo (*m.*) nabob.
nabal (*m.*) turnip field.

nabiça (*f.*) turnip greens; a young turnip.
nabo (*m.*) turnip.—**do-diabo**, (*Bot.*) the white bryony (*Bryonia alba*)—**japonês**, garden radish [= RABANETE].—**selvagem**, the Indian jack-in-the-pulpit (*Arasaema triphyllum*).
nabuco –**ca** (*adj.*) tailless; bobtailed [= SURU].
Nabucodonosor (*m.*) Nebuchadnezzar.
naca, nacada (*f.*) piece, slice.

nação (*f.*) nation, state; people, race. **Nações Unidas,** United Nations.—**s não comprometidas,** unaligned nations.

nácar (*m.*) nacre, mother of pearl; the color bright red; pink.

nacarado –da, **nacarino** –na (*adj.*) nacreous; bright red; rose-colored.

nacela (*f.*, *Arch.*) scotia; (*Aeron.*) nacelle.

nacional (*adj.*) national. **artigo**—, domestic goods; (*m.*) national, native.

nacionalidade (*f.*) nationality.

nacionalismo (*m.*) nationalism.

nacionalista (*adj.*) nationalistic; (*m.,f.*) nationalist.

nacionalização (*f.*) nationalization.

nacionalizar (*v. t.*) to nationalize; to naturalize.

naco (*m.*) piece, chunk.—**de fumo,** plug of tobacco.

nada (*m.*) nothing; nothingness; naught; a worthless something; (*adv.*) nothing, not at all; to no purpose.—**de novo,** nothing new.—**disso!** Nothing of the kind!—**feito,** (*slang*) Nothing doing!—**mais,** nothing else.—**(mais) de (lágrimas),** Let us have no (more) (tears).—**mais que,** nothing but, only, that's all.—**menos,** nonetheless; nothing less; not less (**que,** than).—**obstante,** nevertheless, notwithstanding. **antes de mais**—, before anything else. **Daí não vai sair**—**de bom,** No good will come of it. **dar em**—, to come to naught. **Isso não vai dar em**—. Nothing will come of it. **de**—, don't mention it (after thanks). **Não me faltava mais**—! That's the last straw! **Não sera**—**difícil,** It won't be at all difficult. **Não tenho**—**(que ver) com isto,** It is none of my business. **ou tudo ou**—, all or nothing. **Qual**—! Nothing of the sort! **quando**—, at least. **quase**—, almost nothing, scarcely anything.

nadadeira (*f.*) fish's fin [= BARBATANA].

nadador –dora (*adj.*) swimming; (*m.,f.*) swimmer.

nadadura (*f.*) act of swimming.

nadante (*adj.*) swimming; floating.

nadar (*v.i.*) to swim; to float.—**como um prego,** to float like a brick.—**contra a corrente,** to swim against the tide. **Filho de peixe sabe**—, Like father, like son. **nadando em ouro,** rolling in wealth.

nádega (*f.*) buttock; (*pl.*) rump.

nadegudo –da (*adj.*) having a large buttock.

nadinha (*m.*) almost nothing, a tiny bit.

nadir (*m.*) nadir; lowest point.

nado (*m.*) a swim(ming); a floating.—**de costas,** back stroke.—**de peito,** breast stroke.—**livre,** free style swimming. **a**—, afloat; swimming; (*adj.*) = NATO. Cf. NATAÇÃO.

náfego –da (*adj.*; *m.,f.*, *Veter.*) ragged-hipped (horse).

nafta (*f.*) naphtha.

naftalina (*f.*, *Chem.*) naphthalene, tar camphor.

naftilamina (*f.*, *Chem.*) naphthylamine.

naftiônico –ca (*adj.*, *Chem.*) naphthionic [acid].

naftóico –ca (*adj.*, *Chem.*) naphthoic [acid].

naftol (*m.*, *Chem.*) naphthol.

naftoquinona (*f.*, *Chem.*) naphthoquinone.

nagiagite (*f.*, *Min.*) nagyagite.

nagôs (*m.pl.*) Negroes imported into Brazil from the Yoruba region of the African Slave Coast.

naiá (*f.*) = GUACURI.

náiade, **náiada** (*f.*) naiad, water nymph; (*Bot.*) the southern naiad (*Naias guadalupensis*); (*Zool.*) a fresh-water mussel of the tribe Naiades.

nailon (*m.*) nylon.

naipada (*f.*) a series of cards of one suit.

naipar (*v.i.*) to play cards of the same suit.

naipe (*m.*) suit (of cards).

naja (*f.*) a hooded cobra [= COBRA-CAPELO].

najá (*f.*) the regal maximiliana (palm), c.a. INAJÁ, MARIPÁ.

najadáceas (*f.pl.*, *Bot.*) a family (*Naiadaceae*) of aquatic plants.

nalga (*f.*) = NÁDEGA.

nambi [í] (*m.*) ear [= ORELHA]; (*adj.*) tailless; having a cropped ear; of horses, flop-eared.

nambiquara (*m.,f.*) variant of NHAMBIQUARA.

nambu [ú] (*m.*) yam [= INHAME]; a tinamou (bird), c.a. INHAMBU.

namoração (*f.*) courting [= NAMÔRO].

namorada (*f.*) sweetheart, girlfriend.

namoradeira (*f.*) coquette, flirt; (*adj.*) coquettish, flirtatious.

namoradeiro –ra, **namoradiço** –ça (*adj.*) given to courting and love-making.

namorado (*m.*) suitor, lover, sweetheart, beau, boy friend.

namorador (*adj.*) philandering; (*m.*) philanderer.

namorar (*v.t.*) to court, woo, make love to; to flirt with;

to look at longingly; to sue, pursue.—**se de si,** to become enamored of oneself.

namoricar (*v.t.,v.i.*) to philander, play at courtship (with). Vars. NAMORISCAR, NAMORICHAR.

namorico, **namorilho** (*m.*) amorous play, dalliance, flirtation. Vars. NAMORISCO, NAMORICE, NAMORICHO.

namôro (*m.*) courtship, love-making; love-affair; dalliance; flirtation.—**-de-criança,** calf love.

nana (*f.*) lullaby.

nanã-de-rapôsa (*f.*) = GRAVATÁ-DE-GANCHO.

nandaia (*f.*) = JANDAIA.

nandina (*f.*, *Bot.*) the genus Nandina (sacred bamboo).

nandu [ú] (*m.*) = NHANDU.

nanico –ca (*adj.*) dwarfish, pygmy.

nanismo (*m.*) nanism, dwarfishness.

nanôide (*adj.*) nanoid, dwarfish.

nanosomia (*f.*) nanosomia, dwarfishness.

nanquim (*m.*) nankeen (cloth); India ink; [*cap.*] Nanking.

nanzuque (*m.*) nainsook.

não (*adv.*) no, not; (*m.*) a no, a refusal.—**achar vau,** to find no place to ford a river, or, fig., no means of reaching an end.—**adiantar idéia,** to advance no ideas or suggestions.—**alterar nem uma vírgula,** to change not a single comma.—**apoiado!** not approved! [An exclamation of disapproval of or disagreement with a speaker's remarks.]—**caber em si de contentamento,** to be overjoyed.—**creio,** I don't think so; I don't believe (it).—**criar môfo,** not to let the grass grow under one's feet.—**dar o braço a torcer,** not to admit one's mistake.—**dar palavra,** to utter not a word.—**dar ponto sem nó,** to do nothing without an ulterior motive.—**dar paz nem tréguas,** to give not a moment's peace.—**dar quartel (ao inimigo),** to give (the enemy) no quarter.—**dar sinal de vida,** to give no sign of life.—**dar tino de,** to be unaware of.—**dar uma nota,** not to be able to sing a note.—**deixar pedra sôbre pedra,** to leave no stone unturned.—**dispor da sua vontade,** to have no will of one's own.—**dispor de si (or de um minuto),** to have not a minute to oneself.—**dizer nem sim nem não,** to say neither yes nor no; to remain undecided.—**dizer palavra,** to not speak, remain silent.—**duvidar (de nada),** to have no doubt (about anything).—**é?** Is it not so? Isn't that so? [Corresponds to French *n'est ce pas?*]—**entender nem uma palavra de,** to know nothing about (a subject).—**esperado,** unexpected.—**estar mais no seu poder,** to be powerless to do more.—**estar no seu poder,** not to be within one's power (to do something).—**estar pelos autos,** (*colloq.*) to disagree with something.—**faz mal,** It doesn't matter; never mind.—**há muito,** not (so) long ago.—**ir nada com,** or—**ir à missa com,** to be ill-disposed toward (someone); to be in complete disaccord with (his ideas).—**ligar duas idéias,** not to be able to put two and two together.—**longe de,** not far from.—**mais,** no longer, no more, never more.—**me faltava mais nada!** That's the last straw!—**menos,** not less; equally.—**menos que,** no (not) less than.—**merecer o pão que come,** not to be worth one's salt.—**obstante,** notwithstanding, despite; yet, nevertheless.—**olhar a despesas,** to be heedless of expense; to be a spendthrift.—**olhar a nada,** to heed nothing.—**passar de,** to be no more than; to be naught but.—**pegar a lábia,** of one's sly, honeyed words, to not produce the desired effect.—**pensar nem por sombra em,** to have no slightest thought (idea, intention) of.—**perder o ponto,** to miss no opportunity.—**pestanejar,** not to bat an eye (remain unperturbed).—**poder consigo,** to be too tired, or weak, to lift a finger.—**poder deixar de ser,** to be unavoidable.—**poder mexer as pernas (or os pés),** to be unable to move a muscle.—**poder piar,** not to be able to utter a peep.—**poder ser,** not to be possible. [**Não pode ser,** It can't be; it is impossible.]—**poder ver,** to be unable to "see" (like, admire, accept) someone.—**poder pôr a vista em cima de,** to be unable to catch sight of (find) something or someone.—**poupar ninguém,** to spare no one (in criticism).—**poupar sexo nem idade,** to spare no one (anything) without regard to age or sex.—**pregar ôlho,** not to sleep a wink.—**prestar para nada,** to be good for nothing.—**que eu saiba,** Not that I know of.—**querer negócios com,** not to want to have anything to do with (someone).—**roçar pêlo,** of a racehorse, to take and hold the lead for the entire course; (lit., not to rub his hide against another horse).—**saber onde se meter,** to be perplexed, at a loss, not know which way to turn.—**saber o que quer,** not to know what one wants.—**se dar nada com (or de),** to be indifferent to.—**se dar por entendido,**

to make out that one does not understand.—**se ensaiar para**, not to hesitate about (doing something).—**se fazer mister**, to be unnecessary.—**se poupar a**, to spare oneself nothing.—**sentir a falta de**, to have no lack of; to do well without, feel no need of.—**ser nada a**, to be of no kin to.—**ser para graças**, not to stand for any fooling (playing, teasing).—**servir de nada**, to be of no utility.—**só**, not only.—**tanto assim**, not that much; not as much as (all) that.—**tem de quê**, (*colloq.*) You're welcome; don't mention it.—**temer Deus nem o diabo**, to fear nothing and no one; to be utterly depraved.—**ter a língua limpa**, to be foul-mouthed.—**ter eira nem beira**, to have nothing, be penniless.—**ter estômago para**, to have no stomach for.—**ter freio na língua**, to have an unbridled tongue.—**ter jôgo**, to have a poor hand (at cards).—**ter lugar**, to be out-of-place, out of keeping, inadmissible.—**ter mais que um sôpro de vida**, to be about to expire.—**ter mão de si**, to be unable to contain oneself.—**ter mãos a medir**, to have one's hands full, more than one can handle.—**ter nada com**, to be none of one's affair.—**ter nada em (or por) que se lhe pegue**, to afford no grounds for censure, criticism, etc.; to be irreprehensible.—**ter nome**, to be unutterably vile.—**ter ombros para**, to be incapable of (a task, a job).—**ter onde cair morto**, to have nothing or no place of one's own.—**ter pano para mangas**, to be short of ways and means.—**ter papas (or pevide) na língua**, to speak out, hold nothing back.—**ter paz nem tréguas**, to have not a moment of peace and quiet.—**ter pé**, to be too deep to stand up in, unable to touch bottom (of pool, river, etc.).—**ter pés nem cabeça**, to make no sense.—**ter ponta por onde se lhe pegue**, to have no possible explanation.—**ter por onde se lhe pegue**, to be good for nothing.—**ter preço**, to be priceless; also, to be valueless.—**ter que invejar**, to have no cause for envy.—**ter razão de ser**, to have no reason for being, or for coming to pass.—**ter resultado**, to be of no effect.—**ter segredos para**, to keep no secrets from.—**ter tempo**, to have no time (for leisure).—**ter um momento de seu**, not to have a moment to oneself.—**ter vintém**, to be without a farthing.—**ter vontade sua**, to have no will of one's own.—**tirar nem pôr**, to be indifferent, neutral, neither good nor bad.—**tirar os olhos de**, to keep one's eyes fastened upon.—**tugir nem mugir**, not to let out a peep.—**valer a pena**, not to be worth the trouble.—**valer dois caracóis**, not to be worth a tinker's damn.—**ver dois dedos (or um palmo) adiante do nariz**, not to see two inches in front of one's nose (be quite stupid).—**ver senão pelos olhos de**, to see only through another's eyes, to be guided by him in everything.—**vi ninguém**, I saw nobody. **a**—**ser que**, unless, excepting. [A não ser que chova, irei, I'll go if it doesn't rain.] **À viagem**—**adiantou**, The effort (work, attempt) accomplished nothing. **achar que**—, not to agree. [Acho que **não**, I don't think so.] **agora**—, no more, no longer; not now; not yet. **ainda**—, not yet. **ano sim, ano**—, every other year (or so). **Ela**—**tem nada**, There is nothing the matter with her; or, lit., she hasn't anything. **Êle**—**disse nada**, He said nothing. **Eu**—**disse!** I told you so! **hoje**—, not today. **já**—, no longer. **nem sim nem**—, neither yes nor no. **pois**—, of course, certainly; gladly; why not? **porque**—? Why not? **Que alegria**—**sentiu ela!** How happy she must have felt! **que**—**aquêle**, other than that one. **também**—, neither, not either.

não-combatente (*adj.; m.,f.*) noncombatant.
não-conformista (*adj.; m.,f.*) nonconformist.
não-cumprimento (*m.*) noncompliance.
não-eu (*m., Philos.*) nonego.
não-euclideano -na (*adj.*) non-Euclidean.
não-execução (*f.*) nonexecution; nonfeasance.
não-existência (*f.*) nonexistence.
não-intervenção (*f.*) nonintervention.
não-me-deixes (*m., Bot.*) a groundsel (*Senecio sp.*)
não-me-esqueças (*m., Bot.*) forget-me-not (*Myosotis*).
não-me-toques (*m.,f.*) a touch-me-not (touchy, haughty, aloof) person.
não-pagamento (*m.*) non-payment.
não-pronúncia (*f., Law*) nonindictment.
não-sei-quê (*m.*) a vague something.
não-sei-que-diga (*m.*) used in place of an obscene word or expression.
não-ser (*m.*) nonexistence, nonentity.
não-te-esqueças (-de-mim) = NÃO-ME-ESQUEÇAS.
napéias (*f.pl.*) wood-nymphs.
napeiro -ra (*adj.*) sleepy, lazy.

napelo [ê] (*m.*) common monkshood (*Aconitum napellus*)
napeva (*adj.*) short-legged (said esp. of dogs and chickens)
napiforme (*adj.*) turnip-shaped.
napoleão (*m.*) an old French 20-franc gold coin, bearing a portrait of Napoleon; [*cap.*] Napoleon.
napoleônico -ca (*adj.*) Napoleonic.
Nápoles (*f.*) Naples.
napolitano -na (*adj.; m.,f.*) Neapolitan.
naquela [*em+aquela*], **naquêle** [*em+aquêle*], **naquil** [*em+aquilo*], in that (one), on that (one).
naranazeiro (*m.*) = GUARANÁ.
narandiba (*f.*) orange grove [= LARANJAL].
naraz (*m.*) a thumbing of the nose.
narceína (*f., Chem.*) narceine.
narceja [ê] (*f.*) any snipe, esp. the Paraguayan snipe (*Capella p. paraquaiae*), c.a. BICO-RASTEIRO, CORTA-VENTO, BATUÍRA, MINJOLINHO, AGACHADEIRA, AGACHADA, NARCEJINHA.
narcejinha (*f.*) the Paraguayan snipe (*Capella p. paraguaiae*), c.a. NARCEJA-COMUM, BATUÍRA.
narcisar-se (*v.r.*) to admire oneself (in a mirror).
narcisismo (*m.*) narcissism.
narciso (*m.*) any narcissus or daffodil, esp. poets narcissus (*N. poeticus*); a narcissist.—**da-tarde**, autumn jonquil (*Narcissus serotinus*).—**de-cheiro**, the campernell jonquil (*Narcissus odorus*).—**do-outono** (or—**outoniço** = CÓLQUICO.—**dos-prados**, common daffodil (*Narcissus pseudonarcissus*).
narcolepsia (*f., Med.*) narcolepsy.
narcose (*f.*) narcosis.
narcótico -ca (*adj.; m.,f.*) narcotic.
narcotina (*f., Chem.*) narcotine.
narcotismo (*m.*) narcotism.
narcotização (*f.*) narcotization.
narcotizador -dora (*adj.*) deadening, stupefying.
narcotizar (*v.t.*) to narcotize.
nardo (*m.*) matgrass (*Nardus stricta*); (*Pharm.*) nard.—**da-índia**, spikenard (*Nardostachys jatamansi*).—**do-monte**, Celtic spikenard (*Valeriana celtica*), c.a. ESPIGA-CÉLTICA.—**índico**, spikenard.—**silvestre** = ÁSARO (wild ginger).
narguilé, narguilhé (*m.*) narghile, hookah.
narícula (*f.*) nasal passage; (*pl.*) nostrils.
narigada (*f.*) a hitting with the nose (against the wall etc.).
narigão (*m.*) a big nose.
narigudo -da (*adj.; m.,f.*) big-nosed (person).
narina (*f.*) nostril [= NARÍCULA].
narinari (*f.*) = RAIA-PINTADA.
nariz (*m.*) nose.—**aquilino** (or—**de águia**, or—**de cavalete**), aquiline nose. **dar com o**—**na porta**, to find a door closed to one. **meter o**—**onde não é chamado**, to poke one's nose into another's affairs. **na ponta do**—, before one's very nose. **tapar o**—, to hold one's nose. **torcer o**— to turn up one's nose (at).
narração (*f.*) narration, recital; a narrative, story, tale.
narrado (*m.*) a narrative.
narrador -dora (*adj.*) narrative; (*m.,f.*) narrator.
narrar (*v.t.*) to narrate, relate, recount, tell.
narrativo -va (*adj.*) narrative; (*f.*) a narrative, narration, tale, recital.
narrável (*adj.*) narratable.
nartécia (*f., Bot.*) bog asphodel (*Narthecium*).
nártex [ks], **nártece** (*m., Arch.*) narthex.
naru [ú] (*m.*) = VERME-DA-GUINÉ.
narval (*m.*) narwhal (*Monodon monoceros*), c.a. LICORNE-DO-MAR.
nasal (*adj.; m.,f., Phonet., Anat., Zool.*) nasal (sound, bone).
nasalação (*f.*) nasalizing.
nasalar (*v.t.*) to nasalize.
nasalidade (*f.*) nasality.
nasardo (*m.*) nasard (organ stop).
nascedouro (*m.*) birthplace. Var. NASCEDOIRO.
nascença (*f.*) birth; origin, rise. **de**—, from (by) birth.
nascente (*adj.*) nascent, beginning; (*m.*) the East; (*f.*) water spring.
nascer (*v.i.*) to be born; to come forth, emerge; to begin, originate; to burgeon.—**com uma colher de prata na bôca** (or—**em luvas de pelica**, or—**em berço de ouro**), to be born with a silver spoon in one's mouth.—**empelicado**, to be born lucky. **Pau que nasce torto, tarde ou nunca se endireita**, Just as the twig is bent, the tree's inclined.

nascido -da (*adj.*) born. **bem——**, well-born; born under a lucky star. **recém——**, newborn; (*f.*, *colloq.*) an abscess, boil or tumor.
nascimento (*m.*) birth, origin; race, line. **certidão de—**, birth certificate.
nascituro -ra (*adj.*; *m.,f.*) unborn (child).
nasicórneo -nea (*adj.*; *Zool.*) nasicornous; (*m.*) nasicorn.
nasofaríngeo -gea (*adj.*; *Anat.*) nasopharyngeal.
nassa (*f.*) a funnel-shaped wicker fish trap.
nastro (*m.*) tape.
nata (*f.*) cream; fig., the best of anything; (*Const.*) lime paste—**batida**, whipped cream.—**da terra**, rich soil.
natação (*f.*) swimming. [Verb NADAR].
natadeira (*f.*) a shallow milk pan.
natal (*adj.*) natal, native; (*m.*) birthday; [*cap.*] Christmas Day.
natalício -cia (*adj.*) of or pert. to one's birth or birthday.
natalidade (*f.*) natality, birth rate.
natátil [-teis] (*adj.*) natant, floating.
natatório -ria (*adj.*) natatorial (*m.*) natatorium, swimming pool [= PISCINA].
nateiro (*m.*) silt, warp; soft river mud.
nática, **nátice** (*f.*) a genus (*Natica*) of marine snails.
natimorto -ta (*adj.*) stillborn.
natividade (*f.*) nativity.
nativismo (*m.*) nativism.
nativista (*adj.*; *m.,f.*) (person) prejudiced against foreigners.
nativo -va (*adj.*) native, natural; (*m.,f.*) native [= INDÍGENA].
nato -ta (*adj.*) born; native-born; congenital.
natrão, natro (*m.*, *Min.*) natron.
natrocalcite (*f.*, *Min.*) natrochalcite.
natrojarosita (*f.*, *Min.*) natrojarite.
natrólita (*f.*), **-to** (*m.*, *Min.*) natrolite.
natural (*adj.*) natural, normal; native; ingenuous, artless, spontaneous, unaffected; (*m.*) a native (**de**, of); nature, disposition; what is natural. **ao—**, naturally; of food, cooked plain. [Fr. *au naturel*].
naturalidade (*f.*) naturalness; simplicity; artlessness; native land; naturalization.
naturalismo (*m.*) naturalism.
naturalista (*m.,f.*) naturalist.
naturalístico -ca (*adj.*) naturalistic.
naturalização (*f.*) naturalization.
naturalizado -da (*adj.*) naturalized; (*m.,f.*) a naturalized citizen.
naturalizar (*v.t.*) to naturalize.
naturalizável (*adj.*) that can be naturalized.
naturalmente (*adv.*) naturally; (*interj.*) of course!
natureza [ê] (*f.*) nature; quality, character; temper; disposition.—**morta**, (*Painting*) still life.
nau (*f.*) a large ship; warship.
naufragado (*m.*) the jackass penguin (*Spheniscus magellanicus*) which occasionally strays as far north as Rio de Janeiro—too far to return home—and thus becomes "shipwrecked," whence the name.
naufragar (*v.i.*) to be shipwrecked; to suffer ruin or failure; (*v.t.*) to shipwreck; to ruin.
naufrágio (*m.*) shipwreck; fig., ruin, loss, destruction.
náufrago -ga (*m.,f.*) castaway, shipwrecked person; fig., an outcast; (*adj.*) stranded, shipwrecked.
naupatia (*f.*) seasickness.
náuplio (*m.*, *Zool.*) nauplius.
nauquá (*m.,f.*) an Indian of the Nahukwa, a Cariban tribe of the upper Xingu River; (*adj.*) pert. to or designating this tribe. Var. ANAQUÁ.
náusea (*f.*) nausea, seasickness; queasiness; loathing.
nauseabundo -da, **nauseante** (*adj.*) nauseating; disgusting; nasty.
nauseado -da (*adj.*) nauseated.
nausear (*v.t.*) to nauseate, disgust; to loathe; (*v.r.*) to feel nausea.
nauseativo -va, **nauseoso** -sa (*adj.*) = NAUSEABUNDO.
nauta (*m.*) sailor, seafaring man; navigator.
náutico -ca (*adj.*) nautical; (*f.*) nautical science; seamanship.
náutilo (*m.*, *Zool.*) nautilus, argonaut.
nautilóide (*adj.*) nautiloid.
naval (*adj.*) naval.
navalha (*f.*) razor; (*Mach.*) knife; fig., backbiter, sharptongued person; a cold, cutting wind; bitter cold; tusk of a wild boar; (*Bot.*) a razor sedge; (*Zool.*) a razor clam

[LINGUEIRÃO].—**de-macaco**, a razor sedge (*Scleria*).—**de (ponta e) mola**, a switch blade.
navalhada (*f.*) a slash with a razor.
navalhar (*v.t.*) to cut (slash) with a razor.
navalheira (*f.*, *Bot.*) a razor sedge (*Scleria*).
navalhista (*m.,f.*) a razor-wielder; a stabber.
nave (*f.*) church nave; ship.
navegabilidade (*f.*) navigability; seaworthiness.
navegação (*f.*) navigation; nautical science; a voyage by water; shipping, maritime commerce; a water-borne vessel; "a GAIOLA, boat or LANCHA, a term specifically used by the rubber tappers in the western part of Amazonas." [*GBAT*]—**aérea**, aerial navigation.—**de cabotagem**, coastwise shipping.
navegado -da (*adj.*) navigated; crossed by ships; sailed over.
navegador -dora, **navegante** (*adj.*) navigating; (*m.,f.*) navigator; sailor; traveller by boat.
navegar (*v.i.*) to navigate; to steer; to journey by water; to sail (in).—**a remo e vela**, to leave no stone unturned.—**de ló**, to sail against the wind.—**de vento em pôpa**, to sail with the wind.
navegável (*adj.*) navigable; seaworthy.
naveta [ê] (*f.*) small boat; bobbin (of a sewing machine); (*Art*) navicella; (*Eccl.*) incense boat.
navícula (*f.*, *Anat.*) navicular.
navicular, naviforme (*adj.*) navicular; boat-shaped.
navio (*m.*) ship, boat, vessel.—**a (de) vela**, sailing vessel, schooner.—**a (de) vapor**, steamship.—**aeródromo**, aircraft carrier.—**almirante**, flagship.—**cargueiro**, freighter.—**carvoeiro**, collier.—**costeiro**, coastwise ship.—**couraçado**, battleship, dreadnought.—**de cabotagem**, coastwise ship.—**de carga**, freighter.—**de guerra**, warship, man-of-war; (*Zool.*) = ALBATROZ.—**de linha**, capital ship.—**de pesca de baleia**, whaler.—**de salvamento**, rescue ship.—**em lastro**, a ship under ballast.—**gêmeo**, sister ship.—**graneleiro**, grain vessel.—**hospital**, hospital ship.—**mercante**, merchant vessel.—**mineiro**, mine layer.—**negreiro**, slave ship.—**patrulha**, patrol boat.—**porta-aviões**, aircraft carrier.—**oficina**, repair ship.—**petroleiro**, oil tanker.—**transporte**, troop transport.
Nazaré (*m.*) Nazareth.
nazareno -na (*adj.*; *m.,f.*) Nazarene.
nazi (*adj.*; *m.,f.*) Nazi.
nazismo (*m.*) Nazism.
nazista (*adj.*; *m.,f.*) Nazi.
n/c = NOSSA CARTA (our letter); NOSSA CASA (our firm); NOSSA CONTA (our account).
n/ch. = NOSSO CHEQUE (our check).
N. da R. = NOTA DA REDAÇÃO (editor's note).
N. do A. = NOTA DO AUTOR (author's note).
N. do E. = NOTA DO EDITOR (publisher's note).
N. do T. = NOTA DO TRADUTOR (translator's note).
N.E. = NORDESTE (northeast).
neblina (*f.*) fog, mist, haze.
neblinar (*v.i.*) to mist.
nebular (*adj.*) nebular.
nebulosidade (*f.*) nebulosity.
nebuloso -sa (*adj.*) cloudy; vague, nebulous; (*f.*, *Astron.*) nebula.
necedade (*f.*) nescience, ignorance; stupidity.
necessário -ria (*adj.*) necessary (a, to), requisite, indispensable; inevitable; (*m.*) something necessary; (*f.*, *colloq.*) toilet.
necessidade (*f.*) necessity, need; poverty, want. **A—faz lei**, Necessity knows no law. **É na—que se conhecem os amigos**, A friend in need is a friend indeed.
necessitado -da (*adj.*; *m.,f.*) indigent (person).
necessitar (*v.t.*) to need, want, require.—**a**, to necessitate.—**de**, to have need of.
necrofilia (*f.*, *Med.*) necrophilism.
necrófilo -la (*m.,f.*, *Med.*) necrophile.
necrofobia (*f.*) necrophobia.
necróforo (*m.*) a burying beetle (*Necrophorus*).
necrolatria (*f.*) necrolatry; manes worship.
necrologia (*f.*) necrology; obituary.
necrológico -ca (*adj.*) necrological.
necrologista, necrólogo -ga (*m.,f.*) necrologist; obituarist.
necromancia (*f.*) necromancy.
necromante (*m.,f.*) necromancer.
necromântico -ca (*adj.*) necromantic.
necronita (*f.*, *Min.*) necronite.
necrópole (*f.*) necropolis; cemetery.

necropsia (*f.*) necropsy, post-mortem examination, autopsy [=AUTÓPSIA].

necropsiar (*v.t.*) to dissect (cadavers); to conduct an autopsy upon.

necropsista, necropso –sa (*m.,f.*) anatomist; one who performs autopsies.

necrosar (*v.t.,v.i.*) to necrose.

necrose (*f., Med.*) necrosis.

necrotério (*m.*) morgue.

necrotomia (*f., Med.*) necrotomy.

nectandra (*f.*) a large genus (*Ocotea*) of tropical American trees of the laurel family.

néctar (*m.*) nectar.

nectáreo –rea (*adj.*) nectareous.

nectarífero –ra (*adj., Bot.*) nectariferous.

nectarina (*f.*) nectarine (peach).

nectário (*m., Bot.*) nectary.

nectarizar (*v.t.*) to sweeten as with nectar.

néctria (*f.*) a genus (*Nectria*) of sac fungi.

necturo (*m.*) a genus (*Necturus*) of aquatic salamanders.

nediez (*f.*) sleekness; plumpness.

nédio –dia (*adj.*) sleek, glossy; plump, chubby.

Neemias [e-e] (*m.*) Nehemiah.

neerlandês –desa [e-er] (*adj.*) Dutch; (*m.*) Dutchman; (*f.*) Dutchwoman.

Neerlândia [e-er] (*f.*) Netherlands.

nefando –da, nefário –ria (*adj.*) nefarious, atrocious, heinous, abominable.

nefas (*m.*) that which is not right. **por fas ou por—,** rightly or wrongly; by hook or by crook.

nefasto (*adj.*) ominous; baleful; malign.

nefelibata, nefelíbata (*adj.*) dreamy, visionary; (*m.,f.*) dreamer, impractical visionary.

nefelinito (*m., Petrog.*) nephelinite.

nefelita, nefelina (*f., Min.*) nephelite.

nefelóide (*adj.*) nepheloid, cloudy.

nefelometria (*f., Physical Chem.*) nephelometry.

nefelômetro (*m., Physical Chem.*) nephelometer.

néfila (*f.*) silk spider (*Nephila*).

nefógrafo (*m.*) nephograph.

nefologia (*f., Meteor.*) nephology.

nefoscopia (*f., Meteor.*) nephoscopy.

nefoscópio (*m., Meteor.*) nephoscope.

nefralgia (*f., Med.*) nephralgia.

nefrectomia (*f., Surg.*) nephrectomy.

nefrídio (*m., Zool., Anat.*) nephridium.

nefrita (*f., Min.*) nephrite; jade.

nefrite (*f., Med.*) nephritis.

nefrítico –ca (*adj.*) nephritic.

nefrócito (*m., Zool.*) nephrocyte.

nefródio (*m., Bot.*) a genus (*Dryopteris*) of woodferns.

nefrólito (*m., Med.*) nephrolith, renal calculus.

nefroptose (*f., Med.*) nephroptosis; floating kidney.

nefrose (*f., Med.*) nephrosis.

nefrostoma (*m., Zool., Anat.*) nephrostome.

nefrotomia (*f., Surg.*) nephrotomy.

nega (*f.*) negation; disinclination; (*Const.*) rate of penetration of a pile; zero penetration.

negabelha (*f.*) scurvy grass (*Cochlearia*).

negaça (*f.*) lure, bait; enticement; feint; frustration; a bird called SAÍRA.

negação (*f.*) negation; denial; reluctance.

negaceador –dora (*adj.*) alluring, enticing.

negacear (*v.t.*) to lure, entice, beguile; to inveigle, decoy.

negador –dora (*adj.*) denying; (*m.,f.*) denier.

negalho (*m.*) a bit of thread; a piece of string; a small quantity (of anything).

negar (*v.t.*) to deny, contradict; to negate; to refute; to reject; to disavow, disclaim; to refuse, disallow; to renege (at cards).—**se a,** to refuse to; to dodge.—**se a si mesmo,** to deny oneself.—**fogo,** to misfire.—**a** (or **de**) **pés juntos,** to deny flatly; to swear up and down (on a stack of Bibles) that a thing is not true.

negativa (*f.*) see under NEGATIVO.

negatividade (*f.*) negative state or quality.

negativismo (*m.*) negativism.

negativista (*adj.*) negativistic; (*m.,f.*) negativist.

negativo –va (*adj.*) negative; (*m., Photog.*) negative; (*f.*) negative; negation; denial.

negatório –ria (*adj.*) negatory, denying.

negável (*adj.*) that can be denied, etc. See the verb NEGAR.

neglicência (*f.*) neglect, negligence; shortcoming.

negligenciar (*v.t.*) to neglect; to slight.

negligente (*adj.*) negligent, careless, remiss, lax (**em, in**);

happy-go-lucky; unheeding; slipshod, untidy, slouchy, sloppy.

nêgo (*m.*), **–ga** (*f.*) shortened form of NEGRO , sometimes used as a term of endearment.

negociação (*f.*) negotiation; trading; transaction.

negociador –dora (*adj.*) negociating; trading; (*m.,f.*) negociator; trader, businessman.

negociante (*m.,f.*) trader, businessman, merchant, dealer, shopkeeper.

negociar (*v.t.,v.i.*) to deal (**em, in; com,** with); tò trade, barter, bargain; to carry on business; to negotiate, treat.

negociata (*f.*) shady business, a "deal".

negociável (*adj.*) negotiable, marketable.

negócio (*m.*) business, affair, matter, transaction, deal, trade, bargain; an enterprise; a business house; any subject; a thing, thingumbob.—**da China,** a fine bargain; a very profitable deal.—**de arromba,** a highly profitable business or deal.—**de compadres,** a deal between "pals".—**de dinheiro,** a money matter.—**de ocasião,** a bargain.—**de orelha,** an even trade.—**de pai para filho,** a profitless transaction.—**escabroso,** an underhanded deal, shady business. **a** (or **em**)—**s,** on business. **abandonar os—s,** to retire from business. **Amigos, amigos,—s à parte,** Business is business, friendship is something else. **dar conta do—,** to answer for, take care of, be responsible for (a matter). **estar preso aos—s,** to be a slave (tied down) to business. **fazer bons—s,** to do good business. **fechar um—,** to conclude a bargain; to close a deal. **homem de—s,** a business man. **Não se faz mais—,** Business is at a standstill. **O—foi assim . . . ,** This is the way it was (how it happened, what took place). **o lado mau do—,** the short end of the bargain. **resolver um— amigavelmente,** to settle a matter (difficulty) amicably (in private) (out of court).

negocioso –sa (*adj.*) very busy.

negocista (*adj.*) given to sharp practice, to shady deals; (*m.,f.*) sharper, slicker, "shark".

negra (*f.*) see under NEGRO.

negrada (*f.*) crowd or group of Negroes; (*colloq.*) group of pranksters; bunch, gang.

negral (*adj.*) blackish, murky.

negralhão (*m.*) a strapping Negro [= PRETALHÃO].

negrão (*m., Plant Pathol.*) anthracnose; bitter rot (esp. of grapes).

negralhada, negraria (*f.*) crowd of Negroes. [*Somewhat derogatory.*]

negregado –da (*adj.*) unlucky.

negregoso –sa (*adj.*) very black.

negreiro –ra (*adj.*) of or pert. to Negroes. **navio—,** slave ship; (*m.*) slave trader; (*f.*) a water primrose (*Jussiaea laruoteana*).

negrejar (*v.i.*) to be, appear or become black, dark, gloomy.

negridão (*m.*) blackness, gloom [=NEGRURA].

negrinho (*m.*) a little Negro; "pickaninny"; (*colloq.*) a "small black" (demitasse).—**do pastoreio,** a certain brownie of southern Brazilian folklore.

negrita (*f.*), **–to** (*m.*) boldface type.

negro –gra (*adj.*) negro; black; dark, gloomy; (*m.*) Negro man; slave.—**banto,** a Bantu.—**animal,** animal charcoal.—**de acetileno,** acetylene black.—**de antimônio,** antimony black, antimony trisulfide.—**de carvão,** gas black, carbon black.—**de Espanha,** cork black.—**de ferro,** iron black (powdered pigment).—**de fumo,** lampblack.—**de gás,** gas black.—**de lâmpada,** lampblack.—**de marfim,** ivory black; bone black.—**novo,** raw (newly arrived) slave. **meu—,** old man (term of endearment); (*f.*) Negro woman; the deciding hand or game (after a tie).—**-mina** = CORCOROCA (a fish).

negrófilo –la (*adj.*) negrophile; (*m.,f.*) abolitionist (of slavery).

negróide (*adj.; m.,f.*) negroid.

negror [ô] (*m.*) blackness, darkness.

negrote (*m.*) **–ta** (*f.*) a young Negro.

negrume (*m.*) darkness; gloom.

negrura (*f.*) darkness, blackness; a black deed.

negundo (*m.*) box elder (*Acer negundo*); the negundo chastetree (*Vitex negundo*).

neinei (*m.*) = BEM-TE-VI-DO-BICO-CHATO.

nela [*em*+*ela*] in (on) her (it).

nêle [*em*+*êle*] in (on) him (it).

nelsonito (*m., Petrog.*) nelsonite.

nelúmbio, nelumbo (*m.*) lotus (*Nelumbium*).

nem (*conj., adv.*) neither, nor, not, not even.—**ao menos,**

not even.—**assim**—**assado**, neither this way nor that.
—**bem**, barely, hardly.—**bem**—**mal**, neither well nor
badly; just so-so.—**bom**—**mau**, neither good nor bad.
—**eu**—**éle**, neither I nor he.—**mais**—**menos**, neither
more nor less; just so.—**meio**, not even half; absolutely
none.—**para trás**—**para diante**, neither forward nor
backward.—**peixe**—**carne**, neither fish nor fowl.—**por
isso**, not even so.—**por pensamento**, not even in a
dream.—**por sombras**, not a chance.—**que**, even though;
not even if.—**sempre**, not always.—**sequer**, without
even.—**tanto ao mar**,—**tanto à terra**, (Let's find) a
middle-of-the-road solution.—**todos**, not all; not everyone.—**tudo**, not all.—**um**—**outro**, neither one nor the
other.—**um pio**! Not a peep out of you! **que**—(**uma
criança**), just like (a child).
nemálito (*m.*, *Min.*) nemalite.
nemastomáceas (*f.pl.*) a family (*Nemastomaceae*) of red
algae.
nematelmíntio (*m.*, *Zool.*) a nemathelminth (worm).
nematoblasto (*m.*, *Biol.*) nematoblast.
nematócero –**ra** (*adj.*; *m.*, *Zool.*) nematoceron (fly).
nematocida (*f.*) nematocide.
nematociste (*f.*, *Zool.*) nematocyst.
nematóide (*adj.*; *m.*, *Zool.*) nematoid; nematode.
nembo (*m.*, *Arch.*) pier, pillar.
Nêmese (*f.*) Nemesis.
nemésia (*f.*, *Bot.*) the pouch nemesia (*N. strumosa*).
nemoral (*adj.*) of, pert. to, or inhabiting a wood or grove.
nemorícola (*adj.*) inhabiting groves.
nemoroso –**sa** (*adj.*) tree-shaded; woodsy.
nenê, nenen (*m.*) a baby.
nenén-de-galinha (*m.*) chicken mite.
nenhengatu (*m.*) var. of NHEENGATU.
nenhum [*nem*+*um*] (*pron.*, *masc.*) no, none, not any, not
one, no one, nobody, nothing.—**de nós**, none (neither)
of us.—**dos dois**, neither of the two.—**outro**, nobody
else, no one else. **estar a**—, (*slang*) to be penniless. **de
modo**—, on no account.
nenhuma (*fem. of* NENHUM)—**das duas**, neither of the two.
—**de nós**, neither of us.—**outra**, no one else; no other
one. **sem dúvida**—, without a doubt.
nênia (*f.*) lament for the dead, threnody, dirge.
nenúfar (*m.*) waterlily (*Nymphaea*); cowlily (*Nuphar*).
neocaína (*f.*) = NOVOCAÍNA.
neócito (*m.*, *Biol.*) neocyte.
neoclássico –**ca** (*adj.*) neoclassic.
neocriticismo (*m.*) neocriticism.
neodaruinismo (*m.*) Neo-Darwinism.
neo-escolástica (*f.*) Neo-Scholasticism.
neodímio (*m.*, *Chem.*) neodymium.
neofeto (*m.*) neofetus.
neófito –**ta** (*m.*,*f.*) neophyte.
neofobia (*f.*) neophobia.
neogêneo –**nea** (*adj.*, *Geol.*) Neocene.
neogênese (*f.*) neogenesis.
neogótico –**ca** (*adj.*) Neo-Gothic.
neogrego –**ga** (*adj.*) Neo-Greek.
neo-impressionismo (*m.*, *Painting*) neoimpressionism.
neo-impressionista (*adj.*; *m.*,*f.*, *Painting*) neoimpression-
ist.
neolamarquismo (*m.*, *Biol.*) Neo-Lamarckism.
neolatino –**na** (*adj.*; *m.*,*f.*) Neo-Latin.
neolítico –**ca** (*adj.*) neolithic; (*f.*) Neolithic age.
neologia (*f.*), **neologismo** (*m.*) neologism.
neologista (*adj.*) neologistic; (*m.*,*f.*) neplogist.
néon, neônio (*m.*, *Chem.*) neon.
neoplasia (*f.*, *Physiol.*, *Med.*) neoplasia; neoplasty.
neoplasma (*m.*, *Med.*) neoplasm.
neoplastia (*f.*, *Surg.*) neoplasty; autoplasty.
neopreno (*m.*, *Chem.*) neoprene.
neossina (*f.*, *Biochem.*) neossin.
neotínea (*f.*, *Zool.*) neoteinia.
neotomismo (*m.*) Neo-Thomism.
neotrópico –**ca** (*adj.*) Neotropical.
neovitalismo (*m.*) neovitalism.
neovulcânico –**ca** (*adj.*, *Petrog.*) neovolcanic.
neozóico –**ca** (*adj.*; *Geol.*) Neozoic.
nepa (*f.*, *Zool.*) the genus of water scorpions (*Nepa*).
nepentáceo –**cea** (*adj.*; *Bot.*) nepenthaceous; (*f.pl.*) the
nepenthaceae (pitcher plant or monkey cup family).
nepente (*f.*) nepenthe, care-killing drug; (*Bot.*) a pitcher
plant (*Nepenthes*).
neperiano –**na** (*adj.*; *Math.*) Napierian.
nepídeos (*m.pl.*) the family Nepidae, containing the water

scorpions (*Nepa*) and needle bugs (*Ranatra*).
nepote (*m.*) the Pope's nephew; by exten., a favorite.
nepotismo (*m.*) nepotism, favoritism, patronage.
neptúnio (*m.*, *Chem.*) neptunium.
neque (*m.*, *Geol.*) neck.
nequícia (*f.*) perversity.
nereida, nereide (*f.*) sea nymph.
neres (*adv.*, *slang*) nothing.—**de**—, absolutely nothing.
nerita (*f.*) a genus (*Nerita*) of marine snails.
nerítico –**ca** (*adj.*, *Biol.*) neritic.
nérole, néroli (*m.*) neroli oil.
nervação (*f.*, *Bot.*) nervation, venation.
nervado –**da** (*adj.*) nervate, nerved, veined; ribbed.
nerval, nérveo –**vea** (*adj.*) nerval, neural.
nervino –**na** (*adj.*; *m.*) nervine.
nêrvo [ê] (*m.*) nerve; sinew, tendon; energy, vim; (*Arch.*)
rib; fillet; (*Bot.*) vein.—**ciático**, sciatic nerve.—**espinal**,
the eleventh or spinal accessory nerve.—**frênico**, phrenic
nerve.—**ótico**, optic nerve.—**pneumogástrico**, pneumogastric or vagus nerve.—**s raquidianos**, spinal nerves.—
vago, the vagus.
nervosidade (*f.*) nervous energy; nervousness.
nervosismo (*m.*) nervousness; jitters, heebie-jeebies.
nervoso –**sa** (*adj.*) nervous; energetic; highly strung,
excitable; jittery; skittish; uneasy; sinewy; (*m.*,*f.*) any
unspecified nervous malady; hysteria. **esgotamento**—,
nervous exhaustion, nervous breakdown.
nervudo –**da** (*adj.*) nervy, bold; sinewy.
nervura (*f.*, *Bot.*, *Zool.*) nervure; (*Arch.*) rib.
nescidade (*f.*) = NECEDADE.
néscio –**cia** (*adj.*) nescient, ignorant, stupid; (*m.*,*f.*) fool,
numskull, ignoramus.
nesga [ê] (*f.*) a gore (of cloth, of land); gusset; a nook or
corner.
nespereira (*f.*, *Bot.*) loquat (*Eriobotrya*), c.a. AMEIXA-
AMARELA.
nessa [*em*+*essa*] in (on) that (one).
nesse [*em*+*esse*] in (on) that (one).
nesta [*em*+*esta*] in (on) this (one) .
neste [*em*+*este*] in (on) this (one).
nestor (*m.*) wise old man.
neta (*f.*) granddaughter; fine foam on boiling cane sirup.
neto (*m.*) grandson; (*pl.*) descendants, posterity.
netuniano –**na**, **netunino** –**na**, **netúnio** –**nia** (*adj.*) Nep-
tunian.
Netuno (*m.*) Neptune.
neural (*adj.*) neural.
neuralgia (*f.*) neuralgia.
neurálgico –**ca** (*adj.*) neuralgic.
neurastenia (*f.*) neurasthenia.
neurastênico –**ca** (*adj.*) neurasthenic.
neurectomia (*f.*, *Surg.*) neurectomy.
neurilema (*f.*, *Arat.*) neurilemma. Var. NEVRILEMA.
neurisma (*m.*) = ANEURISMA.
neurite (*f.*, *Med.*) neuritis.
neuro (*m.*, *Anat.*) neuron, nerve cell. Var. NEVRÔNIO.
neuroblasto (*m.*, *Embryol.*, *Zool.*) neuroblast.
neuróglia (*f.*, *Anat.*) neuroglia.
neurografia (*f.*, *Anat.*) neurography.
neurologia (*f.*) neurology.
neurologista (*m.*,*f.*) neurologist.
neuroma (*f.*, *Med.*) neuroma.
neuromério, neurômero (*m.*, *Anat.*) neuromere.
neuromimese (*f.*, *Med.*) neuromimesis.
neurônio (*m.*) = NEURO.
neuroparalisia (*f.*, *Med.*) neuroparalysis.
neuropata, neurópata (*adj.*) neuropathic, neurotic; (*m.*,*f.*)
neuropath, neurotic person.
neuropatia (*f.*, *Med.*) neuropathy.
neuropático –**ca** (*adj.*, *Med.*) neuropathic, neurotic.
neuropatologia (*f.*) neuropathology. Var. NEVROPA-
TOLOGIA.
neuropsicose (*f.*, *Med.*) neuropsychosis; psychoneurosis.
neurópteros (*m.pl.*) the order (*Neuroptera*) which includes
the laced-winged flies, ant lions, etc.
neurose (*f.*, *Med.*) neurosis.—**de guerra**, shell shock.
neurótico –**ca** (*adj.*; *m.*,*f.*) neurotic. Var. NEVRÓTICO.
neurotomia (*f.*, *Surg.*) neurotomy. Var. NEVROTOMIA.
neurotoxina [ks] (*f.*, *Med.*) neurotoxin.
neurotripse (*f.*, *Med.*) neurotripsy.
neutral (*adj.*) neutral [= NEUTRO].
neutralidade (*f.*) neutrality.
neutralização (*f.*) neutralization.
neutralizador –**dora** (*m.*,*f.*) neutralizer.

neutralizar (*v.t.*) to neutralize; to counteract.
neutrino (*m.*, *Physics*, *Chem.*) neutrino.
neutro –**tra** (*adj.*) neutral; neuter; (*m.,f.*) neuter.
neutrófilo –**la** (*adj.; Physiol.*) neutrophile.
nêutron, neutrônio (*m.*, *Physics*) neutron.
nevado –**da** (*adj.*) snow-white; snow-covered; (*f.*) snowfall.
nevão (*m.*) snow storm, blizzard.
nevar (*v.i.*) to snow; to freeze; (*v.t.,v.i.*) to turn or render snow-white.
nevasca (*f.*) snow storm.
neve (*f.*) snow; by exten., snow-whiteness; snow-white hair.—**carbônica**, dry ice.
nêveda (*f.*) the calamint savory (*Satureia calamintha*), c.a. ERVA-DAS-AZEITONAS.—**cataria**, catnip.—**menor**, the catnip savory (*Satureia nepeta*).
neviscar (*v.i.*) to snow lightly.
nevo (*m.*, *Med.*) nevus; (*colloq.*) birthmark [= NEVO MATERNO].
névoa (*f.*) fog, mist; obscurity.
nevoeiro (*m.*) dense fog, heavy mist; obscurity.
nevoento –**ta** (*adj.*) snowy; obscure.
nevra-, nevri-, nevro-, see words beginning with **neura-, neuri-, neuro-**.
nexo [ks] (*m.*) connection (between ideas); tie, bond. **sem** —, incoherent, disconnected.
nhá (*f.*) "missy". Cf. IAIÁ.
nhambibororó, nhambiborororoca (*m.*) = BORORÓ.
nhambicuara (*m.,f.*) an Indian of the Nambicuara, a once large but now virtually extinct tribe of primitives in the northwestern part of Mato Grosso; (*adj.*) pert. to or designating this tribe. Var. NAMBIQUARA.
nhambu [ú] (*m.*) Pará cress spotflower (*Spilanthes oleracea*); also a bird, better known as INHAMBU.
nhamburana (*f.*, *Bot.*) brassbuttons (*Cotula*).
nhamburi [í] (*m.*) a blackberry (*Rubus*).
nhandaia (*f.*) = JANDAIA.
nhandi [í] (*m.*) a pepper (*Piper caudatum*), c.a. PIMENTA-DOS-ÍNDIOS.
nhandu [ú] (*m.*) nandu or rhea (American ostrich), found in southern Brazil; c.a. EMA, NHANDUGUAÇU.
nhanhã, nhanhãzinha, (*f.*) an affectionate form of miss [= IAIÁ].
nhapim (*m.*) = ENCONTRO (a bird).
nheengatu [tú] (*m.*) the language of the Tupi which became and still serves as a lingua franca along the Amazon. Var. NENHENGATU.
nhenhenhém (*m.*) muttering; grumbling; yak-yak-yak.
nhonhô (*m.*) Negro slave corruption of SENHOR (master), equivalent in use and meaning to U. S. slave "massa" (master). Used also to designate the master's young son. Cf. IOIÔ.
nhoque (*m.*) gnòcchi (a sort of Italian dumpling).
nhor-não, nhor-sim (*colloq.*) nossuh, yessuh.
nhu (*m.*) gnu.
nica (*f.*) impertinence; trifle.
nicar (*v.t.*) to peck; to nick.
nicho (*m.*) niche; pigeon hole (in a desk); sinecure.
nicociana (*f.*, *Bot.*) tobacco (*Nicotiana*).
nicocianina (*f.*, *Chem.*) nicotianin.
nicol [-cóis] (*m.*, *Optics*) a Nicol prism.
Nicolau (*m.*) Nicholas; Nicolas.
nicotina (*f.*) nicotine.
nicotínico –**ca** (*adj.*, *Chem.*) nicotinic.
nicotinismo (*m.*) nicotinism.
nicotino –**na** (*adj.*) nicotine.
nicotizar (*v.t.*) to nicotinize.
nicou (*m.*, *Bot.*) a lancepod (*Lonchocarpus nicou*).
nictação (*f.*) winking, blinking.
nictagináceo –**cea** (*adj.*, *Bot.*) nyctaginaceous; (*f.pl.*) the Nyctaginaceae (four-o'clock family).
nictalope (*m.,f.*) nyctalope (one affected with nyctalopia).
nictalopia (*f.*, *Med.*) nyctalopia (night blindness; day sight), or, by confusion, day blindness (hemeralopia).
nictanto (*m.*) night jasmine (*Nyctanthes*), c.a. JASMIN-DA-ARÁBIA.
nictipelágico –**ca** (*adj.; Biol.*) nyctipelagic.
nictipiteco (*m.*) a genus (*Nyctipithecus, syn. Aotus*) of night apes.
nictitropismo (*m.*, *Plant physiol.*) nyctitropism.
nictobata, nictóbata (*m.,f.*) sleepwalker [= SONÂMBULO].
nicuri (*m.*) = ARICURI.
nicurioba, nicuriroba (*f.*) = ACURIROBA.
nidícola (*adj.; Zool.*) nidicolous.

nidificação (*f.*) nestbuilding.
nidificar (*v.t.*) to build a nest.
nidífugo –**ga** (*adj.; Zool.*) nidifugous.
nidoroso –**sa** (*adj.*) rankly odorous.
nidulariáceas (*f.pl.*) the Nidulariacae (family of bird-nest fungi).
nielo (*m.*) niello (black metallic alloy); = NIGELA.
nigela (*f.*) niello, niellowork; (*Bot.*) fennelflower (*Nigella*).
—**damascena**, love-in-a-mist (*N. damascena*).—**dostrigos**, common corn cockle (*Agrostemma githago*), c.a. AXENUS.
nigelar (*v.t.*) to niello.
nigérrimo –**ma** [*absol. superl. of* NEGRO] most black.
nígua (*f.*, *Zool.*) the chigoe (*Tunga, syn. Sarcopsylla, penetrans*), c.a. TUNGA, BICHO-DE-PÉ, PULGA-PENETRANTE
niilismo [i-i] (*m.*) nihilism.
niilista [i-i] (*adj.; m.,f.*) nihilist.
nimbar (*v.t.*) to adorn or crown with a halo.
nimbo (*m.*) nimbus, storm cloud; halo.
nimbuia (*f.*) = RÃ-PIMENTA.
nímio –**mia** (*adj.*) excessive.
ninar (*v.t.*) to lull to sleep.
ninfa (*f.*) nymph; (*pl.*, *Anat.*) labia minora.
ninfala (*f.*) a "four-footed" butterfly (nymphalid).
ninfalídeos (*m.,pl.*) the Nymphalidae (family of "four-footed" butterflies).
ninfeáceo –**cea** (*adj.; Bot.*) nymphaeaceous; (*f.pl.*) the water lily family (*Nymphaeaceae*).
ninfeu –**féia** (*adj.*) nymphean; (*f.*) water lily.
ninfolepsia (*f.*) nympholepsy (frenzy).
ninfomania (*f.*, *Med.*) nymphomania.
ninfose (*f.*, *Zool.*) nymphosis.
ninguém (*pron.*) nobody, no one.—**mais**, nobody else.—**se não êle**, nobody but he. **mais que**—, more than anyone (else). **um joão**—, a nobody.
ninhada (*f.*) brood, litter, covey, nestful.
ninharia (*f.*) trifle, bauble, knickknack.
ninho (*m.*) nest; lair; snug retreat; home.—**alçapão**, trapnest.—**de amores**, love nest.—**de andorinha**, soup birdnest.—**de metralhadoras**, machine-gun nest.—**de ratos**, rats' nest (lit. & fig.).
ninquim (*m.*) = MANGANGÁ-LISO.
ninquim-da-pedra (*m.*) = MANGANGÁ.
niobato (*m.*, *Chem.*) niobate columbate.
nióbico –**ca** (*adj.*, *Chem.*) niobic.
nióbio (*m.*, *Chem.*) niobium.
niobite (*f.*, *Chem.*) niobite, columbite.
niponense (*adj.*) Nipponese.
nipónico –**ca** (*adj.; m.,f.*) Nipponese.
níquel [-queis] (*m.*) nickel (metal, coin).—**bronze**, nickel bronze, German silver, nickel silver.
niquelagem (*f.*) nickel-plating.
niquelar (*v.t.*) to nickel-plate.
niqueleira (*f.*) coin purse.
niquelina (*f.*, *Min.*) niccolite.
niquento –**ta** (*adj.*) fussy, excessively busy with trifles; niggling, caviling.
niquim-da-areia, niquim-do-mar (*m.*) = MOREIATIM.
nirvana (*m.*) nirvana.
nissa (*f.*, *Bot.*) tupelo (*Nyssa*).
nisso [*em* + *isso*] in (on) that; at that (moment); meanwhile.
nistagmo (*m.*, *Med.*) nystagmus.
nisto [*em* + *isto*] in (on) this; at this (moment); meanwhile.
nitente (*adj.*) bright, shining; resistant.
niteroiense (*adj.*) of or pert. to the city of Niteroi (formerly spelled Nictheroy), capital of Rio de Janeiro state; (*m.,f.*) a native or inhabitant of that city.
nitidez [ê] (*f.*) brightness, clearness, distinctness; nicety; neatness.
nítido –**da** (*adj.*) bright; clear; distinct; clear-cut, well-defined.
níton, nitônio (*m.*) niton, radon, radium emanation.
nitralina (*f.*) = SALITRE DO CHILE.
nitraloi (*m.*) Nitralloy (steel).
nitramina (*f.*, *Chem.*) nitramine.
nitranílico –**ca** (*adj.; Chem.*) nitranilic [acid].
nitratina (*f.*) nitratine, native sodium nitrate [= SALITRE DO CHILE].
nitrato (*m.*) nitrate.—**de alumínio**, aluminum nitrate.—**de amônio**, ammonium nitrate.—**de bário**, barium nitrate; nitrobarite.—**de bismuto**, bismuth nitrate.—**do Chile**, Chile saltpeter.—**de estrôncio**, strontium nitrate.—**de guanidina**, guanidine nitrate.—**de mercúrio**, mercuric

nitrate; mercury pernitrate.—**mercurioso,** mercurous nitrate; mercury pronitrate.—**de potássio,** potassium nitrate.—**de prata,** silver nitrate.—**de sódio,** sodium nitrate, cubic niter, soda niter, caliche.—**de tório,** thorium nitrate.

nitreira (f.) niter bed.—**artificial,** manure pile, compost heap.

nitretação (f.) nitriding (casehardening of steel).

nitreto (m., Chem.) nitride.

nítrico -ca (adj.) nitric.

nitrido (m.) neigh, whinny.

nitrificação (f., Bacteriol., Chem.) nitrification.

nitrificadoras (f.pl.) nitrobacteria.

nitrificante (adj.) nitrifying.

nitrificar (v.t., Chem.) to nitrify.

nitrir [25] (v.i.) to neigh, whinny.

nitrito (m., Chem.) nitrite.

nitro (m.) nitro, saltpeter.—**algodão,** nitro-cotton.—**do Chile,** Chile saltpeter.—**cúbico,** cubic niter.

nitrobactérias (f.pl.) nitrobacteria.

nitrobarito (m., Min.) nitrobarite.

nitrobenzeno (m.) nitrobenzene.

nitrobenzina (f.), **nitrobenzol** (m.) nitrobenzene; nitrobenzol.

nitrocalcite (f.) nitro-calcite, calcium nitrate.

nitrocarboneto (m.) calcium cyanide.

nitrocelulose (f.) cellulose nitrate, guncotton.

nitrofórmio (m.) nitroform.

nitrogelatina (f.) nitrogelatin, blasting gelatin.

nitrogênio (m.) nitrogen [= AZOTO].

nitroglicerina (f.) nitroglycerin.

nitroglicol (m.) nitro-glycol.

nitróleo (m.) = NITROGLICERINA.

nitrometana (m.) nitro-methane, nitro-carbinol.

nitrômetro (m., Chem.) nitrometer.

nitromuriato (m.) nitromuriate.

nitroparafina (f.) nitroparaffin.

nitroprussiato (m.) nitroprussiate, nitroprusside.

nitroso -sa (adj.) nitrous.

nitrossulfato (m.) nitrosulphate.

nitroxilo [ks] (m.) nitroxyl, nitryl, the nitro group.

nível [-veis] (m.) level (surface, instrument); state of equality.—**do mar,** sea level. **ao**—, flush, on a level (**de,** with). **passagem de**—, grade crossing.—**de água,** carpenter's level.—**de bôlha de ar,** spirit level.—**de luneta,** surveyor's level.

nivelação (f.) leveling; grading (as of a railroad bed).

nivelador -dora (adj.) leveling; grading; (m.,f.) leveler; grader.

nivelamento (m.) leveling; grading.

nivelar (v.t.) to level; to grade; to raze; to equalize; (v.r.) to put oneself on the same level with.

níveo -vea (adj.) snow-white.

n/1 = NOSSA LETRA (our [promissory] note).

N.N., an abbreviation corresponding to Anon. (anonymous).

N.N.E. = NOR-NORDESTE (north-northeast).

N.N.O. or **N.N.W.** = NOR-NOROESTE (north-northwest).

n.º = NÚMERO (number).

n/o = NOSSA ORDEM (our order—commercial term).

no (contraction of prep. EM + art. O) in the, at the, on the, into the, by the, with the, etc.; (dir. obj. pron. masc.) him, it, you. [Used instead of pron. O when attached to verb forms with a nasal ending; **mandaram-no** instead of **mandaram-o.** Used also when pron. **nos** is followed by -LO(S) or -LA(S); thus: **no-lo(s), no-la(s).**]

nó (m.) knot, tie; hitch, bend; node; joint; knuckle; entanglement; (Naut.) knot; (Astron.) knot.—**ascendente** or **boreal,** (Astron.) ascending node.—**cego,** a tangled knot.—**corredio,** slip knot; running noose.—**de-adão,** Adam's apple.—**de-cachorro,** (Bot.) Brazil thryallis (T. brasiliensis).—**descendente** or **austral** (Astron.) descending node.—**de escota singelo,** hawser bend.—**górdio,** Gordian knot.—**na garganta,** a lump in the throat.—**nas tripas,** (colloq.) intestinal obstruction, volvulus.—**vital,** (Anat.) the olivary body; (Bot.) crown (junction of stem and roots in a seed plant). **não dar ponto sem**—, to take no action unless one is sure of the outcome. **ser cheio de**—s, or **ter**—**pelas costas,** to be given to intricacies and complicated details.

noa [ó] (f., Eccl.) nones.

nobiliário -ria (adj.) nobiliary.

nobilíssimo -ma (absol. superl. of NOBRE) most noble.

nobilitar (v.t.) to ennoble; to exalt.

nobre (adj.) noble, high-born; majestic; illustrious; honorable; (m.) nobleman.

nobreza [ê] (f.) nobility; nobleness.

nobríssimo -ma (adj.) = NOBILISSIMO.

noção (f.) notion, concept, idea.

nocárdia (f., Bacteriol.) a genus (Actinomyces) of bacteria.

nocardiose (f., Med., Veter.) actinomycosis.

nocaute (m.) knock-out (in boxing).—**técnico,** TKO.

nocional (adj.) notional.

nocividade (f.) noxiousness, harmfulness, malignancy.

nocivo -va (adj.) noxious, injurious, harmful, unwholesome, malign.

noctambulismo (m.) noctambulism, somnambulism.

noctâmbulo -la (m.,f.) noctambulist, somnambulist, sleepwalker [= NICTOBATA].

noctidiurno -na (adj.) noctidiurnal.

noctilucina (f., Zool.) noctilucin.

noctívago -ga (adj.) night-wandering; nocturnal; (m., colloq.) nighthawk, night prowler.

noctovisão (f., Physics) noctovision.

noctívolo -la (adj.) night-flying.

nodal (adj.) nodal; knot.

nodicórneo -nea (adj., Zool.) nodicorn.

nodífero -ra (adj.) nodiform.

nodifloro -ra (adj., Bot.) nodiflorous.

nodiforme (adj.) nodiform.

nodo (m.) node (all senses).

nódoa (f.) stain, spot, blemish; blot; disgrace, dishonor.

nodosidade (f.) nodosity; knottiness.

nodoso -sa (adj.) nodous, nodose, knotty; gnarled.

nódulo (m.) nodule.

noduloso -sa (adj.) nodulous, nodulose.

Noêmia (f.) Naomi.

nogado (m.) nougat.

nogal (m.) = NOGUEIRAL.

nogueira (f.) walnut (tree or wood). [The fruit is NOZ.] —**comum,** persian walnut (Juglans regia).—**da-américa** or—**preta,** Eastern black walnut (Juglans nigra).—**da-austrália,** Queenslandnut macadamia (M. ternifolia).—**de-iguape,** candlenut tree (Aleurites moluccana), c.a. NOZ-DA-ÍNDIA, NOZ-DE-BANCUL.—**do-japão,** the maidenhair tree (Ginkgo biloba).—**do-mato,** American muskwood (Guarea trichiloides), c.a. CARRAPETA-VERDADEIRA.

nogueirado -da (adj.) of walnut color.

nogueiral (m.) walnut grove.

noitada (f.) a whole night; a sleepless night; a night out; night work; a night's revel, spree or carousal.

noite (f.) night; nighttime; evening.—**dos tempos,** the dark ages.—**do túmulo** or—**eterna,** death.—**e dia,** night and day.—**fechada,** dark night.—**inquieta,** restless night. —**velha,** late at night. **à**—, at night, in the evening; this evening. **à—calada** (**fechada, cerrada**), in the dead of night. **a—passada,** last night. **à alta**—, late at night. **à meia**—, at midnight. **à** (or **na bôca da**)—, at nightfall. **ante-ontem à**—, night before last. **ao cair da**—, at nightfall. **até altas horas da**—, far into the night; till all hours of the night. **da**—, in the evening, at night. **da—para o dia,** overnight. **de**—, at night, by night, in the nighttime. **durante a**—, in (during) the night. **esta**—, last night; tonight; this evening. **hoje à**—, tonight. **horas mortas da**—, the dead of night. **juntar** (or **ajuntar**) **o dia com a**—, to work day and night. **lá para as tantas da**—, at some time during the night. **na calada da**—, in the dead of night. **na mesma**—, (on) that same night. **ontem à**—, last night; last evening. **passar a—em claro** (or **em branco**), to spend a sleepless night. **por—velha,** late at night. **tôda**—, every night. Var. NOUTE.

noitecer (v.) = ANOITECER.

noitibó (m.) nighthawk (lit. & fig.).

noitinha (f.) dusk, twilight, nightfall. Var. NOUTINHA.

noiva (f.) fiancée; bride.

noivado (m.) wedding day; wedding feast; betrothal; engagement period.

noivar (v.i.) to become engaged, betrothed; to court one's intended; to spend one's honeymoon; to become a newlywed.

noivo (m.) fiancé; bridegroom; (pl.) engaged couple; newlyweds. **ficar**—, to become engaged.

noivinha (f.) = POMBINHA-DAS-ALMAS.

nojado -da (adj.) = ANOJADO.

nojento -ta (adj.) nauseating, disgusting; nasty; noisome; queasy.

nojo [nô] (m.) nausea; disgust, loathing; mourning.

nojoso –**sa** (*adj.*) in mourning; also = NOJENTO.
no-la, fem. form of NO-LO.
nolição (*f.*) unwillingness.
noli-me-tangere (*m.*) = NÃO-ME-TOQUES.
no-lo (*pers. pron.*) it to us; (*pl.*) them to us.
nômade, nômada (*adj.*) nomadic, wandering, vagrant; (*m.pl.*) nomads, gypsies; roamers.
nomadismo (*m.*) nomadism.
nome (*m.*) name, appellation, nickname, surname; noun; reputation; fame, renown.—**apelativo** (or **comum**), common name.—**batismal** (or **de batismo**), baptismal, or Christian, name.—**científico,** scientific name.—**de família,** family name.—**de guerra,** pseudonym.—**feio,** dirty word.—**popular,** or **vulgar,** common name (for plants or animals).—**próprio,** proper name, **dar—,** to name. **dar—s aos bois,** to call a spade a spade. **de—,** by name. **só de—,** in name only. **em—de,** in the name of; in (on) behalf of. **por—,** by name. **sem—,** unspeakable, despicable.
nomeação (*f.*) nomination; appointment; designation. Cf. NOMINAÇÃO.
nomeado –**da** (*adj.*) nominated; designated; named; (*m.*) nominee; appointee; (*f.*) renown, name.
nomeador –**dora** (*adj.*) nominating; (*m.,f.*) nominator.
nomeadura (*f.*) = NOMEAÇÃO.
nomeante (*adj.*) nominating; (*m.,f.*) nominator.
nomear (*v.t.*) to name, term; to label; to call by name; to nominate; to appoint; to designate.
nomenclatura (*f.*) nomenclature.
nômina (*f.*) amulet, phylactery; brass stud.
nominação (*f.*) the giving or assigning of a name or names. [But not nomination in the usual sense, which is NOMEAÇÃO (appointment), or INDICAÇÃO (DE CANDIDATO)]. Cf. NÓMEAÇÃO.
nominal (*adj.*) nominal.
nominativo –**va** (*adj.*) nominative; (*m., Gram.*) nominative case.
nomografia (*f.*) nomography.
nomógrafo –**fa** (*m.,f.*) nomographer.
nomograma (*m.*) nomograph (alignment chart).
nomologia (*f.*) nomology.
nomotésico –**ca** (*adj.*) nomothetic; legislative.
nonada (*f.*) trifle, bagatelle.
nonagenário –**ria** (*adj.; m.,f.*) nonagenarian.
nonagésimo –**ma** (*adj.*) nonagesimal, ninetieth; (*m.*) a ninetieth.
nonágono (*m., Math.*) nonagon [= ENEÁGONO].
nonano (*m., Chem.*) nonane.
nonato –**ta** (*adj.*) delivered by Caesarean section; (*m.*) an unborn calf in a slaughtered cow.
nongentésimo –**ma, noningentésimo** –**ma** (*adj.*) nine-hundredth.
nonílico –**ca** (*adj., Chem.*) nonylic, nonoic.
nonílio (*m., Chem.*) nonyl.
nônio (*m.*) vernier scale.
nono –**na** (*adj.*) ninth; (*m.*) a ninth; (*f., Eccl.*) none.
nontronite (*f., Min.*) nontronite.
nopal (*m., Bot.*) cochineal nopalcactus (*Nopalea cochenillifer*).
nora (*f.*) daughter-in-law; noria (bucket wheel for raising water).
norça-branca (*f., Bot.*) redberry bryony (*Bryonia dioica*), c.a. BRIÔNIA.
nordestal (*adj.*) northeastern.
nordeste (*m.*) the northeast; a northeast wind; that part of Brazil which includes the states of Piauí, Ceará, Rio Grande do Norte, Paraíba, Pernambuco, Alagôas and Sergipe; (*adj.*) northeastern.
nordestear (*v.i.*) to swing northeast; to steer northeast.
nordésteo –**tea** (*adj.*) from the northeast.
nordestia (*f.*) cold northeast wind.
nordestino –**na** (*adj.*) of or pertaining to northeastern Brazil; (*m.,f.*) a Brazilian northeasterner.
nórdico –**ca** (*adj.; m.,f.*) Nordic [= NORRENO].
norite (*f., Petrog.*) norite.
norma (*f.*) norm; rule; (*Bot.*) = ESCUMILHA or EXTREMOSA.
normal (*adj.*) normal; serving as a standard or model; (*f., Math.*) normal.
normalidade (*f.*) normalcy, normality.
normalista (*adj.*) of or pertaining to the ESCOLA NORMAL (normal school for teachers); (*m.,f.*) a graduate or undergraduate of the same.
normalização (*f.*) normalizing.
normalizado –**da** (*adj.*) normalized, back to normal.
normalizar (*v.t.*) to normalize; (*v.r.*) to return to normal.

normando –**da** (*adj.*) Norman; (*m.,f.*) a native of Normandy; (*m.*) Norman French (dialect).
normativo –**va** (*adj.*) serving as an accepted basis for comparison, reference, etc.; standard.
normócito (*m., Anat.*) normocyte.
normógrafo (*m.*) a lettering guide.
nor-nordeste (*adj.; m.*) north-northeast (wind or direction)
nor-noroeste (*adj.; m.*) north-northwest (wind or direction).
noroeste (*adj.; m.*) northwest (wind); (*colloq.*) bad humor.
noroestear (*v.i.*) to swing northwest; to steer northwest.
norreno –**na** (*adj.*) = NÓRDICO.
nortada (*f.*) a cold north wind.
norte (*m.*) the north; the northern regions of Brazil; polestar; general direction. **perder o—,** to lose one's head (presence of mind); (*adj.*) north.
norte-americano –**na** (*adj.; m.,f.*) North American, esp. of, or an inhabitant of, the U.S.A. Cf. ESTADUNIDENSE.
nortear (*v.t.*) to steer (stand) to the north; to guide, direct, show the way; (*v.r.*) to find one's bearings.
norteio (*m.*) landmark.
norteiro –**ra, nortense** (*adj.; m.,f.*) = NORTISTA.
nortista (*adj.*) of or pertaining to northern Brazil; (*m.,f.*) a native or inhabitant of that region, especially of the states of Maranhão, Pará and Amazonas.
noruega (*f.*) cool, damp land sloping away from the sun; cold, sharp wind; [*cap.*] Norway.
norueguense, noruegûes –**guêsa** (*adj.; m.,f.*) Norwegian.
nos (*contraction of prep.* EM + *art.* OS) in (into, on, at) the; (*pers. pron.*) (to) us, (to) ourselves.
nós (*pron.*) we, us.—**mesmos,** we ourselves.—**outros,—todos,** we all; us all. **entre—,** between us, between you and me. **todos—,** all of us.
noseana, noselita, nosita (*f., Min.*) nosean, noselite.
nosocômio (*m.*) hospital.
nosófito (*m., Bot.*) nosophyte.
nosografia (*f.*) nosography.
nosologia (*f.*) nosology.
nossa-amizade (*f., slang*) an endearing term: old dear, old man, chum, pal.
nosso –**sa** (*poss. adj.*) our; (*poss. pron.*) ours. **os—s,** our folks, our people.
nostalgia (*f.*) nostalgia.
nostálgico –**ca** (*adj.*) nostalgic.
nota (*f.*) note, memorandum; notice, attention; musical note; bank note; restaurant check; grade, mark (on school work); formal diplomatic note.—**falsa,** counterfeit bill; (*Music*) sour note.—**marginal,** marginal note.—**promissória,** promissory note.—**tônica,** (*Music*) keynote.—**verbal,** an oral diplomatic communication. **dar—,** to grade (school work). **digno de—,** noteworthy.
notabilidade (*f.*) notability; person of note.
notabilíssimo –**ma** (*absol. superl. of* NOTÁVEL) most notable.
notabilizar (*v.t.*) to make notable; (*v.r.*) to distinguish oneself.
notação (*f.*) notation; annotation.—**léxica (fônica, ortográfica, prosódica),** diacritical mark.—**lógica** (or **sintática),** punctuation mark.
notado –**da** (*adj.*) noted, notable; recorded.
notar (*v.t.*) to note, mark, observe; to denote; to annotate; to record, register. **é de—que,** it is noteworthy that. **fazer—,** to call attention to.
notariado (*m.*) the office of notary.
notário (*m.*) notary.
notável (*adj.*) notable, noteworthy; noted, well-known, conspicuous, outstanding; striking; remarkable; (*colloq.*) amazing.
notícia (*f.*) news, tidings, notice, announcement; information; report.—**s alvissareiras,** glad tidings.—**s de última hora,** last-minute news.—**em primeira mão,** firsthand news. **boas—s,** good news. **dar—s de,** to tell of, speak about, give news of. **uma—,** a piece of news.
noticiador –**dora** (*m.,f.*) advertiser; announcer; (*adj.*) announcing.
noticiar (*v.t.*) to announce, publish, report.
noticiário (*m.*) news section of a newspaper.
noticiarista (*adj.; m.,f.*) news reporter.
noticioso –**sa** (*adj.*) newsy. **agência—,** news agency.
notificação (*f.*) notification; summons.
notificar (*v.t.*) to notify; to summon.
noto (*m.*) south wind. [*Poetical.*]
notocórdio (*m., Anat., Zool.*) notochord.

notodontídeos (*m.pl.*) the family (*Notofontidae*) which includes the puss moths and lobster moths.

notonecta (*f.*), **-to** (*m.*) a genus (*Notonecta*) of aquatic insects called back swimmers.

notoriedade (*f.*) quality of being public, known to all. [But not notoriety, in the sense of bad repute, which is MÁ FAMA.]

notório -ria (*adj.*) well-known, public. [But not notorious, in the sense of ill-famed, which is DE MÁ FAMA.]

nototremo (*m.*) the genus (*Nototrema*) of marsupial frogs.

notra (*f.*) Chilean firebush (*Embothrium coccineum*).

noturnal (*adj.*) nocturnal.

noturno -na (*adj.*) nocturnal, nightly; (*m.*) a night train; (*Music*) nocturne.

noúmeno (*m.*) = NÚMENO.

noute (*f.*) & derivs. = NOITE & derivs.

noutro [*em + outro*] in (on) another.

nov. = NOVEMBRO (November).

nova (*f.*) see under NOVO.

novação (*f.*) innovation; renewal.

novaculito (*m.*, *Petrog.*) novaculite.

Nova Deli (*f.*) New Delhi.

Nova Escócia (*f.*) Nova Scotia.

Nova Gales (*f.*) New South Wales.

Nova Guiné (*f.*) New Guinea.

Nova Inglaterra (*f.*) New England.

Nova Iorque (*f.*) New York.

nova-iorquino -na (*adj.; m.,f.*) New Yorker.

Nova Jérsia (*f.*) New Jersey.

novamente (*adv.*) anew, again, afresh.

Nova Orleães (*f.*) New Orleans.

novar (*v.t.*, *Law*) to renew (a contract).

nova-seita (*m.,f.*, *colloq.*) Protestantism (in Northeastern Brazil).

novato -ta (*adj.*) raw, inexperienced; (*m.,f.*) novice, beginner, tyro; (*m.*) freshman; tenderfoot; greenhorn; rookie; a venomous ant which inhabits the hollow stems of the ant tree, c.a. TAXI, FORMIGA-DE-NOVATO.

Nova Zelândia (*f.*) New Zealand.

nove (*adj.; m.*) nine.

novecentos (*num.*) nine hundred.

novedio -dia (*adj.*) young; (*m.*) bud, sprout.

nove-horas (*f.pl.*, *colloq.*) airs, mannerisms, pretensions; finicalness; overpoliteness.

novel [-véis] (*adj.*) novel, new; green, raw, untrained.

novela (*f.*) a short novel; story, tale.—**policial**, detective story.

novelar (*v.i.*) to write novels.

noveleiro -ra (*m.,f.*) a writer of novels; a newsmonger; (*m.*) scion.

novelesco [ê] (*adj.*) novellike.

novelista (*m.,f.*) novelist; (*adj.*) gossipy.

novêlo (*m.*) skein, ball of yarn, etc.; fig., tangle; plot.—**de linho**, a cactus (*Notocactus haselbergii*); (*pl.*) the European cranberrybush viburnum (*V. opulus*), c.a. SABUGUEIRO-DE-ÁGUA (or DOS PÂNTANOS), and BOLA-DE-NEVE.—**da-china** = HORTÊNSIA (*Hydrangea*).

novembro (*m.*) November.

novena (*f.*) a novena; nine things or people.

noventa (*adj.; m.*) ninety; (*m.*) a, or the, ninetieth.

noviciado (*m.*) novitiate, apprenticeship.

noviciar (*v.i.*) to begin, try out (for the first time).

noviço -ça (*m.,f.*) a novitiate; an apprentice; novice, beginner, rookie; (*adj.*) new (**em**, at), inexperienced, unfledged; = NOVATO.

novidade (*f.*) novelty; recent event; item of news; newness, recentness; (*colloq.*) unforeseen difficulty, mishap. **cheio de—s**, full of airs. **não há—**, no news, nothing new. **sem—s**, uneventful, without incident.

novidadeiro -ra (*m.,f.*) newfangled person; newsmonger; gossiper.

novilha (*f.*) heifer.

novilho (*m.*) bullock, yearling.

novilúnio (*m.*) new moon [= LUA NOVA].

novinho -nha [dim. of NOVO] (*adj.*) quite new, brand new, spic-and-span.

novíssimo -ma (*absol. superl. of NOVO*) very new; latest.

nov.º = NOVEMBRO (November).

nôvo -va [nó] (*adj.*) new, novel, fresh, late, recent, young, modern; unused; inexperienced.—**em fôlha**, brand new. **de—**, anew, again, once more. **mais —**, younger, youngest; newer, newest. **Que há de—?** What's new? **um livro—**, a new book. **um—livro**, another book; (*m.*) recent thing;

new person; new year; (*f.*) a piece of news. **boas—s**, good news.

novocaína (*f.*, *Pharm.*) novocaine.

Novo México (*m.*) New Mexico.

nóxio -xia [ks] (*adj.*) noxious [= NOCIVO].

noz (*f.*) nut; walnut.—**-de-galha**, oak gallnut.—**-da-índia** (or—**-de-bancul**), the candlenut tree (*Aleurites moluccana*), c.a. NOGUEIRA-DE-IGUAPE.—**-do-pará**, the pichurim bean (fruit of the PIXURIM, which see). [Do not confuse with the Pará or Brazil nut, which is CASTANHA-DO-PARÁ.]—**-moscada-do-brasil** = BICUÍBA-REDONDA (a nutmeg tree).—**-vômica**, the nuxvomica poison nut (*Strychnos nuxvomica*). Cf. NOGUEIRA.

n.p. = NOME PRÓPRIO (proper name).

N.P. = NOSSO PADRE (Our Father).

N.R.P. = NOSSO REVERENDO PADRE (Our Reverend Father).

n/s = NOSSO SAQUE (our draft).

N.S. = NOSSO SENHOR (Our Lord).

N.S.ª = NOSSA SENHORA (Our Lady).

N.S.J.C. = NOSSO SENHOR JESUS CRISTO (Our Lord Jesus Christ).

N.S.P. = NOSSO SANTO PADRE (Our Holy Father).

N.SS.P. = NOSSO SANTÍSSIMO PADRE (Our Most Holy Father).

N.T. = NOVO TESTAMENTO (New Testament).

nu -nua (*adj.*) naked, nude, bare; unclad, undressed.—**e cru**, blunt, downright.—**em pêlo**, stark naked. **a ôlho—**, with the unaided eye; (*m.*, *Art.*) a nude.

nuança (*f.*) nuance, shade.

nuaruaque (*adj.*) Arawakan.

nubente (*adj.; m.,f.*) betrothed.

nubiforme (*adj.*) nubiform, cloudlike.

núbil [-beis] (*adj.*) nubile, marriageable.

nubilidade (*f.*) nubility.

nubiloso -sa (*adj.*) cloudy.

nublado (*adj.*) cloudy, overcast; blurred.

nublar (*v.t.*) to cloud; to become cloudy.

nubloso -sa (*adj.*) cloudy.

nuca (*f.*) nape of the neck; (*Anat.*) nucha.

nucela (*f.*, *Bot.*) nucellus.

nucicultor -tora (*m.,f.*) nut grower.

nucicultura (*f.*) nut growing.

nucífero -ra (*adj.*) nuciferous.

nuciforme (*adj.*) nut-shaped.

nucleado -da (*adj.*, *Bot.*) nucleated.

nucleal (*adj.*) nuclear.

nuclear (*adj.*) nuclear; (*v.r.*) to nucleate.

nucleário -ria (*adj.*) nucleary.

nucléase (*f.*, *Biochem.*) nuclease.

nucleico -ca (*adj.*, *Chem.*) nucleic [acid].

nucleífero -ra (*adj.*) nucleiferous.

nucleiforme (*adj.*) nucleiform.

nucleína (*f.*, *Biochem.*) nuclein.

nucleinato (*m.*, *Biochem.*) nucleate.

núcleo (*m.*) nucleus; kernel, core; (*Elec.*) core.

nucleoalbumina (*f.*, *Biochem.*) nucleoalbumin, phosphoprotein.

nucleohistona (*f.*, *Biochem.*) nucleohistone.

nucleolado -da (*adj.*) nucleolated.

nucleolar (*adj.*, *Biol.*) nucleolar.

nucléolo (*m.*, *Biol.*) nucleolus.

nucleomicrosomo (*m.*, *Biol.*) nucleomicrosome, karyomicrosome [= CARIOMICROSOMO].

nucleoplasma (*m.*, *Biol.*) nucleoplasm.

nucleoproteína (*f.*, *Biochem.*) nucleoprotein.

núcula (*f.*) nutlet.

nudez[a] (*f.*) nudity, nakedness.

nudibrânquio -quia (*adj.*, *Zool.*) nudibranch.

nudicaudato -ta (*adj.*, *Zool.*) nudicaudate.

nudicaule (*adj.*, *Bot.*) nudicaul.

nudifloro -ra (*adj.*, *Bot.*) nudiflorous.

nudípede (*adj.*) nudiped.

nudismo (*m.*) nudism.

nudista (*m.,f.*) nudist.

nuelo -la (*adj.*) newborn.

nuga (*f.*) trifle.

nugá (*f.*) nougat.

nugacidade (*f.*) triviality; futility; frivolity.

nugativo -va, nugatório -ria (*adj.*) nugatory; trifling, worthless.

nulidade (*f.*) nullity, invalidity; nonentity; a nobody.

nulificação (*f.*) nullification; nullifying.

nulificador -dora (*adj.*) nullifying.

nulípara (*adj., Med.*) nulliparous.
nulo –**la** (*adj.*) null, void, invalid; vain, useless, of no account; (*m.*) a good-for-nothing.—**de pleno direito,** null and void. **tornar**—, to nullify.
num(a) [*em+um(a)*] in a, on a.
nume (*m.*) numen.—**tutelar,** a tutelary spirit.
númeno (*m., Metaph.*) noumenon.
numeração (*f.*) numeration, numbering.
numerado –**da** (*adj.*) numbered; in numerical order.
numerador –**dora** (*adj.*) numerative; (*m.,f.*) numeràtor; (*f.*) a numbering machine.
numeral (*adj.*) numeral.
numerar (*v.t.*) to number; to enumerate.
numerário –**ria** (*adj.*) nummary, of or pert. to coins or money; (*m.*) coins, money, specie.—**para despesas,** expense money.
numerável (*adj.*) numerable.
numérico –**ca** (*adj.*) numerical.
número (*m.*) number (in any sense); numeral, digit.— **abstrato,** abstract number.—**complexo,** complex n.— **dígito,** digit.—**fracionário** or —**quebrado,** fractional n.— **ímpar,** odd n.—**inteiro,** whole n.—**misto,** mixed n.— **perfeito,** perfect n.—**quadrado,** square n.—**racional,** rational integer.—**redondo,** round n.—**sem conta,** innumerable. **ser um**—, (*colloq.*) to be a laughingstock. **em**—**de,** to the number of. **no**—**dos presentes,** among those present. **um sem**—**de vezes,** countless times.
numerosidade (*f.*) numerousness.
numeroso –**sa** (*adj.*) numerous.
numismata (*m.,f.*) numismatist.
numismático –**ca** (*adj.*) numismatic; (*f.*) numismatics.
numulite (*f., Zool., Paleontol.*) nummulite.
numulítico –**ca** (*adj.; m., Geol.*) nummulitic (limestone).
nunca (*adv.*) never, ever, not ever.—**jamais,** never.—**mais,**

never more, never again, no more.—**por**—, never. **agora ou**—, now or never. **antes tarde do que**—, better late than never. **como**—, as never before. [**Está bonita como**—, I never saw you looking so pretty.] **mais do que**—, more than ever. **melhor que**—, better than ever. **quase**—, hardly ever. **um**—**-acabar de,** a never-ending of.
núncia (*f.*) messenger. Cf. NÚNCIO.
nunciativo –**va** (*adj.*) nunciative, nunciatory.
nunciatura (*f.*) nunciature.
núncio (*m.*) Papal nuncio; a messenger.
nuncupativo –**va** (*adj.*) nuncupative.
nunes (*adj.; colloq.*) odd (not even); (*m.*) odd number.
nupcial (*adj.*) nuptial, bridal.
núpcias (*f.pl.*) nuptials, wedding.
nuquear (*v.t.*) to slaughter cattle by jabbing a prong into the base of the brain.
nutação (*f., Bot., Astron.*) nutation.
nutante (*adj.*) nodding.
nutar (*v.i.*) to nod.
nuto (*m.*) an approving nod of the head.
nutria (*f.*) coypu (*Myocastor coypus*).
nutrição (*f.*) nutrition; nutriment; nourishment; food.
nutricionista (*adj.*) nutritional; (*m.,f.*) nutritionist.
nutrido –**da** (*adj.*) well-fed.
nutriente (*adj.*)=NUTRITIVO.
nutrimental (*adj.*) nutrimental, nutritious.
nutrimento (*m.*) nutriment, nourishment, food.
nutrir (*v.t.*) to nourish, nurture, feed; to cherish; (*v.r.*) to nourish (feed) oneself (**de, com,** with).
nutritivo –**va** (*adj.*) nutritive, nutritious, nourishing.
nutriz (*f.*) wet nurse [=AMA-DE-LEITE].
nuvem (*f.*) cloud; moving throng.
N.W. or **N.O.**=NOROESTE (northwest).

O

O, o, the 14th letter of the Portuguese alphabet.
O.=OESTE (West).
o/=ORDEM ([commercial] order).
o (*art. masc.*) the; (*dir. obj. pron.*) him; (*dem. pron.*)' he (**que,** who); the one (**que,** who, which, that).
ó (*interj.*) Oh! Hey! **Ó de casa!** Hello in there! Anybody home?
oacaju [ú] (*m.*)=CAJUEIRO.
oacauã (*f.*)=ACAUÃ.
oaiana (*m.,f.*) an Indian of a Cariban tribe (Oyana) dwelling on the Jari and Paru Rivers, northern tributaries of the Amazon. Var. OIANA.
Oaio (*m.*) Ohio.
oanaçu [u] (*m.*) a palm (*Orbignya spectabilis*).
oanani [í] (*m.*) the hog-plum or Guiana symphonia (*S. globulifera*).
oasiano –**na, oásico** –**ca** (*adj.*) of, pert. to, or like an oasis.
oásis (*m.*) oasis.
ob.=OBRA(S)=[literary] work(s).
oba (*f.*)=OPA.
obarana (*f.*) the chiro (*Elops saurus*), a tarponlike fish c.a. ROBALO-DE-AREIA.
obcecação (*f.*) obduracy; opinionatedness.
obcecado –**da** (*adj.*) blind, unreasoning; infatuated.
obcecar (*v.t.*) to blind (to the truth); to obfuscate; to lead into error; to root in error.
obcomprimido –**da** (*adj., Bot.*) obcompressed.
obcônico –**ca** (*adj.*) obconical.
obcordado –**da, obcordiforme** (*adj., Bot.*) obcordate.
obducção (*f., Med.*) obduction, autopsy.
obduração (*f.*) obdurateness, obduracy.
obdurado –**da** (*adj.*) obdurate.
obdurar (*v.t.*) to make obdurate; (*v.r.*) to become so.
obeba (*m.*) a drumfish.
obed.=OBEDIENTE (obedient [servant]—used in closing a letter).
obedecedor –**dora** (*adj.*) obeying; obedient.
obedecer (usually with **a**) (*v.i.*) to obey, mind, comply with, yield to.—**à sua inclinação,** to follow one's bent.

obediência (*f.*) obedience, compliance, submission.— **cega,** or **passiva,** blind obedience.
obediente (*adj.*) obedient (**a, to**); compliant (**a,** with); submissive; docile.
obelisco (*m.*) obelisk.
oberado (*adj.*) debt-ridden; overloaded with expenses.
oberar (*v.t.*) to load (**-se,** oneself) with debt.
obesidade (*f.*) obesity.
obeso –**sa** [é] (*adj.*) obese.
óbice (*m.*) impediment, obstacle.
óbito (*m.*) death. **atestado de**—, death certificate.
obituário –**ria** (*adj.; m.*) obituary; (*m.*) mortality, death rate.
objeção (*f.*) objection; opposition, obstacle. **pôr**—**s a,** to object to.
objetar (*v.t.*) to object, produce an argument against, present as an objection, oppose; (*v.i.*) to object to.
objetiva (*f.*) see under OBJETIVO.
objetivação (*f.*) objectifying.
objetivar (*v.t.*) to objectify; fig., to have as an objective; to have in view (a purpose, an end).
objetividade (*f.*) objectivity.
objetivo –**va** (*adj.*) objective, non-subjective; (*m.*) object, end, aim, purpose, goal. **sem**—, aimlessly; (*f.*) lens, object glass.
objeto (*m.*) object, thing; purpose, motive; (*Gram.*) object.—**de estimação,** a prized possession.—**de fantasia,** a curio.—**s de primeira necessidade,** prime necessities.
objurgação (*f.*) objurgation, severe rebuke, upbraiding.
objurgado –**da** (*adj.*) berated, upbraided.
objurgar (*v.t.*) to objurgate, berate, upbraid, scold.
objurgatório –**ria** (*adj.*) objurgatory; (*f.*) objurgation; upbraiding.
oblação (*f.*) oblation, offering, sacrifice.
oblanceolado –**da** (*adj., Bot.*) oblanceolate.
oblata (*f.*) oblation.
oblato (*m., R.C.Ch.*) oblate.
oblíqua (*f.*) see under OBLÍQUO.
obliquângulo –**la** (*adj.*) oblique-angled.

obliquar [9] (*v.i.*) to move in an oblique direction.
obliqüidade (*f.*) obliquity.
oblíquo –qua (*adj.*) oblique, slanting; lopsided, awry; indirect; (*f.*) oblique line.
obliteração (*f.*) obliteration.
obliterado –da (*adj.*) obliterated, effaced, forgotten.
obliterar (*v.t.*) to obliterate; to blot out from memory.
oblívio (*m.*) oblivion, forgetfulness.
oblongo –ga (*adj.*) oblong.
oboé (*m.*, *Music*) oboe.
oboísta (*m.*,*f.*) oboist.
óbolo (*m.*) obolus; fig., alms, dole; widow's mite.
obóveo –vea, oboval, obovalado –da (*adj.*) obovate.
obovóide (*adj.*) obovoid.
obra (*f.*) work, toil, labor; opus; literary composition; scientific achievement; artistic performance; a building under construction or repair; a bowel movement.—capital, masterpiece.—de arte, a work of art; a road structure, such as a bridge or tunnel.—de cantaria, stonework, masonry.—de carregação, a botch job.—de consulta, a reference work.—de empreitada, a contract job; a hurry-up job.—de encomenda, a made-to-measure piece of work.—de fancaria, shoddy work.—de misericórdia, an act of charity.—espúria, spurious work.—grossa, any crude piece of work.—s mortas, (*Naut.*) the part of the hull above the water line.—s pias, good works.—póstuma, a posthumous work.—prima, masterpiece.—s públicas, public works.—s vivas, (*Naut.*) the part of the hull below the water line. Mãos à—! Let's get to work! meter (or pôr) mãos à—, to set to work; to put one's shoulder to the wheel.
obrador –dora (*adj.*) working; (*m.*,*f.*) worker.
obrageiro (*m.*) logger.
obragem (*f.*) work [= OBRA].
obrar (*v.t.*) to produce, originate; (*v.i.*) to work, to act, operate; to defecate.—milagres, to perform miracles.
obreira (*f.*) a woman worker; a worker bee.
obreiro (*f.*) worker, workman, laborer.
obrigação (*f.*) obligation, responsibility, duty; task; bond. Primeiro a—, depois a devoção, Duty before pleasure.
obrigacionista (*m.*,*f.*) bondholder.
obrigado (*adj.*) obliged, compelled; bound; obligatory. Muito —! Much obliged; Thank you. Foi—a falar, He was forced to speak.
obrigar (*v.t.*) to oblige, compel, constrain; to obligate, bind; (*v.r.*) to bind oneself (a, to); to undertake to; to assume an obligation.
obrigatário (*m.*), –ria (*f.*) = OBRIGACIONISTA.
obrigatoriedade (*f.*) obligatoriness.
obrigatório –ria (*adj.*) obligatory, binding, compulsory.
obr.mo = OBRIGADÍSSIMO (most obliged).
obr.o = OBRIGADO (obliged).
obs. = OBSERVAÇÃO (remark).
obscenidade (*f.*) obscenity; an obscene word, expression or act; a lewd picture.
obsceno –na (*adj.*) obscene, lewd; scurrilous.
obscurante (*adj.*) obscuring; (*m.*,*f.*) obscurant.
obscurantismo (*m.*) obscurantism.
obscurantista (*adj.*; *m.*,*f.*) obscurantist.
obscurecer (*v.t.*) to obscure, darken, cloud; to obfuscate; to hide, disguise.
obscurecido –da (*adj.*) obscured; obscure; forgotten.
obscurecimento (*m.*) darkness.
obscuridade (*f.*) obscurity; darkness of meaning; namelessness; seclusion.
obscuro –ra (*adj.*) obscure, dark; unintelligible; secluded.
obsedante, obsediante (*adj.*) obsessive.
obsedar, obsediar (*v.t.*) to beset; to obsess; to importune, harass.
obseqüente (*adj.*) compliant, dutiful.
obsequiador –dora [ze] (*adj.*) accommodating, obliging; (*m.*,*f.*) one who bestows a favor or a present.
obsequiar [ze] (*v.t.*) to favor; to display courtesy (kindness, attention) toward; to present with.
obséquias [zé] (*f.pl.*) obsequies, funeral rites.
obséquio [zé] (*m.*) favor, kindness.
obsequiosidade [ze] (*f.*) kindliness, complaisance. [But not obsequiousness, which is SERVILISMO.]
obsequioso –sa [ze] (*adj.*) courteous, kind, obliging. [But not obsequious, which is SERVIL, SUBSERVIENTE.]
observação (*f.*) observation; annotation; remark, comment.
observador –dora (*adj.*) observing; heedful; observant;

(*m.*,*f.*) observer; spectator: astronomer; weather observer.
observância (*f.*) observance.
observante (*adj.*) observing, obedient; (*m.*) Observant (of St. Francis).
observar (*v.t.*,*v.i.*) to observe, look at; to notice, watch; to obey, comply with; to make a remark (a, to).
observatório (*m.*) observatory; observation post.—meteorológico, weather station.
observável (*adj.*) observable.
obsessão (*f.*) obsession; fixed idea.
obsessivo –va (*adj.*) obsessive [= OBSESSOR].
obsesso –sa (*adj.*) obsessed, tormented, haunted; (*m.*,*f.*) one who is possessed.
obsessor –sora (*adj.*) obsessive; (*m.*,*f.*) one who besets or harasses another.
obsidente (*adj.*) obsessive; (*m.*,*f.*) besieger.
obsidiana (*f.*, *Petrog.*) obsidian.
obsidiar (*v.t.*) to besiege; to beset, haunt; to harass.
obsidional (*adj.*) of or pert. to a siege; besetting.
obsolescência (*f.*) obsolescence.
obsoletar (*v.t.*) to render obsolete.
obsoletismo (*m.*) obsoleteness.
obsoleto –ta (*adj.*) obsolete; outmoded.
obstaculizar (*v.t.*) to hinder, impede.
obstáculo (*m.*) hindrance, impediment, obstacle, difficulty, drawback; hitch, snag, stumbling block; barrier.
obstância (*f.*) obstacle, hindrance.
obstante (*adj.*) hindering, obstructive. nada, or não,—, however, nevertheless, though, notwithstanding, despite.
obstar (*v.t.*) to obstruct, hinder, impede, oppose. Nada obsta que aquilo se faça, There is nothing to prevent its being done.
obstativo –va (*adj.*) obstructive.
obstétrica, obstetrícia (*f.*) obstetrics.
obstetrício –cia (*adj.*) obstetric.
obstétrico –ca (*adj.*) obstetric.
obstetriz (*f.*) midwife [= PARTEIRA].
obstinação (*f.*) obstinacy, doggedness; cussedness; tenaciousness.
obstinado –da (*adj.*) obstinate, stubborn; opinionated.—no êrro, perverse.
obstinar (*v.t.*) to make obstinate; (*v.r.*) to be obstinate, self-willed.—se em, to persist in (error).
obstipação (*f.*, *Med.*) obstipation.
obstrução (*f.*) obstruction; counteraction, opposition.
obstrucionismo (*m.*) obstructionism; filibuster.
obstrucionista (*m.*,*f.*) obstructionist; filibuster.
obstruir [72] (*v.t.*) to obstruct, clog, block; to choke (up); to hinder, impede; to filibuster.
obstrutivo –va (*adj.*) obstructive, hindering.
obstrutor –tora (*adj.*) obstructive; (*m.*,*f.*) obstructor.
obtemperar (*v.i.*) to reply mildly; to acknowledge, agree; to acquiesce, assent; to obey.
obtenção (*f.*) obtainment, attainment, acquisition, acquirement.
obtentor –tora (*adj.*) obtaining; (*m.*,*f.*) obtainer.
obter [78] (*v.t.*) to obtain, attain, get, acquire; to succeed.
obtestar (*v.t.*) to call to witness; to beseech; to provoke, incite.
obtido –da (*adj.*) obtained, achieved.
obtundente (*adj.*) obtundent.
obtundir (*v.t.*) to obtund, blunt, dull, deaden.
obturação (*f.*) obturation, stopping up, closing (of a cavity); filling (of a tooth).
obturador –dora (*adj.*) obturator; (*m.*) obturator, that which closes, (stops, seals, plugs) an opening; shutter (of a camera); (*Ordn.*, *Surg.*, *Anat.*) obturator.
obturar (*v.t.*) to obturate, stop up, seal, close, plug (an opening). —um dente, to fill a tooth, or to have one filled.
obtusado –da (*adj.*) obtuse [leaf, petal].
obtusângulo –la (*adj.*) obtuse-angled.
obtusão (*f.*) obtuseness, stupidity; dullness.
obtusidade (*f.*) obtuseness; dullness.
obtusífido –da (*adj.*; *Bot.*) obtusifid.
obtusifoliado –da, obtusifólio –lia (*adj.*; *Bot.*) obtusifolius.
obtusilobulado –da (*adj.*; *Bot.*) obtusilobous.
obtusirrostro –tra (*adj.*; *Zool.*) obtusirostrate.
obtuso –sa (*adj.*) obtuse, blunt; dull, stupid; thickskulled. ângulo—, obtuse angle.
obumbrado –da (*adj.*) darkened (as by shadow).
obumbrar (*v.t.*) to shade; darken; cloud.
obus [-es] (*m.*) howitzer.

obverso (*m.*) obverse [= ANVERSO].
obviar (*v.t.*) to obviate, preclude, prevent; to oppose; to intervene.
obviável (*adj.*) that can be obviated.
óbvio –via (*adj.*) obvious, evident, plain, clear.
obvir [82] (*v.i.*) to escheat.
oca (*f.*) primitive Ind. hut; wood sorrel (*Oxalis tuberosa*); = OCRA.
ocara (*f.*) open space in an Indian village.
ocarina (*f.*) ocarina, "sweet potato."
ocasião (*f.*) occasion, opportunity; circumstances, juncture; incidental cause; motive, reason. **A—faz o ladrão,** Opportunity makes the thief. **aproveitar a—favorável,** to strike while the iron is hot; to make hay while the sun shines. **em todas as—s,** on all occasions; at all times. **negócio de—,** a rare business opportunity. **por—de,** on the occasion of. **quando se der a—,** when the opportunity presents itself.
ocasional (*adj.*) occasional, incidental; causative.
ocasionar (*v.t.*) to occasion, cause, give rise to.
ocaso (*m.*) setting of the sun; decline; the west; end of life.
occipício (*m.*, *Anat.*) occiput. Var. OCCIPÚCIO.
occipital (*adj.*; *m.*) occipital.
oceânico –ca (*adj.*) oceanic, marine; Oceanian.
oceano –na (*adj.*) oceanic; (*m.*) ocean; fig., immense expanse.
oceanografia (*f.*) oceanography.
oceanográfico –ca (*adj.*) oceanographic.
oceanografista (*m.*,*f.*) oceanographist.
oceanógrafo –fa (*m.*,*f.*) oceanographer.
ocelado –da (*adj.*) ocellated.
océleo –lea (*adj.*, *Zool.*) ocellar.
ocelífero –ra (*adj.*) ocelliferous.
ocelo (*m.*, *Zool.*) ocellus.
ocelote (*m.*) ocelot (*Felis pardalis*).
ocidental (*adj.*) occidental, western.
ocidentalidade (*f.*) occidentality.
ocidentalismo (*m.*) Occidentalism.
ocidentalista (*m.*,*f.*) Occidentalist.
ocidentalização (*f.*) Occidentalization.
ocidentalizar (*v.t.*) to Occidentalize.
ocidente (*m.*) occident, west.
ócimo (*m.*, *Bot.*) basil (*Ocimum*).
ócio (*m.*) idleness; laziness; leisure time, spare time.
ociosidade (*f.*) idleness; laziness; vagrancy.
ocioso –sa (*adj.*) otiose, idle, indolent, lazy; (*m.*,*f.*) idler.
ocípoda (*f.*) a genus (*Ocypode*) of swift-running crabs.
oclocracia (*f.*) mob rule.
oclofobia (*f.*) morbid fear of crowds.
oclusal (*adj.*, *Anat.*, *Dent.*) occlusal.
oclusão (*f.*) occlusion; closing or shutting; (*Chem.*) occlusion; absorption of gases; (*Med.*) occlusion.—**intestinal,** volvulus.—**das coronárias,** coronary occlusion.
oclusivo –va (*adj.*) occlusive.
ocluso –sa (*adj.*) occluded; closed (in, off, up, out).
oclusor –sora (*adj.*) occluding.
ôco –ca (*adj.*) hollow; void; vain, unreal; trivial; useless; (*m.*) hole, hollow.—**da mão,** hollow of the hand.—**do mundo,** faraway lands.
oconita (*f.*, *Elec.*) okonite.
ocorrência (*f.*) occurrence, incident, event.
ocorrente (*adj.*) occurrent.
ocorrer (*v.i.*) to occur, happen, take place, come to pass; to come to mind, present itself.—**a,** to meet (needs, expenses). **não me ocorreu que,** it did not occur to me that. **ocorreu, ocorreram,** there occurred.
ocótea (*f.*, *Bot.*) a large genus (*Ocotea*) of tropical trees and shrubs of the laurel family.
ocotona (*f.*, *Zool.*) the pikas (*Ochotona*).
ocra, ocre (*f.*) ocher.
ocráceo –cea (*adj.*) ocherous.
ócrea (*f.*, *Bot.*) ocrea.
ocreoso –sa (*adj.*) ochraceous, ocherous.
ocrocarpo –pa (*adj.*; *Bot.*) ochrocarpous, yellow-fruited.
ocroíta (*f.*, *Min.*) ochroite, cerite [= CERITA].
ocrólito (*m.*, *Min.*) ochrolite.
ocroma (*f.*) balsa or tropical American corkwood (*Ochroma lagopus*), c.a. PAU-DE-JANGADA.
octaédrico –ca, octaedriforme (*adj.*) octahedral.
octaedrita (*f.*, *Min.*) octahecrite, anatase [= ANATÁSIO].
octaedro (*m.*) octahedron.
octana (*f.*), –no (*m.*, *Chem.*) octane.
octangular (*adj.*) octangular; octagonal.
octílio, octilo (*m.*, *Chem.*) octyl.
octingentésimo –ma (*adj.*) eighthundredth.

octípede (*adj.*; *Zool.*) octipede, eight-footed.
octodáctilo –la (*adj.*; *Zool.*) octodactylous.
óctodo (*m.*, *Elec.*) octode tube.
octófido –da (*adj.*; *Bot.*) octofid.
octófilo –la (*adj.*; *Bot.*) octophyllous.
octogenário –ria (*adj.*; *m.*,*f.*) octogenarian.
octogésimo –ma (*adj.*) eightieth.
octógino –na (*adj.*; *Bot.*) octogynous.
octogonal (*adj.*) octagonal, eight-sided.
octógono –na (*adj.*) octagonal; (*m.*) octagon.
octopétalo –la (*adj.*; *Bot.*) octopetalous.
octópode (*adj.*; *m.*, *Zool.*) octopod; (*m.pl.*) the Octopoda (octopuses, etc.).
octorum, octoruno –na (*adj.*; *m.*,*f.*) = OITAVÃO.
octose (*f.*, *Chem.*) octose.
octossépalo –la (*adj.*; *Bot.*) octosepalous.
octossílabo –ba, octossilábico –ca (*adj.*) octosyllabic.
octostilo (*m.*, *Arch.*) octostyle.
óctuplo –pla (*adj.*) octuple, eight-fold.
oculado –da (*adj.*) having eyes; ocellated, spotted.
ocular (*adj.*) ocular, visual. **globo—,** eyeball. **testemunha—,** eyewitness; (*m.*,*f.*) ocular; eyepiece (of an optical instrument).
oculista (*m.*,*f.*) oculist, eye specialist; optician; (*adj.*) oculistic.
óculo (*m.*) spy glass; a "bull's-eye" window; (*pl.*) eyeglasses, spectacles.—**s de proteção,** goggles.
ocultação (*f.*) occultation, concealment.
ocultador –dora (*adj.*) concealing; (*m.*,*f.*) concealer.
ocultante (*adj.*) concealing.
ocultar [24] (*v.t.*) to conceal, hide, secret; to dissemble, disguise; to keep secret; (*v.r.*) to hide.—**a verdade,** to hold back the truth.
ocultas (*f.pl.*) **às—,** covertly, secretly.
ocultismo (*m.*) occultism.
ocultista (*m.*,*f.*) occultist.
oculto –ta (*adj.*) occult, hidden; mystical.
ocupação (*f.*) occupation, job, position, employment, business; possession, occupancy.
ocupado –da (*adj.*) occupied, taken; busy; active.
ocupador –dora (*adj.*) occupying; (*m.*,*f.*) occupier.
ocupante (*adj.*) occupying; (*m.*,*f.*) squatter.
ocupar (*v.t.*) to occupy; to inhabit, tenant.—**se de,** to busy oneself with.—**se em (com),** to concern oneself with.
odalisca (*f.*) odalisk.
ode (*f.*) ode.—**sinfonia,** symphonic poem.
odiar [16] (*v.t.*) to hate, abhor, detest; (*v.r.*) to hate oneself. **Odiam-se,** They hate each other.
odiento –ta (*adj.*) hateful, spiteful, rancorous.
ódio (*m.*) odium, hate, hatred; spite.—**figadal** (or **de morte**), deep-seated hatred.
odiosidade (*f.*) odiousness, hatefulness.
odioso –sa (*adj.*) odious, hateful; (*m.*) that which is hateful or hate-provoking; odiousness.
odisséia (*f.*) odyssey.
odógrafo (*m.*) odograph.
odologia (*f.*) odology, odic theory.
odometria (*f.*) odometry.
odômetro (*m.*) odometer.
odonatas (*m.pl.*) an order (*Odonata*) of dragonflies.
odontíase (*f.*) odontiasis; teething.
odontoblasta (*m.*, *Anat.*) odontoblast.
odontocetos (*m.pl.*) the Odontoceti (toothed-whales).
odontoclasta (*m.*, *Anat.*) odontoclast.
odontofia (*f.*) teething [= DENTIÇÃO].
odontóforo (*m.*) a genus (*Odontophorus*) of crested tropical quaillike birds.
odontogenia (*f.*, *Biol.*) odontogeny, odontogenesis.
odontoglosso (*m.*) a large genus (*Odontoglossum*) of tropical American orchids.
odontografia (*f.*) odontography.
odontógrafo (*m.*, *Mach.*) odontograph.
odontóide, odontoídeo –dea (*adj.*) odontoid.
odontólite (*f.*, *Dent.*) odontolith, tartar of the teeth; (*Min.*) odontolite.
odontologia (*f.*) odontology.
odontológico –ca (*adj.*) odontological.
odontologista (*m.*,*f.*) odontologist; dentist.
odontóstomo –ma (*adj.*; *Zool.*) odontostomatous, odontostomous.
odor [ôr] (*m.*) odor, smell, scent, fragrance.
odorante, odorífero –ra, odorífico –ca, odoroso –sa (*adj.*)

odorous, odoriferous, fragrant, perfumed, sweet-smelling.
odre (*m.*) wineskin; (*colloq.*) winebibber.
OEA = ORGANIZAÇÃO DOS ESTADOS AMERICANOS (Organization of American States; formerly, Pan American Union).
oeirana (*f.*) a Christmas bush (*Alchornea*); a willow (*Salix*).
oeraponga (*f.*) = ARAPONGA.
oersted (*m.*, *Elec.*) oersted.
oés, short for OESTE (west).
oés-nordeste (*m.*) west-northeast.
oés-noroeste (*m.*) west-northwest.
oés-sudoeste (*m.*) west-southwest.
oés-sueste (*m.*) west-southeast.
oeste (*m.*) west; westward; west wind.—**quarta a noroeste,** west by north.—**quarta a sudoeste,** west by south; (*adj.*) **de—**, west, westerly, western; (*adv.*) **a—, para—**, west, westerly, westward(s).
Of. = OFERECE(M) = offered by.
ofegante (*adj.*) panting, puffing, gasping; out-of-breath; anxious; yearning.
ofegar (*v.i.*) to pant, puff, breathe hard; to gasp; to pant after, thirst for; to be anxious.
ofêgo (*m.*) labored breathing; breathlessness.
ofegoso –sa, ofeguento –ta (*adj.*) = OFEGANTE.
Ofélia (*f.*) Ophelia.
ofender (*v.t.*) to offend, affront; to outrage; to spite; to wound, injure, hurt.—**se com,** to be offended by (with); to resent, take amiss.
ofendido –da (*adj.*) offended; "sore"; (*m.,f.*) offended person.
ofensa (*f.*) offense; wound, injury; affront, outrage; resentment.—**corporal,** bodily injury.
ofensivo –sa (*adj.*) offensive; injurious; aggressive; (*f.*) offense, attack, assault; offensive (position).
ofenso –sa (*adj.*) = OFENDIDO.
ofensor –sora (*adj.*) offending; (*m.,f.*) offender.
oferecedor –dora (*adj.*) offering; (*m.,f.*) one who offers.
oferecer (*v.t.*) to offer, present, proffer.—**se (a, para),** to volunteer; to occur, present itself.
oferecimento (*m.*) offer, proposal, proffer; offering.
oferenda (*f.*) offering; oblation.
oferendar (*v.t.*) to make an offering.
oferente (*adj.*; *m.,f.*) = OFERECEDOR.
oferta (*f.*) offer, bid; promise; gift; offering; l'envoi of a ballade [= ENVIO and REMATE].—**e procura,** supply and demand.
ofertar (*v.t.*) to present, proffer; to give, bestow.
ofertório (*m.*, *Eccl.*) offertory.
oficalcito (*m.*, *Petrog.*) ophicalcite.
oficiador –dora (*adj.*) officiating; (*m.,f.*) officiator, officiant.
oficial (*adj.*) official, formal, authorized; authentic; (*m.*) officer; official; artisan, skilled workman, craftsman, journeyman.—**às ordens,** a subaltern military or naval officer attached to the personal staff of a general, admiral, governor of a state, etc.—**da-sala** = CAPITÃO-DA-SALA (a plant).—**de diligências, de justiça,** a minor court official.—**de pintura,** a master (house) painter.—**de ronda,** officer of the guard.—**de quarto,** officer of the watch.—**diplomado,** a commissioned officer.—**do estado maior,** general staff officer.—**general,** (*Milit.*) general.—**inferior,** (*Milit.*) non-commissioned officer.—**marinheiro,** (*Navy*) petty officer.—**reformado,** retired officer.—**subalterno,** non-commissioned officer. **sub—**, chief petty officer.
oficialato (*m.*) officership.
oficialidade (*f.*) a body or staff of officers.
oficialismo (*m.*) officialdom; bureaucracy.
oficialização (*f.*) act of making official.
oficializado –da (*adj.*) officially established; officially recognized.
oficializador –dora (*adj.*) that makes official.
oficializar (*v.t.*) to make official; to sanction or approve officially.
oficiante (*adj.*) officiating; (*m.,f.*) officiant.
oficiar (*v.i.*) to officiate (at mass); to address an official letter to.
oficina (*f.*) workshop; print shop; machine shop. **navio—**, repair ship.
oficinal (*adj.*) officinal.
ofício (*m.*) art, trade, craft; service; occupation, job, walk of life; an official letter on government business;

(*Eccl.*) office (of the Mass, of the dead, etc.); (*pl.*) rites.—**divinos,** divine offices.
oficioso –sa (*adj.*) obliging, kind, accommodating; gratuitous. [Not an equivalent of officious in the sense of meddlesome, which is INTROMETIDO.] **advogado—**, a court-appointed lawyer. **em caráter—**, unofficially. **fonte—**, an unofficial but (government-) inspired source (of news). **mentira—**, a lie told to protect or benefit another.
oficlide (*m.*, *Music*) ophicleide.
ofídico –ca (*adj.*) ophidian.
ofídio –dia (*adj.*; *m.*) ophidian; (*m.pl.*) the Ophidia (snakes).
ofidismo (*m.*) snake poisoning.
ofiófago –ga (*adj.*) ophiophagous, snake-eating.
ofiolatria (*f.*) ophiolatry, snake worship.
ofiólito (*m.*, *Petrog.*) serpentine.
ofita (*f.*, *Petrog.*) ophite.
ofítico –ca (*adj.*, *Petrog.*) ophitic.
ofiúro (*m.*) an ophiuran (brittle star, basket fish or sea spider).
ófrio (*m.*, *Craniol.*) ophryon.
ófris (*m.*) a hardy terrestrial orchid (*Listera,* syn. *Ophrys*).
oftalmia (*f.*, *Med.*) ophthalmia.
oftálmico –ca (*adj.*) ophthalmic; ocular.
oftalmologia (*f.*) ophthalmology.
oftalmologista, oftalmólogo –ga (*m.,f.*) ophthalmologist.
oftalmômetro (*m.*, *Optics.*, *Physiol.*, *Med.*) opthalmometer.
oftalmoscopia (*f.*) ophthalmoscopy.
oftalmoscópio (*m.*) ophthalmoscope.
oftalmotorrinolaringologista (*m.,f.*) eye, ear, nose and throat specialist.
ofuscação (*f.*) obfuscation.
ofuscar (*v.t.*) to obfuscate, darken, cloud, overshadow, obscure; to dim, dull; to daze, dazzle; to outshine (others); (*v.r.*) to lose prestige.
ogervão (*m.*) = GERVÃO.
ogiva (*f.*, *Arch.*) ogive, pointed arch.
ogival (*adj.*) ogival.
ogiveta (*f.*, *Arch.*) foil.
ogra (*f.*) ogress.
ogro (*m.*) ogre.
Oh (*interj.*) Oh!
ohm (*m.*, *Elec.*) ohm.
ohmamperímetro, ohmamperômetro (*m.*, *Elec.*) ohmammeter.
ohmômetro, ohmímetro (*m.*, *Elec.*) ohmmeter.
oi–, see also under **ou–.**
oiana, variant of OAIANA.
oiça, oiço = OUÇA, OUÇO.
oídio (*m.*, *Plant Pathol.*) oidium, powdery mildew.
oiro (*m.*) & derivs. = OURO & derivs.
oit–, see also **out–.**
OIT = ORGANIZAÇÃO INTERNACIONAL DO TRABALHO (International Labor Organization).
oitante (*m.*, *Geom.*, *Astron.*) octant.
oitão (*m.*) property-line side wall. Var. OUTÃO.
oitava (*f.*) see under OITAVO.
oitavado –da (*adj.*) eight-sided.
oitavão, –vona (*adj.*; *m.,f.*) octoroon.
oitavar (*v.t.*) to divide into eight equal parts; (*Music*) to octave.
oitavo –va (*adj.*; *m.*) eighth; (*f.*) an eighth; a musical octave; one-eighth of an ONÇA, or 3.586 grams; the octave of a church feast; a former Portuguese gold coin; (*Fencing*) octave (a parry).
oitchi [chí] (*m.*, *Bot.*) a wax myrtle (*Myrica*).
oitenta (*adj.*; *m.*) eighty; (*m.*) an, or the, eightieth. **ou oito ou—,** all or nothing.
oitentão, –tona (*f.*) octogenarian.
oiti [tí] (*m.*) any of various tropical trees and plants of the family Rosaceae, esp. *Licania tomentosa*, c.a. OITI-DA-PRAIA, OITIZEIRO; also the fruit of this tree.
oiticica (*f.*) a medium-sized rosaceous tree (*Licania rigida*), native to northeastern Brazil, from whose seeds is extracted the oiticica oil of commerce.
oitiva (*f.*) hearing. **de—,** by hearsay.
oito (*adj.*; *m.*) eight. **ou—ou oitenta,** all or nothing.
oitocentos (*adj.*; *m.pl.*) eight hundred.
ojeriza (*f.*) ill will, antipathy; grudge.
ojerizar (*v.t.*) to dislike, detest (another person).
ojó (*m.*) witch doctor's incantation.
olá (*interj.*) Hello! Hey!

olada (*f.*) right moment. **estar de—**, to be in luck.
olaia, olaeira (*f.*) redbud, Judas tree (*Cercis siliquastrum*).
olandi [í] (*m.*) = GUANANDI, LANTIM.
olaria (*f.*) pottery (factory); brick factory.
Olavo (*m.*) Olaf.
oleáceo –cea (*adj.; Bot.*) oleaceous; (*f.pl.*) the Oleaceae (olive family).
oleado –da (*adj.*) oily; (*m.*) oilcloth.
oleaginoso –sa (*adj.*) oleaginous, oily; unctuous.
oleandrina (*f., Chem.*) oleandrin.
oleandro (*m., Bot.*) oleander (*Nerium*), c.a. ESPIRRADEIRA, OLENDRO, LOENDRO.
olear (*v.t.*) to smear or rub over with oil; to impregnate with oil. [But not to oil, in the sense of lubricate, which is LUBRIFICAR.]
olearia (*f.*) olive oil factory.
oléase (*f., Biochem.*) olease.
oleastro (*m.*) wild common olive (*Olea oleaster*), c.a. OLIVEIRA-BRAVA, AZAMBUJEIRO, ZAMBUJEIRO.
oleato (*m., Chem., Pharm.*) oleate.—**de chumbo**, lead oleate.—**de sódio**, sodium oleate.
olecrânio, olécrano (*m., Anat.*) olecranon.
oleento –ta [e-e] (*adj.*) oily; greasy; [= OLEOSO].
olefina (*f., Chem.*) olefin.
oléico –ca (*adj., Chem.*) oleic.
oleicultura [e-i] (*f.*) olive growing [= OLIVICULTURA].
oleífero –ra, oleificante (*adj.*) oleiferous; producing oil [seeds].
oleína (*f., Chem.*) olein.
oleiro (*m.*) a pottery worker; a baker or oven bird, so called because of its ovenlike nest built of clay; c.a. FORNEIRO, JOÃO-DE-BARRO.
olente (*adj.*) sweet-smelling.
ôleo (*m.*) oil.—**animal**, animal oil, animal fat.—**branco** = COPAÍBA-VERDADEIRA (a tree).—**bruto**, crude oil.—**canforado**, camphorated oil.—**combustível**, fuel oil.—**cru**, crude oil.—**de acetona**, acetone oil.—**de algodão**, cottonseed oil.—**de alizarina**, alizarin oil (sulphonated vegetable oil).—**de amêndoas**, almond oil.—**de amendoím**, peanut oil.—**de antraceno**, anthracene oil.—**de babaçu**, babassu oil, widely used in the manufacture of oleomargarine. [It is expressed from the kernels of *Orbygnia speciosa*, the largest palm in the Amazon basin.]—**de banana**, banana oil (isoamyl acetate).—**de batata**, fusel oil.—**de bergamota**, bergamot oil (used in perfumery).—**de caroço de algodão**, cottonseed oil.—**de cassia**, cassia oil.—**de cedro**, cedarwood oil.—**de côco**, coconut oil or butter.—**de cohune**, cohune(-nut) oil or fat.—**de colza**, rape oil.—**de copaíba**, copaiba oil.—**de eucalípto**, eucalyptus oil.—**de girassol**, sunflower oil.—**de laranja**, orange(-peel) oil.—**de limão**, lemon(-peel) oil.—**de linhaça**, linseed oil.—**de macaco** = CABRIÚVA-DE-MACACO (a tree).—**de macanilha**, oil of the peach-palm (*Gulielma gasipaes*).—**de mamona** or **de rícino**, castor oil.—**de milho**, maize oil, corn oil.—**de murumuru**, oil from the seeds of the murumuru astrocaryum palm (*A. murumuru*).—**de oiticica**, oiticica oil, derived from the seeds of the oiticica tree (*Licania rigida*).—**de oliva**, olive oil [= AZEITE DOCE].—**de palma**, palm (-kernel) oil.—**de parafina**, paraffin oil.—**de pinho**, pine oil.—**de rocha**, petroleum.—**de sapucaia**, sapucaia-nut oil.—**de transformador**, (*Elec.*) transformer oil.—**de tucum**, oil from the seeds of the tucuma astrocaryum palm (*A. tucuma*).—**de tungue**, tung oil.—**de uricuri**, oil from the kernels of the uricury palm (*Scheelea martiana*).—**de vetivert**, vetiver oil.—**de vitríolo**, oil of vitriol; sulfuric acid.—**essencial**, essential oil.—**fixo**, fixed oil.—**graxo** or **gordo**, fatty oil; liquid fat; fixed oil.—**lubrificante**, lubricating oil.—**mineral**, mineral oil.—**pardo** = CABRIÚVA-DE-MACACO (a tree).—**santo**, chrism, consecrated oil.—**secativo** or **secante**, drying oil.—**vegetal**, vegetable oil.—**vermelho**, any of several leguminous trees, esp. *Myrospermum erythroxylum*, which yields a fine-grained aromatic hardwood, very similar to mahogany.
oleoduto (*m.*) pipe line.
oleografia (*f.*) oleograph; oleography.
oleomargárico –ca (*adj., Chem.*) oleomargaric.
oleomargarina (*f., Chem.*) oleomargarine.
oleômetro (*m.*) oleometer.
oleoptênio (*m., Chem.*) elaeoptene.
oleorrefractômetro (*m.*) oleorefractometer.
oleoresina (*f.*) oleoresin.
oleosidade (*f.*) oiliness.

oleoso –sa (*adj.*) oily; greasy.
oleossacareto (*m., Pharm.*) oleosaccharum.
oleostearato (*m., Chem.*) oleostearate.
oleráceo –cea (*adj.*) oleraceous, esculent.
oleum (*m., Chem.*) oleum, fuming sulfuric acid.
olfação (*f., Physiol.*) olfaction.
olfatear (*v.t.*) to smell [= CHEIRAR].
olfato (*m.*) sense of smell; smell.
olga (*f.*) a strip of land; [*cap.*] Olga.
ôlha (*f.*) stew; pot.—**podrida**, Spanish stew; potpourri, hodgepodge.
olhada, olhadela (*f.*) look, glance, squint, ogle.
olhado –da (*adj.*) looked at; (*m.*) the evil eye [= MAU-OLHADO].
olhador –dora (*adj.*) seeing, looking; (*m.,f.*) seer, looker, observer.
olhal (*m.*) archway; touchhole (of an old cannon); (*Naut.*) iron ring to which ropes and cables are fastened.
olhar (*v.t.*) to look at, behold; to view; to look after, care for; to give attention to, consider; to beware of; to look into; (*v.i.*) to bud, sprout. (*v.r.*) to look at oneself (in the mirror); to look at one another; (*m.*) look, mien, aspect; expression of the eyes.—**a**, to look to (towards, at).—**(alguém) de frente**, to look directly at (someone).—**ao longe**, to look afar; to look into the future.—**com bons olhos**, to look upon with favor.—**com desprêzo**, to look at with disdain; to look down upon; sneer at.—**de cima**, to look down on.—**de esguelha** (or de lado, or de viés) **para**, to look askance at, glance at.—**em**, to look on.—**em tôrno de si**, to look about one.—**oblíquo**, side glance.—**para**, to look at.—**para as mulheres**, to ogle the women; leer at them.—**para o dia de amanhã**, or—**para o futuro**, to look out for a rainy day.—**pelo** (or com o) **rabinho do ôlho**, to look out of the corner of one's eye; to glance sideways at.—**por**, to look after, care for.—**por si**, to look out for oneself.—**raivoso**, or—**apunhalador**, a killing look; a dirty look.—**retrospectivo**, a backward glance. **A cavalo dado não se olham os dentes**, One does not look a gift horse in the mouth. **Antes que cases, olha o que fazes**, Look before you leap (into marriage). **atravessar (alguém) com o—**, to pierce (someone) with a look. **com o—desvairado**, wild-eyed. **de—abatido**, tired, worn-looking. **não—a nada**, to look at nothing.
olheiras (*f.pl.*) dark circles under the eyes.
olheiro (*m.*) overseer; in Rio de Janeiro, a public watchman of parked automobiles; a water spring; ant hole.
olhento –ta (*adj.*) having eyes or holes.
olhete [ête] (*m.*) a small eye or opening; kink in a rope or thread; an amber-fish (*Seriola carolinensis*), c.a. ARABAIANA, ÔLHO-DE-BOI.
olhiagudo –da (*adj.*) sharp-eyed.
olhibranco –ca (*adj.*) white-eyed.
olhimanco –ca (*adj.*) cock-eyed; squint-eyed; one-eyed.
olhinegro –gra, olhiprêto –ta (*adj.*) black-eyed.
olhirridente (*adj.*) of smiling aspect; having smiling eyes.
olhizaino –na (*adj.*) squint-eyed.
ôlho [olhos (ó)] (*m.*) eye; eyesight; attention; perception; eye of a tool handle; bud, eye (of a plant).—**clínico**, "clinical eye," i.e., a doctor's ability to diagnose at a glance. [Ter (bom) ôlho clínico, to be shrewd (in any appraisal or conclusion); to size up in a hurry.]—**d'água**, spring (of water).—**da rua**, the middle of the street. [O senhorio o pôs no—da rua, His landlord threw him out. Perdeu o emprêgo, está no—da rua, He lost his job and is on his uppers. Ponha-se no—da rua! Get the hell out of here! pôr alguém no—da rua, to give someone the bounce; to kick someone into the street; to turn someone out of doors.]—**de-boi**, (*Arch.*) oeil-de-boeuf, bull's-eye [but not center of a target which is MÔSCA DO ALVO]; the first Brazilian postage stamp. [It was issued in 1843 and has a design suggestive of a bull's-eye]; the giant hyacinth bean (*Dolichos giganteus*), c.a. MUCUNÃ-DO-MATO; the longan (*Euphoria longan*); (*Zool.*) an amber-fish (*Seriola lalandi*), c.a. ARABAIA, ARABAIANA, PINTAGOLA, TAPIREÇA; another amber-fish (*Seriola dorsalis*), c.a. OLHETE.—**de-cabra**, an early Brazilian postage stamp [1845]; (*Bot.*) kinds of Ormosia; red buckeye (*Aesculus pavia*).—**de-cabra-miúdo**, the least rhynchosia (*R. minima*).—**de-cabra-verde**, an apes-earring (*Pithecellobium langsdorfii*), c.a. RAPOSEIRA.—**de-cão**, (*Zool.*) the common big-eye or catalufá (*Priacanthus arenatus*), c.a. ÔLHO-DE-VIDRO, ÔLHO-DO-DIABO, MARIQUITA, IMPERADOR, PIRANEMA.—**de-fogo**, (*colloq.*) an albino person; a gray mullet (*Mugil brasiliensis*), c.a.

PARATI-FOGO; the head-and-tail light (*Hemigrammus ocellifer*), a popular aquarium fish.—-**de-gato**, (*Bot.*) the nickernut caesalpinia (*C. crista*), c.a. BONDUQUE; (*Min.*) cat's-eye (onyx).—**de lince**, lynx-eyed.—-**de-môcho** =LEITUGA (a plant).—-**de-perdiz**, (*Bot.*) pheasant's-eye adonis (*A. annua*).—**de-pombo**, the crab's-eye rhynchosia (*R. phaseoloides*); the Indian licorice or jequirity rosary pea (*Abrus precatorius*), c.a. JEQUIRITI.—**de-santa-luzia**, (*Bot.*) a spiderwort (*Tradescantia*), c.a. MARIANINHA, TRAPOERABA.—**de-sapiranga**, (*Med.*) ectropion; blepharitis.—**de-sapo**, (*colloq.*) popeye (exophthalmos).—**de-sogra**, lit., mother-in-law's eye: popular name for a confection consisting of a blanched almond resting on a sugared prune, thus suggestive of a baleful eye.—**de-tigre**, tiger's-eye (agate).—**de-vidro**, a squirrel fish (*Myriapristis jacobus*), c.a. FOGUEIRA, VOVÓ; also=ÔLHO-DE-CÃO (above).—**nela!** Keep your eye on her!—**nu**, naked eye.—**pisado**, black-and-blue eye.— **por—, dente por dente**, an eye for an eye, a tooth for a tooth; tit for tat.—**s amendoados**, almond eyes.—**s de sapiranga**, red-rimmed eyes.—**s empapuçados**, puffed eyes.—**s encovados**, hollow eyes.—**s injetados** (or **vermelhos**) bloodshot eyes.—**s fundos**, sunken (hollow) eyes, as of a sick or tired person.—**s papudos**, baggy eyes. —**s rasgados**, large eyes. **a—armado**, with a spyglass. **a—desarmado**, or **a—nu**, with the unaided or naked eye. **a—s cerrados**, with half-closed eyes. **a—s vistos**, patently; before one's very eyes. **abaixar os—s**, to drop (lower) the eyes. **abrir o—**, to keep an eye open, be on the alert. **abrir os—s**, to awaken; to look out for oneself. **abrir os—s alguém**, to open another's eyes; to undeceive (disallusion, disabuse) him. **alargar os—s**, to look off into the distance; to stretch one's eyesight. **ao primeiro lance de—s**, at first glance. **arregalar os—s**, to open wide the eyes; to stare. **até os—s**, up to one's neck; to the limit. **carregação dos—s**, conjunctivitis. **com os—s espantados**, with wild, staring eyes. **comer com os—s**, to gaze upon with lust or avarice. **dar com os—s em**, to catch sight of. **de—s azuis**, blue-eyed. **de um—só**, one-eyed. **enquanto o diabo esfrega um—**, in the twinkling of an eye; in a jiffy; in two shakes of a dog's tail. **estar com os—s em**, to have one's eyes on. **fechar os—s a**, to blink, connive at. **jogar areia nos—s de alguém**, to throw dust in someone's eyes (deceive him). **Longe dos—s, longe do coração**, Out of sight, out of mind. **não pregar—**, not to sleep a wink. **não abrir e fechar de—s**, in the twinkling of an eye. **O que os—s não vêem, o coração não sente**, What you don't know won't hurt you. **passar uma vista de—s em**, to give a quick glance at; to glance over (something). **Quatro—s vêem mais do que dois**, Two heads are better than one. **rabo**, or **rabinho, do—**, corner of the eye. **relancear os—s sôbre**, to glance at. **Tinha os—s rasos de lágrimas**, Her eyes were flooded with tears. **vendar**, or **tapar, os—s**, to blindfold. **ver com bons—s**, to look upon with favor; to approve of. [**não ver com bons—s**, to take a dim view of.]

olhudo -da (*adj.*) big-eyed; (*m.*) fish of the perch family (*Promatomus telescopus*).

olíbano (*m.*) olibanum; (*Bot.*) frankincense (*Boswellia*).

oligarca (*f.*) oligarch.

oligarquia (*f.*) oligarchy; dictatorship.

oligárquico -ca (*adj.*) oligarchic.

oligisto (*m., Min.*) oligist.

oligocarpo -pa (*adj.; Bot.*) oligocarpous.

oligoceno -na (*adj.; Geol.*) Oligocene.

oligocitemia (*f., Med.*) oligocythemia.

oligoclásio (*m., Min.*) oligoclase.

oligoclasita (*f.,m., Petrog.*) oligoclasite.

oligodinâmico -ca (*adj.; Chem., Physiol.*) oligodynamic.

oligófilo -la (*adj.; Bot.*) oligophyllous.

oligofrenia (*f.*) mental deficiency.

oliguria (*f., Med.*) oliguria.

olimpíada, olimpíade (*f.*) Olympiad.

olimpiano -na (*adj.; m.,f.*) Olympian.

olímpico -ca (*adj.*) Olympic.

Olimpo (*m.*) Olympus.

oliniáceo -cea (*adj.; Bot.*) oliniaceous.

olinto (*m.*) a genus (*Olynthus*) of sponges; an ascon.

olira (*f.*) a genus (*Olyra*) of grass.

olisiponense (*adj.*) Lisbonese [=LISBOETA].

oliva (*f.*) olive [poetical; the everyday term is AZEITONA]; olive tree; (*Anat.*) olivary body; (*Zool.*) an olive shell; [*cap.*] Olive.

oliváceo -cea (*adj.*) olivaceous.

olival (*m.*) olive grove.

olivar, olivário -ria (*adj.*) olivary, shaped like an olive.

olivedo [ê] (*m.*) =OLIVAL.

oliveira (*f.*) olive tree (*Olea*).—-**brava**, the wild common olive (*Olea europaea oleaster*), c.a. AZAMBUJEIRO, ZAMBUJO.—-**comum**, the common olive (*Olea europaea*).—-**da-china**, sweet osmanthus (*O. fragrans*).—**de-marrocos**, a false olive (*Elaeodendron*).—**do-paraiso**, oleaster or Russian olive (*Elaeagnus angustifolia*).

oliveiral (*m.*) olive grove [=OLIVAL].

Oliveiros (*m.*) Oliver.

olivel [-véis] (*m.*) =NÍVEL.

olivela (*f.*) a genus (*Olivella*) of olive shells.

olivenita (*f., Min.*) olivenite.

oliveranto (*m., Bot.*) a succulent (*Echeveria elegans*).

Olivério (*m.*) Oliver.

Olívia (*f.*) Olivia.

olivicultor -tora (*m.,f.*) olive grower.

olivicultura (*f.*) olivegrowing [=OLEICULTURA].

olivídeos (*m.pl.*) a family (*Olividae*) of olive shells.

olivífero -ra (*adj.*) oliviferous, producing olives.

oliviforme (*adj.*) oliviform, shaped like an olive.

olivila (*f., Chem.*) olivil.

olivina (*f., Min.*) olivine.

olmedal, olmedo (*m.*) elm grove.

olmeiro, olmo (*m.*) any elm, esp. *Ulmus campestris*.

ológrafo -fa (*adj.*) holographic [will].

olor (*m.*) odor, fragrance. [*Poetical*]

olorado -da, **olorante, olorente** (*adj.*) fragrant; perfumed.

olorífero -ra (*adj.*) =ODORÍFERO.

olorizar (*v.t.*) to render fragrant.

oloroso -sa (*adj.*) fragrant. [*Poetical*]

olvidadiço -ça (*adj.*) easily forgotten; forgetful.

olvidado -da (*adj.*) forgotten.

olvidamento (*m.*) forgetting.

olvidar (*v.t.,v.r.*) to forget.

olvidável (*adj.*) that can be, or should be, forgotten.

olvido (*m.*) forgetfulness; oblivion.

omágua (*m.,f.*) an Indian of the Omagua, a Tupian tribe of the Amazon; (*adj.*) of or pert. to this tribe.

omaso (*m., Zool.*) omasum.

omatídia (*f., Zool.*) ommatidium.

ombrear (*v.t.*) to shoulder (a burden).—**com**, to come up to the shoulder of, i.e., to equal (in merit).

ombreira (*f.*) doorpost, doorjamb; side piece of a window frame; shoulder of a garment; a shrug of the shoulders.

ombrino (*m.*) a food fish of the genus *Umbrina* (family *Sciaenidae*).

ombro (*m.*) shoulder.—**a** (**com, por**)—, shoulder to shoulder.—**armas!** (*Milit.*) Shoulder arms! **dar de** (or **encolher os**)—**s**, to shrug the shoulders.

ombrógrafo (*m., Meteorol.*) ombrograph.

ombrômetro (*m., Meteorol.*) ombrometer, rain gauge.

ômega (*m.*) Omega; fig., the end.

omeleta [lê] (*f.*) omelet.

ômicro[n] (*m.*) omicron.

ominoso -sa (*adj.*) ominous, inauspicious.

ômio (*m., Elec.*) ohm.

omiômetro (*m., Elec.*) ommeter [=OHMÔMETRO or OHMÍMETRO].

omissão (*f.*) omission, neglect, oversight, shortcoming, default.

omisso -sa (*adj.*) remiss, neglectful.

omitir (*v.t.*) to omit, neglect, overlook; to skip, pass without notice.

omni-, see **oni-**.

omofagia (*f.*) omophagia.

omófago -ga (*adj.*) omophagous.

omohioídeo -dea (*adj., Anat.*) omohyoid.

omóide (*m., Zool.*) omoideum.

omoplata (*f., Anat.*) scapula, shoulder blade.

omosterno (*m., Zool.*) omosternum.

o.m.q. = O MESMO QUE (the same as).

onagra (*f.*) an evening primrose (*Oenothera*); (*Zool.*) a female ONAGRO.

onagráceo -cea (*adj.*) onagraceous; (*f.pl.*) the evening primrose family (*Onagraceae*).

onagro (*m.*) onager, wild ass (*Equus onager*) of Asia.

onanismo (*m.*) onanism, masturbation.

onanista (*adj.*) masturbating; (*m.,f.*) masturbator.

onanizar-se (*v.r.*) to masturbate.

onça (*f.*) an old unit of weight (28.69 grams) equivalent to 1/16th LIBRA; also, the ounce avoirdupois (1/16th lb. or 28,3495 grams); any of various wildcats, pumas or

cougars.—**-d'água**, a kind of otter.—**-parda**, or—**-vermelha**, puma, cougar (*Puma concolor*).—**-pintada**, or—**-preta**, the jaguar (*Felis onca*), c.a. JAGUAR, JAGUARA, JAGUARETÊ, ACANGUÇU, CANGUÇU, CANGUÇU-AÇU, PINTADA. **do tempo da**—, from way back (very old).
onceiro (*m.*) wildcat-hunting dog.
oncídio (*m.*) = ONQUÍDIO.
oncinha (*f.*) = FORMIGA-CHIADEIRA.
oncocéfalo (*m.*) = PEIXE-MORCÊGO.
oncocerca (*f.*) a genus (*Onchocercus*) of round worms.
oncografia (*f.*) oncography.
oncologia (*f.*, *Med.*) oncology.
onda (*f.*) wave; billow; breaker, comber; tide, flood, surge; undulation; wave of vibration.—**acústica**, or—**sonora**, sound wave.—**amortecida**, damped wave.—**s caloríficas**, heat waves.—**celeste**, (*Radio*) sky wave.—**contínua**, (*Radio*) continuous wave (C.W.).—**curta**, short wave.—**de calor**, heat wave.—**s dirigidas**, radio beam.—**electromagnética**, electromagnetic wave.—**s hertzianas**, hertzian waves.—**de hiperfreqüência**, ultra high-frequency wave.—**s luminosas**, light waves.—**maré**, tide.—**modulada**, modulated wave.—**refletida**, reflected wave.—**s terrestres**, (*Radio*) ground waves.—**ultra-curta**, ultra-short wave. **ao sabor das**—**s**, at the mercy of the waves. **ir na**—, to be swept along by others; to be taken in.
ondâmetro (*m.*, *Radio*) wave meter.
ondatra (*m.*) muskrat.
onde (*adv.*) where, wherever.—**está o Zèzinho?** Where is Johnnie?—**fica o correio?** Where is the postoffice?—**há um bom café?** Where is there a good coffee shop?—**quer que**, wherever.—**quer que seja**, wherever it may be. **até**—, as far as. **Até**—**?** How far? **De**—**?** Where from? **de**—, whence, from which. **De**—**é o Sr.?** Where are you from? **de**—**em**—, from time to time; now and then. **Não sei para**—**voltar-me**, I don't know which way to turn. **para**—, where, wherever, whither. **por**—, along where, down which way; wherefore; where, wherever.
ondeado **-da** (*adj.*) wavy, billowy.
ondeante (*adj.*) waving, billowing; undulating.
ondear (*v.i.*) to wave, billow, roll; to undulate; (*v.t.*) to wave.—**os cabelos**, to give a (permanent) wave to the hair.
ondim (*m.*), **ondina** (*f.*) undine (water spirit).
ondógrafo (*m.*, *Elec.*) ondograph.
ondômetro (*m.*) ondometer, electric wavemeter; radio wave-length meter.
ondulação (*f.*) undulation; waviness; ripple.—**permanente**, permanent (hair) wave.
ondulado **-da** (*adj.*) wavy; rippled [= ONDEADO].
ondulamento (*m.*) = ONDULAÇÃO.
ondulante (*adj.*) undulant; waving; [= ONDEANTE].
ondular (*v.i.*) to undulate, ripple; (*v.t.*) to wave (the hair); [= ONDEAR].
ondulatório (*adj.*) undulatory.
onduloso **-sa** (*adj.*) undulating.
onerar (*v.t.*) to burden, oppress.
onerosidade (*f.*) onerousness.
oneroso **-sa** (*adj.*) onerous, burdensome, oppressive.
onfacita (*f.*, *Min.*) omphacite.
onfálico **-ca** (*adj.*; *Anat.*) omphalic.
ongleté [lê] (*m.*) graver, burin.
ônibus (*m.*) omnibus. **ponto do**—, bus stop.
onicocriptose (*f.*) ingrown nail.
onicofagia (*f.*) nail-biting.
onicolor (*adj.*) having all colors.
onidirecional (*adj.*, *Radio*) omnidirectional [waves].
oniforme (*adj.*) omnifarious.
onígeno **-na** (*adj.*) omnigenous.
onilíngue (*adj.*) omnilingual.
onímodo **-da** (*adj.*) omnimodous.
onipotência (*f.*) omnipotence.
onipotente (*adj.*) omnipotent; almighty; [*cap.*] (*m.*) the Omnipotent, the Almighty, God.
onipresente (*adj.*) omnipresent; ubiquitous.
oníquio (*m.*, *Zool.*) onychium; pulvillus.
onírico **-ca** (*adj.*) oneiric, pert. to dreams.
onirócrita (*m.*,*f.*) an interpreter of dreams.
oniromancia (*f.*) oneiromancy, interpretation of dreams.
onisciência (*f.*) omniscience.
onisciente (*adj.*) omniscient.
onisciforme (*adj.*; *Zool.*) onisciform.
onisco (*m.*) = ÔNIX (onyx), and BICHO-DE-CONTA (pill bug).
onividência (*f.*) omnividence, omnivision.

onividente (*adj.*) omnivident.
onívoro **-ra** (*adj.*) omnivorous.
ônix [ks] (*m.*) onyx.
onomástico **-ca** (*adj.*) onomastic; (*m.*,*f.*) onomasticon, list of proper names.
onomatologia (*f.*) onomatology; terminology.
onomatopéia (*f.*) onomatopoeia.
onomatopéico **-ca**, **onomatopaico** **-ca**, **onomatópico** **-ca** (*adj.*) onomatopoeic.
onopórdio (*m.*) the cottonthistles (*Onopordon*), esp. *O. acanthium*, the Scotch cottonthistle, c.a. POLIACANTO.
onosmódio (*m.*) marbleseed (*Onosmodium*).
onquídio (*m.*) a genus (*Onchydium*) of marine airbreathing slugs [= ONCÍDIO].
ontem (*adv.*) yesterday.—**à noite**, last night (evening).—**à tarde**, yesterday afternoon. **sòmente**—, only yesterday.
ontogênese, **ontogenia** (*f.*, *Biol.*) ontogeny, ontogenesis.
ontologia (*f.*) ontology.
ontologista (*m.*,*f.*) ontologist.
ONU = ORGANIZAÇÃO DAS NAÇÕES UNIDAS (Organization of United Nations).
ônus [*pl.* ônus] (*m.*) onus, burden, load; responsibility, obligation; heavy taxes. **sem**—, without cost; free of charge.
onze (*adj.*; *m.*) eleven;—**horas**, (*f.*, *Bot.*) rose moss, common portulaca (*P. grandiflora*).—**-letras** (*m.*) pander; (*f.*) procuress.
onzena (*f.*) see under ONZENO.
onzenar (*v.i.*) to practise usury.
onzenário **-ria** (*adj.*) usurious; (*m.*,*f.*) usurer.
onzeneiro **-ra** (*adj.*) usurious; meddlesome; (*m.*,*f.*) usurer; mischief-maker.
onzenice (*f.*) mischief, gossip, tale-bearing.
onzeno **-na** (*adj.*) eleventh [= UNDÉCIMO, DÉCIMO-PRIMEIRO]; (*f.*) eleven percent interest; usury.
ooblástio [o-o] (*m.*, *Biol.*) oöblast.
oocinese [o-o] (*f.*, *Biol.*) oökinesis.
oocinético **-ca** [o-o] (*adj.*) oökinetic.
oocineto [o-o] (*m.*, *Zool.*) oökinete.
oócito [o-ó] (*m.*, *Embryol.*, *Zool.*) oöcyte.
ooforectomia [o-o] (*f.*, *Surg.*) oöphorectomy.
ooforídea [o-o] (*f.*, *Bot.*) oöphoridium.
ooforite [o-o] (*f.*, *Med.*) oöphoritis, ovaritis.
oóforo [o-o] (*m.*) oöphoron, ovary.
oogâmico **-ca** [o-o] (*adj.*; *Biol.*) oögamous.
oogênese [o-o] (*f.*, *Biol.*) oögenesis [= OVOGÊNESE].
oogônio [o-o] (*m.*, *Biol.*) oögonium.
ooleina [o-o] (*f.*), **oolema** [o-o] (*m.*, *Zool.*) oölemma; (*Anat.*) zona pellucida.
oolítico **-ca** [o-o] (*adj.*) oölitic.
oólito [o-ó] (*m.*, *Petrog.*) oölite.
oologia [o-o] (*f.*) oölogy.
oomiceto [o-o] (*m.*, *Bot.*) oömycete.
oosfera [o-o] (*f.*, *Bot.*) oösphere.
oosporângio [o-o] (*m.*, *Bot.*) oösporangium.
oospório [o-o] (*m.*, *Bot.*) oöspore.
ooteca [o-o] (*f.*, *Zool.*) oötheca; (*Bot.*) sporangium.
opa (*f.*) sleeveless surplice.
ôpa (*interj.*) Oh! Wow!
opacidade (*f.*) opacity, opaqueness; darkness.
opacíssimo **-ma** (*absol. superl. of* OPACO) most opaque.
opaco **-ca** (*adj.*) opaque, obscure; drab.
opala (*f.*) opal; very fine muslin.—**comum**, common (resinous, or pitch) opal.—**nobre**, or—**preciosa**, noble, or precious, opal.—**xilóide**, wood opal.
opalescência (*f.*) opalescence, iridescence.
opalescente (*adj.*) opalescent, iridescent.
opalino **-na** (*adj.*) opaline; (*f.*) a genus (*Opalina*) of infusorians parasitic in amphibians.
opção (*f.*) option, choice. **direito de**—, freedom of choice.
ópera (*f.*) opera.—**-bufa**, opera buffa.—**-cômica**, comic opera.
operação (*f.*) operation.—**aritmética**, the process of addition, subtraction, etc.—**de alta cirurgia**, or—**de vulto**, major surgery.—**da talha**, lithotomy.—**de apendicite**, appendectomy.—**de baixa** (or **pequena**) **cirurgia**, minor surgery. **entrar em**—**s**, to open hostilities. **fazer**—, to have an operation; to be operated on. **mesa de**—, operating table, **sala de**—, operating room.
operado **-da** (*m.*,*f.*) one who has had a surgical operation; (*adj.*) operated. **Ela foi**—**ontem**, She was operated on yesterday.
operador **-dora** (*adj.*) operating; (*m.*) operator; surgeon.

—**cinematográfico,** a motion picture operator (projectionist).
operante (*adj.*) operating [=OPERATIVO].
operar (*v.t.*) to work, produce, effect, accomplish; (*v.i.*) to operate (surgically) on; to perform an operation (of any kind); (*v.r.*) to take place. [But not to operate a machine or a business, which is MANEJAR, FAZER FUNCIONAR (UMA MÁQUINA), DIRIGIR (UM NEGÓCIO).]
operariado (*m.*) the laboring classes, wage earners, proletariat.
operária (*f.*) a woman factory worker.
operário (*m.*) worker, workman, operative, (handi)craftsman, artisan.—**especializado** or **técnico,** technician.—**habilidoso,** skilled workman.—**industrial,** factory hand.
operativo –va (*adj.*) operative [=OPERANTE].
operatório –ria (*adj.*) operating.
operável (*adj.*) operable.
operculado –da (*adj., Bot., Zool.*) operculate.
opérculo (*m.*) cover, lid; (*Zool.*) operculum, gill-cover.
opereta [rê] (*f.*) operetta.
operosidade (*f.*) operoseness, toil, labor.
operoso –sa (*adj.*) laborious; industrious.
oph–, see under **of–.**
opiáceo –cea, opiado –da (*adj.*) opiate.
opiânico –ca (*adj., Chem.*) opianic.
opiar (*v.t.*) to opiate.
opiato (*m.*) opiate.
opilação (*f., Med.*) oppilation, obstruction, stopping up; a former name for hookworm disease [= ANCILOSTOMÍASE].
opilado –da (*adj.*) suffering from hookworm disease; (*m.,f.*) one so affected.
opilar (*v.t.*) to oppilate, stop up, obstruct (the liver, etc.).
opilência (*f.*) = EPILEPSIA.
opilião (*m.*) harvestman (daddy-longlegs).
opimo –ma [í] (*adj.*) rich, fertile.
opinante (*adj.; m.,f.*) holding, or one who holds, an opinion.
opinar (*v.i.*) to deem; to hold or express an opinion (sôbre, about); to express oneself.
opinativo –va (*adj.*) opinionative.
opinável (*adj.*) conjectural.
opinião (*f.*) opinion, view, conception. **mudar de—,** to change one's mind. **aferrado à sua—,** of fixed opinions, opinionated.
opiniático –ca (*adj.*) opinionated; conceited.
opinioso –sa (*adj.*) opinionated; stubborn; headstrong.
ópio (*m.*) opium.
opiofagia (*f.*) opium-eating.
opiófago –ga (*m.,f.*) opium eater.
opiomania (*f.*) opiumism.
opiômano –na, opiomaníaco –ca (*adj.*) opium-smoking or -eating; (*m.,f.*) an opium eater, opium smoker.
opíparo –ra (*adj.*) sumptuous, "swell".
opístio (*m., Anat.*) opisthion.
opistódomo (*m., Arch.*) opisthodome.
opistogástrico –ca (*adj.; Anat.*) behind the stomach.
opistoglifa (*f.*) an opisthoglyphous snake.
opistognatismo (*m., Craniology*) opisthognathism.
opistótico –ca (*adj.; Zool.*) opisthotic [bone or element].
opobalsameira (*f.*) Mecca myrrhtree, or balm of Gilead tree (*Commiphora opobalsamum*).
opobálsamo (*m.*) balsam of the balm of Gilead tree.
opodeldoque (*m., Pharm.*) opodeldoc, a soothing balm or liniment.
opoente, oponente (*adj.*) opposing, adverse; (*m.,f.*) opponent.
opopânace, opopânax [ks] (*m., Pharm., Bot.*) opopanax.
opor [63] (*v.t.*) to oppose.—**a,** to set against, put in opposition to; to contrast.—**se a,** to oppose, thwart; to act (go, run) counter to.
oportunidade (*f.*) opportunity, chance; favorable time, occasion.
oportunismo (*m.*) opportunism.
oportunista (*m.,f.*) opportunist; (*adj.*) opportunistic; expedient.
oportuno –na (*adj.*) opportune, appropriate, timely; expedient.
oposição (*f.*) opposition, antagonism; obstacle, hindrance; contrast. **em—a,** against.
oposicionismo (*m.*) obstructionism.
oposicionista (*adj.*) opposing; (*m.,f.*) a member of the opposition, of the "outs" (party out of power). [A member of the "ins" is a SITUACIONISTA.]

opositifloro –ra (*adj., Bot.*) oppositiflorous.
opositifólio –lia (*adj., Bot.*) oppositifolius.
opositipenado –da (*adj., Bot.*) oppositipinnate.
opositipétáleo –lea, oposipétalo –la (*adj., Bot.*) oppositipetalous.
opositipolar (*adj.*) oppositipolar.
opositisépalo –la (*adj., Bot.*) oppositisepalous.
opositor –tora (*adj.*) opposing; (*m.,f.*) opposer; opponent; candidate or competitor for a job.
oposto –ta (*adj.*) opposite, facing, over against; opposed, adverse; contrary; (*m.*) the contrary, opposite. **em sentido—a,** against.
opoterapia (*f.*) = ORGANOTERAPIA.
opressão (*f.*) oppression, hardship; tyranny, persecution; stifling.
opressivo –va (*adj.*) oppressive.
opresso –sa (*adj.*) oppressed.
opressor –sora (*adj.*) oppressing; (*m.,f.*) oppressor.
oprimido –da (*adj.; m.,f.*) oppressed (person).
oprimir (*v.t.*) to oppress; to scourge; to burden (com, with); (*v.i.*) to tyrannize over.
opróbrio (*m.*) opprobrium, ignominy, disgrace; contumely, scurrility.
oprobrioso –sa (*adj.*) opprobrious.
opsiômetro (*m.*) optometer.
optação (*f.*) choice; option.
optante (*adj.; m.,f.*) optant.
optar (*v.i.*) to opt., make a choice, to choose (entre, por, between).
optativo –va (*adj.*) optative.
ó[p]tico –ca (*adj.*) optic; (*m.,f.*) optician; (*f.*) optics. Cf. ÓTICO.
optígrafo (*m.*) optigraph.
optimates (*m.pl.*) optimates (nobles, aristocrats, magnates).
optimismo (*m.*) = OTIMISMO.
optimista (*adj.; m.,f.*) = OTIMISTA.
óptimo –ma (*adj.*) = ÓTIMO.
optoblástio (*m., Anat.*) optoblast.
optofone, optofônio (*m.*) optophone.
optograma (*m., Physiol.*) optogram.
optomeninge (*f., Anat., Zool.*) optomeninx, retina.
optometria (*f.*) optometry.
optometrista (*m.,f.*) optometrist.
optômetro (*m.*) optometer.
optótico –ca (*adj., Med.*) optotypes (reading chart).
opugnação (*f.*) oppugnancy, opposition, antagonism; attack.
opugnador –dora (*adj.*) oppugnant, opposing; antagonistic; contrary; (*m.,f.*) oppugner, opponent, adversary.
opugnar (*v.t.*) to oppugn, assail; to attack; to impugn.
opulência (*f.*) opulence, wealth, affluence; plenty; corpulence.
opulentar (*v.t.*) to enrich; (*v.r.*) to become opulent.
opulento –ta (*adj.*) opulent, rich; luxuriant; profuse; lavish.
opúncia (*f.*) prickly pear, cholla (*Opuntia*).
opunciáceas (*f.pl.*) = CACTÁCEAS.
opuscular (*adj.*) opuscular.
opúsculo (*m.*) opuscule, a small or petty work; a pamphlet.
oquenita (*f., Min.*) okenite.
ora (*adv., conj., interj.*) but, nevertheless, however; therefore; meanwhile; now. **Ora!** Well! Well now! Pooh! Come now! Fiddlesticks!—**bem,—mal,** sometimes well, sometimes badly; up and down (in health).—**bolas!** Nonsense! After all!—**essa!** Well now! That's a good one! The very idea!—**pois,** that being so.—**ri,—chora,** now laughing, now crying.—**se gosto!** Do I like it? What a question!—**um,—outro,** now one, then the other.—**vejamos,** Now let's see. **d'ora em diante,** henceforth. **por—,** for the present; for the time being.
oraca (*f.*) = ALMA-DE-GATO.
oração (*f.*) prayer; sermon; oration, address, speech; clause, sentence, proposition.
oracional (*adj.; Gram.*) of or pert. to a sentence.
oracioneiro –ra (*m.,f.*) one who goes from door to door offering prayers.
oracular (*adj.*) oracular.
oráculo (*m.*) oracle.
orada (*f., colloq.*) a wayside chapel.
orador –dora (*m.,f.*) orator, speaker; preacher.
oral (*adj.*) oral; spoken, verbal; vocal.
orangista (*m.*) Orangeman.
orangite (*f., Min.*) orangite.

orangotango (*m.*) orangutan.

ora-pro-nóbis (*m., R.C.Ch.*) "Pray for us"—refrain of a litany to the Virgin in the liturgy; (*Bot.*) the Barbados gooseberry (*Cereus aculeata*), c.a. ROSA-MADEIRA, JUM-BEBA; the common purslane (*Portulaca oleracea*), c.a. BELDROEGA.

orar (*v.i.*) to make a speech; to preach a sermon; to pray; (*v.t.*) to pray (**a**, to; **por**, for); to beseech.

orate (*m.*) lunatic, maniac, **casa de—s**, madhouse.

oratório –**ria** (*adj.*) oratorical; (*m.*) oratory, small chapel, place for private worship; (*Music*) oratorio; (*f.*) oratory.

orbe (*m.*) orb, sphere, globe.

orbicular (*adj.*) orbicular.

órbita (*f.*) orbit (of planet, etc.); scope (range, field) of personal activity; eye socket; (*Zool.*) the part surrounding the eye of a bird or insect.

orbitário –**ria** (*adj.*) orbital.

orca (*f.*) a killer whale (*Orcimus orca*).

orça (*f.*) guess, estimate; (*Naut.*) tack. **à—s**, roughly, by guess, more or less.

orçador –**dora** (*adj.*) estimating; guessing; (*m.,f.*) estimator.

orçamentário –**ria**, **orçamental** (*adj.*) budgetary. **verba—**, a fiscal appropriation; an item in the budget.

orçamento (*m.*) budget, fiscal estimate; estimated cost. **equilibrar o—**, to balance the budget.

orçaneta [ê] (*f.*) alkanet or dyer's alkanna (*Alkanna tinctoria*) whose root is a source of orcanet or alkannin.

orçanetina (*f., Chem.*) orcanet or alkannin, c.a. ANCUSINA.

orçar (*v.i.*) to estimate, compute, reckon (**em**, **por**, at, at about); to approximate; (*Naut.*) to luff, haul up.

orceína (*f., Chem.*) orcein.

orchata (*f.*) orgeat; a sweet cooling drink made from crushed melon seeds, almonds or barley.

orcina (*f.*), **orcinol** (*m., Chem.*) orcin(e), orcinol.

ordálio (*m.*) ordeal [but only in the primitive sense of a test (by water, fire, etc.) of guilt or innocence. In the modern sense, ordeal is PROVAÇÃO or TRANSE.]

ordeiro –**ra** (*adj.*) orderly; peaceable; (*m.,f.*) peace-loving, law-abiding person.

ordem [-ens] (*f.*) order, disposition, regularity, method; array, arrangement; rule, law; command, mandate; peace, quiet, discipline; religious order; rank, grade; (*Arch.*) order. [An order for goods is not **ordem** but PEDIDO or ENCOMENDA.]—**coríntia**, Corinthian order.— **da jarreteira**, Order of the Garter.—**de despejo**, eviction notice; a court order to vacate premises.—**de prisão**, warrant for arrest.—**do Banho**, Order of the Bath.—**do dia**, order of the day.—**dórica**, Doric order.—**jônica**, Ionic order.—**social**, social order.—**s maiores**, (*R.C.Ch.*) the major (holy, greater, or sacred) orders.—**s menores**, (*R.C.Ch.*) the minor orders.—**toscana**, Tuscan order. **ajudante de—s**, aide-de-camp. **às—s de**, under the orders of; at the disposal of. **às suas—s**, at your service. **até nova—**, until further orders. **por—**, in order, in succession. **sob—s**, under orders.

ordenação (*f.*) ordering; ordinance; (*Eccl.*) ordination.

ordenado –**da** (*adj.*) orderly; ordered; (*m.*) salary; stipend; (*f., Math.*) ordinate.

ordenador –**dora** (*adj.*) ordering; (*m.,f.*) orderer.

ordenança (*f.*) ordinance, regulation, command; (*Milit.*) orderly.

ordenar (*v.t.*) to put in order, arrange, assort, dispose; (*Eccl.*) to ordain; to command, enjoin, direct, bid, give an order to; (*v.i.*) to order; (*v.r.*) to take holy orders (**de**, as); to prepare oneself for (**para**, to).

ordenha (*f.*) milking (of a cow).

ordenhar (*v.t.*) to milk, (a cow, etc.).

ordinal (*adj.*) ordinal.

ordinário –**ria** (*adj.*) ordinary, customary; usual, frequent; commonplace, mediocre, average; bad, of poor quality; vulgar; low, common. **de—**, ordinarily, usually; (*m.*) that which is ordinary or habitual; a high church official; an ordinary of the Mass; (*f.*) (monthly, yearly) expenses; food allowance.

ordoviciano –**na** (*adj., Geol.*) Ordovician.

oréade (*f.*) oread, nymph.

orear (*v.t.*) to sun-dry (washed clothes, meat, etc.).

orégão [-gãos] (*m.*) common origanum, wild marjoram (*Origanum vulgare*).

orelha (*f.*) ear, esp. the external part. [The internal ear is OUVIDO.]; a lug or handle; (*Arch.*) volute (of a capital); (*pl.*) claws of a hammer; plowshares.—**de-burro**, (*Bot.*) prickly comfrey (*Symphytum asperum*); (*pl.*) dunce's

cap.—**de-cabra**, (*Bot.*) roundhead plantain (*Plantago lagopus*).—**de-gato**, (*Bot.*) a St. Johnswort (*Hypericum connatum*).—**de-lebre** = BEIJOS-DE-FREIRA (a plant).— **-de-macaco** = TIMBAÚBA.—**de-monge** = FÔLHA-DA-FOR-TUNA.—**de-negro**, an earpod tree (*Enterolobium ellipticum*), c.a. FAVELA-BRANCA.—**de-pau** = URUPÊ (a shelf fungus).—**de-porco** = CORAÇÃO-MAGOADO (a plant).— **-de-onça** = ABUTUA-GRANDE (a plant).—**de-rato**, a false pimpernel (*Lindernia sp.*); also = DOURADINHA.—**de-rato-dos-herbolários**, chickweed (*Stellaria media*).—**de-sapato**, tongue of a shoe.—**de-toupeira**, a starwort (*Stellaria sp.*), c.a. ALSINA, ESTELÁRIA.—**de-urso**, a glorybush (*Tibouchina sp.*); also, auricula primula.—**de-veado**, pickerelweed (*Pontederia cordata*).—**humana** = ASARO (wild ginger). **à—**, in whispers. **A palavras loucas,—s moucas**, (Turn) a deaf ear to foolish words. **andar**, or **estar**, **com a pulga atrás da—**, to smell a rat (be suspicious). **bater—s**, to run neck-and-neck. **de—s baixas**, abashed (lit., with drooping ears). **de—em pé**, wary, suspicious (lit., with ears pricked). **negócio de—**, an even trade.

orelhado –**da** (*adj.*) eared; (*f.*) an ear-pull.

orelhão (*m.*) an ear-pull.

orelhar (*v.t.*) to seize (an animal) by the ears.

orelheira (*f.*) animal's ears.

orelhudo –**da** (*adj.*) big-eared; bull-headed, "dumb"; (*m.*) a kind of large-eared bat; a donkey.

orélia (*f., Bot.*) common allamanda (*A. cathartica*).

orelina (*f., Chem.*) orellin.

oreodoxa [ks] (*f.*) the royal palm (*Roystonea*).

oreografia (*f.*) = OROGRAFIA.

orexia [ks] (*f.*) orexis (desire; appetite).

orexina [ks] (*f., Chem.*) orexin.

órfã, fem. of ÓRFÃO.

orfanar (*v.t.*) to orphan.

orfanato (*m.*) orphanage; orphan asylum.

orfandade (*f.*) orphanhood; orphans collectively.

orfão [-fãos] –**fã** [-fãs] (*adj.*) orphan; bereft of protection; (*m.,f.*) orphan, half-orphan; hence, one bereft of protection.—**de mãe**, motherless.—**de pai**, fatherless.

orfeão (*m.*) choral society.

orfeico –**ca** (*adj.*) orphean.

orfeonista (*m.,f.*) member of a choral society.

Orfeu (*m.*) Orpheus.

órfico –**ca** (*adj.*) Orphic; Orphean.

orga (*f.*) corn spurry (*Spergula arvensis*).

organdi [í] (*m.*) organdy.

organicismo (*m., Med., Biol., Philos., Social.*) organicism.

orgânico –**ca** (*adj.*) organic.

organismo (*m.*) organism; body.

organista (*m.,f.*) organist, organ player.

organização (*f.*) organization; organism.

organizado –**da** (*adj.*) having organic structure; organized; methodical.

organizador –**dora** (*adj.*) organizing; (*m.,f.*) organizer.

organizar (*v.t.*) to organize, constitute, dispose, arrange; to establish, systematize.

organizável (*adj.*) organizable.

organogenesia, **organogenia** (*f., Biol.*) organogenesis.

organógeno (*m., Chem.*) organogen.

organografia (*f.*) organography.

organóide (*adj.; Med., Zool.*) organoid.

organoléptico –**ca** (*adj.; Physiol.*) organoleptic.

organologia (*f.*) organology.

organometálico –**ca** (*adj.; Chem.*) organometallic.

organonímia (*f., Biol.*) organonymy.

organopatia (*f., Med.*) organopathy; organic disease.

organosol (*m., Phys. Chem.*) organosol.

organoterapia (*f., Med.*) organotherapy [= OPOTERAPIA].

organotropia (*f., Biol.*) organotropy.

organotrópico –**ca** (*adj., Biol.*) organotropic.

organsim, **organsino** (*m.*) organzine (silk thread).

organsinar (*v.t.*) to organsine (silk).

órgão [-gãos] (*m.*) organ, instrument, means; functioning part; a reed organ; a newspaper. **grande—**, pipe organ.

orgasmo (*m.*) orgasm.

orgástico –**ca** (*adj.*) orgastic.

orgia (*f.*) orgy; revelry.

orgíaco –**ca**, **orgiástico** –**ca**, **órgio** –**gia** (*adj.*) orgiastic.

orgulhar (*v.t.*) to make proud.—**se de**, to be proud of; to take pride in; to pride oneself on.

orgulho (*m.*) pride, conceit, vanity; haughtiness; lofty self-respect.—**da posse**, pride of possession.

orgulhoso –**sa** (*adj.*) proud (**de**, of); conceited; vainglorious; haughty (**para com,** toward); "high hat," uppish; high and mighty.

oricalco (*m.*) orichalch (brass alloyed with zinc).

orictologia (*f.*) oryctology (mineralogy; paleontology).

orientação (*f.*) orientation; guidance; bearings, direction.

orientador –**dora** (*adj.*) orienting; (*m.,f.*) one who guides or directs.

oriental (*adj.*) oriental, eastern; Uruguayan; (*m.,f.*) an Uruguayan; (*pl.*) Orientals.

orientalismo (*m.*) orientalism.

orientalista (*m.,f.*) Orientalist.

orientar (*v.t.*) to orient; to guide, direct; (*v.r.*) to get one's bearings; to take stock (of a situation).

oriente (*m.*) orient; [*cap.*] East.—**Extremo,** Far East.—**Médio,** Middle East.—**Próximo,** Near East.

orifício (*m.*) orifice, aperture, hole.

oriflama (*f.*) oriflamme [= AURIFLAMA].

origem (*f.*) origin, source, beginning; cause.

origenismo (*m., Eccl. Hist.*) Origenism.

originador –**dora** (*adj.*) originating; (*m.,f.*) originator.

original (*adj.*) original, primitive; not imitative; creative; novel, new, odd; (*m.*) an original; an eccentric person.

originalidade (*f.*) originality.

originar (*v.t.*) to originate, create.—**-se de,** to arise from.

originário –**ria** (*adj.*) derived from; native of. Êle é—do Rio, he is a native of Rio.

orilha (*f.*) border, edge, fillet.

orindiúva (*f.*) = CRINDIÚVA.

orismologia (*f.*) orismology; terminology of a science.

oriundo –**da** [i-ún] (*adj.*) derived from; originating in or out of; arising from; resulting from.

orixá (*m.*) a pagan divinity or idol, of African ancestry.

oriza (*f.*) rice (*Oryza*); = ARROZ.

orizanina (*f. Biochem.*) oryzanin.

orizicultor –**tora** (*adj.*) rice-growing; (*m.,f.*) rice grower.

orizicultura (*f.*) rice growing.

orizívoro –**ra** (*adj.*) oryzivorous, feeding on rice.

orla (*f.*) border, edge, rim; hem, fringe, edging, selvage; welt; shore; (*Arch.*) fillet. Cf. OURELA.

orladura (*f.*) edging; fringe.

orlar (*v.t.*) to border, edge, hem; to outline.

ornador –**dora** (*adj.*) ornamenting; (*m.,f.*) decorator.

ornamentação (*f.*) ornamentation, decoration, adornment.

ornamental (*adj.*) ornamental.

ornamentalista (*m.,f.*) fancy diver.

ornamentar (*v.t.*) to ornament, decorate.

ornamentista (*m.f.*,) interior decorator; window dresser.

ornamento (*m.*) ornament, decoration, adornment.

ornar (*v.t.*) to adorn, embellish, decorate, bedeck, ornament.

ornatista (*m.,f.*) = ORNAMENTISTA.

ornato (*m.*) ornament, adornment.

ornear, ornejar (*v.i.*) to bray [= ZURRAR].

orneio, ornejo (*m.*) bray [= ZURRO].

ornitodelfo (*m.*) monotreme.

ornitófilo –**la** (*adj.*) ornithophilous, bird-loving; (*m.,f.*) ornithophile, bird lover.

ornitoídeo –**dea** (*adj.*) ornithoid, birdlike.

ornitógalo (*m., Bot.*) star-of-Bethlehem (*Ornithogalum*).

ornitologia (*f.*) ornithology.

ornitologista (*m.,f.*), **ornitólogo** (*m.*) –**ga** (*f.*) ornithologist.

ornitorrinco (*m.*) ornithorhynchus (duck-billed platypus).

ornitotomia (*f.*) ornithotomy, dissection of birds.

ornitúrico –**ca** (*adj., Biochem.*) ornithuric.

oró (*m.*) a bean (*Phaseolus panduratus*).

orobanca (*f., Bot.*) broomrape (*Orobanche*).

orobó (*m.*) Sudan colanut (*Cola acuminata*).

órobo (*m.*) bitter vetch (*Vicia ervilia*), c.a. JERO, ERVILHA-DE-POMBO.

orogenia (*f., Geol.*) orogeny.

orogênico –**ca** (*adj., Geol.*) orogenic.

orognosia (*f.*) orology.

orografia (*f.*) orography.

orógrafo (*m., Surveying*) orograph.

orohidrografia (*f.*) orohydrography.

oróide (*m.*) oroide (copper-zinc alloy).

orologia (*f.*) orology.

orômetro (*m., Meteorol.*) orometer.

orôncio (*m., Bot.*) golden club (*Orontium aquaticum*).

orquestídeos (*m.pl.*) the beach fleas (*Orchestiidae*).

orquestra (*f.*) orchestra.

orquestração (*f.*) orchestration.

orquestrador –**dora** (*adj.*) orchestrating; (*m.,f.*) orchestra-tor.

orquestral (*adj.*) orchestral.

orquestrar (*v.t.*) to orchestrate.

orquialgia (*f., Med.*) orchialgia.

orquidáceo –**cea** (*adj., Bot.*) orchidaceous; (*f.pl.*) the orchid family (*Orchidaceae*).

órquide (*f., Bot.*) the genus Orchis, typifying the orchid family.

orquídea (*f.*) any orchid.

orreta [ê] (*f.*) narrow valley.

orrologia (*f.*) orrhology, serology.

orroterapia (*f.*) orrhotherapy, serum therapy.

ortálide (*f.*) a genus (*Ortalis*) of flies.

orticonoscópio (*m., TV*) orthiconoscope.

ortita (*f., Min.*) orthite.

ortobiose (*f.*) orthobiosis, correct living.

ortocefálico –**ca** (*adj., Cranion.*) orthocephalic.

ortocentro (*m., Geom.*) orthocenter.

ortocinético –**ca** (*adj., Chem.*) orthokinetic.

ortoclásio (*m., Min.*) orthoclase.

ortoclasita (*f., Min.*) orthoclasite.

ortoclorito (*m., Min.*) orthochlorite.

ortocromático –**ca, ortocrômico** –**ca** (*adj., Photog.*) ortho-chromatic.

ortodiagonal (*adj., Cryst.*) orthodiagonal.

ortodontia, ortodontosia (*f.*) orthodontia.

ortodontista, ortodontosista (*m.,f.*) orthodontist.

ortodoxia [ks] (*f.*) orthodoxy.

ortodoxo –**xa** [ks] (*adj.*) orthodox.

ortodromia (*f., Naut.*) great-circle route.

ortoépia, ortoepia (*f.*) orthoepy, correct pronunciation.

ortófiro (*m., Petrog.*) orthophyre.

ortofonia (*f.*) orthophony.

ortofosfórico –**ca** (*adj., Chem.*) orthophosphoric [acid].

ortogênese (*f., Biol.*) orthogenesis.

ortógnato –**ta** (*adj., Craniom.*) orthognathous.

ortogonal, ortógono –**na** (*adj.*) orthogonal.

ortógrado –**da** (*adj.*) orthograde, walking upright.

ortografar (*v.t.*) to write (spell) correctly.

ortografia (*f.*) orthography, correct spelling; (*Drawing*) orthographic projection, esp. of an elevation.

ortográfico –**ca** (*adj.*) orthographic.

ortógrafo –**fa** (*m.,f.*) orthographer.

ortologia (*f.*) orthology.

ortométrico –**ca** (*adj., Cryst.*) orthometric.

ortopedia (*f.*) orthopedics.

ortopédico –**ca** (*adj.*) orthopedic.

ortopedista (*m.,f.*) orthopedist.

ortopinacóide (*m., Cryst.*) orthopinacoid.

ortopiroxênio [ks] (*m., Min.*) orthcpyroxene.

ortoplasia (*f., Biol.*) orthoplasy.

ortóptero –**ra** (*adj.*) orthopterous; (*m.*) orthopteron (cricket, grasshopper, cockroach, etc.); (*m.pl.*) the Orthop-tera.

ortorrômbico –**ca** (*adj., Cryst.*) orthorhombic.

ortoscópico –**ca** (*adj., Optics*) orthoscopic.

ortoscópio (*m., Med., Photog.*) orthoscope.

ortósia (*f.*), –**sio** (*m.*) = ORTOCLÁSIO.

ortospermo –**ma** (*adj., Bot.*) orthospermous.

ortostático –**ca** (*adj.*) orthostatic, standing erect.

ortóstica (*f., Bot.*) orthostichy.

ortostilo (*m., Arch.*) orthostyle.

ortotropismo (*m., Plant Physiol.*) orthotropism.

ortótropo –**pa** (*adj., Bot.*) orthotropous.

oruzu [zú] (*m., Bot.*) a licorice (*Glycyrrhiza astragalina*).

orvalhado –**da** (*adj.*) dew-covered; dewy; (*f.*) morning dew.

orvalhar (*v.t.*) to bedew; to besprinkle; (*v.i.*) to become dewy; to drizzle, mist.

orvalheira (*f.*) a heavy dew.

orvalhinha (*f.*) the roundleaf sundew (*Drosera rotundi-folia*), c.a. ROSELA.

orvalho (*m.*) dew; mist.—**-da-aurora,** the iceplant (*Mesembryanthemum crystallinum*), c.a. GELADA, PRATEA-DA, ERVA-DO-ORVALHO.

orvalhoso –**sa** (*adj.*) dewy; misty.

os (*art.; pron.*) plural of o.

oscilação (*f.*) oscillation; fig., vacillation; (*Stat.*) range.

oscilador –**dora** (*adj.*) oscillating; (*m.*) oscillator.

oscilante (*adj.*) oscillating.

oscilar (*v.i.*) to oscillate, swing, sway; fig., to vacillate, waver.

oscilatoriáceo –**cea** (*adj., Bot.*) oscillatoriaceous; (*f.pl.*) a family (*Oscillatoriaceae*) of blue-green algae.

oscilatório –**ria** (*adj.*) oscillatory.

oscilógrafo (m., Elec.) oscillograph.
oscilograma (m.) oscillogram.
oscilometria (f.) oscillometry.
oscilômetro (m.) oscillometer.
osciloscópio (m., Elec.) oscilloscope.
oscitar (v.i.) to gape, yawn.
osculação (f.) osculation, kissing; (Geom.) osculation.
osculador –dora (adj.) kissing; (Geom.) osculatory.
oscular (v.i.) to osculate, kiss.
osculatório –ria (adj.) osculatory; (m., R.C.Ch.) pax, osculatory.
osculatriz (f., Geom.) osculatrix.
ósculo (m.) kiss; (Zool.) osculum.
osfrese (f.) osphresis, olfaction, sense of smell.
osga (f.) a gecko lizard; (colloq.) deep-seated aversion.
osmandi (m.) Ottoman Turkish (language).
osmanli (m.) Osmanli, Ottoman, a Turk.
osmiato (m., Chem.) osmate.
ósmico –ca (adj., Chem.) osmic; osmious.
osmidrose (f., Med.) osmidrosis, bromidrosis.
ósmio (m., Chem.) osmium.
osmioso –sa (adj., Chem.) osmious.
osmirídio (m., Min.) osmiridium, iridosmine.
osmologia (f.) osmology.
osmometria (f.) osmometry.
osmômetro (m.) osmometer.
osmose (Physical Chem., Physiol.) osmosis.
osmotactismo (m., Biol.) osmotaxis.
osmótico –ca (adj.) osmotic.
osmunda (f.) cinnamon fern (Osmunda).
Osmundo (m.) Osmund; Osmond.
osqueol (m., Anat.) oscheal.
ossada (f.) a pile of bones; bones of a skeleton; ruins, débris.
ossama (f.) heap of bones.
ossamenta (f.) bony structure.
ossaria (f.), ossário (m.) pile of bones; ossuary.
ossatura (f.) bones, skeleton; frame.
osseína (f., Biochem.) ossein.
ósseo –sea (adj.) osseous, bony.
ossicos (m.pl., Anat., Zool.) vomer.
ossículo (m., Anat., Zool.) ossicle; (pl.) ossicles of the middle ear.
ossificação (f.) ossification.
ossificar (v.t.) to ossify.
osso [ôsso; pl.: ossos(ó)] (m.) bone; fig., a difficulty.—s de borboleta, trifles.—coxal or ilíaco, ilium, hipbone.—de correr, marrow bone.—difícil de roer, a hard nut to crack.—-do-pai-joão, (colloq.) tail bone (coccyx).—espactal, any Wormian bone.—inominado, innominate bone.—metacarpiano, metacarpal bone.—metatarsiano, metatarsal bone.—occipital, occipital bone.—s do ofício, the "headaches" (difficulties, problems) inherent in any occupation.—parietal, parietal bone.—zigomático, cheek bone. até a medula dos—s, to the very marrow of one's bones. em carne e—, in flesh and blood; in person.
ossuário (m.) ossuary; charnel house; a common grave.
ossudo –da (adj.) big-boned, bony; gaunt.
ostaga (f.) halyard.
osteína (f.) = OSSEÍNA.
osteíte (f., Med.) osteitis.
ostensível, ostensivo –va (adj.) ostensive, ostensible.
ostentação (f.) ostentation, display, pomp; swank, fanfare.
ostentador –dora (adj.) ostentatious, vainglorious; (m.,f.) such a person.
ostentar (v.t.) to exhibit, display, show off; flaunt; to "sport" (a new hat, etc.).
ostentoso –sa (adj.) ostentatious; garish.
osteoblasto (m., Anat.) osteoblast.
osteoclas[t]ia (f., Surg.) osteoclasis.
osteoclasta (m., Surg.) osteoclast.
osteocola (f.) osteocolla (calcium carbonate).
osteocondral (adj., Anat.) osteochondrous.
osteocondrite (f., Med.) osteochondritis.
osteodentina (f., Zool.) osteodentine.
osteófito (m., Med.) osteophyte.
osteogênese (f., Physiol.) osteogenesis; ossification.
osteóide (adj.) osteoid, like bone.
osteologia (f.) osteology.
osteoma (f., Med.) osteoma.
osteomalacia (f., Med.) osteomalacia; (Veter.) cripples.
osteomielite (f., Med.) osteomyelitis.
osteoplastia (f., Surg.) osteoplasty.

osteoplástico –ca (adj., Surg.) osteoplastic.
osteoporose (f., Med., Physiol.) osteoporosis; (Veter.) bighead.
osteose (f.) ostosis; ossification.
osteotomia (f., Surg.) osteotomy.
osteótomo (m., Surg.) osteotome.
ostiário (m.) ostiary.
ostíolo (m., Bot., Zool.) ostiole.
ostra (f.) oyster.—-americana, the American or Virginia oyster (Ostrea virginica), c.a. GUERIRI, LERIAÇU.—-francêsa, the common European oyster (Ostrea edulis), c.a. OSTRA-CHATA, OSTRA-EUROPÉIA, OSTRA-PÉ-DE-CAVALO.—-dos-mangues, a tree or coon oyster (Ostrea frons or Ostrea arborea).—perlífera, pearl oyster (Pinctada margaritifera).
ostraceiro (m.) the oyster catcher (Haemotopus).
ostráceo –cea (adj.) ostracean, ostraceous.
ostracião (m.) = BAIACU-SEM-CHIFRE.
ostracismo (m.) ostracism.
ostracita (f.) a fossil oyster.
ostraria (f.) oyster bed.
ostreicultura (f.) oyster culture.
ostreídeos (m.pl.) the oyster family (Ostreidae).
ostreiforme (adj.) shaped like an oyster.
ostreiro –ra (adj.) oyster; (m.,f.) oysterer; (f.) oyster bed; also = SAMBAQUI.
ostreófago –fa (adj.) ostreophagous, feeding on oysters; (m.,f.) ostreophagist, oyster-eater.
Osvaldo (m.) Oswald.
otalgia (f., Med.) otalgia, earache.
OTAN = ORGANIZAÇÃO DO TRATADO DO ATLÂNTICO NORTE (NATO—North Atlantic Treaty Organization).
otária (f.) any otary (eared seal).
otário (m., slang) a "sucker" (a person who is easily duped or cheated).
Otava (f.) Ottawa.
Otávia (f.) Octavia.
Otávio (m.) Octavius.
Otelo (m.) Othello.
ótico –ca (adj., Anat.) otic, auricular; also = ÓPTICO (f.) optics.
otimismo (m.) optimism.
otimista (adj.) optimistic; (m.,f.) optimist.
ótimo –ma (adj.; absol. superl. of BOM) very, very good; the best, excellent; grand; tiptop, "tops"; (interj.) Fine! "Swell"!
otite (f., Med.) otitis.
Oto (m.) Otto.
otocisto (m., Zool.) otocyst.
otocônio (m., Anat.) otoconium.
otodinia (f.) earache.
otofônio (m.) ear trumpet.
otólito (m., Anat., Zool.) otolith.
otologia (f.) otology.
otomano –na (adj.) Ottoman, Turkish; (m.,f.) a Turk (f.) ottoman, couch.
otorrino (m.,f.) short for OFTALMOTORRINOLARINGOLOGISTA or OTORRINOLARINGOLOGISTA.
otorrinolaringologia (f.) the branch of medicine dealing with ear, nose and throat.
otorrinolaringologista (m.,f.) ear, nose and throat specialist.
otoscópio (m., Med.) otoscope.
ou (conj.) or, either. ou ela ou êle, either she or he. ou oito ou oitenta, all or nothing. ou seja, or rather.
ouabaína (f., Chem.) ouabain.
ouça, ouças, etc., forms of OUVIR [58]; written also: OIÇA, OIÇAS, etc. (f.) = OUVIDO.
oução (m.) cheese mite.
oura (f.) dizziness, giddiness.
ourama (f.) heap of gold.
ourana (f., Bot.) a willow (Salix).
ourela (f.) edge, border. Cf. ORLA.
ouricana (f.) an arboreal pit viper (Bothrops bilineatus).
ouriçar (v.t.) to bristle.
ouriço (m.) chestnut bur; hedgehog.—-cacheiro, coendou (a small aboreal porcupine of Brazil [genus Coendou] having a prehensile tail); c.a. COANDU, COENDU, CUENDU, CUANDU, CUIM, LUÍS-CACHEIRO; also, the European hedgehog (Erinaceus).—-do-mar, a sea urchin (Echinus esculenta).
ouricuri [urí], ouricurizeiro (m.) = ARICURI.
ourives (m.) goldsmith, jeweler.
ourivesaria (f.) jewelry store.

ouro (*m.*) gold; riches; (*pl.*) diamonds (card suit).—**branco** white gold (an old term for platinum); cotton (as a crop). —**bruto**, native gold.—**de lei**, 18-carat gold.—**em fôlhas**, gold leaf.—**fino**, fine (pure) gold.—**maçiço**, solid gold. —**nativo**, native gold.—**negro**, black gold (at one time, Amazon rubber; now, petroleum).—**ormulu**, ormulu.—**-pigmento**, orpiment.—**verde**, green gold (coffee as a crop).—**virgem**, virgin gold. **a pêso de**—, for its weight in gold. **a preço de**—, at a very high price. **nadando em**—, rolling in wealth. **Nem tudo que reluz é**—, All is not gold that glitters. Var. OIRO.
ouropel [-péis] (*m.*) tinsel; by ext., sham, pretense.
ouro-pretano –**na**, **ouro-pretense** (*adj.*) of or pert. to the city of Ouro Prêto, in the State of Minas Gerais; (*m.,f.*) a native or inhabitant of that city.
ousadia (*f.*) daring, boldness; impudence, "cheek", "nerve", "gall", "brass".
ousado –**da** (*adj.*) bold, daring; impudent, presumptuous.
ousar (*v.t.*) to dare, brave; to venture, make bold.
out. = OUTUBRO (October).
outeiro (*m.*) hillock, knoll, foothill.
outiva (*f.*) **de**—, from hearsay.
outº = OUTUBRO (October).
outonada (*f.*) fall harvest; autumn.
outonal (*adj.*) autumnal.
outoniço –**ça** (*adj.*) autumn; in the autumn of life.
outono (*m.*) autumn, fall.
outorga (*f.*) a grant(ing); a bestowal.
outorgante (*adj.*) granting; bestowing; (*m.,f.*) one who grants or bestows something.
outorgar (*v.t.*) to grant, bestow, confer; to award; to vouchsafe.
outrem (*pron.*) another person or persons; somebody else.
outro –**tra** (*adj.*) other, another, some other; (*pl.*) others. —**coisa**, something else; another thing.—**dia**, the other day.—**mundo**, the next world.—**qualquer**, any other.— **que não**, other than.—**que tal**, another such.—**tanto**, as much again; as much more; twice as much.—**s tantos**, as many more.—**tempo**, in other times; at another time. —**vez**, again, once more, another time. **de**—**maneira**, otherwise. **em**—**parte**, elsewhere. **em**—**tempo**, at another time. **nem um nem**—, neither one nor the other. **nenhum**—, no other, no one else. **no**—**dia**, the other day, recently; the next day. **nós**—**s**, we; we people. **ou, por**—, or, stated another way. **qualquer**—, anyone else, any other. **um ao**—, one to the other. **um e**—, both. **um ou**—, one or the other. **uns e**—**s**, all of them, the whole lot.
outrora (*adv.*) formerly, before; in olden times, long ago, once upon a time, of old, of yore.
outrossim (*adv.*) likewise, also, furthermore, moreover.
outubro (*m.*) October.
ouvarovita (*f., Min.*) uvarovite.
ouvido (*m.*) the sense of hearing; the (inner) ear. Cf. ORELHA.—**absoluto**, (*Music*) absolute pitch.—**externo**, external ear.—**interno**, inner ear.—**médio**, middle ear. **abrir os**—**s**, to give ear, heed. **ao**—, in whispers, in secret. **chegar aos**—**s de**, to reach the ears of. **dar**—(s) **a**, to give ear to, heed, listen to. **de**—, by ear. **de olhos abertos e**—**s atentos**, with eyes and ears open. **duro de**—, hard of hearing. **entrar por um**—**e sair pelo outro**, to go in one ear and out the other. **fazer**—**s moucos**, to turn a deaf ear. **ferir os**—**s**, to grate upon the ear. **Os meus**—**s estão zunindo**, my ears are buzzing. **tapar os**—**s**, to close the ears. **ter bom**—, to have a good ear (for music).
ouvidor (*m.*) listener; auditor; a special magistrate; in Brazil, during colonial days, a justice of the peace appointed and maintained on their properties by the owners of land grants.
ouvinte (*m.,f.*) listener, hearer; auditor (of a class).
ouvir [58] (*v.t.,v.i.*) to hear, listen (to), give ear (to),— (**alguém**) **de confissão**, to hear confession.—**dizer**, or **falar, que**, to hear it said that.—**falar de**, to hear of (about).—**mal**, to be hard of hearing.—**missa**, to hear mass. **Já ouvi falar dêle**, I have heard of him (before). **Não há pior surdo do que aquêle que não quer**—, There is none so deaf as he who will not listen **Quem já ouviu falar em tal coisa!** Who ever heard of such a thing!
ova (*f.*) fish ovary; (*pl.*) roe, spawn. **uma**—! Like hell! [*Defiantly*].
ovação (*f.*) ovation; fish roe, spawn.
ovacionar (*v.t.*) to acclaim, cheer.
ovado –**da** (*adj.*) ovate; (*m., Arch.*) ovolo, echinus, quarter-round.

oval (*adj.*) oval; (*m., Geom.*) oval; (*f., Arch.*) ovolo, echinus, quarter-round.
ovalar (*v.t.*) to make oval.
óvalo, óvano (*m., Arch.*) ovolo; quarter round.
ovante (*adj.*) triumphant.
ovar (*v.i.*) to lay eggs; to spawn.
ovariano –**na**, **ovárico** –**ca** (*adj., Anat., Zool.*) ovarian.
ovariectomia (*f., Surg.*) ovariotomy.
ovário (*m., Anat., Zool.*) ovary.
ovariotomia (*f., Surg.*) ovariotomy.
ovarite (*f., Med.*) ovaritis.
oveiro (*m.*) bird ovary; an egg dish or cup.
ovelha (*f.*) sheep, ewe; member of a spiritual flock.— **desgarrada**, stray sheep.—**tinhosa**, black sheep. **Cada**— **com sua parelha**, Birds of a feather flock together. **Uma**—**má põe o rebanho a perder**, One rotten apple spoils the barrel.
ovelhada (*f.*) a herd of sheep.
ovelheiro (*m.*) sheepherder, shepherd; sheep dog.
ovém (*m., Naut.*) shroud; hawser.
ovencadura (*f., Naut.*) shrouds (collectively).
oveva (*m.*) a drumfish.
ovicápsula (*f., Zool., Anat.*) ovicapsule.
ovículo (*m., Arch.*) oviculum.
ovídeos (*m.pl.*) the Ovidae (sheep and goats).
ovidiano –**na** (*adj.*) Ovidian.
Ovídio (*m.*) Ovid.
oviduto (*m., Anat., Zool.*) oviduct.
ovífero –**ra** (*adj.*) oviferous.
ovificação (*f.*) ovification.
oviforme (*adj.*) oviform, egg-shaped.
ovígeno –**na** (*adj.*) ovigenetic; ovigenic; ovigenous.
ovígero –**ra** (*adj.*) ovigerous.
ovil (*m.*) sheepfold.
ovino –**na** (*adj.*) ovine; of or like sheep.
ovinocultor –**tora** (*m.,f.*) sheep raiser.
ovinocultura (*f.*) sheep raising.
oviparidade (*f.*), **oviparismo** (*m., Zool.*) oviparity.
ovíparo –**ra** (*adj., Zool.*) oviparous.
ovipositor, oviscapto (*m., Zool.*) ovipositor.
ovissaco (*m., Zool., Anat.*) ovisac.
ovívoro –**ra** (*adj.*) ovivorous, feeding on eggs.
ôvo [ovos] (*m.*) egg.—**-de-galo-**, (*Bot.*) cockseggs (*Salpichroa rhomboidea*).—**-de-peru**, a freckle.—**-de-pombo**, a rounded quartz pebble found in diamond-bearing gravel. —**-de-sapo**, aquatic snails' egg cluster.—**s duros**, hard-boiled eggs.—**s escaldados** or **pochados**, poached eggs. —**s estrelados** or **fritos**, fried eggs.—**s mexidos**, scrambled eggs. **batedor de**—**s**, egg beater. **clara de**—, white of egg. **É como o**—**de Colombo**, It's easy when you know how. **fazer**—, to be mysterious.
ovócito (*m., Biol.*) ovocyte.
ovogênese (*f., Biol.*) ovogenesis [= OOGÊNESE].
ovogênico –**ca** (*adj., Biol.*) ovogenetic.
ovogônio (*m., Zool.*) ovogonium [= OOGÔNIO].
ovóide (*adj.*) ovoid.
ovolecitina (*f., Biochem.*) egg lecithin.
ovologia (*f.*) ovology.
ovovitelina (*f., Biochem.*) vitellin.
ovoviviparidade (*f., Zool.*) ovoviviparity.
ovovivíparo –**ra** (*adj., Zool.*) ovoviviparous.
ovulação (*f., Biochem.*) ovulation.
ovulado –**da** (*adj.*) ovulate.
ovulígero –**ra** (*adj.*) ovuligerous.
ovular (*adj.*) ovular.
óvulo (*m.*) ovule; (*Arch.*) ovolo; quarter circle.
oxácido [ks] (*m., Chem.*) oxy-acid.
oxalá (*interj.*) Would to God! Let's hope!—**fosse!** Would that it were so!—**que venha!** I do hope he will come.
oxalato [ks] (*m., Chem.*) oxalate.
oxalemia [ks] (*f., Med.*) oxalemia.
oxálico –**ca** [ks] (*adj., Chem.*) oxalic.
oxalida [ks] (*f.*) the woodsorrel oxalis (*O. acetosella*).
oxalidáceo –**cea** [ks] (*adj., Bot.*) oxalidaceous; (*f.pl.*) the sorrel family (*Oxalidaceae*).
oxalílio [ks] (*m., Chem.*) oxalyl.
oxaliluréia [ks] (*f.*) oxalylurea, parabanic acid.
oxalúrico –**ca** [ks] (*adj., Chem.*) oxaluric.
oxamato [ks] (*m., Chem.*) oxamate.
oxametana [ks] (*f., Chem.*) oxamethane, ethyl oxamate.
oxâmico –**ca** [ks] (*adj., Chem.*) oxamic.
oxamida [ks] (*f., Chem.*) oxamid(e).
oxamite [ks] (*f., Min.*) oxammite, ammonium oxalate.
oxiantraquinona [ks] (*f., Chem.*) oxyanthraquinone.

oxibrometo [ks] (*m.*, *Chem.*) oxybromide.
oxibutírico –ca [ks] (*adj.*, *Chem.*) oxybutyric [acid].
oxicedro [ks] (*m.*) the prickly juniper (*Juniperus oxycedrus*).
oxicefalia [ks] (*f.*, *Craniol.*) oxycephaly.
oxicianeto [ks] (*m.*, *Chem.*) oxycyanide.
oxiclorato [ks] (*m.*, *Chem.*) oxychlorate.
oxicloreto [ks] (*m.*, *Chem.*) oxychloride [= CLORÓXIDO].
oxiclórico –ca [ks] (*adj.*, *Chem.*) oxychloric.
oxicromatina [ks] (*f.*, *Biol.*) oxychromatin.
oxidabilidade [ks] (*adj.*) oxidability.
oxidação [ks] (*f.*) oxidation.
oxidante [ks] (*adj.*) oxidizing; (*m.*) oxidizing agent.
oxidar [ks] (*v.t.*) to oxidize; (*v.r.*) to rust.
oxidase [ks] (*f.*, *Biochem.*) oxidase.
oxidável [ks] (*adj.*) oxidizable.
óxido [ks] (*m.*) oxide.—**argêntico**, silver oxide.—**áurico**, gold oxide.—**básico**, basic oxide.—**de cálcio**, calcium oxide, quick lime.—**de carbono**, carbon monoxide.—**de chumbo**, lead oxide; litharge.—**de cobre**, copper oxide.—**cúprico**, cupric oxide, black oxide of copper.—**cuproso**, cuprous oxide, red oxide of copper, cuprite.—**de estanho**, tin (stannous) oxide.—**estânico**, tin (stannic) oxide; tin anhydride.—**de etileno**, ethylene oxide, oxirane.—**de európio**, europium oxide.—**férrico**, ferric oxide, red iron oxide, Indian red, Venetian red, vitriol red, colcothar.—**de ferro**, or—**ferroso**, iron (ferrous) oxide.—**de magnésio**, magnesium oxide, periclase; magnesia usta; calcinated magnesium oxide.—**mercúrico**, (red) mercuric oxide, montroydite; yellow mercury oxide.—**niqueloso**, nickelous oxide, nickel monoxide; bunsenite.—**nítrico**, nitrogen (nitric) oxide.—**nitroso**, nitrogen monoxide, nitrous oxide.—**de prata**, silver oxide.—**de titânio**, titanium dioxide.—**túngstico**, tungsten trioxide.—**urânico**, uranium trioxide.—**de urânio**, uranium oxide, pitchblende.—**uranoso**, uranium dioxide.—**xântico**, xanthine, ureous acid.—**de zinco**, zinc oxide, zinc white, flowers of zinc, Chinese white.
oxídrico –ca [ks] (*adj.*, *Chem.*) oxyhydric.
oxidrilo [ks] (*m.*, *Chem.*) hydroxyl [= HIDROXÍLIO].
oxidulado –da [ks] (*adj.*, *Chem.*) oxidulated.
oxifenol [ks] (*m.*, *Chem.*) oxyphenol.
oxifílico –ca [ks] (*adj.*, *Biol.*) oxyphilic.
oxífilo –la [ks] (*adj.*; *m.*, *Biol.*) oxyphile.
oxifluoreto [ks] (*m.*, *Chem.*) oxyfluoride.
oxigenação [ks] (*f.*) oxygenation.
oxigenado –da [ks] (*adj.*, *Chem.*) oxygenated.
oxigenador –dora [ks] (*adj.*) oxygenating; (*m.*,*f.*) oxygenator.

oxigenar [ks] (*v.t.*) to oxygenate.
oxigenável [ks] (*adj.*) oxygenizable.
oxigênio [ks] (*m.*) oxygen.
oxigenizar [ks] (*v.t.*) to oxygenize.
oxigenizável [ks] (*adj.*) = OXIGENÁVEL.
oxígnato –ta [ks] (*adj.*, *Zool.*) oxygnathous.
oxígono [ks] (*m.*) a triangle having three acute angles.
oxihematina [ks] (*f.*, *Biochem.*) oxyhematin.
oxihemoglobina [ks] (*f.*, *Biochem.*) oxyhemoglobin.
oxihídrico –ca [ks] (*adj.*, *Chem.*) oxyhydric.
oxiiodeto [ks] (*m.*, *Chem.*) oxyiodide.
oxil [ks] (*m.*, *Chem.*) oxyl.
oxilóbio [ks] (*m.*, *Bot.*) the pointed pod (*Oxylobium*).
oxiluminescência [ks] (*f.*, *Physical Chem.*) oxyluminescence.
oxiluminescente [ks] (*adj.*) oxyluminescent.
oximel [ks] (*m.*, *Pharm.*) oxymel.
oximoro [ks] (*m.*, *Rhet.*) oxymoron.
oxinaftóico –ca [ks] (*adj.*, *Chem.*) oxynaphthoic.
oxineurina [ks] (*f.*, *Chem.*) oxyneurine, betaine, lycine.
oxiópidas, oxiopídeos [ks] (*m.pl.*) a family (*Oxyopidae*) of eight-eyed hunting spiders.
oxipurina [ks] (*f.*) oxypurine.
oxiria [ks] (*f.*) mountain sorrel (*Oxyria*).
oxirrincos [ks] (*m.pl.*) the Oxyrrhyncha (spider crabs, etc.).
oxirrino –na [ks] (*adj.*, *Zool.*) oxyrhine.
oxissal [ks] (*m.*, *Chem.*) oxysalt.
oxissulfureto [ks] (*m.*, *Chem.*) oxysulfide.
oxístomos [ks] (*m.pl.*) the Oxystomata (box crabs, etc.).
oxitocia [ks] (*f.*, *Med.*) oxytocia, quick childbirth.
oxitócico –ca [ks] (*adj.*, *Med.*) oxytocic.
oxitocina [ks] (*f.*, *Biochem.*) oxytocin, a-hypophamine.
oxítono –na [ks] (*adj.*) oxytone; (*m.*) an oxytone word (i.e., one having an acute accent on the last syllable).
oxiúra [ks] (*f.*) = OXIURO.
oxiúro [ks] (*m.*) pinworm (*Oxyuris*).
Oxônia [ks] (*f.*) Oxford.
oxoniano –na [ks] (*adj.*) Oxonian.
oxozone [ks] (*Chem.*) oxozone.
ozocerite (*f.*, *Min.*) ozocerite.
ozonador (*m.*) ozonizer.
ozonide (*f.*, *Chem.*) ozonide.
ozônio, ozone (*m.*, *Chem.*) ozone.
ozonização (*f.*) ozonization.
ozonizar (*v.t.*) to ozonize.
ozonômetro (*m.*) ozonometer.
ozonoscópio (*m.*) ozonoscope.
ozotipia (*f.*, *Photog.*) ozotype.

P

P, p, the 15th letter of the Portuguese alphabet.
p. = PÉ (foot); POR (by); PRÓXIMO (next); PÁGINA (page); PALMO (hand, as a measure); PENCE (British money).
P. = PADRE (Priest); PRAÇA (plaza).
p.ª = PARA (for).
PA = PARÁ (State of).
Pã (*m.*) Pan.
pá (*f.*) shovel, spade; thigh of a steer.—**de lixo**, dustpan.—**de hélice**, propeller blade.—**do forno**, baker's peel.
da—virada, reckless, wild, impetuous, headstrong.
paaguaçu [a-a . . . çú] (*m.*, *Zool.*) a skimmer (*Rhynchops*), c.a. BICO-RASTEIRO.
pabular (*v.i.*) to swagger; boast.
pábulo (*m.*) pabulum.
paca (*f.*) paca, spotted cavy (*Agouti paca*); (*m.*) nincompoop.
pacajá (*m.*,*f.*) an Indian of the Pacajá, a little-known Tupian tribe of the lower Tocantins River, now extinct; (*m.*,*f.*) pert. to or designating this tribe.
pacamão (*m.*) any poison toadfish (genus *Thalasophryne*, family *Batrachoididae*). Cf. MOREIATIM.
pacapeua (*m.*) a swartzpea (*Swartzia racemora*).
pacarana (*f.*) a So. Amer. rodent, of genus *Dinomys*, closely resembling the PACA.
pacatez [ê] (*f.*) tranquillity, placidity.

pacato –ta (*adj.*) peaceable, placid, serene; (*m.*,*f.*) such a person.
pacavaré (*m.*) = LINGUARUDO (a beach snail).
pacavira (*f.*, *Bot.*) a heliconia (*H. pendula*).
pachola (*adj.*) swanky; vain; (*m.*) idler; coxcomb.
pacholar (*v.i.*) to swank, swagger.
pachorra [ô] (*f.*) sluggishness; apathy; deliberateness.
pachorrento –ta (*adj.*) slow, sluggish; laggard; snail-paced; phlegmatic; easygoing.
pachouchada (*f.*) an obscene or stupid remark.
pachuli [í] (*m.*) patchouli (plant, perfume).
paciência (*f.*) patience, resignation; perseverance; solitaire (card game); (*Bot.*) patience dock (*Rumex patientia*).
paciencioso –sa (*adj.*) = PACIENTE.
pacientar (*v.i.*) to be patient, have patience.
paciente (*adj.*) patient, resigned, long-suffering; (*m.*,*f.*) patient (sick person); object or recipient of an action;— distinguished from agent.
pacificação (*f.*) pacification, tranquillization; appeasement
pacificar (*v.t.*) to pacify, allay, tranquillize; to appease; (*v.r.*) to become peaceful.
pacífico –ca (*adj.*) pacific, peaceful; gentle; (*m.*,*f.*) a peaceful person.
pacifismo (*m.*) pacifism.

pacifista (*adj.; m.,f.*) pacifist.
pacivira (*f., Bot.*) a canna (*C. flaccida*).
pacnólito (*m., Min.*) pachnolite.
paço (*m.*) palace, court.
paco (*m.*) a wad of fake money used by swindlers; (*Min.*) paco.—**-catinga**, (*Bot.*) a spiralflag (*Costus pisonis*), c.a. CANA-DO-BREJO, PERINÁ.—**-paco**, (*Bot.*) a false abutilon (*Pseudabutilon*), c.a. MALVA-BRANCA-DO-SALGADO, MAL-VA-DE-PENDÃO, RABO-DE-FOGUETE.—**-seroca** = PACOVÁ, CARDAMOMO-DA-TERRA.
pacoba (*f.*) = PACOVA.
pacobal (*m.*) banana plantation [= BANANAL]. Var. PACOVAL.
pacobeira (*f.*) banana plant [= BANANEIRA]. Var. PACO-VEIRA.
pacoca (*f.*) river rapids.
paçoca (*f.*) a certain Brazilian dish made of bits of meat mixed with manioc meal; in Amazonia, it consists of "roasted Brazil nuts ground up in a mortar with manioc flour, salt and sugar; when uniformly mixed, the product is packed in paper containers and sold in the cities." [*GBAT*]; fig., hodgepodge.
pacote (*m.*) package, bundle; pack; (*pl., slang*) dough (money).
pacotê (*m.*) = BUTUÁ-DE-CORVO.
pacotilha (*f.*) cheap, poorly-made article; a gang of bandits.
pacotilheiro (*m.*) maker of, or dealer in, cheap articles of merchandise.
pacova (*adj.; m.,f.*) a lazy, simple-minded person; (*f.*) a kind of banana.—**-brava** = BANANEIRA-DO-MATO.—**-catinga**, (*Bot.*) parrots heliconia (*H. psittacorum*), c.a. SOROROQUINHA; also = PACOVÁ.—**-de-macaco**, a swartz-pea (*Swartzia langsdorfii*), c.a. PATRONA.—**-sororoca**, a travelerstree (*Ravenala guianensis*).
pacová (*f., Bot.*) any of various renealmias, as *R. aromatica, R. exaltata* (c.a. PACO-SEROCA, PACOVA-CATINGA), *R. occidentalis* (c.a. CARDAMOMO-DA-TERRA); a spiralflag (*Costus spiralis*), c.a. CANA-DE-MACACO.
pacoval (*m.*) var. of PACOBAL.
pacoveira (*f.*) var. of PACOBEIRA.
pacóvio (*m.*) fool, "dope," nincompoop, dunce.
pacto (*m.*) pact, compact, agreement.
pactuante (*adj.*) pact-making; (*m.,f.*) pact-maker.
pactuar (*v.t.,v.i.*) to make a pact (**com**, with).
pactuário -ria (*m.,f.*) a party to a pact or contract.
pacu [ú] (*m.*) a common name for any of numerous small fresh-water fishes of Brazil.
pacuçu [çú] (*m.*) a male PACA.
pacuera (*f.*) viscera (of cattle).
padaria (*f.*) bakery.
padecedor -dora (*adj.*) suffering; (*m.,f.*) sufferer.
padecente (*adj.*) suffering; (*m.,f.*) suffering person; person condemned to death.
padecer (*v.t.,v.i.*) to suffer (**de**, from), endure, bear, undergo; to permit, admit.
padecimento (*m.*) suffering, pain; hardship.
padeiro (*m.*) baker; bread man.
padejar (*v.t.*) to knead dough for bread; (*v.i.*) to work as a baker.
páder (*m., Radio*) padder.
padieira (*f.*) lintel.
padiola (*f.*) stretcher, litter; handbarrow.
padioleiro (*m.*) stretcher-bearer; ambulance man.
padoque (*m.*) paddock.
padrão (*m.*) standard (of weights, measures); guage; model.—**de vida**, standard of living.
padrar-se (*v.r.*) to become a priest.
padrasto (*m.*) stepfather; towering mountain.
padre (*m.*) priest.—**-cura**, parish priest.—**-mestre**, priest-teacher.—**-nosso**, Pater Noster (Our Father).—**-santo**, or **Santo—**, Holy Father (Pope).
padreador -dora (*adj.*) stud; (*m.*) studhorse.
padrear (*v.i.*) of horses, to breed.
padrinho (*m.*) godfather; sponsor; best man (at a wedding); second (of a duel).
padroado (*m.*) patronate; patronage.
padroeiro -ra (*adj.*) patron; patronal; (*m.*) patron saint; patron [but not in the sense of regular customer, which is FREGUÊS]; protector, supporter; (*f.*) patroness.
padronagem (*f.*) pattern; standard.
padronizado -da (*adj.*) standardized. **tipo—**, standard type.
padronizar (*v.t.*) to set the standard for; to standardize.

pág. = PÁGINA (page).
paga (*f.*) pay, wages,
pagã, fem. of PAGÃO.
pagado -da, obsolete though regular p.p. of PAGAR. [The modern form is PAGO.]
pagador -dora (*m.*) payer, paymaster, pay clerk, paying teller; (*adj.*) paying.
pagadoria (*f.*) disbursing office; paymaster's office.
pagamento (*m.*) payment; repayment; instalment payment.—**adiantado**, prepayment.—**atrasado**, payment in arrears.—**à vista**, sight payment; cash payment.—**integral**, payment in full.—**na entrega**, payment on delivery, C.O.D. **condições de—**, terms of payment. **falta de—**, non-payment. **mediante—**, on payment of.
paganal (*adj.*) pagan.
paganismo (*m.*) paganism.
paganizar (*v.t.*) to paganize.
pagante (*adj.*) paying; (*m.,f.*) payer.
pagão [-ãos] (*adj.; m.*) pagan. [Fem. PAGÃ.]
pagar [24] (*v.t.*) to pay (for, up); to settle (for, up); to repay; to retaliate; to remunerate.—**a prestações**, to pay in instalments.—**à vista**, to pay at sight.—**o pato**, to pay the piper.—**adiantado**, to prepay.—**caro**, to pay dear.—**na bôca do cofre**, to pay cash on the barrelhead.—**por conta**, to pay on account.—**na mesma moeda**, to give tit for tat.—**por inteiro**, to pay in full.—**prenda**, to pay a forfeit (in the game of forfeits).—**uma visita**, to pay a visit (to). **Favor com favor se paga**, One good turn deserves another. **Você me paga!** I'll get even with you!
pagável (*adj.*) payable; due.—**à vista**, payable at sight, on demand.—**ao portador**, payable to bearer.
página (*f.*) page (of a book, etc.).—**de rôsto**, title page of a book [= FACHADA or RÔSTO].—**em branco**, blank page. **a—s tantas**, suddenly; at that moment; when least expected. **primeira—**, first or front page.
paginação (*f.*) pagination.
paginar (*v.t.*) to paginate (a book, etc.).
pago -ga (*irreg. p.p. of* PAGAR) paid; (*m.,f.*) pay, wages; (*m.pl.*) one's birthplace, home town or old homestead.
pagode (*m.*) pagoda; spree, revelry, high jinks.
pagodear (*v.i.*) to carouse; to make fun (of).
pagodeira, pagodice (*f., slang*) spree; lark; fun.
pagodista (*m.,f.*) reveler; fun-loving person.
pagodita (*f., Min.*) pagodite, figure stone, agalmatolite.
pagro (*m.*) = PARGO.
paguro (*m.*) a hermit crab (*Pagurus*); = ERMITÃO, EREMITA-BERNARDO.
pai (*m.*) father; forefather; originator; author (*pl.*) parents.—**-adão**, a simple, single-share plow, drawn by 8 to 20 oxen.—**-agostinho**, a tyrant flycatcher (*Myiarchus*), c.a. IRRÉ, MARIA-CAVALHERRA, PAPA-MÔSCAS.—**da mentira**, or—**do mal**, the Devil.—**da pátria**, a national political leader (such as a senator).—**das queixas**, (*colloq.*) a deputy chief of police.—**de chiqueiro**, a ram (billy goat).—**de família**, paterfamilias; a certain type of small-mesh hammock.—**d'égua**, a studhorse; a woman chaser.—**-de-malhada**, a wild young bull that dominates a herd of cattle.—**-de-mel**, a certain wild honey bee.—**-de-santo**, or—**-de-terreiro**, a medicine man.—**-de-todos**, the middle finger.—**-dos-burros**, (*colloq.*) a dictionary.—**-gonçalo**, a hen-pecked husband.—**-joão**, an Uncle Tom (negro).—**-mané**, a dope (stupid person).—**-luís**, weeds, wild growth.—**Natal**, Santa Claus.—**-pedro**, a sparrow (*Arremon taciturnus*), c.a. COROADO.—**-velho**, (student's) pony.
paié (*m.*) var. of PAJÉ.
paina [ái] (*f.*) floss of silk-cotton trees.—**-cipó**, the white bladderflower (*Araujia sericifera*).—**-de-arbusto**, a silk-cotton tree (*Bombax*).—**-de-penas**, a savanna flower (*Echites*), c.a. CAPA-HOMEM, CIPÓ-CAPADOR.—**-de-sêda** = PAINEIRA.—**-do-arpoador**, a silk-cotton tree (*Bombax*).—**-do-campo** = CIPÓ-DE-SAPO.
painço [ã-ín] (*m.*) millet (plant or grain).—**-grande** = CAPIM-GUINÉ (Guinea grass).
paineira (*f.*) the floss-silk tree (*Chorisia speciosa*), c.a. BARRIGUDA, PAINA-DE-SÊDA. [Not to be confused with kapok, which is SUMAÚMA.]—**-loura** = CIPÓ-DE-PENAS.
painel [-néis] (*m.*) panel.
paio -a (*adj.*) gullible; (*m.,f.*) a gullible person; (*m.*) a large pork sausage.
paiol [-óis] (*m.*) powder magazine; corn crib; barn; storehouse; "a part of a Brazil-nut collector's hut, partitioned off for storing the crop." [*GBAT*]
paioleiro (*m.*) storekeeper.

pairar (*v.i.*) to hover (**sôbre, por sôbre, acima de,** over); to flutter; to soar; to impend; to vacillate, waver (**entre,** between); (*Naut.*) to scud; to tack; to lie to.

pairiri [-rirí] (*m.*) = POMBA-DE-BANDO.

país [-es] country, land, nation; region.

paisagem (*f.*) landscape; countryside.—**marinha,** seascape.

paisagismo (*m.*) landscaping.

paisagista (*m.,f.*) landscape painter; landscape architect.

paisano –**na** (*adj.*) civilian; (*m.,f.*) civilian; fellow countryman. **à**—, in civilian clothes. **policial à**—, plain-clothes man (detective).

paixão (*f.*) passion; love; emotion, strong feeling; ardor, vehement desire; wrath; suffering, martyrdom.

paixonite (*f., colloq.*) "crush" (infatuation, attachment).

pajamarioba (*f.*) coffee senna (*Cassia occidentalis*), c.a. FEDEGOSO-VERDADEIRO, TARARUCU.

pajé (*m.*) shaman; witch doctor; medicine man [= PIAGA and MANANGA].

pajear (*v.t.*) to serve as a page; to mind a child (as a nursemaid).

pajelança (*f.*) sorcery; magic cure.

pajem (*m.*) page (attendant); (*f.*) nursemaid.

pajeú (*m.*) sandgrass (*Triplaris*).; (*f.*) long, thin knife.

pajonal (*m.*) grass-covered land.

pal. = PALAVRA (word).

pala (*f.*) visor; eyeshade; setting for a jewel; tongue of a shoe; yoke (of a dress); (*Eccl.*) pall; (*m.*) poncho.

palacete [cê] (*m.*) small palace; fine city house, mansion.

palaciano –**na** (*adj.*) palatial; aristocratic; (*colloq.*) courtly; (*m.*) courtier.

palácio (*m.*) palace.

paladar (*m.*) palate; sense of taste; flavor, taste.

paladim, paladino (*m.*) paladin, knight-errant; champion (of a cause).

paládio (*m.*) palladium, safeguard; (*Chem.*) palladium; [*cap.*] Palladium (statue of Pallas Athene);

palafita (*f., Archaeol.*) palafitte.

palafrém (*m.*) palfrey.

palafreneiro (*m.*) groom, hostler.

palagonito (*m., Petrog.*) palagonite.

palamenta (*f., Naut.*) masts, rigging, equipment.

pâlamo (*m.*) web (membrane between digits and toes).

palanca (*f.*) piling; pile; lever [= ALAVANCA].

palanfrório (*m.*) balderdash; = PALAVREADO.

palangana (*f.*) large platter; large bowl.

palanque (*m.*) raised platform; scaffold; reviewing stand; bandstand [= CORETO]; hitching post; snubbing post; fence post.

palanquear (*v.t.*) to snub (a horse).

palanquim (*m.*) palanquin (covered litter).

palatal (*adj.*) palatal.

palatalizar (*v.t.*) to palatalize.

palatina (*f.*) palatine (a fur piece covering the neck and shoulders).

palatinado (*m.*) palatinate

palatinal (*adj.*) = PALATAL.

palatino –**na** (*adj.*) palatine; palatal; palatial; (*m.*) a palatine (nobleman).

palatite (*f., Med.*) palatitis; (*Veter.*) lampas.

palatizar (*v.*) = PALATALIZAR.

palato (*m.*) palate.

palatodental (*adj., Phonet.*) palatodental.

palatofaríngeo –**gea** (*adj., Anat.*) palatopharyngeal; (*m.*) pharyngopalatinus.

palatolabial (*adj., Anat.*) palatolabial.

palatolingual (*adj., Phonet.*) linguopalatal.

palavra (*f.*) word, term, expression, utterance; warrant, assurance, promise; (*interj.*) I give you my word!—**composta,** compound word.—**dada,** pledged word.—**de advertência,** word of warning.—**de Deus,** the Word of God.—**de elogio,** word of praise.—**de ordem,** word of command.—**de passe,** (*Masonry*) password.—**de rei,** unfailing promise.—**derivada,** (*Gram.*) a derivative.—**divina,** divine word.—**empenhada,** pledged word.—**expletiva,** (*Gram.*) an expletive.—**por palavra,** word for word.—**puxa palavra,** One word leads to another.—, **que não sei,** Honestly, I don't know.—**quebrada,** broken promise.—**s açucaradas,** or—**s de mel,** honeyed words. —**s cruzadas,** crossword puzzle.—**s imundas,** filthy or obscene words.—**s mágicas,** magic words.—**s no ar,** empty words.—**s pesadas,** coarse, offensive language.—**s truncadas,** garbled words. A—**s loucas, orelhas moucas,** Turn a deaf ear to foolish words. **A bom entendedor**

meia—**basta,** A word to the wise is sufficient. **cortar a**—**a,** to cut (someone) off. **cumprir a**—, to keep one's word. **dar a**—, to pledge one's word. **dar a**—**a,** to yield the floor (to another speaker). **de**—, by word of mouth. **dirigir a**—**a,** to address another (person). **em duas** (or **poucas, or quatro)**—**s,** in a word; in short; in brief. **em outras**—**s,** in other words. **em tôda a extensão,** or **na plena acepção, da**—, in the full sense of the word. **empenhar a**—, to pledge one's word. **estar com a**—**na bôca,** to have a word on the tip of one's tongue. **falta de**—, untrustworthiness. **faltar à** (or **voltar com a)**—, to go back on one's word. **Foi escolhido para tomar a**—, He was chosen as spokesman. **homem de**—, a man of his world. **homem de poucas**—**s,** a man of few words. **jôgo de**—**s,** a play on words. **medir** (or **pesar) as**—**s,** to measure (weigh) one's words. **não dizer**—, not to utter a word, remain silent. **não entender**—**de,** to know nothing about (a subject). **passar**—, to pass the word (on, around). **pedir a**—, to ask for the floor. **pessoa de**—, a person of (his) word. **prometer sob**—, to promise on one's word of honor. **Que quer dizer esta**—? What does this word mean? **Santas**—**s!** Blessed words! **ter**—, to keep one's promises. **ter a**—, to have the floor. **ter o dom da**—, or **ter a**—**facil,** to have the "gift of gab". **tirar a**—**da bôca de alguem,** to take the word out of another's mouth. **tomar uma coisa por**—**de evangelho,** to take something as gospel truth. **usar da**—, to take the floor.

palavrada (*f.*) dirty word; coarse expression.

palavrão (*m.*) a big (hard) word; an ugly word; "cuss word".

palavreado (*m.*) loquacity; idle chatter; a jumble of words [= PALAVRÓRIO, PALANFRÓRIO].

palavreador –**dora** (*adj.*) talkative; chattering; (*m.,f.*) talker; chatterer.

palavrear (*v.i.*) to pour forth, be loquacious.

palavrório (*m.*) = PALAVREADO.

palavroso –**sa** (*adj.*) loquacious, garrulous; diffuse; long-winded.

palco (*m.*) stage; platform.

pálea (*f., Eccl.*) pall; (*pl., Bot.*) paleae.

paleáceo –**cea** (*adj., Bot.*) paleaceous.

paleantropologia (*f.*) paleoanthropology.

palear (*v.i.*) to use a shovel.

paleetnologia [e-e] (*f.*) paleethonology.

paleiforme (*adj.*) strawlike; chafflike.

paleio (*m.*) an annoying joke; lark; fun; teasing; a dare; courtship; idle chatter; act of shoveling.

palejar (*v.i.*) to pale.

paleobotânica (*f.*) paleobotany.

paleoceno –**na** (*adj., Geol.*) Paleocene.

paleofitologia (*f.*) paleophytology.

paleogeografia (*f.*) paleogeography.

paleografia (*f.*) paleography.

paleógrafo –**fa** (*m.,f.*) paleographer.

paléola (*f., Bot.*) paleola.

paleolítico –**ca** (*adj.; f.*) paleolithic (period).

paleontografia (*f.*) paleontography.

paleontologia (*f.*) paleontology.

paleontologista (*m.,f.*) **paleontólogo** (*m.*), -**ga** (*f.*) paleontologist.

paleotropical (*adj., Biogeog.*) paleotropical.

paleovulcânico –**ca** (*adj.*) paleovolvanic.

paleozóico –**ca** (*adj.; m., Geol.*) Paleozoic (era).

paleozoologia (*f.*) paleozoology.

palerma (*adj.*) stupid, "dumb," "goofy"; (*m.,f.*) boob, simpleton, fool, nincompoop; lout; loggerhead.

palermar (*v.i.*) to behave like a PALERMA.

palermice (*f.*) foolishness, imbecility.

palescência (*f.*) paleness.

palestino –**na** (*adj.; m.,f.*) Palestinian; (*cap., f.*) Palestine.

palestra (*f.*) chat, informal conversation; an address.

palestrador –**dora** (*adj.*) chatty; (*m.,f.*) one who chats.

palestrante (*m.,f.*) one who chats.

palestr[e]ar (*v.i.*) to chat.

paleta [ê] (*f.*) painter's palette; potter's or sculptor's pallet; clod of beef shoulder; shoulder blade; (*m.,f.*) a killjoy.

paletear (*v.t.*) to spur on (a horse); to inject oneself into another's affairs in order to upset him; to carry a burden on the shoulder.

paletó (*m.*) man's coat.—**saco,** single-breasted sack coat. —**de traspasse,** double-breasted coat.

palha (*f.*) straw (single or in mass); dry grass; sipper; trifle.—**brava,** melic or onion grass (*Melica*).—**de aço,**

steel wool.—-**de-arroz**, common name for cyanite crystals found in diamond beds.—-**de-itália**, Leghorn straw.—-**de milho**, corn husk.—-**de-penacho** = CAPIM-DOS-PAMPAS.—-**de-prata**, a reedgrass (*Calamagrostis montevidensis*).—-**de-santa-fé**, a panicum or witchgrass (*Panicum rivulare*), extensively used in Brazil for thatching.—-**voadora**, Berg panicum (*P. bergi*). **chapéu de**—, straw hat. **dar**—**a (alguém)**,·to beguile, inveigle (someone). **dormir nas**—**s**, to go to sleep at the switch. **por dá cá aquela**—, (to lose one's temper) for little or no reason.

palhabote (*m.*) a two-masted schooner.

palhaçada (*f.*) buffoonery, clowning, capers; group of clowns.

palhaço –**ça** (*adj.*) straw; (*m.*) clown, buffoon.

palhada (*f.*) fodder, hay; idle talk.

palhagem (*f.*) straw pile.

palhal, palhar (*m.*) thatched hut, cabin or cottage.

palharesco –**ca** [ê] (*adj.*) straw.

palhegal (*m.*) grass-covered land.

palheirão (*m.*) large haystack; a large, dull book; a long-winded and confusing speaker.

palheireiro (*m.*) one who sells straw; one who makes cane bottoms for chairs.

palheiro (*m.*) hay loft; haystack; hay rick. **procurar agulha em**—, to look for a needle in a haystack.

palhento –**ta** (*adj.*) strawy; full of straw.

palhêta (*f.*) reed (of musical instrument); vane, fin (as of a turbine); slat (of venetian blind); straw hat.

palhetão (*m.*) bit or web of a key.

palhête (*adj.*) straw-colored; (*m.*) bit of a key; white wine.

palhetear (*v.i.*) to tease, banter, jest with (the person with whom one is talking).

palhiçar (*v.t.*) to thatch with straw.

palhiço –**ça** (*adj.*) made of straw; (*f.*) straw cape; (*m.*) chopped straw; a slender straw.

palhinha (*f.*) split cane for chair bottoms; a rush used for the same purpose; straw hat.

palhoça, palhota (*f.*), **palhote** (*m.*) straw-thatched hut; straw cape.

palhona (*f.*) cane- or rush-bottom chair.

palhoso –**sa** (*adj.*) strawlike.

paliação (*f.*) palliation.

paliador –**dora** (*adj.*) palliating; (*m.*,*f.*) palliator.

paliar (*v.t.*) to palliate; extenuate, excuse; mitigate, alleviate; allay; (*v.i.*) to moderate.

paliativo –**va** (*adj.*) palliative; (*m.*) a palliative agent.

paliçada (*f.*) palisade; stockade.

palidez [ê] (*f.*) paleness, pallor.

pálido –**da** (*adj.*; *m.*) pale, pallid, wan, colorless.

palimpsesto (*m.*) palimpsest.

palíndromo (*m.*) palindrome.

palingenesia (*f.*) palingenesis, rebirth, regeneration.

palinódia (*f.*) palinode; recantation.

pálio (*m.*) a portable canopy carried in street processions; (*R.C.Ch.*) pallium.

palissandra (*f.*), **palissandro** (*m.*) palisander, Brazilian rosewood (*Dalbergia nigra*); also the similar kingwood or violet wood (*D. cearensis*); also = CAROBAGUAÇU (a jacaranda).

palitar (*v.t.*) to pick the teeth.

paliteira (*f.*) = BISNAGA-DAS-SEARAS.

paliteiro (*m.*) toothpick holder.

palito (*m.*) toothpick; (*colloq.*) match. **fazer economia de**—**s**, to be pennywise and pound-foolish.

paliúro (*m.*, *Bot.*) Christ-thorn paliurus (*P. spina-christi*); c.a. ESPINHEIRO-DE-CRISTO.

palma (*f.*) palm; palm leaf; fig., laurels; (*pl.*) hand-clapping. **bater**—**s**, to clap hands. **levar a**—**a**, to carry off the palm, win the prize, take the cake.—-**cristi**, palma Christi (castor-oil plant, c.a. MAMONEIRO).—-**de-santa-rita**, (*Bot.*) gladiolus.—-**de-são-jorge** = SANSEVIÉRIA.—-**de-são-josé**, Easter lily (*Lilium longiflorum*), c.a. AÇUCENA-BRANCA, BASTÃO-DE-SÃO-JOSÉ, COPO-DE-LEITE, LIRIO-BRANCO.

palmáceo –**cea** (*adj.*, *Bot.*) arecaceous, palmaceous; (*f.pl.*) the Arecaceae (palm family).

palmada (*f.*) slap, smack, swat.

palmar (*m.*) grove of palm trees; (*adj.*) palmar; of the breadth of a span; fig., big. **êrro**—, gross blunder; flagrant error. (*v.t.*) = EMPALMAR.

palmares (*m.pl.*) extensive palm-covered land areas in northern Brazil.

palmatífido –**da** (*adj.*, *Bot.*) palmate, palmatifid.

palmatiforme (*adj.*, *Bot.*) palmatiform.

palmatilobado –**da** (*adj.*, *Bot.*) palmatilobate.

palmatinérveo –**vea** (*adj.*, *Bot.*) palmately veined or nerved.

palmatipartido –**da** (*adj.*, *Bot.*) palmatipartite.

palmatoar, palmatoriar (*v.t.*) to punish (school boys) with a PALMATÓRIA.

palmatória (*f.*) a palmer or ferule (for striking school boys on the palm of the hand); (*Bot.*) a prickly pear (*Opuntia*). —**do mundo**, a self-appointed censor; a would-be world reformer. **dar a mão à**—, to acknowledge one's mistake.

palmear (*v.t.*,*v.i.*) to clap (applaud); (*v.t.*) to take hold of; to crumble (tobacco) in the palm; (*Naut.*) to shove off; (*v.i.*) to cover every inch of the ground on foot.

palmeira (*f.*) any palm tree, esp. the following: —**açaí** = ACAÍZEIRO.—-**açaí-da-terra-firme**, an euterpe palm (*E. longispathea*).—-**açaí-mirim**, another euterpe palm (*E. precatoria*), c.a. PALMITO-MOLE.—-**anã**, or—-**das-vassouras**, the dwarf date palm (*Phoenix humilis*).—-**bambu**, the yellow butterfly palm (*Chrysalidocarpus lutescens*).—-**catolé** = ANAJÁ-MIRIM or CÔCO-CATOLÉ.—-**da-igreja**, the date palm (*Phoenix dactylifera*).—-**das-bermudas**, the Hispaniola palmetto (*Sabal umbraculifera*).—-**imperial**, or—-**real**, a royal palm (*Roystonea oleracea*).—-**laca**, a sealing-wax palm (*Cyrtostachys lakka* or *C. rendah*).—-**leque-do-rio-negro** = CARANÁ.—-**marinha** = CABEÇA-DE-MEDUSA (a crinoid).

palmeiral (*m.*) a grove of palm trees [= PALMAR].

palmeirim (*m.*) a palmer (pilgrim); also = ANAJÁ-MIRIM or CÔCO-CATOLÉ (a palm).

palmeirinha (*f.*) = ANAJÁ-MIRIM or CÔCO-CATOLÉ.—-**de-petrópolis**, the Weddell syagrus palm (*Syagrus weddelliana*).

palmejar (*m.*, *Naut.*) a cargo batten.

pálmer (*m.*) thread gauge.

palmeta (*f.*) spatula; inner sole of a shoe; iron wedge for splitting rocks.

palmífero –**ra** (*adj.*) palmy, abounding in palms.

palmiforme (*adj.*) palmiform.

palmilha (*f.*) inner sole of a shoe; sole of a stocking.

palmilhar (*v.t.*,*v.i.*) to tread, tramp, trudge; to trample. —**lugares comuns**, to hash over (discuss) commonplaces.

palmilobado –**da** (*adj.*, *Bot.*) palmilobate.

palminervado –**da** (*adj.*, *Bot.*) palminervate.

palminhas (*f.pl.*) **dar**—**a**, to applaud. **trazer nas**—, to take great care of.

palmípede (*adj.*; *m.*) palmiped, web-footed (animal).

palmira (*f.*) the palmyra palm (*Borassus flabellifer*).

palmital (*m.*) a grove of BABAÇU palms.

palmitato (*m.*, *Chem.*) palmitate.

palmítico –**ca** (*adj.*) palmitic [acid].

palmitina (*f.*, *Chem.*) palmitin.

palmito (*m.*) palm leaf; palm cabbage (the terminal bud of certain palms, used as a vegetable); a palm branch borne on Palm Sunday.—-**amargoso** = COQUEIRO-CATOLÉ and JERIVÁ.—-**do-campo**, the acuma syagrus palm (*S. flexuosa*).—-**doce**, the assai euterpe palm (*E. oleracea*)—-**juçara** = JUÇARA.—-**mole** = PALMEIRA-AÇAÍ-MIRIM.

palmo (*m.*) span (of the hand).—**a**—, inch by inch, foot by foot, step by step.

palmoura (*f.*) a webbed foot. Var. PALMOIRA.

paloma, palomar (*f.*) sailmaker's twine.

palomba (*f.*, *Naut.*) boltrope twine.

palombadura (*f.*, *Naut.*) boltrope tie.

palombeta (*f.*) the bumper (*Chloroscombrus chrysurus*)—a fish of the family Carangidae, c.a. CARAPAU, JUVÁ, VENTO-LESTE, PALOMETA.

palor (*m.*) pallor, paleness [= PALIDEZ].

palpabilidade (*f.*) palpability.

palpação (*f.*) act of touching or feeling; (*Med.*) palpation.

palpadela (*f.*) = APALPADELA.

palpamento (*m.*) = PALPAÇÃO.

palpar (*v.t.*) to palpate [= APALPAR].

palpável (*adj.*) palpable; obvious.

pálpebra (*f.*) eyelid.

palpebral (*adj.*) palpebral.

palpiforme (*adj.*, *Zool.*) palpiform.

palpígero –**ra** (*adj.*, *Zool.*) palpigerous.

palpitação (*f.*) palpitation.

palpitante (*adj.*) palpitating, quivering; stirring, moving, thrilling. **assunto**—, subject of vital interest.

palpitar (*v.i.*) to palpitate, beat, throb; to quiver; to conjecture, guess.

palpite (*m.*) palpitation; (*colloq.*) hunch; suggestion; tip (as on a horse race); (*slang*) an intrusive remark.

palpiteiro (*m.*) tipster.

palpo (*m., Zool.*) palpus.—**s labiais**, labial palpi.—**s maxilares**, maxillary palpi. **em—s** (or **papos**) **de aranha**, in hot water, in the soup, in a fine pickle, in a mess, behind the 8-ball, in a jam, in a spot, "stumped".

palra, palraria (*f.*) chatter, gab, babble.

palrador –**dora** (*adj.*) chattering; garrulous; (*m.,f.*) gabbler, chatterer.

palrar, palrear (*v.i.*) to chatter (as a parrot); to babble, gabble, jabber; to tittle-tattle.

palratório (*m.*) talk; chat; visiting room in a convent or prison [= PARLATÓRIO].

palreiro –**ra** (*adj.*) = PALRADOR.

palrice (*f.*) = PARLA.

paludano –**na** (*adj.*) marshy, boggy.

palude (*m.*) marsh, bog, fen.

paludial (*adj.*) paludal, marshy.

paludismo (*m., Med.*) paludism, malarial disease [= IMPALUDISMO].

paludoso –**sa** (*adj.*) marshy; paludous; malarial.

palúrdio –**dia** (*adj.; m.,f.*) stupid (person).

palustre (*adj.*) swampy, marshy; paludous. **febre—**, malarial fever.

pamonã (*m.*) a native Brazilian dish consisting of corn or manioc meal mixed with beans and meat or fish.

pamonha (*f.*) a sweetish concoction of which green corn paste is the chief ingredient, rolled and baked in fresh corn husks; (*m.*) sluggard; boob, simpleton; a softy [= MOLEIRÃO].

pampa (*adj.*) white-faced [horses, cattle]; (*m.*) pampa, vast treeless, grass-covered plain.

pâmpano (*m.*) tendril; vine shoot; pompano (fish), c.a. GALHUDO.

pamparra (*adj., colloq.*) great, "swell"; luscious; juicy.

pamparrona (*f.*) = GUAIVIRA.

pampeiro (*m.*) strong southwest wind in southeastern Brazil; (*slang*) shindy; free-for-all.

pampilho (*m.*) prod, goad; any of various chrysanthemums.—**das-searas** = ESTRÊLA-DE-OURO.

pamplo (*m.*) = PAMPO.

pampo (*m.*) the common or true pompano (*Trachinotus carolinus*), c.a. PAMPO-DE-CABEÇA-MOLE, PAMPLO, PIRAROBA, SEMENDUARA; the palometa (*T. glaucus*), c.a. PAMPO-ARACANGUIRA, PAMPO-DE-ESPINHA-MOLE, PAMPO-GALHUDO, PAMPO-RISCADO, but better known simply as GALHUDO.—**arabebéu** (or—**gigante**) is the round pompano (*T. falcatus*), c.a. SERNAMBIGUARA.

pamprodá[c]tilo –**la** (*adj., Zool.*) pamprodactyl.

panabásio (*m., Min.*) gray copper ore, tetrahedrite [= TETRAEDRITA].

panaca (*adj.; m.,f.*) knock-kneed (person); dim-witted (person).

panacarica (*f.*) straw canopy on a canoe.

panacéia (*f.*) panacea, cure-all; any allheal (plant).

panacheiro (*m., Bot.*) the showy bottlebrush (*Callistemon speciosus*).

panaço (*m.*) a blow with the flat side of a sword or machete.

panacocó (*m.*) the wamara swartzpea (*Swartzia tomentosa*).

panacu[m] (*m.*) a large wicker basket.

panado –**da** (*adj.*) breaded.

panal (*m.*) cloth, shroud; diaper; cylindrical piece of wood on which a boat is rolled into the water.

panamá (*m.*) Panama hat; public graft; a "milking" or "bleeding" of an enterprise by its management, for personal gain.—**camajondura** = XIXÁ (a plant).

panamenho, panamenho –**nha** (*adj.; m.,f.*) Panamanian.

pan-americanismo (*m.*) Pan-Americanism.

pan-americano –**na** (*adj.*) Pan-American.

panapaná (*f.*) a cloud of butterflies; a bean (*Phaseolus peduncularis*).

panar (*v.t.*) to bread (cutlets, etc.).

panarício, panariz (*m., Med.*) whitlow, felon, paronychia [= PARONÍQUIA].

panascal, panasqueira (*m.*) waste land.

panasco (*m.*) wild parsnip (*Pastinaca sylvestris*); also = CAPIM-PÉ-DE-GALINHA.—**de-tabuleiro** = CAPIM-RABO-DE-RAPÔSA (a grass).

panásio (*m.*) a kick or blow; a blow with the flat of a saber or bush knife; the sound of a gunshot.

panavueiro (*m.*) a cane knife [= FACÃO].

panca (*f.*) a heavy wooden lever. **andar em—s**, to be very busy or in a tight spot. **dar—s**, to be outstanding in something.

pança (*f.*) potbelly, paunch; (*Zool.*) rumen.

pançada (*f.*) a bellyful; a blow on the belly.

pancada (*f.*) blow, stroke, hit, knock, bang; a drubbing; heart beat; "hunch"; mania; sudden downpour; a small vertical waterfall. **esperar pela—**, to wait for something to happen—lit., for the blow to fall; (*m., colloq.*) screwball, crackpot; a roughneck; (*adj.*) batty, "nuts".

pancadão (*m., slang*) curvaceous, attractive woman.

pancadaria (*f.*) shower of blows; brawl, fracas; (*Music*) percussion instruments, collectively.

pancardite (*f., Med.*) pancarditis.

pancrácio (*m.*) simpleton, nitwit; (*Bot.*) the sea daffodil (*Pancratium maritimum*); (*Gr. Antiq.*) pancratium.

pancreadene (*m., Biochem.*) pancreatin.

pâncreas (*m. Anat.*) pancreas; (*Physiol.*) pancreatic juice.

pancreatectomia (*f., Surg.*) pancreatectomy.

pancreático –**ca** (*adj.*) pancreatic.

pancreatina (*f., Biochem.*) pancreatin.

pancresto (*m.*) panacea [= PANACÉIA].

pancromático –**ca** (*adj., Photog.*) panchromatic [= ORTOCROMÁTICO].

pancuã (*m.*) = CAPIM-PANCUÃ.

pançudo –**da** (*adj.*) potbellied, paunchy; parasitic; (*m.*) sponge, parasite.

panda (*f.*) cork float of a fishing net; (*Bot.*) a screw pine (*Pandanus*); (*m., Zool.*) the giant panda.

pandacosta (*f.*) = PANO DA COSTA.

pandanáceo –**cea** (*adj., Bot.*) pandanceous; (*f.pl.*) the screw pine family (*Pandanaceae*).

pandano (*m.*) the common screw pine (*Pandanus utilis*), c.a. VACUÁ.

pandarecos (*m.pl.*) bits, crumbs, scraps, shreds, chips, slivers; smithereens.

pandear (*v.t.*) to puff up or out, cause to swell or expand; to distend, inflate, bloat.

pândega (*f.*) spree, revel, noisy merrymaking, high jinks; lark.

pandegar (*v.i.*) to revel, carouse, make merry, paint the town red.

pândego –**ga** (*adj.*) carousing, reveling, roistering, merrymaking; (*m.*) reveler, carouser, roisterer, cutup.

pandeireiro (*m.*) maker of tambourines; tambourine player.

pandeireta [rê] (*f.*) small tambourine or timbrel.

pandeirinha (*f.*) the little quaking grass (*Briza minor*).

pandeiro (*m.*) tambourine.—**de cordas**, a coil of rope.

pandemia (*f.*) pandemic disease.

pandêmico –**ca** (*adj.*) pandemic.

pandemônio (*m.*) pandemonium; infernal noise; wild uproar.

pandermita, -te (*f., Min.*) pandermite [= PRICEÍTA].

pandiculação (*f.*) pandiculation (a stretching and yawning).

pandilha (*f.*) plot, scheme (for a bad purpose); gang of evildoers; (*m.*) schemer; cheat, rogue.

pandilhar (*v.i.*) to live by scheming and cheating; to loaf.

pandilheiro (*m.*) rogue; loafer.

pândita (*m.*) pundit.

pando –**da** (*adj.*) full, inflated, stretched, extended. **velas —s**, full sails.

pandora (*f., Music*) bandore; (*cap., Gr. Myth.*) Pandora. **boceta de—**, Pandora's box; (*Zool.*) the genus Pandora of marine bivalves.

pandorca, pandorga (*f.*) discordant noises such as a charivari; an obese woman; a paper kite; (*m.,f.*) dumbbell (stupid person).

pandulho (*m.*) fishing net sinker; any weight used as an anchor; (*colloq.*) belly [= BANDULHO].

panduriforme (*adj., Bot.*) panduriform, obovate.

pane (*f.*) failure of an automobile or airplane motor. [Fr. *panne.*]

panegirical (*adj.*) panegyrical.

panegírico –**ca** (*adj.; m.*) panegyric.

panegirista (*m.,f.*) panegyrist.

paneiro (*m.*) pannier, hamper, wicker basket; (*Theater*) curtain handler; seats for passengers in the stern of a small boat; the removable floor boards of a boat; a wicker carriage; a piece of tin or metal sheet on which a mason dumps mortar.

panejar (*v.t.*) to drape; (*v.i.*) of sails, to flap.

panela (*f.*) pot, pan, kettle; pothole; political clique; ants' underground nest.

panelada (*f.*) potful; many pots; air rattles (in the throat and bronchi); a stew made with calves' feet and vegetables.

panelinha (*f.*) small pot; group of political insiders; literary clique.

panema (*adj.*) unlucky, jinxed; (*m.,f.*) victim of bad luck; a hunter or fisherman who returns empty-handed.

pan-eslavismo (*m.*) Pan-Slavism.

panetela (*f.*) panatela (cigar).

pânfila (*f.*) the resurrectionlily (*Kaempferia*); a genus of sawflies (*Pamphilius*).

panfletário –ria (*adj.*) pamphletic; passionate (in speech); (*m.*) pamphleteer.

panfletista (*m.,f.*) pamphleteer; lampooner.

panfleto [ê] (*m.*) pamphlet; lampoon.

pangarave (*adj., colloq.*) vile; mean.

pangaré (*adj.*) of horses, dark-red with lighter muzzle and underbelly; (*m.*) such a horse; an unruly horse.

pangene, pangeno (*m., Biol.*) pangen(e), biophore.

pangênese (*f., Biol.*) pangenesis.

pangermanismo (*m.*) Pan-Germanism.

pango (*m.*) = DIAMBA.

pangolim (*m.*) pangolin (scaly anteater).

panhame (*m.,f.*) an Indian of the Pañame, a tribe of the Maxacalí in Mato Grosso on the upper Mucuri and Suçui-pequeno Rivers; (*adj.*) pert. to or designating this tribe.

pan-helênico –ca (*adj.*) Panhellenic.

pan-helenismo (*m.*) Panhellenism.

paníceo –cea (*adj.*) paniclike [grass].

pânico –ca (*adj.*) panicky; (*m.*) panic. **assoberbado de—,** panic-stricken.

paniconografia (*f.*) paniconography, photozincography.

panícula (*f., Bot.*) panicle.

paniculado –da (*adj., Bot.*) paniculate.

panículo (*m., Anat.*) tela.—**adiposo,** tela subcutanea (panniculus adiposus).

panificação (*f.*) breadmaking; bakery.

panificador (*m.*) breadmaker; baker.

panificar (*v.t.*) to make flour into bread.

paninho (*m.*) a small cloth; fine cotton cloth.

panívoro –ra (*adj.*) panivorous, subsisting on bread.

pano (*m.*) cloth, sail; (*colloq.*) skin blemish; a curtain wall. —**alcatroado,** tarpaulin.—**cru,** unbleached cloth.—**da costa,** a bright cotton cloth worn as a shawl by Negro women in Bahia.—**de bôca,** stage curtain.—**de fundo,** backdrop.—**do telhado,** side (slope) of a roof.—**para as mangas,** plenty to spare, more than enough.—**patente,** madras, shirting.—**s mornos** (or **quentes**), half-measures. **a todo o—,** under full sail; full speed ahead. **estar em—verde,** to have lost all one's money at the gaming table. **saia de quatro—s,** a four-gore skirt. **sem—s quentes,** without mincing words.

panóplia (*f.*) panoply.

panorama (*m.*) panorama.

panorâmico –ca (*adj.*) panoramic.

panqueca [é] (*f.*) pancake; (*colloq.*) idleness.

pânria (*f.*) idleness, loafing; (*m.,f.*) idler, loafer.

pansofia (*f.*) pansophy.

panspermia (*f., Biol.*) panspermy.

pantafaçudo –da (*adj.*) chubby-faced.

pantagruélico –ca (*adj.*) Pantagruelian.

pantalão (*m.*) pantaloon, buffoon.

pantalha (*f.*) lampshade; screen.

pantalonada (*f.*) buffoonery.

pantalonas (*f.pl.*) pantaloons.

pantana (*f.*) squandering, dissipation. **dar em—,** to go to the dogs.

pantanal (*m.*) large swamp; the lowlands of Mato Grosso.

pântano (*m.*) marsh, swamp, morass, bog; mire; river lowlands.

pantanoso –sa (*adj.*) marshy, swampy.

Panteão (*m.*) Pantheon.

pantear (*v.i.*) to utter foolishness; (*v.t.*) to make fun of.

panteísmo (*m.*) pantheism.

panteísta (*adj.*) pantheistic; (*m.,f.*) pantheist.

pantera (*f.*) panther.

pantim (*m.*) **fazer—,** to spread bad news.

pantofobia (*f.*) pantophobia.

pantógrafo (*m.*) pantograph.

pantólogo (*m.*) pantologist.

pantômetro (*m.*) pantometer.

pantomima (*f.*) pantomime.

pantomimar (*v.t.,v.i.*) to pantomime.

pantomimeiro –ra, pantomimo –ma (*m.,f.*) pantomimist.

pantomímico –ca (*adj.*) pantomimic.

pantomórfico –ca (*adj.*) pantomorphic.

pantoscópio (*m., Photog.*) pantoscope.

pantufa (*f.*) house slipper; a big woman, esp. one carelessly dressed.

pantufo (*m.*) pantofle, slipper; (*slang*) fat man; young male termite.

panturra (*f.*) potbelly, paunch; bellyful; fig., pomposity.

panturrilha (*f.*) calf of leg.

paô (*m.*) = PAVÓ or PAVÔ.

pão [pães] (*m.*) bread; loaf of bread; cereals; livelihood; (*Metal.*) sow.—**amanhecido** or—**dormido,** yesterday's bread; day-old bread.—**ázimo,** unleavened bread.—**branco,** white bread.—**caseiro,** homemade bread.—**com manteiga,** bread and butter.—**cotidiano,** or—**de cada dia,** daily bread.—**de açúcar,** sugar loaf.—**de ajunta,** bread made of cornmeal mixed with wheat flour.—**de centeio,** rye bread.—**-de-leite,** English primrose (*Primula vulgaris*).—**-de-ló,** sponge cake.—**-de-ló-de-mico,** a courbaril tree (*Hymenea courbaril*).—**de milho** = CANJICA.—**de munição,** soldiers' coarse bread.—**-de-pássaros,** the goldmoss stonecrop (*Sedum acre*), c.a. PIMENTA-DAS-PAREDES, SAIÃO-ACRE, UVA-DE-CÃO, VERMICULÁRIA-QUEIMANTE.—**-de-pobre,** the manioc plant; lit., the poor man's bread.—**do espírito,** fig., knowledge, learning.—**-durismo,** avarice, stinginess.—**-duro,** a miser; a stingy person.—**e-queijo,** a primula or primrose.—**-grande,** idleness.—**integral,** wholewheat bread.—**negro,** black bread.—**nosso de cada dia,** our daily bread [= PÃO COTIDIANO].—, **pão, queijo, queijo,** clearly, frankly, forthrightly.—**sêco,** dry bread (without butter). —**-porcino,** or—**-de-porco,** sowbread (the common European cyclamen, *C. europaeum*), c.a. ARTANITA, CICLAME-DA-EUROPA, VIOLETA-DOS-ALPES.—**-pôsto,** a herb of the thistle family (*Anacyclus valentinus*).—**torrado,** toast. **a—e agua,** on bread and water; on a strict diet; hard-up. **a—e laranja,** hard-up; on short rations. **côdea do—,** bread crust. **fazer—grande,** to loaf. **ganhar o—,** to earn a living. **miolos de—,** bread crumbs. **O—de cada dia, dai-nos hoje,** Give us this day our daily bread.

pãozeiro (*m.*) bread man [= PADEIRO].

papá (*m.*) = PAPAI.

Papa (*m.*) the Pope; (*not cap., f.pl.*) pap, gruel, mushy food.—**s de linhaça,** linseed poultice. **não ter—s na língua,** to be outspoken.

papa-abelhas (*m.*) = ABELHEIRO.

papa-açaí (*m., Zool.*) the red chatterer (*Phoenicircus carnifex*), c.a. ANAMBÉ, UIRA-TATA, SAURÁ, ARAÇUIRÁ.

papa-areia (*m.,f.*) "sand sucker"—a nickname applied by natives of Pelotas to those of Rio Grande do Sul (city).

papa-arroz (*m.*) a cowbird (*Molothrus sp.*); also, any of numerous unspecified ricebirds of the finch family.

papa-cacau (*m.*) the festive parrot (*Amazona festiva*).

papa-capim (*m.*) any of numerous seedeaters of the genus Sporophila, esp. *S. caerulescens*, c.a. COLEIRA, COLEIRO-VIRADO, and *S. lineola*, c.a. BIGODE, COLEIRINHO. Other common names for seedeaters are: PAPA-ARROZ, PATATIVA, BREJAL, CHORÃO, PIXOXÓ, CABOCLINHO.

papa-ceia (*f., colloq.*) evening star.

papa-côco (*m.*) a squirrel (*Sciurus sp.*).

papaconha (*m.*) = IPECACUANHA.

papada (*f.*) double chin; jowl; dewlap; goitre.

papa-defuntos (*m.*) an armadillo (*Dazypus setosus*); (*colloq.*) a tout for an undertaker.

papado (*m.*) the papacy.

papa-figo (*m.*) bogeyman [= PAPÃO]; any of various birds; (*Naut.*) fore course, main course, any lowest square sail.

papa-filas (*m.*) a type of extra-long bus in service in some of Brazil's larger cities.

papa-fina (*adj.*) savory; excellent; (*m.*) a ridiculous individual.

papa-formigas (*m.*) any of numerous antbirds, esp. the white-winged fire-eye (*Pyriglena leucoptera*), c.a. MÃE-DE-TORÁ; Pelzeln's antcatcher (*Myrmoderus squamosus*); Lichtenstein's antcatcher (*Myrmoderus loricatus*), c.a. TAQUARI; a wryneck (*Jynx*), c.a. PIADEIRA, TORCICOLO.

papagaia (*f.*) a female parrot.

papagaiado –da (*adj.*) pigeon-toed; (*f.*) noisy chatter.

papagaial (*adj.*) of or pert. to parrots.

papagaiar (*v.i.*) to parrot.

papagaieira (*f.*, *Bot.*) the poinsettia, c.a. FÔLHA-DE-SANGUE.

papagaínho (*m.*) Wied's black-eared parrotlet (*Urochroma wiedi*); the caica parrot of Guiana (*Eucinetus caica*).—-roxo = MATICA-PARDA.

papagaio (*m.*) any parrot; a person who parrots another; a paper kite; an accommodation note; a bill of exchange; a parrot fish; a dividing wall or fence between window balconies; a circular letter of instructions; a rider (tacked on to another document); a "hot foot" (given as a practical joke); a scribbled note; (*Zool.*) the Spanish hogfish (*Bodianus rufa*), c.a. PRETUCANO; also, a ray called RAIA-PINTADA; (*Bot.*) the garden balsam (*Impatiens balsamina*); the poinsettia, c.a. FÔLHA-DE-SANGUE, PAPAGAIEIRA; (*interj.*) You don't say! Really now!—-campeiro, the yellow-headed parrot (*Amazona o. ochrocephala*), c.a. AOLO.—-caboclo = PEITO-ROXO.—-da-serra = CHORÃO.—-de-coleira (or—-de-colete), the hawk-headed parrot (*Deroptyus a. accipitrinus*), c.a. NANACÃ, IA-IA, VANAQUIÁ.—-do(s)-mangue(s) and—-poaieiro = CURICA.—-do-mar, a puffin (*Fratercula*).—-imperial = GUARUBA.—-verdadeiro, the blue-fronted parrot (*Amazona a. aestiva*), or the yellow-winged parrot (*Amazona aestiva xanthropteryx*) which differs chiefly in having the front border of wing golden instead of red, c.a. PAPAGAIO-GREGO, AJURU.

papa-gente (*m.*) cannibal; hobgoblin.

papagueador –dora (*adj.*) parroting; (*m.,f.*) parroter.

papaguear (*v.t.,v.i.*) to parrot; (*v.i.*) to talk nonsense.

papa-hóstias (*m.,f., colloq.*) an excessively devout communicant, or a sanctimonious one.

papai (*m.*) papa; kind of catfish.—**Noel**, Santa Claus.

papaia, papaieira (*f.*) the papaya tree [= MAMÃO or MAMOEIRO].

papaína (*f., Chem.*) papain.

papa-jantares (*m.*) sponge, parasite.

papal (*adj.*) papal.

papa-lagartas (*m., Zool.*) Azara's cuckoo (*Coccyzus melacoryphus*), c.a. CHINCOÃ, CUCU.

papa-laranja (*m.*) the blue-and-yellow tanager (*Thraupis b. bonariensis*).

papa-léguas (*m.*) a fast walker; one who covers much ground.

papalva (*f.*) gullible woman.

papalvice (*f.*) naïveté, gullibility.

papalvo (*m.*) simpleton, boob; sucker, greenhorn.

papa-mamão (*m.,f.*) a nickname formerly applied by inhabitants of Recife to those of the neighboring town of Olinda.

papa-mel (*m.*) = IRARA.

papa-mico (*m.*) = GAVIÃO-PEGA-MACACO.

papa-missas (*m.,f.*) a sanctimonious person [= CAROLA].

papa-môscas (*m.,f.*) a simpleton [= TOLO]; (*m.*) a jumping spider (family *Attidae*); the sordid tyrant (*Myiarchus swainsoni*), c.a. IRRÉ, PAI-AGOSTINHO; Lichtenstein's fork-tailed tyrant (*Muscipara vetula*), c.a. TESOURA.—-real, Swainson's royal flycatcher (*Onychorhynchus swainsoni*); a sun bittern called pavão-do-pará; a small fly-catching lizard; (*Bot.*) a sundew (*Drosera*).

papamundo (*m.*) the mamoncillo or Spanish lime (*Melicocca bijuga*).

papança (*f., colloq.*) "grub", "vittles".

papa-novenas (*f.*) a sanctimonious woman.

papão (*m.*) bogeyman, bugbear, ogre, hobgoblin [= BICHO-PAPÃO, PAPA-GENTE, PAPA-FIGO].

papa-ôvo (*m.*) a harmless gopher snake, c.a. PAPA-OVA(S), PAPA-PINTO; either of two birds called MATRACA and BORRALHARA.

papa-peixe (*m.*) a kingfisher (*Ceryle amazona*).

papa-pimenta (*m.*) a rove beetle (*Staphylinus*).

papa-pinto (*m.*) either of two non-venomous Brazilian snakes: *Phrynonax sulphureus* and *Drymarchon corais*; an antbird called BORRALHARA.

papa-piri [rí] (*m.*) the many-colored tyrant bird (*Tachuris r. rubrigastra*).

papar (*v.t.,v.i.*) to gobble (food); to gain by graft or extortion.

paparicar (*v.i.*) to nibble at.

paparicos (*m.pl.*) dainty morsels; pettings, caresses.

papariuba (*f.*) = SIMARUBA-AMARGA.

paparraz (*m.*) the stavesacre larkspur (*Delphinium staphisagria*), c.a. ESTAFISÁGRIA.

paparreta [ê] (*adj.; m.*) = PAPARROTÃO.

paparriba (*adj.*) (lying) belly-up; loafing.

paparrotada, paparrotagem (*f.*) bragging, boasts; swill, hogwash.

paparrotão (*adj.*) boastful; (*m., colloq.*) braggart.

paparrotear (*v.t.,v.i.*) to brag.

paparrotice (*f.*) bragging, boasting.

papa-santos (*m.,f.*) an excessively devout person;—used disparagingly.

papata (*f.*) graft, racket; a profitable deal.

papa-tabaco (*m.*) a stargazer (fish); (*m.,f.*) an inveterate snuff user.

papataoca (*f.*) a black, red-eyed antbird (*Pyriglena leucoptera*), c.a. PAPA-FORMIGA.

papa-terra (*m.,f.*) a clay eater; either of two stingless bees: *Melipona quadriculata*, c.a. GUIRUÇU, ABELHA-MULATA, and *M. capitata*, c.a. MUMBUCA; any of various freshwater fishes; the southern kingfish (*Menticirrhus americanus*), c.a. PIRA-SIRIRICA, CARAMETARA, SAMBE-TARA, JUDEU, TAMBETARA, TREMETARA;—estrêla = VER-MELHO (red snapper); (*Bot.*) a medium-sized tree (*Posoqueria latifolia*) of the Rubiaceae; also, either of two other trees of the same family: *Basanacantha spinosa*, c.a. LIMÃORANA-DA-TERRA-FIRME, and *Chomelia anisomeris*, c.a. LIMÃORANA-DA-VÁRZEA; also = DOURADINHA, AÇUCENA-DO-MATO.

papável (*adj.*) designating a cardinal who is in line for the papacy; by ext., designating anyone eligible to some office or position.

papa-vento (*m.*) any of various Brazilian lizards, esp. *Anisolepis undulatus*, of the iguana family, c.a. LAGAR-TIXA, CALANGO; a paper whirligig (child's toy).

papaveráceo –cea (*adj., Bot.*) papaveraceous, papaverous; (*f.pl.*) the poppy family (*Papaveraceae*).

papaverina (*f., Chem.*) papaverin(e).

papazana (*f., colloq.*) a blowout, big feed [= COMEZAINA].

papeá-guaçu [çú] (*m.*) a whiptree (*Luhea speciosa*).

papear (*v.i.*) to chatter, jabber; to chirp.

papeata (*f.*) hypocritical exhibition of sympathy, sorrow, etc.

papeateiro –ra (*adj.; m.,f.*) given to displaying, or one who displays, phony sentiments.

papeio (*m.*) peep, chirp.

papeira (*f., Med.*) mumps [= CAXUMBA or TRASORELHO]; goitre [= BÓCIO]; (*Veter.*) lumpy jaw, big jaw; (*Bot.*) a tropical shrub of the borage family (*Tournefortia lucidaphylla*).

papel [-péis] (*m.*) paper; role, part; paper money; (*pl.*) documents (passports, etc.).—**almaço**, foolscap paper.—-arroz, the ricepaper plant (*Tetrapanax papyriferus*).—**assetinado**, glazed or glossy paper.—**carbono**, carbon paper.—**cartucho**, cartridge paper; coarse wrapping paper.—**chupão**, blotting paper.—**com brilho**, (*Photog.*) glossy paper.—**couché**, art paper.—**curto**, short-term notes.—**de calcar**, tracing paper.—**de carta**, letter paper; note paper.—**de desenho**, drawing paper.—**de embrulho**, wrapping paper.—**de escrever**, writing paper.—**de filtrar**, filter paper.—**de imprensa**, newsprint.—**de impressão**, printing paper.—**de lixa**, sandpaper.—**de luto**, black-bordered (mourning) note paper.—**de máquina**, typewriter paper.—**de mortalha**, cigarette paper.—**de música**, music paper.—**de pergaminho**, parchment paper.—**de sêda**, tissue paper.—**de segunda via**, copy paper.—**de tornassol**, (*Lab.*) litmus paper.—**de trapo**, rag paper.—**em branco**, blank paper.—**encerado** or **impermeável**, wax paper.—**ferroprussiato**, blueprint paper.—-filtro, filter paper.—**higiênico**, toilet paper.—**longo**, long-term notes.—**manilha**, Manila paper.—**mataborrão**, blotting paper.—**mata-môscas**, flypaper.—**mate**, (*Photog.*) mat paper.—**moeda**, paper currency.—**mofado** or **queimado**, (*colloq.*) a married man.—**pano**, vellum (tracing) cloth.—**paquête**, light, thin paper, as for air mail.—**parafinado**, wax paper.—**pardo**, brown wrapping paper.—**pautado**, ruled paper.—**pergaminho**, parchment paper.—**pintado**, wall paper.—**quadriculado**, graph paper.—**químico**, carbon paper.—**sem brilho**, (*Photog.*) dull-finish paper.—**sensibilizado**, (*Photog.*) sensitized paper.—**vegetal**, translucent tracing paper.—**velino**, vellum paper. **corta**—, paper knife, paper cutter. **desempenhar um**—, to play a part. **fábrica de**—, paper mill. **fazer o**—**de**, to play the part of. **fazer um triste**—, to cut a sorry figure. **fôlha de**—, a sheet of paper. **papagaio de**—, paper kite. **tira de**—, a slip of paper. **u'a mão de**—, a quire of paper.

papelada, papelagem (*f.*) a pile of papers, esp. a disorderly one; a mass of documents.

papelama (*f.*) paper work; red tape; a pile of papers.
papelão (*m.*) cardboard, pasteboard; (*colloq.*) a fool; sorry spectacle; fiasco.—**ondulado**, corrugated paper.
papelaria (*f.*) stationery store; office supply house.
papeleiro –**ra** (*adj.*) of or pert. to the paper industry; (*m.*) stationer; worker in a paper mill; (*f.*) slant-top desk.
papelejo (*m.*) scrap of paper.
papeleta [lê] (*f.*) any small piece of paper; leaflet; a notice posted on a wall; identification paper; patient's chart in a hospital.
papelete, papelico, papelinho (*m.*) scrap of paper, lit. & fig.
papelismo (*m.*) a policy of deficit-financing by means of printing-press money.
papelista (*m.,f.*) one who handles (investigates, archives) papers; one who favors inflationary deficit-financing.
papelório (*m.*) a stack of papers; (*colloq.*) a sorry figure.
papelotes (*m.pl.*) curl papers for the hair.
papelucho (*m.*) scrap of paper; piece of wrapping paper.
papífero –**ra** (*adj., Bot.*) pappiferous.
papiforme (*adj., Bot.*) pappiform.
papila (*f., Anat., Zool., Bot.*) papilla, nipple; papule; pimple.—**mamária**, breast nipple.
papilar (*adj.*) papillary.
papilha (*f.*) cock's wattle.
papilhoso –**sa** (*adj.*) papillose.
papiliforme (*adj.*) papilliform.
papílio (*m.*) swallowtail butterfly (*Papilio*).
papilionáceo –**cea** (*adj.*) papilionaceous, like a butterfly; (*Bot.*) having a corolla somewhat resembling a butterfly; belonging to the Fabaceae; (*f.pl.*) the Fabaceae (peas and beans).
papiliônidas (*f.pl.*), **papilionídeos** (*m.pl.*) the Papilionidae (butterflies).
papiloma (*m., Med.*) papilloma.
papira (*f.*) = TIÉ-FOGO.
papiráceo –**cea** (*adj.*) papyraceous, papery.
papíreo –**rea** (*adj.*) papyrian.
papiri [í] (*m.*) = TAPIRI.
papiro (*m., Bot.*) papyrus (*Cyperus papyrus*).
papisa (*f.*) popess (specif., Pope Joan).
papismo (*m.*) papism.
papista (*adj.; m.,f.*) papist; (*m.*) a small sea catfish; a clay eater.
papo (*m.*) bird's crop or craw; cheek pouch (as of a squirrel); (*colloq.*) stomach; goitre; double chin; jabot; (*Bot.*) pappus.—**branco**, a white-breasted hummingbird (*Leuchloris albicollis*).—**de-anjo** = CANUDO-DE-PITO (a plant).—**de-fogo**, the Brazilian ruby hummingbird (*Clytolaema rubricauda*).—**de-galo** = CIPÓ-MATA-COBRA (a plant).—**de-pavão**, a tree (*Combretum alternifolium*) of the myrobalan family.—**de-peru**, (*Bot.*) a dutchmans-pipe (*Aristolochia*). **bater**—, (*colloq.*) to chat. **De grão em grão a galinha enche o**—, Little and often fills the purse. **estar** (or **ver-se**) **em**—**s** (or **palpos) de aranha**, to be in a fix, in a jam, in a mess, behind the 8-ball. **ficar de**—**para o ar esperando que tudo nos caia dos céus**, to sit with folded hands, waiting for the Lord to provide. **um bate**—, (*slang*) a chat; a "chin-fest," a "bull-session".
papocar (*v.*) = PIPOCAR.
papoula (*f.*) poppy (*Papaver*) (*Naut.*) pulley block.—**da-califórnia**, the California poppy, c.a. GLOBO-DO-SOL.—**das-praias**, yellow hornpoppy (*Glaucium flavium*).—**de-espinho**,—**do-méxico**,—**espinhosa**, the Mexican prickly poppy (*Argemone mexicana*), c.a. CARDO-MARIANO, CARDO-SANTO.—**do-são-francisco**, the Kenaf hibiscus (*H. cannabinus*). Var. PAPOILA.
papua (*adj.; m.,f.*) Papuan.
papuã (*m.*) a signal grass (*Brachiaria plantaginea*), c.a. CAPIM-MARMELADA.
papudo –**da** (*adj.*) double-chinned; goitrous; puffed out (as the breast of a pouter pigeon); puffed up (vain).
pápula (*f., Med.*) papule.
papulífero –**ra** (*adj.*) papuliferous; pimply.
papuloso –**sa** (*adj.*) papulose.
paquê (*m.*) printer's composing stick [= GRANEL].
paquebote (*m.*) packet boat.
paquête (*m.*) steamship; (*colloq.*) menses.
paquicarpo –**pa** (*adj., Bot.*) pachycarpous.
paquicéfalo –**la** (*adj., Anthropom., Zool.*) pachycephalous.
paquiderme (*m.*) pachyderm; (*adj.*) pachydermous.
paquife (*m., Arch.*) ornamental foliage; rosette.
paquímetro (*m.*) pachymeter; a caliper rule.
paquinha (*f.*) a mole cricket [= GRILO-TOUPEIRA].

paquirrizo (*m., Bot.*) the yambean (*Pachyrhizus*).
Paquistão (*m.*) Pakistan.
paquítrico –**ca** (*adj., Zool.*) pachytrichous.
par [-es] (*adj.*) equal, like; on a par; of numbers, even; (*m.*) pair, couple, brace, two of a kind; dance partner; peer.—**do reino**, peer of the realm.—**ou ímpar**, even or odd.—**es ou nunes**, even or odd. **a**—**de**, along with; at the same time as; in view of; well-posted on, acquainted with, informed about, au courant. **acima do**—, above par; at a premium. **ao**—, at par. **aos**—**es**, two by two; in pairs. **de**—**em**—, wide open (as doors). **Isto é um outro**—**de mangas**, That is a horse of another color. **numero**—, even number. **sem**—, peerless, unmatched. **um**—**de contos**, a lot of money.
para (*prep.*) for, to, toward, in, into; (*conj.*) in order to, for the purpose of; about to.—**alí**, over there.—**baixo**, downward.—**cá**, here, over here, this way.—**cá e**—**lá**, here and there, back and forth.—**cima**, upward.—**com**, toward.—**dentro**, to the inside; inward.—**diante**, forward.—**fora**, to the outside.—**inglês ver**, just for show, just to make an impression.—**já**, for now,—**logo**, at once.—**onde**, where.—**que**, so that, in order that.—**que?** What for? Why?—**sempre**, forever. **de lá**—**cá**, since then. **estar**—, to be about to.
paraambôia [a-am] (*f.*) = SURUCUCU-DE-PATIOBA.
parabacu-prêto (*m.*) = SAGUI-DE-CABEÇA-BRANCA.
parabanato (*m., Chem.*) parabanate.
parabânico –**ca** (*adj., Chem.*) parabanic.
parabém (*m.*) = PARABÉNS.
parabéns (*m.pl.*) congratulations, felicitations.
parabiju [ú] (*m.*) = BIJUPIRÁ.
parabiose (*f., Zool.*) parabiosis.
parablasto (*m., Embryol.*) parablast.
parábola (*f.*) parable, allegory; (*Geom.*) parabola.
parabólico –**ca** (*adj.*) parabolic(al).
parabolóide (*adj.; m., Geom.*) paraboloid(al).
pára-brisa(s) (*m.*) windshield.
paração (*f.*) roundup of cattle [= RODEIO].
paracatas (*f.pl.*) clodhoppers (strong, heavy shoes).
paracari [í] (*m.*) iripil-bark tree (*Pentaclethra filamentosa*); = PRACAXI.
pára-centelhas (*m.*) spark arrester [= FAGULHEIRO].
paracentral (*adj., Anat.*) paracentral.
paracêntrico –**ca** (*adj.*) paracentric.
pára-chispas (*m.*) = PÁRA-CENTELHAS.
pára-choque (*m.*) bumper (of automobile, etc.); buffer; shock absorber.
pára-chuva (*m.*) = GUARDA-CHUVA.
paracianogênio (*m., Chem.*) paracyanogen.
paracleto [é] (*m.*) paraclete.
paracronismo (*m.*) parachronism.
paracutaca (*f.*) a swartzpea (*Swartzia*).
paracuuba [u-u] (*f.*) a bitterwood (*Trichilia*); = PRACUUBA.
parada (*f.*) see under PARADO.
paradear (*v.i.*) to vaunt: to boast; brag; to parade.
paradeiro (*m.*) stopping place; destination, bourne; whereabouts; business slump, depression.
paradigma (*m.*) pattern, model, example; (*Gram.*) paradigm.
paradisíaco –**ca** (*adj.*) paradisiacal.
parador (*m., Mach.*) a stop (for arresting or limiting motion).—**de margem**, margin stop (on a typewriter).
parado –**da** (*adj.*) still, motionless; dull, spiritless; (*colloq.*) unrivaled; (*f.*) stop; halt; pause, rest; standstill; stopping place (as for bus or streetcar); a flag stop; parade; bet, stake, wager; parry; show, display; (*slang*) hazard; boast; (*m.*) braggart, boaster.
paradouro (*m.*) place where cattle rest at night; also = PARADEIRO. Var. PARADOIRO.
paradoxal [ks] (*adj.*) paradoxical, contradictory.
paradoxo [ks] (*m.*) paradox.
paraense (*adj.*) of or pert. to Pará; (*m.,f.*) a native or inhabitant of that State.
paraestatal (*adj.*) autarchical, self-governing, economically self-sufficient (said of certain Brazilian government agencies, such as the National Coffee Department).
parafernais (*m.pl., Law*) paraphernalia (personal belongings of a married woman).
parafina (*f.*) paraffin.—**natural**, ozocerite, mineral wax.
parafinar (*v.t.*) to paraffin.
parafínico –**ca** (*adj., Chem.*) paraffinic.
paráfise (*f., Bot.*) paraphysis.
pára-fogo (*m.*) fire screen.
paráfrase (*f.*) paraphrase, exposition; free translation.
parafrasear (*v.t.*) to paraphrase.

parafrasta (*m.,f.*) paraphrast.
parafrástico –ca (*adj.*) paraphrastic.
parafusar (*v.t.*) to screw, bolt; (*v.i.*) to ponder, muse, cogitate.
parafuso (*m.*) screw; bolt; spin (of an airplane).—**batente,** a stop screw.—**com olhal,** eyebolt; screw eye.—**de apêrto,** pressure screw; thumbscrew.—**de Arquimedes,** Archimedean screw.—**de avanço,** feed screw.—**de chamada** or **de reclamo,** a screw for making fine adjustment (as of a telescope).—**de fenda,** wood screw.—**de madeira,** wood screw.—**de montagem,** erection or assembly bolt.—**de orelha,** thumb screw.—**de porca,** bolt having a nut.—**de retenção,** setscrew.—**em gancho,** hook screw.—**fixador,** setscrew.—**micrométrico,** micrometer screw.—**parador,** stop screw.—**Phillips,** Phillips screw.—**regulador,** adjusting screw.—**sem fim,** endless screw. **chave de**—, screw driver. **porca de**—, nut for a bolt. **rôsca de**—, screw thread.
paragão (*m.*) paragon.
paragata (*f.*) = ALPERCATA.
paragem (*f.*) a stopping or stoppage; stopping place. **nestas**—**s,** in these parts, hereabouts.
paraglossa (*f., Zool.*) paraglossa; (*Med.*) paraglossia.
paragnaisse (*m., Petrog.*) paragneiss.
paragoge (*m., Gram.*) paragoge.
paragonita (*f., Min.*) paragonite.
paragrafar (*v.t.*) to divide into paragraphs.
parágrafo (*m.*) paragraph, passage, clause.
paraguaçu [çú] (*m.*) = MACACO-CABELUDO.
Paraguai (*m.*) Paraguay.
paraguaio –aia (*adj.; m.,f.*) Paraguayan [= PARAGUAI-ANO]; (*f., Bot.*) the mercury anchieta (*A. salutaris*), c.a. PIRIGUARA, CIPÓ-SUMÁ.
paraíba (*f.*) a non-navigable stretch of river; (*Bot.*) = SIMARUBA-AMARGA,—-**mirim** = CALUNGA; [*cap.*] a Brazilian state.
paraibano –na [a-i] (*adj.*) of or pert. to the state of Paraíba; (*m.,f.*) a native or inhabitant of that state.
paraíso (*m.*) paradise, Eden, heaven.
parajá (*m.*) a shower which stops (**pára**) as suddenly (**já**) as it started.
paraju [jú] (*m.*) a bulletwood (*Mimusops longifolia*).
paralá[c]tico –ca (*adj.*) parallactic.
pára-lama (*m.*) mud guard; automobile fender.
paralaxe [ks] (*f.*) parallax.
paraldeído (*m., Chem.*) paraldehyde.
paraldol (*m., Chem.*) paraldol.
paralela (*f.*) see under PARALELO.
paralelepípedo (*m., Geom.*) parallelepiped; in Brazil, the common name for paving blocks of that shape.
paralelismo (*m.*) parallelism.
paralelizar (*v.t.*) to render parallel.
paralelo –la (*adj.*) parallel; (*m., Geog.*) parallel; (*f.*) a line or surface parallel to another.
paralelogramo (*m.*) parallelogram.
paralinina (*f., Biol.*) paralinin.
paralisação (*f.*) stoppage, interruption; paralyzation.
paralisar (*v.t.*) to paralyze; (*v.i.,v.r.*) to become paralyzed.
paralisia (*f.*) paralysis, palsy.—**agitante,** (*Med.*) paralysis agitans.—**dos escrivães,** writer's cramp.—**infantil,** infantile paralysis.
paralítico –ca (*adj.; m.,f.*) paralytic.
paralogismo (*m., Logic*) paralogism.
pára-luz (*m.*) lamp shade [= QUEBRA-LUZ].
paramagnetismo (*m.*) paramagnetism.
parambeju (*m.*) = BIJUPIRÁ.
paramécia (*f.*), -cio (*m., Zool.*) paramecium.
paramentar (*v.t.*) to ornament, adorn; (*v.r.*) to attire oneself.
paramento (*m.*) ornament, adornment; apparel; vestment; (*Arch.*) stone or other facing.
paramério, parâmero (*m., Zool.*) paramere.
paramétrico –ca (*adj., Math.*) parametric.
parâmetro (*m., Math.*) parameter.
paramida (*f., Chem.*) paramid(e).
paramnésia, –nesia (*f., Med.*) paramnesia; dèjà vu.
páramo (*m.*) high, treeless plateau in tropical South America; the vault of heaven.
paramorfina (*f., Chem.*) thebaine.
paramorfismo (*m., Min.*) paramorphism.
paramorfo –fa (*adj., Min.*) paramorphous, paramorphic.
paraná (*m.*) "a branch of a river separated from the main stream by an island; a stream that leaves and re-enters

the same river." [*GBAT*]—-**i** = MAITACA-PARDA (a parrot).—-**mirim,** a small PARANÁ.
paranaçu [ú] (*m.*) a black saki monkey (*Pithecia nigra*).
paranaense (*adj.*) of or pert. to the state of Paraná; (*m.,f.*) a native or inhabitant of that State.
parança (*f.*) a stop, rest or pause; repose.
paranéfrico –ca (*adj., Anat.*) paranephric.
paranefrina (*f.*) = ADRENALINA.
paranefro (*m., Anat.*) paranephros.
paranéia (*f.*) = PARANÓIA.
paraninfa (*f.*) godmother; sponsor.
paraninfar (*v.t.*) to sponsor; to stand as godparent to.
paraninfo (*m.*) paranymph; groomsman, best man; sponsor; advocate; one who solicits or speaks for another; the honored spokesman for a graduating class; by ext., godparent.
paranóia (*f., Psychiatry*) paranoia.
paranóico –ca (*adj.; m.,f.*) paranoiac.
parantelia (*f., Meteorol.*) paranthelion.
paranucleína (*f., Biochem.*) paranuclein.
paranúcleo (*m., Biol.*) paranucleus.
parapará (*m., Bot.*) a species of Cordia (*C. tetandra*), c.a. PAU-DE-JANGADA, URUÁ, URUÀZEIRO; the copaia jacaranda [= CAROBA-DO-MATO]; the matchwood (*Didymopanax morototoni*) [= MOROTOTÓ].
parapeito (*m.*) parapet, rampart, breastwork; window sill.—**da lareira,** mantelpiece.
parapétalo –la (*adj., Bot.*) parapetalous.
paraplasma (*m., Biol.*) paraplasm.
parapléctico –ca (*adj., Med.*) paraplegic.
paraplegia, paraplexia [ks] (*f., Med.*) paraplegia.
paraplégico –ca (*adj.; m.,f.*) paraplegic.
parapleura (*f., Zool.*) parapleurum.
parápode (*m., Zool.*) parapodium.
parapsicologia (*f.*) psychical research.
pára-quedas (*m.*) parachute.
pára-quedista (*m.,f.*) parachutist; (*m.*) paratrooper.
parar (*v.i.*) to stop, halt, pause, come to a standstill; (*v.t.*) to stop, stay, check; to discontinue; to parry, ward off; to wager (**em,** on).—**de** + infinitive = to stop + pres. part. [**parar de chover,** to stop raining].—**em,** to remain in (at); to stay put; to stop at; to result in.
pára-raios (*m.*) lightning rod.
parari [rí] (*m.*) a tropical pigeon of genus Zenaida, c.a. AVOANTE, POMBA-DE-BANDO.
pararu [rú] (*m.*) = POMBA-ESPÊLHO.
parasita (*m.*) var. of PARASITO.
parasit[e]ar (*v.i.*) to live as a parasite.
parasitário –ria (*adj.*) parasitic.
parasiticida (*adj.; m.*) parasiticide.
parasítico –ca (*adj.*) parasitic.
parasitismo (*m.*) parasitism.
parasito –ta (*adj.*) parasitic; (*m.*) parasite; sponger, deadbeat; (*f.*) = CHOPIM (a cowbird).
parasitóide (*adj.*) parasitoid.
parasitologia (*f.*) parasitology.
parasitose (*f., Med.*) parasitosis.
pára-sol [pára-sóis] (*m.*) parasol [= GUARDA-SOL].—-**da-china,** Chinese parasol tree (*Firmiana simplex*).
parasselênio, parasselene (*m., Meteorol.*) paraselene.
parassimpático (*m., Anat.*) parasympathetic nervous system.
parassintético –ca (*adj.*) parasynthetic.
parastêmone (*m., Bot.*) parastemon.
parástica (*f., Bot.*) parastichy.
parastilo (*m., Bot.*) parastyle.
paratáctico –ca (*adj., Gram.*) paratactic.
parataxe [ks] (*f., Gram.*) parataxis.
parati [i] (*m.*) a kind of rum; any of various mullets, esp. the white mullet (*Mugil curema*), c.a. PARATI-BÔCA-DE-FOGO, SAÚNA-BÔCA-DE-FOGO, SAÚNA-DO-ÔLHO-VERMELHO, PRATIQUEIRA, MONDEGO, SOLÉ; also = TAINHA-DE-RIO.—**-barbado,** the barbu (*Polynemus virginicus*).—**-fogo,** a gray mullet (*Mugil brasiliensis*), c.a. ÔLHO-DE-FOGO.
paratifo (*m.*), paratifóide (*f.*) paratyphoid fever.
paratireóide (*adj.; m., Anat.*) parathyroid.
paratoma (*m., Zool.*) paratomium.
paratropa (*f.*) paratroops.
paratuberculose (*f., Veter.*) paratuberculosis, Johne's disease.
paratucu [cú] (*m., Bot.*) the orangeleaf tabernaemontana (*T. citrifolia*), c.a. JASMIM-DO-MATO.
paratudo (*m., Bot.*) a senna (*Cassia rugosa*), c.a. BOI-GORDO; a Drimys known as CASCA-DE-ANTA; a globe-

amaranth, c.a. CORANGO, PERPÉTUA-ROXA; a terrestrial orchid (*Ophrys tuberculosa*); see also CAROBEIRA, CORAÇÃO-DA-ÍNDIA, GUAÇATUNGA.

paraturá (*m.*) a cord grass (*Spartina*).

parauaçu [çú] (*m.*) = MACACO-CABELUDO.

paravante (*m.*) foredeck.

pára-vento (*m.*) wind-screen [= GUARDA-VENTO].

parceirada (*f.*) a team of partners (in a game).

parceiro –ra (*m.*,*f.*) partner (in a game); (*adj.*) similar.

parcel [-céis] (*m.*) reef[= RECIFE].

parcela (*f.*) bit, fragment; portion, parcel; item; any one of two or more numbers being added.

parcelar (*v.t.*) to parcel out.

parceria (*f.*) partnership; association; clique. **de—**, in cahoots. **trabalhar de—**, to work on shares.

parche (*m.*) pledget, compress.

parcial (*adj.*) partial, not complete; biassed, unfair; (*m.*,*f.*) partisan.

parcialidade (*f.*) **parcialismo** (*m.*) partiality, unfairness, bias, discrimination.

parcializar (*v.t.*) to render partial or partisan; (*v.r.*) to become so.

parciário –ria (*adj.*; *m.*) partisan; participant.

parcimônia (*f.*) parsimony.

parcimonioso –sa (*adj.*) parsimonious.

parco –ca (*adj.*) frugal, thrifty, saving; scanty.

parda (*f.*) see under PARDO.

pardacento –ta, pardaço –ça (*adj.*) brownish; dusky; drab.

pardal (*m.*), **pardaloca** (*f.*) the common house or English sparrow (*Passer domesticus*).

pardavasco (*adj.*; *m.*,*f.*) mulatto.

pardento –ta (*adj.*) var. of PARDACENTO.

pardieiro (*m.*) dilapidated old house or building.

pardilho –lha (*adj.*) = PARDACENTO.

pardo –da (*adj.*) brown, dark; dark gray; (*m.*,*f.*) mulatto.

pardoca (*f.*) = PARDALOCA.

pardusco –ca (*adj.*) = PARDACENTO.

párea (*f.*) a gauge for casks, barrels, etc.; c.a. PAREIA; (*pl.*) afterbirth [= SECUNDINAS].

parear (*v.t.*) to gauge casks, barrels, etc.

parece-mas-não-é (*f.*, *Bot.*) poinsettia [= FÔLHA-DE-SANGUE].

parecença (*f.*) resemblance, likeness.

parecente (*adj.*) resembling, like [= PARECIDO].

parecer (*v.i.*) to seem, appear, look, appear to be; (*m.*) appearance, mien, aspect; opinion, counsel, judgment. **—se com alguém**, to resemble, look like (someone).— **bem**, to look well, be becoming.—**bem (mal) a**, to seem good (bad) to.—**um sonho**, to seem like a dream. **ao que parece**, seemingly; to outward appearances. **O seu filho parece-se com a Snra.**, Your son take after you. **Os que se parecem andam juntos**, Birds of a feather flock together. **parece-me que**, it strikes me that; it seems to me that; I think that. **Parece-me que sim**, I think so. **Parece que vai chover**, It looks like rain. **Parece-se com a mãe**, She looks like her mother. **Parecem-se como duas gotas d'água**, They are as alike as two peas in a pod. **Que lhe parece?** What do you think? How does it strike you? What's your opinion? **queria lhe—que**, it seemed to him that. **ser do—que**, to be of the opinion that.

parecido –da (*adj.*) similar (a, com, to); like, resembling. **bem—**, goodlooking, handsome. **bem—com**, having a strong resemblance to.

pareci [í] (*m.*,*f.*) an Indian of the Paressi, a recently-extinct Arawakan tribe in the southeast corner of Mato Grosso; (*adj.*) pert. to or designating this tribe. Cf. CABIXI.

paredão (*m.*) a high, thick wall; high, steep river bank.

parede [rê] (*f.*) wall, partition; strike [= GREVE].—**de frontal**, a partition wall.—**de pau a pique**, a wall of wattles and mud.—**de pedra insôssa**, dry masonry wall.—**de tapamento**, partition wall.—**mestra**, main wall.—**nua**, bare wall.—**s meias**, a common wall separating two buildings.—**primária (secundária)**, (*Bot.*) primary (secondary) meristem. **dar com a cabeça na—**, to butt one's head against a wall. **entre quatro—s**, between four walls. **fazer—**, to picket (a struck employer, etc.). **encostar (alguém) à—**, to back (someone) up against the wall; fig., to corner (someone) in an argument. **encostado à—**, with one's back to the wall.

paredista (*adj.*) striking; picketing; (*m.*,*f.*) striker; picket.

paredro (*m.*) important personage; (*colloq.*) political "big shot" [= MANDACHUVA].

paregórico (*adj.*) paregoric. **elixir—**, soothing syrup.

parelha (*f.*) see under PARELHO.

parelheira (*f.*) a harmless Brazilian tree snake (*Philodryas sp.*), c.a. COBRA-CIPÓ.

parelheiro (*m.*) race horse; team horse.

parelho –lha (*adj.*) similar; mated, matched; nip and tuck; even, unbroken; (*m.*) man's two-piece suit; large flat plain; (*f.*) team (of horses, etc.); pair, couple; match (person or thing); running mate; couplet. **correr—com**, to run neck-and-neck with.

parélio (*m.*, *Meteorol.*) parhelion, mock sun.

parencéfalo (*m.*, *Anat.*) parencephalon, cerebellum [= CEREBELO].

parênquima (*m.*, *Zool.*, *Bot.*, *Anat.*) parenchyma; tissue. —**fundamental**, (*Bot.*) fundamental, or ground, tissue.

parenta, fem. of PARENTE.

parental (*adj.*) of or pert. to one's kin. [But not parental, which is RELATIVO AOS PAIS.]

parentalha (*f.*) var. of PARENTELA.

parente –ta (*adj.*) kin; related; (*m.*) any relative; kinsman; (*f.*) kinswoman; (*m.pl.*) kinsfolk, relations, relatives [but not parents, which is PAIS]; (*f.pl.*) the womenfolk of the family (aunts, cousins, etc.).—**s chegados**, close kin.—**(em linha) colateral**, a collateral relation.— **consangüíneo**, a blood relation.—**em linha reta**, a lineal relation.—**longe**, or **longínquo**, a distant relative.—**por afinidade**, a relation by marriage.—**próximo (or chegado)**, a close relative.—**transversal** = PARENTE COLATERAL. **Êle é meu—por parte de pai**, He is a relation on my father's side.

parentear (*v.i.*) to be related (kin).

parentela (*f.*) kinsfolk, kindred; one's relatives collectively.

parentesco [ê] (*m.*) kinship; fig., connection.

parêntese, parêntesis (*m.*) parenthesis (a word, clause, or sentence, inserted in a passage); also, the round brackets ( ) used for this.—**quadrado**, bracket or crotchet [ ].

parentético –ca (*adj.*) parenthetic(al).

páreo (*m.*) horse race; foot race; the winner's prize.

paresia (*f.*, *Med.*) paresis.

parestesia (*f.*, *Med.*) paresthesia.

parga (*f.*) stack, rick (of grain, hay, straw); heap, pile.

pargasita (*f.*), **-to** (*m.*, *Min.*) pargasite.

pargata (*f.*) = ALPERCATA.

pargo (*m.*) a porgy (*Pagrus*); a snapper (*Lutianus*).— **-branco** = RONCADOR (a grunt).—**-ôlho-de-vidro**, the red porgy (*Pagrus pagrus*), c.a. PAGRO.

pari [í] (*m.*) fish weir.

pariá, pária (*m.*) pariah; social outcast.

pariambo (*m.*) = PIRRÍQUIO.

pariatá (*f.*) = MATUPÁ.

pariato (*m.*) peerage.

paricá (*m.*, *Bot.*) the cohoba piptadenia (*P. peregrina*), —**-grande**, a nittatree (*Parkia*); an apes-earring (*Pithecellobium*).

parição (*f.*) parturition (of animals only); foaling; calving.

paricâzinho (*m.*, *Bot.*) sensitive joint vetch (*Aeschynomene virginica*), c.a. CORTICEIRA-DO-CAMPO.

parida (*adj.*; *f.*) (woman or animal) recently delivered of young.

paridade (*f.*) parity; likeness, analogy [= PARECENÇA].

parideira (*adj.*) of animals, old enough to bear young.

parídeos (*m.pl.*, *Zool.*) the *Paridae* (titmice, etc.).

parietal (*adj.*) mural; (*Anat.*, *Zool.*, *Bot.*) parietal; (*m.*, *Anat.*, *Zool.*) parietal bone.

parietária (*f.*, *Bot.*) wall pellitory (*Parietaria officinalis*), c.a. ALFAVACA-DE-COBRA.

parietário –ria (*adj.*) parietal; wall-growing [plants].

parilidade (*f.*) = PARIDADE.

parintintim (*m.*,*f.*) an Indian of the Parintintin, a savage and cannibalistic Tupi-speaking people who for many years were the scourge of other tribes on the Madeira River. It was not until 1922 that the small number remaining was pacified; (*adj.*) pert. to or designating this tribe.

pariparoba (*f.*) = CAPEBA.

paripenado –da (*adj.*, *Bot.*) paripinnate.

parir [59] (*v.t.*,*v.i.*) to bring forth young; to whelp; to foal; to farrow; to calve; to lamb; to kid; to litter.

parisiense (*adj.*; *m.*,*f.*) Parisian.

parissílabo –ba (*adj.*) parisyllabic.

paritá (*m.*) = PARI.

parla (*f.*, *colloq.*) palaver; blather

parlamentação (*f.*) parleying; negotiation.

parlamentar (*adj.*) parliamentary; (*m.*) member of a parliament; (*v.i.*) to parley, treat; to negotiate.
parlamentário –ria (*adj.*) parliamentary; (*m.,f.*) parliamentarian.
parlamento (*m.*) parliament.
parlante (*m., slang*) "mouthpiece" (lawyer).
parlapassada (*f.*) prior agreement.
parlapatão (*m.*) impostor, deceiver; braggart; blatherskite, popinjay; "stuffed shirt".
parlapatear (*v.i.*) to brag, talk big.
parlapatice (*f.*) boasting; claptrap, rubbish.
parlapatório (*m.*) much talking, loquacity.
parlar (*v.i.*) to prate [= PAROLAR].
parlatório (*m.*) parlatory (visiting room in a prison or convent); friendly chat.
parlenga, parlenda (*f.*) empty words, idle talk, palaver.
parlengar (*v.i.*) to indulge in idle, tiresome talk; to blow hard (boast).
parmélia (*f.*) a lichen of the genus Parmelia.
parmesão (*adj.*) Parmesan. queijo—, P. cheese.
parnasiano –na (*adj.; m.,f.*) Parnassian.
Parnaso (*m.*) Parnassus.
pároco (*m.*) parish priest; rector; parson, clergyman, pastor.
paródia (*f.*) parody, travesty; burlesque, take-off.
parodiar (*v.t.*) to parody, imitate, travesty, burlesque.
parodista (*m.,f.*) parodist.
parol [-róis] (*m.*) manager; large kettle for cane syrup; large storage vat for rum.
parola (*f.*) palaver, idle talk.
parolador –dora (*adj.*) palaverous; (*m.,f.*) palaverer.
parolagem (*f.*), parolamento (*m.*) palaverment; gabbling.
parol[e]ar (*v.i.*) to palaver; to chatter; to prate.
paroleira (*f.*) = PAROLA.
paroleiro (*m.*) talker; windbag.
parolice (*f.*) loquacity; palaver; talkativeness.
parolim (*m.*) parlay (bet).
parônimo –ma (*adj.*) paronymous; (*m.*) paronymy.
paroníquia (*f., Med.*) paronychia, whitlow, felon [= PANARÍCIO or PANARIZ]; (*Bot.*) the wall rue (*Asplenium rutamuraria*), c.a. ARRUDA-DOS-MUROS, RUTAMURARIA.—-ouriçada, a nailwort (*Paronychia echinata*).
paronomásia (*f., Rhet.*) paronomasia (punning).
paróquia (*f.*) parish.
paroquial (*adj.*) parochial.
paroquiano –na (*adj.*) parochial; (*m.,f.*) parishioner.
parótico –ca (*adj., Anat., Zool.*) parotic.
parótide, parótida (*f., Anat.*) parotid gland.
parotídeo –dea (*adj.*) parotid.
parotidite (*f., Med.*) parotitis, mumps [= CAXUMBA].
parovaúna (*f.*) = BARAÚNA.
paroxísmico –ca, paroxístico –ca [ks] (*adj.*) paroxysmal.
paroxismo [ks] (*m.*) paroxysm; spasm; (*pl.*) death throes.
paroxítono –na [ks] (*adj.; m.*) paroxytone.
parque (*m.*) park; game preserve.
parquete [ête] (*m.*) parquetry; parquet flooring.
parra (*f.*) grapevine leaf; tendril.
parrado –da (*adj.*) trellised.
parrana (*adj.*) slovenly; slipshod, lackadaisical; (*m.*) slob; slow poke.
parranda (*f.*) gang of swindlers.
parreira (*f.*) trellis.—-brava or—-do-mato, the velvet-leaf or false pareira (*Cissampelos pareira*); the true pareiraroot (*Chondrodendron tomentosum*) which yields the pareira-brava root of pharmacy.—-brava-lisa or —-capeba = CIPÓ-DE-COBRA (a vine).
parreiral (*m.*) grape arbor.
parricida (*m.,f.*) parricide (the criminal).
parricídio (*m.*) parricide (the crime).
parrudo –da (*adj.*) short and fat [= ATARRACADO].
parse (*m.*) Parsee.
part. apass. = PARTÍCULA APASSIVADORA ([*Gram.*] passivating particle).
part. explet. = PARTÍCULA EXPLETIVA ([*Gram.*] expletive particle).
partazana (*f.*) partisan (halberd); (*Bot.*) a cattail (*Typhya dominguensis*) better known as TABUA.
parte (*f.*) part, piece; share, portion; region; party (side in a dispute or dealing); communication, information (oral or written); role; (*Music*) part; (*pl.*) abilities; whims.—alguma, nowhere, anywhere.—dianteira (traseira), front (rear) end.—oficial, official communiqué. à—, apart; aloof; separately, by itself; secretly. à—de, aside from, except. à boa—, in good part. a maior—

(das vezes), most (of the time). da—de, on the part of; from; in the name of; in place of; at the behest of. dar—, to impart, disclose; to inform, report. de—, aside, to one side. de—a—, reciprocally. de outra—, elsewhere. de (sua)—, on his (her) part. em—, partly. em—alguma, nowhere. em alguma—, somewhere. em grande—, largely. em nenhuma—, nowhere. em outra—, elsewhere. em qualquer—, anywhere. em qualquer outra—, anywhere else, elsewhere. em tôda—, everywhere. noutra—, elsewhere. por—de, on the part of. por tôda—, everywhere. por (sua)—, on her (his) part. qualquer—, anywhere. ter—s com (alguém), to have dealings with (someone).
parteira (*f.*) midwife.
parteiro (*m.*) accoucheur, obstetrician.
partejar (*v.t.*) to deliver (a woman) of a child; (*v.i.*) to give birth to.
partenocarpia (*f., Bot.*) parthenocarpy.
partenogênese (*f., Biol., Bot.*) parthenogenesis.
partição (*f.*) partition(ment), division.
participação (*f.*) imparting, communication; participation.—de casamento, wedding announcement.—nos lucros, profit-sharing.
participador –dora, participante (*adj.*) informing; participant; (*m.,f.*) informer; participant.
participar (*v.t.*) to announce, break the news, make known, impart information (a, to).—de (em), to partake of, share in, take part in, participate in.
partícipe (*adj.; m.,f.*) participant.
participial (*adj., Gram.*) participial.
particípio (*m., Gram.*) participle.
partícula (*f.*) particle, bit; (*R.C.Ch.*) the small Host given to each lay communicant; (*Gram.*) particle. —alfa, (*Physics*) alpha particle.
particular (*adj.*) particular, personal, private; specific; minute. em—, privately, in private. [Not an equivalent of particular in the sense of fussy or demanding, which is EXIGENTE.] (*m.*) private individual (person, citizen): (*pl.*) details, particulars.
particularidade (*f.*) particularity, peculiarity; detail, minute circumstance.
particularização (*f.*) act of particularizing.
particularizador –dora (*adj.*) particularizing.
particularizar (*v.t.*) to particularize, specify, itemize; (*v.r.*) to distinguish oneself.
particularmente (*adv.*) privately.
partida (*f.*) see under PARTIDO.
partidão (*m., colloq.*) "big deal"; a good catch; fine marriage; "swell job".
partidário –ria (*m.,f.*) partisan, adherent, supporter; backer; party member; booster.—político, political henchman; (*adj.*) partisan.
partidarismo (*m.*) partisanship.
partidista (*adj.; m.,f.*) strong(ly) partisan.
partido –da (*adj.*) broken, severed; (*m.*) party, faction; handicap given; matrimonial match; legal services on retainer; sugar cane field.—majoritário, majority party. tirar—de, to make capital of; to derive an advantage from. tirar o melhor—duma situação difícil, to make the best of a bad situation. tomar o—de, to take sides with. um bom—a good "catch"; (*f.*) departure; withdrawal; party (meeting of friends); game, match, set; lot, shipment (of merchandise); trick, hoax; taunt; practical joke; false start (of a race horse); armed party.—de cartas, card game.—de desempate, play-off game.—s dobradas, double-entry bookkeeping.—s simples, single-entry bookkeeping. ponto de—, point of departure; starting point. pregar uma—(em alguém) to play a trick or practical joke (on someone).
partidor –dora (*adj.*) apportioning; of racehorses, given to making false starts; (*m.,f.*) one who apportions shares; (*m.*) starting point of a horse race.
partilha (*f.*) partition, division, apportionment; a sharing or dividing up (as of profits).
partilhar (*v.t.*) to share; to divide; to participate.
partimento (*m.*) division; departure.
partir (*v.t.*) to break, rend, fracture [= QUEBRAR]; to part, divide; (*v.i.*) to depart from, leave, go away; to start from; (*v.r.*) to part, come apart, break, split; to take one's leave. a—de hoje, henceforth, from today on, beginning today.
partista (*adj., colloq.*) fussy, full of airs, prissy.
partitivo –va (*adj.*) partitive.
parto (*m.*), parturição (*f.*) parturition, childbirth.

parturiente (*adj.*) parturient; (*f.*) a woman in, or recently in, labor.

paru [ú] (*m.*) the Dutch tonka bean (*Dipteryx odorata*), c.a. CUMARU-VERDADEIRO; any of various fishes, esp. the following:—**-beija-moça**, or—**-listrado**, a butterfly fish (*Pomocanthus arcuatus*), c.a. FRADE.—**branco**, the spadefish (*Chaetodipterus faber*).—**da(s)-pedra(s)**, or—**prêto**, black angelfish (*Pomacanthus rathbuni*), c.a. PRETUCANO.—**dourado**, harvest fish (*Prepilus paru*).—**mulato**, or—**rajado**, butterfly fish (*Chaetodon striatus*).—**soldado** = SOLDADO (fish).

parúlia, parúlide, parúlide (*f.*) gumboil.

parva (*f.*) breakfast, or a light snack before lunch [= DESJEJUA or DEJEJUADOURO]; a small sum of money; a haystack [= PARGA].

parvajola (*m.,f.*) fool.

parvalhão (*m.*), **-lhona** (*f.*) big fool.

parvalhice (*f.*) idiotic remark or behavior.

parvidade (*f.*) littleness; stupidity.

parvifloro -ra (*adj., Bot.*) parviflorous.

parvo -va (*adj.*) small, skimpy; stupid, "goofy"; (*m.,f.*) nitwit, numskull; fool [= TOLO].

pârvoa, another fem. form of PARVO.

parvoeirão (*m.*), **-rona** (*f.*) = PARVALHÃO, -LHONA.

parvoejar (*v.i.*) to talk or behave like a fool.

parvoíce (*f.*) imbecility.

parvolina (*f., Chem.*) parvolin(e).

parvulez[a] (*f.*) childhood; puerility; imbecility.

párvulo -la (*adj.*) tiny; (*m.,f.*) child.

pascácio (*m.*), **-cia** (*f.*) imbecile, halfwit; boob.

pascal (*adj.*) paschal.

pascentar (*v.*) = APASCENTAR.

pascer (*v.t.,v.i.*) to graze, browse; (*v.t.*) to delight; (*v.i.,v.r.*) to delight in.

Páscoa (*f.*) Easter; Passover.

pascoal (*adj.*) = PASCAL.

pascoar (*v.i.*) to celebrate Easter.

pascoela (*f.*) Low Sunday; Easter week.

pascoinha (*f., Bot.*) honey coronilla (*C. glauca*).

pasmaceira (*f.*) stupefaction; apathy, do-nothingness.

pasmado -da (*adj.*) amazed, astonished; witless, dull; (*m.*) an old gate post, or fence post, left standing.

pasmar (*v.t.*) to amaze, astonish, astound; to flabbergast; (*v.i.*) to wonder, be amazed (de, at).

pasmo -ma (*adj.*) amazed; astounded; (*m.*) astonishment, wonder, amazement.

pasmoso -sa (*adj.*) amazing, surprising, wonderful.

paspalhão -lhona (*adj.*) "dumb," oafish; (*m.,f.*) simpleton.

paspalhice (*f.*) foolishness, nonsense; oafishness.

paspalho (*m.*) dunce; fool; oaf.

páspalo (*m.*) paspalum grass.

pasquim (*m.*) pasquinade or lampoon; yellow journal, cheap newspaper.

pasquinada (*f.*) pasquinade, lampoon.

pasquinagem (*f.*) lampoonery.

pasquinar (*v.t.*) to pasquinade, lampoon, satirize, ridicule.

pasquineiro (*m.*) lampooner; yellow journalist.

passa (*f.*) raisin.

passa-culpas (*m.,f.*) a very indulgent, soft-hearted person.

passada (*f.*) see under PASSADO.

passadeira (*f.*) colander, strainer; runner (long narrow carpet); a clothes-pressing machine or shop; a necktie ring; a clasp; (*pl.*) stepping-stones.

passadiço -ça (*adj.*) transitory; (*m.*) passageway, corridor; catwalk; (*Naut.*) bridge; sidewalk; running board.

passadio (*m.*) daily ration; diet.

passadista (*m.,f.*) a person who lives in the past; (*adj.*) old-fashioned, old-fogyish.

passado -da (*adj.*) past, gone (by), over, bygone; ended; last, latter; of fruit, overripe or sun-dried; stunned, amazed; sharp, smart; brassy, cheeky. **ano—**, last year. **bem—**, well-done (cooked); **mal—**, rare, underdone; (*m.*) the past; (*Gram.*) preterit; (*pl.*) predecessors; (*f.*) stride, step, pace; (*pl.*) efforts, pains.

passador -deira (*adj.*) passing; (*m.,f.*) passer; receiver and passer of stolen goods, counterfeit money, etc.; (*m.*) colander, strainer; leather strap used in tightening the cinch; marlinespike, fid.

passadouro (*m.*) passage. Var. PASSADOIRO.

passageiro -ra (*adj.*) transitory, passing, fleeting; (*m.,f.*) passenger, traveller.—**clandestino**, stowaway.

passagem (*f.*) passage; act of passing or crossing; transit; course; way, passageway; fare (ticket); a happening;

portion of a writing, speech, etc.; a repair by darning; "a term which the pilots and navigators of Amazonia apply to certain difficult stretches of a ship's course." [GBAT]—**de nível**, grade crossing.—**inferior**, underpass. **abrir—**, to make way, break through. **dar—**, to afford or permit passage. **de—**, in passing, on the way, passing through. **direito de—**, right of way. **meia—**, half-fare.

passaguá (*m.*) fisherman's small hand net.

passajar (*v.t.*) to repair (clothing) by darning or sewing

passamanar (*v.t.*) to adorn or trim with lace, braid, etc.

passamanaria (*f.*) trimming made of gold, silver, silk, etc.; lace; braid.

passamanes (*m.pl.*) passementerie, lace, braid, trimmings, etc.

passamento (*m.*) passing (death); a passing out (temporary loss of consciousness).

passa-moleque (*m.*) a dirty trick; a double-cross.

passanito (*m., colloq.*) any fellow; a nobody.

passante (*adj.*) passing.—**de**, surpassing; (*m.,f.*) passer-by.

passa-piolho (*m., colloq.*) whiskers that extend under the chin from ear to ear; lit., louse passageway.

passaporte (*m.*) passport; pass; (*colloq.*) full permission.

passar (*v.t.*) to pass, go, (by, past, over, beyond, across, through); to spend (as time); to approve, sanction (as a bill); to pronounce (a sentence); to pass (something) through a sieve; (*v.i.*) to pass, go, move (by, past, beyond, onward); to elapse (as time); to be enacted (as a law); to pass (as in bridge or poker); to be passable (in quality); (*v.r.*) to occur, happen; to go (pass) by.—**a**, to begin to (do something).—**à espada**, to put to the sword. —**a ferro**, to press, iron (clothes).—**à frente**, to outstrip, outrun.—**a fronteira**, to cross the frontier.—**a idade de**, to pass the age of.—**a idade para**, to pass the age limit for.—**a lição**, to assign the lesson.—**a limpo**, to make a clean copy of.—**a mão em**, to steal.—**a noite em claro**, or em branco, to spend a sleepless night.—**a perna em**, to trick, outsmart, outwit (someone).—**a vau**, to ford (a stream).—**adiante**, to outstrip, outrun.—**adiante de**, to get ahead of.—**ao largo de**, to by-pass; to pass wide of.—**as raias**, to exceed the limit; to take advantage of. —**bem**, to live well; to feel well.—**das medidas**, to exceed oneself.—**dos limites**, to go too far.—**de**, to be more than, go beyond.—**de bôca em bôca**, of news, to spread from person to person.—**de mão em mão**, to pass from hand to hand, as a loving cup.—**de moda**, to go out of fashion. —**despercebido**, to go unnoticed.—**dinheiro falso**, to pass counterfeit money.—**fome**, to go hungry; to starve.— **mal**, to have a hard time; to be sick, feel bad.—**o beiço**, (*slang*) to hoodwink.—**o dia (a noite, o verão)**, to spend the day (the night, the summer).—**o tempo**, to pass the time.—**os olhos por**, to glance over (something).—**pelas mãos de todo o mundo**, to pass through many hands. —**por**, to pass as (wise, virtuous, etc.); to endure, undergo; to go by; to pass by (over, through).—**por alto**, to overlook, pass up, omit, take no notice of.—**por cima de**, to transgress, break a rule; to pass over, overlook.— **raspando (um exame, etc.)**, to scrape through (an exam, etc.).—**recibo**, (*colloq.*) to retort.—**revista**, to pass in review.—**sem**, to do without, dispense with.— **tempo**, to spend time. (To spend money is GASTAR DINHEIRO.)—**um carão (um pito, uma descompostura) em alguém**, to give someone a scolding, a "bawling out," a dressing down.—**uma lei**, to enact a law.—**um susto em**, to give someone a fright.—**um telegrama**, to send a telegram.—**uma vista de olhos em**, to give a quick glance at. **A chuva ja passou?** Has it stopped raining? **Como passa?** How are you? **Como tem passado?** How have you been? **em tempos passados**, in times past; in bygone days. **fazer—gato por lebre**, to sell a pig in a poke. **Não passa de sonho**, It is only a dream. **Não passa de um tolo**, He is no better than a fool. **Não havia passado um ano, quando se casaram**, Before a year had passed, they were married. **Não sei o que me passou pela cabeça**, I can't imagine what I was thinking of. **passa a ser (importante)**, it becomes (important). **Passa do tempo**. It is past the time. **Passe bem!** Farewell! Good-bye! **Passe os cobres!** (*slang*) Come across with the dough!

passarada (*f.*) a flock of birds.

passarão (*m.*) a large bird; the wood ibis (*Mycteria americana*), c.a. CABEÇA-DE-PEDRA, CABEÇA-SÊCA.

passaredo [ê] (*m.*) = PASSARADA.

passareira (*f.*) aviary.

passarinha (*f.*) animal's spleen; (*colloq.*) female pudenda.

passarinhada (f.) a flock of birds; a sudden side-stepping by a startled horse.

passarinhagem (f.) bird-trapping.

passarinhão (m.) a sudden jump by a startled horse.

passarinhar (v.i.) to trap birds; to loaf; of a horse, to prance, side-step, toss the head.

passarinheiro (m.) bird trapper; bird fancier; a mettlesome horse.

passarinho (m.) any small bird.—**-de-verão** = VERÃO (a bird).

pássaro (m.) any passerine bird.—**-angu** = JAPACANIM.—**-pêndulo**, a motmot.—**-prêto** = CHOPIM and ARRANCA-MILHO.—**-sol** = ANAMBÉ-GRANDE.—**-trombeta** = AGAMI.—**trepador**, any scansorial bird. **Mais vale um—na mão que dois voando**, A bird in the hand is worth two in the bush.

passaroco (m., colloq.) the blues.

passarola [rô] (f.), **-lo** [rô] (m.) any large bird.

passatempo (m.) pastime, amusement, recreation, sport.—**predileto**, hobby, favorite pastime. **por—**, for fun.

passável (adj.) passable, tolerable, middling, so-so.

passe (m.) pass, permit; free ticket; transference of a ball from one player to another; (pl.) passes with the hands.—**livre**, a professional soccer player's right to switch teams upon expiration of his current contract.

passé (m.,f.) An Indian of the Pasé, an Arawakan tribe between the Rio Negro and Japuará River. [They were considered the most advanced Indians of the middle Amazon region, and highly esteemed by the Portuguese for their good looks and mild disposition]; (adj.) pert. to or designating these people.

passeador –deira (adj.) much given to promenading; (m.,f.) assiduous stroller or promenader.

passeadouro (m.) a promenade or public walk.

passeante (m.,f.) lounger, idler; rambler, stroller; (adj.) idling, strolling.

passear (v.i.) to promenade, stroll, walk, ride (about), for pleasure; (v.t.) to take for a walk; to walk (a horse) for exercise; to pass (the eyes) over a scene; to display, show ostentatiously.

passeata (f.) stroll; public parade (of protest or in celebration of something).—**estudantil**, students' march.

passeio (m.) promenade, walk, ride, stroll, hike, jaunt, outing, excursion; sidewalk, walk, path. **dar um—**, to go for a walk, take a stroll.

passeiro –ra (adj.) slow-paced, slow-moving; of horses, pacing; (m.) a river ferryman; (f.) a place where fruit (esp. grapes) is spread to dry.

passento –ta (adj.) porous, permeable (as unsized paper or cloth).

passe-passe (m., colloq.) prestidigitation; shell game.

passeres (m.pl.) a group (Passeres) of birds.

passibilidade (f.) passibility.

passiflora (f.) the genus (Passiflora) comprising the passionflower and maypop.

passifloráceo –cea (adj.) passifloraceous; (f.pl.) the passionflower family (Passifloraceae).

passilargo –ga (adj.) wide-stepping, long-stepping.

passibilidade (f.) passibility.

passinhas (m., colloq.) one who minces his steps.

passional (adj.; m.) passional.

passionário, passioneiro (m.) passional.

passiva (f., Gram.) passive voice.

passivar (v.t., Gram.) to render (verbs) passive.

passível (adj.) passible.—**de**, capable of, susceptible of, liable to, open to, subject to (cure, error, suffering, emotion, feeling, etc.).

passividade (f.) passiveness, inactivity, inertness; apathy.

passivo –va (adj.) passive, submissive, apathetic; (Gram.) of (in) the passive voice; (m., Com.) liabilities; (Gram.) passive voice.

passo (m.) pace, step, footstep; the length of a step in walking; gait, walk; pass (juncture); narrow pass; pitch (of a screw thread or of an airplane propeller). —**a—**, step by step; slowly.—**acelerado**, quick step.—**de cágado**, snail's pace.—**de urubu malandro**, slow, stealthy stride.—**largo**, long stride.—**s contados**, slowly, little by little. **a—**, slowly. **a—de gigante**, with giant strides. **a—de lêsma**, at snail's pace. **a—e—**, step by step, slowly. **a—igual**, at the same rate (speed). **a—tardo**, with dragging step. **a—s contados**, slowly, cautiously. **a—s lentos**, with slow step. **a—s medidos**, with cautious step. **a cada—**, at every step (turn), continually. **a dois—s de**, a short distance (two steps) from. **a poucos—s**, a few steps away. **a um—de**, on the verge of. **acelerar o—**,

to quicken the step. **acertar o—**, to get in step (with). **andar a—**, (of horses) to pace. **ao—que**, while; at the same time that; during the time that; whereas. **ao** (do) **mesmo—**, at the same time, simultaneously. **conservar o—**, to keep step. **dar um—**, to take a step. **marcar—**, to mark time. **suspender o—**, to stop walking, come to a halt.

pasta (f.) paste; pulp; brief case; portfolio (of a minister of state); a dressed and combed forelock.—**de dente**, toothpaste.—**para soldar**, flux paste for soldering.—**mecânica**, wood pulp made mechanically.—**química**, sulphite or other chemical-process pulp for papermaking.

pastagem (f.) pasture, pasturage, grazing land.

pastar (v.t.,v.i.) to graze, browse; (v.t.) to turn out or lead to pasture.

pastel [téis] (m.) a fried turnover (enclosing ground meat, olives, hardboiled egg, etc.); a tart; pied type; a pastel drawing.—**dos-tintureiros**, (Bot.) dyers' woad (Isatis tinctoria).

pastelaria (f.) pastry shop; pastry-making.

pasteleiro (m.) pastryman.

pastelista (m.,f.) pastel painter.

pasteurelose (f., Med., Veter.) pasteurellosis; (Veter) hemorrhagic septicemia.

pasteurização (f.) pasteurization.

pasteurizadeira (f.), **-dor** (m.) pasteurizer [apparatus].

pasteurizar (v.t.) to pasteurize.

pasticho (m.) pasticcio (olio, potpourri); pastiche (imitation, caricature).

pastifício (m.) paste (macaroni) factory.

pastilha (f.) pastille.

pastinaga (f.) parsnip.

pastinha (f.) lock of plastered hair.

pastinhar (v.i.) to nibble at food.

pasto (m.) pasture, grassland; food.—**-amargo**, a needle-grass (Stipa trichotoma).—**-aranha**, a grama grass (Bouteloua multiseta).—**-borla**, the many-spiked chloris (C. polydactyla).—**-de-areia**, the desert panicum (P. urvilleanum).—**-de-bezerro**, a basketgrass (Oplismenus setarius).—**-de-outono**, a lovegrass (Eragrostis flaccida).—**-salgado**, a dropseed grass (Sporobolus phleoides). **casa de—**, eating-house. **vinho de—**, cheap wine.

pastor [-tôres] (m.) shepherd; herder; parish priest; parson; studhorse.

pastôra (f.) shepherdess.

pastorador (m.) pasture [= PASTAGEM].

pastoral (adj.) pastoral; (f., Eccl.) pastoral letter; (Music) pastorale; eclogue, idyl.

pastoreador (m.) herder. Var. PASTOREJADOR.

pastorear (v.t.) to pasture; to herd. Var. PASTOREJAR.

pastoreio (m.) pasturing of cattle (as a business); pasture land; a herd on pasture. Var. PASTOREJO.

pastorela (f., Music) pastorale; an eclogue.

pastoril (adj.) pastoral; bucolic; (m.) in northeastern Brazil, a certain outdoor folk play, c.a. PASTORINHAS.

pastorizar (v.) & derivs. = PASTEURIZAR & derivs.

pastoso –sa (adj.) pasty, viscous; of voice, thick, husky.

pastrano –na (adj.; m.,f.) rustic.

pata (f.) paw; foot; duck; fluke of an anchor; the bonnethead shark (Sphyrna tiburo), c.a. CAÇÃO-MARTELO, CAÇÃO-PANÃ, CAÇÃO-RODELA.—**anterior (posterior)**, foreleg (hind leg).—**choca**, a female land crab; also (colloq., m.) a sexton.—**d'água**, cormorant [= BIGUÁ].—**de-cavalo** = CAIRUÇU (a plant).—**de-lebre** = PAU-DE-BALÇA.—**de-lôbo**, a clubmoss (Lycopodium).—**de-vaca**, (Bot.) the bell bauhinia (B. forficata).—**maxila**, (Zool.) maxilla of arthropods.—**s natatórias**, flippers, as of seals, turtles, etc. **a—**, afoot. **meter a—**, to commit a faux pas; to "put one's foot in it".

pataca (f.) an old Brazilian silver coin worth 320 RÉIS.

patacão (m.) a large, old Port. copper coin worth 40 RÉIS; in Brazil, an old silver coin worth two MIL-RÉIS; (colloq.) a large, old-fashioned pocket watch; (colloq.) kneecap.

patacho (m., Naut.) a two-masted tender.

pataço (m.) kick by an animal.

patacoada (f.) nonsense; bluster; lie.

patacudo –da (adj., colloq.) "loaded" (with money).

patada (f.) a kick; a stamp of the foot; a pawing, by an animal; (colloq.) blunder, faux pas.

patágio (m., Zool.) patagium.

patagônio –nia, patagão –gona (adj.; m.,f.) Patagonian.

patalear (v.i.) to paw, stamp, kick.

pataluco (m.) the blister buttercup (Ranunculus sceleratus).

patamar (*m.*) stair landing; veranda; a stretch of level roadway.

patamaz (*adj.*) sanctimonious.

patão (*m.*) the Brazilian merganser (*Mergus octosetaceus*).

pataqueiro –ra (*adj.*) cheap, common; of poker, etc., penny-ante; (*m.*) moneyed person; ham actor.

patarata (*f.*) humbuggery; (*m.*) boaster; "dope".

patativa (*f.*) the sweet-singing plumbeous seedeater (*Sporophila p. plumbea*).—**do-sertão**, Temminck's seedeater (*S. falcirostris*); both c.a. PAPA-CAPIM.

patau (*m.*) simpleton, "dope" [= TOLO].

patavina (*f.*) nothing, not a thing.

pataxó (*m.,f.*) an Indian of the Patashó, a tribe of the Maxacalí linguistic family of southern Bahia; (*adj.*) pert. to or designating this tribe.

patchuli [í] (*m.*) patchouli (perfume); (*Bot.*) the patchouli plant (*Pogostemon*).

pate (*m.*) a queen palm (*Arecastrum romanzoffianum botyrophorum*).

pateada, pateadura (*f.*) a stomping of the feet.

patear (*v.i.*) to stomp and whistle (in disapproval); to stamp the foot; to pad (walk); to "flop" (fail).

pateiro (*m.*) duck raiser; lay pantryman in a monastery; retriever dog.

patel [-téis] (*m.*, *Chess*) checkmate.

patela (*f.*) kneecap; quoit; the game of quoits; a limpet; (*Zool.*) patella.

patelar (*adj.*, *Anat.*) patellar. **reflexo**—, knee jerk.

patelha [ê] (*f.*) pintle of a rudder.

patelídeos (*m.pl.*) a family (*Patellidae*) of limpets.

pateliforme (*adj.*, *Zool.*, *Bot.*) patelliform.

pátena, patena (*f.*, *Eccl.*) paten.

patente (*adj.*) patent, open, evident, plain, obvious. **pano**—, calico; (*f.*) patent, privilege, exclusive grant; military commission, rank. **altas**—**s do exército**, high-ranking Army officers.

patentear (*v.t.*) to make patent; to show, unfold, reveal, manifest; to patent (an invention); (*v.r.*) to become evident.

paternal (*adj.*) paternal.

paternidade (*f.*) paternity.

paterno –na (*adj.*) paternal, fatherly; hereditary. **casa**—, family home.

patesca [ê] (*f.*, *Naut.*) snatch block.

pateta (*m.,f.*) simpleton, fool, blockhead, dumbbell, saphead; = TOLO.

patetice (*f.*) stupidity, nonsense.

patético –ca (*adj.*) pathetic; (*m.*) something pathetic.

pati [í] (*m.*) = JERIVÁ.

patibular (*adj.*) of or pert. to the gallows; of criminal mien.

patíbulo (*m.*) gallows, gibbet.

patifa, fem. of PATIFE.

patifão (*m.*) scoundrel.

patifaria (*f.*) rascality, knavery, chicanery.

patife (*m.*) rascal, rogue, scalawag, scamp, scoundrel; (*adj.*) rascally, knavish; pusillanimous.

patilha (*f.*) high, flat, cantle of a saddle; bicycle brake shoe; base of a steel rail.

patim (*m.*) (ice, roller) skate; a small stair-landing.—**do freio**, brake shoe.—**traseiro**,—**da bequilha** or **da cauda**, tail wheel, tail skid (of an airplane).

pátina (*f.*) patina.

patinação (*f.*) skating [= PATINAGEM]; skating rink.

patinador –dora (*adj.*) skating; (*m.,f.*) skater.

patinagem (*f.*) skating.

patinar (*v.i.*) to skate; to become covered with a patina.

patinete [nê] (*m.*) toy scooter.

patinhar (*v.i.*) to slosh, dabble (in water); to play, splash about (in water); of locomotive wheels, to slip (rotate without gripping the rails).

patinho (*m.*) duckling; boob, simpleton.—**d'água**, or—**-de-igapó**, a sun grebe or finfoot, c.a. IPEQUI.

pátio (*m.*) patio; courtyard; inner court; apron (at an airport).—**de recreio**, playground.

patioba (*f.*) a highly poisonous arboreal pit viper (*Bothrops bilineatus*), c.a. SURUCUCU-DE-PATIOBA; (*Bot.*) a palm (*Polyandrococos caudescens*), c.a. BURI, IMBURI, PINDOBA. —**mirim**, a shadowpalm (*Geonoma platicaule*).

pato (*m.*) drake, duck, esp. the domesticated kind; a goose (in the sense of simpleton). [The bird goose is GANSO.]—**arminho**, the black-necked swan (*Cygnus melanocoryphus*), c.a. CISNE-DE-PESCOÇO-PRÊTO.—**de-cabeça-prêta**, the black-headed duck (*Heteronetta atricapilla*).—**de-crista**, the So. Amer. comb duck (*Sarkidiornis sylvicola*).—**do-mato** or—**bravo**, the Muscovy duck (*Cairina moschata*); also = PATO-DE-CRISTA. —**pataca** = ALMA-DE-GATO (a cuckoo). **pagar o**—, to pay the piper.

patoá (*m.*) patois, regional dialect.

patofobia (*f.*) morbid dread of disease.

patogênese, patogenesia, patogenia (*f.*) pathogenesis, pathogeny.

patogenético –ca, **patogênico** –ca (*adj.*) pathogenic.

patognomônico –ca (*adj.*, *Med.*) diacritic, diagnostic.

patola (*f.*) claw (of crabs, etc.); chain hook; (*slang*) "paw" (person's hand); (*m.,f.*) boob; (*adj.*) stupid.

patolar (*v.t.*, *slang*) to grab; to buttonhole (another person).

patologia (*f.*) pathology.

patológico –ca (*adj.*) pathologic(al).

patologista (*m.,f.*) pathologist.

patos (*m.*) pathos.

patota (*f.*) cheating, trickery; thievery.

patotada (*f.*) swindle.

patoteiro –ra (*adj.*) cheating; (*m.*) cheat, crook.

patranha (*f.*) whopper, great lie; rigmarole; cock-and-bull story.

patranheiro –ra (*adj.*) lying; (*m.,f.*) liar.

patrão (*m.*) boss, employer, master; owner, proprietor; patron, protector; skipper; (*Rowing*) coxswain.

pátria (*f.*) see under PÁTRIO.

patriarca (*m.*) patriarch.

patriarcado (*m.*) patriarchate; patriarchy.

patriarcal (*adj.*) patriarchal.

patrício –cia (*adj.*) patrician; (*m.,f.*) fellow-countryman; patrician; [*cap.*] (*m.*) Patrick; (*f.*) Patricia.

patrimonial (*adj.*) patrimonial.

patrimônio (*m.*) patrimony, inheritance, heritage; assets.— **hereditário**, birthright.—**móvel**, movable assets.

pátrio –ria (*adj.*) of or pert. to one's father or fathers or fatherland; (*m.*)—**poder**, a father's legal authority in relation to his minor children.—**s lares**, fatherland; home; (*f.*) fatherland, native country.

patriota (*m.,f.*) patriot.

patriotada (*f.*) a patriotic flurry; a throng of patriots.

patrioteiro –ra (*adj.*) chauvinistic; (*m.*) chauvinist, noisy patriot.

patriotice (*f.*) exaggerated or false patriotism.

patriótico –ca (*adj.*) patriotic.

patriotismo (*m.*) patriotism.

patrística (*f.*, *Eccl.*) patristics; patrology.

patroa (*f.*) lady-of-the-house, mistress, landlady; (*colloq.*) the "missus".

patrocinador –dora (*adj.*) aiding, favoring, supporting; sponsoring; (*m.,f.*) supporter, defender; sponsor.

patrocinar (*v.t.*) to patronize, favor, support, aid, befriend, defend; to sponsor; to back up (a cause or person).

patrocínio (*m.*) sponsorship; patronage; help, support.

patrologia (*f.*, *Eccl.*) patrology.

patrona (*f.*) patroness; cartridge belt [= CARTUCHEIRA]; a viper c.a. JARARACUÇU.

patronado (*m.*) = PATRONATO.

patronagem (*f.*) = PATROCÍNIO.

patronal (*adj.*) patronal.

patronato (*m.*) patronage; an asylum for juveniles.

patronear (*v.t.*) to patronize; to sponsor.

patronímico –ca (*adj.*) patronymic.

patronita (*f.*, *Min.*) patronite.

patrono (*m.*) patron; patron saint.

patrulha (*f.*) patrol. **rádio**—, radio patrol.

patrulhar (*v.t.,v.i.*) to patrol, go the rounds.

patuá (*m.*) wicker basket; leather bag; amulet.

patuarana (*f.*, *Bot.*) the India canna (*C. indica*).

patudo –da (*adj.*) big-pawed, big-footed.

patuléia (*f.*) populace, rabble, riffraff.

pátulo –la (*adj.*) patent, open. [*Poetical*]

patureba (*m.*) dried and salted catfish, c.a. MULATO-VELHO.

paturi [í] (*m.*) the masked duck (*Nomonyx dominicus*), c.a. CANCÃ, POTERI, POTETI.

patuscada (*f.*) jamboree, carousal, merrymaking, revelry, "binge," spree, lark.

patuscar (*v.i.*) to roister, carouse, make merry.

patusco –ca (*adj.*) roistering; waggish; ridiculous; (*m.*) roisterer, wag, joker.

pau (*m.*) stick, rod, club, stake, pole, spar, beam; wood; tree; timber; a beating; horn (of an animal); (*pl.*) clubs (card suit); (*adj.*) boresome, tiresome.—**a-pique**,

(a fence or wall) of wattle and daub (stud and mud).—
-amarelo, Brazilian boxwood or Brazilian stinkwood
(*Euxylophora paraensis*) c.a. PAU-CETIM. It is a "very
large tree; fine, homogeneous wood of average hardness
and regular grain; bright yellow in color, has a satin-
like surface; easily worked. Much sought after for furniture manufacture, floors and cabinet work." [*GUAF*].
—-bala, American muskwood (*Guarea trichilioides*), c.a.
CARRAPETA, JATUAÚBA-BRANCA.—-bálsamo, Brazilian
myrocarpus (*M. frondosus*), c.a. CABRIÚVA.—-branco =
CATANDUBA.—-brasil, the prickly brazilwood (*Caesalpinia echinata*), which yields a valuable timber and
whose heartwood is used in making red and purple
dyes. [This is the national tree of Brazil. Other common
names for it are: IBIRAPITANGA, MUIRAPITANGA, PAU-
ROSADO, PAU-DE-PERNAMBUCO, BRASIL, SAPÃO.]—-cam-
peche, logwood (*Haematoxylon campechianum*), c.a.
CAMPECHE.—-candeia, an ironweed (*Vernonia diffusa*),
c.a. CASCA-PRETA.—-canela, cinnamon-bark tree (*Cinnamomum zeylanicum*), c.a. CANELEIRA.—-cardoso,
a tree fern (*Alsophila atrovirens*).—-carrasco = CATAN-
DUBA.—-catinga = COSTO.—-cavalo, a chaste tree (*Vitex
nigrum*).—-cetim, a white quebracho (*Aspidosperma
eburneum*), c.a. PEQUIÁ-MARFIM; also = PAU-AMARELO.
—-concha = CARVALHO-DO-BRASIL.—-cravo, clove-bark
tree (*Dicypellium caryophyllatum*), c.a. CRAVEIRO-
DO-MARANHÃO.—-da-fumaça, (*colloq.*) a "shooting
iron".—-d'água, a copaiyé tree (*Vochysia thyrsoidea*),
c.a. GOMEIRA; (*colloq.*) a boozer.—-d'arco, a trumpetbush (*Tecoma heptaphylla*), c.a. IPÊ.—-d'arco-
do-campo = CAROBEIRA.—-de-anjo = CANUDO-DE-PITO.—
-de-amarrar-égua, (*colloq.*) an unprincipled person who
will lend himself to anything.—-de-arara, a nitta tree
(*Parkia pendula*); a small rubiaceous tree (*Sickingia
tinctoria*), c.a. ARARIBA, ARARÉUA. (*colloq.*) migrant, esp.
from N.E. Brazil to the south; truck for transporting
migrants.—-de-arrasto, a heavy piece of wood used as a
clog for a grazing horse.—-de-balsa, balsa, bobwood,
or corkwood (*Ochroma pyramidale*, syn. *lagopus*),
c.a. PAU-DE-JANGADA, PATA-DE-LEBRE.—-de bandeira,
flagpole.—-de-bicho = MURUPITA.—-de-bôto, a lancepod
(*Lonchocarpus denudatus*).—-de-breu = ALMECEGUEIRA-
MANSA.—-de-brincos = CONGONHEIRO.—-de-bugre, a
plant (*Lithraea brasiliensis*) of the sumac or cashew
family, c.a. AROEIRA-DE-BUGRE.—-de-cabeleira, a go-
between for lovers; a pander.—-de-cachimbo = CANUDO-
DE-PITO.—-de-caixa, a copaiyé wood tree (*Vochysia
tucanorum*).—-de-cangalha, a sweetleaf (*Symplocos
parviflora*).—-de carga, boom (of a derrick).—-de-
cêra = JENIPAPO-BRAVO.—-de-cinzas = CONGONHEIRO.
—-de-cobra = TALONA.—-de-colher, a tabernaemontana
(*T. echinata*).—-de-cortiça = MALVA-DO-CAMPO.—-de-
cunanã, a succulent (*Euphorbia phosphorea*), c.a.
CUMANÃ.—-de-cutia, a gasparillo (*Esenbeckia grandiflora*).—-de-embira, a Brazilian plant (*Xylopia fruc-
tescens*), of the custardapple family, c.a. COAJERUCU,
PINDAÍBA, SEMENTE-DE-EMBIRA.—-de-formiga, an ant
tree (*Triplaris americana*), c.a. FORMIGUEIRA.—-de-
gasolina = LOURO-INHAMUÍ.—-de-guiné, a custardapple
tree (*Annona acutiflora*).—-de-jangada, a linden (*Apeiba
tibourbou*) whose extraordinarily light wood is used in
building the noted JANGADAS (fishing rafts) of northeastern Brazil; the wood is c.a. APÉ-IBA; a cordia (*C.
tetandra*), c.a. PARAPARÁ; also = PAU-DE-BALSA.—-de-
lacre, a gutta-gum tree (*Vismia sp.*).—-de-lágrima
= CONGONHEIRO.—-de-macaco, a tree (*Posoqueria acutifolia*), c.a. FRUTA-DE-MACACO, BACUPARI-MIÚDO.—-de-
mastro, a copaiyé tree (*Vochysia caerulea*).—-de-mocó,
a tiputree (*Tipuana auriculata*).—-de-morcêgo = AN-
GELIM-DE-FÔLHA-LARGA and ANGELIM-DOCE.—-de-mo-
tamba = CAMACÃ.—-de-novato, an ant tree (*Tripularis
americana*), c.a. FORMIGUEIRA.—-de-óleo, a copal tree,
c.a. COPAÍBA-VERDADEIRA, COPAÍBA-VERMELHA.—-de-
óleo-verdadeiro = CABRIÚVA.—-de-ouro = IPÊ-AMARELO.
—-de-pente = PAU-PEREIRA.—-de-pernambuco = PAU-
BRASIL. — -de-pólvora = CRINDIÚVA. — -de-praga
= CORDÃO-DE-FRADE.—-de-quiabo, a laurel (*Ocotea
bofo*).—-de-rato = CATINGUEIRO-DE-FÔLHA-MIÚDA.—-de-
remo, a snowbell (*Styrax acuminatum*).—-de-rosas, a
tulipwood tree (*Physocalymma scabberimum*), whose
rose-colored wood is used in cabinet-making; c.a. PAU-
ROSA.—-de-salsa, the Surinam calliandra (*C. surinamensis*).—-de-sassafrás, a laurel (*Laurus sassafras*).—
-de-sebo, Chinese tallow tree (*Sapium sebiferum*).—-de-

semana, a tree (*Byrsonima sp.*) of the Barbados cherry
family, c.a. MURICI-CASCUDO.—-de-viola, a fiddlewood
(*Citharexylum cinereum*), c.a. POMBEIRA.—-do-serrote,
a rushpea (*Hoffmannseggia petra*).—-doce, a copaiyé
wood tree (*Vochysia sp.*); a tree of the sapodilla family
(*Glycoxylon sp.*).—-dos-feiticeiros = MUAVE.—-em-ser,
an unpruned ERVA-MATE tree.—-espêto, a shrub
(*Casearia sp.*) of the Indian plum family, c.a. PEQUIÁ-
CAFÉ. - -fava = MANDUIRANA. — -fedorento = JENI-
PAPARANA.—-ferro, any of various ironwoods, esp. the
wamara (*Swartzia tomentosa*), c.a. PANACOCÓ.—-fôfo
= JANGADEIRA.—-forquilha = PAU-PFREIRA.—-gonçalo
= GONÇALO-ALVES.—-jerimum, a plant (*Spinacia gerimu*)
of the goosefoot family.—-lágrima, a copaiyé wood
(*Vochysia sp.*).—-lixa, a lippia (*L. urticoides*) of the
verbena family.—-mamão, a tree (*Maytenus aquifolium*), of the staff-tree family.—-mandado, (*colloq.*) a
stooge.—-mulato-(da-várzea), the mulatto calycophyl-
lum (*C. spruceanum*).—-negro, the lebbek albizzia (*A.
kalkora*).—-papel, a glorybush or spiderflower (*Tibouchina papyrifera*), c.a. ÁRVORE-DO-PAPEL.—-paraíba
= CACHETA.—-para-tôda-obra, Jack-of-all-trades; also
= PAU-PEREIRA.—-para-tudo, a plant (*Simaruba cedron*)
of the quassia family; also = CASCA-DE-ANTA, CHAPADA.—
-pereira or—-pereiro, a white quebracho (*Aspidosperma
macrocarpum*), c.a. GUATAMBU; a Brazilian tree (*Geissospermum vellosii*, family *Apocynaceae*), whose intensely
bitter bark (pereira bark) is used as a tonic and febrifuge;
c.a. CAMARÁ-DE-BILRO, CAMARÁ-DO-MATO, CANUDO-AMAR-
GOSO, PINGUACIBA.—-pintado = ANGELIM-CÔCO.—-pom-
bo, one of the commonest trees in Pará, is *Tapirira
guianensis* (cashew family); c.a. TATAPIRIRICA; yields
good timber for trim, furniture manufacture and carpentry in general.—-prêto, East Indian rosewood
(*Dalbergia latifolia*).—-rainha, the Pará porcupinepod-
tree (*Centrolobium paraense*), c.a. MUIRAQUATIARA.—
-rosa, Ceará rosewood (*Dalbergia cearensis*); a tree
(*Aniba sp.*) of the laurel family; also = PAU-DE-ROSAS.—
-rosa-do-oiapoque, a laurel (*Aniba rosaeodora*).—-rosado
= PAU-BRASIL.—-roxo, a purpleheart (*Peltogyne densi-
flora*), c.a. GUARABU.—-santo, the holywood lignum
vitae (*Guajacum sanctum*); also = MALVA-DO-CAMPO.—
-vintém, a senna (*Schizolobium parahybum*), c.a. BACU-
RUBU.—-violeta, a purpleheart (*Peltogyne sp.*). a meio—,
at halfmast. dar por—s e por pedras, to go from bad to
worse; to jump off the deep end. de—, wooden. jogar
com—s de dois bicos, to play both ends against the
middle; to double-cross (someone); to straddle (an
issue); to sit on the fence. levar—, (*slang*) to flunk an
exam. meter o—em, to cudgel (someone); to backbite;
to flunk (someone); to squander (money). pegar no—
furado, (*colloq.*) to take up arms, enter military service.
tecer (or torcer) os pauzinhos, to pull strings, work the
angles. Quanto maior for o—, maior é a queda, The
bigger they are, the harder they fall. Vamos ver com (or
de) quantos—s se faz uma canôa (or uma cangalha),
We'll see about that! I'll show you (him, her, them)!
paucifloro –ra (*adj.*, *Bot.*) pauciflorous.
paucifólio –la (*adj.*, *Bot.*) paucifolious.
paucinervado –da (*adj.*, *Bot.*) paucinervate.
paucirradiado –da (*adj.*, *Bot.*) pauciradiated.
paul [a-ú; pl. pauis] (*m.*) marshland; tideland; quagmire.
Paula (*f.*) Paula.
paulada (*f.*) a blow with a stick; a drubbing, cudgeling.
paulama (*f.*) a heap of sticks, felled trees, branches, etc.
paula-sousa (*m.*, *colloq.*) buck shot.
paulatino –na (*adj.*) slow, gradual.
paulificação (*f.*, *slang*) annoyance, bore. Que—! What a
bore!
paulificante (*adj.*, *slang*) boring, tedious.
paulificar (*v.t.*,*v.i.*) to bore.
Paulina (*f.*) Pauline.
paulínea (*f.*) a genus (*Paullinia*) of tropical woody vines.
[The seeds of *P. cupana* are the source of GUARANÁ.]
paulista (*m.*) a Paulist; (*m.*,*f.*) a native or inhabitant of
the State of São Paulo; (*adj.*) of or pert. to the State of
São Paulo; (*colloq.*) "from Missouri" (skeptical).
paulistano –na (*adj.*) of or pert. to the city of São Paulo;
(*m.*,*f.*) a native or inhabitant of that city.
paulito (*m.*) a small wooden peg or pin, used in a certain
form of billiards and in other games.
Paulo (*m.*) Paul.
paulo-pires (*m.*) = JOÃO-BÔBO.
paúna (*f.*) = CORAÇÃO-DA-ÍNDIA.

pauperismo (*m.*) pauperism.
paupérrimo -ma (*absol. superl. of* POBRE) most poor.
pausa (*f.*) pause, stop; standstill; (*Music*) rest; rose (of a watering pot) [= CRIVO, RALO].
pausado -da (*adj.*) deliberate, unhurried, leisurely.
pausar (*v.i.*) to pause, stop, delay, rest.
pauta (*f.*) schedule, list; ruler; guide lines; ruling (of paper); (*Music*) staff; (*colloq.*) pact.—**de alfândega**, customs tariff. **em**—, on the agenda; order of the day. **fora da**—, (*Music*) outside the score; by ext., off base; out of line.
pautado -da (*adj.*) of paper, ruled; regular, methodical.
pautar (*v.t.*) to rule (paper); to list (in the customs tariff); to regulate, adjust.
pautear (*v.i.*) to chat, gabble. [= TAGARELAR]
pauzama (*f.*) a heap of wood or sticks.
pauzinho (*m.*) small stick, twig; (*colloq.*) gossip; intrigue. **mexer**, or **tocar, os**—**s**, to pull strings.
pavacaré (*m.*) an olive shell.
pavana (*f., Music*) pavan; (*colloq.*) a dressing down, scolding; a ferrule.
pavão (*m.*) peacock.—**do-mato(-grosso)**, the umbrella bird (*Cephalopterus o. ornatus*), c.a. ANAMBÉ-PRÊTO, TOROPICHI.—**do-pará**, the common sun bittern (*Eurypyga h. helias*), c.a. PAPA-MÔSCAS, PAVÃOZINHO.
pavãozinho (*m.*) = PAVÃO-DO-PARÁ.
paveia (*f.*) sheaf of hay or grain.
pavena (*adj.*) turbulent.
pávido -da (*adj.*) fearful, timid.
pavilhão (*m.*) pavilion, tent; canopy; flag, ensign; banner; ward of a hospital; exhibitor's building; market stall; auricle of the ear; bell (of a trumpet, etc.).
pavimentação (*f.*) paving.
pavimentar (*v.t.*) to provide with a floor or floors; to pave.
pavimento (*m.*) floor, story (of a building); the floor itself; paving, pavement.
pavio (*m.*) wick. **de fio a**—, from beginning to end; from A to Z; from stem to stern; from soup to nuts.
pá-virada (*m.*) reckless, headstrong, person.
pavó, pavô (*m.*) the scutated fruit-crow (*Pyroderus s. scutatus*), c.a. PAÓ.
pavoa (*f.*) pea hen. [peacock = PAVÃO.]
pavoã (*f.*) a water hyacinth (*Eichhornia*).
pavonaço -ça (*adj.*) violet-colored.
pavonada (*f.*) the spreading of a peacock's tail; hence, vaingloriousness; fanfare.
pavonear (*v.t.*) to adorn, bedizen (showily); (*v.i.,v.r.*) to flaunt; to prance, strut, swagger.
pavor (*m.*) terror, fear, fright.
pavoroso -sa (*adj.*) terrifying, dreadful; appalling; (*f.*) an appalling report.
paxá (*m.*) Turkish pasha.
paxicá (*m.*) a dish of fried turtle liver.
paxiúba-manjerona (*f.*) the caryota rufflepalm (*Aiphanes caryotaefolia*).
pax-vóbis [ks] (*m., colloq.*) a simple, good-natured, peace-loving person.
paz (*f.*) peace; public order; calm, tranquillity; quiet; harmony; freedom from war. **deixar em**—, to let alone. **em**—, at peace. **em boa**—, harmoniously. **fazer as**—**es**, to patch up a quarrel, make peace, bury the hatchet. **o ramo de**—, the olive branch.
pázada (*f.*) a shovelful; a blow with a shovel.
PB = PARAÍBA (State of).
P.B. = PÊSO BRUTO (gross weight).
pc. = PACOTE(S) = package(s).
P.D. = PEDE DEFERIMENTO (approval requested).
PE = PERNAMBUCO (State of).
pé (*m.*) foot; paw; hind foot of a horse [the front foot is MÃO]; 12 inches [30.48 centimeters]; base, bottom; pedestal; state of affairs; footing; footstalk; leafstalk; a single vine, shrub, plant or tree; pretext, excuse (for doing something).—**ante pé**, on tiptoe.—**cúbico**, cubic foot.—**d'água**, a heavy downpour.—**de alface, repôlho**, etc., head of lettuce, cabbage, etc.—**de-altar**, altar fees (for a baptism, marriage, etc.).—**de-amigo**, a three-leg hobble for a horse.—**de-anjo**, (*slang*), big foot.—**de-bezerro**, (*Bot.*) taro, elephant's-ear [= TAIOBA].—**de biela**, the large or split end of a piston connecting rod.—**-de-boi**, plodder, hard worker; old fogy, mossback; (*Bot.*) any bauhinia.—**-de-burro**, AÇAFROL.—**-de-cabra**, crowbar; (*colloq.*) Old Nick (the Devil).—**de café**, a single coffee tree.—**-de-cavalo** = CARUÇU (a plant).—**-de-chumbo**, (*colloq.*) a laggard; a derogatory epithet for a

Portuguese; (*Bot.*) the scarlet salvia (*S. splendens*).—**de-galinha**, crow's-foot; (*Bot.*) cocksfoot (*Dactylis*) and other grasses.—**de-galo**, hop (*Humulus*), better known as LÚPULO.—**de-ganso**, (*Bot.*) goosefoot (*Chenopodium*).—**de-gato**, (*Bot.*) pussytoes (*Antennaria*).—**de-leão**, (*Bot.*) lady's-mantle (*Alchemilla*).—**de-lebre**, rabbit-foot clover (*Trifolium arvense*).—**de meia**, a single stocking.—**de-meia**, nest egg (savings).—**de milho**, a stalk of corn.—**de-moleque**, peanut brittle (candy); rough cobblestone pavement.—**de-pato**, (*colloq.*) Old Harry (the Devil).—**de-pau**, a small stingless honeybee (*Melipona nigra*).—**de-peia**, (*colloq.*) Old Scratch (the Devil).—**de-poeira**, a man of low condition.—**de-pombo** = BICO-DE-CEGONHA (a geranium).—**de vento**, gust of wind; squall.—**direito**, height between ceiling and roof; headway, headroom; side wall of a mine gallery; pier (of an arch, etc.).—**duro**, (*colloq.*) rural worker, rustic; yokel.—**fresco**, (*colloq.*) a man of the people, man in the street; barefoot man.—**lamberto**, (*Photom.*) foot-lambert.—**libra**, (*Mech.*) foot-pound.—**libra-segundo**, (*Physics*) foot-pound-second.—**quadrado**, square foot.—**torto**, club foot.—**s chatos**, flat feet. **a**—, on foot. **a firme**, steadfastly, resolutely. **abrir o**—, to run away. **ajudar-se de**—**s e mãos**, to leave no stone unturned, spare no effort (in helping oneself). **andar de**—**coxo**, to limp, hop on one foot. **ao**—**da letra**, literally, to the letter. **ao**—**de**, near, close to. **apertar o**—, to hasten one's steps. **arco do**—, arch of the foot. **arrastar os**—**s**, (*colloq.*) to dance; to drag one's feet; to be on one's last legs. **arredar o**—, to withdraw, step back, budge. [**Não arredo**—**daqui**, I won't budge.] **a terra dos**—**s juntos**, (*colloq.*) the cemetery. **bater (o)**—, to put one's foot down. **bater o**—**no mundo**, to flee. **bicho-de**—, chigoe. **chamar no**—, to hot-foot it. **com (or em)**—**s de lã**, stealthily. **com o**—**nas costas**, (*colloq.*) with the greatest of ease. **com o**—**no estribo**, with one foot in the stirrup; fig., about to depart; about to die. **com um**—**(or os**—**s) na cova**, with one foot in the grave. **dar**—, of a body of water, shallow, fordable. **de**—, on foot, standing; up and about (convalescent); of orders, rules, in effect; of invitations, etc., standing. **de**—**no chão**, barefoot. **de**—**s juntos**, firmly, staunchly. **de quatro**—(or simply **de quatro**) on all fours; crawling. **dedinho do**—, little toe. **do**—**para a mão**, at a moment's notice. **dos**—**s à cabeça**, from head to toe; from top to bottom. **em**—, on foot, standing (up), upright. **em**—**de guerra**, on a war footing. **entrar com o**—**direito**, to get off on the right foot (to a good start). **fazer**—**atrás**, to step back; to hesitate, balk. **ficar de**—, to stand up; to remain standing. [O convite **fica de**—, The invitation stands.] **ficar de**—**atrás com alguém**, to be on one's guard against another person. **ir a**—, to go on foot; to walk. [Você veio **a**—? Did you walk?] **juntar os**—**s**, to turn up one's toes (die). **lamber os**—**s de alguém**, to fawn upon someone. **levantar-se com o**—**esquerdo**, to get up on the wrong side of the bed. **manter**—**firme**, to stand pat. **meter os**—**s pelas mãos**, to go haywire (in speech or behavior); to get hopelessly confused. **não chegar aos**—**s de alguém**, to be far beneath another person (in worth), not able to hold a candle to him. **negar a**—**s juntos**, to deny emphatically (swear on a stack of Bibles). **passear a**—, to go for a walk. **peito do**—, instep. **perder o**—, to lose one's footing; (in water) unable to touch bottom. **planta do**—, sole of the foot. **ponta do**—, toe tip. **pôr de**—, to set upright. **pôr-se de**—, to stand up, jump up. **pôr um**—**na frente do outro**, to set one foot before another. **sem**—**s nem cabeça**, without head or tail; without rhyme or reason. **tirar o**—**da lama** (or do lôdo), to better one's position; to get out from under. **tomar**—, (in water) to touch bottom; also, fig., to get one's bearings. **um**—**de**, a single plant of any kind.
peã (*m.*) paean.
peagem (*f.*) toll, fee.
peal (*m.*) pump (shoe).
pealar (*v.t.*) to rope, lasso.
pealo (*m.*) cattle rope.
peanha (*f.*) pedestal, stand.
peanho (*m.*) the hull of a ship below the water line.
peão (*m.*) foot traveler; foot soldier; pawn; peon, farm hand; muleteer; horse tamer.
pear (*v.t.*) to hobble (horses); to impede (progress).
peba (*m.*) the six-banded armadillo (*Dasypus Sexcinctus*); (*adj.*) squat, shortlegged.

peça (*f.*) piece; part, portion; piece of furniture; room of a house; piece of artillery; document in a dossier; stage play; (*Chess, Checkers*) piece, man; hoax; prank, practical joke; (*v.t.*) a form of PEDIR [60].—**antiaérea,** antiaircraft gun.—**de artilharia,** piece of artillery.—**de vestuário,** garment.—**em um ato,** one-act play.—**sobressalente,** or **para consêrto,** spare part, repair part.—**suplementária,** an attachment. **assistir a uma—,** to see a play (show). **montar uma—,** to stage a play. **por—,** a piece. **pregar uma—em (alguém),** to play a practical joke on (someone). **Quantas—s tem esta casa?** How many rooms in this house?

pecadilho (*m.*) peccadillo.

pecado (*m.*) sin, transgression; offense, misdeed. **estar em—,** to be in a state of condemnation (for sin).

pecador –**dora** (*adj.*) sinful; (*m.,f.*) sinner, wrongdoer.

peçais, peçam, peçamos, forms of PEDIR [60].

pecaminoso –**sa** (*adj.*) sinful.

pecante (*adj.*) peccant; (*m.,f.*) sinner.

pecapara (*f.*) a sun grebe or finfoot (*Heliornis fulica*), c.a. IPEQUI.

pecar (*v.i.*) to sin, trespass, err; of fruits, to wither.

pecari [í] (*m.*) peccary, wild pig.

peças, form of PEDIR [60].

pecável (*adj.*) peccable, liable to sin.

pecha (*f.*) blemish; an opprobrious verbal label.

pechada (*f.*) head-on collision; request for money.

pechar (*v.t.*) to bump, collide with; to ask for money. (*v.r.*) to collide, bump against, run into.

pechblenda (*f.*) pitchblende.

pechincha (*f.*) bargain; find.

pechinchar (*v.t.*) to gain (get profit) unexpectedly or without work; (*v.i.*) to obtain at bargain prices; to dicker, haggle.

pechincheiro –**ra** (*m.,f.*) bargainer; bargain-hunter.

pechiringar (*v.i.*) to give grudgingly; to wager little.

pechisbeque (*m.*) pinchbeck (alloy); tombac.

pechoso –**sa** (*adj.*) faultfinding; faulty.

peciolado –**da** (*adj., Bot.*) petiolated.

peciolar (*adj., Bot.*) petiolar.

pecíolo (*m., Bot.*) petiole, leafstalk.

pêco –**ca** (*adj.*) withered, blighted; fig., mentally stunted; (*m.*) plant blight.

peço, form of PEDIR [60].

peçonha (*f.*) venom, poison; fig., malice, malevolence.

peçonhento –**ta** (*adj.*) venomous; malignant.

pécora (*f.*) drab, wench.

péctase (*f., Biochem.*) pectase.

pectato (*m., Chem.*) pectate.

péctico –**ca** (*adj., Chem.*) pectic.

pectina (*f., Biochem.*) pectin.

pectíneo –**nea** (*adj., Bot., Zool.*) pectinate.

pectinídeos (*m.pl., Zool.*) the Pectinidae (scallops).

pectólita (*f.*), –**to** (*m., Min.*) pectolite.

pectoral (*adj.*) = PEITORAL.

pectose (*f., Biochem.*) protopectin.

pecuário –**ria** (*adj.*) of or pert. to farm animals; (*m.*) cattleman, rancher; (*f.*) animal husbandry.

pecuarista (*m.,f.*) cattle raiser, rancher.

peculador –**dora** (*m.,f.*) peculator, embezzler.

peculato (*m.*) peculation, embezzlement (esp. of public funds).

peculiar (*adj.*) peculiar (**a,** to), special, own; pert. to money reserve. [Not employed in Port. as meaning odd of unusual, which is ESTRANHO, ESQUISITO.]

peculiaridade (*f.*) peculiarity [but only in the sense of being special, not of oddity, which is ESTRANHEZA, ESQUISITICE].

pecúlio (*m.*) savings, nestegg, money reserve.

pecúnia (*f.*) funds, money.

pecuniário –**ria** (*adj.*) pecuniary.

pecunioso –**sa** (*adj.*) moneyed.

pedaço (*m.*) piece, fragment, bite, chunk, slice; (*colloq.*) long time; attractive, provocative woman.—**de asno,** ass, fool.—**de gado,** a few head of cattle.—**de mau caminho,** bad habit, moral defect; lit., a bad piece of road.

pedágio (*m.*) bridge toll.

pedagogia (*f.*) pedagogy.

pedagógico –**ca** (*adj.*) pedagogic(al).

pedagogo –**ga** (*m.,f.*) pedagogue.

pedal (*m.*) pedal.

pedalada (*f.*) act of pedalling; pedal-pushing.

pedalar (*v.t., v.i.*) to pedal.

pedanálise (*f.*) pedanalysis.

pedantaria (*f.*) pedantry.

pedante (*adj.*) pedantic, priggish; (*m.,f.*) pedant, prig, wiseacre.

pedantear (*v.i.*) to pedantize.

pedanteria (*f.*) = PEDANTARIA.

pedantesco –**ca** (*adj.*) pedantesque.

pedantice (*f.*), **pedantismo** (*m.*) pedantism.

pedantizer (*v.*) = PEDANTEAR.

pedantocracia (*f.*) pedantocracy.

pedatilobado –**da** (*adj., Bot.*) pedatilobate.

pedatipartido –**da** (*adj., Bot.*) pedatipartite.

pederasta (*m.*) pederast.

pederastia (*f.*) pederasty.

pedernal (*m.*) flint; (*adj.*) petrous, stony.

pederneira (*f.*) flint.

pedesia (*f., Physics*) Brownian movement, pedesis.

pedestal (*m.*) pedestal, base, support.—**de mancal,** (*Mach.*) a bearing pedestal.

pedestre (*adj.; m.,f.*) pedestrian; **corrida—,** a foot race.

pedestrianismo (*m.*) pedestrianism, walking, hiking.

pedete (*m.*) the jumping hare (*Pedetes*).

pediastro (*m.*) a genus (*Pediastrum*) of free-floating green algae.

pediatra (*m.,f.*) pediatrician, child specialist.

pediatria (*f.*) pediatrics.

pedicelado –**da** (*adj., Bot.*) pedicellate.

pedicelo (*m., Bot.*) pedicel.

pediculado –**da** (*adj.*) having a pedicle.

pedicular (*adj.*) pedicular (lousy); (*m., Bot.*) the European lousewort (*Pedicularis palustris*).

pediculídeos (*m.pl.*) the Pediculidae (lice).

pedículo (*m., Bot.*) pedicel, peduncle.

pedicuro (*m.*) chiropodist, pedicure.

pedida (*f.*) cards drawn, as in poker.

pedido (*m.*) request, demand; petition; application; order, requisition (for goods).—**de casamento,** marriage proposal.—**de demissão,** or **de exoneração,** resignation (from office).—**de informação,** inquiry. **a—de,** at the request of.

pedidor –**dora** (*adj.*) asking; (*m.,f.*) asker, petitioner, applicant.

pediforme (*adj.*) pediform.

pedilúvio (*m.,*) foot-bath.

pedímanos (*m.pl.*) the Pedimana (a division of marsupials).

pedimento (*m.*) petition. [But not a pediment, which is FRONTÃO.]

pedinchão –**chona** (*adj.*) whining, begging; (*m.,f.*) such a person.

pedinchar (*v.t.,v.i.*) to importune, beg.

pedinchice, pedincheira (*f.*) continual begging, importuning.

pedintão –**tona** (*adj.; m.,f.*) = PEDINCHÃO.

pedintaria (*f.*) mendicancy.

pedinte (*adj.*) petitioning; (*m.,f.*) beggar; petitioner.

pedipalpos (*m.pl.*) an order (*Pedipalpida*) of Arachnida.

pedir [60] (*v.t.*) to ask for, apply for, request, seek, solicit; to beg, beseech, petition; to demand; to order (goods). —**a (alguém) para (fazer alguma coisa),** to ask (someone) to (do something).—**a mão de,** to ask the hand of (in marriage).—**a palavra,** to ask for the floor.—**bandeira,** to call for time out.—**consêlho a,** to seek advice from.—**contas a (or de),** to demand an accounting, an explanation.—**demissão,** to resign; to apply for discharge (from office).—**desculpas,** to apologize.—**em casamento,** to ask in marriage.—**emprestado,** to borrow. —**esmolas,** to beg alms.—**informações,** to make inquiries.—**licença a,** to ask permission of.—**misericórdia,** to beg for mercy.—**notícias dum amigo,** to inquire about a friend.—**para,** to ask to.—**para as almas,** to beg alms for the souls in purgatory.—**por,** to ask for.—**segrêdo,** to ask for secrecy.—**uma informação,** to inquire, ask a question.—**vênia a,** to ask permission of.

peditório (*m.*) a soliciting or collection of funds (for charity); importunate request.

pedógrafo (*m.*) pedograph.

pedologia (*f.*) pedology.

pedólogo (*m.*) pedologist.

pedômetro (*m.*) pedometer.

pedomorfismo (*m., Anat.*) pedomorphism.

pedomotor (*m.*) pedomotor.

pedotrofia (*f.*) pedotrophy.

pedra (*f.*) stone, rock; pebble; gem; kidney stone; tombstone; blackboard; chessman or checker; hailstone.—

angular, cornerstone.—**arenosa**, sandstone.—**braba**, (*slang*), a no-good person.—**britada**, crushed rock.—**calcárea**, limestone.—**-da-lua**, moonstone, adularia.—**-das-amazonas**, Amazon stone, amazonite; a kind of talisman—see MUIRAQUITÁ.—**de açúcar**, sugar tablet, lump of sugar.—**-de-águia**, eaglestone [= AETITA].—**de amolar**, whetstone, grindstone.—**-de-anil**, lazulite.—**de ara**, altar stone.—**de areia**, sandstone [= ARENITA].—**-de-bolonha**, Bologna stone.—**-(-de-)bronze**, a kind of Jewstone, c.a. CABO-VERDE.—**de escândalo**, stumbling block (but only in the original sense of cause for scandal or temptation. Cf. PEDRA DE TROPEÇO, below).—**de-ferro**, a certain tree in the State of São Paulo which is taken to indicate fertile soil; also, certain pebbles found in alluvial deposits and taken as an indication of the presence of diamonds or other precious stones.—**de-fogo**, or—**-de-fuzil**, flint.—**s de gêlo**, ice cubes.—**de-judeu**, Jewstone, c.a. CABO-VERDE.—**de moinho**, millstone.—**-de-raio**, aerolite.—**de sangue**, carnelian.—**de-santana**, an iron sulfide found in diamantiferous gravel. —**desgalhada**, rough-hewn stone.—**de toque**, touchstone.—**de tropeço**, stumbling block, obstacle, hindrance. Cf. PEDRA DE ESCÂNDALO, above.—**do-sol**, sunstone, heliolite, aventurine feldspar.—**filosofal**, philosopher's. stone; fig., a hard thing to find.—**fundamental**, foundation stone.—**Imã**, loadstone.—**infernal**, silver nitrate, lunar caustic.—**lascada**, (Stone Age) chipped stone. —**lipes**, copper sulfate, blue vitriol, bluestone.—**litográfica**, lithographic stone.—**-olar**, soft soapstone or talc.—**polida**, neolithic polished stone.—**pomes**, pumice stone.—**preciosa**, precious stone, gem.—**refratária**, refractory stone.—**que rola não cria bolor**, A rolling stone gathers no moss.—**sabão**, soapstone.—**-ume**, alum; (*Bot.*) a myrtle.—**-verde** = MUIRAQUITÁ. **Água mole em —dura tanto bate até que fura**, Constant dripping bores the stone. **andar com a—no sapato**, to smell a rat. **atirar a primeira—**, to throw the first stone. **carvão de—**, coal. **dar por paus e por—s**, to go from bad to worse. **dormir como uma—**, to sleep like a log. **de—e cal**, of stone and mortar; fig., strong, sturdy; firm, steadfast. **Quem com todas as—s bole, uma lhe cai na cabeça**, Jack-of-all-trades, master of none. **Quem tem telhado de vidro, não atira—s no vizinho**, Those who live in glass houses should not throw stones. **ser de—**, to be stony-hearted. **vir, or sair-se, com quatro—s na mão**, to make an angry reply, a savage remark.

pedrado -da (*adj.*) paved with stone; (*f.*) stone-throwing; a stoning.

pedral (*adj.*) pert. to rocks; speckled black and white; (*m.*) "an accumulation of rocks and stones which impede navigation, specifically, stones in a GORGULHO." [*GBAT*]

pedranceira (*f.*) rock pile.

pedraria (*f.*) stone yard; rock work; a quantity of precious stones; "(1) a large extensive rocky area covered by water in flood season but exposed during the dry season (the word is a synonym for PEDRAL); (2) a rock quarry." [*GBAT*]

pedregal (*m.*) stony place.

pedregoso -sa, pedreguento -ta (*adj.*) stony, rocky.

pedregulhento -ta (*adj.*) gravelly.

pedregulho (*m.*) gravel.

pedreira (*f.*) stone quarry.

pedreiro (*m.*) bricklayer; mason; an oven bird, c.a. JOÃO-DE-BARRO.—**pequeno** = CORRUIRA-DO-BREJO.

pedreiro-livre (*m.*) freemason.

pedrês (*adj.*) mottled (black and white).

pedrinhas (*f.pl.*) jacks (children's game).

pedrisco (*m.*) sleet.

Pedro (*m.*) Peter

pedroso -sa (*adj.*) rocky, stony.

pedunculado -da (*adj.*) pedunculate.

pedruncular (*adj.*) peduncular.

pedúnculo (*m., Bot., Zool.*) peduncle.

P.E.F. = POR ESPECIAL FAVOR (by special favor).

pêga (*f.*) in Brazil, a New World oriole (*Icterus*); in Portugal, a magpie (*Pica*); by ext., a chattering woman.

pega (*f.*) handle; catch; opportunity; clash, quarrel; (*slang*) chase; setting (of cement), hardening (of mortar); military draft or roundup of recruits; trap (for the unwary); fetter used on runaway slaves; telephone exchange cord; (*m.*) fracas, knock-down and drag-out fight.

pegada [pègáda] (*f.*) see under PEGADO.

pegadiço -ça (*adj.*) adhesive; catching, contagious; importunate.

pegadilha (*f.*) dissension, quarrel.

pegado -da (*adj.*) stuck (together); caught; near, close by; of a friend, close; (*colloq.*) drunk; **a casa—**, the house next door; (*f.*) footprint, track; (*Soccer*) a catch by the goalkeeper.

pegador -dora (*adj.*) catching; (*m.,f.*) catcher; (*m.*) hide-and-seek; remora (fish).

pegadouro (*m.*) handle, holder. Var. PEGADOIRO.

pegajento -ta (*adj.*) = PEGAJOSO.

pega-fogo (*m.*) country dance.

pegajoso -sa (*adj.*) sticky, adhesive, gummy, viscous.

pega-mão (*m.*) handbag, satchel, grip; a handle.

pegamassa (*f.*) burdock (*Arolium*), c.a. BARDANA-MENOR.

pegamasso (*m.*) sticking paste.

pega-macaco, pega-mico (*m.*) = GAVIÃO-PEGA-MACACO.

peganhento -ta (*adj.*) = PEGAJOSO.

pegão [-gões] (*m.*) buttress; abutment; windstorm; (*Bot.*) beggartick (*Bidens*).

pega-pega (*m.*) quarrel, fight, shindy, free-for-all; (*Bot.*) any bur or bur-bearing plant.

pega-pinto (*m.*) a kind of chicken hawk; (*Bot.*) a spiderling (*Boerhaavia*), c.a. AGARRA-PINTO.

pegar (*v.t.*) to stick, attach (to); to catch (fire, measles, etc.); to nab (a thief); to grasp, seize; (*v.i.*) to cling to; to be catching, contagious; of a fad, to catch on; of a plant, to take root; of a drawer, etc., to stick; (*v.r.*) to adhere, stick.—**se a**, to cling to; to seize upon (make use of).—**se com**, to adjoin (as one building to another).—**se com alguém**, to have it out with someone.—**a**, to stick to; to infect with; to take hold of.—**a+verb** (**comer, correr**, etc.), to start to (eat, run, etc.)—**com**, to adjoin, be contiguous.—**de** (or **em**), to take hold of, grasp, seize. [Pegou da faca, He took hold of his knife.]—**em armas**, to take up arms.—**em cheio**, to hit squarely, catch full on (the nose, the side, etc.).—**fogo**, to catch fire.—**fogo a**, or **em**, to set fire to.—**na palavra**, to take at one's word.—**na pena**, to take one's pen in hand.—**no bico do chefe**, (*colloq.*) to flatter the boss.—**no sono**, to fall asleep.—**o touro à unha**, or **pelos chifres**, to take the bull by the horns. **O apelido pegou**, The nickname stuck. **O carro não pega**, or **não quer—**, The car won't start. **Pegaram-no em flagrante**, They caught him red-handed. **não ter por onde se lhe pegue**, of persons, good-for-nothing. **Não pega!** You're joking! I don't believe it!

pêgas (*m.*) shyster.

Pégaso (*m.*) Pegasus.

pegativo -va (*adj.*) catching; contagious.

pegmatito (*m., Petrog.*) pegmatite.

pegmatóide (*adj., Petrog.*) pegmatoid.

pego (*m.*) deepest part of river, lake, etc.; abyss, chasm.

peguaba (*f.*) = BEGUABA.

peguenhento -ta, peguento -ta (*adj.*) = PEGAJOSO.

peguilhar (*v.i.*) to pick a quarrel.

pegureiro (*m.*) herdsman, shepherd; sheep dog; hunting dog.

peia (*f.*) a fetter, shackle or clog for an animal; fig., any impediment; a rawhide whip [= PEIA-BOI (*m.*)]; a leather strap; (*pl.*) a device of leather straps to assist in climbing coconut trees.

peiote (*m., Bot.*) the mescal-button peyote (*Lophora williamsi*).

peita (*f.*) bribe; sop.

peitar (*v.t.*) to bribe, suborn.

peiteiro -ra (*adj.*) bribing; (*m.*) briber; (*f.*) breastband of harness.

peitica (*f.*) the striped cuckoo (*Tapera naevia*), c.a. SACI; (*colloq.*) a persistently annoying thing or person.

peitilho (*m.*) shirt-front; breastplate; chest protector.

peito (*m.*) chest; breast; bosom; heart.—**de-forno**, "turtle meat seasoned with lemon, salt and pepper, spread out in the shell itself, covered with a thin layer of very finely ground manioc flour and roasted in an oven; this dish is common even in the cities." [*GBAT*]—**do pé**, instep (of foot or shoe).—**ferido** = SACI (a cuckoo). —**roxo**, the vinaceous parrot (*Amazon vinacea*), c.a. ANACÃ, CURRALEIRO, PAPAGAIO-DE-COLEIRA, PAPAGAIO-DE-CABOCLO. **a—descoberto**, with bared breast. **abrir dos—s**, of horses, to jade, tire out; to display unwonted generosity. **amigo do—**, bosom friend. **carregação do—**, bronchitis. **criança de—**, a nursing infant. **de—feito**, resolutely; purposefully. **tomar a—**, to take to heart.

peitoral (*adj.*) pectoral; (*m.*) chest or lung medicine; breastband (of a harness).

peitoril (*m.*) parapet; window sill.

peitudo –da (*adj.*) big-chested; of a woman, big-bosomed; (*slang*) chesty; (*m.*) = CRAVORANA (a ragweed).

peixada (*f.*) fish stew.

peixão (*m.*, *colloq.*) a buxom, comely woman.

peixaria (*f.*) fish market.

peixe (*m.*) fish.——**-agulha**, any needlefish, esp. the timucu (*Strongylura timucu*), c.a. TIMUCU, CARAPIÁ; any garfish, esp. *Belone argalus* and *B. trachura;* the halfbeak (*Hyporhamphus unifasciatus*); any pipefish (*Syngnathus*), c.a. CACHIMBO.——**-anjo**, angelfish (*Squatina sp.*).——**-aranha**, the greater weever (*Trachinus draco*), or the lesser weever (*T. vipera*).——**-arqueiro**, archerfish (*Toxotes jaculator*).——**-azeite**, an amber fish (*Seriola sp.*).——**-beijador**, the kissing gourami (*Helostoma temmincki*).——**-boi**, any manatee (*Trichestus*, syn. *Manatus, sp.*), c.a. MANATIM, VACA-MARINHA; also = BAIACU.——**-borboleta**, butterfly fish (*Chaetodon spp.*).——**-cabra**, a gurnard (*Trigla sp.*).——**-cachimbo**, any pipefish (*Syngnathus*), c.a. CACHIMBO, PEIXE-AGULHA.——**-canga**, hammerhead shark (*Sphyrna sp.*).——**-carlim**, a herring (*Clupea sp.*).——**-cavalo** = PEIXE-GALO.——**-cobra**, an unspecified snakelike fish.——**-cobrelo**, a cusk eel (*Ophidion sp.*).——**-coelho**, rabbit fish (*Chimaera sp.*), c.a. QUIMERA; the smooth puffer (*Lagocephalus laevigatus*), better known as BAIA-CUARÁ.——**-da-china**, a carp (*Cyprinus sp.*).——**-da-cola**, sturgeon (*Acipenser sturio*).——**-de arrasto**, fish taken in a net (i.e., not hooked).——**-de-briga**, Siamese fighting fish (*Betta splendens*).——**-de-são-pedro**, the John Dory (*Zeus faber*) of the Mediterranean, c.a. GALO-DO-MAR, PEIXE-GALO. [The Port. term—St. Peter's fish—is in allusion to the black ring or spot on the sides, said to be the imprint of the Saint's thumb and finger when he once held this fish to remove a coin from its mouth.]——**-diabo**, the caribe (*Serrasalmo sp.*), better known as PIRANHA; an angler fish (*Lophius sp.*) c.a. PEIXE-PESCADOR; also = JAMANTA (the manta).——**-do-paraíso**, a threadfin (*Polynemus sp.*).——**-dourado**, goldfish.——**-doutor**, the sargassum (frog-)fish (*Histrio histrio*).——**-elefante** = PEIXE-COELHO.——**-elétrico**, electric eel, c.a. PORAQUÊ, TREME-TREME.——**-escobar** (or **-escolar**) = ENXOVA-PRETA (the oilfish), c.a. PEIXE-PREGO.——**-espada**, swordfish, c.a. ESPADARTE; the cutlass fish (*Trichiurus lepturus*); the swordtail (*Xiphophorus helleri*).——**-fantasma**, a filefish (*Davidia punctata*).——**-flor** = BABOSA.——**-fôlha**, the triple-tail, c.a. PREJEREBA, PEIXE-SONO; the leaf-fish (*Monocirrhus polyacanthus*).——**-frade**, black angelfish or butterfly fish (*Pomacanthus arcuatus*).——**-frito**, the striped cuckoo (*Tapera n. naevia*), c.a. SACI; the pheasant cuckoo (*Dromococcyx phasianellus*); (*slang*) a runabout roadster.——**-galo**, moonfish (*Argyreiosus vomer* or *Vomer setapinnis*); the look-down (*Selene vomer*), c.a. ARACANGUIRA, CAPÃO, GALO, GALO-BANDEIRA, GALO-DE-PENACHO, TESTUDO; also = GALO-DO-FUNDO and PEIXE-DE-SÃO-PEDRO.——**-gato**, a small S.A. catfish (*Pygidium sp.*); also = BADEJO-PINTADO.——**-lagarto**, a lizard fish—the sand-diver (*Synodus intermedius*)—c.a. TIRAVIRA, LAGARTO-DO-MAR, CALANGO.——**-leque**, a sailfish or marlin (*Istiophorus volador*), c.a. PEIXE-VELA, AGULHÃO-BANDEIRA.——**-lima**, a rattail or grenadier (*Macrorus sp.*).——**-lua**, the huge ocean sunfish (*Mola mola*); the King-of-the-Mackerels (*Ranzania truncata*) also a sunfish.——**-macaco**, a small fresh-water goby (*Eleotris pisonis*), c.a. AMBORÉ; a blenny (*Blennius*); a four-eyes (fish).——**-martelo**, hammerhead shark (*Sphyrna zygaena*), c.a. PEIXE-CANGA, CAÇÃO-MARTELO, CAMBEBA, CAMBEVA, CORNUDA, MARTELO.——**-morcêgo**, any batfish (*Ogcocephalus*), esp. *O. vespertilio*, c.a. MORCÊGO; *O. longirostris* (long-nosed batfish) and *O. radiatus* (short-nosed batfish), both the latter c.a. GUACUCUIA, ONCOCÉFALO, PIRÁ-ANDIRA.——**-mulher**, female manatee.——**-papagaio**, parrot fish, c.a. BUDIÃO.——**-paraíso**, paradise fish (*Macropodus sp.*); a threadfin (*Polynemus sp.*) c.a. PEIXE-DO-PARAÍSO.——**-pegador**, a remora or sucker-fish.——**-pena**, the little-mouth porgy (*Calamus penna*); the grass porgy (*C. arctifrons*).——**-pérsico**, yellow perch (*Perca flavescens*).——**-pescador**, the angler fish (*Lophius gastrophysus* or *L. piscatorius*), c.a. PEIXE-DIABO, PEIXE-SAPO, LÓFIO, DIABO-MARINHO, RÃ-DO-MAR, TAMBORIL, PENADEIRA. XARRÔCO-MAIOR.——**-pica**, a rockling or whistlefish (*Motella mustela*).——**-piolho**, a clingfish, suckfish or remora, c.a. (PEIXE-)AGARRADOR.——**-pombo** = PAMPO.——**-porco**, a filefish (*Monocanthus hispidus*), c.a. NEGRA-MINA.——**-rato** = UBARANA.——**-rapôsa**, a thrasher (*Alopias vulpes*), c.a. PEIXE-ZORRO.——**-rei**, a fish of the wrasse family (*Halichoeres cyno-*

cephalus), closely related to the pudding-wife; a silver-sides of southern South America (*Basilichthys sp.*); also = BIJUPIRÁ.——**-sapo**, a frogfish (*Antennarius scaber*), c.a. ANTENÁRIO, GUAPERVA.——**-roda** = PEIXE-LUA.——**-serra**, any sawfish, esp. *Pristis pectinatus*, c.a. ARAGUAGUÁ, PIRAGUAGUÁ; a swordfish or broadbill (*Xiphius gladius*), better known as ESPADARTE.——**-tigre**, a barracuda (*Sphyraena*), better known as BICUDA.——**-tordo**, a wrasse-fish (*Labrus sp.*).——**-trombeta**, bellows fish (*Macrorhamphosus scolopax*), c.a. BICANÇUDO, CENTRISCO; the cornet fish (*Fistularia tabacaria*), c.a. PETIMBUABA, TROMBETA, AGULHÃO-TROMBETA.——**-vaca**, cowfish, c.a. BAIACU.——**-vela**, sailfish, see PEIXE-LEQUE.——**-vermelho**, goldfish (*Carassius auratus*).——**-vidro**, the East Indian glassfish or X-ray fish (*Ambassis lala*).——**-voador**, any flying fish; a flying gurnard (*Dactylopterus volitans*), c.a. COIÓ, CAJALEÓ, PIRABEBE, VOADOR-CASCUDO.——**-zorro** = PEIXE-RAPÔSA. **como o—dentro d'água**, like a pig in clover; in one's natural element; perfectly at ease. **Filho de—sabe nadar**, or **Filho de—peixinho é**, Like father, like son. **não ser nem—nem carne**, to be neither fish nor fowl; to be neither for nor against (something). **não ter nada com o—**, to have no part in a discussion, not be a party to an argument, not take sides. **vender o seu—**, to look out for one's interests; to declare oneself.

peixeira (*f.*) fishwife; fish knife.

peixeiro (*m.*) fishmonger.

pejado –da (*adj.*) bashful, shy; replete, fraught; burdened; pregnant.

pejar (*v.t.*) to fill; to encumber; (*v.i.*) to become pregnant; of a sugar mill, to shut down; (*v.r.*) to become ashamed.

pejo (*m.*) shame, modesty; bashfulness.

pejorar (*v.t.*) to depreciate, disparage.

pejorativo –va (*adj.*) pejorative, depreciatory; disparaging.

pejoso –sa (*adj.*) bashful.

pela (*contraction of prep.* PER + *archaic art.* LA) by the, at the, for the, in the, through the, toward the, over the, among the, with the, on the, along the, etc.——**calada**, quietly, silently.——**janela (porta)**, through the window (door).——**(or de) manhã**, in the morning.——**palavra**, literally, absolutely.——**pátria**, for the fatherland.——**raiz**, (out) by the root.——**rama**, superficially.——**rua**, along the street.——**segunda vez**, for the second time.——**sonega**, surreptitiously.——**(or à) surdina**, secretly.——**ventura**, per adventure.——**(or por) volta de**, about (near in time).——**s costas**, through the back.——**s mesmas palavras**, literally, word for word.——**s (quatro) horas**, about (four) o'clock Cf. PELO.

péla (*f.*) handball; rubber ball; layer of bark of a cork tree.

pelado –da (*adj.*) hairless; bald; bare; skinned, flayed; penniless; (*m.*) penniless person; a much-grazed pasture; (*f.*) bald spot; kids' or second-rate soccer game.

pelador –dora (*adj.*) hair-removing; skinning; (*m.*) hair-remover; skinner.

peladura (*f.*) hair-removal; baldness; skinning.

pelagem (*f.*) pelage, fur.

pelágia (*f.*) kind of jellyfish [= ÁGUA-VIVA].

pelágio –gia, pelágico –ca (*adj.*) pelagic.

pélago (*m.*) an ocean deep; ocean far from land; depths.

pelagra (*f.*, *Med.*) pellagra.

pelame (*m.*) fur, hair; pelt; pelts collectively.

pelanca (*f.*) dewlap or other fold of loose, pendulous skin; (*m.*, *slang*) old-time reporter.

pelanco (*m.*) fledgling, lit. & fig.

pelanga, pelangana (*f.*) = PELANCA.

pelar (*v.t.*) to skin, flay; to strip, peel off; to scrape or otherwise remove hair or fur; to fleece (plunder, swindle); (*v.r.*) to lose one's hair;——**-se de (or com) mêdo**, to shiver with fright.——**-se por (alguma coisa)**, to be "crazy about" (something).

pelargônio (*m.*, *Bot.*) any pelargonium, c.a. CATINGA-DE-MULATA.

pelaria (*f.*) peltry; fur store.

pele (*f.*) skin, epidermis, hide, pelt; fur piece; fruit skin; rubber biscuit (dark, flat cake of crude Pará rubber). **de—negra**, black-skinned.——**de galinha**, gooseflesh. **enxêrto de—**, skin graft. **ir à—de alguém**, (*colloq.*) to go after another's hide.

peleador –dora (*adj.*; *m.,f.*) rowdy.

pelear (*v.i.*) to fight; to struggle.

pelechar (*v.i.*) to shed fur.

pelega [lê] (*f.*, *colloq.*) a paper bill (money).

pelegada, pelegama (*f.*, *colloq.*) bank roll; a quantity of sheepskins.

pelego (*m.*) a sheepskin which is placed between the rider and the saddle, wool side up; (*colloq.*) political henchman; ward heeler.

peleia (*f.*) = PELEJA.

peleiro (*m.*) furrier.

peleja (*f.*) battle, fight, fray; contest, bout; quarrel.

pelejador –**dora** (*adj.*) fighting, struggling; (*m.*) fighter; rowdy.

pelejar (*v.i.*) to fight; to battle; to dispute.—**com**, to struggle with.—**contra**, to fight against.—**por**, to strive for.

pelerine (*f.*) pelerine, tippet, cape.

peletaria, peleteria (*f.*) fur shop [= PELARIA].

peleteiro (*m.*) = PELEIRO.

pele-vermelha (*m.,f.*) a redskin (Indian).

pelhanca (*f.*) = PELANCA.

peliagudo –**da** (*adj.*) risky.

pelica (*f.*) kid leather.

peliça (*f.*) pelisse, fur-lined garment.

pelicano (*m.*) pelican.

pelico (*m.*) a sac or membrane enveloping a fetus; a shepherd's sheepskin coat.

película (*f.*) pellicle, thin skin or membrane; camera film; motion picture reel.

pelicular (*adj.*) pellicular.

pelinho (*m.*) = ANU-BRANCO.

pelintra (*m.*) a coarse, vulgar, unscrupulous man, who though penniless is a "slick" dresser; (*adj.*) poor but pretentious; stingy; "slick" in dress and actions.

peliose (*f.*, *Med.*) purpura.

pelítico –**ca** (*adi.*, *Petrog.*) pelitic.

peliqueiro (*m.*) one who prepares or deals in kid leather.

pêlo (*m.*) hair, fur, down, fuzz; **a**—, on purpose. **a contra**—, of fur, rubbed the wrong way; against the grain. **em**—, stark naked. **ir ao**—**de (alguém)**, to go after (someone's) hide. **montar em**—, to ride bareback.

pelo (*contraction of prep.* PER + *archaic art.* LO), by the, at the, for the, in the, through the, toward the, over the, among the, with the, on the, along the, etc.—(or **por**) **amor de Deus**, for God's sake.—**ano** (1900), about (1900).—**cabo**, by the handle.—**contrário**, on the contrary.—**corredor**, through the hall.—**correio**, by mail. —**menos**, at (the very) least.—(or **por**) **miúdo**, in detail. —**modo**, by the looks of.—(or **em**) **nome de**, in the name of.—(or **de**) **ordinário**, ordinarily.—**Presidente**, in the name of, or on behalf of, the President.—**(próprio) punho de**, by the hand (in the handwriting) of.—**que**, in view of which, wherefore.—**que respeita a**, as regards, in .espect to.—**sim**—**não**, on account of this or that.—**tato**, by touch, by feel.—**tempo**, nowadays; at the time of. Cf. PELA.

peloponésio –**sia** (*adj.*; *m.,f.*) Peloponnesian.

peloria (*f.*), **pelorismo** (*m.*, *Bot.*) peloria.

pelosidade (*f.*) pilosity, hairiness.

pelosina (*f.*, *Chem.*) pilosine.

peloso –**sa** (*adj.*) hairy; furry [= PELUDO].

pelota (*f.*) pellet; football; leather pad of a truss; hard clay pellet shot with a BODOQUE (Indian bow); boat made of hides.

pelotada (*f.*) a kick on a football.

pelotão (*m.*) platoon.—**de fuzilamento** or **de execução**, firing squad.

pelote (*m.*) jerkin. **em**—, nude.

pelotense (*adj.*) of or pert. to the city of Pelotas in the State of Rio Grande do Sul; (*m.,f.*) a native or inhabitant of that city.

pelotica (*f.*) small juggling ball.

pelotiqueiro (*m.*) juggler.

pelourinho (*m.*) pillory, stocks [= PICOTA]; whipping post; a decorative shaft or column set in a public square of a Portuguese city.

pelouro (*m.*) cannon ball.

peltado –**da, peltiforme** (*f.*, *Bot.*) peltate, shield-shaped.

peltígera (*f.*, *Bot.*) a genus (*Peltigera*) of lichens.

peltinérveo –**vea** (*adj.*, *Bot.*) peltinerved.

peltre (*m.*) pewter.

pelúcia (*f.*) plush.

peludo –**da** (*adj.*) hairy, furry, shaggy; shy, chary; touchy; mongrel; (*m.*) armadillo [= TATUPEBA]; circus roustabout; drunken spree.

pelugem (*f.*) down, fuzz.

peluginoso –**sa** (*adj.*) downy, fuzzy.

pelve (*f.*, *Anat.*) pelvis.—**renal**, pelvis of the ureter.

pélvico –**ca** (*adj.*) pelvic.

pelviforme (*adj.*) pelviform, basin-shaped.

pelvímetro (*m.*) pelvimeter.

pélvis (*f.*) = PELVE.

pena (*f.*) feather, plume; (*Zool.*) penna; quill; writing pen; writer; penalty, punishment; pain, grief; pity, sorrow; regret; peen of a hammer.—**capital**, or—**de morte**, capital punishment.—**de talião**, a retaliatory penalty; "eye for an eye, tooth for a tooth." **cumprir**—**s**, to serve a prison sentence. **dar**—, to arouse pity. **É (uma)**—! It's too bad! **fazer**—, to sadden, hurt. **Não vale a**—, It isn't worth while; the game isn't worth the candle; it's not worth the trouble. **Que pena!** What a pity! What a shame! **sob**—**de**, under penalty of; on condition that. **ter**—**de**, to be sorry for. **valer a**—, to be worth while.

penáceo –**cea** (*adj.*, *Zool.*) pennaceous.

penacheiro (*m.*, *Bot.*) the stiff bottlebrush (*Callistemon rigidus*).

penachinho (*m.*) = CANA-BRAVA.

penacho (*m.*) plume or bunch of feathers, esp. one on a helmet; any ornamental group of feathers; bird's top-knot; pampas grass; fig., leadership.

penadeira (*f.*) = PEIXE-PESCADOR.

penado –**da** (*adj.*) pennate, feathered; grieved; suffering. **alma**—, tormented soul; (*f.*) pen stroke, dash of a pen; penful of ink.

penal (*adj.*) penal, punitive.

penalidade (*f.*) penalty.

penalizado –**da** (*adj.*) full of pity; grieved, distressed.

penalizar (*v.t.*) to pain, grieve, distress; to cause heartache; (*v.r.*) to feel sorry, full of pity. [But not to penalize which is (1) SUJEITAR A PENALIDADE; (2) IMPÔR DESVATAGEM (handicap).]

penalogia (*f.*) penology.

penalógico –**ca** (*adj.*) penological.

penalogista, penálogo –**ga** (*m.,f.*) penologist.

penalti (*m.*) penalty (in sports).

penão (*m.*) pennon, pennant.

penar (*v.t.*) to pain, grieve, distress; (*v.i.*) to suffer heartache; to feel sorrow, pity; (*v.r.*) to grieve, be anguished.

penates (*m.pl.*) penates; fig., household effects; family; home.

penatífido –**da** (*adj.*, *Bot.*) pinnatifid.

penatilobado –**da** (*adj.*, *Bot.*) pinnatilobate.

penca (*f.*) stalk, stem (of bananas, etc.); (*colloq.*) large numbers of anything; big nose. **às**—**s**, in bunches (like bananas). **em**—, **galore**, "lots".

pencudo –**da** (*adj.*, *colloq.*) big-nosed.

pendão (*m.*) pennant, banner, flag, standard; corn tassel.

pendência (*f.*) dispute, squabble; wrangling; duration of a court action.

pendenciar (*v.i.*) to dispute, quarrel, wrangle.

pendenga (*f.*) squabble, wrangle, bickering.

pendente (*adj.*) pendent, hanging, suspended; sloping; pending; in abeyance; (*m.*) pendant; chandelier.

pender (*v.i.*) to hang, be suspended (**de**, from); to sag; to droop; to incline, lean, tilt, (**para**, **sôbre**, toward); to go down [sun].—**da bôca de**, to hang on every word of.—**de um fio**, to hang by a thread.

penderica (*f.*), **penderico, pendericalho, penderucalho** (*m.*) = PENDURICALHO.

pendoado –**da** (*adj.*) of growing corn, having tassels.

pendor (*m.*) slope, incline; leaning, proneness, propensity, penchant.

pêndulo –**la** (*adj.*) pendulous; (*m.*) pendulum; (*f.*) a pendulum clock.

pendura (*f.*) act of hanging (something); a hanging object. **estar na**—, (*colloq.*) to be hard up.

pendurado –**da** (*adj.*) hanging, suspended; pendulous; (*m.*) steep ground.

pendural (*m.*) king post of a roof truss.

pendurar (*v.t.*) to hang, suspend, (**em**, on; **de**, from); (*slang*) to hock (pawn); (*v.r.*) to hang, dangle. [To hang on the gallows is ENFORCAR.]

penduricalho (*m.*) pendant, watch charm, medal, trinket.

pene (*m.*, *Anat.*) penis.

penedia (*f.*), **-dio** (*m.*) pile of big rocks.

penedo (*m.*) big rock, boulder.—**s erraticos**, (*Geol.*) erratic boulders.

penego [nê] (*m.*) feather pillow or cushion.

peneira (*f.*) sieve, bolter, sifter, screen, riddle; (*Locom.*) spark arrester; (*colloq.*) light rain; straw hat.—**de**

carvão, coal screen. **tapar o sol com uma—**, to carry water in a sieve.

peneiração (*f.*) act or operation of sifting or screening.

peneirada (*f.*) a sieveful (of anything); also = PENEIRAÇÃO.

peneirador –**dora** (*m.,f.*) sifter; (*adj.*) sifting, screening.

peneiramento (*m.*) act or operation of sifting or screening; a screening, classification and selection of persons (as for employment).

peneirar (*v.t.*) to sift, bolt, screen; (*v.i.*) to drizzle; to wheel in the sky (as a buzzard); (*v.r.*) to waggle, waddle.

Penélope (*f.*) Penelope.

peneplanície (*f.*, *Geol.*) peneplain.

penetra (*m.,f.*, *slang*) gate-crasher; party-crasher; interloper.

penetrabilidade (*f.*) penetrability.

penetração (*f.*) penetration; insight; acuity; discernment.

penetrador –**dora**, **penetrante** (*adj.*) penetrating, piercing; discerning, acute, searching.

penetrar (*v.t.,v.i.*) to penetrate; (*v.t.*) to enter into; to permeate; to invade; to see through, discern, perceive; (*v.i.*) to pierce.—**-se de**, to be convinced of.

penetrativo –**va** (*adj.*) = PENETRANTE.

penetrável (*adj.*) penetrable, permeable, pervious.

penetrômetro (*m.*) penetrometer.

pênfigo (*m.*, *Med.*) pemphigus.—**foliáceo**, shingles (herpes zoster).

pengüim (*m.*) penguin [= PINGÜIM].

penha (*f.*) rock, cliff.

penhasco (*m.*) massive rock; crag, cliff, bluff.

penhascoso –**sa** (*adj.*) rocky.

penhor [-es] (*m.*) pledge, pawn; deposit; bond.—**de bens móveis**, chattel mortgage. **casa de—es**, pawnshop. **dar em—**, to pledge, pawn, **sob—**, in pawn, pledged.

penhora (*f.*, *Law*) attachment (seizure) of property in satisfaction of a lien.

penhorado –**da** (*adj.*) pledged; fig., obliged, grateful.

penhorante (*adj.*) pledging; obligating.

penhorar (*v.t.*) to pledge; to put under obligation; to distrain (goods); (*v.r.*) to show oneself grateful.

penhorista (*m.,f.*) pawnbroker.

pêni (*m.*) penny.

penicilina (*f.*) penicillin.

penico (*m.*) chamber pot.

pênico –**ca** (*adj.; m.,f.*) Punic [= PÚNICO].

penífero –**ra**, **penígero** –**ra** (*adj.*) feathered.

peninervado –**da** (*adj.*, *Bot.*) penninervate.

peninita (*f.*, *Min.*) penninite.

península (*f.*) peninsula.

peninsular (*adj.*) peninsular.

pênis (*m.*, *Anat.*) penis.

peniscar (*v.t.*) to nibble.

penitência (*f.*) penitence, repentance; penance.

penitencial)*adj.*) penitential.

penitenciar (*v.t.*) to impose a penance on; (*v.r.*) to do penance; to regret, feel sorry. **Penitenciamo-nos êrros cometidos**, We deeply regret our mistakes.

penitenciário –**ria** (*adj.*) penitentiary; (*m.,f.*) inmate of a penitentiary; (*f.*) penitentiary.

penitente (*adj.; m.,f.*) penitent.

peno –**na** (*adj.; m.,f.*) = PÚNICO.

penol (*m.*, *Naut.*) yardarm.

penoso –**sa** (*adj.*) painful, grievous; distressing; grim; troublesome, arduous, difficult, "tough".

pensado –**da** (*adj.*) deliberate, well-considered.

pensador –**dora** (*adj.*) thinking; (*m.,f.*) thinker.

pensamento (*m.*) act of thinking; thought; idea; mind; opinion; meaning.

pensante (*adj.*) thinking, thoughtful.

pensão (*f.*) pension, annuity, income, allowance; board, boardinghouse.—**vitalícia**, life pension. **quarto com—**, room and board.

pensar (*v.t.,v.i.*) to think (**em**, of, about); to cogitate; to reflect (**sôbre**, on); to ponder (**sôbre**, over); to imagine, conceive; to deem, to purpose, intend, design; (*v.t.*) to attend to, care for, wait on; to dress a wound.—**alto**, to think out loud.—**bem (mal) de alguém**, to think good (evil) of someone. **coisa em que—**, food for thought. **Deixe-me—**, Let me think. **dizer o que pensa**, to speak one's mind. **Não penso assim**, I don't agree. **Penso partir amanhã**, I plan (expect, hope, intend) to leave tomorrow.

pensativo –**va** (*adj.*) pensive, thoughtful; wistful.

pênsil [-seis] (*adj.*) pensile, hanging, suspended. **ponte—**, suspension bridge.

Pensilvânia (*f.*) Pennsylvania.

pensionar (*v.t.*) to pay a pension to; to overload with work.

pensionário –**ria** (*adj.*) pension; (*m.,f.*) pensioner.

pensionista (*m.,f.*) pensioner; boarder.

penso –**sa** (*adj.*) hanging, pendulous; awkwardly placed; (*m.*) care (of children, animals); food ration (for farm animals); dressing (for a wound).—**individual**, first-aid kit.

pentadáctilo –**la** (*adj.*) pentadactyl.

pentadecágono (*m.*, *Geom.*) pentadecagon.

pentadelfo –**fa** (*adj.*, *Bot.*) pentadelphous.

pentaedro (*m.*) pentahedron.

pentafilo –**la** (*adj.*, *Bot.*) pentaphyllous.

pentagonal (*adj.*) pentagonal.

pentágono (*m.*) pentagon.

pentagrama (*m.*) pentagram; (*Music*) staff.

pentaídrico –**ca** (*adj.*, *Chem.*) pentahydric.

pentâmero –**ra** (*adj.*) pentamerous; (*m.*) a pentamerous beetle.

pentâmetro –**tra** (*adj.; m.*) pentameter.

pentanal (*m.*) = ALDEÍDO VALÉRICO.

pentandro –**dra** (*adj.*, *Bot.*) pentandrous.

pentangular (*adj.*) pentangular; pentagonal.

pentano (*m.*, *Chem.*) pentane.

pentapétalo –**la** (*adj.*, *Bot.*) pentapetalous.

pentaspermo –**ma** (*adj.*, *Bot.*) pentaspermous.

pentassépalo –**la** (*adj.*, *Bot.*) pentasepalous.

pentassílabo –**ba** (*adj.*) pentasyllabic.

pentastilo (*m.*) a pentastyle building.

Pentateuco (*m.*) Pentateuch.

pentatlo (*m.*) pentathlon.

pentatômico –**ca** (*adj.*, *Chem.*) pentatomic.

pentavalente (*adj.*, *Chem.*) quinquevalent.

pente (*m.*) comb (for the hair); curry comb; card (for wool, etc.); hackle (for flax, hemp, etc.); reed of a loom; (*Anat.*) pubis.—**-de-jacó**, the pilgrim scallop (*Pecten jacobaeus*).—**de cartuchos** or **de balas**, cartridge clip.—**-de-macaco**, (*Bot.*) a monkeycomb (*Pitchecoc-terium*).—**-de-vênus**, (*Bot.*) the Venus-comb shepherds-needle (*Scandix pecten-veneris*).—**dos bichos**, fine-tooth comb (for head lice).—**-fino**, fine-tooth comb; unprincipled opportunist; carping critic; one who picks flaws in everything.

penteadeira (*f.*) vanity (dressing table); headdress.

penteadela (*f.*) a hasty or careless combing of the hair.

penteado (*m.*) coiffure, headdress, hairdo.

penteador –**dora** (*adj.*) combing; (*m.*) a lady's negligee, dressing gown; a hair dresser.

penteadura (*f.*) act of combing.

pentear (*v.t.*) to comb; (*v.r.*) to comb one's hair.

Pentecostes (*m.pl.*) Pentecost.

pentlandita (*f.*, *Min.*) pentlandite.

pêntodo (*m.*, *Elec.*) pentode.

pentose (*f.*, *Chem.*) pentose.

pentosuria (*f.*, *Physiol.*, *Med.*) pentosuria.

penugem (*f.*) down, fuzz, fluff.

penugento –**ta** (*adj.*) downy, fuzzy, fluffy.

penujar (*v.i.*) to begin to be covered with down.

penúltimo –**ma** (*adj.*) penultimate, next-to-the-last.

penumbra (*f.*) penumbra; half-shadow, dimness, twilight.

penumbroso –**sa** (*adj.*) penumbral; shadowy, dimly lit; dusky.

penúria (*f.*) penury, destitution; hardship.

penurioso –**sa** (*adj.*) poverty-stricken. [But not penurious, which is AVARO, SOVINA.]

P.E.O. = POR ESPECIAL OBSÉQUIO (by special kindness).

peoa, peona, fem. of PEÃO.

peonada (*f.*) farm or ranch hands in a group or as a class.

peonagem (*f.*) farm or ranch workers collectively; foot soldiers.

peônia (*f.*, *Bot.*) peony (*Paeonia*).

peperino (*m.*, *Petrog.*) peperino.

peperomia (*f.*, *Bot.*) Sander's peperomia (*P. sandersi*).

pepinal (*m.*) cucumber field.

pepineira (*f.*) cucumber field; cucumber vine; spree; bargain; bonanza; sinecure, snap, "plum".

pepineiro (*m.*) cucumber plant (*Cucumis sativus*).

pepino (*m.*) cucumber (fruit or vine).—**-do-mar**, sea cucumber.

pepita (*f.*) gold nugget.

pepitoso –**sa** (*adj.*) abounding in gold nuggets.

peplo (*m.*) peplos (ancient Greek outer garment); peplum.

peponídeo –**dea** (*adj.*) melonlike (fleshy and full of seeds); = MELONÍDEO.

pepsina (f., *Biochem.*) pepsin.
péptico –ca (*adj.*) peptic.
peptídio (m., *Biochem.*) peptide.
peptizar (*v.t.*, *Physical Chem.*) to peptize.
peptógeno –na (*adj.*) peptogenous.
peptona (f., *Biochem.*) peptone.
peptonato (m., *Biochem.*) peptonate.
peptonizar (*v.t.*) to peptonize.
peptonúria, peptonuria (f., *Med.*) peptonuria.
pepuíra (f.) a stunted chicken.
pequena (f.) see under PEQUENO.
pequenada (f.) a "bunch of kids"; a large family of small children.
pequenez(a) [ê] (f.) littleness, smallness; pettiness.
pequenino –na, pequenito –ta (*adj.*) tiny, wee; (m.,f.) a little one (child).
pequeníssimo –ma (*absol. superl.* of PEQUENO) very small, tiny.
pequenitote (*adj.*) very small; (m.) a very small boy.
pequeno –na (*adj.*) small, little; modest; (m.) child, lad, boy; (f., *colloq.*) girl; girl-friend; sweetheart; (m.pl.) the little people.—caloria, (*Physics*) small calorie.—-hipocampo, (*Anat.*) hippocampus minor.—-lábios, (*Anat.*) labia minora.
pequenote (*adj.*) smallish; (m.) small boy.
pequerrucho –cha (*adj.*) wee, tiny; (m.,f.) a little one, tot.
pequetito –ta (*adj.*) = PEQUENINO.
pequi [í] (m., *Zool.*) a finfoot (*Heliornis fulica*), c.a. IPEQUI, PATINHO-D'ÁGUA; (*Bot.*) a souari nut tree (*Caryocar sp.*) or its fruit; c.a. PEQUIÁ, PEQUIZEIRO.
pequiá (m.) kinds of trees; (*colloq.*) small woven cane basket.—-amarelo, a white quebracho (*Aspidosperma*). —-café, a shrub (*Casearia*) of the Indian plum family, c.a. CAFÉ-BRAVO, PAU-ESPÊTO.—-marfim = PAU-CETIM.
pequice (f.) a trivial or silly remark; inanity.
Pequim (m.) Peking.
pequinês –nêsa (*adj.*) Pekingese; (m.,f.) native of Peking; (m.) Pekingese dog; Pekin duck.
pequito (m.) little one (child).
pequizeiro (m.) = PEQUI (tree).
per (*prep.*) = POR. de—si, by itself (herself, himself).
pêra (f.) pear; goatee; a pear-shaped electric bell button; rubber bulb (as of an atomizer).
perada (f.) pear jam or preserves; pear wine.
perado (m., *Bot.*) the Azores holly (*Ilex perado*).
peral (m.) pear orchard [= PEREIRAL]; (*adj.*) pear(-like).
peralta (m.) dude, dandy, whippersnapper; idler; mischievous child; (f.) prissy (priggish) woman; (*adj.*) mischievous, prankish; dapper.
peraltice (f.) prank; mischievousness; foppery.
peralvilho (m.) popinjay; vain, chattering person; fop, dandy.
perambeira (f.) precipice.
perambulação (f.) perambulation.
perambular (*v.i.*) to perambulate, go about.—pelas ruas, to roam the streets.
perambele (m., *Zool.*) bandicoot.
perante (*prep.*) in the presence of, before.
perau (m.) deep hole; sudden drop (in lake or river bottom); steep hill; steep river bank.
perborato (m., *Chem.*) perborate.
perborina (f., *Chem.*) perborin, sodium perborate.
perca (f., *colloq.*) loss, damage; (*Gram.*) form of PERDER [60]; (*Zool.*) perch, bass.—-amarela, yellow perch (*Perca flavescens*).—-branca, white perch (*Morone*).—-do-mar, a wrasse (*Labrus*).
percais, form of PERDER [60].
percal (m.) percale.
percalço (m.) perquisite; emolument, fee; drawback, disadvantage (of a given office or profession); hitch (in proceedings).
percalina (f.) percaline.
percam, percamos, percas, forms of PERDER [60].
percêbe (m.) = PERCEVE.
perceber (*v.t.*) to perceive, understand; to see through, get the point; to be aware of; to feel, sense; to hear; to descry, discern, distinguish; to draw down a salary or other honorarium.
percebimento (m.) perception.
percebível (*adj.*) perceptible.
percentagem (f.) percentage.
percentil (*adj.*; m.) centile; percentile.
percepção (f.) perception, discernment, apprehension;

awareness; feeling.—de vencimentos, drawing of a salary.
perceptibilidade (f.) perceptibility.
perceptível (*adj.*) perceptible.
perceptivo –va (*adj.*) perceptive.
perceve [cê] (m.) rock barnacle.
percevejo [vê] bedbug (*Cimex*); thumb tack.—-do-sertão = BARBEIRO (bug).—vulgar, common bedbug (*Cimex lectularius*).
percha (f.) acrobat's perch pole; short for GUTA-PERCHA.
percherão –rona (*adj.*; m.,f.) Percheron.
pércidas (m.pl., *Zool.*) the Percidae (perch family).
percilito (m., *Min.*) percylite.
perclorato (m., *Chem.*) perchlorate.
percloreto [ê] (m., *Chem.*) perchloride.
perclórico –ca (*adj.*; *Chem.*) perchloric.
percluso –sa (*adj.*) crippled.
perco, form of PERDER [60].
percóide (*adj.*) percoid.
percóides (m.pl.) the Percoidea (superfamily of perches, sunfishes, seranoids, etc.).
percolação (f.) percolation. Cf. LIXIVIAÇÃO.
percorrer (*v.t.*) to traverse, travel all over; to pass through or over; to go through (as a museum); to search, examine thoroughly; to scour, range over; to glance over, peruse.
percristalização (f., *Chem.*) percrystallization.
percuciente (*adj.*) percussive, percutient.
percurso (m.) course, run, route, way, track. fazer o—entre, to ply between (given points).
percussão (f.) percussion. instrumento de—, percussion instrument.
percussor –sora (*adj.*) percussive, striking; (m.) percussor; firing pin.
percutir (*v.t.*) to percuss.
perda [ê] (f.) loss, damage, waste; leakage.—de núcleo, (*Elec.*) core loss.—de potência, power loss.—dielétrica, (*Elec.*) dielectric loss.—s e danos, indemnity for loss and damage.
perdão (m.) pardon, forgiveness, remission, absolution; (*interj.*) Excuse me!
perde-ganha (m.) a game in which the low scorer is the winner.
perder [60] (*v.t.*) to lose; to forfeit; to be bereaved of (by death); to fail to keep; to cease to have; to leave far behind (in a pursuit, race, etc.); to waste (time, etc.); to be defeated (in a game, battle, etc.); (*v.i.*) to lose, suffer loss; to lose ground, fall behind; to fail to win; (*v.r.*) to get lost; to stray; to ruin oneself; to lose oneself (as in thought).—a cabeça, to lose one's head.—a côr, to grow pale; of a dress, etc., to fade.—a coragem, to lose heart, courage.—a esperança, to lose hope.—a fala, to lose one's voice; to be struck dumb.—a linha, to lose one's decorum.—a luz da razão, to lose the light of reason (one's mind).—a mão, to lose one's chance to play first or to do something else.—a memória, to lose one's memory.—a ocasião, to miss an opportunity.—a paciência, to lose one's patience or temper.—a partida, to lose out (at something).—a pista de, to lose track of.—a prosa, to come down a peg.—a razão, to lose one's mind.—a reputação, to lose one's reputation or credit.—a sela, to lose one's saddle, be unseated.—a tolerância, to lose one's draft deferment because of poor marks.—a tramontana, to lose one's bearings (lit. & fig.); also = PERDER AS ESTRIBEIRAS.—a vez, to lose one's turn or an opportunity.—a vida, to lose one's life.—a vista, to lose one's eyesight, go blind.—a viagem, to lose one's efforts; to waste time.—a voz, to lose one's voice.—as estribeiras, to lose one's head, temper or composure; to fly off the handle; also = PERDER A TRAMONTANA.—caminho, to lose ground; (*colloq.*) to waste one's time. [Cf. PERDER O CAMINHO.]—de ganhar, to fail to profit or to win.—de vista, to lose sight of (lit. & fig.); to forget a face.—na opinião de, to drop in the opinion of another.—o amor a, to lose one's love or liking for.—o ânimo, to lose heart. —o apetite, to lose one's appetite.—o caminho, to lose one's way. [Cf. PERDER CAMINHO].—a cetro, to lose the throne.—o conceito, to lose one's prestige.—o crédito, to lose one's credit or reputation.—o fio, to lose one's train of thought.—o fôlego, to get out of breath.—o leme, not to know which way to turn.—o juízo, to lose one's good sense.—o nome, to lose one's identity; to lose one's reputation.—o norte, to lose one's judgment; to go haywire.—o prumo, to lose one's aplomb; to lose one's balance (fall).—o rasto a, to lose track of.—o ser,

to become lifeless.—**os estribos**, to lose one's foothold in the stirrups; to lose one's composure.—**o (seu) latim**, to waste one's breath; to waste one's efforts in behalf of another.—**o siso**, to lose one's good sense.—**o sono**, to lose sleep, be greatly concerned.—**o sôpro**, to faint.—**o tato**, to lose one's sense of touch; to become lost, confused.—**o tempo**, to waste time.—**o tempo e o feitio**, to lose one's time and effort.—**o tento de**, to neglect (one's obligations).—**o trem**, to miss the train.—**o uso dos sentidos**, to lose the use of one's faculties.—**os sentidos**, to lose consciousness, pass out.—**pé**, to be unable to touch bottom (in water); to lose one's bearings.—**se à (or de) vista**, to disappear from sight.—**se de riso**, to die laughing.—**se em cogitações**, to lose oneself in thought.—**se em divagações**, to ramble.—**se na opinião de**, to lose the esteem of another.—**tempo**, to lose time.—**terra**, to lose sight of land.—**terreno**, to lose ground.—**vazas**, to lose tricks (as at bridge). **a—de vista**, as far as the eye can see. **deitar a—**, to render liable (subject) to loss. **Do prato à bôca se perde a sopa**, There's many a slip twixt the cup and the lip. **Quem muito quer, tudo perde**, To attempt all is to lose all. **saber—**, to be a good loser.
perdestilação (*f.*, *Chem.*) perdistillation.
perdição (*f.*) perdition, doom. **votar à—**, to damn.
perdíceo –cea (*adj.*) partridgelike.
perdida (*f.*) see under PERDIDO.
perdidamente (*adj.*) crazily, wildly, desperately, uselessly.
perdidiço –ça (*adj.*) easily lost.
perdido –da (*adj.*) lost, astray; wrecked; dissipated; depraved; irreclaimable; desperately in love; (*f.*) a loss; a lost (fallen) woman; (*m.*) lost object.—**de amor**, head-over-heels in love; lovesick.—**de riso**, dying of laughter. **uma bala—**, a stray bullet.
perdigão (*m.*, *Zool.*) the dwarf tinamou (*Taoniscus nanus*); Chapman's crake (*Micropygia schomburgkii*); the rufous tinamou (*Rhynchotus rufescens*).
perdigotar (*v.i.*) to splutter.
perdigoteiro –ra (*adj.*) spluttering; (*m.,f.*) one who splutters moistly.
perdigôto (*m.*) chick of a partridge; (*colloq.*) a shower of droplets of saliva (emitted by one who splutters); fine bird shot.
perdigueiro –ra (*adj.*) quail-hunting; (*m.,f.*) pointer or setter (dog).
perdimento (*m.*) losing; loss; perdition.
perdível (*adj.*) losable.
perdiz (*f.*) any of various partridges, esp. the catinga tinamou (*Rhynchotus rufescens calingae*) or the rufous tinamou (*Rynchotus r. rufescens*).—**do-mar**, a pratincole (*Glareola pratincola*).
perdoador –ra (*adj.*) forgiving, forbearing; (*m.,f.*) forgiver.
perdoar (*v.t.*) to pardon, forgive, absolve, condone, overlook; (*v.i.*) to forgive, excuse; (*v.r.*) to forgive oneself.
perdoável (*adj.*) pardonable, excusable.
perdoe (*f.*) a straw bag used by beggars for collecting gifts of food, and by others as a shopping bag.
perdulário –ria (*adj.*) prodigal, wasteful; spendthrift, wastrel.
perduração (*f.*) long duration, continuance.
perdurar (*v.i.*) to perdure, last long, endure. **Não há bem que sempre dure, nem mal que por si perdure**, It's a long lane that has no turning.
perdurável (*adj.*) long-lasting, enduring, abiding.
pereba (*f.*) sore; mange; skin disease.
perebento –ta (*adj.*) mangy; sore-covered.
perecedor –dora, –douro –ra (*adj.*) perishable; mortal.
perecer (*v.i.*) to perish, die.
perecimento (*m.*) perishing; extinction.
perecível (*adj.*) perishable.
peregrim (*m.*) archaic form of PEREGRINO (pilgrim).
peregrinação (*f.*) peregrination; pilgrimage.—**dêste mundo**, life's journey.
peregrinador –dora, –grinante (*adj.*) traveling, wandering; (*m.,f.*) peregrinator, wanderer, wayfarer, pilgrim.
peregrinar (*v.i.*) to travel; to go on a pilgrimage.
peregrino –na (*adj.*) peregrine, exotic; travelling; (*m.,f.*) traveler; pilgrim.
pereira (*f.*, *Bot.*) pear tree (Pyrus).—**bergomota**, the bergomot orange (*Citrus bergamia*).—**branca** or—**vaqueta**, a white quebracho (*Aspidosperma*).—**do-campo**, the peradocampo (*Eugenia klotzschiana*), c.a. CABACINHA-DO-CAMPO.—**do japão**, flowering quince (*Chaenomeles lagenaria*).

pereiral (*m.*) pear orchard.
pereiro (*m.*) pearmain apple; ox goad; (*Bot.*) a white quebracho (*Aspidosperma*) better known as GUATAMBU.
perempção (*f.*, *Law*) peremptory exception, peremptory plea.
perempto –ta (*adj.*, *Law*) quashed.
peremptório –ria (*adj.*) peremptory, decisive.
perene, perenal (*adj.*) perennial, lasting, enduring.
perenidade (*f.*) perenniality.
perenizar (*v.t.*) to perpetuate.
perequação (*f.*, *Stat.*) graduation, smoothing.
perequê (*m.*) rumpus, fracas, shindy.
perereca (*f.*) any of numerous small tree toads (*Hylidae*) and robber frogs (*Leptodactylidae*), c.a. RELA, TANOEIRO; a mosquito (*Culex*), c.a. SOVELA, MURIÇOCA.—**azul**, a large tree frog (*Phyllomedusa bicolor*).—**verde**, a tree frog (*Phyllomedusa burmeisteri*). (*m.*) any lively small animal or person; (*adj.*) restless, fidgety; tiny.
pererecar (*v.i.*) to hop about, bounce about, move from place to place; to flounder.
perereco (*m.*, *colloq.*) rough-and-tumble fight.
pererema (*f.*) a palm (*Syagrus cocoides*).
pererento –ta (*adj.*) white-flecked, white-speckled. **céu—**, cloud-flecked sky.
pereroba (*f.*) = PAMPO-DA-CABEÇA-MOLE.
perequia (*f.*) a shrubby, spinose, tropical cactaceous plant (*Pereskia undulata*).
pereva (*f.*) = PEREBA.
perexi [í] (*m.*) = CAVALHEIRO-DAS-ONZE-HORAS.
perfazer [47] (*v.t.*) to perfect, complete; to accomplish; to make up; to bring up to (the required number, quantity, etc.)
perfazimento (*m.*) completion, perfecting.
perfectibilidade (*f.*) perfectibility.
perfectível (*adj.*) perfectible.
perfeição (*f.*) perfection, excellence.
perfeiçoar (*v.*) = APERFEIÇOAR.
perfeitamente (*adv.*) perfectly; exactly, quite so.
perfeito –ta (*adj.*) perfect; complete; faultless, accomplished.
perfídia (*f.*) perfidy, treachery, foul play.
pérfido –da (*adj.*) perfidious, faithless, traitorous, dastardly; (*m.,f.*) perfidious person.
perfil (*m.*) profile, side view; outline, contour; lineup (of troops); sectional drawing; character sketch.—**do solo**, soil profile. **de—**, in profile.
perfiladora (*f.*) shaper (machine tool).
perfilar (*v.t.*) to draw the profile of; to draw up in a line; to straighten (up); (*v.r.*) to draw oneself up; stand up straight.
perfilhação (*f.*), **perfilhamento** (*m.*) adoption (of a child); espousal (of a cause).
perfilhar (*v.t.*) to adopt (child, principle); (*v.i.*) to sprout.
perfoliado –da (*adj.*, *Bot.*) perfoliate.
perfulgente (*adj.*) refulgent.
perfumado –da (*adj.*) perfumed; fragrant.
perfumador –dora (*adj.*) perfuming; (*m.*) incense burner.
perfumar (*v.t.*) to perfume (**com**, with); (*v.r.*) to put on perfume.
perfumaria (*f.*) perfumery; (*pl.*, *colloq.*) soft drinks.
perfume (*m.*) perfume; fragrance, aroma, pleasant odor.
perfumista (*m.,f.*) perfumer.
perfumoso –sa (*adj.*) odoriferous, perfumed, fragrant.
perfun[c]tório –ria (*adj.*) perfunctory.
perfuração (*f.*) perforation; drilling, boring.
perfurador –dora (*adj.*) piercing, boring; (*m.,f.*) perforator; a perforating drill or puch; boring machine; oil-well drilling rig.
perfurados (*m.pl.*, *Zool.*) the Perforata (corals).
perfurante (*adj.*) perforating, piercing, boring, drilling, punching.
perfurar (*v.t.*) to perforate, pierce, penetrate, bore, drill, punch, prick, puncture.
perfuratriz (*f.*) punch press; drill press.
perfusão (*f.*) perfusion; aspersion.
pergamin[h]áceo –cea (*adj.*) pergamaneous, like parchment.
pergaminharia (*f.*) parchment-making.
pergaminheiro (*m.*) parchment-maker or parchment dealer.
pergaminho (*m.*) parchment; vellum; (*colloq.*) sheepskin (diploma); (*pl.*) titles, honors.—**vegetal**, parchment paper.

pérgula (*f.*) pergola.

pergunta (*f.*) question, interrogation; inquiry.—**de algibeira**, trick question. **Êle me fez muitas—s**, He asked me a lot of questions. **fazer—s**, to ask questions, make inquiries. **submergir de—s**, to deluge with questions.

perguntador –dora (*adj.*) questioning; inquisitive; (*m.,f.*) questioner; inquirer.

perguntante (*m.,f.*) questioner.

perguntar (*v.t.*) to question, query, interrogate; to inquire of; (*v.i.*) to question, ask questions, inquire; (*v.r.*) to ask oneself.—**por (alguém)**, to ask for or about (someone). **Ainda que mal pergunte**, excuse me for asking.

peri [í] (*m.*) peri (an elf or fairy of Persian mythology); gulch, gully; (*Bot.*) a bulrush (*Scirpus riparius*), c.a. CAPIM-DE-ESTEIRA.

periambo (*m.*) = PIRRÍQUIO.

periândrico –ca (*adj., Bot.*) perianthial.

periantã (*m.*) a place abounding in gullies; also = MATUPÁ.

periantado –da (*adj., Bot.*) having a perianth.

periântio, perianto (*m., Bot.*) perianth.

periatã (*m.*) = MATUPÁ.

periblasto (*m., Embryol.*) periblastula.

periblema (*m., Bot.*) periblem.

períbolo (*m., Archit.*) peribolos.

pericardino –na (*adj., Anat.*) pericardial.

pericárdio (*m., Anat.*) pericardium.

pericardite (*f., Med.*) pericarditis.

pericardítico –ca (*adj.*) pericarditic.

pericarpial (*adj., Bot.*) pericarpial.

pericárpico –ca (*adj., Bot.*) pericarpic.

pericárpio (*m., Bot.*) pericarp.

pericentral (*adj.*) pericentral.

pericêntrico –ca (*adj.*) pericentric, pericentral.

perícia (*f.*) skill, dexterity, expertness, know-how. **com—**, adroitly, cleverly.

periciclo (*m., Bot.*) pericycle.

periclásio (*m., Min.*) periclase.

periclina (*f.*) = PERICLÍNIO.

periclinal (*adj., Geol.*) periclinal, quaquaversal.

periclínio (*m., Bot.*) periclinium; (*Min.*) pericline.

periclinita (*f., Min.*) pericline.

periclino (*m.*) = PERICLÍNIO.

periclitante (*adj.*) exposed to danger; in a perilous situation; ramshackle, shaky.

periclitar (*v.i.*) to be exposed to danger; to be in jeopardy; to threaten to fall.

pericondro (*m., Anat.*) perichondrium.

perícope (*f.*) pericope, esp. a selection from the Bible.

pericote (*m.*) a knot of hair at the back; topknot [= COCÓ].

pericrânio (*m., Anat.*) pericranium.

periculosidade (*f.*) hazard, peril; (*Law*) the status of one who, or that which, constitutes a public menace; the danger potential of a lawbreaker.

periderme (*f., Zool., Bot.*) periderm.

peridérmico –ca (*adj.*) peridermic.

peridésmio (*m., Anat.*) peridesmium.

perídio (*m., Bot.*) peridium.

peridíola (*f.*), **–lo** (*m., Bot.*) peridiolum.

peridotite (*f.*), **–to** (*m., Petrog.*) peridotite.

peridoto (*m.*) peridot.

perídromo (*m., Arch.*) peridrome.

periegese (*f.*) periegisis (description of a region).

periélio (*m., Astron.*) perihelion.

periergia (*f.*) excessive refinement of language.

periferia (*f.*) periphery.

periférico –ca (*adj.*) peripheric(al).

perífise (*f., Bot.*) periphysis.

perífrase (*f.*) periphrasis, circumlocution.

perifrasear (*v.t.,v.i.*) to periphrase.

perifrástico –ca (*adj.*) periphrastic.

perigalho (*m.*) pendulous fold of skin on the face or throat; (*Naut.*) boom fall.

perigar (*v.i.*) to be in danger, in peril.

perigênese (*f.*) perigenesis.

perigeu (*m., Astron.*) perigee.

periginia (*f., Bot.*) perigyny.

perígino –na (*adj., Bot.*) perigynous.

perigo (*m.*) peril, danger; risk, hazard. **em—de vida**, in danger of losing one's life. **Não tem—!** No danger of that!

perigônio, perígono (*m., Bot.*) perigonium, perianth.

perigoso –sa (*adj.*) perilous, dangerous, hazardous; (*f., colloq.*) booze.

periguari [arí] (*m., Zool.*) a wing shell (*Strombus*).

perila (*f., Bot.*) an Asiatic mint (*Perilla arguta*).

perilha (*f.*) pearlike ornament.

perilhão (*m., Zool.*) a Tortrix moth.

perilinfa (*f., Anat.*) perilymph.

perimétrico –ca (*adj.*) perimetric(al).

perímetro (*m.*) perimeter.

perimir (*v.t., Law*) to quash; to lapse; to forfeit.

perimísio (*m., Anat.*) perimysium.

periná (*m.*) = CANA-DE-MACACO; PACO-CATINGA.

perineal (*adj., Anat.*) perineal.

períneo (*m., Anat.*) perineum.

perineu (*m.*) = PERÍNEO.

perineuro (*m., Anat.*) perineurium.

periodato (*m., Chem.*) periodate.

periodeto (*m., Chem.*) periodide.

periodicidade (*f.*) periodicity.

periódico –ca (*adj.*) periodic(al); (*m.*) a periodical (publication).

periodismo (*m.*) journalism; periodicity.

periodista (*m.,f.*) journalist, writer (for a periodical).

período (*m.*) period; cycle; term; (*Rhet.*) a complete sentence; (*Math., Geol.*) period. [The period (punctuation mark) is PONTO FINAL.]—**geológico**, geological era.

periodonto (*m., Dent.*) periodontium.

períoplo (*m., Veter.*) periople.

periorbita (*f., Anat.*) periorbit.

periósseo (*m.*) = PERIÓSTEO.

periost[e]al (*adj., Anat.*) periosteal.

periosteíte (*f.*) = PERIOSTITE.

periósteo (*m., Anat.*) periosteum.

periostite (*f., Med.*) periostitis.

perióstraco (*m., Zool.*) periostrachum.

periparoba (*m., Bot.*) a pepper (*Piper umbellatum*).

peripatético –ca (*adj.*) peripatetic; (*m.*) a Peripatetic.

peripatetismo (*m.*) peripateticism.

perípato (*m., Zool.*) peripatus.

peripécia (*f.*) surprising turn of events; happening, incident, esp. an unexpected one.

periperi [í] (*m., Bot.*) a flatsedge (*Cyperus giganteus*).—**açu**, papyrus (*Cyperus papyrus*), c.a. PAPIRO.

peripétalo –la (*adj., Bot.*) peripetalous.

periplaneta (*f., Zool.*) a genus (*Periplaneta*) of large cockroaches.

periplasma (*m., Bot.*) periplasm.

períplo (*m.*) periplus.

períploca (*f., Bot.*) the silkvines (*Periploca*) of the milkweed family.

peripomonga (*f., Bot.*) Johnson grass (*Sorghum halepense*), c.a. CAPIM-MAÇAMBARA.

periprocto (*m., Zool.*) periproct.

peripterado –da (*adj., Bot.*) alate.

períptero (*m., Arch.*) peripteros.

periquécio (*m., Bot.*) perichaetium.

periquitar (*v.t.*) to walk pigeon-toed.

periquiteira (*f.*) = CRINDIÚVA.—**da-mata**, (*Bot.*) a shellseed (*Cochlospermum orinocense*).—**do-campo**, = BUTUÁ-DE-CORVO.

periquitinho (*m.*) = PERIQUITO-VASSOURA.

periquito (*m.*) any parakeet or unspecified small parrot; (*Bot.*) the garden alternanthera (*A. bettzickiana*); a small tin kerosene lamp; a black-and-blue spot on the skin; a topknot [= COCÓ].—**da-campina**, the yellow-winged paroquet of the Amazon region (*Tirica virescens*), c.a. JUPARABA.—**d'anta** = MARIANINHA.—**de-cabeça-preta** = MAIPURÉ.—**do-pantanal**, the green paroquet (*Myopsitta monacha*), c.a. CATORRITA.—**rei**, the golden-headed paroquet (*Eupsittula a. auricapillus*), c.a. JANDAIA, CATURRA, MAITACA-CABEÇA-DE-CÔCO.—**vassoura**, Ridgway's Brazilian parrotlet of southern Brazil (*Psittacula v. vivida*), c.a. TUÍ, TUIM, PERIQUITINHO.—**verdadeiro**, the green paroquet of eastern and southerr Brazil (*Tirica tirica*).

periscópico –ca (*adj.*) periscopic.

periscópio (*m.*) periscope.

perisfera (*f., Biol.*) perisphere.

perispermo (*m., Bot.*) perisperm.

perispérmico –ca (*adj., Bot.*) perispermic.

perisporângio (*m., Bot.*) perispore.

perissarco (*m., Zool.*) perisarc.

perissístole (*f., Physiol.*) perisystole.

perissistólico –ca (*adj., Physiol.*) perisystolic.

perissodá[c]tilo –la (*adj.; m.,f., Zool.*) perissodactyl.

perissologia (*f.*) superfluity of words; pleonasm.

peristalse (*f., Physiol.*) peristalsis.

peristáltico –ca (*adj., Physiol.*) peristaltic.
peristerita (*f.,m.*) peristerite (a gem variety of albite).
peristetio (*m., Zool.*) peristethium.
peristilo (*m., Arch.*) peristyle, colonnade.
perístole (*f., Physiol.*) peristole, peristalsis.
perístomio (*m., Bot., Zool.*) peristome.
peritécio (*m., Bot.*) perithecium.
peritélio (*m., Anat.*) perithelium.
perito –ta (*adj.*) skillful (**em**, at); able, expert (**em**, in, at); (*m.,f.*) an expert, adept; an official appraiser.
peritoneal (*adj.*) peritoneal.
peritônio, peritoneu (*m., Anat.*) peritoneum.
peritonite (*f., Med.*) peritonitis.
peritrófico –ca (*adj., Zool.*) peritrophic.
perítropo –pa (*adj., Bot.*) peritropous.
periuretral (*adj., Anat.*) periurethral.
periuterino –na (*adj., Anat.*) periuterine.
perivascular (*adj., Anat.*) perivascular.
perivesical (*adj., Anat.*) perivesical.
perivisceral (*adj., Anat.*) perivisceral.
perjurar (*v.i.*) to perjure.
perjúrio (*m.*) perjury.
perjuro –ra (*adj.*) perjuring; (*m.,f.*) perjurer.
perlado –da (*adj.*) pearly; pearl-covered.
perlar (*v.t.*) to pearl.
perlaria (*f.*) a quantity of pearls.
perlasso (*m.*) pearlash (purified potash).
perlenda, perlenga (*f.*) = PARLENGA.
perlengar (*v.i.*) to gabble.
perlídeos (*m.pl., Zool.*) the large stone flies (*Perlidae*).
perlítico –ca (*adj.*) perlitic; pearlitic.
perlita (*f., Petrog.*) perlite; (*Metal.*) pearlite.
perlonga (*f.*) undue delay.
perlongar (*v.t.*) to skirt (the edge of); to follow along (a given line); to delay unduly.
perlongo (*m.*) sloping side of a roof.
perlustrar (*v.t.*) to scan, scrutinize.
perluxo –xa [ks] (*adj.*) popular form of PROLIXO; (*m., Bot.*) a passionflower (*Passiflora parahybensis*).
permanecente (*adj.*) permanent, lasting, enduring.
permanecer (*v.i.*) to remain, stay; to last, continue.
permanência (*f.*) permanence, continuance; stay, sojourn.
permanente (*adj.*) permanent, lasting, enduring; (*m.*) a permanent pass; (*f.*) a permanent wave.
permanganato (*m., Chem.*) permanganate.—**de potássio,** potassium permanganate.
permeabilidade (*f.*) permeability.—**magnética,** magnetic permeability.
permeâmetro (*m., Elec.*) permeameter.
permeância (*f., Magnetism*) permeance.
permear (*v.t.*) to permeate, penetrate; (*v.i.*) to pervade.
permeável (*adj.*) permeable, penetrable, pervious.
permeio (*m.*) midst. **de**—, among, between.
permiano –na (*adj.; m., Geol.*) Permian.
permissão (*f.*) permission, consent.
permissível (*adj.*) permissible, allowable, legitimate.
permissivo –va (*adj.*) permissive.
permissor, permissório –ria (*adj.*) permissory.
permitância (*f.*) electrostatic capacity.
permitidor –dora (*adj.*) permissive.
permitir (*v.t.*) to permit, let, allow; to give permission to.
permo-carbônico –ca (*adj., Geol.*) Permocarboniferous.
permuta (*f.*) exchange; substitution.
permutação (*f.*) permutation, alteration, interchange.
permutador –dora (*adj.*) exchanging, interchanging; (*m.*) permuter; (*Elec.*) permutator.
permutamento (*m.*) permutation.
permutante (*adj.*) permuting.
permutar (*v.t.*) to permute; to exchange, barter; to permutate.
permutável (*adj.*) permutable.
perna (*f.*) leg; something that resembles a leg in form or use; strand (of a cable); principal rafter of a gable roof truss; (*slang*) drunken spree.—**base,** (*Aeron.*) base leg.—**-de-moça,** a weakfish (*Cynoscion*), c.a. PESCADINHA.—**-de-pau,** wooden leg; stiff leg; a poor soccer player; a stilt (long-legged wading bird), c.a. MAÇARICÃO; (*pl.*) stilts.—**de rio,** branch of a river.—**de-xis,** (*colloq.*) a knock-kneed person.—**-fina,** dude, coxcomb, popinjay; poltroon.—**-lavada** or—**-lavrada** = GALINHA-DO-MATO (antbird).—**-longa,** a long-legged wading bird.—**-vermelha,** (*Zool.*) a redshank (*Totanus totanus*). **barriga da**—, calf of the leg. **com uma**—**às costas,** with the greatest of ease (i.e., even with a leg around one's

neck). **dar à**—, to shake a leg (walk fast). **dar às**—**s,** to leg it (run away). **estirar as**—**s,** to stretch one's legs. **fazer uma**—, to play a partner's hand; to enter into a deal. **passar a**—**a** (or **em**) **alguém,** to trick (outwit, outsmart) someone.
pernaça (*f.*) fat leg.
pernada (*f.*) long stride, big step; kick; tiring walk.
pernaltas (*f.pl., Zool.*) the Grallatores (wading birds).
pername (*f.*) big (thick) leg.
pernão (*m.*) thick (upper) part of a horse's leg.
pernear (*v.i.*) to kick one's legs; to jump up and down.
perneiras (*f.pl.*) leggings, puttees.
perneta [nê] (*f.*) small leg; (*m.*) one-legged person.
perniaberto –ta (*adj.*) open-legged.
pernibambo –ba (*adj.*) loose-legged.
pernicioso –sa (*adj.*) pernicious; baleful; malign; noxious; (*f., Med.*) pernicious malaria.
pernicurto –ta (*adj.*) short-legged.
pernigrande (*adj.*) big-legged.
pernil (*m.*) shank (of animal's leg); thin leg. **esticar o**—, (*colloq.*) to turn up one's toes (die).
pernilongo –ga (*adj.*) long-legged; (*m.*) a shore bird called MAÇARICÃO; the yellow-fever mosquito (*Aedes aegypti*).
perno (*m.*) bolt, pin, rivet.—**de manilha,** shackle bolt.
pernoita (*f.*), **pernoitamento** (*m.*) = PERNOITE.
pernoitar (*v.i.*) to stay overnight; to spend the night. Var. PERNOUTAR.
pernoite (*m.*) an overnight stay.
pernosticismo (*m.*) pretentiousness; bumptiousness.
pernóstico –ca (*adj.*) affected, pretentious; bumptious; "uppity". Cf. PRONÓSTICO.
pernoutar (*v.*) = PERNOITAR.
pernudo –da (*adj.*) big-legged.
peroba (*adj., colloq.*) boring, tiresome, importuning [=MAÇANTE, CACÊTE]; (*m.,f., colloq.*) bore, pest; (*m., colloq.*) anything big [=BUTELO]; (*f.*) any of various important Brazilian timber trees of the genus Aspidosperma (the whitequebrachos), esp. *A. polyneuron*, having very hard, rose-yellow wood, common in the State of São Paulo; a walking stick made of this wood.—**-branca,** despite the name (white peroba) this is not a true peroba but a tree of the sapodilla family (*Achras zapota* or *Calocarpum sapota*).—**-brava,** this also is not a true peroba but a white alder (*Clethra gonocarpa*).—**-do-pará,** a huge tree whose timber is much used in naval construction.—**-cetim** = GUATAMBU (a tree).
perobal (*m.*) a place abounding in PEROBA trees.
perobeira (*f.*) PEROBA tree.
perobinha (*f.*) = CHAPADA.—**-do-campo,** a medicinal plant (*Sweetia elegans*) of the pea family.
perognato (*m.*) the genus (*Perognathus*) consisting of the pocket mice.
pérola (*f.*) pearl; pearl bead; person of superior qualities; clear drop (as a tear); kind of white grape; kind of pear; a stone fly (*Perla*); (*pl., Arch.*) pearl molding; kind of tea.—**apigentada,** pear-shaped pearl.—**oriental,** Oriental pearl.—**s da aurora,** morning dewdrops. [*Poetical*]—**s de estilo,** beauties of style.—**vegetal,** a leafflower (*Phyllanthus nobilis*), c.a. CATUABA.—**verde,** a lace-winged fly (*Hermerobius perla*).
perolar (*v.t.*) = PERLAR.
peroleira (*f.*) pearl oyster or mussel.
perolífero –ra (*adj.*) pearl-producing [shells].
perolino –na (*adj.*) pearl.
perolizar (*v.t.*) to pearl.
peroneal, perôneo –nea (*adj., Anat.*) peroneal [=PERÔNIO].
perôneo-calcârio –ria (*adj., Anat.*) peroneocalcaneal.
perôneo-tibial (*adj., Anat.*) peroneotibial.
perônio, peroneu (*adj., Anat.*) peroneal; (*m.*) fibula.
peronospora (*f., Bot.*) a genus (*Peronospora*) of downy mildews.
perope (*m., Zool.*) a peropod.
peropode (*adj., Zool.*) peropodous.
peroração (*f.*) peroration.
perorador –dora (*adj.*) perorating; (*m.*) orator.
perorar (*v.i.*) to perorate.
perovaúna (*f.*) a tree (*Melanoxylum brauna*) of the pea family.
peroxidar [ks] (*v.t., Chem.*) to peroxidize.
peroxidase [ks] (*f., Biochem.*) peroxidase.
peróxido [ks] (*m., Chem.*) peroxide.
perpassar (*v.i.*) to pass (**por**, by, through; **além de**, beyond); to go by; to flit.

perpassável (adj.) passable; tolerable.
perpendicular (adj.; f.) perpendicular.
perpendicularidade (f.) perpendicularity.
perpendículo (m.) plumb line.
perpetração (f.) perpetration.
perpetrador –dora (adj.) perpetrating; (m.,f.) perpetrator.
perpetrar (v.t.) to perpetrate, commit (a crime, a wrong).
perpetuação (f.) perpetuation.
perpetuador –dora (adj.) perpetuating (m.,f.) perpetuator.
perpetuamento (m.) = PERPETUAÇÃO.
perpetuar (v.t.) to perpetuate, eternalize, immortalize; (v.r.) to self-perpetuate.
perpetuidade [u-i] (f.) perpetuity.
perpétuo –tua (adj.) perpetual, endless, everlasting; lifelong; (f.) any of the various immortelles or everlastings: Helichrysum, Xeranthemum, Gomphrena, etc.—amarela = HELICRISO.—da-mata, a Brazilian amaranth (Alternanthera brasiliana), c.a. ERVANÇO.—do-mato = MACELADO-MATO.—roxa, a globe amaranth (Gomphrena globosa), c.a. PARATUDO.
perpianho (m., Arch.) perpend stone; bondstone.
perplexidez, perplexão, perplexidade [ks] (f.) perplexity, confusion, bewilderment, doubt.
perplexo –xa [ks] (adj.) perplexed, nonplussed; at wit's end.
perquirição (f.) = PERQUISIÇÃO.
perquiridor –dora (adj.) delving, probing [= PERQUISIDOR].
perquirir (v.t.) to probe, search, seek out, investigate.
perquisição (f.) thorough search, minute investigation [= PERQUIRIÇÃO].
perquisidor –dora (adj.) = PERQUIRIDOR.
perquisitivo –va (adj.) investigative.
perrengue (adj.) cowardly, craven; faint-hearted; lame. andar—, to limp.
perrexil (m., Bot.) the samphire (Crithmum maritimum); c.a. PERREXIL-DO-MAR, FUNCHO-MARINHO.
perrice (f.) stubbornness; malice, spite.
perro –ra [ê] (adj.) stiff; hard to open and close; stubborn; (m.) dog (lit. & fig.); dar-se a—s, to get angry, (f.) = CADELA.
persa (adj.; m.,f.) Persian.
perscrutação (f.) scrutiny, close investigation.
perscrutador –dora (adj.) scrutinizing; (m.,f.) investigator.
perscrutar (v.t.) to scan, subject to scrutiny or close investigation; to search, explore (as, the skies with a telescope); to probe (secrets); to peer into (the future).
persecução (f.) = PERSEGUIÇÃO.
perseguição (f.) pursuit, chase; persecution.
perseguidor –dora (adj.) pursuing; harassing; (m.,f.) pursuer; persecutor.
perseguir [21a] (v.t.) to chase, run after, pursue, follow; to persecute, harass; to obsess; to beset.
pérseo –sea (adj.; m.,f.) = PERSA.
perseverança (f.) perseverance, persistence, stamina; diligence.
perseverante (adj.) persevering, persistent; diligent.
perseverar (v.i.) to persevere, persist (em, in); to be steadfast.
persianas (f.pl.) persiennes (wooden window blinds having movable slats).
persiano –na (adj.; m.,f.) = PERSA.
persicária (f., Bot.) spotted ladysthumb (Polygonum persicaria), c.a. PESSEGUELHA, ERVA-PESSEGUEIRA; the marshpepper smartweed (Polygonum hydropiper).—do-brasil = CAPITIÇOVA.—mordaz = ACATAIA.
pérsico –ca (adj.; m.) = PERSA.
persignação (f.) act of crossing oneself.
persignar-se (v.r.) to cross oneself.
pérsio –sia (adj.; m.,f.) = PERSA.
persistência (f.) persistence, perseverance.
persistente (adj.) persistent, persevering, dogged, tenacious.
persistir (v.i.) to persist (em, in); to continue, last; to persevere, keep on.
Persival (m.) Percival; Parsifal.
persolver (v.t.) to pay off in full.
personado –da (adj.; Bot.) personate, masked [= MASCARINO].
personagem (m.,f.) a personage; character (in novel, play, etc.).
persona-grata (f.) persona grata.
personalidade (f.) personality, individuality; a person; personal criticism.
personalíssimo –ma (absol. superl. of PESSOAL) most personal, very personal.

personalização (f.) personalizing, personification.
personalizar (v.t.) to personalize, personify; to name persons, mention names; (v.i.) to make unflattering personal remarks.
personária (f.) personal power-of-attorney.
personificação (f.) personification.
personificar (v.t.) to personify.
perspé[c]tico –ca (adj.) perspective.
perspe[c]tiva (f.) perspective, projection; prospect, outlook.—aérea, aerial perspective.—axonométrica, axonometric projection, linear perspective.—isométrica, isometric projection.—linear, linear perspective. em—, in prospect, expected.
perspectivar (v.t.) to show (put, draw) in perspective.
perspe[c]tivo –va (adj.) = PERSPÉCTICO.
perspectógrafo (m.) perspectograph.
perspicácia (f.) perspicacity, acumen; insight; discernment; acuteness of sight.
perspicaz (adj.) perspicacious, shrewd, sharp; discerning; keen-sighted.
perspicuidade [u-i] (f.) perspicuity, lucidness.
perspícuo –cua (adj.) clear, lucid, distinct.
perspirar (v.i.) to sweat [= TRANSPIRAR, SUAR].
persuadimento (m.) = PERSUASÃO.
persuadir (v.t.) to persuade, induce, influence (a, to); to convince (de que, that); (v.r.) to persuade oneself.
persuadível (adj.) pursuadable.
persuasão (f.) persuasion; conviction.
persuasível, persuasivo –va (adj.) persuasive.
persuasor –sora (adj.) persuading; (m.,f.) persuader.
persuasório –ria (adj.) persuasive; (f.) persuasive, incentive, inducement.
persulforeto [rê] (m., Chem.) persulfide.
persulfúrico –ca (adj., Chem.) persulfuric.
pertença (f.) an accessory or part of anything; (pl.) belongings.
pertence (m.) part, accessory; attribute; (Law) appurtenance; (pl.) belongings.
pertencente (adj.) pertaining (to); belonging (to).
pertencer (v.i.) to belong to; to (ap)pertain to; to concern, relate to; to behoove, be incumbent on.
pértiga (f.), –go (m.) long pole.
pertinácia (f.) pertinacity; stubborness; obstinacy.
pertinaz (adj.) stubborn; pertinacious; dogged, obstinate.
pertinência (f.) pertinence, relevancy.
pertinente (adj.) pertinent, relevant.
pertinho (adv.) very near.
perto –ta (adv., adj.) near, close, nigh; (m.pl.) close-ups.—de, near(ly), approximately, almost, about, around; near by, close to.—do mar, near the ocean. aqui—, near here. conhecer de—, to know intimately. de—, close(ly), near(ly). muito—, very near. para—, near to. por—, near. seguir de—, to follow close on the heels of.
pertosse (f., Med.) pertussis, whooping cough [= COQUELUCHE].
perturbação (f.) perturbation, disturbance, commotion, turmoil; trouble; jitters.
perturbado –da (adj.) perturbed; upset.
perturbador –dora (adj.) perturbing, disturbing; (m.,f.) perturber, disturber, agitator.
perturbar (v.t.) to perturb, disturb; to vex, trouble; to disquiet; to distract, disconcert; (v.r.) to become upset, perturbed.—o sossêgo, to disturb the peace.—o repouso dos mortos, to disturb the sleep of the dead; to exhume the dead.
perturbativo –va (adj.) disturbing.
perturbatório –ria (adj.) disturbing.
perturbável (adj.) perturbable.
pertusariáceo –cea (adj., Bot.) pertusariaceous; (f.pl.) a family of lichens (Pertusariaceae).
pertussina (f., Pharm.) a cough medicine extracted from thyme.
peru [ú] (m.) turkey; (colloq.) onlooker, kibitzer; the language of the Quechuan Indians of Peru.—bebê, a sea catfish.—de roda, a strutting turkey cock, with tail feathers spread.—enfeitado, a sophomore [Humorous].—de-sol, (Zool.) a trogon.—do-mato, (Zool.) a piping guan (Pipile jacutinga), c.a. JACUTINGA.—selvagem, American wild turkey; also the bustard [= ABETARDA].
perua (f.) turkey hen; (colloq.) drunken spree; (colloq., loose woman; station wagon; small bus.—choca, (Zool.) a trogon, c.a. SURUCUÁ.
peruada (f.) a flock of turkeys.
peruano –na (adj.; m.,f.) Peruvian.

peruar (*v.i.*) to woo; to kibitz; to hang around.
peruca (*f.*) peruke, wig.
perueiro –ra (*adj.*) of or pert. to turkeys.
peruinho-do-campo (*m.*) = SOMBRIO.
pérula (*f., Bot.*) perula.
peruviano –na (*adj.; m.,f.*) = PERUANO.
pervagante (*adj.*) crossing; wandering.
pervagar (*v.t.*) to cross (from one end of the country to the other); to wander aimlessly; to move (the eyes) here and there.
perversão (*f.*) perversion, corruption.
perversidade (*f.*) perversity, perverseness; surliness.
perversivo –va (*adj.*) perverting.
perverso –sa (*adj.*) perverse, bad, wicked; vile, base; malicious; fractious; crooked; (*m.,f.*) such a person.
perversor –sora, **pervertedor** –dora (*adj.*) perverting (*m.,f.*) perverter.
perverter (*v.t.*) to pervert, corrupt; (*v.r.*) to become perverted, depraved.
pervertido –da (*adj.*) perverted, depraved, corrupt.
pervinca (*f., Bot.*) periwinkle (*Vinca*).
pérvio –via (*adj.*) pervious.
pesa-álcool (*m.*) alcoholometer [= ALCOÔMETRO].
pesa-cartas (*m.*) letter scale.
pesada (*f.*) see under PESADO.
pesadão –dona (*adj.*) very heavy; cumbersome; of overweight persons, slow-moving; hulking.
pesadelo [ê] (*m.*) nightmare (lit. & fig.).
pesado –da (*adj.*) heavy, weighty, hefty; burdensome; dull, torpid; serious; onerous, difficult; coarse; (*slang*) out of luck; of weather, sultry, muggy; (*f.*) a weighing; that which is weighed at one time.—**a ouro**, worth its weight in gold.—**de anos**, bowed with age.—**de cuidados**, weighed down with care.
pesador –dora (*adj.*) weighing; (*m.,f.*) weigher; (*f.*) weighing machine.
pesadume (*m.*) weight; burden; grief; sadness, gloom.
pesagem (*f.*) act or operation of weighing; weighing-in place (at racetrack, prizefights, etc.).
pesa-leite (*m.*) lactometer.
pesamenteiro –ra (*m.,f.*) one who habitually joins groups of mourners at the home of a deceased person, ostensibly to offer condolences but in reality to partake of the refreshments which he expects will be served.
pêsames (*m.pl.*) condolences.
pesar [17] (*v.t.*) to weigh; (*v.i.*) to weigh; to ponder, consider.—**as palavras**, to weigh one's words.—**na balança de**—, to weigh heavily in the balance; to carry weight with.—**sôbre os ombros**, to have a burden (of responsibility, etc.) on one's shoulders. **em que pese**, despite, notwithstanding. (*m.*) burden; sorrow; desolation; regret. **apesar dos—es**, notwithstanding, even so, for all that.
pesaroso –sa (*adj.*) sorry, sorrowful; heavy-hearted; rueful; regretful; moody.
pesa-ouro (*m., colloq.*) moneybags (rich person).
pesa-papéis (*m.*) paper weight.
pesa-sais (*m.*) hydrometer for saline solutions.
pesa-vagões (*m.*) a railroad track scale.
pesa-vinho (*m.*) hydrometer for wines.
pesca (*f.*) fishing; catch of fish; investigation. **navio de de baleia**, whaling vessel.
pescada (*f.*) any of the various cods (*Gadus*) and weakfishes (*Cynoscion*).—**-de-angola** = ENXOVA-PRETA (oilfish).
pescadaria (*f.*) fish market.
pescadinha (*f.*) any of the various small cods, hakes (*Merluccius*), and weakfishes (*Cynoscion*).—**branca** (or **-goete**) = GUETE (a croaker).—**-de-rabo-na-bôca**, small fish fried into a curl.
pescado (*m.*) a catch of fish; any food fish.—**congelado**, frozen fish.—**real**, a flounder (*Paralichthys*), c.a. LINGUADO.—**salgado-sêco**, dry salt fish.
pescador –dora (*adj.*) fishing; (*m.*) fisher; fisherman; fishmonger; kingfisher (bird).—**es de homens**, fishers of men (The Apostles); (*f.*) fisherwoman.
pesca-em-pé (*m., Zool.*) the lesser yellow-legs (*Totanus flavipes*).
pescal (*m.*) wedge inserted in the end of tool handle to make it fit tight.
pescanço (*m., colloq.*) a peep or peeping (as at a player's cards, or as through a keyhole).
pescar [2] (*v.t.*) to fish (up, out); to hook, catch; to catch a glimpse of; to catch a sound (hear); to catch (someone) in the act; to fish for (something); to catch on, appre-

hend; to nod; (*slang*) to cheat in exams; (*v.i.*) to fish (as employment).—**corrido**, to know (something) forward and backwards.—**de poita**, to fish while anchored.—**em águas turvas**, to fish in troubled waters.—**os estribos**, to keep reaching for the stirrups with one's toes (when the straps are too long). **Êle não pesca palavra de francês**, He doesn't understand a word of French. **Não pesco nada**, I don't get it.
pescaria (*f.*) fishing; fishing industry; fishing trip; a great quantity of fish.—**de corrico**, troll fishing.—**de poita**, fishing while anchored.—**de sondar**, deep-sea fishing.
pescoçada (*f.*) a blow on the neck.
pescoção (*m.*) a blow on the neck; a seizing and shoving by the scruff [= CACHAÇÃO].
pescocear (*v.t.*) to shake the head (as a horse); to dodge one's duty or obligations; to shove (someone) by the scruff.
pescoceiro (*m.*) a horse which fights the rope around his neck; a dead beat, poor payer.
pescocinho (*m.*) removable white collar (as of a cassock).
pescoço (*m.*) neck; throat; nape; scruff.—**-de-cisne**, swan's neck; (*Bot.*) the common swanorchid (*Cycnoches chlorochilon*).—**-de-ganso**, gooseneck.—**grosso**, (*colloq.*) goiter.
pescoçudo –da (*adj.*) thick-necked.
pesebre (*m.*) crib, rack; manger; stall (in a stable).
pesepelo, pés-e-pêlo (*adv.*) barefoot.
peseta (*f.*) Spanish silver coin; (*colloq.*) a person of small worth.
pesgar (*v.t.*) to line with pitch (the inside of earthen wine jars).
pesista (*m.*) weight-lifter.
pêso (*m.*) weight; gravity; peso (South American or Spanish coin); burden, load; importance; onus; (*slang*) hard luck.—**atômico**, atomic weight.—**bruto**, gross weight.—**dos anos**, the burden of the years.—**específico**, specific gravity.—**líquido**, net weight.—**molecular**, molecular weight.—**morto**, dead weight.—**vivo**, live weight. **a—**, by weight. **arremêsso do—**, shot-putting; hammer throwing. **contra—**, counterweight, counterbalance. **em—**, in a body; wholly, entirely; in full force. [The following is a classification of boxers' or prizefighters' weights:—**-galo**, bantamweight.—**-leve**, lightweight.—**-médio**, middleweight.—**-meio-médio**, light middleweight.—**-meio-pesado**, light heavyweight.—**-môsca**, flyweight.—**-pena**, featherweight.—**-pesado**, heavyweight.]
pespegar (*v.t.*) to apply, deliver (a blow, slap, etc.).—**golpes**, to deal blows; (*v.r., colloq.*) to stick around (wasting another's time, making a bore or nuisance of oneself).
pespêgo (*m., colloq.*) hindrance; bore, nuisance.
pespontar (*v.t.*) to backstitch.
pesponteado –da (*adj.*) done with great care.
pespontear (*v.*) = PESPONTAR.
pesponto (*m.*) backstitch.
pesqueira (*f.*) fishing grounds; fishing nets, traps, tackle, etc.; a fish hawk.
pesqueiro (*m.*) a fishing hook and line; a fishing hole; fishweir.
pesquisa (*f.*) search, inquiry, research, investigation.—**de opinião**, public opinion poll.—**espacial**, space research.
pesquisador –dora (*adj.*) searching, investigating; (*m.,f.*) searcher, investigator, researcher.
pesquisar (*v.t.*) to search, scrutinize, investigate, probe, delve into; pry into; to inquire into; (*v.t.,v.i.*) to research.
pessário (*m., Med.*) pessary.
pessedista (*m.,f.*) a member of the PSD (Partido Social Democrata) in Brazil.
pessegada (*f.*) peach jam; peach preserves.
pessegal (*m.*) peach orchard.
pêssegal (*m.*) peach.
pessegueiro (*m.*) peach tree (*Prunus persica*).—**-bravo** or—**-do-mato** = GINJEIRA-DA-TERRA.—**-da-índia**, mabola persimmon (*Diospyros discolor*).
pessimismo (*m.*) pessimism; gloom, low spirits.
pessimista (*adj.*) pessimistic; (*m.,f.*) pessimist.
péssimo –ma (*superl. of* MAU) very bad; wretched.
pessoa (*f.*) person, individual; personage; (*pl.*) people.—**bem-parecida**, well-appearing person.—**civil**, person having a civil status.—**de bem**, person of fine character.—**de calcanhar rachado**, (*colloq.*) inferior-class person, esp. one who goes barefoot.—**de distinção**, distinguished person.—**de esperança**, person of promise.—**de feliz memória**, person of happy memory.—**de meio-relêvo**,

undistinguished person.—**de pouco mais ou menos,** person of little importance.—**de qualidade,** person of high quality.—**de uma figa,** a no-good person, that so-and-so.—**desconhecida,** a stranger, an unknown.—**esquisitona,** queer, odd, peculiar person.—**do outro mundo,** a person who is "out of this world" (tops).—**do rei,** the person of the king.—**física,** physical or natural person.—**jurídica,** juristic person.—**meã,** middle-class person; average-height person.—**moral,** person having a civil status.—**natural,** a natural or physical person.—**qualificada,** qualified person.—**sem imputação,** person of no consequence.—**sem importância,** person of no importance.—**s de obrigação,** the dependents of a family head.—**s divinas,** the divine Trinity.—**s reais,** members of a royal family.—**tal,** so-and-so.

pessoal (*adj.*) personal, private; (*m.*) personnel; staff; (*colloq.*) folks, people, friends.—**de terra,** ground crew.—**do sereno,** gang of night loafers.

pessoalidade (*f.*) personality.

pessoalizar (*v.*) = PERSONIFICAR.

pessoalmente (*adv.*) personally.

pestana (*f.*) eyelash; fringe of vegetation along a river; flap covering a buttonhole; nut (of a stringed instrument); a double-stop (in playing a stringed instrument); (*colloq.*) forty winks. **queimar as—s,** to burn the midnight oil.

pestane[j]ar (*v.i.*) to blink, wink; to twinkle, gleam.

pestanejo [ê] (*m.*) wink.

pestanudo –da (*adj.*) having large eyelashes.

peste (*f.*) pest, plague, pestilence; vermin; bone; scourge, trouble; stench; a pesterer.—**bovina,** cattle plague.—**branca,** tuberculosis.—**bubônica,** bubonic plague.—**das abelhas,** a certain disease which attacks bees.—**de coçar,** an epizootic disease of central Brazil.—**de passarinho,** an epizootic disease affecting cattle in a certain part of Brazil.—**índica,** an old name for syphilis.—**negra,** the Black Death of the Middle Ages.—**pulmonar,** pulmonary plague.—**suína,** hog cholera.—**russa,** influenza.

pestear (*v.t.,v.i.*) to infect with, or be infected by, the plague (speaking of animals). Cf. EMPESTAR.

pestífero –ra (*adj.*) pestiferous; noxious; (*m.,f.*) one who is infected with the plague.

pestilência (*f.*) pestilence.

pestilencial, pestilencioso –sa, **pestilente, pestilento** –ta (*adj.*) pestilential, pestiferous.

pestilo (*m.*) bolt, door latch.

pestoso –sa (*adj.; m.,f.*) plague-stricken (person).

pêta (*f.*) fib, story, lie; cock-and-bull story; cuttlefish; sharp single or double points on one side of a weeding hoe; sharp hatchetlike edge on the back of a pruning hook; spot in a horse's eye.

pétala (*f.*) petal.

petalado –da (*adj.*) petaled.

petalhada (*f.*) a pack of lies.

petaliforme (*adj.*) petaliform.

petalino –na (*adj.*) petaline.

petalita (*m., Min.*) petalite.

petalóide (*adj.*) petaloid.

petalomania (*f., Bot.*) petalody.

petalostêmone (*m.*) the genus (*Petalostemon*) of prairie clovers.

petar (*v.i.*) to lie, prevaricate; to be a pest.

petarada (*f.*) = PETALHADA.

petard[e]ar (*v.t.*) to blow up with petards.

petardeiro, petardista (*m.*) petardier.

petardo (*m.*) petard; kind of firecracker.

petarola (*f.*) big lie; (*m.,f.*) big liar.

petauróide (*m.*) a genus (*Petaurista*) of flying squirrels.

petear (*v.*) = PETAR.

peteca (*f.*) a sort of shuttlecock, consisting of a leather pad with feathers stuck in it. [It is played by striking it into the air with the palm of the hand]; plaything; toy, trifle.

petecada (*f.*) a game of PETECA.

petecar (*v.t.*) to embellish tawdrily.

peteiro –ra (*adj.*) lying; (*m.,f.*) liar.

peteleco (*m.*) rap, light blow, fillip; by analogy, a slapping down.

petequear (*v.i.*) to play PETECA.

petequeira (*f., Bot.*) a goldentrumpet (*Anemopaegma*).

petéquias (*f.pl.*) spots on the skin in certain fevers.

peteribi [bí] (*m.*) a tree of Cordia (*C. glabrata*).

petição (*f.*) petition, appeal; entreaty, supplication.—**de**

princípio, petitio principii (begging of the question); (*m.*) a large pony.

peticego –ga (*adj.; m.,f.*) nearsighted, blear-eyed (person).

petícia (*f., Bot.*) any Petitia.

peticionar (*v.i.*) to petition.

pectionário –ria (*m.,f.*) petitioner; applicant.

petiço –ça (*adj.*) short-legged; (*m.*) pony.

petiçote (*m.*) small pony.

petigris (*m.*) a Siberian squirrel or its skin.

petim-pau (*m.*) a breadfruit tree of Brazil.

petima (*f.*) = PETUMA.

petimbau (*m.*) a twist of tobacco.

petimboaba (*f.*) a flutemouth fish (*Fistularia*), c.a. TROMBETA, AGULHÃO-TROMBETA, PETUMBO.

petimetre (*m.*) dandy, fop, coxcomb; lady's man; [Fr. *petit-maître*].

petinga (*f.*) a small herring; any minnow used as bait.

petinha (*f.*) a titlark (*Anthus*), c.a. SOMBRIA.

petinho (*m.*) a certain thrush (TURDUS ILIACUS).

petipé (*m.*) architect's scale; map scale.

petisca (*f.*) a game consisting of tossing pebbles at a coin on the ground, the coin going to the one who first hits it.

petiscador (*m.*) nibbler.

petiscar (*v.t.*) to nibble; to taste; to eat tidbits; to strike a spark with flint and steel; to strike with a door knocker; (*v.i.*) to nibble; to knock. **Quem não arrisca, não petisca,** Nothing ventured, nothing gained.

petisco (*m.*) dainty, tidbit, choice morsel; flint for striking steel; (*colloq.*) ridiculous little man; butt.

petisqueira (*f., colloq.*) tidbits.

petisqueiro (*m.*) food closet (= GUARDA-COMIDA].

petitinga (*f.*) a prawn (*Palaemon*); also = MANJUBA (anchovy).

petitório –ria (*adj.*) petitionary; (*Law*) petitory; (*m.,f.*) petition.

petiz (*adj.; m.*) small (child), little (one).

petizada (*f.*) little ones (collectively), small fry.

pêto (*m.*) any of various European woodpeckers of the genus Picus. Cf. PICA-PAU.—**da-chuva** = PIADEIRO.

petrarquista (*adj.; m.*) Petrarchist.

pétrea (*f.*) see under PÉTREO.

petrechar (*v.t.*) to supply, equip.

petrechos (*m.pl.*) tools, implements; supplies, provisions.—**de cozinha,** kitchen utensils.—**de guerra,** war equipment.

petrel (*m.*) petrel.

petrense (*adj., Bot., Zool.*) saxicoline.

pétreo –rea (*adj.*) petrean; rock; rocklike; fig., stony-hearted, callous; (*f., Bot.*) a genus (*Petrea*) of purple wreaths.

petreu (*adj.*) petrean.

petrícola (*f.*) a genus (*Petricola*) of bivalve mollusks.

petrificação (*f.*) petrification; petrified fossil.

petrificado –da (*adj.*) petrified (lit. & fig.).

petrificador –dora, **petrificante** (*adj.*) petrifying.

petrificar (*v.t.*) to petrify; to render hard as rock; to stupefy (with amazement); (*v.r.*) to become petrified (with fear, etc.).

Petrobrás (*f.*) = PETRÓLEO BRASILEIRO S.A. (Brazilian Petroleum Inc.)

petroglifo (*m.*) petroglyph.

petrografia (*f.*) petrography.

petrográfico –ca (*adj.*) petrographic(al).

petrógrafo –fa, **petrografista** (*m.,f.*) petrographer.

petrolaria (*f.*) oil refinery.

petrolato (*m.*) petrolatum.

petroleiro (*m.*) oil tanker.

petroleno (*m., Chem.*) petrolene.

petróleo (*m.*) petroleum.—**bruto,** crude oil.

petrolífero –ra (*adj.*) oil-bearing.

petrologia (*f.*) petrology.

petrológico –ca (*adj.*) petrologic(al).

petrologista (*m.*) petrologist.

Petrópolis (*m.*) Petropolis (fashionable resort and industrial city situated in the hills just north of Rio de Janeiro; [*not cap.*] (*slang*) a heavy walking stick.

petropolitano –na (*adj.*) of, or pert. to, the city of Petropolis in the State of Rio de Janeiro; (*m.,f.*) a native or inhabitant thereof.

petrosal (*m., Anat.*) petrous portion of the temporal bone or capsule of the inner ear.

petroso –sa (*adj.*) petrous.

petrossílex [ks] (*m., Petrog.*) felsite [= FELSITO].

petrossilicoso –**sa** (*adj.*) felsitic.
petrostafilino –**na** (*adj.*, *Anat.*) peristaphyline.
petulância (*f.*) insolence, brashness, impudence, brazenness, impertinence; pertness, sauciness, cheek. [But not petulance, which is RABUGICE, IRRITABILIDADE.]
petulante (*adj.*) brazen, bold-faced, shameless; insolent, fresh, flippant; cocky, uppish. [But not petulant, which is RABUGENTO, BIRRENTO.]
petumbo (*m.*) = PETIMBOABA.
petunce (*m.*) petuntse (China stone used in the manufacture of porcelain).
petúnia (*f.*, *Bot.*) any petunia.—**branca**, the whitemoon petunia (*P. axillaris*).
péua (*f.*, *Bot.*) a bluestem grass (*Andropogon brevifolius*) of Amazonia; also = TACONHAPÉ.
peúca (*f.*) = PIÚCA.
peucédano (*m.*, *Bot.*) hog fennel (*Peucedanum*); c.a. FUNCHO-DE-PORCO.
peúga (*f.*) sock; buskin.
peugada [e-u] (*f.*) footprint; track, clue [= PEGADA].
peúva (*f.*, *Bot.*) a trumpetbush (*Tecoma speciosa*).
peva (*adj.*; *m.*) = PEBA.
pevide (*f.*) pip (seed of orange, apple, etc.); pip, roup (fowl disease); snuff (of a wick); (*slang*) rum.
p. ex. = POR EXÊMPLO (for example).
pexotada (*f.*) fumble.
pexote (*m.*) tyro, beginner, novice, greenhorn.
pexotear (*v.i.*) to play (soccer, etc.) like a novice.
pez [ê] (*m.*) resin, tar, pitch.—**amarelo**, rosin.—**de-borgonha**, Burgundy pitch.—**de hulha**, coal tar.—**líquido**, tar.—**loiro** or **sêco**, colophane; mineral, asphalt.—**negro**, tar.—**resina**, rosin. Cf. ALCATRÃO, BREU, PICHE, RESINA.
pezizáceo –**cea** (*adj.*, *Bot.*) pezizaceous; (*f.pl.*) the family of fungi (*Pezizaceae*) containing the blood cups.
pezizóide (*adj.*, *Bot.*) pezizoid, cup-shaped.
pèzudo –**da** (*adj.*) big-footed.
p. f. = PRÓXIMO FUTURO (near future).
P. F. = POR FAVOR (please).
p. f. v. = POR FAVOR, VOLTE (please return).
pg. = PAGOU (paid).
ph, for words formerly spelled ph–, see f–.
PI = PIAUÍ (State of).
pia (*f.*) wash basin, sink; shell of the giant clam (*Tridacna*); (*Bot.*) an epiphytic American orchid (*Coryanthes macrantha*).—**batismal**, baptismal font.—**da cozinha**, kitchen sink.—**de água benta**, holy water font, stoup.
piã (*m.*, *Med.*) pian, yaws.
piá (*m.*) Indian boy; any non-white boy who works on a ranch.
piaba (*f.*) a small, edible fresh-water fish of Brazil, c.a. PIAVA.
piabanha (*f.*) a large voracious fresh-water Braz. fish (*Megalobrycon piabanha*) prized as a table delicacy.
piabar (*v.i.*) to play penny-ante; to play cards close to the chest.
piabinha (*f.*) a small tropical fish, the yellow tetra (*Hyphessobrycon bifasciatus*).—**branca**, the glow-light tetra, or Rio tetra, or flame fish (*Hyphessobrycon flammeus*), c.a. ENGRAÇADINHO. [Both are popular in home aquaria.]
piaçaba, piaçá (*f.*) the piassava palm (*Attalea funifera*); the Pará piassava (*Leopoldinia piassaba*).—**brava**, an oilpalm (*Elaeis odora*).
piaçava (*f.*) = PIAÇABA.
pia-cobra (*m.*) a bird—Dufresne's masked yellow-throat (*Geothlypis aequinoctialis velata*), c.a. CANÁRIO-DO-SAPÊ, CANÁRIO-DO-BREJO.
piaçoca (*f.*) = JAÇANÃ.
piada (*f.*) quip, witticism, witty remark, joke, wisecrack, gag; chirp, peep (of birds, baby chicks, etc.).—**forte**, coarse jest, spicy joke. Isso é—! you're joking! Cf. PIO.
piadeira (*f.*) the Old World widgeon (*Mareca penelope*); also = PIADEIRO, and ASSOBIADEIRA (a teal).
piadeiro (*m.*) a wryneck (*Jynx torquilla*) allied to the woodpeckers, c.a. PAPA-FORMIGAS, PIADEIRA, PÊTO-DA-CHUVA, TORCICOLO.
piadista (*adj.*) wisecracking; (*m.,f.*) wisecracker.
piado (*m.*) peep, cheep [= PIO].
piafe (*m.*, *Manège*) piaffe, piaffer.
piaga (*m.*) = PAJÉ.
pia-mater (*f.*, *Anat.*) pia mater.
piamente (*adv.*) piously.
piançar (*v.i.*) to yearn, long (**por**, for).
pianino (*m.*) pianette.

pianista (*m.,f.*) pianist.
pianístico –**ca** (*adj.*) pianistic.
pianizar (*v.t.*) to arrange (music) for the piano.
piano (*m.*) piano; (*adv.*, *Mus.*) piano.—**de armário**, upright piano. —**de cauda**, grand piano.—**de grande cauda**, concert grand piano.—**de quarto de cauda**, baby grand piano. **afinar um**—, to tune a piano. **tocar**—, to play the piano.
pianoforte (*m.*) pianoforte.
pianola (*f.*) pianola.
pianolar (*v.i.*) to play a pianola.
pianoma (*m.*, *Med.*) pian (a tumor characteristic of yaws).
piante (*adj.*) peeping, cheeping, chirping.
pião (*m.*) top (spinning toy); plummet.—**de-purga**, the Barbados nut (*Jatropha curcas*).—**roxo**, (*Bot.*) the bellyache nettlespurge (*Jatropha gossypifolia*).
pia-poco (*m.*) = TUCANO-DE-PEITO-BRANCO.
piar (*v.i.*) to peep, cheep, chirp, twitter; (*m.*) peep, cheep. **não**—, (*slang*) not let out a peep. **sem**—, (*slang*) without a peep.
pia-sol (*m.*) = JAÇANÃ.
piastra (*f.*) piaster (Near Eastern coin).
piau (*m.*) large minnow.
piauiense [au-i] (*adj.*) of or pert. to the state of Piauí; (*m.,f.*) a native or inhabitant thereof.
piava (*f.*) = PIABA.
piàzada (*f.*) group of Indian or halfbreed boys.
pica (*f.*, *Zool.*) the pika or little chief hare (*Ochotona princeps*), c.a. LAGOMIS.
picaço –**ça** (*adj.*) having a white face or white feet [horse]; (*m.*) = CARRAPATO-ESTRELA (a tick).
picacuroba (*f.*) = POMBA-AMARGOSA.
picada (*f.*) see under PICADO.
picadão (*m.*) a rough road through virgin territory.
picadeira (*f.*) pickax; bricklayer's hammer; facing hammer.
picadeiro (*m.*) circus ring; riding arena; (*Anat.*) stocks, ways; carpenter's bench-stop.
picadela (*f.*) = PICADA.
picadinho –**nha** (*adj.*) touchy, easily piqued; (*m.*) hash, minced meat; a hopping dance, c.a. PULADINHO.
picado –**da** (*adj.*) pricked, stung; piqued; chopped; pecked; pitted, pock-marked; speckled; tart, sour; choppy [sea]; (*m.*) hash; (*f.*) prick, sting; insect bite; pin prick; puncture (as with a hypodermic needle); a roughhewn trail through woods or forest; dive (of an airplane). —**a prumo**, (*Aeron.*) nose dive.—**de cobra**, snake bite.
picador –**dora** (*adj.*) pricking, stinging; (*m.*) ridingmaster; horseman; a ticket punch; a trail blazer; picador (bullfighter on horseback).
picadura (*f.*) = PICADA.
pica-flor (*m.*) hummingbird [= BEIJA-FLOR].
pica-fumo (*m.*, *colloq.*) pocketknife; a hard-trotting horse; penny pincher.
picana (*f.*) oxgoad [= AGUILHADA].
picancilho (*m.*) the common European nuthatch (*Sitta caesia*) c.a. PICA-PAU-CINZENTO, TREPADEIRA.
picanço (*m.*) any of various birds allied to the woodpeckers.
picante (*adj.*) piquant; pungent; spicy; biting, mordant; piercing; malicious; (*m.*) an appetizer.
picão (*m.*) pickax; stonecutter's pick; a plant c.a. DOIS-AMORES.—**branco**, the littleflower quickweed (*Galinsoga parviflora*), c.a. FAZENDEIRO.—**da-praia** = CARRAPICHO-RASTEIRO.—**de-tropeiro**, a globeamaranth (*Gomphrena paniculata*).—**do-campo** or—**prêto** = CUAMBU (a plant).
pica-osso (*m.*) an Old World vulture (*Vultur monachus*).
picapara (*f.*, *Zool.*) a finfoot (*Heliornis fulica*), c.a. PECA-PERA.
pica-pau (*m.*) any of numerous woodpeckers and other unrelated birds; a muzzleloader (old-fashioned gun).—**amarelo**, the chestnut-winged yellow woodpecker (*Crocomorphus f. flavens*), c.a. IPECUTUAÁ.—**anão**, any piculet (*Picumnus*) esp. *P. temminckii* (Temminck's piculet), *P.c. cirrhatus* (the tufted piculet), *P. pygmaeus* (the pigmy piculet).—**branco**, the white-bellied woodpecker (*Leuconerpes candidus*), c.a. BIRRO.—**de-cabeça-vermelha**, the black-and-white woodpecker (*Scapaneus m. melanoleucos*).—**carijó**, Wagler's woodpecker (*Chrysoptilus m. melanochlorus*) of southeastern Brazil.—**cinzento**, the common European nuthatch (*Sitta caesia*), c.a. PICANCILHO, TREPADEIRA.—**de-bico-comprido**, the long-billed wood-hewer (*Nasica longirostris*)—not related to the woodpeckers.—**de-cabeça-amarela**,

the Brazilian yellow woodpecker (*Celeus f. flavescens*), c.a. JOÃO-VELHO, IPECUATI.—-do-campo, or—-malhado, the pampas flicker (*Soroplex c. campestris*).—-do-mato-virgem, the yellow-fronted woodpecker of southern Brazil (*Tripsurus flavifrons*), c.a. BENEDITO.—-dourado, the gold-backed green woodpecker (*Chloronerpes aurulentus*) of southern Brazil.—-fura-laranja, the golden-naped woodpecker (*Veniliornis affinis*).—-grande, the robust woodpecker (*Phoeoceastes r. robustus*) of southern Brazil, c.a. PICAPAU-SOLDADO.—-vermelho, Buffon's wood-hewer (*Dendrocolaptes c. certhia*)—not related to the woodpeckers.

pica-pauzinho (*m.*) the tufted piculet (*Picumnus c. cirrhatus*).

pica-peixe (*m.*) a small, brightly-colored European kingfisher (*Alcedo hispida*).

picar (*v.t.*) to prick, pierce, stick; to peck; to spur, goad; of insects, to bite, sting; to needle; to nettle; to mince, chop fine; to tear (paper, etc.) into bits; to punch (tickets); to raise a bid; (*v.i.*) to bite, nibble; to burn, smart; of prices, to rise; (*v.r.*) to prick oneself; to take pique.—a curiosidade, to pique the curiosity.—de esporas, to spur.—fumo, to mince twist tobacco with a knife.—o peixe, to set the hook in a fish.—terra, to touch land.

picarço –ça (*adj.*) = PIGARÇO.

picardia (*f.*) meanness; dirty trick; pique.

picardo –da (*adj.; m.,f.*) (person, language) of Picardy.

picaresco –ca [ê] (*adj.*) picaresque; mock-heroic.

picareta [ê] (*f.*) pick, pickax; (*colloq.*) hanger-on, grafter, chiseler.

picaria (*f.*) horsemanship.

pícaro –ra (*adj.*) crafty; mean; ridiculous.

piçarra (*f.*) shale; a mixture of shale, sand and rock; quarry.

piçarral (*m.*) slate quarry.

picauro (*m.*) a pigeon of Amazonia (*Columba plumbea*).

piceno (*m., Chem.*) picene.

píceo –cea (*adj.*) piceous.

pichar (*v.t.*) to paint with pitch.

piche (*m.*) pitch.

pichel [-chéis] (*m.*) mug, tankard, esp. one of pewter.

pichelaria (*f.*) tinsmith's shop.

picheleiro (*m.*) tinsmith.

pichi [chí] (*m., Bot.*) the Peru falseheath (*Fabiana imbricata*).

pichororê (*m.*) = JOÃO-TENENÉM.

pichorra (*f., m.*) large tin, pewter or earthenware jug or pitcher, equipped with a spout; laziness.

pichua (*m.*) a Brazilian euphorbia (*E. portulacoides*).

picídeos (*m.pl.*) the family of birds (*Picidae*) comprising the woodpeckers, piculets and wrynecks.

picles (*m.pl.*) pickles.

picnídio (*m., Bot.*) pycnidium.

picnito (*m., Min.*) pycnite.

picnômetro (*m.*) pycnometer.

picnostilo (*m., Arch.*) a pycnostyle colonnade.

pico (*m.*) peak, summit; crest; spine; sharp point; sting; thorn; a bit (of anything). **um ano e—**, a little more than a year.

picô (*m.*) picot.

picola (*f.*) stonecutter's chisel.

picolé (*m.*) popsicle (ice cream on a stick).

picólico –ca (*adj.; Chem.*) picolinic.

picolina (*f., Chem.*) picoline.

picoso –sa (*adj.*) prickly; sharp; pointed.

picota (*f.*) see under PICÔTO.

picotado –da (*adj.*) picoté.

picotador (*m.*), **-deira** (*f.*) a paper-perforating machine.

picotagem (*f.*) perforation (of paper).

picotar (*v.t.*) to picot; to punch (tickets); to perforate (paper).

picote (*m.*) a kind of coarse cloth; picot; perforated edging of postage stamps.

picotita (*f., Min.*) picotite.

picôto –ta (*adj.*) coarse, made of goat's hair [cloth]; (*m.*) peak, pinnacle; geodesic landmark on a mountain top; (*f.*) stake, post; stocks; pillory [= PELOURINHO]; plunger rod of a pump; guinea fowl [= GALINHA-D'ANGOLA]; a picotah (water-raising device in India).

picrâmico –ca (*adj.*) ácido—, picramic acid.

picrato (*m., Chem.*) picrate.

pícrico –ca (*adj., Chem.*) picric.

picrito (*m., Min.*) picrite.

picroeritrina (*f., Chem.*) picroerythrin.

picrólito (*m., Min.*) picrolite.

picromerite (*f., Min.*) picromerite.

picrotina (*f., Min.*) picrotin.

picrotoxina [ks] (*f., Chem.*) picrotoxin.

pictografia (*f.*) pictograph.

pictográfico –ca (*adj.*) pictographic.

pictograma (*m., Stat.*) pictogram.

pictoresco –ca (*adj.*) = PINTURESCO.

pictórico –ca, pictorial (*adj.*) pictorial.

picu [ú] (*m.*) a type of coarse tobacco.

picuá (*f.*) canvas traveling bag; duffel bag; traveling basket; bamboo cylinder or horn tip, corked at one end, for holding rough diamonds; (*pl.*) household goods.

picuçaroba (*m.*) = POMBA-LEGÍTIMA.

picudo –da (*adj.*) sharp-pointed.

picuinha [u-í] (*f.*) peep, cheep, chirp; taunt, gibe, caustic remark.

picuipeba [u-i] (*f.*) = RÔLO-AZUL.

picuipiúma [u-i] (*m.*) = FOGO-APAGOU.

picumã (*m.*) soot; black cobwebs.

pidão (*m.*), **-dona** (*f.*) person who is always asking for something. Cf. PEDINCHÃO.

piedade (*f.*) piety; pity, compassion, mercy.—filial, filial piety. **sem dó nem—**, pitilessly, ruthlessly.

piedoso –sa (*adj.*) pious; merciful; piteous.

piegas (*adj.*) fussy, finicky; goody-goody; maudlin, "mushy," silly; (*m.,f.*) such a person; fuss-budget.

pieguice (*f.*) slush, mush (maudlin sentiment); silly affectation; finicalness.

pieira (*f.*) wheeze.

piela (*f., slang*) drunkenness.

pielite (*f., Med.*) pyelitis.

piemia (*f., Med.*) pyemia, blood poisoning.

piêmico –ca (*adj.*) pyemic.

piemontês –têsa (*adj.; m.,f.*) Piedmontese.

piemontite (*f., Min.*) piedmontite.

pientíssimo –ma (*absol. superl. of* PIEDOSO) most compassionate; most pious.

pieride (*f.*) any pierid butterfly; (*cap., f.pl.*) Pierides, the Muses.

piério –ria (*adj.*) Pierian.

pierrete (*f.*) pierrette (a female pierrot).

pierrô (*m.*) pierrot.

pietismo (*m.*) pietism.

pietista (*m.,f.*) Pietist; pietist (*adj.*) pietist.

piezoeletricidade (*f.*) piezoelectricity.

piezômetro (*m.*) piezometer.

pifada (*f.*) miscue.

pífano (*m.*) = PÍFARO.

pifar (*v.i., colloq.*) to conk out, fail to function; to get drunk.

pífaro (*m.*) fife; fifer.

pífio –fia (*adj.; colloq.*) cheap, punk, piddling, second-rate; coarse, vulgar.

pifonista (*adj.; m.,f.*) habitual drinker.

pigarço –ça (*adj.; m.*) piebald, mottled, spotted (horse).

pigarra (*f.*) pip, roup.

pigarr[e]ar (*v.i.*) to clear the throat.

pigarro (*m.*) a frog in the throat; a clearing of the throat.

pigídio (*m., Zool.*) pygidium.

pigméia, fem. of PIGMEU.

pigmentação (*f.*) pigmentation.

pigmentado –da (*adj.*) pigmented.

pigmentar (*v.t.*) to pigment.

pigmentário –ria (*adj.*) pigmentary.

pigmento (*m.*) pigment.

pigmeu –méia (*adj.; m.,f.*) pygmy.

pignoratício –cia (*adj., Civil Law*) pignorative, pledging, pawning. **emprestimo—**, collateral loan. **garantia—**, collateral security.

pigope (*m.*) a genus (*Pygopus*) of snakelike lizards.

pigostílio (*m., Zool.*) pygostyle.

piguancha (*f.*) = CHINA; old or useless mare.

piina [i-i] (*f., Biochem.*) pyin.

piíssimo –ma [i-i] (*absol. superl. of* PIO) most pious.

pijama (*m.,f.*) pyjama(s).

pijerecu[m] (*m.*) = COAJERUCU.

pilador –dora (*adj.*) pounding, crushing; (*m.,f.*) pounder, crusher.

pilão (*m.*) a heavy mortar, formed of a solid block of wood, used for pounding corn and other grain; beetle, stamper, crusher; the sliding counterpoise of a steelyard; ram of a pile driver; hard-trotting mule or horse; pylon; riding ring.

pilar (*v.t.*) to pound (grain); (*m.*) pillar, column, pier, post, stanchion.

pilastra (*f.*) pilastre; (*m., Arch.*) pilaster, pier, newel. **Pilatos** (*m.*) Pilate.

pilé (*adj.*) açúcar—, rock candy.

pileca (*f.*) jade, nag.

pilecado –da (*adj.*) tipsy.

píleo (*m., Eccl., Bot.*) pileus.

pileque (*m.*) rubber ring; (*colloq.*) drinking spree. **suspender**, or **tomar, um—**, to get drunk.

pilha (*f.*) pile, heap, stack; an act of thievery.—**elétrica**, electric battery.—**sêca**, dry battery.—**termoelétrica**, thermopile.

pilhagem (*f.*) pillage, looting, plundering; booty.

pilhante (*adj.*) pillaging, looting, plundering; (*m.*) pillager, looter, plunderer, marauder.

pilhar (*v.t.*) to pillage, plunder, loot, ransack; to detect, catch unawares.—**com a bôca na botija**, to catch in the act.

pilha-ratos (*m., Zool.*) the hen harrier (*Circus cyaneus*).

pilheira (*f.*) pile; ash heap.

pilheiro (*m.*) water reservoir.

pilhéria (*f.*) prank; jest, gag; raillery.

pilheriar (*v.i.*) to play jokes; to jest.

pilhérico –ca (*adj.*) waggish.

pilheta [ê] (*f.*) tub.

pilífero –ra (*adj.*) piliferous.

piliforme (*adj.*) piliform.

pilígero –ra (*adj.*) piligerous.

pilô (*m.*) = ANUM-BRANCO.

pilobolo (*m.*) a genus (*Pilobolus*) of saprophytic fungi.

pilocarpidina (*f., Chem.*) pilocarpidine.

pilocarpina (*m., Chem.*) pilocarpine.

pilocarpo (*m.*) a genus (*Pilocarpus*) of the rue family.

pilóia (*f.*) rum [= CACHAÇA].

pilonagem (*f., Aeron.*) a nose-over.

pilonar (*v.i., Aeron.*) to nose-over.

pilono, pilone (*m.*) pylon [= PILÃO].

pilórico –ca (*adj.*) pyloric.

piloro (*m., Anat.*) pylorus.

pilosela (*f.*) hawkweed.—**alaranjada**, the orange hawkweed (*Hieracium aurantiacum*).—**dos-muros**, wall hawkweed (*Hieracium murorum*).

pilosidade (*f.*) pilosity, hairiness.

pilosismo (*m., Bot.*) pilosism (abnormal hairiness).

piloso –sa (*adj.*) pilose, hairy.

pilossebáceo –cea (*adj., Anat.*) pilosebaceous.

pilota (*f., colloq.*) fatigue from much walking; defeat, beating; criticism; bad luck.

pilotagem (*f.*) piloting. **aparelho de—automática**, automatic pilot. **escola de—**, flying school.

pilotar (*v.t.*) to pilot; (*v.i.*) to work as a pilot.

pilotáxico –ca [ks] (*adj., Petrog.*) pilotaxitic.

pilotear (*v.t., colloq.*) to give a beating to (defeat); to win out then deride the loser; to knock (criticize).

pilotis (*m., Arch.*) foundation pile-work; group of piles or stilts on which a building is held above ground level.

pilôto (*m.*) pilot (of a ship in and out of port); airplane pilot, flyer; the common pilot fish (*Naucrates ductor*), c.a. ROMEIRO; (*Naut.*) first mate; a guide; pilot light; (*Bot.*) sunrose (*Halimium lasianthum*).—**adjunto**, copilot.—**bombardeiro**, bomber pilot.—**de planador**, glider pilot.—**de provas**, test pilot.

pilrete (*m.*) midget. [*Disparaging*]

pilriteiro (*m.*) English hawthorn (*Crataegus oxyacantha*), c.a. ESCALHEIRO.

pílula (*f.*) pill; pilule; (*pl., colloq., interj.*) Shucks! **dourar a—**, to sugar-coat the bitter pill. Var. PÍRULA.

pilulador (*m.*) pillmaker.

pilular (*adj.*) pilular; (*v.t.*) to make into pills.

pilularia (*f., Bot.*) the pillworts (*Pilularia*).

piluleiro (*m.*) pill machine; pillmaker.

pilungo (*m.*) plug, nag, old or broken-down horse.

pimárico –ca (*adj., Chem.*) ácido—, pimaric acid.

pimelato (*m., Chem.*) pimelate.

pimélico –ca (*adj., Chem.*) pimelic.

pimelito (*m., Min.*) pimelite.

pimelose (*f.*) = OBESIDADE.

pimenta (*f.*) pepper (fruit, plant, powder); a peppery person; chigger, red bug; a rove beetle (*Staphylinus*), c.a. POTÓ.—**albarrã**, a pricklyash (*Zanthoxylum rhetsa*).—**coroada**, a lidflower (*Calyptranthes aromatica*).—**cumari**, bush redpepper (*Capsicum frutescens*), c.a. CUMARI.—**da-américa**, California peppertree (*Schinus*

mollis).—**d'água**, the bitter smartweed (*Polygonum acre*), c.a. ACATAIA, CATAIA, ERVA-DE-BICHO; a water primrose (*Jussiaea linifolia*), c.a. CRAVINA-D'ÁGUA.—**da-jamaica**, the allspice pimenta (*P. officinalis*), c.a. PIMENTA-DA-COROA.—**das-paredes**, a stonecrop (*Sedum acre*), c.a. PÃO-DE-PÁSSAROS.—**da-terra**, a bitterbark tree (*Xylopia langsdorffiana*) of the custardapple family. — **de-água** = PIMENTA-D'ÁGUA. — **de-bugre** = FRUTA-DE-BURRO.—**de-coroa** = PIMENTA-DA-JAMAICA.—**de-galinha** = CARAXIXU.—**de-gentio** = ENVIRA.—**de-macaco** = FRUTO-DE-BURRO, BREDO-FEDORENTO.—**de-rabo** = PIMENTA-LONGA.—**de-rato**, a nightshade (*Solanum oleraceum*).—**do-diabo**, a redpepper (*Capsicum luteum*). — **do-mato** = FRUTO-DE-MORCÊGO. — **do-pará**, the paracress spotflower (*Spilanthes oleracea*).—**do-reino**, black pepper (*Piper nigrum*)—plant, fruit or powder. — **dos-índios** = FRUTO-DE-MORCÊGO. — **dos-negros**, a bitterbark tree (*Xylopia aromatica*).—**longa**, long pepper (*Piper longum*).—**malagueta**, red (cayenne, chili) pepper (*Capsicum frutescens*).—**vulgar**, common black pepper (*Piper nigrum*).

pimental (*m.*) pepper field.

pimentão (*m.*) a red pepper (*Capsicum cordiforme*).—**comprido** or—**longal** = CORNICABRA.—**doce**, a red pepper (*Capsicum tetragonum*); Jerusalem cherry (*Solanum pseudocapsicum*).—**doce-da-américa**, sweet (bell) pepper (*Capsicum frutescens grossum*).

pimenteira (*f.*) pepper plant; pepperbox; (*Bot.*) a sp. of Cordia c.a. CATINGA-DE-PRÊTO.—**bastarda** or—**do-peru** = AROEIRA.—**da-terra** or—**do-sertão** = FRUTA-DE-BURRO.

pimenteiro (*m.*) pepper plant; one who deals in pepper.—**silvestre**, lilac chastetree (*Vitex agnuscastus*), c.a. ÁRVORE-DA-CASTIDADE.

pimento (*m.*) Jerusalem cherry (*Solanum pseudocapsicum*), c.a. PIMENTÃO-DOCE.

pimpão –pona (*adj.*) blustering; ostentatious; smart, elegant; (*m.,f.*) such a person; (*m.*) goldfish; (*colloq.*) firearm.

pimpar (*v.i.*) to lead a life of pleasure; to show off.

pimpinela (*f.*) any plant of this genus, esp. the anise (*P. anisum*); also, plants of *Sanguisorba* (the burnets) through confusion with pimpernel (an obsolete name for burnets).

pimpol (*m.*) the pipal or bo tree or sacred fig (*Ficus religiosa*) of India.

pimpolhar (*v.i.*) to sprout, bring forth.

pimpôlho (*m.*) scion, shoot, sprout; by ext., a healthy youngster.

pim-pom (*m.*) ping-pong [= PINGUE-PONGUE].

pimponaço –ça (*adj.*) very elegant.

pimpon[e]ar (*v.i.*) to swagger.

pimponente (*adj.*) ostentatious.

pimponete [nê] (*m., colloq.*) dandy, fop.

pimponice (*f.*) swank, swagger.

pina (*f.*) felly or felloe (of a wheel).

pinaca (*f.*) the residue of coconut kernels or of sesame seeds, after the oil has been expressed; an East Indian one-string musical instrument.

pinaça (*f., Naut.*) pinnace; rope for lifting a pile hammer.

pináceo –cea (*adj., Bot.*) pinaceous; (*f.pl.*) the pine family (*Pinaceae*).

pinacóide (*adj., Cryst.*) pinacoid(al).

pinacolina (*f., Chem.*) pinacolin(e).

pinacoteca (*f., Gk. Antiq.*) pinakotheke; hence, art gallery, art museum.

pináculo (*m.*) pinnacle, summit, highest point, acme.

pinador (*m.*) shoemaker's awl; a workman who sets pins, pegs, cotterpins.

pinafres (*m.pl.*) gremlins (in a motor).

pinalado –da (*adj., Bot.*) pinnated, pinnate.

pinambaba (*f.*) coil of fishing line; fishing rig.

pinar (*v.t.*) to set pins and pegs.

pinásio (*m., Arch.*) muntin; sash bar; riser of a stair; chimney stone or block.

pinatífido –da (*adj., Bot.*) pinnatifid.

pinça (*f.*) pincers, tongs; clip of a horseshoe.

píncaro (*m.*) pinnacle.

pincel [-céis] (*m.*) small paint or similar brush; shaving brush; a painter or his style.—**de luz**, a pencil of light.—**de estudante**, a tasselflower (*Emilia*).

pincelada, pincelagem (*f.*) a brush stroke, brush mark.

pincelar (*v.t.*) to paint with a brush.

pincenê (*m.*) pincenez.

pincha-cisco (*m.*) any of various ovenbirds, c.a. VIRA-FÔLHAS, esp. the following: Ménétriès leaf-scraper (*Sclerurus s. scansor*) of southeast to southern Brazil; the Ceará leaf-scraper (*S. s. cearensis*) of northeastern Brazil; the Bahia leaf-scraper (*S. mexicanus bahiae*) of eastern Brazil; the short-billed leaf-scraper (*S. r. rufigularis*) of northern Brazil south of the Amazon; the ochreous-throated leaf-scraper (*S. rufigularis*) of north of the Amazon; the spiny leaf-scraper (*S. caudacutus umbretta*) of eastern and northern Brazil south of the Amazon; and the brown leaf-scraper (*S. caudacutus brunneus*) of upper Amazonia.

pinchão (*m., Bot.*) the rocket salad (*Eruca sativa*).

pinchar (*v.t.*) to pitch (**fora**, out); to heave (**em**, into) to toss (**a**, to; **de**, from); to leap, spring (**de**, from); (*v.i.*) to reel, lurch.

pinchau *m., Sewing*) dart.

pinchicoroto (*m.*) = PAU-DE-FORMIGA.

pincho (*m.*) bound, leap, spring, jump; small pinch bar.

pinda (*f., colloq.*) lack of funds.

pindá (*m.*) Indian term for fishhook; (*Zool.*) an echinoderm.

pindaíba (*f.*) palm-fiber rope; (*slang*) lack of money [**na**—, flat broke]; (*Bot.*) a tree of Rollinia (*R. emarginata*); any of various snowbells (*Styrax*) some of which are called BENJOEIRO; any of several trees of *Xylopia* (Annona family) some of which are called COAJERUCU and ENVIRA.

pindauba [a-u] fishing rod; (*Bot.*) = COAJERUCU.

pindárico -ca (*adj.*) Pindaric; (*colloq.*) magnificent.

pindo (*m.*) the pindo or robust queenpalm (*Arecastrum romanzoffianum australe*), widely cultivated in northern greenhouses for its feathery, graceful foliage; c.a. PINDOBA-DO-SUL.

pindoba (*f.*) the pindova palm (*Attalea humilis*), a nearly stemless palm making dense growths along the Amazon; the leaves are made into mats for thatching—see JAPÁ; another palm (*Polyandrococus caudescens*), c.a. PATIOBA. —**do-sul** = PINDO, JERIVÁ.

pindobinha (*f.*) a shadowpalm (*Geonoma altissima*).

pindonga (*f.*) a gadabout.

pindongar (*v.i.*) to gadabout.

pindorama (*f.*) palm country.

pinduiba [u-i] = CUIA-DO-BREJO.

pinduras (*f.pl., colloq.*) unpaid bills; things in hock; creditors.

piné (*m.*) a kind of kestrel or sparrow hawk.

pinga (*f.*) drop; swallow; booze [= CACHAÇA]; drip. (*m., colloq.*) penniless man. **na**—drunk.

pingadeira (*f.*) drip pan; a dripping; constant expense; (*colloq.*) source of small but steady income (as, royalties on a book); (*colloq.*) runny nose.

pingadela (*f.*) a dripping.

pingado -da (*adj.*) sprinkled, spotted, speckled; (*slang*) drunk.

pingadouro (*m., Arch.*) drip.

pinga-fogo (*adj.*) fiery—said esp. of horses; quarrelsome; provoking; (*m.*) large wasp; troublemaker.

pingalim (*m.*) coachman's long whip. Var. PINGUELIM.

pingante (*adj.*) dripping; (*m., colloq.*) pauper.

pingão -gona (*adj.*) tattered, filthy; stupid; (*m.,f.*) such a person.

pingar (*v.t.*) to sprinkle (**de**, with); to drip (as blood, tears) from; (*v.i.*) to drip; to leak; to sprinkle (rain); to yield small but steady profits. —**miséria**, to live in poverty.

pingente (*m.*) prism of a chandelier; earring; watch charm; (*colloq.*) straphanger; hanger-on; (*adj.*) hanging.

pingo (*m.*) a drop (of liquid); pork or other fat; good saddle horse. —**d'água**, name given by prospectors to hyalites or other colorless pebbles found in diamantiferous gravel; lit., drop of water. —**de chuva**, raindrop. **aos**—**s**, drop by drop. **pôr os**—**s nos ii**, to dot the i's (and cross the t's). **um**—**de gente**, a tiny person.

pingoso -sa (*adj.*) drippy.

pinguaçiba (*f.*) = PAU-PEREIRA.

pinguço -ça (*adj.; colloq.*) tipsy.

pingue (*adj.*) fat; fertile; productive. **lucros**—**s**, fat profits; (*m.*) fat, lard, grease.

pinguela (*f.*) a log or plank across a small stream; trigger of a snare.

pinguelear (*v.i.*) to swing (as from a tree) and jump from one side (of a stream, etc.) to the other.

pinguelo (*m.*) trigger [= GATILHO]; also = PINGUELA.

pingue-pongue (*m.*) ping-pong.

pinguim (*m.*) penguin; (*Bot.*) the pinguin bromelia (*B. pinguin*).

pinguinho (*m.*) droplet, tiny bit, trifle.

pinguite (*f., Min.*) pinguite.

pinha (*f.*) the fruit of the sugarapple or sweetsop tree (*Annona squamosa*); c.a. ATA, FRUTA-DO-CONDE; pine cone; clock (of a stocking); jam (crowd); bunch (of things); (*Bot.*) a nettlespurge (*Jatropha horrida*) better known as QUEIMADEIRA; a custardapple (*Annona*). —**queimadeira** = CANSANÇÃO-DE-LEITE.

pinhal (*m.*) pine forest.

pinhão (*m.*) piñon (edible pine seed); pinion gear; (*Bot.*) any of various nettlespurges (*Jatropha*). —**de-purga** = MEDICINEIRO. —**do-mato** = ANGELIM-DOCE. —**manso**, Barbados nut (*Jatropha curcas*). —**rôto**, the bellyache nettlespurge (*Jatropha gossypifolia*).

pinhé (*m., Zool.*) a caracara (*Milvago chimachima*).

pinheira (*f.*) the sugarapple (*Annona squamosa*), the fruit of which is called ATA, PINHA, FRUTA-DO-CONDE.

pinheiral (*m.*) a pine grove [= PINHAL].

pinheirinho (*m., Bot.*) either of two species of Podocarpus (*P. lambertii* or *P. sellowii*). —**da-água** = CAVALINHO-D'ÁGUA.

pinheiro (*m.*) pine tree. —**baboso**, (*Bot.*) the insectivorous sundew (*Drosophyllum lusitanicum*). —**branco-do-canadá**, Eastern white pine (*Pinus strobus*). —**bravo**, Scotch pine (*Pinus sylvestris*). c.a. PINHEIRO-SILVESTRE. —**calvo**, common bald cypress [= CIPRESTE-CALVO]. —**chorão**, a weeping pine. —**de-alepo**, Aleppo pine (*Pinus halepensis*), c.a. PINHEIRO-BRANCO, PINHEIRO-CASQUINHA, PINHEIRO-DE-JERUSALÉM, PINHEIRO-FRANCÊS. —**de-purga**, the Barbados nut (*Jatropha curcas*), c.a. PURGUEIRA. —**de-riga**, Riga Scotch pine (*Pinus sylvestris regensis*). —**do-brejo**, a tree (*Talauma ovata*) of the magnolia family. —**do-canadá**, Eastern arborvitae (*Thuja occidentalis*), c.a. CIPRESTE. —**do-paraná**, Paraná araucaria (*A. angustifolia*), c.a. PINHEIRO-DE-SÃO-PAULO, PINHEIRO-DO-BRASIL, PINHEIRO-NACIONAL. —**larício**, Corsican pine (*Pinus nigra poiretiana*), c.a. LÁRICE, PINHEIRO-MARÍTIMO. —**manso**, Italian stone pine (*Pinus pinea*).

pinho (*m.*) pine wood; (*colloq.*) a guitar. —**de-flandres**, wood of the Scotch pine. —**do-brejo** = PINHEIRO-DO-BREJO. —**da-paraná** = PINHEIRO-DO-PARANÁ.

pinhões-de-ratos (*m.pl., Bot.*) white stonecrop (*Sedum album*), c.a. ARROZ-DOS-TELHADOS.

pinicão (*m.*), **pinicada** (*f.*) a pinch.

pinicar (*v.t.*) to pinch; to peck.

pinica-pau (*m.*) = PICA-PAU.

pinico (*m.*) sharp point; beak.

pínico -ca (*adj., Chem.*) pinic.

piniforme (*adj.*) piniform.

pinípedes (*m.pl.*) the Pinnipedia (seals and walruses).

pinipicrina (*f., Chem.*) pinipicrin.

pinita (*f.*), -**to** (*m., Min.*) pinite.

pino (*m.*) peg, pin, cotterpin; the highest point. —**de manivela**, crankpin. **a**—, upright. **com o sol a**—, at high noon. **no**—**de**, at the peak of.

pinóia (*m.,f.*) person or thing of little or no consequence; a cocotte.

pinote (*m.*) a horse's curvet, buck or leap.

pinot[e]ar (*v.i.*) to curvet, buck, leap.

pinta (*f.*) spot; pip (of cards or dominoes); mole; complexion; characteristic; the cut of one's jib. —**da-erva**, short-billed rail (*Porzana*). —**cega**, (*f.*) a nighthawk; (*colloq.*) a nearsighted person.

pintadela (*f.*) light coat of paint.

pintadinho (*m.*) = CAÇÃO-PINTO.

pintado -da (*adj.*) painted; colored; spotted; perfect, complete; bold, daring; (*m.*) = SURUBIM; (*f.*) = GALINHA-D'ANGOLA; RAIA-PINTADA; ONÇA-PINTADA.

pintagol [-góis] (*m.*) a cross between a goldfinch (*Spinus*) and a canary, c.a. ARLEQUIM.

pintagola (*f.*) = ÔLHO-DE-BOI (fish).

pintainha [a-i] (*f.*) young pullet.

pintainho [a-i] (*m.*) baby chick [= PINTINHO].

pintalegrete [grê] (*m.*) fop; (*adj.*) foppish.

pintalgado -da (*adj.*) speckled, flecked; piebald; mottled.

pintalgar (*v.t.*) to speckle, mottle.

pinta-monos (*m.*) dauber.

pinta-no-cabo (*m.*) = MARIMBÁ.

pintar (*v.t.,v.i.*) to paint; to portray; (*v.r.*) to make up (the face). —**a manta (o sete, o diabo, o caneco)**, to raise Cain, to raise the devil, to act up, cut up, have a good time; to paint the town red. **vir ao—**, to arrive at just the right moment.

pintassilgo (*m.*) any of various birds, such as the Brazilian siskin (*Spinus magellanicus ictericus*) and the western guira tanager (*Hemithraupis guira guirana*).—**-do-brejo** = JAPACANIM.—**-do-mato-virgem** = TIÉ-TINGA (a tanager).—**-verde,** Allen's siskin (*Spinus magellanicus alleni*), c.a. LUGRE, ABADAVINA.

pinteiro (*m.*) brooder for baby chicks.

pintinho (*m.*) **-nha** (*f.*) baby chick.

pinto (*m.*) young chicken; (*colloq.*) = CRUZADO (Port. coin); (*sl.*) easy thing, snap, breeze; beginner, novice. (*Zool.*) = CAÇÃO-PINTO (a shark).—**-calçudo,** (*colloq.*) boy wearing his first pair of long pants.—**-do-mato,** the Amazonian antthrush (*Formicarius ruficeps amazonicus*), c.a. GALINHA-DO-MATO; the rufous-vented antthrush (*F. a. analis*), c.a. TAUOCA; the Cayenne antthrush (*Myrmornis torquata*.)

pintor (*m.*) **-tora** (*f.*) painter.

pintura (*f.*) painting; picture; depiction, portrayal; face make-up.—**a óleo,** oil painting.—**mural,** a mural.—**s rupestres,** cave drawings.

pinturesco **-ca** [ê] (*adj.*) = PITORESCO.

pínula (*f.*) pinnule; (*Zool., Bot.*) pinnule; pinnula.

pinulado **-da** (*adj., Bot., Zool.*) pinnulate.

pio **-ia** (*adj.*) pious, devout; charitable; compassionate; (*m.*) peep, chirp; bird call (whistle). **não dar um—,** not let out a peep, not utter a sound; (*f.*) see PIA.

pioca (*m.,f.*) = CAIPIRA.

piocianina (*f., Biochem.*) pyocyanin.

piocito (*m.*) pyocyte.

pioemia (*f.*) = PIEMIA.

piogênico **-ca** (*adj.*) pyogenic.

pióide (*adj., Med.*) pyoid; puriform.

piolhada (*f.*) a quantity of lice.

piolharia (*f.*) lice galore; fig., squalor.

piolheira (*f.*) a lot of lice; (*Bot.*) the lousewort; fig., squalid living quarters; (*colloq.*) a "lousy" business.

piolhento **-ta** (*adj.*) lousy; louse-breeding; crummy.

piolho [ô] (*m.*) louse, mite, aphid; shoemakers' tack; (*Bot.*) a tree of the Indian-plum family (*Casearia parvifolia*).—**-branco,** a scale insect which attacks coffee trees.—**-da-cabeça,** head louse (*Pediculus capitis*).—**-da-língua,** a tongue worm (*Linguatulida*).—**-das-abelhas,** bee louse (*Braula coeca*).—**-das-aves,** bird louse.—**-das-virilhas** = PIOLHO-LADRO.—**-de-cobra,** a centipede or millipede; long-winded speech.—**-de-galinha,** chicken louse.—**-de-padre,** (*Bot.*) a beggartick (*Bidens pilosa*).—**-de-queijo-velho,** cheese mite.—**-de-são-josé,** the armored scale insect (*Diaspidine*).—**-de-tubarão,** clingfish, remora, suckfish, c.a. AGARRADOR.—**-do-corpo** or **-do-fato,** body louse (*Pediculus vestimenti*).—**-dos-peixes,** fish louse.—**-dos-vegetais,** plant louse, aphid, scale insect.—**-ladro,** crab louse (*Phthirius inguinalis* or *P. pubis*).

piolhoso **-sa** (*adj.*) louse-infested.

piom-piom (*m.*) = QUEM-QUEM.

pioneiro (*m.*) pioneer, explorer, trail-blazer.

pior (*adj., comp. of* MAU) worse, worst; (*adv. comp. of* MAL) worse; (*m.*) the worst.—**ainda,** even worse.—**que nunca,** worse than ever. **ainda—,** worse yet. **fazer o—,** to do the worst. **de mal a—,** from bad to worse. **na—das hipóteses,** if the worst comes to the worst; supposing the worst. **o—é que,** the worst of it is that.

piora (*f.*), **pioramento** (*m.*) a worsening.

piorar (*v.t.,v.i.*) to worsen, deteriorate.

piorno (*m., Bot.*) a woadwaxen (*Genista*).

piorra [ô] (*f.*) small top, whirligig.

piorréia (*f., Med.*) pyorrhea.

pioscópio (*m.*) a kind of lactoscope.

piose (*f., Med.*) pyosis, suppuration.

piotanina (*f., Pharm.*) pyoctanin.

pioxantose [ks] (*f., Biochem.*) pyoxanthose.

pipa (*f.*) pipe, cask, butt, wine barrel, hogshead; (*colloq.*) a short, fat person; a tosspot; (*m.*) the Surinam toad (*Pipa pipa*), c.a. SAPO-DE-SURINÃ, CURURU-PÉ-DE-PATO.

pipal (*m., Bot.*) India fig (*Ficus indica*).

piparote (*m.*) flip, fillip, flick.

piperáceo **-cea** (*adj., Bot.*) piperaceous; (*f.pl.*) the pepper family (*Piperaceae*).

piperato (*m., Chem.*) piperate.

piperazina (*f., Chem.*) piperazine.

pipérico **-ca** (*adj.*) **ácido—,** piperic acid.

piperidina (*f., Chem.*) piperidine.

piperina (*f., Chem.*) piperine.

piperino (*m., Petrog.*) piperno.

piperioca (*f., Bot.*) a flatsedge (*Cyperus sanguineo fuscus*).

piperonal (*m., Chem.*) piperonal; heliotropine.

pipeta [ê] (*f.*) pipette, pipet.

pipi [pipí] (*m.*) garlic guineahen weed (*Petiveria alliacea*).

pipiar, pipilar (*v.i.*) to peep, chirp, twitter; (*m.*) a peeping, chirping, twittering.

pipilante (*adj.*) chirping.

pipilo (*m.*) chirp.

pipira (*f.*) a woman worker in a textile factory; (*Zool.*) the Brazilian silver-beaked tanager (*Ramphocelus carbo centralis*).—**-encarnada,** the black-throated tanager (*Ramphocelus nigrogularis*).

pipiri [rí] (*m., Bot.*) a beak rush (*Rhynchospora storea*).

pipirioca (*f., Bot.*) a flatsedge (*Cyperus*).

pipitar (*v.i.*) to chirp.

pipitinga (*f.*) = MANJUBA.

pipo (*m.*) keg.

pipoca (*f.*) popcorn.

pipocar (*v.i.*) to pop, crackle.

pipôco (*m.*) a pop; (*colloq.*) shindy, brawl.

pipoquear (*v.*) = PIPOCAR.

pique (*m.*) pike, halberd; children's game of hide-and-seek; a card bearing a pricked design for making bobbin lace; a small prick or puncture; earmark (of cattle).—**vertical,** nose dive. **a—,** vertically; steeply. **a—de,** on the point of; on the verge of; about to (happen); in danger of. **brincar de—,** to play hide-and-seek. **descer em—,** (*Aeron.*) to dive. **ir a—,** to sink, go down, founder. **pau a—,** wattle and daub.

piqueiro (*m.*) picador (in bull fight); pikeman.

piquenique (*m.*) picnic.

piquêta (*f.*) picket (pointed stake). Var. PIQUÉTE.

piquetar (*v.t.*) to mark with stakes.

piquête (*m.*) picket, patrol, guard; shift of workers; strike picket; also = PIQUÊTA.

piquira (*adj.*) of persons, insignificant; of horses, small; (*m.*) small fry (fish); a pony.

pira (*f.*) pyre, funeral pile. **dar o—,** (*slang*) to "beat it".

pirá (*m.*) the Tupian word for fish—used as a combining term for many Braz. fish names.

pirá-açá (*m.*) = CANGULO (triggerfish).

piraaca [a-a] (*m.*) fringed filefish (*Monocanthus ciliatus*).

pirá-andira (*m.*) = PEIXE-MORCÊGO.

pirabebe (*m., Zool.*) a flying gurnard (*Dactylopterus volitans*), c.a. COIÓ, CAJALEÓ, VOADOR-CASCUDO, PEIXE-VOADOR.

pirabeju, pirabiju [ú] (*m.*) = BIJUPIRÁ.

piraboca (*f.*) = PIRAGICA.

piraca (*f.*) = PREJEREBA.

piracambucu (*m.*) = SURUBIM.

piracanto (*m.*) any Pyracantha, esp. the fire-thorn (*P. coccinea*), c.a. ESPINHEIRO-ARDENTE.

piracema (*f.*) "(1) the period of the year (at the end of the dry season) when the fish migrate from the flooded areas in the forest and the lakes to the rivers; (2) a school of fish; (3) the time of the year when the schools of fish go upstream to deposit their eggs." [GBAT]

piracicaba (*f.*) a place where a waterfall or other obstruction acts as a barrier to fish headed upstream.

piracuí (*m.*) dried fish meal; "it keeps for a long time and hence is a favorite food for fishermen, hunters and travelers." [GBAT]. Var. PIRACUÍM.

piracuca (*f.*) = GAROUPA-VERDADEIRA.

piragaia (*f.*) = GAROUPA-DE-SÃO-TOMÉ.

piragica (*f.*) the Bermuda chub (*Kyphosus sectatrix*), c.a. PIRABOCA.

piraguaia (*f.*) = ANCHIETA.

piraf (*m.*) rawhide whip.

piraia (*f.*) = IPECACONHA-DE-FLOR-BRANCA.

piraíba (*m.*) a large smooth-skinned fresh-water Amazonian catfish (*Branchiplatystoma filamentosum*).—**-de-pele,** another fresh-water catfish (*Bagrus reticulatus*).

pirajeva (*f.*) = PREJEREBA.

pirálidas (*f.pl.*), **piralídeos** (*m.pl.*) the Pyralididae (family of moths).

pirambóia (*f.*) the Amazon lungfish (*Lepidosiren paradoxa*), c.a. TRAÍRA-BÓIA, TRARIAMBÓIA, PIRARUCU-BÓIA, CARAMURU.

pirambu [ú] (*m.*) the margate fish (*Haemulon album*), c.a. ARREBENTA-PANELA; also = CORCOROCA (blue-striped grunt), and SARGAÇO-DE-BEIÇO (a fish).

piramembeca (*m.*) = GUETE.

piramidal (*adj.*) pyramidal; fig., immense.

pirâmide (*f.*) pyramid.—**cônica,** a cone.

piramidélidas (*m.pl.*) the Pyramidellidae (family of marine snails).

piramidizar (*v.i.*) to pyramid.

piramido (*m.*), **-dona** (*f., Chem.*) pyramidon.

piranema (*f.*) the catalufa (*Priacanthus arenatus*), a small marine spiny-finned fish, c.a. ÔLHO-DE-CÃO.

piranga (*adj.*) red; shabby; (*f.*) a certain red clay found in Brazil; a funnelvine (*Arrabidaea chica*) from which the Amazon Indians extract a tattooing pigment; the pigment itself, both c.a. CARAJURU; (*Zool.*) a small red-jawed caribe (*Serrasalmo rhomboeus*); a genus of tanagers; (*colloq.*) lack of money.

pirangar (*v.i.*) to beg.

pirangueiro -ra (*adj.*) begging; crazy about fishing; (*m.*) avid fisherman.

piranha (*f., Zool.*) caribe—any of several S.A. fresh-water fishes (genus *Serrasalmo*, family *Characinidae*) remarkable for their voracity.

piranômetro (*m., Physics*) pyranometer.

pirantera (*f.*) a large carnivorous fresh-water dog-fish (*Hydrocyon armatus*).

pirão (*m.*) manioc mush; (*colloq.*) pretty girl.—**de batata**, mashed potatoes.

piraoba (*m.*) Indian name for spring rains (Sept.–Oct.) which in No. Braz. are called CHUVAS-DE-CAJU.

pirapanema (*m.*) place where fish are scarce.

pirapeba (*f.*) fresh-water fish.

pirapebebe (*m.*) = PIRABEBE.

pirapema (*f.*) = CAMURUPI, CAMURUPIM.

pirapua (*f.*) Indian name for whale [= BALEIA].

pirapuia (*f.*) = JURUVA.

piraquara (*m.,f.*) dweller along the Paraíba River in the State of Rio de Janeiro, esp. one who fishes; by exten., any skilled fisherman.

piraqüera (*f.*) Tupian word for night fishing.

piraqui [í] (*m.*) fish meal.

piraquiba (*m.*) a suckfish (remora), c.a. AGARRADOR.

pirar (*v.i., slang*) to scram, beat it.

pirargirite (*f., Min.*) pyrargyrite.

piraroba (*f.*) = PAMPO-DE-CABEÇA-MOLE.

pirarucu [cú] (*m.*) a large-scaled Amazon fish (*Arapaima gigas*, family *Osteoglossidae*), said to be the largest freshwater fish in the world, attaining a length of 15 feet and a weight of 500 lbs.—**boia** = PIRAMBÓIA.

pira-siririca (*f.*) = PAPA-TERRA.

pirata (*m.*) pirate, buccaneer, corsair; pirate-ship; robber; scoundrel; lady-killer, "wolf".

piratagem (*f.*) piracy; robbery; fraud, chicanery.

pira-tan-tan (*m.*) a small Amazon fish (*Copeina arnoldi*) sometimes seen in home aquaria.

pirataria (*f.*) piracy.

piratear (*v.i.*) to pirate.

pirático -ca (*adj.*) piratical.

piraú (*f.*) = POMBA-PEDRÊS.

piraúna (*f.*) a sea drumfish (*Pogonias chromis*), c.a. BURRIQUETE, MIRAGUAIA, VACA; also = GAROUPINHA.

pirca (*f.*) dry stone wall.

pireliometria (*f.*) pyrheliometry.

pireliômetro (*m.*) pyrheliometer.

Pireneus (*m.*) Pyrenees.

pirenina (*f., Biol.*) pyrenin.

pireno (*m., Chem.*) pyrene.

pirenóide (*adj., Bot.*) pyrenoid.

pirenomicetos (*m.pl., Bot.*) the Pyrenomycetes (sphere fungi).

pirento -ta (*adj.*) mangy; (*m.*) saucer, small plate.

pires (*m.*) saucer; small plate.

pirético -ca (*adj.*) feverish.

piretrina (*f., Chem.*) pyrethrin.

píretro (*m.*) pyrethrum (plant and powder).—**da-beira**, a laserwort (*Laserpitium*), c.a. BRUCO.—**do-cáucaso**, Caucasian pyrethrum (*Chrysanthemum marschalli*), c.a. MONSENHOR-AMARELO, MATRICÁRIA.—**partênio**, feverfew chrysanthemum (*C. parthenium*).

pirexia [ks] (*f., Med.*) pyrexia, fever.

piri [rí] (*m., Bot.*) a beak sedge (*Rhyncospora cephalotes*), c.a. CAPIM-DE-BOTA.

pírico -ca (*adj.*) Pyrrhic.

pirídico -ca (*adj., Chem.*) pyridic.

piridina (*f., Chem.*) pyridine.

pirífora (*f.*) = PIRILAMPO.

piriforme (*adj.*) pyriform, pear-shaped.

piriguara (*f., Bot.*) the mercury anchieta (*A. salutaris*), c.a. PARAGUAIA, CIPÓ-SUMÁ.

pirilampe[j]ar (*v.i.*) to flicker as a firefly.

pirilampo (*m.*) firefly, lightning bug [= VAGALUME].

pirimembeca (*f.*) = CANARANA-RASTEIRA.

pirina (*f.*) a syagrus palm (*S. cocoides*).

piripiri [rí] (*m.*) the vulturine parrot (*Gypositta vulturina*) of central and northeastern Brazil.

piriquiteira (*f., Bot.*) a shellseed (*Cochlospermum orinocense*).

piriquitete [tête] (*adj.*) neatly dressed.

piriquiti [tí] (*m., Bot.*) a canna (*C. flaccida*).

piririca (*adj.*) like sandpaper; brazen; (*f.*) ripple; (*Bot.*) a prostrate herb (*Coccocypselum canescens*).

piriricar (*v.i.*) to ripple.

piririguá, piririquia, piritá (*m., Zool.*) a white ani (*Piaya cayana*), c.a. ALMA-DE-GATO, ANU-BRANCO, ANU-DO-CAMPO.

pirita, pirite (*f., Min.*) pyrite, iron pyrites; fool's gold.—**cúprica**, copper pyrites, chalcopyrite.

piritífero -ra (*adj.*) pyritiferous.

piritoedro (*m., Cryst.*) pyritohedron.

piritologia (*f.*) pyritology.

piritoso -sa (*adj., Min.*) pyritous, pyritic.

pirixi [chí] (*m.*) = CAPOTIRAGUÁ.

pirizal (*m.*) place abounding in PIRI.

pirliteiro (*m.*) = ESCALHEIRO.

piroaba (*f.*) = CHUVA-DE-CAJU.

piroantimoniato (*m., Chem.*) pyroantimonate.

piroarseniato (*m., Chem.*) pyroarsenate.

piroarsenito (*m., Chem.*) pyroarsenite.

piroborato (*m., Chem.*) pyroborate.

piroca (*adj.*) bald; (*f., vulgar*) penis.

pirocar (*v.i.*) to grow bald.

pirocatequina (*f., Chem.*) pyrocatechin, pyrocatechinol.

pirocítrico -ca (*adj., Chem.*) pyrocitric.

pirocondensação (*f., Chem.*) pyrocondensation.

pirocloro (*m., Min.*) pyrochlore.

pirocroíta (*f., Min.*) pyrochroite.

piroculu [lú] (*m.*) = SAGÜI-DE-NARIZ-BRANCO.

pirodina (*f., Chem.*) pyrodine.

piroeletricidade (*f., Physics*) pyroelectricity.

pirófano -na (*adj.*) pyrophanous.

pirofilite (*f., Min.*) pyrophyllite.

pirofobia (*f., Med.*) pyrophobia.

pirofórico -ca (*adj.*) pyrophoric.

piróforo -ra (*adj.*) pyrophorous; (*m., Chem.*) pyrophorus.

pirofosfato (*m., Chem.*) pyrophosphate.

piroga (*f.*) pirogue, dugout canoe.

pirogaiacina (*f., Chem.*) pyroguaiacin.

pirogal[h]ato (*m., Chem.*) pyrogallate.

pirogálico -ca (*adj.*) pyrogallic.

pirogalol (*m., Chem.*) pyrogallol.

pirogêneo -nea (*adj., Chem.*) pyrogenous; (*m.*) pyrogen.

pirogênese (*f.*) pyrogenesis.

pirogenético -ca (*adj.*) pyrogenetic.

pirogênico -ca (*adj.*) pyrogenic.

pirognóstico -ca (*adj., Min.*) pyrognostic.

pirográfico -ca (*adj.*) pyrographic.

pirogravura (*f.*) pyrography.

piroláceo -cea (*adj., Bot.*) pyrolaceous; (*f.pl.*) the shinleaf or false wintergreen family (*Pyrolaceae*).

pirólatra (*m.,f.*) pyrolater, fire worshiper.

pirolatria (*f.*) pyrolatry, fire worship.

pirolenhito (*m.*) pyrolignite.

pirólise (*f., Chem.*) pyrolysis.

pirolítico -ca (*adj.*) pyrolytic.

pirolusita (*f., Min.*) pyrolusite; polianite; bogmanganese.

piromagnético -ca (*adj., Physics*) pyromagnetic.

piromancia (*f.*) pyromancy.

piromania (*f., Psychiatry*) pyromania.

piromaníaco (*m.*) **-ca** (*f.*) firebug.

pirometria (*f.*) pyrometry.

pirométrico -ca (*adj.*) pyrometric.

pirômetro (*m.*) pyrometer.—**de irradiação**, radiation pyrometer.—**de Wedgwood**, contraction pyrometer.—**de resistência**, resistance thermometer.—**óptico**, optical pyrometer.—**termoelétrico**, thermoelectrical thermometer.

piromorfita (*f., Min.*) pyromorphite.

piromucato (*m., Chem.*) pyromucate.

piromúcico -ca (*adj., Chem.*) pyromucic.

pirona (*f., Chem.*) pyrone.

piroplasma (*m.*) a genus (*Babesia*, syn. *Piroplasma*) of parasitic protozoans which live in the blood of cattle and other animals.

piroplasmose (f., Med., Veter.) piroplasmosis; babesiacis; Texas fever of cattle, c.a. TRISTEZA.
piropo (m., Min.) pyrope.
piroscopia (f.) pyromancy.
piroscópio (m., Physics) pyroscope.
pirose (f., Med.) pyrosis, heartburn.
pirosfera (f., Geol.) pyrosphere.
pirosmalite (f., Min.) pyrosmalite.
pirossulfúrico –ca (adj., Chem.) pyrosulphuric.
piróstato (m., Physics) pyrostat.
pirostilpnite (f., Min.) pyrostilpnite.
pirotartrato (m., Chem.) pyrotartrate.
piróte (m.) = cocó.
pirotecnia, pirotécnica (f.) pyrotechny; pyrotechnics.
pirotécnico –ca (adj.) pyrotechnical; (m.,f.) pyrotechnist.
pirótico –ca (adj.; m.) pyrotic, caustic.
piroxantina [ks] (f., Chem.) pyroxanthin.
piroxênico –ca [ks] (adj.) pyroxenic.
piroxenite [ks] (f., Petrog.) pyroxenite.
piroxênio [ks] (m., Min.) pyroxene.
piroxilina [ks] (f.), piroxilino [ks] (m.) pyroxylin, soluble guncotton.
pirraça (f.) spite; spiteful taunt; orneriness, foolish stubbornness, pique.
pirraçar (v.t.) to tease, torment, taunt.
pirracento –ta (adj.) spiteful; ornery.
pirralhada (f.) group of children.
pirralho (m.) youngster, kid, tot, moppet, brat, urchin.
pirrica (f.) pyrrhic dance.
pirríquio (m., Pros.) pyrrhic.
pirrocorídeos (m.pl., Zool.) the Pyrrhocoridae (cotton stainers and related bugs).
pirrol (m., Chem.) pyrrole.
pirronice (f.) stubborn skepticism; orneriness.
pirrônico –ca (adj.) skeptical; ornery.
pirronismo (m.) Pyrrhonism, extreme skepticism; (colloq.) orneriness.
pirrotita (f., Min.) pyrrhotite, magnetic pyrites.
pírtiga (f.) pole, shaft.
pírtigo (m.) the free-swinging end of a flail.
piruá (m.) unpopped grains of popcorn.
piruêta (f.) pirouette.
piruetar (v.i.) to pirouette.
pírula (f.) a genus (Pyrula) of marine univalve mollusks; also = PÍLULA.
pirulário (m.) a genus (Pyrularia) of parasitic shrubs of the sandalwood family.
pirulito (m.) all-day sucker, lollipop (taffy on a stick).
pirupiru [rú] (m.) the oyster-catcher (Haematopus ostralegus), c.a. BATUÍRA.
piruruca (f.) coarse sand and gravel.
piruvato (m., Chem.) pyruvate.
pirúvico –ca (adj., Chem.) pyruvic.
pisa (f.) act of treading; pressing of grapes with the feet; beating, trouncing.
pisada (f.) see under PISADO.
pisadela (f.) a treading or trampling.
pisado –da (adj.) stepped on; trampled on; bruised. ôlho—, black eye; (f.) footprint; footstep; tread; treading of grapes; horse's gait.
pisador –dora (adj.) treading, pounding, crushing, trampling; (m.) grape presser.
pisadura (f.) bruise, hurt; footmark; trampling.
pisa-flôres (m.) a man of mincing manners.
pisa-mansinho (adj.; m.,f.) sly (person).
pisamento (m.) = PISADELA.
pisanite (f., Min.) pisanite.
pisano –na (adj.; m.,f.) Pisan.
pisão (m.) fulling mill.
pisar (v.t.) tô step on, tread upon, trample on; to set foot on; to press (grapes) with the feet; to stamp, pound, grind; to crush, bruise, hurt; (v.i.) to step, walk.—aos pés, to tread upon; to humiliate.—no cangote, to humiliate.—o palco, to tread the boards (act on stage).
pisaurídeos (m.pl.) the Pisauridae (hunting spiders).
pisca (f.) see under PISCO.
piscadela (f.), piscado, piscamento (m.) wink(ing), blink(ing).
pisca-pisca (m.) a person who has an eye tic; a blinker signal light.
piscar (v.t.,v.i.) to wink, blink.
piscatório –ria (adj.) piscatorial.
písceo –cea (adj.) piscine.
piscícola (adj.) piscicultural.

piscicultor –tora (m.,f.) pisciculturist.
piscicultura (f.) fish culture.
piscídia (f., Bot.) the genus (Piscidia) of fishfuddle trees.
pisciforme (adj.) fish-shaped.
piscina (f.) swimming pool; watering trough; fish pond; (Eccl.) piscina.
piscívoro –ra (adj.) piscivorous, fish-eating.
pisco –ca (adj.) blinking; half-shut [eye]; nearsighted; (m.) a wagtail (Motacilla).—-chilreiro, a bullfinch (Pyrrhula), c.a. DOM-FAFE.—-ribeiro = PICA-PEIXE. (f.) mote, speck; cigarette butt; (exclam.) Sic 'em!
pisídio (m.) a genus (Pisidium) of fresh-water bivalves.
pisiforme (adj.) pisiform, like a pea in size and shape.
piso (m.) tread, gait; ground, floor, pavement; tread of a stair.
pisoador –dora (m.,f.) fuller (of cloth).
pisoagem (f.), pisoamento (m.) fulling (of cloth).
pisoar (v.t.) to full (cloth).
pisoeiro –ra (m.,f.) = PISOADOR.
pisolítico –ca (adj., Petrog.) pisolitic.
pisólito (m., Petrog.) pisolite.
pisotear (v.t.) to trample upon; to humiliate.
pisoteio (m.) trampling.
pissandô (m.) a palm (Diplothemum littorale).
pissitar (v.i.) of starlings, to chirp, chatter.
pista (f.) track, footprint, trail; clue; race track; riding ring; arena; rink; runway, landing strip; traffic lane. —de vôo, flight deck (of an airplane carrier). seguir uma—, to follow a trail, a clue.
pistácia, pistacha, pistache (f.), pistacho (m.) all names for the pistachio (Pistacia vera), c.a. ALFÓSTIGO; the pistachio nut.
pistacite (f.), –to (m., Min.) pistacite, epidote.
pistão (m.) piston [= ÊMBOLO]; (Music) cornet.
pistar (v.i.) to chirp, twitter.
pistilífero –ra (adj., Bot.) pistilliferous.
pistiliforme (adj.) pistilliform.
pistilo (m., Bot.) pistil.
pistola (f.) pistol; a Roman candle; a pistole (former European gold coin).—automática, automatic pistol.—de graxa, grease gun.
pistolado (m.), –da (f.) a pistol shot.
pistolão (m.) a large Roman candle; (colloq.) the backing of a person of influence; a "big shot" who uses his prestige and influence in behalf of someone seeking a job, a promotion, an appointment, etc.
pistolé (m.) French (drawing) curve.
pistoleiro (m.) pistoleer; gunman.
pistoleta [ê] (f.) small pistol.
pistolóquia (f., Bot.) a dutchmanspipe (Aristolochia pistolochia).
pita (f.) pita hemp fiber; any of various bromeliaceous plants called PITEIRA, CARAGUATÁ, AGAVE, ABECEDÁRIA.
pitada (f.) a pinch of snuff, salt, etc.
pitadear (v.i.) to take snuff.
pitador (m.) pipe smoker.
pitagórico –ca (adj.; m.,f.) Pythagorean.
pitaguar (adj.; m.,f.) variant of POTIGUAR.
pitaiaiá (m.) a cactus of Cereus, c.a. CARDO-ANANÁS, CARDO-DA-PRAIA.
pitança (f.) pittance [but only in the sense of an alms or dole of food].
pitanga (f., Bot.) the pitanga or Brazil cherry (Eugenia uniflora), or its fruit; any of several other related trees. [Cf. PITANGUEIRA] chorar—s, to implore, entreat.
pitangaçu [ú], pitanguá(-açu) [ú] (m.) = BEM-TE-VI-DO-BICO-CHATO.
pitangueira (f., Bot.) the Brazil cherry (Eugenia uniflora), c.a. PITANGA, and other related myrtles.—-de-cachorro, a lidflower (Calyptranthes obscura).—-mulata, an eugenia (E. dasyblastus).
pitão (m.) python; soothsayer.
pitar (v.i.) to smoke, esp. to smoke a pipe.
pitauá (m.) = BEM-TE-VI-DO-BICO-CHATO.
pitecântropo (m.) pithecanthropus.
pitecantropóide (m.) pithecanthropoid.
pitécia (f.) a genus of monkeys (Pithecia) consisting of the sakis.
pitecismo (m.) pithécism.
pitecóide (adj.) pithecoid.
piteira (f.) cigarette or cigar-holder; (colloq.) drunkenness; (Bot.) the century plant (Agave americana), c.a. AGAVE. —-imperial, the giant lily or piteira furcrea (Furcraea gigantea).

pitéu (*m.*) tidbit.
Pita (*f.*) Pythia; [*not cap.*] pythoness.
pitiáceas (*f.pl.*) the Pythiaceae (parasitic fungi).
pítico –**ca** (*adj.*) Pythian.
pitilo (*m.*, *Zool.*) a genus of grosbeaks (*Pitylus*).
pitiríase (*f.*, *Med.*) pityriasis.
pititinga (*f.*) = ALETRIA (sand smelt); MANJUBA (anchovy).
pitiú (*m.*) fish odor; any stench [= PITUÍ]; a certain fresh-water turtle (*Podocnemis unifilis*) c.a. TARECAÍ, TRACAJÁ, CABÉUA; also a terrestrial turtle (*Niconia punctulata*) c.a. JABOTI-APEREMA; also = ANAMBÉ-AÇU (a bird).
pito (*m.*) tobacco pipe; cigarette; a scolding; (*Zool.*) kinds of dragonflies, c.a. LAVANDEIRA, JACINA.
pitoco –**ca** [tô] (*adj.*) bob-tailed; tailless [= SURU].
pitomba (*f.*) fruit of the
pitombeira (*f.*, *Bot.*) the pitomba eugenia (*E. luschnathiana*), c.a. CURUIRI; a certain soapberry (*Sapindus esculentus*); a tropical Am. tree (*Simaba guianensis*), c.a. CAJURANA.
pitômetro (*m.*, *Hydraulics*) pitometer.
piton (*m.*) = PITÃO.
pitonídeos (*m.pl.*) the Pythonidae (family of large O.W. non-venomous snakes).
pitonis[s]a (*f.*) pythoness; fortune-teller.
pitonomorfo (*m.*, *Paleontol.*) pythonomorph.
pitoresco –**ca** [ô] (*adj.*) picturesque.
pitorra [ô] (*f.*) whirligig, top; a squat person.
pitosga (*adj.*; *m.*,*f.*) nearsighted, blinking (person).
pitosporáceo –**cea** (*adj.*, *Bot.*) pittosporaceous; (*f.pl.*) the pittosporum family (*Pittosporaceae*).
pitósporo (*m.*, *Bot.*) the genus Pittosporum; a shrub of this genus, esp. *P. tobira*.
pitote (*m.*) topknot [= COCÓ].
pituá (*f.*) camel's-hair brush.
pituba (*adj.*) white-livered; (*m.*) horse thief.
pituí, pituim (*m.*) strong body odor.
pituíta (*f.*) pituites, mucus, phlegm.
pituitário –**ria** [u-i] (*adj.*, *Anat.*) pituitary. **corpo**—, pituitary body or gland. **glândula**—, pituitary gland. **membrana**—, pituitary membrane.
pituitoso –**sa** [u-i] (*adj.*) pituitous.
pituitrina [u-i] (*f.*, *Biochem.*) pituitrin.
pitumarana (*f.*, *Bot.*) a prairie gentian (*Lisianthus serratus*).
pitura (*f.*) tobacco [= FUMO].
piúca (*f.*) very dry, half-rotted, stick or branch; charred log or tree stump.
pium [i-úm] (*m.*) a buffalo gnat (*Simulium pertinax*).
piuneiro (*m.*) "a kind of cloth used on the upper [Amazon] rivers as a protection against the bite of the PIUM, covering the ears, face—except for the eyes, mouth and nose—the neck and top of the head." [*GBAT*]
piúria, piuria (*f.*, *Med.*) pyuria.
pivô (*m.*) pivot.
pivotante (*f.*, *Bot.*) taproot.
pixaim [a-ím], **pixainho** –**nha** [a-í] (*adj.*) kinky (*m.*) kinky hair.
pixé (*adj.*) smoky; tasting of smoke; (*m.*) bad smell.
pixelar, pixerar (*v.i.*) of cooked food, to taste smoky.
píxide [ks] (*Eccl.*) pyx; (*Bot.*) pysidium.
pixilinga (*f.*) chicken mite [= PIOLHO-DE-GALINHA].
pixote (*m.*) a rock drill.
pixoxó (*m.*) the superciliated seedeater (*Sporophila frontalis*), c.a. PAPA-ARROZ, PAPA-CAPIM, PIXANXÃO, CHÃ-CHÃO; the uniform finch (*Haplospiza unicolor*).
pixuna (*f.*) a kind of small wild rat; (*Bot.*) an eugenia (*E. glomerata*); a seagrape (*Coccolobis pixuna*).
pixurim (*m.*) a lauraceous tropical Am. tree (*Acrodiclidium puchury* or *Nectandra pichurim*) whose beans (pichurim bean = NOZ-DO-PARÁ) are strongly aromatic and used as a substitute for nutmegs; used also by natives along the Amazon as a stimulant tonic. Var. spellings: PICHURIM, PUCHIRI, PUXIRI, PUXURI.
pixurum (*m.*) = MUXIRÃO.
piza (*f.*) Italian pizza.
p.j. = PEDE JUSTIÇA (justice requested).
p.l. = PÊSO LÍQUIDO (net weight).
placa (*f.*) plate (thin, flat sheet or piece of metal or other material, esp. of uniform thickness, as a name plate); (*Electronics*) anode. Cf. CHAPA, PRATO.
placar (*m.*) placard, poster, bill; badge, decoration. [Fr. *placard*]; (*v.*) = APLACAR.
placável (*adj.*) placable.
placenta (*f.*, *Anat.*, *Zool.*, *Bot.*) placenta.

placentação (*f.*, *Anat.*, *Zool.*, *Biot.*) placentation.
placentário –**ria** (*adj.*) placental; (*m.pl.*, *Zool.*) the Placentalia.
placidez [ê] (*f.*) placidity, serenity, peacefulness.
plácido –**da** (*adj.*) placid, tranquil, calm, serene.
plácito (*m.*) sanction; pact.
placóide (*adj.*) placoid, platelike; (*m.pl.*, *Zool.*) the Placodei (a group of fishes).
plaga (*f.*) region, country, parts. [*Poetical.*]
plagiador –**dora** (*m.*,*f.*) plagiarist.
plagiante (*adj.*) plagiarizing.
plagiar (*v.t.*,*v.i.*) to plagiarize.
plagiário –**ria** (*adj.*) plagiaristic; (*m.*,*f.*) plagiarist.
plagiato, plágio (*m.*) plagiary, plagiarism.
plagiocéfalo –**la** (*adj.*) plagiocephalic.
plagioclásio (*m.*, *Min.*, *Petrog.*) plagioclase.
plagioclásico –**ca** (*adj.*) plagioclastic.
plagionita (*f.*, *Min.*) plagionite.
plagióstomo –**ma** (*adj.*, *Zool.*) plagiostome; (*m.pl.*) the Plagiostomi (sharks and rays).
plagiotrópico –**ca** (*adj.*, *Plant physiol.*) plagiotropic.
plagiotropismo (*m.*) plagiotropism.
plagiótropo –**pa** (*adj.*) plagiotropous, plagiotropic.
plaino –**na** (*adj.*) level, flat [= PLANO]; (*m.*) plain, prairie; (*f.*) carpenter's plane.—**mecânica**, planer (machine tool); planing mill.
planada (*f.*) plain, plateau.
planador –**dora** (*adj.*) gliding; (*m.*) glider.
planalto (*m.*) plateau, tableland.
planar (*v.i.*) to plane, soar, glide.
planaria (*f.*, *Zool.*) planarian, flatworm.
plancha (*f.*) = PRANCHA.
plancto, plâncton (*m.*, *Biol.*) plankton.
planctonite (*m.*, *Biol.*) planktont.
planê (*m.*, *Aeron.*) glide.
planeador –**dora** (*adj.*) planning; scheming; (*m.*,*f.*) planner; schemer.
plane[j]ar (*v.t.*) to plan, scheme, project; to design; to frame; to sketch out.
planeio (*m.*) = PLANÊ.
planejador –**dora** (*m.*,*f.*) planner, designer.
planeta (*f.*, *Eccl.*) planeta, chasuble [= CASULA].
planêta (*m.*) planet.
planetário –**ria** (*adj.*) planetary; (*m.*) planetarium.
planetóide (*m.*) planetoid; asteroid.
planeza [ê] (*f.*) flatness, evenness; a plain.
plangência (*f.*) plangency; plaintiveness.
plangente (*adj.*) plaintive, mournful, sad, tearful; whining.
planger (*v.i.*) to mourn, lament; (*v.t.*) to toll mournfully.
planície (*f.*) plain, prairie; lowland.
planiço (*m.*) extensive meadowland.
planígrafo (*m.*) planigraph.
planilha (*f.*) criminal's police record card.—**dactiloscópica**, the same with fingerprints.
planimetria (*f.*) planimetry; mapping.
planímetro (*m.*) planimeter.
planipenes (*m.*) the insect order of Planipennia (ant lions, lace-wings, etc.).
planirrostro –**tra** (*adj.*, *Zool.*) planirostral.
planisférico –**ca** (*adj.*) planispheric(al).
planisfério (*m.*) planisphere.
plano –**na** (*adj.*) plane, level, flat, smooth, even; (*m.*) plane, level surface; plan, diagram; design; scheme, project.—**aerodinâmico**, (*Aeron.*) airfoil.—**de incidência**, (*Optics*) plane of incidence.—**de polarização**, plane of polarization.—**de projeção**, plane of projection.—**de reflexão**, plane of reflection.—**de refração**, plane of refraction.—**de simetria**, plane of symmetry (of a flower).—**de tiro**, (*Gunnery*) plane of sight.—**em relêvo**, relief map.—**focal**, (*Optics*) focal plane.—**horizontal**, ground plan.—**inclinado**, inclined plane; slide, chute. **primeiro**—, foreground. **meio**—, middle ground. **último**—, background.
planococo (*m.*, *Bacteriol.*) a genus (*Planococcus*) of motile cocci.
plano-côncavo –**va** (*adj.*) plano-concave.
plano-convexo –**xa** [ks] (*adj.*) plano-convex.
planoferrite (*m.*, *Min.*) planoferrite.
planografia (*f.*) planography.
planográfico –**ca** (*adj.*) planographic.
planometria (*f.*) planometry.
planômetro (*m.*) planometer; surface plate.
planorbe (*f.*, *Zool.*) a genus (*Planorbis*) of fresh-water snails.

planospório (*m., Bot.*) planospore, zoospore.

planta (*f.*) plant, vegetable; sole of the foot; plot, ground plan. [But not plant, in the sense of factory or equipment for manufacture, which is FÁBRICA, USINA, MAQUINARIA, INSTALAÇÃO, APARELHAGEM.]—**anfíbia**, amphibious plant.—**de estufa**, hothouse plant.—**de-neve**, an iceplant (*Mesembryanthemum crystallinum*), c.a. FÔLHA-DE-GÊLO.—**espontânea**, a volunteer plant.—**feminina**, female plant.—**-milho** = CORTA-JACA (a dance).—**-misteriosa**, a nandina (*N. domestica*).—**paredeira**, (*Bot.*) a wall pellitory.—**s annuais**, annual plants.—**s lenhosas**, woody plants.—**s parasitas**, parasitic plants.—**s parietais**, the wall pellitories.—**s piramidais**, pyramidal plants.—**s rastejantes**, low-growing, ground-hugging plants.—**s sarmentosas**, vines.—**s trepadoras**, climbers.—**-telégrafo**, the telegraph tickclover (*Desmodium gyrans*).—**vivaz**, a perennial plant.

plantação (*f.*) planting; planted land [but not plantation in the sense of a large estate, which is FAZENDA; e.g., coffee plantation is FAZENDA DE CAFÉ].

plantadeira (*f.*) planting machine.

plantador –dora (*adj.*) planting; (*m.,f.*) planter; planting machine; dibble.

plantagem (*f., Bot.*) plantain (*Plantago*), better known as TANCHAGEM.

plantagináceo –cea (*adj., Bot.*) plantaginaceous; (*f.*) the plantain family (*Plantaginaceae*).

plantão (*m., Mil.*) an orderly or his duty; late shift at a hospital, newspaper office, etc.; night editor; night nurse; night watchman. **de—**, on duty.

plantar (*v.t.*) to plant (seeds, cuttings, bushes, trees, potatoes, etc.); to set firmly in the ground (as piles: **plantar estacas**); to implant, engender, inculcate (principles, ideas, knowledge, etc.; as, **plantar a fé, a verdade, os conhecimentos, as ciências**, etc.); to stock or provide with plants (as a garden: **plantar um quintal, um jardim**); (*v.r.*) to plant oneself (stay put a long time in one place; **plantou-se na esquina**, he planted himself on the corner). —**bananeira**, to do a hand stand.—**uma figueira**, to take a tumble; to fall off a horse. **Vá plantar batatas!** Go to the devil! (*adj., Anat., Zool.*) plantar.

plantel [-téis] (*m.*) breeding herd or flock; racing stable.

plantígrado –da (*adj., Zool.*) plantigrade; (*m.pl.*) the Plantigrada.

plantio (*m.*) act of planting; planted place; planting land; = PLANTAÇÃO.

plantívoro –ra (*adj.*) plantivorous.

plantula (*f.*) plantule, plantlet.

plânula (*f., Zool.*) planula.

planura (*f.*) plain, prairie; tableland, plateau; [= PLANÍCIE].

plaquê (*m.*) thin metal plating; plated metal.

plaqueta [ê] (*f.*) booklet.—**sanguínea**, blood platelet.

plasma (*m., Anat., Biol., Min., Physiol.*) plasma.

plasmação (*f.*) plasmation.

plasmado –da (*adj.*) made, molded, formed.

plasmador –dora (*adj.*) forming, molding; (*m.,f.*) former, molder.

plasmar (*v.t.*) to mold, form, shape, model (in clay, etc.).

plásmase (*f., Biochem.*) thrombin.

plasmático –ca (*adj.*) plasmatic.

plasmócito (*m.*) plasmocyte, white blood corpuscle.

plasmodesma (*f., Biol.*) plasmodesm.

plasmódio (*m., Biol.*) plasmodium.

plasmioforáceas (*f.pl., Bot.*) a family (*Plasmodiophoraceae*) of alga fungi.

plasmófago –ga (*adj.*) plamophagous.

plasmólise (*f., Physiol.*) plasmolysis.

plasmolítico –ca (*adj.*) plasmolytic.

plasmópara (*m.*) a genus (*Plasmopara*) of downy mildews.

plasmosoma (*m., Biol.*) plasmosome, nucleolus.

plasmotomiá (*f., Zool.*) plasmotomy.

plasoma (*m., Biol.*) plasome, biophore.

plástica (*f.*) the art of modeling or molding; plastic surgery; the general form of the human body.

plasticidade (*f.*) plasticity.

plasticina (*f.*) plasticine (modeling clay), c.a. PLASTILINA.

plasticizar (*v.t.*) to plasticize.

plástico –ca (*adj.; m.*) plastic.

plastídio (*m., Biol.*) plastid, plastidium.

plastídula (*f.*), **-lo** (*m., Biol.*) plastidule.

plastidular (*adj.*) plastidular.

plastificar (*v.t.*) to plastify, plasticize.

plastilina (*f.*) = PLASTICINA.

plastina (*f., Biol.*) plastin.

plastócito (*m.*) blood platelet.

plastodinamia (*f., Physiol.*) plastodynamia.

plastogamia (*f., Biol.*) plastogamy.

plastogâmico –ca (*adj.*) plastogamic.

plastômetro (*m.*) plastometer.

plastrão (*m.*) plastron; fencer's breast pad; Ascot tie; stiff shirt front.

plataforma (*f.*) platform, stand, dais, stage; terrace; platform of a railway station, of a streetcar, etc.; political platform; flatcar; (*colloq.*) appearance, pretense.—**giratória**, locomotive turntable.

plataleídeos (*m.pl., Zool.*) the spoonbills (*Plataleidae*).

platanáceo –cea (*adj., Bot.*) platanaceous; (*f.pl.*) the plane tree family (*Platanaceae*).

platanal (*m.*) a grove of plane trees.

platanista (*m., Zool.*) platanist, the susu.

plátano (*m.*) the American planetree or sycamore (*Platanus occidentalis*); sometimes, the plantain banana (*Musa paradisiaca*).—**bastardo**, the planetree maple (*Acer pseudoplatanus*).

Platão (*m.*) Plato.

platéia (*f.*) main floor of a theater; the audience on the main floor. **cadeira de—**, orchestra seat.

platelminte (*m.*) = PLATIELMINTE.

platense (*adj.*) Platine, of or pert. to the River Plate; (*m.,f.*) a native or inhabitant of the River Plate region; = PLATINO.

plati [í] (*m.*) the platy or moonfish (*Platypoecilus maculatus*), popular in home aquariums.

platibanda (*f.*) terrace wall; garden fence; flower border; (*Arch.*) platband.

platibásico –ca (*adj.*) platybasic, having a flat base.

platicarpo –pa (*adj., Bot.*) platycarpous.

platicefalia (*f., Craniol.*) platycephaly.

platicéfalo –la (*adj., Craniol.*) platycephalous; (*m.,f.*) a platycephalic (flat-headed) individual; (*Zool.*) a genus (*Platycephalus*) of sculpinlike mail-cheeked fishes.

platicúrtico –ca (*adj., Statistics*) platykurtic, more flat-topped than the Gaussian curve.

platidáctilo –la (*adj., Zool.*) platydactyl(ous).

platielminte (*m., Zool.*) platyhelminth (flatworm).

platifilo –la (*adj., Bot.*) platyphyllous.

platilobulado –da (*adj., Bot.*) platylobate.

platímetro (*m., Elec.*) platymeter.

platimíscio (*m., Bot.*) macawood (*Platymiscium*).

platina (*f.*) platinum; Birmingham platina; platen (of a printing press, typewriter, planer, etc.); stage of a microscope; set of knives in a shredding machine.

platinado –da (*adj.*) platinized; platinumlike. **loura—**, platinum blonde; (*m.pl., Elec.*) distributor points.

platinador (*m.*) one who platinizes or plates articles.

platinagem (*f.*) platinization.

platinar (*v.t.*) to platinize.

platinato (*m., Chem.*) platinate.

platínico –ca (*adj.*) platinic.

platinífero –ra (*adj.*) platiniferous.

platinirídio (*m.*) platiniridium.

platinita (*f.*) platinite (iron-nickel alloy).

platinorródio (*m.*) platinum-rhodium (thermocouple).

platino –na (*adj.; m.,f.*) = PLATENSE.

platinocianeto (*m., Chem.*) cyanoplatinite.

platinóide (*m.*) platinoid.

platinoso –sa (*adj.*) platinous.

platinotipia (*f., Photog.*) the process of making platinotypes.

platípode (*adj., Zool.*) platypod, broad-footed.

platipodia (*f., Med.*) platypodia, flat-footedness.

platirrinia (*f.*) platyrrhinism.

platirrínico –ca (*adj., Anthropom.*) platyrrhinian.

platirrinos (*m.pl.*) a division (*Platyrrhina*) of American monkeys.

platispermo –ma (*adj., Bot.*) having flat seeds; (*m.*) a flat seed.

platissiliquado –da (*adj., Bot.*) having flat siliques.

platitude (*f.*) platitude.

platnerita (*f.*) plattnerite, lead dioxide.

platô (*m.*) plateau.

platônia (*f., Bot.*) the Guiana orange (*Platonia*).

platônico –ca (*adj.*) Platonic; platonic.

platonismo (*m.*) Platonism.

plausibilidade (*f.*) plausibility.

plausível (*adj.*) plausible.

plebe (*f*.) populace, the common herd; the rabble; the rank and file; mob.
plebeidade [e-i] (*f*.) = PLEBEÍSMO.
plebeísmo (*m*.) plebeianism.
plebeizar [e-i] (*v.t*.) to plebianize.
plebeu –béia (*adj*.; *m.,f*.) plebian.
plebiscitário –ria (*adj*.) plebiscitary; (*m.,f*.) plebiscitarian.
plebiscito (*m*.) plebiscite.
plecopteros (*m.pl., Zool*.) the Plectopera (stone flies).
plecto (*m*.) a genus (*Plectus*) of long-eared bats.
plectógnatos (*m.pl., Zool*.) the Plectognathian order of fishes including the filefishes, globefishes, triggerfishes, trunkfishes and sunfishes.
plectranto (*m*.) the genus of spur flowers (*Plectranthus*).
plectro (*m*.) plectrum.
Plêiade (*f*.) Pleiad; [*not cap*.] pleiad, group of illustrious persons; (*m.pl., Astron*.) the Pleiades.
pleiofilia (*f., Bot*.) pleiophylly.
pleistoceno –na (*adj*.) = PLISTOCENO.
pleiteador –dora, **pleiteante** (*adj*.) pleading (at law), disputing, defending, contesting; (*m.,f*.) litigant; pleader; disputant; contestant; rival; applicant.
pleitear (*v.t*.) to plead (a cause); to argue (a lawsuit); to sue; to go to law against; to contest, dispute; to seek, strive for.—**parelhas a**, to vie with (**em**, in).—**por reeleição**, to campaign for reelection.
pleito (*m*.) plea, suit, cause in contest; dispute; campaign for election.
plenamente (*adv*.) fully, completely, entirely; (*m*.) a grade (mark) of 60 to 90 on a student's examination paper.
plenário –ria (*adj*.) plenary, full, complete. **indulgência**—, (*R.C.Ch*.) plenary indulgence; (*m*.) plenary assembly, session, court, etc.; a jury trial; a jury courtroom.
plenicórneo –a (*adj., Zool*.) plenicorn, solid-horned.
plenidão (*f*.) plenitude.
plenilúnio (*m*.) full moon [= LUA CHEIA].
plenipotência (*f*.) full powers, complete authority.
plenipotenciário –ria (*adj*.; *m.,f*.) plenipotentiary.
plenismo (*m*.) plenism.
plenista (*m.,f*.) plenist.
plenitude (*f*.) plenitude, fullness, completeness; repletion.
pleno –na (*adj*.) full, complete, entire, perfect. **em—mar**, on the high sea. **em—verão**, in the middle of summer. **em—dia**, in the full light of day. **Tenho—certeza**, I am quite sure.
pleocroísmo (*m., Cryst*.) pleochroism.
pleomazia (*f., Anat*.) pleomastia.
pleomorfismo (*m., Bot*.) pleomorphism.
pleonasmo (*m*.) pleonasm, redundancy.
pleonástico –ca (*adj*.) pleonastic, redundant.
pleonasto (*m., Min*.) pleonaste.
pleósporo (*m., Bot*.) a genus (*Pleospora*) of sphere fungi.
pleroma (*m., Bot*.) plerome.
plesiomorfismo (*m., Cryst*.) plesiomorphism.
plesiomorfo –fa (*adj., Cryst*.) plesiomorphous.
plesiossauro (*m*.) plesiosaurus.
plessígrafo (*m., Med*.) plessigraph.
plessímetro, **plessômetro** (*m., Med*.) pleximeter.
pletismógrafo (*m., Physiol*.) plethysmograph.
pletodonte (*m*.) a genus (*Plethodon*) of salamanders.
pletora [tó] (*f*.) plethora, superabundance; overfullness.
pletórico –ca (*adj*.) plethoric, overfull; turgid, inflated.
pleura (*f., Anat., Zool*.) pleura.
pleural (*adj*.) pleural.
pleuris (*m*.), **pleurisia, pleurite** (*f., Med*.) pleurisy.
pleurítico –ca (*adj*.) pleuritic; (*m.,f*.) person suffering from pleurisy.
pleurocapso (*m., Bot*.) a genus (*Pleurocapsa*) of bluegreen algae.
pleurocarpo –pa (*adj., Bot*.) pleurocarpous.
pleurococáceo –a (*adj., Bot*.) pleurococcaceous; (*f.pl*.) the Pleurococcaceae (family of green algae).
pleurodiscal (*adj., Biol*.) pleurodiscous.
pleurodonte (*adj., Zool*.) pleurodont.
pleurógeno –na (*adj., Med*.) pleurogenic.
pleuronéctidas (*f.pl*.) **pleuronectídeos** (*m.pl*.) a family (*Pleuronectidae*) of flatfishes.
pleuropneumonia (*f., Med*.) pleuropneumonia.
plevia (*f*.) riffraff, rabble [= RALÉ].
plexiforme [ks] (*adj*.) plexiform.
plexo [ks] (*m., Anat*.) plexus; network,—**braquial**, brachial plexus.—**cervical**, cervical plexus.—**coróide**,

choroid plexus.—**lombar**, lumbar plexus.—**sacrococcigiano**, sacrococcygean plexus.—**sagrado**, sacral plexus—**solar**, solar plexus.
plica (*f*.) plica; pleat; fold; acute accent mark.
plicação (*f*.) plication; a folding.
plicado –da (*adj*.) plicate; plaited; folded.
plicar (*v.t*.) to plicate; to fold; to pleat.
plicatura (*f*.) plicature, plication; pleat.
Plimude (*f*.) Plymouth.
Plínio (*m*.) Pliny.
plinto (*m., Arch*.) plinth.
pliocênico –ca, **plioceno** –na (*adj*.; *m., Geol*.) Pliocene.
pliofilia (*f., Bot*.) pleiophyly.
pliomeria (*f., Bot*.) pleiomery.
plissagem (*f*.) act or operation of plaiting, pleating, gathering, tucking.
plissar (*v.t*.) to plait, fold, pleat, tuck, crease, crimp.
plissé (*m*.) machine pleating.
plistocênico –ca, **plistoceno** –na (*adj*.; *m., Geol*.) Pleistocene.
ploceidas (*f.pl*.), **ploceídeos** (*m.pl*.) the Ploceidae (family of weaverbirds).
plosão (*f., Phonet*.) plosion, explosion.
plosivo –va (*adj., Phonet*.) plosive, explosive.
ploto (*m*.) = ANHINGA.
pluma (*f*.) plume, feather; writing quill.—**da-pérsia**, (*Bot*.) a tansy (*Tanacetum sauveolens*).—**de-capim** = CAPIM-DOS-PAMPAS.
plumaceiro (*m*.) plumassier, one who prepares or deals in ornamental plumes or feathers.
plumacho, plumaço (*m*.) plumage; plume (ornament).
plumagem (*f*.) plumage.
plumbagina (*f*.) plumbagine, the mineral plumbago; in everyday trade, graphite.
plumbagináceo –cea (*adj., Bot*.) plumbaginaceous; (*f.pl*.) the plumbago family (*Plumbaginaceae*).
plumbaginoso –sa (*adj*.) plumbaginous; plumbean.
plumbago (*f., Bot*.) a genus (*Plumbago*) of leadworts; (*Min*.) graphite.
plumbaria (*f*.) lead work.
plumbato –ta (*adj*.) plumbean, plumbeous; (*m., Chem*.) plumbate.
plumbear (*v.t*.) to render leaden in color or appearance.
plúmbeo –a (*adj*.) plumbeous.
plúmbico –ca (*adj., Chem*.) plumbic.
plumbífero –ra (*adj*.) plumbiferous.
plumboargentífero –ra (*adj*.) containing lead and silver.
plumbocuprífero –ra (*adj*.) containing lead and copper.
plumbojarosita (*f., Min*.) plumbojarosite.
plumboso –sa (*adj*.) plumbous.
plumeria (*f., Bot*.) any frangipani (*Plumeria*)
plumetis (*m*.) plumetis, tambour work (embroidery).
plumilha (*f*.) plumelet.
plumípede (*adj*.) plumiped.
plumista (*m.,f*.) one who prepares or deals in feathers.
plumitivo (*m*.) scribbler; literary hack.
plumoso –sa (*adj*.) plumose, feathered, feathery
plum-pudim (*m*.) plum pudding.
plúmula (*f., Bot*.) plumule.
plumulária (*f., Zool*.) a genus (*Plumularia*) of hydrozoans.
plural (*adj*.; *m*.) plural.
pluralidade (*f*.) plurality.
pluralista (*m.,f*.) pluralist.
pluralização (*f*.) pluralization.
pluralizar (*v.t*.) to pluralize.
pluricelular (*adj., Bot*.) pluricellular.
plurivalente (*adj., Biol*.) plurivalent.
plurivalve (*adj., Bot., Zool*.) plurivalve, multivalve.
plúsia (*f*.) a genus (*Plusia*) of moths.
Plutão (*m*.) Pluto.
Plutarco (*m*.) Plutarch; [*not cap*., *fig*.] a biographer.
plúteo (*m., Arch*.) pluteus.
plutocracia (*f*.) plutocracy.
plutocrata (*m.,f*.) plutocrat.
plutônico –ca (*adj., Geol*.) plutonic.
plutônio –nia (*adj*.) plutonian.
plutonomia (*f*.) political economy.
pluvial (*adj*.) pluvial; (*m*.) raincoat.
pluviátil [-teis] (*adj*.) pluvial.
pluviógrafo (*m*.) pluviograph.
pluviômetro (*m*.) pluviometer, rain gauge.
pluvioscópio (*m*.) pluvioscope, rain.
pluvioso –sa (*adj*.) pluvious, rainy.

P.M.= PREFEITURA MUNICIPAL (Municipal Prefecture); PADRE-MESTRE (Father-Teacher).

p.m.e. = POR MERCÊ ESPECIAL (as a special favor).

p.m.o. = POR MUITO OBSÉQUIO (as a great kindness).

p.m.o.m. = POUCO MAIS OU MENOS (a little more or less).

p.m.p. = POR MÃO PRÓPRIA (by [one's] own hand).

P.N. = PADRE-NOSSO (our Father)

P.N.A.M. = PADRE-NOSSO E AVE-MARIA (Our Father and Hail Mary).

pneodinâmica (*f.*, *Physics*) pneodynamics.

pneometria (*f.*) pneometry.

pneu, short for PNEUMÁTICO (rubber tire).

pneuma (*f.*) pneuma; soul, spirit; a breath, breathing.

pneumático -ca (*adj.*) pneumatic; (*f.*) pneumatics; (*m.*) rubber tire.—**balão**, balloon tire.—**careca** or—**com biscoito comido**, a smooth-worn tire.—**reconstituído**, rebuilt tire.—**sobresselente**, spare tire. **arrebentar um**—, to blow out a tire. **bomba para**—, tire pump. **freio**—, air brake.

pneumatóforo (*m.*, *Zool.*) pneumatocyst; (*Bot.*) pneumatophore.

pneumatógeno -na (*adj.*) pneumatogenous.

pneumatografia (*f.*) pneumatography, spirit writing.

pneumatolise (*f.*, *Petrog.*) pneumatolysis.

pneumatologia (*f.*) pneumatology.

pneumatometria (*f.*) pneumatometry, spirometry.

pneumatoquímico -ca (*adj.*) pneumatochemical.

pneumatoterapia (*f.*) pneumatotherapy.

pneumectomia (*f.*, *Surg.*) pneumonectomy.

pneumobacilo (*m.*, *Bacteriol.*) pneumobacillus.

pneumobrânquio -quia (*adj.*, *Zool.*) dipnoous.

pneumocócico -ca (*adj.*) pneumococcic.

pneumococo (*m.*, *Bacteriol.*) pneumococcus.

pneumodinâmico -ca (*adj.*) pneumodynamic.

pneumogástrico -ca (*adj.*, *Anat.*) pneumogastric; (*m.*) the vagus.

pneumografia (*f.*) pneumography.

pneumográfico -ca (*adj.*) pneumographic.

pneumógrafo (*m.*, *Physiol.*) pneumotograph, stethograph.

pneumologia (*f.*, *Anat.*, *Physiol.*) pneumology.

pneumonia (*f.*, *Med.*) pneumonia

pneumônico -ca (*adj.*) pneumonic; (*m.,f.*) person having pneumonia.

pneumonite (*f.*, *Med.*) pneumonitis; pneumonia.

pneumopiotórax [ks] (*m.*, *Med.*) pneumothorax, pyopneumothorax.

pneumopleurisia, pneumopleurite (*f.*, *Med.*) pneumopleuritis, pleuropneumonia.

pneumoterapia (*f.*, *Med.*) pneumotherapy, pneumatotherapy.

pneumotórax [ks] (*m*, *Med.*) pneumothorax.

pneumotoxina [ks] (*f.*, *Immunol.*) pneumotoxin.

pó (*m.*) powder; dust.—**de arroz**, rice powder; face powder.—**de carvão**, founder's coal blacking.—**de face,—de grês**,—**de polir**, metal-polishing powder, tripoli powder. —**de Goa**, (*Pharm.*) Goa powder.—**de mico**, a general term for the fine hairs found on various plants and pods, and which cause an intense stinging or itching.—**de ouro**, gold dust.—**-de-santana**, (*Bot.*) a medicinal laurel (*Nectandra amara*).—**de zinco**, (*Metal.*) blue powder.— **Royal**, baking powder. **estojo de**—or **porta**—, compact, vanity for the purse. Cf. POALHA, POEIRA.

poa (*f.*) the genus (*Poa*) of bluegrasses or meadow grasses; (*Naut.*) bridle.

poáceo -cea (*adj.*, *Bot.*) poaceous; (*f.pl.*) the grass family (*Poaceae*).

poaia (*f.*) any of various medicinal plants.—**-branca** or —**-do-campo**, Mexican clover (*Richardia scabra*), c.a. IPECACUANHA-ONDULADA, IPECACUANHA-BRANCA.—**-da-praia**, a herb of the violet family (*Hybanthus communis*). —**-de-cipó**' or—**-de-minas** or—**-do-rio**, all syns. for CORAL (*Manettia vine*).—**-de-mato-grosso**, the ipecac (*Cephaelis ipecacuanha*).—**-vermelha** = IPECACUANHA-RUBRA.

poaieiro (*m.*) = TROPEIRO (a bird).

poalha (*f.*) fine dust in the air.

poalho (*m.*) fog, drizzle.

pobre (*adj.*) poor, needy, indigent; unhappy, unfortunate; of soil, barren; (*m.,f.*) beggar, pauper; (*m.*) poor man; (*f.*) poor woman; (*pl.*) the poor.—**como Jó**, as poor as a church mouse.—**de mim!** Poor me!—**diabo**, poor devil; underdog.—**homem**, poor man (to be pitied). **cada vez mais**—, poorer and poorer. **o**—**velho**, the poor (unhappy) old man. **o velho**—, the poor (poverty-stricken)

old man. **os**—**s de espírito**, the poor in spirit; (*colloq.*) the weak-minded (people).

pobretão, -tona (*m.,f.*) very poor person; person who cries poor; poor person who makes a show of not being so poor.

pobrete [brê] (*adj.*) somewhat poor; pitiable; (*m.*) poor devil.

pobreza [brê] (*f.*) poverty, want, destitution; penury, pauperism; paucity; barrenness.—**de espírito**, poorness of spirit.—**de faculdades**, weakmindedness.—**de língua**, poorness (inadequacy) of language.—**de sangue**, anemia. —**evangélica**, voluntary renunciation of worldly goods. —**franciscana**, extreme poverty.—**não é vergonha**, Poverty is no disgrace.

pobrezinho (*m.*), -**nha** (*f.*) poor little thing.

poca (*f.*) a kind of bamboo used in basketry.

poça [ô] (*f.*) shallow pool, pond; puddle.

pocaçu [ú] (*m.*) = POMBA-LEGÍTIMA.

poção (*f.*) potion; deep hole in a lake or river.

poceiro (*m.*) well digger.

pochade (*f.*) rough sketch; quick sketch.

pocilga (*f.*) pig sty; filthy hovel; (*slang*) a "dump" (squalid living quarters).

poço [pô; *pl.*: poços(pó)](*m.*) well; minesha ft.—**artesiano**, artesian well.—**de ciencia** or **de saber**, very learned person (sometimes said ironically).—**de petróleo**, oil well.— **de virtude**, person of great virtue.

poda (*f.*) act or operation of pruning. **fazer a**— to backbite.

podadeira (*f.*) pruning shears (hook, knife).

podador -**dora** (*adj.*) pruning; (*m.,f.*) pruner; trimmer.

podadura (*f.*) = PODA.

podagra (*f.*, *Med.*) podagra, gout in the feet.

podágrico -ca (*adj.*) podagric, gouty.

podagro -**gra** (*adj.*) podagrous, gouty; (*m.,f.*) person having the gout.

podal (*adj.*) podal; pedal.

podálico -ca (*adj.*) podalic.

podão (*m.*) pruning hook; awkward person.

podar (*v.t.*) to prune, clip, trim.

podargo (*m.*, *Zool.*) a genus (*Podargus*) of frogmouths or goatsuckers.

podartro (*m.*, *Zool.*) podarthrum.

pôde, form of PODER [62].

podengo (*m.*) harrier, rabbit hound.

poder [62] (*v.t.*) can, may; to have the power, right, ability, permission, means, etc. to (do a thing); to know how to; to be able to; (*m.*) power, ability, faculty, authority, might; sovereign, ruler; (*pl.* -es) delegated powers to act, power of attorney.—**aquisitivo**, purchasing power (of money).—**calorífico**, calorific value.—**com**, to withstand; to stand up under; to be able to manage; to have influence, control (over someone), as in the expression, **Não posso com êle**, I can't do a thing with him.—**de barganha**, bargaining power.—**de emissão**, heat emissivity. —**libertatório**, (*Econ.*) the inherent power of legal tender in the settlement of obligations. **a**—**de**, with the help of; by dint of; at the expense of. **até mais não**—, to the limit, to the utmost, with might and main. **em meu**—, in my possession (keeping). **Não posso deixar de (rir)**, I can't help (laughing). **O mais depressa que puder**, Just as soon as you can. **Pode entrar**, You may come in. **pode ser que**, it may be that; it maý be true. **Pudera!** No wonder! What do you expect? **Salve-se quem puder!** Every man for himself! **só para quem pode**, only for those who can [afford to]. **Querer é poder**, Where there's a will, there's a way.

poderio (*m.*) power, authority.

poderoso -**sa** (*adj.*) powerful, mighty; forceful; forcible; profound, intense. **todo**—, almighty; (*m.,f.,pl.*) the powerful ones.

pódice (*m.*, *Zool.*) podex.

pódio (*m.*) podium.

podoa (*f.*) = PODADEIRA (pruning knife).

podobrânquio -**quia** (*adj.*, *Zool.*) podobranchial; (*f.*) a podobranch.

podocarpo (*m.*, *Bot.*) any plant of the genus Podocarpus (yew family), c.a. PINHEIRINHO.

podocéfalo -**la** (*adj.*, *Bot.*) podocephalous.

podofiláceas (*f.pl.*, *Bot.*) the barberry family (*Berberidaceae*, syn. Podophyllaceae).

podofilina (*f.*), -**no** (*m.*) podophyllum resin extracted from the rootstock of PODOFILO.

podofilo (*m.*) the May apple or mandrake (*Podophyllum peltatum*).
podofiloso –sa (*adj.*, *Veter.*) podophyllous.
podofilotoxina [ks] (*f.*, *Chem.*) podophyllotoxin.
podoftalmários (*m.pl.*, *Zool.*) the Podophtalmaria (stalk-eyed crustacea).
podógino (*m.*, *Bot.*) podogyn, gynophore.
podologia (*f.*) podology.
podômetro (*m.*) pedometer.
podosperma (*m.*, *Bot.*) podosperm, funiculus.
podostemáceo –cea (*adj.*, *Bot.*) podostemaceous; (*f.pl.*) the riverweed family (*Podostemaceae*).
podostemo (*m.*, *Bot.*) a genus (*Podostemon*) of riverweeds.
podovilite (*f.*, *Veter.*) laminitis, founder.
podre [ô] (*adj.*) putrid, rotten; corrupt, depraved.—de rico, filthy rich; (*m.*) rottenness; (*pl.*) defects; private vices.
podridão (*f.*) putridity; moral corruption, rottenness.
podrido –da (*adj.*) putrid; rotten.
podura (*f.*, *Zool.*) the genus (*Podura*) of snow fleas and springtails.
põe, form of PÔR [63].
poedeira (*adj.*; *f.*) egg-laying (hen).
poeira (*f.*) dust; (*colloq.*) disturbance; turmoil; third-rate theater.—s côsmicas, cosmic dusts.
poeirada (*f.*) cloud of dust.
poeirento –ta (*adj.*) dusty, dust-covered.
poejo [ê] (*m.*) pennyroyal mint (*Mentha pulegium*).—da-praia = CARRAPICHO-RASTEIRO and AMOR-DE-NEGRO.—-do-mato = CORAL (Manettia vine).
poem, form of PÔR [63].
poema (*m.*) poem.
põe-mesa (*m.*) = LOUVA-A-DEUS (praying mantis).
poente (*adj.*; *m.*) setting (sun).
poento –ta (*adj.*) = POEIRENTO.
pões, form of PÔR [63].
poesia (*f.*) poetry, verse.
poeta (*m.*) poet, bard, versifier.—das dúzias or de água doce, poetaster.
poetaço, poetastro (*m.*) poetaster, rhymester.
poético –ca (*adj.*) poetic(al); (*f.*) the art of poetry.
poetisa (*f.*) poetess.
poetizar (*v.i.*,*v.t.*) to poeticize.
pogonia (*f.*) a genus (*Pogonia*) of terrestria orchids.
pogoníase (*f.*, *Med.*) pogoniasis.
pogonologia (*f.*) pogonology.
pogrom (*m.*) pogrom.
poial (*m.*) place where anything is usually put; stone bench; horse block.
poído –da (*adj.*) dust-covered; well-worn; shabby, seedy, threadbare.
poinciana (*f.*) = FLAMBOYANT.
poinsetia (*f.*) = FÔLHA-DA-SANGUE.
pois (*adv.*) since, for, as, because, on this account, seeing that, so.—bem, Very well; Well then; All right.—é, Of course; All right; So it is; That's right; That's it.—é isso mesmo! That's just it!—então, Well then; Of course; There you are! [meaning, "Now you see what I mean."] —não, Certainly; Surely; By all means; Of course; Why not.—que, since, because.—sim, Well, All right; (ironically) Certainly! Of course! Absolutely not! Not much! Oh yeah? Oh sure! I wonder?!
poisar (*v.*) & derivs. = POUSAR & derivs.
poita (*f.*) "a stone attached to a rope, used as an anchor by fishermen." [*GBAT*] Vars: POUTA, PUITÁ, TAUAÇÁ.
poitar (*v.t.*) to anchor (a canoe) while fishing.
poja (*f.*, *Naut.*) clew.
pojadouro (*m.*) top round of beef, c.a. CHÃ-DE-DENTRO. Var. POJADOIRO.
pojar (*v.t.*) to land, disembark.
pôjo (*m.*) landing place; resting place.
pojoji [í] (*m.*) a certain dogfish (*Squalus cornubicus*); a certain harbor porpoise (*Phocaena brasiliensis*).
pol. = POLEGADA(S) = inch(es).
póla (*f.*) beating, trouncing.
polaco –ca (*adj.*) Polack, Polish; (*m.*) a Pole; (*colloq.*) any foreigner who sells house furnishings and other goods on the installment plan; (*f.*) a Polish woman; polonaise (dance, music); (*colloq.*) a Slavic prostitute [in allusion to the many such who formerly came to Brazil from Poland, etc.]
polainas (*f.pl.*) leggings, puttees, gaiters, spats.
polanísia (*f.*) the genus (*Polanisia*) of clammyweeds (caper family).

polar (*adj.*) polar.
polaridade (*f.*) polarity.
polarímetro (*m.*) polarimeter.
polariscópio (*m.*, *Optics*) polariscope.
polarização (*f.*) polarization.
polarizador –dora (*f.*) polarizing; (*m.*,*f.*) polarizer.
polarizar (*v.t.*) to polarize; by ext., to give arbitrary direction to. O novo edifício polariza as atenções, The new building draws all eyes.
polarizável (*adj.*) polarizable.
polca (*f.*) polka.
polcar (*v.i.*) to dance the polka.
poldra (*f.*) filly; (*pl.*) stepping stones.
poldro (*m.*) colt.
polé (*m.*) pulley; hoist.
poleame (*m.*, *Naut.*) block and tackle, tackle.
polegada (*f.*) an inch [= 2.54 centimeters.]
polegar (*m.*) thumb; big toe.
poleiro (*m.*) perch; high position; (*colloq.*) "peanut gallery," "buzzards' roost" (top gallery in a theater).
polemicar (*v.i.*) to engage in polemical controversy.
polêmico –ca (*adj.*) polemic, polemical; (*f.*) polemic, controversy; polemics.
polemista (*adj.*) given to polemics; (*m.*) polemician, polemicist, polemist.
polemístico –ca (*adj.*) polemical.
polemoniáceo –cea (*adj.*, *Bot.*) polemoniaceous; (*f.pl.*) a family (*Polemoniaceae*) comprising, among others, the genera *Polymonium*, *Phlox*, *Gilia* and *Cobaea*.
pólen (*m.*) pollen. Var. POLEM.
polenta (*f.*) Italian porridge.
pólex [ks] (*m.*) = POLEGAR (thumb).
polha (*f.*) pullet.
polhastro (*m.*) cockerel.
polia (*f.*) pulley; sheave, block; larva of the larder beetle and other dermestids; white rust (plant disease) or any fungus of the genus *Albugo* (syn. *Cystopus*) causing this disease.—ajustável, or—de expansão, expanding pulley.—escalonada, stepped pulley.—louca, idle pulley.—motriz, or—acionadora, transmission pulley.
poliacanto –ta (*adj.*) polyacanthus, spiny, thorny; (*m.*, *Bot.*) the Scotch cottonthistle (*Onopordum acanthium*), c.a. ONOPÓRDIO.
poliácido –da (*adj.*, *Chem.*) polyacid.
poliactinários (*m.pl.*, *Zool.*) the actinias and other anthozoa having many simple tentacles.
poliacústico –ca (*adj.*) polyacoustic.
polialito (*m.*, *Min.*) polyhalite.
poliandria (*f.*) polyandry; (*Bot.*) a Linnaean class of polyandrous plants.
poliândrico –ca (*adj.*) polyandric.
poliandro –dra (*adj.*; *f.*) polyandrous (woman, plant).
polianita (*f.*, *Min.*) polianite; pyrolusite.
polianto –ta (*adj.*) multiflorous.
poliarquia (*f.*) polyarchy.
poliatomicidade (*f.*, *Chem.*) polyatomicity.
poliatômico –ca (*adj.*, *Chem.*) polyatomic.
polibásico –ca (*adj.*, *Chem.*) polybasic.
polibasita (*f.*, *Min.*) polybasite.
polibóridas (*f.pl.*), poliborídeos (*m.pl.*, *Zool.*) the family (*Polyborinae*) of caracaras or carrion hawks.
polição (*f.*) act or operation of polishing [= POLIMENTO].
policárpico –ca (*adj.*, *Bot.*) polycarpic, sychnocarpous.
policarpo –pa (*adj.*, *Bot.*) polycarpous.
pólice (*m.*) pollex, thumb [= POLEGAR].
policefalia (*f.*) polycephaly.
policefálico –ca (*adj.*) polycephalic.
policéfalo –la (*adj.*) polycephalous.
policelular (*adj.*) policellular.
policêntrico –ca (*adj.*) polycentric.
polichinelo (*m.*) punchinello, a Punch. segredo de—, something everybody knows but of which only the very credulous make a mystery.
polícia (*f.*) the police; police force; polity, government; (*m.*) a policeman.—inglêsa = ROUXINOL (a bird). delegado de—, chief of police.
policial (*adj.*) police; (*m.*) policeman; (*f.*) policewoman.
policiamento (*m.*) policing.
policiar (*v.t.*) to police, control; (*v.r.*) to control (restrain) oneself.
policíclico –ca (*adj.*) polycyclic.
policilíndrico –ca (*adj.*) multicylinder.
policitação (*f.*, *Law*) unaccepted offer or promise.
policladia (*f.*, *Bot.*) polyclady.

policlínico –ca (*adj.*) pertaining to general, or to urban, practice of medicine; (*m.,f.*) a city physician; a general practitioner of medicine; (*f.*) polyclinic; the practice of general medicine.

policoca (*f., Bot.*) a polycoccous fruit.

policônico –ca (*adj.*) polyconic.

policotiledôneo –a (*adj., Bot.*) polycotyledonous; (*m.*) polycotyledon.

policrase (*f., Min.*) polycrase.

policresto –ta (*adj., Pharm.*) polichrestic.

policróico –ca (*adj., Cryst.*) polychroic, pleochroic.

policroísmo (*m., Cryst.*) pleochroism.

policromático –ca (*adj.*) polychromatic; multicolored.

policromia (*f.*) polychromatism; (*Med.*) polychromia.

policrômico –ca (*adj.*) polychromic, polychromatic.

policromismo (*m.*) polychromatism.

policromo –ma (*adj.*) polychrome, polychromatic.

policrono –na (*adj.*) enduring, long-lasting [=DURADOURO].

policultura (*f.*) mixed farming (as distinguished from one-crop farming).

polidactilia (*f.*) polydactyly, polydactylism.

polidactilismo (*m.*) polydactylism.

polidá[c]tilo –la (*adj., Zool.*) polydactyl.

polidez [ê] (*f.*) politeness, civility, urbanity, good breeding.

polidimite (*f., Min.*) polydymite.

polido –da (*adj.*) polished, burnished, bright; polite, refined, well-bred, well-mannered, well-spoken, urbane, courtly.

polidor –dora (*adj.*) polishing; (*m.,f.*) polisher; (*f.*) polishing machine.

poliédrico –ca (*adj.*) polyhedral.

poliedro (*m.*) polyhedron.

poliembrionia (*f., Bot., Embryol.*) polyembryony.

poliergo (*m.*) a genus (*Polyergus*) of Amazon ants.

polietileno (*m., Chem.*) polyethylene.

polifagia (*f., Med.*) polyphagia.

polifásico –ca (*adj.*) polyphase.

polifilogênese (*f., Biol.*) polyphylogeny.

polifiodentes (*m.pl., Zool.*) polyphyodonts.

polifonia (*f.*) polyphony.

polifônico –ca (*adj.*) polyphonic.

polígala (*f., Bot.*) the genus (*Polygala*) typifying the milkwort family, esp. *P. senega*, the Seneca-snakeroot polygala.

poligaláceo –cea (*adj., Bot.*) polygalaceous; (*f.pl.*) the milkwort family (*Polygalaceae*).

poligálico –ca (*adj., Chem.*) ácido—, polygallic acid.

poligamia (*f.*) polygamy.

poligâmico –ca (*adj.*) polygamic.

poligamista (*adj.; m.,f.*) polygamist.

polígamo –ma (*adj.*) polygamous; (*Bot., Zool.*) polygamous individual.

poligenia (*f.*) polygeny, polygenesis.

poligênico –ca (*adj.*) polygenous; polygenic.

poligenismo (*m.*) polygenism.

poligenista (*adj.; m.,f.*) polygenist.

poliginia (*f.*) polygyny.

polígino –na (*adj.*) polygynous.

poliglota (*adj.; m.,f.*) polyglot.

poliglótico –ca (*adj.*) polyglottic, polyglottous.

poliglotismo (*m.*) polyglottism.

poligonáceo –a (*adj., Bot.*) polygonaceous; (*f.pl.*) the buckwheat family (*Polygonaceae*).

poligonal (*adj.*) polygonal.

polígono –na (*adj.*) polygonal; (*m.*) polygon.—côncavo, convexo, curvilíneo, esférico, inscrito, regular = concave, convex, curvilinear, spherical, inscribed, regular polygon. (*Bot.*) a polygony (and plant of the genus *Polygonum*) esp. the prostrate knotweed (*P. avicular*), c.a. SEMPRE-NOIVA, SANGUINÁRIA, SANGUÍNEA.

poligrafia (*f.*) polygraphy.

polígrafo (*m.*) polygraph; polygrapher.

polilépide (*adj., Bot.*) many-scaled.

polilha (*f.*) spore dust; clothes moth.

polimastia (*f., Anat.*) polymastia.

polimastodonte (*m.*) polymastodon.

polimatia (*f.*) polymathy.

polimato –ta (*adj.*) polymath; (*m.,f.*) polyhistor.

polimentar (*v.t.*) to polish [= POLIR].

polimento (*m.*) act of polishing; patent leather.

polímere (*m., Chem.*) polymer.

polimérico –ca (*adj., Chem.*) polymeric.

polimerismo (*m., Chem.*) polymerism.

polimerização (*m., Chem.*) polymerization.

polimerizar (*v.t.,v.i., Chem.*) to polymerize.

polímetro (*m.*) polymeter.

polimiário –ria (*adj., Zool.*) polymyarian.

polimorfia (*f.*) = POLIMORFISMO.

polimórfico –ca (*adj.*) polymorphic.

polimorfismo (*m., Biol.*) polymorphism; (*Cryst.*) pleomorphism.

polimorfo –fa (*adj.*) polymorphous, polymorphic.

polinário –ria (*adj.*) pollinar.

polinêmidas (*f.pl.*), **polinemídeos** (*m.pl., Zool.*) the Polynemidae (threadfins).

Polinésia (*f.*) Polynesia.

polinésico –ca, **polinésio** –sia (*adj.; m.,f.*) Polynesian.

polínico –ca (*adj.*) pollinic.

polinífero –ra (*adj., Bot.*) polliniferous.

polínio (*f., Bot.*) pollinium, pollen mass.

polinização (*f., Bot.*) pollination.

polinizar (*v.t.*) to pollinate.

polinódio (*m., Bot.*) pollinodium.

polinômico –ca (*adj.*) polynomic, polynomial.

polinômio (*m., Alg.*) polynomial.

polinose (*f., Med.*) polinosis, hay fever.

polinoso –sa (*adj.*) pollinose.

pólio (*m., Bot.*) golden germander (*Teucrium polium*).

polioftalmo –ma (*adj.*) polyommatous, having many eyes.

poliomielite (*f., Med.*) poliomyelitis.—anterior aguda, infantile paralysis.

poliorama (*m.*) polyorama.

poliorquia (*f.*) polyorchidism.

poliose (*f., Chem.*) polyose, polysaccharide.

polipedato (*m.*) tree frog.

polipeiro (*m., Zool.*) polyparia, polypary.

polipetalia (*f., Bot.*) polypetaly.

polipétalo –la (*adj.*) polypetalous.

poliplacóforos (*m.pl., Zool.*) the Polyplacophora (chitons).

polipneico –ca (*adj.*) polypnoeic.

pólipo (*m., Med., Zool.*) polyp.

polipodiáceo –cea (*adj., Bot.*) polypodiaceous; (*f.pl.*) the polypody family (*Polypodiaceae*).

polipódio –dia (*adj.*) having many feet; (*m., Bot.*) a genus of ferns (*Polipodium*), the polypodies.

polipóide (*adj.*) polypous.

poliporáceo –cea (*adj., Bot.*) polyporaceous; (*f.pl.*) the polypores or bracket fungi (*Polyporaceae*).

políporo (*m., Bot.*) a genus (*Polyporus*) of pore fungi.

poliposo –sa (*adj.*) polypous.

poliprisma (*m., Optics*) polyprism.

polir [21b] (*v.t.*) to polish (metal, speech); to polish up, improve; (*v.r.*) to take on a polish.—as arestas, to smooth over matters. uma frase polida, a well-turned sentence.

polirrítmico –ca (*adj.*) polyrhythmic.

polirrizo –za (*adj., Bot.*) polyrhizal.

poliscópio (*m., Optics*) polyscope.

polispermia (*f., Med.*) polyspermia; (*Biol.*) polyspermy.

polispermo –ma (*adj., Bot.*) polyspermous.

polísporo –ra (*adj., Bot.*) polyspored, polysporic.

polissacáride (*f., Chem.*) polysaccharide.

polissaco (*m., Bot.*) the earth-balls (*Polysaccum*).

polissépalo –la (*adj., Bot.*) polysepalous.

polissilábico –ca (*adj.*) polysyllabic(al).

polissilabismo (*m.*) polysyllabism.

polissílabo –ba (*adj.; m.,f.*) polysyllable.

polissíndeto[n] (*m., Rhet.*) polysyndeton.

polissulfeto (*m., Chem.*) polysulphide.

polistêmone, polistêmono –na (*adj., Bot.*) polystemanous.

polístico (*m.*) a genus (*Polystichum*) of polypodiaceous ferns.

polistilo –la (*adj.; m., Arch.*) polystyle.

polistireno (*m., Chem.*) polystyrene resin.

polisto (*m., Zool.*) a genus (*Polistes*) of social wasps.

polístomo –ma (*adj., Zool.*) polystomatous.

politeama (*m.*) a variety theatre.

politecnia (*f.*) technology.

politécnico –ca (*adj.*) polytechnic(al); (*f.*) polytechnic school.

politéico –ca (*adj.*) polytheistic.

politeísmo (*m.*) polytheism.

politeísta (*adj.; m.,f.*) polytheist.

politeístico –ca (*adj.*) polytheistic(al).

politelia (*f., Anat.*) polythelia.

politeno (*m., Chem.*) polythene (plastic).

política (f.) politics; political science; polity; astuteness, cunning; civility.
politicagem, politicalha (f.) petty politics; political gang.
politicalhão (m.) politicaster; petty politician.
politicalheiro -ra (adj.) given to petty politics.
politicalho (m.) petty politician.
politicante (adj.) given to petty politics; (m.) petty politician.
politicão (m., colloq.) political big shot.
politicar (v.i.) to politicize.
politicaria (f.) petty politics.
politicastro (m.) politicaster.
político -ca (adj.) political; politic; (m.,f.) politician.
político-econômico -ca (adj.) politico-economical.
politicóide (m.) a hack politico.
politicomania (f.) politicomania.
político-religioso -sa (adj.) politico-religious.
político-social (adj.) politico-social.
politicote (m.) minor politician.
politipar (v.t., Print.) to produce a polytype of.
politipo (m., Print.) polytype.
politiquear (v.i.) to engage in politics; to play politics.
politiqueiro -ra (adj.) given to "politicking"; (m.) petty politician.
politiquete [quê] (m.) minor politician.
politiquice (f.) petty politics or an instance thereof.
politiquilho (m.) politicaster.
politiquismo (m.) petty politics.
politista (m.) partisan politician; professional politician.
politização (f.) politicizing.
politizar (v.t.) to politicize; to train in politics; to bring within the sphere of politics; (v.r.) to become politically aware.
polítomo -ma (adj., Bot.) polytomous.
politonalidade (f., Music) polytonality.
polítono -na (adj.) polytonal.
politriceáceas (f.pl.) a family (Polytrichaceae) of mosses.
polítrico -ca (adj., Zool.) polytrichous; (m., Bot.) the genus (Polytrichum) of haircap mosses.
poliúria, poliuria (f., Med.) polyuria.
polivalente (adj., Chem.) multivalent.
polizóico -ca (adj., Zool.) polyzoic.
polizonada -da (adj.) polyzonal.
polizonite (f., Petrog.) polzenite.
polmo [pôl] (m.) cloudiness (of a liquid).
polo, archaic form of PELO.
pôlo (m.) young kite or hawk.
pôlo (m.) pole (extremity of an axis), [But not an ordinary pole (long, round piece of wood), which is VARA, POSTE, VAREJÃO, MAROMBA, LANÇA.] magnetic pole; (Sports) polo.—**antártico** or **sul** or **austral**, South Pole.—**aquático**, water polo.—**ártico** or **norte** or **boreal**, North Pole.—**negativo (positivo)**, negative (positive) pole.—**magnético**, magnetic pole.
polonês -nesa (adj.) Polish; (m.) Pole; (f.) Polish woman; (Music) polonaise; polonaise (garment). Cf. POLACO.
Polônia (f.) Poland.
polônio (m., Chem.) polonium; also = POLACO,
polpa [ô] (f.) pulp, soft mass.—**de sulfato**, sulphate pulp.
polpação (f.) operation of reducing (wood, etc.) to pulp.
polposo -sa (adj.) pulpy; plump, fleshy.
polpudo -da (adj.) pulpy; of a business, yielding fat profits.
poltrão -trona (adj.) cowardly; (m.) poltroon, craven.
poltrona (f.) armchair, easy chair; an orchestra seat; (adj.) fem. of POLTRÃO.
poltronaria (f.) poltroonery, cowardice.
poltronear (v.i.) to act the coward; (v.r.) to lounge (in an easy chair).
polução (f.) pollution, esp. in the medical sense.
poluição [u-i] (f.) pollution; defilement.
poluir [72] (v.t.) to pollute; to defile; to taint.
poluto -ta (adj.) polluted; defiled.
polvilhação (f.), **polvilhamento** (m.) dusting, spraying.
polvilhadeira (f.) sprayer; duster.
polvilhar (v.t.) to powder, besprinkle; to dust, spray (insecticides, etc.).
polvilho (m.) tapioca; cassava starch; any fine powder.
polvo [pôl] (m.) octopus.
pólvora (f.) gun powder; a tiny midge or gnat; gun powder tea; (Bot.) a bulrush (Scirpus mucronatus).—**sem fumaça**, smokeless powder.
polvorada (f.) blast of gun powder; powder smoke.

polvoraria (f.) powder factory.
polvorento -ta (adj.) pulverulent.
polvorinho (m.) powder horn.
polvoroso -sa (adj.) powdery; dusty; (f., colloq.) commotion, stir, bustle; uproar.
poma (f.) woman's breast. Cf. POMO.
pomacêntridas (f.pl.), **pomacentrídeos** (m.pl.) the Pomacentridae (damselfishes).
pomacentro (m.) a genus (Pomacentrus) of damselfishes.
pomáceo -cea (adj., Bot.) pomaceous.
pomada (f.) pomade, pomatum; salve, ointment; lie; flattery, "soft soap"; vanity. **cheio de—s**, full of airs.
pomadear (v.i.) to put on airs.
pomadista (m.) coxcomb; liar.
pomar (m.) orchard.
pomaré = PUNARÉ (rat).
pomareiro (m.) orchardist.
pomatômidas (f.pl.), **pomatomídeos** (m.pl.) the Pomatomidae (bluefishes).
pomba (f.) any female dove or pigeon. Cf. POMBO.—**-amargosa**, the plumbeous pigeon (Columba p. plumbea), c.a. POMBA-DE-SANTA-CRUZ, POMBA-PRETA, CAÇUIROVA, PICACUROBA.—**cabocla** = JURITI-PIRANGA.—**cascavel**, the scaled dove (Scardafella squammata), c.a. FOGO-APAGOU, POMBA-CARIJÓ.—**de-bando** or—**de-arribação**, the Paraguayan eared dove (Zenaidura auriculata chrysauchenia), c.a. POMBA-DO-SERTÃO, ARRIBAÇÃO, ARRIBAÇÃ, AVOANTE, RABAÇA, REBAÇA, RIBAÇÃ, PARARI, PAIRIRI, BAIRAI, MURITI-CARREGADEIRA, CARDIGUEIRA, CARDINHEIRA.—**de-leque**, fantail pigeon.—**do-cabo**, the Cape pigeon (Daption capensis), c.a. FREIXAS-FRADINHO.—**espêlho**, Geoffroy's dove (Claravis godefrida), c.a. POMBA-AZUL, PARURU, POMBA-PARURU.—**legítima**, the southern rufous pigeon (Columba cayennensis sylvestris), c.a. POMBA-DO-AR, POMBA-GALEGA, POMBA-GEMEDEIRA, POMBA-DE-SANTA-CRUZ, POMBA-VERDADEIRA, CAÇAROBA, CAÇUIROBA, PICUÇAROBA, SAROVA, SAROBA, POCAÇU, PUCAÇU.—**de-papo-de-vento**, pouter pigeon.—**pedrês**, the scaled pigeon (Columba speciosa), c.a. POMBA-TROCAL, PIRAÚ.—**rôla** = ROLINHA.—**trocaz**, the Picazuro pigeon (Columba p. picazuro), c.a. ASA-BRANCA, JACAÇU.
pombal (m.) dovecote.
pombeira (f.) fiddlewood tree (Citharexylum), c.a. PAU-DE-VIOLA; an anchor [= ÂNCORA].
pombeiro (m.) Indian trader; slave trader; headman of bearers on an expedition; stool pigeon; chicken peddler; fish peddler.
pombinha (f.) a little dove or pigeon; rump of beef; (colloq.) the female pudenda; (f.pl.) the butterfly orchids (Oncidium).—**cascavel**, the scaled dove (Scardafella squammata), c.a. POMBA-CARIJÓ, POMBA-CASCAVEL, FOGO-APAGOU.—**das-almas** (Zool.) the gray pepoaza (Xolmis cinerea), c.a. MOCINHA-BRANCA, MARIA-BRANCA, MARIA-É-DIA, PRIMAVERA; the widow pepoaza (Xolmis irupero), c.a. VIÚVA, NOIVINHA; the veiled pepoaza (Xolmis velata), c.a. LAVADEIRA, MOCINHA-BRANCA.
pombinho (m.) dim. of POMBO; (adj.) designating a certain type of wheat.
pombo (m.) male pigeon, dove.—**anambé** = ANAMBÉ-AÇU.—**correio** or **-volante** or **-mensageiro**, carrier (homing) pigeon. Cf. POMBA.
pomicultor (m.) pomiculturist, fruitgrower.
pomicultura (f.) pomiculture, fruitgrowing.
pomífero -ra (adj.) pomiferous.
pomiforme (adj.) pomiform, apple-shaped.
pomo (m.) any pome, esp. an apple; pommel; a woman's breast [Poetical].—**da espada**, sword hilt.—**de-adão**, Adam's apple, c.a. GOGÓ.—**de discórdia**, apple of discord, bone of contention; sore subject.—**do-elefante**, elephant apple (Feronia elephantum).—**proíbido** or **vedado**, forbidden fruit.
pomologia (f.) pomology.
pomológico -ca (adj.) pomological.
pomólogo (m.) pomologist.
pompa (f.) pomp, display, ostentation; pride.
pompeante (adj.) ostentatious.
pompear (v.i.) to flaunt, show off, display ostentatiously.
pompilídeos (m.pl., Zool.) the Pompilidae (burrowing wasps).
pompílio (m.) a genus of wasps (Pompilus) which comprises the tarantula killer.
pompom (m.) pompon; powder puff.
pomposidade (f.) pomposity.

pomposo –sa (*adj.*) pompous, showy, ostentatious; high-sounding; self-important.

pômulo (*m.*) cheek.

ponche (*m.*) punch (beverage); also = PONCHO.

poncheira (*f.*) punch bowl.

poncho (*m.*) poncho; duster (coat).—**dos pobres**, the sun. —**-pala**, a light poncho. **forrar o**—, to line one's pockets. **pisar no**—, fig., to step on another's toes. **por baixo do**—, under the table (in secret). **sacudir o**—, to taunt; fig., to wave a red flag.

ponciana-régia (*f.*) the Royal Poinciana or flamboyant tree (*Delonix regia*), c.a. FLAMBOYANT.

Pôncio (*m.*) Pontius.

ponde, form of PÔR [63].

ponderação (*f.*) act of pondering; careful consideration; deliberation; a well-considered statement.

ponderado –da (*adj.*) considerate, thoughtful, sober, sedate, judicious, deliberate; weighted.

ponderador –dora (*adj.*) pondering; (*m.,f.*) one who ponders, thinks carefully.

ponderar (*v.t.*) to ponder, consider, weigh; to express a considered opinion; to make a thoughtful statement; to weight (statistical data); (*v.i.*) to meditate, muse.

ponderável (*adj.*) ponderable; appreciable; weighable.

ponderoso –sa (*adj.*) ponderous, weighty; important, significant, momentous.

pondo, gerund of PÔR [63].

pônei (*m.*) pony.

ponente (*adj.*) positing; of sun, setting [= POENTE]; (*m.*) western wind.

ponga (*f.*) a thrush (*Turdus rufiventris*).

pongar (*v.i.*) to hop on a moving streetcar.

pongo (*m.*) a stretch of river flowing between high walls; a chimpanzee.

pongueró (*m.*) the India coralbean (*Erythrina indica*).

ponh+verb endings = forms of PÔR [63].

ponjê (*m.*) pongee.

ponta (*f.*) point, sharp end, tip, extreme end; bit, small piece; brad, tack; bit part in a play; (*Elec.*) point; (*pl.*) headwaters. Cf. PONTO.—**de cigarro**, cigarette butt.—**de fuga**, vanishing point.—**de lança**, a bluestem grass (*Andropogon glaucescens*).—**de linha**, end of the line, last stop.—**de Paris**, finishing nail.—**de terra**, point of land. —**-direita**, (*Soccer*) right-end (position or player).—**do nariz**, tip of the nose.—**do pé**, tiptoe.—**dos trilhos**, railhead.—**-esquerda**, (*Soccer*) left-end (position or player). —**limpa**, fully developed horn.—**negra** or **preta**, a certain shark (*Carcharias limbatus*).—**sêca**, dry point (needle, engraving, print).—**troncha**, ear slit, earmark. **à**—**de faca**, strictly, sternly, inflexibly. **andar na**—, to look spruce. **até a**—**dos cabelos**, up to one's ears (or neck); to the limit. **de**—**a**—, from end to end. **estar na**—, to be outstanding. **fazer uma**—, to play a minor role. **na**—**da língua**, on the tip of one's tongue. **na**—**do nariz**, before one's very nose. **na**—**dos dedos**, fig., with great care. **na**—**da unha**, very quickly.

pontaço (*m.*) blow struck with the end of a stick, gun, etc.

pontada (*f.*) twinge, stitch; neuralgia; act of taking a sewing stitch.

pontal (*m.*) spit of land, (*Shipbldg.*) molded depth; depth of hold.

pontalête (*m.*) prop, stay, stanchion, strut, brace.

pontão (*m.*) prop, stay; punt, flatboat; pontoon; small highway bridge; steel lighter (on the Amazon).

pontapé (*m.*) a kick (by a person; the same by an animal is PATADA); fig., offense; blow, reverse, setback; an act of ingratitude. **dar (um)**—**em**, (*colloq.*) to spurn.

pontar (*v.t.*) = APONTAR; (*v.i.*) to work as a (theater) prompter.

pontaria (*f.*) aim, sight; target; act of aiming, sighting, pointing. **dormir na**—, to take slow aim. **fazer**—, to aim (at).

ponte (*f.*) bridge; dental bridge; (*Naut.*) bridge deck; (*Elec.*) jumper; bridge.—**abobadada** or **arqueada**, arch bridge.—**aérea**, air shuttle service.—**com arco de aço**, steel arch bridge.—**de aço**, steel bridge.—**de barcas**, pontoon bridge; bit part in a play.—**de cavaletes**, trestle.—**de concreto armado**, concrete arch bridge.—**de desembarque**, gang plank.—**de traves de aço**, steel truss bridge.—**de varólio**, (*Anat.*) pons Varolii. —**de Wheatstone**, (*Elec.*) W. bridge.—**do comando**, ship's bridge.—**flutuante** or—**de pontões**, pontoon bridge.—**levadiça**, lift bridge, drawbridge.—**pênsil** or **suspênsa**, suspension bridge.—**rolante**, gantry, traveling

crane.—**romana**, masonry arch bridge. **cabeça** or **testa de**—, bridgehead. **vão de uma**—, bridge span.

pontear (*v.t.*) to dot; to baste, stitch; to finger (a musical instrument); (*v.i.*) of a cowboy, to ride at the head of a herd.

pontederiáceo –a (*adj., Bot.*) pontederiaceous; (*f.pl.*) the pickerelweed family (*Pontederiaceae*).

ponteiro –ra (*adj.*) leading, in front; of wind, head; of a hunting dog, disobedient; of a gun, poorly balanced; (*m.*) one who rides at the head of a herd [= CHAMADOR]; pointer (rod); point chisel; puncheon; plectrum; hand (of a clock); (*f.*) tip (as of a cane or umbrella); cigar or cigarette holder [= BOQUILHA]; snapper on the end of a whip; the third or last picking of cotton.

pontel [-téis] (*m.*, *Glass mfg.*) punty, pontee.

pontiagudo –da (*adj.*) sharp; pointed (like a needle).

pontícula (*f.*) a small bridge.

pontificação (*f.*) pontification.

pontificado (*m.*) pontificate.

pontifical (*adj.; m.*) pontifical.

pontificar (*v.t.,v.i.*) to pontificate; (*v.i.*) to pontify.

pontífice (*m.*) pontiff; (*colloq.*) one who plays the pontiff. **Sumo**—, supreme pontiff, the Pope.

pontilha (*f.*) sharp point; narrow gold or silver braid; lace edging; trifle; bullfighter's dagger.

pontilhão (*m.*) a small bridge.

pontilhar (*v.t.*) to dot. **linha pontilhada**, dotted line. **pontilhado de**, dotted with.

pontilhoso –sa (*adj.*) punctilious; strait-laced; touchy.

pontinha [dim. of PONTA] (*f.*) a small point or end; trifle; a touch of anger, jealousy, etc. **da**—, (*slang*) "super," tops.

pontinho [dim. of PONTO] (*m.*) a small stitch, point, dot etc.; (*pl.*) ellipsis [. . .].

pontino –na (*adj.*) Pontine.

ponto (*m.*) point; point at issue, subject-matter; stitch; dot; small round spot; period (punctuation mark); small patch of adhesive plaster; vanishing point (in perspective); site, place; degree, state; end, limit; (*Music*) fret; meeting point; time book; punctilio; (*Theater*) prompter. Cf. PONTA.—**a jour**, hemstitch.—**adiante**, the next stitch.—**anaclástico**, (*Physics*) anaclastic point.—**atrás**, the stitch before this one.—**central**, central meeting point.—**crítico**, critical point.—**culminante**, highest point.—**da questão**, the point at issue.—**de admiração**, or **de exclamação**, exclamation mark [!].—**de apoio**, (*Mech.*) bearing point, point of support, fulcrum; (*Milit.*) point d'appui.—**de brio**, point of honor.—**de cabelo**, point at which a stream of sirup threads.—**de cadeia**, chain stitch.—**de casa**, buttonhole stitch.—**de combustão**, fire point; burning point; ignition point.—**de congelação** or **de congelamento**, freezing point.—**de contacto**, point of contact.—**de destino**, destination point.—**de ebulição**, boiling point.—**de espadana**, point at which a stream of sirup falls in a ribbon.—**de fusão**, melting point.—**de honra**, point of honor.—**de incidência**, the vertex of the angle of incidence.—**de ignição**, ignition point.—**de inflamabilidade**, flash point. —**de inflexão**, (*Arch. & Engin.*) inflection point, point of contraflexure.—**de interrogação**, question mark [?]. —**de intersecção**, point of intersection.—**de liquefação**, point of liquefaction.—**de marca**, cross stitch.—**de margarida**, loop stitch.—**de mira**, gunsight.—**de ossificação**, (*Physiol.*) center of ossification.—**de parada**, bus (train, streetcar) stop.—**de partida**, point of departure, starting point.—**de pérola**, point at which cane sirup begins to bubble.—**de rebuçado**, the density at which a boiling sirup will form sugar crystals; fig., point of perfection.—**de referência**, point of reference; landmark.— **de rocio**, dew point.—**de saturação**, saturation point.— **de secção**, boundary of a bus or streetcar fare zone.—**de suspensão**, point of suspension.—**de sustentação**, point of support.—**de vista**, point of view viewpoint.— **decimal**, decimal point.—**e virgula**, semi-colon [;].—**em branco**, (*Gunnery*) point-blank.—**falso**, sticking plaster. —**final**, end; period [.].—**fraco**, -foible, weakness.— **-limite**, (*Math.*) limit point.—**morto**, dead center; (*Mach.*) upper or lower dead center (of a piston); (*Radio*) dead spot.—**múltiplo**, (*Geom.*) multiple point.—**negro**, black cloud (lit. & fig.).—**por**—, point by point.— **rematado**, hemstitch.—**s cardiais**, cardinal points (of the compass).—**s de reticência**, suspension points [. . .].—**s equinociais**, equinoctial points (vernal, autumnal).—**s estratégicos**, (*Milit.*) strategic points.—

singular, (*Math.*) singular point.—s **naturais**, (*Surg.*) stitches.—s **solticiais**, solsticial points (summer, winter).—**vernal**, vernal equinox.—**vertical**, zenith. **a**—, pointedly; exactly; opportunely. **a (ao)**—**de**, almost, nearly; to (on) the point of; on the verge of; within an ace of. **a**—**que**, so much that; to the point that. **às dez em**—, at ten sharp. **assinar o**—, to sign in on arriving for work (esp. at a Govt. office). **até certo**—, to a certain extent; to a degree. **dar**—**s**, to take stitches. **de**—**em branco**, with great care, accuracy, etc. **dois**—**s**, colon [:]. **dormir no**—, to fall asleep at the switch; to sleep on the job. **em**—, on the dot, exactly on time, punctually. **em algum**, at no point. **em**—**pequeno**, on a small scale. **em bom**—, just right. **entregar os**—**s**, to throw in the sponge, quit, give up. **fazer**—**em**, to hang out at (frequent) a given place. **marcar o**—, to keep score. **não dar**—**sem nó**, to do nothing without an ulterior or selfish motive. **no mesmo**—, at the same moment. **pôr os**—**s nos ii**, to dot the i's (and cross the t's). **sair fora do**—, to digress, stray from the subject. **sob o**—**de vista de**, from the standpoint of. **subir de**—, to increase (go up) a point.
pontoada (*f.*) a jab, as with a cane or umbrella.
pontoneiro (*m.*) pontoon builder.
pontoso -**sa** (*adj.*) punctilious.
pontuação (*f.*) punctuation.
pontual (*adj.*) punctual; prompt; punctilious; precise.—**como um relógio**, as regular as clockwork.
pontualidade (*f.*) punctuality; scrupulosity.
pontuar (*v.t.*) to punctuate.
pontudo -**da** (*adj.*) pointed, sharp; aggressive.
ponxirão (*m.*) = MUXIRÃO.
pôpa (*f.*) poop, stern. **à**—, aft. **de proa à**—, fore and aft; from stem to stern. **motor de**—, outboard motor. **vento em**—, tail wind.
popelina (*f.*) poplin.
poperi [í] (*m.*) shack in which newly-gathered rubber latex is smoked.
popinha (*f.*) = COTOVIA.
poplíteo -**tea** (*adj., Anat.*) popliteal.
popocar (*v.t.,v.i.*) to pop, crack, explode (as fireworks). Cf. PIPOCAR.
populaça (*f.*) populace, rabble, riffraff, mob.
população (*f.*) population.
populacho (*m.*) = POPULAÇA.
popular (*adj.*) popular, of the people; approved, admired (by the people); common, prevailing, current; (*m.*) an everyday citizen, a man of the people.
popularidade (*f.*) popularity.
populário (*m.*) folklore; popular music, poetry, legends, amusements, etc.
popularizar (*v.t.*) to popularize; (*v.r.*) to become popular.
populina (*f., Chem.*) populin.
populista (*adj.; m.*) populist.
populoso -**sa** (*adj.*) populous, thickly settled, crowded.
pôquer (*m.*) poker (the card game).
por (*prep.*) by, for, per, through. [Do not confuse with the verb PÔR.] Cf. PELA, PELO.—**acaso**, perchance, by chance.—**aí**, thereabout.—**aí além**, out there somewhere; out of this world.—**alí**, that way; there somewhere.—**alta noite**, late at night.—**alto**, superficially; without entering into details.—**amor de**, for the love (sake) of.—**amor de Deus**, for God's sake.—**ano**, per year; yearly.—**antecipação**, in anticipation of.—**aqui**, around here; this way.—**aqui assim**, around this way.—**artes de berliques e berloques**, magically, miraculously.—**artes do diabo**, through devilish bad luck.—**assim dizer**, if one may so say; so to speak; almost, more or less.—**atacado**, wholesale.—**baixo (de)**, under, underneath, below, beneath.—**baixo de mão**, underhandedly.—**banda**, on each side.—**bem**, willingly, gladly.—**bem ou por mal**, willingly or not; willy-nilly.—**bem ou por força**, willy-nilly.—**cá**, over here.—**causa de**, because of, by reason of; on account of.—**certo**, surely, certainly.—**cima (de)**, on top of, above, over.—**cima do ombro**, over one's shoulder, disdainfully.—**cinco dias**, for (during) five days.—**comparação com**, in comparison with.—**conseguinte**, consequently; therefore.—**costume**, customarily; habitually.—**dá cá aquela palha**, for a trifling reason or for none at all.—**demais**, vainly, uselessly.—**dentro (de)**, inside (of).—**derradeiro**, lastly, finally, in the last place.—**desazo**, through carelessness; for want of skill.—**descargo de alma**, or **de consciência**, for the sake of one's peace of mind (soul, conscience).—**descuido**, inadvertently; through neglect; through carelessness.—

desenfado, or **desfastio**, for amusement; as a pastime; for fun.—**despedida**, in conclusion; as a last word.—**detrás (de)**, behind; in back (of).—**Deus!** in God's name!—**dia**, per day; by the day.—**diante**, thenceforth; in front.—**enquanto**, yet, still, so far, for the time being.—**entre**, among, between, through.—**escala**, in turn, by turns.—**especial favor**, by courtesy of (the one who delivers a letter, etc.).—**essas e por outras**, for these and other reasons.—**excelência**, par excellence.—**exemplo**, for example; for instance.—**extenso**, in full (without abbreviation).—**extremo**, extremely, exceedingly.—**falar em** (. . .), speaking of (. . .).—**fas ou nefas**, willy-nilly.—**fazer**, still to be done.—**fim**, at last.—**fora (de)**, out, outside (of); without.—**força**, perforce; willingly or unwillingly; needs must.—**gôsto**, voluntarily; gladly.—**graça de Deus**, by the grace of God.—**graus**, gradually, step by step.—**grosso**, in large quantity; wholesale.—**hipótese**, hypothetically, theoretically, supposedly.—**hoje**, for today.—**honra da firma**, noblesse oblige.—**igual**, equally.—**instinto**, instinctively.—**inteiro**, in full, wholly, completely, totally.—**intenção de**, (*R.C.Ch.*) [mass, prayers, etc.] for the special intention of (a particular purpose or person).—**interposta pessoa**, through another person; indirectly.—**intervalos**, at intervals.—**isso (que)**, therefore; that's why; for that reason; because.—**isso mesmo**, for that very reason.—**junto**, wholesale; altogether; all at once.—**largo (or longo) tempo**, for (during) a long time.—**maioria de razão**, for impelling reasons.—**mais que**, however much; howsoever.—(or de) **mão de**, by the hand of.—**mar**, by sea.—**mares nunca dantes navegados**, over seas never before sailed.—**meio de**, by means of.—**menores**, minutely, in detail.—**menos de**, for less than.—**meu mal**, unluckily for me.—**meus pecados**, in punishment of me.—**milagre**, unaccountably, unexplainably.—**milhares**, by the thousands.—**minha vida**, upon my soul (I swear).—**miúdo**, in detail.—(or de) **modo que**, so; so that.—**momentos**, for the moment.—**muito que**, however long; however much; no matter how much.—**muitos anos**, for (during) many years.—**nada**, barely; almost; also: Don't mention it (in reply to a thank-you).—**natureza**, by nature.—**ocasião de**, on the occasion of; at the time that.—**onde**, where; along which.—**ordem**, in orderly fashion.—**ordem de**, by order of.—**outra**, in other words; that is.—(or de) **outro lado**, on the other hand.—**partes**, specifically, in detail.—**perto (de)**, near (to), close (to).—**pessoa**, per person.—**piedade**, for mercy's sake; for pity's sake; for heaven's sake.—**pouco** (or—**pínculas**), nearly, almost.—**preço arrastado**, dirt cheap.—**qualquer preço** (or, **a todo o preço**), at any price.—**quanto**, see PORQUANTO.—**que**, see PORQUE and PORQUÊ.—**rico que seja**, não gosto dêle, However (no matter how) rich he is (may be), I don't like him.—**seca e meca**, from place to place; hither and yon.—**seu turno**, in (his, her, your) turn.—**si**, by oneself.—**sistema**, systematically; habitually.—**sob**, under, underneath.—**sôbre**, upon; over and above.—**sua alta recreação**, spontaneously; for fun.—**sua vez**, in turn.—**tabela**, used in the expression jogar por tabela, meaning to make indirect or oblique reference to someone or something.—**tamina**, a little at a time.—**terra**, by land.—**último**, lastly.—**um ápice**,—**um tris**,—**uma linha**,—**uma mão travessa**,—**uma unha negra**,—**um erre**,—**um és-não-és**, are all expressions meaning within an ace of, within an inch of, within a hair of.—**um fio**, by a thread; almost.—(or de) **um lado**, on one side.—**ventura**, perchance.—**vezes**, at times (same as às vezes).—**via de**, through; by means of.—**via de regra**, as a general rule; usually.—**vias indiretas**, by shady means.—(or em) **virtude de**, by virtue of.—**volta de**, around (near in time). [Por volta das onze, around eleven o'clock.] **A gente nunca sabe o que está**—**acontecer**. One never knows what's going to (what is about to) happen. **aí**—, about; thereabout. **apaixonado**—**ela**, crazy about her. **duas vezes**—**ano**, twice a year. **estar**—(**alguma coisa**), to be for, in favor of (something). **lá**—**baixo**, down over (around) there. **lá**—**cima**, up over (around) there. **nem**—**isso**, not even so. **palavra**—**palavra**, word by word. **pôr**—**escrito**, to put in writing. **tomar**—**tema**, to take as a theme. **um**—**um**, one by one.
pôr [63] (*v.t.*) to place, put, set, (em, sôbre, on); to don, put on (apparel of any kind); (*v.i.*) to lay (eggs); (*v.r.*) to put (place) oneself; of the sun, to set; (*m.*) setting (of the sun). [Do not confuse with prep. POR.] Cf. BOTAR, COLOCAR, METER.—**a bôca em**, to touch with the lips; to

speak ill of.—**a bôca no mundo**, to cry, shout, yell, holler, scream; to lie; to malign (someone).—**a calva à mostra**, (*colloq.*) to show up, expose, unmask (another person). —**acima de tôda prova**, to place (something) beyond all doubt.—**a coberto**, to shelter, protect.—**a culpa em**, to lay the blame on.—**a descoberto**, to uncover, lay bare. —**à disposição de**, to place at the disposal of.—(or **passar**) **à espada**, to put to the sword.—**a esperança em**, to place hope in.—**a faca ao peito**, to intimidate by force or threats.—**a ferros**, to put in irons.—**a língua de môlho**, to fall silent (usually in shame or repentance).—**a mão em**, to touch, place the hand on.—**a mão no fogo por**, to go to bat for; to vouch for.—**a mesa**, to set (lay) the table.—**à morte**, to put to death.—**a navalha na cara**, (*colloq.*) to shave.—**a nu**, to lay bare (facts, etc.).—**a panela no fogo**, to place the pot on the fire.—**a pão e água**, to put on bread and water.—**a pão e laranja**, to place on a starvation diet; to ill-treat.—**a pedra no sapato de**, to arouse suspicion in.—**a pique**, to send (a ship) to the bottom.—**a preço a cabeça de**, to put a price on another's head.—**a proa em**, to sail for.—**a pulga atrás da orelha de**, to arouse suspicion in.—**à rasa**, to malign.—**a saco**, or **a saque**, to sack, plunder.—**a salvo**, to place in safety, out of danger; to salvage; to save.— **à sombra**, [*humorous*] to put in the shade, i.e., in jail.—**a venda**, to place on sale.—**a vida a preço**, to risk one's life.—**à vista**, to make visible, clear.—**água na fervura**, to pour oil on troubled waters.—**ao ar**, to air; to give the air to.—**ao corrente**, to put (someone) au courant.—**ao fato**, to give the facts to.—**ao pescoço**, to place (a scarf, etc.) around the neck.—**aos cuidados de**, to entrust (someone) with.—**as armas em sarilho**, to stack arms.— **as barbas de môlho**, to take precautions against.—**as cartas na mesa**, to lay one's cards on the table.—**as esperanças em**, to place hopes in.—**as mãos**, to place one's hands together (in supplication).—**as mãos em**, to lay hands on.—**as mãos no fogo por**, to swear by (someone).—**as raizes ao sol**, to root up (weeds, etc.).—**as tripas pra fora**, to be sick as a dog.—**atalho**, to impede, bar.—**banda**, to don officer's stripes.—**casa**, to set up housekeeping.—**cêrco** (or **sítio**), to surround, lay siege to.—**côbro a**, to put a stop to.—**claro**, to make clear.—**de acôrdo**, to reconcile, suit (one thing to another). [Cf. **pôr-se de acôrdo**].—**de banda**, to set aside; to place aside; to place askew.—**de castigo**, to place under punishment. —**de lado**, to set aside, relegate.—**de môlho**, to put (something) to soak; to sleep on a matter; in cookery, to marinate.—**de olhos**, (*m.*) act, or way, of looking at (something).—**de parte**, to set aside; to set apart.— **de pé**, to stand (someone or something) up.—**de permeio**, to place among; to interpose.—**de quarentena**, to place in quarantine; to isolate; to withhold judgment.— **do sol**, (*m.*) the setting of the sun.—**de seu bôlso**,—**de sua cabeça**,—**de sua casa**,—**de sua lavra**,—**por sua conta**, all mean to make up, improvise, add details (to a story).—**debaixo dos pés**, to cast underfoot.—**defeitos em**, to find fault with, pick flaws in.—**diante**, to place in front.—**diante dos olhos**, to place before the eyes.— **dúvidas**, to raise doubts, call in question.—**em ação**, to put in motion.—**embargos à execução de**, to offer arguments (in court) in support of a motion for stay of execution (of a sentence).—**em campo**, to put in the field (into play); to put in motion.—**em cena**, to stage a play. —**em côbro** = PÔR CÔBRO A.—**em conselho**, to offer for discussion.—**em contacto**, to bring together.—**em debandada**, to scatter, disperse, put to flight.—**em descoberto** (**conta, crédito**), to overdraw one's account.— **em dúvida**, to raise a doubt concerning.—**em efeito**, to put into effect.—**em embaraços**, to perplex, render indecisive.—**por escrito** (**em escrito, em escritura**), to put in writing.—**em esquecimento**, to forget.—**em evidência**, to make evident; to place in the open, make clearly visible; to stress.—**em execução**, to execute, make effective.—**em face**, to place before, in comparison with.—**em fogo**, to fire, inflame with passion, stir up revolt.—**em fuga** (or **fugida**), to put to flight.—**em leilão**, to put up (sell) at auction.—**em lembrança**, to bring to mind.—**em liberdade**, to set at liberty; to set free.—**em movimento**, to set going, put in motion.—**em ordem**, to put in order. —**em paralelo**, to put side by side (compare).—**em perigo**, to place in danger.—**em polvorosa**, to cause great commotion; to scatter to the winds.—**em posição**, to place in (the right) position.—**em postas**, to slash to pieces.—**em praça**, to put up for sale.—**em prática**, to

put into practice; to make practical use of.—**em pratos limpos**, to "come clean"; to lay the cards on the table.— **em público**, to make public.—**em relêvo**, to bring out into relief; to emphasize, stress.—**em risco**, to risk.—**em silêncio**, to impose silence on.—**em sossêgo**, to impose silence on; to quiet.—**em terra**, to unload, discharge on land.—**em uso**, to put in use; to put to use.—**em ventura**, to risk.—**em vida**, to bring to life.—**em vigor**, to place (law, ruling) in force.—**em vinhas d'alho**, (*Cookery*) to marinate.—**em voga**, to make popular, fashionable, the vogue.—**empenho em**, to take a special interest in.— **entre as estrêlas**, to apotheosize.—**esperança em**, to place hopes in.—**falhas**, to speak ill of someone.—**ferrete em**, to brand, mark with infamy, stigmatize.—**fim a**, to put an end to.—**fim à vida**, to end one's life.—**fora**, to put out; to throw out; to squander.—**freio a**, to put a brake on, restrain.—**impostos**, to lay on taxes.—**jugo em**, to place under a yoke, enslave.—**limites a** (or **em**), to limit.—**longe**, to send afar; to put safely away.—**luto**, to put on mourning.—**mal com**, to set (someone) at odds with (another).—**maluco**, (*slang*) to run (another) crazy. —**mãos em**, to lay hands on.—(or **meter**) **mãos à obra**, to set to work.—**mêdo em**, to instill fear in.—**mel em bôca de asno**, to cast pearls before swine; lit., to put honey in an ass' mouth.—**muito alto a mira** (**o desejo, os olhos**), to put one's sights too high.—**na bôca de**, to place (words) in another's mouth.—**na cabeça**, to place on the head; to put [it] into one's head.—**na cruz**, to crucify.—**na dependura**, to bring about another's ruin. —**na idéia**, to conceive an idea.—**na mesa**, to set on the table.—**na necessidade** (or **na obrigação**) **de**, to place under necessity (or obligation) to.—**na rua**, see PÔR NO ÔLHA DA RUA.—**nas costas**, to place (a burden) on the back, (de, of).—**nas estrelas**, or **nas núvens**, to laud to the skies.—**nas mãos de**, to place in the hands of; to entrust with.—**no andar da rua**, to turn out of doors.— **no canto**, to place on the shelf.—**nódoa em**, to smear, stigmatize.—**no estaleiro**, to put on the shelf; lit., to put in drydock; to reduce to poverty.—**no (extremo) fio**, to reduce to extreme poverty.—**no fogo**, to put on the fire (to cook).—**no índice**, to proscribe.—**no limbo**, to forget. —**no ôlho da rua**, to oust, kick out; to turn out of doors; to bounce, give the boot to; to fire (discharge from a job).—**no papel**, to put down on paper.—**no prego**, (*slang*) to hock, pawn.—**no rol do esquecimento**, to put out of mind, forget.—**no são**, to restore to good health. —**no seguro**, to cover with insurance.—**nos eixos**, to regulate (matters); to straighten (things) out.—**num beco sem saída**, to drive into a corner, into an impasse. —**num caos**, to create chaos.—**o aceite em**, to accept a bill of exchange (by endorsement).—**o caso em si**, to put oneself mentally in another's position.—**óculos**, to wear glasses.—**o dedo em cima**, to put one's finger on (the problem, etc.).—**o dedo na ferida**, to touch a sore spot. —**o fito em**, to aim at.—**o joelho em terra**, to kneel on one knee.—(or **meter**) **ombros a**, to put one's shoulder to (the wheel).—**o nome num documento**, to put one's name on (sign) a document.—**o paletó**, to put on one's coat.—(or **meter**) **o pé em**, to put one's foot in or on.—**o peito à banca**, to keep one's nose to the grindstone.—**o pé no pescoço de**, to put one's foot on another's neck. —**o prêto no branco**, to put down in black and white (in writing).—**o punhal ao peito de**, to put a knife to another's throat, lit. & fig.—**o rosto em**, to turn one's face to (look at).—**objeções a**, to put up objections to. —**o sêlo a** (or **em**), to seal; to close, finish.—**os cornos em**, to make a cuckold of.—**os joelhos no chão**, to kneel. —**os óculos**, to put on one's glasses.—**os olhos no chão**, to drop the eyes.—**os pés à parede**, to stand pat, refuse to budge.—**os pés em**, to set foot in.—**os pés em polvorosa**, to hot-foot it.—**os pés sôbre**, to tread on, subjugate.—**os pontos nos ii**, to dot the i's (and cross the t's).—**os podres para fora**, to spill out one's grievances; to confess.—**ovos**, to lay eggs.—**ovos de ouro**, to lay golden eggs.—**para o lado**, to put to one side.— **patente**, to make manifest.—**pé em terra**, to set foot on land.—**pecha**, to pick flaws.—**pedra em cima de**, to give a quietus to.—**peito à corrente**, to swim against the current.—**ponto em** (or **a**), to put a period (end) to.—**por escrito**, to put in writing.—**preceitos**, to exorcise.— **preço**, to put a price on.—**proa a**, to get set to (do something).—**remate a**, to put on the finishing touches.— **remédio em**, to remedy.—**-se a**+infinitive = to start +present part. [e.g., **pôr-se a andar**, to start walking.

pôr-se a falar, to begin speaking.].—**se à cabeceira**, to exert strong influence over; lit., to take position at the head of the table.—**se a caminho**, to get started, get going, get under way.—**se a cavalo**, to get on horseback.—**se a cavalo em**, to override; fig., to get on someone's back.—**se a gôsto**, to make oneself at home.—**se à ligeira**, or **à vontade**, to change into lighter, less formal dress.—**se à mercê de**, to place oneself at the disposal of, at the mercy of.—**se à mesa**, to sit down at table.——**se a salvo**, to take refuge.—**se à vontade**, to make oneself at home.—**se ao lado de**, to align oneself with; to take sides with; to stand by, side with.—**se ao largo**, to take off; to take to the open sea.—**se aos pés de**, to humble oneself.—**se bem com**, to become reconciled with (someone).—**se bem com Deus**, to get right with God.—**se de acôrdo**, to come to agreement.—**se de alcatéia** or **de atalaia**, to keep a sharp lookout.—**se de cama**, to take to one's bed.—**se de conversa com**, to engage in conversation with.—**se de joelhos**, to get down on one's knees.—**se de luto**, to put on mourning.—**se de mal**, to get in bad (with someone), get oneself disliked.—**se de parte**, to stand to one side, remain neutral.—**se de partida**, to set off on a journey.—**se de (or em) pé**, to get up, stand up, get on one's feet.—**se de prevenção or de vigia**, to keep an eye open.—**se de regresso**, to start back (home).—**se diante de**, to place oneself in front of.—**se em armas**, to take up arms.—**se em campo**, to take to the field; to get (down) to work.—**se em contacto com**, to put oneself in touch with; to get in contact with.—**se em dia com**, to catch up with one's correspondence, bills, etc.; to bring oneself up to date.—**se em guarda**, to be on one's guard.—**se em lugar enxuto**, to get to a safe place; lit., to get to a dry place.—**se em marcha**, to march off; to start out.—**se em mãos de**, to place oneself in the hands of.—**se em pé**, to get on one's feet, stand up; to get out of bed.—**se em têrmos**, to adjust oneself (to a situation).—**se em vias de**, to come within an ace of.—**se fora**, to leave, get out.—**se mal com**, to get in bad with (someone).—**se na moda**, to get in style.—**se nas pontas (or nos bicos) dos pés**, to stand on tiptoes.—**se no mundo**, to run away.—**se ombro a ombro com**, to stand shoulder to shoulder with.—**silêncio a**, to impose silence on.—**sôbre o lado**, to lay (something) on its side.—**sua espada ao serviço de**, to enlist in the service of.—**tacha em**, to pick flaws in (someone); to accuse (someone) of (something specific).—**têrmo**, or **fim, a**, to put a stop (end) to (an abuse, etc.).—**tréguas a**, to call a truce.—**um emplastro**, to apply a plaster.—**um pé falso**, to take a false step.—**um prego na roda**, to freeze (a given state of affairs).—**um refreadouro a**, to put a halter on.—**uma carta no correio**, to mail a letter.—**uma mordaça na bôca de**, to put a gag on (someone).—**uma pedra em cima de**, to stop, hold up, impede (the progress of).—**uma loja**, to open a store (shop).—**vista em**, to look at. **ao—do sol**, at sunset. **do raiar ao—do sol**, from sunrise to sunset. **O homem põe e Deus dispõe**, Man proposes and God disposes. **Ponhamos que assim acontece**, Let us suppose it *does* happen. **Preciso—gravata?** Must I wear a tie? **sem tirar nem—**, precisely, without adding to or taking form.

poranga (f.) = INHAMBU.

porão (m.) hold (of a ship); basement (of a house).

poraquê (m.) an electric eel (*Electrophorus*, syn. *Gymnotus, electricus*), of the Orinoco and Amazon basins, c.a. PEIXE-ELÉTRICO, TREME-TREME. [It grows to be six feet long, and its shock will stun a horse.]

porca (f.) see under PORCO.

porcaço (m.) huge hog.

porcada (f.) swine herd; filth; bungled job.

porcalhada (f.) smut, obscenity.

porcalhão –lhona (adj.) filthy; (m.,f.) filthy person, slob; bungler.

porção (f.) portion, piece, bit; parcel; share, allotment; allowance; lot, batch; large quantity. **uma—de**, a lot of, a large number of.

porcaria (f.) filth; filthy state or act; foul language; mess, bungled job; rubbish.

porcelana (f.) porcelain; (*Zool.*) the genus (*Cypraea*) of mollusks; (*Bot.*) the common purslane (*Portulaca oleracea*), c.a. BELDROEGA.

porcelânico –ca (adj.) porcelainic.

porcelanídeos (m.pl.) the family of porcelain crabs and allied genera (*Porcellanidae*).

porcelanita (f., *Petrog.*) porcelanite.

porcentagem (f.) = PERCENTAGEM.

Pórcia (f.) Portia.

porcino –na (adj.) porcine, swinish [= SUÍNO].

porcionário, porcioneiro (m.) one who receives a portion; portioner; (*Eccl.*) portionist.

porciúncula [dim. of PORÇÃO.] (f.) tiny portion.

porco [pô] **–ca** [pó] (adj.) swinish, filthy; foul, obscene; bungling; (m.) pig, porker, hog, swine; pork; filthy person; the Devil; drunkenness.—**bravo** or **-montês**, wild boar (*Sus scrofa*).—**da-índia** = PORQUINHO-DA-ÍNDIA.—**-da-terra**, aardvark (*Orycteropus*).—**do-mar**, harbor porpoise (*Phocaena*).—**do-mato**, peccary (= CAITITU).—**-espim** or—**-espinho**, porcupine (*Hystrix cristata*).—**-espinho-de-cauda** = OURIÇO-CACHEIRO.—**marinho**, blackfish (*Globicephala melas*).—**-ribeiro**, kingfisher (*Alcedo hispida*), c.a. PICA-PEIXE.—**-sujo**, (*colloq.*) the Devil.—**veado** = BABIRRUSSA; (f.) sow (female hog); nut (for a bolt); slattern.—**acastelada** or **almeiada**, castellated or castle nut.—**alada** or—**borboleta**, wing or thumb nut.—**criadeira**, adult female swine selected for reproduction; sow.—**de borne** or **de terminal**, (*Elec.*) terminal nut.—**de compressão**, jam nut.—**sextavada**, hexagonal nut.—**-marinha**, a hogfish (*Scorpaena*). **E aí que a—torce o rabo**, That's where the shoe pinches.

porejar (v.t.,v.i.) to exude; to ooze.

porém (conj.) but, yet, however, still, nevertheless. Syns: MAS, TODAVIA, CONTUDO, NÃO OBSTANTE, APESAR DISSO.

porfia (f.) contention, wrangling, bickering; pertinacity; stubbornness. **à—**, in a spirit of rivalry.

porfiado –da (adj.) pertinacious, stubborn; of match, race, etc., tight, hard-fought; strenuous; tough.

porfiador –dora (adj.) disputatious; contumacious; (m.,f.) such a one.

porfiar (v.i.) to argue, dispute (stubbornly).—**em**, to persist in (an idea, etc.); to insist on or upon (carrying out a plan).

pórfido (m.) = PÓRFIRO.

porfioso –sa (adj.) contentious, disputatious.

porfirião (m.) an O.W. purple gallinule (*Porphyrio*), c.a. CAMÃO.

porfírico –ca, porfirítico –ca (adj.) porphyritic.

porfirito (m., *Petrog.*) porphyrite.

porfirizar (v.t.) to pulverize.

pórfiro (m., *Petrog.*) porphyry.—**diabásico**, diabase-porphyrite.—**quarzífero**, quartz porphyry.—**sienítico**, syenite porphyry.

porfiróide (adj.) = PORFÍRICO.

poricida (adj., *Bot.*) poricidal.

poríferos (m.pl.) the Porifera (sponges), c.a. ESPONGIÁRIOS.

poriforme (adj.) poriform.

porisma (m., *Geom.*) porism.

porístico –ca (adj.) poristic.

poritídeos (m.pl.) reef-building corals (*Poritidae*).

pormenor [-es] (m.) detail.

pormenorização (f.) a detailing or particularizing.

pormenorizadamente (adj.) in detail, minutely (= MINUCIOSAMENTE].

pormenorizar (v.t.) to detail, relate, particularize.

pornografia (f.) pornography.

pornográfico –ca (adj.) pornographic.

pornógrafo (m.) pornographer.

poro [pó] (m.) pore.

porofilo –la (adj., *Bot.*) porophyllous.

porongo (m.) the common bottle or calabash gourd (*Lagenaria siceraria*), c.a. PORONGUEIRO; a water dipper, bottle, basket or other vessel made from the dry shell of a gourd [= CUIA, CABAÇA]. Vars. PURUNGA, PURUNGO.

poroplástico –ca (adj., *Surg.*) poroplastic—said of a kind of felt used for splints, jackets, etc.

porora [contraction of POR+HORA] (adv.) for the time being, for now [= POR ENQUANTO].

pororoca (f., *Phys. Geog.*) tidal bore at the mouth of the Amazon and other large rivers; "a tidal phenomenon characterized by a large roaring wave several meters high which ascends a river, destroying everything in its path and creating lesser waves in its wake, known as BRASEIROS, which break violently on the shores." [*GBAT*]; (*Bot.*) a sp. of Clusia (*C. volubilis*); a snowbell (*Styrax acuminatum*), c.a. CARNE-DE-VACA; also = JUTAIPEBA.

porosidade (f.) porosity.

porosímetro (m., *Physical Chem.*) porosimeter.

poroso –sa (*adj.*) porous.
porótico –ca (*adj.*) porotic.
porpezita (*f., Min.*) porpezite.
porquanto (*conj.*) considering, since, because, for the reason that, inasmuch as; [= PORQUE, VISTO QUE].
porque (*conj.*) because, since, as, for the reason that, inasmuch as; why, for what cause or reason.
porquê (*adv.*) why? for what reason? on what account? for what purpose? to what end? (*m.*) the why; the cause or reason; the wherefore. **os—s e comos,** the whys and wherefores.
porqueiro –ra (*adj.*) porcine; (*m.*) swineherd; (*f.*) pig pen; filthy house; filth; (*colloq.*) ruckus, brawl.
porquinho (*m.*) piglet.—**-da-índia,** guinea pig [= COBAIA].
porráceo –cea (*adj.*) leek-green.
porrada (*f., coarse slang*) a cudgeling or clubbing; a slew, oodles (of something).
porral (*m.*) a field of leeks.
porrão (*m.*) earthen jug; squat fellow.
porre (*m.*) a drinking spree. **cair no—,** to go on a bender. **cozinhar o—,** to get drunk.
porretada (*f.*) a blow with a stick.
porrete [rê] (*m.*) club, cudgel; (*colloq.*) a sure cure.
porrigem (*f.*), **porrigo** (*m., Med.*) porrigo; tinea [= TINHA].
porriginoso –sa (*adj.*) porriginous.
porrinha (*f.*) a game in which two or more persons try to guess the total number of pennies, for example, held by each, the winner taking all.
porrista (*adj.*) given to sprees; (*m., slang*) boozer.
porro [pô] (*m., Bot.*) leek (*Allium porrum*).
porta (*f.*) door, doorway.—**corrediça** or—**de correr,** sliding door.—**da rua,** street (front) door.—**de carga,** charging door (of a furnace).—**de dois batentes,** folding door.—**de emergência,** emergency exit.—**giratória,** revolving door.—**janela,** French window.—**lateral,** side door.—**s a dentro,** indoors.—**s a fora,** outdoors.—**s secretas or travessas,** occult means, illicit ways. **à—,** at the door (about to enter). **a—s fechadas,** behind closed doors. **abrir a—,** to open the door; fig., to render free of access; to ease the way. **às—s da morte,** at death's door. **bater a—,** to slam the door. **bater à or na—,** to knock at (on) the door. **dar com a—na cara de (alguém),** to slam the door in (another's) face. **dar com o nariz na—,** to find the door closed to one. **de—em—,** from door to door. **vão da—,** doorway, door opening.
porta-algodão (*m.*) cotton holder.
porta-aviões (*m.*) aircraft carrier.
porta-bagagens (*m.*) baggage rack.
porta-bandeira (*m.*) color bearer; flagman.
porta-bombas (*m.*) (bomber) bomb rack.
porta-cartas (*m.*) mailbag; letter holder.
porta-cartões (*m.*) card case.
porta-cartuchos (*m.*) cartridge case.
porta-chapéus (*m.*) hatrack; hatbox.
porta-chaves (*m.*) key ring.
porta-cigarros (*m.*) cigarette case.
porta-cocheira (*f.*) porte-cochere, large gateway.
porta-colo (*m.*) schoolboy's bag.
porta-cruz (*m.*) crucifer (in processions).
portada (*f.*) portal.
porta-diferencial (*m.*) differential gear case.
portador –dora (*adj.*) bearing; (*m.*) bearer, carrier; messenger; porter.
porta-eléctrodo (*m.*) electrode holder.
porta-enxêrto (*m., Hort.*) stock (for grafting), = CAVALO.
porta-escovas (*m., Elec.*) brush holder.
porta-espada (*m.*) saber holder (on a cavalryman's saddle).
porta-estandarte (*m.,f.*) standard-bearer.
porta-ferramenta, porta-ferro (*m.*) toolholder; tool post.
porta-fios (*m.*) thread holder.
porta-fólio (*m.*) portfolio; wallet, pocketbook.
porta-fresa (*m.*) mill holder.
porta-fusível (*m.*) fuse holder.
portagem (*m.*) toll; tollgate.
porta-guardanapo (*m.*) napkin ring.
porta-joias (*m.*) jewel case.
portal (*m.*) portal, doorway.
porta-lanterna (*m.*) lamp-holder.
porta-lápis (*m.*) pencil box.
porta-leque (*m.*) fan case.
porta-livros (*m.*) book ends; book strap.
portaló (*m., Naut.*) gangway.
porta-luvas (*m.*) glove compartment (in an automobile.)

porta-maça (*m.*) mace bearer.
porta-malas (*m.*) baggage compartment (of an automobile).
porta-manta (*m.*) portmanteau.
porta-microfone (*m.*) microphone holder.
porta-mitra (*m., Eccl.*) miter bearer.
porta-moedas, porta-níqueis (*m.*) coin purse.
porta-novas (*m.,f.*) newsmonger, talebearer.
portanto (*conj.*) therefore.
portão (*m.*) a large (iron) gate; front entrance.
porta-objeto (*m.*) stage (of a microscope).
porta-ordens (*m.*) one who carries orders.
porta-paz (*m., R.C.Ch.*) pax, osculatory.
porta-penas (*m.*) penholder.
porta-pneumático (*m.*) tire rack.
porta-pó (*m.*) lady's compact.
portar-se (*v.r.*) to comport, bear, conduct (oneself).—**bem,** to acquit oneself well.—**como uma criança,** to behave like a child.—**direito,** to behave well.—**mal,** to behave badly, misbehave.
porta-rêde (*m.*) net carrier (fishing boat).
porta-relógio (*m.*) watch case.
porta-retratos (*m.*) pictureframe.
portaria (*f.*) reception desk, information desk, front office; vestibule of a convent; a gòvernment directive, edict or regulation.
porta-seios (*m.*) brassière.
porta-sementes (*m.*) plant grown for seeds; seed tree, mother tree.
portátil [-táteis] (*adj.*) portable, light, easily transported.
porta-toalha[s] (*m.*) towel rack.
porta-válvula (*m.*) electronic tube socket.
porta-vento (*m.*) wind trunk (of pipe organ).
porta-voz (*m.*) spokesman; megaphone.
porte (*m.*) act of carrying or transporting; carrying charge; postage; carrying capacity; personal bearing, poise, demeanor; deportment.—**da voz,** timbre or carrying quality of the voice.—**pago,** postpaid. **de grande—,** of large tonnage [vessel].
porteira (*f.*) barrier (as at a R.R. crossing); gate (as in a pasture fence); woman gatekeeper; gatekeeper's wife.
porteiro (*m.*) doorman, gatekeeper; janitor.—**de igreja,** verger.
portela (*f.*) gateway; bend in the road; narrow gorge.
portenho –nha (*adj.*) of, from or pert. to Buenos Aires; (*m.,f.*) a citizen or inhabitant thereof. Vars. BONARENSE, BUENAIRENSE.
portento (*m.*) a marvel; wonderful thing or happening; a prodigy. [Not an equivalent of portent, in the sense of a forewarning of evil, which is PRESSÁGIO.]
portentoso –sa (*adj.*) marvelous, wonderful; prodigious. [But not portentous in the sense of ominous, which is AGOURENTO.]
pórter (*m.*) porter (beer).
pórtico (*m.*) portico, colonnade, arcade.
portinha (*f.*) small door.
portinhola (*f.*) wicket; carriage door; porthole; flap or fly of a garment.
pôrto [portos (pó)] (*m.*) port, harbor; Port wine; fig., shelter, refuge; [*cap.*] Oporto.—**de arribada,** port of refuge.—**de escala,** port of call.—**de mar,** sea port.—**e salvamento,** "happy landings," happy conclusion of any trip or enterprise.—**franco,** free port.—**sêco,** (*colloq.*) large retail store in a seaport town, dealing in all manner of foodstuffs and merchandise. **capitania do—,** harbor master's office. **capitão do—,** harbor master.
pôrto-alegrense (*adj.*) of or pert. to the city of Pôrto Alegre; (*m.,f.*) an inhabitant or native thereof.
Pôrto-príncipe (*m.*) Port-au-Prince.
pôrto-riquenho –nha, **porto-riquense** (*adj.; m.,f.*) Puerto Rican.
portuário –ria (*adj.*) of or pert. to a port or harbor; (*m.*) dock worker.
portucha (*f., Naut.*) grommet.
portuchar (*v.t.*) to reef sails.
portuchos (*m.pl.*) the holes of various shapes and sizes in a goldsmith's drawplate.
portuense (*adj.*) of or pert. to Oporto, Portugal; (*m.,f.*) a native or inhabitant thereof.
portuga (*m.*) Portugee. [*Contemptuous*]
português –guêsa (*adj.; m.,f.*) Portuguese (person, language).
portuguesismo (*m.*) a Portuguese idiom or colloquialism; Portuguese mode of thought or feeling.

portulaca (f.) any plant of this genus, esp. the common purslane (P. oleracea), c.a. BELDROEGA.
portulacáceo –cea (adj., Bot.) portulacaceous; (f.pl.) the purslane family (Portulacaceae).
portulano (m.) portolano (book for navigators).
portunídeos (m.pl.) the lady crabs (Portunidae).
poruca (f.) a type of sieve for coffee beans.
porunga (f.) skin bag for liquids.
poruti [í] (m.) a European swift (Apus squamatus).
porventura (adv.) peradventure, perhaps, perchance.
porvindouro –ra (adj.; m.) future.
porvir (m.) time to come, hereafter, by-and-by; destiny.
pos, form of PÔR [63].
pós (prep.) post [= APÓS].
posar (v.i.) to pose (as a model); to pose affectedly, strike attitudes.
pós-bélico –ca (adj.) post-bellum, post-war.
pós-bôca (f.) the back of the mouth.
poscefálico –ca (Anat.) postcephalic.
poscênio (m.) postscenium, backstage.
poscomunhão (f., R.C.Ch.) Postcommunion.
pós-data (f.) postdate.
pós-datar (v.t.) to postdate.
pós-diluviano –na (adj.) postdiluvian.
pós-dorsal (adj.) postcostal.
pose [ô] (f.) pose, posture; act of posing as a model; (Photog.) exposure.
pós-escolar (adj.) postschool.
pós-escrito –ta (adj.) written after or at the end; (m.) postscript.
posfácio (m.) postface.
pós-glacial (adj., Geol.) postglacial.
pós-graduado –da (adj.) postgraduate.
posição (f.) position, place, site; posture; state, circumstances; incumbency, (public) office; standing, rank, status.—**defensiva,** defensive position.—**esquerda,** awkward position. **em—de sentido,** (Milit.) at attention.
positivar (v.t.) to make positive, real; to determine positively.
positividade (f.) positiveness.
positivismo (m.) Positivism.
positivista (adj.; m.,f.) positivist.
positivo –va (adj.) positive, real, actual; definite, unequivocal; (m.) positive; messenger, bearer, courier, runner.
positron (m., Phys. Chem.) positron; positive electron.
posliminio (m., Law) postliminium.
pós-meridiano –na (adj.) postmeridian.
posmilitar (adj.) after military service.
pós-nominal (adj.) postnominal.
pós-operatório –ria (adj., Med.) postoperative.
posoquéria (f., Bot.) a genus (Posoqueria) of the madder family.
pós-palato –ta (adj., Anat., Zool.) postpalatine.
pospasto (m.) post-prandial course (dessert); = SOBREMESA.
pospelo [ê] (adv.) **a—,** against the fur, against the grain, the wrong way.
pós-perna (f.) buttock (of a horse).
posplioceno –na (adj., Geol.) Pleistocene.
pospontar (v.t.) to backstitch.
posponto (m.) backstitch.
pospor [63] (v.t.) to postpone, delay; to shelve, set aside; to place after.
posposição (f.) postposition.
pospositivo –va (adj.) postpositive; (f.) postpositive particle or word.
posposto –ta (adj.) postponed; placed after.
pós-romano –na (adj.) post-Roman.
possa, possais, possam, possamos, possas, forms of PODER [62].
possança (f.) puissance [= PUJANÇA and POTÊNCIA]; (Geol.) thickness (of strata), depth (of soil).
possante (adj.) puissant, powerful, mighty, strong; high-powered.
posse (f.) possession, tenure, retention; taking of office; a legal title or claim to land; (pl.) possessions, means; potentialities.—**por tolerância,** (Law) tenure at will. **a—do Presidente,** the President's inauguration. **de—de,** in possession of. **tomar—,** to be seated, inaugurated (in office). **tomar—de,** to take possession of. [Not an equivalent of sheriff's posse, which is FORÇA CIVIL DE EMERGÊNCIA ORGANIZADA PELO XERIFE PARA CERCAR UM BANDIDO, MANTER A PAZ, etc.]

possear (v.t.) to take possession of (occupy, squat on) vacant land.
posseiro –ra (adj.; m.,f.) holding, or one who holds, legal title to land and/or improvements thereon; (m.) homesteader.
possessão (f.) possession, ownership; realm, dominion; state of being possessed.
possessivo –va (adj.; m.) possessive.
possesso –sa (adj.) possessed (of the devil); (m.,f.) such a one.
possessor –sora (adj.) possessing; (m.,f.) possessor.
possessório –ria (adj.) possessory; (m., Law) possessory action.
possibilidade (f.) possibility, feasibility; (pl.) potentialities.
possibilitar (v.t.) to make possible.
possível (adj.) possible, feasible; (m.) the possible. **fazer o—,** to do one's utmost. **o mais (breve)—,** as (soon) as possible.
posso, 1st pers. pres. ind. of PODER [62].
possuído –da (adj.) possessed; (slang) stuck-up; (m.pl.) possessions.—**do demônio,** possessed of the devil.
possuidor –dora [u-i] (adj.) possessing; (m.,f.) possessor.
possuir [72] (v.t.) to possess, own; to have; to control.—**-se de,** to take hold of.—**-se do seu papel,** to play one's part (role) exceptionally well.
posta (f.) slice of fish, meat, etc.; (colloq.) soft job; post, mail; post relay station; GBAT: "(1) a school of PIRARUCU; (2) name given in Amazonia to batches of PIRARUCU cut open along their whole length and spread out in the sun to dry." (adj.) irreg. p.p. of PÔR [63].
postal (adj.) postal; (m.) postal card.
postalista (m.,f.) post-office employee.
postar (v.t.) to post (a sentinel, guard); to plant (a spy); to post, mail (a letter); (v.r.) to station oneself.
posta-restante (f.) poste restante, general delivery (at post office).
poste (m.) post, pole, pillar, stake.—**de guia,** landmark.—**de iluminação,** lamppost.—**indicador,** sign post.—**telegráfico,** telegraph pole.
posteiro (m.) watchman on a FAZENDA; cattle herder.
postejar (v.t.) to cut up (fish), slice (meat).
postema (f.) = APOSTEMA.
pós-terciário –ria (adj., Geol.) quaternary.
postergação (f.) a putting off, postponement; neglect.
postergar (v.t.) to leave behind; to leave in arrears; to disregard, slight; to postpone, put off, delay; to neglect, lose sight of.
posteridade (f.) posterity; offspring, progeny.
posterior (adj.) posterior, hind, back; (m., colloq.) the "back side" (rump).
posterioridade (f.) posteriority.
posteriormente (adv.) afterward(s).
póstero –ra (adj.) coming (in the future); (m.pl.) the coming generations.
postiço –ça (adj.) removable; added (to something finished) as an afterthought; inserted artificially. **dentes —s,** false teeth.
postigo (m.) peephole; wicket; shutter.
postila (f.) student's notebook; note, commentary. Var. APOSTILA.
postilhão (m.) postilion; postrider.
postliminio (m.) = POSLIMÍNIO.
pôsto [postos (pó)] (m.) post, place [but not post in the sense of pole, which is POSTE]; station, rank.—**avançado,** (Milit.) advanced post.—**de gasolina,** service station.—**de sentinela,** sentinel's post.—**de socorros,** first-aid (dressing) station.—**hípico,** stud farm.—**meteorológico,** weather station; (adj., irreg. p.p. of PÔR [63]), put, placed; of sun, set.—**que,** although, since, even though, inasmuch as. **bem—,** well-groomed. **isto—,** accordingly.
postônico –ca (adj., Philol.) posttonic.
postre[s] (m.) dessert [= SOBREMESA].
postremo –ma (adj.) last; end; extreme. Vars. POSTREIRO, POSTREMEIRO, POSTIMEIRO, POSTUMEIRO, POSTIMEIRO.
postulação (f.) postulation, supplication.
postulado (m.) postulate, proposition, conjecture.
postulante (m.,f.) postulant; (adj.) postulating.
postular (v.t.,v.i.) to postulate, solicit, supplicate.
póstumo –ma (adj.) posthumous, after death.
postura (f.) posture; bearing; carriage; attitude; stance; the number of eggs laid in a season; a city ordinance.
pós-velar (adj., Phonet.) postvelar.
pós-verbal (adj., Philol.) postverbal.

potabilidade (*f.*) potability.
potagem (*f.*) potage, thick soup.
potâmide (*f.*) water nymph.
potamologia (*f.*) potamology.
potamoplancto (*m.*) potamoplankton; river plankton.
potassa (*f.*) potash.—**cáustica**, caustic potash; lye.—**do comércio**, potassium carbonate, crude potash.
potássico –**ca** (*adj.*) potassic.
potássio (*m., Chem.*) potassium.
potável (*adj.*) potable.
pote (*m.*) pot; pitcher; jug; also (*colloq.*) jug in the sense of jail; (*colloq.*) a squat person.
potéia (*f.*) putty powder.
potência (*f.*) potency, power, might; virility; a power (state, nation); mechanical energy; (*Geol.*) thickness (of strata or soil dikes); = POSSANÇA.—**aérea**, air power.—**ao freio**, brake horsepower.—**aparente**, apparent power.—**colorífica**, heating power; calorific value.—**luminosa**, (*Elec.*) candlepower.
potencial (*adj.; m.*) potential.—**de fogo**, firing power.—**humano**, manpower.
potencialidade (*f.*) potentiality.
potenciar (*v.t., Math.*) to raise the power of a number.
potenciômetro (*m., Elec.*) potentiometer.
potentado (*m.*) potentate, sovereign.
potente (*adj.*) potent, powerful, mighty; strong; influential.
potentéia (*adj.; f., Heraldry*) potent (cross).
potentil[h]a (*f., Bot.*) cinquefoil (*Potentilla*).
potério (*m., Bot.*) burnet (*Poterium*).
poterna (*f., Fort.*) postern.
potestade (*f.*) an angelic or demonic power.
poti [í] (*m.*) = CAMARÃO.
potiche (*m.*) porcelain vase.
potiguar –**guara** (*adj.*) of or pert. to the State of Rio Grande do Norte; (*m.,f.*) a native or inhabitant of that State. [Originally, a member of the Potiguares or Portiguaras or Pitaguares: a large tribal division of the Tupinambá who dominated the coast of what is now the Brazilian states of Paraíba, Ceará, and Rio Grande do Norte.]
potirão, potirom (*m.*) = MUXIRÃO.
potitinga (*m.*) a prawn (*Palaemon*).
potó (*m.*) a rove beetle (*Staphylinus*).
potoca (*f.*) lie, cock-and-bull story.
potocar (*v.i.*) to fib, lie.
potômetro (*m.*) potometer.
potoqueiro –**ra**, **potoquista** (*adj.*) fibbing, lying; (*m.,f.*) fibber, liar.
potra (*f.*) see under POTRO.
potrada (*f.*) herd of colts.
potranca –**co** (*m.,f.*) two-year old (horse).
potrancada (*f.*) herd of colts.
potreação (*f.*) round-up (of horses).
potrear (*v.t.*) to round up (wild) horses; to taunt; (*v.i.*) to blow up (in anger).
potreiro (*m.*) horse trader; corral; an enclosed pasture.
potril (*m.*) corral for colts.
potrilho (*m.*) young colt.
potro –**tra** (*adj.*) unbroken; (*m.*) foal, colt; rack (instrument of torture); (*f.*) filly; foal; rupture, hernia; (*colloq.*) good fortune; haughtiness.
potroso-sa (*adj.*) ruptured.
poucachinho (*adv.; m.*) = POUCOCHINHO.
poucadinho (*adv.*) very little; (*m.*) little bit.
poucha-vergonha (*f.*) shamelessness; shameful behavior; rascality.
pouco –**ca** (*adj.*) little, inconsiderable; (*pl.*) few. [comp. MENOS; superl. POUQUÍSSIMO]; (*m.*) a little, bit, small quantity; short time [dim. POUQUINHO]; (*adv.*) little, slightly, not much, not very.—**a**—, little by little, gradually, by degrees.—**adiante**, a little further on.—**depois**, soon after.—(**me**) **importa**, I don't care; it's all the same to me.—**interessante**, uninteresting.—**mais ou menos**, about, nearly.—**se me dá**, It matters little to me.—**tempo**, a short time.—**s vezes**, seldom. **aos**—**s**, little by little, gradually. **até bem**—, until quite recently. **bem**—, very little. **com**—**prazo**, on short notice. **daquí a**—, soon, presently. **em**—**tempo**, within a short time. **fazer**—**caso de**, to belittle, look down on; to ignore. **há**—, just now, a little while ago. **havia**—, a short time before. **por**—**mais ou nada**, for little or nothing. **Por não segui a carreira médica**, I came very near to following a medical career. **por**—**que não**, nearly, almost,

within a little, within an ace of. **por um**—, for a little while. **por**—**que**, however little. **tão**—, so little. [Cf. TAMPOUCO]. **um**—, awhile; a little. **um**—**de (vinho)**, a little (wine). **um (amigo) como**—**s**, an exceptional (friend).
poucochinho (*adv.*) very little; (*m.*) wee bit.
poule, poula (*f.*) betting ticket on a horse race.
poupa (*f., Zool.*) hoopoe (*Upupa epops*); lapwing (*Vanellus vanellus*); crest, tuft of feathers; topknot; forelock combed up.
poupado –**da** (*adj.*) thrifty, frugal; (*p.p. of* POUPAR) saved; spared. **Vintém**—, **vintem ganho** (or **ganhado**, as the people say), Penny saved, penny earned.
poupador –**dora** (*adj.; m.,).*) thrifty, frugal (person).
poupança (*f.*) thrift; savings; (*colloq.*) stinginess. **alimento de**—, any stimulating drink.
poupar (*v.t.*) to use sparingly; to save, economize, husband; to spare, preserve, save; (*v.i.*) to stint, be sparing; (*v.r.*) to spare oneself (trouble, etc.).—**o castigo a**, to withhold punishment from.—**palavras**, to save words.—**tempo**, to save time.
pouquidade, pouquidão (*f.*) small amount; smallness, littleness; paucity.
pouquinho [dim. of POUCO] (*m.*) a tiny bit.
pouquíssimo –**ma** [absol. superl. of POUCO] very, very little.
pousada (*f.*) act of stopping, alighting. etc.—see the verb POUSAR; lodge, inn; a night's lodging; a place for stopping overnight; a resting place. Var. POISADA.
pousadia (*f.*) lodge, lodging; retirement from office. Var. POISADIA.
pousar (*v.t.*) to place, put (**em**, on, in); to rest (**sôbre**, upon); to set down; (*v.i.*) to repose, rest; to stay overnight; to perch, roost; to alight, settle, come to rest; to stop, halt, pause; (*Aeron.*) to land. Var. POISAR.
pousio –**sia** (*adj.*) uncultivated; (*m.*) fallow land. Var. POISIO.
pouso (*m.*) resting place; anchorage; settling, alighting (of a bird); landing (of an airplane).
pouta (*f.*) = POITA.
povaréu, poviléu (*m.*) = POVOLÉU.
povo [pô; povos (pó)] (*m.*) people, nation; population, persons; the public; populace; (*colloq.*) one's folks.—**de Deus**, God's chosen people (the Jews).
póvoa (*f.*) a small settlement.
povoação (*f.*) population; a settlement; "a stand of rubber trees in the forest." [GBAT]
povoado –**da** (*adj.*) peopled, populated; (*m.*) village, settlement.
povoador –**dora** (*adj.*) populating; (*m.,f.*) settler (on land).
povoamento (*m.*) act of peopling; population; a stand of timber trees.
povoar (*v.t.*) to people, populate, settle; to stock with (fish, game, etc.).
povoléu, povoréu (*m.*) populace, rabble, common herd, rank and file, mob; [= RALÉ].
povoto (*m.*) hedgehog cactus (*Echinopsis*).
powellita (*f., Min.*) powellite.
pòzeira (*f.*) powder box.
pozolana (*f., Petrog.*) pozzuolana.
pp. = PÁGINAS (pages).
p.p. = POR PROCURAÇÃO (by power of attorney); PRÓXIMO PASSADO (recently passed).
PR = PARANÁ (State of).
P.R. = PRÍNCIPE REAL (Royal Prince).
pra, p'ra = PARA.—**lá de**, way beyond; much more than.
praça (*f.*) public square, plaza; open market; an enlisted man (soldier).—**comercial**, trading center.—**de armas**, parade ground.—**de esportes**, athletic or playing field.—**de guerra**, military stronghold.—**forte**, stronghold, fortified city.—**de pré**, private (soldier).—**do comércio**, trading center, marketplace, brokers exchange.—**do martelo**, face of a hammer.—**s de reserva**, reserve forces. **abrir**—, to make way. **assentar**—, to enlist (in the army). **auto de**—, taxi. **boa**—, (*slang*) good Joe, nice guy. **fazer**—**de**, to make a show of, call attention to.
pracari [í] (*m.*) a nitta tree (*Parkia platycephala*), c.a. FAVA-DE-BOLOTA.
pracaxi [í] (*f.*) iripil-bark tree (*Pentaclethra filamentosa*).—**de-fôlha-grande**, owala-oil tree (*P. macrophylla*).
pracear (*v.t.*) to put up for sale; to auction off.
pracejar (*v.t.*) to make a show of; to boast of.
praciano –**na** (*adj.*) city-dwelling; having city manners; (*m.,f.*) such a person.
pracinha (*m.*) Brazilian "G.I.".

pracista (*m.*) a local city salesman; a country dweller who has spent time in the city and acts accordingly.

pracuuba [u-u] (*f.*)—**branca**, a mora (*Mora paraensis*), one of the largest timber trees in the Amazon region.——**cheirosa-da-várzea**, a leguminous medium-sized tree (*LeCointea amazonica*), common along the lower Amazon, whose timber is used for fine inlay work.——**da-terra-firme**, a bitterwood (*Trichilia lecointei*).

pradaria (*f.*) prairie land.

prado (*m.*) meadow, field, grassland; race track, turf.

pradoso –sa (*adj.*) grassy.

praga (*f.*) curse, malediction; plague, scourge; pest; vermin; weeds; [*cap.*] Prague. **rogar—s**, to call down curses on.

pragal (*m.*) waste land.

pragana (*f., Bot.*) awn.

praganoso –sa (*adj., Bot.*) having awns, bearded.

pragmático –ca (*adj.*) pragmatic; (*colloq.*) customary, usual; (*f., colloq.*) social etiquette, formalities.

pragmatismo (*m.*) pragmatism.

pragmatista (*adj.*) pragmatistic; (*m.,f.*) pragmatist.

praguedo [ê] (*m.*) volley of curses, string of oaths.

praguejado –da (*adj.*) plagued, afflicted; sickly.

praguejador –dora (*adj.*) cursing; (*m.,f.*) one who curses.

praguejamento (*m.*) cursing.

praguejar (*v.t.,v.i.*) to curse; (*colloq.*) to go to weeds.

praguento –ta (*adj.*) cursing, imprecatory.

praia (*f.*) beach, seashore.—**de viração**, "a sandbank where edible turtles are caught in great numbers by turning them on their backs as they come out of the water during the summer to lay their eggs on land." [*GBAT*]

praiano –na (*adj.; m.,f.*) beach-dwelling (person).

praieiro (*m.*) beach-dweller; liberal-minded man.

pralina (*f.*) praline.

prancha (*f.*) plank; gang plank; engraved plate. "(1) a single plank used as a gangplank which GAIOLAS carry on board for use in places where there are no docks; (2) same as BOLACHA, a thin sheet of rubber from CAUCHO trees; (3) in Mato Grosso, a canoe with a wooden deck used on some rivers of the Paraguay basin." [*GBAT*]

pranchada (*f.*) a blow with the broad side of a sword.

pranchão (*m.*) large and thick plank.

prancheta [ê] (*f.*) small plank; thin board; surveyor's compass; drawing board; (*Med.*) pledget, compress.

prândio (*m.*) repast. [*Poetical*]

prantaria (*f.*) prolonged wailing.

pranteador –dora (*adj.*) weeping, wailing, mourning; (*m.,f.*) mourner.

pranteadura (*f., colloq.*) wailing; lamentation.

prantear (*v.t.,v.i.*) to mourn; to lament; (*v.i.*) to wail, weep.

prantina (*f.*) weeping and wailing.

pranto (*m.*) weeping, tears; wailing; mourning; lament; elegy.

prasino (*m.*) emerald [= ESMERALDA].

prásio (*m., Min.*) prase.

prasiodímio (*m., Chem.*) praseodymium trioxide.

prasiolito (*m., Min.*) praseolite.

prasóide (*adj., Min.*) resembling prase.

prata (*f.*) silver (metal, coin); silverware; silver jewelry.—**alemã**, German silver [= ARGENTÃO].—**de lei**, sterling silver.—**fulminante**, (*Chem.*) silver fulminate.—**nativa** or **virgem**, native silver.—**viva**, quicksilver.

pratada (*f.*) plateful; a full plate.

pratalhada (*f.*) plateful of food.

pratalhaz, pratarraz, pratázio (*m.*) a large plate, esp. one heaped with food.

prataria (*f.*) silverware; a quantity of plates.

prateação (*f.*) silver plating.

prateado –da (*adj.*) silver-plated; silvery; (*f.*) = ORVALHO-DA-AURORA (iceplant).

prateador –dora (*adj.*) silver-plating (*m.,f.*) silver plater.

prateadura (*f.*) silver plating; (*Plant Pathol.*) silverleaf.

pratear (*v.t.*) to plate with silver; to cover with silver; to make silvery.

prateira (*f.*) silver chest or closet.

prateiro (*m.*) silversmith.

prateleira (*f.*) any shelf, esp. a dish rack.—**da chaminé**, mantel piece.

prateleiro (*m.*) cymbalist.

pratense (*adj.*) of, pert. to, or growing or living in, meadows.

prática (*f.*) practice, use; exercise, drill; habitual doing;

experience, know-how; a short talk; (*Naut.*) pilot's license.

praticabilidade (*f.*) practicability, feasibility.

praticagem (*f.*) piloting (of a ship).

praticante (*adj.*) practicing; (*m.,f.*) practitioner; apprentice.

praticar (*v.t.*) to practice; to do, perform, carry on, act, execute; to perpetrate (a crime); to make, cut (as, notches on a stick or an opening in a wall); (*v.i.*) to act, operate, proceed; to exercise (a profession); to converse, talk.—**desatinos**, to do crazy things. **aprender praticando**, to learn by doing. **Que esporte você pratica?** What sports do you go in for?

praticável (*adj.*) practicable; that can be negotiated (in the sense of traversed, forded, etc.).

prático –ca (*adj.*) practiced, experienced; practical; expedient. **o meio—**, an expedient; (*m.*) an experienced person; harbor pilot; a person who practices a profession for which he is not fully trained; an officer risen from the ranks.

praticola (*adj., Biol.*) pratincolous; of or pert. to meadowlands.

praticultor [ô] (*m.*) grower of fodders.

praticultura (*f.*) growing of cattle feed.

pratilheiro (*m.*) cymbalist.

pratinho (*m.*) small plate; (*colloq.*) butt, laughingstock.

pratiqueira (*f.*) = PARATI (a mullet).

prato (*m.*) plate (food vessel); dish (kind of food); pan (of scales); (*pl.*) cymbals.—**de lentilhas**, mess of pottage.—**de resistência**, pièce de résistance.—**de sobremesa**, dessert dish.—**de tintagem**, ink disk (of a printing press).—**do fonógrafo**, phonograph turntable.—**do meio**, entrée (main dish).—**fino**, a delicacy.—**fundo**, soup plate.—**raso**, dinner plate.—**sopeiro**, soup plate.—**travêsso**, platter. **cuspir no—em que se come**, to bite the hand that feeds one. **Do—à bôca se perde a sopa**, There's many a slip twixt the cup and the lip. **pôr em—s limpos**, to lay the cards on the table; to come clean, make a clean breast (of things).

praxe (*f.*) habit, custom, conventional conduct; praxis. **de—**, usual, customary.

praxista (*adj.*) ceremonious, formal, conventional, (*m.,f.*) one who adheres to ceremony, protocol, formalities, and conventions.

prazentear (*v.t.*) to praise, flatter; (*v.i.*) to engage in pleasantries.

prazenteiro –ra (*adj.*) pleasant, pleasing; jolly; merry, cheerful, gay, goodhumored; likable.

prazer (*m.*) pleasure, delight, enjoyment; fun.—**es físicos**, material pleasures. **Muito—em conhecê-lo**, Happy to meet you! (*v.t.*) [64]) to please—a defective verb used only in the third person.

prazerosamente (*adv.*) gladly, with pleasure.

prazeroso –sa (*adj.*) pleasant; pleasurable; gay.

prazo (*m.*) term, span, period of time, given time, time limit; maturity date. **com pouco—**, on short notice. **conceder—**, to grant a delay. **vencer-se o—**, of a note, etc., to fall due. **vender a—**, to sell on time.

pré (*m.*) soldier's daily pay. **praça de—**, enlisted man.

preá (*m., Zool.*) cavy.

preaca (*f.*) rawhide whip.

preacaa [a-á] (*m., Bot.*) an ironweed (*Vernonia sobrepanda*).

preacada (*f.*) blow with a whip.

preamar (*f.*) high tide.

preâmbulo (*m.*) preamble, preface, introduction.

preanunciação (*f.*) preannouncement.

preanunciar (*v.t.*) to preannounce.

prear (*v.t.*) to catch, grab, seize (as prey).

prebasilar (*adj., Anat.*) prebasilar.

prebenda (*f.*) prebend (stipend of a canon); by ext., a sinecure.

prebendado –da (*adj.*) prebendal; (*m.*) prebendary.

prebixim (*m.*) = TIÉ-TINGA.

preboste (*m.. Mil.*) provost.

precação (*f.*) supplication, entreaty.

precalço (*m.*) = PERCALÇO.

pré-cambriano –na (*adj., Geol.*) pre-Cambrian.

precariedade (*f.*) precariousness.

precário –ria (*adj.*) precarious, unstable, unreliable; ticklish; delicate.

precatado –da (*adj.*) wary.

precatar (*v.t.*) to warn, admonish, caution; (*v.r.*) to take precautions; to be careful, cautious, wary.

precatório –ria (*adj.*) precatory, supplicatory; (*f., Law*) a writ of mandamus.

precaução (*f.*) precaution, caution, forethought.

precaucional (*adj.*) precautional, precautionary.

precaucionar-se (*v.r.*) to take precautions.

precautelar (*v.*) = PRECAVER.

precautório –ria (*adj.*) precautionary. **medicina**—, preventive medicine.

precaver [65] (*v.t.*) to warn, caution, forewarn, put on one's guard (**contra, de,** against); (*v.r.*) to be on one's guard (**contra, de,** against).

precavido –da (*adj.*) on guard, careful, cautious.

prece (*f.*) prayer; plea; (*pl., Eccl.*) preces.

precedência (*f.*) precedence, priority, seniority.

precedente (*adj.*) preceding, previous, prior; (*m.*) precedent.

preceder (*v.t.,v.i.*) to precede, come (go) before; to antecede.

preceito (*m.*) precept, maxim, rule; commandment, dictate.—**cominatório,** (*Law*) an injunction.

preceituar (*v.t.*) to assert (something) as a precept or rule; to ordain, decree; (*v.i.*) to prescribe, give directions.

preceptor (*m.*) preceptor, tutor; mentor; coach.

preceptoral (*adj.*) preceptoral.

precessão (*f.*) precession, precedence.—**dos equinócios,** (*Astron.*) precession of the equinoxes.

precingir (*v.t.*) to gird.

precinta (*f.*) band, strap; (*Naut.*) canvas for wrapping ropes.

preciosidade (*f.*) preciousness; a precious thing; preciosity.

preciosismo (*m.*) preciosity.

precioso –sa (*adj.*) precious, costly; rich; over-refined, over-nice, finical; (*m.*) = SAÍRA (a bird).

precipício (*m.*) precipice, crag, sheer drop; perdition.

precipitação (*f.*) precipitation, a throwing or falling headlong; precipitancy, rash haste, abruptness; (*Chem., Meteor.*) precipitation.

precipitado –da (*adj.*) precipitate, over-hasty, rash, headlong; abrupt, sudden; helter-skelter. **fuga**—, stampede. (*m.*) a rashly hasty person; a hothead; (*Chem.*) a precipitate.

precipitante (*adj.*) precipitating; (*m., Chem.*) precipitant.

precipitar (*v.t.*) to precipitate, throw (hurl) headlong; to hasten, hurry, bring on (sooner); (*Chem.*) to precipitate; (*v.r.*) to rush (dash, fall, plunge) headlong; to hurl oneself upon; to act hastily; to rush to ruin; (*Chem.*) to precipitate.

precipitável (*adj., Chem.*) precipitable.

precípite (*adj.*) precipitate, hasty.

precipitina (*f., Immunol.*) precipitin.

precipitógeno (*m., Immunol.*) precipitinogen.

precipitoso –sa (*adj.*) precipitous, craggy; precipitate, headlong.

precípuo –pua (*adj.*) principal, essential, paramount. **de —importância,** of prime importance; (*m., Law*) the right to a preferential share of an estate.

precisado –da (*adj.; m.,f.*) needy, indigent (person).

precisão (*f.*) precision, preciseness; accuracy; need, necessity.

precisar (*v.t.*) to need, be in need of; to make precise, particularize, state in detail; (*v.i.*) to need, be needful, be necessary; to be in need.—**fatos e datas,** to specify facts and dates.—**de (dinheiro, etc.),** to be in want of, have need of (money, etc.). **Eu preciso ir,** I must go; I am obliged to go. **Precisa-se de (or precisam-se) operários,** Men wanted. **Quando você precisa ir?** When must you go? **Quanto preciso pagar?** How much must I pay?

preciso –sa (*adj.*) needful, requisite; precise, exact, accurate; distinct, well-defined. **É—faze-lo,** It must be done.

precitado –da (*adj.*) aforementioned.

precito –ta (*adj.; m.*) reprobate.

preclaro –ra (*adj.*) pre-eminent, illustrious, renowned; bright, brilliant.

preço [ê] (*m.*) price, value; worth; estimation.—**a varejo,** retail price.—**baixo,** low price.—**de fatura,** billing cost.—**de ocasião,** bargain price.—**fixo,** fixed price.—**-teto,** ceiling price. **a—de ouro,** at a very high price. **a todo**—, at any price. **a vil**—, dirt-cheap. **ao—de,** at the rate (price) of.

precoce (*adj.*) precocious, premature. **diagnóstico**—, early diagnosis; (*adv.*) prematurely.

precocidade (*f.*) precocity, precociousness, prematureness.

precogitar (*v.i.*) to premeditate.

precógnito –ta (*adj.*) known beforehand.

pré-colombiano –na (*adj.*) pre-Columbian.

preconceber (*v.t.*) to preconceive.

preconcebido –da (*adj.*) preconceived.

preconceito (*m.*) preconception; prejudice, bias, superstition.

precondição (*f.*) precondition.

preconização (*f.*) preconization.

preconizador –dora (*adj.*) preconizing; (*m.,f.*) preconizer.

preconizar (*v.t.*) to extol, commend highly (in public); to recommend, advise, counsel; of the Pope, to preconize.

pré-consciente (*m.., Psychoanalysis*) preconscious.

precordial (*adj., Anat.*) precordial.

pré-cristão –tã (*adj.*) pre-Christian.

precursor –sora (*adj.*) precursory; (*m.*) precursor, forerunner; harbinger, herald.

predador (*m.*) predator.

predatório –ria (*adj.*) predatory, plundering.

predecessor (*m.*) predecessor.

predefinição (*f.*) predefinition, predetermination.

predefinir (*v.t.*) to predefine.

predela (*f.*) predella; gradino (altar, painting, sculpture).

predestinação (*f.*) predestination.

predestinado –da (*adj.*) predestinated, predestined, foreordained; (*m.,f., Theol.*) person predestined to eternal life.

predestinar (*v.t.*) to predestinate, predestine, fore-ordain.

predeterminação (*f.*) predetermination.

predeterminante (*adj.*) predetermining.

predeterminar (*v.t.*) to predetermine.

predial (*adj.*) pertaining to buildings; praedial.

prediastólico –ca (*adj., Physiol.*) prediastolic.

prédica (*f.*) sermon, preachment.

predicação (*f.*) preachment; (*Gram.*) predication.

predicado (*m.*) quality, attribute; talent, ability, faculty, endowment; (*Gram.*) predicate.

predicador –dora (*adj.*) preaching; (*m.*) preacher.

predicamento (*m.*) predicament (but only in the sense of a category). [In the sense of plight or predicament, see APURO, ENTALADA, APÊRTO.]

predicante (*adj.*) preaching, predicatory; (*m..f.*) predicant; Protestant preacher.

predição (*f.*) prediction; forecast.—**do tempo,** weather forecast.

predicar (*v.t.*) to preach.

predicativo –va (*adj., Gram.*) predicative; (*m.*) objective complement or predicate.

predicatório –ria (*adj.*) complimentary, encomiastic.

predileção (*f.*) predilection, preference, fondness for; penchant.

predileto –ta (*adj.; m.,f.*) beloved, dear, darling, favorite, pet.

pré-diluviano –na (*adj.*) antediluvian.

prédio (*m.*) building, house; land, property.

predisponência (*f.*) predisponency.

predisponente (*adj.*) predisponent, predisposing.

predispor [63] (*v.t.*) to predispose.—**contra,** to prejudice (prepossess) against.

predisposição (*f.*) predisposition, inclination, bent.—**para,** readiness to.

predisposto –ta (*adj.*) predisposed.

predito –ta (*adj.*) predicted.

preditor (*m.*) predictor.

predizer [41] (*v.t.*) to predict, foretell.

predominação (*f.*) predomination.

predominador –dora (*adj.*) predominating; (*m.,f.*) one who predominates.

predominância (*f.*) predominance, prevalence.

predominante (*adj.*) predominant, prevailing, ruling.

predominar (*v.i.*) to predominate, prevail, preponderate.

predomínio (*m.*) predominancy, preponderance; upper hand; advantage.

pré-dorsal (*adj., Anat.*) predorsal.

preeleitoral [e-e] (*adj.*) pre-election.

preeminência [e-e] (*f.*) pre-eminence, superiority.

preeminente [e-e] (*adj.*) pre-eminent.

preempção [e-e] (*f.*) pre-emption.

preencher [e-e] (*v.t.*) to fill (in, out); to fulfill, perform.—**um cupon,** to fill out a coupon.—**uma fórmula,** to fill in (out) a blank form.—**uma vaga,** to fill a vacancy (position).

preenchimento [e-e] (*m.*) fulfilling; fulfillment.—**de cargo**, filling of an office.
preensão [e-e; *pl.:* preênseis] (*m.*) prehension.
preênsil [e-e] (*adj.*) prehensile.
pré-escolar (*adj.*) preschool.
preestabelecer [e-e] (*v.t.*) to pre-establish.
pré-estreia (*f.*) preview (of a motion picture, etc.) [A Brazilian neologism which is replacing the French *avant-première.*]
preexcelente [e-e] (*adj.*) surpassingly excellent.
preexistência [e-e] (*f.*) pre-existence, previous existence.
preexistente [e-e] (*adj.*) pre-existent.
preexistir [e-e] (*v.i.*) to pre-exist.
pref. = PREFEITO (mayor).
prefação (*f.*) preface.
prefaciador –**dora** (*m.,f.*) writer of a preface.
prefaciar (*v.t.*) to preface.
prefácio (*m.*) preface, preamble, prologue, introduction, foreword; (*Eccl.*) Preface.
prefeito (*m.*) mayor.
prefeitura (*f.*) city hall.
preferência (*f.*) preference; predilection; liking; priority; (*pl.*) likes and dislikes. **de**—, preferably.
preferencial (*adj.*) preferential.
preferido –**da** (*adj.*) preferred, chosen, selected.
preferir [21a] (*v.t*) to prefer, choose, select; to count more desirable, like better. **como**—, as you wish (prefer).
preferível (*adj.*) preferable, more desirable, to be preferred, better.
prefiguração (*f.*) prefigurement.
prefigurar (*v.t.*) to prefigure, foreshadow.
prefixar [ks] (*v.t.*) to prefix.
prefixo –**xa** [ks] (*adj.*) prefixed; (*m.*) a prefix.
prefloração, preflorescência (*f., Bot.*) praefloration, estivation.
prefoliação (*f., Bot.*) praefoliation, vernation —**conduplicada**, conduplicate vernation.—**encaracolada**, involute vernation.—**enrolada**, circinate vernation.—**franzida**, plicate vernation.—**imbricada**, imbricate vernation.—**reclinada**, reclinate vernation.—**valvar**, valvate vernation.
preformar (*v.t.*) to preform.
prefrontal (*adj., Anat., Zool.*) prefrontal.
prefulgente (*adj.*) surpassingly fulgent.
prega (*f.*) pleat, plait, fold, crease.
pregação (*f.*) act of preaching, nailing, etc. See the verb PREGAR; sermon, preachment, exhortation; (*colloq.*) tedious homily.
pregadeira (*f.*) pin cushion.
pregado –**da** (*adj.*) nailed; (*colloq.*) tipsy; pooped, worn out.
pregador –**dora** (*adj.*) nailing; stitching; preaching; (*m.,f.*) nailer; stitcher; preacher; (*colloq.*) sermonizer; (*slang*) liar; beam of a loom.—**de cartazes**, billposter.—**de roupa**, clothespin.
pregadura (*f.*) pattern of (ornamental) nails.
pregagem (*f.*), **pregamento** (*m.*) act or operation of nailing.
pregão (*m.*) street vendor's cry; auction, bidding; (oral) public proclamation; (*pl.*) banns of marriage.
pregar (*v.t.*) to nail; to drive in (a nail, spike, etc.); to fasten or fix (as with nails, pins, stitches); to stick (as with glue); to deliver or deal (a blow); to rivet (the eyes) upon; to deliver or pronounce (as, a sermon); (*v.i.*) to preach, proclaim (the gospel); to exhort.—**aos peixes** or—**no deserto**, to preach or admonish in vain; to cry out in the desert.—**botões em**, to sew on buttons.—**pêtas**, to tell lies, whoppers, cock-and-bull stories.—**sem missão**, to speak without authority.—**um susto a**, to give a fright to.—**uma estopada em**, to inflict a tedious harangue upon.—**uma partida**, or **peça, a**, to play a trick on; to hoax. **É proibido**—**cartazes**, Post no bills. **não**—**ôlho**, not to sleep a wink.
pregaretas (*f.pl.*) Dominican nuns.
pregaria (*f.*) quantity of nails; nail factory; ornamental studding with nails.
pré-glacial (*adj., Geol.*) pre-glacial.
prego (*m.*) nail; [Nail of finger or toe is UNHA.]; (*slang*) pawnshop; a lie.—**-cachorro**, dog spike.—**caibral** or—**de caverna**, spike or very large nail. **dar o**—, to poop out. **dar os**—**s**, to hit the ceiling. **não meter** (or **não botar**)—**sem estôpa**, to do nothing (as an act of kindness, etc.) without an ulterior motive.
pregoar (*v.t.*) to proclaim, blazon. Cf. APREGOAR.

pregoeiro (*m.*) crier; auctioneer; barker, spieler.
pregresso –**sa** (*adj.*) prior, previous; antecedent. **vida**—, former life.
preguari [í] (*m.*) an edible wing shell, the fighting conch (*Strombus pugilis*).
pregueadeira (*f.*), –**dor** (*m.*) a tucking or pleating attachment for a sewing machine.
pregueado –**da** (*adj.; m.*) tucked or pleated (piece of sewing).
preguear (*v.t.*) to pleat, tuck, crease, crimp.
pregueiro (*m.*) one who deals in or manufactures nails.
preguiça (*f.*) laziness, slothfulness, indolence; lassitude; (*Zool.*) a three-toed sloth (*Bradypus tridactylus*), c.a. AÍ; also = SINIMBU (the iguana).—**real**, the unau or two-toed sloth (*Choloepus didactylus*). **ter**—, to be lazy.
preguiçar (*v.i.*) to laze; to lounge; to spend time in idleness; to lie abed.
preguiceiro –**ra** (*adj.*) lazy; sleep-provoking; (*m.*) sleeping cot; (*f.*) easy chair.
preguicento –**ta** (*adj., colloq.*) lazy.
preguiçoso –**sa** (*adj.*) lazy, indolent, sluggish; (*m.*) loafer; lazybones; sluggard; (*f.*) deck chair; a tiny stingless honeybee (*Melipona butteli*) which does not attack robbers of its nest.
preguilha, preguinha (*f.*) tuck, small pleat.
preguntar (*v.*) & derivs. = PERGUNTAR & derivs.
pregustar (*v.i.*) to taste before.
prehabilitar-se (*v.r.*) to prepare oneself beforehand.
pré-helênico –**ca** (*adj.*) pre-Hellenic.
pré-historia (*f.*) prehistory.
pré-historiador (*m.*) prehistorian.
pré-histórico –**ca** (*adj.*) prehistoric(al).
preignição (*f.*) preignition.
pré-incaico –**ca** (*adj.*) pre-Incan.
pré-islâmico –**ca** (*adj.*) pre-Islamic.
preitear, preitejar (*v.i.*) to render homage to.
preito (*m.*) a token of gratitude, esteem, etc.; homage.
prejereba (*f.*) the triple-tail (*Lobotes surinamensis*), c.a. BREJEREBA, DORMINHOCO, FREJEREBA, PEIXE-FÔLHA, PEIXE-SONO, PIRACA, PIRAJEVA.
prejudicado –**da** (*adj.*) damaged, impaired; hurt.
prejudicador –**dora** (*adj.*) damaging; (*m.,f.*) one who damages.
prejudicar (*v.t.*) to damage, hurt, injure, impair; to detract from; (*v.r.*) to suffer damage.
prejudicial (*adj.*) prejudicial, hurtful, detrimental, deleterious; noxious.
prejuízo (*m.*) prejudice, harm, injury; financial loss, setback, misfortune; bias, preconception. **agir em**—**de**, to discriminate against. **causar**—, to cause financial loss. **com**—**para**, in detriment of. **levar um**—, to suffer a loss or damage.
prejulgar (*v.t.*) to prejudge.
prelação (*f.*) preferment.
prelado (*m.*) prelate.
prelatura, prelazia (*f.*) prelacy, prelature.
preleção (*f.*) prelection; lecture to students.
prelecionador –**dora** (*m.,f.*) lecturer, teacher.
prelecionar (*v.t.*) to lecture to; to give a lesson to.—**matemática**, to teach math; (*v.i.*) to discourse in public.
prelibação (*f.*) foretaste, prelibation.
prelibar (*v.t.*) to taste beforehand.
preliminar (*adj.*) preliminary, prefatory; (*m.*) preliminary; introduction.
preliminarista (*m.,f.*) student in a preliminary course.
prélio (*m.*) fight, struggle, battle. [*Poetical*]
prelo (*m.*) printing press. **dar ao**—, to send to press.
prelombar (*adj., Anat.*) prelumbar.
prelúcido –**da** (*adj.*) surpassingly bright.
preludiar (*v.t.*) to prelude; to precede as introductory; to introduce; to foreshadow; (*v.i.*) to prelude; to give or serve as a prelude; to furnish an introduction; to be introductory; (*Music*) to play an introduction or prelude.
prelúdio (*m.*) prelude, introduction, overture; flourish, fanfare.
prema (*f.*) oppression.
prematuração, prematuridade (*f.*) prematureness, prematurity.
prematuro –**ra** (*adj.*) premature; early; precocious.
premedeira (*f.*) treadle.
premediato –**ta** (*adj., Zool.*) premedian.
pré-medico –**ca** (*adj.*) pre-med [college course].
premeditação (*f.*) premeditation.
premeditado –**da** (*adj.*) deliberate.

premeditar (*v.t.*) to premeditate.
premência (*f.*) urgency; act of pressing.
premente (*adj.*) pressing; urgent.
premer (*v.t.*) to press, squeeze; to oppress.
pré-messiânico –ca (*adj.*) pre-Messianic.
premiado –da (*adj.*) prize-winning; winning (lottery ticket).
premiador –dora (*adj.*) rewarding; (*m.,f.*) one who rewards.
premiar (*v.t.*) to award a prize to; to reward, recompense.
pré-militar (*adj.*) premilitary [training].
prêmio (*m.*) premium, reward, prize; award; bonus, bounty; interest, profit.—**de consolação,** booby prize.—**honorífico,** honorary award.—**pecuniário,** pecuniary reward. **ganhar o**—, to carry off the prize.
premir (*v.*) = PREMER.
premissa (*f., Logic*) premise; presupposition.—**maior,** major premise.—**menor,** minor premise.
premoção (*f., Theol.*) premovement.
premolar (*adj.; m.*) premolar (tooth).
premonitório –ria (*adj.*) premonitory.
premonstratense (*m., R.C.Ch.*) Premonstratensian.
premorso –sa (*adj., Bot.*) premorse.
premunição (*f.*) premonition (but only in the sense of previous warning or forewarning). [In the sense of presentiment, the Port. equivalent is PRESSÁGIO or PRESENTIMENTO.]
premunir (*v.t.*) to premonish, forewarn; (*v.r.*) to forearm oneself, be prepared.
premunitivo –va (*adj.*)' premonitive, premonitory; forewarning.
prenanto (*m., Bot.*) rattlesnake root (*Prenanthes*).
pré-natal (*adj.*) prenatal.
prenda (*f.*) gift, present; token; talent, faculty; (*pl.*) accomplishments.—**s de mãos,** manual arts, needlework, embroidery, etc.—**s domésticas,** domestic arts. **jôgo de**—**s,** game of forfeits.
prendado –da (*adj.*) talented, accomplished, gifted.
prendar (*v.t.*) to present with, bestow upon, endow with.
prendedor –dora (*adj.*) binding, fastening; arresting, apprehending; (*m.*) arrester; fastener, holder; clasp, clip; (*Zool.*) remora, c.a. AGARRADOR.
prender [24] (*v.t.*) to bind, tie, fasten; to entangle; to hold, catch; to apprehend, seize; to arrest; (*v.r.*) to get caught, entangled, stuck; to cling (**a,** to); to catch, adhere, stick.
prenhe (*adj.*) pregnant, gravid; in foal; fraught, replete, full. Colloq. var. PRENHA.
prenhez (*f.*) pregnancy.—**molar** = MOLA HIDATIFORME.
prenoção (*f.*) prenotion, preconception.
prenome (*m.*) first or given name.
prenotação (*f.*) prenotation; prognostication.
prenotar (*v.t.*) to note beforehand.
prensa (*f.*) press (compressing machine of any kind); printing press; (*Photog.*) printing frame; (*slang*) a collusive raising of bets by two or more (poker) players—the intended victim gets caught in the squeeze.—**de algodão,** cotton press.—**de aparo,** trimming press.—**de copiar,** copying press.—**de lagar,** wine press; oil press.—**de parafuso,** screw press.—**hidráulica,** hydraulic press.—**tipográfica,** printing press.
prensagem (*f.*) act of pressing or compressing.
prensar (*v.t.*) to press, compress, squeeze.
prenseiro (*m.*), **prensista** (*m.,f.*) presser.
prenunciação (*f.*) prediction, foreboding, foreshadowing.
prenunciador –dora (*adj.*) foretelling, foreboding; (*m.,f.*) one who forebodes.
prenunciante (*adj.*) prenuncial, announcing beforehand.
prenunciar (*v.t.*) to proclaim beforehand; to predict, foretell, forebode, foreshadow.
prenunciativo –va (*adj.*) foreshadowing.
prenúncio (*m.*) prediction; advance sign.
prenupcial (*adj.*) prenuptial, antenuptial.
preocupação (*f.*) preoccupation, prepossession, engrossment, absorption; concern, worry, anxiety.
preocupado –da (*adj.*) uneasy, worried; concerned; anxious.
preocupante (*adj.*) preoccupying; (*m.,f.*) preoccupier.
preocupar (*v.t.*) to preoccupy; to prepossess; to engross, absorb; to obsess; to concern, disquiet; to worry.—**-se (com, de, em, por),** to be anxious about, concerned with; to worry about, worry over.
preopérculo (*m., Zool.*) preopercle, preoperculum.
preopinante (*m.,f.*) previous speaker.

preopinar (*v.i.*) to express one's opinion (ideas) before another (speaker).
preordenação (*f.*) preordination, preordaining, foreordaining.
preordenado –da (*adj.*) preordained; predestined.
preordenar (*v.t.*) to preordain, foreordain.
prepalatal (*adj., Phonet.*) prepalatal.
prepalato (*m., Anat.*) fore part of the hard palate.
preparação (*f.*) preparation (act, process, instance, result or product of preparing).
preparado –da (*adj.*) prepared, ready; well-educated, cultured; (*m.*) pharmaceutical or chemical product.
preparador –dora (*adj.*) preparing; (*m.,f.*) preparer; preparator, lab assistant.
preparamento (*m.*) preparation.
preparar (*v.t.*) to prepare; to fit, adapt, make ready; to get ready beforehand; to provide, equip; to fit out; (*Military command*) Ready!—**o terreno para,** to pave the way for; (*v.r.*) to prepare (oneself), get ready (**para,** to).
preparativo –va (*adj.*) preparatory, preparative; (*m.pl.*) preparations, preparatives.
preparatório –ria (*adj.; m.pl.*) preparatory (studies).
preparo (*m.*) preparation, preparing, making ready; (*colloq.*) ability, competence; (*pl.*) dressmakers' notions; harness, gear.
preponderância (*f.*) preponderance; predominance, supremacy; advantage; (*Ordn.*) preponderance.
preponderante (*adj.*) preponderant; outweighing; over-ruling.
preponderar (*v.t.*) to preponderate, outweigh, prevail, predominate.
prepor [63] (*v.t.*) to preplace; to place ahead of; to prefer.
preposição (*f.*) preposition.
preposicional (*adj.*) prepositional.
prepositivo –va (*adj.; f.*) prepositive (word).
prepósito (*m.*) = PROPÓSITO.
prepóstero –ra (*adj.*) preposterous (but only in the sense of inverted in order). [Preposterous in the ordinary sense of nonsensical is DISPARATADO.]
preposto –ta (*adj.*) placed before; preferred; (*m.*) manager, agent; (*Law*) institor, agent.
prepotência (*f.*) predominance; domineering, despotism.
prepotente (*adj.*) very powerful, superior in force; preponderant; overbearing, despotic.
prepúbico –ca (*adj., Anat., Zool.*) prepubic.
prepúcio (*m., Anat.*) prepuce.
prequeté (*f.*) Amazon Indian sandal or moccasin.
pré-rafaelita (*adj.; m.,f.*) pre-Raphaelite.
pré-renascentista (*adj.*) pre-Renaissance.
pré-romano –na (*adj.*) pre-Roman.
prerrogativa (*f.*) prerogative, privilege.
pres. = PRESIDENTE (President).
prêsa (*f.*) see under PRÊSO.
presbíope (*m.*) a presbyope (farsighted person).
presbiopia (*f., Med.*) presbyopia.
presbiópico –ca (*adj.*) presbyopic, farsighted.
presbita (*adj.; m.,f.*) farsighted (person).
presbiterado or –ato (*m.*) presbyterate, eldership.
presbiteral (*adj.*) presbyterial.
presbiter[i]anismo (*m.*) Presbyterianism.
presbiter[i]ano –na (*adj.; m.,f.*) Presbyterian.
presbitério (*m.*) presbytery.
presbítero (*m.*) presbyter.
presbitia (*f.*), **presbitismo** (*m., Med.*) presbytia, presbyopia, farsightedness.
presb.º = PRÉSBITO (presbyter).
presciência (*f.*) prescience, foreknowledge.
presciente (*adj.*) prescient.
prescindir (*v.t.*) to prescind from; to dispense with, give up, do without; to ignore, leave out of consideration.
prescindível (*adj.*) that can be dispensed with.
prescrever [44] (*v.t.*) to prescribe, lay down (authoritatively); to ordain, dictate; to enjoin; to fix, establish; to advise use of; (*v.i., Law*) to become outlawed (by prescription); to fall into decay (disuse).
prescrição (*f.*) prescript, direction, precept; (*Law*) prescription. [But not a doctor's prescription which is RECEITA.]—**aquisitiva,** acquisitive prescription —**extinta,** extinctive prescription.
prescritível (*adj.*) prescriptible.
prescrito –ta (*adj.*) prescribed; (*Law*) invalidated (by prescription).
presença (*f.*) presence, attendance; air, mien, appearance. —**de espírito,** presence of mind. **à**—**de, b̀efore, in the

presence of, face to face with. **dar pela—de (alguém),** to become aware of (another's) presence. **fazer ato de—,** to put in an appearance.

presencial (*adj.*) present. **testemunha—,** eye witness,

presenciar (*v.t.*) to witness, see, observe; to be present at (an occurrence).

presentâneo –nea (*adj.*) momentary.

presente (*adj.*) present, at hand; current, actual. **ter—que,** to bear in mind that; (*m.*) the present (now); member of an audience; present, gift; (*Gram.*) present tense; (*pl.*) those (persons) present.—**de aniversário,** birthday gift. **dar de—,** to present as a gift. **entre os—s,** among those present.

presentear (*v.t.*) to present (a gift) to. **—com,** to present with.

presépio, presepe (*m.*) stable; manager; crèche; Nativity scene (at Christmas).

preservação (*f.*) preservation, preserving.

preservador –dora (*adj.*) preserving; (*m.,f.*) preserver.

preservar (*v.t.*) to preserve, keep (from evil, harm, danger, etc.). [To preserve food, etc., is CONSERVAR.]

preservativo –va (*adj.; m.,f.*) preservative.

presidência (*f.*) presidency.

presidencial (*adj.*) presidential.

presidenta (*f.*) woman president; president's wife.

presidente (*adj.*) presiding; (*m.*) president; presider, chairman.—**da-porcaria** = CAPITÃO-DAS-PORCARIAS or MACUQUINHO.

presidiar (*v.t.*) to fortify with a garrison.

presidiário –ria (*adj.*) presidial; of or pert. to a presidio; detained in a presidio; (*m.*) inmate of a presidio or penitentiary.

presídio (*m.*) presidio, garrisoned place; fortified military prison.

presidir (*v.i.*) to preside (over), guide, direct.

presilha (*f.*) a tab, flap, loop, strip, etc., for fastening; paper fastener.

prêso –sa (*adj.; irreg. p.p. of* PRENDER) imprisoned, jailed, arrested, caught, seized; manacled; (*colloq.*) married; (*m.,f.*) a prisoner.—**em flagrante,** caught in the act.—**aos negócios,** tied down to business; (*f.*) seizure, capture; plunder, booty; prey, quarry; dam [= REPRÊSA]; fang, tusk, claw; woman prisoner.—**de guerra,** war prize.

pressa (*f.*) haste, dispatch, alacrity; speed; hurry, rush, impetuosity; impatience; urgency. **A—é inimiga da perfeição,** Haste makes waste. **a tôda—,** posthaste. **à(s) —(s),** hurriedly, hastily. **com—,** in a hurry. **dar-se—,** to hurry. **Estou com muita—,** I'm in a great hurry. **Ontem êle estava com tanta—que não pôde esperar,** Yesterday he was in such a hurry that he couldn't wait. **sem—,** leisurely, slowly, unhurriedly. **ter—de,** to be in a hurry to.

pressagiador –dora (*adj.*) presaging, foreboding; (*m.,f.*) soothsayer, presager.

pressagiar (*v.t.*) to presage, forebode; to foretell, bode, betoken.

presságio (*m.*) presage, omen, augury; prediction; conjecture.

pressagioso –sa (*adj.*) foreboding.

pressantificado –da (*adj.*) presanctified, preconsecrated.

pressão (*f.*) pressure; fig., compulsion; a snap button.—**arterial,** blood pressure.—**atmosférica,** atmospheric pressure.—**crítica,** (*Physics*) critical pressure.—**de adução,** intake pressure.—**de caldeira,** boiler pressure.—**de ensaio,** test pressure.—**dinâmica,** (*Hydraulics, Aeron.*) dynamic pressure, impact pressure.—**estática,** static pressure.—**interna,** internal pressure.—**manométrica,** gauge pressure.—**osmótica,** osmotic pressure.—**tributária,** tax pressure.

pressentido –da (*adj.*) anticipated, foreseen; jumpy, nervous, apprehensive, supersensitive.

pressentimento (*m.*) presentiment, foreboding, anticipation; misgiving.

pressentir [21a] (*v.t.*) to have a presentiment of; to foresee; to suspect, surmise; to have a hunch.

pressionar (*v.t.*) to pressure. [*A recent anglicism.*]

pré-sístole (*f., Physiol.*) presystole.

pré-sistólico –ca (*adj.*) presystolic.

pré-socrático –ca (*adj.*) pre-Socratic.

pressupor [63] (*v.t.*) to presuppose, assume, take for granted.

pressuposição (*f.*) presupposition; postulate.

pressuposto –ta (*adj.; p.p. of* PRESSUPOR) pre-supposed; (*m.*) presupposition, conjecture; pretext; design, **pur-**

pose, plan; (*conj.*) presupposing, supposing that.

pressurizado –da (*adj.*) pressurized. [*A recent anglicism.*] **cabine—,** (*Aeron.*) pressurized cabin.

pressuroso –sa (*adj.*) hasty; impatient; eager, keen, willing.

prestação (*f.*) instalment-payment; (*m.*) a peddler who sells dry goods, garments, etc., on the instalment plan; c.a. TURCO DA PRESTAÇÃO, PRESTAMISTA.

prestadio –dia, prestador –dora (*adj.*) usable; having some use; obliging.

prestamista (*m.*) moneylender; pawnbroker; one who derives an income from interest on government securities; merchant who sells on the instalment plan. Cf. PRESTAÇÃO.

prestante (*adj.*) helpful; excellent; worthy; distinguished.

prestar (*v.t.*) to render, give; to lend, afford; (*v.i.*) to be of use; good (fit) for; to serve, be suitable.—**atenção,** to pay attention.—**contas,** to give an accounting, render accounts (**a, to**).—**contas de,** to account for.—**caução,** to give bail.—**compromisso de posse,** to take oath of office.—**exame,** to take an exam.—**homenagem a,** to render homage to.—**juramento,** to take an oath.—**mão forte,** to lend a strong hand.—**ouvidos a,** to give ear, listen to.—**-se a,** to lend oneself (itself) to; to be suitable for.—**-se ao ridículo,** to lend oneself to ridicule.—**serviços a,** to render services to.—**socorro,** to give aid, help. **Não presta para nada,** It is of no use (no good).

prestativo –va (*adj.*) helpful, cooperative.

prestável (*adj.*) useful, serviceable; helpful, obliging.

prestes (*adj.*) ready, willing; (*adv.*) about to, at (on, upon) the point of, soon.—**a chegar,** about to arrive.

presteza [tê] (*f.*) readiness, alacrity, promptness, dispatch.

prestidigitação (*f.*) prestidigitation, sleight-of-hand. Var. PRESTIGIAÇÃO.

prestidigitador (*m.*) prestidigitator [= ILUSIONISTA]. Vars. PRESTIGIADOR, PRESTÍMANO.

prestidigitar (*v.i.*) to perform legerdemain.

prestigiado –da (*adj.*) illustrious, having prestige, influence.

prestigiar (*v.t.*) to give prestige to; to render influential.

prestígio (*m.*) prestige, influence, reputation.

prestigioso –sa (*adj.*) prestigious, having or manifesting prestige, influential.

préstimo (*m.*) worth, merit, utility, usefulness; aid, help. **sem—,** useless, worthless.

prestimoso –sa (*adj.*) helpful; excellent; worthy.

préstito (*m.*) procession, cortège, pageant.

presumido –da (*adj.*) presumptuous; vain, conceited; "stuck-up"; priggish; "fresh"; (*m.,f.*) such a person.

presumidor –dora (*adj.*) presuming; (*m.,f.*) one who presumes.

presumir (*v.t.*) to presume, suppose, assume, surmise; (*v.i.*) to be presumptuous, conceited, **segundo se presume,** supposedly.

presumível (*adj.*) presumable, presumptive, probable.

presunção (*f.*) presumption, conjecture; effrontery; pride; self-conceit; swank.

presunçoso –sa (*adj.*) vain, conceited, stuck-up; uppish; cocky; cocksure; self-important; smug; presumptuous; bumptious.

presunho (*m.*) dewclaw.

presuntivo –va (*adj.*) presumptive.

presunto (*m.*) ham.

preta [ê] (*f.*) see under PRÊTO.

pretalhada, pretaria (*f.*) a group of Negroes; Negroes collectively. [*Derogatory*]

pretalhão, pretalhaz (*m.*) a strapping Negro [= NEGRALHÃO].

pretejar (*v.i.*) to turn dark or black; of a street, to fill with people.

pretendente (*adj.*) pretending to; claiming; (*m.,f.*) pretender, claimant; candidate, aspirant; applicant; (*m.*) suitor.

pretender (*v.t.*) to pretend, lay claim to; to aspire to, aim at; to intend, mean, purpose.—**a mão de,** to aspire to the hand of. [To pretend, in the sense of feign, sham, make believe, is FINGIR, SIMULAR, FAZER DE CONTA.]

pretendida (*f.*) the intended one (fiancée).

pretensão (*f.*) pretention, claim, aspiration; (*pl.*) pretentions, airs, vain boasting.

pretensioso –sa (*adj.*) pretentious, affected; haughty; arrogant; highfalutin; overweening; (*m.,f.*) such a one.

pretenso –sa (*adj.*) supposed; would-be; sham.

preterição (*f.*) preterition; deferment; a passing over; (*Rhet.*) paraleipsis.

preterido –da (*adj.*) deferred, omitted, passed over.

preterir [21a] (*v.t.*) to pretermit, pass over (without mention or notice), omit; to neglect, leave undone; toî ail to promote or to appoint to a given position; to fail to grant a petition; to supplant.

pretérito –ta (*adj.*) bygone, former, past; (*m.*, *Gram.*) preterit.—**imperfeito**, imperfect indicative.—**mais, que perfeito**, pluperfect, past perfect.—**perfeito**, preterit indicative.

preterível (*adj.*) that may be passed over or deferred.

pretermissão (*f.*) pretermission, omission.

pretermitir (*v.t.*) to pretermit.

preternatural (*adj.*) preternatural, supernatural.

preternaturalismo (*m.*) preternaturalism.

pretextar [tês] (*v.t.*) to use or allege (something) as a pretext.

pretexto [tês] (*m.*) pretext, excuse; provocation. **a—de**, under pretext of. **sob o—de**, under the pretense of.

pretibial (*adj.*, *Anat.*) pretibial.

pretidão (*f.*) blackness.

pretinho –nha (*m.,f.*) Negro child.

prêto –ta (*adj.*) black, dark; fig., forbidding, sombre, dismal; (*m.*) a black man, Negro; the color black; (*f.*) Negro woman.—**-aça**, an albino Negro. [Cf. SARARÁ.]—**-mina**, a certain type of robust Negroes captured in the Cape Verde region of Africa and brought to Brazil as slaves.—**-musungo**, an African Negro of noble race, or a semi-civilized one. **As coisas andam pretas**, Things are pretty black. **dar no—para acertar no branco**, to proceed by indirection. **frades—s**, Benedictine monks. **pôr o—no branco**, to set down (something) in writing. **vestir de—**, to wear black.

pretônico –ca (*adj.*, *Philol.*) pretonic.

pretor (*m.*) justice of the peace; Roman praetor.

pretoria (*f.*) magistrate's court.

pretoriano –na (*adj.*) praetorian.

pretório –ria (*adj.*) praetorian; (*m.*) tribunal, court.

pretucano (*m.*) = PAPAGAIO (hogfish), and PARU-DAS-PEDRAS (butterfly fish).

pretume (*m.*), **pretura** (*f.*) = PRETIDÃO.

prevalecente (*adj.*) prevalent, prevailing, rife.

prevalecer (*v.i.*) to prevail (**contra**, against; **sôbre**, over); to predominate, preponderate.—**-se de**, to take advantage of, avail oneself of.—**-se contra**, to set oneself up against—**-se da desgraça alheia**, to take advantage of another's misfortune.

prevalência (*f.*) prevalency.

prevaricar (*v.i.*) to prevaricate (but only in the sense of deviating from rectitude or duty). [The equivalents of the ordinary senses, to lie, is MENTIR, to quibble is TERGIVERSAR.]

prevenção (*f.*) prevention; warning; prejudice.—**contra a tuberculose**, prevention of tuberculosis. **estar de—com**, to be prejudiced against, on one's guard against (another person).

prevenido –da (*adj.*) cautious, wary. **Um homem—vale por dois**, Forewarned is forearmed.

prevenir [21b] (*v.t.*) to prevent, preclude, forestall; to anticipate; to inform, warn, admonish, caution, advise; (*v.r.*) to prepare, take precautions. **Mais vale—do que remediar**, An ounce of prevention is better than a pound of cure; A stitch in time saves nine.

preventivo –va (*adj.*) preventive.

prever [81] (*v.t.*) to foresee, forecast, anticipate; to surmise.

prevertebral (*adj.*, *Anat.*) prevertebral.

prèviamente (*adj.*) previously; in anticipation of.

previdência (*f.*) forethought, foresight, forecast, precaution.—**social**, social welfare.

previdente (*adj.*) foreseeing, forehanded, provident.

prévio –via (*adj.*) previous, prior, former, foregoing. **sem aviso—**, without (prior) notice.

previsão (*f.*) prevision, foresight.—**da ·conjuntura**, business forecast.—**do tempo**, weather forecast.

previsível (*adj.*) foreseeable.

previsor –sora (*adj.*) = PREVIDENTE.

previsto –ta (*adj.*) foreseen.

prezado –da (*adj.*) dear, highly esteemed.—**s Snrs.**, Dear Sirs.

prezar (*v.t.*) to prize, hold dear, value highly, esteem; (*v.r.*) to have self-respect; to pride oneself on.

priacantídeos (*m.pl.*) a family (*Priacanthidae*) of small,

carnivorous tropical marine fishes.

príapo (*m.*) priapus; phallus [= FALO].

priapulídeos (*m.,pl.*, *Zool.*) a family (*Priapulidae*) of worms.

priceita [e-í] (*f.*, *Miner*) priceite, colemanite; pandermite.

prima (*f.*) female cousin; (*Eccl.*) prime (canonical hour); the first (finest) string of a musical instrument. Cf. PRIMO.

primado (*m.*) primacy; primateship.

prima-dona (*f.*) prima donna.

primagem (*f.*, *Marine*) primage.

primar (*v.i.*) to excel (**em**, in), be superior, stand out (**entre**, among), be noteworthy, notable (**por**, for).—**pela virtude**, to excel in virtue.

primário –ria (*adj.*) primary, prime, primal; (*colloq.*) childish, of limited intelligence, narrow-minded; primitive, benighted; (*m.,f.*) such a person.

primarismo (*m.*) childishness, want of intelligence, poverty of intellect, clouded perception, short-sightedness, narrow-mindedness.

primatas, –tes (*m.pl.*, *Zool.*) the Primates.

primavera (*f.*) spring, springtime. [In the southern hemisphere, the season beginning Sept. 22nd and ending Dec. 21st]; fig., youth; (*Zool.*) = POMBINHA-DAS-ALMAS; (*Bot.*) the cardinal starglory (*Quamoclit sloteri*), c.a. FLÔR-DO-CARDEAL; the cowslip primrose (*Primula veris*); the Brazil bougainvillea (*B. spectabilis*).—**-da-vida**, the prime of life.—**-de-caiena**, (*Bot.*) the scarlet starglory (*Quamoclit coccinea*), c.a. JETIRANA.—**-dos-jardins**, (*Bot.*) the oxslip primrose (*Primula elatior*).

primaveral, primaveril, primvero –ra (*adj.*) vernal.

primaz (*m.*) primate, archbishop; (*adj.*) prime, highest.

primazia (*f.*) primacy, excellency, supremacy; advantage; upper hand; rivalry; primateship.

primeira (*f.*) see under PRIMEIRO.

primeiramente (*adv.*) firstly, in the first place.

primeiranista (*m.,f.*) a first-year student, freshman.

primeirissimo –ma (*adj.; colloq.*) foremost, "firstest".

primeiro –ra (*adj.*) first, foremost, prime; primary; primal, primitive; first-born; elementary; (*m.,f.*) the first (one); (*adv.*) first.—**de Abril**, April Fool's day.—**de todos**, ahead of all (others).—**de tudo**, first of all.—**estado**, primitive state; virginity.—**meridiano**, (*Geog.*) first or prime meridian.—**ministro**, prime minister.—**móvel**, prime mover.—**número**, number one, A-1.—**oficial**, top-ranking non-com.—**passo**, first step.—**que**, before.—**raio de luz**, first ray of morning light.—**tenente**, first lieutenant. **ao—**, at first, in the beginning. **ao—aspeto**, at first sight. **ao—lance de olhos**, at first glance. **em—lugar**, in (the) first place. **Mateus,—os teus!** Charity begins at home. **o—do mês**, the first (day) of the month. **os três—s**, the first three. (*f.*) the first (one).—**dama**, leading lady (in a play); first lady (president's wife).—**falange**, (*Anat.*) first phalanx.—**idade**, infancy.—**mocidade**, early youth.—**página**, first page; front page.—**pedra**, cornerstone.—**pessoa**, (*Gram.*) first person.—**via**, the first or original copy (i.e., not a carbon copy).—**s águas**, the first rains of the season.—**s letras**, the three R's.—**s linhas**, first draft. **à—(vista)**, at first (sight). **de—**, tiptop, first-rate (quality).

primevo –va (*adj.*) primeval, primordial.

primícias (*f.pl.*) primitiae, first fruits.

primifalange (*f.*, *Anat.*) first phalanx.

primifalangeta (*f.*, *Anat.*) third phalanx.

primifalanginha (*f.*, *Anat.*) second phalanx.

primigênio –nia, **primígeno** –na (*adj.*) primigenial.

primigesta, primigrávida (*adj.; f.*, *Med.*) (woman) pregnant for the first time.

primina (*f.*, *Bot.*) primine.

primípara (*adj.*, *Med.*) primiparous.

primitiva (*f.*) see under PRIMITIVO.

primitivismo (*m.*) primitivism.

primitivo –va (*adj.*) primitive, original, primordial; ancient; simple (people); (*m.,f.*) a primitive (artist); (*f.*, *colloq.*) the early days, ancient times; the beginning.

primo –ma (*adj.*) prime. **número—**, prime number. **obra—**, masterpiece; (*m.,f.*) cousin.—**coirmão or—germano**, own, first or full cousin; cousin-german.—**segundo or—em segundo gráu**,· second cousin.—**em terceiro gráu**, third cousin.—**longe or longínquo**, distant cousin.—**s cruzados**, a man's son(s) in relation to his sister's daughter(s).—**s direitos**, the children of two brothers, or of two sisters, in relation to each other.

primogênito –ta (*adj.; m.,f.*) first-born (child).

primogenitor –tora (*m.,f.*) primogenitor, ancestor.

primogenitura (*f.*) primogeniture. **direito de—**, birthright.
primor (*m.*) excellence, fineness, perfection; beauty. **a—**, meticulously.
primordial (*adj.*) primordial, primitive; prime.
primordialidade (*f.*) primordiality.
primórdio (*m.*) origin, beginning.
primoroso -sa (*adj.*) perfect, excellent, exquisite, delicate.
prímula (*f.*) the primrose (*Primula*), better known as PRIMAVERA.
primuláceo -cea (*adj.*, *Bot.*) primulaceous; (*f.pl.*) the primrose family (*Primulaceae*).
primulina (*f.*) primuline, a yellow dye.
princeps (*adj.*) first [edition].
princês (*m.*) prince. [*Ironic*].
princesa [ê] (*f.*) princess.—**-da-noite**, (*Bot.*) the Peru cereus (*C. peruvianus*), c.a. FLOR-DO-BAILE, FLOR-DA-NOITE, MANDACARU, JAMACARU, RAINHA-DO-BAILE, RAINHA-DA-NOITE.—**-mafalda**, (*Bot.*) the brushtip sotol (*Dasylirion acrotrichum*).—**real**, princess royal.
principado (*m.*) principality; (*pl.*) in medieval angelology, one of the nine orders of angels.
principal (*adj.*) principal, chief, main, leading; (*m.*) principal; chief; capital sum.
principalidade (*f.*) principality (but only in the sense of state or quality of being principal). Cf. PRINCIPADO.
príncipe (*adj.*) principal; first. **edição—**, first edition; (*m.*) prince; also = VERÃO (a bird).—**consorte**, prince consort. —**da igreja**, prince of the Church (cardinal).—**das trevas**, Prince of Darkness (Satan).—**do ar**, Prince of the Power of the Air (Satan).—**dos Apóstolos**, prince of the Apostles (St. Peter).—**real**, prince royal.—**s de sangue**, princes of the blood royal.
principelho [ê] (*m.*) princeling.
principesco -ca [ê] (*adj.*) princely.
principiador -dora (*adj.; m.,f.*) beginner.
principiante (*adj.*) beginning; (*m.,f.*) beginner, novice; (*m.*) greenhorn; rookie, tyro.
principiar (*v.t.,v.i.*) to begin, start, set about.—**a**, to begin to.—**por**, to begin by.
principículo (*m.*) princekin.
princípio (*m.*) beginning, start; origin; principle, essence; element, component, ingredient; (*pl.*) rudiments.—**vital**, vital principle. **a—**, at first. **ao—**, at first, in the beginning. **no—**, in the beginning. **no—do mês**, at the beginning of the month.
priodonte (*m.*) a giant armadillo (*Priodontes giganteus*).
príono (*m.*) a genus (*Prionus*) of cerambycid beetles.
prior (*m.*) prior, parish-priest. [The adj. prior is PRÉVIO or ANTERIOR.]
priora (*f.*) = PRIORESA.
priorado, priorato (*m.*) priorate.
prioresa [ê] (*f.*) prioress.
prioridade (*f.*) priority.
prisão (*f.*) imprisonment, incarceration; confinement; seizure, capture; apprehension; arrest; prison, jail.—**de ventre**, constipation.—**domiciliar**, house arrest.—**perpétua**, life imprisonment. **mandado de—**, warrant for arrest.
priscar (*v.i.*) to dodge from side to side; (*v.r.*) to leave.
prisco -ca (*adj.*) pristine.—**s eras**, olden times, days of yore; (*m.*) dodge, leap; (*f.*) cigarette butt.
prise (*f.*, *Autom.*) high gear.
prisioneiro (*m.*), **-ra** (*f.*) prisoner; (*m.*) stud bolt.—**de guerra**, prisoner of war.
prisma (*m.*) prism; point of view, bias.
prismático -ca (*adj.*) prismatic.
prismatôide (*adj.*, *Geom.*) prismatoidal.
prismóide (*adj.*) prismoidal.
pristino -na (*adj.*) pristine.
privação (*f.*) privation, deprivation; (*pl.*) hardships, privations.
privado -da (*adj.*) private, confidential; devoid, deprived (**de**, of); (*m.*) confidant, private friend; (*f.*) privy, toilet, water closet [= LATRINA].
privança (*f.*) closeness, intimacy.
privar (*v.t.*) to deprive (**de**, of); to strip (**de**, of).—**com**, to hobnob with, be on intimate terms with, have private dealings with.—**se de**, to abstain from; to deprive oneself of.
privativo -va (*adj.*) privative, causing privation; depriving; private, exclusive, particular, own; (*Gram.*) privative [prefixes and suffixes].
privilegiado -da (*adj.*) privileged; exceptional.

privilegiar (*v.t.*) to privilege, invest with privilege, exempt from burden; to accord special treatment to.
privilégio (*m.*) privilege, prerogative, franchise.—**creditório**, (*Law*) preferred debts.—**de invenção**, or **de invento**, patent.
P.R.J. = PEDE RECEBIMENTO E JUSTIÇA (acceptance and justice requested).
pro, contraction of PARA + O.
pró (*adv.*) pro, for, in favor of, in behalf of; (*m.*) argument, reason, etc., for the affirmative. **os—s e os contras**, the pros and the cons.
proa [ô] (*f.*) prow, bow; (*Rowing*) bow oarsman; (*colloq.*) swagger, swank, airs. **abaixar a—**, to draw in one's horns; to eat humble pie. **castelo de—**, forecastle. **de—à pôpa**, fore and aft; from stem to stern. **figura de—**, figurehead. **sota—**, the oarsman next in line to the bow oarsman. **tirar a—a alguém**, to take the wind out of another's sails; to pull him off his high horse.
proâmnio (*m.*, *Embryol.*) proamnion.
probabilidade (*f.*) probability, likelihood.—**s da vida**, (*Statistics*) probable life, expectation of life.
probabilismo (*m.*) probabilism.
probabilista (*adj.*) probabilistic; (*m..f.*) probabilist.
probante (*adj.*) probative.
probatório -ria (*adj.*) probatory.
probidade (*f.*) probity, uprightness, honesty.
problema (*m.*) problem, question.—**de descida**, (*Aeron.*) landing problem.—**do alojamento**, housing problem.—**indeterminado**, (*Math.*) indeterminate problem. **ladear o—**, to dodge the issue.
problemático -ca (*adj.*) problematic(al), doubtful, dubious, uncertain.
probo -ba (*adj.*) honest, upright.
probóscide, -da (*f.*) proboscis, snout; elephant's trunk; proboscis of insects and worms.
proboscídeo -dea (*adj.*) having a proboscis; (*m.pl.*) the Proboscidea.
proboscidiano -na (*adj.*) proboscidian.
proboscidiforme (*adj.*) proboscidiform.
proc. = PROCESSO (lawsuit); PROCURAÇÃO (power of attorney); PROCURADOR (attorney).
procacia, procacidade (*f.*) insolence; pertness; petulance.
procâmbio (*m.*, *Bot.*) procambium.
procaz (*adj.*) pert; petulant; insolent.
procedência (*f.*) source, origin; derivation from; cogency; validity. **sem—**, without foundation (in fact).
procedente (*adj.*) proceeding from, derived from, arising from; logical; valid.
proceder (*v.i.*) to proceed, arise (**de**, from); to take measures (**contra**, against); to act, conduct oneself.—**a** or **em**, to go ahead with; (*m.*) procedure, conduct.
procedimento (*m.*) procedure, behavior; bearing; process, manner of proceeding; legal action; source.—**vil**, dirty trick.
procedura (*f.*) judicial procedure.
procefálico -ca (*adj.*) procephallic.
procela (*f.*) storm, tempest, esp. at sea; severe disturbance.
procelária (*f.*) a genus (*Hydrobates*) of stormy petrels.
procelarídeos (*m.pl.*, *Zool.*) the family of petrels, fulmars, shearwaters (*Hydrobatidae*).
proceloso -sa (*adj.*) stormy, tempestuous.
prócer[e] (*m.*) head, chief, top-ranking person (in a political party, government, etc.); (*pl.*) nobles.—**político**, political leader.
prócero -ra (*adj.*) important, prominent.
processador (*m.*) court official who prepares and handles the documents in a legal process.
processamento (*m.*) legal processing.
processar (*v.t.*, *Law*) to process; to prepare the papers in a (legal) process; to sue.
processional (*adj.*) processional.
processionar (*v.i.*) to march in procession.
processionário -ria (*adj.*) processional; (*m.*) processional prayer book; (*f.*) larva of the processionary moth.
processo (*m.*) process, procedure; (*Law*) proceeding; lawsuit, trial; the file of papers in a case. **intentar—contra**, to prefer charges against. **ir a—**, to go to court.—**sumário**, summary proceeding or procedure.
processual (*adj.*) processual.
procionídeo (*m.*, *Zool.*) one of the Procyonidae (raccoons, coatis, etc.).
procissão (*f.*) procession (esp. a religious one).
proclama (*f.*) banns (of marriage); proclamation.

proclamação (*f.*) proclamation, announcement, promulgation; edict, manifesto.
proclamador –**dora** (*adj.*) proclaiming; (*m.,f.*) proclaimer.
proclamar (*v.t.*) to proclaim, announce, declare, promulgate; (*v.r.*) to proclaim oneself to be (something).
proclamatório –**ria** (*adj.*) proclamatory.
proclinado –**da** (*adj.*) inclined toward; bent forward.
próclise (*f., Gram.*) proclisis.
proclítico –**ca** (*adj.; m.,f., Gram.*) proclitic (word).
proclive (*adj.*) inclined obliquely forward.
proclividade (*f.*) proclivity.
proclorita (*f., Min.*) prochlorite, clinochlorite.
procônsul (*m.*) proconsul.
proconsulado (*m.*) proconsulate.
proconsular (*adj.*) proconsular.
procoracoidal, procoracoídeo –**dea** (*adj.; m., Zool.*) precoracoid.
procotó (*m.*) = BARBEIRO (insect).
procrastinação (*f.*) procrastination; postponement.
procrastinador –**dora** (*adj.*) procrastinating; (*m.,f.*) procrastinator.
procrastinar (*v.t.*) to put off, postpone, delay, defer; (*v.i.*) to procrastinate.
procriação (*f.*) procreation.—**orientada**, planned parenthood.
procreador –**dora** (*adj.*) procreant; (*m.,f.*) procreator.
procriar (*v.t.*) to procreate, beget, engender; (*v.i.*) to beget offspring; to germinate.
proctoscopia (*f., Med.*) proctoscopy.
procumbente (*adj., Bot.*) procumbent.
procumbir (*v.i.*) to fall forward; to fall dead or wounded.
procura (*f.*) search, quest; demand (for goods, services, etc.). **a**, or **em**—**de**, in search of. **lei de oferta e**—, law of supply and demand.
procuração (*f.*) power of attorney; power of procuration; proxy.—**bastante**, limited p. of a.—**em branco**, blank p. of a.—**especial**, special p. of a.—**geral**, general p. of a.—**particular**, private p. of a.—**público**, notarized p. of a.
procuradeira (*f.*) prying woman.
procurador –**dora** (*adj.*) procuring; searching; (*m.,f.*) procurator, proctor, agent, proxy, attorney [but not procurer (procuress) which is CÁFTEN (CAFTINA)].
procuradoria (*f.*) proctorship; procurator's office.
procurar (*v.t.*) to seek (for), search for, look for; to aim at, strive after; to try, attempt; to call on, go to see (another person); (*v.i.*) to act as an attorney. [This verb is only rarely employed in Port. as an equivalent of procure, in the sense of gain, get, obtain, which translates CONSE-GUIR].—**a quadratura do círculo**, to attempt the impossible (lit., to attempt to square the circle).—**a sua vida**, to search for a way to make a living.—**agradar**, to aim to please.—**agulha em palheiro**, to look for a needle in a haystack.—**com a vista**, to search (for something) with the eyes, look for it.—**Deus**, to search for God.—**dormir**, to try to sleep.—**marido (mulher)**, to look for a husband (wife).—**por**, to make inquiries about (someone).—**sarna para se coçar**, to look for (ask for) trouble. **Procurou levantar-me o ânimo**, He (she) tried to cheer me up.
procustiano –**na** (*adj.*) Procrustean.
prodigalidade (*f.*) prodigality, lavishness, extravagance.
prodigalização (*f.*) lavishing, dissipation.
prodigalizador –**dora** (*adj.; m.,f.*) prodigal.
prodigalizar, prodigar (*v.t.*) to squander, lavish, dissipate.
prodígio (*m.*) prodigy, marvel, wonder.
prodigioso –**sa** (*adj.*) prodigious, marvellous, wonderful, extraordinary; very strange, amazing; huge.
pródigo –**ga** (*adj.*) prodigal, wasteful, wanton, extravagant, lavish. **filho**—, prodigal son; (*m.*) prodigal spendthrift, wastrel, squanderer.
proditório –**ria** (*adj.*) treacherous; traitorous.
prodrômico –**ca** (*adj.*) prodromal, precursory.
pródromo (*m.*) prodromus; prodrome; (*Med.*) premonitory symptom of a disease.
produção (*f.*) production; product, yield, output.—**em série**, mass production.
producente (*adj.*) producing; conclusive.
produtibilidade (*f.*) productibility.
produtível (*adj.*) producible.
produtividade (*f.*) productivity.
produtivo –**va** (*adj.*) productive, fertile, fruitful.
produto (*m.*) product, proceeds, returns; results, fruit.—**bruto**, gross receipts.—**derivado**, by-product.—**s alimentícios**, food products, foodstuffs.—**s de desperdício**,

waste products.—**s gravosos**, products which are overpriced (due to inflation) and thereby unable to compete in foreign markets.—**s químicos**, chemical products.
produtor –**triz** (*adj.*) producing; (*m.,f.*) producer, maker.
produzir [36] (*v.t.*) to produce; make, manufacture; to bring about; to cause to be or to happen; to bring forth; to generate, beget; (*v.i.*) to produce, bear, yield.
produzível (*adj.*) producible.
proeiro (*m.*) bow oarsman.
proejar (*v.i.*) to forge ahead.
proembrião (*m., Bot.*) proembryo.
proembrionário –**ria** (*adj., Bot.*) proembryonic.
proemial (*adj.*) proemial; prefatory.
proemiar (*v.t.*) to preface.
proeminar (*v.i.*) to stand out, project.
proeminência (*f.*) prominence, conspicuousness; protruberance, projection, salient point.
proeminente (*adj.*) prominent, eminent, distinguished; outstanding; jutting, protuberant.
proêmio (*m.*) proem, preface, preamble, foreword.
proemptose (*f., Chron.*) proemptosis.
proesto (*m., Physiol.*) pro-oestrum.
proeza [ê] (*f.*) feat, prowess, accomplishment; deed, exploit; stunt; (*colloq.*) scandalous behavior.
prof. = PROFESSOR (teacher).
prof.ª = PROFESSÔRA (teacher).
profanação (*f.*) profanation, desecration; sacrilege.
profanador –**dora** (*adj.*) profaning; (*m.,f.*) profaner.
profanar (*v.t.*) to profane, desecrate, defile.
profanidade (*f.*) profanity; profanation.
profano –**na** (*adj.*) profane, blasphemous; irreverent; secular, worldly; uninitiated; (*m.,f.*) the profane; outsider.
prófase (*f., Biol.*) prophase.
profecia (*f.*) prophecy, prediction, forecast, presage.
proferir [21a] (*v.t.*) to utter, pronounce.—**sentença**, to pronounce judgment.—**um discurso**, to deliver an address.—**uma conferência**, to give a lecture. **sem palavra**, without uttering a word.
professa (*f.*) see under PROFESSO.
professador –**dora** (*adj.*) professing; (*m.,f.*) one who professes.
professar (*v.t.*) to profess, avow, confess, declare (openly); to teach; to exercise a profession.
professo –**sa** (*adj.; m.,f.*) professed (person); (*f.*) professed nun.
professor (*m.*) teacher, schoolmaster; professor (of religion, of art, of special knowledge, etc.).—**catedrático**, university professor.—**particular**, private tutor.
professôra (*f.*) woman teacher; schoolmistress.
professoraço (*m.*) incompetent but vain teacher.
professorado (*m.*) professorate; professorship; teachers collectively.
professoral (*adj.*) professorial.
professorar (*v.t.,v.i.*) to teach (as a profession).
profeta (*m.*) prophet, seer, soothsayer; (*colloq.*) street lamplighter.
profético –**ca** (*adj.*) prophetic.
profetisa (*f.*) prophetess.
profetismo (*m.*) prophetism.
profetista (*adj.*) prophetic.
profetizador –**dora** (*adj.*) prophesying; (*m.,f.*) prophesier.
profetizar (*v.t.,v.i.*) to prophesy, foretell.
proficência (*f.*) proficiency, skill.
proficiente (*adj.*) proficient, skilled, adept, dextrous.
proficuidade [u-i] (*f.*) profitableness, usefulness.
profícuo –**cua** (*adj.*) profitable, useful.
profilá[c]tica (*f.*) = PROFILAXIA.
profilaxia [ks] (*f.*) prophylaxis.
profissão (*f.*) profession, calling, career, vocation, occupation; declaration, avowal.—**de fé**, profession of faith.—**s liberais**, the liberal professions.
profissional (*adj.; m.,f.*) professional.
profissionalismo (*m.*) professionalism.
profligado –**da** (*adj.*) overthrown, beaten, put to rout; profligate, dissolute.
profligar [3] (*v.t.*) to overthrow; to rout; to defeat; to destroy, demolish; to beat, strike; to try to destroy with arguments; to corrupt, deprave.
profragma (*m., Zool.*) prophragma.
prófugo (*m.*) fugitive; deserter.
profundar (*v.t.*) to deepen, make deeper; to fathom, plumb, sound, penetrate; (*v.i.,v.r.*) to go deep into; to grow deeper.

profundas (*f.pl.*, *colloq.*) the deepest part; the depths (of hell).
profundez(a) (*f.*) = PROFUNDIDADE.
profundidade (*f.*) profundity, depth, deepness. **bomba de—**, depth charge. **cem metros de—**, 100 meters deep.
profundo -da (*adj.*) profound, deep; penetrating; obscure; deep-seated; (*m.*) the deep; profundity; hell; (*adv.*) profoundly.
profundura (*f.*) = PROFUNDIDADE.
profusão (*f.*) profusion, lavishness; abundance.
profuso -sa (*adj.*) profuse, lavish, wasteful; prolix.
progênie (*f.*) lineage; descent; parentage; progeny, offspring; [= PROGENITURA].
progenitor -tora (*m.*,*f.*) progenitor; (*pl.*) ancestors.
progenitura (*f.*) = PROGÊNIE.
proglote (*f.*) tip of the tongue.
proglótide (*f.*, *Zool.*) proglottid.
prognatia (*f.*, *Anat.*, *Zool.*) prognathy.
prognático -ca (*adj.*) prognathic.
prógnato -ta (*adj.*) prognathous.
progne (*f.*) a swallow; springtime. [*Poetical*]
prognose (*f.*, *Med.*) prognosis.
prognosticar (*v.t.*) to prognosticate, foretell, predict; (*v.i.*, *Med.*) to make a prognosis.
prognóstico -ca (*adj.*) prognostic; (*m.*) prognostication, forecast; (*Med.*) prognosis.
programa (*m.*) program, plan, schedule.
programação (*f.*) act of programming.
programador -dora (*f.*) programmer.
programar, programatizar (*v.t.*) to program; to plan.
progredimento (*m.*) act of progressing.
progredir [21b] (*v.i.*) to progress, advance; to make headway.
progressão (*f.*) progression.—**aritmética**, or—**por diferença**, arithmetical progression.—**ascendente (descendente)**, (*Math.*) ascending (descending) series.—**geométrica**, or—**por quociente**, geometrical progression.
progressismo (*m.*) progressism; progressionism.
progressista (*adj.*) favoring, advocating or striving for progress; (*m.*, *f.*) such a person.
progressivo -va (*adj.*) progressive; advancing; developing.
progresso (*m.*) progress, advance(ment); development.—**do tempo**, the course of time.
pró-homem (*m.*) person of great influence in a period of history or of a social movement.
proibição [o-i] (*f.*) prohibition, forbiddance, ban.
proibicionismo [o-i] (*m.*, *Econ.*) protectionism.
proibicionista [o-i] (*adj.*; *m.*,*f.*) protectionist.
proibido -da [o-i] (*adj.*) prohibited, forbidden. **É—pregar cartazes**, Post no bills. **É—fumar**, No smoking.
proibidor -dora [o-i] (*adj.*) prohibiting; (*m.*,*f.*) one who prohibits.
proibir [o-i] (*v.t.*) to prohibit, forbid, inhibit.
proibitivo -va, proibitório -ria [o-i] (*adj.*) prohibitive, prohibitory, forbidding.
proiz [o-íz; pl. **-es**] (*m.*) hawser.
projeção (*f.*) projection, protuberance, extension; bulge, overhang; propulsion, ejection; project, plan; prominence.—**axonométrica**, (*Mech. drawing*) axonometric projection.—**gnomônica**, (*Math.*) gnomonic projection. —**isométrica**, (*Mech. drawing*) isometric drawing.— **oblíqua**, (*Mech. drawing*) oblique projection.—**ortogonal** or **ortográfica**, orthographic projection.
projetação (*f.*) = PROJEÇÃO.
projetador -dora (*adj.*) projecting; (*m.*,*f.*) one who projects.
projetante (*adj.*) projecting; (*f.*) projecting line.
projetar (*v.t.*) to project, propel, eject; to hurl; to plan, scheme, devise; to design; to delineate, draw; (*v.r.*) to throw oneself; to jut (out); protrude; to overhang.— **sôbre**, to cast over or on (as a shadow).
projetil [-tis], **projétil** [-teis] (*adj.*) projectile; (*m.*) projectile; missile.—**foguete**, rocket missile.—**teledirigido** or **teleguiado**, guided missile.
projetista (*adj.*) given to much planning; (*m.*,*f.*) planner, designer, projector, schemer.—**naval**, naval architect.
projetivo -va (*adj.*) projective.
projeto (*m.*) project, scheme, plan, design.—**de lei**, draft (legislative) bill.
projetor (*m.*) projector, searchlight, spotlight.—**de teto**, (*Aeron.*) ceiling projector.
projetura (*f.*) projection, overhang (as of a roof or window balcony).
prol (*m.*) benefit. **em—de**, in behalf of; in favor of; for;

pro; in support of; for the benefit of.
prolábio (*m.*, *Anat.*) prolabium.
prolação (*f.*) act of pronouncing, utterance; (*Mus.*) prolation.
prolapso (*m.*, *Med.*) prolapse.
prole (*f.*) progeny, offspring, issue, descendants.
prolegômenos (*m.pl.*) prolegomena, preliminary observations, introductory discourse.
prolepse (*f.*, *Rhet.*, *Philos.*) prolepsis; presupposition.
proléptico -ca (*adj.*) proleptic.
proletariado (*m.*) proletariat, the laboring classes, wage earners collectively.
proletário -ria (*adj.*; *m.*,*f.*) proletarian.
proletarização (*f.*) proletarization, proletarianization.
proliferação (*f.*) proliferation, rapid growth (of cells).
proliferar (*v.i.*) to proliferate, grow, multiply [cells, germs].
prolífero -ra (*adj.*) proliferous, prolific.
prolificação (*f.*) prolification.
prolificar (*v.i.*) to breed, produce offspring.
prolífico -ca (*adj.*) prolific, fruitful.
prolixidade [ks] (*f.*) prolixity, diffuseness, verbosity.
prolixo -xa [ks] (*adj.*) prolix, diffuse, wordy, long-winded, garrulous.
prologar (*v.i.*,*v.t.*) to prologize.
prologista (*m.*,*f.*) prologist.
prólogo (*m.*) prologue.
prolonga (*f.*) prolongation; (*Mil.*) prolonge.
prolongação (*f.*) prolongation, continuation, extension.
prolongado -da (*adj.*) prolonged, lengthened, protracted; lingering; delayed.
prolongador -dora (*adj.*) prolonging; (*m.*,*f.*) prolonger.
prolongamento (*m.*) prolonging, extension.
prolongar (*v.t.*) to prolong, lengthen, extend, project; (*v.r.*) to continue, last; to extend, stretch; to run alongside of.
prolongável (*adj.*) prolongable.
prolusão (*m.*) prolusion.
promanar (*v.i.*) to emanate, flow; arise, proceed, issue (de, from).
proméria-do-cerrado (*m.*) a treebine (*Cissus elongata*).
promessa (*f.*) promise, word, vow, pledge.
prometedor -dora (*adj.*) promising; (*m.*,*f.*) promiser.
prometéico -ca (*adj.*) Promethean.
prometer (*v.t.*) to promise, pledge, vow; (*v.i.*) to promise; to give ground for expectations.—**mundos e fundos**, or —**mares e montes**, to promise the moon.—**pancadas**, to promise a beating.—**sob palavra**, to promise on one's word.
prometido -da (*adj.*) promised, pledged; betrothed; (*m.*,*f.*) that which has been promised; (*m.*) fiancé; (*f.*) the promised one (fiancée).
prometimento (*m.*) act of promising; promise.
proeminência (*f.*) prominence.
prominente (*adj.*) = PROEMINENTE.
promiscuidade [u-i] (*f.*) promiscuity, promiscuousness.
promiscuir-se [u-ír] (*v.r.*) to mix or mingle promiscuously.
promíscuo -cua (*adj.*) promiscuous, indiscriminate.
promissão (*f.*) promise. **Terra da—**, the Promised Land.
promissivo -va (*adj.*) promissory.
promissor -sora (*adj.*) promising; (*m.*,*f.*) promiser.
promissório -ria (*adj.*) promissory; (*f.*) promissory note.
prominente (*adj.*) promising, promissory; (*m.*,*f.*) promiser.
promoção (*f.*) promotion, elevation, advancement.
promode (*contraction of* POR AMOR DE) for the sake of.
promombó (*m.*) fishing by torchlight (which causes fish to jump into the canoe), and in other ways than by hooking, such as by herding fish into shallow water where they can be scooped up.
promontório (*m.*) promontory, headland.
promorfologia (*f.*, *Biol.*) promorphology.
promotor -tora (*adj.*) promoting, fomenting; (*m.*) promoter.—**público**, public prosecutor, prosecuting attorney.
promotoria (*f.*) public prosecutor's office.
promover (*v.t.*) to promote, forward, advance, further; to foment, foster; to prosecute; to elevate.—**uma ação (contra)**, to bring suit (against).
promulgação (*f.*) promulgation, divulgation.
promulgador -dora (*adj.*) promulgating; (*m.*,*f.*) promulgator, publisher.
promulgar (*v.t.*) to promulgate; publish, make known, blaze abroad.
pronação (*f.*, *Physiol.*) pronation.
pronador (*m.*, *Anat.*) pronator.

pronefro (*m. Embryol.*) pronephros.
prono **-na** (*adj.*) prone.
pronome (*m.*) pronoun.
pronominado **-da, pronominal** (*adj.*) pronominal.
pronóstico **-ca** (*adj.; colloq.*) presumptuous pretentious, affected. Cf. PERNÓSTICO.
pronoto (*m., Zool.*) pronotum.
prontidão (*f.*) promptitude, promptness, readiness, quickness, alertness; (*colloq.*) lack of funds; (*m.*) officer on duty at a police station.
prontificar (*v.t.*) to make ready; (*v.r.*) to volunteer, offer (to do a thing); to declare oneself ready and willing.
pronto **-ta** (*adj.*) prompt, ready, quick, alert; willing, disposed; ready, prepared, finished; (*colloq.*) flat, broke, strapped; (*adv.*) promptly. **de—**, immediately.
pronto-socorro (*m.*) emergency hospital; first-aid clinic.
prontuário (*m.*) handbook; a police dossier.
prônubo **-ba** (*adj.*) matchmaking.
pronúcleo (*m., Biol., Embryol.*) pronucleus.
pronúncia (*f.*) pronunciation, utterance, enunciation, articulation; (*Law*) arraignment; indictment [= DENÚNCIA, ACUSAÇÃO].
pronunciação (*f.*) pronunciation.
pronunciado **-da** (*adj.*) pronounced, strongly marked; distinct; (*Law*) arrainged; indicted.
pronunciamento (*m.*) pronouncement, pronunciamiento, manifesto.
pronunciar (*v.t.*) to pronounce, enunciate, articulate (words); to declaim, make a speech; to assert, declare; (*Law*) to arraign; to indict; [= DENUNCIAR, ACUSAR] (*v.r.*) to declare oneself, express one's opinion, pass judgment (**acêrca de** or **sôbre**, on, about, concerning; **contra**, against; **em favor de**, for, in favor of).
pronunciável (*adj.*) pronounceable.
propadieno (*m., Chem.*) propadiene; allene.
propagação (*f.*) propagation, multiplication; generation, procreation; dissemination, diffusion.
propagador **-dora** (*adj.*) propagating; diffusive; (*m.,f.*) propagator; diffuser.
propaganda (*f.*) legitimate advertising; propaganda. **fazer—**, to advertise.
propagandista (*m.,f.*) propagandist; advertising agent, press agent.
propagar (*v.t.*) to propagate, multiply, increase; to procreate; to disseminate, spread, diffuse; to extend; (*v.r.*) to spread (as fire); to multiply (as rabbits).
propagativo **-va** (*adj.*) propagative.
propágulo (*m., Bot.*) propagulum.
propalação (*f.*) act of divulging.
propalador **-dora** (*adj.*) divulging; (*m.,f.*) divulger.
propalar (*v.t.*) to spread abroad, noise abroad, publish, divulge, disclose.
propanal (*m., Chem.*) propanal, propyl aldehyde.
propanatriol (*m., Chem.*) glycerol, glycerin.
propano, propânio (*m., Chem.*) propane, dimethyl methane.
propanóico **-ca** (*adj.*) = PROPIÔNICO.
propanol (*m.*) propyl alcohol [= ÁLCOOL PROPÍLICO].
propanoma (*f., Chem.*) acetone.
propargílico **-ca** (*f., Chem.*) propargylic.
proparoxítono **-na** [ks] (*adj.; m., Gram.*) proparoxytone (word).
propelir [21a] (*v.t.*) to propel, drive foreward.
propender (*v.i.*) to hang downward or forward; to incline; to be favorably inclined; to tend.
propensão (*f.*) propension, propensity; penchant.
propenso **-sa** (*adj.*) inclined, disposed, favorable, partial.
propiciação (*f.*) propitiation.
propiciador **-dora** (*adj.*) propitiating; (*m.,f.*) propitiator.
propiciar (*v.t.*) to propitiate; to provide, give.
propiciatório **-ria** (*adj.; m.*) propitiatory.
propício **-cia** (*adj.*) propitious, auspicious, favorable, opportune.
propilamina (*f., Chem.*) propylamine.
propilbenzina (*f., Chem.*) propyl benzene.
propileno (*m., Chem.*) propylene, propene.
propilglicol (*m., Chem.*) propylene glycol.
propílio (*m., Chem.*) propyl.
propilito (*m., Petrog.*) propylite.
propina (*f.*) tip, gratuity; esp. of drink money; fee; entrance fee.
propinar (*v.t.*) to offer, give (drink, poison) to.
propínio (*m., Chem.*) propyne, allylene, methyl acetylene.
propinóico **-ca** (*adj., Chem.*) propargylic.

propinol (*m., Chem.*) propargyl alcohol, propiolic alcohol.
propinqüidade (*f.*) propinquity, nearness, proximity.
propínquo **-qua** (*adj.*) near, neighboring; (*m.pl.*) kinsfolk.
propiólico **-ca** (*adj.*) propiolic [acid].
propionato (*m., Chem.*) propionate.
propione (*m., Chem.*) propione, ethyl ketone.
propiônico **-ca** (*adj., Chem.*) propionic [acid].
proplasma (*f.*) proplasm, mold, matrix.
proplástico **-ca** (*adj.*) proplastic; (*m.*) sculptor's clay or wax model; (*f.*) proplastic (art of making molds for casting).
propódio (*m., Zool.*) propodeum.
propodite (*m., Zool.*) propodite.
própole (*f.*) propolis, bee glue. Var. PRÓPOLIS.
propolizar (*v.t.*) to propolize.
proponente (*adj.; m.,f.*) proponent.
proponível (*adj.*) proposable.
propor [63] (*v.t.*) to propose, suggest, offer (for consideration); (*v.r.*) to intend, purpose. **O homem propõe e Deus dispõe**, Man proposes but God disposes.
proporção (*f.*) proportion, relation; ration; rate; dimension; symmetry.—**aritmética**, or—**por diferença**, arithmetical proportion.—**contínua**, harmonic proportion. **à—** proportionally. **à—de**, in proportion to; at the rate of. **à—que**, as, according as, while, at the same time that.
proporcionação (*f.*) proportioning.
proporcionado **-da** (*adj.*) well-proportioned; proportionate; commensurate, adequate.
proporcional (*adj.*) proportional; proportionate.
proporcionalidade (*f.*) proportionality.
proporcionalizar (*v.t.*) to proportionate.
proporcionamento (*m.*) proportionment.
proporcionar (*v.t.*) —**a, com**, to proportion to, adjust to; to give to, provide to; (*v.r.*) to present itself (as, an opportunity).
proporcionável (*adj.*) proportionable.
proposição (*f.*) proposition; proposal; postulate; statement; (*Gram.*) clause; (*Math.*) theorem; problem.
propositadamente (*adv.*) purposely, on purpose.
propositado **-da, proposital** (*adj.*) purposed, intentional, willful, designed, deliberate.
propósito (*m.*) purpose, design, intention; resolution. **a—** (**de**), apropos, to the point, opportunely, seasonably; by the way; speaking of that; in that connection; for the reason that; by reason of the fact that. **com—**, wisely. **de—**, purposely, on purpose, deliberately, intentionally. **fora de—**, out of reason; irrelevant. **sem—**, aimless(ly), unintentional(ly). **ter o—de**, to aim at.
proposta (*f.*) proposal, bid, offer; proposition; thing or person proposed.—**de lei**, legislative bill.
proposto **-ta** (*m.,f.*) thing or person proposed.
pròpriamente (*adv.*) properly; rightly, correctly; individually, personally; intrinsically; inherently.—**dito**, strictly speaking.
propriedade (*f.*) property, possessions (esp. real estate); attribute; propriety, appropriateness.—**alodial**, freehold. —**s físicas**, physical properties. **direitos de—**, property rights.
proprietariado (*m.*) property owners collectively.
proprietário **-ria** (*adj.*) proprietary, proprietorial; (*m.,f.*) proprietor, owner, possessor, esp. of real property.
próprio **-pria** (*adj.*) own (not another's), private, particular, peculiar, individual; proper, fitting, appropriate; real, actual; exact, precise; (*m.*) individual characteristic, special quality, peculiar feature (of something or someone); private courier or messenger.—**de**, pertaining to.— **para**, fit for. **do—punho**, in one's own handwriting. **êle—**, he himself. **por iniciativa—**, on one's own initiative. **por si—**, of his own accord.
propterígio (*m., Zool.*) propterygium.
proptoma, proptose (*f., Med.*) proptosis; exophthalmos.
propugnação (*f.*) propugnation.
propugnáculo (*m.*) fortress, bulwark, defense.
propugnador **-dora** (*adj.*) defending; (*m.,f.*) defender; vindicator; booster.
propugnar (*v.t.*) to defend, uphold.—**por**, to fight for, stand up for; to boost.
propulsão (*f.*) propulsion.—**a jato**, jet propulsion.
propulsar (*v.t.*) to repulse, repel; to propel, drive forward.
propulsionador **-dora** (*adj.*) propelling, driving; (*m.,f.*) one who or that which drives or propels. [But not propeller, which is HÉLICE or PROPULSOR.]
propulsivo **-va** (*adj.*) propulsive, propelling.

propulsor –sora (*adj.*) propelling; (*m.*) propeller.—**helicóide,** ship's propeller. **eixo**—, driving axle.
prorratado –da (*adj.*) prorated.
prorratear (*v.t.,v.i.*) to prorate.
prorrogação (*f.*) prorogation, adjournment, postponement, continuance.—**do estado de sítio,** extension of the state of siege.
prorrogador –dora (*adj.*) proroguing, delaying; (*m.,f.*) one who prorogues.
prorrogar (*v.t.*) to prorogue, postpone, extend the time limit.—**uma letra por trinta dias,** to extend a note for thirty days.
prorrogativo –va, **prorrogatório** –ria (*adj.*) that prorogues.
prorrogável (*adj.*) postponeable.
prorromper (*v.i.*) to burst out.—**em aplausos,** to break out in applause.
Pros. = PROSÓDIA (*Prosody*).
prosa (*adj.; m.,f.*) boastful, vainglorious (person); (*m.*) a blowhard; (*f.*) prose; that which is prosaic; (*colloq.*) chat, chit-chat, chatter; swagger, bluster; dalliance, courtship. **dar uma**—, to hold a friendly chat. **tirar a**—**a (alguém),** to take the conceit out of (someone).
prosador (*m.*), –dora (*f.*) prose writer.
prosaico –ca (*adj.*) prosaic(al), dull, matter-of-fact, humdrum, workaday.
prosaísmo (*m.*) prosaism.
prosaísta (*m.,f.*) prose writer.
prosantera (*f., Bot.*) the mint bush (*Prosanthera*).
prosápia (*f.*) ancestry; family pride; vainglory.
prosar (*v.i.*) to write in prose; to chat.
proscênio (*m.*) proscenium; stage.
proscolécio (*m., Zool.*) proscolex.
proscrever [44] (*v.t.*) to proscribe, banish; to ban, interdict; to condemn.—**de,** to exclude from.
proscrição (*f.*) proscription, banishment, exile; exclusion; expulsion; condemnation.
proscrito –ta (*p.p. of proscrever*) proscribed; (*m.,f.*) exile, banished person; outcast; outlaw.
proscritor (*m.*) proscriber.
proseador –dora (*adj.*) chatty, talkative; (*m.,f.*) talker; loquacious person.
prosear (*v.i.*) to talk, chat, palaver, "jaw".
proseirão (*m.*), –rona (*f.*) prosaic person concerned only with material things.
proselítico –ca (*adj.*) proselytical.
proselitismo (*m.*) proselytism.
prosélito (*m.*), –ta (*f.*) proselyte, convert.
prosênquima (*m., Bot.*) prosenchyma.
proserpínia (*f., Bot.*) mermaid weed (*Proserpinaca*).
prosificação (*f.*) prosification.
prosificar (*v.t.*) to prosify.
prosista (*m.,f.*) prose writer; proser; chatterer; blowhard.
prosodêmico –ca (*adj.*) prosodemic [diseases].
prosódia (*f.*) orthoepy, correct pronunciation, esp. as regards accent. [Not an equivalent of prosody which is VERSIFICAÇÃO, METRIFICAÇÃO.]
prosonomásia (*f.*) prosonomasia.
prosopito (*m., Min.*) prosopite.
prosopografia (*f.*) prosopography.
prosopopéia (*f., Rhet.*) prosopopoeia.
prospecção (*f.*) prospecting (for oil, gold, minerals, etc.).
prospectar (*v.i.*) to prospect.
prosperador –dora (*adj.*) prospering.
prosperar (*v.i.*) to prosper, thrive, flourish, succeed.
prosperidade (*f.*) prosperity, success, felicity, welfare.
próspero –ra (*adj.*) prosperous, successful, flourishing, thriving; propitious, favorable.
prospérrimo –ma, **prosperíssimo** –ma (*absol. superl. of* PRÓSPERO) most prosperous.
prospetivo –va (*adj.*) prospective; (*f.*) = PERSPECTIVA.
prospeto (*m.*) prospect, outlook; prospectus, plan, outline; circular.
prospetor (*m.*) prospector.
prossecução (*f.*) prosecution, pursuit, a carrying on (out), a following out (up).
prossecutor (*m.*), –tora (*f.*) one who prosecutes, pursues, follows, etc. See the verb PROSSEGUIR.
prosseguição (*f.*) = PROSSECUÇÃO.
prosseguidor –dora (*adj.*) prosecuting, pursuing, following, continuing; (*m.,f.*) prosecutor, pursuer, follower.
prosseguimento (*m.*) = PROSSECUÇÃO.
prosseguir [21a] (*v.t.*) to prosecute, pursue; (*v.i.*) to continue; to follow, keep on, go on, go ahead, carry on.
prossilogismo (*m., Logic*) prosyllogism.

prossímio (*m., Zool.*) prosimian, lemur.
próstata (*f., Anat.*) prostate gland.
prostatectomia (*f., Surg.*) prostatectomy.
prostático –ca (*adj.*) prostate; (*m.*) one who suffers from prostatism.
prostatite (*f., Med.*) prostatitis.
prosternar (*v.*) = PROSTRAR.
próstese (*f., Gram.*) prosthesis. Cf. PRÓTESE.
prostibular (*adj.*) of or pert. to brothels.
prostíbulo (*m.*) brothel, bawdyhouse [= BORDEL, LUPANAR].
prostilão (*m., Arch.*) prostyle front.
prostilo (*m., Arch.*) a prostyle building.
próstio (*m., Craniol.*) prosthion.
prostituição [u-i] (*f.*) prostitution, harlotry; perversion, degradation.
prostituidor –dora [u-i] (*adj.*) prostituting; (*m.,f.*) prostituter.
prostituir (*v.t.*) to prostitute, degrade (–se, oneself).
prostituível (*adj.*) capable of being prostituted.
prostituto –ta (*adj.*) prostituted; (*f.*) prostitute, harlot [= MERETRIZ].
prostração (*f.*) prostration; collapse, breakdown; exhaustion.
prostramento (*m.*) = PROSTRAÇÃO.
prostrar (*v.t.*) to prostrate, throw down, overthrow; to bring low; (*v.r.*) to prostrate oneself.
protagão (*m., Biochem.*) protagon.
protagonista (*m.,f.*) protagonist; (*m.*) leading man.
protamina (*f., Biochem.*) protamine.
protandria (*f., Bot., Zool.*) protandry.
protândrico –ca (*adj.*) protandric, protandrous.
protandro –dra (*adj.*) protandrous.
protanopsia (*f.*) protanopia, red blindness.
protanóptico –ca (*adj.*) protanoptic.
protargol (*m., Pharm.*) protargol.
prótase (*f.*) protasis.
protático –ca (*adj.*) protatic.
proteáceo –cea (*adj., Bot.*) proteaceous; (*f.pl.*) the protea family (*Proteaceae*).
proteção (*f.*) protection; safeguard; shelter, refuge; championship, patronage; help, aid, support; (*Econ.*) protection.
protecionismo (*m.*) protectionism.
protecionista (*adj.; m.,f.*) protectionist.
protegedor –dora (*adj.; m.,f.*) protector.
protegedoria (*f., colloq.*) protection.
proteger (*v.t.*) to protect, guard, watch over; to defend, safeguard; to champion, foster.
protegido –da (*adj.*) protected; (*m.*) protegé; (*f.*) protegée; kept woman.
protéico –ca (*adj.*) protean; (*Biochem.*) proteic, proteinaceous.
proteiforme (*adj.*) proteiform, protean.
proteína (*f., Biochem.*) protein.
proteínico –ca (*adj.*) proteinaceous.
protelação (*f.*), **protelamento** (*m.*) a putting off, postponement, procrastination, delay.
protelador –dora (*adj.*) procrastinating; (*m.,f.*) procrastinator.
protelar (*v.t.*) to postpone, put off, delay; to stave off.
protelatório –ria (*adj.*) dilatory. **manobra**—, delaying tactic.
protendido –da (*adj.*) prestressed [concrete]
proteólise (*f., Biochem.*) proteolysis.
proteose (*f., Biochem.*) proteose.
proterandria (*f., Zool.*) protandry.
proterândrico –ca (*adj.*) protandrous.
proterânteo –tea (*adj., Bot.*) proteranthous.
proteróbase (*f., Petrog.*) proterobase.
proteroginia (*Zool.*) protogyny.
proterogínico –ca (*adj.*) protogynous.
proteróglifa (*f.pl.*) one of the Proteroglypha (snakes).
proterozóico –ca (*adj., Geol.*) proterozoic.
prótese (*f., Gram., Surg., Dent.*) prosthesis. Cf. PRÓSTESE
protesista (*m.,f.*) = PROTÉTICO.
protestação (*f.*) protestation; protest.
protestador –dora (*adj.*) protesting; (*m.,f.*) protester.
protestante (*adj.*) protestant (*m.,f.*) one who protests; a Protestant.
protestantismo (*m.*) Protestantism.
protestar (*v.t.*) to protest, declare, assert, affirm, aver; to kick up a row; to protest (a note or draft); (*v.i.*) to protest (against); to dissent; to object.

protesto (*m.*) protest, protestation; objection, "kick," complaint.

protético –ca (*adj., Gram., Surg., Dent.*) prosthetic; (*m.,f.*) prostodontist.

protetivo –va (*adj.*) protective.

protetor –tora (*adj.*) protecting, defending; aiding; (*m.*) protector, patron, supporter; shield, cover; guard; (*f.*) patroness.

protetorado, –to (*m.*) protectorate.

protetoral (*adj.*) protectoral.

protetório –ria (*adj.*) protecting.

proteu (*m.*) a protean person.

prótilo (*m., Chem., Astron.*) protyle.

protíride (*f., Arch.*) prothyride.

prótiro (*m., Arch.*) prothyrum.

protista (*m., Biol.*) protist.

protactínio (*m., Chem.*) protoactinium.

protoblasto (*m., Biol.*) protoblast.

protocanônico –ca (*adj., Biol.*) protocanonical.

protoclástico –ca (*adj., Petrog.*) protoclastic.

protococo (*m.*) a genus (*Protocococcus* syn. *Pleurococcus*) of green algae.

protocolar (*adj.*) protocolar; (*v.t.*) to protocol(ize).

protocolista (*m.,f.*) protocolist.

protocolizar (*v.t.*) to protocolize.

protocolo (*m.*) protocol.

protocone (*m., Zool.*) protocone.

protoconide (*m., Zool.*) protoconid.

protodórico –ca (*adj., Arch.*) proto-Doric.

protofílico –ca (*adj., Chem.*) protophilic.

protófitos (*m.pl.*) the Protophyta (unicellular plants).

protogênico –ca (*adj., Chem.*) protogenic.

protógeno –na (*adj., Bot., Geol.*) protogenic.

protoginia (*f., Bot.*) protogyny.

protógino (*m., Petrog.*) protogine.

protógrafo (*m., Biol.*) protograph.

protohematoblasto (*m., Anat.*) protohematoblast.

protomártir (*m.*) protomartyr.

protomeristema (*m., Bot.*) protomeristem.

protomerita (*m., Zool.*) protomerite.

próton (*m., Physics, Chem.*) proton.

protonema (*f., Bot.*) protonema.

protoneurônio (*m., Anat.*) protoneuron.

protônico –ca (*adj., Philol.*) pretonic.

protonotário (*m.*) prothonotary.

protopapa (*m. Eastern Ch.*) protopope.

protopatia (*f.*) protopathy.

protopina (*f., Chem.*) protopine.

protoplasma (*m. Biol.*) protoplasma.

protoplasmático –ca, **protoplásmico** –ca (*adj.*) protoplasmatic.

protopódio (*m., Zool.*) protopodite.

protoprisma (*m., Cryst.*) protoprism.

protóptero (*m.*) protopterus (a lung fish).

protorosauro (*m., Paleontol.*) protorosaur.

protossifonáceas (*f.pl.*) a family (*Protosiphonaceae*) of green algae.

proterianos (*m.pl., Zool.*) the Prototheria (monotremes).

prototípico –ca (*adj.*) prototypic.

protótipo (*m.*) prototype.

prototropia (*f., Chem.*) prototropy.

protóxido [ks] (*m., Chem.*) protoxide.—**de chumbo,** lead monoxide.—**de cobre,** copper oxide.

protoxilema [ks] (*m., Bot.*) protoxylem.

protozoário –ria (*adj.; m., Zool.*) protozoan; (*m.pl.*) the Protozoa.

protraimento [a-i] (*m.*) protraction.

protrair (*v.t.*) to protract, prolong.

protrusão (*f.*) protrusion.

protuberância (*f.*) protuberance, prominence, projection, bulge, bump.—**anular,** (*Anat.*) the midbrain.—**s solares,** (*Astron.*) solar streamers.

protuberante (*adj.*) protuberant.

protuso –sa (*adj.*) protruding, bulging.

protutor (*m., Law*) protutor.

proustita (*f.*) = PRUSTITA.

prouv+verb endings=forms of PRAZER [64].

prov.=PROVEDOR (purveyor); PROVISÃO (provision, supply); PROVISÓRIO (temporary).

prova (*f.*) proof, demonstration, verification, confirmation, testimony; test, trial; taste, sample; ordeal; examination; proof sheet.—**de carga,** load test.—**dos nove,** fig., acid test, final test.—**s de afeição,** tokens of affection. **à—de água,** waterproof. **à—de bala,** bulletproof.

à—de bomba, bombproof. **à—de chuva,** rainproof. **à—de fogo,** fireproof. **à—de ruído,** soundproof. **a tôda—,** irrefragable. **corrida de—,** test run. **remeter à—,** to send on approval.

provação (*f.*) probation; proving, proof; test, trial, ordeal; hardship.

provado –da (*adj.*) proven; tested.

provador –dora (*adj.*) proving; testing (*m.,f.*) prover; tester.—**de vinho,** winetaster.

provadura (*f.*) trial, test; tasting.

provante (*adj.*) proving.

provar (*v.t.*) to prove, demonstrate; to test, try, assay; to put to the test; to experience, undergo; to taste; to try on (as a garment). [In Port., to prove, in the intransitive sense of turn out to be, is VERIFICAR-SE or DESCOBRIR-SE.].—**à saciedade,** to prove completely, overwhelmingly. **—armas,** to measure arms.—**forças com,** to try forces with.—**fortuna em,** to risk one's chances; to venture.—**lanças,** to cross swords with.

provará (*m., Law*) each of the counts in a bill of indictment.

provatório –ria (*adj.*) = PROBATÓRIO.

provável (*adj.*) probable, likely.

provecção (*f., Philol.*) provection.

provecto –ta (*adj.*) advanced, esp. in years; experienced; accomplished. **de idade—,** of advanced years. **idade—,** old age.

provedor –dora (*m.,f.*) purveyor; provider.

provedoria (*f.*) office of purveyor.

proveito (*m.*) profit, gain; advantage, benefit; boon; utility. **em—comum,** to (our) mutual profit; for (our) common good. **em—de,** to the profit of, in benefit of. **tirar—de,** to gain advantage by; to benefit by; to turn (something) to account.

proveitoso –sa (*adj.*) advantageous profitable.

proveniência (*f.*) provenience, provenance, source, origin.

proveniente (*adj.*) provenient, forthcoming, issuing.—**de,** proceeding from, originating in.

provento (*m.*) benefit, gain; (*pl.*) retirement income, pension.

prover [66] (*v.t.*) to provide, supply, furnish (**de, com,** with); to bestow, confer (**em,** upon).—**a,** or—**acerca de,** to look after, see to, attend to.—**com que,** to see to it that.—**se de,** to provide oneself with.

proverbiador (*m.*) book of proverbs.

proverbial (*adj.*) proverbial.

proverbiar (*v.i.*) to utter proverbs.

provérbio (*m.*) proverb, maxim, adage, saying.

proverbioso –sa (*adj.*) given to using proverbs, sententious.

proverbista (*m.,f.*) person given to using proverbs.

provete [vê] (*m.*) test tube, glass gauge.

providência (*f.*) foresight, prudence; divine Providence; (*pl.*) steps, measures, means.

providencial (*adj.*) providential.

providencialismo (*m.*) providentialism.

providenciar (*v.i.*) to provide, arrange; to take steps, measures; to take care of matters, arrange things; (*v.t.*) to look out for, procure, prepare.

providente (*adj.*) provident, prudent, foresighted.

provido –da (*adj.*) provided for, well-supplied.

próvido –da (*adj.*) provident, prudent; frugal.

provigário (*m.*) provicar.

provimento (*m.*) act or operation of providing or provisioning; purveyance; public appointment or promotion; filling of a vacancy (in office).

província (*f.*) province, territory.

provincial (*adj.; m.*) provincial.

provincialismo (*m.*) = PROVINCIANISMO.

provincializar-se (*v.r.*) to become provincial.

provincianismo (*m.*) provincialism.

provinciano –na (*adj.; m.,f.*) provincial.

provindo –da (*adj.*) proceeding from, coming from.

provir [82] (*v.i.*)—**de,** to derive from; to arise (spring) from; to result from.

provisão (*f.*) provision, supply, store; (*pl.*) provisions.

provisional (*adj.*) provisional.

provisionar (*v.*) = APROVISIONAR.

provisor (*m.*) provisor.

provisório –ria (*adj.*) provisory, provisional, temporary; (*m.*) something temporary; a makeshift; (*Bot.*) a bluestem grass (*Andropogon*), c.a. JARAGUÁ.

provocação (*f.*) provocation, incitement; affront, aggravation.

provocador –**dora** (*adj.*) provoking; provocative; (*m.,f.*) one who provokes.
provocamento (*m.*) = PROVOCAÇÃO.
provocante (*adj.*) provoking.
provocar (*v.t.*) to provoke, excite; to arouse; to stir up, vex; to nettle; to tease; to affront; to cause, promote, bring on; to tempt.
provocativo –**va**, **provocatório** –**ria** (*adj.*) provocative.
proxeneta [ks] (*m.*) go-between, intermediary; pimp, procurer; (*f.*) bawd, procuress.
proximal [x = ss] (*adj.; Anat.*) proximal.
proximidade [x = ss] (*f.*) proximity, nearness; (*pl.*) proximities, neighborhood.
próximo –**ma** [x = ss] (*adj.*) near, close, not distant; proximate; close or next in line; closely related; (*adv.*) near (by), close (by); (*m.*) fellow man.—**a** or **de**, near to, close to.—**futuro**, in the near future; in or of the next or coming month.—**Oriente**, the Near East.—**passado**, the recent past; in or of the month or year preceding this one.—**pretérito**, the immediate past.
pruca (*f.*) round wooden stool.
prudência (*f.*) prudence; discretion; judiciousness; foresight; [*cap.*] Prudence.
prudencial (*adj.*) prudential.
prudente (*adj.*) prudent, careful, provident; expedient; judicious, wise; discreet.
pruinoso –**sa** [u-i] (*adj., Bot.*) pruinose.
pruir (*v.*) = PRURIR.
prumada (*f.*) plumb line.
prumar (*v.i., Naut.*) to take soundings with a plummet.
prumidade (*f.*) state of being plumb.
prumo (*m.*) plummet, plumb; sounding line; fig., common sense, level-headedness. **a**—, perpendicularly.
prunela (*f., Bot.*) the common selfheal (*Prunella vulgaris*), c.a. ERVA-FÉRREA.
pruniforme (*adj.*) pruniform.
prurido (*m., Med.*) pruritus, itching; fig., burning desire.
pruridoso –**sa** (*adj.*) itching; impatient.
pruriente (*adj.*) itching, pruriginous. [But not prurient, which is LASCIVO, LÚBRICO.]
prurigem (*f., Med.*) prurigo.
pruriginoso –**sa** (*adj.*) pruriginous.
prurigo (*m.*) = PRURIGEM.
prurir [25] (*v.t.*) to cause pruritus; to stimulate; (*v.i.*) to itch; to have a burning desire.
prussianismo (*m.*) Prussianism.
prussianização (*f.*) prussianization.
prussianizar (*v.t.*) to Prussianize.
prussiano –**na** (*adj.*; *m.,f.*) Prussian. Var. PRUSSO, –SA.
prussiato (*m., Chem.*) prussiate.—**amarelo**, potassium ferrocyanide.—**vermelho**, potassium ferricyanide.
prússico –**ca** (*adj.*) prussic.
prustita (*f., Min.*) proustite; ruby silver ore.
p.s. = PURO SANGUE (pure-blooded [horse]).
P.S. = PÓS-ESCRITO (postscript).
psamítico –**ca** (*adj.*) psammitic.
psamito (*m., Petrog.*) psammite, sandstone.
psamófilo –**la** (*adj.*) psammophilous.
psamógeno –**na** (*adj.*) psammogenous.
PSB = PARTIDO SOCIALISTA BRASILEIRO (Brazilian Socialist Party).
PSD = PARTIDO SOCIAL DEMOCRÁTICO (Social Democratic Party).
psefite (*f.*), –**to** (*m., Petrog.*) psephite.
pselismo (*m.*) pselism(us).
pseudepígrafo (*m., Biol.*) pseudepigraph.
pseudo-ácido (*m., Chem.*) pseudo acid.
pseudobase (*f., Chem.*) pseudo base.
pseudobulbo (*m., Bot.*) pseudobulb.
pseudocarpo (*m., Bot.*) pseudocarp.
pseudociência (*f.*) pseudoscience.
pseudocotiledone (*m., Bot.*) pseudocotyledone.
pseudocromestesia (*f., Bot.*) pseudochromesthesia.
pseudocumeno (*m., Chem.*) pseudocumene.
pseudodoxo –**doxa** [ks] (*adj.*) pseudodoxal.
pseudo-esfera (*f., Geom.*) pseudosphere.
pseudógina (*f., Zool.*) pseudogyne.
pseudomalaquita (*f., Min.*) pseudomalachite.
pseudomembrana (*f.*) false membrane.
pseudomorfismo (*m., Min.*) pseudomorphism.
pseudomorfo –**fa** (*adj.*) pseudomorphous.
pseudomorfose (*f.*) pseudomorphosis.
pseudonímia (*f.*) pseudonymity.
pseudonímico –**ca** (*adj.*) pseudonymic.

pseudônimo –**ma** (*adj.*) pseudonymous; (*m.*) pseudonym.
pseudoparênquima (*f., Bot.*) pseudoparenchyma.
pseudoperídio (*m., Bot.*) pseudoperidium.
pseudópode, **pseudopódio** (*m., Zool.*) pseudopodium.
pseudoporfírico –**ca** (*adj., Petrog.*) pseudoporphyritic.
pseudoprofeta (*m.*) false prophet.
pseudopurpurina (*f., Chem.*) pseudopurpurin.
pseudo-rainha (*f.*) false queen bee.
pseudoscopia (*f.*) pseudoscopy.
pseudoscópio (*m., Optics*) pseudoscope.
pseudosofia (*f.*) false wisdom.
pseudospermo (*m., Bot.*) pseudospermium.
pseudossolução (*f., Physical Chem.*) pseudosolution.
pseudovulcânico –**ca** (*adj., Geol.*) pseudovolcanic.
pseudoxantina (*f., Biochem.*) pseudoxanthine.
psicagogo (*m.*) psychagogos; necromancer.
psicanálise (*f.*) psychoanalysis.
psicanalista (*adj.*) psychoanalytic(al); (*m.,f.*) psychoanalyst.
psicastenia (*f., Psychiatry*) psychasthenia.
psicastênico –**ca** (*adj.*) psychasthenic.
psichê (*m.*) a cheval glass [French *psyché*]. Cf. PSIQUE.
psicode (*f.*) a genus (*Psychoda*) of midges.
psicodinâmico –**ca** (*adj.*) psychodynamic.
psicofísica (*f.*) psychophysics.
psicofisiologia (*f.*) psychophysiology.
psicogênese (*f.*) psychogenesis.
psicogenia (*f., Psychol.*) psychogenesis.
psicognosia (*f., Psychiatry*) psychognosis.
psicografia (*f., Spiritualism*) spirit writing.
psicógrafo (*m.*) psychograph.
psicolepsia (*f.*) psycholepsy.
psicologia (*f.*) psychology.
psicológico –**ca** (*adj.*) psychologic(al).
psicólogo –**ga** (*m.,f.*) psychologist.
psicometria (*f.*) psychometria.
psicômetro (*m.*) psychometer.
psicomonismo (*m.*) psychomonism, solipsism.
psiconeurose (*f.*) psychoneurosis.
psiconeurótico –**ca** (*adj.*) psychoneurotic.
psicopaníquia (*f., Theol.*) psychopannychy.
psicopata (*adj.*) psychopathic; (*m.,f.*) psychopath.
psicopatia (*f.*) psychopathy.
psicopáptico –**ca** (*adj.*) psychopathic.
psicopatologia (*f.*) psychopathology.
psicopatológico –**ca** (*adj.*) psychopathological.
psicose (*f.*) psychosis.
psicotécnica (*f.*) psychotechnology.
psicoterapia (*f.*) psychotherapy.
psicoterápico –**ca** (*adj.*) psychotherapeutic.
psicótria (*f., Bot.*) the genus (*Psychotria*) of wild coffee.
psicotrina (*f., Chem.*) psychotrine.
psicrometria (*f.*) psychrometry.
psicrômetro (*m.*) psychrometer, hygrometer.
psila (*f.*) jumping plant louse (*Psylla*).
psilídeos (*m.pl.*) a family of jumping plant lice (*Psyllidae*, syn. *Chermidae*).
psílio (*m.*) the leafwort (*Plantago psyllium*).
psilomelanita (*f., Min.*) psilomelane, black hematite.
psilose (*f., Med.*) psilosis; sprue.
psilotáceas (*f. pl., Bot.*) the Psilotaceae (fern allies).
psíloto (*m.*) a genus (*Psilotum*) of tropical fern allies.
psique (*f.*) psyche; [*cap.*] Psyche. Cf. PSICHÊ.
psiquiatra (*m.,f.*) psychiatrist.
psiquiatria (*f.*) psychiatry.
psiquiátrico –**ca** (*adj.*) psychiatric.
psíquico –**ca** (*adj.*) psychic.
psiquídeos (*m.pl.*) the Psychidae (bagworm moths).
psiquismo (*m.*) psychism.
psitáceo –**cea** (*adj.*) psittaceous.
psitacídeos (*m.pl.*) the Psittacidae (parrots).
psitaciformes (*m.pl.*) the Psittaciformes, syn. Psittaci (parrotlike birds).
psitacinita (*f., Min.*) psittacinite.
psitacismo (*m.*) psittacism, parrotlike speech.
psitacista (*adj.*) psittacistic.
psítaco (*m.*) a genus (*Psittacus*) of parrots.
psitacose (*f., Med.*) psittacosis, parrot fever.
psitáculo (*m.*) a lovebird (small parrot) of the genus Psittacula.
psiu! (*interj.*) Pst! (to attract attention or to enjoin silence).
psoas (*m., Anat.*) psoas.
psoríaco –**ca** (*adj.; m.,f., Med.*) psoriatic.

psoríase (*f.*, *Med.*) psoriasis.
psoropta (*m.*) scab mite (*Psoroptes*).
psorospérmia (*f.*, *Zool.*) psorosperm.
psorospermose (*f.*, *Med.*) psorospermosis.
PSP = PARTIDO SOCIAL PROGRESSISTA (Social Progressive Party).
ptármico **-ca** (*adj.*) ptarmic(al), sternutative; (*f.*, *Bot.*) the yarrows or sneezeworts (*Ptarmica*, *syn. Achillea*).
ptármiga (*f.*, *Zool.*) ptarmigan.
PTB = PARTIDO TRABALHISTA BRASILEIRO (Brazilian Labor Party).
pteridófito (*m.*, *Bot.*) pteridophyte.
pterígio (*m.*, *Med.*) pterygium, c.a. UNHA-DO (or -NO) -ÔLHO.
pterigóide, pterigoídeo **-dea** (*adj.*, *Anat.*) pterygoid.
pterigopalatino **-na** (*adj.*, *Anat.*) pterygopalatine.
pterila (*f.*, *Zool.*) pteryla.
ptério, ptérion (*m.*, *Craniol.*) pterion.
pteris (*m.*) a genus (*Pteris*) of coarse ferns or brake.
pterocarpo **-pa** (*adj.*, *Bot.*) pterocarpous; (*m.*) the genus (*Pterocarpus*, *syn. Lingoum*) of padauk trees.
pterocéfalo (*m.*, *Bot.*) the winghead (*Pterocephalus*).
pterócera (*f.*, *Zool.*) the Pterocera (marine snails).
pterodá[c]tilo **-la,** (*adj.*, *Zool.*) pterodactylous; (*m.*) pterodactyl.
pterófilo (*m.*) a name sometimes used for the scalare (*Pterophyllum scalare*), a small Amazon fish better known as ACARÁ-BANDEIRA.
pteróforos (*m.pl.*) the plume moths (*Pterophorus*).
pteróide, pteroídeo **-dea** (*adj.*) winglike; (*Bot.*) fernlike.
pterópode (*adj.; m.*, *Zool.*) pteropod.
pterosáurio (*m.*, *Paleontol.*) pterosaur.
pterospermo **-ma** (*adj.*, *Bot.*) pterospermous.
pterósporo (*m.*, *Bot.*) the pinedrops (*Pterospora*).
ptialina (*f.*, *Biochem.*) ptyalin.
ptialismo (*m.*) ptyalism, salivation.
ptilose (*f.*, *Med.*) ptilosis; madarosis.
ptolemaico **-ca** (*adj.*) Ptolemaic.
ptomaína (*f.*) ptomaine.
ptose (*f.*, *Med.*) ptosis.
pua (*f.*) auger, brace and bit; steel spur for a gamecock; prong; thorn; (*slang*) drunkenness.
puã (*f.*) a kind of small crab (*Callinectes sapidus*).
puava (*adj.*) skittish, wild [= ARUÁ].
puba (*f.*, *m.*) see under PUBO.
pubar (*v.t.*) to ferment (grated manioc); (*v.i.*) to ferment; to spoil.
pube (*m.*) = PÚBIS.
pubente (*adj.*) = PÚBERE.
puberdade (*f.*) puberty.
púbere (*adj.*) pubescent.
pubes (*m.*) = PÚBIS.
pubescência (*f.*) pubescence; down, fuzz.
pubescente (*adj.*) pubescent; downy, fuzzy.
pubescer (*v.i.*) to arrive at puberty; (*m.*) puberty.
pubiano **-na, púbico** **-ca** (*adj.*) pubic.
pubígero **-ra** (*adj.*) hairy.
púbis (*m. or f.*, *Anat.*, *Zool.*) pubis.
publicação (*f.*) publication.
publicador **-dora** (*adj.*) publishing; (*m.,f.*) publisher.
pública-forma (*f.*) certified copy of a document.
publicar (*v.t.*) to publish, make known, make public; to disclose, reveal. [To publish books is EDITAR not PUBLICAR.]
publicidade (*f.*) publicity; advertising.
publicista (*m.,f.*) publicist; political journalist.
publicitário (*m.*) advertising man.
público **-ca** (*adj.; m.*) public. funcionário—, civil service employee. servidor—, public servant.
pubo **-ba** (*adj.*) fermented; spoiled; sore (from work or exercise); (*f.*) manioc mash; dandyism; wet grassland; (*m.*) fat steer.
puça (*f.*, *Bot.*) treebine (*Cissus*).
puçá (*f.*) ornamental cotton fringe; a certain kind of lace; a hand net for catching shrimp and small fish, c.a. JERERÉ; the fruit of or the PUÇAZEIRO.
pucaçu [çú] (*m.*) = POMBA-LEGITIMA.
puçanga (*f.*) household remedy; witchcraft.
puçanguara (*m.*) healer, herb doctor. [= CURANDEIRO].
púcara (*f.*) = PÚCARO.
pucarada (*f.*) mugful, bowlful.
pucarim (*m.*) baked clay dish with handles.
pucarinha (*f.*), **-nho** (*m.*) small mug.

púcaro (*m.*) baked clay cup, mug or dipper with a handle.
puçàzeiro (*m.*) a devil pepper (*Rauwolfia behiensis*), c.a. CASCA-DE-ANTA-BRAVA.
pucheiro (*m.*) meat cooked plain (without seasoning or vegetables).
puchuri [i] (*m.*) = PIXURIM.
puchurim (*m.*) = MUXIRÃO.
pucínia (*f.*) a genus (*Puccinia*) of rust fungi.
puciniáceo **-cea** (*adj.*) pucciniaceous.
pucu [cú] (*m.*) a treebine (*Cissus*).
puçuca (*adj.*) cadging, sponging; (*m.*) cadger, sponger.
puçuquear (*v.t.*) to cadge, sponge.
pucuri-silvestre (*m.*) = PIXURIM.
pud- + verb endings = irreg. forms of PODER [62].
pudendo **-da** (*adj.*) modest, bashful; chaste; ashamed; (*Anat.*) pudendal.
pudente (*adj.*) modest; chaste.
pudibundo **-da** (*adj.*) modest, bashful; demure; shamefaced.
pudicícia (*f.*) pudency, modesty; chastity.
pudico **-ca** [dí] (*adj.*) modest; demure; coy; shy; chaste; pudic.
pudim [also **pudingue**] (*m.*) pudding; (*Geol.*) pudding stone.—de ameixas, plum p.—de creme, custard p.
pudlador (*m.*, *Metal.*) puddling furnace.
pudlagem (*f.*, *Metal.*) puddling.
pudlar (*v.t.*) to puddle (iron).
pudor (*m.*) pudency, modesty; shamefacedness, shyness; chastity.
pudoroso **-sa** (*adj.*) modest; shy.
puera [ê] (*f.*) = IPUEIRA.
puerícia (*f.*) childhood.
puericultor **-tora** (*m.,f.*) one who practices puericulture.
puericultura (*f.*) puericulture, child care.
pueril (*adj.*) of or pert. to a child or children; juvenile; puerile, childish; foolish, silly.
puerilidade (*f.*) puerility, childishness; foolishness.
puérpera (*adj.; f.*) (woman) in childbirth.
puerperal (*adj.*) puerperal.
puerpério (*m.*, *Med.*) puerperium.
pufe (*m.*) bustle; puff, pad, pannier (of a skirt); ottoman seat.
pufino (*m.*, *Zool.*) the shearwaters (*Puffinus*).
púgil [-geis] (*adj.*) pugilistic; (*m.*) pugilist.
pugilar (*v.i.*) to fight with the fists.
pugilato (*m.*) pugilism, boxing; fig., a heated discussion.
pugilismo (*m.*) boxing.
pugilista (*m.*) pugilist; boxer; wrestler.
pugilo (*m.*) a pinch (as of salt or snuff); small quantity um—de amigos, a handful of friends.
pugna (*f.*) fight, combat.
pugnacidade (*f.*) pugnacity.
pugnador **-dora** (*adj.*) pugnacious.
pugnar (*v.i.*) to fight, contend, struggle (com, with; por, for; contra, against).
pugnaz (*adj.*) pugnacious.
puideira (*f.*) polishing powder, abrasive.
puído **-da** (*adj.*) polished; of garments, shiny, threadbare, worn smooth.
puir [67] (*v.t.*) to polish (with an abrasive); to fray, wear out.
puíta (*f.*) a stone or other heavy object used to anchor a fishing boat [= POITA or POUTA]; a drum made from the end of a hollow log [= CUÍCA].
pujança (*f.*) puissance, power, potency; vigor, strength; vigorous growth; (*Geol.*) thickness (of strata and dikes); = POSSANÇA and POTÊNCIA.
pujante (*adj.*) puissant, powerful, mighty, potent; fearless.
pujar (*v.t.*) to overpower; (*v.i.*) to struggle.
pula (*f.*) bet; pool (of bets). Cf. PULE.
pulação (*f.*) act of jumping.
puladinho (*m.*) a popular Brazilian hopping dance [= PICADINHO].
pulador **-dora** (*adj.*) jumping, skipping, hopping; (*m.,f.*) jumper, skipper, hopper.
pulante (*adj.*) jumping, skipping, hopping.
pula-pula (*m.*) the golden-crowned warbler (*Basileuterus culicivorus auricapillus*).
pular (*v.i.*) to jump, leap, spring, vault (over); to hop, skip; to cavort.—à corda, to skip rope.—carniça, to play leapfrog.—de contente, to leap for joy.—de galho, to switch sides.
pulcritude (*f.*) pulchritude.

pulcro -cra (*adj.*) pulchritudinous.

pule (*f.*) a betting pool; a ticket on a horse race. [Fr. *poule*]. Cf. PULA.

púlex (*m.*) a genus of fleas (*Pulex*).

pulga (*f.*) flea.—comum, the common flea (*Pulex irritans*). —-d'água, water flea.—-do-mar, a sand or beach flea.—-penetrante, the chigoe, c.a. NÍGUA, TUNGA, BICHO-DE-PÉ. com a—atrás da orelha, with a flea in the ear.

pulgão (*m.*) the common name for any plant louse.—-branco cottony-cushion scale (*Icerya purchasi*).—-langígero, woolly aphid (*Erisoma lanigerum*).

pulgoso -sa, pulguento -ta (*adj.*) infested with fleas, flea-ridden.

pulguedo (*m.*) many fleas or place where they are.

pulha (*adj.*) slovenly; low, coarse, indecent; (*f.*) coarse joke; vulgar saying; (*m.*) low person, "skunk".

pulhar (*v.i.*) to use low or vulgar language.

pulhastra, pulhastro (*m.*) rotter, blackguard.

pulhice (*f.*), pulhismo (*m.*) dirty trick; vulgar remark; low life.

pulicar (*v.i.*) to hop up and down.

pulicídeos (*m.pl.*) the Pulicidae (family of fleas).

pulim (*m.*) skip, hop.

pulmão (*m.*) lung.—de aço, iron lung.

pulmonados (*m.pl.*) the Pulmonata (snails and slugs).

pulmonar (*adj.*) pulmonary.

pulmonária (*f. Bot.*) the lungworts (*Pulmonaria*); a tree moss (*Lichen pulmonarius*).

pulmonia (*f.*) pop. form of PNEUMONIA.

pulmonífero -ra (*adj.*) having lungs.

pulmonite (*f.*) = PNEUMONIA.

pulmotuberculose (*f.*) tuberculosis of the lungs.

pulo (*m.*) leap, jump; hop; skip; bounce.—de gato, a trick up one's sleeve.—do nove, crooked gambling trick. aos —s, jumping, hopping, skipping, bouncing.

pulôver (*m.*) pull-over (blouse or sweater).

pulpeiro (*m.*) country storekeeper or tavern keeper (in So. Brazil).

pulperia (*f.*) country store or tavern (in So. Brazil).

púlpito (*m.*) pulpit.

pulquérrimo -ma (*absol. superl. of* PULCRO) most beautiful.

pulsação (*f.*) pulsation, beat(ing), throb(bing); thrill.

pulsar (*v.i.*) to pulsate, beat, throb; to pant; (*v.t.*) to strike (keys or strings of an instrument).

pulsátil [-teis] (*adj.*) pulsatile.

pulsatila (*f.*) European pasqueflower (*Anemone pulsatilla*), c.a. FLOR-DA-PÁSCOA.

pulsativo -va (*adj.*) pulsating.

pulsear (*v.i.*) to play at Indian wrestling.

pulseira (*f.*) bracelet.—-relógio, wrist watch.

pulsímetro (*m., Physiol.*) pulsimeter, sphygmograph.

pulso (*m.*) pulse; wrist; force, vigor.—filiforme, thready pulse.—intermitente, intermittent pulse.—irregular, irregular pulse.—lento, slow pulse.—livre, side fees or profits which one is free to accept; spare-time earnings.—regular, regular pulse.—variável, variable pulse.—venoso, venous pulse. a—, by force.

pulsógrafo (*m.*) = PULSÍMETRO.

pulsômetro (*m.*) pulsometer (pump).

pultáceo -cea (*adj.*) pultaceous, of porridgelike consistency.

pululação (*f.*) pululamento (*m.*) pullulation.

pululância (*f.*) vigorous vegetative growth.

pululante (*adj.*) teeming, swarming.

pulular (*v.i.*) to pullulate, gemmate, sprout; to teem, swarm.

pulveráceo -cea (*adj.*) pulvereous, covered with dust.

pulverização (*f.*) pulverization.

pulverizador (*m.*) pulverizer; atomizer.

pulverizar (*v.t.*) to pulverize; to atomize.

pulverizável (*adj.*) pulverable.

pulveroso -sa (*adj.*) pulverous, powdery; dusty.

pulverulência (*f.*) pulverulence; dustiness.

pulverulento -ta, pulveruloso -sa (*adj.*) pulverulent, dusty, dust-covered.

pulvinado -da (*adj.*) pulvinate, pulvillar, cushionlike.

pulvínula (*f., Bot.*) pulvinula.

pum! (*interj.*) Boom!

puma (*m.*) puma, wildcat, mountain lion.

puna (*f.*) the higher Andes; mountain sickness, soroche; (*Bot.*) either of two spp. of fiber-yielding beautyleaf (*Calophyllum inophyllum* or *C. tomentosum*) of the East Indies. [The Brazil beautyleaf is *C. brasiliense*.]—-vermelha, the hazel sterculia (*S. foetida*).

punaré (*adj.*) tan [horse]; (*m.*) a certain large reddish rat; a blenny (small fish).

punção (*f.*) puncture; (*m.*) punch (tool), awl, bodkin.—de bico, or—marcador, prick punch.

punçar, puncejar (*v.*) = PUNCIONAR.

punceta [ê] (*f.*) steel punch.

puncionagem (*f.*) act or operation of punching or puncturing.

puncionar (*v.t.*) to punch, puncture, tap.

pun[c]tura (*f.*) puncture.

pundonor [ô] (*m.*) dignity, decorum; point of honor; face; self-respect; gallantry, chivalry.

pundonorar (*v.i.*) to take offense.

pundonoroso -sa (*adj.*) proud, jealous of honor.

punga (*adj.*) very poor, punk (said esp. of horses); (*m.*) an inferior person or horse; victim of a pickpocket; the pickpocket's loot; (*f.*) a face-to-face bump with another person. Cf. UMBIGADA.

pungarecos (*m.pl.*) quack pharmacist's drugs.

pungência (*f.*) poignancy.

pungente (*adj.*) pungent; poignant; acute.

pungibarba (*adj.; m.*) (youth) whose beard has started to grow.

pungidor -dora (*adj.*) distressing.

pungimento (*m.*) piercing; distress.

pungir [25] (*v.t.*) to prick, sting; to goad, prod, incite; to afflict, distress.

pungitivo -va (*adj.*) pungent; poignant.

pungo (*m.*) the maigre, a large European marine food fish (*Sciaena aquila*).

punguear (*v.t., slang*) to pilfer; to pick pockets.

punguista (*m., slang*) pickpocket; pilferer; quack pharmacist.

punh-+verb endings = irreg. forms of PÔR [63].

punhada (*f.*) cuff (blow with fist).

punhado (*m.*) handful; a few.

punhal (*m.*) dagger, dirk.

punhalada (*f.*) a stab.

punhete (*m.*) mitt [= MITENE].

punho (*m.*) fist; wrist; cuff; grip, handle.—cerrado, closed fist. de (faca) em—, with (knife) in hand. em—, (held) in the hand. escrito de próprio—, written in one's own handwriting.

punibilidade (*f.*) punishability.

púnica (*f.*) see under PÚNICO.

punicáceo -a (*adj., Bot.*) punicaceous; (*f.pl.*) the pomegranate family (*Punicaceae*).

punição (*f.*) punishment; penalty.

punicear (*v.t.*) to make red; to rouge (the face).

puníceo -cea (*adj.*) bright-red or purplish-red (as a pomegranate).

punicina (*f., Chem.*) punicin.

púnico -ca (*adj.*) Punic; treacherous, faithless; (*m.*) Punic language. fé—, Punic faith; (*f.*) the pomegranate (*Punica*). Cf. ROMÃZEIRA.

punidor -dora (*adj.*) punishing; (*m.,f.*) punisher.

punir (*v.t.*) to punish.—de morte, to inflict capital punishment (on).—por, to fight for (rights, honor).

punitivo -va (*adj.*) punitive.

punível (*adj.*) punishable.

puntiforme (*adj., Bot.*) punctiform.

puntilha (*f.*) pointed rod used to slaughter beef cattle by jabbing into the base of the brain.

puntilhaço (*m.*) jab with a PUNTILHA.

puntura (*f.*) puncture; (*pl., Print.*) register points.

punu [nú] (*m.*) a scratchbush (*Urera punu*).

pupa (*f., Zool.*) pupa; a pupa shell.

pupídeos (*m.pl.*) the pupa shells (*Pupidae*).

pupila (*f.*) young orphan girl under the charge of a tutor or guardian; novice; a protegée; (*Anat.*) pupil of the eye.

pupilagem (*f.*) tutelage.

pupilar (*v.t.*) to place (someone) under a guardian or tutor; (*v.i.*) to screech (as peacocks); (*adj.*) pupillary.

pupilo (*m.*) orphan boy in the care of a tutor or guardian; a protegé. [But not pupil, which is ALUNO.]

pupíparo -ra (*adj., Zool.*) pupiparous; (*m.pl.*) the Pupipara (horse, sheep, bird and bat ticks).

pupunha (*f.*) the spiny peachpalm (*Guilielma speciosa*), c.a. PUPUNHA VERDE-AMARELA, PUPUNHEIRA, or its fruit.

pupunharana (*f.*) = CURUARANA.

purágua (*f.*) the uncovered or unlapped part of a roof tile.

puraquê (*m.*) electric eel (*Electrophorus, syn. Gymnotus, electricus*), c.a. PIRAQUÉ.

purê (*m.*) purée.—de batatas, mashed potatoes.

pureza [ê] (*f.*) purity, pureness; clearness; faultlessness; chasteness; (*Bot.*) the moundlily yucca (*Y. gloriosa*).

purga (*f.*) purge; purgative; any of various plants used as a purgative.—**da-praia** = IPECACONHA-DE-FLOR-BRANCA —**de-cabocla** or **-de-caiapó** or **-de-gentio** = CAPITÃO-DO-MATO.—**de-caboclo** = FRUTA-DE-GENTIO.—**de-caitité**, a bitterwood (*Trichilia cathartica*).—**de-carijó** = ESPE-LINA.—**de-cereja**, a cucurbitaceous plant (*Cayaponia cordifolia*).—**de-joão-pais** = BUCHINHA.—**de-pastor**, an apocinaceous plant (*Dipladenia polimorpha*).—**de-veado** or **-de-vento** = GANHA-SAIA.—**do-campo** or **-do-pastor**, a savannaflower (*Echites sp.*); also = IPECACONHA-DE-FLOR-BRANCA.—**dos-paulistas** = BUCHINHA.—**preta** = CIPÓ-CRUZ-VERDADEIRO.

purgação (*f.*) purgation.

purgador (*m.*) worker in a purgery (part of a sugar-house where molasses is drained from the sugar).

purgante (*adj.; m.*) purgative.

purgar (*v.t.*) to purge, cleanse, purify; to defecate (liquors)

purgatina (*f.*), **purgatol** (*m.*) a purging medicine.

purgativo **-va** (*adj.; m.*) purgative.

purgatório **-ria** (*adj.*) purgatorian; (*m.*) purgatory.

purgueira (*f.*) the Barbadosnut nettlespurge (*Jatropha curcas*), c.a. PINHÃO (-DE-PURGA).

puri [í] (*m.*) a kind of manioc; a halfbreed Indian; (*m.,f.*) an Indian of the Purí, a linguistically-independent family formerly one with the Coroado (which see). They occupied the mountainous regions north and west of Rio de Janeiro; (*adj.*) pert. to or designating the Purí.

puridade (*f.*) purity [= PUREZA].

purificação (*f.*) purification, purifying.—**de Nossa Senhora,** Purification of the Virgin Mary (Candlemas Day, Feb. 2nd).

purificador **-dora** (*adj.*) purifying; (*m.,f.*) purifier; finger bowl; (*Eccl.*) purificator, mundatory.—**de ar,** air purifier.

purificante (*adj.*) purifying.

purificar (*v.t.*) to purify cleanse; to deterge; to refine.

purificativo **-va** (*adj.*) purificative.

purificatório **-ria** (*adj.*) purificatory.

puriforme (*adj., Med.*) puriform, like pus.

purina (*f., Chem.*) purine.

purinha (*f.*) = CACHAÇA.

purismo (*m.*) purism.

purista (*adj.; m.,f.*) purist.

puritanismo (*m.*) Puritanism.

puritano **-na** (*adj.; m.,f.*) Puritan (lit. & fig.).

puro **-ra** (*adj.*) pure, clean, unpolluted; chaste; unadulterated; unblemished.

puro-sangue (*adj.; m.*) pure-blooded (horse).

púrpura (*f.*) the color crimson, deep purplish red [but not purple which is ROXO]; cloth dyed purple or crimson, esp. when worn as an emblem of rank or authority; imperial or regal rank or power; the cardinalate; (*Zool.*) a purple or murex shell (*Murex senegalensis*) which yields a purple dye; (*Her.*) purpure; (*Med.*) purpura.—**-de-cássio** or**—mineral,** (*Chem.*) purple of Cassius.—**hemorrágica,** (*Med.*) purpura haemorrhagica, peliosis.—**romana,** the cardinalate.

purpurado **-da** (*adj.*) purpurate, purpureal; purpled; crimson; elevated to the cardinalate; (*m.*) one who has been so elevated.

purpurâmico **-ca** (*adj.*) = PURPÚRICO.

purpurâmida (*f.*) = PURPURINA.

purpurar (*v.t.*) to make crimson; to dress in royal purple; to elevate to the cardinalate.

purpurato (*m., Chem.*) purpurate.

purpure(j)ar (*v.t.*) to make red or crimson; (*v.i.*) to turn red; (*v.r.*) to blush.

purpúreo **-rea** (*adj.*) crimson red, deep purplish-red.

purpúrico **-ca** (*adj., Chem.*) purpuric.

purpurina (*f., Chem.*) purpurin.

purpurizar (*v.*) = PURPUREAR.

púrpuro **-ra** (*adj.*) = PURPÚREO.

purui [í] (*m.*) = AÇUCENA-DO-MATO.—**da-costa** = JENIPAPO-BRAVO.

purulência (*f.*) purulence.

purulento **-ta** (*adj.*) purulent.

purunga (*f.*), **-go** (*m.*) calabash gourd [= PORONGO].

purupaqui (*m., Bot.*) shack-shack crotolaria (*C. incana*).

purupuru [rú] (*m.*) pinta (a skin disease).

pururu [rurú] (*m., Zool.*) the rufous-headed motmot (*Baryphthengus ruficapillus*) c.a. JURUVA.

pururuca (*adj.*) friable; irritable; (*m.*) young coconut; hominy; coarse sand.

pus (*m.*) pus.

pus + verb endings = forms of PÔR [63].

pusilânime (*adj.*) pusillanimous, craven, cowardly; (*m.,f.*) coward, craven.

pusilanimidade (*f.*) pusillanimity, cowardice.

pústula (*f.*) pustule, pimple, blister; (*Bot.*) pustule.

pustulado **-da** (*adj.*) pustuled.

pustulento **-ta, pustuloso** **-sa** (*adj.*) pustulous, pustulate, pustular.

puta (*f.*) a low word for whore.

putativo **-va** (*adj.*) putative, supposed, reputed.

puteal (*m.*) a well curb.

putear (*v.t.*) to upbraid (another person) with vile and offensive references to his ancestry.

pútega (*f., Bot.*) an herb (*Cytinus hypocistis*) which is parasitic on the roots of the cistus; fruit of the rockrose. Cf. HIPOCISTE.

putirão, putirom, putirum (*m.*) "(1) friends and neighbors banded together for cooperative work in clearing land, house building and fishing; (2) reciprocal aid among small farmers." [*GBAT*] Cf. MUXIRÃO.

putório (*m.*) polecat (*Putorius communis*), c.a TOURÃO.

putredinoso **-sa** (*adj.*) proceeding from putrefaction; stinking; rotten.

putrefação (*f.*) putrefaction, decay.

putrefaciente, putrefativo **-va** (*adj.*) putrefactive.

putrefato **-ta** (*adj.*) putrefied, rotten.

putrefator **-tora** (*adj.*) putrefying; (*m., f.*) putrefier.

putrefatório **-ria** (*adj.*) = PUTREFACIENTE.

putrefazer [47] (*v.t., v.i.*) to putrefy, decay, rot.

putrefeito **-ta** (*adj.*) = PUTREFATO.

putrescência (*f.*) putrescence.

putrescente (*adj.*) putrescent.

putrescina (*f., Biochem.*) putrescine.

putrescível (*adj.*) putrescible.

pútrido **-da** (*adj.*) putrid, rotten; corrupt.

putrificar (*v.*) = PUTREFAZER.

putuca (*m., colloq.*) unlucky person.

putumuju [jú] (*m. Bot.*) a macawood (*Platymiscium, praecox*); also = ARARIBÁ-ROSA.—**amarelo** = ARARIBÁ-AMARELO.

puvi [í] (*m.*) = GATURAMO-MIUDINHO.

puxa (*interj.*) Well, I'll be! (expressing amazement); Doggonit! (annoyance); (*m., slang*) flatterer, wheedler.

puxá (*m.*) a kind of dance; asthma.

puxação (*f., colloq.*) asthma.

puxada (*f.*) see under PUXADO.

puxadeira (*f.*) bootstrap; a knob, cord, handle, etc., for pulling something.

puxadinho **-nha** (*adj.*) spruce, dandyish; high-priced; (*m.*) dandy.

puxado **-da** (*adj.*) fastidious, very particular; (*colloq.*) exhausting [work]; stiff, fancy [price]; (*m., Arch.*) wing; (*colloq.*) asthma; (*f.*) a pull or pulling; a lead card; wing of a building; a forced march.

puxador **-dora** (*adj.*) act of pulling; (*m.*) drawer handle, door knob; puller.

puxamento (*m.*) act of pulling; (*colloq.*) asthma.

puxanço (*m.*) act of drawing a billiard ball.

puxante (*adj.*) pulling; pungent, piquant.

puxão (*m.*) a hard pull, tug; yank, jerk, wrench.—**de orelhas,** an ear-pulling.

puxa-puxa (*f.*) taffy, pull candy; (*adj.*) of cane sirup, at the point of threading.

puxar (*v.t.*) to pull, draw (at, on, up, out); to haul, drag (on); to tug (at); to pluck at; to take after (resemble); (*slang*) to flatter.—**a brasa para sua sardinha,** to draw water to one's mill.—**a (da, pela) espada,** to draw out one's sword.—**à fieira,** to draw (wire rods) through a drawplate.—**à mãe,** to take after (resemble) one's mother.—**briga,** to pick a fight.—**conversa,** to strike up a conversation.—**de uma perna,** to limp on one leg.—**para médico,** to incline towards medicine (as a profession).—**pela língua a alguém,** to pump (draw out) a person.—**pelo pé,** to shake a leg (hurry).—**pelos seus direitos,** to stand up for one's rights.—**um assunto,** to bring up a subject.—**uma cadeira,** to draw up a chair. **A criança puxa os pais,** The child is like its parents. **Êle puxou pelo pai,** He takes after his father. **Mentira puxa mentira,** One lie calls for another.

puxa-saco[s] (*m.*) servile flatterer. [*A coarse term.*]
puxavante (*adj., colloq.*) highly-seasoned; thirst-arousing; (*m.*) driving rod (of locomotive); piston rod; horseshoer's butteris; (*colloq.*) kept woman.—de orelha, an ear-pulling.
puxavão (*m.*) a hard pull.
puxa-verão (*m.*) = ROUXINOL.

puxa-vista (*m.*) placard-bearer, sandwich-man.
puxe! (*interj.*) Get out! Beat it! Scram!
puxeira (*f.*) the sniffles (cold in the head).
puxiri [í] (*m.*) = PIXURIM.
puxo (*m., Med.*) tenesmus; labor pain.
puxuri [í] (*m.*) = PIXURIM.
puxurirana (*m.*) a laurel (*Ocotea fragrantissima*).

Q

Q, q, the 16th letter in the Port. alphabet.
q. = QUE (which, that, who).
Q.G. = QUARTEL-GENERAL (General Headquarters).
ql. = QUILATE (carat).
q.^ta, q.^to = QUANTA, -TO (how much).
qua–, for words which cannot here be found, try under CUA- and GUA-.
quacre (*m.*) Quaker.
quacrismo (*m.*) Quakerism.
quaderna (*f.*) the four-spot face of a die.
quacacuja (*m.*) an angler fish (*Lophius vespertilio*), c.a. XARROCO-BICUDO, XARROCO-DO-BRASIL.
quadernado –da (*adj., Bot.*) quaternate [leaves].
quadra (*f.*) a square enclosure; quatrain; quartet; a set or series of four; one side of a square; period, time, season; a court for tennis or other games; a playing card with four spots; a lineal measure of 132 meters; a measure of surface equivalent to 3600 square BRAÇAS or 17,424 sq. mts.; the flag of a flagship; the distance from one street corner to the next in the same block.—da lua, quarter of the moon.—de tênis, tennis court.—do ano, season of the year.
quadrado –da (*adj.*) quadrate, square; squared; uncouth; (*m.*) a quadrate; a squared number; (*pl., Printing*) quads and spaces.
quadrador –dora (*adj.*) squaring; (*m.,f.*) frame maker.
quadradura (*f.*) = QUADRATURA.
quadragenário –ria (*adj.; m.,f.*) (person) in his or her forties.
quadragésimo –ma (*adj.; m.*) fortieth (part). —primeiro, forty-first.—segundo, forty-second, etc.; (*f.*) a space of forty days.
quadrangulado –da, quadrangular (*adj.*) quadrangular.
quadrângulo (*m.*) quadrangle.
quadrantal (*adj.*) quadrantal.
quadrante (*m.*) quadrant; dial. os—s do país, the four corners of the country.
quadrar (*v.t.*) to make square; (*Math.*) to square numbers. —o corpo, to square the shoulders; (*v.i.*) to square, accord, conform, agree, jibe (com, with).
quadrarão –rona (*adj.; m.,f.*) quadroon.
quadrático –ca (*adj.*) quadratic, square.
quadratim (*m., Print.*) quad.
quadratriz (*f., Geom., Math.*) quadratrix.
quadratura (*f.*) quadrature.—do círculo, quadrature (squaring) of the circle. maré de—, neap tide.
quadrela (*f.*) section of a wall; side of a building.
quadrialado –da (*adj.*) four-winged.
quadribásico –ca (*adj.; Chem.*) quadribasic.
quadricapsular (*adj., Bot.*) quadricapsular.
quadricelular (*adj., Bot.*) quadricellular.
quadriceps (*adj., Anat.*) quadricipital.
quadriciclo (*m.*) quadricycle.
quadricípite (*m., Anat.*) quadriceps extensor.
quádrico –ca (*adj., Math.*) quadric.
quadricolor (*adj.*) four-colored.
quadricórneo –nea (*adj., Zool.*) having four horns or antennas.
quadricotiledôneo –nea (*adj., Bot.*) quadricotyledonous.
quadrícula (*f.*) small square.
quadriculado –da, quadricular (*adj.*) checkered. papel—, graph paper.
quadrículo (*m.*) small square.
quadricúspide (*adj.*) quadricuspidal.
quadridentado –da (*adj.*) quadridentate, four-toothed.
quadridigitado –da (*adj.*) quadridigitate, four-fingered.
quadrienal (*adj.*) quadrennial.

quadriênio (*m.*) a period of four years.
quadrífido –da, quadrifendido –da (*adj.*) quadrifid; divided or deeply cleft into four parts (as a petal).
quadrifoliado –da (*adj., Bot.*) quadrifoliolate.
quadrifólio –lia (*adj., Bot.*) quadrifoliate; (*m.*) a zornia (*Z. tenuifolia*).
quadriforme (*adj.*) quadriform.
quadrigêmeo –mea, quadrigêmino –na (*adj.*) quadrigeminal, fourfold.
quadrigeminado –da (*adj., Bot.*) quadrigeminate.
quadrijugado –da (*adj., Bot.*) quadrijugate.
quadril (*m.*) hip; haunch.
quadrilateral (*adj.*) quadrilateral, four-sided.
quadrilátero –ra (*adj.; m.*) quadrilateral.
quadrilha (*f.*) a gang (of evildoers); a quadrille; square dance; a squadron; (*Bull fighting*) cuadrilla.—de cães, pack of dogs.—de ladrões, gang of thieves.
quadrilhado –da (*adj.*) checkered (as graph paper).
quadrilheiro (*m.*) gangster, hoodlum.
quadrilobulado –da, quadrilobado –da (*adj.*) quadrilocular, quadriloculate.
quadrilongo –ga (*adj.; m.*) oblong.
quadrímano –na (*adj.*) having four hands. Cf. QUADRÚMANO.
quadrimembre (*adj.*) quadrimembral.
quadrimestre (*m.*) a period of four months.
quadrimotor (*adj.; m.*) four-motored (airplane).
quadringentésimo –ma (*adj.; m.*) four-hundredth.
quadrinha (*f.*) popular ditty.
quadrinômio (*m., Alg.*) quadrinomial.
quadripartido –da, quadripartito –ta (*adj.*) quadripartite [= QUADRÍFIDO].
quadripenado –da, quadripene (*adj.*) quadripennate.
quadrissilábico –ca, quadrissílabo –ba (*adj.*) quadrisyllabic.
quadrivalente (*adj., Chem.*) quadrivalent.
quadrívio (*m.*) a quadrivial point; (*Med. Hist.*) quadrivium.
quadro (*m.*) a square; framed picture; blackboard; table; list, schedule, statement (of condensed information); roster; scene, tableau; team (of soccer players, etc.); crew; staff; cadre.—a óleo, oil painting.—baixo, (*Arch.*) base block, plinth.—de avisos, bulletin board.—de comando or de instrumentos, instrument panel.—de gênero, a genre painting.—de ligação telefônica, telephone switchboard.—do pessoal, working staff.—-negro or -prêto, blackboard.—nosológico, nosological table.—sinótico, synoptic chart (of business conditions, etc.).—s vivos, living tableaux.
quadrúmano –na (*adj., Zool.*) quadrumanous, four-handed; (*m.pl.*) the Quadrumana.
quadrupedal (*adj., Zool.*) quadrupedal.
quadrupedar (*v.i.*) to go on all four feet.
quadrúpede (*adj.; m.*) quadruped.
quadrúplex (*m., Teleg.*) quadruplex instrument.
quadruplicação (*f.*) quadruplication.
quadruplicado –da (*adj.*) quadruplicate; fourfold.
quadruplicar (*v.t.*) to quadruplicate.
quádruplo –pla (*adj.*) quadruple, fourfold; (*m.*) quadruple, quadruplet. [But quadruplets is QUATROGÊMEOS.]
quaiapá (*m.*) = ESPINHO-DE-JUDEU.
qual [pl. quais] (*pron.*) which, what, who whom, that; (*adj.*) which, what one, what; (*conj.*) as, like as; (*interj.*) Nonsense! Fiddlesticks!—é a altura daquela árvore? How high is that tree? —dêles? Which of them?—história!,—lá!,—nada!, Nonsense! Baloney! Nothing of the sort!—o quê! Not at all! Of course not! No such

thing! Nothing of the sort! I should say not! That's not so! You don't mean it!—**seja**, which is.—**rico**—**nada**! Rich, nothing! **cada**—, each one, each person. **cada**—**mais interessante que o outro**, each more interesting than the other. **de**—, of which. **em época**—**a presente**, at a time such as this; in times like these. **o**—, who, whom, which. **seja**—**fôr**, be whatever it may. **tal**—, just like, just as.

quálé (*m.*) = PAU-TERRA-DO-AMAZONAS.

qualidade (*f.*) quality, attribute, characteristic; character; grade, kind; high social standing. **de boa**—, of good quality. **na**—**de**, in the capacity of, as.

qualificação (*f.*) qualification; classification.

qualificado –**da** (*adj.*) qualified, competent.

qualificador –**dora** (*adj.*) qualifying; classifying; (*m.,f.*) qualifier; classifier.

qualificar (*v.t.*) to qualify, modify.—**de** (**por**, **como**), to classify as, deem, regard; (*v.r.*) to register as a voter.

qualificativo –**va** (*adj.*) qualifying; (*Gram.*) descriptive; (*m.*) qualifying adjective.

qualificável (*adj.*) qualifiable, classifiable.

qualitativo –**va** (*adj.*) qualitative.

qualquer [pl. **quaisquer**] (*adj.*, *pron.*) any, any one, any at all, either, someone (or other).—**coisa**, anything.—**dia**, any day.—**lugar**, anywhere.—**outro**, any other; anyone else.—**parte**, anywhere.—**pessoa**, anybody.—**um**, any one, anyone, anybody. **de**—**maneira**, anyhow. **em**—**caso**, in any case. **em**—**tempo**, at any time. **todo e**—, each and every. **um**—, a nobody. **um** (**livro**)—, any (book) at all.

quando (*adv.*) when, at what time; (*conj.*) when, at what time; at the time that; at any time, whenever; whereas, while on the contrary.—**do seu regresso**, upon his return.—**mais não seja**, at the very least; if for no other reason.—**menos**, when least, at least.—**menos se esperava**, when least expected.—**mesmo**, even when.—**muito**, at (the) most, at the outside, at best.—**não**, if not.—**quizer**, when you like.—**por mais não fosse**, if for no other reason.—**um não quer, dois não brigam**, It takes two to make a fight. **ainda**—, even though, although. **até**—? Till when? For how long? **de**—**em**—, from time to time. **de**—**em vez**, or **de vez em**—, once in a while, now and then, from time to time, occasionally. **desde**—, How long? Since when? **senão**—, then; suddenly; one day.

quanta (*m.pl.*, *Physics*) quanta. **teoria dos**—, quantum theory.

quantia (*f.*) amount, sum (of money).

quântica (*f.*, *Math.*) quantic.

quantidade (*f.*) quantity, sum, amount; measure, number; length, duration.—**de movimento**, (*Mech.*) momentum.—**discreta**, (*Math.*) discrete quantity.—**indeterminada**, (*Math.*) indeterminate quantity.

quantioso –**sa** (*adj.*) pert. to quantity; numerous; valuable; rich.

quantitativo –**va** (*adj.*) quantitative.

quanto –**ta** (*adj.*, *pron.*) all that, everything that, as many as, as much as, as far as; (*pl.*) all those who, all those which; (*interrog.*) How much? (*pl.*) How many? (*adv.*) how greatly.—**a**, as for.—**a isso**, as to that; for that matter.—**a mim**, as for me; as for as I am concerned.—**antes**, as soon as possible, at once, right away.—**é**? How much is it?—**mais**, let alone.—**mais** (. . .), **tanto mais** (. . .), the more (. . .), the more (. . .).—**mais barato, melhor**, the cheaper, the better.—**mais cedo, melhor**, the earlier, the better.—**mais comprido, mais pesado**, the longer, the heavier.—**mais, tanto melhor**, the more, the better.—**mais** (**tem**), **mais** (**quer**), the more (he has), the more (he wants).—**mais trabalho, menos ganho**, The more I work, the less I earn.—**menos**, much less, let alone.—**menos** , **melhor**, the less, the better.—**tempo faz que** (**você não joga tênis**)? How long is it since (you played tennis)? **Quantas vezes**? How many times? **Quantos são**? How many are there? **Quantos somos**? How many are we? **tanto**—, as much as, as far as. **tão**—, as much as. **tão boa, quanto linda**, as good as she is beautiful. **todos quantos**, everyone who, all who. **tudo**—, everything that.

quantum (*m.*, *Physics*) quantum.

quão (*adv.*) how; as.

quapóia (*f.*) waxflower (*Clusia insignis*).

quá-quá-quá (*interj.*) Ha-ha-ha! Ho-ho-ho!

quáquer (*m.*) Quaker [= QUACRE].

quaquerismo (*m.*) Quakerism [= QUACRISMO]

quarador (*m.*) a patch of grass, wood frame, flat rock, or other place, where washed clothes are spread out to bleach in the sun; fig., a sunny place which becomes intolerably hot. [The term is a corrup. of CORADOURO, the correct but little-used form.]

quarango (*m.*) = QUINA-QUINA.

quarar (*v.t.*) to bleach (washed clothes) by sunning. [Corrup. of CORAR which is little used in this sense.]

quárico –**ca** (*adj.*) = QUÁRTZICO.

quarcífero –**ra** (*adj.*) = QUARTZÍFERO.

quarcito (*m.*) = QUARTZITO.

quarço (*m.*) = QUARTZO.

quarçoso –**sa** (*adj.*) = QUARTZOSO.

quarenta (*adj.*; *m.*) forty; fortieth.—**-e-quatro**, a 44 (gun).

quarenta-feridas (*f.*) = ESPINHO-DE-JUDEU.

quarenta-horas (*f.pl.*, *R.C.Ch.*) the forty hours' devotion.

quarentão –**tona** (*adj.*) fortyish; (*m.,f.*) person of about forty.

quarentena (*f.*) quarantine; a period of forty days (as Lent); forty of anything. **de**—, in quarantine.

quarentenar (*v.i.*) to go into (or to be in) quarantine.

quarentenário –**ria** (*adj.*) relative to quarantine; that lasts forty years; (*m.,f.*) one who is quarantined.

quarentona, fem. of QUARENTÃO.

quaresma (*f.*) Lent; (*pl.*, *Bot.*) meadow saxifrage (*S. granulata*).—, or **quaresminha**, **-do-cercado**, a glorybush (*Tibouchina canescens*).

quaresmal (*adj.*) Lenten.

quaresmar (*v.i.*) to observe Lent.

quaresmeira (*f.*) any of various glorybushes, esp. *Tibouchina holosericea*, c.a. ORELHA-DE-URSO.

quaribu [bú] (*m.*) = GUARABU-AMARELO.

quarô (*m.*, *Bot.*) Brazil thryallis (*T. brasiliensis*), c.a. RESEDÁ-AMARELO, TINTUREIRA.

quarta (*f.*) see under QUARTO.

quartã (*adj.*; *f.*) quartan ague or fever.

quarta-feira (*f.*) Wednesday.—**de Cinzas**, Ash Wednesday.

quartado –**da** (*adj.*) quartered.

quartanista (*m.,f.*) a fourth-year student.

quartau (*m.*) pony, small horse.

quartear (*v.t.*) to quarter.

quarteirão (*m.*) a city block; a quarter-hundred.

quartejar (*v.t.*) to divide into quarters.

quartel [-téis] (*m.*) military quarters, barracks; a quarter (of anything); a fourth of normal span of life; (*Mil.*) quarter.—**das escotilhas**, (*Naut.*) hatches.—**de inverno**, winter quarters.—**de um século**, quarter-century.—**-General**, General Headquarters.—**paulista** = ALQUEIRE PAULISTA. **sem**—, without quarter.

quartela (*f.*, *Zool.*) pastern.

quarterão –**rona** (*adj.*; *m.,f.*) quadroon [= QUADRARÃO].

quartetista (*m.,f.*) member of a musical quartet.

quarteto (*m.*) quartet; quatrain.—**de cordas**, string quartet.—**de sôpro**, wind quartet.

quartil (*adj.*, *Astron.*, *Stat.*) quartile.

quartilho (*m.*) a measure of capacity equivalent to a quarter CANADA; also equivalent to the British pint (0.568 liter).

quartinha (*f.*) small water jug.

quartinho (*m.*) cubicle.

quarto –**ta** (*adj.*) fourth; (*m.*) a fòurth or quarter (of anything); a quarter-hour; room in a house; watch (spell of duty); (*Farriery*) quarter (rear side) of a hoof; also, a cracked hoof; (*Printing*) quarto (4 leaves, 8 pages); (*Butchering*) quarter of a carcass; (*f.*) quarter, a fourth part; short for QUARTA-FEIRA (Wednesday); any of various measures; German measles; (*Naut.*) quarter point.—**crescente**, first (crescent) quarter of the moon.—**de banho**, bathroom.—**de brincar**, rumpus room.—**de crianças**, nursery room.—**de círculo**, (*Arch.*) quarter-circle.—**de dormir**, bedroom.—**de hóspedes**, guest room, spare bedroom.—**de modôrra**, (*Naut.*) midwatch.—**de sentinela**, (*Mil.*) sentinel's two-hour watch.—**de serviço**, (*Naut.*) watch (four hours).—**de solteiro**, single bedroom.—**dianteiro**, forequarter (of a carcass).—**e comida**, or —**com pensão**, room and board.—**minguante**, the waning or third quarter of the moon.—**para casal**, double bedroom.—**redondo**, (*Arch.*) quarterround, ovolo.—**traseiro**, hindquarter (of a carcass). **em**—**lugar**, in the fourth place, fourthly. **fazer**—, to stand watch; to attend a wake.

quartola (*f.*) small cask.

quártzico –ca (*adj.*) quartzic.

quartzífero –ra (*adj.*) quartziferous.

quartzite (*m.*), –ta (*f.*) quartzite.

quartzo (*m.*) quartz [= CRISTAL DE ROCHA (rock crystal)]. —**amarelo**, false topaz.—**ametista**, amethyst quartz; violet quartz.—**azul**, blue quartz.—**citrino**, citrine.— **enfumaçado**, smoky quartz.—**hialino**, any colorless and transparent crystalline quartz.—**róseo**, rose quartz.

quartzoso –sa (*adj.*) quartzose, quartzous.

quase (*adv.*) almost, nearly, not quite; scarcely, hardly, barely; quasi.—**nada**, almost nothing; scarcely anything. —**nunca**, almost never; hardly ever.—**quase**, in just a minute, right away.—**que**, almost.—**que não**, barely.— **sempre**, nearly always, most of the time.

quase-contrato (*m., Law*) quasi contract.

quase-delito (*m., Law*) quasi delict.

quase-posse (*m., Law*) quasi possession.

quassação (*f.*) a crushing (of roots, herbs, etc.).

quássia (*f., Bot.*) the Surinam quassia (*Q. amara*); also Jamaica quassiawood (*Picrasma excelsa*).—**-do-pará** = CAFERANA.—**-mineira**, a poison nut (*Strychnos macrocanthos*).

quassina, quassite (*f., Chem.*) quassin.

quassitunga (*f.*) = GUAÇATUNGA.

quaternado –da (*adj., Bot.*) quaternary.

quaternário –ria (*adj.*) quaternary.

quaternidade (*f.*) quaternity.

quaterno –na (*adj.*) quatern, fourfold, quadruple.

quatetê (*m.*) a regional name for the sapucaia tree.

quati (*m., Zool.*) coati, a tropical carnivore related to the raccoon. It has an elongated body, long tail, long and very flexible snout, whence its generic name, Nasua. In Brazil there are two principal species: the red, ringtailed *N. rufa*, and the brown *N. narica*; c.a. URSONARIGUDO.—**-mirim**,—**-puru** = ACUTI-PURU.

quatiara (*f.*) a poisonous pit viper (*Bothrops coatiara*), c.a. CUATIARA, URUTU.

quatindiba (*f.*) = CORINDIBA.

quatorze (*adj.*) fourteen. Var. CATORZE.

quatorzeno –na (*adj.*) fourteenth [= DÉCIMO-QUARTO].

quatreiro (*m.*) cattle rustler.

quatríduo (*m.*) a period of four days.

quatriênio (*m.*) = QUADRIÊNIO.

quatrinca (*f.*) four (cards) of a kind.

quatro (*adj.; m.*) four; fourth. **a—**, by fours; on all fours. —**ventos**, cardinal points. **a—mãos**, for four hands (piano duet). **caír de—**, to come a cropper. **de—pés**, on all fours.

quatrocentão –**tona** (*adj.*) designating persons whose family tree stems from the founding of São Paulo four hundred years ago; (*m.*) four hundred MIL-RÉIS; four hundred RÉIS.

quatrocentismo (*m.*) quattrocentism.

quatrocentista (*adj.*) quattrocento; (*m.,f.*) quattrocentist.

quatrocentos (*adj.; m.*) four hundred.

quatrodobro –bra (*adj.*) fourfold.

quatrolho –lha (*adj.*) having white eyebrows.

quatro-fôlhas (*m., Arch.*) quatrefoil.

quatro-olhos (*m., Zool.*) four-eyes, a top minnow (*Anableps tetrophthalmus*), c.a. ANABLEPSO, TRALHOTO; (*colloq.*) person who wears glasses; also = CATINGUEIRO (a deer).

quatro-patacas (*f., Bot.*) the violet allamanda (*A. violacea*).

quatro-paus (*m.*) the four of clubs.

quaxinduba (*f.*) = GAMELEIRA.—**-preta** = FIGUEIRA-DE-LOMBRIGUEIRA.

quaxinguba (*f.*) = CAUXINGUBA.

q.^do = QUANDO (when).

que (*adj., pron.*) that, which, who; (*interrog.*) What? (*exclam.*) What! (*conj.*) that, than; (*prep.*) but, excepting.—**aconteceu?** What happened?—**Deus te abençoe**, May God bless you.—**dia é hoje?** What day is today?—**é que há?** What is it? What's the matter? What's going on? —**é—houve?** What happened?—**é do Paulo?** Where is Paul? [Cf. CADÊ].—**é dêle?** Where is he? What became of him?—**há?** What's up? What's the matter? What's doing?—**há de novo?** What's new?—**horas são?** What time is it?—**lindo!** (**bom, barato, feio,** etc.), How beautiful! (good, cheap, ugly, etc.).—**não**, other than; and not. —**nem**, just like, than, more than.—**nem uma criança,** just like a child.—**pena!** What a pity! What a shame!— **quer?** What do you expect? What do you want?—**só,** like no other [e.g., **Chato que só êle,** As a bore he has no equal.].—**tal?** What's doing? How are things? What do

you say? How about it? How does it strike you? What do you think of it? [When hyphenated, **que-tal** is an adjective, meaning: identical, exactly the same.].— **vergonha!** For shame!—**vida!** What a life! **assim**—(**êle chegar**), as soon as (he arrives). **bem**—, though, while. **como**—, like, as if. **contanto**—, provided that. **de modo**—, so that. **do**—, than. **Espero**—**sim** (**não**), I hope so (not). **estar**—, to hold (be of the opinion) that. **frio**— **nem gêlo**, cold as ice. **houve tempo em**—, there was a time when. **já**—(**você esqueceu**), since, seeing that (you forgot). **logo**—**você não quer**, since you do not wish it. **nada**—**fazer**, nothing to do (to be done). **nem**—, not even if. **o**—, he who, the one who, which, what, that which. **o**—**quer que**, whatever (may be). **Para**—? What for? What's the use? **por**—, see PORQUE and PORQUÊ. **sem** —(**pedisse**) without (asking). **Tenho**—**ir**, I have to go.

quê (*m.*) something, a little something; something the matter, something wrong. **Não há de**—, It's nothing; Don't mention it; You're welcome. **por**—, see PORQUE and PORQUÊ. **Qual o**—! No such thing! **Tem seus**—**s,** It has its drawbacks.

Quebeque (*m.*) Quebec.

quebra (*f.*) break, rupture; breakage; spoilage; crash, bankruptcy; interruption; hillside.—**fraudulenta**, fraudulent bankruptcy. **de**—, to boot.—**de braço,** Indian wrestling.

quebra-arado (*m., Bot.*) the myrtleleaf heimia (*H. myrtifolia*).

quebra-bunda (*m.*) a disease of horses which causes weakness and lameness of the hindquarters.

quebra-cabeça (*m.,f., colloq.*) problem, poser; riddle, brain-teaser; jigsaw or other puzzle.—**chinês,** Chinese puzzle.

quebrachal (*m.*) grove of quebracho trees.

quebrachamina (*f., Chem.*) quebrachamine.

quebrachina (*f., Chem.*) quebrachine.

quebracho (*m.*) any of various So. Amer. trees, esp. the Lorentz red quebracho (*Schinopsis lorentzii*) and the white quebracho (*Aspidosperma quebracho*).—**crêspo,** a red quebracho (*Schinopsis marginata*).—**vermelho,** the willowleaf red quebracho (*Schinopsis balansae*).

quebra-costas (*m., colloq.*) a steep and slippery road or street.

quebra-costela (*m., colloq.*) a bear hug.

quebrada (*f.*) see under QUEBRADO.

quebra-dedos (*m.*) a fence of woven laths.

quebradeira (*f.*) puzzle; problem; (*colloq.*) bankruptcy.

quebradiço –ça (*adj.*) fragile, brittle, easily broken.

quebrado –da (*adj.*) broken; ruptured; ruined; (*colloq.*) broke, penniless; bankrupt; worn-out, tired out; (*m.*) slope; ravine; fraction; a bankrupt; (*pl.*) change, "chicken feed"; (*f.*) ravine; gorge; slope; bend in the road.

quebrador –dora (*adj.*) breaking; (*m.,f.*) breaker.

quebradura (*f.*) hernia, rupture; break; act of breaking.

quebra-enguiço (*m.*) a rabbit's foot or other good luck charm.

quebra-esquinas (*m., colloq.*) a person who hangs around street corners.

quebra-febre (*f.*) the drug centaurium (*C. umbellatum*), c.a. CENTÁUREA-MENOR.

quebra-fogo (*m.*) fireplace screen.

quebra-foice (*f., Bot.*) either of two calliandras: *C. tweedi* (c.a. MANDARAVÉ) or *C. parvifolia* (c.a. FLOR-DO-CÉU).

quebra-freio (*adj.*) wild, disorderly; (*m.*) a tough.

quebra-gêlo (*m.*) (*Aeron.*) deicer; (*Naut.*) icebreaker.

quebra-lanças (*m.*) ardent supporter of a cause or of another person.

quebralhão –lhona (*adj.; m.,f.*) very bad (person or animal).

quebra-louças (*m.*) bull in a china shop.

quebra-luz (*m.*) lampshade [= ABAJUR]; eye shade.

quebra-machado (*m.*) = GONÇALO-ALVES and CHUPA-FERRO.

quebra-mar (*m.*) breakwater; sea wall.

quebramento (*m.*) = QUEBRA; QUEBREIRA.

quebrança (*f.*) breaking of waves [= ARREBENTAÇÃO].

quebra-nozes (*m.*) nutcracker; also = RENDEIRA (bird).

quebrantado –da (*adj.*) broken, enfeebled; decrepit; damaged.

quebrantamento (*m.*) breaking; prostration, weakness.

quebrantar (*v.t.*) to break (down), batter; to hurt, bruise; to violate, transgress; to control; to exceed; to assuage; to prostrate; (*v.r.*) to grow weak.

quebranto (*m.*) exhaustion, weakness, prostration; a spell of depression, illness, etc., inflicted by another's "evil eye," esp. upon children and animals.

quebra-panela (*f.*) Scotch heather (*Calluna vulgaris*), c.a. QUEIRÓ; a globeamaranth (*Gomphrena demissa*).

quebra-pedra (*f.*) the fly-roost leafflower (*Phyllanthus niruri*), c.a. ARREBENTA-PEDRA; the wall pellitory (*Parietaria officinalis*), c.a. FURA-PAREDES; the pillpod euphorbia (*E. pilulifera*).

quebra-quebra (*m.*) street riot; (*f.*) a certain nonpoisonous colubrid snake—see COBRA-DE-VIDRO.

quebra-queixo (*m.*, *colloq.*) cheap stogy; jawbreaker (candy).

quebrar (*v.t.*) to break (up), shatter; to fracture; to sever, disrupt; to interrupt; to cut short; to violate, infringe; to mitigate; to twist, turn; (*v.i.*) to break; to rupture; to fail (in business); (*v.r.*) to break.—**a cabeça**, to rack (cudgel) one's brains.—**a cabeça a**, to break another's skull.—**a cara a**, to smash another's face.—**a castanha de**, to excel, outstrip (another).—**a palavra**, to break one's word.—**a tigela**, or—**a panela**, to wear something new (suit, dress, shoes, etc.) for the first time.—**as esquinas**, to hang around street corners.—**as relações com**, to break off relations with.—**catolé**, or—**côco**, to misfire.—**de vez com**, to make a clean break with.—**lanças por**, to go all out in behalf of.—**o coração a**, to break another's heart.—**o fio da história**, to interrupt the thread of a story.—**o fio da vida a**, to cut short another's life.—**o gêlo**, to break the ice.—**o jejum**, to break fast [but to breakfast is ALMOÇAR].—**o silêncio**, to break the silence. —**os grilhões**, to strike off the shackles, throw off the yoke.—**uma lança com**, to cross swords with. **o—da barra**, the break of day.

quebra-rabicho (*m.*, *colloq.*) brawl.

quebrável (*adj.*) breakable.

quebra-ventos (*m.*) windbreak.

quebra-vista (*m.*) blinder [= ANTOLHOS].

quebreira (*f.*, *colloq.*) languor, lassitude, weariness, prostration; status of being broke [= PINDAÍBA].

quebro (*m.*) voice inflection; break in the voice; a dodge, turn or twist of the body.

quebuçu [çú] (*m.*) = GUEBUÇÚ.

quecê, quecé (*m.*) = CAXIRENGUENGUE.

queche (*m.*) ketch.

quéchua (*m.*) = QUÍCHUA.

queci-queci [cí] (*m.*) a parrot (*Conurus solstitialis*), c.a. QUIJUBA.

queda (*f.*) a fall or falling; downfall; collapse; drop, tumble; decline, decadence; bent, inclination, knack; (*Elec.*) drop (of potential).—**de água or de rio**, waterfall. —**de braço**, Indian wrestling.—**do ministério**, fall of the government.—**do pêlo**, natural lie of an animal's fur.— **pelas crianças**, fondness for children.—**por or para**, a leaning towards; a bent for. **dar uma—**, to take a tumble.

quedaço (*m.*) spill, bad fall.

quedamento (*m.*) act of remaining still (quiet).

quedar (*v.i.*,*v.r.*) to stay, stop, remain still (quiet).

quéde, quedê, a careless contraction of **que é de?**, meaning, where is (. . .)? what's become of (. . .)? Cf. CADÊ.

quedivo (*m.*) khedive.

quêdo -**da** (*adj.*) quiet, still; stationary, motionless.—**e**— (*adv.*) quietly, softly, stepping lightly.

quefazer[es] (*m.*) thing(s) to be done (duties, chores).

quefir (*m.*) kefir, kumiss.

queijada (*f.*) kind of cheese cake.

queijadeira (*f.*), -**ro** (*m.*) a maker or vender of QUEIJADA.

queijadilho (*m.*) English primrose (*Primula vulgaris*).

queijar (*v.i.*) to make cheese; to turn into cheese.

queijaria (*f.*) cheese factory; cheesemaking.

queijeiro (*m.*), -**ra** (*f.*) cheese maker; cheese merchant.

queijo (*m.*)· cheese. **ser pão pão, — —**, to be forthright, outspoken. **ter, or estar com, a faca e o—na mão**, to have complete control of a situation.

queijoso -**sa** (*adj.*) cheesy [= CASEOSO].

queima (*f.*) act or result of burning; fire; cremation; fire sale; (*Plant Pathol.*) fire blight. **à—roupa**, point-blank.

queimação (*f.*) = QUEIMA; annoyance, nuisance.

queimada (*f.*) see under QUEIMADO.

queimadeira (*f.*) = CANSAÇÃO-DE-LEITE.

queimadeiro (*m.*) burning place.

queimadela (*f.*) = QUEIMADURA.

queimado -**da** (*adj.*) burned; carbonized; scorched; fireblighted or frost-burned [plants]; (*colloq.*) burned up (angry); (*m.*) the odor of scorched food; a kind of

burned-sugar candy; (*f.*) a clearing of land by burning; burned-over land.

queimador -**dora** (*adj.*) burning; (*m.*,*f.*) burner.

queimadouro (*m.*) burning place.

queimadura (*f.*) a burn(ing); plant blight.

queimamento (*m.*) act of burning.

queimante (*adj.*) burning, hot; (*m.*, *slang*) hot rod (pistol).

queimão (*m.*) = QUIMÃO (kimono).

queimar (*v.t.*) to burn (up), consume (with fire); to char, scorch; to sear; to sell out (stock of goods) at reduced prices; (*v.i.*) to burn; to be burning hot; (*v.r.*) to burn (itself, oneself); to sear, wither, dry up; (*colloq.*) to burn up (get angry).—**as pestanas**, to burn the midnight oil. —**campo**, to tell many lies.—**incenso a**, to flatter (someone).—**o seu último cartucho**, to fire one's last shot.— **uma carta**, to bury a card (in the deck).—**-se nos olhos de**, to fall in love with.

queimoso -**sa** (*adj.*) hot, burning.

queir-+verb endings = forms of QUERER [68].

queiró(s) (*m.*) Scotch heather (*Calluna vulgaris*), c.a. QUEBRA-PANELAS, QUEIROGA.

queirosiano -**na** (*adj.*) pert. to or characteristic of the Port. writer Eça de Queirós or his writings [= ECIANO].

queixa (*f.*) complaint, grievance; formal accusation; groan, moan; sickness.—**do peito**, (*colloq.*) pulmonary tuberculosis. **dar satisfação a uma—**, to settle a complaint. **motivo de—**, grounds for complaint.

queixada (*f.*) jaw [= MAXILA]; (*m.*, *Zool.*) the whitelipped peccary (*Tayassus pecari*), c.a. TIRIRICA, QUEIXO-RUIVO, QUEIXADA-RUIVA, TACUITÉ, TAIAÇU-TIRÁGUA. Cf. CAITITU.

queixal (*adj.*) of or pert. to the jaw; (*m.*) molar tooth.

queixar-se (*v.r.*) to complain (**a**, to; **de**, of, about; **contra**, against); to find fault (**de**, with); to grumble; to "gripe"; to groan, moan; to wail. **Vá—ao bispo!** (*scornfully*) Go jump in the lake! Tell it to Sweeney!

queixeira (*f.*) mouth piece of a curb bit.

queixo (*m.*) chin; jaw.—-**branco** = CAITITU.—**de rabeca**, or **de viola**, lantern jaw.—-**ruivo** = QUEIXADA. **bater o—**, to chatter (with cold or fear). **duro de—**, of a horse, hard-mouthed; of a person, stubborn, hard to manage. **ficar de—caído**, to drop one's jaw (in amazement).

queixoso -**sa** (*adj.*) querulous, complaining; whining; plaintive; (*m.*,*f.*, *Law*) complainant; plaintiff.

queixudo -**da** (*adj.*) big-jawed.

queixume (*m.*) complaint, lament; wail; groan.

queixumeiro -**ra** (*adj.*) much given to faultfinding and complaining; (*m.*,*f.*) such a person.

quejando -**da** (*adj.*) such, like.

quela (*f.*, *Zool.*) chela.

quelato (*m.*, *Zool.*) claw, pincer.

quelelê (*m.*) quarrel; fracas.

queleritrina (*f.*, *Chem.*) chelerythrine.

quelha (*f.*), -**lho** (*m.*) flume; chute; trough.

quelícera (*f.*, *Zool.*) chelicera.

quelidônia (*f.*, *Bot.*) the greater celandine (*Chelidonium majus*), c.a. CELIDÔNIA, CERUDA, ERVA-DAS-VERRUGAS, ERVA-ANDORINHA.—-**menor**, the figroot buttercup (*Ranunculus ficaria*), c.a. BOTÃO-DE-OURO.

quelidonina (*f.*, *Chem.*) chelidonine [= ALIDONINA].

quelífero -**ra** (*adj.*, *Zool.*) cheliferous; (*m.*) book scorpion (*Chelifer*).

queliforme (*adj.*) pincerlike.

quelípode (*m.*, *Zool.*) cheliped.

quelóide (*m.*, *Med.*) keloid.

quelônio (*m.*) chelonian, turtle; (*pl.*) the Chelonia or Testudines (turtles or tortoises).

quem (*pron.*) who, the one who, whom, anybody who.—**é?** Who is it? Who is he (she)?—**me dera (morrer)**, Would that I could (die).—**quer vai, quem não quer, manda**, If you want a thing done, do it yourself.—**quer que**, whoever, whosoever.—**será?** Who can it (she, he) be? I wonder who it (he, she) is?—**sabe?** Who knows? **de**—, whose. **por—é (és**, etc.), for goodness' sake, I beg you. **seja—fôr**, whoever it may be.

quem-come-saberá (*f.*) a certain mango of Bahia (*Mangifera indica*).

quem-te-vestiu (*m.*) the black-and-chestnut warbling finch (*Poospiza nigro-rufa*).

quenga (*f.*) a vessel or dipper made from a coconut shell; chicken stew with okra; (*colloq.*) prostitute.

quengo (*m.*) a dipper made from a coconut shell; head; mind.

Quênia (*f.*) Kenya.

quenopodiáceo –cea (adj., Bot.) chenopodiaceous; (f.pl.) the Chenopodiaceae (goosefoot family).

quenopódio (m., Bot.) any goosefoot (Chenopodium), c.a. ANSERINA.

quenquém (m.) the blue-headed jay (Cyanocorax cyanopogon), c.a. CANCÃO, PIOM-PION, GRALHÃO; (f.) a certain ant (Acromyrex nigra).

quentão (m.) rum with gin.

quentar (v.) = AQUENTAR.

quente (adj.) hot, heated, very warm; ardent. **bem—**, quite hot; (m.) warm place; bed.

quentura (f.) heat, warmth.

quepe (m., Mil.) kepi.

quepleriano –na (adj.) Keplerian.

queque (m.) cake.

quer (conj.) or.—**aqui—alí**, either here or there.—**chova— não chova**, whether it rains or not.—**chova—faça sol**, rain or shine.—**queira—não**, willy-nilly. **o que—que**, whatever (may be).

queratina (f., Biochem.) keratin.

qüercina (f., Chem.) quercin.

qüercínias (f.pl.) = CUPULÍFERAS.

qüercite (f., Chem.) quercitol.

qüercitrina (f. Chem.) quercitrin.

qüerco (m.) quercus, oak. [Poetical]

querela (f., Law) complaint, charge; indictment; altercation, wrangle, dispute; (Poetical) plaint.

querelado –da (m. f., Law) defendant, the accused.

querelador –dora, **querelante** (adj.) complaining; (m.,f., Law) plaintiff, complainant.

querelar (v.t., Law) to make a formal charge or lodge a formal complaint (**contra**, against); (v.r.) to complain.

quereloso –sa (adj.) querulous.

querena (f.) hull of a vessel (below the water line); underwater body. **doca de—**, dry dock.

querenado –da (adj.) keeled over.

querenar (v.t.) to careen (a vessel); to keel over.

querença (f.) desire, wish, want; fondness, liking, affection; haunt (of animals); aerie.

querência (f.) place where one was born and reared; "home, sweet home"; place where cattle usually graze or where they were raised; love, desire.

querençoso –sa (adj.) affectionate, loving.

querendão –dona (adj.) of pets or persons, easily adjusting to a new home or new people; affectionate, loving, cheerful.

querente (adj.) desirous of, wishing for, wanting (something).

querê-querê (m.) a damselfish (Abudefduf saxatilis), c.a. SABERÉ, CAMISETA, CAMISA-DE-MEIA, TINHUMA.

querequexé (m.) = CANZÁ, RECO-RECO.

querer [68] (v.t.) to wish, want, desire; to be willing; to will, intend, mean; to like; (m.) wish, desire; intention; love.—**a**, to be fond of.—**bem (mal) a**, to love (hate).— **dizer**, to mean (to say).—**é poder**, Where there's a will, there's a way.—**uma no saco outra no papo**, to attempt two things at once. **ainda quando o quisessem**, even if they (had) wanted to. **bem—a**, to have affection for; to wish well for. **como quer que seja**, however it may be; anyhow. **Como queira** (or **quiser**), As you wish, as you prefer. **Faça como quiser**, Do as you please. **Eu bem quisera se pudesse, mas . . .** , I wish I could, but . . . **Eu só queria ver!** I'd just like to see it! **Não quis (falar)**, He refused (to talk). **o que quer que seja**, anything, whatever it may be. **onde quer que seja**, wherever it may be. **por—**, intentionally, wilfully, on purpose. **Quando um não quer, dois não brigam**, It takes two to start a quarrel. **Que quer?** What do you expect? **Que quer dizer isto?** What does this mean? **Queira (entrar)**, Please (come in). **queira Deus**, please God; God grant. **queira ou não queira**, willy-nilly (also: **quer queira, quer não queira**). **Queiram comparecer**, Kindly appear (come). **Quem quer, vai, quem não quer, manda**, If you want a thing done, do it yourself. **Quem muito quer, tudo perde**, To attempt all is to lose all. **quer me parecer que**, it seems to me that. **quer dizer**, that is to say; in other words. **Quero crer que foi assim, mas . . .** , I would like to believe it was that way, but . . . **.quero dizer**, I mean to say. **quis (fugir)**, he tried (to escape). **sem—**, unintentionally.

querido –da (adj.) dear, beloved; (m.,f.) dear one, darling. **tornar-se—**, to endear oneself.

querimólia (f., Bot.) the cherimoya (Annona cherimola); c.a. ANONA-DO-CHILE.

querite (f.) kerite (insulating material).

quermes (m.) kermes (berry, mineral).

quermesita (f., Min.) kermesite, antimony blende.

quermesse (f.) kermis, charitable bazaar.

quernita (f., Min.) kernite, hydrous sodium borate.

quero-quero (m.) the Brazilian lapwing (Belonopterus cayenensis lampronotus), c.a. TERO-TERO, ESPANTA-BOIADA, GAIVOTA-PRETA.

querosenar (v.t.) to saturate with kerosene.

querosene (m.) kerosene, coal oil; (Bot.) a laurel, c.a. PAU-DE-GASOLINA, LAURO-INHAMUÍ.

querubim (m.) cherub.

querubínico –ca, **querúbico** –ca (adj.) cherubic.

quérulo –la (adj.) querulous; whining.

queru-queru [rú] (m.) the cinnamomeous sparrow hawk (Falco sparverius cinnamominus), c.a. QUIRI-QUIRI.

quesito (m.) query, question.

questã, questan, popular pronunciation of QUESTÃO.

questão (f.) question, interrogation; matter, subject (under discussion); topic; inquiry; dispute, controversy. **—de estado**, a matter of state.—**de fato**, a question of fact.—**de opinião**, a matter of (personal) opinion.—**de ordem**, (Parliamentary Practice) point of order.—**de tempo**, a question of time.—**irritante**, a bone of contention.—**prévia**, (Parliamentary Practice) previous question. **fazer—**, to raise an objection. **fazer—de**, to insist on; to make a point (an issue) of. **ladear a—**, to dodge the question (issue). **resolver uma—**, to settle a matter.

questionabilidade (f.) questionableness.

questionador –dora (adj.) questioning; (m.,f.) questioner.

questionar (v.t.) to call in question, dispute; (v.i.) to wrangle; to bicker.

questionário (m.) questionnaire.

questionável (adj.) questionable, disputable.

questiúncula (f.) question of minor importance.

quetenito (m., Min.) quetenite.

queto, pop. pronunciation of QUIETO.

quetua (f.) a parrot (Pyrrhura roseifrons).

quiabeiro (m., Bot.) okra (Hibiscus esculentus).

quiabento (m.) = CACTO-ROSA.

quiabinho-do-campo (m., Bot.) a piriqueta (P. aurea).

quiabo (m., Bot.) okra (pod or plant).—**-azêdo**, or—**-de-angola**, or—**-róseo**, or—**-roxo** = CARURU-AZÊDO.—**-bravo** = CARRAPICHINHO.—**-cheiroso**, muskmallow (Hibiscus abelmoschus).—**-chifre de veado**, the common okra (Hibiscus esculentus), c.a. QUIABEIRO.

quiaborana (f.) a malvaceous plant of genus Malachra.

quiante (m.) Chianti wine.

quiaquiá (m.) a turtle shell partly filled with pebbles, serving as a rattle.

quiasma (m., Anat., Biol.) chiasma; (Rhet.) chiasmus.

quiastólito (m., Min.) chiastolite.

quibando (m.) a coarse sieve, for rice, coffee, etc.

quibebe [bêbe] (m.) pumpkin purée.

quibungo (m.) Negro dance; hobgoblin; devil; witch doctor; wild animal.

quica (f., Bot.) a palaverde (Cercidium spinosum).

quiçá (adv.) perhaps, maybe; who knows?; peradventure. [from Italian: chi sa?]

quiçaba (f.) earthen pot or water jar. Cf. IGAÇABA.

quiçamba (f.) wicker grain basket.

quicê, quicé (m.) old, broken knife [= CAXIRENGUENGUE].

quíchua (m.) Cuechuan (language); (pl.) Quechuas.

quício (m.) hinge.

quicuta (f.) the cowage velvetbean (Stizolobium pruritum).

quidam [ú-f] (m.) somebody, one unknown, esp. someone of little importance.

qüididade (f.) quiddity.

quiescente (adj.) quiescent.

quietação (f.) a quieting; quietness.

quietar (v.t.) to quiet.

quietarrão –rona (adj.) of persons, very still and quiet.

quietinho –nha (adj.) of children, nice and quiet; still as a mouse.

quietismo (m.) quietism; passiveness.

quietista (adj.; m.,f.) quietist.

quieto –ta (adj.) quiet, still, motionless; calm, silent. **não parar—**, to have the fidgets.

quietude (f.) quietude.

quigombô (m.) = QUINGOMBÔ.

quija (m., Zool.) the copyu (Myocastor coypus), c.a. NUTRIA, RATÃO-DO-BANHADO.

quijuba (m.) a parrot (Conurus solstitialis), c.a. QUECI-QUECI.—**-tuí**, a small parakeet, c.a. GUARAJUBA.

quilaia (*f.*) soapbark tree (*Quillaja saponaria*).
quilanto (*m.*, *Bot.*) any lipfern (*Cheilanthes*).
quilatação (*f.*) assay(ing).
quilatar (*v.t.*) to assay [= AQUILATAR].
quilate (*m.*) carat; degree of perfection.—**métrico**, metric carat [= 200 milligrams = 3.086 grains troy].
quilateira (*f.*) a screen for grading precious stones by size.
quilha (*f.*) keel.—**corrediça**, centerboard.
quiliare (*m.*) 1000 ares [= 24.71 acres].
quilífero –ra (*adj.*, *Physiol.*) chyliferous; (*m.pl.*) chyliferous vessels.
quilificação (*f.*, *Physiol.*) chylification.
quilificar (*v.t.*,*v.i.*, *Physiol.*) to chylify.
quilo (*m.*) short for QUILOGRAMA (kilogram); (*Physiol.*) chyle.
quiloampère (*m.*) kiloampere.
quilocaloria (*f.*, *Physics*) kilocalorie, great calorie.
quilocíclo (*m.*) kilocvcle.
quilognatos (*m.pl.*) = DIPLÓPODES.
quilograma (*m.*) kilogram [= 1,000 grams = 2.204 lbs.].
quilogrâmetro (*m.*, *Mech.*) kilogram-meter.
quilolitro (*m.*) kiloliter [= 1000 liters = 264.17 gals.].
quilombo (*m.*) a hiding place of runaway slaves; a primitive dance.
quilombola (*m.*) a runaway slave hiding in a QUILOMBO.
quilometragem (*f.*) distance in kilometers; act of measuring in kilometers.
quilométrico –ca (*adj.*) kilometric.
quilômetro (*m.*) kilometer [= 1,000 meters = 0.62137 mile].
quiloplastia (*f.*, *Surg.*) chiloplasty.
quilópode (*m.*) chilopod, centipede.
quiloso –sa (*adj.*, *Physiol.*) chylaceous.
quilopoese (*f.*, *Physiol.*) chylopoiesis, chylification.
quilovolt (*m.*) kilovolt.—**ampère**, kilovoltampere.
quilowatt (*m.*) kilowatt.—**hora**, kilowatt-hour.
quimanga (*f.*) a coconut vessel for keeping food.
quimão (*m.*) kimono.
quimase (*f.*, *Biochem.*) rennin.
quimbembe (*adj.*) poorly dressed; poor; (*m.*) thatched hut; (*pl.*) junk; amulets, charms.
quimbembeques (*m.pl.*) trinkets, charms, amulets.
quimbérlito (*m.*, *Petrog.*) kimberlite.
quimboa (*f.*, *Bot.*) a figwort (*Achimenes*).
quimera (*f.*) chimera, creature of the imagination; (*Zool.*) the bottle-nosed chimera (*Callorhynchus callorhynchus*), c.a. PEIXE-ELEFANTE, PEIXE-COELHO.
quimérico –ca (*adj.*) chimerical, unreal.
quimerídeos (*m.pl.*, *Zool.*) the Chimaeridae (fish).
quimerista (*m.,f.*) visionary.
química (*f.*) chemistry.—**agrícola**, agricultural chemistry.—**analítica**, analytical chemistry.—**biológica**, biochemistry.—**biológica animal**, zoochemistry.—**biológica vegetal**, phytochemistry.—**bromatológica**, food chemistry.—**farmacêutica**, pharmaceutical chemistry [= FARMACOLÓGICA].—**física**, physical chemistry.—**fisiológica**, physiological chemistry.—**geológica**, geological chemistry.—**geral**, theoretical chemistry.—**industrial**, industrial or technological chemistry.—**inorgânica**, inorganic chemistry.—**médica**, medical chemistry.—**metalúrgica**, metallurgical chemistry.—**mineral**, inorganic chemistry.—**mineralógica**, mineralogical chemistry.—**orgânica**, organic chemistry.—**sanitária**, sanitary chemistry.—**técnica**, technological or industrial chemistry.
químico –ca (*adj.*) chemical; (*m.*,*f.*) chemist.
químico-analítico –ca (*adj.*) pert. to analytical chemistry.
químico-físico –ca (*adj.*) chemicophysical.
químico-legal (*adj.*) pert. to forensic or legal chemistry.
quimicoterapia (*f.*, *Med.*) chemotherapy.
quimificação (*f.*, *Physiol.*) chymification.
quimificar (*v.t.*, *Physiol.*) to chymify.
quimiotaxia [ks] (*f.*, *Biol.*) chemotaxis.
quimioterapêutica, **quimioterapia** (*f.*) chemotherapeutics, chemotherapy.
quimioterápico –ca (*adj.*) chemotherapeutic.
quimiotrópico –ca (*adj.*, *Biol.*) chemotropic.
quimiotropismo (*m.*, *Biol.*) chemotropism.
quimismo (*m.*) chemism.
quimitipia (*f.*, *Engraving*) chemitype.
quimo (*m.*, *Physiol.*) chyme.
quimonanto (*m.*, *Bot.*) the wintersweet (*Chimonanthus praecox*).
quimono (*m.*) kimono.
quimoso –sa (*adj.*) chymous.

quina (*f.*) sharp edge (as of a table); corner (as of a wall); five-spot (of cards or dice); a row of five numbers on a keno or lotto card; (*Pharm.*) cinchona (bark), Peruvian bark, Jesuits' bark; (*Bot.*) any of numerous bitter-barked South American shrubs and trees, many of which are used locally as a substitute for quinine.—**amarela**, yellowbark cinchona (*C. calisaya*).—**amargosa** = CAFE-RANA.—**bicolorada**, a nightshade (*Solanum pseudo-quina*).—**branca** = FALSA-QUINA.—**brava**, a melastomaceous plant (*Miconia*, syn. *Tamonea, wildenowii*).—**caribé**, the Caribbean princewood (*Exostemma caribaeum*).—**cruzeiro** = CAFERANA and ESPINHO-DE-SÃO-JOÃO.—**da-chapada** = FALSA-QUINA.—**da-serra**, the rubiaceous *Remijia ferruginea*.—**das-três-fôlhas** = GUAMI-XINGA.—**de-cipó**, a poison nut (*Strychnos gardneri*) and a greenbrier (*Smilax fluminensis*).—**de-condamine** = CARQUEJA-AMARGOSA.—**de-cuiabá**, the rubiaceous *Remijia cuyabensis*.—**de-diogo-de-sousa** = QUINA-DO-PIAUÍ.—**de-mato-grosso** = FALSA-QUINA.—**de-periquito** = FALSA-QUINA.—**de-pernambuco**, the rubinaceous *Coutarea hexandra*, c.a. MURTA-DO-MATO.—**de-raiz-preta** = CIPÓ-CRUZ-VERDADEIRA.—**de-santa-catarina** = CAU-AÇU.—**de-são-joão**, a goldenweed (*Aplopappus grandiflorum*).—**de-são-paulo** = QUINA-BICOLORADA.—**do-amazonas** = CAFERANA.—**do-campo** = FALSA-QUINA.—**do-cerrado** = FALSA-QUINA.—**do-mato**, any of various rubiaceous plants of genera Exostemma, Cinchona and Ladenbergia; also the solanaceous *Cestrum pseudo-quina*.—**do-pará**, a plant of the Indian plum family (*Caseria adstringens*); also = CAFERANA.—**do-paraná** = CAUAÇU.—**do-piauí**, any of various rubiaceous plants, genus Exostemma.—**do remígio**, the rubiaceous *Remijia hilarii*.—**do-rio-de-janeiro**, the rubiaceous *Exostemma formosum*.—**do-rio-negro**, the rubiaceous *Ladenbergia lambertiana*.—**falsa** = GUAMIXINGA.—**falsa** = QUINA-DA-SERRA.—**pereira**, a white quebracho (*Aspidosperma illustre*), c.a. TAMBU.—**quina**, the rubiaceous *Cinchona officinalis*; also = GUAMIXINGA and MURTA-DO-MATO.—**verdadeira**, the rubiaceous *Cinchona ledgeriana*, an important source of cinchona bark.—**vermelha**, the redbark cinchona (*C. succirubra*), also an important source of cinchona bark.—**vermelha-do-brasil** = ARA-RIBA-VERMELHA.
quinado –da (*adj.*) grouped by fives; (*Bot.*) quinate; cinchonized; (*m.*) medicinal wine treated with cinchona.
quináldico –ca (*adj.*) quinaldic (acid).
quinaldina (*f.*, *Chem.*) quinaldine.
quinamina (*f.*, *Chem.*) quinamine.
quinanga (*f.*) wooden bucket.
quinaquina (*f.*) = MURTA-DO-MATO.
quinar (*v.t.*) to cinchonize; (*v.i.*) to win at keno.
quinário –ria (*adj.*) quinary.
quinato (*m.*, *Chem.*) quinate.
quinau (*m.*) correction; corrective.
quincaju [jú] (*m.*, *Zool.*) kinkajou (*Potos*, syn. *Cercoleptes caudivolvulus*).
quincalha (*f.*) = QUINQUILHARIA.
quincha (*f.*) thatch roof.
quinchar (*v.t.*) to thatch.
quincunce (*m.*) quincunx: "an arrangement, esp. of trees, with one at each corner and one at the center of a square." [*Webster*]
quincuncial (*adj.*, *Bot.*) quincuncial.
qüindecágono (*m.*, *Geom.*) quindecagon.
quindênio (*m.*) fifteen; fifteen days.
quindim (*m.*) difficulty; shyness; amorous longing; a term of endearment (such as darling); a kind of coconut candy.
quineira (*f.*) quinine bush.
quineto (*m.*, *Pharm.*) quinetum.
qüingentésimo –ma (*adj.*; *m.*) five hundredth.
quingombô (*m.*) okra (pod or plant); any of several other malvaceous plants. Cf. QUIABO.—**de-espinho** = CHIFRE-DE-VEADO.
quinguingu [gú] (*m.*) forced overtime labor (of slaves); hence, any overtime work.
quinhão (*m.*) portion, share, allotment. **dar em**—, to allot to.
quinhentão (*m.*, *colloq.*) formerly, a Brazilian coin of 500 réis or a bill of 500 mil-réis; nowadays, 50 centavos or 500 cruzeiros, respectively.
quinhentismo (*m.*) style, taste, habit, expression, etc. characteristic of the 16th century.

quinhentista (adj.) of or pert. to the 16th cent.; (m.,f.) writer of the 16th cent.
quinhentos (adj.; m.) five hundred.
quinhoar (v.) = AQUINHOAR.
quinhoeiro (m.) share-taker; partner.
quinhonista (m.,f.) shareholder.
quinicina (f., Chem.) quinicine, quinotoxine.
quínico –ca (adj.) quinic. ácido—, quinic acid.
quinidina (f., Chem.) quinidine.
quinina (f., Chem., Pharm.) quinine.
quinínico –ca (adj.) quininic (acid).
quinismo (m., Med.) cinchonism.
quino (m.) keno, lotto, bingo.
quinoa (f.) a goosefoot or pigweed (Chenopodium quinoa), c.a. CAPERIÇOBA-BRANCA.
quinofórmio (m., Pharm.) quinoform.
quinogênio (m., Chem.) quinogen.
quinoidina [o-i] (f., Pharm.) quinoidine.
quinol (m., Chem.) quinol.
quinolina (f., Chem.) quinoline.
quinologia (f.) quinology.
quinologista (m.,f.) quinologist.
quinona (f., Chem.) quinone.
quinotânico –ca (adj., Chem.) quinotannic [acid].
quinotoxina [ks] (f., Chem.) quinotoxine, quinicine.
quinovato (m., Chem.) quinovate.
quinóvico –ca (adj.) quinovic [acid].
quinovina (f., Chem.) quinovin, quinova bitter.
qüinquagenário –ria (adj.; m.,f.) quinquagenarian.
qüinquagésimo –ma (adj.; m.) quinquagesimal; fiftieth (one); a fiftieth; (f.) a space of fifty days; Quinquagesima or Shrove Sunday.
qüinqüengular (adj.) having five angles.
qüinqüecapsular (adj., Bot.) quinquecapsular.
qüinqüedentado –da (adj.) quinquedentate.
qüinqüéfido –da (adj., Bot.) quinquefid.
qüinqüefoliado –da (adj., Bot.) quinquefoliolate; (m.) creeping cinquefoil (Potentilla reptans).
qüinqüelocular (adj., Bot.) quinquelocular.
qüinqüenal (adj.) quinquennial. plano—, five-year plan.
qüinqüenário –ria (adj.) five-year.
qüinqüenio (m.) quinquennium.
qüinqüevalente (adj., Chem.) quinquevalent, pentavalent.
quinquilharias, quinquilherias (f.pl.) gew-gaws, gim-cracks, knickknacks, baubles.
quinquina (f.) = QUINA-QUINA.
quinta (f.) see under QUINTO.
quintã (adj.; f.) quintan (fever).
quinta-coluna (f.) fifth column.
quinta-colunista (m.,f.) fifth columnist.
quinta-essência (f.) quintessence.
quinta-feira (f.) Thursday.
quintal (m.) back yard.—métrico, 100 kilograms [= 220.46 lbs.].
quintalejo (m.) small back yard.
quintanista (m.,f.) a fifth-year student.
quintar (v.t.) to divide into five parts; to take a fifth part or one in five.
quintarola (f., colloq.) small country villa.
quinta-substância (f.) = QUINTA-ESSÊNCIA.
quinteiro (m.) caretaker of a QUINTA.
quintetista (m.,f.) member of a quintet.
quinteto (m.) quintet.
quintil (m., Stat.) quintile.
quintilhão (m.) quintillion.
quintilho (m., Bot.) apple-of-Peru (Nicandra physalodes).
Quintino (m.) Quentin; Quintin.
quinto –ta (adj.; m.,f.) fifth; (f.) country seat, villa, rural residence; short for QUINTA-FEIRA; (Music) fifth; (Fencing) quinte; (m.pl. colloq.) hell.
quintuplicação (f.) quintuplication.
quintuplicado –da (adj.) quintuplicate; fivefold.
quintuplicar (v.t.) to quintuple.
quintuplinérveo –vea (adj., Bot.) quinquenerved, quintu-plenerved, quintuple-ribbed.
quíntuplo –pla (adj.) quintuple; (m.,f.) a fivefold amount.
quinze (adj.; m.) fifteen; fifteenth.—de resto, quinze (card game).
quinzena (f.) a period of fifteen days; fortnight; a tax of a fifteenth; lightweight men's jacket.
quinzenal (adj.) fortnightly.
quinzenalmente (adv.) fortnightly.
quinzenário (m.) fortnightly periodical.

quioiô (m., Bot.) sweet basil (Ocimum basilicum); also = ALFAVACA-DA-GUINÉ.
quiólito (m., Min.) chiolite.
quionablepsia (f.) snow-blindness.
quionanto (m.) fringetree (Chionanthus sp).
quionodoxa [ks] (f., Bot.) glory-of-the-snow (Chonodoxa).
quiosque (m.) kiosk, newstand. [Formerly, in Brazil, a street stand serving bad food and hard liquor.]
quiosqueiro (m.) owner of a kiosk.
quiótomo (m.) = CIÓTOMO.
quipata (f.) quantity of fish shared by lucky fishermen with others less fortunate.
quipateiro (m.) fisherman who receives a QUIPATA; lazy fisherman.
quipos (m.pl.) quipu (Peruvian mnemonic device).
qüiproquó (m.) blunder made by using or putting one thing for another; witticism.
quiquiqui (m.) one who stutters or stammers.
quiquiriqui (m.) trifle; a nobody; a cockadoodle-do.
quirche (m.) kirsch(wasser)—a liqueur.
quirera (f.) cracked corn; hominy grits; (pl.) chicken feed.
quirerar (v.t.) to crack corn.
quiri [rí], quirim (m., Bot.) the Goeldi cordia (C. goeldiana).
quírie, quirieleisão (m., Eccl.) kyrie eleison.
quirina (f., Zool.) a toucan (Ramphastos erythrorhynchus).
quiripiranga (f., Bot.) a caesalpinia (C. ferrea).
quiriquiri [rí] (m.) a small sparrow hawk (Falco sparverius), c.a. GAVIÃO-QUIRIQUIRI, QUERU-QUERU.
quiriri [riri] (adj.) silent, deserted; (m.) dead of night.
quiriripitá (f.) a Brazilian snake closely related to the harmless BOIPEVA, which see; c.a. QUITITIPITÁ.
quiriru [ú] (m.) = ANUM-BRANCO.
quiriívia (f.) = ALQUIRIVIA.
quirognomonia (f.) palmistry.
quirografia (f.) chirography, handwriting.
quirógrafo (m.) chirograph.
quirologia (f.) dactylogy (art of communicating by signs made with the fingers, as by deaf-mutes).
quiromancia (f.) chiromancy, palmistry.
quiromante (m.,f.) chiromancer, fortuneteller.
quiromegalia (f., Med.) chiromegaly.
quirônimo (m., Bot., Zool.) chironym.
quironomia (f.) chironomy; gesture.
quiroplastia (f.) chiroplasty, surgery of the hand.
quirópode (adj., Zool.) chiropodous.
quiropodia (f.) chiropody.
quiropodista (m.,f.) chiropodist.
quiroprática (f.) chiropractic.
quirópteros (m.pl., Zool.) the Chiroptera (bats).
quirospasmo (m.) writer's cramp.
quirotesia (f., Eccl.) chirothesia.
quirótipo (m., Bot., Zool.) chirotype.
quirotonia (f.) chirotony.
quiruá (f., Zool.) the banded cotinga (Cotinga maculata), c.a. CATINGÁ.
quirurgia (f.) & derivs. = CIRURGIA & derivs.
quis-+verb endings = forms of QUERER [68].
quisafu [fú] (m.) = DITEQUE.
quisanana (f., Bot.) a jute (Corchorus tridens).
quisco (m.) a cactus (Cereus pugioniferous).
quisto (m.) cyst, wen.—dermóide, (Med.) dermoid cyst. —sebáceo, sebaceous cyst.
quitação (f.) quittance, discharge, acquittal; release.
quitado –da (adj.) quits.
quitador –dora (adj.) releasing, discharging; (m.,f.) one who releases another (from an obligation).
quitambuera (f.) = CATIMPUERA.
quitamento (m.) quittance [= QUITAÇÃO]; divorce, legal separation [= DESQUITE].
quitança (f.) quittance [= QUITAÇÃO].
quitanda (f.) a small shop or market, esp. one dealing in vegetables, fruits, eggs, etc.; greengrocery.
quitandeira (f.) woman who operates a QUITANDA; street vender of sweets; market woman; fishwife (lit. & fig.).
quitandeiro (m.) greengrocer; operator of a QUITANDA.
quitar (v.t.) to free (of an obligation); to quit, relieve, release (from); (v.r.) to free oneself; to be divorced.
quite (adj.) quit, clear, free; divorced. dar por—(s), to release (from an obligation). estar—, to be paid up (as, in one's club dues).
quiti [tí] (m.) club, cudgel [= CACÊTE].
quitina (f., Biochem.) chitin.
quitinização (f.) chitinization.
quitino-arenoso –sa (adj.) chitino-arenaceous.

quitino-calcário -ria (*adj.*) chitinocalcareous.
quitinógeno -na (*adj.*) chitinogeneous.
quitinóide (*adj.*) resembling chitin.
quitinoso -sa (*adj.*) chitinous.
quititipitá (*f.*) a Brazilian snake closely related to the harmless BOIPEVA, which see; c.a. QUIRIRIPITÁ.
quitoco [tô] (*m.*, *Bot.*) a marsh fleabane (*Pluchea quitoc*), c.a. TABACARANA.
quíton (*m.*) chiton (classical Greek garment); (*Zool.*) a genus (*Chiton*) of limpetlike mollusks.
quitonídeos (*m.pl.*) the chitons (coat-of-mail shells).
quitute (*m.*) tasty dish, delicacy, tidbit.
quituteira (*f.*), **-ro** (*m.*) an expert in preparing tidbits.
quixaba (*f.*) fruit of the QUIXABEIRA.
quixabeira (*f.*) the ibiranira bumelia (*B. obtusifolia*).
quixiligangue (*m.*) trifle [= NINHARIA].
quixiúme (*m.*) = CRICIÚMA.
quixó (*m.*) a trap for small animals.
quixotada, quixotice (*f.*) vain boast.
quixotesco -ca [tê], **quixótico -ca** (*adj.*) quixotic.
quixotismo (*m.*) quixotism.
quizila, -zília (*f.*) tiff; repugnance; annoyance; uneasiness.

quizilar (*v.t.*) to annoy; (*v.i.*) to be annoyed; (*v.r.*) to get angry.
ql. = QUILATE (carat).
quocientar (*v.t.*) to find the quotient of.
quociente (*m.*) quotient.
quodlíbeto (*m.*) quodlibet.
quodore (*m.*) sip of wine; bite of food.
quórum (*m.*) quorum.
quota (*f.*) quota, share, portion, allotment; installment payment, contribution; = COTA.
quotidiano -na (*adj.*) daily [= COTIDIANO].
quotiliquê (*m.*) person or thing of no importance.
quotista (*adj.*) shareholding; (*m.,f.*) shareholder [= COTISTA].
quotização (*f.*) assessment [= COTIZAÇÃO].
quotizar (*v.t.*) to parcel out; to assess (one's share); (*v.r.*) to contribute one's share; to join with others in a common expense; = COTIZAR.
q.v. = VEJA ISSO (*quod vide*, which see); QUANTO SE QUEIRA (*quantum vis*, as much as wanted); QUEIRA VOLTAR (please return).

R

R, r, the seventeenth letter of the Port. alphabet.
R. = REI (King); REPROVADO (failed—school mark); RÉU (defendant); RUA (street).
R.ᵃ = RAINHA (Queen).
R.A., REGIMENTO DE ARTILHARIA (artillery regiment).
rã (*f.*) any frog, but the term is applied also to toads, which properly speaking are SAPOS.—**arbícola**, any tree frog.—**comum**, a robber frog (*Leptodactylus ocellatus*) which appears on restaurant menus in Brazil as **rã-dourada**.—**das-moitas** = PERERECA, RELA, or RUBETA.—**do-mar** = PEIXE-PESCADOR.—**pimenta**, a large robber frog (*Leptodactylus pentadactylus*), c.a. NIMBUIA or JIMBUIA—general throughout Brazil.—**verdadeira**, is *Rana palmipes*, the only true large aquatic frog (*Ranidae*) native to Brazil. [An attempt has been made to introduce the common American bullfrog (*Rana catesbeiana*) into Brazil, where it is called **rã-gigante** or **rã-touro**.]
rabaça (*f.*) a water parsnip (*Sium*).
rabaçá (*f.*) = POMBA-DE-BANDO.
rabaceiro -ra (*adj.*) fond of fruits and vegetables.
rabacuada (*f.*) riffraff.
rabada (*f.*) see under RABADO.
rabadela, rabadilha (*f.*) the tail end of animals.
rabado -da (*adj.*) tailed, caudate; (*f.*) the tail end of anything; a pigtail (of hair); oxtail (used as food).
rabalvo -va (*adj.*) white-tailed; (*f.*) the gray sea eagle (*Haliaeetus albicilla*).
rabanada (*f.*) French toast [= FATIA DOURADA or FATIA DE PARIDA]; a blow with the tail; a gust of wind.
rabanete [nê] (*m.*) radish (*Raphanus*).
rábano, rábão [-bãos] (*m.*) turnip (plant or root).—**aquático**, amphibious marsh cress (*Rorippa amphibia*), c.a. SARAMAGO-DE-ÁGUA.—**bastardo**,—**picante**,—**silvestre-maior**,—**saramago-maior**, are all horseradish (*Armoracia lapathifolia*).
rabão -bona (*adj.*) bobtailed.
rabarbaro (*m.*) = RUIBARBO.
rabavento -ta (*adj.*) having a tail wind.
rabdóide, rabdoídeo -dea (*adj.*) rhabdoid(al), rod-shaped.
rabdomancia (*f.*) rhabdomancy, divination by rods or wands.
rabdomante (*m.*) dowser.
rabdomioma (*f.*, *Med.*) rhabdomyoma.
rabear (*v.t.*) to switch or wag the tail; (*v.i.*) to fidget; to writhe, contort (the body).
rabeca (*f.*) fiddle; a fiddle fish or ray; billiards rest or bridge; (*m.*) fiddler.
rabecada (*f,*) reprimand.
rabecão (*m.*) bass fiddle; (*slang*) black closed vehicle in which cadavers are transported, as to the morgue;

(*students' slang*) the mathematical sign of integration [∫].—**pequeno**, 'cello.
rabeira (*f.*) train (of a gown); tail end.
rabequista (*m.,f.*) fiddler.
rabi [bí] (*adj.*) bobtailed; (*m.*) rabbi [= RABINO].
rábia (*f.*) rabies [= RAIVA].
rabialvo -va (*adj.*) = RABALVO.
rabiar (*v.i.*) to rage.
rabiça (*f.*) plow handle.
rabicho (*m.*) pigtail, queue; crupper (of a harness); (*colloq.*) passion; (*R.R.*) switchback.
rabicó (*adj.*) bobtailed [= SURU].
rábido -da (*adj.*) rabid.
rabijunco (*m.*, *Zool.*) a pintail (*Dafila acuta*), c.a. ARRABIO.
rabil[h]a (*f.*, *Zool.*) the Brazilian gallinule (*Gallinula chloropus galeata*), c.a. ARRIBA-COELHA, FRANGO-D'ÁGUA, FRANGO-DO-RIO, GALINHA-D'ÁGUA, GALINHA-DO-RIO, RABISCOELHA.
rabilongo -ga (*adj.*) long-tailed; (*m.*) a cuckoo, c.a. ALMA-DE-GATO.
rabinado, rabinato (*m.*) rabbinate.
rabinho (*m.*) little tail.
rabínico -ca (*adj.*) rabbinical.
rabinismo (*m.*) rabbinism.
rabinista (*m.*) rabbinist.
rabino (*m.*) rabbi.
rabioso -sa (*adj.*) rabid.
rabipreto -ta (*adj.*) black-tailed.
rabirruivo -va (*adj.*) red-tailed.
rabisca (*f.*) = RABISCO.
rabiscador -deira (*adj.*) scribbling; (*m.,f.*) scribbler.
rabiscadura (*f.*) a scribble or scribbling.
rabiscar (*v.i.*) to scribble, scrawl; to doodle.
rabisco (*m.*) scrawl; (*pl.*) scribblings; doodles.
rabiscoelha = RABILA (gallinule).
rabo (*m.*) tail; handle; (*colloq.*) tail end, rump.—**aberto**, the yellowtail (*Ocyurus chrysurus*), a fish, c.a. CIOBA-MULATA, SAÚBA.—**de-andorinha**, (*Carp.*) dovetail.—**de-aranata** = FETO-MACHO-DO-PARÁ.—**de-arara** = CONGONHEIRO and CURACI.—**de-arraia**, the "sting-ray's tail"—a maneuver in the style of fighting called CAPUEIRAGEM which consists of dropping on the hands and swinging the legs against those of one's opponent to knock him off his feet.—**de-boi** = CAPIM-RABO-DE-BOI.—**de-bugio**, a tree fern (*Alsophila aromatica*).—**de-burro** = CAPIM-RABO-DE-BURRO.—**de cachorro** = CAPIM-RABO-DE-CACHORRO.—**de-camaleão**, (*Bot.*) a mimosa (*Mimosa spp.*).—**de-cavalo** = CAVALINHA.—**de-cavalo-falso**, a swartzpea (*Swartzia jacaranda* or *S. grandiflora*).—**de-cavalo-verdadeiro**, wistaria.—**de-cutia**, the Brazil stifftia (*S. chrysantha*).—**de-escrivão** = ALMA-DE-GATO.

—-**de-foguete** = GUAXIMA-ROXA and PACO-PACO.—-**de-galo**, mare's-tail (cirrus cloud).—-**de-gato**, love-lies-bleeding (*Amaranthus caudatus*), c.a. CAUDA-DE-RAPÔSA; a grevillea (*G. rosea*); a grass called CAPIM-RABO-DE-RATO.—-**de-guaraxaim** = CAPIM-RABO-DE-BURRO. —-**de jacaré**, a whip cactus (*Rhipsalis macrocarpa*).—-**de-lagarto**, a bromeliad (*Bilbergia leopoldi*).—-**de-leque**, a winder (treads of stair steps cut wider at one end than at the other so they can be arranged in circular form).—-**de-macaco**, crested dogtail (*Cynosurus cristatus*); chenille copperleaf (*Acalypha hispida*), c.a. CRISTA-DE-PERU; also the BARAÚNA(-PRETA).—-**de-maré**, a tidal bore.—-**de-minhoto**, dovetail.—-**de-mucura** = CAPIM-DA-PRAIA.—-**de-osso**, a very venomous viper (*Bothrops neuwredii urutu*), similar to the JARARACA.—-**de-palha**, (*colloq.*) moral or ethical defect; (*Zool.*) the red-billed tropic-bird (*Phaethon aethereus*); also birds called RABILONGA and ALMA-DE-GATO.—-**de-rapôsa**, foxtail (*Alopecurus*); a betony or woundwort (*Stachys acymastrum*); either of two bluegrasses called CAPIM-PEBA and CAPIM-AGRESTE-DO-PIAUÍ; a panicum or witchgrass called CAPIM-PALMEIRA; either of two millets called CAPIM-TINGA and CAPIM-VERDE; the love-lives-bleeding (*Amaranthus cristatus*), c.a. CAUDA-DE-RAPÔSA.—-**de-rato**, a panicum or witchgrass (*Panicum vilfrides*); a whip cactus (*Rhipsalis myosurus*); a grass called CAPIM-RABO-DE-RATO.—-**de-rojão** = CUARI-BRAVO.—-**de-saia**, (*colloq.*) a "skirt" (woman).—-**de-tatu**, a quirt or riding crop; (*Bot.*) a Brazilian ladyslipper (*Cypripedium brasiliensis*).—-**de-tesoura** = CENTOPEIA. —-**de-tucano** = CONGONHEIRO. —-**de-zorra-macio** = CAPIM-RABO-DE-RAPÔSA.—-**leva**, donkey's tail (pinned on someone in fun).—-**torto**, a scorpion.—-**do arado**, plow handle.—(or **rabinho**) **do ôlho**, corner of the eye. **de cabo a**—, from head to tail, from end to end, from stem to stern. **É aí que a porca torce o**—, That's where the shoe pinches.

rabona (*f.*) short jacket; also = fem. of RABÃO.

rabonar (*v.t.*) to crop or bob (an animal's tail).

raboso -**sa** (*adj.*) long-tailed.

rabote (*m., Carp.*) a large wooden jack plane.

rabudo -**da** (*m.*) long-tailed.

rabugem (*f.*) grouchiness, ill temper; mange; (*Bot.*) a cordia (*C. obliqua*); a macawood (*Platymiscium floribundum*).

rabugento -**ta** (*adj.*) grouchy, grumpy, crabby, cantankerous; tetchy, peevish, petulant; sullen, sulky, morose.

rabugice (*f.*) petulance; peevishness.

rabujar (*v.i.*) to grumble, grouch; of children, to whine.

rábula (*m.*) pettifogger, shyster.

rabulagem (*f.*) = RABULICE.

rabular (*v.i.*) to pettifog.

rabulice, rabularia (*f.*) pettifoggery.

raça (*f.*) race, breed, strain; lineage.—**s futuras**, the future generations.—**s latinas**, the Latin races. **cavalo de**—, a thoroughbred horse [but not necessarily a race horse, which is CAVALO DE CORRIDA].—**amarela** or **mongólica**, yellow or mongolian race.—**azeitonada** or **malaia**, the brown or Malay or Polynesian race.—**branca** or **caucásica**, the white or caucasian race.—**de víboras**, generation of vipers.—**etiópica**,—**negra** or **preta**, the Negro or Negroid race.—**humana**, the human race, mankind.—**indígena** or **vermelha**, the race of the American Indians.

ração (*f.*) ration, portion, allowance.—**de reserva**, emergency ration. **a meia**—, on half rations; on half pay.

racemado -**da** (*adj., Bot.*) racemose.

racemato (*m., Chem.*) racemate, a racemic compound.

racêmico -**ca** (*adj., Chem.*) racemic.

racemífero -**ra** (*adj., Bot.*) racemiferous.

racemiforme (*adj., Bot.*) racemiform.

racemização (*f., Chem.*) racemization.

racemo (*m., Bot.*) raceme, cluster.

racemoso -**sa** (*adj.*) racemose, racemous.

racha (*f.*) a split, or fissure; splinter.

rachadeira (*f.*) grafter (instrument).

rachadela (*f.*) a split or crack.

rachador -**deira** (*adj.*) splitting; (*m.,f.*) splitter; chopper; hewer of wood.

rachadura (*f.*) cleavage, fissure, split, splitting.

rachar (*v.t.*) to split, cleave; to crack (open); to split, divide (profits, expenses); to insult, abuse; (*slang*) to tie (a football match); (*v.r.*) to split, crack.—**as despesas**, to split expenses.—**lenha**, to chop wood. **argumentos de**—, unanswerable arguments. **vento de**—, furious wind.

racial (*adj.*) racial.

racimo (*m.*) & derivs. = RACEMO & derivs.

raciocinação (*f.*) ratiocination, reasoning.

raciocinador -**dora** (*adj.; m. f.*) reasoning (person).

raciocinar (*v.i.*) to ratiocinate, reason.

raciocínio (*m.*) ratiocination, reasoning.—**cornuto**, dilemma.

racional (*adj.; m. f.*) rational (being).

racionalidade (*f.*) rationality.

racionalismo (*m.*) rationalism.

racionalista (*adj.*) rationalistic; (*m. f.*) rationalist.

racionalização (*f.*) rationalization.

racionalizar (*v.t.*) to rationalize.

racionalmente (*adv.*) rationally.

racionamento (*m.*) rationing.

racionar (*v.t.*) to ration.

racionável (*adj.*) reasonable [= RAZOÁVEL].

racismo (*m.*) racism.

racista (*adj.; m.,f.*) racist.

rad. = RADICAL (radical); RADIOGRAMA (radiogram).

rada (*f.*) roadstead.

radar (*m.*) radar.

radiação (*f.*) radiation.

radiado -**da** (*adj., Bot., Zool.*) radiate; (*m.pl., Zool.*) the Radiata.

radiador (*m.*) radiator.

radial (*adj.*) radial.

radialista (*m. f.*) broadcaster.

radiância (*f.*) radiance.

radiano (*m., Math.*) radian.

radiante (*adj.*) radiant, resplendent; beaming, ecstatic; (*m., Geom.*) radiant.

radiar (*v.t.,v.i.*) to radiate; (*v.i.*) to shine, beam.

radiários (*m.pl., Zool.*) the Radiata.

radiatiforme (*adj., Bot.*) radiatiform.

radiatividade (*f.*) = RADIOATIVIDADE.

radiativo -**va** (*adj.*) = RADIOATIVO.

radiator (*m.*) = RADIOATOR.

radiatro (*m.*) = RADIOTEATRO.

radicação (*f.*) taking root.

radicado -**da** (*adj.*) rooted; inveterate.

radical (*adj.*) radical, ingrained; fundamental; leftist; (*m.*) the root or stem of a word; a radical (in politics); the radical sign in mathematics [$\sqrt{\ }$]; (*Chem.*) radical.—**ácido**, acid radical.

radicalismo (*m.*) radicalism.

radicalista (*adj.*) radical; (*m.,f.*) radicalist.

radicando (*m., Math.*) radicand.

radicante (*adj., Bot.*) radicant.

radicar (*v.t.*) to root; (*v.r.*) to take root; to settle on the land.

radicela (*f., Bot.*) radicel, rootlet.

radicícola (*adj.*) radicicolous.

radicifloro -**ra** (*adj.*) radiciflorous.

radiciforme (*adj.*) radiciform.

radicívoro -**ra** (*adj.*) radicivorous.

radícola (*adj., Zool.*) living on roots.

radícula (*f., Bot.*) radicle.

radiculado -**da** (*adj.*) having roots.

radífero -**ra** (*adj., Chem.*) radiferous.

rádio (*m.,f.*) radio; (*m., Chem.*) radium; (*Anat.*) radius.—**de móvel**, cabinet radio. **anunciador de**—, radio announcer. **companhia**, or **emprêsa, de**—, radio broadcasting company. **feixe de**—, radio beam.

radioactínio (*m., Chem.*) radioactinium.

radioamador (*m.*) radio "ham".

radioatividade (*f., Chem.*) radioactivity. Var. RADIATIVIDADE.

radioativo -**va** (*adj.*) radioactive. Var. RADIATIVO.

radioator (*m.*) radio-actor.

radioatriz (*f.*) radio-actress.

radiobússola (*f.*) radio compass.

radiocárpico -**ca** (*adj., Anat.*) radiocarpal.

radiocomunicação (*f.*) radio communication.

radiocondutor (*m.*) radioconductor.

radiocontrôle (*m.*) radio control.

radiodifundir (*v.t.*) to radiobroadcast.

radiodifusão (*f.*) radiobroadcast(ing).

radiodifusor -**sora** (*adj.; m.*) broadcasting (station).

radioelemento (*m.*) radio(active) element.

radioemissora (*f.*) radio transmitter; broadcasting station.

radioemitir (*v.i.*) to radio.

radioengenharia (*f.*) radio engineering.

radioenigma (*m.*) radio quiz.

radioescuta (*m.,f.*) radio listener.
radiofaixa (*f.*) radio range.
radiofarol [-róis] (*m.*) radio beam; radio beacon.
radiofone (*m.*) radiophone.
radiofonia (*f.*) radiophony.
radiofonização (*f.*) preparation of radio script.
radiofonizar (*v.t.*) to prepare script for radio programs.
radiofonógrafo (*m.*) radio-phonograph.
radiofreqüência (*f.*) radio frequency.
radiogoniometria (*f.*) direction finding.
radiogoniômetro (*m.*) radiogoniometer; direction finder.
radiografar (*v.t.,v.i.*) to radiograph.
radiografia (*f.*) radiography; a radiograph; an X-ray
photograph.—**industrial**, X-ray inspection of metal parts,
etc.
radiografista (*m.,f.*) X-ray technician.
radiograma (*m.*) radiogram.
radiola (*f.*) radio-phonograph.
radiolário (*m.*, *Zool.*) radiolarian.
radiólito (*m.*, *Zool.*) radiolite.
radiologia (*f.*) radiology.
radiologista (*m.,f.*) radiologist.
radioluminescência (*f.*, *Physical Chem.*) radiolumines-
cence.
radiometalografia (*f.*) radiometallography.
radiometria (*f.*, *Physics*) radiometry.
radiômetro (*m.*, *Physics*) radiometer.
radiomicrômetro (*m.*, *Physics*) radiomicrometer.
radioonda [o-o] (*f.*) radio wave.
radiooperador [o-o] (*m.*) radio operator.
radiopatrulha (*f.*) radio patrol.
radioquímico -**ca** (*adj.*) radiochemical; (*m.*) radiochemis-
try.
radioreceptor (*m.*) radio receiver.
radioscopia (*f.*) radioscopy; fluoroscopy.
radioscópico -**ca** (*adj.*) radioscopic(al).
radioso -**sa** (*adj.*) radiant; effulgent; ecstatic.
radiossonda (*f.*) radiosonde, radiometeorograph.
radioteatro (*m.*) radio-theater. Var. RADIATRO.
radiotécnica (*f.*) radiotechnology.
radiotelefone (*m.*) radiotelephone.
radiotelefonia (*f.*) radiotelephony.
radiotelefoto (*m.*) radiophotography.
radiotelefotografia (*f.*) photoradiogram.
radiotelegrafia (*f.*) radiotelegraphy, wireless telegraphy.
radiotelegrafista (*m.,f.*) radio operator; wireless operator.
radiotelegrama (*m.*) radiotelegram; radiogram.
radioterapéutico -**ca** (*adj.*) radiotherapeutic.
radioterapia (*f.*) radiotherapy or radiumtherapy.
radiotório (*m.*, *Chem.*) radiothorium.
radiotron (*m.*) Radiotron (tube).
radiotransmissor (*m.*) radio transmitter.
radiouvinte (*m.,f.*) radio listener.
rádon (*m.*, *Chem.*) radon.
rádula (*f.*, *Zool.*) radula.
Rafael [a-e] (*m.*) Raphael.
rafaméia (*f.*) riffraff [= RALÉ].
rafar (*v.t.,v.r.*) to fray.
rafe (*f.*, *Anat.*, *Bot.*) raphe.
rafeiro (*m.*) sheep dog; watch dog.
ráfia (*f.*) any raffia palm (*Raphia*), or its fiber.
ráfides (*f.pl.*, *Bot.*) raphides.
rafinase (*f.*) raffinase.
rafinose (*f.*, *Chem.*) raffinose.
ragu [ú] (*m.*) ragout, lamb stew.
raia (*f.*) line, stroke, streak; line in the palm of the hand;
racecourse; territorial limit, frontier; paper kite; brand
on a horse; (*slang*) blunder, boner; (*pl.*) the limit of something (as nonsense); (*Zool.*) skate, ray [= ARRAIA].—
-**chita**, a skate (*Raja meta*), c.a. ARRAIA-CHITA.—**comum**,
the European or gray skate (*Raja batis*).—**elétrica**,
electric ray (genus *Torpedo*).—**lixa**, a sting ray (*Dasyatis guttatus*), c.a. JABEBIRETÉ, JABIRETA.—**manteiga** (or
-**amarela** Say's sting ray (*Dasyatis say*), c.a. ARRAIA-
MANTEIGA.—**pintada**, spotted whip ray (*Aetobatus
narinari*), c.a. PAGAIO, NARINARI, PINTADA.—**pregada**,
the thornback (*Raja clavata*).—**prego**, a sting ray
(*Dasyatis hastatus*).—**sapo**, eagle ray (*Myliobatus
freminvillei*), c.a. ARRAIA-SAPO. **fechar a**—, (*slang*) of a
race hose, to come in last. **passar as**—**s**, to go too far.
tocar as—**s**, to reach the limit.
raiado -**da** (*adj.*) striped; streaked; of gun barrel, rifled.
raiamento (*m.*) gun-barrel rifling. **sem**—, smoothbore.
raiar (*v.i.*) to emit rays, gleam; to dawn, grow light; to

radiate; (*v.t.*) to rifle (a gun barrel); to stripe, streak.
do—**ao pôr do sol**, from sunrise to sunset.
raid (*m.*) raid; long excursion as by automobile, or on horseback, etc., in the nature of a sporting event.
raigota [a-i] (*f.*) hangnail.
raigrás (*f.*) rye grass (*Lolium*).
Raimundo (*m.*) Raymond, Raymund.
raineta [ê] (*f.*) reinette (a type of apple); also = PERERECA.
rainha [a-í] (*f.*) queen.—**cláudia**, the Reine Claude greengage plum, c.a. AMEIXA-CARANGUEJEIRA.—**da-holanda**,
the polyanthus narcissus (*N. tazetta*).—**da-noite**, or
-**do-baile**, queen of the night (*Selenicereus grandiflorus*),
c.a. PRINCÊSA-DA-NOITE.—**das abelhas**, queen bee.—
-**das-avencas**, a maidenhair fern (*Adiantum farleyense*).
-**do-abismo**, (*Bot.*) a corytholoma (*C. canescens*).—
-**dos-prados**, the queen-of-the-meadow (*Filipendula
ulmaria*), c.a. ERVA-ULMEIRA, BARBA-DE-BODE.—**mãe**,
queen-mother.—**margarida**, China aster (*Callistephus
chinensis*).
rainúnculo (*m.*) = RANÚNCULO.
raio (*m.*) ray, beam; radius; spoke; flash of lightning;
thunderbolt; sudden stroke of misfortune; obstreperous,
boisterous person, troublemaker.—**s actínicos**, actinic
rays.—**s anódicos**, (*Elec.*) anode rays.—**de ação**,
range, scope, field of action.—**s Becquerel**, (*Physical
Chem.*) B. rays, uranium rays.—**s beta**, (*Physical Chem.*)
beta rays.—**s caloríficos**, heat rays.—**s catódicos**,
(*Physics*) cathode rays.—**de-júpiter**, the Caribbean
spiderlily (*Hymenocallis caribaea*), c.a. LÁGRIMAS-DE-
NAPOLEÃO.—**s gama**, (*Physics*) gamma rays.—**s Grenz**,
grenz rays.—**s Lenard** (*Physics*) L. rays.—**de lua**, moon-
beam.—**luminoso**, light ray.—**de roda**, wheel spoke.—**s
Roentgen**, R. rays, X rays.—**solar**, sunbeam.—**s ultra-
violeta**, ultraviolet rays.—**s de urânio**, uranium rays,
Bequerel rays.—**s X**, X rays.—**s X brandos**, soft X rays.
raion (*m.*) rayon.
raiva (*f.*) rage, fury, anger; hate, aversion; madness;
rabies, hydrophobia; distemper. **com**—, angrily. **Ela
olhou para êle com**—**nos olhos**, She looked daggers at
him. **escumar de**—, to foam at the mouth with rage.
meter—, to anger. **pálido de**—, white with rage.
raivar (*v.i.*) to rage, rave, be furious.
raivoso -**sa** (*adj.*) angry, furious; (*f.*, *Bot.*) a frangipani
(*Plumeria drastica*), c.a. TIBORNA.
raiz [a-í; *pl.* -**es**] (*f.*) root; origin, source; word root;
(*Math.*) root.—**adventícia**, adventitious root.—**aérea**,
aerial root.—**amarela**, (*Bot.*) goldenseal (*Hydrastis
canadensis*), c.a. HIDRASTE.—**amarga** = GENCIANA-BRA-
SILEIRA.—**cúbica**, cube root.—**da-bôlsa**, (*Bot.*) a yam
(*Dioscorea daemona*).—**da-china**, (*Bot.*) chinaroot greenbrier (*Smilax china*).—**da-guiné**, (*Bot.*) a guineahenweed (*Peteveria tetrandra*).—**da-hungria**, (*Bot.*) common
gypsophila (*G. elegans*).—**da serra**, foot of a mountain.
—**de-barbeiro**, (*Bot.*) a savannaflower (*Echites longiflora*).—**de-chá**, (*Bot.*) common dracena or ti palm
(*Cordyline terminalis*), c.a. COQUEIRO-DE-VÊNUS.—**de-
cheiro**, a bluestem grass (*Andropogon squarrosus*).—**de-
cobra**, (*Bot.*) a nettlespurge (*Jatropha elliptica*).—**de-
frade** = CAINCA.—**de-jacaré**, (*Bot.*) Guiana tachia (*Tachia guianensis*).—**de-lagarto** = TIÚ.—**do-brasil**, (*Pharm.*)
Rio, or Brazilian, ipecac.—**do-sol**, (*Bot.*) a dutchmanspipe (*Aristolochia paraensis*).—**doce** = ALCAÇUZ-DA-
TERRA.—**quadrada**, square root. **bens de**—, real estate
raizame (*m.*), **raizada**, **raizama** [a-i] (*f.*) the roots of a
plant; a quantity of roots.
raizeiro [a-i] (*m.*), -**ra** (*f.*) "herb doctor" [= DOUTOR-DE-
RAIZ].
raja (*f.*) stripe, streak.
rajá (*m.*) rajah; also = CIPÓ-MIL-HOMENS (a plant).
rajada (*f.*) a gust of wind; squall; flurry; a burst of oratory.—**de cólera**, burst of anger.—**de eloquência**, burst
of oratory.—**de metralhadora**, a burst of machine-gun
fire.
rajadão (*m.*) a certain type of cattle in Minas Gerais;
also = MATRACA (a bird).
rajado -**da** (*adj.*) striped, streaked; mottled.
rajar (*v.t.*) to stripe, streak; to intermix.
rajeira (*f.*) hawser.
ralação (*f.*) act of grating, etc.;—see the verb RALAR.
rala-côco (*m.*) = MIJA-MIJA.
ralador (*m.*) grater.
raladura (*f.*) any substance after grating (as coconut, nutmeg, etc.).
ralar (*v.t.*) to grate, scrape, rasp; to annoy, irritate; to
harass; (*v.r.*) to chafe, fret, "stew". Var. RELAR.

ralé (f.) riffraff, the masses, the common herd, rabble, mob; the prey of raptorial birds.

raleamento (m.) thinning out (of unripe fruit on trees); disbudding (of flower plants).

ralear (v.t.,v.i.) to thin out.

raleia (f.) = RALÉ.

raleiro (m.) European water rail (Rallus aquaticus).

ralhação (f.) railing, scolding.

ralhador –dora (adj.) faultfinding; scolding; (m.,f.) scolder; faultfinder.

ralhar (v.i.) to rail (**com**, at, against); to scold, chide, berate, upbraid; to nag.

ralho (m.) a scolding, railing or upbraiding; faultfinding; rebuke.

ralídeos (m.pl.) the Rallidae (rails, crakes, coots and gallinules).

raliforme (adj., Zool.) ralliform.

ralo –la (adj.) thin, sparse; weak, watery [coffee, soup, etc.]; (m.) grater, rasp; sieve; strainer; grate; grating; (Zool.) a mole cricket (Gryllus grylloptalpa); (Med.) râle, rhonchus.

rama (f.) branches, foliage; a printer's chase.—**de bezerro** = CATANDUBA. **algodão em—**, raw cotton. **cera em—**, crude beeswax. **pela—**, superficially.

ramado –da (adj.) branched, ramate; (f.) branches, leafage; trellis; bower; pergola.

ramagem (f.) branches, boughs; leaf and flower design on cloth.

ramal (m.) railroad branch line; strand (of yarn or thread); telephone extension line; ramification; string (of beads).

ramalhar (v.i.) to rustle.

ramalhete [lhê] (m.) a bunch of flowers, posy, nosegay; a small branch.

ramalho (m.) large branch or bough.

ramaria (f.) branches, leafage.

rambutão (m.), **–teira** (f., Bot.) rambutan (Nephelium lappaceum).

rameal (adj.) ramal, branch.

rameira (f.) prostitute, drab [= MERETRIZ].

ramela (f.) blear [= REMELA].—**de-cachorro** = GRÃO-DE-PORCO.

rameloso –sa (adj.) blear-eyed.

ramerrão (m.) everyday routine, daily grind, rut.

rami [í] (m.) ramie (Boehmeria nivea), plant or fiber.

ramificação (f.) ramification, subdivision, offshoot; branching.

ramificado –da (adj.) branched; furcate; subdivided.

ramificar (v.t.,v.r.) to ramify, branch (off), subdivide; to furcate.

ramifloro –ra (adj., Bot.) ramiflorous.

ramiforme (adj., Bot.) ramiform.

ramilhete (m.) = RAMALHETE.

raminho (m.) sprig.

ramíparo –ra (adj., Bot.) ramiparous.

ramnáceo –cea (adj., Bot.) rhamnaceous; (f.pl.) the buckthorn family (Rhamnaceae).

ramno (m.) the buckthorn (Rhamnus); = SANGUINHEIRO.

ramnose (f., Chem.) rhamnose.

ramo (m.) branch, limb, bough; offshoot, ramification, subdivision; family branch; a bunch of flowers.—**da paz**, olive branch.—**de negócios**, line of business. **Domingo de—s**, Palm Sunday.

ramoso –sa (adj.) ramose, ramous.

rampa (f.) ramp, incline, slope, gradient; runway; bosh (of a blast furnace), c.a. ETALAGE.

rampante (adj.) rampant (but only in the heraldic sense). [Rampant, in the sense of rank is VIÇOSO, LUXURIANTE; unbridled is DESENFREADO].

rampear (v.t.) to slope.

ramudo –da (adj.) ramose; having dense foliage.

ranário (m.) frog farm.

rançar (v.i.) to grow rancid.

rancharia (f.) a group of huts.

rancheiro (m.) army cook; messmate. [But not rancher, which is CRIADOR DE GADO or VAQUEIRO.]

rancheria (f.), **–rio** (m.) = RANCHARIA.

rancho (m.) a group of people walking or on a junket together; organized group or club of carnival merrymakers who parade through the streets, singing and dancing; soldier's mess; a rude hut where herdsmen or travelers may find rest or shelter. [But not ranch, except in Rio Grande do Sul; elsewhere in Brazil the term for ranch is FAZENDA DE CRIAÇÃO DE GADO.]

rancidez (f.) rancidity.

râncido –da, râncio –cia (adj.) = RANÇOSO.

ranço –ça (adj.) rancid; (m.) rancidity; (fig.) stuffiness, stodginess.

rancor [ô] (m.) rancor, hate, spite, grudge, malice, animosity.

rancoroso –sa (adj.) rancorous, hateful, spiteful.

rançoso –sa (adj.) rancid.

randanito (m., Min.) randannite.

ranfástidas, ranfastídeos (m.pl.) the Ramphastidae (toucans).

ranfoteca (f., Zool.) rhamphotheca.

rangedeira (f., Zool.) a teal (Querquedula sp.).

rangedor –dora, rangente (adj.) creaky, squeaking.

ranger (v.i.) to creak, squeak.—**os dentes**, to grind the teeth.

rangido (m.) a creak or squeak.

rangífer, rangífero (m.) reindeer, caribou [= RENA].

Rangum (m.) Rangoon.

ranhar (v.t.) to scratch [= ARRANHAR].

ranhento –ta (adj.) sniveling, snotty.

ranho (m.) snot.

ranhoso –sa (adj.) snotty.

ranhura (f.) rabbet, channel, groove, slot, slit.—**da chavêta**, (Mach.) keyway.

ranicultura (f.) frog raising.

ranídeos (m.pl.) the Ranidae (frogs).

ranilha (f.) frog of a horse's hoof.

ranino –na (adj., Anat.) ranine.

ranívoro –ra (adj.) frog-eating.

ranu [ú] (m.) = RAMI.

ranunculáceo –cea (adj., Bot.) ranunculaceous; (f.pl.) buttercup family (Ranunculaceae).

ranúnculo (m.) any buttercup (Ranunculus).—**-aquático**, the watercrowfoot buttercup (R. aquatilis).—**-brasileiro** (or—**-dos-prados**), the tall buttercup (R. acris), c.a. BOTÃO-DE-OURO.—**-dos-jardins**, the Persian buttercup (R. asiaticus).—**-rasteiro**, the creeping buttercup (R. repens).

ranzinza (adj.) crabbed, cranky, cantankerous, peevish, grouchy; unruly.

rapa (m.) put-and-take (game of chance) played with a four-sided teetotum; (f.) an earwig (Forficula), c.a. BICHA-CADELA.

rapace (adj.) rapacious.

rapacidade (f.) rapacity.

rapa-cuia (f.) any snout beetle; a small frog which lives in bromeliads, c.a. RAPA-CÔCO.

rapadeira (f.) scraper.

rapadela (f.) act of scraping; scrapings.

rapado –da (adj.) scraped clean; clean-shaven.

rapador (m.) scraper; close-cropped pasture land.

rapadouro (m.) scraper; land which has been grazed clean. Var. RAPADOIRO.

rapadura (f.) scraping; hard square of raw brown sugar eaten as food or candy; (Bot.) a licania, c.a. CARAIPÉ-VERDADEIRO. **entregar a—**, (colloq.) to throw in the sponge.

rapagão (m.) strapping fellow.

rapa-línguas (m.) tongue scraper.

rapão (m.) forest litter.

rapapé (m.) a servile bowing and scraping; kowtow.

rapar (v.t.) to scrape; to shave; [But not to rape, which is ESTUPRAR.]; (v.i.) to paw the ground (as a horse); (v.r.) to shave clean.—**a**, to steal from.

rapariga (f.) in Portugal, girl, young woman; in Brazil, strumpet, wench; servant girl.

raparigaça (f.) healthy, comely girl.

raparigada (f.) bunch of girls.

raparigo (m.) = RAPAZ.

raparigota (f.) lass.

raparigueiro –ra (adj.) woman-chasing; (m.) woman chaser.

rapa-tábuas (m.) second-rate carpenter.

rapa-tachos (m.,f., colloq.) plate licker (hearty eater).

rapaz (m.) lad, youth, young man, young fellow; a snipe called NARCEJÃO.—**feito**, grown young man.

rapazelho, rapazete [zê] (m.) kid, urchin.

rapaziada (f.) bunch of boys or young men; lark, prank.

rapazinho (m.) boy; (Zool.) the spotted sandpiper (Actitis macularia).—**dos-velhos**, the collared puffbird (Bucco capensis), and the Brazilian spotted puffbird (Nystalus m. maculatus); also = JOÃO-BÔBO.

rapazio (m.) boys or young men in general.

rapazola (m.) overgrown boy.

rapazote (*m.*) = RAPAZELHO.
rapé (*m.*) snuff.
rapèzista (*m.,f.*) snuff-taker.
rapidez [ê] (*f.*) speed, rapidity; dispatch.
rápido –da (*adj.*) rapid, fast, quick, speedy; (*adv.*) rapidly; (*m.*) rapids, swift current; a special messenger or express service; a fast long-distance train.
rapina (*f.*) rapine. ave de—, bird of prey.
rapinador –dora (*adj.; m.,f.*) = RAPINANTE.
rapinagem (*f.*) rapine, plunder.
rapinante (*adj.*) plundering; (*m.,f.*) plunderer.
rapinar (*v.t.*) to plunder.
rapineiro –ra (*adj.*) raptorial; (*m.*) bird of prey.
rapinhar (*v.*) = RAPINAR.
rapôncio, raponço (*m.*) the rampion bellflower (*Campanula rapunculus*).
rapôsa (*f.*) female fox; fox skin; foxy person; (*Naut.*) cathead. cova de—, foxhole.
raposeiro –ra (*adj.*) foxy, sly; (*m.,f.*) cunning person; (*f.*) nap; drunkenness; foxhole; (*Bot.*) = ÔLHO-DE-CABRA-VERDE.
raposia, raposice (*f.*) foxiness; cunning.
raposinhar (*v.i.*) to behave cunningly.
raposinho (*m.*) fox club; (*colloq.*) strong body odor.
raposino –na (*adj.*) vulpine.
raposo (*m.*) male fox.—azulado, blue fox (*Alopex lagopus*).
rapsódia (*f.*) rhapsody.
rapsódico –ca (*adj.*) rhapsodical.
rapsodista (*m.,f.*) rhapsodist.
raptador –dora (*adj.; m.,f.*) = RAPTOR.
raptar (*v.t.*) to abduct, seize, kidnap; to ravish; to snatch; to plunder.
rapto –ta (*adj.*) rapt; entranced; (*m.*) abduction, kidnapping; ravishment; rapture; flight (of imagination, etc.); plunder, robbery.
raptor –tora (*adj.*) abducting; ravishing; enrapturing; (*m.,f.*) abductor; (*m.*) ravisher.
raque (*f., Anat.*) rachis, spinal column; (*Bot.*) stalk, stem; (*Zool.*) shaft of a feather.
raqueano –na (*adj.*) rachidian. bulbo—, bulb of the spinal cord. fluido—, spinal fluid.
raquel (*f., Bot.*) Guernseylily nerine (*Nerine sarniensis*); [*cap.*] Rachel.
raqueta [ê] (*f.*) tennis or other racket; snow shoe; hairpin curve.
raquianestesia (*f., Med.*) spinal anesthesia.
raquidiano –na (*adj.*) = RAQUEANO.
ráquis (*f.*) = RAQUE.
raquite (*f., Med.*) rachitis, rickets.
raquítico –ca (*adj.*) rachitic, rickety; (*m.,f.*) one suffering from rachitis or rickets.
raquitismo (*m., Med.*) rachitis, rickets; (*Bot.*) abortion of fruit or seeds.
raramente (*adv.*) seldom, rarely.
rarear (*v.t.*) to rarefy; to make scarce, less numerous; to diminish the number of; (*v.i.*) to become scarce, less numerous; to diminish in number; to become less dense.
rarefação (*f.*) rarefaction.
rarefaciente (*adj.*) rarefactive.
rarefatível (*adj.*) rarefiable.
rarefativo –va (*adj.*) rarefactive [= RAREFACIENTE].
rarefato –ta (*adj.*) = RAREFEITO.
rarefator –tora (*adj.*) rarefying; (*m.*) rarefier.
rarefazer [47] (*v.t.,v.r.*) to rarefy.
rarefeito –ta (*adj.*) rarefied, less dense.
raridade, rareza (*f.*) rareness, scarcity; a rarity.
raro –ra (*adj.*) rare, uncommon, scarce, unusual; unique; sparse; thin. [But not rare in the sense of underdone, which is MAL-PASSADO.] (*adv.*) rarely. de—em—, once in a blue moon.
rasa (*f.*) a measure of grain, salt or the like; a grain strickle.
rasado –da (*adj.*) leveled with a strickle.
rasadura (*f.*) act of strickling grain, etc.
rasante (*adj.*) sweeping, grazing, skimming, touching, flanking.
rasar (*v.t.*) to level; to strickle; to graze, skim; (*v.r.*) to overflow.
rasca (*f.*) a dragnet; small two-master fishing boat; oyster rake; a share in profits; (*colloq.*) drunkenness.
rascadeira (*f.*) currycomb.
rascador (*m.*) rasp; scraper.
rascadura (*f.*) abrasion, scratch.

rascante (*adj.*) of wine, tart, bad-tasting, that scratches the throat.
rascar (*v.t.*) to scratch, scrape; to rasp; to grate.
rascasso (*m.*) a scorpion fish (*Scorpaena porcus*).
rasco (*m.*) oyster rake.
rascunhado –da (*adj.*) sketched, outlined.
rascunhar (*v.t.*) to make a rough sketch or rough notes of; to outline.
rascunho (*m.*) draft, sketch, outline, rough copy
raseiro –ra (*adj.*) shallow; of boats, shallow-draft.
rasgadela (*f.*) = RASGÃO and RASGAMENTO.
rasgado –da (*adj.*) torn, rent; broad, ample; open, spread; extravagant, profuse; lavish; noble, magnanimous.—s cumprimentos, effusive greetings.—s elogios, extravagant praises. olhos—s, large, full eyes; (*m.*) in guitar playing, a sweeping of the strings with the thumb instead of picking them.
rasgador –dora (*adj.*) tearing; (*m.,f.*) one who tears.
rasgadura (*f.*) tear, rent, rip.
rasgamento (*m.*) tearing, ripping.
rasga-mortalha (*f.*) the Paraguayan snipe (*Capella paragusiae*), c.a. AGACHADEIRA.
rasgão (*m.*) rent, tear.
rasgar (*v.t.*) to tear (up), rend, rip (apart); to lacerate; to tear open; to tear asunder; to make an opening (as in a wall); to rip up (a piece of ground); to tear up (a contract); (*v.r.*) to be torn (in two).—a farda a, to strip someone of his uniform.—o pinho, (*colloq.*) to play a guitar. —o véu, to tear the veil (speak out frankly).—sêda, to be excessively polite and complimentary.
rasgo (*m.*) a tear, rip; dash, spirit, verve; a burst of eloquence; flight (of imagination, fantasy, etc.); an impulsive deed.—de chavêta, (*Mach.*) keyway.
raso –sa (*adj.*) even, level; close-cropped; shallow; low. campo—, flat open country. soldado—, private soldier. tábua—, tabula rasa; blank canvas; (*m.*) flat open country.
rasoura (*f.*) strickle; hence, anything that operates to smooth or level; carpenter's rasp.
rasourar (*v.t.*) to strickle; to level.
raspa (*f.*) scrapings, filings; scraper.
raspadeira (*f.*) scraper; eraser; (*Bot.*) a fig (*Ficus asperrima*).
raspadela (*f.*) = RASPAGEM.
raspador –dora (*adj.*) scraping; (*m.,f.*) scraper; (*m., Surg.*) curette.
raspadura (*f.*) scrapings, filings; scraping, rasping, filing; erasure.
raspagem (*f.*) abrasion; act of scraping or rasping.
raspança (*f.*) reprimand, lecture.
raspanete [nê] (*m.*) a dressing down; reprimand.
raspão (*m.*) scratch or scrape on the skin. atingir, or golpear, de—, to sideswipe.
raspar (*v.t.*) to rasp, scrape; to grate; to abrade: to rub out, erase; to scratch (out); (*v.r.*) to betake oneself, scurry, scamper off, decamp, skedaddle, make oneself scarce.—o bigode, to shave off one's mustache. Raspa! (*slang*) Scram!
raspilha (*f.*), raspe (*m.*) cooper's scraper.
raspito (*m., Min.*) raspite.
rasqueiro –ra (*adj.*) scarce, hard to get.
rasqueta (*f.*) deck scraper.
rasquetear (*v.t.*) to currycomb.
rastaqüera (*m.,f.*) parvenu(e), upstart, nouveau riche, showy person, esp. a stranger or one whose claims to rank or wealth are under suspicion. [Fr. *rastaquouère*; Sp. *rastracuero*].
rasteira (*f.*) see under RASTEIRO.
rasteirinha (*f.*) a low-growing malvaceous herb (*Sida procumbens*), c.a. VIOLETA-DO-PARÁ.
rasteiro –ra (*adj.*) creeping, crawling; humble; low (not high); low-growing; abject, scurvy. cão—, a dachshund. planta—, a creeping, trailing plant; (*f.*) a tripping up (of someone).
rastejador (*m.*) tracker, tracer.
rastejar (*v.t.*) to track, trace; (*v.i.*) to creep, crawl; to lower (degrade) oneself.
rastejo [ê] (*m.*) act of crawling.
rastelar (*v.t.*) to comb (flax, hemp, etc.) with a hackle.
rastêlo (*m.*) a hackle or hatchel (for flax, hemp, jute).
rastilha (*f.*) drawknife [= FACA INGLÊSA or CORTACHEFE].
rastilho (*m.*) fuse; track, trail.
rasto (*m.*) track, trace, trail, vestige; clue; scent; spoor, footprint. a, or de, —s, creeping, crawling, dragging

(along the ground). **andar de**—, to creep, crawl. **levar de**—, to drag (along the ground).

rastôlho (*m.*) = RESTÔLHO.

rastrear, rastrejar (*v.*) = RASTEJAR.

rastrilho (*m.*) portcullis; (*Agric.*) harrow.

rastro (*m.*) = RASTO.

rasura (*f.*) erasure; act of scraping or grating.

rasurar (*v.t.*) to scrape; to grate.

rata (*f.*) blunder, boner; female rat. **dar uma**—, to pull a boner. Cf. RATO.

ratada (*f.*) lots of rats; a migration or invasion of rats.

ratafia (*f.*) any sweet liqueur flavored with fruit or fruit kernels.

ratânia (*f.*, *Bot.*) any ratany, esp. the Brazil or Pará ratany (*Krameria argentea*), the source of rhatanyroot used in medicine.

ratão -tona (*adj.*) amusing, droll, facetious, eccentric; (*m.*,*f.*) such a person (a "card", a "character"); a large rat.—**do-banhado**, (*Zool.*) a coypu (*Myocastor coypus*) which yields the fur nutria.

rataplã, rataplão (*m.*) beat or ruffle of a drum.

ratar (*v.t.*) to gnaw, as a rat.

rataria (*f.*) a multitude of rats.

ratazana (*f.*) female rat; a large rat of either sex, esp. the large brown or Norway rat (*Rattus norvegicus*).

rateação (*f.*) = RATEIO.

ratear (*v.t.*) to prorate, divide pro rate; (*v.i.*) of a motor, to miss.

rateio (*m.*) proration, apportionment [= RATEAÇÃO].

rateiro -ra (*adj.*; *m.*,*f.*) ratter.

rati [í] (*m.*) seed of the jequirity rosary pea (*Abrus praecatorius*).

ratice (*f.*) antic, caper, vagary, prank.

raticida (*adj.*) rat-killing; (*m.*) rat poison.

ratificação (*f.*) ratification.

ratificador -dora (*adj.*) ratifying.

ratificante (*adj.*) ratifying.

ratificar (*v.t.*) to ratify, confirm.

ratificável (*adj.*) ratifiable.

ratina (*f.*) a woolen fabric similar to frieze.

ratinar (*v.t.*) to frizz.

ratinhar (*v.t.*) to haggle over; (*v.i.*) to pinch pennies.

ratinheiro -ra (*adj.*) haggling.

ratinho (*m.*) small rat or mouse; child's first tooth.

ratitas (*m.pl.*) the Ratitae (ostriches, emus, cassowaries and moas).

ratívoro -ra (*adj.*) rat-eating.

rato -ta (*adj.*) mouse-colored; eccentric; known, confirmed; (*m.*) any rat or large mouse.—**branco**, white rat or mouse.—**catita**, house mouse [= CAMUNDONGO].—**-cego**, mole.—**d'água**, water rat.—**de-biblioteca**, book worm (person) who haunts the libraries.—**de-cartório**, pettifogger; shyster [= RÁBULA].—**de-faraó** or —**de-egito**, mongoose.—**de-fava**, or—**de-palmatória**, a small cricetine, nest-building rat (*Oryzomys pyrrhorinus*). **-de-hotel**, hotel thief.—**de-palmeira**, a palm squirrel (*Sciurus aestuans*), c.a. ACUTIPURU.—**de-sacristia**, an over-zealous churchgoer.—**de-taquara** or—**dos-banhados**, any of a number of small rice rats, esp. *Oryzomys longicaudatus*.—**do-mato**, any of numerous small, hamsterlike rats or rice rats and mice, esp. of the genus Oryzomys.—**espinho**, hedgehog.—**pardo**, the large brown or Norway rat (*Rattus norvegicus*), c.a. RATO-CINZENTO, RATO-DE-ESGÔTO, RATO-MIGRADOR, RATAZANA. —**prêto**, common black rat (*Rattus r. rattus*), c.a. RATO-DE-CANA, RATO-DOMÉSTICO, RATO-INGLÊS, RATO-ORDINÁRIO, RATO-DE-COURO.

ratoeira (*f.*) rattrap.—**pequena**, mousetrap.

ratonear (*v.i.*) to pilfer.

ratoneiro (*m.*) sneak thief, pilferer.

ratonice (*f.*) petty theft, pilferage.

Raul [a-ú] (*m.*) Ralph.

raucíssono -na (*adj.*) raucous.

ravenala (*f.*) the traveler's tree (*Ravenala*).

ravina (*f.*) small mountain stream; ravine, gulch.—**estreita**, gully.

raviôis, raviões, raviolos (*m.pl.*) Italian ravioli.

razão (*f.*) reason, mind, sense; argument, reasoning; right judgment; cause, motive; rate; ratio; account; (*m.*) ledger.—**das engrenagens**, gear ratio.—**de estado**, reason of state.—**direta**, direct ratio.—**inversa**, inverse ratio. —**pura**, pure reasoning.—**recíproca**, inverse ratio.— **social**, name by which a firm is known.—**suficiente**, (*Logic*) sufficient reason. **à**—**de**, at the rate of. **dar**—**a**, to

concur with. **em**—**de**, on account of; by reason of. **idade da**—, age of discretion. **não ter**—, to be wrong. **por aquela**—, for that reason; for one reason or another. **por razões independentes de nossa vontade,** for reasons beyond our control. **Tem**—, You are (he, she is) right. **ter (bem)**—, to be (quite) right; to have good reason.

razia (*f.*) foray, raid, plundering incursion.

razoado -da (*adj.*) rational, reasonable.

razoador -dora (*adj.*) reasoning; (*m.*,*f.*) one who reasons.

razoamento (*m.*) reasoning; argument.

razoar (*v.i.*) to reason; (*v.t.*) to plead a cause.

razoável (*adj.*) reasonable, sensible, wise; open-minded.

R.e = RÉCIPE (prescription).

ré (*f.*) a female criminal or defendant in a lawsuit; [masc. RÉU]; the stern of a ship. **à**—, astern. **marcha à**—, reverse speed (automobile, locomotive).

reabastecer (*v.t.*) to restock, refurnish, replenish, supply, revictual.—**de combustível,** to refuel.

reabastecimento (*m.*) restocking, replenishment.—**de combustível,** refueling.

reaberto -ta (*irreg. p.p. of* REABRIR) reopened.

reabertura (*f.*) reopening.

reabilitação (*f.*) rehabilitation, restoration, reinstatement.

reabilitar (*v.t.*) to rehabilitate, reestablish, restore, reinstate.

reabitar (*v.t.*) to re-inhabit.

reabituar-se (*v.r.*) to become reaccustomed.

reabrir [26] (*v.t.*) to reopen.

reabsorção (*f.*) reabsorption.

reabsorver (*v.t.*) to reabsorb.

reação (*f.*) reaction; response; a counter tendency (in politics).—**bimolecular,** (*Chem.*) bimolecular reaction.— **em cadeia**, chain reaction.—**de capacidade**, (*Elec.*) capacitive reactance.—**endotérmica,** (*Chem.*) endothermic reaction.—**exotérmica,** (*Chem.*) exothermic reaction.—**induzida,** (*Elec.*) inductive reactance.—**nuclear,** nuclear reaction.—**química,** chemical reaction.—**secundária**, secondary reaction.—**de Wassermann,** (*Med.*) W. reaction.

reacender (*v.t.*) to relight; to rekindle. Cf. REASCENDER.

reaceso -sa (*irreg. p.p. of* REACENDER) relit.

reacionário -ria (*adj.*; *m.*,*f.*) reactionary.

reacusar (*v.t.*) to reaccuse.

readmissão (*f.*) readmission.

readmitir (*v.t.*) to readmit.

readquirir (*v.t.*) to reacquire, regain, recover, retrieve.

reafirmação (*f.*) reaffirmation.

reafirmar (*v.t.*) to reaffirm, restate.

reagente (*adj.*; *m.*, *Chem.*) reagent.

reagir (*v.i.*) to react; to resist, rebel against.

reajustar (*v.t.*,*v.r.*) to readjust.

real (*adj.*) [*pl.*: reais] real, actual, true; royal; of property, real; (*m.*) [*pl.*: réis] a former Brazilian monetary unit [1/1000th of a mil-réis].

realçar (*v.t.*) to enhance, heighten; to intensify, accentuate, emphasize.

realce (*m.*) enhancement; distinction; emphasis; heightened effect. **dar**—**a**, to enhance; to emphasize.

realegrar (*v.t.*) to make happy again; (*v.r.*) to become so.

realejo [lê] (*m.*) a hand (barrel) organ; hurdy-gurdy.— **de bôca**, harmonica [= GAITA DE BÔCA].

realengo -ga (*adj.*) royal; of property, public.

realentar (*v.t.*) to revive.

realeza (*f.*) royalty; reality.

realgar (*m.*, *Min.*) realgar, red arsenic.

realidade (*f.*) reality, actuality. **na**—, really, in reality, actually, as a matter of fact.

realimentação (*f.*, *Elec.*) self-excitation; (*Radio*) regeneration, feedback.

realismo (*m.*) realism.

realista (*adj.*; *m.*,*f.*) realist; royalist.

realistar (*v.t.*) to re-enlist.

realístico -ca (*adj.*) realistic.

realito (*m.*) = MULATA (a fish).

realização (*f.*) realization, achievement, accomplishment, fulfilment; financial transaction; conversion (of goods, etc.) into actual money.

realizado -da (*adj.*) realized; accomplished.

realizador -dora (*adj.*) realizing; (*m. f.*) one who gets things done.

realizar (*v.t.*) to realize, effectuate, fulfill, carry out, accomplish, bring to pass; to convert (checks, etc.) into actual money; (*v.r.*) to take place, come true. [To realize, in the sense of understanding clearly, is PERCEBER, COMPREENDER.]

realizável (*adj.*) realizable; achievable.

realmente (*adv.*) really, actually, indeed; regally, royally.

realugar (*v.t.*) to relet.

reamar (*v.t.*) to love again.

reanimação (*f.*) reanimation.

reanimado –da (*adj.*) reanimated, revived, roused.

reanimar (*v.t.*) to reanimate, revive, enliven, rouse; (*v.r.*) to be encouraged; to rally; to cheer up.

reaparecer (*v.i.*) to reappear.

reaparecimento (*m.*) = REAPARIÇÃO.

reaparelhamento (*m.*) reequipment (as of a railroad).

reaparição (*f.*) reappearance.

reapoderar-se de (*v.r.*) to retake, seize again.

reapossar-se de (*v.r.*) to retake, repossess.

reaprender (*v.t.*) to learn again.

reapresentar (*v.t.*) to present again.

reaquecer (*v.t.*) to reheat.

reaquisição (*f.*) reacquisition. [Verb: READQUIRIR.]

reascender (*v.i.*) to reascend, rise again; (*v.t.*) to raise again. Cf. REACENDER.

reassegurar (*v.t.*) to reassure.

reassentar (*v.t.*) to reseat.

reassinar (*v.t.*) to sign again.

reassumir (*v.t.*) to reassume, regain.

reassunção (*f.*) reassumption.

reata (*f.*) lariat [= ARREATA]; (*pl.*) coils of rope.

reatância (*f.*, *Elec.*) reactance.—**capacitiva**, capacitive reactance.—**indutiva**, inductive reactance.

reatar (*v.t.*) to retie, rebind; to renew (a fight); to re-establish (relations).—**o sono**, to return to sleep.

reativar (*v.t.*) to reactivate; (*v.r.*) to revive.

reatividade (*f.*) reactivity.

reativo –va (*adj.*; *m.*) reactive (agent).

reato (*m.*, *Law*) reatus (state of a defendant).

reator –tora (*adj.*; *m.*,*f.*) reactor, reagent; (*m.*, *Elec.*) reactor; choke coil.

reaver [69] (*v.t.*) to get back, recover, recapture.

reaviar (*v.t.*) to guide anew, redirect; (*v.r.*) to find one's way again.

reavir-se com (*v.r.*) to reconcile oneself with.

reavisar (*v.t.*) to warn again.

reavivar (*v.t.*) to revive (memories).

rebaça (*f.*) = AVOANTE.

rebaixa (*f.*) a lowering (as of prices).

rebaixado –da (*adj.*) lowered; demoted; debased; discredited.

rebaixador –dora (*adj.*) lowering; (*m.*) fillister, molding plane.

rebaixamento (*m.*) a lowering; abasement, debasement; degradation; demotion.

rebaixar (*v.t.*) to lower; to demote; to debase; to discredit; (*v.i.*) to lower, drop; (*v.r.*) to debase (demean) oneself; to eat humble pie.

rebaixe, rebaixo (*m.*) a lowering; depressed part; (*Carp.*) mortise.

rebalçar (*v.i.*,*v.r.*) to stagnate.

rebanhar (*v.*) = ARREBANHAR.

rebanho (*m.*) flock, herd, drove; fig., congregation.—**espiritual**, spiritual flock. **Uma má ovelha põe o—a perder**, One rotten apple spoils the barrel.

rebarba (*f.*) barb; prong of a ring setting; space between lines of print; (*Metal.*) burr, fin, flash.

rebarbar (*v.t.*, *Metal.*) to burr or deburr.

rebarbativo –va (*adj.*) double-chinned; repellent; crabbed.

rebatar (*v.*) = ARREBATAR.

rebate (*m.*) act of striking, repelling, etc.;—see the verb REBATER; tocsin; sudden alarm; presentiment; rebound, repercussion; discount (of notes, bills, etc.); [But not rebate, which is ABATIMENTO].—**falso**, false alarm.

rebatedor –dora (*adj.*) striking, beating; alarming; discounting; (*m.*,*f.*) discounter (of notes, etc.); a soccer player who kicks back the ball without controlling its direction.

rebater (*v.t.*) to beat or strike again; to beat back, repel (the enemy); to parry (a blow); to refute; to rebut; to clinch (a nail); to discount (bills, notes); to kick back (a soccer ball).

rebatido –da (*adj.*) oft-beat; clinched (as a nail); beaten back; of bills and notes, discounted; (*f.*) retort.

rebatimento (*m.*) = REBATE.

rebatizar (*v.t.*) to rebaptize.

rebato (*m.*) door sill; stair step.

Rebeca (*f.*) Rebecca; Rebekah; [*not cap.*] = RABECA.

rebeijar (*v.t.*) to kiss again.

rebel (*adj.*; *m.*,*f.*) rebel [= REBELDE].

rebela (*f.*) rebellion [= REBELIÃO].

rebelador –dora (*adj.*) = REBELDE.

rebelão –lona (*adj.*) of a horse, unmanageable, refractory; of a person, self-willed, deaf to advice.

rebelar (*v.t.*) to incite to rebellion; (*v.r.*) to rebel, revolt (**contra**, against).

rebelde (*adj.*) rebellious, insurgent; disaffected; self-willed, unruly; defiant; rambunctious, ornery; (*m.*,*f.*) rebel; deserter.

rebeldia (*f.*) rebellion; rebelliousness; defiance.

rebelião (*f.*) rebellion, revolt, uprising, insurrection; defiance; disloyalty.

rebém (*m.*) whip, lash.

rebencada (*f.*), **rebencaço** (*m.*) a blow with a riding whip.

rebenque (*m.*) quirt, riding whip.

rebenquear (*v.t.*) to whip.

rebenta-boi (*m.*) = ARREBENTA-BOI and ROSEIRA-CANINA.

rebentação (*f.*) act of bursting; breaking of waves; pounding of surf.

rebentão (*m.*) shoot, offshoot, sprout; plant sucker; scrub vegetation; fig., offspring.

rebentar (*v.i.*) to burst (open); to blow up; to explode; to break; to burst forth, gush out; to break out; to burgeon; (*v.t.*) to break; "bust"; (*v.r.*) to burst, break. —**a chorar**, to burst out crying.—**de**, to burst with (curiosity, laughter, health, etc.).—**de rir**, to split one's sides laughing.—**em blasfêmias**, to burst out in curses. Cf. ARREBENTAR.

rebento (*m.*) bud, sprout, cion; fig., offspring. **lançar—s**, to burgeon.

rebentona (*f.*) burning question; political upheaval.

rebicar (*v.*) = ARREBICAR.

rebique (*m.*) = ARREBIQUE.

rebitadeira (*f.*) = REBITADORA.

rebitador (*m.*) riveter (man or machine).

rebitadora (*f.*) riveting machine, riveting hammer.—**automática**, automatic riveter.—**mecânica**, riveting hammer.

rebitamento (*m.*) **rebitagem** (*f.*) riveting.

rebitar (*v.t.*) to rivet.

rebite (*m.*) rivet.

rêbo (*m.*) piece of rock; rough stone.

reboar (*v.i.*) to re-echo, reverberate, resound.

rebocado –da (*adj.*) plastered, stuccoed; towed (as a trailer).

rebocador –dora (*adj.*) towing; plastering; (*m.*) plasterer; tugboat.

rebocadura (*f.*) act of plastering; act of towing.

rebocar (*v.t.*) [from REBÔCO] to plaster; to daub, coat, cover (as with plaster); [from REBOQUE] to tow, haul, drag.

rebôco (*m.*) plaster.

rebôjo (*m.*) whirlpool, swirl; whirlwind; ocean spray; churning of water, as by a boat's propeller; curve of a waterfall; southwest wind blowing out to sea.

rebolada (*f.*) a growth of native plants; a clump of trees or shrubs.

rebolado (*m.*) a rolling, swinging movement of the hips.

rebolão (*m.*) swaggerer, blusterer; a kind of tick.

rebolar (*v.r.*) to roll, twirl, whirl, spin; to swing the hips (as in a hula dance); (*v.i.*,*v.r.*) to turn on itself; to roll, tumble (as in play); to shake (as the hips).

rebolcar (*v.t.*) to tumble, toss; (*v.r.*) to thrash about.

reboldrosa (*f.*) = REBARDOSA.

rebolear (*v.t.*) to swing, twirl (as a lasso); (*v.r.*) to swing the hips.

reboleira (*f.*) dense growth; clump of woods.

reboliçar (*v.i.*) to squirm, twist and turn.

reboliço –ça (*adj.*) resembling a grindstone; that turns on itself. Cf. REBULIÇO.

rebolir (*v.i.*) to hurry, walk fast; to squirm; (*v.r.*) to swing the hips.

rebôlo (*m.*) grindstone; (*colloq.*) cylinder; a joint of sugar cane for planting.

reboo (*m.*) re-echo, reverberation.

reboque (*m.*) a tow or towing; tow rope; trailer; barge; fig., a dragging along of somebody; (*colloq.*) street walker; "a MONTARIA towed by sailing vessels which ply between the island of Marajó and the opposing coast of Pará." [*GBAT*] **a—**, trailing (behind). **cabo de—**, towline. **carro—**, a trailer. **corda de—**, tow rope. **levar a—**, to take in tow. [Verb: REBOCAR].

reboquear (*v.*) = REBOCAR (to tow).

rebordagem (*f.*) damage (to a ship) by collision; indemnity for such damage.

rebordar (*v.t.*) to re-embroider; to smooth (glass edges).

rebôrdo (*m.*) turned edge; edging.

rebordosa (*f.*) censure, rebuke, reprimand; tough situation; serious illness; a severe setback.

reborquiada (*f.*) a lassoing.

rebotalho (*m.*) scrap, tag end; refuse, leavings; discard. **o—da sociedade (da humanidade)**, the dregs of humanity; the scum of the earth.

rebotar (*v.t.*) to dull (knife, etc.); to beat off (enemy); (*v.r.*) to grow dull (lose interest).

rebote (*m.*) bounce, rebound.

rebradar (*v.t.*) to shout again; to roar.

rebramar (*v.i.*) to thunder; to roar; to shout.

rebramir (*v.i.*) to cry out; to bellow.

rebrilhar (*v.i.*) to shine again and more brightly.

rebrilho (*m.*) intense brightness.

rebuçado –**da** (*adj.*) covered up, wrapped up; disguised; (*m.*) wrapped piece of candy; "an extract of sugar cane hardened in the form of a loaf which is packed in paper; a national candy, but above all Amazonian." [*GBAT*]

rebuçar (*v.t.*) to hide, conceal (as with a veil or muffler); to disguise; (*v.r.*) to cover one's face or mouth (as with a napkin or handkerchief); to disguise oneself.

rebuço (*m.*) high collar of a coat or cloak (one which turns up and serves to conceal or protect the face); lapel; disguise. **falar sem—s,** to speak without mincing words, be outspoken.

rebuliço (*m.*) tumult, commotion, bustle; uproar, hubbub, hell let loose. Cf. REBOLIÇO.

rébus (*m.*) rebus.

rebusca (*f.*), –**co** (*m.*) act of searching, ransacking, etc. See the verb REBUSCAR

rebuscado –**da** (*adj.*) exquisite, highly refined, recherché.

rebuscar (*v.t.*) to search again; to glean; to ransack, rummage; to refine; (*v.r.*) to get fixed up (as with a good deal).

rebusque (*m.*) deal, bargain, arrangement (for mutual advantage).

rebutalho = REBOTALHO.

rec. = RECEITA (revenue; income).

recacho (*m.*) swagger.

recadeiro (*m.*) messenger.

recadista (*m.,f.*) one who goes on errands.

recado (*m.*) message, errand; reprimand; (*pl.*) greetings; also = RECAUS. **dar conta do—**, (*colloq.*) to handle the matter, manage the job, "deliver the goods," "bring home the bacon". **mandar—,** to send word.

recaída (*f.*), **recaimento** [a-i] (*m.*) relapse; setback.

recair [75] (*v.i.*) to fall again; to relapse (**em, into**); to revert (**em,** to); to fall (**sôbre,** upon).

recalcado –**da** (*adj.*) repressed (emotionally); pressed down, crammed; well-trod; oft-repeated.

recalcar (*v.t.*) to trample on, tread upon; to press down, pack, cram; to reiterate; to repress.

recalcitração, recalcitrância (*f.*) recalcitrance.

recalcitrante (*adj.*) recalcitrant.

recalcitrar (*v.i.*) to recalcitrate.—**a,** to manifest stubborn opposition to. (*v.t.*) to retort rudely.

recalescência (*f., Metal.*) recalescence.

recalmão (*m.*) lull between storms.

recalque (*m.*) repression; (*Const.*) settling (as of a wall); (*Psychoanalysis*) repression.

recamar (*v.t.*) to embroider with raised stitches; to adorn, embellish.

recambiar (*v.t.*) to return (something) to the sender; to return an unpaid or unaccepted bill of exchange; (*v.i.*) to turn around.

recâmbio (*m.*) a sending back (of something); expense incurred in returning an unpaid draft.

recamo (*m.*) stud, boss, ornament.

recanto (*m.*) recess, nook, corner; a retreat, place of retirement.—**s da terra**, far corners of the earth.

recapitulação (*f.*) recapitulation.

recapitular (*v.t.*) to recapitulate.

recapturar (*v.t.*) to recapture.

recarregar (*v.t.*) to reload; to load heavily.

recartilha (*f., Mach.*) index plate.

recartilhamento (*m., Mach.*) knurling.

recartilhar (*v.t., Mach.*) to index; to knurl.

recasar (*v.t.,v.i.*) to remarry.

recatado –**da** (*adj.*) modest, proper; restrained, sober.

recatar (*v.t.*) to preserve, guard (in secrecy); to shield (**de, contra,** against); (*v.r.*) to protect oneself (**de,** against).

recativar (*v.t.*) to recapture.

recato (*m.*) cautiousness; circumspection; secrecy.

recauchutagem (*f.*) recapping (of tires).

recauchutar (*v.t.*) to recap (tires).

recaus (*m.pl.*) a saddle with its trappings. Var. RECADOS.

recavar (*v.t.*) to dig over, dig again.

recavém (*m.*) the rear end of a wagon bed.

receado –**da** (*adj.*) feared, dreaded.

recear (*v.t.,v.i.*) to fear, dread. [The noun is RECEIO].—**de,** to be afraid of.—**por,** to fear for.—**-se de,** to be fearful of.

recebedor –**dora** (*adj.*) receiving; (*m.,f.*) receiver; tax collector.

recebedoria (*f.*) tax collector's office; treasurer's office.

receber (*v.t.*) to receive, accept; to admit, take in; to welcome, greet.—**em familia,** to receive informally, as one of the family.—**visitas,** to receive visitors.—**-se (com),** to receive (one another) in marriage.

recebimento (*m.*) receipt; acceptance.

recebível (*adj.*) receivable, acceptable.

receio (*m.*) distrust, misgiving, suspicion; dread, apprehension. [The verb is RECEAR]. **Não tenha—,** Have no fear.

receita (*f.*) revenue, income, receipts; recipe, prescription. —**bruta,** gross income.—**líquida,** net income.—**ordinária,** regular (usual) income.

receitar (*v.t.,v.i.*) to prescribe (a remedy).

recém (*adv.*) newly, recently, lately.

recém-casado –**da** (*adj.; m.,f.*) newlywed.

recém-chegado –**da** (*adj.*) newly arrived; (*m.,f.*) recent arrival, newcomer.

recém-convertido –**da** (*adj.*) newly converted; (*m.,f.*) recent convert.

recém-falecido –**da** (*adj.; m.,f.*) recently deceased (person).

recém-feito –**ta** (*adj.*) recently made or done.

recém-finado –**da** (*adj.*) recently deceased; recently finished.

recém-morto –**ta** (*adj.*) recently dead.

recém-nado –**da**, **recém-nascido** –**da** (*adj.; m.,f.*) newborn (child).

recém-ouvido –**da** (*adj.*) recently heard.

recém-plantado –**da** (*adj.*) newly planted.

recém-vindo –**da** (*adj.; m.,f.*) = RECÉM-CHEGADO.

recender (*v.t.*) to exhale, emit (an aroma); (*v.i.*) to give forth an aroma, smell of.

recendor (*m.*) strong, pleasant aroma.

recenseado –**da** (*adj.*) registered in a census or as a voter.

recenseador –**dora** (*adj.*) census-taking; (*m.,f.*) census taker.

recenseamento (*m.*) census.

recensear (*v.t.*) to take a census.

recente (*adj.*) recent, new, late, fresh.

receoso –**sa** (*m.*) fearful, afraid, apprehensive; distrustful. [The noun is RECEIO.]

recepção (*f.*) reception (of visitors); receiving, acceptance; (*Radio*) reception.—**heteródina,** heterodyne (beat) reception.—**homódina,** homodyne reception.

receptação (*f.*) a receiving of stolen goods.

receptacular (*adj., Bot.*) receptacular.

receptáculo (*m.*) receptacle, vessel, container; reservoir; (*Bot.*) receptacle.

receptador (*m.*), –**dora** (*f.*) fence (receiver of stolen goods).

receptar (*v.t.*) to receive or hide (stolen goods).

receptibilidade (*f.*) receptibility.

receptível (*adj.*) receptible.

receptividade (*f.*) receptivity.

receptivo –**va** (*adj.*) receptive.

receptor –**tora** (*adj.*) receiving; (*m.,f.*) receiver (of telephone, radio, etc.); also = RECEPTADOR.—**de alta fidelidade,** hi-fi receiver. **aparelho—,** a radio receiving set.

recessivo –**va** (*adj.*) recessive, latent, subordinate.

recesso (*m.*) recess, alcove, niche. [School recess is HORA DO RECREIO.]

rechaçar (*v.t.*) to repulse, repel, beat back; to drive out, drive off.

rechaço (*m.*) repulse; rebound.

recheado –**da** (*adj.*) stuffed, crammed.

rechear (*v.t.*) to stuff (a turkey, etc.); (*v.r.*) to fill oneself with riches.

rechego [ê] (*m.*) a hunter's blind.
recheio (*m.*) act of stuffing; forcemeat, stuffing.
rechiar (*v.i.*) to sizzle (as frying eggs); to hiss (as steam).
rechonchudo –**da** (*adj.*) plump, chubby, buxom, rolypoly.
recibo (*m.*) a written receipt. **passar**—, (*colloq.*) to retort.
recidiva (*f.*) return, reappearance, recurrence (of a disease); relapse.
recidivar (*v.i.*) to relapse; to be recurrent.
recidividade (*f.*) relapse, recurrence; recividism.
recidivista (*m.,f.*) recidivist.
recidivo –**va** (*adj.*) recidivous.
recife (*m.*) reef, shoal.—**circular**, atoll. [*cap.*] Recife (Pernambuco).
recifense (*adj.*) of or pert. to the city of Recife; (*m.,f.*) a native or inhabitant of that city.
recifoso –**sa** (*adj.*) reefy.
recinto (*m.*) enclosure, enclosed place; sanctuary.
récipe (*m.*) doctor's prescription.
recipiendário—**ria** (*adj.*) that is to receive (something); (*m.,f.*) one who is to receive (prize, medal, etc.); recipiendary (accepted candidate, as for membership).
recipiente (*adj.*) recipient, receiving, receptive; (*m.*) receiver; receptacle, container.
reciprocar (*v.t.,v.i.*) to reciprocate.
reciprocidade (*f.*) reciprocity.
recíproco –**ca** (*adj.*) reciprocal, mutual; interchangeable; (*m., Math.*) reciprocal.
récita (*f.*) recital, play.
recitação (*f.*) recitation, declamation.
recitado –**da** (*adj.*) recited, rehearsed; (*m. Music*) recitative.
recitador –**dora** (*adj.*) reciting; (*m.,f.*) reciter.
recital (*m.*) a musical recital.
recitante (*m.,f.*) recitalist.
recitar (*v.t.*) to recite, declaim; to narrate, relate, recount.
recitativo –**va** (*adj.; m., Music*) recitative.
reclamação (*f.*) claim, demand; complaint, protest. [But not reclamation (of land), which is ARROTEAMENTO (DE TERRENO INCULTO).]
reclamador –**dora** (*adj.*) demanding; protesting; (*m.,f.*) claimant; protester.
reclamante (*adj.*) claiming; (*m.,f.*) claimer.
reclamar (*v.t.*) to protest, cry out against, complain of or about; to lay claim to, demand; to exact, require; to call for; to urge; (*v.i.*) to protest, complain. [But not to reclaim (land), which is ARROTEAR (TERRENO INCULTO).] —**o que lhe é devido**, to demand one's due.
reclamável (*adj.*) susceptible of demand, protest, or complaint.
reclamo, reclame (*m.*) advertisement, advertising; claim, complaint; whistle used to imitate a birdcall; decoy, lure; (*Print.*) catchword.
reclinação (*f.*) reclining; reclination.
reclinado –**da** (*adj.*) reclined, reclining, recumbent; (*Bot.*) reclining.
reclinar (*v.t.*) to recline, incline, lean (**a, em,** on); to rest, lay, put (**sôbre,** on); (*v.r.*) to recline, rest, lie down; to lounge.
reclusão (*f.*) seclusion; imprisonment.
recluso –**sa** (*adj.*) recluse, shut up, cloistered; (*m.,f.*) recluse; convict; one who leads a retired life.
rec.º = RECEBIDO (received).
recobramento (*m.*) recovery.
recobrar (*v.t.*) to recover, regain, get back; (*v.r.*) to rally, recuperate.—**a razão**, to regain one's reason.—**as forças**, to rally.
recobrável (*adj.*) recoverable.
recobrir [33] (*v.t.*) to re-cover.
recôbro (*m.*) recovery, regaining.
recognição (*f.*) recognition. Cf. RECONHECIMENTO.
recognoscível (*adj.*) recognizable.
recoitar (*v.t.*) to anneal (metals); = RECOZER.
recoleto (*m.*), –**ta** (*f., R.C.Ch.*) a Recollect (monk or nun).
recolhedor –**dora** (*adj.*) gathering; collecting; harboring; withdrawing; (*m.,f.*) one who gathers, collects, etc.; (*m.*) one who rounds up horses.
recolher (*v.t.*) to gather (up, in, together); to harbor, entertain; to collect, garner; to bring in; (*v.i.*) to return (home). **O bonde vai**—, The streetcar is on its way to the carbarn. (*v.r.*) to betake oneself, go; to withdraw; to return home; to retire, go to bed; to withdraw from the world.—**se aos bastidores**, fig., to withdraw from public life.—**se com as galinhas**, to go to bed with the chickens.—**se dentro de si**, to withdraw within oneself.

recolhido –**da** (*adj.*) retired; withdrawn; (*f.*) retirement, withdrawal; (*R.C.Ch.*) lay sister.
recolhimento (*m.*) retirement, withdrawal; retreat, asylum; seclusion, privacy; contemplation, self-communion; couvade.
recolho [cô] (*m.*) heavy breathing; the spout or blowing of a whale.
recolocar (*v.t.*) to restore, put back.
recolonizar (*v.t.*) to recolonize.
recolorir (*v.t.*) to re-color.
recombinar (*v.t.*) to recombine.
recomeçar (*v.t.*) to recommence, begin again, renew, resume.
recomêço (*m.*) recommencement.
recomendação (*f.*) recommendation, counsel, advice; admonition; (*pl.*) commendable qualities; compliments, respects, greetings.—**s em casa**, Remember me to the family. **carta de**—, letter of recommendation (introduction).
recomendado –**da** (*adj.*) recommended; (*m.,f.*) one who is recommended to another.
recomendador –**dora** (*adj.*) recommending; (*m.,f.*) recommender.
recomendar (*v.t.*) to recommend, advise, counsel, suggest; to enjoin; to confide, commit, entrust; to commend; (*v.r.*) to recommend oneself; to present one's compliments.
recomendatório –**ria, recomendativo** –**va** (*adj.*) recommendatory.
recomendável (*adj.*) commendable. **pouco**—, discreditable, unworthy.
recompensa, –pensação (*f.*) recompense, reward; compensation.
recompensador –**dora** (*adj.*) compensating, compensatory; (*m.,f.*) compensator.
recompensar (*v.t.*) to recompense, reward; to pay back; to compensate, make up for.
recompensável (*adj.*) deserving of reward.
recompilar (*v.t.*) to recompile.
recompor [63] (*v.t.*) to recompose, recombine, rearrange; to reset; to reconcile.
recomposição (*f.*) recomposition, reconciliation.
recomprar (*v.t.*) to repurchase.
recôncavo (*m.*) hollow, cave, deep recess; land surrounding a port or city.—**da Bahia**, a large and fertile area on the coast of the State of Bahia. [For centuries a producer of sugar, it is now a source of oil also.]
reconcentração (*f.*) reconcentration.
reconcentrar (*v.t.*) to reconcentrate; (*v.r.*) to concentrate.
reconcertar (*v.t.*) to reconcert; to reharmonize. Cf. RECONSERTAR.
reconciliação (*f.*) reconciliation, restoration of harmony; conciliation.
reconciliado –**da** (*adj.*) reconciled; (*m.,f., Eccl.*) reconcilee.
reconciliador –**dora** (*adj.*) reconciling; (*m.,f.*) reconciler.
reconciliar (*v.t.*) to reconcile; to conciliate.—**se com**, to become reconciled to (with).
reconciliatório –**ria** (*adj.*) reconciliatory.
reconciliável (*adj.*) reconcilable.
recondicionar (*v.t.*) to overhaul, rebuild, recondition.
recôndito –**ta** (*adj.*) recondite, hidden, secret, abstruse; (*m.*) recess, niche, hiding place.
recondução (*f.*) reconveyance; return.
reconduzir (*v.t.*) to return, take back; to reconvey; to re-elect.
reconfessar (*v.t.*) to confess anew.
reconfortante, reconfortador –**dora** (*adj.*) comforting; (*m.,f.*) comforter.
reconfortar (*v.t.*) to comfort, animate, revive, strengthen; (*v.r.*) to take on new life.
reconfôrto (*m.*) comfort, invigoration.
recongraçar (*v.*) = RECONCILIAR.
reconhecedor –**dora** (*adj.*) recognizing; (*m.,f.*) recognizer.
reconhecer (*v.t.*) to recognize (**como**, as); to acknowledge, admit; to show appreciation of; to reconnoiter; (*v.r.*) to declare (confess) oneself (to be something).—**a assinatura**, to witness a signature.—**um filho natural**, to acknowledge one's parenthood of a child.—**um govêrno**, to recognize a government. **não**—, to disown (a child).
reconhecidamente (*adv.*) admittedly.
reconhecido –**da** (*adj.*) recognized; undoubted; grateful.
reconhecimento (*m.*) recognition; gratitude, thankfulness; acknowledgment; reconnaissance; (*Med.*) examination.
reconhecível (*adj.*) recognizable.

reconquistar (v.t.) to regain, recapture, recover.
reconsagrar (v.t.) to reconsecrate.
reconsertar (v.t.) to mend again, repair once more. Cf. RECONCERTAR.
reconsiderar (v.t.) to reconsider.
reconsolidar (v.t.) to reconsolidate.
reconstituição [u-i] (f.) reconstitution.
reconstituido -da [u-i] (adj.) rebuilt, reconditioned; of antique furniture, restored; of imitation gems, synthetic. pneu—, rebuilt tire.
reconstituinte [u-ín] (adj.) reconstituting, rebuilding, restoring; (m., Med.) a tonic.
reconstituir [u-i] (v.t.) to reconstitute; to restore; to reestablish; to rebuild.
reconstrução (f.) reconstruction; rebuilding.
reconstituir (v.t.) to reëstablish.
reconstruir [37] (v.t.) to reconstruct, rebuild; to reform.
recontamento (m.) a re-count; a recounting.
recontar (v.t.) to re-count, count again; to recount, relate.
recontro (m.) reëncounter, clash, combat; a chance meeting.
reconvenção (f. Law) countercharge; countersuit.
reconvir [82] (v.t.) to counterclaim; to countercharge.
recopilação (f.) compilation.
recopilar (v.t.) to compile (data, etc.).
recordação (f.) remembrance, memory; memento, souvenir.
recordar (v.t.) to recall, remember.—-se de, to remember, recollect.
recordativo -va, recordatório -ria (adj.) recordative, commemorative.
recorde (m.) record (in sports).
recordista (adj.) record-holding; (m.,f.) record holder.
reco-reco (m.) a noise like that of frogs croaking; a small dance party; a musical instrument consisting of a length of bamboo with transverse notches cut into it and over which a wand is rubbed to produce the sound; c.a. REQUE-REQUE, CANZÁ, GANZÁ, CARACAXÁ, QUEREQUEXÉ.
recorrente (adj.) having recourse to; appealing; (m.,f., Law) appellant. Cf. RECURRENTE.
recorrer (v.t.) to retrace, go back over; to run over (a book, etc.) for the second time.—a, to resort to, have recourse to; to make use of, fall back on.—a todos os meios, to leave no stone unturned.—de (um tribunal para outro), to appeal from (one court to a higher one).—o passado, to relive the past.
recorrido -da (m.,f., Law) appellee.
recorrível (adj.) appealable.
recortado -da (adj.) scalloped; cut out; (Med.) dissected; (f.) a country dance.
recortar (v.t.) to cut (out), trim, clip (out); to scallop; to pink; to interrupt; to overtrump (a trick).
recorte (m.) a cutout; outline, profile.—de jornal, newspaper clipping. álbum de—s, scrapbook.
recortilha (f.) punch (tool).
recoser (v.t.) to resew. Cf. RECOZER.
recosta (f.) mountain slope [= VERTENTE].
recostado -da (adj.) reclining.
recostar (v.t.) to recline, rest (the head, the body) a, em sôbre, on, against.—-se (a, em, sôbre), to rest, lean back, lean against, lie on (chair, bed, sofa, etc.); to lounge.
recôsto (m.) back of a chair; resting place; also = RECOSTA.
recova (f.) = RECOVAGEM.
récova (f.) pack train [= RÉCUA].
recovagem (f.) transportation of goods and baggage by pack trains; the goods so transported; the price of such service.
recovar (v.t.) to transport (baggage and merchandise) by pack train; (v.i.) to follow the occupation of muleteer.
recoveiro (m.) muleteer [= ALMOCREVE].
recozer (v.t.) to cook again; to anneal (metals). Cf. RECOSER.
recozido -da (adj.) cooked over; of steel, etc., annealed.
recozimento (m.) annealing (of metals).
recreação (f.) recreation; fun; = RECREIO.
recrear (v.t.) to cheer, divert, amuse; (v.r.) to take recreation; to play; have a good time; to relax. Cf. RECRIAR.
recreativo -va (adj.) recreative, diverting.
recreio (m.) recreation, diversion, relaxation; playground. hora do—, school recess time. viagem de—, pleasure trip.
recrementício -cia (adj., Med.) recrementitial.
recremento (m., Med.) recrement.

recrescer (v.i.) to grow again; to grow, swell, expand (in strength).
recriar (v.t.) to re-create. Cf. RECREAR.
recriminação (f.) recrimination, retort, countercharge.
recriminar (v.t.) to recriminate, return an accusation. [The intransitive form is FAZER RECRIMINAÇOES.]
recriminatório -ria (adj.) recriminatory, accusing.
recristalizar (v.t., v.i., Chem.) to recrystallize.
recrudescência (f.) recrudescence, fresh outbreak.
recrudescente (adj.) recrudescent.
recrudescer (v.i.) to recrudesce, break out again, renew activity.
recruta (f.) fresh levy or reinforcement; a draft of cattle; training of recruits; (m.) recruit, rookie; draftee; new member; novice.
recrutamento (m.) recruiting, recruitment; reinforcement.
recrutar (v.t.) to recruit, enlist (troops, new members, etc.); to round up (cattle).
recruzar (v.t.,v.i.) to cross and recross.
recruzamento (m., Biol.) backcross.
rect-, see under RET-.
récua (f.) pack train; a herd of pack animals; goods transported by pack animals; gang, pack (of evildoers). caminho de—, pack trail.
recuada (f.), recuamento (m.) = RECUO.
recuadeira (f.) breeching strap (of a harness).
recuanço (m.) act of backspinning (a billiard ball).
recuar (v.i.) to step (move, go, draw, fall) back; to back away; to retreat, recede; to give ground; to back up; to recoil, flinch.
recúbito (m.) recumbent position.
recultivar (v.t.) to recultivate.
recumbente (adj.) recumbent.
recuo (m.) backward movement; retreat; recoil; (Const.) setback. aos—s, [to move] backwards (by degrees, step by step).
recuperação (f.) recuperation; recovery; salvage.
recuperador -dora (adj.) recuperative; (m.,f.) recuperator; (m., Metal.) recuperative furnace.
recuperar (v.t.) to recuperate, recover, regain, get back, retrieve; to salvage; (v.r.) to recuperate.—o tempo perdido, to make up for lost time.
recuperativo -va (adj.) recuperative.
recuperável (adj.) recoverable.
recurrência (f., Med.) recurrence.
recurrente (adj.) recurrent. Cf. RECORRENTE.
recurso (m.) recourse, resort; expedient; makeshift; aid; judicial appeal; (pl.) resources, means, funds; talents, abilities. em último—, as a last resort. ter—a, to have resort to. ter—s, to be well-off.
recurvado -da (adj.) recurved, bent (over, downwards, backwards).
recurvar (v.t.) to recurve, bend (back, over, down); (v.r.) to bow, bend low.
recusa, recusação (f.) refusal, denial, rejection; rebuff; snub.
recusado -da (adj.) refused, not accepted.
recusador -dora (adj.) refusing; (m.,f.) refuser.
recusante (adj.) refusing.
recusar (v.t.) to refuse, deny, decline; to disallow; to reject, repel.—a porta, or a entrada, a, to deny admission to.—categoricamente, to refuse flatly.—-se a, to refuse to.—-se à evidência, to refuse to face the facts.
recusativo -va (adj.) rejective.
recusável (adj.) admitting of refusal; meriting refusal.
red. = REDUÇÃO (reduction).
redação (f.) redaction; editorial staff; editorial room.
redada (f.) act of casting a net; a netful, catch, haul (of fish); a nestful of fledglings.
redanho (m.) = REDENHO.
redar [39] (v.t.) to regive; to cast a net.
redargüente (adj.) retorting.
redargüição (f.) retort, answer.
redargüidor -dora (adj.) retorting; (m.,f.) retorter.
redargüir [31] (v.t.) to retort, reply; to recriminate.
redator -tora (m.,f.) editor, esp. of a newspaper.—-chefe, editor-in-chief.
redatoriar (v.t.) to edit (a newspaper).
rêde (f.) net; fish net; hair net; wire netting; hammock; network; snare.—de arrasto, trawl/ dragnet.—de difração, (Optics) diffraction grating.—de fundo, deep net.—de sardínia, sardine net.—fole = JERERÉ.—ferroviária, railway network.—nuclear, (Biol.) linin.—rodoviária, highway system.

rédea (*f.*) reins, bridle; fig., control, direction. **à—larga** or **sôlta**, headlong, full tilt; foot-loose. **dar—s sôltas à imaginação**, to give full rein to the imagination.

redeclarar (*v.t.*) to declare anew.

redecretar (*v.t.*) to decree anew.

redeiro (*m.*) net-maker; small river fishing net.

redemoinho [o-í] = REMOINHO.

redenção (*f.*) redemption.

redenho (*m.*) a shrimp net; (*Anat.*) the great omentum.

redente (*m.*, *Fort.*) redan.

redentor –tora (*adj.*) redeeming; (*m.,f.*) redeemer; [*cap.*] (*m.*) the Redeemer. [The verb is REDIMIR or REMIR.]

redentorista (*m.*) a Redemptorist Father.

redescender, redescer (*v.i.*) to redescend.

redescobrimento (*m.*) rediscovery.

redescontar (*v.t.*) to rediscount.

redesconto (*m.*) rediscount.

redestilar (*v.t.*) to redistill.

rédia (*f.*, *Zool.*) redia.

redibição (*f.*, *Civil Law*) redhibition.

redibir (*v.t.*, *Civil Law*) to annul the sale of an article, on account of some material defect.

redigir (*v.t.*) to write, pen, compose; to write newspaper articles, esp. as an editor; to redact.

redil (*m.*) pen; sheepfold; fig., fold, flock, congregation.

redimir (*v.t.*) to redeem, ransom. Cf. REMIR.

redimível (*adj.*) redeemable.

redingote (*m.*) redingote.

redinha (*f.*) a small net.

redintegrar (*v.*) = REINTEGRAR.

redissolver (*v.t.*) to redissolve.

redistribuir (*v.t.*) to redistribute.

redito –ta (*p.p.* of REDIZER) said anew; restated; repeated; (*f.*) repetition.

rédito (*m.*) return; profit.

redivivo –va (*adj.*) revived; (*f.*) the resurrection plant, rose of Jericho (*Anastatica hierochuntica*), c.a. ROSA-DE-JERICÓ.

redizer [41] (*v.t.*) to repeat, say over.

redobrado –da (*adj.*) redoubled.

redobramento (*m.*) a redoubling.

redobrar (*v.t.*) to redouble; to fold again; (*v.r.*) to multiply. **dobrar e—**, of bells, to peal over and over.

redobre (*m.*, *Music*) trill; (*adj.*) redoubled; rascally.

redôbro (*m.*) redoubling; quadruple.

redoiça (*f.*) = RETOUÇA.

redoirar (*v.*) = REDOURAR.

redolente (*adj.*) redolent.

redoma (*f.*) glass bell, bell jar.

redomão –mona (*adj.*) not fully broken in—ref. to a horse, a pair of new shoes, etc.

redondear (*v.t.*) to make round; (*v.i.*) to go around.

redondel [-déis] (*m.*) circular arena.

redondeza [dê] (*f.*) roundness, rotundity; surroundings, environs.

redondilha (*f.*, *Poetry*) roundel.

redondo –da (*adj.*) round, circular, spherical, globular; plump, stout, chubby.

redor (*m.*) circuit; (*pl.*) environs, surroundings. **ao**, or **em—**, about, around, roundabout. **ao**, or **em,—de**, encompassing.

redouça (*f.*) = RETOUÇA.

redourar (*v.t.*) to regild. Var. REDOIRAR.

redução (*f.*) reduction, decrease, abridgment, abatement, lowering; a bringing back (of something) to a former or original place or state; a reducing to zero (of the figures on the keyboard of a calculating machine); a reducer (sleeve, coupling, nipple, etc.); (*Chem.*, *Metal.*) reduction (as of ore).—**ao absurdo**, reduction to an absurdity.

reducente (*adj.*) reducing.

redundância (*f.*) redundancy.

redundante (*adj.*) redundant.

redundar (*v.i.*) to superabound, to redound, result (**de**, from; **em**, in).

reduplicação (*f.*) reduplication, redoubling.

reduplicado –da (*adj.*) reduplicate.

reduplicar (*v.t.*) to reduplicate; to redouble.

redútase (*f.*, *Biochem.*) reductase.

redutibilidade (*f.*) reducibility.

redutível (*adj.*) reducible.

redutivo –va (*adj.*) reductive.

reduto (*m.*) redoubt, fortification.

redutor –tora (*adj.*) reducing; (*m.,f.*) reducer; (*m.*) a reducing sleeve, coupling, or similar device.

redúvio (*m.*) an assassin bug (*Reduvium*).

reduzido –da (*adj.*) reduced, diminished.—**à miseria**, reduced to poverty.

reduzir [36] (*v.t.*) to reduce, diminish, lessen, decrease, cut down, curtail, make less; to subdue, conquer; to convert, change; (*Math.*) to solve, resolve; (*Chem.*) to reduce, oxidize.—**à miséria**, to reduce to want.—**em cinzas**, to reduce to ashes.

reduzível (*adj.*) reducible [= REDUTÍVEL].

reedição [e-e] (*f.*) reissue (of a publication).

reedificar [e-e] (*v.t.*) to rebuild.

reeditar [e-e] (*v.t.*) to reissue, publish again.

reeducação [e-e] (*f.*) re-education.

reeducar [e-e] (*v.t.*) to re-educate.

reeleger [e-e] (*v.t.*) to re-elect.

reeleição [e-e] (*f.*) re-election.

reeleito –ta [e-e] (*adj.*) re-elected; (*m.,f.*) one who has been re-elected.

reembarcar [e-e] (*v.t.*) to reship; to re-embark.

reembolsar [e-e] (*v.t.*) to reimburse.

reembôlso [e-e] (*m.*) reimbursement.

reemergência [e-e] (*f.*) re-emergence.

reemergir [e-e] (*v.i.*) to re-emerge.

reempossar [e-e] (*v.t.*) to re-empower.

reempregar [e-e] (*v.t.*) to re-employ.

reencanar [e-e] (*v.t.*) to reset (bone fracture).

reencarcerar [e-e] (*v.t.*) to re-incarcerate.

reencarnação [e-e] (*f.*) reincarnation.

reencarnar [e-e] (*v.t.*) to reincarnate.

reencenar [e-e] (*v.t.*) to re-stage, repeat a scene or performance.

reencher [e-e] (*v.t.*) to refill.

reenchimento [e-e] (*m.*) a refilling.

reencontrar [e-e] (*v.t.*) to meet again; to find again.

reencontro [e-e] (*m.*) a meeting again; a finding again.

reencordoar [e-e] (*v.t.*) to restring (musical instrument, tennis racket, etc.).

reencorporar [e-e] (*v.t.*) to reincorporate.

reendireitar [e-e] (*v.t.*) to straighten anew.

reengajar [e-e] (*v.t.*) to re-engage, reemploy.

reensair [e-e] (*v.t.*) to rehearse again.

reentendido –da [e-e] (*adj.*) understood anew.

reentrada [e-e] (*f.*) reëntrance.

reentrância [e-e] (*f.*) a reëntering angle or curve.

reentrante [e-e] (*adj.*) reëntrant.

reentrar [e-e] (*v.i.*) to reënter.

reenviar [e-e] (*v.t.*) to send again; to return, send back.

reenvidar [e-e] (*v.*) = REVIDAR.

reerguer [e-e] [5] (*v.t.*) to raise again; (*v.r.*) to rise again.

reescrever [e-e] (*v.t.*) to rewrite.

reesposar [e-e] (*v.t.*) to remarry.

reestabelecer [e-e] (*v.*) = RESTABELECER.

reestampar [e-e] (*v.t.*) to reprint.

reestudar [e-e] (*v.t.*) to re-study.

reexaminar [e-e] (*v.t.*) to reëxamine.

reexpedir [e-e 60] (*v.t.*) to reship.

reexportação [e-e] (*f.*) reëxportation.

reexportar [e-e] (*v.t.*) to reëxport.

ref. = REFORMADO (retired).

refalar (*v.i.*) to speak again.

refazedor –dora (*adj.*) remaking; redoing; (*m.,f.*) remaker.

refazer [47] (*v.t.*) to remake, make over, do over; to re-form, remodel; to repair, restore; (*v.r.*) to rally, be on the mend, recover strength; to refresh oneself.

refazimento (*m.*) remaking; repair; restoration; regaining of health.

refece (*adj.*) base, vile, infamous; easy; dirt-cheap.

refechar (*v.t.*) to close again; to fill cracks (in masonry).

refectivo, -tório (*m.*) a restorative (medicine).

refega (*f.*) = REFREGA.

refêgo (*m.*) plait, tuck.

refeição (*f.*) meal, repast.—**de assobio**, (*colloq.*) a light snack. **fazer as —ções**, to take meals. **hora da—**, mealtime.

refeito –ta (*p.p.* of REFAZER) remade, restored; sturdy.

refeitório (*m.*) refectory, dining hall, mess hall.

refém (*m.*) hostage.

refender (*v.t.*) to split anew; to splinter.

referência (*f.*) reference; allusion, intimation, hint; (*pl.*) information; references.—**cruzada**, cross reference.

referenda (*f.*) countersignature.

referendar (*v.t.*) to countersign.

referente (*adj.*) referent, concerning, relating to.—**a**, regarding.

referido –da (*adj.*) aforesaid, above-mentioned.
referimento (*m.*) referral.
referir [21a] (*v.t.*) to report, relate, tell, recite; to relate, connect (one thing with another).—-se a, to refer to; to allude to, mention.
referver (*v.i.*) to effervesce, fizz; to bubble; to boil again.
refestelar-se (*v.r.*) to loll, stretch out, lean back (as in an easy chair); formerly, to make merry.
refilar (*v.i.*) to bite back; to turn against; to retort.
refiltrar (*v.t.*) to re-filter.
refinação (*f.*) refining; refinery.—eletrolítica, electrolytic refining (of metals).
refinado –da (*adj.*) refined; pure; downright, utter.
refinador –dora (*adj.*) refining; (*m.,f.*) refiner.
refinadura (*f.*) = REFINAÇÃO.
refinamento (*m.*) refining; refinement; subtlety.
refinar (*v.t.*) to refine, purify; to improve, perfect.
refinaria (*f.*) refinery.—de petróleo, oil refinery.
refino (*m.*) = REFINAÇÃO.
refle (*m.*) rifle; saber.
refletido –da (*adj.*) reflected; deliberate; discreet.
refletidor –dora (*adj.; m.,f.*) = REFLETOR.
refletir [21a] (*v.t.*) to reflect; to mirror; to deflect; (*v.i.*) to reflect, ponder, meditate.
refletivo –va (*adj.*) reflective; thoughtful.
reflectômetro (*m.*) reflectometer.
refletância (*f., Photom., Optics*) reflectance.
refletor –tora (*adj.*) reflecting; (*m.,f.*) reflector; headlight. —parabólico, parabolic reflector or headlight.
reflexão [ks] (*f.*) reflection, thought, meditation, cogitation; retort, reply; deflection; (*Physics*) reflection; [*British*] reflexion.
reflexibilidade [ks] (*f.*) reflexibility.
reflexionar [ks] (*v.i.*) to reflect, ponder.
reflexível [ks] (*adj.*) reflexible.
reflexivo –va [ks] (*adj.*) reflexive.
reflexo –xa [ks] (*adj.*) reflex; (*m.*) a reflex.—patelar, knee-jerk. ação—, reflex action; twitch, jerk.
reflorescente (*adj.*) reflorescent.
reflorescer (*v.i.*) to blossom again.
reflorestar (*v.t.*) to reforest.
reflorir [46] (*v.*) = REFLORESCER.
refluência (*f.*) refluence; reflux.
refluente (*adj.*) refluent.
refluir [72] (*v.i.*) to flow back, reflow.
refluxo [ks] (*m.*) reflux, flowing back; ebb of a tide.
refocilar (*v.t.*) to reinvigorate, reanimate; (*v.r.*) to enjoy oneself.
refogado (*m.*) onion and tomato gravy.
refogar (*v.t.*) to stew, simmer; to sauté; to braise.
refolgar (*v.i.*) to rest, take things easy.
refôlgo (*m.*) rest.
refolhar (*v.t.*) to cover with leaves; to cover in folds; to hide
refôlho (*m.*) fold, pleat, tuck.
reforçado –da (*adj.*) reinforced; strapping, strong, husky, stalwart.
reforçar (*v.t.*) to reinforce, strengthen; to reinvigorate, reanimate; (*v.r.*) to grow stronger.
reforço (*m.*) reinforcement; additional troops.
reforma, reformação (*f.*) reform, reformation; the Reformation; renovation; renewal (of a promissory note); retirement (from office).—tributária, tax reform.
reformado –da (*adj.*) reformed; (*m.,f.*) a Protestant; (*m.*) a retired officer.
reformador –dora (*adj.*) reforming; (*m.,f.*) reformer.
reformar (*v.t.*) to reform, rebuild, remodel, renovate, reconstruct; to make over; to restore; to correct, improve, rectify; to retire (from office); to reverse (a legal decision); (*v.r.*) to reform, mend one's ways; to retire (from office).—uma letra, to renew a note (at the bank).
reformativo –va (*adj.*) reformative; reformatory.
reformatório –triz (*adj.*) reformatory; reformative.
reformável (*adj.*) reformable.
reformular (*v.t.*) to reformulate.
refornecer (*v.t.*) to resupply.
refortificar (*v.t.*) to refortify.
refração (*f., Physics*) refraction. dupla—, (*Optics*) double refraction.
refrangência (*f.*) refraction.
refrangente (*adj.*) refrangent, refracting.
refranger (*v.t.*) to refract; (*v.r.*) to be reflected.
refrangibilidade (*f.*) refrangibility.
refrangir (*v.t.*) to wrinkle (the brow).

refrangível (*adj.*) refrangible.
refranzir (*v.t.*) to wrinkle.
refrão [-ãos, -ães] (*m.*) refrain; adage, saying.
refratar (*v.t., Physics*) to refract; (*v.r.*) to be refracted or deflected.
refratário –ria (*adj.*) refractory, obstinate, unruly, willful, stubborn; of ore, bricks, metal, etc., refractory; (*m.,f.*) a refractory (intractable) person.
refrativo –va (*adj.*) refractive.
refrato –ta (*adj.*) refracted.
refratômetro (*m., Physics*) refractometer.
refrator –tora (*adj.*) refractive.
refratura (*f., Med.*) refracture (of a bone, for the purpose of resetting it).
refreado –da (*adj.*) curbed, restrained.
refreador –dora (*adj.*) restraining.
refreamento (*m.*) restraint.
refrear (*v.t.*) to curb, restrain, control; (*v.r.*) to refrain; to hold oneself in check.
refreável (*adj.*) restrainable.
refrega (*f.*) fray, fight, melee, skirmish.—de vento, flurry, gust of wind.
refregar (*v.i.*) to fight.
refreio (*m.*) restraint, curb.
refrém (*m.*) = REFRÃO.
refrescador –dora (*adj.*) refreshing, cooling; (*m.,f.*) that which cools or refreshes.
refrescamento (*m.*) refreshing; refreshment.
refrescante (*adj.*) refreshing, cooling.
refrescar (*v.t.*) to refresh, cool; to revive, brace; (*v.i.*) to grow cool; (*v.r.*) to refresh oneself.
refrêsco (*m.*) refreshment; snack; a cool (soft) drink; (*colloq.*) a thrashing.
refrigeração (*f.*) refrigeration, freezing, chilling, cooling.
refrigerador –dora (*adj.*) refrigerating, chilling, cooling; (*m.*) refrigerator, icebox.—elétrico, electric refrigerator.
refrigerante (*adj.; m.*) refrigerant; cooling (drink).—líquido, coolant.
refrigerar (*v.t.*) to refrigerate, cool, chill; (*v.r.*) to refresh oneself.
refrigério (*m.*) refrigeration; relief from the heat.
refringência (*f., Optics*) refringency, refractivity, refractive power.
refringente (*adj.*) refractive.
refugado –da (*adj.*) refused, rejected, thrown out.
refugar (*v.t.*) to refuse, reject, discard.
refugiado –da (*m.,f.*) refugee.
refugiar-se (*v.r.*) to seek refuge; to take refuge.
refúgio (*m.*) refuge, asylum, haven.
refugir (*v.i.*) to flee again.—de, to flee from.
refugo (*m.*) refuse, waste matter, offal, discard, leavings, rejects, rubbish.
refulgência (*f.*) refulgence.
refulgente (*adj.*) refulgent.
refulgir [50] (*v.i.*) to be refulgent; to shine, glitter.
refundar (*v.t.*) to make deeper; to deepen; to sink.
refundir (*v.t.*) to recast; to remelt.
refusar (*v.*) = RECUSAR.
refutação (*f.*) refutation, confutation, disproof; disavowal.
refutador –dora (*adj.*) refuting; (*m.,f.*) one who refutes.
refutar (*v.t.*) to refute, disprove, rebut; to disavow.
refutável (*adj.*) refutable.
reg. = REGIMENTO (regiment); REGULAR (regular).
rega (*f.*) watering, irrigation, sprinkling; (*colloq.*) rain.
regabofe (*m.*) regalement, feast; "blowout".
regaçar (*v.*) = ARREGAÇAR.
regaço (*m.*) lap.
regador (*m.*) watering can, sprinkler.
regadura (*f.*) = REGA.
regalado –da (*adj.*) regaled; delighted.
regalão –lona (*adj.; m.,f.*) self-indulgent (person).
regalar (*v.t.*) to regale, entertain; to delight; (*v.r.*) to regale oneself; to fare sumptuously; to feel delight.
regalia (*f.*) special privilege, prerogative. [Not an equivalent of regalia, in the sense of emblems or decorations, which are INSÍGNIAS, DISTINTIVOS.]
regalismo (*m.*) royalism.
regalista (*m.,f.*) royalist.
regalo (*m.*) regalement; treat, pleasure; delight; a present; a fur muff.
regalona, fem. of REGALÃO.
reganhar (*v.t.*) to regain.
regar (*v.t.*) to water, irrigate, sprinkle (plants); to wet,

moisten; to wash down (food) with drink; to baste (roasting meat).
regata (*f.*) regatta, boat races.
regatão (*m.*) regrater, middleman, huckster; an itinerant Amazon River trader (often an Armenian) whose mode of transport is a GALEOTA (which see). His wares are the most varied imaginable, ranging from needles to shotguns, from nails to face powder, from guitars to funeral wreaths.
regatar (*v.t.*) to regrate; to buy in quantity to sell at retail, referring esp. to farm products; to trade with natives.
regatear (*v.i.*) to haggle, dicker (over prices); (*v.t.*) to skimp, stint, dole out; to grudge; to wrangle; to decry, run down.
regateio (*m.*) haggling, bargaining.
regateira (*f.*) fishwife.
regateiro (*m.*) huckster.
regato (*m.*) brook, creek.—**marulhante**, gurgling brook.
regedor –**dora** (*adj.*) ruling, governing, directing; (*m.*) ruler; parish administrator.
regelado –**da** (*adj.*) congealed, frozen, icy.
regelador –**dora** (*adj.*) = REGELANTE.
regelamento (*m.*) freezing.
regelante (*adj.*) freezing, congealing.
regelar (*v.t.,v.i.,v.r.*) to freeze, congeal.
regélido –**da** (*adj.*) extremely cold.
regêlo (*m.*) refreezing.
regência (*f.*) regency; (*Gram.*) relationship between words.
regeneração (*f.*) regeneration, reproduction; conversion; (*Elec.*) regeneration; feedback.
regenerador –**ratriz, regenerante** (*adj.*) regenerating; (*m.,f.*) regenerator; (*Mach.*) regenerator; recuperator.—**de calor**, reheating furnace.
regenerar (*v.t.*) to regenerate, reproduce, renovate; to convert, transform.
regenerativo –**va** (*adj.*) regenerative; recuperative.
regeneratriz, fem. of REGENERADOR.
regente (*m.*) regent.—**de orquestra**, conductor of an orchestra.
reger (*v.t.*) to rule, govern, conduct; to guide, direct; to lead (an orchestra).—**uma cadeira na universidade**, to occupy a university chair.
régia (*f.*) see under RÉGIO.
região (*f.*) region.
regicida (*m.,f.*) regicide (the criminal).
regicídio (*m.*) regicide (the crime).
regime, regímen (*m.*) regime, rule; regimen; diet; rate of flow or discharge.—**alimentar**, diet.—**de revoluções**, rate of R.P.M.—**para emagrecer**, reducing diet. **fazer**—, to go on a diet.
regimental (*adj.*) regimental.
regimentar (*adj.*) regimental; pert. to regulation.
regimento (*m.*) regiment; rule, regime.—**interno**, internal rule; by-laws.
régio –**gia** (*adj.*) regal, kingly, royal; (*f.*) royal palace.
regional (*adj.*) regional, sectional, local; (*m.*) a band of regional musicians, such as a hill-billy band.
regionalismo (*m.*) regionalism.
regionalista (*adj.*) regionalistic; (*m.,f.*) regionalist.
regirar (*v.t.*) to turn; (*v.i.*) to whirl.
regiro (*m.*) turn, whirl; circumlocution.
regist[r]ação (*f.*) registration.
regist[r]ador –**dora** (*adj.*) registering; (*m.,f.*) register; registerer; registrar, official recorder; (*m.*) autographic recording instrument. **caixa**—, cash register.
regist[r]ar (*v.t.*) to register, record.
regist[r]o (*m.*) registration; registry; register, record; bookmark; damper, shutter; (*Mach.*) any hand-operated valve for regulating the flow of water, oil, etc., through a pipe; (*Music*) register.—**de gás**, gas meter.—**de som**, sound recording.—**genealógico**, pedigree.—**genealógico de cavalos**, studbook.
reg.º = REGISTRADO (registered); REGULAMENTO (regulation).
rêgo (*m.*) furrow, trench; rut; ditch; groove.—**d'água**, irrigation ditch.
regolfo [gô] (*m.*) backwater.
rególito (*m., Geol.*) regolith.
regoliz (*m.*) = ALCAÇUZ.
regorjear (*v.i.*) to warble.
regorjeio (*m.*) warble.
regougar (*v.i.*) to frown, snarl; to grumble; of foxes, to bark.

regougo (*m.*) bark of a fox; growl.
regozijar (*v.t.*) to gladden, delight; (*v.r.*) to rejoice, take delight (**de, com, in**).
regozijo (*m.*) joy, delight, pleasure, mirth, glee.
regra (*f.*) rule; precept; canon; heed, regard, care; order, method. (*pl.*) menses.—**de falsa-posição**, (*Math.*) rule of false position.—**de proporção**, or—**de três**, rule of proportion; rule of three. **À exceção confirma a—**, The exception proves the rule. **em—**, usually. **estar em—**, or **estar nas—s**, to be in keeping with the rules, the law, the custom, etc. **Não há—sem exceção**, There is an exception to every rule. **(por via) de—**, as a general rule; usually, generally.
regrado –**da** (*adj.*) ruled; regular; orderly.
regrar (*v.t.*) to rule, guide, govern; to rule (mark with lines).—**se por**, to govern oneself by.
regredir [21b] (*v.i.*) to regress.
regressão (*f.*) return; (*Biol., Psychoanalysis, Psychol.*) regression.—**curvilínea**, (*Stat.*) skew regression.
regressar (*v.i.*) to return, go back; (*v.t.*) to return, send back. [But not to regress, which is RETROGRADAR.]
regressivo –**va** (*adj.*) regressive, retrogressive, reactive.
regresso (*m.*) return. **de—**, back (returned).
regreta [grê] (*f., Print.*) reglet.
regrista (*m.,f.*) stickler.
régua (*f.*) ruler, straight edge.—**de cálculo** or **de calcular**, or—**logarítmica**, slide rule.—**-tê**, a T-square.
regueiro (*m.*), –**ra** (*f.*) small brook or creek; drainage ditch; furrow along the backbone.
reguinga (*m.,f.*) objector, one who disagrees on every subject.
reguingar (*v.t.*) to object, retort, disagree.
regulação (*f.*) regulation, adjustment, control.
regulado –**da** (*adj.*) regulated; regular.
regulador –**dora** (*adj.*) regulating; (*m.,f.*) regulator; adjusting device.—**de alimentação**, (boiler) feed-water regulator.—**automático de voltagem**, automatic voltage regulator.—**centrífugo**, (*Mach.*) centrifugal governor.—**de gás**, gas-line pressure governor; automobile gas throttle.—**de induzido**, induction voltage regulator.—**de velocidade**, speed governor.—**de voltagem**, voltage regulator.
regulagem (*f.*) = REGULAÇÃO.
regulamentação (*f.*) regulation.
regulamentar (*v.t.*) to regulate.
regulamento (*m.*) regulation, rule law.
regular (*adj.*) regular, usual, normal; symmetrical; uniform, even; fair, average, pretty good, so-so; (*v.t.*) to regulate; to adjust, arrange, order; to manage, control; (*v.i.*) to run properly (as a watch); (*v.r.*) to be guided (by).—**com**, to be about on a par with (in size, performance, age, etc.).—**o relógio**, to set one's watch. **Êle não regula bem**, He is not quite all there. **não—bem da bola**, to have a screw loose (in the head); to have bats in the belfry.
regularidade (*f.*) regularity.
regularização (*f.*) regularization; (*Const.*) leveling of ground preparatory to building on it.
regularizar (*v.t.*) to regularize.—**uma situação**, to straighten out a situation.
regularmente (*adv.*) normally.—**bem**, fairly well, so-so.
regulável (*adj.*) adjustable.
regulete [lê] (*m., Arch.*) reglet.
régulo (*m.*) kinglet; (*Chem., Metal.*) regulus.
regurgitação (*f.*) regurgitation.
regurgitar (*v.t.*) to regurgitate.
rehabilitar (*v.*) & derivs. = REABILITAR & derivs.
rehabitar (*v.*) = REABITAR.
rehabituar-se (*v.*) = REABITUAR-SE.
rehaver (*v.*) = REAVER.
rei (*m.*) king, sovereign, monarch; (*Cards, Chess*) king. [Queen is RAINHA.]—**dos abutres**, king vulture (*Sarcoramphus papa*).—**dos animais**, king of beasts (the lion).—**dos metais**, king of metals (gold).—**dos-quá** = ARAPAPÁ (a heron).—**dos reis**, King of Kings.—**dos-tuiuius**, wood ibis (*Mycteria americana*), c.a. JABURU.—**s magos**, the Magi. **o—Sol**, Le Roi Soleil (Louis XIV). **sem—nem roque**, haphazardly. **trazer o—na barriga**, to be proud, stuck-up.
reide (*m.*) enemy raid; long excursion, as by automobile or on horseback.
reídeos (*m.pl., Zool.*) the family of rheas (*Rheidae*).
reima (*f.*) olive juice [= ALMOFEIRA]; rheum; bad temper.
reimão (*m.*) stray animal.

reimoso –sa (*adj.*) rheumy; bad for the blood; ill-tempered.

reimersão [e-i] (*f.*) re-immersion.

reimplantação [re-im] (*f.*) reimplantation.

reimplantar [re-im] (*v.t.*) to reimplant.

reimportação [re-im] (*f.*) reimportation.

reimportar [re-im] (*v.t.*) to reimport.

reimpressão [re-im] (*f.*) reprint; reprinting.

reimprimir [re-im] (*v.t.*) to reprint.

reinação (*f.*, *colloq.*) boisterous good time; romp: childish mischief, cutting up; prank.

reinaço (*m.*) rut, oestrus [= CIO].

reinado (*m.*) reign; ascendancy, predominance.

reinador –dora (*adj.*, *colloq.*) of children, mischievous, impish.

Reinaldo (*m.*) Reynold.

reinante (*adj.*) reigning, ruling; (*m.,f.*) ruler.

reinar (*v.i.*) to reign, rule (**sôbre**, over); to prevail, have sway; (*colloq.*) to cut up (as children).

reinauguração [e-i] (*f.*) reinauguration.

reinaugurar [e-i] (*v.t.*) to reinaugurate.

reincidência [re-in] (*f.*) relapse; recurrence; reincidence; backsliding; wilfulness.

reincidente [re-in] (*adj.*) wilful, wayward; relapsing (into error).

reincidir [re-in] (*v.i.*) to relapse, fall back, backslide; to repeat (the same crime, mistake, etc.).

reincitar [re-in] (*v.t.*) to reincite.

reinel (*adj.*) = REINOL.

reineta [nê] (*f.*) reinette (a type of apple).

reinfecção [re-in] (*f.*) reinfection.

reinflamar [re-in] (*v.t.*) to reinflame.

reinfundir [re-in] (*v.t.*) to reinstill.

reingressar [re-in] (*v.t.*) to reënter.

reiniciar [e-i] (*v.t.*) to begin again.

reinício [e-i] (*m.*) new beginning.

reinícola [e-i] (*adj.; m.,f.*) (person) of the realm.

reino (*m.*) realm, kingdom.—**animal**, animal kingdom.—**dos céus**, Kingdom of Heaven.—**eterno**, Realm Eternal. —**mineral**, mineral kingdom.—**vegetal**, vegetable kingdom.

reinoculação [e-i] (*f.*) reinoculation.

reinocular [e-i] (*v.t.*) to reinoculate.

reinol [-nóis] (*adj.*) of the realm.

reinquirir [re-in] (*v.t.*) to cross-examine.

reinscrever [re-in] (*v.t.*) to reinscribe.

reinsistir [re-in] (*v.t.*) to reinsist.

reinstalação [re-in] (*f.*) reinstallation.

reinstalar [re-in] to reinstall.

reinstituição [re-in] (*f.*) reinstitution.

reinstituir [re-in] (*v.t.*) to reinstitute.

reintegração [re-in] (*f.*) reintegration; restoration.

reintegrar [re-in] (*v.t.*) to reinstate, restore.

reintegro [re-in] (*m.*) restoration; lottery prize equal to the price paid for the ticket.

reintroduzir [re-in] (*v.t.*) to reintroduce.

reinvidar [re-in] (*v.t.*) to re-raise a bet (as at poker); to retort; (*v.i.*) to get revenge, get even.

reinvite [re-in] (*m.*) = REVIDE.

reinvocar [re-in] (*v.t.*) to invoke again or anew.

reira (*f.*, *colloq.*) lower backache; (*Veter.*) diarrhea; (*pl.*) lower back; kidneys.

réis (*m.pl.*) plural of REAL [former Braz. monetary unit]. Cf. MIL-RÉIS.

reisado (*m.*), –da (*f.*) in Brazilian folklore, a public merrymaking in celebration of Epiphany (Jan. 6).

reiteração [e-i] (*f.*) reiteration, repetition.

reiteradamente [e-i] (*adv.*) repeatedly.

reiterado –da [e-i] (*adj.*) reiterated, repeated.

reiterar [e-i] (*v.t.*) to reiterate, repeat.

reiterativo –va [e-i] (*adj.*) reiterative.

reiterável [e-i] (*adj.*) reiterable.

reitor (*m.*) ruler; director; head of a university; (*Eccl.*) rector.

reitorado (*m.*) office or dignity of a REITOR.

reitoria (*f.*) term of office of a REITOR.

reiunada [ei-u] (*f.*) stray or government-owned cattle, as a class; large herd of sorry horses.

reiunar [ei-u] (*v.t.*) to earmark stray or government-owned cattle.

reiúno—**na** (*adj.*) furnished by army (soldier's clothing); bad, no-good; (*m.*) stray or government-owned cattle; punk horse; (*f.*) flintlock firearm; congress boot.

reivindicação (*f.*) act of claiming; claim, demand (for

rights, just due, return of property, etc.); (*Civil Law*) revendication, a reclaiming.

reivindicador –dora (*adj.*) demanding, claiming; (*m.,f.*) claimant.

reivindicamento (*m.*) = REIVINDICAÇÃO.

reivindicante (*adj.*) claiming, demanding; (*m.,f.*)claimant.

reivindicar (*v.t.*) to claim, demand (dues, privileges, birthright, property, etc.); to reclaim, regain, take back; (*Civil Law*) to revendicate.

reivindicativo –va, –catório –ria (*adj.*) serving to claim; involving demands.

reixa (*f.*) grille, lattice.

reizete [zê] (*m.*) kinglet.

rejeição (*f.*) rejection; disavowal; disallowance.

rejeitador –dora (*adj.*) rejecting; (*m.,f.*) one who rejects; one who is hard to please.

rejeitar (*v.t.*) to reject, cast aside; to discard; to refuse, spurn; to repudiate; to disallow; to disclaim.

rejeitável (*adj.*) rejectable.

rejubilação (*f.*), **rejúbilo** (*m.*) jubilation.

rejubilar (*v.t.*) to give great joy to; (*v.i.,v.r.*) to rejoice.

rejubiloso –sa (*adj.*) rejoiceful, joyful.

rejuntar (*v.t.*) to seal the joints of.

rejurar (*v.t.*) to swear anew.

rejuvenescência (*f.*) rejuvenescence.

rejuvenescente (*adj.*) rejuvenescent.

rejuvenescer (*v.t.,v.i.*) to rejuvenate.

rejuvenescimento (*m.*) rejuvenation, rejuvenescence.

rela (*f.*) razzle-dazzle (toy noisemaker); a noisemaking contraption for keeping birds out of fruit trees; a bird trap; in Portugal, a tree toad which in Brazil is called PERERECA.

relação (*f.*) list, register, roll; relationship, relation, connection, bearing; recital, report; (*pl.*) connections, contacts; kinship.—**inversa**, inverse ratio. **em**—**a**, regarding. **com**—**a**, with regard to. **ter boas** (or **más**) **relações com alguém**, to be on good (or bad) terms with someone.

relacionação (*f.*) a listing of; relating, report.

relacionado –da (*adj.*) related; having relations with.

relacional (*adj.*) relational.

relacionamento (*m.*) = RELACIONAÇÃO.

relacionar (*v.t.*) to make a list of; to relate, report; to connect, correlate.—**se a** or **com**, to relate to, have to do with.

relacrar (*v.t.*) to reseal with wax.

relambório –ria (*adj.*) dull, insipid; lazy; (*m.*) indolence, inertia; boring talk.

relampadear, relampadejar (*v.*) = RELAMPAGUEAR.

relâmpago (*m.*) flash of lightning.—**de calor**, heat lightning. **de**—, in a flash. **guerra**—, blitzkrieg.

relampagueante (*adj.*) flashing like lightning. Vars. RELAMPEANTE, RELAMPEJANTE.

relampaguear (*v.i.*) to fulgurate; to flash like lightning. Vars. RELAMPAR, RELAMPEAR, RELAMPEJAR.

relançar (*v.*) = RELANCEAR.

relance (*m.*) look, glance.—**de olhos**, quick glance. **de**—, at a glance.

relancear (*v.t.*) to dart the eyes, cast a quick glance (**a, para, por, por sôbre**, at); (*m.*) quick glance.

relapsão (*f.*) relapse, backsliding.

relapsia (*f.*) relapse.

relapso –sa (*adj.*) relapsing, backsliding; recidivous; (*m.,f.*) backslider; recidivist.

relatador (*m.,f.*) relater; narrator.

relatar (*v.t.*) to report, relate, give an account of.

relatividade (*f.*) relativity.

relativismo (*m.*) relativism.

relativista (*adj.*) relativistic; (*m.,f.*) relativist.

relativo –va (*adj.*) relative; comparative; relating to.

relato (*m.*) report, account; story.

relator –tora (*m.,f.*) relater, reporter, narrator; (*Law*) relator.

relatório (*m.*) written report; formal statement,—**meteorológico**, weather report.

relavar (*v.t.*) to wash again.

relaxação (*f.*) relaxation, slackening; laxation; laxity; a letting down.

relaxado –da (*adj.*) lax, remiss; sloppy, frowsy, slovenly, careless; slipshod; slack; relaxed; (*m.,f.*) slouch, slob, slacker.

relaxador –dora (*adj.*) relaxing; (*m.,f.*) one who relaxes or becomes lax.

relaxamento (*m.*) laxity; carelessness; slackness; = RELAXAÇÃO.

relaxante (*adj.*) relaxing, slackening.
relaxar (*v.t.*) to relax, loosen, slacken; to moderate; (*v.i.*) to become lax, unbend, let down; (*v.r.*) to become careless, lax, remiss.—**o ventre**, to loosen the bowels.
relaxidão (*f.*) = RELAXACÃO.
relaxismo (*m.*) laxity, looseness (of morality, of customs, etc.).
relaxista (*adj.*) tending to laxity; (*m.,f.*) one who tends to laxity.
relé (*m., Elec.*) relay.—**de ação retardada**, delayed-action relay.—**de antena**, antenna relay.—**de corrente alternada**, A.C. relay.—**de corrente contínua**, D.C. relay—**diferencial**, differential relay.—**de dupla ação**, double-action relay.—**de tempo**, a timer, or time-delay relay.—**térmico**, temperature relay.
relegação (*f.*) relegation, banishment.
relegar (*v.t.*) to relegate, banish.
releição (*f.*) second reading.
releixar (*v.*) = RELAXAR.
releixo (*m.*) path alongside a wall or ditch; (*Fort.*) berm; overhang of a wall; sharp edge (of a razor, knife, etc.).
relembrador –**dora** (*adj.*) reminding.
relembrança (*f.*) remembrance.
relembrar (*v.t.*) to remember; to remind; to bring to mind, put in mind.
relembrável (*adj.*) rememorable, memorable.
relentar (*v.i.*) to form or fall as dew; (*v.t.*) to bedew; (*v.r.*) to become dew-damp.
relento (*m.*) night air; dew; dew-dampness; night dampness. **dormir ao**— to sleep out of doors, in the open.
reler [38] (*v.t.*) to re-read.
reles [ré] (*adj.*) poor, shabby, inferior, cheap; despicable; disreputable; vulgar; paltry, petty, picayunish.
relesmente (*adv.*) shabbily; despicably.
relevação (*f.*) = RELEVAMENTO.
relevado –**da** (*adj.*) salient, in relief; conspicuous; absolved, pardoned.
relevador –**dora** (*adj.*) absolving; (*m.,f.*) absolver, pardoner.
relevamento (*m.*) remission, absolution, pardon.
relevância (*f.*) importance. [Not an equivalent of relevancy, which is PERTINÊNCIA.]
relevante (*adj.*) outstanding, important; salient, conspicuous. [Not an equivalent of relevant which is PERTINENTE, APROPOSITADO].
relevar (*v.t.*) to cause to stand out (by contrast); to emboss; to relieve; to remit, excuse, pardon; (*v.t.,v.i.*) to behoove.
relevável (*adj.*) pardonable.
relêvo (*m.*) salience; (*Sculpture*) relief, relievo; fig., prominence, conspicuousness. **de**—, outstanding.
rêlha (*f.*) plowshare.
relhaço (*m.*), **relhada** (*f.*) lash with a whip.
relhador (*m.*) long whip.
relhar (*v.t.*) to whip.
relheira (*f.*), –**ro** (*m.*) furrow, rut.
rêlho (*m.*) rawhide whip.
relicário (*m.*) reliquary.
religação (*f.*), **religamento** (*m.*) re-tying.
religar (*v.t.*) to re-tie, bind closely.
religião (*f.*) religion.
religionário –**ria** (*m.,f.*) religionist.
religiosa (*f.*) see under RELIGIOSO.
religiosidade (*f.*) religiousness, religiosity.
religioso –**sa** (*adj.*) religious; (*m.*) a religious.—**eliano**, a Carmelite.—**menor**, Friar Minor; (*f.*) a nun.
relinchão –**chona** (*adj.*) neighing; playful, merry.
relinchar (*v.i.*) to neigh, whinny [= NITRIR; RINCHAR].
relincho (*m.*) whinny, neigh [= RINCHO].
relinga (*f., Naut.*) boltrope.
relíquia (*f.*) relic; memento, souvenir; (*pl.*) remains.
reliquiário (*m.*) relicary [= RELICÁRIO].
relógio (*m.*) watch, clock, timepiece; (*Bot.*) the broomjute sida (*S. rhombifolia*) c.a. GUAXIMA; (*Zool.*) Ridgway's tody-tyrant (*Todirostrum cinereum*) .very similar to TEQUE-TEQUE (*T. poliocephalum*).—**autográfico**, sign-in time clock.—**carimbo**, time stamp.—**cuco**, cuckoo clock.—**de algibeira** or **de bôlso**, pocket watch.—**de estacionamento**, parking meter.—**de fachada**, large clock for the front of a building.—**de gás**, gas meter.—**de mão-de-obra**, labor timing clock.—**de parede**, wall clock.—**de ponto**, time clock.—**de pulso**, wrist watch.—**de repetição**, repeating watch.—**de sol**, sun dial.—**de tôrre**, tower clock.—**elétrico**, electric clock.—**despertador**, alarm

clock.—**-pulseira**, wrist watch.—**-vigia**, night watchman's clock. **acertar o**—, to set a timepiece to the correct time. **adiantar o**—, to set a timepiece ahead. **atrasar o**—, to turn a timepiece back. **dar corda ao**—, to wind a clock or watch. **maquinismo do**—, the works of a timepiece. **mostrador do**—, face or dial of a timepiece. **O**—**não anda**, The clock (or watch) won't go. **O**—**não regula bem**, The watch (or clock) doesn't run well. **ponteiros do**—, clock or watch hands. **vidro do**—, watch crystal.
relojoaria (*f.*) watchmaking; watchmaker's shop.
relojoeiro (*m.*) watchmaker.
relumar (*v.i.*) to sparkle; (*v.t.*) to cause to sparkle.
relumbrar (*v.i.*) to sparkle (as the eyes).
relustrar (*v.t.*) to shine, polish.
relutância (*f.*) reluctance; unwillingness; disinclination; repugnance; (*Elec.*) reluctance, magnetic resistance.
relutante (*adj.*) reluctant, loath, unwilling, averse.
relutar (*v.i.*) to resist, struggle, fight against; to feel reluctance or repugnance.
relutividade (*f., Elec.*) reluctivity.
reluzente (*adj.*) radiant, refulgent, shining.
reluzir [36] (*v.i.*) to shine, glitter, gleam. **Nem tudo que reluz é ouro**, All is not gold that glitters.
relva (*f.*) grass, turf, sward.—**-do-olimpo**, (*Bot.*) common thrift (*Armeria maritima*).—**-dos-caminhos**, bluegrass (*Poa*).—**-turca**, moss saxifrage (*S. hypnoides*). **tabuleiro de**—, a plot of lawn.
relvado (*m.*) grassland; greensward; grassplot, lawn.
relvagem (*f.*), **relval** (*m.*) = RELVADO.
relvão (*m.*) grassland; (*Bot.*) teff (*Eragrostis abyssinica*), c.a. CAPIM-RELVÃO.—**-da-abissínia** = CAPIM-RELVÃO (a grass).
relvoso –**sa** (*adj.*) grassy.
remada (*f.*) oar stroke.
remador –**dora** (*adj.*) rowing; (*m.,f.*) rower; (*m.*) oarsman; (*f.*) oarswoman.
remadura (*f.*) rowing.
remagnetizar (*v.t.*) to remagnetize.
remanchador –**dora** (*adj.*) dawdling; (*m.*) tinsmith's beading or crimping tool.
remanchão –**chona** (*adj.*) slow, sluggish, dawdling.
remanchar [15] (*v.i.*) to dawdle, loiter; (*v.t.*) to waste time; to edge, bead, crimp (tin or sheetmetal work); (*v.r.*) to tarry, linger.
remancho (*m.*) dawdling, wasting of time; procrastination, sluggishness.
remanência (*f.*) remanence; property of being remanent; residual magnetism.
remanente (*adj.*) remanent.
remanescente (*adj.*) remanent, residual, remaining, left over; (*m.*) remainder, residue, remnant; (*pl.*) left-overs, odds-and-ends.
remanescer (*v.i.*) to remain, be left over.
remangar (*v.*) = ARREMANGAR.
remaniscar (*v.i.*) to make a sudden motion.
remansado –**da** (*adj.*) still, calm, slow, quiet.
remansar-se (*v.*) = ARREMANSAR-SE.
remansear (*v.i.,v.r.*) to remain still.
remanso (*m.*) lull, quiet, stillness; repose; backwater, still water; "a backwash or countercurrent along the shore-line of a river caused by a projecting point of land." [GBAT]
remar (*v.t.,v.i.*) to row.—**a chegar**, to row hard.—**à ré**, to row backwards; to back-water.—**certo**, to row in unison.—**contra a maré**, to row against the tide; to struggle against difficulties.—**de esparrela**, to drift.—**enxuto**, to row "dry" (without splashing).—**largo**, to row slowly. **bote de**—, rowboat.
remarcar (*v.t.*) to re-mark; to hallmark (gold and silver articles).
remaridar-se (*v.r.*) to take a new husband.
remartelar (*v.t.*) to re-hammer.
remascar (*v.t.*) to chew again, ruminate; to meditate on, ponder.
remastigação (*f.*) remastication.
remastigar (*v.t.*) to remasticate.
rematado –**da** (*adj.*) downright, utter. **patife**—, utter rascal.
rematador –**dora** (*adj.*) finishing; (*m.,f.*) finisher.
rematar (*v.t.*) to conclude, finish; to cap, crown, complete; to cap the climax; to put on the finishing touch; to finish off (seams).
remate (*m.*) climax; finish, closing chapter; cap, peak;

apogee; coping; envoy of poem [Cf. ENVIO, TORNADA, OFERTA.] **nota de**—, final touch.
remedar (*v.*) = ARREMEDAR.
remedeio (*m.*, *colloq.*) remedy.
remediado –da (*adj.*) remedied; moderately well-fixed, neither rich nor poor; having enough to get by on.
remediar [16] (*v.t.*) to remedy, relieve, palliate; to repair, rectify, amend. **Mais vale prevenir do que**—, An ounce of prevention is worth a pound of cure.
remediável (*adj.*) remediable.
remédio (*m.*) remedy, medicine; cure; help, relief; (*colloq.*) rum [= CACHAÇA].—**caseiro**, household remedy. —**de precaução**, preventive medicine.—**heróico**, heroic drug. **Não há**—, It can't be helped. **Não teve outro**—, He could do nothing else. **O que—não tem, remediado está**, What cannot be cured must be endured. **Que**—! What else could one do!
remêdo (*m.*) = ARREMÊDO.
remeiro (*m.*) an amberfish (*Seriola falcata*), or the banded rudderfish or shark's pilot (*Seriola zonata*).
remela (*f.*) a gummy secretion of the eyelids, blear-eye.
remelado –da, **remelão** –lona, **remeleiro** –ra, **remelento** –ta (*adjs.*) = REMELOSO.
remelar (*v.i.*) to become blear-eyed.
remelexo [lê] (*m.*) an obscene or lascivious dance.
remeloso –sa (*adj.*) blear-eyed.
rememorar (*v.t.*) to remind; remember.
rememorável (*adj.*) memorable.
rememoriar (*v.t.*) to remember.
remendado –da (*adj.*) patched; mended; mottled.
remendagem (*f.*) patching; mending.
remendão –dona (*adj.*) patching, botching, bungling; (*m.*) patcher, botcher, bungler. [See REMENDONA below.]
remendar (*v.t.*) to patch, mend, repair; to piece together. —**a manta**, to patch things up (after a quarrel).
remendeira (*f.*) woman who patches or repairs garments [= REMENDONA].
remendeiro –ra (*adj.*; *m.,f.*) = REMENDÃO.
remendo (*m.*) patch; repair; amendment.
remendona (*f.*) woman who patches (clothing); woman in rags; bungling woman. [see REMENDÃO above.]
rementir (*v.i.*) to lie anew.
rementira (*f.*) big lie.
remerecer (*v.t.*) to highly deserve.
remergulhar (*v.t.*) to resubmerge.
remessa (*f.*) remittance (of money); shipment, consignment (of goods); act of throwing.
remessar (*v.*) = ARREMESSAR.
remêsso –sa (*adj.*) missile; (*m.*) = ARREMÊSSO.
remetedura (*f.*) = ARREMETIDA.
remetente (*adj.*) remitting; (*m.,f.*) remitter; shipper; sender (of a letter, etc.).
remeter (*v.t.*) to remit, send (**a**, to); to hand over, deliver up; to defer, put off; to rush at; (*v.r.*) to defer (to another's judgment).—**se ao silêncio**, to keep silent.—**à prova**, to send on approval.
remetida (*f.*), **remetimento** (*m.*) = ARREMETIDA.
remexedor –dora (*adj.*) stirring, disturbing; jumbling; ransacking.
remexer (*v.t.*) to stir, agitate, disturb; to jumble; to rummage, ransack; (*v.r.*) to bestir oneself; to squirm; to waddle.
remexido –da (*adj.*) stirred again; squirmy, fidgety; mischievous; (*f.*) stirring, rummaging; bustle, confusion.
remição (*f.*) redemption; retrieval; repurchase. [Verb REMIR]. Cf. REMISSÃO.
remido –da (*adj.*) redeemed; paid-up [membership dues].
remiforme (*adj.*; *Zool.*) remiform.
rêmige (*adj.*) rowing; (*m.*) remex [= REMÍGIO].
remidor –dora (*adj.*; *n.,f.*) = REDENTOR.
remígio (*m.*, *Zool.*) remex (flight feather); (*pl.*) remiges.
remigração (*f.*) remigration.
remigrado –da (*adj.*) remigrated; (*m.,f.*) remigrant.
remigrar (*v.i.*) to remigrate.
remilhão (*m.*) corrup. of REMINHOL.
remineralizar (*v.t.*) to remineralize.
reminhol [-óis] (*m.*) large kitchen spoon; large copper spoon used in sugar-making.
reminiscência (*f.*) reminiscence, remembrance, recollection.
remípede (*adj.*, *Zool.*) remiped.
remir [46] (*v.t.*) to redeem, repurchase; to retrieve; to ransom, free, save; to expiate, atone for; (*v.r.*) to redeem oneself. [Noun REMISSÃO] Cf. REDIMIR, REMITIR.

remirar (*v.t.*) to look at again; (*v.r.*) to look at oneself repeatedly (in the mirror); to see oneself again (in one's children).
remissão (*f.*) remission, forgiveness, absolution; moderation, mitigation; cross reference. [Verb REMITIR] Cf. REMIÇÃO.
remissibilidade (*f.*) remissibility.
remissível (*adj.*) remissible, pardonable; remittable.
remissivo –va (*adj.*) remissive, abating; cross indexed.
remisso –sa (*adj.*) remiss, lax, negligent, slow.
remissor –sora, **remissório** –ria (*adj.*) remissive.
remitência (*f.*) remission; (*Med.*) temporary subsidence (of pain, etc.). [But not remittance, which is REMESSA DE DINHEIRO.]
remitente (*adj.*) remittent.
remitir (*v.t.*) to remit, forgive, condone; to diminish, abate; (*v.r.,v.i.*) to abate in force or intensity (as pain or fever). [But not to remit in the sense of sending, which is REMETER.] Cf. REMIR, REDIMIR.
remível (*adj.*) redeemable.
remo (*m.*) oar.—**de galé**, sweep.—**de pá**, paddle [= PAGUIA].
remoalho (*m.*) cud.
remobil[h]ar (*v.t.*) to refurnish.
remoçado –da (*adj.*) young again, rejuvenated.
remoçador –dora, **remoçante** (*adj.*) rejuvenating.
remoção (*f.*) removal.
remocar (*v.t.*) to twit.
remoçar (*v.t.*) to rejuvenate, renew; (*v.i.,v.r.*) to become young or youthful again.
remodelação, –**agem** (*f.*), –**amento** (*m.*) a remodeling.
remodelador –dora (*adj.*) remodeling.
remodelar (*v.t.*) to remodel; to reconstruct.
remoelar (*v.t.*) to ruminate, chew the cud.
remoer [56] (*v.t.*) to regrind; to grind slowly; to ruminate, chew the cud; to brood over; to gall, annoy; (*v.r.*) to chafe, fume, rage.
remoído –da (*adj.*) reground; ruminated; (*m.*) ground cattle feed.
remoinhante [o-i] (*adj.*) whirling, swirling.
remoinhar [o-i] (*v.i.*) to spin, whirl, twirl, eddy, swirl.
remoinho [o-i] (*m.*) whirlpool, vortex; eddy, swirl; whirlwind [= REDEMOINHO].
remolada (*f.*) remolade (a certain sauce for cold meats and fish).
remolar (*m.*) oar maker.
remolaria (*f.*) oar factory.
remolhado –da (*adj.*) wet again; sopping wet.
remolhar (*v.t.*) to wet again, drench; to soak; (*v.r.*) to get wet.
remôlho (*m.*) act of rewetting; condition of anything which is being steeped or soaked; (*colloq.*) any illness which puts one in bed.
remolinito (*m.*) = ATACOMITO.
remondagem (*f.*) act of reweeding.
remondar (*v.t.*) to weed again.
remonta (*f.*) remount, fresh horse; a supply of such horses; (*colloq.*) repair, remodeling; rebuilding; overhaul.
remontado –da (*adj.*) high, towering; lofty, sublime; remote.
remontagem (*f.*) reconstitution.
remontar (*v.t.*) to lift (up), raise (on high); to outfit; to refit, repair; to provide with remounts; to cap (as a column); to return (to the past).
remonte (*m.*) lifting, etc. (see the verb); repair, esp. of shoes.
remoque (*m.*) twit, gibe.
remoquear (*v.t.,v.i.*) to taunt, twit, gibe.
rêmora (*f.*) any remora (suckfish), esp. the shark remora (*Echeneis naucrates*), or the offshore remora (*Remora remora*), both c.a. AGARRADOR, PEIXE-PEGADOR, PIOLHO (-DE-CAÇÃO), PIRAQUIBA.
remorado –da (*adj.*) late, delayed.
remorder (*v.t.*) to bite again (and again); to disparage; to backbite; to torture, afflict (with remorse); (*v.i.*) to ponder; (*v.r.*) to fret oneself.
remordicar (*v.t.*) to nibble at, take small bites of.
remordido –da (*adj.*) bitten often; afflicted (as with remorse); enraged.
remordimento (*m.*) act of biting often; remorse.
remoroso –sa (*adj.*) = REMORADO.
remorso (*m.*) remorse, regrets.
remoto –ta (*adj.*) remote, far off; outlying.

remover (*v.t.*) to remove, transfer shift; to take away, do away with; to dismiss, oust (**de,** from).
removimento (*m.*) removal, removing.
removível (*adj.*) removable.
Rem.ᵗᵉ = REMETENTE (sender).
remudar (*v.t.*) to change again.
remugir (*v.t.*) to low (moo) again and again; to bellow.
remuneração (*f.*) remuneration, pay, reward.
remunerador –dora (*adj.*) remunerating; (*m.,f.*) remunerator.
remunerar (*v.t.*) to remunerate, reward, pay.
remunerativo –va, –tório –ria (*adj.*) remunerative.
remunerável (*adj.*) remunerable.
remuneroso –sa (*adj.*) = REMUNERATIVO.
remurmúrio (*m.*) constant murmuring.
rena (*f.*) reindeer.
renaco (*m.*) = COAJINGUBA.
renal (*adj.*) renal.
Renânia (*f.*) Rhineland.
renantera (*f.*) a genus (*Renanthera*) of orchids.
renascença (*f.*) renascence, rebirth; wool shoddy; [*cap.*] Renaissance.
renascente (*adj.*) renascent.
renascentista (*adj.*) Renaissant; (*m.,f.*) Renaissancist.
renascer (*v.i.*) to be born again; to rejuvenesce; to revive.
renascimento (*m.*) rebirth.
Renata (*f.*) Renée.
Renato (*m.*) René.
renaturação (*f.*, *Chem.*) renaturation (of denatured alcohol).
rencontro (*m.*) = RECONTRO.
renda (*f.*) income, revenue; rent; lace.—**bruta,** gross income.—**do mar,** (*Zool.*) retepore.—**líquida,** net income.—**nacional,** national income. **impôsto de—,** income tax.
rendabilidade (*f.*) income or profits derivable from labor or capital; profit potential; profitability.
rendado –da (*adj.*) lace-trimmed; (*m.*) lace trimming; lacework.
rendar (*v.*) = ARRENDAR.
rendável (*adj.*) income-producing.
rendedouro –ra (*adj.*) profitable. Var. RENDEDOIRO.
rendeira (*f.*) lacemaker; renter; (*Zool.*) a bearded manakin (*Chiro machaeris gutturosus*), c.a. BARBUDINHO, MONO, MONJE, BILREIRA, ATANGARATINGA, RENDEIRO-BARBUDINHO; Desmarest's manakin (*Manacus manacus*), c.a. BARBUDINHO, MONO.
rendeiro (*m.*) tenant farmer; renter; (*Zool.*) = VIUVINHA (a bird).—**bardudinho** = RENDEIRA (a bird).
render (*v.t.*) to render (**a,** to); to subdue, conquer; to take the place of, relieve; to produce, yield (profits, etc.); to give rise to; to lay down (arms); (*v.i.*) of a job, business, investment, etc., to pay; to produce income or profit; to rend, split (as a mast); to suffer a rupture; (*v.r.*) to surrender.—**a alma,** or—**o espírito,** to give up one's soul (die).—**a sentinela,** to relieve the guard.—**graças,** or—**agradecimentos,** to render thanks (**a,** to).
rendição (*f.*) surrender. [But not rendition, which is INTERPRETAÇÃO, EXECUÇÃO.]
rendido –da (*adj.*) overcome; contemplative; ruptured.
rendilha (*f.*) fine lace; tracery.
rendilhado –da (*adj.*) lacy; (*m.*) lace work; laciness; tracery.
rendilhar (*v.t.*) to trim with lace.
rendimento (*m.*) yield, return; profit, interest; income; output; efficiency (of motors and machines); surrender.
rendoso –sa (*adj.*) productive, profitable.
renegação (*f.*) act or fact of renegading; denial.
renegado –da (*adj.*) renegade; (*m.*) renegade; turncoat; worthless fellow.
renegador –dora (*adj.*) renegading; (*m.,f.*) renegade.
renegamento (*m.*) = RENEGAÇÃO.
renegar (*v.t.*) to deny, renounce, disown; to disclaim; to abjure, abnegate. [To renege, in the sense of failing to keep a promise, is FALTAR À PALAVRA; to renege in card playing is RENUNCIAR.]
renete [nê] (*m.*) a smith's drawknife [= PUXAVANTE].
rengo –ga (*adj.*) lame.
renguear (*v.i.*) to limp.
renhideiro (*m.*) cockpit.
renhido –da (*adj.*) hotly contested; nip-and-tuck; relentless; furious; bloody.
renhidor –dora (*adj.*) quarrelsome; (*m.,f.*) one given to quarreling; disputatious person.
renhimento (*m.*) quarrel, fight.

renhir [46] (*v.t.*) to contest, contend for; to engage in a fight; (*v.i.*) to contend; to wrangle.
renículo (*m.*, *Anat.*) reniculus.
reniforme (*adj.*) reniform, kidney-shaped.
rênio (*m.*, *Chem.*) rhenium.
renitência (*f.*) renitency.
renitente (*adj.*) renitent, recalcitrant; obstinate, dogged.
Reno (*m.*) Rhine.
renogástrico –ca (*adj.*, *Anat.*) renogastric.
renointestinal [o-i] (*adj.*, *Anat.*) renointestinal.
renome (*m.*) renown, reputation.
renomear (*v.t.*) to reappoint; to make renowned.
renopulmonar (*adj.*, *Anat.*) renopulmonary.
renova (*f.*) new shoot, sprout.
renovação (*f.*), **renovamento** (*m.*) renovation, renewal.
renovar (*v.t.*) to renovate, renew, repair; to refurbish; to restore; (*v.i.*) to sprout anew; to reappear. (*v.r.*) to become rejuvenated, renewed in strength, regenerated; to reappear.—**conhecimento com,** to renew acquaintance with.
renovável (*adj.*) renewable.
renôvo (*m.*) cion, shoot, sprout.
renque (*m.,f.*) row, rank, tier, file.
rentabilidade (*f.*) = RENDABILIDADE.
rentar (*v.i.*) to pass close to (by); (*colloq.*) to taunt, defy, provoke; (*colloq.*) to flirt, court.
rente (*adj.*) close-cut; close by; prompt; assiduous; (*adv.*) close, close to, even with; of haircut, close.
renteado –da (*adj.*) close-clipped, close-cut.
renteador (*m.*) gallant, suitor.
rentear (*v.t.*) to shear; to trim close, cut short (as the hair); (*v.i.*) to act the gallant; to make love.
renuir [72] (*v.t.*) to renounce; to reject.
renúncia (*f.*) renunciation, rejection, abnegation, disavowal; relinquishment; (*Law*) quitclaim.
renunciação (*f.*) renouncement.
renunciador –dora (*adj.*) renouncing; (*m.,f.*) renouncer.
renunciamento (*m.*) = RENÚNCIA.
renunciante (*adj.*) renouncing.
renunciar (*v.t.*) to renounce, reject; to disown; to abjure; to relinquish, resign; to forego, waive; to renege (at cards).—**ao mundo,** to forsake the world.—**ao trono,** to renounce the throne.
renunciativo –va (*adj.*) renunciative.
renunciatório –ria (*adj.*) renunciatory.
renunciável (*adj.*) renunciable.
renutrir (*v.t.*) to renourish; (*v.i.*) to take nourishment.
reocupação (*f.*) reoccupation.
reocupador –dora (*adj.*) reoccupying.
reocupar (*v.t.*) to reoccupy.
reóforo (*m.*, *Elec.*) rheophore.
reômetro (*m.*, *Elec.*) rheometer; galvanometer.
reordenação (*f.*) reordination.
reordenar (*v.t.*) to reordain.
reorganização (*f.*) reorganization; shake-up.
reorganizador –dora (*adj.*) reorganizing; (*m.,f.*) reorganizer.
reorganizar (*v.t.*) to reorganize.
reoscópio (*m.*, *Physics*) rheoscope, galvanoscope.
reostato, reóstato (*m.*, *Elec.*) rheostat.—**do campo,** field rheostat.
reotaxia [ks] (*f.*, *Biol.*) rheotaxis.
reótomo (*m.*, *Elec.*) rheotome, interrupter.
reotropismo (*m.*, *Biol.*) rheotropism.
reótropo, reotrópio (*m.*, *Elec.*) rheotrope, reversing commutator.
reoxidação [ks] (*f.*) reoxidation.
reoxidar [ks] (*v.t.*) to reoxidize.
reoxigenar [ks] (*v.t.*) to reoxygenate.
rep. = REPROVADO (failed—school mark).
Rep. = REPARTIÇÃO (Department).
repagar (*v.t.*) to repay; to pay well.
repanhar (*v.*) = ARREPANHAR.
reparação (*f.*) reparation, repair, restoration; redress, amends, satisfaction.—**pelas armas,** duel.
reparadeira (*adj.; f.*) (woman who is) observing or "nosey".
reparado –da (*adj.*) repaired.
reparador –dora (*adj.*) repairing; (*m.*) repairer; trouble shooter.
reparar (*v.t.*) to repair, restore; to make amends for, atone for; to observe; (*v.i.*) to notice; (*v.r.*) to seek shelter.—**em,** to notice, mark, pay attention to.—**o tempo perdido,** to make up for lost time.—**para,** to look at.

reparável (*adj.*) reparable.

reparo (*m.*) repair, restoration; help, remedy; notice, attention; remark; gun carriage; shield.

repartição (*f.*) partition, distribution, allotment; government bureau.

repartidor –**deira** (*adj.*) dividing, distributing, sharing; (*m.,f.*) one who divides, shares, etc. (see the verb); (*m., Math.*) divisor; (*f.*) small copper pan used in sugar manufacture.

repartimento (*m.*) compartment; pigeon hole (in a desk); till; a small tributary.

repartir (*v.t.*) to divide (**com**, with; **entre**, among); distribute, allot, apportion; to share; (*v.r.*) to scatter.—**os cabelos**, to part the hair.

repartitivo –**va** (*adj.*) distributive.

repartível (*adj.*) distributable.

repassado –**da** (*adj.*) filled full; saturated; (*m.,f.*) = REPASSE.

repassage (*f., Bot.*) bristly oxtongue (*Picris echioides*).

repassagem (*f.*) = REPASSE.

repassar (*v.t.*) to repass; to review, go over; to soak, drench; to glean; (*v.i.*) to ooze, drip; to become saturated.—**na memória**, to remember.

repasse, repasso (*m.*) a gleaning; a going-over.

repastar (*v.t.*) to pasture again; (*v.i.*) to eat one's fill; (*v.r.*) to enjoy oneself.

repasto (*m.*) repast.

repatriação (*f.*) repatriation.

repatriar (*v.t.*) to repatriate; (*v.r.*) to return to one's homeland.

repedir [60] (*v.t.*) to request again.

repelado –**da** (*adj.*) with hair on end (as a startled cat).

repelão (*m.*) rough push.

repelar (*v.*) = ARREPELAR.

repelência (*f.*) repellency.

repelente (*adj.*) repellent, repulsive, disgusting; gruesome.

repelido –**da** (*adj.*) repelled, repulsed.

repelir [21a] (*v.t.*) to repel, repulse; to oppose, rebuff; to snub, spurn; to reject, refuse.—**a força pela força**, to meet force with force.

repelível (*adj.*) that may be repelled or refused.

repêlo (*m.*) rough push.

repender (*v.*) & derivs. = ARREPENDER & derivs.

repenicar (*v.t.*) to cause to sound, esp. by striking, as a bell, an anvil, etc.; to twang a guitar, etc.; (*v.i.*) to jingle-jangle. Cf. REPICAR.

repensar (*v.t.,v.i.*) to rethink.

repente (*m.*) sudden (impulsive, impetuous, rash, hasty, thoughtless) act or utterance; spurt. **de—**, suddenly, all of a sudden; slapdash, slap-bang.

repentino –**na** (*adj.*) sudden, unexpected, precipitate.

repetinoso –**sa** (*adj.*) impulsive, impetuous, thoughtless.

repentista (*m.,f.*) one who improvises short poems, etc.; one who does or says things on the spur of the moment; one who plays music at first sight.

repercussão (*f.*) repercussion.

repercussivo (*adj.*) repercussive.

repercutir (*v.t.*) to drive or beat back; to reflect; to reverberate, re-echo; (*v.i.*) to rebound; to resound.—**-se em**, to be reflected in, have repercussions in.

repergunta (*f.*) cross-examination.

reperguntar (*v.t.*) to reinterrogate; to cross-examine.

repertório (*m.*) list, index, catalogue, calendar; a collection; repertoire.

repes (*m.*) rep (fabric).

repesar (*v.t.*) to re-weigh; to re-examine.

repetenar-se (*v.*) = REFESTELAR-SE.

repetente (*adj.; m.,f.*) repeating (student).

repetição (*f.*) repetition, recurrence; (*Gun.*) repeater.

repetidor –**dora** (*adj.*) repeating; (*m.,f.*) repeater.

repetir [21a] (*v.t.*) to repeat (say or do again); (*v.r.*) to recur, be repeated. **repetidas vezes**, time after time, again and again, over and over.

repicar (*v.t.*) to mince, chop; to rehash; to ring, chime, peal, toll (bells); to transplant seedlings; (*v.i.*) to ring, peal, toll; of billiard balls, to strike a second time. Cf. REPENICAR.

repimpado –**da** (*adj.*) lolling, lounging, stretched out (in an easy chair); puffed up (with pride).

repimpar (*v.t.*) to cram with food, fill the belly; (*v.r.*) to loll, stretch out (as in an easy chair after dinner).

repimponado –**da** (*adj.*) filled with self-conceit.

repinchar (*v.i.*) to splash; to rebound.

repincho (*m.*) splash; bound.

repintar (*v.t.*) to repaint; to smudge.

repique (*m.*) a pealing (of church bells); a re-striking (of billiard balls).

repiquête (*m.*) rapid pealing of bells; freshet; short dry spell during rainy season; (*pl.*) baffling winds. "(1) in Ceará, a drought with calamitous consequences; (2) in the lower Amazon basin, a rise in the level of the river in November, caused by spring rains in the region of the headwaters." [*GBAT*]—**de chuva**, dearth of rains.

repisar (*v.t.*) to tread again (as grapes); to repeat, reiterate; to hash over; harp on, dwell tediously on (a subject).

repisativo –**va** (*adj.*) repetitious.

repiscar (*v.t.*) to blink the eyes.

replanta (*f.*) a planting or replanting of sparse patches in a field, or of a clearing in the woods; a tree planted in replacement of one cut down.

replantação (*f.*), **replantio** (*m.*) a re-planting.

replantar (*v.t.*) to re-plant.

repleção (*f.*) repletion, surfeit.

repleto –**ta** (*adj.*) replete, full; crammed.

réplica (*f.*) retort, reply, rejoinder, rebuttal, refutation, repartee; (*Fine Arts*) replica, reproduction; (*Music*) replica, repeat.

replicação (*f.*) replication, rejoinder.

replicador –**dora** (*adj.*) replying, rejoining; (*m.,f.*) one who replies, rebuts, retorts.

replicar (*v.t.,v.i.*) to reply, rebut, rejoin, retort; to talk back.

repoisar (*v.*) & derivs. = REPOUSAR & derivs.

repolêgo (*m.*) ornamental fillet.

repolhal (*adj.*) cabbage; (*m.*) cabbage patch.

repolhinho (*m.*) a little cabbage.—**s de Bruxelas**, Brussels sprouts.

repôlho (*m.*) cabbage.—**chinês**, pakchoi, Chinese cabbage (*Brassica chinensis*), ca.. COUVE-CHINÊSA.

repolhudo –**da** (*adj.*) round, plump (as a cabbage).

repolir (*v.t.*) to repolish; to refine, perfect.

repoltrear-se (*v.*) = REFESTELAR-SE.

reponta (*f.*) new point; beginning of flood tide.

repontão –**tona** (*adj.*) recalcitrant; (*m.,f.*) one who talks back when reprimanded.

repontar (*v.i.*) to show, come into view, begin to appear; to talk back, retort, reply in kind; to turn and fight; of the tide, to come in.

repor [63] (*v.t.*) to replace, put back; to restore.

reportação (*f.*) act of turning back, etc.;—see the verb REPORTAR.

reportado –**da** (*adj.*) moderate; patient.

reportagem (*f.*) newspaper reporting; a factual report; a reporter's report; resporters collectively.

reportamento (*m.*) = REPORTAÇÃO.

reportar (*v.t.*) to turn (carry) back (to the past); to obtain, achieve; (*v.t.,v.r.*) to moderate.—**-se a**, to refer, turn to (a page, a list, a report, etc.).

reporte (*m., London stock exchange*) contango, continuation. [But not a report, which is NOTÍCIA, INFORMAÇÃO, RELATÓRIO.]

repórter (*m.,f.*) reporter, news writer.

reposição (*f.*) replacement.

repositório (*m.*) repository.

repostada, repostaça (*f.*) coarse or rude reply.

repostar (*v.t.*) to reply.

reposteiro (*m.*) drapes, hangings, portiere; (*obs.*) housekeeper, steward.

repôsto –**ta** (*adj.*) replaced; restored.

repotrear-se (*v.*) = REFESTELAR-SE.

reposado –**da** (*adj.*) reposing, quiet, calm.

repousante (*adj.*) restful.

repousar (*v.i.*) to repose, rest; to lie, sleep. Var. REPOISAR.

repouso (*m.*) repose, rest; ease, quiet. Var. REPOISO.

repovoar (*v.t.*) to repeople, repopulate; to restock (with animals).

repreendedor –**dora** [e-e] (*adj.*) reprehending; (*m.,f.*) reprehender.

repreender [e-e] (*v.t.*) to reprehend, reprimand, reprove, admonish, chide, censure, take to task.

repreensão [e-e] (*f.*) reprehension, reproof, reprimand, admonition.

repreensível [e-e] (*adj.*) reprehensible, censurable, blameworthy.

repreensivo –**va** [e-e] (*adj.*) that reprehends or conveys reprehension or reproof.

repreensor –**sora** [e-e] (*adj.*) = REPREENSIVO.

repregar (*v.t.*) to renail; to reinforce.

reprêsa (*f.*) dam; body of dammed water; pent-up feeling; stand, pedestal, console.
represado **-da** (*adj.*) repressed; dammed up.
represador **-dora** (*adj.*) that represses, quells; that dams up.
represadura (*f.*), **-amento** (*m.*) act of repressing, etc.;— see the verb REPRESAR.
represália (*f.*) reprisal, retaliation.
represar (*v.t.*) to repress, restrain; to quell; to dam (up).
representação (*f.*) representation, exhibition; acting,performance; protestation, remonstrance; an allowance of money for cost of entertainment while in government or diplomatic service abroad.—**das minorias**, minority representation.—**proporcional**, proportional representation.
representador **-dora** (*adj.*) representing; (*m.,f.*) representer.
representante (*adj.; m.,f.*) representative.
representar (*v.t.*) to represent, exhibit, show; to act (play a role on the stage); to portray, depict; to expostulate; to stand for; to act in the place of; (*v.i.*) to appear; (*v.r.*) to be represented, be shown.
representativo **-va** (*adj.*) representative.
representável (*adj.*) representable.
representear (*v.t.*) to make a return gift to.
reprêso **-sa** (*adj.*) re-arrested; repressed.
repressão (*f.*) repression, suppression.
repressivo **-va** (*adj.*) repressive.
repressor **-sora** (*adj.*) repressing; (*m.,f.*) represser.
reprimenda (*f.*) reprimand, rebuke.
reprimendar (*v.i.*) to reprimand.
reprimir (*v.t.*) to repress, subdue; to quash; to squelch; to quell; to stifle; to restrain, check; to keep back, keep down, keep in.
reprimível (*adj.*) that can be repressed.
reprincipiar (*v.i.*) to begin again or anew.
reprise (*f.*) repeat performance or showing.
reprobatório **-ria** (*adj.*) reprobatory, reprobative.
reprôbo **-ba** (*adj.; m.,f.*) reprobate.
reprochar (*v.t.*) to reproach, rebuke, upbraid.
reproche (*m.*) reproach, rebuke.
reprodução (*f.*) reproduction.
reprodutibilidade (*f.*) reproducibility.
reprodutível (*adj.*) reproducible.
reprodutivo **-va** (*adj.*) reproductive.
reprodutor **-triz** (*adj.*) reproducing; (*m.,f.*) reproducer; (*m.*) stud-horse, bull, etc.; (*f.*) brood mare, cow, etc.
reproduzir [36] (*v.t.*) to reproduce, multiply; to propagate, generate; to copy, imitate.
reproduzível (*adj.*) reproducible.
reprometer (*v.t.*) to repromise.
repromissão (*f.*) a second or new promise; a mutual promise.
reprovação (*f.*) reproval, reproof, disapproval; disapprobation.
reprovado **-da** (*adj.*) reproved; refused rejected; failed, "flunked" (in exam); (*m. f.*) person who flunks an exam.
reprovador **-dora** (*adj.*) reproving; (*m.,f.*) reprover.
reprovar (*v.t.*) to reprove; to take to task; to reject, turn down; to fail, "flunk"; to damn, condemn, disapprove of.
reprovável (*adj.*) reprovable, censurable.
reps (*m.*) = REPES.
reptação (*f.*) = REPTO.
reptador **-dora, reptante** (*adj.*) challenging, defying; (*m.,f.*) challenger.
reptar (*v.t.*) to defy challenge.
reptil [-tis], **réptil** [-teis] (*adj.; m.*) reptile.
repto (*m.*) challenge, defiance.
república (*f.*) republic; (*colloq.*) group of students living together; the place in which they live.
republicanismo (*m.*) republicanism.
republicanizar (*v.t.*) to republicanize.
republicano **-na** (*adj.; m.,f.*) republican.
republicar (*v.t.*) to republish.
repúblico **-ca** (*adj.; m.,f.*) republican.
republiqueta [quê] (*f.*) "banana" republic. [*Derogatory.*]
repudiação (*f.*) repudiation.
repudiada (*f.*) woman who, legally or otherwise, has been ousted by her husband.
repudiador **-dora, repudiante** (*adj.*) repudiating; (*m..f.*) repudiator.
repudiar (*v.t.*) to repudiate, reject; to disown; to disavow; to divorce, put away.
repúdio (*m.*) repudiation; denial; disavowal.

repugnância (*f.*) repugnance, aversion, reluctance; disgust; opposition, contrariness. **sentir—por**, to loathe.
repugnante (*adj.*) repugnant, offensive; nasty; contrary.
repugnar (*v.t.*) to fight against, resist, oppose, repel; to disgust; to cause repugnance to; to feel repugnance for.
repulsão (*f.*) repulse, repulsion, rebuff; repugnance; disgust; abhorrence; hostility; (*Physics*) repulsion.
repulsar (*v.t.*) to repulse, repel.
repulsivo **-va** (*adj.*) repulsive; repellent; obscene.
repulso **-sa** (*adj.*) rejected, spurned, rebuffed; (*f.*) repulse, rebuff; repulsion, repugnance.
repulular (*v.i.*) to bud or sprout again.
repulverizar (*v.t.*) to repulverize.
repurgar (*v.t.*) to repurge.
repurificar (*v.t.*) to repurify.
reputação (*f.*) reputation, fame. **má—**, disrepute.
reputadamente (*adv.*) reputedly.
reputado **-da** (*adj.*) reputed.—**em**, valued at.
reputar (*v.t.*) to repute, regard, reckon, deem; to give a good name to; (*v.r.*) to hold oneself to be, regard oneself as.
repuxadeira (*f.*) stretcher, wire-stretcher.
repuxado **-da** (*adj.*) drawn back; spruce, neat.
repuxão (*m.*) strong pull or jerk.
repuxar (*v.t.*) to pull (jerk, draw) back; to draw tight; to prop, shore up; (*v.i.*) to gush, spout.
repuxo (*m.*) waterspout, water fountain; talus, sloping side of a wall; recoil, kick (of a gun); (*slang*) tough situation.
requebém (*m.*) tail end of an oxcart.
requebrado **-da** (*adj.*) languishing, tender, amorous, sentimental; mincing; (*Bot.*) refracted; (*m.*) voluptuous movement of the body, esp. while dancing.
requebrar (*v.t.*) to court, woo; (*v.r.*) to move the body in a wanton manner while walking or dancing.
requêbro (*m.*) languishing look; sentimental or amorous expression; voluptuous movement; (*Music*) trill.
requeijão (*m.*) curd cheese; milk curds.
requeima[ção] (*f.*) a burning, scorching, or parching (as of plants).
requeimado **-da** (*adj.*) burned, parched, scorched, dried up.
requeimar (*v.t.*) to scorch, parch; to dry up; (*v.i.*) of spices, to bite, smart.
requeira, requeiras, etc., forms of REQUERER [70].
requentado **-da** (*adj.*) reheated (referring esp. to food); warmed-over (as coffee); much discussed, hashed-over.
requentão (*m.*) coffee with cognac; hot toddy.
requentar (*v.t.*) to reheat; to warm over (food); (*v.r.*) of food, to become unpalatable from overheating.
requeredor **-dora, requerente** (*adj.*) petitioning; (*m.,f.*) petitioner, applicant; plaintiff.
reque-reque (*m.*) = RECO-RECO.
requerer [70] (*v.t.*) to request, solicit, petition for; to require, call for, exact, demand.
requerido **-da** (*adj.*) requested, petitioned; required, demanded.
requerimento (*m.*) formal petition; application.
requestar (*v.t.*) to request, solicit (favors); to woo, make love to.
réquiem (*m.*) Requiem (Mass, music).
requietório (*m.*) the grave. [*Poetical*]
requififes (*m.pl.*) finery; affected manners.
requinta (*f.*) high-pitched clarinet; small, high-pitched guitar.
requintado **-da** (*adj.*) exquisite, consummate; of rare excellence or refinement; of speech, manners, style, etc., highly refined, polished, perfected; of persons, highly cultured, accomplished, clever.
requintar (*v.t.*) to perfect, refine to the highest degree (style, manners, speech, etc.).
requinte (*m.*) refinement; height, acme (of perfection, generosity, stupidity, etc.).
requisição (*f.*) requisition, request, demand.
requisitar (*v.t.*) to requisition, demand, press into service; to commandeer.
requisito (*m.*) requisite, requirement.
res. = RESERVA (military reserve).
rés (*adj.*) close, level; (*adv.*) close to.
rês [reses] (*f.*) steer, pig, goat, sheep or other four-footed animal used as food; (*pl.*) livestock, cattle.
rescaldado **-da** (*adj.*) disillusioned; scalded.
rescaldar (*v.t.*) to scald.
rescaldeiro (*m.*) chafer; brazier.

rescaldo (*m.*) reflected heat, as from a furnace; hot cinders; chafer.

rescindir (*v.t.*) to rescind, annul, cancel, repeal.

rescindível (*adj., Law*) defeasible.

rescisão (*f.*) rescission, abrogation, repeal, cancelling (of a contract, etc.).

rescrever [44] (*v.t.*) to rewrite.

rescrição (*f.*) a written money order.

rescrito (*m.*) rescript.

rés-do-chão (*m.*) ground floor.

resedá (*m.*), **reseda** [sê] (*f., Bot.*) common mignonette (*Reseda odorata*), or its flower; also, a perfume made therefrom.—**amarela**, Brazil thryallis (*T. brasiliensis*), c.a. QUARÓ, TINTUREIRA.—**grande**, henna (*Lawsonia inermis*), c.a. RESEDAL.

resedáceo -cea (*adj.; Bot.*) resedaceous; (*f.pl.*) the mignonette family (*Resedaceae*).

resedal (*m., Bot.*) henna (*Lawsonia inermis*), c.a. RESEDÁ-GRANDE.

resenha (*f.*) detailed report; summary; descriptive list; enumeration; inventory.—**de obras e seus autores**, a list of writings and their authors.—**do mercado**, market report.—**semanal**, weekly (news) survey.

resenhar (*v.t.*) to draw up a detailed list or summary of.

reserva (*f.*) reserve, extra supply; military reserve; reservedness, aloofness; reservation, proviso.—**mental**, mental reservation. **de**—, spare, in reserve. **fundo de**—, reserve fund. **pôr de**—, to set aside, store away. **sem**—, unreservedly.

reservação (*f.*) reservation. [But not tract of public land, which is TERRITÓRIO RESERVADO.]

reservado -da (*adj.*) reserved; stiff, standoffish; undemonstrative; secretive; cautious, circumspect; (*m.*) a private booth (as in a restaurant).

reservar (*v.t.*) to reserve, keep (back), hold (back), store up; to withhold; to lay aside, reserve for future use.

reservatório (*m.*) reservoir.—**de água**, water reservoir; water tank.—**de ar**, air tank, chamber, etc.—**de gás**, gasholder.—**de óleo**, oil tank.

reservista (*m., Milit.*) reservist.

resfolegadouro (*m.*) air vent, air hole.

resfol[e]gar (71) (*v.i.*) to pant, puff; to catch one's breath; (*v.t.*) to blow (smoke) as a locomotive.

resfôl[e]go (*m.*) panting, breathing.

resfriadeira (*f.*) cooling place.

resfriado -da (*adj.*) suffering from a cold; chilled; cold, indifferent; (*m.*) common cold.—**do peito**, chest cold. **apanhar um**—, to catch a cold.

resfriador -dora (*adj.*) cooling, chilling; (*m.*) cooler.

resfriamento (*m.*) cooling; head cold.

resfriar (*v.t.*) to cool, chill, to allay, moderate; (*v.r.*) to catch cold; to grow cool; to grow lukewarm.

resgatabilidade (*f.*) redeemability.

resgatador -dora (*adj.*) redeeming, ransoming; (*m.,f.*) redeemer, ransomer.

resgatar (*v.t.*) to ransom, rescue, liberate, redeem; to pay off (a mortgage, note, debt).

resgatável (*adj.*) redeemable.

resgate (*m.*) ransom; redemption, deliverance.

resguardar (*v.t.*) to guard, protect, safeguard; to shield, shelter.

resguardo (*m.*) guard, protection, shield; defense; care, watchfulness; secrecy; discretion; regimen, diet.

residência (*f.*) residence, dwelling, abode, house, home; a railroad division.

residente (*adj.*) resident; residing, dwelling; present, inherent; (*m.*) resident [but only in the sense of a diplomatic agent residing at a foreign seat of government. A resident, in the ordinary sense of dweller, is MORADOR.]

residir (*v.i.*) to reside, dwell, abide, live, inhabit; to inhere.

residual (*adj.*) residual.

residuário -ria (*adj.*) residuary.

resíduo -dua (*adj.*) residual; (*m.*) residue, residuum, remainder.

resignação (*f.*) resignation, renunciation; forbearance, long-suffering.

resignado -da (*adj.*) resigned; uncomplaining.

resignante (*adj.*) resigning; (*m.,f.*) resigner.

resignar (*v.t.*) to resign, quit, renounce; (*v.r.*) to resign oneself, become resigned (**a, em, com**, to).

resignatário -ria (*adj.*) resigning; (*m.,f.*) resigner (of an office).

resignável (*adj.*) that may be resigned.

resiliência (*f.*) resiliency; elasticity.

resiliente (*adj.*) resilient.

resilir (*v.*) = RESCINDIR.

resina (*f.*) resin; rosin.—**amarela**, wood rosin.—**de cumerone**, coumarone resin.—**de pinho líquida**, rosin spirit.—**de sandáraca**, sandarac.—**fóssil**, fossil resin; amber.—**goma**, gum resin.—**sintética**, synthetic resin.

resinação (*f.*) = RESINAGEM.

resinado -da (*adj.*) containing resin.

resinagem (*f.*) extraction of resin; treatment with resin.

resinar (*v.t.*) to extract resin from; to resin; to resinate; to resinify.

resinato (*m., Chem.*) resinate.

resineiro (*m.*) resin extractor.

resinento -ta (*adj.*) resiniferous; resinous.

resinífero -ra (*adj.*) resiniferous.

resinificar (*v.t.*) to resinify.

resiniforme (*adj.*) resinoid.

resino-extrativo -va (*adj.*) resinoextractive.

resinóide (*adj.*) resinoid.

resinoso -sa (*adj.*) resinous.

resistência (*f.*) resistance, opposition; strength, endurance, stamina; (*Elec.*) resistance.—**à tração**, tensile strength.—**dielétrica**, dielectric resistance.—**passiva**, passive resistance. **prato de**—, main dish, pièce de résistance.

resistente (*adj.*) resistant; hardy; tough; stubborn.

resistir (*v.t.*) to resist, oppose, withstand; (*v.i.*) to endure, last.—**ao uso**, to wear well.

resistível (*adj.*) resistible.

resistividade (*f., Elec.*) resistivity.

reslumbrar (*v.i.*) to come to light (as a secret).

resma [ê] (*f.*) ream (of paper).

resmonear, resmunear (*v.*) = RESMUNGAR.

resmungão -gona (*adj.*) grumbling, grouchy; (*m.,f.*) grumbler, grouch.

resmungar (*v.t.,v.i.*) to grumble, mutter, mumble; to "gripe".

resmungo (*m.*) grumble; gripe.

resmuninhar (*v.*) = RESMUNGAR.

reso (*m.*) rhesus monkey.

resolto -ta (*adj.*) resolved; dissolved. [Verb: RESOLVER].

resolubilidade (*f.*) resolubility, resolubleness.

resolução (*f.*) resolution, decision; resolve, intention; firmness, determination; (*Chem., Med., Music*) resolution.—**heróica**, heroic decision.

resolutivo -va (*adj.*) serving to dissolve; operating to resolve; (*m., Med.*) a resolvent or discutient.

resoluto -ta (*adj.*) resolute, staunch, stalwart, sturdy, determined, undaunted, unflinching; dissolved; resolved.

resolutório -ria (*adj.*) serving to resolve.

resolúvel (*adj.*) resoluble.

resolvente (*adj.; m.*) resolvent.

resolver (*v.t.*) to resolve, dissolve; to solve, unravel; to decide, determine; (*v.r.*) to resolve, decide, make up one's mind (**a, to; sôbre**, about).—**se em**, to turn into.—**o assunto**, to decide (settle) a matter.

resolvido -da (*adj.*) resolved, decided upon; resolute.

resolvível (*adj.*) resolvable, solvable.

resorcina (*f., Chem.*) resorcin(ol).

respaldar (*v.t.*) to render smooth (field, roadway, etc.); to repair (a worn or torn page); (*m.*) = ESPALDAR.

respaldo (*m.*) a smoothing (out) of something, as a roadway; upholstered back rest, as in a coach; chair back; saddle gall.

respançar (*v.t.*) to erase [= RASPAR].

respanço (*m.*) erasure [= RASPADURA].

respe (*m.*) rebuke; dressing down.

respe[c]tivo -va (*adj.*) respective, particular, own; several, single, individual.

respeitabilidade (*f.*) respectability.

respeitador -dora (*adj.*) respecting; (*m.,f.*) respecter.

respeitar (*v.t.*) to respect, esteem, honor; to spare, treat with consideration; to heed, consider; to relate to, bear upon.

respeitável (*adj.*) respectable, respected, honorable; considerable, sizable.

respeito (*m.*) respect, esteem, consideration; bearing, aspect, point of view; (*pl.*) respects, compliments, regards.—**a**, concerning. **a**—, in that respect, concerning. **a—de** or **com—a**, concerning, with respect to, about. **falta de**—, disrespect. **que diz—a**, as regards, regarding, respecting.

respeitoso –sa (*adj.*) respectful, deferential, courteous, polite.

respiga (*f.*) a gleaning; (*Carp.*) mortise.—**e mecha,** mortise and tenon.

respigadeira (*adj.*) gleaning; (*f.*) gleaner; mortiser (machine).

respigador –dora (*adj.*) gleaning; (*m.,f.*) gleaner.

respigadura (*f.*) = RESPIGA.

respigão (*m.*) hangnail.

respigar (*v.t.*) to glean; to gather (pick up) here and there.

respigo (*m.*) a gleaning [= RESPIGA].

respingador –dora, **respingão** –gona (*adj.*) surly, recalcitrant; (*m.,f.*) recalcitrant.

respingar (*v.t.*) to spatter, splash; to sputter, spit; to recalcitrate, kick against.

respiração (*f.*) respiration, breathing.

respirador –dora (*adj.*) breathing; (*m.*) respirator.

respiradouro (*m.*) vent, air hole; air shaft.

respiramento (*m.*) respiration; breathing spell.

respirante (*adj.*) respiratory.

respirar (*v.i.*) to breathe, inhale air; to have or enjoy a breathing space, or respite; (*v.t.*) to breathe, exhale; (*m.*) breathing.

respiratório –ria (*adj.*) respiratory. **aparelho**—, (*Anat.*) respiratory system.

respirável (*adj.*) respirable.

respiro (*m.*) breath, breathing; respite, breathing spell; air vent, air hole.

resplandecência (*f.*) resplendence.

resplandecente (*adj.*) resplendent, very bright; shining; splendid.

resplandecer (*v.i.*) to shine resplendently; to be resplendent; (*v.t.*) to reflect resplendently.

resplandente (*adj.*) = RESPLENDENTE.

resplandor (*m.*) = RESPLENDOR.

resplandecer (*v.*) = RESPLANDECER.

resplendência (*f.*) resplendence, splendor, great brightness.

resplendente (*adj.*) resplendent.

resplender (*v.*) = RESPLANDECER.

resplêndido –da (*adj.*) very splendid.

resplendor (*m.*) splendor, brightness, refulgence; glory, fame, renown.

resplendoroso –sa (*adj.*) splendorous.

respondão –dona (*adj.*) churlish, impolite, given to rude answers; (*m.,f.*) an uncivil, discourteous person who indulges in rude answers; a smart aleck.

respondência (*f.*) respondence, respondency.

respondente (*adj.; m.,f.*) respondent.

responder (*v.t.*) to respond, answer, reply, rejoin; to correspond, accord.—**com sete pedras na mão,** to give a rude (coarse, angry) answer.—**por,** to answer (account, be responsible) for.

respondível (*adj.*) answerable.

respondona, fem. of RESPONDÃO.

responsabilidade (*f.*) responsibility, accountability; liability. **lançar a**—**sôbre outrem,** to put the blame on someone else.

responsabilizar (*v.t.*) to hold (make, consider) responsible for.—**se por,** to be responsible for.

responsar (*v.t., Eccl.*) to say responses for the departed; (*colloq.*) to pray to S. Anthony for the return of something lost; to speak evil of others.

responsável (*adj.*) responsible (**por,** for); answerable, liable, accountable.

responsivo –va (*adj.*) responsive.

responso (*m., Eccl.*) response; prayer to S. Anthony for the return of something lost; (*colloq.*) a dressing down, scolding.

responsório (*m., Eccl.*) responsory.

resposta (*f.*) response, answer, reply, rejoinder, retort; (*Fencing*) riposte.—**aguda,** sharp answer.—**ao pé da letra,** literal answer.—**pronta,** ready answer.—**sêca,** dry answer.—**torta,** crooked answer.—**viva,** apt, clever answer. **a modo de**—, by way of answer. **não tem**—, there is no answer. **sempre de**—**engatilhada,** always ready with an answer.

respostada (*f.*) uncivil reply; comeback.

respostar (*v.i.*) to answer discourteously.

resquício (*m.*) dregs, remains, leftovers, leavings; tiny bits; trace, vestige; chink, crack.

ressaber [74] (*v.t.*) to know very well; (*v.i.*) to taste strongly of.

ressabiado –da (*adj.*) skittish, timorous; chary; scared; resentful.

ressabiar (*v.i.,v.r.*) to turn bad-tasting; to become displeased; of animals, to become skittish.

ressabido –da (*adj.*) notorious, well-known; learned, erudite.

ressábio (*m.*) = RESSAIBO.

ressaca (*f.*) a rebounding billow; undertow; (*colloq.*) a hang-over. "(1) a small lake in the winter; a puddle in the process of drying up at the beginning of summer; (2) a small gulf." [*GBAT*]

ressacado –da (*adj.*) suffering from a hang-over; (*m.,f.*) person on whom a bill of exchange is redrawn.

ressacar (*v.t.*) to redraw (a bill of exchange); (*v.r.*) to get a hang-over.

ressaibo (*m.*) rancidity, sour aftertaste; resentment; vestige, trace; ornery behavior of an animal.

ressair [75] (*v.i.*) to go out again; to project above, stand out.

ressalgar (*v.t.*) to resalt.

ressaltado –da (*adj.*) salient.

ressaltar (*v.i.*) of facts, differences, etc., to stand out; to rebound (as a rubber ball); (*v.t.*) to cause to stand out; to throw into relief; to set forth; to emphasize, underscore.

ressalte (*m.*) salience; also = RESSALTO.

ressaltear (*v.t.*) to re-assault.

ressalto (*m.*) protuberance, prominence; bound, rebound; (*Arch.*) projection. **eixo de**—**s,** camshaft. **em**—, protruding.

ressalva (*f.*) reservation, exception; proviso; safety clause; (*Law*) defeasance.—**de entrelinha,** initialing of an insertion by its writer.

ressalvar (*v.t.*) to make a reservation or exception; to insert a proviso or safety clause; to initial an insertion; to safeguard; to make a defeasance.

ressangrar (*v.t.*) to bleed again.

ressaque (*m.*) redraft of a bill of exchange.

ressarcimento (*L.*) indemnification, amends; an offsetting; war indemnity.—**de prejuizos,** indemnity for losses.

ressarcir [46] (*v.t.*) to indemnify, compensate (for); to make amends to; to renew, remodel.

ressaudar [a-u, 10] (*v.t.*) to greet again; to greet one another; (*v.i.*) to respond to a greeting.

ressecar (*v.t.*) to dry again; to dry (up), parch; (*Surg.*) to resect; (*v.r.*) to dry out.

resse[c]ção (*f., Surg.*) resection.

ressêco –ca (*adj.*) very dry.

ressegar (*v.t.*) to mow again.

ressegundar (*v.t.*) to repeat again and again.

ressegurar (*v.t.*) to reinsure.

resseguro –ra (*adj.*) reinsured; (*m.*) reinsurance.

resselar (*v.t.*) to reseal.

ressemear (*v.t.*) to sow again.

ressentido –da (*adj.*) hurt, sore, offended; easily piqued.

ressentimento (*m.*) resentment, pique, umbrage, grudge.

ressentir [21a] (*v.t.*) to feel again.—**se de,** to be resentful of; to feel keenly; to feel the need of; to feel the effects of.—**se do calor,** to feel the heat.

ressequido –da (*adj.*) parched, shriveled up, desiccated.

ressequir [46] (*v.t.*) to desiccate, shrivel, dry up.

resserenar (*v.i.,v.r.*) to grow quiet again.

resservir (*v.t.*) to serve again.

ressoador –dora (*adj.*) resounding; (*m.*) resonator.

ressoamento (*m.*) act of resounding.

ressoante (*adj.*) resounding.

ressoar (*v.t.,v.i.*) to resound, echo, re-echo.

ressoca (*f.*) third cutting of sugar cane.

ressoldar (*v.t.*) to reweld; to resolder.

ressonador –dora (*adj.*) resounding; (*m.,f.*) resounder; resonator.

ressonância (*f.*) resonance.

ressonante (*adj.*) resonant.

ressonar (*v.t.*) to resound; (*v.i.*) to snore.

ressono (*m.*) deep sleep.

ressoprar (*v.t.*) to blow again.

ressorção (*f.*) reabsorption; resorption.

ressorver (*v.t.*) to reabsorb.

ressuar (*v.i.*) to sweat freely.

ressubir (*v.t.,v.i.*) to climb again or anew.

ressudação (*f.*) perspiration, transpiration.

ressudar (*v.t.,v.i.*) to transpire, sweat.

ressumar, ressumbrar (*v.t.*) to sweat, drip, exude; (*v.i.*) to ooze, percolate; to let transpire.

ressunção (*f.*) resumption.

ressupino –na (*adj.*) bent backward; (*Bot.*) resupinate.

ressurgência (f.) resurgence.
ressurgente (adj.) resurgent.
ressurgido –da (adj.) resurrected.
ressurgimento (m.) resurgence; revivification; renascence.
ressurgir (v.i.) to resurge, rise again, come to life.
ressurecto –ta (adj.) resurrected; revived.
ressureição (f.) resurrection, rising; [cap.] the Resurrection.
ressureicionista (m.,f., slang) body snatcher.
ressuscitação (f.) resuscitation; restoration; revival; renewal.
ressuscitamento (m.) = RESSUREIÇÃO.
ressuscitar (v.t.) to resuscitate, bring back to life; to renew, revive; (v.i.) to resurge, rise again.
ressuscitável (adj.) resuscitable.
restabelecedor –dora (adj.) reëstablishing; (m.,f.) reëstablisher.
restabelecer (v.t.) to reëstablish, restore; (v.r.) to rally, be restored to health.
restabelecido –da (adj.) reëstablished; restored to health.
restabelecimento (m.) reëstablishment.—de saúde, recovery of health.
resta-boi (m., Bot.) a restharow (Ononis procurrens).
restante (adj.) remaining, left-over; (m.) remainder.
restar (v.i.) to remain, be left over (behind); to be left (a, to; de, of). Resta-lhe um cruzeiro, He has one cruzeiro left.
restauração (f.) restoration, reëstablishment, renewal, repair.
restaurado –da (adj.) restored; reëstablished.
restaurador –dora (adj.) restoring; (m.,f.) restorer.
restaurante (adj.) restoring; (m.) restaurant; restorer. carro—, dining car.
restaurar (v.t.) to restore, replace; to repair; to reinstate. —se de, to recover from (illness, fatigue).
restaurativo –va (adj.) restorative.
restaurável (adj.) restorable.
reste (m., Billiards) rest, bridge.
restelar (v.) = RASTELAR.
resteva [tê] (f.) stubble.
réstia (f.) a short length of braided rope grass (Restio sp.) used for stringing heads of onions, garlic, etc.; ray of light.
restício (m.) small remainder.
restilação (f.) redistillation.
restilar (v.t.) to redistill.
restilo (m.) redistillation; (colloq.) = CACHAÇA.
restinga (f.) sand bank; salt marsh; shelf, reef; a long strip of wooded land bordering a river or the sea coast; spit of land. "(1) in northern Brazil, a stretch of beach, recently covered by mud, which usually rises up out of the water parallel to the coast; isolated, long, recently formed lowland." [GBAT]
réstio (m.) a genus (Restio) comprising the cordleaf or rope grass.
restionáceas (f.pl.) a family (Restionaceae) of rushlike herbs.
restituição [u-i] (f.) restitution, restoration, return.
restituidor –dora [u-i] (adj.) restoring; (m.,f.) one who makes restitution.
restituir [72] (v.t.) to restore, return, refund, give back; to replace, put back; to reinstate; to repair, restore; to compensate, make amends for.—se em, to reinstate oneself in (power, another's graces, etc.).
restituitório –ria [u-i], restitutório –ria (adj.) restitutory.
restituível (adj.) returnable, restorable.
resto (m.) rest, remainder, residue, left-over; (Billiards) cue rest; (pl.) ruins; mortal remains; scraps.—s de cozinha, (Archaeol.) kitchen midden. de—, besides, moreover, for that matter; actually, in fact, really. quanto ao—, as for the rest.
restolhada (f.) a quantity of stubble; rustling noise.
restolhal (m.) stubble field.
restolhar (v.i.) to make a noise as of walking on dry leaves, twigs, etc.; to search among leftovers; (v.t.) to glean.
restôlho (m.) stubble; stubble field; a rustling noise.
restribar (v.i.,v.r.) to stand firm, "pat"; to resist stubbornly.—se em, to stand firmly on.
restrição (f.) restriction, limitation; shortage (of supply). —mental, mental reservation.
restringência (f.) stringency.
restringente (adj.; m.) astringent.
restringir (v.t.) to restrict, limit, confine; to restrain; to

curtail; to cramp; (v.r.) to be limited; to limit oneself.— —se aos fatos, to stick to the facts.
restritivo –va (adj.) restrictive; (f., Gram.) restrictive clause.
restrito –ta (adj.) restricted, limited.
restrugir (v.i.) to resound, echo loudly.
restucar (v.t.) to replaster.
resultado (m.) result, outcome, consequence, effect, end; conclusion. não dar—, to result in nothing.
resultante (adj.) resultant; (f., Mech.) resultant force.
resultar (v.i.) to result.—de, to result from, follow from, ensue from, be derived from.—em, to result in, end in.
resumido –da (adj.) resumed; reduced; abbreviated.
resumir (v.t.) to summarize, epitomize; to make an abstract of; to sum up.—a, to reduce to. (v.r.) to be brief. —se a, to limit oneself to.—se em, to be reduced to. [To resume, in the sense of reassume, is REASSUMIR.]
resumo (m.) résumé, summary, abstract. em—, in short; briefly.
resvaladiço –ça, resvaladio –dia (adj.) slippery; (m.) a slippery place.
resvaladouro (m.) a slide, skid; steep place.
resvaladura (f.), resvalamento (m.) a slip(ping).
resvalar (v.i.) to slip, slide, glide, skid.
resvalo (m.) a slipping or sliding; a steep place.
reta (f.) straight line; a stretch of track or road; stretch of a racecourse.
retábulo (m., Eccl.) retable.
retaco –ca, retacado –da (adj.) squat, thickset, stubby.
retaguarda (f.) rear, rear guard.
retal (adj.) rectal.
retalhação (f.) a shredding of substances.
retalhadista (adj.) retailing; (m.,f.) retailer.
retalhado –da (adj.) shredded, slashed, cut (into pieces).
retalhar (v.t.) to cut (into pieces); to slash; to shred; to cut up; to sell at retail; to sterilize (but not geld) a horse.
retalhista (adj.) retailing; (m.,f.) retailer.
retalho (m.) piece, remnant, scrap, shred, slice, fraction; a patch of cloth. a—, at retail. colcha de—s, crazy quilt.
retaliação (f.) retaliation, reprisal, retribution; tit for tat.
retaliar (v.t.,v.i.) to retaliate.
retaliativo –va (adj.) retaliatory.
retama (f., Bot.) woadwaxen (Genista), c.a. GIESTA.
retambana (f., colloq.) a dressing down, bawling out.
retamente (adv.) uprightly, honestly.
retangular (adj.) rectangular; right-angled.
retângulo –la (adj.) rectangular; (m.) rectangle.
retardação (f.) retardation, delay, slowdown; lag.
retardado –da (adj.) (mentally) retarded; slow, delayed; postponed; (m.,f.) mentally retarded person.
retardador –dora (adj.) retarding, delaying; (m.) decelerator.
retardamento (m.), retardança (f.) = RETARDAÇÃO.
retardão –dona (adj.) slow-moving, easy-going; (m.,f.) slow poke.
retardar (v.t.) to retard, delay; to defer; to impede, hinder; to decelerate, slow down; (v.r.) to linger, loiter, tarry.
retardatário –ria (adj.) late, tardy; (m.,f.) latecomer; straggler; laggard.
retardativo –va (adj.) delaying, hindering, impeding.
retarde (m.) = RETARDAÇÃO.
retardio –dia (adj.) tardy, late; slow.
retelhar (v.t.) to re-roof.
retém (m.) retention; spare; depot.
retemirábile (m.) rete mirabile (network of blood vessels).
retemperar (v.t.) to re-temper; to strengthen, fortify, invigorate; to rebuild, reform.
retenção, retência (f.) retention, holding, keeping; retentiveness; detention.
retencionário –ria (m.,f.) one who retains something by right.
retencionista (m.,f.) one who retains something in his possession.
retenida (f., Naut.) guy.
reteno (m., Chem.) retene.
retensivo –va (adj.) retentive.
retentividade (f.) retentiveness.
retentivo –va (adj.) retentive; (f.) retentiveness, remembrance.
retentor –tora (adj.) retaining; (m.,f.) one who retains; (Mach.) retainer; keeper (any of various devices to keep something in position); (Magnetism) keeper; (Elec.) armature.

retentriz (*adj.*) retentive; (*f.*) retentiveness.
reter [78] (*v.t.*) to retain, hold back, keep (in possession), withhold; to restrain, hold in; to remember; to detain; (*v.r.*) to detain oneself; to contain oneself.
retesado –da (*adj.*) taut, stiff, tense, tight.
retesador –dora (*adj.*) stiffening, tightening.
retesar (*v.t.*) to stretch, tighten; (*v.r.*) to stiffen.
retêso –sa (*adj.*) taut, tight, stiff.
reticência (*f.*) reticence, reserve in speech, a keeping silent; (*pl. Print.*) ellipses.
reticencioso –sa (*adj.*) reticent.
reticente (*adj.*) reticent, silent, mum; (*m.,f.*) one who remains silent.
retícula (*f.*) = RETÍCULO.
reticulação (*f.*) reticulation, network.
reticulado –da, **reticular** (*adj.*) reticulate, reticular, net-like.
reticulados (*m.pl., Zool.*) the Foraminifera.
retículo (*m.*) a small net; (*Optics*) a reticle (cross hair); (*Bot.*) reticulate venation of leaves; (*Zool.*) reticulum (second stomach of ruminants).
retidão (*f.*) rectitude, uprightness.
retido –da (*adj.*) retained; restrained; detained.
retifica (*f., Mach.*) grinder.
retificação (*f.*) rectification, rectifying.
retificado –da (*adj.*) rectified, corrected; of alcohol, etc., redistilled, purified.
retificador –dora (*adj.*) rectifying; (*m.,f.*) rectifier; (*Radio*) detector.
retificar (*v.t.*) to rectify, straighten; to correct, adjust, set right; (*Chem.*) to purify, redistill (alcohol, etc.); (*Radio*) to detect; (*v.r.*) to regulate (improve) oneself.
retificativo –va (*adj.*) serving to rectify.
retificável (*adj.*) rectifiable.
retiforme (*adj.*) retiform, reticular, netlike.
retígrado –da (*adj.*) rectigrade.
retilíneo –nea (*adj.*) rectilineal, rectilinear.
retilinidade (*f.*) rectilinearity.
retina (*f.*) retina (of the eye).
retináculo (*m., Anat., Bot., Zool.*) retinaculum.
retinérveo –vea (*adj., Bot.*) retinerved, net-veined.
retingir [24] (*v.t.*) to re-dye; to recolor.
retiniano –na, **retínico** –ca (*adj., Anat.*) retinal.
retinim (*m.*) jingle (sound).
retininte (*adj.*) jingling, tinkling.
retinir (*v.i.*) to jingle (as spurs); to tinkle; to clang, jangle, ring; to resound; (*m.*) the sound of jingling, tinkling, ringing, etc.
retinite (*f., Med.*) retinitis.
retinito (*m., Min.*) retinite.
retinol (*m.*) retinol, codol.
retinoscioscopia (*f., Physiol.*) retinoscopy, skiascopy.
retinóspora (*f., Bot.*) the sawara false cypress (*Chamaecyparis pisifera*).
retintim (*m.*) a jingling; a tinkling, clanging, ringing sound (as of coins, spurs, anvil).
retintinir (*v.i.*) to jingle, tinkle, ring, clang.
retinto –ta (*adj.*) deep-dyed. **prêto**—, coal black; (*m.*) any very dark color.
retirado –da (*adj.*) retired, secluded, solitary, sequestered; (*f.*) retiral, departure, withdrawal; (*Milit.*) retreat; place of refuge, retreat; a partner's monthly draw. **bater em**—, to beat a retreat.
retiramento (*m.*) a withdrawal into seclusion. [But not retirement from business or profession, which is RE-FORMA or APOSENTADORIA.]
retirante (*adj.*) retiring, retreating; (*m.,f.*) a migrant from the drought areas of northeastern Brazil; (*f., Bot.*) a starbur (*Acanthospermum hispidum*), c.a. CARAPICHO-RASTEIRO.
retirar (*v.t.*) to take (draw, pull) back (**de**, from); to retract (something said); (*v.i.,v.r.*) to withdraw (**de**, from); to retreat; to retire (**para**, to; **de**, from).—-**se de roldão**, to retreat pell-mell.
retiro (*m.*) retreat (place of seclusion); retreat (withdrawal of troops); "(1) in Maranhão, a hut located at some distance from cattle ranches suitable as a dormitory for the cowboys; (2) on Marajó, a FAZENDA where cattle are kept for a certain part of the year; a large shed at some distance from the regular household, where plantations are located." [*GBAT*]
retirrostro –tra (*adj.*) having a straight beak.
retisseriado –da (*adj., Bot.*) rectiserial.
retitude (*f.*) = RETIDÃO.

reto –ta (*adj.*) right, straight, rectilinear, upright, erect, plumb; fair, square, just, honest. **ângulo**—, right angle; (*m.*) rectum.
retocação (*f.*) = RETOQUE.
retocado –da (*adj.*) retouched, refinished.
retocador –dora (*adj.*) retouching; (*m.,f.*) retoucher.
retocamento (*m.*) = RETOQUE.
retocar (*v.t.*) to retouch, touch up, finish, perfect.
retocele (*f., Med.*) rectocele, hernia of the rectum.
retoiçar (*v.*) & derivs. = RETOUÇAR & derivs.
retomada (*f.*) a retaking.
retomar (*v.t.*) to retake, recover, regain.
retoque (*m.*) retouching, finishing touch.
retor (*m.*) rhetor; rhetorician.
retorcedeira (*f.*) twisting machine.
retorcer (*v.t.*) to re-twist; to twist back; (*v.r.*) to wiggle; to writhe; to dodge (questions).—**a bôca**, to twist the lips.—**o caminho**, to turn back.—**os olhos**, to turn up the eyes.
retorcido –da (*adj.*) twisted, gnarled, kinked; of style, labored, forced.
retórica (*f.*) see under RETÓRICO.
retoricão (*m.*) a would-be rhetorician.
retoricar (*v.i.*) to speak or write rhetorically.
retoricismo (*m.*) a passion for rhetoric.
retórico –ca (*adj.*) rhetorical; oratorical; glib, fluent; bombastic; (*m.,f.*) rhetorician, declaimer, or a would-be such; (*f.*) rhetoric, art of discourse; artificial eloquence of language; (*colloq.*) woman given to rhetorical speech.
retornar (*v.i.*) to return.—**a**, to return (go or come back) to; to restore, give back, send back.—**a si**, or **sôbre si**, to recover oneself, regain one's courage.
retôrno (*m.*) a return, a going or coming back; barter, exchange; a giving back, reward.
retorquir, retorqüir [25] (*v.t.,v.i.*) to retort, reply, return.
retorsão (*f.*) retortion.
retorto –ta (*adj.*) gnarled, twisted, bent down; (*f.*) retort, still.
retostar (*v.t.*) to toast again.
retouça (*f.*) child's swing. Var. RETOIÇA.
retouçar (*v.i.,v.r.*) to swing; to frolic, gambol, romp, skylark, cavort, cut capers. Var. RETOIÇAR.
retouço (*m.*) frolic, gambol, skylark, caper. Var. RETOIÇO.
retovado –da (*adj.*) rascally; (*m.*) rascal, scoundrel.
retovaginal (*adj.; Anat.*) rectovaginal.
retovesical (*adj.; Anat.*) rectovesical.
retôvo (*m.*) leather covering.
retração (*f.*) retraction, act of retracting or drawing back or in. [But not retraction in the sense of disavowal, which is RETRATAÇÃO.]; (*Concrete*) shrinkage.
retrá[c]til (*adj.*) retractile.
retraduzir (*v.t.*) to retranslate.
retraído –da (*adj.*) withdrawn, drawn back; fig., restrained, shy, reserved, undemonstrative, uncompanionable.
retraimento [a-i] (*m.*) withdrawal, a drawing back; retreat, solitude; reserve, shyness; a shrinking.
retrair [75] (*v.t.*) to withdraw, draw back (in, away), hold back; (*v.r.*) to shrink, withdraw, retire; to quail, flinch. —-**se do mundo**, to withdraw from society.—**a promessa**, to go back on a promise.
retranca (*f.*) crupper; (*Naut.*) boom; (*slang*) brunt.
retrança (*f.*) dense crown of a tree.
retrançar (*v.t.*) to rebraid.
retransir (*v.t.*) to penetrate, touch, affect (the heart, soul).
retratação (*f.*) retractation, retraction, withdrawal of promise, statement, etc.; picture-taking; new treatment (of a subject).
retratado –da (*adj.*) pictured, mirrored, photographed portrayed; retracted, withdrawn; treated again or anew.
retratador –dora (*adj.*) photographing; retracting, recanting; (*m.,f.*) picturetaker; recanter.
retratar (*v.t.*) to picture, paint, portray, photograph; to mirror, reflect; to retract, withdraw (consent, promise, etc.); to treat (a subject) again or anew; (*v.r.*) to recant; to go back on one's word; to be portrayed; to be mirrored, reflected.
retratável (*adj.*) suitable to be photographed; retractable; retractible; retreatable.
retratista (*m.,f.*) photographer, picturetaker.
retrativo –va (*adj.*) retractive.
retrátil (*adj.*) retractile. Var. RETRÁCTIL.
retrato (*m.*) picture, painting, portrait, photograph; por

trayal, description.—**a** (or **de**) **corpo inteiro,** full-length portrait. **tirar o—,** to have one's picture taken.
retravar (*v.t.*) to begin anew.
retrazer [79] (*v.t.*) to bring again.
retremer (*v.i.*) to tremble.
retreta [trê] (*f., Milit.*) evening roll call; public band concert; also = RETRETE.
retrete [trê] (*f.*) water closet, toilet, privy.
retribuição [u-i] (*f.*) recompense, reward. [But not retribution in the sense of punishment, which is CASTIGO or PUNIÇÃO.]
retribuidor –**dora** [u-i] (*adj.*) rewarding; reciprocating; (*m.,f.*) rewarder; one who returns a favor.
retribuir [72] (*v.t.*) to pay back; to give in return; to requite; to reciprocate. **não retribuido,** unrequited.
retrilhar (*v.t.*) to tread again or anew (as, the path of virtue).—**as pegadas de,** to follow in another's footsteps.
retrincado –**da** (*adj.*) fraudulent, dèceitful; sly, secretive.
retrincar (*v.t.*) to lock up again; to gnash the teeth; to misconstrue; (*v.i.*) to take amiss; to murmur.
retriz (*f.*) rectrix (large tail feather).
retro –**tra** (*adv.*) backwards; (*m.*) the front side of a printed sheet; (*interj.*) Back!
retroação (*f.*) retroaction; (*Elec.*) feedback.
retroagir (*v.i.*) to retroact.
retroar (*v.i.*) to resound, thunder again.
retroatividade (*f.*) retroactivity.
retroativo –**va** (*adj.*) retroactive.
retrocarga (*f.*) breech loading.
retrocedência (*f.*) retrocedence.
retrocedente (*adj.*) retrocendent; (*m.,f.*) one who, or that which, retrocedes.
retroceder (*v.i.*) to retrocede, recede, retrograde.
retrocedimento (*m.*) = RETROCESSO.
retrocessão (*f.*) = RETROCESSO; (*Law, Med.*) retrocession.
retrocessivo –**va** (*adj.*) retrocessive.
retrocesso (*m.*) retrocession; retrogression; back-spacer on typewriter.
retrocruzamento (*m.*) backcross (of a hybrid.).
retrodatar (*v.t.*) to date back.
retroflexão [ks] (*f., Med.*) retroflexion.
retroflexo –**xa** [ks] (*adj.*) retroflex, bent backward.
retrogradação (*f.*) retrogradation.
retrogradar (*v.i.*) to retrograde; to regress; to retrace one's steps.
retrógrado –**da** (*adj.*) retrograde, backward; (*m.,f.*) retrograde.
retrogredir (*v.i.*) to retrogress.
retrogressão (*f.*), **retrogresso** (*m.*) retrogression; setback.
retropropulsão (*m.*) jet propulsion; backward reaction.
retrorso –**sa** (*adj.*) retrorse, turned backward.
retrós [retroses] (*m.*) silk embroidery thread.
retrosarias (*f.pl.*) (dressmaker's) notions.
retrospe[c]ção (*f.*) retrospection, a looking back.
retrospe[c]tivo –**va** (*adj.*) retrospective.
retrospe[c]to (*m.*) retrospect, reminiscence.
retrotrair [75] (*v.t.*) to make retroactive; to retract.
retrovender (*v.t.*) to sell with the right of repurchase.
retroversão (*f.*) retroversion; retranslation.
retrucar (*v.i.*) to retort, reply; to talk back; to raise the bet (at cards).—**na mesma moeda,** to reply in kind.
retruque (*m.*) retort; comeback; (*Billiards*) rebound, "kiss".
retumbante (*adj.*) resounding; rumbling.
retumbar (*v.i.*) to resound, reverberate; to rumble; (*v.t.*) to re-echo.
returetral (*adj., Anat.*) recto-urethral.
retuterino –**na** (*adj., Anat.*) recto-uterine.
returno (*m.*) return match.
retuso –**sa** (*adj.; Bot.*) retuse.
réu (*m.*) defendant, the accused; criminal, convict, culprit. [Fem. RÉ].
reubárbaro, reubarbo (*m.*) = RUIBARBO.
reuma (*f.*) rheum.
reumático –**ca** (*adj.*) rheumatic; (*m.,f.*) one who suffers from rheumatism.
reumatismo (*m.*) rheumatism; rheumatoid arthritis.
reumoso –**sa** (*adj.*) rheumy.
reunião [e-u] (*f.*) reunion, meeting, assembly; festive gathering.—**de cúpula,** summit meeting.—**conjunta,** joint meeting.
reunificar [e-u] (*v.t.*) to reunify.
reunir [e-u] [20] (*v.t.*) to (re)unite, (re)join; to (re)connect; to gather, collect; to amass; to bring together; to assem-

ble, rally; to embody; to combine; to reconcile, harmonize; to add, annex; (*v.r.*) to meet (come, flock, get) together, convene, cluster.
Rev. = REVISTA (Review [magazine]); REVERENDO (Reverend)
revacinar (*v.t.*) to revaccinate; (*v.r.*) to be revaccinated.
revalidação (*f.*) revalidation.
revalidador –**dora** (*adj.*) revalidating.
revalidar (*v.t.*) to revalidate.
revalorização (*f.*) revalorization.
revalorizar (*v.t.*) to revalorize.
revancha (*f.*) revenge; return match. [French: *revanche.*]
revel [-véis] (*adj.*) rebel, contumacious; (*m.,f.*) rebel; defaulter.
revelação (*f.*) revelation, striking disclosure; discovery.
revelado –**da** (*adj.*) revealed; disclosed.
revelador –**dora** (*adj.*) revealing; (*m.*) revealer; (*Photog.*) developer.
revelar (*v.t.*) to reveal, disclose; to display; to unearth; to expose, divulge; to show, betray; to develop (a photograph); (*v.r.*) to reveal itself (or oneself); to appear.
revelatriz (*adj.*) revealing; (*f.*) revealer.
revelável (*adj.*) revealable.
revelho –**lha** (*adj.; m.,f.*) very old (person).
revelia (*f.*) default, non-appearance (in court); contumacy. **à—de,** without the knowledge (consent, approval) of. **deixar um negócio correr à—,** to let a matter take care of itself. **julgamento à—,** judgment by default.
revelim (*m., Fort.*) ravelin.
revenda (*f.*) resale.
revendedor –**dora** (*adj.*) reselling; (*m.,f.*) reseller; middleman.
revender (*v.t.*) to resell.
revendição (*f.*) = REVENDA.
revendível (*adj.*) resalable.
revenir (*v.t.*) to temper (steel).
rever [81] (*v.t.*) to see again; to review, re-examine; (*v.r.*) to see oneself again (as in one's children); to look at oneself again (in the mirror).—**as provas,** to proofread.
reverberação (*f.*) reverberation.
reverberante (*adj.*) reverberating; reflecting heat or light.
reverberar (*v.t.*) to reverberate. [But only in the sense of reflecting light or heat. In the sense of reëchoing sound, see REBOAR, RETUMBAR.]; (*v.i.*) to reflect.
reverberatório –**ria** (*adj.*) reverberatory.
reverbério (*m., colloq.*) a bawling out.
revérbero (*m.*) reverberation; reflection; light reflector; street light.
reverdecer (*v.t.*) to make green again; to clothe with verdure; to give new life to; (*v.i.*) to turn green again; to come to life again.
reverência (*f.*) reverence, veneration; bow. **fazer—s,** to bow and scrape.
reverencial (*adj.*) reverential.
reverenciar (*v.t.*) to reverence, revere, venerate.
reverencioso –**sa** (*adj.*) reverential.
reverendíssimo –**ma** (*adj.*) most reverend; [*cap.*] (*m.*) Right Reverend; (*f.*) His (Your) Reverence.
reverendo –**da** (*adj.*) reverend, venerable; (*m.*) a priest.
reverente (*adj.*) reverent, reverential.
reverificação (*f.*) reverification; recheck.
reverificador –**dora** (*adj.*) rechecking; (*m.,f.*) rechecker.
reverificar (*v.t.*) to verify again; to recheck.
revernizar (*v.t.*) to revarnish.
reversão (*f.*) reversion, return.
reversibilidade (*f.*) reversibility.
reversível (*adj.*) reversible.
reversivo –**va** (*adj.*) reversive.
reverso –**sa** (*adj.*) reversed; contrary, adverse; perverse; (*m.*) reverse, contrary, opposite; tail (of a coin).—**da mão,** back of the hand. **o—da medalha,** fig., the other side of an argument, subject or situation. **Todas as coisas tem seu—,** There are two sides to every question.
reverter (*v.i.*) to revert, return (**a, para,** to); to come or go back (**a, para,** to).—**em proveito** (or **benefício**) **de,** to revert to the benefit of.
revertível (*adj.*) revertible.
revés [-veses] (*m.*) reverse, opposite, contrary; a backhand stroke; mishap; disaster; hardship; rebuff; a set-back, reverse of fortune; (*pl.*) ups and downs. **ao—,** on the contrary; against the grain; upside down. **ao—de,** to the contrary of; opposed to. **sofrer um—,** to meet with a mishap, a set-back.
revessa (*f.*) countercurrent; valley of a roof.

revêsso -sa (*adj.*) reversed; twisted, tortuous; of wood, knotty, hard to work.
revestimento (*m.*) revetment, retaining wall; facing of brick, stone, etc.; coating.—**antioxidante**, rustproofing. —**de gêsso**, plaster cast.—**de asfalto**, asphalt layer.
revestir [21a] (*v.t.*) to don, put on; to clothe (**de, com**, with); to revet, face (embankment, etc.) with masonry; to coat, cover, overlay; to invest, endow (with authority, etc.).—**-se de**, to assume, take on (importance, authority); to put on (airs); to cover oneself with (glory).
revezadamente (*adv.*) by turns.
revezador -dora (*m.,f.*) alternate, substitute, proxy; "pinch-hitter".
revezamento (*m.*) rotation, alternation. **corrida de—**, relay race. **turma de—**, relay team.
revezar (*v.t.,v.i.*) to alternate; (*v.t.*) to spell (relieve), as at work; (*v.r.*) to take turns; to rotate.
revibrar (*v.t.*) to vibrate again and again.
reviçar (*v.t.,v.i.*) to revive.
revidar (*v.t.*) to reply in kind; to strike back; to pay back (insults, injuries, etc.); to raise the bet (as in poker).
revide (*m.*) a reply in kind; reprisal, retaliation; requital; raising of a bet (in poker).
revigorador -dora (*adj.*) reinvigorating.
revigoramento (*m.*) reinvigoration.
revigorante (*adj.*) reinvigorating.
revigorar (*v.t.*) to reinvigorate, reanimate, make strong again; (*v.i.,v.r.*) to grow strong again.
revigorizar (*v.*) & derivs. = REVIGORAR & derivs.
revinda (*f.*) return.
revindicar (*v.*) = REIVINDICAR.
revingar (*v.t.*) to revenge again or anew; (*v.i.*) to take new revenge.
revir [82] (*v.i.*) to come again, return.
revira (*f.*) a Negro dance.
reviramento (*m.*) complete reversal; flip-flop.
revirão (*m.*) welt (of a shoe).
revirar (*v.t.*) to turn, twist, bend around; to turn inside out; to turn over and over; to roll (the eyes); (*v.i.*) to turn around.—**o caminho**, to turn back.—**se contra**, to turn against.—**se sôbre os calcanhares**, to turn on one's heels.
reviravolta (*f.*) a reversal of rotation, backspin; spinning; whirling; pirouette; about-face; flip-flop.
revisão (*f.*) revision, review; proofreading.
revisar (*v.t.*) to revise, review, re-examine; to proofread.
revisionismo (*m.*) revisionism.
revisionista (*adj.; m.,f.*) revisionist.
revisitar (*v.t.*) to revisit.
revisível (*adj.*) revisable; reviewable.
revisor -sora (*adj.*) revising; reviewing; (*m.,f.*) proofreader; reviewer, examiner; checker.
revisório -ria (*adj.*) revisory.
revista (*f.*) see under REVISTO.
revistar (*v.t.*) to review, survey, inspect; to examine, investigate; to search, ransack; to overhaul.
revisto -ta (*adj.*) reviewed; checked; corrected; proofread; (*f.*) review, (re-)survey; revue, musical comedy; periodical, magazine; military inspection, parade; search, investigation; overhauling.
revitalizar (*v.t.*) to revitalize.
revivente (*adj.*) reviving.
reviver (*v.i.*) to revive, return to life, rise; to reawake, recall; to recover, bring into use; (*v.t.*) to reanimate; to relive (in memory).
revivescer (*v.*) = REVIVER.
revivificação (*f.*) revivification, revival; (*Physical Chem.*) reactivation, as of charcoal.
revivificar (*v.t.*) to revivify; (*Physical Chem.*) to reactivate (charcoal, etc.).
Rev.ᵐᵒ = REVERENDÍSSIMO (Most Reverend).
Rev.º = REVERENDO (Reverend).
revoada (*f.*) a flight of birds; a flock of birds in flight.
revoar (*v.i.*) to fly (again, back); to soar.
revocação (*f.*) revocation.
revocar (*v.t.*) to call back; to evoke; to revoke.
revocatório -ria (*adj.*) = REVOGATÓRIO.
revocável (*adj.*) revocable; (*Law*) defeasible.
revogabilidade (*f.*) revocability.
revogação (*f.*) revocation, repeal; (*Law*) defeasance.
revogado -da (*adj.*) revoked; annulled; cancelled.
revogador -dora (*adj.*) revoking; (*m.,f.*) revoker.
revogante (*adj.*) revoking.
revogar (*v.t.*) to revoke, repeal, annul, quash.

revogativo -va (*adj.*) revocative.
revogatório -ria (*adj.*) revocatory.
revogável (*adj.*) revocable.
revolta (*f.*) revolt, rebellion, uprising; revulsion; of land, a second turning over.
revoltado -da (*adj.*) revolting, insurgent; revolted; (*m.,f.*) revolter, rebel; one who is revolted.
revoltante (*adj.*) revolting, disgusting; gruesome.
revoltar (*v.t.*) to revolt, repel, shock; to disgust; to incite to revolt (**contra**, against); (*v.i.*) to return; (*v.r.*) to revolt, rebel, mutiny; to be indignant.—**para**, to turn again to (toward).
revoltear (*v.t.,v.i.,v.r.*) to turn over and over or around and around.
revolteio (*m.*) a turning around movement.
revôlto -ta (*adj.*) disturbed, disarranged, disordered; turbulent, agitated; tempestuous, wild, stormy [sea]; bent, twisted; disheveled, tousled [hair].
revoltoso -sa (*adj.*) rebellious, mutinous; (*m.,f.*) rebel, insurgent, revolter.
revolução (*f.*) revolution, rotation, gyration; revolt, rebellion; insurrection; coup d'état; revulsion, repugnance.
revolucionado -da (*adj.*) revolutionized.
revolucionador -dora (*adj.*) revolutionizing.
revolucionamento (*m.*) revolutionizing.
revolucionar (*v.t.*) to revolutionize; (*v.r.*) to revolt.
revolucionário -ria (*adj.; m.,f.*) revolutionary.
revoluteante (*adj.*) revolving, whirling, swirling.
revolutear (*v.i.*) to revolve, whirl; swirl, eddy; of birds, to soar, wheel; (*m.*) act of revolving.
revoluto -ta (*adj.*) revolved.
revolutoso -sa (*adj.; Bot.*) revolute.
revolver (*v.t.*) to stir, mix; to rummage; to jumble (up); to agitate, toss; to turn over (the soil, the pages of a book); to roll (the eyes); to revolve in the mind; (*v.i.*) to rotate; to revolve about (the sun); (*v.r.*) to roll, heave (as the sea); of time, to roll by.—**céus e terra**, to turn heaven and earth, leave no stone unturned.—**na fantasia, no pensamento**, to turn (something) over and over in the mind.
revólver (*m.*) revolver, pistol.
revolvido -da (*adj.*) revolved, stirred, agitated.
revolvimento (*m.*) revolving; revolution.
revulsão (*f., Med.*) revulsion, counterirritation. [Not revulsion in the sense of sudden violent change of feeling, which is REVOLTA, INDIGNAÇÃO.]
revulsar (*v.t., Med.*) to counterirritate.
revulsivo -va (*adj.; m.,f., Med.*) revulsive (medicine or agent).
rexenxão (*m.*) = GRAÚNA.
réxia [ks] (*f., Bot.*) meadow beauty (*Rhexia*).
reza (*f.*) prayer; praying.
rezadeiro -ra (*adj.*) pious; (*m.,f.*) one given to much praying; (*f., colloq.*) fortuneteller.
rezado -da (*adj.*) prayed; said in secret; much talked of. **missa—**, Low Mass.
rezador -dora (*adj.*) praying; (*m.,f.*) quack healer.
rezar (*v.t.,v.i.*) to pray; (*colloq.*) to mutter; of a notice, regulation, etc., to read (thus and so).—**o terço**, to tell one's beads.
rezina (*adj.; m.,f.*) pigheaded (person).
rezinga (*f.*) grumbling; bickering.
rezingão -gona, rezingueiro -ra (*adj.*) grumbling, bickering, grouchy; peevish; (*m.,f.*) such a person.
rezingar (*v.i.*) to grumble, find fault; to bicker.
rh+vowel, see under r+vowel.
ri, ria, riais, riam, ríamos, rias, forms of RIR [73].
ria (*f.*) estuary; (*Geog.*) ria.
riachão (*m.*) a large, running creek.
riacho (*m.*) small stream, creek, brook.
riacolito (*m., Min.*) rhyacolite.
riamba (*f.*) = DIAMBA.
riba (*f.*) high river bank; a type of coffee-husking machine. **em—**, on top.
ribaçã (*f.*) = AVOANTE.
ribada (*f.*) long, high river bank.
ribaldaria, ribaldia (*f.*) rascality, skullduggery. [Not ribaldry, which is LINGUAGEM INDECENTE.]
ribaldo -da (*adj.*) rascally; (*m.*) rascal, scalawag. [But not ribald, which is GROSSEIRÃO, INDECENTE.]
ribalta (*f.*) footlights.
ribamar (*m.*) seashore.
ribanceira (*f.*) river bluff, high bank, steep slope; brink.
ribeira (*f.*) riverside; river bank; stream.

ribeirada (*f.*) fast-running stream.

ribeirão (*m.*) wide stream; diamond field.

ribeirinho **–nha** (*adj.*) living or situated in a river or on its banks; riparian; (*f.*) brook; (*pl.*) wading birds.

ribeiro (*m.*) creek, brook; valley of a roof.

ribésia (*f.*, *Bot.*) currant or gooseberry (*Ribes*).

ribesiáceas (*f.pl.*) the currant or gooseberry family (*Grossulariaceae*).

ribete [bê] (*m.*) hemming tape.

riboflavina (*f.*, *Biochem.*) riboflavin, vitamin B₁.

ribombância (*f.*) booming, thundering.

ribombante (*adj.*) booming, thundering, rumbling. Var. RIMBOMBANTE.

ribombar (*v.i.*) to thunder, boom, resound, roll, rumble. Var. RIMBOMBAR.

ribombo (*m.*) clap of thunder, or similar loud noise. Var. RIMBOMBO.

riça (*f.*) a frizzle-feathered chicken.

ricaço **–ça** (*adj.*) rolling in riches; (*m.*,*f.*) rich person; a moneybags.

rica-dona (*f.*) wife or heiress of a rich man.

ricanho **–nha** (*adj.*; *m.*,*f.*) rich but stingy (person).

riçar (*v.t.*) to curl, frizzle, crimp (the hair).

Ricardo (*m.*) Richard.

richárdia (*f.*) a genus (*Zantedeschia*, syn. *Richardia* [Kunth]) of callalilies.

richardsônia (*f.*) the Mexican clover genus (*Richardia* [Houst.] syn. *Richardsonia*).

ricina (*f.*, *Chem.*) ricin(e).

ricinelaídico **–ca** (*adj.*) ácido—, ricinelaidic acid.

ricínico **–ca** (*adj.*) ácido—, ricinic acid.

ricinina (*f.*, *Chem.*) ricinine.

ricino (*m.*) castor-oil plant [=MAMONA]; a tick [=CAR-RAPATO].—**maior**, the Barbados nut (*Jatropha curcas*), c.a. PURGUEIRA. **óleo de**—, castor oil.

ricinodendro (*m.*) the manketti nut (*Ricinodendron*).

ricinoleato (*m.*, *Chem.*) ricinoleate.

ricinólico **–ca** (*adj.*, *Chem.*) ricinoleic.

ricinolina (*f.*, *Chem.*) ricinolein.

rico **–ca** (*adj.*) rich, well-to-do; splendid, sumptuous; fruitful, luxuriant; precious; noble. **podre de**—, "filthy rich". (*m.*,*f.*) a rich person. **os**—**s**, the wealthy (as a class).

riço **–ça** (*adj.*) frizzly, curly; (*m.*) rat (hair pad).

ricochet[e]ar (*v.i.*) to ricochet.

ricochête (*m.*) a ricochet, skip, jump.

rico-homem (*m.*) grandee.

ricto, ríctus (*m.*) rictus; grin.

ride, rides, forms of RIR [73].

ridência (*f.*) cheerfulness.

ridente (*adj.*) smiling, pleased.

ridicularia (*f.*) a trifle; something ridiculous.

ridicularizador **–dora** (*adj.*) = RIDICULIZADOR.

ridicularizar, ridiculizar (*v.t.*) to ridicule, deride, laugh at; to banter, chaff; (*v.r.*) to make oneself ridiculous.

ridiculez[a] (*f.*) ridiculousness.

ridiculismo (*m.*) something ridiculous.

ridiculização (*f.*) ridiculing.

ridiculizador **–dora** (*adj.*) ridiculing.

ridiculizante (*adj.*) ridiculing.

ridiculizar (*v.*) = RIDICULARIZAR.

ridículo **–la** (*adj.*) ridiculous, ludicrous; outlandish; "batty"; (*m.*,*f.*) ridiculous act, thing or person.

rididico (*m.*) the yellow-fronted woodpecker (*Tripsurus flavifrons*). Cf. PICA-PAU.

rido, form of RIR [73].

rieira (*f.*) rut [= RELHEIRA].

rieis, riem, forms of RIR [73].

rifa (*f.*) raffle.

rifada (*f.*) a number of cards of the same suit.

rifador **–dora** (*adj.*) raffling; (*m.*,*f.*) raffler.

rifão (*f.*) proverb, adage, maxim.

rifar (*v.t.*) to raffle (off); (*v.i.*) to whinny.

rifle (*m.*) rifle [=REFLE].

rigeza (*f.*) = RIJEZA.

rigidez (*f.*) rigidity, stiffness; severity, strictness; (*Physiol.*) rigor.—**cadavérica**, rigor mortis.

rígido **–da** (*adj.*) rigid, stiff; unbending; severe, stern; harsh; stringent; strait-laced.

rigodão (*m.*) rigadoon (dance or music).

rigoliz (*m.*) = ALCAÇUZ.

rigolene, rigoleno (*m.*), **rigolina** (*f.*, *Chem.*) rhigolene, cymogene.

rigor [ô] (*m.*) rigor, rigidness; rigorousness; severity,

harshness; strictness, exactness; inclemency; (*Bot.*) the prince's-plume lady's-thumb (*Polygonum orientale*). **a**—, strictly; formally dressed. **de**—, required by etiquette. **traje de**—, formal dress.

rigorismo (*m.*) rigorism.

rigorista (*adj.*) rigoristic; (*m.*,*f.*) rigorist.

rigorosidade (*f.*) rigorousness.

rigoroso **–sa** (*adj.*) rigorous, strict, harsh; rugged; stringent; strait-laced; exact, precise.

rijeza [ê] (*f.*) rigidness; firmness.

rijo **–ja** (*adj.*) rigid, stiff, hard; harsh, unyielding, inflexible; tough; stalwart; strong, sturdy; intense; of flesh or muscles, hard, firm, solid.

ril (*m.*) reel (dance).

rilada (*f.*, *colloq.*) kidney stew; suet.

rilha-boi (*m.*) = RESTA-BOI.

rilhador **–dora** (*adj.*) gnawing; (*m.*.,*f.*) gnawer.

rilhadura (*f.*) gnawing.

rilhar (*v.t.*) to gnaw; to grind, grit, (the teeth).

rim [rins] (*m.*) kidney; (*Arch.*) spandrel; (*Bot.*) a Brazilian variety (*Gossypium brasiliense*) of sea-island cotton.

rima (*f.*) rhyme; pile, stack, heap; chink, crack; (*pl.*) verses.

rimador **–dora** (*adj.*) rhyming; (*m.*,*f.*) rhymester.

rimar (*v.t.*,*v.i.*) to rhyme.

rimbombar (*v.*) & derivs. = RIBOMBAR & derivs.

rimel (*m.*) mascara.

rimos, form of RIR [73].

rinal (*adj.*, *Anat.*) rhinal, nasal, narial.

rinanto (*m.*) the common rattleweed (*Rhinanthus crista-galli*), or other plant of this genus.

rincão (*m.*) a far-off, secluded place, esp. a wooded one; valley of a roof; a grooving plane.

rinchada (*f.*) horse laughter.

rinchão (*m.*) garlic mustard (*Sisymbrium officinale*); a false valerian (*Stachytarpheta caiennensis*).

rinchar (*v.i.*) to neigh, whinny [= RELINCHAR].

rinchavelhada (*f.*) horselaugh, guffaw.

rinchavelhar (*v.i.*) to guffaw, horselaugh.

rincho (*m.*) neigh, whinny [= RELINCHO].

rindo, form of RIR [73].

rincobdelídeos (*m.pl.*) an order of leeches (*Rhynchobdellida*).

rincóforo **–ra** (*adj.*; *Zool.*) rhynchophorous, having a beak; (*m.pl.*) the snout beetles (*Rhynchophora*).

rincósia (*f.*) the crab's-eye rhynchosia (*R. phaseoloides*), or other plant of this genus.

ringente (*adj.*; *Bot.*) ringent.

ringir (*v.i.*) to creak; (*v.t.*) to grit (the teeth).

ringue (*m.*) prize ring.

rinha (*f.*) cockfight; cockpit. **galo de**—, gamecock.

rinhadeiro (*m.*) cockpit.

rinhão (*m.*, *colloq.*) kidney.

rinhar (*v.i.*) to fight (as cocks).

rinismo (*m.*) nasal twang.

rinite (*f.*, *Med.*) rhinitis.

rinobatídeos (*m.pl.*) the family which comprises the guitar fishes (*Rhinobatidae*).

rinóbato (*m.*) the typical genus of guitar fishes (*Rhinobatus*).

rinocero[n]te (*m.*) rhinoceros.

rinofaringe (*f.*, *Anat.*) rhinopharynx.

rinolifídeos (*m.pl.*) a family (*Rhinolophidae*) of leaf-nosed or horseshoe bats.

rinologia (*f.*) rhinology.

rinologista (*m.*,*f.*) rhinologist.

rinoplastia, rinoplástica (*f.*) rhinoplasty.

rinoplástico **–ca** (*adj.*) rhynoplastic.

rinóptero (*m.*) the genus (*Rhinoptera*) to which the cow-nosed rays belong.

rinoscopia (*f.*, *Med.*) rhinoscopy.

rinoscópio (*m.*, *Med.*) nasoscope [= NASOSCÓPIO].

rinoteca (*f.*, *Zool.*) rhinotheca.

rinque (*m.*) rink.

rio, form of RIR [73].

rio (*m.*) river.—**abaixo**, downstream.—**acima** or **arriba**, upstream. **leito do**—, river bed. **vau de**—, ford, river crossing.

rio-grandense-do-norte (*adj.*) of or pert. to the state of Rio Grande do Norte; (*m.*,*f.*) a native or inhabitant of that state.

rio-grandense-do-sul (*adj.*) of or pert. to the state of Rio Grande do Sul; (*m.*,*f.*) a native or inhabitant of that state.

riólito (*m., Petrog.*) rhyolite.
rio-platense (*adj.; m.,f.*) = PLATENSE.
ripa (*f.*) lath; batten; (*Bot.*) = BURITIZINHO.
ripada (*f.*) a blow with a lath; a dressing down, bawling out; shot, slug (of liquor).
ripado (*m.*) lath house (for growing plants); lathwork; battens under roof tiles.
ripador (*m.*) a ripple (for flax) [= RIPANÇO].
ripadura, ripagem (*f.*), **ripamento** (*m.*) rippling of flax.
ripal (*adj.*) designating lath nails.
ripançar (*v.t.*) to ripple (flax).
ripanço (*m.*) ripple (for flax); garden rake; couch, sofa; (*Bot.*) = RAPANÇO.
ripar (*v.t.*) to cover or line with laths; to nail battens on; to rip (wood) into strips; to ripple (flax); to rake (the ground); to strip a branch of its fruit with one movement of the hand; to clip a horse's mane; to rip out hair; to pilfer.
ripário –ria (*adj.*) riparian.
riparografia (*f.*) rhyparography.
ripeira (*f.*) lath, narrow strip.
ripícola (*adj.*) riparian.
ripídio (*m., Bot.*) rhipidium.
ripidolito (*m., Min.*) ripidolite.
ripina (*f.*) the double-toothed hawk (*Harpagus bidentatus.*)
rípio (*m.*) a stone chip; rubble; fig., an expletive (word used to fill up space).
ripo (*m.*) a hatchel (for flax).
riposta (*f., Fencing*) riposte.
ripostar (*v.i.*) to utter a quick retort; (*Fencing*) to riposte.
riqueza [ê] (*f.*) riches, wealth; richness, abundance.
rir [73] (*v.i.,v.r.*) to laugh.—**a bandeiras despregadas,** to laugh uproariously; to shriek with laughter; to split one's sides laughing; to cackle.—**até chorar,** to cry laughing. —**à custa de,** to laugh at another's expense.—**até morrer,** to die laughing.—**amarelo,** to laugh on the wrong side of one's face; to give a sickly smile.—**às gargalhadas,** to guffaw.—**de,** to laugh at; to sneer at.—**-se (de),** to laugh (at). **dar para—,** or **faz—,** to give cause for laughter. **de—,** (*adj.*) laughable. **Eu até ri,** (*ironically*) I had to laugh. **olhos que riem,** smiling eyes. **Ri melhor quem ri por último,** He laughs best who laughs last. **Ri-se o sujo do mal lavado,** The pot calls the kettle black.
ris, form of RIR [73].
risada (*f.*) laughter, loud laugh.
risadinha (*f.*) giggle.
risão –sona (*adj.*) given to laughing much and easily.
risca (*f.*) scratch, line, stripe; hair parting line; furrow; nick (on type).—**de dois fios,** the equals sign [=].—**de quadratim,** the dash sign [—].—**(or traço) de união,** hyphen.—**s do espetro,** lines of the spectrum.—**suplementar,** a second nick on type. **seguir à—,** to follow (instructions, etc.) to the letter; to hew to the line.
riscado –da (*adj.*) striped; (*m.*) striped cotton cloth. **entender do—,** (*slang*) to know what something is all about.
riscador –dora (*adj.*) striping; (*m.,f.*) striper; scriber; scratch awl; (*m.*) a fish called CARAPICU.
riscadura (*f.*), **riscamento** (*m.*) striping [= RISCA].
riscar (*v.t.*) to scratch (out), cross out (off); to delete; to delineate, trace; to mark (with a line or lines); to scribe; to blot out, erase (from memory); to expel (from membership).—**da ata,** to strike from the minutes.—**um fosforo,** to strike a match. [To risk is ARRISCAR.]
risco (*m.*) risk, hazard, chance; jeopardy; trace, mark, scratch, line; score mark. **com,** or **sob,—de,** at the risk of. **a todo—,** at any risk.—**de união,** hyphen.
riscoso –sa (*adj.*) risky [= ARRISCADO].
risibilidade (*f.*) risibility.
risinho (*m,*) feigned laughter.
risível (*adj.*) risible, laughable, ludicrous.
riso (*m.*) laugh, laughter, smile, grin.—**alvar,** silly laugh or giggle.—**amarelo,** sickly grin.—**homérico,** guffaw.— **sardônico,** sardonic laugh.—**sêco,** dry laughter, **um frouxo de—,** a fit of laughter.
risonho –nha (*adj.*) laughing, smiling, gay, cheerful.
risório –ria (*adj.*) risorial; (*m., Anat.*) risorius.
risota (*f.*) laughter, esp. of a jeering nature.
risote (*adj.*) jeering; (*m.,f.*) one who jeers or scoffs.
risoto [sô] (*m.*) risotto (rice cooked with chicken, meat, etc.).
rispidez[a] [ê] (*f.*) severity, harshness, gruffness.
ríspido –da (*adj.*) severe, harsh, gruff.
risse, riste, ristes, forms of RIR [73].

riste (*m.*) a rest to support or couch the butt of a spear or lance. **de dedo em—,** with upheld or pointing finger. **de lança em—,** with lance at rest. **de orelha em—,** of an animal, with ears pointing.
ritaforme (*m., Zool.*) the cinereous harrier (*Circus cyaneus cinereus*).
ritidoma (*m., Bot.*) rhytidome.
ritingerito (*m., Min.*) ritingerite.
ritismo (*m.*) a genus of fungi (*Rhytisma*) forming tar spots on leaves.
ritmar (*v.t.*) to give rhythm to; (*v.i.*) to sound in cadence.
rítmico –ca (*adj.*) rhythmical; (*f.*) rhythmics.
ritmizar (*v.t.*) to give rhythm to.
ritmo (*m.*) rhythm, cadence; rate.
ritmômetro (*m.*) rhythmometer.
ritmopéia (*f.*) rhythmopoeia.
rito (*m.*) rite, ritual, ceremony.
ritual (*adj.; m.*) ritual.
ritualismo (*m.*) ritualism.
ritualista (*adj.*) ritualistic; (*m.,f.*) ritualist.
ritumba (*f.*) African tom-tom.
riu, form of RIR [73].
rival (*adj.; m.,f.*) rival.
rivalidade (*f.*) rivalry, competition.
rivalizar (*v.t.*) to rival.—**com,** to compete with, vie with.
rivícola (*adj.; Bot.*) riparian.
rivina, rivínia (*f.*) the genus (*Rivina*) of rouge plants.
rivulária (*f., Bot.*) the type genus (*Rivularia*) of a family (*Rivulariaceae*) of fresh-water blue-green algae.
rixa (*f.*) quarrel, brawl, wrangle, squabble, scuffle, row, fracas, "rumpus"; riot.
rixador –dora (*adj.; m.,f.*) quarrelsome (person).
rixar (*v.i.*) to quarrel, fight, come to blows.
rixoso –sa, rixento –ta (*adj.*) quarrelsome, pugnacious, rowdy.
rizadura (*f., Naut.*) reefing.
rizagra (*f.*) dentist's root-extracting forceps.
rizanto –ta (*adj.; Bot.*) rhizanthous.
rizar (*v.t.,v.i., Naut.*) to reef.
rizes (*m.pl., Naut.*) reef points.
rizicultor (*m.*) rice grower.
rizicultura (*f.*) rice growing.
rizina (*f.*), **–no** (*m., Bot.*) rhizine, rhizoid.
rizóbio (*m.*) any bacterium of the genus Rhizobium.
rizocárpico –ca (*adj.; Bot.*) rhizocarpic, rhizocarpous.
rizocárpio, rizocarpo (*m.*) any plant of the Salviniales (fern allies).
rizocéfalos (*m.pl.*) an order (*Rhizocephala*) of crab parasites.
rizóctone (*f.*) a rhizoctonia fungus.
rizófago –ga (*adj.*) rhizophagous.
rizófilo –la (*adj.*) rhizophilous.
rizoflagelado –da (*adj.; m., Zool.*) rhizoflagellate.
rizoforáceo –cea (*adj.; Bot.*) rhizophoraceous; (*f.pl.*) the mangrove family (*Rhizophoraceae*).
rizóforo –ra (*adj.; Bot.*) rhizophorous; (*m.*) the genus (*Rhizophora*) of true mangroves.
rizógeno –na (*adj.*) = RIZÓGONO.
rizógono –na (*adj.; Bot.*) rhizogenic, rhizogenous.
rizóide (*m., Bot.*) rhizoid.
rizoma (*m., Bot.*) rhizome, rhizoma.
rizomatoso –sa (*adj.; Bot.*) rhizomatous.
rizomélico –ca (*adj.; Anat.*) rhizomellic.
rizomorfo –fa (*adj.; Bot.*) rhizomorphous, rootlike.
rizópode (*adj.; m., Zool.*) rhizopod; (*m.pl.*) the Rhizopoda, a division of Protozoa.
rizopódio –dia (*adj.*) rhizopodal.
rizostoma (*m.*) a rhizostome jellyfish.
rizostomídeos (*m.pl.*) a division (*Rhizostomae* or -*stomata*) of jellyfishes.
rizóstomo –ma (*adj.; Zool.*) rhizostomatous.
rizotaxia [ks] (*f., Bot.*) rhizotaxy.
rizotomia (*f., Surg.*) rhizotomy.
rizotônico –ca (*adj.; Pron.*) stressed on the first or root syllable.
R J = RIO DE JANEIRO (State of).
RN = RIO GRANDE DO NORTE (State of).
robalete [lê] (*m., Naut.*) bilge keel; (*Zool.*) a snook (*Centropomis ensiferus*), c.a. CAMORIM-SOVELA, CAMORIM-PEBA.
robalo (*m.*) in Brazil: the snook, a pikelike marine fish (*Centropomis undecimalis*) highly esteemed for food; c.a. ROBALO-BICUDO, ROBALO-FLECHA, CAMURI(M), CAMURIM-AÇU, CAMORIM. In Portugal, the term designates *Labrax*

lupus, a European wrasse.—**-de-areia**, the chiro, a tarpon-like fish (*Elops saurus*).
róber (*m.*) rubber (at bridge or whist).
Roberta (*f.*) Roberta.
Roberto (*m.*) Robert; Rupert.
roberval (*f.*) Roberval's balance.
robina (*f.*, *Biochem.*) robin.
robínia (*f.*, *Bot.*) a locust (*Robinia*).—**-comum**, black locust (*R. pseudoacacia*), c.a. FALSA-ACÁCIA.—**-híspida**, rose acacia locust (*R. hispida*).—**-viscosa**, the clammy locust (*R. viscosa*).
robinina (*f.*, *Chem.*) robinin, robinoside.
robissão (*m.*) = SOBRECASACA.
roble (*m.*) oak tree—better known as CARVALHO; the antarctic false beech (*Notofagus antarctica*).
robledo [ê] (*m.*) oak grove.
robô (*m.*) robot.
roboração (*f.*) roboration, strengthening.
roborado -da (*adj.*) corroborated.
roborante (*adj.*) roborant, strengthening.
roborar (*v.t.*) to roborate, strengthen; corroborate.
roborativo -va (*adj.*) roborative, corroborative.
roboredo (*m.*) = ROBLEDO.
robóreo -rea (*adj.*) roborean, oaken. [*Poetical*]
roborite (*f.*) roburite (a mining explosive).
roborizar (*v.*) = ROBORAR.
robustecedor -dora (*adj.*) fortifying, strengthening.
robustecer (*v.t.*) to make robust; to strengthen, vitalize; to confirm, corroborate; (*v.r.*) to grow robust.
robustez[a], robustidão (*f.*) robustness, vigor, strength, stamina.
robusto -ta (*adj.*) robust, strong, stout, hale, hardy, sturdy, able-bodied, rugged.
roca (*f.*) distaff; toy rattle on a stick; a pole with a gadget on the end, for picking fruit; a large rock; an ornamental slash or slit (in a garment).—**-de-eva**, (*Bot.*) the saffron tritonia (*T. crocata*).—**-de-vênus**, common torchlily (*Kniphofia uvaria*).—**forte**, rock fortress.
roça (*f.*) country, rural regions; backwoods plantation; field; act of clearing land by chopping down wild growth; land so cleared and planted, esp. land planted with manioc; in general, "country" as opposed to "city".
roçada (*f.*) act of clearing land of brushwood; cleared land.
roçadela (*f.*) clearing of land, removal of brushwood.
roçado (*m.*) cleared land; cleared field.
roçadoura (*f.*) a kind of long-handled scythe for cutting underbrush.
roçadura (*f.*) a skin abrasion; also = ROÇADELA.
roçagar (*v.t.,v.i.*) to drag (as a gown) over the ground; (*v.i.*) to rustle.
roçagem (*f.*) clearing of land for planting.
rocal (*adj.*) hard as rock; (*m.*) string of beads.
rocalha (*f.*) beads.
rocalhoso -sa (*adj.*) rocky, craggy.
rocambole (*m.*) roly-poly (pastry).
roçamento (*m.*) = ROÇADURA.
rocar (*v.i.*, *Chess*) to castle [= ENROCAR].
roçar (*v.t.*) to grub land for planting; to graze (touch lightly); to rub, scrape against, chafe, fray.
rocaz (*adj.*) = ROCHAZ.
rocedão (*m.*) shoemaker's thread.
rocega (*f.*) a dragging or sweeping (of river or harbor bottom); a drag cable; (*Naut.*) a sweep.
rocegar (*v.t.*) to drag or sweep the bottom (of a harbor, lake, etc.).
roceiro -ra (*adj.*) of or pert. to the ROÇA; (*m.*) man who clears and cultivates land; backwoodsman; "(1) a person from the interior of the country corresponding to the peasant of Europe; (2) a person who immediately shows by his mannerisms that he comes from the settlements, towns and cities of Amazonia; (3) a small planter." [*GBAT*]—**-planta** = SACI (a cuckoo); (*f.*) an angledozer (ground scraper); also an ant called SAÚBA or FORMIGA-DE-ROÇA.
rocela (*f.*) a maritime genus (*Roccella*) of rock-inhabiting lichens which yield rocellin and other dyes.
rocélico -ca (*adj.*, *Chem.*) ácido—, roccellic acid.
rocelina (*f.*) roccellin(e)—a red dye.
rocha (*f.*) rock, crag, large boulder.—**-ácida**, acid igneous rock.—**-básica**, basic igneous rock.—**-calcárea**, limestone.—**-de intrusão**, intrusive rock.—**-filoniana**, dike rock.—**holocristalina**, holocrystalline igneous rock.—**ígnea**, igneous rock.—**negra**, basalt.—**neutra**, neutral or intermediate rock.—**petrolífera**, oil rock.—**viva**, living rock.

—**vulcânica**, volcanic rock. **cristal de**—, rock crystal (quartz).
rochaz (*adj.*) rock-inhabiting.
rochedo [ê] (*m.*) crag, cliff, steep rock.—**auditivo**, (*Anat.*) temporal bone.
rochoso -sa (*adj.*) rocky.
rociado -da (*adj.*) wet, as with dew.
rociar (*v.i.*) to dew; (*v.t.*) to bedew, besprinkle.
rocim (*m.*) jade, nag, small horse.
rocinante (*m.*) nag, sorry horse; small horse.
rocinha (*f.*) "(1) a dwelling located on the outskirts of the city of Belém do Pará; (2) an ancient upper-class dwelling of Pará." (*GBAT*)
rocio (*m.*) dew [= ORVALHO].
rocioso -sa (*adj.*) dewy.
rococó (*adj.*) rococo, florid; by ext., old-fashioned, ugly, in poor taste; (*m.*) rococo ornamentation.
rocororé (*m.*) = COROTÉU.
roda (*f.*) wheel; circle; disk; round slice; lottery wheel; circuit, circumference; social circle; a turn-box set in the door or wall of a convent (used for passing things in and out); a similar device in the wall of an asylum, in which are placed unwanted infants; by ext., a foundling asylum; a torture wheel. (*Naut.*) stem or stern post.—**da fortuna**, wheel of fortune; also = COURAMA (airplane).—**de água**, water wheel.—**de alcatruzes** or **de caçambas**, bucket wheel.—**de balança**, balance wheel.—**de bequilha** (*Aeron.*) tail wheel.—**de esmeril**, emery wheel.—**de oleiro**, potter's wheel.—**-de-pau**, (*colloq.*) a clubbing or cudgeling.—**de tensão** (*Mach.*) tension roller.—**dentada**, cogwheel, gear, rack, pinion.—**diplomática**, diplomatic circles.—**do arado**, gauge wheel of a plow.—**do leme**, (*Naut.*) steering wheel.—**dos expostos**, or—**de misericórdia**, a turn-box in the wall of a convent, hospital or asylum in which unwanted infants are abandoned.—**excêntrica**, cam or eccentric wheel.—**fronteira**, front wheel.—**gigante**, Ferris wheel.—**hidráulica**, water wheel.—**louca**, idle pulley.—**traseira**, rear wheel.—**viva**, bustle, stir, commotion. **à**—**(de)**, around, about. **afastamento das**—**s**, wheelbase. **alta**—, high society. **andar à**—, to go around and around. **brincar de**—, to play ring-around-a-rosy, etc. **cadeira de**—**s**, wheel chair. **cubo da**—, wheel hub. **de**—, around, about. **em**—**de**, around. **fazer**—, to turn handsprings; of a peacock, to spread the tail. **fazer alguém andar com a cabeça à**—, to turn a person's head. **meter na**—, to place (an unwanted infant) in the turn-box of an asylum.
rodada (*f.*) a turn of a wheel; a round (of drinks); a falling forward (of a horse); a hot reception (one in which the person is sent packing); an athletic tournament.
rodagem (*f.*) set of wheels; wheeling. **estrada de**—, highway.
rodágio (*m.*) road toll.
rodamontada (*f.*) rodomontade.
Ródano (*m.*) Rhone.
rodante (*adj.*) rolling. **material**—, (*R.R.*) rolling stock.
rodapé (*m.*) valance; part of a "boiler-plate" serial carried by a newspaper at the bottom of an inside page; footnote; (*Arch.*) baseboard.
rodar (*v.i.*) to turn, revolve, roll, rotate; to run on wheels; to wheel; (*v.t.*) to tumble, roll down; to rake.—**sôbre os calcanhares**, to turn on one's heels. (*v.t.*) to cause to turn; to rake up.—**um filme**, to "roll" a motion picture camera.
rodear (*v.t.*) to surround (com, with), encircle, encompass; to skirt, go or pass around; to use circumlocution.—**com a vista**, or **com os olhos**, to look around, take in with the eyes.—**-se de**, to surround oneself with (amigos, friends).
rodeio (*m.*) circumlocution; evasion, subterfuge; quirk; rodeo, roundup. **declarar**, or **falar**, **sem**—**s**, to speak out, get right to the point. **fazer**—**s**, to beat about the bush; to hem and haw.
rodeira (*f.*) rut.
rodeiro (*m.*) axle; a pair of wheels on the same axle.
rodela (*f.*) a small wheel; a ring; a washer; a tall tale. **uma**—**de limão**, a round slice of lemon.
rodelo [ê] (*m.*) a shoe patch.
Rodésia (*f.*) Rhodesia.
rodeta [ê] (*f.*) a small wheel.—**da cauda**, tail wheel (of an airplane).
ródico -ca (*adj.*, *Chem.*) rhodic.
rodilha (*f.*) rolled cloth pad placed under an object carried on the head; mop, swab.
rodinha (*f.*) small wheel; pinwheel (firework).

ródio (*m.*, *Chem.*) rhodium.
rodite (*f.*, *Min.*) rhodite.
rodízio (*m.*) water wheel; scheduling of work; round, turn, rotation; caster (small swiveled wheel); crooked swap; collusion, connivance.
rodizite (*f.*, *Min.*) rhodizite.
rodizônico -ca (*adj.*, *Chem.*) rhodizonic.
rôdo (*m.*) a wooden rake (without teeth) for raking up grain, coffee beans, etc., into piles; hoelike scraper. **a—,** plentifully, abundantly.
rodobacteriáceas (*f.pl.*) a family (*Rhodobacteriaceae*) of bacteria.
rodocrosita (*f.*), **-to** (*m.*, *Min.*) rhodochrosite [= DIA-LOGITO].
rododendro (*m.*, *Bot.*) rhododendron.
rodofilidáceas (*f.pl.*) a family (*Rhodophyllidaceae*) of red algae.
rodolego [ê], **rodoleiro** (*m.*) = CARRAPATO-ESTRÊLA.
Rodolfo (*m.*) Rodolph(us); Rudolph(us).
rodolita (*f.*, *Min.*) rhodolite.
rodomeláceas (*f.pl.*) a family (*Rhodomelaceae*) of red algae.
rodonita (*f.*), **-to** (*m.*, *Min.*) rhodonite.
rodopiante (*adj.*) swirling, eddying; wheeling (in graceful circles, as a vulture in the sky).
rodopiar (*v.i.*) to swirl, twirl, spin, eddy.
rodopio (*m.*) swirl(ing), twirl(ing) spin(ning).
rodopsina (*f.*, *Physiol.*) rhodopsin, the visual purple.
rodouça (*f.*) = RODILHA.
rodovalho (*m.*) = LINGUADO (a flounder).
rodovia (*f.*) highway.—**encascalhada,** gravel road.
rodoviário -ria (*adj.*) highway. **rêde—,** highway network.
rodriguézia (*f.*) a genus (*Burlingtonia*) of orchids.
Rodrigo (*m.*) Roderic(k).
rodura (*f.*) act of raking; raked-up heap (of grain, coffee, salt, etc.).
roedor -dora (*adj.*) rodent; gnawing; biting; corroding; (*m.*, *Zool.*) a rodent; (*pl.*) the Rodentia.
roedura (*f.*) gnawing; corrosion.
roeméria (*f.*) Asia poppy (*Roemeria*).
roentgen (*m.*) roentgen (international unit of X radiation).
roentgenfotografia (*f.*) an X-ray photograph.
roentgenologia (*f.*) roentgenology.
roentgenologista (*m.,f.*) roentgenologist.
roentgenoterapia (*f.*, *Med.*) roentgenotherapy, treatment by X-rays.
roer [56] (*v.t.*) to gnaw, nibble (at), crunch; to corrode, erode, eat away.—**a corda,** to renege, go back on one's word; to stand (someone) up, fail to show up.—**as unhas,** to bite the fingernails.—**na consciência,** to prey on the conscience.—**os ossos,** to take the leavings; to do the work but receive none of the profit. **Ficou roendo os ossos,** He (she, you) was (were) left holding the bag. **um osso difícil de—,** a hard nut to crack.
rogação (*f.*) entreaty [= RÔGO]; (*pl.*, *Eccl.*) rogations.
rogado -da (*adj.*) begged, entreated, implored, etc. See the verb ROGAR.
rogador -dora (*adj.*) entreating; imploring; interceding; (*m.,f.*) supplicant; intercessor.
rogar (*v.*) to beg, beseech, pray (for), implore, entreat.—**a,** to pray to, implore, plead with.—**pragas,** to call down curses on. **fazer-se—**(or **rogado**), to seek to be coaxed; to play hard to get.
rogativo -va (*adj.*) supplicating, beseeching, entreating; (*f.*) supplication.
rogatório -ria (*adj.*) suppliant; (*f.*) petition.
Rogério (*m.*) Roger.
rôgo (*m.*) entreaty, supplication, prayer, appeal, plea, petition. **a—de,** at the earnest request of.
rojão (*m.*) a dragging (along the ground) or the sound so produced; slow playing of a fiddle; forced march, long pull; long stretch (of work); bullfighter's lance; sky-rocket, or the noise it makes when rising; cracklings [= TORRESMO]; (*Bot.*) a marigold (*Tagetes minuta*), c.a. CUARI-BRAVO.
rojar (*v.t.*) to drag, draw slowly; to scrape, rub, graze; to hurl (rocks, etc.); to throw (flowers, etc.); to hurl to the ground; (*v.i.*) to creep, crawl; to trail along the ground; to drag; to grovel; (*v.r.*) to drag oneself along; to throw oneself to the ground or at someone's feet.—**-se no pó,** to grovel in the dust (at someone's feet).
rôjo (*m.*) a dragging or trailing (along the ground); the sound so produced. **de—,** dragging along the ground.

rojoada (*f.*) fireworks display.
rol [róis] (*m.*) roll, list, roster.—**da roupa,** laundry list.
rôla (*f.*) any of numerous small doves and pigeons, esp. the talpacoti dove (*Columbigalla talpacoti*) c.a. RÔLA-CABOCLA, RÔLA-CALDO-DE-FEIJÃO, RÔLA-GRANDE, RÔLA-ROXA, RÔLA-SANGUE-DE-BOI, ROLINHA, APICUÍ; the cinereous dove (*Claravis pretiosa*), c.a. RÔLA-AZUL, PICUÍ-PEBA, JURITI-AZUL; the grayish ground dove (*Columbigalla passerina griseola*), c.a. RÔLA-PEQUENA; the mauve-spotted ground dove (*Uropelia campestris*), c.a. RÔLA-VAQUEIRA; the scaled dove (*Scardafella squammata*) c.a. FOGO-APAGOU, RÔLA-CASCAVEL.
rola-bosta (*m.*) tumblebug.
rolador (*m.*) roller.
rolagem (*f.*) rolling; (*Aeron.*) taxi-ing.
rolamento (*m.*) act of rolling.—**cilíndrico,** roller bearing.—**de agulhas** or **de bastões,** needle, or pin, bearing.—**de esferas,** ball bearing.—**de roletes,** roller bearing.
rolandiano -na, rolândico -ca (*adj.; Anat.*) Rolandic. **sulco—,** fissure of Rolando, central sulcus.
Rolando (*m.*) Rowland.
rolante (*adj.*) rolling, turning, revolving.
rolão (*m.*) wheat middlings, bran; heavy wooden roller; a long rolling billow; a certain gray pigeon sought as game; a bugaboo; riffraff.
rolar (*v.t.,v.i.*) to roll, turn, revolve; (*v.i.*) to whirl; to swirl; to tumble, fall over; to run (on wheels); to coo (as a dove); (*v.t.*) to bowl, impel forward.
roldana (*f.*) sheave; grooved pulley.
roldão (*m.*) confusion, milling around. **de—,** tumultuously; pell-mell; headlong, tumbling, crashing.
roleta [lê] (*f.*) roulette.
rolete [lê] (*m.*, *Mach.*) follower.
rôlha (*f.*) cork, stopper; fig., a gag on free speech.
rolhador (*m.*) bottle corker, corking machine.
rolhar (*v.*) = ARROLHAR.
rolharia (*f.*) cork factory or industry.
rolheiro -ra (*m.,f.*) cork maker; (*m.*) sheaf of grain.
roliço -ça (*adj.*) roundish, round, rolling; roly-poly, plump, chubby, rotund.
rolimã (*m.*) ball bearing. [Corruption of French *roulement*. More usual: ROLAMENTO (or MANCAL) DE ESFERAS.]
rolinha (*f.*) the talpacoti dove (*Columbigallina t. talpacoti*) c.a. POMBA-RÔLA, RÔLA-GRANDE, RÔLA-ROXA, RÔLA-CALDO, RÔLA-CABOCLA, RÔLA-SANGUE-DE-BOI, RÔLA-VERMELHA, RÔLA-DE-FEIJÃO, APICUÍ; also, the blue-eyed dove (*Oxyphelia cyanopsis*) found only in Brazil.
rôlo (*m.*) roll (of paper, etc.); roller (as of a printing press, etc.); dirt roller, steam roller; billow; bundle; male pigeon; riot, row, fracas; rough-and-tumble fight; a certain type of feminine hair-do [= COCÓ].—**de massas,** or **para massa,** rolling pin.
Roma (*f.*) Rome.
romã (*f.*) pomegranate; Roman woman.
romaico -ca (*adj.; m.*) Romaic.
romana (*f.*) steelyard.
romance (*m.*) romance, novel; romantic love affair.—**policial,** detective story; (*adj.*) = ROMÂNICO.
romancear (*v.t.,v.i.*) to romance.
romanceiro (*m.*) collection of romances, novels, popular poems and songs, representative of a people; (*adj.*) = ROMÂNTICO.
romancista (*m.,f.*) novelist.
romanço (*m.*) the Romance languages collectively.
romaneio (*m.*) packing list; shipping list.
romanesco -ca [ê] (*adj.*) romanesque, fanciful; romantic.
romani [í] (*m.*) Romany (language of the gypsies).
românico -ca (*adj.*) Romance; (*m.*) Romance languages; Romance architecture.
romanista (*m.,f.*) Romanist.
romanizar (*v.t.*) to Romanize.
romano -na (*adj.; m.,f.*) Roman.
romano-bizantino -na (*adj.*) Romano-Byzantine.
romanticismo (*m.*) romanticism.
romanticista (*adj.; m.,f.*) romanticist.
romântico -ca (*adj.*) romantic, fanciful, sentimental, fantastic; (*m.,f.*) a romantic.
romantismo (*m.*) romanticism.
romantizar (*v.t.,v.i.*) to romanticize.
romaria (*f.*) pilgrimage, procession; by ext., any throng of persons going in the same direction, as to a football game, etc.
romãzeira (*f.*) pomegranate (*Punica granatum*).
rômbico -ca (*adj.*) rhombic.

rombiforme (*adj.*) rhombiform.
rombo -ba (*adj.*) blunt, obtuse; dull-witted; (*m.*) rhombus; hole, opening (as made by breaking in a door, a safe, a wall, the side of a ship); embezzlement.
romboédrico -ca (*adj.*) rhombohedric, rhombohedral.
romboedro (*m.*) rhombohedron.
romboidal (*adj.*) rhomboidal; (*m., Anat.*) rhomboideus.
rombóide (*adj.*) rhomboid; (*m.*) rhomboid; (*Anat.*) rhomboideus [= MÚSCULO ROMBÓIDE].
rombudo -da (*adj.*) very blunt (lit. & fig.).
romeina (*f., Min.*) romeine.
romeira (*f.*) woman pilgrim.
romeiro (*m.*) pilgrim; (*Zool.*) pilot fish (*Naucrates ductor*), c.a. PILOTO.
romeíto (*m., Min.*) romeíte.
romeno -na (*adj.; m.,f.*) Rumanian.
Romeu (*m.*) Romeo.
rompante (*adj.*) arrogant, haughty; impetuous; furious; (*m.*) impetuosity; fury; fit of anger, bluster; (*Arch.*) springer of an arch.
rompão (*m.*) calk (of a horseshoe).
rompedeira (*f.*) blacksmith's chisel for hot iron; cold chisel; locksmith's punch.
rompedor -dora (*adj.*) breaking; (*m.,f.*) breaker; (*m.*)—de concreto, concrete "buster."
rompedura (*f.*) breaking, breakage; break; tear.
rompe-gibão (*m., Bot.*) a thorny bumelia (*B. sertorum*).
rompente (*adj.*) breaking; tearing; (*Heraldry*) rampant.
romper (*v.t.*) to break (open, through, down); to split, burst; to disrupt; to rend, part; (*v.i.*) to burst out (forth); to erupt; to break off (relations) with.—**as leis**, to break the law.—**dentes**, to teethe.—**com alguém**, to break with (have a falling out with) someone.—**o silêncio**, to break the silence.—**obstáculos**, to overcome obstacles. **ao—da aurora**, at daybreak. **Rompeu-se o feitiço**, The spell is broken.
rompimento (*m.*) breaking, rupture, breach.
ronca (*f.*) snore; drone; roar; grunt; boast, bravado; foghorn; a drubbing. **meter a—**, to backbite.
roncada (*f.*) nap [= SONECA].
roncador -deira (*adj.*) snoring; droning; roaring; boastful; (*m.,f.*) snorer; boaster; (*Zool.*) the barred grunt (*Conodon nobilis*), c.a. CORÓ, FERREIRO, COROQUE, PARGO-BRANCO.
—**tobaca** = CORVINA-RISCADA (a croaker).
roncadura (*f.*) snoring.
roncante, roncão -cona (*adj.*) snoring.
roncar (*v.i.*) to snore; to drone; to grunt (as a pig); to roar (as a motor); to rumble; to bluster; (*v.t.*) to boast of; to threaten.—**grosso**, (*slang*) to talk tough, to talk big.
roncear (*v.i.*) to plod, trudge; to kill time; to loiter.
ronceirismo (*m.*) indolence; fogyism.
ronceiro -ra (*adj.*) slow, indolent, laggard, snail-paced.
roncinado -da (*adj.*) = RUNCINADO.
ronco (*m.*) snore; roar; rumble; growl, snarl; grunt (of a pig); purr (of a cat); drone of a bagpipe; (*Med.*) ronchus.
roncolho (*adj.*) having only one testicle; badly castrated.
ronda (*f.*) patrol, watch; beat, circuit, rounds; prowl.
rondador (*m.*) night watchman; prowler.
rondar, rondear (*v.t.*) to patrol, go the rounds; to lurk, prowl about; (*v.i.*) of the wind, to haul round to; to shift; veer.
rondel [-déis] (*m., Pros.*) rondel, rondeau.
rondó (*m., Pros.*) rondeau, rondel; (*Music*) rondo.
rongó (*f., colloq.*) prostitute [= MERETRIZ].
ronha (*f., Veter.*) scabies; (*colloq.*) wile.
ronhento -ta, ronhoso -sa (*adj.*) scabietic.
ronquear (*v.t.*) to clean and pack (fish).
ronqueira (*f.*) wheeze.
ronquejador (*m.*) blusterer.
ronquejar (*v.i.*) to roar.
ronquenho -nha (*adj.*) wheezy.
ronquidão (*m.*) wheeziness; hoarseness.
ronquido -da (*adj.*) wheezy; (*m.*) wheeze.
ronrom (*m.*) purring of a cat.
ronronar (*v.i.*) to purr (like a cat).
ropálico -ca (*adj.; Pros.*) rhopalic.
ropalóceros (*m.pl.*) a division (*Rhopalocera*) of butterflies.
roque (*m., Chess*) rook, castle. **sem rei nem—**, without rhyme or reason.
roquefort (*m.*) Roquefort cheese.
roquete [quê] (*m.*) ratchet; (*Eccl.*) rochet.
roquinha (*f.*) toy rattle on a stick.
roquinho (*m.*) a petrel (*Oceanodroma*).
ror [ô] (*m., colloq.*) lots, a heap.

rorante (*adj.*) roral, roric, dewy. [*Poetical*]
rorejar (*v.t.*) to let fall (drops); to bedew; (*v.i.*) to transpire (moisture).
rorela (*f.*) = ROSELA.
rórico -ca (*adj.*) roric, dewy.
rorífero -ra (*adj.*) roriferous, generating dew. [*Poetical*]
rorocoré (*m.*) = COROTÉU.
rorqual (*m.*) finback whale or rorqual (*Balanaeoptera physalus*).
rosa (*adj.*) rose; rose-colored, pink; (*f.*) rose (flower, bush, emblem, diamond, or color); rosette; (*Arch.*) rose window; (*Med.*) erysipelas; (*Naut.*) compass rose; (*Music*) rose of a lute or similar instrument; (*pl.*) joys; rosary. [*cap.*] Rose.—**albardeira**, common name for peony.—**-almiscarada**, muskmallow (*Hibiscus abelmoschus*).—**-amarela**, sweetbrier (*Rosa eglanteria*).—**-amélia** = ROSA-DE-CEM-FÔLHAS.—**branca**, the cottage rose (*Rosa alba*).—**canina** = ROSA-DE-CÃO.—**chá**, tea rose.—**cruz** (or **-cruzista**), Rosicrucian.—**da-china**, Chinese rose (*Rosa chinensis*); also the cottonrose hibiscus (*H. mutabilis*), c.a. ROSA-DE-SÃO-FRANCISCO, AURORA, INCONSTANTE-AMANTE.—**da-índia**, the Aztec marigold (*Tagetes erecta*), c.a. ROSA-DE-OURO, but better known as CRAVO-DE-DEFUNTO.—**damascena**, damask rose (*Rosa damascena*).—**da-montanha**, the glory flamebean (*Brownea grandiceps*).—**da-turquia**, the Jerusalem thorn (*Parkinsonia aculeata*) better known as ESPINHO-DE-JERUSALÉM.—**de-agulha**, compass rose.—**de-cachorro**, the so-called brier-rose or roseleaf raspberry (*Rubus rosaefolius coronarius*).—**de-cão** (or **rosa-canina**), the dog rose (*Rosa canina*) c.a. ROSEIRA-CANINA.—**de-cem-fôlhas**, the cabbage rose (*Rosa centifolia*). c.a. ROSA-AMÉLIA, ROSA-PÁLIDAS.—**de-guel(d)res**, cranberrybush viburnum (*V. opulus*).—**de-jericó**, rose of Jericho, the resurrection plant (*Anastatica hierochuntia*), c.a. REDIVIVA; also, a cow's-eye (*Odontospermum pygmaeum*).—**de-lôbo**, peony.—**de-musgo**, climbing Japanese rose (*Rosa multiflora*); the Aztec marigold (*Tagetes erecta*), c.a. ROSA-DA-ÍNDIA, but better known as CRAVO-DE-DEFUNTO and CRAVO-FÉTIDO-DA-ÍNDIA; (*R.C.Ch.*) golden rose.—**de-são-francisco** = ROSA-DA-CHINA (hibiscus).—**de-toucar**, cabbage rose (*Rosa centifolia*).—**de-vênus**, common torchlily or redhot poker (*Kniphofia uvaria*).—**do-campo**, the spearleaf pavonia (*P. hastata*).—**do-céu**, the rose-of-heaven (*Lychnis coelirosa*) c.a. VISCÁRIA.—**do-japão**, common name for camellias and hydrangeas.—**do-mar**, sea anemone.—**dos-ventos**, mariner's compass card.—**do-ultramar**, hollyhock (*Althaea rosea*).—**louça**, another name for the cottonrose hibiscus (*H. mutabilis*), c.a. ROSA-PAULISTA.—**madeira**, the Barbados-gooseberry (*Pereskia aculeata*, a cactus), c.a. ORA-PRO-NÓBIS, JUMBEBA.—**marinha**, another name for the hollyhock (*Althaea rosea*), c.a. ROSA-DO-ULTRAMAR, MALVAÍSCO, MALVA-ROSA.—**mijona** = ROSA-DE-CACHORRO.—**moscada** (or **rosa-musqueta**), the musk rose (*Rosa moschata*).—**náutica** = ROSA-DOS-VENTOS.—**paulista** = ROSA-LOUÇA.—**primitiva**, another name for the dog rose (*Rosa canina*).—**rubra**, the French rose (*Rosa gallica*).
rosaça (*f., Arch.*) rosette; rose window; rosace [= ROSÁCEA].
rosáceo -cea (*adj.*) rosaceous; (*f.pl.*) the rose family (*Rosaceae*); (*m.*) a top minnow, c.a. BARRIGUNDINHO; (*f.*) = ROSAÇA.
rosadinha (*f.*) an ironwood or jungleplum (*Sideroxylon resiniferum*).
rosado -da (*adj.*) roseate, rosy, rosaceous.
rosal (*m.*) = ROSEIRAL.
rosália (*f.*) mountainrose coralvine (*Antigonon leptopus*), c.a. CORAL, AMOR-AGARRADO; [*cap.*] Rosalie.
rosanilina (*f., Chem.*) rosaniline.
Rosalinda (*f.*) Rosalind.
Rosalina (*f.*) Rosaline.
Rosamunda (*f.*) Rosamond; Rosamund.
rosar (*v.t.*) to rose, render rose-colored; (*v.r.*) to turn red; to redden, blush.
rosário (*m.*) rosary (prayer of devotion, beads); chaplet (third of a rosary), c.a. TERÇO; endless or bucket conveyor; string, series of things; trotline.—**de-jambu**, (*Bot.*) a eugenia (*E. racemosa*).
rosassolis (*m.*) rosa solis (a cordial).
rosbife (*m.*) roastbeef.
rôsca (*f.*) screw thread; spiral, as of a corkscrew or auger; coil, as of a snake; rusk (twist of bread); larva of an owlet moth; (*colloq.*) drunken spree.—**de adução**, screw

conveyor.—**de parafuso,** screw thread.—**sem fim,** worm gear.—**soberba,** lag thread. **tampa com**—, screw cap.

roscar (*v.t.*) to thread (i.e., form a thread on a bolt, screw, pipe, etc.); to screw.

róscido –da (*adj.*) roscid, dewy. [*Poetical*]

roscioso –sa (*adj.*) dewy.

roscoélita (*f.*), **–to** (*m., Min.*) roscoelite.

roseira (*f.*) rosebush.—**-canina,** the dog rose (*Rosa canina*), c.a. ROSA-DE-CÃO.—**-do-japão,** common name for the camellia plant.

roseiral (*m.*) rose garden; place where roses grow.

roseirista (*m.,f.*) rosarian, rose fancier.

rosela (*f.*) the roselle (*Hibiscus sabdariffa*), c.a. CARURU-AZÊDO; the roundleaf sundew (*Drosera rotundifolia*), c.a. ORVALHINHA, RORELA.

roselha [ê] (*f.*) wrinkleleaf rockrose (*Cistus crispus*).

roselita (*f.*), **–to** (*m., Min.*) roselite.

rôseo –sea (*adj.*) rose, rosy; rose-scented.

roséola (*f., Med.*) roseola, rose rash; rubella, german measles.

roseta [ê] (*f.*) rosette; rowel.—**-de-pernambuco,** a cactus (*Rhipsalis sarmentosa*).—**-de-santa-catarina,** a nailwort (*Paronychia rosela*).

rosete [sê] (*adj.*) rosyish.

rosetear (*v.t.*) to spur with a rowel.

rosicler (*adj.*) rose-pink; (*m.*) ruby silver, pyrargyrite; the color rose-red; string of pearls.

rosilho –lha (*adj.; m.,f.*) strawberry roan (horse). Cf. RUÃO.

rosmaninho (*m.*) lavender (*Lavandula*); bushmint (*Hyptis*).

rosmaro (*m.*) rosmarine—an old name for the walrus, now called MORSA or VACA-MARINHA.

rosnadela, **–dura** (*f.*), snarl, growl.

rosnador –dora (*adj.*) snarling, growling.

rosnar (*v.t.,v.i.*) to snarl, growl; to mutter.

rosnento –ta (*adj.*) growling.

rosólico –ca (*adj.; Chem.*) rosalic.

rosquear (*v.*) = ROSCAR.

rosquilha (*f.*), **–lho** (*m.*) ring-shaped biscuit.

rosquinha (*f.*) a beach snail (*Tegula viridula*).

rossio (*m.*) public square.

rossolis (*m.*) rosolio, rossolis (liqueur).

rostear (*v.t.*) to face.

rostelo (*m., Bot., Zool.*) rostellum.

rostir (*v.t.*) to hit in the face.

rosto [rôs] (*m.*) face, countenance; title page; head (of a coin). **—a**—, face to face. **de**—, facing. **fazer**—, to face. **lançar em**—, to twit, taunt.

rostrado –da (*adj.*) rostrate, having a rostrum or beak.

rostral (*adj.*) rostral.

rostrária (*f.*) = TRISSETO.

rostriforme (*adj.*) rostriform.

rostro (*m.*) rostrum [but not in the modern sense of pulpit or platform, which is TRIBUNA or PÚLPITO]; (*Anat., Zool., Bot.*) rostrum.

rota (*f.*) rout, defeat; route, itinerary, course; rattan [= ROTIM]; Sacred Roman Rota.—**aérea,** airline.—**batida,** (*Naut.*) direct route.—**marítima,** sea route.—**mercante,** merchant sea lane, **de,** or **em,—batida,** in full flight.

rotação (*f.*) rotation, revolution, spin, gyration; succession, sequence, round.—**à direita,** clockwise movement.—**à esquerda,** counter-clockwise movement.—**cultural,** (*Agric.*) crop rotation. **motor de alta**—, high-speed motor.—**por minuto,** revolutions per minute.—**por segundo,** revolutions per second.

rotacismo (*m.*) rhotacism.

rotacista (*adj.*) rhotacistic.

rotador (*m., Anat.*) rotator; (*Zool.*) rotifer; (*pl.*) the Rotifera.

rotala (*f., Bot.*) a genus (*Rotala*) which includes the toothcup (*R. ramosior*).

rotâmetro (*m.*) rotameter.

rotante (*adj.*) rolling.

rotar (*v.i.*) to rotate.

rotariano –na (*adj.*) Rotarian; (*m.*) a Rotarian (member of the Rotary Club).

rotativamente (*adv.*) by turns; in rotation.

rotativo –va (*adj.*) rotative; (*f.*) rotary printing press.

rotatório –ria (*adj.*) rotatory; (*m.*) rotifer [= ROTADOR].

rotear (*v.*) = ARROTEAR; MAREAR.

roteiro (*m.*) route, intinerary; log book; bearings, directions; schedule; agenda; list of things to do or see, or of topics for discussion; norm; sea chart.

rotenona (*f., Chem.*) rotenone.

Roterdão (*m.*) Rotterdam.

rotífero –ra (*adj.*) wheeled; (*m., Zool.*) rotifer; (*pl.*) the Rotifera [= ROTADORES].

rotiforme (*adj.*) wheel-shaped.

rotim (*m.*) rattan palm (*Calamus*); a rush used for mats, chair bottoms, etc.

rotina (*f.*) routine procedure; well-trod path.

rotineiro –ra (*adj.*) routine; hidebound, old-fogyish; workaday; (*m.,f.*) such a person; (*f.*) = ROTINA.

rôto –ta (*irreg. p.p. of* ROMPER) broken, rent, tattered, torn; (*m.*) tatterdemalion. **Ela é um saco**—, She can't keep a secret. **Ri o—do esfarrapado,** The pot calls the kettle black.

rotogravura (*f.*) rotogravure.

rotoína (*f.*) = ESCOPOLEINA.

rotor (*m., Mach., Elec.*) rotor.

rotoscópio (*m.*) stroboscope.

rótula (*f.*) kneecap, patella; lattice, trellis; window shutter.

rotulagem, rotulação (*f.*) labeling.

rotular (*v.t.*) to label; (*adj.*) rotular.

rótulo (*m.*) label; inscription.

rotunda (*f.*) rotunda; (*R.R.*) roundhouse.

rotundidade (*f.*) rotundity.

rotundifólio –lia (*adj.; Bot.*) rotundifolious.

rotundo –da (*adj.*) rotund; plump.

rotura (*f.*) = RUPTURA.

rouba (*f.*) = ROUBO.

roubador –dora (*adj.*) robbing; (*m.,f.*) robber.

roubalheira (*f.*) a huge gyp or swindle; embezzlement of public funds.

roubar (*v.t.*) to rob, plunder, strip, take from; to embezzle. **—a,** to steal from.

roubo (*m.*) robbery; plunder; exorbitant price.

rouco –ca (*adj.*) hoarse, husky; raucous.

roufenhar (*v.i.*) to speak with a twang.

roufenho –nha (*adj.*) twangy; raucous, hoarse; wheezy.

roupa (*f.*) clothing, clothes, garments, dress, garb, wearing-apparel.—**branca,** or—**de baixo,** or—**inferior,** underwear, undergarments.—**de banho,** bathing suit.—**de cama,** bedclothes, bed linen.—**de dormir,** night clothes, nightdress, nightgown.—**domingueira,** Sunday clothes.—**feita,** ready-made clothing.—**sob medida,** made-to-measure clothing.—**suja,** soiled clothes, laundry.—**s menores,** underclothes.—**usada,** secondhand clothing. **a queima**—, at close range; point-blank. **rol da**—, laundry list. **terno de**—, three-piece suit.

roupagem (*f.*) clothing, clothes; apparel; drapery; show, pretense.

roupão (*m.*) bathrobe, dressing gown.

rouparia (*f.*) clothing; clothes closet.

rouparelheiro (*m.*) old clothes man.

roupeiro (*m.*) clothes closet; also, the man in charge of the locker room at a club.

roupeta [ê] (*f.*) cassock; by ext., a priest.

roupinha (*f.*) bodice.

rouqueira (*f.*) = ROUQUIDÃO.

rouquejante (*adj.*) croaking.

rouquejar (*v.i.*) to croak; to talk hoarsely.

rouquenho –nha, roquento –ta (*adj.*) hoarse.

rouquice, rouquidão (*f.*) hoarseness.

rouquido (*m.*) hoarse wheeze.

rouxinol [-óis] (*m.*) in Portugal, the nightingale, which does not occur in Brazil but where the term is used to designate three other birds called SOLDADO, ENCONTRO and CORRUÍRA; philomel (in poetical use); fig., a songstress.—**-do-campo,** the Cayenne red-breasted blackbird (*Leistes m. militaris*), c.a. POLÍCIA-INGLÊSA, PUXA-VERÃO, TEM-TEM-DO-ESPÍRITO-SANTO. **—-do-rio-negro,** the moriche oriole (*Icterus chrysocephalus*), c.a. TEM-TEM.

Roxane (*f.*) Roxana.

roxeado –da (*adj.*) purplish.

roxear (*v.*) = ARROXEAR.

roxinho (*m.*) = GUARABU.—**-do-pará** = GUARABU-AMARELO.

roxo –xa [rô] (*adj.*) purple.—**de frio,** blue with cold.—**-forte,** rum.—**-rei,** red ocher.

R.P. = REPÚBLICA PORTUGUÊSA (Republic of Portugal); REVERENDO PADRE (Reverend Father).

R.P.M. = REVERENDO PADRE-MESTRE (Reverend Father-Teacher).

r.p.m. = ROTAÇÃO POR MINUTO (revolutions per minute).

r.p.s. = ROTAÇÃO POR SEGUNDO (revolutions per second).

RS = RIO GRANDE DO SUL (State of).

rs. or **R.ˢ** = RÉIS (monetary unit).

R.S.A. = RECOMENDADA A SANTO ANTÔNIO (recommended to St. Anthony).

rua (*f.*) street; (*exclam.*) Get out!—**de uma mão (só)**, one-way street.—**sem saída**, blind street. **andar na**—, to be out of work, down and out. **andar pelas**—**s**, to walk the streets. **arrastar pela**—**da amargura**, to blemish, besmirch. **pôr no ôlho da**—, to oust, turn out of doors. **ser posto na**—, to be fired (from one's job).

ruaça (*f.*) = ARRUAÇA.

ruaceiro (*m.*) = ARRUACEIRO.

ruamom (*m.*, *Bot.*) a poison nut (*Strychnos rouhamon*).

ruão (*adj.*; *m.*) roan (horse); (*cap.*) Rouen (France).

ruar (*v.i.*) to spend time in the streets.

rubefação (*f.*) rubefaction.

rubefaciente (*adj.*; *m.*) rubefacient.

rubelita (*f.*), **-to** (*m.*, *Min.*) rubellite.

rubente (*adj.*) reddish.

rubéola (*f.*, *Med.*) rubella; German measles.

ruberítrico **-ca** (*adj.*, *Chem.*) ruberythric.

rubescência (*f.*) rubescence.

rubescente (*adj.*) rubescent.

rubeta [ê] (*f.*) = PERERECA.

rubi [í] (*m.*) ruby; ruby spinel; the color ruby.—**almandino**, almandine, ruby spinel.—**da-boêmia**, Bohemian ruby (a rose-red variety of quartz).—**da-sibéria**, or **-de-madagascar**, rubellite (ruby-red tourmaline).—**do-brasil** = TOPÁZIO-QUEIMADO.—**do-cabo**, Cape ruby—a ruby-colored garnet.—**espinélio**, spinel ruby.—**falso**, or **-ocidental**, a rose-red variety of quartz.—**oriental**, the true, or Oriental, ruby.—**negro** = ALABANDINA.—**-topázio**, the ruby-and-topaz hummingbird.

rúbia (*f.*, *Bot.*) a genus (*Rubia*) of madders.

rubiáceo **-cea** (*adj.*; *Bot.*) rubiaceous; (*f.*, *colloq.*) coffee; (*f.pl.*) the madder family (*Rubiaceae*).

rubião (*m.*) rubine (a dye).

rubicano **-na** (*adj.*) rubican [horse].

Rubicão (*m.*) Rubicon; fig., obstacle. **passar o**—, to cross the Rubicon; take an irrevocable step; burn one's bridges.

rubicundo **-da** (*adj.*) rubicund, ruddy, red.

rubidez [ê] (*f.*) redness [= RUBOR].

rubídio (*m.*, *Chem.*) rubidium.

rúbido **-da** (*adj.*) ruby. [*Poetical*]

rubificação (*f.*) rubification.

rubificante (*adj.*) = RUBEFACIENTE.

rubificar (*v.t.*,*v.i.*) to redden.

rubiginoso **-sa** (*adj.*) rusty, rust-colored.

rubim (*m.*) = CORDÃO-DE-FRADE.

rubinegro **-gra** (*adj.*) red-and-black.

rubirrostro **-tra** (*adj.*; *Zool.*) red-beaked, red-faced.

rubixá (*m.*) = JAPU.

rublo (*m.*) Russian ruble.

rubo (*m.*) brier; blackberry; any species of *Rubus* (blackberry).

rubor (*m.*) redness, blush; bashfulness, modesty, shame.

ruborescer, ruborizar (*v.t.*) to make red; (*v.r.*) to redden, blush.

rubrica (*f.*) rubric; instructions to actors (in the MS of a play); abbreviated signature; autograph initials; flourish (on the end of a signature); red ocher; red chalk.

rubricador **-dora** (*adj.*) rubric(al); (*m.*,*f.*) rubricator.

rubricar (*v.t.*) to rubricate, rubricize; to sign or initial the pages of a book or document.

rubricista (*m.*,*f.*) rubrician, rubricist.

rubricolo **-la** (*adj.*, *Zool.*) red-necked.

rubricórneo **-nea** (*adj.*) having red antennae or feelers.

rubriflor **-flora** (*adj.*) red-flowered.

rubrigastro **-tra** (*adj.*, *Zool.*) red-bellied.

rubrípede (*adj.*; *Zool.*) red-footed.

rubrirrostro **-tra** (*adj.*, *Zool.*) red-beaked; red-faced.

rubro **-bra** (*adj.*) ruby-red, blood-red.—**branco**, (*m.*) the color of iron at white heat.—**negro**, (*adj.*) red-and-black.

rubrostigma (*m.*) a small tropical aquarium fish (*Panchas lineatus*).

ruço **-ça** (*adj.*) brownish; gray; faded; having very light brown hair; (*m.*) a wet, heavy fog.

rucuri [í] (*m.*) = GUACURI.

rude (*adj.*) rude, crude, rustic; rough, coarse, uncouth; blunt, gruff, brusque, harsh.

rudentura (*f.*, *Arch.*) rudenture.

rudez[a] [ê] (*f.*) rudeness, incivility; abruptness.

rudimentar (*adj.*) rudimental, elementary; embryonic.

rudimento (*m.*) rudiment, first principle; embryo.

rueiro **-ra** (*adj.*) of the street; fond of walking the streets.

ruela (*f.*) little street, alley.

rufar (*v.t.*) to ruffle, beat (a drum); to furnish with ruffles.

rufião [-fiães, -fiões] (*m.*) ruffian; hooligan; pl ug-ugly, bully; pander; stud horse.

ruficarpo **-pa** (*adj.*, *Bot.*) ruficarpous.

ruficórneo **-nea** (*adj.*, *Zool.*) ruficornate.

ruflar (*v.t.*) to ruffle, rustle, flutter; (*v.i.*) to ruffle, flutter; to swish.

rufo (*m.*) ruffle, roll (of a drum); ruffle (of a garment, etc.); (*m.*) coarse or middle-cut file; [*cap.*] Rufus.

ruga (*f.*) wrinkle; furrow; pleat.

ruge-ruge (*m.*) rustling sound (as of silk).

rugido (*m.*) roar (of a lion); bellow.

rugidor **-dora** (*adj.*) roaring, bellowing.

rugir (*v.i.*) to roar, bellow, howl; to rustle; (*m.*) roar.

rugosidade (*f.*) rugosity.

rugoso **-sa** (*adj.*) rugose, wrinkled; rugged.

ruibarbo (*m.*, *Bot.*) rhubarb (*Rheum*).—**do-brejo** = BARIRIÇO.—**da-china**, sorrel rhubarb (*Rheum palmotum*).—**do-campo** = BATATINHA-DO-CAMPO, BUTUÁ-DE-CORVO.

ruído (*m.*) noise, sound; din, clamor, clatter; renown; show, pomp.—**do trânsito**, street (traffic) noises. **à prova de**—, soundproof.

ruidoso **-sa** [u-i] (*adj.*) noisy; loud, boisterous, showy, pompous; spectacular, sensational.

ruim [u-ím] (*adj.*) bad, evil; vile, mean; poor, inferior.

ruína (*f.*) ruin, destruction; doom; bane; a has-been; (*pl.*) ruins.

ruinar (*v.*) = ARRUINAR.

ruindade [u-in] (*f.*) evil, badness, malignity.

ruinoso **-sa** [u-i] (*adj.*) ruinous; ruined.

ruir [25] (*v.i.*) to crash to earth, fall, tumble, topple. **fazer** —**a sala**, to bring down the house.

ruiva (*f.*) see under RUIVO.

ruivacento **-ta** (*adj.*) reddish.

ruivinho (*m.*) peccary [= CAITITU].

ruivo **-va** (*adj.*) reddish-yellow, auburn; red-haired; (*m.*,*f.*) red-headed person; (*m.*) a three-awn grass (*Aristida capillacea*); (*f.*) red sunset or sunrise; European redwing (a thrush); (*Min.*) rutile (when found in the diamond fields); (*Bot.*) common madder (*Rubia tinctorum*).—**-brava** = GRANZA-BRAVA.—**da-índia** or **-da-sibéria**, the India madder (*R. cordifolia*).—**-dos-tintureiros**, common madder (*R. tinctorum*),

rulhar (*v.*) = ARRULHAR.

ruma (*f.*) heap, pile [= RIMA]; (*interj.*) an oxcart driver's shout of command to his oxen.

rumar (*v.t.*) to steer, guide.—**para**, to head for, go in the direction of (toward).

rumado (*m.*, *Bot.*) the cluster fig (*Ficus glomerata*).

rume, rúmen (*m.*, *Zool.*) rumen.

ruminação (*f.*) rumination, chewing the cud; meditation, reflection.

ruminador **-dora** (*adj.*) ruminating, ruminant.

ruminadouro (*m.*) = RUMEN.

ruminal (*adj.*) ruminant.

ruminante (*adj.*; *m.*) ruminant; (*pl.*, *Zool.*) the Ruminantia.

ruminar (*v.t.*) to ruminate, chew the cud; (*v.i.*) to ponder, meditate; to brood over.

rumo (*m.*) rhumb (any of the points of the mariner's compass); bearing, course, direction.—**a**, in the direction of, toward.—**estimado**, dead reckoning. **(de)**—**a**, toward, headed for, bound for.—**de**, toward. **sem**—, adrift.—**de vida**, way of life.

rumor (*m.*) noise, rumbling; murmur; rumor, hearsay.

rumorar (*v.*) = RUMOREJAR.

rumorejante (*adj.*) murmuring, rustling.

rumorejar (*v.i.*) to purl, murmur; to rustle; (*v.t.*) to rumor, noise abroad.

rumorejo [ê] (*m.*) purling, babbling, rustle; hum of voices.

rumorinho (*m.*) murmur.

rumoroso **-sa** (*adj.*) widely (loudly, hotly) debated; highly controversial; much talked about; noisy.

runas (*f.pl.*) runes.

runcinado **-da** (*adj.*; *Bot.*) runcinate.

rúnico **-ca** (*adj.*) runic.

rupestre (*adj.*) rupestral, rupestrian, rupicolous. **pinturas** —**s**, cave pictures.

rupia (*f.*) rupia (a Port. colonial coin corresponding to the Indian rupee); (*Med.*) rupia.

rúpia (*f.*) the genus (*Ruppia*) which contains the widgeon, tassel, or ditch, grass (*R. maritima*).

rupícola (*adj.; Bot., Zool.*) rupicolous; (*f.*) the genus (*Rupicola*) containing the cock-of-the-rock.

rúptil (*adj.; Bot.*) dehiscing irregularly.

ruptura (*f.*) rupture, disruption; breach (of contract); quarrel, rift; (*Med.*) hernia; fracture.

rural (*adj.*) rural. **caminho—,** country road.

ruralismo (*m.*) ruralism (in art).

ruralista (*adj.; m.,f.*) ruralist (in art).

ruralizar (*v.t.*) to ruralize.

rurícola (*adj.*) living in the country.

rusco (*m.*) = GILBARBEIRA.

rusga (*f.*) row, fracas; tiff, squabble, spat.

rusgar (*v.i.*) to tiff, squabble.

rusguento -ta (*adj.*) quarrelsome; faultfinding.

russalhada (*f.*) a bunch of Russians. [*Derogatory*

russianizar (*v.t.*) to Russianize.

russiano -na (*adj.; m.,f.*) = RUSSO.

russificar (*v.t.*) to Russify.

russo -sa (*adj.; m.,f.*) Russian.

russófilo -la (*adj.; m.,f.*) Russophile.

russófobo -ba (*adj.; m.,f.*) Russophobe.

rússula (*f.*) a genus (*Russula*) of white-spored agaricaceous fungi, some species of which are edible.

rusticar (*v.i.*) to rusticate; (*v.t., Masonry*) to rusticate.

rusticidade (*f.*) rusticity.

rústico -ca (*adj.*) rustic, rural, country; loutish; boorish; (*m.*) a rustic, bumpkin, hick, yokel, lout; a peasant.

ruta (*f., Bot.*) a genus (*Ruta*) of the rue family.—**-murária,** the wall rue (*Asplenium rutamuraria*), c.a. ARRUDA-DOS-MUROS, PARONÍQUIA.

rutabaga (*f., Bot.*) rutabaga (*Brassica napobrassica*).

rutáceo -cea (*adj.; Bot.*) rutaceous; (*f.pl.*) the rue family (*Rutaceae*).

Rute (*f.*) Ruth.

rútela (*f., Zool.*) a rutelian (goldsmith beetle).

rutenense (*adj.*) Ruthenian.

rutênico -ca (*adj.; m.,f.*) Ruthenian.

rutênio (*m., Chem.*) ruthenium.

rutenos (*m.pl.*) the Ruthenians or Little Russians.

ruterfordito (*m., Min.*) rutherfordite.

rútila (*f.*) = RUTÍLIO.

rutilação (*f.*) glittering, shining; brightness, brilliancy.

rutilância (*f.*) brightness, brilliancy.

rutilante (*adj.*) shining, glittering, bright, radiant.

rutilar (*v.i.*) to shine, gleam, glitter, blaze.

rutílio, rutilo (*m., Chem.*) rutile, titanium dioxide.

rutim (*m.*) a bramble palm (*Desmonchus polyacanthus*).

rutina (*f., Chem.*) rutin.

ruvinhoso -sa (*adj.*) rusty; worm-eaten; ill-humored; coarse-mannered; petulant.

S

S, s, the 18th letter of the Port. alphabet.

S. = SÃO, SANTO, SANTA (Saint); SUL (south).

s/ = SEM (without); SEU(S) or SUA(S) = your [letter, etc.]; SÔBRE (on [followed by name of bank on which a check is drawn]).

s/a = SEU ACEITE (your acceptance [of a draft]).

S.A. = SOCIEDADE ANÔNIMA (joint stock company, corporation); SUA ALTEZA, (His [Her] Highness).

sã (*adj.*) fem. of SÃO; (*f.*) the larder beetle (*Dermestes lardarius*).

saã (*m., Zool.*) a marmoset (*Callithrix nigrifrons*), c.a. SAUÁ.

Saará (*m.*) Sahara.

sabá (*m.*) Sabbath.

sabácia (*f., Bot.*) the genus *Sabatia* (rose gentian).

sabacu[-de-coroa] (*m.*) = MATIRÃO.

sabadear (*v.i.*) to keep the Sabbath.

sábado (*m.*) Saturday; Sabbath.—**de aleluia,** or—**Santo,** Holy Saturday.—**gordo,** the last Saturday before Easter.

sabão (*m.*) soap [for kitchen or laundry; toilet soap is SABONETE]; (*colloq.*) a dressing down, scolding; (*Bot.*) the southern soapberry (*Sapindus saponaria*).—**de barba,** shaving soap.—**-de-soldado,** a soapberry (*Sapindus divaricatus*).—**-dos-vidreiros,** bog manganese. **água de—,** soapsuds. **bôlha de—,** soap bubble. **pedra-—,** soapstone.

sabático -ca (*adj.*) sabbatical.

sabatina (*f.*) a weekly school test or review (on Saturdays); fig., a discussion; question-period (following a lecture); roundtable discussion, open forum.

sabe-a-tôda (*m., colloq.*) a know-it-all, wise guy.

sabável (*adj.*) pleasing to the taste.

sabedor -dora (*adj.*) knowing; aware; proficient.—**de,** cognizant of; (*m.,f.*) a knowing person.

sabedoria (*f.*) wisdom, sapience; knowledge, learning; reason; (*Bot.*)—**legítima** = SABOEIRA-LEGÍTIMA.

sabela (*f., Zool.*) a genus (*Sabella*) of annelids.

sabelária (*f., Zool.*) a genus (*Sabellaria*) of annelids.

sabença (*f., colloq.*) wisdom; learning.

saber [74] (*v.i.*) to know, have knowledge of; to be aware of; to understand; to know how to; to be sure or certain of; to be capable of. [Cf. CONHECER] (*m.*) knowledge, learning, wisdom.—**+inf.** = to know how+inf. [saber ler, escrever, cantar, etc., to know how to read, write, sing, etc.]—**a,** to smack of, taste like.—**a quantas andam,** to know what's what.—**as linhas como que se cose,** to know what one is doing.—**com quem (se) está falando,** to know whom (one) is talking to.—**de,** to hear about;

to find out about; to know about.—**de cor,** to know (something) by heart.—**de cor e salteado,** to know (something) upside down and backwards.—**na ponta da língua,** to have (something) on the tip of one's tongue. —**o que está dizendo,** to know what one is talking about. —**perder,** to be a good loser.—**ser homem,** to display manliness, strength, courage, guts.—**viver,** to know how to live (wisely, enjoyably). **a—,** to wit, namely, viz. **ao que sabemos,** as far as we know. **como se sabe,** as is well-known. **dar a—,** to give out information; to let (someone) know (something). **Ela não sabe de nada,** She hasn't heard yet; she mustn't be told. **Ela não sabe nada,** She doesn't know (can't learn) anything. **Eu não sei (falar) inglês,** I can't speak English. **fazer—,** to inform, make known. **Já sei!** Yes, I know! I know! Of course! **Já se sabe,** Of course; that's understood. **não querer—de,** not to want to hear of (about); not to want to become involved with. **não —de si,** to be confused, not know what one is doing. **não—a quantas anda,** not to know what one is about. **Não se pode—,** You (one) cannot tell (know). **Não sei que dizer,** I don't know what to say. **Pelo que sei,** As far as I know. **procurar—se,** to try to find out if. **Que eu saiba, não,** Not that I know of. **Quem sabe?** Maybe so; Perhaps; Who knows? **sabendo de,** on learning that. **Sei lá!** How should I know! I haven't the slightest idea! **Só sei dizer que,** I can only say that . . . ; All I know is . . . **Soube (que não era verdade),** He (she) found out (that it wasn't true). **Tanto quanto eu saiba,** Not as far as I know. **um não-sei-quê,** an indefinable (vague) something. **vir a—se que,** to become (known) known that.

saberé (*m.*) = QUERÊ-QUERÊ.

sabiá (*m. or f.*) any of a number of thrushes widely scattered throughout Brazil, where it is a favorite songbird. [Every schoolchild learns the CANÇÃO DO EXILO (Song of Exile) written by Antonio Gonçalves Dias, which begins: *Minha terra tem palmeiras, onde cantá o sabiá,* In my homeland there are palm trees, where sings the **sabiá**]. In addition to the thrushes (*Turdus*), the name **sabiá** is applied to some mockingbirds (*Mimus*), and to some other birds, as shown below; (*Med.*) thrush, c.a. BOQUEIRA, CANTO-DE-BÔCA.—**-barranco** (or -cinzento, or -poca), Azara's thrush (*Turdus leucomelas*).—**-branco** (or -pardo), the dusky thrush (*Turdus amaurochalinus*).—**-coleira** (or -branco, or -da-mato, or -poca), the rusty-flanked thrush (*Turdus albicollis*).—**-da-campina** = TRINCA-FERRO.—**-da-capoeira** (or -da-mata, or -verdadeiro), the sabian thrush (*Turdus fumigatus*), c.a.

CARAXUÉ-DA-MATA.—**da-lapa** (or **-poca**), the Bahian white-necked thrush (*Turdus albicollis crotopezus*).—**da-praia** (or **-da-restinga**, or **-piri**), the blue-gray mockingbird (*Mimus gilvus*).—**do-banhado**, the La Plata ground finch (*Emgernagra platensis*).—**do-brejo** = JAPACANIM.—**do-campo** (or **-do-sertão**), the Brazilian mockingbird (*Mimus saturninus*), c.a. ARREBITA-RABO, GALO-DO-CAMPO.—**do-mato-grosso** = TROPEIRO.—**guaçu** = JAPACANIM.—**laranjeira** (or **-cavalo**, or **-gongâ**, or **-laranja**, or **-piranga**, or **-ponga**, or **-verdadeiro**), the rufous-bellied thrush (*Turdus rufiventris*), c.a. UIRAXUÉ. [This is the best-known species in Brazil, and is believed by some to be the subject of the verse mentioned above.]—**pimenta** = TRINCA-FERRO.—**prêto** (or **-una**), the Brazilian gray ouzel (*Platycichla flaviceps*), reputed to be the best singer among the sabiás.—**tropeiro** = TROPEIRO.

sabiacica (m.) the blue-bellied parrot (*Triclaria cyanogaster*), c.a. ARAÇUAIAVA.

sabichã (*adj.; f.*) = SABICHONA.

sabichão (m.) wiseacre, know-it-all, "wise guy," smart-aleck, prig. **fazer-se de—**, to look wise.

sabichar (*v.i.*) to pry about, nose around.

sabichona (*adj.; f.*) bluestocking (woman).

sabidas (*f.pl.*) **às—**, openly, aboveboard. **às não—**, covertly, secretly.

sabido –**da** (*adj.*) known; knowing, learned, wise; cunning, shrewd, sharp.

sabino –**na** (*adj.; m.*) Sabine (people, language); (*f.*) Savin juniper (*Juniperus sabina*); Japanese snakegourd (*Tricosanthes cucumeroides*).

sábio –**bia** (*adj.*) wise, sagacious; judicious; scholarly; (m.) sage, savant, scholar, man of learning.

sabitu [ú] (m.) the male SAÚVA ant

sabível (*adj.*) knowable.

sable (m., *Heraldry*) sable (the color black).

saboaria (*f.*) soap factory; soap warehouse.

saboeira (*f.*) soap dish; (*Bot.*) southern soapberry (*Sapindus saponaria*).—**legítima**, bouncingbet (*Saponaria officinalis*), c.a. ERVA-SABOEIRA, SABEDORIA-LEGÍTIMA.

saboeirana (*f., Bot.*) a swartzpea (*Swartia sp.*).

saboeiro (m.) soapmaker; soap dealer; soap dish; (*Bot.*) a saman tree (*Samanea multiflora*), c.a. FAVEIRA-DO-MATO; southern soapberry (*Sapindus saponaria*), c.a. SABÃO-DE-MACACO, SABÃO-DE-SOLDADO, SABONETEIRO, SABOEIRA.

saboiano –**na** (*adj.; m.,f.*) Savoyard.

saboneira (*f.*) = ERVA-SABOEIRA.

sabonete [nê] (m.) toilet soap; (*colloq.*) a remonstrance (mild "SABÃO").

saboneteira (*f.*) soap dish, soap holder.

sabor [ô] (m.) savor, taste, flavor; relish; sort, nature; style, character; whim, caprice; spice, sparkle. **ao—de**, at the mercy (whim, discretion, pleasure) of. **sem—**, savorless.

saborear (*v.t.*) to savor, relish, taste, enjoy; to add flavor to; (*v.r.*) to enjoy oneself.

saboroso –**sa** (*adj.*) savory, palatable, tasty, luscious, delicious; pleasant.

sabotagem (*f.*) sabotage.

sabotar (*v.t.*) to sabotage.

sabre (m.) saber.

sabugar (*v.t.*) to flog.

sabugo (m.) corncob; elderberry tree; root of a fingernail; pith; a cactus, c.a. CACTO-TREPADOR.

sabugueirinho (m.) = ENGOS.

sabugueiro (m., *Bot.*) European elder (*Sambucus nigra*).—**d'água**, or—**dos-pantanos**, the European cranberry-bush viburnum (*V. opulus*), c.a. NOVÉLOS, BOLA-DE-NEVE.—**do-campo**, a button plant (*Spermacoce centranthoides*), c.a. GUAICURU-DO-CAMPO.

sabujar (*v.t.*) to flatter, fawn upon.

sabujo (m.) hound, hunting dog; heeler, servile follower; toady, lickspittle.

sabuloso –**sa** (*adj.*) sabulous, sandy, gritty.

saburra (*f.*) a foul coating of the tongue.

saburrar (*v.t.*) to ballast a ship.

saburroso –**sa**, **saburrento** –**ta** (*adj.*) coated, furred [tongue].

sac. = SACERDOTE (priest).

saca (*f.*) sack, bag; esp. a large one; act of drawing out (cork, etc.).—**de café**, bag of coffee. Cf. SACO.

saca-balas (m., *Surg.*) a crow's-bill (kind of forceps for extracting bullets, etc.).

saca-bocados (m.) a blanking punch or die; paper punch.

saca-boi (m.) cow-catcher (on a locomotive).

saca-buxa (*f.*) sackbut (medieval trombone).

sacaca (*f.*) sorcery, magic; (*Bot.*) a croton, c.a .CAJUCARA.

sacada (*f.*) see under SACADO.

sacadela (*f.*) tug, pull, jerk.

sacado –**da** (*m.,f.*) drawee (of a demand for payment); (m.) = TIPISCA; (*f.*) balcony; a sackful.

sacador –**dora** (*adj.*) drawing; (*m.,f.*) drawer (of a demand for payment).

saca-estrepe-de-campinas (m., *Bot.*) a globethistle (*Echinops*).

sacaí (m.) twigs, dry branches, kindling.

sacaibóia (*f.*) = COBRA-CIPÓ.

sacalão (m.) pull, jerk; a sudden pull-up on the reins.

saca-molas (m.) dentist's extracting forceps; (*colloq.*) tooth-puller (second rate dentist).

sacana (m.) person of low character; pederast; kidder.

saca-nabo (m.) piston rod (of a marine pump).

sacanagem (*f.*) low trick; pederasty; foolery.

sacanga (*f.*) kindling wood, dry twigs.

sacão (m.) jump, plunge (of a horse).

sacar (*v.t.*) to draw (out), take out, extract; to draw against credit.—**a descoberto**, to overdraw (against credit).—**de**, to draw (something) out quickly (as a knife or sword).—**sôbre**, to draw on (credit).

saca-rabo (m.) a mongoose or ichneumon, c.a. MANGUSTO.

sacárase (*f., Chem.*) saccharase.

sacarato (m., *Chem.*) saccharate, sucrate.

sacaria (*f.*) a quantity of sacks.

saçaricar (*v.i., slang*) to wiggle, wriggle, writhe, squirm, esp. while dancing.

sacárico –**ca** (*adj., Chem.*) saccharic.

sacáride (*f., Chem.*) saccharide.

sacarífero –**ra** (*adj.*) sacchariferous.

sacarificação (*f.*) saccharification.

sacarificar (*v.t.*) to saccharify.

sacarímetro (m.) saccharimeter [= SACARÔMETRO].

sacarina (*f.*) saccharin.

sacarínico –**ca** (*adj.*) saccharinic.

sacarino –**na** (*adj.*) saccharine, sugary.

sácaro (m., *Bot.*) the genus Saccharum (sweet cane, sugar cane).

sacaróide (*adj.*) saccharoid, crystalline, granular.

saca-rôlha[s] (m.) corkscrew; (*Bot.*) a screw tree (*Helicteres*).

sacarose (*f., Chem.*) sucrose; cane sugar; beet sugar.

sacaroso –**sa** (*adj.*) sugary.

saca-saia (*f.*) = CORREIÇÃO.

saca-trapo (m.) = MALVA-CAJUÇARA.

sacerdócio (m.) priesthood; priestly power, qualities or mission.

sacerdotal (*adj.*) sacerdotal, priestly.

sacerdotalismo (m.) sacerdotalism.

sacerdote (m.) priest, cleric.

sacerdotisa (*f.*) priestess.

sacha (*f.*) act of hoeing or grubbing; hoe [= ENXADA].—**rosa**, a cactus (*Pereskia sacharosa*).—**uva**, Magellan barberry (*Berberis buxifolia*).

sachadela (*f.*) a weeding or light cultivation with a hoe.

sachador –**dora** (*adj.*) weeding, hoeing; (m.) weeder, hoer.

sachadura (*f.*) a weeding or hoeing.

sachar (*v.t.*) to weed, hoe, grub up.

sacho (m.) weeding hoe.

sachola (*f.*) garden hoe.

sacholar (*v.t.*) to hoe or weed with a light hoe.

saci [í] (m.) In Brazilian folklore, a small one-legged negro who pesters wayfarers at night or sets traps for them; c.a. SACI-CERERÊ, SACI-PERERÊ; (*Zool.*) the striped cuckoo (*Tapera naevia*), c.a. PEITICA, MATI-TAPERÊ, MATINTA-PEREIRA, PIRIRIGUÁ, FEM-FEM, MATIMPERERÊ, PEIXE-FRITO, SÊCO-FICO, PEITO-FERIDO; or the southern striped cuckoo (*Tapera naevia chochi*). c.a. SEM-FIM, ROCEIRO-PLANTA.

saciado –**da** (*adj.*) sated.

saciamento (m.) = SACIEDADE.

saciar (*v.t.*) to satiate; to cloy; (*v.r.*) to become satiated.

saciável (*adj.*) satiable.

saciedade (*f.*) satiety, satiation; surfeit.

saco (m.) sack, bag; sac.—**de água quente**, hot-water bag.—**de café**, small cloth bag for percolating coffee [but not sack of coffee, which is SACA DE CAFÉ.]—**de mão**, handbag, grip.—**de viagem**, travelling bag.—**folicular**, (*Anat.*) dental follicle.—**rôto**, (*colloq.*) a blabbermouth.—

sinovial, (*Anat.*) synovial capsule.—**vitelino**, (*Embryol.*) yolk sac. Cf. SACA.

sacola (*f.*) pouch; saddlebag.

sacolejar (*v.t.*) to shake (up and down); to jolt.

sacopari [í] (*m.*, *Bot.*) the bakupari rheedia (*R. brasiliensis*).

sacramental (*adj.*) sacramental.

sacramentar (*v.t.*, *Eccl.*) to administer the sacraments to; (*v.r.*) to receive the sacraments.

sacramentário (*m.*, *Eccl.*) sacramentarian; [*cap.*] (*R.C.Ch.*) Sacramentary.

sacramento (*m.*) sacrament.

sacrário (*m.*) sacrarium; sanctuary; shrine.

sacratíssimo –**ma** (*absol. superl. of* SAGRADO) most sacred.

sacrificador –**dora**, **sacrificante** (*adj.*) sacrificing; (*m.,f.*) sacrificer.

sacrifical (*adj.*) sacrificial.

sacrificar (*v.t.*) to sacrifice, immolate; to surrender, forego; (*v.r.*) to sacrifice oneself (**por**, for).

sacrificatório –**ria** (*adj.*) = SACRIFICAL.

sacrifício (*m.*) sacrifice, offering; surrender; atonement.

sacrifículo (*m.*) acolyte.

sacrilégio (*m.*) sacrilege, profanation, desecration.

sacrílego –**ga** (*adj.*) sacrilegious.

sacrilíaco –**ca** (*adj.*) = SACRO-ILÍACO.

sacripanta (*adj.*) villainous; blustering; cowardly; (*m.,f.*) vile wretch; boastful coward. Var. SACRIPANTE.

sacrista, pop. form of SACRISTÃO.

sacristã (*f.*) sacristan's wife; sexton's wife; woman who cleans and cares for the vestry.

sacristão [-tãos, -tães] (*m.*) sacristan; sexton.

sacristia (*f.*) sacristy, vestry.

sacro –**cra** (*adj.*) sacred; of or pert. to the sacrum ; (*m.*, *Anat.*) sacrum.

sacro-ciático –**ca** (*adj.*, *Anat.*) sacrosciatic.

sacro-coccígeo –**gea** (*adj.*, *Anat.*) sacroccocygeal.

sacro-colégio (*m.*, *R.C.Ch.*) college of cardinals.

sacro-espinhal (*adj.*, *Anat.*) sacrospinal.

sacro-femoral (*adj.*, *Anat.*) sacrofemoral.

sacro-ilíaco –**ca** (*adj.*, *Anat.*) sacroiliac.

sacro-lombar (*adj.*, *Anat.*) sacrolumbar.

sacrospinal (*adj.*) = SACRO-ESPINHAL.

sacrossanto –**ta** (*adj.*) sacrosanct.

sacro-vertebral (*adj.*, *Anat.*) sacrovertebral.

sacubaré (*m.*) an orchid (*Cryptopodium sp.*).

sacudidela (*f.*) a shake; jolt; shaking; (*colloq.*) a spanking.

sacudido –**da** (*adj.*) shaken, jerked; free, unrestrained; strong, handsome; expert; capable.

sacudidor –**dora** (*adj.*) shaking; (*m.,f.*) shaker.

sacudidura (*f.*), **sacudimento** (*m.*) a shaking; shake-up.

sacudir [22] (*v.t.*) to shake (up, off, out); to agitate; to jar, jolt; to beat; (*v.r.*) to shake oneself; to quake; to waggle, wiggle.—**a cabeça**, to wag the head.—**a poeira do corpo a**, or—**o pó a**, to give (someone) a dusting (beating).—**a poeira dos pés**, or—**o pó dos sapatos**, to shake the dust off one's feet.—**o jugo**, to throw off the yoke.—**o sono**, to shake off sleep.

saculiforme (*adj.*) sac-like.

sáculo (*m.*) sac, saccule; (*Anat.*) sacculus.

sacupari [í] (*m.*) = SACOPARI.

sacupema (*f.*, *Zool.*) a guan (*Penelope guan*).

sádico –**ca** (*adj.*) sadistic; (*m.,f.*) sadist.

sadio –**dia** (*adj.*) sound, healthful, wholesome.

sadismo (*m.*) sadism.

sadista (*adj.*: *m.,f.*) sadist.

saduceu (*m.*) Sadducee.

safa (*interj.*) Doggone! Good heavens! Goodnight! Goodness gracious!

safadagem (*f.*) low behavior.

safadeza [ê], **safadice** (*f.*) dirty trick; immorality.

safadismo (*m.*) vulgar speech, coarse manners, low behavior.

safado –**da** (*adj.*) worn out, worse for wear; (*colloq.*) shameless; barefaced; immoral; irate, indignant; (*m.*) low, vulgar man. **terra**—, impoverished land.

safanão (*m.*) a shake, shove, push; jerk, yank.

safar [24] (*v.t.*) to pull off, remove (as a shirt); to set free (as a vehicle or vessel which has got stuck); (*v.r.*) to take (oneself) off, beat it, run away, make oneself scarce.—**se de uma dificuldade**, to get out of a difficulty.

safardana (*m.*) a low good-for-nothing.

sáfaro –**ra** (*adj.*) wild, waste, barren [land].

safeno –**na** (*adj.*, *Anat.*) saphenous; (*f.*) saphena.

sáfico –**ca** (*adj.*) Sapphic.

safio (*m.*) a small conger eel.

safira (*f.*) sapphire; the color sapphire blue.—**do-brasil**, blue tourmaline.

safirina (*f.*, *Min.*) sapphirine.

safismo (*m.*) Sapphism, Lesbianism.

safista (*f.*) Sapphist.

safo –**fa** (*irreg. p.p. of* SAFAR) clear, free; gone; escaped; worn out, worn smooth; (*f.*) [*cap.*] Sappho.

safra (*f.*) harvest, crop; harvest time; a large anvil.

safranina (*f.*, *Chem.*) safranine.

safrão (*m.*, *Naut.*) the afterpiece or after-timber of a rudder built of wood.

safreiro (*m.*) harvest hand.

safrejar (*v.i.*) to run a sugar mill; to operate a still.

safrol (*m.*, *Chem.*) safrole.

saga (*f.*) saga.

sagacidade (*f.*) sagacity; discernment; wits.

sagacíssimo –**ma** (*absol. superl. of* SAGAZ) most sagacious.

saganho (*m.*) the hairy rockrose (*Cistus hirsutus*).—**ouro**, the false sunrose (*Halimium alyssoides*).

sagaz (*adj.*) sagacious, shrewd, clever, astute, keen, wise, smart, sharp.

sagenito (*m.*, *Min.*) sagenite.

sagina (*f.*) a genus (*Sagina*) of pearlworts or pearlweeds.

sagitado –**da** (*adj.*) sagittate.

sagital (*adj.*) resembling an arrow or arrowhead; (*Anat.*, *Zool.*) sagittal.

sagitaria (*f.*) arrow, arrowhead; (*Bot.*) arrowhead.

sagração (*f.*) consecration.

sagrado –**da** (*adj.*) sacred, holy; (*m.*) holy thing or place; (*m.pl.*)—**s apóstolos**, Holy Apostles; (*f.*) —**família**, Holy Family; (*f.pl.*)—**s letras**, Holy Writ.

sagrar (*v.t.*) to consecrate, dedicate; to hallow, sanctify.—**se campeão**, to become champion.

sagu [ú] (*m.*) sago flour; palm wine.—**do-jardim**, (*Bot.*) the sago cycas (*C. revoluta*) which yields a coarse sago and is widely grown in Brazilian parks and gardens.—**verdadeiro**, the true sago palm (*Metroxylon rumphii*).

saguão (*m.*) lobby, foyer, entrance hall, vestibule; indoor patio, courtyard.

saguaraji [í] (*f.*) a timber-yielding species of colubrina (*C. rufa*).

saguaritá (*m.*) a marine snail or whelk (*Purpura*, syn. *Thais*, *haemastoma*), c.a. MUÇARETE.

sagüeiro (*m.*) either the sago palm (*Metroxylon rumphii*), or the sago cycas (*C. revoluta*).

sagüi [m.] (*m.*) any of numerous Amazonian saki monkeys (*Pithecia*) and marmosets (*Callithrix*) or tamarins (*Tamarin*), esp.—**de-cabeça-branca**, a white-headed saki (*Pithecia pithecia*), c.a. PARABACU-PRÊTO.—**de-cabeça-dourada**, a golden-headed saki (*P. chrysocephala*).—**de-nariz-branco**, a black saki with white nose (*P. albinasa*), c.a. PIROCULU, CUXIÚ-PRÊTO-DE-NARIZ-BRANCO; (*colloq.*) a grotesque, queer-looking person.

S.A.I. = SUA ALTEZA IMPERIAL (His [Her] Imperial Highness).

saí (*m.*) any of a number of honey creepers or sugarbirds, and small tanagers, among them the chestnut-vented ateleodacnis (*A. speciosa*); the East Brazilian green honey creeper (*Chlorophanes spiza axillaris*); the white-vented dacnis (*D. lineata*); the blue honey creeper (*Cyanerpes cyaneus*), c.a. SAPITICA, which is considered by some to be one of the most beautiful birds on earth. It is a deep blue, with a light blue cap, and satin yellow on the wings.—**açu-azul**, the bishop tanager (*Thraupis episcopus*), or the blue-gray tanager (*Thraupis episcopus coelestis*).—**açu-pardo** = SANHAÇO-DE-COQUEIRO.—**azul** or—**bicudo**, the Paraguayan dacnis (*D. cayana*), c.a. SAÍRA.—**andorinha**,—**buraqueira**,—**arara**, are all the eastern swallow-tanager (*Tersina viridis*).—**de-fogo** = CANÁRIO-DO-MATO.—**de-sete-côres** = SAÍRA-DE-SETE-CÔRES.—**mirim** = MACACO-DE-CHEIRO, a squirrel monkey. Cf. SAÍRA.

saia (*f.*) skirt, petticoat; gown.—**de baixo**, underskirt.—**de balão**, hoop skirt.—**de-cunhã**, (*Bot.*) the heartkey serjania (*S. glabrata*).—**rodada**, full skirt. **andar atrás de**—**s**, to run after women. **Êle está sempre nas**—**s dela**, He is tied to her apron strings.

saião-acre (*m.*, *Bot.*) a stonecrop (*Sedum acre*), c.a. PÃO-DE-PÁSSAROS.

saib+verb endings = pres. subj. forms of SABER [74].

saibo (*m.*) bad taste.

saibro (*m.*) coarse river sand; fine gravel.

saibroso –**sa** (*adj.*) gravelly, sandy.

saído –da (*adj.*) gone out; forward, bold; outjutting; (*f.*) an outgoing, exit, departure; a coming out; issue, outflow; output; egress, outlet; outgo, sale, exportation (of goods); recourse, way out; an "out" (loophole); makeshift. **beco sem—**, blind alley; impasse, deadlock. **rua sem—**, blind (dead end) street. **dar—a**, to start off, fire the opening gun; in bookkeeping, to record outgoing items of money, merchandise, etc.

saídor –dora [a-i] (*adj.*) outgoing.

saimel (*m.*, *Archit.*) springer.

saimento [a-i] (*m.*) exit; funeral cortège; brass, effrontery.

saimiri (*m.*) a squirrel monkey (*Callithrix sciura*).

sainete [nê] (*m.*) pleasing thing or gesture; cutting remark; short farce.

saiote (*m.*) petticoat.—**de escocês**, kilt.

sair [75] (*v.i.*) to go out (**de**, of); to issue (**de**, from); to get out (**de**, of); to leave, depart (**de**, from); to result in; to appear; to sprout; (*v.r.*) to escape (**de**, from); to leave, go away.—**a alguém**, to take after (resemble) someone. [**Saiu à mãe**, She looks like her mother.]—**a campo**, to take to the field; to make a field trip.—**à francesa**, to take French leave.—**à luz**, to appear, be published.—**ao encontro do inimigo**, to sally forth against the enemy.—**às carreiras**, to rush out pellmell.—**(-se) bem**, to come off well, succeed.—**branco**, to come out blank.—**caro**, to come out dear; to cause many headaches; fig., to cost a lot.—**(-se) com**, to come out with (an unexpected remark, an oath, etc.).—**da linha**, of a train, streetcar, etc., to jump the track; fig., to get out of line (in decorum).—**de banda**, to slip away; to sneak out.—**de casa**, to leave the house, go out of doors; to leave home.—**de mansinho**, to sneak out.—**do atoleiro**, to escape from danger, or to get out of a bad situation; lit., to pull (oneself) out of a swamp or mud hole.—**do sério**, to drop one's serious demeanor.—**dos limites**, to exceed, go beyond (one's authority, etc.).—**-se bem**, to come out well, end up successfully.—**se mal**, to come off badly, fail.—**-se com quatro pedras na mão**, to make an angry remark, a savage reply.—**-se de um apêrto**, to get out of a scrape, out of a tight spot.—**vendendo os arreios**, of a horse, to run away. **Acaba de—**, He (she) has just gone out (just left). **Daí não vai —nada de bom**, No good will come of it. **Êle me saiu um sem-vergonha!** He turned out to be a rascal. **fazer—**, to eject, force out. **O tiro saiu pela culatra**, the charge (accusation) backfired; lit., the gun backfired. **Saí de casa às oito**, I left home at eight. **Saiu-lhe o melhor prêmio**, He (she) won the best prize.

saíra (*f.*) Any of a number of tanagers of the genus Calospiza, among them the chestnut-backed tanager (*C. castanonota*), c.a. PRECIOSO; the Brazilian turquoise tanager (*C. brasiliensis*); the western paradise tanager (*C. chilensis coelicolor*), c.a. SETE-CÔRES; the red-rumped tanager (*C. chilensis chilensis*); the spotted tanager (*C. punctata punctata*), c.a. NEGAÇA.—**-açu**,—**guaçu**,—**sapucaia**, all = VÍUVA; the yellow tanager (*C. cayana flava*).—**-de-sete-côres**, the greenheaded tanager (*C. seledon*), c.a. SAÍ-DE-SETE-CÔRES, or SETE-CÔRES.—**militar**, the red-necked tanager (*C. cyanocephala*).—**verde**, the yellow-breasted tanager (*C. desmaresti*).—**vermelha** = CANÁRIO-DO-MATO. Cf. SAÍ.

sairuçu (*m.*) = SANHAÇO-FRADE.

sal [sais] (*m.*) salt; wit, humor, sparkle, esprit; (*pl.*) smelling salts.—**amargo**, or—**de Epsom**, or—**inglês**, Epsom salts.—**amoníaco**, sal ammoniac, ammonium chloride.—**ático**, Attic wit.—**comum**, or—**de cozinha**, common table salt.—**-gema**, or—**de rocha**, rock (native) salt.—**de azêdas**, oxalic acid.—**de Glauber**, Glauber's salt.—**de Rochelle**, R. salt.—**microcósmico**, microcosmic salt.

sala (*f.*) large room, hall, parlor, anteroom.—**de armas**, fencing room.—**de aulas**, classroom.—**de baile**, ballroom.—**de bolão**, bowling alley.—**de composição**, typesetting shop.—**de entrada**, entrance hall.—**de espera**, waiting room.—**-de-estar**, living room.—**de estudo**, study hall.—**de jantar**, dining room.—**de operações**, operating room.—**de refeições**, dining room, dining hall. —**de visitas**, parlor, drawing room. **fazer—**, to entertain visitors; to be nice, polite (to someone).

salacidade (*f.*) salaciousness.

salada (*f.*) salad.

saladeira (*f.*) salad bowl.

saladeirista (*m.*) owner of a CHARQUEADA.

saladeiro (*m.*) = CHARQUEADA.

salafrário (*m.*) rascal, rogue, scoundrel.

salamaleque (*m.*) salaam; kowtow; by ext., exaggerated politeness in greeting.

salamandra (*f.*) salamander; fig., a fire-eater (fireman).

salamanta (*f.*) = JIBÓIA-VERMELHA.

salame (*m.*) salame; salaam.

salão (*m.*) large hall; saloon [but only in the sense of ballroom, drawing room, or the like. In the ordinary sense, a saloon is BAR or BOTEQUIM]; a salon (art exhibit); sandy clay; "(1) hard river bottom consisting of sand and clay; (2) a very viscous type of clay which slides down from the BARRANCOS forming a second ledge adjacent to the river banks proper, visible only during the low water season." [*GBAT*]—**de barbeiro**, barber shop.—**de beleza**, beauty parlor.—**de bilhares**, billiard room.—**de dança**, ballroom.—**nobre**, auditorium.

salariado –da (*m.,f.*) wage earner.

salário (*m.*) wages, pay [but not salary, which is ORDENADO].

salaz (*adj.*) salacious.

salchicha (*f.*) & derivs. = SALSICHA & derivs.

saldar (*v.t.*) to settle, pay, adjust (accounts).—**contas**, to settle accounts (lit. & fig.).

saldo –da (*adj.*) settled, liquidated; (*m.*) balance, remainder, surplus; remnants (of merchandise); fig., revenge, requital.—**a favor**, or—**positivo**, credit balance.— **contra**, or—**negativo**, debit balance.

salé (*f.*, *colloq.*) salted meat; corned beef.

saleiro –ra (*adj.*) of or pert. to salt; (*m.*) salt shaker; salt lick; salt dealer; salt maker; deer's horn bud.

salema (*f.*) the porkfish (*Anisotremus virginicus*); also = CANHANHA.

salepo (*m.*) salep; (*Bot.*) male orchis (*O. mascula*).

salesiano –na (*adj.; m.*) Salesian.

saleta [ê] (*f.*) small hall, waiting room.

salga (*f.*) act or place of salting.

salgação (*f.*) salting; sorcery.

salgadeira (*f.*) salting trough; (*Bot.*) Mediterranean sagebrush (*Atriplex halimus*).

salgadiço –ça, **salgadio –dia** (*adj.*) salty; (*m.*) salt marsh.

salgado –da (*adj.*) salty, salted; witty; expensive; (*m.pl.*) salt marsh. **Panela que muitos mexem ou sai insonsa ou sai—**, Too many cooks spoil the broth.

salgador –dora (*adj.*) salting; (*m.,f.*) salter, one who salts meat, etc.

salgadura (*f.*) = SALGA.

salgagem (*f.*) addition of salt to cattle fodder.

salgalhada (*f.*) salmagundi, mixture, medley, hodgepodge.

salgar (*v.t.*) to salt; to season with salt.—**o galo**, (*colloq.*) to drink an eye opener.

salgueirinha (*f.*, *Bot.*) purple lythrum (*L. salicaria*).

salgueiro (*m.*) the Babylon weeping willow (*Salix baby lonica*), c.a. SALGUEIRO-CHORÃO, CHORÃO-SALGUEIRO, SALGUEIRO-DA-BABILÔNIA; the Trinidad tournefortia (*T. hirsutissima*).—**branco**, white willow (*Salix alba*).— **-do-mato** = CANGALHEIRO.—**dos-rios**, Humboldt willow (*Salix humboldtiana*).—**francês**, the common osier or basket willow (*Salix viminalis*).—**mainato**, a mangrove (*Rhizophora mucronata*).—**prêto**, the tealeaf willow (*Salix phylicifolia*).

salicáceo –cea (*adj.*, *Bot.*) salicaceous; (*f.pl.*) the willow family (*Salicaceae*).

salicária (*f.*) = SALGUEIRINHA.

salicilamida (*f.*, *Chem.*) salicylamide.

salicilato (*m.*, *Chem.*) salicylate.

salicílico –ca (*adj.*, *Chem.*) salicylic.

saliciloso –sa (*adj.*) **ácido—**, salicylic acid.

salicilúrico –ca (*adj.*, *Biochem.*) salicyluric.

salicina (*f.*, *Chem.*) salicin.

salicional (*f.*, *Music*) salicional.

salicórnia (*f.*) the genus (*Salicornia*) of glassworts or marsh samphires.

salicultura (*f.*) saltmaking.

saliência (*f.*) salience, projection, overhang.

salientar (*v.t.*) to make clear (noticeable, striking, emphatic); to emphasize, stress; to enhance; to highlight; to underscore; (*v.r.*) to distinguish oneself.

saliente (*adj.*) salient, projecting, jutting; outstanding, prominent; conspicuous; forward, bold [= ESPEVITADA].

salífero –ra (*adj.*) salt-bearing, saliferous.

salificação (*f.*, *Chem.*) salification.

salificar (*v.t.*, *Chem.*) to salify.

saligenina (*f.*, *Chem.*) saligenin.

salina (*f.*) salina, saltworks.

salinação, salinagem (*f.*) salination.
salineiro –ra (*adj.*) of or pert. to a saltworks; (*m.*) one who manufactures or deals in salt; (*m.,f.*) worker in a saltworks.
salinidade (*f.*) salinity.
salino –na (*adj.*) saline.
salinômetro (*m.*) salinometer.
salisbúria (*f., Bot.*) the ginkgo.
salitral (*m.*) niter deposit.
salitre (*m.*) potassium nitrate, niter, saltpeter.—do Chile, sodium nitrate.
salitreira (*f.*) niter bed.
salitroso –sa (*adj.*) nitrous.
saliva (*f.*) saliva, spit, spittle.
salivação (*f.*) salivation.
salival (*adj.*) salivary.
salivante (*adj.*) salivant.
salivar (*adj.*) salivary. **glândulas—es,** salivary glands; (*v.i.*) to salivate.
salivoso –sa (*adj.*) salivous.
salmão (*m.*) salmon.—**pequeno** = SALMONETE.—**rei,** the king or quinnat salmon (*Oncorhynchus*).—**truta,** the European sea trout (*Salmo trutta*).
salmear (*v.t.*) to sing psalms; (*v.i.*) to chant, intone.
salmeira (*f., Zool.*) scallop (*Pecten*).
salmiaque (*m., Min.*) sal ammoniac.
sálmico –ca (*adj.*) psalmic.
salmista (*m.,f.*) psalmist.
salmo (*m.*) psalm.
salmodia (*f.*) psalmody.
salmodiar (*v.i.*) to chant, intone.
salmonete [nê] (*m.*) a surmullet or goatfish (*Mullus surmuletus*), c.a. SARAMONETE, SALMÃO-PEQUENO, SALMONEJO.
salmonídeo –dea (*adj.*) salmonoid; (*m.pl.*) a family (*Salmonidae*) of salmons and trouts.
salmoura (*f.*) pickle brine.
salmourar (*v.t.*) to pickle, corn.
salobre, salobro –bra (*adj.*) salty; brackish.
saloio (*adj.*) yokel-like; (*m.*) a peasant from around Lisbon; yokel, rustic.
salol (*m., Chem.*) salol, phenyl salicylate.
Salomão (*m.*) Solomon.
salpa (*f., Zool.*) a genus (*Salpa*) of oceanic tunicates; c.a. DESMOMIÁRIO, TÁLIA.
salpicador –dora (*adj.*) speckling; spattering.
salpicadura (*f.*), **salpicamento** (*m.*) a speckling; a splashing; or spattering.
salpicão (*m.*) a kind of pork sausage.
salpicar (*v.t.*) to splash, spot, spatter, speck, sprinkle (**de, com,** with); to mottle.
salpico (*m.*) spot, speck, speckle; splash.
salpídeos (*m.pl., Zool.*) the family of tunicates (*Salpidae*) consisting of the genus *Salpa*.
salpiglossa (*f., Bot.*) the genus Salpiglossis.
salpimenta (*adj.; f.*) salt-and-pepper.
salpimentar (*v.t.*) to salt-and-pepper; to tongue-lash.
salpinge (*f., Anat.*) salpinx.
salsa (*f.*) common parsley; sauce, condiment; (*Bot.*) the Surinam calliandra (*C. surinamensis*).—**americana,** sarsaparilla.—**branca** = ALGODÃO-BRAVO (a morning glory).—**crêspa,** curly garden parsley (*Petroselinum crispum*).—**d'água,** a pennywort (*Hydrocotyle natans*).—**da-praia,** soilbind morning glory (*Ipomoea pes-caprae*).—**do-campo** = CRAVORANA (a ragweed).—**do-rio-grande-do-sul,** a wirevine (*Muehlenbeckia sagittifolia*).—**leitosa,** hemlock waterdropwort (*Oenanthe crocata*).—**selvagem,** foolsparsley (*Aethusa cynapium*).—**vulgar,** common garden parsley (*Petroselinum crispum latifolium*).
salsada (*f.*) mess, muddle; confusion.
salsaparrilha (*f.*) sarsaparilla (plant or root).—**do-reino** or—**indígena,** (*Bot.*) Eurasian greenbrier (*Smilax aspera*), c.a. LEGAÇÃO.—**indiana,** India sarsaparilla (*Hemidesmus indicus*).
salseira (*f.*) sauce dish.
salseiro (*m.*) downpour, shower; (*colloq.*) riot, row, brawl.
salsicha (*f.*) sausage.
salsicharia (*f.*) sausage factory; sausage goods [= CHARCUTARIA].
salsicheiro –ra (*m.,f.*) one who makes or deals in sausages [= CHARCUTEIRO]; pork-butcher.
salsifi [fí] (*m.*) = ESCORCIONEIRA.
salsinha (*f., colloq.*) a "pansy" (effeminate man).

salso –sa (*adj.*) salty. [*Poetical*]
sálsola (*f.*) the common saltwort or Russian thistle (*Salsola kali*).
salsugem (*f.*) mud of a salt flat; saltness; (*Med.*) impetigo.
salta (*f.*) salta: "A game like halma played by two, each having 15 men, on a board of 100 squares." [*Webster*]
salta-caminho (*m.*) = TICO-TICO.
salta-caroço (*m.*) freestone peach.
salta-cavalo (*m.*) a whiptree (*Luhea grandiflora*).
saltado –da (*adj.*) jutting, projecting; (*f.*) saltation; jump, leap; assault; a hop (short, quick trip).
saltador –dora (*adj.*) saltant; jumping; leaping; dancing; (*m.,f.*) jumper; leaper; vaulter; dancer; (*pl., Zool.*) the Saltatoria (grasshoppers, locusts, crickets).
salta-marquês (*m.*) grasshopper [= GAFANHOTO].
salta-martim (*m.*) a click or snapping beetle.
salta-martinho (*m.*) a Brazilian poison nut (*Strychnos brasiliensis*).
saltante (*adj.*) saltant, leaping, jumping, dancing.
saltantes-picados (*m.pl.*) loaded dice.
saltão –tona (*adj.*) jumping; (*m.,f.*) jumper; (*m., colloq.*) grasshopper.—**da-praia,** beach flea, sand hopper.
salta-pocinhas (*m., colloq.*) a man who minces his steps.
saltar (*v.t.,v.i.*) to leap, jump (over), vault, bound (across), spring.—**ao pescoço de alguém,** to fall on someone's neck.—**aos ares,** to go up in the air, blow up (become angry).—**à vista,** or **aos olhos,** to strike the eye.—**da cama,** to jump out of bed.—**da cama com o pé esquerdo,** to get out of bed on the wrong foot (or on the wrong side).—**de capitão a general,** to jump from the rank of captain to that of general.—**do cavalo, do bonde, etc.,** to jump off a horse, alight from a streetcar, etc.—**em paraquedas,** to bail out (from an airplane).—**em terra,** to disembark, go ashore.—**fora de,** to get loose, out of place.—**fora dos trilhos,** to jump the rails.—**lugares or postos,** to skip a place or rank.—**na sela,** to spring into the saddle.—**pela janela,** to jump out the window.—**por cima de tudo,** to override.—**um obstáculo,** to hurdle an obstacle.—**uma página,** to skip a page.—**uma parede,** to vault over a wall. fazer—**os miolos,** to blow out one's brains. fazer—**uma ponte,** to blow up a bridge. **uma bola que salta,** a bouncing ball.
saltarelo (*m.*) saltarello (a dance).
saltaricar, saltarilhar, saltarinhar (*v.i.*) to hop, skip.
saltatriz (*adj.*) jumping; leaping; dancing; (*f.*) ballet dancer.
salteado –da (*adj.*) assaulted, assailed; alternated, interpolated; (*f.*) assault.
salteador –dora (*adj.*) assaulting; (*m.*) footpad; highwayman, outlaw, brigand.
salteamento (*m.*) assault [= SALTEADA].
saltear (*v.t.*) to assault, set upon; to take by surprise; to skip (as pages in a book); (*v.t.*) to startle.
salteio (*m.*) assault.
salteira (*f.*) heel lift (of a shoe).
saltério (*m.*) psaltery; Psalter; (*Zool.*) omasum; tripe [= FOLHOSO, DOBRADA].
salticídeos (*m., Zool.*) a family of saltigrade spiders.
saltígrado –da (*adj., Zool.*) saltigrade.
saltimbanco (*m.*) mountebank.
saltitante (*adj.*) saltatory, skipping, hopping, tripping, frisky, lively, jumpy.
saltitar (*v.i.*) to skip (about), hop (about).
salto (*m.*) leap, spring, jump, vault, bound; bounce; heel (of a shoe).—**à** (or **de**) **vara,** pole vaulting.—**de** (or **em**) **altura,** high jump.—**de anjo,** swan dive.—**de borracha,** rubber heel.—**de extensão,** or—**à distância,** or—**em comprimento,** broad jump.—**mortal,** somersault, back flip.—**s ornamentais,** fancy diving. dar—**s,** to leap. dar um—, to go in a hurry. um—**no escuro,** a leap in the dark.
salubérrimo –ma (*absol. superl. of* SALUBRE) most salubrious.
salubre (*adj.*) salubrious, salutary.
salubridade (*f.*) salubriousness, healthfulness.
salutar (*adj.*) salutary, wholesome.
salva (*f.*) salvo, volley; gun salute; simultaneous discharge (of guns, rockets, fireworks, etc.); burst (of shouts, cheers, laughter, etc.); round (of applause); salver, tray; proviso, exception, reservation; pretext, excuse.—**de palmas,** or **de aplausos,** round of applause.—**de gargalhadas,** burst of laughter.—**imperial,** a 101-gun salute.—**real,** a 21-gun salute; (*Bot.*) any of various herbs and shrubs, esp.—**bastarda,** or **-brava,** the wood

germander (*Teucrium scorodonia*), c.a. ESCÓRDIO.—**das-boticas,** or—**verdadeira,** garden sage (*Salvia officinalis*).—**de-marajó,** or—**do-campo,** or—**do-pará,** a bushmint (*Hyptics incana*).—**de-pernambuco,** a thistle (*Calcalia odorifera*).—**do-brasil,** the cardinal salvia (*S. fulgens*).—**do-rio-grande,** the lemon-verbena lippia (*Lippia citriodora*).—**do-mar** = BATATA-DO-MAR.—**larga,** silver sage (*Salvia argentea*).

salvabilidade (*f.*) savableness.

salvação (*f.*) salvation; deliverance; that which delivers from danger; the means of preservation; redemption; salvage; salutation, greeting.

salvádego (*m.*) salvage (compensation paid for saving ship or cargo); a vessel employed in salvaging another.

salvados (*m.pl.*) salvaged goods.

salvador –**dora** (*adj.*) saving; (*m.,f.*) savior; saver.

salvadorenho –**nha** (*adj.; m.,f.*) = SALVATORIANO.

salvagem (*f.*) salvage rights.

salvaguarda (*f.*) safeguard; safe-conduct; shield.

salvaguardar (*v.t.*) to safeguard; to shield.

salvamento (*m.*) salvation, rescue; deliverance; salvage.

salvante (*adj.*) saving; (*prep.*) save, excepting.

salvar [24] (*v.t.*) to save, rescue (**de,** from); to preserve; to salvage; to greet, salute, hail; to impose a condition or exception (as a safeguard); to leap over (a ditch, etc.); (*v.r.*) to save oneself, escape. **Salve-se quem puder!** Every man for himself!—**as aparências,** to save appearances.

salvatela (*f., Anat.*) salvatella.

salvatério (*m.*) salvation; an out (means of escape).

salvatoriano –**na** (*adj.; m.,f.*) Salvadorian [= SALVA-DORENHO].

salvável (*adj.*) savable.

salva-vidas (*m.*) life saver.

Salve (*interj.*) Hail!

Salve-rainha (*interj.*) Hail Mary; Ave Maria.

salveta [ê] (*f.*) garden sage (*Salvia officinalis*).

sálvia (*f.*) = SALVA-DAS-BOTICAS.

salvina (*f.*) a bushmint (*Hyptis recurvata*).

salvínia (*f.*) a genus (*Salvinia*) of fern allies.

salvináceo –**cea** (*adj., Bot.*) salvinaceous; (*f.pl.*) the salvinia family (*Salviniaceae*).

salvo –**va** (*irreg. p.p. of* SALVAR) safe; saved.—**seja!** God forbid! **a**—, in safety; safely. **a**—**de,** safe from. **em**—, in a safe place. **são e**—, safe and sound.

salvo (*prep.*) save, except, unless.—**êrro,** barring a mistake.—**êrro ou omissão,** errors and omissions excepted. [Eng. abbrev. E.O.E. = Port. abbrev. S.E.O.].

salvo-conduto (*m.*) safe-conduct (pass).

samambaia (*f., Bot.*) any of various polypodies; also a bromelia: the treebeard tillandsia (*T. usneoides*).—**açu,** a dicksonia fern (*D. selloviana*), c.a. XAXIM.—**cheirosa,** a woodfern (*Dryopteris patens*).—**chorona,** or —**paulista,** the jointed polypody (*Polypodium subauriculatum*).—**cumaru,** a Brazilian polypody (*Polypodium brasiliense*).—**do-brejo,** a marattia fern (*M. cicutaefolia*).—**douradinha,** a spleenwort (*Asplenium auritum*), c.a. DOURADINHA.—**verdadeira,** the common brake or bracken (*Pteridium aquillinum*).

samambaial (*m.*) a place abounding in SAMAMBAIAS.

samango (*m.*) lazy man.

samanguaiá (*m.*) a round clam (*Venus flexuosa*).

samaqui [í] (*m.*) = SAMBAQUI.

sâmara (*f., Bot.*) samara.

samário (*m., Chem.*) samarium.

samarita (*m.*) Samaritan.

samaritano –**na** (*adj.; m.,f.*) Samaritan (man, woman, language); (*f.*) a nurse.

samarra (*f.*) sheepskin garment.

samarreiro (*m.*) dealer in sheepskins.

samaúma, samaumeira [a-u] (*f., Bot.*) the kapok ceiba (*C. pentandra*), c.a. SAMAÚVA, SUMAÚMA. Cf. PAINEIRA.

samauqui [í] (*m.*) = SAMBAQUI.

samaúva (*f.*) = SAMAÚMA.

samba (*m.*) a popular Brazilian dance of African origin.

sambacaeta (*m., Bot.*) a hyssop (*Hyssopus cryspapilla*), c.a. ALFAZEMA-DE-CABOCLO.

sambacuim [u-ím] (*m.*) the silverleaf pumpwood (*Cecropia palmata*), c.a. MATATAÚBA.

sambador –**dora** (*m.,f.*) one who dances the samba.

sambaíba (*f.*) a pumpwood (*Cecropia concolor*); any of several other Brazilian trees.

sambaibinha [a-i] (*f.*) = CIPÓ-CABOCLO.

sambamba (*f.*) = CHARQUE.

sambaqui [í] (*m.*) prehistoric shellmound or kitchen midden found on the coast of Brazil. Syns. CERNAMBI, SARNAMBI, MINA DE CERNAMBI, CASQUEIRO, CONCHEIRA, OSTREIRA, SAMAUQUI, BERBIQUEIRA, CAIEIRA, CALEIRA.

sambar (*v.i.*) to dance the samba.

sambarca (*f.*) breastband (of a harness).

sambaúva (*f.*) = SAMBAÍBA.

sambenito (*m.*) sanbenito (yellow garment worn by condemned victims of the Inquisition).

sambernardo (*m.*) St. Bernard dog [= SÃO-BERNARDO].

sambetara (*f.*) = PAPA-TERRA.

sambista (*m.,f.*) a composer or dancer of sambas.

sambladura (*f., Carp.*) a rabbet, scarf or other joint.

samblar (*v.*) = ENSAMBLAR.

sambuco (*m.*) sambuk: "a small kind of Arab dhow." [*Webster*]

sambunigrina (*f., Chem.*) sambunigrin.

samburá (*m.*) round wicker basket; creel [= COFO].

SAMDU = SERVIÇO MÉDICO DOMICILIAR DE URGÊNCIA (Emergency Home Medical Service).

samiresito (*m., Min.*) samiresite.

samito (*m.*) samite (ancient heavy silk fabric).

samouco (*m.*) Canary Islands wax myrtle (*Myrica faya*).

samovar (*m.*) samovar.

sampaulino –**na** (*adj.; m.,f.*) of, or a native of, São Paulo, Cf. PAULISTA.

sampana (*f.*) sampan.

Samuel (*m.*) Samuel.

samurai (*m.*) samurai.

sanã (*f.*) the white-throated rail (*Porzana albicollis*), c.a. SANÃ-DE-SAMAMBAIA, SARACURA-SANÃ, FRANGO-D'ÁGUA.

sanambaia (*f.*) oriental waterfern (*Ceratopteris thalictroides*).

sanamento (*m.*) = SANEAMENTO.

sanamunda (*f.*) = ERVA-BENTA.

sananduí (*m.*) a coralbean (*Erythina falcata*).

sananduva (*f.*) = CORTICEIRA.

sanar (*v.t.*) to cure, heal; to remedy. Cf. SANEAR.

sanativo –**va** (*adj.*) sanatory.

sanatório (*m.*) sanatorium, sanitarium.

sanável (*adj.*) curable.

sanca (*f., Arch.*) cove; cavetto.

sancadilha (*f.*) a tripping up of another person; a wedge.

sanção (*f.*) sanction, approval; penalty or reward; confirmation, ratification.

sancionador –**dora** (*adj.*) sanctioning; (*m.,f.*) one who sanctions.

sancionar (*v.t.*) to sanction, approve, ratify.

sanco (*m.*) shank (of bird or animal).

sancristão (*m.*) pop. form of SACRISTÃO.

sancristia (*f.*) pop. form of SACRISTIA.

sandália (*f.*) sandal.

sândalo (*m.*) sandalwood (*Santalum*).—**branco,** white sandalwood (*S. album*), c.a. SÂNDALO-AMARELO, SÂNDALO-CITRINO.—**vermelho,** the sandalwood padauk (*Pterocarpus santalinus*).

sandará (*m., Bot.*) the smooth terminalia (*T. glabra*).

sandáraca (*f.*) sandarac resin.

sandaracina (*f., Chem.*) sandaracin.

sandejar (*v.i.*) to play the fool.

sandeu (*m.*) fool, idiot, nincompoop, moron. [Fem. SANDIA]

sandice (*f.*) foolishness, fatuity; drivel.

sandim (*m.*) Italian buckthorn (*Rhamnus alaternus*).

sandio –**dia** (*adj.*) foolish, nonsensical; (*f.*) fool (fem. of SANDEU).

sanduíche (*m.*) sandwich.—**americano,** ham-and-egg sandwich. **homem**—, sandwich man.

saneador –**dora** (*adj.*) sanitizing; curing; (*m.,f.*) one who sanitizes.

saneamento (*m.*) sanitation; remedying; ironing out of difficulties.

sanear (*v.t.*) to make sanitary; to cure, heal; to remedy, repair. Cf. SANAR.

sanedrim (*m.*) = SINEDRIM.

sanefa (*f.*) valance.

sanfeno (*m., Bot.*) common sainfoin (*Onobrychis viciaefolia*), c.a. ESPARZETA.—**de-espanha,** the sulla sweetvetch (*Hedysarum coronarium*).

sanfona (*f.*) accordion [= ACORDEÃO]; hurdy-gurdy; (*colloq.*) a nobody; (*slang*) billfold.

sanfonina (*f.*) concertina.

sanfoninar (*v.i.*) to play the accordion.

sanga (*f.*) deep erosion gully.

sangangu [ú] (*m.*, *colloq.*) brawl; angry mob.

sangradouro (*m.*) drainage ditch; trench, canal; spillway; bleeder valve.

sangrar (*v.t.,v.i.*) to bleed; (*v.t.*) to tap (rubber trees).

sangrento –ta (*adj.*) bleeding, bloody, gory; rare [roast beef].

sangria (*f.*) a bleeding; bloodletting; bloodshed; extortion.

sangue (*m.*) blood; consanguinity.—**arterial**, arterial blood.—**azul**, blue blood.—**-de-boi** = TIÊ-SANGUE, VERÃO (birds).—**-de-dragão** or **-de-drago**, dragon's blood (a resin).—**-de-tatu**, a type of red soil suitable for coffee-growing.—**frio**, cold blood (lit. & fig.).—**misturado**, mixed blood.—**quente**, warm blood.—**suor e lágrimas**, "blood, sweat and tears."—**venoso**, venous blood. **a—frio**, in cold blood. **banco de—**, blood bank. **banhado em—**, bathed in blood; blood-drenched. **de—quente**, hot-tempered. **esvair-se em—**, to bleed to death. **intoxicação do—**, blood poisoning. **fazer ferver o—**, to make the blood boil. **ter—de barata**, to be meek, mild, spiritless, tamely submissive, lily-livered.

sangueira (*f.*) pool of blood.

sanguentado –da (*adj.*) = ENSANGUENTADO.

sanguento –ta, **sangüento** –ta (*adj.*) bloody; sanguinary.

sanguessuga (*f.*) a leech (lit. & fig.).

sanguícola (*adj.*) sanguicolous.

sanguífero –ra (*adj.*) sanguiferous.

sanguinário –ria, **sangüinário** –ria (*adj.*) sanguinary, bloodthirsty; cruel, inhuman; (*f.*) prostrate knotweed (*Polygonum aviculare*), c.a. CORRIOLA-BASTARDA, SEMPRE-NOIVA.—**-do-canadá**, bloodroot (*Sanguinaria canadensis*).

sanguíneo –nea, **sangüíneo** –nea (*adj.*) sanguine; full-blooded; blood red; bloody. **vaso—**, blood vessel; (*m.*) a full-blooded, red-faced person.

sanguinheiro (*m.*) the glossy buckthorn (*Rhamnus frangula*).

sanguinho (*m.*) bloodtwig dogwood (*Cornus sanguinea*).

sanguinidade (*f.*) = CONSANGÜINIDADE.

sanguinolento –ta, **sanguinoso** –sa (*adj.*) bloody, blood-stained; sanguinary, bloodthirsty.

sanguissedento –ta (*adj.*) bloodthirsty. [*Poetical*]

sanguissorba (*f.*, *Bot.*) any burnet of this genus.

sanha (*f.*) anger, rage, fury.

sanhaço (*m.*) any tanager, esp. of genus Thraupis; c.a. SANHAÇU.—**-de-coqueiro** (or **-de-mamoeiro**) the palm tanager (*Thraupis palmarum*), c.a. SAÍ-AÇU-PARDO; also = BICO-DE-VELUDO.—**-do-coqueiro**, the sayaca tanager (*Thraupis sayaca*).—**-de-fogo** = CANÁRIO-DO-MATO.—**-de-encontros** (or **-da-serra**) the archbishop tanager (*Thraupis ornata*).—**-frade**, the white-capped tanager (*Stephanophorus diadematus*), c.a. AZULÃO, AZULÃO-DE-CABEÇA-ENCARNADA, AZULÃO-DA-SERRA, CABEÇA-ENCARNADA, LINDO-AZUL, SANHAÇU, GURANDI-AZUL, SAIRUÇU, CAIRÉ.—**-tinga** = TIETINGA.

sanhaçu [çú] (*m.*) = SANHAÇO.

sanharão, **sanharó** (*m.*) = TORCE-CABELO.

sanhoso –sa (*adj.*) irascible; choleric.

sanhudo –da (*adj.*) angry; irascible; frightful.

sanícula (*f.*, *Bot.*) the European sanicle (*Sanicula europaea*).—**-dos-montes**, the meadow saxifrage (*Saxifraga granulata*), c.a. SAXIFRAGA-BRANCA.

sanidade (*f.*) sanitation, hygiene. **departamento de—**, public health department. [But not sanity, which is JUÍZO PERFEITO.]

sanidina (*f.*, *Min.*) sanidine.

sânie (*f.*, *Med.*) sanies, ichor.

sanificação (*f.*) sanification.

sanificar (*v.t.*) to make healthful; to sanitate.

sanioso –sa (*adj.*; *Med.*) sanious.

saníssimo –ma (*absol. superl. of* SÃO) most healthful.

sanitário –ria (*adj.*) sanitary, hygienic.

sanitarista (*adj.*, *m.*,*f.*) sanitarian.

sanja (*f.*) ditch, trench, drain.

sanjar (*v.t.*) to provide (land) with ditches.

Sansão (*m.*) Sampson, Samson.

sânscrito (*m.*) Sanskrit.

sanseviéria (*f.*) any of various plants of the genus *Sansevieria*, c.a. BASTÃO-DE-SÃO-JORGE, ESPADA-DE-SÃO-JORGE, PALMA-DE-SÃO-JORGE, RABO-DE-GATO.

santa (*f.*) see under SANTO.

santa-bárbara (*f.*) powder magazine; (*exclam.*) Good heavens!

santa-fé (*f.*) a panic grass (*Panicum rivulare*), extensively used in Brazil for thatching.

santafèzal (*m.*) tract abounding in SANTA-FÉ grass.

santaláceo –cea (*adj.*, *Bot.*) santalaceous; (*f.pl.*) a family (*Santalaceae*) typified by the sandalwoods.

santalina (*f.*, *Chem.*) santalin.

santalol (*m.*, *Chem.*, *Pharm.*) santalol.

santa-luzia (*f.*) ferule [= PALMATÓRIA]; also, a moraceous tree (*Sorocea spinosa*).

santanário –ria (*adj.*; *m.*,*f.*) = SANTARRÃO.

santantoninho (*m.*, *colloq.*) a much-petted person.

santantônio (*m.*) pommel of a saddle.

santão –tona (*adj.*) = SANTARRÃO.

santarrão –rona (*adj.*) sanctimonious; goody-goody; (*m.*,*f.*) hypocrite; pietist; pious fraud; prudish person.

santa-vitória (*f.*) ferule [= PALMATÓRIA].

santelmo (*m.*) St. Elmo's fire, corposant.

santidade (*f.*) sanctity, saintliness; [*cap.*] **Sua—**, His Holiness (the Pope).

santificação (*f.*) sanctification.

santificado –da (*adj.*) sanctified, hallowed. **dia—**, religious feast day.

santificador –dora (*adj.*) sanctifying; (*m.*,*f.*) sanctifier.

santificante (*adj.*) sanctifying.

santificar (*v.t.*) to sanctify, make holy; to hallow.

santificável (*adj.*) sanctifiable.

santilão –lona (*adj.*; *m.*,*f.*) = SANTARRÃO.

santimônia (*f.*) sanctimoniousness.

santimonial (*adj.*) sanctimonious.

santinho (*m.*) small image of a saint.

santíssimo –ma (*absol. superl. of* SANTO) most holy; [*cap.*] (*m.*, *Eccl.*) the consecrated Host.

santista (*adj.*) of or pert. to Santos, Brazil; (*m.*,*f.*) a native or inhabitant of that city.

santo –ta (*adj.*) saintly, holy, sacred; blessed; pious; virtuous; livelong, blessed (day, night); (*m.*,*f.*) saint; saintly person.—**casa** = CASA DA MISERICÓRDIA.—**Família**, the Holy Family.—**ofício**, the Holy Office (of the Inquisition).—**Padre**, the Holy Father (Pope).—**Sacrifício**, Sacrifice of the Mass.—**Sepulcro**, Holy Sepulcher.—**Sínodo**, Holy Synod.—**s óleos**, chrism, holy oil.—**de casa não faz milagre**, A prophet is not without honor save in his own country.—**do pau ôco**, a holy terror (unruly child); a pious hypocrite.—**-e-senha**, watchword, password, countersign. **despir um—para vestir outro**, to rob Peter to pay Paul. **fazer-se de—**, to play the saint.

santolina (*f.*) cypress lavendercotton (*Santolina chamaecyparissus*).

santonina (*f.*, *Bot.*) santonica (*Artemisia cina*); (*Chem.*, *Pharm.*) santonin.

santono (*m.*, *Bot.*) the palimara alstonia (*A. scholaris*).

santuário (*m.*) sanctuary shrine.

são [sãos] **sã** [sãs] (*adj.*) sound, hale, hearty, healthy; sane; able-bodied; wholesome, entire; unbroken; undecayed.—**e salvo**, safe and sound; (*m.*) healthy man; soundness, healthiness; (*v.i.*) form of SER [76].

São, abbrev. of SANTO (Saint). [The form **São** is used instead of **Santo** when the saint's name begins with a consonant; thus: **São Paulo**, **São José**, **São João**, but **Santo Antônio**, **Santo Amaro**, etc. The fem. form is always SANTA: SANTA MARIA, SANTA ANA.]

são-bernardo (*m.*) = SAMBERNARDO.

são-gonçalo (*m.*) an outdoor nighttime revel in honor of this saint; (*colloq.*) one who proposes marriage in behalf of another.

são-pauleiro (*adj.*) designating a migrant laborer who leaves Bahia to work on farms in São Paulo.

são-salavá (*m.*) a woods spirit (in the Brazilian folklore).

sapa (*f.*) a sapping or undermining; a spade.

sapador (*m.*, *Milit.*) sapper.

sapar (*v.t.*) to sap, dig, undermine.

saparia (*f.*) a quantity of frogs; frogs collectively.

saparrão (*m.*) a big frog; a big fat man.

sapata (*f.*) low shoe; bracket; footing of a wall; hopscotch; brake shoe; (*Naut.*) small deadeye.

sapatada (*f.*) a blow with a shoe or slipper, or with the hand; a cat's slap with its paw.

sapataria (*f.*) shoe store; shoemaking; shoe factory.

sapateado (*m.*) tap dance, clog dancing.

sapateador –dora (*adj.*) stomping; clogging; (*m.*,*f.*) tap dancer.

sapatear (*v.i.*) to stomp; to tap-dance.

sapateira (*f.*) cobbler's wife; shoe closet.

sapateiro (*m.*) shoemaker, cobbler.

sapateta [tê] (*f.*) house slipper; noise of footsteps.
sapatilho (*m., Mach.*) thimble; (*Naut.*) bull's-eye.
sapatinho (*m.*) little shoe; lady's evening slipper; baby's bootee; (*Bot.*) a slipper-flower (*Pedilanthus retusus*).—**-de-judeu**, (or **-do-diabo**, or **-dos-jardins**), the Jewbush or redbird slipper-flower (*Pedilanthus tithymaloides*), c.a. DOIS-AMÔRES; also, the common coralbean (*Erythrina corallodendron*), c.a. MULUNGU.—**-de-vênus**, a calceolaria.
sapato (*m.*) low shoe, oxford shoe. Cf. CALÇADO.—**de baile**, pump.—**de duas côres**, two-tone shoe.—**-de-vênus**, (*Bot.*) a ladyslipper (*Cyprepedium calceolus*).—**ferrado**, hobnailed shoe.—**plataforma**, wedge shoe.—**raso**, a loafer type of shoe.—**s de defunto**, dead-men's shoes (contingent inheritance).—**s de tênis**, sneakers.—**s de verniz**, patent-leather shoes. **É ahi que aperta o—**, That's where the shoe pinches. **estar com a pedra no—**, to smell a rat.
Sape! (*interj.*) Scat! Scram!
sapé (*m.*) the Brazil satintail or sape grass (*Imperata brasiliensis*) extensively used for thatching; also = CAPIM-SAPÉ, CAPIM-SAPÉ-MACHO, CAPIM-PEBA; in Paraná, the term refers also to dried pine branches, such as are found on the ground under the trees.—**-de-capueira**, a bluestem grass (*Andropogon holcoides*).—**gigante** = CAPIM-JARAGUÁ.—**-macho**, a giant reed (*Arundo*).
sapear (*v.t.*) to look on (from the outside); to kibitz.
sapeca (*adj.*) flirtatious; forward, bold (referring to women); (*f.*) process of toasting or parching (MATE leaves); a drying, singeing or searing (of meat or game); a thrashing; a scorching rebuke; cash (Chinese coin); a coquette, flirt.
sapecação (*f.*) a scorching or singeing; process of parching (MATE leaves).
sapecadouro (*m.*) a place where MATE leaves are parched before grinding into tea.
sapecar (*v.t.*) to scorch, singe, sear; to parch (MATE leaves); to thrash; (*v.i.*) to flirt.
sape-sape (*m.*) the soursop (*Annona muricata*), c.a. CORAÇÃO-DA-ÍNDIA.
sapèzal, **sapèzeiro** (*m.*) an area overgrown with SAPÉ grass; poor land.
sápido **-da** (*adj.*) having strong savor or (agreeable) flavor; palatable.
sapiência (*f.*) sapience, wisdom.
sapiente (*adj.*) sapient, wise, knowing.
sapindáceo **-cea** (*adj., Bot.*) sapindaceous; (*f.pl.*) the soapberry family (*Sapindaceae*).
sapinho (*m.*) little frog.—**s de leite**, (*Med.*) stomatomycosis (small white patches occurring in the mouths and fauces of young children, characteristic of thrush).—**-roxo**, (*Bot.*) the red sand spurry (*Spergularia rubra*).
sapiranga (*f., Med.*) blepharitis with loss of eyelashes.
sapiraquento **-ta** (*adj.*) having no eyelashes.
sapiroca (*adj.*) of eyes and eyelids, red, swollen; having no eyelashes; of horses, white-eyed; (*m.*) inflammation of the eyelids.
sapítaca (*f.*) frog; woman who wiggles as she walks; a suggestive dance.
sapitica = SAÍ, SAÍRA.
sapo (*m.*) any toad, esp. of the genus *Bufo*, but the term is applied also to frogs, which, properly speaking, are RÃS; tadpole; kinds of fish; (*slang*) a kibitzer; (*colloq.*) a streetcar inspector; tip given by a winner at gambling. Cf. RÃ, PERERECA, INTANHA.—**antanha** or—**-de-chifre**, a large Brazilian horned frog (*Ceratophrys counta*), c.a. SAPO-BOI.—**aranzeiro**, a toad (*Bufo calamita*).—**boi**, a toad (*Bufo paracnemis*) closely resembling the marine toad (*B. marinus*), c.a. SAPO-GIGANTE; also = SAPO-CURURU and INTANHA.—**cururu**, the agua or marine toad (*Bufo marinus*), the most common and most widely distributed toad in Brazil; c.a. CURURU, SAPO-BOI, XUÉ-(-GUAÇU).—**de-surinã**, the Surinam toad (*Pipa pipa*), c.a. PIPA, CURURU-PÉ-DE-PATO.—**ferreiro** = FERREIRO.—**-do-mar**, a puffer (fish), c.a. BAIACU.—**e-cobra**, an orchid (*Stanhopea graveolens*).—**pipa-da-guiana**, = SAPO-DE-SURINÃ.
sapó (*m., Metal.*) sow.
sapodilha (*f.*) = SAPOTILHA.
sapogenina (*f., Chem.*) sapogenin.
sapóleo (*m.*) any scouring powder. [Derived from Sapolio.]
saponáceo **-a** (*adj.*) saponaceous.
saponária (*f., Bot.*) a genus (*Saponaria*) of soapworts.

saponarina (*f., Chem.*) saponarin.
saponário **-ria** (*adj.*) soapy.
sapônase (*f.*) = LIPASE.
saponificação (*f.*) saponification.
saponificador **-dora** (*adj.*) saponifying.
saponificar (*v.t.*) to saponify.
saponificável (*adj.*) saponifiable.
saponina (*f., Chem.*) saponin.
saponita (*f.*), **-to** (*m., Min.*) saponite.
sapopema, **sapopemba** (*f.*) large prop root.
saporífero **-ra**, **saporífico** **-ca** (*adj.*) saporific.
sapota (*f., Bot.*) the sapote (*Calocarpum sapota*); c.a. SAPOTA-GRANDE, UNIQUÉ.—**branca**, the white sapote (*Casimiroa edulis*).—**grande**, the Guiana-chestnut (*Pachira aquatica*), c.a. CASTANHEIRO-DO-MARANHÃO.—**negra**, or—**preta**, a persimmon (*Diospyros sapota*).
sapotáceo **-cea** (*adj., Bot.*) sapotaceous; (*f.pl.*) the sapodilla family (*Sapotaceae*).
sapotaia (*f., Bot.*) the dog caper (*Capparis flexuosa*), c.a. FEIJÃO-DE-BOI.
sapoti [í] (*m.*) sapodilla fruit.
sapotizeiro (*m., Bot.*) sapodilla (*Achras sapota*).
saprema (*f.*) fulcrum.
sapremia (*f., Med.*) sapremia.
saprófago **-ga** (*adj., Zool.*) saprophagous; (*m.,f.*) saprophagan.
saprófilo (*adj., Bot.*) saprophilous; saprophytic.
saprófito (*m., Biol., Bot.*) saprophyte.
saprógeno **-na** (*adj.*) saprogenic, saprogenous.
saprolégnia (*f., Bot.*) a genus (*Saprolegnia*) of water molds.
saprólito (*m., Petrog.*) saprolite.
sapropélico **-ca** (*adj., Biol.*) sapropelic.
SAPS = SERVIÇO DE ALIMENTAÇÃO E PREVIDÊNCIA SOCIAL (Food and Social Security Service).
sapucaia (*f.*) any of several large trees of the genus *Lecythis* in Amazonia, esp. *L. paraensis*, the curious woody capsules ("monkeypots") of which contain 30 to 40 of the edible and highly valued paradise or sapucaia nuts.—**açu**,—**-de-castanha**,—**grande**, all = FRUTA-DE-MACACO.
sapucaieira[-mirim] (*f.*) = SAPUCAIA.
sapucainha [a-í] (*f.*) a tall tree (*Carpotroche brasiliensis*) of central and southern Brazil, the nut of which yields an oil used as a substitute for chaulmoogra oil in the treatment of leprosy; c.a. CANUDO-DE-PITO, PAU-DE-CACHIMBO.
sapudo **-da** (*adj.*) squat, thick, froglike—referring to persons.
sapupema (*m., Bot.*) a white quebracho (*Aspidosperma nitidum*), c.a. CARAPANAÚBA.
sapupira (*f.*) the alcornoco of Brazil (*Bowdichia virgilioides*) whose bark (alcornoque) is used as a remedy for consumption, and other trees of this genus.—**da-mata** = SUCUPIRA-AMARELA. — **-do -campo** = SUCUPIRA-DO-CAMPO.
sapuruna (*f.*) = CORCOROCA.
sapuva (*f.*) = GINJEIRA-DA-TERRA.
sapuvão (*m.*) = CATINGA-DE-NEGRO.
saque (*m.*) [from SACAR] bank draft; [from SAQUEAR] sack, booty; spoliation, plunder.
saqué (*m.*) Japanese sake.
saqueador **-dora** (*adj.*) sacking, pillaging, plundering; (*m.,f.*) sacker, plunderer, marauder.
saquear (*v.t.*) to sack, plunder, despoil, pillage, loot.
saqueio (*m.*) sack, plunder.
saqui [í] (*m.*) saki: "Any of several So. Amer. monkeys of the genus *Pithecia*, having a bushy non-prehensile tail and long hair which usually forms a beard on the chin and a ruff around the neck." [*Webster*] Cf. SAGÜI.
saquiada (*f.*) sackful.
saquim (*m.*) kosher butcher's knife.
saquinho (*m., dim. of* SACO) a small sack or bag; a sachet bag.
saquista (*m.*) maker of bags for shipping coffee.
S.A.R. = SUA ALTEZA REAL (His [Her] Royal Highness).
Sara (*f.*) Sarah; Sara; (*m.*) Sahara.
sarabanda (*f.*) saraband (slow, stately Spanish dance); rebuke, curtain lecture.
sarabandear (*v.i.*) to dance the saraband.
sarabatana (*f.*) speaking trumpet; Indian blowgun.
sarabulhento **-ta** (*adj.*) pimply.
sarabulho (*m.*) roughness on surface of earthenware; fig., pimple, blister.
sarabulhoso **-sa** (*adj.*) pimply.
saracotear (*v.i.*) to shake the hips; to ramble, saunter

along; (v.r.) to walk or dance with a waggling, wiggling, swaying or waddling motion.

saracoteio (m.) a shaking or wagging; a wiggling or swaying movement of the body, esp. of the hips.

saracura (f., colloq.) long-legged woman; (Bot.) a trumpet-creeper (Bigonia hirtella).—**-do-norte**, a water primrose (Jussiaea angulata); (Zool.) any of various wood rails (Aramides), esp. Spix's wood rail (A. mangle), c.a. SARACURA-DO-MANGUE (or -DA-PRAIA); the Cayenne wood rail (A. cajanea), c.a. SERICÓIA, SERICORA, TRÊS-POTES; the ypecaha wood rail (A. ypecaha), c.a. SARA-CURAÇU; the saracura wood rail (A. saracura); the white-throated rail (Porzana albicollis), c.a. SANÃ, FRANGO-D'ÁGUA.—**-da-canarana**, the purple gallinule (Porphyrula martinica), c.a. FRANGO-D'ÁGUA-AZUL.—**-sanã**, the blackish rail (Rallus nigricans) or the white-throated rail (Porzana albicollis).

sarado –da (adj.) healed; cured of illusions; sharp, rascally; brave; greedy.

saragaça (f.) = SARGAÇO.

saraiva (f.) hail; fig., a hail or shower of anything.

saraivada (f.) hail storm; a pelting (with anything).

saraivar (v.i.) to hail; (v.t.) to pelt, as with hail.

saramago (m.) wild radish (Raphanus raphanistrum).—**-de-água**, amphibious marsh cress (Rorippa amphibia).—**-maior**, horse radish, c.a. RÁBANO-BASTARDO.

sarambé (m.) boob, fool, sap.

sarampo (m.) measles.—**alemão**, German measles, c.a. RUBÉOLA.

saramposo –sa (adj.) having measles.

saranda (adj.) loafing; (m.) loafer.

sarandalhas (f.pl.), **-lhos** (m.pl.) remains, leavings, riff-raff.

sarandi [í] (m.) waste land; small rocky river island; any of various leafflowers (Phyllanthus).

sarapanel [-panéis] (m., Arch.) a three-centered or basket-handle arch.

sarapantar (v.) = ASSARAPANTAR.

sarapatel [-patéis] (m.) a dish made of sheep's or pig's viscera and blood; by ext., hodgepodge. Cf. SARRABULHO.

sarapilheira (f.) = SERAPILHEIRA.

sarapintado –da (adj.) spotted, speckled, flecked; pied, piebald; motley.

sarapintar (v.t.) to spot, dot, speckle; to mottle.

sarapueira (f.) mat of fallen leaves on forest floor; forest litter.

sarar (v.t.) to heal, cure, remedy; to mend, correct; (v.i.) to get well, be healed (de, of).

sararã (m.,f.) a person of mixed negro blood, having very light, often freckled, skin, bluish-green eyes and reddish kinky or curly hair; (adj.) designating such a type of person. Cf. AÇA.

sararaca (f.) a type of harpoon-arrow employed along the Amazon for taking fish and turtles.

sarau (m.) soirée, evening party; evening concert.

sarbacana (f.) sarbacane, blowgun.

sarça (f.) brier, bramble; blackberry bush.—**-amoreira** = AMOREIRA-DO-BRASIL.—**-ardente**, a cotoneaster (C. pyracantha).—**-de-moisés**, the scarlet firethorn (Pyracantha coccinea), c.a. ESPINHEIRO-ARDENTE.—**-idéia**, the red raspberry (Rubus idaeus).

sarçal (m.) brier patch.

sarcasmo (m.) sarcasm; scorn; cutting jest.

sarcástico –ca (adj.) sarcastic, taunting.

sarcoblasto (m., Biol.) sarcoblast.

sarcocárpio, sarcocarpo (m., Bot.) sarcocarp.

sarcocola (f.) sarcocolla gum.

sarcocolina (f.) sarcocollin.

sarcode (m., Biol.) sarcode.

sarcoderma (f., Bot.) sarcoderm.

sarcódico –ca (adj., Biol.) sarcodic.

sarcódio (m.) = SARCODE.

sarcófaga (f.) a genus (Sarcophaga) of flesh flies.

sarcofagia (f.) the practice of eating flesh.

sarcófago –ga (adj.) sarcophagous; (m.) sarcophagus.

sarcóideo –dea, **sarcóide** (adj., Biol.) sarcoid.

sarcolema (m., Anat.) sarcolemma.

sarcólito (m., Min.) sarcolite.

sarcologia (f.) sarcology.

sarcólogo –ga (m.,f.) sarcologist.

sarcoma (f., Med.) sarcoma.

sarcomatose (f., Med.) sarcomatosis.

sarcomatoso –sa (adj., Med.) sarcomatous.

sarcomério (m., Anat.) sarcomere.

sarcoplasma (m., Anat.) sarcoplasm.

sarcopta (m.) itch mite.

sarcoptídeos (m.pl.) the family (Sarcoptidae) of itch mites.

sarcorranfo (m.) the typical genus (Sarcorhamphus) of true condors.

sarcose (f., Bot.) an abnormal formation of bark.

sarcosina (f., Chem.) sarcosine.

sarçoso –sa (adj.) thorny.

sarcrólito (m., Min.) sarcrolite.

sarda (f.) spanish mackerel, c.a. SOROROCA; (pl.) freckles.

sardácata, sardágata (f.) sardachate: "A variety of agate containing sard." [Webster]

sardanisca, sardanita (f.) any small lizard.

sardão (m.) the O. W. green lizard (Lacerta viridis).

Sardenha (f.) Sardinia.

sardento –ta (adj.) freckled.

sardinha (f.) a sardine, or any of various herring-like fishes; (slang) a razor or dagger.—**-lage**,—**-do-lage**,—**-bandeira**,—**-facão**,—**-larga**,—**-gato**,—**-de-galha**, are all the thread herring (Opisthonema oglinum), c.a. SARGO, CAIÇARA.—**-prata**, an anchovy (Lycengraulis grossidens), c.a. MANJUBA.—**-verdadeira**, the true sardine (Sardinella aurita or allecia) which occurs in large schools off the coast and in the bay of Rio de Janeiro. **tirar a—com a mão do gato**, to use someone as a cat's-paw [alluding to the fable of the monkey using the cat's paw to draw the roasting chestnuts out of the fire].

sardinheiro –ra (adj.) sardine; (m.) sardine vender; (f.) sardine woman; sardine net; sardine fishery.

sárdio (m.) sard (a variety of carnelian).

sardônia (f.) blister buttercup (Ranunculus scleratus).

sardônico –ca (adj.) sardonic, derisive; (f.) sardonyx, c.a. SARDÔNIX.

sardoso –sa (adj.) freckled.

sarg. = SARGENTO (sergeant).

sargaça (f.) African false sunrose (Halimium halimifolium).—**-híspida**, the lime lithodora (L. fruticosa), c.a. ERVA-DAS-SETE-SANGRIAS, SARGACINHA.

sargaço (m.) floating seaweed, gulfweed; (Zool.)—**-de-beiço**, the pompon or black margate grunt (Anisotremus surinamensis), c.a. SARGO, PIRAMBU.—**-vesiculoso** = BODELHA. **mar de—**, Sargasso Sea.

sargento (m.) sergeant; carpenter's clamp, screw clamp; (Zool.) = GALHUDO (a fish).—**-instructor**, drill sergeant.—**-mor**, sergeant-major.

sargo (m.) a porgy, sea bream.—**-de-dente**, the sheepshead (Archosargus probatocephalus).

sarigüê (m.), **sarigüêia** (f.) = GAMBÁ.

sarilhar (v.) = ENSARILHAR.

sarilho (m.) reel; windlass, winch; a gyration on the horizontal bar; the gear of a waterwheel; mêlée, hubbub, confusion, disorder; (Milit.) stack. **fazer um—**, to raise a fuss.

sarja (f.) serge (fabric); (Med.) a small incision.

sarjação (f., Med.) scarification.

sarjadeira (f., Med.) scarificator.

sarjador –dora (adj.) scarifying; (m., Med.) scarifier.

sarjadura (f.) = SARJAÇÃO.

sarjar (v.t., Med.) to scarify; to score.

sarjeta [ê] (f.) gutter.

S.A.R.L. = SOCIEDADE ANÔNIMA DE RESPONSABILIDADE LIMITADA (a joint stock company of limited liability).

sarmentáceo –cea (adj., Bot.) sarmentacous, sarmentose.

sarmento (m., Bot.) sarmentum, runner.

sarmentoso –sa (adj., Bot.) sarmentose, having runners.

sarna (f.) itch, scabies; mange; (m.,f., colloq.) a person who clings tenaciously and annoyingly to another. **procurar—para se coçar**, to ask for (look for) trouble.

sarnambi [í] (m.) = SAMBAQUI.

sarnento –ta, **sarnoso** –sa (adj.) having the itch; mangy.

saroba, sarova (f.) = POMPA-LEGÍTIMA.

sarpar (v.) = ZARPAR.

sarrabulho (m.) pig's blood (preserved for the kitchen); a dish made of liver, blood, pork fat, etc.; hubbub, fracas. Cf. SARAPATEL.

sarracênia (f.) the genus (Sarracenia) of pitcherplants.

sarraceniáceo –cea (adj., Bot.) sarraceniaceous.

sarraceno –na (adj.; m.,f.) Saracen.

sarrafaçal (m.) botcher, bungler.

sarrafaçar (v.i.) to botch, bungle; to scarify.

sarrafão (m.) light wooden beam [= VIGOTA].

sarrafascada (f.) brawl.

sarrafear (v.t.) to rod (level) newly-applied plaster.

sarrafo (*m.*) picket, lath.

sarrapiá (*m.*) a tonkabean (*Dipteryx sp.*).

sarro (*m.*) tartar (in wine casks or on the teeth); fur on the tongue; the nicotine deposited on the inside of pipe stems; any of various small tropical armored catfishes (*Corydoras spp.*) popular in home aquaria.

sarsaparrilha (*f.*) = SALSAPARRILHA.

sartã (*f.*) frying pan [= SERTÃ].

sartório (*m.*, *Anat.*) sartorium, c.a. COSTUREIRO.

saruê (*m.*) opossum [= GAMBÁ].

saruga (*f.*, *Bot.*) awn.

S.A.S. = SUA ALTEZA SERENÍSSIMA (His Most Serene Highness).

sassafraz (*m.*) sassafras; also = CASCA-PRECIOSA (a tree).

sassolita (*f.*, *Min.*) sassolite.

Satanás (*m.*) Satan.

satânico –ca (*adj.*) satanic, devilish, diabolic.

satélite (*m.*) satellite; vassal, hanger-on; any of certain minerals or pebbles found in alluvial deposits and said to indicate the presence of diamonds; (*adj.*, *Anat.*) satellite.

S.At.g. = SANTO ANTÔNIO TE GUIE (may Saint Anthony guide you).

sátira (*f.*) satire; lampoon

satirão (*m.*) hazel sterculia (*S. foetida*); a chaste tree (*Vitex leucoxylon*).

satirião (*m.*, *Bot.*) two species of *Orchis*: *O. incarnata*, called SATIRIÃO-BASTARDO, and *O. mascula*, the male orchis, called SATIRIÃO-MACHO.

satiríase (*f.*, *Med.*) satyriasis.

satírico –ca (*adj.*) satiric(al); (*m.*,*f.*) satirist.

satirídeos (*m.pl.*) a family (*Agapetidae*) of butterflies.

satírio (*m.*) = SATIRIÃO (orchid).

satirista (*m.*,*f.*) satirist.

satirizar (*v.t.*) to satirize.

sátiro (*m.*) satyr; a lecherous man; a satyr butterfly.

satisfação (*f.*) satisfaction, gratification; pleasure; redress, indemnification; discharge, settlement; (*pl.*) amends, apologies; explanations. **dar—a uma queixa,** to settle a complaint. **dar uma—,** to offer an apology.

satisfatório –ria (*adj.*) satisfactory; tolerable, fair.

satisfazer [47] (*v.i.*) to give satisfaction; (*v.t.*) to satisfy; (*v.r.*) to be satisfied.—**a fome,** to appease hunger.—**as necessidades,** to meet the needs.—**uma dívida,** to pay a debt.—**uma obrigação,** to fulfill an obligation.

satisfeito –ta (*adj.*) satisfied, gratified, pleased, content; fulfilled, answered, met. **dar-se por—,** to be satisfied, content.

sativo –va (*adj.*) that is sown or planted.

sátrapa (*m.*) satrap; despot, sybarite.

satrapia (*f.*) satrapy.

saturação (*f.*) saturation.

saturado –da (*adj.*) saturated; replete, full.

saturador –dora (*adj.*) saturating; (*m.*,*f.*) saturator.

saturagem (*f.*) = SEGURELHA.

saturamento (*m.*) = SATURAÇÃO.

saturante (*adj.*) saturating.

saturar (*v.t.*) to saturate, drench, soak, imbue; to impregnate; to sate, cloy, (*v.r.*) to become sated.

saturável (*adj.*) saturable.

saturnal (*adj.*) Saturnian; saturnalian; (*f.*) revel, orgy; (*pl.*) saturnalia.

saturnino –na (*adj.*) Saturnine; leaden. [But not saturnine in the sense of gloomy, which is SOTURNO, SOMBRIO, LÚGUBRE.]

saturnismo (*m.*) lead poisoning.

saturno –na (*adj.*) saturnalian; [*cap.*] (*m.*) Saturn.

sauá (*m.*) a marmoset (*Callithrix nigrifrons*), c.a. SAÁ.

saúba (*f.*) = SAÚVA.

saubal [a-u] (*m.*) = SAUVAL.

saúco (*m.*) the coffin of a horse's hoof.

saudação [a-u] (*f.*) salutation, greeting; a bow; a lifting of the hat.

saudade [a-u] (*f.*) longing, yearning (for someone); "memory imbued with longing"; fond remembrance; nostalgia, homesickness; [in these senses usually plural]; (*Bot.*) the sweet scabious (*Scabiosa atropurpurea*), c.a. SAUDADE-DA-VIÚVA, SUSPIRO-DOS-JARDINS; a goldenhair plant (*Chrysocoma cimosa*), c.a. SAUDADE-DO-BREJO; a milkweed (*Asclepias umbellata*), c.a. SAUDADE-DA-CAMPINA, CEGA-ÔLHO.—**s de casa,** or **da família,** or **da terra,** homesickness.—**s perpétuas,** (*Bot.*) the common immortelle (*Xeranthemum annum*). **matar as—s,** to satisfy one's longings (for someone or some place). **ter —s de,** to miss, long for (someone or something).

saudador –dora [a-u] (*adj.*) greeting; (*m.*,*f.*) one who greets.

saudante [a-u] (*adj.*) greeting.

saudar [a-u] (*v.t.*) to greet, salute; to hail, welcome.

saudável [a-u] (*adj.*) healthful, wholesome, salutary.

saúde (*f.*) health, vigor; a toast (the drinking of a health); (*exclam.*) Farewell! **estar bem de—,** to be in good health. **vendendo—,** bursting with health. **Você está vendendo—,** You look the picture of health.

saudosismo [a-u] (*m.*) a longing for the return of former days, esp. as under a given political regime.

saudosista [a-u] (*adj.*) yearning, longing; (*m.*,*f.*) one who advocates the return of a former regime.

saudoso –sa [a-u] (*adj.*) longed-for; of fond memory; heartfelt; nostalgic; regretful.

sauí (*m.*) a small, sluglike caterpillar; the same also as SAGÜI, SAGÜIM and SAUIM (monkeys).

sauiguaçu [çú] (*m.*) a titi monkey (*Callicebus*).

saúna (*f.*) any of various mullets, esp. of the fantail (*Mugil trichodon*); also = TAINHA-DE-RIO.—**ôlho-de-fogo** (-vermelho), the white mullet (*Mugil curema*), c.a. PARATI.

sauni [í] (*m.*) = JUIZ-DO-MATO.

saurá (*m.*) = ANAMBÉ.

sáurio (*m.*) saurian.

saurófago –ga (*adj.*) saurophagous.

saúva (*f.*) any of a number of leaf-cutting or umbrella ants of the genus *Atta*, esp. *A. cephalotes*, which is widely distributed in Brazil. [They live in immense subterranean colonies and cause great damage to agriculture. There is a saying that unless Brazil finishes the **saúva**, the **saúva** will finish Brazil: **O Brasil ou acaba com a saúva ou a saúva acaba com o Brasil.**] Other vernacular names are: CABEÇUDA, CARREGADEIRA, FORMIGA-CARREGADEIRA, FORMIGA-DE-MANDIOCA, FORMIGA-DE-ROÇA, ROCEIRA. The males are called: BITU, ESCUMANA, SABITU, SAVITU, VITU; the females: IÇÁ and TANAJURA.

sauval, saubal, sauveiro (*m.*) the underground nest of SAÚVA ants.

savacu-de-côroa (*m.*) = MATIRÃO.

savana (*f.*) savannah.

savate (*f.*) savate (French boxing).

saveiro (*m.*) a kind of long and narrow fishing boat; the boatman; lighter, barge.

savelha [ê] (*f.*, *Zool.*) a menhaden (*Brevoortia tyrannus aurea*).

savitu [ú] (*m.*) a male SAÚVA ant.

saxão –xona [ks] (*adj.*; *m.*,*f.*) Saxon.

saxátil [ks] (*adj.*) saxatile, saxicoline.

saxicava [ks] (*f.*) a genus (*Saxicava*) of rock-boring mollusks.

saxícola [ks] (*adj.*) saxicoline, saxatile.

saxicolídeas [ks] (*f.pl.*) a family (*Saxicolidae*) of O.W. passerine birds including the stonechats and allied species.

saxífraga (*f.*) see under SAXÍFRAGO.

saxifragáceo –cea [ks] (*adj.*, *Bot.*) saxifragaceous.

saxífrago –ga [ks] (*adj.*) saxifragous; (*f.*, *Bot.*) the genus of saxifrages (*Saxifraga*).—**-branca,** the meadow saxifrage (*S. granulata*), c.a. SANÍCULA-DOS-MONTES.—**-doreino,** the saxifrage pimpinella (*P. saxifraga*).

saxofone, saxofôno [ks] (*m.*) saxophone.

saxofonista [ks] (*m.*,*f.*) saxophonist.

saxônio –nia [ks] (*adj.*; *m.*,*f.*) Saxonian.

saxonito [ks] (*m.*, *Petrog.*) saxonite.

saxoso –sa [ks] (*adj.*) rocky [= PEDREGOSO].

saxotrompa [ks] (*m.*) saxotromba; saxhorn.

sazão (*m.*) season (of year); harvest season; fit time.

sazonação (*f.*) ripening; seasoning.

sazonado –da (*adj.*) ripe; mature; seasoned; mellow.

sazonador –dora (*adj.*) ripening; seasoning.

sazonamento (*m.*) = SAZONAÇÃO.

sazonar (*v.t.*) to ripen; to season; (*v.i.*) to ripen; (*v.r.*) to ripen; to become seasoned (experienced).

sazonável (*adj.*) about to ripen; seasonable.

sc. = SACO (sack, bag).

s/c = SUA CARTA (your letter); SUA CONTA (your account); SUA CASA (your house).

S.C. = SENTIDAS CONDOLÊNCIAS (deep-felt condolences).

SC = SANTA CATARINA (State of).

s.d. = SEM DATA (undated).

S.E. = SUESTE (southeast); SUA EMINÊNCIA (His Eminence); SALVO ÊRRO (save error).

SE = SERGIPE (State of).

se (*conj.*) if, whether (or not), provided, though, in case that.—**ao menos,** if only.—**bem que,** even though, although. [Frequently used to emphasize verbs and other parts of speech, esp. in conversation. **Gosta?** Do you like it? **Ora se gosto!** Do I! Of course I like it]; (*sing. & pl. reflexive pers. pron.*) (to) himself, herself, itself, oneself, yourself, themselves, yourselves. Cf. SI.

sé (*f.*) see, diocese. **a Santa—,** the Holy See.

sê, imperative form of SER [76].

seara (*f.*) grain field; harvest. **Isto é—alheia,** This is out of my field (not in my line).

sebáceo –cea (*adj.*) sebaceous, fatty.

sebácico –ca (*adj., Chem.*) sebacic.

sebastião (*m.*) smooth dogfish (*Mustelus canis*), c.a. CAÇÃO-ANGOLISTA, CAÇÃO-TORRADOR, CACÃO-FIUSO, BO-DINHO, TOLO, JOÃO-DIAS; also = BACURAU and TROPEIRO (birds); [*cap.*] Sebastian.

sebe (*f.*) fence; screen.—**viva,** hedge (of plants).

sebento –ta (*adj.*) greasy, dirty.

sebereba (*f.*) = CHIBÉ.

sebesta (*f.*) sebesten plum.

sebesteiro (*m.*) the sebesten-plum cordia (*C. myxa*).

sebífero –ra (*adj.*) sebiferous.

sebite, sebito (*m.*) = CAGA-SEBINHO.

sebiubu [bú] (*m.*) a frangipani (*Plumeria phagedenica*).

sebo (*m.*) suet, tallow, fat; (*colloq.*) secondhand book store; (*interj.*) Nuts!

seborreia (*f., Med.*) seborrhea.

seborréico –ca (*adj.*) seborrheic.

seboso –sa (*adj.*) sebaceous; greasy; dirty, filthy.

sec. = SECANTE (secant).

séc. = SÉCULO (century).

seca (*f.*) act of drying; (*colloq.*) long, boring talk; chatter; formality; (*m.*) annoying or boring person.

sêca (*f.*) see under SÊCO.

secação (*f.*) drying; siccation.

secadeira (*f.*) drier; drying place.

secador –dora (*adj.*) drying; long-winded; (*m.,f.*) drier.

secadouro (*m.*) drying place.

secagem (*f.*) process of drying.

secale (*m., Bot.*) rye.

secalose (*f., Chem.*) secalose.

sêcamente (*adv.*) drily, coldly, curtly (referring to manner of speaking).

secante (*adj.*) annoying; boring; drying; secant, cutting; (*m.*) annoying person; paint drier; (*f., Geom., Trig.*) secant.

seção (*f.*) var. of SECÇÃO.

secar (*v.t.*) to dry; to drain; to desiccate, parch; to furl (sails); (*v.i.*) to dry (up, out); (*v.r.*) to become dry; to wither; to become angry (**a, com,** with).

secativo –va (*adj.; m.*) siccative, disiccant.

secatório –ria (*adj.*) siccative; (*f.*) pruning shears.

se[c]ção (*f.*) section; cross section; cutting, severance; segment; division; government office or department.

se[c]cional (*adj.*) sectional.

se[c]cionar(*v.t.*) to section.

secessão (*f.*) secession.

sécio –cia (*adj.*) coquettish; (*f., Bot.*) china aster (*Callistephus chinensis*).

seclusão (*f.*) seclusion.

sêco –ca (*adj.*) dry; arid, parched; barren; curt, crusty; thirsty; longing, craving; **ama—,** a dry nurse (as opposed to AMA-DE-LEITE, wet nurse); (*f.*) drought; long dry spell; (*m.pl.*) dry foodstuffs (as opposed to MOLHADOS, liquids). **armazém de—s e molhados,** grocery store.

sêco–fico (*m.*) = SACI (bird).

secr. = SECRETÁRIO (secretary).

secreção (*f.*) secretion, discharge.—**interna,** internal secretion.

secreta (*m.*) secret (police) agent; (*f., Liturgics*) silent prayer. [But not a secret, which is SEGREDO.]

secretar (*v.*) = SEGREGAR.

secretaria (*f.*) secretariat; government bureau; ministry.

secretária (*f.*) secretary; writing-desk.

secretariado (*m.*) secretariat.

secretariar (*v.i.*) to act as secretary.

secretário (*m.*) secretary; minister of state.—**de Embaixada,** Embassy Secretary.—**de Estado,** Secretary of State, Minister of State.—**de Legação,** Legation Secretary.—**de redação,** secretary of a newspaper.—**particular,** private secretary.

secreto –ta (*adj.*) secret, hidden; occult; secluded; (*adv.*) secretly. Cf. SECRETA above.

secretório –ria (*adj.; m.*) secretory (organ or gland).

sectário –ria (*adj.*) sectarian; (*m.*) sectarian; henchman.

sectarismo (*m.*) sectarianism.

séctil [-teis] (*adj.*) sectile.

sectilidade (*f.*) sectility.

sector (*m.*) = SETOR.

secular (*adj.*) secular, temporal; laical; age-old, long-enduring, centuried; (*m.*) a layman.

secularidade (*f.*) secularity.

secularismo (*m.*) secularism.

secularizar (*v.t.*) to secularize.

século (*m.*) century.

secundar (*v.t.*) to second, back up; to repeat.

secundário –ria (*adj.*) secondary, subordinate.

secundina (*f., Bot.*) secundine; (*pl., Med., Veter.*) secundines, afterbirth.

secura (*f.*) dryness; thirst.

securígero –ra (*adj.*) securigerous; (*f., Bot.*) the genus (*Securigera*) of hatchet vetches.

sêda (*f.*) silk; (*pl.*) bristles.—**animal,** real silk.—**crua,** or **—em rama,** raw silk.—**frouxa,** embroidery silk.—**-vegetal** = LINHO-DA-NOVA-ZELÂNDIA. **bicho da—,** silkworm. **papel de—,** tissue paper.

sedação (*f., Med.*) sedation.

sedalha (*f.*) = SEDELA.

sedante (*adj.*) sedative.

sedar (*v.t.*) to quiet, as pain or passion.

sedativo –va (*adj.; m.*) sedative.

sede [sé] (*f.*) seat, site; see, diocese.

sêde (*f.*) thirst; desire, craving.—**de sangue,** blood-thirstiness. **com—,** thirsty; (*v.i.*) imperative form of SER [76].

sedeiro (*m.*) hackle or hatchel (for flax, hemp, or jute).

sedela (*f.*) fishing line; snell [= SEDALHA].

sedenho (*m., Med., Veter.*) seton.

sedentariedade (*f.*) sedentariness.

sedentário –ria (*adj.*) sedentary; inactive; (*m.,f.*) such a person.

sedento –ta (*adj.*) thirsty; athirst, eager, avid.—**de sangue,** bloodthirsty.

sêde-sêde (*m.*) = SACI (bird).

sedeúdo –da (*adj.*) silken; hairy.

sédia (*f.*) rich armchair.

sedição (*f.*) insurrection, tumult, riot, rebellion, sedition. —**militar,** mutiny.

sedicioso –sa (*adj.*) seditious, mutinous; refractory, rebellious; (*m.*) an insurgent; rioter.

sedimentação (*f.*) sedimentation.

sedimentado –da (*adj.*) of long standing, deeply rooted [habits, etc.].

sedimentar, sedimentário –ria (*adj.*) sedimentary.

sedimento (*m.*) sediment.

sedinha (*f., Bot.*) a globe amaranth (*Gomphrena holosericea*).

sedoso –sa (*adj.*) silky.

sedução (*f.*) seduction, attraction, allurement; temptation; lure; seducement.

sédulo –la (*adj.*) sedulous, assiduous.

sedutor –tora (*adj.*) seductive, tempting, attractive; (*m.*) seducer; (*f.*) a seductive woman.

seduzimento (*m.*) = SEDUÇÃO.

seduzir [36] (*v.t.*) to seduce, lead astray; to decoy, entice, inveigle; to lure; to beguile; to deprive of chastity.

seduzível (*adj.*) seducible.

seg. = SEGUINTE (next); SEGUNDO (second).

sega, segada (*f.*) harvest(ing); harvest season.

sêga (*f.*) colter (of a plow).

segadeira (*f.*) scythe.

segador –dora (*adj.*) harvesting; reaping; (*m.,f.*) harvester, reaper.

segadouro –ra (*adj.*) harvesting, reaping; ready for harvesting.

segar (*v.t.*) to harvest, reap, mow.

sege (*f.*) an old-fashioned chaise.

segmentação (*f.*) segmentation.

segmentador –dora (*adj.*) segmenting.

segmentar (*v.t.*) to segment; (*adj.*) segmental.

segmentário –ria (*adj.*) segmentary.

segmento (*m.*) segment, division, section; (*Geom.*) segment.—**de êmbolo,** piston ring.

segredar (*v.i.,v.t.*) to whisper; (*v.t.*) to insinuate, inspire slyly.

segredeiro –ra (*adj.*) whispering; secretive.

segredista (*adj.; m.,f.*) secretive, whispering (person).

segrêdo (*m.*) a secret; a mystery; a confidence; secret combination of a safe; a hidden spring.—**de estado,** state secret.—**de polichinelo,** something everybody knows but of which only the very credulous make a mystery.—**do êxito,** secret of success.—**inviolável,** inviolable secret.—**político,** political or state secret.—**profissional,** professional secret.—**s da natureza,** secrets of Nature. **em**—, in secret, secretly.

segregação (*f.*) segregation; secretion.

segregar (*v.t.*) to segregate, set apart; to seclude; to dissociate; (*Physiol., Biol.*) to secrete, discharge.

segregativo **-va** (*adj.*) segregative; (*Physiol., Biol.*) secretory.

seguida (*f.*) see under SEGUIDO.

seguidamente (*adv.*) continually, continuously, constantly, time after time.

seguidilha (*f.*) seguidilla (Spanish dance and its music).

seguidinho **-nha** (*adv.*) frequently.

seguido **-da** (*adj.*) followed; following; next; continuous. **dias**—**s,** day after day; (*f.*) act of following. **em**—, after, afterwards, then, soon after(ward), immediately, right away.

seguidor **-dora** (*adj.*) following; (*m.,f.*) follower, partisan; (*Mach.*) cam follower.

seguilhote (*m.*) unweaned whale calf.

seguimento (*m.*) a following (after); pursuit, chase; sequence; continuation; sequel.

seguinte (*adj.*) following, ensuing, next after, succeeding, sequent, subsequent. **o dia**—, the next day; (*m.*) what follows; the following.

seguir [21a] (*v.t.*) to follow; to come or go after (behind, in the wake of); to go with, accompany; to go in pursuit of (a criminal, etc.); to chase, hunt; to proceed along (a given course); to pursue (a calling); to watch, attend closely, keep up with; to take (as leader); to heed, obey, observe, be guided by; to copy after, take after; (*v.i.*) to proceed, go ahead; to follow; (*v.r.*) to follow (in order), succeed, ensue; to result (**de,** from).—**a,** to come after.—**a sua inclinação, o seu gênio, os seus apetites,** to follow one's bent, one's nature; to yield to one's appetites.—**as pisadas,** or **as pegadas, de alguém,** to follow in another's footsteps.—**de perto,** to follow closely.—**disfarçadamente,** to shadow, keep under surveillance.—**o inimigo,** to pursue (chase) the enemy.—**o bom caminho,** to take the right path, do the right thing.—**os conselhos da mãe,** to take, heed (her, his, your) mother's advice.—**para o sul,** to proceed south.—**pelo primeiro train,** to leave by the first train. [The purists object to the use of the verb.]—**-se a,** to follow, come after.—**o seu caminho,** to go on one's way.—**um entêrro,** to accompany a funeral.—**um exemplo,** to follow an example.—**viagem, caminho,** to go on, continue on one's way. **a**—, following, in succession, next, then. **fazer**—, to forward, send on. **segue-se que,** it follows that. **Siga por êste caminho,** Go along this road. **Siga por êsse caminho,** You're on the right track.

segunda (*f.*) second proof sheet; (*Autom.*) second speed; (*Music*) second; (*adj.*) fem. of SEGUNDO.

segunda-feira (*f.*) Monday.

segundanista (*m.,f.*) second-year student; sophomore.

segundar (*v.t.*) to repeat [= SECUNDAR].

segundário **-ria** (*adj.*) = SECUNDÁRIO.

segundo (*prep.*) according to.—**a imprensa,** according to the press.—**a opinião geral,** according to general opinion.—**o costume,** according to custom; as usual.—**se afirma,** or—**se pretende,** allegedly. (*adv.*) secondly; (*m.*) a second (of time); (*adj.; fem.* **segunda**) second, secondary; other, another.—**estado,** matrimony.—**infância,** second childhood.—**intenção,** real intention (not the ostensive one).—**pessoa,** (*Gram.*) second person.—**primo,** second cousin.—**prova,** second proof.—**saia,** overskirt.—**tenor,** second tenor.—**via,** second sheet; second (or carbon) copy.—**vista,** second sight.—**s vistas,** afterthoughts; mental reservations. **de**—**classe,** second-class; second-rate. **de**—**mão,** secondhand. **em**—**lugar,** in (the) second place. **em**—**mão,** at secondhand.

segundogênito **-ta** (*adj.; m.,f.*) second-born (child).

segura (*j.*) see under SEGURO.

segurado **-da** (*adj.*) insured; (*m.,f.*) an insured person; a policyholder.

seguramente (*adv.*) assuredly; safely; securely.

segurança (*f.*) security, safety; assurance, certainty; reliability, reliance; aplomb. **aparelho de**—, safety device.

caixa de—, safe; safe deposit box; strong box. **com**—, assuredly.

segurar [24] (*v.t.*) to hold, grasp, seize; to fasten, make secure; to make sure; to assure, warrant; to insure. Cf. ASSEGURAR.

segurável (*adj.*) insurable.

segurelha [ê] (*f.*) sweet basil (*Ocimum basilicum*).—**-do-inverno,** winter savory (*Satureia montana*).—**-dos-jardins,** or—**-do-verão,** summer savory (*Satureia hortensis*).

segureza [ê], **seguridade** (*f.*) = SEGURANÇA.

seguro **-ra** (*adj.; irreg. p.p.* of SEGURAR) secure; safe, dependable, free from danger; sure, certain; firm, fast; stingy, miserly; (*adv.*) safely, securely; (*f.*) cooper's adze; (*m.*) insurance, assurance, security.—**contra acidentes,** accident insurance.—**contra fogo,** fire insurance.—**de vida,** life insurance. **apólice de**—, insurance policy. **companhia de**—, insurance company. **fazer um**—, to take out insurance. **O**—**morreu de velho,** Better safe than sorry; Discretion is the better part of valor.

sei, I know. [Verb SABER (76)]

seibo (*m.*) a coralbean (*Erythrina falcata*).

seio (*m.*) bosom; breast; loop, curve; a bay of the sea; depths, innermost recesses; womb; intimate privacy; midst.—**basilar,** (*Anat.*) basilar sinus.

seira (*f.*) wicker or rush basket.

seis (*adj.*) sixth; (*m.*) the number six; the six spot (dominos, cards, dice); the sixth one.

seisavo (*m.*) a sixth.

seiscentésimo **-ma** (*adj.*) sixhundredth.

seiscentista (*adj.*) of the 1600's; (*m.,f.*) a 17th century writer.

seiscentos (*m.pl.*) six hundred.

seistil (*m.*) a sixth.

seita (*f.*) sect, faction.

seiva (*f.*) sap; life blood; vim, vitality.

seivoso **-sa** (*adj.*) sappy.

seixebra (*f.*) = ESCÓRDIO.

seixo (*m.*) pebble.

seixoso **-sa** (*adj.*) pebbly.

sej + verb endings = present subjunctive forms of SER [76].

seja (*conj.*) be it.—**quente,**—**frio,** be it hot, (or) be it cold; (*interj.*) So be it!—**assim,** All right, let it be so; (*adv.*)—**como fôr,** Be that as it may.—**o que fôr,** Come what may.

sela (*f.*) saddle.—**turca,** or **túrcica,** or **turquesa,** (*Anat.*) sella turcica.

selado **-da** (*adj.*) saddled; saddlebacked; sealed; stamped; (*f.*) saddleback (low point in the crest of a ridge); (*m.*) side curve of the waist; inner or curved side of the foot.

selador **-dora** (*adj.*) saddling; sealing; (*m.,f.*) saddler; sealer; stamper.

seladouro (*m.*) place on a horse's back on which the saddle rests; cut of the waistline of a garment.

seladura (*f.*) act of saddling; sway-back.

selagem (*f.*) placing of stamps or seals on letters or documents.

selagina (*f.*) = SELAGO.

selaginela (*f.*) a genus (*Selaginella*) of fern allies.

selaginláceo **-a** (*adj., Bot.*) selaginellaceous.

selagito (*m., Petrog.*) selagite.

selago (*m.*) the fir clubmoss (*Lycopodium selago*).

selagote (*m.*) a crude type of saddle used in the interior of Brazil.

seláqueo **-quea** (*adj.*) of fishes, cartilaginous; (*m.pl., Zool.*) the order Selachii (sharks, rays, etc.).

selar (*v.t.*) [from SELA] to saddle; [from SÊLO] to seal; to close, fasten; to stamp (for mailing).

selaria (*f.*) saddlery.

seleção (*f.*) selection, choice; picked team.—**manual,** hand sorting.—**natural,** natural selection, "survival of the fittest."

selecionado (*m.*) picked team (as of soccer players).

selecionador **-dora** (*adj.*) selecting, choosing; (*m.,f.*) selector, chooser.

selecionar (*v.t.*) to select, choose, screen, pick out, cull;

seleiro **-ra** (*adj.*) of riders, good in the saddle; of horses, used to the saddle; (*m.,f.*) saddler.

selenato, seleniato (*m., Chem.*) selenate, seleniate.

seleneto (*m., Chem.*) selenide.

selênico **-ca** (*adj., Chem.*) selenic.

selenífero **-ra** (*adj., Chem.*) seleniferous.

selênio (*m., Chem.*) selenium.

selenioso –sa (*adj.*, *Chem.*) selenious.
selenita (*m.*) moon dweller; (*f.*, *Chem.*, *Min.*) selenite.
selenocêntrico –ca (*adj.*, *Astron.*) selenocentric.
selenodonte (*adj.; m.*, *Zool.*) selenodont.
selenografia (*f.*, selenography.
selenologia (*f.*) selenology.
seleta (*f.*) see under SELETO.
seletar (*v.t.*) to select.
seletividade (*f.*, *Radio*) selectivity.
seletivo –va (*adj.*) selective.
seleto –ta (*adj.*) select, choice; (*f.*) a collection of literary gems; a choice variety of pear and of orange.
seletor –tora (*adj.*) selecting; (*m.*) selector.
self-indução (*f.*, *Elect.*) self-induction.
selha [ê] (*f.*) wooden tub.
selim (*m.*) an English saddle.—**de bicicleta**, bicycle saddle.
selista (*m.,f.*) stamp collector or dealer.
sêlo (*m.*) seal; official seal; postage stamp. Cf. ESTAM-PILHA.—**de consumo**, excise stamp tax.—**de estampilha**, tax stamp.—**-de-salomão**, (*Bot.*) the drug Solomon seal (*Polygonatum officinale*).—**de verba**, a written notation on a document attesting to the fact that the corresponding tax has been paid.—**postal**, postage stamp.
selote (*m.*) a small saddle of the English type [= SELIM].
selva (*f.*) jungle, forest, woods—esp. the Amazon rain forest.
selvagem (*adj.*) savage, uncultivated; uncivilized, wild, untamed; barbarous; (*m.,f.*) savage, barbarian.
selvageria (*f.*) = SELVAJARIA.
selvagíneo –nea (*adj.*) wild, untamed—referring esp. to jungle animals.
selvagismo (*m.*) savagery; savages collectively.
selvajaria (*f.*) savagery, barbarism.
selvático –ca (*adj.*) wild, savage; jungle.
selvícola (*adj.; m.,f.*) = SILVÍCOLA.
selvoso –sa (*adj.*) of land, having woods or jungles.
sem. = SEMANA (week); SEMELHANTE (similar); SEMESTRE (semester).
sem (*prep.*) without, lacking, destitute of. [See also compound words beginning with sem-].—**amigos**, friendless.—**casa**, homeless.—**cerimônia**, at ease, informally, without fuss or feathers; also, impudently. [Cf. SEM-CERIMÔNIA].—**cessar**, unceasingly; continually.—**conta**, innumerably.—**costura**, seamless [= INCONSÚTIL].—**de-longas**, without "stalling"; without delay.—**demora**, without delay, immediately.—**descanso**, without rest; uninterruptedly.—**destino**, aimlessly; destination unknown.—**dificuldade**, easily; willingly.—**dinheiro**, penniless.—**discernimento**, without thinking; unthinkingly.—**distinção**, indiscriminately.—**distinção de**, without regard to; regardless of.—**dizer palavra**, without uttering a word; silently.—**dúvida**, indubitably.—**embargo**, although, notwithstanding.—**embargo de**, in spite of.—**emprêgo**, jobless.—**endereço certo**, no fixed address.—**escolha**, at random; also, without choice (the right to choose).—**fala**; mutely; speechless.—**falta**, without fail; infallibly.—**fim**, (*adj.*) endless; (*adv.*) endlessly. [Cf. SEM-FIM]—**fio**, wireless.—**fome**, not hungry. [O menino está sem fome, The kid has no appetite; he won't eat.]—**jeito**, clumsy, all thumbs; awkward.—**mais nem menos**, without so much as; just like that.—**mais tardar**, without further delay.—**medida**, unstintingly.—**mêdo**, fearless(ly).—**mêdo de errar**, without fear of contradiction; with absolute certainty.—**número**, innumerably. [Cf. SEM-NÚMERO.]—**pensar**, unthinkingly.—**pés nem cabeça**, without head or tail.—**pestanejar**, without batting an eye.—**piedade**, pitilessly, inexorably.—**prejuízo de**, without prejudice to.—**quantia**, countlessly.—**que**, unless; without, in the absence of.—**que ninguém soubesse**, without anyone knowing.—**querer**, without wishing to, unthinkingly; accidentally. [Foi sem querer, It was an accident! He (she, you) didn't mean to do it!]—**receio**, unhesitatingly.—**remédio**, irremediably; inevitably; hopeless(ly)—**remissão**, implacably; unforgivably.—**reserva**, unreservedly, unconditionally.—**resguardo**, unreservedly, frankly.—**rumo**, at random; haphazard.—**têrmo**, interminably. [Cf. SEM-TÊRMO].—**tino**, carelessly.—**tirar nem pôr**, without change; exactly; verbatim.—**tugir nem mugir**, without uttering a word. **ficar—jeito**, to feel awkward, embarrassed. **passar—(alguma coisa)**, to do without, get along without (something).
S. Em.ᵃ = SUA EMINÊNCIA (His Eminence).

semafórico –ca (*adj.*) semaphoric.
semáforo (*m.*) semaphore.
semana (*f.*) week.—**da Paixão**, Passion week.—**donzela** = **solteira**.—**dos nove dias**, a week that will never come to pass.—**furada**, a broken week, i.e., one having a holiday in it.—**inglêsa**, a five-and-a-half days workweek (ending Saturday noon).—**Santa**, Holy week.—**solteira**, a week having no saint's day in it. **a—que vem**, the coming week, next week. **a—passada**, last week. **a—próxima**, next week. **a—seguinte**, the following week. **daquí a uma—**, a week from now. **de duas em duas—s**, every two weeks. **dentro de uma—**, within a week, inside of a week. **dia da—**, day of the week. **dia de—**, weekday. **duas vezes por—**, twice a week. **faz uma—**, a week ago. **fim de—**, week end. **há uma—**, a week ago. **havia uma—**, a week earlier (prior). **na—passada**, last week. **na—que vem**, next week. **todas as—s**, every week.
semanal (*adj.*) weekly.
semanalmente (*adv.*) weekly; from week to week; every week.
semanário (*m..*) a weekly publication.
semântico –ca (*adj.*) semantic; (*f.*) semantics.
semasiologia, sematologia (*f.*, *Philol.*) semasiology, semantics.
semblante (*m.*) countenance, face, visage; aspect, mien.
sem-cerimônia (*f.*) unceremoniousness, informality, unconventionality; rudeness, abruptness; offhandedness. Cf. SEM CERIMÔNIA.
sem-cerimonioso –sa (*adj.*) informal; unceremonious; unconventional.
sêmea (*f.*) wheat bran; bran bread.
semeação (*f.*) act of sowing.
semeada (*f.*) a sown field.
semeadeira (*f.*) sowing machine.
semeador –dora (*adj.*) sowing; (*m.*) sower; sowing machine.
semeadura (*f.*) sowing.—**a lança**, broadcast sowing.
semear (*v.t.*) to sow, scatter seed; to disseminate, spread abroad.—**a cizânia**, to sow discord.
semelhança (*f.*) resemblance, similarity, likeness, semblance, similitude, analogy. **à—de**, in the likeness of; similar to.
semelhante (*adj.*) similar, like, analogous; any such; (*m.,f.*) fellow creature.
semelhar (*v.t.,v.r.*) to resemble, look like.
sêmen [pl. semens] (*m.*) seed; semen, sperm.
sêmen-contra, semencina (*f.*, *Pharm.*) semen contra, semencinae, santonica, Levant wormseed; (*Bot.*) Levant wormwood (*Artemisia cina*).
semenduara (*f.*) = PAMPO-DE-CABEÇA-MOLE.
semente (*f.*) seed; origin.—**de embira** = PAU DE EMBIRA.—**de paraíso** = MANIGUETE.
sementeiro –ra (*adj.*) seeding, sower; (*m.,f.*) seeder, sower; (*m.*) seed bag; (*f.*) seeding, sowing; seeding time; a seed field.
sementina (*f.*) = SÊMEN-CONTRA.
semestral (*adj.*) semestral, semi-annual.
semestralmente (*adv.*) half-yearly.
semestre (*m.*) semester.
sem-fim (*m.*) endless quantity, number, space, etc.; a cuckoo, c.a. SACI. Cf. SEM FIM.
semi-aberto –ta (*adj.*) half-open, ajar.
semi-aço (*m.*) semisteel.
semi-aderente (*adj.*, *Bot.*) semiadherent.
semi-amplexicaule [ks] (*adj.*, *Bot.*) semiamplexicaul.
semi-anão –nã (*adj.*) half-dwarf.
semi-animal (*adj.*) semianimal.
semiânime, semiânimo –ma (*adj.*) half-dead.
semi-anual (*adj.*) semiannual.
semi-anular (*adj.*) semianular.
semi-ânuo –nua (*adj.*) = SEMI-ANUAL.
semi-automático –ca (*adj.*) semiautomatic.
semibárbaro –ra (*adj.*) semibarbarous.
semibrasileiro –ra (*adj.*) almost Brazilian.
semibruto (*m.*) half-brute.
semiburlesco –ca [lê] (*adj.*) semiburlesque.
semicadáver (*m.*) half-dead person.
semícapro (*m.*) faun, satyr.
semichas (*f.pl.*, *colloq.*) spillage, excess (as of wine being poured into a measure).
semicientífico –ca (*adj.*) semiscientific.
semicilíndrico –ca (*adj.*) semicylindric(al).
semicilindro (*m.*) semicylinder.
semicircular (*adj.*) semicircular.

semicírculo (*m.*) semicircle.
semicircunferência (*f.*) semicircumference.
semicivilizado –da (*adj.*) half-civilized.
semiclausura (*f.*) semiclosure.
semicólon (*m.*) = PONTO-E-VIRGULA.
semicolonial (*adj.*) semicolonial.
semicolosso (*m.*) a somewhat colossal thing or person.
semicômico –ca (*adj.*) semicomic.
semicondutor (*m., Elec.*) semiconductor.
semiconfuso –sa (*adj.*) somewhat confused.
semiconvergente (*adj.; Math.*) semiconvergent.
semicristão –tã (*m.,f.*) a semi-Christian.
semicrítico –ca (*adj.*) half-critical.
semicúbico –ca (*adj.; Math.*) semicubical.
semicúpio (*m.*) sitz bath.
semicúpula (*f., Arch.*) semicupola.
semidefunto –ta (*adj.*) half-dead.
semidéia (*f.*) = SEMIDEUSA.
semidesperto –ta (*adj.*) half-awake.
semideus (*m.*) demigod.
semideusa (*f.*) demigoddess.
semidiáfano –na (*adj.*) semidiaphanous.
semidiâmetro (*m., Math., Astron.*) semidiameter.
semidisco (*m.*) semidisk.
semiditongo (*m.*) a rising diphthong or a falling one.
semidiurno –na (*adj.*) semidiurnal.
semidivino –na (*adj.*) semidivine.
semidobrado –da (*adj.*) semidouble.
semidoido –da (*adj.*) half-crazy.
semidúplex (*adj.*) semiduplex.
semi-elíptico –ca (*adj.*) semielliptical.
semi-enterrado –da (*adj.*) half-buried.
semi-esfera (*f.*) hemisphere.
semi-esferoidal (*adj.*) semispheroidal.
semi-estragado –da (*adj.*) somewhat spoiled.
semifabuloso –sa (*adj.*) semifabulous.
semifavor (*m.*) small favor.
semifendido –da (*adj.*) semisegmented.
semífero –ra (*adj.*) semiferal.
semifilosófico –ca (*adj.*) semiphilosophic(al).
semifinal (*adj.; f.*) semifinal (sporting match).
semiflósculo (*m., Bot.*) semifloret.
semiflosculoso –sa (*adj.; Bot.*) semifloscular (-lose, -lous).
semifluido –da (*adj.*) semifluid.
semigasto –ta (*adj.*) half-worn.
semiglobuloso –sa (*adj.*) semiglobular.
semigótico –ca (*adj.*) semi-Gothic.
semi-histórico –ca (*adj.*) semihistorical.
semi-homem (*m.*) halfman.
semi-humano –na (*adj.*) half-human.
semi-improviso (*m.*) an almost improvised speech.
semi-internato (*m.*) a day school at which pupils take their meals.
semi-interno –na (*m.,f.*) a day student who takes his or her meals at school.
semilíquido –da (*adj.*) semiliquid.
semilocular (*adj.; Bot.*) semilocular.
semilouco –ca (*adj.*) half-crazy.
semilouro –ra (*adj.*) blondish.
semilunar (*adj.*) semilunar; (*m., Anat.*) semilunar bone.
semilunático –ca (*adj.*) half-lunatic.
semilúnio (*m., Astron.*) semilunation.
semimédico (*m.*) a non-graduate physician.
semimembranoso –sa (*adj.; Anat.*) semimembranous.
semimetal (*m., Chem.*) semimetal.
semimetálico –ca (*adj.*) semimetallic.
semimorte (*f.*) moribundity.
semimorto –ta (*adj.*) half-dead.
seminação (*f., Bot.*) the natural dispersal of seeds; (*Med.*) coitus.
seminal (*adj.*) seminal.
seminário (*m.*) seminary; seminar; seed plot.
seminarista (*m.,f.*) seminarist.
seminase (*f., Biol.*) seminase.
seminífero –ra (*adj.; Bot., Zool., Anat.*) seminiferous.
seminíparo –ra (*adj.; Anat., Zool.*) seminiferous.
semino (*m.*) a fishing-net float.
seminu –nua (*adj.*) half-naked.
seminulífero –ra (*adj.*) seminuliferous.
semínulo (*m.*) seminule.
seminume (*m.*) = SEMIDEUS.
semi-oficial (*adj.*) semiofficial.
semiologia (*f.*) semiology.
semi-onda (*f., Elec.*) half-wave.

semi-opala (*f.*) semiopal.
semi-orbicular (*adj.; m., Anat.*) semiorbicular (muscle).
semi-oval (*adj.*) semioval.
semipagão –gã (*m.,f.*) semipagan.
semiparente (*adj.*) having some kinship with another.
semipedal (*adj.*) semipedal.
semipenumbra (*f.*) half shadow.
semiperiferia (*f.*) semiperiphery.
semiperíodo (*m.*) = SEMI-ONDA.
semipermeável (*adj.*) semipermeable.
semipetalóide (*adj.; Bot.*) semipetaloid.
semipleno –na (*adj.*) half-full; of proof, incomplete, less than full.
semipolítico –ca (*adj.*) semipolitical.
semiporcelana (*f.*) semiporcelain.
semiprova (*f.*) incomplete proof.
semipútrido –da (*adj.*) semiputrid.
semiquadrado –da (*adj.; Astron.*) semiquartite, semi-quadrate.
semiquietismo (*m.*) semiquietism.
semiquietista (*adj.; m.,f.*) semiquietist.
semi-reboque (*m.*) half-trailer.
semi-racional (*adj.*) very stupid.
semi-radiado –da (*adj.; Bot.*) semiradiate.
semi-real (*adj.*) half-real.
semi-regular (*adj.; Geom.*) semiregular.
semi-rei (*m.*) half-king.
semi-reto –ta (*adj.*) half-straight; right-angled.
semi-roliço –ça (*adj.*) semiround, semicylindrical.
semi-rôto –ta (*adj.*) half-broken.
semisfera (*f.*) = SEMI-ESFERA.
semi-sábio –bia (*adj.*) half-informed.
semi-sagitado –da (*adj.*) semisagittate.
semi-secular (*adj.*) half-century.
semi-segredo (*m.*) semisecret.
semi-selvagem (*adj.*) semisavage.
semi-serpente (*adj.*) half-serpent.
semi-silvestre (*adj.*) semiwild [plants, flowers].
semi-soberania (*f.*) incomplete sovereignty.
semi-som (*m.*) semivowel.
semita (*adj.*) Semitic; (*m.,f.*) Semite.
semitangente (*f., Math.*) semitangent.
semitendinoso (*m., Anat.*) semitendinosus.
semítico –ca (*adj.*) Semitic.
semitismo (*m.*) Semitism.
semitista (*m.,f.*) Semitist.
semitoar (*v.t.*) to intone (as a prayer).
semitofolia (*f.*) exaggerated anti-Semitism.
semitom (*m., Music*) semitone.
semitrágico –ca (*adj.*) almost tragic.
semitranquilo –la (*adj.*) neither tranquil nor agitated.
semitranslúcido –da (*adj.*) semitranslucent.
semitransparência (*f.*) semitransparency.
semitransparente (*adj.*) semitransparent.
semiverdade (*f.*) half-truth, semitruth.
semíviro (*m.*) halfman, eunuch.
semivítreo –trea (*adj.*) semivitreous.
semiviver (*v.i.*) to half-live.
semivoar (*v.i.*) to fly low.
semivocálico –ca (*adj., Phonet.*) semivocal.
semivogal (*f., Phonet.*) semivowel.
sem-justiça (*f.*) an injustice.
sem-luz (*m.,f.*) one who lives in darkness (blind person).
sem-modos (*m.,f.*) ill-mannered person.
sem-nome (*adj.*) nameless; anonymous; that cannot be described.
sem-número (*m.*) a great number (of anything).
sêmola, semolina (*f.*) semolina, wheat middlings; rice starch.
semostração (*f.*) showing off of self; ostentation; vanity.
semostrador –deira (*adj.*) given to exhibitionism.
semovente (*adj.; m.,f.*) self-propelled, self-moving (creature). bens—s, livestock.
sem-par (*adj.*) peerless.
sem-pátria (*m.,f.*) person without a country.
sempiternal (*adj.*) = SEMPITERNO.
sempiternamente (*adv.*) sempiternally.
sempiterno –na (*adj.*) sempiternal, everlasting.
sempre (*adv.*) always, ever, evermore, forever; really; yet, still; (*m.*) the ages.—que, provided (that); whenever, as often as. como—, as always, as usual. de—, as always. história de—, same old story. nem—, not always. para—, forever. para tôdo o—, for ever and ever. quase—, nearly always.

sempre-lustrosa (f.) Brazil bougainvillea (*B. spectabilis*).
sempre-noiva (f.) = POLÍGONO (knotweed).
sempre-viva, sempre-verde (f.) strawflower (*Helichrysum bracteatum*); the common immortelle (*Xeranthemum annum*); also = FLOR-DE-CETIM.
sem-pudor (m.) want of shame or modesty.
sem-razão (f.) an illogical (senseless, unreasonable) act or statement; a wrong.
sem-sal (adj.) insipid.
sem-segundo –da (adj.) unmatched, unique, peerless.
sem-têrmo (adj.) endless; interminable. Cf. SEM TÊRMO.
sem-vergonha (adj.) shameless; (m.,f.) shameless person; (f.) shamelessness.
sem-vergonhez[a], –nhice (f.), –nhismo (m.) shamelessness; shameful behavior.
sen. = SENO (sine).
sena (f.) the six-spot (cards or dice); (pl.) the double-six (domino); all sixes (dice); (Bot.) senna (*Cassia spp.*).—-do-reino, the honey cronilla (*C. glauca*).
SENAC = SERVIÇO NACIONAL DE APRENDIZAGEM COMERCIAL (National Service for Commercial Apprenticeships).
senado (m.) senate.
senador –dora (m.,f.) senator.
senadoria (f.) senatorship.
SENAI = SERVIÇO DE EDUCAÇÃO NACIONAL E APREDIZAGEM INDUSTRIAL (National Service of Industrial Education and Apprenticeship).
senaíto (m., Min.) senaite: "after J. de Costa Sena, Brazilian mineralogist. A titanite of iron, manganese, and lead occurring in black rounded crystals and fragments (favas) in the diamond-bearing sands of Minas Gerais, Brazil." [*Webster*]
senal (adj.) designating a very small rough diamond.
senão (conj.) otherwise, else, or else; but; except, unless. [Do not confuse with se não, if not.] (prep.) but, except, excepting; (m.) fault, defect, flaw.—quando, suddenly; then; one day.—que, but also, but rather.—também, but also.
senário (m.) senary, group of six.
senarmontita (f., Min.) senarmontite.
senatoria, senatória (f.) senatorship.
senatorial, senatório –ria (adj.) senatorial.
senatriz (f.) senator's wife.
senciente (adj.) sentient, feeling.
sencilha (f.) money loaned to a card player by a kibitzer.
sencilheiro (m.) money lender, esp. one who lends to card players.
senda (f.) path, trail, lane, walk way; routine, rut, groove.
sendeiro (m.) sorry nag, jade; a small but strong pack animal; a low, despicable person; a parasite.
sendo, pres. part. (gerund) of SER [76].
sene (m., Bot.) any of various species of *Cassia* (senna).—-da-europa, or—-falso, or—-vesiculoso, = ESPANTA-LOBOS or COLÚTEA.
sêneca (f., Bot.) either of two species of polygala: *P. virginiana* or *P. grandiflora*.
senécio (m., Bot.) the genus (*Senecio*) of groundsels.
senectude (f.) senility, old age.
sênega (f., Bot.) the seneca-snakeroot polygala (*P. senega*).
senegalês –lêsa, senegalesco –ca [lês] (adj.; m.,f.) Senegalese.
senegina (f., Chem.) senegin.
senembi, senembu, vars. of SINIMBU.
senescal (m.) seneschal.
senescência (f., Biol.) senescence.
senescente (adj.) aging.
senga (f.) leavings; screenings; oyster and clam shells.
sengar (v.t.) to sift, screen.
senha (f.) sign, password, countersign; receipt, voucher; theater ticket stub.
senhor [ô] (m.) seigneur, seignior, feudal lord or landowner; nowadays, any gentleman; Mr., sir. [Used in formal conversation as the equivalent of "you". O senhor tem passado bem? Have you been well?]—de baraço e cutelo, feudal lord having the power of life and death over his vassals; a highhanded person.—de engenho, owner and master of a large sugar plantation complex.—de si, master of self.—-velho, a slave's former master. Nosso—, Our Lord. O—, the Lord, God. o—da casa, head of the house, host.
senhora [ó or ô] (f.) lady, dame; wife, lady of the house; Mrs.; you (in formal speech). [A senhora é muito bondosa, You are very kind.] Nossa—, Our Lady.

senhoraça (f., colloq.) a would-be grande dame.
senhoraço (m.) a would-be grandee.
senhorear (v.t.) to master, conquer; to reign over, dominate.
senhoria (f.) seigniory; lordship, ladyship; dominion; landlord. Vossa—, Your Lordship.
senhoriagem (f.) seigniorage.
senhorial (adj.) seigniorial; manorial.
senhoril (adj.) lordly; ladylike.
senhorinha (f.) a young unmarried woman.
senhorio (m.) seigniory; domain, sway; manor; landlord.
senhorita (f.) small woman; also = SENHORINHA.
senil (adj.) senile, aged.
senilidade (f.) senility, old age.
sênior (adj.) senior, older, elder; a holder of first prizes in sports.
seno (m., Math.) sine.
senoidal (adj.) sine-shaped.
senóide (f.) sine wave.
sensabor (adj.; m.,f.) insipid, flat (person).
sensaborão –rona (adj.; m.,f.) very dull, insipid (person)
sensaboria (f.) insipidity, flatness, dullness; unpleasantness.
sensação (f.) sensation, feeling; a sensational event, situation, etc.
sensacional (adj.) sensational; lurid; thrilling.
sensacionismo (m.) sensationalism.
sensatez [têz] (f.) wisdom, good judgment, good sense.
sensato –ta (adj.) sensible, judicious, wise, well-balanced, levelheaded.
sensibilidade (f.) sensibility, feeling, susceptibility, sensitiveness, delicacy; (Radio) sensitivity.
sensibilizador –dora, sensibilizante (adj.) emotionally touching or moving; (Chem., Photog.) sensitizing.
sensibilizar (v.t.) to touch, move (someone) emotionally; (Chem., Photog.) to sensitize; (v.r.) to be touched (emotionally).
sensitivo –va (adj.) sensitive; (f.) the sensitive plant (*Mimosa pudica*), c.a. DORMIDEIRA, MALÍCIA-DE-MULHER, JUQUIRÁ-RASTEIRO, VERGONHOSA.—-mansa = CORTICEIRA-DO-CAMPO.
sensitômetro (m., Optics.) sensitometer.
sensível (adj.) sentient; impressionable; perceptible; appreciable, considerable; tenderhearted, compassionate; highly sensitive; touchy; sore; (Radio) sensitive.—redução nos preços, a substantial price reduction.
senso (m.) sense, reason, judgment, soundness.—comum, common sense.—estético, aesthetic feeling.—íntimo, inner conscience.
sensório –ria (adj.) sensory; (m., Anat.) sensorium.
sensual (adj.) sensual; (m.,f.) sensualist.
sensualidade (f.) sensuality; voluptuousness.
sensualismo (m.) sensualism.
sensualista (adj.; m.,f.) sensualist.
sentada (f.) sudden stop by a running horse.
sentador –dora (adj.) that sits; of a horse, given to sudden stops while running.
sentar (v.t.) to seat, place; (v.r.) to sit down.—à mesa, to sit at table.—praça, to enlist (as a soldier). Cf. ASSENTAR.
sentença (f.) maxim, axiom; dictum; sentence, decision, award, judgment; (Gram.) proposition.—absolutória, (Law) acquittal. Cada cabeça, cada—, Everyone to his own taste.
sentenciado –da (adj.) sentenced; (m.,f.) one who has been condemned.
sentenciar (v.t.) to pass sentence upon, judge, condemn; (v.i.) to make a decision; to pass an opinion.
sentencioso –sa (adj.) sententious; terse, to the point, pithy; cocksure.
sentido –da (adj.) sorry, grieved; sad, sorrowful; hurt, offended; (m.) sense, meaning; feeling, sensation, perception; each of the five senses; aim, direction, course; (Milit.) Attention! —acomodatício, a non-literal interpretation of passages of Scripture.—figurado, figurative meaning.—obtuso, obtuseness, dullness.—próprio, proper sense or meaning.—restrito or rigoroso, restricted sense or meaning.—vulgar, common meaning. em—contrário, in the opposite direction. em—lato, in a broad sense. em—oposto a, against. em posição de—, standing at attention. ficar—, to be offended, hurt. no—de que, to the end that; with a view to. os cinco—s, the five senses. perder os—s, to lose consciousness. sem—, unconscious; senseless, unintelligible.

sentimental (*adj.*) sentimental, tender, romantic; maudlin. **um caso**—, a love affair.
sentimentalidade (*f.*) sentimentality.
sentimentalismo (*m.*) sentimentalism.
sentimentalista (*adj.*; *m.*,*f.*) sentimentalist.
sentimento (*m.*) sentiment, sensibility; sense, perception; grief; feeling; tender feeling; notion, judgment; (*pl.*) good instincts; condolences.—**de culpa**, guilty feeling.—**s nobres**, noble sentiments.
sentina (*f.*) bilge; latrine [= PRIVADA].
sentinela (*f.*) sentinel, sentry; (*Bot.*) a paspalum grass (*P. parviflorum*). **de**—, on sentry (guard) duty; on the lookout. **fazer quarto de**—, to stand watch. **render**—, to relieve the watch.
sentir [21a] (*v.t.*) to sense, feel, perceive, be aware of; to understand, appreciate, know; to experience; to feel sorry for, regret; to hear; to smell; to resent; (*v.r.*) to feel hurt, offended.—**se à vontade**, to feel at home, at ease. —**se bem (mal)**, to feel well (bad).—**se magoado**, to feel hurt.—**alívio**, to feel better.—**amor, ódio, etc., por alguém**, to have a feeling of love, hate, etc., toward someone.—**falta de**, to feel the lack or absence of; to miss (someone).—**frio, fome, etc.**, to feel cold, hungry, etc.—**saudades de**, to miss, long for (someone). **O que os olhos não vêem, o coração não sente**, What you don't know won't hurt you.
senzala (*f.*) plantation slave quarters.
S.E.O. = SALVO ÊRRO OU OMISSÃO (save error or omission).
sépala (*m.*, *Bot.*) sepal.
sepalóide (*adj.*, *Bot.*) sepaloid.
separação (*f.*) separation (all senses).—**de bens**, separation of property as between husband and wife.—**de pessoas e bens**, legal separation of spouses and their property.
separado –**da** (*adj.*) separate; separated. **em**—, separately.
separador –**dora** (*adj.*) separating; (*m.*,*f.*) separator; (*m.*) milk separator.
separar (*v.t.*) to separate (all senses).—**se de**, to separate oneself from, withdraw from; to part from.
separata (*f.*) reprint (of articles).
separatismo (*m.*) separatism.
separatista (*adj.*; *m.*,*f.*) separatist.
separativo –**va** (*adj.*) separative.
separatório –**ria** (*adj.*; *m.*) separatory (funnel).
separável (*adj.*) separable; detachable.
sépia (*f.*) sepia.
sepícola (*adj.*, *Bot.*) sepicolous.
sépio (*m.*) cuttlebone.
sepíola (*f.*) a genus (*Sepiola*) of small cuttlefishes.
sepiostário (*m.*) sepiostaire, cuttlebone.
sepsia (*f.*, *Med.*) sepsis.
sepsina (*f.*, *Biochem.*) sepsine.
septicemia (*f.*, *Med.*) septicemia, blood poisoning.
septicêmico –**ca** (*adj.*) septicemic.
septicida (*adj.*, *Bot.*) septicidal.
séptico –**ca** (*adj.*) septic.
septicolor (*adj.*) septicolored.
septifoliado –**da** (*adj.*, *Bot.*) septifolius.
séptil (*adj.*, *Bot.*) septile.
septífrago –**ga** (*adj.*, *Bot.*) septifragal.
septo (*m.*, *Biol.*, *Bot.*, *Anat.*, *Zool.*, *Physics*) septum; (*Mach.*) baffle plate.
sepulcral (*adj.*) sepulchral, funereal.
sepulcro (*m.*) sepulchre, tomb, grave.— **s caiados**, whited sepulchres, hypocrites.
sepultar (*v.t.*) to bury, inter; to cover up, hide, conceal. —**se em vida**, to bury oneself; withdraw from the world.
sepulto –**ta** (*adj.*, *irreg. p.p. of* SEPULTAR) buried.
sepultura (*f.*) sepulture, grave, tomb; act of burying.
sepultureiro (*m.*) grave-digger [= COVEIRO].
sequacidade (*f.*) sequacity, sequaciousness.
sequaz (*adj.*) sequacious; sectarian, partisan; (*m.*) follower; hanger-on, henchman.
sequeiro –**ra** (*adj.*) of land, dry, parched; (*m.*) dry land; place where anything is put out to dry; (*f.*) = SECA (annoyance).
seqüela (*f.*) act of following; sequel; sequela; consequence; band, gang.
seqüência (*f.*) sequence, succession, series; in cards, a sequence of one suit.—**máxima**, ace-high straight.
seqüente (*adj.*) = SEGUINTE.
sequer (*adv.*) so much as, even. **nem**—, not even, without even, without so much as.

seqüestração (*f.*) sequestration; kidnaping.
seqüestrador –**dora** (*adj.*) sequestering; (*m.*,*f.*) one who sequesters; abductor, kidnaper.
seqüestrar (*v.t.*) to sequester, seize; to abduct; to seclude.
seqüestro (*m.*) sequestration; seizure; (*Surg.*) sequestrum; (*Law*) sequestration.
sequidão (*f.*) = SECURA.
sequilho (*m.*) rusk, dry biscuit; dried fruit.
sequioso –**sa** (*adj.*) thirsty; eager, greedy, avid.
sequista (*adj.*; *m.*,*f.*, *colloq.*) boring, tiresome (person).
séquito, séquito (*m.*) entourage, retinue; escort; following.
sequóia (*f.*) the genus (*Sequoia*) consisting of the big trees and redwoods of California.
ser [76] (*v.i.*) to be [Unlike ESTAR (to be) which expresses a temporary state or condition, **ser** usually denotes permanency, or an inherent or characteristic quality of persons and things. It serves also as an auxiliary verb when combined with the past participle of the main verb.]; (*m.*) a being [pl. SERES].—**alguém**, to be somebody (important).—**breve**, to be brief.—**capaz de**, to be able to; to be capable of; to be apt to.—**contra**, to be against, opposed to.—**da gema**, to be genuine.—**de opinião**, or **parecer, de que**, to be of the opinion that.—**de sobra**, to be in excess.—**do contra**, (*slang*) to be contrary; to be grouchy, fussy, demanding.—**doente**, to be a sick(ly) person; to be sickness-prone; to be an invalid. [Cf. ESTAR DOENTE, to be (temporarily) sick.]—**mau de contentar**, to be hard to please.—**mister**, to be needed, necessary— applied to actions, not people. [**É mister agir corajosamente**, Courageous action must be taken.]—**nada**, to be nothing.—**o mesmo**, to be the same.—**pau para tôda obra**, to lend oneself to anything.—**rei de si mesmo**, or —**senhor das suas ações**, or—**senhor de si**, to be master of oneself.—**sem querer**, inadvertently; accidentally.— **útil**, to be useful, come in handy.—**um ótimo cartaz**, to be a drawing card. **A música é assim**, The tune goes like this. **a não**—**que**, unless; except that. **ainda que fosse**, even if it were so. **Antes fosse!** Would that it had been! I wish it (I, he, she, you) were. **Assim seja, Amen**; I hope so. **Como foi que . . . ?** How comes it that . . . ? How did it happen that . . . ? **É**, Yes, that's right. **É boa!** That's a good one [of a joke, remark, etc.]; or, She's quite a dish! **É isso mesmo!** That's just it! **É minha vez**, It's my turn. **É que**, It's just that (. . .). [**É que não tenho dinheiro**, The fact is I'm broke]. **É sempre assim**, It never fails; It always happens that way. **É você?** Is that you? **era uma vez**, once upon a time there was. **fôsse como fôsse**, anyway, besides, be that as it may; in any (either) case. **fôsse de quem fôsse**, whose ever. **fôsse qual fôsse**; whichever; whoever, **fôsse por que fôsse**, somehow or other; It doesn't matter why. **isto é**, that is. **Não é?** Isn't it so? Aren't you (they, we)? Isn't he (she)? [Corresponds to French *N'est-ce pas?*] **não**—**por querer**, not purposely. **não fôra êle**, had it not been for him, if he hadn't (done something). **não fôsse**, were it not for. **onde quer que seja**, wherever it may be. **Oxalá fôsse!** Would that it were so! I wish (I, he, she, it) were! **pode**—**que**, maybe; it may be that. **por quem quer que fôsse**, by anyone whosoever. **quando por mais não fôsse**, if for no other reason. **Quem será?** I wonder who he (she, it) is? Who can he (she, it) be? **Se fôsse eu, eu não faria isso**, If it were I, I would not do that. **Se eu fôsse você, eu não faria isso**, If I were you, I would not do that. **se não fôsse que**, were it not that. **se não fôsse por você**, but for you. **seja (isso) como fôr**, be that as it may; in any case; at any rate. **sendo assim**, that being so, that being the case; in that case. **sendo que**, seeing that; and furthermore. **Será que (. . .)?** I wonder if (. . .)? Can it be that (. . .)? **Somos quatro**, There are four of us. **tal como deve**—, as it should be.
seráfico –**ca** (*adj.*) seraphic, angelic.
serafim (*m.*) seraph.
serão (*m.*) night work; overtime work; an evening party at home.
serápia (*f.*) a genus (*Epipactis*, *syn. Serapias*) of hardy terrestrial orchids.
serapilheira (*f.*) burlap.
sereia (*f.*) siren (lit. & fig.); mermaid; (*colloq.*) bathing beauty; an eellike salamander (family *Sirenidae*); siren of fire and police vehicles. Cf. SIRENA.
sereíba (*f.*) the false mangrove (*Laguncularia racemosa*).
sereibatinga [e-i] (*f.*) the black mangrove (*Avicennia marina*).

serelepe (adj.) lively, frisky, airy; (m.) a lively person; kind of chipmunk or ground squirrel.

serenada (f.) damp night air; mist, drizzle; serenade.

serenagem (f.) act of quieting or tranquillizing.

serenar (v.t.) to render serene, calm, peaceful; (v.i.) to mist, drizzle; to dance quietly, smoothly; (v.r.) to grow calm, quiet.—os ânimos, to quiet (lull, tone down) animosities; pour oil on troubled waters.

serenata (f.) serenade.

serenatista (m.,f.) serenader [=SERESTEIRO].

serenidade (f.) serenity, tranquillity.

sereníssimo -ma (absol. superl. of SERENO) most serene; [cap.] (m.) Serenissimo: "a title of honor given to certain persons of royal rank or to sovereign states." [Webster]

sereno -na (adj.) serene, calm, tranquil; sedate; clear, bright, unclouded; (m.) damp night air, mist; open-air, out-of-doors; (colloq.) group of persons who gather at night to observe from the outside the festivities taking place inside a house.

seresma [rês] (f.) hag; (m.) fool; scarecrow.

seresta (f.) serenade [=SERENATA].

seresteiro (m.) serenader [=SERENATISTA].

sergipano -na, sergipense (adj.) of or pert. to Sergipe; (m.,f.) a native or inhabitant of that State.

seriação (f.) seriation.

seriado -da (adj.) seriate.

seriadamente (adv.) seriatim, serially.

serial (adj.) serial; seriate. [A serial story is FOLHETIM; a serial moving picture is FILME EM SÉRIE or UM SERIADO.]

seriamente (adj.) seriously; earnestly; sternly.

seriar (v.t.) to arrange in series.

seriário -ria (adj.) seriary.

seribolo [bô] (m.) brawl; disorder, confusion.

seríceo -cea (adj.) sericeous, silky. [Poetical]

sericícola (adj.) sericultural; (m.,f.) sericulturist; breeder of silk worms.

sericicultor -tora (adj.) sericultural; (m.,f.) sericulturist.

sericicultura (f.) sericiculture.

sericífero -ra (adj.) silk-producing [glands of silk worms.]

sericígeno -na (adj.) silk-producing [worms].

sericina (f., Biochem.) sericin, silk gelatin, silk glue.

sericita, -te (f.), -to (m., Min.) sericite.

sericitaesquisto, sericitaxisto (m., Min.) sericite schist.

sérico -ca (adj.) silken; of or pert. to serum.

sericocarpo (m.) the genus (Sericocarpus) of white-topped asters.

sericóia, sericora (f.) = SARACURA.

sericultor (m.) = SERICICULTOR.

sericultura (f.) = SERICICULTURA.

seridó (m.) a certain cotton-growing zone in Paraíba and Rio Grande do Norte; the long-staple cotton grown there.

série (f.) series; row, string; (Biol., Chem., Math.) series. —descontínua, (Stat.) broken series. produção em—, mass production.

seriedade (f.) seriousness; gravity, solemnity; integrity.

seriema (f., Zool.) the crested seriema of southern Brazil (Cariama cristata).

serigado (m., Zool.) any of various groupers, esp. of genus Epinephelus.—-cherne, or—-tapoan, = CHERNE-PINTADO.—-prêto = BADEJO-FERRO.—-sabão = BADEJO-SABÃO.

serigola (f.) iron ring in a bull's nose; throatlatch of a bridle.

serigote (m.) a type of Brazilian saddle with high bow and cantle.

serigrafia (f.) silk-screen process.

serigueiro (m.) silkman. Var. SIRGUEIRO.

seriguilha (f.) a kind of rough woolen cloth.

serímetro (m.) serimeter.

seringa (f.) rubber syringe; rubber latex.—hipodérmica, hypodermic syringe.

seringação, seringadela (f.) act of syringing or squirting.

seringada (f.) a squirt.

seringador -dora (adj.; m.,f., slang) boring, annoying (person); (m.,f.) one who uses a syringe; (m.) land bordering a lake or river.

seringal (m.) a stand of rubber trees or a forest region where they are found; a riverside plantation.

seringar (v.t.) to syringe; to squirt; (slang) to bore, annoy.

seringarana (f., Bot.) Brazil sapium (S. biglandulosum), c.a. MURUPITA.

seringatório (m.) a "shot" of medicine.

seringueira (f., Bot.) Pará rubber tree (Hevea brasiliensis); common names of other species are:—-barriguda, (H.

spruceana).—-branca, (H. randiana).—-chicote, (H. benthamiana).—-itaúba, (H. lutea).—-tambaqui, (H. mycrophylla).—-vermelha, (H. guaianensis).

seringueiro (m.) rubber-gatherer; rubber-tapper; exploiter of a rubber plantation.

sério -ria (adj.) serious, solemn; earnest, grave, sober; important, momentous; upright, conscientious; (adv.) really, truly. falando a—, all joking aside. levar or tomar (alguém ou alguma coisa) a—, to take (someone or something) seriously.

seriola (f.) the genus (Seriola) of amber-fishes.

serisse (f.) the Malabar simaltree (Salmalia malabarica).

seritipia (f.) silk screen printing process.

serjânia (f., Bot.) supplejack (Serjania).

sermão (m.) sermon; reprimand, lecture; annoying harangue.

sermoa (f., colloq.) a poor sermon.

sermonar (v.) = PREGAR.

sermonear (v.i.) to preach.

sernambi [í] (m.) any of various marine bivalves, esp. Lucina, syn. Phacoides, pectinatus, Anomalocardia brasiliana (c.a. SERNAMBITINGA), and Mesodesma mactroides (c.a. MOÇAMBIQUE and MAÇAMBIQUE).

sernambiguara (f.) the round pompano (Trachinotus falcatus), c.a. GARABEBEL, PAMPO, PAMPO-ARABEBÉU, PAMPO-GIGANTE, TAMBÓ.

seroada (f.) a long period of overtime night work.

seroar (v.i.) to work at night.

serôdio -dia (adj.) late (tardy in appearing).

serolina (f., Biochem.) serolin.

serolipose (f., Biochem.) serolipase.

serologia (f.) serology.

serológico -ca (adj.) serologic(al).

seromuscular (adj.) seromuscular.

serosa (f., Embryol., Anat.) serosa.

serosidade (f.) serosity; (Physiol.) serosity.

seroso -sa (adj., Physiol.) serous.

seroterpêutica (f., Med.) serotherapeutics.

seroterapia (f., Med.) serum therapy [=SOROTERAPIA].

serotino -na (adj.) late, slow.

serpão (m., Bot.) mother-of-thyme (Thymus serpyllum), c.a. SERPIL, SERPILHO, SERPOL; other plants of this genus.

serpeante (adj.) winding, meandering; twining, coiling.

serpear (v.i.) to crawl (as a snake); to wind, turn, twist, meander; to wriggle, wiggle, squirm.

serpejante (adj.) = SERPEANTE.

serpejar (v.) = SERPEAR.

serpentante (adj.) = SERPEANTE.

serpentão (m.) serpent (an old wooden musical wind instrument of serpentine form).

serpentar (v.) = SERPEAR.

serpentária (f.) any of various plants used against snakebite, such as the common stinkdragon (Dracunculus vulgaris), c.a. DRAGONTÉIA; the Texas snakeroot (Aristolochia reticulata), or the Virginia snakeroot (A. serpentaria), both c.a. SERPENTINA.

serpentário (m.) the secretary bird (Sagittarius serpentarius); a serpentarium.

serpente (f.) serpent, snake; a coil; a hag.—-de faraó; (Chem.) Pharaoh's serpent (mercury thiocyanate).

serpenteante (adj.) serpentine, winding, twisting [= SERPEANTE].

serpentear (v.i.) to serpentine, wind, twist; to meander [= SERPEAR].

serpenticida (adj.) serpenticidal.

serpentífero -ra (adj.) serpentiferous.

serpentiforme (adj.) serpentiform.

serpentinita (f., Min.) serpentine.—fibrosa, chrysotile.—lamelosa, antigorite.

serpentino -na (adj.) serpentine; (f.) worm or coil of a still; serpentin (rolled paper streamer); girandole (firework; candle holder); (Min.) serpentine; (Bot.) the viviparous bistort (Polygonum viviparum); also = SERPENTÁRIA.—-de aquecimento, heating coil.—-de esfriamento, cooling coil.

serpiginoso -sa (adj., Med.) serpiginous.

serpil, serpilho, serpol (m.) = SERPÃO.

sérpula (f., Zool.) a genus (Serpula) of marine annelids.

serra (f.) saw; mountain range; (Zool.) the common bonito (Sarda sarda), c.a. SERRA-DE-ESCAMA.—-abaixo, southern part of the state of Rio de Janeiro; the coastal area in southern Brazil lying east of Serra do Mar.—-acima, northern part of the state of Rio de Janeiro.—-braçal, two-handed saw.—-circular, circular saw; buzz saw.—-de escama, a mackerel (*Scomber scomber*).—**de fita**, band saw.—**garoupa** = CORTA-GAROUPA (a shark).—**de mão**, handsaw.—**-pinima** = SOROROCA (Spanish mackerel).—**tico-tico**, jig saw; scroll saw.

serrabulho (*m.*) = SARRABULHO.

serração (*f.*) act or operation of sawing.

serradela (*f.*, *Bot.*) the common serradella (*Ornithopus sativus*); also = SERRAÇÃO.

serrado -da (*adj.*) serrate.

serrador -dora (*adj.*) sawing; (*m.*) sawyer.

serradura (*f.*) sawdust; also = SERRAÇÃO.

serragem (*f.*) = SERRAÇÃO; SERRADURA.

serralha (*f.*, *Bot.*) the common sowthistle (*Sonchus oleraceus*).—**-preta**, prickly sowthistle (*S. asper*).

serralhar (*v.i.*) to work as a locksmith or metalworker; to clatter; (*v.t.*) to file, grind, work, smooth (metal).

serralharia (*f.*) metalworker's or locksmith's shop.

serralheiro (*m.*) locksmith; metalworker.—**de chapa**, sheetmetal worker.

serralho (*m.*) seraglio, harem; fig., brothel.

serrana (*f.*) mountain woman; country woman; country dance.

serrania (*f.*) cordillera, chain of mountains.

serrânidas, serraníideos (*m.pl.*) a family (*Serranidae*) of marine, carnivorous, perchlike fishes.

serrano -na (*adj.*) mountain; (*m.*) mountaineer; country man; peasant.

serra-osso (*m.*, *colloq.*) shindig, hoedown.

serra-pau (*m.*) any of various wood-boring beetles.

serra-perna (*f.*) = ARROZ-BRAVO.

serrar (*v.t.*,*v.i.*) to saw; (*v.t.*) to shuffle (a deck of cards).—**de cima**, (*colloq.*) to be on top, have the upper hand, call the tune.

serraria (*f.*) sawmill; sawhorse.

serrasalmo (*m.*) a genus (*Serrasalmo*) of voracious freshwater fishes which includes the PIRANHAS (caribes).

serra-serra (*f.*) the blue-black grassquit (*Volatinia jacarina*), c.a. TIZIU, ALFAIATE, VELUDINHO, JACARINA.

serrátil [-teis] (*adj.*) serriforme.

serrazina (*adj.*; *m.,f.*) (act of) nagging, pestering, annoying; (*m.,f.*) nagger.

serrazinar (*v.t.*) to nag, pester, annoy.

serreado -da (*adj.*) serrate.

serrear (*v.t.*) to serreate.

serricórneos (*m.pl.*) a division of beetles (*Serricornia*) having serrate antennas.

serridênteo -tea (*adj.*) serrate-dentate.

serriforme (*adj.*) serriform.

serrilha (*f.*) serration, serrated edge; milled edge of a coin.

serrilhado -da (*adj.*) serrated; knurled.

serrilhador (*m.*) knurling machine.

serrilhar (*v.t.*) to knurl.

serrípede (*adj.*, *Zool.*) serriped.

serrirrostro -tra (*adj.*, *Zool.*) serratirostral.

serrotar (*v.t.*) to cut with a handsaw.

serrote [*dim. of* SERRA] (*m.*) handsaw; small mountain range.

sertã (*f.*) griddle; frying pan [= SARTÃ].

sertanejar (*v.i.*) to live in the SERTÃO.

sertanejo -ja [nê] (*adj.*) of or pert. to the SERTÃO; rude; rustic; (*m.,f.*) one who lives in the SERTÃO; frontiersman; inlander; (*colloq.*) hillbilly.

sertania (*f.*) the hinterland of Brazil.

sertanista (*m.,f.*) a person with extensive first-hand knowledge of the Brazilian SERTÃO.

sertão (*m.*) hinterland, back country, wilderness, remote interior (of Brazil).

sertulária (*f.*, *Zool.*) a genus (*Sertularia*) of hydrozoans.

serubuna (*f.*) = SERUTINGA.

sérum (*m.*) = SÔRO.

serunterapia (*f.*) = SEROTERAPIA.

serutinga (*f.*, *Bot.*) black mangrove (*Avicennia marina*), c.a. SERUBUNA, SEREIBATINGA.

serva (*f.*) see under SERVO.

servente (*adj.*) serving; (*f.*) servant; (*m.*) servitor; helper; waiter; cleaner; janitor; office boy.—**de pedreiro**, hod carrier.

serventia (*f.*) usefulness; use, utility; utilization; servitude; help; passageway.

serventuário (*m.*) one who serves.

serviçal (*adj.*) useful, helpful; accommodating, obliging; (*m.*) servitor; worker for wages.

serviço (*m.*) service; help; work.—**ativo**, (*Mil.*) active duty.—**doméstico**, house work.—**externo**, outside work.—**militar**, military service.—**obrigatório**, compulsory military service.—**s públicos**, public utilities.—**salariado**, work for wages. **a—de**, in the service of. **ao—de**, at the service of. **de—**, on duty.

servidão (*f.*) servitude, slavery, bondage; right of way; right of passage.

servido -da (*adj.*) served; worn, used.

servidor -dora (*adj.*) serving; (*m.,f.*) servitor, servant.

servil (*adj.*) servile, slavish, cringing.

servilismo (*m.*) servility.

servimento (*m.*) serving; service.

sérvio -via (*adj.*; *m.,f.*) Serbian.

serviola (*f.*, *Naut.*) cathead, anchor beam.

servir [21a] (*v.i.*) to serve; to perform duty, obey; to be of use; to fit; to suit, be suitable; to attend, wait on; to help, minister to; to supply with (food, drink); (*v.r.*) to help oneself (de, to); to employ, use, make use (de, of).—**à mesa**, to wait on table.—**à pátria**, to serve one's country.—**de**, to serve as, do duty for.—**na marinha**, to serve in the navy. **De que serve isto?** What is this good for? **Esta casa nos serve muito bem**, This house suits us very well. **Estes sapatos não me servem, são muito grandes**, These shoes don't fit me, they are too large. **Isso não serve**, It won't do. **Não serve para nada**, It's of no use for anything. **Qualquer coisa servirá**, Anything will do. **Sirva-se de café**, Help yourself to coffee.

servível (*adj.*) serviceable, useful.

servo -va (*adj.*) in bondage; (*m.,f.*) serf; hireling; servant.

servomotor (*m.*, *Mach.*) servomotor.

serzir (*v.t.*) to darn; to fine-draw (torn fabric).

sésamo (*m.*, *Bot.*) sesame (*Sesamum*), c.a. GERGELIM.

sesamoídeo -dea (*adj.*; *m.*, *Anat.*) sesamoid (bone or cartilage).

sesbânia (*f.*) a genus (*Sebania*) of the pea family.

sesgo -ga [ê] (*adj.*) biased, oblique, on a slant.

sésia (*f.*) a genus (*Sesia*) of clearwing moths.

sesmaria (*f.*) barren, uncultivated land; a land grant in colonial Brazil.—**do campo**, an old land measure.

SESP = SERVIÇO ESPECIAL DE SAÚDE PÚBLICA (Special Public Health Service).

sesquiáltero -ra (*adj.*, *Math.*) sesquialteral, having the ratio of 1½ to 1.

sesquióxido (*m.*, *Chem.*) sesquioxide.—**de alumínio**, aluminum oxide.—**de antimônio**, antimony oxide.—**de chumbo**, lead sesquioxide.

sesquipedal (*adj.*) sesquipedalian.

sesquiquadrado (*m.*, *Astron.*) sesquiquadrate.

sesquissulfeto (*m.*, *Chem.*) sesquisulfide.

sesquiterpeno (*m.*, *Chem.*) sesquiterpene.

sessão (*f.*) session, sitting; meeting; term; seance; each of two or more daily showings of a play, picture, etc. **encerrar**, or **levantar**, **a—**, to close or adjourn the meeting. **suspender a—**, to recess the meeting.

sessenta (*adj.*) sixty.

sessenta-e-dois (*m.*) = GALINHA-CHOCA.

sessenta-feridas (*f.*) = ESPINHO-DE-JUDEU.

sessentão -tona (*adj.*) sixtyish; (*m.,f.*) sexagenarian.

séssil [sésseis] (*adj.*, *Bot.*, *Zool.*) sessile.

sessilifloro -ra (*adj.*) sessile-flowered.

sessilifoliado -da (*adj.*) sessile-leaved.

sesta (*f.*) siesta; midday or afternoon rest or nap [= CODORNO, TORA]; the heat of the day.

sesteada (*f.*) act of taking a siesta; place where herdsmen and wayfarers stop at noontime for food and a siesta.

sestear (*v.i.*) to snooze, nap.

sestro -tra (*adj.*) left; sinister; (*m.*) addiction; bad habit; mania; fate. **à sestra**, on the left (side, hand).

sesúvio (*m.*, *Bot.*) a genus (*Sesuvium*) of succulents.

set. = SETEMBRO (September).

seta (*f.*) arrow, dart; hand, pointer (of a clock); (*Bot.*) Old World arrowhead (*Sagittaria sagittifolia*), c.a. FLECHA.

setáceo -cea (*adj.*) setaceous, bristlelike.

setada (*f.*) an arrow wound or thrust.

setária (*f.*) the genus (*Setaria*) of millets and bristle-grasses. [The Brazil bristlegrass is *Setaria rariflora*.]

sete (*adj.*) seven; seventh; (*m.*) seven; the seven-spot (card); the seventh in a series; [*cap.*] Seth.—**de Setembro**, Brazilian national holiday in commemoration of Dom Pedro I's declaration of independence from Portugal on Sept. 7, 1822. **as—maravilhas do mundo**, seven wonders of the world.—**pecados mortais**, seven deadly sins. **pintar o—**, to raise hell (the devil, Ned, Cain, the mischief, etc.).

setear (*v.t.*) to wound with an arrow.

setecentos –tas (*adj.*) seven hundred.
sete-côres (*m.*) any of various brilliantly colored tanagers of genus *Calospiza*, esp. the rainbow tanager (*C. tricolor*), c.a. SAÍ or SAÍRA.
sete-e-meio (*m.*) a card game like blackjack.
sete-em-rama (*m.*, *Bot.*) tormentilla cinquefoil (*Potentilla erecta*)
sete-estrêlo (*m.*) popular name for the Pleiades.
seteira (*f.*) embrasure; loophole.
seteiro (*m.*) archer, bowman.
setembrino –na (*adj.*) Septembrian.
setembro (*m.*) September.
setemesinho –nha (*adj.*, *colloq.*) of infants, born the seventh month.
setenado –da (*adj.*, *Bot.*) septenate; (*m.*) septennate.
setenal (*adj.*) septennial.
setenário –ria (*adj.*) septenary, septennial; (*m.*) septenary.
setenial (*adj.*) septennial.
setênio (*m.*) septennium.
setenta (*adj.*) seventy.
setentrião (*m.*) the far north; north pole; north wind.
setentrional (*adj.*) septentrional, northerly, northern; (*m.*,*f.*) a person from the far north.
sete-sangrias (*f.*) a sweetleaf (*Symplocos parviflora*), c.a. PAU-DE-CANGALHA.
sete-virtudes (*m.*, *colloq.*) rum [= CACHAÇA].
setia (*f.*) water trough, chute, flume.
setífero –ra (*adj.*) setiferous.
setígero –ra (*adj.*) setigerous.
setim (*m.*) satin. [A variant and disputed spelling is CETIM.]
sétimo –ma (*adj.; m.*) seventh; (*f.*, *Music*) seventh.
setíneo –nea (*adj.*) satiny.
setingentésimo –ma (*adj.; m.*) seven-hundredth.
setinoso –sa (*adj.*) silken, like satin.
set.º = SETEMBRO (September).
setor (*m.*) sector (all senses).
setuagenário –ria (*adj.; m.,f.*) septuagenarian.
setuagésimo –ma [zi] (*adj.; m.*) seventieth; (*f.*) septuagesima Sunday (the third before Lent).
seu [*fem.* sua] (*masc. poss. pron. & adj.*) his (own), its (own), your (own), yours, their (own), theirs; (*m.*) that which is yours. **ter de—**, to be well-fixed. **os—s**, your (his, her) family or people; (*abbrev.*) a colloquial form of SENHOR: **"seu" Pedro**; also, a form of you, when used in denunciation: **"seu" cachorro!** (you dog!).
seu-vizinho (*m.*, *colloq.*) the ring finger.
sevadilha (*f.*) = ESPIRRADEIRA.
sevandija (*f.*) vermin, parasites; (*m.*) sponger, parasite, hanger-on; a lickspittle.
sevandijar-se (*v.t.*) to cringe, fawn, crawl, grovel.
sevandijaria (*f.*) servility, obsequiousness.
severidade (*f.*) severity, austerity; harshness; strictness, rigorousness.
severo –ra (*adj.*) severe (**com**, with; **para com**, toward); austere, rigorous; grim; exact, strict; stringent; hard, harsh; simple, restrained [taste, style].
sevícia (*f.*) maltreatment, abuse, cruelty; corporal punishment. [Usually plural.]
seviciamento (*m.*) brutal treatment (as of prisoners).
seviciar (*v.t.*) to treat cruelly (in physical sense only).
Sevilha (*f.*) Seville.
sevilhano –na (*adj.; m.,f.*) Sevillian.
sevo –va (*adj.*) cruel, brutal.
S. Ex.ª = SUA EXCELÊNCIA (His [Her] Excellency).
S. Ex.ª Rev.ma = SUA EXCELÊNCIA REVERENDÍSSIMA (His Most Reverend Excellency).
sexagenário –ria [ks] (*adj.; m.,f.*) sexagenarian.
sexagesimal [ks] (*adj.*) sexagesimal.
sexagésimo –ma [ks] (*adj.; m.,f.*) sixtieth; [*cap.*] (*f.*) Sexagesima (the second Sunday before Lent).
sexangulado –da, sexangular, sexângulo –la [ks] (*adj.*) sexangular, hexagonal.
sexcentésimo –ma [ks] (*adj.; m.*) six hundredth.
sexdigital [ks] (*adj.*) having six toes or fingers.
sexenal [ks] (*adj.*) sexennial.
sexênio [ks] (*m.*) sexennian.
sexlocular [ks] (*adj.*, *Bot.*) sexlocular.
sexo [ks] (*m.*) sex; privates. **o belo—**, the fair sex. **o—devoto**, nuns collectively. **o—forte**, the stronger sex. **o—fraco**, the weaker sex.
sexta [ex = ês] short for SEXTA-FEIRA (Friday); (*f.*, *Music*) sixth; (*Eccl.*) sext.

sextafeira [ex = ês] (*f.*) Friday; (*colloq.*) a kept woman. [*cap.*]—**Santa, or—da Paixão**, Good Friday.
sextanista [x = s] (*m.,f.*) a sixth-year student.
sextante [x = s] (*m.*) sextant (all senses).
sextavado –da [x = s] (*adj.*) six-sided, hexagonal.
sexteto [x = s] [tê] (*m.*) sextet.
sextil [x = s] (*adj.; m.*, *Astrol.*) sextile.
sextilão = SEXTILIÃO.
sextilha [x = s] (*f.*) sextain, six-line stanza.
sextina [x = s] (*f.*, *Poetry*) sestina.
sexto –ta [ex = ês] (*adj.; m.,f.*) sixth
sextogênito –ta [x = s] (*adj.; m.,f.*) sixth-born (child).
sêxtuor [x = s] (*m.*, *Music*) sextet.
sêxtuplo –pla [x = s] (*adj.; m.*) sextuple.
sexual [ks] (*adj.*) sexual.
sexualidade [ks] (*f.*) sexuality.
sexualismo [ks] (*m.*) sexualism.
sezão [-zões] (*m.*) intermittent fever; ague; malaria.
sezonático –ca (*adj.*) malarial.
s/f = SEU FAVOR (your favor [letter]).
sfalerita (*f.*, *Min.*) sphalerite, blende, zincblende.
s.f.f. = SE FAZ FAVOR (if you please).
S.G. = SUA GRAÇA (His [Her] Grace); SUA GRANDEZA (His [Her] Highness).
S.H. = SUA HONRA (His [Her] Honor).
si (*pers. pron.*) himself, herself, itself, oneself, yourself, yourselves, themselves. Cf. SE. **dar por—**, to regain one's senses. **dar sinal de—**, to show signs of life. **de—para—**, to oneself. **para—**, to himself. **por—mesmo**, by himself, herself, etc. **por—próprio**, of his (her, etc.) own accord. **satisfeito com—próprio**, self-satisfied.
siá, short for SINHÁ.
siagro (*m.*) a genus (*Syagrus*) of palms.
sialagogo –ga (*adj.*, *Med.*) sialagogic; (*m.*) sialagogue, ptyalagogue.
sialismo (*m.*) ptyalism, salivation.
sialoína (*f.*, *Biochem.*) ptyalin.
sialologia (*f.*, *Anat.*) sialology.
siamês –sa (*adj.; m.,f.*) Siamese.
Sião (*m.*) Zion; Siam.
siba (*f.*) cuttlefish (*Sepia*).
sibarita (*adj.*) sybaritic; (*m.,f.*) sybarite.
sibarítico –ca (*adj.*) sybaritic, voluptuous.
siberiano –na (*adj.; m.,f.*) Siberian.
siberite (*f.*), –**to** (*m.*, *Min.*) siberite.
sibila (*f.*) sibyl; (*colloq.*) witch.
sibilação (*f.*) sibilation, hissing; whistling; (*Med.*) a sibilant râle.
sibilador –dora (*adj.*) hissing; whistling; (*m.,f.*) sibilator; whistler.
sibilamento (*m.*) = SIBILAÇÃO.
sibilância (*f.*) sibilance.
sibilante (*adj.*) sibilant; whistling.
sibilar (*v.i.*) to whistle; to hiss.
sibilino –na (*adj.*) sibylline; mysterious; enigmatic.
sibilismo (*m.*) sybillism.
sibilo (*m.*) a hiss; a whistle.
sicário –ria (*adj.*) murderous; (*m.*) hired assassin, hatchetman.
sicativo –va (*adj.; m.*) siccative.
siciliano –na (*adj.; m.,f.*) Sicilian.
sicofanta (*m.,f.*) traducer, calumniator. [Not sycophant, which is BAJULADOR.]
sicômoro (*m.*) sycamore.—**-bastardo**, the China tree (*Melia azedarach*), c.a. AMARGOSEIRA, CINAMOMO.—**-figueira**, the sycamore fig (*Ficus sycomorus*).
sicônidas, siconídeos (*m.pl.*) a family (*Syconidae*) of calcareous sponges.
sicônio, sícono (*m.*, *Bot.*) syconium.
sicose (*f.*, *Med.*) sycosis.
sicrano (*m.*) Richard Roe. [John Doe is FULANO.]
siçuíra (*f.*) = ENXUÍ.
sícula (*f.*, *Paleontol.*) sicula.
sicupira (*f.*) a locust tree (*Robinia coccinea*); the Guiana ormosia (*O. coarctata*).—**-amarela** = SUCUPIRA-AMARELA.
sida (*f.*) the genus Sida of tropical herbs or shrubs.
sideral (*adj.*) sidereal.
siderar (*v.t.*) to benumb, paralyze, stupefy, stun.
siderita (*f.*, *Bot.*) the genus (*Sideritis*) of ironwound worts; (*m.*, *Min.*) siderite; (*Med.*) = SIDEROSE.
siderocromo (*m.*, *Min.*) chromite.
siderografia (*f.*) siderography.
sideromelana (*f.*, *Petrog.*) sideromelanc.
sideronatrite (*f.*, *Min.*) sideronatrite.

sideroscópio (*m.*) sideroscope.

siderose (*f., Med.*) siderosis.

sideróstato (*m., Astron.*) siderostat.

siderotecnia (*f.*) siderurgy.

siderurgia (*f.*) the metallurgy of iron and steel.

sido, past part. of SER [76].

sidra (*f.*) cider.

siegesbéquia (*f., Bot.*) the common St. Paul's wort (*Siegesbeckia orientalis*).

sienito (*m., Petrog.*) syenite.

sifão (*m.*) siphon.

sifiligrafia (*f.*) syphilography.

sifilígrafo (*m.*) a specialist in syphilis.

sifilis (*f., Med.*) syphilis. [Some common names for this disease are: AVARIOSE, GÁLICO, LUES, VENÉREO. For others, see under MAL.]

sifilítico –**ca** (*adj.; m.,f., Med.*) syphilitic.

sifilografia (*f.*) = SIFILIGRAFIA.

sifilóide (*f., Med.*) syphiloid skin eruption.

sifonagem (*f.*) siphonage.

sifonária (*f.*) a genus (*Siphonaria*) of limpet-like marine gastropods.

sifonianos (*m.pl., Zool.*) the division Siphonata.

sifonóforo (*m., Zool.*) a siphonophore.

sifonóide (*adj.*) like a siphon.

sifônulo (*m., Zool.*) siphuncle.

sigilar (*v.t.*) to sigillate; (*adj.*) sigillary.

sigilo (*m.*) secret; secrecy.

sigla (*f.*) sigla.

sigmóide (*adj.*) sigmoid.

sigmoídeo –**dea** (*adj., Anat.*) sigmoid.

signa (*f.*) ensign, flag, banner.

signatário –**ria** (*adj.; m.,f.*) signatory.

significação (*f.*) signification, meaning, sense, import.

significado (*m.*) meaning (of words).

significador –**dora** (*adj.*) signifying.

significante (*adj.*) significant.

significar (*v.t.*) to signify, denote, betoken, mean.

significativo –**va** (*adj.*) significant.

signo (*m.*) sign of the zodiac.—**-de-salomão**,—**-salmão**, —**-saimão**,—**-salomão**, Solomon's seal. **sob o—de**, under the spell of.

sílaba (*f.*) syllable.

silabação (*f.*) syllabication.

silabar (*v.i.*) to syllabize; to spell.

silabário (*m.*) first book in reading.

silábico –**ca** (*adj.*) syllabic.

sílabo (*m.*) syllabus [referring only to a list of errors condemned by the Pope. In the ordinary sense of compendium, the Port. equivalent is COMPÊNDIO or RESUMO.]

silagem (*f.*) ensilage; silage.

silena (*f., Bot.*) the genus (*Silene*) of catchflys, campions, wild pinks, etc.

silenciador –**dora** (*adj.*) silencing; (*m.,f.*) silencer; muffler.

silenciar (*v.i.*) to become or remain silent; (*v.t.*) to silence.

silêncio (*m.*) silence, stillness, quiet. **um—de pedra**, a stony silence.

silencioso –**sa** (*adj.*) silent, still, quiet, noiseless; mute, mum; (*m.*) muffler (of an automobile); a silent person; (*f.*) a silent sewing machine.

silente (*adj.*) silent. [Poetical form of SILENCIOSO.]

silepse (*f., Gram.*) syllepsis.

siléptico –**ca** (*adj.*) sylleptic(al).

siler (*m., Bot.*) a laserwort (*Laserpitium siler*).

silesiano –**na** (*adj.; m.,f.*) Silesian.

sílex [ks] (*m.*) flintstone.—**xiloide**, petrified wood.

silfa (*f.*) a genus (*Silpha*) of clavicorn beetles.—**sepultadora**, a burying beetle (*S. vespilla*).

sílfide (*f.*) sylph; slender, graceful young woman.

silfídeos (*m.pl.*) the family (*Silphidae*) which comprises the burying and carrion beetles.

silha (*f.*) row of beehives.

silhão (*m.*) sidesaddle.

silhar (*m.*) ashlar, squared block of stone.

silhueta [ê] (*f.*) silhouette.

sílica (*f., Chem.*) silica, silicon dioxide, silicic anhydride.

silicalcário –**ria** (*adj.*) silicicalcareous.

silicane (*m.*) silicane, silicon hydride.

silicatação (*f., Chem.*) silication.

silicatização (*f., Chem.*) silicatization, silicification.

silicatizar (*v.t.,v.i.*) to silicify.

silicato (*m., Chem.*) silicate.—**de etilo**, ethyl orthosilicate. —**de sódio**, sodium silicate.

sílice (*m.*) silex, flint [= SÍLEX].

silícico –**ca** (*adj., Chem.*) silicic.

silic[i]eto (*m., Chem.*) silicide.

silicífero –**ra** (*adj.*) siliciferous.

silicificação (*f., Chem.*) silicification.

silicificar (*v.t.*) to silicify.

silício (*m., Chem.*) silicon.—**-alumínio**, aluminum-silicon alloy.—**-alumínio-ferro**, silicon-aluminum-iron alloy.—**-manganês**, silicomanganese.

silicioso –**sa** (*adj.*) siliceous.

silicocalcáreo –**rea** (*adj.*) silicicalcareous.

silicoclorofórmio (*m., Chem.*) silicochloroform.

silicone (*m., Chem.*) silicone.

silicose (*f., Med.*) silicosis.

sílico-spiegel (*m., Min.*) silicon spiegel.

silicotúngstico –**ca** (*adj., Chem.*) silicotungstic.

silícula (*f., Bot.*) silicle.

siliculoso –**sa** (*adj., Bot.*) siliculose, siliculous.

silificação (*f.*) silicification.

silificar (*v.t.,v.i.*) to silicify.

silimanite (*f., Min.*) fibrolite.

silindra (*f.*) the sweet mockorange (*Philadelphus coronarius*).

síliqua (*f., Bot.*) silique, pod.

siliqüiforme (*adj., Bot.*) siliquiform.

siliquoso –**sa** (*adj., Bot.*) siliquose.

silo (*m.*) silo.

silogismo (*m.*) syllogism.

silogístico –**ca** (*adj.*) syllogistic.

silogizar (*v.t.,v.i.*) to syllogize.

silômetro (*m.*) sillometer.

silundo (*m.*) silundum, silicon carbide, carborundum.

siluriano –**na** (*adj.; m.*) Silurian.

silurídeos (*m.pl.*) a family (*Siluridae*) of European freshwater catfishes.

siluro (*m.*) the genus (*Silurus*) which includes the European sheatfish (*S. glanis*).—**elétrico**, the electric catfish (*Melepterurus electricus*).

silva (*f.*) blackberry vine, bramble.—**branca** = AMOREIRA-DO-BRASIL.—**das-amoras**, European blackberry (*Rubus fruticosus*).—**framboesa**, the red raspberry (*Rubus idaeus*).—**macha**, the dog rose (*Rosa canina*).

silvado (*m.*) bramble patch; bramble hedge.

silvanita, **-te** (*f.*), **-to** (*m., Min.*) sylvanite.

silvano –**na** (*adj.*) sylvan.

silvão (*m., Bot.*) dog rose (*Rosa canina*).

silvar (*v.i.*) to whistle; to hiss. Cf. SIBILAR.

silvato (*m., Chem.*) sylvate, abietate.

silvedo (*m.*) = SILVADO.

silveira (*f.*) bramble; brier patch; dish of roast chopped meat and scrambled eggs.

silvestre (*adj.*) sylvestral, sylvan; wild, uncultivated.

silvestreno (*m., Chem.*) sylvestrene.

Sílvia (*f.*) Sylvia; [*not cap.*] = ANEMONA-DOS-BOSQUES.

silvíadas (*m.pl., Zool.*) a family (*Sylvidae*) of O.W. or true warblers.

silvícola (*adj.*) silvicolous (*m.,f.*) aborigine; savage.

silvicultor (*m.*) silviculturist, forester.

silvicultura (*f.*) silviculture.

silvina (*f., Min.*) sylvite, potassium chloride [= SILVITA]; (*Bot.*) a polypody, c.a. ERVA-SILVINA.—**de-fôlhagrande** = FETO-MACHO-DE-MINAS.—**grande**, a polypody (*Polypodium lycopodioides*).

silvita (*f.*) = SILVINA.

silvo (*m.*) a whistle; shrill sound; a snake's hiss.

silvoso –**sa** (*adj.*) brambly, full of briers.

sim (*adv.; m.*) yes. **achar**, or **crer**, **que—**, to think so. **ano—**, **ano não**, every other year or so. **Claro que—**, Of course. **dar o—**, to give consent. **dizer que—**, to say yes. **Isso—**! That's the stuff! **nem—nem não**, neither yes nor no. **Pois—**! Not much! [ironically]; also, simply, All right.

simaba (*f.*) a genus (*Simaba*) of South American trees. [The fruit of one (*S. cedron*) is employed as an antidote to snake bite and as a remedy for hydrophobia.]

Simão (*m.*) Simon.

simaruba (*f.*) a genus (*Simarouba*) of the ailanthus family. —**amarga**, the Orinoco simarouba or mountain damson (*S. amara*), the bark of which is a bitter tonic; c.a. MARUPÁ, PARARIÚBA, PARAÍBA.—**copaia**, or—**falsa**, = CAROBA-DO-MATO.—**mirim** = CALUNGA.—**versicolor** = PÉ-DE-PERDIZ, PARAÍBA-DO-BRASIL.

simarubáceo –**cea** (*adj.*) simaroubaceous; (*f.pl., Bot.*) the ailanthus family (*Simaroubaceae*).

simbaibinha [a-i] = CIPÓ-DE-CABOCLO.

simbionte (*m., Biol.*) symbiont.

simbiose (*f., Biol.*) symbiosis.
simbiota (*m., Biol.*) symbiote, symbient.
simbiótico –ca (*adj., Biol.*) symbiotic.
simbólico –ca (*adj.*) symbolic(al); (*f.*) symbolics.
simbolismo (*m.*) symbolism.
simbolista (*adj.; m.,f.*) symbolist.
simbolização (*f.*) symbolization.
simbolizar (*v.t.,v.i.*) to symbolize; to typify.
símbolo (*m.*) symbol, emblem, token.
simbologia (*f.*) symbology.
simbológico –ca (*adj.*) symbological.
Simeão (*m.*) Simeon.
simetria (*f.*) symmetry, harmony, proportion, shapeliness.—**binária** (quaternária, senária, ternária); (*Cryst.*) binary (tetragonal, senary or hexagonal, ternary) symmetry.
simétrico –ca (*adj.*) symmetrical.
simetrizar (*v.t.*) to symmetrize.
simiesco –ca [ê], **simiano** –na (*adj.*) simian.
simiídeos [i-í] (*m.pl.*) family (*Simiidae*) of anthropoid apes.
similar (*adj.*) similar, like; homogeneous.
similaridade (*f.*) similarity, likeness.
símile (*m.*) simile, comparison; (*adj.*) similar.
similitude (*f.*) similitude, resemblance [= SEMELHANÇA].
símio –mia (*adj.*) simian; (*m.,f.*) monkey.
simira (*f.*) a wild coffee of Brazil (*Psychotria simira*).
simongoiá (*m.*) = CERNAMBI.
simonia (*f.*) simony.
simonte (*adj.*) of or pert. to snuff; (*m.*) snuff.
simpatia (*f.*) sympathy, compatibility, congeniality; instinctive liking for, affinity; charm, appeal, attractiveness; thoughtfulness. [But not sympathy in the sense of commiseration, which is COMPAIXÃO, CONDOLÊNCIA.] **atrair—s**, to arouse the liking and admiration (not the sympathy) of others. [Anton. ANTIPATIA]
simpático –ca (*adj.*) sympathetic (to one); charming, attractive, prepossessing, pleasing, likeable, delightful, engaging; of a nature or taste congenial to one. [Not an equivalent of sympathetic in the sense of compassionate, which is CONDOÍDO.] Anton. ANTIPÁTICO.
simpatizante (*m.,f.*) sympathizer.
simpatizar (*v.t.*)—**com**, to take an instinctive liking to; to like, be attracted to, at first meeting; to be in congenial accord with. [But not to sympathize with someone, which is CONDOER-SE DE ALGUÉM.]
simpétalo –la (*adj., Bot.*) sympetalous, gamopetalous.
simpiezômetro (*m.*) sympiesometer.
simplé[c]tico –ca (*adj., Petrog., Zool.*) symplectic.
simples (*adj.*) simple; single, unblended; bare, mere; plain, unadorned; ordinary; artless; guileless; simple-minded, naïve; clear, uninvolved; (*m.,f.*) a simpleton; (*m., Const.*) centering [= CIMBRE].
simplesite (*f., Min.*) symplesite.
símplex [ks] (*adj., Teleg.*) simplex.
símplices (*m.pl.*) simples (medicinal plants).
simplicidade (*f.*) simplicity, clearness; plainness, naturalness; artlessness, sincerity; simple-mindedness.
simplicíssimo –ma (*absol. superl. of* SIMPLES) most simple.
simplificação (*f.*) simplification.
simplificador –dora (*adj.*) simplifying; (*m.,f.*) simplifier.
simplificar (*v.t.*) to simplify.
simplificativo –va (*adj.*) simplificative.
simplismo (*m.*) simplism; oversimplification.
simplista (*adj.*) simplistic; oversimplified. (*m.,f.*) simplicist.
simplicáceo –a (*adj., Bot.*) symplocaceous; (*f.pl.*) the symplocos or sweetleaf family (*Symplocaceae*).
simplocarpo (*m.*) a genus (*Symplocarpus*) of bad-smelling swamp herbs. [*S. foetidus* is the skunk cabbage.]
simploce (*f., Rhet.*) symploce.
simplócio (*m.*) the annulus of a fern sporagium.
simploco (*m.*) a genus (*Symplocos*) of sweetleafs.
simplório –ria (*adj.*) simple, witless, "goofy"; (*m.,f.*) simpleton, fool, "sap".
simpósio (*m.*) symposium. [But only in the ancient Greek sense of a post-banquet party. There is no single Port. word equivalent to symposium in the modern sense.]
simulação (*f.*) simulation, feigning, sham, make-believe; affectation.—**de doença**, malingering.
simulacro (*m.*) simulacrum, sham, pretense; copy, imitation, substitute; image.—**de ataque**, a feint.
simulado –da (*adj.*) simulated, make-believe; sham.

simulador –dora (*adj.*) simulating; feigning; (*m.,f.*) simulator; faker; malingerer.
simular (*v.t.*) to simulate, feign, sham, pretend; to act the part of.
simúlia (*f.*) a genus (*Simulium*) of black flies and buffalo gnats.
simuliídeos [i-í] (*m.pl.*) the family (*Simuliidae*) of black flies and buffalo gnats.
símulo –la (*adj.*) simulatory; (*m.,f.*) simulator; (*Bot.*) the simulo caper (*Capparis coriacea*).
simultâneamente (*adj.*) simultaneously.
simultaneidade (*f.*) simultaneousness.
simultâneo –nea (*adj.*) simultaneous, concurrent, synchronous.
simum (*m.*) simoon.
sin. = SINALEIRO (flagman).
sina (*f.*) fate, doom, destiny; curse; spell, "jinx".
sinagoga (*f.*) synagogue.
sinaíto (*m., Petrog.*) sinaite.
sinal (*m.*) sign; signal; mark, indication; token, manifestation; sign board; earnest money; down payment; portent, omen; a mole (skin blemish); birthmark; beauty spot.—**aberto**, (*adj.*) green (go) traffic light.—**da cruz**, sign of the Cross.—**de advertência**, traffic signal.—**de alerta**, warning signal.—**de direção**, guidepost.—**de nascença**, birthmark.—**de viação**, road sign.—**diretivo de rádio**, radio beam.—**fechado**, red (stop) traffic light.—**por bandeirola**, wigwagging.—**ortográfico**, punctuation, accent or other mark used in writing or printing. **sinais particulares**, scars, moles and other marks of identification. **dar—de si**, to show signs of life, of coming to. **fazer—**, to signal. **Muito trovão é—de pouca chuva**, A barking dog seldom bites. **por—(que)**, at that; by the way.
sinalar (*v.*) = ASSINALAR.
sinalbina (*f., Chem.*) sinalbin.
sinalefa (*f., Gram.*) synaloepha.
sinaleira (*f.*) traffic light or signal.
sinaleiro (*m.*) signalman; flagman.
sinalgia (*f., Med.*) referred pain.
sinalização (*f.*) signaling; system of road signs or traffic signals.
sinalizar (*v.t.*) to equip with (road) signs or (traffic) signals.
sinamina (*f., Chem.*) sinamine.
sinângio (*m., Bot.*) synangium.
sinânteo –tea (*adj., Bot.*) synanthous.
sinantéreo –rea (*adj., Bot.*) synantherous.
sinantrose (*f., Chem.*) synanthrose, levulin.
sinapato (*m., Chem.*) sinapate.
sinápico –ca (*adj., Chem.*) sinapic, sinapinic.
sinapina (*f., Chem.*) sinapine.
sinapismo (*m., Med.*) sinapism; mustard plaster.
sinapizar (*v.t.*) to sinapize.
sinapolina (*f., Chem.*) sinapoline.
sinapse (*f., Physiol.*) synapse; (*Biol.*) synapsis.
sináptase (*f., Chem.*) synaptase, emulsion.
sinartrose (*f., Anat.*) synarthrosis.
sina-sina (*f.*) Jerusalem thorn (*Parkinsonia aculeata*).
sincalina (*f., Chem.*) sincaline.
sincarpado –da (*adj., Bot.*) syncarpous.
sincárpio, sincarpo (*m., Bot.*) syncarp.
sinceiro (*m.*) = SALGUEIRO-BRANCO.
sincelo (*m.*) icicle.
sinceridade (*f.*) sincerity, honesty, frankness, genuineness.
sincero –ra (*adj.*) sincere, honest, open, frank, artless, guileless.
sincipúcio (*m., Anat.*) sinciput.
sinclinal (*adj., Geol.*) synclinal.
sinclinório (*m., Geol.*) synclinorium.
sincondrose (*f., Anat.*) synchondrosis.
sincopado –da (*adj.*) syncopated.
sincopal (*adj.*) syncopal.
sincopar (*v.t.*) to syncopate (words, music).
síncope (*f., Med.*) syncope.—**cardíaca**, heart stroke; (*Gram.*) syncope; (*Music*) syncopation.
sincopizar (*v.t.*) to syncopate.
sincotiledôneo –nea (*adj., Bot.*) syncotyledonous.
sincrético –ca (*adj.*) syncretic.
sincretismo (*m.*) syncretism.
sincretista (*adj.; m.,f.*) syncretist.
sincretizar (*v.t.*) to syncretize.
sincripta (*f.*) a plantlike flagellate (*Syncrypta volvox*).

síncrise (f., Rhet.) syncrisis.
sincrocíclotron (m.) synchrocyclotron.
sincrônico –ca = SÍNCRONO.
sincronismo (m.) synchronism.
sincronístico –ca (adj.) synchronistic.
sincronização (f.) synchronization; timing.
sincronizador (m.) synchronizer.
sincronizar (v.t.) to synchronize; to time.
síncrono –na (adj.) synchronal, synchronous.
sincronógrafo (m., Teleg.) synchronograph.
sincronologia (f.) synchronology.
sincroscópio (m., Elec.) synchroscope.
sincroton (m., Physics) synchroton.
sindactilia (f., Zool., Med.) syndactylia, syndactilism.
sindá[c]tilo –la (adj.) syndactyl.
sindesmose (f., Anat.) syndesmosis.
sindesmótico –ca (adj.) syndesmotic.
sindicação (f.) inquiry, investigation, esp. of a judicial nature [= SINDICÂNCIA].
sindicado –da (adj.) investigated; (m.) one who has been investigated; office or term of a syndic.
sindicador –dora (adj.) investigating; (m.,f.) investigator.
sindical (adj.) syndical; of or pert. to a trade union.
sindicalismo (m.) syndicalism; trade-unionism.
sindicalista (m.,f.) syndicalist; trade-unionist.
sindicalizar (v.t.) to organize into (form) a labor union.
sindicância (f.) investigation, inquiry, probe [= SINDICAÇÃO].
sindicar (v.t.) to investigate, probe, inquire into; to organize into a trade or labor union.—os fatos, to investigate the facts.
sindicatado –da (m.,f.) member of a labor union.
sindicato (m.) syndicate; pool; labor union.
sindicatório –ria (adj.) of or pert. to a syndicate or to a labor union; (m.,f.) member of a syndicate or of a labor union.
síndico (m.) syndic; magistrate; resident manager of a co-operative apartment building.—de massa falida, or de uma falência, assignee in bankruptcy.
síndroma, –me (f., Med.) syndrome.
sinéctico –ca (adj., Math.) synectic, holomorphic.
sinectria (f., Zool.) synechthry.
sinecura (f.) sinecure.
sinecurismo (m.) sinecurism.
sinecurista (m.,f.) sinecurist.
sinédoque (f., Rhet.) synecdoche.
Sinedrim, Sinédrio (m.) Sanhedrin.
sineiro –ra (adj.) having bells; (m.,f.) bell ringer; (m.) bell maker; a thrush (Turdus tiniens); (f.) bell tower; cork float.
sinema (m., Bot.) synema.
sinergia (f., Med.) synergy.
sinérgico –ca (adj.) synergetic.
sinérgide, sinergídea (f., Bot.) synergid.
sinergismo (m., Theol.) synergism.
sínese (f., Gram.) synesis.
sinestesia (f., Physiol., Psychol.) synesthesia.
sinêta (f.) small bell, hand bell.
sinête (m.) signet, seal; signet ring.
sinfilia (f., Zool.) symphily.
sinfinoto –ta (adj., Zool.) symphysis.
sínfise (f., Anat., Zool.) symphysis.
sínfito (m., Bot.) comfrey (Symphytum officinale).
sinfonia (f.) symphony.—de câmara, chamber music.
sinfônico –ca (adj.) symphonic; symphonious.
sinfonista (m.,f.) symphonist.
sinfornia (f.) a honeysuckle (Lonicera symphoricarpus).
singamia (f., Biol., Bot.) syngamy.
síngamo (m.) gapeworm (Syngamus trachealis), c.a. FORQUILHA.
singamose (f.) the gapes (a disease of poultry and other birds, caused by the gapeworm); c.a. GAPE.
Singapura (f.) Singapore.
singelez[a] [lê] (f.) simplicity, artlessness, naïveté; sincerity; innocence.
singelo –la (adj.) simple, naïve, guileless, sincere; single.
singenciana (f.) = GENCIANELA.
singenito (m., Min.) syngenite.
singnátidas (f.pl.), singnatos (m.pl.) the family (Syngnathidae) of sea horses and pipefishes.
singradura (f., Naut.) a day's sail or run; sailing course.
síngrafo (m., Civil Law) syngraph.
singrar (v.i.) to sail; to plow the seas.

singular (adj.) single, sole, unique; individual; private; singular, odd, queer, freakish; (Gram.) singular.
singularice (f., colloq.) queerness.
singularidade (f.) singularity; oddity.
singularizar (v.t.) to singularize; to single out; to particularize; (v.r.) to distinguish oneself.
sinhá (f.) "Missus" (negro slave corruption of SENHORA). —moça = SINHÀZINHA.
sinhàzinha [dim. of SINHÁ] (f.) "missy" [= SINHÁ-MOÇA].
sinhô (m.) "Massa" (negro slave corruption of SENHOR). —moço = SINHÔZINHO.
sinhôzinho [dim. of SINHÔ] (m.) "young Massa" [= SINHÔ-MOÇO].
sinigrina (f., Chem.) sinigrin.
sinimbu [ú] (m.) the common edible iguana of tropical America (Iguana iguana), c.a. SENEMBU, SINUMBU, PAPA-VENTO, CAMELEÃO, PREGUIÇA.
sinistra (f.) see under SINISTRO.
sinistrado –da (adj.) damaged, wrecked, ruined; (m.,f.) person who has suffered losses and damages.
sinistrar (v.i.) to suffer loss or damage, referring esp. to insured property.
sinistrino (m., Chem.) sinistrin.
sinistro –tra (adj.) sinister, ominous, dreadful, baleful; grim; on the left; (f.) left hand; (m.) disaster, damage, wreck, loss, esp. of insured property.—maritimo, maritime disaster.
sinistrogiro –ra (adj.) sinistrogyric, moving toward the left.
sinistrorso –sa (adj., Bot.) sinistrorse.
sino (m.) bell.—de mergulhar, diving bell; = SIGNO; = GÔLFO.
sinodal (adj.) synodal.
sinódico –ca (adj.) synodic(al).
sínodo (m.) synod.
sinologia (f.) sinology.
sinólogo (m.) sinologue.
sinonimia (f.) synonymy, being synonymous; use of synonyms.
sinonímica (f.) synonymy, study of synonyms.
sinonimista (m.,f.) synonymist.
sinônimo –ma (adj.) synonymous; (m.) synonym.
sinopite (f., Min.) sinopite.
sinopse (f.) synopsis, summary.
sinóptico –ca (adj.) synoptic(al). quadro—, a synoptic chart (of business conditions, etc.).
sinoptizar (v.t.) to synopsize.
sinosteologia (f.) synosteology, arthrology.
sinóvia (f., Anat.) synovia, synovial fluid.
sinovial (adj., Anat.) synovial; (f.) synovial capsule.
sinovite (f., Med.) synovitis.
sinsépalo –la (adj., Bot.) synsepalous, gamosepalous.
sintático –ca (adj.) syntactic(al).
sintaxe [x = ss] (f.) syntax.
sintáxico –ca (adj.) = SINTÁTICO.
síntese (f.) synthesis.
sintético –ca (adj.) synthetic(al).
sintetizar (v.t.) to synthesize.
sintoísmo (m.) shintoism.
sintoma (m.) symptom, indication, sign.
sintomático –ca (adj.) symptomatic(al), indicative.
sintomatologia (f.) symptomatology.
sintomia (f.) brevity; conciseness.
sintonina (f., Biochem.) syntonin.
sintonização (f.) syntonization; tuning (of a radio).
sintonizar (v.t.) to syntonize, tune (radio).
sintrófico –ca (adj., Biol.) syntrophic.
sinuado –da (adj., Bot.) sinuate.
sinuca (f., colloq.) tight spot, pretty pickle, nice mess [from British snookered].
sinumbu [bú] (m.) var. of SINIMBU.
sinuosidade (f.) sinuosity.
sinuoso –sa (adj.) sinuous, winding.
sinusite (f., Med.) sinusitis.
sinusoidal (adj.) sine-shaped.
sinusóide (f., Math.) sine curve.
siobinha (f.) = VERMELHO-HENRIQUE.
sionismo (m.) Zionism.
sionista (adj.; m.,f.) Zionist.
sipoúba (f.) a nitta tree (Parkia discolor), c.a. JIPOÚBA
sire (m.) sire, sir.
sirena (f.) siren, nymph; = SEREIA.
sirênico –ca (adj.) sirenic, seductive, alluring.
sirenídeo –dea, sirênio –nia (m.) sirenian.

sirga (*f.*) hawser, tow rope, warping rope; warping, towing, hauling.
sirgar (*v.t.*) to warp, tow (ship, etc.); to haul.
sirgo (*m.*) silkworm; thick, smooth woolen cloth.
sirgueiro (*m.*) = SERIGUEIRO.
siri [rí.] (*m.*) any of various crabs of the family *Portunidae*.
síria (*f.*) see under SÍRIO.
siríaco –ca (*adj.; m.,f.*) Syrian.
sirigaita (*f.*) a wren; (*colloq.*) a lively, spirited woman, esp. one who gads about; a coquettish young woman; a minx; a hussy.
siringe (*f., Zool.*) syrinx.
siringina (*f., Chem.*) syringin.
siringomielia (*f., Med.*) syringomyelia.
sírio –ria (*adj.; m.,f.*) Syrian; (*m.*) a sack for manioc meal; [*cap.*] Syrius (dog star); (*f.*) [*cap.*] Syria.
siriri [sirirí] (*m.*) Azara's kingbird (*Tyrannus melancholicus*); the white-throated kingbird (*T. albogularis*); also = SUIRIRI.—**tinga,** the solitary flycatcher (*Myiodynastes solitarius*), c.a. BEM-TE-VI-PRÊTO, BEM-TE-VI-RISCADO; also = SURURU (a mussel); also = PANTUFO (a male termite).
siririca (*f.*) = BEM-TE-VI.
siriú (*f.*) = JURUVA.
siroco [rô] (*m.*) sirocco.
sirtes (*f.pl. or m.pl.*) quicksands; fig., dangers.
sisa (*f.*) a transfer tax.
sisal (*m., Bot.*) sisal agave (*A. sisalana*); henequen agave (*A. fourcroydes*).
sisar (*v.t.*) to impose a transfer tax on; to pad an expense account; to steal.
sisgola (*f.*) throatlatch (of a bridle).
sísmico –ca (*adj.*) seismic.
sismografia (*f.*) seismography.
sismógrafo (*m., Physics*) seismograph.
sismograma (*m., Physics*) seismogram.
sismologia (*f.*) seismology.
sismológico –ca (*adj.*) seismological.
sismométrico –ca (*adj.*) seismometric.
sismômetro (*m.*) seismometer.
sismometrógrafo (*m.*) seismometrograph.
siso (*m.*) good sense, prudence, judgment. **dente do—,** wisdom tooth.
sissarcose (*f., Anat.*) syssarcosis.
sistáltico –ca (*adj.*) = SISTÓLICO.
sistema (*m.*) system; organism, organization; scheme, plan, arrangement; method, routine.—**assimétrico** or **triclínico,** (*Cryst.*) asymmetric or triclinic system.—**C.G.S.,** (*Physics*) C.G.S. system.—**circulatório,** (*Anat.*) circulatory system.—**das ondulações,** wave theory (of light).—**da vida vegetativa,** or—**nervoso simpático,** (*Anat., Physiol.*) autonomic nervous system.—**de arrefecimento,** cooling system.—(**métrico**) **decimal,** decimal (metrical) system.—**nervoso,** nervous system.—**protetor,** protective tariffs.—**quadrático,** (*Cryst.*) tetragonal system.—**vascular,** vascular system.—**venoso,** venous system.
sistemático –ca (*adj.*) systematic(al), methodical, orderly; systemic; (*f.*) taxonomy.
sistematização (*f.*) systematization.
sistematizar (*v.t.*) to systematize, systemize.
sistematologia (*f.*) systematology.
sístole (*f., Physiol., Biol., Pros.*) systole.
sistólico –ca (*adj.*) systolic.
sisudez[a] [ê] (*f.*) prudence, wisdom; gravity, seriousness; dignified bearing.
sisudo –da (*adj.; m.,f.*) pensive, unsmiling, serious, sober (person); wise, prudent (person).
sitiado –da (*adj.; m.,f.*) besieged (person, place).
sitiador –dora (*adj.*) besieging.
sitiante (*adj.*) besieging; (*m.*) besieger; one who owns and/or lives on a SÍTIO (farm).
sitiar (*v.t.*) to besiege, beleaguer, lay siege to; to surround.
sítio (*m.*) location; place, spot, locality; the country; a country place; small farm or ranch; siege. **cá por estes—s,** in these parts, hereabouts. **do—,** from the country.
sitioca (*f.*) small farm.
sitiofobia (*f., Med.*) sitophobia.
sitiologia (*f.*) sitology; dietetics.
sitiomania (*f., Med.*) sitomania.
sitiotoxismo [ks] (*m.*) food poisoning.
sito –ta (*irreg. p.p. of* SITUAR) situated; located.
situação (*f.*) act of placing or locating; situation, position, location; circumstances, condition, state of affairs. **em**

boa—, well-to-do, well-fixed. **em má—,** in a bad fix. **naquela—,** at that moment. **regularizar uma—,** to straighten out a situation.
situacionismo (*m.*) the dominant or reigning political power.
situacionista (*m.,f.*) member of the "ins" (party in power);—in contrast to OPOSICIONISTAS, the "outs".
situar (*v.t.*) to place, put.
sizígia (*f., Astron.*) syzygy. **maré de—,** spring tide.
sizígio (*m., Bot.*) syzygium.
s/l = SEU LANÇAMENTO (your [bookkeeping] entry).
s.l.n.d. = SEM LUGAR NEM DATA (without place or date).
S.M. = SUA MAJESTADE (His [Her] Majesty).
S.M.I. = SUA MAJESTADE IMPERIAL (His [Her] Imperial Majesty).
S.M.J. = SALVO MELHOR JUÍZO (save better judgment).
smoking [simôquim] (*m.*) tuxedo, dinner jacket.
s.° = SERVO (servant).
s/o = SUA ORDEM (your [commercial] order).
só (*adj.*) alone, single, sole, only; lone, lonely, solitary; companionless; (*adv.*) only, merely.—**de nome,** in or by name only.—**mesmo,** just, only.—**se,** only if. **a—s,** all alone. **Noã—êle como também você,** Not only he but you too. **por si—,** by himself; alone; in itself. **que—êle,** like no (none) other. **Enfim, sós!** Alone at last!
soaberto –ta (*adj.*) ajar, half-open.
soabrir [26] (*v.t.*) to half-open [= ENTREABRIR].
soado –da (*adj.*) sounded, struck (as a bell); sounding; much-discussed; (*f.*) sound, report, clap; rumor; fame.
soagem (*f., Bot.*) common viper's-bugloss (*Echium vulgare*).
soalhado –da (*adj.*) having two or more floors; (*m.*) flooring.
soalhar (*v.t.*) to jingle (as a tambourine); to provide with a floor [= ASSOALHAR].
soalhas (*f.pl.*) metallic disks or jingles of a tambourine.
soalheiro –ra (*adj.*) sunny, sun-drenched; (*f.*) sun's heat; noonday heat; (*m.*) sunny spot.
soalho (*m.*) a wooden floor.—**da bôca,** the sublingual region or floor of the mouth.
soante (*adj.*) sounding. **bem—,** well-sounding, melodious.
soar (*v.t.,v.i.*) to sound, ring, chime; to please; to suit.
sob [ô] (*prep.*) sub, under, beneath.—**color,** or **côr, de,** under pretense of.—**emenda,** subject to correction.—**espécie,** under pretense of.—**juramento,** under oath.—**os auspícios de,** under the auspices of.—**palavra,** on one's word.—**pena de,** on pain of. **feito—medida,** made-to-measure.
sobdominante (*adj.; f., Music*) subdominant.
sobejado –da (*adj.*) more than enough; leftover.
sobejamente (*adv.*) excessively.
sobejar (*v.i.*) to be left over; to be more than enough.
sobejo –ja [ê] (*adj.*) leftover; surplus; excessive; (*adv.*) excessively; (*m.pl.*) leftovers; surplus.
soberania (*f.*) sovereignty, supreme power.
soberano –na (*adj.*) sovereign, supreme; (*m.,f.*) sovereign, supreme ruler; (*m.*) sovereign (a gold coin of Great Britain, worth one pound sterling).
soberba (*f.*) see under SOBERBO.
soberbia (*f.*) haughtiness; loftiness.
soberbo –ba (*adj.*) superb, sublime; tiptop; supercilious, haughty, lofty, overbearing; disdainful; self-important; exalted, proud; (*m.,f.*) a vainglorious person; (*f.*) pride, haughtiness, superciliousness, arrogance.
sobestar [45] (*v.i.*) to be under, inferior in position.
sobexposição (*f., Photog.*) underexposure.
sóbole (*f., Bot.*) soboles, sucker, stolon.
sobpor [63] (*v.t.*) to place below (beneath).
sobra (*f.*) surplus, excess; (*pl.*) leftovers; overage; odds and ends. **de—,** spare, extra; galore, in abundance, in profusion; plenty of, more than enough; left over. **ficar de—,** to be left over.
sobraçar (*v.t.*) to carry under the arm (as a book, bundle, umbrella, etc.).—**se com,** to walk arm in arm with.
sobradado –da (*adj.*) having two or more floors; having wooden floors.
sobrado –da (*adj.*) plentiful; left over; (*m.*) wooden floor; upper story; a house of two or more stories; large plantation owner's home.
sobrançaria (*f.*) disdain; haughtiness. Var. SOBRANCERIA.
sobrancear (*v.t.*) to tower, overlook, overtop.
sobranceiro –ra (*adj.*) towering, overlooking, lofty; over-

lying; proud, haughty, disdainful.—**a,** commanding, dominating, overlooking (from a superior position).
sobrancelha (f.) eyebrow [= SUPERCÍLIO, SOBROLHO].
sobrancelhudo –da (adj.) having heavy eyebrows.
sobranceria (f.) = SOBRANÇARIA.
sobrante (adj.) leftover; surplus.
sobrar (v.i.) to be left over; to be more than enough; to exceed. **Sobraram cinco,** There were five left over.
sobrasil (m., Bot.) a peltophorum (P. dubium), c.a. FARINHA-SÊCA.
sôbre (prep.) over, above; on, upon; in addition to, besides; more than; about, concerning. **por—,** above, besides.
sobreabundar (v.) & derivs. = SUPERABUNDAR & DERIVS.
sobreaguado –da (adj.) inundated.
sobreagudo –da (adj.) very sharp.
sobreanca (f.) = CHAIREL.
sobrearco (m.) lintel.
sobreaviso –sa (adj.) warned; (m.) precaution. **de—,** on (one's) guard; on the alert.
sobrecana (f., Veter.) splint.
sobrecarga (f.) overload; surcharge; surcingle; (m.) supercargo.
sobrecarregar (v.t.) to overload; to overburden; to surcharge; to supercharge.
sobrecarta (f.) = SOBRESCRITO.
sobrecasaca (f.) a Prince Albert or similar frock coat.
sobrecenho (m.) frown, scowl.
sobrecéu (m.) canopy, tester.
sobrecheio –cheia (adj.) overfull.
sobrecincha (f.) a long girth which passes over the saddle.
sobrecomum (adj., Gram.) having the same form for both genders; e.g., ARTISTA; [= COMUM-DE-DOIS].
sobrecurva (f., Veter.) curb.
sobredito –ta (adj.) above-mentioned; aforesaid.
sobredourar (v.t.) to overgild.
sobreentender [e-e] (v.) = SUPERINTENDER.
sobreestadia [e-e] (f.) demurrage (of a vessel in port).
sobreestar [e-e] (v.) = SOBRESTAR.
sobreexaltação [e-e] (f.) superexaltation.
sobreexaltar [e-e] (v.t.) to superexalt.
sobreexcedente [e-e] (adj.) surpassing.
sobreexceder [e-e] (v.t.) to superexceed, surpass, outdo, outstrip.
sobreexcelência [e-e] (f.) superexcellence.
sobreexcelente [e-e] (adj.) of surpassing excellence, superexcellent.
sobreexcitação [e-e] (f.) superexcitation.
sobreexcitar [e-e] (v.t.) to overexcite.
sobrefusão (f., Physical Chem.) superfusion.
sôbre-humano –na (adj.) superhuman.
sobreintender [e-i] (f.) = SUPERINTENDER.
sobreiro (m.) Hispania oak (Quercus hispanica); Brazil roupala (R. brasiliensis); raintree saman (Samanea saman). Var. SOVEIRO.
sobrejacente (adj.) superjacent, overlying [rocks].
sobrelevar (v.t.) to tower above; to rise above; to raise, lift up; to surmount, triumph over; (v.r.) to stand out.
sobreloja (f., Arch.) mezzanine, entresol.
sobrelotação (f.) overload.
sobrelotar (v.) = SUPERLOTAR.
sobremaneira (adv.) exceedingly, greatly.
sobremão (m., Veter.) splint on a foreleg. **de—,** well and carefully done.
sobremaravilhar (v.t.) to wonder greatly about.
sobremesa [ê] (f.) dessert.
sobremodo (adv.) much, greatly; excessively; unusually.
sobrenadante (adj.) floating, swimming.
sobrenadar (v.i.) to float, swim.
sobrenatural (adj.) supernatural; uncanny; (m.) the supernatural.
sobrenaturalidade (f.) supernaturalism.
sobrenome (m.) surname.
sobrenumerável (adj.) numberless, countless.
sobreolhar (v.t.) to look down upon; to look at over the shoulder.
sobreosso (m., Veter.) splint.
sobrepaga (f.) extra payment; bonus.
sobrepairar (v.t.) to hang over, hover over.
sobreparto (adv.) after parturition; (m.) period of recovery following childbirth.
sobrepeliz (f., Eccl.) surplice.
sobrepensado (adv.) aforethought, premeditated, intentional.

sobrepensar (v.t.) to think much about, reflect on.
sobrepesar (v.t.) to overload; to weigh, ponder; (v.i.) to weigh upon the heart.
sobrepêso (m.) excess weight; counterweight.
sobrepor [63] (v.t.) to superpose; to superimpose; to overlay.—**a,** to value (something) above another.—**se a,** to overcome.
sobreporta (f.) door transom.
sobreposição (f.) superposition; overlap.
sobreposse (adv.) overmuch, excessively, too. **trabalhar—,** to overwork.
sobreposto –ta (adj.) superposed; added; (m.) ornamental overlay.
sobrepratear (v.t.) to silver; to silverplate.
sobrepujamento (m.), **sobrepujança** (f.) act of surpassing, overshadowing, outclassing, overcoming.
sobrepujante (adj.) surpassing, excelling.
sobrepujar (v.t.) to surpass, excel, outclass, overshadow, outshine, eclipse; to outdo; to outstrip; to overcome; (v.i.) to stand out.
sobrequilha (f., Naut.) keelson.
sôbre-renal (adj.; Anat.) suprarenal.
sôbre-rosado –da (adj.) pinkish.
sôbre-saia (f.) overskirt.
sôbre-saturacão (f.) supersaturation.
sôbre-saturar (v.t.) to supersaturate.
sobrescrever [44] (v.t.) = SOBRESCRITAR.
sobrescritar (v.t.) to superscribe; to address (a letter, etc.).
sobrescrito (m.) envelope; superscription, address.
sôbre-solar (v.t.) to resole (shoes).
sobressair [75] (v.t.) to stand out, project; to overhang; to be prominent or conspicuous; to overtop.
sobressalente (adj.; m.) = SOBRESSELENTE.
sobressaltado –da (adj.) startled, frightened, surprised. **acordar—,** to wake with a start.
sobressaltar (v.t.) to surprise, take unawares; to startle, frighten; to pass beyond; to skip (jump) over; (v.r.) to start, be startled; to take alarm.
sobressalto (m.) alarm, fright; surprise, start; sudden dread; shock.
sobressarar (v.i.) to get partly well; (v.t.) to palliate (a disease).
sobresselente (adj.) salient; outstanding; surplus; spare; (m.) that which stands out; a spare something; spare part. Var. SOBRESSALENTE.
sobrestante (adj.) overlooking (as from a height); (m.) overseer.
sobrestar [45] (v.i.) to come to a stop; to forbear, desist; to be imminent; (v.t.) to put a stop to (work).
sobrestimar (v.t.) to overestimate; to overrate.
sôbre-substancial (adj.) supersubstantial, spiritual.
sobretarde (f.) gloaming; (adv.) at dusk.
sobretaxa (f.) surtax.
sobretensão (f., Elec.) excess voltage.
sobretudo (m.) overcoat; (adv.) above all, before all else, especially.
sobrevento (m.) squall.
sobrevigiar (v.t.) to watch over.
sobrevir [82] (v.i.) to supervene, follow upon; to befall.
sobrevirtude (f.) nun's veil.
sobrevivência (f.) survival.
sobrevivente (adj.) surviving; (m.,f.) survivor.
sobreviver (v.i.) to survive.
sobrevoar (v.t.) to fly over; to skim over the surface.
sobriedade (f.) sobriety, temperance; moderation.
sobrinha (f.) niece.—**neta,** grandniece.
sobrinho (m.) nephew.—**neto,** grandnephew.
sôbrio –bria (adj.) sober, temperate, abstemious; frugal.
sobr.º = SOBRINHO (nephew).
sôbro (m.) the cork oak (Quercus suber), or its wood.
sob-roda (f.) bump or hole in the road.
sobrolho [brô] (m.) eyebrow [= SOBRANCELHA].—**carregado,** scowl. **carregar o—,** to scowl.
Soc. = SOCIEDADE (partnership).
soca (f.) the second cutting or harvesting of sugar cane, rice, tobacco, etc. (Bot.) rhizome.
socado –da (adj.) squat, thickset; pounded.
socador –dora (adj.) hard-trotting [horse].
socadura (f.) act of pounding, tamping, etc. See the verb SOCAR.
socairo (m.) the loose or slack part of a rope; cave; foot of a hill.
socalcar (v.t.) to tamp (earth), tread (grapes).
socalco (m.) terrace, ledge.

socapa (*f.*) false appearance. **à—**, furtively; on the sly. **rir à—**, to laugh up one's sleeve; to chuckle.

socar (*v.t.*) to strike, hit (with the fist), "sock"; to pound, beat; to tamp, ram; to knead; (*v.i.*) to sprout again after cutting (as sugar cane).

socava (*f.*) underground hole.

socavão (*m.*) cave; hideaway.

socavar (*v.t.*) to undermine, undercut; (*v.i.*) to dig.

sócia (*f.*) woman partner; companion. Cf. sócio.

sociabilidade (*f.*) sociability; good-fellowship.

social (*adj.*) social.

socialismo (*m.*) Socialism.

socialista (*adj.; m.,f.*) Socialist.

socialização (*f.*) socialization.

socializar (*v.t.*) to socialize.

sociável (*adj.*) sociable.

sociedade (*f.*) society; social mode of life; company, companionship; any social community; social high life, fashionable world; association (of persons); a partnership. **—anônima**, corporation, joint-stock company.**—de consumo**, consumers' cooperative.**—de socorros mútuos**, mutual aid society.**—em comandita**, limited partnership.

sócio (*m.*) member; associate, partner, copartner.**—benemérito**, a most distinguished member (of a club or association).**—comanditário**, silent partner.**—de mérito**, or **honorário**, honorary member.

sociologia (*f.*) sociology.

sociológico **-ca** (*adj.*) sociological.

sociólogo **-ga** (*m.,f.*) sociologist.

soco (*m.*) sock (in the sense of a "shoe worn by actors of comedy in ancient Greece and Rome"); by ext., comedy or a matter of minor importance; nowadays, a wooden shoe or clog, better known as TAMANCA or TAMANCO; (*Arch.*) socle.

sôco (*m.*) clout, cuff; a "sock" (blow with the fist).— **inglês**, boxing [= BOXE].

socó (*m.*) any of various herons and bitterns.**—azul**, or **—-beija-flor** = GARÇA-DE-GUIANA.**—-boi**, the tiger heron (*Tigrisoma lineatum* or *T. brasiliense*), c.a. ALCARAVÃO, MARIA-MOLE; the neotropical bittern (*Botaurus pinnatus*).**—-estudante** = SOCÒZINHO.**—-mirim** = SOCOÍ. **—-vermelho** = GARÇA-VERMELHA (a bittern).

soçobra (*f.*) = SOÇÔBRO.

soçobrar (*v.t.*) to upset, overturn, turn upside down; (*v.i.*) to capsize, turn turtle; to go under; (*v.r.*) to become upset.

soçôbro (*m.*) act of capsizing, foundering, sinking; shipwreck.

socoí (*m.*) the cocoi heron (*Ardea cocoi*), c.a. JOÃO-GRANDE, MANGUARI, MAGUARI, TABUJAJÁ; the black-browed night heron (*Nycticorax n. hoactli*), c.a. DORMINHOCO, TAQUARI, ARAPAPÁ-DE-BICO-COMPRIDO, GARÇA-CINZENTA, GUACURU; the undulated bittern (*Zeibrilus undulatus*); the variegated bittern (*Ixobrychus involucris*).**—-vermelho** = GARÇA-VERMELHA (a bittern).

socopo (*m.*) coaster (for a glass).

socorrer (*v.t.*) to succor, help, befriend; to rescue.**—-se (de)**, to have recourse to; to resort to.

socorro [cô] (*m.*) succor, aid, relief, help; (*interj.*) Help! **em—de**, to the aid of. **hospital de pronto—**, emergency hospital. **monte de—**, a remedial loan association. **primeiros—s**, first aid.

socovão (*m.*) deep cellar.

socòzinho (*m.*) the striated heron (*Butorides striatus*), c.a. SOCÓ-ESTUDANTE, SOCÓ-MIRIM, ANA-VELHA, MARIA-MOLE.

socrático **-ca** (*adj.*) Socratic.

soda (*f.*) sodium hydroxide, caustic soda; soda water; (*Bot.*) Russian thistle (*Salsola*).**—de comércio**, soda ash. **—Solvay**, sodium carbonate, washing soda.

sodalício (*m.*) sodality.

sodálita (*f., Min.*) sodalite.

sodamida (*f., Chem.*) sodamide.

sódico **-ca** (*adj.; Chem.*) sodic.

sódio (*m., Chem.*) sodium.**—prússico**, sodium cyanide.

sodomia (*f.*) · sodomy.

sodomita (*m.,f.*) sodomite.

sodomítico **-ca** (*adj.*) sodomitical.

soer [77] (*v.i.*) to be wont to [= COSTUMAR].

soerguer [5] (*v.t.*) to lift slightly; (*v.r.*) to raise oneself to a half-lying or sitting position.

soez [ê] (*adj.*) mean, low, vile, base, scurrilous.

sofá (*f.*) sofa, couch, divan, davenport.**—-de-arrasto**, or **—-rasteiro**, a floor mat of plaited rushes [= ESTEIRA].

Sofia (*f.*) Sophia; Sophie; [*not cap.*]**—-dos-cirurgiões**, the pinnate tansy mustard (*Descurainia pinnata*); a kind of corvina or croaker (*Pachyrus francisci*).

sofisma (*m.*) sophism; (*colloq.*) deception; quibble.

sofismador **-dora** (*adj.*) given to sophism.

sofismar (*v.t.,v.i.*) to employ sophism; to quibble.

sofista (*m.,f.*) sophist.

sofística (*f.*) sophistic; sophistry.

sofisticação (*f.*) sophistication, sophistry; adulteration, debasement. [But not sophistication in the everyday, sense of "worldly wiseness," which is EXPERIÊNCIA DO MUNDO; TRAQUEJO SOCIAL.]

sofisticado **-da** (*adj.*) sophistical; adulterated. [But not sophisticated in the everyday sense of worldly-wise, which is DESILUDIDO, EXPERIENTE, SABIDO.]

sofisticaria (*f.*) sophistry; quibbling.

sofístico **-ca** (*adj.*) sophistical; caviling.

sofito (*m., Arch.*) soffit.

sofralda (*f.*) foothill.

sofraldar (*v.t.*) to lift (something) in order to see what lies beneath; (*v.r.*) to lift one's dress or other garment.

sofrê (*m.*) a handsome black, yellow and white oriole (*Icterus, syn. Xanthornus, jamacaii*) of northeastern Brazil, having a fine, powerful song, in whose first notes the Brazilian hears the word SOFRER (to suffer)—whence the bird's name; c.a. CONCRIZ, CORRUPIÃO, JOÃO-PINTO. [It is a popular cage bird.]

sofreamento (*m.*), **sofreada**, **sofreadura** (*f.*) act of curbing, checking, restraining.

sofreador **-dora** (*adj.*) curbing, restraining; (*m.,f.*) one who, or that which, curbs or restrains.

sofrear (*v.t.*) to rein (in), pull (up) on the reins; to curb, check, restrain; (*v.r.*) to hold oneself back.

sofredor **-dora** (*adj.*) suffering; (*m.,f.*) sufferer.

sôfrego **-ga** (*adj.*) greedy, ravenous; eager, avid; hasty, impatient.

sofreguidão (*f.*) greediness; avidity; eagerness, impatience.

sofrenaço (*m.*) a strong pull on the reins.

sofrenar (*v.t.*) to pull up on the reins.

sofrer (*v.i.*) to suffer, submit, endure; (*v.t.*) to suffer, undergo, experience; to tolerate.**—do coração**, to have heart trouble.**—o diabo**, to go through hell.

sofrido **-da** (*adj.*) long-suffering; uncomplaining.

sofrimento (*m.*) suffering, endurance; pain, distress, anguish; hardship.

sofrível (*adj.*) sufferable, endurable; passable, so-so, pretty good.

Sofrônia (*f.*) Sophronia.

soga (*f.*) hemp rope; lariat; ditch.

sogra (*f.*) mother-in-law.

sôgro (*m.*) father-in-law; (*pl.*) parents-in-law.

sói, form of SOER [77].

sois, form of SER [76].

soja (*m.*) soybean [= FEIJÃO-SOJA].

sol [sóis] (*m.*) sun; sunshine; (*Music*) sol; (*Chem.*) sol.— **abrasador**, burning sun.**—a pino**, high noon.**—dabolívia**, a flamebean (*Brownea ariza*).**—levante**, rising sun.**—-nado**, or **-nascente**, sunrise.**—poente**, or **-ponente**, setting sun.**—-pôsto**, sunset.**—vertical**, overhead sun. **banho de—**, sun bath. **de—a—**, from sunrise to sunset. **fazer—**, to be sunny. **luz do—**, sunlight. **nascer do—**, sunrise. **pôr do—**, sunset. **queimadura de—**, sunburn. **raio de—**, sunbeam. **relógio de—**, sundial.

sola (*f.*) sole leather; shoe sole; sole of the foot.

solama (*f.*) burning sun; heat of the sun; = SOLÃO.

solanáceo **-cea** (*adj., Bot.*) solanaceous; (*f.pl.*) the nightshade or potato family (*Solanaceae*).

solancar (*v.i.*) to toil, drudge, work hard (as from sunup to sundown).

solandra (*f.*) the showy chalicevine (*Solandra grandiflora*).

solandre (*m., Veter.*) a dry or scurfy eruption, similar to molanders, occurring on the hind leg of a horse, in front of the hock.

solanina (*f., Chem.*) solanine.

solano (*m.*) the genus (*Solanum*) of nightshades.**—-dacarolina**, the Carolina horsenettle (*S. carolinense*).

solão (*m.*) sandy or clayey soil; burning sun [= SOLAMA].

solapa (*f.*) hidden opening in the earth, as a cave with a large rock at the entrance. **à—**, secretly.

solapado **-da** (*adj.*) undermined; hidden.

solapador **-dora** (*adj.*) sapping, undermining; (*m.*) sapper.

solapamento (*m.*) act of sapping or undermining; (*R.R.*) washout.

solapão (*m.*) a large cavity in the earth formed by erosion.

solapar (*v.t.*) to sap, undermine; to hide, disguise; (*v.r.*) to hide as in a cave or burrow. Var. ASSOLAPAR.

solapo (*m.*) a hole washed out under the roots of a tree on a river bank.

solar (*adj.*) solar; sole; manorial; (*m.*) manor house; large plantation-owner's house; land held by the nobles, in distinction from church lands or crown lands; (*pl.*) sun worshipers; (*v.t.*) to sole (shoes); to talk alone with someone; (*v.i.*) to play a solo; to win at solo (card game); to fly solo.

solarengo –ga (*adj.*) manorial; (*m.*) lord of the manor; tenant-farmer of a manor.

solário (*m.*) solarium; sundial.

solarômetro (*m.*, *Navig.*) solarometer.

solavancar (*v.i.*) to jolt, bump, jog.

solavanco (*m.*) jolt, jar, jerk, bump, jog.

solda (*f.*) solder; weld; (*Bot.*) white bedstraw (*Galium mollugo*), c.a. MOLUGEM.—**autógena**, autogenous welding. —**de arco (elétrico)**, arc welding.—**elétrica**, electric welding.—**forte**, brazing.—**por pontos**, spot welding.— **por resistência**, resistance welding.

soldada (*f.*) see under SOLDADO.

soldadeiro –ra (*adj.*) wage-earning; (*m.,f.*) wage-earner.

soldadesco –ca [ê] (*adj.*) of or pert. to soldiers; (*f.*) soldiery.

soldadinho (*m.*) a little soldier.—**de chumbo**, tin soldier (lit. & fig.).

soldado –da (*adj.*) welded; soldered; (*f.*) wages; (*m.*) soldier; policeman; (*Zool.*) the superciliated red-breasted starling (*Leistes militaris superciliaris*); the white-billed cacique (*Archiplanus albirostris*), c.a. MELRO, ROUXINOL, PÉGA; also = CAPITÃO and ENCONTRO (birds); the rock beauty (*Holocanthus tricolor*), a fish, c.a. PARU-SOLDADO, VIGÁRIO.—**de fortuna**, soldier of fortune.—**de leva**, or **de manada**, a soldier who has been impressed into service. —**de fogo**, fireman [= BOMBEIRO].—**de infantaria**, infantryman.—**gregal**, or **raso**, buck private.

soldador –dora (*adj.*) welding; (*m.,f.*) welder.

soldadura, soldagem (*f.*) soldering; welding.

soldar (*v.t.*) to solder; to weld.—**forte**, to braze.

sôldo (*m.*) soldier's pay. **a**—, mercenarily. **a**—**de**, in the pay of.

soldra (*f.*, *Veter.*) stifle (joint).

solé (*m.*) = PARATI.

solecismo (*m.*) solecism; error.

solecista (*m.,f.*) solecist.

solecizar (*v.i.*) to solecize.

soledade (*f.*) solitude; loneliness.

soleira (*f.*) threshold; door sill; carriage step.

sólen (*m.*) a genus (*Solen*) of razor clams.

solene (*adj.*) solemn, sober, grave; formal; impressive; self-important.

solenidade (*f.*) solemnity, seriousness; impressiveness; formal ceremony.

solenídeos (*m.pl.*) a family (*Solenidae*) of marine clams which includes the razor clams.

solenização (*f.*) solemnization.

solenizar (*v.t.*) to solemnize.

solenóide (*m.*) solenoid.

solércia (*f.*) cunning, craft, guile; sharp practice.

solerte (*adj.*) sly, crafty; skillful; (*m.f.*) schemer.

soleta [ê] (*f.*) inner sole of a shoe.

soletração (*f.*) spelling.

soletrar (*v.t.*) to spell out (orally); to read slowly and with difficulty.

solevantar, solevar (*v.t.*) to lift up a little; (*v.r.*) to raise oneself with difficulty.

solferino (*m.*) solferino, fuschsine; solferino red.

sôlha (*f.*, *Zool.*) plaice, flounder, flatfish (*Pleuronectes*).— **-reis**, sturgeon.

sôlho (*m.*) = SOALHO.

solicitação (*f.*) solicitation; request; entreaty; (*pl.*) demands, duties, obligations; unwelcome invitations.

solicitador –dora (*adj.*) soliciting; (*m.*) solicitor (legal agent).

solicitante (*m.,f.*) solicitant, petitioner; applicant.

solicitar (*v.t.*) to solicit, seek, endeavor to obtain; to ask, request (earnestly, urgently); to petition, apply for; to draw on, out, together, etc., by physical attraction, force, or means; (*v.i.*) to tout for; to serve as a solicitor or legal agent.—**a** or **para**, to press, urge, appeal to; to tempt, lure on; to incite. —**a** or **de**, to ask of.

solícito –ta (*adj.*) solicitous, helpful, anxiously willing;

apprehensive (of, about), concerned (about, for); careful.

solicitude (*f.*) solicitude, care, concern; carefulness; eagerness.

solidão (*f.*) solitude, isolation; seclusion; lonely place; wilderness.

solidar (*v.t.*) to solidify; to corroborate.

solidariedade (*f.*) solidarity; sympathy, condolence.

solidário –ria (*adj.*) characterized by, or manifesting, solidarity; sympathetic, understanding.

solidéu (*m.*) skullcap; woman's small hat.

solidez [ê] (*f.*) solidity; strength.

solidificação (*f.*) solidification.

solidificar (*v.t.*) to solidify; (*v.r.*) to set (harden).

sólido –da (*adj.*) solid, hard; dense, compact; strong; substantial; (*Printing*) unleaded; (*m.*) a solid.—**de revolução**, (*Math.*) solid of revolution.

solidônia (*f.*, *Bot.*) a spiderling (*Boerhaavia*), c.a. PEGA-PINTO.

soliloquiar (*v.i.*) to soliloquize.

solilóquio (*m.*) soliloquy.

solimão (*m.*, *colloq.*) corrosive sublimate, bichloride of mercury; by ext., any deadly poison.

solinhar (*v.t.*) to hew (stone, wood, etc.) to the line.

sólio (*m.*) throne; fig., regal power.

solipa (*f.*) = CHULIPA.

solípede (*adj.*) solipedal, solidungulate; (*m.pl.*) the Solidungula (horses, zebras, asses).

solipsimo (*m.*, *Philos.*) solipsism.

solista (*m.,f.*) soloist.

solitário –ria (*adj.*) solitary, lonely; secluded; desolate; unsociable; (*m.*) hermit; solitaire (piece of jewelry, but not the card game, which is PACIÊNCIA); (*f.*) tapeworm (*Taenia*); a solitary cell.

solito –ta (*adj.*) = SÓZINHO.

sólito –ta (*adj.*) wonted, accustomed.

solitude (*f.*) = SOLIDÃO.

solo (*m.*) soil; solo (performance, flight, card game).

sol-pôsto (*m.*) sunset.

solsticial (*adj.*) solstitial.

solstício (*m.*) solstice.

sôlta (*f.*) see under SÔLTO.

soltar [24] (*v.t.*) to loosen, unloose, unfasten, untie; to let loose, let go, free; to release, slacken; to release, relinquish; to unfurl (sails); to let out (a cry, groan, etc.); (*v.r.*) to get loose.—**a língua**, to loosen the tongue.—**a rédea**, to slacken the reins.—**as asas a**, to give wings to (imagination).—**a trela a**, to slip the leash of.—**a voz**, to give voice.—**piadas**, to wisecrack.—**suspiros**, to let out sighs. —**uma risada**, to let out a laugh, give way to laughter.

solteira (*f.*) see under SOLTEIRO.

solteirão (*m.*) a confirmed bachelor.

solteiro –ra (*adj.*) single, unmarried; (*m.*) a bachelor; (*f.*) a spinster; a fish c.a. XARELETE; another called GUAIVIRA.

solteirona (*f.*) old maid.

sôlto –ta (*adj.*) loose, free.—**de língua**, glib; indiscreet. **dormir a sono**—, to sleep like a log. **verso**—, blank verse; (*f.*) a hobble (for a horse); feed pasture; act of freeing. **à**—, foot-loose. **às sôltas**, at large, on the loose.

soltura (*f.*) act of loosening or setting free; loose behavior. —**de ventre**, loose bowels, diarrhea.

solubilidade (*f.*) solubility.

solubilizar (*v.t.*) to solubilize.

soluçante (*adj.*) sobbing; hiccuping.

solução (*f.*) solution; solving (of a problem); explanation, elucidation; dissolution.

soluçar (*v.i.*) to sob; to hiccup; of ship or waves, to toss, heave.

solucionar (*v.t.*) to solve; to work out.

soluço (*m.*) hiccup; sob; a tossing or heaving (of ship or waves).

solutivo –va (*adj.*) solvent.

soluto –ta (*adj.*) loose; dissolved; (*m.*, *Physical Chem.*) solute.

solúvel (*adj.*) soluble; solvable; resolvable.

solvabilidade (*f.*) solvability; solubility.

solvável (*adj.*) = SOLVÍVEL.

solvência (*f.*) solvency.

solvente (*adj.; m.*) solvent (person, action).

solver (*v.t.*) to solve, explain; to resolve; to dissolve; to liquidate (an obligation).

solvível (*adj.*) solvent (financially).

som (*m.*) sound; noise; voice. **em alto e bom**—, loud and clear.

soma (*f.*) sum, sum total; amount; (*Biol.*) soma.

somar (*v.t.*) to add (up, up to). **máquina de—**, adding machine.
somático **-ca** (*adj.*) somatic.
somatógeno **-na** (*adj.*, *Biol.*) somatogenic.
somatologia (*f.*) somatology.
somatológico **-ca** (*adj.*) somatologic(al).
somatopleura (*m.*, *Embryol.*) somatopleure.
sombra (*f.*) shade, shadow; darkness; trace, tinge; a "has been"; phantom; bodyguard; light-shade. **à—**, in the shade (**de**, of); (*colloq.*) in jail. **de boa—**, pleasant-looking. **de má—**, evil-looking. **na—**, (*colloq.*) in hock. **nem por—**, not by the remotest chance.
sombral (*m.*) shady place.
sombreado **-da** (*adj.*) shady.—**por árvores**, shaded by trees; (*m.*) shading (in a picture).
sombrear (*v.t.*) to shade, screen; to darken.
sombreireiro **-ra** (*m.*) one who makes or sells SOMBREIROS; (*f.*) hat box.
sombreiro **-ra** (*adj.*) shade-giving; (*m.*) shady tree, wall, etc.; a broad-brimmed hat.
sombrejar (*v.t.*) to shade.
sombrinha (*f.*) small parasol; (*pl.*) magic lantern pictures.
sombrio **-bria** (*adj.*) somber, shady, shadowy; dark, dim, gloomy, dismal; overcast; glum, sullen, morose, grim, frowning; melancholy, depressing; (*m.*) the yellowish pipit (*Anthus lutescens*), c.a. SOMBRIA, COTOVIA, PERUINHO-DO-CAMPO.
sombroso **-sa** (*adj.*) somber; shady.
someiro (*m.*, *Arch.*) impost of an arch; wind chest of an organ.
somenos (*adj.*) ordinary, inferior, of little worth. **de—**, unimportant.
sòmente (*adv.*) only, merely, solely.—**isso?** Is that all? **não—**, not only.
somiticaria, somitiquice (*f.*) stinginess.
somítico **-ca** (*adj.*) stingy, miserly; (*m.*) miser [= AVARO].
somito (*m.*, *Anat.*, *Zool.*) somite.
somos, form of SER [76].
sonâmbula (*f.*) see under SONÂMBULO.
sonambular (*v.i.*) to somnambulate, walk when asleep.
sonambulismo (*m.*) somnambulism, sleepwalking.
sonâmbulo **-la** (*adj.*) somnambulistic; (*m.*,*f.*) somnambulist, sleepwalker; (*f.*, *Bot.*) = AÇAFROEIRA-DA-TERRA.
sonância (*f.*) sonance.
sonante (*adj.*) sonant. **moeda—**, coins.
sonata (*f.*, *Music*) sonata; (*colloq.*) catnap, snooze.
sonatina (*f.*, *Music*) sonatina.
sonda (*f.*) sounding lead; plummet; (*Surg.*) sound, probe; catheter; a sounding; a probe (investigation); a well drill or drilling rig (as for oil).
sondá (*f.*) a long, heavy fishing line.
sondagem (*f.*) a sounding; act of sounding out; a "feeler"; drilling (as for oil).
sondar (*v.t.*) to sound, fathom; to probe; to sound out; to test, try; to drill (as for oil).
sondareza [ê] (*f.*) sounding line.
sondável (*adj.*) soundable; fathomable.
soneca (*f.*) a nap, forty winks. **tirar uma—**, to take a snooze.
sonegação, sonega (*f.*) dishonest concealment (as of taxable income); a holding out (as of taxes); theft.
sonegado **-da** (*adj.*) purloined, filched; (*m.pl.*) items wrongfully concealed or withheld (as from an inventory).
sonegador **-dora** (*adj.*; *m.*,*f.*) that, or one who, conceals, withholds, purloins, etc. See the verb SONEGAR.
sonegamento (*m.*) = SONEGAÇÃO.
sonegar (*v.t.*) to conceal, suppress, withhold (taxes, property) with wrongful intent; to purloin, filch; (*v.r.*) to dodge (duty, orders).
soneira (*f.*) = SONOLÊNCIA.
sonet[e]ar (*v.i.*) to write sonnets.
sonetista (*adj.*) sonnet-writing; (*m.*,*f.*) sonneteer.
sonêto (*m.*) sonnet.
songamonga (*m.*, *f.*) a sly, cunning person; a dissembler.
songuinha (*m.*,*f.*) a slyboots.
sonhado **-da** (*adj.*) dreamed of, longed for; unreal, fancied.
sonhador **-dora** (*adj.*) dreaming; dreamy; (*m.*,*f.*) dreamer.
sonhar (*v.i.*) to dream; to imagine, fancy.—**com**, to dream about (of); to wish for.
sonho (*m.*) dream; reverie, fantasy; a kind of cruller.—**acordado**, day dream.—**de ópio**, pipe dream.—**s de ouro**,

golden dreams; also, a wild coffee (*Psychotria gardneriana*).
sônico **-ca** (*adj.*) sonic.
sonido (*m.*) sound; noise.
sonífero **-ra** (*adj.*) somniferous; (*m.*) a soporific.
soniloquo (*m.*), **-qua** (*f.*) one who talks while asleep.
sono (*m.*) sleep, slumber.—**cheio**, sound sleep.—**crepuscular**, twilight sleep.—**da morte**, the sleep of death.—**das plantas**, (*Plant Physiol.*) nyctitropism.—**de chumbo**, leaden sleep.—**do repouso**, eternal rest.—**dos justos**, the sleep of the just.—**dos mortos**, the sleep of the dead.—**do trespasse**, the sleep of death.—**do túmulo**, the sleep of the grave.—**estival**, (*Zool.*) estivation.—**eterno**, eternal sleep.—**hibernal**, (*Zool.*) hibernation.—**inquieto**, restless sleep.—**leve**, light sleep. **com—**, sleepy, drowsy. **conciliar o—**, to fall asleep. **doença do—**, sleeping sickness. **dormir à—sôlto**, to sleep like a log. **ferrar no—**, to fall sound asleep. **pegar no—**, to fall asleep. **sem—**, sleepless. **ter—**, to be sleepy.
sonolência (*f.*) somnolence, sleepiness, drowsiness.
sonolento **-ta** (*adj.*) somnolent, sleepy, drowsy.
sonometria (*f.*, *Acoustics*) audiometry.
sonômetro (*m.*, *Acoustics*) audiometer.
sonoridade (*f.*) sonority.
sonoro **-ra** (*adj.*) sonorous; vibrant; (*Phonetics*) sonorant, sonorous.
sonorosidade (*f.*) sonorousness.
sonoroso **-sa** (*adj.*) sonorous
sonsice (*f.*) wile, guile, cunning [= SONSA]
sonsinho **-nha** (*adj.*) wily, cunning
sonso **-sa** (*adj.*) sly, wily, cunning, artful; (*f.*) wile, guile, cunning [= SONSICE]
sopa [ô] (*f.*) soup; sop; a bus (in northeastern Brazil); (*slang*) cinch, pushover.—**juliana**, or—**de legumes**, vegetable soup. **Do prato à bôca se perde a—**, There's many a slip 'twixt the cup and the lip.
sopapear (*v.t.*) to slap, buffet, cuff.
sopapo (*m.*) a slap, blow [= BOfETÃO].
sopé (*m.*) foot, base, bottom.—**de montanha**, foot of a mountain.
sopear (*v.t.*) to trample under foot; to check, rein; to repress.
sopeiro **-ra** (*adj.*) pert. to soup; fond of soup; (*m.*,*f.*) one who is fond of soup; (*f.*) soup tureen.
sopesar (*v.t.*) to weigh by hand; to heft; to balance in the hand.
sopetear (*v.t.*) to sop, "dunk" (bread, etc.).
sopitado **-da** (*adj.*) drooping; drowsy; effeminate
sopitar (*v.t.*) to put to sleep, lull, quiet; to quell; to repress; to weaken, enfeeble; to raise hopes.
sopor (*m.*) sopor, lethargic sleep; stupor.
soporativo **-va**, **soporífero** **-ra**, **soporífico** **-ca** (*adj.*; *m.*) soporific.
soporizar (*v.*) = SOPITAR.
soprador **-dora** (*adj.*) blowing; (*m.*,*f.*) blower.
sopramento (*m.*) a blowing.
soprano (*m.*) soprano (voice or singer); treble; (*f.*) a woman soprano.—**ligeiro**, coloratura soprano. **meio—**, mezzo-soprano.
soprar (*v.t.*) to blow on (out, up).—**a**, to whisper (something) to someone; to prompt (a student); (*v.i.*) to blow.
sôpro (*m.*) puff, whiff, breath; aura; a blowing; blast, gust.—**anfórico**, (*Med.*) amphoric respiration.—**no coração**, heart murmur, **instrumento de—**, wind instrument.
soquear (*v.t.*) to sock (hit with the fist); to pound.
soqueira (*f.*) brass knuckles; sugar cane stumps left in the ground after harvesting, and from which new plants will sprout.
soquete [quê] (*m.*) ramrod; socket wrench; paver's beetle; tamper; a light jab; socket of a light bulb or radio tube; (*colloq.*) meat stew; ankle-length sock.
soquetear (*v.t.*) to tamp, pound.
S.or = SÊNIOR (Senior).
Sor. = SOROR (Sister).
sorbato (*m.*, *Chem.*) sorbate.
sórbico **-ca** (*adj.*; *Chem.*) sorbic.
sorbita (*f.*, *Metal.*) sorbite.
sorbitol (*m.*, *Chem.*) sorbitol.
Sorbona (*f.*) Sorbonne.
sorda [ô] (*f.*) a dish of manioc meal mixed with beef juice and eggs
sordícia, -cie (*f.*) = SORDIDEZ.
sordidez[a] [ê] (*f.*) sordidness; squalor.

sórdido -da (*adj.*) sordid, filthy; nasty; low, vile; squalid; niggardly.

sorgo [ô] (*m.*) sorghum.—**-de-alepo**, Johnson grass (*Sorghum halepense*), c.a. MAÇAMBARÁ.—**-de-vassoura**, little bluestem grass (*Andropogon scoparius*).

sorites (*m., Logic*) sorites.

sôrna (*adj.*) indolent, sluggish; (*m.,f.*) lazy person; (*f.*) indolence, sluggishness.

soro [só] (*m., Bot.*) sorus.

sôro (*m.*) serum.—**do leite**, whey.

soroca (*f.*) a cave-in; jaguar's lair.

sorocabano -na (*adj.*) of or pert. to the city of Sorocaba in the state of São Paulo; (*m.,f.*) a native or inhabitant of that city; [*cap.*] (*f.*) short for ESTRADA DE FERRO SOROCABANA (Sorocabana Railway).

sorocabuçu [çú] (*m.*) a large cave-in.

sorologia (*f.*) serology.

sorologista (*m.,f.*) serologist.

sorongo (*m.*) a Brazilian negro dance of African origin.

soror [-es] (*f.*) Sister (nun).

sororó (*m., slang*) death rattle; the Spanish mackerel (*Scomberomorus maculatus*), c.a. CAVALA-PINTADA, SARDA, SERRA-PINIMA, and (when young) ESCALDA-MAR.

sorose (*f., Bot.*) sorosis.

soroso -sa (*adj.*) serous.

sorrateiro -ra (*adj.*) sly, sneaky.

sorrelfa (*f.*) false pretense, duplicity; (*m.,f.*) skinflint. **olhar à—**, to look askance at. **pela**, or **à—**, underhandedly; secretly; on the sly.

sorridente (*adj.*) smiling, cheery, gay, in good spirits.

sorrilho (*m.*) = CANGAMBÁ.

sorrir [73] (*v.i.*) to smile (**a**, upon; **de**, at); (*v.r.*) to smile.—**amarelo**, to give a sickly smile.

sorriso (*m.*) smile.—**amarelo**, sickly smile.

sorte (*f.*) fate, destiny; fortune, lot; mode, manner; sort, kind.—**grande**, grand prize. **A—está lançada**, The die is cast. **andar com falta de—**, to be down on one's luck. **arriscar**, or **experimentar, a—**, to try one's luck, take a chance. **Cabra de—**! (*slang*) You lucky dog! **com—**, lucky. **dar—**, to bring good luck. **de—que**, so that. **de tal —que**, in such a way that. **estar com** (or **em**)—, to be in luck. **estar de pouca—**, to be down on one's luck. **falta de—**, no luck. **má—**, bad luck. **maré de—**, wave of good luck; bonanza. **por—**, [chosen] by lot. **Sujeito de—**! Lucky stiff! **Tem muita—em estar vivo**, He is lucky to be alive. **Tenha boa—**! Good luck to you! **tentar a—**, to try one's luck. **tirar a—**, to draw lots; toss a coin. **tirar a—grande**, to win the grand prize; to hit the jackpot. **tôda—**, all kinds. **uma—**, godsend, windfall.

sorteado -da (*adj.*) chosen by lot; assorted. **ser—**, to be drafted (for military service); (*m.*) a conscript, "draftee".

sorteamento (*m.*) = SORTEIO.

sortear (*v.t.*) to cast or draw lots; to allot; to raffle.

sorteio (*m.*) a raffle or other drawing of lots.—**militar**, draft, selective service.

sortido -da (*adj.*) stocked; assorted; (*m.*) = SORTIMENTO; (*f.*) sortie.

sortilégio (*m.*) sortilege; sorcery.

sortílego (*m.*) sorcerer.

sortimento (*m.*) assortment.

sortir (*v.t.*) to supply, provide (**de**, with); to mix, vary (colors, goods, etc.).

sorubim (*m.*) = SURUBIM.

soruma (*f.*) = DIAMBA.

sorumbático -ca (*adj.*) melancholy, sad, somber; glum, gloomy; moody.

sôrva (*f.*) fruit of the SORVEIRO.—**-do-peru**, a starapple (*Chrysophyllum excelsum*).

sorvar (*v.i.,v.r.*) of fruit, to begin to spoil.

sorvedouro (*m.*) whirlpool, maelstrom, vortex.

sorveira (*f.*) the servicetree mountainash (*Sorbus domestica*); the couma sorva or cow tree (*Couma utilis*).

sorver (*v.t.*) to sip; to suck up (down); to absorb.

sorvetaria (*f.*) = SORVETERIA.

sorvete [vê] (*m.*) sherbet; ice cream.—**de casquinha**, ice-cream cone.

sorveteira (*f.*) ice-cream freezer.

sorveteiro (*m.*) ice-cream peddler.

sorveteria (*f.*) ice-cream shop.

sôrvo (*m.*) sip; gulp; draught; also = SORVEDOURO.

sós, a—, quite alone; by oneself.

sósia (*m.*) double, counterpart (of another person).

soslaio (*m.*) obliquity. **de—**, aslant, obliquely, sideways, askance.

sossega (*f.*) act of tranquilizing.

sossegado -da (*adj.*) quiet, calm, peaceful, tranquil.

sossegador -dora (*adj.*) tranquilizing.

sossegar (*v.t.*) to quiet, tranquilize, lull; (*v.i.,v.r.*) to grow quiet.

sossêgo (*m.*) quiet, calm, tranquility; act of tranquilizing.

sosso [sôs] (*m.*) stone used in building a dry-masonry wall.

sota (*f.*) queen (of cards); spell (period of rest); (*pl.*) the lead horses; (*m.*) coachman; outrider. **dar— e ás**, to outwit, outsmart.

sotaina (*f., Eccl.*) soutane; cassock; (*colloq.*) a priest.

sótão [-ãos] (*m.*) attic, garret. **macaquinhos no—**, bats in (one's) belfry.

sota-pilôto (*m.*) second pilot.

sota-proa (*m., Rowing*) the number two oarsman.

sotaque (*m.*) foreign accent.

sotaventear (*v.t., Naut.*) to steer leeward; (*v.i.*) to fall off to leeward [= SULAVENTEAR].

sota-vento (*m., Naut.*) lee [= SULAVENTO]. **a—**, leeward.

sota-voga (*m., Rowing*) the oarsman next to the stroke.

sotéia (*f.*) roof terrace [= AÇOTÉIA].

soterrado -da (*adj.*) buried in the earth.

soterramento (*m.*) burial.

soterrâneo -nea (*adj.*) subterranean [= SUBTERRÂNEO.]

soterrar (*v.t.*) to bury in the ground.

sotilicário (*m.*) a penguin (*Aptenodytes demersa*).

soto-capitão (*m., Naut.*) first mate, second in command.

soto-mestre (*m., Naut.*) undermaster.

soto-ministro (*m.*) steward in a monastery.

sotopor [63] (*v.t.*) to put under; to omit; to postpone.

sotoposto -ta (*p.p. of* SOTOPOR) placed beneath.

sotreta (*adj.; m.*) no-good (thing, animal, or person).

soturnidade, soturnez (*f.*) saturninity.

soturno -na (*adj.*) saturnine, gloomy, moody; morose; taciturn; doleful; silent, secretive.

sou, form of SER [76].

soub+verb endings, forms of SABER [74].

soutien (*m.*) brassière [= PORTA-SEIOS].

souto (*m.*) coppice.

sova (*f.*) a beating, drubbing, thrashing; (*colloq.*) hard wear.

sovaco (*m.*) armpit [= AXILA].

sovado -da (*adj.*) beaten, battered; tired, worn out.

sovaqueira (*f.*) armpit [= SOVACO]; underarm perspiration or its odor; (*Veter.*) cinch gall.

sovaquinho (*m.*) disagreeable underarm odor.

sovar (*v.t.*) to knead; to belabor, beat, lambaste; (*colloq.*) to subject to hard wear.

sovela (*f.*) shoemaker's awl; broach; a bird called AL-FAIATE; a mosquito of genus *Culex*, c.a. MURIÇOCA, PERERECA. **a—**, bristling.

sovelar (*v.t.*) to pierce with an awl.

sovereiro (*m.*) = SOBREIRO.

sovi [í] (*m., Zool.*) a pileated tinamou (*Crypturellus soui*); the plumbeous kite (*Ictinia plumbea*), c.a. GAVIÃO-POMBO.

soviético -ca (*adj.*) sovietic.

sovietismo (*m.*) sovietism, Bolshevism.

sovina (*adj.*) mean, niggardly; closefisted; (*m.,f.*) tightwad, skinflint; (*f.*) a wooden pin; a pointed instrument.

sovinar (*v.t.*) to pierce, as with an awl; to annoy.

sovinice (*f.*) meanness; stinginess.

sòzinho -nha (*adj.*) all alone, quite alone.

SP = SÃO PAULO (State of).

speiss (*m., Metal.*) speiss.

sperrilita (*f., Min.*) sperrylite.

SPI = SERVIÇO DE PROTEÇÃO AOS ÍNDIOS (Indian Welfare Service).

spiegeleisen (*m., Metal.*) spiegeleisen.

squiascópio (*m., Med.*) skiascope.

squíatron, squiatrônio (*m., Elec.*) skiatron.

S.R. = SUA RESIDÊNCIA (your residence).

Sr. = SENHOR (Mr.).

Sr.ª = SENHORA (Mrs.).

S. Rev.ª = SUA REVERÊNCIA (His Reverence).

Sr.ta = SENHORITA (Miss).

SS. = SANTÍSSIMO -MA (Most Holy).

S.S. = SUA SANTIDADE (His Holiness).

S.S.ª = SUA SENHORIA (His Lordship).

SS.AA. = SUAS ALTEZAS (Their Highnesses).

SS.AA.II. = SUAS ALTEZAS IMPERIAIS (Their Imperial Highnesses).
SS.AA.RR. = SUAS ALTEZAS REAIS (Their Royal Highnesses).
S.S.E. = SU-SUESTE (south-southeast).
SS.MM. = SUAS MAJESTADES (Their Majesties).
SS.MM.II. = SUAS MAJESTADES IMPERIAIS (Their Imperial Majesties).
S.S.W. or **S.S.O.** = SU-SUDOESTE (south-southwest).
stefanita (*f., Min.*) stephanite.
STF = SUPREMO TRIBUNAL FEDERAL (Federal Supreme Court).
stolzita (*f., Min.*) stolzite.
sua, fem. of SEU.
suã (*f.*) loin of pork; the dried backbone of a pig or other small animal, used as a whip.
suaçu [çú] (*m.*) a Tupian word meaning deer—used alone or in combination.
suaçuapara (*m.*) a small, white-spotted deer (*Odocoileus suacuapara*), c.a. CARIACU, VEADO-GALHEIRO, VEADO-DO(S)-MANGUE(S).
suaçucatinga (*m.*) = CATINGUEIRO.
suaçupita (*m.*) = VEADO-MATEIRO.
suaçutinga (*m.*) = CATINGUEIRO.
suadela (*f.*) act of sweating.
suado –da (*adj.*) wet with sweat; designating something achieved after much effort.
suador –dora (*adj.*) sweating; (*adj.; m.*) sudorific.
suadouro (*m.*) act of sweating; a spell of sweating; a sudorific; saddlecloth; horse's back.
suante (*adj.*) sweating.
suão (*m.*) a hot south wind.
suar (*v.i.*) to sweat; to toil, drudge; (*v.t.*) to exude. [The noun sweat is SUOR].—**em bicas,** to sweat copiously.—**sangue,** to sweat blood (fig.).
suarda (*f.*) suint; yolk (in sheep's wool).
suarento –ta (*adj.*) sweaty, sweat-covered.
suasivo –va, **suasório** –ria (*adj.*) = PERSUASIVO.
suástica (*f.*) swastika.
suave (*adj.*) suave, pleasant; mild, sweet; soft, gentle; soothing.
suavidade (*f.*) suave or smoothly agreeable quality (of persons, manner, etc.); sweetness and gentleness of nature; kindness of spirit; pleasantness, charm, grace, of voice and manner; loveliness, beauty, harmony, of form and color; inward joy and peace of mind.
suavizar (*v.t.*) to assuage, soothe, allay, ease.—**a voz,** to soften the voice.
subácido –da (*adj.*) subacid.
subaéreo –rea (*adj.*) subaerial.
subagente (*m.*) subagent.
subagudo –da (*adj.*) subacute.
subalimentação (*f.*) undernourishment.
subalimentado –da (*adj.*) underfed, undernourished.
subalimentar (*v.t.*) to underfeed, undernourish.
subalterno –na (*adj.*) subaltern; subordinate; inferior; secondary; (*m.*) a subaltern.
subaquático –ca (*adj.*) subaquatic, underwater.
subáqüeo –qüea (*adj.*) subaqueous.
subarbusto (*m.*) subshrub, undershrub.
subarrendador –dora (*adj.*) subletting; (*m.,f.*) sublessor; sublessee.
subarrendamento (*m.*) a subletting.
subarrendar (*v.t.*) to sublet, sublease.
subarrendatário –ria (*m.,f.*) sublessee.
subatômico –ca (*adj., Chem., Phys.*) subatomic.
subaxilar [ks] (*adj., Bot.*) subaxillary.
sub-bibliotecário –ria (*m.,f.*) assistant librarian.
subcarbonato (*m., Chem.*) subcarbonate.
subcarbonífero –ra (*adj., Geol.*) subcarboniferous.
subcaudal (*adj., Zool.*) subcaudal.
subcaulescente (*adj., Bot.*) subcaulescent.
subchefe (*m.*) subchief.
subclasse (*f.*) subdivision.
subclavicular (*adj., Anat.*) subclavian.
subcloreto (*m., Chem.*) subchloride.
subcomissão (*f.*) subcommission.
subcomissário (*m.*) subcommissioner.
subconsciência (*f.*) subconsciousness.
subconsciente (*adj.; m.*) subconscious.
subcontratar (*v.t.*) to subcontract.
subcorrente (*f.*) undercurrent.
subcostal (*adj., Anat., Zool.*) subcostal.
subcutâneo –nea (*adj.*) subcutaneous.

subdelegação (*f.*) subdelegation.
subdelegado (*m.*) subdelegate.
subdiácono (*m.*) subdeacon.
subdiretor (*m.*) subdirector; assistant manager.
súbdito –ta (*adj.; m.,f.*) = SÚDITO.
subdividido –da (*adj.*) subdivided.
subdividir (*v.t.*) to subdivide.
subdivisão (*f.*) subdivision.
subentender (*v.t.*) to perceive, understand; to suppose.
subentendido –da (*adj.*) implied; (*m.*) implication.
súber (*m., Bot.*) suber, cork tissue.
suberato (*m., Chem.*) suberate.
subérico –ca (*adj., Chem.*) suberic.
suberina (*f., Biochem.*) suberin.
suberite (*f., Zool.*) a genus (*Suberites*) of sponges.
suberização (*f., Bot.*) suberization.
suberizar (*v.t.*) to suberize.
suberoso –sa (*adj.*) suberose, having a corky tissue.
subescapular (*adj., Anat.*) subscapular.
subespécie (*f.*) subspecies.
subestação (*f.*) substation.
subestimar (*v.t.*) to underestimate, underrate.
subestrutura (*f.*) substructure, understructure.
subfamília (*f.*) subfamily.
subgênero (*m., Biol.*) subgenus.
subgerente (*m.,f.*) assistant manager.
subgrupo (*m.*) subgroup.
subículo (*m., Bot.*) subiculum.
subida (*f.*) see under SUBIDO.
subideira (*f.*) = ARAPAÇU-GRANDE.
subido –da (*adj.*) high, lofty; sublime; great; high-priced; (*f.*) ascent; upward slope, up grade.
subimento (*m.*) ascent; increase; excess.
subinflamação (*f.*) mild inflammation.
subinspetor (*m.*) subinspector.
subinte (*adj.*) climbing, ascending.
subir [22] (*v.i.*) to climb, mount, ascend (**a, até, para,** to; **por,** by); to rise; (*v.t.*) to climb, go up; to raise, elevate.—**a (na, pela) escada,** to climb the stairs.—**a fêsto,** to go straight up.—**a serra,** (*colloq.*) to get on one's high horse.—**ao trem,** to board the train.—**ao trono,** to mount the throne.—**de preço,** to go up in price.—**no bonde,** to board the streetcar.—**no conceito público,** to rise in public esteem.—**os preços,** to up the prices.—**para,** to go on or into (a vehicle).—**-se a um cavalo,** to get up on a horse.
subitanteidade (*f.*) suddenness.
subitâneo –nea (*adj.*) = SÚBITO.
súbitas, used in the phrase **a**—, suddenly.
súbito –ta (*adj.*) sudden; unexpected; (*m.*) something sudden or unexpected; a sudden attack; (*adv.*) **de**—, suddenly.
subjacente (*adj.*) underlying.
subjetivar (*v.t.*) to subjectivize.
subjetividade (*f.*) subjectivity.
subjetivismo (*m., Metaph.*) subjectivism.
subjetivo –va (*adj.*) subjective.
subjugação (*f.*) subjugation.
subjugador –dora (*adj.*) subjugating; (*m.,f.*) subjugator.
subjugante (*adj.*) subjugating, dominating.
subjugar (*v.t.*) to subjugate, conquer, subdue; to overcome; to subject; (*v.r.*) to contain oneself; to subject oneself (**a,** to).
subjuntivo –va (*adj.*) subjunctive; (*m.*) subjunctive mood; (*f.*) subjunctive vowel.
sublevação [sub-le] (*f.*) uprising, insurrection; upheaval.
sublevar [sub-le] (*v.t.*) to raise up; to stir up revolt; (*v.r.*) to rise up, revolt.
sublimação (*f.*) sublimation.
sublimado –da (*adj.*) sublimate; (*m., Chem.*) a sublimate.—**corrosivo,** corrosive sublimate.
sublimar (*v.t.*) to sublimate; (*v.r.*) to become sublime, exalted.
sublimatório (*m., Chem.*) sublimatory.
sublime (*adj.*) sublime, exalted, lofty, noble; (*m.*) the sublime.
sublimidade (*f.*) sublimity.
sublinear [sub-li] (*adj.*) sublinear.
sublingual [sub-lin] (*adj., Anat.*) sublingual.
sublinha [sub-li] (*f.*) an underline.
sublinhar [sub-li] (*v.t.*) to underline, underscore; to emphasize.
sublocação [sub-lo] (*f.*) sublease; act of subletting.
sublocador –dora [sub-lo] (*m.,f.*) sublessor.

sublocar [sub-lo] (v.t.) to sublet, sublease.
sublocatário -ria [sub-lo] (m.,f.) sublessee.
sublunar [sub-lu] (adj.) sublunary.
submarginal (adj., Zool., Bot.) submarginal.
submarinho –nha (adj.; m.) = SUBMARINO.
submarinista (m.) submariner.
submarino –na (adj.) submarine, undersea, underwater; (m.) submarine, undersea boat. caça—, sub-chaser.
submaxilar [ks] (adj., Anat.) submaxillary.
submental (adj., Anat., Zool.) submental.
submergido –da (adj.) submerged; submersed.
submergir [24] (v.t.) to submerge, submerse; to sink; to deluge, inundate; to drown; (v.i.,v.r.) to submerge; to sink.
submergível, submersível (adj.) submersible; (m.) submarine.
submersão (f.) submersion.
submerso –sa (irreg. p.p. of SUBMERGIR) submerged; sunken.
submeter (v.t.) to subdue.—a, to submit (something) to (someone, for approval, etc.); (v.r.) to submit (oneself; a, to); to knuckle under; to yield.
submicroestrutura (f., Metal.) submicroscopic structure.
subministrar (v.t.) to supply; furnish.
submissão (f.) submission, yielding; obedience, acquiescence; submissiveness.
submisso –sa (adj.) submissive, compliant; obedient, resigned.
submucoso –sa (adj., Anat.) submucous; (f.) submucosa.
submúltiplo –pla (adj., m.) submultiple.
subnasal (adj.) subnasal.
subnitrato (m., Chem.) subnitrate.
subnormal (f., Geom.) subnormal.
subnutrição (f.) undernourishment.
subnutrido –da (adj.) undernourished, underfed.
subnutrir (v.t.) to undernourish, underfeed.
suboccipital (adj., Anat.) suboccipital.
subocular (adj., Anat., Zool.) subocular.
suboficial (m.) petty officer; noncommissioned officer.
suborbicular (adj., Anat., Zool.) suborbital.
subordem (f.) suborder.
subordinação (f.) subordination; subservience.
subordinado –da (adj.) subordinate, subsidiary, dependent, inferior, secondary; (m.) subordinate; underling; (f., Gram.) subordinate clause.
subordinar (v.t.) to subordinate, subject, make subservient; (v.r.) to submit, yield.
subornação (f.), subornamento (m.) = SUBÔRNO.
subornador –dora (adj.) suborning; (m.,f.) suborner.
subornar (v.t.) to suborn.
subôrno (m.) subornation; bribery; graft.
subóxido [ks] (m., Chem.) suboxide.
subparágrafo (m.) subparagraph.
subperitoneal (adj., Anat., Med.) subperitoneal.
subprefeito (m.) subprefect.
subprefeitura (f.) subprefecture.
subproduto (m.) subproduct, byproduct.
sub-repção (f.) subreption.
sub-reptício –cia (adj.) subreptitious; surreptitious.
sub-rés-do-chão (m.) basement.
sub-rogação (f.) subrogation; surrogation.
sub-rogado –da (adj.) surrogate.
sub-rogar (v.t.) to subrogate; surrogate.
subscrever [44] (v.t.,v.i.) to subscribe; to underwrite; (v.r.) to sign one's name.
subscrição (f.) subscription.
subscritar (v.t.) to subscribe, sign.
subscritor –tora (m.,f.) subscriber, signer. [But not subscriber to periodical, which is ASSINANTE.]; underwriter.
subse[c]ção (f.) subsection.
subsecretário –ria (m.,f.) subsecretary.
subseqüência (f.) subsequence; sequel.
subseqüente (adj.) subsequent, following, ensuing.
subserviência (f.) subservience.
subserviente (adj.) subservient, obsequious, servile.
subsidiado –da (adj.) subsidized.
subsidiar (v.t.) to subsidize.
subsidiário –ria (adj.) subsidiary.
subsídio (m.) subsidy; allowance; lawmaker's salary.
subsistência (f.) subsistence.
subsistente (adj.) subsistent.
subsistir (v.i.) to subsist, exist; to obtain a livelihood; to persist, endure.—de, to live on (off of).

subsolo (m.) subsoil, substratum; underground construction.
substabelecer (v.t.) to substitute; to subrogate.
substância (f.) substance, essence.
substancial (adj.) substantial.
substancialidade (f.) substantiality.
substancioso –sa (adj.) substantial; nourishing.
substantivar (v.t.) to change into, or use as, a substantive, or noun.
substantivo –va (adj.; m.) substantive.
substituição [u-i] (f.) substitution, exchange, replacement.
substituído –da (m.,f.) one who has been replaced by another.
substituinte [u-ín] (adj.) substituting; (m.,f.) one who replaces another.
substituir [72] (v.t.) to substitute; to replace; to supersede; to supplant.—a, com, em, por, to put (something or someone) in the place of; to substitute (something or someone) by or with, instead of for (something or someone) [—vinho por cerveja means to take beer instead of wine, not the opposite, as in English]. (v.r.) to replace oneself by, or be put in place of, another.
substituto –ta (adj.; m.,f.) substitute; makeshift.
substrução (f.) substructure, underpinning, foundation.
subtrutura (f.) understructure.
subtangente (f., Geom.) subtangent.
subtendente (adj.) subtendent; (m.) chord of an arc.
subtender (v.t.) to subtend.
subtensa (f.) chord of an arc.
subterfúgio (m.) subterfuge, evasion, pretext.
subterrâneo –nea (adj.) subterranean, underground; (m.) subway (underground railway); subterranean cave.
subtérreo –rea (adj.) subterraneous.
subtil (adj.) & derivs. = SUTIL & DERIVS.
subtipo (m.) subtype.
subtítulo (m.) subtitle.
subtração (f.) subtraction; a theft.
subtraendo (m., Math.) subtrahend.
subtrair [75] (v.t.) to subtract, take away; to embezzle.—-se a, to escape from, avoid.
subtrativo –va (adj.) subtractive.
subtribu (f.) subtribe.
subtropical (adj.) subtropical.
subulado –da (adj., Bot., Zool.) subulate, awl-shaped.
suburbano –na (adj.) suburban.
subúrbio (m.) suburb; (pl.) outskirts.
subvenção (f.) subvention.
subvencionar (v.t.) to grant a subvention to; to subsidize.
subversão (f.) subversion, overthrow, upset.
subversivo –va (adj.) subversive.
subverter (v.t.) to subvert, overturn, destroy, overthrow, upset; to pervert.
suc. = SUCURSAL (branch); SUCESSOR(ES), (successor(s).
sucapé (m.) = CAPIM-PUBA.
sucata (f.) scrap iron.
su[c]ção (f.) suction.
sucedâneo –nea (adj.) substitute; (m.) succedaneum, substitute.
suceder (v.i.) to happen, occur, befall, betide, take place, come to pass.—a, to succeed, follow, come after; to take the place of. suceda o que—, come what may. sucede que, it (so) happens that.
sucedido –da (adj.) that occurred; (m.) an occurrence, happening, incident [= SUCESSO]. bem-—, successful. mal-—, unsuccessful.
sucessão (f.) succession; happening.
sucessivamente (adv.) successively; seriatim.
sucessivo –va (adj.) successive, sequent, consecutive.
sucesso (m.) event, occurrence; result, outcome; success, favorable issue; prosperity.
sucessor –sora (adj.) succeeding, following; (m.,f.) successor, follower, heir.
súcia (f.) gang, band, mob (of thieves, etc.).
sucinato (m., Chem.) succinate.
sucínico –ca (adj., Chem.) succinic [acid].
sucinita (f., Min.) succinite.
súcino (m.) succin, amber.
sucinto –ta (adj.) succinct; terse.
súcio (m.) rascal; a no-good.
suco (m.) juice; sap; (slang) anything that is "swell".
sucoso –sa (adj.) juicy, succulent.
súcrase (f.) invert sugar.
sucrosa (f.) sucrose, cane sugar, saccharose.

suçuarana (f.) puma, cougar (*Puma concolor*).
súcubo (m.) succubus.
sucuíba (f., *Bot.*) a frangipani (*Plumeria phagedenica*).
suculência (f.) succulence.
suculento -ta (adj.) succulent; luscious.
sucumbido -da (adj.) depressed, discouraged.
sucumbir (v.i.) to succumb, yield, submit; to give in; to die.
sucupira (f.) any of various timber trees of the pea family, esp.—**amarela** (*Bowdichia nitida*), c.a. SICUPIRA-AMARELA, SUPUPIRA-DA-MATA, whose wood of rich dark brown with light streaks is used for fine furniture, pianos, etc. [The furniture, fixtures and interior trim of the municipal library in São Paulo are of this wood.]— **-do-campo**, is the alcornoco (*Bowdichia virgiloides*) whose bark is used as a remedy for consumption; c.a. SUCUPIRAÇU, SUCUPIRA-BRANCA, SUCUPIRA-DA-PRAIA, SAPUPIRA-DO-CAMPO.
sucuri [i] (f.) the South American anaconda or water boa (*Eunectes murinus*), c.a. SUCURIJU, SUCURIÚ, SUCURUJU, SUCURUJUBA, BOIUNA, BOIÇÚ, BOI-AÇU, BOI-GUAÇU, VIBORÃO, BOITIAPÓIA, etc. [Although it is the second largest of world snakes (the Regal Python of Malasia being first) it does not attain a proven length of more than 25 ft., contrary to popular belief which attributes to it twice that many.]—**amarela**, the yellow anaconda (*Eunectes notaeus*).—**de-galha-preta** = CORTA-GAROUPA (a shark).
sucursal (f.) branch (of a business); (adj.) succursal.
sucuru [rú] (m.) = JOÃO-BÔBO.
sucussão (m.) succussion.
sucutuba (adj.; *colloq.*) succulent; good.
sudação (*Med.*) diaphoresis; sweating.
sudanês -nêsa (adj.; m.,f.) Sudanese.
Sudão (m.) Sudan.
sudário (m.) sweat cloth; burial shroud.
sudatório -ria (adj.) = SUDORÍFERO.
sudeste (adj.; m.) = SUESTE.
súdito -ta (adj.) subject (under the power or dominion of another); (m.,f.) subject (one owing allegiance to a sovereign power); vassal. Var. SÚBDITO.
sudoestada (f.) strong southwest wind.
sudoeste (adj.; m.) southwest.
sudorífero -ra (adj.) sudoriferous; (m.) a sudorific agent.
sudorífico -ca (adj.; m.) sudorific.
sudoríparo (adj.) sudoriparous.
sué (f.) a tomato (*Lypersicon luberosum*).
suécio -cia (adj.) Swedish [iron]; (f.) smith's swage block; [*cap.*] Sweden.
sueco -ca (adj.) Swedish; (m.,f.) a Swede; (m.) Swedish language.
sueira (f., *colloq.*) hard work.
suelto (m.) brief paragraph on editorial page [= VÁRIA and TÓPICO].
suestada (f.) strong southeast wind.
sueste (adj.; m.) southeast; (m.) southeast wind; sou'wester (hat).
suéter (m.) sweater.
suf. = SUFIXO (suffix).
suficiência (f.) sufficiency, adequacy; ability, capacity; self-sufficiency, self-importance.
suficiente (adj.) sufficient, adequate, enough, ample; able, competent.
sufixar [ks] (v.t.) to suffix.
sufixo [ks] (m.) suffix.
sufocação (f.) suffocation.
sufocador -dora, **sufocante** (adj.) suffocating; sweltering.
sufocar (v.t.,v.i.) to suffocate; to stifle; (v.t.) to strangle to death; (v.r.) to strangle, choke.
sufocativo -va (adj.) suffocative.
sufragâneo -nea (adj.; m., *Eccl.*) suffragan.
sufragar (v.t.) to vote for; to side with; to pray or give alms for the dead.
sufrágio (m.) suffrage, vote, voting; approval; intercessory prayer.
sufragista (adj.; m.,f.) suffragist; (f.) suffragette.
sufumigar (v.t.) to suffumigate.
sufusão (f., *Med.*) suffusion.
sugação (f.) act of sucking.
sugador -dora (adj.) sucking; (m.,f.) sucker.
sugadouro (m.) insect's proboscis.
sugar (v.t.) to suck (up); to bleed, extort money from.
sugerir [21A] (v.t.) to suggest, recommend; to hint at.
sugerível (adj.) that can or may be suggested.

sugestão (f.) suggestion, hint, reminder.
sugestibilidade (f.) suggestibility.
sugestionador -dora (m.,f.) one who suggests or inspires
sugestionamento (m.) act of suggesting.
sugestionante (adj.) that suggests.
sugestionar (v.t.) to influence by suggestion.
sugestionável (adj.) suggestible, easily influenced by suggestion.
sugestivo -va (adj.) suggestive.
suiá (m.,f.) an Indian of the Suya, a tribe of the Northwestern Ge on the upper Xingu River; (adj.) pert. to or designating this tribe.
suíça(s), see under SUÍÇO.
suicida [u-i] (m.,f.) one who commits suicide; (adj.) suicidal.
suicidar-se [u-i] (v.r.) to commit suicide.
suicídio [u-i] (m.) suicide; self-destruction.
suíço -ça (adj.; m.,f.) Swiss; (f.pl.) side whiskers; [f., *cap.*] Switzerland.
suídeos (m.pl.) the Suidae (swine family).
suiná (f., *Bot.*) the common coralbean (*Erythrina corallodendron*), c.a. CORTICEIRA.
suiná [u-i], **suinara** [u-i], **suindá** [u-in], **suindara** [u-in] (f.) all names for the Brazilian barn owl (*Tyto perlata*), c.a. CORUJA-DAS-TORES, SONDAIA.
suíno -na (adj.) swinish; (m.) a hog.
suinocultor [u-i] (m.) hog raiser.
suinocultura [u-i] (f.) hog raising.
suiriri [rirí] (m.) the fire-crowned tyrant (*Machetornis rixosa*), c.a. SUIRIRI-DO(S)-CAMPO(S), BEM-TE-VI-DE-COROA; the yellow-browed tyrant (*Satrapa icterophrys*), c.a. SUIRIRI-AMARELO.
suíte (f., *Music*) suite; (m., *slang*) **dar o**—, to scram, get away.
sujar (v.t.) to soil, dirty, stain; to pollute, defile, sully; (v.i.) to defecate.
sujeição (f.) subjection; submission; bondage.
sujeira (f.) filth, dirt; low behavior.
sujeita (f.) see under SUJEITO.
sujeitador -dora (adj.; m.,f.) that, or one who, subjects, etc.; —see the verb SUJEITAR.
sujeitar [24] (v.t.) to subject, subdue, subjugate; to dominate; to subordinate; (v.r.) to submit, yield (**a**, to).
sujeito -ta (*irreg. p.p. of* SUJEITAR) subjected, enslaved; submissive; subject to, exposed, liable; (m.) fellow, "guy," "customer"; subject (of a state); topic, subject-matter; (*Gram.*) subject.—**de sorte!** Lucky dog!— **estranho**, queer fellow.—**original**, a "character". **bom**—, good fellow (not a bad sort). **certo**—, a certain (unnamed) person. (f.) a colloquial and somewhat derogatory term for an unnamed woman. **aquela**—, that hussy. **uma**—**qualquer**, some dame or other.
sujidade (f.) dirt, filth; foul matter.
sujo -ja (adj.) soiled, dirty, grimy; slovenly, untidy; foul, nasty; untrustworthy; (m.) second growth (on cleared land); (*colloq.*) the Devil. **O**—**ri-se do mal-lavado**, The pot calls the kettle black.
sul (m.) south; south wind; (adj.) south, southern.
sula (f., *Bot.*) sulla sweetvetch (*Hedysarum coronarium*).
sul-americano -na (adj.; m.,f.) South American.
sulão (m.) = SULVENTO.
sulaque (m.) steam chest (of a steam engine).
sulaventear (v.i., *Naut.*) to fall off to leeward [= SOTA-VENTAR].
sulavento (m.) = SOTA-VENTO.
sulcar (v.t.) to plow, make furrows in; to wrinkle (the brow); to groove.—**os mares**, to plow the oceans.
sulco (m.) furrow; groove; rut; wrinkle; wake, trail; river bed.—**de roda**, wheel rut.
suleiro -ra (adj.; m.,f.) = SULISTA.
sulfácido (m., *Chem.*) sulphacid.
sulfanilimida (f., *Pharm.*) sulphanilimide.
sulfapiridina (f., *Pharm.*) sulphapyridine.
sulfarseniato (m., *Chem.*) sulpharseniate.
sulfarsênico -ca (adj., *Chem.*) sulpharsenic.
sulfarsenieto (m., *Chem.*) sulpharsenite.
sulfarsenioso -sa (adj., *Chem.*) sulpharsenious.
sulfatação (f.) sulphation (on the plates of a storage battery).
sulfatar (v.t.) to spray (plants) with copper sulphate.
sulfatiazol (m., *Pharm.*) sulphatiazole.
sulfatizar (v.t.) to sulphate.
sulfato (m.) sulphate.—**de alumínio**, aluminum sulphate, alunogenite.—**de amônio**, ammonium sulphate.—**de**

bário, barium sulphate, barite.—**básico de chumbo**, basic lead sulphate, lanarkite.—**de cádmio**, cadmium sulphate.—**de cálcio**, calcium sulphate; gypsum.—**de chumbo**, lead sulphate, anglesite.—**de cobalto**, cobalt sulphate.—**de cobre**, copper sulphate, blue vitriol, bluestone.—**dimetílico**, methyl sulphate.—**de estrôncio**, strontium sulphate, celestite.—**férrico**, ferric sulphate.—**ferroso**, ferrous sulphate, melanterite, copperas.—**de magnésio**, magnesium sulphate, epsom salt, epsomite.—**manganoso**, manganese sulphate.—**de metilo**, methyl sulphate.—**de níquel**, nickel sulphate.—**de sódio**, sodium sulphate; Glauber's salt.—**de tálio**, thallium sulphate.—**de zinco**, zinc sulphate.

sulfêto (*m.*) sulphide.—**de amônio**, ammonium sulphide.—**de antimônio**, antimony trisulphide, stibnite, antimony glance.—**de arsênico**, arsenic sulphide, orpiment, king's gold.—**de bário**, barium monosulphide.—**de cádmio**, cadmium sulphide; greenockite; orient yellow; aurora yellow.—**de hidrogênio**, hydrogen sulphide, sulphuretted hydrogen.—**de prata**, silver sulphide, acanthite.—**vermelho de mercúrio**, red mercuric sulphide, cinnabarite, chinese red, vermillion.

sulfidrato (*m.*) hydrosulphide.
sulfídrico –**ca** (*adj.*, *Chem.*) hydrosulphuric.
sulfito (*m.*) sulphite.—**de cálcio**, calcium sulphite.—**de sodio**, sodium sulphite.
sulfobenzóico –**ca** (*adj.*) sulphobenzoic [acid].
sulfocianeto (*m.*) sulphocyanide.
sulfonato (*m.*) sulphonate.
sulfônico –**ca** (*adj.*) sulphonic.
sulfosol (*m.*) sulfosol, sodium sulphide.
sulfovínico –**ca** (*adj.*) sulphovinic [acid].
súlfur (*m.*) = ENXÔFRE.
sulfuração (*f.*) sulphuration.
sulfurar (*v.t.*) to sulphurate.
sulfúreo –**rea** (*adj.*) sulphureous.
sulfurêto (*m.*) = SULFÊTO.
sulfúrico –**ca** (*adj.*) sulphuric.
sulfurino –**na** (*adj.*) sulphur-yellow.
sulfuroso –**sa** (*adj.*) sulphurous.
sulimão (*m.*) = SOLIMÃO.
sulino –**na** (*adj.*; *m.*,*f.*) = SULISTA.
sulipa (*f.*) = CHULIPA.
sulista (*adj.*; *m.*,*f.*) (person) from southern Brazil (as opposed to NORTISTA].
sul-rio-grandense (*adj.*) of or pert. to Rio Grande do Sul; (*m.*,*f.*) a native or inhabitant of that state. Cf. GAÚCHO.
sultana (*f.*) sultana; the sultana bird (*Porphyrio*); the basketflower centaurea (*C. americana*); the sultan snapweed (*Impatiens sultani*).
sultanado (*m.*) sultanate.
sultão (*m.*) sultan.
sulvento (*m.*) south wind [= SUL, SULÃO].
suma (*f.*) summary; sum. **em**—, in short; briefly.
sumaca (*f.*) smack (fishing vessel); also = CHARQUE.
sumagre (*m.*, *Bot.*) Sicilian sumac (*Rhus coriaria*).
sumamente (*adv.*) supremely.
sumanta (*f.*, *colloq.*) a beating or trouncing [= SURRA].
sumaré (*m.*) an orchid (*Cyrtopodium punctatum*), c.a. BISTURI-DO-MATO, RABO-DE-TATU.—**de-pedras**, is *C. andersoni*.
sumarento –**ta** (*adj.*) juicy [= SUMOSO, SUCOSO].
sumàriamente (*adv.*) summarily.—**vestida**, scantily dressed.
sumariar (*v.t.*) to summarize.
sumário –**ria** (*adj.*) summary, brief, concise; without delay or formality; (*m.*) a summary or summation.
sumaúma, **sumaumeira** [a-u] (*f.*) the kapok ceiba or silk-cotton tree (*Ceiba petandra*). Cf. PAINEIRA.—**do-igapó** = BUTUÁ-DE-CORVO.
sumauveira (*f.*) = CORTICEIRA.
sumbaré (*m.*, *colloq.*) dalliance, courtship [= NAMORO].
sumiço (*m.*), **sumição** (*f.*) disappearance.
sumidade (*f.*) highness; summit.—**s médicas**, medical authorities.
sumidiço –**ça** (*adj.*) that disappears easily.
sumido –**da** (*adj.*) disappeared; low (not loud); hidden, sunk; tenuous; faint. **olhos**—**s**, hollow eyes.
sumidouro, **sumidoiro** (*m.*) sinkhole; drain, gutter, sewer; also = ITARARÉ.
sumidura (*f.*) = SUMIÇO.
sumir [22] (*v.t.*) to cause to vanish; to submerge; to hide; to squander; (*v.r.*) to vanish, disappear; to fade away;

to drop out of sight; (*colloq.*) to scram. **Suma-se daqui!** Get out of here!
sumo –**ma** (*adj.*) highest, supreme; paramount.—**sacerdote**, high priest; (*m.*) juice [= SUCO]; the summit.
SUMOC= SUPERINTENDÊNCIA DA MOEDA E DO CRÉDITO (Superintendency of Money and Credit).
sumoso –**sa** (*adj.*) = SUMARENTO.
sumpes (*m.*, *colloq.*) shindig, hoedown [= ARRASTA-PÉ].
sumptuário –**ria** (*adj.*) = SUNTUÁRIO.
sumptuosidade (*f.*) = SUNTUOSIDADE.
sumptuoso –**sa** (*adj.*) = SUNTUOSO.
súmula (*f.*) summary, brief, résumé.
sunga (*f.*) bloomers for a child; swim trunks.
sungar (*v.t.*) to hitch up (pants, skirt); to lift (something which has slipped down); to snuffle (instead of blowing the nose).
suntuário –**ria** (*adj.*) sumptuary. Var. SUMPTUÁRIO.
suntuosidade (*f.*) sumptuousness. Var. SUMPTUOSIDADE.
suntuoso –**sa** (*adj.*) sumptuous, costly; luxurious; gorgeous. Var. SUMPTUOSO.
suor [ó] (*m.*) sweat, perspiration; (*colloq.*) hard work.—**de alambique**, (*colloq.*) rum [= CACHAÇA].—**frio**, cold sweat. "**sangue,—e lágrimas,**" "blood, sweat and tears." [The verb is SUAR.]
sup. = SUPERLATIVO (superlative).
sup.e = SUPLICANTE (suppliant).
supedâneo (*m.*) footstool.
superabundância (*f.*) superabundance; oversupply.
superabundante (*adj.*) superabundant, excessive.
superabundar (*v.i.*) to superabound.
superacidez [ê] (*f.*) excessive acidity.
superado –**da** (*adj.*) outdone, etc. See the verb. **ser**—, to come off second-best.
superalimentar (*v.t.*) to supercharge (a motor); to overfeed.
superante (*adj.*) surpassing; excelling.
superaquecer (*v.t.*) to superheat; to overheat.
superaquecimento (*m.*) overheating.
superar (*v.t.*) to outdo, outrival, outstrip, "beat", surpass; to surmount, triumph over; to overcome, conquer.
superável (*adj.*) superable, surmountable; that can be beaten (outdone).
superavit (*m.*) surplus (on a balance sheet).
superciliar (*adj.*, *Anat.*, *Zool.*) superciliary.
supercílio (*m.*) eyebrow. [*Poetical*]
supercilioso –**sa** (*adj.*) having thick eyebrows; supercilious.
supercompressor (*m.*) supercharger.
superdimensionado –**da** (*adj.*) oversized.
superestimar (*v.t.*) to overrate.
superestrutura (*f.*) superstructure.
superexcitar (*v.*) = SOBREEXCITAR.
superfetação (*f.*, *Physiol.*, *Bot.*) superfetation.
superficial (*adj.*) superficial; perfunctory; shallow, frivolous; slight.
superficialidade (*f.*), –**lismo** (*m.*) superficiality, shallowness.
superfície (*f.*) surface, exterior, face, area.—**de reação**, (*Aeron.*) airfoil.
superfino –**na** (*adj.*) superfine.
superfluidade [u-i] (*f.*) superfluity.
supérfluo –**flua** (*adj.*) superfluous, needless, useless.
superfosfato (*m.*) superphosphate.
superheteródino –**na** (*adj.*; *Radio*) superheterodyne.
super-homem (*m.*) superman.
superintendência (*f.*) superintendence, -cy.
superintendente (*adj.*; *m.*,*f.*) superintendent.
superintender (*v.t.*) to superintend, supervise, manage.
superior (*adj.*; *comp. of* ALTO) superior, higher, better, greater, ultra.—**a**, above. **leito**—, upper berth. (*m.*) superior (person higher in rank); head of a monastery.
superiora (*f.*) mother superior.
superioridade (*f.*) superiority.
superlativo –**va** (*adj.*; *m.*) superlative.
superlotar (*v.t.*) to overload; overcrowd.
supermercado (*m.*) supermarket.
superno –**na**, **supernal** (*adj.*) supernal.
superpopulação (*f.*) over-population.
superpor (*v.*) = SOBREPOR.
superprodução (*f.*) overproduction.
super-realismo (*m.*) surrealism.
super-realista (*adj.*; *m.*,*f.*) surrealist.
super-regeneração (*f.*, *Radio*) superregeneration.

supersaturação (*f.*) supersaturation [= SÔBRE-SATU-RAÇÃO].
supersaturar (*v.t.*) to supersaturate [= SÔBRE-SATURAR].
supersensível (*adj.*) supersensible.
supersônico –ca (*adj.*) supersonic.
superstição (*f.*) superstition.
supersticiosidade (*f.*) superstitiousness.
supersticioso –sa (*adj.; m.,f.*) superstitious (person).
supérstite (*adj.*) surviving.
superstrutura (*f.*) superstructure.
superumeral (*adj.*) superhumeral.
supervenção (*f.*) supervention.
superveniência (*f.*) supervenience.
superveniente (*adj.*) supervenient.
supervisionar (*v.t.*) to supervise.
supervivência (*f.*) = SOBREVIVÊNCIA.
supervivente (*adj.; m.,f.*) = SOBREVIVENTE.
supetão, used only in the expression **de—**, all of a sudden.
supimpa (*adj.; colloq.*) splendid, excellent, "swell" [= ÓTIMO].
supinação (*f., Physiol.*) supination.
supinador (*m., Anat.*) supinator.
supino –na (*adj.*) supine.
supl.= SUPLEMENTO (supplement).
suplantar (*v.t.*) to supplant, replace, supersede; to crush (grapes) with the feet.
suplementar (*adj.*) supplementary; additional.
suplementário –ria (*adj.*) supplementary.
suplemento (*m.*) supplement; addendum.
suplente (*adj.*) substituting; (*m.,f.*) substitute, proxy, alternate; pinch hitter.
súplica, suplicação (*f.*) supplication, prayer, entreaty; petition, appeal.
suplicante (*adj.*) suppliant (*m.,f.*) supplicant, suitor, petitioner; (*m., colloq.*) John Doe.
suplicar (*v.t.,v.i.*) to supplicate, entreat.
suplicatório –ria (*adj.*) supplicatory; (*f.*) entreaty; petition.
súplice (*adj.*) suppliant, imploring, beseeching, pleading.
supliciado –da (*adj.*) punished, executed; (*m.*) an executed criminal.
supliciar (*v.t.*) to punish, execute; to torture.
suplício (*m.*) torture; death sentence, capital punishment.
supor [63] (*v.t.*) to suppose, presuppose, presume, take for granted.
suportar (*v.t.*) to support; to bear (weight), hold up; to tolerate, put up with; to suffer, undergo, endure, withstand; to bear up under. [To support in the sense of providing for is SUSTENTAR; to substantiate is CORROBORAR; to aid, abet, back is PATROCINAR.]
suportável (*adj.*) supportable, endurable, bearable, toler-.able.
suporte (*m.*) support, prop, brace. [But not support in the sense of sustenance, which is SUSTENTO, nor of backing, which is APOIO.]—**do mancal**, bearing base.—**de motor**, motor base.
suposição (*f.*) supposition, surmise, conjecture; assumption.
supositício –cia, **supositivo** –va (*adj.*) supposititious, sham, feigned; supposed.
supositório (*m., Med.*) suppository.
suposto –ta (*adj.*) supposed, imagined; reputed; bogus; (*m.*) supposition; (*conj.*)—**que**, even supposing, even if, although, granting that.
supra-auricular (*adj.; Zool.*) supra-auricular.
supra-axilar [ks] (*adj.; Bot.*) supra-axillary.
suprabranquial (*adj.; Zool.*) suprabranchial.
supracaudal (*adj.; Zool.*) supracaudal.
supracitado –da (*adj.*) above-mentioned.
supraclavícula (*f., Zool.*) supraclavicle.
supraclavicular (*adj.; Anat.*) supraclavicular.
supracomissura (*f., Anat.*) supracommissure.
supracondução (*f., Elec.*) supraconduction.
supracondutor (*m., Elec.*) supraconductor.
supradito –ta (*adj.*) = SOBREDITO.
supradorsal (*adj.; Zool.*) supradorsal.
supralabial (*adj.; Anat., Zool.*) supralabial.
supralateral (*adj.; Zool.*) supralateral.
supraliminal (*adj.; Psychol.*) supraliminal.
supramaxilar [ks] (*adj.; Anat.*) supramaxillary.
supramental (*adj.; Anat.*) supramental.
supramolecular (*adj.*) supramolecular.
supramundano –na (*adj.*) supramundane.
supranasal (*adj.; Anat., Zool.*) supranasal.

supranatural (*adj.*) supranatural.
supranaturalismo (*m.*) supranaturalism.
supranaturalista (*m.,f.*) supranaturalist.
supranumerado –da (*adj.*) above-numbered.
supranumerário –ria (*adj.; m.,f.*) supernumerary.
supraoccipital (*adj.; Anat., Zool.*) supraoccipital.
supraocular, supraorbital (*adj.; Anat., Zool.*) supraocular; supraorbital.
supra-realismo (*m.*) = SUPER-REALISMO.
supra-realista (*adj.; m.,f.*) = SUPER-REALISTA.
supra-renal (*adj.; Anat.*) suprarenal, adrenal.
supra-renina (*f., Pharm., Biochem.*) adrenaline.
suprascâpula (*f., Zool.*) suprascapula.
suprascapular (*adj.; Anat., Zool.*) suprascapular.
supra-sensível (*adj.*) = SUPERSENSÍVEL.
supraspinal (*adj.; Anat.*) supraspinal.
supra-segmental (*adj.; Anat.*) suprasegmental.
supra-solar (*adj.; Astron.*) suprasolar.
supra-sumo (*m.*) the height, the peak (of anything).
supratemporal (*adj.*) Zool.) supratemporal.
supratonsilar (*adj.; Anat.*) supratonsilar.
supraversão (*f., Anat.*) supraversion.
supravital (*adj.; Biol.*) supravital.
supremacia (*f.*) supremacy.
supremo –ma (*adj.*) supreme, highest, utmost, paramount; (*m., colloq.*) Supreme Court.
supressão (*f.*) suppression. Verb: SUPRIMIR.
supresso –sa, irreg. p.p. of SUPRIMIR.
supressor –sora [ô] (*adj.*) suppressive; (*m.*) suppressor.
supressivo –va, **supressor** –sora, **supressório** –ria (*adj.*) suppressive.
supridor –dora (*adj.*) supplying; (*m.,f.*) supplier.
suprimento (*m.*) supply(ing); supplement.—**em dis-ponibilidade**, available supply. [Verb: SUPRIR.]
suprimir (*v.t.*) to suppress, hold back, keep from appearing; to eliminate, do away with, abolish; to silence.
suprir (*v.t.*) to supply; to make up for, take the place of.
suprível (*adj.*) suppliable.
supupara (*f., colloq.*) rum [= CACHAÇA].
supuração (*f.*) suppuration.
supurante (*adj.*) suppurating.
supurar (*v.i.,v.t.*) to suppurate.
supurativo –va, **supuratório** –ria (*adj.; m.*) suppurative.
sura (*f.*) calf of leg; fermented palm juice; (*adj.*) fem. of SURU.
sural (*adj.; Anat.*) sural.
surdear (*v.i.*) to play deaf.
surdescente (*adj.*) deafening.
surdez [ê] (*f.*) deafness.
surdina (*f., Music*) mute. **à (em, na)—**, softly, quietly; in a whisper; on the sly.
surdir (*v.i.*) to issue (forth); of water, to well up.
surdo –da (*adj.*) deaf; muffled, quiet; dulled; implacable, inflexible; (*Phonet.*) surd, voiceless; (*m.,f.*) deaf person.
surdo-mudez [ê] (*f.*) deaf-muteness.
surdo-mudo –da (*adj.; m.,f.*) deaf-mute.
surgidouro, –doiro (*m.*) anchorage.
surgir [24] (*v.i.*) to arise, appear, loom; to spring up, crop up; to emerge.—**à mente**, to come to mind.
suri [i] (*adj.*) tailless [= SURU]; sleeveless.
suro –ra, **surote** (*adj.*) = SURU.
surpreendente (*adj.*) surprising, remarkable, extraordinary, wonderful, astonishing.
surpreender (*v.t.*) to surprise, take unawares; to astonish, astound, amaze; (*v.r.*) to be surprised. **surpreendido com a bôca na botija**, caught redhanded.
surprêso –sa (*adj.*) surprised, astonished; (*f.*) surprise, astonishment, amazement; unexpected occurrence. **de—**, unawares.
surra (*f.*) a beating; a thrashing; a spanking.—**de língua**, a tongue lashing.
surrado –da (*adj.*) threadbare, worn-thin, seedy; "corny"; beaten, thrashed; curried [leather].
surrador –deira (*adj.*) thrashing, beating; tanning; (*m.,f.*) thrasher; currier.
surrão (*m.*) shepherd's leather bag; filthy person; filthy garment. **arrastar—**, (*colloq.*) to bluster.
surrar (*v.t.*) to curry (leather); to beat, thrash, whip; (*v.r.*) of garments, to wear thin.
surrealismo (*m.*) = SUPER-REALISMO.
surrealista (*adj.; m.,f.*) = SUPER-REALISTA.
surriada (*f.*) volley; foam of breakers; (*colloq.*) taunt.
surribar (*v.t.*) to cultivate the soil.
surripiar, surripilhar (*v.t.*) to purloin, pilfer, filch, "swipe".

surro (*m.*) grime; filth; trash.

surrupiar (*v.*) = SURRIPIAR.

surtida (*f.*) sortie, sally, dash.

surtir (*v.t.*) to cause, occasion, give rise to, bring about. —**bem** (**mal**), to turn out well (badly).—**efeito**, to produce the desired result.

surto **-ta** (*adj.*) at anchor; (*m.*) burst (of interest, enthusiasm); flight, soaring (of ambition); outbreak (of an epidemic).

suru (*adj.*) tailless; bobtailed; (*m.*) a kite without a tail.

suruanã (*f.*) the large green or scaly marine turtle, (*Chelonia mydas*).

suruba (*adj.*) good; strong; (*f.*) a big walking stick.

surubim, surubi (*m.*) "an edible fish (*Platystoma fasciatum*) which weighs as much as 20 kilos; it can be caught both by net and by line and is an excellent source of food." [*GBAT*]. C.a. LOANDO, LOANGO, PINTADO, PIRACAMBUCU.

surucuá (*m.*, *Zool.*) any of a number of trogons.—**de-barriga-amarela**, the green-backed trogon (*Trogon strigilatus*), c.a. PERUA-CHOCA; the orange-breasted trogon (*Trogonurus aurantius*), both of southeastern and southern Brazil.—**de-barriga-vermelha**, the surucura trogon (*Trogonurus surrucura*) of southern Brazil; the black-tailed trogon (*Curucuius melanurus*) of northern Brazil; the black-throated trogon (*Trogonurus curucui*) of northeastern to southern Brazil; and the purple-breasted trogon (*Trogonurus variegatus*) of northeastern to southern Brazil, c.a. PERUA-CHOCA, DORMINHOCO.

surucucu [cucú] (*m.*) the bushmaster (*Lachesis muta*), a spectacular and highly dangerous equatorial viperine snake. It attains a length of 12 ft. and is the largest of the poisonous snakes in Brazil. Other common names are: SURUCUCU-PICO-DE-JACA, SURUCUTINGA, SURURUCUTINGA, URICANA.—**de-patioba**, or—**pindoba**, or—**pinta-de-ouro**, a 3 ft. green pit viper (*Bothrops bilineatus*), one of the JARARACAS, c.a. COBRA-VERDE, COBRA-PAPAGAIO, JURICANA, PATIOBA, PARÁ-AMBÓIA.—**do-pantanal** = BOIPEVAÇU.—**dourado**, or—**tapete**, = JARARACUÇU.

suruje (*m.*) termite mound.

surumbamba (*m.*) brawl; riot.

sururina (*f.*) the pileated tinamou (*Crypturus soui*), a partridgelike bird, c.a. TURIRI.

sururu [rurú] (*m.*) an edible mussel (*Mytilus falcatus*), c.a. SIRIRI; also = BACUCU; (*colloq.*) brawl, riot; roughhouse; fracas.

sururuca (*f.*) a coarse sieve; a passionflower.

sururucurana (*f.*) = COBRA-D'ÁGUA.

Sus! (*interj.*) Courage! Take heart!

susceptância (*f.*, *Elec.*) susceptance.

susce[p]tibilidade (*f.*) susceptibility; touchiness.

susce[p]tibilizar (*v.t.*) to offend slightly; (*v.r.*) to feel offended.

susce[p]tível (*adj.*) susceptible; touchy.—**de**, capable of; admitting of; (*m.,f.*) a touchy person.

suscitação (*f.*) arousal, stimulation, etc., See the verb.

suscitar (*v.t.*) to excite, rouse, stimulate.—**dúvidas**, to raise doubts.

suserania (*f.*) suzerainty.

suserano (*m.*) suzerain.

suspeição (*f.*) suspicion.

suspeita (*f.*) see under SUSPEITO.

suspeitar (*v.t.*) to suspect, distrust; to surmise, conjecture.

suspeito **-ta** (*adj.*) suspect, regarded with suspicion; disreputable; (*m.,f.*) one who is suspect; (*f.*) suspicion, distrust, misgiving; surmise, guess, "hunch". **afastar**—**s**, to allay suspicion. **campo para**—**s**, ground for suspicion.

suspeitoso **-sa** (*adj.*) suspicious, distrustful; also = SUSPEITO.

suspender [24] (*v.t.*) to hang (**de**, from); to interrupt, discontinue, leave off; to dismiss temporarily; to stop temporarily; to delay, postpone.—**a sessão**, to adjourn the meeting.—**o passo**, to halt one's steps.—**os pagamentos**, to stop payments.—**se dos lábios de alguém**, to hang on another's every word.

suspensão (*f.*) suspicion, hanging; interruption, suspense; delay, postponement; abeyance; cessation; temporary dismissal (as from a job).—**de armas**, suspension of fighting, armistice.—**de Cardan**, Cardan's suspension (as for a magnetic needle).—**de garantias**, suspension of civil rights (as during an insurrection).—**de pagamentos**, stoppage of payments (as due to bankruptcy).—**de roda**, (*Autom.*) wheel suspension.

suspensivo **-va** (*adj.*) suspensive.

suspenso **-sa** (*irreg. p.p. of* SUSPENDER) suspended, hanging; interrupted; stopped; delayed. **em**—, in suspense, in abeyance.

suspensório **-ria** (*adj.; m.*) suspensory; (*m.pl.*) suspenders.

suspicácia (*f.*) distrust; wariness.

suspicaz (*adj.*) suspicious, questionable; distrustful.

suspirado **-da** (*adj.*) sighed for, longed for.

suspirar (*v.t.,v.i.*) to sigh (**por**, for); to pine (**por**, for).

suspiro (*m.*) sigh; vent in a cask; breather vent (as in the crankcase of a motor); a dainty made of white of egg and sugar; (*Bot.*) sweet scabiosa (*S. atropurpurea*), c.a. ESCABIOSA, PERPÉTUA; (*pl.*) common four-o'clock (*Jalapa mirabilis*), c.a. BOAS-NOITES.

suspiroso **-sa** (*adj.*) sighing; lamenting.

sussurante (*adj.*) murmuring, whispering; purling, rippling; humming, droning.

sussurrar (*v.t.,v.i.*) to murmur, whisper; to rustle; to hum, drone; to ripple.

sussuro (*m.*) murmur; rustle; a humming or droning; act of whispering.

sustança, sustância (*f.*, *colloq.*) strength, vigor; elegance; also = SUBSTÂNCIA.

sustar (*v.t.*) to stop, arrest, halt; (*v.i.*) to stop.

sustenido (*m.*, *Music*) sharp.

sustentação (*f.*) act of sustaining or upholding; sustenance.

sustentáculo (*m.*) support, prop, stay.

sustentador **-dora** (*adj.*) sustaining, supporting; (*m.,f.*) sustainer, supporter.

sustentante (*adj.*) sustaining.

sustentar (*v.t.*) to sustain; to prop, uphold; to justify, confirm, establish; to maintain, defend; to endure, brave; to bear, suffer, undergo; to preserve, keep alive, to support, provide for; to nourish, supply with food; to strengthen, fortify, bolster, buttress; (*v.r.*) to maintain oneself (**a, em,** in [a given position]; **de, com,** with).

sustentável (*adj.*) sustainable, maintainable.

sustento (*m.*) sustenance, nourishment; support, maintenance.

suster [78] (*v.t.*) to sustain, hold up; to restrain, hold back; to restrict; (*v.r.*) to contain oneself.

susto (*m.*) scare, fright; fear.

sustoso **-sa** (*adj.*) fearful.

su-sueste (*adj.; m.*) south-southeast.

suta (*f.*) a bevel square; (*colloq.*) a surprise house-raising party or other neighborly "bee".

sutache (*m.*) braid.

sutambaque (*m.*) = SOBRECASACA.

sutar (*v.t.*) to join (pieces) by bevelling.

sutil [-tis] (*adj.*) subtle. Var. SUBTIL.

sútil [-teis] (*adj.*) done by stitching.

sutileza [ê], **sutilidade** (*f.*) subtlety; shade of meaning. Vars. SUBTILEZA, SUBTILIDADE.

sutilizar (*v.t.*) to subtilize, rarefy, refine; (*v.i.*) to use subtlety. Var. SUBTILIZAR.

sutinga (*f.*) a variety of manioc.

sutura (*f.*) suture; seam.

suturar (*v.t.*) to suture.

suxar (*v.t.*) to slacken, loosen.

suxo **-xa** (*adj.*) slack.

S.V. = SOTAVENTO (leeward).

S.W. or **S.O.** = SUDOESTE (southwest).

T

T, t, the 19th letter of the Port. alphabet.
T. = TARA (tare); TRAVESSA (Lane—name of a street).
t = TONELADA (ton).
t. = TÊRMO (term); TOMO (tome).
taba (*f.*) Indian settlement.
tabacal (*m.*) tobacco field.
tabacarana (*f.*) a knotweed (*Polygonum hispidum*) c.a.
FUMO-BRAVO-DO-AMAZONAS—yields a dyestuff; also
= QUITOCO.
tabacaria (*f.*) tobacco shop; cigar store.
tabaco (*m.*) tobacco; snuff [= RAPÉ].—**-bom** = BACURAU
(a nighthawk).—**-de-fôlha-larga,** common tobacco
(*Nicotiana tabacum*).—**-do-méxico,** or—**-de-fôlha-de-
couve,** Aztec tobacco (*Nicotiana rustica*).—**em fôlha,**
leaf tobacco.—**-indiano,** Indian-tobacco lobelia (*L.
inflata*).
tabagismo (*m., Med.*) tobaccoism.
tabaiacu [cú] (*m.*) long, low-lying reef [= TACI].
tabanídeo (*m.*) horsefly [= MUTUCA].
tabaque (*m.*) an Indian drum made from a piece of hollow
log, c.a. TAMBAQUE, CURIMBÓ, CURIMBU.
tabaquear (*v.t.,v.i.*) to take snuff; to smoke.
tabaqueiro –ra (*adj.*) tobacco; snuff; tobacco-using; snuff-
using; (*m.,f.*) one who uses tobacco or snuff; tobacco
pouch or horn; snuffbox; (*m., colloq.*) a wide nose; (*f.,
colloq.*) nostrils.
tabaquista (*m.,f.*) one who uses tobacco or snuff.
tabaréu (*m.*) raw recruit; greenhorn; rustic, "hick"
[= CAIPIRA].
tabaroa (*f.*) country woman.
tabatinga (*f.*) a certain type of variously-colored sedimentary clay, used in pottery; c.a. TAUATINGA, TOBA-
TINGA.
tabatingal (*m.*) a large area of TABATINGA.
tabe (*f., Med.*) tabes, locomotor ataxia.
tabebuia (*f.*) a trumpet tree (*Tabebuia spp.*).
tabefe (*m.*) a kind of custard; whey; (*colloq.*) blow, slap.
tabeira (*f., Arch.*) baseboard.
tabela (*f.*) table (of contents, etc.), list, chart, schedule;
billiard-table cushion; bulletin board.—**de horário,**
timetable. **por**—, indirectly.
tabelar (*adj.*) tabular; (*v.t.*) to list prices; to put on a
price list.
tabelião [-ães] (*m.*) notary public.
tabeliar (*v.i.*) to exercise the office of notary.
tabelioa (*adj.*) large, crude [handwriting]; usual, routine
[words, expressions, as in official documents]; (*f.*)
notary's wife.
tabelionado, –nato (*m.*) notary's office.
taberna (*f.*) low tavern [= BAIÚCA, BODEGA, LOCANDA,
TASCA]; cheap eating-place [= LOCANDA, TASCA]. Var.
TAVERNA.
tabernáculo (*m.*) tabernacle.
tabernal (*adj.*) tavern; filthy. Var. TAVERNAL.
tabernário –ria (*adj.*) tavern.
taberneiro –ra (*m.,f.*) tavernkeeper. Var. TAVERNEIRO.
tabes (*f.*) = TABE.
tabescente (*adj.*) tabescent.
tabético –ca (*adj.*) tabetic.
tabi [í] (*m.*) tabby, watered silk.
tabica (*f.*) a wedge inserted in the end of a log being sawed
lengthwise; a withe or slender switch; a bean pole (very
thin person).
tabicada (*f.*) a switching (birching).
tabicar (*v.t.*) to provide with a TABICA (wedge), or a
TABIQUE (partition wall).
tábido –da (*adj.*) rotten; tabid, tabescent.
tabique (*m.*) an indoor partition; (*Biol., Bot.*) septum.
tabla (*f.*) sheet, plate; (*adj.*) flat-cut [diamond].
tablada (*f.*) cattle fair.
tablado (*m.*) stage, dais; raised platform, scaffold; boxing
ring; bridge floor.
tablilha (*f.*) billiard-table cushion; fig., indirect method.
taboca (*f.*) any of several bamboos of the genus Guadua;
a carpenter ant (*Camponotus abdominalis*), c.a. JEJÁ; a
small retail store; a segment of bamboo filled with powder, for use in fireworks; (*slang*) a disappointment.—
-gigante, a large bamboo (*Guadua superba*) of the upper

Amazon region, whose stalks sometimes attain a height
of 20 meters and a diameter of from 15 to 20 cms; c.a.
TAQUARAÇU. "Stalks are employed as upright timbers,
forming part of house frames; for ladders and as con-
duits; raw material for wooden lathing, baskets and
light construction; cellulose for paper manufacture;
seeds edible and nutritious; the hollow interior of the
young stalks contains drinking water, which at times,
however, is a bit mucilaginous." [*GUAF*]
tabocal (*m.*) an area abounding in bamboo [= TAQUARAL].
tábola (*f.*) = TÁBULA.
taboquear (*v.t., colloq.*) to jilt; to deceive; to break one's
word to.
taboquinha (*f.*) a panic grass (*Panicum latifolia*); also
= CANA-DE-PASSARINHO.
tabu [ú] (*m.*) taboo; cane sirup spoiled in the processing;
also = TABUA (cattail).
tabua [ú] (*f., Bot.*) a cattail (*Typha dominguensis*), c.a.
PARTAZANA; a joint vetch (*Aeschynomene sp.*); a flatsedge (*Cyperus giganteus*) of the Amazon region.
tábua (*f.*) board; plank; table (of figures, prices, etc.); list,
chart, gaming table; the smooth flat side of the neck of a
horse or other animal; a fish c.a. GUAIVIRA; (*colloq.*) refusal of a marriage proposal.—**de abatimento,** or **de
bolina,** (*Naut.*) leeboard.—**de beira,** (*Carp.*) eaves board.
—**s de comutação,** (*Life Ins.*) commutation tables or
columns.—**de engomar,** ironing board.—**de harmonia,**
sounding board (of a piano).—**de mármore,** slab of
marble.—**de mesa,** leaf of a table.—**de multiplicação,**
multiplication table.—**de Pitágoras,** Pythagorean table.
—**de salvação,** fig., life preserver (last resort).—**rasa,** a
blank canvas; a tabula rasa; fig., an ignorant person.—**s
da Lei,** Tablets of the Law (Ten Commandments).—**s de
fôrro,** ceiling boards. **agarrar-se à primeira**—, to catch
at the first straw. **dar**—**a,** to jilt; to disappoint. **fazer**—
rasa, to wipe the slate clean; to turn over a new leaf.
levar—, to suffer a severe letdown.
tabuada (*f.*) table of figures; multiplication table; tabular
logarithms; (*colloq.*) list, index.
tabuado (*m.*) board floor; wooden partition.
tabual (*m.*) an area abounding in cattails.
tabuão (*m.*) plank, heavy board; foot bridge.
tabuinha [u-í] (*f.*) slat; (*pl.*) venetian blinds.
tabujajá (*m.*) a heron (*Ardea cocoi*), c.a. SOCOÍ.
tábula (*f.*) round piece used in playing checkers; formerly,
a table, esp. a gaming table [= TÁVOLA]
tabulado (*m.*) wooden partition; board flooring; an improvised stage.
tabulador (*m.*) tabulator key (of a typewriter).
tabular (*adj.*) tabular.
tabuleiro (*m.*) a tray, esp. one used by street venders;
chessboard; garden bed; cane field; a low, treeless tableland; salt pan; stair landing; floor of a bridge; "a high
beach, at times following the shore, at times in the middle of the river, where turtles deposit their eggs."
[*GBAT*].—**de instrumentos,** instrument panel.—**de
relva,** a lawn.—**de xadrez,** chessboard.
tabuleta [ê] (*f.*) a sign or signboard (on the front of a
building); directory of names (in a building); name
plate; a doctor's or lawyer's "shingle".
taca (*f.*) leather strap; a blow; (*Bot.*) Fiji-arrowroot tacca
(*T. pinnatifida*). **meter a**—(or **a ronca**) **em,** to backbite.
taça (*f.*) cup; trophy cup; goblet.
tacaca (*f.*) offensive body odor.
tacacá (*m.*) "a porridge made of tapioca flavored with
TUCUPI which has been boiled up with garlic, salt,
shrimp, etc.; it is served in small gourds, and is considered a delicacy by the inhabitants of Pará and Amazonas." [*GBAT*]
tacacàzeiro (*m.*) any of several tropical trees of the genus
Sterculia (chocolate family) esp. *S. pruriens*, whose seeds
yield a clear, yellow, odorless oil.
tacada (*f.*) stroke (with a cue, golf stick, etc.).—**em falso,**
miscue. **de uma**—, at a single stroke; at one sitting.
tacanhice, tacanharia, tacanhez[a] (*f.*) narrow-mindedness; niggardliness.
tacanho –nha (*adj.*) short in stature; stingy, miserly;
narrow-minded, hidebound; dim-witted.

tacaniça (*f.*) eaves; hip rafter.
tacão (*m.*) shoe heel.
tacape (*m.*) Indian club.
tacar (*v.t.*) to brandish; to strike with a cue; to lash with a strap; to throw, hurl.
tacha (*f.*) tack, small nail; blemish; fault; boiler for cane juice.
tachã (*f.*) the southern screamer (*Chauna torquata*), c.a. ANHUPOCA, ANHUMAPOCA, XAIÁ, XAJÁ, TAJÃ.
tachá (*m.*) = GUARANDI.
tachada (*f.*) boilerful; full boiler.
tachão (*m.*) large spot or blemish; ornamental stud or boss.
tachar (*v.t.*) to stigmatize.—**de**, to brand as; (*v.r., slang*) to get drunk.
tachear (*v.t.*) to tack; to stud with tacks.
tacheiro (*m.*) worker in a sugar mill.
tachim (*m.*) case in which to keep a book with a fine binding.
tachinho (*m.*) small tack.
tacho (*m.*) large pan; copper boiler.
tachonar (*v.t.*) to stud with brass tacks.
taci [í] (*m.*) = TABAIACU.
tácito –**ta** (*adj.*) tacit, implied, unspoken.
taciturnidade (*f.*) taciturnity, reserve.
taciturno –**na** (*adj.*) taciturn, reserved, closemouthed; glum, morose; sullen.
taco (*m.*) billiard cue; golf stick; hockey stick; polo mallet; wooden plug; dowel; wood flooring block; a clever man; bit, bite or piece (of something).
tacógrafo (*m.*) tachograph.
tacometria (*f.*) tachometry.
tacômetro (*m.*) tachometer, speed counter, speedometer.—**registrador**, a recording tachometer.
taconhapé (*m.,f.*) one of the Taconhapé or Tucunapèua, an extinct Tupian tribe who lived on the Iriri River, a tributary of the lower Xingu. Called also Péau, they are reported to have been the most tractable Indians of the entire region, as well as honest, industrious and at peace with their neighbors; (*adj.*) pert. to or designating these people.
táctil [-teis] (*adj.*) = TÁTIL.
tactilidade (*f.*) = TATILIDADE.
tacto (*m.*) = TATO.
tactura (*f.*) = TATURA.
tacuaré (*m.*) = TAMACUARÉ.
tacuera (*f.*) = CABACEIRO-AMARGOSO.
tacuité (*m.*) = QUEIXADA.
tacuru [rú], **tacuri** [rí] (*m.*) huge ant hill. Var. TUCURI.
tacuruba, tacurua (*f.*) a cooking trivet formed of rocks or clay balls. Var. ITACURUBA.
tacuruzal (*m.*) area abounding in large ant hills.
tael [taéis] (*m.*) tael (Chinese coin).
tafetá (*m.*) taffeta.
tafiá (*m.*) rum [= CACHAÇA].
tafona (*f.*) = ATAFONA.
taful [-fuis] (*adj.*) dandyish; (*m.*) dandy, fop; professional gambler.
tafulão (*m.*) seducer of women.
tafular (*v.i.*) to live like a TAFUL.
tafulhar (*v.*) = ATAFULHAR.
tafulho (*m.*) plug or cork.
tafulo (*m., colloq.*) sweetheart, lover.
tagant[e]ar (*v.t.*) to whip, lash.
tagarela (*adj.*) garrulous; (*m.,f.*) prattler; gossip; chatterbox; blabbermouth; tattler.
tagarelar (*v.i.*) to jabber, chatter, babble, gabble; to tittle-tattle, gossip; to wag one's tongue.
tagarelice (*f.*) garrulity, talkativeness, babbling, blather; hot air.
tagetes (*m.*) marigold (*Tagetes*); c.a. CRAVO-DE-DEFUNTO.
tágico –**ca** (*adj.*) of or pert. to the Tejo (Tagus River) in Portugal. [*Poetical*]
tágide (*f.*) a nymph of the Tejo (Tagus River).
taguá (*m.*) = TUÁ and MARFIM-VEGETAL.
taguicati [í] (*m.*) = QUEIXADA.
taiã (*m.*) taro [= TAIOBA].—**-jararaca**, (*Bot.*) Brazil dragonaroid (*Dracontium asperum*), c.a. TAJÁ-DE-COBRA.
taiaçu [ú] (*m.*) a tiger-bittern (*Tigrisoma lineatum* or *T. fasciatum*); the white-lipped peccary (*Tayassu albirostris*).
taiaçuíra (*m.*) the rufous-winged ground cuckoo (*Neomorphus rufipennis*).
taiaçutirágua (*f.*) = QUEIXADA.

taifa (*f.*) ship's stewards, collectively.
taifeiro (*m.*) ship's steward.
tailleur (*m.*) woman's tailored suit or dress.
tainha [a-í] (*f.*) any mullet esp. the Brazilian mullet (*Mugil brasiliensis*), c.a. TAINHA-DE-CORSO, TAINHA-VERDADEIRA, TAINHA-CURIMÃ, TAINHA-SÊCA, CAMBIRA.—**-de-rio**, a mullet of southern Brazil (*Mugil liza*), c.a. TAINHA, TAINHOTA, TAPUGI, TAMATARANA, PARATI, URICHOCA, SAÚNA.
tainheira [a-i] (*f.*) mullet net; mullet-fishing canoe.
tainhota [a-i] (*f.*) = TAINHA-DE-RIO.—**-voadeira**, a flying fish (*Cypselurus speculiger*).
taioba (*f.*) elephant's-ear taro (*Colocasia antiquorum*), c.a. TAIÁ, TALO, TARRO, JARRO, TAIOVA, PÉ-DE-BEZERRO; the primrose malanga (*Xanthosoma violaceum*); [*colloq.*, in Rio de Janeiro] second-class streetcar.
taiobal (*m.*) a field of taro.
taipa (*f.*) partition; screen; mud wall; lath-and-plaster wall; horse's hoof. **casa de—**, mud (wattle and daub) hut.
taipal (*m.*) mud wall; plaster wall; screen; wooden form for concrete; (*pl.*) outside shutters.
taipar (*v.t.*) to build mud walls; to partition with walls.
taipeira (*f.*) = MANDURI and GUARAPU-MIUDO.
taira [a-í] (*f.*, *Zool.*) the tayra. [*Webster:* "A long-tailed musteline mammal (*Tayra barbara*) of South and Central America, allied to the grison. It resembles the North American fisher in size, but has short fur and is black with a grayish head."]
Taiti [a-i] (*m.*) Tahiti.
taititu (*m.*) = CAITITU.
tajã (*m.*) = TACHÃ.
tajá (*m.*, *Bot.*) the common caladium (*C. bicolor*), c.a. TINHORÃO.—**-de-cobra**, the Brazil dragonaroid (*Dracontium asperum*), c.a. TAIÁ-JARARACA.
tajaçu [ú] (*m.*) = CAITITU.
tajaçuíra (*f.*) = MÃE-DE-PORCO.
tajaçutirágua (*f.*) = QUEIXADA.
tajurá (*m.*) = TINHORÃO.
tal (*adj.*) such, like, similar; this; that; (*adv.*) so, thus; (*pron.*) this, that; (*m.,f.*) the one (person).—**como**, just as.—**como deve ser**, just as it should be.—**e coisa**, this and that.—**ou qual**, this or that; one or another; some sort of.—**pai,—filho**, Like father, like son.—**qual**, just as, just like.—**qual vez**, once in a while. **a—ponto que**, to such an extent that. **de—maneira que**, in such a manner that. **de—modo que**, so much so that. **É—a sua bondade, que todos a estimam**, She is so kind everyone loves her. **em—caso**, in that case; in such a case. **Fulano de—**, John Doe. **o—**, that person; that one. **o—sujeito**, that fellow. **outro que—**, another such. **Que—?** Well? How does it strike you? What do you say? What do you think? **Que —um jôgo de tênis?** How about a game of tennis? **um—**, such a. **um—de X**, a certain X (person's name).
tala (*f.*) splint; splice; leather strap; (*R.R.*) fishplate; (*pl.*) fix, "hot water".
talabartaria, talabarteira (*f.*) harness shop; saddlery.
talabarte (*m.*) baldric.
talabarteiro (*m.*) harness maker; saddler.
talaço (*m.*) a strapping or whipping.
talagada (*f.*) swig.
talagarça (*f.*) cross-stitch canvass (for embroidery).
talambor [ô] (*m.*) secret lock.
tálamo (*m.*) nuptial bed; (*Anat.*) thalamus; (*Bot.*) a torus or receptacle.
talante (*m.*) will, pleasure.
talão (*m.*) heel; ogee molding; ticket stub; stub in a check book; stub of a branch after pruning; bead of a pneumatic tire.—**de bagagem**, baggage check.—**de cheques**, check book.
talar (*adj.*) heel; heel-length; (*m.pl.*) talaria (Mercury's winged shoes); (*v.t.*) to trench; to lay waste.
talássico –**ca** (*adj.*) thalassic.
talassografia (*f.*) oceanography.
talassômetro (*m.*) tide gauge.
tálcico –**ca** (*adj.*) talcose.
talcito (*m.*, *Petrog.*) talc schist.
talco (*m.*) talc; talcum powder; tinsel.
talcoclorito (*m.*) talcochlorite.
talcoesquisto (*m.*) = TALCOXISTO.
talco-micáceo –**cea** (*adj.*) talcomicaceous.
talcoso –**sa** (*adj.*) talcous, talcose.
talcoxisto (*m.*, *Petrog.*) talc schist.
taleiga (*f.*) sack, esp. one for grain, meal or flour. Cf. SACA, SACO.

taleira (*f.*) an angle iron, brace or bracket.
talentaço, talentão (*m., colloq.*) great talent; highly-talented man.
talento (*m.*) talent, faculty, aptitude; high mental ability; ancient weight and money; (*colloq.*) muscularity.
talentoso –sa (*adj.*) talented, gifted; clever.
talha (*f.*) a cut; act of cutting, carving or engraving; a deal at cards; ship's tackle; block and tackle; tally stick; large earthenware jug or pot. **operação da—,** (*Surg.*) lithotomy.
talhada (*f.*) a cut or slice of something; (*colloq.*) rebuke, reprimand.
talhadão (*m.*) crack in the surface of the earth; entrance to a cave; river bed between high walls.
talhadeira (*f.*) cleaver, chopping knife; chisel.—**a frio,** cold chisel.
talha-dente (*m.*) smilograss (*Oryzopsis miliacea*).
talhadia (*f.*) a stand of trees from which only the renewed branches are taken by wood choppers; wood chopping.
talhadiço –ça (*adj.*) of vegetation, that can be cut down or chopped out.
talhado –da (*adj.*) cut, sliced, chopped; cut to measure. **leite—,** sour milk. (*m.*) "a stretch of river with high banks on either side; that is, a place where the river has cut through a cliff." [*GBAT*]
talhador –dora (*adj.*) cutting; carving; (*m.,f.*) cutter, carver; meat cutter, butcher; cleaver, chopper.
talhadura (*f.*) = TALHAMENTO.
talha-frio (*m.*) a woodworking chisel.
talha-mar (*m.*) cutwater (fore part of a ship's stem, or the V-shaped edge of a pier facing upstream); (*Zool.*) the black skimmer (*Rhynchops nigra*), c.a. CORTA-MAR, BICO-RASTEIRO.
talhamento (*m.*) act of cutting, slicing, carving, etc. See the verb TALHAR.
talhão (*m.*) planting field; piece of whole meat.
talhar (*v.t.*) to cut, slash, gash, slice, chop; to carve, chisel; to cut out (cloth); to tailor; to fashion, form, shape by cutting; to whittle.—**se,** to split; to curdle.—**pedras,** to hew stones.
talharim (*m.*) vermicelli, noodles. [Ital. *taglierini*]
talhe (*m.*) cut, form, shape, figure.
talher (*m.*) knife, fork and spoon; a table place setting (cover) for one person.
talhinha (*f.*) a small block and tackle.
talho (*m.*) a cut or act of cutting; tree pruning; meat cutting; butcher shop; butcher's block; form, shape.—**da vida,** mode of living.—**s de sal,** salt beds. **vir a—(de foice),** to come up at the right moment.
tália (*f.*) any plant of the genus Thalia (arrowroot family); (*Zool.*) any member of the genus Salpa.
taliáceos (*m.pl., Zool.*) the Thaliacea (order of tunicates).
talião (*m.*) retaliation, a return of evil for evil.
tálico –ca (*adj.; Chem.*) thallic.
talictro (*m.*) meadow rue (*Thalictrum*). Var. TALITRO.
talim (*m.*) sword belt, baldric [= BOLDRIÉ].
talina (*f., Chem.*) thalline; (*Bot.*) flameflower (*Talinum*).
talinga (*f., Naut.*) clinch knot.
talingadura (*f., Naut.*) clinching of a rope.
talingar (*v.t., Naut.*) to clinch (a rope).
tálio (*m., Chem.*) thallium.
talionar (*v.t.*) to punish by retaliation.
talionato (*m.*) retaliation, esp. of an "eye for an eye, a tooth for a tooth".
talioso –sa (*adj., Chem.*) thallous.
talipote (*m.*) talipot palm.
talisca (*f.*) crevice, chink; fragment, splinter; (*Carp.*) spline.
talismã (*m.*) talisman.
talitro (*m.*) = TALICTRO.
tálitro (*m.*) knuckle; a rap with the knuckles. Var. TÁLITRE.
Talmude (*m.*) Talmud.
talmúdico –ca (*adj.*) Talmudic(al).
talmudista (*m.,f.*) Talmudist.
talo (*m.*) stalk, stem; petiole; shaft of a column; (*Bot.*) thallus; also = TAIOBA.
talocha (*f.*) mason's float [= ESPARAVEL].
talocrural (*adj.; Anat.*) talocrural.
taloescafoídeo –dea (*adj.; Anat.*) taloscaphoid.
talófito (*m., Bot.*) thallophyte.
talona (*f.*) Java devilpepper (*Rauwolfia serpentina*), c.a. PAU-DE-COBRA.
talonavicular (*adj.; Anat.*) talonavicular.

talonear (*v.t.,v.i.*) to whip.
talpária (*f., Veter.*) poll evil.
talpídeos (*m.pl.*) a family (*Talpidae*) of moles.
taluda (*f.*) see TALUDO.
taludamento (*m.*) act of making a slope.
taludão (*m.*) a strongly-developed lad.
taludar (*v.t.*) to give a slope or slant to.
talude (*m.*) slope, slant; sloping bank; batter (of a wall).
taludo –da (*adj.*) having a strong stalk; full-grown, well-developed; (*f., slang*) the grand (lottery) prize.
talvegue (*m., Physiog.*) thalweg.
talvez [ê] (*adv.*) perhaps, maybe.
tamacarica (*f.*) deck awning.
tamacuaré (*m.*) a small Brazilian lizard (*Enyalius sp.*) of the iguana family, c.a. LAGARTIXA, TACUARÉ. Cf. TAMAQUARÉ.
tamanca (*f.*) a low, wide-mouthed sabot, wooden shoe or clog, worn by Portuguese peasant women; brake shoe. **pôr-se,** or **ter-se, nas suas—s** (or **tamanquinhas**), to balk, not yield. **trepar-se nas—,** to get angry. Cf. TAMANCO.
tamancada (*f.*) a blow with a sabot.
tamancão (*m.*) = CACHETA.
tamancaria (*f.*) a shop where wooden shoes are made and/or sold.
tamanco (*m.*) a kind of open, low-heeled or heelless shoe having a wooden sole and leather toe covering, common among the working classes in Portugal and Rio de Janeiro; wooden axle-bearing of an oxcart; brake shoe [= BREQUE and CEPO]. **trepar-se nos—s,** to get peeved. Cf. TAMANCA.
tamancudo –da (*adj.*) rough, coarse [person].
tamanduá (*m.*) anteater, ant bear; c.a. PAPA-FORMIGAS. **—bandeira,** the great anteater (*Myrmecophaga jubata* or *M. tridactyla*), c.a. TAMANDUÁ-AÇU, TAMANDUÁ-CAVALO, JURUMI, JURUNA.**—mirim,** the little anteater (*Myrmecophaga tetradactyla*), c.a. COLÊTE, JALECO, MELETE, MIXILA.
tamanduaí (*m.*) a small, slothlike, two-toed arboreal anteater of Brazil (*Cyclothurus,* or *Cyclopes, didactylus*), c.a. TAMANDUÀZINHO. [It has a prehensile tail.]
tamanhão –nhona (*adj.; m.,f.*) very large (person).
tamanhinho –nha (*adj.*) tiny.
tamanho –nha (*adj.*) so big, so great, such big, such, so much; (*m.*) size, dimensions.—**natural,** life size. **de—avantajado,** good-sized.
tamanquear (*v.i.*) to wear clogs; to make a clatter while walking with clogs.
tamanqueira (*f.*) a pricklyash (*Zanthoxylum rhoifolium,* family *Rutaceae*), c.a. TAMANQUEIRA-DA-TERRA-FIRME, ESPINHO-DE-VINTEM.**—de-leite,** a Brazilian tree (*Zshokkea lastescens,* family *Apocynaceae*) which yields a chicle latex.
tamaquaré (*m.*) any of a number of trees of the genus Caraipa (family *Clusiaceae, syn. Guttiferae*), yielding strong, hard and valuable wood. The principal species are *Caraipa psidifolia,* a small tree with white, highly perfumed flowers, and *C. fasciculata,* a large tree with brownish wood, yielding a balsam resin.**—grande** is *Caraipa grandifolia,* very common in the region of the Amazon estuary.**—muido** is *C. minor.* Cf. TAMACUARÉ.
tâmara (*f.*) fruit of the date palm.**—da-terra** = JERIVÁ.
tamaral (*f.*) a grove of date palms.
tamarana (*f.*) = CUIDARU.
tamareira (*f.*) the date palm (*Phoenix dactylifera*).**—anã,** the dwarf Roebelen date palm (*Phoenix humilis loureiri*).
tamarga, tamargueira (*f.*) the French tamarisk (*Tamarix gallica*) or the African tamarisk (*T. africana*).
tamari [rí] (*m.*) any of numerous South American marmosets of the genus Leontocebus (syn. Midas)—the tamarins—better known in Brazil as SAGÜI.
tamaricáceo –cea (*adj.; Bot.*) tamaricaceous; (*f.pl.*) the Tamaricaceae (tamarisk family).
tamarinada (*f.*) a cooling drink made with the fruit of the tamarind.
tamarindal (*m.*) a grove of tamarinds.
tamarindeiro (*m.*), **-ra** (*f.*) = TAMARINDO.
tamarindo (*m.*) the tamarind (*Tamarindus indica*); also its fruit. Other common names are: JUBAÍ, TAMARINEIRA, TAMARINEIRO, TAMARINHEIRO, TAMARINHO.
tamarisco (*m.*) tamarisk seed.
tamariz (*f.*) = TAMARGUEIRA.
tamaru [rú] (*m.*) a mantis crab (*Squilla mantis*).
tamarutaca (*f.*) a large mantis crab (*Squilla empusa*), c.a.

TAMBARUTACA, TAMBURUTACA, LAGOSTA-GAFANHOTO, MÃE-DO-CAMARÃO, ESQUILA.

tamatarana (*f.*) a gray mullet (*Mugil lisa*), c.a. TAINHA-DE-RIO.

tamati [tí] (*m.*) a cockle (*Cardium muricatum*) c.a. MIJA-MIJA.

tamatiá (*m.*) the tropical American boatbill (*Cochlearius cochlearius*), c.a. ARAPAPÁ.—**-aquático-do-pará**, the boat-billed heron (*Cancroma cochlearius*), c.a. CANCROMA.——**-barbudo**, a barbet or puffbird (*Bucco philippinensis*).——**-do-brasil**, a Brazilian barbet or puffbird (*Bucco capensis*).

tamatião (*m.*) a night heron; also = JOÃO-BOBO.

tambaca (*f.*) tombac (copper and zinc alloy), c.a. TAMBAQUE.

tambaco, tambacoli [í] (*m.*) = TAMPAFOLE.

tambaque (*m.*) = TABAQUE and TAMBACA.

tambaqui [í] (*m.*) "a fish (*Myletes bidens*) which is a common article of food in Amazonia, found in lakes, IGARAPÉS and IGAPÓS." [*GBAT*]

tambarutaca (*f.*) = TAMARUTACA.

tambatajá (*m.*) = TINHORÃO.

tambataruga (*f.*) = ESPINHO-DE-VINTÉM.

também (*adv.*) also, too, likewise, besides, moreover, as well.—**não**, nor either, neither. **senão**—, but also.

tambetara (*f.*) = PAPA-TERRA.

tambo (*m.*) dairy farm; cow barn.

tambó (*m.*) = SERNAMBIGUARA.

tambor [ô] (*m.*) drum cylinder; tumbling barrel; eardrum; drummer.—**basco**, tambourine.—**de freio**, brake drum.——**mor**, drum major.

tamborete [rê] (*m.*) taboret; stool.

tamboril (*m.*) tambourin or tabor [= TAMBORIM]; an angler fish, c.a. PEIXE-PESCADOR, DIABO-MARINHO; an earpod tree (*Enterolobium maximum*).—**-bravo**, the Paraná peltophorum (*P. vogelianum*), c.a. FARINHA-SÊCA.

tamborilada (*f.*) a playing or rolling of drums.

tamborilar (*v.i.*) to drum with the fingers; to repeat a thing over and over.

tamborileiro (*m.*) drummer.

tamborilete [ête] (*m.*) a little drum.

tamborim (*m.*) = TAMBORIL.

tambotá (*m.*) a small armored catfish (*Callichthys callichthys*), seen in home aquaria.

tambu [ú] (*m.*) a drum; a wood beetle; a plant called QUINA-PEREIRA

tamburi [í] (*m.*, *Bot.*) the timbouva earpod tree (*Enterolobium timbouva*).

tamburipará, tamburupará (*m.*) = TANGURUPARÁ.

tamburutaca (*m.*) = TAMARUTACA.

tamearama (*f.*) a Brazilian scratchbush (*Dalechampia brasiliensis*), c.a. URTIGA-TAMEARAMA, CAAJAÇARA.

tametara (*f.*) = TEMBETÁ.

tâmia (*f.*) genus (*Tamias*) of ground squirrels and chipmunks.

tamiarama (*f.*) = CIPÓ-TRIPA-DE-GALINHA.

tamina (*f.*) slave's daily food ration; the vessel used to dole it out; daily public water ration during a drought. **por**—, a little at a time.

tamís (*m.*) a fine sieve or strainer made of silk or cloth; tammy cloth.

Tamisa (*f.*) Thames.

tamisar (*v.t.*) to sift, sieve, strain; to bolt (flour).

tamnófilo (*m.*) a genus (*Thamnophilus*) of neotropical, hook-billed ant shrikes.

tamo (*m.*, *Bot.*) common black bryony (*Tamus communis*).

tamoio -**moia** (*m.*,*f.*) an Indian of the Tamoyó, a sub-division of the Tupinambá who dominated the area of what is now the state of Rio de Janeiro; (*adj.*) pert. to or designating these people.

tampa (*f.*) lid, cover.—**com rôsca**, screw cap.

tampafole (*m.*, *Zool.*) a piddock—the ribbed pholas or angel's wings (*Barnea costata*).

tampão (*m.*) a large lid or cover; manhole cover; stopper bung, plug; stopgap, makeshift. (*Surg.*) tampon. **estado** —, buffer state.

tampar (*v.t.*) to cover with a lid. Cf. TAPAR.

tampinha (*f.*) a children's game played with bottle caps.

tampo (*m.*) barrelhead; toilet seat cover; the front or back of a stringed instrument.

tamponamento (*m.*) act of plugging; (*Surg.*) tamponment.

tamponar (*v.t.*) to plug, stop; (*Surg.*) to tampon. Cf. TAPAR.

tampouco (*adv.*) neither.

tamuripará, tamurupará (*m.*) = TANGURUPARÁ.

tanacetina (*f.*, *Chem.*) tanacetin.

tanaceto (*m.*, *Bot.*) common tansy (*Tanacetum vulgare*), c.a. TANÁSIA.

tanado -**da** (*adj.*) of the color tan.

tanagem (*f.*) = CURTIMENTO.

tanagrídeo (*m.*, *Zool.*) any tanager; (*pl.*) the family Thraupidae (syn. Tanagridae).

tanajuba (*f.*) = GUARUBA.

tanajura (*f.*) female flying ant [= IÇÁ and SAÚVA.]

tanar (*v.*) = CURTIR.

tanásia (*f.*) = TANACETO.

tancagem (*f.*, *Agric.*) tankage (fertilizer).

tanchagem (*f.*) the rippleseed plantain (*Plantago major*). ——**aquática**, the grass waterplantain (*Alisma plantago*). ——**rabo-de-rato**, mousetail plantain (*Plantago myosurus*).

tanchão (*m.*) grapevine stake; a slip or plant cutting [= CHANTÃO].

tanchar (*v.t.*) to stake (plants); to plant (cuttings).

tandem (*m.*) tandem bicycle.

tanduju [jú] (*m.*) a fish—the northern stargazer (*Astroscopus guttatus*), c.a. MIRACÉU.

tang. = TANGENTE (tangent).

tanga (*f.*) loincloth, breechcloth, G-string; sarong; hammock fringe.

tangar (*v.t.*) to cover (-se, oneself) with a TANGA; (*v.i.*) to dance the tango.

tangará (*m.*) Azara's long-tailed manakin (*Chiroxiphia caudata*), c.a. ATANGARÁ, DANÇADOR, DANÇARINO; the blue-backed manakin (*C. pareola*), c.a. CABEÇA-ENCARNADA, RENDEIRA, UIRAPURÚ-DE-COSTA-AZUL; the queen manakin (*C. regina*).—**-de-cabeça-encarnada**, or **-de-cabeça-vermelha**, the red-headed manakin (*Pipra erythrocephala cubrocapilla*), c.a. CABEÇA-ENCARNADA.

tangaracá-açu [çú] (*m.*) = COURADÃO.

tangarana (*f.*) an anttree (*Triplaris schomburgkiana*), c.a. TAXI.—**-açu**, a seagrape (*Coccolobis crescentiaefolia*).

tangaràzinho (*m.*, *Zool.*) the military manakin (*Ilicura militaris*).

tangedor (*m.*) player (of an instrument); driver (of animals).

tange-fole (*m.*) one who works the bellows in a black-smith's shop; fig., one who stimulates a gossiper.

tangência (*f.*) tangency.

tangencial (*adj.*) tangential.

tangenciar (*v.t.*) to touch (as a straight line in relation to a curve or surface); to graze (touch lightly).

tangente (*adj.*) tangent, touching; (*f.*) a tangent; a straight stretch of road; (*colloq.*) a loophole, an "out".

tanger (*v.t.*) to play (a musical instrument); to strike (a gong); to pluck (a harp); to drive, prod (animals); (*v.i.*) of bells, to toll, sound, ring out; to play [music].—**a**, to refer to. **tangendo sempre na mesma corda**, always harping on the same string. **tangido de casa**, driven from home.

Tânger (*pn.*) Tangier.

tangerina (*f.*) a tangerine or mandarin orange, c.a. BERGAMOTA, VERGAMOTA, LARANJA-CRAVO, MEXERICA, MANDARINA, MIMOSA, LARANJA-MIMOSA.

tangerineira (*f.*) any of several varieties of mandarin orange or tangerine trees, c.a. BERGAMOTA, VERGAMOTA, LARANJA-CRAVO, MEXERICA, MEXERIQUEIRA.

tangerino (*m.*) Tangerine (a native or inhabitant of Tangier); c.a. TINGITANO; a cow-puncher.

tange-tange (*m.*, *Bot.*) a lupine (*Lupinus unijugata*).

tange-viola (*m.*, *colloq.*) any "long-horned" cerambycid beetle, c.a. TOCA-VIOLA.

tangível (*adj.*) tangible, palpable.

tanglomanglo (*m.*) hoodoo, Jonah, bad luck [= CAIPORISMO].

tango (*m.*) tango.

tanguista (*m.*,*f.*) tango-dancer.

tangurupará (*m.*) the black nun bird (*Monasa niger*), c.a. TAMBURIPARÁ, TAMBURUPARÁ, TAMURIPARÁ, TAMURUPARÁ; also = JUIZ-DO-MATO.

tanibuca (*f.*) "the pole or paddle on which rubber is coagulated in the smoking process." [*GBAT*]; (*Bot.*) a terminalis (*T. tanibouca*).

tânico -**ca** (*adj.*) tannic.

tanino (*m.*) tannin.

tanoar (*v.i.*) to cooper.

tanoaria (*f.*) cooperage.

tanoeiro (*m.*) cooper; also = PERERECA (a tree toad).
tanque (*m.*) tank, vat; pool, reservoir; tank truck; concrete wash tub; (*Milit.*) tank.—**de água**, water tank; cistern.—**de gasolina**, motor fuel tank—**de lastro**, ballast tank.
tantã (*m.*) tomtom; gong; (*adj.*) daft; doting, senile.
tantalato (*m.*, *Chem.*) tantalate.
tantálico –**ca** (*adj.*, *Chem.*) tantalic.
tantalita (*f.*, *Min.*) tantalite.
tantalizar (*v.t.*) to tantalize.
tântalo (*m.*, *Chem.*) tantalum.
tantas-folhas (*f.pl.*) tripe [= FOLHOSO, DOBRADINHA]; (*Zool.*) manyplies, omasum.
tantinho (*m.*) a tiny bit.
tantíssimo –**ma** (*absol. superl. of* TANTO) most numerous; most high (in degree).
tanto (*adj.*, *fem.* **tanta**) so much, as much; (*pl.*) so many, so much; odd (left over, indeterminate). [**Vinte e tantos**, twenty odd]; (*adv.*) so, to such a degree, in such a manner; so much; so often; (*m.*) sum, quantity.—**assim que**, so much so that.—**como**, as much as.—(**êle**) **como** (**eu**) **estávamos lá**, Both (he) and (I) were there.—**faz que**, it makes no difference whether.—**mais quanto** (**que**), all the more because.—**mais** (**tem**) **quanto mais** (**quer**), The more (she has), the more (she wants).—**melhor**, so much the better; all the better.—**pior**, so much the worse.— **por tanto**, as between this and that; things being equal. —**quanto**, as much as, so far as.—**s quantos**, as many as. —**que**, so much that.—**se me dá**, It's all the same to me. —**tempo**, so long (a time).—**um como outro**, both of them; the one as well as the other.—**s dêstes como daquêles**, as many of these as of those.—**s vezes**, so many times, so often.—**um como outro**, as much one as the other; both one and the other. **a fôlhas—s**, at a given moment; lit., on such and such a page. **a—s horas**, at such and such a time. **Água mole em pedra dura,— bate até que fura**, Dripping water bores the stone. **algum—**, a little, somewhat. **duzentos e—s**, two hundred odd. **lá para tantas da noite**, sometime during the night. **Não é—assim**, It is not so bad as all that. **outro—**, as much again. **outros—s**, as many again; as many more. **quanto mais** (...)—**mais** (...), the more (...), the more (...). **se—**, at most, if that much. **um—**, somewhat, a little, to a degree. **um—ou quanto** (**importante**), more or less (important). **um homem e—!** quite a man! **uns—s**, a few.
tão (*adv.*) so, such, a, so very, so much. Cf. TANTO.— (**longe**) **que**, so (far) that.—**de pressa que**, as soon as.— **pouco**, so little.—**só**, only (because).—**sòmente**, only. **Era—boa, quão** (**quanto, como**) **formosa**, She was as good as she was beautiful. **um dia—quente**, such a warm day.
taoca (*f.*) a cowfish or trunkfish (*Lactophrys*), c.a. PEIXE-VACA, BAIACU (-DE-CHIFRE); the driver ant.
tão-badalão, tão-balalão (*m.*) dingdong.
tapa (*f.*) tampion (gun plug); the outside horny part of a hoof; a blindfold put on a wild mule or horse being harnessed; (*m.* or *f.*) rap, slap, cuff, clout; a spat; a clincher, poser; (*f.*) a sole (genus Achirus) c.a. LINGUADO (-LIXA); the tonguefish (*Symphurus plagiusa*), c.a. LÍNGUA-DE-MULATA, SOLHA.
tapa-bôca (*m.*) a slap or blow on the mouth (to stop further talk); a woolen muffler.
tapaciriba (*f.*) = ESPORA-DE-GALO.
tapado –**da** (*adj.*) stopped, plugged; covered with a lid; closed tight; (*colloq.*) dense, thick, stupid; long-drawn out [conversation]; (*m.*) a woman's winter coat; (*f.*) fenced grounds; a hunting preserve.
tapador (*m.*) stopper, cover, lid [= TAMPA].
tapadura (*f.*) a stopping, plugging or covering; a hedge or screen; also = TAPAMENTO.
tapagem (*f.*) a method of fishing which consists of closing with a net the outlet of a pond, etc., against which the fish are then driven and gathered up; also = TAPADURA and TAPAMENTO.
tapaiúna (*f.*) a very large Amazonian tree (*Dicorynia ingens*) of the senna family, yielding a dense, dark reddish-brown timber.
tapajônia (*f.*) the drainage region of the Topajós river and its tributaries.
tapamento (*m.*) act of plugging or stopping; a screen or hedge.
tapa-nuca (*f.*) a short cape attached to the back of headgear to afford shade for the nape.

tapanhuna (*m.*,*f.*) one of the Tapanhunha, an extinct tribe who lived on the Arinos River, a tributary of the upper Tajajós in Mato Grosso; (*adj.*) pert. to or designating this tribe.
tapa-ôlho (*m.*, *colloq.*) an eye-closing blow.
tapar (*v.t.*) to cover (with a lid); to stop (up), close (up) with a cork, plug, etc.; to hide, dim; to shut off (with a fence, hedge, etc.); to blindfold.—**a bôca**, to shut the mouth.—**a bôca, or os lábios, a**, to cause another to shut up.—**o nariz**, to hold one's nose.—**o sol com uma peneira**, to carry water in a sieve.—**os ouvidos**, to close one's ears. —**um buraco**; to plug or fill a hole; (*colloq.*) to fill a want; to pay a debt; to patch (something) up.
tapeação (*f.*) act of fooling, tricking, etc. See the verb TAPEAR.
tapeacuaçu [çú] (*m.*) a whiptree (*Luhea speciosa*). Cf. AÇOITA-CAVALOS.
tapeador –**dora** (*adj.*) duping, cheating, tricking; (*m.*,*f.*) trickster, one who fools, deceives, hornswoggles.
tapear (*v.t.*) to hoodwink, hornswoggle, fool, trick, deceive; to slap; to guide (a horse) by slaps on the neck, while riding him without saddle or bridle.
tapeçaria (*f.*) tapestry, drapery, hangings; rugs, carpets; fig., verdure; grass-covered, flower-covered, landscape.
tapeceiro (*m.*) one who makes and/or sells rugs and carpets.
tapejara (*m.*) guide, scout [= BAQUEANO, VAQUEANO]; pilot (of a boat); an old hand (at anything); (*adj.*) daring. Var. TAPIJARA.
tapema, tapena (*m.*) = GAVIÃO-TESOURA.
tapera (*f.*) a place in ruins; an abandoned or ruined house or settlement; a country estate which has been completely abandoned and in ruins; a tumble-down shack; (*adj.*) blind in one eye or in both; "screwball," "nuts".
taperá (*f.*) = ANDORINHA-DO-CAMPO.
taperebá (*m.*) = CAJÀZEIRA.—**-açu** or—**-cedro**, a large tree (*Poupartia amazonica*) of the cashew family, whose edible fruit closely resembles the CAJÁ.—**-do-sertão** = CAJÁ-MANGA.
taperebàzinho (*m.*, *Bot.*) variegated leafcroton (*Codiaeum variegatum*). Var. TAPERIBÀZINHO.
taperibá (*m.*) = TAPEREBÁ.
taperu [ú] (*m.*) bot; maggot. Var. TAPURU.
taperuçu [çú] (*m.*) a swift (*Chaetura zonaris*), c.a. ANDORINHÃO.
tapetar (*v.*) = ATAPETAR.
tapête (*m.*) a rug or carpet; fig., a lawn or flowered field.
tapiaçu [u] (*m.*) = TAPIÇUÁ.
tapiá-guaçu [çú] (*m.*, *Bot.*) Poirets copperleaf (*Acalypha poireti*); a Christmasbush (*Alchornea iricurana*), c.a. FÔLHA-REDONDA; a whiptree (*Luhea speciosa*).
tapiara (*f.*) a mullet; (*m.*) rascal, sharper.
tapichi [chí] (*m.*) unborn calf found in a slaughtered cow.
tapiçuá (*f.*) a stingless bee (*Melipona tubiba*), c.a. TUBIBA, TAPIAÇU.
tapicuru [rú] (*m.*) the Brazilian barefaced ibis (*Phimosus infuscatus nudifrons*); the Cayenne ibis (*Mesembrinibis cayennensis*); the glossy ibis (*Plegadis falcinellus*).
tapieira (*f.*) a stingless bee (*Trigona flavipennis*).
tapiira [i-í] (*f.*) = ANTA [tapir].
tapijara (*f.*) = TAPEJARA.
tapioca (*f.*) tapioca.
tapiolita (*f.*, *Min.*) tapiolite.
tapir (*m.*) tapir (*Tapirus terrestris*, *etc.*), better known as ANTA.
tapiranga (*f.*) = TIÉ-SANGUE.
tapirapé (*m.*,*f.*) an Indian of a practically extinct Tupi-Guarani-speaking group in the northeast corner of Mato Grosso; (*adj.*) pert. to or designating this group.
tapireça (*f.*) = ÔLHO-DE-BOI (fish).
tapiri [rí] (*m.*) thatched hut or shed, c.a. ITAPIRI, PAPIRI.
tapiriba (*f.*) = CAJÀZEIRA.
tapiti (*m.*) small harelike rodent (*Sylvilagus brasiliensis*) common in southern Brazil; c.a. COELHO-DO-MATO, COELHO-SELVAGEM.
tapiucaba [i-u] (*m.*) a wasp (*Polybia dimidiata*).
tapiz (*m.*) = TAPÊTE.
tapizar (*v.t.*) to carpet.—**-se de**, to become carpeted with (grass, leaves, flowers, etc.).
tápsia (*f.*, *Bot.*) gargan deathcarrot (*Thapsia garganica*).
tapucaja (*f.*) = JABURU.
tapugi [í] (*m.*) = TAINHA-DE-RIO.
tapuia, tapuio (*m.*,*f.*) a term formerly considered practically synonymous with Ge, but now simply a blanket

term used to designate any non-Tupi Indian, or a mestizo with straight black hair; (adj.) Tapuyan.

tapulho (m.) a stopple or plug.

tapume (m.) hedge, fence, palisade, barrier, screen [= TAPAGEM].

tapuru [rú] (m.) = MURUPITA (a tree) and TAPERU (a maggot).

taquara (f.) any bamboo, esp. of the smaller species [= TOBOCA]; a bird called JURUVA (q.v.).—**açu** or—**-mansa,** = CANAFLECHA.—**-do-reino** = CANA-DO-REINO. —**-sêca,** a stick insect [= MANÉ-MAGRO].

taquaral (m.) = TABOCAL.

taquari [í] (m.) a bamboo (Chusquea spp.); a panic grass (Panicum horizontale); pipe stem; a small or medium-sized succulent tree of the spurge family (Mabea augustifolia); also = PAPA-FORMIGAS (an antbird) and SOCOÍ (a heron); (adj.) small-bore [gun].—**-de-cavalo** = CAPIM-RABO-DE-MUCURA.—**-do-mato** (or—**-de-cavalo**) = CAPIM-DE-BEZERRO.—**-ubá** = CANA-DO-REINO.

taquariço –**ça** (adj.) slender as a bean pole.

taquarinha (f.) = CAPIM-DE-PASSARINHO and CAPIM-LAN-CÊTA.

taquaruçu [çú] (m.) = TABOCA-GIGANTE.

taqueira (f., Billiards) cue rack.

taqueômetro (m., Surveying) tachymeter.

taquímetro (m.) tachometer, speed counter.

taquicardia (f., Med.) tachycardia.

taquidrita (f., Chem.) tachydrite.

taquigênese (f., Biol.) tachygenesis.

taquigrafar (v.t.) to write in shorthand.

taquigrafia (f.) tachygraphy; shorthand; stenography.

taquígrafo (m.), –**fa** (f.) tachygrapher; stenographer.

taquilito (m., Petrog.) tachylyte.

taquimetria (f.) tachymetry.

taquímetro (m.) tachymeter (speed indicator). Cf. TAQUEÔMETRO.

taquino (m.) a genus (Tachina) of flies.

taquiri [rí] (m.) a young heron.

tara (f.) tare (deduction from gross weight); flaw, crack; fault, defect; taint.

tarado –**da** (adj.) defective; physically impaired; moronic; morally degenerate.

taraguira (f.) a South American iguanid (Tropidurus torquatus), c.a. PAPA-VENTO, CALANGO, LAGARTO.

taraíra (f.) = TRAÍRA.

tarambola (f.) a golden plover (Charadrius pluvialis), c.a. DOURADINHA.

taramela (f.) wooden door latch (the kind held in place by a nail, around which it spins); fig., the tongue; a tongue-wagging person.

taramel[e]ar (v.i.) to wag the tongue, jabber, gabble, prate.

tarantela (f.) tarantella (Italian dance).

tarantismo (m., Med.) tarantism.

tarântula (f.) tarantula (spider).

tarar (v.t.) to tare (ascertain, note, allow for, or mark, the tare of).

tarara (f.) a winnowing machine.

tararucu [cú] (m., Bot.) the coffee senna (Cassia occidentalis), c.a. FEDEGOSO (-VERDADEIRO), PAJAMARIOBA.

tarasca (f.) = ARAPAÇU-GRANDE.

tarauaxi [í] (m.) iripil bark tree (Pentaclethra filamentosa).

taraxaco (m.) common dandelion (Taraxacum officinale), c.a. DENTE-DE-LEÃO.

tarca (f.) a tally stick.

tardada (f.) a delay or act of delaying.

tardador –**dora** (adj.) delaying, slow; (m.,f.) delayer.

tardamento (m.), **tardança** (f.) tardiness, lateness, delay; slowness.

tardar (v.t.) to delay; (v.i.) to delay; to be tardy, late in coming, long in happening; to tarry, linger.—**em (a) chegar,** to be late (long) in arriving. **Não tardou (muito) que (chegasse),** It wasn't (very) long before (he arrived). **no mais—,** at the latest. **sem (mais)—,** without (further) delay.

tarde (adv.) tardily, late; (f.) afternoon. **à—,** in the afternoon. **amanhã à—,** tomorrow afternoon. **Antes—do que nunca,** Better late than never. **antes que seja demasiado—,** before it is too late. **Boa—!** Good afternoon! **chegar—,** to arrive late. **(cinco horas) da—,** (five) P.M. **de—,** in the afternoon. **É—,** It is late. **hoje à—,** this afternoon. **Já vai—!** It's high time! **mais cedo ou mais—.** sooner or later; eventually. **mais—,** later; afterwards,

ontem à—, yesterday afternoon. **todas as—s,** every afternoon.

tardeza [ê] (f.) tardiness, lateness.

tardígrado –**da** (adj.) tardigrade [Poetical]; (m., Zool.) one of the Tardigrada.

tardinha (f.) late afternoon.

tardinheiro –**ra** (adj.) slow, sluggish, lazy.

tardio –**dia** (adj.) slow; tardy.

tardo –**da** (adj.) slow-paced; lazy.

tardoz (m.) backing of a wall.

tarecaí = PITIÚ.

tareco (m.) foolish person; prankish person; piece of junk; (pl.) sticks of furniture.

tarefa (f.) task, duty, chore, job, stint, assignment; a land measure.—**sem remate,** endless task.

tarefeiro (m.) one who assumes a task; one who contracts to do a specific piece of work in a given time.

tarelar (v.) & derivs. = TAGARELAR & DERIVS.

tareoqui [í] (m.) = MATA-PASTO.

tarifa (f.) tariff.—**alfandegâria,** customhouse tariff.

tarifar (v.t.) to tariff.

tarifário –**ria** (adj.) tariff. **acôrdo—,** tariff agreement.

tarima (f.) a carpet-covered dais under a canopy.

tarimba (f.) soldier's wooden bunk; fig., army life. **ter—,** to have long practice or experience (in a trade or profession).

tarimbar (v.i.) to serve in the army.

tarimbeiro –**ra** (adj.) coarse, rude; (m.) an officer who has risen from the ranks.

tarioba (f.) a marine mussel (Iphigenia brasiliana).

taripicu-grande (m.) = CAPIM-MARAJÓ.

tarja (f.) an ornamental painted or carved border (on something); black border on stationery as a sign of mourning; a targe (round shield).

tarjar (v.t.) to provide with an ornamental edge or border.

tarjeta [ê] (f.) narrow border; small iron door bolt.

tarlatana (f.) tarlatan; buckram.

taro (m.) = INHAME-BRANCO.

taropé (m.) = CAIAPIÁ (an herb).

taroque (m.) = CORNIMBOQUE.

tarrafa (f.) a circular fishing net; (colloq.) a torn or ragged coat; "in northern Brazil, a kind of lace woven from cotton, linen or silk thread." [GBAT]

tarraxa (f.) screw; wedge; bolt; pipe threader; holder for taps and dies.

tarraxar (v.) = ATARRAXAR.

tarraxo (m.) screw; bolt; peg; wedge.

tarro (m.) milk pail; (Bot.) = TAIOBA.

társeo –**sea** (adj., Anat.) tarsal; (m.) tarsus (of the eyelid).

tarsiano –**na, társico** –**ca** (adj., Anat., Zool.) tarsal.

tarso –**sa** (adj.) tarsal; (m., Anat., Zool.) tarsus.

tarsometatarsiano –**na** (adj., Anat., Zool.) tarsometatarsal.

tartã (m.) tartan, plaid.

tartago (m.) the moleplant or caper euphorbia (E. lathyrus), c.a. LÁTIRE or LATÍRIDE.

tartamel[e]ar (v.) = TARTAMUDEAR.

tartamelo –**la** (adj.; m.,f.) = TARTAMUDO.

tartamudear (v.i.) to stutter, stammer; to sputter; to quaver [= TARTAMEL(E)AR].

tartamudez [ê] (f.) speech difficulty (stammering, faltering, etc.).

tartamudo –**da** (adj.) stammering, gagging, etc.; (m.,f.) stammerer, stutterer; one who is tongue-tied [= TARTA-MELO].

tartarato (m., Chem.) tartrate.

tartárico –**ca** (adj., Chem.) tartaric.

tartarizar (v.t., Chem.) to tartarize.

tártaro (m.) tartar (of teeth; of wine); boiler scale; a Tartar; Tartarus (Hades); also = TÁTARO.—**emético,** (Chem.) tartar emetic. **cremor de—,** cream of tartar.

tartaroso –**sa** (adj.) tartarous.

tartaruga (f.) any turtle, esp. a sea turtle.—**de-couro,** or—**-marinha,** the huge leatherback or trunk turtle (Dermochelys coriacea) measuring up to six feet and weighing a half-ton or more.—**do-mar,** or—**-verde,** the large green turtle (Chelonia mydas), c.a. JURUCUÁ.—**-grande-do-amazonas,** a large semi-aquatic fresh-water turtle (Podocnemis expansa) of great economic importance in the Amazon region as a source of meat, eggs and oil.—**-verdadeira,** or—**-imbricada,** or—**-de-pente,** the hawksbill turtle (Eretmochelys imbricata), the principal and best source of the tortoise shell of commerce. [It is not used as food.]

tartrazina (f., Chem.) tartrazine, hydrazine yellow.
tartufo (m.) tartufe, hypocrite; false friend.
tarubá (m.) "a fermented drink made from BEIJÚ dissolved in water." [GBAT]
tarugar (v.t.) to dowel.
tarugo (m.) dowel, wooden pin; a squat man.
tarumã (m.) any of various chaste trees (Vitex) esp. V. multinervis, c.a. GUABIROBA-BRAVA, IPÊ-DO-CÓRREGO, MARIA-PRETA.—-frondoso is Vitex orinocensis, a large tree whose wood is suited for piling, shoring and railroad ties.—-grande-do-campo or—-tuíra is Vitex flavens, a small or medium-sized tree yielding a tough timber for piling, railroad ties, etc.
tasca (f.) low tavern, cheap eating place [= TABERNA]; a beating [= SURRA]; scutching (of flax, hemp, etc.); a piece or bite of anything.
tascadeira (f.) woman who scutches flax, etc.
tascante (m.) tavernkeeper; (adj.) scutching.
tascar (v.t.) to scutch flax, etc.; to champ (as a horse); to beat, thrash (someone); to give to another a piece of something one is eating.
tasco (m.) woody fiber of flax, hemp, etc.
tasimetria (f.) tasimetry.
tasímetro (m.) tasimeter.
tasna, tasneira (f., Bot.) the ragwort groundsel (Senecio jacobaea).
tasneirinha (f., Bot.) the common groundsel (Senecio vulgaris), c.a. ASPELINA, SENÉCIO.
tasqueiro (m.) tavernkeeper [= TABERNEIRO].
tasquinha (f.) a small scutch. [Dim. of TASCA]
tasquinhar (v.t.) to swingle (beat) flax, etc.; (v.i.) to nibble; to backbite.
tassalho (m.) a large slice, cut, piece (of something to eat).
tasto (m.) fret (of a lute, guitar, etc.).
tataíra (f.) = CAGA-FOGO or ABELHA-CAGA-FOGO.
tatajuba (f.) a large or very large tree (Bagassa guianensis) of the mulberry family, c.a. TATAJIBA, TATAÚBA, TATA-REMA, TUIJUBA, JATAÍBA.—-de-espinho = LIMÃORANA.
tatajupoca (f.) = GUARAPARIBA.
tatalar (v.i.) to clack, click (as dice being shaken or bones rattled); to whir; (m.) a whirring sound, as of flapping wings.
tatamba (m.,f.) an inarticulate or tongue-tied person [= TATIBITATE]; a simpleton [= TOLEIRÃO].
tatambuera (f.) = GANGÃO.
tatapirica (f.) = PAU-POMBO.
tataporas (f.pl.) = CATAPORAS.
tataravô (m.), -avó (f.) = TETRAVÔ, -vó.
tatarema, tataúba (f.) = TATAJUBA.
tate (interj.) Watch out! (adv.) thus it was; it so happened.
tateante (adj.) groping, touching, feeling, fumbling.
tatear (v.t.) to feel, handle, probe; to test, sound; (v.i.) to grope, feel one's way.
tatera (f.) the southern swallow-wing puffbird (Chelidoptera tenebrosa brasiliensis), c.a. MIOLINHO. Cf. ANDOR-INHA-DA-MATA.
tatibitate (adj.; m.,f.) inarticulate, shy, timid; "dumb" (person).
tátil [-teis] (adj.) tactile. Var. TÁCTIL.
tatilidade (f.) tactility. Var. TACTILIDADE.
tato (m.) tactus, sense of touch; feeling; fig., tact. Var. TACTO.
tatu [tú] (m.) any armadillo; a type of Brazilian hog; a palm-thatched rain shelter; a tree called PAU-MARFIM-VERDADEIRO; (pl.) brothers having no sister, or sisters having no brother—in allusion to the fact that all the young in any litter of armadillos are always of one sex.—-bola, an apar or three-banded armadillo (Tolypeutes tricinctus) c.a. APAR, TATUAPARA.—-canastra, the rare giant armadillo (Priodontes giganteus), c.a. TATUAÇU.—-china, a seven-banded armadillo (Dasypus septemcinctus).—-de-focinho-comprido = TATUETÊ.—-de-rabo-mole, the tatouay (Cabassous unicinctus) having 12 or 13 movable scutes, c.a. TATU-XIMA.—-do-sul = TATUPEBA. —-fôlha = TATUETÊ. —-galinha = TATUETÊ.—-mijão, the runt in a litter of armadillos.—-peludo = TATUPEBA.—-verdadeiro = TATUETÊ.—-vespa = TATU-CABA.—-xima = TATU-DE-RABO-MOLE. rabo de—, a rawhide quirt.
tatuaçu (m.) = TATU-CANASTRA.
tatuagem (f.) tattooing; tattoo mark.
tatuaíva (m.) = TATUPEBA.
tatuapara (m.) = TATU-BOLA.
tatuar (v.t.) to tattoo.

tatucaba (m.) a wasp (Synoeca surinama), c.a. TATU-VESPA, CABATATU.
tatuetê (m.) a 9-banded armadillo (Dasypus novemcinctus) c.a. TATU-GALINHA, TATU-VERDADEIRO, TATU-FÔLHA, TATU-DE-FOCINHO-COMPRIDO.
tatupeba (m.) a hairy six-banded armadillo, the payou or peludo (Dasypus sexcinctus or D. vilosus), c.a. TATUAIVA, TATU-PELUDO, TATU-DO-SUL, PELUDO, PEBA.
tatuquira (m.) any bloodsucking sand fly of the genus Phlebotomus, esp. P. squamiventris.
tatura (f.) act of touching or feeling. Var. TACTURA.
taturana (f.) a caterpillar of the flannel moth, c.a. BICHO-CABELUDO, LAGARTA-DE-FOGO; a wasp; an albino person.
tatuzinho (m.) a small armadillo; a wood louse or pill bug, c.a. BARATINHA.
tauá (m.) unfertile soil which underlies the rich top layer of MASSAPÊ; a "yellowish argillaceous stone of iron peroxide, used to color pottery; an ink made from the same material." [GBAT]
tauaçu [çú] (m.) = POITA.
tauari [í] (m.) any of several Amazonian trees of the sapucaia-nut family (Lecythidaceae), esp. Couratari tauary or C. guianensis, which is "a very large tree with near-white sapwood; heartwood reddish; density .51. Uses: timber for furniture manufacture; the natives prepare extensive sheets which they use as a substitute for cigarette paper from parts of the bark." [GUAF]
tauatinga (f.) = TABATINGA.
tauismo (m.) taoism.
taumasite (f., Chem.) thaumasite.
taumaturgia (f.) thaumaturgy; magic.
taumaturgo -ga (m.,f.) thaumaturge.
tauoca (f.) the rufous-vented antthrush (Formicarius a. analis), c.a. PINTO-DO-MATO.
taurino -na (adj.) taurine.
taurocola (f.) taurocol (glue made from a bull's hide, etc.).
taurocolato (m., Biochem.) taurocholate.
taurocólico -ca (adj., Biochem.) taurocholic.
tauromaquia (f.) bullfighting.
tautocronismo (m., Math.) tautochronism.
tautôcrano -na (adj., Math.) tautochronous.
tautofonia (f.) tautophony.
tautologia (f.) tautology.
tautológico -ca (adj.) tautological.
tautomeria (f., Chem.) tautomerism.
tautossilábico -ca (adj., Phonet.) tautosyllabic.
taúva (f.) = CARRAPÊTA.
tauxia (f.) damascene.
tauxiado -da (adj.) inlaid.
tauxiar (v.t.) to damascene; to inlay.
tavanês -nêsa (adj.) reckless, rash, heedless.
tavão (m.) horsefly, gadfly (Tabannus), c.a. MOSCARDO.
taverna (f.) & derivs. = TABERNA & DERIVS.
távola (f.) = TÁBULA.
taxa (f.) a tax or surcharge. [Cf. IMPOSTO]; rate of interest, etc.; official (fixed) price.—de câmbio, rate of exchange.—de insalubridade, extra wages paid for work in hazardous or unhealthy surroundings (as in a mine, tunnel, swamp, etc.).—de inscrição, entrance fee.—de juro, rate of interest.—de mortalidade, death rate.—de natalidade, birth rate.
taxação (f.) rate fixing, price fixing; taxation.
taxáceo -cea [ks] (adj., Bot.) taxaceous; (f.pl.) the Taxaceae (yew family).
taxador (m.) rate fixer; appraiser.
taxar (v.t.) to fix the price or rate of; to place a value upon; to tax.—de, to tax with, charge with, accuse of.
taxativamente (adv.) positively, decidedly.
taxe [ks] (f., Surg.) taxis.
taxi [shí] (f.) an anttree (Triplaris schomburgkiana), c.a. TANGARANA; the Guiana tachia (T. guianensis); a tree (Sclerolobium goeldianum) of the senna family; a venomous ant which inhabits the hollow stems of the anttree and repels intruders, c.a. NOVATO, FORMIGA-DE-NOVATO.—-preta, the Surinam anttree (Triplaris surinamensis).—-preta-da-mata, a large or very large tree (Tachigalia myrmecophila) with whitish hard wood which gives off a nauseous odor, and whose almost black bark is used in tanning.
táxi [ks] (m.) taxicab.
taxia (f., Biol.) taxis.
taxidermia [ks] (f.) taxidermy.
taxidermista [ks] (m.,f.) taxidermist.
taxímetro [ks] (m.) taximeter; taxicab.

taxinomia [ks] (f.) taxonomy.
taxinômico –ca [ks] (adj.) taxonomic.
taxuri [í] (m.) = FRUXU.
taylorismo (m.) management by the Taylor system.
tchã (m.) = TIÊ-PRÊTO.
tcheco –ca (adj.; m.,f.) Czech (person, language).
tcheco-eslovaco ᵣ-ca (adj.; m.,f.) Czechoslovakian.
Tcheco-eslováquia, Tchecoslováquia (f.) Czechoslovakia.
te (pron.) you [= TU]; to you [= A TI].
tê (m.) the letter T. régua——, a T-square.
té (prep.) short form of ATÉ. Té logo! So long!
teáceo –cea (adj., Bot.) theaceous; (f.pl.) the Theaceae (tea family).
teantropia (f.) theanthropism.
tear (m.) a loom; the works of a timepiece.
teatinar (v.i.) to stray, wander.
teatino –na (adj.) stray, vagrant; (m.) a vagrant; a wanderer; (m.,f., R.C.Ch.) Theatine (order).
teatrada (f., colloq.) a show.
teatral (adj.) theatrical; fig., showy, ostentatious.
teatralidade (f.) theatricality.
teatrista (adj.) theatergoing; (m.,f.) theatergoer.
teatro (m.) theater; the stage; dramatic works collectively. —de variedades, vaudeville theater.—lírico, lyrical theater.
teatrólogo (m.), –ga (f.) playwright.
tebaína (f., Chem.) thebaine.
tebaísmo (m.) opiumism.
tebas (adj.; m., slang) big, important, bold (man).
teca (f., Bot.) theca, spore case; common teak (Tectona grandis); an angelin tree (Andira racemosa).
tecedeira, fem. of TECEDOR.
tecedor –deira (adj.) weaving; intriguing; (m.,f.) weaver; a weaver of intrigues; (m.) heddle of a loom.
tecedura (f.) weaving; web; plot, scheme.
tecelagem (f.) weaving; the textile industry.
tecelão (m.) weaver. [Fem. teceloa]
tecer (v.t.) to weave (yarns, cloth, a plot, etc.); (v.i.) to weave; to move from side to side; to intrigue; (v.r.) to become woven or interwoven.—considerações sôbre (or em tôrno de), to discuss, comment on, make remarks about.—considerações severas, to set forth severe criticisms.—os seus pauzinhos, (slang) to pull strings.
tecido –da (adj.) woven; (m.) textile, cloth; tissue.—adiposo, (Anat.) adipose tissue.—celular, (Anat., Bot.) cellular tissue; (Petrog.) granular texture.—conetivo or conjuntivo, (Anat.) connective tissue.—de algodão, cotton cloth.
tecla (f.) key (of a piano, typewriter, etc.); a hairstreak butterfly (genus Thecla).—de espacejamento, spacing key.—de retrocesso, back-spacing key.—seletor, tab key. bater sempre na mesma—, to harp on the same string.
teclado (m.) keyboard.
teclar (v.i.) to strike the keyboard.
técnico –ca (adj.) technical; (m.,f.) technician; (f.) technics; technique; know-how.
tecnocracia (f.) technocracy.
tecnografia (f.) technography.
tecnologia (f.) technology.
tecnológico –ca (adj.) technological.
tecnólogo (m.), –ga (f.) technologist.
teco-teco (m.) small single-motor airplane.
tecto, var. of TETO.
te[c]tônica (f.) tectonics.
te[c]triz (f.) a quill feather.
tecum (m.) palm-leaf fiber.
tedeum [-uns] (m., Eccl.) Te Deum.
tédio (m.) tedium; ennui.
tedioso –sa (adj.) tedious; irksome.
têem, form of TER [78]
Teerão [e-e] (m.) Teheran.
tefe-tefe (m., colloq.) heart beat; a heaving or panting; passion; (adv.) trippingly.
tefrito (m., Petrog.) tephrite.
tefroíta (f., Min.) tephroite.
tefrose (f.) tephrosis, incineration.
tefrósia (f.) the white tephrosia (T. candida) planted as a green manure.
tegão [-gãos] (m.) grain hopper [= TREMONHA].
tegme, tégmen (m., Bot.) tegmen, endopleura.
tegmina (f., Zool.) tegmen.
tegui [í] (m.) = TOVACA.
tégula (f., Zool.) tegula.

tegumentar (adj.) tegumentary.
tegumento (m., Bot., Anat., Zool.) integument.
teia (f.) web, texture, tissue; weft, woof; network; mesh; plot, intrigue.—de aranha, spider web; (Bot.) the spider-web houseleek (Sempervivum arachnoideum).
teinoscópio (m.) teinoscope; a prism telescope.
teiforme (adj.) theiform; (Pharm.) brewed (as tea).
teilorita (f., Min.) taylorite.
teima (f.) wilfulness, obstinacy.
teimar (v.i.) to insist (em, in); to persist (em, in); to argue (com, with).—em não morrer, to die hard. O pensamento teimou, The thought persisted.
teimosia, teimosice (f.) stubborn insistence; wilfulness, obstinacy, stubbornness.
teimoso –sa (adj.) insistent, obstinate; stiffnecked; wilful; self-willed, headstrong; opinionated.—como uma pedra, as stubborn as a mule. (f.) = CACHAÇA.
teína (f., Chem.) theine.
teirô (m.,f.) squabble; argument; doubt, suspicion.
teiru [ú] (m.) Indian file.
teísmo (m.) theism.
teísta (adj.) theistic; (m.,f.) theist.
teitei (m.) = GATURAMO.
teiú (m.) a tegu or teiid lizard (Teius teyou), c.a. TEJU, LAGARTIXA, LAGARTO-VERDE; also = TEIÚ-AÇU (the common tegu); (Bot.) a nettlespurge (Jatropha opifera).
teiú-açu [çú] (m.) the common tegu (Tupinambis teguixin), a large carnivorous lizard known throughout Brazil, and c.a. LAGARTO, TEIÚ, TEIÚ-GUAÇU, TEJUAÇU, JACURUARU.
teiú-guaçu [çú] (m.) = TEIÚ-AÇU.
teixo (m.) the English yew (Taxus baccata).
tejadilho (m.) shed roof, pent roof, canopy.
Tejo (m.) Tagus (River).
teju, tejuaçu (m.) = TEIÚ, TEIÚ-AÇU.
tel. = TELEFONE, TELEGRAMA.
tela (f.) web, network; fabric; painter's canvas; a canvas (finished painting); woven wire fencing; moving picture screen.
telagarça (f.) = TALAGARÇA.
telamão, télamon (m., Arch.) telamon.
telangiectasia (f., Med.) telangiectasis.
telão (m.) drop curtain.
telar (v.t.) to provide (doors and windows) with wire screening.
telautógrafo (m.) telautograph.
telecomando, telecontrôle (m.) remote control.
telecriptógrafo (m.) telecryptograph.
telectroscópio (m.) telelectroscope.
telefonada (f.) a telephone call.
telefonar (v.t.,v.i.) to telephone.
telefone (m.) telephone.
telefonema (m.) a telephone call. dar um—, to make a phone call.
telefonia (f.) telephony.
telefônico –ca (adj.) telephonic. lista—, telephone directory.
telefonista (m.,f.) telephone operator; switchboard operator.
telefoto (m.) telephoto.
telefotografia (f.) telephotography.
telega (f.) telega (4-wheeled Russian wagon).
telegonia (f., Genetics) telegony.
telegrafar (v.t.,v.i.) to telegraph.
telegrafia (f.) telegraphy.
telegráfico –ca (adj.) telegraphic.
telegrafista (m.,f.) telegraph operator.
telégrafo (m.) telegraph.—sem fio, wireless telegraph.
telegrama (adj.) telegram.
teleguiado (m.) guided missile.
teleinterruptor (m.) remote-control switch.
telelétrico –ca (adj.) telelectric.
telemanômetro (m., Elec.) telemanometer.
telemecânico –ca (adj.) telemechanic; (f.) telemechanics.
telemetria (f.) telemetry.
telemétrico –ca (adj.) telemetric(al).
telêmetro (m.) telemeter; range finder.
telemetrógrafo (m.) telemetrograph.
telencéfalo (m., Anat., Embryol.) telencephalon.
teleneurone (m.) teleneuron.
teleologia (f.) teleology.
teleológico –ca (adj.) teleological.
teleósteo –tea (adj., Zool.) teleostean; (m.) teleost.
telepatia (f.) telepathy.

telepático –ca (*adj.*) telepathic.
telescópia (*f.*) telescopy.
telescópico –ca (*adj.*) telescopic.
telescópio (*m.*) telescope.
telescritor (*m.*) telescriptor (a form of teletypewriter).
telespectroscópio (*m.*, *Astrophysics*) telespectroscope.
telessinal (*m.*) TV signal.
telestereoscópio (*m.*) telestereoscope, a binocular telescope.
telestúdio (*m.*) TV studio.
teletécnico (*m.*) TV technician.
teletermômetro (*m.*, *Physics*) telethermometer.
teletipo (*m.*) teletype.
teletransmissão (*f.*) TV transmission.
teletransmissor (*m.*) TV transmitter.
teletransmissora (*f.*) TV station.
telev. = TELEVISÃO (TV).
televisado –da (*adj.*) televised.
televisão (*f.*) television.
televisar (*v.t.*) to televise.
televisor (*m.*) TV receiver.
televisora (*f.*) TV station.
telha [ê] (*f.*) a roofing tile; (*colloq.*) kink, odd notion.—de espigão, ridge tile.—de vidro, glass tile.—-vã, a roof with no ceiling; roof tiles laid without mortar. Deu-me na—fazer isso, It came into my head to do that. ter uma —de menos, (*slang*) to have a screw loose. Cf. LADRILHO.
telhado (*m.*) roof; tile roof; (*colloq.*) a craze of some sort. —de vidro, bad reputation.
telhador (*m.*) roofer.
telhadura (*f.*) roofing; roof tile factory.
telhal (*m.*) tile kiln.
telhão (*m.*) a large tile.
telhar (*v.t.*) to cover (a roof) with tiles.
telheira (*f.*) tile factory; brickyard.
telheiro (*m.*) a maker of roofing tiles; an open tile-covered shed.
telso (*m.*, *Zool.*) telson.
telurato (*m.*, *Chem.*) tellurate.
telureto (*m.*, *Chem.*) telluride.
telúrico –ca (*adj.*) telluric, terrestrial.
teluridrico –ca (*adj.*, *Chem.*) telluridic [acid].
telúrio (*m.*, *Chem.*) tellurium.—negro, (*Min.*) black tellurium.
telurita (*f.*, *Min.*) tellurite.
teluroso –sa (*adj.*, *Chem.*) tellurous.
tem, form of TER [78]
tema (*m.*) theme, topic; thesis; text; school exercise, written composition; stem of a word.
temão (*m.*) tiller; (*Agric.*) beam (of a plow); tongue, pole or shaft of a vehicle.
temário (*m.*) list of topics to be discussed at a conference.
temático –ca (*adj.*) thematic.
tembataia (*f.*) the darkleaf malanga (*Xanthosoma atrovirens*).
tembé, tembê (*m.*) precipice.
tembé (*m.*,*f.*) An Indian of a very small Tupi-Guarani-speaking group in the state of Pará, closely related to the Guajajara in the adjoining state of Maranhão, together with whom they form the Tenetehara; (*adj.*) pert. to or designating the Tembé.
tembetá (*m.*) The Tupian designation for an ear plug or labret, different in size and shape, however, from the BOTOQUE of the Botocudo.
temblar (*v.t.*) to tune (an instrument) with or by another.
temente (*adj.*) fearful.—a Deus, God-fearing.
temer (*v.t.*,*v.i.*,*v.r.*) to fear, be afraid (de, of).
temerário –ria (*adj.*) rash, reckless, foolhardy, daredevil.
temeridade (*f.*) temerity, rashness, foolhardiness; derring-do.
temeroso –sa (*adj.*) fearful, dreadful; timorous, afraid.
temido –da (*adj.*) feared; frightening; timid, fearful.
temível (*adj.*) fearful, direful.
temor [ô] (*m.*) fear, dread; awe. sem—de êrro, without fear of contradiction.
temos, form of TER [78].
tempão (*m.*) a long time.
têmpera (*f.*) seasoning (of food); temperature (of the air); temperament, mettle; a tempera painting; (*Metal.*) degree of temper, hardness, toughness; act of quenching [but not of tempering, in the sense of drawing back or annealing, which is REVENIDO].—pela água, water quenching. —ao ar, air quenching.—pelo óleo, quenching in oil.

temperado –da (*adj.*) seasoned, spiced; temperate, moderate; (*Metal.*) hardened, toughened.
temperador –dora (*adj.*) seasoning; tempering, moderating.
temperamento (*m.*) temperament, constitution; temper; seasoning.
temperança (*f.*) temperance, moderation.
temperante (*adj.*) tempering; moderating; seasoning.
temperar (*v.t.*) to season, spice, flavor; to mix in due proportion; to moderate, soften; (*Metal.*) to harden by quenching. [But not to temper (draw back) which is REVENIR]; (*Music*) to temper.
temperatura (*f.*) temperature; fever.—crítica, (*Metal.*) critical temperature; arrestation point.
têmpero (*m.*) any seasoning or condiment; taste, relish.
tempestade (*f.*) tempest, storm.—em copo d'água, tempest in a teacup; much ado about nothing.
tempestivo –va (*adj.*) timely; well-timed.
tempestuar (*v.i.*) to storm.
tempestuosidade (*f.*) tempestuousness.
tempestuoso –sa (*adj.*) tempestuous.
templário (*m.*) Knight Templar.
templo (*m.*) temple, church.
tempo (*m.*) time; duration; spell, season; period, age, epoch; opportunity; proper time; weather; (*Music*) tempo; (*Gram.*) tense.—das chuvas, rainy season.—de indulto por boa conduta, time off for good behavior (in prison).—de sobra, time to spare.—(s) houve em que, there was a time when.—-quente, hot time, brawl; also = SACI (a bird).—s idos, bygone days.—variável, unsettled weather.—s d'antanho, the good old days. a—, on time; in time. a—integral, full-time. a medida que o tempo passa, as time goes by. a, or em, seu—, at the proper time; in due season. a um—, at one (and the same) time; altogether and simultaneously. antes do—, untimely; prematurely. ao—, out in the weather; at the time. ao mesmo—, at the same time; simultaneously. ao—que, while. ao—em que, at the same time that. aproveitamento de—, making good use of time. àquele—, at that time. até há pouco—, until recently. através dos —s, across the ages; through the years. bom—, good weather. com o—, in the course of time. dar—, to afford time. dar—ao tempo, to bide one's time. de—s em—s, from time to time. depois de passado muito—, after a long time had passed. em—recorde, in record time. em—s de, in times of. em—s passados, in bygone days. em—s que correm, in these days; nowadays. em—s que vão longe, in olden times; a long time ago; in the good old days. em bom—, in good time. em seu—, in due time. estar em—, to be in season; to be on time. fora de—, out of season; ill-timed. ganhar—, to gain time. gastar—, to waste time. há—s (atrás), some time ago. há muito—, long ago. há pouco—, recently. Há quanto—? How long ago? Há quanto—o Snr. está esperando? How long have you been waiting? Há quanto—(or quanto—faz que) você não joga tênis? How long is it since you played tennis? Há quanto—isto aconteceu? How long ago did this happen? Isto aconteceu há muito—, This happened a long time ago. levar—, to take time. mais a—, sooner. mau—, bad weather. meio—, half time. muito—, (for) a long time. Não faz muito—, Not long ago. naquele—, at that time. no—da onça, long, long ago; way back when. O—abrandou depois da chuva, The weather cooled off after the rain. O—urge, Time is pressing. Os—s estão difíceis, Times are hard. Passa do—, It is past the time. passado algum—, some time later passar—, to spend time. perder—, to lose time. por muito—, for much longer. pouco—, a short time. predição, or previsão, do—, weather forecast. primeiros—s da mocidade, early youth. Quanto—, How long? tanto—, so long (a time).
temporada (*f.*) season, spell; a long time.—lírica, opera season.
temporal (*adj.*) temporal, worldly, secular. poder—, temporal power (of the Pope). (*m.*) tempest, storm; commotion, disturbance; (*Anat.*) temporal bone.
temporalidade (*f.*) temporality, temporariness.
temporão [-rãos] –ra [-rãs] (*adj.*) untimely, premature, unseasonable, early.
temporário –ria (*adj.*) temporary, transitory; makeshift.
têmporas (*f.*) temples (sides of the forehead).
temporização (*f.*), temporizamento (*m.*) temporization; procrastination.
temporizar (*v.i.*) to temporize.

tem-tem (*m.*) toddling (of a child); any of various birds c.a. GATURAMO and ROUXINOL; a harrier-hawk (*Micrastur*).—**-de-estrêla** or—**-verdadeiro** = GATURAMO-VERDADEIRO.—**-do-espírito-santo**, the purple honey creeper (*Cyanerpes c. caeruleus*).

tem-tenzinho (*m.*) = CAURÉ.

temulência (*f.*) intoxication.

temulento –ta (*adj.*) intoxicated.

ten. = TENENTE (lieutenant).

ten.-c.[el] = TENENTE-CORONEL (lieutenant-colonel).

tenacidade (*f.*) tenacity, perseverance, doggedness; adhesiveness; fig., closefistedness.

tenacíssimo –ma (*absol. superl. of* TENAZ) most tenacious.

tenáculo (*m.*, *Surg.*) tenaculum.

tenalha (*f.*, *Fort.*) tenaille.

tenalhão (*m.*, *Fort.*) tenaillon.

tenantita (*f.*, *Min.*) tennantite, binnite.

tênar (*m.*, *Anat.*) thenar.

tenardita (*f.*, *Min.*) thenardite; sodium sulfate.

tenaz (*adj.*) tenacious, stubborn, obstinate, unyielding, dogged; adhesive; fig., closefisted; (*f.*) blacksmith's tongs.

tenca (*f.*, *Zool.*) the tench (*Tinca tinca*).

tenção (*f.*) intention, design, purpose. Cf. TENSÃO.

tencionar (*v.t.*) to intend.

tenda (*f.*) tent; market stall; small shop.—**de oxigênio**, oxygen tent. **armar**—, to set up shop.

tendal (*m.*) a deck awning; a place where meat and fish are hung on horizontal poles to dry; a drying platform for cacao beans; a place where sheep are shorn; a place where clothes are laid out to dry.

tendão (*m.*, *Anat.*) tendon, sinew.—**de Aquiles**, Achilles' tendon.

tende, form of TER [78].

tendeiro (*m.*) small shopkeeper.

tendência (*f.*) tendency, inclination, propensity.—**da conjuntura**, business trends.

tendencioso –sa (*adj.*) having a hidden design or motive, esp. an evil one; biased.

tendente (*adj.*) tending, prone to.

tender (*v.t.*) to extend (as, the hand); to fill, spread (sails); to roll out (dough); (*v.i.*) to tend, incline (**a**, **para**, **to**, toward).

tênder [-es] (*m.*, *R.R.*, *Naut.*) tender.

tendes, form of TER [78].

tendinha (*f.*) a small tent; a small, cheap shop.

tendo, gerund of TER [78].

tendilhão (*m.*) field tent.

tendinoso –sa (*adj.*) tendinous; sinewy.

tenebroso –sa (*adj.*) tenebrous; dark; gloomy; appalling.

tenência (*f.*) lieutenancy; lieutenant's quarters; (*colloq.*) vigor; prudence; one's usual manner or habits. **tomar —de,** to take stock of (a situation).

tenené (*m.*) = JOÃO-TENENÉM.

tenente (*m.*) lieutenant; deputy.—**-coronel**, lieutenant colonel. **primeiro—**, 1st lieutenant or lieutenant (j.g.). **segundo—**, 2nd lieutenant or ensign. **capitão—**, lieutenant (senior grade).

tenesmo (*m.*, *Med.*) tenesmus.

Tenessi [í] (*m.*) Tennessee.

tenh + verb endings = forms of TER [78].

tênia (*f.*, *Zool.*) taenia, tapeworm.

teníase (*f.*, *Med.*) taeniasis.

tenífugo –ga (*adj.*; *m.*, *Med.*) taeniafuge.

tenioide (*adj.*, *Zool.*) taenioid.

tênis (*m.*) tennis.—**de convés**, deck tennis.—**de mesa**, table-tennis (ping-pong). **quadra de—**, tennis court.

tenista (*m.*,*f.*) tennis player.

tenito (*m.*, *Min.*) taenite; kamacite.

tenor [ô] (*m.*) tenor (voice, singer).

tenorita (*f.*, *Min.*) tenorite.

tenossinite (*f.*, *Med.*) tenositis, inflammation of a tendon.

tenotomia (*f.*, *Surg.*) tenotomy.

tenro –ra (*adj.*) tender, soft, delicate; young, immature.—**idade**, tender age.—**s anos**, tender years.

tenrura (*f.*) tenderness.

tens, form of TER [78].

tensão (*f.*) tension; tenseness, strain.—**arterial**, arterial pressure.—**elétrica**, voltage.—**de superfície**, surface tension. **alta—**, high tension. Cf. TENÇÃO.

tensímetro (*m.*) tensimeter; manometer.

tensiômetro (*m.*, *Mach.*) tensiometer.

tensivo –va (*adj.*) tensive.

tenso –sa (*adj.*) tense, taut; stretched tight; intent, rapt.

tensor –sora (*adj.*) tensive; (*m.*, *Anat.*) tensor; (*Arch.*) tie beam; (*Mach.*) radius rod; tension rod; tension pulley; tension roller; (*Math.*) tensor.

tenta (*f.*, *Surg.*) probe.

tentação (*f.*) temptation; allurement.

tentaculado –da (*adj.*) tentacled, tentaculate.

tentacular (*adj.*) tentacular.

tentaculífero –ra (*adj.*) tentaculiferous; (*f.pl.*, *Zool.*) the Tentaculifera.

tentaculiforme (*adj.*) tentaculiform.

tentáculo (*m.*) tentacle; feeler; tentaculum.

tentador –dora (*adj.*) tempting; (*m.*) tempter; (*f.*) temptress.

tentame, tentâmen (*m.*) an attempt; an undertaking.

tentamento (*m.*) = TENTAÇÃO and TENTATIVA.

tentar (*v.t.*) to try, test, prove; to attempt, essay, venture; to tempt, entice, lure; (*v.r.*) to fall for temptation.—**a sorte**, to try one's luck.—**a Deus**, to tempt Providence.—**a fortuna**, to seek one's fortune.—**a paciência de alguém**, to try someone's patience.—**contra a vida de alguém**, to make an attempt on someone's life.—**os mares**, to defy the seas.

tentativa (*f.*) an attempt, effort, trial; temptation.

tenteador –dora (*adj.*) probing; groping; fumbling; (*m.*,*f.*) one who probes, gropes, fumbles.

tentear (*v.t.*) to probe; to sound, explore; to grope, fumble; to cut-and-try.

tentilhão (*m.*) a finch [= ABADAVINA].

tento (*m.*) care, attention; good sense; painter's maulstick; counter (piece for keeping score); (*Soccer*) goal; score; a leather thong.—**-azul**, the soaptree apes-earring (*Pithecellobium trapezifolium*), a medium-sized Amazonian tree with porous, soft and silky wood.—**-carolina**, (*Bot.*) = CAROLINA.—**-grande**, (*Bot.*) an ormosia (*O. nitida*). **a—**, warily. **tomar—**, to take careful notice. **marcar o—**, to keep score.

tênue (*adj.*) tenuous, slender; small, minute; subtle, rarefied.

tenuidade [u-i] (*f.*) tenuity.

Teobaldo (*m.*) Theobald.

teobroma (*m.*) the genus (*Theobroma*) of chocolate trees.

teobromina (*f.*, *Chem.*) theobromine.

teocale (*m.*, *Archaeol.*) teocalli.

teocracia (*f.*) theocracy.

teocrata (*m.*,*f.*) theocrat.

teocrático –ca (*adj.*) theocratic.

Teodora (*f.*) Theodora.

Teodoro (*m.*) Theodore.

teofania (*f.*) theophany.

Teófilo (*m.*) Theophilus.

teogonia (*f.*) theogony.

teologia (*f.*) theology.

teológico –ca (*adj.*) theological.

teologizar (*v.i.*) to theologize.

teólogo (*m.*) theologian.

teor [ô] (*m.*) tenor, meaning, intent, gist; manner, course; chemical content.—**alcoólico**, alcohol content. **de alto—**, high-grade [ore].

teorema (*m.*) theorem.

teorético –ca (*adj.*) theoretical.

teoria (*f.*) theory; theoria; procession.

teórico –ca (*adj.*) theoretical; (*f.*) = TEORIA.

teorista (*m.*,*f.*) theorist.

teorizar (*v.t.*,*v.i.*) to theorize.

teosinto (*m.*, *Bot.*) Mexican teosinte (*Euchlaena mexicana*).—**-de-guatemala** = CAPIM-DE-VENEZUELA.

teosofia (*f.*) theosophy.

teosófico –ca (*adj.*) theosophic(al).

teosofista, teósofo –fa (*m.*,*f.*) theosophist.

tepidez [ê] (*f.*) tepidity, lukewarmness.

tépido –da (*adj.*) tepid, lukewarm.

teque-teque (*m.*) a street peddler of dry goods and notions who uses a clacker to advertise his approach; (*Zool.*) the diminutive gray-headed tody-tyrant (*Todirostrum poliocephalum*), c.a. FERREIRINHO, JOÃO-DE-CRISTO, PAPA-SEBO.

ter [78] (*v.t.*) to have; to possess, own; to keep, hold; to contain; to get, gain; to bear, beget (offspring); (*v.r.*) to hold oneself (upright or in check); to hold (consider) oneself (to be something). [In addition to its principal function as a verb, **ter** serves also as an auxiliary in forming compound tenses, having in this respect supplanted HAVER: **Eu tenho telefonado todos os dias,** (I have telephoned every day); **Tem feito muito frio,** (It has been very cold), etc. **Ter** has also supplanted HAVER, in colloquial speech at least, in the sense of "to be, to exist": **Aqui tem telefone?** (Is there a telephone here?) instead of the correct but stilted: **Há telefone aqui?**] Cf. HAVER.—**a+verb=**to have to+verb [but the more usual form is ter **de** or ter **que. Tenho de** (or tenho que) **sair,** (I must go out), instead of tenho a sair].—**a certeza de,** to be certain of.—**a consciência elástica,** or **larga,** to have an elastic conscience.—**a consciência tranqüila,** to have a clear conscience.—**a faca e o queijo na mão,** fig., to hold all the trumps.—**à mão,** to have at hand.—**a mesma idade,** to be (of) the same age.—**a palavra,** to have the floor.—**a palavra de alguém,** to have someone's word.—**ares de,** to look like. [**Tem ares de patife,** He looks like a crook.].—**as cartas na mão,** to hold the winning hand.—**as costas quentes,** to have the backing of a powerful person.—**assunto,** to have something to talk about.—**boa aceitação,** to meet with approval; to find a ready market.—**bom êxito,** to have (meet) with success.—**cabeça para,** to have a head (aptitude) for.—**cara de,** to look like; to appear to be. [**Tem cara de tolo,** He looks like a fool. Also applied to inanimate things: **Esta casa tem cara de ser mal-assombrada,** This house looks as if it might be haunted. **Êste presunto tem** (or, **está com) cara de velho,** This ham looks stale.]—**ciumes de,** to be jealous of.—**com,** to have to do with. [**Isto nada tem com aquilo,** This has nothing to do with that. **Você nada tem com isso,** It's none of your business.]—**consciência de,** to be aware of.—**cuidado,** to be careful. [**Tenha cuidado!** Take it easy! Be careful!]—**culpa de,** to be to blame for; to be guilty of. [**Você é que tem culpa,** It's your fault.]—**de+infinitive=**to have (a definite obligation) to, be obliged to, must. [**Tem de pagar,** He (she, you) must pay. Cf. TER QUE.]—**dedo,** to have a knack for. Cf. TER JEITO.—**de memória,** to know by heart.—**de seu,** to be well off [or, negatively, **não ter de seu,** to have nothing. **Êle nada tem de seu,** He hasn't a nickel to his name.].—**direito a,** to have a right to (something).—**direito de,** to have a right to (do something).—**dó de,** to feel sorry for.—**dom da palavra,** to have a talent for speech; or, *colloq.*, to have the gift of gab.—**dono,** to be owned (by someone).—**dúvida,** to be in doubt, have doubts, be uncertain.—**em (pouco, muito, nada, etc.),** to consider (it) to be (little, much, nothing, etc.).—**em conta,** to make allowances for.—**em alta conta,** to have a high regard for.—**em mente,** to bear in mind.—**em vista,** to have in view; to have as a purpose.—**fé em,** to have faith in.—**inveja de,** to be envious of.—**lugar,** in idiomatic usage, this is a gallicism [French *avoir lieu*], meaning to take place, happen. Strictly speaking, however, it means to have place, be admissible, opportune.—**macaquinhos no sótão,** to have bats in the belfry.—**mania de,** to have a mania for; to be crazy about (something); to be obsessed with; to have the nasty habit of; to be stubbornly compulsive about.—**mãos largas,** to be openhanded, liberal.—**mêdo de,** to be afraid of.—**mêdo da própria sombra,** to be afraid of one's own shadow.—**muito que (a, para) fazer,** to have much to do.—**muito que dizer (contar, comunicar),** to have lots to say (relate, tell).—**na palma da mão,** to hold in the palm of the hand, lit. & fig.—**necessidade de,** to have need to.—**notícias de,** to hear from or about.—**o hábito** (or **o costume) de,** to be in the habit of.—**o juizo perfeito,** to be sane.—**o propósito de,** to intend to; to purpose.—**o sono leve (pesado),** to be a light (heavy) sleeper.—**para+verb=ter que+verb.**—(or **achar) para si,** to have one's own opinion. [**Eu tenho para mim,** I rather suspect . . .].—**partes com,** to have dealings with.—**partes com o diabo,** to have a pact with the devil.—**pena de,** to feel sorry for; to be reluctant to (do something).—**por,** to consider, judge. [ter (**algo) por incorreto,** to consider (something) to be wrong.]—**por fim,** to have as an end, as an objective.—**prazer em,** to be happy to; to enjoy (doing something).—**presente que,** to keep in mind that.—**que+infinitive=**to be (more or less) obliged to; must. [**Tenho que sair,** I must go out.]—**que dizer,** to have something to say about; find fault with.—**que fazer,** to have something to do.—**raiva de (alguém),** to hate (someone); to be angry at (someone) for a while.—**relações com,** to have intercourse with; to be on terms of close friendship with; to visit back and forth with.—**remédio,** to be remediable. [**Não tem remédio,** It can't be helped.]—**sangue de barata,** to have a yellow streak;

also, to be as cold as a fish (unemotional).—**sangue quente,** to be hot-headed.—**saudades de,** to miss, long for (someone or something).—**-se na conta de (escritor, juiz,** etc.), to look upon oneself as (a writer, judge, etc.).—**tempo,** to have time (**para, de,** for, to).—**um gesto,** to make a move; to display an attitude.—**uma telha demais** (or **de menos),** to have a screw loose (in the head).—**vontade de,** to want to, have a notion to, be anxious to; to feel like; to be in the mood for.—**vontade forte,** to be strong-willed. **A casa tem goteiras,** The house leaks; The house develops leaks all the time. **Aí tem (o livro),** There is (the book). **Aqui tem (o livro),** Here is (the book). **Aqui tem cachorro?** Is there a dog here? **Como é que você tem coragem de . . . ?** (1) I admire your courage in . . . ; (2) How could you do [such a thing]? **Ela tem cada uma!** She's full of tricks (fun)! She does the darndest things! She's impossible! Isn't that just like her? **Ela teve um acesso de riso,** She couldn't stop laughing. **Êle tem muito do pai,** He takes after his father in lots of ways. **Êle tem que ir à cidade amanhã,** He has to go downtown tomorrow. **Eu não tenho coragem de,** I'm not brave enough to; I don't have the heart to; I couldn't (do that). **Eu não tenho nada com isso,** That is no business of mine; that's your lookout. **nada—que ver com,** to have nothing to do with, not be concerned with. **Não tem dúvida,** There is no doubt about it. **não—eira nem beira,** of a person, to be good for nothing; to have no prospects; to be poverty-stricken. **não—jeito para,** to have no knack or talent for something; to be no good at (it). **não—nada com,** to be none of one's affair; to have no interest in. **não—por onde,** to see no way to (do something). **Não tem importância,** It doesn't matter. **Não tem jeito mesmo,** "No can do"; It's hopeless, no use trying; also, He's incorrigible. **Não tem pé nem cabeça,** I can't make head or tail of it; It makes no sense at all. **Não tem perigo,** There is no danger. **Não tem perigo!** (1) Don't you worry! (2) You won't catch *me* doing that! (3) Fat chance! **não tem senão,** has done nothing but. **Não tenha dúvidas,** Have no doubts, rest assured. **Não tenho coisa nenhuma que ver com isso,** I have absolutely nothing to do with it; I'm not involved; I "wash my hands." **Não tive outro remédio,** I could do nothing else. **Quantos anos tem (. . .)?** How old is (. . .)? **Que é que você tem?** What's the matter with you? What ails you? What's wrong? **Que idade tem você?** How old are you? **Que tem isso?** What does that matter? **Que tem você que fazer agora?** What have you to do now? **Tem graça,** That's funny. **Tem jeito de estrangeiro,** He looks (or acts) like a foreigner. **Tem (tenha) modos!** Behave yourself! **Tem muita gente aqui,** There are a lot of people here. **Tem os olhos azuis,** She has blue eyes. **Tem sorte,** he (she) is lucky; You are lucky. **Tenha a bondade (or a gentileza) de+verb=**Please+verb. **Tenha juizo!** Be sensible! Behave yourself! **Tenha paciência,** Have patience; or, Now, honestly! Come, now! **Tenho de (or que) estudar,** I've got to study. **Tenho muita pressa,** I'm in a great hurry. **Tenho muito que fazer,** I have lots to do. **Tenho para mim que . . . ,** Something tells me that . . . **Tenho plena certeza,** I am quite sure. **Tenho receio disso,** I'm afraid of that. **Terei que falar com êle,** I shall have to speak to him. **Você não tem razão,** You're wrong. **Você não tem vergonha?** Aren't you ashamed of yourself? **Você tem as horas?** Do you have the time? **Você tem razão,** You're right. **Você terá (or tem) cem cruzeiros que me empreste (or para me emprestar)?** Could you lend me 100 cruzeiros?

terapeuta (*m., f.*) therapeutist; therapist.

terapêutico -ca (*adj.*) therapeutic; (*f.*) therapeutics.—**ocupacional,** occupational therapy.

terapia (*f.*) =TERAPÊUTICA.

teratia (*f.*) monstrosity.

teratóide (*adj.*) teratoid.

teratologia (*f., Biol.*) teratology.

teratoma (*f., Med., Plant Pathol.*) teratoma.

térbio (*m., Chem.*) terbium.

têrça (*f.*) a third part; (*Eccl., Mus., Fencing*) tierce; (*Arch.*) purlin. Cf. TÊRÇO. (*adj.*) third (used only in **têrça-feira** and **têrça parte).** Cf. TERCEIRO.

terçã (*f.*) tertian fever.

terçado (*m.*) a machete (large heavy knife) used for tapping rubber trees, cutting through vines, etc.; a sword having a wide short blade.

terça-feira (*f.*) Tuesday.—**gorda,** Shrove Tuesday.

terçar (*v.t.*) to mix three of anything (as, cement, sand and gravel); to divide something into three parts; to cross swords.—**por**, or **em favor de**, to intercede in behalf of.
terceira (*f.*) see TERCEIRO.
terceiranista (*m.,f.*) a third-year student.
terceiro –**ra** (*adj.*) third; (*m.,f.*) the third one; third person; (*f.*) a woman go-between; (*Music*) third.—**via**, third copy.
tercêto (*m.*) tercet; triplet (in music).
terciário –**ria** (*adj.; m.*) tertiary.
tercina (*f., Bot.*) tercine.
têrço (*m.*) a third of anything ; (*R.C.Ch.*) chaplet (third of a rosary); (*Arch.*) the lower or upper third of a column; (*Naut.*) the middle third of a ship; (*Agric.*) a third share; leather bag. Cf. TÊRÇA.
terçó (*m.*) tercel (the male of various hawks, esp. of the peregrine falcon and the goshawk).
terçol [-çóis] (*m., Med.*) chalazion; sty.
terçolho (*m., colloq.*) = TERÇOL.
terébico –**ca** (*adj., Chem.*) terebic.
terebinteno (*m., Chem.*) terebentene, pinene.
terebintina (*f.*) turpentine.
terebinto (*m., Bot.*) the terebinth pistache (*Pistacia terebinthus*).
térebra (*m., Zool.*) a genus (*Terebra*) of marine gastropods.
terebração (*f.*) a piercing pain.
terebrante (*adj.*) boring, piercing; (*m.pl., Zool.*) the Terebrantia (sawflies, horntails, etc.).
terebrar (*v.t.*) to bore with a gimlet; to perforate.
terebrátula (*f., Zool.*) a lamp shell and others of the genus Terebratula.
terecaí (*m.*) a turtle (*Podocnemis unifilis*).
terédone (*m.*) the ship worm (*Teredo navalis*). Vars. TEREDO, TEREDEM.
tereftalato (*m., Chem.*) terephthalate.
teremembé (*m., f.*) an Indian of an extinct non-Tupi tribe who formerly lived on the coast of what is now Ceará; (*adj.*) pert. to or designating these people.
teremim (*m.*) theremin (an electronic musical instrument).
terém-terém (*m.*) = QUERO-QUERO.
tereno (*m.*) = GATURAMO-REI.
terereca (*m.,f.*) big talker but small doer.
teres [têl] (*m.pl.*) possessions, means.
Teresa (*f.*) Teresa, Theresa
tereterê (*m.*) miry ground.
teréu-teréu (*m.*) = QUERO-QUERO.
tergal (*adj., Zool.*) tergal, dorsal.
tergeminado –**da** (*adj., Bot.*) tergeminate.
tergito (*m., Zool.*) tergite.
tergiversação (*f.*) tergiversation; subterfuge, evasion.
tergiversar (*v.i.*) to tergiversate; to quibble.
tergo (*m., Zool.*) tergum.
teriatria (*f.*) veterinary science.
teriatro (*m.*) veterinary [= VETERINÁRIO].
term. = TERMINAÇAO (termination).
termal (*adj.*) thermal.
termas (*f.pl.*) hot springs.
termestesia (*f., Physiol.*) thermesthesia.
termia (*f.*) thermal unit.
térmico –**ca** (*adj.*) thermic.
terminação (*f.*) termination, end, conclusion; ending; suffix.
terminal (*adj.*) terminal; limiting. (*m., Elec.*) terminal.
terminália (*f., Bot.*) the genus (*Terminalia*) typifying the myrobalan family (*Terminaliaceae*).
terminante (*adj.*) terminating; conclusive, decisive; determinate.
terminantemente (*adv.*) categorically.
terminar –*(v.t.)* to terminate, conclude, close, bring to an end; to finish, complete; to bound, limit; (*v.i.*) to end, cease.—**em**, or **por**, (of words) to end in or with (a vowel, etc.).—**por**, to end up in or by.—**-se com**, to be bound or limited by.
terminativo –**va** (*adj.*) terminative.
término (*m.*) terminus, end, limit.—**feliz**, happy ending.
terminologia (*f.*) terminology.
térmion (*m., Physics*) thermion.
térmite, térmita (*f.*) termite; (*Metal.*) thermite.
têrmo (*m.*) term, limit, boundary; span, spell, period of time; end, finish; word, expression, phrase; (*Math.*) term of a fraction, etc.; (*Logic*) term of a syllogism; (*pl.*)

manners. [Terms in the sense of conditions is CONDIÇÕES.]
—**médio**, average; median; (*Logic*) middle term. **a—**, in full. **ao—**, finally; at last. **ao—de**, at the end of. **approximar-se do—**, to draw to a close. **em—s**, in proper form; within limits **em—s genéricos**, in general terms. **meio—**, halfway; the middle ground; compromise. **pôr —a**, to put an end to; to finish; to cut short.
termo [é] (*m.*) thermos bottle.
termoacoplamento (*m., Elec.*) thermocouple.
termoamperímetro (*m., Elec.*) thermoammeter.
termobarômetro (*m., Physics*) thermobarometer.
termocautério (*m., Surg.*) thermocautery.
termocinemática (*f.*) thermokinematics.
termocorrente (*f., Physics*) thermocurrent.
termocrôico –**ca** (*adj., Physics*) thermochroic.
thermocrose (*f., Physics*) thermocrosy.
termodifusão (*f.*) thermal diffusion.
termodinâmico –**ca** (*adj.*) thermodynamic; (*f.*) thermodynamics.
termoelemento (*m., Elec.*) thermoelement.
termoeletricidade (*f.*) thermoelectricity.
termoelétrico –**ca** (*adj.*) termoelectric(al).
termoeletrômetro (*m.*) thermoelectrometer.
termoeletromotriz (*adj.*) thermoelectromotive.
termoestábil (*adj., Biochem.*) thermostable.
termoestesia (*f.*) thermesthesia, sensitiveness to heat.
termoestesímetro (*m., Physiol.*) thermesthesiometer.
termófilo –**la** (*adj., Biol.*) thermophilic.
termofone (*m.*) thermophone.
termogalvanômetro (*m., Elec.*) thermogalvanometer.
termogêneo –**nea** (*adj.*) thermogenous, thermogenic.
termogénese, termogenia (*f.*) thermogenesis.
termogênico –**ca** (*adj.*) thermogenic.
termógeno –**na** (*adj.*) thermogenous.
termografia (*f.*) thermography.
termógrafo (*m.*) thermograph.
termolábil (*adj., Biochem.*) thermolabile.
termólise (*f., Chem.*) thermolysis.
termologia (*f.*) thermology.
termoluminescência (*f., Physics, Chem.*) thermoluminescence.
termomagnético –**ca** (*adj.*) thermomagnetic; pyromagnetic.
termomagnetismo (*m.*) thermomagnetism.
termometria (*f.*) thermometry.
termométrico –**ca** (*adj.*) thermometric(al).
termômetro (*m.*) thermometer.—**centígrado**, Centigrade thermometer.—**de álcool**, spirit thermometer.—**de Fahrenheit**, F. thermometer.—**de Réaumur**, R. thermometer.—**registrador**, a recording thermometer.
termometrógrafo (*m.*) thermometrograph.
termomultiplicador (*m., Physics*) a thermopile.
termonatrito (*m., Min.*) thermonatrite.
termoneutralidade (*f., Chem.*) thermoneutrality.
termopilha (*f., Physics*) thermopile.
termoplástico –**ca** (*adj.*) thermoplastic.
termoplegia (*f.*) heatstroke.
termopolipnéia (*f., Physiol.*) thermopolypnea.
termoquímica (*f.*) thermochemistry.
termorregulador (*m., Physics*) thermoregulator; thermostat.
termorresistente (*adj.*) heat-resistant.
termoscópico –**ca** (*adj.*) thermoscopic.
termoscópio (*m., Physics*) thermoscope.
termossifão (*m.*) thermosiphon.
termossistáltico –**ca** (*adj., Physiol.*) thermosystaltic.
termostático –**ca** (*adj., Physics*) thermostatic.
termóstato (*m.*) thermostat.
termostável (*adj., Biochem.*) thermostable.
termotaxia [ks] (*f., Biol., Physiol.*) thermotaxis.
termotensão (*f.*) thermotension.
termoterapia (*f., Med.*) thermotherapy.
termotropismo (*m., Biol.*) thermotropism.
ternado –**da** (*adj., Bot.*) ternate.
ternário –**ria** (*adj.*) ternary.
terneiro (*m.*) young calf.
terno –**na** (*adj.*) tenderhearted; affectionate; touching, pathetic; (*m.*) a threesome; three of anything forming a group; a trio; a man's (three-piece) suit; a trey or three-spot (card, die, domino).—**de missa**, Sunday suit.
ternura (*f.*) tenderness, kindness, gentleness; fondness.
tero-tero (*m.*) the Cayenne lapwing or spur-winged plover (*Belonopterus cayennensis*), c.a. TÉU-TÉU, QUERO-QUERO.
terpeno (*m., Chem.*) terpene.

terpileno (*m.*, *Chem.*) terpilene.
terpineno (*m.*, *Chem.*) terpinene.
terpineol (*m.*, *Chem.*) terpineol.
terpinol (*m.*, *Chem.*) terpinol.
terra (*f.*) earth, world; soil, ground; land; loam, dirt; native land; country, region, province; nation.—**a terra**, pedestrian, dull, commonplace.—**alheia**, foreign land.—**apurada**, rich soil.—**arável**, arable land.—**caída**, an extensive caving-in of the high banks of a river.—**cansada** or **safada**, worn-out land.—**cozida**, terra cotta [= TERRACOTA].—**da Promissão**, the Promised Land.—**de infusórios**, or—**fóssil**, infusorial earth; kieselguhr.—**de planta**, farming soil.—**de siena**, raw sienna.—**s devolutas**, unused public lands.—**firme**, terra firma; "an elevated portion of the terrain, above the inundation level." [*GBAT*].—**natal**, native land.—-**nova**, a Newfoundland dog; [*cap.*] Newfoundland.—-**roxa**, a rich red soil, especially valuable in the growing of coffee.—**vegetal**, rich loam; leaf mould, humus.—**virgem**, virgin land. **em**—, ashore; aground. **fio**—, ground wire. **por**—, on the ground. **saltar em**, or **descer à**,—, to go ashore.
terraço (*m.*) terrace, flat house top [= EIRADO, TERRADO]; a nearly level strip of high land bordering a sea, lake or river.
terracota (*f.*) terra cotta.
terral (*adj.*) land; (*m.*) a land breeze.
terramoto (*m.*) var. of TERREMOTO.
terrão (*m.*) var. of TARRÃO.
terraplenagem (*f.*) operation of moving, filling in and levelling with earth.
terraplenar (*v.t.*) to fill and level low ground.
terrapleno (*m.*) filled and levelled ground.
terrazo (*m.*) terrazzo.
terreal (*adj.*) earthy; terrestrial, worldly.
terreiro (*m.*) terrace; public square; flat open terrace on which coffee beans, etc., are spread to dry; cleared land in front of a farm house; any locale where voodoo rites are practiced; backyard, esp. a planted one.
terremoto (*m.*) earthquake. Var. TERRAMOTO.
terreno -na (*adj.*) terrestrial; earthy; mundane; (*m.*) terrain; plot of ground; tract of land; field or sphere of activity, knowledge, etc.; (*Geol.*) terrane.—**concertado**, fairly level land.—**de aluvião**, alluvial soil.—**undante**, undulating terrain. **despachar**—, to burn up the ground (speed). **preparar o**—**para**, to pave the way for; lit., to prepare the ground for.
térreo -rea (*adj.*) earthy; terrestrial; on the ground. **andar**—, ground floor.
terrestre (*adj.*) terrestrial; worldly; overland [transport].
terriço (*m.*) rich loam, humus, leaf mould.
terrícola (*adj.*, *Bot.*, *Zool.*) terricolous.
terrificante, terrífico -ca (*adj.*) terrifying, appalling.
terrígeno -na (*adj.*) terrigenous.
terrina (*f.*) soup tureen.
territorial (*adj.*) territorial.
territorialidade (*f.*) territoriality.
território (*m.*) territory.
terrível (*adj.*) terrible, awful.
terroada (*f.*) = TORROADA and ATERROADA.
terror [ô] (*m.*) terror; dismay.
terrorismo (*m.*) terrorism.
terrorista (*adj.*) terroristic; (*m.*,*f.*) terrorist.
terrorizar (*v.t.*) to terrorize [= ATERRORIZAR].
terroso -sa (*adj.*) earthy; earth-colored.
terso -sa (*adj.*) smooth, polished; pure, correct. [But not terse in the sense of brief and to the point, which is LACÔNICO.]
tertúlia (*f.*) an informal party or social gathering; a literary discussion.
tervalente (*adj.*, *Chem.*) trivalent.
tes. = TESOUREIRO (treasurer).
tese (*f.*) thesis. **em**—, in general; in theory.
têso -sa (*adj.*) tense, tight, taut; stiff, hard, rigid; (*slang*) broke, hard-up; (*m.*) steep hill; "a tongue or spit of land connecting dry ground which is separated by swampy or flooded terrain; an elevated bit of land not inundated during a flood; a dry meadow in the VÁRZEA." [*GBAT*]
tesoira (*f.*) & derivs. = TESOURA & DERIVS.
tesoura (*f.*) scissors, shears; cross-reins; truss of a gable roof; (*colloq.*) backbiter; (*Zool.*) the swallow-tailed flycatcher (*Muscivora tyrannus*), c.a. PIRANHA, PIRANHA-UIRA; Lichenstein's fork-tailed tyrant (*Muscipara vetula*), c.a. PAPA-MÔSCAS; the strange-tailed tyrant (*Yetapa risora*); the cock-tailed tyrant (*Alectrurus tri-*

color), c.a. GALITO; a fiddler crab (*Uca maracoani*); an earwig; a frigate bird [= ALCATRAZ]. Var. TESOIRA.
tesourada (*f.*) a cut or snip with the scissors. Var. TESOIRADA.
tesourão (*m.*) a steel shear; (*Zool.*) = GAVIÃO-TESOURA. Var. TESOIRÃO.
tesourar (*v.t.*) to scissor; to shear; to backbite. Var. TESOIRAR.
tesouraria (*f.*) treasury. Var. TESOIRARIA.
tesoureiro (*m.*) treasurer. Var. TESOIREIRO.
tesourinha (*f.*) a bird—the swallow-tailed chatterer (*Phibalura flavirostris*). Var. TESOIRINHA.
tesouro (*m.*) treasure; treasury; precious thing or person. Var. TESOIRO.
tessela (*f.*) tessella.
tesselário (*m.*) a maker of tesserae; one who tesselates.
téssera (*f.*) tessera.
test. = TESTEMUNHA (witness).
testa (*f.*) brow, forehead; (*Bot.*) testa, episterm.—**de ferro**, dummy, figurehead, straw man, stooge.—, or **cabeça, de ponte**, bridgehead. **à**—, at the front; in command. **à**—**de**, at the head of.
testáceo -cea (*adj.*) testaceous, brick-red.
testador -dora (*adj.*) will-making; (*m.*) testator; (*f.*) testatrix.
testamental (*adj.*) testamentary.
testamentário -ria (*adj.*) testamentary (*m.*,*f.*) a legatee.
testamenteiro (*m.*) executor of a will.
testamento (*m.*) testament, will.—**místico**, a sealed and secret will.—**ológrafo**, holographic will.
testada (*f.*) that portion of a road or street lying in front of a building. **varrer a**—, to disclaim all responsibility.
testante (*adj.*; *m.*,*f.*) = TESTADOR.
testar (*v.t.*) to will, bequeath (**a**, to); to test; (*v.i.*) to make one's will.
teste (*m.*) test.
testeira (*f.*) a front or forepart; frontage, façade; part of a nun's headdress which covers the forehead; headstall of a bridle; also = TESTICO.
testemunha (*f.*) witness; (*pl.*) landmarks.—**auricular**, or —**de ouvido**, earwitness.—**ocular**, or—**de vista**, eyewitness.—**falsa**, false witness.—**presencial**, personal witness.
testemunhador -dora (*adj.*) witnessing; (*m.*,*f.*) witnesser.
testemunhar (*v.t.*) to bear witness to, testify to, confirm, corroborate; to witness, observe, mark, notice; (*v.i.*) to manifest, evince; to serve as witness.
testemunhável (*adj.*) corroborative, confirmatory.
testemunho (*m.*) testimony, witness, evidence, proof.—**auricular**, hearsay evidence. **dar**—, to bear witness; to give evidence. **em**—**de**, in witness of, as evidence of.
testico (*m.*) either end of a two-handed saw, c.a. TESTEIRA or CABECEIRA.
testicondo -da (*adj.*, *Zool.*) testicond.
testículo (*m.*, *Anat.*, *Zool.*) testicle.—-**de-cão**, or -**de-perro**, (*Bot.*) the male orchis (*O. mascula*), c.a. BEXIGA-DE-CÃO.—-**de-frade** = AGNOCASTO.
testicular (*adj.*) testicular.
testificação (*f.*) testification.
testificador -dora, testificante (*adj.*) testifying; (*m.*,*f.*) testifier.
testificar (*v.t.*) to testify, bear witness to; to affirm, declare.
testilha (*f.*) quarrel.
test.º = TESTAMENTO (will).
testo -ta [é] (*adj.*) resolute; serious.
têsto (*m.*) a lid or cover for an iron or clay vessel.
testudinídeos (*m.pl.*) the Testudinidae (family of turtles).
testudo -da (*adj.*) hardheaded, stubborn; (*m.*) a turtle; also = PEIXE-GALO (a fish).
tesura (*f.*) tautness, stiffness, rigidness.
têta (*f.*) teat, tit, nipple.
tetania (*f.*, *Med.*) tetany.
tetânico -ca (*adj.*) tetanic.
tetanizar (*v.t.*, *Physiol.*) to tetanize.
tétano (*m.*, *Med.*, *Physiol.*) tetanus; trismus, lockjaw.
tetanomotor (*m.*, *Physiol.*) tetanomotor.
tetanotoxina [ks] (*f.*, *Biochem.*) tetanus toxin.
tetéia (*f.*) charm, trinket, bauble; a precious (darling) person.
tetérrimo -ma (*absol. superl. of* TETRO) exceedingly dark; most horrible.
tetéu (*m.*, *Zool.*) = QUERO-QUERO.—-**de-savana**, a stone curlew (*Burkinus*).

tetibrânquios (*m.pl.*, *Zool.*) a suborder of gastropods (*Tectibranchia*) which includes the bubble shells (genus *Bulla*) and the sea hares (genus *Tethys*).

tetigoniídeos [i-í] (*m.pl.*) a family (*Locustidae*, *syn. Tettigoniidae*) of grasshoppers.

tetipoteira (*f.*) a grape (*Vitis arbustiva*).

tetis (*m.*) any sea hare (genus *Tethys*).

teto (*m.*) ceiling; roof, shelter.—**absoluto**, (*Aeron.*) absolute ceiling. **preço——**, ceiling price. **sem——**, without a roof (over one's head).

tetrabrânquios (*m.pl.*, *Zool.*, *Paleontol.*) the Tetrabranchia.

tetrabrometo (*m.*, *Chem.*) tetrabromide.

tetracíclico –ca (*adj.*, *Bot.*, *Chem.*) tetracyclic.

tetracloretano (*m.*, *Chem.*) acetylene tetrachloride.

tetracloreto (*m.*, *Chem.*) tetrachloride.

tetracoco (*m.*, *Bacteriol.*) tetracoccus.

tetradá[c]tilo –la (*adj.*, *Zool.*) tetradactylous.

tetradimita (*f.*, *Min.*) tetradymite.

tetraédrico –ca (*adj.*) tetrahedral.

tetraedro (*m.*, *Geom.*) tetrahedron.

tetraexaedro (*m.*) = TETRAHEXAEDRO.

tetrafilo –la (*adj.*, *Bot.*) tetraphyllous, four-leaved.

tetraedrita (*m.*, *Min.*) tetrahedrite, gray copper ore [= PANABÁSIO].

tetrafásico –ca (*adj.*, *Elec.*) four-phase.

tetrafilar (*adj.*) four-wire.

tetrágenos (*m.pl.*, *Bacteriol.*) tetracocci.

tetragonal (*adj.*) tetragonal. **sistema——**, (*Cryst.*) tetragonal system.

tetrágono –na (*adj.*) tetragonal, four-sided. (*m.*, *Geom.*) tetragon.

tetragrama (*m.*) tetragram.

tetrahexaedro (*m.*, *Cryst.*) tetrahexahedron.

tetralogia (*f.*) tetralogy.

tetrâmero –ra (*adj.*) tetramerous.

tetrâmetro (*m.*) tetrameter.

tetramina (*f.*, *Chem.*) tetramine.

tetrandro –dra (*adj.*, *Bot.*) tetandrous, having four stamens.

tetra-nitro-anilina (*f.*, *Chem.*) tetranitroaniline, T.N.A.

tetrapétalo –la (*adj.*, *Bot.*) tetrapetalous.

tetrapode (*adj.*) tetrapod, having four feet.

tetrapolar (*adj.*, *Biol.*) tetrapolar; (*Magnetism*) four-pole.

tetráptero –ra (*adj.*, *Bot.*, *Zool.*) tetrapterous.

tetraspérmeo –mea, **tetraspermo** –ma (*adj.*, *Bot.*) tetraspermal, four-seeded.

tetrasporângio (*m.*, *Bot.*) tetrasporangium.

tetrásporo (*m.*, *Bot.*) tetraspore.

tetrassépalo –la (*adj.*, *Bot.*) tetrasepalous.

tetrassílabo –ba (*adj.*) tetrasyllabic(al); (*m.*) tetrasyllable.

tetrastáqueo –quea (*adj.*, *Bot.*) tetrastichous.

tetrástico –ca (*adj.*) four-ranked; having four lines or verses.

tetratiônico –ca (*adj.*, *Chem.*) tetrathionic.

tetratômico –ca (*adj.*, *Chem.*) tetratomic; quadrivalent.

tetravó (*f.*) great-great-great-grandmother.

tetravô (*m.*) great-great-great-grandfather.

tetraz (*m.*) cock-of-the-wood, capercaillie (*Tetrao urogallus*).

tetrazona (*f.*, *Chem.*) tetrazone.

tétrico –ca (*adj.*) sad, gloomy, dismal; frightful, awful; macabre, gruesome; austere; stern, harsh.

tetrilo (*m.*, *Chem.*) tetryl.

tetro –tra (*adj.*) dark, somber; frightful.

tétrodo (*m.*, *Elec.*) tetrode.

tetrose (*f.*, *Chem.*) tetrose.

tetróxido [ks] (*m.*, *Chem.*) tetroxide.

teu (*fem. tua*] (*poss. pron.*) thy, thine—familiar form of your, yours. Cf. VOSSO. **os——s**, your (own) folks.

téu (*m.*) = TOVACA.

teucrieta [ê] (*Bot.*) germander speedwell (*Veronica chamaedrys*).

têucrio (*m.*, *Bot.*) germander (*Teucrium*).

teúdo –da (*adj.*) designating a kept woman.

teurgia [e-ur] (*f.*) theurgy.

teurgista [e-ur] (*m.,f.*) theurgist.

téu-téu (*m.*) the Guianan thick-knee or stone curlew (*Burhinus bistriatus vocifer*); also = QUERO-QUERO.

teuto –ta (*adj.*) Teutonic, German.

teutônico –ca (*adj.*) Teutonic.

teve, form of TER [78].

tevê (*f.*) TV (television).

têxtil [x = z; pl. -teis] (*adj.*) textile, weavable [but not a textile, which is TECIDO or PRODUTO TÊXTIL.]

têxto [x = z] (*m.*) text.

textual [x = z] (*adj.*) textual.

textura [x = z] (*f.*) texture.

texugo (*m.*) a badger; (*colloq.*) a well-fed person.

tez [ê] (*f.*) complexion (of the face); skin.

T.G. = TIRO DE GUERRA (a school for military reservists).

ti (*pron.*) when preceded by a prep. (except COM) it is a form of TU (thee, you). **a**, **de**, **em**, **para**, **por**, **etc.**,**——**, to, from, in, for, by, etc., you. [COM + TI = CONTIGO]

tia (*f.*) aunt.—**-avó**, great-aunt, grandaunt. **ficar para——**, to remain unmarried, be an old maid.

tiã-tiã-prêto (*m.*) = ALFAIATE (the bird).

tiacê (*f.*) an attalea palm (*A. humboldtiana*).

Tiago (*m.*) James.

tiamina (*f.*, *Biochem.*) thiamine chloride, antiberiberi vitamin (B₂).

tiaporanga (*f.*, *colloq.*) drunkenness.

tiara (*f.*) tiara (the Pope's triple crown); fig., the papal position or dignity.

tiazina (*f.*, *Chem.*) thiazine.

tiazole (*m.*, *Chem.*) thiazole.

tibetano –na (*adj.*; *m.,f.*) Tibetan.

tíbia (*f.*, *Anat.*) tibia.

tibial (*adj.*, *Anat.*) tibial.

tibiez, **tibieza** [ê] (*f.*) lukewarmness, half-heartedness [= ENTIBIAMENTO].

tíbio –bia (*adj.*) tepid; lukewarm, healf-hearted; also = TIPIU (a finch).

tiborna (*f.*) hot bread soaked in new olive oil; a mixture of food and drink; (*Bot.*) a frangipani (*Plumeria drastica*), c.a. RAIVOSA.

tibuna (*f.*) = BÔCA-DE-BARRO.

ticaca (*f.*) = GAMBÁ.

tiburo (*m.*) = GUIAVIRA.

tição (*m.*) firebrand; dark or dirty person; devil; disagreeable or evil person.

Ticiano (*m.*) Titian.

tico (*m.*) a bit of anything; a nervous tic, twitch. Var. TIQUE.

tiçoeiro (*m.*) iron poker.

ticonha (*f.*) an eagle ray (*Rhinoptera jussieui*).

ticopá (*f.*) a grunt (*Pomadasis crocro*).

tico-tico (*m.*) any unspecified sparrow, but esp. the Brazilian sparrow (*Zonotrichia capensis matutina*), c.a. MARIA-JUDIA, SALTA-CAMINHO, JESUS-MEU-DEUS. [This well-behaved and beloved little Brazilian bird is gradually retreating before the onslaught of the rude and pugnacious PARDAL (English sparrow) which someone mistakenly imported into the country a number of years ago.]; also, a jig saw.—**-do-biri**, the black-faced spinetail (*Phleocryptes melanops*), c.a. CACHIMBÓ.—**-do-campo**, the grasshopper sparrow (*Myospiza humeralis*), c.a. MANIMBÉ, CANÁRIO-PARDO; also, Cabanis' warbling finch (*Poospiza lateralis cabanisi*).—**-do-mato**, the half-collared sparrow (*Arremon taciturnus*), c.a. JESUS-MEU-DEUS.—**-rei**, the southern crested finch (*Coryphospingus cucullatus rubescens*), and the pileated finch (*C. pileatus*), both c.a. CARDEAL, VINTE-UM-PINTADO, GALO-DO-MATO.

ticuna (*f.*) = CURARE.

tido –da (*p.p. of* TER) owned; held, considered.

tié (*m.*) any of various birds of the tanager family.—**-detopête**, the four-colored red-crested tanager (*Trichothraupis melanops*).—**-do-mato-grosso**, the rare and beautiful red ant tanager (*Habia rubica*).—**-galo**, the scarlet-crested tanager (*Tachyphonus cristatus*).—**-guaçu-paroá** = CARDEAL.—**-piranga** = CANÁRIO-DO-MATO.—**-prêto**, the red-crowned tanager (*Tachyphonus coronatus*), c.a. TCHÁ, GUARANDI-PRÊTO; also = GUARANDI.—**-sangue**, the saddle tanager (*Ramphocelus bresilius dorsalis*) of southern Brazil, c.a. TIÉ-FOGO, TIÉ-PIRANGA, TIÉ-VERMELHO, SANGUE-DE-BOI, TAPIRANGA, CANÁRIO-BAETA.

tiemanita (*f.*, *Min.*) tiemannite; mercuric selenide.

tietê (*m.*) = GATURAMO-SERRADOR.

tieteí (*m.*) = GATURAMO.

tietinga [ê] (*m.*) the handsome greater magpie tanager (*Cissopis leveriana major*) c.a. SANHAÇO-TINGA, PRE-BEXIM, ANICAVARA, PINTASSILGO-DO-MATO-VIRGEM.

tifa (*f.*, *Bot.*) the genus (*Typha*) of cattails.

tifáceo –cea (*adj.*, *Bot.*) typhaceous; (*f.pl.*) the cattail family (*Typhaceae*).

tifia (*f.*) a shining black wasp (*Tiphia sp.*).

tífico –**ca** (*adj., Med.*) typhic; typhoid.
tiflite (*f., Med.*) typhlitis.
tiflologia (*f.*) typhlology.
tiflose (*f., Med.*) typhlosis, blindness.
tifo (*m., Med.*) typhoid fever.—**abdominal**, typhoid fever.—**bilioso**,—**da américa**,—**ictérico**,—**icteróide**, all = FEBRE AMARELA (yellow fever).—**exantemático**, typhus; spotted fever.
tifóide, tifoídeo –**dea** (*adj.*) typhoid. **febre**—, typhoid fever.
tifolisina (*f., Immunol.*) typholysin.
tifoso –**sa** (*adj.*) typhous; (*m.,f.*) a typhoid patient.
tifotoxina [ks] ((*f., Biochem.*) typhotoxine.
tigela (*f.*) small bowl or porringer; tin cup used to collect rubber latex as it flows from the tree. **de meia**—, very mediocre; small; petty. **quebrar a**— (or **a panela**), to wear something (new dress, shoes, etc.) for the first time.
tigelada (*f.*) a bowlful.
tigmotaxia [ks] (*f., Biol.*) thigmotaxis; stereotaxis.
tigmotropismo (*m., Biol.*) thigmotropism; stereotropism.
tigrado –**da** (*adj.*) spotted like a tiger.
tigre (*m.*) tiger; a tigerish person; (*slang*) a first-year medical student; or a student who repeats a class; in the days of slavery, a barrel in which feces were collected; the slave who attended to this; a small tropical catfish (*Corydoras paleatus*) often seen in home aquaria.—**-d'água**, a South American terrapin (*Chrysemys d'orbignyi*). [The name derives from its spotted carapace, not from any exhibition of tigerish traits.]—**da-américa**, the jaguar.—**das-pereiras**, a pear sawfly.—**do-mar**, the barracuda.
tigreza [ê] (*f.*) tigeress.
tigrídia (*f.*) the tigerflower (*Tigridia pavonia*).
trigrino –**na** (*adj.*) tigrine; tigerish.
tigüera, tiguera (*f.*) a cornfield, or any field, which has been harvested.
tijoleira (*f.*) tile brick; large brick.
tijoleiro (*m.*) brickmaker; brickkiln.
tijolo [jô; *pl.*: jó] (*m.*) brick; a brick of candy or sweet paste.—**burro**, raw brick.—**esmaltado**, enamelled brick.—**perfurado**, cored brick.—**refratário**, fire brick.—**vidrado**, glazed brick. **fazer**—, to flirt; to be dead and buried.
tijuca (*f.*) = ASSOBIADOR (a bird) and TIJUCO.
tijucada (*f.*), **tijucal** (*m.*) morass. Vars. TUJUCADA, TUJUCAL.
tijuco (*m.*) morass; mud; "dark grey mud with very fine plastic texture consisting of silt carried down by the rivers." [GBAT]
tijupá (*m.*) an inverted V-shaped straw hut; an Indian hut; awning on a canoe.
til (*m.*) tilde: a diacritical mark [⌣].
tilaíto (*m., Petrog.*) tilaite.
tilar (*v.*) = TILDAR.
tilasito (*m., Min.*) tilasite.
tílburi (*m.*) tilbury.
tildar (*v.t.*) to place a tilde over (a vowel).
tília (*f., Bot.*) a genus (*Tilia*) of lindens.
tiliáceo –**cea** (*adj., Bot.*) tiliaceous; (*f.pl.*) the linden family (*Tiliaceae*).
tilintar (*v.t., v.i.*) to clink, jingle, tinkle; to ring (as a coin).
timacetina (*f., Pharm.*) thymacetin.
timão (*m.*) beam of a plow, pole (of a vehicle); tiller; helm; fig., control, management; a long nightgown.
timbale (*m.*) timbal, kettledrum; (*Cookery*) timbale.
timbaleiro (*m.*) tympanist.
timbaúba (*f.*) an alumbarktree (*Stryphnodendron guianense*), a valuable tree of French Guiana, where it is called "*Bois Serpent*".
timbaúba (*f.*) = FAVA-DE-RÔSCA.
timbaúva (*f.*) a soapbark tree (*Quillaja brasiliensis*), c.a. PAU-DE-SABÃO; also = TIMBOÚVA.
timbira (*m.,f.*) An Indian of the Timbira, a tribe of the Northwestern Ge in Maranhão and Piaui; (*adj.*) pert. to or designating this tribe.
timbó (*m.*) an Amazon woody vine (*Paullinia pinnata*), the bitter bark of which contains a fish poison; c.a. CURURU-APÉ; a lancepod (*Lonchocarpus nicou*), c.a. TIMBÓ-MACAQUINHO; a fishfuddle tree (*Piscida erytharia*); a bladderflower (*Araujia sericifera*), c.a. CIPÓ-DE-SAPO; the meadow rue paullinia (*P. thalictrifolia*), c.a. CAMAÍUA.—**açu** or—**de-jacaré**, a jewelvine (*Derris guianensis*).—**amarelo**, a supplejack (*Serjania ovali-*

folia), c.a. CIPÓ-TIMBÓ.—**boticário**, a lancepod (*Lonchocarpus peckolti*).—**bravo** = CIPÓ-DE-TIMBÓ.—**caá**, a tephrosia (*T. nivens*), c.a. AJARÉ.—**cabeludo** = GUARUMINA.—**catinga** or—**taturuaia**, a lancepod (*Lonchocarpus floribundus*).—**cipó** = CURURU-APÉ.—**da-mata**, an earpod tree (*Enterolobium schomburgkii*), c.a. FAVA-DE-RÔSCA; also, a piptadenia (*P. recurva*).—**das-piranhas** = CIPÓ-DE-MACACO.—**de-caiena**, the fishdeath tephrosia (*T. toxicaria*).—**de-peixe** = GUARUMINA, CIPÓ-TIMBÓ.—**do-campo** = CIPÓ-D'ÁGUA.—**do-rio-de-janeiro**, the clammy ground cherry (*Physalis heterophylla*), c.a. BATETESTA, CANAPU.—**fedorento** = CIPÓ-TIMBÓ.—**titica**, the heartleaf ampelopsis (*A. cordata*).—**legítimo** = CIPÓ-TIMBÓ.—**manso** = DRAGÃO-FEDORENTO.—**miúdo**, a supplejack (*Serjania communis*).—**urucu** or—**vermelho**, a lancepod (*Lonchocarpus urucu*).
timboína (*f., Chem.*) timboin.
timborana (*f.*) a lancepod tree (*Lonchocarpus discolor*); an earpod tree called FAVA-DE-RÔSCA, which see.
timboúva (*m.*) an earpod tree (*Enterolobium timbouva*), c.a. ORELHA-DE-PRÊTO, TIMBORIL, TIMBAÚBA. [It is a beautiful timber tree and is used for street planting in Buenos Aires; its red, easily-worked wood is used for furniture and interior woodwork.]
timbòzinho (*m., Bot.*) an indigo (*Indigofera lespedezoides*).
timbrar (*v.t.*) to mark or emboss with coat of arms, seal, emblem, etc.—**de**, to dub, name, call.—**em**, to pride oneself on.
timbre (*m.*) seal, mark, emblem, insignia; stamp; crest (on a coat of arms); justifiable pride; a timbrel; (*Music*) timbre, tone color.
timbri (*m.*) the mountain persimmon [*Diospyros montana*).
timbroso –**sa** (*adj.*) punctilious; meticulous.
timbu [ú] (*m.*) = GAMBÁ.
timbuar (*v.i., colloq.*) to have a relapse.
time (*m.*) team, esp. of soccer players.
timeleáceo –**cea** (*adj., Bot.*) thymelaeaceous; (*f.pl.*) the mezereum family (*Thymelaeaceae*).
timeléia (*f., Bot.*) a daphne (*D. thymelaea*).
timélia (*f., Zool.*) a genus (*Timalia*) of babbling thrushes typifying the family Timaliidae.
tímico –**ca** (*adj., Anat.*) thymic.
timicuí (*m.*) a small tick (insect).
timidez [ê] (*f.*) timidity, shyness, diffidence.
tímido –**da** (*adj.*) timid, fearful; shy, diffident; bashful; (*m.,f.*) a timid person.
timina (*f., Chem.*) thymine.
timiose (*f., Med.*) thymiosis.
timo (*m., Anat.*) thymus; (*Bot.*) thyme [= TOMILHO].
timol [-móis] (*m., Chem.*) thymol.
timoneiro (*m.*) helmsman, steersman; by ext., guide, ruler. **Na hora da tempestade não se muda o**—, Don't swap horses in the middle of the stream.
timorato –**ta** (*adj.*) timorous.
Timóteo (*m.*) Timothy; [*not cap.*] timothy grass.
timpanal, timpânico –**ca** (*adj.; m., Anat., Zool.*) tympanic.
timpanilho (*m., Print.*) tympan.
timpanismo (*m.*) -**nite** (*f., Med.*) tympanites; meteorism.
timpanítico –**ca** (*adj., Med.*) tympanitic.
tímpano (*m.*) a kind of Persian water-raising wheel; (*Anat., Zool.*) tympanum; (*Arch.*) tympanum; panel; spandrel; (*Print.*) tympan; (*Music*) timbal, kettledrum.
timucu [cú] (*m.*) = PEIXE-AGULHA.
tina (*f.*) tub, trough, vat.
tinada (*f.*) tubful.
tinalha (*f.*) small tub.
tinamu [ú] (*m., Zool.*) any tinamou.
tincal (*m., Min.*) tincal (crude native borax), c.a. ATINCAL.
tinção (*f.*) = TINTURA.
tinéia (*f.*) a tineid moth.
tineídeos (*m.pl.*) a family (*Tineidae*) of small moths, such as the cloth moths.
tineta (*f., colloq.*) whim, fancy, kink, odd notion.
tingido –**da** (*reg. p.p. of* TINGIR) dyed. Cf. TINTO.
tingidor –**dora** (*adj.*) dyeing; (*m.,f.*) dyer.
tingidura (*f.*) = TINTURA.
tingir [24] (*v.t.*) to dye, tint; to tinge; to stain.
tingua-aba (*m.*) = CAFERANA.
tinguaciba (*f.*) a pricklyash (*Zanthoxylum sp.*), c.a. ESPINHO-DE-VINTÉM.—**do-pará** = CAFERANA.
tinguaçu [çú] (*m.*) a bird—the gray-throated attila (*Attila rufus*), c.a. CAPITÃO-DE-SAÍRA; also, a cuckoo called ALMA-DE-GATO.

tinguaíte -ta (*m.*, *Petrog.*) tinguaite.

tingui [guí] (*m.*) a lupine (*Lupinus cascavella*) used as a fish poison; also = CONAMBI and CIPÓ-DE-TIMBÓ.——**-capeta**, a supplejack (*Serjania erecta*).—**-da-praia** = CALÇÃO-DE-VELHO.—**-das-piranhas** = CIPÓ-DE-MACACO.. —**-de-cipó**, a paullinia (*P. trigonia*).—**-de-peixe**, a jacquinia (*J. tingui*) used as a fish poison.

tinguijada (*f.*) poisoning of fish as a means of taking them.

tinguijar (*v.t.*) to poison fish; to place fish poison in a river, etc.; to dump industrial wastes into a river; (*v.i.*) to be poisoned (referring to fish).

tinh + verb endings = forms of TER [78].

tinha (*f.*, *Med.*) tinea; ringworm.—**-verdadeira**, or **-favosa**, favus.

tinhorão (*m.*, *Bot.*) common caladium (*C. bicolor*), c.a. ARÁ, TAJÁ, TAMBATAJÁ.

tinhoso -sa (*adj.*) mangy, scabby; repugnant; (*m.*, *colloq.*) the Devil; (*m.*,*f.*) one suffering from tinea.

tinhuma (*f.*) = QUERÊ-QUERÉ.

tinido (*m.*) tinkling (as of glass); ringing (as of metal); jingling (as of spurs).

tininte (*adj.*) tinkling; jingling.

tinir [25] (*v.i.*) to tinkle; to jingle.—**de frio (mêdo)**, to tremble, shiver with cold (fear). **estar a—**, to be penniless, broke.

tino (*m.*) judgment, discernment, good sense, prudence; tact; intuition; wits.

tinote (*m.*) a small tub.

tinta (*f.*) see TINTO.

tintagem (*f.*) inking of a printing press.

tintar (*v.t.*) to ink a printing press.

tinteira (*f.*) ink fountain of a printing press; (*Bot.*) a seagrape (*Coccolobis excelsa*) which yields a dyestuff; also = MUTUTI.—**-do-campo**, a waterprimrose (*Jussiaea lithospermifolia*).

tinteiro (*m.*) inkwell, inkstand; (*Print.*) ink fountain. **ficar no—**, to remain unsaid, be forgotten.

tintim-por-tintim (*adv.*) minutely; point by point; in full detail.

tintinabular (*v.t.*,*v.i.*) to tintinnabulate.

tintinar (*v.*) = TILINTAR.

tinto -ta (*adj.*; *irreg. p.p. of* TINGIR) dyed; tinted; stained; of wine, red. Cf. TINGIDO. (*f.*) ink; paint; dye; (*Bot.*) the littleflower wildtobacco (*Acnistus parciflorus*); small amount, dash, trace; also used as a combining term for many varieties of Portuguese red grapes.—**a óleo**, oil paint.—**da China**, —**de Cantão**, —**de Nanquim**, —**oriental**, India ink.—**de escrever**, writing ink.—**de imprimir**, or **de imprensa**, printer's ink.—**de pintar**, paint.—**fresca**, wet paint.—**indelével**, indelible ink.—**simpática**, sympathetic ink. **meia—**, halftone.

tintômetro (*m.*, *Physics*) tintometer; colorimeter.

tintorial, **tintório** -ia (*adj.*) tinctorial.

tintura (*f.*) dyeing; tincture; paint; (*pl.*) smattering.

tinturaria (*f.*) dyeing and cleaning establishment; the cleaner's; the dyer's.

tintureiro -ra (*adj.*) dyeing; (*m.*,*f.*) dyer and cleaner; (*m.*) a variety of red grapes; (*colloq.*) Black Maria (police wagon), c.a. VIÚVA-ALEGRE; (*f.*, *Bot.*) a dividivi (*Caesalpinia tinctoria* or *C. coriaria*); also = ERVA-DOS-CANCROS (a peaberry), QUARÓ, and RESEDÁ-AMARELO.—**vulgar** = CARURU-DE-CACHO (a jute); (*Zool.*) the tiger shark (*Galeocerdo arctivus* or *G. maculatus*).

tio (*m.*) uncle; (*pl.*) uncles and aunts.—**-avô**, great uncle, granduncle.

tioálcool (*m.*, *Chem.*) thioalcohol; mercaptan.

tiobenzóico -ca (*adj.*, *Chem.*) thiobenzoic [acid].

tiocianato (*m.*, *Chem.*) thiocyanate.

tiociânico -ca (*adj.*, *Chem.*) thiocyanic [acid].

tioéter (*m.*, *Chem.*) thioether.

tiofeno (*m.*, *Chem.*) thiophene; thiofuran.

tiofenol (*m.*, *Chem.*) thiophenol; phenyl mercaptan.

tiom-tiom (*m.*) = BACURAU.

tiônico -ca (*adj.*, *Chem.*) thionic.

tionina (*f.*, *Chem.*) thionine; Lauth's violet.

tiopirina (*f.*, *Chem.*) thiopyrine.

tiosinamina (*f.*, *Chem.*) thiosinamine, allyl thiourea.

tiossulfato (*m.*, *Chem.*) thiosulfate.—**de chumbo**, lead thiosulfate.—**de sódio**, sodium thiosulfate; Hypo.

tiossulfúrico -ca (*adj.*, *Chem.*) thiosulfuric [acid].

tipa (*f.*, *slang*) a "dame," esp. one of easy virtue.

tipi [pí] (*m.*) = CARURU-DE-CACHO, GUINÉ, ERVA-PIPI.

típico -ca (*adj.*) typical, representative, symbolic.

tipió (*m.*) a small finch or canary bird (*Sicalis luteola* or *S. arvensis*).

tipiri [rí] (*m.*) = ARARIBÁ-ROSA.

tipisca (*f.*) an inland body of water formed by the overflowing of the Amazon and other rivers [= SACADO].

tipiti [tipití] (*m.*) a long, elastic, plaited cylinder of JACITARA-palm bark used by Brazilian Indians in expressing the poisonous juice from grated manioc root. [It operates on the principle of the Chinese "torture tube".] ; by analogy, a tight spot.

tipitinga (*adj.*) muddy [water].

tipiu (*m.*) a bird—the misto yellow finch (*Sicalis luteola luteiventris*), c.a. TIBIO.

tiple (*m.*,*f.*) = SOPRANO.

tipo (*m.*) type, model; representative; printing type; (*colloq.*) odd, eccentric person, a "character"; a fellow, "guy," "customer".—**padronizado**, standard type. **um—de**, a sort of.

tipocromia (*f.*) color-printing.

tipografar (*v.t.*) to print.

tipografia (*f.*) typography; printing plant.

tipográfico -ca (*adj.*) typographic.

tipógrafo (*m.*) typographer, printer; typesetter, compositor.

tipóia (*f.*) an arm sling; an old hammock; a hammock swung from a pole and thus carried on the shoulders of bearers; a rickety old cart; a tent or shelter made of foliage.

tipolitografia (*f.*) typolithography.

tipometria (*f.*, *Print.*) typometry.

tipuana (*f.*) the common tiputree (*Tipuana tipu*).

típula (*f.*) a crane fly ("daddy longlegs") of the genus Tipula.

tipulídeos (*m.pl.*, *Zool.*) the Tipulidae (family of crane flies).

tiquara (*f.*) any cooling drink; also = CHIBÉ.

tique (*m.*) tic, bad habit; a bit of something.—**-taque**, tick-tock. **nem—nem taque**, nothing .

tiquinho (*m.*) a little bit or piece of something. [Dim. of TICO].

tiquira (*f.*) "alcoholic spirits distilled from manioc." [*GBAT*]

tira (*f.*) a strip (of paper, cloth, etc.); ribbon, band; (*slang*) police detective.

tira-bragal (*m.*) truss (for hernia).

tiração (*f.*) logging (in Amazonia).

tira-cisma (*m.*) a heavy pocketknife, sometimes used as a weapon; any weapon or whip carried as a warning to would-be aggressors.

tiracolo (*m.*) a baldric, shoulder belt. **a—**, slung over the shoulder and across the chest (as a bandoleer).

tirada (*f.*) act of taking, drawing, pulling, etc. See the verb [TIRAR]; a long stretch of road; a considerable length of time; an extensive passage or quotation; a tirade; exportation of foodstuffs.

tiradeira (*f.*) a chain or strap connecting the yoke of a pair of oxen to that of another pair behind; a fishing line with many hooks; a woman who shells cacao pods; (*pl.*) traces (of a harness).

tiradela (*f.*) = TIRADURA.

tira-dentes (*m.*, *colloq.*) dentist [lit., tooth puller]; [*cap.*, *not hyphenated*] nickname of Joaquim José da Silva Xavier (1748-1792), Brazilian martyr in the cause of independence.

tiradoura (*f.*) shaft of a cart; beam of a plow. Var. TIRADOIRA.

tiradura (*f.*) act of pulling, etc. See the verb [TIRAR].

tira-dúvidas (*m.*) someone who, or something which, removes doubt, settles a matter.

tirafundo (*m.*) a long auger; a screw bolt for fastening rails to crossties. Var. TIREFÃO.

tiragem (*f.*) circulation, number printed (of newspapers, books, etc.), printing, presswork; draft (of a chimney); the drawing of metal; the drawing of lots; a drawing off or out of anything.—**forçada**, forced draft.

tira-linhas (*m.*) draftsman's ruling pen.

tirambóia (*f.*) = JAQUIRANABOIA.

tiramento (*m.*) = TIRADURA.

tirana (*f.*) see TIRANO.

tiranete [nê] (*m.*) petty tyrant, martinet.

tirania (*f.*) tyranny, despotism; oppression; (*colloq.*) ingratitude.

tirânico -ca (*adj.*) tyrannical, despotic; oppressive; overbearing.

tiranizar (*v.t.*) to tyrannize.
tirano –na (*adj.*) tyrannical; (*m.*) tyrant, despot; bully; (*f.*) shrew, termagant; a kind of fandango; (*colloq.*) a hoe.
tira-nódoas (*m.*) spot remover.
tirante (*adj.*) drawing, pulling; (*prep.*) except; (*m.*) strap or trace (of a harness); a tie-rod; a tie-beam; driving rod (of a locomotive or steam engine).—**a**, like, resembling. —**a verde, azul**, etc., greenish, bluish, etc.
tirão (*m.*) a strong pull, jerk, tug; an apprentice.
tirapé (*m.*) shoemaker's stirrup.
tira-peia (*f.*) = JARARACA-PINTADA.
tira-prosa (*f.*, *colloq.*) a "tough guy" [= VALENTÃO].
tirar (*v.t.*) to take (away, off, out); to draw out (sword); to pull (cart); to remove (coat); to extract (tooth); to draw (profits); to attract (as a magnet); (*v.i.*) to withdraw.—**a**, to deprive of.—**a limpo**, to make a clean copy of; to get at the bottom of (a situation).—**a mesa**, to clear the table.—**a sardinha com a mão do gato**, to use someone' as a cat's-paw [alluding to the fable of the monkey using the cat's paw to draw the roasting chestnuts out of the fire].—**a sorte**, to draw lots; to try one's luck.—**a sorte grande**, to win the grand (lottery) prize; to hit the jack pot.—(**as**) **conseqüências**, to draw inferences.—**a sela**, to unsaddle.—**água de pedra**, to get blood from a turnip. —**baforadas**, to puff (a cigar, etc.).—**de**, to take from; to infer from.—**do êrro**, to disabuse (someone).—**a farinha**, (*colloq.*) to start a fight; to get even.—**férias**, to take a vacation.—**fogo**, to strike sparks.—**leite de vaca morta**, to cry over spilled milk.—**notas altas**, to get high (school) marks.—**o(s) boi(s) da linha**; to remove obstacles; lit., to get the cow(s) off the track.—**o cavalo da chuva**, (*colloq.*) to put the cards on the table.—**o chapéu**, to take off one's hat.—**o corpo fora**, to side-step.—**o retrato**, to have one's picture taken.—**partido de**, to turn to account; to make capital of; to take advantage of; to benefit by.—**um curso**, to take a course (of study).—**um fiapo com**, to engage in a flirtation with.—**uma conclusão**, to draw a conclusion.—**uma cópia de**, to make a copy of.—**uma fatura**, to make out an invoice.—**vantagem de tudo**, to turn everything to account. **Ninguem me tira isso da cabeça**, No one can convince me otherwise. **sem—nem pôr**, precisely, without exaggeration.
tira-teimas (*m.*) a clincher, decisive argument; by ext., a dictionary, or (*slang*) a club.
tira-testa (*f.*) front of a bridle.
tiratron, tiratrônio (*m.*, *Elec.*) thyratron.
tiravira (*f.*) parbuckle; (*Zool.*) the saury (*Scombresox saurus*), a slender, long-beaked fish, c.a. AGULHÃO-ATUM; the lizard fish (*Synodus foetens*), or the sand-diver (*S. intermedius*), c.a. LAGARTO-DO-MAR, PEIXE-LAGARTO, CALANGO.
tirefão (*m.*) = TIRAFUNDO.
tireoaritenoideu (*adj.*, *Anat.*) thyroarytenoid.
tireoepiglótico –ca (*adj.*, *Anat.*) thyroepiglottic.
tireohioideu (*adj.*, *Anat.*) thyrohyoid.
tireóide (*adj.*, *f.*, *Anat.*) thyroid (gland).
tireoidectomia (*f.*, *Surg.*) thyroidectomy.
tireóideo –dea, **tireoideu** (*adj.*, *Anat.*) thyroid.
tireoidina (*f.*, *Med.*) thyroid extract.
tireoidite (*f.*, *Med.*) thyroiditis.
tirete [rê] (*m.*) hyphen [= HÍFEN or TRAÇO DE UNIÃO].
tiriba (*m.*) any Brazilian parrot of the genus Pyrrhura [c.a. MEREQUÉM], esp. Azara's paroquet (*Pyrrhura chiripepe*) of southern Brazil, c.a. PERIQUITO.—**grande**, the red-eared paroquet of southeastern Brazil (*Pyrrhura cruentata*), c.a. FURA-MATO, TIRIBINHA, TIRIBAÍ.—**pequeno**, the white-eared paroquet of southeastern Brazil (*Pyrrhura leucotis*), c.a. FURA-MATO. Var. TIRIVA.
tiribaí (*m.*), **tiribinha** (*f.*) = TIRIBA-PEQUENO.
tiriri (*m.*) = JOÃO-TENENÉM.
tiririca (*f.*) a wild pig [= QUEIXADA]; permanently turbulent stretches of water in the Pará River; "brambles overhanging river banks which impede navigation" [*GBAT*]; (*Bot.*) a flatsedge (*Cyperus*), c.a. CAPISCABA-MIRIM; a razor sedge (*Scleria tenacissima*).—**falsa** = FALSA-TIRIRICA; (*m.*, *slang*) thief; pickpocket; (*adj.*, *colloq.*) irate, riled up, burned up.
tiririal (*m.*) a place abounding in sedges.
tiritante (*adj.*) shivering (with cold).
tiritar (*v.i.*) to shiver, shake (with cold).
tiriva (*m.*) = TIRIBA.
tiro (*m.*) a shot; act of shooting; discharge of a gun; firing distance; target range; a telling remark; trace of a

harness; act (by animals) of drawing a vehicle; a team of draft animals; (*slang*) criminal hold-up.—**ao alvo**, target practice.—**cego**, point-blank shot.—**de guerra**, military training school.—**de misericórdia**, coup de grâce; finishing stroke.—**de revólver**, pistol shot.—**livre**, (*Soccer*) free kick. **dar um—na praça**, (*slang*) to declare fraudulent bankruptcy. **O—saiu pela culatra**, the charge (scheme, plot) backfired.
tirocínio (*m.*) apprenticeship; early training; military training for promotion.
tiróglifo (*m.*) a genus (*Tyroglyphus*) of mites which includes the cheese mites.
tirolês –lesa (*adj.*; *m.*,*f.*) Tyrolese; (*f.*) Tyrolienne (song).
tirólito (*m.*, *Min.*) tyrolite.
tirosina (*f.*, *Biochem.*) tyrosin(e).
tirosínase (*f.*, *Biochem.*) tyrosinase.
tirotear (*v.t.*,*v.i.*) to volley.
tiroteio (*m.*) volley; gun fight; steady stream of words.
tirotóxico [ks] (*m.*, *Biochem.*) tyrotoxicon.
tirrênio –nia, **tirreno** –na (*adj.*) Tyrrhenian, Etruscan.
tirso (*m.*, *Bot.*, *Gk. Relig.*) thyrsus.
tirsóide (*adj.*, *Bot.*) thyrsoid.
tisana (*f.*) ptisan, tisane.
tisanopteros (*m.pl.*, *Zool.*) the Thysanoptera (thrips).
tisanuros (*m.pl.*, *Zool.*) the Thysanura (bristletails).
tísico –ca (*adj.*; *m.*,*f.*) consumptive; (*f.*) phthisis; consumption, tuberculosis of the lungs.—**galopante**, galloping consumption.—**pulmonar**, pulmonary tuberculosis.
tisna (*f.*) a blackening; lampblack or other blackening substance.
tisnado –da (*adj.*) blackened; grimy; sunburned; swarthy.
tisnar (*v.t.*) to blacken (with soot); to smudge; to scorch.
tisne (*m.*) grime; soot; smudge; stain; moral blot.
Titã (*m.*) Titan; [*not cap.*] a titan crane.
titanato (*m.*, *Chem.*) titanate.
titânico–ca (*adj.*) titanic.
titanífero –ra (*adj.*, *Chem.*) titaniferous.
titânio (*m.*, *Chem.*) titanium.—**oxidado**, titanium dioxide. —**oxidado ferrífero**, titanic iron ore; ilmenite.—**silício calcário**, titanite, sphene.
titanita (*f.*, *Min.*) titanite, sphene.
titela (*f.*) breast of chicken, etc.; hence, the best part of anything.
titeragem (*f.*) puppetry.
títere (*m.*) marionette, puppet.
titia (*f.*) auntie.
titilação (*f.*) titillation.
titilador –dora (*adj.*) titillating.
titilamento (*m.*) = TITILAÇÃO.
titilar (*v.t.*) to titillate.
titímalo (*m.*, *Bot.*) a spurge (*Tithymalus sp.*).
titio (*m.*) uncle.
Tito (*m.*) Titus.
titração (*f.*, *Chem.*, *Immunol.*, *Physiol.*) titration.
titrimetria (*f.*, *Chem.*) titrimetry.
titubeação (*f.*) titubancy.
titubeante (*adj.*) staggering; tottering; unsteady; vacillating; timid.
titubear (*v.i.*) to stagger; totter; to reel or stammer as one tipsy; to falter, hesitate.
titulagem, titulometria (*f.*, *Chem.*) volumetric analysis.
titular (*adj.*) titular; honorary; (*m.*) titled person; cabinet member; titular head of a department; (*v.t.*) to title; to entitle.
título (*m.*) title, caption, name; label, inscription; reputation; reason; right; title of rank; a note, policy, bond, stock or similar certificate.—**ao portador**, a deed, stock certificate, etc., payable to bearer. **a—de**, under pretense of; as; by way of; in the guise of. **A—de quê?** By what right? On what grounds? **a justo—**, deservedly.
tiú (*m.*, *Bot.*) a nettlespurge (*Jatropha elliptica*), c.a. GAFANHOTO, JALAPÃO, RAIZ-DE-LAGARTO; also = CAIAPIÁ.
tiúba (*f.*) = CACHAÇA.
tiv+verb endings = FORMS of TER [78].
tixotrópio [ks] (*m.*, *Chem.*) thixotropy.
tiziu (*m.*) = ALFAIATE (bird).
tlintlim (*m.*) tinkle-tinkle.
tlintar (*v.i.*) to tinkle, jingle (as coins).
tmese (*f.*, *Gram.*) tmesis.
toa [ô] (*f.*) towrope; act of towing. **à—**, (*adv.*) aimlessly; at random; **à—**, (*adj.*) worthless; careless, thoughtless.
toada (*f.*) sound, tone, noise; rumor, hearsay; tune. **nesta (naquela)—**, in this (that) way, manner; at that rate. **numa—**, (*colloq.*) without stopping.

toadeira (*f.*) a harpooned whale which continues to sound.

toadilha (*f.*) a little tune.

toalete = TOILETTE.

toalha (*f.*) towel.—**de água,** sheet of water.—**de altar,** altar cloth.—**de mesa,** tablecloth.

toalheiro (*m.*) towel rack; towel supplier, manufacturer or seller.

toalhete [êt] (*m.*) small hand towel.

toalhinha (*f.*) small towel; nun's coif.

toante (*adj.*) tonant; designating words whose tonic vowels, as a minimum, rhyme with each other; as: *casa* and *fada,* but also *casa* and *mato.*

toar (*v.i.*) to sound, resound, thunder; to match, harmonize with; to tune in with.—**com,** to jibe with.

tobatinga (*f.*) = TABATINGA.

tobô (*m., colloq.*) a big diamond.

tobogã (*m.*) toboggan; a playground slide.

toca (*f.*) burrow; a "dump" (squalid living quarters).

tocada (*f.*) see TOCADO.

tocadela (*f.*) a touch or act of touching; (*colloq.*) = TOCATA.

toca-discos (*m.*) a record player.

tocado –**da** (*adj.*) tipsy; touched (in the head); (*f.*) tryout of a race horse.

tocador –**dora** (*adj.*) touching; playing [music]; driving [cattle]; (*m.,f.*) player (of piano, etc.); (*m.*) muleteer; cattle driver.

tocadura (*f.*) = TOCADELA.

tocaia (*f.*) ambush; hunter's blind; a lying in wait; a stalking (of game or enemy).

tocaiar (*v.i.*) to waylay; to stalk (game or enemy).

tocaio (*m.*) namesake [= XARÁ].

tocajé (*m., Bot.*) the Brazil roupala (*R. brasiliensis*).

toca-lápis (*m.*) the leg of a bow compass which carries a pencil.

tocamento (*m.*) = TOQUE.

tocante (*adj.*) touching; concerning; moving, affecting. **no—a,** as regards; with respect to; concerning; touching on; relating to.

tocar (*v.t.*) to touch; to feel of; to play upon (musical instrument); to execute (a piece of music); to ring (bells, telephone, etc.); to touch (the heart); to impress, inspire; to touch, be contiguous to (as one house to another); to drive (animals); to drive (animals or people) out or away; to run (someone) out of town or off the land; (*v.r.*) to touch.—**a,** to fall to the share or lot of; to be the turn of; to devolve upon; to refer to.—**a meta,** or **o têrmo,** to reach the end.—**com,** to pertain to.—**em,** to touch, call at (a port); to strike on; to touch upon (a subject).—**de leve,** to touch lightly upon.—**de perto,** to strike closely; to concern greatly.—**música,** to play music.—**na corda sensível de alguém,** to touch a person's soft spot.—**na honra de alguém,** to touch upon another's honor.—**para diante,** to drive ahead.—**viola sem corda,** to talk without saying anything. **O navio toca em Santos,** The ship touches at Santos. **Toque!** Hurry up! Get along! Drive on! **ondas tocadas pelo vento,** waves driven by the wind.

tocari [í] (*m.*) = CASTANHA-DO-PARÁ.

tocarola (*f., colloq.*) a handshake; a noisy or inharmonious playing of music.

tocata (*f.*) a playing of musical instruments; a musical rendition; a toccata.

toca-viola (*m.*) = TANGE-VIOLA.

tocha (*f.*) large ornamental candle; torch, flambeau; firebrand; a tree whose top has snapped off.

tocheiro (*m.*), –**ra** (*f.*) large candleholder.

tôco (*m.*) tree stump; stump of an arm or leg; stub (of a cigarette, candle, pencil, etc.); a short club.—**môcho,** (*slang*) a lottery ticket on which the number has been fraudulently altered to correspond to a prize-winning number and as such sold to a "sucker." **um—de gente,** a (cute) child.

tocologia (*f.*) obstetrics; midwifery.

tôda (*adj.*) fem. of TODO.

toda [ó] (*f.*) = TODEIRO.

todavia (*adv.*) nevertheless, notwithstanding, however, yet, still, even so.

todeiro (*m., Zool.*) any tody (*Todus spp.*).

todo [tô] (*adj., fem.* **tôda**) all; whole, complete, entire; every. Cf. TUDO. (*m.*) the whole, all, entirety, aggregate; (*pl.*) everyone, everybody. (*adv.*) all, entirely.—**ano** (or —**s os anos**), every year [but **todo o ano,** or **o ano todo,** is the whole year, all year (long)].—**e qualquer,** each and every.—**homem,** every man.—**s os homens,** all men.—**o mundo,** or **tôda a gente,** everybody. [Corresponds to Fr.

tout le monde.]—**-poderoso,** all-powerful. [O **Todo-poder-oso,** the Almighty.]—**s êles** (or **êles todos**) **foram,** All of them (they all) went.—**s quantos,** all (those) who; as many as.—**s de uma vez,** all the at same time; all at once. —**s nós,** all of us.—**s os dias** (or **todo dia**), every day; daily [but **todo o dia,** or **o dia todo,** is the whole day; all day long]. **a nossa família tôda,** our whole family. **ao—,** in all; all in all; all told. **de—,** or **de todo em todo,** quite, wholly. **de tôda sorte,** of all sorts. **em—caso,** in any case; at all events. **Ela é tôda ouvidos,** She is all ears. **Tôda casa se queimou** (or **tôdas as casas se queimaram**), every house burned; all the houses were burned. [But **tôda a casa se queimou,** is: the whole house was burned.] **tôda espécie de,** every kind of; all kinds of.

toé (*m., Bot.*) a datura (*D. insignis*), c.a. MARICAUA—a solanaceous tropical plant with large, showy, solitary, whitish flowers.

toeira (*f.*) a guitar string, esp. the third or fourth lowest of a 12-string instrument.

toesa [ê] (*f.*) an old French linear measure (*toise*) of six French feet (*pieds de roi*) corresponding to almost seven U.S. or British feet; (*colloq.*) a big foot.

tofo (*m., Med.*) tophus.

toga (*f.*) toga; gown, garb; fig., magistracy.

togado –**da** (*adj.*) wearing a toga; magisterial; (*m.*) a judge.

toiceira (*f.*) = TOUCEIRA.

toicinho (*m.*) pork fat.—**americano,** bacon. Var. TOU-CINHO.

toilette (*f.*) French word used mainly in the French sense of clothes, dress; act of dressing, washing, etc.; (*m.*) washstand, dressing table, dressing room. [Sometimes used as an equivalent of American "toilet"]. Var. TOALETE.

toirada (*f.*) = TOURADA.

toirear (*v.*) = TOUREAR.

toireiro (*m.*) = TOUREIRO.

toiro (*m.*) = TOURO.

toitear (*v.*) = TOUTEAR.

toitiço (*m.*) = TOUTIÇO.

tojal (*m.*) furze-covered waste land.

tojeira (*f.*), –**ro** (*m.*) person who gathers furze for fuel.

tojo (*m., Bot.*) common gorse or furze (*Ulex europaeus*), c.a. TOJO-ARNAL or TOJO-ORDINÁRIO.—**gatanha-maior,** a woadwaxen (*Genista falcata*).—**molar,** dwarf gorse (*Ulex nanus*).

tojoso –**sa** (*adj.*) gorsy, furzy.

tolano (*m., Chem.*) tolan; diphenyl acetylene.

tolaz (*adj.*) stupid, foolish; (*m.,f.*) dupe, gull.

tolda (*f.*) an awning; quarter-deck; locomotive cab.

toldar (*v.t.*) to provide with an awning; to darken, cloud; to obscure, blur, befog; to muddy; (*v.r.*) to become cloudy; to become tipsy.

tôldo (*m.*) an awning; a settlement of half-civilized Indians.

toledana (*f.*) a Toledo sword blade.

toleima (*f.*) foolishness; folly.

toleirão –**rona** (*adj.*) very foolish; (*m.,f.*) fool, nincompoop, booby.

tolejar (*v.i.*) to speak or behave foolishly.

tolerabilidade (*f.*) tolerability.

tolerada (*f.*) a licensed prostitute.

tolerância (*f.*) tolerance, open-mindedness; toleration, sufferance; (*Mach.*) tolerance.

tolerante (*adj.*) tolerant, forbearing, indulgent; broad-minded.

tolerantismo (*m.*) toleration, both official and private, as to religious matters.

tolerar (*v.t.*) to tolerate, allow, indulge; to brook, put up with, bear with.

tolerável (*adj.*) tolerable, bearable; passable, not too bad.

tolete [lê] (*m.*) tholepin; a roller made of wood or other material; a roll of tobacco; a pointed stick used by Indians in catching alligators.

toleteira (*f.*) oarlock; rowlock.

tolher (*v.t.*) to hinder, hamper, impede; to bar, restrain; to prevent (**a, de,** from); to paralyze; to cramp; (*v.r.*) to become disabled, helpless.—**se de mêdo,** to become frozen with fear.

tolhido –**da** (*adj.*) paralyzed, disabled, helpless; numb.

tolice (*f.*) follishness, folly, stupidity; blunder; nonsense, tommyrot, piffle, poppycock; (*inter.*) Fiddlesticks!

tolo –**la** (tô] (*adj.*) foolish, idiotic, silly, simple-minded

daft, crazy; (*m.,f.*) fool, blockhead, "dumb bell," "dope"; (*m.*) = SEBASTIÃO (a dogfish).
tolontro (*m.*) bump, lump.
tolu [ú] (*m.*) tolu balsam.
tolueno (*m., Chem.*) toluene.
toluidina (*f., Chem.*) toluidine.
toluol (*m.*) = TOLUENO.
tolva (*f.*) hopper (for sand, gravel, etc.).
tom (*m.*) tone; intonation, accent, inflection; sound, note; tension, elasticity; tenor, drift; mood, temper; color, shade; (*Music*) key.
tomado –da (*adj.*) taken; seized; (*colloq.*) tipsy; (*m.pl.*) tucks, folds; (*f.*) act of taking, seizure, capture; an electric outlet (for plugging in a fan, heater, radio, etc.).—**de ar,** air intake.—**de posição,** taking of a stand.
tomadura (*f.*) saddle gall.
tomar (*v.t.*) to take (in all the usual senses); to take (something) into one's hands or possession; to seize, grasp; to capture; to usurp; to receive or accept; to take (food, drink); to take up (space); to take (a given road).—**a alça,** to sight a gun.—**à boa (má) parte,** to take (something said or done) in the right (wrong) way.—**a liberdade de,** to take the liberty of.—**a mal,** to take amiss.—**a palavra,** to take the floor.—**a peito,** to take (something) to heart.—**a vez de,** to take the place or turn of.—(**algo**) **a sério,** to take (something) seriously.—**assento em,** to take one's seat (as in Congress).—**banho de mar,** to go sea bathing.—**como alvo,** to take as an objective.—**conhecimento de,** to take notice of.—**conselho,** to take counsel.—**conta de,** to take charge (control, possession) of; to take care of.—**conta de si,** to recover oneself; to regain one's self-possession.—**conta dum assunto,** to dwell at length upon a subject.—**cuidado,** to be careful.—**de assalto,** to take by storm.—**em consideração,** to take into consideration.—**em conta,** to take into account.—**emprestado,** to borrow (something).—**estado,** to marry, settle down.—**fogo,** to catch fire, lit. & fig.—**gôsto por,** to develop a fondness for.—**impulso,** to gather momentum.—**juízo,** to behave; to settle down.—**marido (mulher),** to take a husband (wife).—**o comando,** to assume control.—**o freio nos dentes,** to take the bit in one's teeth.—**o véu,** to take the veil.—**para (or por) espôsa,** to take as wife.—**parte em,** to take part in.—**o partido de,** to take the side of, side with.—**pelo caminho da direita,** to take the righthand road.—**por hipótese,** to assume (as a hypothesis).—**por modêlo,** to take as a model (pattern, standard).—**por testemunha,** to call as witness.—**posse,** to be seated (inaugurated) in office.—**posse de,** to take possession of.—**satisfações,** to demand satisfaction of.—**-se de** (**ira, paixão, ódio,** etc.), to be overcome with (anger, passion, hate, etc.).—**-se de afeição por,** to take a strong liking to.—**-se de encantos por,** to be enchanted by, fall in love with.—(**alguma coisa**) **sôbre si,** to take (something) upon oneself.—**um copo de leite,** to take a glass of milk.—**um chope,** to have a glass of beer.—**uma bebida,** to have a drink.—**uma carraspana,** (*slang*) to go on a bender.—**uma decisão (deliberação, resolução),** to reach (make) a decision.—**uma providência,** to take steps (measures), do something about.—**vulto,** to grow in size, in volume. **ir—fresco.** to go for an airing. **Toma-lá, dá-cá,** give-and-take. **Tomara!** Would to God! Let's hope! **Tomara que não!** I hope not!
tomatada (*f.*) tomato paste.
tomate (*m.*) tomato (plant or fruit).—**-bravo,** cutleaf nightshade (*Solanum triflorum*).—**-cheiroso,** a treetomato (*Cyphomandra fragrans*).—**-chimango,**—**-da-serra,**—**-francês** = TOMATEIRO-DA-SERRA.—**-de-sodoma,** apple-of-Sodom nightshade (*Solanum sodomeum*), c.a. TOMATEIRO-DO-DIABO.—**-do-amazonas,** Amazon tomato (*Lycopersicon humboldtii*).—**-grande,** common tomato (*Lycopersicon esculentum*).—**-pêra,** pear tomato (*Lycopersicon pyriforme*), c.a. TOMATE-PIRIFORME.—**-redondo,** cherry tomato, (*Lycopersicon cerasiforme*).
tomateiro (*m.*) –**ra** (*f.*) any tomato plant.—**-da-serra,** the treetomato (*Cyphomandra betacea*), c.a. TOMATE-CHIMANGO, TOMATE-DE-ÁRVORE, TOMATE-FRANCÊS.—**-do-diabo** = TOMATE-DE-SODOMA.—**-grande,** the common tomato (*Lycopersicon esculentum*.).—**-redondo,** the cherry tomato (*Lycopersicon cerasiforme*).—**-pêra,** the pear tomato (*Lycopersicon pyriforme*).
tomba (*f.*) shoe patch; title of a book printed separately and pasted on the book's spine; (*Bot.*) = ESPELINA.
tombac (*m.*) tombac (copper-base alloy). Var. TOMBAQUE.
tombada (*f.*) = VERTENTE.

tombadilho (*m.*) quarter-deck.
tombador –dora (*adj.*) tumbling; (*m.,f.*) one who tumbles, etc. See the verb [TOMBAR]; (*m.*) steep hillside; a steep flattopped hill near a river's edge; workman who feeds sugar cane to the mill.
tombamento (*m.*) a fall or act of falling, tumbling, etc. See the verb [TOMBAR].
tombaque (*m.*) = TOMBAC.
tombar (*v.t.,v.i.*) to tumble, topple; (*v.t.*) to fell; to overthrow; to record (charters, title deeds); (*v.i.*) to drop; to fall (down, over).
tombo (*m.*) a fall or tumble; an upset; a high and heavy waterfall; (*colloq.*) a person's natural bent, nature or ability; a collection or register of charters, title deeds, etc. **aos—s,** falling, tumbling. **dar o—em alguém,** to bring about another's downfall; to cause him loss or damage. **levar um—,** to take a spill.
tômbola (*f.*) tombola, esp. at a charity bazaar; lotto, bingo.
tômbolo (*m.*) tombolo. ["A sand-and-gravel bar or reef which connects an island with the mainland." *Webster*]
tome-juízo (*m.*) = CACHAÇA.
tomento (*m.*) tow, hurds, scutch (of flax, hemp, jute, etc.); (*Bot.*) tomentum.
tomentoso –sa (*adj., Bot.*) tomentose.
tomilho (*m., Bot.*) common thyme (*Thymus vulgaris*), c.a. TIMO.
tomismo (*m.*) Thomism.
tomista (*m.,f.*) Thomist.
tomo (*m.*) tome, volume, book.
ton. = TONEL or TONÉIS = tun(s), cask(s).
tona (*f.*) a natural integument; as, the tunic of a seed; pellicle; fig., surface. **à—,** afloat. **vir à—,** to come to the surface.
tonal (*adj.*) tonal.
tonalidade (*f.*) tint, shade; (*Music*) tonality.
tonalito (*m., Petrog.*) tonalite.
tonante (*adj.*) thundering; thunderous.
tondinho (*m., Fine Arts*) tondino; (*Anat., Zool.*) ankle [= TARSO].
tonel [-néis] (*m.*) tun, large cask, hogshead, vat; (*colloq.*) tosspot, sot, guzzler.
tonelada (*f.*) ton.—**americana,** short ton (2,000 lbs.).—**inglêsa,** long ton (2,240 lbs.)—**métrica,** metric ton (1,000 kilograms, 2,204.6 lbs.).
tonelagem (*f.*) tonnage.
tonelaria (*f.*) = TANOARIA.
tôni (*m.*) clown; stooge.
tônica (*f.*) see TÔNICO.
tonicidade (*f.*) tonicity.
tônico –ca (*adj.*) tonic; (*f., Music*) keynote; (*Gram.*) tonic vowel.
tonificar (*v.t.*) to tone up, invigorate, strengthen (**-se,** oneself).
toninha (*f.*) = MARSOPA (porpoise).
tonite (*f.*) tonite (an explosive).
tonitruante, tonítruo –trua, tonitruoso –sa (*adj.*) thundering; thunderous.
tono (*m.*) tone; aria; (*Physiol.*) tonus.
tonógrafo (*m., Physiol.*) tonograph.
tonometria (*f.*) tonometry.
tonômetro (*m.*) tonometer.
tonoplasto (*m., Biol.*) tonoplast.
tonos (*m.*) strain, tone, mode; muscular tension.—**ocular,** intraocular tension.
tonose (*f., Biol.*) increase or decrease in osmotic pressure.
tonotaxia [ks] (*f., Biol.*) tonotaxis.
tonsila (*f.*) = AMÍGDALA.
tonsilite (*f., Med.*) tonsillitis.
tonsura (*f.*) tonsure.
tonsurar (*v.t.*) to tonsure.
tontear (*v.i.*) to talk nonsense; to suffer dizziness.
tonteira (*f.*) = TONTICE; TONTURA.
tontice (*f.*) nonsense, foolishness.
tontina (*f.*) a tontine (annuity).
tonto –ta (*adj.*) giddy, dizzy; foolish; crazy; flighty; muddleheaded; (*m.,f.*) a fool.
tontura (*f.*) dizziness; dizzy spell; daze.
topada (*f.*) a trip or stumble. **dar uma—,** to stub one's toe (*lit. & fig.*).
topador –dora (*adj.*) stumbling; (*slang*) designating a person who accepts any bet or challenge.
topar (*v.t.*) to meet, encounter, run across; to cover (a bet); to bet the limit.—**a parada,** to call a bet; to take on

(accept) a challenge.—**com,** to meet up with; to come (run) across (upon); —**em,** to stumble on (*lit. & fig.*). —**em cheio,** to hit (fall) squarely on. **Eu topo,** I'm game.

topa-tudo (*m.*) a person who is always ready to undertake anything; one who accepts any challenge, whom nothing fazes.

topázio (*m.*) topaz.—**falso,** or **ocidental,** false topaz—a yellow variety of quartz changed in color by heating.— **oriental,** Oriental topaz (yellow sapphire).—**queimado,** yellow topaz made red by heating.

tope (*m.*) clash, jar, collision; top, summit; masthead; stumbling block; cockade.

topetada (*f.*) a butt with the head.

topetar (*v.t.*) to butt, strike (with the head); to top.

topete [pé or pê] (*m.*) topknot; pompadour; forelock; (*colloq.*) impudence, "brass," "cheek," "nerve," "gall". **abaixar o—,** to come down a peg.

topetuda (*f.*) = MARIA-É-DIA.

topiaria (*f.*, *Gardening*) topiary work.

tópico –ca (*adj.*) topical; (*m.*) topic; a brief paragraph on the editorial page of a newspaper [= SUELTO and VÁRIA]; (*Med.*) a topical remedy.

topinambo (*m.*, *Bot.*) Jerusalem artichoke (*Helianthus tuberosus*).

tôpo (*m.*) crest, top, summit; butt end. **de—,** suddenly.

Topogr. = TOPOGRAFIA (*Topography*).

topografia (*f.*) topography.

topográfico –ca (*adj.*) topographic(al).

topógrafo (*m.*) topographer.

toponímia (*f.*) toponymy.

topônimo (*m.*) toponym, place name.

toque (*m.*) touch, contact; stroke; bugle call; playing (of an instrument); handclasp; a retouching; bouquet (of wine); trace, dash (of something); rotten spot (on fruit); test, assay; artistic touch; lady's toque; (*Aeron.*) touch-down; (*Med.*) a swabbing.—**toque,** quickstep.—**de alvorada,** (*Milit.*) reveille.—**de caixa,** drumbeat.—**de clarim,** bugle call.—**de recolher,** curfew; call to quarters. —**de silêncio,** (*Milit.*) taps; lights out.—**militar,** bugle call. **a—de caixa,** posthaste. **pedra de—,** touchstone.

toqueiro (*m.*) "a SERINGUEIRO who sells his products to an AVIADO in the forest for whatever price it will bring." [*GBAT*]

Tóquio (*m.*) Tokyo, Tokio.

tora (*f.*) log; a chat; (*slang*) a nap [= SESTA]; [*cap.*] the Torah; (*Bot.*) the sickle senna (*Cassia tora*). **tirar uma—,** to take forty winks.

torácico –ca (*adj.*) thoracic.

toracolombar (*adj.*, *Anat.*) thoracolumbar.

toracoplastia (*f.*, *Surg.*) thoracoplasty.

torado –da (*adj.*) cut up into logs; tailless; bobtailed [= SURU]; (*f.*) a piece of log.

toral (*m.*) the butt end of a spear or lance.

torar (*v.t.*) to cut up into logs or pieces.

tórax [ks] (*m.*, *Anat.*, *Zool.*) thorax.

torbanito (*m.*) torbanite, boghead coal.

torbernita (*f.*, *Min.*) torbernite; copper uranite.

torça (*f.*) lintel; an oblong, squared piece of stone.

torçal (*m.*) silk cord.

torção (*f.*) torsion; twisting. **momento de—,** (*Mech.*) torque.

torce-cabelo (*m.*) any of various small stingless bees of Trigona and Melipona, c.a. ARAPUÃ, IRAPUÃ, ENROLA-CABELO, SANHARÃO, SANHARÓ, TUJUMIRIM.

torcedeira (*f.*) twisting machine.

torcedela (*f.*) = TORCEDURA.

torcedor –dora (*adj.*) twisting; (*m.*) twister; spindle; twisting machine; (*m.,f.*, *colloq.*) rooter.

torcedura (*f.*) twist; act of twisting; wrench, sprain; fig. subterfuge, evasion. Syns. TORCEDELA, TORÇO, TORCIMENTO.

torcer (*v.t.*) to twist; to wring; to wrench; to distort (the meaning); (*colloq.*) to root for, pull for (someone to win); (*v.r.*) to writhe (as in pain); to squirm.—**a bôca,** to make a wry face.—**a orelha e não sair sangue,** to rue, repent of.—**a roupa,** to wring out wet clothes.—**o caminho,** to take a different road.—**o nariz a,** to turn up one's nose; to sniff at.—**o pé,** to sprain one's foot.—**o pescoço dum frango,** to wring a chicken's neck.—**o sentido,** to twist the meaning.—**os seus pauzinhos,** to pull strings. **É aí que a porca torce o rabo,** That's where the shoe pinches. **não dar o braço a—,** to refuse to admit or confess anything; not to "let on" (as when in pain).

torcicolo (*m.*) crick, wry neck; roundabout speech; (*Zool.*)

a wryneck (*Jynx torquilla*), c.a. PAPA-FORMIGAS, PIADEIRA.

torcido –da (*adj.*) twisted; tortuous, crooked; winding; (*f.*) a wick; act of rooting (at a soccer game, etc.); a group of rooters.

torcimento (*m.*) = TORCEDURA.

torcímetro (*m.*) torsion meter.

torço [tô] (*m.*) in Bahia, a shawl wrapped around the head in the manner of a turban; also = TORCEDURA.

torcular (*m.*, *Anat.*) torcular; *confluens sinuum*.

tórculo (*m.*) a screw press, as for wine.

tordilho –lha (*adj.*) dapple-gray [horse].

tordo [tôr] (*m.*) any thrush of the genus Turdus; a Mediterranean wrasse (*Labrus sp.*).—**dos-remedos,** mockingbird (*Mimus polyglottos*).—**-marinho,** the small European kingfisher (*Alcedo hispida*), c.a. PICA-PEIXE.—**-menor-contador,** the redwing (*Turdus musicus*), c.a. TORDO-BRANCO.—**-pisco,** a water ouzel (*Cinchus sp.*).—**visgueiro,** the missel thrush (*Turdus viscivorus*).

torém (*m.*) = UMBAÚBA.

torênia (*f.*, *Bot.*) the blue torenia (*T. fournieri*), c.a. AMOR-PERFEITO-DA-CHINA.

torga (*f.*), **torgo** (*m.*) = URZE.

tori [í] (*m.*) torii (Japanese gateway).

tória (*f.*, *Chem.*) thoria; thorium oxide.

toriado –da (*adj.*, *Elec.*) thoriated.

torianita (*f.*, *Min.*) thorianite.

tórico –ca (*adj.*, *Geom.*) toric; (*Chem.*) thoric.

tório (*m.*, *Chem.*) thorium.

torita (*f.*, *Min.*) thorite.

tormenta (*f.*) storm, tempest, gale; fig., turmoil, turbulence, trouble.

tormento (*m.*) torment, agony, torture; anguish, distress.

tormentório –ria, **tormentoso** –sa (*adj.*) stormy.

torna (*f.*) something given to boot.

tornada (*f.*) a returning; l'envoi of a sestina, etc. Cf. OFERTA, ENVIO, REMATE.

tornado (*m.*) tornado.

tornar (*v.i.*) to turn back (**a, para,** to); to return; (*v.t.*) to reply; to return, give back (**a,** to); to translate (**em,** into); to render, make, change, convert (something into something); (*v.r.*) to return, turn back (**a, para,** to); to turn, change (**em,** into); become.—**a**+infinitive = infinitive+again. [e.g., **tornar a bater,** to strike again.]—**à baila,** to bring back for discussion.—**a empregar capital,** to reinvest capital.—**exequível,** to render possible of execution.—**a si,** to regain consciousness.—**nulo,** to render void. **Tudo se torna fácil quando se quer,** Where there's a will there's a way.

tornassol [-ssóis] (*m.*) sunflower [= GIRASSOL]; heliotrope; (*Chem.*) litmus. **papel de—,** litmus paper.

torna-viagem (*f.*) return trip.

torneado –da (*adj.*) well-turned (phrase, ankle, etc.).

torneador –dora (*adj.*) lathe-turning; (*m.*) turner.

tornear (*v.t.*) to turn (on a lathe); to shape (mold) gracefully (neatly); to encompass; to joust, tilt.

tornearia (*f.*) turnery.

torneio (*m.*) act of turning (something) on a lathe; turning of a phrase; tourney, tournament or joust; contest; a verbal tilt.

torneira (*f.*) faucet, spigot, tap.

torneiro (*m.*) wood turner; lathe operator.

torneja [ê] (*f.*) axle pin.

tornejar (*v.t.*,*v.i.*) to turn or curve (as a road).

tornel [-néis] (*m.*) swivel.

tornilheiro –ra (*adj.*) deserting; (*m.*) deserter.

torninho (*m.*) small vise.

torniquete [ête] (*m.*) turnstile; tourniquet; small vise; rack (instrument of torture); (*colloq.*) a tough spot.

tôrno (*m.*) lathe; faucet, spigot; wooden peg; a turn around.—**de bancada,** bench vise.—**de fiar,** spinning wheel.—**de repuxar,** a mandrel, or spinning, lathe.—**mecânico,** a power lathe.—**revólver,** a turret, or capstan, lathe. **em—(de, a),** around, about, all-around. **em—da cidade,** round about town. **olhar em—(de si),** to look about (one).

tornozelo [ê] (*m.*) ankle; tarsus.

toro (*m.*) log; torso; (*Arch.*, *Math.*) torus.

toró (*m.*) downpour; drizzle; (*adj.*) having a finger, or a part of one, missing.

torocana (*f.*) Indian log drum. Var. TROCANO.

toroidal (*adj.*, *Elec.*) toroidal. **bobina—,** toroid coil.

tóron (*m.*, *Chem.*) thoron.

toronja (*f.*) grapefruit.

torom-torom (*m.*) = TRONTRON.
toropixi [xí] (*m.*) = ANAMBÉ-PRÊTO.
torp. = TORPEDEIRO (torpedo boat).
torpe [ô] (*adj.*) base, shameful, vile, sordid; scurrilous; indecent, obscene; low, mean; torpid.
torpedeamento, torpedagem (*f.*) torpedoing.
torpedear (*v.t.*) to torpedo.
torpedeiro (*m.*) torpedo boat.
torpedo [ê] (*m.*) torpedo.
torpeza [ê], **torpidade, torpitude** (*f.*) turpitude, depravity, vileness, scurrility.
tôrpido –da (*adj.*) torpid; numb; = ENTORPECIDO.
torpor [pôr] (*m.*) torpor; stupor.
torque (*m., Mech.*) torque.
torquês (*f.*) pincers.
torra (*f.*) a toasting or roasting; a carbon diamond of poor quality [= MELÊ]; drainage of paddy fields.
torração (*f.*) act of toasting, roasting (as of coffee), parching, scorching; (*colloq.*) a fire sale.
torradeira (*f.*) toaster.
torrado –da (*adj.*) toasted, scorched, browned, parched; (*f.*) piece of toast.
torrão (*m.*) clod; hard lump of soil; piece of farming land; "a stone-like block of TABATINGA clay which has broken off from the river banks of the upper tributaries and lies in midstream, hardened over a long period of time." [GBAT].—**de açúcar**, lump of sugar.—**natal**, native sod.
torrar (*v.t.*) to toast, brown, parch; (*colloq.*) to sell at a fire sale.—**café**, to roast coffee.
tôrre (*f.*) tower; steeple; belfry; (*Chess*) rook, castle.—**de água**, water tower.—**de borbulhamento**, (*Petrol.*) bubble tower, bubble column.—**de tiro**, gun turret.
torreado –da (*adj.*) tower-shaped.
torreante (*adj.*) towering.
torreão (*m.*) turret.
torrear (*v.i.*) to tower.
torrefação (*f.*) roasting, esp. of coffee beans.
torrefator –tora (*adj.*) roasting; (*m.*) roaster, esp. of coffee beans.
torrefazer (*v.t., Metal.*) to roast (ores).
torrencial (*adj.*) torrential.
torrente (*f.*) torrent.
torresmo (*m.*) crackling (crisp, browned pork fat).
tórrido –da (*adj.*) torrid, hot, burning.
torrificar (*v.t.*) to torrefy, roast, parch, scorch.
torrinha (*f.*) the "peanut gallery" (in a theater).
torroada (*f.*) "in Maranhão, a path through a swamp which is drying up; in Pará, a highland full of good rubber stands; an elevated piece of ground." [GBAT]
torsiógrafo (*m.*) torsiograph; torsion meter.
torso (*m.*) torso.
torto [tôr], –ta [tór] (*adj.*) crooked, bent; twisted, awry, lopsided; wrong. **a**—**e a direito**, indiscriminately, blindly; without thinking. **a**—**ou a direito**, by hook or by crook; rightly or wrongly; willy-nilly. **Pau que nasce**—, **nunca ou tarde se endireita**, Just as the twig is bent, the tree's inclined. (*f.*) pie; tart.—**de caroço de algodão**, cottonseed cake.
tortulho (*m.*) young mushroom; a squat person; a bundle of dried and inflated entrails (for sausage making).
tortuosidade (*f.*) tortuosity, sinuosity.
tortuoso –sa (*adj.*) tortuous, crooked, sinuous; circuitous, devious.
tortura (*f.*) torture, agony; anguish; tortuosity.
torturante (*adj.*) agonizing, grievous; galling; nerve-racking.
torturar (*v.t.*) to torture, torment; cause to suffer agony or anguish.
torunguenga (*adj.*) fearless; (*m.*) fearless man; man skilled in the use of any weapon; skillful guitar or accordion player. Var. TOURUNGUENGA.
torvação (*f.*) disturbance, upset, perturbation.
torvar (*v.t.*) to disturb, upset; (*v.i.,v.r.*) to become perturbed or irritated.
torvelinhar (*v.i.*) to swirl, eddy.
torvelin[h]o (*m.*) whirlwind; eddy, swirl; whirlpool.
tôrvo –va (*adj.*) appalling; grim, of forbidding look; frowning; moody.
tosa (*f.*) act of shearing sheep; (*colloq.*) a drubbing; a rebuke.
tosador –dora (*adj.*) shearing; (*m.,f.*) shearer.
tosadura (*f.*) act of shearing.
tosão (*m.*) fleece; a net used in trout fishing.

tosar (*v.t.*) to shear, clip; to browse, crop; to nibble; to beat, trounce.
toscanejar (*v.i.*) to nod, dose, drowse. Var. TOSQUENEJAR.
tôsco –ca (*adj.*) rough, rugged, unpolished; unformed; coarse, crude; clumsy, ungainly.
tosquenejar (*v.*) = TOSCANEJAR.
tosquia (*f.*) shearing, clipping; sheep-shearing time; (*colloq.*) a harsh dressing-down.
tosquiadela (*f.*) a shearing; a light going-over; a reprimand; a trouncing.
tosquiado –da (*adj.*) sheared, cropped short.
tosquiador (*m.*) shearer.—**de ovelhas**, sheep shearer.
tosquiar (*v.t.*) to shear (sheep, hair, etc.); to clip closely; (*colloq.*) to trim, skin, fleece (someone) in a deal.
tosse (*f.*) a cough or act of coughing.—**comprida**,—**convulsa**,—**de guariba**, whooping cough [= COQUELUCHE].—**de cachorro**, hoarse, hacking cough.—**sêca**, dry cough.
tossegoso –sa (*adj.*) coughing.
tossidela (*f., colloq.*) a cough or coughing.
tossido (*m.*) a cough given to attract another's attention.
tossir [21a] (*v.i.*) to cough; (*v.t.*) to cough up.
tosta (*f.*) a piece of toast.
tostadela (*f.*) a light toasting.
tostado –da (*adj.*) toasted, browned.
tostão (*m.*) a Brazilian "nickel," formerly 100 RÉIS, now 10 CENTAVOS. **sem**—, penniless.
tostar (*v.t.*) to parch, toast, brown; to singe, scorch; (*v.r.*) to become scorched or toasted.
toste (*m.*) toast (drink).
total (*adj.; m.*) total.
totalidade (*f.*) totality, entirety. **a quase**—, almost all.
totalitário –ria (*adj.*) totalitarian.
totalitarismo (*m.*) totalitarianism.
totalitarista (*adj.; m.,f.*) totalitarian.
totalizar (*v.t.*) to totalize.
totem, tôteme (*m.*) totem.
totêmico –ca (*adj.*) totemic.
totemismo (*m.*) totemism.
touca (*f.*) toque, bonnet, hood; nun's coif.—**-de-viúva** = FLOR-DE-VIUVA, CAPELA-DE-VIÚVA, COROA-DE-VIÚVA.
toucá (*m.*) = CASTANHEIRO-DO-PARÁ.
touça (*f.*) a withe employed as a barrel hoop; a thicket.
toucado (*m.*) headdress, coiffure, hairdo.
toucador (*m.*) dressing table, vanity; dressing room.
toucar (*v.t.*) to dress the hair of; to adorn, embellish; (*v.r.*) to comb and dress one's hair.
touceira (*f.*) clump of trees; clump of roots; live tree stump. Var. TOICEIRA.
toucinho (*m.*) = TOICINHO.
toupeira (*f.*) a ground mole; a person with small, blinking eyes; (*slang*) a dull-witted person; a "dumbbell".
toupeirinha (*f.*) a mole cricket.
tourada (*f.*) herd of bulls; bullfight. Var. TOIRADA.
tourear (*v.t.*) to fight or bait bulls; to harass; to woo; to challenge; (*v.i.*) to egage in bullfighting. Var. TOIREAR.
toureiro (*m.*) bullfighter. Var. TOIREIRO.
tourejão (*m.*) axle pin.
touro (*m.*) bull; (*pl.*) bullfight. Var. TOIRO.—**de capa**, a bull ready for castration. **pegar o**—**pelos chifres**, or **pegar o**—**à unha**, to take the bull by the horns.
tourunguenga (*adj.; m.*) = TORUNGUENGA.
touruno –na (*adj.*) of bulls, improperly or incompletely castrated.
touta (*f., colloq.*) topknot; noodle (the head); nape. Var. TOITA.
toutear (*v.i.*) to talk or act foolishly. Var. TOITEAR.
toutiço (*m.*) back part of the head; nape; the head. Var. TOITIÇO.
toutinegra (*f.*) the blacktop (*Sylvia atricapilla*) and other European warblers and gnatcatchers of the family Sylviidae, some of which occur in Brazil, though they seem to have no common name there. The Brazilian species are: *Polioptila d. dumicola* (the brush-loving gnatcatcher); *P. dumicola berlepschi* (Berlepsch's gnatcatcher); *P. lactea* (the cream-bellied gnatcatcher); *P. plumbea atricapilla* (the white-bellied gnatcatcher). Var. TUTINEGRA.
tovaca (*f., Zool.*) the short-tailed antthrush (*Chamaeza b. brevicauda*), and the rufous-tailed antthrush (*C. r. ru-. ficauda*).
tovacaçu [çú] (*m.*) = GALINHA-DO-MATO.
toxemia [ks] (*f., Med.*) toxemia; blood poisoning.
toxicdiade [ks] (*f.*) toxicity.
tóxico –ca [ks] (*adj.*) toxic; narcotic; (*m.*) toxin; poison.

toxicologia [ks] (f.) toxicology.
toxicológico –ca [ks] (adj.) toxicological.
toxicólogo (m.), –ga (f.) [ks] (toxicologist.
toxicômano (m.), –na (f.) [ks] drug addict.
toxicomania [ks] (f.) drug addiction.
toxidez [ks] (f.) toxicity.
toxina [ks] (f.) toxin.
toxiquemia (f.) = TOXEMIA.
toxóide [ks] (m., Immunol.) a toxoid; = ANATOXINA.
trabalhadeira (f.) a diligent housewife; (adj.) hard-working.
trabalhado –da (adj.) worked; wrought.
trabalhador –dora (adj.) laborious, industrious, hard-working; diligent; (m.) worker, workman, laborer; a jackass employed in the breeding of mules.
trabalhão (m.) hard (heavy) work; big bother.
trabalhar (v.i.) to work, labor, toil; to exert oneself; to run, go, function (as a machine, etc.); to perform (on the stage); (v.t.) to work, manipulate, shape, form, mold (a material); to cause to labor.—como um burro, to work like a dog, like a Trojan.—de dia, to work in the day-time.—de noite, to work at night.—de parceria, to work on shares.—do raiar ao pôr do sol, to work from sunrise to sunset.—em rodízio, to take turns at work.—por contra própria, to work for oneself.—sobreposse, to overwork. fazer—, to start, set going; to cause to run (go, function). maquinaria para—madeira, woodworking machinery.
trabalheira (f.) hard work, drudgery; bother.
trabalhismo (m.) laborism.
trabalhista (adj.) of or pert. to labor, labor unions, labor party, etc.
trabalho (m.) work, labor, toil; effort, exertion; occupation, employment; result of work, performance, achievement; stress; (Mech.) work.—braçal, manual labor.—de casa, home work.—de sapa, an undermining of another's reputation, etc.—escravo, slave labor.—reles, drudgery.—s manuais, manual arts. companheiro de—, fellow-worker. estar com—até os olhos, to be up to one's ears in work. O—está bem adiantado, The work is well advanced. sem—, out of work.
trabalhoso –sa (adj.) laborious, difficult, irksome, fatiguing.
trabecula (f., Anat.) trabecula.
trabelho [ê] (m.) a toggle, such as a stick used in tightening the cord of a bucksaw.
trabucar (v.t.) to attack with a catapult; to sink (ships); to stir up, agitate; (v.i.) to work hard; to make a noise as by pounding; of ships, to go down.
trabuco (m.) catapult; blunderbuss [= BACAMARTE]; (colloq.) a big cigar, esp. a cheap one.
trabuzana (f., colloq.) a storm; a spell of sickness or of indigestion; drunken spree; shindy, free-for-all; (m., colloq.) tough, rowdy, bully [= VALENTÃO] Var. TRIBUZANA.
traça (f.) a clothes moth (Tinea), or silverfish (Lepisma); by ext., anything which gradually consumes or wastes something else; a tracing, sketch, rough draft; aspect.
traçado –da (adj.) delineated; moth-eaten; (m.) a design, sketch, tracing, drawing.
traçador –dora (adj.) tracing; (m.) tracer; lumberman's (crosscut) saw.
tracajá (m.) any semi-aquatic fresh-water turtle of Podocnemis and Emys, esp. P. cayennensis, prized for its meat and eggs.
tracalhaz, tracanaz, (f., colloq.) a big slice or piece of something.
traçanga (f.) a carpenter ant (Camponotus abdominalis).
tração (f.) traction.
traçar (v.t.) to trace, draw, sketch; to delineate, outline; to plan, map out; to rule (paper); of moths, to eat (clothes, etc.).
tracejar (v.i.) to trace, draw lines; (v.t.) to outline, delineate.
traço (m.) trace, streak, line; stroke of a pen, pencil, etc.; trait, feature; lineament, outline; trace, vestige; point of intersection (of two lines); proportion of sand, cement, gravel, etc., in concerte.—de união, hyphen [-]; connecting link. duplo—, the equals sign [=].
tracoma (f., Med.) trachoma.
tracomatoso –sa (adj.) trachomatous.
trad. = TRADUÇÃO (translation).
tradar, tradear (v.t.) to bore with a large auger.
tradescância (f., Bot.) the Virginia spiderwort (Tradescantia virginiana).

tradição (f.) tradition.
tradicional (adj.) traditional.
tradicionalismo (m.) traditionalism.
tradicionalista (adj.; m.,f.) traditionist.
trado (m.) a large auger; a broach.
tradução (f.) translation.—literal, literal translation.—livre, free translation.
tradutor –tora (adj.) translating; (m.,f.) translator.—juramentado, sworn translator.
traduzir [36] (v.t.) to translate (em, into; para, to; de, from); to interpret; (v.r.) to become manifest.
traduzível (adj.) translatable.
trafegar (v.i.) to plod, toil.—com, to trade with.—por, to cross; come and go. Var. TRAFEGUEAR.
tráfego (m.) traffic, trade, barter; transport, transit; traffic department; drudgery.—engarrafado, traffic jam.—preferencial, traffic having the right of way.
traficância (f.) roguery, swindling.
traficante (adj.) dishonest, fraudulent; (m.,f.) swindler, crook; (obs.) merchant.
traficar (v.i.) to traffic, trade; to have underhanded dealings.
tráfico (m.) traffic, trade, esp. of an illicit nature.
traga, –gas, –gamos, –gais, –gam, regular forms of TRAGAR, and irreg. forms of TRAZER [79].
tragacanto (m.) tragacanth (gum or plant, esp. Astragalus gummifer).
tragada (f.) a draft of tobacco smoke; a swig of liquor.
tragadeiro (colloq.) gullet, gorge, throat [= GOELA]; also = TRAGADOURO.
tragador –dora (adj.) swallowing; engulfing; (m.,f.) swallower.
tragadouro (m.) pit, gulf; abyss. Var. TRAGADOIRO.
tragamento (m.) act of swallowing, etc. See the verb TRAGAR.
traga-mouros (m.) bully, hoodlum, ruffian. Var. TRAGA-MOIROS.
tragar (v.t.) to devour, gulp down, swallow; to swallow up, engulf; to swallow (something) as being true; to put up with, bear meekly; (v.i.) to inhale tobacco smoke. tragado pelo mar, pela selva, etc., swallowed up by the sea, by the jungle, etc. Não posso—aquêle sujeito; I can't stomach that fellow.
tragédia (f.) tragedy; shocking event.
trágico –ca (adj.) tragic; (m.) tragedian; (f.) tragedienne.
tragicomédia (f.) tragicomedy.
tragicômico –ca (adj.) tragicomic.
trago (m.) a gulp, swallow, swig, draft; (Anat.) tragus; (v.) pres. ind. of TRAGAR and TRAZER [79].
tragueado –da (adj.) half-drunk.
traguira (f.) baby trout.
trágus (m., Anat.) tragus [= TRAGO].
traição (f.) treachery, treason, perfidiousness; (colloq.) a surprise house-raising or other neighborly "bee".
traiçoeiro –ra (adj.) treacherous, traitorous, perfidious, untrustworthy; guileful; tricky.
traidor –dora (adj.) treacherous; unsafe; (m.,f.) traitor; double-crosser.
traineira (f.) trawler; a large net, esp. for sardines.
trair [75] (v.t.) to betray; to be false to; to double-cross; to reveal, expose (unintentionally); (v.r.) to betray one-self.—um segrêdo, to disclose a secret.
traíra-bóia, trairambóia [a-i] (f.) = PIRAMBÓIA.
trajar (v.t.) to wear, don, put on; (v.r.) to dress oneself.
traje (m.) dress, clothing, garb, apparel, attire; suit. Var. TRAJO.—à paisana, civilian clothes; mufti.—de banho, bathing suit.—de cerimônia, formal attire.—de fantasia, fancy dress.—de montar, riding habit.—de passeio, de rua, street clothes; informal dress.—de rigor, formal evening attire.—domingueiro, Sunday clothes.—s menores, underclothes.
trajeto (m.) passage, course, route, way; flight; loosely, trajectory; trip, journey; act of passing along a given route. Var. TRAJECTO.
trajetória (f.) trajectory. Var. TRAJECTÓRIA.
tralha (f.) net, mesh [= TRALHO]; (Naut.) boltrope; useless old things [= TRALHADA]. tôda a—, the whole caboodle.
tralhada (f.) = TRALHA, CACARÉUS.
tralhar (v.t.) to cast a small fishing net.
tralho (m.) = TRALHA.
tralhoada (f.) hodgepodge, farrago, jumble.
tralhoto [lhô] (m.) four-eyes (a top minnow, Anableps tetrophthalmus), c.a. QUATRO-OLHOS, ANABLEPSO.

trama (*f.*) woof, weft; weave; scheme, plot, conspiracy; collusion; crooked deal, racket; roof frame. **gasto até à—,** threadbare, worn thin. **urdidura e—,** warp and woof.

tramagueira (*f.*) = CORNO-GODINHO.

tramanzola (*m.,f.*) easy-going, overgrown young person.

tramar (*v.t.*) to weave; to scheme, plot; (*v.i.*) to conspire.

trambalear, –balhar, trambecar (*v.i.*) to stagger, stumble, tumble.

trambelho (*m.*) = TRABELHO.

trambolhada (*f.*) a quantity of things together (bunch of keys, string of fish, etc.).

trambolhão (*m.*) a heavy fall, a crashing down; (*colloq.*) a jolt.

trambolhar (*v.i.*) to stagger about; to stammer.

trambôlho (*m.*) clog (fastened to the leg of an animal); any trammel or impediment; awkward or difficult situation; person whose gait is impeded by obesity.

tramela (*f.*) = TARAMELA.

tramista (*m.*) crook, swindler.

trâmite (*m.*) path; way, course.—**s legais,** legal channels.

tramóia (*f.*) trick, imposture, swindle.

tramoieiro (*m.*) swindler, cheater.

tramontana (*f.*) tramontana (north wind); tramontane (polestar); course, direction. **perder a—,** to lose one's bearings.

tramontar (*v.i.*) of the sun, to set behind the mountains; (*m.*) a setting of the sun behind mountains. Cf. TRANS-MONTAR.

trampolim (*m.*) spring board.

trampolina, –nada, –nagem, –nice (*f.*) trickery, cheating; swindle, fraud.

trampolinar (*v.i.*) to cheat, swindle.

trampolineiro –ra (*adj.*) swindling, cheating, crooked; (*m.,f.*) one who swindles, cheats, tricks; a double-crosser; [= TRAPACEIRO].

tramposear (*v.i.*) to intrude; (*v.t.*) to cheat.

trâmuei (*m.*) tramway.

tranar (*v.t.*) to swim across; to cut through. Cf. TRANS-NADAR.

tranca (*f.*) door bar; by ext., any bar, hindrance, obstruction; breast band (of a harness); (*m.*) a stingy person or one of low character; (*adj.*) miserly; mean.

trança (*f.*) braid of hair; silk or gold braid; scheme, plot; shindy, free-for-all.

trancaço (*m.*) a cold in the head [= CORIZA].

trançadeira (*f.*) a hair ribbon.

trancado –da (*adj.*) bolted, barred, guarded, locked up; (*f.*) blow with a heavy stick; a weir.

trançado (*m.*) plait or braid.

trançador –dora (*adj.*) plaiting, braiding; (*m.*) plaiter (of leather, horse hair, etc.); one who schemes and plots.

trancafiar (*v.t., colloq.*) to lock up (in jail); to put under lock and key.

trancão (*m.*) bump, jolt.

trancar (*v.t.*) to bar, bolt, lock up; in a soccer game, to jolt an opposing player away from the ball; (*v.r.*) to shut oneself up.

trançar (*v.t.*) to braid, plait; (*colloq.*) to crisscross.

tranca-ruas (*m.*) bully, rowdy.

tranca-trilhos (*m.*) barrier at a railroad crossing.

trancelim (*m.*) gold braid; gold chain; ribbon.

trancha (*f.*) tinsmith's edging tool.

trancinha (*f.*) small plait or braid; tress; narrow gold or silk braid; (*colloq.*) intrigue [= MEXERICO]; (*m.,f.*) intriguer; (*adj.*) given to intrigues.

tranco (*m.*) jolt, bump, shove, jostle; jog, slow trot. **aos—s e barrancos,** by fits and starts.

trancucho –cha, trancudo –da (*adj.*) tipsy.

trangla (*f.*) stair carpet rod.

tranquear (*v.i.*) to jog, trot along.

tranqueira (*f.*) stockade; trench; heap of brush, branches, etc.

tranqueta (*f.*) door bar; latch.

tranquia (*f.*) barrier.

tranquibérnia, –bernice (*f.*) trick, fraud, trap.

tranquilidade (*f.*) tranquility, peace, quiet; stillness, calmness.

tranquilizador –dora (*adj.*) tranquilizing; lulling; (*m.,f.*) tranquilizer.

tranquilizar (*v.t.*) to tranquilize, quiet, still; to allay, soothe; (*v.r.*) to calm down, grow quiet.

tranquilo –la (*adj.*) tranquil, quiet, peaceful, undisturbed; unconcerned. **Fique—,** Calm yourself.

tranquitana (*f.*) = TRAQUITANA.

transação [za] (*f.*) transaction; business deal; (*m.,* slang) a sharper.

transacionar [za] (*v.i.*) to transact (business).—**com,** to trade (do business) with.

transalpino –na (*adj.*) transalpine.

transandino –na (*adj.*) trans-Andean.

transatlântico –ca (*adj.*) transatlantic; (*m.*) transatlantic steamer.

transato –ta (*adj.*) past; previous. Var. TRANSACTO.

transator –tora (*adj.*) transacting; (*m.,f.*) transactor. Var. TRANSACTOR.

transbordar (*v.*) & derivs. = TRASBORDAR & DERIVS.

transcendência (*f.*) transcendence, -cy.

transcendental (*adj.*) transcendental.

transcendentalismo (*m., Philos.*) transcendentalism.

transcendente (*adj.*) transcendent.

transcender (*v.t.*) to transcend, surpass, excel.

transcondutância (*f., Elec.*) transconductance.

transcontinental (*adj.*) transcontinental.

transcorrer (*v.t.*) to elapse, go by. **Transcorre hoje o aniversário natalício do Senhor Fulano,** Today is So-and-So's birthday.

transcrever [44] (*v.t.*) to transcribe, copy.

transcrição (*f.*) transcription; transcribing.

transcrito –ta (*adj.*) transcribed; (*m.*) transcript.

transcritor –tora (*adj.*) transcribing; (*m.,f.*) transcriber.

transcursar (*v.t.*) to pass or go beyond; (*v.i.*) to elapse.

transcurso (*m.*) passage (of time, of a given date).

transdutor (*m., Physics*) transducer.

transe [ze] (*m.*) throes, anguish, agonizing moment, crisis; ordeal; predicament. **a todo—,** at all costs; at all hazards.

transepto (*m., Arch.*) transept.

transeunte [ze-un] (*adj.*) transient, transitory; (*m.,f.*) passer-by [= VIANDANTE, PASSANTE].

transferência (*f.*) transference, transfer; assignment.

transferidor –dora (*adj.*) transferring; (*m.*) transferer; (*Math., etc.*) protractor.

transferir [21a] (*v.t.*) to transfer; to assign; to postpone.

transferível (*adj.*) transferable.

transfiguração (*f.*) transfiguration; [*cap.*] Transfiguration (of Jesus).

transfigurado –da (*adj.*) transfigured, changed, transformed; (*m.*) transformation.

transfigurador –dora (*adj.; m.,f.*) that, or one who, transfigures.

transfigurar (*v.t.*) to transfigure, transform.

transfixar [ks] (*v.t.*) to transfix, pierce through, impale.

transformação (*f.*) transformation.

transformador –dora (*adj.*) transforming; (*m.*) transformer; (*Elec.*) transformer.—**aumentador,** step-up transformer.—**blindado,** shell transformer.—**de instrumentos,** instrument transformer.—**elevador de tensão,** step-up transformer.—**com núcleo de ferro,** iron-core transformer.—**de voltagem,** voltage transformer.—**redutor de tensão,** step-down transformer.

transformante (*adj.*) transforming.

transformar (*v.t.*) to transform, transfigure, transmute, convert; (*v.t.*) to change (**em,** into).

transformativo –va (*adj.*) transformative.

transformável (*adj.*) transformable.

transformismo (*m.*) transformism.

transformista (*adj.; m.,f.*) transformist; (*m.,f.*) quick-change artist.

trânsfuga (*m.,f.*) deserter; turncoat; apostate.

transfugir (*v.i.*) to desert.

transfundir (*v.t.*) to transfuse.

transfusão (*f.*) transfusion.—**de sangue,** blood transfusion.

transgredir [21b] (*v.t.*) to transgress, infringe; to overstep.

transgressão (*f.*) transgression, infringement; trespass.

transgressor –sora (*adj.*) transgressing; (*m.,f.*) transgressor, wrongdoer.

transição [zi] (*f.*) transition, passage, shift.

transido –da [zi] (*adj.*) numb (**de,** with—fear, cold, pain, etc.).

transigência [zi] (*f.*) compromise; give-and-take; mutual concession.

transigente [zi] (*adj.*) willing to compromise.

transigir [zi] (*v.i.*) to compromise, settle differences, come to terms.

transigível [zi] (*adj.*) that can be compromised.

transir [46] (v.t.) to penetrate; pierce; (v.i.) to be numb, paralyzed (with cold, fear, etc.).

transitar [zi] (v.i.) to transit, pass (por, over, through, across).

transitável [zi] (adj.) passable.

transitivo –va [zi] (adj.) transitive.

trânsito [zi] (m.) transit, passage (through, over); flow of people passing by; street traffic; surveyor's transit.

transitoriedade [zi] (f.) quality of that which is transitory, fleeting.

transitório –ria [zi] (adj.) transitory, passing, fleeting.

translação (f.) translation (in the sense of transfer or removal. A rendering from one language into another is TRADUÇÃO.); metaphor; (Mech.) translation.

transladação (f.) = TRASLADAÇÃO.

translato –ta (adj.) metaphoric; also = TRASLADADO.

transliteração (f.) transliteration.

transliterar (v.t.) to transliterate.

translucidez (f.) translucency, semi-transparency.

translúcido –da (adj.) translucent, semi-transparent, pellucid; diaphanous.

transluzimento (m.) transparency; diaphaneity.

transluzir [36] (v.t.) to shine through (between); (v.i.) to come to light, become known; (v.r.) to reveal itself.

transmeável (adj.) permeable.

transmigração (f.) transmigration.

transmigrador –dora, transmigrante (adj.; m.,f.) transmigrant.

transmigrar (v.t.,v.i.) to transmigrate.

transmigratório –ria (adj.) transmigratory.

transmissão (f.) transmission; transmittal.—radiofônica, radio broadcast.

transmissível (adj.) transmissible.

transmissor –sora (adj.) transmitting; (m.) transmitter (in any sense); (f.) radio broadcasting station.—de ondas curtas, (m.) short-wave transmitter.

transmitir (v.t.) to transmit, send over (out), pass on (along); to let (light, etc.) through; to transfer, convey; (Radio) to broadcast.

transmontano –na (adj.) tramontane [= TRAMONTANO].

transmontar (v.t.) to cross over mountains; to surpass; (v.i.) to go down behind the mountains (referring to the sun); (v.r.) of the sun, to set. Cf. TRAMONTAR.

transmudação (f.), –mudamento (m.) transmutation. Var. TRANSMUTAÇÃO.

transmudar (v.t.) to transmute, change, transform. Var. TRANSMUTAR.

transmutável (adj.) transmutable.

transnadar (v.t.) to swim across [= TRANAR].

transoceânico –ca (adj.) transoceanic.

transparecer (v.i.) to appear, show, be evident (em, in).

transparência (f.) transparency; (Photog.) slide.

transparente (adj.) transparent, translucent; manifest, patent; (m.) window shade.

transpassar (v.) = TRASPASSAR.

transpiração (f.) transpiration, perspiration.

transpirar (v.t.,v.i.) to transpire, exhale; (v.t.) to perspire; [to sweat is SUAR]; (v.i.) to leak out, come to light, become known [but not to come to pass, happen, occur, which is ACONTECER].

transpirável (adj.) transpirable.

transplantação (f.) transplantation [= TRANSPLANTE].

transplantador –dora (adj.) transplanting; (m.) transplanter (person, tool, or machine).

transplantar (v.t.) to transplant.—se para, to move to.

transplante (m.) = TRANSPLANTAÇÃO.

transpor [63] (v.t.) to cross over, traverse, pass through; to transpose.—a porta, to cross a threshold.—um obstáculo, to hurdle an obstacle.

transportação (f.) transportation [= TRANSPORTE].

transportamento (m.) transportation; transport (ecstasy, rapture).

transportador (m.) transporter; conveyor.—de gravidade, gravity conveyor.

transportar (v.t.) to transport, haul, carry, convey; to entrance, enrapture; to transpose; (v.r.) to be transported.

transportável (adj.) transportable; conveyable; portable.

transporte (m.) transportation, conveyance; naval transport (ship); transport, rapture; in bookkeeping, amount carried forward; (Geol.) transportation.—por água, water transportation.

transposição (f.) transposition.

transposto –ta (adj.) transposed.

transtornado –da (adj.) upset, disturbed.

transtornar (v.t.) to overturn; to upset, disturb, discompose; to derange, unsettle; to throw into disorder.

transtôrno (m.) disturbance, unsettlement; upset; disappointment; trouble; derangement.

transubstanciação [ssu] (f.) transubstantiation.

transubstanciar [ssu] (v.t.) to transubstantiate.

transudação [ssu] (f.) transudation.

transudar [ssu] (v.t.,v.i.) to transude.

transudato [ssu] (m., Physiol.) transudate.

transumância [zu] (f.) the seasonal moving of sheep from or to the mountains.

transunto [ssún (m.) copy of a writing or document.

transvariação (f., Stat.) overlapping.

transvasar (v.t.) to pour out of one vessel into another.

transvazar (v.t.) to decant, pour out, empty; (v.r.) to spill.

transverberar (v.t.) to reflect (light, color); to manifest.

transversal (adj.) transverse, cross, oblique; (f.) a transversal line; a line of collateral kinsmen; (m., Anat.) transversalis.

transverso –sa (adj.) transverse, lying across, athwart; (m.) a transverse muscle.

transvestir (v.t.) to transvest, disguise.

transviado –da (adj.) wayward.

transviar (v.t.) to lead astray; (v.r.) to stray.

tranvia (f.) tramway.

trapa (f.) pitfall; a lifting cable; the Trappist order.

trapaça, trapaçaria (f.) swindle, fraud, cheat, trickery; skin game; skulduggery; double cross.

trapacear (v.t.,v.i.) to cheat, bamboozle, swindle, gyp.

trapaceiro –ra (adj.) deceitful, fraudulent; (m.) trickster, cheat, swindler, crook, sharper, slicker [= TRAMPOLINEIRO].

trapagem (f.) rag pile.

trapalhada (f.) a heap of rags; fig., a jumble, hodgepodge; rigmarole; entanglement, imbroglio. Que—! What a mess!

trapalhão –lhona (adj.) clumsy, blundering; ragged; (m.,f.) blunderer; fumbler; tatterdemalion, ragamuffin.

trapalhice (f.) tatters; a swindle; a blunder.

trape (m., Geol.) trap, specif., oil trap.

trapear (v.i.) to flap (as a sail).

trapeira (f.) trap; pitfall; (Arch.) lucarne, dormer, gablet; (colloq.) jumble, confusion.

trapeiro (m.) ragman, rag picker.

trapejar (v.i.) to flap; to rattle.

trape-zape (m.) the sound made by swords clashing.

trapeziforme (adj.) = TRAPEZÓIDE.

trapézio (m.) trapeze; (Geom.) trapezium; (Anat.) trapezium, trapezoid.

trapezista (m.,f.) trapeze artist.

trapezoedro (m., Cryst.) trapezohedron.

trapezoidal (adj.) = TRAPEZÓIDE.

trapezóide (adj.) trapezoid [= TRAPEZOIDAL, TRAPEZIFORME]; (m., Geom.) trapezium [U.S.A.]; trapezoid [Great Britain]; (Anat., Zool.) trapezoid.

trapiche (m.) water-front warehouse.

trapicheiro (m.) owner or superintendent of a TRAPICHE.

trapista (adj.; m.) Trappist.

trapo (m.) rag, tatter; a tattered suit.

trapoeraba (f., Bot.) a spiderwort (Tradescantia diuretica). c.a. ANDACA, ÔLHO-DE-SANTA-LUZIA.—-azul = CAPIM-GOMOSO.—-vermelha, red spiderwort (Tradescantia rubra).

trapoerabarana (f.) a dayflower (Commelina deficiens); also = CAPIM-GOMOSO.

trápola (f.) trap, snare.

traque (m.) firecracker.—de chumbo, torpedo (a firework), c.a. ESTALO, CHUMBINHO.

traqueal (adj.) tracheal.

traqueano –na (adj., Anat., Zool.) tracheal; (Zool.) having tracheae.

traquéia (f., Anat., Zool.) trachea, windpipe; (Bot.) trachea; tracheid.

traqueíte (f., Med.) tracheitis.

traquejado –da (adj.) skilled, practiced, experienced.

traquejar (v.t.) to chase, pursue; to beat (woods).

traquejo [ê] (m.) skill, practice, experience.

traqueotomia (f., Surg.) tracheotomy.

traquete [ête] (m., Naut.) foresail; a simple square sail for a small fishing boat.

traquina (adj.; m.,f.) = TRAQUINAS.

traquinada (f.) hullabaloo; children's misbehavior; plot, scheme.

traquinagem (f.) = TRAQUINICE.

traquinar (*v.i.*) of children, to misbehave, cut up; to fidget.

traquinas (*adj.*) of children, mischievous, impish, naughty; fidgety; (*m.,f.*) a naughty, mischievous, prankish child or adult; [= TRAQUINA, TRAQUINO].

traquinice (*f.*) mischievousness; misbehavior (of children); [= TRAQUINADA].

traquitana (*f.*, *colloq.*) a rattletrap. Var. TRANQUITANA.

traquitanda (*f.*) = ALMANJARRA.

traquítico –ca (*adj.*, *Petrog.*) trachytic.

traquito (*m.*, *Petrog.*) trachyte.

trás (*adv.; prep.*) behind, back, after [= ATRÁS]. **andar para**—, to walk backwards **ano**—**ano**, year after year. **de**—, from behind. **de frente para**—, from front to rear. **mais para**—, further back. **para**—, backward(s); behind, back. **por**—**de**, behind.

trasanteontem (*adv.*) day before the day-before-yesterday; three days ago. Var. TRASANTONTEM.

trasbordamento (*m.*) overflow, overflowing. **rocha de**—, (*Geol.*) effusive rock. Var. TRANSBORDAMENTO.

trasbordante (*adj.*) overflowing, full to overflowing, brimful. Var. TRANSBORDANTE.

trasbordar (*v.t.*) to spill over; (*v.i.*) to overflow.—**de alegria**, to be overjoyed. Var. TRANSBORDAR.

trasbôrdo (*m.*) overflow; transshipment of passengers and freight from one train to another (around a washout or other obstruction in the line). Var. TRANSBÔRDO.

traseiro –ra (*adj.*) hind, hindmost, rear, back; (*f.*) rear, hind part; (*m.*, *colloq.*) the behind (rump). **lanterna**—, tail light.

trasfega, –**gadura** (*f.*), –**fêgo** (*m.*) decantation.

trasfegar (*v.t.*) to decant (liquids).

trasfogueiro (*m.*) backlog; andiron.

trasfoliar (*v.t.*) to copy (a drawing or the like) by tracing the lines through a transparent sheet.

trasgo (*m.*) hobgoblin; sprite; pixy; a mischievous person.

trasladação (*f.*) removal, transfer; translation.—**de propriedade**, conveyance of property. **comando de**—, (military aviation) ferrying command.

trasladado –da (*adj.*) removed, transferred; translated.

trasladar (*v.t.*) to transfer; to postpone; to transcribe; to paraphrase.—**a (para)**, to remove to.—**a (em, para)**, to translate (in any sense) to.

traslado (*m.*) transcript, copy; transfer; removal; translation; paraphrase.

traslar (*m.*) the back part of a hearth.

trasmontano –na (*adj.; m.,f.*) tramontane [= TRANSMONTANO]; specif., pert. to, or a native or inhabitant of, the province of Trás-os-Montes in the north of Portugal.

trasorelho [ê] (*m.*, *Med.*) parotitis; mumps [= CAXUMBA].

traspassação (*f.*), –**passamento** (*m.*) act or instance of crossing over, etc. See the verb TRASPASSAR.

traspassar (*v.t.*) to cross (over); to pass (over, through); to transfix; to pierce (through); to transgress, trespass; to postpone; to transfer or sublet (property); to exceed, overstep (one's authority); to copy, transcribe; to translate (language); (*v.r.*) to faint; to die.—**-se de**, to be filled with (awe, fear, respect, etc.).

traspasse (*m.*) the act or an instance of passing over, transferring, etc. See the verb TRASPASSAR; specif., a transfer or sublease (of property); death.

traspasso (*m.*) piercing pain; great grief; delay, postponement; also = TRASPASSE.

trastalhão (*m.*), –**lhona** (*f.*) big rascal.

trastaria (*f.*) heap of old furniture.

traste (*m.*) household utensil or piece of furniture, esp. an old one and of little value; rascal; worthless fellow.

trastejão (*m.*), –**jona** (*f.*) = TRASTALHÃO, –LHONA.

trastejar (*v.i.*) to deal in second-hand furniture and the like; to manage household affairs; to act in a rascally manner; to turncoat; (*v.t.*) to furnish (a house, etc.).

trat. = TRATAMENTO (treatment).

tratadista (*m.,f.*) writer of a treatise.

tratado (*m.*) treaty, pact; treatise.

tratador –dora (*adj.*) that treats or cares for; (*m.*) caretaker; hostler.—**de fazenda**, ranch hand.

tratamento (*m.*) treatment (in any sense); mode of address; daily food.—**térmico**, (*Metal.*) heat treatment.

tratantada, -**tice** (*f.*) swindle, piece of crooked business; a gyp; rascality.

tratante (*adj.*) crooked, rascally; (*m.,f.*) crook; sharper; (*m.*) scalawag, scamp.

tratar (*v.t.*) to treat; to deal with; to treat of, discuss; to care for (medically); to transact; to negotiate, arrange

for; (*v.r.*) to treat (take care of) oneself.—**(alguém) de cima para baixo**, to talk down to (someone).—**com**, to deal with; to treat with (respect, etc.).—**de** , to speak of; to care for; to deal with; to seek to; to address as.—**de negócios**, to attend to business.—**de potência a potência**, to deal with (one another) as equals.—**de um assunto**, to deal with a matter.—**o preço**, to agree on the price.—**por**, to address (someone) as.—**por alto**, to deal with superficially.—**-se por tu**, to use TU (the familiar form of you) in addressing one another. **De que se trata?** What is it about? **O assunto de que se trata**, the business in hand; the subject dealt with. **trata-se de**, it is a question of. **Tratou de arranjar emprêgo**, He went about looking for a job.

tratável (*adj.*) treatable; tractable; pleasant, affable.

tratear (*v.t.*) to mistreat.

tratista (*adj.; m.,f.*) = TRATANTE.

trato (*m.*) treatment, usage, handling, dealing; manner of dealing (with other persons); therapy; a contract; lapse of time; extent, course; board, fare; tract of land; (*R.C.Ch.*) tract; (*pl.*) ill-treatment. **dar**—**s à bola**, (*colloq.*) to cudgel one's brains. **sem**—, unkempt; uncaredfor.

trator (*m.*) tractor.—**agrícola**, farm tractor.—**de esteira**, caterpillar tractor.

traulitadas (*f.pl.*) slaps, cuffs.

trauma (*m.*) = TRAUMATISMO.

traumático –ca (*adj.*) traumatic.

traumatismo (*m.*, *Med.*) traumatism; trauma.

trauta (*f.*) spoor.

trautear (*v.t.,v.i.*) to hum (a tune); (*colloq.*) to pester; to gyp; to scold.

Trav. = TRAVESSA (Lane—name of a street).

trava (*f.*) act of restraining, etc. See the verb TRAVAR; fetter for an animal [= PEIA]; lock for a wheel [= TRAVÃO].

travação (*f.*) act or an instance of restraining, etc. See the verb TRAVAR; [= TRAVAMENTO].

travadeira (*f.*) = TRAVADOURA.

travado –da (*adj.*) closely tied, joined, linked or locked; close, intimate; restrained; joined (as battle); tonguetied; fierce, hotly contested; of a horse, hobbled or trammeled.—**de dificuldades**, beset with difficulties.

travador –dora (*adj.*) hampering, etc. (see the verb); (*m.,f.*) one who hampers, etc. (see the verb); also = TRAVADOURA.

travadoura (*f.*) a saw set [= TRAVICHA, TRAVADEIRA]; a bondstone; also = TRAVADOR. Var. TRAVADOIRA.

travadouro (*m.*) pastern (of a horse's foot). Var. TRAVADOIRO.

travagem (*f.*, *Veter.*) a disease which causes swollen gums and loss of teeth.

travamento (*m.*) = TRAVAÇÃO.

travanca (*f.*) obstacle, impediment; stumbling block.

travão (*m.*) fetter or shackle for an animal; a device to lock a wheel.

travar (*v.t.*) to bind, tie, join, dovetail; to check, restrain, hamper, impede; to clog, block; to lock (as a wheel); to set (the teeth of a saw); to clasp, grip; to embitter; (*v.i.*) to taste acrid (as a green persimmon); (*v.r.*) to mingle (as pleasure and pain); to be joined (as in battle).—**batalha**, to join battle.—**combate**, to join combat.—**conversa**, to join in conversation with.—**de**, to take hold of.—**espadas**, to cross swords.—**o passo**, to drag one's feet.—**relações**, to establish relations with.—**-se com**, to struggle with.

trave (*f.*) heavy wooden beam; girder; also = TRAVA.

travejamento (*m.*) framework; beams, girders, rafters, collectively.

travejar (*v.t.*) to provide with beams; to frame (a building).

travela (*f.*) = BICHA-AMARELA.

travento –ta (*adj.*) tart; acrid [= TRAVOSO].

travertino (*m.*, *Min.*) travertine.

través (*m.*) bias, slant. **de**—, (*adv.*) across, athwart. Cf. ᐧATRAVÉS.

travessa (*f.*) crosspiece, cross beam; lintel; railroad crosstie; bolster; cross street or alley; connecting passageway; platter; bar pin (for the hair); also = TRAVESSIA.

travessão (*m.*) a dash [—]; large beam; turbulent cross wind; beam of a scale; (*Music*) bar, division; [GBAT: "(1) a river crossing, such as is provided by a sand spit or a series of stones; (2) a stretch of quiet water extending along the course of a river; (3) in Pará and Goiás, a kind of reef that stretches from one bank of the river to the other and is divided into several sections in which rather deep channels are formed through which canoes can pass; (4) a sand bank or heap of rocks which crosses a river and can be used in fording."] (*adj.*) of wind, cross and turbulent.

travessar (*v.*) = ATRAVESSAR.

travesseiro (*m.*) pillow; bolster; pillow case. [In Portugal, the noun is fem., TRAVESSEIRA].

travessia (*f.*) a crossing or act of crossing (an ocean, a continent, etc.); strong head wind; long stretch of lonely road; a buying up of merchandise (to corner the market).

travesso –**sa** (*adj.*) transverse, lying athwart.

travêsso –**sa** (*adj.*) mischievous, naughty; playful, prankish; cross, fretful; restless.

travessura (*f.*) prank, antic; frolic; escapade; mischief; naughtiness.

travicha (*f.*) = TRAVADOURA.

travo, travor (*m.*) tartness; bitterness; acridity; unpleasant aftertaste.

travoso (*adj.*) = TRAVENTO.

trazedor –**dora** (*adj.*) bringing; (*m.,f.*) bringer.

trazer [79] (*v.t.*) to bring (in any sense); to bring about; to wear, have on; to carry (upon the person).—**à baila**, to bring (a matter) up for discussion.—**à cinta**, to wear (knife, pistol) at the belt.—**à memória**, to call to mind. —**consigo**, to bring (something) with one.—**de ôlho**, to be wary of.—**de presente**, to bring (something) as a gift. —**em mente**, to bear in mind.—**na bôca**, to mention frequently.—**na mão**, to carry in the hand.—**no coração**, to carry in the heart (love intensely).—**os olhos em**, to keep the eyes on.—**pelo beiço**, to lead (someone) by the nose.—**para cima da mesa**, to bring out a matter (for discussion).—**um vestido vermelho**, to wear a red dress.

trazida (*f.*), **trazimento** (*m.*) a bringing, carrying, bearing.

trecentésimo –**ma** [zi] (*adj.; m.,f.*) three hundredth.

trecho [ê] (*m.*) space, distance, interval; passage (musical or literary).

treco (*m., slang*) thing; situation.

trécula (*f.*) a rattle for frightening birds away from plants and fruit trees.

trêfego –**ga** (*adj.*) unruly; restless; mischievous; naughty; frisky, sprightly; sly, tricky.

trégua (*f.*) truce; respite, lull.

treinador (*m.*) trainer; coach.

treinagem (*f.*), **treinamento** (*m.*) training.

treinar (*v.t.*) to train, drill; (*v.r.*) to practice, exercise. Var. TRENAR.

treino (*m.*) training; drill, practice. Var. TRENO.

trejeitar, –**tear** (*v.i.*) to grimace, make faces.

trejeito (*m.*) grimace.

trela (*f.*) dog leash; (*colloq.*) a chat; gossip; leave, license. **dar**—**a**, (*slang*) to encourage another to talk, flirt, etc.; to lead him on; to encourage familiarity.

treler [38] (*v.i.*) to encourage familiarity; to gossip; to butt in; not know what one is doing or saying; to argue.

trelho [ê] (*m.*) dasher of a churn. **sem**—**nem trabalho**, without rhyme or reason.

treliça (*f.*) truss (of a bridge); trestlework (of a viaduct).

trem (*m.*) railway train; a set of gears; the insides of a clock; bags, luggage; retinue; kitchen and household utensils, collectively; carriage, coach; (*pl.*) a person's "things".—**blindado**, armored train.—**cargueiro**, freight train.—**da alegria**, (*slang*) gravy train.—**de aterragem** (or **de pouso**), landing gear (of an airplane).—**laminador**, rolling mill.—**subterrâneo**, subway train.

trema (*m.*) dieresis (''), [= ÁPICES, DIÉRESE].

tremar (*v.t.*) to mark with a dieresis; to unravel.

trematôdeo (*m., Zool.*) any member of the Trematoda.

tremebundo –**da** (*adj.*) trembling; trembly; tremulous; tremendous (in the sense of frightful).

tremedal (*m.*) quagmire, morass, bog.

tremedeira (*f.*) tremor, trembling, quaking; chills and fever; last moments of a dying person.

tremedor –**dora** (*adj.*) trembling.

tremelica (*adj.; m.,f.*) scary (person).

tremelicante (*adj.*) = TREMELICOSO.

tremelicar (*v.i.*) to shiver; to quake.—**as pestanas**, to flutter the eyelashes.

tremelicoso –**sa** (*adj.*) shivery; tremulous; = TREMELICANTE.

tremelique (*m.*) act of trembling, shivering, quaking.

tremeluzente (*adj.*) twinkling, blinking, flickering, glimmering.

tremeluzir [36] (*v.i.*) to twinkle, blink, wink, flicker, glimmer.

tremembé (*m.*) swamp land, marsh, quagmire.

tremendo –**da** (*adj.*) tremendous; terrible, dreadful; extraordinary.

tremente (*adj.*) trembling, quaking, shivering.

tremer (*v.i.*) to tremble, shudder, shiver, quiver, quake.

tremetara (*f.*) = PAPA-TERRA.

treme-treme (*m.*) the electric ray (*Narcine brasiliensis*), c.a. ARRAIA-ELÉTRICA; also = PORAQUÊ, PEIXE-ELÉTRICO; (*Bot.*) a quakinggrass (*Briza viridis*).

trêmito (*m.*) = FRÊMITO.

tremó (*m.*) pier (portion of wall between doors or windows); pier glass.

tremoceiro (*m., Bot.*) lupine.—**-amarelo**, European yellow lupine (*L. luteus*).—**-branco**, white lupine (*Lupinus albus*).—**-de-flor-azul**, blue-flowered lupine (*L. varius*).

tremoço (*m.*) lupine (seed or plant).

tremolita (*f., Min.*) tremolite.

tremonha (*f.*) hopper, as for grain, coal, gravel, ore, etc. [= TEGÃO].

tremor (*m.*) tremor, quiver, quake, shiver, thrill; fright [= TEMOR].—**da terra**, earthquake [= TERREMOTO].—**dos artistas**, stage fright.

trempe (*f.*) trivet; (*colloq.*) a trio or threesome; a JANGADA of only three logs instead of the usual five.

tremular (*v.t.*) to wave (as a flag); to shake (as the head); (*v.i.*) to flutter (as a flag); to glimmer (as stars); to waver, hesitate.

tremulina (*f.*) glimmer; glimmering.

trêmulo –**la** (*adj.*) tremulous; shaky; hesitant; wavering; timid; (*m., Music*) tremolo.

tremura (*f.*) tremor; (*pl.*) the shivers.

trena (*f.*) tapeline; a hair ribbon.

trenar (*v.*) & derivs. = TRINAR & DERIVS.

trenó (*m.*) sled or sleigh.

trenodia (*f.*) threnody, dirge.

trepa (*f., colloq.*) a rebuke; a trouncing.

trepação (*f.*) malicious gossip; jeering.

trepada (*f.*) a climb; a slap.

trepador –**deira** (*adj.*) that climbs; maligning; (*f.*) a climbing plant; a woodpecker called PICA-PAU-CINZENTO; the hedge glorybind (*Convolvulus sepium*); (*m.,f.*) one who maligns others; a climber (bird).

trepa-moleque (*m.*) a high comb; the wood ibis [= JABIRU]; a rove beetle (*Staphylinus*), c.a. POTÓ.

trepanar (*v.t., Surg.*) to trepan; to trephine.

trépano (*m., Surg.*) trepan; trephine.

trepar (*v.t.*) to clamber up, climb up (a tree, ladder, mountain, etc.); (*colloq.*) to malign; (*v.i.*) of plants, to climb.—**em seus tamancos**, to rise up, get mad.

trepidação (*f.*) trepidation, tremor; quaking.

trepidante (*adj.*) tremulous.

trepidar (*v.i.*) to feel trepidation; to hesitate (**em**, to); to tremble, shake. **não**—**em dizer**, not hesitate to say.

trépido –**da** (*adj.*) trembling; timorous.

tréplica (*f.*) rejoinder.

treplicar (*v.t.,v.i.*) to rejoin.

treponemo (*m.*), –**ma** (*f., Bacteriol.*) a genus (*Treponema*) of spirochetes.

três (*adj.*) three; (*m.*) the number three; the trey (cards, dice, dominos). **às duas por**—, suddenly; unexpectedly. **Dois é bom**—**é demais**, Two is company, three is a crowd. **regra de**—, the rule of three.

tresandar (*v.t.*) to turn back (as the hands of a clock); to upset, disturb; to exhale (offensive odors); (*v.i.*) to reek (**de**, of).

trescalar (*v.t.*) to emit a strong odor; (*v.i.*) to give forth a strong aroma.

tresdobrado –**da** (*adj.*) triplicate [= TRIPLICADO].

tresdobrar (*v.t.,v.i.*) to treble, triple.

tresdôbro (*m.*) treble, triple.

três-estrelinhas (*f.pl.*) three asterisks [***] used in printing and writing instead of actual names of persons and places, or after paid newspaper articles.

tresfolegar (*v.i.*) to pant.

tresloucado –**da** (*adj.; m.,f.*) crazed, deranged, distraught (person).

tresloucar (*v.t.*) to make crazy; (*v.i.*) to go crazy.

tresmalhado –**da** (*adj.*) strayed, runaway. **gado**—, stray cattle.

tresmalhar (*v.t.*) to drop a stitch (in knitting); to lose, let escape (as game); to run off (as cattle); (*v.i.*) to stray (from the herd); (*v.r.*) to escape (through a net); to stray; to get lost.

tresmalho (*m.*) trammel (fish net); disappearance; stampede.

três-marias (*f.pl.*) jackstones (children's game); (*Astron.*) Orion's Belt; (*Bot.*) bougainvillea; also = BOLEADEIRAS.

tresnoitar (*v.i.*) to stay awake all night; (*v.t.*) to keep awake. Var. TRESNOUTAR.

trespassar (*v.*) = TRASPASSAR.

três-potes (*m.*) = SARACURA.

tresvariado –da (*adj.*) raving.

tresvariar (*v.i.*) to rave.

tresvario (*m.*) raving; delirium.

treta [ê] (*f.*) feint, sham attack; (*pl.*) smooth talk.

treteiro (*m.*) rascal, smooth talker.

trevas (*f.pl.*) darkness; fig., ignorance; (*R.C.Ch.*) the Tenebrae. **ao caír das—**, at nightfall.

trevinho-do-campo (*m.*) = CARRAPICHO-DE-BEIÇO-DE-BOI.

trevo [ê] (*m.*) clover.—**-aquático**, common bogbean or buck bean (*Menyanthes trifoliata*), c.a. TRIFÓLIO.—**-azêdo**, creeping oxalis (*O. corniculata*).—**-azul**, the bluewhite trigonella (*T. caerulea*).—**-cervino**, the hemp eupatorium (*E. cannabium*), c.a. TREVO-DE-SEARA, EUPATÓRIO-COMUM, EUPATÓRIO-DE-AVICENA.—**-cheiroso** = ANAFA.—**-da-flórida**, Cherokee tickclover (*Desmodium tortuosum*).—**-de-carvalho** = ANAFA.—**-de-cheiro**, sweet clover (*Melilotus*), c.a. TREVO-REAL, MELILOTO.—**-de-serra**, a sweetclover (*Melilotus parviflora*).—**-do-campo** = AMOR-DO-CAMPO.—**-do-egito**, Egyptian clover (*Trifolium alexandrinum*).—**-dos-prados**, red clover (*Trifolium pratense*), c.a. TREVO-VERMELHO.—**-maçaroca**, fineleaf clover (*Trifolium angustifolium*).—**-namorado**, low hop clover (*Trifolium procumbens*).—**-rasteiro**, the toothed burclover (*Medicago hispida denticulata*).

trevoso –sa (*adj.*) dark; gloomy.

treze (*m.*) thirteen; (*adj.*) thirteenth [= DÉCIMO-TERCEIRO].—**-de-maio**, an epithet sometimes applied to Negroes. [The reference is to the date—May 13, 1888—on which slavery was abolished in Brazil.]

trezeno –na (*adj.*) thirteenth [= TÉRCIO-DECIMO, TREDÉCIMO, DÉCIMO-TERCEIRO]; (*f.*) a group or unit of thirteen; a period of thirteen days.

trezentos (*m.*) three hundred.

triácido –da (*adj.*, *Chem.*) triacid.

tríade, triada (*f.*) triad (in any sense).

triagem (*f.*) switching (of railroad cars); sorting, (of data, papers, etc.); screening (as of immigrants).

triangulação (*f.*, *Surveying*) triangulation.

triangulador (*m.*) triangulator.

triangular (*adj.*) triangular; (*v.t.*) to triangulate.

triângulo (*m.*, *Geom.*, *Music*) triangle.—**-acutângulo**, acute-angled triangle.—**-curvilíneo**, curvilinear triangle.—**de reversão**, a railroad Y.—**-equilátero**, equilateral triangle.—**-escaleno**, scalene triangle.—**-esférico**, spherical triangle.—**-isóceles**, isosceles triangle.—**-obtusângulo**, obtuse-angled triangle.—**-oxígono** = TRIANGULO ACUTÂNGULO.—**-plano**, plane triangle.—**-retângulo**, right-angled triangle.

triarquia (*f.*) triarchy, triumvirate.

triásico –ca (*adj.*, *Geol.*) Triassic.

triatômico –ca (*adj.*, *Chem.*) triatomic, trivalent.

tribásico –ca (*adj.*, *Chem.*) tribasic.

tríbade (*f.*) tribade.

tribadismo (*m.*) tribadism.

tribal (*adj.*) tribal.

tribo (*f.*) tribe; clan.

triboeletricidade (*f.*) triboelectricity.

tribofar (*v.i.*) to rig a horse race; to cheat at games of any sort.

tribofe (*m.*) rigging of a horse race; cheating, crookedness, swindling, of any sort; dalliance, amorous toying.

tribofeiro (*m.*) cheat, trickster, sharper, crook.

tríbraco (*m.*, *Pros.*) tribrach.

tribulação (*f.*) tribulation, suffering, affliction, woe.

tríbulo (*m.*) the puncture vine (*Tribulus terrestris*), c.a. ABRÔLHO.—**-aquático**, the water caltrop or water chestnut (*Trapa natans*), c.a. ABRÔLHO-AQUÁTICO, CASTANHA-D'ÁGUA.

tribuna (*f.*) tribune, rostrum, speaker's platform, pulpit; public speaking, oratory.

tribunado (*m.*) tribunate.

tribunal (*m.*) tribunal; court; bar, bench.

tribunato (*m.*) = TRIBUNADO.

tribuno (*m.*) tribune; demagogue.

tributar (*v.t.*) to impose a tax or other charge on; to assess; to pay as tribute; to pay tribute to; (*v.r.*) to contribute.

tributário –ria (*adj.*; *m.,f.*) tributary. **reforma—**, tax reform.

tributo (*m.*) tribute, tax, duty, toll; contribution.

tribuzana (*f.*) = TRABUZANA.

trica (*f.*) trick, flimflam; trifle.—**s e futricas**, intrigues, meddling.

tricentenário –ria (*adj.*; *m.*) tricentennial, tercentenary.

tricentésimo –ma (*adj.*) three-hundredth.

triciclo (*m.*) tricycle.

tricípite (*m.*, *Anat.*) triceps.

triclínico –ca (*adj.*, *Cryst.*) triclinic.

tricloretelino (*m.*, *Chem.*) trichloroethylene.

tricloreto (*m.*, *Chem.*) trichloride.—**-etílico**, ethylene trichloride.

tricô (*m.*) jersey or other knitted cloth. [French *tricot*]. **agulha de—**, knitting needle.

tricociste (*f.*, *Zool.*) trichocyst.

tricóide (*adj.*) trichoid, hairlike.

tricologia (*f.*) trichology.

tricolor [lôr] (*adj.*) tricolor.

tricorne (*adj.*) tricorn.

tricórnio (*m.*) tricorn hat.

tricosana (*f.*, *Chem.*) tricosane.

tricotar, tricotear (*v.i.*) to knit.

tricotomia (*f.*) trichotomy.

tricromático –ca (*adj.*) trichomatic.

tricrômico –ca (*adj.*) trichromic.

tricúspide (*adj.*) tricuspid.

tridáctilo –la (*adj.*, *Zool.*) tridactyl.

tridecano (*m.*, *Chem.*) tridecane.

tridentado –da (*adj.*) tridentate.

tridente (*adj.*; *m.*) trident.

tridi [dí] (*m.*) = MACUQUINHO.

tridimita (*f.*, *Min.*) tridymite.

triduano –na (*adj.*) lasting three days.

tríduo (*m.*) a span of three days; (*R.C.Ch.*) triduum.

triécico –ca (*adj.*, *Bot.*) trioecious.

triedro –dra (*adj.*) trihedral; (*m.*) trihedron.

trielina (*f.*) = TRICLORETILENO.

trienado (*m.*) = TRIÊNIO.

trienal (*adj.*) triennial.

triênio (*m.*) triennial [= TRIENADO].

trifacial (*adj.*, *Anat.*) trifacial, trigeminal [= TRIGÊMEO].

trifânio (*m.*, *Min.*) triphane; spodumene.

trifásico –ca (*adj.*, *Elec.*) three-phase. **correntes—s**, three-phase currents. **motor—**, three-phase motor.

trífido –da (*adj.*) trifid [= TRIGÊMINO].

trifilar (*adj.*; *Elec.*) three-wire.

trifilita (*f.*, *Min.*) triphylite.

trifilo –la (*adj.*, *Bot.*) triphyllous, three-leaved.

trifloro –ra (*adj.*, *Bot.*) trifloral, three-flowered.

trifoliado –da (*adj.*, *Bot.*) trifoliate.

trifólio (*m.*) clover [= TREVO]; trefoil; a pencilflower (*Stylosanthes sp.*).

trifoliose (*f.*, *Veter.*) trifoliosis.

trifório (*m.*, *Arch.*) triforium.

triforme (*adj.*) triform.

trifurcar (*v.t.*) to trifurcate.

trigal (*m.*) wheat field.

trigêmeo –mea (*adj.*) designating a triplet; (*Anat.*) trigeminal [= TRIFACIAL]; (*m.,f.*) a triplet; (*pl.*) triplets.

trigêmino –na (*adj.*) = TRÍFIDO.

trigésimo –ma (zi] (*adj.*; *m.*) thirtieth.—**-primeiro**, **-segundo**, etc. thirty-first, -second, etc.

trígino –na (*adj.*, *Bot.*) trigynous.

tríglifo (*m.*, *Arch.*) triglyph.

triglota (*adj.*; *m.,f.*) trilingual (person).

trigo (*m.*) wheat.—**-cachudo**, Poulard wheat (*Triticum turgidum*).—**-candial**, einkorn (*Triticum monococcum*).—**de prioste**, choice wheat.—**-duro**, durum wheat; macaroni wheat.—**-grama** = GRAMA-DE-PONTA.—**-mouro**, = buckwheat, c.a. TRIGO-PRÊTO, TRIGO-SARRACENO.—**-ordinário**, common wheat (*Triticum aestivum*).—**-selvagem** = GRAMA-DE-PONTA. **separar o joio do—**, to separate the tares from the wheat.

trigonal (*adj.*) trigonal.

trígono –na (*adj.*) trigonous; (*m.*, *Astrol.*) trigon.

trigonelina (*f.*, *Chem.*) trigonelline; caffearin; gynesin.

trigonometria (*f.*) trigonometry.

trigonométrico –ca (*adj.*) trigonometric(al).

trigrama (*m.*) trigraph.

trigueiro –ra (*adj.*; *m.,f.*) brunet; brunette. Cf. MORENO.

triguenho –nha (*adj.*) pert. to or like wheat.
triguilho (*m.*) chaff.
triidrato [i-i] (*m., Chem.*) trihydrate.
triídrico –ca [i-í] (*adj., Chem.*) trihydric.
triidroxipropano [i-i . . . ks] (*m., Chem.*) trihydroxypropane; glycerol.
trijugado –da (*adj., Bot.*) trijugate.
trilar (*v.t., v.i.*) to trill, warble.
trilátero –ra, **trilateral** (*adj.*) trilateral, three-sided.
trilha (*f.*) act of threshing, flailing (grain); trail, track; footsteps (in the sense of example).—**sonora**, sound track.
trilhada (*f.*) = TRILHA.
trilhadeira (*f.*) threshing machine.
trilhado –da (*adj.*) well-known; well-trod. **caminho—**, beaten track.
trilhador –dora (*adj.*) threshing; (*m.*) thresher.
trilhadura (*f.*), **trilhamento** (*m.*) threshing; trail.
trilhão (*m.*) trillion.
trilhar (*v.t.*) to thresh, flail (grain); to tread, trample; to tread upon, crush; to tread, follow (a path); to tramp, travel on foot.
trilheira (*f.*) a path through the woods.
trilho (*m.*) steel rail; track, trail; churn; thresher.
trilião (*m.*) = TRILHÃO.
trilinear (*adj.*) trilinear; three-line.
trilingüe (*adj.*) trilingual.
trílito (*m., Archaeol.*) trilithon.
trilo (*m.*) musical trill; warble.
trilobado –da (*adj.*) trilobate.
trilobite (*m.*) trilobite.
trilocular (*adj.*) trilocular.
trilogia (*f.*) trilogy; triad.
trim. = TRIMESTRE (trimester).
trimaculado –da (*adj.*) trimacular.
trimegisto (*m.*) 36-point type.
trimensal (*adj.*) occurring, done, or coming, thrice-monthly. Cf. TRIMESTRAL.
trimérico –ca (*adj., Chem.*) trimeric.
trímero –ra (*adj.*) trimerous; (*m., Chem.*) trimer.
trimestral (*adj.*) trimestral; trimonthly. Cf. TRIMENSAL.
trimestralidade (*f.*) quarter-annual payment.
trimestre (*m.*) trimester, quarter year, the period of three months; (*adj.*) = TRIMESTRAL.
trimétrico –ca (*adj.*) trimeter.
trímetro (*m.*) trimeter.
trimorfismo (*m.*), **trimorfia** (*f., Cryst.*) trimorphism.
trimorfo –fa (*adj.*) trimorphous.
trinado (*m.*) act of trilling, warbling [= TRINO].
trinar (*v.t., v.i.*) to trill; to warble.
trinca (*f.*) set of three (of anything); three cards of a kind; street gang; chink or crack (as in a plate); a scratch.
trincado –da (*adj.*) split, cracked, chipped (as a dish); (*f.*) a bite or nibble.
trincadura (*f.*) chink.
trinca-espinhas (*m., colloq.*) a spindle-legs, bean pole (tall, thin man.).
trinca-ferro (*m.*) a bird—the lesser buff-throated saltator (*Saltator maximus*), c.a. SABIÁ-PIMENTA, SABIÁ-DA-CAMPINA, GARGANTA-DE-FERRO.
trincafiar (*v.t., Naut.*) to lash; in shoemaking, to sew.
trincafio (*m.*) shoemaker's thread; string, etc., which one twists around the end of a bolt before screwing on the nut; (*Naut.*) a lash.
trincal (*m.*) = TINCAL.
trincanises (*m.pl., Naut.*) scuppers.
trinca-nozes (*m.*) = CRUZA-BICO.
trincar (*v.t.*) to chew, bite, munch, crunch; to nibble, chew on; (*v.i.*) to make a crackling or snapping sound (as of nuts cracked with the teeth); (*v.r.*) to get angry.
trincha (*f.*) a carpenter's or similar adz; a wood (or other) shaving, thin slice; nail puller; jimmy (short crowbar); wide paint brush.
trinchador –dora (*adj.*) carving; (*m.,f.*) carver.
trinchante (*m.*) carving knife; carving set; carving table; (*m.,f.*) carver; (*adj.*) carving.
trinchar (*v.t.*) to carve (meat).
trincheira (*f.*) trench; parapet.
trinchete [chê] (*m.*) shoemaker's blade.
trincho (*m.*) trencher; act of carving (meat).
trinco (*m.*) door or gate latch; a snap (clicking sound). **chave de—**, latchkey.
trincolejar (*v.*) = TILINTAR.

trindade (*f.*) trinity; [*cap.*] the Trinity.
trineto (*m.*) great-great grandchild.
trinfar (*v.i.*) to chirp, twitter [= TRISSAR]; (*m.*) chirp, twitter [= TRISSO].
trinitrina (*f., Chem.*) trinitrin; nitroglycerin.
trinitrocelulose (*f., Chem.*) nitrocellulose.
trinitrocresol (*m., Chem.*) trinitrocresol.
trinitrofenol (*m., Chem.*) trinitrophenol; picric acid.
trinitrotolueno (*m., Chem.*) trinitrotoluene.
trinitroxileno (*m., Chem.*) trinitroxylene.
trino –na (*adj.*) three in one, triune.
trinômio (*m.*) trinomial.
trinque (*m.*) spruceness.
trinta (*adj.; m.*) thirty; thirtieth.
trintanário (*m.*) footman.
trintão –tona (*adj.*) thirtyish; (*m.,f.*) one in his or her thirties. Var. TRINTENÁRIO.
trintar (*v.i., colloq.*) to reach thirty (years of age).
trinta-réis (*m.*) = ANDORINHA-DO-MAR (a tern).
trintário (*m., R.C.Ch.*) month's mind; trental.
trintena (*f.*) thirty of anything; a thirtieth.
trintenário –ria (*adj.; m.,f.*) = TRINTÃO –TONA.
trintídio (*m.*) a thirty-day period; a commemoration on the thirtieth day after a person's death.
trio (*m.*) trio.
triocular (*adj.*) triocular.
tríodo (*m., Elec.*) triode.
trióico –ca (*adj., Bot.*) trioecious.
triolé (*m.*) triolet.
trional (*m., Chem.*) trional.
triose (*f., Chem.*) triose.
trióxido [ks] (*m., Chem.*) trioxide.
trioximetileno [ks] (*m., Chem.*) paraformaldehyde.
tripa (*f.*) gut, intestine; tripe; (*Newspaper slang*) padding, space-fillers; (*Naut.*) jeer of mainsail; (*pl.*) entrails; (*slang*) guts.—**de-galinha**, a rosewood (*Dalbergia gracilis*); also = CARACOL (a bean) and URTIGA-DE-CIPÓ (a spurge). **comer à—fôrra**, to eat to overfullness. **falar pelas—s de Judas** to talk the hind legs off a mule. **fazer das—s coração**, to take heart; to put on a bold front; to display "guts". **viver à—fôrra**, to live on the fat of the land.
tripagem, tripalhada (*f.*) a quantity of intestines.
tripango (*m., Zool.*) trepang, sea cucumber, c.a. BICHO-DO-MAR, HOLOTÚRIA.
tripanossomíase (*f., Med.*) trypanosomiasis.—**americana**, Chagas' disease.
tripanossomo (*m., Zool.*) trypanosome.
tripartido –da (*adj.*) tripartite.
tripartir (*v.t.*) to divide into three parts.
tripé (*m.*) tripod.
tripeça (*f.*) three-legged stool.
tripeiro (*m.*) seller of tripe and other animal viscera [= BUCHEIRO, FATEIRO].
tripes (*m., Zool.*) thrips.
tripétalo –la (*adj., Bot.*) tripetalous.
tripetrepe (*adv.*) on tip-toe, quietly.
triple (*adj.; m.*) = TRIPLO.
triplicado –da (*adj.*) tripled; triplicate.
triplicar (*v.t., v.i., v.r.*) to triple.
triplicata (*f.*) third (carbon) copy.
tríplice (*adj.*) = TRIPLO.
triplicidade (*f.*) triplicity.
triplo –pla (*adj.; m.*) triple; treble; triplicate; three-ply.
tripó (*m.*) tripod.
trípode (*adj.; m.*) three-legged (stool).
trípoli (*m.*) tripoli, rottenstone, infusorial earth [= DIATOMITO, TERRA DE INFUSÓRIOS].
tripsina (*f., Biochem.*) trypsin.
triptana (*f., Chem.*) triptane.
tríptico (*m.*) triptych.
tripudiar (*v.i.*) to dance (up and down); to rejoice; to exult; to gloat (com, over); to live in debauchery; (*v.t.*) to stamp the foot (while dancing).
tripúdio (*m.*) act of dancing; exultation; gloating; debauchery.
tripulação (*f.*) ship's crew.
tripulante (*m.*) crew-member, seaman.
tripular (*v.t.*) to man (a ship); to run (a ship).
triquestroques (*m.*) pun; play on words [= TROCADILHO].
triquetraque (*m.*) tricktrack (a variety of backgammon); a repeating firework.
triquetraz (*m.*) mischievous child [= TRAQUINAS].
tríquetro –tra (*adj.*) triquetrous; (*m.*) triskelion [= TRÍSCELO].

triquíase (*f.*, *Med.*) trichiasis.
triquina (*f.*, *Zool.*) trichina.
triquinado –da, –noso –sa (*adj.*) trichinous.
triquinose (*f.*, *Med.*) trichinosis.
trirradiado –da (*adj.*) triradiate.
trirregno (*m.*) triarchy.
trirreme (*f.*) trireme (galley).
triságio (*m.*, *Eccl.*) Trisagion.
trisanual (*adj.*) triennial.
trisarquia (*f.*) triarchy.
trisavô (*m.*) great-great-grandfather.
trisavó (*f.*) great-great-grandmother.
triscar (*v.i.*) to brawl; (*v.t.*) to graze.
tríscelo (*m.*) triskelion.
trismo (*m.*, *Med.*) trismus, lockjaw.
trispermo –ma (*adj.*, *Bot.*) trispermous, three-seeded.
trissar (*v.i.*) to twitter [= GRINFAR].
trissecar (*v.t.*) to trisect.
trisse[c]ção (*f.*) trisection.
trisse[c]tor –tora (*adj.*) that trisects; (*m.*) trisector.
trissépalo –la (*adj.*, *Bot.*) trisepalous.
trisseto (*m.*, *Bot.*) a genus (*Trisetum*) of forage grasses, c.a. ROSTRÁRIA.
trissilábico –ca (*adj.*) trisyllabic.
trissílabo –ba (*adj.*, *m.*) trisyllable.
trisso (*m.*) swallow's chirp.
trissulco –ca (*adj.*) trifid.
trissulfeto, trissulfureto (*m.*, *Chem.*) trisulphide.
Tristão (*m.*) Tristam, Tristan.
triste (*adj.*) sad, mournful; unhappy, wretched; depressed, dejected, glum, blue, in the dumps; dreary, gloomy, dismal, cheerless, drab; (*m.*,*f.*) an unhappy person. **fazer um papel**—, to cut a sorry figure.
triste-pia (*m.*) the common American bobolink (*Dolichonyx oryzivorus*) which winters as far south as southern Brazil.
triste-vida (*f.*) = BEM-TE-VI.
tristeza [tê] (*f.*) sorrow, unhappiness, sadness, melancholy, the blues; Texas (tick) fever (of cattle), c.a. MAL-TRISTE, FEBRE DO TEXAS, PIROPLASMOSE; also, a virus disease which destroyed millions of citrus fruit trees in the State of Sao Paulo between 1940 and 1950.—**s não pagam dívidas**, Care killed the cat.
trístico –ca (*adj.*) tristichous; (*Bot.*) arranged in three vertical rows.
tristimania (*f.*) chronic sadness.
tristonho –nha (*adj.*) dejected, unhappy, glum, "blue".
tristura (*f.*) = TRISTEZA.
Tritão (*m.*) Triton (the sea demigod); [*not cap.*] (*Zool.*) a triton (newt of genus *Triturus*); a large marine shell of genus *Triton*.
triteísmo [e-i] (*m.*, *Theol.*) tritheism.
tritíceo –cea (*adj.*) pert. to, or like, wheat.
triticultor –tora (*m.*,*f.*) wheat grower.
tricultura (*f.*) wheat growing.
trítio (*m.*, *Chem.*) tritium.
tritongo (*m.*) triphthong.
tritopina (*f.*, *Chem.*) tritopine; laudanidine.
trituração (*f.*), **trituramento** (*m.*) trituration.
triturar (*v.t.*) to triturate, grind to powder.
triunfador –dora [i-un] (*adj.*) triumphant. (*m.*,*f.*) one who triumphs.
triunfal [i-un] (*adj.*) triumphal.
triunfante [i-un] (*adj.*) triumphant, exultant.
triunfar [i-un] (*v.i.*) to triumph (over); prevail (over); to win; to exult (over); (*v.t.*) to cause to triumph; (*v.r.*) to be triumphant; to glory in.
triunfo [i-un] (*m.*) triumph, jubilation, exultation; conquest, victory.
triunvirado, –to [i-un] (*m.*) triumvirate.
triúnviro (*m.*) triumvir.
trivalência (*f.*, *Chem.*) trivalence, –cy.
trivalente (*adj.*, *Chem.*) trivalent.
trivial (*adj.*) commonplace, trite, hackneyed; trivial, trifling, petty; (*m.*) plain, everyday, home-cooked dishes.
trivialidade (*f.*) triviality.
trívio (*m.*) crossroads; (*Zool.*) trivium.
triz (*m.*) used in the expression: **por um triz**, within an ace of. **escapar por um**—, to escape by the skin of one's teeth. (*f.*) = ICTERÍCIA (jaundice).
troada (*f.*) thunder, rumbling.
troante (*adj.*) thundering.

troar (*v.i.*) to thunder, boom, roar, rumble; (*m.*) thunder [= TROADA].
troca (*f.*) exchange, truck, barter. **em**—**de**, in exchange for.
troça (*f.*) scoffing, derision; raillery, banter; joke; revelry, spree.
trocadilhar (*v.i.*) to make puns.
trocadilhista (*m.*,*f.*) punster.
trocadilho (*m.*) pun, play on words.
trocado (*adj.*) exchanged.
trocador –dora (*adj.*) exchanging; (*m.*,*f.*) exchanger; (*f.*) change-maker (machine for dispensing change).
trocaico –ca (*adj.*; *Pros.*) trochaic.
trocano (*m.*) = TOROCANA.
trocanter [tér] (*m.*, *Anat.*, *Zool.*) trochanter.
troca-pernas (*m.*, *colloq.*) loafer [= VAGABUNDO].
trocar (*v.t.*) to exchange, barter, trade, swap (one thing for another); to change, remove for other, replace by other.—**de roupa**, to change clothes.—**dinheiro**, to change money (into smaller units).—**nomes**, to confuse names.—**o bem pelo mal**, to exchange good for evil.—**pernas**, (*colloq.*) to walk.—**prisioneiros**, to exchange prisoners. **Vou me**—, I'm going to change (my clothes).
troçar (*v.t.*) to scoff, gibe, mock.—**de**, to make fun of.
trocarte (*m.*, *Surg.*) trocar.
troca-tintas (*m.*) dauber (bad painter); botcher.
trocável (*adj.*) exchangeable; changeable.
trochar (*v.t.*) to rifle (a gun barrel).
trôcho (*m.*) a rough stick.
trocisco (*m.*, *Pharm.*) troche.
trocista (*adj.*) given to scoffing, joking, making fun of; (*m.*,*f.*) mocker; funster; wag; joker.
tróclea (*f.*, *Anat.*) trochlea.
troclear (*adj.*) trochlear.
trocleartrose (*f.*, *Anat.*) a trochoid, or pivot-joint, articulation.
trôco (*m.*) exchange; change (money).—**miúdo**, small change. **a**—**de**, in exchange for, in place of. **a**—**de quê?** What on earth for? **dar o**—, (*slang*) to pay back in the same coin; to give tit for tat.
troço [tró] (*m.*) any "thing"—esp. an old and useless one; (*slang*) a big shot.
trôço (*m.*) cudgel; stick of wood; a body of troops or of people.
trocoídeo –dea (*adj.*, *Geom.*, *Anat.*) trochoid.
troféu (*m.*) trophy; (*slang*) thingamajig.
trófico –ca (*adj.*, *Physiol.*) trophic.
trofoneurose (*f.*, *Med.*) trophoneurosis.
troglodita (*adj.*; *m.*,*f.*) troglodyte.
Tróia (*f.*) Troy.
trole (*m.*) railroad handcar [c.a. DRESINA in Paraná]; buckboard; trolley wire.
trôlha (*f.*) mortarboard; (*colloq.*) a blow or slap; (*m.*) bricklayer; hod carrier.
tromba (*f.*) elephant's trunk; snout; proboscis; (*colloq.*) mug (face).—**d'água**, water spout; cloud burst.—**de-elefante**, (*Bot.*) an agave (*A. attenuata*). **de**—, out of temper. **fazer**—, (*colloq.*) to thrust out the lips (pout).
trombeta [ê] (*f.*) trumpet, bugle, horn; the jimsonweed datura (*D. stramonium*), c.a. ESTRAMÔNIO; the flute-mouth or tobacco-pipe fish (*Fistularia tabacaria*), c.a. PEIXE-TROMBETA; muzzle for a horse; (*m.*) trumpeter, bugler.—**azul**, common morning-glory, c.a. TROMBE-TINHA.—**bastarda**, or—**inglêsa**, coaching horn.—**do-juízo-final** = TROBETÃO-AZUL.—**falante**, or—**marinha**, speaking trumpet, megaphone.
trombetão-azul (*m.*, *Bot.*) angel's-trumpet or floripondio (*Datura arborea*), c.a. CÁLICE-DE-VÊNUS.
trombetão-roxo (*m.*, *Bot.*) the Hindu datura (*Datura metel*), c.a. TROMBETA-DO-JUÍZO-FINAL.
trombetear (*v.t.*,*v.i.*) to trumpet; (*v.i.*) to blare as a trumpet.
trombeteiro (*m.*) trumpet player; a kind of mosquito; a trumpeter-bird, c.a. JACAMIM.
trombetinha (*f.*) = TROMBETA-AZUL.
trombo (*m.*, *Med.*) thrombus.
trombone (*m.*) trombone; trombonist; also = AGAMI.—**de pistões**, valve trombone.—**de vara**, slide trombone.
trombose (*f.*, *Med.*) thrombosis.
trombudo –da (*adj.*) having a trunk or snout; (*colloq.*) sullen, scowling, grouchy.
trompa (*f.*) horn (musical instrument); muzzle for a horse.—**de caça**, hunting horn.—**de Eustáquio**, (*Anat.*) Eustachian tube.—**de Falópio** or—**uterina**, (*Anat.*)

Fallopian tube.—**de orquestra** or—**de pistões,** French horn.

tromp[e]ar (*v.t.*) to bump into.

trompázio (*m.*) bump, collision; blow.

tromtrom (*m., Zool.*) the Brazilian antpitta (antbird) (*Grallaria berlepschi*), c.a. TOROM-TOROM.

trona (*f., Min.*) trona, urao.

tronante (*adj.*) thundering.

tronar (*v.i.*) to thunder [= TROVEJAR].

troncho –cha (*adj.*) mutilated; twisted; (*m.*) stump, stub.

tronchuda-maior (*f.*) kale (*Brassica oleracea acephala*), c.a. HÔRTO-DA-BEIRA.

tronco (*m.*) tree trunk; body trunk, torso; stocks (for punishment); family tree; (*Geom.*) frustum.

troncudo –da (*adj.*) large, bulky; powerful, muscular.

troneira (*f., Fort.*) embrasure for a gun.

trono (*m.*) throne (lit. & fig.)

tronqueira (*f.*) gate post made of a small log; "a collection of heavy timbers which by chance have become vertically embedded in the bottom of the river, constituting great obstacles to navigation." [*GBAT*]

troostita (*f., Min., Metal.*) troostite.

tropa (*f.*) troop, throng; troops, soldiers, army.

tropacocaína (*f., Chem., Pharm.*) tropacocaine.

tropear (*v.i.*) to work as a TROPEIRO.

tropeção (*m.*) stumble, trip.

tropeçar (*v.i.*) to stumble (**em,** on, upon, against); to trip (**em,** over); to err, blunder.

tropêço (*m.*) hitch, hindrance, stumbling block.

trôpego –ga (*adj.*) halt, disabled, hobbling, shaky.

tropeiro (*m.*) a driver of pack animals; drover (dealer in cattle); (*Zool.*) a bird—the gray screaming pika (*Lipaugus cineraceus*), c.a. SEBASTIÃO, BASTIÃO, SABIÁ-DO-MATO-GROSSO, SABIÁ-TROPEIRO, VIRAÇU, POAIEIRO.

tropel [péis] (*m.*) crowd, throng; uproar, tumult, confusion; noisy agitation (of a throng); tramping of feet; clatter of hoofs. **em—,** pell-mell.

tropelia (*f.*) confusion, tumult; lark, prank; damage.

tropeoláceo –cea (*adj., Bot.*) tropaeolaceous; (*f.pl.*) the nasturtium family (*Tropaeolaceae*).

tropical (*adj.*) tropical.

tropicar (*v.i.*) to stumble repeatedly.

trópico –ca (*adj.*) tropic; tropical; (*m., Geog.*) tropic; (*pl.*) the tropics; (*Zool.*) a tropic bird (*Phaëthon sp.*).

tropidina (*f., Chem.*) tropidine.

tropina (*f., Chem.*) tropine.

tropismo (*m., Biol.*) tropism.

tropo (*m., Rhet.*) trope, figure of speech.

tropologia (*f.*) tropology.

tropopausa (*f., Meteorol.*) tropopause.

troposfera (*f., Meteorol.*) troposphere.

troquel [-quéis] (*m.*) a die for stamping coins or medals.

troqueu (*m., Pros.*) trochee.

troquilídeo (*m.*) trochilus, hummingbird.

tróquilo (*m., Arch.*) cavetto, scotia.

trotador –dora (*adj.*) trotting; (*m.*) trotter.

trotão –tona (*adj.*) trotting; (*m.*) trotting horse.

trotar (*v.i.*) to trot; to ride (a horse) at a trot.

trote (*m.*) trot; (*colloq.*) hazing (of new students).—**largo,** a lope. **dar um—em alguém,** to banter, rag, rib (someone); to haze (a new student); to "kid" someone over the telephone by disguising one's voice.

trotear (*v.*) = TROTAR.

troteiro (*adj.; m.*) = TROTADOR.

trotil, trotol (*m.*) = TRINITROTOLUENO.

troux-+verb endings = forms of TRAZER [79].

trouxa (*adj.*) foolish, credulous, fatuous; (*f.*) a pack or bundle of clothes; a frump; (*m.,f.*) booby; sap, sucker (dupe). **bancar o—,** to play the fool; to be a "sucker". **sempre com a—nas costas,** always on the move, esp. moving from one house to another.

trouxe-mouxe, used in the expression: **a—,** in disorder, pell-mell, helter-skelter.

trova (*f.*) popular song or tune.

trovador (*m.*) troubadour; bard.

trovão (*m.*) a clap of thunder. **Muito—é sinal de pouca chuva,** A barking dog seldom bites.

trovar (*v.i.*) to compose or sing folk tunes; (*v.t.*) to express in song.

trovejar (*v.i.*) to thunder and lightning; (*v.t.*) to utter threateningly, fulminate; (*m.*) thunder.

troviscado –da (*adj.*) half-drunk, tipsy.

troviscar (*v.i.*) to thunder lightly; (*v.i.,v.r., colloq.*) to get a little drunk.

trovisco (*m., colloq.*) a beating; (*Bot.*) the spurgeflax daphne (*D. gnidium*), the fruit of which is called GRÃO-GNÍDIO.

trovoada (*f.*) thunderstorm; (*colloq.*) shindy, free-for-all [= RÔLO]; (*Zool.*) the ferruginous antcatcher (bird) (*Myrmoderus ferrugineus*).

trovoar (*v.i.*) to thunder [= TROVEJAR].

trovoso –sa (*adj.*) thundering; thunderous.

truanaz (*m.*) = TRUÃO.

truanêsco –ca (*adj.*) buffoon.

truania, truanice (*f.*) buffoonery, or an instance of it.

truão (*m.*) buffoon; clown.

trucar (*v.i.*) to bet (in a card game).—**de falso,** to bluff (as in poker or otherwise).

trucidar (*v.t.*) to murder ruthlessly; to wipe out; to decapitate.

truculência (*f.*) truculence, fierceness, savageness; cruelty.

truculento –ta (*adj.*) truculent, fierce, savage; cruel.

trufa (*f.*) truffle [= TÚBERA].

trufeiro (*m.*) truffler.

trugimão (*m.*) = TURGIMÃO.

truirapeva [u-i] (*f.*) a fierce-looking but harmless small lizard (*Heplocercus spinosus*) of the iguna family.

truísmo (*m.*) truism.

trumaí (*m.,f.*) an Indian of the Trumaí, an isolated linguistic family of the upper Xingu River in Mato Grosso; (*adj.*) pert. to or designating this tribe.

truncado –da (*adj.*) truncate; truncated; lopped off; maimed. **palavras—s,** garbled words.

truncar (*v.t.*) to truncate, cut off, lop; to garble (words), mutilate (a text).

trunfa (*f.*) headdress resembling a turban; mop of hair.

trunfar (*v.i.*) to deliver a blow; to be important.

trunfo (*m.*) trump card; (*colloq.*) bigwig. **ter todos os—s na mão,** to hold all the trump cards (lit. & fig.).

truque (*m.*) a kind of card game; a type of long billiard table; various shots at billiards; (*colloq.*) trick, wile; gimmick; a fake; truck of a railroad car; an open railroad freight car. [From British truck; an American truck (British lorry) is CAMINHÃO.]—**com baralho,** card trick. —**de mágico,** sleight-of-hand trick. **conhecer todos os —s,** to know all the tricks.

truste (*m., Com.*) trust.

truta (*f.*) trout.

truxu [xú] (*m.*) = FRUXU.

truz (*m.*) knock, rap, blow. **de—,** excellent, first-rate; very desirable.

tsé-tsé (*f.*) tsetse fly [= CECÉ].

T.S.F. = TELEFONIA SEM FIOS, TELEGRAFIA SEM FIOS (wireless telephony or telegraphy).

t.te = TENENTE (lieutenant).

t.te-c.el = TENENTE-CORONEL (lieutenant-colonel).

tu [*pl.* vós] (*pron.*) thou; you (familiar form). [Corresponds to Fr. *tu*, German *du*.] Cf. VOCÊ.

tua, fem. form of TEU.

tuba (*f.*) tuba (wind instrument); (*m.*) tuba player.

tubagem (*f.*) tubing; pipes.

tubarão (*m.*) any large shark [= CAÇÃO]; (*colloq.*) profiteer. —**sombreiro,** a mackerel-shark (*Isurus oxyrhynchus*).

tubeira (*f.*) nozzle; end of a tube.

tubel [-béis] (*m., Metal.*) scale.

túbera (*f.*) truffle [= TRUFA].

tuberculado –da, tubercular (*adj.*) tubercular (but only in the sense of having tubercles).

tuberculina (*f., Med.*) tuberculin.

tubérculo (*m.*) tubercle (in any sense).

tuberculose (*f., Med.*) tuberculosis.

tuberculoso –sa (*adj.*) tubercular, tuberculous; (*m.,f.*) a tuberculous person.

tuberosa (*f., Bot.*) tuberose (*Polianthes tuberosa*), c.a. ANGÉLICA.

tuberosidade (*f.*) tuberosity.

tuberoso –sa (*adj.*) tuberous.

tubiba (*f.*) = TAPIQUÁ.

tubífero –ra (*adj.*) tubiferous.

tubifloro –ra (*adj., Bot.*) having a tubular corolla.

tubiforme (*adj.*) tubulate.

tubixaba (*m.*) tribal chief [= MORUBIXABA].

tubo (*m.*) tube; pipe.—**Bourdon,** Bourdon tube.—**de admissão** intake tube or pipe.—**de arejo** = TUBO DE VENTILAÇÃO.—**de caldeira,** boiler flue.—**de ensaio,** test tube.—**de lixo,** garbage chute.—**de rádio** = VÁLVULA ELECTRÓNICA.—**electrônico** = VÁLVULA ELECTRÔNICA.—

fotoelétrico, photoelectric cell.—inconsútil, seamless tube or pipe; c.a. TUBO SEM COSTURA.—lança-torpedos, torpedo tube.—pitot, (*Hydraulics*) Pitot's tube.—s seríferos, silk glands (of the silk worm). corta——s, pipe cutter.

tubulação (f.) tubulation; pipes or piping; tubes or tubing.

tubulado –da (*adj.*) tubulate.

tubuladura (f.) tubulure.

tubular (*adj.*) tubular.

tubulifloro –ra (*adj.*, *Bot.*) tubuliflorous.

túbulo (*m.*) tubule.

tubuloso –sa (*adj.*) tubulous.

tubulura (f., *Chem.*) tubulure.

tubuna (f.) saddle gall [= CUERA]; a stingless bee (*Trigona bipunctata*), c.a. MANDAGUARI.

tucajé (*m.*) = CARVALHO-DO-BRASIL.

tucanaçu [çú] (*m.*, *Zool.*) the large toco toucan (*Rhamphastos toco*) widely distributed in Brazil; c.a. TUCANO-GRANDE.

tucano (*m.*, *Zool.*) any toucan (*Rhamphastos*).—de-bico-prêto, the ariel toucan (*R. ariel*).—de-bico-verde, the red-breasted toucan (*R. discolorus*).—de-peito-amarelo, the sulfur and white-breasted toucan (*R. vitellinus*).—de-peito-branco, the red-billed toucan (*R. monilis*) c.a. TUCANO-CACHORRINHO, PIA-POCO, QUIRINA.—grande = TUCANAÇU.

tucanuí (*m.*) = ARAÇARI-DO-MINHOCA.

tuchos (*m.pl.*, *Autom.*) tappets.

tuco-tuco (*m.*) a small burrowing, gopherlike rodent (*Ctenomys brasiliensis*, family *Octodontidae*), c.a. CURURU.

tucum (*m.*) a Brazilian spiny club palm (*Bactris setosa*) whose fiber is used in hammock-weaving, c.a. TUCUN-ZEIRO. —bravo, —do-amazonas = CUMARI. —do-brejo = COQUINHO-BABÁ.

tucumã (f.) the tucuma palm (*Astrocaryum tucuma*); any spiny club palm (*Bactris setosa*); also species of *Acrocomia*.—piranga = CUMARI.

tucuna (*m.,f.*) an Indian of the Tucuna, a jungle tribe of enigmatic linguistic stock on the northern side of the Solimões-Amazon River; (*adj.*) pert. to or designating the Tucuna.

tucunapéua, variant of TACONHAPÉ.

tucunzeiro (*m.*) = TUCUM.

tucupi [í] (*m.*) a condiment made of manioc juice and pepper.

tucuri [í] (*m.*) = TACURU.

tudesco –ca [ê] (*adj.; m.,f.*) German [= ALEMÃO].

tudo (*pron.*) all, everything. Cf. TODO.—junto, all together.—mais, everything else.—menos, all but, everything but (except).—nada, almost nothing, a tiny bit.—quanto, all that; everything that.—que há de bom, everything good there is. antes de—, first of all; before all else. ao fim de—, after all. estar por—, to agree with everyone and everything. Nem—que luz e ouro, All is not gold that glitters. ou—ou nada, all or nothing.

tufão (*m.*) typhoon; gale.

tufar (*v.t.*) to puff up (out); (*v.i.*) to swell (out); to flare out; (*v.r.*) to become puffed up.

tufo (*m.*) tuft, bunch, cluster; a bulge; (*Geol.*) tufa; tuff.

tufoso –sa (*adj.*) tufted; puffed out.

tugir [25] (*v.i.*) to speak in a whisper; (*v.t.*) to utter any slight sound, as a whisper. sem—nem nugir, without a peep; without saying a word.

tugue (*m.*) thug.

tugúrio (*m.*) cabin, hut, shack; country house; hideout.

tuí, tuim (*m.*) = PERIQUITO.

tuia (f., *Bot.*) arborvitae (*Thuja*); also = CIPÓ-QUINA.

tuição [u-i] (f., *Law*) defense.

tuidara [u-i] (f.) an owl [= CORUJA].

tuim [u-í] (*m.*) = PERIQUITO.

tuiuiú (*m.*) the wood ibis (*Mycteria americana*, sym. *Tantolus locutor*), c.a. TUIUPARA, TUIÚ-QUARTELEIRO, CABEÇA-DE-PEDRA.

tujucada (f.) = TIJUCADA.

tujucal (*m.*) = TIJUCAL.

tujumirim (*m.*) = TORCE-CABELO.

tule (*m.*) tulle, fine silk net.

tulha (f.) granary; drying ground for fruit; bunker.

túlio (*m.*, *Chem.*) thulium.

tulipa (f., *Bot.*) any tulip (*Tulipa*).—da-áfrica, bell flambeau tree (*Spathodea campanulata*), c.a. ESPATÓDEA.

tumba (f.) tomb; tombstone; bier; (*m.,f.*) ill-fated person, esp. at gambling.

tumbice (f., *colloq.*) bad luck, esp. at gambling.

tumefacção (f.) tumefaction.

tumefaciente (*adj.*) tumefacient.

tumefazer, tumeficar (*v.t.*) to tumefy.

tumescer (*v.*) & derivs. = INTUMESCER & DERIVS.

tumidez [ê] (f.) tumidity.

túmido –da (*adj.*) tumid, swollen; fig., puffed up, pompous.

tumor (*m.*, *Med.*) tumor.—benigno, non-malignant tumor. —branco, tuberculosis.—maligno, malignant tumor.

tumoroso –sa (*adj.*) tumorous.

túmulo (*m.*) tomb, sepulcher, burial vault.

tumulto (*m.*) tumult, uproar; hullabaloo, hubbub, bedlam; ruckus, shindy, row, disturbance; agitation of mind.

tumultuar (*v.t.*) to stir up a tumult; (*v.i.*) to become tumultous.

tumultuário –ria, tumultuoso –sa (*adj.*) tumultuous.

tuna (f.) idleness; a roving band of student musicians; a cactus c.a. NOPAL. [Tuna fish is ATUM.]

tunal (*m.*) = NOPAL.

tunante (*adj.*) idle; drifting; (*m.,f.*) idler; drifter.

tunar (*v.i.*) to idle; to drift.

tunda (f.) a thrashing; fig., harsh criticism.

tundá (*m.*) a full skirt with several underskirts; (*slang*) the buttocks; a lump or swelling, esp. on the back.

tundra (f.) tundra.

túnel [-neis] (*m.*) tunnel.—aerodinâmico or—de vento wind tunnel.

tunga (f., *Zool.*) the chigoe (*Tunga*, syn. *Sarcopsylla*, *penetrans*), c.a. NÍGUA, BICHO-DE-PÉ, PULGA-PENE-TRANTE.

tungar (*v.i.*) to wrangle; (*v.t.*) to beat (someone); to trick, cheat; (*colloq.*) to dunk (a piece of bread).

tungstato (*m.*, *Chem.*) tungstate.

tungstênio (*m.*, *Chem.*) tungsten.

túngstico –ca (*adj.*) tungstic.

tungstita (f., *Min.*) tungstite.

tungue (*m.*, *Bot.*) tung oil tree (*Aleurites fordi*).

túnica (f.) tunic; (*Bot.*, *Zool.*, *Anat.*) a tunic or tunica.

tunicado (*m.*, *Zool.*) one of the Tunicata.

tunicela (f.) a small or short tunic; (*R.C.Ch.*) tunicle. Var. TUNIQUETE.

tuparapo, tuparobá (*m.*) = CAFERANA.

tupé (*m.*) "a term used by small proprietors to designate mats made of PURUMÃ splints for drying cacao." [GBAT]

tupi [í] (*m.,f.*) any Tupian Indian, esp. a member of the tribes forming the northern division of the Tupian stock dwelling along the Amazon, Tapajós and Xingu Rivers; (*m.*) the name of a Caingang tribe; the language of the Tupi, called also NHEENGATU or NENHENGATU, which became and still serves as a lingua franca along the Amazon; (*adj.*) Tupian.

tupia (f.) shaper (woodworking machine); jack (weight lifter).

tupieiro (*m.*) operator of a wood-shaping machine.

tupinambá (*m.,f.*) an Indian of any of a large group of closely related, fierce, cannabalistic tribes, now extinct, who in the 16th century were masters of almost the whole of the Brazilian shore from north to south; (*adj.*) pert. to or designating the Tupinambá.

tupinambo, –bor (*m.*) the Jerusalem artichoke sunflower (*Helianthus tuberosus*), c.a. GIRASSOL-BATATEIRO. Var. TUPINAMBA.

tupiniquim (*m.,f.*) an Indian of an extinct tribe of the Tupinambá which occupied a narrow strip on the southernmost coast of what is now Bahia, in the region of Porto Seguro. The name is applied as a nickname to present-day inhabitants of that region; (*adj.*) pert. to or designating the Tupiniquim.

tupitixa (f.) = GUAXIMA.

tupixaba (f., *Bot.*) sweet broomwort (*Scoparia dulcis*).

tupurapo (*m.*) = CAFERANA.

turari [í] (*m.*, *Bot.*) a supplejack (*Serjania erecta*).

turba (f.) mob, rabble, crowd, people.

turbação (f.) turbamento (*m.*) disorder, commotion, disturbance.

turbador –dora (*adj.*) disturbing; (*m.,f.*) disturber.

turbamulta (f.) turbulent multitude; mob.

turbante (*m.*) turban.

turbar (*v.t.*) to disturb, trouble; to darken, dim; (*v.r.*) to be troubled. Cf. TURVAR.

turbativo –va (*adj.*) disturbing.

turbelário (*m.*, *Zool.*) planarian (flatworm).

turbidímetro (*m.*) turbidimeter.

túrbido –da (*adj.*) turbid.

turbilhão (*m.*) whirlwind, whirlpool, vortex, maelstrom; eddy, swirl.

turbilhonar (*v.i.*) to whirl, spin.

turbina (*f.*) turbine.—**de água,** water turbine.—**de gás,** gas turbine.—**de vapor,** steam turbine.—**eólica,** modern windmill (with vane).—**hydráulica,** hydraulic turbine.

turbinado –da (*adj.,* Anat., Zool., Bot.) turbinate.

turbinagem (*f.*) any spinning or whirling process, as of a centrifuge. (*Sugar mfg.*) turbinage.

turbiniforme (*adj.*) turbiniform.

turbinoso –na (*adj.*) spinning, revolving, whirling.

turbo-acionado –da (*adj.*) turbo-driven.

turbo-alternador (*m.*) turbodynamo.

turbo-bomba (*f.*) turbopump.

turbo-compressor (*m.*) turbocompressor; supercharger.

turbo-dínamo (*m.*) turbodynamo.

turbo-excitador (*m.*) turboexciter.

turbo-gerador (*m.*) turbogenerator.

turbo-oxigenador [ks] (*m.,* Aeron.) exhaust-driven supercharger.

turbulência (*f.*) turbulence; uproar, turmoil; boisterousness.

turbulento –ta (*adj.*) turbulent, obstreperous; boisterous, rowdy; (*m.,f.*) such a person.

turco –ca (*adj.*) Turkish; (*m.,f.*) a Turk; (*m.*) the Turkish language. In Brazil, the term TURCO is colloquially applied to any native of the Middle East (Syrians, etc.), esp. those engaged in the dry goods business; (*Naut.*) bitt; davit.—**da prestação** = MASCATE.

turcomano (*m.*) Turkoman.

turdídeo –dea (*adj.,* Zool.) turdoid, thrushlike.

turfa (*f.*) peat.

turfe (*m.*) the turf (race track); also, horse racing as a sport.

turfeira (*f.*) peat bog.

turfista (*m.,f.*) a votary of the turf, or horse racing.

turgência (*f.*) = TURGIDEZ.

turgente (*adj.*) = TÚRGIDO.

turgescência (*f.*) turgescence.

turgescente (*adj.*) turgescent.

turgescer (*v.i.,v.r.*) to become turgid; (*v.t.*) to make turgid.

turgidez [ê] (*f.*) turgescence.

túrgido –da (*adj.*) turgid.

turgimão (*m.*) dragoman. Var. TRUGIMÃO.

turião (*m.,* Bot.) turion.

turibular (*v.t.*) to thurify, cense; fig., to flatter.

turíbulo (*m.*) thurible, censer.

turiferário (*m.,* Eccl.) thurifer.

Turim (*m.*) Turin.

turiri [rirí] (*f.*) = SURURINA.

turismo (*m.*) touring, tourism.

turista (*m.,f.*) tourist.

turivara (*m.,f.*) an Indian of the Turivara, a tribe which lived on the Capim River in Pará; (*adj.*) pert. to or designating this tribe.

turma (*f.*) band, group; division (of a school class); a work crew, squad, gang or shift.—**de revezamento,** relay team.

turmalina (*f.,* Min.) tourmaline.—**comum,** or—**negra,** common black tourmaline; schorl.—**de magnésio,** or—**parda,** brown tourmaline.

turmalinita (*f.,* Petrog.) tourmalite.

turmeiro (*m.*) member of a road gang; section hand.

túrnepo (*m.,* Bot.) —**amarelo,** bird rape (*Brassica campestris*).—**branco,** common white turnip (*Brassica rapa*).

turnerita (*f.,* Min.) turnerite.

túrnia (*f.*) a rushlike herb (*Thurnia sphaerocephala*).

turnicídeos (*m.pl.*) the family (*Turnicidae*) containing the button quails or hemipodes.

turno (*m.*) shift (at work); bout, round, inning; school period (hour). **por—,** by turns. **por seu—,** in his (her) turn.

turquesa [ê] (*f.,* Min.) turquoise.—**oriental,** blue Persian turquoise.

turquesado (*adj.*) turquoise-colored.

turqui [í] (*adj.*) Turkish-blue.

Turquia (*f.*) Turkey.

turra (*f.*) a butt (with the head); controversy. **andar às—s com,** to be at sixes and sevens with (someone).

turrão –rona (*adj.*) hard-headed.

turrar (*v.i.*) to butt (with the head); to wrangle.

turriculado –da (*adj.;* Zool.) of shells, turreted.

turriforme (*adj.*) tower-shaped.

turrista (*m.,f.*) person given to wrangling.

turucué (*m.*) = CURUTIÉ.

turumbamba (*m.,* slang) brawl, fracas, row.

turuna (*adj.*) strong, fearless, powerful.

turundumdum (*m.*) shindy, free-for-all [= RÔLO].

tururi [rí] = CASTANHA-DO-PARÁ.

tururié (*m.*) = CURUTIÉ.

tururim (*m.,* Zool.) a small tinamou (*Crypturellus soui albigularis*).

turvação (*f.*), **turvamento** (*m.*) a clouding (as of the weather, of wine, of the eyes, etc.).

turvar (*v.t.*) to make turbid; to cloud; to muddle; (*v.i.,v.r.*) to become turbid; to become cross or grouchy. Cf. TURBAR, TORVAR.

turvo –va (*adj.*) turbid; unsettled, confused; cloudy, overcast. **pescar em águas turvas,** to fish in troubled waters.

tussilagem (*f.,* Bot.) a coltsfoot (*Tussilago integerrima*), c.a. UNHA-DE-CAVALO.

tussor [ó] (*m.*) tussah silk.

tuta-e-meia (*f.,* colloq.) trifle.

tutano (*m.*) marrow, medulla, pith; essential part.

tutear (*v.t.*) to thee-and-thou, address familiarly as **tu;** (*v.r.*) so to address one another; [= ATUAR]. [Fr. tutoyer].

tutela (*f.*) tutelage, protection, guardianship.

tutelado –da (*adj.*) protected (as by a guardian); (*m.,f.*) ward (of a guardian).

tutelar (*adj.*) tutelary; (*v.t.*) to tutor [= TUTORAR].

tutinegra (*f.*) = TOUTINEGRA.

tutor (*m.*) legal guardian (but not tutor in the sense of private teacher, which is PROFESSOR PARTICULAR). [Fem. tutora, tutriz]. Also, stake for a plant or sapling.

tutorar (*v.*) = TUTELAR.

tutoria (*f.*) tutorship (but only in the sense of guardianship); tutelage.

tutriz, fem. of TUTOR.

tutu [tutú] (*m.*) a dish made of beans, pork and manioc meal; a hobgoblin [= PAPÃO]; a big shot [= MANDA-CHUVA]; a bird called JURUVA.

tutumumbuca (*m.*) = MANDACHUVA.

tutunqué (*m.*) = MANDACHUVA.

tuvira (*f.*) a So. Amer. fresh-water eel (*Giton,* syn. *Carapus, fasciatus*) of the family Gymnotidae.

tuxaua (*m.*) tribal chief; political boss.

tuzina (*f.*) a beating, trouncing.

tzar (*m.*) = CZAR.

tzigano –na (*adj.; m.,f.*) gypsy (musician).

U

U, u (*m.*) the 20th letter of the Port. alphabet.

u'a, contraction of **uma.** [Used generally when the next word begins with **ma;** e.g., **u'a mão** instead of **uma mão; u'a mata** instead of **uma mata.**]

uacanga (*f.,* Bot.) a shadow palm (*Geonoma princeps*).

uacari [í] (*m.*) any of several short-tailed ouakari monkeys (genus Cacajao), esp. the following:—**branco,** a white ouakari (*C. calvus*).—**de-cabeça-preta,** a black-headed ouakari (*C. malanocephalus*), c.a. MACACO-COTÓ, MACACO-MAL-ACABADO.—**prêto,** a black ouakari (*C. roosevelti*).—**vermelho,** a redbearded ouakari (*C. rubicundus*), c.a. MACACO-INGLÊS.

uacima-da-praia (*f.*) = MALVA-RELÓGIO-GRANDE.

uaicima (*f.,* Bot.) the cadillo (*Urena lobata*), c.a. GUAXIMA also = MALVA-CAJUÇARA.

uaiapuçá (*m.*) = MACACO-CABELUDO.

uaimiri[m] (*m.*) dart used in a blowgun.
uapé, uapê (*m.*) = VITÓRIA-RÉGIA.
uapuçá (*m.*) a titi monkey (*Callicebus*); also = MACACO-CABELUDO.
uaraná (*m.*) = GUARANÁ.
uarema (*f.*) = ANGELIM-CÔCO.
uarubé (*m.*) manioc juice used in making TUCUPI.
uaturá (*m.*) "a basket carried on one's back and fastened around the head with a tumpline, used to carry farm products." [*GBAT*]
uau [uaú] (*m.*) = JURUVA.
uauaçu [çú] (*m.*) = BABAÇU.
uaurá, variant of VAURÁ.
ubá (*f.*) a primitive dugout canoe; also = CANAFRECHA.
ubacaba (*m., Bot.*) a guava (*Psidium radicans*).
ubarana (*f.*) the ten-pounder (*Elops saurus*)—a marine fish—c.a. UBARANA-AÇU.—-mirim (or—-branca, or—-de-bôca-pequena), a ten-pounder (*Elops lacerta*), c.a. JURUMA.—-rato, (or—-focinho-de-rato) the bonefish (*Albula vulpes*), c.a. PEIXE-RATO.
ubatã (*m.*) = ADERNO.
uberdade (*f.*) fruitfulness, fertility; plenty.
úbere (*adj.*) fertile; fruitful; copious; plenteous; abundant; [= UBERTOSO]; (*m.*) udder; teat. Var. UBRE.
ubérrimo -ma (*absol. superl. of* ÚBERE) most fertile.
ubertoso -sa (*adj.*) = ÚBERE.
ubiqüidade, ubiquação (*f.*) ubiquity, ubiquitousness.
ubíquo -qua (*adj.*) ubiquitous.
ubiraçoca (*f.*) teredo, shipworm [= GUSANO].
ubre (*m.*) teat; udder [= ÚBERE].
ubuçu [çú] (*m.*) = BUÇU.
ucasse (*m.*) ukase, lit. & fig.
ucha (*f.*) grain hutch.
uchão (*m.*) pantryman; butler; [= DESPENSEIRO].
ucharia (*f.*) royal pantry; storehouse.
ucraniano -na (*adj.; m.,f.*) Ukranian.
ucuquirana (*f.*) a large or medium-sized sapotaceous Amazon tree (*Ecclinusia balata*), whose latex yields balata; c.a. COQUIRANA.
ucuuba [u-u] (*f.*) a nutmeg (*Myristica sebifera*), c.a. CANANGA, UCUUBEIRA.—-branca, "a common tree (*Virola surinamensis*) growing on both low, inundated land and on the uplands, which annually bears seeds yielding from 25 to 35 liters of oil used for candles and soap." [*GBAT*]—-preta or—-vermelha, a similar tree (*Virola sebifera*).
udenista (*m.,f.*) a member of UDN.
UDN = UNIÃO DEMOCRÁTICA NACIONAL (National Democratic Union).
udômetro (*m.*) = PLUVIÔMETRO.
udu (*m.*) = JURUVA.
u.e. = USO EXTERNO (external use).
ué, uê (*interj.*) Well! I'll be darned!
ufa (*interj.*) Whew!
ufanar (*v.t.*) to make proud; (*v.r.*) to become proud, boastful (de, of); to pride oneself on.
ufania (*f.*) pride, conceit, vanity; self-complacency, boastfulness.
ufano -na (*adj.*) proud, boastful, vainglorious; self-complacent; self-satisfied.
ufanoso -sa (*adj.*) proud, conceited; boastful.
u.i. = USO INTERNO (internal use).
ui (*interj.*) Oh! (expressing pain, surprise, disapprobation).
uiqué (*m.*) sapota (the fruit).
uiraçu [çú] (*m.*) = HARPIA.
uirapiana (*f., Zool.*) the great jacamar (*Jacamerops aurea*).
uirari [rí] (*m.*) = CURARE.
uiraponga (*f.*) = ARAPONGA.
uirapuru [rú] (*m.*) any wren of genus Leucolepis, esp. the organ bird (*L. a. arada*); the gray-flanked musician wren (*L. arada griseolateralis*); Todd's musician wren (*L. arada interposita*); the musician wren (*L. arada modulatrix*). Variant names are IRAPURU, ARAPURU, MÚSICO, MANDINGUEIRO. [This last derives from MANDINGA (magic, witchcraft) and has reference to the magical powers which one can achieve by killing one of these little birds while it is singing, then preserving its body by drying or stuffing. It then becomes a sort of potent "rabbit's foot"].—-de-cabeça-amarela, yellow-headed manakin (*Pipra chrysocephala*).—-de-costa-azul = TANGARÁ.
uirari [rí] (*m.*) = CURARE.
uiratauá (*m.*) = CORRUPIÃO.
uiratatá (*f.*) = ANAMBÉ.

uiraxué (*m.*) = SABIÁ-LARANJEIRA.
uiriri [rirí] (*m.*) = ANDORINHA-DO-CAMPO, ANDORINHÃO.
uiruuetê [u-u] (*m.*) = GAVIÃO-REAL.
uiruucutim [u-u] (*m.*) = GAVIÃO-PEGA-MACACO.
uísque (*m.*) whisky.
uíste (*m., Cards*) whist.
uivada (*f.*) howl.
uivador -dora (*adj.*) howling; (*m.,f.*) howler.
uivar (*v.i.*) to howl; to wail; lament.
uivo (*m.*) howl(ing), ululation.
ulano (*m.*) uhlan.
úlcera (*f.*) ulcer.—de Baurú, tropical boil.
ulceração (*f.*) ulceration.
ulcerar (*v.t.,v.i.,v.r.*) to ulcerate.
ulcerativo -va (*adj.*) ulcerative.
ulceroso -sa (*adj.*) ulcerous.
ulexina [ks] (*f., Chem.*) ulexine, cytisine.
ulexita [ks] (*f., Min.*) ulexite, boronatrocalcite.
uliginoso -sa (*adj.*) muddy; oozy; swampy.
ulissiponense (*adj.; m.,f.*) = LISBOETA.
ulna (*f., Anat.*) ulna [= CÚBITO]; an ell.
ulmáceo -cea (*adj., Bot.*) ulmaceous; (*f.pl.*) the elm family (*Ulmaceae*).
ulmária (*f.*) queen-of-the-meadow or European meadowsweet (*Filipendula ulmaria*), c.a. RAINHA-DOS-PRADOS, ERVA-ULMEIRA, BARBA-DE-BODE.
ulmeira (*f.*) = ULMÁRIA.
ulmeiro (*m.*) = OLMO.
úlmico -ca (*adj.*) humic [acid].
ulmina (*f., Chem.*) ulmin.
ulmo (*m.*) = OLMO.
ulótrico -ca (*adj.*) ulotrichous (having woolly or kinky hair); (*m., Bot.*) a genus (*Ulothrix*) of green algae; (*m.pl., Anthropol.*) the Ulotrichi.
ulterior (*adj.*) ulterior, beyond; further, later.
ulteriormente (*adv.*) afterward(s).
ultimação (*f.*) final stage of completion; conclusion, finishing.
ultimado -da (*adj.*) ended, concluded, finished; closed [piece of business].
ultimamente (*adv.*) lately, of late, recently, not long ago.
ultimar (*v.t.*) to bring to a conclusion, finish; (*v.r.*) to come to an end.
últimas (*f.pl.*) see under ÚLTIMO.
ultimato (*m.*) the ultimate; an ultimatum.
último -ma (*adj.*) last; latest; hindmost; final, ultimate; utmost, extreme; (*m.,f.*) the last one; the lowest (worst) one; (*f.pl.*) extreme degree. **às últimas**, to the extreme. **dizer as últimas (a alguém)**, to address supreme insults (to someone). **em—lugar**, in last place. **na—análise**, in the final analysis. **nas últimas**, in the last or extreme stages (of poverty or disease); almost done for, on one's last legs. **por—**, finally, at last.
ultrabasita (*f., Min.*) ultrabasite.
ultracentrifugador (*m., Physical Chem.*) ultracentrifuge.
ultracurto -ta (*adj.*) ultrashort [waves].
ultrafiltração (*f., Physical Chem.*) ultrafiltration.
ultrafreqüência (*f., Radio*) ultra-high frequency, U.H.F.
ultrajador -dora (*adj.*) = ULTRAJANTE; (*m.,f.*) insulter.
ultrajante (*adj.*) outrageous; insulting.
ultrajar (*v.t.*) to outrage, insult, affront.
ultraje (*m.*) outrage, affront.
ultrajoso -sa (*adj.*) outrageous, insulting.
ultramar (*m.*) distant lands; overseas possessions; ultra marine (blue pigment).
ultramarino -na (*adj.*) ultramarine, overseas.
ultramicrômetro (*m.*) ultramicrometer.
ultramicroscópio (*m.*) ultramicroscope.
ultromicroscópico -ca (*adj.*) ultromicroscopic.
ultramontanismo (*m.*) ultramontanism.
ultramontano -na (*adj.; m.,f.*) ultramontane.
ultrapassar (*v.t.*) to go beyond, exceed the limits of, overstep, overreach; to surpass; to overtake, pass.—de dez por cento, to exceed by ten per cent.
ultra-som (*m.*) supersonic vibrations and waves.
ultrasônico -ca (*adj.*) supersonic.
ultravioleta (*adj.*) ultraviolet.
ultravírus (*m., Bacteriol.*) ultravirus.
ululação (*f.*) ululation, howling; wailing.
ululador -dora (*adj.*) howling; (*m.,f.*) howler.
ululante (*adj.*) ululant, howling; wailing.
ulular (*v.i.*) to ululate, howl; to whine; to wail; to yell.
ululo (*m.*) = ULULAÇÃO.
um [pl. uns; fem. uma(s)] (*m.,f.*) one; (*adj.*) one, single;

(pl.) some, any, a few, about, several; *(art.)* a, an.—**a um**, one by one.—**ao outro**, one to the other; each to the other; to each other.—**demais**, one too many.—**dos que**, one of those who (which).—**e outro**, both.—**é pouco, dois é bom, três é demais**, One isn't enough; two's company; three's a crowd.—**outro**, another, one other, another one, one more.—**por um**, one by one; one after the other.—**só**, just one; but one. **à uma**, as with one accord. **à uma hora**, at one o'clock. **a uma hora daqui**, one hour's distance from here. **cada**—, each one. **daqui a uma hora**, one hour from now. **há uma hora**, an hour ago. **Falta**—, There's one missing. **qualquer**—, anyone; either one. **Quando**—**não quer, dois não brigam**, It takes two to make a quarrel. **Sobra**—, There's one left over; one too many. **Tanto faz**—**como o outro**, One's as good as the other. **uma e outro pessoa**, an occasional person. **uma ou** (or **que**) **outra vez**, once in awhile; now and then. **uns, umas**, some, a few, about, several. **uns e outros**, all of them; the whole lot. **uns poucos**, a few.

umari [í] *(m.)* = ANGELIM-DE-ESPINHO.
umbamba *(f., Bot.)* a bramble palm (*Desmoncus midentum*) c.a. JACITARA.
umbaru [rú] *(m.)* the kenaf hibiscus (*H. cannabinus*), c.a. CÂNHAMO-BRASILEIRO.
umbaúba *(f.)* the silverleaf pumpwood or trumpet tree (*Cecropia palmata*) c.a. IMBAÍBA, IMBAÚBA, IMBAÚVA, AMBAÚBA, AMBAÍBA, EMBAÚBA, ÁRVORE-DA-PREGUIÇA, TORÉM. " . . . it has a hollow stem which roars like a cannon when on fire." [*GBAT*]
umbela *(f.)* umbrella [= GUARDACHUVA]; *(Bot.)* umbel. Var. UMBRELA.
umbelifero –ra *(adj., Bot.)* umbelliferous; *(f.)* an umbellifer (any plant of the carrot family); *(f.pl.)* the parsley or carrot family (*Umbelliferae*, syns. *Ammiaceae, Apiaceae*).
umbeliferona *(f., Chem.)* umbelliferone.
umbigada *(f.)* a face-to-face (lit., navel-to-navel) bump into another person. Var. EMBIGADA.
umbigo *(m., Anat.)* umbilicus, navel.
umbilicado –da *(adj.)* umbilicate.
umbilical *(adj.)* umbilical.
umbráculo *(m., Bot.)* umbraculum.
umbral *(m.)* jamb; threshold.
umbrátil [-teis] *(adj.)* umbratile.
umbrela, var. of UMBELA.
umbrífero –ra *(adj.)* umbriferous; umbrageous.
umbro *(m.)* staghound; Umbrian.
umbroso –sa *(adj.)* umbrageous, shady.
umbu [bú] *(m.)* = IMBU.
umbuia *(f.)* = IMBUIA.
umburana *(f.)* = IMBURANA.
umbuzada *(f.)* = IMBUZADA.
umbuzeiro *(m.)* = IMBUZEIRO.
ume *(m.)* alum [= ALUME].
umedecedor *(m.)* humidifier.
umedecer *(v.t.)* to moisten, wet, dampen; *(v.i.,v.r.)* to get wet.
umedecimento *(m.)* a moistening.
umeral, umerário –ria *(adj., Anat., Zool.)* humeral.
úmero *(m., Anat., Zool.)* humerus; brachium.
umidade *(f.)* humidity, dampness.
úmido –da *(adj.)* humid, damp, moist.
umirirana *(f.)* a species of the copaiyé family (*Qualea retusa*). It is a "medium-sized tree with [hard] light brown wood whose fibers are coarse and interwoven." [*GUAF*]. Used for heavy construction work and for furniture.
unau *(m.)* a two-toed sloth of Amazonas (*Choloepus didactylus*), c.a. PREGUIÇA.
unanimar *(v.t.)* to make unanimous.
unânime *(adj.)* unanimous.
unanimidade *(f.)* unanimity.
unção *(f.)* unction, act of anointing; also unction in the sense of "a soothing, sympathetic, and persuasive quality in discourse."
úncia *(f.)* inch [= POLEGADA].
uncial *(adj.)* uncial.
unciforme *(adj.)* unciform, hook-shaped; *(m., Anat.)* unciform bone.
uncinado –da *(adj., Biol.)* uncinate, hooked.
uncinaríase *(f., Med.)* uncinariasis, ancylostomiasis, hookworm disease [= ANCILOSTOMÍASE, OPILAÇÃO, AMARELÃO].
undante *(adj.)* undulant.

undécimo –ma *(adj., m.)* eleventh [= DÉCIMO-PRIMEIRO].
undoso –sa *(adj.)* wavy.
ungido –da *(adj.)* anointed.
ungir [25] *(v.t.)* to anoint; to consecrate by unction.
úngüe *(m., Amat.)* the lachrymal bone (*os unguis*) Var. ÚNGÜIS.
ungueal *(adj., Anat., Zool.)* ungual.
ungüentáceo –cea, **ungüentário** –ria *(adj.)* unguentary.
ungüento *(m.)* unguent, ointment, salve.
ungii, ungui [í] *(m.)* a dish of beans and manioc meal [= TUTU].
unguiculado –da *(adj., Zool.)* unguiculate, clawed; *(m.)* one of the Unguiculata.
ungüinoso –sa *(adj.)* unguinous, oily.
úngüis *(m.)* = ÚNGÜE.
úngula *(f., Geom.)* ungula.
ungulado –da *(adj., Zool.)* ungulate; *(m.)* one of the Ungulata.
unha *(f.)* fingernail; toenail; claw; talon; hoof; *(Zool., Bot.)* unguis.—**d'anta** = CHAPADA.—**de-boi**, *(Bot.)* the bell bauhinia (*B. forficata*).—**de-boi-do-campo** = CATINGA-DE-TAMANDUÁ.—**de-cavalo**, *(Bot.)* a coltsfoot (*Tussilago sp.*), c.a. TUSSILAGEM.—**(s)-de-fome**, pennypincher.—**de-gato**, the catclaw acacia (*A. greggi*); the catclaw mimosa (*M. biuncifera*), c.a. JAGUARIPE; also = CIPÓ-DE-GATO.—**de-vaca** = UNHA-DE-BOI. —**de-vaca-roxa** = CATINGA-DE-TAMANDUÁ.—**de-velha**, or -**de-velho**, the short razor clam (*Tagelus gibbus*); also = LONGUEIRÃO.—**do martelo**, claw of a hammer.—**do-** (or **no-**) **ôlho**, *(colloq.)* pterygium (an eye disease).—**encravada**, ingrowing toenail. **à**—, with the bare hands. **defender com**—**s e dentes**, to fight tooth and nail; to defend to the last ditch. **fazer as**—**s**, to "do" (trim and clean) the nails. **lamber as**—**s**, to lick one's fingers. **pegar o touro à**—, to take the bull by the horns. **ser**—**e carne com alguém**, to be hand and glove with someone.
unhada *(f.)*, **unhaço** *(m.)* a nail scratch.
unhão *(m.)* a splice or splicing of a rope.
unhar *(v.t.)* to scratch with the nails or claws; *(v.i.)* to steal.
unheira *(f.)* saddle gall [= CUERA].
unheiro *(m.)* hangnail; whitlow.
união *(f.)* union, uniting, joining, junction, coupling; alliance, confederation; marriage. **traço**, or **risca, de**—, hyphen.
uniaxial [ks] *(adj.)* uniaxial.
unicelular *(adj., Biol.)* unicellular.
unicidade *(f.)* uniqueness.
único –ca *(adj.)* only, only one, sole, single, alone, one and only; unique, singular, exceptional, unmatched, unexampled.
unicolor *(adj.)* of but one color; monochromatic.
unicorne *(adj.)* one-horned; *(m.)* unicorn.
unicórnio *(m.)* unicorn.—**do-mar**, narwhal.
unicúspide *(adj.)* single-pointed.
unidade *(f.)* unit; integer; digit; oneness; unity; military or naval unit.
unidirecional *(adj.)* unidirectional.
unido –da *(adj.)* united, joined.
unificação *(f.)* unification.
unificador –dora *(adj.)* unifying; *(m.,f.)* unifier.
unificar *(v.t.)* to unify, unite.
unifilar *(adj.)* unifilar.
unifloro –ra *(adj., Bot.)* uniflorous.
unifoliado –da *(adj., Bot.)* unifoliate.
uniforme *(adj.)* uniform, unvarying, even, alike; *(m.)* uniform.
uniformidade *(f.)* uniformity, sameness.
uniformizar *(v.t.)* to render uniform; *(v.r.)* to put on a uniform.
unigênito –ta *(adj.)* only-begotten; *(m.)* only-begotten son; Christ.
unijugado –da *(adj., Bot.)* unijugate [leaf].
unilateral *(adj.)* unilateral, one-sided.
unilíngüe *(adj.)* unilingual.
unilobado –da, **unilobulado** –da *(adj.)* unilobed.
unilocular *(adj., Bot., Zool.)* unilocular.
unimolecular *(adj.)* monomolecular.
unioculado –da, **uniocular** *(adj.)* one-eyed.
unionismo *(m.)* unionism.
unionista *(adj., m.,f.)* unionist.
uníparo –ra *(adj., Zool.)* uniparous; *(f., Bot.)* a uniparous cyme.
unipedal *(adj.)* having but a single foot.

unipessoal (*adj.*) unipersonal.
unipétalo -la (*adj., Bot.*) unipetalous.
unipolar (*adj., Physics*) unipolar; monopolar.
unipolaridade (*f.*) unipolarity.
unir (*v.t.*) to unite; to join, connect; to amalgamate, consolidate, blend; to couple, link, marry; to reconcile.—**se a (com)**, to come together with, join oneself to (with).
unirrefringente (*adj.*) isotropic.
unissexuado -da, unissexual [ks] (*adj.*) unisexual.
unissonância (*f.*) unity of sound or pitch.
unissonante (*adj.*) unisonant.
uníssono -na (*adj.*) unisonous, unisonal; (*m.*) unison.
unitário -ria (*adj.*) unitary; (*m.,f.*) Unitarian.
unitarismo (*m.*) Unitarianism.
unitivo -va (*adj.*) unitive.
Univ. = UNIVERSIDADE (University).
univalente (*adj., Chem.*) monovalent.
univalve (*adj.*) univalve, univalved.
univalvular (*adj.*) univalvular.
universal (*adj.; m.*) universal.
universalidade (*f.*) universality.
universalismo (*m.*) universalism.
universalização (*f.*) universalization.
universalizar (*v.t.*) to universalize.
universidade (*f.*) university.
universitário -ria (*adj.*) of or pert. to a university; (*m.,f.*) a university student or teacher.
universo (*m.*) universe.
uno -na (*adj.*) one; unique.
unóculo -la (*adj.*) one-eyed.
uns, pl. of UM.
untadela (*f.*) smear(ing).
untadura (*f.*) = UNTURA.
untanha (*f.*) = SAPO-ANTANHA.
untar (*v.t.*) to anoint; to smear, daub; to grease.—**com manteiga**, to butter.
unto (*m.*) grease, fat, lard.
untuosidade (*f.*) unctuosity.
untuoso -sa (*adj.*) unctuous; fig., full of unction, bland, suave.
untura (*f.*) act of anointing; ointment, unguent.
upa (*interj.*) Up! (*f.*) a rearing up (of a horse).
ura [*f.*] bot [= BERNE].
uracaçu [çú] (*m., Zool.*) the redthroated caracara (*Daptrius americanus*).
úraco (*m., Anat.*) urachus.
uraçu [çú] (*m.*) = CUTUCURIM.
uralita (*f., Min.*) uralite.
uranato (*m., Chem.*) uranate.
uranilo (*m., Chem.*) uranyl.
uraninita (*f., Min.*) uraninite.
urânio (*m., Chem.*) uranium.
uranita (*f., Min.*) uranite.
Urano (*m., Astron.*) Uranus.
uranofotografia (*f.*) uranophotography.
uranografia (*f.*) uranography.
uranologia (*f.*) uranology.
uranômetro (*m.*) uranometry.
urarema (*f., Bot.*) an angelin tree (*Andira stipulacea*).
urarirana (*f.*) ringed kingfisher (*Ceryle torquata*); a certain shrub (*Paullinia alata*).
úrase (*f., Biochem.*) urase, urease.
urato (*m., Chem.*) urate.
urbanidade (*f.*) urbanity, courtesy.
urbanismo (*m.*) city planning.
urbanita (*adj.; m.,f.*) urbanite.
urbanizar (*v.t.*) to urbanize.
urbano -na (*adj.*) urban; urbane, suave, well-mannered.
urceolado -da, urceolar (*adj.; Bot.*) urceolate.
urcéolo (*m., Bot.*) urceolus.
urco (*m.*) a fine, big horse.
urdideira (*f.*) a woman warper or weaver; warp beam or frame.
urdidor -deira (*adj.*) warping; (*m.*) warper; fig., schemer.
urdidura (*f.*), urdimento, urdume (*m.*) act or operation of warping.
urdir (*v.t.*) to warp (yarn); to scheme, plot, intrigue.
uréia (*f., Biochem.*) urea; carbamide.
uremia (*f., Med.*) uremia.
urente (*adj.*) burning, stinging.
ureter [tér] (*m., Anat., Zool.*) ureter.
urético -ca (*adj., Med.*) uretic.
uretra (*f., Anat.*) urethra.
uretral (*adj.*) urethral.

uretrite (*f., Med.*) urethritis.
uretroscopia (*f., Med.*) urethroscopy.
uretroscópio (*m., Med.*) urethroscope.
urgebão, urgevão (*m.*) European verbena (*V. officinalis*), c.a. VERBENA-OFICINAL, VERBERÃO.
urgência (*f.*) urgency.
urgente (*adj.*) urgent, pressing. **entrega—**, special delivery (of mail, etc.).
urgir [25] (*v.i.*) to be urgent, pressing; to urge. **O tempo urge**, Time is pressing.
Urias (*m.*) Uriah.
uribaco (*m.*) = CORCOROCA.
uricana (*f., Bot.*) a shadow palm (*Geonoma pumila*); also = SURUCUCU (a snake).
urichoca (*f.*) = TAINHA-DE-RIO.
úrico -ca (*adj.*) uric [acid].
uricuri [curí] (*f.*) the uricury syagrus palm (*Syagrus coronata*), c.a. ARICURI, OURICURI.
uricuriroba (*f.*) = ARICURIROBA.
urina (*f.*) urine.
urinação (*f.*) urination.
urinar (*v.i.*) to urinate.
urinário -ria (*adj.*) urinary.
urinífero -ra (*adj.*) uriniferous.
uriníparo -ra (*adj.*) uriniparous.
urinol [-nóis] (*m.*) urinal; chamber pot.
urinoso -sa (*adj.*) urinous.
uritutu [tutú] (*m.*) = JURUVA.
uriunduba [i-un] (*f., Bot.*) a star tree (*Astronium sp.*), c.a. AROEIRA.
urna (*f.*) urn; ballot box.
urobilina (*f., Biochem.*) urobilin.
urobilinogênio (*m., Biochem.*) urobilinogen.
urocinanogênio (*m., Biochem.*) urocyanogen.
uroclorálico -ca (*adj., Chem.*) urochloralic [acid].
urocroma (*m., Biochem.*) urochrome.
urodelo -la (*m., Zool.*) caudate; (*m.*) one of the Caudata; a tailed amphibian.
uroeritrina (*f., Biochem.*) uroerythrin.
urofeína (*f., Biochem.*) urophein.
urogáster (*m., Anat., Embryol.*) urogaster.
urogastro (*m., Zool.*) urogaster.
urogênico -ca (*adj., Physiol., Med.*) urogenous.
urogenital (*adj., Anat., Zool.*) urogenital.
uroglaucina (*f., Biochem.*) uroglaucin.
urohial (*m., Zool.*) urohyal.
urolagnia (*f.*) urolagnia.
urólito (*m., Med.*) urolith.
urologia (*f.*) urology.
urológico -ca (*adj.*) urological.
urologista (*m.,f.*) urologist.
uroluteína (*f., Biochem.*) urolutein.
uromelanina (*f., Biochem.*) uromelanin.
uromice (*m., Bot.*) a very large genus (*Uromyces*) of rusts.
uropigial (*adj., Zool.*) uropygial.
uropígio (*m., Zool.*) uropygium.
urópode (*m., Zool.*) uropod.
uroscopia (*f., Med.*) uroscopy.
urosteólito (*m., Biochem.*) urostealith.
urotóxico -ca [ks] (*adj., Physiol.*) urotoxic.
urotoxia [ks] (*f., Physiol.*) urotoxy.
uroxantina [ks] (*f., Biochem.*) uroxanthin, indican.
urrar (*v.i.,v.t.*) to howl (as a wolf); to bellow (as a bull); to roar (as a lion); to bawl.
urro (*m.*) roar, bellow, howl; cry.
ursa (*f.*) female bear.—**Maior (Menor)**, (*Astron.*) Great (Little) Bear.
ursada (*f., colloq.*) false friendship; a double-crossing; dirty trick.
ursídeo -dea (*adj.*) ursine; (*m.pl., Zool.*) the bear family (*Ursidae*).
ursinho (*m.*) toy bear.
ursino -na (*adj.*) ursine, bearlike.
urso (*m.*) bear; fig., gruff, surly person; (*colloq.*) false friend.—**-branco**, polar bear.—**-do-bôlso**, the koala (*Phascolarctos cinereus*).—**-escuro**, brown bear.—**-narigudo** = COATI.—**-negro**, black bear.
U.R.S.S. = UNIÃO DAS REPÚBLICAS SOCIALISTAS SOVIÉTICAS (USSR: Union of Soviet Socialist Republics).
urticação (*f., Med.*) urtication.
urticáceo -cea (*adj., Bot.*) urticaceous; (*f.pl.*) the nettle family (*Urticaceae*).
urticante (*adj.*) urticant, stinging, itching.
urticar (*v.t.*) to sting, as with nettles.

urticária (*f., Med.*) urticaria, hives, nettle rash.
urtíceas (*f.pl.*) = URTICÁCEAS.
urtiga (*f.*) a genus (*Urtica*) of nettles; also = CANSANÇÃO-DE-LEITE.—**amarela**, the archangel deadnettle (*Lamium galeobdolon*).—**branca** = URTIGA-MORTA.—**brava** = CANSANÇÃO.—**cansanção** = CANSANÇÃO-DE-LEITE.—**da-china**, the ramie or Chinese silk plant (*Boehmeria nivea*).—**de-cipó**, a spurge (*Euphorbia urens*), c.a. TRIPA-DE-GALINHA [lit., chicken entrails]; another euphorbia (*Dalechampia brasiliensis*), c.a. TAMEARANA; the cowitch dalechampia (*D. tiliafolia*), c.a. CIPÓ-TRIPA-DE-GALINHA and TAMIARANA.—**de-espinho**, a rattlepot (*Alectorolophus spinosus*).—**de-mamão** = CANSANÇÃO-DE-LEITE.—**de-papel**, the African falsenettle (*Boehmeria platyphylla*).—**do-mar**, a stinging jellyfish; a sea anemone.—**-fogo** or—**grande** = CANSANÇÃO.—**-maior** = URTIGÃO.—**-morta**, the white deadnettle (*Lamium album*), c.a. URTIGA-BRANCA, LÂMIO-BRANCO.—**-tamiarana** = CIPÓ-TRIPA-DE-GALINHA and TAMEARANA.—**-vermelha** = CANSANÇÃO.
urtigação (*f.*) urtication.
urtigal (*m.*) a place abounding in nettles.
urtigante (*adj.*) urticant; (*Zool.*) adapted for stinging.
urtigão (*m.*) the bigsting nettle (*Urtica dioica*); either of two scratchbushes (*Urera armigera* or *U. baccifera*), the latter c.a. CANSANÇÃO; a Chile nettle (*Loana parviflora*), c.a. CANSANÇÃO.
urtigar (*v.t.*) to urticate; to nettle; (*v.r.*) to get stung by nettles.
urtigueira (*f.*) = URTIGAL.
urtiguinha (*f.*) a scratchbush (*Urera subpeltata*).—**-de-cipó** = CIPÓ-URTIGUINHA.
uru [urú] (*m.*) the capueira partridge (*Odontophorus capueira*) and others of that genus, c.a. CAPOEIRA, CORCOVADO; "a splint or straw basket with a top, used in small boats and in huts for storing small articles." [GBAT]
uruá (*m., Bot.*) the onion cordia (*C. alliodora*); also = ARUÁ (a snail).
uruâzeiro (*m.*) = PARAPARÁ.
urubamba (*f.*) = JACITARA.
urubu [bú] (*m.,f.*) an Indian of the Urubu, a Tupian tribe with remnants living on the upper Gurupi River in Maranhão; (*adj.*) pert. to or designating this tribe; (*m.*) the very common Brazilian black vulture (*Coragyps atratus*).—**caçador**, the turkey vulture (*Cathartes aura*), c.a. URUBU-CAMPEIRO, URUBU-DE-CABEÇA-VERMELHA, URUBU-GAMELEIRA, URUBU-JEREBA, URUBU-MINISTRO, URUBU-PERU, URUBUPEBA, JEREBA, CAMIRANGA.—**de-cabeça-amarela**, the yellow-headed turkey vulture (*Cathartes urubutinga*), c.a. URUBUTINGA.—**rei**, king vulture (*Sarcorhamphus papa*), c.a. URUBU-RUBIXÁ.
urubucaá [ca-á] (*m.*) = ANGELICÓ.
urubupeba (*m.*) = URUBU-CAÇADOR.
urubutinga (*m.*) = URUBU-CAÇADOR.
urubuzinho (*m.*) = ANDORINHA-DA-MATA.
urucaca (*f.*) hag.
urucari [í] (*m., Bot.*) a palm (*Scheelea martiana*), c.a. URUCURI.
urucu [cú] (*m.*) the fruit of the annatto tree (*Bixa orellana*) from whose pulp is extracted annatto dye; the dye itself.
uruçu [çú] (*m.*) a large, black, stingless honeybee (*Melipona nigra*), c.a. GARAPU, GUARAPU, GUARAPU, GUARAIPO, PÉ-DE-PAU.—**mirim** = GUARAPU-MIRIM.
urucubaca (*f.*) bad luck; black-and-white checkered cloth.
urucuera (*f.*) = CABORÉ-DO-CAMPO.
urucurana (*f.*) = MUIRÁ-GONÇALO.
urucuri (*m.*) = URUCARI.
urucuréia, urucuria = CORUJA-DO-CAMPO.
urucuzeiro, urucueiro (*m.*) the annatto tree (*Bixa orellana*), c.a. URUCUUBA.
Uruguai (*m.*) Uruguay.
uruguaio –guaia (*adj.; m.,f.*) Uruguayan.
urumbeba, urumbeva (*m.*) a person easily duped or imposed upon; a "sucker"; a yokel.
urumutum (*m., Zool.*) a curassow (*Nothocrax urumutum*), c.a. MUTUM.
urundeúva (*f.*) a large star tree (*Astronium urundeuva*) whose wood is used for heavy constructions; c.a. AROEIRA-DO-SERTÃO, AROEIRA-PRETA.
urupê (*m.*) a red bracket or shelf fungus (*Polyporus sanguineus*), c.a. ORELHA-DE-PAU ("wooden ear") and PIRONGA.

urupema (*f.*) a fiber sieve or sifter, esp. for manioc meal, c.a. ARUPEMBA, URUPEMBA, GUARUPEMA, JURUPEMA.
urupuca (*f.*) a bird trap, c.a. ARAPUCA; a sort of small wooden cage placed around young coffee plants.
ururuca (*f.*) = CONGONHEIRO.
urutaí (*m.*) = MAÚ.
urutau (*m., Zool.*) the giant potoo (*Nyctibius griseus*), or the grand potoo (*N. grandis*) c.a. MÃE-DA-LUA, CHORA-LUA, MANDALUA, IBIJAÚ-GUAÇU.
urutaurana (*m.*) = APACANIM.
urutu [tú] (*m. or f.*) either of two dangerously poisonous Brazilian vipers: a large, heavy, handsomely-marked lance-head type of pit viper (*Bothrops alternata*), c.a. CRUZEIRO, CRUZEIRA, COTIARA; or Maximilian's viper (*Bothrops neuweidii*), c.a. JARARACA-PINTADA, JARARACA-DO-RABO-BRANCO, CRUZEIRA. Also, a sea catfish.—**-dourado**, or—**estrêla** = JARARACUÇU.
urze (*f.*) kinds of heath or heather.—**das-camarinhas** = CAMARINHEIRA.
urzela (*f., Bot.*) litmus roccella (*R. tinctoria*).
usado –da (*adj.*) used; in use, accustomed; worn (out); secondhand. **não—**, not used, unused. **pouco—**, little used.
usagre (*m., Med.*) impetigo.
usança (*f.*) usage, custom.
usar (*v.t.*) to use; to employ, put to use; to wear, have on; to use up; to wear out; to be accustomed to.—**da palavra**, to speak at a meeting.—**de**, to make use of.—**(de) meios legais**, to employ legal means.—**de misericórdia**, to use mercy.—**gravata**, to wear a necktie.
usável (*adj.*) usable.
useiro –ra (*adj.*) usual, customary, wonted.—**e vezeiro**, used to doing the same thing over and over.
usina (*f.*) factory, mill, works, manufacturing establishment.—**de açúcar**, sugar mill.—**de montagem**, assembly plant.—**elétrica**, power plant.—**hidrelétrica**, hydroelectric station.
usinado –da (*adj.*) machine-made.
usinar (*v.t.*) to machine-make; to finish by machine.
usineiro –ra (*adj.*) of or pert. to a sugar mill; (*m.*) owner of a sugar mill.
úsnea (*f., Bot.*) a genus (*Usnea*) of lichens.
usneáceo –cea (*adj., Bot.*) usnaceous; (*f.pl.*) a family (*Usnaceae*) of fruticose lichens.
uso (*m.*) use, employment, application; exercise, practice; usage, custom. **ao—antigo**, in the old-fashioned way. **em—**, in use. **fora de—**, out of use. **O—faz o mestre**, Practice makes perfect.
USP = UNIVERSIDADE DE SÃO PAULO.
ustão (*f.*) act of burning; state of being burned; cauterization.
ustório –ria (*adj.*) having the quality or power of burning.
ustulação (*f.*) ustulation.
ustular (*v.t.*) to scorch, roast, dry (ores and other substances).
usual (*adj.*) usual, customary, familiar, frequent, habitual. accustomed, everyday.
usuário –ria (*adj.*) designating one having the right of use; useful; (*m.*) user.
usucapiente (*adj.; m.,f., Law*) usucapient.
usucapir (*v.t., Law*) to usucapt.
usufruir [25] (*v.t.*) to usufruct, enjoy the fruits of.
usufruto (*m.*) usufruct; fruition.
usufrutuário –ria (*adj., Law*) usufructuary; (*m.,f.*) one having the usufruct of property.
usura (*f.*) usury.
usurar (*v.i.*) to practice usury.
usurário –ria (*adj.*) usurious; (*m.,f.*) usurer.
usurpação (*f.*) usurpation.
usurpador –dora (*adj.*) usurping; (*m.,f.*) usurper.
usurpar (*v.t.*) to usurp, arrogate, appropriate unlawfully to encroach on or upon.
Utá (*m.*) Utah.
utensílio (*m.*) utensil, tool, implement.
uterino –na (*adj.*) uterine.
útero (*m., Anat., Zool.*) uterus, womb.
útil [-teis] (*adj.*) useful, advantageous, utilitarian, serviceable, helpful.
utilidade (*f.*) utility, usefulness, advantageousness; expediency.
utilitário –ria (*adj.*) utilitarian; expedient.
utilitarismo (*m.*) utilitarianism; expediency.
utilização (*f.*) utilization.

utilizar (*v.t.*) to utilize, put to use, make use of, turn to account, take advantage of.—-se de, to make use of.
utilizável (*adj.*) utilizable.
Utopia (*f.*) Utopia; [*not cap.*] utopia.
utópico –ca (*adj.*) Utopian; utopian.
utopista (*adj.; m.,f.*) Utopian; utopian.
utricular, utriculariforme (*adj.*) utricular, baglike.
utrículo (*m.*) small sac or bag; (*Anat., Bot.*) utricle.
utriculoso –sa (*adj.*) utricular.
utriforme (*adj.*) utriform.
utuaba (*f., Bot.*) a muskwood (*Guarea purgans*).
utuapoca (*f., Bot.*) a muskwood (*Guarea spicoeflora*).
uva (*f.*) grape.—-brava = CIPÓ-DE-FOGO.—-de-cão, the bitter-sweet nightshade (*Solanum dulcamara*), c.a. PÃO-DE-PÁSSAROS.—-de-cão-menor, a stonecrop (*Sedum acre*).—-de-gentio = ABUTUA.—-de-espinho = ESPINHO-DE-SÃO-JOÃO.—-do-mato = ABUTUA-GRANDE.—-do-monte, the myrtle whortleberry (*Vaccinium myrtilus*), c.a. ARANDO.

—-espim, the European barberry (*Berberis vulgaris*).—-sêca = ABUTUA.
uvada (*f.*) grape jam or preserves.
uvaia, uvaieira (*f., Bot.*) the uvalha eugenia (*E .uvalha*).
uvarovita (*f., Min.*) uvarovite.
úvea (*f., Anat.*) uvea.
uveíte (*f., Med.*) uveitis.
uvífero –ra (*adj.*) bearing fruit in bunches, as grapes.
uviforme (*adj.*) grapelike.
úvula (*f., Anat.*) uvula; c.a. CAMPAINHA.
uvular (*adj.*) uvular.
uvulite (*f., Med.*) uvulitis.
uxoriano –na [ks] (*adj.*) uxorial. bens—s, wife's property.
uxoricida [ks] (*f.*) uxoricide (wife killer).
uxoricídio [ks] (*m.*) uxoricide (wife killing).
uxório –ria [ks] (*adj.*) uxorial.
uzarina (*f., Chem.*) uzarin.
uzífur, uzífuro (*m.*) cannabar [= CINABRE].

V

V, v, the 21st letter of the Port. alphabet.
v. = VAPOR (steamer); VOCÊ (you); VOLT (volt); VERSO (verse); VIDE, VEJA (see).
v/ = VOSSO(S), VOSSA(S), (your).
V. = VISTO (visaed).
V.ª = VIÚVA (widow); VILA (Villa).
V.A. = VOSSA ALTEZA (Your Highness).
vá, imperative of IR [53].
vaca (*f.*) cow; pool (joint gambling venture); a drumfish (*Pogonias chromys*), c.a. PIRAÚNA, MIRAGUAIA, BURRIQUETE.—-leiteira, milch cow; also (in Rio de Janeiro) a retail milk truck.—-loura, an oil beetle (*Meloe sp.*); a stag beetle (*Lucanus cervus*); the yellow meal or darkling beetle (*Tenebrio molitor*), c.a. ABADEJO.—-marinha, sea cow, manatee, c.a. PEIXE-BOI; a walrus, c.a. MORSA.—-sem-chifre = BAIACU-SEM-CHIFRE (a swellfish). fazer uma—, to form a pool; to take up a collection. voltar, or tornar, à—fria, to rehash an old subject.
vacada (*f.*) herd of cows.
vacagem (*f.*) large number of cows.
vacal (*adj.*) indecent.
vacância (*f.*) vacancy.
vacante (*adj.*) vacant; unoccupied; in abeyance. bens—s, unclaimed inheritance.
vacar (*v.i.*) to be vacant; to be on vacation; to be unoccupied.
vacaraí (*m.*) = TAPICHI.
vacaria (*f.*) herd of cows; cow barn; cows collectively.
vacatura (*f.*) = VACÂNCIA.
vacê, pop. form of VOCÊ.
vacilação (*f.*) vacillation; oscillation; hesitation.
vacilante (*adj.*) vacillating; hesitant; shaky, unsteady.
vacilar (*v.i.*) to vacillate, sway, waver; to totter; to oscillate; to hesitate, dillydally.
vacilatório –ria (*f.*) vacillatory.
vacina (*f.*) vaccinia, cowpox; vaccine; vaccination.—antivariólica, vaccination against smallpox.—terapêutica, vaccine therapy.
vacinação (*f.*) vaccination.
vacinador –dora (*adj.*) vaccinating; (*m.,f.*) vaccinator; (*m.*) vaccine point.
vacinal (*adj.*) = VACÍNICO.
vacinar (*v.t.*) to vaccinate.
vaciniáceo –cea (*adj., Bot.*) vaccineaceous; (*f.pl.*) the blueberry or cranberry family (*Vacciniaceae*).
vacínico –ca (*adj.*) vaccinal; vaccinial.
vacínio (*m.*) the genus (*Vaccinium*) of blueberries.
vacinogênico –ca (*adj.*) vaccinogenic.
vacinoterapia (*f.*) vaccine therapy.
vacu [ú] (*m.*) = BACU.
vacuá (*f.*) common screwpine (*Pandanus utilis*), c.a. PANDANO.
vacuidade [u-i] (*f.*) vacuity, emptiness; fig., vanity.
vacum (*adj.*) bovine; (*m.*) bovine cattle.
vácuo –cua (*adj.*) vacuous, void, empty; (*m.*) vacuum, empty space.

vacuolar (*adj., Biol.*) vacuolar.
vacuolização (*f., Biol.*) vacuolation.
vacúolo (*m., Biol.*) vacuole.
vadeação (*f.*) fording of a stream. [Do not confuse with VADIAÇÃO.]
vadear (*v.t.*) to ford a stream. [Do not confuse with VADIAR.]
vadeável (*adj.*) fordable.
vades, form of IR [53].
vadeoso –sa (*adj.*) of a stream, having sand bars or other shallow crossings.
vadiação (*f.*) idleness, loafing.
vadiagem, vadiice (*f.*) vagrancy, vagabondage; idleness; the class of vagrants; truancy.
vadiar (*v.i.*) to loaf; to bum around; to dawdle, esp. at school.
vadio –dia (*adj.*) idle, lazy; vagrant; truant; (*m.*) loafer; street bum; vagrant; drone, sluggard; idler.
vaga (*f.*) wave, billow, breaker; vacancy, unfilled position; void; leisure. preencher uma—, to fill a (vacant) position.
vagabundagem (*f.*) vagabondage; vagrancy.
vagabundear (*v.i.*) to loaf, be an idler; to roam, wander.
vagabundo –da (*adj.*) vagrant; vagabond; truant; (*colloq.*) of wretched quality, third-rate, no-good. cargueiro—, tramp steamer. (*m.*) loafer, bum, hobo, tramp, vagrant, vagabond, ne'er-do-well; (*f.*) a certain ponerine ant.
vágado (*m.*) dizziness; faint.
vagalhão (*m.*) large wave, billow.
vaga-lume (*m.*) firefly; (*colloq.*) usher in a motion-picture theater.
vagante (*adj.*) vagrant; vacant.
vagão (*m.*) railway freight car or passenger coach.—de carga, freight car.—dormitório, sleeping car.—fechado, boxcar.—plataforma, flatcar.—-restaurante, dining car.
vagar (*v.i.*) to roam, wander; to drift; to loiter, idle; to become vacant; (*m.*) spare time, leisure; deliberateness.
vagarento –ta (*adj.*) = VAGAROSO.
vagareza [ê] (*f.*) want of hurry; slowness.
vagaroso –sa (*adj.*) slow, slow-moving, sluggish, unhurried, deliberate.
vagatura (*f.*) = VACÂNCIA.
vagem (*f.*) string bean; green bean; pod.
vagido (*m.*) cry of a newborn child; fig., wail(ing).
vagina (*f., Anat., Bot.*) vagina.
vaginal (*adj.*) vaginal; sheathlike.
vaginite (*f., Med.*) vaginitis.
vagínula (*f.*) a little sheath; (*Bot.*) vaginula.
vaginulado –da (*adj.*) vaginulate.
vagir (*v.i.*) to pule, whimper, whine; (*m.*) wail(ing).
vago –ga (*adj.*) vagrant; fickle; vague; vacant, unoccupied; disengaged; (*m.*) vagueness. horas—s, spare time. nervo—, (*Anat.*) vagus.
vagonete [nê] (*m.*) ore cart; dump cart.
vagotonia (*f., Physiol., Med.*) vagotonia.

vagueação (*f.*) act or instance of wandering; vagrancy; vagary.

vaguear (*v.i.*) to roam, wander; to stray, straggle; to stroll (about); to ramble; to float, drift.

vagueza [ê] (*f.*) vagueness.

vai, vais, forms of IR [53].

vaia (*f.*) hoot, jeer, boo.

vaiar (*v.t.,v.i.*) to hoot (at); jeer (at); to boo.

vaidade (*f.*) vanity; emptiness, foolishness, futility; self-conceit; idle show, display.

vaidoso –sa (*adj.*) vain, conceited; vainglorious; proud, haughty; self-satisfied; cocky.

vaivém (*m.*) any to-and-fro motion (as of a piston rod); any coming and going (of persons); a battering ram; vicissitude. **os vaivéns da fortuna,** the ups and downs of fortune.

vai-volta (*m.*) a box which is used over and over for transporting cadavers to the potter's field.

vala (*f.*) ditch, trench.—**comum,** common grave; potter's field.

valada (*f.*) a big ditch.

valadio –dia (*adj.*) having drainage ditches; laid without mortar [Spanish roof tiles].

valado (*m.*) a surrounding ditch or trench; a rampart.

valão (*adj.; m.*) Walloon.

valar (*v.t.*) to provide with a ditch or trench (for drainage or as an enclosure).

Valdemar (*m.*) Waldemar.

valdevinos (*m.*) loafer, vagrant; pauper; scalawag.

vale (*m.*) valley; an IOU; a voucher.—**de lágrimas,** vale of tears.—**postal,** postal money order.

valedio –dia (*adj.*) valid; that can serve as legal tender.

valeira (*f.*), –ro (*m.*) ditch; gutter.

valência (*f., Chem.*) valence.

valenciana (*f.*) Valenciennes lace.

valentão –tona (*adj.*) swaggering; **à valentona,** by brute force. (*m.*) ruffian, tough, braggart, bully; "bad man".

valente (*adj.*) valiant, brave, intrepid, dauntless; (*m.*) a valiant man.

valentia (*f.*) valor, prowess, daring; heroic act.

valer [80] (*v.t., v.i., v.r.*) to be worth; to be of the value of; to be equal in value to; to count (have value); to merit, deserve; to help, succor; to be of use.—**a pena,** to be worth while.—(-**se**) **contra,** to prevail against.—**se de,** to avail oneself of; to make use of; to resort to; to take advantage of.—**mais,** to be worth more.—**por,** to be the equal of, worth as much as. **a or para**—, really; very; in earnest; to beat the band. **"A honra vale mais que a vida,"** Honor is worth more than life itself. **Assim não vale!** (or simply: **não vale**), No fair! That's not cricket! **fazer**—**os seus direitos,** to assert one's rights. **fazer-se**—. to establish one's worth; to make oneself felt. **Mais vale prevenir do que remediar,** An ounce of prevention is worth a pound of cure. **Mais vale um pássaro na mão que dois voando,** or **Mias vale um toma que dois te darei,** A bird in the hand is worth two in the bush. **Não vale a pena,** It doesn't pay; It's not worth while; The game is not worth the candle. **O silêncio vale ouro,** Silence is golden. **ou coisa que o valha,** or what amounts to the same thing; or something similar; or something like it. **pelo que valha,** for what it may be worth; as far as it goes. **que não vale nada,** worthless; good-for-nothing. **que não vale um caracol,** not worth a tinker's damn. **Vale a pena,** It is worth while. **Vale a pena fazer isso,** That's worth doing. **vale dizer,** that is to say; in other words. **Vale por dois,** He is as good as two. **Vale tudo!** anything (everything) goes! **Valha-me Deus!** God help me! **valha a verdade,** truth to tell; let truth prevail; let it be said. **Vale tudo!** anything goes!

valeriana (*f., Bot.*) common valerian (*Valeriana officinalis*).

valerináceo –cea (*adj.; Bot.*) valerianaceous; (*f.pl.*) the valerian family (*Valerianaceae*).

valerianato (*m., Chem.*) valerate.

valeriânico –ca (*adj.; Chem.*) **ácido**—, valeric acid.

valeta [ê] (*f.*) street gutter; roadside ditch.

valete (*m.*) knave, jack (playing card), c.a. CONDE.

valetudinário –ria (*adj.*) valetudinarian, sickly.

valha, valhas, etc., pres. subj. forms of VALER [80].

valhacouto (*m.*) asylum, sanctuary.

valho, form of VALER [80].

valia (*f.*) value, worth; intrinsic value; real worth; estimation, valuation; price; merit. **de**—, valuable.

validação (*f.*) validation.

validade (*f.*) validity.

validar (*v.t.*) to validate; to give legal force to; to acknowledge (a legal document); (*v.r.*) to become valid.

validez [ê] (*f.*) validity.

valido –da (*adj.*) favorite; (*m.*) protégé; (*f.*) protégée.

válido –da (*adj.*) valid, having legal strength; efficacious, powerful; sound; able-bodied.

valimento (*m.*) worth, worthiness; value; prestige.

valioso –sa (*adj.*) valuable, precious; worthy.

valise (*f.*) valise, travelling bag, suitcase, grip.

V.-alm. = VICE-ALMIRANTE (vice admiral).

valo (*m.*) rampart; earthworks; trench; arena, lists; a certain type of fishnet.

valor (*m.*) value, worth; price; valor, prowess; merit, excellence; (*Music*) duration; (*pl.*) securities; valuables.— **empenhado,** hypothecated or collateral security.— **mediano,** (*Stat.*) median. **dar**—**a,** to value. **sem**—, valueless, worthless.

valorização (*f.*) valorization.

valorizar (*v.t.*) to valorize; to boost prices; (*v.r.*) to increase in value.

valoroso –sa (*adj.*) valorous, brave, stout, doughty.

valquírias (*f.pl.*) valkyries.

valsa (*f.*) waltz.

valsar (*v.i.*) to waltz.

valsista (*m.,f.*) waltzer; (*adj.*) waltzing.

valuação (*f.*) valuation.

valverde [vê] (*m., Bot.*) the belvedere summer cypress (*Kochia scoparia*), c.a. BELVERDE; the butter-and-eggs toadflax (*Linaria vulgaris*), c.a. LINÁRIA-COMUM.

válvula (*f., Anat., Mach.*) valve; (*Radio*) tube.—**de admissão** or **de entrada,** intake valve.—**de borboleta,** butterfly valve.—**de escape,** relief valve.—**de segurança,** safety valve.

valvulado –da (*adj.*) having valves.

vamirim (*m.*) = GUAMIRIM.

vamos, form of IR [53].

vampírico –ca (*adj.*) vampiric.

vampiro (*m.*) vampire, ghoul; bloodsucker, human leech extortioner; a vampire bat; a "vamp" (temptress).

vanádio (*m., Chem.*) vanadium.

vanaquiá (*m.*) = PAPAGAIO-DE-COLEIRA.

vancê, pop. form of VOCÊ.

vandalismo (*m.*) vandalism.

vândalo (*m.*) vandal.

vanglória (*f.*) vainglory, vanity, empty boasting.

vangloriar (*v.t.*) to inspire vainglory in; (*v.r.*) to boast, swagger; to talk big; to pride oneself on or upon; to sing one's own praises, blow one's own horn.

vanglorioso –sa (*adj.*) vainglorious, conceited.

vanguarda (*f.*) vanguard; forefront. **literatura de**— avant-garde writing.

vanilina (*f.*) vanillin.

vaníloquo, vaniloqüente (*adj.*) of words, vain, empty.

vantagem (*f.*) advantage, upper hand; odds; benefit, gain; boon; feat. **contar**—**s,** to boast, swagger. **levar**—, to gain the upper hand. **levar a**—, to have the whip hand. **Qual é a**—? What's the advantage? What does one gain by that? **tirar**—**de,** to take advantage of, profit by.

vantajoso –ja (*adj.*) advantageous, profitable, beneficial, favorable.

vão [vãos] **vã** [vãs] (*adj.*) vain, empty; useless; conceited; false; hollow; (*m.*) empty space; opening in wall for door or window; span of a bridge.

vápido –da (*adj.*) vapid, insipid. [*Poetical*]

vapor [-es] (*m.*) vapor, steam; steamship, steamer. **cavalo**—, horsepower.

vaporar (*v.t.*) to exhale, emit (as vapor); to reek; (*v.r.*) to evaporate.

vaporização (*f.*) vaporization.

vaporizador –dora (*adj.*) vaporizing; (*m.*) vaporizer atomizer.

vaporizar (*v.t.*) to vaporize; (*v.r.*) to evaporate.

vaporoso –sa (*adj.*) vaporous, misty; fanciful; vain.

vaqueano (*m.*) one who knows his way about; an old hand (at anything); = TAPEJARA.

vaqueirada (*f.*) a group of cowpunchers.

vaqueirar (*v.i.*) to work as a cowboy.

vaqueiro –ra (*adj.*) of or pert. to cattle; (*m.*) cowboy, cowpuncher; herdsman.

vaquejada (*f.*) round-up of cattle.

vaquejador (*m.*) cattle trail.

vaqueta [ê] (*f.*) thin leather used for lining; umbrella rib drum stick.

vaquilhona (*f.*) young heifer.
vara (*f.*) pole, shaft, staff; rod, wand, cane; switch, stick; shoot, withe; judgeship; jurisdiction; scourge, punishment; a lineal measure of 1.10 meters or 43.31 in.—**de condão,** magic wand.—**de foguete** = CUARI-BRAVO (a marigold).—**de porcos,** a herd of swine.—**real,** royal scepter. **camisa de onze—s,** tight spot; awkward fix. **salto de—,** pole vault(ing).
varação (*f.*) portage.
varada (*f.*) a whack with a stick.
varador (*m.*) gauger (of casks, etc.).
varadouro (*m.*) a place where boats are beached for repairs. Var. VARADOIRO.
varal (*m.*) shaft (of a cart, etc.); pole a (of litter, sedan chair, etc.); clothesline; a place where clothes or jerky (beef) are spread to dry.
varanda (*f.*) veranda, porch; balcony; terrace; dining room.
varandim (*m.*) narrow balcony; low window grating.
varão (*m.*) a man; a male; a "he-man"; (*adj.*) male.
varapau (*m.*) long pole; (*m.,f.,colloq.*) a "bean pole" (very thin person).
varar (*v.t.*) to beat with a cane; to broach a boat; to pierce through; to drive out or away; to ford a stream; to go beyond. (*v.i.*) to run aground.—**por,** to push or dash through. **varado por uma bala,** pierced by a bullet.
varedo [ê] (*m.*) roof timbers.
vareio (*m.*) derangement, delirium; a beating; reprimand.
vareiro (*m.*) poler of a boat.
vareja (*f.*) blowfly, botfly, c.a. MÔSCA-VAREJEIRA.
varejadura (*f.*), **varejamento** (*m.*) act of flailing, etc. See the verb VAREJAR.
varejante (*m.*) retailer [= VAREJISTA].
varejão (*m.*) punting pole.
varejar (*v.t.*) to beat, flail, (a carpet, etc.); to gauge (contents or capacity of a pipe, cask, etc.); to knock down (fruit) with a long pole; to batter (with gun fire); to ransack; (*v.i.*) of wind, to bluster.
varejeira (*f.*) = VAREJA.
varejista (*adj.; m.,f.*) retail (merchant).
varejo (*m.*) a legal search or inspection; severe criticism; retail trade. **a—,** at retail. **loja de—,** retail store. **preço a—,** retail price.
vareque (*m.*) varec, seaweed.
vareta [ê] (*f.*) slender stick, switch; ramrod; leg of a draw ing compass; (*Bot.*) = ALHO-DO-MATO and BATATINHA-DO-CAMPO.
vareteiro (*m., Bot.*) seron (*Phyllostylon brasiliensis*).
varga (*f.*) wet meadowland; a kind of fish net.
varge, várgea, vargem (*f.*) = VÁRZEA.
vargedo (*m.*) extensive meadowlands.
vária (*f.*) see under VÁRIO.
variabilidade (*f.*) variability.—**relativa,** (*Stat.*) relative variability.
variação (*f.*) variation; variance.
variado –**da** (*adj.*) varied, varying, diverse; motley; variegated; (*colloq.*) fickle.
variante (*adj.*) variant, varying; (*f.*) variation; change in direction of a road; variant spelling, etc.
variar (*v.t.*) to vary, alter, change; to diversify; to variegate; to alternate; (*v.i.*) to be at variance, disagree; to deviate, swerve; to be fickle; to go out of one's mind; (*v.r.*) to vary.
variável (*adj.*) variable, changeable; fickle, inconstant.
varicela (*f.*) chicken pox, c.a. CATAPORA(S).
varicocele (*f., Med.*) varicocele.
varicoso –**sa** (*adj.*) varicose.
variedade (*f.*) variety, variation, variance, diversity; varied assortment; (*pl.*) variety show.
variegação (*f.*) variegation.
variegado –**da** (*adj.*) variegated; motley.
variegar (*v.t.*) to variegate; to diversify; to vary.
varina (*f.*) Portuguese fishwife (from Ovar).
varinha [dim. of VARA] (*f.*) wand.—**de condão,** magic wand.
varino (*m.*) long, narrow boat.
vário –**ria** (*adj.*) various, several, sundry, divers; varied; diverse; variegated; at variance; (*f.*) brief paragraph on editorial page [= SUELTO, TÓPICO].
varíola (*f.*) smallpox.—**discreta,** (*Med.*) discrete smallpox.
variolar (*adj.*) variolar.
variolóide (*f.*) varioloid, mild smallpox.
varioloso –**sa** (*adj.*) variolous; (*m.,f.*) a victim of smallpox.

variômetro (*m., Elec.*) variometer; (*Aeron.*) climb indicator.
variz (*f., Med.*) varix, varicose vein; (*Zool.*) varix (of a shell).
varja (*f.*) = VÁRZEA.
varonia (*f.*) masculinity; virility, manhood.
varonil (*adj.*) virile, manly.
varonilidade (*f.*) virility, masculinity.
varrão, varrasco (*m.*) boar (adult male swine), esp. one selected for reproduction [= BARRÃO].
varredeira (*f., Naut.*) studding sail; c.a. CUTELO, VAR-REDOURA.
varredela (*f.*) a sweeping; a clean sweep.
varredor –**dora** (*adj.*) sweeping; (*m.,f.*) sweeper.
varredoura (*f.*) wholesale slaughter, havoc; = VARRE-DEIRA.
varredura (*f.*) act or operation of sweeping; sweepings.
varrer (*v.t.*) to sweep (up, off, away, out).—**a testada,** to clear one's conscience.
varrição (*f.*) act of sweeping.
varrido –**da** (*adj.*) swept, brushed; stark crazy.—**do juízo,** stark mad.—**pelo vento,** wind-swept. **doido—,** complete lunatic. (*m.*) = VARREDURA.
várzea (*f.*) meadow, plain; low grassy land bordering a stream or body of water.
vás, form of IR [53].
vasa (*f.*) slime, mud, ooze, mire; silt.
vasca (*f.*) seizure, convulsion, spasm.—**s da morte,** death throes; dying gasps.
vascaíno –**na** (*adj.*) of or pert. to the Vasco da Gama soccer club in Rio de Janeiro; (*m.,f.*) a member or fan of that club.
vascolejador –**dora** (*adj.*) shaking; (*m.,f.*) shaker.
vascolejamento (*m.*) act or operation of shaking.
vascolejar (*v.t.*) to shake (a bottle of medicine, etc.); to stir up.
vasconço (*m.*) the Basque language; fig., gibberish.
vascular (*adj., Biol., Bot., Med., etc.*) vascular.
vascularidade (*f.*) vascularity.
vasculhadeira (*f.*) woman sweeper. Var. BASCULHADEIRA.
vasculhador –**dora** (*adj.*) sweeping; (*m.*) sweeper; one who pries into the affairs of others; dust mop. Var. BASCUL-HADOR.
vasculhar (*v.t.*) to sweep and dust walls and ceilings with a long broom; fig., to pry into every nook and corner; to rummage, ransack; to forage; (*Milit.*) to mop up. Var. BASCULHAR.
vasculho (*m.*) a long-handled broom for sweeping walls and ceilings.
vasento –**ta** (*adj.*) miry, slimy [= VASOSO].
vasilha (*f.*) vessel (for liquids); barrel, cask.
vasilhame (*m.*) a quantity of vessels.
vaso (*m.*) vase, vessel, receptacle; flower pot; (*Anat., Zool.*) duct, tube, vessel.—**de capitel,** (*Arch.*) the bell of a Corinthian or composite capital.—**de eleição,** God-chosen vessel (person).—**de guerra,** man-of-war.—**de rio,** river bed.—**sanguíneo,** blood vessel.—**s seminíferos,** (*Anat., Zool.*) seminiferous tubules.
vasomotor (*adj., Physiol.*) vasomotor.
vasoso –**sa** (*adj.*) = VASENTO.
vasquear (*v.i.*) to become scarce; to experience mortal agony.
vasqueiro –**ra** (*adj.*) that causes convulsions; scarce, uncommon; troublesome; critical, difficult [times]; cross-eyed; one-eyed [= VESGUEIRO].
vasquejar (*v.i.*) to suffer convulsions, death throes.
vasquim (*m.*) waist (upper part) of a woman's dress.
vassalagem (*f.*) vassalage.
vassalo –**la** (*adj.; m.,f.*) vassal.
vassoura (*f.*) broom; (*m.*) clerk whose job it is to sweep out the store or office; (*Bot.*) = CALÇÃO-DE-VELHO, CAR-QUEJA-AMARGA, MALVA-RELÓGIO-GRANDE. Var. VASSOIRA. —**de-ferro** = CHILCA.—**do-campo,** the clammy hopseed bush (*Dodonaea viscosa*).—**nêles!** Out with them!—**nova varre bem,** A new broom sweeps clean.—**vermelha** = FAXINA.
vassourada (*f.*) a blow with a broom; a broom stroke; a sweeping up; a house-cleaning (political or other). Var. VASSOIRADA.
vassoural (*m.*) an area abounding in sida, esp. *S. carpini-folia.* Var. VASSOIRAL.
vassourar (*v.t.*) to sweep (up.). Var. VASSOIRAR.
vassoueiro (*m.*) broommaker; broom seller. Var. VASSOIREIRO.
vassourinha (*f.*) little broom; whiskbroom; (*Bot.*) = CAL-

CÃO-DE-VELHO; MALVA-RELÓGIO-GRANDE. Var. VASSOI-RINHA.—**de-botão**, a buttonbush (*Cephalanthus occidentalis*).—**de-varrer**, sweet broomwort (*Scoparia dulcis*), c.a. TAPIXABA.—**do-mato** = FAXINA.

vastidão, vasteza (*f.*) vastness; wilderness.

vasto –ta (*adj.*) vast; very extensive.

vatapá (*m.*) a Braz. dish made of manioc meal, mixed with fish or meat, and seasoned.

vate (*m.*) seer; bard.

vaticano –na (*adj.*) vaticanal; (*m.*) [*cap.*] Vatican; [*not cap.*] a large Amazon River steamboat having two stacks and two propellers, and displacing up to 1,000 tons. It is a modern outgrowth of the GAIOLA (which see); (*f.*) [*cap.*] the Vatican library.

vaticinação (*f.*) = VATICÍNIO.

vaticinador –dora (*adj.*) prophesying; (*m.*) prophet; (*f.*) prophetess.

vaticinante (*adj.*) prophesying.

vaticinar (*v.t.*) to vaticinate, prophesy, foretell; to guess.

vaticínio (*m.*) prophesy, prediction.

vatídico –ca (*adj.*) prophetic; oracular.

vau (*m.*) ford, river crossing; fig., opportunity; (*Naut.*) beam; (*pl.*) cross timbers. **errar o—**, to lose out, come off badly, miss a chance.

vaurá (*m.,f.*) an Indian of the Waura, an Arawakan tribe on the upper Xingu River in Mato Grosso; (*adj.*) pert. to or designating this tribe. Var. UAURÁ.

vavavá, vavavu (*m.*) hubbub, rumpus.

vaza (*f.*) a trick (round of cards); ornamental carving. **cortar as—s à alguém**, to clip another's wings; take the wind out of his sails. **não perder—**, to miss no trick; to overlook no opportunity.

vaza-barris (*m.*) a place where shipwrecks occur.

vazador –dora (*adj.*) that empties, etc. See the verb VAZAR; (*m.*) one who or that which empties, pours, etc. See the verb; a leather punch.

vazadouro (*m.*) drain, sewer.

vazadura (*f.*), **vazamento** (*m.*) act of emptying or draining.

vazante (*adj.*) that drains or empties; (*f.*) "(1) low damp land; (2) a wide river valley; (3) any lowland which is inundated at the time of river floods; (4) in northeast Brazil, plant cultivation as practiced on the river bed and on the sides of water-holes during the dry season; (5) low water-mark." [*GBAT*]

vazão (*f.*) an ebbing and flowing; emptying; outgo; rate of flow; fig., a way out (solution).

vazar (*v.t.*) to empty (de, of; em, in); to pour (liquid metal); to hollow out (something); to put out (an eye); (*v.i.*) to leak, ooze out; to flow (out, away); (*v.r.*) to drain.

vaziar (*v.*) = ESVAZIAR.

vazio –zia (*adj.*) empty; vacant; devoid of; (*m.*) vacuum [= VÁCUO]; (*pl.*) flanks (of a horse, etc.).

vb. = VERBO (verb).

v/c = VOSSA CONTA (your account).

vê, form of VER [81].

veação (*f.*) hunting; venison.

veada (*f.*) doe.

veadeiro (*m.*) deer hound; deer hunter.

veado (*m.*) any deer. [The tendency is to use CERVO instead of VEADO, because of an obscene slang connotation of the latter word.]—**campeiro** (or -baio, or -branco), a pampas deer (*Ozotoceros bezoarticus*), c.a. GUAÇUTI.—**galheiro** or—**do(s)-mangue(s)**, a marsh deer (*Odocoileus suacuapara*), c.a. SUAÇUAPARA, CARIACU.—**galheiro-grande** = CERVO.—**mateiro** (= *pardo*), a brocket (*Mazama rufa*), c.a. GUAÇU-ETÊ, GUAÇUPITA, GUARAPARÁ, GUATAPARÁ, SUAÇUETÊ, SUAÇUPITA.—**negro** (or -roxo), a brocket (*Mazama rondoni*), c.a. FOBOCA, GUARAPU.—**virá**, a brocket (*Mazama simplicicornis*), c.a. CATINGUEIRO, GUAÇUBIRÁ, SUAÇUTINGA, VIRÁ, VIROTE.

vector (*m.*) vector. Var. VETOR.

veda, vedação (*f.*) act of impeding, forbidding, stopping, etc. See the verb VEDAR; barrier, rail; screen; fence.

vedado –da (*adj.*) forbidden; closed off, walled off.

vedar (*v.t.*) to forbid; to stop, check; to block, bar; to hedge off; (*v.i.,v.r.*) to stop.

vêde, vêdes, forms of VER [81].

vedeta [dê] (*f.*) lookout place or man, esp. a mounted sentry; mosquito (speed) boat; the star (in a cast of actors).—**da-praia**, a sandpiper, **em—**, standing out (of line).

vêdo (*m.*) barrier, fence, rail.

vedor (*m.*) overseer; dowser.

veeiro (*m.*) vein or fissure (in rock or earth); line of cleavage (in a crystal).

veem, form of VIR [82].

vêem, form of VER [81].

veemencia (*f.*) vehemence; eagerness; boisterousness; force, might.

veemente (*adj.*) vehement, impetuous; ardent, eager, keen.

vegetação (*f.*) vegetation; plants. **vegetações, adenóides**, adenoids.—**rasteira**, underbrush.

vegetal (*adj.*) vegetal; (*m.*) vegetable.

vegetar (*v.i.*) to vegetate.

vegetariano –na (*adj.*; *m.,f.*) vegetarian.

vegetativo –va (*adj.*) vegetative.

veia (*f.*) vein, blood vessel; rib of a leaf; bent, disposition.—**axilar**, axillary vein.—**artéria**, pulmonary artery.—**s ázigas**, azygos veins.—**braquial**, brachial vein.—**cava, vena cava.—da arca** or—**real** = SALVATELA.—**frênica**, phrenic vein.—**s leônicas**, ranine veins (of the tongue).—**s medianas**, median veins.—**pilórica**, pyloric vein.—**porta**, portal vein.—**s superficias**, superficial veins.—**suprarrenal**, suprarenal vein.—**s titilares**, costoaxillary veins.—**traqueal**, tracheal vein. **estar de—**, to be in the mood; to be inspired. Cf. VEIO.

veicular [e-i] (*adj.*) vehicular; (*v.t.*) to transport in vehicles; to transmit.

veículo (*m.*) vehicle; means or medium of conveyance, transmission, or communication; (*Pharm.*) vehicle; (*colloq.*) menses.

veiga (*f.*) lowland; fertile plain; = VÁRZEA.

veio (*m.*) vein, lode, seam, streak; grain (of wood); steel shaft; fig., essence. Cf. VEIA; (*v.*) form of VIR [82].

veja, vejais, vejam, vejamos, vejas, vejo, forms of VER [81].

vela (*f.*) sail; candle; wake [= VELADURA].—**da-pureza**, the moundlily yucca (*Y. gloriosa*).—**de ignição**, spark plug.—**de espicho**, a kind of lateen sail.—**internacional**, (*Photom.*) international candle.—**latina**, lateen sail. **à—**, under sail. **acender uma—a Deus e outra ao diabo**, to be two-faced, double-dealing; to play both ends against the middle; to carry water on both shoulders. **fazer-se à** (or **de**)—, to set sail. **luz de—**, candlelight. **navio de—**, sailing vessel.

velacho (*m.*) foresail; nickname.

velado –da (*adj.*) veiled, shrouded.

velador –dora (*adj.*) watching; (*m.,f.*) watcher; (*m.*) large wooden candleholder.

veladura (*f.*) act of veiling; glazing (of a painting).

velame, velâmen (*m.*) set of sails; a cloak or covering; disguise; (*Bot.*) velamen.

velamento (*m.*) act of hiding or covering.

velar (*v.t.*) to veil, cover, cloak; to watch, keep an eye upon; (*v.i.*) to keep awake, keep vigil (as at a wake); (*adj., Phonet.*) velar.—**pelos interesses de**, to watch out for the interests of.—**por**, to watch over.

velarizar (*v.t., Phonet.*) to velarize.

velatura (*f.*) glazing of a picture.

veleidade (*f.*) velleity, mere wish; whim; fancy; want of common sense.

veleiro (*m.*) sailing vessel; sailmaker.

velejar (*v.i.*) to sail.

veleta [lê] (*f.*) weather vane; fickle person.

velha (*f.*) see under VELHO.

velhacaço –ça (*adj.; m.*) = VELHACO.

velhacada, –cagem (*f.*) = VELHACARIA.

velhacão (*m.*) consummate scoundrel; big crook.

velhacar (*v.t.,v.i.*) to trick, cheat, swindle.

velhacaria (*f.*) rascality; crookedness; skulduggery.

velhaco –ca (*adj.*) scoundrelly, crooked; foxy, guileful, shifty; (*m.*) crook, slicker, scalawag, rascal. **Para—, —e meio**, Set a thief to catch a thief.

velhada (*f.*) old man's talk or behavior; group of old people; old folks collectively.

velhaquear (*v.i.*) to act like a VELHACO; of a horse, to buck; (*v.t.*) to cheat, trick, deceive (someone).

velharia (*f.*) act, saying, habit, etc., typical of old folks; any old thing; corny expression, joke, etc.; (*pl.*) antiques.

velhice (*f.*) old age; old people as a class; old person's crabbedness.

velhinho –nha (*adj.*) quite old; (*m.*) little old man; (*f.*) little old woman; also = VIUVINHA (a bird).

velho –lha (*adj.*) old; aged, elderly; ancient; old-fashioned; not new, worn out; experienced; (*m.*) old man; (*m.pl.*) old folks; the aged; (*f.*) old woman. **mais—**, older;

senior. **o—**, (*colloq.*) the old man (father). **O seguro morreu de—**, Better safe than sorry. **um—cacête** (or **chato**), an old fogy; a graybeard.

velhote (*m.*) a man past middle age; an old sport.

velhusco –ca, velhustro –tra (*adj.; m.*) = VELHO; VELHOTE.

velino (*m.*) parchment paper.

velo (*m.*) fleece; wool.

velocidade (*f.*) velocity, speed, swiftness, fleetness.— **angular**, (*Physics*) angular velocity.—**ascencional**, (*Aeron.*) rate of climb.—**de aterrisagem**, (*Aeron.*) landing speed.—**de cruzeiro**, cruising speed.—**relativa**, (*Aeron.*) air speed. **em plena—**, at full speed. **indicador de—**, speed indicator.

velocímetro (*m.*) speedometer; velocimeter.

velocino (*m.*) sheepskin.—**de ouro**, Golden Fleece.

velocípede (*m.*) velocipede, tricycle.

velocíssimo –ma (*absol. superl. of* VELOZ) most speedy; very fast.

velódromo (*m.*) velodrome.

velório (*m.*) wake (vigil over a corpse).

veloso –sa (*adj.*) woolly, shaggy.

veloz (*adj.*) swift, speedy, fast, flying.

veludilho (*m.*) velveteen; (*Bot.*) common feather cockscomb (*Celosia cristata*); c.a. VELUDO, CRISTA-DE-GALO.

veludíneo –nea (*adj.*) velvety [= AVELUDADO].

veludinha (*f.*) velours.

veludinho (*m.*) = ALFAIATE (bird).

veludo (*m.*) velvet; velure; velvety object or surface; (*Bot.*) a pavonia (*P. malacophylla*); also = VELUDILHO and CARURU-VERMELHO.—**branco** = CELÓSIA-BRANCA.— **-de-penca** = CAUDA-DE-RAPÔSA.—**piquê**, corduroy.

veludoso –sa, velutíneo –nea (*adj.*) velvety.

vem, form of VIR [82].

V.Emª = VOSSA EMINÊNCIA (Your Eminence).

vem-vem (*m.*) = GATURAMO.

venábulo (*m.*) javelin, spear.

venado –da (*adj.*) veined.

venal (*adj.*) venal; venous.

venalidade (*f.*) venality; mercenariness.

venatório –ria (*adj.*) of, or pert. to, hunting.

vencedor –dora (*adj.*) victorious, winning, conquering; (*m.,f.*) winner; victor.

vencer (*v.t.*) to conquer, vanquish; to defeat; to surmount, overcome; to subdue; (*v.i.*) to win by victory; to gain by effort; to earn (as a salary); to succeed; (*v.r.*) to conquer oneself; of a note, etc., to mature, fall due.

vencido –da (*adj.*) conquered, defeated, overcome; of a note or other obligation, past due, unpaid, outstanding; (*m.,f.*) one who has been defeated. **dar-se por—**, to admit defeat, quit, give up, throw in the sponge.

vencimento (*m.*) conquering; victory; pay, wage, salary; maturity or due date (of an obligation). **dar—a**, to cope with. **fôlha de—s**, payroll. **no—**, at maturity.

vencível (*adj.*) conquerable.

venda (*f.*) a sale; small grocery store; blindfold.—**a retro**, a sale conditioned on the seller's right of repurchase. **à—**, on sale; for sale.

vendar (*v.t.*) to blindfold.

vendaval (*m.*) gale.

vendável (*adj.*) having a ready market. Cf. VENDÍVEL.

vendedor (*m.*) seller; salesman. [Fem. VENDEDEIRA.]—**a domicílio**, house-to-house salesman.—**ambulante**, hawker, street peddler.

vendeiro (*m.*) small grocer.

vender (*v.t.*) to sell; to trade, barter; to hawk, peddle; to betray (take a bribe for).—**a consciência**, to bribe one's conscience.—**a dinheiro**, to sell for cash.—**a prestações**, to sell on installment payments.—**a retalho or a varejo**, to sell at retail.—**a vida. caro**, to sell one's life dear.— **farinha**, (*colloq.*) to go about with the shirttail showing. —**fiado**, to sell on credit.—**muito caro o seu peixe**, to drive a hard bargain.—**por atacado**, to sell at wholesale. —**saúde**, to glow with health. [**Você está vendendo saúde**, You are the picture of health.] **ter para dar e—**, to have more than enough.

vendeta (*f.*) vendetta, blood feud.

vendido –da (*adj.*) sold; bribed.

vendilhão (*m.*), **–lhona** (*f.*) peddler.

vendível (*adj.*) salable. Cf. VENDÁVEL.

vendo, pres. part. (gerund) of VER [81].

venefício (*m.*) criminal poisoning.

veneno (*m.*) venom, poison; spite, malice.

venenoso –sa (*adj.*) venomous, poisonous; malicious.

venera (*f.*) badge, emblem; insignia, decoration; formerly, pilgrim's scallop shell.

venerabilidade (*f.*) venerability.

venerabundo –da (*adj.*) reverent.

veneração (*f.*) veneration, reverence; worship.

venerado –da (*adj.*) revered.

venerador –dora (*adj.*) venerating; (*m.,f.*) venerator.

venerando –da (*adj.*) = VENERÁVEL.

venerar (*v.t.*) to venerate, revere.

venerável (*adj.*) venerable.

venéreo –rea (*adj.*) venereal; (*m., colloq.*) syphilis.

vênero –ra (*adj.*) of or pert. to Venus [*Poetical*]

veneta (*f.*) fit of madness; conniption; sudden notion; whim; vagary. **cheio de—s**, capricious. **dar na—**, to be struck with an idea.

Veneza (*f.*) Venice.

veneziano –na (*adj.; m.,f.*) Venetian; (*f.*) wooden window shutter having louvered slats.

venezuelano –na (*adj.; m.,f.*) Venezuelan.

venh-+verb endings, forms of VIR [82].

vênia (*f.*) permission, leave; forgiveness, indulgence; a bow. **fazer—**, to bow the head. **pedir—**, to beg leave; to ask forgiveness.

venial (*adj.*) venial.

venialidade (*f.*) veniality.

ven. or = VENERADOR (venerator).

venoso –sa (*adj.*) venous; veiny.

vens, form of VIR [82].

venta (*f.*) nasal cavity, nostril; (*pl.*) nose. **nas—s de**, (*colloq.*) right in front of, under the nose of.

ventanejar (*v.i.*) of the wind, to blow hard.

ventania (*f.*) a high wind.

ventanilha (*f.*) pocket of a billiard table.

ventar (*v.i.*) of the wind, to blow.

ventarola (*f.*) palm-leaf fan or one like it.

ventilação (*f.*) ventilation.

ventilador –dora (*adj.*) ventilating; (*m.*) ventilator; electric fan; air shaft.

ventilar (*v.t.*) to ventilate; to discuss, debate; to winnow.

vento (*m.*) wind, breeze; windiness; flatulence.—**cortante**, a cutting (biting) wind.—**de proa**, head wind.—**de través**, cross wind.—**em pôpa**, tail wind.—**s alísios or alisados**, trade winds.—**-leste**, (*Zool.*) = PALOMBETA (a fish). **ao—**, to the wind. **aos quatro—s**, to the four winds. **Bons—s o levem!** Good luck to you! **contra—**, head wind. **de—em pôpa**, splendidly, "famously". **fazer—**, to blow, be windy. **pé (golfada, lufada, rabanada) de—**, a gust of wind, squall.

ventoinha [o-i] (*f.*) weather vane, weathercock; fig., fickle person; (*Zool.*) a lapwing or pewit (*Vanellus vanellus*), c.a. ABIBE.

ventosidade (*f.*) flatulence.

ventoso –sa (*adj.*) windy, gusty; airy, inflated; (*f.*) cupping glass; (*Zool.*) sucker (as of a leech or octopus).

ventral (*adj.*) ventral.

ventre (*m.*) belly, paunch; (*Anat.*) venter; uterus, womb; bulge; antinode.—**livre**, the boon granted to women slaves in Brazil, during the days of the Empire, that their children would be born free. **prisão de—**, constipation, costiveness.

ventricular (*adj.*) ventricular.

ventrículo (*m., Anat., Zool.*) ventricle; ventriculus.

ventrilho (*m.*) bellyband (of a harness).

ventriloquia (*f.*) ventriloquism.

ventríloquo [quo=co] (*m.*) ventriloquist.

ventrudo –da (*adj.*) big-bellied, pot-bellied.

ventura (*f.*) good fortune, happiness; chance, venture, risk; luck (good or bad). **à—**, haphazardly. **por—**, perchance, peradventure.

venturoso –sa (*adj.*) fortunate, happy; risky.

vênula (*f.*) venule, veinlet.

venulado –da (*adj.*) veined.

Vênus (*f., Roman Relig.; Astron.; Zool.*) Venus; by ext., a beautiful woman.

venusto –ta (*adj.*) beautiful, graceful.

ver [81] (*v.t.,v.i.*) to see; (*v.t.*) to behold, descry, witness; to look at; to discern, perceive, comprehend; to ascertain; to make a call upon, visit; to notice, observe; to attend to, take care of; (*v.r.*) to see oneself; to find oneself (in a given situation).—**a mal**, to see evil in (everything).—**com bons olhos**, to look with kindly eyes upon, approve of.—**com os próprios olhos**, to see for oneself, with one's own eyes.—**dobrado**, to see double.—**para crer**, Seeing is believing.—**-se a braços com**, to find oneself swamped, up to one's neck (in something, as work), or saddled with a job, obligation, etc.—**se ao espelho,** to see oneself in the mirror.—**se em apêrto,** to find oneself in a tight spot.—**se em talas,** to find oneself in a fix, in a jam.—**tudo côr-de-rosa,** to see everything through rose-colored glasses. **a meu—,** as I see it. **a seu—,** in his (their) opinion. **ao—,** on seeing. **Assinar e beber não se faz sem—,** Look before you leap. **bem se vê que,** it's plain to see that; it's quite clear (evident) that. **Bons olhos o vejam!** You're a sight for sore eyes! Welcome! **coisa de se—,** a thing to be seen. **como se vê desta carta,** as we see from this letter. **deixar—,** to show, make clear. [**Deixe—,** Let me see.]. **Está vendo?** See? I told you so! **Eu não vejo bem,** I can't see very well; I have poor eyesight. **Eu só queria—!** I'd just like to see it! **fazer—,** to demonstrate, make evident, clear; to point out; to remind. **ficar a—navios,** to be left holding the bag. **Isso nada tem que—com a questão,** That has nothing to do with the question. **já se vê,** of course, naturally. **Já se viu isso?!** Did you ever?! **maneira de—,** way of looking at things; point of view. **não—um palmo adiante do nariz,** not to see the nose on one's face. **não tem que—,** there can be no question. **não—com bons olhos,** to dislike; to take a dim view of. **Não tenho nada que—com isso,** It is none of my business. **O que os olhos não vêem, o coração não sente,** Out of sight, out of mind. **Ora veja!** Just fancy! Just imagine! **pelo que vejo,** from what I can see; apparently. **Quarto olhos vêem mais do que dois,** Two heads are better than one. **Que prazer em vê-lo!** It is good to see you! **Quem vê cara não vê coração,** The face alone does not reveal the heart. **só para inglês—,** just for show; just to make an impression. **ter que—com alguém,** to have business to attend to with someone. **Vá—,** Go and see. **Vamos—,** Let's see; Let's go see. **Vamos—com quantos paus se faz uma canoa!** We'll see about that! I'll show him!**Vamos a—,** Let's see. **Veja o que faz,** Watch out what you do. **Veja só!** Just imagine! Just think! **vê-se obrigado,** he (she) is obliged. **Você já viu que desafôro?** Have you ever seen [can you imagine] so much nerve (brass)?

veracidade (*f.*) veracity, truthfulness, truth.
vera-efígie (*f.*) faithful portrait; exact copy.
veranear (*v.i.*) to spend the summer.
veraneio (*m.*) a spending of the summer; summer holiday or vacation.
veranico, veranito (*m.*) cool summer; a hot spell during the winter season.
veranista (*m.,f.*) person on a summer holiday or vacation.
verão (*m.*) summer [In the southern hemisphere, from Dec. 21 to Mar. 21]; summertime; (*Zool.*) the scarlet flycatcher (*Pyrocephalus rubinus*), c.a. PASSARINHO-DE-VERÃO, SANGUE-DE-BOI, PRÍNCIPE, MÃE-DO-SOL, MIGUIM. **passar o—,** to spend the summer. **pleno—,** midsummer. **Uma andorinha não faz—,** One swallow does not a summer make. (*v.*) form of VER [81].
veras (*f.pl.*) verities. **com tôdas as—,** in all truth.
verascópio (*m., Photog.*) verascope.
veratrato (*m., Chem.*) veratrate.
verátrico –**ca** (*adj., Chem.*) veratric.
veratrina (*f., Chem.*) veratrine.
veratro (*m., Bot.*) white false helebore (*Veratrum album*), c.a. HELÉBORO-BRANCO.
veraz (*adj.*) veracious, truthful.
verba (*f.*) item, entry, article, separate paragraph; appropriation, fund, allotment.—**de representação,** allowonce (to high government officers, ambassadors, etc.) for official entertainment.—**orçamentária,** budgetary item; fiscal appropriation. **uma conta com discriminção de—s,** an itemized bill.
verbal (*adj.*) verbal; oral.
verbalismo (*m.*) verbalism.
verbalista (*adj.*) verbalistic; (*m.,f.*) verbalist.
verbalizar (*v.i.*) to express verbally; (*Gram.*) to convert into a verb.
verbasco (*m., Bot.*) mullein (*Verbascum*); Brazilian butterflybush (*Buddleia brasiliensis*), c.a. CALÇÃO-DE-VELHO, BARBASCO.
verbena (*f., Bot.*) verbena.—**cidrada** or **odorífera,** lemon verbena lippia (*L. citriodora*), c.a. LÚCIA-LIMA.—**falsa** = GERVÃO.—**oficinal** European verbena (*V. officinalis*), c.a. VERBERÃO, URGEBÃO.
verbenáceo –**cea** (*adj., Bot.*) verbenaceous; (*f.pl.*) the Verbenaceae.
verberação (*f.*) verberation.

verberar (*v.t.*) to verberate, beat, strike; to berate, censure, criticize; (*v.i.*) to reverberate.
verberão (*m.*) = VERBENA-OFICINAL.
verbesina (*f.*) a genus (*Guizotia*) of tropical herbs of the Compositae, esp. *G. abyssinica*, the seeds of which yield an oil.
verbete [bê] (*m.*) note; small piece of paper on which one jots down a note; article in a dictionary or encyclpoedia.
verbiagem (*f.*) verbiage, wordiness.
verbo (*m.*) verb; [*cap.*] the Word, Logos.
verborragia, verborréia (*f.*) verbosity, prolixity, logorrhea.
verbosidade (*f.*) verbosity, verboseness.
verboso –**sa** (*adj.*) verbose, wordy, talkative, loquacious, long-winded.
verdacho –**cha** (*adj.*) greenish.
verdade (*f.*) truth; a truth; truthfulness. **a dizer,** or **para falar, a—,** to tell the truth; properly speaking. **de—,** real, really, truly; sure enough. **Diga de—,** Tell (me) the truth. **É—,** It's true; That's right. **É a—,** It is the truth. **em—,** in truth; truly; in fact; as a matter of fact. **faltar com a—,** not to speak the truth. **na—,** in truth; in fact; actually; truly. **Não é—?** Isn't it (so)? Doesn't it? [Corresponds to Fr. *n'est ce pas?*] **tomar uma coisa por—eterna,** to accept a thing as gospel truth. **uma—evidente por si mesma,** a self-evident truth.
verdadeiro –**ra** (*adj.*) true, truthful, veracious; real, genuine, veritable, actual, legitimate, authentic.
verdascada (*f.*) a switching or caning.
verdascar (*v.t.*) to switch, cane.
verdasco –**ca** (*adj.; m.*) very tart (wine); (*f.*) switch (flexible whip).
verde (*adj.*) green, verdant, emerald; unripe, immature; of meat, fresh; young, tender; (*m.*) the color green; green fodder.—**bexiga,** dark green.—**claro,**—**gaio,**—**mar** light green.—**crê,** green-gold.—**escuro,**—**fundo,**—**montanha,**—**negro,** dark green.—**paris,** Paris green.
verdeal (*adj.*) greenish.
verdecer (*v.i.*) to grow green; to show green.
verdeia (*f.*) white wine with a greenish hue.
verdeio (*m.*) green fodder.
verdejante (*adj.*) that is growing or showing green.
verdejar (*v.i.*) to grow green; to show green.
verdete [dê] (*m.*) verdigris.
verdoengo –**ga, verdolengo** –**ga** (*adj.*) greenish; not quite ripe.
verdor (*m.*) verdure, greenness.
verdoso –**sa** (*adj.*) greenish, verdant.
verdugo (*m.*) hangman, executioner; flange of a railroad car wheel; (*Naut.*) strake.
verdura (*f.*) verdure; (*pl.*) vegetables, greens.
verdureiro (*m.*) green grocer; vegetable huckster. Var. VERDULEIRO.
vereação (*f.*) a town or city council; the office, or term of office, of a councilman.
vereador (*m.*) councilman, alderman.
vereamento (*m.*) function of a town council.
verear (*v.t.,v.i.*) to function as a council or councilman.
vereda [rê] (*f.*) path, lane, walk.
veredicto (*m.*) verdict, finding, decision, judgment.
vêrga (*f.*) slender rod, pole, shaft, stick, switch; (*Naut.*) spar, yard; lintel; furrow.—**vêrga** = CATINGA-DE-NEGRO.
vergal (*m.*) trace (part of harness).
vergalhada (*f.*) a lashing with a whip; rascality.
vergalhão (*m.*) large whip; heavy iron bar.
vergalhar (*v.t.*) to whip.
vergalho (*m.*) whip, quirt; pizzle.
vergame (*m.*) a ship's spars.
vergamota (*f.*) = BERGAMOTA, TANGERINA.
vergão (*m.*) weal, welt.
vergar (*v.t.*) to bend, curve, crook; (*v.i.*) to bow, stoop; to sag, sway.
vergasta (*f.*) a slender switch; a whip.
vergastada (*f.*) a whip lash.
vergastar (*v.t.*) to switch, whip, flog.
vergel [-géis] (*m.*) garden; orchard.
Vergílio (*m.*) Virgil, Vergil.
vergonha (*f.*) shame; feeling of shame; embarrassment; disgrace; dishonor; ignominy. **É uma—,** It's a downright shame. **Pobreza não é—,** Poverty is no disgrace. **Que—!** What a shame! **Que pouca—!** How shameless! How disgraceful! **ter—,** to be ashamed; to be shy. **Você não tem—?** Aren't you ashamed of yourself? Have you no shame?

vergonheira (f.) shameful procedure; disgraceful behavior.

vergonhoso –**sa** (adj.) shameful; disgraceful; disreputable; (f.) the sensitive plant, c.a. SENSITIVA.

vergôntea (f.) shoot, scion; offspring; (Naut.) spar.

vergueiro (m.) slender rod or switch; wooden handle of smith's chisel; (Naut.) rudder chain.

veridicidade (f.) veridicalness.

verídico –**ca** (adj.) truthtelling; truthful; veracious.

verificação (f.) verification; confirmation.—**de contas**, checking of accounts.

verificador –**dora** (adj.) verifying, confirmatory; (m.,f.) verifier, checker.

verificar (v.t.) to verify, prove to be true, corroborate; to ascertain, find out; (v.r.) to happen, take place, occur. **Verificou-se que o boato era falso**, The rumor proved to be false.

verificável (adj.) verifiable.

verme (m.) worm; grub, larva.—**da-guiné**, the Guinea worm (Dracunculus medinensis), c.a. NARU.—**roedor**, larva of clothes moth.—**solitário**, tapeworm.

vermelhaço –**ça** (adj.) very red; ruddy.

vermelhão (m.) cinnabar; vermilion; a blush.

vermelhar, –**lhear**, –**lhejar** (v.t.,v.i.) to redden.

vermelhecer (v.i.) to grow red.

vermelhidão (m.) redness; flush.

vermelinha (f.) three-card monte.

vermelho –**lha** (adj.) red; ruddy; fig, revolutionary; (m.) the color red; (Zool.) any of various snappers of genus Lutianus, esp. the red snapper (L. aya), c.a. VERMELHO-DE-FUNDO, ACARÁ-AIA, CARANHA, CARAPITANGA, CARAPUTANGA, DENTÃO, ACARAPITANGA, CHERNE-VERMELHO, PAPA-TERRA-ESTRÊLA; also = GALHUDO.—**henrique**, the spot snapper (L. synagris), c.a. ARICÓ, ARIOCÓ, AREOCÓ, VERMELHO-ARICÓ, VERMELHO-VERDADEIRO, CARANHO (-VERDADEIRO), SIOBINHA.—**paramirim** = MULATA (vermilion snapper).

vermicida (adj.; f.) vermicide.

vermiculado –**da** (adj.) vermiculate; wormlike.

vermiculária (f., Bot.) goldmoss sedum (S. acre), c.a. VERMICULÁRIA-QUEIMANTE, PÃO-DE-PÁSSAROS.

vermículo (m.) a small worm.

vermiculoso –**sa** (adj.) vermiculate.

vermiculura (f., Arch.) vermiculated work.

vermiforme (adj.) vermiform.

vermífugo –**ga** (adj.; m.) vermifuge.

verminação (f.) vermination.

verminado –**da** (adj.) vermin-ridden; vermin-eaten.

vermineira (f.) worm-breeding place.

verminoso –**sa** (adj.) verminous; wormy.

vermiola (f.) = BICHA-AMARELA.

vermis (m., Anat.) vermis.

vermívoro –**ra** (adj.) feeding on worms.

vermizela (f.) a wireworm or other worm destructive to the roots of plants.

vermute (m.) vermouth.

vernação (f., Bot.) vernation.

vernaculidade (f.), –**lismo** (m.) purism; purity of speech or language.

vernaculista (m.,f.) vernacularist.

vernaculização (f.) vernacularization.

vernacularizar (v.t.) to vernacularize.

vernáculo –**la** (adj.; m.) vernacular, indigenous; pure, correct (language) without foreign words or expressions; puristic (person); (m.) indigenous or native language.

vernal (adj.) vernal.

vernalização (f., Agric.) vernalization.

vernante (adj.) flourishing in spring.

verniz (m.) varnish; fig., polish, refinement; whitewash of wrongdoing. **sapatos de**—, patent leather shoes.

verno –**na** (adj.) = VERNAL.

vero –**ra** (adj.) true [= VERDADEIRO].

Verônica (f.) Veronica; [not cap.] a woman who in street processions carries a veronica; (Bot.) the genus (Veronica) of speedwells; a rosewood (Dalbergia subcymosa).—**oficinal**, the drug speedwell (Veronica officinalis), c.a. CHÁ-DA-EUROPA.

verossímil, verossimilhante (adj.) verisimilar.

verossimilhança, verossimilitude (f.) verisimilitude.

verrina (f.) lampoon; diatribe; bitter criticism.

verrineiro, verrinista (m.) lampooner; bitter critic.

verrucífero –**ra** (adj.) having warts.

verruciforme (adj.) wartlike.

verrucoso –**sa** (adj.) warty.

verruga (f.) wart.—**do-peru**, (Med.) verruga peruana, Oroya fever.

verrugoso –**sa**, –**guento** –**ta** (adj.) warty.

verruma (f.) auger; bit; gimlet.

verrumão (m.) a large auger.

verrumar (v.t.) to bore a hole in (with an auger); to torment, torture; (v.i.) to bore holes (with or as with an auger); to rack one's brains.

versado –**da** (adj.) versed, practiced, conversant, proficient, adept; well-read.

versal (adj.; m.) capital (letter).

versalete [lê] (m.) small capital letter.

versalhada (f.) doggerel verse.

Versalhes (f.) Versailles.

versão (f.) version, translation, rendition; a particular account of some matter; (Med.) version (of a fetus in the uterus).

versar (v.t.) to turn over, examine (something); to study (something); to treat of, deal with (a subject); to put into verse; (v.i.) to write verses.—**acêrca de** (or **em**, or **sôbre**), to deal with, treat of.—**em**, to train, exercise (in a subject); to turn on, hinge on (ref. to a difficulty or problem). **A carta versava assim**: The letter ran thus:

versaria (f.) doggerel [= VERSALHADA].

versátil [-sáteis] (adj.) versatile (but only in the sense of fickle, mercurial, erratic). [There is no single-word equivalent in Port. for versatile in the ordinary sense of many-sided in abilities.]

versatilidade (f.) inconstancy, fickleness.

versejador –**dora** (adj.) versifying; (m.,f.) versifier, poetaster.

versejar (v.i.,v.t.) to versify.

verseto [sê] (m., Bible, Music) verse [= VERSÍCULO].

versicolor (adj.) versicolor.

versículo (m.) versicle, esp. a Bible one.

versificação (f.) versification.

versificador –**dora** (adj.) versifying; (m.,f.) versifier.

versificar (v.t.,v.i.) to versify [= VERSEJAR].

verso (m.) verse, line of poetry; the reverse, as of a coin or page.—**s brancos** or **sôltos**, blank verse.

vértebra (f.) vertebra.

vertebrado –**da** (adj.; m.) vertebrate.

vertebral (adj.) vertebral.

vertedor –**dora** (adj.) spilling; (m.) water pitcher.

vertedouro (m.) spillway; a utensil for bailing water out of a boat. Var. VERTEDOIRO.

vertedura (f.) act or operation of spilling or pouring; overflow.

vertente (adj.) spilling, pouring; under discussion; (f.) watershed; slope of a roof.

verter (v.t.) to spill; pour out; shed; to fill to overflowing; (v.i.) to overflow; to spill.—**de**, to spring from.—**em** (or **para**), to translate into.—**lágrimas**, to shed tears.—**no oceano**, to empty into the ocean.—**sangue**, to spill blood.

vertical (adj.) vertical, perpendicular, upright, plumb; (f.) a vertical line.

verticalidade (f.) verticality.

vértice (m.) vertex, top, summit; apex; crown of the head. —**da cunha**, spearhead.

verticidade (f.) verticity (tendency to turn, as of a magnetic needle).

verticilado –**da** (adj., Bot.) verticillate.

verticilo (m., Bot., Zool.) verticil, whorl.

vertigem (f.) dizziness, giddiness; (Med.) vertigo; (Veter.) staggers.

vertiginoso –**sa** (adj.) vertiginous, dizzy, giddy.

verve (f.) verve.

vês, form of VER [81].

vesânia (f.) mental illness.

vesano –**na** (adj.) mentally ill.

vesgo –**ga** (adj.; m.,f.) cross-eyed (person).

vesguear (v.i.) to squint.

vesgueiro –**ra** (adj.) squint-eyed; cross-eyed.

vesguice (f., Med.) strabismus.

vesicação (f., Med.) vesication.

vesical (adj., Anat.) vesical.

vesicante, vesicatório –**ria** (adj.; m.) vesicant, vesicatory.

vesicar (v.t., Med.) to vesicate, blister.

vesículo (f.) vesicle, sac, cyst; blister; fish's air bladder. —**biliar**, gall bladder, c.a. BÔLSA DO FEL.

vesicular, vesiculoso –**sa** (adj.) vesicular.

vespa [ê] (f.) wasp, hornet; waspish person.—**caçadora**, any spider wasp, such as the tarantula killer, c.a.

CAVALO-DE-CÃO.—**s-da-areia,** sand wasps of the genus *Ammophila* (syn. *Sphex*); c.a. AMÓFILOS.
vespão (*m.*) a large, strong, pugnacious hornet (*Vespa crabro*); also = MARIMBONDO-CAÇADOR and CAVALO-DO-CÃO.
vespeiro (*m.*) hornet's nest (lit. & fig.).
Vésper (*m.*) Vesper, evening star; Venus.
véspera (*f.*) vesper, evening; eve, day before; (*pl.*) vespers. —**de Natal,** Christmas Eve. **às,** or **em,—s de,** on the eve of (lit. & fig.). **nas—s de,** just before.
vesperal (*adj.*) vesper, evening; (*m.*) a book for vespers; (*colloq.*) matinée.
Véspero (*m.*) = VÉSPER.
vespertino **–na** (*adj.*) vespertine; (*f.*) evening star; (*m.*) evening newspaper.
vespídeo (*m., Zool.*) any vespid.
vessar (*v.t.*) to plow deeply.
vessigão (*m., Veter.*) thoroughpin.
vestal (*adj.; f.*) vestal (virgin); (*colloq.*) prude.
veste (*f.*) vestment; garment; (*pl.*) clothing, apparel; regalia.—**talar,** a talar or ankle-length robe or academic gown.
véstia (*f.*) a short, loose jacket; leather jacket.
vestiaria (*f.*) vestry; vestment; wardrobe.
vestiário (*m.*) cloakroom; wardrobe master.
vestibular (*adj.*) vestibular. **exame—,** college entrance exam. **curso—,** pre-college course.
vestíbulo (*m.*) vestibule, foyer, entrance hall, lobby; (*Anat., Zool.*) vestibule.
vestido (*m.*) dress; gown; garment.
vestidura (*f.*) garment; garb, dress; investiture.
vestígio (*m.*) vestige, sign, trace; track, footprint.
vestimenta (*f.*) clothes, apparel, garb; priestly vestments.
vestir [21a] (*v.t.*) to dress, clothe (**de, com,** with); to embellish (**de,** with); (*v.r.*) to dress.—**-se de branco,** to dress in white. **despir um santo para—outro,** to rob Peter to pay Paul.
vestuário (*m.*) wardrobe, apparel, clothing, raiment.
vet. = VETERINÁRIO (veterinary).
vetar (*v.t.*) to veto; by ext., to forbid.
veterano **–na** (*adj.*) veteran; (*m.*) veteran; old-timer.
veterinário **–ria** (*adj.*) veterinary; (*m.*) veterinary; (*f.*) veterinary medicine.
vetiver (*m.*) the khuskhus (*Vetiveria zizanioides*), an East Indian grass cultivated in the tropics, and whose fragrant roots yield an essential oil; c.a. CAPIM-DE-CHEIRO, CAPIM-VETIVER.
veto (*m.*) veto.
vetor (*m.*) = VECTOR.
vetusto **–ta** (*adj.*) ancient, old, time-honored; venerable.
véu (*m.*) veil; all of a sheep's wool sheared at one time.—**de ombros,** or—**umeral,** (*R.C.Ch.*) humeral veil.—**do cálice,** (*R.C.Ch.*) paten veil.—**do paladar,** (*Anat., Zool.*) velum, soft palate.
V.Ex.ᵃ = VOSSA EXCELÊNCIA (Your Excellency).
vexação (*f.*) vexation, annoyance, chagrin.
vexado **–da** (*adj.*) vexed, chagrined.
vexador **–dora** (*adj.*) = VEXATÓRIO; (*m.,f.*) vexer.
vexame (*m.*) vexation, annoyance; chagrin.
vexante (*adj.*) = VEXATÓRIO.
vexar (*v.t.*) to vex, annoy, pester, harass, trouble; to chagrin; (*v.r.*) to suffer chagrin.
vexativo **–va, –tório** **–ria** (*adj.*) vexing.
V.Ex.ᵃ Rev.ᵐᵃ = VOSSA EXCELÊNCIA REVERENDÍSSIMA (Your Most Reverend Excellency).
vexilo [ks] (*m., Bot.*) vexillum, banner, standard.
vez [ê] (*f.*) time, occasion; season, spell, turn, inning; epoch; move (as in a game).—**por outra,** now and then; once in a while. **ainda uma—,** once more. **alguma—,** some time or other. **algumas—,** sometimes; now and then. **às—es,** at times. **às mais das—es,** in most cases. **cada—,** every time; always. **cada—mais,** more and more. **cada—mais fraco,** weaker and weaker. **cada—melhor,** better and better. **cada—menos,** less and less. **cada—pior,** worse and worse. **cada—que,** every time that; whenever. **certa—,** once; one time. **da última—,** last time; the last time. **de—,** for good (and all); once for all. **de—em quando,** now and then; once in a while; from time to time. **de—que,** since; seeing that; in view of that. **de quando em—,** once in a while; occasionally. **de uma—por tôdas,** once for all. **desta (dessa)—,** this time; last time. **duas—es,** twice. **duma só—,** all at once; at one stroke. **duma—para sempre,** once for all. **É a—dêle,** It is his turn; It's his move. **em—de,** instead of. **era uma—,**

once upon a time there was. **fazer a—de,** to serve as; to take the place of. **mais de uma—,** more than once. **mais uma—,** again; once more. **mais vêzes,** more often. **matar de—o assunto,** to settle the matter once for all. **menos que da outra—,** less (or fewer) than the other time. **muita(s)—(es),** often; many times; many a time. **na maioria das—es,** most of the time; more often than not. **no mais das—es,** more often than not; for the most part. **outra—,** again; anew; once more. **outras—es,** at other times; on other occasions; or else. [Outras vezes êle ficava calado, Or else he'd just keep silent.] **pela última—,** for the last time. **por—es,** at times. **por (sua) vez,** in (his, her, your, its) turn. **Quantas—es?** How often? How many times? **raras—es,** rarely; seldom; infrequently. **repetidas—es,** again and again; over and over; many times. **tantas—es,** so many times; so (very) often. **tôda—que,** or **tôdas as—es que,** whenever; every time [that]. **todos de uma—,** all at once (at the same time). **um de cada—,** each one in his turn; one at a time. **uma—,** once; once upon a time; (*adv.*) first. [Uma—p'ra cá, depois p'ra lá, First this way, then that way.] **uma—ou** (or **por**) **outra,** once in a while; now and then. **uma—por tôdas,** once for all. **uma ou duas—es,** once or twice. **uma—que,** if; seeing that; since; because; as long as. [Pode levar o carro uma vez que prometa devolvê-lo logo, You can take the car as long as you promise to return it soon.] **Uma—na vida, outra na morte,** Once in a blue moon. **uma porção de—es,** lots of times. **várias—es,** several times.
vezeiro **–ra** (*adj.*) in the habit of.
vêzo (*m.*) any habit, esp. a bad one.
v.g. = POR EXEMPLO (for example).
V.G. = VOSSA GRAÇA (Your Grace); VOSSA GRANDEZA (Your Highness).
V.H. = VOSSA HONRA (Your Honor).
v.i. = VELA INTERNACIONAL (international candle).
vi, via, forms of VER [81].
via (*f.*) way, road, route; mode, manner; carbon copy; (*prep.*) via, by way of.—**Ápia,** Appian Way.—**expressa,** express highway.—**láctea,** or—**de-são-tiago,** Milky Way.—**permanente,** railroad right of way.—**-sacra,** Way of the Cross.—**s de aproximação** or **de acesso,** approaches (as to a bridge.)—**s de fato,** blows, beatings.—**s marítimas,** sea lanes. **em—s de,** on the way to, about to (happen); in course of. (**por**)—**de regra,** generally, as a rule.
viabilidade (*f.*) viability.
viação (*f.*) transit system; means of transportation.
viador (*m.*) traveler, passenger.
viaduto (*m.*) viaduct.
viagear (*v.i.*) to travel as a salesman.
viageiro **–ra** (*adj.*) pert. to travel; (*m.,f.*) traveler.
viagem (*f.*) voyage, trip.—**de ida e volta,** round trip.—**de núpcias,** wedding trip.—**de regresso,** return trip. **companheiro de—,** fellow traveler. **de—,** traveling, away on a trip.
viajante (*adj.*) traveling; (*m.,f.*) traveler; (*m.*) traveling salesman.
viajar (*v.i.,v.t.*) to travel.
viajor [ô] (*m.*) traveler [= VIAGEIRO].
viam, víamos, forms of VER [81].
vianda (*f.*) viand, article of food (esp. meat).
viandante (*adj.*) wayfaring; (*m.,f.*) wayfarer; traveler.
viandeiro **–ra** (*adj.*) wayfaring; fond of food; (*m.,f.*) wayfarer; (*m.*) glutton.
vias, form of VER [81].
viático (*m.*) money or provisions for a journey; (*Eccl.*) viaticum.
viatura (*f.*) any vehicle.
viável (*adj.*) passable; transitable; practicable; viable.
víbora (*f.*) viper; fig., a venomous person; a harmless alligator lizard (*Diploglossus fasciatus*, family *Aguidae*), c.a. BRIBA; also a skink (MABUYA MABOUYA).—**-cornuta,** horned viper (*Cerastes cornutus*).
viborão (*m.*) = SUCURI.
vibração (*f.*) vibration, oscillation; thrill.
vibrador (*m.*) electric buzzer.
vibrante (*adj.*) vibrant.
vibrar (*v.t.,v.i.*) to vibrate; (*v.i.*) to quiver, thrill; (*v.t.*) to brandish; to strike (the strings of a guitar, etc.).—**de entusiasmo,** to vibrate with enthusiasm.—**impropérios,** to hurl invectives at.—**o auditório,** to thrill the audience. —**um golpe,** to deal a blow.
vibrátil [-teis] (*adj.*) vibratile.

vibratilidade (*f.*) vibratility.
vibratório –**ria** (*adj.*) vibratory.
vibrião (*m., Bacteriol.*) any bacterium of the genus Vibrio. —**colérico** is *Vibrio comma* (syn. *Spirillum cholorae asiaticae*), which causes Asiatic cholera.
vibrissas (*f.pl., Anat., Zool.*) vibrissae; hair in the nostrils.
viburno (*m., Bot.*) any viburnum, esp. *V. lentago* (nanny-berry viburnum) and *V. prunifolium* (blackhaw viburnum), both c.a. ESPINHEIRO-PRÊTO.
viçar (*v.i.*) to grow rank [= VICEJAR].
vicarial (*adj.*) vicarial.
vicariato (*m.*) vicariate.
vicário –**ria** (*adj.*) vicarious.
vice-almirante (*m.*) vice-admiral.
vice-chanceler (*m.*) vice-chancellor.
vice-cônsul (*m.*) vice-consul.
vice-consulado (*m.*) vice-consulate.
vice-governador (*m.*) vice-governor.
vicejante (*adj.*) luxuriant, rank; thriving.
vicejar (*v.i.*) to flourish; to grow luxuriantly; to cause to luxuriate.
vice-legado (*m.*) vice-legate.
vicênio (*m.*) a period of twenty years.
Vicente (*m.*) Vincent.
vice-presidência (*f.*) vice-presidency.
vice-presidente (*m.*) vice-president.
vice-rei (*m.*) viceroy.
vice-reinado (*m.*) viceroyalty.
vice-reitor (*m.*) vice-rector.
vice-versa (*adv.*) vice versa.
viciação (*f.*) vitiation.
viciado –**da** (*adj.*) vitiated; habit-bound; addicted. **jogador**—, confirmed gambler.
viciador –**dora** (*adj.*) vitiating; habit-forming; (*m.,f.*) vitiator.
viciamento (*m.*) = VICIAÇÃO.
viciar (*v.t.*) to vitiate; to demoralize, corrupt; to defile; to adulterate; to debase (currency); to make void; (*v.r.*) to become depraved.
vicinal (*adj.*) vicinal.
vício (*m.*) vice, failing, weakness, besetting sin; bad habit; addiction; depravity, immorality; rut, oestrus.
vicioso –**sa** (*adj.*) vicious; corrupt; defective.
vicissitude (*f.*) vicissitude, change, variation; reverse (of fortune).
viço (*m.*) luxuriance, rank growth; exuberance.
viçoso –**sa** (*adj.*) luxuriant, rank, lush; flourishing; exuberant.
vicunha (*f.*) vicuña (the animal or cloth made from its wool).
Vid. = VIDE (see).
vida (*f.*) life; lifetime; manner of life; calling, career; animation, vivacity, spirit; a biography; life after death. —**acidentada**, checkered career.—**animal**, animal existence.—**aventurosa**, eventful life.—**de sempre**,—**eterna**, eternal life.—**privada**, private life.—**social**, social life; society. **a carestia da**—, the high cost of living. **aborrecido da**—, fed up. **a luta pela**—, hard work; sweat and toil; the struggle for life. **A**—**dêle é isso: de casa p'ro trabalho, do trabalho p'ra casa**, That's all he lives for, his home and his job. **A**—**é um buraco sem fundo** [a wryly humorous expression], Life is a bottomless pit; "you can't win." **A**—**lá é muito cara?** Does it cost a lot to live there? **A**—**não vale nada**, Life just isn't worth living. **acabar com a**—, to commit suicide. **andar com a**—**atrapalhada**, to be beset with personal problems. **Cada qual com a sua**—, Live and let live. **Cada qual é que sabe da sua**—, Well, it's his (her) life. **cair na**—, to fall into prostitution. **com**—, alive. **Como é a**—**lá nos Estados Unidos?** What's it like to live in the States? **É a**—(or, **a vida é essa**, or **assim é a vida**, or **são coisas da vida**), That's life (for you)! **em**—, during life. **estar bem de**—, to be well-off. **falar da**—**alheia**, to gossip about others. **fazer**—**nova**, to turn over a new leaf. **fazer a**—, to lead the life of a prostitute. **ganhar a**—, to earn a living. **Isso lá é**—? Hell, that's no way to live! **Isto é**—? This is *living?* **levar a**—**na macióta**, (*slang*) to lead an easy life. **levar uma**—**de cachorro**, to lead a dog's life. **levar uma**—**desordenada**, to lead a wild life; or, to have exceedingly involved affairs (of all kinds). **má**—, prostitution. **Meta-se com sua**—! Mind your own business! Keep your nose out of my affairs! **mudar de**—, to change one's mode of living. **mulher da**—, a prostitute. **na flor da**—, in the prime of life. **não ter amor à**—, to be reckless of danger.

padrão de—, standard of living. **para tôda a**—, for life. **Que**—**ela tem!** Boy, is she full of life! **Que tal a**—**de casado?** Well, how do you like being married? **seguro de**—, life insurance. **sem**—, lifeless; insipid (ref. to a woman, a show, a color, a picture). **ter êxito na**—, to get on in the world. **tôda a**—, (*adv., colloq.*) ceaselessly; without stopping. [O Sr. vá tôda a vida por esta rua, que no fim encontra a praça, Just keep on going up this street, as far as you can go, and you'll run into the square.] **um boa**— (*colloq.*) a high liver. **uma rapariga da**—**airada**, trull, strumpet.
vidão (*m.*) easy life; soft living.
vide (*f.*) shoot or twig of grape vine.—**branca**, (*Bot.*) the virgin's-bower or traveler's-joy (*Clematis vitalba*), c.a. CIPÓ-DO-REINO.
videiro –**ra** (*adj.*) watchful, prudent; (*m.,f.*) one who watches his affairs; (*f.*) European grape vine (*Vitis vinifera*).
vidência (*f.*) clairvoyance.
vidente (*adj.; m.,f.*) clairvoyant.
vidoca (*f.*) = VIDÃO.
vidoeiro (*m., Bot.*) any birch (*Betula*), c.a. BÉTULA.
vidraça (*f.*) window pane; window sash.—**de guilhotina**, a sash window.
vidraçaria (*f.*) the glazier's.
vidraceiro (*m.*) glazier. **massa de**—, putty.
vidrado –**da** (*adj.*) glazed; glassy, dim; (*m.*) glaze.
vidrar (*v.t.*) to glaze; to render glassy.
vidraria (*f.*) glass factory; china shop.
vidreiro (*m.*) glass worker.
vidrento –**ta** (*adj.*) glassy; brittle.
vidrilho (*m.*) long glass bead.
vidrino –**na** (*adj.*) made of glass; glassy.
vidro (*m.*) glass; small bottle; glass pane.—**bisotê**, beveled glass.—**de aumento**, magnifying glass.—**de moscóvia**, Muscovy glass; muscovite mica.—**do-ar**, a swallow-tailed butterfly (*Papilio proterilans*).—**fôsco** or **esmerilhado**, ground glass.—**solúvel**, (*Chem.*) water glass. **bolinhas de**—, marbles. **corta**—, glass cutter. **Quem tem telhado de**—**não atira pedras no vizinho.** Those who live in glass houses should not throw stones.
vidrioso –**sa** (*adj.*) glassy [= VIDRENTO].
vidual (*adj.*) of or pert. to widowhood or to widows.
vieira (*f.*) a scallop (ornament).
víeis, form of VER [81].
viela (*f.*) narrow way, alley.
viemos, vier, etc., forms of VIR [82].
vienense (*adj.; m.,f.*) Viennese.
vienês –**nesa** (*adj.; m.,f.*) = VIENENSE.
viés (*m.*) bias, slant; (*Sewing*) bias binding. **ao** or **de**—, on the bias. **olhar de**—**para**, to look askance at.
Vig. = VIGÁRIO (Vicar).
viga (*f.*) beam, girder.—**mestra**, main beam.—**transversal**, cross beam. **alma da**—, web of an I-beam.
vigairaria (*f.*) vicariate.
vigamento (*m.*) framework of beams.
vigar (*v.t.*) to provide with beams; to place on beams; = TRAVEJAR.
vigararia (*f.*) = VIGAIRARIA.
vigarice (*f.*) skin game, gyp.
vigário (*m.*) vicar; a fish called PARATUCANO; another called SOLDADO; a joint of sugar cane used for planting; c.a. CABOJE; (*colloq.*) a smart rascal.—**de Cristo**, the Pope. **conto do**—, confidence game.
vigarista (*m.*) swindler, confidence man, crook, gyp artist.
vigência (*f.*) state of being in force; period of validity.
vigente (*adj.*) actual, present; in force.
viger (*v.i.*) to be in force, valid.
vigésimo –**ma** (*adj.; m.*) twentieth.
vigia (*f.*) vigil, watch; lookout; watchfulness; peephole; (*Naut.*) porthole; (*pl.*) underwater reefs; (*m.*) watchman; sentry.
vigiador –**dora** (*adj.*) watching; (*m.*) watcher; guard.
vigiante (*adj.*) vigilant [= VIGILANTE].
vigiar (*v.t.*) to watch, keep on eye on; to watch over; (*v.i.*) to keep vigil; to stand guard.—**por** (or **sôbre**), to take care of, care for, watch out for, look out for.
vigíl [-geis] (*adj.*) watchful; wide-awake.
vigilância (*f.*) vigilance, watchfulness; supervision.
vigilante (*adj.*) vigilant, watchful, careful; on the alert; (*m.,f.*) vigilant person.
vigilar (*v.*) = VIGIAR.
vigilenga (*f.*) in Pará, a small, undecked, almost circular

river fishing boat, usually black, with red sails remindful of a bat's wing.

vigilengo (*m.*) one who fishes in a VIGILENGA.

vigor (*m.*) vigor, force, might, potency; pep, vim; validity. **em—**, in force, in effect. **entrar em—**, to become effective. **pôr em—**, to put in effect.

vigorante (*adj.*) ruling, effective, in force.

vigorar (*v.i.*) to be in force, in effect; (*v.t.*) to invigorate.

vigorizar (*v.t.*) to invigorate.

vigoroso **-sa** (*adj.*) vigorous, lusty, sturdy, hardy; hale, hearty; trenchant.

vigota (*f.*), **-te** (*m.*) small beam or rafter.

vil (*adj.*) vile, base, mean, paltry; cheap, sorry; (*m.,f.*) vile person. **procedimento—**, dirty trick. **a preço—**, dirt-cheap.

vila (*f.*) town, village; villa.

vilanesco **-ca** (*adj.*) loutish, boorish, churlish.

vilania (*f.*) villainy; turpitude.

vilão [-lãos, -lões, -lães] (*m.*) villager; peasant; countryman; villain; (*adj.*) rustic. [fem. VILÃ or VILOA].

vilegiatura (*f.*) country holiday; a sojourn in the country.

vilela, vileta [ê̞ta] (*f.*) small village.

vileza [lê] (*f.*) vileness, baseness, meanness; turpitude.

Vilfredo, Vilfrido (*m.*) Wilfred, Wilfrid.

vilificar (*v.t.*) to vilify.

vilipendiar (*v.t.*) to vilipend; to depreciate; to slight, despise.

vilipêndio (*m.*) contempt, scorn.

vilipendioso **-sa** (*adj.*) slanderous; calumniatory.

vilosidade (*f.*) villosity.

viloso **-sa** (*adj.*) villous, hairy, woolly.

vilota (*f.*) = VILETA.

vim, form of VIR [82].

vime (*m.*) a pliant withe or osier for basket and wickerwork.

vimeiro (*m.*) = SALGUEIRO.

vimíneo **-nea, viminoso** **-sa, vimoso** **-sa** (*adj.*) made of wickers.

vimos, form of VER [81] and of VIR [82].

vim-vim (*m.*) = GATURAMO.

vináceo **-cea** (*adj.*) vinaceous; wine-colored.

vinagre (*m.*) vinegar; a vinegary person.

vinagreira (*f.*) vinegar cruet; (*Bot.*) = FANFÃ and ALGODÃO-DO-BREJO.

vinagreiro (*m.*) vinegar merchant.

vincar (*v.t.*) to crease.

vincendo **-da** (*adj.*) coming due (as a note).

vincetóxico (*m., Bot.*) any milkvine of *Vincetoxicum*.

vincilho (*m.*) fiber cord.

vinco (*m.*) crease, seam, wrinkle, dent, scratch; track of a wagon wheel.

vinculação (*f.*) entailment.

vinculado **-da** (*adj.*) closely bound; under commitment; of property, entailed.—**ao sexo,** (*Biol.*) sex-linked.

vinculador **-dora** (*adj.*) entailing; binding; (*m.,f.*) one who or that which entails or binds.

vinculagem (*f., Biol.*) linkage.

vincular (*v.t.*) to bind, tie, link; to pledge; to entail (property); to perpetuate; (*adj.*) entailing, binding.

vínculo (*m.*) vinculum, bond of union, tie; an entailed estate.

vinda (*f.*) advent, arrival. **idas e—s,** goings and comings.

vindecaá (*m., Bot.*) a galangal (*Alpinia*); a panic grass (*Panicum brevifolium*).

vindes, form of VIR [82].

vindicação (*f.*) claim, demand; vindication.

vindicador **-dora** (*adj.*) vindicating; (*m.,f.*) vindicator.

vindicar (*v.t.*) to vindicate. Cf. VINGAR.

vindicativo **-va** (*adj.*) vindicatory.

vindima (*f.*) vintage, grape crop, gathering of grapes; harvest. **festa da—,** grape festival.

vindimador (*m.*) vintager.

vindimar (*v.t.*) to gather grapes; to do away with (kill).

vindita (*f.*) legal punishment; revenge; retaliation.

vindo (*past and pres. part. of* VIR [82]) coming; arrived.—**de,** proceeding from.

vindouro **-ra** (*adj.*) coming, future, hereafter; (*m.,f.*) a newcomer.

víneo **-nea** (*adj.*) vinous; wine-colored.

vingador **-dora** (*adj.*) avenging; vindictive; (*m.,f.*) avenger.

vingança (*f.*) vengeance, revenge.

vingar (*v.t.*) to avenge, revenge; to take satisfaction for; to reach, arrive at, attain to; (*v.i.*) to win out, be success-

ful; to thrive, flourish; (*v.r.*) to take vengeance (**de, contra,** on). Cf. VINDICAR.

vingativo **-va** (*adj.*) vengeful, vindictive, spiteful.

vinh+verb endings=forms of VIR [82].

vinha (*f.*) vineyard.—**d'alhos,** marinade for meat and fish of garlic, vinegar and spices.

vinhaça (*f.*) drunkenness.

vinháceo **-cea** (*adj.*) winy.

vinhado (*m.*) a cage bird.

vinhão (*m.*) wine of superior quality used for blending.

vinhateiro (*m.*) winegrower.

vinhático (*m.*) a tropical tree (*Plathymenia reticulata*) of the mimosa family; the goldwood ape's-earring (*Pithecellobium vinhatico*) and others of this genus.—**de-espinho,** an ape's-earring (*Pithecellobium tortum*).—**do-campo,** an earpod tree (*Enterolobium ellipticum*), c.a. FAVELA-BRANCA.

vinhedo (*m.*) large vineyard.

vinheiro (*m.*) winegrower.—**do-campo** = GOMEIRA.

vinheta (*f.*) vignette.

vinhetista (*m.,f.*) vignettist.

vinho (*m.*) wine.—**tinto,** claret.

vinhoca (*f.*) cheap wine.

vinícola (*adj.*) winegrowing.

vinicultor (*m.*) viniculturist; wine maker; winegrower.

vinicultura (*f.*) viniculture; wine making; winegrowing.

vinífero **-ra** (*adj.*) wine-producing.

vinificação (*f.*) vinification; wine making.

vinificador (*m.*) vinificator.

vinoso **-sa** (*adj.*) vinous.

vinte (*adj.; m.*) twenty.—**e-um,** blackjack (card game).—**e-um-pintado** = TICO-TICO-REI (a finch).—**pés** = ACUNÃ. **dar no—,** to hit the nail on the head; to guess rightly.

vintém (*m.*) an old minor coin of Brazil, worth 20 RÉIS; a penny.—**poupado,—ganho** (or, as the people say, **ganhado,** to rhyme with **poupado**), Penny saved, penny earned. **sem—,** penniless.

vinteno **-na** (*adj.*) twentieth; (*f.*) a score (20).

viola (*f.*) a type of small guitar; viola, c.a. VIOLETA; an angelfish (*Squatina sp*); a guitar fish (*Rhinobatus parcellens*), c.a. ARRAIA-VIOLA, GUITARRA; a bird called JAPACANIM; violet (plant or flower).—**bastarda,** the viola bastarda.—**de amor,** the viola d'amore.—**de arco,** an old name for the violin.—**de braço,** the viola da braccio.—**de gamba,** the viola da gamba.—**francesa,** Spanish guitar. **meter a—no saco,** to clam up, remain silent. **tocar—sem corda,** to talk foolishness.

violação (*f.*) violation, infringement, transgression; profanation; rape.—**da ordem,** breach of the peace.

violáceo **-cea** (*adj.*) violaceous; (*f.pl., Bot.*) the violet family (*Violaceae*).

violador **-dora** (*adj.*) violating; (*m.,f.*) violator; (*m.*) ravisher.

violal (*m.*) violet bed.

violão (*m.*) Spanish guitar.

violar (*v.t.*) to violate; to break (laws); to disregard (promises, vows); to commit rape on, ravish, outrage; to profane, desecrate.

violável (*adj.*) violable.

violeiro (*m.*) guitar maker; guitar player; a bird called CUITELÃO.

violência (*f.*) violence; unjust or brute force; impetuosity, vehemence; outrage, assault; profanation, infringement; (*Law*) coercion, forcible constraint.

violentador **-dora** (*adj.*) violating; (*m.,f.*) violator.

violentar (*v.t.*) to coerce, constrain forcibly; to do violence to; to violate, force; to ravish, rape; to injure by violence; (*v.r.*) to force oneself (against one's will).

violento **-ta** (*adj.*) violent; furious, severe, vehement; fierce, raging, outrageous. **morte—,** violent death.

violeta [lê] (*f.*) violet (plant, flower, color); the color purple; viola, c.a. VIOLA; [*cap.*] Violet.—**africana,** African violet (*Saintpaullia spp.*).—**brava,** the dog violet (*Viola canina*), c.a. BENEFE.—**d'água,** water hyacinth (*Eichhornia spp.*).—**da-lua,** the dollar plant (*Lunaria annua*).—**do-brasil,** Brazilian violet (*Viola gracillima*).—**do-brejo,** a bladderwort (*Uticularia sp.*).—**do-pará,** a low-growing malvaceous herb (*Sida procumbens*), c.a. RASTEIRNHA.—**dos-alpes,** the European cyclamen (*C. europaeum*), c.a. CICLAME-DA-EUROPA.—**tricolor,** the pansy, c.a. AMOR-PERFEITO.

violetista (*m.,f.*) viola player.

violina (*f., Chem.*) violine.

violinista (*m.,f.*) violinist.

violino (*m.*) violin; violinist.

violonista (*m.,f.*) guitar player.

viomal (*m., Bot.*) a centaurea (*C. sempervirens*); the blueweed or common viperbugloss (*Echium vulgare*); both c.a. LAVAPÉ, and the latter, VIPERINA.

vipéreo –rea (*adj.*) = VIPERINO.

viperídeos (*m.pl.*) a family of poisonous, viviparous snakes, the Viperidae.

viperina (*f.*) = LAVAPÉ.

viperíneos (*m.pl.*) the vipers (*Viperinae*).

viperino –na (*adj.*) viperine; venomous.

vir [82] (*v.i.*) to come; to approach; to arrive; to come to pass, come about. [Sometimes employed as an auxiliary verb: O sol vinha nascendo, The sun was rising.]—**a,** to arrive at, come to; to happen to; to succeed in.—**a (um) acôrdo,** to arrive at (an) agreement.—**a uma conclusão,** to come to a conclusion.—**à baila,** to come up in discussion.—**a furo,** to come to light.—**à mão,** to come to hand; to be handy.—**à memória,** to come to mind.—**a propósito,** to be appropriate; to arrive at the opportune moment.—**a saber,** to find out. [veio a saber que, he (she) learned, found out, that.[—**a saber-se,** to come to be known.—**a ser,** to mean, to become, to come to be; to amount to.—**a significar,** to come to mean.—**a talho de foice,** to come at just the right time.—**ao mundo,** to come into the world, to be born.—**às mãos (de alguém);** to come to hand; to come into (someone's) hands. [Veio-me às mãos, It came into my hands.]—**buscar,** to come for (to get).—**da cidade,** to come (return) from the city.—**com rodeios,** to beat about the bush.—**com quatro pedras na mão,** to make an angry remark, a savage reply; to fly off the handle at very slight provocation.—**de,** to return from, come from; to proceed (arise, issue, flow) from.—**de**+inf. = to have just+past part. [o telegrama que venho de ler, the telegram I have just read.] **A que vem a pergunta?** Why the question? **Aí vem!** There he (she, it) is! He (she, it) is on the way! **em dias que estão por—,** in (the) days to come (ahead). **Isto vem de longe,** This is nothing new (referring to a behavior-pattern, or to a specific, but peculiar, act). **mandar—,** to send for; to order (at a restaurant, bar, etc.). **não saber o que (algo) venha a ser,** not to know what (something) really is (like). **Não veio ninguém,** Nobody came. **não—ao caso,** to be neither here nor there. **Não vem ao caso,** It is irrelevant. **o ano que vem,** the coming year. **O Sr. de onde vem?** Where are you [coming] from? **que der e vier,** whatever may happen; come what may. [para o que der e vier, to be on the safe side.] **que vem a ser,** which is; that is; which turned out to be. **Que vem a ser isso?** What is that? What does that mean? What's the meaning of this? **tempo virá em que,** the time will come when. **um ir e—de gente,** a constant coming and going of persons. **Vamos! Come! Let's go! Let's begin! Vamos embora! Let's leave! Let's go! Come on! Vem cansado,** He is all in (tired). **Vem chorando,** She comes crying. **Venha! Come along! Venha aqui! Come here! venha o que vier,** come what may. **Venho à sua presença,** I come to you [a rather old-fashioned phrase still used in letters that are more formal than the average; or by a humble employee timidly approaching the boss, etc.]

vira (*f.*) welt of a shoe; also a form of VER [81].

virá (*m.*) = VEADO-VIRA; form of VIR [82].

vira-bosta (*m.*) tumblebug; also = CHOPIM, GRAÚNA, ARRANCA-MILHO (birds).

virabrequim (*m.*) automobile crankshaft.

viração (*f.*) a cool (fresh, gentle) breeze; sea breeze; afternoon fog in summer.

vira-casaca (*m.*) a turncoat.

viraçu [ú] (*m.*) = TROPEIRO (a bird).

virada (*f.*) a turning (back, around, over).

viradela (*f.*) see under VIRADO.

viradinho (*m.*) a dish of beans, crackling, manioc meal and eggs [= VIRADO].

virado –da (*adj.*) turned (over, around, back, away, inside out, upside down); playful, prankish.—**da bola,** (*colloq.*) "nuts". (*m.*) = VIRADINHO; (*f.*) a turn or turning (back) = VIRADELA; (*slang*) in sports, an upset (defeat of a contestant favored to win).

virador (*m.*) hawser, cable; tow rope; a railroad Y; a locomotive turntable [= GIRADOR].

vira-fôlhas (*m.*) = PINCHA-CISCO.

viragem (*f.*) turning, change of direction; (*Aeron.*) a banking turn; (*Photog.*) developer.

virago (*f.*) a masculine-mannered, masculine-looking woman. [Not a virago in the sense of termagant, which is BICHA, MULHER RABUGENTA (TURBULENTA, QUEIXOSA).]

vira-lata (*m., colloq.*) cur, mutt, mongrel street dog—lit., one who overturns garbage cans in search of food; fig., a down-and-outer.

viram, víramos, forms of VER [81].

viramento (*m.*) a turn or turning.

vira-mundo (*m.*) heavy shackle used on slaves.

virar (*v.t.*) to turn; to invert, turn over, turn upside down; to turn around; to divert, deflect, turn away; to turn inside out; (*v.i.*) to turn into, be changed to; (*v.r.*) to turn; to turn (oneself) around.—**a cabeça a alguém,** to turn a person's head.—**a cara,** to turn away (from something); to pretend not to see; to snub; to "cut dead". —**a casaca,** to become a turncoat.—**a esquina,** to turn the corner.—**a manivela,** to turn a crank.—**a proa,** to change direction; to change the subject.—**ao sul,** to turn south.—**as costas a alguém,** to turn one's back on another person.—**bicho,** to become wild (angry).—**de cabeça p'ra baixo,** to turn upside down.—**frege,** to make an uproar.—**na cama,** to roll over in bed; to toss and turn.—**o feitiço contra o feiticeiro,** to turn the tables, have the laugh, on someone.—**os calcanhares,** to take to one's heels.—**para o norte,** to turn north.—**pelo avêsso,** to turn inside out.—**(-se) contra,** to turn against.—**-se para alguém,** to turn to someone (as for help, or to say something, ask a question, etc.). **Êle virou outro,** He's no longer the same person. **O barco virou,** The boat capsized. **Vire à direita,** Turn to the right.

viras, virdes, víreis, virem, vires, forms of VER [81].

viravolta (*f.*) a complete turnabout; flipflop.

virente (*adj.*) verdant; flourishing.

virgem (*f.*) virgin; maiden, damsel; [*cap.*] Virgin Mary; (*adj.*) virgin(al), chaste, pure; new, maiden. **floresta—,** virgin forest.

virginal (*adj.*) virginal.

virginidade (*f.*) virginity.

Virgínia (*f.*) Virginia.—**Ocidental,** West Virginia.

vírgula (*f.*) comma. [Used also as a decimal mark; thus 2.03 in U.S. = 2,03 in Brazil.]—**dobrada,** paired quotation marks. [" . . . "]. **ponto e—,** semicolon.

virgular (*v.t.*) to insert commas; to punctuate.

víride (*adj.*) green [= VERDE].

viril (*adj.*) virile, manly, vigorous, robust.

virilha (*f., Anat.*) groin.

virilidade (*f.*) virility, manly vigor.

virilismo (*m., Med.*) virilism.

viripotente (*adj.*) marriageable; sexually mature.

virola (*f.*) ferrule.

viroso –sa (*adj.*) virulent, poisonous, noxious.

virote (*m.*) a short arrow; cross guard of a sword hilt; a deer, c.a. GUAÇU-BIRÁ, VEADO-VIRÁ, CATINGUEIRO.

virtual (*adj.*) virtual; potential.

virtualidade (*f.*) virtuality.

virtude (*f.*) virtue, uprightness, probity, moral excellence; merit, worth; efficacy, potency; chastity; (*pl.*) an order of angels. **em—de,** by virtue of; as a result of. **um poço de—,** a paragon of virtues.

virtuose [ô] (*m.,f.*) virtuoso.

virtuosidade (*f.*) virtuosity.

virtuoso –sa (*adj.*) virtuous, righteous, upright; (*m.*) virtuoso.

virulência (*f.*) virulence; acrimony.

virulento –ta (*adj.*) virulent; acrimonious.

vírus (*m.*) virus.—**filtrável,** filterable virus.

visagem (*f.*) grimace; scowl; (*colloq.*) a spook.

visão (*f.*) vision, sight; apparition, chimera, dream.

visar (*v.t.*) to aim at (a target); to have in view, seek, strive for; to turn the gaze upon; to visa (a pass port); to "O.K." (any document).

viscária (*f., Bot.*) the rose-of-heaven (*Lychnis coelirosa*), c.a. ROSA-DO-CÉU.

víscera (*f.*) a visceral organ; (*pl.*) viscera.

visceral, visceroso –sa (*adj.*) visceral.

visceralmente (*adv.*) deeply, profoundly, intimately.

viscidez [ê] (*f.*) = VISCOSIDADE.

víscido –da (*adj.*) = VISCOSO.

visco (*m.*) mistletoe; birdlime; fig., lure, bait.

viscondado (*m.*) viscountcy.

visconde (*m.*) viscount.

viscondessa (*f.*) viscountess.
viscosidade (*f.*) viscosity; stickiness; sticky substance.
viscosímetro (*m.*) viscosimeter.
viscoso -ca (*adj.*) viscous, sticky; slimy.
viseira (*f.*) visor; protection; disguise. **de—caída**, scowling, frowing.
visgueiro (*m.*, *Bot.*) any of various nitta trees (*Parkia*).
visguento -ta (*adj.*) = VISCOSO.
visibilidade (*f.*) visibility.
visionar (*v.t.*) to envision; (*v.i.*) to have a vision.
visionário -ria (*adj.*; *m.,f.*) visionary; utopian.
visita (*f.*) visit, call; visitor; (*colloq.*) menses; (*pl.*) regards, greetings.—**de cerimônia**, formal call.—**de médico**, hurried visit. **de—**, on a visit. **fazer uma—**, to pay a call. **retribuir uma—**, to return a call.
visitação (*f.*) visitation, visit.
visitador -dora (*adj.*) visiting; (*m.,f.*) visitor.
visitante (*m.,f.*) visitor; (*adj.*) visiting.
visitar (*v.t.*) to visit, call on; to go to see; to inspect, examine.
visível (*adj.*) visible, seeable, perceptible, discernible; conspicuous, manifest.—**a olho nú**, visible to (with) the naked eye.
vislumbrar (*v.t.*) to glimpse, catch a glimpse of; to conjecture, guess at; to hint at, give an inkling of; (*v.i.*) to glimmer; to begin to appear.
vislumbre (*m.*) glimmer, gleam; glimpse; hint, faint idea.
viso (*m.*) sign, indication; glimpse; hint; hillock.
visonha (*f.*) frightful vision.
visório -ria (*adj.*) = VISUAL.
víspora (*f.*) lotto, keno.
visse, vísseis, vissem, víssemos, visses, forms of VER [81].
vista (*f.*) sight, vision, eyesight; the eyes; range of vision; view, vista, scene; opinion, conception, point of view; (*pl.*) views, intentions.—**curta**, myopia, near-sightedness; fig., short-sightedness, lack of foresight.—**desarmada**, unaided eye. **à—**, at sight; on demand; in sight, visible, plain. **à—de**, in view of; in the presence of. **à—disto**, therefore, consequently. **à primeira—**, at first sight. **à simples—**, with the naked eye; intuitively. **aguçar a—**, to keep a sharp lookout; to keep one's eyes peeled. **amor à primeira—**, love at first sight. **ao primeiro lance de—s**, at the very first glance. **Até a—**, Au revoir, So long; I'll be seeing you soon. **até onde a—alcança**, as far as eye can see. **baixar a—**, to drop (lower) the eyes. **conhecer de—**, to know by sight. **dar na—**, to strike the eye. **dar uma—de olhos**, to give a quick glance (at). **em—de**, in view of. **fazer—grossa a**, to overlook, let pass, wink at, connive at. **haja—**, keep in mind; witness. **Longe da—, longe do coração**, Out of sight, out of mind. **pagamento à—**, payment at sight. **pagar à—**, to pay at sight (on demand). **perder de—**, to lose sight of. **perder-se de—**, to disappear from view. **ponto de—**, point of view. **ter em—**, to have in mind.
viste, vistes, forms of VER [81].
visto -ta (*adj.*; *p.p.* of VER [81]) seen; visaed; received, accepted; skilled; (*m.*) a visa; an O.K. on documents.—**que**, seeing that, since, inasmuch as, considering, in view of the fact that. **bem—**, welcome; well-beloved. **está—que**, why of course, naturally.
vistoria (*f.*) an official inspection, review or survey.
vistoriar (*v.t.*) to inspect; to overhaul.
vistoso -sa (*adj.*) eye-catching, eye-filling, showy, colorful, striking in appearance; good-looking; smart, elegant; tawdry, garish.
visual (*adj.*) visual.
visualidade (*f.*) visuality; mirage, changing scene.
visualização (*f.*) visualization.
vit. = VITICULTURA (viticulture).
vitáceas (*f.pl.*, *Bot.*) the grape or vine family (*Vitaceae*).
vital (*adj.*) vital, essential, paramount.
vitalício -cia (*adj.*) lifelong.
vitalidade (*f.*) vitality, vital power.
vitalismo (*m.*) vitalism.
vitalista (*adj.*) vitalistic; (*m.,f.*) vitalist.
vitalizar (*v.t.*) to vitalize.
vitamina (*f.*) vitamin(e).
vitando -da (*adj.*) to be avoided; abominable.
vitela (*f.*) heifer, calf; veal; calf leather.
vitelino -na (*adj.*; *Biochem.*) vitelline; (*f.*) vitellin. **saco,—** (*Embryol.*) yolk sac.
vitelo (*m.*) young male calf; (*Embryol.*) vitellus.
viticola (*adj.*) viticultural; (*m.,f.*) viticulturist.
viticultor (*m.*) viticulturist, winegrower.

viticultura (*f.*) viticulture, winegrowing. Cf. VINICULTURA.
vitiligem (*f.*) vitiligo (*m.*, *Med.*) vitiligo [= LEUCODERMIA]; (*colloq.*) = CALOR DE FÍGADO.
vítima (*f.*) victim; sufferer, prey; sacrifice.
vitimar (*v.t.*) to victimize.
vito (*m.*, *Med.*) St. Vitus's dance, chorea.
vitória (*f.*) victory, conquest; victoria (carriage); (*Bot.*) royal water platter (*Victoria regia*); [*cap.*] Victoria.
vitoriano -na (*adj.*) Victorian.
vitoriar (*v.t.*) to applaud vigorously, greet noisily; to acclaim.
vitorioso -sa (*adj.*) victorious, triumphant; winning.
vitral (*m.*) stained glass window.
vítreo -trea (*adj.*) vitreous; clear, transparent.
vitrescível (*adj.*) vitrifiable.
vitrificar (*v.t.*) to vitrify.
vitrificável (*adj.*) = VITRESCÍVEL.
vitrina (*f.*) show window; glass showcase.
vitriólico -ca (*adj.*) vitriolic.
vitríolo (*m.*, *Chem.*) vitriol.
vitróla (*f.*) Victrola, phonograph.—**automática**, jukebox.
vitrolizar (*v.t.*) to vitrolize.
vitu [ú] (*m.*) a male SAÚVA ant.
vitualhas (*f.pl.*) victuals.
vituperação (*f.*) vituperation, upbraiding, severe censure.
vituperador -dora (*adj.*) vituperative; (*m.,f.*) vituperator, reviler.
vituperar (*v.t.*) to vituperate, upbraid; to rail against; to vilify, revile; to taunt.
vitupério (*m.*) vituperation; reproach; taunt; disgrace, shame.
vituperioso -sa (*adj.*) shameful.
viu, form of VER [81].
viúva (*f.*) widow; (*adj.*) widowed. Cf. VIÚVO.—**alegre**, Merry Widow; (*colloq.*) Black Maria (police wagon); (*pl.*, *Bot.*) the common throatwort (*Trachelium caeruleum*); (*Zool.*) the dark-backed tanager (*Pipraeidia melanonota*), c.a. SAÍRA-AÇU, SAÍRA-GUAÇU, SAÍRA-SAPUCAIA; the long-tailed tyrant (*Colonia colonus*); also = POMBINHA-DAS-ALMAS.
viuvar [i-u] (*v.*) = ENVIUVAR.
viuvez [i-u . . . ê] (*f.*) widowhood.
viuvinha [i-u] (*f.*) a little widow; a bird—the white-bellied marsh-tyrant (*Arundinicola leucocephala*), c.a. VELHINHA, RENDEIRO, LAVADEIRA-DE-NOSSA-SENHORA; the spectacled tyrant (*Lichenops perspicillata*); any of various plants, c.a. AMOR-AGARRADO, CAPELA-DE-VIUVINHA, CORAL, FLOR-DE-VIÚVA (which see).
viúvo (*m.*) widower; (*adj.*) widowed. Cf. VIÚVA.
viva (*m.*) hurrah, cheer, shout of joy.—**o Presidente!** Long live the President!
vivacidade (*f.*) vivacity, vivaciousness, sprightliness, alacrity, snap.
vivandeira (*f.*) a woman who follows an army and sells to the troops provisions and the like. [Fr. *vivandière*].
vivaz (*adj.*) vivacious; long-lived; jaunty; (*Bot.*) perennial.
vivedouro -ra (*adj.*) long-lived. Var. VIVEDOIRO.
viveirista (*m.*) nurseryman.
viveiro (*m.*) vivarium (warren, aviary, fish hatchery, aquarium, etc.); plant nursery, seed bed, hotbed.
vivência (*f.*) mode of life; experience.
vivenda (*f.*) dwelling-place, place of abode; mode of life.
vivente (*adj.*) living, alive; (*m.,f.*) a living creature.
viver (*v.i.*) to live, exist, be alive; to live on, survive; to enjoy life; (*v.t.,v.r.*) to live.—**à custa dos outros**, to live on others; to mooch, sponge, bum.—**à custa de**, to sponge on.—**à larga**, to live wantonly, extravagantly.—**a trabalhar**, to work all the time.—**à tripa fôrra,—na fartura**, to live high, in ease and plenty, in clover.—**aborrecido**, to be continually distressed, annoyed, etc.—**ao Deus dará**, or—**como Deus é servido**, to live from hand to mouth, from one day to the next; barely to manage.—**bem**, to live comfortably.—**bem com**, to live harmoniously with (somebody).—**chorando, rindo, etc.**, to be continually crying, laughing, etc.—**como cão e gato**, to live like cats and dogs.—**de**, to live (feed) on; to earn a livelihood by; to live off (some scheme or expediency, or a rich widow . . . , i.e., not necessarily to *earn* a living).—**de brisas**, or **de nada**, to live on little or nothing.—**de expedientes**, to live by one's wits.—**de pão e água**, to live on bread and water.—**de suas mãos**, to earn one's own living.—**em**, to live (dwell, reside) in; to be constantly in (trouble), or at (a doctor's office), or

on (someone's doorstep).—**em família,** to live together (as a family).—**no astral,** to live with one's head in the clouds.—**no seu canto,** to keep to oneself.—**sôbre si,** to pay one's own way. **deixar—quem vive,** to live and let live. **Êle vive assim,** He's always like that; He's always doing that. **Êle vive por graça de Deus,** Only by God's mercy does he keep alive. **saber—,** to know how to live (wisely, enjoyably). **Viva** (. . .)! Long live (. . .)!

víveres (*m.pl.*) victuals, provisions.

viveza [vê] (*f.*) liveliness, vivacity.

Viviana (*f.*) Vivian, Vivien.

vividez [ê] (*f.*) vividness.

vivido –da (*adj.*) said of one who has much experience of life.

vívido –da (*adj.*) vivid.

vivificação (*f.*) vivification.

vivificante (*adj.*) vivifying.

vivificar (*v.t.*) to vivify; to pep up; to revive; (*v.i.*) to impart life; to quicken.

viviparidade (*f.*) viviparousness.

vivíparo –ra (*adj.*) viviparous.

vivise[c]ção (*f.*) vivisection.

vivise[c]cionista (*m.,f.*) vivisector, vivisectionist.

vivo –va (*adj.*) live, living, alive; active, lively, brisk, alert, quick; spry, sprightly; bright, vivid; keen, ardent; (*m.*) living creature, esp. man; (*pl.*) piping, fluting.—**alma,** not a soul. **à—força,** by main force. **à—voz,** viva voce, orally. **alma—,** living soul. **ao—,** to the life; vividly. **cal—** quick lime. **carne—,** quick flesh. **côr—,** bright color. **dar no—,** to sting to the quick. **língua—,** living language. **mais morto que—,** more dead than alive. **os—s,** the living. **os—s e os mortos,** the quick and the dead. **retrato—,** a striking likeness.

vivório (*m.*) cheers, shouts, hurrahs.

vizindário (*m.*), **vizinhada** (*f.*) the neighbors.

vizinhança (*f.*) vicinity; neighborhood; neighbors; proximity.

vizinhar (*v.t.*) to border upon; to approach; (*v.r.*) to become a neighbor.—**com,** to be contiguous to; to be a neighbor to.—**de,** to draw near to.

vizinho –nha (*adj.*) nigh, near, adjoining; near-by; neighboring, next-door. (*m.,f.*) neighbor.

vizir (*m.*) vizier. **grão-—,** Grand Vizier.

V.M. = VOSSA MAJESTADE (Your Majesty); VIRGEM MÁRTIR (Virgin Martyr).

vm.ce = VOSSEMECÊ or VOSMECÊ (you).

V.M.ce = VOSSA MERCÊ (Your Honor, Your Lordship).

v.° = VERSO (over [other side]).

v/o = VOSSA ORDEM ([Com.] your order).

voador –dora (*adj.*) flying; fleet; (*m.,f.*) flier; flying acrobat; (*m.*) any flyingfish, esp. Exocoetus volitans (or evolans).—**-cascudo,** the flying robin or batfish (*Dactyloperus volitans*), c.a. COIÓ, CAJALÉU, PIRABEBE. **peixe-—,** flying fish.

voadouros, -doiros (*m.pl., Zool.*) the primary quills of a bird's wing.

voadura (*f.*) act of flying; a flight.

voagem (*f.*) chaff.

voante (*adj.*) fleeting.

voar (*v.i.*) to fly, soar; to depart, vanish; to flee; to flit; to burst, explode; (*v.t.*) to send (something) flying.—**baixinho,** (*colloq.*) to find oneself in a bad fix as to money, job, etc., and obliged to retrench; lit., to fly very low.—**em** (or **para**) **cima de,** (*slang*) to beset, lay siege to (as in wooing).—**em socorro de,** to fly to the aid of. **—uma pedra,** to let fly (throw) a stone. **fazer—,** to blast, blow up.

vocabular (*adj.*) vocabular.

vocabulário (*m.*) vocabulary.

vocábulo (*m.*) vocable, word.

vocação (*f.*) vocation, inner call, summons; special fitness or talent; (*Theol.*) vocation. [But not vocation in the sense of profession, trade, etc., which is PROFISSÃO, OCUPAÇÃO.]

vocacional (*adj.*) vocational.

vocal (*adj.*) vocal.

vocálico –ca (*adj.*) vocalic.

vocalização (*f.*) vocalization.

vocalizador –dora (*adj.*) vocalizing; (*m.,f.*) vocalist.

vocalizar (*v.t.,v.i.*) to vocalize.

vocalizo (*m., Music*) vocalise.

vocativo (*m., Gram.*) vocative case.

você [contraction of VOSSA MERCÊ] (*pron.*) you. [This is the informal, familiar form of the pronoun used in addressing one's equals or social inferiors.] Cf. TU, VÓS.

vociferação (*f.*) vociferation, clamor.

vociferador –dora, vociferante (*adj.*) vociferant.

vociferar (*v.i.*) to vociferate, roar out; to rave, bluster; to clamor, bawl.—**contra,** to rant (rail, inveigh) against.

voçoroca (*f.*) a cave-in caused by heavy rains.

vodca (*f.*) vodka.

vodu [ú] (*m.*) voodoo.

voejar (*v.i.*) to flit, flutter [= ESVOAÇAR].

voejo [ê] (*m.*) a flitting or fluttering; flour dust.

vog. = VOGAL (vowel).

voga (*f.*) act of rowing; gliding, floating; vogue, fashion; (*Rowing*) stroke (oarsman). **a—surda,** with muffled oars. **sota-—,** the oarsman next to the stroke.

vogal (*adj.*) vocal; vowel; (*f., Phonet.*) vowel; (*m.,f.*) voting member (of an association, etc.).

vogante (*adj.*) rowing; sailing; floating; drifting.

vogar (*v.i.*) to row; to sail; to float, drift, glide; to be in vogue; (*v.t.*) to navigate; to impel by rowing.

vo-la(s), fem. form of VO-LO(S).

volácio (*m.*) = BOI-GORDO (a shrub).

volante (*adj.*) volant, flying, able to fly; mobile, fickle, flighty. **hospital—,** mobile hospital unit. (*m.*) flywheel; steering wheel; voile, veiling; a dart, arrow or shuttlecock; the game of badminton; a light, easily-moved table; a flunky; automobile racing driver; (*pl.*) fliers (leaflets dropped by airplane).

volantim (*m.*) tightrope walker; acrobat [= FUNÂMBULO]; footman who walks or runs beside his master's horse or carriage [= ANDARILHO].

volataria (*f.*) falconry.

volatear (*v.i.*) = ESVOAÇAR.

volátil [-teis] (*adj.*) volatile, fickle, unsteady; (*m.*) flying bird.

volatilidade (*f.*) volatility.

volatilizar (*v.t.,v.i.,v.r.*) to volatalize.

volatim (*m.*) = VOLANTIM.

voleibol (*m.*) volleyball.

volfrâmio (*m., Chem.*) wolframium, tungsten.

volibol (*m.*) = VOLEIBOL.

volição (*f.*) volition.

volitante (*adj.*) volitant, flying.

volitar (*v.i.*) = ESVOAÇAR.

volitivo –va (*adj.*) volitive.

vo-lo(s) (*pers. pron. masc.*) it to you; (*pl.*) them to you. [The fem. form is VO-LA(S).]

volt (*m., Elect.*) volt.

volta (*f.*) return, a coming or going back; turn, twist, bend, crook, coil, loop, bight, curve; rebound; repercussion, recoil, reaction; rebuttal; exchange, change, alteration; restitution, restoration; short walk, stroll; (*Music*) refrain.—**e meia,** frequently; at every turn; every now and then. **à—,** at the time of return. **à—de,** around. **às—s com,** busy with; struggling with; at odds with. **cortar (uma)—,** (*colloq.*) to withstand hardship, hard work, suffering, etc. **dar—a um argumento,** to twist an argument around. **dar—ao juízo,** to go crazy. **dar—ao mostrador,** to sleep the clock around. **dar uma—,** to go for a stroll. **de—,** back, returned. **de—a,** back to. **em—,** around. **em—de,** around, roundabout. **estar de—,** to be back (returned). **fazer-se na—do mar,** of a ship, to move out to sea. **ida e—,** round trip. **Na—jogamos pôquer,** On the way back we played poker. **numa—de mão,** in two shakes of a dog's tail. **pela—do correio,** by return mail. **por—de,** about, around (somewhere near). **por—de uma hora,** around one o'clock. **por—dos quinze anos,** around fifteen years of age.

volta-face (*f.*) an about-face.

voltagem (*f.*) voltage.

voltaico –ca (*adj.*) voltaic.

voltaísmo (*m., Elec.*) voltaism.

voltâmetro (*m., Elec.*) voltameter. Var. VOLTOMETRO.

voltar (*v.i.,v.t.*) to return, come back, get back, go back, turn back (**a, para,** to; **de,** from); (*v.i.*) to turn (**a, para,** to, toward; **contra,** against); (*v.t.*) to restore (**a, to**); to turn over (the soil); (*v.r.*) to turn (**contra,** against; **para,** towards); to turn over (as in bed); to turn around; to return.—**a+inf.** = to+inf. again. [**voltar a (chamar),** to (call) again.]—**à baila,** to come up again for discussion. **—a cabeça,** to turn one's head.—**à carga,** to insist upon. **—a si,** regain one's composure.—**à vaca fria,** to get back to the subject.—**(as) costas a,** to turn one's back on.—**atrás,** to unsay, take back (one's words); lit., to turn around and go back.—**o miolo** (or **o juízo**) **a alguém,** to turn another's head.—**para trás,** to turn back, go back. —**para casa,** to return home.—**sôbre si** (or **sôbre os seus passos**), to retrace one's steps, turn back. **não saber para onde**—-**se,** not to know which way to turn. **Voltou às duas horas,** He returned at two o'clock.

voltarete [rê] (m.) omber. [Webster: "A [card] game of Spanish origin, very popular in the 17th and 18th centuries. It is played by three persons, usually, and with a Spanish pack."]

volteada (f.) roundup of cattle; turn, stroll.

volteador –dora (adj.) that swings, turns, etc. See the verb VOLTEAR; (m.,f.) tumbler, acrobat; (m.) railroad car or dump car tipple.

voltear (v.t.) to go (swing, circle) around; to wave, swing (as the arms); (v.i.) to wheel, revolve; to fly about (in circles); (v.i.) to vault, tumble.

volteio (m.) twist, turn (as of an acrobat); spin.

voltejar (v.) = VOLTEAR.

voltômetro (m., Elec.) voltmeter; voltammeter. Var. VOLTÍMETRO. Cf. VOLTÂMETRO.

volubilado –da (adj.) twining.

volubilidade (f.) fickleness, inconstancy. [But not volubility, in the sense of glibness or loquacity, which is FLUÊNCIA, LOQUACIDADE.]

volume (m.) volume, bulk, mass; book, tome; package; piece of luggage; fullness of tone.

volumetria (f., Chem., Physics) volumetry.

volumétrico –ca (adj., Chem., Physics) volumetric.

volúmetro (m.) volumeter.

volumoso –sa (adj.) voluminous, large, bulky; full, great; of many volumes.

voluntariado (m.) volunteers, collectively or as a class.

voluntário –ria (adj.) voluntary, spontaneous; willing; (m.,f.) volunteer.

voluntarioso –sa (adj.) willful, headstrong, obstinate.

voluntarismo (m., Philos.) voluntarism.

volúpia (f.) voluptuousness; pleasure.

volu[p]tuário –ria (adj.) voluptuous, sensual.

volu[p]tuosidade (f.) voluptuousness, sensuality.

volu[p]tuoso –sa (adj.) voluptuous, sensual; pleasure-loving.

voluta (f.) volute, spiral, swirl, whorl; scroll-like ornament (in architecture); scroll of a violin, 'cello, etc.; (Zool.) volute shell; (pl.) scrollwork.

volutear (v.) = VOLTEAR.

volúvel (adj.) changeable, unstable, fickle; (Bot.) volubile, twining. [But not voluble in the sense of fluent or glib, which is FLUENTE, LOQUAZ.]

volva [ô] (f., Bot.) volva.

volver (v.t.) to turn (as the eyes or face); to turn over, revolve (in the mind); to turn round, roll; to return (**a, para,** to); (v.i.) of years, to roll by; (v.r.) to turn (oneself) around.—**direita!** Right turn! (military command).

volvo [vôl] (m., Med.) volvulus. Var. VÓLVULO.

vólvulo (m.) coil of a snake; also = VOLVO.

vômer (m., Anat.) vomer.

vomeriano –na (adj.) vomerine.

vômica (f., Med.) vomica.

vomição (f.) = VÔMITO.

vomitado (m.) that which is vomited.

vomitador –dora (adj.) vomiting; (m.,f.) vomiter.

vomitar (v.t.) to vomit, spew; to belch forth; (colloq.) to spill a secret.

vomitivo –va (adj.; m.) emetic.

vômito (m.) vomit; act of vomiting.—-**negro,** black vomit (yellow fever).

vomitório –ria (adj.) vomitory, emetic; (m., colloq.) third degree (severe examination to extort a confession).

vontade (f.) will, volition; wish, desire, want; mind, intention; (pl.) desires, whims, fancies.—**férrea,** or—**de ferro,** iron will. **à**—, at ease; as much as you like; capriciously, arbitrarily. **à**—**de,** at the will of; in keeping with the wish(es) of. **à**—**do freguês,** as you like it; lit., as the customer wishes. **A**—**tudo pode,** Where there's a will, there's a way. **abrir a**—**de comer,** to whet the appetite. **boa**—, good will. **com**—, resolutely. **com**—**de,** of a mind to. **com**—**ou sem ela,** willy-nilly. **contra a**—, reluctantly, unwillingly. **de boa**—, gladly, willingly. **de má**—, grudgingly. **estar à**—, to be at ease, at home, comfortable. **estar com**—**de,** to feel like; to have a mind to. **Esteja à**—, Make yourself at home. **fazer a**—**de,** to give in to; to do the wishes of. **força de**—, will power, determination. **má**—, ill will, grudge. **mais à**—, easier,

more comfortable. **não ter**—**de fazer algo,** not to feel like doing something. **pôr alguém à**—, to set another at ease, make him feel welcome. **sentir-se à**—, to feel at home, at ease. **ter**—**de,** to want to.

vôo (m.) flight; flying, soaring; fleeing, hasty departure.— **às cegas,** blind flying.—**de prova,** test flight.—**de reconhecimento,** reconnaissance flight.—**orbital,** global flight.—**rasante,** low-level flight.—**sem escalas,** nonstop flight.

voquisiáceo –cea (adj., Bot.) vochysiaceous; (f.pl.) the copaiyé family (Vochysiaceae).

vorá (m.) = ARAMÁ.

voracidade (f.) voracity, ravenousness.

voragem (f.) vortex, whirlpool, maelstrom; gulf, abyss.

voraz (adj.) voracious, ravenous, greedy; insatiable.

vórmio (m., Anat.) Wormian bone.

vórtice (m.) vortex.

vorticoso –sa (adj.) vorticose, vortical, whirling.

vos (pers. pron. pl.) indirect object: to you, to yourselves; direct object: you, yourselves. [Singular: TE]

vós (pers. pron. 2nd pers. pl.) you; ye. [This is the formal form of you. Cf. TU, VOCE.]

vosmecê, contraction of VOSSEMECÊ.

vossemecê (pron.) you. [Old-fashioned respectful mode of address to parents and superiors. From VOSSA MERCÊ, Your Grace.]

vossência, contraction of VOSSA EXCELÊNCIA, Your Excellency.

vosso –sa (poss. adj.) your; (pron.) yours. [This is the formal form. Cf. TEU, SEU.]

votação (f.) voting; votes.

votado –da (adj.) elected, voted for, voted on.

votante (adj.) voting; (m.,f.) voter.

votar (v.t.,v.i.) to vote (**em, por,** for; **em favor de,** in favor of; **contra,** against).—-**se a,** to devote (dedicate) oneself to.—**à perdição,** to damn.

votivo –va (adj.) votive.

voto [vó] (m.) vote, ballot, poll; suffrage; vow.—**de Minerva** or **de qualidade,** deciding vote cast by presiding officer. **fazer**—**s por** (or **que**), to hope that. **fazer**—**s pela felicidade ou boa saúde de alguém,** to wish someone happiness or good health.

vou, form of IR [53].

vouapa (f.) = ESPADEIRA.

vovô (m.) granddad. [From AVÔ.]

vovó (f.) grandma [from AVÓ]; also = ÔLHO-DE-VIDRO (squirrel fish).

voz (f.) voice, articulate sound; cry (of animals); speech; tone, expression; say, option; rumor.—**ativa,** active voice.—**de cana rachada,** a rasping voice.—**de comando,** word of command.—**de pipia,** falsetto voice.—**do povo,** the people's voice; popular opinion.—**nasal,** nasal vowel; nasal tone.—**oral,** vowel.—**passiva,** passive voice.— **pública,** public fame.—**velada,** veiled, husky voice. **à boa**—, loudly, out loud. **à meia**—, in an undertone; in a whisper. **à viva**—, by word of mouth. **a uma**—, in one voice; unanimously. **ao alcance da**—, within earshot. **dar**—**de prisão a,** to place (someone) under arrest. **de viva**—, viva voce. **em alta**—, aloud. **em**—**alta,** aloud; out loud; in a loud voice. **em**—**baixa,** in a low tone; in an undertone. **fazer**—**grossa,** to talk big. **levantar a**—, to lift the voice. **Mais são as**—**es que as nozes,** The game is not worth the candle. **porta**—, spokesman; megaphone. **ter**—**ativa no assunto** (or **no capítulo**), to have an active voice in the matter.

vozeada (f.) = VOZEARIA.

vozeamento (m.) = VOZEARIA.

vozear (v.i.) to clamor, cry out, shout; (m.) a cry or shout.

vozearia (f.) hullabaloo, hubbub, uproar.

vozeio (m.) clamor, outcry.

vozeirão (m.) thundering voice.

vozeria (f.), –rio (m.) = VOZEARIA.

V.Rev.ª = VOSSA REVERÊNCIA (Your Reverence).

V.Rev.ma = VOSSA REVERENDÍSSIMA (Your Most Reverend).

V.S. = VOSSA SENHORIA (Your Honor, Your Lordship); VOSSA SANTIDADE (Your Holiness).

V.S.ª = VOSSA SENHORIA (Your Honor, Your Lordship).

V.s.f.f. = VOLTE, SE FAZ FAVOR (Please return).

V.T. = VELHO TESTAMENTO (Old Testament).

vulcânico –ca (adj.) volcanic.

vulcanismo (m.) volcanism.

vulcanite (f.) vulcanite.

vulcanização (*f.*) vulcanization.
vulcanizar (*v.t.*) to vulcanize.
vulcanologia (*f.*) volcanology.
vulcão [-cões, -cãos] (*m.*) volcano.
vulgacho (*m.*) populace, rabble, riffraff; the masses.
vulgar (*adj.*) vulgar [but only in the senses of common, ordinary, popular, well-known, commonplace, hackneyed, trite. Cf. BAIXO, CHULO, GROSSEIRO for equivalents of coarse or low.] **língua—**, the vernacular.
vulgaridade (*f.*) vulgarity, commonness, coarseness; platitude.
vulgarismo (*m.*) vulgarism, unrefined speech.
vulgarização (*f.*) vulgarization.
vulgarizar (*v.t.*) to vulgarize, popularize; (*v.r.*) to become commonplace.
Vulgata (*f.*) the Vulgate.
vulgo -ga (*m.*) the common people; the common herd; (*adv.*) commonly. **Fulano, vulgo Sicrano,** Doe, alias Roe.
vulnerário -ria, (*adj.*) vulnerary.
vulnerável (*adj.*) vulnerable.

vulpinita (*f., Min.*) vulpinite.
vulpínia (*f.*) foxtail grass (*Alopecurus*).
vulpino -na (*adj.*) vulpine; of or like a fox.
vulto (*m.*) face, form, figure; appearance; indistinct shape; bulk, volume; important figure (person).
vultoso -sa (*adj.*) bulky.
vulturino -na (*adj.*) vulturine, vulturous.
vulva (*f., Anat.*) vulva.
vulvar (*adj.*) vulvar.
vulvuterino -na (*adj., Anat.*) vulvouterine.
vurapiá (*f.*) = GRÃO-DE-GALO.
vurmo (*m.*) pus.
vurmoso -sa (*adj.*) purulent.
vv. = VERSOS (verses).
Vva. = VIÚVA (Widow).
VV.AA. = VOSSAS ALTEZAS (Your Highnesses).
VV.Ex.ªˢ = VOSSAS EXCELÊNCIAS (Your Excellencies).
VV.MM. = VOSSAS MAJESTADES (Your Majesties).
VV.SS. or **VV.S.ªˢ** = VOSSAS SENHORIAS (Your Lordships).

W

W, w, this letter is no longer a part of the official Portuguese alphabet, but has been replaced by U and V. It is still used, however, in proper names and international symbols.
W = WATT INTERNACIONAL (international watt); OESTE (west); VOLFRÂMIO (wolfram, tungsten).
w = WATT.
W.C. = RETRETE or PRIVADA (water closet).
W.N.W. = OÉS-NOROESTE (west-northwest).
W.S.W. = OÉS-SUDOESTE (west-southwest).

X

X, x, the 22nd letter of the Portuguese alphabet. It has five different sound values: *sh* (as in LUXO), *ks* (as in FIXO), *s* (as in EXCELENTE), *z* (as in EXATO), and *ss* (as in PRÓXIMO). The letter itself is called **xis** (sheez). Look under **ch** for words formerly spelled with **x,** and viceversa.
xá (*m.*) shah.
xábega (*f.*) a sweep net; fishing smack.
xabraque (*m.*) shabrack. [*Webster*: "A saddlecloth, often of goatskin, used by European light cavalry."]
xácara (*f.*) ballad, pop. narrative poem or song. Cf. CHÁCARA.
xacriabá (*m.,f.*) an Indian of the extinct Shacriabá, a tribe of the Central Ge which once inhabited the southern part of the Tocantins-San Francisco watershed between Goiás and Bahia; (*adj.*) pert. to or designating this tribe. Cf. ACUÉ.
xadrez [ê] (*m.*) chess; chessboard; plaid or checkered cloth; (*Naut.*) grating; (*colloq.*) jail. **de—,** checkered.
xadrezar (*v.t.*) to checker.
xadrezista (*m.,f.*) chess player [= ENXADRISTA].
xaguão (*m.*) = SAGUÃO.
xaiá, xajá (*f.*) = TACHÃ.
xale (*m.*) shawl; shoulder scarf.
xalmas (*f.pl.*) rack (spreading framework) set on a wagon for carrying hay or the like in large loads. Var. XELMA.
xamã (*m.*) shaman.
xaminismo (*m.*) shamanism.
xamanista (*adj.; m.*) shamanist.
xamanístico -ca (*adj.*) shamanistic.
xambioá (*m.,f.*) one of the Xambioá, a virtually extinct tribal group of the Carajá (which see); (*adj.*) pert. to or designating the Xambioá.
xampu (*m.*) shampoo.
Xangai (*f.*) Shanghai.
xangô (*m.*) voodooism; one of the more powerful but secondary gods.
xanteína (*f., Chem.*) xanthein.
xantelasma, xanteloma (*m., Med.*) xanthoma of the eyelid.
xântio (*m., Bot.*) cocklebur (*Xanthium*).

xantofila (*f., Biochem.*) xanthophyll.
xantogênico -ca (*adj.*) xanthogenic.
xantungue (*m.*) Shantung (pongee).
xapacura (*m.,f.*) an Indian of any of the Chapacuran tribes along the Guaporé River where it forms the frontier with Bolivia; (*adj.*) pert. to or designating these tribes.
xaque-mate (*m.*) = XEQUE-MATE.
xará (*m.,f.*) namesake.
xarda (*f.*) czardas (Hungarian dance).
xarelete [lê] (*m.*) the hard-tailed jack (*Caranx crysos*), c.a. CAVALO, XARÉU-DOURADO (or -PEQUENO), XERELETE, XERERETE, SOLTEIRA; when young: CHUMBERGA.
xaréu (*m.*) the common jack (*Caranx hippos*), c.a. XARÉU-RONCADOR (or -VAQUEIRO), CABEÇUDO, CORIMBAMBA, GUIARÁ; leather covering for horse's hindquarters.——**dourado** (or -**pequeno**) = XARELETE.
xarife (*m.*) = XERIFE.
xaroco (*m.*) = SIROCO.
xaropada (*f.*) cough syrup, or a dose of it; (*colloq.*) boresome discourse.
xaropar (*v.t.*) to treat, as with cough syrup.
xarope (*m.*) any medicated syrup.
xaroposo -sa (*adj.*) syrupy.
xarroco (*m.*) a genus (*Lophius*) of angler fishes, c.a. DIABO-MARINHO.——**bicudo,** or——**do-brasil** = QUACACUJA.——**maior,** angler fish (*Lophius piscatorius*), c.a. TAMBORIL, RÃ-DO-MAR, PEIXE-PESCADOR.——**menor,** a stargazer (URANOSCOPUS SCABER).
xauim [au-ím] (*m.*) = SAGÜI.
xavaé, variant of JAVÉ.
xavante (*m.,f.*) an Indian of the Shavante (or Chavante), a fierce tribe of the Central Ge west of the upper Araguaya River in Mato Grosso. The same name is applied also to other tribes not related to this one, notably a group of isolated speech on the Tietê River in the State of São Paulo; (*adj.*) pert. to or designating the Xavante. Cf. ACUÉ.
xaveco (*m.*) a small old, poorly-built boat; (*Naut.*) xebec (a Medit. sailing vessel); (*colloq.*) an old tub; a trivial

thing or person; a hag; (*slang*) a lost bet which the dealer or croupier neglects to rake in.

xaxim (*m.*, *Bot.*) a dicksonia tree fern (*D. sellowiana*), c.a. SAMAMBAIAÇU.

xelim (*m.*) shilling.

xelma (*f.*) = XALMAS.

xenartro (*m.*, *Zool.*) one of the Xenarthra (anteaters, sloths, armadillos).

xenófilo –la (*adj.*) fond of strangers.

xenofobia (*f.*) xenophobia.

xenófobo –ba (*adj.*; *m.,f.*) xenophobe.

xenomórfico –ca (*adj.*, *Petrog.*) xenomorphic.

xenônio (*m.*, *Chem.*) xenon.

xepa [ê] (*f.*) chow (army food); (*slang*) a newspaper which is sold for the second time.

xepeiro (*m.*) a soldier who lives in quarters; a person who lives from hand to mouth; an urchin who picks up old newspapers and resells them.

xeque (*m.*) sheik; (chess) check; (*fig.*) parliamentary move which threatens to topple the government.— **descoberto**, (*Chess*) discovered check.—**-mate**, checkmate.—**-xeque** = CORAÇÃO-DA-ÍNDIA. Cf. CHEQUE.

xerafim (*m.*) a silver coin formerly current in Portuguese India.

xerelete [lê] **xererete** [ête], (*m.*) = XARELETE.

xerém (*m.*) coarse cracked corn left in the sieve when making cornmeal; (*Zool.*) the tiny hairy hermit hummingbird (*Glaucis hirsuta*), perhaps the smallest bird in the world.

xerengue (*m.*) = CAXIRENGUENGUE.

xerente (*m.,f.*) an Indian of the Sherente, a tribe of the Central Ge on both sides of the Tocantins River in Mato Grosso; (*adj.*) pert. to or designating this tribe. Cf. ACUÉ.

xereré (*m.*) = XIXIXI.

xerêta (*m.,f.*) newsmonger; busybody; flatterer.

xeret[e]ar (*v.t.,v.i.*) to flatter.

xerez [rêz] (*m.*) sherry wine.

xerife (*m.*) sheriff. Var. XARIFE.

xerimbabo (*m.*) a wild animal raised as a pet [= MUMBAVO].

xerofagia (*f.*) xerophagy (very strict fast).

xerófilo –la (*adj.*, *Bot.*) xerophilous.

xerófito –ta (*adj.*, *Ecology*) xerophytic.

xeroftalmia (*f.*, *Med.*) xerophthalmia.

xerose (*f.*, *Med.*) xerosis.

xexeu (*m.*) = JAPIM and ENCONTRO.

xícara (*f.*) cup, teacup, coffee cup [= CHAVENA].

xicarada (*f.*) a cupful.

xicriabá (*m.,f.*, *adj.*) = ACUÉ.

xifofilo –la (*adj.*, *Bot.*) xiphophyllus.

xifóide, xifoídeo –dea (*adj.*, *Anat.*, *Zool.*) xiphoid.

xifópagos (*m.pl.*) Siamese twins.

xilarmônico (*m.*) xylophone [= XILOFONE, XILOFONO].

xilema (*m.*, *Bot.*) xylem [= LENHO].

xilênio, xileno (*m.*, *Chem.*) xylene, dimethylbenzene.

xilindró (*m.*, *slang*) hoosegow, jug, cooler (jail).

xilo (*m.*) cotton plant.

xilocarpo (*m.*, *Bot.*) xylocarp.

xilócopo –pa (*adj.*) xilotomous [= XILÓTOMO].

xilofagia (*f.*) eating, boring, or destroying of wood.

xilófago –ga (*adj.*) xylophagous; (*m.*, *Zool.*) a xylophagan (wood-eating insect); (*pl.*) the Xylophaga (a division of weevils).

xilófilo –la (*adj.*; *Bot.*, *Zool.*) xylophilous.

xilofone, xilofono (*m.*) = XILARMÔNICO.

xilofonista (*m.,f.*) xylophonist.

xilografia (*f.*) xylography.

xilógrafo (*m.*) xylographer.

xilogravura (*f.*) xylograph; woodcut.

xilóide (*adj.*) xyloid; ligneous.

xiloidina (*f.*) xyloidin.

xilologia (*f.*) xylology

xilótomo –ma (*adj.*) = XILÓCOPO.

ximango (*m.*, *Zool.*) the chimango (*Milvago chimango*), a caracara of Brazil. [Because of its fondness for ticks, which it picks off the sides and bellies of cattle, it is called also CARRAPATEIRO.]

ximarona (*f.*, *Bot.*) a viper's-bugloss (*Echium plantagineum*).

ximbé, ximbeva (*adj.*) snub-nosed.

ximbica (*f.*) a popular card game.

ximbo (*m.*) stray horse.

ximbra (*f.*) a game played with marbles [= GUDE].

xingação, **–gadela** (*f.*), **–gamento** (*m.*) act of scolding, abusing, bawling out.

xingar (*v.t.*) to call names, rail at, abuse, scold.

xingatório –ria (*adj.*) scolding, abusive.

xingo (*m.*) words used in scolding or abusing (someone).

xintã (*m.*) = INHAMBU-XINTÃ.

xintó, xintoísmo (*m.*) Shinto.

xintoísta (*adj.*; *m.,f.*) Shintoist.

xipaia (*m.,f.*) an Indian of the Shipaya, a Tupian tribe closely related to the Juruna and living in Pará between the lower Tapajós and Xingu Rivers; (*adj.*) pert. to or designating this tribe.

xiquexique (*m.*) a cactus (*Pilocereus gounellei*); a rattlebox (*Crotolaria*), c.a. CHOCALHO-DE-CASCAVEL; also = CANÁRIA. **—-do-sertão**, a pricklypear (*Opuntia brasiliensis*).

xira (*f.*) = CORCOROCA.

xirianã (*m.,f.*) an Indian of the Shirianá, a warlike and linguistically independent tribe of forest nomads in the region of the Serra Parima between Brazil and Venezuela; (*adj.*) pert. to or designating these people.

xiridáceo –cea (*adj.*; *Bot.*) xyridaceous; (*f.pl.*) the yellow-eyed grass family (*Xyridaceae*).

xirimbambada (*f.*, *colloq.*) brawl, shindy.

xiririca (*f.*) river rapids.

xiriuba, **–beira** (*f.*, *Bot.*) a dodder (*Cuscuta umbellata*), c.a. CIPÓ-CHUMBO.

xisto (*m.*) schist (or any schistose rock, such as slate, shale, etc.).

xistóide (*adj.*; *Petrog.*) schistoid.

xistosidade (*f.*, *Petrog.*) foliation.

xistoso –sa (*adj.*) schistose.

xixá (*m.*, *Bot.*) chicha. [*Webster:* "A So. Amer. tree (*Sterculia chicha*) bearing edible seeds or nuts."]

xixarro (*m.*) the widely known saurel (*Trachurus trachurus*); the goggler or big-eyed scad (*Trachurops crumenophthalmia*).**—-calabar** (or **-cavala**), the mackerel scad (*Decapterus macurellus*), c.a. CARAPAU, CAVALINHA. **—-pintado** (or **-branco**, or **-de-ôlho-grande**), the round scad (*Descapterus punctatus*).

xixixi (*m.*) fine drizzle.

xô (*interj.*) Whoa!

xô (*interj.*) Shoo!

xocrém (*m.,f.*) any Indian of the Shokleng-Caingang of Santa Catarina, called also Botocudo and Bugre (which see); (*adj.*) pert. to or designating the Xocrém.

xodó (*m.*) dalliance; courtship; sweetheart; apple of the eye; gossip.

xorte (*m.*) shorts.

xorumela (*f.*) trifle.

X.P.T.O. (*adj.*) A-number-one, first-class, excellent.

xucrice (*f.*), **xucrismo** (*m.*) roughness; boorishness.

xucro –cra (*adj.*) awkward, clumsy, rough; wild, savage; of horses, unbroken.

xué(-guaçu) (*m.*) = SAPO-CURURÚ.

xumberga (*f.*) drunkenness.

xuri (*m.*) = EMA.

Y

Y, y, This letter is no longer included in the official Portuguese alphabet but has been replaced entirely by the letter I, except in proper names and international symbols.

Z

Z, z, *(m.,f.)* the 23rd letter of the Port. alphabet.
zabelê *(m.)* = JAÓ.
zabucaí *(m.)* = GALO (moonfish).
zabumba *(m.)* big bass drum; *(Bot.)* jimson weed *(Datura stramonium)*, c.a. ESTRAMÔNIO.
Zacarias *(m.)* Zacharias, Zachariah, Zachary, Zechariah.
zaga *(f., Soccer)* fullback position.
zagal *(m.)* shepherd; herdsman [= PASTOR].
zagala *(f.)* shepherdess [= PASTÔRA].
zagueiro *(m., Soccer)* fullback (player); c.a. BEQUE.
zagunchada *(f.)* a spear thrust; fig., a dig (cutting remark).
zagunchar *(v.t.)* to spear; fig., to taunt, deride. Var. ZARGUNCHAR.
zaguncho *(m.)* spear. Var. ZARGUNCHO.
zãibo **–ba** *(adj.)* twisted; knock-kneed; cockeyed. Var. ZAIMBRO.
zaino **–na** *(adj.)* of a horse, dark chestnut all over (without white spots); of a bull, dull black; deceitful, untrustworthy.
zambo *(m.)* offspring of a Negro man and an Indian woman.
zambro **–bra** *(adj.)* knock-kneed.
zambujeiro, zambujo *(m.)* the wild variety of the true olive, c.a. AZAMBUJEIRO, AZAMBUJO.
zanaga *(adj.)* cross-eyed; one-eyed.
zanga *(f.)* anger; aversion.
zangado **–da** *(adj.)* angry; annoyed.
zangão [-gãos, -gões], **zângão** [-gãos] *(m.)* drone (bee); fig., an idler, sponger; canvasser, runner, drummer.
zangar *(v.t.)* to anger, irritate, displease.—**-se com**, to get angry with.
zangarelha *(f.)*, **–lho** *(m.)* dragnet.
zangarilhar *;v.i.)* to walk backwards and forwards.
zangarrear *(v.i.,v.t.)* to strum, plunk, twang (stringed instrument).
zangarreio *(m.)* a strumming.
zanguizarra *(f.)* hubbub, racket; idle thrumming (of a guitar); shrill sound.
zangurriana *(f.)* monotonous chanting; *(colloq.)* drunkenness.
zangurrina *(f., colloq.)* drunkenness.
zanho **–nha** *(adj.)* hypocritical.
zanolho **–lha** *(adj.; m.,f.)* cross-eyed (person); = ZAROLHO.
zanzar *(v.i.)* to wander aimlessly about.
zanzo *(m., Bot.)* the broomjute sida *(S. rhombifolia)*, c.a. RELÓGIO, GUAXIMA, VASSOURA.
zape *(m.)* a blow or slap; *(interj.)* Bang!
zápete *(m.)* the four of clubs in a card game called TRUQUE.
zarabatana *(f.)* blowgun [= ESGARAVATANA].
zaragata *(f.)* hubbub.
zaragatoa *(m.)* a swab or small brush for applying medicine, as to the throat.—**-maior**, shrubby plantain *(Plantago cynops)*.—**-menor**, flaxseed plantain *(P. psyllium)*.
zaranza *(adj.; m.,f.)* scatterbrained (person).
zaranzar *(v.i.)* to loiter, dawdle; to putter about.
zarco **–ca** *(adj.; f.)* blue-eyed (woman). **cavalo—**, horse with white spots around the eyes.
zarcão *(m.)* red oxide of lead.
zarelha [ê] *(f.)* busybody.
zarelhar *(v.i.)* to intrude, butt in.
zarelho [ê] *(m.)* meddler; prankish boy; scatterbrain.
zargo **–ga** *(adj.)* (horse) having one or both eyes white.
zarguncho *(m.)* & derivs. = ZAGUNCHO & DERIVS.
zarolho **–lha** *(adj.)* cross-eyed; one-eyed.
zarpar *(v.t.,v.i.)* to weigh anchor; to put out to sea.
zarzuela *(f.)* zarzuela (Spanish vaudeville).
zás(-trás) *(interj.)* Bang!
Zé *(m.)* a familiar nickname—short for JOSÉ. Also, ZEQUINHA, ZEZINHO.
zêbra *(f.)* zebra; *(colloq.)* stupid person; prisoner's striped uniform.
zebrado **–da** *(adj.)* striped like a zebra.
zebral, zebrário **–ria, zebrino** **–na** *(adj.)* zebrine.
zebrar *(v.t.)* to provide with stripes like those of a zebra.
zebróide *(adj.)* zeboid; *(m.)* a zebrula; *(colloq.)* a dope (stupid person).
zebu *(m.)* zebu, humped cattle *(Bos indicus)*.

zebueiro, zebuzeiro *(m.)* one who raises or deals in zebu cattle.
zedoária *(f., Bot.)* zedoary turmeric *(Curcuma zedoaria)*.
zé-dos-anzóis *(m.)* any fellow.
zefir *(m.)* zephyr cloth.
zéfiro *(m.)* zephyr.
zelação *(f.)* shooting star.
zelador *(m.)* caretaker; janitor; keeper; custodian.
zelar *(v.t.)* to watch over; to take care of.—**pelos seus interesses**, to look after one's interests.
zêlo *(m.)* zeal, ardor, fervor *(pl.)* jealousy.
zeloso **–sa** *(adj.)* zealous; jealous.
zenital *(adj.)* zenithal.
zênite *(m.)* zenith (lit. & fig.).
zeólito *(m.)* zeolite.
zepelim *(m.)* zeppelin airship; *(Zool.)* the three-line pencil fish *(Nannostomus trifasciatus)* seen in home aquaria.
zé-pereira *(m.)* a Carnival personification of the Brazilian man-in-the-street; a certain noisy marching chant and rhythmic drum beat to which Carnival merrymakers keep time while parading through the streets.
zé-povinho, zé-povo *(m.)* riff-raff, lower classes; the "little man," the man-in-the-street.
zé-pregos *(m.)* a male turtle [= CAPITARI].
Zequinha *(m.)* = ZÉ.
zero *(m.)* zero; nothing; a person of no importance.
zetacismo *(m.)* zetacism.
zetético **–ca** *(adj.; f., Math., Philos.)* zetetic (search, inquiry, investigation).
zé-tranquilino *(m.)* a certain type of dagger having an ornamental silver handle and made from a sword blade.
zeugma *(f., Gram., Rhet.)* zeugma.
Zezinho *(m.)* = ZÉ.
zigodáctilo **-la** *(adj.)* zygodactil.
zigofiláceo **–cea** *(adj.; Bot.)* zygophyllaceous.
zigoma *(m., Anat.)* zygoma; cheekbone.
zigomático **–ca** *(adj.)* zygomatic.
zigomorfo **–fa** *(adj.; Bot.)* zygomorphic.
zigospório *(m., Bot.)* zygospore.
zigoto *(m., Biol.)* zygote.
ziguezague *(m.)* zigzag.
ziguezagueante *(adj.)* zigzagging.
ziguezaguear *(v.i.)* to zigzag; *(Aeron.)* to hedge-hop.
zímase *(f., Biochem.)* zymase.
zimbo *(m.)* cowrie shell.
zimbório *(m., Arch.)* dome.
zimbrar *(v.t.)* to beat, whip, strike; to equip a snare drum with strings; *(v.i.)* to rock ; of a ship, to pitch.
zimbro *(m., Bot.)* any juniper; c.a. ZIMBREIRO, JUNÍPERO.
zímico **–ca** *(adj.)* zymotic.
zimogenia *(f., Biochem.)* zymogenesis.
zimogênico **–ca** *(adj.)* zymogenic.
zimologia *(f.)* zymology.
zimoscópio *(m., Biochem.)* zymoscope.
zimose *(f.)* zymosis, fermentation.
zimotecnia *(f.)* zymotechnics.
zimótico **–ca** *(adj.)* zymotic.
zincagem *(f.)* operation of coating with zinc.
zincar *(v.t.)* to zincify.
zinco *(m., Chem.)* zinc. **fôlha de—**, a sheet of corrugated galvanized steel (used for roofing).
zincografia *(f.)* zincography.
zinga *(f.)* an oar used as a sweep or scull; a long pole used for propelling a boat or raft.
zingamocho *(m.)* weather vane; pinnacle.
zingar *(v.i.)* to scull.
zíngaro *(m.)* a gypsy musician.
zingiberáceo **–cea** *(adj.; Bot.)* zingiberaceous; *(f.pl.)* the ginger family *(Zingiberaceae)*.
zingrar *(v.t.)* to mock, taunt, deride.
zinho *(m.,f. slang)* any "guy" or "gal" (esp. boy or girl friend).
zínia *(f., Bot.)* zinnia.
zinideira *(f.)* a toy bull-roarer.
zinido *(m.)* shrill, chirr (as of a cicada).
zinir *(v.)* = ZUNIR.
zircão *(m.)* zircon (semi-precious stone).
zircônio *(m., Chem.)* zirconium.

zirro (*m.*) = GAIVÃO.
zizânia (*f.*) = CIZÂNIA.
ziziar (*v.i.*) to chirr as a cicada [= FRETENIR].
zoada (*f.*) a humming or buzzing, as of bees.
zoantário (*m., Zool.*) one of the Zoantharia (corals, sea anemones).
zoar (*v.i.*) to hum or buzz, as bees.
zodiacal (*adj.*) zodiacal.
zodíaco (*m.*) zodiac.
zóico –ca (*adj., Zool.*) zoic.
zoilo (*m.*) a bitter, envious, unjust critic.
zombador –dora (*adj.*) jeering, sneering; (*m.,f.*) one who jeers, etc. See the verb ZOMBAR.
zombar (*v.t.,v.i.*) to jeer, gibe, deride, razz, make fun of. —com (or de), to laugh at, poke fun at.
zombaria (*f.*) banter, derision, raillery, ridicule, mockery.
zombetear (*v.*) = ZOMBAR.
zombeteiro –ra (*adj.; m.,f.*) = ZOMBADOR.
zona (*f.*) zone, region; (*colloq.*) red-light district.—de silêncio, (*Aviation radio*) skip distance.—-zóster, (*Med.*) herpes zoster, shingles.
zonchar (*v.i.*) to pump.
zoncho (*m.*) pump handle.
zonzo –za (*adj.*) dizzy, giddy; addlebrained.
zoófilo –la (*adj.*) zoöphilous.
zoofítico –ca (*adj.*) zoöphytic(al).
zoófito (*m.*) zoöphyte.
zoofobia (*f.*) zoöphobia.
zoogeografia (*f.*) zoögeography.
zoolgéia (*f., Bacteriol.*) zoögloea.
zoografia (*f.*) zoögraphy.
zoóide (*adj.*) zoöidal.
zoologia (*f.*) zoölogy.
zoológico –ca (*adj.*) zoölogical, **jardim—**, zoölogical garden (a zoo).
zoólogo (*m.*) zoölogist.
zoomorfismo (*m.*) zoömorphism.

zooquímica (*f.*) zoöchemistry.
zoosporângio (*m., Bot.*) zoösporangium.
zoospório (*m., Bot., Zool.*) zoöspore.
zootecnia (*f.*) animal husbandry; zoötechny.
zootomia (*f.*) zoötomy.
zootomista (*m.,f.*) zoötomist.
zopo –pa [zô] (*adj.*) faltering; (*m.,f.*) one who stumbles or falters, owing to old age or sickness.
zorô (*m.*) a dish of shrimp and okra.
zorra (*f.*) see under ZORRO.
zorrilho (*m.*) = CANGAMBÁ.
zorro –ra [zô] (*adj.*) sly, crafty; sluggish; (*m.*) fox; rascal; (*f.*) a low truck or dray for heavy hauling; a sledge for hauling rocks or logs; an old vixen (she-fox).
zóster (*m., Med.*) herpes zoster, shingles.
zote (*m.*) fool, idiot.
zuarte (*m.*) nankeen (cloth); blue denim.
zuavo (*m.*) zouave.
zuir [u-i] (*v.i.*) to buzz.
zumbaia (*f.*) kowtow.
zumbaiar (*v.t.*) to kowtow to; to flatter.
zumbi [bí] (*m.*) zombi.
zumbido (*m.*) drone, buzz.
zumbir (*v.i.*) to drone; to buzz.
zunir [25] (*v.i.*) to whistle through the air (as an arrow); to buzz, whir, drone; of wind, to whine.
zunzum (*m.*) a buzzing, humming; a rumor.
zunzunar (*v.i.*) to drone.
zupa (*interj.*) Whang!
zupar (*v.t.*) to whale, hit, "sock".
Zurique (*m.*) Zurich.
zurrapa (*f.*) cheap wine.
zurrar (*v.i.*) to bray.
zurro (*m.*) a braying.
zurzidela (*f.*) a whipping.
zurzir (*v.t.*) to thrash, whip, beat, trounce; fig.; to give a tongue lashing to.

APPENDIX

VERB MODELS *by* JAMES S. HOLTON

REGULAR VERBS

1. Conjugations of regular verbs

A. Simple Tenses (Tempos Simples)

IMPERSONAL INFINITIVE (INFINITIVO IMPESSOAL)

passar	**bater**	**partir**

PERSONAL INFINITIVE (INFINITIVO PESSOAL)

passar	bater	partir
passares	bateres	partires
passar	bater	partir
passarmos	batermos	partirmos
passardes	baterdes	partirdes
passarem	baterem	partirem

GERUND (GERÚNDIO)

passando	batendo	partindo

PAST PARTICIPLE (PARTICÍPIO PASSADO)

passado	batido	partido

INDICATIVE (INDICATIVO)

PRESENT (PRESENTE)

passo	bato	parto
passas	bates	partes
passa	bate	parte
passamos	batemos	partimos
passais	bateis	partis
passam	batem	partem

IMPERFECT (PRETÉRITO IMPERFEITO)

passava	batia	partia
passavas	batias	partias
passava	batia	partia
passávamos	batíamos	partíamos
passáveis	batíeis	partíeis
passavam	batiam	partiam

PRETERITE (PRETÉRITO PERFEITO)

passei	bati	parti
passaste	bateste	partiste
passou	bateu	partiu
passamos	batemos	partimos
passastes	batestes	partistes
passaram	bateram	partiram

PLUPERFECT (PRETÉRITO MAIS-QUE-PERFEITO)

passara	batera	partira
passaras	bateras	partiras
passara	batera	partira
passáramos	batêramos	partíramos
passáreis	batêreis	partíreis
passaram	bateram	partiram

FUTURE (FUTURO IMPERFEITO)

passarei	baterei	partirei
passarás	baterás	partirás
passará	baterá	partirá
passaremos	bateremos	partiremos
passareis	batereis	partireis
passarão	baterão	partirão

CONDITIONAL (CONDICIONAL IMPERFEITO)

passaria	bateria	partiria
passarias	baterias	partirias
passaria	bateria	partiria
passaríamos	bateríamos	partiríamos
passaríeis	bateríeis	partiríeis
passariam	bateriam	partiriam

IMPERATIVE (IMPERATIVO)

Singular:

passa	bate	parte

Plural:

passai	batei	parti

SUBJUNCTIVE (SUBJUNTIVO)

PRESENT (PRESENTE)

passe	bata	parta
passes	batas	partas
passe	bata	parta
passemos	batamos	partamos
passeis	batais	partais
passem	batam	partam

IMPERFECT (PRETÉRITO IMPERFEITO)

passasse	batesse	partisse
passasses	batesses	partisses
passasse	batesse	partisse
passássemos	batêssemos	partíssemos
passásseis	batêsseis	partísseis
passassem	batessem	partissem

FUTURE (FUTURO IMPERFEITO)

passar	bater	partir
passares	bateres	partires
passar	bater	partir
passarmos	batermos	partirmos
passardes	baterdes	partirdes
passarem	baterem	partirem

B. Compound Tenses (Tempos Compostos)

INDICATIVE (INDICATIVO)

PERFECT (PRETÉRITO PERFEITO COMPOSTO)

tenho passado	tenho batido	tenho partido
etc.	etc.	etc.

(Note that compound tenses may be formed also with the appropriate tense of the auxiliary **haver** [52] instead of **ter** [78].)

PLUPERFECT (MAIS-QUE-PERFEITO COMPOSTO)

tinha passado	tinha batido	tinha partido
etc.	etc.	etc.

FUTURE PERFECT (FUTURO PERFEITO COMPOSTO)

terei passado	terei batido	terei partido
etc.	etc.	etc.

CONDITIONAL PERFECT (CONDICIONAL PERFEITO COMPOSTO)

teria passado	teria passado	teria partido
etc.	etc.	etc.

SUBJUNCTIVE (SUBJUNTIVO)

PERFECT

tenha passado	tenha batido	tenha partido
etc.	etc.	etc.

PLUPERFECT

tivesse passado	tivesse batido	tivesse partido
etc.	etc.	etc.

FUTURE PERFECT

tiver passado	tiver batido	tiver partido
etc.	etc.	etc.

	Present Indicative	*Present Subjunctive*	*Preterite Indicative*
2. Verbs in **-car** change **c** to **qu** before **e**. Example: **ficar**.	regular	fique fiques fique fiquemos fiqueis fiquem	fiquei ficaste ficou ficamos ficastes ficaram
3. Verbs in **-gar** change **g** to **gu** before **e**. Example: **chegar**.	regular	chegue chegues chegue cheguemos chegueis cheguem	cheguei chegaste chegou chegamos chegastes chegaram
4. Verbs in **-ger** and **-gir** change **g** to **j** before **a** or **o**. Example: **corrigir**.	corrijo corriges corrige corrigemos corrigeis corrigem	corrijá corrijas corrija corrijamos corrijais corrijam	regular
5. Verbs in **-guer** and **-guir** change **gu** to **g** before **a** or **o**. Example: **distinguir**.	distingo distingues distingue distinguimos distinguis distinguem	distinga distingas distinga distingamos distingais distingam	regular
6. Verbs in **-çar** change **ç** to **c** before **e**. Example: **começar**.	regular	comece comeces comece comecemos comeceis comecem	comecei começaste começou começamos começastes começaram
7. Verbs in **-cer** and **-cir** change **c** to **ç** before **o** or **a**. Example: **esquecer**.	esqueço esqueces esquece esquecemos esqueceis esquecem	esqueça esqueças esqueça esqueçamos esqueçais esqueçam	regular
8. Verbs in **-guar** add an acute accent or a dieresis over the **u** before **e** depending on whether it is stressed or unstressed. Example: **averiguar**. But note that usage and authorities are at variance concerning the accentuation of **aguar, desaguar, enxaguar**, and **minguar**. These words are commonly stressed: **deságuo, deságuas**, etc.	regular	averigúe averigúes averigúe averigüemos averigüeis averigúem	averigüei averiguaste averiguou averiguamos averiguastes averiguaram
9. Verbs in **-quar** are few, little used, and mostly defective. Two exist which have full conjugations. They take an acute accent or dieresis over **u** before **e** according as **u** is stressed or not. In Brazil, usage is commonly as shown in the examples, although there is disagreement as to accentuation.	apropínquo apropínquas apropínqua apropinquamos apropinquais apropínquam	apropínqüe apropínqües apropínqüe apropinqüemos apropinqüeis apropínqüem	apropinqüei apropinquaste apropinquou apropinquamos apropinquastes apropinquaram
	obliquo obliquas obliqua obliquamos obliquais obliquam	obliqúe obliqúes obliqúe obliqüemos obliqüeis obliqúem	obliqüei obliquaste obliquou obliquamos obliquastes obliquaram
10. Saudar, abaular and certain verbs with **iu** where hiatus is to be made, as **enviuvar**, add an acute accent in the present tenses to indicate hiatus.	saúdo saúdas saúda saudamos saudais saúdam	saúde saúdes saúde saudemos saudeis saúdem	

	Present Indicative	Present Subjunctive	Preterite Indicative
11. Similarly, verbs with **ai** or **ui** bear an accent on the **i** to indicate hiatus. But note that **bainhar** and its compounds, although similarly pronounced, do not bear a written accent.	arraígo arraígas arraíga arraigamos arraigais arraígam	arraígue arraígues arraígue arraiguemos arraigueis arraíguem	
12. Verbs in **-oar** bear a circumflex accent over the **o** when it is followed by **o**. Example: **soar**.	sôo soas soa soamos soais soam		

RADICAL-CHANGING VERBS

	Present Indicative	Present Subjunctive	Preterite Indicative
13. Verbs in **-ear** change stem **e** to **ei** in root-stressed forms. Note that the **e** of this diphthong is close. Example: **cear**.	ceio ceias ceia ceamos ceais ceiam	ceie ceies ceie ceemos ceeis ceiem	
14. **Idear** and **estrear** change **e** to **éi** under the above conditions, the accent denoting open vowel quality.			
15. **Remanchar** is popularly though incorrectly conjugated as if it were **remanchear**. See **13** above.			
16. Verbs in **-iar** are regular, with a few exceptions: **ansiar, odiar, incendiar, mediar,** and **remediar** are conjugated as in **13** above. With regard to certain others, some hesitancy exists, the regular forms being more widely accepted as correct.	odeio odeias odeia odiamos odiais odeiam	odeie odeies odeie odiemos odieis odeiem	
17. In **-ar** verbs with the stem vowel **e**, this **e** is given an open quality whenever stressed. (For exceptions see **13** above and A and B below.) Example: **levar**.	lęvo lęvas lęva levamos levais lęvam	lęve lęves lęve levemos leveis lęvem	
A. Verbs ending in **-echar, -exar, -ejar** (excepting **invejar**) and **-elhar**, retain close **e** throughout, as do the verbs **chegar** and its compounds, **pesar** when it means "to grieve," **ensebar** and **amancebar**.			
B. If the stem vowel is followed by **m** or **n** it will be pronounced as a nasal close e); *e.g.*, **sentar, remar, ordenhar**.			

18. Similarly, **-ar** verbs with stem vowel **o** have open **o** when stressed. Example: **mofar**.
  A. Excepted are those verbs in which a nasal follows the stem vowel, which then is pronounced as a nasal close **o**: **abandonar, tomar**.
  B. Also excepted are verbs in **-oar** (see **12** above) and the verb **afofar** which retain close **o**.
	mǫfo
	mǫfas
	mǫfa
	mofamos
	mofais
	mǫfam
		mǫfe
		mǫfes
		mǫfe
		mofemos
		mofeis
		mǫfem	

19. In **-er** verbs with stem vowel **e**, the quality of the vowel sound changes regularly as shown (ę indicates close, ę open quality.) A. If a nasal follows **e** the quality will be close in all forms; *e.g.*, **vender, tremer**.	escręvo escręves escręve escrevemos escreveis escręvem	escręva escręvas escręva escrevamos escrevais escręvam	

	Present Indicative	Present Subjunctive	Preterite Indicative
20. Similarly, in **-er** verbs with stem vowel **o**. Example: **mover.** A. As in 19A, a following nasal keeps the stem vowel close and nasal; *e.g.*, **esconder, comer.** B. For further irregularities of verbs in **-oer**, (**roer, moer, doer** and compounds), see **56** below.	mǫvo mǫves mǫve movemos moveis mǫvem	mǫva mǫvas mǫva movamos movais mǫvam	
21. In **-ir** verbs with stem vowel **e** or **o**, there are two types.			
A. **e** changes to **i** and **o** to **u** in 1st singular present indicative and all of the present subjunctive. The quality of stressed **e** or **o** is open unless followed by a nasal. Examples: **ferir, dormir.**	fíro fęres fęre ferimos feris fęrem	fíra fíras fíra fíramos fírais fíram	
	durmo dǫrmes dǫrme dormimos dormis dǫrmem	durma durmas durma durmamos durmais durmam	
B. **e** changes to **i** and **o** to **u** when stressed, and in all of the present subjunctive. Examples: **agredir, sortir.**	agrído agrídes agríde agredimos agredis agrídem	agrída agrídas agrída agrídamos agrídais agrídam	
	surto surtes surte sortimos sortis surtem	surta surtas surta surtamos surtais surtam	
22. A few **-ir** verbs with stem vowel **u** change **u** to **o** in certain forms. Example: **subir.**	subo sǫbes sǫbe subimos subis sǫbem		
23. Verbs with stem diphthong **oi** not followed by a consonant (*e.g.* **boiar, apoiar**) take an acute accent and have open **o** in root-stressed forms.	bóio bóias bóia boiamos boiais bóiam	bóie bóies bóie boiemos boieis bóiem	

IRREGULAR VERBS

24. The following verbs have a regular and an irregular form of the past participle. The regular form is preferred in compound tenses, the irregular form to form the passive voice, with certain exceptions which are indicated. Only the irregular form is listed.

aceitar	aceito, aceite[1]	frigir	frito
acender	aceso	ganhar	ganho[6]
afetar	afeto	gastar	gasto[7]
aspergir	asperso	imergir	imerso
assentar	assente, assento[2]	imprimir	impresso
bem-querer	benquisto	incorrer	incurso
benzer	bento	inserir	inserto
concluir	concluso[3]	isentar	isento
corrigir	correto	juntar	junto
defender	defeso[4]	limpar	limpo
destingir	destinto	malquerer	malquisto
eleger	eleito	matar	morto
emergir	emerso	morrer	morto
encher	cheio[5]	ocultar	oculto
entregar	entregue	pagar	pago[7]
envolver	envolto[5]	prender	prêso
enxugar	enxuto	retingir	retinto
erigir	ereto	romper	rôto[5]
espargir	esparso	safar	safo
exaurir	exausto	salvar	salvo
expelir	expulso	segurar	seguro
expressar	expresso	soltar	sôlto
exprimir	expresso	submergir	submerso
expulsar	expulso	sujeitar	sujeito
extinguir	extinto	surgir	surto
fartar	farto	suspender	suspenso
findar	findo	tingir	tinto

[1] The popular variant *aceite* is used mainly in Portugal.
[2] The irregular form is rare.
[3] *Concluso* is exclusively a legal term.
[4] *Defendido* = defended; *defeso* = prohibited.
[5] The regular form is also commonly used in the passive.
[6] *Ganhado* is archaic except in fixed expressions.
[7] *Gastado* and *pagado* are archaic.

DEFECTIVE AND IRREGULAR VERB MODELS

Impersonal Infinitive, Gerund, Past Participle	Present Indicative	Imperfect Indicative	Preterite	Simple Pluperfect	Future Indicative	Conditional	Present Subjunctive	Imperfect Subjunctive	Future Subjunctive	Imperative	Remarks
25 abolir / abolindo / abolido	..... aboles abole abolimos abolis abolem	regular	regular	regular	regular	regular	*lacking*	regular	regular	regular	Regarding **explodir** and **fundir**, some admit **expludo** and **fundo**, but not the pres. subj.
26 abrir / abrindo / aberto	regular	regular	regular	regular	regular	regular	regular	regular	regular	regular	
27 adequar / adequando / adequado	.... adequamos adequais	regular	regular	regular	regular	regular	*lacking*	regular	regular	adequai	Defective. Very rare except for infinitive and past participle.
28 antiquar / antiquando / antiquado	.... antiqua antiquamos antiquais	regular	regular	regular	regular	regular	*lacking*	regular	regular	antiquai	Like **adequar**, but 3rd singular present indicative is sometimes found.
29 apiedar / apiedando / apiedado	apiado apiadas apiada apiedamos apiedais apiadam	regular	regular	regular	regular	regular	apiade apiades apiade apiademos apiadeis apiadem	regular	regular	apiada apiedai	
30 aprazer / aprazendo / aprazido	aprazo aprazes apraz aprazemos aprazeis aprazem	regular	aprouve aprouveste aprouve aprouvemos aprouvestes aprouveram	aprouvera aprouveras aprouvera aprouvéramos aprouveram	regular	regular	regular	aprouvesse aprouvesses aprouvesse aprouvéssemos aprouvésseis aprouvessem	aprouver aprouveres aprouver aprouvermos aprouverdes aprouverem	regular	Note that **comprazer** does not follow this model. See **54.**
31 argüir / argüindo / argüido	arguo argüis argüi argüimos argüis arguem	argüía argüías argüía argüíamos argüíeis argüíam	argüi argüiste argüiu argüimos argüistes argüiram	argüíra argüíras argüíra argüíramos argüíreis argüíram	argüirei argüirás argüirá argüiremos argüireis argüirão	argüiria argüirias argüiria argüiríamos argüiríeis argüiriam	argua arguas argua arguamos arguais arguam	argüísse argüísses argüísse argüíssemos argüísseis argüíssem	argüir argüires argüir argüirmos argüirdes argüirem	argüi	
32 caber / cabendo / cabido	caibo cabes cabe cabemos cabeis cabem	regular	coube coubeste coube coubemos coubestes couberam	coubera couberas coubera coubéramos coubéreis couberam	regular	regular	caiba caibas caiba caibamos caibais caibam	coubesse coubesses coubesse coubéssemos coubésseis coubessem	couber couberes couber coubermos couberdes couberem	*lacking*	

Impersonal Infinitive, Gerund, Past Participle	Present Indicative	Imperfect Indicative	Preterite	Simple Pluperfect	Future Indicative	Conditional	Present Subjunctive	Imperfect Subjunctive	Future Subjunctive	Imperative	Remarks
33 **cobrir** cobrindo coberto	cubro cobres cobre cobrimos cobris cobrem	regular	regular	regular	regular	regular	cubra cubras cubra cubramos cubrais cubram	regular	regular	regular	See also 21A
34 **computar** computando computado	.... computamos computais computam	regular	regular	regular	regular	regular	regular	regular	regular	regular	
36 **conduzir** conduzindo conduzido	conduzo conduzes conduz conduzimos conduzis conduzem	regular	regular	regular	regular	regular	regular	regular	regular	regular	
37 **construir** construindo construído	construo construis or construís construi or constrói construímos construis construem or constroem	regular	construí construíste construiu construímos construístes construíram	construíra construíras construíra construíramos construíreis construíram	regular	regular	construa construas construa construamos construais construam	construísse construísses construísse construíssemos construísseis construíssem	construir construíres construir construirmos construirdes construírem	construi or constrói construí	
crer crendo crido	creio crês crê cremos credes crêem	regular	cri crêste creu cremos crêstes creram	crera creras crera crêramos crêreis creram	regular	regular	creia creias creia creiamos creiais creiam	cresse cresses cresse crêssemos crêsseis cressem	regular	crê crede	
39 **dar** dando dado	dou dás dá damos dais dão	regular	dei deste deu demos destes deram	dera deras dera déramos déreis deram	regular	regular	dê dês dê demos deis deem	desse desses desse déssemos désseis dessem	der deres der dermos derdes derem	regular	
41 **dizer** dizendo dito	digo dizes diz dizemos dizeis dizem	regular	disse disseste disse dissemos dissestes disseram	dissera disseras dissera disséramos disséreis disseram	direi dirás dirá diremos direis dirão	diria dirias diria diríamos diríeis diriam	diga digas diga digamos digais digam	dissesse dissesses dissesse disséssemos dissésseis dissessem	disser disseres disser dissermos disserdes disserem	dize dizei	
42 **embair** embaindo embaído	.... embaimos embais	regular	regular	regular	regular	regular	*lacking*	regular	regular	embaí	

Impersonal Infinitive, Gerund, Past Participle	Present Indicative	Imperfect Indicative	Preterite	Simple Pluperfect	Future Indicative	Conditional	Present Subjunctive	Imperfect Subjunctive	Future Subjunctive	Imperative	Remarks
33 cobrir cobrindo coberto	cubro, cobres, cobre, cobrimos, cobris, cobrem	regular	regular	regular	regular	regular	cubra, cubras, cubra, cubramos, cubrais, cubram	regular	regular	regular	See also 21A
34 computar computando computado	....., ..., computamos, computais, computam	regular	regular	regular	regular	regular	regular	regular	regular	regular	
36 conduzir conduzindo conduzido	conduzo, conduzes, conduz, conduzimos, conduzis, conduzem	regular	regular	regular	regular	regular	regular	regular	regular	regular	
37 construir construindo construido	construo, construis or construóis, construói or construói, construímos, construís, construem or construoem	regular	construí, construíste, construiu, construímos, construístes, construíram	construíra, construíras, construíra, construíramos, construíreis, construíram	regular	regular	construa, construas, construa, construamos, construais, construam	construísse, construísses, construísse, construíssemos, construísseis, construíssem	construir, construíres, construir, construirmos, construirdes, construírem	construí or construói, construí	
crer crendo crido	creio, crês, crê, cremos, credes, crêem	regular	cri, crêste, creu, crêstes, cream	crera, creras, crera, crêramos, crêreis, cream	regular	regular	creia, creias, creia, creiamos, creiais, creiam	cresse, cresses, cresse, crêssemos, crêsseis, cressem	regular	crê, crede	
39 dar dando dado	dou, dás, dá, damos, dais, dão	regular	dei, deste, deu, demos, destes, deram	dera, deras, dera, déramos, déreis, deram	regular	regular	dê, dês, dê, demos, deis, dêem	desse, desses, desse, déssemos, désseis, dessem	der, deres, der, dermos, derdes, derem	regular	
41 dizer dizendo dito	digo, dizes, diz, dizemos, dizeis, dizem	regular	disse, disseste, disse, dissemos, dissestes, disseram	dissera, disseras, dissera, disséramos, disséreis, disseram	direi, dirás, dirá, diremos, direis, dirão	diria, dirias, diria, diríamos, diríeis, diriam	diga, digas, diga, digamos, digais, digam	dissesse, dissesses, dissesse, disséssemos, dissésseis, dissessem	disser, disseres, disser, dissermos, disserdes, disserem	dize, dizei	
42 embair embaindo embaído	....., ..., embaímos, embaís, ...	regular	regular	regular	regular	regular	*lacking*	regular	regular	embaí	

Impersonal Infinitive, Gerund, Past Participle	Present Indicative	Imperfect Indicative	Preterit	Simple Pluperfect	Future Indicative	Conditional	Present Subjunctive	Imperfect Subjunctive	Future Subjunctive	Imperative	Remarks
51 grassar / grassando / grassado	..... / grassa / ..... / grassam	grassava / grassavam	grassou / grassaram	grassara / grassaram	grassará / grassarão	grassaria / grassariam	grasse / grassem	grassasse / grassassem	grassar / grassarem	*lacking*	
52 haver / havendo / havido	hei / hás / há / havemos / haveis / hão	regular	houve / houveste / houve / houvemos / houvestes / houveram	houvera / houveras / houvera / houvéramos / houvéreis / houveram	regular	regular	haja / hajas / haja / hajamos / hajais / hajam	houvesse / houvesses / houvesse / houvéssemos / houvésseis / houvessem	houver / houveres / houver / houvermos / houverdes / houverem	há / havei	
53 ir / indo / ido	vou / vais / vai / vamos / ides / vão	ia / ias / ia / íamos / íeis / iam	fui / fôste / foi / fomos / fôstes / foram	fôra / fôras / fôra / fôramos / fôreis / foram	regular	regular	vá / vás / vá / vamos / vades / vão	fôsse / fôsses / fôsse / fôssemos / fôsseis / fôssem	fôr / fôres / fôr / formos / fôrdes / forem	vai / ide	
54 jazer / jazendo / jazido	jazo / jazes / jaz / jazemos / jazeis / jazem	regular	regular	regular	regular	regular	regular	regular	regular	regular	The forms jaço, jasço, jaça, jasca, jouvera, and jouvesse are archaic.
55 mobiliar / mobiliando / mobiliado	mobílio / mobílias / mobília / mobiliamos / mobiliais / mobíliam	regular	regular	regular	regular	regular	mobílie / mobílies / mobílie / mobiliemos / mobilieis / mobíliem	regular	regular	mobília / mobiliai	Irregular only in the accentuation of the present tenses and the imperative.
56 moer / moendo / moído	môo / móis / mói / moemos / moeis / moem	moía / moías / moía / moíamos / moíeis / moíam	moí / moeste / moeu / moemos / moestes / moeram	moera / moeras / moera / moêramos / moêreis / moeram	regular	regular	regular	moesse / moesses / moesse / moêssemos / moêsseis / moessem	regular	mói / moei	
57 moscar / moscando / moscado	musco / muscas / musca / moscamos / moscais / muscam	regular	regular	regular	regular	regular	musque / musques / musque / mosquemos / mosqueis / musquem	regular	regular	musca / moscai	A regular variant, muscar, is also to be found.
58 ouvir / ouvindo / ouvido	ouço or oiço / ouves / ouve / ouvimos / ouvis / ouvem	regular	regular	regular	regular	regular	ouça or oiça / ouças or oiças / ouça or oiça / ouçamos or oiçamos / ouçais or oiçais / ouçam or oiçam	regular	regular	ouça or oiça / ouvi	

DEFECTIVE AND IRREGULAR VERB MODELS (continued)

Impersonal Infinitive, Gerund, Past Participle	Present Indicative	Imperfect Indicative	Preterite	Simple Pluperfect	Future Indicative	Conditional	Present Subjunctive	Imperfect Subjunctive	Future Subjunctive	Imperative	Remarks
59 **parir** parindo parido	pairo pares pare parimos paris parem	regular	regular	regular	regular	regular	paira pairas paira pairamos pairais pairam	regular	regular	regular	This verb is not ordinarily used in **those** forms whose endings do not begin with **i**. Cf. **46**.
60 **pedir** pedindo pedido	peço pedes pede pedimos pedis pedem	regular	regular	regular	regular	regular	peça peças peça peçamos peçais peçam	regular	regular	regular	
61 **perder** perdendo perdido	perco perdes perde perdemos perdeis perdem	regular	regular	regular	regular	regular	perca percas perca percamos percais percam	regular	regular	regular	
62 **poder** podendo podido	posso podes pode podemos podeis podem	regular	pude pudeste pôde pudemos pudestes puderam	pudera puderas pudera pudéramos pudéreis puderam	regular	regular	possa possas possa possamos possais possam	pudesse pudesses pudesse pudéssemos pudésseis pudessem	puder puderes puder pudermos puderdes puderem	regular	
63 **pôr** pondo **pôsto**	ponho pões põe pomos pondes põem	punha punhas punha púnhamos púnheis punham	pus puseste pôs pusemos pusestes puseram	pusera puseras pusera puséramos puséreis puseram	regular	regular	ponha ponhas ponha ponhamos ponhais ponham	pusesse pusesses pusesse puséssemos pusésseis pusessem	puser puseres puser pusermos puserdes puserem	põe ponde	Note that the inflected forms of the past participle are not accented and have open **o: posta, postos, postas.**
64 **prazer** prazendo prazido	..... praz ..... prazem	prazia praziam	prouve prouvem	prouvera prouveram	prazerá prazerão	prazeria prazeriam	praza prazam	prouvesse prouvessem	prouver prouverem	*lacking*	For compounds of **prazer**, see **30**.
65 **precaver** precavendo precavido	.... precavemos precaveis	regular	regular	regular	regular	regular	*lacking*	regular	regular	precavei	Not a compound of **ver** or **vir**, and forms based on those verbs, though found, are not considered correct.
66 **prover** provendo provido	provejo provês provê provemos provedes proveem	regular	regular	regular	regular	regular	proveja provejas proveja provejamos provejais provejam	regular	regular	provê provede	Though a compound of **ver**, **prover** does not follow it in several of its tenses.

Impersonal Infinitive, Gerund, Past Participle	Present Indicative	Imperfect Indicative	Preterite	Simple Pluperfect	Future Indicative	Conditional	Present Subjunctive	Imperfect Subjunctive	Future Subjunctive	Imperative	Remarks
67 puir puindo puido	.... puis pui puímos or poímos puís or poís puem	regular	regular	regular	regular	regular	*lacking*	regular	regular	regular	A variant **poir** may be found with stem vowel o in all forms except those shown in **the** present tense.
68 querer querendo querido	quero queres quer queremos quereis querem	regular	quis quiseste quis quisemos quisestes quiseram	quisera quiseras quisera quiséramos quiséreis quiseram	regular	regular	queira queiras queira queiramos queirais queiram	quisesse quisesses quisesse quiséssemos quisésseis quisessem	quiser quiseres quiser quisermos quiserdes quiserem	quere querei	See **24** for the past participles of **bem-querer** and **malquerer**.
69 reaver reavendo reavido	.... reavemos reaveis	regular	reouve reouveste reouve reouvemos reouvestes reouveram	reouvera reouveras reouvera reouvéramos reouvéreis reouveram	regular	regular	*lacking*	reouvesse reouvesses reouvesse reouvéssemos reouvésseis reouvessem	reouver reouveres reouver reouvermos reouverdes reouverem	reavei	Some writers do not conjugate this verb in the preterite, the pluperfect, the imperfect subjunctive, or the future subjunctive
70 requerer requerendo requerido	requeiro requeres requer or requere requeremos requereis requerem	regular	regular	regular	regular	regular	requeira requeiras requeira requeiramos requeirais requeiram	regular	regular	requere requerei	
71 resfolegar resfolegando resfolegado	resfólego resfólegas resfólega resfolegamos resfolegais resfólegam	regular	regular	regular	regular	regular	resfólegue resfólegues resfólegue resfoleguemos resfolegueis resfóleguem	regular	regular	resfólega resfoleguei	Some writers recommend the form **resfolgar.**
72 restituir restituindo restituido	restituo restituis restitui restituímos restituís restituem	regular	regular	regular	regular	regular	regular	regular	regular	restitui restitui	
73 rir rindo rido	rio ris ri rimos rides riem	regular	regular	regular	regular	regular	ria rias ria riamos riais riam	regular	regular	ri ride	
74 saber sabendo sabido	sei sabes sabe sabemos sabeis sabem	regular	soube soubeste soube soubemos soubestes souberam	soubera souberas soubera soubéramos soubéreis souberam	regular	regular	saiba saibas saiba saibamos saibais saibam	soubesse soubesses soubesse soubéssemos soubésseis soubessem	souber souberes souber soubermos souberdes souberem	regular	

DEFECTIVE AND IRREGULAR VERB MODELS (continued)

Impersonal Infinitive, Gerund, Past Participle	Present Indicative	Imperfect Indicative	Preterite	Simple Pluperfect	Future Indicative	Conditional	Present Subjunctive	Imperfect Subjunctive	Future Subjunctive	Imperative	Remarks
75 sair [a-i]	saio	saía	saí	saíra	sairei [a-i]	sairia [a-i]	saia	saísse	sair [a-i]		The group ai forms a diphthong in those forms which do not bear a written accent, or in which the hiatus is not indicated in brackets.
saindo [a-i]	sais	saías	saíste	saíras	sairás [a-i]	sairias [a-i]	saias	saísses	saíres [a-i]	sai	
saído [a-i]	sai	saía	saiu [a-i]	saíra	sairá [a-i]	sairia [a-i]	saia	saísse	sair [a-i]		
	saímos	saíamos	saímos	saíramos	sairemos [a-i]	sairíamos [a-i]	saiamos	saíssemos	sairmos		
	saís	saíeis	saístes	saíreis	saireis [a-i]	sairíeis [a-i]	saiais	saísseis	saírdes [a-i]	saí	
	saem [a-e]	saíam	saíram	saíram	sairão [a-i]	sairiam [a-i]	saiam	saíssem	saírem		
76 ser	sou	era	fui	fôra	regular	regular	seja	fôsse	fôr		
sendo	és	eras	fôste	fôras			sejas	fôsses	fôres	sê	
sido	é	era	foi	fôra			seja	fôsse	fôr		
	somos	éramos	fomos	fôramos			sejamos	fôssemos	formos		
	sois	éreis	fôstes	fôreis			sejais	fôsseis	fôrdes	sêde	
	são	eram	foram	foram			sejam	fôssem	forem		
77 soer	sóis	regular	regular	regular	regular	regular	*lacking*	regular	regular	sói	
soendo	sói										
soído	soemos									soei	
	soeis										
	soem										
78 ter	tenho	tinha	tive	tivera	regular	regular	tenha	tivesse	tiver		
tendo	tens	tinhas	tiveste	tiveras			tenhas	tivesses	tiveres	tem	
tido	tem	tinha	teve	tivera			tenha	tivesse	tiver		
	temos	tínhamos	tivemos	tivéramos			tenhamos	tivéssemos	tivermos		
	tendes	tínheis	tivestes	tivéreis			tenhais	tivésseis	tiverdes	tende	
	têm	tinham	tiveram	tiveram			tenham	tivessem	tiverem		
79 trazer	trago	regular	trouxe	trouxera	trarei	traria	traga	trouxesse	trouxer		The x appearing in certain forms of this verb is pronounced ss.
trazendo	trazes		trouxeste	trouxeras	trarás	trarias	tragas	trouxesses	trouxeres	traze	
trazido	traz		trouxe	trouxera	trará	traria	traga	trouxesse	trouxer		
	trazemos		trouxemos	trouxéramos	traremos	traríamos	tragamos	trouxéssemos	trouxermos		
	trazeis		trouxestes	trouxéreis	trareis	traríeis	tragais	trouxésseis	trouxerdes	trazei	
	trazem		trouxeram	trouxeram	trarão	trariam	tragam	trouxessem	trouxerem		
80 valer	valho	regular	regular	regular	regular	regular	valha	regular	regular	regular	
valendo	vales						valhas				
valido	vale						valha				
	valemos						valhamos				
	valeis						valhais				
	valem						valham				
81 ver	vejo	regular	vi	vira	regular	regular	veja	visse	vir		
vendo	vês		viste	viras			vejas	visses	vires	vê	
visto	vê		viu	vira			veja	visse	vir		
	vemos		vimos	víramos			vejamos	víssemos	virmos		
	vêdes		vistes	víreis			vejais	vísseis	virdes	vêde	
	vêem		viram	viram			vejam	vissem	virem		
82 vir	venho	vinha	vim	viera	regular	regular	venha	viesse	vier		
vindo	vens	vinhas	vieste	vieras			venhas	viesses	vieres	vem	
vindo	vem	vinha	veio	viera			venha	viesse	vier		
	vimos	vínhamos	viemos	viéramos			venhamos	viéssemos	viermos		
	vindes	vínheis	viestes	viéreis			venhais	viésseis	vierdes	vinde	
	vêm	vinham	vieram	vieram			venham	viessem	vierem		